Oxford Dictionary of
National Biography

Volume 38

Oxford Dictionary of National Biography

IN ASSOCIATION WITH
The British Academy

From the earliest times to the year 2000

Edited by
H. C. G. Matthew
and
Brian Harrison

Volume 38
Meyrick–Morande

OXFORD
UNIVERSITY PRESS

OXFORD
UNIVERSITY PRESS

Great Clarendon Street, Oxford OX2 6DP

Oxford University Press is a department of the University of Oxford.
It furthers the University's objective of excellence in research, scholarship,
and education by publishing worldwide in

Oxford New York

Auckland Bangkok Buenos Aires Cape Town
Chennai Dar es Salaam Delhi Hong Kong Istanbul Karachi
Kolkata Kuala Lumpur Madrid Melbourne Mexico City Mumbai Nairobi
São Paulo Shanghai Taipei Tokyo Toronto

Oxford is a registered trade mark of Oxford University Press
in the UK and in certain other countries

Published in the United States
by Oxford University Press Inc., New York

British Library Cataloguing in Publication Data
Data available

Library of Congress Cataloging in Publication Data
Data available: for details see volume 1, p. iv

ISBN 0-19-861388-1 (this volume)
ISBN 0-19-861411-X (set of sixty volumes)

Text captured by Alliance Phototypesetters, Pondicherry
Illustrations reproduced and archived by
Alliance Graphics Ltd, UK
Typeset in OUP Swift by Interactive Sciences Limited, Gloucester
Printed in Great Britain on acid-free paper by
Butler and Tanner Ltd,
Frome, Somerset

LIST OF ABBREVIATIONS

1 *General abbreviations*

AB	bachelor of arts
ABC	Australian Broadcasting Corporation
ABC TV	ABC Television
act.	active
A$	Australian dollar
AD	*anno domini*
AFC	Air Force Cross
AIDS	acquired immune deficiency syndrome
AK	Alaska
AL	Alabama
A level	advanced level [examination]
ALS	associate of the Linnean Society
AM	master of arts
AMICE	associate member of the Institution of Civil Engineers
ANZAC	Australian and New Zealand Army Corps
appx *pl.* appxs	appendix(es)
AR	Arkansas
ARA	associate of the Royal Academy
ARCA	associate of the Royal College of Art
ARCM	associate of the Royal College of Music
ARCO	associate of the Royal College of Organists
ARIBA	associate of the Royal Institute of British Architects
ARP	air-raid precautions
ARRC	associate of the Royal Red Cross
ARSA	associate of the Royal Scottish Academy
art.	article / item
ASC	Army Service Corps
Asch	Austrian Schilling
ASDIC	Antisubmarine Detection Investigation Committee
ATS	Auxiliary Territorial Service
ATV	Associated Television
Aug	August
AZ	Arizona
b.	born
BA	bachelor of arts
BA (Admin.)	bachelor of arts (administration)
BAFTA	British Academy of Film and Television Arts
BAO	bachelor of arts in obstetrics
bap.	baptized
BBC	British Broadcasting Corporation / Company
BC	before Christ
BCE	before the common (*or* Christian) era
BCE	bachelor of civil engineering
BCG	bacillus of Calmette and Guérin [inoculation against tuberculosis]
BCh	bachelor of surgery
BChir	bachelor of surgery
BCL	bachelor of civil law

BCnL	bachelor of canon law
BCom	bachelor of commerce
BD	bachelor of divinity
BEd	bachelor of education
BEng	bachelor of engineering
bk *pl.* bks	book(s)
BL	bachelor of law / letters / literature
BLitt	bachelor of letters
BM	bachelor of medicine
BMus	bachelor of music
BP	before present
BP	British Petroleum
Bros.	Brothers
BS	(1) bachelor of science; (2) bachelor of surgery; (3) British standard
BSc	bachelor of science
BSc (Econ.)	bachelor of science (economics)
BSc (Eng.)	bachelor of science (engineering)
bt	baronet
BTh	bachelor of theology
bur.	buried
C.	command [identifier for published parliamentary papers]
c.	*circa*
c.	*capitulum pl. capitula*: chapter(s)
CA	California
Cantab.	Cantabrigiensis
cap.	*capitulum pl. capitula*: chapter(s)
CB	companion of the Bath
CBE	commander of the Order of the British Empire
CBS	Columbia Broadcasting System
cc	cubic centimetres
C$	Canadian dollar
CD	compact disc
Cd	command [identifier for published parliamentary papers]
CE	Common (*or* Christian) Era
cent.	century
cf.	compare
CH	Companion of Honour
chap.	chapter
ChB	bachelor of surgery
CI	Imperial Order of the Crown of India
CIA	Central Intelligence Agency
CID	Criminal Investigation Department
CIE	companion of the Order of the Indian Empire
Cie	Compagnie
CLit	companion of literature
CM	master of surgery
cm	centimetre(s)

Cmd	command [identifier for published parliamentary papers]	edn	edition
CMG	companion of the Order of St Michael and St George	EEC	European Economic Community
		EFTA	European Free Trade Association
Cmnd	command [identifier for published parliamentary papers]	EICS	East India Company Service
		EMI	Electrical and Musical Industries (Ltd)
CO	Colorado	Eng.	English
Co.	company	enl.	enlarged
co.	county	ENSA	Entertainments National Service Association
col. *pl.* cols.	column(s)	ep. *pl.* epp.	*epistola(e)*
Corp.	corporation	ESP	extra-sensory perception
CSE	certificate of secondary education	esp.	especially
CSI	companion of the Order of the Star of India	esq.	esquire
CT	Connecticut	est.	estimate / estimated
CVO	commander of the Royal Victorian Order	EU	European Union
cwt	hundredweight	ex	sold by (*lit.* out of)
$	(American) dollar	excl.	excludes / excluding
d.	(1) penny (pence); (2) died	exh.	exhibited
DBE	dame commander of the Order of the British Empire	exh. cat.	exhibition catalogue
		f. *pl.* ff.	following [pages]
DCH	diploma in child health	FA	Football Association
DCh	doctor of surgery	FACP	fellow of the American College of Physicians
DCL	doctor of civil law	facs.	facsimile
DCnL	doctor of canon law	FANY	First Aid Nursing Yeomanry
DCVO	dame commander of the Royal Victorian Order	FBA	fellow of the British Academy
DD	doctor of divinity	FBI	Federation of British Industries
DE	Delaware	FCS	fellow of the Chemical Society
Dec	December	Feb	February
dem.	demolished	FEng	fellow of the Fellowship of Engineering
DEng	doctor of engineering	FFCM	fellow of the Faculty of Community Medicine
des.	destroyed	FGS	fellow of the Geological Society
DFC	Distinguished Flying Cross	fig.	figure
DipEd	diploma in education	FIMechE	fellow of the Institution of Mechanical Engineers
DipPsych	diploma in psychiatry		
diss.	dissertation	FL	Florida
DL	deputy lieutenant	*fl.*	*floruit*
DLitt	doctor of letters	FLS	fellow of the Linnean Society
DLittCelt	doctor of Celtic letters	FM	frequency modulation
DM	(1) Deutschmark; (2) doctor of medicine; (3) doctor of musical arts	fol. *pl.* fols.	folio(s)
		Fr	French francs
DMus	doctor of music	Fr.	French
DNA	dioxyribonucleic acid	FRAeS	fellow of the Royal Aeronautical Society
doc.	document	FRAI	fellow of the Royal Anthropological Institute
DOL	doctor of oriental learning	FRAM	fellow of the Royal Academy of Music
DPH	diploma in public health	FRAS	(1) fellow of the Royal Asiatic Society; (2) fellow of the Royal Astronomical Society
DPhil	doctor of philosophy		
DPM	diploma in psychological medicine	FRCM	fellow of the Royal College of Music
DSC	Distinguished Service Cross	FRCO	fellow of the Royal College of Organists
DSc	doctor of science	FRCOG	fellow of the Royal College of Obstetricians and Gynaecologists
DSc (Econ.)	doctor of science (economics)		
DSc (Eng.)	doctor of science (engineering)	FRCP(C)	fellow of the Royal College of Physicians of Canada
DSM	Distinguished Service Medal		
DSO	companion of the Distinguished Service Order	FRCP (Edin.)	fellow of the Royal College of Physicians of Edinburgh
DSocSc	doctor of social science		
DTech	doctor of technology	FRCP (Lond.)	fellow of the Royal College of Physicians of London
DTh	doctor of theology		
DTM	diploma in tropical medicine	FRCPath	fellow of the Royal College of Pathologists
DTMH	diploma in tropical medicine and hygiene	FRCPsych	fellow of the Royal College of Psychiatrists
DU	doctor of the university	FRCS	fellow of the Royal College of Surgeons
DUniv	doctor of the university	FRGS	fellow of the Royal Geographical Society
dwt	pennyweight	FRIBA	fellow of the Royal Institute of British Architects
EC	European Community	FRICS	fellow of the Royal Institute of Chartered Surveyors
ed. *pl.* eds.	edited / edited by / editor(s)		
Edin.	Edinburgh	FRS	fellow of the Royal Society
		FRSA	fellow of the Royal Society of Arts

FRSCM	fellow of the Royal School of Church Music
FRSE	fellow of the Royal Society of Edinburgh
FRSL	fellow of the Royal Society of Literature
FSA	fellow of the Society of Antiquaries
ft	foot *pl.* feet
FTCL	fellow of Trinity College of Music, London
ft-lb per min.	foot-pounds per minute [unit of horsepower]
FZS	fellow of the Zoological Society
GA	Georgia
GBE	knight or dame grand cross of the Order of the British Empire
GCB	knight grand cross of the Order of the Bath
GCE	general certificate of education
GCH	knight grand cross of the Royal Guelphic Order
GCHQ	government communications headquarters
GCIE	knight grand commander of the Order of the Indian Empire
GCMG	knight or dame grand cross of the Order of St Michael and St George
GCSE	general certificate of secondary education
GCSI	knight grand commander of the Order of the Star of India
GCStJ	bailiff or dame grand cross of the order of St John of Jerusalem
GCVO	knight or dame grand cross of the Royal Victorian Order
GEC	General Electric Company
Ger.	German
GI	government (*or* general) issue
GMT	Greenwich mean time
GP	general practitioner
GPU	[Soviet special police unit]
GSO	general staff officer
Heb.	Hebrew
HEICS	Honourable East India Company Service
HI	Hawaii
HIV	human immunodeficiency virus
HK$	Hong Kong dollar
HM	his / her majesty('s)
HMAS	his / her majesty's Australian ship
HMNZS	his / her majesty's New Zealand ship
HMS	his / her majesty's ship
HMSO	His / Her Majesty's Stationery Office
HMV	His Master's Voice
Hon.	Honourable
hp	horsepower
hr	hour(s)
HRH	his / her royal highness
HTV	Harlech Television
IA	Iowa
ibid.	*ibidem*: in the same place
ICI	Imperial Chemical Industries (Ltd)
ID	Idaho
IL	Illinois
illus.	illustration
illustr.	illustrated
IN	Indiana
in.	inch(es)
Inc.	Incorporated
incl.	includes / including
IOU	I owe you
IQ	intelligence quotient
Ir£	Irish pound
IRA	Irish Republican Army
ISO	companion of the Imperial Service Order
It.	Italian
ITA	Independent Television Authority
ITV	Independent Television
Jan	January
JP	justice of the peace
jun.	junior
KB	knight of the Order of the Bath
KBE	knight commander of the Order of the British Empire
KC	king's counsel
kcal	kilocalorie
KCB	knight commander of the Order of the Bath
KCH	knight commander of the Royal Guelphic Order
KCIE	knight commander of the Order of the Indian Empire
KCMG	knight commander of the Order of St Michael and St George
KCSI	knight commander of the Order of the Star of India
KCVO	knight commander of the Royal Victorian Order
keV	kilo-electron-volt
KG	knight of the Order of the Garter
KGB	[Soviet committee of state security]
KH	knight of the Royal Guelphic Order
KLM	Koninklijke Luchtvaart Maatschappij (Royal Dutch Air Lines)
km	kilometre(s)
KP	knight of the Order of St Patrick
KS	Kansas
KT	knight of the Order of the Thistle
kt	knight
KY	Kentucky
£	pound(s) sterling
£E	Egyptian pound
L	lira *pl.* lire
l. *pl.* ll.	line(s)
LA	Lousiana
LAA	light anti-aircraft
LAH	licentiate of the Apothecaries' Hall, Dublin
Lat.	Latin
lb	pound(s), unit of weight
LDS	licence in dental surgery
lit.	literally
LittB	bachelor of letters
LittD	doctor of letters
LKQCPI	licentiate of the King and Queen's College of Physicians, Ireland
LLA	lady literate in arts
LLB	bachelor of laws
LLD	doctor of laws
LLM	master of laws
LM	licentiate in midwifery
LP	long-playing record
LRAM	licentiate of the Royal Academy of Music
LRCP	licentiate of the Royal College of Physicians
LRCPS (Glasgow)	licentiate of the Royal College of Physicians and Surgeons of Glasgow
LRCS	licentiate of the Royal College of Surgeons
LSA	licentiate of the Society of Apothecaries
LSD	lysergic acid diethylamide
LVO	lieutenant of the Royal Victorian Order
M. *pl.* MM.	Monsieur *pl.* Messieurs
m	metre(s)

m. *pl.* mm.	membrane(s)	ND	North Dakota
MA	(1) Massachusetts; (2) master of arts	n.d.	no date
MAI	master of engineering	NE	Nebraska
MB	bachelor of medicine	*nem. con.*	*nemine contradicente*: unanimously
MBA	master of business administration	new ser.	new series
MBE	member of the Order of the British Empire	NH	New Hampshire
MC	Military Cross	NHS	National Health Service
MCC	Marylebone Cricket Club	NJ	New Jersey
MCh	master of surgery	NKVD	[Soviet people's commissariat for internal affairs]
MChir	master of surgery		
MCom	master of commerce	NM	New Mexico
MD	(1) doctor of medicine; (2) Maryland	nm	nanometre(s)
MDMA	methylenedioxymethamphetamine	no. *pl.* nos.	number(s)
ME	Maine	Nov	November
MEd	master of education	n.p.	no place [of publication]
MEng	master of engineering	NS	new style
MEP	member of the European parliament	NV	Nevada
MG	Morris Garages	NY	New York
MGM	Metro-Goldwyn-Mayer	NZBS	New Zealand Broadcasting Service
Mgr	Monsignor	OBE	officer of the Order of the British Empire
MI	(1) Michigan; (2) military intelligence	obit.	obituary
MI1c	[secret intelligence department]	Oct	October
MI5	[military intelligence department]	OCTU	officer cadets training unit
MI6	[secret intelligence department]	OECD	Organization for Economic Co-operation and Development
MI9	[secret escape service]		
MICE	member of the Institution of Civil Engineers	OEEC	Organization for European Economic Co-operation
MIEE	member of the Institution of Electrical Engineers		
		OFM	order of Friars Minor [Franciscans]
min.	minute(s)	OFMCap	Ordine Frati Minori Cappucini: member of the Capuchin order
Mk	mark		
ML	(1) licentiate of medicine; (2) master of laws	OH	Ohio
MLitt	master of letters	OK	Oklahoma
Mlle	Mademoiselle	O level	ordinary level [examination]
mm	millimetre(s)	OM	Order of Merit
Mme	Madame	OP	order of Preachers [Dominicans]
MN	Minnesota	op. *pl.* opp.	opus *pl.* opera
MO	Missouri	OPEC	Organization of Petroleum Exporting Countries
MOH	medical officer of health	OR	Oregon
MP	member of parliament	orig.	original
m.p.h.	miles per hour	OS	old style
MPhil	master of philosophy	OSB	Order of St Benedict
MRCP	member of the Royal College of Physicians	OTC	Officers' Training Corps
MRCS	member of the Royal College of Surgeons	OWS	Old Watercolour Society
MRCVS	member of the Royal College of Veterinary Surgeons	Oxon.	Oxoniensis
		p. *pl.* pp.	page(s)
MRIA	member of the Royal Irish Academy	PA	Pennsylvania
MS	(1) master of science; (2) Mississippi	p.a.	per annum
MS *pl.* MSS	manuscript(s)	para.	paragraph
MSc	master of science	PAYE	pay as you earn
MSc (Econ.)	master of science (economics)	pbk *pl.* pbks	paperback(s)
MT	Montana	*per.*	[during the] period
MusB	bachelor of music	PhD	doctor of philosophy
MusBac	bachelor of music	pl.	(1) plate(s); (2) plural
MusD	doctor of music	priv. coll.	private collection
MV	motor vessel	pt *pl.* pts	part(s)
MVO	member of the Royal Victorian Order	pubd	published
n. *pl.* nn.	note(s)	PVC	polyvinyl chloride
NAAFI	Navy, Army, and Air Force Institutes	q. *pl.* qq.	(1) question(s); (2) quire(s)
NASA	National Aeronautics and Space Administration	QC	queen's counsel
NATO	North Atlantic Treaty Organization	R	rand
NBC	National Broadcasting Corporation	R.	Rex / Regina
NC	North Carolina	*r*	recto
NCO	non-commissioned officer	*r.*	reigned / ruled
		RA	Royal Academy / Royal Academician

RAC	Royal Automobile Club	Skr	Swedish krona
RAF	Royal Air Force	Span.	Spanish
RAFVR	Royal Air Force Volunteer Reserve	SPCK	Society for Promoting Christian Knowledge
RAM	[member of the] Royal Academy of Music	SS	(1) Santissimi; (2) Schutzstaffel; (3) steam ship
RAMC	Royal Army Medical Corps	STB	bachelor of theology
RCA	Royal College of Art	STD	doctor of theology
RCNC	Royal Corps of Naval Constructors	STM	master of theology
RCOG	Royal College of Obstetricians and Gynaecologists	STP	doctor of theology
RDI	royal designer for industry	*supp.*	supposedly
RE	Royal Engineers	suppl. *pl.* suppls.	supplement(s)
repr. *pl.* reprs.	reprint(s) / reprinted	s.v.	*sub verbo* / *sub voce*: under the word / heading
repro.	reproduced	SY	steam yacht
rev.	revised / revised by / reviser / revision	TA	Territorial Army
Revd	Reverend	TASS	[Soviet news agency]
RHA	Royal Hibernian Academy	TB	tuberculosis (*lit.* tubercle bacillus)
RI	(1) Rhode Island; (2) Royal Institute of Painters in Water-Colours	TD	(1) *teachtaí dála* (member of the Dáil); (2) territorial decoration
RIBA	Royal Institute of British Architects	TN	Tennessee
RIN	Royal Indian Navy	TNT	trinitrotoluene
RM	Reichsmark	trans.	translated / translated by / translation / translator
RMS	Royal Mail steamer		
RN	Royal Navy	TT	tourist trophy
RNA	ribonucleic acid	TUC	Trades Union Congress
RNAS	Royal Naval Air Service	TX	Texas
RNR	Royal Naval Reserve	U-boat	*Unterseeboot*: submarine
RNVR	Royal Naval Volunteer Reserve	Ufa	Universum-Film AG
RO	Record Office	UMIST	University of Manchester Institute of Science and Technology
r.p.m.	revolutions per minute		
RRS	royal research ship	UN	United Nations
Rs	rupees	UNESCO	United Nations Educational, Scientific, and Cultural Organization
RSA	(1) Royal Scottish Academician; (2) Royal Society of Arts	UNICEF	United Nations International Children's Emergency Fund
RSPCA	Royal Society for the Prevention of Cruelty to Animals		
		unpubd	unpublished
Rt Hon.	Right Honourable	USS	United States ship
Rt Revd	Right Reverend	UT	Utah
RUC	Royal Ulster Constabulary	*v*	verso
Russ.	Russian	v.	versus
RWS	Royal Watercolour Society	VA	Virginia
S4C	Sianel Pedwar Cymru	VAD	Voluntary Aid Detachment
s.	shilling(s)	VC	Victoria Cross
s.a.	*sub anno*: under the year	VE-day	victory in Europe day
SABC	South African Broadcasting Corporation	Ven.	Venerable
SAS	Special Air Service	VJ-day	victory over Japan day
SC	South Carolina	vol. *pl.* vols.	volume(s)
ScD	doctor of science	VT	Vermont
S$	Singapore dollar	WA	Washington [state]
SD	South Dakota	WAAC	Women's Auxiliary Army Corps
sec.	second(s)	WAAF	Women's Auxiliary Air Force
sel.	selected	WEA	Workers' Educational Association
sen.	senior	WHO	World Health Organization
Sept	September	WI	Wisconsin
ser.	series	WRAF	Women's Royal Air Force
SHAPE	supreme headquarters allied powers, Europe	WRNS	Women's Royal Naval Service
SIDRO	Société Internationale d'Énergie Hydro-Électrique	WV	West Virginia
		WVS	Women's Voluntary Service
sig. *pl.* sigs.	signature(s)	WY	Wyoming
sing.	singular	¥	yen
SIS	Secret Intelligence Service	YMCA	Young Men's Christian Association
SJ	Society of Jesus	YWCA	Young Women's Christian Association

2 Institution abbreviations

All Souls Oxf.	All Souls College, Oxford
AM Oxf.	Ashmolean Museum, Oxford
Balliol Oxf.	Balliol College, Oxford
BBC WAC	BBC Written Archives Centre, Reading
Beds. & Luton ARS	Bedfordshire and Luton Archives and Record Service, Bedford
Berks. RO	Berkshire Record Office, Reading
BFI	British Film Institute, London
BFI NFTVA	British Film Institute, London, National Film and Television Archive
BGS	British Geological Survey, Keyworth, Nottingham
Birm. CA	Birmingham Central Library, Birmingham City Archives
Birm. CL	Birmingham Central Library
BL	British Library, London
BL NSA	British Library, London, National Sound Archive
BL OIOC	British Library, London, Oriental and India Office Collections
BLPES	London School of Economics and Political Science, British Library of Political and Economic Science
BM	British Museum, London
Bodl. Oxf.	Bodleian Library, Oxford
Bodl. RH	Bodleian Library of Commonwealth and African Studies at Rhodes House, Oxford
Borth. Inst.	Borthwick Institute of Historical Research, University of York
Boston PL	Boston Public Library, Massachusetts
Bristol RO	Bristol Record Office
Bucks. RLSS	Buckinghamshire Records and Local Studies Service, Aylesbury
CAC Cam.	Churchill College, Cambridge, Churchill Archives Centre
Cambs. AS	Cambridgeshire Archive Service
CCC Cam.	Corpus Christi College, Cambridge
CCC Oxf.	Corpus Christi College, Oxford
Ches. & Chester ALSS	Cheshire and Chester Archives and Local Studies Service
Christ Church Oxf.	Christ Church, Oxford
Christies	Christies, London
City Westm. AC	City of Westminster Archives Centre, London
CKS	Centre for Kentish Studies, Maidstone
CLRO	Corporation of London Records Office
Coll. Arms	College of Arms, London
Col. U.	Columbia University, New York
Cornwall RO	Cornwall Record Office, Truro
Courtauld Inst.	Courtauld Institute of Art, London
CUL	Cambridge University Library
Cumbria AS	Cumbria Archive Service
Derbys. RO	Derbyshire Record Office, Matlock
Devon RO	Devon Record Office, Exeter
Dorset RO	Dorset Record Office, Dorchester
Duke U.	Duke University, Durham, North Carolina
Duke U., Perkins L.	Duke University, Durham, North Carolina, William R. Perkins Library
Durham Cath. CL	Durham Cathedral, chapter library
Durham RO	Durham Record Office
DWL	Dr Williams's Library, London
Essex RO	Essex Record Office
E. Sussex RO	East Sussex Record Office, Lewes
Eton	Eton College, Berkshire
FM Cam.	Fitzwilliam Museum, Cambridge
Folger	Folger Shakespeare Library, Washington, DC
Garr. Club	Garrick Club, London
Girton Cam.	Girton College, Cambridge
GL	Guildhall Library, London
Glos. RO	Gloucestershire Record Office, Gloucester
Gon. & Caius Cam.	Gonville and Caius College, Cambridge
Gov. Art Coll.	Government Art Collection
GS Lond.	Geological Society of London
Hants. RO	Hampshire Record Office, Winchester
Harris Man. Oxf.	Harris Manchester College, Oxford
Harvard TC	Harvard Theatre Collection, Harvard University, Cambridge, Massachusetts, Nathan Marsh Pusey Library
Harvard U.	Harvard University, Cambridge, Massachusetts
Harvard U., Houghton L.	Harvard University, Cambridge, Massachusetts, Houghton Library
Herefs. RO	Herefordshire Record Office, Hereford
Herts. ALS	Hertfordshire Archives and Local Studies, Hertford
Hist. Soc. Penn.	Historical Society of Pennsylvania, Philadelphia
HLRO	House of Lords Record Office, London
Hult. Arch.	Hulton Archive, London and New York
Hunt. L.	Huntington Library, San Marino, California
ICL	Imperial College, London
Inst. CE	Institution of Civil Engineers, London
Inst. EE	Institution of Electrical Engineers, London
IWM	Imperial War Museum, London
IWM FVA	Imperial War Museum, London, Film and Video Archive
IWM SA	Imperial War Museum, London, Sound Archive
JRL	John Rylands University Library of Manchester
King's AC Cam.	King's College Archives Centre, Cambridge
King's Cam.	King's College, Cambridge
King's Lond.	King's College, London
King's Lond., Liddell Hart C.	King's College, London, Liddell Hart Centre for Military Archives
Lancs. RO	Lancashire Record Office, Preston
L. Cong.	Library of Congress, Washington, DC
Leics. RO	Leicestershire, Leicester, and Rutland Record Office, Leicester
Lincs. Arch.	Lincolnshire Archives, Lincoln
Linn. Soc.	Linnean Society of London
LMA	London Metropolitan Archives
LPL	Lambeth Palace, London
Lpool RO	Liverpool Record Office and Local Studies Service
LUL	London University Library
Magd. Cam.	Magdalene College, Cambridge
Magd. Oxf.	Magdalen College, Oxford
Man. City Gall.	Manchester City Galleries
Man. CL	Manchester Central Library
Mass. Hist. Soc.	Massachusetts Historical Society, Boston
Merton Oxf.	Merton College, Oxford
MHS Oxf.	Museum of the History of Science, Oxford
Mitchell L., Glas.	Mitchell Library, Glasgow
Mitchell L., NSW	State Library of New South Wales, Sydney, Mitchell Library
Morgan L.	Pierpont Morgan Library, New York
NA Canada	National Archives of Canada, Ottawa
NA Ire.	National Archives of Ireland, Dublin
NAM	National Army Museum, London
NA Scot.	National Archives of Scotland, Edinburgh
News Int. RO	News International Record Office, London
NG Ire.	National Gallery of Ireland, Dublin

NG Scot.	National Gallery of Scotland, Edinburgh
NHM	Natural History Museum, London
NL Aus.	National Library of Australia, Canberra
NL Ire.	National Library of Ireland, Dublin
NL NZ	National Library of New Zealand, Wellington
NL NZ, Turnbull L.	National Library of New Zealand, Wellington, Alexander Turnbull Library
NL Scot.	National Library of Scotland, Edinburgh
NL Wales	National Library of Wales, Aberystwyth
NMG Wales	National Museum and Gallery of Wales, Cardiff
NMM	National Maritime Museum, London
Norfolk RO	Norfolk Record Office, Norwich
Northants. RO	Northamptonshire Record Office, Northampton
Northumbd RO	Northumberland Record Office
Notts. Arch.	Nottinghamshire Archives, Nottingham
NPG	National Portrait Gallery, London
NRA	National Archives, London, Historical Manuscripts Commission, National Register of Archives
Nuffield Oxf.	Nuffield College, Oxford
N. Yorks. CRO	North Yorkshire County Record Office, Northallerton
NYPL	New York Public Library
Oxf. UA	Oxford University Archives
Oxf. U. Mus. NH	Oxford University Museum of Natural History
Oxon. RO	Oxfordshire Record Office, Oxford
Pembroke Cam.	Pembroke College, Cambridge
PRO	National Archives, London, Public Record Office
PRO NIre.	Public Record Office for Northern Ireland, Belfast
Pusey Oxf.	Pusey House, Oxford
RA	Royal Academy of Arts, London
Ransom HRC	Harry Ransom Humanities Research Center, University of Texas, Austin
RAS	Royal Astronomical Society, London
RBG Kew	Royal Botanic Gardens, Kew, London
RCP Lond.	Royal College of Physicians of London
RCS Eng.	Royal College of Surgeons of England, London
RGS	Royal Geographical Society, London
RIBA	Royal Institute of British Architects, London
RIBA BAL	Royal Institute of British Architects, London, British Architectural Library
Royal Arch.	Royal Archives, Windsor Castle, Berkshire [by gracious permission of her majesty the queen]
Royal Irish Acad.	Royal Irish Academy, Dublin
Royal Scot. Acad.	Royal Scottish Academy, Edinburgh
RS	Royal Society, London
RSA	Royal Society of Arts, London
RS Friends, Lond.	Religious Society of Friends, London
St Ant. Oxf.	St Antony's College, Oxford
St John Cam.	St John's College, Cambridge
S. Antiquaries, Lond.	Society of Antiquaries of London
Sci. Mus.	Science Museum, London
Scot. NPG	Scottish National Portrait Gallery, Edinburgh
Scott Polar RI	University of Cambridge, Scott Polar Research Institute
Sheff. Arch.	Sheffield Archives
Shrops. RRC	Shropshire Records and Research Centre, Shrewsbury
SOAS	School of Oriental and African Studies, London
Som. ARS	Somerset Archive and Record Service, Taunton
Staffs. RO	Staffordshire Record Office, Stafford

Suffolk RO	Suffolk Record Office
Surrey HC	Surrey History Centre, Woking
TCD	Trinity College, Dublin
Trinity Cam.	Trinity College, Cambridge
U. Aberdeen	University of Aberdeen
U. Birm.	University of Birmingham
U. Birm. L.	University of Birmingham Library
U. Cal.	University of California
U. Cam.	University of Cambridge
UCL	University College, London
U. Durham	University of Durham
U. Durham L.	University of Durham Library
U. Edin.	University of Edinburgh
U. Edin., New Coll.	University of Edinburgh, New College
U. Edin., New Coll. L.	University of Edinburgh, New College Library
U. Edin. L.	University of Edinburgh Library
U. Glas.	University of Glasgow
U. Glas. L.	University of Glasgow Library
U. Hull	University of Hull
U. Hull, Brynmor Jones L.	University of Hull, Brynmor Jones Library
U. Leeds	University of Leeds
U. Leeds, Brotherton L.	University of Leeds, Brotherton Library
U. Lond.	University of London
U. Lpool	University of Liverpool
U. Lpool L.	University of Liverpool Library
U. Mich.	University of Michigan, Ann Arbor
U. Mich., Clements L.	University of Michigan, Ann Arbor, William L. Clements Library
U. Newcastle	University of Newcastle upon Tyne
U. Newcastle, Robinson L.	University of Newcastle upon Tyne, Robinson Library
U. Nott.	University of Nottingham
U. Nott. L.	University of Nottingham Library
U. Oxf.	University of Oxford
U. Reading	University of Reading
U. Reading L.	University of Reading Library
U. St Andr.	University of St Andrews
U. St Andr. L.	University of St Andrews Library
U. Southampton	University of Southampton
U. Southampton L.	University of Southampton Library
U. Sussex	University of Sussex, Brighton
U. Texas	University of Texas, Austin
U. Wales	University of Wales
U. Warwick Mod. RC	University of Warwick, Coventry, Modern Records Centre
V&A	Victoria and Albert Museum, London
V&A NAL	Victoria and Albert Museum, London, National Art Library
Warks. CRO	Warwickshire County Record Office, Warwick
Wellcome L.	Wellcome Library for the History and Understanding of Medicine, London
Westm. DA	Westminster Diocesan Archives, London
Wilts. & Swindon RO	Wiltshire and Swindon Record Office, Trowbridge
Worcs. RO	Worcestershire Record Office, Worcester
W. Sussex RO	West Sussex Record Office, Chichester
W. Yorks. AS	West Yorkshire Archive Service
Yale U.	Yale University, New Haven, Connecticut
Yale U., Beinecke L.	Yale University, New Haven, Connecticut, Beinecke Rare Book and Manuscript Library
Yale U. CBA	Yale University, New Haven, Connecticut, Yale Center for British Art

3 Bibliographic abbreviations

Adams, *Drama*	W. D. Adams, *A dictionary of the drama*, 1: *A–G* (1904); 2: *H–Z* (1956) [vol. 2 microfilm only]
AFM	J O'Donovan, ed. and trans., *Annala rioghachta Eireann / Annals of the kingdom of Ireland by the four masters*, 7 vols. (1848–51); 2nd edn (1856); 3rd edn (1990)
Allibone, *Dict.*	S. A. Allibone, *A critical dictionary of English literature and British and American authors*, 3 vols. (1859–71); suppl. by J. F. Kirk, 2 vols. (1891)
ANB	J. A. Garraty and M. C. Carnes, eds., *American national biography*, 24 vols. (1999)
Anderson, *Scot. nat.*	W. Anderson, *The Scottish nation, or, The surnames, families, literature, honours, and biographical history of the people of Scotland*, 3 vols. (1859–63)
Ann. mon.	H. R. Luard, ed., *Annales monastici*, 5 vols., Rolls Series, 36 (1864–9)
Ann. Ulster	S. Mac Airt and G. Mac Niocaill, eds., *Annals of Ulster (to AD 1131)* (1983)
APC	*Acts of the privy council of England*, new ser., 46 vols. (1890–1964)
APS	*The acts of the parliaments of Scotland*, 12 vols. in 13 (1814–75)
Arber, *Regs. Stationers*	F. Arber, ed., *A transcript of the registers of the Company of Stationers of London, 1554–1640 AD*, 5 vols. (1875–94)
ArchR	*Architectural Review*
ASC	D. Whitelock, D. C. Douglas, and S. I. Tucker, ed. and trans., *The Anglo-Saxon Chronicle: a revised translation* (1961)
AS chart.	P. H. Sawyer, *Anglo-Saxon charters: an annotated list and bibliography*, Royal Historical Society Guides and Handbooks (1968)
AusDB	D. Pike and others, eds., *Australian dictionary of biography*, 16 vols. (1966–2002)
Baker, *Serjeants*	J. H. Baker, *The order of serjeants at law*, SeldS, suppl. ser., 5 (1984)
Bale, *Cat.*	J. Bale, *Scriptorum illustrium Maioris Brytannie, quam nunc Angliam et Scotiam vocant: catalogus*, 2 vols. in 1 (Basel, 1557–9); facs. edn (1971)
Bale, *Index*	J. Bale, *Index Britanniae scriptorum*, ed. R. L. Poole and M. Bateson (1902); facs. edn (1990)
BBCS	*Bulletin of the Board of Celtic Studies*
BDMBR	J. O. Baylen and N. J. Gossman, eds., *Biographical dictionary of modern British radicals*, 3 vols. in 4 (1979–88)
Bede, *Hist. eccl.*	*Bede's Ecclesiastical history of the English people*, ed. and trans. B. Colgrave and R. A. B. Mynors, OMT (1969); repr. (1991)
Bénézit, *Dict.*	E. Bénézit, *Dictionnaire critique et documentaire des peintres, sculpteurs, dessinateurs et graveurs*, 3 vols. (Paris, 1911–23); new edn, 8 vols. (1948–66), repr. (1966); 3rd edn, rev. and enl., 10 vols. (1976); 4th edn, 14 vols. (1999)
BIHR	*Bulletin of the Institute of Historical Research*
Birch, *Seals*	W. de Birch, *Catalogue of seals in the department of manuscripts in the British Museum*, 6 vols. (1887–1900)
Bishop Burnet's History	*Bishop Burnet's History of his own time*, ed. M. J. Routh, 2nd edn, 6 vols. (1833)
Blackwood	*Blackwood's [Edinburgh] Magazine*, 328 vols. (1817–1980)
Blain, Clements & Grundy, *Feminist comp.*	V. Blain, P. Clements, and I. Grundy, eds., *The feminist companion to literature in English* (1990)
BL cat.	*The British Library general catalogue of printed books* [in 360 vols. with suppls., also CD-ROM and online]
BMJ	*British Medical Journal*
Boase & Courtney, *Bibl. Corn.*	G. C. Boase and W. P. Courtney, *Bibliotheca Cornubiensis: a catalogue of the writings … of Cornishmen*, 3 vols. (1874–82)
Boase, *Mod. Eng. biog.*	F. Boase, *Modern English biography: containing many thousand concise memoirs of persons who have died since the year 1850*, 6 vols. (privately printed, Truro, 1892–1921); repr. (1965)
Boswell, *Life*	*Boswell's Life of Johnson: together with Journal of a tour to the Hebrides and Johnson's Diary of a journey into north Wales*, ed. G. B. Hill, enl. edn, rev. L. F. Powell, 6 vols. (1934–50); 2nd edn (1964); repr. (1971)
Brown & Stratton, *Brit. mus.*	J. D. Brown and S. S. Stratton, *British musical biography* (1897)
Bryan, *Painters*	M. Bryan, *A biographical and critical dictionary of painters and engravers*, 2 vols. (1816); new edn, ed. G. Stanley (1849); new edn, ed. R. E. Graves and W. Armstrong, 2 vols. (1886–9); [4th edn], ed. G. C. Williamson, 5 vols. (1903–5) [various reprs.]
Burke, *Gen. GB*	J. Burke, *A genealogical and heraldic history of the commoners of Great Britain and Ireland*, 4 vols. (1833–8); new edn as *A genealogical and heraldic dictionary of the landed gentry of Great Britain and Ireland*, 3 vols. [1843–9] [many later edns]
Burke, *Gen. Ire.*	J. B. Burke, *A genealogical and heraldic history of the landed gentry of Ireland* (1899); 2nd edn (1904); 3rd edn (1912); 4th edn (1958); 5th edn as *Burke's Irish family records* (1976)
Burke, *Peerage*	J. Burke, *A general [later edns A genealogical] and heraldic dictionary of the peerage and baronetage of the United Kingdom* [later edns *the British empire*] (1829–)
Burney, *Hist. mus.*	C. Burney, *A general history of music, from the earliest ages to the present period*, 4 vols. (1776–89)
Burtchaell & Sadleir, *Alum. Dubl.*	G. D. Burtchaell and T. U. Sadleir, *Alumni Dublinenses: a register of the students, graduates, and provosts of Trinity College* (1924); [2nd edn], with suppl., in 2 pts (1935)
Calamy rev.	A. G. Matthews, *Calamy revised* (1934); repr. (1988)
CCI	*Calendar of confirmations and inventories granted and given up in the several commissariots of Scotland* (1876–)
CClR	*Calendar of the close rolls preserved in the Public Record Office*, 47 vols. (1892–1963)
CDS	J. Bain, ed., *Calendar of documents relating to Scotland*, 4 vols., PRO (1881–8); suppl. vol. 5, ed. G. G. Simpson and J. D. Galbraith [1986]
CEPR letters	W. H. Bliss, C. Johnson, and J. Twemlow, eds., *Calendar of entries in the papal registers relating to Great Britain and Ireland: papal letters* (1893–)
CGPLA	*Calendars of the grants of probate and letters of administration* [in 4 ser.: England & Wales, Northern Ireland, Ireland, and Éire]
Chambers, *Scots.*	R. Chambers, ed., *A biographical dictionary of eminent Scotsmen*, 4 vols. (1832–5)
Chancery records	chancery records pubd by the PRO
Chancery records (RC)	chancery records pubd by the Record Commissions

CIPM	*Calendar of inquisitions post mortem*, [20 vols.], PRO (1904–); also *Henry VII*, 3 vols. (1898–1955)
Clarendon, *Hist. rebellion*	E. Hyde, earl of Clarendon, *The history of the rebellion and civil wars in England*, 6 vols. (1888); repr. (1958) and (1992)
Cobbett, *Parl. hist.*	W. Cobbett and J. Wright, eds., *Cobbett's Parliamentary history of England*, 36 vols. (1806–1820)
Colvin, *Archs.*	H. Colvin, *A biographical dictionary of British architects, 1600–1840*, 3rd edn (1995)
Cooper, *Ath. Cantab.*	C. H. Cooper and T. Cooper, *Athenae Cantabrigienses*, 3 vols. (1858–1913); repr. (1967)
CPR	*Calendar of the patent rolls preserved in the Public Record Office* (1891–)
Crockford	*Crockford's Clerical Directory*
CS	Camden Society
CSP	*Calendar of state papers* [in 11 ser.: *domestic, Scotland, Scottish series, Ireland, colonial, Commonwealth, foreign, Spain* [at Simancas], *Rome, Milan,* and *Venice*]
CYS	Canterbury and York Society
DAB	*Dictionary of American biography*, 21 vols. (1928–36), repr. in 11 vols. (1964); 10 suppls. (1944–96)
DBB	D. J. Jeremy, ed., *Dictionary of business biography*, 5 vols. (1984–6)
DCB	G. W. Brown and others, *Dictionary of Canadian biography*, [14 vols.] (1966–)
Debrett's Peerage	*Debrett's Peerage* (1803–) [sometimes *Debrett's Illustrated peerage*]
Desmond, *Botanists*	R. Desmond, *Dictionary of British and Irish botanists and horticulturists* (1977); rev. edn (1994)
Dir. Brit. archs.	A. Felstead, J. Franklin, and L. Pinfield, eds., *Directory of British architects, 1834–1900* (1993); 2nd edn, ed. A. Brodie and others, 2 vols. (2001)
DLB	J. M. Bellamy and J. Saville, eds., *Dictionary of labour biography*, [10 vols.] (1972–)
DLitB	Dictionary of Literary Biography
DNB	*Dictionary of national biography*, 63 vols. (1885–1900), suppl., 3 vols. (1901); repr. in 22 vols. (1908–9); 10 further suppls. (1912–96); *Missing persons* (1993)
DNZB	W. H. Oliver and C. Orange, eds., *The dictionary of New Zealand biography*, 5 vols. (1990–2000)
DSAB	W. J. de Kock and others, eds., *Dictionary of South African biography*, 5 vols. (1968–87)
DSB	C. C. Gillispie and F. L. Holmes, eds., *Dictionary of scientific biography*, 16 vols. (1970–80); repr. in 8 vols. (1981); 2 vol. suppl. (1990)
DSBB	A. Slaven and S. Checkland, eds., *Dictionary of Scottish business biography, 1860–1960*, 2 vols. (1986–90)
DSCHT	N. M. de S. Cameron and others, eds., *Dictionary of Scottish church history and theology* (1993)
Dugdale, *Monasticon*	W. Dugdale, *Monasticon Anglicanum*, 3 vols. (1655–72); 2nd edn, 3 vols. (1661–82); new edn, ed. J. Caley, J. Ellis, and B. Bandinel, 6 vols. in 8 pts (1817–30); repr. (1846) and (1970)
DWB	J. E. Lloyd and others, eds., *Dictionary of Welsh biography down to 1940* (1959) [Eng. trans. of *Y bywgraffiadur Cymreig hyd 1940*, 2nd edn (1954)]
EdinR	*Edinburgh Review, or, Critical Journal*
EETS	Early English Text Society
Emden, *Cam.*	A. B. Emden, *A biographical register of the University of Cambridge to 1500* (1963)
Emden, *Oxf.*	A. B. Emden, *A biographical register of the University of Oxford to AD 1500*, 3 vols. (1957–9); also *A biographical register of the University of Oxford, AD 1501 to 1540* (1974)
EngHR	*English Historical Review*
Engraved Brit. ports.	F. M. O'Donoghue and H. M. Hake, *Catalogue of engraved British portraits preserved in the department of prints and drawings in the British Museum*, 6 vols. (1908–25)
ER	*The English Reports*, 178 vols. (1900–32)
ESTC	*English short title catalogue, 1475–1800* [CD-ROM and online]
Evelyn, *Diary*	*The diary of John Evelyn*, ed. E. S. De Beer, 6 vols. (1955); repr. (2000)
Farington, *Diary*	*The diary of Joseph Farington*, ed. K. Garlick and others, 17 vols. (1978–98)
Fasti Angl. (Hardy)	J. Le Neve, *Fasti ecclesiae Anglicanae*, ed. T. D. Hardy, 3 vols. (1854)
Fasti Angl., 1066–1300	[J. Le Neve], *Fasti ecclesiae Anglicanae, 1066–1300*, ed. D. E. Greenway and J. S. Barrow, [8 vols.] (1968–)
Fasti Angl., 1300–1541	[J. Le Neve], *Fasti ecclesiae Anglicanae, 1300–1541*, 12 vols. (1962–7)
Fasti Angl., 1541–1857	[J. Le Neve], *Fasti ecclesiae Anglicanae, 1541–1857*, ed. J. M. Horn, D. M. Smith, and D. S. Bailey, [9 vols.] (1969–)
Fasti Scot.	H. Scott, *Fasti ecclesiae Scoticanae*, 3 vols. in 6 (1871); new edn, [11 vols.] (1915–)
FO List	*Foreign Office List*
Fortescue, *Brit. army*	J. W. Fortescue, *A history of the British army*, 13 vols. (1899–1930)
Foss, *Judges*	E. Foss, *The judges of England*, 9 vols. (1848–64); repr. (1966)
Foster, *Alum. Oxon.*	J. Foster, ed., *Alumni Oxonienses: the members of the University of Oxford, 1715–1886*, 4 vols. (1887–8); later edn (1891); also *Alumni Oxonienses … 1500–1714*, 4 vols. (1891–2); 8 vol. repr. (1968) and (2000)
Fuller, *Worthies*	T. Fuller, *The history of the worthies of England*, 4 pts (1662); new edn, 2 vols., ed. J. Nichols (1811); new edn, 3 vols., ed. P. A. Nuttall (1840); repr. (1965)
GEC, *Baronetage*	G. E. Cokayne, *Complete baronetage*, 6 vols. (1900–09); repr. (1983) [microprint]
GEC, *Peerage*	G. E. C. [G. E. Cokayne], *The complete peerage of England, Scotland, Ireland, Great Britain, and the United Kingdom*, 8 vols. (1887–98); new edn, ed. V. Gibbs and others, 14 vols. in 15 (1910–98); microprint repr. (1982) and (1987)
Genest, *Eng. stage*	J. Genest, *Some account of the English stage from the Restoration in 1660 to 1830*, 10 vols. (1832); repr. [New York, 1965]
Gillow, *Lit. biog. hist.*	J. Gillow, *A literary and biographical history or bibliographical dictionary of the English Catholics, from the breach with Rome, in 1534, to the present time*, 5 vols. [1885–1902]; repr. (1961); repr. with preface by C. Gillow (1999)
Gir. Camb. opera	*Giraldi Cambrensis opera*, ed. J. S. Brewer, J. F. Dimock, and G. F. Warner, 8 vols., Rolls Series, 21 (1861–91)
GJ	*Geographical Journal*

Gladstone, *Diaries* — *The Gladstone diaries: with cabinet minutes and prime-ministerial correspondence*, ed. M. R. D. Foot and H. C. G. Matthew, 14 vols. (1968–94)

GM — *Gentleman's Magazine*

Graves, *Artists* — A. Graves, ed., *A dictionary of artists who have exhibited works in the principal London exhibitions of oil paintings from 1760 to 1880* (1884); new edn (1895); 3rd edn (1901); facs. edn (1969); repr. [1970], (1973), and (1984)

Graves, *Brit. Inst.* — A. Graves, *The British Institution, 1806–1867: a complete dictionary of contributors and their work from the foundation of the institution* (1875); facs. edn (1908); repr. (1969)

Graves, *RA exhibitors* — A. Graves, *The Royal Academy of Arts: a complete dictionary of contributors and their work from its foundation in 1769 to 1904*, 8 vols. (1905–6); repr. in 4 vols. (1970) and (1972)

Graves, *Soc. Artists* — A. Graves, *The Society of Artists of Great Britain, 1760–1791, the Free Society of Artists, 1761–1783: a complete dictionary* (1907); facs. edn (1969)

Greaves & Zaller, *BDBR* — R. L. Greaves and R. Zaller, eds., *Biographical dictionary of British radicals in the seventeenth century*, 3 vols. (1982–4)

Grove, *Dict. mus.* — G. Grove, ed., *A dictionary of music and musicians*, 5 vols. (1878–90); 2nd edn, ed. J. A. Fuller Maitland (1904–10); 3rd edn, ed. H. C. Colles (1927); 4th edn with suppl. (1940); 5th edn, ed. E. Blom, 9 vols. (1954); suppl. (1961) [see also *New Grove*]

Hall, *Dramatic ports.* — L. A. Hall, *Catalogue of dramatic portraits in the theatre collection of the Harvard College library*, 4 vols. (1930–34)

Hansard — *Hansard's parliamentary debates*, ser. 1–5 (1803–)

Highfill, Burnim & Langhans, *BDA* — P. H. Highfill, K. A. Burnim, and E. A. Langhans, *A biographical dictionary of actors, actresses, musicians, dancers, managers, and other stage personnel in London, 1660–1800*, 16 vols. (1973–93)

Hist. U. Oxf. — T. H. Aston, ed., *The history of the University of Oxford*, 8 vols. (1984–2000) [1: *The early Oxford schools*, ed. J. I. Catto (1984); 2: *Late medieval Oxford*, ed. J. I. Catto and R. Evans (1992); 3: *The collegiate university*, ed. J. McConica (1986); 4: *Seventeenth-century Oxford*, ed. N. Tyacke (1997); 5: *The eighteenth century*, ed. L. S. Sutherland and L. G. Mitchell (1986); 6–7: *Nineteenth-century Oxford*, ed. M. G. Brock and M. C. Curthoys (1997–2000); 8: *The twentieth century*, ed. B. Harrison (2000)]

HJ — *Historical Journal*

HMC — Historical Manuscripts Commission

Holdsworth, *Eng. law* — W. S. Holdsworth, *A history of English law*, ed. A. L. Goodhart and H. L. Hanbury, 17 vols. (1903–72)

HoP, *Commons* — *The history of parliament: the House of Commons* [*1386–1421*, ed. J. S. Roskell, L. Clark, and C. Rawcliffe, 4 vols. (1992); *1509–1558*, ed. S. T. Bindoff, 3 vols. (1982); *1558–1603*, ed. P. W. Hasler, 3 vols. (1981); *1660–1690*, ed. B. D. Henning, 3 vols. (1983); *1690–1715*, ed. D. W. Hayton, E. Cruickshanks, and S. Handley, 5 vols. (2002); *1715–1754*, ed. R. Sedgwick, 2 vols. (1970); *1754–1790*, ed. L. Namier and J. Brooke, 3 vols. (1964), repr. (1985); *1790–1820*, ed. R. G. Thorne, 5 vols. (1986); in draft (used with permission): *1422–1504*, *1604–1629*, *1640–1660*, and *1820–1832*]

IGI — *International Genealogical Index*, Church of Jesus Christ of the Latterday Saints

ILN — *Illustrated London News*

IMC — Irish Manuscripts Commission

Irving, *Scots.* — J. Irving, ed., *The book of Scotsmen eminent for achievements in arms and arts, church and state, law, legislation and literature, commerce, science, travel and philanthropy* (1881)

JCS — *Journal of the Chemical Society*

JHC — *Journals of the House of Commons*

JHL — *Journals of the House of Lords*

John of Worcester, *Chron.* — *The chronicle of John of Worcester*, ed. R. R. Darlington and P. McGurk, trans. J. Bray and P. McGurk, 3 vols., OMT (1995–) [vol. 1 forthcoming]

Keeler, *Long Parliament* — M. F. Keeler, *The Long Parliament, 1640–1641: a biographical study of its members* (1954)

Kelly, *Handbk* — *The upper ten thousand: an alphabetical list of all members of noble families*, 3 vols. (1875–7); continued as *Kelly's handbook of the upper ten thousand for 1878* [1879], 2 vols. (1878–9); continued as *Kelly's handbook to the titled, landed and official classes*, 94 vols. (1880–1973)

LondG — *London Gazette*

LP Henry VIII — J. S. Brewer, J. Gairdner, and R. H. Brodie, eds., *Letters and papers, foreign and domestic, of the reign of Henry VIII*, 23 vols. in 38 (1862–1932); repr. (1965)

Mallalieu, *Watercolour artists* — H. L. Mallalieu, *The dictionary of British watercolour artists up to 1820*, 3 vols. (1976–90); vol. 1, 2nd edn (1986)

Memoirs FRS — *Biographical Memoirs of Fellows of the Royal Society*

MGH — Monumenta Germaniae Historica

MT — *Musical Times*

Munk, *Roll* — W. Munk, *The roll of the Royal College of Physicians of London*, 2 vols. (1861); 2nd edn, 3 vols. (1878)

N&Q — *Notes and Queries*

New Grove — S. Sadie, ed., *The new Grove dictionary of music and musicians*, 20 vols. (1980); 2nd edn, 29 vols. (2001) [also online edn; see also Grove, *Dict. mus.*]

Nichols, *Illustrations* — J. Nichols and J. B. Nichols, *Illustrations of the literary history of the eighteenth century*, 8 vols. (1817–58)

Nichols, *Lit. anecdotes* — J. Nichols, *Literary anecdotes of the eighteenth century*, 9 vols. (1812–16); facs. edn (1966)

Obits. FRS — *Obituary Notices of Fellows of the Royal Society*

O'Byrne, *Naval biog. dict.* — W. R. O'Byrne, *A naval biographical dictionary* (1849); repr. (1990); [2nd edn], 2 vols. (1861)

OHS — Oxford Historical Society

Old Westminsters — *The record of Old Westminsters*, 1–2, ed. G. F. R. Barker and A. H. Stenning (1928); suppl. 1, ed. J. B. Whitmore and G. R. Y. Radcliffe [1938]; 3, ed. J. B. Whitmore, G. R. Y. Radcliffe, and D. C. Simpson (1963); suppl. 2, ed. F. E. Pagan (1978); 4, ed. F. E. Pagan and H. E. Pagan (1992)

OMT — Oxford Medieval Texts

Ordericus Vitalis, *Eccl. hist.* — *The ecclesiastical history of Orderic Vitalis*, ed. and trans. M. Chibnall, 6 vols., OMT (1969–80); repr. (1990)

Paris, *Chron.* — *Matthaei Parisiensis, monachi sancti Albani, chronica majora*, ed. H. R. Luard, Rolls Series, 7 vols. (1872–83)

Parl. papers — *Parliamentary papers* (1801–)

PBA — *Proceedings of the British Academy*

Pepys, *Diary*	*The diary of Samuel Pepys*, ed. R. Latham and W. Matthews, 11 vols. (1970–83); repr. (1995) and (2000)
Pevsner	N. Pevsner and others, Buildings of England series
PICE	*Proceedings of the Institution of Civil Engineers*
Pipe rolls	*The great roll of the pipe for . . .*, PRSoc. (1884–)
PRO	Public Record Office
PRS	*Proceedings of the Royal Society of London*
PRSoc.	Pipe Roll Society
PTRS	*Philosophical Transactions of the Royal Society*
QR	*Quarterly Review*
RC	Record Commissions
Redgrave, *Artists*	S. Redgrave, *A dictionary of artists of the English school* (1874); rev. edn (1878); repr. (1970)
Reg. Oxf.	C. W. Boase and A. Clark, eds., *Register of the University of Oxford*, 5 vols., OHS, 1, 10–12, 14 (1885–9)
Reg. PCS	J. H. Burton and others, eds., *The register of the privy council of Scotland*, 1st ser., 14 vols. (1877–98); 2nd ser., 8 vols. (1899–1908); 3rd ser., [16 vols.] (1908–70)
Reg. RAN	H. W. C. Davis and others, eds., *Regesta regum Anglo-Normannorum, 1066–1154*, 4 vols. (1913–69)
RIBA Journal	*Journal of the Royal Institute of British Architects* [later *RIBA Journal*]
RotP	J. Strachey, ed., *Rotuli parliamentorum ut et petitiones, et placita in parliamento*, 6 vols. (1767–77)
RotS	D. Macpherson, J. Caley, and W. Illingworth, eds., *Rotuli Scotiae in Turri Londinensi et in domo capitulari Westmonasteriensi asservati*, 2 vols., RC, 14 (1814–19)
RS	Record(s) Society
Rymer, *Foedera*	T. Rymer and R. Sanderson, eds., *Foedera, conventiones, literae et cuiuscunque generis acta publica inter reges Angliae et alios quosvis imperatores, reges, pontifices, principes, vel communitates*, 20 vols. (1704–35); 2nd edn, 20 vols. (1726–35); 3rd edn, 10 vols. (1739–45); facs. edn (1967); new edn, ed. A. Clarke, J. Caley, and F. Holbrooke, 4 vols., RC, 50 (1816–30)
Sainty, *Judges*	J. Sainty, ed., *The judges of England, 1272–1990*, SeldS, suppl. ser., 10 (1993)
Sainty, *King's counsel*	J. Sainty, ed., *A list of English law officers and king's counsel*, SeldS, suppl. ser., 7 (1987)
SCH	Studies in Church History
Scots peerage	J. B. Paul, ed. *The Scots peerage, founded on Wood's edition of Sir Robert Douglas's Peerage of Scotland, containing an historical and genealogical account of the nobility of that kingdom*, 9 vols. (1904–14)
SeldS	Selden Society
SHR	*Scottish Historical Review*
State trials	T. B. Howell and T. J. Howell, eds., *Cobbett's Complete collection of state trials*, 34 vols. (1809–28)
STC, 1475–1640	A. W. Pollard, G. R. Redgrave, and others, eds., *A short-title catalogue of . . . English books . . . 1475–1640* (1926); 2nd edn, ed. W. A. Jackson, F. S. Ferguson, and K. F. Pantzer, 3 vols. (1976–91) [see also Wing, *STC*]
STS	Scottish Text Society
SurtS	Surtees Society
Symeon of Durham, *Opera*	*Symeonis monachi opera omnia*, ed. T. Arnold, 2 vols., Rolls Series, 75 (1882–5); repr. (1965)
Tanner, *Bibl. Brit.-Hib.*	T. Tanner, *Bibliotheca Britannico-Hibernica*, ed. D. Wilkins (1748); repr. (1963)
Thieme & Becker, *Allgemeines Lexikon*	U. Thieme, F. Becker, and H. Vollmer, eds., *Allgemeines Lexikon der bildenden Künstler von der Antike bis zur Gegenwart*, 37 vols. (Leipzig, 1907–50); repr. (1961–5), (1983), and (1992)
Thurloe, *State papers*	*A collection of the state papers of John Thurloe*, ed. T. Birch, 7 vols. (1742)
TLS	*Times Literary Supplement*
Tout, *Admin. hist.*	T. F. Tout, *Chapters in the administrative history of mediaeval England: the wardrobe, the chamber, and the small seals*, 6 vols. (1920–33); repr. (1967)
TRHS	*Transactions of the Royal Historical Society*
VCH	H. A. Doubleday and others, eds., *The Victoria history of the counties of England*, [88 vols.] (1900–)
Venn, *Alum. Cant.*	J. Venn and J. A. Venn, *Alumni Cantabrigienses: a biographical list of all known students, graduates, and holders of office at the University of Cambridge, from the earliest times to 1900*, 10 vols. (1922–54); repr. in 2 vols. (1974–8)
Vertue, *Note books*	[G. Vertue], *Note books*, ed. K. Esdaile, earl of Ilchester, and H. M. Hake, 6 vols., Walpole Society, 18, 20, 22, 24, 26, 30 (1930–55)
VF	*Vanity Fair*
Walford, *County families*	E. Walford, *The county families of the United Kingdom, or, Royal manual of the titled and untitled aristocracy of Great Britain and Ireland* (1860)
Walker rev.	A. G. Matthews, *Walker revised: being a revision of John Walker's Sufferings of the clergy during the grand rebellion, 1642–60* (1948); repr. (1988)
Walpole, *Corr.*	*The Yale edition of Horace Walpole's correspondence*, ed. W. S. Lewis, 48 vols. (1937–83)
Ward, *Men of the reign*	T. H. Ward, ed., *Men of the reign: a biographical dictionary of eminent persons of British and colonial birth who have died during the reign of Queen Victoria* (1885); repr. (Graz, 1968)
Waterhouse, *18c painters*	E. Waterhouse, *The dictionary of 18th century painters in oils and crayons* (1981); repr. as *British 18th century painters in oils and crayons* (1991), vol. 2 of *Dictionary of British art*
Watt, *Bibl. Brit.*	R. Watt, *Bibliotheca Britannica, or, A general index to British and foreign literature*, 4 vols. (1824) [many reprs.]
Wellesley index	W. E. Houghton, ed., *The Wellesley index to Victorian periodicals, 1824–1900*, 5 vols. (1966–89); new edn (1999) [CD-ROM]
Wing, *STC*	D. Wing, ed., *Short-title catalogue of . . . English books . . . 1641–1700*, 3 vols. (1945–51); 2nd edn (1972–88); rev. and enl. edn, ed. J. J. Morrison, C. W. Nelson, and M. Seccombe, 4 vols. (1994–8) [see also *STC, 1475–1640*]
Wisden	*John Wisden's Cricketer's Almanack*
Wood, *Ath. Oxon.*	A. Wood, *Athenae Oxonienses . . . to which are added the Fasti*, 2 vols. (1691–2); 2nd edn (1721); new edn, 4 vols., ed. P. Bliss (1813–20); repr. (1967) and (1969)
Wood, *Vic. painters*	C. Wood, *Dictionary of Victorian painters* (1971); 2nd edn (1978); 3rd edn as *Victorian painters*, 2 vols. (1995). vol. 4 of *Dictionary of British art*
WW	*Who's who* (1849–)
WWBMP	M. Stenton and S. Lees, eds., *Who's who of British members of parliament*, 4 vols. (1976–81)
WWW	*Who was who* (1929–)

Meyrick, Edward (1854–1938), entomologist, was born at Ramsbury, Wiltshire, on 24 November 1854, the eldest son of the Revd Edward Meyrick and his wife, Mary. He was educated at Marlborough College and he went on to read classics at Trinity College, Cambridge, graduating in 1877. He spent the first ten years of his working life teaching classics in Australia and New Zealand, dividing his time between the King's School, Parramatta, Sydney, and the cathedral grammar school, Christchurch. In 1887 he returned to Marlborough, where he taught classics until his retirement in 1914. In 1892 he married Antonia, daughter of Heinrich Eckhard of the Rhenish palatinate. The couple had three sons and two daughters.

Meyrick is justly considered the father of modern Microlepidoptera systematics—the classification and nomenclature of the smaller moths—but the influences that drew him to collect and study these insects are unclear. Before his departure for the Antipodes in 1877 he had published only four brief notes on British species, but in Australia and later in New Zealand he began assiduously to collect specimens and information. With his first taxonomic paper, on new species and genera of Microlepidoptera from Australia, he embarked in 1879 on a course of scientific publication that lasted until his death in 1938. In his first twenty years of research he concentrated on the Australasian fauna, but by 1900 had extended his scope to cover the Microlepidoptera of the world, especially of the tropics.

Meyrick was one of the world's most prolific entomological authors, publishing at least 439 books and papers. To cope with a proportion of this vast output he founded his own one-author journal, *Exotic Microlepidoptera*, in 1912. He formally described probably more than 20,000 species of Lepidoptera new to science, more than 14,000 of them Microlepidoptera. Meyrick applied his knowledge and love of the classics to scientific nomenclature, and the results may be seen in the elegant and imaginative scientific names, rarely duplicated, that he proposed for new taxa. His ideas on the higher classification of the Lepidoptera as a whole were encapsulated in *A Handbook of British Lepidoptera* (1895), a revised edition of which appeared in 1928, and his paper in *The Zoologist* in 1898. This copious output increased with Meyrick's retirement from teaching and continued up to the day of his death. His personal collection comprised some 100,000 specimens, predominantly type-material; he bequeathed it to the British Museum (Natural History), London, in 1939, along with his ledgers and notebooks. His legacy was, however, more than just an enormous collection and innumerable descriptions of new species and genera.

J. F. G. Clarke gives a detailed appraisal of Meyrick's work, reserving severe criticism for his ideas of classification and his catholic view of genera. He quotes a typically robust letter from Meyrick castigating the young American entomologist August Busck for unnecessary splitting of genera: 'you wish to separate them on account of differences; I wish to unite them on account of resemblances … every beginner and every specialist (i.e., everyone of narrow views) is on your side … My views are wider and I know I am right'. It is easy, from such extracts, to label Meyrick as a difficult and bombastic man, but to his many correspondents Meyrick was prompt, courteous, conscientious, and generous, with a keen but never malicious sense of humour. Busck wrote a fulsome obituary of Meyrick. Clarke's dismissal of Meyrick's abilities as a systematist has been challenged by G. S. Robinson.

Meyrick had a clear understanding of the evolutionary implications of classification. His undoubted aim was a phylogenetic classification in the modern sense of the term. That he did not achieve it fully may be attributed to three factors. First, he perhaps never realized the danger of plesiomorphic similarity. This was a trap into which he was drawn repeatedly, especially in his early work, grouping taxa that shared primitive rather than derived characteristics (symplesiomorphy) in contravention of modern cladistic theory. Second, he gave disproportionate weight to one particular character-set, that provided by wing venation, to the virtual exclusion of all others. Third, he actually saw very little of the detailed structure of the insects on which he worked. His aid to magnification, a hand-lens, was woefully inadequate. Nevertheless, he had a remarkable aptitude for species recognition and incredible powers of recall, offering a one-man identification service covering some 70,000 species. Meyrick made errors, but it is an unending source of wonder to entomologists at the end of the twentieth century that most of his taxonomic opinions have survived the test of time and modern techniques. He was very nearly a cladist—'unite them on account of resemblances' has a splendid ring, even though the heresy of symplesiomorphy was never wholly expunged. He has left an extraordinary legacy. His synthesis of generic affinities and family groups among the smaller moths largely stands today.

Elected FRS in 1904, Meyrick was awarded the Captain Scott memorial medal of the South African Biological Society in 1927 for his contributions to South African entomology. He died at the Savernake Hospital, Marlborough, on 31 March 1938.   GADEN S. ROBINSON

Sources A. Busck, 'Edward Meyrick, FRS, 1854–1938', *Proceedings of the Entomological Society of Washington*, 40 (1938), 177–9 · J. F. G. Clarke, *Catalogue of the type specimens of Microlepidoptera in the British Museum (Natural History), described by Edward Meyrick*, 1 (1955) · J. S. Dugdale, *Fauna of New Zealand*, 14 (1988), 1–262 [biographical notes, Australasian bibliography] · T. B. Fletcher, 'Edward Meyrick', *Entomologist's Record*, 50 (1938), 49–51 · T. B. Fletcher and A. J. T. Janse, 'List of publications by the late Edward Meyrick', *The moths of South Africa*, ed. A. J. T. Janse, 4/1 (1942) · A. W. Hill, *Obits. FRS*, 2 (1936–8), 531–48 · A. J. T. Janse, 'Edward Meyrick, BA, FRS, FRES, FZS', *Journal of the Entomological Society of Southern Africa*, 1 (1939), 151–5 · G. S. Robinson, 'Edward Meyrick: an unpublished essay on phylogeny', *Journal of Natural History*, 20 (1986), 359–67 · W. H. T. Tams, 'Edward Meyrick, BA, FRS', *The Entomologist*, 71 (1938), 121–2 · L. Vári and J. F. G. Clarke, 'Additions to the E. Meyrick bibliography', *Exotic Microlepidoptera*, ed. E. Meyrick, 1 (1969), 1–5 · *CGPLA Eng. & Wales* (1938)

Archives NHM, drawings and papers | Oxf. U. Mus. NH, letters and postcards to Sir E. B. Poulton and MS article; letters to Arthur Sidgwick

Likenesses W. Stoneman, photograph, 1921, NPG · portrait, repro. in Clarke, *Catalogue of the type specimens of Microlepidoptera* ·

portrait, repro. in Fletcher, 'Edward Meyrick' · portrait, repro. in Hill, *Obits. FRS*

Wealth at death £44,543 0s. 9d.: probate, 13 May 1938, *CGPLA Eng. & Wales*

Meyrick, Frederick (1827–1906), Church of England clergyman and author, was born at Ramsbury, Wiltshire, on 28 January 1827, the youngest son of Edward Graves Meyrick (*c*.1790–1839), vicar of Ramsbury, and his wife, Myra, *née* Howard. He claimed descent from the ancient family of Meyricks of Bodorgan, Anglesey, through Rowland Merrick (or Meyrick), bishop of Bangor (1559–66). Educated first at Ramsbury School, he won a scholarship at Trinity College, Oxford, where he matriculated on 12 June 1843, graduating BA in 1847 and proceeding to an MA in 1850. Elected fellow of Trinity in 1847, two years later he was president of the undergraduate debating society, the Oxford Union. Following his ordination in 1850 he became tutor, dean, and bursar of Trinity College, and was select preacher for the University of Oxford for 1855–6, 1865–6, and 1875–6. He was also appointed a preacher at the Chapel Royal, Whitehall, in 1856–7.

During 1849–50, and again in 1851, Meyrick travelled on the continent with private pupils, closely observing ecclesiastical affairs. One result was the publication of his first book, *The Practical Working of the Church of Spain* (1851). Another was the establishment in 1853 of the Anglo-Continental Society (of which he remained secretary until 1898) to promote the principles of the English church on the continent through the publication of literature and to help forward the internal reformation of national churches.

In 1859 Meyrick married Marion S. Danvers who, with their two sons and five daughters, survived him. He was also appointed an inspector of schools in 1859 and resigned his fellowship in the following year. During the next decade he made about 3000 visits to schools and parsonages in the course of his work. In 1868 he was instituted to the rectory of Blickling with Erpingham, Norfolk, where he spent the rest of his life. From 1868 until 1885 he served the bishop of Lincoln, Christopher Wordsworth, as examining chaplain, and in 1869 became a non-resident canon of Lincoln.

Meyrick's interest in continental church affairs was rekindled by the controversy surrounding the First Vatican Council in 1869–70. He visited the liberal Catholic and anti-infallibilist Ignaz von Döllinger at the time of his excommunication in 1871, and helped to organize the Bonn conferences of 1874 and 1875 on the reunion of churches where Anglicans met leaders of the schismatic Old Catholics and representatives of the Orthodox churches. He was the initiator and editor of the *Foreign Church Chronicle and Review* (1877–99), which publicized the views of the Anglo-Continental Society and monitored the progress of the Old Catholics. During 1886–7 he served as principal of Codrington College, a theological training institution in Barbados. In 1892 and 1894 he accompanied the archbishop of Dublin, Lord Plunket, on visits to Spain for the aid of the reformed church; when protests arose over Plunket's consecration of Juan Cabrera as bishop in the

Frederick Meyrick (1827–1906), by unknown photographer

latter year, he drew up an address in support of the archbishop's action. At the close of his life, in 1904–5, he joined with Henry Wace, the evangelical dean of Canterbury, in issuing an appeal to churchmen to refrain from promulgating any practices or doctrines which were not generally accepted during the first few centuries of the church.

Meyrick was an old-fashioned high-churchman, adhering firmly to the authority of scripture, to the English prayer book, and to the English Reformation, and with a deep mistrust of both Roman Catholicism and ritualism. A wide traveller, an accomplished linguist, and a clever disputant, his ecclesiastical advancement was hindered by both his delicate health and his controversial zeal. He was the author of more than forty books and pamphlets, as well as numerous articles in dictionaries and periodicals, many of them of a polemical nature and displaying his close interest in a broad range of theological topics. However, his most significant contribution to theological literature was probably as a translator into Latin and other languages of the works of Andrewes, Cosin, and other standard English divines. He died at Blickling, Norfolk, on 3 January 1906, where a window to his memory was installed in the parish church.   STEPHEN GREGORY

Sources F. Meyrick, *Memories of life at Oxford* (1905) · Crockford (1905) · *The Guardian* (10 Jan 1906) · Foster, *Alum. Oxon.* · *Men and women of the time* (1899) · A. T. C. Pratt, ed., *People of the period: being a collection of the biographies of upwards of six thousand living celebrities*, 2 (1897) · *The Times* (4 Jan 1906) · *The Times* (17 Jan 1906) · J. Foster,

Oxford men and their colleges (1893) • M. Pawley and B. C. Pawley, *Rome and Canterbury through four centuries: a study of the relations between the church of Rome and the Anglican churches, 1530–1973*, 2nd edn (1981) • *DNB*
Archives LPL, corresp. relating to Anglo-Continental Society | BL, corresp. with W. E. Gladstone, Add. MS 44251
Likenesses Art Repro. Co., photogravure, NPG • photograph, NPG [*see illus.*]
Wealth at death £21,156 11s. 9d.: resworn probate, 26 Feb 1906, *CGPLA Eng. & Wales*

Meyrick, Sir Gelly (*c.*1556–1601), conspirator, was the eldest son of Rowland *Meyrick (1504/5–1566), bishop of Bangor. Although descended from an ancient family of north Wales and ultimately bishop there, Gelly's father had made his career in south Wales, where he had married Katherine (*d.* 1598), second daughter of Owen Barrett of Gelliswic, Pembrokeshire. Meyrick was almost certainly given the unusual forename of Gelly in token of his maternal grandfather's estate of Gelliswic. After his father's death on 24 January 1566 Meyrick and his three younger brothers and two sisters grew up in Pembrokeshire. According to a story later related by Sir Anthony Ashley, who had by then become his enemy, Meyrick was left impoverished by his father's death, when he was about nine years old, and he was initially taken into service as an act of charity by George Devereux of Lamphey, Pembrokeshire, uncle to Robert Devereux, second earl of Essex. However, Ashley's account of Meyrick's catching Devereux's attention as a boy 'playing at whippergundy (a Welsh play) in a poor red pair of hose' (*Salisbury MSS*, 13.584) is probably a malicious invention. Both the Meyrick and Barrett families had already become strongly associated with the Devereux family, who dominated south Wales. Meyrick's father had been an ally of Essex's great-grandfather in the early 1550s and Meyrick's uncle Edmund Meyrick served as chaplain to both Essex's father and to Essex himself.

Meyrick became a close attendant upon Essex in October 1579, when the earl was a student at Cambridge. For the next two years, while Essex remained at university, Meyrick was chiefly responsible for the hiring and keeping of horses for the earl. In December 1583, when he was styled as a gentleman of Hasguard, Pembrokeshire, Meyrick was granted a lion's head crest for his family coat of arms. This grant may have been connected to his marriage about this time to Margaret, daughter of Ieuan Lewis and widow of John Gwyn. The match brought him two stepsons and control of two important estates in Radnorshire, Gladestry and Builth. When Essex joined the earl of Leicester's expedition to the Low Countries in 1585–6 Meyrick organized supplies for the household which accompanied Essex to war. Once Essex came of age, in November 1586, Meyrick became increasingly involved in the management of his estates and financial affairs. He was regularly named in grants and property transactions for Essex from 1588. Although named as comptroller of the earl's household in a lawsuit of 1593, Essex's accounts for 1592–3 describe Meyrick as steward of the earl's household and receiver-general of his rents and revenues.

Meyrick's influence among Essex's inner circle seems to have grown considerably in the mid-1590s, especially after Essex secured advancement into royal service for Robert Wright and Thomas Smith. His loyalty and ability to mobilize support among the Welsh gentry gave him a special role in expanding Essex's power base in Wales. Meyrick helped to ensure that Essex's followers had a stranglehold over local government and parliamentary representation in south Wales. He was himself MP for Carmarthen Boroughs in 1589 and knight of the shire for Pembrokeshire in 1597. The marriage of his daughter Margaret to John Vaughan of Golden Grove, Carmarthenshire, in 1598–9 was typical of the way that Meyrick's efforts served both his master and his own family. Although local rivals complained about the rapacity and monopolistic tendencies of 'Lord Meryke' and his associates, Essex supported him to the hilt. In Radnorshire, which lay adjacent to his own lands in Herefordshire, Essex helped Meyrick to build upon the lands and local power which he had gained by his marriage through a series of royal grants. An arrangement with the earl of Shrewsbury and the queen allowed Meyrick to seat himself at nearby Wigmore Castle. In 1598 Essex even succeeded in having him appointed as a deputy lieutenant for Radnorshire over the strident objections of the earl of Pembroke, lord president of Wales. Meyrick also became *custos rotulorum* for the county by 1599. Although Essex failed to get him appointed receiver for Cheshire and north Wales (because the holder of the office recovered from his sickness), Meyrick cast an imposing shadow across much of Wales during the late 1590s.

Meyrick also proved a loyal and aggressive servant of Essex in other spheres. Whenever Essex went to war Meyrick accompanied him and helped to organize supplies, pay, and the disposal of prizes. This exposed Meyrick to sickness when Essex went to Normandy in 1591, but such service brought its reward when Meyrick was knighted after the capture of Cadiz in June 1596. Returning to England at the end of July he became involved in a bitter dispute with Sir Anthony Ashley about prize goods. Meyrick's secret haul included hides shared with his brother Francis (an army officer) and pillars for constructing his own tomb. In 1597 Meyrick's fierce partisanship for Essex on the Azores expedition prompted him to criticize Sir Walter Ralegh and (unsuccessfully) demand his court martial. Two years later he accompanied Essex on his disastrous expedition to Ireland, which entrenched in him (as with many other followers of the earl) a deep sense of alienation from the court. Returning to England before his master, like Henry Cuffe, Meyrick viewed the subsequent arrest and detention of Essex with dismay and joined with certain other Essexians such as the earl of Southampton, Sir Charles Danvers, and Cuffe to plot his master's escape and vindication. In contrast to those friends and servants of Essex who argued that the earl could only recover his fortunes by placating the queen, Meyrick believed that Essex's plight required resolute action. This belief was perhaps encouraged by his awareness of the crippling burden of Essex's debts, in which he was himself deeply enmeshed by numerous deeds and bonds.

By the end of 1600, following months of dilatory plotting, Meyrick and his associates seem to have begun rallying Welsh support for decisive action. However, Meyrick's plans were poorly co-ordinated with those of Southampton's circle and were entirely pre-empted by the panic of Saturday, 7 February 1601, which saw Essex commit himself to entering London on the following day. In company with a group of gentlemen supporters of Essex, Meyrick spent the Saturday afternoon at the Globe Theatre watching a performance of Shakespeare's *Richard II*, which had apparently been requested by Sir Charles Percy. It was subsequently alleged by the authorities that Meyrick himself was responsible for paying the players 40 shillings for reprising this play 'so old & so long out of use' (PRO, SP 12/278/85), even though the surviving evidence does not prove the claim. Meyrick did not join the march into the City on the next morning, but was ordered to hold Essex House as a place of potential retreat, a precaution which soon proved all too necessary. Following Essex's surrender Meyrick was imprisoned in Newgate, initially in heavy irons. This regime was moderated on 17 February, three days before he was moved to the Tower. On 5 March he was tried at Westminster Hall and charged with rebellion on the grounds that he had fortified Essex House against the queen's forces, provided munitions for the earl's men, and helped to arrange the performance of the play. It was also alleged that Meyrick had extorted protection money from recusants in Wales. Unlike Cuffe he made little effort to defend himself: 'I must die and not unwillingly; for the tree being fallen, the branches must not stand' (*State trials*, 1.1449).

Meyrick was hanged, drawn, and quartered at Tyburn on 13 March 1601; he was allowed to die by strangulation. Cuffe died with him. Resolute to the end, he made only a short speech at the gallows, clearing Lord Mountjoy of complicity in his actions. Litigation over Meyrick's estate, and how much he had concealed from the crown's agents, continued for many years after his death, but reached no satisfactory conclusion. His son Rowland and daughter Margaret Vaughan were restored in blood and name in May 1606.   PAUL E. J. HAMMER

Sources Longleat House, Wiltshire, Devereux MSS · Cecil MSS, Hatfield House, Hertfordshire · PRO, SP 12; SP 15 · PRO, C 66, C 67, C 78 · PRO, E 134, E 178 · *Calendar of the manuscripts of the most hon. the marquis of Salisbury*, 24 vols., HMC, 9 (1883–1976) · PRO, PROB 11/114, sig. 83; PROB 11/127, sig. 51 · *State trials*, vol. 1 · F. Jones, 'Gelliswick and its families', *Archaeologia Cambrensis*, 129 (1980), 133–50 · F. Jones, 'The Vaughans of Golden Grove', *Transactions of the Honourable Society of Cymmrodorion* (1963), 96–145 · W. Camden, *The history of the most renowned and victorious Princess Elizabeth*, 4th edn (1688) · *DWB* · HoP, *Commons, 1558–1603* · Wood, *Ath. Oxon.*, new edn · R. Fenton and F. Fenton, *A historical tour through Pembrokeshire*, 2nd edn (1903) · *Heraldic visitations of Wales and part of the marches … by Lewys Dwnn*, ed. S. R. Meyrick, 2 vols. (1846)
Archives Longleat House, Wiltshire, Devereux MSS 1–3
Wealth at death est. several thousand pounds

Meyrick, Sir George Eliott Tapps-Gervis-, third baronet (1827–1896), landowner and developer, was born at Dover on 1 September 1827, the only son among the four children of Sir George William Tapps-Gervis, second baronet (1795–1842), and Clara, daughter of Augustus Eliott Fuller, landowner, of Rosehill, Hurst Green, Sussex. The third baronet adopted the name Meyrick in 1876 in compliance with the will of Owen Fuller Meyrick, a relative of his mother, from whom he inherited the 17,000 acre estate of Bodorgan, Anglesey.

The lands in Hampshire on which Bournemouth was to be built were inherited by Sir George Ivison Tapps (1753–1835), the first baronet (created 1792). As lord of the manor of Christchurch, he was one of the instigators and principal beneficiaries of the 1802 Christchurch Enclosure Act. Settlement at Bournemouth started with the purchase from him in 1810 of a tract of seaside land by Captain Lewis Tregonwell, who built a house for himself on the west bank of the Bourne Stream. The development of a resort on Sir George's estate on the opposite bank was put in hand in 1834, when he obtained a loan of £40,000 from the earl of Arran and John Augustus Fuller, into whose family his son had married, on the mortgage of the Tapps-Gervis estate at Hinton Admiral near Christchurch.

The first baronet died in 1835 and the estate passed to his son, Sir George William Tapps-Gervis, member of parliament for New Romney (1826–32) and Christchurch (1832–7), who had assumed the surname Gervis in addition to his patronymic. Building got under way in 1837, following the laying out of the 108 acre East Cliff estate as a prestigious neighbourhood of large detached villas. It was interrupted by the second baronet's death in 1842, since his successor was a minor and it was necessary to secure a private act of 1846 to circumvent encumbering entails on the estate. Building at East Cliff proceeded slowly in the 1840s and 1850s, but accelerated in the 1860s. Other parts of the Meyrick estate were developed from the 1870s.

The third baronet, Sir George Eliott Tapps-Gervis-Meyrick, was educated at Christ Church, Oxford, from 1846 to 1849. In the latter year he married Fanny (*d.* 1892), daughter of Christopher Harland of Ashbourne, Derbyshire, and they had three daughters and one son. He subsequently played an important role in fostering the growth of the fledgeling resort. He was one of the sponsors of the Bournemouth Improvement Act of 1856, which established an improvement commission, the town's first local government authority. As lord of the manor he had a permanent place on the board of commissioners, though he rarely attended, and another place was reserved for his agent; from 1847 to 1870, this was the well-known architect Decimus Burton.

Sir George was also closely associated with the building of Bournemouth's pier in 1861, a vital amenity for a nineteenth-century seaside resort. Initially he opposed the building of the 'direct line' railway connection because of its intrusion through his holdings. However, he was persuaded to change his mind by the proprietor of the Royal Bath Hotel, Sir Merton Russell Cotes, who acted as a go-between for those at Hinton Admiral and the local tradesmen, in view of the benefits to the resort from the drastic cut in travelling time to London.

Under the terms of the Christchurch Enclosure Act, certain areas were set aside as commons under the trusteeship of the lord of the manor. The transformation of these commons into local authority parks was a contentious local issue that soured relations between Sir George and the townsfolk. Bournemouth's incorporation as a borough in 1890 settled the matter in the townsfolk's favour. Thereupon Sir George co-operated fully, and the first of the new parks, which opened in 1894, was named Meyrick Park in his honour.

In politics Sir George was a Conservative, being president of the Bournemouth and Christchurch Constitutional Conservative Club, and his London club was the Conservative Club. He divided his time between his lands in Hampshire, Sussex, and his large estate in north Wales. In 1878 he was high sheriff of Anglesey. He was also a Hampshire magistrate and patron of two livings. He died at Hinton Admiral on 7 March 1896 and was buried there four days later. He was succeeded by his son and heir, Sir George Augustus Eliott Tapps-Gervis-Meyrick (1855–1928), fourth baronet. RICHARD ROBERTS

Sources R. Roberts, 'Leasehold estates and municipal enterprise: landowners, local government and the development of Bournemouth, 1850 to 1914', *Patricians, power and politics in nineteenth century towns*, ed. D. Cannadine (1982), 175–218 • D. S. Young, *The story of Bournemouth* (1957) • J. Soane, 'The significance of the development of Bournemouth, 1840–1940', PhD diss., University of Surrey, 1977 • C. H. Mate and C. Riddle, *Bournemouth, 1810–1910* (1910) • *Bournemouth Visitors' Directory* (11 March 1896) [obituary] • 'The Meyrick estate', *Bournemouth Times* (14 May 1921) • Boase, *Mod. Eng. biog.* • Foster, *Alum. Oxon.* • Walford, *County families* (1920)
Archives Meyrick estate office, Hinton Admiral, Hampshire, Meyrick estate MSS
Wealth at death £19,755 7s. 1d.: probate, 31 March 1896, CGPLA Eng. & Wales

Meyrick, John (1537/8–1599), bishop of Sodor and Man, was the illegitimate son of Owen ap Hugh ap Meyrick of Bodorgan, Anglesey, and Gwenllian, daughter of Evan of Penrhyndeudraeth, Merioneth. The Meyricks prospered under the Tudors, and in Gwynedd came to be second in influence only to the Bulkeleys; Roland Meyrick, bishop of Bangor, was also a scion of this family. John had two half-brothers, William (*d.* 1605), who became chancellor of the diocese of Bangor, and Maurice (1563–1640), who was registrar of Oxford University from 1600 to 1608.

In 1550, at the age of twelve, John Meyrick became a scholar at Winchester College, whose register lists him as hailing from Mold. He took up a scholarship at New College, Oxford, where he graduated BA on 12 December 1558 and MA on 26 June 1562, serving as junior proctor in 1565. He was a fellow of the college from 1557 to 1572. Between 1570 and 1574 he held the college living of Hornchurch. In 1575 he was nominated by Henry Stanley, fourth earl of Derby, to the bishopric of Sodor and Man, in the province of York, in succession to John Salesbury. As a result of the vacancy caused by Grindal's translation from York, it proved necessary to obtain the queen's assent twice, on 5 November 1575 (when she made it clear that in accepting Meyrick's elevation she was not countenancing any diminution of her own authority in the church) and again on 8 April 1576; it was as the new archbishop of Canterbury that on 15 April 1576 Grindal consecrated Meyrick at Lambeth.

In the Isle of Man the bishops were powerful figures and sat on the island's council. In 1580 Meyrick presided over the earliest court session of the bishop's barony for which records are extant. On 9 November 1585 he sent some impressions of the island to William Camden, who soon afterwards published extracts from them in his *Britannia*. These were in part a response to claims made in Raphael Holinshed's *Chronicles of England* that Man was populated by strange species, and that its people, little removed from savagery, were ruthlessly milked by their lord, the bishop's patron, Henry, earl of Derby. Meyrick was most anxious to dispute these charges. The island, he protested, was 'very fortunate in its expenses … for the earl expends the greater part of his yearly rent in defraying them'; the people, or at least the wealthier farmers, resembled those of Lancashire, and were 'extremely religious' and 'most readily conform without a single exception to the formularies of the Church of England' (Oliver, 95, 98).

These last remarks may well be connected with Meyrick's visit to Anglesey two or three years earlier, when he had found several of his friends in prison, possibly the victims of the anxieties of the authorities—fuelled by tension with Spain—concerning recusancy and other manifestations of disloyalty. These often focused on remote and vulnerable areas such as Anglesey—and the Isle of Man. Despite Bishop Meyrick's testimony as to the warmth of Manx protestant sentiment, it was still found necessary in 1594 for juries to be empanelled to deal with several symptoms of religious insufficiency, notably among 'all such as carry bells or banners before the dead or pray upon the graves of the dead' (Moore, 1.352). Meyrick often returned to his native Anglesey, and it was from there that on 4 April 1590 he wrote to Lord Burghley, giving a vivid description of the poverty which, thanks to loans made to imprisoned friends and to the depredations of the tax assessors, it was now his lot to endure: his income from the bishopric of £90 per annum was quite inadequate, and his own estates were in ruin. 'I have neither house nor home here … but three travelling nags to carry me to and from the waterside', where he lay, 'sick and waiting for passage' back to his duties on the isle (Strype, 4.18). John Meyrick died on 7 November 1599. STEPHEN WRIGHT

Sources A. W. Moore, *A history of the Isle of Man*, 1 (1900); repr. (1992) • T. F. Kirby, *Winchester scholars: a list of the wardens, fellows, and scholars of … Winchester College* (1888) • J. Strype, *Annals of the Reformation and establishment of religion … during Queen Elizabeth's happy reign*, new edn, 4 (1724), 18–19 [correct version of letter to Burghley in Lansdowne MS 63, fol. 81] • J. R. Oliver, ed., *Monumenta de Insula Manniae, or, A collection of national documents relating to the Isle of Man*, 1, Manx Society, 4 (1860), 87–99 [checked against MS Cotton Julius F10, fols. 124–5] • D. Sylvester, *A history of Gwynedd* (1983), 73, 79 • G. Williams, *Recovery, reorientation and reformation: Wales, c.1415–1642*, History of Wales, 3 (1987) • Bishop Burnett, BL, Lansdowne MS 982, fols. 274–5 [relies chiefly on Wood] • B. Coward, *The Stanleys, lords Stanley and earls of Derby, 1385–1672: the origins, wealth and power of a landowning family*, Chetham Society, 3rd ser., 30 (1983) • Wood, *Ath. Oxon.* • *Fasti Angl.* (Hardy)

Archives BL, letter to Burghley, Lansdowne MS 63, fol. 81 · BL, impression of Isle of Man sent to William Camden, Cotton Julius F10, fols. 124–5

Meyrick, Sir John (*c*.1559–1638/9), diplomat and merchant, was the second son of William Meyrick of London. William Meyrick was an original member of the Muscovy Company, acting as its London agent from 1560 to 1563, later serving as the chief agent in Russia for a period after 1575. John Meyrick's youth was spent at the factory of English merchants in Moscow. In 1584 he was appointed the company's agent in Yaroslavl, before succeeding Robert Peacock as the company's chief agent in Russia in 1587 or 1588. It is likely that about this time Meyrick married Frances Cherry, the daughter of Francis Cherry and his first wife, Margaret.

With the company's position in Russia contingent upon the good will of the tsar, Meyrick found himself increasingly embroiled in diplomatic affairs. In 1595 Tsar Feodor I heard reports from the papal legate in his demesne that England was deliberately aiding the Turks in their struggle against other Christian princes. Meyrick was summoned to answer these charges and though he replied that such matters did not pertain to merchants, the tsar told him to relay his concerns to Queen Elizabeth. However, the queen was loath to reply and so Lord Burghley instructed Meyrick to persuade the tsar that the reports of the legate were unfounded. The tsar remained unconvinced and in 1597 prohibited all foreign merchants from entering his dominions beyond the waterside; only Meyrick was exempted from this decree.

Back in England in 1600, Meyrick became one of the original subscribers to the East India Company. But with the rise to the throne of Boris Godunov, an ambassador was dispatched to England to negotiate the possibility of a marriage between the tsar's son and a daughter of the earl of Derby. While these negotiations came to nought because of the difference in age between the two children, Meyrick and his father-in-law, Francis Cherry, wrote to Sir Robert Cecil advising him to keep the issue of marriage open by dispatching an embassy which would present a number of unsuitable matches to the tsar. They feared that were no offer made, the company's privileged commercial position would be placed in jeopardy. To this end, Meyrick himself was sent to Moscow in early 1602.

According to Meyrick's subsequent account of the negotiations, he met the tsar on the evening of 12 February 1602, presenting him with a letter from the queen expressing her desire for a marriage alliance and suggesting again the daughter of the earl of Derby, whom she described as being of royal blood and possessing more land than any other of her subjects. Meyrick, though, argued against such a union on the basis of age and presented the tsar with a chart explaining the pedigree of the English royal family. The meeting concluded amicably with the tsar's cursing the machinations of the pope to procure the queen's death. Nevertheless, Meyrick was detained in Moscow while the tsar negotiated a marriage alliance between his daughter and the brother of the king of Denmark. On 22 June Meyrick was granted a final audience with the tsar and entrusted with the sons of four gentlemen who were to be educated in England. He left Moscow on 24 July and was in England two months later, at which point he promptly wrote to Cecil arguing that the queen should write to the tsar announcing that she had discovered a girl of eleven or twelve years old of noble descent who would make a perfect match for the tsar's son.

Meyrick was soon back in Russia and in 1603 forwarded a Russian Bible and a copy of the *Canones patrum Muscov.* as a gift to the Bodleian Library in Oxford. In the confusion in Moscow after the death of Boris Godunov in 1605, an impostor named Dmitry seized the throne; nevertheless, Meyrick was able to secure protection for English commerce in the region from him. When Basil Shuysky became tsar the subsequent year, Meyrick was again successful in effecting a renewal of these privileges. However, with the political landscape turbulent, he was often forced to leave Moscow and in late 1606 he returned to England to render a report of the situation.

In 1610 Meyrick became a shareholder in Henry Hudson's plan to discover a north-west passage to China and Japan. In June 1614 he was again appointed ambassador to the tsar's court and instructed to use his influence to reduce the anarchy prevailing in the Russian government. On 13 June, before his departure, he was knighted by James I at Greenwich. Travelling with a large retinue and a substantial sum of money to be advanced to the tsar and his ministers if need be, Meyrick's mission proved a success. Mikhail Romanov was able to consolidate his position as tsar and Meyrick embarked on negotiations to conclude the protracted war between Russia and Sweden. On 27 February 1617 he helped secure the peace of Stolbovo between the two countries, which bore his signature as one of the contracting parties, and in November that year he returned to England with an ambassador from the tsar, bearing an array of lavish gifts for the king, including white hawks and live sables. In June 1620 he was sent back to Russia to negotiate a commercial treaty with three other ambassadors; three years later, these negotiations bore fruit and Meyrick became one of the signatories to the first commercial agreement between the two nations. He was still in Moscow in 1628, but had then become governor of the Muscovy Company. In 1633 he invested £256 in a voyage to Greenland, though at his death this had yet to see any return. In his will, dated 20 October and 30 December 1638, he asked to be buried in the parish church of St Andrew Undershaft in London and bequeathed £100 to the Merchant Taylors' Company, with a further £300 to be lent to scholars in the company's school. He left no children, and an estate worth over £6200 was divided between nieces, nephews, godchildren, and other friends and relatives. He died soon afterwards, the will being proved on 1 February 1639.

RICHARD RAISWELL

Sources S. R. Meyrick, 'Report of Sir J. Merick's mission to Moscow', *GM*, 1st ser., 94/2 (1824), 226–9 · W. D. Macray, *Annals of the Bodleian Library, Oxford*, 2nd edn (1890) · T. S. Willan, *The early history of*

the *Russia Company, 1553–1603* (1956) · *Collectanea Topographica et Genealogica*, 3 (1836), 158–9 · *APC, 1613–14, 1616–17, 1619–25, 1628–9* · *CSP for., 1588* · *CSP col.*, vol. 2, *1573–1616* · *CSP dom., 1611–23; 1631–3* · *DNB* · T. S. Willan, *The Muscovy merchants of 1555* (1953) · will, PRO, PROB 11/179, fols. 267–9
Archives BL, MS Cotton Nero B. viii
Wealth at death £6200 legacies: will, PRO, PROB 11/179, fols. 267–9

Meyrick [Merrick], **Sir John** (c.1600–1659), parliamentarian army officer, was the fifth son of Sir Francis Meyrick of Fleet (d. 1603) in the parish of Monkton, Pembrokeshire, and his wife, Anne Laugharne, daughter of Francis Laugharne of St Bride's in the same county. His grandfather was Rowland *Meyrick, bishop of Bangor. His father served under the second earl of Essex, and his uncle, Sir Gelly *Meyrick, was steward of Essex's Welsh lands and was executed for complicity in Essex's rebellion in 1601. Through his mother Meyrick was a kinsman of the parliamentarian commander in South Wales, Rowland *Laugharne, and when he came to make his will in 1653 Meyrick named among its overseers both Laugharne and another kinsman, the royalist commander Richard *Vaughan, earl of Carbery, whom Laugharne had defeated.

John Meyrick matriculated at Christ's College, Cambridge, in April 1615, before emulating his father and uncle by pursuing a military career. He accompanied his patron, the third earl of Essex, to Flanders in 1620, served as a lieutenant in the Palatinate, and was recommended for a captaincy in Mansfeld's United Provinces expedition of 1624. He was probably knighted upon his return from the expedition against Spain in 1625. Having been commissioned in Morgan's regiment in Swedish service in 1630, he was wounded at Maestricht on 17 August 1632. He returned to England, and became financially engaged as an adventurer to Greenland during the 1630s, in which capacity he prosecuted two London merchants in the court of king's bench. His first wife was Alice (d. after 1632), daughter of Sir Edward Fitton, baronet of Gawsworth, Cheshire, and his wife, Anne, daughter of James Barret of south Wales. Their son, Essex Meyrick, was still aged under twenty-one in 1653.

Sir John Meyrick's service under Essex, who was also Staffordshire's lord lieutenant, facilitated Meyrick's election to the Short Parliament for Newcastle under Lyme, Staffordshire. Between June and October 1640 he commanded a regiment in the second bishops' war, and despite re-election to the Long Parliament on 13 October he remained occupied with military duties until spring 1641.

Meyrick was among Staffordshire's three parliamentarian MPs at the outbreak of civil war; his military experience and Essex's patronage elevated him to sergeant-major-general of parliament's main field army. He was also a colonel of foot, lord president of the council of war, and from 4 July 1642 a member of the committee of safety. He engaged in equipping the army, to which he made a significant financial contribution himself. His regiment of London greycoats forced the surrender of Portsmouth on 7 September, but was absent at Worcester during the battle of Edgehill. During the king's march on London in

November Meyrick commanded 5000 men facing the royalist vanguard on the road between Brentford and Hammersmith. When Meyrick brought orders for Hampden's regiment to withdraw, his friend Bulstrode Whitelocke, present among them, suggested to him there was treachery in the high command. As a result of this exchange, on 17 November the House of Commons had to discountenance rumours that Meyrick had slandered them.

By 1643 Meyrick's regiment was serving in the west and some of its companies were among defeated parliamentarians at Launceston in Cornwall on 25 April. Clarendon noted that during that spring Meyrick was replaced as sergeant-major-general by Sir Philip Skippon 'without the cheerful concurrence of the earl of Essex; though Sir John Merrick, who had executed that place by his lordship's choice from the beginning, was preferred to be general of the ordnance' (Clarendon, 7.26). Maintaining close relations with Essex, Meyrick subsequently served at the relief of Gloucester and first battle of Newbury. Some time after December 1643 he married his second wife, Jane (d. 1660), widow of Sir Peter Wyche, ambassador at Constantinople, and daughter of William Meredith of Wrexham, Denbighshire.

On 10 June 1644 Meyrick headed the new committee for associating the counties of Pembroke, Carmarthen, and Cardigan. He participated in Essex's disastrous southwestern campaign, and on 1 September 1644 accompanied him during his escape to Plymouth on a fishing boat. That December he attended the earl's late-night conference at Essex House to discuss proceedings against Cromwell: a meeting attended by the Scottish commissioners and by Denzil Holles, Sir Philip Stapleton, Meyrick, and 'others of [Essex's] speciall & most intimate friends' (*Diary of Bulstrode Whitelocke*, 161).

Surrendering his commissions upon the self-denying ordinance, Meyrick was occasionally required to attend the committee of both kingdoms. In September 1646 he carried the gorget on the pall's left side during Essex's public funeral. On 21 November the House of Commons ordered £1500 be paid to Meyrick to settle part of his pay arrears. Named on the assessments committees for Staffordshire and Pembrokeshire during 1647 and 1648, he was also included on Richard Baxter's list of commanders who were 'moderate Episcopal conformants', but 'Meyrick was rather a Presbyterian with a leaning toward Independency' (Keeler, *Long Parliament*, 273).

On 6 December 1648 Meyrick was secluded from parliament by Pride's Purge, and despite offers of parole from Fairfax, he was not released from confinement until 20 December. He was not readmitted to parliament and henceforth took no prominent part in public affairs. He died in retirement in Pembrokeshire in 1659.

ANDREW J. HOPPER

Sources Keeler, *Long Parliament* · E. Hyde, earl of Clarendon, *The history of the rebellion and civil wars in England*, new edn, 7 vols. (1839), vols. 4, 7 · *CSP dom., 1633–45* · *DNB* · M. A. E. Green, ed., *Calendar of the proceedings of the committee for advance of money, 1642–1656*, 3 vols., PRO (1888) · J. Moone, 'A brief relation of the life and memoirs of John Lord Belasyse', *Calendar of the manuscripts of the marquess of Ormonde*, new ser., 2, HMC, 36 (1903), 376–99 · C. H. Firth and R. S.

Rait, eds., *Acts and ordinances of the interregnum, 1642–1660*, 1 (1911) · P. Young, *Edgehill: the campaign and battle* (1967) · Venn, *Alum. Cant.* · *The diary of Bulstrode Whitelocke, 1605–1675*, ed. R. Spalding, British Academy, Records of Social and Economic History, new ser., 13 (1990), vol. 1 · D. H. Pennington and I. A. Roots, eds., *The committee at Stafford, 1643–1645*, Staffordshire RS, 4th ser., 1 (1957) · will, PRO, PROB 11/292, sig. 309 · HoP, *Commons, 1558–1603*, vol. 3 · *JHC*, 2–3 (1640–44) · W. Notestein, 'The establishment of the committee of both kingdoms', *American Historical Review*, 17 (1911–12), 477–95 · D. Underdown, *Pride's Purge: politics in the puritan revolution* (1971) · M. A. E. Green, ed., *Calendar of the proceedings of the committee for compounding … 1643–1660*, 1, PRO (1889)

Archives Pembrokeshire RO, Haverfordwest, family papers, D/BUSH | PRO, Commonwealth Exchequer papers, SP 28

Wealth at death lands in Pembrokeshire to son; £500 to each of two daughters; annuities totalling £100 p.a.; £100 to widow: will, PRO, PROB 11/292, sig. 309

Meyrick [*née* Nason], **Kate Evelyn** (1875–1933), night-club owner, was born on 7 August 1875 at 24 Cambridge Terrace, Kingstown, Dublin, the younger daughter of John William Washington Nason (*c*.1842–1876), a physician of Kingstown, who was heir to property at Newtown, near Rathcormack, co. Cork, and Sarah Frances, *née* Bateman. Her widowed mother married a Lancashire clergyman and died when Kate was seven. Having returned to Ireland, Kate Nason lived with her grandmother in a house called Fairyland, where she was educated by governesses. About 1890 she attended Alexandra College, Dublin.

On 12 December 1899 Kate Nason married Ferdinand Richard Holmes Merrick, a Dublin physician (1868?–1940). They adopted the spelling of Meyrick about 1903, and had three sons and three daughters. He practised medicine at Southsea before moving to Basingstoke, where he received nerve cases. The marriage became strained after ten years of dreary, irksome respectability, and about 1912 she left with her children, drifting for a year from one seaside town to another. Afterwards the Meyricks were reconciled. During the war she took lessons in hypnotism and practised suggestive therapeutics on her husband's shell-shocked and chronic nerve patients. Her children stated that he spent all her money, 'thus forcing her to work for her children, that Mrs Meyrick never spent money on herself, that the father did nothing for them, meant nothing to them' (*Diaries of Sir Robert Bruce Lockhart*, 1.241).

A new enthusiasm for dancing clubs marked the end of the war. Following the final collapse of her marriage in 1919, Kate Meyrick moved to London, where she managed and part-owned Dalton's club in Leicester Square. Under the licensing laws of this period, closing-up time was 10 p.m., but Ma Meyrick had no truck with these puritanical austerities. Accordingly the police raided Dalton's, she was fined £25 for keeping disorderly premises, and the club closed shortly afterwards. Next she took an interest in a Charing Cross Road club before, in 1921, opening her own night club, the 43, in Gerrard Street, Soho. She enjoyed the excitement of club life, including the management of her staff. Initially she organized subscription dances, selling 10*s*. tickets to include food and non-alcoholic drinks, but then began supplying alcohol in defiance of the Licensing Act of 1921. The first raid on the 43 (February 1922) was led by Sergeant George Goddard.

In 1924 the purity-campaigning home secretary Sir William Joynson-Hicks set out to suppress London night clubs, which were mostly run by Italians. The authorities distrusted the clubs' undermining of social barriers. The 43's regulars included 'officers of distinguished regiments, members of the peerage, experienced Men about

Kate Evelyn Meyrick (1875–1933), by unknown photographer [centre, with four of her children: (left to right) Nancy, Anne, May (the countess of Kinnoull), and Gordon]

Town or rich young City magnates' (Meyrick, 89). They mingled not only with the dancers and provincial businessmen on a spree in London, but also with criminals and delinquents. Despite repeated police raids for drinking out of hours, the clubs' clientele was not deterred by these efforts to turn night life into a crime.

The 43, which Evelyn Waugh depicted as the Old Hundredth in *A Handful of Dust* (1934), was raided by Goddard in July 1924. Mrs Meyrick, however, would not submit to 'the kill-joys' (Meyrick, 118). Following another raid, she was in November 1924 sentenced to six months for selling liquor without a licence. Sir Chartres Biron, the Bow Street magistrate who sentenced her, recalled this 'very remarkable woman' with respect. 'She was a lady, of good appearance and charming manners, and conducted her various clubs with more decorum than many, but with also a fine contempt for the law' (Biron, 334). In addition to the 43, she owned other clubs, notably the Silver Slipper in Regent Street, and the Manhattan in Denman Street, together with an interest in the Folies Bergères in Newman Street. Her celebrity was enhanced in 1926 when her second daughter married the twenty-sixth Baron de Clifford; two years later her eldest daughter married the fourteenth earl of Kinnoull. The Silver Slipper was raided on Christmas eve 1927; the 43 and Manhattan in May 1928. As a result, she was again sentenced to six months for selling drinks after hours. Her profits in the mid-1920s were considerable. A good week at the Silver Slipper yielded £1000, of which half was profit. On boat race night of 1927 she took £600 at the 43. Under the guidance of the financier Alfred Loewenstein she amassed investments worth £150,000, and altogether made about £500,000. However, the value of her holdings plummeted while she was in prison, and she lost her residual fortune to swindlers or in unsuccessful ventures.

A month after her release in November 1928 Meyrick and an Italian club owner were charged under the Prevention of Corruption Act. Sergeant Goddard, who held £12,000 in notes and other investments, was alleged to have extracted £100 weekly from her to forestall further raids. After trial in January 1930 before Sir Horace Avory, she was sentenced to fifteen months' hard labour for bribery and corruption. Once released, she resumed her old business, but Lord Byng of Vimy, the commissioner of Metropolitan Police appointed by Joynson-Hicks, was successfully throttling London night life. Following further raids, Meyrick was reimprisoned from July to December 1930, and finally from May to October 1931. Conditions at Holloway having weakened her health, she died aged fifty-seven of broncho-pneumonia following influenza on 19 January 1933 at her home, 3 Park Square West, Regent's Park, London, and was buried four days later after a funeral service at St Martin-in-the-Fields, London.

RICHARD DAVENPORT-HINES

Sources K. E. Meyrick, *Secrets of the 43* (1933) • R. Blythe, *The age of illusion* (1963) • C. Biron, *Without prejudice: impressions of life and law* (1936), 334–5 • *The diaries of Sir Robert Bruce Lockhart*, ed. K. Young, 1 (1973), 221, 241 • *The Times* (22–30 Jan 1929) • H. A. Taylor, *Jix, Viscount Brentford* (1933) • G. Lang, *Mr Justice Avory* (1935), 292–6 • 'The Goddard case', *The Spectator* (2 Feb 1929), 147 • Loelia, duchess of Westminster, *Grace and favour* (1961), 108–9 • Lord Kinross, *Society racket* (1933) • d. cert. • Burke, *Gen. Ire.* • b. cert.

Likenesses photograph, 1930, Hult. Arch.; repro. in Blythe, *Age of illusion*, facing p. 23 • photograph, NPG [*see illus.*] • photographs, repro. in Meyrick, *Secrets* • photographs, Hult. Arch.

Wealth at death £771 8s. 1d.: probate, 14 March 1933, *CGPLA Eng. & Wales*

Meyrick, Rowland (1504/5–1566), bishop of Bangor, born at Bodorgan in the parish of Llangadwaladr, Anglesey, was the second son of Meurig ap Llywelyn ap Heylin, rector of Aberffraw, and Margaret, daughter of Rowland ap Hwyl. Rowland's grandfather had fought with Henry Tudor at Bosworth and his father had obtained a crown lease of Aberffraw (where the princes of Gwynedd had had their seat) and built a house at Bodorgan. According to Wood he was educated 'at St Edward's Hall [Oxford], a noted place for civilians, sometime situated near St Edward's Church' (*DNB*), although Yardley gives New Inn Hall as his place of education. He graduated BCL in 1531, BCnL in 1534, and DCL in 1537–8. He was principal of New Inn Hall from 1534 to 1536 before following his father into the church. In 1541 he was made precentor of Llanddewibrefi in St David's, in 1544 he was made vicar of Stoke by Nayland, Suffolk, and in 1547 was appointed chancellor of Wells. His position made Meyrick principal official in the consistory court and his appointment was probably influenced by his legal knowledge. He was also a Cardiganshire JP.

Meyrick had already been promoted to be chancellor and canon of St David's by Bishop William Barlow, who was assembling a group of enthusiastic young reformers in his diocese before 1548. However, Barlow was soon replaced by Robert Ferrar who was highly critical of the 'great spoil being made' by the chapter, and accused Meyrick, in particular, of 'shameless whoredom' (*Acts and Monuments*, 7.17). After initial hostilities Ferrar appointed Meyrick commissary in the archdeaconry of Cardigan, but he was removed from his position about November 1550 as new disagreements appeared. It was in such circumstances that friends of Ferrar brought a suit in the court of augmentations alleging that Meyrick's living of Llanddewibrefi was a collegiate church. It had been deemed not to be so when such foundations were confiscated in 1549, and after a long legal battle Meyrick successfully defended this decision. The Marian period saw the downfall of both sides. Ferrar was burnt at the stake for his reforming opinions and Meyrick was alone among his enemies in not seeking his pardon. Meyrick himself was deprived of his livings on the grounds of heresy and marriage. However, he managed to get his own nominee installed in his place at Eglwys Ail by fiercely arguing against the bishop's nominee.

With the accession of Queen Elizabeth, Meyrick not only resumed his positions but saw his fortunes sharply rise. Initially he was appointed to the commission to enforce the use of the prayer book, promulgate the royal injunctions, and administer the oath to the clergy under the Act of Supremacy. He was one of five commissioners, and the area over which they had charge amounted to all four Welsh dioceses, plus the marcher ones of Hereford and Worcester. On 21 December 1559, when Yardley gives his age as fifty-four, Meyrick was consecrated bishop of Bangor, having first been nominated shortly before the death of Edward VI. He was licensed to hold other livings *in commendam*, owing to the poverty of his see; this included most of his St David's income amounting to £80 per annum. In 1562 he became rector of Llanbedrog, Caernarvonshire. His appointment as bishop and others made at the same time were part of a changing pattern whereby Welshmen were appointed to Welsh sees. He appointed his brother Edmund as archdeacon of Bangor.

Meyrick married Katherine (*d.* 1598), daughter of Owen Barrett of Gelliswic, parish of Hasguard, Pembrokeshire. They had six sons and two daughters, of whom Gelly *Meyrick and Francis were knighted by Essex. Through the latter Meyrick was grandfather to Sir John Meyrick. Meyrick died on 24 January 1566, although by Yardley's time the inscription on his tomb in Bangor Cathedral was 'all torn away' (Yardley, 147).   MIHAIL DAFYDD EVANS

Sources G. Williams, *Wales and the Reformation* (1997) · G. Williams, 'The protestant experiment in the diocese of St David's, 1534–55', *Welsh Reformation essays* (1967), 111–39 · G. Williams, 'The Elizabethan settlement of religion in Wales and the marches, 1559–60', *Welsh Reformation essays* (1967), 141–53 · E. A. Lewis and J. C. Davies, *Records of the court of augmentations relating to Wales and Monmouthshire* (1954) · *Heraldic visitations of Wales and part of the marches … by Lewys Dwnn*, ed. S. R. Meyrick, 2 vols. (1846) · A. J. Brown, *Robert Ferrar: Yorkshire monk, Reformation bishop and martyr in Wales, c.1500–1555* (1997) · A. I. Pryce, *The diocese of Bangor in the sixteenth century* (1923) · E. Yardley, *Menevia sacra*, ed. F. Green (1927) · *The acts and monuments of John Foxe*, new edn, ed. G. Townsend, 8 vols. (1843–9) · *DNB*

Meyrick, Sir Samuel Rush (1783–1848), antiquary and historian of arms and armour, born on 26 August 1783, was the only surviving son of John Meyrick (*d.* 1805), FSA, agent, of Great George Street, Westminster, and Peterborough House, Fulham, and of his wife, Hannah (*d.* 1832), daughter and coheir of Samuel Rush of Ford House, Hertfordshire, and Chislehurst, Kent. He matriculated from Queen's College, Oxford, in 1800 and graduated BA in 1804, then proceeded MA and BCL in 1810, and DCL in 1811. On 3 October 1803 he married Mary (*c.*1784–1818), the daughter of James Parry of Llwyn Hywel, Cardiganshire. This early marriage offended his father, who arranged that his property should bypass his son and devolve to his son's children. There was in the event only one son, Llewelyn (1804–1837), who died unmarried before his father; the property then passed to Sir Samuel.

Meyrick practised until 1823 as an advocate in the ecclesiastical and admiralty courts and in London lived first at 3 Sloane Terrace, Chelsea, and afterwards at 20 Upper Cadogan Place. In 1810 he published his first work, *The History and Antiquities of the County of Cardigan*. He is said to have planned a history of the monarchs of Britain, but his next major publication combined the interest in early British history with that which was to become his main subject of study. With Charles Hamilton Smith, he joined in the production of a work on *The costume of the original inhabitants of*

Sir Samuel Rush Meyrick (1783–1848), by unknown engraver

the British islands, from the earliest periods to the sixth century (1815), illustrated by twenty-four colour plates.

Meyrick was elected FSA in 1810, and for some years took an active part in the proceedings of the society. His contributions to *Archaeologia* between 1818 and 1830 were primarily concerned with his collecting and antiquarian interests: all were original, and one—'Description of the engravings on a German suit of armour made for King Henry VIII, in the Tower of London' (*Archaeologia*, 22, 1829)—is probably the earliest detailed examination of a single armour to have been written. He also assisted Thomas Dudley Fosbroke in his *Encyclopaedia of Antiquities* (1823–5) and published contributions to the *Gentleman's Magazine* and other learned journals.

It was during these years that Meyrick began to acquire the collection of arms and armour for which he became famous. His obituary in the *Gentleman's Magazine* describes it at this time as filling not only 'the garrets, the staircase and the back drawing room' but as even encroaching 'upon the bedrooms'. From the beginning it was conceived of as a scientific collection and it was regularly made available to students. In 1825 it was visited by the artists Eugène Delacroix and Richard Bonnington, who both drew items from the collection and made use of them in later works. Meyrick was also involved in the antiquarian world of the day and, among others, helped Sir Walter Scott to collect arms and armour to decorate his new house at Abbotsford.

In 1824 Meyrick published his great work on arms and

armour, in three lavishly illustrated volumes, entitled *A critical inquiry into antient armour as it existed in Europe, but particularly in England, from the Norman conquest to the reign of King Charles II*. In 1826 he was consulted by the authorities at the Tower of London as to the arrangement of the national collection of arms and armour, which he had severely criticized in his *Inquiry*, and in 1828, at the command of George IV, he arranged the collection at Windsor Castle. In January 1832, in recognition of this work, William IV conferred the Hanoverian order upon him and he was knighted on 22 February following.

In 1823 Meyrick became acquainted with James Robinson Planché, who asked for advice on the armour and costumes suitable for a new production of *King John*, and he introduced him to Francis Douce. Planché, in his *Recollections* (Planché, 1.54–5), warmly acknowledges the valuable assistance he received from both in his efforts for the reform of theatrical costume.

About 1827 Meyrick, having failed to purchase the ruins of Goodrich Castle, near Ross, Herefordshire, bought the hill opposite. He chose Edward Blore, a fellow member of the Society of Antiquaries, as his architect: the first stone was laid on St George's day 1828 and the shell of Goodrich Court was completed by April 1831. The public rooms of the house were designed specifically to display the Meyrick collection of arms and armour: its projected arrangement is shown in Joseph Skelton's series of *Engraved illustrations of antient arms and armour, from the collection at Goodrich Court, from the drawings and with the descriptions of Dr. Meyrick* (2 vols., 1830), and later descriptions show that the final arrangement followed the Skelton designs closely. In 1834 Francis Douce bequeathed to him a part of his collection of antiquities and they were added to the displays. Meyrick published 'A catalogue of the museum' bequeathed to him by Francis Douce, in the *Gentleman's Magazine* in 1836.

Although he had spoken of his project as a 'summer residence', Meyrick seems to have settled permanently at Goodrich Court. In 1834 he served the office of high sheriff of Herefordshire, and made his year in office conspicuous by the revival of javelin-men and other pageantry. He assisted in the formation of the British Archaeological Association in 1843 and presided over its Gloucester congress in 1846. According to Planché during these years:

> His precision was equalled by his punctuality. During his brief visits to London all his movements were regulated by the clock, and no persuasion could induce him to stay anywhere five minutes beyond the time he had prearranged to remain. (Planché, 2.146)

Meyrick contributed the descriptions to Henry Shaw's *Specimens of Ancient Furniture* (1836) and edited a new edition of John Carter's seminal but disorganized *Specimens of the Ancient Sculpture and Paintings now Remaining in England* (1838). His last published work was an edition of Lewis Dwnn's *Heraldic Visitation of Wales*, for the Society for the Publication of Ancient Welsh Manuscripts (1846).

Meyrick died at Goodrich Court on 2 April 1848, and was buried in the churchyard of St Giles's Church there. His property was left to his second cousin Lieutenant-Colonel Augustus Meyrick. The armour was exhibited in Manchester in 1857 and at the South Kensington Museum in 1868, being arranged on both occasions by Planché. The museum failed to buy the collection when it was offered for £50,000, and about 1871 Colonel Meyrick's son and heir sold both the armoury and the art treasures at Goodrich Court. Many of the pieces were bought by the Paris dealer and collector Frederic Spitzer, and some were later acquired by Sir Richard Wallace and are now in the Wallace Collection. Goodrich Court itself was demolished in 1950.   SARAH BARTER BAILEY

Sources GM, 2nd ser., 30 (1848), 92–5 · Foster, *Alum. Oxon.* · T. D. Fosbroke, *The Wye tour* (1833) · C. Nash, *The Goodrich Court guide* (1845) · J. R. Planché, *Recollections and reflections*, rev. edn (1901) · H. Meller, 'The architectural history of Goodrich Court, Herefordshire', *Transactions of the Woolhope Naturalists' Field Club*, 42 (1976–8), 175–85, esp. 125–84 · C. Blair, *The Meyrick Society, 1890–1990* (1991) · C. Wainwright, *The romantic interior: the British collector at home, 1750–1850* (1989) · Royal Armouries, London · DNB

Archives BL, collections relating to archery, Add. MS 28801 · NL Wales, corresp., collections, and literary MSS · Queen's College, Oxford, catalogue of names of sheriffs of north and south Wales | Bodl. Oxf., Phillipps-Robinson MSS, corresp. with Sir Thomas Phillipps · Bodl. Oxf., letters to J. J. Skelton · Cardiff Central Library, letters to Angharad Llwyd, mainly relating to Welsh pedigrees · NL Scot., letters to Sir Walter Scott · NL Wales, letters to Cambrian Archaeological Association · Royal Armouries, London · S. Antiquaries, Lond., description of Margam Abbey · U. Southampton L., business letters to J. C. Isaac · Wallace Collection, London · Yale U., Beinecke L., letters to T. J. Pettigrew

Likenesses W. Brockedon, chalk drawing, c.1830, NPG · J. Skelton, engraving (after H. P. Briggs), repro. in A. E. Evans and E. Evans, *Catalogue of engraved British portraits* (1853), 11, 278 · engraving, NPG [see illus.]

Meyrick, Sir William (1595/6–1669), civil lawyer and judge, was born in West Meon, Hampshire, the son of Maurice Meyrick (d. 1640) of Bodeon, Anglesey, steward of New College and registrar of Oxford University and half-brother of Bishop John Meyrick of Sodor and Man, and Jane, daughter of Lewis Evans. Meyrick was elected a scholar at Winchester College in 1608 (aged twelve), and from there proceeded to New College, Oxford, where he was admitted on 21 October 1614, and elected a full fellow on 16 July 1616. He graduated BCL on 18 April 1621. He resigned his fellowship in 1626, was granted the degree of DCL on 30 June 1627, and was admitted a member of Doctors' Commons on 2 February 1628. By 1629 he had married Sarah (d. 1663), daughter of James Dodwell of Oxford, and the widow of Robert Beesley of Oxford, for on 29 October 1629 the burial in St Benet Paul's Wharf, London, was recorded of a stillborn child. In 1638 he was renting a house assessed at £30 in St Peter's Hill in St Peter Paul's Wharf. In 1640 Meyrick was admitted an honorary member of Lincoln's Inn at the request of Charles Jones, reader of the inn.

Meyrick was active as an advocate in the civil courts between 1628 and 1640, and on 28 September 1641 he was appointed judge of the prerogative court of Canterbury. Some controversy occurred over his appointment by Archbishop Laud. On 26 October 1641 the House of Lords received a petition from Arthur Duck DCL claiming a prior appointment by virtue of a patent issued by Laud. Laud claimed in turn that he had cancelled his patent to Duck and appointed 'a very worthy man' (*JHL*, 4.409) in his place. The case was eventually referred to the law courts. On 18 May 1643 the House of Lords was informed that Meyrick had joined Charles I at Oxford and revoked 'all the substitutions I have made' (*JHL*, 6.51), thereby paralysing probate in areas held by parliament. Parliament responded on 1 November 1644 with an ordinance constituting Sir Nathaniel Brent judge in his place.

Meyrick was reinstated as judge of the prerogative court following the Restoration, and knighted on 8 November 1661. His wife was buried on 27 February 1663 in St Peter Paul's Wharf. Meyrick made his will in June 1665, making several bequests, including £100 to his 'dear friend' Lady Parry, and to several members of Doctors' Commons. The remainder went to his brother and executor, Benjamin, as at least two daughters, Joan and Katherine, had predeceased him. Meyrick died on 3 February 1669, and was buried on the 11th in St Benet Paul's Wharf.

STUART HANDLEY

Sources B. P. Levack, *The civil lawyers in England, 1603–1641* (1973) · G. D. Squibb, *Doctors' Commons: a history of the College of Advocates and Doctors of Law* (1977), 173 · will, PRO, PROB 11/329, fol. 154r–v · *GM*, 1st ser., 95/1 (1825), 406–7 · J. Haydn, *The book of dignities: containing rolls of the official personages of the British empire* (1851), 421 · C. H. Firth and R. S. Rait, eds., *Acts and ordinances of the interregnum, 1642–1660*, 3 vols. (1911), 1.564–6 · Foster, *Alum. Oxon.* · W. A. Littledale, ed., *The registers of St Bene't and St Peter, Paul's Wharf, London*, 4, Harleian Society, register section, 41 (1912), 14, 18, 62, 231 · *JHL*, 4 (1628–42), 406, 409, 429; 6 (1643–4), 51; 7 (1644–5), 43 · T. F. Kirby, *Winchester scholars: a list of the wardens, fellows, and scholars of … Winchester College* (1888), 163 · T. C. Dale, ed., *The inhabitants of London in 1638*, 1 (1931), 179

Mhic an Bhaird, Diarmaid mac Laoisigh (*fl.* 1675–1695). *See under* Mac an Bhaird family (*per. c.*1400–*c.*1695).

Mhic Bhruaideadha, Domhnall mac Dáire (*fl.* 1558–1570). *See under* Mac Bruaideadha family (*per.* 1558–1636).

Miall, Edward (1809–1881), politician, journalist, and Congregational minister, was born on 8 May 1809 at Portsmouth, one of several children of Moses Miall (*d.* 1829), a general merchant and later a schoolmaster, and his wife, Sarah, daughter of George Rolph. The family moved to Hammersmith, and then to north London, where Moses opened a school, in which, after a short time at St Saviour's Grammar School, Edward became an assistant when not more than sixteen. Because the school proved unsuccessful, Edward transferred in 1827 to teach, first at Bocking, Essex, and then at Nayland, Suffolk. He absorbed Shakespeare and the English poets, also composing verse of his own. Under the influence of letters from his family, he experienced evangelical conversion and on his eighteenth birthday signed, in the manner recommended by Philip Doddridge, a formal dedication of his life to Christ. Inspired by the example of his older brother James (who was already in the Congregational ministry) in 1828 he entered Wymondley College (then located near Stevenage in Hertfordshire) to train for the same career—a decision he later seems to have regretted as precipitate. After only

Edward Miall (1809–1881), by Henry John Whitlock

three years of the five-year course, he left in November 1831 to be ordained as minister of the Congregational church at Ware, Hertfordshire. Shortly afterwards, on 25 January 1832, he married Louisa, eldest daughter of Edward Holmes of Enfield, and niece of the theological tutor at Wymondley, Thomas Morell. They had two sons and three daughters.

Congregational minister and journalist In 1834 Miall moved to the more prestigious Bond Street Congregational chapel in Leicester. Briefly, during 1835, he was attracted by the thought of serving as a missionary in southern Africa, but from the following year he became committed to the struggle against church rates—the annual levies on all householders, including dissenters, for the upkeep of the parish churches. Together with his friend James Philippo Mursell, minister of the adjacent Harvey Lane Baptist Church, Miall formed a Voluntary Church Society on the model of one already existing at Birmingham, with disestablishment of the Church of England as its eventual goal and resistance to local church rates as its immediate object. Alongside twenty others, he was summoned for non-payment, declined to appear before magistrates in a spiritual case, and suffered the distraint of some of his goods. The publicity surrounding the controversy helped ensure that from 1837 onwards the majority in Miall's parish vestry voted down a church rate. From 1838 he was further radicalized by the prosecution and subsequent imprisonment of a member of his congregation, William Baines, for non-payment, and, with provincial disdain for the capital, became ever more dissatisfied with the caution and deference to the government of the metropolitan leaders of dissent, especially Josiah Conder, editor of *The Patriot*. The Leicester party determined to replace Conder's magazine as the mouthpiece of dissent, and so, in default of anyone else, Miall undertook to raise the capital for a weekly newspaper and to become its editor. He resigned his pulpit in 1840—an action that was widely censured as a desertion of his spiritual calling—and, after moving to the London suburb of Stoke Newington, he issued the first copy of *The Nonconformist* on 14 April 1841.

The newspaper launched a shrill attack on the principle of a national establishment of religion. 'A state church!', ran an editorial. 'Have they never looked into that dark, polluted, inner chamber of which it is the door? Have they never caught a glimpse of the loathsome things that live, and crawl, and gender there?' (E. Miall, *The Nonconformist's Sketch Book*, 1842, 17). There were subordinate assaults on aristocratic power, the supine dissenting leadership, and the folly of nonconformist subservience to the whigs. The first of several collections of leading articles appeared in 1842 as *The Nonconformist's Sketch Book*; in a reissue of 1867 Miall expressed the wish that he had been more charitable. In its first year *The Nonconformist* also carried a series on 'Reconciliation between the middle and working classes' in which Miall coined the phrase 'complete suffrage' for universal male enfranchisement. The series, issued as a pamphlet with the same title and an introduction by Joseph Sturge, became the rallying call for an effort to achieve co-operation between Anti-Corn Law Leaguers and Chartists. Although the league stood aside, Miall put his newspaper at the disposal of Sturge's Complete Suffrage Union, launched in April 1842 to achieve class collaboration in the spirit of the gospel. Toying with the six points of the Charter, however, reduced circulation, and in the autumn of 1842 Miall publicly warned against Sturge's new policy of civil disobedience until parliamentary reform was granted. With the take-over of its December conference by Feargus O'Connor, the Complete Suffrage Union was crippled. Believing that no landlord parliament would concede repeal of the corn laws, Miall turned to organizing nonconformist opinion against the established church.

The Disruption of the Church of Scotland and the successful agitation against the pro-Anglican education clauses of the Factories Bill (both of which Miall applauded in his columns during 1843) provided a favourable opportunity. Miall proposed a national dissenting convention, which duly assembled in London, with some 700 delegates, from 30 April to 2 May 1844. The British Anti-State Church Association was established with Miall as one of the three secretaries. Its tracts and lectures were to mobilize many of the younger Congregationalists and Baptists, especially the ministers, in its cause. In 1845

Miall denounced the Maynooth grant, though contributing to the division of the protestant ranks by urging the withdrawal of all state support for religion. He was the first, in September 1845, to stand as a parliamentary candidate under Anti-State Church Association auspices, coming a poor third in a by-election at Southwark. At the 1847 general election, standing against a Conservative, a whig and a Chartist at Halifax, he was perhaps over-confident and suffered another defeat. In the same year he joined Chartist leaders in creating the National Alliance for Promoting the Real Representation of the People in Parliament, which achieved little before merging with the short-lived People's League in 1848. In that year he travelled as a representative of Sturge's League of Universal Brotherhood to visit the Paris republican government. He returned to Paris in 1849 to address the peace congress sponsored by the league and the Peace Society, also speaking at the successor congresses in Frankfurt (1850), London (1851), and Edinburgh (1853). In 1852 Miall was at last returned to parliament, representing John Bright's Rochdale.

In 1849 Miall had published a substantial work, *The British Churches in Relation to the British People*. It revealed his debt to the moral government theology of Joseph Bellamy; and its catalogue of the hindrances to effective Christian mission earned him the enmity of John Campbell, the Congregationalist editor of the popular *British Banner*. Miall's *Bases of Belief* (1853), arguing that Christianity corresponds to the needs of human nature, was adopted by several colleges as a textbook. During the controversy among Congregationalists over the undoctrinal sentimentalities of T. T. Lynch's *The Rivulet* (1855–7), Miall at first ignored the discussion and then emerged prominently on the liberal side against John Campbell.

Campaigns for disestablishment Miall's main energies nevertheless continued to be poured into the Anti-State Church Association—from 1853 the Society for the Liberation of Religion from State Patronage and Control, or Liberation Society for short. In that year he successfully suggested the creation of parliamentary and electoral subcommittees that enhanced the society's political impact. In 1856 his motion (with a view to disestablishment) that the Commons should consider the state of the Irish church, failed by 163 votes to 93. This proposal, together with increased local opposition, lost him the Rochdale seat in 1857. From 1858 to 1861 he served on the Newcastle commission investigating popular education. Together with Goldwin Smith, he submitted a minority report arguing against all state involvement in schooling, a position he was to recant in 1867. In 1862 he published *The Title Deeds of the Church of England to her Parochial Endowments*, contending that church endowments were public property that parliament could disperse. Seeing no prospect of political progress under Palmerston's administration, in 1863 he initiated a new Liberation Society strategy based on the training of public opinion to influence the selection of parliamentary candidates. In 1865 he came close to securing nomination for Manchester, and in the following year a lecture tour played a significant part in the mobilization of Welsh nonconformity in the Liberal interest. After twice, in 1867 and 1868, unsuccessfully contesting Bradford, where his brother James was a Congregational minister, Miall returned to the Commons as its MP, on 12 March 1869.

His first speech, on the Irish Disestablishment Bill, proved disappointing and, despite contacts with Bright, Miall exerted no influence over its passage during 1869. In the following year he denounced in the Commons the Education Bill introduced by his Bradford colleague W. E. Forster—because it gave public money to denominational schools—only to earn a sharp rebuke from Gladstone. His own preferred education policy was for the state to support only secular instruction. Miall's finest hour, the culmination of the Liberation Society's efforts, came when he proposed English disestablishment, on 9 May 1871. 'Miall, fear God', urged his fellow-liberationist MP George Hadfield, 'and you need not fear any man' (Miall, 320). Although the vote was lost by 89 to 374, *The Times* predicted that the establishment would not outlast the century. Miall chaired the first session of a Manchester conference that in January 1872 voiced nonconformist dissatisfaction with Liberal policy, especially on education. Although a Commons resolution in July in favour of investigating church finances gained 96 supporters against 295 opponents, church defenders were rallying and *Punch* depicted Gladstone applying a fire extinguisher to Miall. In May 1873 his motion for English and Scottish disestablishment failed by 61 to 356. He retired from parliament with rheumatism in 1874, but nevertheless drew up a five-year strategy for the Liberation Society and continued to edit *The Nonconformist* until, by 1877, it was transferred to his brother Charles. In his last years he also contributed regularly to the *Illustrated London News*. His wife died in January 1876, and in 1881 he moved from London, where he had lived in suburban Tottenham, Holloway, Upper Norwood, and Forest Hill, to Greystone Lodge, Sevenoaks. Here Miall suffered from shivering and swelling of the legs with general debility, and died on 29 April 1881. He was buried in Honor Oak cemetery.

Miall's *An Editor off the Line* (1865), a collection of reflective essays, gives the impression of a hard-working mid-Victorian, a believer in progress, the sanctity of childhood, and the elevating power of mountain scenery. He was also an advocate of voluntary moral limits on commercial gain and the creation of labour exchanges. Thin and agile, he loved walking and music making at home. His reserve made him an unexciting platform orator, but his spiritual-intellectual written sermons, 'as clear, sometimes as cold, as ice' (J. E. Ritchie, *The London Pulpit*, 1854, 130), were appreciated by London congregations. His greatest achievement was the rousing of younger nonconformist ministers to political action, a development that shaped the late Victorian Liberal Party.

D. W. Bebbington

Sources A. Miall, *Life of Edward Miall* (1884) · *The Monthly Christian Spectator*, 2 (Oct 1852), 577–86 · J. S. Newton, 'The political career of Edward Miall, editor of the Nonconformist and founder of the Liberation Society', diss., U. Durham, 1975 · A. Temple Patterson, *Radical Leicester: a history of Leicester, 1780–1850* (1954) · A. Tyrrell, *Joseph Sturge and the 'moral radical party' in early Victorian Britain* (c.1987) · E. Miall, *An editor off the line: or wayside musings and reminiscences* (1865) · C. Binfield, *So down to prayers: studies in English nonconformity, 1780–1920* (1977) · *The Times* (2 May 1881)
Archives DWL, letters and papers | BL, Cobden MSS · BL, Gladstone MSS · BL, Sturge MSS · priv. coll., Sturge MSS
Likenesses Ape [C. Pellegrini], chromatograph caricature, NPG; repro. in *VF* (29 July 1871) · Mayall, carte-de-visite, NPG · P. Naumann & R. Taylor & Co., group portrait, wood-engraving (*Our literary contributors—past and present*), BM, NPG; repro. in *ILN* (14 May 1892) · H. J. Whitlock, carte-de-visite, NPG [*see illus.*] · wood-engraving, NPG; repro. in *ILN* (7 May 1881) · woodcut (after photograph by Mayall), NPG; repro. in *Cassell's Illustrated Family Paper* (2 April 1859)
Wealth at death under £2000: probate, 19 May 1881, *CGPLA Eng. & Wales*

Miantonomo (1600?–1643), leader of the Narragansett Indians, was the nephew of the Narragansett Indians' principal sachem, Canonicus, and by the 1630s had emerged as co-sachem with his ageing uncle, whom he succeeded upon the latter's death. The Narragansetts' early relations with Plymouth Colony, founded in 1620, were abrasive, perhaps because of Plymouth's relationship with their rivals the Wampanoag. In the 1620s Narragansetts traded with itinerant Dutch merchants who visited the Connecticut river valley, exchanging wampum and furs for highly coveted European trade goods, including textiles, glass beads, metal pots, and steel weapons. After the founding of the Massachusetts Bay Colony in 1629 the Narragansetts also established a trade connection with the English. Miantonomo was far less suspicious than Canonicus of the puritans and used his influence within the tribe to secure acceptance of an alliance with Massachusetts. He also welcomed prominent English refugees from puritan oppression, granting asylum and land to both Roger Williams and Samuel Gorton. The colony of Rhode Island, known to the puritans as the 'place of the otherwise-minded', was founded within Narragansett territory.

The pro-English policy championed by Miantonomo was opposed by some of the powerful lesser sachems, who were probably responsible for the killing of John Oldham, a prominent Massachusetts Bay trader and ship captain, off Block Island. Miantonomo, determined to remain at peace with the English, led a band of 200 Narragansett warriors against the Block Islanders. He later paid the eastern Niantics to execute a sachem who was said to have led the raiding party that murdered Oldham. After the Massachusetts Bay Colony dispatched an army to punish the Block Islanders and attack the Pequots, whom they believed guilty of several earlier killings of Englishmen, the Pequots sent a delegation to the Narragansetts to ask that they join in a war against the English. Some of the Narragansett leaders were impressed by the Pequot portrayal of the English as a deadly threat to their continued existence. But Miantonomo, after first considering neutrality, urged the Narragansetts to ally themselves with the English against their traditional rivals and enemies the Pequots. His arguments prevailed and Narragansett warriors accompanied the English army that laid waste Pequot country in 1637.

Despite their invaluable aid to the puritans in the Pequot War, Miantonomo and the Narragansetts did not fare well in the post-war settlement. Involved in a power struggle with the Mohegan sachem Uncas, who had also fought against the Pequots, Miantonomo fell out of favour with the English. Puritan authorities distrusted the Narragansetts as too powerful and independent. They were more comfortable with Uncas, who was far more compliant than the proud and headstrong Narragansett leader. Puritan authorities also resented Miantonomo's hospitality to exiled English freethinkers such as the Gortonites. They took seriously rumours of his treachery circulated by Uncas and by another rival sachem, Wyandanch of the Montauk, which alleged that Miantonomo intended to use former Pequot warriors to mount a war of extermination against the English.

Years later Lion Gardener, one of the English commanders during the Pequot War, wrote that Miantonomo had given a speech on Long Island in which he exhorted the warriors to unite to kill all of the English, 'men, women and children'. Unless they were exterminated, Miantonomo allegedly warned,

> we shall all be gone shortly, for you know our fathers had plenty of deer and skins, our plains were full of deer, as also our woods, and of turkies, and our coves full of fish and fowl. But these English having gotten our land, they with scythes cut down the grass, and with axes fell the trees; their cows and horses eat the grass and their hogs spoil our clam banks, and we shall all be starved.

Although often quoted by historians, the authenticity of the speech cannot be confirmed. The leaders of the puritan colonies investigated charges against Miantonomo, but could find no firm evidence that he was plotting against the English. There was proof, however, that he had tried to arrange for the assassination of Uncas. Shortly afterwards, in July and August 1643, the Narragansetts and the Mohegans fought a war. Miantonomo was captured by Uncas, who took him to Hartford, Connecticut, where he was kept under guard while Uncas sought a decision on his fate from the commissioners of the United Colonies then meeting in Boston. In September 1643, the commissioners, after acknowledging rumours that Miantonomo had 'engaged in mischievous plots to root out the English nation', determined that as long as he lived, their great friend Uncas would be unsafe. They therefore condemned Miantonomo to death, and turned him over to Uncas for execution, with the proviso that he be killed humanely. Somewhere near Hartford Uncas dispatched his rival with a tomahawk blow to the head.

ALFRED A. CAVE

Sources C. Orr, ed., *History of the Pequot war: the contemporary accounts of Mason Underhill* (Cleveland, Ohio, 1897) · A. B. Forbes, ed., *Winthrop papers, 1623–30*, 5 vols. (Boston, 1931) · *John Winthrop's journal: 'History of New England', 1630–1649*, ed. J. K. Hosmer, 2 vols. (1908) · G. W. Lafantasie, ed., *The correspondence of Roger William*, 2 vols. (1988) · W. Bradford, *History of Plymouth plantation, 1620–1647*, ed. W. C. Ford, 2 vols. (1912) · A. A. Cave, *The Pequot war* (Amherst, Mass., 1996) · A. T. Vaughan, *New England frontier* (New York, 1995) · N. Salisbury, *Manitou and Providence* (1982) · F. Jennings, *The invasion of America* (1976) · E. S. Johnson, 'Some by flatteries and others by threatenings', PhD diss., University of Massachusetts, 1993 · J. W. De Forest, *History of the Indians of Connecticut* (Hartford, 1852) · J. A Sainsbury, 'Miantonomi's death and New England politics, 1630–1645', *Rhode Island History*, 30 (1971), 111–13

Archives Mass. Hist. Soc., Winslow MSS · Mass. Hist. Soc., Winthrop MSS

Michael Blaunpayn. *See* Cornwall, Michael of (*fl.* 1243–1255).

Michael of Canterbury. *See* Canterbury, Michael (*fl.* 1275–1321).

Michel, Jean Baptiste (1738/1748–1804). *See under* Boydell, John, engravers (*act.* 1760–1804).

Michel, Sir John (1804–1886), army officer, born on 1 September 1804, was the eldest son of General John Michel (*d.* 1844) of Dewlish and Kingston Russell, Dorset, and his second wife, Anne, daughter of Henry Fane MP, of Fulbeck, Lincolnshire, and granddaughter of the eighth earl of Westmorland. The father, who had no children with his first wife, entered the army in February 1781, and in the same year was a subaltern in the 51st foot at the defence of Minorca, of which he was one of the last survivors. He was lieutenant-colonel commanding the 30th light dragoons in 1794–6 and the 14th light dragoons in 1799–1806, and afterwards held a brigade command in Ireland; he was promoted lieutenant-general in June 1814 and general in January 1837. He died, aged seventy-nine, in April 1844, reportedly leaving considerable wealth.

John Michel was educated at Eton College (1820–23). On 3 April 1823 he obtained an ensigncy by purchase in the 57th foot, passing through the 27th to the 64th, joining it at Gibraltar, and obtaining his lieutenancy in it on 28 April 1825. He purchased an unattached company on 12 December 1826, and on 15 February 1827 exchanged back to the 64th at Gibraltar. On 8 February 1832 he entered the senior department of the Royal Military College, Sandhurst, and on 7 November 1833 passed his examination and received a first certificate. He then rejoined his regiment, and served with it in Ireland until February 1835, when he exchanged to the 3rd foot (the Buffs) in Bengal. He was aide-de-camp to his uncle General Sir Henry Fane GCB, while commander-in-chief in India in 1835–40. While in India Michel married, on 15 May 1838, Louisa Anne, only daughter of Major-General H. Churchill, then quartermaster-general of the queen's troops in India; they had two sons and three daughters. On 6 May 1840 he was promoted to a majority by purchase in the 6th foot, over the heads of many old officers in the regiment, provoking much criticism.

On 15 April 1842, a few weeks after the arrival of the regiment in England, Michel purchased the lieutenant-colonelcy. He commanded the 6th at home and at the Cape until 1854. He was in command of a brigade during the Cape Frontier War of 1846–7, and during part of the war of 1852–3 was in command of the 2nd division of the army in the Waterkloof; at the close he was made CB. He became brevet colonel on 20 January 1854, and was appointed to command the York recruiting district, but exchanged to half pay 98th foot, on appointment as chief of the staff of the Turkish contingent in the Crimean War, with the local rank of major-general in Turkey, a post he held until the end of the war; he received the order of the Mejidiye (second class). In 1856 he was appointed to a brigade at Fort Beaufort, Cape of Good Hope, at a time of great danger and threatened war, owing to the expected fulfilment in February 1857 of an old African prophecy of the destruction of the Europeans.

The danger was hardly over before Michel was ordered to China for a command there. On 10 July 1857, however, he was shipwrecked in the steamer *Transit* in the Strait of Sunda, and taken to Singapore. His services were subsequently diverted to India during the Indian mutiny, and he was placed on the Bombay staff on 18 February 1858. In June 1858 the troops in Rajputana were concentrated at Nasirabad and Neemuch, under Major-General H. G. Roberts, Bombay army, those at Mhow consisting of a brigade under Brigadier Honner. The latter, reinforced from Bombay, were formed into a division, as the Malwa field force, under Michel, the command of the troops in Rajputana being added in August 1858 when Roberts was promoted to the command in Gujarat. Michel became major-general on 26 October 1858. Impressed with the necessity of cutting off from the towns the bodies of mutineers under Tantia Topi, Rao Sahib, and other leaders, and compelling them to seek the jungles, Michel adopted a strategy which proved successful, despite serious physical obstacles—the rains at this season had converted the soil of Malwa into black mud and the heat was phenomenal. He distributed his troops in lightly equipped columns at salient points in Rajputana and Malwa, with orders to pursue the rebels without intermission. Starting himself from Mhow, Michel came up with Tantia Topi at Beorora on 15 September 1858. Tantia and the cavalry fled, pursued by the British cavalry. The infantry and guns made a stand but did not await the British onset, and leaving thirty guns behind them, 8000 troops were put to flight without the loss of a man. Michel again defeated Tantia at Mingrauli on 9 October, then marched against Rao Sahib the next day, and defeated him at Sindwaha on 15 October; on 5 December he annihilated one wing of Tantia's force near Saugor, the other escaped and crossed the Narbada into Nagpur. Other defeats of rebel forces followed, and they began to lose heart and creep away to their homes. Between 20 June 1858 and 1 March 1859 the field force traversed an aggregate distance of over 3000 miles, of which Michel himself marched 1700. The operations ended with the capture of Tantia Topi, who was taken by a small column under Brigadier Meade, at once tried by court martial, and hanged on 18 April 1859 for being in arms against the British. The legality of the sentence was questioned, but Tantia was considered to have been one of the most bloodthirsty of Nana Sahib's advisers.

Michel was made KCB in March 1859. He remained in command of the Mhow division until the end of 1859, when he was appointed to the army under Sir James Hope Grant, going to the north of China. He commanded the 1st division at the action at Sinho, and at the occupation of Peking (Beijing) on 12 October 1860. His division on 18 October burnt the summer palace at Peking in reprisal for Chinese atrocities against British, Indian, and French captives. At the close of the campaign Michel was made GCB for his 'zeal, skill, and intrepidity'. He was appointed colonel of the 86th (Royal County Down) regiment (later 2nd Irish rifles) on 19 August 1862; he became lieutenant-general on 25 June 1866, and general on 28 March 1874. He was selected to command the troops in the first autumn manoeuvres in the south of England in 1873, and in 1875 was appointed commander of the forces in Ireland and was sworn of the Irish privy council. He held the Irish command from 1875 to 1880, his social qualities and wealth making him popular. He was made field marshal on 27 March 1885, and was a JP for Dorset. Michel was an active, spare-built man, somewhat below average height, impetuous and warm-hearted, a keen sportsman, and an energetic and capable officer. He died at his seat, Dewlish House, near Dorchester, Dorset, on 23 May 1886, and was survived by his wife.

H. M. CHICHESTER, *rev.* ROGER T. STEARN

Sources Burke, *Gen. GB* (1886) • *Hart's Army List* (1885) • 'Tantia Topee', *Blackwood*, 88 (1860), 172–94 • *Army and Navy Gazette* (25 May 1886) • G. B. Malleson, *History of the Indian mutiny, 1857–1858: commencing from the close of the second volume of Sir John Kaye's History of the Sepoy War*, 3 vols. (1878–80) • C. Hibbert, *The great mutiny, India, 1857* (1978) • C. Hibbert, *The dragon wakes: China and the West, 1793–1911* (1970) • T. A. Heathcote, *The military in British India: the development of British land forces in south Asia, 1600–1947* (1995) • E. M. Spiers, *The late Victorian army, 1868–1902* (1992) • *Dod's Peerage* (1878) • Boase, *Mod. Eng. biog.* • *GM*, 2nd ser., 22 (1844) • Burke, *Peerage* (1879) • H. E. C. Stapylton, *The Eton school lists, from 1791 to 1850*, 2nd edn (1864)
Archives NAM, letter-book
Wealth at death £7939 7s. 3d.: probate, 6 July 1886, *CGPLA Eng. & Wales*

Michelborne, Sir Edward (*c.*1562–1609), soldier and adventurer, was the eldest son of Edward Michelborne (*d.* 1587), landowner, of Clayton, Sussex, and his first wife, Jane, daughter of Thomas Farnfold (or Parsons) of Steyning, Sussex. He is not to be confused with his kinsman, the Latin poet Edward *Michelborne (1564/5–1626). He entered Gray's Inn in 1580.

Nothing is known of Michelborne's early life. He married Anne Shelley of Pelham, Sussex, and had two sons, Edward (*b.* 1586/7) and Richard. Although in 1591 he was commander of a company of English infantry in the Netherlands, by 1593 he had returned home and was elected MP for Bramber, Sussex, for the parliament of that year. About 1595, while living in London, he became one of the clients of Robert Devereux, second earl of Essex. In 1597 he commanded the *Moone*, a warship in Essex's expedition to the Azores (the 'Islands voyage'). The next year he was back in the Netherlands, as captain of a company of 150 foot. Most of the English companies were transferred to Dutch pay at the end of 1598 and the following spring Michelborne left the Netherlands again. He joined Essex on his ill-fated Irish campaign and was knighted by him at Dublin in the summer of 1599. Then, in 1601, he was among those arrested after Essex's attempted coup. Michelborne was imprisoned in the Marshalsea and was lucky to escape with just a £200 fine—he claimed he had gone to Essex House only to hear a sermon.

Michelborne's interests had already shifted from military duties to commerce with the East Indies. Another patron, Thomas Sackville, first Baron Buckhurst, twice attempted (in 1599 and 1600) to obtain for him command of an East India Company trading venture to Asia. The governors refused, but agreed to let him invest. However, when Michelborne, following Essex's fall, was temporarily financially embarrassed and could not make his agreed payment, the company governors promptly blackballed him. Michelborne was made a gentleman pensioner by James VI and I and royal favour allowed him to thwart the East Indies merchants' ill will. In June 1604 he obtained from the king a licence 'to discover the countries of Cathay, China, Japan, Corea, and Cambaya, and to trade there' (*CSP dom.*, 1603–10, 121): surely the first reference in English official documents to Cambodia, if not to Korea and Japan. It superseded all previous grants, allowing Michelborne to interlope on the East India Company's turf. He sailed from Plymouth on 1 December 1604 in ships he and his associates had built: the *Tiger* and the *Tiger's Whelp*. The celebrated navigator John Davis was his pilot. In October 1605 there were rumours that Michelborne had been killed by the Spanish on the high seas, but in fact about that time he was ruthlessly sacking Dutch settlements in what is now Indonesia; he later plundered Chinese shipping. On 9 July 1606, after a voyage that soured locals' attitudes to English merchants, he arrived home.

In January 1609 Michelborne was busy making arrangements to export more plunder obtained by his ships, but he fell ill. On 22 March he made his will and on 27 April he died: the will was proved the same day by his heir. Michelborne left substantial properties (and a debt of £400, owed him by Buckhurst, now first earl of Dorset) to his family and £75 to the poor. He was buried in Hackney, where he owned a house.   D. J. B. TRIM

Sources HoP, *Commons, 1558–1603*, 3.45–6 · *CSP dom.*, 1598–1601; 1603–10 · *Calendar of the manuscripts of the marquis of Bath preserved at Longleat, Wiltshire*, 5 vols., HMC, 58 (1904–80), vol. 5 · C. R. Markham, *The fighting Veres: lives of Sir Francis Vere … and Sir Horace Vere* (1888) · W. B. Bannerman, ed., *The visitations of the county of Sussex … 1530 … and 1633–4*, Harleian Society, 53 (1905) · BL, Add. MS 5753 · Nationaal Archief, The Hague, Archief van de staten-generaal, 5883-ii · *DNB*
Wealth at death left £75 cash to poor of four local parishes; was owed £400 by earl of Dorset; left lands to sons: HoP,*Commons, 1558–1603*, 3.46 citing PRO, PROB 11/113/33; C 142/314/111

Michelborne, Edward (1564/5–1626), Latin poet, was a member of an extended family with lands in Hampshire and Sussex, and was brought up as a Roman Catholic. He matriculated as a commoner of St Mary Hall, Oxford, on 27 March 1579, aged fourteen, and later migrated to Gloucester Hall, where he was 'many years' a commoner (Foster, *Alum. Oxon.*, 3.1007). He took no degree, for religious reasons, but resided in Oxford, where he had a wide circle of literary friends, and himself established a reputation as the 'most noted Latin poet of his time in the university' (Wood, *Ath. Oxon.: Fasti*, 1.428). He joined several other members of Gloucester Hall in writing introductory verses for Peter Bales's *Arte of Brachygraphie* (1597); he provided two poems, of eleven and four lines, both in the scazon, or limping iambic, metre. The earth has no parallel for the Balesian shorthand, he wrote, the virtues of which readily recommend it: 'laudibus suis semet / Commendat Orbi'.

In later life Michelborne contributed to some Oxford commemorative verse collections. For *Justa Oxoniensium* (1612) he wrote twenty lines of elegiacs for Prince Henry (sig. K2v): there is lamentation everywhere, except in heaven, which has made a profitable acquisition. Two volumes of 1613 attracted his attention; in the *Epithalamia* for the marriage of Princess Elizabeth he has three poems, totalling twenty-six lines of elegiacs and six scazontes (sig. F1v–2r). He is still described as 'ex' Gloucester Hall (a word which often implies current residence), though in 1597 we find 'olim' (which does not). *Bodleiomnema* (1613), for Oxford's own academic hero, called forth his longest set, five poems in four metres (including twenty-one hendecasyllables, a total of seventy-one lines). Finally in 1624 Michelborne sent eighteen iambics, and a twelve-line epode, for *Camdeni insignia*; the longer poem is a dignified acceptance of death, which the supreme dictator has decreed for all on land and sea (though Camden lives on in his *Britannia*); but the epode is a neat, light-hearted 'dialogismus', with Saturn's sister consoled by the survival of 'Degoreius' (Wheare) and 'Brianus' (Duppa) as Camden's successors (*Camdeni insignia*, sig. C1r–v).

Charles Fitzgeffrey's *Affaniae* (1601) is dedicated to Michelborne and his brothers, Laurence and Thomas, with affectionate Catullan hendecasyllables from 'Hilarius Verus' to 'Candidissime millium trecentum / Edoarde' ('Edward, the most candid man among 300,000'), to whom Michelborne replies in elegiacs. Thomas Campion was another close literary friend, with four poems to Edward in his *Epigrammata* (1619), and one each to his brothers; Campion engages Edward in bawdy banter, 'tento nolles parsisse Priapo' ('don't spare the rod'; Campion, 1.180); he offers a moving tribute to Edward's sister, dead within six months of marriage (ibid., 2.77); and, in lively hendecasyllables, congratulates him on avoiding London's distractions, except for three or four visits in a year (ibid., 2.121). Whenever Campion is sick of his own affairs, he writes, he turns to Michelborne's manuscript poetry (ibid., 1.192); why, he asks, does Michelborne insist on suppressing its publication?

Eighteen years earlier Fitzgeffrey expressed similar sentiments, calling Michelborne a hard-hearted parent of the fruits of his genius (sig. D5v–6r): that epigram forms part of a group that sets Michelborne alongside Campion, Sidney, Spenser, Daniel, and Drayton. Though he perhaps lacked Campion's brilliance and sure touch, Michelborne was clearly a significant figure in Oxford's neo-Latin culture, a gentleman amateur who could participate freely when he chose, while religion barred him from a formal role in the university. He died at Oxford on 27 December 1626, and was buried in the church of St Thomas the Martyr. D. K. MONEY

Sources Wood, *Ath. Oxon.: Fasti* (1815), 428 · Foster, *Alum. Oxon.* · *DNB* · P. Bales, *Arte of brachygraphie* (1597) · C. Fitzgeffrey, *Affaniae* (1601) · T. Campion, *Epigrammata* (1619)

Michelborne, John. *See* Mitchelburne, John (1648–1721).

Michele, Charles Eastland de (1809–1898), newspaper proprietor and consul, was born at 63 Charlotte Street, Portland Place, London, on 27 February 1809, the youngest of five children, and the third son of Henry de Michele (1774–1828) and his wife, Susan Manning (1770–1854). His grandfather was Italian-born. Michele was educated at Westminster School from 1822 and practised as a solicitor until he became editor and part proprietor of the *Morning Post*, buying shares in the newspaper after the death of its owner, Nicholas Byrne, in 1832. He increased his holding to one-tenth in 1834. In 1841 Michele became the major shareholder, owning 121 of 240 shares, with overall control of the newspaper. On 28 February 1835 he married Mary, daughter of John Llewelyn of Morriston Hall, Swansea. Between 1836 and 1848 they had four sons and four daughters.

The *Morning Post*, founded in 1772 by a group of tradesmen, was politically Conservative, articulating and representing the interests of Britain's landowners and fashionable society. According to the obituary of William Byrne, Michele's business partner, Byrne expanded the range of the paper beyond political reporting to reflect his interests in science and the arts. As editor Michele may also have contributed to the process, but his impact on the political direction of the paper was more profound. When the Protectionist Party, led by his friend Lord George Bentinck, opposed Sir Robert Peel's revision of the corn laws and the trend towards free trade, Michele championed their cause.

Dismayed, Byrne sought to revise their partnership agreement in 1844, claiming that Michele had sacrificed the paper's independence, reducing its circulation and profits. The issue was resolved in June 1845 when Michele bought out Byrne with money borrowed on a mortgage from T. B. Crompton, the Lancashire paper manufacturer who supplied the *Morning Post*. Michele invested in new machinery for the offices in Wellington Street and improved the premises, but in 1849 Crompton, citing his own trading difficulties, called in the mortgage. Michele turned to his political friends for financial assistance but they could raise only a few hundred pounds. The *Morning Post* passed to Peter Borthwick, beginning his family's long association with the paper.

The loss of the *Morning Post* in 1849 was the defining moment in Michele's life. His subsequent appointment as Britain's consul to St Petersburg was viewed with suspicion by the tories, but there is nothing in Michele's many accounts of his departure from the *Morning Post* to support their claims that he was being rewarded for not opposing Palmerston or being removed because he had 'inconvenient information' (Koss, 79–81). Fresh disaster beset Michele in the aftermath of the Crimean War. Since 1728 the salary of the post had been combined with duties levied on British shipping on the authority of the Russia Company, but neither British traders nor the Russia Company wished to resume the arrangement, which was subsequently prohibited by parliament. Without the levy, Michele's income was reduced by half, compounding the losses sustained during the war when he and his family had had to live on half pay in Brussels. Michele appealed to successive foreign secretaries (including Lord Malmesbury, whose assistance he had sought to maintain ownership of the *Morning Post*), and to Napoleon III, whose cause he had backed during the emperor's exile in England. Eventually awarded a pension, Michele retired from the consular service in 1866. His ill-fated involvement in public and official life left him in financial difficulties for many years.

On his retirement Michele invested in a London cement firm, Francis & Co., which his youngest child, Vitale, an engineer, managed, later becoming a partner. Reading was Michele's main leisure activity. He occasionally held play-readings at the consulate, and often copied extracts from newspapers and books into his diaries. He died at his home, Old Palace Gardens, Weybridge, Surrey, on 19 February 1898 from a renal coma, and was buried in Weybridge cemetery, his will stipulating that his burial should be as simple as possible. Among his papers in the Bodleian Library are two photographs of him as a consul and a photograph of a miniature on ivory of Mary de Michele.

HELEN LANGLEY

Sources Bodl. Oxf., MSS De Michele · S. E. Koss, *The rise and fall of the political press in Britain*, 2 vols. (1981–4); repr. (1990) · W. Hindle, *The Morning Post, 1772–1937: portrait of a newspaper* (1937) · R. Lucas, *Lord Glenesk and the Morning Post* (1910) · S. Morrison, *The English newspaper* (1932) · W. C. Price, *The literature of journalism, an annotated biography* (1959) · Bodl. Oxf., MSS Kimberley · Bodl. Oxf., MSS Crampton · 'Peel, Sir Robert', *DNB* · d. cert. · copy of will, 1897, Bodl. Oxf., MS Eng. misc. b. 431, fol. 23 · *Benjamin Disraeli letters*, ed. J. A. W. Gunn and others (1982–), vol. 3, appx I, p. 418, n. 1
Archives Bodl. Oxf., corresp., diaries and papers | Bodl. Oxf., Clarendon MSS · Bodl. Oxf., letters to Sir John Crampton · Bodl. Oxf., letters to Lord Kimberley · U. Southampton L., letters to Lord Palmerston
Likenesses photograph, 1860, Bodl. Oxf. · de Dresde, portrait, 1860–69 · Mayall, portrait, 1861, Bodl. Oxf. · photograph (after miniature on ivory), Bodl. Oxf.; presented to V&A, 1930
Wealth at death £19,284 4s. 10d.: probate, 15 April 1898, CGPLA Eng. & Wales

Michelham. For this title name *see* Stern, Herbert, first Baron Michelham (1851–1919) [*see under* Stern family (*per. c.*1830–1964)].

Michell, Anthony George Maldon (1870–1959), mechanical engineer, was born on 21 June 1870 in Islington, London, the second son and youngest of five children of John Michell and his wife, Grace Rowse. Of Cornish and perhaps Huguenot extraction, his parents were reared near Tavistock in Devon. Energetic and serious-minded people, unscholastic but serious-minded, they emigrated to Australia about 1855 and settled in the small goldmining community of Maldon, north-west of Melbourne. To further the education of their sons (George had been born during a visit to England), they moved to Melbourne, where George and his elder brother, John Henry (1863–1940), attended South Yarra state school. In 1884 the family returned to England and Michell completed his schooling at the Perse School, Cambridge, while John Henry Michell was becoming successively senior wrangler, Smith's prizeman, and fellow of Trinity. About 1890 the family returned to permanent residence in Melbourne, where Michell took courses in civil and mining engineering at the university. After completing his studies with great distinction (BCE 1895, MCE 1899), he became pupil assistant and later partner with Bernhard Alexander Smith in his engineering practice.

In 1903 Michell commenced an independent practice centred on hydraulic engineering; this involved extensive travel in Victoria and Tasmania. *Inter alia* he was consultant to the Mount Lyell Copper Mining Company, which made one of the first hydroelectric installations in Australia, designer of the pumping machinery for the Murray valley irrigation works, and investigator (1919) for the Victorian government of the hydroelectric possibilities later developed on the Kiewa River. Along with this activity he pursued his ideas for mechanical inventions, which probably had begun to germinate before 1900. His international reputation was established through his invention of the Michell thrust block, a device for supporting a rotating propeller or turbine shaft against a large longitudinal force externally applied to it. This invention, patented in 1905, was based on theoretical investigations regarding fluid motion and the principles of lubrication. It revolutionized thrust technology, especially in the field of marine propulsion, and made possible much of the modern development of steam and water turbines and of large fast ships. Of his other inventions the most striking and potentially revolutionary was the Michell crankless engine, which was patented in 1917. Michell gave up his Victorian practice in 1925 to concentrate on the manufacture of this engine. He spent some years travelling in Britain, Europe, and the United States, before returning permanently to Melbourne about 1933.

In 1934 Michell was elected FRS; in 1938 he was awarded the Kernot memorial medal of the University of Melbourne, and in 1943 the James Watt international medal of the Institution of Mechanical Engineers, London. He wrote little beyond his book, *Lubrication: its Principles and Practice* (1950), a major work, published when he was eighty, and three theoretical papers reprinted in 1964 along with those of his brother. Many of his results in theoretical and experimental mechanics were published only in the specifications of his dozen or more patented inventions.

Michell's achievements rested on the rare combination of mathematical and theoretical power with mechanical flair and inventiveness, all of which he had in high degree; his own assessment of their relative importance is shown on the title-page of his book on lubrication, where he quoted Leonardo da Vinci's 'theory is the captain, practice the soldiers'. But his achievements rested equally on his character, in the formation of which family influence was very strong. In work and conduct he adhered firmly to the highest standards; he found refreshment from contact with nature and simple country life which were essential to his mental health and comfort. Hence came his ideal, 'that the products of mechanical art should be truly serviceable and durable, and hence of necessity simple in construction, however recondite in theory'. A reticent man, who sought only a small circle of friends, Michell displayed always a direct quiet manner and genuine courtesy and modesty. His conversation was (in his latter years at any rate) rather deliberate, underpinned by wide knowledge and keen intelligence, with sometimes a flash of dry humour. He never married. His mental capacity failed at the end; he died at Camberwell, Melbourne, on 17 February 1959 and was buried in Boroondara cemetery. The A. G. M. Michell award was created in 1978 by the Institution of Engineers, Australia, to perpetuate his memory.

T. M. CHERRY, rev.

Sources T. M. Cherry, *Memoirs FRS*, 8 (1962), 91–103 · *The Times* (21 Feb 1959), 10a · *AusDB*
Likenesses photograph, Institution of Mechanical Engineers, London
Wealth at death £174,009: *AusDB*

Michell, Charles Cornwallis [*formerly* Charles Collier Michell] (**1793–1851**), army officer and engineer, was born at Exeter on 29 March 1793, the second son, fourth of six children, of Lieutenant Sampson Michell RN (1755–1809) and Ann (1765–1838), daughter of Samuel Shears MD, of Bedminster, near Bristol. Michell's marriage certificate (1814) shows that he was baptized Charles Collier; only later being known as Charles Cornwallis. According to a mistaken statement in the *Dictionary of National Biography* Cornwallis 'became attached to him through some confusion with Cornwall, the name of the county in which he was born'. This may have occurred during his time in the Portuguese service, though possibly he found this name more euphonious than the relatively humble Collier.

Michell entered the Royal Military Academy, Woolwich, as a cadet on 28 April 1807 and was commissioned second-lieutenant, Royal Artillery, on 2 October 1809. The next year, through the influence of his father's cousin, Colonel Rufane Shaw Donkin, Michell was seconded to the Portuguese army in the Peninsula. He commanded an artillery company at the siege and capture of Badajoz (March–April 1812), and a field battery of 9-pounders at the battles of Vitoria (21 June 1813) and Toulouse (10 April 1814). During the latter he was wounded and 'greatly distinguished' himself. Meanwhile, on 16 March 1813 he had been promoted first-lieutenant in the Royal Artillery, though a captain in the Portuguese army. For his services in the Peninsula Michell was awarded a gold medal for Vitoria with a clasp for Toulouse and the military general service medal for Badajoz.

While Michell was quartered at Toulouse he met and eloped with Anne d'Arragon, the fourteen-year-old daughter of a retired French army officer, whom he married on 10 October 1814. They had four daughters, Louisa, Julia, Eveline Marie (b. 16 April 1821), and Anne (b. 28 Oct 1829).

On 4 September 1817 Michell was promoted captain in the Royal Artillery and placed on half pay. However, he remained attached to the Portuguese army, serving on the staff of Marshal William Carr Beresford, for some years in Brazil and France, until 1820, when he retired to Nantes, France. There he and his growing family lived in near poverty on only £120 per year. On 25 March 1824 Michell was appointed military drawing master at the Royal Military College, Sandhurst, before becoming professor of fortification at the Royal Military Academy, Woolwich, in September 1825. He was promoted brevet major on 5 January 1826.

In April 1828 Michell was appointed surveyor-general and civil engineer of the Cape Colony at a salary of £700 per year, he and his family reaching Cape Town in October. Almost immediately Michell turned his attention to improving the roads and mountain passes of the colony. Within three years, aided by military and convict labour, passes over the Hottentots Holland (1830) and Houwhoek (1831) mountains had been constructed, the former named Sir Lowry's Pass after the governor, Sir Lowry Cole. During the following decade two further passes were designed by Michell, the Montagu Pass (1847) and Michell's Pass (1848). In 1836 he devised a plan to improve Table Bay harbour (which in the event was not begun owing to a lack of funds), and in 1844 he chaired a commission which made fresh recommendations for its improvement. He designed and supervised the construction of two lighthouses on the South African coast, at Mouille Point (1842) and Cape Agulhas (1848). He also designed the Cape Recife lighthouse, near Port Elizabeth (1851). In his capacity as civil engineer Michell thus proved active and effective, but as surveyor-general he was less successful. His department's dilatoriness in attending to the surveying and granting of title deeds to farms on the frontier districts was one of the causes of the great trek, which led to the founding of the Orange Free State and South African (Transvaal) republics.

Michell served in the Cape Frontier War of 1834–5 as deputy quartermaster-general to the army under the command of the governor, Sir Benjamin D'Urban, and was appointed a KH (1836). On 23 November 1841 he advanced to brevet lieutenant-colonel. For his earlier services in Portugal he was made a knight of the order of St Benedict of Avis (1844) and a commander of the order of the Tower and Sword (1846). A petition to the Colonial Office after his retirement for a knighthood was unsuccessful.

Michell was an accomplished musician and linguist, fluent in French and Portuguese, with a working knowledge of Cape Dutch (Afrikaans). He was also a talented architect and artist, designing the Anglican churches at Rondebosch, Cape Town (1834), and Bathurst, eastern Cape (1837), and the commercial exchange, Port Elizabeth (1843). Several of his drawings were used to illustrate the book *Excursions in Western Africa and Narrative of a Campaign in Kaffir-Land* (1837) by Sir James Edward Alexander, who married Michell's third daughter. A number of his caricature drawings of Cape Town personalities are in the Museum Africa, Johannesburg. He was widely popular,

and on his retirement as surveyor-general received an address from the inhabitants of Cape Town.

In December 1847 Michell suffered a severe stroke, which affected his speech and ability to write, leading to a grant of twelve months' sick leave in England. His health did not improve, and he tendered his resignation in August 1848. On retirement Michell lived at Eltham, Kent, where he died on 28 March 1851; on 4 April he was buried at St Mary's Church, Bexley. His wife survived him for less than two years, dying on 3 January 1853, and was buried beside her husband. Michell was regarded by a contemporary as 'one of the tallest and handsomest men in the Peninsular Army' (*Colburn's United Service Magazine*, 121). His masonic diploma of Lodge Charity, Exeter (1820), gives his height as just under 6 foot, with dark hair and hazel eyes.

F. G. RICHINGS

Sources *Colburn's United Service Magazine*, 2 (1851), 119–22 • *DSAB* • J. E. Alexander, *Excursions in western Africa and narrative of a campaign in Kaffir-land*, 2 vols. (1837) • C. C. Michell, 'On the roads and kloofs in the Cape Colony', *Journal of the Royal Geographical Society*, 6 (1836), 168–74 • G. C. Boase, *Collectanea Cornubiensia: a collection of biographical and topographical notes relating to the county of Cornwall* (1890) • E. Wood, *From midshipman to field marshal*, 2 vols. (1906) • H. E. Wood, *Winnowed memories* (1917) • L. C. Duly, *British land policy at the Cape, 1795–1844* (1968) • L. S. Challis, 'British officers serving in the Portuguese army, 1809–1814', *Journal of the Society for Army Historical Research*, 27 (1949), 50–60 • R. Lewcock, *Early nineteenth century architecture in South Africa: a study of the interaction of two cultures, 1795–1837* (1963) • J. Burman, *So high the road: mountain passes of the western Cape* (1963) • H. Williams, *Southern lights: lighthouses of southern Africa* (1993) • *DNB*

Archives government archives depot, Cape Town, South Africa **Likenesses** photograph, *c.*1815 (after painting), University of Natal, Durban, South Africa, Campbell collections, Sir Evelyn Wood MSS

Michell, Edward Thomas (1786–1841), army officer, entered the Royal Military Academy, Woolwich, on 27 January 1802, and passed out as second lieutenant Royal Artillery on 8 September 1803. He became first lieutenant on 13 September 1803, second captain on 11 August 1811, brevet major on 17 March 1814, first captain on 29 August 1825, brevet lieutenant-colonel on 22 July 1830, and regimental lieutenant-colonel on 11 June 1838. He was detached from his company at Gibraltar to Spain in 1810, and commanded a guerrilla division in the Sierra de Ronda; he was present at the capture of Ronda, the battle of El Brosque and Bornos, and the night attack on Arcos and its capture. He commanded the artillery of the British force occupying Tarifa in 1810–12, was shot through the shoulder at the battle of Barossa, and was praised for his skilful handling of the artillery at the final defence of Tarifa in December 1811. In 1812 he was engaged at the attack on the forts of Salamanca, the battle of Salamanca, and minor actions.

From December 1813 to May 1814 Michell served in the Low Countries at Merxem, the bombardment of Antwerp, and the attack on Bergen-op-Zoom. During these operations he once extinguished a lighted shell that had fallen into a wagonload of ammunition. He volunteered to lead one of the assaulting columns at Bergen-op-Zoom, where he was severely wounded. He was British commissioner with local rank of colonel with the Spanish armies during the latter part of the Carlist War (August 1839 to December 1840), and received the Spanish decorations of St Fernando, Charles III, and Isabella the Catholic.

Michell was then dispatched to Syria, with local rank of brigadier-general, to command the detachments of Royal Artillery and sappers and miners sent with Admiral Stafford's fleet to assist the Turks in driving the Egyptian army out of Syria. With the other British officers he accompanied the Turks, under General Jochmus, in their advance from Jaffa towards Gaza, and was present at the battle of Medjdel on 15 January 1841, which compelled the Egyptians to retreat. The British advised the immediate seizure of Gaza, 6 miles distant. Jochmus prevaricated over the bad state of the roads, and two days later news arrived of the convention concluded by Napier at Alexandria, ending the war.

Michell, who was made CB on 19 July 1838 and was in receipt of £300 a year for wounds, was popular with his fellow officers and his men. He was described as an open-hearted, frank old soldier, small in stature, with a stoop from the effects of an old wound and a keen, clear eye. Michell died on 24 January 1841 of fever caused by sleeping in his wet clothes on the night after the battle of Medjdel. He was buried by the British sappers in a grave in the left flank of the Sir Sidney Smith bastion of the fortress of Jaffa. By permission of the Turkish authorities a large white marble tablet, subscribed for by the British officers who served with him in Syria, was afterwards placed near the grave.   H. M. Chichester, *rev.* James Falkner

Sources *Army List* • *Naval and Military Gazette* (20 Feb 1841) • *Hart's Army List* • J. Kane, *List of officers of the royal regiment of artillery from the year 1716 to the year 1899*, rev. W. H. Askwith, 4th edn (1900) • W. F. P. Napier, *History of the war in the Peninsula and in the south of France, from the year 1807 to the year 1814*, new edn, 6 vols. (1851) • J. A. Browne, *England's artillerymen* (1865) • *Corrections and additions to the Dictionary of National Biography*, Institute of Historical Research (1966)

Michell, Francis (*b.* *c.*1556, *d.* in or after **1628**), administrator, was probably of an Essex family, but his parents are unknown. He matriculated, aged eighteen, at Magdalen Hall, Oxford, about 1574 and seems to have been subsequently employed as private secretary to a succession of noblemen. In a letter to secretary Conway (February 1626) he speaks of having served 'six great persons' in that capacity, but only gives the name of Lord Burgh, lord deputy of Ireland. He was secretary from 1594 to 1597 to Sir William Russel, lord deputy of Ireland, and was probably in the employment of William Davison and Lord Salisbury; possibly in the service of the latter he visited Rome, where he was imprisoned by the inquisition. He appears to have performed services in Scotland on behalf of James VI before that king's accession to the English throne. Doubtless through the favour of one of his patrons he secured (25 May 1603) the grant in reversion of the office of clerk of the market for life. He seems to have returned from abroad, where he had been travelling for six years, about 1611, and subsequently to have lived in Clerkenwell as a JP for Middlesex. There is an entry in the register of St James,

Clerkenwell, dated 16 August 1612, of the marriage of Francis Michell and Sisley Wentworth.

In 1618 the king adopted the policy of extending and more vigorously enforcing existing patents. On 6 April 1618 the original patentee surrendered by agreement the gold and silver thread patent; fresh patents were immediately granted, and a commission was issued for the discovery and punishment of offenders. Michell was appointed a member of this commission, and he and one Henry Tweedy were throughout the subsequent proceedings the acting commissioners. Their duties were to guard against the importation, or unauthorized manufacture, of gold and silver thread, and any two or more of them were granted the power of imprisonment. These powers, however, proved insufficient, and on 20 October 1618 a fuller commission was issued with the name of Sir Giles Mompesson added. Michell had exceeded his authority under the first commission and now, stimulated by the activity of Mompesson, he exercised his powers corruptly and with considerable harshness for two years, thereby incurring great odium. The result was an outburst of public feeling against the enforcement of the obnoxious patent. A parliamentary committee of inquiry into monopolies reported that the enforcement of the patent involved serious grievances. Yet it was as one of the patentees for ale houses that Michell was called to the bar of the Commons to answer alleged abuses. Appearing on 23 February 1621, '[h]e, by rash words, presented the Commons with a welcome, if unexpected, opportunity to evade the legal complications involved in reviving Parliamentary judicature' (Russell, 105). Dismissing the principal allegation against him—namely that his patent derogated from the authority of local justices—Michell, who in December 1620 had been knighted, was accordingly committed by the House of Commons to the Tower for contempt, and travelled thither 'on foot and bareheaded' (*CSP dom.*, 1621, 106).

Michell's treatment in respect of the ale-house patent was highly controversial—the authority for the Commons' action was dubious. However, there was no denying his culpability in the principal matters against him. On 6 March 1621 he confessed before the Commons that he had received £100 per annum for executing the commission for gold and silver thread. On 26 April 1621 he was tried at the bar of the House of Lords, the chief accusations against him being that he had erected an office and kept a court and exacted bonds, and that he had taken money in a suit to compound the same. On 4 May 1621 the lord chief justice sentenced him to degradation from knighthood, a fine of £1000, disability to hold or receive any office in future, and imprisonment during the king's pleasure in Finsbury gaol, 'in the same chamber where he provided for others, the tower where he now remains being a prison too worthy of him'. On 23 June the portion of the sentence relating to degradation from knighthood was carried out with all formalities publicly in Westminster Hall, and Michell was proclaimed by the herald as 'no knight but arrant knave'. The king, however, granted the commissioner's petition for release from prison, dated 30 June 1621 (not impossibly in order to avoid his testifying against Buckingham, leading proponent of the patents policy). Evidently Sir Robert Cotton had spoken up in Michell's favour at the hearing before the king which led to his release as well as the remission of his fine. In the Lords, Prince Charles, Buckingham, and the earl of Arundel had all opposed degradation from knighthood, too.

Shortly after his release Michell petitioned the king for means to live, and at the same time he wrote to Prince Charles and Buckingham begging their support; to the latter he hinted that he was deserving of his especial favour, 'as he [Buckingham] could not but commiserate, knowing wherefore his sufferings were inflicted' (BL, Cotton MS Julius C.III. fol. 254), but the favourite declined to become a suitor on his behalf. In December 1623 Michell was in trouble for an attack he had made in writing on his old enemies, Lord Coke and Sir Dudley Digges, and narrowly escaped examination before the Star Chamber. At this time he was beset with financial difficulties, and in the same year petitioned the council for protection from his creditors, 'having lost most of his estate in his trouble' (DNB). In July 1625 he presented a petition to the Commons for release of an unjust information made against him in their house in 1620, and he begged for leave to discourse to a committee the 'slights and practises' then used (BL, Harley MS 161, fol. 96). On the accession of Charles I he represented, in a carefully framed petition, that he had screened the principals (notably Sir Edward Villiers) against whom the attack of the Commons had been directed; and the house, he complained, after 'failinge against Cedars then oppressed your supplicant, a poore shrubb, to his utter undoinge' (PRO, SP 16/21/105). His petitions were ungranted in March 1628, when he wrote to a friend that if it were necessary for him to come to London for the prosecution of his suit 'he will teach his old limbs so weary a tedious journey' (BL, Cotton MS Julius C.III. fol. 256). No more is heard of Michell after this date and his date of death remains unknown.

WILLIAM CARR, rev. SEAN KELSEY

Sources E. R. Foster, 'The procedure of the House of Commons against patents and monopolies, 1621–4', Conflict in Stuart England, ed. W. Aiken and B. D. Henning (1960), 57–85 · C. G. C. Tite, Impeachment and parliamentary judicature in early Stuart England (1974) · C. Russell, Parliaments and English politics, 1621–1629 (1979) · W. A. Shaw, The knights of England, 2 (1906), 176 · Foster, Alum. Oxon. · CSP dom., 1621 · JHL, 3 (1620–28)

Michell, Henry (1713/14–1789), classical scholar, was born at Lewes, Sussex. He was educated locally before entering Clare College, Cambridge, on 18 May 1732. He graduated BA (1735), MA (1739), and became a fellow of the college (1738–40). In 1739 he was presented to the rectory of Maresfield in Sussex, and in 1744 to the vicarage of Brighton with the rectory of West Bletchington united. In 1741 he married Faith (d. in or after 1789), only daughter of the Revd Francis Reade of Bedford; they had sixteen children. Michell lived in Brighton for the rest of his life, enjoying ample means, the friendship of many men of note, and the reputation of an accomplished Greek and Latin scholar. Such were Michell's talents and so admirable his character that he was thought 'formed for the higher

sphere than the parochial duties of a county town' (GM). In fact he played an important part in the rapid development of Brighton, and for a short time included the second duke of Wellington among his pupils. In 1766 Michell published De arte medendi apud priscos musices, with a later 1783 edition dedicated to the earl of Shelburne; this was followed by De jure colonias inter et metropolin (1777). Michell died at Brighton on 31 October 1789, aged seventy-five, and was buried in the parish church, where an inscription was set up to his memory. His wife and seven of his children survived him. At his death he left with other manuscripts a translation, with notes, of Voltaire's Le dîner du comte de Boulainvilliers, 1768, par Mons. St. Hiacinte.

A. F. POLLARD, rev. PHILIP CARTER

Sources Nichols, Lit. anecdotes, 4.447 · Nichols, Illustrations, 4.866–70 · GM, 1st ser., 59 (1789), 1055 · Venn, Alum. Cant. · J. E. Wilmot, Memoirs of the life of the Right Honourable Sir John Eardley Wilmot, 2nd edn (1811) · will, PRO, PROB 11/1185, fols. 156v–158v · N&Q, 12th ser., 1 (1916), 476, 517 · N&Q, 12th ser., 2 (1916), 35, 98 · N&Q, 13th ser., 1 (1923), 289, 395
Likenesses E. Scott, stipple (after C. Sherriff), BM, NPG

Michell, John (1724/5–1793), astronomer, was described as of Nottinghamshire on 17 June 1742, when he was admitted to Queens' College, Cambridge. He was elected a Bible clerk there on 23 January 1747, graduated (in mathematics) as fourth wrangler in 1748, was elected to a fellowship in 1749, and proceeded MA in 1752 and BD in 1761. Between 1751 and 1760 he held various college offices, including those of lecturer in Hebrew, arithmetic, geometry, and Greek. From 20 March 1760 to June 1763 he was rector of St Botolph's, Cambridge. He resigned his fellowship of Queens' on 8 April 1764. His membership of the Royal Society dated from 12 June 1760, but his name does not appear in the lists until 1762, in which year he was appointed Woodwardian professor of geology at Cambridge.

Michell published at Cambridge in 1750 A Treatise of Artificial Magnets (2nd edn 1751, translated into French 1752), in which he described the mode of making artificial magnets by 'double touch' and stated the law of variation of magnetic action according to the inverse squares of distances. He communicated to the Royal Society his observations of the comet of January 1760, made at Cambridge with a Hadley's quadrant, and shortly afterwards Conjectures Concerning the Cause, and Observations upon the Phenomena of Earthquakes (1760), in which he put forward the theory of their origin through the elastic force of subterraneanly generated steam. A Recommendation of Hadley's Quadrant for Surveying followed in 1765, and A Proposal of a Method for Measuring Degrees of Longitude upon Parallels of the Equator in 1767.

On 7 and 14 May 1767 there was read to the Royal Society Michell's paper entitled An enquiry into the probable parallax and magnitude of the fixed stars from the quantity of light which they afford us, arguably the most innovative and perceptive contribution to stellar astronomy to be published in the eighteenth century. He used a pioneering probability argument to show that most double stars were not formed of two independent elements that chanced to lie in the same direction from earth, but were two companion stars bound together by an attractive force. The same was true of a star cluster such as the Pleiades, and Michell investigated the possibility of our sun's belonging to some similar association. He anticipated the presence of an element in stellar proper motions due to the sun's motion in space, and foresaw that the distances of objects affected by this 'secular parallax' could be deduced from its amount. He finally pointed out the law connecting the visibility of small stars with telescopic aperture and the information on stellar distances that could result.

In 1779 William Herschel, ignorant of Michell's 1767 paper, began searching for double stars on the assumption that they were each formed of two independent elements. In 1783, therefore, Michell presented a second paper to the Royal Society on his argument that most double stars were two companion stars bound together by an attractive force. In the same paper he speculated about stars so massive that their gravitational pull prevented light from leaving them, the first consideration of the 'black holes' of modern cosmology.

Shortly before his death Michell devised a method and completed an apparatus for weighing the earth by means of the torsion balance, of which he was the original inventor. This apparatus passed from the hands of William Hyde Wollaston to those of Henry Cavendish (1731–1810), who successfully carried out in 1798 the experiments planned by Michell.

In 1767 Michell became rector of Thornhill, Yorkshire, where he lived for the rest of his life. He married Anne Brecknock, perhaps a local lady; she pastured a flock of sheep on the 1½ acres called Gonston Ing, which Michell held on Thornhill Common. Their daughter Mary married Thomas Turton of Leeds. Michell died on 21 April 1793 and was buried at Thornhill on 27 April. His wife and daughter survived him. His scientific instruments were presented after his death to Queens' College, Cambridge.

A. M. CLERKE, rev. MICHAEL HOSKIN

Sources private information (1894) · R. McCormmach, 'John Michell and Henry Cavendish: weighing the stars', British Journal for the History of Science, 4 (1968–9), 126–55 · Z. Kopal, 'Michell, John', DSB · C. L. Hardin, 'The scientific work of John Michell', Annals of Science, 22 (1966), 27–47 · will, PRO, PROB 11/1232, sig. 274 · J. Charlesworth, ed., The register of the parish of Thornhill, 3 vols. (1907–15)

Michell, Sir Lewis Loyd (1842–1928), banker in South Africa, was born at Plymouth on 11 August 1842, the second son of John Michell, solicitor, of Ilfracombe, a member of an old Cornish family, and his wife, Mary Elizabeth, née Bryan. He was named after the banker Lewis Loyd (father of Samuel Jones Loyd, first Baron Overstone), with whose help he was sent to school at Christ's Hospital, London. In 1859 he entered Bolitho's Bank at Penzance, and after four years' training there was transferred to the London and South African Bank. In 1864 he was sent to Port Elizabeth, Cape Colony, where he remained for twenty-one years. In 1871 he married Maria Agnes, daughter of

Edward Philpott, magistrate at Uitenhage. They had four sons and three daughters.

In 1873 Michell left the London and South African Bank in order to become manager of the Standard Bank of South Africa at Port Elizabeth. His life at Port Elizabeth seems to have been peaceful enough, until the outbreak in 1880 of the First South African War. At the conclusion of that war, in 1881, he met presidents Kruger and Brand and secured the insertion in the Pretoria convention of a clause safeguarding banking interests in the Transvaal. In 1885 Michell was transferred to Cape Town, which then became his permanent headquarters. It was at about this time that Michell met Cecil Rhodes, then a dynamic force on the Kimberley diamond fields and a prominent young member of Cape Colony's parliament. Among so many of his other projects, Rhodes was in a year to acquire control over all the diamond diggings and, overnight, to become one of the wealthiest men in the British empire. Although Rhodes was always guided in his diamond consolidation efforts by the astute financial brain of Alfred Beit, advice from a steady banker in Cape Town would also have been welcome. Rhodes never had a good head for figures and required a reliable money man; Michell was that person and in time even became a close confidant.

Michell was Rhodes's senior by a decade, and was married; even so, like so many others in South Africa, he worshipped the young visionary imperialist, 'I loved Rhodes', he said, 'as I have never loved any other man.' Rhodes never loved Michell in return, but he welcomed his counsel on innumerable occasions. By 1891 Rhodes was prime minister of Cape Colony. Two years earlier banks had collapsed throughout the colony, as had banks in London and on the continent. Only Michell's Standard Bank had survived. The legislation of 1891 to reform banking in the Cape and prevent future collapses was shaped by Michell, by treasury minister John Xavier Merriman, and by Rhodes. For the next decade, until Rhodes's death in 1902, Michell held his general power of attorney, acting for him in particular with regard to the affairs of the British South Africa Company. Rhodes, who had early premonitions of his death, asked Michell to become one of his executors. Together they shared ideas about the lofty goals of what became the Rhodes scholarships. For that reason, and others, Rhodes insisted that, upon his death, Michell should promise to succeed him as chairman of De Beers Consolidated Mines and become a director of the British South Africa Company.

Meanwhile Michell's influence in the banking world steadily increased. In 1893 he attended a conference called to consider the adoption of a single coinage for South Africa. The conference broke down, as Willem Leyds, who represented the Transvaal, insisted that the proposed coinage should bear the head of President Kruger. It was on the occasion of this conference that Kruger asked Michell why he could not speak Dutch, an attack which Michell countered by suggesting that, as the president had been born at Colesberg, in British territory, he should be familiar with the English language. In 1895 Michell became sole general manager in South Africa of the Standard Bank.

Throughout the Second South African War of 1899–1902 Michell directed the financing of the army's requirements in South Africa on behalf of the British War Office. At the close of the war, in fulfilment of his promise to Rhodes, Michell retired from the Standard Bank, and was appointed chairman of De Beers Consolidated Mines and a director of the British South Africa Company.

Michell was knighted in 1902 in recognition of his services as chairman of the Cape martial law board, which had been appointed to consider the cases of British subjects who had been guilty of treasonable practices during the war. He was elected a member of the Cape house of assembly, and in 1903 became minister without portfolio in Leander Starr Jameson's cabinet. Parliamentary life, however, in no way appealed to him, and in 1905 he resigned his seat, and also the chairmanship of De Beers. From this time his attention was chiefly concentrated on the business of the Rhodes Trust and of the British South Africa Company, which entailed frequent visits to London and Rhodesia, although his interest in public affairs was by no means diminished. Together with Sir William Milton and Sir Charles Coghlan he represented Rhodesia at the national convention (October 1908 – May 1909) which preceded the formation of the Union of South Africa.

In 1910 Michell published his biography of Rhodes, with the object, as he said, of showing that Rhodes was a great Englishman. His two-volume *Life of the Rt. Hon. Cecil John Rhodes* (1910) was not the first of the biographies of Rhodes, but it was the fullest and the best before Basil Williams's *Rhodes* was published in 1923. It was the work of an unabashed admirer, and based as much on first- and secondhand conversation and observation as on any particular research. Yet Michell's reasonable, anodyne account succeeded in shaping and warping the world's view of Rhodes for several, if not many, generations. Naturally, Michell avoided or glossed over those aspects of Rhodes's life which were capable of being criticized. He even sought to downplay Rhodes's role in the Jameson raid, and the extent to which that event hardened the anti-British feelings of Afrikaners.

At this period Michell's health was giving him cause for anxiety, and in 1917 he resigned his position of Rhodes trustee. With advancing age his activities naturally decreased, but he retained to the last his directorship of the British South Africa Company and his close connection with all Rhodesian affairs. He died at his home, Ednight, Duke Road, Rondebosch, Cape Province, on 29 October 1928, survived by his wife and five of their children.   D. CHAPLIN, rev. ROBERT I. ROTBERG

Sources L. Michell, *Life of the Rt. Hon. Cecil John Rhodes*, 2 vols. (1910) · R. I. Rotberg, *The founder: Cecil Rhodes and the pursuit of power* (1988) · private information (1937) · personal knowledge (1937) · J. A. H., 'Michell, Lewis Lloyd', *DSAB* · *CGPLA Eng. & Wales* (1929) · *DNB*
Archives Bodl. RH, British South Africa Co. MSS · National Archives of South Africa, Cape Town, 'Sixty years in and out of South Africa' [unpublished autobiography] · National Archives of Zimbabwe | BL, corresp. with Lord Selborne, Add. MS 46003 · Bodl. RH, Rhodes MSS · Derbys. RO, Gell MSS · National Archives of Zimbabwe, corresp. with Francis Chaplin
Likenesses portrait, repro. in *British South Africa Annual* (1916–17) · portrait, repro. in *South African Who's Who* (1927) · portrait, repro. in *Men of the times: old colonialists of the Cape Colony and Orange River Colony* (Johannesburg, 1906) · portrait, repro. in H. A. Chilvers, *The story of De Beers* (1939)
Wealth at death £2147 10s. 4d. effects in England: probate, 2 Jan 1929, *CGPLA Eng. & Wales*

Michell, Matthew (1705?–1752), naval officer, was the first son of Christopher Michell of Chitterne, Wiltshire, and Anne Willys of London. He went to sea in 1713 at the age of eight, was commissioned as lieutenant in the navy in 1729, and received his first command, of the bomb-vessel *Terrible*, in 1738. In 1740 he was appointed captain of the *Pearl* (40 guns), which on 18 September sailed for the South Sea as part of Commodore George Anson's squadron. On 3 November he replaced Captain Norris as commander of the *Gloucester* (50 guns), a ship which suffered terrible damage and casualties in rounding the Horn. It says much for Michell's tenacity that the *Gloucester* eventually made its rendezvous with Anson at Juan Fernández in July 1741, though so weak were the remnants of the crew that the vessel took more than four weeks to make harbour after first sighting the island.

Although the ship was repaired, and additional men sent on board, the *Gloucester* seems never to have recovered from its ordeal. In March 1742 Michell wrote that he had lost almost 300 men, only eighty surviving of those who had sailed from England. As the *Gloucester* struggled across the north Pacific it lost its mainmast and with 7 foot of water in the hold was in sinking condition. Only sixteen men and eleven boys were able to get on deck. On 13 August the ship was blown up, and its crew taken on board Anson's *Centurion*. 'Thus ended the *Gloucester*,' its purser wrote, 'a ship justly esteemed the beauty of the English navy' (Williams, 128).

For Michell, now a supernumerary on the *Centurion*, further hardships and dangers lay ahead. In rare references to him in the journals he is described, together with the other officers, as working like a seaman as the crew tried to keep the *Centurion* afloat. When the ship reached Macao, Michell was allowed to take passage for England. He thus missed the dramatic climax of the voyage— Anson capturing the Acapulco galleon in June 1743. Even so the returning officers received an enthusiastic welcome, as the report of Anson's brother shows: 'The Captains of your squadron have been sought for and pointed out in particular places as a spectacle, most graciously received by the Admiralty' (Williams, 180).

Michell did not spend long on land. In October 1743 he was appointed to the *Worcester*; and in 1745 he was made commodore of the Downs squadron. In 1747 his cruisers off the coasts of Flanders and Zealand played an important role in the restoration of the Stadholderate, and in May 1747 Count William Bentinck wrote to the earl of Sandwich that Michell's 'diligence, activity, prudence, and spirit are quite remarkable, and will gain him universal admiration' (BL, Add. MS 32808, fol. 197). A rather different picture emerges in Michell's letters, which show him in poor health with his 'South-Sea distemper [scurvy]', and disillusioned with 'this Cursed Station' (BL, Add. MS 15956, fols. 254v–255, 258). On 16 March 1748 he was elected MP for Westbury, and resigned his commission. And on 4 March 1749 he married Frances, daughter of John Ashfordby of Cheshunt, Hertfordshire, who brought with her, it was said, a fortune of £20,000; they had one son and one daughter. Michell died on 29 April 1752, reportedly in the prime of life.   GLYNDWR WILLIAMS

Sources R. S. Lea, 'Michell, Matthew', HoP, *Commons* · R. Walter and B. Robins, *A voyage round the world … by George Anson* (1748) · G. Williams, ed., *Documents relating to Anson's voyage round the world, 1740–1744*, Navy RS, 109 (1967) · N. A. M. Rodger, 'Instigators or spectators? The British government and the restoration of the Stadholderate in 1747', *Tijdschrift voor Geschiedenis*, 106 (1993), 497–514 · BL, Add. MS 32808, fol. 197; Add. MS 15956, fols. 254v–255, 258
Archives BL, letters, orders, etc., relating to Michell's period as commander of the Downs squadron, Add. MS 15956, fols. 240–261 · NMM, letters, orders, etc., relating to Michell's period as commander of the Downs squadron, SAN/V/46 · PRO, letters, orders, etc., relating to Michell's period as commander of the Downs squadron, ADM 1/2101, 2103, 2104 · PRO, Michell's log of the *Gloucester*, 1740–42 on Anson's voyage, ADM 51/402

Michell, Nicholas (1807–1880), writer, was born at Calenick, near Truro, on 4 June 1807, the son of John Michell (1774–1868), and his wife, Elizabeth. His father was a prominent tin smelter and chemist, and one of the discoverers of tantalite. After attending the Truro grammar school Nicholas Michell was employed in the office of his father's smelting works at Calenick, and afterwards in London. On 3 August 1836 Michell married Maria (c.1813–1887), second daughter of John Waterhouse of Halifax, Yorkshire; they had two children, both of whom died in infancy.

Michell had written poems from an early age, was encouraged by Thomas Campbell and other literary men, and contributed to the *Forget-me-Not*, the *Keepsake*, and other annuals. While working in London he met Charles Dickens and William Makepeace Thackeray at a party given by Harrison Ainsworth, but it was not until after the publication of his *Ruins of many Lands* in 1849 that Michell succeeded in attracting much public attention. This work took as its subject the existing remains of ancient people and kingdoms in the Old and New worlds. He went on to produce several further volumes of poetry, mainly on historical or mythological subjects. Examples include his *Spirits of the Past* (1853, later reprinted as *Famous Women and Heroes*, 1871), and *The Immortals, or, Glimpses of Paradise* (1870). He sometimes also used his native Cornwall as a setting for his works, for instance in *Sybil of Cornwall* (1869). A collected edition of his poetry appeared in 1871. Michell also wrote several novels, but these did not obtain as large a circulation as his poems. He died at his home in Tehidy Terrace, Falmouth, on 6 April 1880, and was buried in St Kea churchyard on 12 April.

G. C. BOASE, *rev.* MEGAN A. STEPHAN

Sources 'Nicholas Michell', *Men of the West*, 4 (April 1877), 17–20 · Boase & Courtney, *Bibl. Corn.*, 1.352–4 · Allibone, *Dict.* · BL cat., [CD-ROM] · Boase, *Mod. Eng. biog.* · IGI
Likenesses H. Adlard, stipple, BM, NPG

Wealth at death under £7000: probate, 10 May 1880, *CGPLA Eng. & Wales*

Michell, Richard (1805–1877), college head, was born in Bruton, Somerset, the third son of Edward Michell of Bruton and Ann Clements of Wyke Champflower, also in Somerset. He was educated at Bruton grammar school before proceeding in 1820 to Wadham College, Oxford, where his uncle, Dr Richard Michell (1766–1826), was a fellow of some distinction. Obtaining a first class in the classical school (BA 1824, MA 1827, BD 1836, and DD 1868), Michell became a remarkably successful private tutor. Many of his pupils afterwards distinguished themselves in the learned professions or politics; they included the future lords Selborne and Sherbrooke, bishops Charles Wordsworth, James Fraser, and John Pelham, deans R. W. Church and H. G. Liddell, and Professor J. A. Froude. At the previously unprecedented age of twenty-four he was appointed a classical examiner, an office which he frequently held afterwards. He was admitted to the Middle Temple in 1827, but was ordained in 1831, having been elected fellow of Lincoln College in 1830. There he acted as bursar in 1832, and as tutor from 1834 to 1848, continuing to teach for the college after he had relinquished his fellowship on his marriage on 14 July 1841 to Amelia, youngest daughter of Thomas Blair. In 1839 he was elected in convocation, by a very large majority, the first praelector of logic, on the revival of university teaching of that subject in Oxford. This office he held for ten years. He was in 1842 an unsuccessful candidate for the headmastership of Rugby. In 1849 he delivered the Bampton lectures, taking as his title *The Nature and Comparative Value of the Christian Evidences*. In 1849 also Michell was appointed public orator of the university, and he retained that office until his death. His orations delivered at the annual act or encaenia, alternately with the professor of poetry, were notable for their excellent Latinity and conservative sentiment. They were published in 1878, soon after his death, by his eldest son, Edward Blair Michell, with valuable notes. The work forms a sort of running commentary on the history of the university for nearly thirty years. In 1856 Michell became rector of South Moreton, Berkshire, a living in the gift of Magdalen Hall, but did not reside there. On the formation of the new hebdomadal council under the act for reforming the university in 1854, Michell was elected to a seat, and retained it by frequent re-elections until 1872.

In 1848 Michell became vice-principal of Magdalen Hall (later Hertford College), of which Dr John David Macbride was then principal. Michell succeeded William Jacobson, afterwards bishop of Chester, who had been appointed regius professor of divinity. The hall, under the guidance of these three remarkable officers, held an important place in the university, and produced during the sixty years of its existence many distinguished men, but its very limited staff was too small for its numbers and position. In 1868 Michell succeeded Dr Macbride in the principalship, and he then began to agitate for the conversion of the hall into a college. The design assumed a definite shape in 1873, was approved by convocation, and the expenses required for passing the bill through parliament paid by subscription among the members of the hall. Before the act was passed, however, Michell received a munificent offer from T. C. Baring MP, to endow the college with a large number of fellowships and scholarships, mostly limited to members of the Church of England. This offer was accepted, and the new foundation took the name of Hertford College. Michell became the first principal of the new college in 1874, and died at his lodgings there on 29 March 1877.

Michell was a leading manager of the tory party in Oxford. In religion he was more or less of the evangelical school. In person he was a commanding figure. Of his several children, one daughter, Mary, married the third duke of Sutherland, and subsequently Sir Albert Rollit.

MONTAGU BURROWS, rev. M. C. CURTHOYS

Sources personal knowledge (1894) · Boase, *Mod. Eng. biog.* · Foster, *Alum. Oxon.* · V. Green, *The commonwealth of Lincoln College, 1427–1977* (1979) · J. S. Reynolds, *The evangelicals at Oxford, 1735–1871: a record of an unchronicled movement*, [2nd edn] (1975) · J. Hutchinson, ed., *A catalogue of notable Middle Templars: with brief biographical notices* (1902) · Ward, *Men of the reign*
Archives Bodl. Oxf., corresp. · Hertford College, Oxford, corresp. and papers relating to election of Lord Derby as chancellor of Oxford University, and to foundation of Hertford College
Likenesses portrait (after Edis, 1860), Hertford College, Oxford · portrait, repro. in *The Graphic*, 15 (1877), 356
Wealth at death under £35,000: probate, 4 May 1877, CGPLA Eng. & Wales

Michie, Alexander (1833–1902), writer on China, born at Earlsferry, Fife, on 1 March 1833, was the only son of Alexander Michie, a weaver, and his wife, Ann Laing. On his father's death his mother married again; Robert Thin MD (*d.* 1867), and George Thin MD, of London, were Michie's stepbrothers. Educated for commercial life at Kilconquhar School in Scotland, Michie was for some time a bank assistant at Colinsburgh; but in 1853 he left Scotland to join Lindsay & Co., merchants at Hong Kong. His ability and expertise caused him to make rapid progress, and in 1857 he became a partner of his firm and its representative at Shanghai. Subsequently he transferred his services successively to Chapman, King & Co., to Dyce, Nichol & Co., in which he obtained a partnership, and finally to the leading Chinese firm, Jardine, Matheson & Co. He was a prominent member of the chamber of commerce, Shanghai, and was for some years its chairman.

Michie was active in acquiring commercially valuable information. After the drafting of the treaty of Tientsin (Tianjin), ratified in 1860, which proposed to open new ports in the north of China, Michie engaged in a secret trading expedition to the Gulf of Pecheli (Beizhili) in the spring of 1859, and was one of the first European traders to gain direct knowledge of Weihaiwei, Chefoo (Yantai), Newchwang (Yingkou), and other places on that then unexplored coast. In 1861 he helped the British Admiral Sir James Hope, in his negotiations with the Taiping insurgents. He went up the Yangtze (Yangzi) River with the expedition to protect British trade, and at Nanking (Nanjing), Michie, with Lieutenant-Colonel Wolseley and J. P. Hughes, vice-consul designate of Kiukiang (Jiujiang), was

allowed to land. They remained for some weeks as the voluntary guests of the rebels, acquiring useful information about their strength and intention. In 1863 Michie returned briefly to England by the unusual route of Siberia. He described in the *Journal of the Geographical Society* his journey between Tientsin and Mukden (Shenyang), and in 1864 published *The Siberian Route*, a description of the journey from Peking (Beijing) to St Petersburg. He married, on 16 December 1866, Ann, daughter of Charles Morley Robinson of Forest House, Leytonstone, Essex; they had one daughter and one son, Alexander, who became an official in the Chinese customs service.

In 1869 Michie, on behalf of the Shanghai chamber of commerce, accompanied Swinhoe, a consul in Taiwan, on an expedition into western China. A revision of the treaty of Tientsin was contemplated, and Michie and his companion undertook to study the conditions of trade in the districts likely to be affected. After passing through the canal district of the Yangtze valley, he explored Szechwan (Sichuan) and submitted a valuable report. He returned to China in 1883 after some years' residence in London and settled at Tientsin, where he engaged in private business, as well as acting as correspondent of *The Times*. He was a frequent contributor to *Blackwood's Edinburgh Magazine* and other journals, and for some years he also edited the *Chinese Times*, published at Tientsin. In 1895 he was special correspondent for *The Times* during the Sino-Japanese War. Subsequently he left China for England, only returning in 1901 to visit his daughter, who with her husband had been imprisoned in the legations at Peking. In *The Englishman in China in the Victorian Era* (2 vols., 1900), Michie supplied a clear and comprehensive account of European relations with China through the Victorian era. The central figure of the narrative is Sir Rutherford Alcock, a leading English diplomatist in China. Michie's criticisms of English diplomacy and English officials were the fruit of personal observation and first-hand knowledge. He also published *Missionaries in China* (1891) and *China and Christianity* (1900). Michie died, after a brief illness, on 7 August 1902 at the Hotel Cecil, London, and was buried at Highgate cemetery.

S. E. FRYER, rev. CHANDRIKA KAUL

Sources *The Times* (12 Aug 1902) · *GJ*, 17 (1901), 217 · *GJ*, 20 (1902), 348 · S. L. Poole, *Life of Sir Harry Parkes* (1894) · H. Keppel, *A sailor's life under four sovereigns*, 3 vols. (1899) · private information (1912) · WWW
Archives NL Scot., corresp. with Blackwoods
Wealth at death £20,123 6s. 11d.: probate, 3 Sept 1902, CGPLA Eng. & Wales

Mickle, William Julius [*formerly* William Meikle] (1734/5–1788), poet and translator, was born at Parsonage House, Langholm, Dumfriesshire, on 29 September 1734 or 28 September 1735. His father, Alexander Meikle (*d.* 1757), was parish minister for Langholm (1717–46) and later a brewery proprietor in Edinburgh. Alexander's second wife, Julia, daughter of Thomas Henderson of Ploughlands, Dalmeny, was probably the mother of his seven known children. William Meikle attended Langholm grammar school until the family moved to Edinburgh; he studied at the Edinburgh high school from about 1746 until the early 1750s. His first known surviving poem was drafted in 1751 and his first known published poem was printed in 1757. Meikle burned much of his juvenilia. After leaving school he worked as a clerk in the family brewery, where he became chief partner, and owner after his father's death in 1757. He unsuccessfully fought financial collapse from February 1762 to March 1763. He secretly left home on 25 April 1763, and travelled to London to become an author. For the next two years he depended on his brothers for support, and wrote various magazine pieces. He adopted the Anglicized spelling Mickle about 1762, and styled himself William Julius Mickle from *c*.1768.

About this time Mickle was considering a mercantile career in Jamaica, with the East India Company, or as a merchant's clerk in Carolina. Instead he became corrector of the Clarendon Press, Oxford, and held the position from 1765 to 1772. His search for a literary patron met with limited success. He courted Lord Lyttelton from 1763 to 1765, and dedicated *The Lusiad* to the duke of Buccleuch in 1776. His best patron was Commodore George Johnstone, who supported him from 1765–72 until the early 1780s. Though offered a place in the church by Bishop Lowth, Mickle missed his hoped-for royal literary pension.

Mickle's first poetical work to gain attention was the neo-Spenserian poem *The Concubine* (1767; later retitled *Sir Martyn*). In the following year he published *A letter to Mr Harwood, wherin some of his evasive glosses, false translations, and blundering criticism, in support of the Arian heresy, contained in his liberal translation of the New Testament, are pointed out and confuted*. In spring 1772 he moved to the home of Robert Tomkins, in Forest Hill, and attempted to live solely from income as a poet. From 1763 to 1776 Mickle pursued his ambition of having a verse tragedy performed on the London stage. He repeatedly rewrote the script for 'The siege of Marseilles', but the managers at Drury Lane and Covent Garden refused to stage the play, causing Mickle to become involved in a feud with David Garrick. Despite the 'Siege' fiasco, Mickle undertook another ambitious scheme: his *Lusiad*. He was an enthusiastic admirer of Luís de Camões's epic poem *Os Lusíadas* (1572). Mickle's translation was published by subscription as *The Lusiad, or, The Discovery of India* (1776); the first book had been published 'as a specimen', probably in 1770. Mickle's fluency in Portuguese has been questioned, and indeed his *Lusiad* was an adaptation of Camões's epic in his own style, with ample poetic licence. *The Lusiad* was his greatest success since *The Concubine* nearly a decade earlier, and it netted him nearly £1000 from the sale of the copyright. It remained the major translation of *The Lusiad* from 1776 into the mid-nineteenth century. In 1779 he published a pamphlet defending the East India Company against Adam Smith.

Despite the profits from *The Lusiad*, Mickle was drained by lack of employment, old debts, and supporting two sisters. Fortunately, in May 1779 his patron Commodore Johnstone made him secretary of HMS *Romney* and squadron (spring 1779) and purser of HMS *Brilliant*. The squadron mainly let Mickle remain onshore in Portugal. Portugal was remoralizing as well as lucrative. Portuguese notables welcomed the translator of their national epic, and elected him to their new Academia Real. While in Lisbon he wrote *Almada Hill* (1781). In England in November 1780 Mickle returned as purser to HMS *Brilliant* and was appointed joint prize agent for the prizes won by the squadron. This enabled him to pay off his debts, settle annuities on his sisters, and to marry, on 3 June 1782, Mary Tomkins (*b.* 1748), Robert Tomkins's daughter. The match brought Mickle a substantial fortune, and a son, Charles Julius Mickle, who was baptized on 1 November 1784.

Mickle spent much of the period 1782–8 at his new home at Wheatley, Oxfordshire, revising and correcting his works. Except for *The Prophecy of Queen Emma* (1782), a satire on the American War of Independence, he produced few new poems in these final years. He did, however, contribute essays to the *European Magazine*. His final new poem was 'Eskdale Braes' (1788). Mickle died on 25 October 1788, after a short illness, while visiting the Tomkinses in Forest Hill. He was buried in the parish churchyard on 30 October, and was survived by his wife. *The Poetical Works of William Mickle, with a Life of the Author* appeared in 1799.

Mickle's works reveal several influences, including the night-piece and the pastoral, but most notably the Gothick or neo-medieval revival of Spenserian diction. Many of his poems, as well as his translation and tragedy, were set in the middle ages or Renaissance, and Southey claimed that Mickle combined the pursuits of an antiquary with those of a poet. Several of Mickle's poems were resolutely political in a whiggish or patriot idiom.

Mickle was an *assimilé* Scot who Anglicized his name and lived almost half his life in London and Oxford. He is usually grouped with Anglo-Scottish poets who elected to write in metropolitan (or even faux-medieval) English rather than Scots or Gaelic. He wrote more poems on English historical themes than Scottish ones, and even those mostly employed metropolitan English diction. Yet memories of his Eskdale birthplace remained strong in his mind.

Tributes by friends stressed Mickle's bashfulness, shyness, reticence, charity, and honesty, and praised his genius and ingenuousness. Though prone to melancholia after reversals, he was also capable of an even-tempered cheerfulness. More critical observers noticed his awkwardness, called him silent or dry, lamented his refusals to heed advice, and deplored his sense of injury and vendetta. His temperament was generally serious, though works such as *Voltaire in the Shades* (1770) do show signs of humour. Indeed, Mickle possessed enough mordant Scots sarcasm to have written a new *Dunciad* had he wished.

Mickle wished only to be a poet: 'I desire no secondary fame' (Mickle to James Boswell, 8 July 1769). He accomplished his aim of becoming a standard anthologized British poet during his own lifetime, and remained canonical and anthologized into the first quarter of the nineteenth century.   J. J. CAUDLE

Sources I. Reed, 'Anecdotes of William Julius Mickle, esq.', *European Magazine*, 1 (June 1782), 451–2 · I. Reed, 'An account of the life and writings of William Julius Mickle', *European Magazine*, 16 (Sept–Nov 1789), 155–7 · 'William Julius Mickle, esq., poet; Wheatly, nr. Oxford; 25 Oct 1788', *Scots Magazine* (1788), 570 · *GM*, 1st ser., 58 (1788), 1029, 1121–2 · [R. Churton], 'Tribute to Mr Mickle', *GM*, 1st ser., 61 (1791), 801 · J. Ireland, 'Anecdotes of William Julius Mickle', preface to [W. J. Mickle], *Poems and a tragedy*, ed. J. Ireland (1794) · *DNB* · R. Anderson, *The works of the British poets: with prefaces, biographical and critical* (1795–1807) · J. Sim, 'Life of the author', preface to [W. J. Mickle], *Poetical works*, ed. J. Sim (1806) · J. Robertson, 'Mickle', *Lives of the Scottish poets, with portraits and vignettes* (1822), pt 4, 3.96–127 · F. Brady, 'Mickle, Boswell, Garrick and "The siege of Marseilles"', *Transactions of the Connecticut Academy of Arts and Sciences*, 46 (1987), 235–97 · M. Letzring, 'Mickle, Boswell, liberty and the "Prospects of liberty and of slavery"', *Modern Language Review*, 69 (1974), 489–500 · M. E. Taylor, *William Julius Mickle (1734–1788): a critical study* (Washington, 1937) · M. J. Scott, 'James Thomson and the Anglo-Scots', *The history of Scottish literature*, ed. C. Craig, 2: 1660–1800, ed. A. Hook (1987), pp. 82–3 · D. D. Eddy and J. D. Fleeman, 'A preliminary handlist of books to which Dr. Samuel Johnson subscribed', *Studies in Bibliography*, 46 (1993), 187–220 · P. F. Malamud, 'Mickle's quarrel with Garrick over "The siege of Marseilles"', MA diss., Columbia University, 1971 · S. G. West, 'A study of the life and works of William Julius Mickle (1734–1788), translator of *The Lusiad*', MA diss., U. Lond., 1932 · *Fasti Scot.*, new edn, 2.237 · parish register, Forest Hill, 24 July 1748 [birth: Mary Tomkins, wife]

Archives NL Scot., poems, letters and papers · Yale U., Beinecke L., corresp. and literary papers | BL, corresp. with Lord Lyttleton, RP 272 [copies] · BL, letters to his brother and sisters, RP 256 [copies] · Yale U., Beinecke L., corresp. with James Boswell

Likenesses W. H. Worthington, line engraving, pubd 1821 (after J. Thurston), NPG · C. Bestland, stipple (after O. Humphry), BM, NPG; repro. in *European Magazine* (1789) · O. Humphry, chalk drawing, BM · W. Skelton, line engraving (after S. Taylor), BM · engraving, repro. in Sim, 'Life of the author', frontispiece

Wealth at death all his debts were discharged: [W. J. Mickle], *Poetical works*, ed. J. Sim (1806), lii

Micklem, Charles (1882–1955), stockbroker, was born on 17 January 1882 at The Lodge, Herne Hill, London, the fifth of eight sons of Leonard Micklem and his wife, Dora Emily, *née* Weguelin. Leonard Micklem appears to have been a country gentleman of leisure until the 1880s, when (probably because of the demands of his large family) he went into the City as a company secretary. Dora Micklem's father had been governor of the Bank of England. Charles Micklem was educated at Wellington College, and at Hertford College, Oxford. He entered the stock exchange in 1904 as an unauthorized clerk to the brokers Billett, Campbell, and Grenfell. He became a member of the stock exchange in 1909, and by 1912, with much ability but with little capital, he had moved to Cazenove and Akroyds on a half-commission basis. He was made a salaried partner there in 1913 and in the inter-war years he worked closely with another important City stockbroker, Claud *Serocold. The two were responsible for the promotion of Cazenoves 'from somewhere in the middle of the first division of stockbrokers to a position at or near the top of the league' (Kynaston, 99). Serocold, shrewd and able, created introductions and opportunities, while Micklem, detailed and able, realized them. He was 'the outstanding stockbroker of the inter war Stock Exchange' (ibid., 104).

Micklem's parents had originally intended him to follow a military career but medical reasons had made this impossible. Active service in the First World War offered him the opportunity to fulfil that ambition. He served, reaching the rank of major, with the Royal Marine Artillery, howitzer brigade, in Gallipoli and in France; he was twice mentioned in dispatches, and in January 1919 he was awarded the DSO. He also studied, successfully, for a law degree during his military service.

At the end of the war Micklem returned to Cazenove and Akroyds. On 10 November 1920 he married Diana Gertrude May Loyd (*b*. 1889/90), daughter of Graham Loyd JP. There were two sons and four daughters of the marriage; and from 1930 Micklem and his family lived at Long Cross House, near Chertsey, Surrey. Micklem had the house built and its estate offered him the opportunity to put into practice his interest in farming and agricultural affairs.

Micklem built Cazenove's success on corporate work. Early on he realized the opportunities which lay in the promotion of investment trusts, which enjoyed a revival and greater stability in the 1920s. But he was especially good at building relationships with industrialists and with issuing houses, and in the 1930s he won for his firm its paramount role in company finance.

Micklem had a dry sense of humour and great charm, often hidden under a reserve of severity. It won him many friends in the City, including such influential men as Alfred Wagg, and his contacts extended far beyond his own family, who were also not without sway in the City: two of his brothers were on the board of the mining company Selection Trust, and one of them was much involved in the establishment of Cull & Co., which became a significant finance house; another brother, Robert, became chairman of Vickers-Armstrongs in 1946. As a young man Charles Micklem was a keen athlete, and his charm was best described by his obituarist who noted that he had such a way of defeating his opponents at squash, tennis, or golf that he left them with the impression that they had after all won the game!

Micklem's personal austerity was well known in the firm, and he set high standards of professional and personal conduct for himself and for Cazenove and Akroyds; he made it clear that no member of the firm should do business with any person or institution attached to any taint, however slight, of dubiety. Outside the City he was, again, a much respected figure; a strong sense of duty led him to serve as a JP and as high sheriff of Surrey in 1938. He took a keen interest in Guildford Cathedral and was a generous contributor to charitable causes. He was the largest individual subscriber to the Wellington College centenary fund.

At Cazenoves Micklem took the strain of keeping the firm going during the Second World War, and he saw it through the difficult immediate post-war years. He became senior partner in name as well as in practice in 1947 when Claud Serocold retired. However, by the early 1950s Micklem himself was frail and increasingly remote from his other, younger partners. Micklem retired in August 1954 and died from diabetes at St Peter's Hospital,

Chertsey, on 26 January 1955, survived by his wife. A memorial service was held for him at St Michael's Church, Cornhill, with an impressive City gathering.

JUDY SLINN

Sources D. Kynaston, *Cazenove & Co.: a history* (1991) · *The Times* (4 Feb 1955) · *WWW* · *CGPLA Eng. & Wales* (1955) · b. cert. · m. cert. · d. cert.
Likenesses oils, Cazenove and Co., London; repro. in Kynaston, *Cazenove and Co.*
Wealth at death £373,917 6s. 10d.: probate, 6 April 1955, *CGPLA Eng. & Wales*

Micklem, Gerald Hugh (1911–1988), golf administrator, was born at Coldblow, Burgh Heath, Banstead, Surrey, on 14 August 1911, the son of Hugh Micklem, a stock jobber, and his wife, Isabella Mary Sechiari. After schooling at Winchester College, he entered Trinity College, Oxford, in 1930, where he graduated with a fourth in philosophy, politics, and economics in 1933. He then, like his father before him, had a successful career in the city as a stockbroker. Along with his inherited wealth this allowed him to retire early to live in a luxurious house near Sunningdale, a golf club he had joined as a youth. During the Second World War he served with the Grenadier Guards in the western desert and suffered a hand injury, fortunately not severe enough to affect his golf adversely.

Although Micklem gained an Oxford blue for golf, he did not emerge as a prominent amateur player until his mid-thirties, when he was runner-up in the 1946 English amateur stroke-play championship and winner of the English amateur championship at Ganton the following year, a title he won again at Royal Birkdale in 1953. Between 1947 and 1955 he played four times in the Walker cup, the biennial competition between British and American amateurs, missing out only in 1951. At this time, as in its professional equivalent the Ryder cup, the United States was dominant and Micklem secured only one victory—in the foursomes in 1953. He was also non-playing captain twice, in 1957 and 1959. He represented England in home internationals nine times. He took a keen interest in the annual President's Putter competition for Oxbridge blues and, from 1941, played in thirty-six consecutive events. Although he won only the 1953 final, he reached the semi-final stage twelve times and overall won 76 of the 111 matches in which he played. Fittingly, he became president of the Oxford and Cambridge Golfing Society.

Micklem later devoted himself to the administration of golf at local, national, and international level. As captain and committee member of his beloved Sunningdale, he helped restore the club to its premier status after the Second World War. From 1985 to his death he was president of Sunningdale, where in 1987 he hosted the Walker cup, the first occasion on which it was held at an inland club rather than on a links course. At various times he chaired the Royal and Ancient rules of golf committee, selection committee, and championship committee, in which latter role he widened the television exposure of the Open,

expanded the concept of corporate hospitality, and modernized the marketing of the championship. In 1968 he was elected captain of the Royal and Ancient, the seventh Sunningdale member to gain that honour. He also served as president of the English Golf Union and president of the European Golf Association. His services to golf brought him the Bobby Jones and Walter Hagen awards from the United States and his appointment as CBE in 1969.

Micklem was abrasive and arrogant, at times downright rude to those who disagreed with him or whom he regarded as not knowing their place. He stood no nonsense, not even from the most famous players. In the world match-play championship of 1966 he took over as referee after Jack Nicklaus had disagreed vehemently with a decision of the official in charge of his match: no more was heard from the 'Golden Bear'. Yet Micklem was a generous benefactor to many young players and, as captain of Sunningdale, he was responsible for building a new clubhouse for the Artisan Club, basically to enable working men to play at private clubs in return for maintenance work on the course and elsewhere.

Micklem never married. He died of a cerebrovascular accident on 21 May 1988 at St Peter's Hospital, Chertsey, Surrey.

WRAY VAMPLEW

Sources *The Times* (23 May 1988), 18 · J. Whitfield, *Sunningdale golf club, 1900–2000* (2000) · J. Behrend, *The amateur* (1995) · R. Green, *Illustrated encyclopedia of golf* (1994) · P. Alliss, *The who's who of golf* (1983) · B. Ferrier and G. Hart, eds., *The Johnnie Walker encyclopedia of golf* (1994) · J. Sheridan, *Sheridan of Sunningdale* (1967) · archives of the Professional Golfers' Association, The Belfry, Sutton Coldfield · b. cert. · d. cert.
Archives Professional Golfers' Association, The Belfry, Sutton Coldfield · Royal and Ancient Golf Club, St Andrews · Sunningdale Golf Club, Berkshire
Likenesses photograph, repro. in Green, *Illustrated encyclopedia of golf* · photograph, repro. in Ferrier and Hart, *Johnnie Walker encyclopedia of golf*
Wealth at death £3,264,609: probate, 11 July 1988, *CGPLA Eng. & Wales*

Micklem, Nathaniel (1888–1976), theologian and college head, was born at Fairlight, Willesden Lane, Brondesbury, Middlesex, on 10 April 1888, the eldest of the four sons of Nathaniel Micklem (1853–1954) QC and his wife, Ellen Ruth Curwen (1857–1952). His father, who was among the first generation of nonconformists to take degrees at Oxford, had a distinguished career as a lawyer and MP; his mother had studied music in Germany. The family moved to Boxmoor, Hertfordshire, when the young Micklem was six. In 1901 he entered Rugby School, from where he won a classical scholarship to New College, Oxford. Before going up to Oxford in 1907 he spent two terms at Marburg, where he gained fluency in German and laid the foundations of the theological thinking which was to be the mainspring of his life.

At Oxford Micklem's oratorical gifts led to his election as president of the union. A natural advocate, he had a questing mind which found expression in elegant speech and writing. Though briefly tempted to enter politics, he

Nathaniel Micklem (1888–1976), by Elliott & Fry

was drawn to the ministry, particularly through the influence of his father's friend R. F. Horton. At the end of his classical course in 1911 he entered Mansfield College, Oxford, where he studied under the principalship of W. B. Selbie, breaking in the middle for an extended visit to India with Horton. During his undergraduate years he had already met and formed lifelong friendships with the future leaders of other denominations through the Intercollegiate Christian Union (later the Student Christian Movement) and the Free Church Fellowship.

Micklem was ordained as a Congregational minister on 5 October 1914 at Highbury Chapel, Bristol, where for two years he was assistant to Arnold Thomas. At the end of that period he married Agatha Frances Silcock (c.1893–1961) of Bath in 1916, with whom he was to have three sons and to enjoy a happy and cultured family life. A short ministry in Withington, Manchester, was soon terminated because of the pacifist views which he then held. He and his wife went out to France to run a YMCA camp behind Dieppe for six months in 1917. The following year he was appointed chaplain at Mansfield College, but in 1921 moved to Birmingham to teach Old Testament studies at the Selly Oak Colleges, where he published his first books.

After six years in Birmingham Micklem was invited to teach New Testament at Queen's Theological College, Kingston, Ontario. Here he spent a very happy and fruitful four years in the United Church of Canada. By the time he returned to England (with an honorary DD from Queen's University) his theological thinking had reached a turning point. He had now abandoned his earlier liberal position: reason was no longer for him the source, but rather the expression, of faith.

In 1931 Micklem returned to Mansfield College as vice-principal on the understanding that he would succeed Selbie as principal in the following year. During his years as principal (1932–53) he exercised a profound influence on the Congregational denomination through his teaching and conduct of college worship and through his writing. His leading of college worship, drawing on sources from many Christian traditions and using liturgical as well as extempore forms of prayer, had a profound influence on his students, and through them on the whole denomination and beyond. In 1936 he edited *Christian Worship: Studies in its History and Meaning*, essays by past and present members of Mansfield, which illustrated the richness of the college's liturgical studies and practice.

Micklem was appalled at the vagueness of the theological liberalism of many in his denomination. In *What is the Faith?* (1936) and in his regular column in the *British Weekly* (under the name Ilico) he tried to recall his fellow Congregationalists to their reformed heritage of 'orthodox Christianity'. His views were not supported by all the members of his college, and this led to much unfortunate tension, both within the college's senior common room and with the college council.

In the mid-1930s Micklem was alerted to what was happening in Germany, and in 1937 paid the first of two pre-war visits to the German Confessing church. He brought back to England some of that church's clandestine literature, which he later gave to the Bodleian Library. In 1939 he wrote *National Socialism and the Roman Catholic Church* for Chatham House, warning that a 'ferocious and illimitable anti-Semitism' was an integral element of German national socialism. The situation in Germany led him to abandon his earlier pacifism. During the war he broadcast a weekly programme about Christians in occupied Europe.

Micklem's interest in politics had continued, and his thinking now turned more frequently to the relations between theology and law, and between religion and politics. *The Theology of Politics* was published in 1941, and later his Wilde lectures of 1949 were published in 1952 as *Law and the Laws*.

In 1944 Micklem was elected chairman of the Congregational Union. After the war he played a leading part in the free church response to the archbishop of Canterbury's appeal for unity in 1946. He was joint chairman of the Anglican and free church committee which produced *Church Relations in England* (1950). He had a great influence on the debates and negotiations which finally led to the formation of the United Reformed church (a union of Congregationalists and Presbyterians) in 1972.

Micklem retired from Mansfield in 1953. After a prolonged visit to the United States, he and his family settled in Princes Risborough, until he moved with his eldest son's family to Abingdon in 1972. He devoted some of his time in retirement to public affairs, serving as president of the Liberal Party in 1956–7, and continued to hope for greater unity among Christians. His intellectual vigour remained strong, and he wrote a series of books of mature reflection particularly directed to those who found faith difficult; in 1957 he published an autobiography, *The Box and the Puppets*, though his most profound reflections on life had already been expressed in poetry, notably *The Labyrinth*, published in 1945. In 1974 he was made a Companion of Honour. He died at home, Sheepstead House, Abingdon, on 26 December 1976; and his cremation took place at Oxford crematorium the following January. His memorial in Mansfield College chapel reads: 'Salem caritate condiens, fide sapientiam.' ELAINE KAYE

Sources N. Micklem, *The box and the puppets* (1957) · Mansfield College council minutes, annual reports and magazines, Mansfield College, Oxford · E. Kaye, *Mansfield College, Oxford: its origin, history and significance* (1996) · N. Goodall, 'Nathaniel Micklem C.H.', *Journal of the United Reformed Church History Society*, 1 (1973–7), 286–95 · *The Times* (29 Dec 1976) · personal knowledge (2004) · *CGPLA Eng. & Wales* (1977)
Archives BLPES, corresp. relating to unemployment · Mansfield College, Oxford, archive
Likenesses A. Utin, oils, 1953, Mansfield College, Oxford · Elliott & Fry, photograph, NPG [*see illus.*]
Wealth at death £33,245: administration, 11 Feb 1977, *CGPLA Eng. & Wales*

Micklethwaite, Sir John (*bap.* 1612, *d.* 1682), physician, was the son of Thomas Micklethwaite (*d.* 1663), from 1613 the rector of Cherry Burton, Yorkshire, and his first wife, Mary (*née* Maxfield) (*d.* 1623). He was baptized on 23 August 1612 in the church of Bishop Burton, 3 miles from Beverley, Yorkshire. His sister Mary later became the mother of the physician Phineas Fowke. Micklethwaite attended school in Beverley, where he was a classmate of another prominent Yorkshire physician, Robert Wittie. In 1627 Micklethwaite matriculated as pensioner at Queens' College, Cambridge, his father's former college. He received his BA there in 1631 and an MA in 1634. On 15 December 1637 he entered the University of Leiden as a medical student, and subsequently took an MD at Padua in 1638. He eventually incorporated on this degree at Oxford on 14 April 1648. After leaving Padua he appears to have practised medicine in London, where he met and married Ann Clarke, daughter of the physician John *Clarke (1582?–1653). On 12 February 1644 Micklethwaite was nominated by the Long Parliament as physician to St Bartholomew's Hospital, in place of William Harvey, 'who had withdrawn himself from his charge and is retired to the party in arms against the Parliament'. Micklethwaite did not, however, become physician at St Bart's until 26 May 1648, when he was appointed assistant physician to his father-in-law, Dr Clarke. He became full physician on Clarke's death, on 13 May 1653, and continued in that office until his own death in 1682. Micklethwaite was also physician to Christ's Hospital, a position to which he probably succeeded on the death of Sir Edward Alston in 1669.

Micklethwaite had a distinguished career in the College of Physicians. He was elected a fellow on 11 November 1643; delivered the Goulstonian lectures in 1644; was selected censor seven times; and served as treasurer from 1667 to 1675, and as president from 1676 to 1681. Less well known are Micklethwaite's strong ties to English puritanism and religious dissent. His father-in-law, who was president of the college from 1645 to 1649, was also the most zealous Presbyterian in the college. In 1642 his father, the Revd Thomas Micklethwaite, was appointed a member of the Westminster assembly of divines, which tried unsuccessfully to bring a Presbyterian church settlement to

Sir John Micklethwaite (*bap.* 1612, *d.* 1682), by unknown artist

England. At the Restoration, after nearly fifty years as rector of Cherry Burton, he was ejected from his living for nonconformity. John Micklethwaite's brother-in-law, the Revd Luke Clayton (*d.* 1674), suffered the same fate. In 1665 another ejected Presbyterian minister, the Revd Gilbert Rule, dedicated his medical thesis at Leiden to Micklethwaite at Bart's and to Thomas Wharton at St Thomas's Hospital.

Among Micklethwaite's close friends and admirers were the Presbyterian leader Richard Baxter, who stayed in the physician's house whenever he went to London, and the Presbyterian minister Thomas Jacombe, who asked at his death to be buried as close to Micklethwaite's body as was convenient. Charles Goodall of the college, who knew him well, wrote that 'his piety towards God, and charity to the poor was exemplary' (Goodall, *Epistle Dedicatory*). An elegy of 1682 referred to him as 'a great physician and a pious Soul' and concluded: 'Art without virtue 'tis an empty thing' (*Elegy*, 1682). And finally to the consternation of Anglican authorities, Micklethwaite and other influential college fellows, such as Alston and Thomas Coxe, supported the granting of medical licences by the College of Physicians to a number of ejected dissenting ministers desperate for a livelihood.

Like most English Presbyterians, political or religious, Micklethwaite welcomed the restoration of Charles II. His medical treatment of the king, seriously ill at Windsor in 1681, earned him the monarch's gratitude and a knighthood. Micklethwaite died in London, of acute cystitis, on Saturday 29 July 1682, and was buried on 2 August in St

Botolph's, Aldersgate, where a monument with a long inscription by Thomas Flatman was erected to his memory. He was survived by his wife, Ann, and six daughters, all of whom were generously provided for in his will (PRO, PROB 11/370, sig. 100). He left no writings.

WILLIAM BIRKEN

Sources An elegy to commemorate and lament the death of ... Sir John Micklethwaite (1682) · Munk, Roll · C. Goodall, Epistle dedicatory (1684) · P. Barwick, The life of ... Dr John Barwick, ed. and trans. H. Bedford (1724) · W. Birken, 'The dissenting tradition in English medicine of the seventeenth and eighteenth centuries', Medical History, 39 (1995), 197–218 · Venn, Alum. Cant. · C. Hart, 'John Clarke, MD', St Bartholomew's Hospital Journal, 55 (1951), 34–40, 47 · D'A. Power, Selected writings, 1877–1930 (1931), 140 · RCP Lond., 156 · G. W. Marshall, 'Additions to Le Neve's Pedigrees of the knights [pt 2]', The Genealogist, 1 (1877), 147–54 · A. F. Mitchell and J. Struthers, eds., Minutes of the sessions of the Westminster assembly of divines (1874) · DNB · Calamy rev.

Likenesses oils, RCP Lond. [see illus.]

Wealth at death lands in Cherry Burton, Yorkshire; houses in the Old Bailey, London, and elsewhere in the city; stock in the East India Company; disbursements totalling £6600: will, PRO, PROB 11/370, sig. 100

John Thomas Micklethwaite (1843–1906), by George Charles Beresford

Micklethwaite, John Thomas (1843–1906), architect and ecclesiologist, was born at Rishworth House, Wakefield, Yorkshire, on 3 May 1843, the son of James Micklethwaite of Hopton, Mirfield, worsted spinner and colliery owner, and his wife, Sarah Eliza Stanway of Manchester. After private education at Tadcaster and Wakefield, and subsequently in the engineering and applied science department of King's College, London, which in 1901 granted him an honorary fellowship, there was anxiety about his eyesight; holy orders were considered as an alternative to architecture, but in 1862 he became a pupil of George Gilbert Scott, and formed a lifelong friendship with a fellow pupil, Somers Clarke (1841–1926). In February 1866 he was a founder member of the Spring Gardens Sketching Club, which published eight folio volumes of architectural lithographs before disbanding in 1890. He began independent practice in 1869 and was in constant collaboration with Somers Clarke, who was his partner from 1876 until his retirement from active work in 1892.

An earnest churchman and a master of historic ritual, Micklethwaite brought sympathy and knowledge to bear on his works as a designer. His buildings, though not strikingly original, were scholarly, dignified, and convincing. The individual responsibilities of Micklethwaite and his partner are not always easy to distinguish. Of their joint works the churches of St John, Gainsborough, Lincolnshire (1881–2), St Paul, Wimbledon Park, Surrey (1888, 1896), and All Saints, Brixham, Devon (1892–1906), as well as the enlargement of the parish church at Brighton, were all designed and begun by Clarke and completed by Micklethwaite after 1892. At Brighton Micklethwaite modified his colleague's design, and at All Saints', Wimbledon (1891–3), Micklethwaite, besides completing Clarke's plans, designed the screens and furniture. The church at Stretton was designed by Clarke and carried out by Micklethwaite in 1895–7.

Among the works which were distinctly or exclusively Micklethwaite's are: St Hilda's Church, Leeds (1876–81); St

Bartholomew's, East Ham (1901–2; dem.); St Peter's, Bocking, Essex (1896–7); the rebuilding (tower excepted) of St Paul's, Morton, near Gainsborough (1891–3); St Saviour's, Luton (1897–1905); and the restoration of Madingley church, Cambridgeshire. His ecclesiological skill was often in demand for the completion or furnishing of chancels and the like, for example at St John's, Wakefield, where he showed sympathy with the classical style. The screens and rood of St Mary Magdalene, Munster Square, London, are of his design. He was often engaged in restoration, as at: Kirkstall Abbey, Yorkshire; the churches of Oundle, and Thornhaugh, Northamptonshire; Orford, Suffolk; Winchelsea, Sussex; West Malling, Kent (where he replaced a Georgian nave); Lydbury North, Shropshire; and All Saints', Great Sturton, Lincolnshire. The York county council appointed him, with W. H. Brierley, to restore Clifford's Tower at York. At Ranworth, Norfolk, he repaired the celebrated screen, and at St Andrew's, Cherry Hinton, Cambridgeshire, he restored the chancel. Though not a member, he was frequently consulted by the Society for the Protection of Ancient Buildings, for whom he carried out a sensitive restoration of Inglesham church which paid equal respect to every period of the building's history. Of Micklethwaite's less frequent domestic and secular work there are examples in the addition to and reorganization of the interiors at Stapleford Park, Leicestershire, in the Jacobean style (1894–8), and the technical schools at Wimbledon.

Micklethwaite's critical knowledge of Westminster Abbey and his affection for the fabric were recognized by his appointment as surveyor to the dean and chapter on the death of J. L. Pearson in 1898. Works of renewal on the south transept and west front were carried out during his period of office in collaboration with W. D. Caroe FSA. As custodian of the abbey he aimed at conservation: with the possible exception of the decoration on the west side of the Confessor's shrine carried out at the time of the coronation of Edward VII (when he also designed some of the vestments for the ceremonial), he made few if any attempts at conjectural restoration. In 1900 he was appointed architect to St George's Chapel, Windsor.

Throughout his career Micklethwaite devoted himself to archaeological enquiry and writing as well as to architectural work. In 1870, when he wrote a paper on the chapel of St Erasmus in Westminster Abbey, he was elected fellow of the Society of Antiquaries, and he became a vice-president of the society in 1902. In 1872, while working on St Albans Abbey under Scott's direction, he pieced together the fragments of the saint's shrine and re-erected it. In 1874 he published *Modern Parish Churches: their Plan, Design and Furniture*, which argued that the arrangement of churches should be conditioned by an understanding of medieval liturgy. For him the building was a shelter for the liturgy, which would dictate its plan and form. Among his more important monographs were two essays on Saxon churches and two on Westminster Abbey, all in the *Archaeological Journal*, one on the sculptures of Henry VII's Chapel in *Archaeologia*, and a treatise on the Cistercian plan in the *Yorkshire Archaeological Journal*. He was also an authority on the Carthusian order.

Micklethwaite was one of the founders of the Alcuin Club, the Henry Bradshaw Society, and the St Paul's Ecclesiological Society. His tract *The Ornaments of the Rubric* was the first publication of the Alcuin Club in 1897. He was a member, and in 1893 master, of the Art Workers' Guild, and took a leading part in the affairs of the Archaeological Institute, of which he was elected a member in 1875 and became vice-president. In 1874 he issued, with Somers Clarke, a pamphlet, *What shall be Done with St Paul's?*, a practical assessment of ritual requirements, utility, and architectural dignity which would have left Wren's choir intact. He assisted the Society for the Protection of Ancient Buildings and the Society of Antiquaries with their (unsuccessful) protests in 1896 against Pearson's proposals to demolish and rebuild parts of the west front of Peterborough Cathedral, and joined in attempts to curb Lord Grimthorpe's proposals for St Albans Abbey.

Throughout his life Micklethwaite retained his Yorkshire patriotism and trenchant mode of expression. After some years of failing health, he died, unmarried, on 28 October 1906 at his residence, 27 St George's Square, Westminster, and on the 31st was accorded the honour of burial in the west cloister, Westminster Abbey.

PAUL WATERHOUSE, *rev.* DONALD FINDLAY

Sources W. Lethaby, *The Athenaeum* (10 Nov 1906), 589 · W. Niven, 'The late John Thomas Micklethwaite', *Archaeological Journal*, 64 (1907), 58–62 · J. Avebury, *Proceedings of the Society of Antiquaries of London*, 2nd ser., 21 (1905–7), 435–6 · *The Builder*, 91 (1906), 516 · private information (1912) · W. Niven, *ArchR*, 20 (1906), 317 · *CGPLA Eng. & Wales* (1906)
Archives BL, ecclesiological collections, Add. MSS 37504–37510 | Northampton Central Library, corresp. with Sir Henry Dryden
Likenesses G. C. Beresford, photograph, NPG [*see illus.*] · photograph, repro. in Incorporated Church Building Society, *Occasional notes on church furniture and arrangement*, repr. (1908), frontispiece
Wealth at death £12,265 12*s.* 9*d.*: probate, 18 Dec 1906, *CGPLA Eng. & Wales*

Micklethwaite, Paul (1588/9–1639), Church of England clergyman, was the younger son of Thomas Micklethwaite (*d.* in or before 1599), vicar of Plumstead, Kent. After attending the King's School, Canterbury, in 1606 at the age of seventeen he was admitted as a scholar at Gonville and Caius College, Cambridge, following in the footsteps of his elder brother, Elias. After graduating BA in 1610 he migrated to Sidney Sussex College, where he was nominated a Smith's fellow on 19 April 1611. While at Sidney he proceeded MA (1613), BD (1620), and DD (1628). He established a reputation as a preacher in both Cambridge and London, and in 1628 he resigned his fellowship on being appointed master of the Temple by Charles I. In 1630 he succeeded Samuel Brooke, master of Trinity College, Cambridge, as a royal chaplain, having deputized for Brooke previously.

Micklethwaite's appointment as master of the Temple was at the petition of the benchers of the Inner and Middle Temple, who had been impressed by his performance as lecturer at the Temple since January 1627. However, he soon became embroiled in a series of interrelated disputes with the benchers about precedence and the ordering of services at the Temple Church. The first sign of difficulties appeared in November 1628, when Micklethwaite reopened the question of the order to be followed when administering communion to members of both the Inner and the Middle Temple, who had earlier agreed that between them there was to be no precedence. In 1629 it was Micklethwaite's own precedence that became the subject of a quarrel. On the feast of All Saints he insisted on a position of honour at the table in Inner Temple hall, removing the purse customarily placed opposite the lord keeper's seat and sitting in Lord Keeper Coventry's place. As a result he was requested by the benchers of the Inner Temple 'to forbear the hall till he was sent for' (Inderwick, lxxxiii). Even more extravagant was his demand for tithes of men's gains, including 10 per cent of lawyers' fees. Despite petitions to the king and hearings in Star Chamber his claims to jurisdiction and precedence were not supported. There was a more sympathetic response to his requests for improvements in the conduct of divine service. In 1637, following yet another petition to the king, the altar was replaced at the east end, arrayed as in the Chapel Royal, with candles burning on it during services. The pulpit was removed from the centre to the side of the church. Steps were taken to prevent secular use of the church. A further indication of royal approval was his appointment to the livings of Herstmonceaux, Sussex, in 1637, and Sandy, Bedfordshire, early in 1639. The quarrel with the benchers ended only with Micklethwaite's death, probably in London, on 7 August 1639. It is not known where he was buried; significantly, his name does not appear in the burial register of the Temple Church.

Despite Micklethwaite's fame as a preacher, none of his sermons was ever published. The gist of one is given by Fuller in his *Church History*, in the course of his discussion of the sabbatarian debates of the late 1620s (Fuller, 146–7). Micklethwaite was of the opinion that gentlefolk were obliged to a stricter observance of the Lord's day, since 'such as are not annihilated with labour, have no title to be recreated with liberty'. Micklethwaite's views on another controversial topic are preserved in an 'Answer to a friend that desired to be resolved about bowing before the holy table or altar', which survives in two seventeenth-century copies (CUL, MSS Dd.5.31 and Mm.4.24). In this he argues that the table or altar is a monument of God's presence, similar to the Jewish ark, and thus deserving of gestures of adoration. The tenor of Micklethwaite's arguments in this pamphlet, together with his actions at the Temple Church, mark him as a moderate Laudian, as does his friendship with John Pocklington, who in 1639 described him as 'a right man for the Church' (PRO, SP 16/414/25). However, his bequest of mourning rings to his friends Ralph Brownrig, bishop of Exeter, and Richard Holdsworth is a reminder that his theological background was more strictly Calvinist.

Micklethwaite is best remembered for his bequest to Sidney Sussex College of his collection of Hebrew books, amounting to seventy-three volumes, virtually all of which survive. His donation reveals a profound interest in Jewish studies. In addition to the biblical and grammatical works commonly owned by scholars in this period, there are works on halachah, the Talmud, philosophy, ethics, liturgy, and history. Several of the books came from the libraries of earlier English Hebraists, such as John Dee and Hugh Broughton. Most of the famous Italian Hebrew presses are represented, and there are also rare items from Jewish printers in eastern Europe. Nothing is known to survive of the rest of his library, or of his papers, which passed with the residue of his estate to his nephew Nathaniel Micklethwaite, who in 1635 was apprenticed to a London linen draper. NICHOLAS ROGERS

Sources F. A. Inderwick and R. A. Roberts, eds., *A calendar of the Inner Temple records*, 2 (1898), lxxxi–xcv • Venn, *Alum. Cant.* • Sidney Sussex College, Cambridge, box 9/6a; MR 41 • PRO, PROB 11/182, fols. 386–386v • *CSP dom., 1628–9*, 256; *1629–31*, 384–5, 396 • T. Fuller, *The church-history of Britain*, 11 pts in 1 (1655), cent. 17, 146–7 • CUL, MSS Dd.5.31, fols. 181–182v; Mm.4.24, 122–4 • Sidney Sussex College, Cambridge, MS 91, pp. 100–01 • A. Milton, 'The Laudians and the Church of Rome, *c.*1625–1640', PhD diss., U. Cam., 1989, 11, n.37
Archives Sidney Sussex College, Cambridge, Hebrew books from library | CUL, MSS Dd.5.31, fols. 181–182v; Mm.4.24, pp. 122–4

Mickleton, Christopher (*bap.* 1612, *d.* 1669), lawyer, was born in Mickleton, North Riding of Yorkshire, and baptized on 28 June 1612 at Romaldkirk, the son of John Mickleton (*c.*1575–1636) and his wife, Helen Harker (*c.*1580–1622). The family was of modest status and his elder brother, William, was illiterate. He received a legal training, probably by serving as clerk to an established practitioner, and became a member of Clifford's Inn. He was practising as an attorney in the palatine courts of Durham by the middle 1630s.

Early in his career Mickleton was one of several lawyers representing the inhabitants of his native village in litigation with their landlords Talbot and Thomas Bowes, which affected the titles to over seventy holdings. This was decided in the tenants' favour in January 1646 but Mickleton was still engaged in work arising from the case

as late as 1655. On the establishment of the parliamentarian regime in the early 1640s he acquired a number of offices of local importance. The most significant of these were his role as one of two clerks to the sequestrators of royalist property for co. Durham, his appointment as under-sheriff in November 1647, and his position as clerk of the peace. In January 1649, however, he was himself sequestered and deprived of his offices, on the grounds that he had helped in provisioning the royalist army. It is not known whether this charge had any basis in fact, but on 17 February 1651 he was discharged from delinquency and subsequently became prothonotary, or clerk, of the Durham court of pleas, and possibly deputy registrar of the Durham court of chancery, offices of which the duties included custody of the court records. In 1654 the Durham local courts were abolished by act of parliament, and it was perhaps in order to strengthen his position in the London legal world that he was admitted to the Inner Temple in 1654; he does not appear to have been called to the bar.

In or before 1637 Mickleton married Mary (*c.*1615–1644), daughter of Thomas King, of Shields. Following her death he married, probably in 1645, Anne Dodshon of Stranton, near Hartlepool. Two children of the first marriage, including his eldest son James *Mickleton (1638–1693), and four of the second, reached adulthood.

There is no evidence that Mickleton had any strong sympathy with the puritan view. He was certainly not subservient to the parliamentarian authorities, as is shown by his stubborn and courageous defence of the tenants of Weardale, co. Durham, against their landlord, Sir Arthur Hesilrige, the governor of Newcastle and a member of the council of state. Hesilrige sought to undermine the customary tenure by which the tenants held their land, and Mickleton was so effective in his conduct of the tenants' case that in 1656 Hesilrige lodged a complaint against him. On investigation it was reported that Mickleton had 'shewn himselfe faithfull to his clyents', that he 'has the greatest practice of any attorney in the country', and that Hesilrige's complaint was purely malicious (Thurloe, *State papers*, 5.229, 234). The Weardale tenants finally won their case when Hesilrige withdrew in 1658.

At the Restoration Mickleton failed to secure reappointment to the position of prothonotary. On surrendering the post he stressed that he was not prepared to hand over the rolls of the court without proper authority, because they were 'the common assurances of severall men's estates in this County, which I have bene carefull, during all these late times of trouble to preserve' (Durham University, Cosin letter-book 2/17). He continued to practise as an attorney in the Durham courts and king's bench.

Mickleton died on 26 August 1669, survived by his second wife. The nature of his illness is not known, but it was a long one, since his will dated 4 May 1669 includes a legacy to his nurse. His estate was of about the size one would expect for a successful professional man who had invested wisely. He had substantial landholdings in his second wife's native village of Stranton, and a number of properties in or near Durham. There were also some substantial debts due to him, suggesting that his business included lending money to his clients. He made provision for each of his children except James, who was totally disinherited following an argument over property. He was buried in Durham Cathedral on 29 August, and was described in the register as very expert in law. A monument to him in the cathedral no longer exists. It is clear, from the offices he held and the cases he is known to have undertaken, that Mickleton was outstandingly skilful in organizing large quantities of documents. He preserved much of the archival material essential to the functioning and history of the Durham courts through the civil war and interregnum, and established a tradition of collecting manuscripts which continued through several generations of his family. His son James assembled a vast collection of legal and antiquarian manuscripts, which was later added to by James's grandson James *Mickleton (1688–1719) [see under Mickleton, James (1638–1693)] and by members of the Spearman family, who were related by marriage.

SHEILA DOYLE

Sources S. Doyle, 'The Barrington manuscripts: from Durham to the Inner Temple', Law Librarian, 23/2 (1992), 66–74 · J. L. Drury, 'A chest of manuscripts from Mickleton in Teesdale', Durham Archaeological Journal, 1 (1984), 73–9 · J. L. Drury, 'Sir Arthur Hesilrige and the Weardale chest', Transactions of the Architectural and Archaeological Society of Durham and Northumberland, new ser., 5 (1980), 125–37 · A. Hesilrige, complaint laid against Christopher Mickleton, Bodl. Oxf., MS Rawl. A. 34, fol. 758 · C. Mickleton, letters to Bishop J. Cosin, U. Durham L., archives and special collections, Cosin letter-book 2/5–11, 2/17–18 · R. Surtees, The history and antiquities of the county palatine of Durham, 4/2 (1840), 140 · will, 4 May 1669, Borth. Inst., Prog. Mar. 1669 · M. A. E. Green, ed., Calendar of the proceedings of the committee for advance of money, 1642–1656, 3, PRO (1888), 1409 · admissions register, Inner Temple, London, ADM/1/3, 18 Feb 1654 · G. J. Armytage, ed., The baptismal, marriage, and burial registers of the cathedral church … at Durham, 1609–1896, Harleian Society, register section, 23 (1897), 96 · IGI

Archives Bowes Museum, Barnard Castle, MSS · U. Durham L., antiquarian collections | U. Durham, Weardale MSS

Wealth at death extensive land at Stranton, co. Durham; freehold property in Durham, incl. minimum of nine houses; land at Medomsley, co. Durham; leaseholds at Hurworth and Hamsteels, co. Durham; money on loan; £233 6s. 8d. liabilities: will, Prog. Mar. 1669, Borth. Inst., 4 May 1669

Mickleton, James (1638–1693), antiquary and lawyer, was born in Durham on 19 April 1638, the eldest son of Christopher *Mickleton (bap. 1612, d. 1669), attorney, of Durham, and his first wife, Mary King (c.1615–1644). He was educated at Durham School, admitted to Gray's Inn in 1652, and to Christ's College, Cambridge, and the Inner Temple in 1656. He was called to the bar in 1663. He was appointed keeper of the seal of the county palatine of Durham in 1689.

Mickleton was married on 29 April 1660 to Frances Hall (bap. 1634, d. 1690). His father, Christopher, marked the occasion by transferring to him the ownership of the family home of Crook Hall, on the outskirts of Durham, but friction soon arose between father and son over the right to occupy the property, resulting in rancorous litigation. James was totally excluded from his father's will, which described him as 'ungratefull, unthankfull, abusive and disobedient' (will of Christopher Mickleton).

Like many lawyers, James Mickleton collected manuscripts both for their practical value as legal records and for their absorbing antiquarian interest. As he himself expressed it, 'There is a certain pleasure & delight in hearing & discoursing of Matters that have been in old times before us wch mightily provoked me to look into Antiquity' (Mickleton and Spearman MS 1, fol. [3]). He had a circle of friends with similar interests to his own, among whom was John Davies of Kidwelly, who dedicated to him his edition of The Ancient Rites … of Durham (1672), an important account of the pre-dissolution regime and buildings of Durham Cathedral. Mickleton probably became acquainted with Davies through his brother-in-law John Hall, Davies's patron.

Mickleton died on 3 August 1693, and was buried in Durham Cathedral on 4 August. The value that he attached to his manuscript collections can be judged from his will, in which he left detailed instructions as to how they were to be cared for. Certain major compilations were left to trustees, in the hope that they could eventually be published, while the remainder of his local history collection was left to his only surviving son, Michael (1663–1711). His collection of printed and manuscript law books he left to James [see below], the eldest of Michael's ten children. Michael seems to have been a disappointment to his father. He was called to the bar in 1684 and married Elizabeth (1667–1704), the daughter of John Spearman, a prominent Durham lawyer. However, he did not pursue a legal career or share in his father's antiquarian pursuits, and it was the younger James Mickleton who continued the family interest in manuscript collecting.

James Mickleton (1688–1719) was born on 27 March 1688 and baptized in Durham Cathedral on 2 April 1688. In 1705 he was admitted to the Inner Temple; in 1709 he became a member of Furnival's Inn and in 1716 he migrated to Gray's Inn, which became his normal London residence. He was called to the bar in 1718. Mickleton was married in 1711 or 1712 to Hannah Eden (b. 1686), daughter of his grandfather's close friend Sir Robert Eden. Little is known of this marriage. It seems to have ended on Hannah's death, no later than the spring of 1718. There were no surviving children.

Ownership of his grandfather's legal and antiquarian manuscript collections, together with an easy social manner, gave Mickleton ready access to antiquarian circles, and although he undoubtedly made some effort to study law he gradually became preoccupied with social life and historical studies. His acquaintances included Humfrey Wanley, library keeper to Lord Harley, and John Anstis, Garter king of arms. He assisted Wanley in tracking down works suitable for the Harleian Library, and gave help to Anstis in his researches into heraldry. Meanwhile he continued to add to his own collections, and in 1716 acquired, as a gift from a great-uncle, the library of his great-grandfather Christopher Mickleton. In July 1717 he was one of twenty-three members present at the inaugural meeting of the Society of Antiquaries at the Mitre tavern.

Mickleton's income was not equal to his social aspirations, and by November 1719 he was in deep financial difficulties. The bookseller Richard Sare described his state in a letter to Wanley: 'he was … surrounded with Dunns, running into every ones Debt that wou'd lend him money; the Thoughts whereof made him fly to Drinking, so that he was seldom sober' (BL, Harley MS 3781, fol. 25). According to Sare, he had met with a repulse in his courtship; probably he had unsuccessfully attempted to extricate himself by the well-established expedient of an advantageous marriage. On 25 November 1719 his drowned body was found in the Thames. The verdict of the inquest was the charitable one of 'accidental death', but all the circumstances suggest the likelihood of suicide. He was buried in St Clement Danes, Strand.

On James Mickleton's death the family manuscript collections were bought by his uncle, Gilbert Spearman, also an antiquary, who added his own family's manuscripts. The combined collection passed down the Spearman family until 1817, when it was presented to Shute Barrington, bishop of Durham. Barrington caused the collection to be divided. The legal manuscripts were given to the library of the Inner Temple, where they became known as the Barrington manuscripts, and the antiquarian material was presented to the dean and chapter of Durham, and eventually passed to Durham University as the Mickleton and Spearman collection.

The volumes that the elder James Mickleton wished to be published were never printed in the form that he envisaged. However, his manuscripts and those of his grandson continue to be used as a source for legal and historical research in a way that amply fulfils his intention in forming the collections.   SHEILA DOYLE

Sources S. Doyle, 'The Barrington manuscripts: from Durham to the Inner Temple', *Law Librarian*, 23/2 (1992), 66–74 · Venn, *Alum. Cant.*, 1/3.183 · R. Surtees, *The history and antiquities of the county palatine of Durham*, 4/2 (1840), 140 · will, Borth. Inst., Prog. Mar. 1669 [Christopher Mickleton] · will, U. Durham L., archives and special collections, Durham probate records, 1694, T77 · A. Collins, *The English baronetage*, 3 (1741), 547 · U. Durham L., archives and special collections, Mickleton and Spearman MS 1 · R. Sare, letter to Humfrey Wanley, BL, Harley MS 3781, fol. 25 · J. Mickleton the younger, letter to John Anstis, BL, Stowe MS 749, fol. 19 · J. Evans, *A history of the Society of Antiquaries* (1956), 51–2 · diary of Sir Henry Ellis, BL, Add. MS 36653/1, 22 Nov 1816, 26 April 1817, and 29 May 1817 [as regards the transmission of the MS collections] · IGI
Archives BL, account of his manuscript collections, Stowe MS 1056 · U. Durham L., antiquarian collections | Bodl. Oxf., collections for Durham diocese, MS Willis 35 · Inner Temple, London, Barrington MSS · U. Durham L., annotated copy of John Davies, *Ancient rites and monuments of…Durham*
Wealth at death over £1000—legacies and house (Crook Hall): will, U. Durham L., archives and special collections, Durham probate records, 1694, T77 · Crook Hall (mortgaged); extensive debts for rent, dues to Gray's Inn and other debts 'too many to be mentioned'; James Mickleton jun.: letter from R. Sare to H. Wanley, BL, Harley MS 3781, fol. 25

Mickleton, James (1688–1719). *See under* Mickleton, James (1638–1693).

Mico [Meco], **Richard** (c.1590–1661), musician and composer, was the eldest of four sons and five daughters of Walter Mico of Taunton in Somerset, who was probably involved in the cloth trade, and his wife, Margery (d. 1616), from an Oxfordshire family named Awdrey. His younger brother Walter Mico (1595–1647) described their parents, in a statement made on his admission to the Jesuit English College in Rome, as protestants of the middling sort, but not unlearned. Although there are no surviving records of Mico's early life, it is likely that he was, like Walter, educated at the grammar school in Taunton.

Mico's first known employment began in 1608, when he was appointed resident musician at Thorndon Hall in Essex, the seat of John, first Lord Petre. His immediate employer was John Petre's son, Sir William Petre, and his principal responsibility seems to have been the musical education of the family's children. He also took charge of all the musical instruments: an inventory dated 1608, and signed by Mico, lists five viols, lutes, virginals, and an organ, as well as printed music and manuscript part-books. No resident musician had been employed at Thorndon Hall since 1593, but at about that time William Byrd had taken up residence nearby and had begun a long and close association with the Petres; another inventory for 1608 lists 'Mr Birds chamber'. There is no evidence that Byrd actually taught Mico, but he must have been very closely involved in the choice of a new resident musician. Mico's wages on first appointment were £10 per annum, somewhat above average for this type of post, implying that, although probably still under twenty, he was already seen as an exceptionally able musician. The Petre family, like William Byrd, were Catholics: Mico was to convert to Catholicism by 1614. In 1628 he married Ann Lambe, a maid.

It is likely that all of Mico's surviving compositions date from his period at Thorndon Hall. A total of forty-one pieces survive, all for consorts of between two and five viols, with or without organ. The majority are fantasias (or 'fancies') and pavans, and are stylistically very conservative for this period. His fantasias, for example, are almost consistently contrapuntal, with scarcely any element of chordal texture. Moreover they contain no triple-time writing, which the more madrigalian composers often used to provide passages of homophonic relief. Apart from fantasias and pavans, Mico also wrote one In nomine and a piece entitled 'Latral'. This latter work, a musical response to part of a madrigal by Monteverdi ('Vattene pur, crudel'), demonstrates great technical and imaginative resource, and seems to have no direct parallel among English consort music of this period.

Mico was evidently a highly accomplished organist, for in 1630, on the death of Richard Dering, he was appointed organist to Queen Henrietta Maria. His musical activities in this post would have been very different from those at the Petre residence, with a greater emphasis on sacred music, both at the chapel of St James's Palace and at the chapel of Somerset House. In 1634 he registered a coat of arms, and in 1639 was referred to as 'Richard Mico of London gent'. He held his post in the queen's household until her flight to the Netherlands in 1642. No record of him during the civil war period has been found, but he probably remained in London, where the next reference to him is in 1651. In 1658 he was in receipt of a life annuity of £20 from the Petre family. He survived to see the Restoration but died the following year, and was buried in St Paul's, Covent Garden, on 10 April 1661.

ANDREW J. HANLEY

Sources *Richard Mico: consort music*, ed. A. Hanley, Musica Britannica, 65 (1994) • J. Bennett and P. Willetts, *Chelys*, 7 (1977), 24–46 • R. Thompson, 'A further look at the consort music manuscripts in Archbishop Marsh's library, Dublin', *Chelys*, 24 (1995), 3–18 • A. Kenny, ed., *The responsa scholarum of the English College, Rome*, 1, Catholic RS, 54 (1962), 294–5 • T. M. McCoog, *English and Welsh Jesuits, 1555–1650*, 2, Catholic RS, 75 (1995), 205
Archives Archbishop Marsh's Library, Dublin, Z.3/4.7–12 • Royal College of Music, London, MS 1197

Micron, Marten [Martin Micronius] (1523–1559), protestant minister and theologian, was born in Ghent, Flanders. Little is known of his early life, though he seems to have converted to the Reformation before his departure from the Netherlands in 1546. He studied first in Strasbourg and then in Basel, where he matriculated in the university and embarked on the practice of medicine. His first published work, *In libros de placitis Hippocratis et Platonis argumenta* (1549), was a medical textbook. In 1548 he moved to Zürich to study theology. He became an intimate of Heinrich Bullinger, and seems to have known Calvin. He also became a close friend of the English exile John Hooper, and when Hooper returned to England in March 1549 Micron travelled with him. In London Micron became a prominent figure in the Dutch immigrant community, and with the foundation in 1550 of the London stranger churches, he was named by the royal charter as one of the two ministers to the Dutch congregation. He preached the first sermon at the inauguration of the new church at Austin Friars on 12 December 1550.

In this short but turbulent first phase of the London stranger church's existence Micron played a crucial role. The church was buffeted both by internal dissensions (not least surrounding Micron's fellow minister, Gualter Delenus) and by the hostility of prominent members of the English privy council. Most perilously these included Nicholas Ridley, the new bishop of London, who not surprisingly resented the existence of an independent church inside his diocese but outside his jurisdiction. At times it seemed as if the young church might not survive. In these difficult circumstances Micron was a tower of strength. In close partnership with the church's superintendent, John à Lasco, he worked tirelessly to establish and define the doctrine and pattern of worship of the new church. Two shorter catechisms, *De kleyne cathechismus oft kinderleere* (1552) and *Een corte undersouckinghe des gheloofs* (1553), are normally regarded as his work. Together with Jan Utenhove's longer catechism, they established a carefully graduated hierarchy of religious instruction for new and intending members of the church. In 1552 he also published *Een clear bewijs van het recht gebruyck des nachtmaels Christi*, a statement of the church's eucharistic doctrine which incorporated a fierce attack on the mass.

Finally, in 1554 he published a Dutch version of the church's church order, the *Christlicken ordinancien*.

The church order of the stranger churches, in this and John à Lasco's longer Latin version (*Forma ac ratio*, 1555), would have a profound influence on later Calvinistic church orders, and Micron's part in its conception is worthy of closer investigation. The church order took as its basis the two orders of Calvin devised for his small French refugee church in Strasbourg, and later in Geneva. But although it followed these churches in articulating a classic fourfold order of ministry, it also adopted several features more characteristic of worship in Zürich—including a version of the Zürich *Prophezie*, collective exercises in public speaking and exegesis under the correction of the city's leading ministers—and Emden. The church order also adopted a strikingly democratic procedure for the election of ministers and a strong emphasis on congregational discipline, and embraced a eucharistic theology closer to that of Zürich than Geneva. This latter feature almost certainly derived from Micron. In London he preserved his close allegiance to Zürich: his friend and colleague Jan Utenhove praised his preaching as 'populair, op de manier van de Zurichers' (Nauta and others, 2.328), and his theological writings betray nothing of the disorderly eclecticism of his colleague à Lasco. To the extent that the *Forma ac ratio* served as a model for future English congregations, both in the Marian exile churches and in the London underground congregation, this owes much to the vision and careful ecclesiology of Micron.

The death of Edward VI in 1553 brought an untimely end to the experiment of the stranger churches. À Lasco, Micron, and 175 of their closest colleagues took ship for Denmark, assured, as they thought, of a welcome from the Lutheran state. But news of their strong adherence to reformed doctrine had gone before them, and the king was persuaded to refuse them a refuge. Micron travelled overland to Lübeck, and thence to Emden; his colleagues, meanwhile, resumed a cruel winter journey through northern Germany. In Wismar they encountered the Anabaptist patriarch Menno Simons, who issued a challenge to debate: Micron hastened back from Emden to represent the exiles. The two debates that followed focused on corporality of the word; both men later published accounts, Micron's as *Een waerachtigh verhael der t'zamensprekinghen* ('A true account of the debate') (1556). From Wismar the exiles journeyed to Lübeck, and thence to Hamburg, where new disputes with the prominent Lutheran minister Joachim Westphal resulted in their once again being denied entry to the city. The bedraggled refugees finally found a friendly welcome in Emden, no doubt assured since Micron's earlier visit. Micron himself accepted a post in nearby Norden, where on 20 May 1554 he was established as minister.

The last years of Micron's life were occupied in pastoral responsibilities and with energetic authorial works. Aside from the *Christlicken ordinancien*, and the tract against Menno, he also collaborated with his new Norden colleague in the production of a new exposition of eucharistic theology, the *Kort underricht* (1554). He also contributed to the emerging genre of martyrology the *Waerachteghe historie van Hoste vander Katelyne* (1555), a moving account of the short life and execution of a former member of the London congregation and fellow inhabitant of Ghent, arrested on a missionary journey back to Flanders. Micron died of plague in Norden on 12 September 1559, shortly before the formal reopening of the London foreign churches.

Micron's direct contact with England was therefore short, but influential. Apart from the enduring influence of his Dutch church order, two of his works were translated into English: *A Short and Faithful Instruction, Gathered out of Holy Scripture* (1556), a translation of the *Kort underricht* of 1554 (STC, 1475–1640, 17864), and *Differences between the True Christ of Holy Scripture and their Counterfeited Christ*, a series of antitheses taken from the Vander Kateleyne narrative, recently discovered in a unique English broadsheet of 1561 and identified as the work of Micron (STC, 1475–1640, 17863.7). The translator of the *Short and Faithful Instruction* was Thomas Cottisford, a member of the English exile church in Emden, not Thomas Cranmer as hypothesized in the *Short-Title Catalogue*. The will of Micron's London colleague Jan Utenhove makes reference to writings of Micron that might be found among his papers; presumably this is a reference to manuscripts, but if so, their present location is unknown. Micron himself seems to have left no family. There is no mention of a wife in the Dutch church records, and no indication that he married in the latter phase of his life, in East Friesland.

Andrew Pettegree

Sources D. Nauta and others, eds., *Biografisch lexicon voor de geschiedenis van het Nederlandse protestantisme*, 3 vols. (Kampen, 1978–88) · J. H. Gerretsen, *Micronius: zijn leven, zijn geschriften, zijn geestesrichting* (1895) · A. Pettegree, *Foreign protestant communities in sixteenth-century London* (1986) · J. Lindeboom, *Austin friars: history of the Dutch Reformed church in London, 1550–1950*, trans. D. de Iongh (1950) · A. Pettegree, *Emden and the Dutch revolt: exile and the development of reformed protestantism* (1992) · R. Leaver, 'A unique broadsheet in the Scheide Library, Princeton', *Papers of the Bibliographical Society of America*, 83 (1989), 337–52 · R. A. Leaver, 'Goostly Psalmes and Spirituall Songes': English and Dutch metrical psalms from Coverdale to Utenhove, 1535–1566 (1991) · STC, 1475–1640, nos. 16571a, 15260.7, 17863.3, 17863.5, 17863.7, 17864, 17864.5, 18812

Middiman, Samuel (1750–1831). *See under* Boydell, John, engravers (*act.* 1760–1804).

Middleditch, Edward Charles (1923–1987), painter, was born on 23 March 1923 at 1 Park Avenue, Chelmsford, Essex, the younger son and second of three children of Charles Henry Middleditch, cabinet-maker and bat trimmer, and his wife, Esme Buckley. In the mid-1920s the family moved to the St Anne's district of Nottingham, where Edward went to Mundella School, but they returned to Chelmsford in 1939, where he attended King Edward VI Grammar School.

On leaving school Middleditch worked in an office until he joined the army in 1942, and two years later he was commissioned in the Middlesex regiment, eventually reaching the rank of captain. He saw active service in Normandy during the winter campaign of 1944–5, and was wounded fighting in the Ardennes in 1945, when he was awarded the MC. His interest in art was first marked by the purchase, when on leave in Paris, of a book on Goya. After convalescence in England he was posted to Burma, arriving in India in August 1945. He was then sent to west Africa and was invalided home from Nigeria in 1947 with malaria, and demobilized. That year he married Jean Kathleen (d. 1979), a student of engraving, daughter of Frank Joseph Thomas Whitehouse, assistant controller in the London and North Eastern Railway. They had one daughter.

In 1948 Middleditch attended classes in painting and drawing at the Regent Street Polytechnic. With an ex-serviceman's grant he was accepted by the painting department of the Royal College of Art in September of that year, and he graduated in 1952. The strongest influences on him were Ruskin Spear, who taught him to admire and to some degree emulate the sombre tones of Walter Sickert, and John Minton, who introduced him to modern French art. His friends and contemporaries at the RCA included Derrick Greaves, John Bratby, Jack Smith, and Malcolm Hughes.

In 1950 Middleditch exhibited and sold an oil painting, *Trafalgar Square*, at the Royal Academy, and the following year he showed views of the Thames in the exhibition 'Artists of fame and promise' at the Leicester Galleries. His pictures in the 'Young contemporaries' exhibition of 1952 attracted the attention of John Berger, who wrote in the *New Statesman and Nation* (19 January 1952) that they were 'the most outstanding of all' in the exhibition. His stark picture *Baby* (1952) was bought by the Arts Council, and his *Crowd, Earls Court* (1954) reflected the austere mood of the time. Although, through friendship, he was associated with the group labelled 'kitchen sink painters' by David Sylvester in *Encounter*, few of Middleditch's paintings, then or later, were of domestic subjects. Rather, his melancholy paintings (such as *Sheffield Weir II*, which was bought for the Tate Gallery from his first one-man exhibition in March 1954 at Helen Lessore's Beaux Arts Gallery) were mostly of landscape and cityscape. Characteristic of this period is the dark, bleak, elegiac *Dead Chicken in a Stream* (1955; Tate collection).

In 1955 Middleditch was included in 'Giovani pittori', an exhibition which travelled from Rome to Paris under the auspices of the Congrès pour la Liberté de la Culture, and won second prize in the *Daily Express* 'Young artists' exhibition. With Bratby, Greaves, and Smith he represented Britain at the twenty-eighth Venice Biennale in 1956. He visited Spain for the first time in 1957, and the Middleditch and Greaves families then began to share a large house in Buckinghamshire.

Middleditch taught at the Chelsea School of Art from 1958 until 1963, and at Regent Street Polytechnic, the Cambridge School of Art, and St Martin's School of Art during the 1960s. In 1962 he was awarded a Gulbenkian Foundation scholarship. He moved to Boxford, Suffolk, and was appointed head of the department of fine art at Norwich School of Art in 1964. A gifted teacher and administrator, he had a profound influence on students. On his retirement in 1984 he became in 1985 keeper of the

Royal Academy Schools, having been elected ARA in 1968 and RA in 1973.

From the 1960s Middleditch frequently painted flowers, and over the years the mood and colour of his painting lightened and became more decorative, without losing its serious commitment to the evocation of nature. At Norwich he made many silk-screen prints, and in 1981 he published *Books and Folios, Screenprints by Derrick Greaves, Robert Medley and Edward Middleditch*.

Middleditch dressed informally; his rounded forehead was furrowed under a widow's peak of hair, and deep creases from the side of his nose to his mouth were evidence, perhaps, of the injuries and illnesses he had suffered. Ill health forced Middleditch to retire as keeper of the Royal Academy in 1986, and he died in Chelmsford on 29 July 1987, at the time of his major retrospective exhibition, mounted by the South Bank Centre, London.

ALAN WINDSOR, *rev.*

Sources L. Morris, *Edward Middleditch: the South Bank Centre* (1987) · *The Times* (31 July 1987) · private information (1996) · *CGPLA Eng. & Wales* (1987)

Wealth at death £39,058: probate, 7 Dec 1987, *CGPLA Eng. & Wales*

Middlemore, George (*d.* 1850), army officer, received a commission as ensign in the 48th foot on 16 January 1793. He was made lieutenant of an independent company on 15 April 1793 and on 30 October 1793 lieutenant. He was promoted captain-lieutenant on 15 October 1794 and captain on 1 September 1795. He commanded a company in the 86th, which after service in Ireland embarked as marines in HMS *Brunswick* (74 guns, Captain Lord Charles Fitzgerald) and served in the channel with Admiral Cornwallis in 1795, and afterwards with Lord Duncan in the North Sea. He subsequently served with his regiment at the Cape in 1796–8 and Madras in 1799. (The regiment was not at the capture of Seringapatam as sometimes stated.) Service in Bombay and Ceylon followed, and in 1801 he accompanied the expedition up the Red Sea to Egypt, where he commanded the regiment's grenadier company. He took part in an arduous march across the desert from Quseir to Qena and was in command of a party which dug a vital well near Moilah. With Colonel Ramsay he went on a mission to the Turkish capitan pasha regarding plots against the Mamelukes. After the return of his regiment to India he served at Madras as aide-de-camp to Sir David Baird, with whom he went back to Britain. This was a difficult assignment due to Baird's strong character, but Middlemore discharged his duties to great satisfaction. On 14 September 1804 he was promoted to a majority in the 48th regiment at Gibraltar. He served with it in Portugal in 1809; at the battle of Talavera, when Colonel Donellan was mortally wounded, he commanded it during the greater part of its famous advance to the aid of the guards, which contributed so much to the victory. On that occasion the regiment won its badge of the Star of Brunswick. Wellington recommended Middlemore for promotion as 'an excellent officer'.

Following a brief period on half pay Middlemore received a gold medal for Talavera, and was created CB on 4 June 1815. He was promoted to lieutenant-colonel of the 48th on 2 November 1809, exchanged to half pay of the 8th garrison battalion on 28 June 1810, returned to full pay of the 48th on 21 March 1811, and on 24 October 1811 again exchanged to half pay of the 12th garrison battalion through ill health. He was appointed assistant quartermaster-general in the Severn district in 1813, and in 1814 became inspecting field officer at Nottingham. He was promoted colonel on 12 August 1819 and became a major-general in 1830, and for five years commanded the troops in the West Indies, where he travelled widely and instituted reforms to the benefit of soldiers and the civilian population alike. In 1836 he was made governor of the island of St Helena, and held that post at the time of the removal of the remains of Napoleon I in 1840. He was made a lieutenant-general in 1841 and was colonel in succession of the 76th and 48th regiments. He died at Tunbridge Wells on 18 November 1850. His son, Lieutenant-Colonel R. F. Middlemore (captain, half pay, 91st regiment), was his aide-de-camp at St Helena.

H. M. CHICHESTER, *rev.* JAMES FALKNER

Sources *Army List* · *Hart's Army List* · R. Cannon, ed., *Historical record of the eighty-sixth, or royal county Down regiment of foot* (1842) · *GM*, 2nd ser., 35 (1851), 95 · T. Hook, *Life of Gen. Sir David Baird*, 2 vols. (1832) · W. F. P. Napier, *History of the war in the Peninsula and in the south of France*, 3rd edn, 6 vols. (1834–40) · *Corrections and additions to the Dictionary of National Biography*, Institute of Historical Research (1966)

Middlemore [Middlemere], **Richard** (*c*.1602–1667), Jesuit, was born in Staffordshire, the son of William Middlemere. He studied humanities at the English College, St Omer, and was sent in 1621 to the English College of the Jesuits at Valladolid. It was there that he joined the Society of Jesus in 1623. He was sent to the noviciate at Watten in Flanders in 1624 and was professed of the four vows on 25 March 1624. He served on the English mission from 1631 to 1646. He lived at the residence of the Blessed Stanislaus, which included Devon and Cornwall, being recorded there from 1631 to 1636 and 1642 to 1645, at the house of probation of St Ignatius (1638–41) and at the College of the Holy Apostles in 1641. He appears at Ghent in 1646. He was appointed professor of moral theology and controversy at Liège in 1649. His two published works, both printed at Liège in 1656, are *Lapis Lydius controversiarum modernarum Catholicos inter at Acatholicos* and *Pia exercitatio divini amoris*, the former 'another attempt at a brief controversial compendium', which 'breaks no new ground' but which was printed in a manner which 'made it pocket-portable for priests' (Clancy, *Literary History*, 137). He returned to England and died in London on 26 November 1667.

THOMPSON COOPER, *rev.* RUTH JORDAN

Sources Gillow, *Lit. biog. hist.*, 2.533–4 · G. Holt, *St Omers and Bruges colleges, 1593–1773: a biographical dictionary*, Catholic RS, 69 (1979), 117 · T. M. McCoog, *English and Welsh Jesuits, 1555–1650*, 2, Catholic RS, 75 (1995), 193 · D. A. Bellenger, ed., *English and Welsh priests, 1558–1800* (1984) · T. H. Clancy, *English Catholic books, 1641–1700: a bibliography* [1974], 123 · E. Henson, ed., *The registers of the English College at Valladolid, 1589–1862*, Catholic RS, 30 (1930), 139 · T. H. Clancy, *A literary history of the English Jesuits: a century of books, 1615–1714* (1996)

Archives Archivum Romanum Societatis Iesu, Rome

Middlesex. For this title name *see* Cranfield, Lionel, first earl of Middlesex (1575–1645); Sackville, Charles, sixth earl of Dorset and first earl of Middlesex (1643–1706).

Middleton. *See also* Myddelton.

Middleton, Anne (*d.* 1658), benefactor, was probably born at Shipton by Beningbrough, in the North Riding of Yorkshire, near York. She may have been a member of the Nelson family. She seems to have married Peter Middleton (*d.* 1652), tanner, the son of Thomas Middleton, tanner, of York soon after he obtained his freedom of the city *per patres* in 1595. They had no children. She spent all her married life in the parish of St Mary, Bishophill Senior, where her husband first served as overseer of the poor in 1598 and as churchwarden in 1617, and where for over twenty years from 1612 he audited the churchwardens' accounts. Listed as among the hundred or so leading citizens of York in 1603, he was elected a chamberlain the following year. Although frequently deputed to oversee church attendance in Micklegate ward, he advanced only slowly through the civic hierarchy, not becoming sheriff until 1618; thereafter he regularly attended council meetings as one of the Twenty-Four from 1618 until 1646.

Peter Middleton made his will in October 1623, almost thirty years before he died. Virtually ignoring his own relations apart from his sister Anne Witney and her daughter, he conferred all his property and goods upon his wife and her heirs. At some date after this Peter and Anne Middleton settled their mansion house in Skeldergate upon Anne's kinsman John Ellerker of York, gentleman. In 1645 and 1648 Peter Middleton added codicils to his will leaving £10 apiece to his sisters Susan, Alice, and Mary, and the children of his dead sister Frances, and £4 to the poor of each of the four wards of the city. He died in 1652.

Anne Middleton made her own will in August 1655, three years after Peter's death and two and a half years before her own. In marked contrast to her husband she showered legacies upon her relatives and friends, giving £100 each to the children of John Ellerker by his first and second marriages and a further £100 to her half-sister's daughter, Jane, wife of John Jefferson, who together with Isabel Thornton, the wife of her cousin William Thornton, shared the greater part of her household possessions. The children of William Nelson of Helperby, her heir at law, received £10 apiece, the two children of Thomas Nelson of Helperby 20 nobles, John Steadman her kinsman 20 nobles, her cousin Sarah Calvert £10. In total her legacies to family and friends amounted to about £1400. She then bestowed £100 upon the lord mayor and corporation of York to apprentice freemen's children, a further £40 to set the poor people of the city on work, 100 marks to be spent on silver plate, and no less than £2000 to build a hospital for twenty freemen's widows, each having an annual pension of £4 for life. She also remembered those North Riding parishes with which she seems to have had particular family connections. She donated £50 to the churchwardens and overseers of Brafferton and Helperby

to be lent at 12 per cent interest to honest poor men of the parish, the resulting moneys to be distributed to the poor every Christmas eve, and a further £10 towards providing a clock for Brafferton church. A bequest of £1000 to erect a free grammar school in Shipton and supply £40 annually for the schoolmaster's salary completed her benefactions. All this money for charity she expected to be raised out of debts owing to her at her death. This implies that she had at least £4735 out on loan: an enormous sum and testimony both to her wealth and to the scale of her involvement in the classic propertied widow's occupation of moneylending. Having bequeathed copyhold land in Cawood to John Ellerker, more land and tenements in Bishop Monkton to Richard Allanson's three sons, and a messuage in Brotherton to her kinsman William Kay, she divided the residue of her estate between John Ellerker and William Nelson, whom she named as her executors. Since Nelson died before the grant of probate on 21 April 1658, responsibility for establishing her charities devolved upon Ellerker.

Anne Middleton died in the parish of St Mary, Bishophill Senior, and was buried under the great blue stone in the choir of St Mary's on 17 March 1658. She was one of the greatest benefactors to York and its hinterland in the seventeenth century. In the mid-eighteenth century the corporation began referring to her as Lady Anne Middleton, a courtesy title not accorded her in her lifetime (since her husband never rose to be lord mayor), and as Lady Anne Middleton she has been popularly known ever since. After alterations to her hospital in 1771 the trustees placed her effigy over its door. At Shipton the grammar school did not survive for long before being converted into an elementary school and rebuilt in the Victorian period. It is now a house, while her hospital, rebuilt in 1828, has become a hotel. Financially, however, Shipton children and York widows still benefit substantially from her foundations.

CLAIRE CROSS

Sources Anne Middleton's will, 1655, PRO, PROB 11/274 [microfilm], fols. 201–3 [Wootton quire 131] · Peter Middleton's will, 1623, PRO, PROB 11/224 [microfilm], fol. 267 [Bowyer quire 228] · R. H. Skaife, 'Civic officials of York and parliamentary representatives', York City Reference Library [Victorian MS], 1.125–6; 2.506–8 · housebook, 1592–8, York City Archives, vol. 31 · housebook, 1598–1605, York City Archives, vol. 32 · housebook, 1605–12, York City Archives, vol. 33 · housebook, 1613–25, York City Archives, vol. 34 · housebook, 1625–37, York City Archives, vol. 35 · housebook, 1637–50, York City Archives, vol. 36 · housebook, 1650–63, York City Archives, vol. 37 · St Mary, Bishophill Senior, register and churchwardens' accounts, 1612–46, Borth. Inst., PRY/M Bp 5 · F. Drake, *Eboracum, or, The history and antiquities of the city of York* (1736) · F. Collins, ed., *Register of the freemen of the city of York*, 2, SurtS, 102 (1900) · *VCH Yorkshire*, vol. 1 · *VCH Yorkshire North Riding*, vol. 2 · *VCH Yorkshire City of York* · E. Brunskill, *Some York almshouses* (1960) · J. E. Andrews, 'Notes on the history of Ann Middleton's Hospital, Skeldergate, 1659–1973', 1993, York City Archives · *An inventory of the historical monuments in the city of York*, Royal Commission on Historical Monuments (England), 3 (1972) · J. C. H. Aveling, *Catholic recusancy in the city of York, 1558–1791*, Catholic RS, monograph ser., 2 (1970) · C. B. Norcliffe, 'Paver's marriage licences [pts 1–3, 7]', *Yorkshire Archaeological and Topographical Journal*, 7 (1881–2), 289–304; 9 (1885–6), 55–70, 362–79; 11 (1890–91), 209–45

Archives York City Archives, housebooks, vols. 31–36

Likenesses stone effigy, 1771, Skeldergate Hospital; repro. in *An inventory of the historical monuments in the city of York*, pl. 151
Wealth at death £4735—minimum in cash (out on loan); also lands, property, and possessions: will, PRO, PROB 11/274, sig. 131

Middleton, Arthur (1681–1737), planter and politician in America, was born in Charles Town, South Carolina, the son of Edward Middleton, planter, and his wife, Sarah Fowell. His father had emigrated from England to Carolina in 1678 and founded the Middleton dynasty of wealthy planter–politicians whose influence has been felt in every era of South Carolina history.

Middleton was educated first in South Carolina, and in 1697 went to England but did not attend university. Instead he was probably apprenticed in relatives' counting houses in London and was trained as a merchant. He returned to South Carolina in 1703 or 1704 and soon thereafter entered politics. Middleton was a member of the South Carolina Commons house of assembly (1706–9, 1716–21) and of the proprietors' council (1711–16), the upper chamber of Carolina's general assembly. From his post in the general assembly he was a leader of opposition against the government of the lords proprietors of Carolina. In December 1719 Middleton was president of an extra-legal convention of the people, which deposed proprietary governor Robert Johnson and petitioned George I to assume royal governance of the province.

The revolution succeeded, and Middleton played important political roles in the new royal government. Sir Francis Nicholson, the first royal-appointed governor of Carolina, named Middleton to the royal council. Middleton presided over the council from 1721 to 1736 and became acting governor in 1725, when Nicholson left the colony. He held that post until 1730, when George II appointed Robert Johnson, the deposed former proprietary governor, to succeed Nicholson.

There was considerable unrest in South Carolina during Middleton's term as acting governor. The unity among planters and Charles Town merchants that had accomplished the revolution of 1719 broke down and the colony split into two factions over currency questions and political prerogatives. Middleton had limited success in mediating between the factions and in a two-year period was forced to dissolve the general assembly five times.

Governor Robert Johnson arrived in Charles Town, South Carolina's metropolis, in December 1730 and took up the reins of government that had been pulled from his hands in 1719. Middleton returned to his seat on the royal council and served until his death in 1737. Any recriminations from the 1719 coup were forgotten as the two men collaborated to stabilize political and economic conditions in the colony.

During his public career Middleton augmented his landholding in low-country South Carolina. He owned houses and lots in Charles Town and in Dorchester, a town on the Ashley River. His principal plantation, The Oaks, was near Goose Creek off the Cooper River. There he grew rice, South Carolina's major cash crop in the eighteenth century and the source of the Middletons' great wealth for two centuries.

Middleton was representative of Carolina planter aristocrats who took their political values from the British squirearchy and their economic entrepreneurship from West Indian planters. As was appropriate to his status, Middleton took an active role in local politics and administration. He was a vestryman of St James's, Goose Creek Church of England parish (1707–8), was a free school commissioner (1710, 1712), in 1712 served on commissions to construct a state house and to found a provincial library, was a tax assessor (1715–16), and served in the militia during the Yemassee War (1715–17).

Arthur Middleton married twice. He wed first Sarah (*d.* 1721), daughter of Jonathan Amory, of Charles Town. Eight children were born to the marriage but five died in infancy. His son, Henry Middleton (1717–1784), founded Middleton Place on the Ashley River and a grandson, Arthur Middleton (1742–1787), was a signatory of the Declaration of Independence. After the death of Sarah, Middleton married a widow, Sarah Wilkinson Morton, in 1723. The couple had no children. Arthur Middleton died in Charles Town on 7 September 1737 and, according to family tradition, was buried behind the chancel in the parish church of St James's, Goose Creek. In his will he bequeathed more than 18,000 acres of land to his heirs.

ALEXANDER MOORE

Sources A. Moore, 'Middleton, Arthur', *ANB* · G. W. Lane, 'The Middletons of eighteenth-century South Carolina: a colonial dynasty, 1678–1787', PhD diss., Emory University, Atlanta, Georgia, 1990 · M. E. Sirmans, *Colonial South Carolina: a political history, 1663–1763* (Chapel Hill, NC, 1966) · *The Saumarez papers: materials relating to South Carolina drawing from the Middleton family in the Ipswich and East Suffolk Record Office* (1974) [microfilm] · will, South Carolina department of archives and history, Columbia, South Carolina, wills, inventories and miscellaneous records, Charleston county, 70 (1736–40), 479–84
Archives Suffolk RO, Ipswich, papers [microfilm]
Likenesses J. Herbert, portrait, 1716 (*Plat of the Oaks*), Charleston Museum, South Carolina
Wealth at death 18,000 acres of land: will, South Carolina Archives and History Center, Columbia

Middleton, Cecil Henry (1886–1945), horticulturist and broadcaster, was born on 22 February 1886 in the Northamptonshire village of Weston by Weedon, the son of John Robert Middleton and his wife, Sarah Davis. His father was head gardener to Sir George Sitwell, and Middleton grew up alongside Edith, Osbert, and Sacheverell. At an early opportunity he entered his father's trade: by the age of thirteen he was working on the estate, and at seventeen, with 50 *s*. in his pocket, he left for London.

Middleton worked in the seed trade, studied at evening classes, and became a student gardener at Kew. On 10 August 1912 he married Rosa Annie (*b.* 1880/81), daughter of George Joseph Jenkins, a hat shape maker. During the First World War he was engaged on food production in the horticultural division of the Board of Agriculture and Fisheries. Having obtained the national diploma for horticulture, he joined Surrey county council as an instructor. It was in this capacity that, in 1931, he was approached to broadcast for the first time.

The BBC had broadcast gardening talks from within a few months of its inception in 1922. They ranged from the loftier traditions of the subject, represented by speakers such as Vita Sackville-West and Marion Cran, to a short weekly bulletin of practical advice compiled by the Royal Horticultural Society. This was entirely impersonal, read by an anonymous announcer, and peppered with Latin names. With broadcasting approaching maturity, this was deemed unsatisfactory, and the BBC asked the society to recommend potential speakers. Middleton's name was put forward, and he duly appeared at the microphone on 9 May 1931. His opening words, 'Good afternoon. Well, it's not much of a day for gardening, is it?', demonstrated the unaffected conversational style of the born broadcaster which was to make Middleton one of the best-loved speakers of the golden age of radio.

Initially, Middleton was one of a pool of speakers operating under the auspices of the Royal Horticultural Society. In September 1934 he was given his own weekly series, *In the Garden*. Originally transmitted on Friday evenings, the programme was transferred to Sunday afternoons in October 1936. It continued, with summer breaks, until Middleton's death, and was heard at its peak by three-and-a-half million listeners.

It was clear that many of Middleton's listeners were not gardening enthusiasts, but were attracted by the personality of the speaker. The writer and critic Wilfrid Rooke Ley summed up his appeal:

> It is the art of Mr Middleton to address himself to the lowest common denominator of horticultural intelligence without the faintest hint of superiority or condescension. He will assume that your soil is poor, and your pocket poor. All he asks is that your hopes are high and your Saturday afternoons at his service … he has the prettiest humour. He stands for common sense and has the gift of consolation. (*Catholic Herald*, 27 Sept 1935)

Middleton published a number of books. The first, a collection of broadcast talks on gardening, appeared in 1935. Later works included *Colour All the Year in my Garden* (1938), *Digging for Victory* (1942), and an encyclopaedia of gardening (1944).

Despite his modesty, Middleton was fiercely proud of the tradition he represented, deploring the caricature of gardeners as 'funny old men with battered hats and old moth-eaten trousers, and with whiskers and very little intelligence' (BBC WAC, transcript of broadcast talk, 24 May 1935). No one could have applied this description to the neat, bespectacled Middleton who claimed:

> Generally speaking, they're very much as other men are— perhaps a little better in many ways: wholesome, decent living people who love their work—usually straight and often deeply religious people, perhaps without knowing it, and certainly without shouting about it. They work hand in hand with Nature and they know that their work is under the direct supervision of the Great Architect. (ibid.)

Middleton broadcast additionally to schools, in *Children's Hour*, and was the first television gardener—a garden being created at Alexandra Palace for this purpose in 1937. During the war he lent his support to the Dig for Victory campaign, by broadcasting and lecturing around the country. He died suddenly on 18 September 1945 as he left his home, 17 Princes Avenue, in Surbiton. His wife survived him. Ten years later a memorial gate was erected by public subscription at the entrance to the garden of the BBC building at 12 Cavendish Place, central London. Since 1990 the Middleton Gate has been at the BBC Written Archives Centre in Caversham, Berkshire.

JEFF WALDEN

Sources A. Briggs, *The history of broadcasting in the United Kingdom*, rev. edn, 5 vols. (1995) · P. Scannell and D. Cardiff, *A social history of British broadcasting*, [1] (1991) · *The Times* (19 Sept 1945) · *Catholic Herald* (27 Sept 1935) · b. cert. · m. cert. · d. cert. · *CGPLA Eng. & Wales* (1946) · interview, BBC WAC [transcripts]
Archives FILM BFI NFTVA, news footage
Wealth at death £17,560 10s. 5d.: probate, 15 Feb 1946, *CGPLA Eng. & Wales*

Middleton, Charles, styled second earl of Middleton and Jacobite first earl of Monmouth (1649/50–1719), politician, was the youngest of the three surviving children of John *Middleton, first earl of Middleton (c.1608–1674), soldier and politician, and his first wife, Grizel (d. 1666), daughter of James Durham of Pitkerro. Most of his early years were spent outside Scotland. From 1652 to 1660 he was brought up at the exiled court of Charles II. After the Restoration, when his father was given a Scottish peerage and appointed high commissioner to the Scottish parliament, Middleton was known by the courtesy title of Lord Clermont and went to live for three years in the palace of Holyroodhouse. His father's fall from power in 1663 resulted in another move away from Scotland, this time to London, where the Middletons settled permanently.

Early career Although his uncle Alexander Middleton was principal of King's College, Aberdeen, there is no evidence that Clermont returned to Scotland to be educated. In 1669, when his father went to be governor of Tangier, he was briefly attached to the English embassy to France, and thereafter embarked on a military career. He succeeded to his father's peerage in July 1674, and was commissioned lieutenant-colonel of the Holland regiment in September of that year. England had recently made peace with the Dutch, and remained neutral for the rest of the Franco-Dutch War, but Middleton was posted as a volunteer with the French in 1677 and served in Flanders the following year, until peace was signed at Nijmegen.

The turning point of Middleton's career came in 1679–80. James, duke of York, had gone to Edinburgh to escape the exclusion crisis, and a group of Scottish nobles had formed 'the party' to oppose John Maitland, duke of Lauderdale, the powerful secretary of state for Scotland. As the latter had been responsible for the fall of his father in 1663, Middleton returned to Scotland and attached himself to this group, hoping to secure the patronage of the king's brother. His name was soon put forward as a possible successor to Lauderdale, but although Charles II refused, and eventually gave the secretaryship to Alexander Stewart, fifth earl of Moray, he compensated Middleton by sending him in June 1680 to be his envoy to the imperial court in Vienna.

Middleton's instructions were to obtain an alliance with

Charles Middleton, styled second earl of Middleton and Jacobite first earl of Monmouth (1649/50–1719), by Nicholas Dixon, *c.*1665–70

Leopold I, an impossible task so long as England's naval power was crippled by the crisis over the succession. Although his mission was a failure, it enabled him to gain valuable administrative experience, and he was better qualified for high office when he returned to Edinburgh in July 1681. There he rapidly became a favourite with the duke and duchess of York, before returning to London at the beginning of 1682, followed soon afterwards by the duke himself. Middleton accompanied the duke back to Edinburgh in May and was with him when his frigate the *Gloucester* was shipwrecked off Yarmouth. Soon afterwards he was made a member of the Scottish privy council. But York was keen that Middleton should succeed Moray as secretary for Scotland, and sent him back to Whitehall. This time Charles II compromised, and on 26 September 1682 Middleton was appointed joint secretary with Moray.

Shortly afterwards, during the winter of 1682–3, Middleton married Catherine, a daughter of Robert Brudenell, second earl of Cardigan. Born in 1648 or 1649, she was no longer young, but she brought her husband some valuable connections with the English aristocracy, notably her nephew Charles Talbot, twelfth earl (later duke) of Shrewsbury. She was also a Catholic, and by marrying her Middleton (himself sceptical about religion) consolidated his position with the duke and duchess of York. The marriage was a success, and their first child, John, Lord Clermont, was born and baptized into the Church of England in November 1683. A daughter, Catherine, was born in August 1685.

Secretary of state in England   Although Middleton was involved in the intrigues of the 'secret committee' of the Scottish privy council, his future now lay in England, where he was made a privy councillor in July 1684. The following month he replaced Sidney Godolphin, first Baron Godolphin, as secretary of state for the northern department, and handed over his joint Scottish secretaryship to John Drummond, later earl of Melfort. He was at the same time appointed an extraordinary lord of session, though he resigned the post in February 1686 in favour of his brother-in-law Patrick Lyon, third earl of Strathmore and Kinghorne.

Middleton remained secretary of state for four and a half years, continuing in office when the duke of York succeeded as James II in February 1685, and transferring to the more prestigious southern department in September 1688. As MP for Winchelsea he was entrusted with the chief management of the House of Commons in the parliament of 1685, a particularly difficult task once it became clear that the king wished to repeal the discriminatory laws against dissenters and Catholics. He was a member of the Commons committee that drew up the address to the king against the employment of Roman Catholic officers, but otherwise during and after the parliamentary session loyally carried out the king's religious policies. He was regarded as a moderate and, unlike his fellow secretary of state Robert Spencer, second earl of Sunderland, showed no interest in converting to Catholicism to retain royal favour. He was one of the many officials present at the birth of James Francis Edward, prince of Wales, at St James's Palace in June 1688.

The invasion by William of Orange in November 1688 brought to an end Middleton's political career in England. He accompanied James II to Salisbury and then returned with him to Whitehall, where Lady Middleton gave birth to their third child, Charles, on 4 December. He does not seem to have been informed of the king's secret plans to escape to France, but when news arrived that James had been captured by a rabble of Kentish fishermen, he insisted that guards should be sent to protect him. He was one of the four nobles appointed by the council of peers to attend the king, and accompanied him back to Whitehall. Middleton remained conspicuously loyal to James throughout the crisis and helped arrange for his move to Rochester a few days later. There he advised James not to leave the country. When the king decided that he would nevertheless escape to France, it was to Middleton that he addressed his letter explaining his 'reasons for withdrawing himself from Rochester'.

Middleton was not a member of the convention that assembled in January 1689, and took no part in the debates that resulted in the transfer of the crown to William and Mary. He was replaced as secretary of state by his nephew Lord Shrewsbury, and retired to his house at Winchester, where he lived mainly for the next three years. His youngest child, Elizabeth, was born in June 1690. In May 1692, during the Franco-Jacobite invasion scare, he was arrested, but he was released three months later.

Secretary of state to James II in exile By 1692 James II's principal adviser and secretary of state at St Germain was the earl of Melfort, a Catholic, who maintained that a Jacobite restoration would be achieved only through military conquest and that political concessions and compromises would be of no help in bringing one about. He had advised the king to issue an uncompromising declaration in April 1692. Middleton disagreed with Melfort, hoping (like most Anglicans) for a restoration on terms which would safeguard the monopoly of the Church of England, with a general pardon and no further measures to advance religious toleration. In 1693 he sent an emissary to St Germain with propositions for a new declaration and promising to join the king in exile if they were accepted. James II gave a positive reply and Middleton secretly left England, reaching St Germain on 13 April 1693. The new moderate declaration, in which James promised to renounce his prerogative of suspending the law and to accept all the legislation passed since 1689 which parliament might present to him, was dated 17 April.

Middleton was appointed joint secretary of state with Melfort, and took responsibility for the Jacobite correspondence with England and Scotland, leaving Melfort in charge of negotiations with the French court and Rome. But the Jacobites in England made it clear that they were reluctant to correspond with St Germain so long as the more hard-line Melfort retained his position. Realizing that the latter was an obstacle to a restoration, Louis XIV asked James II to dismiss him and send him away from the court. This took place in June 1694, leaving Middleton as James II's undisputed chief minister, in charge of all negotiations with the French court as well as the correspondence with Great Britain. The Roman correspondence was entrusted to the queen's secretary, John Caryll, with whom Middleton enjoyed good relations. Meanwhile, in England he was tried for treason and outlawed on 23 July 1694, and attainted on 2 July 1695.

Middleton was highly regarded at both St Germain and Versailles, but his personal life was not easy. His wife had remained with their children in London, and although she sent their two daughters to be educated as Catholics at nearby Poissy in 1695, he was not informed. He disliked the Château de St Germain, where he had a large apartment, and likened its architecture to that of the Bastille. His hopes for another attempt to invade England, which he felt should involve a landing in the north near Newcastle, collapsed in 1696 when Louis XIV and the English Jacobites reached an impasse over whether an invasion should be preceded or succeeded by a rising. When the treaty of Ryswick was signed in 1697 Middleton was left as secretary of state to a king who would never be restored, and with relatively little official correspondence to conduct.

Fortunately for Middleton he was financially secure. He not only had an annual pension from James II of 6172 livres, but received the income from his Scottish estates at Fettercairn and Old Montrose. These had been confiscated by William III in August 1695, but granted to a friend named Charles Straton, who took possession of them in

July 1696 and forwarded the money to Middleton's banker in Paris. The return of peace facilitated travel between England and France, and Lady Middleton arrived at St Germain in July 1699, bringing their two sons with her. She was appointed governess to Princess Louise-Marie in July 1700, which brought an additional annual salary of 4116 livres.

Middleton remained secretary of state until James II died at St Germain in September 1701. He then hoped to resign his post, but by the king's will he was appointed a member of the regency council to assist Mary of Modena during the minority of James III (James Francis Edward Stuart), and he was persuaded to remain in office. At the same time he was given a Jacobite title in the English peerage as earl of Monmouth, though he rarely used it.

Conversion to Catholicism Middleton experienced an important crisis in his private life during the summer of 1702. On his deathbed James II had urged him to become a Catholic. In the months which followed, a number of apparently miraculous cures took place which were believed to have been through the intercession of the late king. Middleton seems to have been troubled by this, particularly when his close friend Archbishop Noailles of Paris commissioned the *curé* of St Sulpice to institute proceedings towards the canonization of the king in June 1702. Two weeks later his elder daughter, Catherine, left her convent school at Poissy and married Sir John Gifford, bt (d. 1707), a groom of the bedchamber to James III. Middleton's family were all present but he did not attend the Catholic ceremony, even though he gave her a generous dowry of 60,000 livres (Archives Nationales, Paris, Minutier Central Et LXV/154). Shortly afterwards Lord Clermont fell ill and, seemingly at the point of death, was converted to Catholicism by Dr Thomas Witham, the superior of the English College of St Gregory at Paris. When his son quickly recovered his health, Middleton felt that James II had interceded again and on 20 August, while in Paris, he asked Dr Witham to receive him into the Catholic church as well.

Knowing that his conversion would make him unacceptable to many English Jacobites, and that it might be regarded by the French court as a cynical attempt to strengthen his position, Middleton remained in Paris and urged Mary of Modena to let him retire, but neither she nor Louis XIV would agree. He visited St Germain for ten days in October, but it was not until 27 November that he eventually resumed his office.

Secretary of state to James III By this time the War of the Spanish Succession had begun, and France was again willing to give military support to a Jacobite restoration. James Drummond, fourth earl and Jacobite first duke of Perth, who had been governor to James III since 1696, strongly favoured an invasion of Scotland with a French army, but Middleton, who hoped for a peaceful restoration, was less enthusiastic. He felt that the Scottish nobles were divided among themselves, and argued that an invasion, if successful, might force the government in

London to make peace with France, thus depriving the Jacobites of further military assistance. The result might be civil war in both England and Scotland.

The rivalry between Middleton and Perth steadily increased after 1703. The queen and Caryll supported Middleton, so Perth began to argue that he neglected his duties. Perth was supported by Colonel Nathaniel Hooke, whom the French sent as an emissary to Scotland and who began to spread unfounded rumours that Middleton and Caryll were both traitors, trying to prevent a Jacobite restoration. Certain disaffected people at the French court were willing to believe this, but James III, who achieved his majority in June 1706, showed his opinion by offering Middleton the Garter, an honour which he declined.

When the Franco-Jacobite invasion of Scotland was eventually launched in March 1708, Middleton was among those who accompanied James III, while his two sons, then aged twenty-four and nineteen, sailed in one of the other ships. The French admiral failed to make a landing, and Middleton returned with James to France, but the ship carrying his sons was captured. They had taken service with the French army and were treated as prisoners of war rather than rebels, but they remained in the Tower of London until released on parole in 1711, and did not return to France until June 1713.

A partial reconciliation between Middleton and Perth was achieved when the former's younger daughter, Elizabeth, married the latter's youngest son, Lord Edward Drummond, in November 1709. About the same time the two men were able to agree that a new history of Scotland was badly needed, free of 'groundles fables and … antimonarchicall and republican maxims' (Stuart papers, 130/78). On their advice James III ordered Thomas Innes to write the history, eventually published in 1729 as *A Critical Essay on the Ancient Inhabitants of the Northern Parts of Britain or Scotland*.

The failure to invade Scotland had left Middleton with very little correspondence as secretary of state. He accompanied James to the French army in Flanders for the campaigns of 1708 and 1709, but remained at St Germain in 1710. In 1711, when the new tory government opened peace negotiations, the two men spent the summer months touring the eastern French provinces. Caryll died in September and Middleton took over the Roman correspondence, thus further consolidating his position as James III's chief adviser.

Middleton's work was considerably increased during and after the negotiations for the treaty of Utrecht, when there was a large group of Jacobite MPs in the House of Commons, and when some tory ministers were attempting to negotiate a peaceful Jacobite restoration after the death of Queen Anne. Middleton delegated part of it to his under-secretary, David Nairne. The Jacobite court had moved to Bar-le-Duc, where it was hoped by English Jacobites and sympathetic tories that James III would convert. Regarding the recently converted Middleton as an obstacle to achieving this, they insisted that James should replace him with an Anglican secretary of state, and in December 1713 Middleton was at last allowed to resign. He returned to St Germain, where Mary of Modena appointed him master of the horse. James III, who had no intention of converting, resented his loss and appointed Lord Clermont to be a gentleman of the bedchamber.

Retirement and death Middleton enjoyed his retirement at St Germain, and wrote, 'je m'amuse a la lecture des choses que j'avois appris au College' (BL, Add. MS 31257, fol. 179): 'I occupy my time in reading the things that I learned when I was at school'. However, his political career was not yet over. In November 1714, after the succession of George I and the fall of the tory ministry, he was recalled to Bar-le-Duc and remained there until November 1715, when James left to join the Jacobite rising in Scotland. He joined James in Scotland in January 1716, but returned with him to France the following month. In June 1716 he replaced the duke of Perth, who had recently died, as lord chamberlain to Mary of Modena, and continued to serve her until her death in May 1718. He and his wife lived in a very large apartment on the second floor of the south wing of the château, adjacent to that of the queen and originally intended for the children of the kings of France.

Middleton's last years were saddened by the failure of the 'Fifteen, when his son Lord Clermont was arrested *en route* for Scotland and imprisoned in the Tower from November 1715 to May 1716. He then followed James to Avignon and then Urbino, where he was supplanted by the newly exiled Jacobites from Scotland. The death of Mary of Modena in May 1718 left Middleton and his wife (a lady of the bedchamber since the death of Princess Louise-Marie in 1712) without the chief source of their income in France, but in November 1718 the French government granted them an annual pension of 3000 livres each. When Middleton died on 9 August 1719, aged sixty-nine, he left all his possessions to his wife, who died on 11 March 1743 at St Germain, at the age of ninety-four. He was buried at the parish church of St Germain on the day of his death. Lord Clermont, who never married, had already inherited the estates in Scotland which the first earl had left to his second wife. Middleton's younger son, Charles, died unmarried in September 1738, and when Clermont (who, as a Jacobite, ignored the attainder and called himself third earl of Middleton) died in November 1746 all Middleton's titles became extinct. Of his daughters, Catherine had two children from her first marriage and one from her second, to General Michael *Rothe, and died in June 1763; Elizabeth had no children and died in August 1774.

Middleton was an attractively amusing and witty man, whom even one of his enemies described as 'one of the politest gentlemen in Europe' and 'one of the pleasantest company in the world' (Middleton, 7). David Nairne commented to James III shortly after his death that 'your Majesty never had nor can have a more dissinterested servant and of more true honour, merit and loyalty' (Stuart papers, 44/66). His reputation, however, was undermined in the late nineteenth century by the publication of Colonel Hooke's *Correspondence*, containing his unfounded allegations that Middleton was a traitor serving the government in London. Various French sources, notably the enormously influential *Mémoires* of Saint-Simon, repeated and thus seemed to confirm what Hooke had said. Recent research has totally discredited such allegations, and Middleton is now regarded as a man who combined absolute loyalty with political moderation.

EDWARD CORP

Sources G. H. Jones, *Charles Middleton: the life and times of a Restoration politician* (1967) · D. Middleton, *The life of Charles, second earl of Middleton* (1957) · D. Nairne, diary, NL Scot., MS 14266 · Royal Arch., Stuart papers, vols. 1–44 · Gualterio papers, BL, Add. MSS 20297, 31253–31257 · E. Corp, 'An inventory of the archives of the Stuart court at Saint-Germain-en-Laye, 1689–1718', *Archives*, 23 (1998), 118–46 · C. E. Lart, *The parochial registers of Saint-Germain-en-Laye: Jacobite extracts*, 2 vols. (1910–12) · R. Beddard, ed., *A kingdom without a king: the journal of the provisional government in the revolution of 1688* (1988) · J. Gibson, *Playing the Scottish card: the Franco-Jacobite invasion of 1708* (1988) · D. Szechi, *Jacobitism and tory politics, 1710–1714* (1984) · E. Gregg, 'The politics of paranoia', *The Jacobite challenge*, ed. E. Cruickshanks and J. Black (1988), 42–56 · *Correspondence of Colonel N. Hooke*, ed. W. D. Macray, 2 vols., Roxburghe Club, 92, 95 (1870–71) · L. de Rouvroy, duc de Saint-Simon, *Mémoires*, ed. A. de Boisliste, 41 vols. (1879–1930), vol. 12, p. 449; vol. 15, pp. 416–18, 433–4 · B. D. Henning, 'Middleton, Charles', HoP, *Commons, 1660–90* · GEC, *Peerage* · *Scots peerage*, 6.186–9

Archives BL, papers with Kenelm Digby and Wynne family papers, Add. MSS 41803–41846 · Bodl. Oxf., letters, Carte MSS 180, 208, 212, 238, 256 | BL, letters to F. A. Gualterio, Add. MSS 20297, 31257 · Royal Arch., Stuart papers, vols. 1–44

Likenesses N. Dixon, miniature on vellum, *c*.1665–1670, FM Cam. [*see illus.*] · G. Kneller, oils, *c*.1682–1683, repro. in Middleton, *Life of Charles*, frontispiece; priv. coll.

Wealth at death see will, 7 July 1719, Archives Départementales des Yvelines, B. 537 Saint-Germain-en-Laye, repr. in Lart, *The parochial registers*, vol. 2, pp. 150–56

Charles Middleton, first Baron Barham (1726–1813), by M. Bourlier, pubd 1809 (after John Downman)

Middleton, Charles, first Baron Barham (1726–1813), naval officer and administrator, the twelfth child and second son of Robert Middleton, a collector of customs at Bo'ness in Linlithgowshire, and his wife, Helen, the daughter of Charles Dundas of Arniston, was born at Leith on 14 October 1726. His grandfather, George Middleton (*d.* 1726), and great-grandfather, Alexander Middleton (*d.* 1684), were successively principals of King's College, Aberdeen.

Early career Middleton entered the Royal Navy in April 1741 as captain's servant to Samuel Mead, captain in turn of the *Sandwich* and *Duke* (both 90 guns). As Mead approached retirement, Middleton was transferred to the frigate *Flamborough* (20 guns), where for four years he served successively as servant, midshipman, and master's mate. He passed his lieutenant's examination on 4 October 1745 and the following day was appointed to the frigate *Chesterfield* (40 guns), in which he served until 1749, mainly in the channel and then, after 1748, on the west coast of Africa. Off Sierra Leone, while the officers were on shore, the ship was seized by mutineers, but by good fortune at sea she was regained for the crown and taken to the West Indies, where the officers, including Middleton, rejoined the ship.

In July 1749 Middleton was placed on half pay and, though credited with six months' service in a guardship in 1752, he did not receive a further commission for service at sea until January 1753. He then had almost ten years'

continuous service, initially plying between Portsmouth and Gibraltar, but with the outbreak of the Seven Years' War he was present in the *Anson* (60 guns) at Edward Boscawen's interception of three, and capture of two, French ships of 64 guns attempting to get into Louisburg. The remainder of the war was principally spent off the Leeward Islands. At the end of January 1757 Middleton was the focus of a rowdy complaint against the stoppage of a sailor's rum ration. Records of the event reveal for the first time Middleton's short temper and readiness to resort to physical violence. The complainant was court-martialled for making a disturbance, but Middleton left the ship within a month of the incident and was elevated to the command of the sloop *Speaker*. After being transferred to another sloop, *Barbados*, he achieved post-rank on appointment to the frigate *Arundel* in 1759. There again, on new year's day 1760, Middleton used physical violence to terminate a dispute with the ship's carpenter, only to receive insolence, for which the latter was punished by sentence of court martial.

From July 1760 Middleton commanded the *Emerald* (28 guns) in the Leeward Islands, where he took sixteen prizes, including five privateers, and received a gold-hilted sword from the merchant community of Barbados in gratitude. The *Emerald* was paid off in October 1761, and from March 1762 Middleton spent a year on the Normandy coast in the frigate *Adventure*. In December 1761 he had married Margaret Gambier (*d.* 1792), the niece of Captain Mead, whom he had met twenty years earlier on board the *Sandwich*. According to Middleton's would-be biographer, John Deas Thompson, Margaret had declined another proposal of marriage and defied her father in order to wait for Middleton. She had gone to live with her friend Elizabeth

Bouverie, at Teston in Kent. With peace in prospect, in 1763 Middleton declined another seagoing appointment and joined Margaret and Elizabeth at Teston, and for the next twelve years lived the life of a country gentleman, farming the land belonging to Elizabeth Bouverie.

Comptroller of the navy Hitherto Middleton's naval career had been worthy but undistinguished. On the outbreak of the American War of Independence in 1775 he obtained command of a guardship at the Nore, conveniently close to Teston. He was given a larger one a year later, and in 1778 he was appointed to command a ship of 50 guns then under construction. But in August 1778, without trial or experience in a subordinate post, he was appointed comptroller of the navy. Why the first lord of the Admiralty, Lord Sandwich, should have raised him from relative obscurity to a key post in naval administration has been a source of speculation. However, Middleton enjoyed useful political connections: he was linked by his mother to the Dundas clan, and his wife brought him an association with the Pitts. Akin to the first lord, he was also a proprietor of East India Company stock, and, also like Sandwich, he subscribed to the organization of Concerts of Ancient Music at which they may have met. Furthermore, his brother-in-law, Captain James *Gambier (1723–1789), was a proven naval administrator whom Sandwich employed to sound Middleton out.

In August 1778 the management of the navy demanded administrative abilities of the first order. The Navy Board, of which Middleton was now the leading member, was responsible for the dockyards, manning, and financial procedures. The Navy Office had a staff of about a hundred and worked with the Board of Admiralty, the Treasury, and Victualling and Ordnance boards. Middleton's first task was to grasp a daunting volume of board correspondence, which he did virtually single-handedly. Robert Gregson, a clerk in the Navy Office, who assisted the clerk of the acts at the board, reported in a letter to Lord Shelburne, dated 20 December 1789, that Middleton was 'the most indefatigable and able' comptroller he had known:

> The load of business he goes through at the Board, at the Treasury, Admiralty and his own house, is astonishing, and what I am confident no other man will be able to execute … Upon the whole the weight of business falls upon a few, and of those few, chiefly upon the Comptroller and Secretary, who have piles of papers before them a foot high, to digest and minute, while two or three at the board are looking on or reading newspapers, who if they were to assist, the business would go on smoother and easier.   (Rodger, 161)

In addition he attended the Admiralty for confidential briefings several times a week. One particular source of frustration was the unco-ordinated and economically unrealistic bidding of four government departments—the Navy Board, Victualling Board, Ordnance Board, and Treasury—for the hire of transports to carry on the war in America. To reduce this competition for ships, Middleton proposed that the Navy Board hire ships for all four departments, and in 1779, as a step in that direction, the Navy Board took over the acquisition of army victuallers from the Treasury. By now the war in America had reached a critical stage. The declaration of hostilities against Great

Britain by Spain as well as France gave the Bourbon powers a 44 per cent superiority in ships of the line. In 1778 the Navy Board had been permitted belatedly to begin a programme of new building. By 1783, thirty-three new ships of the line had been launched, the majority from merchant shipbuilding yards.

Meanwhile Middleton proposed an increase in Britain's capability at sea without the necessity of raising the number of ships it maintained in commission. Owing to the frequency with which ships had to be refitted, the British force spent a significant proportion of its time at dockyards, or making its way to and from them. The eastern, inland yards were particularly difficult to access. To reduce the time committed to refitting Middleton proposed that ships of the line should be sheathed with copper, which, unlike the fir currently used, resisted the adherence of weed and mollusc. Equally important, it permitted ships to sail faster, increasing their capacity to attack or escape the enemy. Hitherto, copper sheathing had been resisted on account of the electrolytic action on iron hull fastenings. However, Middleton advocated the insulation of the hull from the sheathing by means of a coating of white lead and a layer of thick tarred paper, a method employed by a Liverpool shipbuilder. In February 1779 Middleton persuaded the Admiralty to try the technique on two battleships. The innovation earned immediate praise. Sea officers claimed great advantage in speed and manoeuvring from the copper bottoms. In late May all ships of the line refitting were ordered to be coppered. By 1781, 313 ships had been metal sheathed, including eighty-two ships of the line. It was only in 1783 that the failure of the insulation process was revealed, so that, post-war, the hull fastenings of the entire coppered fleet had to be renewed.

To enhance the firepower of ships in commission, Middleton advocated use of the carronade, under trial at Woolwich in July 1779 after successful use by a Liverpool privateer. Although they were initially distrustful of the technique, naval officers were won over during 1780, as was Lord Sandwich. However, it was not until 1782 that Middleton was able to persuade naval members of the Board of Admiralty to permit its use. The carronade had an immediate demoralizing effect on opponents and certainly added to the potential firepower of the British navy before the peace was signed in 1783.

In April 1782 Sandwich, along with the ministry as a whole, was forced to resign for his conduct of the sea war. Sandwich's reputation as an inefficient war minister persisted for nearly two hundred years, partly due to Middleton's criticism of his management in papers that were published by the Navy Records Society at the beginning of the twentieth century. As early as 1779 Middleton had directly rebuked the first lord for the disabled state of the dockyards from want of attention to appointments, for lack of system in the disposition of the fleet, for the loss of discipline in the navy, and for not himself working longer hours. Middleton claimed that the Navy Office and the Admiralty were 'so nearly connected that I must be wilfully blind not to see the sad management that prevails at present'; 'unless a new plan is adopted, and your lordship gives your whole time to the business of the admiralty, the misapplication of the fleet will bring ruin upon this country' (*Letters and Papers*, 2.3–5). In 1781 he had deliberately quarrelled with Sandwich over the latter's refusal to permit the Navy Board greater influence in the appointment of dockyard officers. Nevertheless, despite these difficulties, Sandwich appears to have appreciated Middleton's professional merits, and on 23 October 1781 he was created a baronet. Furthermore, the comptroller's experience of Sandwich's successors at the Admiralty led him to make 'a proper sense of distinction' between their respective abilities, and in 1789 he unreservedly encouraged Sandwich to return as first lord.

Naval reformer The non-political status of his office permitted Middleton to remain in post at the conclusion of the American War. He immediately turned his mind to the necessity for reform as demonstrated by the demands of war. In his private time, he revised to 1767 the standing orders to the dockyards and the system of accounts, by which the Navy Board controlled much of the business of naval administration. In this he was encouraged by the wider political movement for economical reform. The commission on fees, gratuities, perquisites, and emoluments in the public offices, appointed in 1785, gave Middleton a vehicle by which to advance his proposals, the most important of which was an extension of the comptroller's official superintending power, the appointment of a sea officer to preside at the Navy Board as deputy comptroller, and for the clerk of the acts to become secretary of the board, which, he argued, for some work should be divided into committees. Lord Howe, first lord at the Admiralty (1783–8), was unsympathetic to his proposals. Moreover, George III's illness in 1789 postponed implementation of the recommendations of the fees commission to such an extent that Middleton was driven in March 1790 to resign.

In 1784 Middleton had been elected MP for Rochester and served as a loyal supporter of William Pitt and Henry Dundas. In six years he spoke only seven times, and then only on naval matters—as on 30 March 1786, when he criticized the bill to disenfranchise voters employed in naval and ordnance yards, an important section of his own constituents. However, conscious of the time taken up by business on behalf of constituents, as well as the conflict of interest he frequently faced, he wrote to Pitt on 24 September 1789 of the 'impropriety of my representing a borough so intimately connected with the civil departments of the navy' (*Letters and Papers*, 2.328). He resigned from the Commons in 1790.

During the 1780s Middleton's main achievement was to ensure that the fleet was repaired and rebuilt to a state of readiness for war. He aimed for ninety ships of the line and ninety frigates fit for service at sea by the end of 1786. In this task he benefited from the support of Pitt, who sometimes visited him at the Navy Office to review progress. Between 1783 and 1789 twelve new ships of the line were built and sixty-five repaired. This quiet but essential work permitted diplomacy by deterrence during the Spanish alarm of 1790. When war did break out in 1793 Britain's strength in ships of the line was exactly equal to the combined strength of France and Spain. It was a long-term achievement that fulfilled the recommendations for forethought and preparation which Middleton repeatedly urged on his political superiors.

On 24 September 1787 Middleton was promoted rear-admiral, in spite of opposition from Lord Howe, who would have preferred to see him made a dockyard commissioner. He became in due course a vice-admiral on 1 February 1793 and admiral on 1 June 1795. In May 1794 he was appointed third naval commissioner at the Board of Admiralty, and in March 1795 first commissioner. Recalling the blockade strategy mounted in the Seven Years' War, he was able to prepare on paper for the logistical demands that would be made on the British fleet over the next twenty years. At the change in first lord of the Admiralty in December 1794, Dundas recommended to Lord Spencer Middleton's 'great official talents and merits', but observed that he was 'a little difficult to act with from an anxiety, I had almost said an irritability of temper, and he requires to have a great deal of his own way of doing business in order to do it well'. In the event, Middleton and Spencer did not get on. Spencer excluded Middleton from his own inner committee of Admiralty advisers, and in November 1795 the comptroller resigned over the disrespect accorded to senior flag officers in the Caribbean to suit the appointment of a junior, a perception that mirrored Middleton's own sense of neglect at the hands of a relatively inexperienced political administrator.

Middleton went back to farming at Teston for eight years. When Pitt returned to office and Dundas (now first Viscount Melville) became first lord of the Admiralty in May 1804, Middleton offered memoranda of advice. In addition, he proposed that the task of revising the dockyards' standing orders, begun in the 1780s, could be resumed with the help of the digest still in his possession. By September 1804 Middleton's friend John Deas Thompson, the naval officer for Leith, was installed at the Admiralty and was charged with concentrating into one list all the standing orders issued by the Navy Board since 1793, then abstracting them under various heads into one of the digest books brought from Teston. By November 1804 the work had reached a stage at which Middleton also wanted to revise the orders under which sea officers acted, accounts and procedures to be included. The scope of the project was deemed sufficient for a commission for revising and digesting the civil affairs of the navy. It was established by letters patent under the great seal in January 1805 with Middleton as chairman.

This new post gave Middleton the opportunity to create order in the navy. His recommendations to the commissioners on fees for reform in the Navy Office had largely been effected in 1796. However, the commission's recommendations for the dockyards had been revised by Sir Samuel Bentham as inspector-general of naval works in collaboration with Evan Nepean, Admiralty secretary, before they were adopted in 1801. Middleton believed his recommendations had been 'sadly garbled' and altered 'to the views of interested individuals'. Conveniently, the new commission of revision replaced Lord St Vincent's commission to inquire into irregularities, frauds, and abuses practised in the naval departments, which, by finding grounds for prosecuting administrative malefactors, had proved a political embarrassment. Indeed, its tenth report on the office of treasurer of the navy obliged Melville to resign as first lord early in April 1805, eventually to be impeached for failing to prevent the paymaster of the navy mixing public funds with his own money in a private account in contravention of an act of 1782.

First lord and final years Middleton, though now aged seventy-nine, was asked to replace Melville. Rewarded with a peerage on 1 May 1805, the new Baron Barham of Teston turned his mind once more to operations at sea. His appetite for work was unabated and he became immersed in strategic details. Already by 1805 extensive instructions, covering every eventuality, had been compiled to direct squadrons blockading the ports of France and Spain. But Middleton's annotations on letters received indicate a grasp of the logistics at individual ship level. Justly, he has been credited with orchestrating the campaign of Trafalgar. The painstaking thoroughness he brought to administration, and the discipline he demanded in the dispatch and execution of orders, was complemented by the seaman's appreciation of the demands of ship management. It was appropriate that on 26 October, Cuthbert Collingwood's congratulations for 'the most complete victory that ever was obtained over an enemy' went to Barham.

Following William Pitt's death on 3 February 1806, Barham resigned with the rest of the government on 10 February. He was worn out. Since becoming first lord he had taken a back seat in the work of the commission for revising the civil affairs of the navy, leaving its management largely to John Fordyce, one of the other commissioners, who aimed to permit Britain to 'provide for a much greater navy than it ever had before', one 'on which our existence depends, more absolutely if possible than it ever did before'. Fordyce and John Deas Thompson, overseen by Barham, eventually generated thirteen reports, of which eleven were adopted by the end of 1809, the year in which the size of the Royal Navy approached almost one thousand ships. In some respects the reports marked a new departure in naval administration: the Navy Board claimed that the eighth report on the dockyards contained directions for alterations that amounted to a total change of system. But their recommendations also arrested changes based on the management principles advocated and partly introduced by Samuel Bentham. The fourth report registered the Navy Board's opposition to Bentham's post at the Admiralty, and in 1807 he was removed from it to a junior position at the board, from which in 1813 he was ousted altogether.

Barham died on 17 June 1813 aged eighty-six. His legacy remains the reports of the commission of revision. They were probably his most important contribution to the long-term development of the Royal Navy, for their recommendations proved the platform upon which the navy operated during the first three decades of the nineteenth century. But if his professional influence is clear, an assessment of the means employed in his professional life provides a more complex picture. Barham was a supreme example of the sort of reformer—dynamic, efficient, and tireless—who takes everything into his own hands. Much of this self-belief derived from his profound evangelical Anglicanism, to which he had converted, possibly at the time of his marriage, from the Church of Scotland. Such expressions of faith were at this time rare among naval officers and often provoked hostility and accusations of Wesleyan Methodism. However, Barham's remained a far more censorious and Calvinistic form of evangelicism, which prompted Hannah More to describe him on first meeting in 1776 as 'a stern and simple Captain' (Talbot, 14). Professionally it was manifest in his outspoken, righteous, and priggish attacks on insubordination among his men and on the perceived incompetence of superiors such as Lord Sandwich. At times his career suffered as a consequence. Nevertheless, Barham was motivated above all by a desire to maintain and improve efficiency in the management of the navy, and he contributed both to its technological development and to its administrative foundation, an organizational capacity which, in some respects, puts him on a par with Samuel Pepys. Lady Barham having died in 1792, he was survived by their daughter, Diana *Noel, who in 1780 had married Gerard Noel Edwardes. In 1798 the latter succeeded to the estates of his maternal uncle, the earl of Gainsborough, and by royal licence assumed the name Noel. On Barham's death Noel succeeded to the baronetcy, and Diana to the barony *suo jure*, which passed in 1823 to her eldest son, Charles Noel Noel.   ROGER MORRISS

Sources *Letters and papers of Charles, Lord Barham*, ed. J. K. Laughton, 3 vols., Navy RS, 32, 38–9 (1907–11) · J. E. Talbot, *The pen and ink sailor: Charles Middleton and the king's navy, 1778–1813* (1998) · D. Syrett, *Shipping and the American War, 1775–1783: a study of British transport organisation* (1970) · R. J. B. Knight, 'The introduction of copper sheathing into the Royal Navy, 1779–1786', *Mariner's Mirror*, 59 (1973), 299–309 · R. J. B. Knight, 'Sandwich, Middleton and dockyard appointments', *Mariner's Mirror*, 57 (1971), 175–92 · R. A. Morriss, *The Royal dockyards during the revolutionary and Napoleonic wars* (1983) · I. Lloyd-Philips, 'Lord Barham at the admiralty, 1805–6', *Mariner's Mirror*, 64 (1978), 217–33 · PRO, ADM 1/5296, fol. 183 · PRO, ADM 1/5299, pt 1, fol. 30 · R. J. B. Knight, ed., *Portsmouth Dockyard papers, 1774–1783: the American War* (1987) · P. L. C. Webb, 'The rebuilding and repair of the fleet, 1783–1793', *BIHR*, 50 (1977), 194–209 · *The private papers of John, earl of Sandwich*, ed. G. R. Barnes and J. H. Owen, 4 vols., Navy RS, 69, 71, 75, 78 (1932–8) · N. A. M. Rodger, *The insatiable earl: a life of John Montagu, fourth earl of Sandwich* (1993) · *DNB*

Archives NMM, papers | BL, letters to Lord Collingwood, Add. MS 40096 · BL, letters and memoranda to Lord Melville, Add. MS 41079 · BL, corresp. with Lord Nelson, Add. MSS 34902–34936 · NA Scot., corresp. with Lord Melville · NMM, letters to Lord Sandwich · NRA, priv. coll., letters to Lord Shelburne · PRO, letters to second earl of Chatham, PRO 30/8 · PRO NIre., corresp. with Lord Castlereagh

Middleton, Christopher (d. 1628), translator and poet, matriculated as a sizar of St John's College, Cambridge, in Easter term 1587. He graduated BA c.1600, and may be identical with the Christopher Middleton who graduated BD from St John's in 1619 and who was incorporated BD at Oxford on 13 July 1619. It is unlikely that he is the same Christopher Middleton, a gentleman of Cheshire, who matriculated from Brasenose College, Oxford, on 12 December 1580, aged twenty, since he is never styled a gentleman in his publications and, in one of his works, describes himself as a young man, which would not suit a 35-year-old in 1595 (Orme, 93). Nothing is known about his parents.

Middleton's literary activity seems to have been confined to the 1590s. His first work, *A short introduction for to learn to swimme, gathered out of Master Digbies booke of the art of swimming*, was published in 1595 and was a translation and abridgement of Everard Digby's *De arte natandi* which appeared in 1587, the year that Middleton entered St John's. It included woodcuts illustrating different swimming strokes such as 'To swim like a dog' (sig. F4) and 'To swimme on the back' (sigs. C2v–C3r). Middleton declared that his intention was to gather Digby's work 'into a brief compendium for their better understanding that are ignorant in the Latin tongue' and 'to uncurtain that to the view of all which was only appropriated to a few' (Orme, 116).

The Historie of Heaven: Containing the Poetical Fictions of All the Starres in the Firmament and a prose romance, *The Nature of a Woman*, were both published in 1596. The latter, by C. M., was published in two separate parts and has been attributed to Christopher Marlowe; but the fact that both the *Historie* and the *Nature of a Woman* were printed by Clement Knight supports the possibility of Middleton's authorship (*STC, 1475–1640*, 2.129; Orme, 92). *The Famous Historie of Chinon of England* was published in 1597, and *The Legend of Humphrey Duke of Glocester* in 1600. The latter was dedicated to Sir Jarvis Clifton, and was prefaced with poems by Robert Allott, Michael Drayton, and John Weever. Allott and Weever attended Cambridge in the 1590s which would seem to support our identification with the Cambridge Middleton. These men evidently formed a literary clique. Weever's *Epigrammes* (1599) included an epigram addressed to Drayton and another to Allott and Middleton jointly, and the *Legend of Humphrey* was perhaps influenced by Drayton's historical poems. Allott's *Wits Theater of the Little World* (1599) was printed for N. L., who is possibly the Nicholas Ling for whom Middleton's *Legend of Humphrey* was printed the following year. In 1612 Middleton became rector of Aston-le-Walls, Northamptonshire, and was buried there on 5 February 1628.

NICHOLAS D. SMITH

Sources DNB • N. Orme, *Early British swimming, 55 BC–AD 1719: with the first swimming treatise in English, 1595* (1983) • Venn, *Alum. Cant.* • Foster, *Alum. Oxon.* • *STC, 1475–1640* • E. Brydges, *Censura literaria: containing titles, abstracts, and opinions of old English books*, 10 vols. (1805–9) • A. F. Griffiths, *Bibliotheca Anglo-poetica* (1815) • J. Ames, *Typographical antiquities, being an historical account of printing in England* (1749) • T. Warton, *The history of English poetry*, new edn, ed. W. C. Hazlitt, 4 vols. (1871) • Cooper, *Ath. Cantab.*

Middleton, Christopher (d. 1770), explorer in Canada, was born at Newton Bewley, near Billingham, co. Durham. He served on privateers during the War of the Spanish Succession (1702–13), and was then engaged in the Spanish and Spanish American trades before sailing to Hudson Bay in 1721 as second mate on one of the Hudson's Bay Company supply vessels. One reason for this move to northern waters was Middleton's interest in the northwest passage, whose entrance had long been thought to lie somewhere along the west coast of Hudson Bay. In all, Middleton made sixteen voyages in the company's service, twelve of them as captain. He was already a proficient navigator with a strong scientific bent at the time of his first voyage to Hudson Bay, where he began a series of observations on the variation of the magnetic needle; these were published in 1726 in the *Philosophical Transactions* of the Royal Society. In 1735 Middleton's paper attracted the attention of Arthur Dobbs, who had made little progress in his efforts to persuade the Hudson's Bay Company to search for the north-west passage. He turned to Middleton, who seemed the ideal choice because he was interested in northern exploration, expert in ice-navigation, and one of the first seamen to use Hadley's quadrant; moreover his reputation was such that in 1737 he was to be elected FRS.

In May 1740 Dobbs's efforts met success when the Admiralty agreed to send an expedition to Hudson Bay the following year in search of the passage. In March 1741 Middleton received a commission in the Royal Navy as captain of the *Furnace* (a bomb-vessel converted to a sloop for the voyage), and relinquished his post with the Hudson's Bay Company. Accompanied by the *Discovery* pink (commanded by William Moor, Middleton's cousin and former chief mate), the *Furnace* sailed for Hudson Bay in June 1741. Middleton's instructions directed him to look for a passage near latitude 65° N, where Dobbs felt that the tidal observations of Luke Foxe in 1631, and those of company sloops in the early 1720s, hinted at some great opening that would lead to the Pacific. The expedition, equipped at Middleton's insistence with the latest navigational instruments, was the first in a long sequence of naval ventures sent out to find the north-west passage. Although a few experienced company hands were on board, many of the crews were brought in by the press-gang, and were 'ailing, having scarce any Cloths' (14 March 1741, PRO, ADM 2/473). The Hudson's Bay Company was outraged at what it saw as Middleton's desertion, and only after government pressure agreed to instruct its factors in Hudson Bay to give the discovery vessels 'the best Assistance in your Power' (Middleton, *Reply*, Appendix, 6).

The expedition did not reach the west coast of Hudson Bay until late July 1741, and amid fog and ice Middleton decided to seek shelter at Fort Prince of Wales, Churchill. This was the farthest north of the Hudson's Bay Company posts, and the wintering there of Middleton's crews in the semi-derelict 'Old Fort' broke their spirit. Ten men died of scurvy, and many others were ill or disabled by frostbite. The ships could neither be cut clear from the ice nor made ready to sail until 1 July 1742. By 12 July they had travelled farther north than previous explorers, and discovered in latitude 65°10′ N a large inlet that Middleton named after Sir Charles Wager, first lord of the Admiralty. Driving ice trapped the ships in Wager Bay for three weeks, during which time it became clear that it was not the entrance to a strait leading to the west. In early August the ships got clear of the inlet and headed north through Roe's Welcome, where a strong flood tide raised hopes that they had found the passage. On 6 August the crews saw land on all sides; the Welcome was a closed inlet, and a disappointed Middleton named its northern extremity Repulse Bay. The flood tide came, not from the Pacific, but from the ice-choked waters of Foxe basin by way of Frozen Strait. It was time to abandon the search. The master of the *Furnace* recounted how when the 'poor scorbutick Creatures heard it was agreed to return from the Frozen Strait, they were overjoy'd' (Middleton, *Vindication*, 163). On the grim homeward voyage there were times when only two men on the *Furnace* were fit to take the wheel, and the officers did the work of seamen to keep the vessel afloat.

Within a month of the expedition's return Middleton read before the Royal Society his 'Account of the extraordinary degrees and surprising effects of cold in Hudson's-Bay', an impressive blend of firsthand experience and scientific observation that won Middleton's paper the society's annual Copley medal. It was an appropriate tribute to an explorer who had accomplished useful survey work in difficult conditions along the west coast of Hudson Bay, and who had made the first reasonably accurate chart of the region. Dobbs, however, was not convinced, and in the spring of 1743 alleged that Middleton had deliberately concealed the entrance of a passage through Wager Bay. For Dobbs the question of a passage was now part of a larger scheme to break the trading monopoly of the Hudson's Bay Company, and Middleton's refusal to admit that he had found a passage was put down to bribery by the company. This malicious accusation marked the beginning of a dispute that led to an inconclusive investigation by the Admiralty, and the publication of no fewer than five books and pamphlets by Middleton and three by Dobbs. Not until the end of this wearisome paper war in 1745 was Middleton offered another command by the Admiralty, and then only of the tiny *Shark* sloop. His pleas for 'the command of a Ship of Force, by which I may hope to retrieve the Fortune I ruin'd, In my former attempt to be of Service to my Country' (1 Feb 1747, PRO, ADM 1/2105) were ignored. When peace came in 1748 Middleton was placed on the half pay list, where he remained until his death at Norton, co. Durham, on 12 February 1770. There is some uncertainty about Middleton's last years. In 1784 the *Monthly Review* claimed that he had died 'in the utmost penury and distress', having sold his Copley medal; but Middleton's will, drawn up only a few weeks before his death, provided for the distribution of his books and instruments, the Copley medal, and an unspecified amount in South Sea annuities to his second wife, Jane, and four children, of whom details are unknown. Middleton's first wife had died in May 1741. Whatever the circumstances in which Middleton lived during his enforced retirement, the promise of his early years and his skill as a navigator and explorer make the story of his wasted career after 1742 a sad one.

GLYNDWR WILLIAMS

Sources W. Barr and G. Williams, eds., *The voyage of Christopher Middleton, 1741–1742* (1994), vol. 1 of *Voyages in search of a northwest passage, 1741–1747* · G. Williams, *The British search for the northwest passage in the eighteenth century* (1962) · G. Williams, 'Middleton, Christopher', *DCB*, vol. 3 · 'Christopher Middleton', *James Isham's observations on Hudsons Bay*, ed. E. E. Rich and A. M. Johnson (1949), 325–34 · C. Middleton, 'New and exact table … shewing the variation of the magnetical needle … 1721 to 1725', *PTRS*, 34 (1726–7), 73–6 · C. Middleton, 'Account of the extraordinary degrees and surprising effects of cold in Hudson's-Bay', *PTRS*, 42 (1742–3), 157–71 · C. Middleton, *A vindication of the conduct of Captain Christopher Middleton* (1743) · C. Middleton, *A reply to the remarks of Arthur Dobbs* (1744) · A. Dobbs, *Remarks upon Capt. Middleton's defence* (1744) · W. Hutchinson, *The history and antiquities of the county palatine of Durham*, 3 (1794) · J. Brewster, *The parochial history and antiquities of Stockton upon Tees*, 2nd edn (1829) · *Monthly Review*, 70 (1784) · register of commissions and warrants, PRO, ADM 1/2105; 2/473 · will, PRO, PROB 11/963

Archives NMM, journal of the voyage of HMS *Furnace* · PRO, half-pay and death, ADM 25/35–78 · PRO, journal, ADM 51/379, I–III · PRO, letters, ADM 1/2099, 2100, 2105 · Provincial Archives of Manitoba, Winnipeg, Hudson's Bay Company archives, service with Hudson's Bay Company; Hudson's Bay Company and Middleton expedition, A 1/34–35, A 1/120–22; A 2/1

Middleton, Conyers (1683–1750), Church of England clergyman and author, was born at either York or Richmond, in Yorkshire, on 27 December 1683, the son of William Middleton (*c*.1646–1714), rector of Hinderwell, near Whitby, Yorkshire, and his second wife, Barbara Place (*d*. 1700). William Middleton left Hinderwell to a curate when he went to live in York, but not having sufficient means to afford city life he returned to Hinderwell for the last fourteen years of his life, and died on 13 February 1714; his wife had died on 8 August 1700. A son by the first marriage and two others, besides Conyers, by the second apparently were spendthrifts and caused their father financial worries in later years.

Education and early career Having received his early education at the cathedral school at York, under Mr Thomlinson's tutelage, Conyers Middleton was admitted pensioner at Trinity College, Cambridge, on 18 March 1699 and matriculated in that year. Named scholar in 1701, he graduated BA in 1703 and proceeded MA in 1706, having been elected a fellow of the college in 1705. He was ordained deacon in 1707 and priest in 1708. Though disappointed in not receiving the preferments that he had expected Middleton held a number of clerical appointments: he was rector of St Clement's, Norwich (1720–25), of Coveney, Cambridgeshire (1725–8), and of Hascombe, Surrey, from 1747 to his death. Except possibly at Coveney he was non-resident.

Nothing is recorded about Middleton's early years in Yorkshire, but after leaving for Cambridge in early 1699 he

Conyers Middleton (1683–1750), by John Giles Eccardt, 1746

never returned, except for one visit about 1744. Nevertheless, to the end his speech revealed a strong Yorkshire dialect. In the preface to his *Life of Cicero* he remarks on the lasting effects of a classical education:

> The scene of it is laid in a place and age, which are familiar to us from our childhood: we learn the names of all the chief actors at school, and chuse our several favourites according to our tempers or fancies: and, when we are least able to judge of the merit of them, form distinct characters of each, which we frequently retain through life. (p. xvi)

As a young man, being very fat and suffering from a nervous disorder in his face, Middleton resorted to a severe dietary regimen that left him thin and in delicate health. An intimate friend, the antiquarian William Cole, observed that he was:

> a most regular and temperate man; never spent an evening from home, never touched a drop of wine, or anything that was salt, or high seasoned; but was one of the most sober, well-bred, easy and companionable men I ever conversed with. (Walpole, *Corr.*, 308)

Though Middleton did meet friends at a coffee house in the evenings he otherwise spent most of his time at home. Except while travelling he was always seen dressed in his gown and cassock, and regularly attended St Michael's Church, Cambridge, with his family. Furthermore, according to Cole his conversation never hinted of any irreverence toward religion or the established church. Appearances notwithstanding, in 1734 he confessed to Lord Hervey:

> Sunday is my only day of rest, but not of liberty; for I am bound to a double attendance at church, to wipe off the stain of infidelity. When I have recovered my credit, in which I

make daily progress, I may use more freedom. (Chalmers, 145)

He 'was immoderately fond of music, and was himself a performer on the violin' (Walpole, *Corr.*, 310); this avocation earned him the contempt of his nemesis at Cambridge, Richard Bentley, master of Trinity College, who derided him for being 'a fiddler' rather than a scholar (Nichols, *Lit. anecdotes*, 5.406).

Family Testimonies about Middleton's family relationships are spare but very positive. An old widow, Mrs Tiplady, who was servant to William Middleton during his last years, reported that Middleton was 'a free good-natured man; that he yearly visited his old father from Cambridge'. She also remarked that 'he was particularly kind to her, for her care of his father' (Nichols, *Lit. anecdotes*, 5.405).

Though he died childless Middleton was married three times; he was a devoted husband to all his wives and was laid to rest with them in his church at Cambridge. Aged twenty-eight he married Sarah Drake, the thirty-six-year-old daughter of Thomas Morris, of Mount Morris in Horton, Kent, and widow of Robert Drake, recorder of Cambridge. Sarah brought Middleton a handsome fortune, which enabled him to quit his fellowship at Trinity College and dwell in a fine house in the best part of town. Sarah died in 1731, at the age of fifty-seven. In 1734 Middleton married his twenty-seven-year-old cousin Mary Place (1707–1745), daughter of the Revd Conyers Place of Dorchester who died eleven years later, on 26 April 1745. While believing that the first two wives showed signs of madness Cole leaves no doubt about the emotional intensity of these relationships.

On 5 July 1747 Middleton married his third wife, Anne Wilkins (*d.* 1760), the widow of a failed Bristol bookseller and the daughter of a Welshman, John Powell, of Boughroyd, near Radnor. In contrast to the first two wives Anne was beautiful, sensible, and a gifted harpsichordist who regularly performed in concert with her husband and his niece at their home. But gossips delighted in her playing shuttlecock with:

> some young gentlemen of her former acquaintance, two in particular … while the good Doctor was writing against the Fathers and miracles in his study overhead, little suspecting that without any miracle he was in great danger of being made a father, without his participation. (Walpole, *Corr.*, 310–11)

Whatever the truth of these slurs Middleton had delivered Anne from a destitute life into one of affluence, and at his death he left her his entire estate, apart from a small portion to his nieces and small legacies to his second wife's brother and sister-in-law and one of his servants.

Perhaps to compensate for being childless Middleton aspired to be a model surrogate parent to various female dependants in his extended family. In a letter to William Warburton, while still finishing his *Life of Cicero*, he mentioned plans to publish the work by subscription as a means of finding more support for the two nieces currently living with him, and added: 'they are fine Children, and have gained already so much upon our Affections, that instead of being a Burthen, we begin to think them a Blessing to us' (C. Middleton, *Miscellaneous Works*, 4 vols., 1752, 2.477). Perhaps his most significant legacy as a family man was his lasting intellectual influence on the bluestocking Elizabeth Montagu, *née* Robinson, whose maternal grandmother was Sarah Drake, Middleton's first wife. Elizabeth's early years were well spent at Middleton's home in Cambridge, where she listened to the conversation of 'divines, scholars, philosophers, travellers, men of the world who were, together, or in turn, to be met with at Dr. Middleton's house' (Doran, 4–5).

Conflict with Richard Bentley Throughout most of his life at Cambridge, Middleton was a valiant combatant in the bitter war fought against the tyrannical master of Trinity College, Richard Bentley. Upon assuming power in 1700 Bentley, the friend and admirer of Isaac Newton, was ambitious to reform his college after what has been described as 'the most calamitous decline in the history of the university' (Westfall, 136) during the politically turbulent seventeenth century, and to promote research, especially in the physical sciences. But his open contempt of the college fellows brought him into continual turmoil with them during the forty years of his administration. In 1709, three years after receiving the MA, Middleton joined other fellows of his college in a petition to John Moore, bishop of Ely, as the college visitor, against Bentley; but his marriage soon afterwards terminated his fellowship. It was not until 1717, after being created, among over thirty other scholars, doctor of divinity, by mandate, during George I's visit to Cambridge, that Middleton returned to the dispute with Bentley.

When Bentley, as divinity professor, demanded that each of the new doctors pay him 4 guineas as a fee, many of them, including Middleton, were outraged and complied only on the condition that the money be returned if it was later determined to be an unjust assessment. But when Bentley still refused to return the money after being found to have acted unfairly Middleton began a suit against him in the vice-chancellor's court to recover his portion of the fee paid. Bentley's behaviour was so contemptuous of the university's authorities that finally, on 18 October 1718, he was stripped of his degrees and reduced to the extremity of petitioning the king for help in the dispute. At this point Middleton, among other complainants, thought it necessary to bring the scholars' grievances before the public. In 1719 he produced four pamphlets, the first of which, *A full and impartial account of all the late proceedings in the University of Cambridge, against Dr. Bentley*, reveals his early power as a controversialist:

> The acrimonious and resentful feeling which prompted every line is in some measure disguised by the pleasing language, the harmony of the periods, and the vein of scholarship which enlivens the whole tract. Middleton's management of the subject is uncommonly artful. (Monk, 67)

After Arthur Ashley Sykes had entered the fray, in defence of Bentley, Middleton answered with yet more intense sarcasm. Since the pamphlets were anonymous Bentley chose to identify John Colbatch, a fellow of Trinity

and Middleton's friend, as the author of *A True Account of the Present State of Trinity College*, and when Bentley initiated a suit for libel Middleton published an advertisement (9 February 1720), declaring himself to be sole author of the piece. At this point Bentley prosecuted him in the court of king's bench, shrewdly leaping upon a passage in the pamphlet that seemed to reflect on the justice system of the country. Despite the upheaval in his college Bentley continued to pursue his scholarship and published proposals for an edition of the New Testament, which spurred Middleton to write yet another caustic attack on every paragraph of his enemy's pamphlet. Some contemporaries believed that Middleton's attack had quashed Bentley's plans, but Bentley's biographer regarded this claim as a commonplace error. Obviously seething with rage, Bentley replied so abusively—although against Colbatch rather than Middleton—that he was reprimanded by the fellows. Nevertheless, in the long run the court of king's bench consistently favoured Bentley, and in 1724 forced the university to reinstate all the degrees that had been removed from him six years earlier by the senate.

In the end Middleton was compelled by Chief Justice Pratt to apologize to Bentley and to pay not only his own court costs but a portion of his adversary's, the total of which must have been enormous, since the college also paid £150 toward the expenses. But to ameliorate Middleton's humiliation and also to get even with Bentley the senate voted by a large majority, on 14 December 1721, to create a new position for him in the university library, with the title 'Protobibliothecarius' and an annual income of £50, a position that he held to the end of his life.

In his new capacity Middleton again attacked Bentley, in 1723, on the pretext of his keeping some valuable manuscripts at his home, but the action once more invoked the wrath of the court of king's bench, and resulted in a £50 fine and a year's probation. Demoralized and in poor health, after being given leave of absence by the university Middleton departed for Rome in August 1723 and remained there until Easter 1724. Upon his return and the renewal of his law suit, in February 1726, he finally retrieved his 4 guineas from Bentley, with 12s. for costs.

A letter from Rome The sojourn in Rome marked a crucial stage in Middleton's scholarly development. While there he enjoyed sumptuous hotel accommodation and spent lavishly on collecting antiquities, which he later described in print and sold in 1744 to Horace Walpole. However, the significant achievement of this immersion in classical culture was his *Letter from Rome*, published in 1729, which argued vigorously that many customs and rituals in the Roman Catholic church derived from ancient pagan religion. Though not an original view, as Middleton admits in the preface, the autobiographical form, anecdotal reference, and crisp style gave the work a personally authentic tone of an English protestant bemused at an exotic spectacle: 'the whole form and outward dress of their worship seemed so grossly *idolatrous and extravagant*, beyond what I had imagined, and made so strong an impression on me, that I could not help considering it with a particular regard' (C. Middleton, *Miscellaneous Works*, 3.68).

Middleton argued that pagan rituals such as the use of incense, holy water, and lamps and wax candles were incorporated in the early Christian church; by 'substituting their *Saints* in the place of the *old Demigods*' the Catholics 'have but set up *Idols of their own*' (C. Middleton, *Miscellaneous Works*, 3.83). Moreover just as the pagan Romans used a public whore to represent the goddess of liberty so Christian artists used their mistresses as models for pictures and sculptures of saints. Middleton found especially revolting the more extreme ascetic practices of the Catholic penitents:

> In one of these *processions*, made lately to St. *Peter's* in the time of *Lent*, I saw that *ridiculous penance* of the *flagellantes*, or *self-whippers*, who march with *whips* in their hands, and lash themselves as they go along, on the bare back, till it is *all* covered with blood; in the same manner, as the *fanatical Priests* of *Bellona* or the *Syrian Goddess*, as well as the votaries of *Isis*, used to slash and cut themselves of old, in order to please the *Goddess, by the sacrifice of their own blood*: which *mad piece of discipline* we find frequently mentioned, and as oft ridiculed by the ancient writers.   (ibid., 100–01)

He claimed that not only the Catholic priesthood but the office of the pope was based on pagan Rome's customs:

> the *sovereign Pontif*, instead of deriving his succession from *St. Peter*, (who, if ever he was at *Rome*, did not reside there at least in any worldly *pomp* or *splendour*) may with more reason, and a much better plea, style himself the *Successor* of the *Pontifex Maximus*, or *chief Priest of old Rome*; whose *authority* and *dignity* was the greatest in the *Republic*; and who was looked upon as the *arbiter* or *judge of all things*, civil as well as sacred, human as well as divine.   (ibid., 114–15)

In anticipation of his further writings Middleton alluded briefly to 'the *pretended miracles*, and *pious frauds* of the *Romish Church*' (ibid., 102), which resembled the impostures in ancient Rome that appealed to the credulity of the poor and ignorant populace.

The deistical controversy: Daniel Waterland After his first wife's death, in 1731, Middleton was named Woodwardian professor of geology, and gave lectures on the value of studying fossils to question the biblical account of the flood. On his second marriage, in 1734, he disqualified himself for this post and abandoned geology. By this time, however, he had gravely offended the church hierarchy by attacking one of its most respected members, Daniel Waterland. After Waterland's work *Scripture Vindicated* appeared in reply to *Christianity as Old as the Creation* (1730), by the deist Matthew Tindal, Middleton produced his anonymous *Letter to Dr. Waterland* (1731), which advised against trying to defend the historical accuracy of the Bible and advocated challenging Tindal's reliance on a 'religion of nature'. To answer the deist Middleton argued that, since right reason was never found to be a sufficient guide, many heathens regarded this inadequacy 'as the very cause of the invention and establishment of *Religion*' (C. Middleton, *Miscellaneous Works*, 2.166).

Not surprisingly the argument that religion was 'invented' to compensate for the weakness of reason disturbed the Anglican orthodoxy; Zachary Pearce, later

bishop of Rochester and dean of Westminster, issued *Reply to a 'Letter to Dr Waterland'*, setting forth many falsehoods by which the letter-writer endeavours to weaken the authority of Moses (1731), which deplored Middleton's irreverence towards Moses as well as to Waterland. While quickly responding with *A Defence of the Letter to Dr. Waterland* (1731) and also with *Some Further Remarks on a Reply to the Defence*—in response to Pearce's *Reply*, which finally insinuated his infidelity—Middleton refused to retract anything: 'Tis not my design to destroy or weaken any thing but those senseless systems and prejudices, which some stiff and cloudy Divines will needs fasten to the body of Religion, as necessary and essential to the support of it' (C. Middleton, *Miscellaneous Works*, 2.182). When his authorship of this pamphlet became known Middleton came under attack from enemies at the university. In his reply to Pearce's second pamphlet, *Some Further Remarks* (1732), he clarified his argument still further and declared once again his sincerity as a Christian. Nevertheless, he was reproached for apostasy by the high-churchman Richard Venn. Furthermore an anonymous pamphlet by Philip Williams, public orator at Cambridge, demanded that the *Letter to Dr. Waterland* be burnt and the author banished unless he confessed his infidelity and formally recanted. In response Middleton reacted with his scornful *Remarks on some Observations* (1733):

> Strange, that a man can be so silly as to imagine, that were I disposed to recant, I should not do it in my own words, rather than his! But I have nothing to recant on the occasion; nothing to confess.   (C. Middleton, *Miscellaneous Works*, 2.315)

Though for some years thereafter Middleton avoided further theological controversy the damage to his standing within the church had been done, and he attributed the loss of a valuable friend, Edward Harley, second earl of Oxford, to the suspicion of his infidelity.

Life of Cicero After the loss of Lord Oxford's friendship, in 1734 John Hervey, Baron Hervey of Ickworth, became Middleton's most congenial patron, for they shared an interest in music, classical studies, and rational theology. Hervey, as the great whig courtier in Robert Walpole's government, opened the way to great influence beyond the walls of Cambridge. Another patron, Thomas Townshend, MP for Cambridge University (1727–74), also gave Middleton valuable support by financing a biography of the great Roman philosopher and orator Marcus Tullius Cicero (106–43BC).

Almost from the outset of their friendship Hervey was keenly interested in Middleton's plans to write a life of Cicero, and over the years continually cajoled or scolded him into completing the work. As their correspondence concerning the Roman senate reveals, Hervey may have also contributed significantly to the interpretation of Cicero's character. By August 1738 Middleton reported to him that a readable draft was finished and that it would be posted to him in sections for his perusal.

Throughout the body of his narrative Middleton portrayed Cicero 'as a great Magistrate and Statesman, administering the affairs and directing the counsils [sic] of a mighty empire' (C. Middleton, *The History of the Life of*

Cicero, 3 vols., 1741, 1.157), and readers at the end of Walpole's long service in the government would readily see the historical parallel. As testimony to Cicero's political skill Middleton emphasized the Roman consul's deft manoeuvring to force Catiline into open rebellion against the state rather than play into the hands of 'the whole faction [who] were prepared to raise a general clamour against him, by representing his *administration as a Tyranny, and the plot as a forgery contrived to support it*' (ibid., 198). Equally praiseworthy in Middleton's view was Cicero's determination to stay independent of the powerful triumvirate formed by Crassus, Pompey, and Caesar. Cicero was particularly suspicious of Caesar's ambition to wrest total control of the republic. Though allowing for Cicero's depression and irresolute behaviour when events came to the crisis that forced him into exile Middleton stressed that it was on the advice of Cato and Hortensius that he fled Rome.

Perhaps Lord Hervey's greatest service to Middleton in this project was his insistence on producing the book by subscription and, with Townshend's support, avidly campaigning for as many signatures as possible. Hervey ensured that the royal court and the most influential members of the government subscribed, and in the end attracted more than 1800 subscribers. Hervey himself ordered twenty-five sets of the large paper edition, his wife two, and his homosexual lover Stephen Fox five. The third duke of Marlborough and Thomas Townshend bought ten sets each; the duke of Newcastle, Arthur Onslow, and Sir Robert Walpole ordered five each.

Middleton's *Life of Cicero* brought him substantial financial rewards and enabled him soon afterwards to purchase a 'rude farm' and turn it into an 'elegant habitation' where he enjoyed his summers; when Thomas Gray arrived at Cambridge in 1742 he regarded Middleton's house as 'the only easy Place one could find to converse in' (Gray). Despite the popularity of the biography it has been tainted since at least 1782, when Joseph Warton declared it to be a plagiarism of *De tribus luminibus Romanorum* (1634), by William Bellenden (*d.* 1633?): 'In this book *Middleton* found every part of Cicero's own history, in his own words, and his works arranged in chronological order, without farther trouble' (J. Warton, *Essay on Pope*, vol. 2, 1782, 323). A few years later Samuel Parr supported Warton's findings:

> I [am] vehemently displeased that a man, possessed of an elegant and enlightened mind, should deprive Bellendus of the fame he merited. For I assert, in the most unqualified terms, that Middleton is not only indebted to Bellendus for many useful and splendid materials, but that, wherever it answered his purpose, he has made a mere transcript of his work. (Parr, 7)

Though Middleton did own a copy of Bellenden's rare work Paul Henry Maty attested: 'I have been told by a gentleman who lived much with him at the time, that he did see it, but did not find it much to his purpose' (Nichols, *Lit. anecdotes*, 415–16). Yet throughout the nineteenth and twentieth centuries Middleton's reputation as a plagiarist has gone unchallenged. M. L. Clarke, however, found that Middleton neither drew upon Bellenden's quotations of

Cicero nor imitated his form of biographical narrative (Clarke). Nevertheless the one incontrovertible fact is that Middleton chose not to acknowledge Bellenden by name as a previous modern who had arranged Cicero's writings to tell the story of his life and times.

Final years: the free inquirer In 1741 the friendship between Middleton and Warburton came to an end over a disagreement about the former's claim that the Catholic religion derived from the ancient heathens. When, at the conclusion of the fourth book of *The Divine Legation*, in 1741, Warburton remarked that 'many able Writers have employed their Time and Learning to prove *Christian Rome* to have borrowed their Superstitions from the *Pagan City*', thus betraying 'the grossest ignorance of human nature' (Warburton, 4.356–7), Middleton took it as a personal attack and replied in a postscript to the fourth edition of *A Letter from Rome*, which appeared in the same year. Since Warburton had at first defended Middleton's *Letter from Rome* as well as his own *Divine Legation* from the accusations of heresy that William Webster published in the *Weekly Miscellany* perhaps he came to see his erstwhile friend as the uncompromising freethinker that he always was.

To his unsympathetic contemporaries Middleton's final years testified to the bitterness of an ambitious clergyman who had been passed over for preferment. After he had failed to win the post of master of the Charterhouse, even with Walpole's efforts on his behalf, the story goes that he was subsequently driven to attack anyone at all who tried to defend orthodoxy. As if to prepare the ground for a frontal barrage, in 1747 he launched first *An Introductory Discourse to a Larger Work Concerning the Miraculous*, which predictably stirred up his enemies. Then, two years later, he delivered his most relentless attack on the credibility of the church fathers, *A Free Inquiry into the Miraculous Powers*. In the spirit of John Locke, whose *Third Letter on Toleration* is evoked in the preface, Middleton argued eloquently against the testimonies of miracles given by patristic authorities and later writers. Without raising any heretical doubts about miracles in the apostolic period he boldly proclaimed his 'honest and disinterested view, to free the minds of men from an inveterate imposture, which, through a long succession of ages, has disgraced the religion of the Gospel, and tyrannized over the reason and senses of the Christian world' (C. Middleton, *Miscellaneous Works*, 1.xxiii). What especially alarmed Middleton's more orthodox Christian contemporaries was his exposé of the

> quackery and imposture, as it was practised by the primitive wonder-workers; who, in the affair especially of casting out Devils, challenge all the world to come and see, with what a superiority of power they could chastise and drive those evil spirits out of the bodies of men, when no other *Conjurers*, *Inchanters*, or *Exorcists*, either among the Jews or the Gentiles, had been able to eject them. (ibid., 17)

Middleton's last published work, *An examination of the lord bishop of London's discourses concerning the use and intent of prophecy, with a further inquiry into the Mosaic account of the Fall*

(1750), which dissected Sherlock's answer to the free-thinker Anthony Collins, first published in 1725, seemed to provide final proof of the author's motivations: 'spleen and personal enmity' (Chalmers, 142).

When his health began to fail Middleton used his remaining years to answer two of his adversaries in a pamphlet published posthumously: *A Vindication of the Free Inquiry from the Objections of Dr. Dodwell and Mr. Church* (1751). For some reason, however, he chose not to answer his most formidable critic, John Wesley, whose *Letter to Middleton* (1749) stressed that without the 'inner spirit' and reliance on 'internal evidence of Christianity' the English people in a century or more would 'be fairly divided into real Deists and real Christians' (Wesley, 225). To judge by Middleton's 'A preface to an intended answer to all the objections made against the free inquiry', however, it seems unlikely that he was convinced by Wesley's stress on the inner light. In a letter to Hervey of 1733 he admitted that he was too much of a heathen to countenance the evangelical claims: 'It is my misfortune to have had so early a taste of Pagan sense, as to make me very squeamish in my Christian studies' (Chalmers, 145).

Middleton's endless quarrel with Bentley brought out a zest for attacking dogmatism in all quarters, so that in the end his formidable power as a writer was largely negative. In 1736 he wrote to Warburton:

> As for myself, I can safely swear with *Tully*, that I have *a most ardent Desire to find out the Truth*: But as I have generally been disappointed in my Enquiries, and more successful in finding what is false than what is true, so I begin, like him too, to grow a mere Academic [sceptic], humbly content to take up with the *probable*. (C. Middleton, *Miscellaneous Works*, 2.467)

His success in finding out the 'false' helped to change the course of theological debate in his own period and afterwards. Modern scholars have recognized his importance to the rise of 'higher criticism' of the Bible (Stromberg, 78). This disposition proved useful for non-theological controversies as well. Against the popular notion at the time that William Caxton had been preceded by a printer at Oxford, Middleton published *A Dissertation Concerning the Origin of Printing in England* (1734–5), which argued vigorously that Caxton had introduced the printing press to England.

Middleton died in Hildersham, Cambridgeshire, on 28 July 1750, 'of a slow hectic fever and disorder in his liver'. He was buried in the parish of St Michael, Cambridge, on 31 July. His biography of Cicero was a benchmark in what has been called 'the rise of modern paganism' (Gay, title-page). Passing through nine editions within the eighteenth century and numerous other editions and reprints in the nineteenth century, it was his most enduring literary achievement. Probably a large part of its appeal derives from its providing an ideal of good citizenship and political independence for aspirants in the British parliamentary system. For instance when in 1790 Nicolas de Azara, the Spanish ambassador in Rome, published a lavishly illustrated Spanish translation it was well received,

and in 1804 it was reprinted. The Spain of the Enlightenment needed a model to emulate, and Middleton's *Life of Cicero* provided the text.   JOHN A. DUSSINGER

Sources Walpole, *Corr.*, 15.305–15 · A. Chalmers, ed., *The general biographical dictionary*, new edn, 22 (1815), 131–45 · Venn, *Alum. Cant.* · Nichols, *Lit. anecdotes*, 5.405–23 · J. H. Monk, *The life of Richard Bentley, DD*, 2nd edn, 2 vols. (1833) · Dr Doran [J. Doran], *A lady of the last century (Mrs Elizabeth Montagu) illustrated in her unpublished letters: collected and arranged, with a biographical sketch and a chapter on blue stockings* (1873) · J. M. Levine, '"Et tu Brute?" History and forgery in 18th-century England', *Fakes and frauds: varieties of deception in print and manuscripts*, ed. R. Myers and M. Harris (1989), 71–97 · M. L. Clarke, 'Conyers Middleton's alleged plagiarism', *N&Q*, 228 (1983), 44–6 · R. Browning, *Political and constitutional ideas of the court whigs* (1982) · *Correspondence of Thomas Gray*, ed. P. Toynbee and L. Whibley, 3 vols. (1935), 1.328 · R. S. Westfall, 'Isaac Newton in Cambridge: the restoration university and scientific creativity', *Culture and politics from puritanism to the enlightenment*, ed. P. Zagorin (1980), 135–64 · R. N. Stromberg, *Religious liberalism in eighteenth-century England* (1954) · W. Warburton, *The divine legation of Moses demonstrated, on the principles of a religious deist, from the omission of the doctrine of a future state in the Jewish dispensation, the second volume, in two parts* (1741) · G. M. Trevelyan, *Trinity college: an historical sketch* (1946), 51–68 · J. S. Watson, *The life of William Warburton, D.D., lord bishop of Gloucester from 1760 to 1779: with remarks on his works* (1863) · A. W. Evans, *Warburton and the Warburtonians: a study in some eighteenth-century controversies* (1932) · W. Bellenden, *De tribus luminibus Romanorum* (1634) · [S. Parr], *A free translation of the preface to Bellenenus, containing animated strictures on the great political characters of the present time* (1788) · [J. Wesley], *A letter to the Reverend Dr. Conyers Middleton, occasioned by his late Free inquiry* (1749) · P. Gay, *The enlightenment: an interpretation* (1966)

Archives BL, corresp. (extracts), Add. MS 4478, fols. 67–103b · BL, corresp. and papers, Add. MSS 32457–32459 · BL, note on his death and the disposition of his MSS, Add. MS 35379, fol. 269 | BL, letters to T. Birch, Add. MS 4314, fols. 16–30 · BL, letters to Dr Colbatch and Dr Crosse, Add. MS 22908, fols. 122, 134 · BL, letter to first Lord Hardwicke, Add. MS 35589, fol. 329 · BL, letters to second Lord Hardwicke, Add. MS 35605, fols. 52, 227, 231, 240, 242, 358 · BL, letters to Lord Hervey, Extr. Stowe MS 305, fol. 306 · BL, letters to second Lord Oxford, Add. MS 70410 · BL, letters to Bishop Warburton, Egerton MS 1953 · Suffolk RO, Bury St Edmunds, corresp. with Lord Hervey

Likenesses G. Pozzo, medal, 1724, BM · oils, *c.*1730–1735, CUL · J. G. Eccardt, oils, 1746, NPG [*see illus.*] · J. Faber junior, mezzotint, pubd 1751 (after J. G. Eccardt), BM, NPG · Ravenet, engraving (after portrait prefixed to C. Middleton *Miscellaneous works*) · Wedgwood, portrait (after G. Pozzo) · portrait, repro. in C. Middleton, *Miscellaneous works*, 4 vols. (1752)

Wealth at death considerable properties in Cambridge and annuities for wife and niece: will, 23 July 1750

Middleton, David (*d.* 1615), mariner, was born in the parish of St Peter, Chester, son of John Middleton, merchant, and his wife, Katherine (*d.* 1588), daughter of Thomas and Margaret Bavand. There were at least nine children in the family, three of whom (John, Sir Henry *Middleton, and David) served the East India Company as sea captains. David Middleton married Alice and had three children, Henry, John, and Elizabeth; a fourth child may have been born after he made his will in March 1614. His widow married John Cannon, and was still alive in 1639.

In 1601–2, Middleton made his first voyage to the West Indies with Michael Geare, an experienced reprisal captain. The *Archangel* and the *James* captured a ship off Cape San Antonio in January 1602, and Middleton returned to

Dartmouth in the prize. His next chronicled expedition was in 1604–6, when he sailed in the *Red Dragon* as personal assistant to his brother Henry, general of the East India Company's second voyage. The *Red Dragon* made for the Moluccas, the first English vessel to attempt trade there. Amid rivalry between the Dutch and the Portuguese, David Middleton was used as an emissary in the delicate negotiations required to secure a lading of cloves. He appears to have been a very confident man, able to charm men such as the king of Tidore, although less popular with some of his East India Company contemporaries who regarded him as too headstrong.

The fleet returned in May 1606 laden with spices. Although the *Susan* was lost coming home, the venture was deemed successful and, in recognition of his part, David Middleton was given command of the *Consent*, a new pinnace of 115 tons, for the company's third voyage in 1607. Middleton left behind the *Dragon* and *Hector* soon after setting sail in March and made quickly for Bantam. The *Consent* arrived in the Moluccas early in January 1608, and Middleton spent his days negotiating with the Spanish for the right to trade, while buying cloves secretly at night. In April Middleton sailed to Butung where he obtained a lading of cloves and some slaves amid a round of reciprocal entertainment and exchange of gifts with the king. The *Consent* arrived at Dartmouth in January 1609. 50 tons of cloves which had cost less than £3000 were sold for £36,000, and Middleton was rewarded with a gratification of £250.

Middleton was immediately appointed commander of the *Expedition* for the company's fifth voyage which sailed in April 1609. The ship anchored at Bantam on 7 December, narrowly missing the *Hector* still on her way back from the third voyage. The *Expedition* reached Butung in January 1610 only to find that a fire had destroyed the king's store of spices, wood, and cloth. Middleton therefore went on to the Banda Islands, where the Dutch at first believed him to be a pirate with no commission. He offered £1000 together with the chain around his neck for a lading and entertained important Dutchmen, but his charm and powers of persuasion did not work: the governor had ships of his own to lade and dared not give the English permission to trade for spices. Middleton then secured his crew's agreement to go to Pulo Ai and to fight the Dutch if necessary. A harbour was found for the *Expedition* at Ceram while Middleton went to buy spices at Ai and organize their shipment. It was rumoured that the Dutch were offering a reward to be rid of Middleton: their problem was nearly solved when a storm drove his skiff ashore in Ceram's cannibal territory, and he almost drowned swimming across a river infested with alligators. Having left instructions ordering a voyage to Sukadana in Borneo for diamonds, Middleton sailed from Bantam in November 1610. The *Expedition* reached England in summer 1611 with more than 139 tons of nutmeg and over 36 tons of mace.

In March 1614 the East India Company appointed Middleton general of the next voyage despite criticism of his conduct and private trade dealings. The *Samaritan*, the *Thomas*, and the *Thomasine* sailed from England in May 1614 intending to trade among the Portuguese in the Moluccas. Middleton arrived at Bantam in February 1615 and was distraught to learn of the death of his brother Henry. He decided to return home in the *Samaritan* with a lading of pepper, and sailed from Bantam on 3 April 1615. The *Samaritan* disappeared, possibly wrecked off the coast of Madagascar. When news of the ship's loss reached London, Middleton's family became involved in a lengthy dispute with the company over moneys said to be owing to Sir Henry and to David. The company was not inclined to be generous: the loss of the *Samaritan* and her valuable cargo was reckoned to have cancelled out any claim based on David Middleton's earlier successful and profitable voyages.   Margaret Makepeace

Sources S. Purchas, *Hakluytus posthumus, or, Purchas his pilgrimes*, bks 2–5 (1625); repr. Hakluyt Society, extra ser., 15–18 (1906) · W. Foster, ed., *The voyage of Sir Henry Middleton to the Moluccas, 1604–1606* (1943) · *CSP col.*, vols. 2–3 · F. C. Danvers and W. Foster, eds., *Letters received by the East India Company from its servants in the east*, 6 vols. (1896–1902), vols. 1–3 · G. Birdwood, ed., *The register of letters … of the governour and company of merchants of London trading into the East Indies, 1600–1619* (1893) · W. Foster, *England's quest of Eastern trade* (1933) · will of David Middleton, 1614, PRO, PROB 11/131, sig. 31 · W. Myddelton, *Pedigree of the family of Myddelton* (1910) · K. R. Andrews, *Elizabethan privateering: English privateering during the Spanish war, 1585–1603* (1964) · will of John Middleton, 1601, PRO, PROB 11/102, sig. 75
Archives BL OIOC, letters to East India Company, E/3/2
Wealth at death bequests totalling £1555 10s.; wife and elder son shared household goods and plate; elder son received residue of estate: will, PRO, PROB 11/131, sig. 31

Middleton [*née* Butler], **Dorothy** (1909–1999), geographer and writer, was born on 9 November 1909 in Lahore, Punjab, daughter of Sir Montagu Sherard Dawes *Butler (1873–1952), who had a distinguished career in the Indian Civil Service, and Anne Gertrude (1876–1954), daughter of George Smith, teacher and geographer, and youngest sister of George Adam *Smith, geographer and Old Testament scholar. Together with her sister Iris and brothers Richard Austen *Butler and J. P. (Jock), Dorothy had the usual upbringing of a British administrative family working in the raj—governess, private boarding-school (in Hove), a spell with a French family with attendance at the local lycée, and a finishing school in Paris—before returning to India where her father was by now governor of the Central Provinces. Something of the family's life at the time is conveyed in the biography of her brother R. A. Butler by Anthony Howard (1987). Substantial family photograph albums provide a colourful record of the social life that Dorothy shared—though not always entirely willingly. After India there followed a brief contact with the Isle of Man, where Sir Montagu was governor-general (1933–7). Whereas her brothers had been to university, Dorothy settled down to a secretarial course at Pitman's, in London, which led to a post with the National Council of Social Service. She shared a flat with her cousin Janet Adam Smith, who was assistant editor of *The Listener* and was one of a group of friends who were at the start of their careers in journalism, at the BBC, and at Chatham House.

There were regular reunions with friends from India, army officers, and civil servants home on leave.

On 30 April 1938 at the register office, Cambridge, Dorothy married Laurence Henry Neave Middleton (1905–1982), a lawyer with a firm of family solicitors in London. During the war Dorothy worked at the central office of information. Then, in 1945, when the Middletons were settled in Sydney Street, Chelsea, she met an old friend of her husband, Laurence Kirwan, at that time secretary and, later, director of the Royal Geographical Society (RGS). The result was an invitation to become assistant editor of the *Geographical Journal*, a post which was to prove a turning point in her life. It led to an active career as an author and eventually to a position as an esteemed senior figure in the society. In fact, if not in name, Dorothy was the editor of the journal for twenty years. The Hakluyt Society, on the council of which she served as the representative of the RGS for many years, also benefited considerably from her editorial experience.

In 1958 Dorothy made her mark as joint author with A. A. Thomson of the book *Lugard in Africa*. It was the beginning of a concern for a continent which, in a way, replaced her connection with India. One notable manifestation of it was her 1969 edition of A. J. Mounteney Sephson's *Diary* for the Hakluyt Society, regarded by some as her best work. The knowledge that she acquired on Africa led to a definitive chapter on the exploration of the continent in the society's authoritative *History of Exploration* (1991). It also brought her on to the platform of the society to address a large audience on a controversial BBC television series on the search for the source of the Nile. The BBC producer declared: 'I had expected Mrs Middleton to put the boot in … but I never expected it to be put in so elegantly' (Janet Adam Smith, memorial address, 1999). It was a measure of the confidence that she developed that she subsequently competed in the BBC television programme *Mastermind*.

Women explorers in Africa had already caught Dorothy's imagination while she was working on the Lugard book and she was to become an authority on the subject. Her book *Victorian Lady Travellers* (1965) was elegant and humorous in style but Dorothy's more serious side was shown by her inclusion among the travellers of the little-known Kate Marsden, who died forgotten after efforts to damage her reputation. Dorothy's aim was to restore her reputation as a traveller, not to dwell on any personal unhappiness. The book was followed by a series of articles and popular lectures on the achievements of women travellers and Dorothy contributed entries on some of the most important of them to the *Oxford Dictionary of National Biography*. Dorothy was amused that her close association with these women gave her a reputation for being a radical feminist, a role which she took some pleasure in refuting. Her scholarship, her knowledge of family papers and the RGS archive, and her library underpinned the work of more radical followers who acknowledged her help in their books.

Dorothy was made an honorary fellow of the RGS (1971), a member of its council (1973–6), and an honorary vice-president (1987). When, 150 years after its foundation, the Geographical Club, a dining club, ceased to be a male preserve, she was one of the first women to be elected. During the latter years of her association with the RGS it underwent a transformation, as academic and educational objectives overtook its historical role as a focus of exploration. Although she knew more than most fellows about the icons of the society's past association with exploration—its museum items, archives, pictures, and photographs—Dorothy was happy to see the development of a strong scientific approach to the society's field activities and to help with the subsequent publication of substantial research monographs.

As with Mary Kingsley, Dorothy's 'judgement was informed', her opinions 'her own and little influenced by current fashion' (D. Middleton, *Victorian Lady Travellers*, 1982, 149). These were qualities greatly admired by those with whom she worked. She also had a flair for gaining the confidence of all sorts of men and women. One day she could be the 'mother confessor' of a distinguished mountaineer; the next, the confidante of a member of the house staff. All this was inseparable from her strong and reassuring personality. Her husband died in 1982. They had no children, but Dorothy was a much-loved aunt and great-aunt. In the last years of her life her eyesight began to fail. She continued to work using enlarged typescripts but falls left her increasingly and frustratingly incapacitated. She died at her home, 74 Royal Hospital Road, Chelsea, on 3 February 1999, and her body was cremated after a funeral service at Christ Church, Chelsea, on 12 February. Her spirit will long haunt Lowther Lodge, the Victorian house of the RGS in Kensington Gore, to the ambience of which in their time her lady travellers themselves contributed. W. R. MEAD

Sources private information (2004) [J. Adam Smith, I. Portal] · tape of reminiscences, RGS · personal knowledge (2004) · *The Times* (10 Feb 1999) · *The Independent* (8 Feb 1999) · *The Hakluyt Society Annual Report for 1998* (1999), 18 · W. R. Mead, 'Dorothy Middleton, 1909–1999', *GJ*, 165 (1999), 246–7 · *WWW*, 1929–40 [Montagu Butler] · d. cert. · m. cert. · A. Howard, *RAB: the life of R. A. Butler* (1987)
Archives RGS, MSS | SOUND RGS, tape of reminiscences [transcribed]
Likenesses photograph, repro. in Mead, 'Dorothy Middleton', *GJ*, 247 · photograph, repro. in *The Times* · photograph, repro. in *The Independent*

Middleton, Erasmus (*bap.* 1739, *d.* 1805), Church of England clergyman and Methodist sympathizer, was born in Horncastle, Lincolnshire, and baptized there on 30 May 1739, son of Erasmus Middleton, an upholsterer of the town, and his wife, Ann Wilson. He attended Kingswood School, Bristol, and, on 4 June 1767, matriculated at St Edmund Hall, Oxford. He was the most prominent of the six undergraduates tried by the proctors and expelled from the university, on 11 March 1768, for publicly praying and preaching at Methodist meetings. The incident, which Middleton would later 'wish to bury in Silence' (Middleton, 4.511), caused some controversy at the time, eliciting the publication of some satirical verses and sermons, and a flurry of pamphlets, including one by George Whitefield. Though there was substance to the charges brought against the students, of illiteracy in the learned languages as well as Methodist tendencies, these had been initiated by the Revd John Higson, the unstable vice-principal of St Edmund Hall and the students' tutor, perhaps for personal motives. Middleton was able to translate from Greek before the proctors but failed to translate the convoluted Latin of the university's statutes. Without having been ordained he had officiated in the chapel of ease at Chieveley in Berkshire, which caused the bishop of Hereford to refuse him holy orders. On another occasion Middleton missed one of Higson's lectures on the Thirty-Nine Articles; furthermore a student testified that he 'despised the prayers of the Church of England' (*Hist. U. Oxf.* 5: *18th-cent. Oxf.*, 5.461). Middleton also taught in one of Wesley's schools, though his Calvinist belief was more evangelical than Wesleyan.

After his expulsion Middleton enrolled at King's College, Cambridge, though he does not appear to have graduated there. He was supported in his study by a dissenting banker named Fuller, and obtained ordination in the Church of Ireland from the bishop of Down. He became, in succession, minister of an episcopalian congregation in Dalkeith, Edinburghshire; curate at St Luke's, Chelsea, in London, where the parishioners applied unsuccessfully to have him appointed their minister on the death of William Cadogan in 1797; lecturer of St Benet Gracechurch and St Helen, Bishopsgate, also in London; and curate of St Margaret's Chapel, Westminster. He succeeded Augustus Montague Toplady as editor of the *Gospel Magazine* and published his ambitious work *Biographia evangelica* (1779–86), which contains biographies of such diverse 'evangelists' as Wycliffe, George Herbert, Archbishop Leighton, Richard Baxter, and Ezekiel Hopkins. Though useful, its style is 'particularly disagreeable' (*GM*, 1st ser., 75, 1805, 490). He also wrote several sermons and part of the *New Dictionary of Arts and Sciences* (1778).

On 1 February 1804 Middleton was presented by the Fuller family to the rectory of Turvey in Bedfordshire. He was also chaplain to Jean, fifth countess of Crawford and Lindsay. Middleton and his wife, Margaret, who came from the ducal family of Gordon, had at least two daughters, Elizabeth and Margaret Ann. His wife predeceased him about April 1803; he died on 25 April 1805. His *Versions and Imitations of Psalms* (1806) and *Life of Luther* (1807) appeared posthumously.   ADAM JACOB LEVIN

Sources S. L. Ollard, *The six students of St Edmund Hall expelled from the University of Oxford in 1768* (1911) · *Hist. U. Oxf.* 5: *18th-cent. Oxf.* · *IGI* · will, PRO, PROB 11/1425, sig. 373 · *GM*, 1st ser., 75 (1805), 490 · L. E. Elliott-Binns, *The early evangelicals: a religious and social study* (1953) · Allibone, *Dict.* · E. Middleton, ed., *Biographia evangelica*, 4 vols. (privately printed, London, 1779–86) · J. Foster, ed., *Index ecclesiasticus, or, Alphabetical lists of all ecclesiastical dignitaries in England and Wales since the Reformation* (1890), 122 · *DNB*

Archives Bodl. Oxf., Montagu MS d. 14, fols. 236–8 · Bodl. Oxf., St Edmund Hall MS 56, fols. 20 ff. · Bodl. Oxf., Western MSS 25442

Likenesses engraving, 1805 (after Ridley?), repro. in Ollard, *Six students*, following p. 42 · A. Smith, line engraving, pubd 1821, NPG · W. Ridley, stipple, BM; repro. in *Evangelical Magazine*, 13 (1805) · line engraving, BM, NPG; repro. in *Gospel Magazine* (1778)

Wealth at death stock in bank; books; household furniture and goods: will, PRO, PROB 11/1425, sig. 373

Middleton, George (1692–1747), banker, was born in the summer of 1692, in Edinburgh, the fifth of the eighteen children of Dr George Middleton, principal of King's College, Aberdeen, and his wife, Janet Gordon of Seton, who died in 1753 at the age of 101. Young George was well educated, with access to his father's well-stocked college library. He served his apprenticeship as a goldsmith in Edinburgh and in 1703 joined John Campbell, a Scottish goldsmith banker in the Strand, London; in 1708 he became his partner. After Campbell's death on 15 November 1712 George married Campbell's daughter Mary (*d.* 1764)—a sweet, sprightly lady, appropriately nicknamed Honey. They had two daughters, Elizabeth (*d.* 1746), who married in 1731 Patrick Craufurd MP, of Auchenames, and Margaret, who married in 1768 John Dalrymple, fifth earl of Stair. Elizabeth had two sons, James and John.

Middleton was regarded with respect and affection by his family and a wide circle of friends. Campbell's was a whig bank under the patronage of the second duke of Argyll and his brother, Lord Ilay, later third duke. Most of George's friends were whigs and supporters of the Hanoverians. His eldest brother, Colonel John (1678–1739), became a general in Argyll's army, and friend of the most powerful men in Scotland. Yet some of his relatives were active Jacobites. His father's first cousin John, the second earl of Middleton (1650–1719), was an adviser to James II. He had been imprisoned as a Jacobite in 1693, escaped, and joined James II at his court in St Germain. He was involved in the failed Jacobite invasion in 1708. His sons were captured and imprisoned in the Tower, but the earl remained a loyal minister at the court at St Germain until his death. These relatives and other Jacobite friends caused the whig banker some embarrassment, but with tact and good humour he maintained friendly relations with all.

Like many bankers at this period, Middleton undertook many different responsibilities: he was paymaster to the duke of Argyll's regiment of horse, to his brother John's regiment of foot, to the earl of Stair's dragoons, to the Royal regiment and 4th troop of Horse Guards. He also sometimes acted as an estate agent for his customers. His chief pride, however, was in his craft as a goldsmith, and he signed himself 'goldsmith banker'. John Campbell had left Middleton very much in charge at the end of his life, so it was he who was responsible for the making of ten gold collars of the Order of the Thistle for Queen Anne, between the years 1707 and 1709. In 1716 he sold a magnificent service of gilt to the prince of Wales, later George II.

As a banker Middleton had the advantage of the patronage of the duke of Argyll and leading whigs; he was respected and trusted at home and abroad. But between 1719 and 1723, when the South Sea Bubble burst in England and the Mississippi adventure sponsored by John Law collapsed in France, he had to endure, as he wrote, 'a fiery trial' (Healey, 49). By nature cautious, nevertheless he was mesmerized by the financial success in France of his brilliant compatriot John Law, whose brother William, a banker in Paris, was an old friend. John Law had made a spectacular leap from international gambler to banker to the duke of Orléans, regent of France, in 1718. In December 1719 he was made controller of French finance: he was now 'King Law'. He had created, in 1717, the Compagnie d'Occident, which he hoped would rival the British East India Company. This Mississippi project aimed to create a French kingdom named Louisiana after the French king, which would stretch from Canada to the Gulf of Mexico. By skilful manipulation Law encouraged a manic rush for shares. George Middleton, on William Law's advice, speculated. The shares and John Law's reputation collapsed as quickly as they had risen. By December 1720 Law's company was closed, and he escaped, but his brother William was imprisoned. Middleton was caught in their ruin. He had not only lost money on his own account, but he had also covered John Law on a speculative gamble on the future of the East India Company. When this failed and Law could not pay his debts, Middleton was obliged to stop payment. His 'shop' did not re-open until 5 September 1723.

Middleton's troubles were compounded by the collapse of the South Sea Bubble in England. In 1711 the South Sea Company had been promoted by the earl of Oxford and the tory government to fund the national debt of £10 million, which had built up during the war with France. The ever-increasing value of its shares caused a rush to invest, when, as Middleton wrote, 'people were running madder every day' (Healey, 45). However, when the bubble burst, many were ruined; as Middleton put it to the duke of Argyll: 'Five goldsmiths broke in one day' (ibid., 49). Middleton was not himself deeply involved, but many of his customers were. Patiently he pursued his debtors until he was able, as he wrote, 'to begin the world anew' (ibid., 55).

With the help of his influential Scottish friends, the duke of Argyll, Lord Ilay, and Lord Milton, Middleton rebuilt his business. They kept him informed of the negotiations for the foundation of the Royal Bank of Scotland in 1727. Middleton in that year took in John Campbell's son George as a partner, and his own nephew David Bruce entered the partnership in 1740. In 1739 he moved into grander premises at 59 Strand. But years of stress had undermined his health. After a long illness he died at Bath on 17 January 1747.

In 1755 George Campbell took in as partner James Coutts, son of the lord provost of Edinburgh, John Coutts, a director of the Royal Bank of Scotland. Coutts married Polly Peagrum, George Campbell's niece, in May 1755, and on Campbell's death inherited the bank. Thomas Coutts joined his brother on 1 January 1761. The bank founded by John Campbell in 1692 and revived by George Middleton was to become the prestigious Coutts & Co., which remained at 59 Strand.   EDNA HEALEY

Sources Coutts & Co., archives and letter books · E. Healey, *Coutts & Co., 1692–1992: the portrait of a private bank* (1992) · S. G. Checkland, *Scottish banking: a history, 1695–1973* (1975) · C. Mackay, *Extraordinary popular delusions and the madness of crowds* (1841); repr. (1932) · *The Royal Bank of Scotland, 1727–1977* (1977) · A. Thiers, *The Mississippi bubble: a memoir of John Law* (1864)

Archives Coutts & Co. archives

Wealth at death left £20,000 capital to son and daughter: Coutts & Co., archives; Healy, *Coutts & Co.*, 63

Middleton, George Humphrey (1910–1998), diplomatist, was born on 21 January 1910 at 47b Welbeck Street, Marylebone, London, the son of George Close Middleton, insurance broker and banker, and his wife, Susan Sophie, formerly Elphinstone, *née* Harley. He spent much of his boyhood in Paris, where his father was chief representative of Lloyds Bank. He went to school at St Lawrence College, Ramsgate, and read French (in which he was bilingual) and Spanish at Magdalen College, Oxford, graduating with a third-class degree in 1931. He then spent a year in Heidelberg, learning German.

Middleton entered the consular service in 1933, serving initially as vice-consul in Buenos Aires (1933–4). While there he married, on 29 October 1934, Elizabeth Rosalie Okeden (Tina) Pockley, detective novelist (as Elizabeth Antill), and daughter of Harry Pockley, of Roma Downs, Roma, Queensland, Australia. There were no children of the marriage. Middleton then filled vice-consular posts in Asuncion (1934–6), New York (1936–9), Lemberg (1939), Cluj (1939–40), Genoa (1940), and Madeira (1940–43). There followed a short spell in the Foreign Office before he was transferred to Washington as second secretary in 1944. He was promoted first secretary there in 1945. This service in Washington marked him out for higher things.

In 1947, by which time the consular and diplomatic services had been amalgamated in the foreign service, Middleton was appointed assistant head of the personnel department in the Foreign Office. He became head of that department in 1949, with promotion to counsellor. With the post-war reconstruction examinations in process to fill the gaps left by an absence of regular recruitment during the war, this was a post of considerable importance, which Middleton filled admirably. One of his achievements was to secure cancellation of the unkind and pointless ban on the adoption of children by foreign service officers. He also inaugurated a far-sighted policy of appointing senior ex-consular officers to a spell of duty in the Foreign Office, to contribute to the unification of the service. He was made a CMG in 1950.

In 1951 Middleton was transferred to Tehran as counsellor, and there had to cope with the problem of the nationalization of the Anglo-Iranian Oil Company by Prime Minister Mossadeq. With the ambassador withdrawn, he became chargé d'affaires from 28 January 1952 to 31 October 1952, when the staff of the embassy was expelled, with Middleton organizing a cross-desert convoy via Baghdad and Damascus to Beirut. He next served, on secondment to the Commonwealth Relations Office, as deputy high commissioner in New Delhi from 1953 to 1956, a well-earned promotion. It was followed by his appointment as ambassador to the Lebanon, the first of his posts in the Arab world. There, using his fluent French (he was not an Arabist), he had to cope with the virulent anti-British riots that followed the ill-fated British invasion of Port Said in the Suez campaign. He was made a KCMG in the new year's honours list of 1958.

Further promotion followed when Middleton was made political resident in the Persian Gulf in 1958. This was an important post, supervising British relations with all the sheikhdoms in the Persian Gulf and with the sultanate of Oman. It fell to Middleton on 19 June 1961 to sign the treaty recognizing the independence of Kuwait, by now a major oil producer with growing investments in the City of London. This event stimulated an Iraqi claim to sovereignty over Kuwait, and in early July 1961 Middleton had to mastermind the landing of British forces in Kuwait to ward off an Iraqi invasion.

This success marked the end of Middleton's service in the Persian Gulf. He returned to Buenos Aires as ambassador to Argentina from 1961 to 1964. He then served in the senior Arab post, Cairo, as ambassador to the United Arab Republic from 1964 to 1966, when he was expelled on the breach of diplomatic relations in a widespread African protest at British policy towards Ian Smith's unilateral declaration of independence in Rhodesia. He was appointed briefly to the *ad hoc* committee on United Nations finances but retired early from the foreign service in 1966.

Middleton's marriage had been in trouble towards the end of his foreign service career. He was divorced on 1 November 1971 and on 10 November that year he married Marie Elizabeth Camille Françoise Middleton, who had also been divorced. She was the daughter of George Sarthou, medical practitioner; she had changed her name to Middleton by deed poll before the marriage. With her Middleton had a son, George Alexander, to add to a stepson and a stepdaughter.

Middleton was in demand after his retirement in a variety of commercial and industrial posts. These included consultant in the Industrial Reorganization Corporation (1967–8), and directorships of Overseas Medical Supplies Ltd, Britarge Ltd, and Décor France Ltd. He was chairman of the executive committee of the British Road Federation in 1972, and chief executive of the British Industry Roads Campaign from 1969 to 1976. Towards the end of his life he chaired Mondial Expatriate Services Ltd, from 1988 to 1991. He was a fellow of the Royal Society of Arts. He also chaired the Bahrain Society, the Anglo-Peruvian society, and the British Moroccan Society. He was made a commander of the order of merit of Peru and a chevalier of the Lebanon's national order of the Cedar. In his last years he suffered from cancer of the colon. He died at his home, 1 Carlyle Square, Chelsea, London, on 12 February 1998, and was survived by his wife, son, and two stepchildren.

FRANK BRENCHLEY

Sources *Daily Telegraph* (16 Feb 1998) · *The Guardian* (19 Feb 1998) · *The Times* (2 March 1998) · *WWW* · Burke, *Peerage* · *FO List* · personal knowledge (2004) · private information (2004) · b. cert. · certificate of decree absolute [first marriage] · m. cert. [Marie Middleton: second marriage] · d. cert.
Likenesses photograph, 1952, repro. in *Daily Telegraph* · photograph, repro. in *The Guardian* · photograph, repro. in *The Times*
Wealth at death under £180,000: probate, 22 May 1998, *CGPLA Eng. & Wales*

Middleton, Sir Gilbert (*d.* 1318), rebel, was the son of Gilbert of Middleton, and grandson of Richard of Middleton, chancellor at the end of Henry III's reign. His father was dead by 1291, when Gilbert became a ward of William of Felton, a royal squire. His lands, acquired through inheritance and marriage, lay in Northumberland. He came of age in 1300, and took part in the Scottish campaign that year. By 1313 he was a member of the royal household, serving in the garrison at Berwick. A petition complained that he would not accept the jurisdiction of the warden of the town, since he was in receipt of the royal livery. Two years later, in 1315, he was listed as a royal household knight; he served in the garrison at Alnwick in the same year. He was still serving the king in the northern marches early in 1317, when he received £42 13s. 4d. in wages for himself and his men.

On 1 September 1317, just south of Durham, Middleton and an armed band attacked and robbed the party bringing Louis Beaumont for his consecration and enthronement as bishop at Durham. The crime was regarded as particularly appalling since the party included two cardinals, Gaucelin de Jean and Luca Fieschi. Louis and his brother Henry were taken prisoner and led to Mitford Castle, which was under Middleton's command. The cardinals were given horses and allowed to proceed to Durham. They stayed there for several days, and on 7 September were escorted south by Thomas, earl of Lancaster. Louis Beaumont was freed by 17 October, but Middleton continued in rebellion. Walter Selby in Northumberland and Goscelin d'Eyville in north Yorkshire joined in what threatened briefly to become a major uprising. Middleton exacted money by questionable means, forcing the community of the see of Durham to agree that he should be paid 500 marks as a fine 'for a certain transgression committed against me' (Durham Cath. CL, MC 5033). The rising did not last long. In mid-December, William Felton, son of Middleton's former guardian, with other Northumbrian landowners, captured Mitford Castle, and with it Middleton, by trickery.

Various explanations for Middleton's rebellion have been suggested. The disputed election to the see of Durham created several rivalries, and it may be that the earl of Lancaster was particularly incensed at the rejection of his candidate. The earl's role, however, appears to have been more that of mediator than instigator. Scottish involvement in the affair can be explained by the fact that the cardinals were empowered to excommunicate Robert I, king of Scots. It seems likely that Robert Sapy, keeper of the temporalities of Durham during the vacancy, had been anxious to delay Beaumont's installation. On 25 April 1317 Sapy had entered into an agreement with John Eure, then keeper of Mitford, which was designed to ensure that Eure would prevent Beaumont taking over the see until after Michaelmas. If he failed to do so, Eure promised to compensate Sapy for his losses. However, by 1 September circumstances had changed, for on 4 May a royal writ had ordered the temporalities to be handed over to Beaumont. A later account, by Thomas Grey, suggested that Middleton acted because his cousin, Adam Swinburne, had been arrested for speaking harshly to the king about the state of the northern marches. Swinburne was not in fact Middleton's cousin, but he was a household knight, and he was in custody in Nottingham at the time of the attack on the cardinals. Robert Sapy was also a household knight, as was John Lilburn who joined Middleton in the attack. It seems possible that the origins of the incident lay in the discontentment felt by a group of northern knights within the royal household.

After his capture, Gilbert Middleton was taken south by sea to London, and was tried for treason before the king on 26 January 1318. He was condemned to be hanged, drawn, and quartered. His trial and execution for treason needs to be set in the context of his career as a royal household knight; it was the fact that he was in a special relationship to the king, as well as the fact that two cardinals were among his victims, that made his offence so heinous.

MICHAEL PRESTWICH

Sources A. E. Middleton, *Sir Gilbert de Middleton: and the part he took in the rebellion in the north of England in 1317* (1918) · M. C. Prestwich, 'Gilbert de Middleton and the attack on the cardinals, 1317', *Warriors and churchmen in the high middle ages*, ed. T. Reuter (1992), 179–94 · Durham Cath. CL, MS MC 5033 · W. Stubbs, ed., *Chronicles of the reigns of Edward I and Edward II*, 2 vols., Rolls Series, 76 (1882–3)

Middleton, Henry (*b.* in or before **1546**, *d.* **1587**), printer, was probably the son of the printer William *Middleton (*d.* 1547), and was probably born in London. He was admitted to the freedom of the Stationers' Company on 17 February 1567 by patrimony, without having been an apprentice, and commenced business in partnership with Thomas East near the church of St Dunstan-in-the-West, Fleet Street. Their earliest known book, Phaer's *Regiment of Life*, was printed in 1567. In 1571 their press was in London Wall, near the sign of the Ship. In 1572 Middleton left East and set up his press at the sign of the Falcon in Fleet Street, and also opened a shop for the sale of his books in St Dunstan's Churchyard. He married, on 20 April 1572, Helen or Ellen, widow of the stationer William Griffith.

The earliest book with Middleton as sole printer was Bull's *Christian Praiers and Holy Meditations* (1570), followed in 1572 by Cato's *Disticha de moribus*, but mostly he was fully employed by Ralph Newbery, John Harrison, George Bishop, Christopher Barker, and other booksellers, printing in English and Latin. A report on London printing offices made to the bishop of London in May 1583 states that Middleton had then three presses at work. The most important books printed by him were the works of Sallust, in Latin (1573), Gascoigne's *Glasse of Governement* (1575), Sir Humphrey Gilbert's *Discourse of a Discoverie for a New Passage to Cataia* and Lambard's *Perambulation of Kent* (1576), several translations from Calvin, *The Heidelberg Catechism* (1578), the Bible and the works of Virgil, both in Latin, Bedford's *English Medicines*, and Bishop Hooper's *Certeine Expositions upon the Psalmes* (1580), Laurence Humphrey's *Jesuitismus* (1582), Cicero's *De officiis* and Sir Thomas Smith's *De republica Anglorum* (1584), Ovid's *Metamorphoses*, in Latin, and Archbishop Sandys's *Sermons* (1585), and Lambard's *Duties of Constables* (1587).

Middleton was admitted into the livery of the Stationers' Company on 1 July 1577, serving as renter warden from 1582 to 1584, and as under-warden in July 1587. He married a second time, to widow Jane Sutton, on 20 December 1584. He died in September 1587 and was buried at St Dunstan's on 9 September. He had made a nuncupative will on 6 September 1587 which was later the subject of litigation between his widow's next husband, Richard Ayres, and Richard Brown. His widow appears to have carried on the business until 4 March 1588, when she was forbidden by the company to print anything more. The printing house was sold in 1588 to Robert Robinson for £200. R. E. GRAVES, *rev.* ANITA McCONNELL

Sources J. Ames, T. F. Dibdin, and W. Herbert, eds., *Typographical antiquities; or, The history of printing in England, Scotland and Ireland*, 4 vols. (1810–19), vol. 3, pp. 547–54 · C. H. Timperley, *A dictionary of printers and printing* (1839), 396 · Arber, *Regs. Stationers*, 1.344; 2.474, 865 · CLRO, repertory 16, fol. 206*r* · parish register, Fleet Street, St Dunstan-in-the-West, GL, MS 10342 [marriage, burial] · PRO, PROB 11/71, sig. 53 · R. L. Steele, 'Printers and books in chancery', *The Library*, new ser., 10 (1909), 101–6 · J. L. Chester and J. Foster, eds., *London marriage licences, 1521–1869* (1887)

Middleton, Sir Henry (*d.* **1613**), East India Company sea captain, was born in the parish of St Peter, Chester, one of at least nine children in the family of John Middleton, merchant, and his wife, Katherine (*d.* 1588), daughter of Thomas and Margaret Bavand. His brothers John and David also served as company captains, and a number of Middleton's relations were subscribers and directors. There is no evidence that Henry Middleton ever married.

In October 1600 the East India Company was organizing its first voyage under James Lancaster. On the recommendation of his elder brother John, second in command to Lancaster, Henry Middleton was appointed to oversee the works at Woolwich on the ship *Scourge of Malice* (soon renamed *Red Dragon* or *Dragon*). He was chosen in November to sail as one of the company's factors (mercantile agents).

The *Dragon*, *Ascension*, *Hector*, and *Susan* left England in April 1601. Many men died from scurvy or dysentery before the ships arrived at Aceh in Sumatra in June 1602. Lancaster secured a local trade agreement with the king, but decided to send the *Susan* to Priaman on the western coast of Sumatra for a lading, entrusting Henry Middleton to be captain and chief merchant in place of John Hayward, who had died. Middleton managed to procure substantial quantities of both pepper and cloves before sailing for England while Lancaster and Henry's brother attempted to establish trade at Bantam in Java. The *Ascension* and *Susan* arrived home safely in the summer of 1603, followed in September by the *Dragon* and *Hector*, bringing news of John Middleton's death at Bantam.

The East India Company court of directors was sufficiently impressed by Henry Middleton's abilities to name him general of the second voyage. He sailed in April 1604 accompanied by his brother David as an unofficial assistant. On arrival at Bantam on 23 December the majority of Middleton's crews were sick or dying. In spite of his own poor health, Middleton at once exerted himself to foster good relations with the local dignitaries and visited the young sultan of Bantam to present gifts and a letter from James I. The *Hector* and *Susan* were sent home with pepper, while Middleton took the *Dragon* and *Ascension* eastwards in quest of cloves and nutmeg, anchoring off Amboina on 10 February 1605. He contacted the Portuguese fort and secured the right to trade, but the price asked for spices was too high. The Dutch then took control and all opportunity to do business was lost. Middleton proposed sending the *Ascension* to the Banda Islands for nutmeg and mace while he went in the *Dragon* to the Moluccas for cloves. His advisory council argued that it would be dangerous for the ships to separate and feared that the *Dragon* would not reach the Moluccas because of the monsoon. However, Middleton managed to overcome his colleagues' opposition, and the ships went their different ways on 18 February. The *Dragon* braved the monsoon and on 18 March became the first English merchant vessel to reach the Moluccas.

Middleton managed to buy cloves but was hampered by the need to negotiate with both the sultan of Ternate, who was allied with the Dutch, and the sultan of Tidore, who was allied with the Portuguese. When war broke out in May, Middleton and his brother acted as mediators for Tidore while trying to persuade Ternate to allow the establishment of an English factory. The company might have won a trade monopoly by pledging to protect Ternate from both Portuguese and Dutch aggression, but Middleton had no authority to agree to this. He sailed for Bantam in mid-June, carrying letters for James I from both rulers holding out hopes of future trade.

The *Dragon* reached Bantam on 24 July and was joined by the *Ascension* bearing a cargo of mace and nutmeg. The ships started homewards on 6 October. Near Table Bay the *Dragon* met the *Hector* still on her voyage home and crippled by high mortality. The *Susan* had lost company in June and was never seen again. However, when the three remaining ships arrived home in May 1606, the cloves and nutmeg found a ready market and the expedition was deemed a success. Middleton presented the letters and gifts sent by the eastern rulers to King James at Greenwich on 25 May, and received a knighthood in recognition of his endeavours.

Sir Henry was approached in November 1607 to lead the company's fourth voyage, but after some deliberation he declined the offer. In 1610 he accepted the appointment of general of the sixth voyage, commanding the newly launched *Trades Increase*, the *Peppercorn*, and the *Darling*. The fleet sailed on 1 April 1610 with instructions to try to establish trade at Surat in western India.

On arrival at Socotra in October Middleton was advised to trade at Aden and Mocha. The English anchored off Aden on 7 November and quickly reached an agreement whereby the *Peppercorn* stayed to do business there while the *Trades Increase* and *Darling* sailed on to Mocha. Having been assured that it was customary for commanders to go ashore before business could be transacted, Sir Henry landed at Mocha on 20 November and was greeted with great pomp by the aga, who persuaded him to stay in the town. On the evening of 28 November the Turks attacked the English, killing eight. Middleton was knocked unconscious and robbed of money and three gold rings before being imprisoned, chained by the neck to seven of his men. The *Darling* meanwhile successfully repelled three boatloads of soldiers.

The following morning the aga informed Middleton that it was unlawful for any Christian to venture so close to the Turks' holy city. Sir Henry was unchained from the others, but fettered and manacled and kept apart from his companions with very little communication with his ships. On 22 December he and his men began the journey across the mountains to San'a' to appear before the pasha. The ride took fifteen days: Middleton bought his men furred gowns as their thin clothing was inadequate protection against the cold, especially when sleeping on the frozen ground. After an interview with the pasha Middleton was sent to lodgings with a few companions while the rest of the Englishmen were put in prison.

In March 1611 Middleton and his men returned to Mocha to be kept as hostages against the safe arrival of the ships coming from India to trade. Sir Henry had to swallow his pride and feign friendship towards the aga, biding his time until May when he decided to escape. He plied his guards with alcohol and arranged to be carried down to the sea in an empty barrel. Fifteen of his men escaped with him to the *Darling*, but others were stranded. The *Darling* and *Trades Increase* blockaded the port and Middleton threatened to fire all the ships in the road and bombard the town unless all his men and goods held on shore were returned. The blockade was lifted after the men were released on 26 May, and Middleton then began negotiating for restitution of his goods and for payment of damages. The last instalment was received on 2 July and the fleet moved into the open sea hoping to capture a ship coming to Mocha from Suez with a rich cargo in which the pasha was rumoured to have invested heavily, but the ship passed at night.

On 9 August Middleton's fleet sailed for India via Socotra, arriving at Surat on 26 September only to find the Portuguese gathered there in strength to prevent it from trading. Sir Henry therefore refused to let any Indian boats enter the river until all the Englishmen at Surat and Cambay had been allowed aboard his vessels. There were skirmishes with the Portuguese in October and November, and the local people were forbidden to supply the English with victuals.

By December 1611 Middleton's frustration at the lack of progress was making him increasingly unable to control his volatile temper. Delays necessitated additional costs for wages, provisions, and ship maintenance, and the success of the voyage was threatened as well as Middleton's reputation. He therefore landed 200 armed men at Surat in January to ensure that the English factors and their goods were safely brought aboard, and in February he sailed for Dabul, where a small amount of trade was quickly completed. The council decided that the fleet should return to the Red Sea to capture the Indian ships heading for Mocha and force them to exchange commodities such as calico and indigo for English cloths and other wares. Middleton's arrival put an abrupt end to the trade negotiations of John Saris, general of the eighth voyage. Saris had been Middleton's subordinate on the second voyage but was no longer prepared to defer to him, instead demanding a share of Sir Henry's proceeds. After several fierce arguments between the two commanders, Middleton angrily agreed to allow the eighth voyage one third of the spoils and one quarter of the ransom extracted from the Indian captains.

On 19 October 1612 Middleton anchored at Sumatra with the *Trades Increase* and *Peppercorn* to rejoin the *Darling*, which had been sent on ahead to procure pepper before Saris arrived. By the end of December all Middleton's ships were gathered at Bantam. Seeking an impressive cargo and determined not to be outshone by Saris, who was preparing to go to Japan in the *Clove*, Middleton proposed a voyage to Amboina, the Banda Islands, and Borneo. Since the *Trades Increase* was worm-eaten and in need of extensive repairs, the *Darling* was sent for Amboina, and the *Peppercorn* sailed for England, delivering her cargo safely in October to give some reassurance to subscribers. Middleton stayed at Bantam to oversee the careening of the *Trades Increase*, only to see most of her crew die as the ship lay damaged by fire with her main mast broken. He died on 24 May 1613, broken-hearted at this latest cruel turn of events in his troubled voyage.

News of Middleton's death and the destruction of the *Trades Increase* reached London in June 1614. It fell to David Middleton's wife, Alice, during her husband's absence at sea to prove Sir Henry's will and to settle his accounts with the company. The will provided for substantial bequests to his siblings, as well as numerous smaller amounts to friends and family. The residue of the estate went to David Middleton and his son Henry.

MARGARET MAKEPEACE

Sources W. Foster, ed., *The voyage of Sir Henry Middleton to the Moluccas, 1604–1606* (1943) • S. Purchas, *Hakluytus posthumus, or, Purchas his pilgrimes*, bks 2–3, 5 (1625); repr. Hakluyt Society, extra ser., 15–16, 18 (1905) • F. C. Danvers and W. Foster, eds., *Letters received by the East India Company from its servants in the east*, 6 vols. (1896–1902), vols. 1–2 • *CSP col.*, vol. 2 • G. Birdwood and W. Foster, eds., *The register of letters etc. of the governor and company of merchants trading into the East Indies, 1600–1619* (1893) • C. R. Markham, ed., *The voyages of Sir James Lancaster, kt., to the East Indies, with abstracts of journals of voyages to the East Indies* (1877) • H. Stevens, ed., *The dawn of British trade to the East Indies as recorded in the court minutes of the East India Company, 1599–1603* (1886) • W. Myddleton, *Pedigree of the family of Myddleton* (1910) • W. Foster, *England's quest of Eastern trade* (1933) • will, PRO, PROB 11/123, sig. 55 • *The journal of John Jourdain, 1608–1617*, ed. W. Foster, Hakluyt Society, 2nd ser., 16 (1905) • E. M. Satow, ed., *The voyage of Captain John Saris to Japan, 1613* (1890)

Archives BL OIOC, letters • BL OIOC, original corresp., ref IOR: E/3

Likenesses oils, NPG • portrait, NPG, Macdonnell collection, book illustration

Wealth at death bequests amounting to £965, plus 40 marks; unknown residue left to brother and nephew: will, PRO, PROB 11/123, sig. 55

Middleton, James Smith [Jim] (1878–1962), political organizer, was born on 12 March 1878 at Primrose Terrace, Clarborough, near Retford, Nottinghamshire, one of three children born to Alfred Edward Middleton (d. 1924), printers' assistant, telegrapher, newspaper accountant, and journalist, and his wife, Martha Odam (d. 1921), formerly a straw-plaiter of Luton. Middleton's father was a cockney, born and educated in Camden Town, who sold newspapers from the age of nine. Working in a printers and as a messenger boy (in Luton) he learned telegraphy and developed his journalistic skills. He worked for the *Retford and Gainsborough Times* before moving to Inverness to work on *The Highlander*, produced by John Murdoch of the crofters' movement. Employed on a series of other short-lived radical newspapers, Alfred Middleton moved to Whitehaven, Ipswich, Rochdale, and Workington (twice), where the family finally settled in 1888 after purchasing the declining *Workington Star* (which they turned into a labour journal). Both parents remained close to their son, who wrote them an almost daily letter until his father's death.

Jim Middleton (as he was always known) was educated at a series of elementary schools. He left a private school in Workington at the age of twelve and worked on his father's newspaper. He was apprenticed to a printer at fourteen. At eighteen he found religion, joining the Young People's Society of Christian Endeavour, and remained a Presbyterian until the Second South African War. He joined the Independent Labour Party at an early age, and became secretary of the Workington Trades Council in 1900, at the age of twenty-two, and secretary of the local branch of the Labour Representation Committee shortly after. Through his political work he met the first of his three wives, Mary Muir (1870–1911), daughter of Martha and Walter Muir of Maryport (formerly of Ayrshire). She was a parlourmaid, who shared his political activism, and they married on 2 July 1900. She became involved in the Women's Labour League, being especially concerned with children's welfare.

In 1902, following a bitter dispute over the reporting of a local event, Middleton left Workington to work as a compositor–reporter on the *Harringay Mercury*. Already in correspondence with Ramsay MacDonald, secretary of the Labour Party, he became the party's first assistant secretary. Initially working on a part-time basis from a bedroom in MacDonald's house, Middleton and his wife became close to MacDonald and his politically active wife, Margaret. The assistant secretary was a dogsbody, since the fledgeling party could afford few other staff. Middleton wrote, typed, and posted endless letters to local parties and trade unions, playing a key role in the development of Labour's organization and writing many unsigned newspaper articles. He was not an orator, a policy maker, or a fierce apparatchik. A slight, humorous, blue-eyed, fair-haired man—'fair-minded and gentle-natured', according to the normally critical Beatrice Webb (*Diary*, 20 March 1918)—he was none the less a powerful influence on Labour's politics over the next forty years.

Middleton was sympathetic to the careful and moderate political strategy which Ramsay MacDonald devised for the young Labour Party. He was also a loyal friend to his leader. The tragedy of their wives' deaths (Mary Middleton collapsed in March 1910 and died in April 1911 of a 'wasting disease') brought the two men even closer together. Middleton remained a friend to MacDonald and his children, despite the later strains on their relationship. In June 1913 Middleton married his first wife's nurse, Alice Todd (1878–1935), a far more domestic woman, whose interests were in the home and gardening. They had one child, Margaret, who in time graduated from the University of Bristol, became a paediatrician, and married a Dr Eastwood.

Middleton worked to enforce MacDonald's policy against his radical critics before 1914, and to keep them from deserting Labour during the war. In personal letters he attacked the immorality of war and the impact which it had on the families left behind. He helped establish the War Emergency Workers' National Committee, which campaigned for better conditions on the home front and aimed to preserve human decency and dignity for soldiers, workers, and their families. He wanted Labour to keep its distance from the coalition government and its policies. Inspired by the Russian Revolution, he noted a change in the public mood, seeing a 'great chance for a new world after this' (Middleton to his parents, 10 June 1917, Middleton MSS, Ruskin College, MID 14/9).

Despite his views on the war, Middleton was not a frustrated radical. A party man who lived for the movement's success, his loyalty to MacDonald was also based on their shared convictions. Both men favoured enlightened state enterprise and efficient public services in the early 1920s; Middleton wrote very positive copy on MacDonald and on party policy for Herbert Tracey's *Book of the Labour Party* (1925). Middleton was cheered by the party's 1928 manifesto, *Labour and the Nation*, although by this time he was less close personally and politically to MacDonald. To Middleton's disquiet, MacDonald handled colleagues badly when forming his cabinets. Despite this, MacDonald confided in Middleton during the 1929–31 government. In return Middleton shielded his leader and friend, eventually expressing his 'awe' at the heroism of MacDonald's personal sacrifice in 1931, when he left Labour to form the National Government. Typically, Middleton retained his instinctive loyalty to the party and did not follow.

In 1934, when Arthur Henderson was obliged to resign, Middleton succeeded him as Labour Party secretary, and remained in post for the next ten years. Throughout the 1930s he opposed working with the Communist Party against fascism, and any suggestion of a 'popular front' as advocated by many on the left. He even declined to attend the funeral of an old friend, Tom Mann, since he knew the funeral oration would be used to attack Labour policy. He acted as the disciplinary mouthpiece of the party on many occasions, warning activists who participated in meetings or movements alongside communists and expelling those who persisted. He believed dissidents were ignoring conference policy and detracting attention from Labour's construction of a positive, energetic, and practical socialism. Converts to the party, such as Stafford Cripps, found Middleton willing to exploit rank-and-file suspicion of

affluent socialists if this would minimize their support. However, Middleton also attempted to persuade even quite unimportant critics in constituency parties with reasoned argument, writing lengthy and personally composed letters. Middleton's lifelong commitment to the party and often tactful approach commanded respect from many, but not all, Labour insiders. Henderson and Dalton saw Middleton as inefficient and pedestrian. Although both were flawed judges, his well-meaning and earnest actions evidently grated with more dynamic rivals. He retired in 1944.

After the death of his second wife, Alice, in June 1935, Middleton married, on 1 May 1936, Lucy Annie Cox (1894–1983) [*see* Middleton, Lucy Annie], a Keynsham-born teacher who, like his first wife, was politically active; she became Labour MP for Plymouth South in 1945. Their relationship had begun in 1931, and was carried on in secret for five years. Their passionate correspondence, and Middleton's explanation of the relationship to his daughter in 1936, illustrate a little-studied but not uncommon aspect of politicians' lives.

Throughout the 1930s Middleton had written many articles for party publications. He continued to write biographical studies and obituaries of party pioneers for trade union and other journals after he retired, and advised the Labour Party historians Frank Bealey, Henry Pelling, and John Saville in the 1950s. His deep commitment to the party and its history was matched only by his commitment to his wife. He acted as her election agent in her Plymouth constituency and helped organize the local party. Handicapped in later years by a heart condition, he rarely went out, and died at his home, 7 Princes Road, Wimbledon, Surrey, on 18 November 1962.

DUNCAN TANNER

Sources Ruskin College, Oxford, J. S. Middleton MSS · J. S. Middleton MSS, People's History Museum, Manchester, Labour Party archives · People's History Museum, Manchester, Labour Party archives, NEC MSS · *The Thistle*, 12 (1928) · *DNB* · PRO, J. R. MacDonald MSS · *The political diary of Hugh Dalton, 1918–1940, 1945–1960*, ed. B. Pimlott (1986) · D. Marquand, *Ramsay MacDonald* (1977) · D. M. Tanner, *Political change and the labour party, 1900–18* (1990) · R. McKibbin, *The evolution of the labour party, 1910–1924* (1974) · B. Pimlott, *Labour and the left in the 1930s* (1977) · *The diary of Beatrice Webb*, ed. N. MacKenzie and J. MacKenzie, 4 vols. (1982–5), vols. 3–4 · b. cert.
Archives JRL, Labour History Archive and Study Centre, corresp. and papers · People's History Museum, Manchester, Labour Party archives, MSS · Ruskin College, Oxford, corresp. and papers | Bodl. Oxf., Attlee MSS, corresp. with Clement Attlee · Internationaal Instituut voor Sociale Geschiedenis, Amsterdam, corresp. mainly with Max Beer · PRO, J. R. MacDonald MSS · U. Warwick Mod. RC, TUC archives
Wealth at death £2907 2s.: administration, 18 April 1963, *CGPLA Eng. & Wales*

Middleton, John (d. 1429), physician, was one of several physicians who were also bureaucrats, and who served noble patrons while receiving incomes from the church. A fellow of University College, Oxford, by 1381, Middleton was MA by 1383, and may be the John Middleton who rented a room in Durham College before 1390. No medical degrees are recorded, even though Middleton practised medicine on behalf of royal patrons. Indeed this was a common situation among learned practitioners, implying that formal medical qualification was not considered necessary by élite patrons. He may be the John Middleton who in 1388 was granted absence for theological study from his benefice in Oddington, Gloucestershire, for seven years, as long as he was ordained subdeacon within the year. Middleton the physician was ordained deacon in 1391 and was given a canonry at Beverley shortly afterwards. This benefice was gained amid prolonged litigation with Nicholas Ryssheton, who was in the end forced to renounce it. Middleton seems to have held the living until his death and apparently never proceeded to the priesthood.

Middleton's career as a physician is first noticed on the fine rolls in 1385, when as king's physician he was given custody of the Benedictine alien priory of Blyth in Nottinghamshire. Possession of the priory was the subject of litigation, since Middleton had unseated the previous holder, who in turn had Middleton deposed. In 1388 Richard II appointed a commission to investigate an assault against his physician, which had taken place at Blyth. Difficulties over the income from the priory may have been the occasion of a grant made to Middleton by Richard in 1392, compensating him for some unspecified loss of past income. Middleton was still in possession of the priory in 1397. He also attended Henry, earl of Derby, in 1387, treating him for 'pokkes'. A payment on behalf of Master John Middleton to his London apothecaries for medical supplies for the king is recorded among the issues of the exchequer.

By the last decade of the fourteenth century, Middleton had achieved a substantial income under Richard's patronage. In the year ending 30 September 1393 he received over £10 as a member of the royal household. In 1395 he received a lifetime annuity of £40, which was increased to 100 marks in 1396. These incomes, which were until such time as he received a benefice of 200 marks, were confirmed in 1397 and 1399. Also in 1396, Richard gave Middleton a messuage in London to be held without rent during the minority of the heir. In 1398 Middleton became warden of St Nicholas's Hospital, York, which he held until his death and which was, yet again, the subject of fierce litigation.

John Middleton was a very common name and there are often problems of identification. It is possible that the king's doctor was identical with the John Middleton who became archdeacon of Norfolk in 1395 (though the archdeacon was styled king's clerk and not physician) and who, under the title Master John Middleton, archdeacon of Norfolk, accompanied Richard to Ireland. The same problem bedevils attempts to trace the physician's career after 1399, but it would appear that his later years were occupied with ecclesiastical duties. Middleton enjoyed a number of benefices under Henry IV and his successors, but was apparently no longer employed as royal doctor. He died in 1429.   FAYE GETZ

Sources C. H. Talbot and E. A. Hammond, *The medical practitioners in medieval England: a biographical register* (1965) · H. E. Ussery, *Chaucer's physician: medicine and literature in fourteenth-century England* (1971) · C. Rawcliffe, 'The profits of practice: the wealth and status of medical men in later medieval England', *Social History of Medicine*, 1 (1988), 61–78 · Emden, *Oxf.*, 2.1276–7 · F. Devon, ed. and trans., *Issues of the exchequer: being payments made out of his majesty's revenue, from King Henry III to King Henry VI inclusive*, RC (1837)

Middleton, John, first earl of Middleton (*c.*1608–1674), army officer, was the eldest son of Robert Middleton (*d.* 1645), laird of Caldhame, Mearns, Kincardineshire, and his wife, Helen Strachan, a daughter of Alexander Strachan of Thornton in the same shire. The family had owned the lands of Middleton, Kincardineshire, from which they took their surname, since before 1154. The future earl began his military career as a pikeman in Sir John Hepburn's infantry regiment in France some time after 1631. He returned home to join the covenanters' army and to get married. In July 1639 he married Grizel Durham (*d.* 1666), the twice-widowed daughter of Sir James Durham of Pitkerro (her previous husbands were Sir Alexander Fotheringham and Sir Gilbert Ramsay of Balmain). They were to have a son, Charles *Middleton, second earl of Middleton, and two daughters, Lady Grisel, who married the ninth earl of Morton in September 1666, and Lady Helen, who married the third earl of Strathmore and Kinghorne.

As a captain under James Graham, fourth earl of Montrose, Middleton distinguished himself in the storming of the Brig of Dee on 19 June 1639. His service during the second bishops' war is unknown, but must have been sufficiently impressive as he joined the English parliamentarian army as a colonel in 1642. He earned a reputation for bravery and generosity during his English campaigns. In late 1643 he served in Sir William Brereton's invasion of north Wales and in August 1644 he was appointed Sir William Waller's major-general of horse. He later became a lieutenant-general. Following the self-denying ordinance, which had a provision for purging foreign officers from the parliamentarian ranks, Middleton resigned his commission.

The war against Montrose Subsequently Middleton raised a regiment of horse, 'all for the most part of our owne nation' (Scotland), partially at his own expense (at least £1000), and on 5 May received permission to join the army of the solemn league and covenant from the Scottish commissioners in London. Middleton and his regiment reached the army on 20 June. He entered the Scottish army not only as a colonel, but also as a major-general of horse. Amid the civil war raging in Scotland, soldiers of his former commander Montrose killed his father in his own house in 1645. Middleton subsequently wreaked considerable vengeance for that act. His regiment was part of the body of 5000 cavalry led north under Lieutenant-General David Leslie to dispose of Montrose, who had become master of Scotland for the king. In the covenanter victory at Philiphaugh on 12 September Middleton served as second in command. For his actions the estates voted him 25,000 merks Scots. He led an army of 800 cavalry into Aberdeenshire and Banffshire in October, then lifted the royalist siege of Spynie Palace in Moray. On 4 February

John Middleton, first earl of Middleton (c.1608–1674), studio of Sir Peter Lely

1646 the estates appointed him commander-in-chief in Scotland and renewed his commission as a major-general of horse. In mid-April he took the field with 800 foot and 600 horse, and returned to Aberdeenshire and Banffshire. Later in the month he successfully led 800–900 horse to raise Montrose's siege of Inverness. Having captured various Mackenzie strongholds, he returned south and seized the royalist base at Fyvie Castle on 29 February. After the king ordered Montrose to disband his army the estates authorized Middleton to negotiate the conditions.

On 22 July 1646 the two commanders had a long meeting in a meadow near the Water of Isla in Forfarshire. There Middleton granted the marquess and his followers more favourable terms than met the approval of the commission of the general assembly of the Church of Scotland. On 29 January 1647 the estates appointed him major-general of horse in the (Scottish) New Model Army and he received command of one of the army's staff troops of horse. In a final effort to rid the highlands of royalist forces Middleton began a campaign in late February. On 3 March his force appeared outside Montrose's castle of Kincardine and commenced a siege. The castle surrendered on 16 March and Middleton levelled it to the ground and had twelve Irish soldiers of the garrison shot. With Lieutenant-General Leslie he pursued the royalist Gordons in March and April, then continued the campaign after his superior departed for Argyll. In July Middleton joined Leslie on Jura with his troops, and accompanied him on the marches through Mull and Moidart. He returned to the lowlands some time in August. Meanwhile

on 24 March the estates had voted to provide him with a gold chain worth £2666 13s. 4d. The final four months of 1647 and the first two of 1648 provided Middleton with his first break from active service in five years.

Preston to Worcester In 1648 Middleton began to follow a more politically conservative course. In late March he refused to sign the original draft of the kirk party officers' Tailors' Hall petition opposing the estates' acceptance of the engagement to restore Charles I to freedom. Middleton altered the document to favour parliament's position, which traded the covenanter movement's insistence upon the permanent establishment of presbyterianism in England for a three-year trial. He subsequently persuaded most of the army to accept the change of political course. On 4 May the estates made Middleton colonel of a horse regiment to be raised from Roxburghshire and Peeblesshire. A week later he received a commission as major-general of horse in the engager army; on 10 June he gained a further promotion to lieutenant-general. On his march south he encountered 2000 kirk party rebels in arms against the engagement at Mauchline Moor, Ayrshire. In the ensuing skirmish on 12 June Middleton was wounded. On 8 July he led the vanguard of the army into Cumberland. In the engager councils of war during the campaign he unsuccessfully argued for the Yorkshire route as opposed to the Lancashire one accepted by James Hamilton, first duke of Hamilton, and commander-in-chief. Later he and Lieutenant-General James Livingston, first earl of Callendar, persuaded Hamilton to divide the infantry and cavalry to provide for better logistic support at the price of leaving the army vulnerable to Cromwell's approaching force. Following the destruction of their English royalist allies at Preston, Middleton commanded the engager rearguard on 18–19 August, fighting bravely at Standish and Wigan, before deserting Lieutenant-General William Baillie and the infantry. Middleton fell prisoner in Cheshire to the parliamentarians after his horse had fallen on him. He was confined initially at Hull, then Newcastle. He was afterwards allowed to reside in Berwick, and then, as some say, broke his parole and returned to Scotland. In mid-April 1649 he joined Pluscardine's rising for Charles II. On 9 May he submitted and was allowed to return home on 'giving assurance of his dutiful carriage in time coming'. The general assembly threatened him with excommunication for his engager and royalist activities. Middleton appeared before it and pleaded his cause, receiving permission to sign 'the declaration and acknowledgment' prescribed for adherents of 'the engagement' or 'in the late rebellion in the north' (Balfour, 4.419).

In June 1650 Middleton joined the king on his landing in Scotland, but was refused a commission in the army of the covenants. In October he and Lewis, second marquess of Gordon, raised the Gordons to oppose the kirk party. On 21 October Middleton defeated a force of kirk party horse in the battle of Newtyle, Forfarshire, but he failed in his attacks on the covenanters in Bog of Gight and Strathbogie/Huntly Castle. His former superior Leslie marched against him, and as Charles urged Middleton to submit, and the estates offered an indemnity, he agreed to terms in the treaty of Strathbogie on 4 November (Balfour, 4.160). The commission of the church, however, prematurely took action, and on a motion on 24 October made by James Guthrie, the radical minister of Stirling, and carried by the votes of the elders, resolved on his excommunication. This was opposed by many of the leading ministers, and the committee of estates urged delay; but Guthrie carried out the sentence on the following Sunday. At its next meeting the commission resolved to correct what it had done so rashly, and Middleton, having done penance in sackcloth in St Mary's Kirk, Dundee, on 12 January 1651, was restored to communion and the right to hold state offices. As a result of his public humiliation Middleton harboured an intense personal hatred of presbyterians for the rest of his life. In May the committee of estates commissioned him a colonel of a horse regiment, and on 17 May he received command of the 4th cavalry brigade, which contained four regiments. Before and during the Worcester campaign, on which he was a major-general, he became a highly popular member of the officer corps thanks to his convivial drinking habits. At the battle of Worcester on 3 September Middleton commanded the western wing of the Scottish army. Although wounded in the fighting he escaped with David Leslie and 1000–1200 horse. On 9 September Colonel John Birch captured him and most of the fleeing Scots at Blackstone Edge Moor between Parsdale and Halifax. Following imprisonment in Liverpool, his former comrades in arms sent him to the Tower of London. Cromwell wished to try him for treason, but he escaped in his wife's clothes and joined the king at Paris in 1652.

Exile and restoration Middleton resumed his role as an active supporter of the royal cause. In late 1653 Charles II appointed him captain-general of the forces raised in the highlands by William Cunningham, eighth earl of Glencairn. Middleton took command at Dornoch, Sutherland, in late February 1654. General George Monck, the English commander in Scotland, and Colonel Thomas Morgan marched against him with large forces. On 10 July Morgan surprised Middleton at Dalnaspidal, near Lochgarry. Middleton's cavalry fled and his foot deserted in the ensuing catastrophe. Middleton escaped with difficulty and joined the king at Cologne some time after 15 March 1655. Predictably Cromwell excluded him from the Act of Indemnity in 1654. Meanwhile in the exiled court he became a protégé of the royal councillor and anti-presbyterian Sir Edward Hyde. In 1656 Charles made him an earl. He also received the colonelcy of the Scots foot raised in Flanders in that year. On 24 September 1656 he received a royal appointment as ambassador to the Jews of Amsterdam, and to Danzig and Poland with the aim of raising troops, but he dismissed them owing to a lack of money. He visited Danzig in 1657–8; on his way west in 1658 he stayed with the electors of Brandenburg and Saxony. Afterwards he resided with the king in Brussels, and on his own in Amsterdam. He returned to the exiled court in the summer of 1659. At the Restoration he returned to England with the king. His peerage was then confirmed by letters patent on 1 October 1660 under the title earl of Middleton, Lord Clermont and Fettercairn. He readily entered into a conspiracy with many Scottish nobles against the presbyterian party (Buckroyd, 16). His favour with Clarendon (the former Sir Edward Hyde) and the king gained him appointments as commander-in-chief in Scotland, governor of Edinburgh Castle, and lord high commissioner to the Scottish parliament. He arrived at Holyroodhouse in late December, having been escorted from Musselburgh by many nobles, gentry, and a thousand mounted men.

On 1 January 1661 Middleton opened the Scottish parliament with great state. He quickly implemented a pro-episcopalian and absolutist regime. His passage of the Acts Rescissory, which annulled all the legislation of the previous twenty-eight years, placed the estates in thrall to the monarchy and debilitated the cause of constitutionalism for nearly three decades. On 11 May he presided at the funeral of Montrose, whose scattered limbs had been collected and buried with full honours in St Giles's, Edinburgh—a fitting ceremony for the resuscitation of Scottish royalism. Middleton led the prosecution of Archibald Campbell, marquess of Argyll, who was executed on 27 May—symbolizing the destruction of the constitutionalist/covenanter party. His personal animosity towards James Guthrie, the force behind his excommunication, led the minister to the same fate. In mid-June Middleton steered the privy council to petition the king for the restoration of episcopacy owing to secret instructions from Clarendon. Armed with that resolution he returned to London and personally urged that policy on the king. Now he assured Charles that bishops were 'desired by the greater and honester part of the nation' (*Burnet's History*, 1.234). John Maitland, earl of Lauderdale, a friend of the king and secretary of state for Scotland, thought differently. The feud that ended with Middleton's downfall began over this policy dispute.

In 1662 Middleton continued to ride the wave of extreme royalism. He served as commissioner of the May 1662 parliament, and in July became an extraordinary lord of session. At the end of September he and the privy council met at Glasgow (popularly called the 'Drunken Parliament'). According to contemporary rumour most of the councillors were drunk when they passed the act which deprived the clergy who refused to conform to episcopacy of their benefices. The council also established monetary penalties for nonconforming protestants. During the period of his dominance in Scotland (from 1662 to early 1663) he wrote *For the Good of the Publick* (n.d.). At court, Lauderdale so successfully retailed stories of the earl's extremely rigorous acts that Middleton became alienated from Whitehall. Middleton's removal from office was expedited by his attempt to exclude royal favourites Lauderdale and Sir Robert Moray from public office. On 11 February 1663 he was ordered to London to meet the accusation of Lauderdale who charged him with withholding letters from the king on public affairs, consenting to measures without royal authority, taking bribes from presbyterians to exempt them from fines, and other lapses.

In March Middleton lost all his offices, and retired to the house of Thomas Dalmahoy, an old Scottish comrade in arms, near Guildford, Surrey. He had a pension from the crown of £1000 sterling p.a. (albeit one frequently in arrears) and the rents from his estates, of about the same value: nevertheless he certainly had financial problems. He was governor of Rochester from 1663 to 1667, and on 30 June 1666 he became lieutenant-general of the Kent militia. Pepys, seeing him in the aftermath of the Dutch raid on the Medway, noted: 'He seems a fine soldier, and so everybody says he is; and a man like … most of the scotch gentry (as I observe), of few words' (Pepys, 8.307). Following the death of his first wife in September 1666 at Cranston, Middleton married on 16 December 1667 Martha Carey (1635/6–1706), daughter and coheir of Henry *Carey, second earl of Monmouth. In the spring of 1667 Pepys reported that Middleton, 'a man of moderate understanding, not covetous, but a soldier-of-fortune and poor' was for certain appointed governor of Tangier, (ibid., 167), a post which he probably owed to the influence of the duke of York. His patent was not issued until May 1668 and he did not set sail until September 1669, in the meantime having importuned Pepys for advances on his pay. The latter, getting to know him, found him 'a shrowd man, but a drinking man, I think, as the world says—but a man that hath seen much of the world'. They talked of the Dutch war, which Middleton said that he had always disliked, 'and did discourse very well of it, I saying little, but pleased to hear him talk and to see how some men may by age come to know much, and yet by their drinking and other pleasures render themselfs not very considerable'. Pepys met Middleton a couple of times before learning that this was 'the great major-Generall Middleton, that was of the Scottish army in the beginning of the late war against the King' (ibid., 9.325, 328).

At Tangier Middleton seems to have been a conscientious and able governor, extending the fortifications of the town ahead of the permission and authorized funding from England, and maintaining the hospitality that his position required, if also showing at times bad temper as much as affability. He was also frequently ill, and it was while suffering from the flux that he had the fall which brought about his death on 3 July 1674. Getting up in the middle of the night looking for a light he tripped up over the sickbed attendant who was sleeping in his doorway: Middleton 'in the dark stumbled over him and broke his arm close by the shoulder, and in two or three days died of the fever, which the pain, and his former weakness caused' (Jones, 24). Middleton had been engaged in buying up the jointure of his wife's stepmother to obviate terms in his 1667 marriage settlement which would effectively have disinherited his son. Moreover, his expenses as governor were great (while the crown's payments to him were also heavily in arrears). Middleton died heavily in debt to both the crown and to Scottish creditors.

Conclusion Middleton was one of the most successful Scottish professional soldiers. He earned a solid reputation for force of character, courage, and ability as a commander. His patron Clarendon says he was 'as courtly a person as ever that nation [Scotland] bred, of great modesty, courage, and judgement, worthy of any trust' (Clarendon State Papers, 4.145). Sir George Mackenzie, the noted lawyer and equally extreme royalist, described him as of 'heroic aspect, courage, and generosity, manly, eloquent, and as more pitied in his fall than envied in his prosperity'. Baillie, on his appointment as royal commissioner in 1661, wrote that 'his wisdom, sobriety, and moderation have been such as make him better beloved, and reputed as fit for that great charge as any other we could have gotten' (Letters and Journals of Robert Baillie, 3.443–4). Others took a harsher view. Burnet, a conservative whig, observed 'He and his company were delivered up to so much excess, and such a madness of frolic and intemperance, that as Scotland had never seen any thing like it' (Burnet's History, 1.363), a view echoed in Walter Scott's Tales of a Grandfather. His reputation is forever black among presbyterians for his apostasy and persecuting inclinations; for episcopalians the corrupt and inebriated nature of his regime made him a problematic hero. EDWARD M. FURGOL

Sources The letters and journals of Robert Baillie, ed. D. Laing, 3 vols., Bannatyne Club, 73 (1841–2) • APS, 1643–60, i–ii, 7 • J. Turner, Memoirs of his own life and times, 1632–1670, ed. T. Thomson, Bannatyne Club, 28 (1829) • J. Balfour, Works, 4 vols. (1823–5) • H. W. Meikle, ed., Correspondence of the Scots commissioners in London, 1644–1646, Roxburghe Club, 160 (1917) • P. Gordon, A short abridgement of Britane's distemper, ed. J. Dunn, Spalding Club, 10 (1844) • Calendar of the Clarendon state papers preserved in the Bodleian Library, 2: 1649–1654, ed. W. D. Macray (1869) • Burnet's History of my own time, ed. O. Airy, new edn, 2 vols. (1897–1900) • Scots peerage • J. Buckroyd, Church and state in Scotland, 1660–1681 (1980) • A. F. Mitchell and J. Christie, eds., The records of the commissions of the general assemblies of the Church of Scotland, 3 vols., Scottish History Society, 11, 25, 58 (1892–1909) • Pepys, Diary • G. Hilton Jones, Charles Middleton: the life and times of a Restoration politician (1967), 1–25 • GEC, Peerage

Archives BL, corresp. and papers relating to Tangier, Sloane MSS 1958, 3510–3514 | NL Scot., letters relating to politics

Likenesses G. Kneller, oils, Castle Ward, Co. Down • studio of P. Lely, portrait; Phillips, 28 April 1992, lot 6 [see illus.]

Wealth at death debts of £6534 owing to treasury were discharged in 1679; there were arrears owing to Middleton of £3345 3s.: Jones, Charles Middleton, 24

Middleton, John (1827–1856), landscape painter, was born in the parish of St Stephen, Norwich, on 9 January 1827. His father was a painter–decorator and his mother exhibited flower paintings at the Norwich Society of Artists. He was taught to paint by the landscape painter John Crome, and later by Henry Bright, and became a friend of many of the Norwich school of landscape painters, including Thomas Lound. Apart from two years in London from 1847, he spent his life in Norwich, where he helped to run the family business.

Middleton exhibited fourteen landscapes at the Royal Academy between 1847 and 1855. He was particularly drawn to woodland scenes, and he also produced studies of plants and grasses. His Landscape with Trees and Farm Buildings is in the Victoria and Albert Museum, London. John Middleton died, unmarried, of consumption on 11 November 1856 in Surrey Street, Norwich.

ANNE PIMLOTT BAKER

Sources H. A. E. Day, East Anglian painters, 2–3: The Norwich school of painters (1979), 268–78 • D. P. Clifford, Watercolours of the Norwich

School (1965), 75–8 · Wood, *Vic. painters*, 3rd edn · Mallalieu, *Watercolour artists*, vols. 1–2 · Graves, *RA exhibitors* · *Norwich Mercury* (15 Nov 1856) · Redgrave, *Artists*
Likenesses photograph, repro. in Day, *Norwich school of painters*, 347 · photograph, BM

Middleton, John Henry (1846–1896), archaeologist and art historian, was born at York on 5 October 1846, the only surviving child of John Middleton (d. 1885), architect, of York, and Maria Margaret, his wife, daughter of James Pigott *Pritchett, architect, of York, and his first wife, Peggy Maria Terry. As a child he was taken by his parents to Italy, where he acquired a love of that country and its language, which lasted throughout his life. On their return his parents settled at Cheltenham, where his father practised as an architect, and where Middleton himself was educated, first at a preparatory school, and afterwards at Cheltenham College. In 1865 he was matriculated at Exeter College, Oxford. Middleton, though far from being an eccentric recluse, or of as weakly a constitution as his appearance seemed to denote, displayed from his youth an acutely nervous and fastidious temperament, liable to strong emotions and to deep depression. This was accentuated in 1866 by the shock caused by the sudden death of a close friend at Oxford, which brought on a severe and painful illness that confined him to his room for five or six years and prevented him from graduating in the ordinary way. During this period, however, by assiduous reading and study he laid the foundations of that remarkable, painstaking, and accurate knowledge of art and archaeology, for which he was afterwards so highly distinguished.

On his recovery Middleton started off on a series of travels of an arduous and adventurous nature. He visited America, crossing it to Salt Lake City and the Rocky Mountains, and descending into Mexico. He travelled in Greece, Asia Minor, Egypt, and north Africa. He undertook a special journey to Fez in Morocco to study the philosophy of Plato as taught there, and disguised as a pilgrim not only gained admission into the Great Mosque, which no non-Muslim had previously succeeded in doing, but was also presented to the sultan as one of the faithful. On his return he adopted the profession of an architect, studied for a time in the office of Sir George Gilbert Scott, and became a partner in his father's business at Storey's Gate, Westminster. The profession was, however, never congenial to him, and after his father's sudden death in February 1885 he placed the business in thorough working order, and disposed of it to others.

Middleton had never ceased to pursue his favourite studies of art and archaeology, and even went through a course in the schools of the Royal Academy. His extensive and accurate knowledge became well known, and brought him many friends, among others William Morris, with whom Middleton travelled in Iceland. In June 1879 he was elected a fellow of the Society of Antiquaries, and was a frequent contributor to their *Proceedings* and their publications; he was elected a vice-president of the society in 1894. He was also a considerable contributor to the *Encyclopaedia Britannica* (9th edn), as well as to many weekly and other periodicals. He made a special study of the antiquities of Rome, and in 1885 published these as *Ancient Rome*, a revised edition of which appeared in 1888. In 1892 he followed this with another work, *Remains of Ancient Rome*. In these works Middleton was a pioneer of the serious and scientific study of Roman antiquities. In 1886 he was elected Slade professor of fine art at Cambridge, and given the honorary degree of MA at Cambridge in 1886, and at Oxford in 1887, followed by those of LittD at Cambridge in 1893, and DCL at Oxford in 1894; he was also honoured with a doctor's degree at the University of Bologna. He was twice re-elected to the professorship. In 1888 he was elected a fellow of King's College, Cambridge. In 1889 he was appointed director of the Fitzwilliam Museum at Cambridge, a post which offered him opportunities for a further display of his knowledge in *Engraved Gems of Classical Times* (1891), *Illuminated MSS of Classical and Mediaeval Times* (1892), and a catalogue of *The Lewis Collection of Gems* (1892). Middleton was also appointed a lecturer at the Royal Academy in London. In 1892 he was selected to fill the important post of art director of the South Kensington Museum, a department then sadly in need of reform and reorganization. Several reforms of great importance were at once initiated and carried out by Middleton at South Kensington. In December 1892 he married Bella, second daughter of William J. Stillman, American correspondent of *The Times* at Rome. They had one child.

The strain of difficult and uncongenial departmental work at South Kensington brought on threatenings of the disease from which he had suffered in his early youth, and for which he had frequently to resort to opiates. An accidental overdose of morphia cut short his life at the Residences, South Kensington Museum, on 10 June 1896. His body was cremated at Woking, and the remains interred at Brookwood cemetery.

L. H. CUST, rev. RICHARD SMAIL

Sources Venn, *Alum. Cant.* · Boase, *Mod. Eng. biog.*
Archives BL, notes and drawings for his *Remains of Ancient Rome*, Add. MSS 35032–35037 · S. Antiquaries, Lond., notebooks and papers · V&A · V&A NAL, working notes | BL, letters to J. T. Micklethwaite, Add. MSS 37504–37508
Wealth at death £18,372 4s. 11d.: probate, 12 Aug 1896, CGPLA Eng. & Wales

Middleton, Joshua (1647–1721), Quaker minister, was born at Darlington, co. Durham, the son of John (or Joshua) Middleton and his wife, Elizabeth. His family were the Middletons of Silksworth, co. Durham, a younger branch of the Middletons of Belsay Castle, Northumberland. Gilbert Middleton, mayor of Newcastle upon Tyne in 1530, was a direct ancestor.

Middleton's parents were strict presbyterians who brought him up with much care in their faith. Despite this, in early adulthood he joined the Society of Friends, who had attracted many families of importance in the northern counties at that time. Shortly after joining the society Middleton became a minister and travelled in many parts of England and Scotland, entertaining Thomas Story and many other travelling Friends at his home. He lived first at Raby, near Staindrop, co. Durham, and afterwards at Newcastle.

Middleton married Dorothy (d. 1688), daughter of Timothy and Katherine Draper of Newcastle, on 18 February 1673. She died fifteen years later, on 27 June 1688. His second marriage, on 9 September 1697, was to Jane (1655/6–1738), daughter of Gilbert Molleson of Aberdeen, and sister of Christian, wife of the Quaker apologist Robert Barclay.

A testimony from members of his quarterly meeting describes Middleton as 'a man of a meek and peaceable spirit, and much beloved among all sorts of people'. It goes on to say that he was always eager 'to compose differences' and was 'liberal to the poor, and a great promoter of such liberality'. He was praised for 'his care of the churches' and for his good example 'by his constant attendance of monthly, and quarterly meetings, though often under much weakness' (Bevan, 307). Middleton's only work was *A tender and compassionate call to prophane swearers and takers of the holy name of God in vain*, first published in 1708 and reprinted three times.

Middleton died in 1721 and was buried at Gateshead, co. Durham, on 25 January. His eldest son, Joshua, married Isabella, daughter of John Doubleday of Alnwick Abbey, Northumberland. A second son, John, was burnt to death at his lodgings in the Cross Keys inn, Gracechurch Street, London. A daughter, Elizabeth, married Peregrine Tyzack of Norwich. Through his youngest daughter, Hannah, Middleton became the ancestor of the Gurneys, Hoares, Frys, and a host of other Quaker families. On 21 July 1713 she married Joseph Gurney of Keswick Hall, Norfolk, brother of John *Gurney. Hannah Middleton Gurney was a woman of extraordinary beauty; a lady who may have been her appears in a portrait painted by Richard Houston, an engraving of which was published by Thomas Bakewell on 28 May 1748, entitled *The Fair Quaker*. This became extremely popular as a typical illustration of the costume of the Society of Friends.

CAROLINE L. LEACHMAN

Sources J. G. Bevan, *Piety promoted … the tenth part*, 2nd edn (1811), 306–10 · D. Gurney, ed., *The record of the house of Gournay*, 4 vols. (1848–58) · digest registers of births, marriages, and burials, RS Friends, Lond. · picture catalogue, RS Friends, Lond. · *A journal of the life of Thomas Story: containing an account of his remarkable convincement of, and embracing the principles of truth, as held by the people called Quakers*, ed. J. Wilson and J. Wilson (1747), 585, 596 · J. Smith, ed., *A descriptive catalogue of Friends' books*, 2 (1867), 175 · bond to execute will, 1721, Borth. Inst.

Middleton [*née* Cox], **Lucy Annie** (1894–1983), socialist propagandist and politician, was born at Albert Road, Keynsham, Somerset, on 9 May 1894, the third of four children of Sidney John Cox (1864–1949), a wire drawer, and his wife, Ada, *née* Britten, both of whom were of rural working-class origins. Lucy was educated at the local elementary and higher grade schools and then gained a scholarship to study at Colston Girls' School, Bristol. After training to be a teacher at Bristol University she worked for ten years in various schools in the west of England. She had developed an interest in politics from her father, a radical Liberal, and in 1916 joined the Independent Labour Party (ILP). In 1919 she became secretary of the Keynsham branch and attended annual conferences, speaking in 1924 on grants for divisional councils and on disarmament.

During the early 1920s Lucy Cox worked with Bristol socialists to develop a programme of municipal reforms, forming a close friendship with the conscientious objector and later MP Walter Ayles. She also held office in local Labour Party organizations in Somerset, and on their behalf travelled all over the west country, speaking to and organizing local groups. In 1924 she was appointed secretary of the No More War movement, a post she held for eight years. For three years she edited the *New World*, a journal devoted to international and peace issues. She later described these as the 'happiest and most rewarding years of my life' (*Labour Woman*, July 1971).

During the 1920s Lucy Cox became well known in socialist and peace circles, gaining a reputation as an effective platform speaker. She qualified as an advertising consultant and became a member of the Institute of International Affairs. Her growing expertise in international and colonial issues was recognized when she was invited to become a political adviser to Hindu minorities at the round-table conference on Indian constitutional reform held in 1932. The early 1930s marked a shift in her activities. She sought a career in parliament and stood unsuccessfully as a candidate for Paddington South in 1931 and for Pudsey and Otley in 1935. She also became a national propagandist for the Labour Party. During this period she met, and began a relationship with, James Smith (Jim) *Middleton (1878–1962), the secretary of the Labour Party. His second wife died in 1935, and the couple were married at the Caxton Hall, Westminster, on 1 May 1936 in a ceremony witnessed by Lucy's sister Eveline and by Walter Ayles.

Lucy and Jim Middleton spent the rest of their lives working for the Labour Party. Their marriage, based as it was on shared interests and political commitment, was extremely close and happy. Jim Middleton claimed that 'everything about us seems to chime. We have the same interests, we share and share in mind and thought, openly and frankly. There is never a jar or misunderstanding' (Bloomfield). There were no children from the marriage, but after initial difficulties Lucy developed a good relationship with her stepdaughter Margaret, Jim's daughter from his second marriage.

In the late 1930s Lucy was adopted as the Labour candidate for Plymouth Sutton (the seat held by Nancy Astor), and she won the seat in the Labour victory of 1945. Jim, who had retired in 1944, acted as her election agent and gave considerable support in helping to further her career. As an MP she took a particular interest in the development of peace and international understanding. During the Second World War she had attempted to maintain links with German emigrés, and in 1942 she established an international women's group to include German women. After 1945 she became a member of the executive committee of the British section of the Inter-

Parliamentary Union and travelled all over Europe to attend their conferences. In 1949 she presented a report to the conference on social services as they affected women and children, and in the same year she visited Germany twice. On the first occasion both Lucy and Jim were invited by socialist women's organizations to address Social Democrats in cities throughout the country and on the second Lucy went on her own, on behalf of the Foreign Office, to speak to German men and women engaged in social and political work in the western zone. Her other main interest was post-war reconstruction and she was appointed as chair of the Committee on War Damaged Areas.

Lucy Middleton lost her seat in the general election of 1951, which saw the return of a Conservative government. She contested the Sutton constituency on one further occasion, in 1955, but was again unsuccessful. Although this marked the end of her parliamentary career, she remained active in Labour politics and in public life. She travelled the country with her husband speaking to local Labour groups, and they both continued to attend Labour Party annual conferences. Between 1958 and 1968 Lucy was also a director and foundation chair of War on Want. As Jim's health began to deteriorate, however, Lucy took time out to nurse him, which she did devotedly until his death from heart disease on 18 November 1962. She then immersed herself in a variety of activities connected with the labour movement. At different times in her life she had engaged in journalism. During the 1940s, for instance, she had published and edited *Labour Candidate*, a journal of the Society of Labour Candidates. In the 1960s and 1970s she wrote frequently for *Labour Woman*, including articles on current political affairs such as 'Homes for our people' and 'Social security', book reviews, and biographical sketches of female pioneers. Both Lucy and Jim had long shared a keen interest in the history of the labour movement and from the 1960s onwards Lucy helped to found labour history groups, corresponded regularly with the editors of the *Dictionary of Labour Biography*, and from 1969 was vice-president of the Trade Union, Labour and Cooperative Democratic History Society. She also edited a collection of essays, *Women and the Labour Movement* (1977), a celebratory account of how women had contributed to the development of Labour politics.

In common with many women active in Labour politics in the 1930s and 1940s Lucy Middleton did not focus on women's rights issues but argued that improvements in women's lives could best be achieved through the social reform programme of the Labour Party, to which she showed unwavering loyalty. In her election literature, for instance, she claimed that she was fighting the Sutton division 'not as a woman, but as a Socialist' (*Daily Herald*, 25 March 1938). On the other hand she was also keen that women's political abilities should be recognized and encouraged. When she was asked to stand for Sutton she was pleased that she had received the invitation before she married because 'I felt it would be the last time I would be asked to do anything political in my own recognisance

... I was very glad they invited me when I was Lucy Cox' (*The News*, 7 Oct 1977).

Lucy Middleton remained active in Wimbledon Labour politics until almost the end of her life, despite suffering from cataracts. At various times she was chair and then vice-president of the Wimbledon divisional Labour Party, and she chaired the Merton women's council of the Labour Party. By October 1983, however, declining health forced her to enter Wandle Valley Hospital, Carshalton, where she died on 20 November 1983 from a cerebral thrombosis and Parkinson's disease.   JUNE HANNAM

Sources C. M. Bloomfield, 'James Smith Middleton', Ruskin College library, Oxford, Middleton papers · L. Cox, 'About myself' [election leaflet, 1935] · W. T., 'Lucy Middleton', 1935, Ruskin College library, Oxford, Middleton papers, Mid 117/5 · 'Lucy Middleton', Ruskin College library, Oxford, Middleton papers, Mid 117/Q5 [unsigned biography] · *Labour Woman* (July 1971) · E. H. T. Robinson, 'J. S. Middleton', Ruskin College library, Oxford, Middleton papers, Mid 36 · b. cert. · m. cert. · d. cert. · *The Labour who's who* (1927)

Archives Bodl. RH, corresp. on colonial issues · Ruskin College, Oxford, corresp. and papers

Likenesses photograph, 1931, Ruskin College library, Oxford, Middleton papers, election leaflet · photograph, in or before 1978, repro. in *The News* (21 July 1978)

Wealth at death £64,027: probate, 23 Feb 1984, *CGPLA Eng. & Wales*

Middleton, Marmaduke (d. 1593), bishop of St David's, was the second son of Marmaduke Middleton of Cardiganshire (descended from the Middletons of Middleton in Westmorland) and his wife, Isabella, daughter of John Staveley. He was educated at Oxford but did not graduate. He later held livings in Ireland at Coolock and Dunboyne, co. Dublin, and Killare, Meath.

On 11 April 1579 Middleton was nominated by the crown to the diocese of Waterford and Lismore, where English influence was strong. In Ireland, as later in Wales, he was strongly opposed to Catholic practices. He was soon in conflict with the citizens of Waterford. Feeling ran high and on 7 December Sir William Pelham, lord justice of Ireland, advised that he be translated to Ferns. The mayor of Waterford accused him of being a man of bad life, and of plundering the cathedral church, but fearing to press their charges in Dublin he and his fellow citizens did not substantiate their claims. Middleton corresponded regularly with Sir Francis Walsingham and had the support of Lord Grey and other leading officials. He was acquitted with great credit, and he still hoped to secure Ferns. In June 1580 he wrote to Walsingham describing conditions in Waterford: 'There is no difference between the clergy and the laity here, for they have joined together to prevent her Majesty's most godly proceedings' (Bagwell, 3.463). The diocese was impoverished; all the livings were in temporal hands. Grey and Archbishop Loftus commended his 'zeal and worthiness' to Walsingham and declared that 'he cometh to Her Majesty for succour' (*Irish Patent Rolls, 1574–85*, 317). He returned to England in September 1581.

Middleton was subsequently appointed to the see of St David's on 30 November 1582, thus relinquishing his Irish diocese. He was created DTh of Oxford on 27 April 1583, apparently in recognition of his services in Ireland, convocation allowing the degree in the hope that he might appoint more Oxford graduates in his diocese. In his primary visitation in 1583 Middleton noted 'there is used in most parts of my diocese an infinite number of popish ceremonies and other things, contrary to the laws of God and the Queen's Majesty's most godly proceedings'. His injunctions provided the essential corrections. By carrying them out, as he told his people:

> you shall not only obey God's commandments, observe her Highness' laws, and discharge your own duties, but shall greatly benefit the Commonweal, increase true religion, and maintain the country in all virtue and godliness, where heretofore it hath been for the most part trained up in erroneous opinions, idolatrous amity, and wicked superstition.   (Kennedy, 3.145)

The state of his cathedral prompted him to urge clerics to 'persuade their parishioners (being sick making their last wills and testaments) to give something to the repairing of the decayed Cathedral Church' (ibid., 141).

In Middleton's own person, however, virtue, godliness, and a genuine interest in his cathedral church were not often apparent. His predecessor, Richard Davies, had left the diocese impoverished and his episcopal residences in sad disrepair. Middleton's inadequate financial administration depleted still further his slender resources. He was critical of impropriators and clerics alike, 'for simony hath been so common a custom with them that they are neither afraid nor yet ashamed to make public bargains thereof' (Williams, 298). Yet he himself continued to use dubious methods to acquire preferment.

Middleton did not refute the accusation, given prominence by Martin Marprelate, that he was a bigamist with two wives, Elizabeth Gigge and Ales Prime. He was certainly guilty of simony. He sought to settle lands of the bishopric on his son, Richard. Conflict with leading laymen, notably Sir John Perrott, led to accusations that Middleton dismissed as 'odious and scandalous libels' (Williams, 330), but the complaints had a firm basis in fact. He came close to embezzlement in 1590–91 when he was charged with forging a will; and for this financial irregularity he was fined in the court of Star Chamber, deprived of office by the high commission and, it was said, formally divested of his episcopal robes and priestly vestments. He has been described as 'the worst of contemporary bishops and one of the few Anglican diocesans ever to be dismissed from his see for his misdeeds' (ibid., 297).

Middleton died on 1 November 1593 and was buried in St George's Chapel, Windsor. Richard *Middleton, archdeacon of Cardigan, may have been his son, though his arms did not match those of the bishop. A Christopher Middleton, parson of Llanarthne, Carmarthenshire, may have been another son or a nephew.   DAVID WALKER

Sources E. Yardley, *Menevia sacra*, ed. F. Green (1927), 100–03 · W. P. M. Kennedy, ed., *Elizabethan episcopal administration*, 3, Alcuin Club, Collections, 27 (1924), 139–52 · *The Marprelate tracts, 1588–1589*, ed. W. Pierce (1911), 215; and see 96 and 186 · *Calendar of the Irish patent rolls of James I* (before 1830), 1574–85 · Emden, *Oxf.*, 2.145 · B. Willis, *A survey of the cathedral church of St David's* (1717), 123 · CSP *dom.*, 1581–90 · G. Williams, *Wales and the Reformation* (1997) · R. Bagwell, *Ireland under the Tudors*, 3 (1890); repr. (1963), 463 · *DNB* · F. O. White, *Lives of the Elizabethan bishops* (1950)

Middleton, Nathaniel (1750–1807), East India Company servant, was one of the several children of the Revd Samuel Middleton (1703–1758), the incumbent at Whitmore, Staffordshire, from 1738 to 1758, and his wife, Mary (*fl.* 1715–1755). Two of his brothers, who were also covenanted company servants, were baptized in the parish of Trentham, Staffordshire (of which Whitmore was a chapelry), but his own early records are apparently not extant. The parish registers are defective, nothing is known of his education, and his petition to become a writer is not in the company archives. However, it can be assumed that he would have followed a course in merchant's accounts and bookkeeping, as required by the company.

Middleton was noted as being already in India when listed among forty-five writers destined for service in Bengal in a general letter from the court of directors to Fort William dated 7 December 1769. After acting as an assistant at Cossimbazar and Murshidabad he was chosen by Warren Hastings in 1773 as his representative at the court of the nawab wazir of Oudh, Shuja ud-Daula, at Lucknow. His appointment owed something to his eldest brother, Samuel, who had been in India since 1753 and was well regarded by Hastings. The integrity of Oudh was the cornerstone of Hastings's plans for the defence of Bengal and, as the man on the spot, Middleton was a major player in the negotiations concerning the use of British troops in Oudh's dispute with the Rohillas. With the arrival in Calcutta of General John Clavering, Colonel George Monson, and Philip Francis on 19 October 1774 as members of the newly constituted Bengal supreme council, Hastings's policies towards Oudh and the Rohillas were overthrown. Within a week the new councillors had obliged him to recall Middleton from Lucknow and to put in his place John Bristow, Francis's nominee. Monson's death in September 1776 gave Hastings a casting vote in council, which he used in December to oust Bristow and reinstate Middleton, despite the strong disapproval of the East India Company directors. To indulge Sir Eyre Coote, who had come out to replace Clavering, Hastings appointed Charles Purling resident in October 1779. Pressure from Francis brought the restoration of Bristow after only a year, although his remit was restricted to political negotiations, Middleton being deputed to try to disentangle the wazir's disordered revenue affairs. However, he again assumed overall responsibility when Bristow was once more removed in May 1781.

On his death in 1775 Shuja ud-Daula had been succeeded by his ineffectual son Asaf ud-Daula. During 1777 Middleton persuaded the wazir to accept Hastings's plan to transfer the troops in his service to the company, a move which entailed the virtual occupation of his country. However, power did not reside in the wazir alone. A rival centre of power existed in the persons of the two begums, the widows of his father and grandfather, who felt threatened by the company's incremental encroachment on the wazir's sovereignty, especially in respect of their *jagirs*

Nathaniel Middleton (1750–1807), by Tilly Kettle, *c*.1784 [centre, with Nawab Asaf ud-Daula (seated) and his ministers Haidar Beg Khan and Hasan Reza Khan]

(grants of land from which the beneficiary derived income), which the wazir might have claimed for himself had he not specifically agreed not to do so. Moreover, interventions by both Middleton and Bristow had made the company party to these guarantees. In September 1781, anxious for the settlement of the wazir's debts to the company, Hastings concluded the treaty of Chunar, which withdrew all guarantees from *jagirs* in Oudh, thus opening the way for Asaf ud-Daula to recover the begums' *jagirs* and to use the proceeds to discharge his debts. But Asaf ud-Daula failed to act, and in early December Hastings instructed Middleton to order the wazir to resume the *jagirs* even though the begums had brought in troops to defend them. By the end of the month Hastings was exasperated by the absence of any material progress and by Middleton's apparent want of resolution. He ordered military action to suppress disturbances in the *jagirs* and at least encouraged, if he did not directly or indirectly demand, the seizure of treasure in the possession of Bahu Begam, the wazir's mother. It has been suggested, however, that Middleton's hesitancy was the caution of an experienced resident unconvinced that extreme measures would for practical if not moral reasons yield more treasure more quickly. Nevertheless, in January and February 1782 Middleton and a military force ferreted out from the palace at Fyzabad and from 'the most secret Recesses' (Torrington, 2.825) in houses nearby some 55 lakhs (£550,000). It was an unedifying operation in which 'some few Severities' (ibid., 2.824) were employed. The begum's two eunuchs were put in irons and the wazir's servants were allowed access 'to inflict corporal Punishment' (ibid., 2.878). They remained in confinement until

December, when they were released, leaving a small balance of the debt still unpaid. During May, Hastings decided to accept a donation of 10 lakhs which the wazir had offered earlier in the year. His loss of confidence in Middleton and his deputy, Richard Johnson, was signalled by the dispatch of his military secretary, Major William Palmer, as negotiator. Middleton felt slighted and contemplated resignation, but in July he informed John Macpherson that 'I shall most chearfully continue my station … as long as it may be Mr. Hastings's desire that I should do so' (BL OIOC, MS Eur. G9, p. 51). Hastings ordered his recall in September, blaming him for neglect and failure to carry out his duties. His replacement (yet again he was succeeded by Bristow) in fact pre-empted the receipt of an order to that effect from the directors dated 28 August 1782.

It is scarcely surprising that Middleton eventually forfeited Hastings's trust. Complaisant, but wanting in depth and agility of mind, he did not possess the ingenuity needed to handle the conflicts generated by a masterful and intransigent governor-general and an incompetent yet wily wazir. On the other hand, he displayed a real interest in Indian art and built up a large collection of Indian miniatures, Persian manuscripts, and natural history drawings by Indian artists. He married Anne Frances Morse (1758–1823) on 26 October 1780. They had ten children. He also had three natural children born in India.

Middleton resigned the service and returned to England in 1784, where he set up house in Wimpole Street, London. In 1788 he purchased Townhill, an estate near Southampton, to which he added part of Bitterne Manor, which he called Midanbury. In the proceedings to impeach Hastings, in which he was a principal witness, Middleton's 'total want of recollection respecting any fact or circumstances which he conceived could tend to the prejudice of his patron was so very marked and determined that he acquired the nickname "Memory Middleton"' (*Memoirs of William Hickey*, 3.155), although Edmund Burke observed that 'notwithstanding his extreme Caution, and his wonderful powers of evasion, he brings out something New at every examination' (Burke to Henry Dundas, 5 April 1787, *Correspondence*, 5.320–21). His allegiance had not been shaken by Hastings's charges regarding his conduct at Lucknow, and in 1795 he loaned his accuser £2000 in the aftermath of his trial.

In 1793, with the fortune that he had acquired in India, Middleton went into partnership with his deputy from Lucknow, Richard Johnson, Alexander Davison, a corrupt government contractor who eventually became the principal partner, Josiah Wedgwood, and two others to establish a banking house. It did not flourish. Lady Jerningham, whose son married Middleton's daughter Emily, wished that 'Mr. M. had been Satisfied with the million he was supposed to bring back from India, without engaging in a Paltry Banking House' (Castle, 1.243). Middleton's eldest son later wrote that between 1803 and 1807 his father had put £47,900 into the bank and that after his death the administrator of his will had put in a further £61,000 (Middleton, *Letter-Books*, 1.149).

Middleton died of 'a cold which fixed on his lungs' (Farington, *Diary*, 14.5089–90) on 7 November 1807 at 30 St James's Square, London, where he had lived since 1804. His remains were deposited in the family vault at St Mary's Church, Battersea, on 14 November 1807. His will was not discovered until nine years after his death, by which time the bank was in such serious financial straits that Thomas Coutts & Co. were called in to save it from collapse.   T. H. BOWYER

Sources P. J. Marshall, *The impeachment of Warren Hastings* (1965) · K. Feiling, *Warren Hastings* (1954) · F. W. Torrington, ed., *Trial of Warren Hastings: minutes of the evidence*, 10 vols. (Dobb's Ferry, NY, 1974) · N. Middleton's correspondence, 1782–3, BL OIOC, MS Eur. G9 · R. B. Barnett, *North India between empires: Awadh, the Mughals and the British, 1720–1801* (1980) · G. F. Osborn, ed., 'Index to the letterbooks of Hastings Nathaniel Middleton, 26 Aug 1816–20 July 1821', 1978, City Westm. AC, WBA 796 · H. N. Middleton, letter-books, 1782–1821, City Westm. AC · Farington, *Diary*, vol. 14 · S. Weitzman, *Warren Hastings and Philip Francis* (1929) · *The correspondence of Edmund Burke*, 5, ed. H. Furber and P. J. Marshall (1965) · *GM*, 1st ser., 77 (1807), 1084 · *Memoirs of William Hickey*, ed. A. Spencer, 3 (1923) · M. Archer, *India and British portraiture, 1770–1825* (1979) · E. Castle, ed., *The Jerningham letters, 1780–1843*, 2 vols. (1896)
Archives BL OIOC, home misc. series, corresp. · BL OIOC, corresp., MS Eur. G9 | BL, corresp. with Warren Hastings, Add. MSS 29132–29194 · BL, Impey corresp., Add. MSS 16259–16264
Likenesses T. Kettle, oils, *c*.1773; Hartnolle Eyres, London, in 1977 · T. Kettle, group portrait, oils, *c*.1784, priv. coll. [*see illus.*]
Wealth at death over £61,000: Middleton, 'Letter-books', vol. 1 p. 149

Middleton, Patrick (1662–1736), Scottish Episcopal clergyman and Jacobite sympathizer, details of whose parents and upbringing are unknown, matriculated at St Leonard's College in 1676 and graduated MA from the University of St Andrews on 24 July 1680. He received a testimonial for licence on 7 August 1684 and became minister of Leslie in the presbytery of Kirkcaldy soon afterwards. On 13 April 1689 the convention of estates published a proclamation against offering any recognition to James VII and insisted on public prayers for William and Mary. Like many other ministers Middleton defied these injunctions and was cited for disobedience to the law. As a result he was deprived of his benefice by the Scottish privy council on 22 August 1689. Despite this penalty Middleton was unabashed in his open Jacobitism and continued to hold services without prayers for the new joint sovereigns. In December 1692 the Scottish privy council finally lost patience and discharged him from exercising any part of the clerical function.

Middleton seems to have looked for other employment. In 1697 he is described as 'waiting on Lord Glamis' (University of St Andrews Archives, SS110.AO4.22); by 1702 he was acting as factor to Patrick, Lord Kinnaird, in Dundee, while continuing proudly to style himself by his pre-revolution title as 'minister of Leslie' (NA Scot., RD2/92). By 1712 he was back in Edinburgh as a colleague of Andrew Cant in the largest meeting-house in the city. As an unreconciled opponent of the Hanoverian succession he could not take advantage of the 1712 Scottish Toleration Act, though like other Edinburgh clergy he prayed for Queen Anne in 1713. The aftermath of the Jacobite rising of 1715 brought fresh prosecutions against Middleton, who in 1716 was holding services in the Skinner's Close meeting-house, Edinburgh, when he was fined £20 for not praying for the king. On 19 June 1717 he was convicted a second time of that offence and for preaching to Episcopalian congregations without authorization by a protestant bishop as the 1712 act stipulated. He was fined another £20 and forbidden to preach or exercise any part of his ministry.

Middleton, nevertheless, remained an important figure in Edinburgh nonjuring circles. Between 1720 and 1732 no fewer than forty-eight illegal marriages conducted by him came to the attention of South Leith kirk session. In 1722 he was assisting Bishop Andrew Cant at Carrubber's Close Chapel, Edinburgh. Both men were sympathetic to the usages party among the nonjurors, and Middleton was forced from his place about 1726 because of the congregation's support for the nomination of John Gillan, of the opposing non-usages party, to a bishopric. Chronically short of money Middleton was living about 1730–31 in the Holyrood Abbey enjoying the debtors' sanctuary within its bounds.

About this time he moved to Bristol to live with John Middleton, his son by his first marriage to Margaret Orme. He married, probably on 24 August 1731, his second wife, Margaret Forbes, *née* Crawford (*d.* 1750), widow of John Forbes of Knaperny. Middleton died in Bristol on 19 July 1736. Five years later his *Enquiry into the Inward Call to the Holy Ministry* was posthumously published at Cambridge, and a second edition appeared at Bristol in 1743. His son, John, became a well-known obstetric physician in Bristol, and his daughter married Dr George Cheyne.

NIGEL ASTON

Sources *Fasti Scot.*, new edn, 5.509 · E. W. M. Balfour-Melville, ed., *An account of the proceedings of the estates in Scotland, 1689–1690*, 1, Scottish History Society, 3rd ser., 46 (1954), 36 · *Reg. PCS*, 3rd ser., vol. 14 · J. P. Lawson, *History of the Scottish Episcopal church* (1843) · B. Lenman, 'The Scottish Episcopal clergy and the ideology of Jacobitism', *Ideology and conspiracy: aspects of Jacobitism, 1689–1759*, ed. E. Cruickshanks (1982), 36–48 · P. W. J. Riley, *King William and the Scottish politicians* (1979) · W. L. Mathieson, *Scotland and the union* (1905) · M. E. Ingram, *A Jacobite stronghold of the church: being the story of old St. Paul's, Edinburgh* (1907) · J. Holloway, *Old St. Paul's* (1989) · J. S. Marshall, ed., *Calendar of irregular marriages in the South Leith kirk session records, 1697–1818*, Scottish RS, 95 (1968), 18–35 · G. Lockhart, *The Lockhart papers*, 2 (1817) · R. Chambers, *Domestic annals of Scotland from the Reformation to the revolution*, 3 vols. (1858–61), vols. 2–3 · U. St Andr. L., SS110.AO4.22 · NA Scot., register of deeds, RD2/92, fol. 56; GD48/1070; CC8/5/4, 503–4
Archives NA Scot., register of deeds, RD2/92, fol. 56; GD48/1070; CC8/5/4, 503–4 · U. St Andr., archives, SS110.AO4.22
Wealth at death over £1960 owed to him: NA Scot., CC 8/8/114/1, vol. 114, pt 1

Middleton, Richard of [Richard de Mediavilla] (*d.* 1302/3), Franciscan friar, theologian, and philosopher, was born about the middle of the thirteenth century in either England or France. The issue of his country of origin has given rise to much discussion, and remains unresolved, but it is at least possible that he was a member of the Northumberland family of Menevill or Meynil, whose name was Latinized as Mediavilla. It is certain, however, that he studied at

Paris, where he formed part of the so-called neo-Augustinian movement, defending the philosophy and theology of Augustine against the inroads of Aristotelianism, during the years 1276–87. He probably studied under William of Ware and Matteo d'Acquasparta, usually viewed as principal figures in this movement. However, a number of his theses step outside the ordinary confines of this tradition flowing from Bonaventure, for he often sides with the Aristotelian movement as manifested in the works of Thomas Aquinas, especially when dealing with the nature of knowledge.

Middleton's *Commentary on Peter Lombard's 'Sentences'* was probably begun in 1281 and was completed in 1284, when he became regent master of the Franciscan school in Paris, a post he held until 1287. The chief characteristic of his *Commentary* is its sober assessment of many of the positions of Thomas Aquinas. However, the tone of his eighty *Quodlibet Questions*, produced during his regency, is much more critical and on many issues shows a strong anti-Thomist reaction. In this they have more in common with his disputed questions, which were argued after the condemnations of 1277 but before his *Sentences* commentary. The latter commentary has been edited along with his *Quodlibet Questions*. A small number of his disputed questions have also been edited, as have six of his sermons.

Middleton's link to the neo-Augustinian movement is seen especially in his treatment of the will, even though he does not entirely follow his teachers, Ware and Acquasparta. For Middleton the will is much more noble than the intellect, since it is much more noble to love God than to understand him. Understanding without the corresponding love separates man from God. However, the key to the will's nobility is its freedom. The intellect is forced by evidence when evidence is given; the will also is forced by its nature to seek the good, but it is free in choosing the means to its predetermined goal. Even if the intellect were prudent enough to show man the best means to his goal, he would not be forced to adopt them. 'For although the intellect, like a servant with a lamp, points out the way, the will, like the master, makes the decisions and can go in any direction it pleases' (Stegmüller, 722).

The superiority of the human will over the intellect further manifests itself in Middleton's conception of the nature of theology. Certainly, the study of the scriptures attempts to clarify human knowledge of both creator and creatures; principally, however, it aims to stimulate man's affections. Middleton believes that scripture prescribes laws, forbids, threatens, attracts man through promises, and shows him models of behaviour that he should follow or avoid. The study of scripture perfects the soul, moving it toward the good through fear and love. It is more of a practical science than a speculative endeavour. A theology that is speculative is one that models itself on the theology of the metaphysician or philosopher and tends to reduce Christian faith to reason.

The influence of Aquinas is more in evidence in Middleton's theory of knowledge. Middleton rejects the illumination theory of Bonaventure and his more loyal followers. Man's intellectual knowledge can be explained, he argues, by the abstraction performed by the agent intellect from the singulars experienced by the human senses. In short, human individuals know, and they know by means of their own intellectual efforts, not by some special divine illumination. Unlike those who endorse the illumination theory, Middleton contends that there is no direct knowledge of spiritual beings, including God. God is not the first thing known. He can be known only by starting with creatures and by reasoning about their origins or final end.

Middleton died in Rheims on 30 March 1302 or 1303.

S. F. Brown

Sources E. Hocedez, *Richard de Middleton: sa vie, ses oeuvres, sa doctrine* (Louvain and Paris, 1925) · D. E. Sharp, 'Richard of Middleton', *Franciscan philosophy at Oxford*, British Society of Franciscan Studies, 16 (1930), 211–76; repr. (1966) · F. -X. Putallaz, *Figure Francescane alla fine del XIII secolo* (1966), 76–7, 87–8 · R. Schönberger and B. Kible, *Repertorium edierter Texte des Mittelalters* (Berlin, 1994), nn. 17415–29 · E. Hocedez, 'Les *Quaestiones disputatae* de Richard de Middleton', *Recherches de Science Religieuse*, 6 (1916), 493–513 · W. Lampen, 'Richard de Mediavilla', *La France Franciscaine*, 13 (1930), 388–90 · R. Zavalloni, *Richard de Mediavilla et la controverse sur la pluralité des formes*, Philosophes Médiévaux, 2 (1951) · P. van Veldhuijsen, 'Richard of Middleton contra Thomas Aquinas on the question whether the created world could have been eternally produced by God', *The eternity of the world in the thought of Thomas Aquinas and his contemporaries*, ed. J. B. M. Wissink (1990) · M. G. Henninger, 'Hervaeus Natalis, b.1250/60; d. 1323, and Richard of Mediavilla, b.1245/49; d.1302/07', *Individuation in scholasticism: the later middle ages and the Counter-Reformation, 1150–1650*, ed. J. J. E. Gracia, 299–318 · F. A. Cunningham, 'Richard of Middleton, O. F. M. on *esse* and essence', *Franciscan Studies*, new ser., 30 (1970), 49–76 · Emden, *Oxf.*, 2.1253–5 · F. Stegmüller, ed., *Repertorium commentariorum in sententias Petri Lombardi*, 1 (Würzburg, 1947), 722

Middleton, Richard (*d.* 1641), Church of England clergyman, was perhaps the son of Marmaduke *Middleton (*d.* 1593), bishop of St David's. He graduated BA from Jesus College, Oxford, on 13 July 1586. He was probably presented to the vicarage of Llanarthne, Carmarthenshire, in 1588, and the following year was installed as prebend of Brecon, and as archdeacon of Cardigan, both in the diocese of St David's. Between 1617 and the institution in 1624 of his successor, John Roche, Middleton was also rector of Tenby, Pembrokeshire.

In 1614 Middleton was put forward by Robert Birkhead, a leading citizen of Leeds, as a candidate for the vicarage there, in succession to Robert Cooke and in opposition to the latter's brother Alexander Cooke, who was backed by most influential parishioners and by the archbishop of York, Toby Matthew. The issue was eventually resolved in the court of chancery, where the presiding judge, Sir Francis Bacon, ruled that Birkhead and his supporters held the advowson only in trust, and ordered the confirmation of Cooke. Birkhead had been confident, because his candidate had already been appointed chaplain to the young Prince Charles. Middleton's *The Carde and Compasse of Life* (1613) suggests that he had already been accepted as such, for it is a manual of advice to the young prince, and in its prefatory address he makes reference to Sir Robert and Lady Elizabeth Carey, in whose household Charles was educated.

In his preface to *The Heavenly Progresse* (1617), Middleton advised Prince Charles that 'Kings and potentates must not consider ... how great they are, but how good they are or should be, nor how potent, but how pious' (sig. A5), for:

> great princes and peers, nay such as are peerless here, must die; and though they differ from all others in their pomp, honours, pleasures, and greatness, in their apparel, meat, attendance, and all, shining like the stars; yet is their end like to the beggars at their gates.   (sig. B3r)

The prevalence of such religious sentiments among divines who surrounded the young Charles is well known. Middleton, at least, had a political standpoint to match, to judge from 'The institution and description of a good prince', Pliny's panegyric on the emperor Trajan, which appears at the end of the *Carde and Compasse*. This opens with a striking epigram: 'He is a good prince, under whom it is lawful (without danger) to inveigh against wicked princes'. Under the protective armour of fifteen centuries of classical authority, there shelter several injunctions highly topical in 1613: 'Let not a good prince permit himself to forbid that which the Senate commands to be done ... A good prince is not above the laws: but the laws are above a good prince'. And if the prince's exchequer should:

> invade or occupy what is not his own, it must be granted to take a course against it, by like right as against other citizens ... Those that are free, take it ill, if any of their fathers inheritance be drawn from them by the Exchequer, as a twentieth part: therefore that tribute, or such like extraordinaries imposed, must be remitted.   (Middleton, *Carde*, 223, 230–32)

In Middleton's *The Key of David* (1619) is an image engraved by R. Elstrack, in which the author appears as a middle-aged man, with a ruff and a long beard. It may be that he remained single for many years. In *Goodness the Blessed Man's Badge*, also issued in 1619, Middleton entreats Lady Olyffe Stapylton that 'this little piece of coin [be] laid up in your closet as acknowledgement of a greater debt'; 'long acquainted with as great a measure of goodness in you as I shall ever hope again to find in any', he hopes she will find a marriage partner, 'though the tooth of envy bite never so deep' (preface, sig. A4). Middleton himself did marry, but all that is known of his wife, Margaret, is that she was buried at Ecton on 20 June 1635 and that her husband's will, proved on 26 March 1642, mentions no children.

Middleton retained his post as archdeacon of Cardigan for forty years until 1629. In that year, on 5 March, by exchange with William Parker, who had held it since September 1619, he acquired the rectory of Ecton, Northamptonshire, said in 1641 to have been worth the very large sum of £240 per annum. In the year of his arrival, as recorded in the parish register, 'did our pastor Mr Middleton, his Majesty's chaplain ... appoint a monthly communion, and the overplussage of the charge thereof, that should be more than quarterly communions he was pleased to pay himself' (Longden, vol. 9, s.v. Middleton). In

1630 Middleton provided a new clock for the church. He died on 16 November 1641 and was buried the following day at Ecton.   STEPHEN WRIGHT

Sources Foster, *Alum. Oxon.* · H. I. Longden, *Northamptonshire and Rutland clergy from 1500*, ed. P. I. King and others, 16 vols. in 6, Northamptonshire RS (1938–52), vol. 9 · *Fasti Angl.* (Hardy), vol. 1 · R. Thoresby, *Vicaria Leodiensis, or, The history of the church of Leedes in Yorkshire* (1724) · R. Marchant, *The puritans and the church courts in the diocese of York, 1560–1642* (1960) · B. Howells, ed., *Early modern Pembrokeshire, 1536–1815* (1987), vol. 3 of *Pembrokeshire county history* · R. Middleton, *Carde and compasse of life* (1613) · R. Middleton, *Goodness the blessed man's badge* (1619)

Likenesses R. Elstrack, engraving, BM, NPG; repro. in R. Middleton, *Heavenly progress* (1617) · R. Elstrack, engraving, repro. in R. Middleton, *The key of David* (1619)

Middleton, Richard William Evelyn (1846–1905), political agent, was born in Putney, Surrey, on 16 February 1846, the younger son of Alexander Middleton (*d.* 1846), Admiralty clerk, and his wife, Elizabeth, daughter of Richard Neave, secretary to the Royal Hospital, Chelsea; they had two sons and one daughter. After a private education Middleton entered the navy in 1860 at the age of thirteen. In January 1873 he was promoted navigating lieutenant and his last service posting was in 1876. In 1877 he married Emily Florence, daughter of Colonel J. W. Rickards, which marked his virtual retirement from service, though he remained on the active list until 1882. In that year he was appointed honorary secretary of the Point House Club, Blackheath, one of the first of a new kind of Conservative political club, and in 1883 he became Conservative agent for the West Kent constituency. His model of the type of full-time professional party agent was the Middlesex agent Wollaston Pym, who set new standards of assiduity and expertise. So impressively did Middleton perform in coping with the cumulatively intricate effects of the Corrupt Practices Act of 1883, the third Reform Act of 1884, and the Redistribution Act of 1885, that, at the instance of the 'Kent gang' of party managers (Lord Abergavenny, Sir William Hart Dyke, and the chief whip, Aretas Akers-Douglas), he was in 1885 offered the post of principal agent and command of the party's 'out of doors' headquarters, Central Office, in succession to G. C. T. Bartley (1842–1910).

Bartley, like his predecessor J. E. Gorst, had seen the principal agentship as a step in a tory democrat political career, and Central Office as a fulcrum for levering the party in a generally conformable democratic direction. Middleton possessed the invaluable attribute of having no political ambitions. He was an organizational technician of high competence with healthily modest notions of what central party organization of itself could achieve in shaping the course of elections. He was well aware of the extent to which his reputation for success in his profession depended on the advantageous turn for Conservatism in the terms of political trade of his times. A shift towards Conservatism in many middle- and lower-middle-class and artisan constituencies had been observable since 1868 and by the 1880s, with the emphasis given to suburban representation by the Redistribution Act, had become the most telling psephological fact of British politics. The

Richard William Evelyn Middleton (1846–1905), by Elliott & Fry

complex registration arrangements left intact in 1884 by the third Reform Act helped Middleton and his team of constituency agents to perfect their expertise in keeping registers tight and polls low, which in turn reinforced Conservative advantage. Nor was Middleton unwilling candidly to concede benefits accruing from unpopular or controversial Liberal policies: he declared that he was 'grateful' when Gladstone adopted home rule for Ireland; grateful also when Gladstone endorsed the Newcastle programme in 1891; and 'deeply grateful' when the Liberals attacked the House of Lords and took up the local veto on liquor licences.

It is one thing to be offered advantages; it is quite another to have the wit to exploit them to optimum effect. It was Middleton's skill as an electioneering manager to optimize the prevailing benefits available to the Conservative Party in the epoch of unionism, empire, and what was widely deplored as the 'age of plutocracy'. Of businesslike habits, energetic yet tactful in his dealings with the constituencies, urbane in his relationship with both superiors and subordinates, he was well prepared by his naval background to navigate the shoals and shallows and currents of new and uncharted political seas. Accorded the courtesy rank of captain and the colloquial sobriquet of Skipper, he worked harmoniously in trio with Akers-Douglas and with Salisbury's principal private secretary, Schomberg McDonnell (1861–1915), through whom he enjoyed direct access to the 'Old Man'. Middleton took 'great satisfaction' from having Salisbury's confidence, and Salisbury is recorded as declaring, 'Douglas and Middleton have never put me wrong.'

At Central Office (then in St Stephen's Chambers, Westminster Bridge), cramped and 'squalid', with a 'surprisingly small' permanent staff, Middleton's managerial expertise reflected the emerging characteristics of the new age of 'mass' politics. Central Office eclipsed the whip's office as the hub of the Conservative machine. Salisbury's accolade on Middleton in 1896 as 'chief wire-puller of the party' was only half joking. In his comprehensive reorganization of the party's constituencies in

1886–7 Middleton erased the traditional demarcation between counties and boroughs. He dovetailed the National Union apparatus into his new decentralized regional system of divisional subagencies. He worked pertinaciously, on the other hand, to bring the Scottish and Irish organizations under his effective supervision. As honorary secretary of the union he kept a firm grip on it, arranging for his agents to be delegates *ex officio* and setting one of his ablest subordinates, A. E. Southall, to run it from offices on the floor above Central Office as a propaganda medium. Middleton was always wary of the Primrose League as tending to amateurish meddling; he was wary also of the Liberal Unionists, with whom he dealt with strict propriety, fearful of what he held to be the weakly over-generous dispositions of Salisbury and, particularly, Balfour. He took a great interest in London county council politics and represented Dulwich on the council in 1898–9. He shrewdly kept fences well mended with the police and the drink trade, and solicitously cultivated the 'new journalism' represented most famously by the Harmsworths and the *Daily Mail*. A criticism increasingly levelled at him within the party was his partiality for a type of Conservative candidate distinguished mainly by wealth and a ready 'generosity', who put himself entirely in the hands of his agent.

Above all Middleton was concerned to raise the status of his agents by encouraging full-time, professionally qualified men to replace the old breed of part-time electioneering attorneys. He was instrumental in founding in 1891 the Society of Conservative Agents, and began the provision of superannuation and other benefits. To the historians of the Conservative agents, Elton Halliley and Arthur Fawcett, Middleton's was ever the 'revered and honoured name'. In 1894 he launched the Association of Conservative Clubs.

The reputation of Middleton and Central Office—already raised by their success in the 1892 election in blocking Gladstone's chances of a majority without Irish support—was 'made' by the greater achievement in 1895 of gaining a small but telling overall Conservative majority within the Unionist coalition. Lord Londonderry hailed Middleton on behalf of the National Union as the 'brilliant agent', who had done 'more than anybody else to secure the great victory we have achieved'. Fears that financial exigency and his large family (five sons and two surviving daughters) might lead to Middleton's being lured away by business interests led to a subscription being raised in the party. On 19 March 1896, at the Constitutional Club, Salisbury presented Middleton with a cheque for £10,000 subscribed by over 4000 admirers in 'acknowledgement of eleven years, energetic and successful organizing as head agent of the Conservative party'.

With the unprecedented 'double' of Unionist triumph in the 'khaki' election of 1900, and with Conservatism's electoral ascendancy so manifest in the metropolitan–home counties–Lancashire axis, Middleton's reputation attained its ultimate lustre. That much was fragile in that ascendancy was soon to be exposed. It became clear also that Central Office's efficiency depended too much on

Middleton's force of character and personal assiduity; his principal agentship faithfully reflected the weaknesses as well as the strengths of the era of Salisburian Conservatism. Like Salisbury, however, Middleton did not survive to witness the catastrophe of 1906. His stockily energetic appearance had for long belied uncertain health. After a series of breakdowns he was obliged to retire in July 1903, and he died at 6 Grand Parade, Eastbourne, after a long illness, on 26 February 1905.   R. T. SHANNON

Sources A. C. Biscoe, *The earls of Middleton and the Middleton family* (1876) · WWW · P. Cohen, *Disraeli's child: a history of the conservative and unionist party organization*, 1964, Conservative Central Office Library
Archives CKS, Chilston MSS; out–letter book · Hatfield House, Hertfordshire, Salisbury MSS
Likenesses Elliott & Fry, photograph, NPG [*see illus.*] · Spy [L. Ward], lithograph, repro. in *VF* (18 April 1901), p. 806
Wealth at death £29,484 4s. 1d.: probate, 8 June 1905, *CGPLA Eng. & Wales*

Middleton, Thomas (*bap.* **1580**, *d.* **1627**), playwright, was baptized on 18 April 1580 in St Lawrence Jewry, London, the first son and oldest surviving child of William Middleton (*d.* 1586), gentleman and bricklayer, and Anne (*c.*1538–1602?), daughter of William Snow.

Early years and education Middleton's parents lived, and Thomas was probably born, in a house on the corner of Ironmonger Lane and Cateaton Street. William Middleton had moved to London as a young man; on 23 April 1568 his coat of arms was certified by the Garter king of arms, making his son Thomas 'a gentleman born'. William and Anne were married on 17 February 1574; their only other child to survive to adulthood was Avis, baptized on 3 August 1582. William was a fairly prosperous member of the Honourable Company of Tilers and Bricklayers.

When Thomas was about five or six his father died (20 January 1586). The net worth of his estate was valued at just over £335. On 7 November 1586 Anne married Thomas Harvey (1559?–1606?), a young but indigent gentleman grocer; Harvey had returned to England after 'one whole yeare & more in very miserable Case' as chief factor in Sir Walter Ralegh's abortive colony at Roanoke, having 'spent or lost whatsoever he embarked & shipped' (PRO C516/48, Chancery 2 Eliz. S16/48). Less than two weeks after their wedding, husband and wife began fighting over the trust Anne had created to protect her children's inheritance. So began fifteen years of lawsuits. Harvey spent years at a time abroad, months at a time in debtors' prison. The struggle for conjugal mastery rippled outwards, as neighbours, friends, tenants, and relatives joined the tug-of-war. Thomas Middleton is first named as a party to a lawsuit in 1597; as late as 1606 he was called as a witness by his sister and her second husband over her share of their father's estate, twenty years after the father's death. Middleton's astute satire of the legal profession, from the character Tangle in *The Phoenix* to 'the wilderness of law' in *A Game at Chess* (II.i), surely has its origin in this extensive early experience of a 'law-tossed' world, where 'what one court orders is by another crossed' (III.iii).

In April 1598 Middleton matriculated at Queen's College, Oxford. One of his fellow students there was Thomas Overbury; allusions to Overbury's murder and the resulting trials (1613–16) have been detected in several Middleton plays. Middleton was still a student on 28 June 1600, but by February 1601 was 'in London daylie accompaning the players'. He left Oxford without a degree, and it is tempting to read autobiographically his account of a poor scholar who 'daily rose before the sun, talked and conversed with midnight, killing many a poor farthing-candle', reading Aristotle, but who—'unfruitfully led to the lickerish study of poetry, that sweet honey-poison that swells a supple scholar with unprofitable sweetness and delicious false conceits'—eventually became 'one of the Poor Knights of Poetry' (*Father Hubburd's Tales*, 1604, 1239–86). But Middleton had enlisted in that bedraggled regiment of poets even before he matriculated.

First writings Dedicated to the earl of Essex, the 4166 lines of *The Wisdom of Solomon Paraphrased* were published in spring 1597. Bullen called this inaugural work 'the most damnable piece of flatness' he had ever read (*Works*, ed. Bullen, 8.297). Such defects are hardly surprising; precocious poets are usually precocious in small doses. But isolated stanzas seldom satisfied Middleton. He later wrote an epitaph on Richard Burbage (1619) and an encomium on John Webster's 'masterpiece of tragedy' *The Duchess of Malfi* (1623), but he dedicated most of his energy to larger works.

Two more books were published while Middleton was still an Oxford student. *Microcynicon: Six Snarling Satyres* was publicly burnt on 4 June 1599, shortly after publication, as part of an ecclesiastical attack on satire. In that genre Middleton's immediate predecessors were Joseph Hall and John Marston, and both influenced this self-consciously little octavo by a young micro-cynic. But the self-deprecating character of its title signals a fundamentally different persona, which must reflect a real difference in its author's personality. Unlike Marston or Hall (or Ben Jonson and Thomas Dekker, later), Middleton did not parody the personal or literary habits of fellow writers. Instead he told dramatic stories about emblematic sinners (including himself).

In *The Ghost of Lucrece* (1600) Middleton again took up a major genre of the 1590s: the Ovidian female complaint, epitomized by Shakespeare's then-popular *Rape of Lucrece*. Like his other early poems it demonstrates Middleton's command of the rhetorical tropes emphasized by humanist educators, and the tension—engendered by the grammar-school curriculum—between Christian and pagan models of experience. Unlike them, it successfully creates character almost entirely through speech.

After leaving Oxford, Middleton switched from élite to popular genres. On 21 April 1601, having come of age, he collected the £25 reserved for him by the City of London since his father's death; with Harvey's final legal victory over his mother, nothing remained of his inheritance, and he needed to earn a living. By 3 August he had sold *The Penniless Parliament of Threadbare Poets*, made the subject of a parliamentary inquiry later that year. Unlike his earlier publications (which all died after one edition), this comic pamphlet was reprinted long and often. It initiated Middleton's fascination with almanacs, which also produced *Plato's Cap Cast at the Year 1604* and the greatest English mock-almanac, *The Owl's Almanac* (1618).

Pamphlets might make money, but plays made more. By 22 May 1602 Middleton was writing for Shakespeare's chief rivals, the Admiral's Men. With Dekker, Michael Drayton, Anthony Munday, and John Webster, he shared £8 for 'Caesar's Fall, or, Two Shapes'. That tragedy is lost, as is 'The Chester Tragedy'—apparently the first play Middleton wrote single-handed, for which he received £7 (3 October–9 November). On 14 December he pocketed 5s. for a new prologue and epilogue for a court revival of Robert Greene's *Friar Bacon and Friar Bungay*. The young Middleton obviously had absorbed Greene's work: *The Ghost of Lucrece* borrows material from *Ciceronis amor*, and *The Black Book* takes its title and some of its underworld subject matter from Greene's cony-catching pamphlets.

Middleton's first plays, like his first poems, belong to genres developed by others, and draw upon classical sources or recent English writers. His work shows no familiarity with modern European literature until *A Mad World, my Masters* of 1605, which recasts Pietro Aretino's pornographic classic *Gli ragionamenti* for its hilarious sick-room scene; thereafter, his reading became increasingly cosmopolitan (including Cervantes, Machiavelli, Giambattista della Porta, Cinzio, Bandello, and others not available in English).

By 1602 Middleton had established his credentials as a commercial playwright, working alone or with others. He collaborated repeatedly with the same writers throughout his career; all were committed protestants. Middleton was brought up in a parish dedicated to the reformed religion, and his own Calvinism is evident throughout his career, from *Wisdom of Solomon* to *A Game at Chess*. Indeed, Margot Heinemann characterized Middleton as a 'Puritan' dramatist (*Puritanism and Theatre*, 1980). But none of his closest associates was a presbyterian or separatist, and Middleton often satirized puritans. Calvinism was compatible with a life in the theatre; puritanism was not. But with the rise of Arminianism under James I, the Calvinism dominant in the English church in 1580 or even 1609 was forced on to the defensive. In the 1620s Middleton's religious politics became increasingly oppositional, not because he had changed but because the national church and royal family were moving away from Calvinist positions.

By collaborating with Dekker in 1602 Middleton at the outset of his career alienated, accidentally or deliberately, Jonson. Jonson and Dekker had caricatured each other in *Poetaster* and *Satiromastix* (late 1601), the central exchange of fire in the so-called 'War of the Theatres'; that dispute was both personal and aesthetic—and perhaps also religious, since Jonson was a professed Catholic at the time. Given Middleton's long and fruitful association with Dekker, Jonson's persistent hostility is hardly surprising: 'a base fellow', he called Middleton in 1619 (*Conversations with Drummond*), and in 1626 maliciously imagined that 'the

poore English-play' *A Game at Chess* was being used for toilet paper (*The Staple of News*, III.ii). Jonson's friend Chapman went out of his way to disparage Middleton as 'a poore Chronicler of a Lord Mayor's naked *Truth* … Whose Raptures are in every Pageant seen' (*The Odyssey*, 1614, dedication). The specific irritant, in each case, was Middleton's popular success, in bitter contrast to the public's indifference towards Jonson and Chapman. Middleton turned the other cheek.

Marriage and maturity Middleton's friend Dekker described 1603 as 'the wonderful year', and it was certainly so for Middleton. The accession of James I created the political and cultural climate in which he wrote all his mature work. Most immediately, it led to his commission to write the speech delivered at one of the seven arches of triumph, part of the City of London's 'magnificent entertainment', officially welcoming the new monarch.

The change of reign also inspired Middleton's first surviving play, *The Phoenix*, successful enough to be 'presented before his Majesty' in the new court's first winter theatrical season. Middleton's episodic panorama belongs to a group of disguised duke plays (including Marston's *The Fawn* and Shakespeare's *Measure for Measure*) written for rival companies in 1603–4, which adopt the conventions of the new Italian genre of tragicomedy to comment on English social and political life at a moment of profound but uncertain transition. Middleton's mercenary Captain, who matter-of-factly sells his wife to finance another voyage, has often been taken as a portrait of his stepfather, the would-be pirate-colonist.

The union of England and Scotland under one king coincided, for Middleton, with a more personal union. He married, c.1603, the London-born Magdalen (Mary) Marbeck (1575–1628), granddaughter of the famous protestant musician John *Marbeck and niece of the chief physician to Elizabeth I, Roger Marbeck. She was the daughter and coheir of Edward Marbeck (d. 1581), one of the six clerks in the court of chancery. Middleton presumably met her through her less distinguished brother, the minor actor Thomas Marbeck (b. 1577), who like Middleton was working for the Admiral's Men in 1602. The couple's only child, Edward, born between November 1603 and November 1604, lived until 1649. From 1608 until their deaths, they lived in Newington Butts, Surrey, a suburban village not far from the theatres in Southwark, and they may have lived there from the beginning of their marriage. A major outbreak of plague in London in 1603 certainly supplied incentives for leaving the capital; Middleton's sister's first husband (Allen Waterer) and two of her children were among the victims.

Dekker considered 1603 'wonderful', despite the bubonic epidemic, because he survived it. So did Middleton. But although the plague did not kill them, it did imperil their livelihood. In spring 1603, hoping to limit the contagion, municipal authorities closed the theatres, which apparently did not reopen until April 1604. Unable to sell their work to theatres, Middleton and Dekker sold it to publishers. Together they vigorously memorialized the effects of the 1603 plague on Londoners in Dekker's *News from Gravesend* (which contains *c.*100 lines by Middleton) and Middleton's *The Meeting of Gallants at an Ordinary* (which contains *c.*100 lines by Dekker). Middleton also published in spring 1604 two literary pamphlets, entirely his own. *Father Hubburd's Tales* uses fable to portray the oppression of the weak and poor; it combines poetry with prose, satire with compassion, literary criticism with social and economic awareness. *The Black Book* is a sequel to Thomas Nashe's *Pierce Penniless* (1592), in which Lucifer rises in person to answer Pierce's (Nashe's) supplication to the devil. 'It is the best of the imitations of Nashe's grotesque manner', as one modern critic has written, but Middleton's more disciplined intelligence supplies 'a clearer narrative and dramatic framework than Nashe' (N. Rhodes, *Elizabethan Grotesque*, 1980, 57–8). He does so in part by describing Nashe's (Pierce's) down-and-out life. The earlier pamphlet laments Nashe's death: 'Thy name they bury, having buried thee; Drones eat thy honey: thou wert the true bee. Peace keep thy soul!' (*Hubburd*, 278–80). Since Nashe lived until 1601, Middleton almost certainly knew him personally.

But Middleton's compassion and admiration for the older writer was not blind: even Nashe is accused of 'bitterness' and 'railing', his dispute with Harvey as wastefully vicious as Jonson's clash with Dekker. Middleton did not idealize his own profession. His dramatic portraits of writers—George Pyeboard in *The Puritan*, Lapet in *The Nice Valour*, the Fat Bishop in *A Game at Chess*—are theatrically appealing and vivacious, but none is innocent or objective. Writers, like other mortals, are sinful and implicated; writing is an inky 'black art' (*Hubburd*, 530).

The Black Book was entered for publication on 22 March 1604; earlier that month, Dekker and Middleton were advanced £5 for 'their play called the patient man and the honest whore' (*Henslowe's Diary*). The result was popular enough to be published within months of its première, to inspire a sequel (apparently by Dekker alone), and to remain in print and on stage for thirty years. Middleton's hand is most apparent in the scenes involving Candido, the paradoxically and comically original 'patient man', who equates true masculinity with imperturbable nonviolence.

Honest Whore was performed by Prince Henry's Men, playing outdoors at the Fortune Theatre; *The Phoenix* was performed by an all-boy company playing indoors at St Paul's, to a smaller audience paying higher prices for admission. From 1603 to 1606 Middleton wrote for Paul's Boys five brilliant comedies; unlike Jonson, he clearly preferred the acting of Paul's Boys to the more aggressive 'bitternesse, and liberall invectives' of the rival children's company at the Blackfriars (T. Heywood, *Apology for Actors*, 1612, sig. G3v). But he was never limited to one company or one genre. While writing for Paul's Boys he sold a comedy to Prince Henry's Men, a tragedy to the Blackfriars Boys ('The Viper and her Brood', 7 May 1606, now lost), and three tragedies to the King's Men. Middleton always remained a free agent, working for at least seven acting companies; his plays exploited the varied artistic opportunities offered by different casts, theatres, and audiences.

Michaelmas Term (1604), the first play Middleton set in contemporary London, was—if not the first—among the earliest English plays explicitly and systematically to represent the present to itself. The result is what Swinburne called 'an excellent Hogarthian comedy' (Steen, 165), or what Theodore Leinwand characterizes as 'profound comic urban sociology' (*Collected Works*, ed. Taylor). Its legal title acknowledges the importance, especially in the more élite theatres, of spectators from the inns of court (always an important constituency for Middleton's work).

A Trick to Catch the Old One (1605) has been the most generally admired of Middleton's early comedies; performed at St Paul's, the Blackfriars, and at court, it was later plagiarized by Lording Barry, Phillip Massinger, and Aphra Behn. Combining figures from Roman comedy with the prodigal son of morality plays and English literature's first accurate portrayal of a terminal alcoholic, it dramatizes the pursuit of credit, financial and sexual; its clever courtesan, Jane, uses her status as a seemingly wealthy widow and her precise knowledge of the law to outmanoeuvre a greedy suitor, in ways that surely owe something to Middleton's mother. *Trick* shares with *A Mad World, my Masters* (1605) a young male protagonist, like Middleton himself, whose father is dead, and whose paper status as a gentleman clashes with his actual lack of cash. In *Trick*, a rich uncle (Pecunius Lucre) refuses to support the youth's feckless lifestyle; Middleton's well-heeled and well-connected uncle Roger Marbeck died in 1605, bequeathing 'his neece Myddletoune' (Thomas's wife) a mere £5 (PRO, PROB 11/106/62).

In that same summer, news pamphlets describing Walter Calverley's murder of two of his children inspired Middleton to write *A Yorkshire Tragedy*. Like Calverley in 1605, Middleton's stepfather in 1595 had allegedly attempted to murder his wife (Middleton's mother), so the playwright had firsthand experience of conjugal violence. The King's Men performed his ten relentless scenes as 'One of the Four Plays in One'. Middleton's brutal domestic tragedy was thus originally only one act of a four-act anthology or variety show, and the subject, genre, and authorship of the other parts remain unknown; but Middleton's portrayal of the psychotic Husband, maddened by the disparity between his status and his income, seems to have caught Shakespeare's attention. Probably immediately afterwards, Middleton collaborated with the older playwright, writing about a third of *Timon of Athens*, including the bitterly comic central sequence where Timon's creditors turn their backs on him. Usually the most successful scenes of the play in performance, these apply classical tragedy techniques and materials developed in Middleton's recent city comedies. Timon lives in an almost entirely male world, like that of *Michaelmas Term*, where intense homosocial and homoerotic relationships dwarf marriages or families. But the relationship between Shakespeare and Middleton did not last beyond one play.

Having written parts of two tragedies for the King's Men, Middleton was well positioned to sell them *The Revenger's Tragedy* (1606). The tragedy was his reply to *Hamlet*, not hesitant but hectic—'hurry, hurry, hurry!'—ironic and obscene, tragic and blackly comic. It is driven by one of the longest, most complex roles in the early modern repertory, that of Vindice (almost certainly played by Richard Burbage).

Meanwhile Middleton was still writing London comedies for boy actors. At St Paul's, *The Puritan Widow* (1606) targeted the mercenary hypocrisy (and gullibility) of separatists. This satire may have had a personal edge: the brother of Avis's first husband was Roger Waterer, active for at least twenty years in the radical Brownist sect, but also accused of having defrauded Avis in the first weeks of her widowhood. In a sermon preached at Paul's Cross on 14 February 1608, W. Crashaw denounced Middleton's play for giving 'hypocrites' the 'names of two churches of God', but also more generally for irreligiously bringing religion on stage—especially objectionable when performed by the cathedral's own choirboys. It may have been the company's last play. Certainly, Middleton's next comedy, *Your Five Gallants* (1607), was written for the Blackfriars company.

In the first scene of *Gallants*, a pawnbroker worries about plague-infected clothing. The authorities kept the theatres closed for all but eight of the thirty-six months from January 1608 to December 1610. Predictably, Middleton had financial problems: he was in custody for debt (£5) on 23 December 1608, sued for debt by another party early in 1609 (£16), and on 18 July 1609 still owed a Westminster innholder £7 9s. During these lean years Dekker again produced amusing pamphlets, but Middleton's two surprising publications were less entertaining; both had different dedications in different extant copies, a trick Middleton never tried elsewhere, and further evidence of financial strain. In *Sir Robert Sherley his Entertainment in Cracovia* (spring 1609), he translated and adapted a Latin text published in Poland, urging a European alliance with Persia against the Turks—the first evidence of Middleton's interest in European politics. Later in 1609 appeared *The Two Gates of Salvation*, reissued as *The Marriage of the Old and New Testament* (late 1620), then again as *God's Parliament House* (1627). An original exploration of biblical typology, this remarkable text deploys an apparently unique six-column polyphonic layout in the service of a Calvinist reading of scripture. In 1609 this was orthodox enough—Middleton cited Joseph Hall's passion sermon—but by 1627 the same text seemed allied with unprecedented parliamentary opposition.

From this pamphlet period only one play survives, *The Bloody Banquet* (1608–9), co-written with Dekker. A tragedy of adultery and cannibalism, popular enough to remain in the repertory for three decades, the play survives only in a posthumously adapted text. Dekker flunked tragedy, but Middleton's complex and sympathetic portrayal of the

Young Queen marks a fundamental shift from all his earlier male-dominated work.

Thirty-something Middleton's new interest in women characters explodes in three plays written in 1611. His finest collaboration with Dekker, *The Roaring Girl, or, Moll Cutpurse*, for the first time gave Middleton top billing. This proto-feminist classic put on the Fortune stage a sympathetic impersonation of a living woman, the determinedly independent cross-dressing Mary Frith (who also made a cameo appearance, perhaps becoming the first Englishwoman to perform on the commercial stage). *No Wit Help Like a Woman's* was premièred at the same theatre a few months later, and was apparently played at court on 29 December; James Shirley revived it in 1638 in Dublin, and in 1677 it was adapted (by Aphra Behn, Thomas Betterton, or both). On 31 October, G. Buc licensed, for the King's Men, an untitled tragedy, based on Cervantes. Buc misleadingly labelled it 'The Second Maiden's Tragedy'; *Collected Works* prefers *The Lady's* (or *Ladies'*) *Tragedy*; the complex tragic centrality of its women and its influence on Webster's *Duchess of Malfi* are not in doubt.

Either Middleton did nothing in 1612, or what he did is lost. But 1613 was a turning point in his career. *A Chaste Maid in Cheapside* is now generally regarded as his comic masterpiece. It was performed at the Swan in spring 1613 by Lady Elizabeth's amalgamated company, whose many boy actors enabled Middleton to put eleven speaking female characters on stage simultaneously. Later in 1613 *Wit at Several Weapons* marked Middleton's collaborative début with William Rowley, the fat and jolly leading comic actor of Prince Charles's Men (who merged with Lady Elizabeth's company at about this time).

The jubilantly oversexed London of these 1613 comedies contrasts remarkably with *The Triumphs of Truth*, Middleton's first lord mayor's pageant, performed that October for his wealthy namesake, Sir Thomas Middleton. With Dekker in prison for debt, Middleton beat out Munday for the commission, creating the most expensive and elaborate lord mayor's pageant ever produced (described by the Russian ambassador Alexis Ziuzin). This success in turn led to Middleton's commissions, that year, for the lost 'The Masque of Cupids' and a brief show celebrating completion of the New River project. Thus began Middleton's productive association with the City of London. It was followed by *Civitatis amor* (the City's celebration of the investiture of Prince Charles, 1616), and two more lord mayor's shows (1617, 1619).

After *The Triumphs of Truth* Middleton never wrote another London comedy on his own, though he did collaborate with Rowley on one more and with Webster on another. *More Dissemblers besides Women* (1614?) and *The Widow* (December 1615?) were his first comedies since *Honest Whore* (1604) to be set elsewhere; like his tragicomedy *The Witch* (mid-1615?), they return to Italy. This change of official residence may have been prompted in part by Middleton's new relationship with the governors of London, or by the fact that all three were written for the King's Men (who acted none of his city comedies), but—like all stylistic evolution—it probably had multiple causes. The city comedies for Paul's Boys were all written in Middleton's mid-twenties, with the brilliant surface virtuosity and drive of absolute youth, in exhilarated command of materials within the narrow circle of its own ego and experience. From that centre Middleton moved gradually outwards, first beyond his own sex, eventually beyond his own neighbourhood to the larger European world. He never lost his lewd, ironic, grounded, comic genius, but the later comedies and tragicomedies achieve a wider emotional range and a more complex orchestration of tones. *The Widow* in particular plays the entire keyboard, and was widely admired from the seventeenth to nineteenth centuries. In *The Roaring Girl* Middleton had compared 'the fashion of playmaking' to alterations in apparel: tastes change. After 1614 audiences rejected Jonson's obdurate city comedies; Middleton stopped writing them.

About this time, Middleton's sensitivity to the public pulse was acknowledged by the King's Men. He was apparently the only playwright trusted by Shakespeare's company to adapt Shakespeare's plays after his death. Perhaps in autumn 1616 he updated *Macbeth*, in part by adapting material from *The Witch*, acted earlier that year but perhaps suppressed (because of its allusions to the Overbury trials). In October 1621 he made alterations to *Measure for Measure*, changing the setting to Vienna, adding the song, and expanding Lucio's role.

Rowley and his company provided a theatrical alternative to the King's Men, and he proved a more flexible collaborator than Dekker. He moved with Middleton into tragicomedy, first with their hit *A Fair Quarrel* (1614–16?), which was performed at court. There Middleton's compelling dramatic exploration and critique of the machismo of duelling may have led to a commission to write *The Peacemaker* (1618). Published anonymously, licensed by James I, that pamphlet rapidly went through five editions. It echoes the king's enthusiasm for international peace and hostility to duelling, but links these into a more general argument for the reformation of manners, imagining a new man whose masculinity is defined by non-violence.

Middleton and Rowley—and Rowley's mentor, Thomas Heywood—next wrote *The Old Law* (1618–19), a tragicomedy of euthanasia later adapted by Trollope. It champions the common law over arbitrary prerogative. As one critic facetiously suggested in 1885, if 'Shakespeare was Bacon, we can only say that it is quite certain that Middleton was [Edward] Coke' (Steen, 149). Perhaps not coincidentally, Middleton's *Masque of Heroes* was performed at the Inner Temple early in 1619 (with Rowley playing Plumporridge). The legal community's increasing enthusiasm for Saxon precedents may explain Middleton's turn to fifth-century history for his last play of the decade. Performed by the King's Men, *Hengist, King of Kent* (1619–20?) is, in some scenes, a tragic history, which includes a unique and chilling episode of marital rape. But the play was better known in the seventeenth century as *The Mayor of Queenborough*, after the protagonist of its comic scenes. The confusion

over titles accurately reflects Middleton's challenge to genre.

Final decade Middleton next worked on a commission for both court and city. He and Rowley co-wrote *The World Tossed at Tennis* for Prince Charles's Men to perform at Denmark House for Prince Charles. But it transferred to the Swan, for the first time successfully bringing 'A Courtly Masque' into commercial playhouses for popular audiences. Middleton's relationship with Charles in *Tennis* reflected the domestic and foreign policy problems created by the outbreak of the Thirty Years' War; those issues profoundly affected his work in the 1620s, through the celebration of the White Knight in *A Game at Chess* to the disappointments of 1626–7.

While collaborating with Rowley for Charles, Middleton was composing for Mayor William Cokayne (whose inaugural pageant he had written and produced six months before) the first of his ten *Honourable Entertainments* (April 1620–April 1621). His appointment as the first salaried city chronologer (6 September 1620) transformed his status, and prompted much of his subsequent work: his lost manuscript 'Annals' (1620 or later), four more mayors' pageants, various occasional poems and entertainments, and his lost manuscript 'Farrago' (describing political events, 1625–7). What Jonson was for Jacobean court masques, Middleton was for Jacobean civic revelry: its dominant, and most inventive, practitioner.

Meanwhile, Middleton kept writing successful plays, alone and in collaboration. *Women Beware Women* probably belongs to 1621; 'Never came *Tragedy* off with more applause', the playwright Nathaniel Richard testified in 1657. In late 1621 or early 1622 Middleton rejoined Webster to produce *Anything for a Quiet Life* for the King's Men. By 7 May 1622 he and Rowley had finished *The Changeling*, performed by William Beeston's company at the Phoenix; its title does not signal genre, and although since the nineteenth century it has been recognized as a tragic masterpiece, in the seventeenth it was most often remembered for its comic scenes. *The Nice Valour* (September 1622?) contains the period's most popular theatrical song (the beautifully melancholy 'Hence all ye vain delights'); a prologue written for a posthumous revival explains that Middleton hated writing prologues 'to a Play well made', and claims that 'our Poet ever writ Language so good, mixt with such sprightly wit, He made the Theatre so soveraigne With his rare scenes'. For *The Spanish Gypsy* (9 July 1623), Middleton collaborated with Rowley, his old partner Dekker, and Dekker's new partner John Ford; performed at the Phoenix, and also at court (5 November, for Prince Charles), the play was so popular that it provoked contempt—or envy—for its 'Gipsie Iigges' and 'other Trumpery' (Steen, 39).

Middleton's greatest theatrical triumph was also his last. The King's Men performed *A Game at Chess* at the Globe for an unprecedented run of nine consecutive days (5–14 August 1624) before it was closed by the privy council after the Spanish ambassador complained. The biggest box-office success and most talked-about dramatic work of its era, Middleton's modern history play survives in more manuscripts than any other play, and was the first single play printed with engraved title-pages. It is *sui generis*: an allegorical representation of English history in the 1620s and of the origin of modern party politics, a work of astonishing originality in conception, executed with an unsurpassed verbal and theatrical command. Accounts of it were dispatched to Brussels, The Hague, Madrid, Florence, Rome, and Venice. Middleton went into hiding, pursued by a warrant; his son, Edward, was arrested and brought before the privy council; Middleton himself claimed, in a poem to King James, that he was imprisoned 'in the Fleet'. None of his extant plays can be convincingly dated after August 1624, and he was probably released on condition that he stopped writing for the stage.

Middleton's relationship with the City of London also deteriorated, perhaps because he was sick or depressed. Plague prevented a lord mayor's show in 1625. He and his usual partner Garrett Christmas were employed to prepare London's official coronation pageant, but what plague delayed was finally aborted by royal indisposition. In January 1626 the court of aldermen received complaints 'of abuses and badd workmanshipp in and about the contrivings and payntings of the pagents' (Report 40, fol. 84). On 1 February the common council resolved to end Middleton's annual salary (of £10) 'unless he give this Court satisfaction according as was intended he should do when the said pension was first granted him' (Report 41, fols. 216–219). On 25 May the earl of Pembroke ordered the lord mayor to 'remove the said Pageants' (*Remembrancia*, 6.86); in June the aldermen ruled that 'noe further moneys' be paid to Middleton and Christmas for the three coronation pageants (Report 40, fol. 256). The Drapers' Company commissioned Middleton and Christmas to produce the 1626 lord mayor's show, but on 31 December the two complained to the court of assistants that they had not been paid by the drapers, who replied that payment had been 'putt of[f] in regarde of the ill performance' of the pageant (Robertson and Gordon, 110); in the end they were paid, at an unspecified date, £25 (17 per cent) less than in 1623.

Middleton was writing until the end. His (lost) 'Farrago' included an account of 'Habeas Corpus 1627' (Oldys); the opening rounds of the historic five knights case began in late June 1627. On 4 July 1627 Middleton was buried in St Mary's churchyard, Newington. His impoverished widow survived him by only a year.

Personality and achievement Middleton and Shakespeare were the only writers of the English Renaissance who created plays that are still considered masterpieces in all four major dramatic genres: comedy, history, tragedy, and tragicomedy. Middleton wrote successful dramatic texts for more theatrical venues than any of his contemporaries. The first anthology of memorable passages from English drama (by John Cotgrave, 1655) quoted the Middleton canon more often than the works of any other

playwright. On and off the commercial stage, Middleton mastered more genres than any English writer of his time.

Hazlitt, who began the resurrection of Middleton's reputation, praised his scenes as 'an immediate transcript from life' (*Specimens*, 1808). What the cultural arbiters of Middleton's lifetime admired in Sidney or du Bartas was aristocratic artifice, consciously modelled upon the monumentality of texts more than a millennium old. Middleton learned to listen instead to the transience of the vernacular. But to call him a transcriber or—as T. S. Eliot did—'merely a great recorder' (*Selected Essays*, 1932) is to misrecognize art as artlessness. No English writer before Middleton had ever achieved such complex sustained transparency, such seemingly unconstructed representations of the shifting currents of speech.

This misunderstanding of his life's work originated in ignorance of his life. Eliot's massively influential essay of 1927 asserted that Middleton had 'no point of view', no 'peculiar personality'; 'He is merely the name which associates six or seven great plays.' The central facts of Middleton's life were established (by Mark Eccles) only four years later, in 1931; the chronology of his work did not begin to be understood until 1937. Middleton's seeming impersonality itself reflects a personality, a decision to reject the selfish rant of battling parents and battling poets. Aged about twenty, he called himself 'Thomas Medius & Gravis Tonus', punning on his surname (*Lucrece*, 69–70); *medius* means 'in the middle' but also 'middling, ordinary' and 'neutral, ambiguous'—and 'central', and 'the common good'. *Gravis* teeters, ambiguously, between 'impressive' and 'base'. He yokes opposites. 'Was ever such a contrariety seen?' (*Old Law*, II.i).

The engraved half-length frontispiece printed in 1657 almost certainly derives from one of the portrait miniatures fashionable in Middleton's lifetime, an object of intimacy and vanity, often encased in a jewelled setting. With a finely shaded face, shoulder-length curls, and a trim beard, the Calvinist Middleton—whom Caroline puritans 'seemd much to Adore' (Steen, 54)—looks sexier and more stylish than any authenticated likeness of any other early playwright. His dark gown could be legal or academic, classical or modish, masculine or effeminate, warm or swank. His left arm propped akimbo on his hip, he wears his crown of laurel as casually as one might a low-slung feathered hat.

Less egotistical than Jonson, Middleton did not collect his own 'Works'; unlike Shakespeare, he was not owned by a single company of actors, who could publish all his plays in posthumous folio. Consequently his work was not collected until 1840, and it took another century and a half of scholarship to define a reliable canon. He was first identified as the adapter of *Macbeth* in 1869 (by W. G. Clark and W. A. Wright), and his authorship of the anonymously published *Revenger's Tragedy* was not recognized until 1926 (by E. H. C. Oliphant), and not generally accepted until the 1980s. His sociable muse long made it difficult to separate him from his collaborators, or to differentiate 'Middleton' from 'Middleton's workshop'. His determined peacefulness left Jonson's hostility unanswered, his modesty let subsequent critics take literally his own self-deprecating remarks about his work. A better estimate is given by an anonymous epigram printed in 1640 (*Wits Recreations*, sig. B7v): 'Facetious *Middleton*, thy witty Muse Hath pleased all, that books or men peruse.'   GARY TAYLOR

Sources *The collected works of Thomas Middleton*, ed. G. Taylor [forthcoming] · M. Eccles, 'Thomas Middleton a Poett', *Studies in Philology*, 54 (1957), 516–36 · M. Eccles, 'Middleton's birth and education', *Review of English Studies* (1931), 431–41 · W. B. Bannerman, ed., *The visitations of the county of Surrey* (1899) · A. W. H. Clarke, ed., *The register of St Lawrence Jewry* (1940) · parish register, Newington, St Mary's, LMA, X92/60, 4 July 1627 [burial] · GL, MS 9168.13, fol. 248v · *The works of Thomas Middleton*, ed. A. H. Bullen, 8 vols. (1885–6) · *Henslowe's diary*, ed. R. A. Foakes and R. T. Rickert (1961) · W. Oldys, manuscript note, BL; in G. Langbaine, *An account of the English drammatick poets* (1691) · J. Robertson and D. J. Gordon, eds., 'A calendar of dramatic records in the books of the livery companies of London, 1485–1640', *Malone Society Collections*, 3 (1954) · S. Steen, *Ambrosia in an earthern vessel: three centuries of audience and reader response to the works of Thomas Middleton* (1992) · S. Schoenbaum, 'A new Middleton record', *Modern Language Review*, 55 (1960), 82–4
Likenesses line engraving, 1657, BM; repro. in Middleton, *Two new plays* (1657) [Folger] · C. Rolls, line engraving, pubd 1821 (after J. Thurston), NPG

Middleton, Thomas (*d.* 1672), naval official, whose origins are unknown, served in the army, perhaps first in the king's cause against the Scots in 1640, and then for parliament in the civil war. Possibly he was the captain of this name in Ballard's regiment of 1642 and eventually attained the rank of colonel. It is certain that by the 1650s he was a shipowner, trading and sometimes sailing to the Americas, where he acquired substantial property. In 1651 he was among purchasers of Shelter Island near New Haven. In December 1657, while resident at Stratford, Essex, he had a share in a Caribbean venture. He may have been the Thomas Middleton nominated a militia commissioner for Southwark in July 1659, and in February 1660 he was nominated a commissioner of the army and navy, and in March a militia commissioner for Essex. He may also have been the Thomas Middleton of Southwark who in December 1660 was bound in £300 surety for good behaviour. His colonial interests qualified him for appointment to the council for foreign plantations on 7 January 1661.

Middleton's nomination as navy commissioner at Portsmouth was made by 4 November 1664 and he had arrived at the yard by 17 November, though his patent was delayed (and he was hesitant to begin work) until 3 January 1665. His salary of £350 per annum was backdated to 10 November 1664. Sir William Coventry welcomed him as 'able and diligent' (*CSP dom.*, 1664–5, 76). Middleton was soon to find much at fault. He scoffed at captains who were prepared to sign whatever papers their officers presented to them, and at the Ordnance board for wasting his time with a scheme for wadding guns with tobacco. But chiefly he was exasperated by lack of funds. He had to buy stores with his own money, on one occasion pawning his plate to prevent

the fleet lying idle for lack of oil (he 'had rather drinke in a horneing cupp then that the kings shipps should stay heere'; Pepys, *Diary*, 8.143 n. 1). He lent the dockyard men 10s. each to keep them at work. When they eventually mutinied, in November 1665, he grabbed the ringleader's cudgel and thrashed him with it, put three others in the stocks, and had no further trouble. Despite his severity (he envisaged hanging deserters in every town along the Portsmouth Road) he was occasionally criticized for indulgence to boatswains and masters attendant. Astonishingly he gave his workforce two days' holiday on 3 June 1666 when the fleet was fighting the toughest battle of the century. Following that defeat, the yard officers were blamed by the generals. Middleton was himself at odds with the commander-in-chief at Portsmouth, about alleged delay in contacting Rupert when the fleet was divided. But overall his record was good, and on 5 October 1667, the day of Sir William Batten's death, he was recommended as his successor as surveyor of the navy ('a most honest and understanding man'; ibid., 8.462).

Middleton's patent was issued on 25 November and he took his seat at the Navy Board on 19 December. Pepys at first thought him a great improvement on Batten. Trouble arose a year later when Middleton accused Pepys's trusted clerk Will Hewer of bribery. Pepys came powerfully to his man's defence before the board on 18 December, whereupon Middleton collapsed 'calm as a lamb' (Pepys, *Diary*, 9.395), burning his letter of complaint. For a while Middleton was careful to read the smallest paper on his desk ('it may be a bill of sale of myself for ought I know'; *Samuel Pepys and the Second Dutch War*, 172). Pepys would still find fault with his bookkeeping, and a 'silly' proposal to make captains indent for all stores (Pepys, *Diary*, 9.460). But Middleton could also advise expertly on the relative durability of cordage in hot and cold climates, and his tales of Barbados, Venice, and elsewhere made him 'mighty good company' and 'droll upon the road' (ibid., 9.499, 501). On 19 September 1668 he responded to the duke of York's inquiry into naval reforms. His wife Elizabeth died on 10 February 1669; he subsequently married again. This second wife, also named Elizabeth, survived him. On 21 June 1672 he was transferred to the resident commissionership at Chatham, where he had spent much of his time as surveyor. He died between 5 and 16 December 1672, leaving estates in Barbados, Antigua, and New England. Trinity House, of which he was an elder brother, had a residuary interest. His son Benjamin was executor, and the overseers included Nehemiah Bourne, republican navy commissioner and a fellow New Englander. Middleton, whom Shaftesbury counted among his friends, was reckoned 'a known protestant zealot' (Jackson, 54–5). The austerity of his character was tempered by a waspish humour, mainly directed at 'silly commanders' who knew their minds 'much as a horse, when he hath oysters in his manger, knoweth how to eat them' (Pepys, *Diary*, 7.334; *CSP dom.*, 1666–7, 96).   C. S. KNIGHTON

Sources Pepys, *Diary*, 5.314; 7.333–4; 8.142–3, 275, 462, 575, 582; 9, 267, 388, 390–95, 444, 452, 460, 499, 500–01; 10.245 · *Samuel Pepys*

and the Second Dutch War: Pepys's navy white book and Brooke House papers, ed. R. Latham, Navy RS, 133 (1995), 157–8, 165, 172, 184–5, 194–6, 199, 264 [transcribed by W. Matthews and C. Knighton] · G. Jackson, *Naval commissioners … 1660–1760*, ed. G. F. Duckett (1889), 8–9, 54–5, 94 · J. M. Collinge, *Navy Board officials, 1660–1832* (1978), 122 · *CSP dom.*, 1656–7, 484; 1657–8, 243; 1660–61, 426; 1664–5, 76, 79–80, 98, 192, 195, 516; 1665–6, 32, 53, 427, 430; 1666–7, 96; 1667–8, 55; 1668–9, 195; 1672, 551 · *CSP col.*, 5.2, 14–15, 18, (nos. 3, 39, 40, 41, 52) · W. A. Shaw, ed., *Calendar of treasury books*, 3, PRO (1908), 1331 · W. R. Chaplin, 'Nehemiah Bourne', *Publications of the Colonial Society of Massachusetts*, 42 (1952–6), 28–155, esp. 138 · E. Peacock, ed., *The army lists of the roundheads and cavaliers*, 2nd edn (1874), 43, 69, 88 · J. R. Tanner, ed., *A descriptive catalogue of the naval manuscripts in the Pepysian Library at Magdalene College, Cambridge*, 1, Navy RS, 26 (1903), 13, 15–16, 118, 164; 4, Navy RS, 57 (1923), 287 · J. D. Davies, *Gentlemen and tarpaulins: the officers and men of the Restoration navy* (1991), 146 · Magd. Cam., Pepys Library, MS 2242, 90–91 · J. R. Powell and E. K. Timings, eds., *The Rupert and Monck letter book, 1666*, Navy RS, 112 (1969), 206 · J. H. Wilson, *The ordeal of Mr Pepys's clerk* (1972), 38 · will, PRO, PROB 11/340, sig. 152

Wealth at death plantations in Barbados, Antigua, and New England: will, PRO, PROB 11/340, sig. 152

Middleton, Thomas Fanshaw (1769–1822), bishop of Calcutta, only son of Thomas Middleton, rector of Kedleston, Derbyshire, was born at Kedleston on 26 January 1769. He entered the school at Christ's Hospital, London, on 21 April 1779, and became a 'Grecian' (top scholar). Among his peers were Samuel Taylor Coleridge and Charles Lamb, who describes him in *Christ's Hospital Five-and-Thirty Years Ago* as 'a scholar and a gentleman in his teens', whose manner at school was 'firm, but mild and unassuming'. Middleton was always grateful to Christ's Hospital, and shortly before his death he gave a donation of £400 and was elected a governor of the institution.

Middleton went on to Pembroke College, Cambridge, in 1788, and graduated BA in January 1792 as fourth in the list of senior optimes. He became MA in 1795, DD in 1808, was ordained deacon in March 1792 by Dr Pretyman, bishop of Lincoln, and became curate of Gainsborough, Lincolnshire. During this time he edited, and in great part wrote, a weekly periodical called the *Country Spectator*, which appeared from 9 October 1792 to 21 May 1793. This periodical—an echo of the work of Addison and Steele—attracted the attention of Dr John Pretyman, archdeacon of Lincoln and brother of Bishop Pretyman, and he made Middleton tutor to his sons, first at Lincoln and then at Norwich. In 1795 Middleton was presented by Dr Pretyman to the rectory of Tansor, Northamptonshire, and in 1802 to the consolidated rectory of Little and Castle Bytham, Lincolnshire. In 1797 he married Elizabeth, eldest daughter of John Maddison of Alvington; they had no children.

Middleton next began his work on the Greek article, being incited by a controversy on this subject, in which Granville Sharp, Wordsworth (master of Trinity), and Calvin Winstanley engaged between 1798 and 1805. His *Doctrine of the Greek article applied to the criticism and the illustration of the New Testament* appeared in 1808. It was praised in *Quarterly Review* (1809, 2.187–203) as a learned and useful work, and went through five editions. In 1809 Middleton

Thomas Fanshaw Middleton (1769–1822), by Henry Hoppner Meyer, pubd 1815 (after John Jackson)

obtained a prebendal stall at Lincoln, and in 1811 he exchanged his livings at Tansor and Bytham for the vicarage of St Pancras, London, and the rectory of Puttenham, Hertfordshire. In 1812 he became archdeacon of Huntingdon. On his removal to London in 1811 he undertook the editorship of the new series of the *British Critic* and took an active part in the proceedings of the Society for Promoting Christian Knowledge. He endeavoured, unsuccessfully, to raise funds for a new church in St Pancras parish.

The act of 1813 which renewed the charter of the East India Company erected their territories into one vast diocese, with a bishop (of Calcutta) and three archdeacons. The number of Anglican clergy in India was then very small. The bishopric, the salary of which was £5000, was offered to Middleton. He was consecrated at Lambeth Palace, London, on 8 May 1814, and reached Calcutta on 28 November 1814. There were some anxieties about Indian resistance to the appointment and he arrived without ceremony and was not granted an official residence. Although this fear proved groundless, Middleton's efforts to impose order and dignity on the Anglican church in India created tension between himself and the Church of Scotland minister (whose post had also been authorized in the 1813 charter renewal), the Church Missionary Society, and the Bible Society. It also brought him into conflict with officials of the East India Company, who resisted his attempts to control the movements and work of company chaplains. Middleton's reserved and haughty manner did little to assuage the situation. Much of the difficulty stemmed from the ambiguities of his letters patent which did not clarify his position *vis-à-vis* the company and the various groups of Christians working in India. The Anglican missionaries in India, who were not licensed by Middleton yet carried out most of their work among Europeans rather than the Indian population, were most affected by Middleton's determination to impose church order and by his view that Indians were not ready for the Bible. Middleton's frequently expressed view was that the 'fabric of idolatry' in India would never be shaken merely by the preaching of missionaries but that a general diffusion of knowledge and the arts was first necessary. This would pave the way for Christianity. He maintained that the first duty of the Anglican church was to bring the European inhabitants of India under its influence by setting high standards of moral and religious life. Thus, in 1815 he organized the Free School and the orphan school at Calcutta, and in May of the same year he formed a diocesan committee of the Society for Promoting Christian Knowledge, a society which had placed £1000 at his disposal for the furtherance of its views. On 18 December 1815 Middleton left Calcutta to make his primary visitation, a journey of about 5000 miles. He traversed southern India and visited Bombay, Goa, Ceylon, and the Syrian Christians at Cochin. The purpose of the visitation was to encourage and to bring order to his diocese, not to make converts.

On 15 December 1820 Middleton laid the foundation stone of Bishop's Mission College, on a site within 3 miles of Calcutta. The establishment of this college was his favourite scheme. The institution was to consist of a principal and professors, and of students who, it was hoped, would become missionaries and schoolmasters in India. On 19 April 1821 the bishop again visited Cochin to ascertain the condition of the Syrian church there, and in December he held his third visitation at Calcutta. He died there on 8 July 1822 of a fever, in the ninth year of his episcopate, and was survived by his wife. He was buried in Calcutta Cathedral.

Middleton bequeathed 500 volumes from his library to the principal, or the principal professor, of Bishop's College. The Society for the Propagation of the Gospel, to which he left £500, joined the Society for Promoting Christian Knowledge in subscribing for a monument to him in the nave of St Paul's Cathedral in London. This memorial—a marble group by J. G. Lough—shows Bishop Middleton blessing two Indian children kneeling before him. In accordance with Middleton's will all his writings in manuscript were destroyed, including a memoir on the Syrian church. While in India he had collected Syriac manuscripts and learnt Hindustani, but gave up the study of Greek. His *Sermons and Charges* were published, with a memoir, in 1824, by Archdeacon Bonney. Middleton was a fellow of the Royal Society from 1814, and a vice-president of the Asiatic Society from 1815.

Middleton was a stout man of handsome and vigorous appearance; his voice was clear and sonorous, and his preaching impressive. J. W. Kaye called him 'a cold and stately formalist' who had 'an overweening sense of the dignity of the episcopal office', though he admitted that the bishop was not actuated by personal vanity, and that

the externals of religion had been too much neglected in India before his arrival (Kaye, 312–14). As an organizer Middleton was cautious, able, and active. He was a devoted and conscientious bishop and laid the foundations on which his successors could build.

W. W. WROTH, *rev.* PENELOPE CARSON

Sources C. W. LeBas, *The life of the Rt. Rev. Thomas Fanshaw Middleton DD*, 2 vols. (1831) · Venn, *Alum. Cant.* · *The Christ's Hospital book*, revised edn (1958) · S. Neill, *A history of Christianity in India, 1707–1858* (1985) · H. Cnattingius, *Bishops and societies: a study of Anglican colonial and missionary expansion, 1698–1850* (1952) · M. E. Gibbs, *The Anglican church in India, 1600–1970* (1972) · J. W. Kaye, *Christianity in India* (1859), 312–14 · C. Lamb, 'On Christ's Hospital, and the character of the Christ's Hospital boys', *Christ's Hospital: recollections of Lamb, Coleridge, and Leigh Hunt*, ed. R. Brimley Johnson (1896), 30 · will, PRO, probate 11/1671, fol. 348
Archives BL OIOC | Bodl. Oxf., letters to William Wilberforce · Bodl. RH, Society for the Propagation of the Gospel Archives
Likenesses T. A. Dean, engraving, repro. in LeBas, *Life*, frontispiece · J. G. Lough, marble statue on monument, St Paul's Cathedral, London · H. H. Meyer, stipple (after J. Jackson), BM, NPG; repro. in *Contemporary portraits* (1815) [*see illus.*]
Wealth at death see will, 13 Jan. 1821, PRO probate 11/1671, fol. 348

Middleton [Myddylton], **William** (*d.* 1547), printer, of whose parentage nothing is known, succeeded to the printing house of Robert Redman at the sign of the George, next to the church of St Dunstan-in-the-West in Fleet Street, London, and continued Redman's business as a printer of law books.

The earliest issues from Middleton's press were Richard Whitforde's *Dyvers Holy Instrucyons and Teachynges Very Necessarye for the Helth of Mannes Soule*, and the *Perutilis tractatus* of John Perkins, a law book in Norman French, both printed in 1541. On 5 July that year he was made free of the Stationers' Company by redemption. About 1542 he printed in folio *The great boke of statutes conteynyng all the statutes made in the parlyamentes from the begynnynge of the fyrst yere of the raigne of kynge Edwarde the thyrde tyll the begynnyng of the xxxiiii yere of … kyng Henry the viii*, as far as the end of the twenty-first year of Henry VIII, the volume being completed with the acts of the subsequent sessions printed annually by the king's printer, Berthelet. Middleton printed altogether some thirty-eight works of law, medicine, and on miscellaneous subjects. Among these last was the well-known *Playe called the Foure PP: a Very Merry Interlude*, written by the buffoon John Heywood.

Middleton used two devices. The smaller consists of a shield bearing a rebus on his name, with supporters. The larger, of which there are three sizes, has the shield with the rebus hanging from a tree, and supported by two nondescript male and female figures, having at their feet a scroll, which, in the smallest of the three devices, bears the printer's name. Middleton died in London between 4 and 13 June 1547. His widow, Elizabeth, married the stationer William Powell, who carried on the business until at least 1566. Henry *Middleton (*d.* 1587) was probably his son.   R. E. GRAVES, *rev.* ANITA McCONNELL

Sources J. Ames, T. F. Dibdin, and W. Herbert, eds., *Typographical antiquities, or, The history of printing in England, Scotland and Ireland*, 4 vols. (1810–19), vol. 3, pp. 547–54 · C. H. Timperley, *Encyclopaedia of*

literary and typographical anecdote, 2nd edn (1842); repr. (1977), 297–8 · City of London RO, repertory 10, fol. 213*r* · will, PRO, PROB 11/31, sig. 39 · J. L. Chester and G. J. Armytage, eds., *Allegations for marriage licences issued by the bishop of London*, 2 vols., Harleian Society, 25–6 (1887)

Middleton, William (*d.* 1613), pamphleteer, was a native of Shropshire. He matriculated as a sizar of Queens' College, Cambridge, in October 1567, received the degree of BA in 1570–71, and was elected a fellow of his college on 28 June 1572. He may well have been a difficult person with whom to get along, however, and in 1574 the president and fellows denied him permission to proceed to the degree of MA at Cambridge, though no reason was given. As a result Middleton instead went to Oxford, and took the degree of MA there. Apparently some of his former colleagues at Cambridge wrote to friends at Oxford, attempting to discredit him. Once he had been granted the degree he returned to Cambridge, but the bishop of Chester, the president of Queens' College, and several fellows, refused to recognize the validity of the Oxford degree. In July 1575 Middleton was deprived of his fellowship for not having commenced MA within the period prescribed by the college statutes. Middleton appealed to William Cecil, Lord Burghley, the chancellor of the university; on Burghley's insistence, Middleton was restored to his fellowship but did not receive the seniority he also requested. He incorporated MA at Cambridge in 1576, and proceeded BTh in 1582.

In 1585 Middleton was involved in further controversy when he was called before the president of his college and admonished for causing contention between the president and the fellows. Middleton was warned to cease from such dealings in the future. He vacated his fellowship in or about 1590. For many years he held the rectory of Hardwick, Cambridgeshire, though it is not known when he received the position. He also married; his wife, Helen, would be his executor. At the end of Elizabeth's reign he was elected master of Corpus Christi College, Cambridge. When the previous master, John Jegon, had become bishop of Norwich, instead of seeing to the election of the candidate desired by John Whitgift, archbishop of Canterbury, Jegon had put his younger brother Thomas into the position. Elizabeth had removed Thomas Jegon, hence Middleton's appointment. The fellows of the college, however, were upset by the imposition of Middleton and wanted Jegon restored to the position. When James I became king in 1603 Middleton was removed and Thomas Jegon restored. Middleton petitioned the king, begging to be allowed to retain possession and asking for help with his recalcitrant fellows, but to no avail.

Middleton apparently wrote a number of tracts, but only one is extant, *Papisto mastix, or, The Protestants Religion Defended* (1606), a learned anti-Catholic pamphlet published soon after the Gunpowder Plot of 1605. He dedicated the work to Dr Humphrey Tendall, and to the fellows of Queens' College. Middleton described his work as 'A Briefe Answere to a Popish Dialogue between two Gentlemen: the one a Papist, the other a Protestant'. The

dialogue to which he referred apparently has not survived, but Middleton presented his work also as a dialogue. He died on 14 June 1613, and was buried in Hardwick churchyard, where a monument was erected to his memory. CAROLE LEVIN

Sources *CSP dom.*, 1603–10, p. 8 · Cooper, *Ath. Cantab.*, 2.446 · J. Heywood and T. Wright, eds., *Cambridge University transactions during the puritan controversies of the 16th and 17th centuries*, 1 (1854), 177–84 · W. Middleton, 'Papisto mastix', or, The protestants religion defended (1606) · P. Milward, *Religious controversies of the Jacobean age* (1978), 156 · W. G. Searle, *The history of the Queens' College of St Margaret and St Bernard in the University of Cambridge*, 2 vols., Cambridge Antiquarian RS, 9, 13 (1867–71), 324–31 · Wood, *Ath. Oxon.*, new edn, 1.649 · will, Cambs. AS, VC 23:245

Middleton [*née* Cumbers], **Yevonde Philone** [*known as* Madame Yevonde] (**1893–1975**), photographer, was born Yevonde Philone Cumbers on 5 January 1893 at The Cottage, St Julian's Road, Streatham Common, London, the daughter of Frederick Cumbers, a director of Johnstone and Cumbers, manufacturers of printing inks, and Ethel Westerton. In 1899 the family moved to Bromley in Kent. Educated with her sister Verena both at home and at a succession of day schools and boarding-schools, at fourteen Yevonde finally found a school which suited her: Lingholt, a progressive boarding-school at Hindhead in Surrey. Two years later the sisters were sent to a convent school in Verviers in Belgium; again unhappy, Yevonde instigated a move to Paris where she and Verena studied at the Sorbonne and lodged at a supervised boarding house for women students. At seventeen and 'finished', Yevonde returned to the family home in Bromley.

In 1910 while still a student on the continent, Yevonde joined the women's suffrage movement, and on her return to Britain she continued to promote female emancipation. In defiance of her genteel upbringing she decided to take up a profession and, after seeing an advertisement for a photographer's apprentice in *The Suffragette*, settled upon photography. She approached Lallie Charles, one of the leading portrait photographers of the day, and was accepted for three years' tuition at Charles's studio at 39A Curzon Street in London's Mayfair. Six months before completing her apprenticeship, and only ever having taken one photograph, Yevonde left Charles's employ and—in 1914, with a loan from her father—opened her own studio at 92 Victoria Street, London.

Madame Yevonde, as she called herself, began by imitating Lallie Charles but quickly developed her own signature style. She used dramatic lighting against a dark background and printed on sepia-toned platinotype paper to give a more modelled effect. In 1916 she temporarily gave up her studio to work as a land girl. After her return to photography, Yevonde's portraits of celebrities began to appear regularly in society magazines, such as *The Bystander*, and the new fashion magazines. Her reputation was such that in 1922 she was commissioned to take the official engagement portrait of Lord Louis Mountbatten and Edwina Ashley (now in the National Portrait Gallery).

In 1921 Yevonde moved into larger premises at 100 Victoria Street. In that same year she became the first woman

Yevonde Philone Middleton [Madame Yevonde] (1893–1975), self-portrait, 1940

to address the congress of the Professional Photographers' Association. She was given as her subject 'Photographic portraiture from a woman's point of view', and chose to discuss the work of women photographers past and present. Her claim that women made better portraitists than men caused a minor controversy when her lecture was published in the *British Journal of Photography* (29 April 1921). She later lectured on photography as a profession for women at the second annual conference of the Business and Professional Women's Federation held in Paris in 1936.

The 1920s saw Yevonde producing creative figure compositions in addition to her commercial portrait work. Examples appeared in the society and fashion journals, in *Photograms of the Year* for 1921 and 1923, and at leading photographic exhibitions. She was also making her name in the new field of advertising photography with her distinctive series of advertisements for Eno's Fruit Salts. It was in the 1930s, however, that she began to produce the photographs for which she is best remembered. In the early 1930s Yevonde began to work with Dr D. A. Spencer's Vivex colour process, building upon her earlier mastery in monochrome of costume, staging, and lighting effects to create intensely vibrant portraits and still lifes. In 1932 she mounted at the Albany Gallery in London a one-woman exhibition of her work, said to be the first in England to include colour portrait photographs. In 1933 she moved to a new studio at 28 Berkeley Square in Mayfair. There she exhibited her 'Goddesses and Others' photographs in

1935. The costumes worn by society women to a charity fancy-dress ball provided the starting point for this series of inventive and often surrealist tableaux, the props for which included a stuffed bull's head, rubber snakes, and a revolver. The sitters for these dramatically modern reinterpretations of classical female icons included Mrs Anthony Eden, the Hon. Mrs Bryan Guinness (Lady Diana Mosley), and the duchess of Wellington.

Yevonde was committed to colour photography at a time when it was not considered a serious medium of expression. She did, however, receive some contemporary recognition for her work in this field. A number of the images from the 'Goddesses' series were identified in *The Times* as 'among the best direct colour photographs we have seen' (11 July 1935), and two of Yevonde's photographs taken aboard the *Queen Mary* for *Fortune* magazine in 1936 were shown in the exhibition 'Photography 1839–1937' at the Museum of Modern Art in New York. In 1940 she was elected as a fellow of the Royal Photographic Society for her work in colour photography.

The end of the 1930s was significant for Yevonde not only because of the approaching war: her husband, the playwright and journalist Edgar Charles William Middleton (c.1895–1939), whom she married on 13 February 1920, died in April 1939. A year later the Vivex factory closed, bringing to an end her work in colour. In 1940 Yevonde published her frank and self-deprecating autobiography *In Camera*. She also produced one of her last works in colour: an allegorical self-portrait in which the photographer, distinctively dark-haired and snub-nosed, holds up a black and white negative (Yevonde Portrait Archive).

After her husband's death Yevonde moved from their London home at 3 Dr Johnson's Buildings in the Inner Temple to Dolphin Square in Pimlico, and then, to escape the bombing of London, to Farnham in Surrey. After the war she moved back to the capital, to 33 Bedford Gardens in Kensington, and in 1955 she moved her studio to 16A Trevor Street in Knightsbridge. Throughout the 1950s and 1960s, working in black and white, she continued to photograph leading artists, actors, and writers and to exhibit her work. In June 1973 the Royal Photographic Society mounted a one-woman exhibition celebrating Yevonde's sixty years as a portrait photographer. Two years later, on 22 December 1975, she died of breast cancer in St Stephen's Hospital, Fulham, in London. The main archive of her work is held at Compton, Hampshire, with smaller collections in the National Portrait Gallery and the Royal Photographic Society collection at the National Museum of Photography, Film and Television, Bradford.

JULIET HACKING

Sources R. Gibson and P. Roberts, *Madame Yevonde: colour, fantasy and myth* (1993) · Madame Yevonde, *In camera* (1940) · K. Salway, *Goddesses and others: Yevonde: a portrait* (1990) · Madame Yevonde, 'Photographic portraiture from a woman's point of view', *British Journal of Photography* (29 April 1936), 251–2 · b. cert. · m. cert.
Likenesses Madame Yevonde, self-portrait, photograph, 1925, National Museum of Photography, Film and Television, Bradford, Royal Photographic Society collection · Madame Yevonde, self-portrait, photograph, 1937, Yevonde Portrait Archive, Compton, Hampshire · Madame Yevonde, self-portrait, photograph, 1940,

Yevonde Portrait Archive, Compton, Hampshire [*see illus.*] · Madame Yevonde, self-portrait, photograph, Yevonde Portrait Archive, Compton, Hampshire

Midgley, Henry Cassidy [Harry] (1892–1957), politician, was born on 8 September 1892 at 59 Seaview Street, Belfast, the third of the five children of Alexander Midgley (1860–1899), labourer, and his wife, Elizabeth Cassidy (*c*.1862–1929). Harry Midgley's parents were both natives of Lurgan, co. Armagh. They moved to Belfast in 1890 after some years spent in Australia, and Alexander Midgley found work in the Harland and Wolff shipyard. The family home was in working-class north Belfast, an area with which Harry Midgley was to be identified politically. Alexander Midgley underwent a religious conversion late in life after attending a mission meeting at Duncairn Gardens Methodist Church. His death at a relatively young age left his wife to raise five children (two girls preceded Harry and two boys followed) against a background of severe economic privation for the family. Harry's education was limited to attendance at Duncairn Gardens national school until the age of twelve. Two years later, after some work experience in a grocery store, he began an apprenticeship as a joiner in the shipyard.

It was also about this time that Midgley took a precocious interest in politics and met the British Labour leader Keir Hardie when the latter was in Belfast. Midgley duly joined the Independent Labour Party which had a presence in the city. His emergence as a public figure occurred after the First World War, in which he fought and out of which experience he produced a small book of poems, *Thoughts from Flanders* (1924). In 1920 he became an organizer for the Irish Linenlappers' and Warehouse Workers' Union, relatively secure employment to support his wife, Eleanor, *née* Adgey (1895–1965), whom he had married on 22 August 1918, and the four children he was to father during the 1920s. Politically, Midgley's brand of fiery evangelical socialism and his considerable oratorical skills were expressed within the Belfast Labour Party (BLP), which had grown after the war in accordance with a general mood of labour unrest.

However, the BLP buckled against the storm of the sectarian violence which accompanied the birth of the new Northern Ireland state and upheavals in other parts of Ireland in the period 1920–22. Labour representatives were perceived, for the most part correctly, as strongly opposed to partition and in favour of Irish home rule, and loyalist attacks rendered it hazardous to build up a party organization for some years. In this climate Midgley displayed courage in standing for the Northern Ireland parliament in 1921 (on an explicitly anti-partitionist platform) and for Westminster in 1923 and 1924. All attempts were unsuccessful but he was elected to the Belfast corporation for the Dock ward of the city (in which he resided) in 1925. Eventually he was returned for Dock to the Northern Ireland parliament in 1933, by which time he was the recognized leader of the Northern Ireland Labour Party (NILP). Midgley presided over a party severely strained by division over the 'national question', and handicapped by its inability to set an agenda around the politics of class interest as in Britain. Even the socialist *cause célèbre*, the Spanish Civil War, brought local difficulties for Midgley. His support for the Spanish republic resulted in bitter dispute with the Catholic church, and the withdrawal of support by Catholic voters cost him his seat in the Northern Ireland election of 1938.

Midgley retreated in disgust to a brand of protestant communalism, and was emboldened by a remarkable by-election triumph in the largely protestant working-class constituency of Willowfield in Belfast in 1941. He left the NILP in 1942 having failed to commit the party explicitly to a pro-British stance on the constitution and the war effort, and having witnessed his nationalist-oriented rival Jack Beattie elected leader. Midgley formed his own pro-Union Commonwealth Labour Party (CLP), and in 1943 accepted the invitation of the new Ulster premier, Basil Brooke, to join the government. He was the first non-Unionist Party cabinet minister, and was a token outsider in an administration meant to appear broad-based to the British government. Nevertheless, he performed his duties first as minister of public security and then as minister of labour (1944–5) with some flair. Midgley resigned to fight—and retain—his seat in the 1945 election in the CLP interest, but two years later took the final step into the ranks of the Unionist Party. Membership of the Orange order, virtually *de rigueur* in the party, duly followed.

In 1949 Midgley found himself back in office as minister of labour, and a year later was moved to the post of minister of education. The latter appointment involved a personal political dilemma, Midgley having strongly opposed the 1947 Education Act which remained for him now to administer. He had been outraged at the act's provision for increased state funding for voluntary schools, in effect those run (with no external control) by the Catholic church. The controversy surrounded him for the rest of his life, and Midgley fanned the flames periodically with flagrantly sectarian speeches. By this time he was displaying the kind of crusading zeal of his socialist years in the cause of Ulster's British connection, but arguably remained to the left on issues such as welfare. His time as minister of education saw the notable expansion of a schools building programme and the raising of the school leaving age to fifteen. It was appropriate that at the end of his career he should have been associated with educational reforms such as he had fought for throughout his life. On 29 April 1957 Midgley died in the Musgrave Clinic, Belfast, after being taken ill at a conference of the Ulster Teachers' Union. He was buried on 1 May in Belfast. His wife survived him.

Midgley's career, spanning as it does so much of the political spectrum, is one of the most interesting in Northern Ireland's history. It highlights the problems of Labour in gaining a significant foothold in a deeply tribal political culture, and the dilemmas accompanying the quest for power and influence.   GRAHAM WALKER

Sources G. S. Walker, *The politics of frustration: Harry Midgley and the failure of labour in Northern Ireland* (1985) · T. Cradden, *Trade unionism,*

socialism and partition (1993) • b. cert. • m. cert. • d. cert. • PRO NIre., Midgley MSS • *CGPLA NIre.* (1957)
Archives PRO NIre., MSS, D4089
Likenesses photograph, repro. in Walker, *Politics of frustration*
Wealth at death £1338 17s.: probate, 2 Aug 1957, *CGPLA NIre.*

Midgley, Robert (1654/5–1695), writer and physician, was born at Adel, near Leeds, the son of Samuel Midgley. On 27 June 1671, aged sixteen, he was admitted a sizar of Christ's College, Cambridge; he proceeded MB in 1676 and MD in 1687, and was admitted on 22 December 1687 as a candidate of the Royal College of Physicians. He resided in the parish of Bassishaw, London, officiating as licenser of books in 1686 and subsequent years. John Dunton had this to say of Midgley, in his capacity as licenser of books, in his *Life and Errors of John Dunton*, to be taken with a grain of salt:

> He was a contemporary Licenser with Mr. Fraser, and had his Deputation from the Bishop of London. His humour was constantly kind and agreeable, his aspect cheerful and strangely obliging. He licensed for me 'Mr. Jay's Tragedies of Sin', 'Barlow's Treatise of Fornication', and other Divine Essays that were out of Mr. Fraser's province. He was a good Physician, and very *high* for the Church; yet (to do Mr. Midgley justice) censoriousness and speaking unhandsomely about persons, or believing easily any ill reports of those that dissented from him, were vices his soul abhorred. In a word, he was a man of singular modesty; and, living a pious life, when he lay on his death-bed, he expressed no concern to live, nor fear to die; he kept nothing in reserve for his last hours, and, being ripe for death, could not be surprized. (1818 edn, 1.267)

Midgley was one of the translators of the eight-volume Plutarch's *Moralia* (1684–1704) and was responsible for 'Why the Oracles Cease to Give Answers' in volume 4 and 'Plutarch's consolatory letter to his wife' in volume 5. In 1687 he translated Antonio Maria Graziani's *De bello Cyprio libri quinque* (1624) as *The History of the War of Cyprus*. The same year he saw published his *New treatise of natural philosophy, freed from the intricacies of the schools, adorned with many curious experiments, both medicinal and chymical, as also with several observations useful for the health of the body*, to be followed, two years later, by *Popery banished. With an account of their base cheats, especially making the word of God of no effect*. His last known work was the 'Key to Hudibras', a copy of which he gave to Sir Roger L'Estrange and which is printed in Samuel Butler's *Posthumous Works*. In 1685, when Midgley became licenser, he served with L'Estrange, licenser of the press.

The publishing history and Midgley's role in the authorship of *The Turkish Spy* have never been fully established. Giovanni Paolo Marana, a Genoese refugee at the court of Louis XIV, published the first volume in Italian in 1683. A French version, *L'espion du grand seigneur* (1684–6), in three volumes and 102 letters, attributed to Marana, reached nine volumes in various editions by 1756. The expanded English version, in eight volumes and 600 letters, titled *Letters Writ by a Turkish Spy*, was published in the years 1687 to 1694. A footnote in Nichols's *Literary Anecdotes* (1.413), concerning the authorship of *The Turkish Spy*, reads:

> the following memorandum was taken from a copy of the original conveyance in the hands of the late Mr. Charles

Bathurst, bookseller in London, in May 1767: 'Dr. Robert Midgely, of the parish of St. Michael Bassishaw, London, conveys 27th Dec. 1693, to Jos. Hindmarsh, Rd. Sare, and Henry Rhodes [a subsequent publisher of some of the volumes], all the copy-right in the *Turkish Spy* in 8 volumes'. He first says: *translated, written, and composed, by himself.* Afterwards: *written originally in Arabick, translated into Italian, and from thence into English.* Last of all, he calls himself the sole author of these copies or books. He sold the copy for 209*l.* 11*s.* 9*d.*

All this is very detailed, but not definite proof of Midgley's authorship.

According to John Dunton, William Bradshaw, a hack writer who had worked for him before absconding with money and books, was the probable author of *The Turkish Spy*. Dunton also stated that Midgley had employed Bradshaw in a work which would take years to finish, and if he, Dunton, had not recognized Bradshaw's style in the first volume of the work, Midgley would have been thought the author of all the volumes (Nichols, *Lit. anecdotes*, 1.414). The editors of *Biographia Britannica* attribute at least the first volume of *The Turkish Spy* to Sir Roger Manley, father of Mrs Manley, novelist and journalist. The attribution doubtless derives from the statement in Mrs Manley's life, published as *The Adventures of Rivella* (1714), where she writes, of *The Turkish Spy*:

> I must likewise tell you that our Governour [her father] was the Genuine Author of the first Volume of that admir'd and successful Work. An Ingenious *Physician*, related to the Family by Marriage, had the Charge of looking over his Papers amongst which he found that Manuscript, which he easily reserved to his proper Use; and both by his own Pen, and the assistance of some others, continu'd the Work until the Eighth Volume, without ever having the Justice to Name the Author of the First. (p. 15)

A footnote in Henry Hallam's *Introduction to the Literature of Europe … * (1872 edn, 4.355) quotes a manuscript note in the 1732 edition of *The Turkish Spy* in the British Museum to the effect that Midgley, 'related to the Manley family by marriage' found Sir Roger's manuscript of the first volume and 'both by his own pen and the assistance of some others continued the work until the eighth volume' (verbatim from *The Adventures of Rivella*). Midgley:

> married the daughter of an attorney who was executor to Sir Robert Manley, the father of Mary de la Rivière Manley; this is of some importance for Dr. Midgley's life, and gives Mary Manley's comments on the *Turkish Spy* special interest, if not total reliability. (private information)

At present, the problem of the authorship of the work is still unsolved, although the *British Library Catalogue of Printed Books*, under Midgley, has him as the probable author of it and of a historical preface and index to each volume. There is a theory that Dunton's William Bradshaw is actually John Bradshaw (*fl.* 1679), a profligate political writer and attempted murderer, the author of *The Jesuits Countermin'd, or, An Account of a New Plot … * (1679). Dunton, an employer of many names and pseudonyms, is supposed actually to have been writing of John Bradshaw, not William. The fact that *The Jesuits Countermin'd* was not published by Dunton casts doubt on the theory.

The Turkish Spy is, however, of greater importance than the problem of its authorship, as it is the first example of a literary genre, the description of a country and its customs, people, and institutions laid bare in a series of letters by a foreigner. Notable among other examples of the genre are Charles de Secondat, baron de Montesquieu's *Lettres persanes* (1727), Jean-Baptiste de Boyer, marquis d'Argen's *Lettres juives* (1738) and *Lettres chinoises* (1739), and Oliver Goldsmith's *The Citizen of the World* (1762). Midgley died in 1695. ARTHUR SHERBO

Sources DNB · *The life and errors of John Dunton*, [rev. edn], ed. J. B. Nichols, 2 vols. (1818) · H. Hallam, *Introduction to the literature of Europe*, 4 vols. (1872) · Nichols, *Lit. anecdotes* · BL cat. · private information (2004) [Christopher Lee] · Munk, *Roll*

Midlane, Albert (1825–1909), hymn writer, was born at Carisbrooke, Isle of Wight, on 23 January 1825, the posthumous child and youngest of the large family of James Midlane (*d*. October 1824) and his wife, Frances Lawes, a member of the Congregational church then under Thomas Binney. After completing his schooling at Newport, Midlane was employed for some three years in a local printing office, then became an ironmonger's assistant, and ultimately was in business for himself as tinsmith and ironmonger. His religious training was in the Congregational church and its Sunday school, in which he became a teacher; he stated that instead of listening to sermons he studied the hymnbook. Subsequently he joined the Plymouth Brethren. Prompted by his Sunday school teacher, he began to write verse as a child, contributing to magazines under the name Little Albert. His first printed hymn, written in September 1842, appeared in the *Youth's Magazine* in November of that year. His first widely used hymn, 'God bless our Sunday schools' (sung to the tune of the national anthem), was written in 1844. The hymn for which he is best known, 'There's a friend for little children', was composed on 7 February 1859, and was translated into a dozen languages, including Chinese and Japanese; it was included in the supplement to *Hymns Ancient and Modern* (1868), when Sir John Stainer wrote the tune 'In Memoriam' for it. The hymn demonstrated not only Midlane's winsome religious emotion, but also his passionate love of children. His output of hymns was amazing, amounting to over 700 compositions, with many published in magazines and in very numerous tiny collections; for the year 1908 he wrote that he counted 'just upon 200 published compositions, which is about the annual average'. This total, however, included verses on national and local topics in the *Isle of Wight County Press* and other periodicals, as well as historical prose. For some time he edited a local magazine, *Island Greetings*. He did not accept remuneration for his writing, and having become guarantor for a friend he was reduced to bankruptcy. Admirers throughout the country, in conjunction with the Sunday School Union, raised a sum which enabled the bankruptcy to be annulled and provided an annuity for Midlane and his wife. He died at Forest Villa, South Mall, Newport, Isle of Wight, on 27 February 1909, as the result of an apoplectic seizure, and was buried in Carisbrooke cemetery. He was survived by his wife, Miriam Granger, and two sons and one daughter.

ALEXANDER GORDON, *rev.* LEON LITVACK

Sources J. Julian, ed., *A dictionary of hymnology*, rev. edn (1907); repr. in 2 vols. (1915) · *The Times* (1 March 1909) · *Isle of Wight County Press* (6 March 1909) · E. Routley, *An English-speaking hymnal guide* (1979) · M. Frost, ed., *Historical companion to 'Hymns ancient and modern'* (1962)

Midleton. For this title name *see* Brodrick, Alan, first Viscount Midleton (1655/6–1728); Brodrick, (William) St John Fremantle, first earl of Midleton (1856–1942).

Midleton [Myddelton], **William** (*c*.1550–1596?), poet and sailor, was the fourth son of Ffowc Midleton (*d*. 1571), a gentleman of Archwedlog, Llansannan, Denbighshire, and Alis (*d*. 1590/91), daughter of Maredudd ap Gronw. Sources that make him the son of Richard Myddelton, governor of Denbigh Castle, are mistaken; Myddelton was his uncle, his father's brother. Midleton's upbringing familiarized him with Welsh literary culture; his mother's family patronized poets, and he probably knew the humanist William Salesbury, also of Llansannan. Wood's claim that he was educated at Oxford cannot be authenticated. By 1575 Midleton was in the service of Henry Herbert, earl of Pembroke, writing a Welsh elegy for Katherine Talbot, Herbert's second wife, who died in that year. He was still in Herbert's service in 1583 when he addressed a letter from Wilton to the grammarian Siôn Dafydd Rhys (Dr John Davies). In 1585 he was a captain in Leicester's army in the Netherlands, being possibly associated with Sir Philip Sidney, Herbert's brother-in-law, whom he may have known since his days at Wilton.

In 1589 Midleton accompanied the Portuguese expedition led by Drake and Norris, his cousin, the London merchant Thomas Myddelton (son of Richard Myddelton of Denbigh) lending him money to levy a company of soldiers. This association flourished further when Midleton, on returning from Portugal, embarked on a privateering career, captaining his cousin's ships. On 15 October 1589 he reached Plymouth in the *Elizabeth and Mary* with a captured Brazilman whose cargo, including sugar and cotton wool, was worth £2700. In 1590, in Myddelton's *Riall* of Weymouth, he and other privateers captured two argosies bound for Florence from Lisbon. The cargo of the *Ugiera Salvagina*, Midleton's share of the spoil—mostly oriental goods, including pepper, spices, rubies, diamonds, pearls, and ivory—was worth a massive £13,000. In 1591, again in the *Riall*, Midleton captured a French ship carrying oil. Interestingly, an eighteenth-century manuscript (NL Wales, Panton MS 7, fols. 57–9, which uniquely among older narratives correctly associates Midleton with Llansannan) claims that he, with another Welsh poet and privateer, Thomas Prys, and Thomas Coet, were 'the first that smoaked Tobacco publickly at London', having obtained it from a ship they had taken between the Canaries and Africa.

In 1595 Midleton sailed with Drake and Hawkins on their ill-fated voyage to Panama, captaining the *Salomon*

Bonaventure of London. In the Canaries misfortune befell the *Salomon*, its captain of soldiers being killed and the ship's surgeon captured during a shore raid. In Panama, while anchored at Escudo de Veragua in the Mosquito Gulf, an island 'full of Tarrtasis and Aligators' (Paris, Bibliothèque Nationale, MS anglais 51, fol. 15v), Midleton finished his metrical psalms, *Psalmae y brenhinol brophwyd Dafydh* (24 January 1596). On the return passage his ship only narrowly survived a Spanish attack off the Isla de Pinos, Cuba. An elegy by Edward Kyffin implies that Midleton died 'close to landing' while returning from the Indies. He was paid, however, like the expedition's other captains until June 1596, and was not named in casualty lists. This could be because he died so close to port as not to be reckoned a casualty of the expedition proper.

As well as his poems in manuscript Midleton was the author of three published volumes. *Bardhoniaeth, neu, Brydydhiaeth* (1593) was a manual of Welsh prosody, meant to provide basic instruction for those eager to compose poetry in accordance with humanist concepts of cultivated gentility. His Welsh metrical version of the Psalms was more ambitious. A printed fragment entitled *Rhann o psalmae Davyd, a phropwyti eraill* survived in the binding of a Latin volume of 1595, indicating that Midleton had published some psalms before completing his work at Escudo in 1596. The completed version, *Psalmae y brenhinol brophwyd Dafydh*, appeared posthumously in 1603, its publication by the London printer Thomas Salisbury being subsidized by an interest-free loan from Thomas Myddelton. Unlike Edmwnd Prys's psalms of 1621 Midleton's were not meant for congregational singing. They combined piety with a deliberate display of the variety of Welsh versification: Midleton used forty-three different metres, including variants of the standard twenty-four metres, some devised by himself. His work invites comparison with the similarly metrically diverse psalms of Sir Philip Sidney, probably begun at Wilton during Sidney's visits to his sister Mary, third wife of Henry Herbert. Midleton may have known of Sidney's endeavour, seeking afterwards to emulate him in Welsh.

Midleton contributed an appendix illustrating metrics to Siôn Dafydd Rhys's grammar *Cambrobrytannicæ … linguæ institutiones* (1592). He also knew Hugh Holland, who addressed him in Latin verse before he sailed for Panama.

GRUFFYDD ALED WILLIAMS

Sources *Barddoniaeth neu brydyddiaeth: gan Wiliam Midleton*, ed. G. J. Williams (1930) · G. A. Williams, 'Wiliam Midleton, bonheddwr, anturiwr a bardd', *Transactions of the Denbighshire Historical Society*, 24 (1975), 74–116 · G. A. Williams, 'Wiliam Midleton, Elizabethan poet and privateer', *Maritime Wales*, 1 (1976), 11–21 · A. H. Dodd, 'Mr Myddelton, the merchant of Tower Street', *Elizabethan government and society: essays presented to Sir John Neale*, ed. S. T. Bindoff, J. Hurstfield, and C. H. Williams (1961), 249–81 · K. R. Andrews, *Elizabethan privateering: English privateering during the Spanish war* (1964) · K. R. Andrews, *The last voyage of Drake and Hawkins*, Hakluyt Society, 2nd ser., 142 (1942) · G. J. Williams, 'William Midleton and Thomas Prys', *BBCS*, 11 (1941–4), 113–14 · G. A. Williams, 'Psalmae Wiliam Midleton', *Ysgrifau Beirniadol*, 17 (1990), 93–113 · W. Williams, 'Three fragments', *Journal of the Welsh Bibliographical Society*, 4 (1932–6), 257–65 · NL Wales, Panton MS 7

Midlothian. For this title name *see* Primrose, Archibald Philip, fifth earl of Rosebery and first earl of Midlothian (1847–1929); Primrose, (Albert Edward) Harry Mayer Archibald, sixth earl of Rosebery and second earl of Midlothian (1882–1974).

Miege, Guy (*bap.* 1644, *d.* in or after 1718), author and lexicographer, was baptized in Lausanne, Vaud, Switzerland, on 30 May 1644, a younger son of Sebastian Meyjoz (*d.* after 1674) or Meige and his wife, Esther Blevet. Admitted as a student to the Académie de Lausanne in 1659, he left in January 1661 and in March arrived in London.

Here Miege soon found powerful patrons to forward his education, indulge his 'constant inclination to travel' (Miege, *A Relation*, preface), and establish him in a career as a writer. Within a few months he joined the household of Thomas Bruce, first earl of Elgin, and for two years 'improved [his] stock of learning' (Miege, *Utrum horum?*, 26) with the earl's eldest grandson, Edward Bruce. When the young man died Miege obtained appointment as under-secretary to Charles Howard, earl of Carlisle, in his embassy to Muscovy, Sweden, and Denmark, and in July 1663 joined an entourage which included Andrew Marvell as chief secretary. With Carlisle's express permission, Miege wrote an account of the journey, subsequently published as *A Relation of Three Embassies* (1669), which is both an attempted vindication of the ambassador's conduct in the face of Russian criticism and a lively source of impressions of Russian society and culture. He considered Muscovy a beautiful country, but found its inhabitants, in contrast to the Swedes, coarse, austere, and ignorant of learning. Exhibiting a characteristic commitment to protestantism and to constitutional monarchy, he was not impressed by a religion 'that obliges its Professors to severe mortification' or by icons, 'very ill-drawn, and in flat painting', and dismissed a monarchy that was 'despotical and absolute' (Miege, *A Relation*, 57, 70, 73).

Having accompanied Carlisle home via Denmark, Germany, and France, Miege arrived back in England in January 1665. During another trip to France and Switzerland between April 1665 and 1668, he finished the *Relation*, published additionally as *La relation des trois ambassades* in Paris and Amsterdam in 1669 and 1672. Also in 1672 *La vie du General Monck*, his translation of Thomas Gumble's biography, appeared in London and Rouen, dedicated to the duke of Albemarle.

From the late 1670s, when he was living in Panton Street, London, teaching French and geography, Miege rapidly established a considerable reputation as a lexicographer and grammarian. French language reforms effected by the Académie Française inspired his *New Dictionary French and English* (1677), dedicated to the young Charles Lennox, duke of Richmond, son of Charles II and Louise de Keroualle. This was complemented by *A New French Grammar* (1678), dedicated to 'Gilbert Gerard-Cosin', grandson of Bishop John Cosin, to whom he had previously taught French and Latin. Reissued many times, most notably as *The Grounds of the French Tongue* (1687), this work was the most influential French grammar for several generations. In contrast, *The English Grammar* (1688), written in his customarily fluent and accessible style, was not apparently popular, although distinguished by remaining 'the only grammar of English written in English by a non-native speaker' (foreword to 1969 edition). However, his *Nouvelle méthode pour apprendre l'Anglois* (1685) was immediately successful and ran to over twenty editions up to 1795. The original edition incorporated Miege's *Nouvelle nomenclature Francoise et Angloise* (1685), containing dialogues discussing distinctive features of contemporary English life: coffee houses and clubs are approved, but the weather is uncertain, the sun 'little seen' and the air 'gross and thick' (pp. 88–9).

Combining talents as a social observer and a translator, Miege exhibited wider interests. *A New Cosmography, or, The Survey of the Whole World* (1682) and *The Present State of Denmark* (1683), occasioned by the marriage of Princess Anne and dedicated to her husband Prince George, were followed by translations into French in 1684 of the observations of Robert Boyle and others on water desalination and into English of French fairy stories. An attempt to launch a newsletter, represented by *L'etat Present de l'Europe* (25 September 1682) was not apparently repeated.

Having published anonymously *A Complete History of the Late Revolution* (1691), which depicted 'the growth of Popery under … King Charles', 'our imminent ruin in his Popish Successor', and 'our wonderful and happy deliverance by the Prince of Orange', Miege reiterated these sentiments in *The New State of England* (1691). Dedicated to Thomas Osborne, earl of Danby, and consciously modelled on Thomas Smith's *De republica Anglorum* 'improved and fitted to the present times', it described English society, topography, and government, and celebrated at length 'a free People … averse from Slavery' (2.6), with a genius for invention, pre-eminent in experimental philosophy, divinity, and literature. The Church of England was 'the best Reformed Religion and the most agreeable to the primitive times of Christianity', excelling in its public worship (2.65); the exclusion of dissenters was regrettable, but the fault lay with the papists, and Miege was optimistic about greater comprehension in future. He upheld the monarchy as established in 1688–9, the king within the law as against James II 'who strikes at the very foundations of government' (2.79, 96); parliament was 'one of the most August Assemblies in the World', and Charles I's attempt to break its privileges a fundamental error (3.1).

The book was generally well received, but John Chamberlayne, in issuing a new edition of his father Edward Chamberlayne's *Angliae notitiae, or, The Present State of England* of 1669, accused Miege of plagiarism and, as a foreigner, of presumption. He defended himself vigorously against both in *Utrum horum? Tyranny or Liberty; Oppression or Moderation* (1705). Dedicated to George Neville, Lord Abergavenny, 'a true Supporter of the Prerogative Royal, but with a due Tenderness of the People's Liberty', it detected, with the accession of Queen Anne, a high-

church plot 'to a new Revolution, like to make us as Miserable, as we became happy by the last' (p. 1). Dismissing Chamberlayne's work as out of date, prone to error and scurrilous in its treatment of dissenters, Miege recounted his education, travels, and credentials as an author, proclaimed his 'particular veneration for the true and moderate Church of England' (p. 24), and asserted 'none can be a greater Admirer of the English Constitution than my self' (p. 44).

Approval of the Act of Union prompted Miege to expand his work into *The Present State of Great Britain* (1707), while the 1715 edition included a discussion of George I's dominions in Germany. In dedicating the latter to Archbishop Thomas Tennison, whose political and religious stance clearly matched his own, Miege paid tribute to his 'Zeal to the King' and 'Steadiness to the Constitution' as well as to his humanity, generosity and piety, expressing his 'deep Sense of Gratitude for your Favours to me in particular'.

The last work bearing Miege's name was the *Nouvelle double grammaire* published with Abel Boyer in Amsterdam and Rotterdam in 1718 and described as the 'last edition'. The date and place of his death are unknown.

VIVIENNE LARMINIE

Sources Archives Cantonales Vaudoises, Lausanne, Eb 71/3, 34 · Archives Cantonales Vaudoises, Lausanne, Bdd 106, p. 97 · L. Junod, *Album studiosorum academiae Lausannensis, 1537–1837*, 2 (Lausanne, 1937), 44, 46, 50 · G. Miege, *A relation of three embassies* (1669) · G. Miege, *A new French grammar* (1678) · G. Miege, *A complete history of the late revolution* (1691) · G. Miege, *The first part of the new state of England* (1691) · G. Miege, *Utrum horum? Tyranny or liberty; oppression or moderation* (1705) · G. Miege, *The present state of Great Britain and Ireland* (1715)

Mierdman, Steven [*pseud.* Niclaes van Oldenborch] (*c.*1510x12–1559), printer and bookseller, was born in Hooge Mierde in North Brabant, in the Netherlands, the youngest son of Aert Aertszoon Mierdmans (Nuyts), yeoman farmer. In 1539 he sold his inheritance to his eldest brother, in presumably the same year that he went to Antwerp. There he may have been engaged as an apprentice in the printing house of Mattheus Crom [*see below*]. On 3 June 1543 he married Crom's younger sister Elizabeth and was admitted to the freedom of the city. About the same time he entered into partnership with Crom, subsequently took over the direction of his business, and started to produce books under his own name. This marked the beginning of a remarkable career devoted to the distribution of Reformation literature both in the Low Countries and in England. In Antwerp, Mierdman printed Dutch evangelical texts and various English religious books. The latter group includes works by George Joye, John Bale, and John Frith, and translations of works by Erasmus and Calvin. One of his first books was Francisco de Enzinas's Spanish translation of the New Testament (1543), which caused him much trouble and brought the translator into prison. Like Crom, Mierdman made use of the pseudonym Niclaes van Oldenborch (for some time taken for the name of a real person), and several other fictitious names.

In 1546 the emperor Charles V strengthened the government's supervision of the printing press. This may explain why Mierdman moved to London in 1546–7, together with his wife, taking with him his printing equipment. In 1549 he was entered in the returns of aliens as living in the parish of St Mary-at-Hill, Billingsgate ward, and in 1550 he was granted a royal licence to print books and was made a denizen. In the same year he joined the Dutch church at Austin Friars. The output of his London press, where he employed at least three men, amounted to more than eighty books. Many were published by Hugh Singleton, John Day, Richard Jugge, or Mierdman's fellow countryman Walter Lynne (Van Lin). Mierdman produced texts by German and English reformers, but also the Bible translations by Tyndale and Coverdale, as well as works commissioned by the refugee churches which flourished during the reign of Edward VI.

This prolific period came to an end on the accession of Mary Tudor. Mierdman fled again to the continent and settled at Emden in East Friesland in December 1553, where he was entered as a citizen in the following April. Although he was not able this time to bring with him his materials (which were disposed of in London to Richard Jugge and John Cawood), he managed to set up a press. From this Emden press there came no more English books, and only a small number of Dutch ones. Among these were two Bible translations (1556, 1558), published in partnership with Jan Gailliart, who had unorthodox leanings. These bibles were a commercial success, but evoked protests from the Reformed consistory. Moreover Mierdman printed anonymously some writings by the Anabaptist Dirk Philips. At the same time his church's official commissions were being given to the other Emden printers Nicholas Hill (Van den Berghe) and Gilles van der Erven (Ctematius).

Mierdman made his will in Emden on 6 January 1559 and presumably died shortly afterwards, leaving a substantial sum to the church's poor. His wife died in Emden on 26 April 1573, also leaving a donation to the church. There were no children.

Mierdman's partner as an evangelical printer, **Mattheus Crom** (c.1505x10–1546?), was born in Antwerp, the second of three sons and third of five children of Peeter Crom, locksmith, and Martine van Roye. He matriculated at Louvain University in 1523. Probably several years later he settled at Antwerp as a printer. He was housed 'in den Ketel', later 'int Huys van Delft', both in the Cammerstraat. The first books with his imprint appeared in 1537, but some books dated 1536 have been attributed to his press as well. Probably he took over the business of his elder sister Geertruyt's husband Lubbaert Tymmerman de Letterghieter, who died in 1537. Crom printed about seventy-five books, often omitting his imprint or using a false name. He played an important role in the distribution of early evangelical or explicitly protestant texts, for the greater part devotional works for the Dutch market. Many of these Dutch texts cannot easily be related to a specific religious doctrine, but in 1539 Crom also printed two works by the Anabaptist leader Menno

Simons. Apart from some Latin, French, and Spanish works he also printed a number of English books: a few editions of the New Testament, and tracts by radical English reformers. Some of his books, including Coverdale's New Testament of 1538, are illustrated with woodcuts after drawings by Lieven de Witte. In 1542 Crom was admitted a member of the St Lucas Guild. The next year his position was threatened by a Louvain heresy trial, where he was mentioned as a seller of prohibited books.

After 1543, when Steven Mierdman took over the direction of his business, no more books were published with Crom's imprint. A document from among the Antwerp public records shows that Crom was still alive in January 1545, but in September 1546 his elder sister was granted a licence as bookseller, from which may be deduced that he had died earlier that year and that she carried on her late brother's business. Crom was unmarried.

WILLEM HEIJTING

Sources A. Rouzet, M. Colin-Boon, and others, *Dictionnaire des imprimeurs, libraires et éditeurs des XVe et XVIe siècles dans les limites géographiques de la Belgique actuelle* (Nieuwkoop, 1975) · W. Heijting, 'Early Reformation literature from the printing shop of Mattheus Crom and Steven Mierdmans', *Dutch Review of Church History*, 74 (1994), 143–61 · A. Pettegree, *Foreign protestant communities in sixteenth-century London* (1986), 90–92 · A. Pettegree, *Emden and the Dutch revolt: exile and the development of reformed protestantism* (1992), 16, 20, 90–99 · P. Valkema Blouw, 'The Van Oldenborch and Vanden Merberghe pseudonyms, or, Why Frans Fraet had to die', *Quaerendo*, 22 (1992), 165–90, 245–72 · H. F. Wijnman, 'The mysterious sixteenth-century printer Niclaes van Oldenborch: Antwerp or Emden?', *Studia bibliographica in honorem Herman de la Fontaine Verwey*, ed. [S. van der Woude] (1968), 448–78 · H. F. Wijnman, 'De Antwerpse hervormingsgezinde drukker Mattheus Crom en zijn naaste omgeving', *De Gulden Passer*, 40 (1962), 105–24 · STC, 1475–1640 · C. Clair, 'On the printing of certain Reformation books', *The Library*, 5th ser., 18 (1963), 275–87 · M. Tielke, ed., *Biographisches Lexikon für Ostfriesland*, 1 (1993) · E. G. Duff, *A century of the British book trade* (1972) · E. J. Worman, *Alien members of the book-trade during the Tudor period* (1906) · W. de Vreese, 'Levensbericht van Th. J. I. Arnold', *Jaarboek der Koninklijke Vlaamsche Academie voor Taal- en Letterkunde*, 15 (1901), 149–252 · H. R. Hoppe, 'The birthplace of Stephen Mierdman, Flemish printer in London, c.1549–c.1552', *The Library*, 5th ser., 4 (1949–50), 213–14 · I. Veldman and K. van Schaik, *Verbeelde boodschap: de illustraties van Lieven de Witte bij 'Dat leven ons heeren'* (1537) (1989) · C. Clair, 'A misdated testament printed by Crom', *The Library*, 5th ser., 17 (1962), 155–6

Miers, Sir **Anthony Cecil Capel** (1906–1985), naval officer and submariner, was born on 11 November 1906 at Birchwood, Inverness, the younger son and second of three children of Captain Douglas Nathaniel Carleton Capel Miers, Queen's Own Cameron Highlanders, who was killed in France in September 1914, and his wife, Margaret Annie Christie. He was educated at Stubbington House in Gosport, Edinburgh Academy, and Wellington College from which he entered the navy as a special entry cadet in 1924.

Miers joined the Submarine Service in April 1929 where he made his mark as totally loyal, outstandingly keen, fearless, hot-tempered, and incautiously outspoken. A prescient training officer wrote that he would either be awarded the VC or a court martial: in the event he got both, the latter in 1933 for self-confessedly striking a rating. Miers, who came to be known as Gamp on the lower deck and Crap by officers for reasons that have never been convincingly explained, was fiercely competitive at sea, ashore, and on the playing field. He was a good athlete, a tennis and squash player, and a fine rugby footballer. His vigorous single-minded aim at all times was to win. He was not a good loser, but his sheer determination to beat the opposition was to overcome all obstacles in war. The men who served him had complete confidence in him and forgave his impetuous outbursts; but, undeniably, those who sought a calmer life avoided his company. Nobody could be indifferent to his presence. He was wholeheartedly supportive to subordinates, provided they were efficient and stood up to him, albeit at some risk of fisticuffs.

Miers's first submarine command was *L54* (1936–7). Then, after a spell of general service in the battleship *Iron Duke*, he qualified on the staff course (1938) before joining, as a lieutenant-commander, the seagoing staff of the commander-in-chief, Home Fleet (1939–40), where he was mentioned in dispatches. He returned to submarines in 1940 to command the new HMS *Torbay* on 12 November. It was in this submarine that Miers gained lasting fame for varied patrols in the Mediterranean over the next two intensely active years. He was promoted to commander in December 1941, again mentioned in dispatches, decorated twice with the DSO (1941 and 1942), and finally invested with the VC (1942).

The VC was richly deserved. On 20 February 1942 *Torbay* sailed from Alexandria for her tenth patrol. Bad luck dogged Miers for several days and his frustration reached full fury when, out of position owing to an earlier fruitless hunt, he was unable to close on an important troop ship convoy. Angry with himself, he coldly decided to attack the convoy at its destination—within the well-protected enemy harbour of Corfu Roads. Accordingly, he took *Torbay* right inside the harbour and remained in this highly hazardous situation for some seventeen hours. In fact, by the time he got there, the convoy had departed; but two supply ships lay at anchor and these went down to his torpedoes.

In 1941, off Crete, Miers ordered the machine-gunning of German soldiers who had taken to a rubber float while their caique was sunk by *Torbay* crewmen with a demolition charge. Accounts of this controversial incident vary: but, whether the shooting can be justified in retrospect or not, Miers was always determined to neutralize as many of the enemy as possible, and, in this case, he reported that he was preventing them from regaining their ship. It has otherwise been said that he was intent on the soldiers taking no further part in the war—either in some kind of action against his own submarine or on the nearby shore against the remaining allied troops there.

In December 1942 Miers was sent as submarine liaison officer to the American Pacific Fleet where he was made an officer of the Legion of Merit. In July 1944 he became commander of the eighth submarine flotilla based on Perth, Western Australia; and here, on 20 January 1945, Miers married Patricia Mary, daughter of David McIntyre Millar, of the Chartered Bank of India, Australia, and China, who was serving in the Women's Royal Australian Naval Service. They had a daughter and a son.

Miers was promoted to captain in December 1946 and, gaining a pilot's A licence, went on to command the naval air station HMS *Blackcap* (1948–50), HMS *Forth* and the 1st submarine squadron (1950–52), the Royal Naval College, Greenwich (1952–4), and the aircraft-carrier HMS *Theseus* (1954–5). In 1955 he was made a burgess and freeman of Inverness and in 1966 a freeman of the City of London. He was promoted to rear-admiral on 7 January 1956 and became flag officer, Middle East, until he retired on 4 August 1959. He was appointed CB in 1958 and KBE in 1959.

Thereafter Miers maintained a large number of business, sporting, and charitable interests. Most notably, he joined National Car Parks as director for development co-ordination in 1971; he became president of the Royal Navy Lawn Tennis Association and of the Royal Navy Squash Rackets Association; and for many years he was national president of the Submarine Old Comrades' Association. He died at his home, 8 Highdown Road, Roehampton, London, on 30 June 1985.

RICHARD COMPTON-HALL, *rev.*

Sources W. Jameson, *Submariners VC* (1962) · P. Chapman, *Submarine Torbay* (1989) · *The Times* (2 July 1985) · WWW · CGPLA Eng. & Wales (1985) · S. W. Roskill, *The war at sea, 1939–1945*, 3 vols. in 4 (1954–61) · PRO, ADM 013 843/41 [HMS *Torbay* patrol report, 28 June–15 July 1941, with comments of Admiral (S) and admiralty depts]
Archives CAC Cam., papers | SOUND IWM SA, oral history interview
Likenesses J. Galsworthy, drawing, RN Submarine Museum, Gosport, Hampshire
Wealth at death £121,350: probate, 22 Aug 1985, CGPLA Eng. & Wales

Miers, Sir Henry Alexander (1858–1942), mineralogist and university administrator, was born in Rio de Janeiro on 25 May 1858, the third son and fifth of the eight children (three of whom died in infancy) of Francis Charles Miers, civil engineer, and his wife, Susan Mary, daughter of Edward Wynn Fry, general merchant, of Handsworth, Staffordshire. John *Miers, the engineer and botanist, was his grandfather, and Francis Place his great-grandfather. In 1860 his father retired and settled at Beckenham, Kent.

Miers gained a classics scholarship to Eton College in 1872. In 1876 he won the public schools gold medal of the Royal Geographical Society and in 1877 was elected a scholar in classics at Trinity College, Oxford, where he formed a lifelong friendship with the musician Basil Harwood. At Oxford he studied classics, science, and mathematics, being placed in the second class of the honour school of mathematics in 1881.

Miers's life falls into three distinct phases: of the student, the professor, and the administrator. On taking his degree he turned to crystallography and mineralogy, and

Sir Henry Alexander Miers (1858–1942), by Sir William Rothenstein, 1917

after studying for three months under Paul Heinrich Groth at Strasbourg, was employed in the department of mineralogy of the British Museum at South Kensington from 1882 to 1895. He also taught crystallography at the Central Technical College from 1886 to 1895. Outside his routine museum duties he made a special study of the crystal forms of different minerals and wrote many original papers.

The second phase opened with his election in 1895 to the Waynflete chair of mineralogy at Oxford with a fellowship at Magdalen College. There his first task was to organize a laboratory for teaching and research; later he began to serve on committees, an activity which duly increased as his versatility and practical ability came to be realized. He nevertheless maintained his own researches, studying the growth of crystals and devising new methods of investigation. His book, *Mineralogy: an Introduction to the Scientific Study of Minerals* (1902; 2nd edn, 1929), was a masterly survey of the state of knowledge at the time, made many years before the development of X-ray crystallography revealed the arrangement of atoms in crystals.

The third phase opened with Miers's appointment as principal of the University of London in 1908, an appointment due to his proven administrative ability rather than his eminence in the scientific world. It ushered in the least happy and productive time of his life. Immersed in routine affairs and constantly confronted with conflicts of interests in the university, he had little time for scientific work. Nevertheless, from the point of view of the university, no better appointment could then have been made. Scrupulously fair, always conciliatory, and anxious to extract the best from the views of opposing parties, he held the university together at a time when it was threatening to fall apart. The outbreak of war prevented the reforms recommended by the Haldane commission, enabling him to accept in 1915 the offer of the vice-chancellorship of the University of Manchester. The offer was made more attractive by the creation for him of a special chair of crystallography, giving him thereby a welcome opportunity to return to his scientific and educational interests.

Miers published few original papers after 1908. His influence on science was mainly indirect, through his pupils, in his constant readiness to help others and in his interest in their work. His suggestion to William Ramsay that he should investigate the gas evolved when the mineral cleveite was heated led in 1895 to the discovery that the rare element helium exists on the earth.

After his retirement from Manchester in 1926 Miers devoted much of his time to museums, as a member of the royal commission which reported in 1929–30, of the standing commission, and as president for five years of the Museums Association. He was also a member of the royal commission on the universities of Oxford and Cambridge (1919–22).

Miers was an ideal chairman of committees. He could gently guide discussion into relevant channels, and was then content to let it follow its course. He had none of the fiery zeal of his great-grandfather, and his quietness brought him trust and affection wherever he went. His keenly adventurous spirit led him in 1888 to go on a balloon flight during which he narrowly escaped death. He enjoyed travel, and acquired, by visits abroad, an unrivalled knowledge of the museums of other countries. In 1903 he went to South Africa at the invitation of the Rhodes trustees to report on educational problems, and in 1918 he was in the United States as chairman of an educational mission representing the British universities.

Of the many honours bestowed upon Miers perhaps the most singular was that after he had left Oxford he remained as an active fellow of Magdalen until the end of his life. He was elected an honorary fellow of Trinity in 1931 and FRS in 1896, and knighted in 1912. Honorary degrees were conferred upon him by the universities of Oxford, Manchester, Sheffield, Christiania, Liverpool, and Michigan. He was an honorary member of many scientific societies at home and abroad, and a Wollaston medallist of the Geological Society of London. He was president of the geological section of the British Association in 1905 and the educational section in 1910, and of the Mineralogical Society, 1904–9. He was also a fellow of Eton College.

In person Miers was short and wiry, and preserved a boyish appearance until an advanced age. He needed no more than four hours' sleep a night. He was seldom ill, and always cheerful, even when failing eyesight handicapped him severely in the closing years of his life. He was a modest man and a delightful companion of young and old. He died, unmarried, at his London home, 18 Aberdare Gardens, West Hampstead, on 10 December 1942. His name is commemorated in the mineral miersite.

H. T. Tizard, *rev.*

Sources T. Holland, *Obits. FRS*, 4 (1942–4), 369–80 · *The Times* (12 Dec 1942) · C. C. J. Webb, *Oxford Magazine* (18 Feb 1943) · private information (1959) · personal knowledge (1959) · *CGPLA Eng. & Wales* (1943)
Archives Bodl. Oxf., corresp., diaries, and papers · JRL, papers · NHM, diaries, notebooks, and papers · NRA, priv. coll., letters and papers | BL, letters to Albert Mausbridge, Add. MSS 65257B–65258 | FILM BFI NFTVA, news footage
Likenesses W. Rothenstein, pencil drawing, 1917, NPG [*see illus.*] · W. Stoneman, photograph, 1933, NPG · H. Campbell, portrait, after 1959 (posthumous; after photograph), U. Lond., Senate House
Wealth at death £40,968 4s. 2d.: probate, 2 March 1943, *CGPLA Eng. & Wales*

Miers, John (1789–1879), botanist and civil engineer, was born on 25 August 1789, the son of John Miers, a London jeweller and miniaturist of Yorkshire extraction, whose business he joined at an early age. Awakened to an interest in science, he then acquired on the side a sufficient knowledge of chemistry and mineralogy to mix freely with the leading up-and-coming specialists in those subjects and to devote his scanty leisure to experiments aimed at establishing the elementary composition of various gases. One of these was nitrogen, on which he published a two-part paper in Thomson's *Annals of Philosophy* in 1814. In the face of Davy's conclusion that this was a simple body, which was then not yet established fact, Miers believed he had demonstrated that it was, on the contrary, a compound.

In 1818 Miers married Annie (or possibly Queenie) (*b. c.*1796). Determined to strike out on his own in business, he responded to an invitation to apply his expertise to developing the rich mineral wealth of newly independent Chile. This came from the admiral of its fleet, Lord Cochrane, the scientifically minded son of the renowned chemist, the ninth earl of Dundonald. Assured by Chile's representatives in London that copper of excellent grade could be had there for half its price in Britain, that coal and wages were even cheaper, and that there was a good demand for rolled sheet copper along the Pacific coast, Miers sent out the necessary heavy machinery and set sail with his bride for Buenos Aires. In May 1819 the couple made the arduous journey from there across the pampas and the cordilleras to Chile, in the course of which his wife fell seriously ill with puerperal fever. On arriving, Miers quickly became convinced that the local mining methods would make the venture unprofitable. Few business decisions in history can have proved so ill judged, for by mid-century Chilean copper was being extracted so economically that it was accounting for almost a third of world output.

Miers was, however, essentially a scientist, and may not have been cut out for managing a large industrial enterprise; he was soon investigating the local natural history

John Miers (1789–1879), by Maull & Polyblank, 1855

instead. The flora, then still little known, attracted him in particular and he drew and dissected the plants he collected. By 1825 his wide-ranging curiosity had produced material enough for a substantial book and that June he returned to London to arrange for its publication, using the few months' stay also to make the acquaintance of several leading botanists. *Travels in Chile and La Plata*, which appeared the next year in two volumes, was to bring him a lasting reputation as the foremost authority on the geography and way of life of that region.

Miers next moved to Buenos Aires, having been awarded a contract by the government of the Argentine confederation to supply and erect the machinery for a national mint. In bringing his wife and children from Chile to join him he crossed the continent in both directions, collecting extensively on the pampas. However, the political situation in Argentina was unsettled, and this may have been the cause of the family's removing in or about 1831 to Rio de Janeiro, where Miers obtained a similar contract from the government of Brazil and thereafter practised as an engineer more generally. Though his years there proved anxious and burdensome professionally, he nevertheless found time for further extensive natural history collecting.

Retirement from business in 1838 took Miers back to London for good. From then on virtually all his time and thoughts were given over to working up his rich botanical collections. Elected to the Linnean Society almost at once, he was eventually to publish almost eighty papers on these, most in the society's journals, the last appearing in his eighty-ninth year. Many of the papers were subsequently grouped together and republished as two books: *Illustrations of South American Botany* (2 vols., 1850–57) and *Contributions to the Botany of South America* (3 vols., 1867–71). They included a number of illustrations mostly lithographed by himself from his original drawings.

The third volume of Miers's *Contributions* was a monograph of the Menispermaceae, a large tropical family containing many species of medicinal value, and was perhaps his most important work. Unfortunately, though, his zeal and conscientiousness were let down by poor judgement as a classifier. Like other recruits to taxonomy from the physical sciences, he did not have a sufficiently sound eye for which characters are significant and for the range of variation to which natural groupings of plants and animals are prone. As a result a large number of the new species and, to a lesser extent, genera and even orders that he described have not been accepted by later workers. His dogged belief to the last in the fixity of species was doubtless a contributory factor in this. Interpreting what he understood by his names has luckily been rendered simple by the availability of his meticulously documented specimens, over 25,000 of which he bequeathed to the British Museum. The fact that forty-three of his species are regarded as valid in the latest authoritative account of the flora of Chile (Marticorena and Rodríguez) nevertheless testifies to the magnitude of his pioneer contribution.

Genial, kindly, and straightforward, Miers became a valued recruit to the councils of London scientific societies, being four times elected to that of the Linnean and once to that of the Royal, of which he became a fellow in 1843. His lasting loyalty to the humbler Botanical Society of London, which he served continuously as a vice-president for at least ten years, probably reflected a fellow-feeling with its largely self-educated membership.

Spared infirmity until he was almost ninety, Miers died at his Kensington home, 84 Addison Road, on 17 October 1879, leaving a sizeable fortune. His wife having predeceased him, he was survived by a daughter and two sons, one of whom followed him with distinction as a civil engineer in South America. Two grandsons followed him in a complementary direction by joining the natural history staff of the British Museum; one of them, Henry Alexander Miers (1858–1942), later became Waynflete professor of mineralogy at Oxford.

Miers is commemorated in three genera of plants. The lily-like *Miersia* of Chile and Bolivia was named by Lindley in 1826, shortly after the two first met. To this Urban later added *Miersella*, tropical American saprophytes allied to orchids, and Engler, *Miersophyton*, appropriately a member of the Menispermaceae, the family which Miers had made his own.   D. E. ALLEN

Sources *Annals and Magazine of Natural History*, 5th ser., 4 (1879), 469–71 · *Journal of Botany, British and Foreign*, 18 (1880), 33–6 · *Nature*, 20 (1879), 614 · H. F. Bain and T. T. Read, *Ores and industry in South America* (1934) · J. Miers, *Travels in Chile and La Plata*, 2 vols. (1826) · A. E. Gunther, *The founders of science at the British Museum, 1753–1900* (1980), 152–3 · W. T. Stearn, *The Natural History Museum at South Kensington: a history of the British Museum (Natural History), 1753–1980* (1981), 295 · C. Marticorena and R. Rodríguez, eds., *Flora de Chile*, 1 (1995), 20 · census returns, 1841

Archives NHM, corresp. and papers · Oxf. U. Mus. NH, Hope Library, entomological catalogues · RBG Kew, herbarium · U. Cam., herbarium · U. Glas., herbarium · Wellcome L., papers relating to meteors | RBG Kew, letters to Sir William Hooker

Likenesses Maull & Polyblank, photograph, 1855, NPG [*see illus.*] · Maull & Fox, photograph, in or before 1863 (overpainted in oils), Linn. Soc.; repro. in *Literary and scientific portrait club* (1863) · lithograph, repro. in *Journal of Botany*, 33

Wealth at death under £60,000: probate, 29 Oct 1879, *CGPLA Eng. & Wales*

Mifflin, Thomas (1744–1800), revolutionary army officer and politician in the United States of America, was born on 10 January 1744 in Philadelphia, the eldest son of John Mifflin, wealthy merchant and later Pennsylvania provincial councillor, and his wife, Elizabeth Bagnell. His father's progenitors were Quakers from England. Thomas graduated from the College of Philadelphia in 1760, and then after apprenticeship formed a successful mercantile partnership with his brother George. After he became heavily involved in public affairs he invested in only occasional mercantile ventures. On 4 March 1767 he married his cousin Sarah Morris (1747–1790), daughter of Morris Morris jun., Quaker merchant. The couple had one daughter.

Mifflin took a leading role in Pennsylvania's anti-British resistance because he believed men of property were obligated to channel resistance carefully. In 1769–70 he served on Philadelphia's committee to superintend non-importation of goods dutied by the Townshend Acts. In 1772 he won election to the assembly on the ticket of the pro-resistance Patriotic Society, and became a top-ranking leader in the house. During the tea crisis of 1773 he was again very active. The assembly chose him as a delegate to the continental congress in 1774, and in December 1774 re-elected him as delegate to the second continental congress. In April 1775 Mifflin raised volunteers for defence against the British. Four months later George Washington made Colonel Mifflin quartermaster-general of the continental army. The Philadelphia monthly meeting disowned him in July, and he never became religiously affiliated again.

Mifflin, brigadier-general by May 1776, was a successful battlefield commander at Trenton and Princeton in early 1777, but he found his quartermaster duties onerous and frustrating, and so he submitted his resignation as quartermaster-general in October 1777. In August 1778 congress began investigating Mifflin for corruption and neglect of duty, but the charges were not substantiated. Offended, Mifflin resigned his major-general's commission. Washington's friends also accused him of plotting to replace the commander-in-chief with Horatio Gates, victor at Saratoga, or perhaps himself. Mifflin grumbled at Washington's mistakes and missed opportunities, but no evidence has shown him involved in any plan to remove the commander.

Thomas Mifflin (1744–1800), by John Singleton Copley, 1773 [with his wife, Sarah Morris]

the rioters. In 1798, abandoning his Francophile sympathies, he co-operated with the administration of the federalist John Adams in defence preparations against the French.

In 1799 Mifflin was elected to the Pennsylvania legislature, although he was drinking heavily and becoming increasingly unwell. He died on 20 January 1800 while attending the legislature's sessions in Lancaster. Because he lived on his government salaries and loans from friends, his estate was small and Pennsylvania provided his funeral; he was buried in the Lutheran church in Lancaster.   BENJAMIN H. NEWCOMB

Sources K. R. Rossman, *Thomas Mifflin and the politics of the American revolution* (1952) · J. K. Alexander, 'Mifflin, Thomas', *ANB* · R. L. Brunhouse, *The counter-revolution in Pennsylvania, 1776–1790* (1942) · P. H. Smith and others, eds., *Letters of delegates to congress, 1774–1789*, 26 vols. (1976–2000) · J. H. Peeling, 'Mifflin, Thomas', *DAB* · R. A. Ryerson, *The revolution is now begun: the radical committees of Philadelphia* (1978) · W. W. Hinshaw, *Encyclopedia of American Quaker genealogy*, ed. [T. W. Marshall and others], 7 vols. (1936–50), vol. 2 · G. Mackinney and C. F. Hoban, eds., *Votes and proceedings of the house of representatives of the province of Pennsylvania*, 8 vols. (1754–76), vol. 6 · *Minutes of the supreme executive council of Pennsylvania* (1851–3)

Archives Hist. Soc. Penn., society collection · Hist. Soc. Penn., Irvine MSS · National Archives and Records Administration, Washington, DC, MSS · NYPL, Reed MSS

Likenesses J. S. Copley, double portrait, oils, 1773, Hist. Soc. Penn. [*see illus.*] · G. Stuart, oils, 1795, priv. coll. · C. W. Peale, oils, Independence Hall National Historical Park · J. Trumbull, oils, priv. coll.

Wealth at death debtor; few assets: Rossman, *Thomas Mifflin*

Mifflin returned to state politics in 1778, winning election to the assembly. He opposed the egalitarian unicameral Pennsylvania constitution, and contributed to the formation of the Republican (anti-constitutionalist) Society. In November 1782 and again in the next year he was elected to the confederation congress by the now republican assembly. In December 1783 congress elected him its president. He succeeded in the difficult task of assembling nine state delegations to ratify the treaty of peace with Britain in early 1784. He was ousted as a delegate in 1784 by the constitutionalists, but a republican resurgence made him assembly speaker (1785–8) and then supreme executive council president (1788–90).

Mifflin was also a delegate to the federal constitutional convention of 1787, and presided over the Pennsylvania constitutional convention of 1790. In both of these he was not an active speaker or floor leader. Both documents established what his experience had led him to demand— a bicameral legislature and a stronger executive. Pennsylvanians overwhelmingly elected him their first state governor in October 1790. He was re-elected for the maximum three terms in 1793 and 1796.

Although formerly of the more conservative party in Pennsylvania, Mifflin by 1793 was a democratic-republican follower of Thomas Jefferson, chiefly because Mifflin was pro-French. He at first opposed the use of force against the Whiskey rebels in Pennsylvania in 1794, advocating to President Washington that judicial process be attempted. When this failed, Mifflin avidly recruited volunteers for the militia detachments to be sent against

Mijn, Heroman van der (c.1684–1741), portrait painter, was born in Amsterdam, the son of Andries Heerenszoon van der Mijn (b. 1655) and his wife, Trijntje Hendricks (b. 1658). He entered the studio of Ernst Stuven and on 26 April 1706 married Susanna Bloemendael (b. 1682). He worked as a flower painter in Amsterdam at least until 1709. Three years later he is recorded briefly in Antwerp before moving to Düsseldorf, where he was employed by Johann Wilhelm, elector palatine. There he painted a number of history pieces. By 1717 he had returned to Antwerp, where he began to specialize in portraiture. There William Leathes, the British ambassador in Brussels, commissioned a portrait and a number of history pictures from him (all Christchurch, Ipswich). In 1721, or shortly afterwards, with the recommendation of Lord Cadogan, who was Leathes's superior, he moved to London. Vertue considered him 'a very Laborious neat painter' (Vertue, *Note books*, 3.34); his portraits, for instance that of Carew Hervey Mildmay (1733; Gov. Art Coll., HM Embassy, Bonn), are typified by their high finish and complex iconography. By 1728 mounting debts forced him to sell his work at auction and part with a large house in Soho Square. Shortly afterwards, Brownlow, eighth earl of Exeter, used van der Mijn's meticulous technique to restore his grandfather's collection of paintings at Burghley House, Northamptonshire, and a number of his still-life paintings remain in that collection. In 1734, now working in a house in Prince's Street, Cavendish Square, he was visited by William IV, prince of Orange, recently married to George II's daughter Princess Anne. In 1736, to escape his debts, van der Mijn returned to the Low Countries with the royal couple, and he painted a portrait of the prince (Groninger Museum, Groningen), the following year. Before long he fell out of favour with his patron and returned to London, where he died in November 1741.

Heroman van der Mijn travelled to London with his sister Agatha (*b.* 1705?), who was a painter of flowers and still life. Five of van der Mijn's sons—Gerhardt (*b.* 1706), Andreas (*b.* 1714, *d.* after 1777), Frans (1719–1783), Robert (*b.* 1724, *d.* after 1764), and George (1726/7–1763)—and his daughter Cornelia (*b.* 1709, *d.* after 1772) also practised painting, many of them specializing in still life. Frans van der Mijn achieved some success as a portraitist in London and also in Norwich, where he resided for several years. In 1763 he became a member of the Free Society of Artists in London. He died in Moorfields, London, on 20 August 1783.   HUGH BELSEY

Sources A. Staring, 'De van der Mijns in Engeland', *Nederlands Kunsthistorisch Jaarboek* (1966), 171–203 • A. Staring, 'De van der Mijns in Engeland', *Nederlands Kunsthistorisch Jaarboek* (1968), 201–44 • M. Beal, 'Bolingbroke and Mildmay in 1733: an allegorical portrait by Herman van der Mijn', *British Journal for Eighteenth-Century Studies*, 21 (1998), 55–72 • Vertue, *Note books*, 3.34–5, 64, 69, 72, 87, 94, 99 • J. Kerslake, 'The duke of Chandos' missing duchess', *National Trust Studies* (1981), 138–49
Likenesses H. van der Mijn, self-portrait, oils; Christies, 11 June 1948, lot 148

Mikardo, Ian [*known as* Mik] (1908–1993), politician, was born in Portsmouth on 9 July 1908, the son of Moshe (Morris) Mikardo, a tailor, and his wife, Bluma. Both his parents came to Britain in the massive Jewish exodus from the tsarist empire in the last decades of the nineteenth century and the first of the twentieth: his mother from the village of Yampol, in the western Ukraine, and his father (who arrived in Britain at the time of the Second South African War) from Kutno, a textile-manufacturing town west of Warsaw. When Morris Mikardo disembarked in London his total possessions consisted of the clothes that he stood up in, plus a little bag containing a change of shirt and underclothes, his accessories for prayer, and one rouble. He initially settled in the East End of London, intending, like many Russian Jews, to move on to the United States. He was, however, unable to scrape together the money for the fare, and left for Portsmouth (where there was work tailoring for the navy) with his wife in 1907.

Mikardo recalled that the language of the family in those early days was Yiddish. When he went to school—first the Beneficial Society school, then Omega Street school, both in Portsmouth—he had only a few words of English, which put him at a disadvantage with his classmates. His mother wanted him to become a rabbi, and next sent him to Aria College in Portsmouth, which had been set up 'for the training and maintenance of young men, natives of the County of Hampshire, as Jewish Divines on orthodox principles' (Mikardo, 30). He attributed his capacity to draft a document, at which he was superb,

Ian Mikardo (1908–1993), by Walter Bird, 1967

to the rigours of Aria College and, subsequently, to an outstanding Latin master at Portsmouth southern secondary school for boys.

Leaving school at 15, Mikardo shuffled from job to job, his greatest pleasure being to support a great Portsmouth football side. In 1930 he met Mary (*b.* 1907), the daughter of Benjamin Rosetsky, and as he put it, 'found a new family in hers' (Mikardo, 44). They married at Mile End and Bow District synagogue on 3 January 1932, and joined the Labour Party and Poale Zion, the Zionist workers' movement, which was affiliated to the party. All his life they were immersed in Jewish causes, and help for Israel, which they often visited. Nevertheless, Mik—as he was universally called in the labour movement—was very much an 'internal Israeli', worked with Mapam (the united workers' party), and abhorred anything which smacked of gratuitous provocation of the Palestinian Arabs.

Mikardo's crucial break came when he stumbled on an advertisement for a seminar in 1931 on what was then called 'scientific management'. He had already seen enough in his various jobs in factories, warehouses, and marketing and distribution agencies, to satisfy himself that there was much room for improvement in the management of industries and commercial organizations. His enrolment in that seminar led to nearly sixty years of activity with the Association of Supervisory Staffs, Executives and Technicians (later the Association of Scientific, Technical and Managerial Staffs, of which he was president from 1968 to 1973). He spent the rest of the 1930s as a management consultant, and during the Second World War worked as an administrator in the aircraft-building industry. In 1944 he published *Centralised Control of Industry*, advocating the extension into peacetime of wartime controls on industry.

In 1944 Mikardo was adopted as the Labour candidate for Reading, regarded at the time as a safe Conservative seat. He quickly introduced a more 'scientific' approach to canvassing, dividing the electorate into 'fors', 'againsts', and 'don't knows', and concentrating his activists' efforts on persuading the fors to vote and converting the 'don't knows'; the 'Reading system', as it came to be called, was subsequently adopted by all the major parties. In the same year as his adoption, he achieved overnight fame in the labour movement. At the London conference of the party he moved a resolution, in effect restating the fundamental principles of the party and committing a Labour government to extensive nationalization. 'If L Plates had existed in those days I'd have been wearing one', he later wrote (Mikardo, 76). His motion was supported by the formidable Bessie Braddock and was carried by a large majority against the wishes of the party leadership. As he left Methodist Central Hall, Herbert Morrison put a hand on his shoulder and said, 'Young man, you did very well this morning. That was a good speech you made—but you realise, don't you, that you've lost us the General Election?' (ibid., 77). That 'misjudgement' was followed by Labour's victory in 1945 and Mikardo's election, by a majority of 6390, as MP for Reading.

Despite his new-found prominence in the labour movement, Mikardo was not invited to become a minister in the Attlee government. Indeed, Attlee believed that both he and Austen Albu were unsuitable, apparently on racial grounds: 'They both belonged to the Chosen People, and he did not think that he wanted any more of them!' (B. Pimlott, *Hugh Dalton*, 1985, 596). Mikardo's chances of a ministerial career were further diminished by his close association with the Bevanite left of the parliamentary party: he often contributed to *Tribune*, was one of fifteen signatories of the *Keep Left* pamphlet (1947), which criticized the government's timidity, and—with Sir Richard Acland, Michael Foot, and others—wrote its successor, *Keeping Left* (1950). He also wrote *The Second Five Years* (1948), setting out a radical programme for a second post-war Labour administration.

Mikardo held his Reading seat through the general elections of 1950, 1951, and 1955—and in the last year published *Electioneering in Labour Marginal Constituencies*—but in the general election of 1959 he was defeated by 3942 votes. He also lost his seat on the national executive committee of the Labour Party (to which he had first been elected in 1950) in the same year, though he returned in 1960, and remained a member until 1978. While out of parliament he focused his considerable energies on the development of his private business as an entrepreneur specializing in trade with the Soviet bloc, ably assisted by his secretary, Jo Richardson. His business activities led him to establish close relations with officials from the Soviet Union and eastern Europe, which reinforced the

suspicion with which he was viewed by his Conservative opponents, and by many on the right wing of the Labour Party.

Mikardo returned to parliament as MP for the safe Labour seat of Poplar in the East End of London in the general election of 1964. He retained the seat (renamed Tower Hamlets, Bethnal Green, and Bow in 1974, and Bow and Poplar in 1983) until his retirement in 1987. He took a special interest in the problems of the many Bangladeshi families arriving in his constituency, whose children often had only a very few words of English. He saw them harassed by having to study the usual range of school studies while still unfamiliar with the language of their teachers and textbooks. Mindful of his own problems as a Yiddish speaker half a century earlier, he persuaded education ministers in the Labour government to allocate extra funds to local authorities where lack of English among immigrant children was a substantial problem. Mikardo was a popular local MP, and very active on behalf of his constituents. He was much less popular with the leadership of his party, and with Harold Wilson in particular; he was highly critical of the latter's policy on the Vietnam conflict, steadfastly opposed all forms of income policy, and was a firm and highly effective opponent of Barbara Castle's proposals for trade union reform outlined in the government white paper *In Place of Strife*. Indeed by 1970 'he had become—from his power base in the Tribune group—in effect the leader of the internal opposition to the government' (*The Times*, 7 May 1993). Denied ministerial preferment, he nevertheless made a significant impact as chairman of the select committee on nationalized industries, from 1966 to 1970. In the opinion of one House of Commons clerk, he 'was simply the most skilful operator in committee that any of us ever saw' (*The Independent*, 7 May 1993).

Mikardo served highly effectively as chairman of the national executive committee of the Labour Party in 1970–71, and as chairman of the Parliamentary Labour Party from March to November 1974; he was also chairman of the international committee of the Labour Party from 1973 to 1978, and vice-president of the Socialist International from 1978 to 1983. During the Labour administrations of Harold Wilson and James Callaghan in 1974–9 he was again marginalized, and in 1978 he lost his seat on the national executive committee to a younger firebrand of the left, Neil Kinnock. He re-emerged as campaign manager for his old ally Michael Foot, who in November 1980 defeated Denis Healey for the leadership of the party, by ten votes; but after the party's disastrous performance in the general election of 1983 under Foot, he had little sympathy either for his successor, Neil Kinnock, or for his predominantly Bennite opponents on the left. After his retirement from the Commons, at the general election of 1987, he published his beautifully written autobiography under the apt title *Back-Bencher*.

With heavy jowls, thick black-rimmed spectacles, and bushy eyebrows which remained stubbornly black long after the rest of his hair had gone white, Mikardo was a gift to caricaturists. Winston Churchill once quipped: 'I'm told he's not as nice as he looks' (*The Times*, 7 May 1993). In fact, he was genial and approachable, with a sharp wit and a talent for self-parody. He was well known as a Commons 'character', and was for many years the house's unofficial bookmaker; fascinated by the mathematics of probability, he even published a pamphlet on the bookmaker's trade, *It's a Mug's Game* (1951). He inspired devotion among his constituency activists, as two socialists from Reading testified after his death:

> At first we were not unduly impressed. No overwhelming charm of manner or appearance, a harsh, somewhat adenoidal voice, and yet, within minutes he had won our respect and, soon after, even a grudging affection. Whatever the topic—the National Health Service, education, social deprivation, nationalisation or socialism itself—he inspired others. He knew where he was going and we wanted to go with him … above all Mik had that rarest of qualities among professional politicians—integrity.   (*The Independent*, 22 May 1993)

He was devoted to his wife Mary (who was progressively disabled after a major heart attack in 1959), and to their two daughters, Ruth and Judy. In his final years he moved to Cheadle, Cheshire, in order to be near the latter. Suffering from sarcoma and chronic obstructive airways disease, he died on 6 May 1993 at the Stepping Hill Hospital, Stockport, after a stroke.   TAM DALYELL

Sources I. Mikardo, *Back-bencher* (1988) · *The Times* (7 May 1993) · *Daily Telegraph* (7 May 1993) · *The Guardian* (7 May 1993) · *The Independent* (7 May 1993), (22 May 1993) · *The Herald* (7 May 1993) · *WWW* · personal knowledge (2004) · private information (2004) · m. cert. · d. cert.
Archives Labour History Archive and Study Centre, Manchester, papers | Labour History Archive and Study Centre, Manchester, corresp. with Morgan Phillips
Likenesses W. Bird, photograph, 1967, NPG [*see illus.*] · photograph, repro. in *The Times* · photograph, repro. in *Daily Telegraph* · photograph, repro. in *The Guardian* · photograph, repro. in *The Independent* · photographs, repro. in Mikardo, *Back-bencher*, following p. 124 · photographs, Hult. Arch.
Wealth at death £107,176: *The Times* (5 Aug 1993)

Milbanke, Mark (*c.*1720–1805), naval officer, was the third son of Sir Ralph Milbanke, fourth baronet (*d.* 1748), of Halnaby, Yorkshire, and his second wife, Anne, daughter of Edward Delavall of South Dissington in Northumberland. Milbanke entered the Royal Naval Academy at Portsmouth on 23 February 1737, and studied there for three years before serving in the *Tilbury*, the *Romney* with Captain Thomas Grenville, and the *Princess Mary* with Captain Thomas Smith. On 22 March 1744 he passed his lieutenant's examination, and was, according to his certificate, more than twenty.

On 20 April 1744 Milbanke was promoted lieutenant of the *Anglesea*, and in December he was appointed to the *Royal Sovereign*. On 13 September 1746 he was promoted to command the sloop *Serpent*, and on 21 May 1748 he was posted captain of the frigate *Inverness*, though in her he saw no active service, and he spent the peace on half pay.

In 1755 Milbanke commanded the *Romney*, and in July 1756 he was appointed to the *Guernsey* (50 guns), in which in 1758 he went out to the Mediterranean. In the summer of 1759 he was sent on a mission to the emperor of Morocco, and was thus absent from his ship in the action off Lagos on 20 August. He continued in the *Guernsey* until the peace in 1763 which he spent on half pay. At some stage he married Mary, *née* Webber (*d.* 1812); they had three children.

In 1775–6 Milbanke commanded the *Barfleur*, guardship at Portsmouth; in 1777–8 the *Princess Royal*; and afterwards the *Namur*. After his promotion to rear-admiral of the white on 19 March 1779 he occasionally acted as commander-in-chief at Plymouth, in the absence of Lord Shuldham. Milbanke was advanced to vice-admiral of the blue on 26 September 1780, and in the spring of 1782 he was appointed to a command in the fleet under Lord Howe, with whom he served in the North Sea, and afterwards in the relief of Gibraltar. From 1783 to 1786 he was port-admiral at Plymouth, and during the years 1790 to 1792 he was commander-in-chief at Newfoundland. On 1 February 1793 he was promoted admiral but he was to have no active command during the French Revolutionary Wars. From 14 September 1799 to 24 March 1803 he was commander-in-chief at Portsmouth. Milbanke's son Ralph (*d.* 1823), a captain in the navy, retired from the active list in 1804. The younger of his two daughters, Elizabeth Mary, married William Huskisson. There is an unflattering character sketch of Mark Milbanke by his secretary, Joseph Harris, published in *The Naval Atalantis* under Harris's pseudonym, Junior Nauticus. Milbanke died on 10 June 1805.   J. K. LAUGHTON, *rev.* ROGER MORRISS

Sources J. Charnock, ed., *Biographia navalis*, 6 (1798), 81 · J. Barrow, *The life of Earl Howe* (1835) · corresp. as commander-in-chief at Newfoundland and Portsmouth, corresp. with admiralty, his lieutenant's certificate, PRO

Milbanke, Ralph Gordon Noel King, second earl of Lovelace (1839–1906), mountaineer, was born on 2 July 1839 at 10 St James's Square, London, the second son of William King-Noel, first earl of Lovelace (1805–1893), and Augusta Ada, *née* Byron (1815–1852), the only legitimate child of Lord Byron. Though nearly a quarter of a century had passed, the shock waves from Byron's disastrously incompatible marriage to Annabella Milbanke remained destructive: her rationalism could no more abide his romantic theatricality than could his self-centred soul tolerate her coldly mathematical mind. Continuing family quarrels meant that the unfortunate Ralph was soon controlled by his grandmother Lady Byron, becoming 'her principal educational experiment' (Lovelace, 3). Her horror of public schools (which she blamed for Byron's bisexuality) ensured that Ralph was educated entirely by private tutors, including Dr William Carpenter—with whom his mother had an affair. Yet his grandmother let him enter unfashionable University College, Oxford, in 1859. On her death in May 1860 he left Oxford when told that he could not retain his rooms during vacations. Effectively homeless, he travelled abroad, including a year in Iceland. In 1861 he adopted the Milbanke surname as directed by his grandmother's will. When his tragic elder brother Byron Noel, Viscount Ockham, died aged twenty-six (1 September 1862), Ralph approached the House of Lords committee of privileges and succeeded, in May

1864, as thirteenth Baron Wentworth, the ancient barony inherited through Lady Byron. Thus 'for thirty years [he] was in the somewhat unusual position of sitting in [the Lords] contemporaneously with his own father' (ibid., 9).

Having read Byron's poetry, Wentworth was keen to discover the truth about his grandfather's relationship with Augusta Leigh. Attempts to do so from 1865 onwards were thwarted by Lady Byron's trustees, who denied him access to her correspondence for the crucial years 1815–16. He was particularly upset by the publication of Teresa Guiccioli's 1868 memoir, *Lord Byron jugé par les témoins de sa vie*, and by Harriet Beecher Stowe's 'Lady Byron vindicated', British publication of which by Macmillan he failed to prevent in 1869. Only thirty-six copies were made of his 1887 book *Lady Noel Byron and the Leighs* which included the unusual title-page warning: 'STRICTLY PRIVATE … No publication of the contents of this volume may take place without authorisation in writing from Lord Wentworth or Lady Noel Byron's other representatives.' It was not until the death on December 1893 of his father, aged eighty-nine, that Ralph gained unrestricted access to the Lovelace papers. In May 1896 he accepted John Murray IV's offer to be honorary 'editor in chief' of a new edition of Byron's *Letters and Journals*, really the work of Rowland E. Prothero. The contract was terminated in 1899 when Lovelace tried 'to restrain Mr Murray from publishing any letters from Byron to Augusta whatsoever' (Lovelace, 138). In December 1905 he privately published *Astarte: a Fragment of Truth Concerning Lord Byron*, giving some of the 200 copies to friends as diverse as the military historian John Fortescue, Swinburne, Lady Gregory, William de Morgan, and Henry James. *Astarte*, effectively the voice of Lady Byron's spirit, was important as long as the Lovelace papers remained inaccessible to scholars; it provided a rose-coloured glimpse.

On 25 August 1869 Ralph married Fanny (1853–1878), daughter of the Revd George Heriot, mother of his only child, Ada Mary Milbanke (1870–1917). They separated in 1871, Ada thereafter being brought up by her aunt Lady Anne Blunt. Again Ralph embarked on 'a long period of aimless wandering' abroad (Lovelace, 46). He was happiest among mountains and their peasant inhabitants. Though never a member of the Alpine Club, he was an inspired climber, first to reach the summit of the Aiguille Noire de Peuteret (5 August 1877), also scaling Pta Giordani (4046 metres, 6 September 1877). In the former case he cut the very top off the mountain and brought it back to his hotel where a Niçoise lady friend, Jola Caccia-Raynaud, was asked to tread symbolically on it (Palazzi-Lavaggi, 141). He then named that peak the Jola (3772 metres). In 1865 he had witnessed the retrieval of the bodies of Lord Francis Douglas's companions from the Matterhorn (4477 metres), but successfully conquered it himself on 30 August 1872. As late as 1897, aged fifty-eight, he could scale the Aiguille de Grépon (3482 metres).

After his estranged wife's death in 1878 Wentworth was able to marry again, this time happily; he wed Mary Caroline Wortley (1848–1941) on 30 December 1880. Politically he was heavily influenced by his brother-in-law Wilfrid

Scawen Blunt, opposing General Graham's Suakim expedition (1884) and defending Arabi Pasha in the House of Lords. He succeeded his father as second earl of Lovelace on the latter's death in 1893 and was among the 41 peers who voted in favour of Gladstone's Home Rule Bill of that year when 419 were 'non-contents'.

Lovelace died very suddenly on 28 August 1906 at his home, Ockham Park, near Ripley, Surrey, and his ashes were interred in the King family vault at All Saints' Church, Ockham, six days later after cremation at Woking. His only daughter succeeded to the Wentworth barony, his half-brother the Hon. L. F. King-Noel becoming third earl of Lovelace. His second wife published a memoir of him in 1920 and brought out a public edition of *Astarte* in the following year, including 'many additional letters'. RALPH LLOYD-JONES

Sources Mary, countess of Lovelace, *Ralph, earl of Lovelace: a memoir* (1920) · Contessa Carolina Palazzi-Lavaggi, *Ricordi Alpini* (1890) · GEC, *Peerage*, new edn, vol. 8 · Burke, *Peerage* (1999) · Burke, *Peerage* (1932) · Burke, *Peerage* (1884) · B. Wooley, *The bride of science: romance, reason and Byron's daughter* (1999) · R. Milbanke, *Lady Noel Byron and the Leighs; some authentic records of certain circumstances in the lives of Augusta Leigh, and others of her family, that concerned Anne Isabella, Lady Byron, in the course of forty years after her separation* (privately printed, limited to only 36 copies, 1887) · R. Milbanke, *Astarte: a fragment of truth concerning George Gordon Byron, sixth Lord Byron* (privately printed, limited to 200 copies, 1905) · R. Milbanke, *Astarte: a fragment of truth etc.; new edition, with many additional letters, edited by Mary countess of Lovelace* (1921) · R. Milbanke, 'Ascent of the Jola', *Alpine Journal*, 9 (Aug 1878) · *The Times* (30 Aug 1906) · *The Times* (3 Sept 1906) · *The Times* (10 Sept 1906) · E. Pyatt, *Guinness book of mountains and mountaineering* (1980)

Archives BL, letters · Bodl. Oxf., corresp. and papers · John Murray, London, letters

Likenesses photographs, repro. in Lovelace, *Ralph, earl of Lovelace*

Wealth at death £380,976 15s.: probate, 22 Dec 1906, CGPLA Eng. & Wales

Milbourn, John (*fl.* 1763–1816), artist, was a student of Francis Cotes RA. Of his parents, nothing is known. In 1767 he accompanied the pastellist John Russell to Guildford, possibly as his assistant. He was awarded a small premium by the Society of Arts in 1764 before entering the Royal Academy Schools in February 1769, where he won a silver medal in 1770. He exhibited four crayon portraits at the Royal Academy between 1763 and 1774. As an artist Milbourn appears to have been extremely versatile, working as a scene-painter in Covent Garden, London, between 1783 and 1789 as well as practising as a picture restorer. Ellis Waterhouse has ascribed a group of grisaille religious scenes in the chapel at Greenwich Hospital (rebuilt after a fire in 1779) to his hand, and Horace Walpole described him in 1795 as 'A drawing master in the New Road, Marylebone' (Walpole, *Corr.*, 113). He is also cited as having copied a portrait of Frances Jenningson, duchess of Tyrconnell, for Walpole's collection at Strawberry Hill. It appears that he was for a time acting as drawing-master at 'Mrs. Stephenson's school in Queen's Square and at other schools which produced him 5 or £600 pr. annm' before the school closed, leaving him without employment (Farington, *Diary*, 14.4914). During the late eighteenth and early nineteenth centuries Milbourn was an active and ubiquitous member of London's artistic community. He was a friend of Paul Sandby as well as an associate of the history painter Edward Edwards, who according to Farington's account dramatically expired in Milbourn's arms in 1806. He was also appointed as a mourner at the funeral of the engraver Giuseppi Marchi. Farington notes that Milbourn had a wife who predeceased him, as well as four sons; one 'A Captain of Engineers in India, another a clerk at the Bank ... and a third who is a Lieutenant in the Navy' (ibid.).   HALLIE RUBENHOLD

Sources B. Stewart and M. Cutten, The dictionary of portrait painters in Britain up to 1920 (1997) · Waterhouse, 18c painters · E. Croft-Murray, Decorative painting in England, 1537–1837, 2 (1970) · Farington, Diary, 8.2923–4, 2928–9; 9.3258; 14.4914 · Walpole, Corr., vol. 2 · Redgrave, Artists · The exhibition of the Royal Academy (1763–74) [exhibition catalogues] · Premiums offered by the Society for the Encouragement of Arts (1764) · Graves, RA exhibitors · S. C. Hutchison, 'The Royal Academy Schools, 1768–1830', Walpole Society, 38 (1960–62), 123–91, esp. 133

Milbourne, Luke (*bap.* 1622, *d.* 1668), clergyman and ejected minister, was born at Loughborough, Leicestershire, and baptized on St Luke's day, 18 October 1622. On 8 March 1634 he was admitted as a sizar at Emmanuel College, Cambridge; he graduated BA in 1638. He was ordained by Matthew Wren, bishop of Ely, and first settled at King's Lynn, either as curate or schoolmaster. Thence he removed to the perpetual curacy of Honiley, Warwickshire, where he lived at the manor of Wroxhall, succeeding Ephraim Hewet, or Huit, who had emigrated to America. Here, on 28 May 1648, with his wife, Phoebe, he baptized a daughter, Elizabeth, and then on 14 March 1650 Luke *Milbourne (*d.* 1720), later a Cambridge scholar.

Edmund Calamy reports that Milbourne's presbyterian royalism earned him abuse from the soldiers, an interview with their general, and a narrow escape from imprisonment; he kept 30 January, the date of the king's execution, as a fast day for the rest of his life. Milbourne felt able to take the covenant, but refused the engagement to the Commonwealth, and was lucky to be able to retain his cure. A presbyterian by persuasion, he was a member of the classis of Kenilworth. Following a dispute between John Bryan and a baptist lay preacher, John Onley, which went badly for the former, Milbourne was one of thirteen ministers who in July 1656 signed an order forbidding further disputations without prior permission of the classis. His cure of Wroxhall, worth £6 13s. 4d. per annum, but augmented by the patron and tenants to £40, was exempt from episcopal jurisdiction. It was a donative in the gift of the Burgoyne family, latterly Sir Roger Burgoyne, whom Milbourne probably served as chaplain. In these circumstances he 'might have kept in with a little conformity' but chose to suffer ejection under the Act of Uniformity of 1662 (Calamy, *Abridgement*, 2.747).

After moving to Coventry with his wife and six children, Milbourne declined to teach and was prevented by the authorities from taking boarders for the grammar school. After the coming of the Five Mile Act he was forced to leave the city and moved to Newington Green, near London, where his wife kept a school. Milbourne died in 1668 and was buried on 10 March in the churchyard of St Michael's, Coventry. He had twenty children, of whom only four, including Luke, also curate of Wroxhall, survived him. His widow, Phoebe, was granted the administration of his estate, valued by inventory at £282 5s. 8d., on 28 September 1670.   STEPHEN WRIGHT

Sources Calamy rev., 349–50 · Venn, Alum. Cant. · J. T. Cliffe, The puritan gentry besieged, 1650–1700 (1993) · A. Hughes, Politics, society and civil war in Warwickshire, 1620–1660 (1987) · E. Calamy, ed., An abridgement of Mr. Baxter's history of his life and times, with an account of the ministers, &c., who were ejected after the Restauration of King Charles II, 2nd edn, 2 vols. (1713) · E. Calamy, A continuation of the account of the ministers ... who were ejected and silenced after the Restoration in 1660, 2 vols. (1727) · will, Lichfield Joint RO, B/C/11/1670
Likenesses oils, Exeter College, Oxford
Wealth at death £282 5s. 8d.: Birmingham Administration, cited in Calamy rev.; will, Lichfield Joint RO, B/C/11/1670

Milbourne, Luke (1649–1720), poet, was born in Wroxhall, Warwickshire, the son of Luke *Milbourne (*bap.* 1622, *d.* 1668), clergyman, and his wife, Phoebe, schoolmistress. In 1665 he entered Pembroke College, Cambridge, where he graduated MA in 1670. While at university he contributed Latin verses to *Lacrymae Cantabrigienses* (1670) on the death of Charles II's sister Henrietta, duchess of Orléans. After graduating Milbourne appears to have held chaplaincies to the English merchants at Hamburg and Rotterdam. In 1672 he became vicar of St Stephen by St Albans, and on 12 May 1676 he married Loise Goldinge. Milbourne became rector of Osmandiston, Norfolk, in 1677, a post he retained until 1702. During this period he appears to have held a further living, in Yarmouth. Here he became acquainted with Rowland Davies, afterwards dean of Cork. Davies makes a number of references to Milbourne in his journal, including the following entry made in 1689:

> After sermon I went with Mr Reynolds and Mr J. Ellys to Mr Milbourn's, where we drank a flask of Florence with him, and then I read his satire made upon Ostia, and then I came home. (*Journal of Rowland Davies*, 66)

This satire would seem to have been a lampoon on Yarmouth (*Journal of Rowland Davies*, 41).

In 1688 Milbourne was appointed lecturer of St Leonard, Shoreditch, and in 1704 he succeeded Samuel Harris as rector of St Ethelburga, Bishopsgate, London. He was 'the priest of the church of England and rector of a church in the city of London' who, in a published letter (1713) to Roger Laurence, author of *Lay Baptism Invalid*, refuted the validity of lay baptism by the authority of Calvin and of French protestant writers. Milbourne's sympathies were generally with the high-church party, and he was a supporter of Henry Sacheverell. In sermons such as *The Christian Subject's Duty to his Lawful Prince* (1716) Milbourne made frequent reference to the martyrdom of Charles I, and in 1713 he preached a sermon strongly criticizing the rule of William, calling him a tyrant. These views attracted the displeasure of Bishop Kennett, who wondered 'why he did not stay in Holland and why he is suffered to stay in England?' (Kennett, 333).

Milbourne is best known for his *Notes on Dryden's Virgil*, published in 1698. Here he claims that Dryden has transformed his author into 'a Virgil of another stamp, of a coarser allay; a silly, impertinent, nonsensical writer, of a various and uncertain style' (p. 4). After some general criticisms of the translation, Milbourne offers a detailed list of pedantic objections to Dryden's versions of the *Eclogues* and *Georgics*. Of a passage in Eclogue 3, for example, he remarks that it contains 'nothing of Virgil's spirit or pastoral style, but pure Ovid, or somewhat looser than he' (p. 60). At the end of the volume Milbourne offers his own version of Eclogues 1 and 4, as well as book 1 of the *Georgics*. The opening lines of this translation give some indication of Milbourne's poetic style:

> What makes the richest tilth, beneath what signs
> To plough, and when to match your elms and vines?
> What care with flocks, and what with herds agrees,
> And all the management of frugal bees,
> I sing Maecenas!

'To call them execrable is a kindness', asserts a twentieth-century critic, Harry Solomon, of these translations (Solomon, 194). It seems likely that Milbourne's animosity towards Dryden was fuelled by the neglect of his own translation of *Aeneid* book 1, published in 1688. A favourable, if belated, notice of this work did appear in the *Gentleman's Journal* (August 1692, 17). The reviewer claims that Milbourne's 'lofty pen vyes with the most majestic of our age', and suggests that the translation would have received more attention had it not appeared at the time of the revolution. Dryden defended himself vigorously against Milbourne's attack in his preface to *Fables Ancient and Modern*, treating his criticisms with scorn:

> I am satisfied however, that while he and I live together, I shall not be thought the worst poet of the age … He has taken some pains with my poetry; but nobody will be persuaded to take the same with his.　(*Works of John Dryden, Poems*, 4.1461)

Dryden condemns Milbourne's character as well as his verse, hinting that he lost his living for libelling his parishioners. If this is the case it would seem to be the Yarmouth living that was forfeited, for he retained his rectorship of St Ethelburga until his death. Pope was a champion of Dryden's cause: he made Milbourne a priest of Dulness in the *Dunciad* (2.311–14) and censured his captious remarks on Dryden in the *Essay on Criticism* (462–3). Milbourne died in London on 15 April 1720.　SARAH ANNES BROWN

Sources The works of John Dryden, ed. W. Scott, 18 vols. (1808), vol. 1, pp. 394–404 · Venn, *Alum. Cant.*, 1/3 · A. Chalmers, ed., *The general biographical dictionary*, new edn, 32 vols. (1812–17) · W. Kennett, *The wisdom of looking backwards* (1715) · BL cat. · Journal of the Very Rev. Rowland Davies, ed. R. Caulfield, CS, 68 (1857) · F. L. Colvile, *The worthies of Warwickshire who lived between 1500 and 1800* [1870] · H. M. Solomon, *Sir Richard Blackmore* (1980) · The poems, ed. J. Kinsley (1958), vol. 4 · Gentleman's Journal (Aug 1692) · L. Milbourne, Notes on Dryden's Virgil (1698) · DNB · IGI
Archives Birm. CA, sermons and discourses
Likenesses oils, Exeter College, Oxford

Milbourne, Richard (d. 1624), bishop of Carlisle, was born in London and grew up at Talkin, in Cumberland. From 1579 he was a student at Queens' College, Cambridge, graduating BA in 1582, and proceeding MA in 1585 and DD in 1601. He was a fellow of Queens' from 1582 to 1592, and was incorporated at Oxford in 1594. About this time he married, and among his children was Leonard, who eventually followed him first to Queens' and then into the ministry. Milbourne was rector of Sevenoaks, Kent, from 1591 to 1616, on the presentation of Archbishop Whitgift, and also rector of Cheam, Surrey, from 1611, and vicar of Goudhurst, Kent, from 1612 to 1613. His only publication was a sermon, *Concerning Impositions of Hands* (1607), preached at St Mary's Cray during Archbishop Bancroft's visitation to Canterbury diocese, in which Milbourne defended the rite of confirmation from the attacks of puritan critics.

Milbourne's career prospered once he became chaplain in 1610 to Prince Henry, who, according to Anthony Wood, admired Milbourne above all his chaplains for his conduct, scholarship, and preaching; doubtless it was through Henry's influence that Milbourne received the deanery of Rochester, on the crown's nomination, in 1611. Following Henry's death in 1612, Milbourne became a senior chaplain to Prince Charles, who may have been responsible for Milbourne's elevation to the bishopric of St David's in 1615. His consecration took place at Lambeth in July 1615, but he remained parson of Sevenoaks until 1616, and appears briefly in the diary of Lady Anne Clifford, wife of the local magnate, the earl of Dorset, supporting her during a dispute over her inheritance.

In June 1621 Milbourne was promoted to the bishopric of Carlisle. Few traces remain of Milbourne's time as bishop in either of his two sees, though he appears to have resided in his dioceses. At Carlisle in 1622 he recruited Isaac Singleton, a former chaplain of Bishop King of London, to be his chancellor and his archdeacon of Carlisle (1623). Milbourne did not attend the parliament of 1624, probably owing to ill health, and on his death that May was buried in the churchyard of Carlisle Cathedral.

KENNETH FINCHAM

Sources R. Milbourne, *Concerning impositions of hands* (1607) · Venn, *Alum. Cant.* · Wood, *Ath. Oxon.*, new edn, 1.268 · K. Fincham, *Prelate as pastor: the episcopate of James I* (1990) · P. E. McCullough, *Sermons at court: politics and religion in Elizabethan and Jacobean preaching* (1998) [incl. CD-ROM] · The diaries of Lady Anne Clifford, ed. D. J. H. Clifford (1990) · Bodl. Oxf., MS Rawl. D. 912, fol. 617v · Fasti Angl., 1541–1857, [Canterbury], 55 · register of Whitgift, LPL, 1, fol. 493r · J. Hacket, *Scrinia reserata: a memorial offer'd to the great deservings of John Williams*, 2 pts (1693), pt. 1, p. 207
Wealth at death intestate; administration granted to son: PRO, PROB 6/11, fol. 112

Milburg. See Mildburg (d. in or after 716).

Milburn [née Bagnall], **Clara Emily** (1883–1961), housewife and diarist, was born on 24 June 1883 at 4 Springfield Place, Hannall Lane, Coventry, the daughter of Frank Bagnall, iron turner, and his wife, Harriett, née Gibson. She lived with her parents until her marriage, on 21 June 1905, to John (Jack) Milburn (1876–1955), an engineer who worked with her brother Frank at the Coventry factory of Alfred Herbert Ltd. Clara and Jack Milburn made their first home in Warwick Avenue, Coventry. They were soon joined by a maid, (Caroline) Kate Taylor, who stayed in their employment almost continuously for the next forty-seven years, becoming a close family friend. On 18 May 1914 their only child, Alan John, was born, and in September of that year the Milburns moved to Canley Corner, a large detached house they had had built beside the main road between Coventry and Kenilworth. In 1931 they moved again, to Burleigh, a spacious detached house at Balsall Common, roughly 6 miles west of Coventry and 3 from the village of Berkswell, where Clara Milburn spent much of her time. A public-spirited and energetic woman, she was a stalwart member of the Women's Institute, a friend of Coventry Cathedral, and a regular worshipper at her local church. The family was well off and could afford to run two motor cars, an Austin Morris and a Rover; when old enough, Alan had his own MG sports car.

Clara Milburn's first experience of an air raid was in 1916, when German Zeppelins obliged her to take her baby son to the safety of the cellar. At the outbreak of the Second World War Alan was twenty-five and a territorial second lieutenant in the 7th battalion of the Royal Warwickshire regiment. After attending Birmingham University he had followed his father to Alfred Herbert Ltd, where he worked as a draughtsman. His regiment was already at its holding camp at Arundel, Sussex, late in August 1939, and for his mother the days passed 'in a sort of evil dream' (*Mrs Milburn's Diaries*, 13). She spent Sunday 3 September, when war was declared, helping to organize the local reception of evacuees, and clearing her son's room in readiness for one of the two teachers she had promised to take in. They arrived later that day bearing their rations of Nestlé condensed milk and Fray Bentos corned beef, but that night, when spirits most needed lifting, Clara provided 'a good old Sunday roast beef and Yorkshire pudding and an extra good apple tart' (ibid.).

On 5 January 1940 Alan Milburn's unit prepared to leave for service overseas. Prompted by Alan's departure Clara began, in February, a diary of 'Burleigh in wartime'. Five years and fifteen exercise books later she had compiled a vivid account of the war, augmented with newspaper cuttings, maps, telegrams, and letters. She avidly followed the war on all its fronts, her radio tuned to the BBC, and listened with growing anxiety to the news of the evacuation of the British army from Dunkirk in June 1940. Her worst fears were realized when news arrived that Alan was missing: she had to wait several weeks before receiving confirmation, in mid-July, that he had been taken prisoner. For the rest of the war she lived for his letters, and prayed for the day when he would return.

The diary describes a home life transformed utterly by war. 'Life is certainly queer now,' Clara wrote in July 1941, 'with coupons for clothes … and very ordinary commodities like potatoes kept in the shops for regular customers only!' (*Mrs Milburn's Diaries*, 103). There was an abundance of condiments and sauces, but little to put them on. Clara bore the privations of the war with determined cheerfulness, even petrol rationing, which she felt acutely. Later she offered her services to the Women's Voluntary Service driving pool: 'Anything to get a legitimate run in the car these days!' (ibid., 151). She undertook a variety of war work with the local Red Cross committee and Women's Institute, and also helped with logistical support for the Women's Land Army stationed nearby.

Clara Milburn's patriotism was of the uncomplicated kind: she gave her husband a union flag for his birthday, thought Winston Churchill 'a great man', Neville Chamberlain 'steel-true and blade-straight', and anyone who made a point of listening to Lord Haw-Haw 'a bit queer' (*Mrs Milburn's Diaries*, 30, 65, 34). To her, the government meant the Conservative Party: she considered the 'Labour lot' inferior and suspected Ernest Bevin of doing 'his utmost to provoke class-consciousness and set employee against employer' (ibid., 144). But she was far from being immune from class-consciousness herself, and was always aware of breeding, whether of dogs or people. From October 1940 enemy bombing forced the Milburns to take frequent refuge in their garden dugout shelter. They stayed there for ten hours on the night of 14–15 November, which witnessed the destruction of Coventry. Clara lost a close school friend in the raid, and as well as the human cost she felt the loss of the fourteenth-century cathedral.

In March 1941 tragedy struck the Milburn household when Peggy Bagnall, the wife of Clara's nephew, was killed in the London blitz. On the day when she heard the news Clara was due to appear as Britannia at an entertainment at the Women's Institute. That evening she bravely took up her shield and trident, and donned her helmet, deciding that 'it is best to go on with whatever is one's job at the moment' (*Mrs Milburn's Diaries*, 87), but the death of someone so young hit her hard: 'They seem the ones so fitted to build a better world after this madness is over' (ibid.). News of German and Japanese atrocities enraged her and her anger was intensified as the first news of the concentration camps broke. She listened excitedly to the radio broadcasts of D-day, and on 10 June 1944 drove blood donors to Warwick Hospital, where casualties from Normandy were arriving. Her diary ends two days after the German surrender, with the completion of her personal war story: 'Thursday 10th May, He came!' (ibid., 300). Initially she did not recognize her son in the dark of Leamington railway station, but soon all of Balsall Common knew of his return.

Alan Milburn married in September 1946, and his wife, Judy, remembered her mother-in-law as a loving but strong-willed woman who could be 'firm, and even difficult': 'When I was expecting our first child she drummed it into me that I just *must* have a boy, another Milburn boy' (*Mrs Milburn's Diaries*, 303). But Clara quickly reconciled herself to a granddaughter. As her son's family life was beginning, her own was ending. She was dealt a double blow in 1955 when her husband died in January, followed by her former maid Kate Taylor in July. Not wanting to live alone at Burleigh she moved to a smaller house in Kenilworth, opposite her son and daughter-in-law. Much of her interest in life died when Alan was fatally injured in a car crash in November 1959. The sense of waste was intensified by the thought of all the years he had spent in German captivity. Clara Milburn died eighteen months later on 29 May 1961, at 93 Holly Walk, Leamington.

Clara Milburn's diary stayed in the family, and the enthusiasm of a family friend, Christopher Morgan, led to its being published in 1979. It gives a fascinating account of the impact of world events in a middle-class English home, but of even greater interest is its account of the war on the home front. This was a battle in which Clara Milburn was herself a participant, though she seldom acknowledged it. It fell to others to draw attention to the sacrifice of ordinary people such as her, and in a broadcast in July 1940 Churchill spoke of the 'unknown warriors' in a war of 'peoples and of causes' (Gilbert, 520). His theme was echoed in a speech in January 1942 by the Liberal politician Lady Violet Bonham Carter, who identified the 'unknown warrior' as the housewife herself:

> There is no roll of honour to record her deeds. She wears no medals on her breast. But without her patient gallantry and grit, without her unflinching staunchness and devotion, the life of the nation could not be carried on for a single day. (Bonham Carter papers)

MARK POTTLE

Sources *Mrs Milburn's diaries: an Englishwoman's day-to-day reflection, 1939–1945* (1979) · b. cert. · m. cert. · d. cert. · A. Calder, *The people's war: Britain, 1939–1945* (1969) · M. Gilbert, *The Churchill war papers*, 2: *Never surrender: May 1940–December 1940* (1994) · V. Bonham Carter, speech to women's parliament, 16 Jan 1942, Bodl. Oxf., MSS Bonham Carter

Wealth at death £3512 19s. 8d.: probate, 22 Aug 1961, *CGPLA Eng. & Wales*

Milburn, Colin (1941–1990), cricketer, was born on 23 October 1941 in the Richard Murray Hospital, Consett, co. Durham, the only child of Jack Milburn (1910–1985), an electrician, and his wife, Bertha Clarke (b. 1918). He was raised in the neighbouring pit village of Burnopfield, where his father was a revered professional in the local Tyneside senior league. He attended Burnopfield primary school, Annfield Plain secondary modern school, and Stanley grammar school. Introduced to cricket at an early age, his enthusiasm and ability were such that by the age of thirteen he was playing in the Burnopfield first eleven. Inheriting his father's vast physique and dynamic approach to the game, he believed that it was important to dominate from the first ball and many a seasoned professional fell victim to his natural instincts. But for all his extraordinary power, he was not simply a compulsive hitter equipped with a razor-sharp eye. He had a superb technique, a perfect sense of timing, and a full range of shots in addition to his talents as a medium-pace seamer and a fearless short leg.

After some spectacular performances for Chester-le-Street, Milburn made his début for Durham in 1959, while still at Stanley grammar school, against the Indians at Sunderland. A typically pugnacious century won him wider notice. In 1960 Northamptonshire duly signed him, after offering him 10s. a week more than Warwickshire. He soon became something of a national hero as his audacious strokeplay, beaming features, bulky figure, and charismatic personality brought a whiff of glamour to this unfashionable club. A scintillating start to the 1963 season took him to the brink of the test team, but two low scores for MCC against the West Indians dented his prospects. In

Colin Milburn (1941–1990), by unknown photographer, 1962

keeping with his flamboyant style Milburn's county form remained inconsistent, although on his day he was the most feared batsman in England. In 1965 he helped Northamptonshire to second place in the county championship and then in 1966, his *annus mirabilis*, he scored nearly 2000 runs with six centuries, two of them before lunch, hit thirty-one sixes, and finished second in the national batting averages.

Chosen in 1966 for the first test against West Indies at Old Trafford, Milburn was ignominiously run out in the first innings without scoring but made amends in the second with a typically defiant 94 as England were trounced. In the next test at Lord's, he rode to his country's rescue with a thrilling 126 not out to secure them a draw. He had become 'one of the few personalities the public craved to see' (*Wisden*, 1967, 81). After a gutsy performance at Headingley, when he batted with a badly bruised arm, he was unfortunate to be dropped for the final test, allegedly because his size impeded his fielding. He responded with a whirlwind 203 against Essex at Clacton, putting on 293 with Roger Prideaux for the first wicket.

Milburn wintered in Australia (1966–7), playing for Western Australia in the Sheffield shield, and briefly returned to the test fold in 1967 for one match each against India and Pakistan. Selected for the winter tour to West Indies, he won many new friends by his ebullience, but indifferent form kept him on the sidelines. After his return to favour against Australia at Lord's in 1968 was marked by a memorable 83, injury prevented him from playing in the next two tests. He was controversially omitted from the tour to South Africa, which ironically never took place because of the furore surrounding the late inclusion of Basil D'Oliveira.

After repairing once again to Perth in 1968–9, Milburn enjoyed a prodigious season for Western Australia, the apogee of which was an awesome 243, his highest score ever, against Queensland in Brisbane, made in just under four hours. No sooner had he finished in Australia than he was flown to Pakistan in an emergency to strengthen the ill-fated MCC tour and made an imperious 139 in the Karachi test before it was abandoned because of political unrest. It proved to be his last test innings.

Back in England, Milburn started the 1969 season auspiciously, suggesting that his batting had acquired a new maturity. Then tragedy struck. Returning to Northampton from a night out, on 23 May, he was involved in a serious car accident which cost him the sight of his left eye (the leading one for a right-hand batsman) and seriously impaired the other one. He accepted his lot uncomplainingly but for all his great fortitude it was a crushing blow from which he never recovered. In 1973–4 an attempted comeback proved too taxing and he retreated briefly to cricket in the local leagues. Thereafter, he did a variety of jobs within cricket but although his genial humour continued to win him friends wherever he went, his life lacked direction. On 28 February 1990 he collapsed in Newton Aycliffe, co. Durham, and died of a heart attack in an ambulance, on the way to hospital in Darlington. He was forty-eight and unmarried. He was buried at Burnopfield on 6 March. 'He was nearing his peak when his injury removed him from the scene he had illuminated during a period of depressing mediocrity', declared *Wisden* (1991, 1273). His statistics were unusual for, in his nine tests, he averaged 46.71 with the bat, comfortably exceeding his first-class average of 33.07 from 13,262 runs and 23 centuries. He also took 99 first-class wickets with his medium-pace bowling at 33.03 and held 224 catches.

MARK PEEL

Sources M. Peel, *Cricketing Falstaff: a biography of Colin Milburn* (1998) · C. Milburn, *Largely cricket* (1968) · C. Martin-Jenkins, *World cricketers: a biographical dictionary* (1996) · *Wisden* (1991) · *The Times* (1 March 1990) · M. Engel, *The Guardian* (1 March 1990)
Likenesses photograph, 1962, Empic Sports Photo Agency, Nottingham [*see illus.*] · photograph, *c.*1966, Sport and General, London · photograph, *c.*1966, repro. in *Wisden* (1967) · photographs, 1968–70, Hult. Arch.
Wealth at death under £100,000: administration, 6 June 1990, *CGPLA Eng. & Wales*

Milburn, John Edward Thompson [Jackie] (1924–1988), footballer, was born on 11 May 1924 at 14 Sixth Row, Ashington, Northumberland, the eldest of three children of Alexander (Alec) Milburn and his wife, Annie (Nance) Thompson (*c.*1900–*c.*1982). His father was a coalminer from a family with a strong footballing tradition. Jackie's great-grandfather 'Warhorse' Milburn had played in goal for Northumberland in the 1880s, and several uncles were professional footballers. In their turn the sons of his cousin Cissie, Jack and Bobby Charlton, grew up nearby and idolized Jackie.

Milburn followed a well-trodden path to professionalism from kicking a ball around the back lanes to playing for his elementary school, Hirst East, in Ashington, where his natural athleticism stood out. His father even beat him for getting too big-headed after winning all his events at the school sports day—an incident, recalled in his autobiography, to which he attributed a subsequent lack of confidence which others took for modesty. At fourteen the depression drove him south to work as a kitchen boy

John Edward Thompson [Jackie] **Milburn** (1924–1988), by unknown photographer, 1955

in a country house near Dorking, but seeing a nearby football match made him homesick. He ran away, straight back to Ashington and a job filling bags of sugar in a grocer's shop. With the approach of war in 1939, the mines took on more labour and at fifteen and a half he became an apprentice fitter, which he remained throughout the war.

Jackie continued playing football with local sides before getting a trial for Newcastle on the basis of a letter written by a friend. The game went down in Geordie folklore as the young Milburn arrived early and sat on the steps of St James's Park with 'a pie and a bottle of pop' before scoring six goals in the second half in a pair of borrowed boots. He was immediately signed by Stan Seymour, the Newcastle manager, and scored with his first kick in his first home game in 1943. Seventy or so of the Milburn clan and friends crammed into the little terrace house in Ashington for a party to celebrate. He was not officially released from mining duties until 1948, by which time he had moved from playing as a winger and inside forward to wearing the famous number 9 shirt. He scored a hat-trick in his first game at centre forward in October 1947 and finished as top goalscorer in the season when Newcastle won back their place in the first division, watched by an average crowd of over 56,000—a record for the Football League.

Always known as Wor Jackie, Milburn became the best known Geordie of his day. He got his first England cap in

1948 and went on to play thirteen times for his country, scoring ten goals. While training with England he met Laura Easton Blackwood, a Scottish girl, the daughter of John Blackwood, hairdresser's assistant. They were married on 16 February 1948 and he remained devoted to her for the rest of his life. Milburn was tall and lean, a handsome man and a spectacular player who could shoot with either foot and had a flair for the big occasion. JET, an alternative nickname taken from his initials, would suddenly sprint at terrific speed from deep positions, leaving defenders yards behind and occasionally ending up in the crowd. His first goal in the 1951 cup final against Blackpool was a solo break of 50 yards. His shooting power brought him the second, winning goal, a fierce shot from long range from a clever back-heel by Ernie Taylor, a goal which Stanley Matthews later called 'the finest ever scored at Wembley' (Kirkup, 69). The team returned to extraordinary public rejoicing as tens of thousands lined streets bedecked in black and white to welcome home a team still largely composed of local players. These scenes were repeated the following year when Milburn played in the side which defeated Arsenal at Wembley—the first consecutive cup final victories for sixty years. Wor Jackie slipped from favour as England centre forward but was confirmed as a Tyneside hero with a third cup final victory in 1955, when he scored an outstanding headed goal after only 45 seconds, the fastest Wembley goal until 1997 and from a player who hated heading the ball.

Milburn began to lose some of his exceptional speed and retired from Newcastle in 1957, at the age of thirty-three, having made 492 appearances for the club, and having scored 238 goals. He became player–manager of Linfield in Northern Ireland, then moved briefly to the English southern league, before becoming manager of Ipswich in 1963, when Alf Ramsey took over the England team. Jackie was too nice to take hard decisions over players and lacked the funds to maintain the club's success. He resigned the following year and returned to Tyneside, where his local fame got him a job as a football reporter, and he settled down to write a weekly column for the *News of the World* for over twenty years. This kept him intimately involved in football, identified with the club and in the public eye without having to bear the responsibility for Newcastle's failures. On the tenth anniversary of his retirement a crowd of 44,000 saw a testimonial in which Milburn's pals from the famous cup final teams played alongside the Charlton brothers and the great Hungarian Puskas.

The Milburn legend began to take on a new significance in popular memory. As football on Tyneside was beset by hooligan problems on the terraces and vastly increased wage demands from players who performed poorly, the character and achievements of Wor Jackie stood out as a reminder of better times. Tyneside itself went into a downward spiral of unemployment and despair with the closure of the shipyards and the pits. Milburn's strong roots in the mining community, his modesty and decency, his friendliness and devotion to the area, combined to turn him into a much loved and honoured local figure. In 1981 he became the first footballer to be made a freeman of the city, an honour he shared with one of his fans, Cardinal Hume, who observed 'a quality of goodness about him which inspired others' (Kirkup, 172). He was the subject of several feature articles, radio programmes, and in 1981 of *This is your Life* on television. In 1987 he received an award from the Sports Council for his lifelong work for sport in the region. But he was never the kind of man to seek a place for himself on the honours list and died just as this kind of recognition began to become more commonplace among footballers.

Jackie was always a heavy smoker—he was even known to light up at half-time—and he developed lung cancer in 1988. His death from the disease, at his home, 2 Bothal Terrace, Ashington, on 9 October 1988, which took the public by surprise, revealed the full extent of popular adulation. Thousands lined the streets for his funeral four days later, which was reported in the national press and on television, as it moved from the simple house in Ashington where he had lived to a packed Newcastle Cathedral. His ashes were scattered on St James's Park. A public subscription for a statue launched by the local paper was soon fully subscribed. A bronze of him, running with the ball at his feet, now stands outside Newcastle's ground while Ashington, not to be outdone, unveiled an 8 foot likeness of their unassuming hero in the town centre in 1995, amid choruses of the 'Blaydon Races' from his surviving teammates, friends, and family. Buses, trains, and council estates along with a new stand in St James's Park were named after him; and in 1991 the Jackie Milburn Memorial Trust was set up to help the young disabled in the region. There was a musical about his life and an award-winning television documentary. Over the years his achievements as a player were embellished by his qualities as a man, especially as a devoted husband, father of three, and grandfather. His long and happy marriage—the family caravan on the coast, playing golf together at Morpeth, Laura's home cooking—was a great source of strength and stability to him, especially in later life, and was turned into a symbol of vanishing family values as divorce rates shot up and a more permissive culture took hold. Media nostalgia was kind to Milburn—he became one of their own—but he earned his fame both as Newcastle's most successful modern player and as an antidote to the Andy Capp image of northern masculinity.

RICHARD HOLT

Sources J. Milburn, *Golden goals* (1957) · M. Kirkup, *Jackie Milburn in black and white: a biography* (1990) · b. cert. · m. cert. · d. cert. · R. Holt, 'Football and regional identity in the north-east of England: the legend of Jackie Milburn', *Football and regional identity in Europe*, ed. S. Gehrmann (1997) · J. Gibson, *Wor Jackie: the Jackie Milburn story* (1990) · A. Appleton, *Hotbed of soccer: the story of football in the north east* (1960) · P. Joannou, *United, the first hundred years: the official history of Newcastle United* (1991) · R. Colls and B. Lancaster, eds., *Geordies: roots of regionalism* (1992) · local press (Oct 1988)
Archives FILM BFI NFTVA, *This is your life* ITV, 1981 · BFI NFTVA, documentary footage · BFI NFTVA, sports footage | SOUND 'A place in the heart', Radio Newcastle (c.1986)

Likenesses portrait, 1949, repro. in *The book of British sporting heroes* (1998) · photographs, 1951–5, Hult. Arch. [*see illus.*] · photographs, repro. in Kirkup, *Jackie Milburn in black and white* · two statues, outside St James's Park, Newcastle upon Tyne

Wealth at death under £70,000: probate, 30 Dec 1988, *CGPLA Eng. & Wales*

Milchsack [*née* Duden], **Lisalotte** [Lilo] (1905–1992), promoter of Anglo-German relations, was born in Frankfurt am Main, Germany, the daughter of Dr Paul Duden (1868–1954), an industrial chemist, and his wife, Johanna Bertha, *née* Nebe (1875–1947). Her grandfather was the lexicographer Konrad Duden (1829–1911), author of the Duden dictionary. She studied history at the universities of Frankfurt, Geneva, and Amsterdam before marrying Hans Milchsack (*d.* 1984), a Düsseldorf businessman and the owner of an inland shipping navigation company; they had two daughters.

The Milchsacks were early opponents of the Nazi regime: in January 1932 Hans walked out in protest during a meeting at the Industrieclub in Düsseldorf where Hitler was speaking, and as early as 1935 Lilo was telling her English friends that Hitler's policies were leading to war. During the war her husband was able to help some of the Dutch workers in his factory in the Netherlands, and in 1945, because of his anti-Nazi record, he was appointed burgomaster of Düsseldorf-Wittlaer by the Americans.

In 1947 Lilo Milchsack was introduced to Robert Birley, educational adviser to the military governor of the British zone from 1947 to 1949, and when she began holding meetings in 1948 with the idea of forming some kind of association, Birley, who by now had moved from Berlin to Düsseldorf, was a great support. The Deutsch-Englische Gesellschaft (Anglo-German Association) was founded in her house in Wittlaer in March 1949 out of a desire for reconciliation between Germany and England, and with the aim that Germany should rebuild a democratic society through studying British institutions, with the help of close personal contacts with Britain. As Birley put it in 1947: 'we can offer the strength of our own traditions to Germany … Germans now … hunger for contacts with the outside world, from which they have cut themselves off for so long' (Uhlig, 167). The association was intended as an informal and independent political forum, where leading German and English politicians, journalists, academics, and others prominent in public life could meet and hold joint discussions. As a means of encouraging frank discussion, she established the rule that names would not be mentioned in press reports.

Lilo Milchsack was director of the Deutsch-Englische Gesellschaft from 1949 to 1977 and chairperson from 1977 to 1982. She organized in 1950 the first of what became annual four-day conferences at Königswinter, on the Rhine, south of Bonn: the theme of the first conference was social work and that of the second press responsibility. Although Birley had returned to England in 1949 to take up his appointment as headmaster of Eton College, he tried to attend every Königswinter conference, and he chaired many of them. Over the years the conferences covered more general topics such as East–West relations

and the Atlantic alliance. Lilo Milchsack also started 'Young Königswinter' conferences, to bring together young people in their twenties from the two countries in order to develop mutual understanding. The Königswinter conferences were described by Chancellor Helmut Schmidt in 1980 as 'a kind of college of higher education in politics'. He also said that 'at Königswinter you have always been able to balance intellectual potential and warmth of heart, in short, to create a human atmosphere' (Uhlig, 200). This was largely because of the strength of Lilo Milchsack's personality and vision and the combination of her organizational ability and her gift for friendship.

Lilo Milchsack retired as chairperson in 1982 but remained as honorary chair for the rest of her life, and she continued to participate in the conferences. She was awarded the Grosses Bundesverdienstkreuz in 1959 by the German government, and, after being appointed honorary CBE in 1958 and honorary CMG in 1968, she was created an honorary DCMG in 1972, the first German so appointed. As Sir Alec Douglas-Home said in 1971, 'Germany and Britain started this century in discord. We enter its last quarter in total trust' (Uhlig, 158). The Königswinter conferences played a large part in the development of this trust. Lilo Milchsack died on 7 August 1992 in Düsseldorf.　　　　　　　　　　　　ANNE PIMLOTT BAKER

Sources R. Uhlig, *Die Deutsch-Englische Gesellschaft, 1949–1983* (1986) · A. Hearnden, *Red Robert: a life of Robert Birley* (1983) · *The Times* (15 Aug 1992) · *WW*

Likenesses photograph, 1985, repro. in www.deg-Koenigswinter.de/lilo_milchsack.htm, official website of the DEG

Mildburg [St Mildburg, Milburg, Milburga] (*d.* in or after **716**), abbess of Much Wenlock, is identified in the Kentish royal legend as one of the daughters of Merewalh, subking of the Magonsæte, and probably a member of the Mercian royal family, and his wife, Domne Eafe ('Domneva'), niece of King Eorcenberht of Kent; their other daughter, *Mildrith, was abbess of Minster in Thanet, which Domneva founded after separating from Merewalh and returning to Kent.

In the 670s or 680s Mildburg became abbess of Much Wenlock, Mercia, in her father's kingdom, which had been founded under the tutelage of St Botwulf's Minster at Iken, East Anglia. An Abbess Liobsind, involved in the foundation of Wenlock and perhaps its first head, had a Frankish name: it seems likely that Merewalh planned his daughter's career by establishing an aristocratic double house on the then dominant Frankish model, to which her succession as abbess may have been virtually automatic. Extracts from charters preserved in the later 'Testament of St Mildburg' show her acquiring other estates for Wenlock from Magonsætan and Mercian rulers and aristocrats. The visions of a brother 'in Abbess Mildburg's minster' in 715–16 attracted the interest of Boniface and of Abbess Hildelith of Barking.

Mildburg illustrates the generation of princess–saints who ruled so many of the major late seventh-century minsters. The Wenlock material, slight though it is, is interesting as evidence for the wide nexus of influences in the monastic culture of the time: this double house on the Welsh border was founded from an East Anglian base under Frankish influence, was ruled by the sister of the abbess of one of the main Kentish royal minsters, and maintained contacts with Barking in the lower Thames and with Boniface, the apostle of Germany.

Wenlock remained a double community in 901, and Mildburg's relics there are mentioned in the earlier part of the Old English list of resting places; there are thus strong grounds for presuming a continuity of the cult. The eleventh-century *Vita beate ac Deo dilectae virginis Mildburgae* contains the 'Testament', a version of her family's genealogical legend, and some miracle stories, but adds no reliable information about her life. Another tract describes the miraculous 'invention' of her relics in Holy Trinity Church at Wenlock in 1101. Her feast was observed on 23 February, that of her translation on 25 June.

JOHN BLAIR

Sources H. P. R. Finberg, *The early charters of the west midlands*, 2nd edn (1972), 197–216 · P. Sims-Williams, *Religion and literature in western England, 600–800* (1990) · D. W. Rollason, *The Mildrith legend: a study in early medieval hagiography in England* (1982) · A. J. M. Edwards, 'An early twelfth-century account of the translation of St Milburga of Much Wenlock', *Transactions of the Shropshire Archaeological Society*, 57 (1961–4), 134–51

Mildenhall [Midnall], **John** (d. 1614), merchant, of unknown parentage, first comes to our attention in two documents included in Samuel Purchas's collection of voyages (Purchas, 297–304). One is a concise account of his outward route as far as Kandahar, starting with his departure from London for Constantinople aboard the *Hector* on 12 February 1599 and describing how he joined a great caravan of 600 people in Aleppo on 7 July 1600. The second document is a letter from Mildenhall to Richard Staper, a prominent London merchant connected with the Levant and East India companies for whom Mildenhall may formerly have worked. Dated 3 October 1606 and written from Qazvin in north-western Persia, it reports 'the successe of this my Voyage unto the Court of the Great King of Mogor and Cambaia' (Purchas, 299). From Lahore, reached in 1603, Mildenhall was escorted to Agra, capital of the Mughal emperor Akbar, and treated with every courtesy as an envoy from Elizabeth I. He was eventually invited to state his business and declared his queen wished her subjects to enjoy the same trade favours as the Portuguese. Although given a friendly hearing, he made little headway and believed the Jesuits and others at Akbar's court conspired against him. After months of waiting, in which he learned Persian, he was eventually granted privileges 'to my owne contentment and, as I hope, to the profit of my Nation'. Mildenhall also obtained the approval of Prince Salim (soon to become the emperor Jahangir) before leaving; he arrived back in London in late 1608 or early 1609.

Armed with the concessions from the Mughal emperor, Mildenhall then applied for an official post in the East India Company but was turned down as being 'for divers respects ... not fitting to be ymployed in the service of the Compagnie' (Foster, 'Midnall travels though Persia', 181).

So he returned to the Levant, part of the funding and stock for his venture being provided by Richard Staper and three other London merchants. The intention may have been to research a new trade route to Persia via the Black Sea and Georgia, but the attempt ended early and in scandal when he was denounced as a Persian spy; the English ambassador in Constantinople had to intervene strongly on his behalf. Mildenhall then set out east again from Aleppo. Nothing was heard of him for so long that the English trading community there became suspicious, and in 1613 Richard Steele and Richard Newman were sent to find him. They recovered goods and money from him near Esfahan to the value of 9,000 piastres, which Newman took back to Aleppo, while Steele accompanied Mildenhall to India.

In 1614 Mildenhall fell ill in Lahore. Steele continued to Ajmer, seat of Jahangir's court, while Mildenhall followed slowly. He reached Ajmer in April and died in June; he is said to have made a Frenchman his executor on condition the latter married his daughter and brought up his son—children born to a wife in Persia. Thomas Kerridge, the East India Company's local representative, reports that the Frenchman also burned Mildenhall's books and papers and as his estate, valued around £500, was seized by the Mughal authorities, Kerridge and Steele had dreadful trouble proving that any assets should go to Mildenhall's original backers, only part of his debt having been repaid earlier via Newman.

Mildenhall was buried in the Roman Catholic cemetery at Agra, the first Christian cemetery in northern India. His tomb is the earliest English monument in India. Whatever his original intentions had been for the disposal of his property, Mildenhall's estate was administered in London by Maurice Abbot, East India Company merchant, and Nicholas Seaton.

JENNY MARSH

Sources S. Purchas, *Hakluytus posthumus, or, Purchas his pilgrimes*, bk 2 (1625); repr. Hakluyt Society, extra ser., 15 (1905), 297–304 · F. C. Danvers and W. Foster, eds., *Letters received by the East India Company from its servants in the east*, 6 vols. (1896–1902), vol. 2 · W. Foster, 'Midnall travels through Persia to India', *England's quest of eastern trade* (1933), 173–82 · W. Foster, ed., *The travels of John Sanderson in the Levant, 1584–1602* (1931) · administration, PRO, PROB 6/9, fol. 33r · N. Steensgaard, *The Asian trade revolution of the seventeenth century: the East India companies and the decline of the caravan trade* (1974) · R. Nath, *Agra and its monuments* (1997), 179–80

Wealth at death approx. £500: Thomas Kerridge, letter, in *Letters received*, vol. 2, p. 141

Mildert, William Van (1765–1836), bishop of Durham, was born on 6 November 1765 at his father's residence in Blackman Street, Southwark, London, the fourth child and second son of Cornelius Van Mildert (1722–1799), gin distiller, and his wife, Martha, *née* Hill (1732–1804). He was baptized on 8 December by the rector of Newington, Samuel Horsley. Cornelius Van Mildert was the great-grandson of an Amsterdam merchant who migrated to London around 1670. His father Abraham and grandfather Daniel were deacons of the Dutch Reformed church at Austin Friars; Cornelius himself was a devout Anglican and fringe associate of the writer and pamphleteer William Stevens

(1732–1807). He achieved little commercial success. Martha was the only daughter of William Hill of Vauxhall, Surrey, merchant and financier; her brother's influence with the Grocers' Company won William Van Mildert his first important preferment.

Van Mildert was interested in his Dutch antecedents, touring the Low Countries in July–August 1792, but regarded himself emphatically as an Englishman. He attended St Saviour's School, Southwark, until, aged about thirteen, he persuaded his father to let him seek holy orders. Although Horsley advised against 'diverting the boy from trade' (Ives, 6), about 1779 Van Mildert entered Merchant Taylors' School to prepare for university. He was a commoner at the Queen's College, Oxford, from 1784, graduating BA in November 1787 and proceeding MA in July 1790. On 18 May 1788 he was ordained deacon to the Oxford curacy of Monk Sherborne, Hampshire, and Lewknor, Oxfordshire, moving in 1789 to become curate of Newchurch and Bonnington, on Romney Marsh in Kent.

Ordained priest on 10 December 1789, in 1790 he became curate of Witham, Essex. There he courted Jane (1760–1837), third daughter of General Douglas, a former aide-de-camp to George II. Her brother Philip, master of Corpus Christi College, Cambridge, from 1795, doubted Van Mildert's financial soundness, but in 1795 Van Mildert was instituted to the small living of Bradden, Northamptonshire, by Cornelius Ives, his cousin and brother-in-law, and he married Jane on 22 December. They never had children; Jane's nieces Mary and Helen Margaret became their foster-daughters and her nephew Henry was among Van Mildert's principal protégés.

In July 1796, sponsored by his uncle William Hill, Van Mildert became chaplain to the Grocers' Company and rector of St Mary-le-Bow, Cheapside, London. There was no habitable parsonage, so he rented 14 Ely Place, Holborn, just outside the parish boundary. In 1800 he was prosecuted for technical non-residence and, although Archbishop Moore of Canterbury spoke on his behalf and the court accepted that he was performing all his duties, Van Mildert was found guilty. His case was cited in parliament and the press as demonstrating the injustice of the legal situation and the urgent need for reform.

In London, Van Mildert became an active member of the high-church campaigning group known as the Hackney Phalanx. He was elected to William Stevens's exclusive Nobody's Club in 1802, co-edited a two-volume anthology of reprinted tracts, *The Churchman's Remembrancer* (1802–8), and was briefly editor of the *British Critic*, bought about 1811 to promote the group's viewpoint. He served as treasurer of the Society for Promoting Christian Knowledge from 1812 to 1815 and helped to found the National Society (1811) and the Church Building Society (1818).

Van Mildert's Boyle lectures of 1802–5 (published in 1806), which depicted Judaism, Islam, popery, freemasonry, and the French Revolution as elements in a conspiracy masterminded by Satan, established him among the foremost conservative theologians of his day. Their footnotes are particularly extensive. Van Mildert's knowledge of divinity was such that when his friends read snippets from obscure theological works and challenged him to name the author he was seldom caught out. From 1812 to 1819 he was preacher of Lincoln's Inn, and his 1812 sermon on the assassination of Spencer Perceval achieved wide circulation. He was Bampton lecturer in 1814, and in 1823 published a ten-volume edition of the works of Daniel Waterland.

In March 1807 Van Mildert became chaplain to his wife's kinsman the fourth duke of Queensberry, an appointment which entitled him to hold two benefices in plurality. In April Archbishop Manners-Sutton made him vicar of Farningham, Kent. The parsonage was uninhabitable, and the building work ran dramatically over budget. In 1810 Van Mildert escaped bankruptcy only because his Hackney Phalanx associates paid his debts. He gave up Ely Place and lived economically at Farningham: in 1813 a messenger from Lord Liverpool could find no servant but 'a female presiding at the churn' who made him keep the churn moving while she fetched her master (Churton, 1.138). Liverpool's offer of the regius professorship of divinity at Oxford and the rectory of Ewelme in Oxfordshire was gratefully accepted. As regius professor Van Mildert also became BD, DD, and a canon of Christ Church.

Consecrated bishop of Llandaff on 31 May 1819, Van Mildert unlike his predecessors resided in the diocese each summer from 1821, renting Coldbrook House near Abergavenny since the bishop's palace was in ruins. He proved a conscientious diocesan and able administrator, serving on a Queen Anne's Bounty committee to assist benefices under £50 yearly value and on the Church Building Commission. In 1820 he declined the archbishopric of Dublin, instead becoming dean of St Paul's *in commendam* with Llandaff. In November 1820 he was notified of Queen Caroline's intention to attend worship at St Paul's in thanksgiving for her deliverance from the bill of pains and penalties. Van Mildert, whose support for the bill had caused disturbances at Ewelme, outraged *The Times* by the curtness of his acknowledgement. His absence from the service was noted. On 25 March 1826 Van Mildert accepted Liverpool's offer of the palatine bishopric of Durham. He poured Durham's vast revenues into church building, parsonage building, augmenting small stipends, and establishing parish schools. In 1827 he hosted a resplendent banquet for the duke of Wellington, then making a triumphal tour of the north-east, but deliberately blunted the political edge of the festivities by also honouring Sir Walter Scott.

As a parliamentarian he was eloquent, respected, and consistently unsuccessful. Although his close friend Charles Lloyd cajoled him into supporting the 1828 repeal of the Test and Corporation Acts, Van Mildert resisted Catholic emancipation to the end. His bitter public clash with Lloyd during the 1829 Lords debate contributed to Lloyd's early death. Burned in effigy at his castle gates in November 1831 for opposing parliamentary reform, Van Mildert was prominent in co-ordinating episcopal resistance to the 'Irish Church Spoliation Bill' (the Irish Church

Temporalities Bill) of 1833. His refusal to compromise even with tory political necessity guaranteed his omission from Peel's 1835 ecclesiastical commission and may explain why in 1828 Wellington, though regarding Van Mildert as the prime candidate for the archbishopric of Canterbury, recommended the king to choose William Howley instead.

In June 1831 Archdeacon Thorp of Durham suggested to Van Mildert that founding a university at Durham would 'give to the Dean & Chapter strength of character & usefulness', help preserve ecclesiastical revenues from the threat of reform, and pre-empt moves to establish a London-style secular university at Newcastle upon Tyne, (Thorp to Van Mildert, 11 June 1831, Oxford, Balliol College, MS Jenkyns IV A). Van Mildert championed the proposal with the dean and chapter, the Grey government, and ultimately in parliament. Besides his advocacy and munificent financial contributions—the dean and chapter collectively provided £3000 per annum, the bishop £2000 with many additional specific benefactions—Van Mildert secured most of his fellow bishops' agreement to accept Durham degrees as qualification for holy orders. He also recruited H. J. Rose as Durham's first professor of divinity. The Durham University Bill became law in July 1832 and the university admitted its first students in October 1833.

Van Mildert was of medium height and slight build, with an expressive face, 'well able, when it behoved him, to assume a highly imposing step and mien' (Ives, 153). His health was never robust and he was known for the austerity of his diet. Following a surgical operation in 1824 his last years were narrowed by constant pain. His wife, after a stroke in 1833 which affected her personality, lived at Harrogate until her death in 1837. Van Mildert died at Auckland Castle, co. Durham, on 21 February 1836, collapsing after a minor illness into a week of steadily deepening stupor followed by a peaceful death. Although he wished to be buried in the Auckland chapel with sumptuous ceremonial, he was entombed in a vault in front of Durham Cathedral's high altar. Shortly after Van Mildert's death the bishopric was stripped of its palatine status and the remnant of its ancient secular powers.

E. A. Varley

Sources E. Churton, ed., Memoir of Joshua Watson, 2 vols. (1861) · C. Ives, 'Memoir of the author', in Sermons on several occasions and charges by William Van Mildert, ed. C. Ives, 1 (1838) · P. W. L. Adams, A history of the Douglas family of Morton in Nithsdale (1921) · E. Hughes, ed., 'The bishops and reform, 1831–3: some fresh correspondence', EngHR, 56 (1941), 459–90 · The Times (24 Feb 1836) · Durham Chronicle (26 Feb 1836) · Durham Advertiser (26 Feb 1836) · GM, 2nd ser., 5 (1836), 425–7 · E. A. Varley, The last of the prince bishops: William Van Mildert and the high church movement of the early nineteenth century (1992) · G. F. A. Best, 'The mind and times of William Van Mildert', Journal of Theological Studies, new ser., 14 (1963), 355–70 · A. Bradshaw, 'William Van Mildert's visit to the Netherlands in 1792', Durham University Journal, 71 (1978–9), 45–53

Archives U. Durham L., archives and special collections, papers relating to him and his family; family and business corresp. and papers · Van Mildert College, Durham, corresp. and papers | Balliol Oxf., papers relating to Durham University · BL, corresp. with Sir Robert Peel, Add. MSS 40272–40416 · Bodl. Oxf., MSS Norris · LPL, letters to Christopher Wordsworth · U. Durham L., archives and special collections, corresp. with second Earl Grey; corresp. with Samuel Smith; corresp. with Charles Thorp

Likenesses T. Lawrence, oils, 1829, Bishop Auckland Palace, Durham · T. Lupton, engraving, pubd 1831 (after T. Lawrence) · J. Gibson, marble memorial statue, 1836, Durham Cathedral · G. Hayter, group portrait, oils (The trial of Queen Caroline, 1820), NPG · R. J. Lane, lithograph (after statue by J. Gibson) · miniature (as young man), University College, Durham

Wealth at death bequests to family members: Adams, History

Mildmay, Sir Anthony (c.1549–1617). See under Mildmay, Sir Walter (1520/21–1589).

Mildmay, Anthony Bingham, second Baron Mildmay of Flete (1909–1950), jockey, was born in London on 14 April 1909, the only son and younger of the two children of Francis Bingham Mildmay, first Baron Mildmay of Flete (1861–1947), and his wife, Alice Lilian, daughter of Charles Seymour Grenfell, of Elibank, Taplow, a kinsman of Lord Desborough. Mildmay was educated at Eton College and Trinity College, Cambridge, where he took his degree. Like his father, while an undergraduate he hunted and played polo for the university. He also rode in point-to-point races but showed surprisingly little of the promise which might have been expected from one who was later to hold his own with the best amateur and professional riders of his day.

His father entered parliament in 1885 as Liberal member for the Totnes division of Devon, but, opposing home rule, subsequently sat as a Unionist until in 1922 he retired and was raised to the peerage. He served with distinction in the Second South African War and the First World War, was sworn of the privy council in 1916, and was lord lieutenant of Devon (1928–36). He took an active part in public life and his many interests ranged from matters of public health to the breeding of light horses and hunters and of south Devon cattle. Mildmay did not share his father's interest in politics and in 1930 joined Baring Brothers, the banking firm of which his uncle, Alfred Mildmay, was the senior partner. Work at the bank allowed him no time for hunting, so he decided to keep some steeplechase horses at Fairlawne, Peter Cazalet's home near Tonbridge. He rode in exercise gallops every morning before leaving for the City, and used his free days from the bank to ride in races under National Hunt rules. Thus began his notable career as an amateur rider, a career made all the more remarkable by his build which was hardly that of a jockey; he was 6 feet 2 inches in height and very long of limb, but his weight was under 10 stone.

As steeplechasing had now become the ruling passion of his life, Mildmay decided, during the summer of 1933, to give up his City career. He realized that he could only become a successful jockey by devoting most of his time to riding, so accordingly, in the autumn, he started a market garden and farm on his father's estate at Shoreham, Kent; he continued to live for most of the year at Fairlawne, only a few miles away, and settled down to the life of an amateur steeplechase jockey, riding both his own horses and the mounts of other owners. The trainer's licence was held by Harry Whiteman, though the real power at Fairlawne was Peter Cazalet, who took over the licence after the Second World War.

Mildmay's first winner was Good Shot, at Wye in the spring of 1933, the year of his first ride in the Grand National. By 1935 he was riding regularly and also taking the inevitable falls. These included a particularly serious one in the foxhunters' chase at Liverpool when he broke a vertebra, three ribs, and an arm, and cracked his skull. Despite this he was back in the saddle a few months later, and in the Grand National of 1936 rode his father's tubed and entire horse Davy Jones, considered by many to be a doubtful stayer. Carrying 10 stone and starting at 100–1, he led from the first jump and would probably have won had not the buckle of his reins broken at the second last fence. This caused him to lose control and run out at the last. In the next season he rode twenty-one winners to be joint leading amateur rider.

On the outbreak of war in 1939 Mildmay served in the Royal Artillery until he joined the commandos in 1940. In 1941 he transferred to the Welsh Guards, and later served as a captain in the guards armoured division from the invasion of Normandy until the end of the war. He was wounded and mentioned in dispatches. On returning to race-riding, stronger in physique and more determined than ever to make himself into a first-class jockey, he was soon, as an amateur, in a class by himself, and could hold his own with the best professionals, particularly in long-distance steeplechases. In 1945–6 he rode eleven winners to be leading amateur for the season. The following season he finished fourth in the list of winning jockeys, and was champion amateur, with thirty-two winners. He was leading amateur again in 1947–8, with twenty-two winners, 1948–9, with thirty, and 1949–50, with thirty-eight winners. In the Grand National of 1948 he rode

Cromwell into third place and might well have won if the recurrence of an old neck injury had not made him powerless to assist his horse for the last half mile. On Cromwell again in 1949 he finished fourth after starting favourite. If this was a disappointment there were compensations from his wins in other famous races. Among these were the Grand Sefton chase at Liverpool (on his own horse), the National Hunt chase at Cheltenham, and on one memorable afternoon both the household brigade cup and the Royal Artillery past and present steeplechase. In 1947 he succeeded his father as second baron and had by that time become such a favourite with the racing crowd that 'Come on, Lordy' was soon a familiar cry on any racecourse.

Throughout his career on the turf Mildmay was a well-known and popular figure. This was not only due to his skill in the saddle, but to his courage and strength of character. He was not a particularly strong rider in a finish but Cazalet regarded him as the best schooling rider he had known. By his example and work he helped to raise National Hunt sport to a position which it had never held before. He was elected a member of the National Hunt committee in 1942 and appointed a steward (1944–7 and 1949–50). He was elected a member of the Jockey Club in 1949, the year in which he became manager to the queen and Princess Elizabeth when, very largely as a result of his suggestion, they began to own steeplechase horses.

His career by this time was almost over. When not riding he spent as much time as possible in Devon on the Flete estate. He lived at Mothecombe, a beautiful Queen Anne house on the estate near the sea, and it was while bathing from there that he was drowned in the early morning of 12 May 1950. He was unmarried, and the title became extinct. Memorial races were named after him at Cheltenham,

Anthony Bingham Mildmay, second Baron Mildmay of Flete (1909–1950), by Sir Alfred Munnings, 1937 [*The Hon. Anthony Mildmay on Davy Jones*]

Sandown Park, Plumpton, and Newton Abbot, and at Aintree a new steeplechase course was called the Mildmay course. Fittingly the first running of the Mildmay memorial chase at Sandown Park was won by his old mount, Cromwell. P. V. F. CAZALET, *rev.* ROGER MUNTING

Sources *The Times* (15 May 1950) • M. Seth-Smith and others, *The history of steeplechasing* (1966) • *Steeplechasing*, The Lonsdale Library of Sports and Games, 32 (1954) • P. Smyly, ed., *Encyclopaedia of steeplechasing* (1979) • *WWW*, 1941–50 • personal knowledge (1959) • private information (1959)

Archives FILM BFI NFTVA, home footage

Likenesses A. Munnings, portrait, 1937 (on Davy Jones), priv. coll. [*see illus.*]

Wealth at death £1,173,628 19*s.* 11*d.*: probate, 21 June 1950, *CGPLA Eng. & Wales*

Mildmay [*née* Sharington], **Grace**, **Lady Mildmay** (*c.*1552–1620), memoirist and medical practitioner, was the second daughter of Sir Henry Sharington (*d.* 1581), of Lacock Abbey, Chippenham, Wiltshire, and his wife, Anne (*d.* 1607), daughter of Robert Paget, alderman of London. Her father, who was formerly from East Dereham in Norfolk, inherited Lacock Abbey from his brother William Sharington (*d.* 1553), vice-treasurer of the Bristol mint. Grace was the second of four children. Her younger brother William did not survive infancy and her elder sister Ursula died in 1576, leaving Grace and her younger sister Olive as coheirs.

Grace was educated at home with her two sisters by a Mistress Hamblyn, a relative of the family brought up by Lady Sharington. The governess took great pains with the character and moral training of her charges, and taught Grace some basic medical skills. Grace married in 1567 Anthony *Mildmay (*c.*1549–1617) [*see under* Mildmay, Sir Walter], eldest son of Sir Walter *Mildmay, chancellor of the exchequer, and founder of Emmanuel College, Cambridge, and his wife, Mary Walsingham. The couple resided at Apethorpe, Northamptonshire, and had one child, Mary (1581/2–1640), who married Francis Fane, later first earl of Westmorland, in February 1599. Sir Anthony and Lady Mildmay endured considerable financial strain in their marriage. Not only was no marriage settlement drawn up, but they also became embroiled in expensive and lengthy litigation to gain control of their respective inheritances. Lady Mildmay and her sister Olive were in dispute from early 1581 until late 1609. Lady Mildmay challenged her father's last will, a nuncupative one, which left to Olive the largest share of the estate. Olive was reluctant to relinquish any land to her sister, but eventually the estate was divided equally between the two sisters. Anthony and his younger brother Humphrey quarrelled because Anthony, wishing to provide for his wife and daughter, wanted to break the entail of their father's will, under which his brother was the heir, since Anthony had no son. Sir Anthony won the case, although his victory cost him his brother's friendship.

Anthony Mildmay had not been eager to marry, 'being then more willing to travel to get experience of the world than to marry so soon' (Pollock, 32). After the wedding Anthony was active in royal service and often away from home. Lady Mildmay divided her time between reading

Grace Mildmay, Lady Mildmay (*c.*1552–1620), by unknown artist

the Bible, praying, playing the lute, drawing, needlework, and medical activities. She was an accomplished musician, able to set songs of five parts. Her proficiency in this regard was recognized in the musical world: a galliard, 'My Lady Mildmay's Delight', attributed to the lutenist Robert Johnson, was named after her (Morrongiello). She was also an acclaimed cook. James VI of Scotland dined at Apethorpe while on his journey to take the throne of England, and enjoyed the dinner, since 'everything that was most delicious for taste proved more delicate by the art that made it seem beauteous to the eye, the lady of the house being one of the most excellent confectioners in England' (Aikin, 1.86). Now James I, he visited again in 1612; in appreciation of the Mildmays' hospitality, he gave the timber for the buildings on the east and south sides. A stone statue of James I on the south side of the courtyard at Apethorpe commemorates his generosity.

Lady Mildmay's medical activities were as sophisticated as her culinary ones and more extensive. She was not unusual in providing medical care: women were expected to be conversant with basic medical treatments, and capable of ministering to their family. However, Lady Mildmay's surviving medical papers reveal that she was engaged in far more than a family-based activity. The papers are not a jumble of cookery and simple herbal recipes, as would be typical, but contain a sophisticated analysis of the causes and treatment of various diseases, accompanied by instructions for the large-scale manufacture of medicines, many of them based on minerals and chemicals. Her understanding of the causes of illness was Galenic in orientation, based on the theory of humours, and was also derived from Christian teachings. She aimed to 'bring the body and parts thereof into an union in itself, by little and little' (Pollock, 110).

Lady Mildmay practised medicine on a large, expensive, and systematic scale. Commonly used medications, like aqua vitae or metheglin, were prepared in bulk, 10 gallons at a time. One balm required 159 different seeds, roots, spices, and gums, as well as 13 lbs of sugar and nuts and 8¼ gallons of oil, wine, and vinegar. She also practised chemical medicine of the Paracelsian kind, using metals and minerals, such as gold, pearls, turbith, sulphur, and antimony in her salves, cordials, and potions. She experimented with the manufacture and administration of the medicines until she had discovered the most effective method. Her still room had thirty-one large bottles of cordials and oils, all clearly labelled, shelves of powders and pills, a black chest full of ingredients, and sheaves of medical papers (over two thousand loose papers, as well as books, were bequeathed to her daughter, Mary). It is not known who her patients were, but she was prepared to treat individuals of either sex and any age, and she had remedies for a wide range of ailments, both mental and physical. There is no evidence that she received any payment for her work. Except that she refused to perform surgery, the type of care she offered was similar to that dispensed by licensed physicians and earned the praise of some of them. Richard Banister, in a denunciation of women who were active in the medical sphere, exempted 'the right religious and virtuous lady, the Lady Mildmay, of Apethorpe'. Her 'cures were attended with due care, and ended with true charity', and she possessed 'good judgement in many things' (Banister, no. 279).

Lady Mildmay grew up as a member of the protestant church. Her mother introduced her to the habit of meditating privately every day in order to commune with God, strengthen her faith, and remind herself of God's favours to her. In later life, convinced of her elect status, Lady Mildmay composed a work of 912 folios of spiritual meditations, which cover many topics, the most frequent themes being Christ as the resurrection and the life, and that God would never abandon the faithful. These meditations are an important source for determining what protestantism was for a lay person in post-Reformation England, and also for examining the role of religion in the life of a woman. They illustrate the doctrinal ambiguity of early protestantism, underline the importance of faith, and reveal the educated laity's understanding of key concepts.

Lady Mildmay's meditations also contain material not recorded elsewhere: on the midlands rising of 1607 and on the earl of Exeter's scheme for draining the fens in Holland, Exeter. Her husband was also involved in both these events.

Lady Mildmay's memoirs constitute one of the earliest existing autobiographies written by a woman in her own hand. A contemporary portrait depicts her as stern, with an upright bearing, plainly dressed in black, with her hand resting on her medical and musical papers. Her medical work is an example of the important contribution women made to the case of the sick in sixteenth- and early seventeenth-century England. Lady Mildmay died on 27 July 1620 at Apethorpe and was buried in the church there.   LINDA A. POLLOCK

Sources L. Pollock, *With faith and physic: the life of a Tudor gentlewoman, Lady Grace Mildmay, 1552–1620* (1993) • R. Warnicke, 'Lady Mildmay's journal: a study in autobiography and meditation in Reformation England', *Sixteenth Century Journal*, 20 (1989), 55–68 • R. Weigall, 'An Elizabethan gentlewoman: the journal of Lady Mildmay, *c.* 1570–1617', *QR*, 215 (1911), 119–38 • K. H. Rogers, ed., *Lacock Abbey charters*, Wilts RS, 34 (1979) • S. E. Lehmberg, *Sir Walter Mildmay and Tudor government* (1964) • *The reports of Sir Edward Coke*, 2nd edn (1680) [Co Rep] • L. Aikin, *Memoirs of the court of King James I* (1822) • R. Banister, *A treatise of one hundred and thirteene diseases of the eyes, and eye-liddes, the second time published, with some profitable additions of certaine principles and experiments* (1622) • H. A. St John Mildmay, *A brief memoir of the Mildmay family* (1913) • T. E. Vernon, 'Inventory of Sir Henry Sharington', *Wiltshire Archaeological and Natural History Magazine*, 63 (1968), 72–82 • J. Bridges, *The history and antiquities of Northamptonshire*, ed. P. Whalley, 2 vols. (1791) • O. Barron, 'The Fanes', *The Ancestor*, 12 (1905), 4–17, esp. 5 • C. Morrongiello, 'Edward Collard: the complete compositions', *Lute Society Editions* (1996) • will, PRO, PROB 11/36

Archives BL, Add. MS 34218, fol. 59 • Lacock Abbey, Chippenham, Wiltshire • Northants. RO, corresp., W/A vol. 55 • Northants. RO, details of the legal dispute, W/A box 2 • Northants. RO, medical notes and papers • Northants. RO, papers, W/A vols. 15, 17, 35 • PRO, court of wards | BL, Lansdowne MS 991, fols. 268–272 • PRO, petition of Sir Walter Mildmay, SP12 151/8

Likenesses double portrait, marble effigy on funeral monument (with her husband Sir Anthony), Apethorpe church, Northamptonshire • portrait, repro. in Barron, 'The Fanes', 6; now destroyed • portrait, NPG [*see illus.*]

Wealth at death see will, PRO, PROB 11/36; *CSP dom.*, 1598–1601, 163

Mildmay, Henry (*c.*1594–1664/5?), politician and courtier, was the second son of Humphrey Mildmay (*c.*1552–1613) of Danbury Place, Essex, and Mary (1560–1633), daughter of Henry Capel of Hadham, Hertfordshire. Tutored by the puritan Martin Holbeach, he was admitted in 1610 to Emmanuel College, Cambridge—the college founded by his grandfather, Sir Walter *Mildmay—and graduated BA in 1612. Although he was admitted to Gray's Inn in 1620, this was purely honorific, and he had by this stage secured significant positions in the administration and at court. In 1617, the year he was knighted by James I, he was made sewer and cupbearer of the household, and in the following year was made master of the jewel house, with the assistance of the duke of Buckingham. Such offices helped provide the foundation of Mildmay's wealth, as did his marriage on 5 April 1619 to Anne (*d.* 1657), daughter of William Halliday, a London alderman and governor of the East India Company, which brought a dowry of £3000. By 1620 Mildmay had established a grand estate at Wanstead, Essex, although his subsequent career would be surrounded by allegations of financial impropriety, which has led to his being described as a 'rapacious scoundrel' (Brunton and Pennington, 126), who was 'chiefly motivated by personal greed' (Underdown, 51). It remains unclear, however, whether he was any more ruthless than other professional office-holders, or whether such comments are founded upon later royalist diatribes against a man whose desertion from the Stuarts seemed explicable only in terms of a desire for personal financial reward. Although royalists dubbed him Sir Whimzy Mildmay it is certainly possible to demonstrate that his loyalty to the crown, and to his patron Buckingham, was eroded significantly long before 1640, and on the basis of an attachment to advanced godly protestantism.

Mildmay was returned for Maldon, his local constituency, in the 1621 parliament, but demonstrated less enthusiasm for its proceedings than for colonial adventures, with which he became associated as a member of the committee of the Virginia Company in 1622. He was narrowly defeated at the Maldon election in 1624 but secured a parliamentary seat at Westbury in Wiltshire, and displayed his dependence upon, and allegiance to, Buckingham through his prominent role in plans to raise money for war with Spain. However, that he was no mere creature of the king's favourite is evident from his having joined those who detected a Catholic conspiracy in England, who sought firm policies regarding domestic recusants, and who sought to investigate Samuel Harsnett, bishop of Norwich. In the 1625 parliament Mildmay once again represented Maldon, and although he sought to defend Buckingham against his critics he was nevertheless prepared to recognize his patron's faults, and emerged as a critic of the Arminian tendency within the church, and as one who was concerned about Charles I's new Catholic wife. Mildmay was appointed a commissioner for the forced loan in 1626, but he was largely inactive in this regard and he was not present in the 1626 parliament, which saw the impeachment of his master, Buckingham. By the time Mildmay returned to the Commons in 1628, once more representing Maldon, the break with Buckingham was evidently complete and he participated in attacks upon the Arminians on religious and secular grounds, hinting that Buckingham was the leader of the faction. Although concerned to secure finance for European wars in defence of protestantism, Mildmay was ambiguous on whether supply should precede alleviation of grievances, and he evidently did not consider that parliament was capable of raising sufficient funds. Although not in the vanguard of attacks upon church policy in the 1629 session, he nevertheless continued to support action on church matters, not least against John Cosin, rector of Brancepeth, Durham.

Mildmay was returned to both the Short and Long parliaments as member for Maldon, where he was now high steward. He rapidly emerged as a supporter of further reformation in the church, in terms of the removal of images and idols, and support for consideration of the London petition for root and branch reform. He also advocated regulation of church courts, and harsh penalties for recusants. He was prepared to defend specific courtiers impeached by parliament, such as Lord Keeper Finch, and he was one of those who opposed the attainder of Strafford. Being a Straffordian is not always significant as an indicator of civil-war allegiance, and Mildmay's defection from the royal cause occurred long before May 1641, and as such may be attributed to conviction as much as opportunism or greed. More significant was his support

for the Scots from early 1641 and his willingness to oppose the Book of Common Prayer, and it was as a supporter of reform that he was nominated to the recess committee in 1641. Thereafter he proved zealous in attempts to raise money for parliament, not least in order to finance the war effort against the Irish rebels, with which he was also involved. That Mildmay's career between the opening of the Long Parliament and the outbreak of war was not merely a reflection of his desire to avoid being called to account for earlier illegality, not least as a monopolist, is evident from his subsequent career. Although his status as a prominent courtier ensured his nomination as a commissioner of array in 1642, Mildmay not only supported the parliamentarian cause, but also quickly became identified as one of the fiery spirits in the Commons who sought a vigorous pursuit of the war and settlement only on harsh terms.

Mildmay was involved in parliament's attempts to win the support of the Scots in 1642, and upon the outbreak of war became a zealous member of the administration in Essex. At Westminster he emerged as a prominent member of the faction which pressed for an aggressive policy of war, and he attacked those suspected of being willing to enter a process of negotiations with the king. Although his nomination as a commissioner for exclusion from the sacrament (1646) and church government (1648), as well as his nomination as an elder in the Essex classis, suggests presbyterianism, Mildmay's religious views were probably in sympathy with congregationalists and he acted as patron to clerics such as Leonard Hoar, who later became president of Harvard College. During the late 1640s Mildmay also flirted with Levelleresque politics, not least in expressing hostility to the House of Lords and their creatures in the Commons, such as Oliver Cromwell. On balance, however, his allegiance lay with the Independent grandees, as is evident from his role as a hostage left with the Scots in December 1646 after he had fled to the army in the wake of the presbyterian counter-revolution and the 'forcing of the houses' in July 1647, and his praise for the Scottish faction headed by Argyll in early 1648. His hostility to the eleven members was evident from his later claim that it would be 'a very wicked thing' for them to be 'called home again (after breach of trust) to sit among the trustees of the people', given that 'the godly party had considered them as enemies to the public interest, and publicly accused them, and it was their mercy to permit them to be banished and not to proceed to a trial' (*Mercurius Pragmaticus*, 38, 12–19 Dec 1648, sig. Ddd2v). Mildmay also served as a member of the revenue committee after 1645, although this was naturally interpreted by royalists as another profitable position which he was concerned not to lose, and as providing an explanation of his attitude to the king, which was reckoned to be a mixture of fear and guilt. That Mildmay was hostile to Charles is evident from his opposition to a negotiated settlement in 1648, and his claim that the king was 'no more to be trusted than a lion that had been enraged and let loose again at liberty' (*Mercurius Pragmaticus*, 36/7, 5–12 Dec 1648, sig. Ccc3).

It was as one of the 'Independent beagles' that Mildmay

adopted a hard-line policy towards those members secluded at Pride's Purge, and he rapidly registered his dissent from the vote to prolong negotiations with the king (21 December 1648). He also sat as a commissioner for the trial of Charles I, but although he attended seven meetings of the commissioners in the painted chamber he was present on only one day of the trial, and was absent on the day of sentencing and failed to sign the death warrant, although he was later listed among the *Regicides. Mildmay, who provided the republican government with the royal jewels and plate, proved an enthusiastic participant in the Rump; his zeal for committee-work is inexplicable simply in terms of personal greed and continued long after he had been awarded £2000 in respect of an earlier loan made to Charles I. Mildmay served on the army committee for the duration of the republic, and was elected to all but one of the councils of state between the trial and the dissolution of parliament in April 1653. His allegiance lay with the civilian republicans, and he displayed hostility to the Levellers and opposed leniency for the plotters associated with Christopher Love. Mildmay's other contributions included assisting the spy-master Thomas Scot, and he was lauded by at least one contemporary for having 'made as wise, as faithful improvement of his intelligence to the good of the whole in apparent peril as any one man in this republic' (E. Grey, *Vox coeli*, 1649, 35).

That Mildmay would not trim his sails in order to curry favour with, and secure rewards from, any political regime is apparent from his withdrawal from Westminster during the protectorate, when he appears neither to have sought nor secured election to parliament. He only returned to public life with the recall of the Rump in 1659, remaining in the Commons until the readmission of the secluded members in mid-February 1660. On the eve of the Restoration and in order to avoid an investigation into his stewardship of the royal jewels, he ignored the order to attend a committee during the Convention Parliament in May 1660, and attempted to escape to the continent, although he was seized at Rye. He was excepted from pardon and stripped of his knighthood, offices, and estate in July 1661. He was also sentenced to life imprisonment, and to be drawn on a sledge to Tyburn each 27 January, despite a petition in which he insisted that he had attended the high court of justice in order to save the king's life. In March 1664 he was ordered to be transported to Tangier, but died at Antwerp, probably between April 1664 and May 1665; his deathbed scene was recorded for posterity, possibly to confute the popular notion that no regicide could die a natural death.   J. T. PEACEY

Sources D. Brunton and D. H. Pennington, *Members of the Long Parliament* (1954) · C. H. Firth and R. S. Rait, eds., *Acts and ordinances of the interregnum, 1642–1660*, 3 vols. (1911) · D. Underdown, *Pride's Purge: politics in the puritan revolution* (1971) · B. Worden, *The Rump Parliament, 1648–1653* (1974) · G. E. Aylmer, *The state's servants: the civil service of the English republic, 1649–1660* (1973) · C. Russell, *The fall of the British monarchies, 1637–1642* (1991) · *JHC*, 1 (1547–1628); 7 (1651–9) · *CSP dom.*, 1625–6 · H. A. St John Mildmay, *A brief memoir of the Mildmay family* (1913) · J. G. Muddiman, *The trial of King Charles the First* (1928) · *The journal of Sir Simonds D'Ewes from the first recess of the Long Parliament to the withdrawal of King Charles from London*, ed. W. H. Coates (1942) · *The journal of Sir Simonds D'Ewes from the beginning of the Long Parliament to the opening of the trial of the earl of Strafford*, ed. W. Notestein (1923) · W. H. Coates, A. Steele Young, and V. F. Snow, eds., *The private journals of the Long Parliament*, 3 vols. (1982–92) · *Mercurius Pragmaticus*, 36–8 (1648) · *DNB*

Archives Som. ARS, papers relating to the jewel house, DD/MI/19

Likenesses oils, c.1664, repro. in Mildmay, *Brief memoir of the Mildmay family*

Mildmay, Sir Walter (1520/21–1589), administrator and founder of Emmanuel College, Cambridge, was born in 1520 or 1521 (a portrait of him painted in 1574 states his age to be fifty-three), the youngest of five sons of Thomas Mildmay (c.1488/9–1551), a mercer of Chelmsford in Essex, and his wife, Agnes Read (d. 1557). His older brothers were Edward (d. 1549), the landowner and MP Thomas Mildmay (b. in or before 1515, d. 1566), of Moulsham in Essex, William (d. 1570), and John (d. 1580). Despite the family's later claims to ancient lineage they appear to have been immediate descendants of a yeoman farmer of Great Waltham, Essex, and Mildmay's father owned a stall in the market place at Chelmsford. Mildmay had at least three sisters, including Thomasin Mildmay (d. in or before 1563), who married first Anthony Bourchier (b. in or before 1521, d. 1551) in or before 1541, then William *Thomas (d. 1554) in or before 1553.

Education and early career, 1538–1547 Walter Mildmay was a fellow-commoner at Christ's College, Cambridge, by 1538, and in 1546 was admitted to Gray's Inn. None of his brothers appears on the rolls of admission for either Oxford or Cambridge University or the inns of court. He did not take a degree at Cambridge, where he remained for roughly two years, and there is no evidence to suggest that he devoted much time or attention to the course of study at Gray's Inn, though a descendant recounted a legend that Mildmay was the person 'who first hit upon the method of cutting off an entail', and he was certainly well versed in the law (Mildmay, 37).

By the time he was admitted to Gray's Inn, Mildmay was already involved heavily in royal financial administration. The development of new revenue courts to handle the acquisition by Henry VIII of huge amounts of ex-monastic land and the continuing Tudor interest in fiscal reform to realize greater income for the crown provided the perfect opportunity for the energetic and intelligent Mildmay. His career as one of the leading financial experts of the second half of the sixteenth century began in 1540 with appointment as clerk in the court of augmentations, a post he likely received through the patronage of his older brother Thomas Mildmay, an auditor of the court. In May 1543 Walter Mildmay was appointed jointly with Francis Southwell to the post of auditor of prests and foreign accounts in the court of general surveyors, and both men were put to work on raising and disbursing revenue related to the war with France. Mildmay travelled to France in 1544 with Sir Richard Rich, the treasurer of the war.

1545 was an important year for Mildmay. He was returned to parliament for the first time, for Lostwithiel, a

Sir Walter Mildmay (1520/21–1589), by unknown artist, 1588

duchy of Lancaster seat in Cornwall. He probably owed his return to his brother-in-law, Bourchier, auditor and councillor to Katherine Parr. He was also appointed, with his brother, as a co-auditor for the court of augmentations for Cambridgeshire, Essex, Hertfordshire, Huntingdonshire, Middlesex, Norfolk, Suffolk, and London. The auditor's office was no sinecure, but required a man with experience in fiscal affairs. Mildmay must have made a strong and immediate impression; by the end of that year he was one of the three main officers of the court, and on 10 September 1546 was appointed for life as auditor of crown lands north of the Trent for the duchy of Lancaster. Early in 1546 he was put to work on the special commission that developed the recommendations for the reorganization of the court of augmentations in January 1547. Their work consisted of attempting to clear debts, root out corruption, and investigate negligence in the revenue departments, and Mildmay appears to have had a major role in the tedious business of debt collection, and of developing the plans for reconstitution. The investigations resulted in the reorganization of the courts of augmentations and general surveyors into one new court of augmentations and general surveyors. Mildmay's diligence was rewarded with his appointment on 1 January 1547 as one of the two surveyors for the new court, a post second only to the

chancellor, Sir Edward North, in importance. This type of reforming investigation into revenue business and administration was a recurrent theme in Mildmay's career, and his growing experience made him increasingly important and valued by the monarch.

On 25 May 1546 Mildmay married Mary (1527/8–1577), daughter of William Walsingham of Scadbury in Chislehurst, Kent, and his wife, Joyce. Therefore, Sir Francis *Walsingham (c.1532–1590) was his brother-in-law. Mildmay appears to have very much ruled his wife's life. She was regarded as virtuous, dutiful, and chaste. The couple had two sons, Sir Anthony Mildmay (c.1549–1617) [see below] and Humphrey (c.1552–1613), father of the politician and courtier Sir Henry *Mildmay (c.1594–1664/5?). Both attended Peterhouse, Cambridge, and were admitted to Gray's Inn. The marriage also produced three daughters: Martha, who married Sir William Brouncker of Melksham in Wiltshire in January 1569; Winifred (d. before 1618), who married Sir William Fitzwilliam of Dogsthorpe in Northamptonshire in September 1569; and Christian (d. 1627), who married Charles Barrett of Aveley in Essex in June 1578 and then Sir John *Leveson (1555–1615) of Halling in Kent in July 1586.

Service under Edward VI and Mary I, 1547–1558 Between 22 February and 1 March 1547 Edward VI knighted Mildmay. The manuscript that supplies his name gives no precise date for his knighting, and says that some of the knights named were dubbed on 22 February, while others were made 'at other tymes duryng the utas of the seid noble solempnisacion' (*Literary Remains*, ed. Jordan, 1.ccci, cccvi). Unlike many leading Tudor royal servants Mildmay was never granted higher honour than a knighthood, despite his long and faithful service to Edward and Mary I, and the obvious favour in which Elizabeth I held him. The memoirs of his daughter-in-law Grace *Mildmay, *née* Sharington (c.1552–1620), hints that the lack of higher honour may have been in deference to Mildmay's wishes rather than oversight or lack of appreciation of his service. Grace, Lady Mildmay, described her father-in-law as a faithful but humble royal servant, a man of piety who refused to enrich himself at the crown's expense, and avoided elevation to the peerage.

Modern historians comment frequently and with admiration on the volume of work that Mildmay accomplished, in excellent order, and in relatively short periods of time, such as the massive inventory of Henry's goods, undertaken in September 1547, for which he was one of the commissioners, and for which he may have done the majority of the work. One particular coffer of jewels belonging to Katherine Parr was delivered directly to Mildmay and two of his fellow commissioners for them to 'make parfecte Inventory of all suche thinges as they founde in the same' (Starkey, 94). Mildmay was named of the quorum of the peace for Essex on 26 May 1547. His expertise drew him into a particularly contentious commission early in the reign. In April 1548 Mildmay, with Robert Keilwey, surveyor of liveries in the court of wards and liveries, was given the thankless task of collating the results of kingdom-wide surveys of chantry properties and making final decisions as to the fate of the properties and the distribution of their assets. The dispersal of lands, funds, or goods dedicated solely to the maintenance of propitiatory masses was a necessary part of doctrinal reformation, encompassing the casting off of purgatory. The contentious issue was that of the proper use of the spoils of this cull. Sympathetic courtiers, local corporations, and country gentry petitioned for the entirety of the sums to be retained for charitable and municipal uses such as refounding grammar schools formerly supported by chantries and poor relief. Those who supported the government's interests desired most of the proceeds to be put to crown use, especially to prosecute the war in Scotland, and as a means of avoiding direct taxation. On 11 August Mildmay was appointed to a commission to assign pensions to the former chantry priests.

Mildmay was well suited to the task of the commission. His protestantism made him eager to remove the vestiges of such a strongly Catholic doctrine as purgatory, yet his subsequent foundations appear to indicate deep support for the professedly educational motives of the Act for the Dissolution of the Chantries (1 Edw. VI c. 14). Thomas and Sir Walter Mildmay, with two other men, petitioned to form a corporation with the object of refounding a grammar school in Chelmsford because the two grammar schools there had been dissolved as a result of the Chantries Act. Their petition was granted on 10 February 1551. The new school, called the King Edward VI Grammar School, was in its turn funded by other confiscations. The first schoolhouse was the refectory of the former monastery of the black friars at Chelmsford, which was part of a property purchased after the dissolution of the monasteries, along with the manor of Moulsham, by Thomas Mildmay, who was succeeded by his son on 22 January 1551. The corporation paid £2 per annum in rent and the Mildmay family retained their connections with the school for many years, Thomas Mildmay bequeathing a yearly rent of £13 6s. 8d. to support it from the tithes of Terling parsonage. Sir Walter Mildmay's later foundation of Emmanuel College, Cambridge, from the proceeds gained from the suppressed Dominican friary was his greatest single contribution to education, and in his will he left the college £200 and a bequest of plate. He also left a gift of plate to his former place of study, Christ's College.

By 1549 Mildmay's reputation as a fiscal expert was well established among privy councillors and his talents made him indispensable, despite the regime change on 13 October. From late 1548 onwards Sir William Paget urged Edward Seymour, duke of Somerset and lord protector, to employ Sir Anthony Aucher, Sir Edward Wotton, and Mildmay to bring order to the crown's hopelessly muddled financial affairs. Nothing seems to have come of it. John Dudley, duke of Northumberland, appointed Mildmay to a commission in late 1551 or early 1552 to press for the payment of long-standing debts to the king. Mildmay's expertise, enthusiasm, and honesty were much in demand during fiscal investigations conducted between 1547 and 1554, and he was named to at least thirty-five special commissions. Many of these were geared towards the

collection of Edward's debts, a chronic problem for the late medieval and early modern exchequer and chamber finance departments. Mildmay may have been one of the guiding hands in the commission of March 1552 charged with reviewing and rationalizing the revenue courts and general crown financial administration. He was certainly one of the most active commissioners. The commission's report was made on 10 December. The first part gave an account of royal income and expenditure and of the state of the revenue courts. The second part laid out the nature of abuses and problems in those courts and how best to rectify them, and provided an overall plan for reform of fiscal bureaucracy in order to produce more income and eliminate sinecures. This included the simple expedient of eliminating courts or reincorporating some into the exchequer. Of the nine men appointed to that commission Mildmay had the greatest expertise in financial affairs, and undoubtedly the other commissioners relied on him to resolve the minutiae of their work. The suggestions put forward by this commission were finally incorporated into the dissolution of the court of augmentations under Mary in 1554, and its absorption into the exchequer along with the court of first fruits and tenths. Upon this event Mildmay was rewarded with a generous pension of £200 per annum for life.

Mildmay's career under Mary received a slight check, particularly in his parliamentary appearances. He had been returned for Lewes in Sussex in 1547 through the patronage of Katherine Parr's husband, Thomas Seymour, Baron Seymour of Sudeley, and for Maldon in Essex in March 1553 through his own influence (having also been returned through Northumberland's client, Sir John Gates, as knight of the shire for Lancaster). Though he gained a seat for Peterborough, Northamptonshire, in Mary's first parliament of October 1553, his overt resistance in the House of Commons to the Catholic restoration ended any political career he may have pursued in her reign. He was removed from the quorum of the peace in February 1554. Perhaps his loyalty was put to the test by a privy council order to him in March 1557 to 'send hither under salfe custodie' his servant, Thomas Penny, first searching his chambers for 'suche bookes, lettres and writings as he shal finde whiche concerne not his accompte or service' (*APC*, 6.62). If such is the case Mildmay must have complied with royal wishes as in April Penny was committed to Newgate prison for seditious writings, but was released the following September after giving a recognizance for good behaviour. Mildmay's mother died and was buried at Chelmsford on 5 October. Mildmay was too valuable an administrator to be left out of fiscal business; he continued to serve on various commissions, and on 9 January 1558 was appointed 'treasurer for our present service beyond the seas', and entrusted with £5000 to carry to Dunkirk for the army that was ordered to Calais (*CSP dom.*, 1553–8, 689–90). Calais fell before the expedition could sail, and Mildmay was ordered to return to the queen with the remains of the money. He was then ordered again to Dunkirk when Mary decided to send a select force to join Philip's army in an attempt to recover Calais. That force was subsequently dismissed on 30 January. Mildmay was returned as knight of the shire for Northamptonshire in 1558, retaining the seat in every subsequent parliament until his death. In March 1558 he was appointed to a commission to 'consider the state of our finances and revenues and devise means how we might be furnished of treasure for the service in hand' (ibid., 729). Mary died before any of the resolutions of this commission could be put into practice.

Chancellor of the exchequer and privy councillor, 1559–1589

Mildmay's particular talents for carrying out surveys and inventories rapidly and efficiently were called immediately into service by Elizabeth I's privy council. On 22 December 1558 he was requested to contact all necessary sources to amass a record of the names of all the queen's 'hed farmours' and copyholders and send it on to the privy council 'with all convenyent spede' (*APC*, 7.27–9). The following day he was also appointed to a committee of the privy council to discover what demesne lands had been granted by Mary. However, this was not the greatest of the duties to be given to the skilled and patient Mildmay. On 5 February 1559, at the particular suit of William Paulet, first marquess of Winchester and lord treasurer, Mildmay was appointed chancellor of the exchequer. In 1559 he was added to the commissions of the peace for Middlesex and Northamptonshire and about 1564 for Huntingdon. In July or August 1566 he became a privy councillor and in January 1567 was named under-treasurer of the exchequer.

Mildmay is generally credited, along with Winchester, with masterminding the exchequer reforms of the late sixteenth century, and he increasingly performed the day-to-day duties of the senior exchequer offices, while Winchester immersed himself more and more in the formation of policy. This was a reading of roles that continued under the next lord treasurer, William Cecil, Baron Burghley. Though Winchester pushed hard for a radical overhaul of exchequer practice, including restoring the 'ancient course' in order to eliminate wasteful expenditure and corruption, it was Mildmay, with Burghley, who actually instigated the necessary reforms after the financial crisis of 1571 that effectively ended the marquess's career. Mildmay, despite orders to the contrary from Winchester, essentially purged the exchequer of receipt of multiple, and ineffective, systems of accounting and money keeping, established checks on tellers, and moved superfluous cash to a deposit treasury. Mildmay's reforms were not perfect, and after his death they were subject to revision by successors eager to prove their ideas superior, but under his administration Elizabeth's deposit treasury accumulated funds as substantial as those achieved under Henry VII, the monarch held up in the late Elizabethan period as the exemplar of fiscal solvency. Mildmay provided continuity during the tumultuous conclusion of Winchester's tenure and the beginning of Burghley's. It was also Mildmay who was among those burdened with the task of resolving one of the most serious issues facing the Elizabethan government, that of the debased coinage. He had participated in the debasement and recoinage of

1551, and on 29 October 1560 was named to the commission to examine the issues of recoinage which oversaw the process during 1561.

Mildmay, however, was far more than a gifted accountant. The influence of his brief Cambridge education and of his circle of university educated friends and family is evident in his manuscript 'Memorial' of precepts to his heir, Anthony Mildmay, which was written in 1570 when his son was about twenty-one. This work includes language and concepts familiar from the discourse of the university educated royal servants of the sixteenth century, men like Burghley and Walsingham. Mildmay's endowments to Christ's College suggest a strong interest in humanist studies. He provided a yearly endowment for a Greek lectureship on 10 March 1569 and donated several works of the great philosophers Plato, Aristotle, and Cicero, some in Greek. He had already assisted his brother-in-law Thomas with the publication in 1550 of the *Principal Rules of the Italian Grammar*, which was a guidebook for the Englishman eager to sharpen his skills in Italian. He was the author of several Latin poems, of which no copies are extant, and allegedly of a book entitled *A Note to Knowe a Good Man* (Mildmay, 41; Roberts, sig. A4r). His interest in old manuscripts and his literary patronage can also be inferred by a translation dedicated to him of part of the widely disseminated text *Secretum secretorum* by Jenkin Gwynne, a surveyor in the court of exchequer and, according to the book's dedication, a long-time client of Mildmay. Gwynne stated that he translated the medical portion of the document as a gesture of thanks to Mildmay, who was then suffering from some illness.

Mildmay was also a remarkably skilled orator. A family history states 'he was the first to make a speech of two hours' duration' (in parliament), and it must be a credit to his talent that he continued to be sought after as a parliamentary speaker (Mildmay, 44). Though he did not achieve fame as a speaker in the 1572 parliament he was among those men named to confer upon and offer their opinions to the Commons on the bill against Mary, queen of Scots, perhaps because he had earlier provided a well-developed set of arguments to the privy council regarding her place of residence and had interviewed her with Cecil in 1570. In the 1576 parliament he came into his own as the Commons' most effective, and effecting, speaker. His speech supporting a supply bill was an excellent demonstration of his masterful technique, as he painted a picture of the debt and despair of the kingdom under Edward and Mary and Elizabeth's great skill in freeing herself of this and establishing a peaceful and happy realm, 'delivered from the bondage of Rome'. He then moved to caution the Commons that they must remain ready for challenges, and keep in mind that the taxes granted to the queen never produced all they were supposed to, that she was often put to expense for special causes, and furthermore lived without extravagance and without resorting to debased coinage, land sales, or loans (Lehmberg, *Mildmay*, 131–4). Mildmay summed up by exhorting the house to grant the requested subsidy so that Elizabeth

Be not unfinished of that which shalbe sufficient to
mainteyne both her and us against the privy or open malice
of enemyes. Wherein lett us so proceed, as her Majestie may
fynde how much wee thinke ourselves bound to God, that
hath given us so gracious a Queen to reigne over us.
(ibid., 133)

It was a remarkable exposition of the argument for
taxes for possible defence which was popular with the
Tudor monarchs, as well as a royal panegyric. Although it
generated only the usual sums this may be put down more
to a parliament weary of taxation than to an ineffective
speech. Mildmay's parliamentary speeches regarding the
queen were ideal material for William Camden and his fellow purveyors of the Gloriana mythos. His deference to,
and praise of, Elizabeth were unstinting: she was generous, compassionate, and wise, and problems were never
to be related to her reign but to either misguided forebears, or potentially troublesome successors. Mildmay's
oratorical skills continued to be exploited in the Elizabethan parliaments, and were particularly effective in
softening up the membership on the issue of supply.

Mildmay's bond with Burghley, a near neighbour in
Northamptonshire since 1550, was based on a long-
standing friendship as well as a comfortable and mutually
agreeable professional relationship, particularly under
Elizabeth, when they worked closely over royal finance.
Their acquaintance may have begun at Cambridge among
the circle of scholars around Sir John Cheke, though evidence for Mildmay's inclusion in this group is circumstantial. His relationship with Burghley was warm and familiar; he was godfather to Anne Cecil in 1556 and Sir Philip
Hoby wanted both men to spend Christmas 1557 with him
at Bisham in Berkshire. In business they seem to have
been a well-matched pair, with Mildmay handling administration and execution of the myriad daily duties in the
exchequer, while Burghley dealt with policy decisions and
political issues. Mildmay was not excluded from the policy
discussions with his friend, however; the two men appear
frequently paired in commissions such as that to review
the victualling of Elizabeth's forces in Ireland, to examine
a suit which touched upon her inheritance, or to develop
suggestions for combating robbers and unlicensed beggars.

Perhaps the most significant, and thankless, task with
which Burghley and Mildmay were entrusted was their
commission in late 1570 to visit Mary, queen of Scots, at
Chatsworth in Derbyshire, where she was under the gentle keepership of George Talbot, sixth earl of Shrewsbury.
This was carried out in the aftermath of the assassination
of James Stewart, earl of Moray, on 21 January and Burghley and Mildmay were to negotiate terms for Mary's possible release from captivity in England and restoration to
the Scottish throne. A letter of Burghley to Sir William
Norris of 25 September stated that neither Mildmay nor
he relished the commission. Although they succeeded in
gaining agreement from Mary to a list of articles prepared
by Elizabeth and the privy council, the Scottish government would not consider the idea of a restoration, nor any
move that potentially negated her abdication, and the

entire exercise came to naught. It was not Mildmay's first
involvement in the affairs of the controversial Scottish
queen, and for nearly twenty years he was intermittently
drawn into issues involving Mary's fate. In October 1569
he had presented to the privy council a carefully weighed
and balanced discussion of the arguments over whether
Mary should be returned to Scotland or retained in English captivity. Mildmay was present at the trial of Thomas
Howard, fourth duke of Norfolk, on 16 January 1572 for
treason in compassing Elizabeth's deposal and death in
conspiracy with Mary. When Mary was removed to Fother-
inghay Castle in Northamptonshire in September 1586
Mildmay was charged by Burghley 'to provyde for hir
bestowyng', while Sir Amias Paulet was given the charge
of actually conveying her there (Read, 49). In 1583 Mildmay was again sent to Mary to enter into negotiations for
her release, with the same frustrating results, and he was
also sent in October 1586 to deliver to her the letter from
Elizabeth informing the former queen of Scots of her
impending trial.

Though Mildmay's career was largely focused on fiscal
matters he participated in his fair share of arbitrations
and examinations in matters both great and small
brought before the privy council. In November 1576
Burghley, Walsingham, and he were recruited to examine
a search carried out by the recorder of London on the Portuguese ambassador, Francisco Giraldi, which apparently
included the rough handling of the ambassador's family,
and the seizure of a host and chalice from his home. Giraldi was not satisfied with the punishment of the
recorder, and the queen wished to know more fully the
circumstances of the incident to ascertain whether or not
the ambassador's continued complaints were justified.
Other items of business included a supplication by the
town of Dedham in Essex against a local attorney, Miles
Laken, for 'sundry misdemeanors'; by the father of a murdered man for justice against the murderer; and by a
woman seeking security for her portion against the wastefulness of a lunatic husband (APC, 9.345; 10.189, 209–10). In
November 1578 Mildmay headed a committee that was
given the task of reviewing the queen's revenue collection in Ireland with an eye to improving the yields and to
making necessary reorganization of Irish exchequer practice. The privy council also solicited his opinion in December 1578 on the proper fineness for English coinage in an
effort to address the problem of debasement. His most
notable local office was that of joint lord lieutenant of
Huntingdon during the northern rebellion of 1569 and
sole lord lieutenant from 1587 until his death.

**Lifestyle, religion, and the foundation of Emmanuel College,
Cambridge** In April 1551 Mildmay acquired his seat of
Apethorpe in Northamptonshire in exchange with
Edward for property in Gloucestershire and Berkshire.
The manor and park had briefly been the property of Princess Elizabeth, and the house was a large, rambling building dating mainly from before 1530. Mildmay also had a
house at Hackney in Middlesex and another in Smithfield
in the parish of St Bartholomew-the-Great, which he purchased from Rich (now first Baron Rich). He did little

building of his own on Apethorpe, besides adding a stone chimney-piece dated 1562 with his arms, motto, *virtute non vi*, and initials, and placing his arms above the exterior gateway. Elizabeth visited the manor on her summer progress of 1566, dining with Mildmay, but he does not appear to have attempted to aggrandize himself or his home at this time or any other. Grace, Lady Mildmay, described her father-in-law as a pious, humble, and prudent man, 'wise, eloquent and methodical in all his speeches', and said that he would not permit irreverent discussion of the queen or 'matters of state', or blasphemy at his table, nor allow men to speak ill of others (Pollock, 31–2). Yet, despite his daughter-in-law's complimentary comments on his humility, and her insistence that he shunned elevation to the peerage, in 1583 the family pursued a more respectable lineage. Mildmay's son Anthony Mildmay presented to Clarenceux herald a claim for the restitution of arms that connected the family with one Hugh de Mildemay, who lived during the reign of Stephen. This information was found in some newly 'discovered' papers. Mildmay had already received a new creation of arms in 1552, at which time he had produced no such papers. The 'auntient credible and authenticall' documents which supported this claim are undoubted forgeries created to justify Mildmay's claim, probably the reason they were not advanced in 1552 (BL, Harley MS 245, fols. 142r–144r). It is possible that the leading spirit in this endeavour was not Mildmay himself but his heir. Anthony Mildmay and his wife appear to have fretted about the smallness of the income allowed them by Mildmay, and subsequently about the portion of the estate that was granted away from them on his death. Further testament to this desire for status is the exquisite and colourful portrait of Anthony Mildmay by Nicholas Hilliard of about 1585 that contrasts sharply with the sombre ones of his father, the splendid, highly decorated tomb for his wife and him in Apethorpe church, and that of his father, which apparently ignored Sir Walter Mildmay's request for a simple monument. Perhaps Anthony Mildmay's work as a diplomat gave him an appetite for grander fare than his puritan father and he sought the evidence for a better pedigree, though Sir Walter Mildmay would certainly have known of the spurious claim of arms.

Sir Walter Mildmay is counted among the puritan gentry of Northamptonshire, though only one of the livings in his possession, Warmington, was consistently awarded to puritan ministers and he appears to have drawn back from association with radicals. In fact, he is characterized by one historian as 'representative of the moderate reforming wing of puritanism' (Sheils, 39, 99, 102). Mildmay could be outspoken in the political arena in defence of the Church of England and in disparagement of Catholicism, as in the case of his defamatory comments regarding François, duc d'Alençon, when that prince was suitor to Elizabeth, and his insistence that marriage between them was an offence to the queen's role as head of the church. A long, heavily annotated document by Thomas Radcliffe, third earl of Sussex, which contains the arguments in favour of the French marriage was challenged by

Mildmay, whose counter-arguments and comments were, according to one historian, 'a veritable debate on paper' (Lehmberg, *Mildmay*, 52). Mildmay objected to the marriage on a number of grounds, but repeatedly he stressed the danger that would result from the queen permitting her husband to worship in a manner that was not permitted to her subjects, and thereby establishing grounds for the indulgence of Catholic beliefs. However, he was not fanatically determined to root out or punish heretics; his passion in decrying the French match was undoubtedly engendered by the certain and unwelcome influence of the proposed bridegroom on the queen and her government if the marriage took place.

Other roles Mildmay carried out included appointment to a commission for uniformity in religion for London and Middlesex by 1573 and to the occasional commission to enquire into religious matters, such as that of August 1579, with Burghley, to examine certain people in Northamptonshire concerning lack of uniformity and for taking the sacraments. In August 1581 Mildmay, Sir Henry Darcy, and Sir Edmund Montaigne were ordered to the residence of a follower of Edmund Campion to search for his servant, Ralph Emerson, for illicit books and papers supposedly sent there, and to examine the residents on the matter. Mildmay himself was entrusted with questioning William Vaux, third Baron Vaux of Harrowden, whom Campion had named as one of his protectors. When Edmund Grindal, archbishop of Canterbury, aroused Elizabeth's enmity in 1576 with his insistence on the need for prophesyings Mildmay acquiesced with her opinion that such meetings offered too great an opportunity for the formation of radical views, despite his own strongly held feelings about the need for religious instruction and improved preaching. His conduct in these affairs, as well as his actions in regard to his servant, Penny, bear out the notion that Mildmay did not support radicalism as a means of advancing protestantism.

Mildmay's efforts to advance puritanism appear to have been largely concentrated on reform, particularly in the area of ministerial education, and a belief that better preaching was necessary for advancement of the gospel. His foundation at Cambridge, Emmanuel College, was meant to help accomplish that objective. On 12 June 1583 he purchased the site of the dissolved house of the Dominicans on what is now St Andrew's Street for £550. He obtained a licence from the queen to establish a new college there on 11 January 1584. As many of the original buildings were used as possible, including the chapel, which was converted into the college hall, but new work was also constructed under the supervision of Ralph Symons of Westminster and was completed in 1588. Others were eager to contribute towards the foundation, including Sir Henry Killigrew, Sir Wolstan Dixie, and Dr Edward Leeds. The initial foundation provided for three fellows and four scholars but subsequent benefactions soon increased these to fourteen and fifty respectively. On 1 October 1585 the college statutes were produced, based closely on those of Christ's College. Emmanuel College was firmly puritan in outlook but the intention was to provide a more highly educated protestant clergy, with better training in preaching, a natural reflection on the founder, who understood, and relied upon, the persuasive power of effective speech. The statutes were designed to promote a spartan and disciplined regimen, and the only studies permitted besides theology were Latin and Greek. The famous story is often repeated that Elizabeth remarked to Mildmay 'Sir Walter, I hear you have erected a Puritan foundation', and his politic reply was, 'no, madam, far be it from me to countenance anything contrary to your established laws; but I have set an acorn which, when it becomes an oak, God alone knows what will be the fruit thereof' (Lehmberg, *Mildmay*, 226). There is little doubt that both Mildmay and the college's first master, Laurence Chaderton, were completely loyal to the monarch and government. Elizabeth herself contributed an annuity for the support of the students during the initial founding of the college and the first of these matriculated in November 1584. Mildmay's other charitable activities are reflected by bequests in his will: one for £40 for the 'releife of the pore children' at Christchurch Hospital in London, and another £40 'to the prisoners in London and the suburbs of the same'. Closer to home he bequeathed £40 'to the pore houshowlders at Apethorpe and other places in Northampton', £20 each to benefit the same in Danbury and Chelmsford in Essex, and in the parishes of St Bartholomew and St Botolph, Aldersgate, in London. The most intriguing bequest is that of £100 'unto the porest of my kinfolkes', leaving it to his executors, Walsingham, Edward Carey, and William Dodington, to designate who these people were .

Legacy Mildmay was 'one of the most highly paid Elizabethan officials', receiving salaries, pensions, and emoluments of as much as £500 per annum, and perhaps that much again in fees (Lehmberg, *Mildmay*, 52). Towards the end of his life his landed estates were worth about £550 per annum. However, Lady Mildmay's autobiography claims that Mildmay kept her husband short of funds during his lifetime, giving the couple only £130 per annum for their upkeep, and failing in his promise to leave them his entire estate on his death. Anthony Mildmay received roughly half his father's estimated wealth of £20,000, while Humphrey Mildmay got about a quarter of it. Mildmay's will contains a lengthy series of bequests of money and plate to friends, family, fellow members of the exchequer, godchildren, prisoners, and the poor. It also includes a large and detailed list of his various nephews, nieces, and grandchildren, and he was generous in providing bequests to them all, including marriage portions for his nieces.

Mildmay also left rich gifts to his government colleagues and to the queen herself. His executors were commanded to purchase a jewel worth £100 as a gift for Elizabeth, jewels of lesser value for Sir Christopher Hatton and Henry Hastings, third earl of Huntingdon, and to deliver a gold covered vessel to Burghley, his long-time associate. His two sons were given his silver cups and seals, and his armour, munitions and tents, and to Humphrey Mildmay

he left his clothing, his books and a silver set of weights and balances. Mary, Anthony Mildmay's daughter, must have been a favoured grandchild. To her Mildmay left a gold chain, a diamond ring, and a 'longe glasse of christall garnished with silver and guilte whiche was given me by Thomas late Duke of Norfolk', a melancholy gift considering it was probably among those pieces bequeathed to Mildmay by Norfolk just prior to his execution in 1572 (PRO, PROB 11/74, sig. 51). Mary Mildmay had died on 16 March 1577 and Mildmay himself died at his house in Smithfield on 31 May 1589.

Camden described Mildmay as a man of 'valour, prudence, piety, and munificence', fit to be ranked among the great men of his age (*VCH Northamptonshire*, 2.544). Mildmay's will requested that his burial avoid 'vaine funerall pompe' and asked for the superfluous cost to be given to 'pore preachers, pore schollers, and poore needye people'. He also commanded his executors to 'make over me and my good wife a descrit tombe with as meane a charge as conveniently may be'. Despite these strictures he was buried in an elaborate marble tomb in St Bartholomew. His virtues were celebrated shortly after his death by an elegiac poem written by Henry Roberts in his *Fames Trumpet Sounding*, which honoured both Mildmay and Sir Martin Calthrop, lord mayor of London, both of whom died in 1589. The poem is dedicated to Anthony Mildmay, and Roberts asserted that he was following the example of the Greeks and Romans who composed 'eloquent Oracions in the decaseds just commendation' on the deaths of great men. The poem is elaborate, florid in its praise, and somewhat inaccurate, but the verse on the title-page before the dedication is simple and worth repeating:

> Loe heere a Mildmay milde, a Counsellor most grave,
> A Worthy man in all his deeds, as one could wish or have:
> A Phoenix in this life, to God and Prince most just,
> In Commons cause and publicks weale, a man of perfect
>   trust.
> (Roberts, sig. A1r)

Sir Anthony Mildmay (c.1549–1617), landowner and diplomat, was born on 8 September about 1549, the elder son and heir of Sir Walter Mildmay and his wife, Mary. He matriculated as a fellow-commoner from Peterhouse, Cambridge, at Easter 1562. Mildmay delivered a successful oration to the queen when she visited the college on 9 August 1564 and may have met her again when she stayed with his father at Apethorpe in summer 1566. Like his father he left Cambridge without taking a degree. In 1567 he married Grace [*see* Mildmay, Grace (c.1552–1620)], memoirist and medical practitioner, the second daughter and coheir of Sir Henry Sharington of Lacock in Wiltshire and his wife, Anne. The couple had one daughter, Mary (1581/2–1640), who subsequently married Francis *Fane, later first earl of Westmorland (1583/4–1629) [*see under* Fane, Sir Thomas]. Mildmay served against the northern rebellion in 1569 and was returned as MP for Newton in Lancashire in 1571, perhaps at the behest of Sir Ralph Sadler, chancellor of the duchy of Lancaster, but he made no impression in the Commons. He accompanied his uncle Walsingham and William Brooke, tenth Baron

Cobham, on their special embassy to the Low Countries between 12 June and 7 October 1578. The following year he was named JP for Northamptonshire and was admitted to Gray's Inn. He was added to the commission of the peace for Wiltshire in 1583 and was sheriff of Northamptonshire from 1580 to 1581 and from 1592 to 1593. As a result of his marriage and his father's influence he was returned as the junior knight of the shire for Wiltshire in 1584 but again made little mark on the house, although he was a member of the subsidy committee appointed on 24 February.

Mildmay held the reversion to his father's office of auditor north of the Trent for the duchy of Lancaster and succeeded him on 12 July 1589. He surrendered the position on 6 July 1594 and was appointed on 27 August 1596 as ambassador extraordinary to France with Gilbert Talbot, seventh earl of Shrewsbury, receiving a knighthood and a diet of £6 per day. He complained about his unsuitability for the role and he was certainly inexperienced. Shrewsbury and he had an audience with Henri IV at Rouen on 9 October. Mildmay was appointed resident ambassador on 27 August with a diet of £3 6s. 8d. per day and Shrewsbury's embassy ended on 22 October. He presented his credentials on 9 October. John Chamberlain described how he 'always knew him to be *paucorum hominum*, yet he hath ever showed himself an honourable fast frend where he found vertue and desert' (*Letters Written by John Chamberlain during the Reign of Queen Elizabeth*, ed. S. Williams, CS, old ser., 79, 1861, 2). Like his father Mildmay was a noted puritan and the French king found him ungenial and cold, making the embassy difficult. During an interview in March 1597 Henri ordered him to leave the chamber and threatened to strike him. However, the main problem was that Mildmay's mission was to keep the French in the war against Spain and to persuade Henri to recapture Calais, all but impossible tasks for the ambassador. He turned to Robert Devereux, second earl of Essex, to procure his recall, and his embassy ended in mid-August 1597. He turned down an invitation to resume his position the following year. In January 1598 he replaced Thomas Cole as MP for Westminster through the patronage of Burghley. Mildmay was more active during this session and served on various committees. Despite this he failed to secure a seat in April 1603.

Mildmay's remaining years were relatively quiet ones, spent mainly on his estates. He made his last will on 14 February 1615 and appointed his 'welbeloved wyfe' as his sole executor, leaving her, among other things, his 'Caroche', plate, jewels, household goods, and remaining chattels (PRO, PROB 11/130, sig. 100). He remembered various kinsmen and friends, including his son-in-law. Mildmay died on 2 September 1617 and was buried after an elaborate funeral at Apethorpe church in a tomb costing £1000, selling the manor of Great Leistrop in Leicestershire to pay for it and to clear his debts. His widow died on 27 July 1620 at Apethorpe and was buried beside her husband.
L. L. FORD

Sources HoP, *Commons, 1509–58*, 2.600–02 · HoP, *Commons, 1558–1603*, 3.49–56 · J. Foster, *The register of admissions to Gray's Inn, 1521–1889, together with the register of marriages in Gray's Inn chapel, 1695–1754* (privately printed, London, 1889) · Venn, *Alum. Cant.* · *VCH Northamptonshire* · *APC, 1556–78*, 6–10, 13 · S. Bendall, C. Brooke, and P. Collinson, *A history of Emmanuel College, Cambridge* (1999) · H. A. St J. Mildmay, *A brief memoir of the Mildmay family* (1908) · *CSP dom., 1553–8* · W. J. Sheils, *The puritans in the diocese of Peterborough, 1558–1610* (1979) · M. E. Finch, *The wealth of five Northamptonshire families, 1540–1640*, Northamptonshire RS, 19 (1956) · F. Stubbings, ed. and trans., *The statutes of Sir Walter Mildmay Kt chancellor of the exchequer and one of her majesty's privy councillors; authorised by him for the government of Emmanuel College founded by him* (1983) · will, PRO, PROB 11/74, sig. 51 [Sir Walter Mildmay] · will, PRO, PROB 11/130, sig. 100 [Sir Anthony Mildmay] · D. E. Hoak, *The king's council in the reign of Edward VI* (1976) · *Literary remains of King Edward the Sixth*, ed. J. G. Nichols, 2 vols., Roxburghe Club, 75 (1857) · W. S. Hudson, *The Cambridge connection and the Elizabethan settlement of 1559* (Durham, NC, 1981) · D. Starkey, *The inventory of King Henry VIII* (1998) · W. C. Richardson, *History of the court of augmentations, 1536–1554* (Baton Rouge, LA, 1961) · S. E. Lehmberg, *Sir Walter Mildmay and Tudor government* (Austin, TX, 1964) · S. E. Lehmberg, *The later parliaments of Henry VIII, 1536–1547* (1977) · J. E. Neale, *Elizabeth I and her parliaments, 1559–1581* (1953) · W. K. Jordan, *Edward VI, 1: The young king* (1968) · S. Alford, *The early Elizabethan polity: William Cecil and the British succession crisis, 1558–1569* (1998) · *A collection of eighteen rare and curious historical tracts and pamphlets* (1884–6) · C. Read, ed., *The Bardon papers: documents relating to the imprisonment and trial of Mary, queen of Scots*, CS, 3rd ser., 17 (1909) · E. R. Adair, 'William Thomas: a forgotten clerk of privy council', *Tudor studies presented … to Albert Frederick Pollard*, ed. R. W. Seton-Watson (1924), 133–60 · W. T. MacCaffrey, *The shaping of the Elizabethan regime: Elizabethan politics, 1558–1572* (1968) · L. Pollock, *With faith and physic: the life of a Tudor gentlewoman, Lady Grace Mildmay, 1552–1620* (1993) · M. A. Manzaloui, 'Tyrocaesar: a manual for Sir Walter Mildmay', *Manuscripta*, 19 (1975), 27–35 · N. Williams, *All the queen's men: Elizabeth I and her courtiers* (1972) · G. R. Elton, *England under the Tudors* (1955) · J. A. Guy, *Tudor England* (1988) · P. Williams, *The Tudor regime* (1979) · H. Roberts, *Fames trumpet sounding* (1589) · S. Zweig, *Mary queen of Scotland and the Isles* (1935) · *DNB* · R. Weigall, 'An Elizabethan gentlewoman: the journal of Lady Mildmay, c. 1570–1617', *QR*, 215 (1911), 119–38

Archives BL, exchequer accounts and papers, Add. MSS 34215–34216 · HLRO, speeches [photocopy] · Northants. RO, official accounts and papers; political papers | BL, Harley MSS, corresp.

Likenesses oils, 1574, Emmanuel College, Cambridge · oils, 1579, Emmanuel College, Cambridge · oils, 1588, Emmanuel College, Cambridge [*see illus.*]

Wealth at death approx. £550 p. a.; value of Apethorpe: Pollock, *With faith and physic*, p. 9 · bequests of approx. £7532, and estate worth roughly £20,000: will, Pollock, *With faith and physic*, p. 9

Mildrith [St Mildrith, Mildred] (*fl.* 716–c.733), abbess of Minster in Thanet, appears in an apparently genuine witness list from a council presided over by King Wihtred of Kent at Bapchild in 716 (*AS chart.*, S 22), and this is the earliest documentary reference to her, since a charter referring to her as abbess and purporting to date from 696 is now regarded as a forgery. After 716 she is named in a series of charters from Minster in Thanet which appear to be authentic or based on authentic materials. In 724 King Wihtred's son Æthelberht granted her various lands in the Weald of Kent (*AS chart.*, S 1180); in 727 she received from King Eadberht I of Kent an area of land probably in Blean Wood near Canterbury (*AS chart.*, S 26), and she was the recipient of remission from toll payable on ships, recorded in a charter dated 716 or 717 but probably referring to about 733, and another dated 737 or 738 but probably referring to 716 or 717 (*AS chart.*, S 86, 87). It is clear therefore that Mildrith was the head of an abbey favoured by the kings of Kent and of a commercial importance which continued under her successors, as is shown by remissions of toll granted to Abbess Eadburh in 748 and to Abbess Sigeburh in the early 760s (*AS chart.*, S 91, 29). The earliest charters for Minster in Thanet were granted to Mildrith's predecessor Æbbe, and these had included substantial grants, one being of 44 hides (S 10, 11, 13–15).

Alongside the evidence of this series of charters must be set that of a series of related hagiographical texts, ranging in date from possibly as early as the eighth century to the end of the eleventh, with derivative texts from later centuries. The earliest of these texts set Mildrith in the context of a complex of royal saints of Kent, East Anglia, and Mercia, and name her mother as Domne Eafe, daughter of Eormenred (said to have been king of Kent and son of King Eadbald), and her father as Merewalh, king of the Magonsæte. Her siblings included St *Mildburg of Much Wenlock. Her mother, Domne Eafe (presumably the Æbbe named in the charters), is described as the founder of Minster in Thanet, said to have been endowed by King Ecgberht of Kent as a wergild for her brothers Æthelberht and Æthelred, murdered at Eastry by his counsellor Thunor. Domne Eafe is said to have sent Mildrith overseas for her education. Eleventh-century texts from St Augustine's Abbey, Canterbury, including one by the hagiographer Goscelin, tell stories relating to her time abroad, during which she is said to have been at the Frankish abbey of Chelles. According to these, she had to be rescued by her mother when the abbess, Wilcoma, tried to force her to marry one of her kinsmen. Miracles are associated with this: Mildrith miraculously escaped death in the oven to which the irate abbess consigned her; and on her return to Ebbsfleet she left the print of her foot permanently in the rock where she disembarked. It is clear that her cult developed after her death, for the hagiographical texts refer to a translation of her remains by her successor Eadburh. In 1030 Ælfstan, abbot of St Augustine's Abbey, translated the relics of Mildrith to his own church, and with them either purchased or laid claim to the former properties of Minster in Thanet, which must have suffered very considerably in the viking invasions. Following the translation, Mildrith's cult acquired some importance at the Canterbury abbey; her relics were enshrined in the crypt of the new Norman church, and Goscelin wrote a tract rebutting the claims of the newly founded St Gregory's Priory, Canterbury, to possess them. Mildrith's feast day was on 13 July, her translation feast on 18 May. There exist few dedications of churches to her, but those in Canterbury itself and Tenterden, Kent, may be pre-conquest.

DAVID ROLLASON

Sources D. W. Rollason, *The Mildrith legend: a study in early medieval hagiography in England* (1982) · S. E. Kelly, ed., *Charters of St Augustine's Abbey, Canterbury, and Minster-in-Thanet*, Anglo-Saxon Charters, 4 (1995) · D. W. Rollason, 'Goscelin of Canterbury's account of the translation and miracles of St Mildrith (BHL 5961/4): an edition with notes', *Mediaeval Studies*, 48 (1986), 139–210 · M. L. Colker, 'A hagiographic polemic', *Mediaeval Studies*, 39 (1977), 60–108 · R. Sharpe, 'Goscelin's St Augustine and St Mildreth: hagiography and liturgy in context', *Journal of Theological Studies*, new ser., 41 (1990), 502–16 · *AS chart.*, S 10–11, 13–15, 18, 22, 26, 29, 86, 87, 91, 1180 · S. Kelly, 'Trading privileges from eighth-century England', *Early Medieval Europe*, 1 (1992), 3–28

Miles, Sir (Arnold) Ashley (1904–1988), microbiologist, was born on 20 March 1904 in York, the second of three children and only son of Harry Miles, draper, and his wife, Kate Elizabeth Hindley. At Bootham School in York, a Quaker foundation that he remembered with great affection, he received a good grounding in both scientific subjects and literature. From there he gained an exhibition to King's College, Cambridge, where his leanings towards pathology and bacteriology were encouraged by Henry Roy Dean, the professor of pathology, and Everitt G. D. Murray. He obtained second classes in both parts of the natural sciences tripos (1924 and 1925). After qualifying in medicine (MRCS LRCP, 1928) at St Bartholomew's Hospital, Miles gave a remarkable foretaste of his academic abilities by obtaining in 1929 membership of the Royal College of Physicians while still a house physician (FRCP, 1937).

In 1929 Miles was appointed demonstrator at the London School of Hygiene and Tropical Medicine; this step was decisive in shaping his future career as a microbiologist with a strong interest in immunity to infection. His first researches, on the antigens of *Brucella*, were continued, in association with N. W. Pirie, when he returned two years later to Cambridge, as a demonstrator. In 1935 he became reader in bacteriology at the British Postgraduate Medical School, Hammersmith, and then, at the early age of thirty-three, was appointed in 1937 to the chair of bacteriology at University College Hospital medical school. Soon afterwards the outbreak of war brought many new responsibilities and difficulties. As well as continuing his professorial duties Miles was a sector pathologist in the Emergency Medical Service, acting director of the Graham Medical Research Laboratories, and director of the Medical Research Council's wound infection unit in Birmingham. This last proved the most important post of all, for his researches on wound infections in collaboration with R. E. O. Williams resulted in effective recommendations for their control in surgical, industrial, and military contexts.

After the war Miles was appointed in 1946 deputy director of the National Institute for Medical Research and head of its department of biological standards, and took a prominent part in the work of the relevant national and international organizations. His own researches, some of which were published in collaboration with his wife, centred on the mechanisms of inflammation and immunity.

In 1952 Miles was appointed director of the Lister Institute of Preventive Medicine, a private organization funded by endowments, grants, and the manufacture and sale of vaccines and antisera; it also housed several Medical Research Council units. In the same year he became MD and professor of experimental pathology in the University of London. In addition to directing these manifold activities and continuing his own investigative work, Miles characteristically shouldered other burdens, some of which alone would have occupied most of the time of lesser men. This capacity for work on a heroic scale, combined with his clear and incisive thinking, made him much in demand on boards and committees. He was elected a fellow of the Royal Society in 1961 and served for five years both as a vice-president and as biological secretary. His command of written English was superb, and as well as publishing more than 140 papers on his own work, he was joint editor, with Sir Graham Wilson, of no fewer than five editions of *Topley and Wilson's Principles of Bacteriology and Immunity*.

After his official retirement from the Lister in 1971 he spent four years on laboratory studies at the Clinical Research Centre, after which he was invited in 1976 to become deputy director of the department of medical microbiology at the London Hospital medical college. His last few years were marred by the results of a disabling stroke, despite which he continued to work until a few months before his death.

Miles's contributions to biomedical science were recognized by his appointment as CBE (1953) and a knighthood (1966); and by honorary fellowships of the Royal College of Pathologists (1969); King's College, Cambridge (1972); the Institute of Biology (1975); the Infectious Diseases Society of America (1979); and the Royal Society of Medicine (1981). He also received a number of honorary memberships of learned societies and was made an honorary DSc of the University of Newcastle upon Tyne (1969).

In addition to his other attainments Miles had a wide knowledge of literature and music, and was an accomplished pianist. His ability to converse knowledgeably on these and other topics, including, for example, botany and the detailed anatomy of the Lake District, made him a delightful companion. His formidable intellectual capacity, set off by his large frame and imposing presence, could be daunting to students and junior staff; but he was a kindly person, who was intolerant only of those who contravened his own standards of personal and scientific integrity.

In 1930 Miles married a medical laboratory technician, Ellen Marguerite (d. January 1988), daughter of Harald Dahl, a Norwegian shipbroker, of Cardiff, and his French wife, Sofie Magdalene Hesselberg. Ellen was the sister of the writer Roald Dahl. They had no children. Miles died on 11 February 1988 at his home, 7 Holly Place, Hampstead, London.   LESLIE COLLIER, *rev.*

Sources A. Neuberger, *Memoirs FRS*, 35 (1990), 303–26 · personal knowledge (1996) · *CGPLA Eng. & Wales* (1988)
Archives Wellcome L., corresp. with Sir Ernst Chain · Wellcome L., corresp. with Sir Graham Selby Wilson
Likenesses Harrods, photograph, Wellcome L.
Wealth at death £547,412: probate, 24 June 1988, *CGPLA Eng. & Wales*

Miles, Bernard James, Baron Miles (1907–1991), actor and theatre manager, was born on 27 September 1907 at 1 Poplar Terrace, New Road, Hillingdon, Uxbridge, Middlesex, the son of Edwin James Miles, market gardener, and his wife, Barbara Hooper, *née* Fletcher, a Scottish cook. Brought up in a strict Baptist household, he learned from

Bernard James Miles, Baron Miles (1907–1991), by unknown photographer, 1971

his parents the value of thrift and hard work, as well as a wealth of ancient countryside lore which he later used in a triumphant series of music-hall monologues about life on a farm.

Educated at Uxbridge county school, Miles won a scholarship to Pembroke College, Oxford, and worked briefly as a schoolmaster in Yorkshire. He abandoned this career in 1930 when he made his stage début as the Second Messenger in a Baliol Holloway revival of Shakespeare's *Richard III*. In 1931 he married the actress Josephine Wilson (d. 1990), who gave him unstinting support. They had two daughters and a son. The carpentry Miles had learned from his father came in useful during several subsequent years travelling the country with repertory companies, when his responsibilities ranged from building scenery to playing small parts. Towards the end of the 1930s he began to make a name in London, in music-halls and late-night cabaret theatres, where he perfected his comic monologues in *Late Joys* (1939) and three Herbert Farjeon revues.

During the war Miles found film fame in Noël Coward's *In Which We Serve* (1942) but also frequently toured with the Old Vic as Iago and directed John Mills in *Men in Shadow* (1942), later following Mills in the leading role. As the war ended he was back with the Old Vic company at the New Theatre for the 1947–8 season, playing the Inquisitor in *Saint Joan* and Christopher Sly in *The Taming of the Shrew*.

From the late 1940s Miles's energies were focused on

building the first Mermaid Theatre in his own garden in St John's Wood, a wooden playhouse faithfully replicating Shakespeare's Globe long before the birth of Sam Wanamaker's similar project. In its first (1951) season he played Caliban in *The Tempest* and, as producer and director, persuaded Kirsten Flagstad and Maggie Teyte to sing Purcell's *Dido and Aeneas*. The Mermaid then found a temporary home at the Royal Exchange in the City, before Miles and his equally tireless wife finally settled it in Puddle Dock, the first theatre to have been opened in the City for 300 years. They spent six years building the new Mermaid and it eventually opened in May 1959 with a triumphant Lionel Bart musical, *Lock up your Daughters*, based somewhat loosely on Henry Fielding's *Rape upon Rape*. Though he was to suffer all the architectural and financial problems only too familiar to anyone trying to build a theatre in Britain, or merely to keep one open, Miles's years at the Mermaid saw triumphant revivals of *Treasure Island* (in which he was always a definitive Long John Silver) and long-running musical celebrations of the songs of Noël Coward and Cole Porter. The Mermaid also gave birth to *Side by Side by Sondheim* in the late 1970s, and more classically was the venue for many notable Bernard Shaw and Shakespeare revivals, some of the latter in relatively modern dress. For his services to the theatre Miles was appointed CBE in 1953, knighted in 1969, and given a life peerage as Baron Miles of Blackfriars in 1979.

Miles was an old-fashioned actor, and was often out of tune also with modern directing techniques, but his ability to keep the Mermaid going on knife-edge finance, and frequently to retrieve it from the jaws of bankruptcy, was always admirable. If he sometimes cast himself in wildly unsuitable roles (Oedipus, for instance, or John Gabriel Borkman) he was nevertheless a memorable Schweyk in *Schweyk in the Second World War* (1963) and a formidable Falstaff in both parts of *Henry IV* (1970).

Like Joan Littlewood at the Theatre Royal a little further beyond the City in Stratford East, Miles worked with very slender resources and often scant critical acclaim; sadly, what should have been a triumphant rebuilding project when the Mermaid moved a few hundred yards inland in 1981 ended in bankruptcy, and in Miles's forced resignation as artistic director of the theatre he had built and still so loved. He and his wife had invested all their own money in the rebuilding project, and were forced to sell their London home to meet their debts. Following the death of his wife in 1990, Miles was moved into a nursing home with nothing more than his state pension, though funds were raised for him by an all-star *Bernard Miles Celebration* at the Mermaid on 3 March 1991, at which he made his last public appearance in a wheelchair, having recently fallen and broken a leg. He died at the Thistle Hill Nursing Home, Knaresborough, Yorkshire, on 14 June 1991. He was survived by his son and one daughter, his other daughter, Sally (who had joined her parents in the management of the Mermaid Theatre), having died of motor neurone disease.

Miles can still be seen in such major movies as Noël Coward's *In Which We Serve* (1942), Alfred Hitchcock's *The Man Who Knew Too Much* (1956), John Huston's *Moby Dick* (1956), Basil Dearden's *The Smallest Show on Earth* (1957), and Charles Crichton's *Battle of the Sexes* (1960). He was a pioneer of the 'talking' gramophone record in the 1940s; his *Over the Gate* monologues, of a mythical Buckinghamshire farmer, were released on several bestselling 78 r.p.m. discs (and he would also occasionally perform them live in the dying days of the music-hall). These were, for their time, if not scandalous then at least lusty, and during his management of the Mermaid Theatre in a still repressive theatrical era (when the lord chamberlain had to approve all scripts) he did his best to move the barriers of sexual tolerance slightly forward, in an always Falstaffian manner. He was also known to television audiences for a lengthy series of commercials on behalf of the Egg Marketing Board. Nevertheless his real legacy was the Mermaid Theatre. Though still standing just north of its original Puddle Dock site, the Mermaid enjoyed little success after he left it, and endured several periods of prolonged closure.

SHERIDAN MORLEY

Sources B. Miles and J. Wilson, *The Mermaid Theatre* (1951) · G. Frow, *The Mermaid 10: a review of the theatre, 1959–1969* (1969) · *The Times* (15 June 1991) · *The Independent* (15 June 1991) · *The Independent* (20 June 1991) · *The Independent* (25 June 1991) · *The Independent* (1 July 1991) · *WWW*, 1991–5 · b. cert. · d. cert.
Archives GL, corresp. and publishers | BFI, corresp. with Ivor Montagu · NL Wales, letters to G. E. Evans
Likenesses D. Levine, pen drawing, 1967, NPG · R. Noakes, bronze head, 1969, NPG · photograph, 1971, Hult. Arch. [*see illus.*] · photograph, repro. in *The Times* · photograph, repro. in *The Independent* (15 June 1991)
Wealth at death approx. £125,000: probate, 8 Oct 1991, CGPLA Eng. & Wales

Miles, Charles Popham (1810–1891). *See under* Miles, William Augustus (1753/4–1817).

Miles, Edward (1752–1828), miniature painter, was born on 14 October 1752 in Yarmouth, Norfolk; nothing is known about his parents. At an early age he became an errand boy for Dr Giles Wakeman, a Yarmouth surgeon, and through his encouragement took up painting. In 1771 Miles moved to London, where he began to make miniature copies of paintings by Reynolds, to whom he was introduced. He entered the Royal Academy Schools on 20 January 1772, when his age was recorded as '19 14 Octr last' (Hutchison, 137). He was subsequently to become a gifted but minor artist. Between 1775 and 1797 he exhibited some fifty-three miniature portraits at the Royal Academy, moved his studio between Norwich and London, established his reputation, and had his own portrait painted (1782) by his friend Sir William Beechey. He also became acquainted with Sir Thomas Lawrence. By 1792 he had been appointed miniature painter to the duchess of York, and in 1794 to Queen Charlotte. Among those whose portraits he painted during his English period were: Queen Charlotte (1794); William IV, when duke of Clarence (*c*.1792–1793); Edward, duke of Kent (*c*.1791); Augustus Frederick, duke of Sussex (*c*.1792–1793); Princess Augusta (*c*.1794); Princess Sophia (*c*.1794; two versions); Richard, first Earl Howe (*c*.1794)—all in the Royal Collection; Spencer Perceval (priv. coll.); George III; William

Frederick, duke of Gloucester; Lord and Lady Vernon; Lord and Lady Harcourt; Lady Chatham; Miss Maltby; and Fanny Kemble. Miles's miniatures, usually oval and on ivory, conform to a personal style which is characterized by a precise treatment of facial features juxtaposed with a softer finish to the hair and clothes. His figures are often light and depicted with yellowish colouring and faint shadows. They are set against uniform backgrounds created from crossed brushstrokes that tend to be green and which lighten to the lower right.

In 1797 Miles moved to St Petersburg, where he stayed for ten years and became court painter to tsars Paul and Alexander I. His portrait of the latter was presented to the earl of Liverpool, while that of Alexander's sister Grand Princess Maria Pavlovna found its way, through royal marriage, to the Dutch royal collection. Other works included portraits of Yekaterina Semyonovna Vorontsova (the future Lady Pembroke); Alexander I's mother, Maria Feodorovna, his sisters Elena and Ekaterina, and his wife, Tsarina Elizabeth.

In 1807 Miles settled in Philadelphia, where he stayed until his death there on 7 March 1828. In 1810 he became a co-founder and fellow of the Society of Artists of the United States (from 1813 the Columbian Society of Artists), with whom he regularly exhibited. His American portraits include Bishop White and a sketch of revolutionary general and secretary of war Henry Knox. However, his American period is mainly marked by pictures of friends and by his teaching of drawing; his pupils included James Reid Lambdin. Miles appears to have married and certainly had one son. In the 1920s his descendant Susan S. Miles contributed a number of his miniatures to exhibitions in the Albertina, Vienna (1924) and the Metropolitan Museum, New York (1927).   JEREMY HOWARD

Sources DAB · Graves, *RA exhibitors*, 5 (1906), 242 · Thieme & Becker, *Allgemeines Lexikon*, 557 · B. S. Long, *British miniaturists* (1929); repr. (1966), 297 · catalogue and microfiche, Courtauld Inst., Witt Library, no. 2381 · R. Walker, *The eighteenth and early nineteenth century miniatures in the collection of her majesty the queen* (1992) · D. Foskett, *Miniatures: dictionary and guide* (1987), 299–300, 600 · L. R. Schidlof, *The miniature in Europe in the 16th, 17th, 18th, and 19th centuries*, 2 (1964), 558–9 · S. C. Hutchison, 'The Royal Academy Schools, 1768–1830', *Walpole Society*, 38 (1960–62), 123–91, esp. 137

Miles, Eustace Hamilton (1868–1948), sportsman, writer, and food reformer, was born on 22 September 1868 at West End House, 6 Belsize Grove, Hampstead, the younger son of William Henry Miles, bookseller and later publisher, of Simpkin, Marshall & Co., and his wife, Mary M'Connell. He had at least one sister.

Miles was educated at Heath Mount preparatory school, Eastbourne College, and Marlborough College (1882–1887), where he co-edited the *Marlburian* with the future novelist E. F. Benson (1867–1940), who became a close friend. Unlike Benson's more sentimental Marlborough involvements, which he portrayed in an intense, crypto-erotic light in *David Blaize* (1916), his relationship with Miles appears to have been one of straightforwardly unromantic comradeship. The two played tennis and squash rackets together, and both went up to King's College, Cambridge, in October 1887, Miles with a minor scholarship which he exchanged for a full college scholarship two years later. In part one of the classical tripos, Miles's was among the more distinguished firsts of his year, but he gained only a second class in part two; he graduated in 1891. During the next fifteen years, until his marriage in 1906, he was known chiefly as an amateur athlete, and as author of various 'how to' or 'teach yourself' books on subjects as diverse as philology, sport, and the nutrition and general education of boys.

Miles stated in his *Who's Who* entry that he taught as an assistant master at Rugby School, but this is not confirmed by the school's own records. Better documented are his sporting successes: he was English amateur real tennis champion (1898–1903, 1905–6, 1909–10) and amateur champion of America at squash rackets and real tennis (1900). He was amateur world champion at rackets (1902), and also for real tennis (1898–1903, and 1905). In addition, he was four times world doubles champion at rackets (1902, 1904, 1905–6). With Benson, whose interests were in golf and figure-skating, he edited a number of sporting books (1902–5) in Hurst and Blackett's Imperial Athletic Library, and collaborated with him on *The Mad Annual* (1903), a humorously satirical compilation of a distinctly juvenile kind. In 1903 he was assistant editor of the *Magazine of Sport and Health*.

Early in 1906 Miles married Dorothy Beatrice (Hallie) Killick, daughter of the rector of St Clement Danes Church in London. Over the next thirty years she collaborated closely with her husband in the health-food shop and vegetarian restaurant, with associated enterprises for physical, mental, and spiritual self-training, which began operation the same year from premises at 40–42 Chandos Street, Charing Cross. Within a few years Eustace Miles's Restaurant, which he promoted as a 'restaurant with ideals', had established a distinctive reputation, and it was wryly celebrated in E. M. Forster's *Howards End* (1910). The heroine of the novel, Margaret Schlegel, wonderfully captures the milieu:

> 'Next time,' she said to Mr Wilcox, 'you shall come to lunch with me at Mr Eustace Miles's.'
>
> 'With pleasure.'
>
> 'No, you'd hate it,' she said, pushing her glass towards him for some more cider. 'It's all proteids and body-buildings, and people coming up to you and beg pardon, but you have such a beautiful aura.' (chap. 17)

Theosophists, simple-lifers, aspiring writers, healers, and others of an idealistic bent were all encouraged to visit Miles's premises. He opened lecture-rooms, an advice bureau, a 'Normal Physical School' and 'School of Cookery', and a publishing business which produced a steady stream of his works, in the form of pamphlets (Milestones) dispensing advice on health, including nervous problems, books on food reform, fitness, the sporting spirit, and mental concentration, and a monthly (later quarterly) magazine. Mrs Miles's literary contributions emphasized the spiritual side of the movement. Bland, tasteless, and excessively simple by late twentieth-century standards, the recipes which Miles shared with his public were intended to provide a balanced, meat-free diet, and relied largely on the use of proprietary protein supplements such as Emprote combined with such humble dishes as lentil salad or scrambled eggs on toast. Husband and wife reiterated the beliefs of the food reform movement of the period, which crusaded against the wastefulness, indigestibility, and general harmfulness to health of the traditionally heavy, rich meat diet of the Edwardian upper and middle classes and of their counterparts elsewhere in the western world.

Although essentially a figure of the pre-1914 era with its enthusiasms and strong theoretical beliefs, Miles continued to expand business operations after the First World War. By 1929, in addition to the Chandos Street restaurant and a long-established vegetarian guest house at Carshalton, Surrey, he owned the Milestone Restaurant in the King's Road, Chelsea, and health-food shops in Bloomsbury and in the north and south London suburbs. None of these activities made him rich, however, and his estate at death was less than £200. Miles died at 38 Palace Road, Streatham, London, on 20 December 1948.

BRIGID ALLEN

Sources WWW · B. Masters, *The life of E. F. Benson* (1991) · *The Eustace Miles Monthly* [later *The Eustace Miles Quarterly*] (1916–36) · G. W. De Lisle and H. W. Simpkinson, eds., *Marlborough College register, from 1843 to 1889 inclusive*, 3rd edn (1890) · marriage index for 1906, St Catherine's House · *Encyclopaedia Britannica*, 14th edn (1929) · E. M. Forster, *Howards End* (1910), 150 · Venn, *Alum. Cant.* · J. J. Withers, *A register of admissions to King's College, Cambridge, 1797–1925* (1929) · d. cert.
Likenesses photograph, repro. in *Eustace Miles Quarterly* (in or before 1930)
Wealth at death £175 1s. 2d.: administration with will, 19 April 1950, *CGPLA Eng. & Wales*

Miles, Frederick George (1903–1976), aircraft designer and manufacturer, was born on 22 March 1903 in Worthing, Sussex, the oldest of the four sons of Frederick G. Miles, laundry proprietor of Portslade, Shoreham Harbour, Sussex, and his wife, Esther, *née* Wicks. He left school in Brighton in 1916 at the age of thirteen, while his father was away fighting in France, and started a motorcycle rental business.

Miles became interested in flying in 1922 and with the help of friends designed and built a small biplane, the Gnat, in his father's laundry. In 1928 he persuaded Cecil Pashley, a pilot who owned an Avro, to go into partnership with him and start a flying school and joyriding business, the Gnat Aero Company Ltd, in Shoreham. Pashley taught Miles to fly and the enterprise expanded as they bought derelict aircraft and undertook aircraft repairs; it soon split into two companies, the Southern Aero Club Ltd, and Southern Aircraft Ltd.

In 1931 Miles went to South Africa intending to emigrate, but the following year he returned and married the recently divorced Maxine Frances Mary (known as Blossom), daughter of Sir Johnston Forbes-*Robertson, the actor–manager. She and her first husband, Inigo Brassey Freeman-Thomas, Viscount Ratendone, had joined the Southern Aero Club in 1930, and Miles had taught them

both to fly. Miles and Blossom had one son and one daughter.

Blossom Miles persuaded her husband to design an aeroplane and together they produced the Miles M1 Satyr, a single-seat biplane, in 1932. The following year the Hawk, designed by Miles and Blossom, who performed the stress analysis, was built by Phillips and Powis at Woodley, near Reading. Following the success of the Hawk, which was faster, cheaper, and easier to fly than the De Havilland Moth, previously the most popular private plane, they joined Phillips and Powis and Miles became technical director and chief designer. The company concentrated on light aircraft and in October 1934 its Falcon broke the light aeroplane record for the journey from Australia to England. In 1935 the firm had a number of successes in the king's cup air race, and in 1936 Colonel Charles Lindbergh asked Miles to build him a fast, long range, light aeroplane for European business trips. This became the Mohawk, first flown in 1937.

In 1935 the decision was taken to become a public company, with Rolls-Royce Ltd providing the financial backing. In 1936 Miles became chairman and managing director, with his brother George as technical director and chief designer. In the same year Phillips and Powis began to produce training planes for the Air Ministry, and the Miles Magister remained a standard trainer for the RAF throughout the Second World War, with more than 1200 built. In 1938 the ministry placed a £2 million order for the Miles Master, and an average of seven Masters were built a week, with more than 3000 produced altogether.

In 1941 Rolls-Royce, no longer interested in the manufacture of airframes, withdrew its capital, and Miles bought financial control of the company. In 1942 it was admitted to full membership of the Society of British Aircraft Manufacturers, and the company was renamed Miles Aircraft Ltd in 1943. At its peak the company had 6000 employees. Miles and his wife started the Miles Aeronautical School for sixteen- and seventeen-year-olds to train as technicians and draughtsmen, which lasted until 1948.

Miles's most significant contribution to aeronautical progress was his design of a supersonic aircraft, the M52. In October 1943, in top secrecy, Sir Stafford Cripps, minister of aircraft production, awarded him the contract to design and produce a supersonic aircraft, powered by a Whittle engine. In February 1946, when the prototype was almost ready, the contract was cancelled by Ben Lockspeiser, controller of scientific research at the Ministry of Aircraft Production, following the discovery that scientists at the German research establishment at Volkenrode, near Brunswick, had shown that aircraft drag at high speeds could be reduced by sweeping back the wings. This was something that British scientists had not appreciated, and it was decided to cancel any high-speed projects that did not incorporate swept-back wings. In addition, Lockspeiser had never believed that manned supersonic flight would be possible. Miles was required to send all his technical information and drawings to the United States, to NASA (the US National Aeronautics and Space Administration), and as a result the Bell X-1, a straight-winged plane, was the first manned aircraft to break the sound barrier, on 14 October 1947. Meanwhile a £500,000 contract was awarded to Barnes Wallis, head of research at Vickers, to design a scale model, powered by a rocket motor, to be tested with models dropped from bombers at 30,000 feet. The tests were a failure and in 1948 the contract was cancelled; in 1955 it was recognized in the white paper on the supply of military aircraft that the decision to abandon research on supersonic flight in manned aircraft seriously delayed the progress of aeronautical research in the UK. It was also generally accepted that the M52 would have been capable of reaching supersonic speeds.

Difficulties after the war with the return to the production of civil aircraft led to the collapse of Miles Aircraft Ltd in 1948. Miles started a new business at Redhill, and in 1949 moved back to Shoreham to start F. G. Miles Engineering Ltd. In 1961 the firm joined the newly formed Beagle Group of aircraft companies, with Miles as deputy chairman and George Miles as chief engineer of the Beagle-Miles subsidiary. After the collapse of the Beagle Group in 1969 he became chairman and managing director of Miles-Dufon Ltd, making flight simulators, and of Miles Hivolt Ltd.

Miles died on 15 August 1976 at the Larkspur Nursing Home in Worthing, Sussex. He was cremated at Worthing on 20 August. His widow died in 1984.

ANNE PIMLOTT BAKER

Sources D. L. Brown, *Miles Aircraft since 1925* (1970) · J. C. Temple, 'Miles, Frederick George', *DBB* · A. H. Lukins, *The book of Miles Aircraft* (1946) · P. King, *Knights of the air: the life and times of the extraordinary pioneers who first built British aeroplanes* (1989) · D. Wood, *Project cancelled*, 2nd edn (1986) · D. Edgerton, *England and the aeroplane: an essay on a militant and technological nation* (1991) · G. Riley, ed., 'Blossom Miles', *Vintage Aircraft*, 31 (July 1984), 8–9 · D. L. Brown, 'Wings over Sussex [pt 2]', *Aeroplane Monthly*, 7 (1979), 514–19 · *The Times* (17 Aug 1976) · *CGPLA Eng. & Wales* (1976) · Burke, *Peerage*
Likenesses photographs, 1933–9, repro. in Brown, *Miles Aircraft since 1925*, 20, 33 · photograph, repro. in Lukins, *Book of Miles Aircraft*, introduction · photographs, repro. in Temple, *Frederick George Miles*
Wealth at death £224,761: probate, 1976, *CGPLA Eng. & Wales*

Miles, George Francis [Frank] (1852–1891), portrait and landscape painter, was born at Bingham, Nottinghamshire, on 22 April 1852, the sixth and youngest son of Robert Henry William Miles, rector of Bingham, and his wife, Mary Ellin, daughter of the Revd J. J. Cleaver (afterwards Peach). Miles was tall and good-looking. His mother was an artist and his father supported Miles financially. In 1874 Miles entered the Royal Academy Schools; that same year he exhibited the first of twenty-one paintings at the academy, *A Study of Reflections*, the last being sent in 1887. At about the time he was a student, Miles visited Paris with his friend, the sculptor and author Lord Ronald Gower; however, no other details of this trip are known. In 1880 Miles won the Royal Academy Turner medal for landscape for *An Ocean Coast, Llangraviog, Cardiganshire*. This early promise was noted by Ruskin in a letter to the writer J. E. C. Bodley, commenting: 'With his love for his mother and his ability to paint clouds he must get on' (Ellmann, 105). While contemporary critics praised his landscapes,

Miles was best-known for his portraits of leading men and sketches of society beauties for *Life* magazine, including the mistresses of the prince of Wales. Reproductions of his Lillie Langtry drawings were best-sellers. His partial colour-blindness often led Miles to work in pencil.

Miles exhibited at the newly opened Grosvenor Gallery, where he combined his roles of socialite and aesthete in the company of Wilde and Whistler. All three were lampooned in the contemporary play about aesthetic dandies called *The Grasshopper*. Miles lived with Wilde, first off the Strand at 13 Salisbury Street in 1879, and then between 1880 and 1881 at 44 Tite Street, Chelsea, in a house Miles had commissioned from E. W. Godwin. Artistically, Miles followed Whistler's aestheticism. *For Pity and Love are akin* (exh. RA, 1882; ex Sothebys, 27 March 1996) depicts the former flower-girl Sally Higgs in pastel colour harmonies, using the flattened perspective and oriental flora of Japanese art. When his work became unfashionable Miles turned increasingly to gardening, introducing several varieties of Japanese flower to England.

Despite his impeccable public reputation, Miles's private life was unconventional. He was almost arrested for his relationships with under-aged girls and cohabited with his young model Higgs. After reading Wilde's *Poems* (1881) Miles's father insisted that Wilde leave 44 Tite Street. The financially dependent Miles acquiesced, but his mental health was shattered. On 27 December 1887 he was admitted to Brislington Lunatic Asylum, triggering premature obituaries and ending his exhibiting career. The *Dictionary of National Biography*'s suggestion that Miles was to marry is unsubstantiated. He died on 15 July 1891 and was buried at Almondsbury near Bristol.

MATTHEW C. POTTER

Sources R. Ellmann, *Oscar Wilde* (1988) · Graves, *RA exhibitors* · *DNB* · sale catalogue (1996) [Sothebys, 27 March 1996] · L. Lambourne, *The aesthetic movement* (1996), 85, 163 · *Art Journal*, new ser., 11 (1891), 288 · *Magazine of Art*, 11 (1887–8), xxiv · *Magazine of Art*, 14 (1890–91), xliv · E. M. Ward, *Recollections of a savage* (1923), 109–12 · 'Frank Miles: a Victorian artist', *Old Lady of Threadneedle Street* (June 1939), 140–41 · D. Buttery, '"La Belle Châtelaine": portraits of Frances Evelyn, fifth countess of Warwick', *Apollo*, 142 (Oct 1995), 17–22 · S. P. Casteras and C. Denney, eds., *The Grosvenor Gallery* (1996) · F. Harris, *My life and loves*, new edn, ed. J. F. Gallagher (1964) · b. cert. · d. cert.
Archives U. Cal., Los Angeles, letter to Oscar Wilde · U. Cal., Los Angeles, letter to Mrs George Boughton
Likenesses photograph, NPG

Miles, Henry (1698–1763), dissenting minister and writer on science, was born at Stroud, Gloucestershire, on 2 June 1698. Nothing is known of his parentage and early life except that his parents were members of the Church of England. Although his early education was limited he avidly read the works of the puritans, which led him to become a dissenter. In the early 1720s he prepared for the Independent ministry, probably at an Independent academy in London, as he was a Trotman grantee in 1723. He was soon known as a diligent student of wide learning. In 1726 he became minister at Tooting, where he remained for the rest of his life. Ordained in 1731, in 1737 he became assistant to Samuel Chandler at the Old Jewry chapel in

London. He held the double appointment until 1744. At this period he was classed as both a Presbyterian and an Independent.

Miles had an extensive knowledge not only of Latin and Greek but also of the oriental languages, with a taste for natural history, botany, and electricity. In 1743 he was elected a fellow of the Royal Society, and he submitted numerous papers in the period 1741–54. His topics ranged from the effect of electricity and the weather to the flow of blood in fishes. In the year of his election he submitted papers entitled 'Of eels in vinegar', and 'Improvement in cider and perry'. In 1744 he was made DD by the University of Aberdeen. He took great care in the preparations of his sermons and almost lived in his study. He loyally served his country congregation:

> Few ministers had so many attempts made upon, or so much importunity used with them, to remove them to some of the most considerable congregations in London. But being absolutely insensible to all secular motives, devoted to his studies, and to the people who had first chose him, and in love with retirement, he preferred spending his days out of the noise and tumult of the world. (Furneaux, 35)

He was a highly regarded figure among the leaders of dissent.

Late in life Miles married Emma Woods (1709/10–1790), who 'devoted herself and a very ample fortune, to render his declining days as easy, as his increasing weakness and bodily infirmities would permit' (Furneaux, 36). He died at Tooting on 10 February 1763 and was buried in Bunhill Fields, London. As a Coward trustee he bequeathed his books to its academy in London, which had to move to larger premises in Hoxton Square in order to accommodate them.

ALAN RUSTON

Sources P. Furneaux, *A sermon occasioned by the death of the Reverend Henry Miles* (1763), 32–9 · private information (2004) [librarian, Royal Society, London] · W. Wilson, *The history and antiquities of the dissenting churches and meeting houses in London, Westminster and Southwark*, 4 vols. (1808–14), vol. 2, p. 384 · DNB · will, PRO, PROB 11/885, sig. 140 · J. A. Jones, ed., *Bunhill memorials* (1849), 176 · E. E. Cleal, *The story of congregationalism in Surrey* (1908), 210–11 · J. H. Thompson, *A history of the Coward Trust: the first two hundred and fifty years, 1738–1988* (1998), 23 · T. G. Crippen, 'London Congregational Board', *Transactions of the Congregational Historical Society*, 2 (1905–6), 50–60, esp. 57, 59 · A. Peel, 'The Throckmorton Trotman Trust, 1664–1941', *Transactions of the Congregational Historical Society*, 14 (1940–44), 70–93, esp. 89 · GM, 1st ser., 60 (1790), 670 · J. Waddington, *Surrey Congregational history* (1866), 312–13 · *Calendar of the correspondence of Philip Doddridge*, ed. G. F. Nuttall, HMC, JP 26 (1979), nos. 509, 538, 546, 600, 687, 957, 966, 1218

Archives DWL, notebooks and letters · DWL, scriptural notes | BL, corresp. with Thomas Birch, Add. MS 4314 · BL, letters to Andrew Millar, catalogue of works of Robert Boyle, Add. MS 4229

Wealth at death see will, PRO, PROB 11/885, sig. 140

Miles [*née* Guest], **Jane Mary** [Jenny] (*c*.1762–1846), pianist and composer, was born about 1762, probably in Bath: her father, Thomas Guest (*fl.* 1760–1800), was a tailor there. Nothing more is known of her parents other than that her father played a role in Bath's musical community by renting rooms to musicians as well as occasionally selling musical compositions and tickets to concerts. Jenny's musical instructors in Bath included Thomas Orpin, her first teacher, and Thomas Linley. By her seventh birthday she had made such remarkable progress with her keyboard studies under Orpin that 'A Lady' felt compelled to publish a poetic tribute that concluded with the prescient observation:

> With envy, Orpin, you may view
> Your pupil—she'll tutor you.
> (*Bath Chronicle*, 12 May 1768, 3)

Her subsequent teachers included Johann Christian Bach, Antonio Sacchini, and Venanzio Rauzzini. Beginning in the late 1770s her frequent performances in London, Bath, and the west country resulted in glowing critical assessments of her skill and musicianship: one enthusiastic admirer hailed her as the 'British Caecilia' (*Bath Chronicle*, 10 May 1781, 2). Fanny Burney, who heard her in Bath, praised Miles as the best performer she had heard since leaving London and described her as 'very young [18], but far from handsome; she is, however, obliging, humble, unassuming, and pleasing' (*Diary and Letters*, 1.358–9). Members of the royal family and professional classes, as well as musicians, were among the nearly 500 subscribers to her first publication, *Six sonatas for the harpsichord or piano forte, with an accompaniment for a violin or German flute*, op. 1 (1783). The sonatas were subsequently published in Paris (1784) and Berlin (1785). Her marriage on 29 August 1789 (St George, Hanover Square) to Abraham Allen Miles (*c*.1760–1832), an accountant with London Assurance House, did not impede her musical activities. In 1804 she was appointed instructor to Princess Amelia and, in 1806, to Princess Charlotte; Miles retained the latter position until the prince regent's dismissal of the princess's staff in 1814. She published a sonata for piano and violin in 1809; beginning in 1820 and continuing for about ten more years, she published at least fifteen additional compositions.

Abraham Miles died in 1832, and near the close of her own life Miles moved to Blackheath to live with her daughter, Louisa, and son-in-law, John Lawrence. Their child, Louisa Cecilia Lawrence, is the likely dedicatee of Miles's last work, *The Field Daisy*. Following a 'long and tedious malady' (according to one obituary) Miles died at 8 Eliot Place, Blackheath, on 20 March 1846 and was interred a week later beside her husband in a chancel vault in the church of St Edmund, King and Martyr, Lombard Street, London.

Technically quite difficult, Jane Miles's works reflect the prevailing musical tastes of their times. The op. 1 sonatas embrace the *galant* style popular during the late eighteenth century, while her works from the 1820s—with such titles as 'La Georgiana', 'La Jeanette', and 'La jolie Julienne'—suggest the milieu of the Romantic salon. Whether early or late, Miles's compositions conform to period expectations in that they entertain and charm more than they ennoble and challenge.

DANIEL M. RAESSLER

Sources D. M. Raessler, 'Jane Mary Guest', *Music Review*, 49 (1988), 247–53 · K. E. James, 'Concert life in eighteenth-century Bath', PhD diss., U. Lond., 1987 · A. M., 'Death of Mrs Miles, the musician, formerly of Bath', *Bath Herald* (28 March 1846), 3 · will, proved, 6 July 1840, PRO · *Diary and letters of Madame D'Arblay (1778–1840)*, ed. C. Barrett and A. Dobson, 1 (1904), 340, 358–9 · *Musical World* (4

April 1846), 161 · 'To Mr Orpin, on hearing Miss Guest (a child of six years old) perform upon the harpsichord', *Pope's Bath Chronicle* (12 May 1768), 3 · *European Magazine and London Review*, 6 (1784), 6–7 · J. Boswell, *The life of Samuel Johnson*, 2 vols. (1791) · *Royal Kalendar* (1807–14) [establishment of Princess Charlotte] · parish records (burials), St Edmund, King and Martyr, London, 1846 · *Bath Chronicle* (10 May 1781), 2 · *Bath rate books* (1766–8) · *Bath Herald* (15 Dec 1832) · D. M. Raessler, 'Guest, Jane Mary', *New Grove*, 2nd edn

Miles [Myles], **John** (1620/21–1683), Particular Baptist minister and founder of the Baptist movement in south Wales, was born at Newton, Herefordshire. He had a profound sympathy and identification with the ministry in Wales, and a family of Miles was one of some substance in Llanigon, in the county of Brecknockshire. For these reasons, the place of his birth has long been considered to be the hamlet of Newton, in Clifford parish, in Herefordshire, but very near Hay-on-Wye in Brecknockshire. He was the son of Walter Miles, described as 'plebs' in the records of Brasenose College, Oxford, where John Miles matriculated in March 1636. Thereafter, John disappears from view until 1649, although it has been thought possible that he served in the parliamentary armies, perhaps as a chaplain. In the spring of 1649 Miles was in London, where he attended the church meeting at the Glasshouse, Broad Street, a building erected by a Venetian glass maker and later to become Pinners' Hall. Presumably after their baptism by total immersion, Miles and Thomas Proud were encouraged by the Glasshouse congregation to return to Wales to proselytize. The theory has been aired—but not clinched—that Miles had some connection with the Mansel family of Oxwich and Margam, Glamorgan: a suggestion attractive because it would explain both Miles's involvement with the Glasshouse, probably once part of the glass-making enterprises of Sir Robert Mansel, and his arrival in the Gower, heartland of the Mansels' territories in south Wales.

Be that as it may, by October 1649 Miles had established a Baptist church at Ilston, Gower, where leading supporters of parliament in south Wales, such as Jenkin Franklen, John Price of Gelli-hir, and Rowland Dawkins, were resident protectors and sympathizers, even if only the first of these was a member. Forty-three members were baptized at Ilston between October 1649 and October 1650, and a total of 261 by August 1660. In January 1650 Miles wrote to some sympathizers in his native parish to promise to preach there and to confront the ministers with established reputations already in the region: Walter Cradock, Vavasor Powell, and Jenkin Jones. The main matter in contention between them was the doctrine of believers' baptism by total immersion, and after some months of manoeuvrings between the Baptists and their Independent rivals the Llanigon congregation swung over decisively to Miles. The ordinance of adult believers' baptism helped define membership of the church in a way which had eluded the followers of Cradock and Powell, and gave his churches a sense of permanent fellowship. Furthermore, his energy and organizing ability enabled the Ilston congregation, meeting probably in the parish church there, to plant offshoots in Gelli-gaer and St Brides Minor, settlements in mid-Glamorgan which soon united

to form a single meeting at Llanharan. A preaching rota agreed by the Ilston members produced many converts at Carmarthen; by means of house meetings the congregations were kept in fellowship, and by general meetings of the churches' ministers and lay people the local Baptist causes were able to succour each other. Internal discipline was maintained by suspensions and excommunications from membership. On 7 November 1651 Miles was formally appointed pastor of the Ilston church; as there were by this time further new meetings at Aberafan and Llangennech, elders were ordained at the satellite congregations. By March 1653 the peculiar centrality of the Ilston meeting had weakened as the movement prospered elsewhere in south Wales, and primacy of authority passed to the general meeting in its dealings with churches at Abergavenny, Llantrisant, and Hay-on-Wye.

At the same time as Miles was taking on the Independents at Llanigon, he was named as an approver in the Act for the Propagation of the Gospel in Wales, in February 1650. Like others of the 'Welsh Saints', such as Morgan Llwyd, Henry Walter, and Walter Cradock, Miles found nothing incompatible in receiving state maintenance while promoting the notion of gathered churches of restricted membership. At some point prior to 31 July 1656 he was appointed lecturer at Llanelli, Carmarthenshire, while from 1657 to 1660 he held the living of Ilston. Although he promoted imaginative and effective strategies towards evangelizing, he was not considered a particularly powerful preacher, and in his theology he was decidedly orthodox. In answer to the perceived growing threat from the Quakers, in 1656 he published *An Antidote Against the Infection of the Times*, a stern affirmation of Calvinist orthodoxy against the 'foul dunghil' of Quakerism (Miles, 19). Indeed, the Baptist movement he founded in four counties was of the Particular (Calvinist) persuasion, which bore a closer resemblance to Presbyterianism than any other strand of religious thought current in contemporary south Wales. In 1656 he signed the pro-Cromwellian *Humble Representation and Address* against Vavasor Powell's withering criticisms of the government in *A Word for God*.

At the Restoration, by 23 July 1660, Miles was ejected from the living of Ilston. The Baptist church there moved to the secluded ruins of the chapel of St Cenydd in the parish for three years. At some point subsequently Miles and a number of his followers emigrated to Massachusetts, where they established a church at Rehoboth. The date of their sailing is in doubt, since records survive of the excommunication of Miles and his wife Katherine in the archdeaconry court of Brecon in May 1664 and of his land transactions as late as July 1665. Nothing is known of his first wife apart from her forename, but by 1666 Miles had married for a second time, his new wife being Anne Humphrey (d. 1693), granddaughter of Thomas Clinton, third earl of Lincoln; and certainly by March 1666 Miles had arrived at Rehoboth. He and his followers were later fined by the Plymouth county court for meeting for worship without approval. From there they moved south to found the town of Swansey (from 1903 renamed Swansea), in what had been called Wannamoisett until Miles was granted the land, on 30 October 1667. He served as minister at Swansey and, from 1673 to his death, as schoolmaster there, but had to flee the town, during 'King Philip's War' with the Native Americans, in 1675. Miles kept lands in Carmarthenshire, and on the other side of the Atlantic kept black slaves at Swansey; he died there on 3 February 1683 and was buried at Barrington, Rhode Island. A memorial enclosure of the ruins of the chapel of St Cenydd, Ilston, dedicated to the memory of Miles and his church there, was unveiled by David Lloyd George on 13 June 1928. STEPHEN K. ROBERTS

Sources B. G. Owens, ed., *The Ilston book: earliest register of Welsh Baptists* (1996) · M. John, ed., *Welsh Baptist studies* (1976) · D. R. Phillips, 'Cefndir hanes eglwys Ilston, 1649–60', *Trafodion Cymdeithas Hanes Bedyddwyr Cymru* (1928), 1–107 · J. Miles, *An antidote against the infection of the times*, ed. T. Shankland, Welsh Baptist Historical Society, 1 (1904) · R. T. Jones and B. G. Owens, 'Anghydffurfwyr Cymru, 1660–1662', *Y Cofiadur*, 32 (1962), 3–91 · B. R. White, ed., *Association records of Particular Baptists of England, Wales, and Ireland to 1660*, pt 1 (1971) [S. Wales and Midlands] · *DWB* · T. Richards, *A history of the puritan movement in Wales* (1920) · T. Richards, *Religious developments in Wales, 1654–1662* (1923) · T. M. Bassett, *The Welsh Baptists* (1977) · *DNB* · Foster, *Alum. Oxon.*

Archives Brown University, Providence, Rhode Island, John Hay Library, Ilston church book, 1649–Sw[ansea], Rare Books MSS · NL Wales, Llanwenarth church book, MS 409

Wealth at death £260 7s. 6d.: inventory, 18 May 1683, Plymouth court, Massachusetts

Miles, Dame Margaret (1911–1994), headmistress, was born on 11 July 1911 at 12 Walton Park, Walton, Liverpool, the second of four children of the Revd Edwin Griffith Miles, Presbyterian minister, and his wife, Annie, *née* Jones, a graduate of Aberystwyth and former schoolmistress. Margaret had an elder sister and two younger brothers. During the First World War the family stayed with her maternal grandmother in north Wales, where she attended the Bala elementary school. Her father was gassed and for the sake of his health the Miles family then settled in Felixstowe on the Suffolk coast. From a mixed county secondary school there Miles won a 'war victim' scholarship to Ipswich high school, a Girls' Public Day School Trust school, where she became head girl and excelled at sport. Her last sixth-form year was spent at Croydon high school, after her father moved to a church in Cheam.

Schoolteaching was not the career Margaret Miles would have chosen, but the Board of Education grant that financed her university education was conditional on a pledge to teach for at least four years. Dreams of medicine or social work had therefore to be abandoned. At Bedford College, London (1930–33), she read first sociology, then (when told that was not a suitable teaching subject) history, graduating with a second class. She became a vice-president of the National Union of Students and president of Bedford's Student Union, and in 1933 she captained the British women's tennis team at the international student games. There followed a year of postgraduate training at the London Institute of Education, an anxious search for a job, and a brief spell teaching in a Swiss finishing school, before she was appointed history mistress at Westcliff

High School for Girls, in 1935. From this conventional local education authority grammar school she moved in 1939 to a progressive independent girls' boarding-school, Badminton School, which attracted her by its internationalist ethos. An active supporter of the League of Nations Union, it was there that she became associated with the Council for Education in World Citizenship (and also formed her lifelong friendship with Naomi Mitchison, whose daughters were at Badminton). She was seconded as assistant lecturer to the department of education at the University of Bristol (1944–6) and at the age of thirty-five became headmistress of a girls' grammar school, Pate's School, Cheltenham (1946–52).

It was, however, Margaret Miles's second headship (1952–73), at Putney County School for Girls, which in 1955 became Mayfield School (a girls' comprehensive with 2000 pupils), that gave her a mission in education and made her reputation as an outstanding headmistress. Mayfield was one of the showpieces of London education and she became a leading advocate of the large neighbourhood school as the only way of making good the ideal of secondary education for all. Her two books, the autobiographical … *And Gladly Teach* (1966) and *Comprehensive Schooling* (1968), convey the challenge involved in creating a new kind of school, offering a first-rate, modern education to children of all abilities. But the idea of the comprehensive school caused much apprehension and controversy. Miles's enthusiasm, charm, and sheer efficiency won over the staff and parents at Mayfield, and her wit and authority as a speaker and broadcaster were appreciated by a wider public. To the Association of Headmistresses, however, she was a *bête noire*; a long-standing member of its executive committee, she was defeated when she stood for election as president. As chair of the Campaign for Comprehensive Education from 1972 and its president in the last fifteen years of her life, she made a forceful case for abolishing all selection in secondary education: 'Co-existence with grammar schools is NOT practically possible for a "Comprehensive" School' (Miles, 'The background to education in inner London; a hundred years of English education', in R. Ringshall and others, *The Urban School: Buildings for Education in London, 1870–1980*, 1983, 10).

Much of Miles's time—too much, according to some colleagues—was taken up by committee work. This included membership of the Schools' Broadcasting Council, the Independent Television Authority's educational advisory council, the General Advisory Council of the BBC, the National Advisory Council for the Training and Supply of Teachers, and the councils of the Royal Society of Arts and the British Association. She was a governor of Bedford College from 1947 until the college merged with Royal Holloway in 1985, becoming vice-chair of its council and an honorary fellow, and was also a council member and honorary fellow of Chelsea College. Her DBE, awarded in 1970, she claimed not to take very seriously, but accepted it as good for the school, the comprehensive ideal, and women. In 1973 the University of Kent made her an honorary DCL. Active as ever after her retirement, she took on more work that reflected her international interests, chairing an advisory committee on development education at the overseas development ministry and serving on the Central Bureau for Educational Visits and Exchanges. In 1985 she served as vice-chair of the educational advisory committee of the UK national commission for UNESCO. In her seventies, when she moved to her family home in Machynlleth, she learned to speak Welsh, chaired the local branch of the Council for the Preservation of Rural Wales, and captained the Aberdyfi ladies' golf team.

Miles never married and, with her 'cut-glass' accent and background in 'good' girls' schools, she appeared the 'quintessential British headmistress … stout of shoe, bobbed of hair, square of face, and sensibly suited at all times' (*The Independent*, 30 April 1994). She was, however, an enthusiast for modernity and change, including co-education. She was passionately opposed to nuclear weapons and regarded herself as a left-wing socialist, but as 'a doer rather than a thinker' (BBC interview, 5 April 1981). In public and professional life she was known for her courage and humour, pragmatism and common sense. Eventually immobilized by strokes and Parkinson's disease, she died at the Bay Nursing Home, Pier Road, Tywyn, Merioneth, on 26 April 1994. A memorial service was held at St James's, Piccadilly, London, on 24 October 1994.   JANET HOWARTH

Sources M. Miles, … *And gladly teach: the adventure of teaching* (1966) · Dame Margaret Miles file, Royal Holloway College, Bedford Centre for the History of Women · *The Independent* (30 April 1994) · *The Times* (29 April 1994) · *The Guardian* (28 April 1994) · *Daily Telegraph* (6 May 1994) · *Wandsworth Borough News* (6 May 1994) · *Times Educational Supplement* (28 July 1967) · *Times Educational Supplement* (16 Nov 1973) · *WWW*, 1991–5 · M. Miles and N. Mitchison, 'Friends', interview, BBC, 5 April 1981, BL NSA, 4900WR · booklet, opening of new buildings by Dame Margot Fonteyn de Arias, Mayfield School, West Hill, London SW15, 23 July 1956, Battersea Public Library · private information (2004) · b. cert. · d. cert.
Archives Royal Holloway College, Bedford Centre for the History of Women | SOUND BL NSA
Likenesses photographs, 1930, Royal Holloway College, Bedford Centre for the History of Women · photograph, 1967, repro. in *Times Educational Supplement* (28 July 1967) · photograph, 1973, repro. in *Times Educational Supplement* (16 Nov 1973) · photograph, repro. in *The Times* · photograph, repro. in *The Guardian*
Wealth at death £151,801: probate, 31 Aug 1994, CGPLA Eng. & Wales

Miles [*née* Hatfield], **Sibella Elizabeth** (*bap.* 1800, *d.* 1882), poet, was baptized on 28 September 1800 at Falmouth, the daughter of John Westby Hatfield (1766/7–1839), auctioneer, and his wife, Sibella (1763/4–1832). Nothing is known of Sibella Elizabeth's education, but she ran a girls' boarding-school in Penzance before her marriage on 13 August 1833 at Madron, Penzance, Cornwall, to Alfred Miles (1796–1851), a royal naval commander. They had two children, Frederick Arundel Miles (*d.* 1862), who in 1852 helped his mother to complete the index to her husband's second edition of Horsburgh's *Indian Directory* (1841), and Helen Jane Arundel Miles, who became an illustrator after her training in South Kensington, which was interrupted by the illness and early death of her brother.

Sibella Elizabeth Miles had first established herself as a published poet and writer under her maiden name, Sibella Elizabeth Hatfield. In 1826, her first volume of verse was published, *The Wanderer of Scandinavia, or, Sweden Delivered*, about the life and achievements of Gustavus Vasa. This volume was produced by private subscription, and the list of about three hundred subscribers included the names of James Silk Buckingham, Sir Humphry Davy, Sir Walter Scott, and Robert Southey. She contributed work to the *Forget-me-Not* from 1825, and the *Selector, or, Cornish Magazine* (1826–8), and two further volumes preceded her marriage: *Moments of Loneliness* (1829), which included a poem on the death of her only brother, and *Fruits of Solitude* (1831). Both contained prose and poetry. Most of the pieces are essentially occasional writing, appealing strongly to the sentiments, and they were popular with her contemporary readers. Miles's first publication after her marriage was anonymous, *An Essay on the Factory Question* (1844). This was 'occasioned by the recent votes in the House of Commons' (title-page) and is an indignant outcry against the failure of parliament to reduce the working hours of women and children in factories to ten hours a day. By 1846 Miles was using her married name in publications: she contributed an introduction and three ballads to *Original Cornish Ballads* (1846), but was identified by the editor as 'Mrs Miles, formerly Miss S. E. Hatfield'. She also contributed leading articles to the *Penzance Journal* (1846–50). In *Leisure Evenings, or, Records of the Past* (1860), another collection of prose and verse, the title-page identifies the writer as 'Mrs Alfred Miles (Late S. E. Hatfield'. Other publications included *Hymn of Thanksgiving for the Recovery of the Prince of Wales* (1872) and an introduction to an edition of the *Te Deum* (1877), illustrated by her daughter, as well as contributions to periodicals, including the *People's Magazine* (1867) and the *Church of England Magazine* (1869).

Miles moved to live in London, but she never managed to produce any substantial writing, and died at her home, 54 South Lambeth Road, Pimlico, on 29 March 1882. Her work has not survived her period, and even within it she was of very minor repute, not warranting even passing mention in *Poets and Poetry of the Century* (1891–7), edited by her husband's namesake, but no relation, Alfred H. Miles.
                                    ROSEMARY SCOTT

Sources Boase, *Mod. Eng. biog.* · Boase & Courtney, *Bibl. Corn.* · E. C. Clayton, *English female artists*, 2 (1876), 110–11 · O'Byrne, *Naval biog. dict.* · census returns for London, 1881

Miles, William (1780–1860), army officer, the eldest son of Captain Miles of the Royal West Middlesex militia (*d.* 1820), obtained a cadetship in 1799. He became an ensign on 6 March 1800, and a lieutenant in the 1st Bombay native infantry (Bombay Grenadiers) on 20 March. He joined his regiment in 1801 at Alexandria, where it formed part of the force sent from India under Sir David Baird to help ensure the expulsion of the French. On arrival in India he took part in operations against Baroda and in 1804 at Bharatpur. He became captain on 27 March 1815, and in the same year was made commandant of the British guard at Baroda. In 1817 he captured the fortified town of Palanpur, reinstating the rightful heir; afterwards he acted for some years as political superintendent of the state.

In 1820, acting as political agent with Colonel Barclay's expedition, Miles concluded a treaty with the raja of Radhanpore. He became major on 21 May 1821, and on 1 May 1824 was appointed lieutenant-colonel, 1st Bombay European regiment. In 1826 he concluded a treaty with the chiefs of Suigam, in Gujarat, formerly noted freebooters, who after the treaty became peaceful cultivators. He was subsequently resident in Cutch and political agent in Gujarat. He became brevet colonel on 1 December 1829, and retired from the command of the 9th Bombay native infantry on 28 July 1834.

In 1838 Miles published a translation of the *Shajrat ul atrak*, or genealogical tree of the Turks and Tartars, the chief value of which, according to the introduction, is its details of Ghengis Khan and his successors. He also translated for the Oriental Translation Fund works by Ali Kirmana' Husain, as *History of Hyder Naik* (1842) and *History of the Reign of Tipú Sultan* (1844). Miles was promoted major-general on 28 November 1854. He died at North Villa, Regent's Park, London, on 21 May 1860. His wife, Ann Hurd, and their son, Thomas, a lieutenant in the 73rd foot, survived him.   H. M. CHICHESTER, rev. JAMES LUNT

Sources W. W. Hunter, *The imperial gazetteer of India*, 9 vols. (1881); 2nd edn 14 vols. (1885–7) · J. Philippart, *East India military calendar*, 3 vols. (1823–6) · W. Miles, trans., *Shajrat ul atrak* (1838) · K. Husain Ali, *The history of Hyder Naik*, trans. W. Miles (1842) · K. Husain Ali, *The history of the reign of Tipú Sultán*, trans. W. Miles (1844) · P. Cadell, *History of the Bombay army* (1938) · C. E. Buckland, *Dictionary of Indian biography* (1906) · Boase, *Mod. Eng. biog.* · *CGPLA Eng. & Wales* (1860)
Archives BL OIOC, diary and papers, MSS Eur E 202–203, F 73–74
Wealth at death under £35,000: probate, 27 Sept 1860, *CGPLA Eng. & Wales*

Miles, William Augustus (1753/4–1817), political writer, born on 1 July in either 1753 or 1754, was the son of Jefferson Miles (d. 1763), proofmaster-general. As a boy he ran away from a school near Portsmouth, supposedly to support the cause of John Wilkes. After travelling in America in the 1760s he returned to England and was appointed in 1770 to the Ordnance office, but he soon quarrelled with his superiors and resigned, afterwards exposing their corrupt practices in the *Letters of Selim*. In 1772 he married his first wife, details of whom are unknown; they had a daughter, Theodosia, the following year. Also in 1773 Miles published his *Letter to Sir John Fielding* with a postscript to David Garrick protesting against the suppression of John Gay's *The Beggar's Opera*. Miles won the friendship of Garrick, and through Garrick's influence he obtained a civil appointment in the Royal Navy. Miles served under Vice-Admiral Sir George Rodney in the West Indies during the American War of Independence, was in Newfoundland in 1779, and, two years later, was a prisoner of war in St Lucia. Soon after his release he left the service. In August 1782 he was in Dublin and was corresponding with Lord Temple, who had just been appointed lord lieutenant, hoping to obtain political employment. Though backed by Lord Shelburne, he failed, and in January of the following year he went to the continent, settling at Seraing, near Liège, in the Southern Netherlands, in order to economize and to

educate his daughter. There he became intimate with two successive prince-bishops of Liège. Between 1784 and 1785 he wrote for the *Morning Post*, signing his contributions Neptune and Gracchus. Miles wrote in support of William Pitt's ministry and condemned the prince of Wales and his supporters. Miles was undeterred in his propaganda efforts by the fact that he lived abroad, although he admitted that it caused some problems when he sent a piece for publication to Lord Temple in the autumn of 1785 along with the following note:

> You will perceive that at this distance, and without facts to go upon, I am restricted in my information on home politics. Like the spider, I spin from myself: would to Heaven I could resemble it further, and entangle the factious fly in my patriotic web.   (Miles to Pitt, *Correspondence*, 1.18)

By the time he wrote to Pitt in November, Miles probably had some justification in saying that 'my pen has been indefatigable in your service' (Miles to Pitt, 30 Nov 1785, PRO, 30/8/159). This no doubt prompted Pitt's decision to give him money. Miles was in Givet in 1787 when British agents were trying to discover the extent of French preparations for war. His activities appear to have done little but arouse suspicions among the French. It is not clear at this point whether he was employed by the British government, or if he was merely working as a freelance in the hopes of some favour or reward. Obliged to move to Brussels on account of the Liège revolution, Miles lived there during 1788, still holding confidential relations with the British government. In 1789 he made a vain attempt to persuade Pitt to interfere in the affairs of Liège. Miles became well known as a spy during the French Revolution. He also become involved in some private business in attempting to find the abducted son of an Irish peer, a matter in which the Foreign Office had been asked to help. On 5 March 1790 Miles had an interview with Pitt, and in July he was sent to Paris to work against the conclusion of the 'family compact' with Spain. At Paris he came to know Mirabeau, Lebrun, Lafayette (whom he had met during his naval experiences in America), and other leading politicians. Ostensibly in favour of the revolution, he was even allowed membership of the Jacobin Club. In April 1791 he left Paris for London. Pitt offered him a pension of £300 a year for his past services and Miles acted as intermediary between the agents of the French republic in London and the ministry, seeking to prevent war. By 1792, the year his first wife died, he was receiving £500 a year to work for the government.

In 1794 Miles issued *A Letter to Earl Stanhope on his Political Conduct in Reference to the French Revolution* (1794), with notes and postscript, and *A Letter to the Duke of Grafton*, in which Lafayette was defended from the charges made against him by Edmund Burke on 17 March in the House of Commons. By 1794 Miles had become extremely critical of Pitt's conduct of the war and his payments seem to have been stopped. He appears to have become overly confident and to have had a misguided sense of his own importance. According to John Ehrman, 'Like many intelligent, ambitious men who attain and remain on the fringe of affairs, he was easily led to magnify his contribution'

(Ehrman, *Reluctant Transition*, 252). In 1795 Miles published anonymously his *Letter to the Prince of Wales on the Subject of the Debts Contracted by him since 1787*. This went through thirteen editions. Lord Thurlow moved in the House of Lords for the author's name to be made public. With no government salary, and under increasing political pressure, Miles retired to Froyle in Hampshire. He continued to write, however, and in 1796, in a *Letter to H. Duncombe, Esq., Member for the County of York*, he answered Burke's *Letter to a Noble Lord*, the pamphlet reaching a fourth edition within the year.

Miles returned to London early in 1800, but in 1803 he retired to a house on Brownsea Island in Poole harbour that was lent to him by his friend Charles Sturt. In this year he also married Harriet Watkinson (*d.* 1872); the couple had five sons, including Charles Popham Miles [*see below*]. On Pitt death's in 1806 Miles sought employment from the new ministry and he was promised the consul-generalship at Corfu, but Charles James Fox's death prevented the fulfilment of this promise. Miles now busied himself again in writing for the press, and his *Letters of Neptune* on parliamentary reform appeared in the *Independent Whig*. He also wrote in favour of Francis Burdett's candidature for Westminster in 1807 and he contributed to *The Statesman*. In July Miles obtained an interview with the prince of Wales through Lord Moira, and in the following year he published his *Letter to the Prince of Wales, with a Sketch of the Prospect before him*. In 1812 Miles retired to Hythe, near Southampton, and he corresponded with, among others, Samuel Whitbread and Lord Moira. On 23 April 1816 he started for Paris, in order to collect materials for a history of the French Revolution, and he stayed a month at Château Lagrange with Lafayette. Miles died at Paris on 25 April 1817.

Miles's three eldest sons served in the army. His fourth son, **Charles Popham Miles** (1810–1891), Church of England clergyman, attended Morpeth grammar school and then served in the East India Company's navy as a midshipman, before entering Gonville and Caius College, Cambridge, in October 1833 where he graduated BA in 1838 and MA in 1851. He was ordained in May 1838, then became chaplain of the Sailors' Home, Wells Street, at London docks, held several curacies, and in 1843 succeeded Robert Montgomery as incumbent of St Jude's, Glasgow. In 1844 Miles's benefice was withdrawn from episcopal jurisdiction after a dispute with the bishop of Glasgow. While at Glasgow, Miles graduated MD. From 1858 to 1867 he was principal of the Malta protestant college, and from 1867 to 1883 rector of Monkwearmouth, co. Durham, where he restored the old Saxon church. In 1872 he was made an honorary canon of Durham. In addition to editing the correspondence of his father in 1890, he published several religious treatises and pamphlets on Scottish episcopacy. One of the earliest fellows of the Linnean Society, he also wrote a paper 'The marine zoology of the Clyde', published in the *Annual Report of the British Association*. In later years Miles lived at St Julian's, Hatherley Road, Kew Gardens, Surrey. He died when on a visit to The Delles, Great Chesterford, Essex, on 10 July

1891, and was buried there. Miles's only daughter was married to M. Richard Waddington, whose brother was a well-known diplomatist and statesman.

G. LE G. NORGATE, *rev.* HANNAH BARKER

Sources *The correspondence of William Augustus Miles on the French Revolution, 1789–1817*, ed. C. P. Miles, 2 vols. (1890) • J. Ehrman, *The younger Pitt*, 1: *The years of acclaim* (1969) • J. Ehrman, *The younger Pitt*, 2: *The reluctant transition* (1983) • H. V. Evans, 'William Pitt, William Miles and the French Revolution', *BIHR*, 43 (1970), 190–213 • PRO, 30/8/159 • A. Aspinall, *Politics and the press, c.1780–1850* (1949) • H. Barker, *Newspapers, politics and public opinion in late eighteenth-century England* (1998) • Hansard • CGPLA Eng. & Wales (1891)
Archives Hunt. L., letters | BL, letters to Lord Grenville, Add. MS 59021 • BL, letters to Sir R. M. Keith, Add. MSS 35537–35540 • BL, letters to earl of Liverpool, Add. MS 38210 • BL, corresp. with W. Windham, Add. MSS 37876; 37886 • NL Scot., letters to Hugh Elliot; corresp. with Robert Liston • NMM, letters to Lord Sandwich • priv. coll., letters to Lord Lansdowne • PRO, Chatham MSS, corresp. with W. Pitt, PRO 30/8/159
Wealth at death £11,902 4*s.* 2*d.*—Charles Popham Miles: probate, 19 Aug 1891, CGPLA Eng. & Wales

Miley, John (1805?–1861), Roman Catholic priest, a native of co. Kildare, was educated at St Patrick's College, Maynooth, ordained in 1830, and appointed to the pro-cathedral, Dublin. He resided at the Irish College at Rome from 1833 to 1835, devoting himself mainly to the study of theology and the history of the papacy. On his return to Ireland in 1835 he was appointed curate of the metropolitan parish, Dublin.

Miley was an ardent admirer of Daniel O'Connell, and warmly defended his attitude on several political issues, including national education, on which Miley published several pamphlets, and the Catholic Bequest Bill in 1838. He visited O'Connell during his imprisonment in Richmond gaol in 1844 and came to national prominence in September upon O'Connell's release, being chosen to preach at the mass of thanksgiving at the pro-cathedral. In his sermon he praised the repeal cause as sacred, and attributed O'Connell's release from prison to the intervention of the Blessed Virgin Mary. He was greatly troubled by the rupture between O'Connell and the Young Ireland party, and in December 1846 he worked hard to effect a reconciliation between him and Smith O'Brien. Miley suggested to O'Connell that he undertake a Roman pilgrimage after doctors ordered that he take a rest and have a change of scene because of his ill health. With the permission of Archbishop Murray he accompanied O'Connell as his private chaplain to Italy in 1847, and tended him in his last days. In obedience to O'Connell's injunction he carried his heart to Rome and, having seen it placed with impressive ceremonies in the church of St Agatha, he returned with his friend's body to Ireland. Miley preached O'Connell's funeral sermon in Marlborough Street Church.

In 1849 Miley was appointed rector of the Irish College in Paris. He proved to be an ineffective disciplinarian and a poor judge of character, being constantly in dispute with the students, his staff, and the board of Irish bishops. Miley argued that the only way to regain authority in the college was to transfer the appointments of staff away from the board of Irish bishops and back to the rector. He was supported by the archbishop of Dublin, Paul Cullen, but opposed by the majority of the Irish bishops, who felt that the rector was largely responsible for the problems at the college. Miley felt that most of his staff were attempting to undermine his control.

The situation was at its worst between 1854 and 1858 when Father Patrick Lavelle served as professor of philosophy at the college. Lavelle made life very difficult for Miley and on occasions hit the rector. When Miley complained to the board of Irish bishops he failed to get satisfaction, as they were unhappy with him because of his refusal to carry out many of their instructions. Matters came to a head in March 1858 when Miley, with Cullen's approval, refused to allow Lavelle and another staff member, Father John Rice, entry into the college as they returned from saying mass in a nearby convent. Both professors eventually entered the college and Miley was forced to call in the French authorities to have them removed. This episode resulted in the board of Irish bishops' having to close the college in May 1858.

In the subsequent investigation Miley was blamed for most of the problems. Despite this censure Paul Cullen succeeded in having Miley appointed administrator in October 1858, when the college came under the control of the Vincentian order. However, Miley soon was in conflict with the Vincentians over reducing the budget which they had submitted for the running of the college. Relations between the two sides deteriorated, and in June 1859 Cullen, fearing that a second major scandal at the college would undermine his authority within the Irish church, persuaded Miley to resign, threatening to recall him if he did not do so.

Miley was subsequently appointed parish priest of Bray, one of the most prosperous parishes in the archdiocese of Dublin, and died there on 18 April 1861. He was an accomplished orator and preacher, and the author of *Rome under Paganism and the Popes* (1848), *History of the Papal States* (1850), *Temporal Sovereignty of the Popes* (1856), and *L'empereur Napoléon III et la papauté* (1859).

ROBERT DUNLOP, rev. GERARD MORAN

Sources *Freeman's Journal* [Dublin] (19 April 1861) • P. MacSuibhne, *Paul Cullen and his contemporaries*, 4 vols. (1962–77) • E. Larkin, *The making of the Roman Catholic church in Ireland, 1850–1860* (1980) • W. J. Fitzpatrick, *The life, times and correspondence of the Right Rev. Dr Doyle, bishop of Kildare and Leighlin*, new edn, 2 vols. (1880) • D. J. Hickey and J. E. Doherty, *A dictionary of Irish history* (1980) • F. Ó Fearghail, 'A stormy decade in the Irish College, Paris, 1849–1859', *The Irish-French connection, 1578–1978*, ed. L. Swords (1978) • G. Moran, *Patrick Lavelle: the rise and fall of an Irish nationalist, 1825–1886* (1994) • P. J. Hamell, 'Maynooth students and ordinations, 1795–1895', *Irish Ecclesiastical Record*, 5th ser., 108 (1968), 407–16

Archives Irish College, Paris | BL, corresp. with R. R. Madden, Add. MS 43684 • Irish College, Rome, Tobias-Kirby MSS

Likenesses J. P. Haverty, group portrait, lithograph with watercolour, pubd 1845 (after drawing, exh. 1854), NG Ire.

Wealth at death under £1000: probate, 13 Dec 1862, *CGPLA Ire.*

Milford. For this title name *see* Philipps, Wogan, second Baron Milford (1902–1993).

Milford, David Sumner (1905–1984), rackets and hockey player, was born in Oxford on 7 June 1905, the second of three children and younger son of Sir Humphrey Sumner *Milford (1877–1952), publisher, and his first wife, Marion Louisa (*d.* 1940), daughter of Horace Smith, Metropolitan Police magistrate. He was educated first at West Downs School, Winchester, where it was said he never missed the chance of hitting a ball against a wall with whatever weapon came to hand, then at Rugby School, where he not only began his remarkable career as a games player but also won the public schools rackets championship with C. H. Goodbody. He went on to New College, Oxford, where he obtained a third class in classical honour moderations (1926) and a fourth in *literae humaniores* (1928). In 1928 he joined the staff at Marlborough College, where he taught Latin and geography for thirty-five years.

In 1930 Milford first became British amateur rackets champion; he went on to win this championship seven times. In all he won the British amateur doubles eleven times, ten of them partnered by John Thompson, a colleague of his at Marlborough. He also won the Noel Bruce old boys' championship on twelve occasions: four times with Cyril Simpson before the Second World War and eight times afterwards, with Peter Kershaw. But his real triumph was in 1937, when he won the world championship in New York and at the Queen's Club, London, defeating the American challenger Norbert Setzler by 7 games to 3. He held the title until 1947, when he retired. At rackets he was outstanding. He had a good eye and fleetness of foot, and extraordinary anticipation. He could fashion unorthodox strokes, in particular a deadly angled drop shot, which is most difficult to achieve when the ball moves as fast as it does at rackets. He often paid tribute to Harry Gray, his coach at Rugby, and Walter Laurence, the Marlborough professional.

When Milford arrived at New College, he played hockey and was at once recognized as a player of promise. He first got his blue in 1927, and played in three successive university matches against Cambridge. In 1930 he was chosen to play for England at inside left; later occasionally he played at centre forward, and became an automatic choice for the side. The qualities he had at rackets he showed too on the hockey field. He was extremely energetic and hard-working: he seemed to be all over the field and available to take a pass, from which he usually scored a goal. His splendid stickwork and ball control were confusing to his opponents and he was almost at his best when the ground was wet or bumpy. When at Marlborough he wrote two books on hockey which in their day were standard works on the game. He was also a good cricketer—a slow left-arm bowler and a very useful middle-order batsman. Once when playing for Wiltshire against Dorset he made 150 on a dangerous wicket, when the rest of the side was struggling to reach double figures. He also played lawn tennis for Wiltshire for many years.

Milford was 5 feet 11 inches in height, very slim and wiry, with good hands and wrists. His lack of physique often caused comment. Once, while visiting an osteopath about a strained shoulder, when he was at the height of his powers, the man looked him over and suggested that he should think of taking up some game to improve his strength. On another occasion a club secretary watching him play golf remarked: 'I don't believe that boy has a joint in his body.' He was a person of many interests. He was an excellent bridge player because he was quick-minded and also enjoyed a gamble. He sang madrigals with local enthusiasts and later in life took up bird-watching. Like many good games players he was modest. He was also rather shy: he disliked pushing himself forward, or speaking in public, which was perhaps unusual for a schoolmaster. Nevertheless, he was friendly and good-tempered.

In 1930 Milford married Elizabeth Mary, a granddaughter of the composer Sir John Stainer and daughter of John Frederick Randall Stainer, chief inspector at the passport office. They had a daughter (Marion, a professional singer) and three sons. Milford died on 24 June 1984, after playing three sets of tennis. His wife survived him.

D. M. GOODBODY, rev.

Sources *The Times* (26 June 1984) · personal knowledge (1990) · private information (1990) [John Thompson, Peter Kershaw, J. B. H. Bisseker, and the Milford family] · *CGPLA Eng. & Wales* (1984)
Wealth at death £33,214: probate, 3 Sept 1984, *CGPLA Eng. & Wales*

Milford, Sir Humphrey Sumner (1877–1952), publisher, was born at East Knoyle, Wiltshire, on 8 February 1877, the youngest of the ten children of the rector, Canon Robert Newman Milford (*b. c.*1829), and his wife, Emily Sarah Frances, daughter of Charles Richard *Sumner, bishop of Winchester. He was a scholar of Winchester College and of New College, Oxford, taking firsts in classical moderations and *literae humaniores*; his tennis-playing skills matched his academic abilities. In 1900 he became assistant to Charles Cannan, secretary to the delegates of the Oxford University Press. Cannan transferred him to the London office in Paternoster Row in 1906. Succeeding Henry Frowde as manager of the London business and publisher to the University of Oxford in 1913, Milford held the post until his retirement in 1945. He was president of the Publishers' Association from 1919 to 1921, and supervised the office's move to Amen House in Warwick Square in 1924. Four years later, Oxford made him an honorary DLitt on the completion of the first edition of the *Oxford English Dictionary*. His knighthood followed in 1936. Milford married twice. His first wife, whom he married on 24 April 1902, was Marion Louisa, daughter of Horace Smith, a Metropolitan Police magistrate. She died in 1940, and on 5 February 1947 Milford married Rose Caroline (*b.* 1890/91), the widow of Sir Arnold Wilson and daughter of Charles Hensley Henson, stockbroker. The first marriage produced a daughter and two sons, Robert Humphrey and David Sumner *Milford, seven times British amateur rackets champion. Having lived latterly at the White House, Drayton St Leonard, Oxfordshire, Milford died in the Acland Nursing Home, Oxford, on 6 September 1952.

The scale of Oxford University Press activities increased dramatically during Milford's tenure. When Cannan appointed him, the press was a relatively specialized concern which depended on sales of academic works, bibles, and prayer books. By the time Milford retired, he had helped to transform this business into a leading publishing house with a vast list of works aimed at scholar and general reader alike: Oxford's first *General Catalogue* (1916) ran to 576 pages. It was also a global organization. Milford encouraged his editor E. C. Parnwell to travel through Africa and the Far East in 1928, investigating avenues for educational publishing in those areas. From this came Oxford's overseas education department, E. S. Hornby's seminal Oxford *Advanced Learner's Dictionary*, and the press's wide-ranging involvement in English language teaching around the world.

Cannan had seen great possibilities if the London office began publishing on its own account. Milford became his lieutenant in this scheme, and the two maintained a close, even hermetic, friendship among their associates until Cannan died in 1919. Soon Milford's name became a familiar mark on Oxford books, distinguishing London volumes from the Clarendon Press imprint that appeared on works which the delegates supervised at Oxford. Milford's brand of mild despotism drew other Oxford men to his staff, including Charles Williams and Gerard Hopkins, nephew of Gerard Manley Hopkins. Milford was quick to make other contacts. His London neighbours included Ernest Hodder Williams, and Milford soon entered into an agreement with Hodder and Stoughton to publish children's literature. Among other works, this produced the successful books written by Herbert Ely and Charles L'Estrange under the pen-name Herbert Strang. The joint venture also led to a new list of medical works from Oxford, with the delegate Sir William Osler as its advisory editor. Milford's first publication in this series for practitioners was Osler's seven-volume *System of Medicine* in 1907.

Milford continued the press's expansion after Cannan's death. In 1923 his great interest in music and hymnbooks encouraged the formation of the press's music department under Hubert Foss. Despite this, literature remained Milford's first love. An insatiable reader of detective stories, he edited *The Oxford Book of English Verse of the Romantic Period* (1928), and produced scholarly volumes of Cowper, Leigh Hunt, and Browning. The latter became one of the most cited authors in *The Oxford Dictionary of Quotations* (1941), a volume which was Milford's idea, and which was produced entirely at Amen House.

Milford favoured both literary resurrections and discoveries. Oxford University Press purchased the World's Classics list from Grant Richards in 1906, and Milford used this as the foundation for a hugely popular series that reflected his own catholic tastes. The World's Classics introduced Tolstoy to English readers, and also acquainted them with novels by Constance Holme. Milford insisted that several of Anthony Trollope's works be reissued as well, and the World's Classics played a large part in restoring the novelist's reputation.

Milford was equally astute with new titles. In 1918 he published *The Poems of Gerard Manley Hopkins*, a volume undervalued until its second edition in 1930. He also 'discovered' Flora Thompson, author of *Lark Rise to Candleford*. It says much for the breadth of Milford's mentality that his colleagues could never decide whether this, or Toynbee's *A Study of History*, was the most important book he had published.

Milford worked a six-day week and proved tenacious in defending his business. He steered the press through the depression of the 1930s while resisting calls for its rationalization. In addition, when it was offered the *Dictionary of National Biography* in 1917, Milford was eager to accept it. Cannan resisted. It seemed too costly. Others shared his opinion: the dictionary appeared a white elephant. Milford replied: 'Very likely; but that is the sort of animal that ought to be in our stable' (Sutcliffe, 186). The phrase was characteristic of the man—polished and literary, but brooking no disagreement.   MARTIN MAW

Sources P. Sutcliffe, *The Oxford University Press: an informal history* (1978) · *The Times* (8 Sept 1952) · *The Periodical*, 26 (1946), 4-page supplement following p. 158 · *The Periodical*, 29 (1952–3), 285–9 · N. Barker, *The Oxford University Press and the spread of learning, 1478–1978* (1978) · *WWW*, 1951–60 · *DNB* · *CGPLA Eng. & Wales* (1952)
Archives Oxford University Press, archives, letter-books | Bodl. Oxf., corresp. with R. W. Chapman · Bodl. Oxf., corresp. with L. G. Curtis · Bodl. Oxf., corresp. with Gilbert Murray · U. Sussex, letters to J. G. Crowther
Likenesses photograph, c.1913, repro. in Sutcliffe, *Oxford University Press*, facing p. 245 · painting, priv. coll. · photographs, Oxford University Press, London
Wealth at death £12,197 0s. 2d.: probate, 8 Dec 1952, *CGPLA Eng. & Wales*

Milford, (Theodore) Richard (1895–1987), Church of England clergyman and philanthropist, was born on 10 June 1895 at Yockleton Hall in Shropshire, the eldest of three sons (there were no daughters) of Robert Theodore Milford, schoolmaster, and his wife, Elspeth Barter, granddaughter of George *Moberly, bishop of Salisbury. Both sides of his family contained notable academics and clerics. Milford went to Clifton College, where the traditional classical education was enhanced by a strong interest in music, unusual at that time. When the First World War broke out in 1914 Milford volunteered for the army and was posted to the 19th Royal Fusiliers and then (1915–19) commissioned in the Oxford and Buckinghamshire light infantry, with whom he saw active service in Mesopotamia, with two spells of leave in India. He was sent to Cairo to train for the Royal Flying Corps in 1918, but was invalided home in 1919.

In 1919 Milford went to Magdalen College, Oxford, where he took a first in *literae humaniores* in 1921. His connection there with the Student Christian Movement (SCM) led him to India, where he taught at Alwaye College in Travancore (1921–3) and St John's College, Agra (1923–4), with a two-year spell in Liverpool as local SCM secretary (1924–6) and a year at Westcott House (1930–31), Cambridge, training for ordination. In 1932 he married Nancy Dickens Bourchier, daughter of Ernest Hawksley, solicitor, and great-granddaughter of Charles Dickens; they had two daughters.

Milford was made priest in Lucknow, India, in 1934. When he returned to England in 1935 he worked again for the SCM (until 1938), stimulating many young minds as the study secretary. At the same time (1935–7) he was a curate at All Hallows, Lombard Street, London. His first wife died in 1936 and in 1937 he married Margaret Nowell Smith, daughter of Nowell Charles Smith, headmaster of Sherborne School and former fellow of New College, Oxford; they had a son, who died in infancy, and two daughters.

In 1938 Milford became vicar of St Mary's, the Oxford University church, where he stayed until 1947. Here a group, the Colloquy, gathered round him to discuss philosophical and theological topics. His rigorous, logical mind and fearless questioning had a lasting influence on its members, many of whom attained later distinction.

Perhaps Milford's most important contribution at this time was the part he played in the founding of Oxfam. Dick (he was never known by any other name) Milford and a few others met in the old library at St Mary's on 5 October 1942, in response to the idea brought to him by Henry Gillett, a Quaker, that in spite of the blockade something should be done to help the victims of starvation in Greece. The result was the foundation of the Oxford Committee for Famine Relief, later known as Oxfam. Many obstacles had to be overcome to get the government to agree to this idea. He remained chairman until 1947, returned for a second period from 1960 to 1965, and continued taking an active interest until his death.

In 1947 Milford was appointed canon and chancellor of Lincoln Cathedral, with special responsibility for religious education in the diocese, including the Scholae Cancellarii, the theological college at which successive ordinands profited from his pithy teaching. In 1958 Milford became master of the Temple. Here the social and intellectual climate was in total contrast to all that had gone before and he found himself at times in conflict with the benchers, notably in 1960 when he appeared for the defence in the crown prosecution unsuccessfully brought under the obscenity laws against the publishers of the unexpurgated edition of *Lady Chatterley's Lover*, by D. H. Lawrence, which had been banned since 1928. These London years also gave further scope for a varied ministry of preaching and counselling. In 1968 he retired to Shaftesbury, where his activities included running a group studying Teilhard de Chardin, with whose evolutionary philosophy and devotional intensity he found himself very much in sympathy.

Milford's influence was out of all proportion to his published work. *Foolishness to the Greeks* (1953), based on talks for a university mission, illustrates his style of Christian apologetic; *The Valley of Decision* (1961), the result of a working party of the British Council of Churches, explores the moral dilemma posed by atomic weapons; articles, broadcasts, and addresses make up the rest except for a little book of verse (*Belated Harvest*, 1978) and some early memoirs published privately in his old age.

Milford was a handsome and gifted man with a first-class mind, dry wit, boundless intellectual curiosity which never left him, and wide interests including chess, music, and sailing. Though discriminating, he was a man of simple tastes. Milford died in Shaftesbury where his home was Spring Hill, 1 Kingsman Lane, on 19 January 1987.

OLIVER TOMKINS, *rev.*

Sources *The Times* (22 Jan 1987) · private information (1996) · personal knowledge (1996) · *CGPLA Eng. & Wales* (1987)
Wealth at death £16,446: probate, 16 Dec 1987, *CGPLA Eng. & Wales*

Milford Haven. For this title name *see* Mountbatten, Louis Alexander, first marquess of Milford Haven (1854–1921); Mountbatten, Victoria Alberta Elisabeth Mathilde Marie, marchioness of Milford Haven (1863–1950); Mountbatten, George Louis Victor Henry Sergius, second marquess of Milford Haven (1892–1938).

Miliband, Ralph [*formerly* Adolphe] (**1924–1994**), political theorist, was born Adolphe Miliband on 7 January 1924 in Brussels, the elder of two children of Samuel Miliband (1895–1966), a leather artisan, and his wife, Renée, *née* Steinlauf (1901–1975). His parents, who were both Jewish, had moved from Poland to Belgium after the First World War, and married in 1923. His father had been a member of the Jewish Bund in Warsaw, and Miliband himself joined the socialist-Zionist youth organization Hashomer Hatzair ('Young Guard') in Brussels. Miliband escaped to Britain with his father in May 1940, just before the Belgian surrender to Germany, but his sister, Nan, was too young to undertake the journey and remained with their mother. Although they avoided deportation by taking refuge in a farm, the separation, and the fact that several relatives and his best friend, Maurice Tran, were victims of the holocaust, affected Miliband deeply.

After arriving in London as a sixteen-year-old refugee, with only a rudimentary grasp of English, Miliband was initially employed removing furniture from bombed houses, but soon received a grant from a refugee organization to resume his education. He matriculated in the summer of 1941, and was admitted to the London School of Economics (LSE), then based in Cambridge, in the autumn. Already a socialist, he attracted the attention of Harold Laski, who became his mentor and friend, and an important influence over his thinking. In 1943, with Laski's help, he joined the Belgian section of the Royal Navy, where his main function was to intercept German radio communications. In 1946 he returned to the LSE to complete his degree and, after graduating with first-class honours the next year, he stayed on and began his doctorate, 'Popular thought in the French Revolution'.

Miliband was appointed to an assistant lectureship in the department of government at the LSE in 1949 but, after Laski's death in March 1950, he became rather isolated and began to lose interest in his PhD, which he did not finish until 1956. The constraining atmosphere of the cold war also inhibited him. Critical of the Communist Party, and never a Trotskyist, he was a rather sceptical supporter of the Bevanite left in the Labour Party. However, he wrote very little during this period and it was only with the formation of the 'new left' after the mass exodus from

Ralph Miliband (1924–1994), by unknown photographer

the Communist Party in 1956, that he found kindred spirits with whom to associate and developed more self-confidence. In particular, he became friendly with the two former communist historians, E. P. Thompson and John Saville, and joined them on the editorial board of the *New Reasoner* in 1958. His circle of associates widened further when this journal merged with the *Universities and Left Review* to form the *New Left Review* in 1960. Moreover, on 14 September 1961 he married Marion Kozak (*b.* 1934), daughter of David Kozak, steel manufacturer, a graduate of international history from the LSE, from a Polish Jewish background. Together they soon established a home in Primrose Hill, London, which became a meeting-point for socialist intellectuals from all over the world. Their son David was born in 1965, followed by Edward four years later.

Miliband's first major book, *Parliamentary Socialism* (1961), was a trenchant critique of the Labour Party. From an implicitly Marxist position the book claimed that, throughout its history, Labour had failed to exploit the potential for radical change because its constitutionalism had prevailed over its socialism. The book was highly influential because it argued so clearly and forcefully, with thorough historical substantiation, and without adopting a polemical tone or sectarian position. Miliband now emerged as an important figure on the intellectual left. Good-looking, with a gift for irony, and a superb command of English with traces of a Belgian-French accent, he was also a compelling speaker. However, the depth of his convictions made him refuse to compromise and by the mid-1960s he had abandoned his earlier hopes that the Labour Party might yet be transformed into a vehicle for socialism. Subsequently, he sought a renewal of the left through a regeneration of ideas and movements outside the party. One organ to which he attached enormous importance in this respect was the annual *Socialist Register*, which he established in 1964 with John Saville, and which he continued to edit until his death. Always international in outlook and with a network of like-minded intellectuals, Miliband hoped that the *Socialist Register* would reinvigorate the left, both in Britain and elsewhere, by drawing on the highest level of independent Marxist scholarship throughout the world.

Miliband's second major work, *The State in Capitalist Society* (1969), was a highly ambitious comparative study in Marxist political sociology, which sought to refute pluralist theory, the prevailing paradigm in Anglo-American political science. Whereas pluralism emphasized the extent to which power was dispersed in liberal-democratic societies, Miliband attempted to demonstrate its concentration in a dominant class and the organic links between this class and the state. This book, which led to a celebrated theoretical debate with the Greek Marxist Nicos Poulantzas, enhanced Miliband's international reputation, and stimulated new thinking about the state in both Marxist and non-Marxist circles.

By now Miliband was alienated from the authorities at the LSE, particularly as a result of their handling of the student protests of the late 1960s, and in 1972 he moved to Leeds University as professor of politics and head of department. However, his time there was again difficult. He had a major heart attack almost immediately after the move, there was opposition to his appointment, and he was ill suited for an administrative role. After resigning in 1978, he subsequently divided his time between North America, where he held a succession of chairs, and London. His major works in the 1970s and 1980s were *Marxism and Politics* (1977), which provided a synthesis of theory and historical experience, arguing for a Marxism untainted by the Soviet model, and *Capitalist Democracy in Britain* (1982), which combined an analytical framework with detailed political insights, providing an exposure of the limitations of British democracy. Although he remained dubious about the Labour Party, from the early 1980s Miliband was close to Tony Benn and worked with a variety of groups that were attempting to revitalize socialism both inside and outside the party. However, the rise of neo-liberalism and the collapse of the Soviet bloc posed major problems for the left, and his last book, *Socialism for a Sceptical Age* (1994), was an attempt to understand the era without abandoning his fundamental ideas. He thus acknowledged the failures of socialist systems in practice, the weaknesses of traditional parties, and the positive features of new social movements, but he continued to argue that a revitalized form of socialism offered the only hope for the future.

Throughout his life Miliband remained faithful to beliefs that he had first developed as a young man. His intellectual honesty, deep convictions, and eagerness to engage in debate made him an inspiring teacher and his lectures were attended by scores of students who were not even taking his subject. These qualities also contributed to the development of independent thinking within Marxist circles and an engagement with Marxist ideas in the wider international academic community. Refusing to take refuge in esoteric jargon or partisan dogma, he confronted counter-arguments and sought to persuade people of the essential validity of his position through reasoned argument. The clarity and directness of his style meant that his writing was unusually persuasive and, because his Marxism was coupled with a burning commitment to democracy and free speech, he was able to influence an audience well beyond those who were already committed to the left.

After his cardiac symptoms worsened Miliband had a heart by-pass operation in 1991. However, this was unsuccessful, and he died in London on 21 May 1994. He was buried there six days later. He was survived by his wife and two sons.   MICHAEL NEWMAN

Sources private information (2004) · M. Newman, *Ralph Miliband and the politics of the new left* (2002) · priv. coll., R. Miliband MSS · L. Panitch, 'Ralph Milibrand: socialist intellectual, 1924–1994', *Why not capitalism?*, ed. L. Panitch and others (1995) · R. Blackburn, 'Ralph Miliband, 1924–1994', *New Left Review*, 206 (July/Aug 1994) · L. Chun, *The British new left* (1993) · M. Kenny, *The first new left* (1995) · *The Times* (10 June 1994) · *The Independent* (24 May 1994) · b. cert.
Archives priv. coll. | FILM BBC WAC · BFI NFTVA | SOUND City University of New York, interview recordings, 30 Sept 1992 · Sussex tapes 1991
Likenesses photograph, News International Syndication, London [*see illus.*] · photograph, repro. in *The Independent*
Wealth at death £353,000: probate, 23 Nov 1994, *CGPLA Eng. & Wales*

Mill [*née* Hardy; *other married name* Taylor], **Harriet** (1807–1858), advocate of sexual equality, was born on 10 October 1807 at 18 Beckford Row, Walworth, in south London, daughter of Harriet (*née* Hurst) and Thomas Hardy (*d.* 1849), surgeon and 'man-midwife' of Walworth. Harriet Hurst's family lived in Walworth; they were of cavalier stock and very proud of their lineage. Thomas Hardy's family were of the gentry, with lands in Yorkshire, which Thomas was to inherit in 1836. At the time of his daughter's birth Thomas had been for five years a member of the Royal College of Surgeons and was practising in Walworth. Harriet was the middle child, with five brothers and a younger sister; only with her youngest brother, Arthur, did Harriet remain on good terms. She appears to have been educated at home; at least no outside schooling is known. On 14 March 1826, at the age of eighteen, she married John Taylor (1796–1849) of Islington, eleven years her senior and a partner in a family firm of wholesale druggists in the City of London; they had three children: Herbert (*b.* 1827), Algernon (*b.* 1830), and Helen *Taylor (1831–1907). The Taylors' first home was at 4 Christopher Street, Finsbury, close to the family firm and the Unitarian chapel at South Place, which they attended. At the end of 1832 they moved to 17 Kent Terrace, Regent's Park.

Although there is a tradition that Harriet Hardy married John Taylor solely to escape from a home dominated by an irascible father, the few extant letters from the first years of their marriage show great affection between Harriet and John Taylor, and affection would appear to have remained the hallmark of all the years of what was to become an unconventional domestic life. They remained

Harriet Mill [Taylor] (**1807–1858**), by unknown artist, *c*.1834

on friendly terms, celebrating together family events and writing frequently, especially when she was travelling.

In the early years of their marriage Harriet and John Taylor had, through their Unitarian connections, become the centre of a small circle of radicals; in this group Harriet Taylor was an outspoken and passionate advocate of completely equal rights for women and men. One of their circle was William Johnson Fox, minister at South Place Chapel and editor of the advanced and feminist *Monthly Repository*, and it was he, probably near the end of 1830, who was asked to bring John Stuart *Mill (1806–1873) to one of the frequent dinners at the hospitable and congenial Taylor home. Fox's daughter gave in her memoirs a description of Harriet Taylor as she remembered her in these years:

> Mrs. Taylor at this date, when she was, perhaps about five and twenty years of age, was possessed of a beauty and grace quite unique of their kind. Tall and slight, with a slightly drooping figure, the movements of undulating grace. A small head, a swan-like throat, and a complexion like a pearl. Large eyes, not soft or sleepy, but with a look of quiet command in them. A low sweet voice with very distinct utterance emphasized the effect of her engrossing personality. Her children idolized her. (Hayek, 25)

And not only her children; John Stuart Mill too idolized her. The attraction between Harriet Taylor and John Stuart Mill was immediate, intellectually fired by their shared views about social, educational, and political reform, especially the removal of the legal disabilities imposed on women. It was for them both an intimate and lasting friendship at first sight.

In 1833 Harriet Taylor and Mill travelled to Paris together; after some weeks she decided a complete break

with her husband would bring 'insupportable unhappiness' (Mill to W. J. Fox, 5 or 6 Nov 1833; *Collected Works*, 12.188). Some time in the late 1830s John Taylor agreed to her having her own establishment, and she moved with her daughter, first (probably for only a short time) to Keston Heath, Bromley, Kent, and in the late 1830s to Walton-on-Thames, 17 miles south-west of London in Surrey. (Algernon seems to have lived with them at least part of the time in his earlier years; Herbert lived with his father.) John Taylor stayed in Kent Terrace; John Stuart Mill remained at home in Kensington with his parents and siblings. Trying to avoid the gossip this *déménage à trois* excited, and suffering from ill health, Harriet Taylor lived away from society, seeing only a few close friends including, of course, John Stuart Mill frequently, and her husband occasionally. As her lungs became worse, she made a number of tours in Europe seeking a warmer, drier climate, accompanied by her daughter and sometimes by Mill; she also spent part of several winters in the south of England.

In May of 1849, when John Taylor told her he was dying of cancer, Harriet Taylor returned to Kent Terrace to nurse him until his death two months later. After a suitable interval she married John Stuart Mill on 21 April 1851. They lived in Blackheath Park, south-east of London; Helen also lived there, continuing to take care of her mother and the household. In October 1858, after Mill's retirement from the East India Company on its being taken over by the crown, the Mills travelled to the south of France for her health. But to no avail: Harriet Mill died of a haemorrhage of the lungs on 3 November 1858 at the Hotel de l'Europe, Avignon. Mill wrote: 'while she lived, she never sought to be known beyond her small circle of intimates' (Mill to A. Ruge, 2 March 1859; *Collected Works*, 15.598).

It is not easy to estimate the importance and influence of a reclusive woman who wrote little; if there had been no John Stuart Mill, Harriet Mill would not be remembered. But there was, and her influence on and through Mill was great, changing his reasoned conviction that 'complete equality in all legal, political, social and domestic relations … ought to exist between men and women' into a crusade for the improvement of mankind. He had held these advanced views before he met her, but it was she who showed him the practical consequences of the lack of equality, 'the mode in which the consequences of the inferior position of women intertwine themselves with all the evils of the existing society and with the difficulties of human improvement' (*Collected Works*, 1.252). This aspect of her influence is not unexpected, for her early essay on marriage, written probably for Mill in 1834 and not for publication, shows a young woman more strongly influenced by the Romantic movement than by any formal education, but acutely aware of the everyday effects on women and on men, especially in the married state, of women's social inequality. There can be little reason to doubt that it was she who convinced Mill that the complete equality of the sexes before the law—the argument later developed in *The Subjection of Women*—was the next immediate and essential rung on the ladder to the hoped-for heaven that was their shared vision.

The little that Harriet is known to have published does not refute Mill's estimate of her influence on him, although it makes credence in her genius difficult. She wrote eleven pieces for the *Monthly Repository* (one in 1831 and ten in 1832): critical notices, poems and mood pieces, reviews and historical essays, all short. Her most substantial essay, *The Enfranchisement of Women*, was published under John Stuart Mill's name in the *Westminster Review* (55, 1851, 298–311); in it she claimed for women 'their admission, in law and in fact, to equality in all rights, political, civil, and social, with the male citizens of the community'. She argued that without equality between the sexes, society would remain tyrannical and corrupt; this argument was to be developed in the Mills' joint productions.

Harriet published nothing else on her own, but she unquestionably wrote or dictated part of the letters they wrote together to the newspapers (mostly to the *Morning Chronicle*) in 1846 and the early 1850s in response to reported cases of domestic brutality. There is evidence from these letters and also from drafts surviving in their papers that at this time they were attempting to work out together the practical consequences of sexual inequality, which Harriet Mill had touched on in *The Enfranchisement*. In the letters they emphasized the importance of domestic practices in corrupting or improving society. They had come to believe that the prevalence and acceptance of domestic brutality, especially among the English working classes, and its lenient treatment in the courts helped explain empirically why some hopes held nearly twenty years earlier by the band of visionaries writing for the *Monthly Repository* had not materialized. Women's legal inequality resulted in injustice and tyranny in the home, reflected not only in the relations between husbands and wives but also in the treatment and upbringing of children. These brutal qualities, imbibed from birth, permeated social attitudes at all levels and in all areas. They were convinced that the slavery in family life was the root cause for the failure of reforms to effect fundamental improvements in society and that thus it had a profound, historically crucial, effect on society.

Harriet Mill's share in and influence on John Stuart Mill's major works cannot be documented precisely with chapter and verse. She read and commented on the draft of his *Principles of Political Economy* (1848): Mill's dedication of the book to her—a dedication John Taylor would not allow to be printed (*Collected Works*, 3.1026, n. 2)—and his attribution to her prompting of the chapter 'On the probable futurity of the working classes' bear ample testimony to her part in this work. And one can attribute to her at least the heightening of his awareness that

> From an imperfection in our language … there is often almost a necessity for using the masculine *pronoun* where both sexes are equally concerned, but seldom the masculine *substantive*. The effect upon the mind of this phraseology is bad; it encourages the habit of *passing by* one-half of the race as not concerned in its highest interests. (*The Examiner*, 1 June 1834)

Although Mill continued in his own work to sanction the practice, a silent but significant change occurred at the time of his marriage. In the revision for the third edition of his *Logic* (1851) and of his *Principles of Political Economy* (1852) he systematically altered, in gender-neutral contexts, 'men' to 'people' or 'mankind' (to him evidently a neutral term), and 'a man' and 'he' to 'a person'. He also added an explicit footnote in that edition of the *Logic* referring 'to the almost universal habit, of thinking and speaking of one-half the human species as the whole' (*Collected Works*, 8.837 n).

As their health, particularly Harriet's, became of increasing concern, they planned together the future publications on which John Stuart Mill should work, one of them being *On Liberty* (1859). On it Harriet's influence is usually acknowledged—certainly it contains ideas she expressed in her earliest unpublished writings; but of the works which Mill wrote after his wife's death *The Subjection of Women* (1869) shows most undeniably her influence. The argument of the book is simple and straightforward, and is clearly a fulfilment of the idea, which Mill attributes to her early influence on him and which they had been developing together in the 1850s,

> That the principle which regulates the existing social relations between the two sexes—the legal subordination of one sex to the other—is wrong in itself, and now one of the chief hindrances to human improvement; and that it ought to be replaced by a principle of perfect equality, admitting no power or privilege on the one side, nor disability on the other. (*Collected Works*, 21.259)

There are strong echoes of Harriet Mill's phrasing in her early unfinished pieces on marriage in *The Enfranchisement*, and in the newspaper letters they wrote together; the themes of male tyranny, domestic slavery, the husband's ownership of his wife and family, and domestic brutality set the tone of *The Subjection of Women*:

> [H]owever brutal a tyrant she may unfortunately be chained to—though she may know that he hates her, though it may be his daily pleasure to torture her, and though she may feel it impossible not to loathe him—he can claim from her and enforce the lowest degradation of a human being, that of being made the instrument of an animal function contrary to her inclinations. (*Collected Works*, 21.285)

Harriet Mill's posthumous influence can also be seen in the activities of John Stuart Mill and her daughter Helen Taylor in furthering the suffrage cause. John Stuart Mill's amendment to the second Reform Bill on 27 May 1867, to replace the word 'man' with 'person', bears a singular resemblance to his earlier amendments to his own editions, and the arguments are many of them similar to those in Harriet Mill's article (but it must be said these arguments were the common coin of many suffragists by the 1860s). John Stuart Mill was honorary president of the first London suffrage society, and both he and Helen Taylor worked hard behind the scenes and spoke at public meetings for the society. The bond that joined John Stuart Mill and his stepdaughter and motivated them was their common devotion to Harriet Mill. John Stuart Mill bought a house overlooking her grave in Avignon, where they lived for six months of each year. There and in London

John Stuart Mill and Helen Taylor laboured to advance the ideas they had shared with 'her'. Mill and Taylor stood together at the graveside when the huge slab of finest Carrara marble was lowered onto the top of Harriet Mill's grave. There Mill had writ in stone:

To the beloved memory of Harriet Mill, the dearly beloved and deeply regretted wife of John Stuart Mill. Her great and loving heart, her noble soul, her clear, powerful and original comprehensive intellect made her the guide and support, the instructor in wisdom and the example of goodness, as she was the sole earthly delight, of those who had the happiness to belong to her. As earnest for the public good as she was generous and devoted to all who surrounded her, her influence has been felt in many of the greatest improvements of the age and will be in those still to come. Were there but a few hearts and intellects like hers this earth would already become the hoped-for heaven. She died, to the irreparable loss of those who survive her, at Avignon, Nov. 3 1858.

ANN P. ROBSON

Sources *Sexual equality: writings by John Stuart Mill, Harriet Taylor Mill, and Helen Taylor*, ed. A. P. Robson and J. M. Robson (1994) • *John Stuart Mill and Harriet Taylor: their correspondence and subsequent marriage*, ed. F. A. Hayek (1951) • M. St J. Packe, *The life of John Stuart Mill* (1954) • J. Kamm, *John Stuart Mill in love* (1977) • *The collected works of John Stuart Mill*, ed. J. M. Robson and others, 33 vols. (1963–91) **Archives** BLPES **Likenesses** oils, *c*.1834, NPG [*see illus.*] • two miniatures, *c*.1844, BLPES **Wealth at death** under £100: probate, 9 Dec 1858, CGPLA Eng. & Wales

Mill, Henry (*bap.* 1683, *d.* 1770), surveyor and engineer, was baptized on 12 April 1683 in the church of St Ann Blackfriars, London, the son of Andrew and Dorothy Mill. He was of the Mill family of Camois Court, Sussex, and a collateral descendant of Sir Hugh Myddleton. It was probably owing to this connection that he was appointed engineer to the New River Company in 1720. He had by then received a liberal education and acquired a knowledge of mechanics as well as experience in hydraulics, having undertaken the water supply to Houghton Hall, in Norfolk, for Sir Robert Walpole.

Mill's interest in mechanics led to his filing two patents, one in 1706 for improvements in carriage springs, the other in 1714 for an apparatus 'for impressing or transcribing of letters singly or progressively one after another, so neat and exact as not to be distinguished from print, very useful in settlements and public records' (patent no. 395, 1714, Spec.). Mill's specification did not detail the workings of this device, which some have claimed as the first proposal for a typewriter, nor is it known if he pursued either of these ideas.

One of Mill's first tasks for the New River Company, which conveyed fresh water from Hertfordshire to the cities of London and Westminster, was a survey in 1723 of the course of the river, which followed the ground contour for nearly 39 miles from the source to Islington, a distance of only 20 miles as the crow flies. Mill appears to have done something to shorten its course. He was unmarried and lived for most of his life in lodgings in the Strand, close to the company's offices off Fleet Street. His assistant there

was Robert Mylne FRS, who rebuilt the offices after a disastrous fire in 1769 when many records perished. When a stroke incapacitated Mill in his old age, Mylne acted on his behalf, and when Mill died after some fifty years in the company's service, succeeded him as engineer.

Mill died at his lodgings in the Strand on 26 December 1770, following another stroke. His effects were sold at auction on 18–19 April 1771. These included the furniture and ornaments appropriate to a tastefully furnished bachelor home and a multitude of timepieces—two clocks, a large striking watch, and ten other watches, several with precious metals—besides his extensive collection of surveying apparatus. He was buried, as he had requested, in Breamore churchyard, near Salisbury, where a long epitaph was set up in his memory.

ANITA McCONNELL

Sources GM, 1st ser., 49 (1779), 537–9 • private information (1894) • W. Betham, *The baronetage of England*, 5 vols. (1801–5) • H. W. Dickinson, *Water supply of Greater London* (1954), 40 • [S. Paterson], *A catalogue of the genuine household furniture, philosophical and mathematical instruments … of Henry Mill* (1771) [sale catalogue, London, 18–19 April 1771] • parish register (baptism), 12 Apr 1683, London, St Ann Blackfriars

Mill, Hugh Robert (1861–1950), geographer, was born on 28 May 1861 at Sutherland Street, Thurso, Caithness, the tenth of the eleven children of James Mill (1808–1873), physician and farmer, and his wife, Harriet Gordon (1824–1911), elder daughter of the Revd George Davidson of Latheron, Caithness, and his wife, Maria Serena. His parents were both Scottish. Mill was educated at home from the age of nine as he suffered from tuberculosis. He moved with his widowed mother to Edinburgh in 1877 and attended evening classes at the Watt Institution and School of Art. His interests included chemistry, meteorology, oceanography, and the polar regions, but geography came to dominate his life. Even so, it was chemistry that took Mill in 1880 to Edinburgh University, from where he graduated in 1883. In the following year he was awarded one of three fellowships provided by the Scottish marine station (recently set up at Granton, on the Firth of Forth) and was appointed chemist and physicist there, working mainly on the chemistry and temperature of coastal waters. For this work he was in 1885 elected FRS Edinburgh and in 1886 was awarded the degree of DSc by Edinburgh University.

During his time at Granton, Mill's interests grew: in meteorology, by being put in charge of observations under the supervision of Alexander Buchan, and by contact with John Aitken, who was working on the part played by nuclei on rain formation, as well as experimenting with thermometer screens; in oceanography and geography, through contact with world leaders who came to the station, and in writing a short history of oceanography as an introduction to the narrative of the *Challenger* expedition, and in helping to found the Scottish Geographical Society; and in polar studies through friendship with the station's director, John Murray. By 1887 the hold of chemistry had begun to wane and Mill looked towards geography for a living. He became a lecturer in physiography at Heriot-Watt College and an extension lecturer at the universities of Edinburgh and St Andrews. In 1888 his *Elementary Commercial Geography* was published, and in 1891 *The Realm of Nature*—a textbook of physical geography that Mill considered his best work. He married his second cousin Frances (*d*. 1929), daughter of Dr Francis Robertson MacDonald, on 18 April 1889.

Mill moved to London in 1892 on appointment as librarian to the Royal Geographical Society. He hoped that the post would give him the livelihood he could not expect from marine research while allowing him to pursue his scientific interests, especially into the influence of topography on mobile populations, and to promote a more rigorous approach to geography in schools and among the public. At the Royal Geographical Society, he not only arranged new subject and author catalogues but also assisted in organizing and advising on Antarctic research, including the scientific equipping of ships and preparation of the bibliography in *The Antarctic Manual for the Use of the Expedition of 1901*. However, he was himself barred from participating by defective sight. While at the society, in 1893 he became recorder of section E (geography) of the British Association, with the task of arranging subjects and speakers, and he also began to assist the newly formed Geographical Association, whose aim was to improve the teaching of geography in schools. He assisted in the pioneer mapping of the depths of English lakes, and he put forward an ambitious plan to prepare a geography of Britain based on the records of the Ordnance Survey and incorporating agricultural and meteorological statistics, but it failed to get support.

In 1900 Mill was awarded the degree of LLD by the University of St Andrews, and in the same year he resigned as librarian to become, in the following year, joint director of the British Rainfall Organization, the body which directed and collated the meteorological observations from some 3000 volunteer observers throughout the British Isles. He planned to give it new life by making scientific research its main aim, particularly the problem of topographic control of rainfall distribution. His other interests remained, however, for in the same year he became president of section E of the British Association, as well as British representative on the International Council for the Study of the Sea, whose aim was to frame rules for ensuring the permanence of the fisheries in the North Sea and the Atlantic margin. In 1903 Mill became sole director of the British Rainfall Organization, but by 1910, because of failing health, he had to transfer the organization's assets to trustees. This gained time for research, including a start on a 50-year average rainfall map, which, however, had to be abandoned. In the meantime he was elected president of the Royal Meteorological Society (1907–8). He also made a significant contribution to polar history in *The Siege of the South Pole: the Story of Antarctic Exploration* (1905), a result of thirty years' reading. Following the sinking of the *Titanic* in 1912 Mill advised the government that a ship should monitor the ocean north of the shipping route during the ice season and provide warnings. His plan was adopted.

In 1919 Mill retired and he concentrated his interests in polar regions. He was an acknowledged expert on Antarctic exploration though he had never been to polar regions, and became a friend, adviser, and inspirer of many explorers, as well as a storehouse of information. Having become a friend of Ernest Shackleton since instructing him on meteorological and oceanographic observations on the way to Madeira at the start of Scott's 1901–4 expedition, Mill wrote *The Life of Sir Ernest Shackleton* (1923). He acquired an extensive library of books on the Antarctic, principally accounts of individual expeditions but also historical and descriptive works. These he later deposited at the Scott Polar Research Institute. In 1932 he was made commander of the Norwegian order of St Olav for help in polar exploration. Mill's geographical connections continued. He was elected vice-president of the Royal Geographical Society (1927–32) and president of the Geographical Association (1933); in his presidential addresses (1933 and 1934) he gave the final form of his ideas on the nature of geography. He was then almost blind—an affliction that had caused him to decline the presidency of the Royal Geographical Society in 1933. (He had been awarded its Victoria medal in 1915.) Nevertheless, he was able to prepare his last major publication, *The Record of the Royal Geographical Society 1830–1930*. Eight years after the death of his first wife he married his former secretary, Alfreda, daughter of Frederick Dransfield of Darton, Yorkshire, on 21 August 1937.

Mill wrote an autobiography, which was published in 1951, soon after his death on 5 April 1950 at his home, Hill Crest, Dormans Park, Sussex. His second wife survived him. Just before his death Mill was awarded the first Hugh Robert Mill medal (1950), created by the Royal Meteorological Society in his honour. Mill was one of several Scottish geographers of the late nineteenth and early twentieth centuries who regarded geography as a sternly practical pursuit which brought scientific rigour to the study of the mutual relations of land and people.

DAVID E. PEDGLEY

Sources H. R. Mill, *An autobiography* [1951] · H. R. Mill, 'Meteorological memories', *Quarterly Journal of the Royal Meteorological Society*, 67 (1941), 315–26 · H. R. Mill, 'Acknowledgement of presentation of Hugh Robert Mill medal and prize', *Quarterly Journal of the Royal Meteorological Society*, 76 (1950), 505–6 · R. N. R. Brown, 'Hugh Robert Mill', *Geography*, 35 (1950), 124–6 · G. R. C. [G. R. Crone], 'Hugh Robert Mill', *GJ*, 115 (1950), 266–7 · J. M. W. [J. M. Wordie], 'Hugh Robert Mill: an appreciation', *Polar Record*, 6 (1951–3), 5–6 · E. L. H. [E. L. Hawke], *Quarterly Journal of the Royal Meteorological Society*, 76 (1950), 356–8 · D. N. Livingstone, *The geographical tradition* (1992)

Archives RGS, corresp. · Scott Polar RI, corresp. and papers | Meteorological Office, Bracknell, Berkshire, National Meteorological Library and Archive, fee book as member of Royal Meteorological Society · NL Scot., corresp. with J. G. Bartholomew · NL Scot., corresp. with Sir Patrick Geddes and Sir J. M. Wordie · Scott Polar RI, letters to William Spiers Bruce

Likenesses Debenham & Gould, photograph, *c*.1930, Scott Polar RI · two photographs, *c*.1930, RGS · photograph, *c*.1940, Scott Polar RI · photograph, Scott Polar RI · photograph, Royal Meteorological Society, Reading, Berkshire · photograph, University of Strathclyde, Glasgow, Royal Scottish Geographical Society

Wealth at death £20,004 6s. 10d.: probate, 15 June 1950, *CGPLA Eng. & Wales*

Mill, Humphrey (*fl.* **1639–1646**), poet, was probably a younger brother of Thomas Mill or Mille (1604–1650), the son of William Mille of Grattam, Sussex, who matriculated at Queen's College, Oxford, on 8 December 1620. Humphrey Mill published *Poems Occasioned by a Melancholy Vision, or, A Melancholy Vision upon Divers Theames Enlarged* (1639). This work, which the author describes as 'the first fruits of his poore indeavours in this kinde', is dedicated to Thomas, earl of Winchilsea. It has an engraved title by Droeshout. A more interesting work is his poem which investigates and comments on the suspicious or criminal behaviour of those who plied their trade at night. It is entitled *A nights search. Discovering the nature and condition of all sorts of night-walkers; with their associates. As also the life and death of many of them together with divers fearful and strange accidents occasioned by all such ill livers; digested into a poem* (1640). This is dedicated to the earl of Essex and contains commendatory lines by the author's brother, Thomas Mill MA (Oxford), Thomas Heywood, Thomas Nabbs, Robert Chamberlain, Richard Broome, and others. It has also an engraved title in compartments.

Mill had sufficient material to publish in 1646 *The second part of the nights search discovering the condition of the various fowles of night, or, The second great mystery of iniquity exactly revealed* .... This is dedicated to Robert, earl of Warwick, and has an engraved title in compartments, one of which contains a portrait of the author. It must have been popular for it went into a second edition in 1652. The 'night-walker' was a title with an extremely broad term of reference which stretched to cover a multitude of characters and situations, mainly concerned with disreputable careers and personalities. By the 1640s, when Mill was writing, the title was closely associated with 'lewd women wandring the streets', and therefore a badge of disordered femininity in seventeenth-century London. Mill's work, therefore, is a valuable contemporary discourse communicating several anxieties, all of which were of essential concern to the ordering of early modern society.

GEORGE THORN-DRURY, *rev.* JOANNA MOODY

Sources Watt, *Bibl. Brit.* · W. T. Lowndes, *The bibliographer's manual of English literature*, ed. H. G. Bohn, [new edn], 2 (1864), 1549 · F. W. Bateson, *The Cambridge bibliography of English literature*, 1 (1940), 477 · P. Griffiths, 'Meanings of night walking in early modern England', *Seventeenth Century*, 13 (1998), 212–38 · Foster, *Alum. Oxon.*
Likenesses etching, BM, NPG; repro. in H. Mill, *The second part of the nights search* (1646)

Mill, James (*fl.* **1744**), writer on India, details of whose parentage and upbringing are unknown, in 1744 submitted to Francis II, grand duke of Tuscany and husband of the empress Maria Theresa, a plan for the conquest of India, Francis being then commander of the imperial forces pitted against the Turks. Mill's proposal (which appears in the appendix of William Bolts's *Considerations on India Affairs*, 1772) claimed that the Mughal empire was both extremely wealthy and poorly defended. It was, he argued, possible for a force of no more than three ships and 1500–2000 men to secure Bengal. Mill spoke of the British government's willingness to co-operate in return for a share of the wealth, though he advised Francis that the East India Company be kept out of negotiations. Nothing is known of Mill's career; in April 1743 the *Gentleman's Magazine* (13.275) noted the promotion of a 'James Mills esq' as captain and second in command of the East India Company's military in Bengal. Bolts described Mill as a colonel with twenty years' service in India.

H. M. CHICHESTER, *rev.* PHILIP CARTER

Sources W. Bolts, *Considerations on India affairs, particularly respecting the present state of Bengal and its dependencies* (1772) · *GM*, 1st ser., 13 (1743), 275

Mill, James (**1773–1836**), political philosopher, was born on 6 April 1773 at Northwater Bridge, in the parish of Logie Pert, Forfarshire, Scotland. He was the son of James Mill (*d.* 1808), formerly known as Milne, a country shoemaker and small-holder, and his wife, Isabel Fenton Mill (1755–1801), daughter of a farmer from Kirriemuir. Socially ambitious, and believing that she had married beneath her station, she changed the family name from the Scottish Milne to the more English-sounding Mill, and resolved to raise her first-born son to be a gentleman.

Early years and education Mill's mother kept him away from other children, demanding that he spend most of his waking hours immersed in study. Unlike his younger brother William and sister May, he was exempted from household chores. Study was his only occupation. A similar regimen was later imposed upon his own first-born son, John Stuart *Mill. By his seventh year he had shown a talent for elocution, composition, arithmetic, and languages, Latin and Greek in particular. A star pupil, he received special attention at the parish school. At the age of ten or eleven he was sent to Montrose Academy, where he excelled in his studies. It was there that Mill met his lifelong friend and later political ally, the radical politician Joseph Hume (1777–1855). Some time before leaving Montrose Academy at the age of seventeen, Mill was persuaded by his mother and the parish minister to study for the ministry. He was assured of support for his studies by Jane Stuart, wife of Sir John Stuart of Fettercairn and patron of a local charity founded for the purpose of educating poor but promising boys for the Presbyterian ministry. She and Sir John were just then looking for a tutor for their fourteen-year-old daughter Wilhelmina. They offered the post to James Mill; he accepted; and when the Stuart family moved to Edinburgh, he accompanied them.

After enrolling in Edinburgh University in the autumn of 1790, Mill pursued a full course of studies while presiding over the education of young Wilhelmina. Each experience made its mark. The Scottish universities at Edinburgh and Glasgow (and to a lesser extent Aberdeen and St Andrews) had been the centre of the Scottish Enlightenment and were still the premier universities in Britain. At Edinburgh Dugald Stewart, under whom Mill studied, carried on the tradition of Scottish moral philosophy. Mill's course of studies also comprised history, political economy, and the classics, including his favourite author, Plato. He was also a keen student of the natural sciences, and formed a lasting friendship with Thomas Thompson,

James Mill (1773–1836), by unknown artist

the eminent chemist. Mill's mind never lost the impress of his Scottish education, which was remarkable both for its range and its rigour.

From 1790 to 1794 Mill served Wilhelmina Stuart as tutor, companion, and confidant. Her admiration grew apace and quite likely turned to love, and the feeling was apparently reciprocated. As his biographer rather coyly observes, the beautiful Wilhelmina 'had reached an interesting age, and made a lasting impression on his mind' (Bain, 24). But that match was not to be. However promising his prospects, Mill was no aristocrat, a social fact that he was not allowed to forget. In 1797 Wilhelmina married Sir William Forbes, seventh baronet, of Pitsligo. She died in 1810, calling out Mill's name 'with her last breath' (*DNB*). Mill never forgot her; he spoke of her always with wistful affection and named his first-born daughter after her.

After receiving his undergraduate degree in 1794 Mill began studying for the ministry. Licensed to preach in 1798, he was for a time an itinerant preacher whose sermons were said to be learned but largely incomprehensible to his hapless parishioners. Belonging as he did to the liberal wing of the Scottish church, Mill's sermons lacked the fire and enthusiasm of his evangelical brethren. 'I've heard him preach', said Sir David Brewster, 'and no great han' he made o't' (Bain, 22). Unable to secure a permanent position, Mill was forced to support himself by tutoring the sons and daughters of several noble families. The experience embittered him. He harboured ever after a hatred for hereditary aristocracy. Mill had by the early 1800s become restless and disillusioned, and in 1802

he left for London, hoping to begin a career outside the kirk. He travelled in the company of his friend and patron Sir John Stuart, who was about to take his seat in parliament as MP for Kincardineshire.

When Mill left for London he was twenty-nine and, his biographer says,

> a youth of great bodily charms. One of my lady informants spoke of him with a quite rapturous admiration of his beauty. His figure and proportions were fine; the short breeches of the time showed a leg of perfect form. His features beamed with expression. Nothing was wanting that could prepossess people's favourable regards.　(Bain, 35)

Mill was of middling height (5 feet 8 inches) and sinewy stature. He had a prominent forehead, curly brown hair, and large and lively light grey eyes set in an expressive face. He was energetic to the point of nervousness, impatient, and constitutionally incapable of rest, still less of relaxation. Intellectually, he was well armed and unable to suffer fools gladly, or at all.

Life in London Arriving in London, Mill was full of schemes for improving his situation. He briefly considered a career as a lawyer and then as a teacher. Nothing came of these, however, and he had to eke out a precarious living as a freelance journalist and literary hack. He contributed articles to the *Anti-Jacobin Review*, edited by John Gifford, and subsequently became editor of the fledgeling *Literary Journal* and then the *St James's Chronicle*. He lived frugally, his only entertainments being long walks and, as Sir John Stuart's guest, watching debates from the gallery in the House of Commons. The latter kindled a passion for politics that never left him.

Mill's political views were almost certainly more radical—that is, egalitarian and democratic—than those of the journals for which he wrote. He had a slightly freer hand in writing penny pamphlets, the first of which was *An Essay on the Impolicy of a Bounty on the Exportation of Grain* (1804). This was followed a year later by his translation of C. Viller's *The Reformation* (1805), a work whose anti-Catholic and anti-clerical leanings were very much to Mill's taste, as his copious notes attest. Mill's mature religious views veered sharply away from the orthodoxy of his youth. He had the dissenter's distaste for creeds, oaths, and dogmas of every description. But, more than that, he became a thoroughgoing sceptic who saw religion, suitably reformed, as an instrument of political education and social control (see Ball, chap. 6).

Two years after his arrival in London, Mill was well established if not yet prosperous, earning approximately £500 annually. In 1804 he became engaged to Harriet Burrow (1783–1854), daughter of a widow who ran a lunatic asylum in Hoxton. When they married on 5 June 1805 Mill was thirty-one and she twenty-two and exceptionally beautiful, if not especially bright. The couple rented a house at 12 Rodney Terrace, Pentonville, from Mill's mother-in-law, for £50 per year. On 20 May 1806 Mrs Mill gave birth to their first child, a son named John Stuart in honour of his father's Scottish patron. John Stuart Mill was the first of a brood of nine 'brats' produced by a father who strongly favoured birth control and recommended abstinence as the best method. The others were: Wilhelmina Forbes, named after Sir John and Lady Jane Stuart's only daughter (*d.* 1861); Clara; Harriet; James Bentham (*d.* 1862), who was named after Jeremy Bentham and entered the Indian Civil Service in 1835; Jane, named after Lady Jane Stuart; Henry (*d.* 1840), whom his eldest brother called 'the noblest and worthiest of us all'; Mary; and George Grote (*d.* 1853), named after Mill's friend George Grote, the historian of Greece, who followed his father and eldest brother into the India Office.

Mill's marriage was not a happy one. He had little patience with his slow-witted wife, and hardly more for his children. Tutored daily by his father from the age of three, John was in turn expected to teach his younger brothers and sisters. Each was examined rigorously and regularly by their father, and the children, like their mother, lived in dread of his rebuke. Although the elder Mill mellowed in his later years, as his fear of financial ruin abated, his older children remembered him mainly for his stern temper. John Stuart Mill remarks that his father's 'temper was constitutionally irritable' and recalls growing up 'in the absence of love and in the presence of fear' (J. S. Mill, 32–3). And his sister Harriet wrote of their mother and father

> living as far apart under the same roof, as the north pole from the south; from no 'fault' of my mother certainly; but how was a woman with a growing family and a very small means (as in the early years of their marriage) to be anything but a German Hausfrau? How could she intellectually become a companion for such a mind as my father? *His* great want was 'temper'.   (F. A. Hayek, *John Stuart Mill and Harriet Taylor*, 1951, 286)

Mill's relations with his family in Scotland were similarly strained. His mother had died shortly before he left Scotland; soon thereafter his father became paralysed (possibly the result of a stroke) and, because he had given security to a friend, bankrupt. Mill's brother William died in 1803, leaving his sister May to look after their ailing father until his death in 1808. Although Mill paid off his father's debts and sent such money as he could to relieve their distress, his sister complained that it was not enough. Given Mill's own straitened circumstances, however, he appears to have acted honourably and even generously.

In stark contrast with Mill's difficult relations with his family were those he had with his friends. He was a genial and generous friend with a wide and remarkably diverse circle of acquaintances. He counted among his friends and allies Henry Brougham, David Ricardo, Joseph Hume, Albany Fonblanque (the editor of *The Examiner*), Henry Bickersteth, the political activist Francis Place, the Quaker editor of *The Philanthropist* William Allen, and John Black, editor of the *Morning Chronicle*. He had a profound impact on several younger men, including the historian of Greece George Grote, John and Charles Austin, William Ellis, Walter Coulson, John Arthur Roebuck, William Molesworth, and Charles Buller. As John Black recalled in 1836:

> Mr. Mill was eloquent and impressive in conversation. He had a great command of language, which bore the stamp of his earnest and energetic character. Young men were particularly fond of his society and it was always to him a source of great delight to have an opportunity of contributing to form their minds and exalt their characters. No man could enjoy his society without catching a portion of his elevated enthusiasm. Many of the men in whom the country now places its warmest hopes benefited largely by the enlightened society of Mr. Mill.   (Bain, 457)

Mill's *History of British India*   In 1806 Mill began writing his monumental *History of British India*. He expected the project to take three years; in the event it took twelve, finally appearing in three fat volumes early in 1818. It was an immediate success, and secured for Mill what he had long lacked: a modicum of prosperity. Better still, it led—with help from Joseph Hume and Ricardo—to his appointment in 1819 as assistant (later chief) examiner of correspondence at the British East India Company at an annual salary of £800, which, by the time of his death in 1836, had risen to £2000.

Mill's *History of British India* begins with a remarkable preface. He says that his never having been to India and knowing none of the native languages are an advantage, and a guarantee of his objectivity. But, far from being objective, his is, as he says, a 'critical, or judging history' whose judgements on Hindu customs and practices are particularly harsh. He denounces their 'rude' and 'backward' culture for its ignorance, superstition, and mistreatment of women, and leaves no doubt that he favours a thoroughgoing reform of Indian institutions and practices. Many a critic has complained that Mill's *History* is dry and largely devoid of human interest. Riveting narrative was not his forte, nor does he paint memorable, or even interesting, portraits of Robert Clive, Warren Hastings, and the other larger-than-life characters who figure in the history of British India. His is a story of ideas and institutions, of historical stages and processes, more than of flesh-and-blood human beings and the din of battle. But, because it filled a need and there were no comparable competitors in the field, this monochromatic *History* was to go through many editions and became the standard nineteenth-century reference work on the subject.

Benthamite propagandist   In late 1807 or early 1808 Mill entered into the most important political and philosophical alliance of his life. He met Jeremy Bentham, the brilliant, eccentric, and reclusive utilitarian philosopher and legal reformer. Despite differences of age, temperament, and background, the two were alike in favouring religious toleration, legal reform, and freedom of speech and press; both feared that the failure to reform the British political system—by, among other things, extending the franchise—would give rise to reactionary intransigence on the one hand, and revolutionary excess on the other. In other respects, however, the two men were vastly different. Bentham, a wealthy bachelor, was a closeted philosopher who fancied himself a modern lawgiver and man of the world. Mill, poor, harried, and hard-working, was by far the more practical and worldly of the two. Bentham soon saw Mill as an indispensable ally and, wishing to have him nearer at hand, invited him and his family to spend summers with him at his country homes at Barrow Green House, near Oxted, Surrey, and later at Ford Abbey, near Chard, in Somerset. The rest of the year was spent in London, where Bentham let Mill a nearby house in Westminster at 1 Queen Square (later 40 Queen Anne's Gate) for £50 per year. Such intimacy, although mutually advantageous, was also a source of some friction. Mill, swallowing his pride and subordinating his will to Bentham's, became Bentham's chief disciple. It cannot have been easy work.

The critic William Hazlitt, upon learning that one of Bentham's books had been translated into French, quipped that someone should translate Bentham into English. That, in effect, is exactly what Mill did. He (and later his eldest son) edited and revised a number of Bentham's scattered and often inchoate manuscripts, including the *Introduction to the Rationale of Evidence* and the *Table of the Springs of Action*. Mill was an energetic organizer and motivator-in-chief. As Halévy notes, 'Bentham gave Mill a doctrine, and Mill gave Bentham a school' (Halévy, 251). Moreover, Mill contributed numerous reviews and articles in the utilitarian cause to the *Edinburgh Review*, *The Philanthropist*, and other periodicals. The topics ranged widely, from jurisprudence and penal reform to political economy and electoral reform, from the evils of established religion to the reform of English education. Mill's most substantial articles appeared in the supplements to the fourth, fifth, and sixth editions of the *Encyclopaedia Britannica* (1816–23) and several of these—'Government', 'Jurisprudence', 'Liberty of the press', 'Prisons and prison discipline', 'Colony', 'Law of nations', and 'Education'— were collected in his *Essays* (1823).

The most famous, or notorious, of Mill's essays on which his modern reputation chiefly rests is the *Essay on Government*. First published in 1820, it is at once a practical and a theoretical document. Practically, it is a defence of representative government and the extension of the franchise. Theoretically, it purports to provide a logical demonstration of the superiority of utilitarian political principles and practices. Mill argues that government is a means of maximizing happiness and minimizing pain. Pleasures and pains come either from our fellow human beings or from nature. The role of government 'is to increase to the utmost the pleasures, and diminish to the utmost the pains, which men derive from one another' (J. Mill, 4). Yet, 'the primary cause of government' is to be found in nature, from which humans must, through labour, wrest 'the scanty materials of happiness' (pp. 4–5). Nature and human nature conspire to make government necessary. It is human nature not only to desire happiness but to satisfy that desire with as little effort as possible. Labour being the means of obtaining happiness, and our own labour being painful to us, we will labour as little as possible and try, if we can, to live off the labour of others. To the degree that others enjoy the fruits of my labour, my main incentive for working—namely, my own happiness—is diminished. The primary problem in designing workable political institutions is to maximize the happiness of the community by minimizing the extent to which

some of its members may encroach upon, and enjoy, the fruits of other people's labour. This problem cannot be solved, Mill maintains, in a monarchy (where a single ruler exploits his subjects) or in an aristocracy (where a ruling élite exploits the common people). Nor can communal happiness be maximized in a direct democracy, since the time and effort required for political participation would be subtracted from that available for engaging in productive labour, thereby diminishing the net wealth and happiness of the community. The only system that serves that end is representative democracy, in which citizens elect representatives to deliberate and legislate on their behalf and in their interest. Representative government—'the grand discovery of modern times' (p. 21)— allows the interests of the many to be represented efficiently and expeditiously by the few. But how can representatives be made to rule on the people's behalf rather than their own? Mill answers that a greatly expanded franchise, frequent elections, and short terms in office make it unlikely that elected representatives will legislate only for their own benefit. For representatives are drawn from the ranks of the people, to which they can, after serving their time in office, expect to return. Therefore representatives have every reason to promote the people's interests as their own. In a properly structured system, there will be an 'identity of interests' between representatives and their constituents. The aim of reform should be to re-jig institutions to bring about this identity of interests.

In the midst of writing his *Essay on Government* Mill attempted to reassure his nervous editor, Macvey Napier: 'You need be under no alarm about my article on Government. I shall say nothing capable of alarming even a whig' (Mill to Napier, 10 Sept 1819, BL, Add. MS 34612, fols. 287–288). Mill was quite mistaken; his article alarmed almost everyone: whigs, tories, even his fellow utilitarians. The whigs, who also favoured reform, feared that Mill's radically democratic and egalitarian programme would undermine their more modest proposals for piecemeal reform. In order to ensure some reform, they were prepared to tolerate a severely limited franchise and rotten boroughs, among other political ills, and actively to advocate 'virtual representation'—the view that representatives elected by the virtuous and responsible few may best represent the interests of the many. This, Mill countered, is a recipe for misgovernment, corruption, and the triumph of the aristocratic interests of the few at the expense of the many. The public interest can be represented only in so far as the public, or a very large portion of it, has the vote. Mill insists that each individual is the best judge of his own interests. And since the public interest is simply the sum of all individual interests, it follows that the wider the franchise, the more truly representative the government.

Mill's criticisms hit their target. Too influential to ignore, his *Essay on Government* became the target of whig polemicists, the most notable of whom was the historian Thomas Babington Macaulay. Macaulay's 'Mill on government', published in the March 1829 issue of the *Edinburgh Review*, is a brilliant broadside consisting of logical criticism, irony, mordant wit, and droll parody. Focusing mainly on what would now be termed 'methodological' matters, Macaulay defends the 'historical' or 'inductive' approach to the study of politics against Mill's abstract, ahistorical, and 'deductive' method. Although angered by Macaulay's attack, Mill forgave his attacker and subsequently supported his appointment to the governing board of the East India Company. For his part, Macaulay came to regret the tone of his article, for which he 'later … made the most ample and honourable amends' (J. S. Mill, 95).

While tories and whigs thought Mill's *Essay on Government* wildly and even dangerously democratic, many of Mill's fellow philosophical radicals—including Bentham, John Stuart Mill, and William Thompson—believed that he should have advocated an even more radical extension of the franchise. Although acknowledging Mill's essay 'as a masterpiece of political wisdom' (J. S. Mill, 63), they were appalled by what was quite clearly a political concession regarding a highly controversial question: the enfranchisement of women. Mill publicly advocated extending the franchise to include all male heads of household over the age of forty, leaving them to speak for and represent the interests of younger men and all women:

> One thing is pretty clear, that all those individuals whose interests are indisputably included in those of other individuals, may be struck off without inconvenience. In this light may be viewed all children, up to a certain age, whose interests are involved in those of their parents. In this light, also, women may be regarded, the interest of almost all of whom is involved either in that of their fathers or in that of their husbands.   (J. Mill, 27)

As his eldest son later remarked, this was 'the worst [paragraph] he ever wrote'. Many of Mill's critics were quick to seize upon it, if only because it clearly contradicts two of Mill's oft-stated premises, namely, that each individual is the best judge of his or her own interests and that anyone having unchecked power is bound to abuse it. As William Thompson argued in his *Appeal of One Half the Human Race* (1825), Mill's premises pointed to the widest possible extension of the franchise, and not to the exclusion of 'one half the human race' who happen to have been born female.

Few, if any, of Mill's other essays proved so controversial as his *Essay on Government*. That essay—and Macaulay's attack—earned for its author an indelible reputation as an egregious simplifier of complex matters. Mill himself remained unrepentant. He saw himself as a theorist, and the point and purpose of theory, in his view, was to simplify. Whether his theory of government was a masterpiece of political wisdom or an oversimplification remains a matter of some controversy.

In addition to being (after Bentham) philosophical radicalism's leading theorist, Mill served the cause of reform on other fronts. He, like Bentham, advocated the abolition of slavery abroad and the radical reform of schools, prisons, and the church at home. With Mill's energy and Bentham's financial backing, utilitarian schemes for legal, political, penal, and educational reform gained an ever wider audience and circle of adherents. Mill was a strong believer in the importance of education,

and particularly in the political education of the poor. In addition to reading, writing, and arithmetic they should be taught to think clearly and critically, to distrust established (and especially ecclesiastical) authority, and to learn the leading principles of political economy. To that end Mill put his pen and his formidable organizational talents in the service of the Lancasterian schools for educating the poor outside the purview of the Church of England. Mill was a moving force in the founding of the Society for the Diffusion of Useful Knowledge and the launching of the *Westminster Review* in 1824. He was also involved in the foundation of University College, London. Intellectually and institutionally, Mill helped to make Bentham's ideas and schemes more palatable and popular than they might otherwise have been. But he also influenced Bentham's ideas in a number of ways. Mill helped Bentham to understand the part played by economic factors in social life and political institutions. More important, perhaps, was Mill's having 'converted' Bentham to the democratic cause.

While maintaining a united front for political purposes, Mill and Bentham became increasingly estranged. The old man was irascible and difficult to work with, and Mill on more than one occasion reluctantly accepted financial help and personal rebuke from him. With the publication of his *History of British India* in 1818, and his appointment at India House a year later, Mill became financially independent and no longer looked to Bentham for financial support. Their precarious friendship was for all but political purposes ended a decade before Bentham's death in 1832.

Later years If Mill pushed his children and his associates hard, he pushed himself even harder. By 1820 he held three jobs: one as first assistant examiner of correspondence at India House, where he worked from four to ten hours daily; another as the leading propagandist for political reform along philosophic radical lines; and a third as a theorist and independent author who displayed a daunting intelligence and a dazzling range of interests. Mill's topics ranged from education and psychology to political economy, to penology and prison reform, to the law and history, and to political theory. On these and other topics he wrote five books and more than a thousand essays and reviews. (For a full listing of Mill's literary labours, see Fenn, appx II.) Mill did not know how not to work hard. But his labours began to take their toll on his strong physical frame. In 1822 he suffered the first of many debilitating attacks of gout. He subsequently showed signs of pulmonary distress.

In the early 1820s Mill was a founder (with his friend David Ricardo) and active member of the Political Economy Club, which provided a forum for debating free trade and other issues. He had previously persuaded Ricardo to write his classic work on that subject, *Principles of Political Economy and Taxation* (1817), whose principles Mill subsequently expounded in his *Elements of Political Economy* (1821). His economic theory is in the main a distillation of the free market, anti-mercantilist views of Adam Smith and Ricardo, among others. In 1822 Mill began work on his *magnum opus* in associationist psychology and philosophy of mind, the *Analysis of the Phenomena of the Human Mind* (2 vols., 1829). In this work he maintains that the human mind is a store of 'associations' of ideas derived from experience (for example, between 'burn' and 'fire'). Reasoning, remembering, and other mental phenomena consist of calling up and recombining these associations. The purpose of education is to instil and reinforce the right sorts of associations. In 1823 he contributed a controversial article to the first number of the *Westminster Review*, attacking the *Edinburgh Review* for its timid 'trimming' on reform and other pressing political matters. In that same year Ricardo died, leaving Mill distraught to a degree that astonished and alarmed his friends. Ricardo and Mill had first met in 1811 and had quickly become fast friends and political allies. Mill subsequently persuaded the shy and diffident Ricardo to stand for parliament, to which he was elected in 1819, serving until his death four years later. Ricardo's death was a blow from which Mill never fully recovered.

By 1822 Mill's growing affluence enabled him to take a house at Dorking, where for several years his family stayed for as long as six months at a time, with the paterfamilias joining them for weekends and over the six-week summer holiday. He later moved his summer residence from Dorking to Mickelham and, in 1830, his main residence from Queen Square in Westminster to a house in Vicarage Place, Church Street, Kensington.

By the late 1820s it appeared that some sort of constitutional reform was inevitable. But exactly what sort it was to be, and how far it was to go, remained a matter of intensely partisan controversy. It was in this context that Macaulay's aforementioned attack on Mill appeared in the 1829 *Edinburgh Review*. Although ailing, Mill joined the fray. He refused to reply to Macaulay directly (although a thinly veiled reply appeared later in his *Fragment on Mackintosh*). Mill made two contributions to the debate preceding the 1832 Reform Act. The first was an article on 'The ballot' in the *Westminster Review* (July 1830), in which Mill knocked down arguments against extending the franchise and defended the secret ballot. Mill's second, and much longer, contribution was his *Fragment on Mackintosh* (1835). Sir James Mackintosh (1765–1832) was an ageing whig polemicist with a plodding and often pompous prose style, who delighted in skewering Bentham and the philosophic radicals. Mill's *Fragment* is an extended critique of Mackintosh's last and most systematic work, the *Dissertation on Ethical Philosophy* (1830). Mackintosh singles out Mill's *Essay on Government* for special censure, and Mill returns the favour. With its withering sarcasm and unremitting ridicule, Mill's *Fragment* is a disagreeable and intemperate book. But it makes an effective case for utilitarian politics and moral philosophy. The *Fragment* was to have been Mill's *pièce de résistance* and main contribution to the debate leading up to the Reform Act of 1832. In the event, Mackintosh died just before it was to appear, and Mill, fearing a backlash, delayed publication until 1835.

By the mid-1830s Mill's powers, both physical and mental, had begun to fail him. Although he continued to write, none of his later articles displays the philosophical firepower of the earlier essays. In August 1835 his lungs began to haemorrhage. After an apparent recovery, the condition recurred and in June 1836 he suffered a severe attack of bronchitis. Knowing the end was near, he remained calm and strangely cheerful. On 23 June 1836 Mill died in London. He was buried two days later in Kensington church.

TERENCE BALL

Sources A. Bain, *James Mill* (1882) · J. S. Mill, *Autobiography*, ed. J. Stillinger (1969) · J. Mill, *Political writings*, ed. T. Ball (1992) · W. Thomas, *The philosophic radicals: nine studies in theory and practice, 1817–1841* (1979) · E. Halévy, *The growth of philosophic radicalism*, trans. M. Morris (1928) [Fr. orig., *La formation du radicalisme philosophique*, 3 vols. (1901–4)] · L. Stephen, *The English utilitarians*, 2 (1900) · J. Hamburger, *James Mill and the art of revolution* (1963) · T. Ball, *Reappraising political theory* (1995) · R. A. Fenn, *James Mill's political thought* (1987) · DNB

Archives BLPES, corresp. and papers · London Library, commonplace books | BL, letters to Macvey Napier, Add. MSS 34611–34615 · BL, corresp. with Francis Place, Add. MSS 35144–35153 · CUL, corresp. with David Ricardo · Derbys. RO, letters to Sir R. J. Wilmot-Horton · LUL, letters to Society for the Diffusion of Useful Knowledge · NL Scot., letters to Sir John Stuart · UCL, letters to Jeremy Bentham; letters to Lord Brougham

Likenesses Perugini, oils?, Hult. Arch.; repro. in Bain, *James Mill* · drawing, NPG [*see illus.*]

Mill, John (1644/5–1707), Church of England clergyman and college head, was born in Hardendale, a hamlet of Shap parish, Westmorland, the son of Thomas Mill (*b. c.*1617x19, *d.* in or after 1707), a weaver of Shap, and his first wife. His family moved to High Knipe in Bampton parish, Westmorland, and he was educated at Bampton School. After matriculating at Queen's College, Oxford, on 14 November 1661, aged sixteen, he proceeded BA on 3 May 1666 and MA on 9 November 1669. On 9 July 1666 he was selected to deliver the 'oratio panegyrica' at the opening of the Sheldonian Theatre; his Latin and English verses addressed to Dr Thomas Barlow were bound up in Simon Ford's *Conflagration of London Poetically Delineated* (1667). Mill was elected a fellow of his college on 17 October 1670, and was ordained in the same year.

Upon Thomas Lamplugh's elevation to the episcopate as bishop of Exeter in 1676, Mill was chosen as his chaplain. In due course, on 29 October 1677, he was made a prebendary of Exeter. In August 1678 he was reported to be 'seeking for preferment at Court having displeased the Provost' (Fox, 11). He proceeded BD on 8 July 1680. On 22 August 1681 he was nominated by his college to the rectory of Bletchingdon, Oxfordshire, worth a nominal £150 per annum. He proceeded DD on 8 December 1681, and was duly instituted rector of Bletchingdon on 3 February 1682. Mill relinquished his Queen's fellowship about the end of August 1682. By 1682 he was also a royal chaplain.

On 6 May 1684 Mill married Priscilla (1649–1685), youngest daughter of Sir William Palmer, of Old Warden, Bedfordshire, and Dorothy Bramston (the surname of his bride being rendered Bramston in Westminster Abbey registers), with a portion of £3000. Mill had been Palmer's chaplain, but the union was not blessed with longevity as

John Mill (1644/5–1707), by unknown artist

his wife died on 1 April 1685 and was buried at Bletchingdon on 14 April. Also in April he was elected clerk of the convocation for Oxford diocese. On 5 May 1685 he was elected principal of St Edmund Hall, probably owing to the influence of the vice-chancellor, William Lancaster, provost of Queen's College. Henceforth most of his duties at Bletchingdon were performed by his curate, one Langhorne, the son of his half-sister.

The revolution of 1688 saw Mill initially adopting a loyalist approach, holding true to the doctrine of passive obedience and non-resistance. He was elected to convocation in 1689 as a proctor of the Oxford clergy, which suggests that he was an unbending high-churchman. However, Mill took the oaths to the new regime, thereby retaining his offices and earning a certain notoriety in the rhyme 'wilt thou take the oaths, little Johnny Mill? No, No, that I won't, Yes but I will' (*Remarks*, 1.189–90). His political vacillations also accounted for his nickname: Johnny Wind-Mill. In 1701 he wrote the preface to Thomas Benson's *Vocabularium Anglo-Saxonicum*, part of his consistent encouragement of Anglo-Saxon scholarship which had at its root the need to demonstrate the antiquity of the church in the face of Catholic challenges to its authority.

By Queen Anne's reign Mill had abandoned toryism and had become a rare whiggish figure in Oxford. After initially supporting the bill against occasional conformity, Mill changed his tune when he realized that the court opposed it. In November 1703 he was one of the college heads who attempted to curb the popularity of the writings of John Locke and Jean Le Clerc, proposing that such works should not be read by tutors to their pupils. This failed ordinance was supported by Mill not because he was opposed to the works of 'the new philosophy', but because he felt that 'there was a great decay of logical exercises in the university' (*Correspondence of John Locke*, 8.269) occasioned by too much study of the new works. On 12 August 1704 he was presented by the queen to a prebend of Canterbury, after which he resigned his Exeter prebend in August 1705. Mill's house was often one of the few illuminated in honour of the military exploits of John Churchill, first duke of Marlborough, which is perhaps one reason why in February 1706 Thomas Hearne described him as 'now one of the rankest Whigs in England' (*Remarks*, 1.189–90). However, Hearne could also show some appreciation of Mill, writing after Mill had donated books worth £10: 'he is a person not only of great learning, but a great patron of it, when the humour takes him' (ibid., 2.289–90). Some criticism also attached itself to Mill over the neglect of his duties at St Edmund Hall: White Kennet opined that Mill 'was so much taken up with the one thing his Testament that he had not leisure to attend to the discipline of the House which rose and fell according to his different vice principals' (Fox, 22).

On 12 June 1707 Mill's long-term academic project was published: his Greek edition of the New Testament, with variant readings and a prolegomena. Mill had begun this work about 1677, taking over the preparatory work undertaken by Dr John Fell, and the printing of the text and apparatus had begun in 1686. The work was dedicated to the queen. The text was taken from Robert Estienne's edition of 1550, but the variant readings were added at the foot of each relevant page. Mill had spent years collating English and continental manuscripts for the purpose. The prolegomena, running to 168 pages, consisted of a canon of the New Testament, then the history of the transmission of the text to posterity and of Mill's text, with a list of authorities used.

On 21 June 1707 Mill was 'seized with a kind of apoplectical fit' (*Remarks*, 2.22), 'although he had a great swelling in his throat' (Fox, 33), and he died, probably in Oxford, on 23 June. He was buried on 25 June at Bletchingdon. He died intestate, administration being granted to his aged father in July. For Abel Boyer he was 'a person of great learning, and particularly well versed in the oriental languages, of which he left a noble specimen, in the Greek Testament, he published a fortnight before he died' (Boyer). By September 1707 there was news of another edition based on Mill's work being prepared for publication by Ludolph Kuster. It was published in 1710, with further editions in 1723 and 1746. Despite Boyer's encomium one of Mill's weaknesses was his relative unfamiliarity with oriental languages. His work came under attack from Dr Daniel Whitby in *Examen variantium lectionum J. Millii* (1709), and then by Anthony Collins in *Discourse of Free Thinking*, both of whom argued that the great number of readings overwhelmed the authority of the text. It was defended with vigour by Richard Bentley, whose early scholarship Mill had encouraged.   STUART HANDLEY

Sources A. Fox, *John Mill and Richard Bentley: a study of the textual criticism of the New Testament, 1675–1729* (1954) · Foster, *Alum. Oxon.* · *Fasti Angl., 1541–1857*, [Canterbury], 23 · *Fasti Angl.* (Hardy), 1.425 ·

J. L. Chester, ed., *The marriage, baptismal, and burial registers of the collegiate church or abbey of St Peter, Westminster*, Harleian Society, 10 (1876), 23 · *Remarks and collections of Thomas Hearne*, ed. C. E. Doble and others, 11 vols., OHS, 2, 7, 13, 34, 42–3, 48, 50, 65, 67, 72 (1885–1921), vols. 1–2 · *Hist. U. Oxf.*, vols. 4–5 · J. R. Magrath, ed., *The Flemings in Oxford*, 3 vols., OHS, 44, 62, 79 (1903–24) · A. Boyer, *Political state of Great Britain*, vol. 6 (1708), p. 380 · *The correspondence of John Locke*, ed. E. S. de Beer, 8 vols. (1989), vol. 8 · J. Gregory, *Restoration, reformation and reform, 1660–1828* (2000), 57 · IGI

Archives Bodl. Oxf., papers for edition of Epistle of Barnabas · Queen's College, Oxford, papers
Likenesses oils, Queen's College, Oxford; copy, St Edmund Hall, Oxford [*see illus.*] · oils, second version, St Edmund Hall, Oxford

Mill, John Stuart (1806–1873), philosopher, economist, and advocate of women's rights, was born on 20 May 1806 at 13 Rodney Street, Pentonville, London. He was the eldest of the nine children of the Scottish-born utilitarian philosopher and Benthamite reformer James *Mill (1773–1836), and his wife, Harriet, *née* Burrow (1782–1854). His paternal grandfather, a Calvinist village shoemaker in Forfarshire, had married the clever and socially ambitious daughter of a farmer who had once been a Jacobite. His grandparents on his mother's side managed a private lunatic asylum in Hoxton, then a rural suburb on the outer edge of north-east London. The child was named after his godfather, Sir John Stuart of Fettercairn, whose patronage had helped James Mill to study at Edinburgh University and later to seek his fortunes in England.

Despite what he called the 'uneventfulness' of his career, few lives have been more closely scrutinized than that of John Stuart Mill. This attention has stemmed partly from the unusual circumstances of his upbringing and marriage, partly from the detailed narrative of his own mental development that Mill left in his *Autobiography*, and partly from the continuing interest in his political, philosophical, and popular writings still widely felt by readers in many countries at the end of the twentieth century. Mill's *Autobiography*, composed mainly during the 1850s, but not published until after his death in 1873, was a pioneering essay in the literary genre of psychological self-analysis. But it was also a somewhat disingenuous work, in that it left out as much as it revealed, it was carefully revised at the time of writing by Mill's wife, Harriet Taylor, *née* Hardy [*see* Mill, Harriet (1807–1858)], and it recounted with great lucidity and certainty a series of multi-faceted events many of which had occurred years or even decades earlier. The *Autobiography* conveniently divided Mill's life into three developmental phases. The first phase, his childhood and early youth, had been dominated by the all-encompassing personality, philosophy, and educational theories of his father. The second phase was the mental crisis of his early manhood, as an outcome of which he had at least partly rejected utilitarianism, and sought new avenues of friendship and personal enlightenment in poetry, German Romanticism, and philosophical high toryism. During the third phase further horizons were opened by the influence of his soulmate and eventual wife, Mrs Taylor. To these three phases may be added the period, covered more briefly in the *Autobiography*, in

John Stuart Mill (1806–1873), by unknown photographer

which Mill after the death of his wife for a time played an active role in radical and parliamentary politics. In this latter phase he also published the series of popular writings on social and political theory for which he is best-known to posterity, most notably *An Essay on Liberty* and *The Subjection of Women*. At all stages the interpreter of Mill's life is faced with three underlying questions: namely, how accurate was the account in the *Autobiography*, how significant were the events and influences that it glossed over, and what was the relationship between Mill's personal history and the different phases in the evolution of his opinions and ideas?

Childhood and early youth The earlier years of John Mill's life were spent in circumstances of 'rigid frugality', both economic and emotional. In the 1800s his father's ambitions for a public career were constantly thwarted by the unorthodoxy of his views on politics and religion, while the continual birth of children, combined with obligations to hard-up Scots relatives, meant that money in the Mill household was always in short supply. The family lived in cramped, cheaply rented accommodation owned by Mrs Mill's mother, first in Pentonville and then in Newington Green; then in 1814 they moved to a more spacious house in Queen Square subsidized by Jeremy Bentham. The Mill parents were an ill-matched pair: James Mill, dry, sardonic, and short-tempered, was immersed in abstract logic and political reform, while his wife, acknowledged in her youth as a woman of exceptional beauty and good nature, was gradually reduced to the role of housemaid and 'squah' and submerged in domesticity. John later recalled himself as growing up 'in the absence of love and the presence of fear'. His father was 'constitutionally irritable' and lacking in tenderness, while his mother, crushed under her husband's scarcely veiled contempt, was unable to meet the emotional, rather than merely practical, needs of her growing brood of children (*Collected Works*, 1.52–3). References to Mrs Mill in her son's draft autobiography, though expunged from the published version, bore witness to his lifelong grievance against her shallowness of feeling and lack of 'strong good sense' (ibid., 1.612).

Among the children themselves, John later implied, relations were less warm and intimate than might have been expected in such an extensive family; and he portrayed himself as having been on occasion actively disliked by his younger brothers and sisters. If this was so (and some contemporary accounts suggest a quite different view) it was almost certainly linked to the remorseless application of James Mill's educational theories. The elder Mill was a disciple not just of Bentham and utilitarianism, but of Hartley and Locke: he believed with Locke that the human mind came into the world as a *tabula rasa* on which knowledge and disposition were subsequently engraved by the experience of the senses; and he believed with Hartley that human behaviour could be indefinitely moulded and modified by the deliberate application of 'associationist' psychology. It may initially have been domestic economy that induced James to undertake the education of his own children; but, faced in his eldest son with a child of quite unusual mental ability, it soon became a matter of prolonged intellectual obsession for him. The young John was set to learn Greek at the age of three, and by the time he was eight had studied the Greek texts of Aesop's fables, Xenophon's *Anabasis*, Herodotus, parts of Lucian, Diogenes Laertius, and six of Plato's dialogues. Extensive reading among Scottish and English historians was also prescribed, and between the ages of four and nine the boy walked every day with his father in the lanes of Hornsey, recounting what he had learned from the works of Hume, Robertson, Millar, Gibbon, Burnet, Hooke, and Watson's *Philip the Second*. Arithmetic 'was the task of the evenings, and I well remember its disagreeableness' (*Collected Works*, 1.9). During his eighth year he progressed to Euclid, algebra, and Latin. By his twelfth birthday he had started on Aristotle, Sophocles, and Euripides, had finished the Greek texts of the *Iliad* and the *Odyssey*, and had read much of Virgil, Horace, Ovid, Terence, and Cicero, though 'Tacitus I do not think I meddled with till my thirteenth year' (ibid., 1.14). For his own pleasure, and 'in imitation of my father', the young Mill started work on his own histories of Holland, Rome, India, and even a 'universal' history. He also composed dramas on historical subjects, and devoured works on physics and chemistry. At twelve he moved on to logic, using as textbooks Aristotle's *Organon* and Hobbes's *Computatio, sive, Logica*, and at thirteen to political economy. At his father's insistence he also undertook 'one of the most disagreeable of my tasks' (ibid., 1.17): the composition of verses in English, a skill valued by James Mill not for its own sake but as a useful exercise in rhetoric. In addition he was

from the age of eight actively involved in assisting with James Mill's own writing—correcting proofs of articles and later of *The History of British India*. He enjoyed music, and became an excellent if unorthodox performer on the piano, which throughout life was to be his only manual skill (many years later his instinctive scorn for phrenology was confirmed when one of its exponents diagnosed his cranium as showing peculiar aptitude for manual dexterity). In all these matters his father:

> demanded of me not only the utmost that I could do, but much that I could by no possibility have done … He was often, and much beyond reason, provoked by my failures in cases where success could not have been expected; but in the main his method was right. (ibid., 1.8–33)

From an early age Mill was required not merely to pursue his own self-education, but to help his father teach his eight siblings. On at least one occasion Mrs Mill refused John a holiday because he could not be spared from instructing the younger children. An account by Francis Place dating from 1814 (when John was eight) recorded that the boy worked alone with his father from 5 to 9 a.m., then assisted James until noon with the lessons of two younger sisters. 'There is not a moment's relaxation … no fault however trivial escapes [James's] notice; none goes without reprehension or punishment.' On one occasion all three children were kept at their books until 6 p.m. without a midday meal: 'the fault today is a mistake in one word' (Packe, 32–4). These duties increased after 1818, when James Mill obtained a full-time post with the East India Company, and John's letters show that even into his thirties he was still actively instructing two of the younger brothers, then studying at the recently founded University College.

Despite these unusual pressures, however, Mill's boyhood afforded some remarkable routes of entry into the outside world, and he certainly felt in later life that the mixture of rigorous tutelage and self-teaching had been an immense intellectual asset. Notwithstanding his financial difficulties James Mill was to become the close associate of the leading radical intellectuals of the age, many of whom were frequent visitors in the Mill domestic circle. These included not just Jeremy Bentham, who was James's mentor and patron from 1808, but the economist David Ricardo, the legal philosopher John Austin, the classical historian George Grote, the radical artisan Francis Place, and many others. From 1812 the summer months, albeit without remission of study, were passed at Bentham's country house at Ford Abbey (a setting that Mill later recalled as having awakened his fondness for picturesque surroundings); and in 1820, at the age of fourteen, he spent a year in the south of France in the much more relaxed household of Bentham's brother, the naval architectural engineer General Sir Samuel Bentham. There, to the amazement of Sir Samuel's family, he continued to study for nine hours a day. But the visit was to be of seminal importance in laying the foundations of his lifelong enthusiasm for French society and culture, and in extending his knowledge—through attending lectures at the

University of Montpellier—of debates in the natural sciences. He also discovered the pleasures of mountain walking, and, through the influence of Sir Samuel's son George Bentham, of collecting botanical specimens—both to become the leisure pursuits of a lifetime.

On Mill's return to England it might have been expected that he would prepare for university, particularly since his godfather, Sir John Stuart, had left a legacy of £500 to pay for his education at Cambridge. James Mill obstinately refused to allow this, however, on the ground that his son 'already knew more than he could learn at Cambridge' (Packe, 49). A year later, through the invitation of Charles Austin (younger brother of the legal philosopher), John was to star as a visiting speaker at the Cambridge Union, where he 'left a great impression' by his 'massive power in disputation, uttered from a flimsy body in the creaking tones of sixteen' (ibid., 52). But James insisted that he remain at home, to continue the education of the younger children, to prepare for a career in the law, and to resume his work as James's own amanuensis. In winter 1821–2 he began to read for the bar, was privately tutored in Roman law and Blackstone's *Commentaries* by John Austin, and for the first time studied the legal and political theories of Jeremy Bentham, published in their French form by Dumont under the title *La traité de législation*. Despite his supposedly Benthamite upbringing this was the first time John Mill had directly encountered the works of the great man, and he later recalled it as 'an epoch in my life; one of the turning points in my mental history'. For the first time the 'greatest happiness principle', taught by his father as an abstract Platonic dogma, 'burst upon me with all the force of novelty' as a principle that laid the axe to all conventional maxims of public and private morality.

> The feeling rushed upon me, that all previous moralists were superseded and here indeed was the commencement of a new era in thought … The 'principle of utility' … gave unity to my conception of things. I now had opinions; a creed, a doctrine, a philosophy … a religion; the inculcation and diffusion of which could be made the principal outward purpose of a life. (*Collected Works*, 1.57–9)

Mill's personal conversion to Benthamism heralded a hyperactive period in his life in many spheres. Early in 1823 he gave up the bar, and was appointed to a full-time junior clerkship in his father's department at the India Office (where he was to remain, progressing upwards to the post of examiner, for the whole of his professional career). This, however, was to prove the least of his new activities, for throughout life he was to find official duties 'an actual rest from the other mental occupations which I have carried on simultaneously with them' (*Collected Works*, 1.85). Both during and outside office hours he continued to assist James Mill with his writings on political economy and on the analysis of mind. He began to associate much more closely with the major figures in his father's circle, and also acquired a younger circle of his own (Roebuck, Buller, Tooke, Romilly, Charles Austin, and others) who formed the nucleus of the group later known as the philosophical radicals. In 1823 he spent two nights

in gaol, having been prosecuted by the Middlesex magistrates for distributing Malthusian birth-control literature in the servants' basements of large houses—the first public statement of what was to become his lifelong conviction that the best cure for lower-class poverty was family limitation. In winter 1822–3 he formed a Utilitarian Society, a small coterie of young men dedicated to 'Utility as their standard in ethics and politics', who for the next four years met fortnightly to discuss questions 'conformably to the premises thus agreed on' (ibid., 1.81). The membership of this society overlapped with that of another informal group, which met at Grote's house for early morning discussions of mental philosophy. From 1825 Mill also attended the London Debating Society, where utilitarians and political economists were locked in combat with whigs, tories, followers of Samuel Taylor Coleridge, and disciples of Robert Owen. He began to publish reviews and essays in his own right, first in *The Traveller* and the *Morning Chronicle*, and then more substantially in the *Westminster Review*, founded in 1823 by Bentham and others as a radical alternative to the whig *Edinburgh* and the tory *Quarterly*. In 1824–6 he acted as Bentham's research assistant in preparing the eight-volume *Rationale of Judicial Evidence*, a work of massive erudition, logical power, and stylistic complexity, that was to become the *locus classicus* of Benthamite legal theory. Looking back in later years, Mill recalled the mid-1820s as the high tide of the utilitarian school: a period when the Benthamite critique of law and government came together with political economy, Hartleian metaphysics, and Malthus's population theory, to pose what seemed an irresistible challenge to established aristocratic interests in society, church, and state. Within government itself, a new generation of reformist ministers headed by Canning and Peel showed signs of being susceptible to new currents of thought, while outside government a highly articulate school of brilliant young men dedicated themselves to far-reaching strategies of moral, legal, and social reform. Of these young men Mill himself, his 'mind directly formed' by his father, his 'object in life' defined for him by Bentham, seemed predestined to be the natural leader and most powerful intellectual force.

The 'mental crisis', 1826–1827 The halting of Mill's career as a 'mere reasoning machine' of Benthamite utilitarianism was intimately linked with what he later termed his mental crisis of 1826–7. 'The time came', he recorded, 'when I awakened … as from a dream'. Normal pleasures became 'insipid or indifferent' to him, and he found himself in a 'dull state of nerves', which he compared to the feelings of a convert to Methodism smitten by conviction of sin. He asked himself whether the instant fulfilment of all his plans for human betterment would give him happiness, 'and an irrepressible self-consciousness distinctly answered, "No!". At this my heart sank within me: the whole foundation on which my life was constructed fell down.' There followed 'the dry heavy dejection of the melancholy winter of 1826–7', in which he could find no comfort in books and dared not tell his father of his distress: the systematic pursuit of happiness in which he had been trained from infancy now seemed to 'fearfully undermine all desires', while the 'analytic habits' that were the corner-stone of his father's educational theory were 'a perpetual worm at the root both of the passions and of the virtues'. Desperately asking himself how he could go on living, he concluded that 'I did not think I could possibly bear it beyond a year'. From the depths of his depression, however, a 'small ray of light broke in upon my gloom'. He read the passage in *Mémoires d'un père*, by Jean-François Marmontel, describing how the boy Marmontel had resolved by a 'sudden inspiration' that he would take the place of his dead father and make up to his family for all that they had lost. Unexpectedly touched by this story, Mill found himself 'moved to tears'. He gradually recovered the capacity for feeling, and once again found enjoyment, 'not intense, but sufficient for cheerfulness, in sunshine and sky, in books, in conversation, in public affairs' (*Collected Works*, 1.137–49). Thereafter he pursued a much modified version of the philosophy of hedonism, resolving to find happiness 'by the way' rather than making it a 'principal object'—a principle re-affirmed thirty years later in his *Utilitarianism*, where he claimed that 'conscious ability to do without happiness gives the best prospect of realising such happiness as is attainable'.

The precipitants of Mill's mental crisis have been the subject of speculation for well over a century. Late-Victorian commentators suspected either fatigue from prolonged overwork, or a secularized variant of a religious loss of faith. Twentieth-century interpreters looked to more subliminal or sexual explanations—to a suppressed desire for the death of his father (mirrored in the Marmontel memoir), or to the plight of a young man emerging from adolescence into adulthood who had been totally sealed off from contact with the female sex. A more recent account emphasizes the shock to Mill's mental system dealt by the London Debating Society, where for the first time he met clever people with well-worked-out philosophies quite different from his own—to whom extreme utilitarianism appeared both morally repulsive and irresistibly comic. A well-publicized financial scandal of 1825–6, when certain prominent Benthamites were found to have lined their pockets from a Greek independence loan, tarnished the movement's reputation for incorruptible high-mindedness, and may well have contributed to the young Mill's disenchantment.

All these explanations have some plausibility, and are not inherently incompatible with each other. Certainly Mill had experienced his discovery of Benthamism in 1821 as akin to a spiritual revelation; and it seems not unlikely that his nausea with Benthamism in 1826 had something of the character of a religious de-conversion. On the other hand, later glimpses of his struggles with the 'awful shadow [of] Necessity' (*Collected Works*, 1.175, 12.476–7) suggest that it was not so much finding Benthamism false but fearing that parts of it might indeed be true that generated his deepest depression. Mill's relations with women will be discussed more fully below; but his long-drawn-out, guilt-ridden resentment against James Mill can

clearly be seen in draft sections excised from the published *Autobiography*. The numerous re-draftings of passages relating to 1824, which refer to John's behind-the-scenes work in preparing James's assault on the *Edinburgh Review*, suggest that he had begun to find his father's meticulous control over everything he thought and wrote increasingly irksome and oppressive. Another relevant factor is that the aspect of Bentham's thought which Mill most admired was its power as a machine tool of practical reform, and his experience was by no means untypical of those who throw themselves into heroic programmes of social reformation. Edwin Chadwick, John Ruskin, C. S. Loch, Beatrice Webb, William Beveridge—to name but a few—all experienced rather similar episodes of psychic trauma when the goals that they were fighting for turned unexpectedly into sinks of desolation.

More prosaically, it was perhaps scarcely surprising that a young man of Mill's wide-ranging intelligence should gradually have become aware of alternatives to the doctrines cherished by his father. In later life Mill recalled a lurking discontent with James's views from the time of the *Essay on Government*, written in 1820, which had treated in dismissive terms the political claims of women. But it was not until 1829, when Macaulay published his famous critique of the *Essay*—dismissing as grotesquely unhistorical its deduction of 'the whole science of Politics' from axioms of unvarying human behaviour—that John Mill's dissent from his father's position began to take coherent shape. In the meantime, during recovery from his breakdown he found for the first time that he could read English poetry for pleasure, particularly Wordsworth, in whose *Intimations of Immortality* he found experiences and sensibilities that matched his own. He began to detach himself from the *Westminster Review* circle, finding the philosophical radicals increasingly sectarian and narrow. Instead he started to learn German, studied the writings of Coleridge and of the French Saint-Simonians, and began to associate with leading disciples of the 'metaphysical' school, notably F. D. Maurice, John Sterling, and Thomas Carlyle.

Mill's interest in the philosophy of Coleridge, regarded in the 1820s as the leading English exponent of the continental reaction against the philosophy of the Enlightenment, was recorded in his essay on Coleridge, published in 1840. Mill there rejected Coleridge's *a priori* theory of knowledge, but wrote warmly of many aspects of his social, political, and religious thought. Coleridge's 'speculative' toryism, with its stress on historical survival as evidence of the viability of beliefs and institutions, he portrayed as a healthy 'counterpole' to the 'shallow empiricism' of Enlightenment thought and the critical methodology of Bentham. He warmly praised Coleridge's emphasis on active government, on the pivotal role of a national 'clerisy', and on rationality and open-mindedness in theological doctrine. And he concurred in Coleridge's view that disciplined popular education, a supra-rational focus on national identity, and a 'strong and active principle of cohesion' were the three indispensable ingredients in holding the 'social union' together (*Mill on Bentham and Coleridge*, 120–24). In his *Autobiography* Mill implied that this essay had been unduly generous to Coleridge at the expense of Bentham; but, if anything, the essay of 1840 rather understated the degree of his adherence to Coleridgean principles over the previous decade. In letters to Sterling, written in the late 1820s and early 1830s, Mill placed Coleridge above all other contemporaries as a systematic and creative thinker. And while dissenting from Coleridge's religious beliefs, he strongly praised the Coleridgean doctrine 'that it is good for man to be ruled; to submit both his body & mind to the guidance of a higher intelligence & virtue'—very favourably contrasting it with the 'narrow views & mischievous heresies' of individualist liberalism (*Collected Works*, 12.84). After meeting Wordsworth he recorded that 'all my differences with him, or with any other philosophic Tory, would be differences of matter-of-fact or detail, while my differences with radicals & utilitarians are differences of principle' (ibid., 12.81). Benthamism he continued to respect as a guide to reformist legislation; but he dismissed it as wholly inadequate as an ethical and psychological theory or as a framework for 'consideration of the greater social questions—the theory of organic institutions and general forms of polity' (ibid., 10.9).

Mill's attraction to organic and idealist thought was fostered by his relationship with F. D. Maurice and John Sterling, whom he met at the London Debating Society in 1828. He admired and befriended both men, but with Maurice the Coleridgean doctrine took perhaps too ecclesiastical a turn for Mill's predominantly secular taste. With the captivating and unorthodox Sterling, however, he 'soon became very intimate, and was more attached to him than I have ever been to any other man'. Like Mill himself, Sterling was moved by 'an equal devotion to the two cardinal points of Liberty and Duty', and although 'he and I started from intellectual points almost as wide apart as the poles … the distance between us was always growing less' (*Collected Works*, 1.161–2). Sterling had some acquaintance with German thought, and was probably the main channel through which Mill absorbed aspects of Kant and Hegel: when, some years later, he tried to read these theorists in German he found that 'je possédais déjà tout ce qu'ils avaient d'utile pour moi' ('I already possessed everything they may have had that was of use to me'; ibid., 13.576). Another influential friend was Thomas Carlyle, the great scourge and satirist of Benthamism, who was helped by Mill in promoting his literary career and jumped to the conclusion that he had found a new 'mystic' disciple. Carlyle was deluding himself, however, for the main group of thinkers apart from the Coleridgeans who attracted Mill in this period were followers of the French philosopher Saint-Simon. In 1828 he met at the London Debating Society a young Saint-Simonian, Gustave D'Eichthal, who subsequently corresponded with him about Saint-Simon's ideas and introduced him to Saint-Simonian activists in Paris, among them the reformist society known as *Aide-toi et le Ciel t'aidera* ('Heaven helps those who help themselves'). Like the Coleridgeans, the Saint-Simonians taught that history

was not static but dynamic, and that institutions which appeared to be corrupt and decadent were not intrinsically so, but had in the past served a progressive social purpose. They believed that civilization moved in cycles of 'organic' and 'critical' epochs—the former being periods of intellectual unity and coherence, the latter periods in which old-established creeds broke down and new creeds had to be formulated to take account of new empirical knowledge. The most ambitious Saint-Simonian was the young Auguste Comte, who had already sketched out his 'law of the three stages', whereby both human knowledge and social organization were portrayed as evolving historically from the 'theological' stage, via the 'metaphysical' stage, through to the 'positive' phase of the future. In this latter epoch all supernatural speculation would become redundant, as all branches of humane knowledge—moral, psychological, social, and historical—acquired the precision and mutual coherence of the most advanced areas of physical science.

Mill was deeply impressed, both by the interpretation the Saint-Simonians seemed to offer of the fast-changing society that he saw around him, and by the very utopianism with which they proclaimed the attainability of a new moral world. Their belief in a *pouvoir spirituel* seemed to fit closely with Coleridge's intellectual 'clerisy', while their emphasis on the evolutionary role of history seemed a necessary counterweight to utilitarian abstraction. Though he refused formally to join the Saint-Simonians (rejection of dogmatic sects being part of his reaction against Benthamism) Mill's new beliefs were nurtured by his visit to Paris during the revolution of 1830, and further developed in the articles that he wrote in support of the rising reform agitation in Britain. He was intrigued also by the intellectual possibilities afforded by a positivist social science. Dimly he began to imagine a way out of the impasse created by his own reaction against Benthamism, and by Macaulay's discrediting of James Mill's deductive and ahistorical method. Before these ideas could be fully developed, however, his life took a new and unexpected turn in the form of his budding relationship with Mrs Harriet Taylor.

Mill and Mrs Taylor Opinions differ about whether Mill had shown any romantic interest in women before he met Harriet Taylor. There is some slight evidence to suggest that he had felt an adolescent *tendresse* for the dashing Sarah Austin, wife of the legal philosopher; and a rumour emanating from Greville claimed that he had fallen briefly in love with Lady Harriet Baring. In the late 1820s he became closely acquainted with William Johnson Fox, editor of the Unitarian *Monthly Repository* and minister of the South Place Chapel; and again there were rumours that Mill had been in love with Fox's ward, the musician and composer Eliza Flower. But others thought differently: his friend Roebuck observed that Mill was 'utterly ignorant of what is called society' and that 'of *woman* he was a child' (Kamm, 32). Certainly Mill himself, nurtured alongside the rather bleak relationship of his parents, had no anticipation of finding happiness in marriage. In April 1829 he had commented to Sterling on his expectation of 'the comparative loneliness of my probable future lot', linking it to the limpness of feeling from which he had suffered since his crisis three years before. He linked it also to the loss of a sense of comradeship and close intimacy that he felt had been present throughout the earlier part of his life: a comment that can only refer to the termination of such a relationship with his own father (*Collected Works*, 12.30).

Harriet Taylor in 1830 was twenty-two years old, the mother of two children, and wife to a liberally minded Unitarian businessman, John Taylor, who was a member of William Fox's congregation at South Place. Harriet, who was renowned within her circle for her cleverness and beauty, confided to Fox that she was troubled by intellectual problems that she could not discuss with her amiable but uncerebral husband. Fox is said to have replied that 'John Mill was the man among the human race to relieve in a competent manner her dubieties and difficulties'. Some time in the early autumn of 1830 a dinner was therefore arranged at the Taylors' house to which Mill was invited, along with Fox, Harriet Martineau, Roebuck, and George Graham. According to Carlyle (who was not invited, but later gossiped relentlessly with those who were) Mill,

> who up to that time, had never so much as looked at a female creature, not even a cow, in the face, found himself opposite those great dark eyes, that were flashing unutterable things while he was discoursin' the utterable concernin' all sorts o' high topics.   (Kamm, 32)

Mill by the end of the evening was passionately in love, and was to remain so until Harriet's death twenty-eight years later.

Mill's relationship with Harriet Taylor, both before and after their eventual marriage in 1851, was the subject of endless speculation among their contemporaries, and has been no less so among historians. In the *Autobiography* Mill made three major assertions about Mrs Taylor and her role in his life. He implied that prior to the death of her first husband, his own association with her had been one of the utmost delicacy and propriety, designed in no way to infringe on the honour of Mr Taylor: it had been simply a marriage of true minds, proving that intellectual, spiritual, and moral union could far transcend the banal intimacy of mere sex. He maintained secondly that Harriet herself was a creature of quite outstanding mental and creative power, whose talents far exceeded his own as a thinker, Carlyle's as a poet, and Shelley's as a transcendent genius; in an era more hospitable to the claims of women she would have been a towering figure in public and intellectual life. And thirdly, he claimed that, with the sole exception of *A System of Logic* (where her role was confined to 'minor matters of composition'), she had contributed substantially to all his mature writings and had personally inspired or redrafted large parts of them (*Collected Works*, 1.191–9, 255–9).

Each of these claims is of some importance in unravelling the course of Mill's own life history. The first claim, that their relationship during John Taylor's lifetime was wholly asexual, seems to have been universally accepted by contemporaries, even by those most prone to prurience and gossip. No one ever suggested that Harriet's youngest child, Helen, born in 1832, was the daughter of anyone other than John Taylor. Nevertheless, the *Autobiography* greatly simplified and smoothed over much of the trauma and uncertainty of the strange triangular relationship that was to be sustained for nineteen years. Three years after their first meeting Harriet Taylor left her husband and travelled to Paris, where she was joined by Mill for a period of six weeks; and there was clearly some prospect at this time, and for several years thereafter, that the separation from John Taylor might become permanent. Mill himself absolutely refused to contemplate the possibility that he should remove himself forever from Harriet's life, but at the same time he was not wholly free from periodic pangs of anxiety about possible adverse consequences for his own public position. 'Good heaven', she wrote to him on one such occasion, 'have you at last arrived at fearing to be "*obscure and insignificant*"! What *can* I say to that but "by all means pursue your brilliant and important career"' (Hayek, 99). Harriet herself was immensely moved by John Taylor's generous conduct; and she was stricken also by the contemplation that, if she abandoned him permanently for Mill, 'I should spoil four lives and injure others' (Kamm, 42). The upshot was that she returned to her husband, not to their former intimacy but with a 'real intention' of his 'being with her as a *friend* and *companion*'.

Over the next few years an accommodation was reached whereby Harriet spent much of her time at a house in the country provided by her husband, where Mill could visit her unobtrusively. On occasions when he visited the Taylor household in Regent's Park, John Taylor contrived always to be absent at his club. Mill himself continued to reside quietly with his family, who since James's appointment to the India Office had lived in a large house in Vicarage Square, Kensington. After James's death in 1836 he moved with his mother and unmarried brothers and sisters to a smaller establishment in Kensington Square (portrayed by visitors at the time as a very harmonious and close-knit family circle). From 1837 to 1840 Mill was the proprietor of the *London and Westminster Review*, which had absorbed the old *Westminster* but now attracted articles from contributors far beyond the confines of philosophical radicalism. Mrs Taylor was rumoured to be the 'Armida', or *mauvaise esprit* of this enterprise, but the only evidence of her involvement shows her using her connection with Mill to support her husband's sponsorship of Italian political refugees. Mill and Harriet for a time attended functions together in London, but this caused so much comment and embarrassment that they gradually withdrew almost completely from joint appearances in public (though they were present together at the first of Carlyle's famous lectures on heroes and hero-worship in May 1840). They often travelled together incognito on the continent, concealing their whereabouts even from Mill's closest family.

These tripartite arrangements continued throughout the 1840s until John Taylor fell ill with cancer. Harriet, who appears to have been genuinely fond of her husband, nursed him through his final illness until his death in July 1849. She and Mill were married on 21 April 1851 at the registrar's office in Melcombe Regis, Mill formally declaring that, as he and his new wife wholly disapproved of 'the marriage relation as constituted by law', he proposed to 'disclaim and repudiate all pretence to have acquired any *rights* whatever by virtue of such marriage' (Hayek, 168). Their union precipitated a major breach between Mill and most of his family, including his mother, whom Mill accused of being insultingly slow to acknowledge his new wife. He and Harriet set up home in Blackheath Park, where they continued to live in great seclusion, again punctuated by frequent visits to the continent. Throughout their marriage Harriet was the dominant partner in all practical affairs—Mill, who had been waited on by his mother and sisters for forty-five years, proving utterly incapable of dealing with such matters as summoning cabs, reserving seats on trains, getting the house cleared of rats, and negotiating publishers' royalties. Both before and after their marriage he and Harriet were troubled by bouts of prolonged ill health. Mill had collapsed with a nervous illness after his father's death in 1836, which left him for the rest of his life with severe facial twitching and recurrent depression; and from the early 1840s he was suffering from consumption, a disease endemic in the Mill family. Their longest separation came in 1854–5, when Mill spent six months travelling in Italy and Greece, much of the time on foot, hoping to effect a remission of his illness (a project that met with some success). Harriet suffered from chronic bronchitis and may also have contracted consumption from Mill, and much of her incessant travelling both in England and abroad was linked to, if not wholly explained by, her search for a climate that would suit her health. She and Mill were engaged in such a search, hoping to find a retirement home in southern France, when Harriet, attacked by sudden congestion of the lungs, died unexpectedly at Avignon on 3 November 1858.

Mill's claims for his wife's intellect and character were expressed most fulsomely in the *Autobiography*, and were for long regarded as the understandable but exaggerated tributes of a stricken and sorrowing widower. Contemporaries acknowledged Harriet's compelling personality and conversational sharpness; but none except Mill perceived her as a great creative genius and moral giant. The discovery of the fact that many of the tributes in the *Autobiography* were composed while Harriet was still alive, some being actually revised by her, has tended to reinforce a feeling among more recent commentators that she was not fully worthy of Mill's rapturous admiration. In the letters between them that have survived there is overwhelming evidence of their mutual devotion, but little comparable with the detailed exchange of ideas on philosophy, religion, politics, economics, and ethics that filled his letters to other correspondents such as Sterling, d'Eichthal, Carlyle, Tocqueville, and Comte. This is perhaps scarcely surprising, since daily intimacy drives out the need to express ideas in letters, and there was a similar paucity of intellectual topics in earlier letters to his father (undoubtedly the most powerful mental influence on his early youth).

This leaves open, however, the question of what the nature of Harriet's intellectual, as opposed to emotional, influence on Mill actually was. Mill's claim that in a more auspicious climate Harriet would herself have been recognized as a major thinker does not wholly ring true, since—despite the barriers against clever women that undoubtedly existed in the 1830s—Harriet Taylor was probably better placed than almost any woman in England to overcome them. The circle in which she and John Taylor moved actively encouraged the creative activity of women; and Harriet, who was beautiful and financially secure, would have been in no worse a position to make her mark than, for example, a fellow member of Fox's congregation, the plain and deaf Harriet Martineau. As Mrs Taylor she contributed in the early 1830s to the *Monthly Repository*, and there was no reason why she should not have continued to write if she had wished to do so. Moreover, it seems almost inconceivable that, if she had really been the prime author of any of Mill's works, her name would not have appeared on the title-page, at least as co-author. Before John Taylor's death there was a reason for reticence in the avoidance of gossip (Taylor on this ground objected strongly to Mill's attempt in 1848 to dedicate to Harriet his *Principles of Political Economy*). But this can scarcely have been the case with writings of the 1850s—still less so with those works, substantially attributed to her by Mill, that were published only after her death.

What then *was* Harriet Taylor's influence on the substance of Mill's thought? Despite his exaltation of her talents, Mill's own accounts of Harriet's role in his mental life were not unambiguous. The sketch of an ideal female partner in *The Subjection of Women* (1869) envisaged a critical, empirical, practical role for a woman as helpmate to 'a man of theory and speculation' who was engaged in formulating 'comprehensive truths of science and laws of conduct' (*Collected Works*, 21.306), a portrait that presumably reflects Mill's own understanding of his own relations with Harriet. And in the *Autobiography* he denied that she had ever fundamentally 'altered the path' of his opinions. When he first met her, he recalled, 'the only actual revolution which has ever taken place in my modes of thinking, was already complete' (ibid., 1.199); it was much more a question of striking out 'more boldly' down channels along which he was moving already. This new departure did not happen overnight, his early mental relations with Harriet being confined to fostering his interest in Romantic poetry. But gradually, he recalled, his 'mental progress … went hand in hand with hers' (ibid., 1.237), until by the early 1840s he had 'no further mental changes to tell of, but only, as I hope, a continued mental progress' (ibid., 1.229). By then he had 'completely turned back' from the 'excess' of his reaction against Bentham. He had renounced the shallow reformism and tolerance of the *status quo* that he believed had characterized his flirtation with German philosophy. And 'in addition to this, our opinions were now far *more* heretical than mine had been in the days of my most extreme Benthamism' (ibid., 1.239). The principle of private property, cherished by Benthamites and the older political economists, was now discarded, and the 'social problem of the future' was redefined as 'how to unite the greatest individual liberty of action, with a common ownership of the globe'. And, similarly, the mechanistic principle of numerical democracy was now viewed by Mill and his wife as heavily qualified by the need for moral transformation of both leaders and masses. In all these matters, Mill concluded, and 'in all that concerned the application of philosophy to the exigencies of human society and progress, I was her pupil, alike in boldness of speculation and cautiousness of practical judgment' (ibid., 1.199, 237–9).

These rather conflicting accounts (of Harriet as faithful research assistant, but also as intellectual master) suggest that her challenge to Mill's mental outlook was perhaps more fundamental than he cared to admit or was even aware of; that it may have amounted not just to a radicalization of specific opinions, or the contribution of a useful helpmate, but to a wider change of underlying sentiment and social philosophy. In the absence of evidence about their intimate conversations, this view must remain conjectural; but there are many archival fragments that point in the same direction. By the time of their first meeting Harriet already held views that, though much less systematically developed than Mill's, were in many respects different from his and certainly far more radical. While he had long inclined towards *ralliement* and reconciliation between the partial truths of different parties, her vision of right and wrong was much more absolute and exacting. In an essay for the *Monthly Repository* (composed at a time when Mill himself was still warmly inclined towards social organicism and historic continuity) she had denounced root and branch the sinister 'conformity plan' imposed by the 'phantom power' of social opinion, through the arbitrary imposition of 'some standard of right or duty erected by some or other of the sets into which society is divided like a net—to catch gudgeons' (Hayek, 275–9). There were even some fundamental differences in their views on women. In the essays on divorce which they wrote for each other's benefit some time in 1831–2, both argued that existing marriage laws were wholly unreasonable, and that to secure their economic independence women needed education on the same basis as men. But Mill suggested that liberalized divorce laws were mainly required by 'higher natures', and that for people in general there was some danger that 'giving facilities for retracting a bad choice' might actively encourage irresponsible entry into marriage. He also thought that, even when relations between the sexes had been reformed, most wives and mothers would continue to be occupied in the home: 'it does not follow that a woman should *actually* support herself because she should be *capable* of doing so: in the natural course of events she will not', an opinion later echoed in *The Subjection of Women* (Hayek, 65; *Collected Works*, 21.298). Harriet by contrast argued for total civic equality between men and women,

the opening of all occupations and public offices to both alike, and 'doing away with all laws whatever relating to marriage' (Hayek, 77–8). Shortly after this exchange of views, she wrote to Mill with some indignation suggesting that in intellectual concerns he was withholding from her his full confidence: 'in this, as in all these important matters there is no medium between the *greatest, all*, and none—anything less than all being insufficient. There might be just as well none' (ibid., 47). Mill protested that this was not so; but since his interest in 'speculative toryism' at this time was still powerful, his reticence about some of his deepest opinions is unsurprising. His fostering of conservative as well as radical opinion in the *London and Westminster*, and indeed his own writings for the review, indicate that his Coleridgean sympathies were still active in the late 1830s. Over the years, however, his correspondence with Harriet suggests that on a wide range of issues he was gradually brought round to her ways of thought. When she dissented from his views on such questions as Comtism, Fenianism, atheism, communism, Greek history, and the moral perfectibility of the human race, Mill almost invariably conceded that he was in the wrong and promised to think again: 'by thinking sufficiently I should probably come to think the same—as is almost always the case, I believe always when we think long enough' (ibid., 135).

These developments were paralleled by Mill's changing relationships with other figures to whom he had once been close. During the 1830s and early 1840s he severed relations with, or drifted away from, many members of the powerful intellectual circles of his youth—Roebuck and Grote, John and Sarah Austin, Sterling and Maurice, Thomas and Jane Carlyle. This happened for a variety of reasons—Roebuck was dismissed for advising Mill against his liaison with Harriet, while the Grotes and the Austins were suspected of malicious gossip. Friendship with the Carlyles miraculously survived the famous incident of March 1835 when Mill arrived at Carlyle's house, speechless with distress, to confess that a maid had accidentally burned the manuscript of Carlyle's *French Revolution*. Carlyle at the time behaved with impeccable forbearance, and only later came to suspect—and to spread disgruntled rumours suggesting—that the real culprit had been Harriet. By the late 1830s Mill's friendship with Carlyle, though never entirely broken off, had markedly waned—more than twenty years before the great issues of political principle that were to divide them in later life. For Sterling Mill retained a lifelong affection, and in 1838 he was an original member of the notorious Sterling Club, founded by Sterling for discussion of heterodox opinions. But this most charismatic of his former associates was now chronically ill and often out of the country. Their friendship was renewed in 1840 when they spent several weeks together at Falmouth in the company of Henry, Mill's dying younger brother. Mill afterwards wrote to Sterling that 'we have been more to each other lately than ever before', but confessed that 'even now I am very far from appearing to you as I am, for though there is nothing that I do not desire to show, there is much that I never do show, and much that I think you cannot even guess' (*Collected Works*, 13.428–9). Whether this was a reference to Harriet or to his intellectual differences with Sterling is impossible to say. But in all these connections a complicating factor was Harriet's jealousy of rival spheres of influence and inability to tolerate people who disagreed with her: 'near relationships to persons of the most opposite principles to my own produces excessive embarrassment' (Hayek, 130). This was evident in her disparaging references not merely to 'the vapid and sentimental egoists', Sterling and Carlyle, but to newer influences in Mill's intellectual orbit such as Auguste Comte and Alexis de Tocqueville—the former a 'dry root of a man … not a worthy coadjutor & scarcely a worthy opponent', the latter 'a notable specimen of … the gentility class—weak in moral, narrow in intellect, timid, infinitely conceited & gossiping' (ibid., 114, 156). By the mid-1840s Mill had been won round to the view that on 'cardinal points of human opinion, agreement of conviction and feeling' was an 'essential requisite of anything worthy the name of friendship, in a really earnest mind' (*Collected Works*, 1.237). Whatever the substantive content of Harriet's contribution may have been, her influence therefore served gradually to isolate Mill from direct intellectual interchange with many of his former associates.

Science and logic   From childhood Mill had been fascinated by the human mind and the foundations and processes of knowledge. Even in the depths of his mental crisis and subsequent attraction to Romantic thought, he seems never substantially to have departed from the views— transmitted via his father from the inheritance of Thomas Hobbes—that knowledge was rooted in material sensations, and that genuine scientific propositions were deductive in character, rather than (as was claimed by Kantians, natural theologians, and the school of Reid and Dugald Stewart) derived from *a priori* categories or from intuition and common sense. These views were forged and sharpened not merely by his early reading in logic but by daily exposure to the economic reasoning of his father and Ricardo, and by the austere legal positivism in which he had been trained by Austin and Bentham.

Nevertheless, there was more wavering in his opinions than Mill was later willing to admit; and the unravelling of his views is complicated by the varying ways in which both he and his antagonists used terms like *a priori*, *deduction*, and *induction*. Confusingly, both the sense-data school and the intuitionists claimed to be supporters of *induction*, but disagreed about its place in the sequence of scientific thought. The former school (usually, though not always) held that general deductive laws could be built up from evidence initially supplied by induction, derived from 'observation of what passes in our own minds' and the 'general tendencies' of human nature. The latter school (usually, though not always) saw induction as the process that retrospectively tested *a priori* hypotheses generated within the mind itself. Mill's thinking in this area over many years indicated some degree of uncertainty on a number of issues. In 1827 he was impressed by the argument of Richard Whately's *Logic* that knowledge derived

from induction could never 'be built up into a regular demonstrative theory like that of the syllogism'. The major shock to his inherited views came, however, in 1829 from Macaulay's onslaught on James Mill's *Essay on Government*. It was Macaulay's dismissal of his father's deductive approach to history—in combination with the historical theories of his Coleridgean and Saint-Simonian friends— that encouraged John Mill to think for a time of exploring these problems by writing a philosophical history of the French Revolution. In the early 1830s he collected many materials for this work, but in the end was happy to pass them on to Carlyle, feeling that his own talents were essentially analytical—and in particular that thinking about thought, 'the science of science itself', was his peculiar forte.

Mill initially pursued his enquiries in a deliberately open-minded, 'non-sectarian' spirit, hoping to reach a position in which the partial truths contained in rival schools might be resolved or synthesized. In the early 1830s he was already working on the theory of syllogisms that was to be propounded twelve years later in book two of his *System of Logic*. The *Autobiography* recorded that he 'could make nothing satisfactory of Induction, at this time'; but manuscript sources show him arguing, against Whately, that induction was 'as much entitled to be called Reasoning, as the demonstrations in Euclid' (*Collected Works*, 1.191, 8.961). His 'Remarks on Bentham's philosophy' in 1833, though more concerned with ethics than theories of knowledge, appeared to make a number of concessions to the intuitionist and anti-deductivist schools—particularly his criticism of Bentham's dismissal of character and conscience, and his rejection of Bentham's claim to have discovered a universal spring of human action that operated regardless of specific variations in history and culture, time and place. In this essay Mill also questioned the view that there was any necessary connection between a thinker's philosophical views and his or her attitudes to practical politics (*Collected Works*, 10.17–18n). But a year later his essay entitled 'On the definition of political economy' asserted the opposite view: 'systematic differences of opinion' in any sphere could always be traced back to 'a difference in their conceptions of the philosophic method' (ibid., 4.324).

Mill's views began to take shape more firmly, however, as certain leading members of the intuitionist school went on the polemical offensive—and as philosophers of all schools in the 1830s and 1840s became increasingly driven by the passionate quest for a holistic theory of knowledge. Mill was wrong in claiming in later years that intuitionism at this time had been all-powerful; but it was, none the less, strongly represented in certain powerful institutions, most notably the University of Cambridge, where it was closely linked with natural theology, the ethical teachings of Bishop Butler, and the promotion of induction as the practical investigative handmaid of certain categorical assumptions about the noumenal, natural, and social worlds. In 1834 a lecture published by a leading proponent of this school, Adam Sedgwick, linked defence of induction to a broader attack on both the 'self-ish' morals of the utilitarians, and their abstract, deductionist methodology. Sedgwick's lecture was mainly concerned with natural science, but it included the claim, in echo of Macaulay, that the facts of history were the only valid basis for a general understanding of politics and society—evoking from Mill the sharp retort that 'not only is history not the source of political philo-sophy, but the profoundest political philosophy is requis-ite to explain history … History is not the foundation, but the verification of the social science' (*Collected Works*, 10.44–5). His essay 'On the definition of political economy' also firmly restated the superior status of deductive rea-soning: mere inductive verification *a posteriori* was 'no part of the business of science at all, but the *application* of science' (ibid., 4.325).

Mill continued to mull over these questions for more than a decade. In the late 1830s his ideas were further crys-tallized, both positively and negatively, by the writings of Auguste Comte and William Whewell. From 1837 he was reading the first five volumes of Comte's *Cours de philoso-phie positif*, and his correspondence with Comte in 1841–2 (when his own study was far advanced) shows him eagerly awaiting the sixth volume and declaring himself Comte's disciple. The differences between them, he assured Comte, stemmed almost entirely from the fact that public opinion in England was too immature to tolerate a wholly non-religious, explicitly positivist philosophy. At the other extreme his ideas were powerfully influenced by two works from the second great Cambridge intuitionist, Whewell, *The History of the Inductive Sciences* (1837) and *The Philosophy of the Inductive Sciences* (1840). These two monu-mental works, designed to expose the logical fallacies of the tradition of Locke, aimed to hitch Baconian inductionism to the *a priori* reasoning of Immanuel Kant. Like Kant, Whewell argued that there were certain neces-sary truths about the phenomenal universe—such as the existence of space, time, causality, and geometric forms—that could only be assumed and not proven. Such assump-tions were essential to the formulation of general hypoth-eses, which could then be verified by inductive observa-tion and experiment. Much of practical science, Whewell implied, consisted simply of inspired guesswork, fol-lowed up by meticulous case-by-case investigation. All sys-tematic knowledge consisted of an interaction between 'metaphysical ideas' and 'inductive movement'; without the former the latter was pointless, since 'in no case can experience prove a proposition to be *necessarily* or *univer-sally* true' (Whewell, 1.62). Whewell's examples were taken largely from mathematics and natural philosophy; but since the early 1820s he had been a recurrent critic of the deductive method of Ricardo and James Mill, and his books were widely viewed, by Whewell himself as well as by others, as a further skirmish in the war against sensa-tionalist theories of mind and abstract political economy.

Whewell's studies provided Mill with a mass of practical examples of scientific method, sifted for him by Alexan-der Bain, who was later to be his first biographer and chief philosophic disciple. Whewell's *Philosophy* in particular

acted as a timely catalyst that helped him to weld together his own still somewhat disparate thoughts on scientific reasoning. The result was *A System of Logic, Ratiocinative and Inductive*, published after twelve years' gestation in 1843. Mill began his book with the assertion that he was not con-cerned with the contested territory of epistemology, but only with the structure of logical argument. This austere agenda proved, however, impossible to observe at every point, and the text frequently spilt over into deep ques-tions of human understanding. Throughout his work Mill concurred with Whewell that knowledge was a unity, but he claimed much more explicitly than Whewell that social knowledge was comparable in kind, if not necessar-ily in degree, with knowledge in the natural sciences. He agreed also about the importance of induction, but dis-agreed fundamentally about the relation of inductive knowledge to general propositions in either natural or social science. For Whewell, the very possibility of scien-tific enquiry was rooted in certain inherently untestable *a priori* assumptions, armed with which it was possible to make sense of empirical data and only thus to formulate general laws. For Mill general propositions (other than those that were purely syllogistic) were deductions, them-selves initially derived by inference from induction, with-out reference at any stage to categorical ideas. The latter he portrayed as having throughout history seduced human minds into the error of believing that there were universal 'substances', over and above the sum of the spe-cific cases which such categories were supposed to repre-sent. Substances were the sirens that lured unwary logi-cians to their doom, down false trails such as animism, mysticism, the Platonic theory of forms, linguistic and mathematical essentialism, the Christian doctrine of human nature, and—closer to Mill's own day—the common-sense philosophy of Thomas Reid and Dugald Stewart and the idealism of Kant. In Mill's view the study of the phenomenal world was a self-contained process of inference between induction and deduction, the latter being the formulation of general laws out of conjunctions of the more particular 'empirical' laws derived from the former. The stage to which a particular science had devel-oped and the general conditions under which it operated determined whether inference from deduction or induc-tion took priority. Such inference he claimed was the basis of all scientific, as opposed to merely imaginative, thought about everything from mathematics and celestial mechanics through to mankind living in society and the individual human mind. Even concepts relating to objects imperceptible in nature, such as perfect circles and lines without breadth, could ultimately be traced back, not to axiomatic truths, but to a mental process of neutralizing non-relevant sense-data (just as non-wealth-producing motives and passions were excluded by economists from study of the pursuit of wealth).

Mill's account of geometry challenged the wellnigh uni-versal view that mathematical theorems were intrinsic-ally axiomatic rather than inductive. But the most contro-versial parts of his thesis, as Mill himself intended, were those that related to the deductive character of social and moral science; and much of book six of the *Logic* was devoted to anticipating possible objections in this area. These objections related primarily to four interrelated problems: free will, the nature of mind, sociological method, and the precise character of deductive reasoning in relation to such volatile and variable subject matter as the working of human society. In defending the compatibility of social laws with free will, Mill was deeply concerned to dissociate himself from the currently vociferous Owenite view that human character was the creature of social forces and that individuals therefore had no choice and no responsibility for their own deeds. Instead he claimed that law-like regularities in human behaviour in no way precluded the possibility of free will. 'The causes … on which action depends' were 'never uncontrollable', and human beings could actively participate in the formation of their own characters; they could choose whether or not they wished to follow the guidance of social laws (*Collected Works*, 8.840–42). The study of mind was imperfectly developed, but was, he claimed, no different in principle from the study of other complex phenomena. As with astronomy, however, the scope for induction and experiment in the study of mind was limited; it could only advance by grafting elementary (inductive) psychology onto the still embryonic (deductive) study of 'Ethology' or the science of character, which was concerned with formulating 'general laws of human nature' (ibid., 8.861–74). Laws relating to individual behaviour would also be the basis of the study of 'human beings united together in the social state', since 'human beings in society have no properties but those which are derived from, and may be resolved into, the laws of the nature of individual man' (ibid., 8.879).

Such an assertion sounded like an echo of the widely condemned reductionism of the *Essay on Government*; but Mill went on to reject his father's 'geometric' method as a model for social science, on the ground that geometry took no account of 'conflicting forces'. He also rejected a 'chemical' model for social science, arguing that (unlike physical elements transformed into compounds) human beings were simultaneously *both* participants in the social organism *and* irreducibly separate and autonomous entities. The appropriate method for social enquiry was the 'Concrete Deductive Method … of which astronomy furnishes the most perfect, natural philosophy a somewhat less perfect, example' (*Collected Works*, 8.894). Here Mill admitted a provisional role for 'a system of deductions *a priori*', though he insisted that 'the ground of confidence in any concrete deductive science is not the *a priori* reasoning itself, but the accordance between its results and those of observation *a posteriori*' (ibid., 8.896–7), a caveat with which many of his opponents would surely have agreed. Sociology's reliance on such retrospective induction meant that it could not be a 'science of positive predictions' but only of general 'tendencies', the latter constantly liable to disruption by the fact that so many countless threads of social causation were constantly mingled together. The main goal of the social sciences should therefore be, not to assert universal causal laws, but the

much more limited methodological goal, of 'teach[ing] us how to frame the proper theorem for the circumstances of any given case' (ibid., 8.898–900).

A further complication was that human societies did not merely differ within themselves, and from each other, but also changed over time, thus producing a degree of complexity that 'could not possibly be computed by human faculties from the elementary laws which produce it' (*Collected Works*, 8.913–15). The proper procedure here, Mill suggested, was to supplement concrete deduction by the inverse deductive method proposed by Comte. Comte's *Cours de philosophie positif* had argued that historical laws were deductive propositions or hypotheses derived from the 'empirical laws of society'. These empirical laws were of two kinds: those which showed how societies were held together ('social statics') and those which demonstrated how societies underwent change ('social dynamics'). To illustrate the kind of laws comprised under the former, Mill quoted the long passage in his own 'Essay on Coleridge', where he had identified the three preconditions of social union in all known historical societies, among them a sense of transcendent origin or purpose (*Mill on Bentham and Coleridge*, 120–24). On social dynamics he was somewhat more equivocal: societies everywhere seemed to be demonstrating 'certain general tendencies', such as the shift from military to industrial organization, the predominance of masses over individuals, and the ascendancy of minds over bodies; but these tendencies had not yet advanced beyond the status of limited empirical laws. What was needed, Mill conjectured, was an 'element in the complex existence of social man' that could both interpret the sequence of social causation and itself be a prime agent of future social change. And, by a happy 'consilience', it so happened that just such an element did in fact exist (*Collected Works*, 8.914–15)! The combined evidence of history and human nature proved that 'the speculative faculties of mankind' were not merely the necessary medium of social understanding, but, increasingly, were themselves 'predominant … almost paramount, among the agents of social progression' (ibid., 7.924–30).

On its initial publication in 1843 *A System of Logic* attracted little public comment, a silence that betokened, according to one contemporary, R. H. Hutton, not lack of interest but sheer terror among the book-reviewing community at the thought of incurring the crossfire of Mill's dialectical powers. Within a very few years, however, it was to become one of the most influential and controversial works of the mid-nineteenth century. Despite Mill's earlier intention of reconciling rival positions, his correspondence with Comte suggests that by the early 1840s he had come to see his book not just as a disinterested work on scientific method but as a polemical attack on the very possibility of metaphysics and theology, at least as conceived by most practitioners of those disciplines in the early Victorian era. Over the next three decades, however, its arguments were to be assimilated in the most unlikely quarters. The book appeared in eight different editions over the course of Mill's lifetime, that of 1851 being, under

Harriet's tutelage, the most heavily revised. The edition of 1862 included an additional chapter on Buckle's *History of Civilization in England* (1857 and 1861), which expounded more fully Mill's thesis that history was the product of dialectical interplay between psycho-social conditions and men's 'own peculiar characters'. After the mid-1840s Mill gradually withdrew from his correspondence with Comte, increasingly perturbed by his former mentor's anti-feminism, constant requests for financial help, and (something Mill appears not to have noticed before) lack of interest in proof and induction. But, despite excision of the first edition's flattering references to Comte, later editions were if anything even *more* positivist in sentiment than that of 1843—incorporating long passages from Comte's predictions of global convergence towards a heavily industrialized, politically collectivized, and culturally homogenized society of the future. Mill himself clearly hoped that the development of a more precise social science would be a central theme of his own future work in systematic theory, and for some time after publication of the *Logic*, he was exploring ideas for a projected work on ethology and the study of national character. But the project made little progress, and in the mid-1840s he returned to his earlier studies of the one area of social science in which deductive theory had already made significant headway—the study of political economy.

Political economy Mill had drafted a series of theoretical essays on economic problems in the early 1830s, only one of which had been published at the time. In 1844 they appeared as a single volume, *Some Unsettled Questions on Political Economy*, which was to become the nucleus of a much larger enterprise. Mill's writings on economic theory demonstrated, perhaps even more clearly than book six of the *Logic*, some of his core preoccupations both as a social philosopher and as a theorist of scientific method. These were, in particular, his hope of synthesizing universal societal 'laws' with the variegated facts of history; his concern to reconcile necessity with human autonomy and free will; and his belief that the advance of knowledge required a high degree of artificial conceptual abstraction. His early essays largely accepted the theoretical model that he had learned as a child from his father and Ricardo. Within this model it was assumed, for purposes of scientific analysis, that rational pursuit of wealth could be isolated as the mainspring of human behaviour, that the economy was an integrated self-correcting system, and that distribution of rewards was inexorably determined by the relative availability of the three prime factors of production (land, labour, and capital). Consistent with these views, Mill's early essays condemned all forms of monetary expansion not guaranteed by gold reserves; denied the possibility of deliberately 'creating' employment by either government expenditure or expansion of private consumption; and defended the principles of 'workhouse-test' and 'less-eligibility' as the indispensable safeguards of rational work incentives, promoted by the new poor law of 1834.

Even in his early writings, however, there were fleeting

signs of discontent with the deterministic and ahistorical character of Ricardo's and James Mill's ideas. His espousal of Place's campaign for birth-control, for example, was propelled not simply by the practical view that large families necessarily brought poverty to working-class households, but by the more theoretical belief that labour in general could enhance its share of wealth by deliberately increasing its own scarcity. His 1834 essay on Harriet Martineau appeared to endorse his father's geometric method, by claiming that, just as 'he who has solved a certain number of algebraic equations, can without difficulty solve others, so he who knows the economy of England, or even Yorkshire, knows that of all nations actual or possible'. But he qualified this claim by suggesting that it applied only to 'method of investigation', that local circumstances were variable, and that the economist should 'have sense enough not to expect the same conclusion to issue from varying premises' (*Collected Works*, 4.226). This paradox of universality of method / relativity of circumstance came increasingly to characterize Mill's writings on practical economic problems. His essays on Ireland, for example, argued that abstract poor law principles suited to the way labourers behaved in industrialized England were totally unsuited to the way labourers behaved in agricultural Ireland, where they would inevitably promote fraud, dependence, and explosion of population—though a sceptic might note that Mill never visited Ireland or the industrialized regions of England, and that his personal experience of the way labourers behaved in both countries was virtually nil.

Recurrent debate about the condition of labour was nevertheless the crucible that in the mid-1840s persuaded Mill to attempt to write a major synoptic work that would expand and bring up to date the classic treatises of Smith and Ricardo. The sufferings of the working classes during the 'hungry forties' led to many outraged attacks on political economy by high tories, socialists, and Christian philanthropists, who condemned its doctrines of Malthusian determinism and political non-intervention. In an article entitled 'The claims of labour' in the *Edinburgh Review* for 1845, Mill dismissed such critics as paternalists and 'State Puseyites', who wanted to restore the working classes to feudal subjection; but he was nevertheless troubled that 'the hard, abstract mode of treating such questions … has brought discredit upon political economists & has enabled those who are in the wrong to claim … exclusive credit for high & benevolent feeling' (*Collected Works*, 4.364). Resolving to rescue political economy from this discredit, he set to work to compose his great treatise, *Principles of Political Economy with some of their Applications to Social Philosophy*, published early in 1848.

Mill's *Principles* substantially restated the theorems about optimum conditions for production, circulation of money, and utilization of land, labour, and capital that he had learned from his father and Ricardo. Like them he portrayed the laws of political economy, not as the ideological underpinning of current economic arrangements, but as a critical, progressive science which—if fully incorporated into policy—would dissolve the bastions of feudalism and monopoly that still dominated many areas of economic life. Like his predecessors he assumed a global framework for assessing comparative advantage; and like them he envisaged that removal of all impediments to true economic laws must ultimately lead, like the removal of friction in mechanics, to the onset of a 'stationary state'. But as its title implied, the *Principles* set these laws in a much more overtly social context than had been employed by Mill's predecessors. It suggested, for example, that there was nothing to fear in the eventual stationary state, because it could come about only after the prior abolition of monopolies, which would have put an end to structural—as opposed to meritorious—inequalities of income and wealth (it was something quite different from the 'Chinese stationariness' that Mill was later to deplore in his political writings). Mill argued also that certain features of economic law—such as the tendency of wages never to rise permanently above subsistence—could be circumvented by improvements in social organization and the growth of human capital. Such developments were most clearly predicted in the chapter 'On the probable futurity of the labouring classes', which Mill attributed to the inspiration of Harriet Taylor; and, although no archival evidence proves her authorship, the vocabulary used in the chapter (and even more so in later editions) seems to suggest that her involvement was far from passive. This chapter reiterated Mill's dismissal of the claim of philanthropists that economic improvement depended on fulfilment of personal obligations from rich to poor. In an echo of his Coleridgean phase, he admitted the attractions of 'a form of society abounding in strong personal attachments and disinterested self-devotion', but concluded that the age of paternal government—'the whole fabric of patriarchal or seigneurial influence'—was now irrevocably past. Newspapers, Chartism, and the downward percolation of the 'principles of the Reformation', all meant that 'the poor have come out of leading-strings, and cannot any longer be treated like children' (*Collected Works*, 4.760–63). The way ahead lay not in philanthropy and personal obligation, but in education, association, and co-operation—the latter to be not the paternalist egalitarian co-operativism of Robert Owen, but self-governing co-operatives of independent members, each entitled to a return proportionate to what they had put in. Under such a system the interests of employers and workers would gradually shade into one another, thus doing away not just with residual patriarchy, but with the structural segregation of classes implicitly entailed in the theory of Ricardo (*Collected Works*, 4.766–9).

From the moment of publication, Mill's *Principles* was hailed as a classic, far more congenial to the public than earlier economic textbooks, and far more readable than the *Logic*. Yet in Mill's eyes it was out of date almost before it appeared, because of the eruption in 1848 of the 'year of revolutions', which brought with it widespread experimentation in co-operative, socialist, and public works schemes in many parts of Europe. Mill later claimed that,

if he and Harriet had anticipated the changes in public opinion that occurred in that year, they would have composed the *Principles* in much more ambitious and 'socialist' terms; and certainly the third edition of 1852 was much more explicit about the extent of their shift towards such themes as co-operative partnership, common ownership of landed property, and the evils of 'division of the human race into two hereditary classes, employers and employed' (*Collected Works*, 4.790–96). The third edition also developed much more fully a theme only hinted at three years earlier, of the parallels between the servitude of workers under capitalist production and the 'patriarchal despotism' imposed on those, mostly women, who were confined to the home. Yet despite Mill's increasing identification of himself as a socialist, there was little change in his views on the role of the state, which he saw as largely confined to the traditional liberal agenda of maintaining a sound currency and to the more radical liberal agenda of dismantling or taxing monopolies. Later editions elaborated his ideas on the export of capital (necessary in advanced countries to counteract diminishing returns) and his theory of taxation (opposed to progressive income tax as liable to reduce incentives, but in favour of heavy duties on land, development values, and inherited wealth). An edition of 1865 greatly extended the discussion of recent working-class experiments in co-operation, friendly societies, and self-help; and the final revision of 1871 included a tentative reference to his abandonment of Ricardo's doctrine of the wages fund, which had denied the possibility of an artificial increase in real wages without automatic reduction in the volume of employment. In his introduction to the 1871 edition Mill remarked that the time was not yet ripe for the full incorporation of such lines of thought in a general treatise on political economy. But his revisions were widely read as giving countenance to militant trade unionism, and he was obliged to resign from the ultra-orthodox Political Economy Club which he had joined forty years before.

Liberty and virtue Despite its immense popularity, Mill's *Principles* still left largely unsolved many of the issues raised by his own *Logic*, chief among them the relation of individuals to society, and the question of how a social science, comparable in certainty with celestial mechanics, could also take account of historical contingency and particularity. The revised editions of the *Principles* suggest that over time Mill became less interested in economics as an abstract science, and more interested in its prescriptive use as a tool of civic morality and social policy. This shift away from scientific method towards morals and politics may well have been influenced by his wife, since there can be no doubt that her interests lay more in the latter areas. Because of Mill's ill health, and his promotion in 1856 to the chief examinership at the East India Company, he published little during the 1850s other than journalistic pieces. The last two years of his official life, falling in the aftermath of the Indian mutiny, were spent defending the administrative record of the company (which he portrayed as a regime of enlightened paternal government for the benefit of India) against proposals for a transfer to direct rule from Britain (which he portrayed as inevitably leading to rule in the interests of the governing power). Nevertheless, the eight years of his marriage were a fertile seedbed for Mill's later thought; and, despite prolonged sick leave and official pressures, he was continuously engaged in drafting the works that were eventually to appear as *On Liberty*, *Representative Government*, *Utilitarianism*, *The Subjection of Women*, and the *Autobiography*. His first publication after Harriet's death was the pamphlet *Thoughts on Parliamentary Reform*, which favoured a system of plural voting based on level of education (his own particular concern) and opposed the secret ballot—the latter a view 'in which she had rather preceded me' (*Collected Works*, 1.261). But the chief monument to her memory Mill saw as his essay *On Liberty*, 'so much of which was the work of her whom I had lost … I have made no alteration or addition to it, nor shall I ever' (ibid.).

A draft paper on liberty had been sketched out in 1854, in response to *The Sphere and Duties of Government*, a translation of the work by Alexander von Humboldt originally published in the 1790s; but it was while travelling in Italy and Greece early in 1855 that Mill conceived the idea of a more ambitious work. 'Almost all the projects of social reformers these days are really *liberticide*—Comte's particularly so', he wrote to Harriet from Rome; and a few weeks later from Naples, continued 'I shall think seriously about the book on Liberty since my darling approves of the subject' (Hayek, 216, 221). The final version appeared in 1859, within a few months of Harriet's death. Though lacking 'the inestimable advantage of her revision' (*Collected Works*, 18.216), its language and sentiments—particularly its critique of custom, patriarchy, 'intrusive' piety, and the tyranny of public opinion—certainly bore many hallmarks of her particular concerns. The text began with an attempt to dissociate the work from the deadlock of free will *versus* structural determinism that had dogged Mill's earlier social writings. Its subject matter was not the 'so-called Liberty of the Will, so unfortunately opposed to the misnamed doctrine of Philosophical Necessity'; rather it was 'Civil, or Social Liberty: the nature and limits of the power which can be legitimately exercised by society over the individual' (ibid., 18.217). In this latter sphere, the lines of historical development that Mill as a social scientist had portrayed as universal, progressive, and largely beneficent, now reappeared as menacing, morally coercive, and tending to 'render mediocrity the ascendant power among mankind' (ibid., 18.268). Threats to personal liberty from tyrants, Mill argued, were no longer a problem in advanced societies, but were being replaced by pressure of public opinion—'a social tyranny more formidable than many kinds of political oppression', because more insidious and tending to enslavement of 'the soul itself'. Throughout Europe, business, philanthropy, education, fashion, and communications were all combining to subvert the 'plurality of paths' that had

been the glory of European civilization, and to replace it with the 'Chinese ideal of making all people alike' (ibid., 18.274). Such trends were reinforced by the quietism of traditional Christianity, the 'bigotry' of contemporary Christian revivalism, and the emergence of newer religions more repressive than the systems they sought to replace—a trend exemplified by the later doctrines of Comte (ibid., 18.222–7, 254–7). Everywhere, Mill claimed, original thought was being stunted and truths glossed over by the race towards uniformity, while in planning their private lives, men were submitting like machines to unreflecting custom, exercising no other faculty 'than the ape-like one of imitation' (ibid., 18.262–3). The result was that 'mind itself is bowed to the yoke; even in what people do for pleasure, conformity is the first thing thought of' (ibid., 18.265). And even in England:

> the greatness … is now all collective; individually small, we only appear capable of anything great by our habit of combining … it was men of another stamp than this that made England what it has been; and men of another stamp will be needed to prevent its decline.   (ibid., 18.272)

Mill's antidote for these tendencies was rooted, he claimed, not in any abstract right to freedom, but in 'utility in the largest sense, grounded in the permanent interests of man as a progressive being' (*Collected Works*, 18.224). In the spheres of thought and belief, suppression of any kind was manifestly both dangerous and absurd, as demonstrated by the historical fates of Socrates and Jesus Christ. In the sphere of action, 'the fact of living in society renders it indispensable that each should be bound to observe a certain line of conduct towards the rest' (ibid., 18.276); but in balancing 'individual independence and social control', a clear distinction needed to be drawn between actions that were other- and self-regarding. In the former case, behaviour that involved fulfilment of obligations or avoidance of harm to others was the rightful subject of social regulation. But in the latter case, the individual was the only legitimate judge of his or her own best interests; in the private sphere, whether comprising flights of sublime inspiration or acts of gross indecency, 'all errors which he is likely to commit against advice and warning are far outweighed by the evil of allowing others to constrain him to what they deem his good' (ibid., 18.277). Moreover, individuality was far more than simply an assertion of the individual's right to freedom: it was also, paradoxically, the medium of the highest collective good. The constant enhancement of individuality made each person not merely 'more valuable to himself', but 'more valuable to others', and thus rendered the human race itself 'infinitely better worth belonging to' (ibid., 18.266).

Mill's *On Liberty* aroused a stir of comment on publication and, perhaps more than any other of his works, has been viewed by posterity as the kernel of his social philosophy. None the less, it needs to be set in the context of Mill's other writings of the period, which drew on 'principles … I have been working up during the greater part of my life' (*Collected Works*, 19.373), and which, much more clearly than *On Liberty*, reflected the goal of higher synthesis between conflicting doctrines that had beckoned him on since his mental crisis thirty years before. Moreover, even in *On Liberty* itself there was more qualification and ambiguity than either critics or admirers were prepared to concede. Mill's catalogue of other-regarding acts, that could justly be regulated by both law and public opinion, was much more extensive than the fire of his libertarian rhetoric led some readers to suppose. It included, for example, any form of self-injury, or injury to a person's own property, that might harm his dependants, undermine his performance of social duties, or 'diminish ... the general resources of the community'. If his actions offered a bad example to others, he 'ought to be compelled to control himself, for the sake of those whom the sight or knowledge of his conduct might corrupt or mislead' (ibid., 18.280). Offences against decency, not in themselves indictable, might nevertheless be prohibited if done in public, as 'a violation of good manners' (ibid., 18.295). Despite a plea for marriage to be dissolvable by 'nothing more than the declared will of either party', this plea was heavily qualified by references to the moral aspect of contractual obligation and duties to third parties (ibid., 18.301). Although idleness *per se* was nobody else's business, idleness that led to failure to support oneself or one's children might legitimately be dealt with by forced labour. Laws in other countries that prohibited marriage unless parties could prove they had means to support a family were 'not objectionable as violations of liberty' (ibid., 18.304). Individual citizens were at all times perfectly entitled to express their disapproval of the acts of others, either by pointing out their faults, or by shunning them and warning others against them. None of the arguments for non-interference countenanced 'misapplied notions of liberty' in the rearing of children; instead, the whims of parents should be set aside and the state should 'require and compel' the education (preferably private) of all children, to prepare them for their duties as citizens and freemen (ibid., 18.301–4). All these caveats indicate some degree of tension between Mill's championship of individuality, privacy, and self-development, and the rival claims of a quite different ethic, hinted at in *On Liberty* but elaborated much more fully in the almost exactly contemporaneous *Utilitarianism* and *Considerations on Representative Government*.

Mill's *Representative Government*, published in 1861, linked many of his long-standing political concerns with a number of more immediate issues. It surveyed the political institutions most appropriate for different kinds of society; and at the same time addressed certain questions about franchise and civil service reform, and colonial and federal government that were specific themes in British politics in the late 1850s and 1860s. As a treatise in political thought its frame of reference was eclectic. Despite Mill's reaction against Comte, the assumption of a close, predetermined, connection between political institutions, physical environment, and mental stage of advancement reflected his debt to Comtean thought, as did his continuing emphasis on the explanatory power of variations in national character. His discussion of organic and mechanical models of constitutions echoed his earlier thoughts on the polarity of Coleridge and Bentham. Bentham's influence was clearly apparent in his advocacy of an impartial, well-informed, civil service recruited by open competition; while Coleridge's influence was equally apparent in the claim that, alike in bureaucracies and voting systems, superior intellect should carry more weight than property or mere power of numbers. Perhaps the most striking strain in *Representative Government*, however, was the salience of a number of classical republican themes that had not been particularly prominent in Mill's earlier writings. These themes stemmed partly from Mill's long-standing interest in Plato (whom he tended to treat as an honorary utilitarian, unwisely prone to metaphysical metaphors) and partly from Grote's *History of Greece* (1846–53), which likewise found many utilitarian resonances in the institutions of Athens and Sparta. Mill had reviewed Grote's volumes in several journals, on each occasion vividly contrasting the culture of active citizenship, political education, and exaltation of 'public interest' in Periclean Athens, with the largely private and personal preoccupations of the average citizen of his own day.

These arguments were now spelt out much more fully in *Representative Government*, where Mill tried to project into modern indirect democracy some of the principles of direct democracy embodied in the practices of fourth-century Athens. As suggested by Grote's *History*, he argued that active participation in civic affairs was itself a crucial form of popular political education. Despite the contrast between ancient and modern systems, service on juries and boards of guardians offered opportunities for Athenian style public service that should be open to everyone entitled to vote. Moreover, the very act of voting was likely to bring about mental improvement and unawakened civic capacity among women, manual labourers, and other members of the politically excluded classes. The ballot, favoured by many radicals as a safeguard against improper pressures, was condemned by Mill as the negation of civic virtue, since anyone vulnerable to improper pressures was self-evidently unworthy to have the vote. Voting itself should be undertaken, not as an expression of private interest, but as an affirmation of the public good; the voter's choice was 'not a thing in which he has an option; it has no more to do with his personal wishes than the verdict of a juryman' (*Collected Works*, 19.489). The right and duty of citizenship could and should be exercised without reference to property, gender, status, or class. Nevertheless, it could not be automatically extended to all, but was dependent on possession of a minimum degree of education and independence. Education was a prerequisite since 'power over others, over the whole community' should not be exercised by those with no understanding of what they were doing. Taxation was another prerequisite, since non-taxpayers could not be trusted with management of other people's money; therefore 'a direct tax, in the simple form of a capitation, should be levied on every grown person in the community', and the vote should be denied to tax refusers, undischarged bankrupts, and recipients of poor relief. Such conditions, Mill claimed, would 'leave the suffrage accessible to all who are in the normal condition of a human being' (ibid., 19.472). In addition, plural voting should be allowed for the better educated, both to protect the interests of minorities and to improve the quality of public decisions—though 'deference to mental superiority is not to go to the length of self-annihilation' (ibid., 19.510). Minorities would also be secured by a system of proportional representation, proposed by his friend Thomas Hare some years before. Civic competence throughout society was to be fostered by a massive extension of municipal democracy, manned mainly by local ratepayers but leavened as far as possible by 'the presence … of a higher order of characters … inspiring them with a portion of their own enlarged ideas, and higher and more enlightened purposes' (ibid., 19.534–45). The result, Mill concluded, would be to subvert the prevailing culture of passive contentment ('unmanliness and want of spirit') and replace it by 'the ideally best form of government' in which every citizen would share in sovereignty and 'take an actual part in the government, by the personal discharge of some public function local or general' (ibid., 19.399–412).

The third of Mill's major political tracts, *Utilitarianism*, appeared two years later. Though originally serialized for a popular readership in *Fraser's Magazine* (October–December 1861), it was nevertheless a more subtle and original work than either of its partners. It picked up the threads of Mill's earlier interest in the long-standing debate between intuitionist and sensationalist philosophies, and applied it to criteria of right and wrong. Mill's 'Essay on Bentham's philosophy' in 1833 had hinted that utility as a touchstone itself shared many of the properties that Benthamites condemned as intuitive (it was deemed to be self-evident, and could not be inferred from anything else). In *Utilitarianism* he now inverted this argument by suggesting that intuitive categories themselves often shared the properties of utility: indeed, 'I might go much further, and say that to all those *a priori* moralists who deem it necessary to argue at all, utilitarian arguments are indispensable' (*Collected Works*, 10.207). As an example he cited Kant's categorical imperative (that moral acts should 'admit of being adopted as a law by all rational beings') as a rule wholly consistent, if not indeed identical with, the dictates of utility. Utility itself, no less than any other 'ultimate end', was not susceptible of proof; and like any other ultimate end it had to be judged by what was capable of proof, namely consequences. This did not mean, as its critics claimed, that utility sanctioned selfishness, expediency, and instant gratification. On the contrary, no less than the ethics of Kant, utilitarianism judged actions by their conformity to a general rule whose frame of reference was the benefit of mankind in general: 'the standard is not the agent's own greatest happiness, but the greatest amount of happiness altogether' (ibid., 10.213). Utilitarians were as prepared for self-sacrifice as any Stoic or transcendentalist, their only caveats being that sacrifice should not be pointless but for the 'sum total of happiness'. Nor did utility merely sanction crude material pleasures, since it was quite compatible with utility to differentiate quality of pleasure: 'better to be a human being satisfied than a pig dissatisfied; better to be Socrates dissatisfied than a fool satisfied' (ibid., 10.212).

Mill's account of utility thus challenged three of Bentham's fundamental positions: that 'public interest' was ultimately reducible to the arithmetical sum of private satisfactions; that the ends of utility were morally neutral; and that it was impossible to distinguish between 'higher' and 'lower' pleasures. On the contrary, utility fostered, no less than other ethical theories, the highest forms of virtue, since love of virtue was itself the most intense form of happiness, and 'the mind is not in a right state … not in the state most conformable to the general happiness, unless it does love virtue in this manner' (*Collected Works*, 10.235). Under the present 'wretched social arrangements' only some were aware of the greater happiness-producing potential of the higher faculties; and while such inequalities continued, Socrates would have to judge for the pig. But in Mill's view there was 'absolutely no reason in the nature of things why an amount of mental culture sufficient to give an intelligent interest in these objects of contemplation, should not be the inheritance of every one born in a civilised country' (ibid., 10.215–16). Nor was there any reason to suppose that, globally as well as nationally, existing inequalities would not eventually pass away, bringing all mankind within the framework of the utilitarian/Kantian calculus: 'so it has been with … slaves and freemen, nobles and serfs, patricians and plebeians; and so it will be, and in part already is, with the aristocracies of colour, race, and sex' (ibid., 10.259). The teachings of Comte showed that, even without divine sanction, there would be no difficulty about endowing 'the service of humanity' with all the 'psychological power and social efficacy of a religion'—the only danger being, not that such a religion might be too weak, 'but that it should be so excessive as to interfere unduly with human freedom and individuality' (ibid., 10.232).

Westminster and women Mill's three classic treatises of 1859–63 therefore left him with something of a dilemma, as the champion both of privacy, spontaneity, and absolute personal choice, and of communitarianism, public spirit, and the sovereignty of higher over lower goals. This dilemma reflected a long-standing tension in Mill's own inclinations, since throughout life he cherished privacy, quietude, intimate friendships, and refined tastes, yet was constantly sucked into the public sphere by the pull of duty, reformism, moral indignation, and a sense of inner mission about his own role as one of the tiny élite to whom it was given both to 'see' and to 'feel' the 'futurity of the species' (*Collected Works*, 21.294). This pull between private and public roles became more acute after Harriet's death, as Mill felt himself called not merely to write about, but to act on, many of the causes they had shared together. In these his new companion was to be his stepdaughter Helen Taylor, who was twenty-seven when her mother died. Helen in the 1850s had fought a long battle with Harriet to be allowed to train for the stage, and had achieved some limited success in provincial repertory. In 1859, however, despite her strongly independent views, she seemed more than happy to slide into her mother's role as Mill's helpmate, amanuensis, and housekeeper of his homes in Blackheath and Avignon. Surprisingly, given Harriet's views on women's education, Helen had had very little formal schooling; but she was soon taking an active role in the editing of Mill's manuscripts,

> which I go over five or six times, putting in words here, stops there; scratching through whole paragraphs; asking him to write whole new pages in particular places where I think the meaning is not clear; condensing, enlarging, polishing, etc. (Packe, 481)

Helen was much more interested in active politics than her mother, and was also more hospitable, with the result that Mill began to resume contact with many old and newer friends—the Grotes, the Bains, the Amberleys, the Fawcetts, Herbert Spencer, John Morley, Moncure Conway, and many others.

It was through the medium of this expanding circle that Mill became involved in many contentious radical causes of the 1860s, among them land reform in Ireland, the Amberleys' campaign for birth-control, Thomas Hare's campaign for proportional representation, and the embryonic movement for women's suffrage. He wrote extensively in support of the North in the American civil war, and in 1866 was to become a very active chairman of the controversial Jamaica committee, which pressed for the prosecution of Governor Eyre—a move denounced by a rival faction, headed by Carlyle, to whom Eyre was a national hero. In 1865 Mill was invited to stand as a Liberal candidate for Westminster in the forthcoming general election, an invitation he felt to be 'one of those calls upon a member of the community by his fellow citizens, which he was scarcely justified in rejecting' (*Collected Works*, 1.273). He accepted on the understanding that, as a matter of principle, he would not campaign or incur election expenses, and he held only two election meetings, one for registered electors, the other for persons without the vote. At the latter he won credit for honesty with his audience by confessing to having written that the British working classes, 'though differing from those of some other countries in being ashamed of lying, are yet generally liars' (ibid., 1.274–5). The election was accompanied by a great surge in the sale of his political, economic, and philosophical works, many of them now reprinted for the first time in cheap popular editions.

Mill was elected with a majority of 700, and, after a shaky start, became a respected speaker in the Commons, particularly with carefully prepared speeches on the great issue of the day, parliamentary reform, in which he pressed for the adoption of his favourite scheme of cumulative voting. On several matters he proved to be markedly at odds with advanced radical opinion, notably in his support for capital punishment, high defence spending, and reduction of the national debt; but on other issues he felt

it his duty to go out of his way to espouse unpopular radical causes, such as defence of the Fenians and Irish land reform, resistance to the extradition of political refugees, and promotion of women's rights. On 20 May 1867 he forced a debate on an amendment to Disraeli's Suffrage Bill, proposing the substitution of 'person' for 'men'—an action he later regarded as 'the only really important public service I performed in the capacity of a member of Parliament' (*Collected Works*, 1.285). A year later he presented to parliament a petition demanding amendment of the law relating to married women's property. He lost his seat in the general election of 1868, after a rather muddled controversy over his contribution to the election expenses of Charles Bradlaugh (an action portrayed by opponents as violating his own declared principle of three years before).

Mill withdrew from Westminster with something of a sense of relief, and thereafter spent much of his time in Avignon, preparing an edition of his father's *Essay on Mind*, revising his own earlier works, and answering the objections of his critics. For the rest of his life his political energies were concentrated almost exclusively on issues relating to the cause of women. In 1869 he published the last of his great political tracts, *The Subjection of Women*, which had originally been drafted in 1861. As with his other mature political writings, the question must be asked: how far was this tract his own work and how far did it reflect the thought of Harriet—and also, in this case, that of his stepdaughter Helen Taylor? In his *Autobiography* Mill gave three slightly different answers to this question. In a long footnote he stated that the abstract principles of the *Subjection* were his own, but the 'perception of the vast practical bearings of women's disabilities' came from Harriet, an account that reflected his broader perception of their respective roles within their marriage (*Collected Works*, 1.253). In a discarded fragment he also ascribed to Harriet the grasping of the more strategic fact that women's freedom was 'the great question of the coming time: the most urgent interest of human progress' (ibid., 1.252). In the main text of the *Autobiography* he stated that the writing of the treatise had initially been suggested by Helen, and that the published version 'was enriched with some important ideas of my daughter's, and passages of her writing'; in the parts composed by himself, 'all that is most striking and profound belongs to my wife', stemming from the 'innumerable conversations and discussions on a topic which filled so large a place in our minds' (ibid., 1.252–3, 265). These references suggest some confusion about the work's genesis, and in the absence of other corroboration the biographer is thrust back on the content and style of the published text. *The Subjection of Women* certainly showed many substantive signs of Harriet's influence, and drew on the arguments for women's enfranchisement she had set out in her classic *Westminster Review* article of 1851. The critique of views that afforded women superior moral status as a compensatory placebo for inferior legal power directly echoed Harriet's curt dismissal of these visions of women as a 'sentimental priesthood'. There was also clear reference back to their essays on divorce composed in 1831–2—the *Subjection* combining both Harriet's argument for opening careers and public offices to women, and Mill's own argument that even under conditions of total equality most women would probably choose the option of managing a home. The detailed references to matrimonial violence, and to the sexual despotism legally practised by the most brutish of men, derived from articles relating to contemporary court cases that Harriet and Mill had composed jointly during the 1850s.

Yet there can be little doubt that the main structure of the text of *The Subjection of Women* was the work of Mill himself, if only because it was the most elaborately rhetorical of all his writings, and drew on all the vast battery of classical and scholastic devices for the advancement of a cause that he had learned at his father's knee from the age of three. It also closely fused the arguments in Mill's other works about the problematic balance between individual and society, and the conjunction of private and public virtue. In no area of life was the repression of 'natural freedom' by the 'despotism of custom' to be seen as so all-encompassing as in society's thinking about women. Women's case for equality rested above all on the fact that their status under existing laws was the only remaining residue of personal bond-service, now universally acknowledged as incompatible with full humanity. That status had survived because—alone among the various forms of servitude—it conferred domination, not on a single ruler or ruling class but on the whole male sex: 'The clodhopper exercises … his share of power equally with the highest nobleman' (*Collected Works*, 21.268). Even married to a good husband, a wife was little more than a domestic 'uncle Tom'; married to a bad one, she was the 'body-servant of a despot' (ibid., 21.284–5). Such an anomaly went against the whole modern current of private rights and free personality; but it also damaged and corrupted the public sphere, by fostering a spirit of patronage and clienthood, confining virtue exclusively to private life, and depriving society of the talents and public services of half the human species. Claims about women's superior moral qualities were a mere 'empty compliment, which must provoke a bitter smile from every woman of spirit, since there is no other situation in life in which it is … considered quite natural and suitable, that the better should obey the worse' (ibid., 21.320). Claims about their inferior mental qualities could not be scientifically substantiated, because—except for a tiny handful of (often successful) female rulers—history had never tested them out. 'What, in unenlightened societies, colour, race, religion … are to some men, sex is to all women; a peremptory exclusion from almost all honourable occupations' (ibid., 21.340).

In the short term Mill's *The Subjection of Women* proved the most unpopular and bitterly contested of all his writings. It was widely denounced both by a majority who saw it as subversive of familial and social stability, and by a minority who disliked Mill's picture of companionate marriage, his very limited endorsement of divorce, and his belief that even liberated women would opt for homes and children. It was the only one of his published works on which he made a financial loss, even though pirated popular editions soon began to circulate widely in Europe and America. Among campaigners for women's suffrage, however, it rapidly became a sacred text and gave him a position of heroic, almost apostolic, authority within the nascent women's movement. This role was not confined to his theoretical works, but for a time involved him in somewhat uneasy participation in practical organization. Mill and Helen had been involved since 1867 in setting up a provisional women's franchise committee, which in 1868 became the London National Society for Women's Suffrage, and similar societies were founded at the same time in Manchester and Edinburgh. These societies mobilized support from middle-class women in many parts of the country, and were to become the spearhead of the women's suffrage campaign. Nevertheless, their early activities were fraught with internal divisions, over such questions as the terms on which women should claim the vote, the role to be played by male sympathizers, and the attitude of the suffrage campaign to the other great women's crusade of the period, the campaign for repeal of the Contagious Diseases Acts (CDA). In these disputes Mill played a prominent but somewhat erratic role that was not always congenial to other leaders of the women's movement. Faithful to the opinions of Harriet, he tried to insist that, in their day-to-day management, women's organizations had to be run exclusively by women, a principle resisted by cautious pragmatists like Millicent Fawcett and Emily Davies, who valued active co-operation with influential men. Mill at first supported, but then retreated from, co-operation with the contagious diseases campaign, on the ground that prurient and fanatical elements were discrediting the primary objective of gaining the vote. Within the National Society for Women's Suffrage he began to lobby for exclusion of CDA activists; and when in 1872 a Women's Suffrage Bill received fewer votes in parliament than his own amendment of 1867, he blamed the failure on the repealers and 'the total want equally of good taste and good sense with which they conduct the proceedings' (Kamm, 190). Such attitudes dismayed those of Mill's disciples who viewed him above all as the champion of personal liberties; they demonstrated once again the awkward tensions between Mill as the champion of resistance to convention, and his rather different role as the promoter of an austere, rational, self-disciplined, public sphere.

Agnosticism, positivism, Christianity Mill in his *Autobiography* portrayed himself as 'one of the very few examples, in this country, of one who has, not thrown off religious belief, but never had it' (*Collected Works*, 1.44). He had been brought up against the backcloth of his father's conclusions that orthodox Christian doctrine was immoral, that dogmatic atheism was absurd, and that 'concerning the origin of things nothing whatever can be known' (ibid., 1.41). Throughout his life Mill underwent nothing that he regarded as a religious experience, and he believed that such experiences in others were rooted either in ignoble feelings of fear or in a noble but misidentified quest for the beautiful and the sublime. Much of his aversion to intuitive and idealist modes of thought, even when practised by secular thinkers, was rooted in the suspicion that they were liable to slide inexorably into some form of mysticism and superstition. He opposed notions of 'natural' conscience in man, insisting that the moral sense was entirely the product of social conditioning (a claim that sat rather uneasily with his equally strong view that people could choose to alter their own characters). His writings on logic, economics, and politics were widely regarded by contemporaries not just as exercises in secular science but as veiled attacks on Christian orthodoxy, and there were occasions on which Mill himself seemed to endorse this view.

Nevertheless, Mill's polemic against both religion in general and Christianity in particular was less sustained and less uniformly hostile than was often supposed. During his Saint-Simonian phase he came to view ecclesiastical institutions not as his father had done as instruments of state terror, but as bodies that had played an indispensable role in the past development of mental and cultural progress; and the early stages of his enthusiasm for Comte were fuelled by the hope that Comte had discovered an ethical and scientific substitute for orthodox Christianity. In the 1830s and 1840s he was visibly impressed by the efforts of churchmen like Whately, Baden Powell, and W. G. Ward to align Christianity to developments in modern knowledge, and he was impressed also by the attempts of the Tractarians to reconstitute a sense of organic Christian community (though he was convinced that in modern circumstances they were bound to fail). Bain's claim that Mill never read a work of theology is clearly false. He had a deep and detailed knowledge of the Bible and of the history of theological argument from the early church fathers through to F. D. Maurice and J. H. Newman, Schleiermacher and Strauss; and part of his irritation with Christianity as a working philosophy stemmed from the fact that many of its adherents seemed to know far less about the subject than he knew himself. Moreover, the circles in which he moved were not so much anti-religious as heterodox and proto-modernist. The dearest friend of his youth, J. H. Sterling, though wildly unorthodox, was nevertheless an ordained Anglican clergyman who combined day-to-day sacramental piety with private pursuit of uninhibited modernist speculation. Fragments of evidence relating to Harriet Taylor's views on religion seem to indicate that, although profoundly hostile to ecclesiastical establishments and formal doctrine, she was sympathetic to the freethinking ethical transcendentalism taught by William Fox and his successors at the South Place Chapel. Her daughter Helen combined absolute commitment to free choice in religion with a private attraction to Roman Catholicism: when, during the Bradlaugh expenses dispute, Helen remonstrated with Mill for publicly denying that he was an atheist, her anger stemmed not from her own personal views but from what she saw as Mill's betrayal of the liberal principle that the public had no right to question a politician's private beliefs.

These affinities with persons of diffuse, unorthodox, radical, religious sympathies provide a context for Mill's meditations on religion, which moved a long way from the pessimistic agnosticism inherited from his father. The correspondence of his middle life reveals his deep interest in debate about the intellectual possibility of belief, not just in contemporary discussion, but in the writings of Catholic authors of the seventeenth century such as Bellarmine, Bossuet, Fénélon, and Suarez. In Mill's view, evidence of the supernatural origins of Christianity was everywhere crumbling under the heel of historical criticism, thrusting religious belief back on claims about the intrinsic excellence of its ethics and metaphysics, claims that directly meshed with his own primary concerns. Like his father before him Mill found that the existence of evil made it logically impossible to envisage a divine being who was both ethically righteous and omnipotent; but unlike James Mill he was able to conceive of an *ideal* Perfect Being' of whose existence there was 'enough in the course of Nature (when once the idea of Omnipotence is discarded) to give to that belief a considerable degree of support'. Human apprehension of that being was however circumscribed by the theory of inference set out in *A System of Logic*, which limited knowledge properly so-called to objects susceptible to induction and deduction: it was this logical constraint that determined Mill's 'position in respect to Theism: I think it a legitimate subject of imagination, and hope, and even belief (not amounting to faith) but not of knowledge' (*Collected Works*, 15.755). There were nevertheless many hints in Mill's writings that he saw his purpose as being not to subvert Christian belief but to strengthen it, by offering the possibility of an alliance with 'good ethics and good metaphysics', and leaving 'Xtianity to reconcile itself with them the best way it can. By that course, in so far as we have any success, we are at least sure of doing something to improve Christianity' (ibid., 15.646). Many of his later works referred to the teaching of Christ as a standard of ethical perfection never yet acknowledged by Christians; and although he had nothing but contempt for the crude rapprochement between Christianity and utility offered by Archdeacon Paley, his own *Utilitarianism* claimed to offer a higher synthesis, not just between utility and Kantianism but between utility and the ethics of the New Testament. This synthesis Mill saw as embodying 'the doctrine of loving one's neighbour as oneself, this being of course understood not of the feeling or sentiment of love, but of perfect ethical impartiality between the two' (ibid., 15.762).

Such aspirations help to explain Mill's growing interest in religion in his later years; not, as cynics at the time implied, as a sentimental hope of reunion with his wife, but as a natural extension of his long-standing interest in ethics and theories of knowledge. His study of Comte in 1865 attacked the fetishism, manic asceticism, and spiritual autocracy of Comte's later writings; but he nevertheless defended the principle of Comte's endeavour to transform positivism into an organized religion, and claimed that more orthodox creeds would be 'made better in proportion as, in their practical result, they are brought to coincide with that which he aimed at constructing' (*Collected Works*, 10.335). The quest for an ethically compelling, rationally defensible, restatement of religious truth also lay behind the work that many regarded as his most serious onslaught on transcendental belief, *The Examination of Sir William Hamilton's Philosophy*, published in 1865. Hamilton, an Edinburgh professor of metaphysics who had died in 1856, was famous for his doctrine of the 'relativity of human knowledge', a doctrine that sounded superficially not unlike the principle affirmed by Mill's own epistemological school, that knowledge was limited to whatever could be derived from evidence of the senses. Certainly Mill began his study of Hamilton's works in the belief that Hamilton had deployed Scottish common-sense philosophy to demolish the rationalist idealism of post-Kantian German philosophers like Hegel and Schelling. But in fact Hamilton had developed quite the opposite view; he had claimed that there was a noumenal world of 'things in themselves', imperceptible by the senses and inaccessible also to 'immediate or intuitive' reasoning. The fact of unknowability Hamilton portrayed, not as a ground for scepticism, but—to Mill's disgust—as the ground for 'a great mass of Belief, differing from Knowledge in the mode but not in the certainty of conviction … respecting the attributes of the Unknowable' (*Collected Works*, 15.816–17). This doctrine had been deployed by Hamilton's disciple Henry Mansel in his Bampton lectures, to suggest that God was absolute, infinite, utterly unfathomable by 'vulgar Rationalism', and vested with moral attributes wholly different in kind from, and apparently contrary to, the moral attributes of mankind. In the realm of the absolute the 'infliction of physical suffering, the permission of moral evil, the adversity of the good, the prosperity of the wicked' were all compatible with the infinite goodness of God, though not in the least compatible with the goodness of human beings (ibid., 9.100–01). Such a doctrine seemed to Mill to confirm his lifelong suspicion that idealist metaphysics was not merely intellectually false but morally evil. 'The question it involves', he declared:

> is, beyond all others which now engage speculative minds, the decisive one between moral good and evil for the Christian world … All trust in a Revelation presupposes a conviction that God's attributes are the same, in all but degree, with the best human attributes … I will call no being good, who is not what I mean when I apply that epithet to my fellow-creatures; and if such a being can sentence me to hell for not so calling him, to hell I will go. (ibid., 9.90, 102–3)

Mill's attack on Hamilton and Mansel shocked some Christians, but brought him virtually into the Christian fold with many others—most notably with disciples of his old friend and debating opponent F. D. Maurice, the apostle of incarnationalism and of the immanent 'Kingdom of Christ'. Mill's *Hamilton* did not, however, mark any change in his religious views, but simply a clearer statement than hitherto of the direction in which he had been trying to steer moral philosophy since the 1840s. It made no difference at all to his advocacy of the claims of Bradlaugh, nor to the tenor and argument of his posthumously published essay 'Theism' (composed 1868–70), which was to prove

his last sustained work. In this essay he expounded the view, mentioned often in private correspondence in his later years, that religious belief—though by its nature outside the boundaries of genuine knowledge—was a legitimate construct of the imagination linked to the conception of a morally perfect being. (To Mill, the term imagination never implied falsehood, but simply, as in aesthetics, a faculty wholly outside the realm of knowledge and science.) This perfect being could take many forms—creator, judge, nature, pure abstraction—but it was 'the God incarnate, more than the God of the Jews or of Nature, who being idealized has taken so great and salutary a hold on the modern mind' (*Collected Works*, 10.487). Such an imaginative construction seemed to Mill 'excellently fitted to aid and fortify that real, though purely human religion, which sometimes calls itself the Religion of Humanity and sometimes that of Duty'; it was 'a part of wisdom to make the most of any, even small, probabilities on this subject, which furnish imagination with any footing to support itself upon' (ibid., 10.488, 483). Even without such exiguous probabilities, 'we venture to think that a religion may exist without belief in a God, and that a religion without a God may be, even to Christians, an instructive and profitable object' (ibid., 10.332).

Death and posthumous reputation Mill's last years were spent partly in London, partly in Avignon, always in the company of the devoted Helen Taylor, often visited by Bain, Hare, the Fawcetts, and John Morley. One of his last public appearances was before the royal commission on contagious diseases (1871), where he argued that, whether the acts were retained or repealed, the key principle was even-handed treatment for both sexes. At his house in Avignon he was befriended by a young protestant pastor, Louis Rey, and his wife, whose undoctrinal Christianity closely coincided with Mill's own undoctrinal agnosticism. In April 1873 he contracted erysipelas, an inflammation of the skin endemic in the Avignon region, and died on 7 May 1873. His last words to his stepdaughter were 'you know that I have done my work' (Packe, 507). In England, the billboards of popular newspapers announced his death in many cities, a tribute accorded to no other English philosopher. Moves were set in hand to have him interred in Westminster Abbey, but before this could be arranged he was buried as he had wished in Avignon in the tomb that he had built for Harriet. A modestly religious service was conducted by Pastor Rey, who nevertheless crushed rumours of a deathbed conversion by insisting that Mill had died, as he lived, an agnostic.

Mill was a national legend long before his death, simultaneously both revered and deplored by large numbers of his fellow citizens. To Gladstone he was the 'Saint of Rationalism', to Disraeli 'the finishing governess', to F. H. Bradley 'the moral Nautical Almanack', to a young liberal of the next generation, L. T. Hobhouse, 'the greatest and best man of this century' (Packe, 51–5; Bradley, 101; Collini, 54). Even in his lifetime different strands in his thought encapsulated some of the most powerful cross-currents of the Victorian age—positivism and idealism, free-market capitalism and the rise of collectivism, mass democracy and the republic of civic virtue. Within the Victorian and post-Victorian women's movement he was to be a profoundly ambiguous figure, venerated for his promotion of female suffrage, less unanimously admired for his constructions of sex and gender. His writings on ethics and religion were to be a powerful force for translating religious belief into the purely private sphere and generating a pervasive culture of 'agnosticism'. But at the same time many of his views about ethics and the nature of belief were to be widely incorporated into late nineteenth-century Christian apologetics, and by the 1890s *A System of Logic* had joined Butler's *Analogy* as one of the two most commonly prescribed books for courses on moral theology. The reputation of Mill's other works has ebbed and flowed over the course of the last century. The *Principles of Political Economy* was an instant success, but declined in popularity at the end of the nineteenth century with the rise of marginalism and collectivism (even though Mill's ideas about monopoly and unearned increment were to play an important part in the economic doctrines of Fabianism and new liberalism). Mill's *Logic* failed to generate a new theory and methodology of the social sciences; indeed its methodological individualism has been blamed for the failure of sociological theory to seed itself deeply in twentieth-century British culture. On the other hand, its powerful social environmentalism was a major influence on the development of the applied social sciences and social policy from the mid-nineteenth century down to the present day. Mill's *On Liberty* was frequently dismissed in the Edwardian era as atomistic, anti-statist, and out-of-date, but it acquired a wholly new significance in the age of totalitarian dictatorship, and was to be reborn yet again during the libertarian movements of the 1960s. As a philosophical work its emphasis on the autonomy of the individual has been seen as a tacit resort to the kind of essentialism that Mill had always claimed to reject; a point that might also be made about his conceptions of character and the laws of human nature. Works like *Utilitarianism* and *Representative Government* have acquired a new salience with the emergence of liberal communitarianism since the 1980s; and the endemic tension in Mill's thought between private liberty and civic duty has many resonances in current Anglo-American political philosophy. Pinpointing Mill's precise identity on the political spectrum was a problem in his lifetime and has been so ever since—his allegiance being claimed by free-marketeers and collectivists, social democrats and liberal conservatives, paternalists and libertarians.

Mill left an estate of £14,000, of which £6000 was bequeathed to women's education and £1000 to other charities. Part of his library and private papers were left to Somerville College, Oxford, much of the rest eventually being acquired by the British Library of Political Science. A portrait by G. F. Watts, painted in 1873, is in the National Portrait Gallery. An earlier portrait by Cunningham, which has not survived, was painted during his visit to Falmouth in 1840, and reproduced in several cameo copies.

JOSE HARRIS

Sources *The collected works of John Stuart Mill*, ed. J. M. Robson and others, 33 vols. (1963–91) • M. St J. Packe, *The life of John Stuart Mill* (1954) • *Mill on Bentham and Coleridge*, ed. F. R. Leavis (1950) • *John Stuart Mill and Harriet Taylor: their correspondence and subsequent marriage*, ed. F. A. Hayek (1951) • J. Kamm, *John Stuart Mill in love* (1987) • W. Thomas, *The philosophic radicals: nine studies in theory and practice, 1817–1841* (1979) • A. Ryan, *The philosophy of John Stuart Mill* (1970) • S. Hollander, *The economics of John Stuart Mill*, 2 vols. (1985) • S. Collini, D. Winch, and J. Burrow, *That noble science of politics* (1983) • W. Whewell, *The philosophy of the inductive sciences*, new edn, 2 vols. (1847) • F. H. Bradley, *Ethical studies*, 1959 edn (1876) • S. Collini, *Liberalism and sociology: L. T. Hobhouse and political argument in England* (1979)

Archives BL, letters to his father; French travel, journal, Add. MS 31909 • BL, papers relating to his memorial, 1873, Add. MSS 44095, 44103, 44141, 44207, 44439, 44440 • BL, revised MS of 'A system of logic', Add. MSS 41624–41627 • BLPES, corresp. and papers • Bodl. Oxf., journal of a tour of Yorkshire and the Lakes, 1831 • Hunt. L., letters • King's AC Cam., corresp. • Somerville College, Oxford, his personal library, with annotations • Trinity Cam., corresp. • U. Leeds, Brotherton L., letters • University of Illinois, Urbana-Champaign, MSS of his autobiography, letters • University of Toronto, Thomas Fisher Rare Book Library, speech notes • Yale U., Beinecke L., corresp. and papers | BL, letters to Sir Charles Dilke, Add. MS 43897 • BL, corresp. with W. E. Gladstone, 1859–69, Add. MSS 44392, 44401–44402, 44407, 44409–44411, 44413, 44421 • BL, letters to George Grote and his wife, Add. MS 46691 • BL, corresp. with Thomas Hare, Add. MS 43773 • BL, letters to Macvey Napier, Add. MSS 34621–34626 • BL, corresp. with Florence Nightingale, Add. MS 45787 • BLPES, letters to Leonard Courtney • BLPES, letters to Macrae Moir • Bodl. Oxf., letters to Sir William Napier • Co-operative Union, Manchester, Holyoake House archive, corresp. with George Jacob Holyoake • Cornell University, Ithaca, New York, letters to William Christie • Herts. ALS, letters to Lord Lytton and Albany Fonblanque • Johns Hopkins University, Baltimore, corresp. • Maison d'Auguste Comte, Paris, corresp. with Auguste Comte • NL Aus., letters to John Chapman • NL Scot., corresp. with Thomas Carlyle • Northwestern University, Chicago, Illinois, corresp. with Herbert Spencer • RS, corresp. with Sir John Herschel • UCL, letters to Edwin Chadwick • UCL, letters to Augustus De Morgan • UCL, corresp. with George Croom Robertson • University of Melbourne, letters to John Plummer

Likenesses J. and C. Watkins, photographs, 1865, NPG • G. F. Watts, oils, 1873, City of Westminster, London; replica, NPG • T. Woolner, bronze statue, *c*.1878, Victoria Embankment Gardens, London • H. Furniss, pen-and-ink drawing, NPG • A. Legros, bronze medallion (posthumous), Man. City Gall. • P. A. Rajon, etching (after Cunningham, 1840), Westminster City Hall, London • Spy [L. Ward], caricature, watercolour and pencil drawing, NPG • Spy [L. Ward], chromolithograph caricature, NPG; repro. in *VF* (29 March 1873) • J. Watkins, cartes-de-visite, NPG • daguerreotype, NPG [*see illus.*]

Wealth at death under £14,000: probate, 5 Sept 1873, *CGPLA Eng. & Wales*

Mill, William Hodge (1792–1853), orientalist, son of John Mill of Dundee and his wife, Martha, *née* Hodge, was born on 18 July 1792 at Hackney, Middlesex. He was educated chiefly in private under Dr Belsham, a Unitarian preacher, and in 1809 proceeded to Trinity College, Cambridge, where he graduated BA as sixth wrangler in 1813. He was elected fellow on 1 October 1814, and proceeded MA in 1816. He took deacon's orders in 1817, and priest's in the following year. Continuing to live in Cambridge, he appears to have devoted himself especially to oriental studies.

In 1820 Mill was appointed the first principal of Bishop's

College, Calcutta, then just founded, under the superintendence of Bishop Thomas Fanshaw Middleton. He assisted in the publication of works in Arabic, of which he had already gained some knowledge, studied the local languages and Sanskrit, and co-operated in the work of the Sanskrit and other colleges. He was also a leading member and vice-president from 1833 to 1837 of the Asiatic Society of Bengal, and appears to have been regularly consulted on all discoveries relating to Sanskrit or Arabic scholarship. He energetically supported the society's *Journal*, contributing to several of its earliest volumes. He gave valuable assistance by his decipherments of several important inscriptions, then little understood, especially those on the pillars at Allahabad and Bhitari.

Mill's health obliged him to return to Europe in 1838. At his departure an address was voted to him by the Asiatic Society. Resuming his theological career in 1839 he was appointed chaplain to William Howley, archbishop of Canterbury, and Christian advocate on the Hulse foundation at Cambridge. In 1848 he became regius professor of Hebrew there, with a canonry at Ely. His lectures were chiefly on the text of the Psalms. He died on 25 December 1853 at Brasted, Kent, a living to which he had been presented by the archbishop in 1843. He was buried in Ely Cathedral on new year's eve. A portion of a window in the chapel of Trinity College, Cambridge, was subsequently (1862) filled with stained glass to his memory.

Mill's chief work is *Christa-Sangita* (Calcutta, 1831), a remarkable translation of the gospel story into the metre and style of the Sanskrit Puranas. It was originally suggested to Mill by a Hindu pandit, who was the main author of the first canto. He translated several other Christian texts into Sanskrit and Arabic. Mill also published many theological lectures and sermons.

CECIL BENDALL, *rev.* PARVIN LOLOI

Sources GM, 2nd ser., 41 (1854), 205 · *Journal of the Royal Asiatic Society of Great Britain and Ireland*, 15 (1855), ii–v · *Journal of Bengal Asiatic Society* · Venn, *Alum. Cant.* · J. Haydn, *A dictionary of biography, past and present*, ed. B. Vincent (1877) · C. E. Buckland, *Dictionary of Indian biography* (1906)
Archives Bodl. Oxf., collections, papers, travel journals · LPL, letters and papers
Likenesses F. Chantrey, marble bust, exh. RA 1840, India; at Royal Asiatic Society, India, in 1938; plaster model, AM Oxf. · J. B. Philip, recumbent effigy, 1860, Ely Cathedral · F. Chantrey, pencil drawing, NPG

Millais, Sir John Everett, first baronet (1829–1896), painter, was born on 8 June 1829 in Portland Street (probably at no. 30), Southampton, and baptized on 27 December in the same year at All Saints' Church, Southampton. He was the third of the three surviving children of John William Millais (1800–1870) and his wife, Mary (1789–1864). The son of a lawyer in St Helier, Jersey, John William Millais pursued no profession and normally described himself as a gentleman; he was a keen amateur musician. Mary Millais, his senior by eleven years, was the daughter of Richard Evamy, a saddler, brewer, and hop merchant of Southampton. She was the widow of Enoch Hodgkinson, a draper, and had two sons from her first marriage, Clement (1818–1893) and Henry (1820–1885). John William and

Sir John Everett Millais, first baronet (1829–1896), by George Frederic Watts, 1871

Mary Millais were married in Southampton on 24 September 1822. Their first two children to survive infancy were Emily Mary (1823–1909), who was to marry the actor Lester Wallack and live in New York, and William Henry (1828–1899), who also became an artist.

Early years, 1829–1848 Millais spent some of the happiest years of his childhood in his father's homeland, Jersey in the Channel Islands, and would always describe himself proudly as a Jerseyman. His family had moved from Southampton to St Helier, Jersey, by 1831; from about 1834 they spent a period living at Dinan in France for the benefit of his mother's health, and they were back in St Helier by 1837. Millais had already shown remarkable artistic talents and from that year took lessons with a local drawing master named Bessell. He also received guidance from the German artist Edward Henry Wehnert, who lived in St Helier at the time, and encouragement from two prominent men on the island, Sir Hilgrove Turner and Philip Raoul Lemprière, seigneur of Rozel.

In 1838, acting on Sir Hilgrove Turner's advice, Millais's parents moved to London so that their gifted son could be trained for a professional career as an artist. After periods at several different addresses in the area of the British Museum, they took a lease on 83 Gower Street, where they lived from 1844 to 1854. The young Millais attended Henry Sass's academy, which prepared boys for entrance into the schools of the Royal Academy, and in 1839–41 he won prizes in the annual drawing competitions for young artists run by the Society of Arts. On 12 December 1840, aged eleven, he became the youngest student ever admitted to the Royal Academy Schools. There he enjoyed a reputation as a prodigy. In 1843 he won a silver medal for the best drawing from the antique, and in 1846 made his début at the Royal Academy's annual exhibition with his highly accomplished though conventional painting *Pizarro Seizing the Inca of Peru* (V&A). From 1846 he attended the life academy at the schools, and he demonstrated his thorough grounding in figure drawing in *The Tribe of Benjamin Seizing the Daughters of Shiloh in the Vineyards* (priv. coll.), which won him the gold medal for best historical painting in 1847. For a period in the later 1840s Millais spent one day a week at the house of the lawyer-cum-art dealer Ralph Thomas, who paid him an annual sum, first £100 and later £150, for painting small genre pictures to add to his stock.

The Pre-Raphaelite Brotherhood, 1848–1854 At the Royal Academy Schools, Millais became close friends with his fellow student William Holman Hunt. He was moved by Hunt's seriousness and idealism, and came to share some of his radical views about the state of British art. The academy remained under the intellectual sway of Sir Joshua Reynolds, its first president. In his famous *Discourses on Art*, Reynolds encouraged young British artists to follow in the Renaissance tradition, to revere Raphael, and to aspire to the classical ideal—that perfect beauty never found in nature but attainable by the artist through careful selection and improvement. Hunt and Millais reacted against this view and resolved to paint people and things just as they found them, observing the particular features of actual models in detail. Taking heart from the truth to nature they saw in art from before the time of Raphael, they and five like-minded colleagues, including Dante Gabriel Rossetti, decided to call themselves the Pre-Raphaelite Brotherhood (PRB); the other members were the relatively minor artists Thomas Woolner and James Collinson, along with William Michael Rossetti and F. G. Stephens, who were to have distinguished careers as art critics. The excited discussion that led to the formation of the PRB took place at Millais's house in Gower Street in September 1848.

Already a name in artistic circles, and far ahead of his friends in his painting technique, Millais rapidly put Pre-Raphaelite ideas into practice at a high professional level and, for better or worse, brought the PRB much public attention. His first major painting in the new style was *Isabella* (exh. RA, 1849; Walker Art Gallery, Liverpool), a subject from John Keats's poem 'Isabella, or, The Pot of Basil'. It shows the use of portraiture as an antidote to idealization, the stiffness of pose intended to recall medieval art, the minute, all-over detail, and the high colour key that characterized early Pre-Raphaelitism. He intended his painting of *Christ in the Carpenter's Shop* (exh. RA, 1850; Tate collection), with its ungainly Christ, emaciated Virgin Mary, and Joseph with dirty fingernails, as a realistic corrective to traditional 'Raphaelite' images of the holy family. It was received by the critics with almost universal disgust, as a piece of wilful blasphemy, and attacked by Charles Dickens in *Household Words*. 'You will have the goodness to discharge from your minds all Post-Raphael

ideas', Dickens warned his readers, 'and to prepare yourselves, as befits such a subject—Pre-Raphaelly considered—for the lowest depths of what is mean, odious, repulsive, and revolting' (15 June 1850, 265).

Millais's friendships with his fellow artists were especially important at this difficult moment in his career. His most intimate companions were Holman Hunt and Charles (or Carlo, as Millais affectionately called him) Collins, the highly sensitive, ascetic younger brother of the novelist Wilkie Collins. He also received much needed moral and material support from his patrons. Among these was James Wyatt, a frame-maker, printseller, and art dealer of Oxford. Wyatt invited Millais to stay at his home on several occasions between 1846 and 1850, bought his painting *Cymon and Iphigenia* (1848; priv. coll.), commissioned a pair of family portraits, owned several other small oils, and kept a large number of drawings given to him by the artist as expressions of friendship. Another was Thomas Combe, also of Oxford, who was printer to the university and superintendent of the Clarendon Press. Millais and Charles Collins spent several weeks in Oxford as Combe's guest between September and November 1850. Combe and his wife, Martha, were devout Christians and staunch supporters of the Oxford Movement, and the Pre-Raphaelites' belief in the purity of art before the high Renaissance resonated with their nostalgia, as high-church Anglicans, for pre-Reformation England. They bought Millais's painting *The Return of the Dove to the Ark* (1850–51), and, through Millais's efforts, works by Collins, Holman Hunt, and Rossetti; their collection remains intact as the Combe bequest at the Ashmolean Museum, Oxford.

In summer 1851 Millais began his masterpiece of outdoor Pre-Raphaelite painting, and now the most familiar of his early works, *Ophelia* (exh. RA, 1852; Tate collection), which shows the pathetic derangement of the heroine of *Hamlet* as she sinks 'to muddy death' in a brook. He painted the background of painstakingly observed plants and flowers, some chosen for their symbolic significance, from a spot on the Hogsmill River, near Ewell in Surrey. He had often been to Ewell to visit the family of William Charles Lemprière, younger brother of Philip Raoul Lemprière of Jersey. On this occasion he was accompanied by Holman Hunt and stayed with him in lodgings; as he worked on *Ophelia* by the river, Hunt painted *The Hireling Shepherd* (1851–2; Manchester City Galleries) in a nearby field. His background took some four months to complete, and he added the figure of Ophelia in his studio in Gower Street during the following winter. As a model he used Elizabeth Siddall, the favourite model and eventually the wife of D. G. Rossetti. According to the biography of Millais by his son John Guille Millais, Siddall posed in a bath full of water kept warm by lamps underneath. One day the lamps went out and she caught a severe cold, at which her father threatened the artist with legal action until he agreed to pay her doctor's bills (*Life and Letters*, 1.144).

From 1852, when he showed *Ophelia* and *A Huguenot, on St Bartholomew's day, refusing to shield himself from danger by* wearing a Roman Catholic badge (priv. coll.) at the Royal Academy exhibition, Millais enjoyed increasing public and critical acclaim. With its touching subject of ill-fated lovers in a historical conflict, A Huguenot was especially popular, preparing the way for his election as an associate of the Royal Academy on 7 November 1853. He went on to paint several variations on the same general theme, including The Proscribed Royalist, 1651 (exh. RA, 1853; priv. coll.), The Order of Release, 1746 (exh. RA, 1853; Tate collection), and The Black Brunswicker (exh. RA, 1860; Lady Lever Art Gallery, Port Sunlight). He also caught the popular imagination with a scene of a heroic fireman carrying children from a burning house, The Rescue (exh. RA, 1855; National Gallery of Victoria, Melbourne).

The Pre-Raphaelites admired the writings of the great critic John Ruskin, who, in turn, had championed their work against the attacks of the press. Millais and Ruskin met, and Ruskin's attractive young wife, Effie, posed as the model for the loyal Jacobite wife in The Order of Release. Euphemia Chalmers Gray (1828–1897), usually known as Effie, was the eldest child of George Gray, a writer to the signet, and his wife, Sophia Jameson; she had married Ruskin in 1848. In June 1853, after The Order of Release was finished and on display at the Royal Academy exhibition, Millais and the Ruskins left together for a visit to Scotland. Ruskin regarded Millais as a potential successor to his beloved Turner, and hoped through his friendship, patronage, and instruction to mould him as such. In Scotland he would encourage him in the painting of the kind of natural subject matter that he most associated with Turner, the rocks and running water of a mountain landscape. The party stayed largely at the village of Brig o' Turk in the Trossachs, and Millais painted a waterfall in nearby Glenfinlas as the background to a portrait of Ruskin for the latter's father (priv. coll.).

During the four rainy months the Millais–Ruskin party spent in Scotland, Millais and Effie Ruskin often found themselves alone together. He gave her drawing lessons, teasingly referred to himself as her 'Master', and nicknamed her 'The Countess'. By the time the party broke up in October, they had clearly fallen in love. On 25 April 1854 Effie left Ruskin, and on 15 July she was granted a decree of nullity dissolving the marriage on the grounds of non-consummation. Though he finished the portrait in 1854, Millais regarded Ruskin with growing contempt. Ruskin wrote to him in a friendly tone after hanging the portrait in his parents' house in December that year but Millais rebuffed him: 'I can scarcely see how you conceive it possible that I can desire to continue on terms of intimacy with you' (Lutyens, Millais and the Ruskins, 248).

Perth, 1855–1861 Millais and Effie Ruskin kept in contact, first indirectly through her mother, then by affectionate exchanges of letters, and on 3 July 1855 they were married; the ceremony took place at Effie's parents' home, Bowerswell, in Perth. Effie was to be an important presence in Millais's life. She assisted him in his work, helping him to find models and props, carrying out historical research, and dealing with some of his business correspondence. As his success grew she encouraged him to move in high social circles rather than bohemian ones; she ran large and impressive households in Kensington, and entertained in some style. For his part Millais seems to have taken naturally to the role of the middle-class Victorian family man, doting father, and provider. Although there is nothing to suggest that the marriage was remarkably happy or unhappy, it arose in painful circumstances, and both Millais and Effie remained conscious of a lingering stigma. At the height of his fame they became friendly with the prince and princess of Wales, but it was not until Millais made a special appeal from his deathbed that Effie was allowed to be presented to the queen.

Millais and Effie had eight children. The first born was Everett Millais (1856–1897), who became an authority on dog breeding; he succeeded his father as baronet. George Gray Millais (1857–1878) died while a student at Cambridge, as a result of complications after contracting typhoid fever. Effie Gray Millais, later Mrs William James (1858–1911), was one of her father's favourite models and appears in a number of his paintings. Mary Hunt Millais (1860–1944) was especially close to her father and helped him with his work; she never married. Alice Caroline Millais, later Mrs Charles Stuart-Wortley and Lady Stuart of Wortley (1862–1936), inherited her father's love of music and enjoyed a long, deeply affectionate friendship with the composer Elgar. Sir Geoffroy William Millais, fourth baronet (1863–1941), was an intrepid traveller and photographer. John Guille Millais (1865–1931) became a naturalist, wildlife artist, and author, writing a two-volume biography of his father. Sophia Margaret Millais, later Mrs Douglas MacEwen (1868–1907), also sat to her father as a model.

To escape the initial bitterness and gossip surrounding their marriage, Millais and Effie spent the first six years of their life together chiefly in Perth. From 1855 to 1857 they rented Annat Lodge, and from 1857 to 1861 they stayed with Effie's parents at Bowerswell. Millais's years in Perth form a distinct phase in his development as an artist. Perhaps to distance himself from the aesthetic of tight observation so closely associated with Ruskin, he experimented with paintings in which specific detail and narrative are suppressed in the interests of a general mood. His masterpiece in this vein was Autumn Leaves (exh. RA, 1856; Manchester City Galleries), which shows Effie's younger sisters Sophie and Alice, along with two other local girls, building a bonfire of leaves at sunset in the garden at Annat Lodge. This was followed by other melancholy twilight scenes, A Dream of the Past: Sir Isumbras at the Ford (exh. RA, 1857; Lady Lever Art Gallery, Port Sunlight) and The Vale of Rest (exh. RA, 1859; Tate collection). Both proved difficult to sell, however, and Millais reverted, generally speaking, to more accessible, easily likeable subject matter.

Millais's closest male friend at this stage of his life was John Leech, the Punch draughtsman; though twelve years his senior, Leech was probably the closest friend he ever had. The two men admired each other's work, shared much the same sense of humour, and were both passionate sportsmen. They were on fairly close terms by 1853, when Millais sent Leech comic drawings from Brig o' Turk to be engraved for *Punch*, and their friendship was sealed in 1854 when Leech introduced Millais to foxhunting. In some ways he filled the void in Millais's life after his old friend and Pre-Raphaelite comrade-in-arms Holman Hunt left London on his first trip to the Holy Land in January that year. Both enjoyed the Garrick Club; when Millais was elected to membership in 1855, his seconders included Leech, W. M. Thackeray, and Wilkie Collins. He and Leech took fishing and shooting trips in Scotland, the basis for some of the adventures of Leech's beloved *Punch* character Mr Briggs. Leech's death in 1864 left Millais devastated; he was a pallbearer at the funeral and wept openly as the coffin was lowered into the grave.

In 1856 *A Huguenot* and *The Order of Release* became the first of Millais's works to be published as engravings. The selling of copyrights to the publishers of engravings was to be an important source of income for Millais. His main publishers were Henry Graves & Co., who published *A Huguenot*, *The Order of Release*, and eleven other paintings between 1856 and 1870, and Thomas Agnew & Sons—also his principal dealers—who published twenty-two paintings between 1873 and 1890. Millais's increasing success in the engravings market was symptomatic of a general shift in his career and patronage. During the 1850s and 1860s he changed from the embattled Pre-Raphaelite who enjoyed the patronage of sympathetic individuals with whom he was on close terms—notably James Wyatt, Thomas Combe, and Ruskin—to the most popular artist of his day, taken up by the major art dealers, first Ernest Gambart then Agnew's, and through them reaching leading collectors such as B. G. Windus, Thomas Plint, William Graham, Samuel Mendel, and Albert Grant.

Though always primarily a painter, Millais was a leading figure in the boom in wood-engraved book and magazine illustrations that took place in the 1850s and 1860s. His first important commission was for designs for Edward Moxon's edition of Tennyson (published 1857), illustrated by members of the Pre-Raphaelite Brotherhood and others. From 1859 he contributed regularly to the magazine *Once a Week*, and from 1860 he illustrated a series of Anthony Trollope's novels: *Framley Parsonage* (published in the *Cornhill Magazine*, 1860–61); *Orley Farm* (published in parts, 1861–2); and *The Small House at Allington* (*Cornhill Magazine*, 1862–4). His career as an illustrator reached its climax with *The Parables of our Lord and Saviour Jesus Christ*, which appeared first in *Good Words* in 1863, then as a separate volume in 1864. He increased his return on many of his more successful illustrations by painting versions in watercolour for sale to dealers and collectors. After the *Parables* were published his output in illustrations fell off. No doubt he became more conscious of the inferior professional status of this kind of work after his election as a Royal Academician in 1863.

Return to London, 1861–1877 Millais rented houses in London during the winter months of 1857–8 and 1859–60, and moved back there for good in 1861. By the end of that year he and his family were living at 7 Cromwell Place, Kensington, where they remained until 1877. The most important new development in Millais's painting in the early 1860s was the beginning of a line in sweet, simple pictures of pretty children, for which his own children—and later grandchildren—were often the models. His first success in this vein was *My First Sermon* (Guildhall Art Gallery, London), which shows his daughter Effie sitting attentively in a pew. The great popularity of this work at the Royal Academy exhibition of 1863 helped secure his election as a Royal Academician on 18 December that year. The diploma picture he submitted to the academy in 1868 was also a child subject, *A Souvenir of Velasquez* (RA). Even the serious, historical subjects that he continued to paint for the rest of his career, though less often than in his youth, tended to feature children. They included *The Boyhood of Raleigh* (1869–70; Tate collection), *The Princes in the Tower* (1878; Holloway collection, Royal Holloway, University of London), and *An Idyll, 1745* (1884; Lady Lever Art Gallery, Port Sunlight).

In the 1860s Millais developed a painterly technique and a taste for the old masters that ran contrary to the Pre-Raphaelite principles of his youth. His later style pays homage to Velázquez, to Frans Hals, and above all to English portraiture of the previous century. In 1868, with his pendant paintings *Stella* (Manchester City Galleries) and *Vanessa* (Walker Art Gallery, Liverpool), he began a line in paintings of attractive young women in eighteenth-century fancy dress, helping to foster an eighteenth-century revival—part of the broader trend in British art known as the aesthetic movement—that affected art, architecture, and fashion alike. His triple portrait *Hearts are Trumps* (1872; Tate collection) is a variation on a theme from Sir Joshua Reynolds's portrait *The Ladies Waldegrave* (NG Scot.) and *Cherry Ripe* (1879; priv. coll.) alludes to the same artist's *Penelope Boothby* (priv. coll.). Reynolds—whom the Pre-Raphaelite Brotherhood had reviled as 'Sir Sloshua'—became Millais's artistic touchstone, especially when it came to the depiction of children. Reynolds's own *Discourses* urged the modern artist to make quotations and borrowings from the art of the past; in painting 'souvenirs' of his portraits Millais was following him in both practice and theory. On 13 May 1871 *Vanity Fair* published an 'Ape' caricature of Millais with the caption 'A converted pre-Raphaelite'.

Millais fostered his growing feeling for the old masters by visits to museums on the continent. In 1865, for instance, he travelled via Paris and Switzerland to Italy, staying for periods in Venice, Florence, and Rome; and in 1875 he visited the Netherlands and admired the works of Rembrandt and Frans Hals. Though devoted to the work of Velázquez, he never went to Spain.

Among his painter contemporaries there was no one whose career Millais followed with a keener eye than that central figure of the aesthetic movement, James Abbott McNeill Whistler, and in certain works of the 1860s and 1870s he plays interesting pictorial variations on Whistlerian themes. His portrait of Nina Lehmann (1868–9; priv. coll.) refers to Whistler's *Symphony in White, No. 1: the White*

Girl (1861–2; National Gallery of Art, Washington); his portrait of Isabella Heugh (1872; Musée d'Orsay, Paris) to Whistler's famous portrait of his mother (1871; Musée d'Orsay); his portrait of Thomas Carlyle (1877; NPG) to Whistler's portrait of the same sitter (1872–3; Glasgow Museums and Art Galleries). The gesture was part compliment, part challenge. In his plays on Whistler, Millais was always looking to offer a corrective, to demonstrate by means of comparison and contrast a more robust, more British type of aestheticism. In the same spirit, he painted *An Idyll, 1745* as a response in terms of British history to Frederic Leighton's classical and sensual *Idyll* of 1880–81 (priv. coll.).

Beginning with *Chill October* (1870; priv. coll.), which shows a windswept backwater of the River Tay near Perth, Millais expressed his taste for the landscape of Scotland in a series of large views remarkable for their bleakness and atmosphere of melancholy. The unrelieved marshland of *Murthly Moss* (1887; priv. coll.) and the impenetrable undergrowth of *Dew Drenched Furze* (1889–90; priv. coll.) are characteristic of the inhospitable, not obviously picturesque scenery he delighted in painting. Free from the self-conscious traditionalism that marks much of his later work, these landscapes possess a grandeur and sense of mystery that he seldom achieved with other types of subject.

The landscapes of Millais's later career were rooted in his experiences as a sportsman. He enjoyed deerstalking, shooting, and fishing with a passion, and from the time he lived in Perth would take a sporting holiday in some part of Scotland almost every year. In the summer and autumn of 1873 he rented St Mary's Tower, Birnam, from the duke of Rutland for the first of many long Scottish holidays with his family. He and his family returned regularly to Birnam, a few miles above Perth on the Tay, and from 1881 to 1890 rented Birnam Hall (also known as Dalpowie) and the shootings and rod fishings on the Murthly estate from Sir Archibald Stewart of Grantully. Typically Millais would leave London for the north in August each year, and might stay for three or four months. 'He knew by heart, as one may say, every bit of the ground and every turn of the river, and his love of the place increased year by year', his son John Guille Millais recalled. 'Except for deerstalking—and for this, as time went on, he felt himself getting a bit old—Murthly had everything that a sportsman could desire' (*Life and Letters*, 2.148).

Palace Gate, 1877–1896 In 1873 Millais bought a site on Palace Gate in Kensington and engaged the architect Philip Hardwick to build him a new house. No. 2 Palace Gate was finished in 1876 and the Millais family moved in during the early months of 1877. Designed in a truly palatial, Italianate style, the house reflected the artist's growing wealth and social standing. On arriving there for a sitting for his portrait, Thomas Carlyle is said to have remarked: 'Millais, did painting do all that? … Well, there must be more *fools* in this world than I had thought!' (D. A. Wilson and D. W. MacArthur, *Carlyle in Old Age*, 1934, 406). The decorations included a fountain with a black marble seal sculpted by Joseph Edgar Boehm. The most notable works

of art other than Millais's own were a marble *Leda and the Swan* bought in Florence as a Michelangelo in 1865 (V&A, now attributed to Bartolomeo Ammanati) and Van Dyck's *Time Clipping the Wings of Cupid*, bought at the Marlborough sale at Christies in 1886 (Musée Jacquemart-André, Paris). The studio was hung with tapestries, and contained an important early seventeenth-century German cabinet.

During his nineteen years at Palace Gate, Millais's affluent and generally happy family life was punctuated by the marriages of five of his children and the births of ten grandchildren. On the darker side, the most painful personal misfortune of this later part of his life was without doubt the loss of his son George, aged only twenty, in 1878. Another cause of deep distress was the mental illness suffered by Effie's sister Sophie for many years before her death in 1882, aged thirty-eight.

In his professional life, Millais's first allegiance was to the Royal Academy. He fulfilled his teaching duties as an academician, served on the hanging committee for the annual academy exhibition, and regarded that exhibition as the main forum in which to show his own work. Nevertheless, from 1877 he also exhibited regularly at the Grosvenor Gallery, the alternative venue to the Royal Academy that became so closely associated with the aesthetic movement, and particularly with Whistler, Edward Burne-Jones, and G. F. Watts. The exhibition of twenty of Millais's paintings held in 1881 at the Fine Art Society, a Bond Street dealer and publisher, was his first retrospective. But the largest held during his lifetime, comprising 159 works, was at the Grosvenor in the early months of 1886. The new exhibiting institution that was least to his taste was the New English Art Club, founded in 1886 to offer exhibition opportunities for artists influenced by French *plein-air* painting. In a rare statement of his ideas, 'Thoughts on our art of to-day', published in the *Magazine of Art* in 1888, he regretted that young British artists should 'persist in painting with a broken French accent, all of them much alike, and seemingly content to lose their identity in their imitation of French masters' (Spielmann, 16). For him part of the essence of Britishness was being an individual; the truly British painter, Gainsborough or Constable for instance, developed a technique that was British not only in its freedom and naturalness, but also in being wholly and unmistakably his own.

By the time of Millais's move to Palace Gate, his occasional work as a portraitist had increased to become an impressive and highly lucrative portrait practice, and he painted the best-known images of many of the most prominent figures of the Victorian age. In addition to Thomas Carlyle, his sitters included Lillie Langtry, whom he greatly admired and portrayed as *A Jersey Lily* (1877–8; Jersey Museums Service); Gladstone (1878–9; NPG; 1884–5; priv. coll., on loan to Eton College; 1885; Christ Church, Oxford); Disraeli (1881; NPG); Tennyson (1881; Lady Lever Art Gallery, Port Sunlight); and Henry Irving (1883; Garrick Club, London). In the male portraits, Millais's animated brushwork suggests vigour and dynamism on the part of the sitters, and the plain backgrounds against which they are painted—recalling Rembrandt, Hals, and

Velázquez—create a sense of inner power, both mental and spiritual. His aim in much of his portraiture seems to have been to carry on the tradition forged by old masters he admired, but with a modern, realist inflection: for all the allusions to the art of the past, the physical fact of the sitter's presence, posing for the portrait, is allowed to come through. He painted his female sitters with an evident delight in the colours and textures of their dresses, which he treated with a display of painterly bravura. Among the most fluent examples are his portraits of two women artists who were members of his social circle, Louise Jopling (1879; priv. coll.) and Kate Perugini (1880; priv. coll.), exhibited at the Grosvenor Gallery in 1880 and 1881 respectively.

As Millais painted his first portrait of Gladstone in 1878–9, the two men discovered that they liked and admired one another, and began a lifelong friendship. (Though careful never to disclose his political allegiances, Millais almost certainly voted Liberal.) In the following years Gladstone entertained Millais at both 10 Downing Street and Hawarden, and on 16 July 1885 he set a seal on Millais's position as the country's most popular and respected artist by having him created a baronet. This made him the first artist since Sir Godfrey Kneller and the first native British artist ever to be given a hereditary title. His baronetcy was just the most prestigious among many honours Millais received, both at home and abroad. In 1878 he won a gold medal for the works he showed at the Universal Exhibition in Paris and was made an officer of the Légion d'honneur. He was made a DCL by Oxford University (1880) and awarded the German order of merit (1882), the Belgian order of Leopold (1895), the Italian order of St Maurice and St Lazarus (1896), and honorary membership of academies of art throughout Europe.

In his later work Millais returned again and again to the theme of childhood. His child subjects were especially in demand in the form of reproductive prints, and the most successful of his whole career was the colour print of *Cherry Ripe*, his Reynoldsian study of a girl in an eighteenth-century mob cap; this was published in 1880 in the Christmas supplement to the *Graphic* magazine, which sold 600,000 copies. Later his painting *Bubbles* (1886; priv. coll.), for which his grandson Willie James was the model, became famous when it was purchased by A. and F. Pears and mass-reproduced as an advertisement for their soap; it remains the work for which he is most widely known today.

Millais was unembarrassed by his popularity and wealth. 'There is something romantic in the connection of Genius and a garret, and the poor Poet Musician & Painter are the pets of the philanthropic dilettanti', he lamented in an unpublished open letter 'To the Art Student' (Millais papers, Pierpont Morgan Library, New York). In 1885 the novelist Margaret Oliphant recorded a conversation between Millais and two friends who were eminent men in medicine and the law, respectively Sir Henry Thompson and Sir Henry James, on the subject of incomes. Thompson and James remarked that doctors at the top of their profession could earn £15,000 and lawyers £20,000.

Millais claimed that a painter could earn as much as £25,000. 'For the last ten years I should have made £40,000 had I not given myself a holiday of four months in the year: what I did actually make was £30,000, so that I gave an estimate considerably under the fact!' (*The Autobiography and Letters of Mrs Oliphant*, ed. Mrs H. Coghill, 1899, 325–6). Millais was paid most handsomely for his occasional ventures into large, many-figured historical compositions such as *An Idyll, 1745*, for which Frederick Wigan paid him £5000. But the majority of his works were single portraits, landscapes, and the 'fancy pictures' of children and young women, and for these he was paid less. His fee for a commissioned three-quarter length portrait, for example, was normally £1000.

Appearance, character, last years, posterity As a boy Millais's delicate features and thick, curly hair gave him an angelic appearance, and he remained classically handsome into manhood. He usually wore sideburns but not beard or moustache. His chiselled profile and high, domed forehead can be seen in what is probably the best portrait of him, painted by G. F. Watts in 1871 (NPG). He was tall and, in his youth, so slight in physique that he referred to himself as 'a specimen of a living paper-knife' (*Life and Letters*, 1.91). He dressed fashionably, disdaining bohemian and aesthetic affectations. By all accounts he was frank, straightforward, and unpretentious by nature. In their descriptions of Millais and his paintings alike, his contemporaries often used the term 'manly'. He was lively and amusing company, and an affectionate friend. Aside from art, the pleasures closest to his heart were sport and music. His musical tastes were wide-ranging, although he particularly admired Bizet and Wagner; when Wagner visited London in 1877, he was proud to entertain him on a visit to the studio. He preferred informal musical parties to concert-going and opera-going, and would often have one of his daughters play favourite pieces on the piano as he worked.

Although the quality of his art declined in his last years, and with it his critical reputation, Millais remained one of the most loved and respected men in the profession, matched in prestige only by Frederic Leighton, who since 1878 had been president of the Royal Academy. When Leighton was abroad for his health and unable to attend the academy's annual banquet in 1895, Millais presided in his place. Leighton died early in the following year and it was no surprise when, on 20 February 1896, Millais was elected his successor as president. He accepted with some reluctance since he was already seriously ill himself. For over three years he had suffered from a failing voice caused by cancer of the larynx, almost certainly the result of his pipe smoking. By 11 May, when the famous surgeon Frederick Treves performed an emergency tracheotomy in the early hours of the morning to enable him to breathe, it was clear that he was on his deathbed. Now communicating by writing on a slate, he expressed a dying wish that Effie should be received at court; this was granted and Princess Louise presented her to the queen at Windsor Castle. Millais died at home on the afternoon of 13 August 1896, aged sixty-seven.

The funeral took place on 20 August. The pallbearers were the artist's old friend Holman Hunt; Archibald Primrose, fifth earl of Rosebery; George Howard, twelfth earl of Carlisle; Henry Manners, marquess of Granby; Viscount Wolseley; Sir Henry Irving; Sir George Reid, president of the Royal Scottish Academy; and, representing the Royal Academy, P. H. Calderon. On its way from Palace Gate to St Paul's Cathedral the funeral procession halted at the Royal Academy, where it was joined by a body of academicians and associates. Millais was buried in the crypt in Artists' Corner, next to J. M. W. Turner.

Sales of the works by Millais remaining in his studio, proof engravings after his paintings, works by other artists in his collection, furniture from the studio, and various other items of furniture, porcelain, faience, and so on, were held at Christies in May 1897, March 1898, and July 1898. In September 1897 the net value of his personal estate was resworn at £98,228 16s. 6d. His eldest son, Everett, who succeeded him as baronet, died from pneumonia on 7 September 1897 and was succeeded by his own son, John Everett, aged eight. Later in the same year, on 23 December, the artist's wife, Effie, died at Bowerswell in Perth, aged sixty-nine; she was buried near by in Kinnoull churchyard. A large commemorative exhibition of Millais's works was held at the Royal Academy between January and March 1898, and the two-volume *Life and Letters* by his son John Guille Millais—which remains the fullest source of information on Millais—appeared in 1899.

Since his death Millais's reputation has declined and revived along with that of Victorian art generally. His work continued to enjoy a popular following, and for many it became a touchstone of Englishness in art. The National Art-Collections Fund based its campaign to buy *Christ in the Carpenter's Shop* for the Tate Gallery in 1921 on an appeal to cultural patriotism. 'May it be given to the NACF to save for us this "little bit of England"', wrote the artist D. Y. Cameron in a letter of support used in the publicity material. To the more sophisticated taste of the modernist artists and critics, however, Millais's love of the pathetic storyline and his devotion to naturalism and detail were anathema. With their contempt for Victorian respectability, their emphasis on the pure artistic concerns of form and colour, and their reverence for the French avant-garde from Manet to Cézanne, influential writers on art such as Clive Bell condemned most Victorian paintings as vulgar and merely illustrative. Between the two world wars Millais's critical fortunes reached their lowest ebb.

The sheer material success Millais enjoyed, coupled with the eagerness to please that is evident in some of his later work, can still weigh decisively against him; some critics and art historians continue to present his career as a triumph of Mammon over art. Since the 1940s, however, the number of exhibitions and publications featuring his works, as well as the prices they have commanded on the market, suggest a growing appreciation for his achievements. The 1960s saw the beginning of a general Pre-Raphaelite revival, and in 1967 there was a Millais exhibition at the Royal Academy and the Walker Art Gallery,

Liverpool, the first major retrospective since 1898. His work featured prominently in the large Pre-Raphaelites exhibition held at the Tate Gallery in 1984, and in 1999 the National Portrait Gallery, London, devoted an exhibition to his work as a portraitist. The paintings of the early, Pre-Raphaelite period are still regarded as Millais's chief contribution to the history of British art. But certain of his later works that were once written off in the general opprobrium, notably the portraits and the large Scottish landscapes, began to attract more favourable reassessment in the late twentieth century.

MALCOLM WARNER

Sources J. G. Millais, *The life and letters of Sir John Everett Millais*, 2 vols. (1899) • Morgan L., Millais papers • Morgan L., Bowerswell papers • family papers and memorabilia, priv. coll. [Geoffroy Richard Everett Millais] • W. H. Hunt, *Pre-Raphaelitism and the Pre-Raphaelite Brotherhood*, 2 vols. (1905) • Hunt. L., Holman Hunt collection • [L. Parris], ed., *The Pre-Raphaelites* (1984) [exhibition catalogue, Tate Gallery, London, 7 March – 28 May 1984] • M. Warner, 'The professional career of John Everett Millais to 1863, with a catalogue of works to the same date', PhD diss., Courtauld Inst., 1985 • P. Funnell, ed., *Millais: portraits* (1999) [exhibition catalogue, NPG, 19 Feb – 6 June 1999] • M. G. Bennett, *PRB, Millais, PRA* (1967) [exhibition catalogue, Walker Art Gallery, Liverpool, and RA, Jan–Apr 1967] • M. Lutyens, *Millais and the Ruskins* (1967) • W. E. Fredeman, *Pre-Raphaelitism: a bibliocritical study* (1965) • *The P. R. B. journal: William Michael Rossetti's diary of the Pre-Raphaelite Brotherhood, 1849–1853*, ed. W. E. Fredeman (1975) • 'Letters from Sir John Everett Millais (1829–1896) and William Holman Hunt (1827–1910) in the Henry E. Huntington Library, San Marino, California', ed. M. Lutyens, *Walpole Society*, 44 (1972–4), 1–93 • M. Lutyens, ed., *John Everett Millais' illustrated edition of 'The parables of our lord'* (1975) • G. H. Fleming, *That ne'er shall meet again: Rossetti, Millais, Hunt* (1971) • C. Donovan and J. Bushnell, *John Everett Millais, 1829–1896: a centenary exhibition* (1996) [exhibition catalogue, Southampton Institute] • M. Warner, *The drawings of John Everett Millais* (1979) [exhibition catalogue, Arts Council of Great Britain] • G. Millais, *Sir John Everett Millais* (1979) • M. H. Spielmann, *Millais and his works: with special reference to the exhibition at the Royal Academy, 1898* (1898) • W. Armstrong, 'Sir John Everett Millais, royal academician: his life and work', *Art Annual* (1885) [Christmas number of the *Art-Journal*] • R. Thomas, *Serjeant Thomas and Sir J. E. Millais, bart., P. R. A.* (privately printed, 1901) • parish register, Southampton, All Saints' Church, 27 Dec 1829 [baptism] • Burke, *Peerage* • S. Trombley, *Sir Frederick Treves* (1989) • *CGPLA Eng. & Wales* (1896) • 'Passages from the notebooks of Sir Frederick Treves [pt 1]', *Annals of the Royal College of Surgeons of England*, 28 (1961), 384–8

Archives FM Cam., letters • Hunt. L., letters • Morgan L., papers | BL, letters to the brothers Dalziel, Add. MS 38794 • BL, letters to W. E. Gladstone, Add. MSS 44442–44522 • Bodl. Oxf., letters to Sir William Harcourt • Bodl. Oxf., letters to F. G. Stephens • Hunt. L., letters, mainly to William Holman Hunt • JRL, letters, mainly to Manchester City Art Gallery • Morgan L., Bowerswell papers • Northumbd RO, Newcastle upon Tyne, letters to Sir Matthew Ridley • NPG, letters to George Frederic Watts • NRA, priv. coll., letters to John Swinton • priv. coll., Geoffroy Richard Everett Millais collection, family papers and memorabilia • Tate collection, letters to John Alfred Vinter

Likenesses C. A. Collins, pencil, ink, and wash drawing, 1850, AM Oxf. • J. E. Millais, self-portrait, group portrait, pen and ink, c.1851 (*Miss Sm-th's party*), Winnipeg Art Gallery, Canada • C. R. Leslie, oils, 1852, NPG • W. H. Hunt, pastel and chalk drawing, 1853, NPG • J. E. Millais, two self-portraits, pen-and-ink sketches, 1853, Athenaeum, London • J. E. Millais, self-portrait, double portrait, chalk drawing, 1854 (with his mother), AM Oxf. • A. Munro, plaster plaques, c.1854, AM Oxf., NPG • H. Watkins, photograph, 1856–9, NPG • W. H. Hunt, chalk drawing, c.1860, NPG • J. E. Boehm, plaster statuette, 1863, NPG · R. Lehmann, crayon drawing, 1868, BM · H. Nelson O'Neil, group portrait, oils, 1869 (*The billiard room of the Garrick Club*), Garr. Club · G. F. Watts, oils, 1871, NPG [*see illus.*] · N. de Keyser, group portrait, oils, 1878 (*Les grands artistes, école du XIXème siècle*), Musée Chéret, Nice · J. E. Millais, self-portrait, oils, 1878, Wightwick Manor, Wolverhampton · J. E. Millais, self-portrait, oils, 1880, Uffizi Gallery, Florence · G. Reid, oils, 1880, Aberdeen Art Gallery · J. E. Boehm, plaster bust, 1882, V&A; related bronze bust, exh. RA 1883, RA · J. E. Millais, self-portrait, oils, 1883, Aberdeen Art Gallery · F. Holl, oils, exh. RA 1886, RA · E. Onslow Ford, bronze bust, 1895, RA; related plaster bust, NPG; bronze cast, NPG · T. B. Wirgman, pencil drawing, 1896, NPG · Ape [C. Pellegrini], caricature, watercolour study, NPG; repro. in *VF* (13 May 1871) · T. Brock, bronze statue, Tate collection · V. Brooks, chromolithograph (after J. Ballantyne), NPG · R. Cleaver, group portrait, pen and ink (*Hanging committee, Royal Academy, 1892*), NPG · C. W. Cope, drawing, FM Cam. · Elliott & Fry, photographs, NPG · Fradelle & Marshall, photographs, NPG · G. Grenville Manson, group portrait, watercolour (*Conversazione at the Royal Academy, 1891*), NPG · H. Jamyn Brooks, group portrait, oils (*Private view of the Old Master exhibition, Royal Academy, 1888*), NPG · C. S. Keene, pencil drawing, NPG · Lock & Whitfield, photographs, NPG · A. F. Mackenzie, photographs, NPG · G. Pilotell, drypoint, BM, NPG · R. Potter, photographs, NPG · R. W. Robinson, photographs, NPG · Spy [L. Ward], pencil caricature, Garr. Club; repro. in *The Graphic* (22 Aug 1896) · J. & C. Watkins, photographs, NPG · D. Wilkie Wynfield, photographs, NPG · Window & Grove, photographs, NPG

Wealth at death £98,228 16*s*. 6*d*.: resworn probate, Sept 1897, *CGPLA Eng. & Wales* (1896)

Ray Milland (1907–1986), by unknown photographer, *c.*1930

Milland, Ray [*real name* Alfred Reginald Jones] (1907–1986), film actor, was born on 3 January 1907 at 5 Exchange Road, Neath, Glamorgan, the son of Alfred Jones, a steel mill superintendent who had fought at the siege of Mafeking, and his wife, Elizabeth Annie Truscott. Following his mother's remarriage he was known as Jack Mullane, after his stepfather. While attending Radur school he spent a summer as a shipping clerk and returned from one tramp steamer expedition with a collection of tattoos and a severe case of septicaemia. Brief spells at King's College, Cardiff, and the University of Wales followed. Then in 1925 he joined the Household Cavalry.

Thanks to his friendship with the actress Estelle Brody, Mullane was already considering a theatrical career when his military prospects took a distinct downturn. Having over-imbibed before escorting a ceremonial procession for the king of Afghanistan, he allowed his horse, B63, to bolt.

> I went right through the mounted band, who were helpless because their reins are fastened to their stirrups. The drum horse, who was at least nineteen years old, ended up in the memorial fountain, and I finished up in Buckingham Palace courtyard, alone and without a friend in the world. (Milland, 82)

He was confined to barracks for three weeks.

Having bought himself out of the blues, Mullane made his screen début as an extra in *Piccadilly* (1929), under the name Spike Milland (after the mill pools in which he had played as a boy). Further films followed, including *The Flying Scotsman* (1929), in which he assumed the lead after Cyril McLaglen broke his leg, and *The Informer* (1929), in which his sharpshooting skills were employed to provide the special effects.

Milland also spent time on stage, most notably in a touring production of *The Woman in Room 13* (1930). Again slightly tipsy, during a performance in Southport he tripped over a piece of carpeting and landed in the orchestra pit. Then, during the final act, his front dental bridge popped out and landed in a large copper bowl with a clang that brought the house down. In spite of such mishaps, fame still beckoned and Milland made his Hollywood bow in *Son of India* (1931). In July of that year he married Malvina Weber, with whom he had a son, Daniel, and an adopted daughter, Victoria. But MGM cancelled his contract in 1932 and he resorted to working in a gas station before signing for Paramount.

Bolero (1933) began a twenty-one-year association with the studio, although Milland's first lead was in Universal's *Alias Mary Dow* (1935). Despite starring in a trio of jungle pictures with Dorothy Lamour, a couple of Bulldog Drummond adventures, and *Beau Geste* (1939), he was best-known for playing suave second leads in light dramas and comedies, such as *We're not Dressing* (1934) and *Easy Living* (1937); in the latter, he for once actually got the girl. But the supercilious nonchalance masked self-doubt—'I never liked acting. it always embarrassed me' (*Evening News*, 8 Jan 1974). However, following acclaim for *Arise, my Love* (1940), he was allowed to diversify, battling with a giant squid in Cecil B. DeMille's *Reap the Wild Wind* (1942), romancing Ginger Rogers in *The Major and the Minor* (1942), and confounding the Nazis in Fritz Lang's adaptation of Graham Greene's *Ministry of Fear* (1944). A more tangible contribution to the war effort, however, was his service as a civilian primary flight instructor for the US army.

The high point of Milland's career was undoubtedly Billy Wilder's *The Lost Weekend* (1945). His penetrating and disturbingly realistic performance as the alcoholic Don Birnam landed him not only the best actor prize at Cannes but also an Academy award and a new contract, which made him Paramount's best-paid star. His new status also brought him a wider choice of material—costume dramas like *Kitty* (1945), thrillers like *The Big Clock* (1948), and even a western, *Bugles in the Afternoon* (1952). He also sought novelty projects, such as Russel Rouse's almost wordless crime caper, *The Thief* (1952), and Alfred Hitchcock's 3-D classic, *Dial M for Murder* (1954). There was even a brief dalliance with television, in which he played a college professor in *Meet Mr McNulty* (1953–4).

Milland's split from Paramount in 1953 finally enabled him to direct. But of *A Man Alone* (1955), *Lisbon* (1956), *The Safecracker* (1958), *Panic in Year Zero* (1962), and *Hostile Witness* (1968), none found critical or commercial favour. No longer a fixture on the A list, he appeared in a series of low-budget horrors, with *The Premature Burial* (1962) and *X—the Man with X-Ray Eyes* (1963) achieving cult status. His return to the genre, a decade later, was much less auspicious, as he settled for misfires like *The Thing with Two Heads* (1972) and *Terror in the Wax Museum* (1973).

Dispensing with the toupee he had worn since the late 1940s, Milland broke out of a sequence of television films to play Ryan O'Neal's father in *Love Story* (1970) and its sequel, *Oliver's Story* (1978). Indeed, he quite enjoyed essaying elder statesmen, as he no longer had 'to deal with that youth syndrome anymore … and the constant dreary effort to appear dashing' (Milland, 259). Cameos followed in *Aces High* and *The Last Tycoon* (both 1976), and he rounded off his 133-feature career with a direct-to-video effort, *The Gold Key* (1985). The author of over 100 short stories, with little time for the glitz and gossip of Tinseltown, he died of lung cancer on 10 March 1986 in Torrance, California. His wife survived him.

DAVID PARKINSON

Sources R. Milland, *Wide-eyed in Babylon* (1974) [autobiography] · *The international dictionary of films and filmmakers*, 2nd edn, 3: *Actors and actresses*, ed. N. Thomas (1992) · D. Thomson, *A biographical dictionary of film* (1991) · *The Times* (12 March 1986) · *Evening News* (8 Jan 1974) · *New York Times* (25 June 1972) · *The Guardian* (15 April 1975) · *Daily Mail* (14 Dec 1973)
Archives FILM BFI NFTVA, news footage · BFI NFTVA, performance footage | SOUND BL NSA, oral history interviews · BL NSA, performance recordings
Likenesses photograph, c.1930, Hult. Arch. [*see illus.*] · photographs, Hult. Arch.

Millar, Andrew (1705–1768), bookseller, was born on 8 October 1705 at Port Glasgow, Renfrewshire, and baptized there on 16 October, the third of fourteen children of the Revd Robert *Millar (1672–1752) and his wife, Elizabeth (*bap.* 1679, *d.* 1759), daughter of John Kelso, customs surveyor of Port Glasgow, and Mary Hamilton, his wife. Andrew's brothers entered the Presbyterian ministry, medicine, or the navy; his Kelso cousins were Ayrshire gentry and army officers.

In 1709 Robert was translated to Paisley Abbey, where Andrew probably attended the ancient grammar school until 1720, when he was apprenticed to the Edinburgh bookseller James McEuen. By 1727, when he appeared for him in *Eyre* v. *Baskett and others*. (PRO, C 11/2726/57), charged with selling piratical Scotch bibles, he was working at his master's Westminster branch 'at Buchanan's Head, against St. Clement's Church in the Strand' (*Daily Journal*, 4–11 Nov 1727), and he had taken over McEuen's shop and sign by February 1728. In 1728–9 he also conducted sales of libraries, with catalogues. Edinburgh books, sometimes reissued with cancel title-pages under Millar's imprint, bulked large in his initial stock, his father's influential *History of the Propagation of Christianity* among them. From this time until the end of 1738 James Thomson wrote a full quarter of Millar's imprints—nearly all printed by Henry Woodfall at nearby Temple Bar—and three-fifths of his copyrights. His first best-seller, a sensational three-part *Defence of F. John Baptist Girard* (October–November 1731), reportedly grossed 700 guineas (*The Bee*, 3, 1791, 127–31).

Millar became free of the Stationers' Company by redemption on 5 December 1738, though his freedom of London was delayed until 1744 (CLRO, CF 1/670 [old no. 120]). He was a vendor for the Society for the Encouragement of Learning (1739–49) and London agent for the Foulis press in Glasgow from 1741 and for Alexander Kincaid in Edinburgh from 13 July 1748, when he received the freedom of the city gratis (Scottish RS, 62, 1930, 139). In 1742 he moved to a better location, 'opposite to Katherine Street in the Strand' (*Daily Post*, 10 Sept 1742), near the bookshops of the Tonsons, François Changuion, and later John Nourse, and his trade began to shift from retailing to publishing. A decade later he was advertising a hundred titles, distributed among 'Poetry', 'Divinity', 'History', 'Entertainment' (i.e. novels), 'Physic', and science (*London Evening-Post*, October 1752). As early as Fielding's *Amelia* (1751) Millar inaugurated biennial pre-publication sales of his editions to the London trade, usually in November (*Library*, 24, 1969, 241–3). In 1763 he and William Strahan, his favoured later printer, were the first Scotsmen ever elected to the Stationers' court of assistants.

On 23 April 1730, at St Luke's, Chelsea, Millar married Jane (1710–1788), daughter of Andrew Johnston, a Westminster printseller, with a dowry of £500 (PRO, PROB 11/668, fol. 287); of their three children only Andrew survived infancy, to die in 1750, aged five and a half. Millar bound three apprentices: Robert Spavan (1730), who worked as his shopman until 1749; John Kelsey (1744), who was never freed; and Thomas Cadell (1758), his successor. Other 'assistants' were Thomas Becket, who left in 1760, and Millar's warehousemen Samuel Bladon and Robert Lawless. Cadell was running the shop by summer 1764 (BL, Add. MS 6858, fols. 33–4) and by July 1766 Millar would advertise 156 titles as 'sold by T. Cadell' (*London Chronicle*).

'Though himself no great judge of literature' Millar sensibly guided his purchase of copyrights by the advice of 'very able men' (Boswell, *Life*, 1.287)—and women, 'for Miller durst not contradict his wife in any thing' (*Beattie's London Diary*, 53). He paid his authors handsomely: £250 for Thomson's *Liberty* (1735–6), £600 for Fielding's *Tom Jones* (1749), and over £4000 for Hume's entire *History of England* (1754–62). He was also one of the first booksellers to advance money for unwritten titles, notably Johnson's

Dictionary and Hume's *Tudors*. Unmindful of former favours Millar led the Stationers' war against Scottish reprints with a spate of lawsuits in the court of session in 1739 that closed in the House of Lords in 1751. His only victory, *Millar v. Taylor* (king's bench, 1766–9), was posthumous and soon overruled by the House of Lords, but litigation had postponed defeat. Irish 'pirates' posed a lesser threat, and indeed Millar sent advance sheets of *Tom Jones* to William Smith for reprinting in Dublin.

Enlisting editors like Thomas Birch, David Mallet, Patrick Murdoch, and Arthur Murphy, Millar actively enhanced the prestige of his older properties: James Harrington (1737), Milton's prose (1738), Sir Francis Bacon (1740), and Robert Boyle (1744). Share sales of his recensions perpetuated canons of Fielding 'the novelist' and Thomson the 'Druid' (later a 'pre-Romantic') down to the twentieth century. He promoted such lavish private publications as William Hunter's *Anatomy of the Gravid Human Uterus* (1774, but proposed 1752), Robert Wood's *Ruins of Palmyra* (1753), Mallet's works of Bolingbroke (1754), and Thomas Hollis's republican reprints.

Before the sale of Millar's copyrights on 13 June 1769, his executor Cadell skimmed off 'Stock and Copies' nominally valued at £1225 (BL, Add. MS 48808, pp. 14, 23), though copyright in Robertson, Hume, and Richard Burn alone had cost Millar over £7200. The remainder realized about £8500; in literature the richest titles were Thomson, Fielding, and Young; in language Johnson's *Dictionary* and the grammars of Bishop Lowth and Louis Chambaud; in science and mathematics James Ferguson and Colin Maclaurin; in technology Hannah Glasse's cookery book. Reference works numbered shares in Chambers's *Cyclopaedia*, Thomas Birch's enlarged translation of Bayle's *Dictionary*, and the voluminous *Universal History*.

After a lingering illness Millar died at his home, 25 Pall Mall, on 8 June 1768. The *London Chronicle* (7–9 June 1768) anticipated Johnson's tribute that he had 'raised the price of Literature'. His £60,000 estate, £40,000 of it in Treasury bonds (*Gazetteer*, 9 June 1768), included a carriage, an Adam house (Survey of London, 29, 1960, 325–6), and a tradesman's country box at Kew, but prosperity had not altered Millar's manners or appearance. Hume joked about his superfluous thrift (*Letters of David Hume*, 1.310–11); he was 'habitually and equably drunk' (Boswell, *Life*, 3.389), with 'the dross of a bookseller about him' (*The Bee*, 6, 1791, 285). At Harrogate in 1763, in an 'old well m[end]ed Suit of Cloathes', Millar received two London newspapers; 'Good Company' smiled and nicknamed him Peter Pamphlet (*Autobiography*, ed. Burton, 222), after the shabby, newsmongering hero of Murphy's *Upholsterer* (1758). Millar's bequests commemorated a strongly commercial and national band of friends: Hume, Murdoch, Burn, Fielding's sons, Sir Andrew Mitchell, and Millar's godsons Spavan, Becket, and Strahan. He was buried at Chelsea; his widow, who married Sir Archibald Grant of Monymusk at St James Westminster on 24 May 1770 and died on 25 October 1788, was buried beside him.

HUGH AMORY

Sources *Fasti Scot.*, new edn, vol. 3 · J. Paterson, *History of the counties of Ayr and Wigton*, 1 (1863), 743–5 · Nichols, *Lit. anecdotes*, 3.386–9 · A. Millar, *Books printed for and sold by Andrew Millar, at Buchanan's Head, over-against St. Clement's Church without Temple-Bar* (1730?) [bound in copies of Thomson's *Spring* (1728) at the Humanities Research Center, U. Texas, and Bod.] · *A catalogue of the copies and shares of copies of the late Mr. Andrew Millar* (1769) [unique copy, partly priced, at John Murray Ltd; sale catalogue, 13 June 1769] · Boswell, *Life* · *The letters of David Hume*, ed. J. Y. T. Greig, 2 vols. (1932) · *New letters of David Hume*, ed. R. Klibansky and E. C. Mossner (1954) · *James Beattie's London diary, 1773*, ed. R. S. Walker (1946) · *Autobiography of the Rev. Dr. Alexander Carlyle … containing memorials of the men and events of his time*, ed. J. H. Burton (1860); repr. as *Anecdotes and characters of the times*, ed. J. Kinsley (1973) · R. J. Goulden, *The ornament stock of Henry Woodfall, 1719–1747* (1988) · G. Abbattista, 'The business of Paternoster Row: towards a publishing history of the *Universal history* (1736–65)', *Publishing History*, 17 (1985), 5–50 [appends provisional list of Millar's imprints, 1738–64] · W. McDougall, 'Copyright litigation in the court of session, 1738–1749', *Edinburgh Bibliographical Society Transactions*, 5/5 (1971–87), 2–31 · H. Amory, 'Andrew Millar and the first recension of Fielding's *Works* (1762)', *Transactions of the Cambridge Bibliographical Society*, 8 (1981–5), 57–78 · register of births and baptisms, Port Glasgow, General Register Office for Scotland, Edinburgh · will, dated 20 Feb 1768, proved, 17 June 1768, PRO, PROB 11/940, sig. 250 [abstracted in V. L. Oliver, *The history of the island of Antigua*, 2 (1896), 265; registered in the commissariat of Edinburgh, 11 Sept 1782, for £5 interest owing by his cousin Capt. John Kelso (d. Aug. 1782) on a bond of £2472, NA Scot., CC 8/8/125/2, fols. 423r–430v] · Dame J. Grant's will (dated 12 Oct 1787 with codicil, 10 June 1788, proved 6 Nov 1788), PRO, PROB 11/1171, sig. 536 [abstracted in V. L. Oliver, *The history of the island of Antigua*, 2 (1896), 265] · R. Myers, ed., *Records of the Stationers' Company, 1554–1920* [1984–6] [microfilm] · D. F. McKenzie, ed., *Stationers' Company apprentices*, [3]: *1701–1800* (1978) [abstracts from court bks and apprentice memorandum bks] · W. Strahan, ledgers, including memoranda on the Millars on 48803A, fol. 103v, BL, Add. MSS 48800–48808 [in R. Austen-Leigh, 'William Strahan and his ledgers', *The Library*, 4th ser., 3 (1922–3), 279; see also microfilm edn, ed. P. Hernlund (1989)] · R. D. Harlan, 'William Strahan: eighteenth century London printer and publisher', PhD diss., U. Mich., 1960 [incl. best conspectus of the archive] · inland revenue board returns on apprentices, PRO [indexed by I. Maxted, *The British book trades, 1710–1777* (1983)]

Archives BL, letters to Thomas Birch, Add. MSS 4256, 4314, 4475, 4477 · BL, Sir A. Mitchell, corresp., Add. MS 6858, fols. 28–34 · BL, Society for the Encouragement of Learning, corresp., Add. MS 6190 · NA Scot., letters to Andrew Mitchell · NL Scot., Culloden MSS, corresp., MSS 2968–2970 · NL Scot., David Hume MSS, corresp., MS 23156

Wealth at death £60,000; incl. £40,000 'in the funds': *Gazetteer and New Daily Advertiser* (9 June 1768)

Millar, Eric George (1887–1966), librarian, was born in Fulham, London, on 24 October 1887, the elder child and only son of George Thomas John Millar (1855–1889), barrister, and his wife, Edith Mary (1862–1942), daughter of Thomas Anstey Guthrie of Kensington. His father died only weeks before the birth of a daughter and his subsequent development was very strongly influenced by his mother's eldest brother, Thomas Anstey *Guthrie the younger (F. Anstey, the humorous writer). He was educated at Charterhouse and at Corpus Christi College, Oxford (1906–10), before joining the staff of the manuscripts department of the British Museum in the autumn of 1912.

Millar had already begun to study illuminated manuscripts, with the encouragement of two established scholars, M. R. James, a friend of his uncle, and Sydney Cockerell. Both were to become close personal friends. He became involved in the work of the New Palaeographical Society and the Société Française de Reproductions de Manuscrits à Peintures. His career was interrupted in 1915, when he enlisted in the Buffs; he served with the 4th battalion in northern India for almost three years before discharge late in 1919. This experience encouraged a lasting taste for Buddhist art. On return he embarked upon a series of publications including a study of the Lindisfarne gospels (1923), a pioneering two-volume survey of English medieval illuminated books (1926–8), and a catalogue of the manuscript collection of A. Chester Beatty (1927–30). It was a source of lifelong regret that the sale of the collection prevented the completion of this ambitious project. His work, meticulous in detail and economic in words, broke new ground and laid solid foundations for later scholars, particularly those who followed him in the investigation of English illumination, an area not well served by previous generations. Millar was elected a fellow of the Society of Antiquaries in 1921, received a DLitt from Oxford University in 1931, and was promoted deputy keeper of his department in 1932. Also in 1932 he published a study of the Luttrell psalter, newly acquired for the nation. His routine departmental work was wide-ranging and included the compilation of a handlist of the Ashley collection of literary manuscripts which, though never published, has remained an essential working tool for well over fifty years. He delivered the Rhind lectures at Edinburgh in 1933 and was Sandars reader in bibliography at Cambridge in 1935. In 1936 he became secretary of the Roxburghe Club; he collaborated with James in a volume on the Bohun manuscripts in that year and published the Rutland psalter in 1937. In 1940 he was seconded to the Ministry of Home Security, before returning to the museum to take up the keepership in 1944. During his three years as head of department he oversaw the return of the collections from their wartime places of safe keeping. Retirement produced a further sequence of Roxburghe Club volumes, the St Trond Lectionary (1949), the York psalter (1952), La Somme le Roy (1953), and the Alnwick Bestiary (1958). He also wrote a monograph on the Parisian miniaturist Honoré for Faber in 1959.

The York psalter and Honoré's Somme le Roy were the two gems of Millar's private collection, both ultimately bequeathed outright to the British Museum, together with his collection of John Downman's portrait drawings, in memory of his mother. The acquisition of manuscripts, portrait miniatures, watercolours, and drawings was a lifelong passion. He bought the first of the sixty-seven medieval manuscripts known to have passed through his hands as early as 1911 and the last in 1957. His collection also embraced the work of modern scribes and illuminators and included a range of literary autographs, many acquired from his uncle's friends. His drawings and watercolours were mainly works by nineteenth- and twentieth-century illustrators, including Punch artists who had been associated with F. Anstey. Many of these were crowded onto the walls of his living-rooms. Virtually the whole of this material, including the twenty medieval books in his possession at the end of his life, was willed to the British Museum.

Eric Millar was a heavily built and not notably agile man. His warm personality and his consistent generosity with his time and expertise made him many friends of all ages, both personal and professional. He was noted for his fund of lively reminiscences and his taste for boyish, unsophisticated jokes. He was particularly popular with children, for whose enjoyment his garden in Wiltshire was laid out. He never married, and shared a home at 28 Pembroke Gardens in Kensington with his mother until her death in 1942. Thereafter he divided his time between his leisure retreat, the Summer House at Dinton, near Salisbury, and a Victorian studio at 28 Holland Park Road, London. In 1943 he became a member of the Athenaeum, where he enjoyed meeting and entertaining his friends, who were also on occasion treated to lavish 'nursery' teas at his home. For most of his life he was an enthusiastic trout fisherman. He was also a keen photographer, adept with both still and movie cameras. He greatly enjoyed listening to the music of Wagner. He died at West Suffolk Hospital at Bury St Edmunds on 13 January 1966, having collapsed during a stay with friends, and was cremated. His ashes were buried at Dinton with the remains of his mother and his sister.   JANET BACKHOUSE

Sources British Museum Quarterly, 33 (1968–9) · WWW, 1961–70 · T. A. Guthrie, A long retrospect (1936) · The Times (15 Jan 1966) · Book Collector, 15 (1966), 65–6 · private information (2004) · CGPLA Eng. & Wales (1966)
Archives BL, corresp., etc. relating to binding of Codex Sinaiticus · BL, corresp., papers, MSS collections, Add. MSS 54229–54323 · University of Toronto, corresp. | BL, corresp. with Sir Sydney Cockerell, Add. MS 52737 · BL, corresp. with J. W. Hely Hutchinson, Add. MS 48353B [partly copies] · BL, corresp. with Society of Authors, Add. MSS 63304–63305
Likenesses photograph, c.1947, BL · W. A. Sillince, cartoon, 1953, BL
Wealth at death £15,502: probate, 23 May 1966, CGPLA Eng. & Wales

Millar, Frederick Robert Hoyer, first Baron Inchyra (1900–1989), diplomatist and civil servant, was born on 6 June 1900 in Montrose, the third son and youngest of three children of Robert Hoyer Millar, timber merchant, of Blair Castle, Culross, Perthshire, and his wife, Alice Anne Combe, daughter of Dr James Simson. Frederick (known as Derick) was educated at Wellington College and New College, Oxford, where he took a second-class honours degree in modern history in 1922 and an MA in 1954 on his election as an honorary fellow of the college. He played rugby for the university without, however, getting a blue.

In 1922 Millar was an honorary attaché at the British embassy in Brussels. In the following year he entered the diplomatic service as a third secretary, first at Berlin and then in Paris. He returned to the Foreign Office in 1928 and moved to Cairo as second secretary in 1930.

In 1931 Millar married (Anna Judith) Elizabeth (known as Bunchie), daughter of Reneke de Marees van Swinderen, the Netherlands minister in London, and his

American wife. Bunchie was a strong and attractive character and a great help to her husband in his career. They had two sons and two daughters.

Millar returned to London in 1934 as assistant private secretary to the secretary of state and, since there was then no personnel department, was responsible for dealing with all appointments in the Foreign Office and diplomatic service. Millar managed this task with sympathy and skill. His judgement of men and events was eminently sound.

In 1939 Millar went to Washington as a first secretary and head of Chancery. It was a critical time. Both the ambassador and his minister were Christian Scientists and, during the final illness of the ambassador, the eleventh marquess of Lothian, Millar was in a difficult position. He also had to deal with the rapid build-up of the British departmental and military representation in Washington and the initial problems of the ambassadorship of the first earl of Halifax. He became counsellor in 1941 and was secretary of the British civil secretariat in Washington in 1943–4. His administrative skills and his Washington connections served him in good stead in this testing period.

In 1944 Millar became counsellor and in 1947 assistant under-secretary in the Foreign Office. He returned to Washington as minister in 1948. He played an important part in the establishment and early years of NATO, becoming in 1950 its UK deputy and in 1952 the permanent representative on the NATO council. In 1953 he was appointed UK high commissioner in Germany, where he had an influential role during the transition from allied control to diplomatic recognition, and in 1955 he became the first post-war ambassador at Bonn.

An excellent administrator and effective operator in the foreign service, in 1957 Millar returned to the Foreign Office as permanent under-secretary of state and head of the diplomatic service, at a time when the foreign service had been badly shaken and divided by the Suez crisis. His robust but sympathetic manner and his administrative ability soon restored morale and made him an outstanding and popular head of the service. He retired in 1961, when he was created a hereditary peer as Baron Inchyra. He took his title from Inchyra House, his Perthshire home, and sat on the cross-benches. He was king-at-arms of the Order of St Michael and St George, and became a member of the queen's bodyguard for Scotland. He was also a governor of Wellington College for many years.

On his retirement from the foreign service Inchyra accepted a number of appointments in banking, finance, industry, and insurance. He was also chairman of the British Red Cross and of the Anglo-Netherlands Society in London. In between these activities and in his final retirement he energetically pursued his favourite sport of shooting. He was appointed CVO (1938), CMG (1939), KCMG (1949), and GCMG (1956).

In appearance Inchyra was very tall and rather portly with a florid complexion and a bald head. He generally moved slowly in a dignified manner. He was a good companion, and had been a popular figure in Oxford and a member of the Bullingdon Club. In April 1989 he was incapacitated by a massive stroke, but lingered on until he died at the Royal Infirmary, Perth, on 16 October 1989. He was succeeded in the barony by his elder son, Robert Charles Reneke Hoyer Millar (*b.* 1935).

SHERFIELD, *rev.*

Sources *The Times* (19 Oct 1989) · *FO List* (1961) · personal knowledge (1996) · private information (1996)
Archives U. Birm. L., corresp. with Lord Avon
Likenesses group portrait, photograph, 1951 (*Nato meeting*), Hult. Arch.
Wealth at death £814,236.23: confirmation, 21 Feb 1990, *CCI*

Millar, Gertrude [Gertie; *married names* Gertrude Monckton; Gertrude Ward, countess of Dudley] (**1879–1952**), actress, was born at 21 Grunwith Street, Manningham, Yorkshire, on 20 February 1879, the third daughter of a thirty-year-old Bradford worsted-stuff worker and dressmaker, Elizabeth Miller. Her father's name does not appear on her birth certificate, but at her marriage she claimed he was John Millar, a wool merchant. She first went on the stage as a child at Christmas 1892, appearing as the girl babe, Lily, to the Harold of Annie Holmes in *The Babes in the Wood* at St James's Theatre, Manchester. She soon moved from such seasonal engagements into musical comedy, taking the part of Phyllis Crosby in the musical-comedy drama *A Game of Cards* at Shodfriars Hall, Boston, in 1897 and the following year touring with such shows as the endlessly travelling *The New Barmaid* (as the lady journalist, Dora, played in London by Lottie Collins), as principal *ingénue* in the no. 3 circuit *The Silver Lining*, and as the actressy 'other woman', Sadie Pinkhose, in the only slightly successful *The Lady Detective*. She also put in a first appearance in the London suburbs when she played Dandini in *Cinderella* at the Grand Theatre, Fulham (1899).

The tall, pixie-faced young actress with the little chirpy singing voice took the step that would lead her to stardom when she joined the touring company of the Gaiety Theatre musical *The Messenger Boy* in 1900, playing the part of Isabel Blyth. The role—a wholly incidental one with a featured number—had been created at the Gaiety by a pretty little dancer who sang a little called Rosie Boote. Rosie and Rosie's song, 'Maisie', had proved to be one of the highest highlights of hugely popular *The Messenger Boy*, but Rosie had now gone newsworthily from the Gaiety to marry a marquess, and the house's producer, George Edwardes, was looking for a replacement to fill a similar spot in the theatre's new show, *The Toreador* (1901). One of the show's composers, Lionel Monckton, saw Gertie playing Isabel on the road and took a fancy to her, and as a result she was brought from the provinces to appear at the Gaiety Theatre itself. Cast as Cora, the little bridesmaid to the principal *ingénue*, Marie Studholme, she squeaked out a little song written for her by the admiring Monckton warning the boys to 'Keep off the grass', made every bit as much of a hit as Miss Boote had done, and proved to be quite the most popular among the four new featured ladies brought to the Gaiety for the show. Her role was soon expanded. Monckton wrote her a song describing how 'Captivating

Gertrude [Gertie] **Millar** (1879–1952), by Bassano, 1912

Cora' makes the bride look small, the rising composer Paul Rubens turned out the winsome and slightly suggestive 'I'm not a simple little girl', the role of the unplotworthy bridesmaid grew to unintended proportions, and Gertie Millar was established as a Gaiety Theatre star. She also, on 20 December 1902, married (John) Lionel Alexander *Monckton (1861–1924).

Over the next dozen years Gertie Millar reigned as one of London's outstanding musical-theatre favourites, as Edwardes cast her first in a run of shows at the Gaiety—as the Hon. Violet Anstruther, the unchallenged leading lady alongside such top comics as Teddy Payne, Connie Ediss, and George Grossmith, in *The Orchid* (1903), where she introduced 'Little Mary', 'Liza Ann', and 'Come with me to the zoo'); as Rosalie, who had nothing to do with the plot but sang another bundle of songs and duos by Monckton ('Alice sit by the fire', 'The Delights of London') in *The Spring Chicken* (1905), which, abnormally for the Gaiety, had a strong plot; and in the title role of Lally in Edwardes's attempt at a return to burlesque with *The New Aladdin* (1906). Unwell when this last show was produced, she was replaced by Lily Elsie, but she returned and took over the part two months into the run, at which stage the role of Lally was vastly increased in size. But the show did not succeed. Edwardes then returned to musical comedy, and Gertie featured alongside her fellow stars Payne and Grossmith as Mitzi, the innkeeper's daughter, in *The Girls of Gottenberg* (1907). The men had the plot, but Gertie got a barrelful of songs, ranging from a merry duo about 'Two Little Sausages' with Payne to some Wagnerian parody in

'Rhinegold'. It was not the best Gaiety score, but the leading lady did well enough with it for *The Times* to notice that 'Miss Gertie Miller showed that her resources are not so limited as previous performances seemed to show' (*The Times*, May 1907). Her resources, in terms of substantial singing and acting talents, were indeed limited, but Gertie Millar never aspired to either. She made her name on that mixture of *ingénue* charm and *soubrette* vivacity which had been established in the theatre's earlier musical comedies by Ellaline Terriss as the standard for the Gaiety's leading ladies, and her appeal was one of personality and charm rather than of talent in performance.

Following his triumph with *The Merry Widow*, starring Gertie's erstwhile replacement Lily Elsie, Edwardes mounted an English version of the next big continental hit of the day, *Ein Walzertraum*, at the Hicks Theatre in 1908 as *A Waltz Dream*. He took Gertie from the Gaiety to star as the little orchestra leader, Franzi, but his touch let him down. Emily Soldene, the prima donna turned journalist, sighed in print: 'Lovely music, but no-one to sing it' (*Sydney Evening News*, April 1908). Gertie's voice might have been up to 'Two Little Sausages', but Oscar Straus's music was something else. She left the failing production in mid-run and returned to Gaiety-weight fare, repeating her *Girls of Gottenberg* part on Broadway (1908). She then returned to London and took up what would prove to be her most successful Gaiety role of all, the made-to-measure part of the Yorkshire shopgirl Mary Gibbs, in *Our Miss Gibbs* (1909). Failure and *A Waltz Dream* were forgotten as she reached the peak of her already considerable career as a musical-comedy player and a public favourite. Monckton supplied her with a lively set of songs, including 'Yorkshire', 'Our farm', and one of her most memorable numbers, 'Moonstruck' ('Moon, moon, aggravating moon, why do you tease me so'), and Gertie and the show both scored first-rate hits.

With the end of the run of *Our Miss Gibbs*, however, came the end of Gertie Millar's reign at the Gaiety. Edwardes now shifted Monckton and his new show down to the Adelphi Theatre. *The Quaker Girl* (1910) gave the pair a second major hit, and Gertie perhaps her greatest triumph of all as Prudence Pym, the Quaker who sets off a Parisian fashion for demure garb, saves the face of a misbehaved French minister, and catches herself an American fairy prince (played by slightly singing *Merry Widow* star Joe Coyne) in the space of two acts. The vocal values of the piece were ensured in the other roles, thus giving Gertie and Joe's contribution of charm a solid musical background and the show a slightly more substantial feeling than those at the Gaiety. Monckton supplied his wife with 'The Quaker Girl', 'The Little Grey Bonnet', and 'Tony from America' to add to her popular-song list.

Gertie next played in another continental operetta, Edwardes's Daly's Theatre remake of Lehár's *Zigeunerliebe* as *Gipsy Love* (1912). Since the music of the show was far beyond her, he fabricated the personality role of Lady Babby to her measure. It was a bad idea, but the suffering show had a fair enough run. She then moved back to the Adelphi for a less successful second teaming with Coyne in *The Dancing Mistress* (1912, Nancy Joyce), returned to Daly's to play the *soubrette* part in Edwardes's rather drastic but nevertheless decidedly successful remake of the Hungarian hit *Leányvásár* (*The Marriage Market*, 1914), and took the role of Nan, originally created by the much more capable singer Evie Greene, in a revival of *The Country Girl* (1914).

The advent of the revue and the death of George Edwardes caused Monckton and his wife to turn away from musical comedy. In the early part of the First World War she appeared in his *Bric à Brac* (1915) and *Airs and Graces* (1917), both of which did well. She then returned to musical comedy, appearing in two shows (without Monckton's music) mounted by producers whose successes came almost exclusively in the world of revue. C. B. Cochran's *Houp-La* (1916) and André Charlot's *Flora* (1918) were both resounding flops. Perceiving that they were not at home in the now changed and changing world of the musical theatre, the Moncktons retired into private life. Shortly after her husband's death, on 30 April 1924 Gertie married William Humble *Ward, second earl of Dudley (1867–1932), a colonial governor. She never lost her enthusiasm for the theatre, which had given her a career of almost unalloyed success, even in its radically altered post-war form, and she was much in evidence at first nights up to the end of what Alan Dent called 'her charmed and charming life' (*DNB*). Incapacitated by illness in 1950, she spent her last days with her cat, Wendy, at Orchard Cottage, Chiddingfold, Surrey, where she died on 25 April 1952.

KURT GÄNZL

Sources K. Gänzl, *The encyclopedia of the musical theatre*, 2 vols. (1994) · K. Gänzl, *The British musical theatre*, 2 vols. (1986) · *DNB* · b. cert. · m. cert. · *The Times* (26 April 1952) · Burke, *Peerage* (1967) · *The Era* (1898–1918) · census returns for Manningham, 1881 · J. Parker, ed., *Who's who in the theatre*, 6th edn (1930)
Likenesses Bassano, photograph, 1912, NPG [*see illus.*] · H. van Dusen & Hassall, lithograph, NPG · postcards, NPG
Wealth at death £52,354 8s. 3d.: probate, 24 July 1952, *CGPLA Eng. & Wales*

Millar, James (1762–1827), physician and writer, born at Ayr on 4 February 1762, distinguished himself in classics and science at Glasgow University, graduating MA in 1788. For some years he worked as a tutor in Jamaica, and afterwards as chaplain at Glasgow University. After moving to Edinburgh, he graduated MD in 1795 and became a fellow of the Royal College of Physicians of Edinburgh. He frequently lectured on natural history and chemistry, and was one of the physicians at the Edinburgh Dispensary, where he caught a fever from which he died on 13 July 1827. He was considered generous and unconcerned with his own advancement. As a result his family were left badly provided for after his death.

Millar was the editor of the fourth edition of the *Encyclopaedia Britannica* (1810) and the last fifteen volumes of the fifth edition of the same work (1817), and wrote extensively for both editions. He also planned and edited a more popular dictionary of arts, sciences, and literature, the *Encyclopaedia Edinensis* (6 vols., 1827). From 1807 he was a contributor to several periodical journals in Edinburgh

James Millar (1762–1827), by John Henning

and London. One of his best-known publications was *Observations on the advantages and practicability of making tunnels under navigable rivers, particularly applicable to the proposed tunnel under the Forth* (1807), written in conjunction with William Vazie. His other publications are chiefly based on his articles contributed to the encyclopaedias, on the subjects of botany and chemistry.

GORDON GOODWIN, *rev.* MYFANWY LLOYD

Sources *GM*, 1st ser., 97/2 (1827), 276–7 · Irving, *Scots.* · Allibone, *Dict.* · [J. Watkins and F. Shoberl], *A biographical dictionary of the living authors of Great Britain and Ireland* (1816)
Likenesses J. Henning, crayon drawing, Scot. NPG [*see illus.*]

Millar, John (1733–1805), physician, was born in Scotland and graduated MD at Edinburgh in 1757. He commenced practice at Kelso, but on being appointed physician to the Westminster General Dispensary in August 1774, he settled in Pall Mall, London. He also became an active promoter of the Medical Society of London, which had been formed in 1773. Millar married Isabella Brisbane; they had two sons. Eccentric and irritable, Millar was considered to be an excellent physician, especially for women and children. His works include *Observations on the Asthma and on the Hooping Cough* (1769), which was praised by Benjamin Rush, and *A Discourse on the Duty of Physicians* (1776). He also published a number of other works on clinical and professional topics. Millar died a few months after the death of his eldest son, on 25 February 1805, at Shepherd Street, Mayfair, Westminster.

GORDON GOODWIN, *rev.* MICHAEL BEVAN

Sources *GM*, 1st ser., 75 (1805), 384 · *Catalogue of the library of the Royal Medical and Chirurgical Society of London: [with] additions to the library* (1844–75)

Millar, John (1735–1801), jurist, was born on 22 June 1735 at the manse, Kirk o' Shotts, Lanarkshire, the eldest of the four children of James Millar (1701–1785), a Church of Scotland minister, first of Shotts, then of Hamilton. His mother was Ann, the daughter of Archibald Hamilton of Westburn and the first cousin of Dr William Cullen. Upon his parents' move to Hamilton in 1737, Millar went to live with his paternal uncle John Millar, who farmed the family estate of Milheugh, Blantyre, and who taught the boy until he could be sent to the grammar school in Hamilton (1742) and then to the University of Glasgow (1746). Cullen seems to have kept an eye on the boy, and in time James Watt (later the famous engineer) became a close friend.

After the usual arts course, which normally lasted four years, Millar was meant to follow his father and study for the ministry, but he was disinclined and opted to study law with Hercules Lindesay instead. Upon the arrival of Adam Smith as professor in 1751, Millar audited his classes in logic and in moral philosophy, and the two men formed a lasting friendship. This influence was decisive for Millar's intellectual outlook. It is not known when he completed his studies, but he passed advocate in February 1760 and before that time had spent about two years as a tutor in the house of Henry Home, Lord Kames. He practised law in Edinburgh for little over a year, showing considerable promise, before accepting the regius chair of civil law at Glasgow in 1761 (royal letter of warrant 15 June; he was admitted to the chair on 15 July) in succession to Lindesay, who had died on 2 June. Millar's appointment had been orchestrated by Kames and Smith, using the patronage of George James Hamilton, seventh duke of Hamilton, a minor whose interest was managed by John Stuart, third earl of Bute, then at his apogee as mentor to George III. Millar's motive in changing his career is said to have been the need for economic security arising from his marriage to Margaret Craig (c.1736–1795) at Glasgow on 10 October 1759. They had thirteen children, two of whom died in infancy.

When Millar took over Lindesay's chair there were usually three or four students in law, occasionally none at all. After a few years Millar regularly had ten times that number, and Glasgow was soon recognized as 'famous as a school for Law, as Edinburgh … for medicine' (R. Heron, *Journey through Western Scotland in 1792*, 2 vols., 1793, 2.418). There were several reasons for this success. Millar was a forceful and engaging teacher who followed his talent for extempore speech by lecturing in English in all his courses, despite attempts by the faculty of advocates to get the university to force him to follow tradition and teach (that is, dictate) in Latin. Millar also supplemented his classes through informal discussion with interested students. Furthermore, he expanded the curriculum significantly to encompass law both as a vocational study and as an advanced liberal arts course. Clearly, he struck a balance that was right for the student market, and he did so within a few years of his appointment. The statutory duty of the professor was to teach Roman law. This was done partly by a shorter course on Justinian's *Institutes*, which

John Millar (1735–1801), by James Tassie, 1796

was—or was meant to be—taught twice during the academic year; and partly by a course on the *Digest*, which took the whole academic year. In 1765 Millar turned the second of the annual courses on the *Institutes* into a presentation of natural jurisprudence modelled on the theory of his mentor, Adam Smith, who had resigned in 1764. This innovation may also have been a reaction to the appointment of Thomas Reid as Smith's successor. In 1765 Millar had also added a course on Scots law, which at least by 1767 had become two separate courses on public and private law. The former was renamed as lectures on government and became a general course on that topic. Finally, in the last years of his teaching, perhaps not until 1798–9, Millar added a course on English law.

The theoretical core of Millar's work was Humean and, more directly, Smithian, as he himself stressed. On the basis of a spectator theory of the moral sentiments, Millar followed Hume and Smith in drawing a sharp distinction between justice and the other virtues. Justice is a 'negative' virtue in that it tells us what not to do, and it stands out because it is generally more precise and because breaches of it tend to be met with much sharper reactions, from both victim and spectators, than infringements of other virtues. Resentment at injury when regulated by impartial spectators is the foundation for the judicial settlement of disputes, and those areas of life which are protected by such resentment are our rights. This Smithian division of jurisprudence into 'actions' and 'rights' was basic to all Millar's legal thought. It was a scheme which invited historical explanation of how rights and actions had been formed and re-formed during the life of the species. Millar excelled in continuing this part of Smith's theory, using the so-called four-stages theory of society as a general framework.

Millar's jurisprudence had a lasting influence on Scots law through one of his pupils, David Hume, a future professor of Scots law in Edinburgh, who had been sent to study with Millar by his uncle, the philosopher David Hume. The younger Hume, an avid tory, was unsympathetic to Millar's politics and seems to have been uninterested in philosophy. Nevertheless, the influence of Millar's teaching can be detected in Hume's lectures on Scots law, in which he used Millar's Smithian jurisprudence as the analytical framework, altering it by reversing Millar's treatment of real (that is, property) rights and personal rights (that is, those between individuals arising out of contracts or wrongs or in some other way).

Millar's published works sprang from his teaching. *Observations Concerning the Distinction of Ranks in Society* (1771) was a pioneering attempt at a historical sociology of social authority, taking up, in turn, familial relations, age, work relations, and political and martial leadership. *An Historical View of the English Government from the Settlement of the Saxons in Britain to the Accession of the House of Stewart* (1787) was intended as a modern whiggish correction to Hume's *History of England*. The full scope of this became clear only with the posthumous third edition, which took the story up to 1688 and also included a volume of essays dealing with the post-revolutionary political debate.

In addition to his teaching and writing, Millar was active in the administration of his university and in its underlying politics. He opposed the appointment of Thomas Reid to succeed Smith as professor of moral philosophy in 1765. The antagonism was purely philosophical and was pursued over the years within the Glasgow Literary Society, where Millar, a particularly faithful member, saw himself as representative of what he called 'the true old Humean philosophy' (John Millar to David Douglas, 10 Aug 1790, University of Glasgow Library, Gen. MS 1035/178). Among the few surviving letters are courteous ones to Edmund Burke on his election to the rectorship at Glasgow. For some years after his appointment Millar also continued some legal practice, though eventually this was restricted to private arbitration.

Apart from his teaching and writing, however, it was politics that interested Millar more than anything else. He was a Rockingham whig who, in time, became a faithful follower of Charles James Fox, undergoing a common development from belief in a 'union of talents and rank' to a desire for parliamentary reform based upon 'a much more general diffusion of political power' (Craig, cii–ciii). This cause underlay his correspondence with Christopher Wyvill on the advancement of economical reform, which was published in Wyvill's *Political Papers* (vol. 6, 1794, pp. 95–108). He was a pronounced supporter of American independence and active in the campaign against the slave trade. He was also an active member of the Society of Friends of the People and spoke out in favour of the early phase of the French Revolution while it could be seen as an attempt at constitutional reform on whig principles. Consistent with this, he also opposed the war against France. His eldest son, also John, and others of his former students, notably Thomas Muir of Huntershill, took his political ideas in a more radical direction and paid the price of emigration to America and transportation to Australia, respectively. Millar's political involvement can be traced to two anonymous pamphlets, *Letters of Crito, on the Causes, Objects, and Consequences of the Present War* (1796, first as letters in the *Scots Chronicle*) and *Letters of Sidney, on Inequality of Property, to which is added A Treatise of the Effects of War on Commercial Prosperity* (1796, first, in part, as letters in the *Scots Chronicle*). The latter may be by John Craig but its contents derive from Millar's work. In addition, Millar wrote for the *Analytical Review*, though his articles have not been identified with certainty. In his lectures on property, Millar had formulated some of the ideas on utility which two of his closest disciples, James Maitland, eighth earl of Lauderdale, and John Craig subsequently developed.

Described as 'a fine muscular man, somewhat above the middle size, with a square chest and shapely bust, a prominent chin, grey eyes that were unmatched in expression, and a head that would become a Roman senator' (W. Beattie, *Life and Letters of Thomas Campbell*, 3 vols., 1849, 1.158–60), Millar remained active and vigorous until his death. He was an eager hobby farmer and spent his summers at the small family estate, Milheugh, Lanarkshire, which he inherited from his uncle and improved according to the fashions of the day. It was here that he prepared his lectures and wrote his books, which were read to and discussed by his family, whose lively intellect was noted by visitors. When in town he lived in one of the professors' houses and, as was common, took in student boarders to supplement his income. This further boosted his reputation as a mentor for his students. Millar taught many prominent politicians and lawyers, English and Scots, including William Lamb and Frederick Lamb, the second and third viscounts Melbourne; William Windham; and a son of the prime minister Shelburne. Adam Smith, following the example of Kames and Hume, entrusted to Millar the education of a young relative, and Francis Jeffrey defied his tory father and attended Millar's lectures by stealth.

Millar's eldest son, John (1760–1795), followed in his father's footsteps as a lawyer. He produced a study of insurance before a combination of depression and fear of reprisals for his radical politics drove him to migrate to America, where he died of sunstroke soon after arriving in 1795, the same year as his mother had died. The second son, James (1762–1831), became professor of mathematics at Glasgow; the third and fourth sons were William *Millar (d. 1838), later an army officer who achieved distinction during the Peninsular War, and Archibald. All four sons were educated at Glasgow. One daughter, Agnes, married James *Mylne (1757–1839), professor of moral philosophy at Glasgow; another, Margaret, married John

*Thomson (1765–1846), professor of surgery at Edinburgh. The other four daughters remained unmarried: Millar provided for them in his will by allowing them to live at Milheugh. Millar died of pleurisy at Milheugh on 30 May 1801, and was buried at High Blantyre, Lanarkshire.

Millar's literary executors were his son James Millar, his son-in-law James Mylne, and his nephew John Craig. The latter two issued the posthumous third edition of the *Historical View of the English Government* and a new edition of the *Origin of the Distinction of Ranks*, which carried a substantial biography by Craig. While Millar's refined use of Scottish conjectural history had some influence on early nineteenth-century historiography, notably on James Mill's *History of British India* (1817), the *Historical View* was too confined to the political world of the era before the French Revolution to retain a significant role. The work on social ranks influenced the developing field of anthropological studies and historical jurisprudence. Not least, and as mentioned already, Millar had an indirect impact on Scots law and, in the early decades of the nineteenth century, on political economy. As with his intellectual master, Adam Smith, however, the full scope of Millar's project disappeared from view because so much of the theoretical structure remained the privileged information of his students.   KNUD HAAKONSSEN and JOHN W. CAIRNS

Sources J. Millar, *Observations concerning the distinction of ranks in society* (1771); 2nd edn (1773); 3rd edn (1779) [repr. in W. C. Lehmann, *John Millar of Glasgow, 1735–1801* (1960)]; 4th edn as *The origin of the distinction of ranks, or, An inquiry into the circumstances which give rise to influence and authority in the different members of society* (1806) • J. Millar, *An historical view of the English government from the settlement of the Saxons in Britain to the revolution of 1688, to which are subjoined some dissertations connected with the history of the government from the revolution to the present time*, 4 vols. (1803) • J. Millar, 'Lectures on government, 1787–88', U. Glas. L., Gen. MSS 289–91 • J. Millar, 'Lectures on civil law', U. Glas. L., Hamilton papers, 117, 1798 • [J. Millar], 'Lectures on the institutions of the civil law, by Professor John Millar, Glasgow, 1794', U. Edin. L., MSS Dc 2.45–6 • J. Craig, 'Account of the life and writings of John Millar, Esq.', in J. Millar, *The origin of the distinction of ranks, or, An inquiry into the circumstances which give rise to influence and authority in the different members of society*, 4th edn (1806), i–cxxiv • W. C. Lehmann, *John Millar of Glasgow, 1735–1801: his life and thought and his contributions to sociological analysis* (1960) • *Letters of Sidney, on inequality of property, to which is added A treatise of the effects of war on commercial prosperity* (1796) • *Letters of Crito, on the causes, objects, and consequences of the present war* (1796) • J. Cairns, '"As famous a school for law as Edinburgh for medicine": the Glasgow law school, 1761–1801', *The Glasgow Enlightenment*, ed. A. Hook and R. Sher (1995), 133–59 • J. Cairns, 'John Millar, Ivan Andreyevich Tret'yakov, and Semyon Efimovich Desnitsky: a legal education in Scotland, 1761–1767', *Russia and Scotland in the Enlightenment*, ed. T. Artemieva, P. Jones, and M. Mikeshin (2001), 20–37 [Proceedings of the International Conference, 1–3 September 2000, Edinburgh] • K. Haakonssen, 'John Millar and the science of a legislator', *Natural law and moral philosophy: from Grotius to the Scottish Enlightenment* (1996), 154–81 • J. Cairns, 'From "speculative" to "practical" legal education: the decline of the Glasgow law school, 1801–1830', *Tijdschrift voor Rechtsgeschiedenis*, 62 (1994), 331–56 • J. Cairns, 'Rhetoric, language and Roman law: legal education and improvement in eighteenth-century Scotland', *Law and History Review*, 9 (1991), 31–58 • 'John Millar's lectures on Scots criminal law', *Oxford Journal of Legal Studies*, 8 (1988), 364–400 • J. Millar, *Disputatio juridica, ad tit. 3. lib. XXVI. Pand. 'De confirmando tutore vel curatore'* (1760)

Archives NA Scot., 332/C3/903, 1063, 1254/1–5 • NA Scot., GD 170/1990 • NL Scot., Adv. MS 29. x. 2, vol. ii; MS 124 • NL Scot., lecture notes • NRA, priv. coll., letters to William Adam • U. Aberdeen, lecture notes • U. Edin. L., La. II. 588, La. II. 475, Dc. 4. 41[108] • U. Edin. L., lecture notes • U. Glas., Archives and Business Records Centre, 11553, 32001, 58307, 58312 • U. Glas. L., lecture notes | U. Glas. L., Murray 660; Gen. MSS 1035/180, 502/36–40, 1035/149, 1035/178

Likenesses J. Tassie, paste medallion, 1796, Scot. NPG [*see illus.*]

Millar, Robert (1672–1752), Church of Scotland minister and historian, was the son of the Revd Andrew Millar of Neilston, Renfrewshire. He was educated at Glasgow University and was licensed to preach by the presbytery of Paisley on 3 February 1697. While the minister of Port Glasgow, where he had been ordained on 18 August 1697, he married, on 10 June 1702, Elizabeth Kelso (d. 1759), daughter of John Kelso of Kelsoland in the borders. They had eight surviving children: Andrew *Millar, a London bookseller; John (d. 1738) and Henry (d. 1771), who followed him into the ministry; Anna (d. 1768) and Elizabeth (d. 1798), who both married Paisley ministers, one of whom, James Hamilton, was his successor; Archibald (d. 1766), a naval officer; Robert, a physician who went abroad; and William, who practised medicine in Antigua and later acquired the Walkinshaw estate near Paisley. On 28 December 1709 Millar moved to the first charge at Paisley where he ministered for the rest of his life.

In 1723 Millar published at Edinburgh his major work, *The History of the Propagation of Christianity, and Overthrow of Paganism*, two large volumes dedicated to the earl of Dundonald, Lord Cochran of Paisley, and William, Lord Ross. The widespread support that Millar's book engendered among clergy and laymen in the Church of Scotland is indicated by the impressive list of nearly 500 subscribers prefixed to the first edition, including several university principals and many professors. From a foundation in Christian apologetics directed against the English deists, the work develops into a global history of evangelism that displays considerable learning and commitment. As stated in the preface the four components in the author's design are to stimulate thankfulness to God for delivering Christians from 'miserable Darkness and Idolatry'; to trace the history of the propagation of Christianity by divine providence 'down to the present time'; to move readers to pity the heathens 'who make up so great a Part of the World'; and to incite Christians with missionary 'Fervour and Zeal'. In sending a copy of the book to Cotton Mather of Boston, from whose work on American missions Millar is said to have borrowed 'almost verbatim' (De Jong, 114), the church historian Robert Wodrow asserted, in a letter of 29 July 1724, that Millar 'is a serious, diligent, and laborious minister, and his book will show his acquaintance with learning, in most of its valuable branches' (*Correspondence of the Rev. Robert Wodrow*, 3.154). A second edition was published in London in 1726, and a third by the author's son Andrew in 1731, in addition to a Dutch translation. It was enormously influential among Scottish missionaries and has been called one of the formative influences in the eighteenth century by a leading historian of Scottish revivalism (Fawcett, 215).

In 1730 Millar published in Edinburgh, also by subscription, his second major work, *The history of the church under the Old Testament … to which is subjoined, a discourse to promote the conversion of the Jews to Christianity*, which may be seen as an extension of his earlier history of Christian conversion among pagans. Although no publisher is named on the title page, an advertisement for the book that appears at the end of the third edition of *The History of the Propagation of Christianity* states that it was 'Printed for A. Millar'. Robert Millar published nothing else before his death on 16 December 1752. In 1782 two pamphlets based on his *History of the Church* appeared in Edinburgh under his name, one on the life of Herod and the other (which was reprinted in Glasgow in 1786) on the history of the Jews from the death of Herod to the destruction of Jerusalem. In 1789 *The Whole Works of the Reverend Robert Millar* was published in Paisley in eight octavo volumes.

RICHARD B. SHER

Sources G. Crawfurd and W. Semple, *The history of the shire of Renfrew* (1782) · R. E. Davies, 'Robert Millar: an eighteenth-century Scottish latourette', *Evangelical Quarterly*, 62 (1990), 143–56 · J. A. De Jong, *As the waters cover the sea: millennial expectations in the rise of Anglo-American missions, 1640–1810* (1970) · A. Fawcett, *The Cambuslang revival: the Scottish evangelical revival of the eighteenth century* (1971) · J. Foster, 'A Scottish contributor to the missionary awakening: Robert Millar of Paisley', *International Review of Missions*, 37 (1948), 138–45 · I. D. Maxwell, 'Millar, Robert', *DSCHT* · *Fasti Scot.*, new edn, 3.166 · *The correspondence of the Rev. Robert Wodrow*, ed. T. M'Crie, 3 vols., Wodrow Society, [3] (1842–3)

Millar, William (*d.* 1838), army officer, third son of John *Millar (1735–1801), professor of law, and his wife, Margaret, *née* Craig, received a direct appointment as second lieutenant, Royal Artillery, on 24 May 1781. His promotions were: first lieutenant in 1787, captain lieutenant in 1794, captain in 1799, major (brevet 1805) in 1806, lieutenant-colonel in 1806, colonel (brevet 4 June) on 14 June 1814, major-general in 1831, colonel commandant in 1834, and lieutenant-general in 1837. He served eighteen years in the West Indies, and was present at the capture of most of the French islands during the early part of the revolutionary wars. In 1804, on the rebuilding of Woolwich arsenal after the great fire of 1802, he was appointed second assistant inspector (at £200 per annum) under Colonel Fage in the royal carriage department; he was promoted first assistant inspector in 1806.

Millar was one of the officers to whose skill and exertions during the Peninsular War the services were indebted for their material. With imperfect mechanical resources they produced supplies of a quality which was admired by other armies, and which at the close of the war led to the French commission of Baron Dupin to inquire into the system that produced such results. Millar was the originator of the 10 inch and 8 inch shell-guns which formed a large part of British armaments from 1832 until after the Crimean War. He was among the first to perceive the advantages of large-calibre shell-guns, and as early as 1820, two years before the publication of General Henri Paixhans's *Nouvelle force maritime*, brought forward his first 8 inch shell-gun. He also invented the compass

saw used at Woolwich, 'applicable to all purposes of circular cutting, or any irregular sweeps' (Hogg, 1.616). He was appointed inspector-general of artillery in 1827, and director-general of artillery in January 1833.

Millar died from self-inflicted injuries near Hastings, on 14 March 1838. He had previously exhibited symptoms of suicidal mania. He was married and left a grown-up family.   H. M. CHICHESTER, *rev.* ROGER T. STEARN

Sources J. Kane, *List of officers of the royal regiment of artillery from 1716*, rev. edn (1869) · *Official catalogue of the Museum of Artillery in the Rotunda, Woolwich* (1906) · O. F. G. Hogg, *The Royal Arsenal: its background, origin, and subsequent history*, 2 vols. (1963) · F. P. C. Dupin, *Voyages dans la Grande Bretagne*, 6 vols. (1820–24) · H. Douglas, *A treatise on naval gunnery* (1861) · *Naval and Military Gazette* (17 March 1838) · *Naval and Military Gazette* (24 March 1838) · F. L. Robertson, *The evolution of naval armament* (1921) · A. D. Lambert, *The last sailing battlefleet: maintaining naval mastery, 1815–1850* (1991)

Millard, Charles Killick (1870–1952), public health official and advocate of voluntary euthanasia, was born at Costock, Nottinghamshire, on 14 August 1870, one of nine children of Charles Sutton Millard (1834–1912), rector of Costock, and his wife, Mary Harriet Killick. He was educated at Trent College, Long Eaton, where he gained his senior school certificate. For two years he was articled pupil to a general practitioner in Ludlow, Shropshire, before going on to study medicine at Edinburgh University, where he won a medal in physiology. In 1892 he spent six months in Bethnal Green as a pupil to the medical officer of health (MOH), before becoming assistant to the MOH for Shropshire, in March 1894. In the same year he became assistant medical officer at Birmingham's hospitals for fever and smallpox; he was subsequently appointed to the position of medical superintendent. His experience with the treatment of infectious disease led him to espouse views that were seen as decidedly contentious; for instance he opposed hospital isolation as a means of reducing mortality from scarlet fever, believing it to be ineffective. Such controversial views became a hallmark of his career. In 1899 he was appointed MOH for Burton upon Trent. On 24 August that year he married Annie Susan (*b.* 1873/4), daughter of the Revd John Longley; they had four children.

In 1901 Millard became MOH for Leicester, a position that he retained until he retired in 1935. He held numerous positions within the Leicester region: president of the Leicester Literary and Philosophical Society, the Leicester Rotary Club, the Leicester Temperance Society, the Leicester Band of Hope Union, and the Leicester Medical Society; chairman of the Leicester and Rutland division of the British Medical Association; and vice-president of the public health section in 1922 and 1932. During his time as MOH for Leicester he gained a wide reputation as a maverick, opposing the policy of compulsory smallpox vaccination on sophisticated though controversial epidemiological grounds. He also helped to pioneer experimental farm colonies for consumptives as a method of treating tuberculosis, promoted the consumption of horseflesh as a substitute for other meats during wartime shortages, and advocated prohibition. While at Leicester he expanded public health services and public housing, and established a birth control clinic. He was also one of the principal figures responsible for persuading the Eugenics Society to advocate birth control between the wars; this was just one aspect of his broader eugenic outlook, which included the advocacy of sterilization for the mentally incompetent. He was later described as 'a sort of George Bernard Shaw among his public health contemporaries, causing them to think furiously even if they did not always agree with him' (*Public Health*). He published several works, including *The Vaccination Question in the Light of Modern Experience* (1914), *Population and Birth Control* (1917), and *Euthanasia* (1931).

From his retirement until his death Millard promoted the legalization of voluntary euthanasia. This had been prompted by his work with cancer patients and his belief that there was still a great deal of suffering that medicine was unable to relieve. These views were first advanced in his presidential address to the annual general meeting of the Society of Medical Officers of Health in 1931. In 1935, with Charles John Bond, senior consulting surgeon at the Leicester Royal Infirmary, Millard founded the Voluntary Euthanasia Legalisation Society, the first euthanasia movement in the modern world. The following year a bill drafted by the society and introduced to the House of Lords by Lord Ponsonby of Shulbrede (in place of Lord Moynihan, who was to have introduced it) was defeated after a vigorous debate on 1 December 1936. Defective circulation forced Millard to resign from the position of honorary secretary of the society. He died at his home, The Gilroes, Groby Road, Leicester, on 7 March 1952. Despite his failure to achieve legalization Millard brought the hitherto taboo subject of voluntary euthanasia into the open, and made possible a more frank and open discussion of many contentious social and medical issues among the medical and legal professions, religious leaders, and the general public.   N. D. A. KEMP

Sources *BMJ* (22 March 1952) • *The Lancet* (22 March 1952) • *Public Health* (April 1952) • *Leicester Evening Mail* (8 March 1952) • *Leicester Mercury* (8 March 1952) • *WWW* • Voluntary Euthanasia Society archives • *CGPLA Eng. & Wales* (1952) • m. cert. • d. cert.
Archives Leics. RO • Wellcome L., papers | BL, corresp. with Marie Stopes, Add. MS 58564 • Wellcome L., Voluntary Euthanasia Society collection, CMAC/SA/VES
Wealth at death £16,119 12s. 5d.: probate, 28 April 1952, *CGPLA Eng. & Wales*

Miller. *See also* Millar.

Miller, Andrew (*d.* 1763), mezzotint engraver, was probably born in London, of Scottish descent. He was a pupil of John Faber the younger, who worked in the Covent Garden area of Westminster. In 1737 Miller launched a career in plagiarism with a copy of Faber's portraits of Maria Clementina as a pair to an apparently original but politically inflammatory portrait of her husband, the Jacobite pretender James III. In 1738 he began to publish his own plates from the sign of the Coffin in Wytch Street, Strand, before moving to Exeter Court in 1739. Two years later he left London for Dublin where, initially, he worked for the printseller John Brooks. In 1743, however, he established

himself at the Golden Head, Fleet Street, Dublin, where he launched a proposal to publish twelve mezzotint heads, most of which were copies of engravings recently published in London. In the following year he moved to Hog Hill in Dublin, where he remained until his death. He published most of his own plates, with the exception of a few published from Michael Ford's address before Miller and Ford became bitter rivals. They quarrelled in the press in 1747–8 about the respective merits of their portraits of Lord Boyne. Miller's next foray into the press brought him more trouble. In 1749 he published some paragraphs in *Esdall's Newsletter* voicing his support for the views of Charles Lucas, advocate of the political rights of citizens. For this, and the portrait of *Charles Lucas a Free Citizen and Sometime one of the Commons of Dublin* under the motto 'Truth and Liberty', he was brought before the House of Commons during a purge of trouble-makers in December 1749, and ordered to be committed to Newgate prison.

Miller produced more than sixty portraits, and an unknown number of decorative subjects. A high proportion of his output consisted of copies of London-published prints of celebrities and attractive designs intended for the wall. These included several copies of portraits of David Garrick as well as good original prints of Jonathan Swift (1743–4) and George Whitfield (1751). Miller was said to have shortened his life by intemperance and he published no prints after 1756. He died at his home at Hog Hill, Dublin, on 5 September 1763 and was buried at St Andrew's on 8 September. He left a wife, Anne (*d.* 1767), and several children.

TIMOTHY CLAYTON and ANITA McCONNELL

Sources J. T. Gilbert, *History of the city of Dublin*, 3 vols. (1854–9), 3.318, 330, 361–2 [repr. 1972] • C. E. Russell, *English mezzotint portraits and their states*, 2 vols. (1926) • W. G. Strickland, *A dictionary of Irish artists*, 2 (1913); repr. with introduction by T. J. Snoddy (1989), 109–15

Miller [*née* Riggs], **Anna, Lady Miller** (1741–1781), poet and salon hostess, was born in London, the daughter of Edward Riggs (*d.* 1748) and his wife, Margaret Pigott, of the ancient house of Chetwynd, Shropshire. From her grandfather Edward Riggs of Riggsdale, co. Cork, for many years a member of the Irish House of Commons, and a commissioner of revenue and a privy councillor in Ireland, she inherited much wealth. Her father became a commissioner of customs in London in 1741. Horace Walpole described her mother in 1765 as 'an old rough humourist, who passed for a wit' (*Letters*, 6.170).

In August 1765 Anna Riggs married Captain John Miller (*c.*1744–1798) [*see* Miller, Sir John Riggs], a member of a poor Irish family seated at Ballicasey, co. Clare; they had one daughter and one son. During the Seven Years' War he rose from the rank of cornet in the light dragoons in 1760 to that of captain in the 113th foot, resigning the latter commission at the peace of 1763. His wife brought him a large fortune, and he adopted her maiden surname before his own in 1780. At extravagant cost he built a house at Batheaston, near Bath, and laid out a garden of which Horace Walpole gives a detailed description (*Letters*, 5.20). The expenses incurred soon necessitated a retreat to France, in order to economize. In 1770–71 Anna Miller and her husband made a tour of Italy. In 1776 the sprightly letters that she sent during her travels to a friend were published anonymously in three volumes as *Letters from Italy, describing the manners, customs, antiquities, paintings … of the country, in 1770–1*. A second edition, in two volumes, appeared in 1777. The book enjoyed some reputation. Horace Walpole remarked, however, 'The poor Arcadian patroness does not spell one word of French or Italian right through her three volumes of travel' (*Letters*, 6.332).

Soon after returning to Batheaston, John Miller was created an Irish baronet (in 1778), and his wife, henceforth known as Lady Miller, instituted a literary salon at her villa. It bore some resemblance to the later follies of the Della Cruscans, which Gifford satirized in the *Baviad*. She invited everyone of wit and fashion in Bath, including Samuel Johnson, Hester Thrale, Horace Walpole, Fanny Burney, Anne Seward, and Mary Delaney, to meet once a fortnight at her house in Batheaston. An antique vase that had been purchased in Italy—it was dug up at Frascati in 1759—was placed on a modern altar decorated with laurel, and each guest was invited to place in the urn an original bout-rimé. A committee was appointed to determine the best three productions, and their authors were then crowned by Lady Miller with wreaths of myrtle. The practice was continued until Lady Miller's death. The urn was then purchased by Edwyn Dowding, of Bath, and placed by him in the public park of the town. The society became famous, and was much laughed at. Anthony Morris Storer, writing to George Selwyn, said, 'Their next subject is upon Trifles and Triflers … You may try your hand at an ode, and I do not doubt but you may be crowned with myrtle for your performance' (Jesse, 3.266).

Between 1775 and 1781 selections of the compositions were published under the title of *Poetical Amusements at a Villa Near Bath*. The edition was sold out within ten days. A new edition appeared in 1776 with a second volume of poems. Horace Walpole called the book 'a bouquet of artificial flowers, and ten degrees duller than a magazine' (*Letters*, 6.169, 178). A third volume was published in 1777, and a fourth in 1781. The profits of the sale were applied to charity. Among the contributors were the duchess of Northumberland (who wrote on the topic of a buttered muffin), Lord Palmerston, Lord Carlisle, Anstey, Mason, David Garrick, Anna Seward, and Lady Miller herself, to whom most of the writers paid extravagant compliments. Dr Johnson held the collection in high contempt (*Boswell's Life of Johnson*, 2.336), but Sir Walter Scott states in his 1810 biography of Anna Seward, prefixed to her works, that her poetical power was brought to light by Lady Miller, an obligation that Seward acknowledged in her 'Poem to the Memory of Lady Miller'.

Besides the works already mentioned, a volume by Lady Miller, entitled *On Novelty and on Trifles and Triflers*, appeared in 1778. Lady Miller died suddenly on 24 June 1781 at Hotwells, Bristol, and was buried in Bath Abbey. On her monument by Bacon, erected in 1785, is an epitaph, in verse, composed by Anna Seward.

Sir John Riggs Miller, who inherited his wife's fortune, went on to marry, on 25 March 1786, the widow of Sir Thomas Davenport. He sat in parliament from 1784 to 1790, as member for Newport in Cornwall, and made various unsuccessful efforts to reform the system of weights and measures, corresponding on the subject with Talleyrand. He settled in Bloomsbury Square and became known in London society as an inveterate gossip and newsmonger, and was a well-known figure in many London clubs. He died suddenly on 28 May 1798, and was succeeded in the baronetcy by his son from his first marriage, John Edward Augustus Miller (1770–1825), on whose death the baronetcy became extinct.

ELIZABETH LEE, *rev.* REBECCA MILLS

Sources R. A. Hesselgrave, *Lady Miller and the Batheaston literary circle* (1927) · J. Robinson, ed., *Wayward women: a guide to women travellers* (1990), 186 · Blain, Clements & Grundy, *Feminist comp.* · J. Todd, ed., *A dictionary of British and American women writers, 1660–1800* (1984) · *N&Q*, 2nd ser., 5 (1858), 495 · *N&Q*, 3rd ser., 8 (1865), 192 · *GM*, 1st ser., 11 (1741), 387 · *GM*, 1st ser., 68 (1798), 626–7 · *GM*, 1st ser., 95/2 (1825), 286 · *GM*, 1st ser., 51 (1781), 295 · *GM*, 1st ser., 55 (1785), 746 · Watt, *Bibl. Brit.*, vol. 2 · Allibone, *Dict.* · J. Collison, *The history of Somersetshire* (1799), 1.103 · *The letters of Horace Walpole, earl of Orford*, ed. P. Cunningham, 9 vols. (1857–9) · J. H. Jesse, *George Selwyn and his contemporaries, with memoirs and notes*, 4 vols. (1843–4) · *Boswell's Life of Johnson*, ed. G. B. Hill, 6 vols. (1887) · HoP, *Commons*

Likenesses J. Bacon sen., medallion on monument, Bath Abbey

Miller, Deborah. *See* Churchill, Deborah (1677/1682–1708).

Miller, Edward (1735–1807), musician, was born in Norwich on 30 October 1735 and was baptized on 30 November 1735 in St Peter Mancroft, Norwich, the second son and fourth child of Thomas Miller (1692/3–1764), a pavior, and his wife, Elizabeth Bacon (*d.* 1756). His brother was the bookseller Thomas *Miller. He was taught music by Charles Burney at King's Lynn. After going to London in his teens, Miller played the flute in performances under Handel. He must also have acquired considerable keyboard skill, as on 19 August 1756, on the recommendation of so considerable a musician as James Nares, Miller was appointed organist of St George's, Doncaster, at an annual salary of £30. He soon came to identify strongly with the West Riding of Yorkshire, volunteering for the militia in 1757. His role in musical life there increased: he took responsibility for the Doncaster town band in 1763. On 15 February 1763 he married Elizabeth Lee (1744/5–1773); they had ten children, only one of whom, William Edward (1766–1839), musician and Church of England clergyman, survived their father. Elizabeth Miller died, probably in childbirth, on 14 August 1773, aged twenty-eight.

Miller also took part in music-making at Nether Hall with Robert Copley and his friends, a group of gentleman amateurs who performed with some professional support. In 1760 they welcomed the German William Herschel, then a young bandsman, who impressed them with his skill on the oboe and violin. At Nether Hall Miller came into contact with Thomas Gray and with his friend the Revd William Mason, precentor of York Minster, whose wide cultural interests included music. Though Miller remarked on the scant success of his efforts to teach compositional skills to Mason, he dedicated his op. 3—a collection of songs—to him about 1770. In 1786, thanks to Mason's good offices, Miller was formally registered at Pembroke College when he took the MusD degree at Cambridge; a manuscript setting of canticles preserved in Cambridge University Library was probably his doctoral exercise. By this time Miller had established a great reputation across Yorkshire and beyond. Doncaster had recognized his importance to the borough by raising his salary to 40 guineas in 1767 and making him a freeman in 1774. In 1784, anticipating the Handel commemoration concerts in London, he wrote *Letters on Behalf of Professors of Music Residing in the Country*, pleading for the establishment of a 'New Musical Fund' for the benefit of impoverished musicians outside the capital. The idea was taken up, and on 12 April 1787 he participated with the composer Philip Hayes and the violinist William Cramer in the first of several concerts supporting the cause at the King's Theatre, Haymarket, London. On 2 May 1789 George III received Miller and others to discuss the fund. Miller's main theatre of activity remained outside London: he was a leading light in music festivals in Doncaster in 1787, in Sheffield in 1788, and at Louth in Lincolnshire in 1791.

During the 1770s Miller formed a relationship with Elizabeth Brailsford, with whom he had two sons, Isaac Brailsford (1778–1846) and Edward Brailsford, who both received £300 in his will. Isaac was trained as a child of the Chapel Royal under Edmund Ayrton, became organist at Bradford, and succeeded his father at Doncaster in 1807. On 27 December 1796 Miller married his second wife, Margaret Edwards (*d.* 1838), apparently an aspiring actress who had approached him for lessons. They had no children.

Many of Miller's publications reflect his occupation as a music teacher. They include collections of songs, some with instrumental obbligato, works for flute (or violin) and keyboard, a set of lessons for guitar (an instrument which was in fashion in polite society in the late eighteenth century), and a progressive elementary instructional manual, *The Institutes of Music*, for the harpsichord or the pianoforte (an instrument then beginning its advance to universal favour). First published in 1771, it went through successive editions which are evidence of its popularity. Responding to the demand for congregational music, Miller published in 1790 *The Psalms of David*. George III was a subscriber and presented him with £25 in recognition of his work in 1792. He also wrote hymn tunes: to the most famous of them, 'Rockingham', which is nowadays associated with Isaac Watts's 'When I survey the wondrous cross', he gave the name of his patron, Charles Watson-Wentworth, second marquess of Rockingham. 'Unveil thy bosom, faithful tomb' (*c.*1800), Miller's arrangement of Handel's 'Death March' to Watts's words, is a typical emotionally charged 'gallery' anthem. Patriotic and masonic songs were among Miller's last compositions.

Though poor at first, Miller was able to start investing in land improvement schemes in the Doncaster area from the mid-1760s. Although the returns from farming were disappointing initially, Miller profited from the enterprise in the long run. In old age, after reducing his teaching commitments, he compiled *The History and Antiquities of Doncaster* (1804). He died in Doncaster on 12 September 1807, and was buried at St George's, Doncaster, probably on 17 September 1807. He was survived by his second wife, his surviving son by his first marriage, his two illegitimate sons, and his son-in-law and nephew, William Richard Beckford *Miller (1769–1844), publisher, who had married his daughter Mary (1769–1791).   CHRISTOPHER SMITH

Sources F. Fowler, J. E. Day, and L. Smith, *Edward Miller, organist of Doncaster: his life and times* (1979) · E. Miller, *The history and antiquities of Doncaster and its vicinity: with anecdotes of eminent men* (1804) · parish register, Norwich, St Peter Mancroft · W. R. B. Miller, 'An account of the parentage and family of Dr Edward Miller', 1840, priv. coll. · *DNB* · will, PRO, PROB 11/1470, sig. 904
Likenesses T. Hardy, stipple, BM, NPG
Wealth at death two bequests of £300: will, PRO, PROB 11/1470, sig. 904

Miller, Edward (1915–2000), historian, was born on 16 July 1915 at Acklington Park, Northumberland, the son of Edward Miller, shepherd, and his wife, Mary Lee Fowler. As a child he wanted to become a vet, but the outstanding aptitude for history that he displayed at King Edward VI Grammar School, Morpeth, led to his winning an exhibition (later raised to a scholarship) to study that subject at St John's College, Cambridge, from October 1934.

Immediately after graduating with a double starred first in 1937 Miller was elected to the Strathcona research studentship at St John's. He specialized in medieval history and initially worked under the guidance of Helen Cam. In 1939 his college made him a research fellow, but he joined the Durham light infantry the following year, ultimately reaching the rank of staff major in the Allied Control Commission for Germany (British element) in 1945. On 14 June 1941 he married Fanny Zara Salingar (*b.* 1921/2), with whom he had a son, John, later professor of history at London University.

Ted Miller returned to St John's College in 1946 and settled down to life as a Cambridge history don. Within the university he was assistant lecturer until 1950, and then lecturer; within the college he was director of studies in history (1946–55) and tutor (1951–7). His easy manner and obvious enjoyment of teaching made him popular with students, who remembered his irreverent humour and distinctive chuckle.

In 1951 Miller published *The Abbey and Bishopric of Ely*, a book that examined the land holdings of Ely Cathedral from the tenth century to the early fourteenth. Having grown up on a farm he appreciated the practical side of agriculture and focused on the peasants whose labours had sustained the clergy. The social and economic history of medieval England would remain his principal academic interest. He especially valued discussing his research with M. M. Postan, the Cambridge economic historian.

Miller's next major work was a study of York in the Middle Ages for a volume of the Victoria county history of

Yorkshire (1961). After finishing *Portrait of a College* (1961), his history of St John's, he took up fresh administrative duties as warden of Madingley Hall, Cambridge University's department of continuing education, but he still found time to join Postan and E. E. Rich in editing volume 3 (1963) of the *Cambridge Economic History of Europe*, for which he wrote a chapter on the economic policies of medieval governments. From this period also date some short yet significant journal articles: 'The English economy in the thirteenth century' in *Past and Present* (1964), and 'The fortunes of the English textile industry during the thirteenth century', in the *Economic History Review* (1965).

From 1965 until 1971 Miller was professor of medieval history at Sheffield University. He continued to identify with the north of England and supported the journal *Northern History*. He went back to Cambridge, however, to be master of Fitzwilliam College (1971–81), which had received its charter in 1966. His sociability and moderation helped to promote collegiate solidarity, as did his keen support for Fitzwilliam's sporting endeavours; cricket and rugby were lifelong passions. He served as a deputy vice-chancellor of the university and as chairman of the library syndicate, while also chairing the Victoria county history committee (1972–9) and the History of Parliament Trust (1975–89). Miller, sturdy and round-faced, was not a controversialist. His writings offered cautious conclusions that recognized the limits of knowledge. Written in collaboration with John Hatcher, *Medieval England: Rural Society and Economic Change, 1086–1348* (1978) argued that the economy was expanding to the limits of its resources by 1300. It soon became a standard textbook for students. A companion volume by the same authors, *Medieval England: Towns, Commerce and Crafts, 1086–1348*, followed in 1995.

Having retired from Fitzwilliam College in 1981, when he became a fellow of the British Academy, Miller moved into 36 Almoners Avenue, Cambridge. Continuing his scholarly work on England in the twelfth and thirteenth centuries, he was co-editor of the second edition of volume 2 (1987) of the *Cambridge Economic History of Europe* and editor of the third volume (1991) of the *Agrarian History of England and Wales*, covering the period 1348 to 1500.

Edward Miller died in Addenbrooke's Hospital, Cambridge, on 21 December 2000, after an academic career that had efficiently combined research with administration and teaching and contributed much to the status of Cambridge as a centre for the study of English society in the middle ages. His wife survived him.

JASON TOMES

Sources *The Independent* (6 Jan 2001) · *Daily Telegraph* (11 Jan 2001) · *The Guardian* (9 Feb 2001) · *The Times* (8 March 2001) · R. Britnell and J. Hatcher, eds., *Progress and problems in medieval England: essays in honour of Edward Miller* (1996) · WW · b. cert. · m. cert. · d. cert.
Likenesses photograph, repro. in Britnell and Hatcher, eds., *Progress and problems*, frontispiece

Miller, Emanuel (1892–1970), psychiatrist, was born on 26 August 1892 at 80 Church Street, Spitalfields, London, the second son in the family of four daughters and three sons of Abram Miller, a dealer in furs, and his wife, Rebecca Finglestein, who were both from Jewish families originating in Russian Lithuania. Miller attended Parminters School from 1902 until 1909 and from the City of London School went to St John's College, Cambridge, in 1911. There he gained an exhibition and a first-class mark in the natural sciences tripos in the May examinations of his first year, and a second class in both part one and part two, in which he read the moral sciences tripos. College records show that Miller was religiously observant in so far as he took his examinations under special conditions to avoid taking them on the sabbath. Miller's tutor thought that he could make a promising career in the Indian Civil Service but his interests already tended towards the mixture of the humanities and sciences involved in the study of medicine. Miller studied at the London Hospital; he achieved his licence to practise, the diploma of the conjoint board, in 1918 but more importantly chose to return to Cambridge to study for the diploma of psychological medicine (DPM), which he took in 1921.

In 1924–5 Miller lectured to students themselves pursuing the DPM at Cambridge University, but most of his working life was spent teaching through clinical practice and example. He practised across the range of activities, with a special interest in children but also working occasionally in what was then called mental deficiency, and in neurology. In 1929 he became a member of the Royal College of Physicians. Miller's approach to psychiatry had a strong psychoanalytic and sociological bent. He was the psychiatrist to and director of the first child guidance clinic to open in England, which he founded at the Jewish Hospital in east London, working with the psychologist (as he then was) Meyer Fortes and a leading psychiatric social worker, Sybil Clement Brown. When some of those interested in this type of work with children combined to create the Child Guidance Council, Miller became a member of its governing body. Miller believed that psychoanalytically informed work would help to prevent delinquency and neurosis spreading from the youthful individual to the adult. He published *Types of Mind and Body* in 1926 and two extremely influential and much cited articles in 1931 on the psychopathology of childhood and illusion and hallucination. He also wrote a moving but professional account of the state of psychotherapy in 1931 and in *The Generations* (1938), the most sociologically inclined of all his writings, his rallying call for mental health to lead social reform for a better future. Some obituarists record a rabbinical quality to Miller's writing and his learning was worn well and deployed gracefully to illustrate points of argument. In *Types of Mind and Body* he discusses poetry in order to reject banal physiology in favour of a more sophisticated psychological discourse.

On 15 August 1933 Miller married Betty Spiro (1910–1965), an author, daughter of Simon Spiro JP. A son, Jonathan Wolfe, was born in July 1934 and a daughter, Sarah, in March 1937. Miller accumulated work in the period, working in neurology for the Ministry of Pensions at the child guidance unit in the West End Hospital for Nervous Diseases, as a consultant at the expanding Tavistock Clinic, and in a mental deficiency hospital in Roehampton. The flavour of domestic life can be seen in two of his wife's fictions: *A Room in Regent's Park* (1942) reflects 'living on the job in the medical district' (Miller, xi) and their life at 23 Park Crescent, while *On the Side of the Angels* (1945) includes a description of wartime psychiatric work. Miller served with the Royal Army Medical Corps as a lieutenant-colonel from 1939 until 1945, initially at the military hospital in Tooting in surgical neurology, then as army psychiatrist to the directorate of medical research and statistics in 1943. At the outbreak of war he helped unite several mental health bodies to form the Campaign for Mental Health, with a journal initially called *Mental Health*. He edited one of the major texts on the subject, *Neurosis in War* (1940).

After the war Miller returned to Queen's Grove, St John's Wood. In 1948 he became joint editor of the *British Journal of Criminology*, holding the post until the year of his death. From 1945 he taught generations of psychiatrists at the leading hospital in the field, the Maudsley, and founded both a journal which perhaps most directly summed up his project of uniting the sciences of the psyche, the *Journal of Child Psychology and Psychiatry*, and the Association of Child Psychology and Psychiatry (ACPP). Miller edited *Foundations of Child Psychiatry* in 1967. His writing was characteristic of the most effective period of British eclecticism in relation to psychoanalytic thinking, where the insights of Freudian and Kleinian analysis could be combined with positivist medicine and enrich each other rather than engage in sterile debates based on a narrow definition of utility. Miller remained firmly medical in his approach to child guidance, seeing the clinic as the setting for a psychotherapeutic encounter. This was the approach generally adopted in child guidance after the National Health Service organized medical work separately from the more psychological work of testing and assessment.

Freud's ambition that psychotherapy could turn neurosis into 'ordinary everyday unhappiness' seems particularly pertinent to Emanuel Miller, who developed severe and painful rheumatoid arthritis during the war and also, according to Edward Glover, frequently suffered from profound depression. Miller's wife died on 24 November 1965, but he nevertheless managed to remain intensely productive and creative. A true humanist, he studied Jewish scripture, was fluent in Hebrew, and was a talented painter. He wrote beautifully, and was admired and loved by his patients and his students. Glover wrote that 'One cannot but be impressed by the unanimity with which correspondents express their admiration for his qualities of heart as well as mind' (Glover, 12). Miller's own account of a good life in *The Generations* sums him up:

> It is only given to a few to sit back at the end of life and survey the spiritual and material wealth which they know they are leaving behind ... The artist leaves his pictures, the scientist his contributions to knowledge, ... the statesman the institutions he helps to build. But for every man less

endowed who feels contributions are but as eddies of dust which whirl and fall, there are left children who come, and remain after him. (p. 210)

Miller's sense both of posterity and disappointment was strong, and he was often very sad. He was extremely proud of his children, and of the institutions he had helped to create. The range of his interests is shown by some of his bequests such as those of art and art books to the Tel Aviv Art Museum; medical objects to the Royal Society; Jewish books to the Herbert Loewe Memorial Library; and money to St John's College, Cambridge, for a biennial prize for essays on the philosophy of science, and the ACPP. Miller died in St George's Hospital, Westminster, on 29 July 1970 and was buried on 30 July in the Jewish cemetery at Bushey, Hertfordshire.   D. Thom

Sources admission records, tutors' notes, press cuttings, St John Cam., Archives · *The Times* (30 July 1970) · *The Times* (4 Aug 1970) · *BMJ* (8 Aug 1970) · *The Lancet* (8 Aug 1970) · E. Glover, 'In piam memoriam Emanuel Miller', *British Journal of Criminology*, 2 (1970), 4–13 · *WW* · S. Miller, 'Introduction', in B. Miller, *On the side of the angels* (1985) · m. cert. · d. cert.

Likenesses photograph, repro. in *BMJ* · photograph, repro. in *The Lancet*

Wealth at death £56,808: probate, 4 Dec 1970, *CGPLA Eng. & Wales*

Miller, Florence Fenwick (1854–1935), journalist and public lecturer, was born on 5 November 1854 in London, the eldest in the family of two sons and one daughter of Captain John Miller (1817–1895), a sea captain in the merchant marine, and his wife, Eleanor, formerly Estabrook (1823–1890), daughter of Simon Fenwick, a railway engineer. She was privately educated, then in 1871 joined Sophia Jex-Blake's group at the University of Edinburgh seeking a medical degree; here she passed part of the preliminary examination in medicine. Following the failure of the attempt to get Edinburgh to grant medical degrees to women, she returned to London and in November entered the new Ladies' Medical College. She completed the course of study with honours in April 1873, but practised only briefly.

In 1876 Fenwick Miller campaigned and was elected as a representative for the borough of Hackney on the London school board. She served three consecutive terms from 1877 to 1885, and was noted for her fearlessness and power of debate. Her reputation as a lecturer grew through her appearances before the London Dialectical Society and the Sunday Lecture Society from 1873 to 1883. From the mid-1870s, she made annual lecture tours throughout England and Scotland, a female pioneer in this field, often speaking to audiences of several thousand people on a variety of literary and social topics. Her work for the early suffrage campaigns also began in the mid-1870s, when she lectured widely for the cause in London, Manchester, Birmingham, and elsewhere. She firmly believed in suffrage for married women and was one of the founders of the Women's Franchise League in 1889.

It was as a pioneer woman journalist that Fenwick Miller earned her most lasting renown, sometimes using the pseudonym Filomena. Early in her career she contributed frequently to such journals as *Fraser's Magazine*, *Lett's*

Illustrated Household Magazine, *Belgravia*, and *The Governess*. In March 1886 she became a columnist for the *Illustrated London News*, writing the 'Ladies' notes', an influential post which she held until 1918. She also wrote for the *Lady's Pictorial*, *Women's World*, the *Young Woman*, and *The Echo*, among others. In 1890 she became editor of *Outward Bound*, a quarterly journal for colonists, and *Homeward Bound*, 1892, for those who were returning. Perhaps her greatest accomplishment came between 1895 and 1899 when she assumed the editorship and proprietorship of the *Woman's Signal*, one of the most influential and outspoken feminist periodicals. She was on the staff of the *London Daily News* from 1902 to 1904. In 1890 she was elected a member of the Institute of Journalists.

In 1893 Fenwick Miller travelled to the United States, to the world fair in Chicago, the Columbian Exposition, as a foreign correspondent for *The Echo*, and as an official delegate to the World's Congress of Representative Women. Here she became closely associated with such leaders of the American suffrage movement as Susan B. Anthony, Rachel Foster Avery, May Wright Sewall, Carrie Chapman Catt, and Anna Howard Shaw. She visited the United States a second time in 1902, as a founding member, with Susan B. Anthony, of the International Council of Women, and took an active part in the growth of the international suffrage movement.

Many of Fenwick Miller's books were on physiology, which drew on her medical training, including: *The House of Life* (1878), *An Atlas of Anatomy* (1879), *Animal Physiology for Elementary Schools* (1882), and the first two books in the series Hughes Natural History Readers (1884). She also published the first full biography of Harriet Martineau (1884); an anonymous three-volume novel, *Lynton Abbott's Children* (1879); and an influential social text, *Readings in Social Economy* (1883).

On 28 April 1877 Fenwick Miller married Frederick Alfred Ford (1849–1910), a stockbroker's clerk and the son of Frederick Alfred Ford, publisher. Because her public reputation was already established, she kept her own name, henceforth being addressed as Mrs Fenwick Miller. After her marriage attempts were made to unseat her from the London school board because of the alleged illegality of her name, but they failed, thus establishing that a British woman has no legal obligation to take her husband's name. There were two daughters of the marriage, which ended in separation. The elder daughter, Irene, in 1906 became the first woman in London to be arrested in the cause of militant suffragism. Florence Fenwick Miller died on 24 April 1935 at 45 Cromwell Road, Hove, Sussex and was cremated.

ROSEMARY T. VAN ARSDEL

Sources *WWW* · F. Hays, *Women of the day: a biographical dictionary of notable contemporaries* (1885) · F. F. Miller, 'An uncommon girlhood', MS autobiography, priv. coll. · R. T. Van Arsdel, 'Mrs Florence Fenwick Miller: feminism and the *Woman's Signal*, 1895–1899', *Victorian Periodicals Review*, 15 (1982) · P. Hollis, *Ladies elect: women in English local government, 1865–1914* (1987) · Women's Franchise League: *report of the proceedings of the inaugural meeting* (1889) · *CGPLA Eng. & Wales* (1935) · R. T. Van Arsdel, 'Victorian periodicals yield their secrets: Florence Fenwick Miller's three campaigns for the London school board', *History of Education Society Bulletin*, 38 (1986), 26–42 · d. cert.

Archives priv. coll., 'An uncommon girlhood', MS autobiography

Wealth at death £6477 5s. 9d.: resworn probate, 15 July 1935, *CGPLA Eng. & Wales*

Miller, Sir Francis Norie-, first baronet (1859–1947), insurance company manager, was born on 11 March 1859 at Cheshunt, Hertfordshire, the son of Henry Miller, a Scot, and chief of the statistical department, HM customs, and his wife, Ann Norie. He was educated privately and trained for the law, but instead began his insurance career in the London office of London and Lancashire Fire Insurance Company. In 1880 he joined Ocean Accident and Guarantee, and in 1882 he became chief clerk in the accident and guarantee department of Employers' Liability Assurance. On 16 January 1884 Norie-Miller married Grace Harvey Day, daughter of the Revd H. J. Day, vicar of Cheshunt. They had two sons and a daughter. In 1885 he became assistant secretary of Mercantile Accident and Guarantee of Glasgow. In February 1887, aged only twenty-seven, he was appointed secretary of General Accident and Employers' Liability Assurance Association of Perth, recently founded by a group of local businessmen and landowners. He remained with the company for the rest of his career, as manager from 1891, as a board member from 1918, as managing director (1933–9), as chairman (1933–44), and as honorary governor from 1938 until his death.

When Norie-Miller joined General Accident, accident insurance was still in its infancy. His achievement was to develop his company into one of Britain's greatest composite insurers. Beginning from a two-room office in Perth, he swept out all but one of the old officials, cancelled doubtful risks, and, travelling throughout the country, appointed 800 new agents in his first year. With great energy and determination, he was alert to new market opportunities, demonstrating competitive panache in underwriting new forms of insurance, diversifying across all markets, discounting premium rates, and cross-subsidizing one branch of business by profits made in another.

In 1887 Norie-Miller introduced coupon insurance by providing free cover against injury from railway accidents for anyone carrying a particular publisher's diary. Burglary, fire, and motor insurance were commenced in the 1890s. No-claims bonuses were pioneered as a competitive device, and in the 1920s a hugely successful scheme was introduced whereby a year's free motor insurance was offered with every new Morris sold. By the 1930s General Accident had become Britain's largest corporate motor insurer. In 1899 business was commenced in the United States. By 1914 a worldwide network of offices had been established. Norie-Miller was also the driving force behind this organization. He crossed the Atlantic eight times during the First World War, and by 1935 he had made thirty-nine business trips to the United States alone.

A prominent figure in the civic life of Perth, Norie-Miller

served as a magistrate for forty-seven years. He was a director of Perth Royal Infirmary for thirty-two years, and chairman for over twenty-one years of Perth school board and the county education authority. In 1907 he was made an honorary fellow of the Educational Institute of Scotland. He was a regular worshipper at St Ninian's Cathedral, Perth. He was awarded the Médaille du Roi Albert by the king of the Belgians for his work for Belgian refugees during the 1914–18 war. In 1933 he became a freeman of the city of Perth. At a by-election in 1935 he was elected member for Perth, after a joint invitation to stand from the local Liberal and Conservative parties, but he did not contest the subsequent general election that year. In 1936 he was created a baronet in recognition of his services to Perth.

Norie-Miller's elder son, Claud, was killed on active service in the Mediterranean in 1917. The younger son, Stanley, succeeded his father as general manager of General Accident in 1933. Grace died in 1931, and in 1934 Norie-Miller married his secretary, Florence Jean Belfrage McKim. He enjoyed the countryside, shooting, fishing, golf, and poetry. He died at his home at Cleeve, Cherrybank, near Perth, on 4 July 1947, aged eighty-eight, and was buried at St Ninian's. He was survived by his second wife. His son Stanley succeeded to the baronetcy.

ROBIN PEARSON

Sources O. M. Westall, 'Norie-Miller, Sir Francis', *DSBB* · *The Times* (5 July 1947) · *Post Magazine and Insurance Monitor* (12 July 1947) · *The Insurance News*, 25 (July–Aug 1947) · *The Insurance Index* (July 1947) · *WWW* · O. M. Westall, 'The invisible hand strikes back: motor insurance and the erosion of organised competition in general insurance, 1920–38', *Business History*, 30 (1988), 432–50 · W. A. Dinsdale, *History of accident insurance in Great Britain* (1954) · R. B. Caverly and G. N. Bankes, *Leading insurance men of the British empire* (1892), 137
Likenesses photograph, *c.*1892, repro. in Caverly and Bankes, *Leading insurance men of the British empire* · M. Grixoni, portrait, 1932, General Accident plc, Perth
Wealth at death £209,100 0s. 3d.: Westall, 'Norie-Miller, Sir Francis'

Miller, George (1764–1848), Church of Ireland clergyman, was the eldest son of Stephen Miller, a general merchant. He was born in Dublin on 22 October 1764. He was educated locally; among his schoolfellows and childhood friends were Theobald Wolfe Tone (1763–1798), later a United Irishman, and Charles Kendal Bushe (1767–1843), later chief justice of the king's bench, Ireland.

In July 1779 Miller entered Trinity College, Dublin, where he was elected a scholar in 1782, graduated BA in 1784, took holy orders and a fellowship, and proceeded MA in 1789, graduated BD in 1794, and proceeded to a DD in 1799. After a visit to England in 1793, he returned to Ireland, where he married, in 1794, Elizabeth (1774/5–1840). They had six sons and eight daughters. The family settled in Dublin, where Miller taught privately and occupied himself with writing philosophical and theological works, until 1803, when he accepted the college living of Derryvullane in the diocese of Clogher. In 1796 he delivered, but did not publish, a course of lectures on the Donnellan foundation 'On the causes which impeded the further progress of Christianity'. In 1797 he published a critical edition of Dionysius Longinus's *De sublimitate*, and in 1799 his own *Elements of Natural Philosophy*. An enthusiastic member of the historical society founded by Grattan, Miller was assistant professor of modern history from 1799 until 1803, and from 1803 to 1811 was lecturer in modern history at the University of Dublin. Although his lectures did not make much impact at first, they grew steadily in popularity, and were eventually published as *Lectures on the Philosophy of Modern History* (1816–28). Though not as sweeping as their title suggests, these lectures were clearly set out and showed breadth of reading. A revised abridgement of the published lectures edited by Bohn, entitled *History Philosophically Illustrated from the Fall of the Roman Empire to the French Revolution*, was published in 1832, and reached a third edition in 1848–9 and a further edition in 1852.

In 1817 Miller was appointed headmaster of the Royal School, Armagh, a post which he held until shortly before his death. While teaching at the school his theological and political views shifted from an Arian and liberal position to strongly protestant and conservative ones. In 1825 he published a pamphlet called *Observations on the doctrines of Christianity in reference to Arianism, illustrating the moderation of the established church, and on the Athanasian creed, purporting to prove that it is not damnatory, nor metaphysical, nor contradictory* (1825); and in 1826 *The Athanasian Creed: with Explanatory Observations*. To the celebrated dissertation by Edward Hawkins, *A dissertation upon the use and importance of unauthoritative tradition, as an introduction to the Christian doctrines, including the substance of a sermon upon 2 Thess, 11:15* (1819), which heralded the beginning of what was to become the Oxford Movement, Miller responded with a defence of the protestant position in *An historical review of the plea of tradition as maintained in the Church of Rome: with strictures on Hawkins's dissertation*. He also issued a manifesto against the proposed emancipation of Roman Catholics from their legal disabilities, entitled *The policy of the Roman Catholic question discussed in a letter to the Right Hon. W. C. Plunket* (1826). In October 1840 he published a trenchantly protestant *Letter to the Rev. E. B. Pusey, D.D., in Reference to his Letter to the Lord Bishop of Oxford*, which may have been one of the provocations to elicit J. H. Newman's contentiously Catholic Tract 90, to which he made a further reply in *A second letter to the Rev. E. B. Pusey in reference to his letter to the Rev. R. W. Jelf, D.D., canon of Christ Church* (1841). Miller was a member of the Royal Irish Academy, and three of his papers were included in the society's *Transactions*. He was also a contributor to the *British Critic*, *Blackwood's Edinburgh Magazine*, the *Irish Ecclesiastical Journal* (1840–46), and the *British Magazine* (1845–6). Besides these contributions he also published various sermons and other miscellaneous items on historical and theological subjects.

In 1843 Miller was appointed vicar-general of the diocese of Armagh, having already acted as its surrogate; he performed the job ably and helped to settle legal points concerning marriage and divorce. He died in Armagh on 6

October 1848, and was buried in St Mark's churchyard, Armagh. For the last forty years of his life he had been a strict vegetarian.   J. M. RIGG, rev. DAVID HUDDLESTON

Sources 'Our portrait gallery, no. XIX', *Dublin University Magazine*, 17 (1841), 674–92 · J. B. Leslie, *Clogher clergy and parishes* (1929), 160 · A. J. Webb, *A compendium of Irish biography* (1878), 340 · N&Q, 4th ser., 3 (1869), 187–8 · N&Q, 3 (1851), 136–7 · N&Q, 7 (1853), 527, 631 · D. Bowen, *The protestant crusade in Ireland, 1800–70* (1978) · GM, 2nd ser., 30 (1848), 551 · [J. H. Todd], ed., *A catalogue of graduates who have proceeded to degrees in the University of Dublin, from the earliest recorded commencements to … December 16, 1868* (1869), 398 · Burtchaell & Sadleir, *Alum. Dubl.* · *Memoirs and correspondence of Viscount Castlereagh, second marquess of Londonderry*, ed. C. Vane, marquess of Londonderry, 12 vols. (1848–53), vol. 2, pp. 302–7 · *Thirty years' correspondence between John Jebb and Alexander Knox*, ed. C. Forster, 2 vols. (1834), vol. 1, p. 374 · 'Memoir of the author', G. Miller, *History, philosophically illustrated, from the fall of the Roman empire, to the French Revolution*, 3rd edn (1849), vol. 4, pp. ix–xlvi
Archives TCD | LPL, letters to Charles Golightly
Likenesses T. Kirk, marble bust, TCD · J. Kirkwood, etching, NPG · J. Kirkwood, etching (after C. Grey), NG Ire.; repro. in *Dublin University Magazine*

Miller, Henry George (1913–1976), neurologist, was born on 13 December 1913 in Chesterfield, Derbyshire, the only son of John Miller, engineer (who died when Henry was aged four) and his wife, Mabel Isobel, *née* Bainbridge. The family later moved to Stockton-on-Tees, where Henry attended the secondary school. He enrolled at the Newcastle College of Medicine (University of Durham) in 1931, qualifying MB, BS in 1937.

After graduation Miller held house appointments at the Royal Victoria Infirmary (RVI), Newcastle upon Tyne, and then worked for a year in pathology at the Johns Hopkins Hospital in Baltimore in the USA, before becoming house-physician at the Hospital for Sick Children, Great Ormond Street, London (1939). He then returned to Newcastle as medical registrar to work with Professor F. J. Nattrass and became interested in neurology, acquiring the MD (Durham) and MRCP (1940). In 1942 he married Eileen Cathcart Baird, gynaecologist, daughter of George Gibson Baird, engineer, of Tynemouth; they had two sons and two daughters.

From 1942 to 1945 Miller served in the Royal Air Force, first as a general-duties medical officer in Bomber Command, then as a neuropsychiatry specialist, when he was much influenced by Charles Symonds. He obtained a diploma in psychological medicine in 1943. After demobilization he worked in London at the National Hospital, Queen Square, and at Hammersmith Hospital, and in 1947 was appointed assistant physician to Dr A. G. Ogilvie at the RVI, where he further developed his neurological interests and established a flourishing private practice. In 1956 he became the first consultant neurologist to the RVI, establishing a department which achieved an international reputation. In 1953 he was elected FRCP, in 1961 became a reader in neurology, and in 1964 a professor. In 1962 he was appointed clinical subdean and played a major part in revising the medical curriculum. When the University of Newcastle became independent he was its first public orator from 1963 to 1966, and in 1966 became

dean of medicine. Two years later he was appointed vice-chancellor, in which capacity he served until his death.

While Miller wrote on many aspects of neurology and psychiatry (which he regarded as 'neurology without physical signs'), his major research interest was in multiple sclerosis and he was chairman of the medical panel of the UK Multiple Sclerosis Society and honorary clinical adviser to the Medical Research Council's demyelinating diseases unit. He was also president of the Association of Physicians of Great Britain and Ireland in 1973–4. He received the John Rowan Wilson award for his book *Medicine in Society* in 1974. In 1967–71 he was director of the British Medical Association planning unit.

Known in his registrar days as Henry 'Gorgeous' Miller, he was notable, even in 1947, for his elegant attire. His energy, drive, intuitive clinical ability, abounding flow of language with (at times) slightly wounding wit, and, above all, his generosity to friends and colleagues were extraordinary. In his presence no meeting was dull and, as vice-chancellor of the university, he had great skill with students; whether with senior academics, students, porters, clerks, or visitors, he was unpredictable and irreverently cheerful. Miller died at home, the vice-chancellor's lodge, 15 Adderstone Crescent, Jesmond, Newcastle upon Tyne, on 25 August 1976 from the heart disease which had dogged his latter years.   WALTON OF DETCHANT, rev.

Sources S. Lock and H. Windle, eds., *Remembering Henry* (1977) · Munk, *Roll* · personal knowledge (1993) · *Medical Directory* (1962) · CGPLA Eng. & Wales (1977)
Likenesses portrait, repro. in Lock and Windle, eds., *Remembering Henry*
Wealth at death £14,257: probate, 3 Feb 1977, CGPLA Eng. & Wales

Miller, Hugh (1802–1856), geologist, evangelical journalist, and writer, was born on 10 October 1802 in Church Street, Cromarty, the first of three children of Hugh Miller (*bap.* 1754, *d.* 1807), shipmaster in the coasting trade, and Harriet Wright (*bap.* 1780, *d.* 1863), both of trading and artisan families in the small Scottish coastal burgh of Cromarty. His father died in a shipwreck in 1807 and Miller was brought up by his mother and uncles James and Sandy (Alexander) Wright. Miller proved an intelligent child and keen reader, but idle and insubordinate at school. He was expelled, aged about sixteen, for brawling with the teacher. Miller rejected his uncles' advice to return to school (which would have enabled him to attend university and enter a profession). Instead he chose to become a stonemason, so that he could pursue his literary interests in the winter close season.

The young stonemason Apprenticed to an uncle from February 1820 to November 1822, Miller worked as a peripatetic stonemason and quarrier in Ross and Cromarty, and Niddrie near Edinburgh. He faced hard physical labour and squalid conditions in the grim 'bothy' accommodation provided by the landowners, recorded in the tale of the laird who deliberately left a hovel unrefurbished for the occasional 'drove of pigs or a squad of masons' (Miller, *Schools*).

Miller returned to Cromarty in 1825, ill with 'stone-

Hugh Miller (1802–1856), by David Octavius Hill and Robert Adamson, c.1843

cutter's malady', probably pneumoconiosis or tuberculosis. After a partial recovery he started lighter work as a monumental mason, meanwhile furthering his literary ambitions. An abortive attempt at publishing verse (*Poems of a Journeyman Mason*, 1829) confirmed that his talents lay in prose, and he contributed articles, notably on the herring fishery, to the *Inverness Courier* and other periodicals.

Cromarty lay on the ethnic frontier between lowlanders and Gaelic highlanders. Miller, an archetypal lowlander, was unable to speak Gaelic. He was fascinated by the area's traditional history and folklore and preserved much that would otherwise have been lost, notably in his first book *Scenes and Legends of the North of Scotland* (1835) where, as elsewhere, he paints a delightfully affectionate picture of his birthplace.

Miller's long-standing interest in local geology ripened into serious study. In 1830 he discovered remarkable fossil fishes in the Old Red Sandstone at Cromarty. His intelligent observations were inevitably restricted by isolation from the geological community and specialist literature. When he made contact with other geologists in the 1830s, the importance of his finds became clear, and eventually Louis Agassiz incorporated them in the key palaeontological work *Poissons fossiles du Vieux Grès Rouge* (1844–5), notably the placoderms *Coccosteus milleri* and *Pterichthys milleri* (later *Coccosteus cuspidatus* and *Pterichthyodes milleri*).

Miller became accountant for the Commercial Bank in

Cromarty in 1834, enabling him to marry Lydia Falconer Fraser (*bap.* 1812, *d.* 1876) [*see* Miller, Lydia Mackenzie Falconer], the daughter of an Inverness merchant, at Cromarty on 7 January 1837. Theirs was a love match reinforced by intellectual compatibility, and Lydia, once a teacher and later a writer of children's stories, took an active interest in Miller's writings. The first of their five children, Elizabeth, died in infancy; her gravestone was the last Miller ever carved. Their eldest surviving child was the writer Harriet Miller *Davidson.

'Evangelical' journalism By family tradition and personal conviction, Miller was one of the non-intrusionists ('evangelicals') who sought to restore the Church of Scotland's freedom from secular interference, especially landowners' imposition of their chosen ministers against the wills of the congregations. As a result of his polemic *Letter to Lord Brougham*, prompted by the infamous Auchterarder case, leading evangelicals recruited Miller to edit a new newspaper friendly to their cause. He thus moved to Edinburgh to become founding editor, and later proprietor, of *The Witness*, which appeared bi-weekly in January 1840 and soon reached the highest circulation among Edinburgh newspapers.

A brilliant journalist, Miller combined straight news with comment and criticism on a wide range of matters, by no means confined to church politics. He often adopted a personal and even autobiographical strain, illuminating his arguments with anecdotes from his own experiences. Stylistically he was influenced by his boyhood favourites, the eighteenth-century Augustan writers such as Addison and Pope.

Miller's vigorous polemic, often attacking opponents personally, suited the robustly controversial journalism of the time. A self-avowed 'old whig', Miller was liberal in his sympathies, and always quick to denounce oppression and exploitation. Unusually, he blamed the poverty of highlanders and the Irish, not on their own indolence, but on the impossible situation imposed on them by oppressive landowners, and he was among the first to denounce the highland clearances. Some of his books were first published in instalments in *The Witness*, and others are compilations of his articles. His journalism has gained new value as contemporary comment on rural Scotland's transformation by the lowland agricultural revolution, and the near-destruction of Gaelic culture in the highlands and islands. However, as his perceptive critic W. M. Mackenzie said, 'on all subjects his mind had been made up before he left Cromarty' (Mackenzie, 242). Perhaps prejudiced by his fellow masons at Niddrie, whom he considered spendthrift and dissolute, he failed—admittedly as did many others—to comprehend the new phenomenon of urban Scotland and its industrial working classes. He remained unsympathetic to trade unions, and vehemently hostile to Chartism and socialism, while simultaneously condemning the oppressions that brought them into being.

Miller mobilized the remarkable popular support that enabled the Disruption of May 1843, when Thomas Chalmers led a mass walk-out of the evangelical wing from the Church of Scotland to form the Free Church. Indeed, together with Chalmers, he has been given credit for enabling the Disruption, upholding high principle arguably at the cost of destroying the unity of the national church. *The Cruise of the Betsey* (1858) vividly portrays one minister tending his Hebridean parish from a floating manse, the 'Free Church Yacht *Betsey*'. However, Miller had little influence on Free Church policy after 1843. His characteristic editorial independence fell foul of the dominant faction led by Robert Candlish, and he had to fight off an attempt to impose direct control in 1847.

Continuing interest in geology Miller was put forward for the professorship of natural sciences at Edinburgh University in 1854 but was beaten by Edward Forbes, one of the new professional scientists. Indeed Miller, although a thoughtful and excellent field observer and collector, made no lasting theoretical contribution to geology. He wrote few formal scientific papers, undoubtedly restricted by his Cromarty isolation and pressure of work in Edinburgh. He always continued to collect fossils, seeking out new sites around his home, especially on the raised beaches of the Forth, and during his summer vacations. His direct contributions to science remain the sites he discovered. His collection of fossils, perhaps the best ever made from Scotland as a whole, later went to the National Museums of Scotland.

Miller made a further, unquantifiable, but perhaps critical, contribution to academic geology in the public support for the science that his brilliant popularization helped to develop. With *The Old Red Sandstone* (published in 1841, after first appearing serially in *The Witness* in 1840), based on his Cromarty work, and other books, Miller became the leading popular expounder of geology in the 1840s and 1850s. His protégé Archibald Geikie, later director-general of the geological survey, commented: 'His books were to be found in the remotest log-hut of the Far West, and on both sides of the Atlantic ideas of the nature and scope of geology were largely drawn from them' (Leask, 149).

Miller's writings were classic Victorian natural history. His strongly personal, and often autobiographical, prose took the reader by the hand through a mixture of straight narrative illuminated with homely but pithy analogies, and eidetic—at times hallucinatory—descriptions of present and past landscapes. Miller never forgot his sense of wonder at the romance and beauty of science. He adopted a form of traditional Paleyan natural theology, demonstrating the divine creator's power and wisdom by exploring the aesthetic and functional design of fossils in loving detail: he could and did find God in a fish's scale. Miller's unimpeachable Christian credentials helped confirm geology—once an 'infidel science'—as a morally and physically improving outdoor recreation.

Miller also tackled the great question of the time, taking full part in the public debate on pre-Darwinian evolutionary ideas, provoked notably by Robert Chambers's *Vestiges of the Natural History of Creation* (1844). In *Footprints of the Creator* (1849) and *The Testimony of the Rocks* (1857) Miller argued that the appearance of complex animals early in the fossil record refuted such naïve ideas of simple progression from primitive to advanced organisms. This valid objection was not refuted until after Miller's death, by Charles Darwin's non-progressionist theory of natural selection.

Miller also disliked evolutionary theories because they reduced humans to animals (either humans had no souls, or animals did have souls, yet animals were not responsible moral beings). Miller nevertheless pragmatically reconciled science and religion, which were, to him, two facets of the same divine truth. He was vehemently opposed to allowing religious dogma to override clear scientific evidence, for instance over the age of the Earth, where he regarded Genesis as a vision of creation rather than a literal account.

Miller's writings about geology were no mere secondary popularization of scientific technicalities. He wrote on the world as he saw it, creating superb literature in the broadest Victorian sense, as he did with other key issues of the time. This is reflected in his autobiography, *My Schools and Schoolmasters* (1852), a wonderfully evocative and dryly witty classic of self-help which exhorts readers to learn from his example, both good and bad, even under the most unpromising conditions: 'life itself is a school, and Nature always a fresh study'. An earlier memoir (1829, published 1995) is less mature but in some ways franker.

Final years Tellingly, Miller's autobiography ends with the move to Edinburgh. Perhaps he would have had a happier, if quieter, life if he had ignored this call of duty and remained at Cromarty. He apparently became increasingly isolated at Edinburgh because of his robust journalism, factional problems within the Free Church, and his pride (and diffidence) which led him to shy away from being lionized and to decline many social invitations except for those from a few friends who shared his interests. In Edinburgh, Miller famously eschewed urban dress in favour of the heavy tweed suit and grey plaid (woollen overblanket) of the Scottish lowland countryman, expressing his independence and pride in his origins; this garb was also comfortable and conveniently practical for impromptu fossilizing forays. Tall and robust, with a shock of sandy hair over sapphire blue eyes, and sidewhiskers, and retaining his broad Cromarty speech, Miller delighted in trials of physical prowess with his friends. Nevertheless, he became increasingly unwell, and old illness, especially his lung problem, flared up with chronic overwork. He therefore took summer breaks, tramping Scotland in all weathers seeking fossils, as related in *The Cruise of the Betsey*. *First Impressions of England and its People* (1847) relates a gentler trip in 1845 to the haunts of his favourite pastoral writers, as well as quarries and museums.

On the night of 23/24 December 1856, seemingly in a moment of unbearable depression and believing that he was going mad, Miller shot himself at his home, Shrub Mount, Portobello, Edinburgh. He had been suffering a personality change with nightmares and perhaps hallucinations, arising possibly from neurological disease—

there was a vague autopsy report of brain disease—or simply from overwork and chronic illness. His confused suicide note prompted recurrent speculation of a final madness triggered by childhood memories of Gaelic legends, and in P. Bayne's otherwise conventionally pious *Life and Letters* (1871) his widow publicly blamed Miller's mother for filling his childish head with such demonic nonsense.

The huge attendance at his funeral (he was buried at the Grange cemetery, Edinburgh, on 29 December) showed the enormous public respect in which Miller was held. His books, supplemented by reprints of his collected journalism, sold well for many years but gradually slipped out of print during the twentieth century as both the Disruption and the pre-Darwinian geologists became less apparently relevant. Miller became almost forgotten outside Cromarty and geology, until the late twentieth-century revivals in Scottish history and culture, and simultaneously the history of pre-Darwinian science, brought him back to full attention as a superb writer and a major player and commentator in the development of modern Scotland.

M. A. TAYLOR

Sources H. Miller, *My schools and schoolmasters* [1852] · H. Miller, *Hugh Miller's memoir: from stonemason to geologist*, ed. M. Shortland (1995) · M. Shortland, ed., *Hugh Miller and the controversies of Victorian science* (1996) [incl. bibliography] · P. Bayne, *Life and letters of Hugh Miller*, 2 vols. (1871) · W. M. Mackenzie, *Hugh Miller: a critical study* (1905) · *The centenary of Hugh Miller, being an account of the celebration held at Cromarty on 22nd August, 1902* (1902) · W. K. Leask, *Hugh Miller* (1896) · M. McK. Johnston, *A genealogical chart relating to Hugh Miller and his wife Lydia Mackenzie Falconer Fraser* (1994) · H. Miller, *A noble smuggler and other stories*, ed. M. Gostwick (1997) · L. M. Mackay, ed., 'Mrs Hugh Miller's journal', *Chambers's Journal*, 6th ser. (1902), 305–8, 369–72, 461–4, 513–16 · private information (2004) · S. M. Andrews, *The discovery of fossil fishes in Scotland up to 1845, with checklists of Agassiz's figured specimens* (1982) · d. cert. · L. Borley, ed., *Hugh Miller in context: geologist and naturalist, writer and folklorist* (2002) · K. Fenyő, *Contempt, sympathy and romance: lowland perceptions of the highlands and the clearances during the famine years, 1845–1855* (2000) · J. A. Secord, *Victorian sensation: the extraordinary publication, reception, and secret authorship of 'Vestiges of the natural history of creation'* (2000) · E. Sutherland, *Lydia, wife of Hugh Miller of Cromarty* (2002) **Archives** Hugh Miller's Cottage, Cromarty, geological specimens, MSS, and personalia · Museums of Scotland, Edinburgh, geological collection · NL Scot., corresp. and papers · U. Edin., New Coll. L., MSS **Likenesses** D. O. Hill and R. Adamson, calotypes, *c*.1843, Scot. NPG [*see illus.*] · J. G. Tunny, carte-de-visite, *c*.1854, NL Scot., Scot. NPG · A. H. Ritchie, statue, 1858, Cromarty · D. O. Hill, group portrait, oils, 1867 (*Signing the deed of demission*), Free Church of Scotland College, Edinburgh; repro. in S. Stevenson, *David Octavius Hill and Robert Adamson* (1981) · A. Paton, marble statue, 1869, National Museums of Scotland · W. Brodie, marble bust, Scot. NPG; repro. in H. Smailes, *The concise catalogue of the Scottish National Portrait Gallery* (1990), 208, 211 · Vincent Brooks, Day and Son, lithograph (after W. Bonnar, *c*.1836), repro. in Bayne, *Life and letters*, vol. 1 · F. Croll, line engraving, BM, NPG; repro. in *Hogg's Instructor* · A. Rae, carte-de-visite, NPG · J. Sartain, mezzotint (after W. Bonnar), NPG; repro. in *Eclectic Magazine* **Wealth at death** £7788 9s. 10d.; plus property: inventory, NA Scot.

Miller, Hugh Crichton- (1877–1959), psychotherapist, was born on 5 February 1877 in Genoa, Italy, the first of four children born to Donald Miller (*b*. 1838), the Presbyterian chaplain there, and his second wife, Mary Wotherspoon. In 1889 Crichton-Miller was sent to Fettes College in Edinburgh. He then entered Edinburgh University in 1893, graduating MA in 1898 and MD in 1901. In 1903, following an eight-year engagement, he married Eleanore Jean (1876–1954), daughter of Sheriff Lorimer QC of Edinburgh; they had six children, including Donald Crichton-Miller, who became headmaster of Fettes and Stowe School.

Following a brief period as resident house surgeon and house physician at Edinburgh's Royal Infirmary (1900–01), Crichton-Miller entered general practice and combined his love of Scotland and Italy by working in the summers in Aviemore and in the winters in San Remo. Studying the many hypochondriacs led to his reputation as a specialist in nervous disorders. Since there were then no treatments for functional nervous disorders, he gave up general practice and as an advocate of the new psychology settled in London in 1911, established a consulting practice, and opened Bowden House, a private nursing home at Harrow specializing in treating neuroses. He published *Hypnotism and Disease* (1912). During the First World War, Crichton-Miller served in Alexandria, where he was in charge of functional nervous disorders, and later at the 4th London General Hospital, as consultant in shell-shock. The large numbers of shell-shocked troops provided a valuable spur to the medical deployment of psychotherapeutic techniques in the immediate post-war period. It was within this context that Crichton-Miller gained backing for a clinic specializing in nervous disorders, the Tavistock Clinic, which he founded in 1920. In 1926 he established the first child guidance training team. Effective in delegating, he was a careful mentor and inspiring lecturer, and synthesized a variety of approaches.

Over the next thirteen years Crichton-Miller published a range of texts exploring the social and medical aspects of the new psychology: *The New Psychology and the Teacher* (1921), *The New Psychology and the Parent* (1922), *The New Psychology and the Preacher* (1924), *Insomnia: an Outline for the Practitioner* (1930), *Marriage, Freedom and Education* (1931), *Psychoanalysis and its Derivatives* (1933). Formal recognition of his expertise came with his election as president of the psychiatric section of the Royal Society of Medicine (1938), president of the International Society for Psychotherapy (1938), and fellow of the Royal College of Psychiatry (1939). Unfortunately illness caused him to curtail his professional activities during the 1940s. He resigned his posts at the Tavistock and the Stanborough Hospital (1941); in 1945, two years after the death of his son, he relinquished his London practice, and he retired as medical director of Bowden House in 1952. He died of Parkinson's disease on 1 January 1959 at Bowden House.

K. LOUGHLIN

Sources *Hugh Crichton-Miller, 1877–1959: a personal memoir by his friends and family* (1961) · E. F. Irvine, *A pioneer of the new psychology: H. C. M. 1877–1959* (1963) · *The Lancet* (10 Jan 1959), 104–5 · H. V. Dicks, *Fifty years of the Tavistock Clinic* (1970) · *BMJ* (10 Jan 1959), 116–17 · *WWW*

Archives BL, corresp. with Society of Authors, Add. MSS 63230
Likenesses photographs, repro. in *Hugh Crichton-Miller*
Wealth at death £3048 4s. 4d.: probate, 9 April 1959, *CGPLA Eng. &
Wales*

Miller, J. (*fl.* 1780), architectural draughtsman, is an
obscure figure who has been connected, sometimes incor-
rectly, with a variety of publications. He was muddled in
Samuel Redgrave's *Dictionary of Artists of the English School*
(1874) with 'J. Miller, Architect', author of *The Country
Gentleman's Architect* (1787), a book of designs for cottages,
farmhouses, villas, and lodges. It is not known what his
forename was or what relationship, if any, there was
between him and 'J. Miller, Esq.' who is described on the
title-page as the author of *Andrea Palladio's Elements of Architecture* (1759), a reissue of a book on perspective written by
William Halfpenny and first published under his name in
1751.

There are also a number of engravings of architectural
and antiquarian subjects signed J. Miller and John Miller:
J. Miller's name appears on some plates in James Paine's
*Plans, Elevations and Sections of Noblemen and Gentlemen's
Houses* (1767, 1783) and the anonymous *Ruins of Paestum*
(1767); John Miller executed several plates for Nicholas
Revett's *Ionian Antiquities* (1769). To confuse matters fur-
ther, the prolific Nuremberg draughtsman and engraver
Johann Sebastian Müller occasionally signed himself John
Miller and J. Miller.   EILEEN HARRIS

Sources Colvin, *Archs.*, 652 · E. Harris and N. Savage, *British architectural books and writers, 1556–1785* (1990), 316 · Waterhouse, *18c
painters*, 241

Miller, James (1704–1744), playwright and satirist, was
born at Bridport, Dorset, on 11 August 1704, the eldest son
of John Miller (*d.* 1743), rector of nearby Compton Valence,
and his wife, Ellen Bruce (*d.* 1731). In 1726, aged twenty-
two, he was admitted to Wadham College, Oxford. Before
this he had been placed with 'a Merchant, his near Relation, in the City' (Mottley, 260). Rawlinson suggests that
Miller was apprenticed to a sugar-baker, whose money he
embezzled (Rawlinson, MS J⁰45, fol. 31). He certainly made
enemies at Oxford, who may have instigated this asper-
sion. John Miller had seven other children, and probably
could not send James to university until he had acquired
his second benefice, at Upcerne, in 1725. The Millers had
married in Old Jewry in the City, so the mercantile relative
was probably on the mother's side.

James Miller was ordained and became lecturer of Trinity Chapel, Conduit Street, and preacher at Roehampton
Chapel, probably residing at Chelsea, roughly halfway
between. At university Miller had written a lively comedy,
The Humours of Oxford, which ran for several nights at
Drury Lane in 1730. It featured a ridiculous blue stocking,
Lady Science, and a university fellow, steeped in vice,
based, somewhat recklessly, on Robert Thistlethwayte,
then warden of Wadham, who was the son of the patron
of John Miller's living at Compton Valence. In 1731 he published *Harlequin-Horace*, a witty inversion of the *Ars poetica*,
attacking pantomime and opera and exuberantly depicting a topsy-turvy theatrical world. Alexander Pope
approved, as did his disciples on the *Grub-Street Journal* (59,

60, and 66; 18 and 25 February and 8 April 1731). Miller
must have married his wife, Dorothy, about this time,
since in 1754 their son, John, a surgeon's mate in the navy,
published his own *Poems on Several Occasions*. To earn
money Miller collaborated with Henry Baker in a translation of Molière (*Select Comedies*, 8 vols., 1732), and went on
to adapt plays by Molière and other, mainly French, dramatists, for the London stage. He freely combined elements from various sources, often adding original topical
material, and strengthening character and verisimili-
tude.

Henry Baker's son David Erskine Baker records that
Edmund Gibson, bishop of London, rebuked Miller for his
theatrical involvement (Baker, 1, sig. Yv). Impetuously,
Miller then inserted a Juvenalian diatribe against Gibson,
Walpole's chief ecclesiastical ally, into his Horatian poem
Seasonable Reproof (1737), which had already been set up in
type. Preferment in the church was thereafter not probable. In 1738 Miller antagonized the students of the Temple by representing in an after-piece, *The Coffee House*, the
widow and daughter who ran their favourite establishment. The play's attractions included songs from Kitty
Clive, Theophilus Cibber as himself, and a poet, Bays,
dressed like Richard Savage, but, like most of Miller's subsequent efforts, it was damned.

Political satire in Miller's plays intensified, until by 1740
his 'Camp Visitants' proved too daring for performance in
its depiction of the troops waiting for deployment in the
controversially postponed war with Spain (Hunt. L., Lar-
pent collection). His poem *Of Politeness* (1738) examines
false taste and its moral consequences, exemplified in the
career of a beau. Pope drew on this in considerable detail,
in 1742, in 'one of the best things in my new addition to
the *Dunciad*' (Spence, 1.150). In 1740 Miller's *Are these Things
so?*, a challenge to Walpole spoken in the persona of Pope,
caused a sensation. Six replies quickly appeared, including one by Miller, *The Great Man's Answer*, where, in confident colloquial verse, Walpole condemns himself by his
own best arguments. The following year, 1741, Miller dedicated his *Miscellaneous Works* to the opposition's figurehead, Frederick, prince of Wales. *Harlequin-Horace* had
lampooned the Italian operas of Handel, but Miller
admired the sacred oratorios in English, and himself furnished the libretto for *Joseph and his Brethren* (1744). Miller's
text has been condemned by modern critics, but his contemporaries approved of it, and the oratorio was counted
a success. Even here Miller maintained his opposition
stance: Joseph is portrayed as a perfect prime minister, 'by
Pow'r unstain'd' (pt 2, scene 1), in implicit contrast to Walpole.

When John Miller died, in December 1743, James succeeded to the living at Upcerne, but did not live to benefit
from it. He remained in town for the staging of his adaptation of Voltaire's *Mahomet* in 1744. John Hoadley, another
clerical dramatist, completed it, as Miller was ill. Its prologue indicates that Miller saw the play as an attack on
'Bigots' in the priesthood. He died in Chelsea, probably at
Cheyne Walk, on the morning of its third performance, 27

April, aged thirty-nine. Dorothy Miller devoted the proceeds of a later benefit to the settling of her husband's debts.

Baker described Miller as a master of ready repartee, ardent in friendship but quick to take offence, naturally cheerful, but in later life depressed by adverse circumstances (Baker, 2, sig. Y2r). Theophilus Cibber recounts (Cibber, 5.332–3) that, for his wife's sake, Miller was once tempted by a large offer from ministry agents, but as she rejected the idea with indignation, he remained true to his principles, to the end.   PAULA O'BRIEN

Sources P. J. O'Brien, 'The life and works of James Miller, 1704–1744', PhD diss., U. Lond., 1979 [incl. full bibliography] • P. Stewart, 'The dramatic career of James Miller', PhD diss., U. Texas, 1939 • [D. E. Baker], *The companion to the play-house*, 2 vols. (1764) • R. Shiels, *The lives of the poets of Great Britain and Ireland*, ed. T. Cibber, 5 vols. (1753) • R. Rawlinson, MS notes for a new edition of Wood's *Athenae Oxonienses*, Bodl. Oxf., MSS Rawl. J°45, fol. 318; J°7, fol. 34 • [J. Mottley], *A compleat list of all the English dramatic poets*, pubd with T. Whincop, *Scanderbeg* (1747) • R. Smith, *Handel's oratorios and eighteenth-century thought* (1995) • *The Twickenham edition of the poems of Alexander Pope*, ed. J. Butt and others, 11 vols. in 12 (1939–69) • *The correspondence of Alexander Pope*, ed. G. Sherburn, 5 vols. (1956) • J. Spence, *Observations, anecdotes, and characters, of books and men*, ed. J. M. Osborn, new edn, 2 vols. (1966) • S. Johnson, *An account of the life of Mr Richard Savage*, ed. C. Tracy (1941) • *The autobiography and correspondence of Mary Granville, Mrs Delany*, ed. Lady Llanover, 1st ser., 3 vols. (1861) • *DNB* • parish register, Dorset, Compton Valence, 11 Aug 1704 [baptism] • parish register, Dorset, Upcerne, Dec 1743 [burial; John Miller] • parish register, Dorset, Upcerne, 1731 [burial; Ellen Miller] • admissions register, Wadham College, Oxford • *General Advertiser* (28 April 1744)

Wealth at death apparently died in debt; widow and family left almost destitute after settling debts with proceeds of a benefit performance (which brought in over £100), and a subscription for Miller's collected sermons: Baker, *The companion*, vol. 1, sig. N3r, and vol. 2, sig. Y2v

Miller, James (1812–1864), surgeon, born at the manse, Essie, Forfarshire, on 2 April 1812, was the third son of the Revd James Miller (1777–1860), and Barbara, daughter of the Revd Dr Martin, of Monimail in Fife. He was taught by his father, and in 1824 went to St Andrews University, where in three winter sessions he completed his general education. In 1827 he became a pupil of Dr Ramsay of Dundee, but later in the same year he transferred to Mr Mackenzie of Edinburgh and began to study medicine. He obtained the licence of the Royal College of Surgeons of Edinburgh in 1832, and he was subsequently elected a fellow. He acted for many years as an assistant to Robert Liston, and when Liston moved to London in 1834 Miller acquired the more lucrative part of his practice. On 11 July 1836 Miller married Penelope Garden Campbell Gordon. A daughter married Sir Patrick Heron *Watson.

In 1842 Miller was appointed professor of surgery in the University of Edinburgh, in succession to Sir Charles Bell. In 1848 he was surgeon-in-ordinary in Scotland to Queen Victoria and Prince Albert. At Edinburgh he was also surgeon, and later consulting surgeon, to the Royal Infirmary and was appointed surgeon to Chalmers Hospital and to the Sick Children's Hospital. He also served as professor of pictorial anatomy to the School of Design at the Royal

Institution. He was a fellow of the Royal Society of Edinburgh and president of both the Medico-Chirurgical and the Harveian societies. Although he held the position of professor of surgery in Edinburgh, Miller practised both as a physician and as an operating surgeon, and it is remarkable that, in spite of his long association with Liston, Miller was conservative in his methods, even in his youth, resorting to the knife only when all other treatment had failed. He was a dexterous operator, and especially prided himself on his lithotomies.

At the disruption of the Presbyterian church in Scotland, Miller, like his father, who since 1827 had been minister of Monikie, sided with the Free Church party, and rendered it substantial service by speech and pen. In his later years he devoted much of his time to religious and social questions, and became an ardent advocate of temperance. He died at Pinkhill, near Corstorphine, Edinburgh, on 17 June 1864, and was buried in the Grange cemetery in Edinburgh on the 22nd.

Miller was best known for his *Principles of Surgery* (1844) and *Practice of Surgery* (1846), which ran concurrently through several editions in Edinburgh and in America. They were finally amalgamated into *A System of Surgery* (1864). It is by these works that Miller became extensively known as a surgeon outside Edinburgh University. He also wrote the articles on surgery in the seventh and eighth editions of the *Encyclopaedia Britannica*, and he wrote numerous pamphlets and addresses on social, religious, and professional topics.

D'A. POWER, *rev.* KAYE BAGSHAW

Sources *Edinburgh Medical Journal*, 10 (1864–5), 92–6 • *Medical Times and Gazette* (25 June 1864), 705–6 • *BMJ* (1864), 698 • private information (1894)

Likenesses T. Duncan, oils, exh. 1845, Royal College of Surgeons, Edinburgh • J. Harris, oils, 1855, Royal College of Surgeons, Edinburgh • J. Steell, bust, 1894, Medical Mission House, Edinburgh • D. O. Hill and R. Adamson, two photographs, NPG • J. D. Panerb?, stipple (after Moffat), Wellcome L. • D. J. Pound, stipple and line engraving (after photograph by Moffat), NPG • lithograph (after W. Stewart), Wellcome L. • stipple, Wellcome L.

Miller, Sir James (1905–1977), builder and local politician, was born on 16 March 1905 in Morningside, Edinburgh, the second of the three sons of James Miller (*d.* 1922), architect. He was educated at George Heriot's School, Edinburgh, and at the age of fourteen was apprenticed to his father, while studying architecture in the evenings at Edinburgh College of Art.

After his father's death Miller, at the age of seventeen, took over the firm, turning his attention to building inexpensive private houses. In 1927 he built a development of twelve semi-detached bungalows, which sold quickly, despite their relatively high price of £840 each, and went on to produce a highly successful design, the two-bedroom 'Type A' bungalow, built of reconstituted stone and concrete, which cost only £475, with a deposit of £25 and weekly payments of 17s. The business grew rapidly as developments went up in all parts of Edinburgh. He increased the range of designs to six, while buying land on the outskirts of the city for future developments, and he formed a partnership with his younger brother, John Manson Miller.

In 1933 Miller married Ella Jane, daughter of John Stewart, an Edinburgh butcher. They had three sons and one daughter. The business was converted into a limited liability company, James Miller & Partners Ltd, in 1934, with all the shares owned by Miller and his two brothers, and it went on to become the largest housebuilding company in Edinburgh. As well as building private houses and flats, the company managed garages, cinemas, and dance-halls, and Miller was also a director of the builders' merchant John and James Lawrence, an important supplier of precast stone.

During the Second World War the business undertook government contracts, building airfields and factories, and in 1941 embarked on open-cast mining contracts in Yorkshire for the government. Offices in London and Wakefield were opened, and in 1942 it took over L. J. Speight & Partners, a contracting firm in London. After the war James Miller & Partners built thousands of council houses for local authorities all over the country. Miller designed a new, non-traditional house, built of brick or concrete with standardized components produced in his own factories at Craigleith and Granton: 7000 were built in the early 1950s. In the later 1950s Miller, who was in charge of the housing side of the business, designed new houses for the private market, while his brother John expanded the company's mining concerns in Yorkshire and Northumberland, and handled the contracting. Two of Miller's sons were taken into the business.

During the 1960s a group structure began to evolve, and in 1970 the Miller Group was formed, including Miller Construction and Miller Homes Northern. Miller retired from the day-to-day management of the company, and established Heritable Development Consultants, which was later incorporated into the Miller Group. He resigned his Miller Group directorships in 1973, and his son James became managing director of James Miller & Partners while his son Roger became managing director of Miller Homes Northern.

Miller was elected a member of Edinburgh town council in 1936, serving until 1954. He was a JP from 1942. He held various offices, including that of city treasurer in 1946, and he was lord provost of the City of Edinburgh in 1951–4. In 1953 he was knighted, and the honorary degree of LLD was conferred on him by Edinburgh University. A businessman in London as well as Scotland, Miller was an alderman for Bishopsgate in 1957–72, and served as lord mayor of London in 1964–5: during that year he devoted himself full-time to his official functions, and left his brother and sons to run the business. He was the first, and only, person to have held the offices of both lord provost of Edinburgh and lord mayor of London. He was made GBE in 1965.

Miller was a keen sailor, and after the death of his youngest son in a road accident in 1966 he gave £75,000 towards the cost of building the training ship the *Malcolm Miller*. He also bought the former Clyde puffer *Auld Reekie*, and fitted it out as a training ship. Despite his London interests in the latter part of his life, Miller remained firmly based in Scotland: he loved highland gatherings, and was chieftain of the highland gathering at the Festival of Scotland held in Richmond, Surrey, in 1973. It was he who instituted the highland games at Murrayfield in Edinburgh. He died on 20 March 1977 in Edinburgh, survived by his wife. His remains were cremated at Warriston on 23 March.   ANNE PIMLOTT BAKER

Sources N. J. Morgan, 'Miller, Sir James', *DSBB* · *WWW* · *The Scotsman* (21 March 1977) · *The Times* (21 March 1977) · NA Scot., SC 70/1/3277, p. 64 · NA Scot., SC 70/1/3365, p. 245 · NA Scot., SC 70/1/3463, p. 179 · NA Scot., SC 70/1/3661, p. 11
Likenesses photograph, repro. in Morgan, 'Miller, Sir James'
Wealth at death £347,223.80: confirmation, 8 June 1977, NA Scot., SC 70/1/3277, p. 64 · eik additional estate, 17 Oct 1978, NA Scot., SC 70/1/3365, p. 245 · £1805: eik additional estate, 29 Nov 1979, NA Scot., SC 70/1/3463, p. 179 · £5: eik additional inventory, 15 Dec 1981, NA Scot., SC 70/1/3661, p. 11

Miller, James Arthur (1855–1939), rugby administrator and schoolmaster, was born in Leeds on 19 January 1855, the son of Joseph Miller, an engineer, and his wife, Elizabeth. He first played rugby in the 1870s as a pupil at Leeds middle class school, an Anglican establishment which specialized in science and technology. He later returned as the school's science master, a role in which he enjoyed great popularity with the boys. He played rugby for Yorkshire as a forward five times between 1879 and 1881, but it was as an administrator of the game that he made his mark.

An official with Leeds St John's Club, which later became Leeds Rugby League Club, Miller was elected secretary of the Yorkshire Rugby Union (YRU) in 1889, and sought to steer a middle course between the amateurism of the Rugby Football Union (RFU) and calls for outright professionalism. In 1891, recognizing that pure amateurism was unworkable in the predominantly working-class environment of northern rugby, he proposed relaxing the RFU's amateur regulations to allow players to be paid for time lost at work through playing rugby, or 'broken time'. In the same year he also argued for a reduction in the number of players in a rugby team from fifteen to thirteen, in order to make the game more attractive and to help it counter the growing popularity of soccer. Ignored by the rugby union authorities at the time, the thirteen-a-side proposal was adopted in 1906 by the Northern Union as a basic rule of rugby league.

The debate on payments for play came to a head at the September 1893 RFU general meeting. Miller proposed the motion 'that players be allowed compensation for bona-fide loss of time', arguing that working-class players were constantly called upon to lose their wages in order to play the game at the highest levels yet were refused recompense for the loss of time involved. But his motion was lost by 282 votes to 136, and the RFU consequently amended its constitution to allow membership only to those clubs 'entirely composed of amateurs'. The die was cast for the great rugby split of 1895.

During his presidency of the YRU (1892–5), Miller's loyalty to the RFU led him to oppose the 1895 formation of the Northern Union. He subsequently became one of the most unyielding defenders of pristine amateurism, steadfastly opposing any attempts to compromise with the new union. Despite having a leg amputated and almost losing his life following an explosion at Roundhay Park in Leeds in 1910, he continued to serve on the YRU committee for another thirty years, and was appointed treasurer in 1922. Ironically, his life ended in disgrace over money, after he was sentenced to six months' imprisonment in 1927 for using his position to embezzle over £1000 from the YRU. He died, almost completely unnoticed and unmourned, at St James's Hospital, Leeds, on 10 March 1939, and was buried at Lawnswood cemetery in north Leeds three days later.   TONY COLLINS

Sources *Yorkshire Evening Post* (11 March 1939) · 'Sad case of rugby official', *Yorkshire Evening Post* (4 Oct 1927) · 'Memories of Leeds middle class school', *Yorkshire Weekly Press* (26 Sept 1908) · 'Former pupils of Leeds middle class school', *Yorkshire Weekly Press* (9 Dec 1922) · 'Yorkshire Rugby Union AGM', *Yorkshire Post* (15 June 1897) · 'Roundhay Park explosion', *Yorkshire Post* (28 June 1910) · 'The Yorkshire rugby Union football committee drawn and no-quartered', *The Yorkshireman* (March 1892)
Wealth at death £27 15s. 9d.: probate, 24 July 1939, CGPLA Eng. & Wales

Miller, Sir James Percy, second baronet (1864–1906), racehorse owner, was born at Manderston, Berwickshire, on 22 October 1864. He was eldest surviving son of the three sons and two daughters of Sir William Miller, first baronet (1809–1887), a merchant trading in Russia, who was MP for Leith (1859–64) and Berwickshire (1873–4), and his wife, Mary Anne Leith (d. 1912). He was educated at Eton College and the Royal Military College, Sandhurst, before gaining a commission in the army, becoming a captain in the 14th hussars on 8 September 1888. On his father's death (10 October 1887) he succeeded to the baronetcy. He married, on 19 January 1893, Eveline Mary (1864–1934), daughter of Alfred Nathaniel Holden Curzon, fourth Baron Scarsdale.

Miller enjoyed racing and was very successful on the turf. During the seventeen years he had horses in training he won 161 races worth £114,005. At different times his horses won all the classic races. Initially he had raced steeplechasers but in 1889 began on the flat, purchasing from Sir Robert Jardine and the trainer John Porter the two-year-old Sainfoin for £6000 and half the Derby stakes as a contingency. Sanfoin won the Derby, but had an undistinguished subsequent career, and was not initially a success at stud. In 1894 Miller bought the mare Roquebrune as a yearling for £4305 and later won with her the New Stakes at Ascot, and the Zetland Stakes at Doncaster. In 1895 he won the Oaks with La Sagesse, trained by Martin Gurry at Abingdon Place, Newmarket, and in 1898 he won the Cesarewitch with Chaleureux, who was a top-class handicapper and the future sire of the Derby and Oaks winner Signorinetta. Miller's horses were by now trained at Beverley House, Newmarket, by George Blackwell.

In 1899 Roquebrune was mated with Sainfoin at Miller's Hamilton stud farm. She produced the most famous of Miller's horses, Rock Sand, who won sixteen of his twenty starts. In 1903 Rock Sand, usually ridden by Blackwell's American stable jockey Danny Maher, became the tenth horse to win the triple crown. Although this was admittedly a poor year, Rock Sand was considered unbeatable. Only four horses faced him when he won the St Leger. However, in one of the most famous races of the period, he was defeated by Ard Patrick and Sceptre in the Eclipse stakes at Sandown Park, which indicated that his merits were overrated. The horse had bad joints and Blackwell had to work hard to keep him sound and fit to race. In the three years Rock Sand was in training the horse won stakes of £45,618, and Miller headed the list of winning owners in 1903 and 1904; Rock Sand then went to stud, where he made a significant contribution to breeding.

Miller was elected a member of the Jockey Club in 1903 and was one of its junior stewards for 1906. In December 1905 he broke up the Hamilton stud, auctioning off most of his mares. Roquebrune was sold to a Belgian breeder for 4500 guineas.

Miller, who was a JP and deputy lieutenant for Berwickshire, was major of the Lothians and Berwickshire imperial yeomanry, and served in South Africa (1900–01) with the 6th battalion, imperial yeomanry. He was mentioned in dispatches and received the DSO. From 1897 he was master of the Northumberland and Berwickshire foxhounds. He died at Manderston, his Berwickshire home, on 22 January 1906 from pneumonia, which had developed from a chill caught in the hunting field. He was buried at Christ Church, Duns, Berwickshire. He left no children, and was succeeded in the baronetcy by his brother John Alexander.   M. J. HUGGINS

Sources *The Times* (23 Jan 1906) · *The Sportsman* (23 Jan 1906) · J. Porter, *John Porter of Kingsclere* (1919), 124–5 · 'Obituary of Rock Sand', *Bloodstock Breeders' Review* (1914); repr. in L. Rasmussen and M. Napier, eds., *Treasures of the Bloodstock Breeders' Review* (1990), 463–7 · *Ruff's Guide to the Turf* (1889–1906) · Burke, *Peerage* (1907)
Likenesses Lib [L. Prosperi], caricature, lithograph, 1890, NPG; repro. in *VF* (6 Sept 1890)
Wealth at death £324,536 17s. 3d.: confirmation, 9 April 1906, CCI

Miller [*formerly* Müller], **Johann Samuel** [John Samuel] (1779–1830), naturalist and museum curator, was born on 26 February 1779 in Danzig, the only son of Johann Beniamin Müller and his first wife, Eleonor Lehman. He came to England in 1801 and settled in Bristol. He Anglicized his surname to Miller (and sometimes Anglicized his forenames, too) and a few years later was described as an accountant or merchant's clerk; a subsequent attempt to establish himself as a commission agent apparently failed. On 12 October 1806 he married Margaret James (d. 1836), of Bedminster, Bristol. They had a daughter (who died in infancy) and three sons. Their sons Edmund G. Müller and William James *Müller (1812–1845) were both artists—the latter in particular achieved distinction as a draughtsman and painter. By the time of Miller's death the family were living at 13 Hillsbridge Place (later renamed Clarence Road), Bristol.

In 1823 Miller was appointed first curator of the Bristol

Institution, a post he held until his death. He was interested in a range of natural history topics including geology, botany, and conchology, and published a number of scientific papers, including descriptions of newly discovered species of British molluscs and, most importantly, the pioneering study *A Natural History of the Crinoidea* (1821). He received considerable encouragement and support from many of his contemporaries, including the geologists William Buckland, William Daniel Conybeare, and Sir Henry Thomas De la Beche. However, his research on crinoids brought him into conflict with George Cumberland. It is also clear from comments by H. Jelly and J. B. Pentland that his work was not held in universal high regard.

Miller was unstinting in the service of the Bristol Institution, and it was as a result of his efforts that the museum (a precursor of the municipal museum) became firmly established. His extensive private collection was purchased by the institution after his death, with some of his papers, but no trace was found of the manuscripts of a supplement to *A Natural History of the Crinoidea*, or of a major account of the corals on which he was known to have been working.

Miller was elected an associate of the Linnean Society in 1817. He died in Bristol on 25 May 1830, and was survived by his wife and sons. His family continued to live at 13 Hillsbridge Place until the death of his widow in 1836.

M. D. CRANE, rev.

Sources *Philosophical Magazine*, new ser., 9 (1831) • H. Jelly, *Bath and Bristol Magazine, or, Western Miscellany*, 2 (1833) • W. A. Sarjeant and J. B. Delair, 'An Irish naturalist in Cuvier's laboratory: the letters of Joseph Pentland, 1820–1832', *Bulletin of the British Museum (Natural History) Historical Series*, 6 (1980), 245–319 • City Museum and Art Gallery, Bristol, Geology dept. MSS • R. N. James, *Painters and their works* (1896–7) • L. C. Sanders, *Celebrities of the century: being a dictionary of men and women of the nineteenth century* (1887) • C. G. E. Bunt, *The art and life of William James Müller* (1948)
Archives Bristol City Museum and Art Gallery, papers • Bristol RO, corresp. | FM Cam., notes and letters to William Baker

Miller, John (1805–1883), civil engineer, was born on 26 July 1805 at Ayr, son of James Miller, builder, and his wife, Margaret Caldwell. He had at least one brother; their father is presumed to have been Scottish. John Miller was educated at Ayr Academy. Alternative accounts state that at the age of twelve and a half he entered the office of C. D. Gairdner, solicitor and estate factor, or that he was apprenticed to the town clerk of Ayr with a view to becoming a lawyer: one appointment may have succeeded the other. In 1823, however, he moved to Edinburgh and was employed in the office of Thomas *Grainger, who had been in business as a surveyor and civil engineer since 1816. In 1825 Grainger took Miller into partnership.

Several authorities state that Miller attended Edinburgh University, without specifying dates. He cannot be clearly identified from surviving university records, but he might have been the John Miller who matriculated in law in 1823, or more probably he was one of two John Millers who matriculated in arts (which included engineering) in 1826.

John Miller's introduction to railway engineering came with the construction of the Monkland and Kirkintilloch Railway between 1823 and 1826; this was followed by the Garnkirk and Glasgow Railway, opened in 1831. Subsequently, Grainger and Miller worked individually on separate projects, though the partnership was dissolved only in 1845. John Miller became a member of the Institution of Civil Engineers in 1832. He married on 1 December 1834 Isabella (b. c.1802), daughter of Duncan Ogilvie of Perth, a merchant. They had at least five children—four daughters and a son, also called John.

Miller was engineer to the Dundee and Arbroath Railway, built between 1836 and 1838 and, more importantly, to the Glasgow, Paisley, Kilmarnock, and Ayr Railway (GPKA), built between 1837 and 1843. More importantly still, he was engineer for the Edinburgh and Glasgow Railway, authorized in 1838 and opened in 1842: this was a line very much in the Stephenson tradition, with extensive engineering works to provide a near-level route.

By then Miller was the leading railway engineer in Scotland, and he thus found himself immensely busy during the railway mania of the mid-1840s. In 1845 alone he deposited plans before parliament for more than 1500 miles of railway. He successfully completed the North British Railway (Edinburgh–Berwick), the Edinburgh and Hawick Railway, the Glasgow, Dumfries, and Carlisle Railway (in effect an extension of the GPKA), the Dundee and Perth Railway, the Stirling Midland Junction Railway (a short but important link from Polmont to Larbert), and several lesser lines. He was also engineer to the proposed Direct Northern Railway, one of several contenders for the route from London to York.

Exhausted, perhaps, and with his fortune certainly made, John Miller retired in 1850 at the age of forty-five. He was said to have been arrogant and his estimates always low; nevertheless, some of his railways remained of vital importance 150 years later. His great viaducts continued to carry trains, notably the 26 arch Avon Viaduct and the curving 36 arch Almond Viaduct on the Edinburgh and Glasgow line. His Ballochmyle Viaduct, south of Kilmarnock, had a central, semicircular masonry arch of 181 feet in diameter, the largest in Britain—though Miller himself considered his greatest work to be the nearby Lugar, or Templand, Viaduct, with its 14 arches carrying the railway 150 feet above the Lugar water.

Miller had been elected a fellow of the Royal Society of Edinburgh in 1841. By 1865 he had left the established Church of Scotland to support the Free Church. He stood unsuccessfully for parliament in 1852 and 1865, but was a Liberal MP for the city of Edinburgh from 1868 until 1874. Much of his time was devoted to running the extensive estates he had bought: Leithenhopes in Peeblesshire and Drumlithie in Kincardineshire. He became a JP and a deputy lieutenant. He died a widower, after a short illness, on 8 May 1883, at his residence, 2 Melville Crescent, Edinburgh.

P. J. G. RANSOM

Sources C. J. A. Robertson, *The origins of the Scottish railway system, 1722–1844* (1983) • *Engineering* (25 May 1883) • *PICE*, 74 (1882–3), 286–9 • *The Scotsman* (9 May 1883) • J. R. Hume, 'Scottish Region', *The railway heritage of Britain*, ed. G. Biddle and O. S. Nock (1983), 121–52 •

Boase, *Mod. Eng. biog.* • J. Simmons, *The railways of Britain* (1961) • D. Martin, *The Monkland & Kirkintilloch railway* (1976) • D. Martin, *The Garnkirk & Glasgow railway* (1981) • *WWBMP*, vol. 1 • J. Foster, *Members of parliament, Scotland … 1357–1882*, 2nd edn (privately printed, London, 1882) • J. Bateman, *The great landowners of Great Britain and Ireland*, 4th edn (1883) • J. R. Hume, *The industrial archaeology of Scotland*, 1 (1976) • b. cert. • d. cert.
Likenesses W. and T. Bonnar, engraving (Miller as a young man; after R. G. Baird), BM • photograph (Miller as an old man), repro. in *Railway Magazine* (April 1899), 326
Wealth at death £37,475 19*s.* 8*d.*: confirmation, 15 Sept 1883, *CCI*

Miller, John Cale (1814–1880), Church of England clergyman, was born in Margate on 11 October 1814, the only son of John and Mary Miller of 25 Bow Street, London. His father was a bookseller and publisher who came to be employed by the American embassy. Miller was educated at the Western Grammar School, Brompton, London, and matriculated at St John's College, Oxford, in 1832. He won a scholarship to Lincoln College, where he graduated BA (first class) in 1835 and MA in 1838. In 1857 he was awarded the Oxford degrees of BD and DD. In June 1836 he married Elizabeth Edwards of Winchester; they had a family of four sons and six daughters. Miller was ordained deacon in 1837 and priest in 1838. As the curate of the chapel of ease of Bexleyheath (1837–9) he was described in his ordination papers as being 'over impatient'. Between 1839 and 1841 he was the assistant minister to Thomas Vores of Park Chapel, Chelsea, and an assistant secretary of the Church Missionary Society. He succeeded Vores as minister of Park Chapel in 1841.

For twenty years, from 1846 to 1866, Miller was the rector of St Martin's, Birmingham, where he was the leader of the evangelical clergy and exercised a powerful influence over the life of the inhabitants of the city. His Liberal politics were ideally suited to Birmingham, and he drew together Jews and Christians of all denominations in philanthropic enterprises. Miller was a founder of the Midland Institute, a governor of the King Edward Grammar School, and supported the formation of free libraries. He is also credited with beginning what developed into the worldwide Sunday hospital movement: from 1859 the Birmingham churches and chapels adopted a particular Sunday on which to preach sermons and to collect money for the support of the city hospitals. In twenty-one years more than £95,000 was collected on Hospital Sunday. This movement helped to draw together the different denominations, and Miller was held in high regard by the leading nonconformists of Birmingham, J. A. James, R. W. Dale, and George Dawson. Miller regretted the celebration of the bicentenary of the 1662 Ejection on the grounds that it would not advance Christian unity.

Miller was active in his large parish, where he was assisted by a team of curates, scripture readers, and district visitors. In the late 1840s there were about 2000 baptisms and 550 weddings held each year. It became something of a model parish, with 'day schools, night schools, Sunday schools, Ragged schools, adult schools, reading rooms, libraries and working men's associations' (*Birmingham Daily Post*, 25 April 1866). Miller believed that the Church of England had failed to be 'the church of the people, the church of the poor,' and stated: 'if we do not obtain the confidence of the labouring classes, we labour in vain' (*Abstract of Report … of the Church Pastoral Aid Society*, 1854, 20). He tried through a variety of means to win converts from among the 'home heathen'. He established a working men's association which ran religious and secular self-improvement classes and awarded prizes to its members, and he promoted a working men's parochial mission. From 1852 he began holding afternoon and then evening communion services, and four years later he began holding shorter services. He held open-air services, conducted lunchtime services for businessmen, and was an early exponent of Sunday evening communion services. He tried to restore the parish church in 1847 but insufficient funds were available and he was able to complete only modest improvement and rebuilding. Miller described himself as 'a good beggar' and during his incumbency more than £18,000 was collected after sermons. When he left Birmingham a large public meeting was held in the town hall, and he was presented with 1000 guineas from the city and 600 guineas and silver plate from his congregation.

In 1866 Miller became the vicar of St Alfege, Greenwich, and rural dean of Greenwich. He had been an honorary canon of Worcester since 1852, and in 1871 he became a canon residentiary of Worcester, which was exchanged for a canonry of Rochester in 1873. From 1877 he was an examining chaplain to the bishop of Rochester, A. W. Thorold. In Greenwich, Miller promoted the Sunday hospital movement and supported the Royal Kent Dispensary (founded in 1783). After his death the dispensary was united with what became known as the Miller Hospital (opened in 1885 and closed in 1973). His work in education continued, and between 1870 and 1872 he was a member for Greenwich on the London school board.

Miller was one of the leading members of the evangelical party, a convinced protestant, and loyal churchman. He was a member of the Church Association and an outspoken critic of Romanism both inside and outside the Church of England. He was equally opposed to theological liberalism and maintained that 'we must neither be Romanized nor Germanized' (J. C. Miller, *Two Farewell Sermons*, 1866, 43); he also believed that the comprehensiveness of the Church of England should not be taken too far. He was a powerful orator, many of whose sermons were published. Much in demand as a preacher, he spoke at Oxford for his friend A. M. W. Christopher and was a select preacher at the university in 1869. He preached the annual sermons for the Church Pastoral Aid Society (1855) and the Church Missionary Society (1858), and often spoke at their meetings. He took a prominent part at the Islington clerical meeting and was a frequent speaker at convocation. Miller died of Bright's disease after an illness of six weeks at the vicarage in Greenwich, on 11 July 1880, and was buried at Shooters Hill cemetery on 16 July. He requested that there be no eulogy at his funeral, and none was given. There were two memorials to him: the Miller Hospital,

Greenwich, and the open-air Miller pulpit at the base of the tower of St Martin's, Birmingham, which was dedicated in 1898.   A. F. MUNDEN

Sources *Birmingham Daily Post* (25 April 1866) · *Birmingham Daily Post* (13 July 1880) · *The Times* (12 July 1880) · *Kentish Mercury* (17 July 1880) · J. Poland, *Records of the Miller hospital and Royal Kent dispensary* (1893) · D. E. H. Mole, 'John Cale Miller: a Victorian rector of Birmingham', *Journal of Ecclesiastical History*, 17 (1966), 95–144 · *Abstract of report and speeches at the 19th annual meeting of the Church Pastoral Aid Society* (1854), 20 · *CGPLA Eng. & Wales* (1880)

Likenesses C. Baugniet, lithograph, 1846, BM · T. Spencer, portrait, 1884; now lost · D. J. Pound, stipple and line engraving (after photograph by Mayall), NPG; repro. in D. J. Pound, *Drawing room portrait gallery of eminent personages* (1859–60) · H. J. Whitlock, two cartes-de-visite, NPG

Wealth at death under £8000: probate, 7 Aug 1880, *CGPLA Eng. & Wales*

Miller, John Frederick (*fl.* 1772–1796). *See under* Miller, John Sebastian (1715–1792).

Miller, Sir John Riggs, first baronet (*c.*1744–1798), writer on weights and measures, was born John Miller at Drumlin, co. Clare, Ireland, the second son of John Miller and his wife, Anne, the daughter of Thomas Browne of New Grove, co. Clare. Educated at Dalston School and Eton College (1752–1760), he entered the army in 1760 as a cornet in the light-dragoons and reached the rank of captain in the 113th foot; he saw action in Germany (Emsdorf, 1760) and France (Belleisle, 1761) and retired in 1763. Although he had been admitted to the Middle Temple on 1 August 1757, there is no evidence that he studied there. He matriculated from Trinity Hall, Cambridge, in 1761 but did not graduate. When in August 1765 he married Anna (1741–1781) [see Miller, Anna, Lady Miller], the daughter and heir of Edward Riggs, of the Middle Temple, he added her surname before his own, and so became known as John Riggs Miller. From about 1780 he hyphenated the two names, giving Riggs-Miller, but by 1790 had reverted to Riggs Miller. The couple had a son and a daughter. With his wife's fortune and the income from his family's estates, which he inherited in July 1762, Riggs Miller built an expensive house at Batheaston, Somerset, where they held literary meetings. These took place every fortnight and were in the form of literary competitions, whereby prizes were awarded to the finest compositions drawn from a Roman vase decked in pink ribbons and myrtles; the salon was thus dubbed 'Lady Miller's Vase', and, though satirized, attracted authors such as David Garrick and Christopher Anstey. Riggs Miller was created a baronet on 24 August 1778. Following the death of his wife on 24 June 1781, he married, on 9 September 1795, Jane, the widow of Sir Thomas Davenport (1734–1786), MP, and the daughter of Robert Seel of Liverpool; they had no children.

Riggs Miller served as MP for Newport, Cornwall, from 1784 to 1790. On 5 February 1790, after making widespread enquiries into the matter, he proposed in the Commons that British weights and measures should be reformed. News of his proposal reached Talleyrand in France, who was making a similar suggestion there, and who formed the impression from Riggs Miller's speech that Britain was on the verge of an actual reform. In a document placed before the French national assembly on 9 March 1790 he referred to the discussions in the British parliament, and proposed that Britain should be invited to collaborate with France in the determination of the length of the seconds pendulum which was to be the fundamental unit of length in a new system (later to become the metre). He sent a copy of his document to Riggs Miller, who in turn referred to Talleyrand's letter in a further speech to the Commons on 13 April 1790. On 8 May 1790 the national assembly adopted a decree initiating the reform of weights and measures in France and proposing that Britain's collaboration in the scientific work should be invited. On 22 May 1790 France's ambassador in London formally conveyed the proposal to the British foreign secretary, but was rebuffed. Shortly afterwards Riggs Miller published the texts of his and Talleyrand's speeches, together with their correspondence; this appears to have been his only publication. In his second speech to the Commons he had stated that he would return to the reform of Britain's weights and measures on a future occasion, but parliament was dissolved in the same year (1790), and he was not re-elected. In 1793 France adopted the metric system, without British collaboration.

Riggs Miller died on 28 May 1798 and was buried in Bath Abbey.   VICTOR MAYES

Sources M. M. Drummond, 'Miller, Sir John', HoP, *Commons, 1754–90* · R. A. Austen-Leigh, ed., *The Eton College register, 1753–1790* (1921) · GEC, *Baronetage* · *The parliamentary register, or, History of the proceedings and debates of the House of Commons*, 27 (1791), 5 Feb, 13 April 1790 · H. McLeod, 'Notes on the history of the metrical measures and weights', *Nature*, 69 (1903–4) · J. Collinson, *The history and antiquities of the county of Somerset*, 1 (1791) · G. P. Judd, *Members of parliament, 1734–1832* (1955) · A. Barbeau, *Life and letters at Bath in the XVIIIth century* (1904) · Venn, *Alum. Cant.*

Miller, John Sebastian [*formerly* Johann Sebastian Müller] (1715–1792), engraver and botanist, was born in Nuremberg, Germany, where his father was a gardener at the Stromerischen Garten. He is said to have trained under Christoph Weigel (who died in 1725, however) and, more plausibly, with Martin Tyroff (*b.* 1704). In 1744 with his brother Tobias, an architectural engraver, he emigrated to England where, by July, he was working for the art dealer Arthur Pond on various landscape prints, his major work being a set of large capriccio views in Rome after Paolo Pannini (1744–7). He also worked for other publishers: in March 1747 an allegorical piece featuring medallion portraits of the royal family and dedicated 'To all True Britons, Lovers of Liberty and the Present Succession' celebrated the survival of the Hanoverian regime. Soon Miller was publishing on his own account. His first advertised publication, in April 1748, was a large print of a 'Tyger' after the Augsburg artist Johann Elias Ridinger. He maintained an energetic and varied practice, engraving and often designing a large number of book illustrations including illustrations to Thomson, Swift, Dryden, Young, Milton, Evelyn, and Gray with vignettes for Baskerville's editions of Horace and Virgil. He engraved twenty-six plates of furniture and his brother Tobias twenty-three for

Thomas Chippendale's *Director* (1753) and he worked for the University of Oxford on engravings of the Arundel marbles (1763–4) and on some almanacs. He also painted, exhibiting a series of paintings of Oxfordshire landscapes in 1764 and 1766.

By the 1760s Miller was established as a leading designer and engraver of historical and portrait prints. The publisher John Boydell commissioned him to engrave for his prestigious *Collection of Prints Engraved after the most Capital Paintings in England*. But like his contemporary William Hogarth, Miller was cynically dismissive of the Englishman's blind veneration for art by dead foreigners. He painted three fake 'Spanish old masters' that he claimed to have acquired from the collection of Friedrich Carl Schönborn. Then he exhibited (1765) and published engravings of them. In 1767 he wrote to the German journalist Christoph von Murr to let him into his private joke:

> They are all three my own Composition, Painting and Engraving. Neither Pantoja, nor Murillo did ever see anything of them. They are three humbuggs for our English Connoisseurs. I had a fancy to see how far their knowledge will penetrate. I sold the Pictures to a Cunning Collector, and to this day they do not know the thrift—We have fools in England, as well, as in Germany, who will allow nothing but what has dead names to it.   (Murr, 11–12)

In England the imposture seems never to have been exposed. Miller's prints continued to be listed in John Boydell's catalogues as works by Murillo and Pantoja. Despite this sceptical attitude to London's connoisseurs, Miller was an enthusiastic champion of the virtues of British life. In 1780 he painted, exhibited, engraved, and published a print of *The Confirmation of Magna Carta* by Henry III, reminding his adopted compatriots that 'it is this Law that constitutes an Englishman, and as such that thou art distinguished from all men on Earth'.

Throughout his life Miller's career had a second strand. His principal passion had always been botany, or so he claimed in the preface to his most significant work, *An Illustration of the Sexual System of Linnaeus* (1770–77). There he spoke of his 'early inclination to Botany' and his 'desire of rendering his Profession as an Engraver subservient to the Cultivation of his favourite Science'. His first major contribution to the illustration of this science came with his plates for Philip Miller's *Figures of the most beautiful, useful and uncommon plants, described in the gardener's dictionary* (1758). In 1759, with Philip Miller's support, he proposed 'one hundred prints, exhibiting a curious collection of Plants and Insects', but this project failed after ten plates had been published. *The Sexual System of Linnaeus*, Miller's greatest work, was launched in 1770 with the support of Gowin Knight, librarian of the British Museum, and completed in parts in 1776. The first two numbers were sent to Linnaeus in December 1770 and received his enthusiastic endorsement. The three folios issued in 1777 contained 108 coloured plates, 109 uncoloured, and 109 sheets of letterpress in Latin and English. In a highly decorated frontispiece Miller depicted himself facing Linnaeus in homage. This portrait was taken by C. J. Maillet in 1787, reversed, and published in a French edition of Philip Miller's *Gardener's Dictionary* with the caption 'Directeur du jardin de botanique des apothecaires de Chelsea' in the mistaken belief that it represented the dictionary's author. Miller published an octavo edition of this work in 1779 and in 1780 attempted to launch another ambitious series dealing with new plants, but of this only seven plates were published. He engraved all the plates to Lord Bute's nine-volume *Botanical Tables* (1785), and there is a further series of unpublished botanical drawings made for Bute in 1783 and 1784 in the Natural History Museum, London.

Miller married three times and had twenty-nine children. Five were still alive in 1783; his third wife had died in 1779. He died at Lambeth, London, in June 1792. Only his eldest son, **John Frederick Miller** (*fl.* 1772–1796) and his second son, James Miller, followed their father's profession, and it was probably through the elder Miller's acquaintance with Joseph Banks that John Frederick was taken into Banks's employment. He drew many of the artefacts collected on James Cook's *Endeavour* voyage of 1768–71 and both brothers were to have accompanied Banks on Cook's second voyage. When that plan foundered, John Frederick accompanied Banks on his travels to the Orkneys, Hebrides, and Iceland in 1772; his drawings are now in the Natural History Museum, London. He subsequently published some of his engravings made from the Iceland drawings without Banks's permission, and allowed other plates to be used by Thomas Pennant to illustrate his *Arctic Zoology* (1784–7). In 1786–92 he published forty-three plates with descriptions, entitled *Various Subjects of Natural History*, and in 1796 he illustrated George Shaw's *Cimelia physica*, both works treating rare quadrupeds, birds, and plants. James Miller joined the navy and served with Rodney's fleet in 1782 during the victory over the French in the Caribbean before sailing to America.

TIMOTHY CLAYTON

Sources C. G. von Murr, 'Nachrichten von dem berühmten Maler, Kupferstecher, und Botaniker, Herrn Johann Miller, Mitglied der königl. Gessellschaft der Künste in London', *Journal zur Kunstgeschichte und zur allgemeinen Litteratur* [Nuremberg], 11 (1783), 3–22; 13 (1784), 134; 15 (1787), 9; 16 (1788), 22 • Graves, *Soc. Artists*, 103 • H. Hammelmann, *Book illustrators in eighteenth-century England*, ed. T. S. R. Boase (1975), 63–4 • D. Alexander, 'Canaletto and the English print market', *Canaletto and England*, ed. M. Liversidge and J. Farrington (1993), 39–40 [exhibition catalogue, Birmingham Gas Hall Exhibition Gallery, Birmingham, 14 Oct 1993 – 9 Jan 1994] • L. Lippincott, *Selling art in Georgian London: the rise of Arthur Pond* (1983) • L. Lippincott, 'Arthur Pond's journal ... 1734–1750', *Walpole Society*, 54 (1988), 220–333 • H. Petter, *The Oxford almanacks* (1974) • J. C. Smith, *British mezzotinto portraits*, 3 (1880), 941 • A. Paterson, 'Philip Miller: a portrait', *Garden History*, 14/1 (1986), 40–41 • R. Joppien and B. Smith, *The art of Captain Cook's voyages*, 2 vols. (1985), vol. 1, p. 74

Likenesses J. S. Miller, self-portrait, engraving, repro. in *Illustration of the sexual system* (1777)

Miller, Josiah (1832–1880), biographer, was born on 8 April 1832 at Putney, Surrey, the son of the Revd Edward Miller. When he was thirteen he was articled to an engineering surveyor at Westminster, but gave up his articles to enter Highbury College, where he studied for the Congregational ministry. He graduated BA with first-class honours in 1853 and MA in 1855 at London University. He was appointed pastor at Dorchester in 1855 and at Long Sutton, Lincolnshire, in 1860. In 1861 he married Harriette Anne, the eldest daughter of H. M. Aldridge of Poole, Dorset. They had at least two sons. In 1868 he was appointed minister at Newark, Nottinghamshire, but he gave this post up when he became secretary of the British Society for the Propagation of the Gospel among the Jews. He later succeeded the Revd J. Robinson as secretary to the London City Mission.

Miller's main works include *Our hymns: their authors and origin, being biographical sketches of the principal psalm and hymn writers (with notes on their psalms and hymns)* (1866), intended as a companion to the *New Congregational Hymn Book*, and *Singers and songs of the church, being biographical sketches of the hymn-writers in all the principal collections* (1869). Miller died on 22 December 1880 at his home, 77 Fortress Road, Kentish Town, London, and was buried at Abney Park on 28 December 1880.

THOMPSON COOPER, rev. ANNE PIMLOTT BAKER

Sources *Congregational Year Book* (1882), 319–20 · *Congregational Year Book* (1861) · Boase, *Mod. Eng. biog.* · *The Nonconformist* (30 Dec 1880), 1334 · *CGPLA Eng. & Wales* (1881)
Wealth at death under £1500: probate, 4 March 1881, *CGPLA Eng. & Wales*

Miller, Josias (1683/4–1738), comic actor and singer, was born between August 1683 and August 1684 and may have been related to another Miller, possibly called Patrick, who operated fair booths at the turn of the century; his name is also given as Joseph. Practically nothing is known about Joe Miller's early life. He first appeared on the cast lists at Lincoln's Inn Fields as Watchman in David Crawford's *Love at First Sight* on 25 March 1704. A second appearance in August 1705 as Julio in A. Chaves's *The Cares of Love* is suggested by the playbill and first edition. Miller then disappeared from the London theatre until the season of 1709–10, when he joined the Drury Lane company to play Teague in Robert Howard's *The Committee*. He took on other comic and low-life roles that season, with Jeremy in William Congreve's *Love for Love*, Clip in John Vanbrugh's *The Confederacy*, Guzman in William Mountfort's *The Successful Strangers*, the singing Pedlar in John Fletcher and William Rowley's *The Maid of the Mill*, and the second Sailor in Susannah Centlivre's afterpiece *A Bickerstaff's Burial*, and he shared a benefit with another performer of similar range, Mr Knapp.

Miller again disappears from London theatre records until 1715. Highfill, Burnim, and Langhans suggest that he spent the intervening years playing in the provinces. He rejoined the Drury Lane company for the 1715–16 season and remained a member there until 1730, building a reputation mainly in comic roles. In a later petition against the managers he recalled the terms of his articles of employment at Drury Lane, where he was sworn in on 12 March 1717 at the modest salary of £4 per week. However, he also received solo benefits for most seasons at Drury Lane. His portfolio of roles included comic leads and character

parts, but he was not unwilling to take on tiny roles, usually in more serious plays. Among characters he made his own were Tallboy in Richard Brome's *The Jovial Crew*, Kate Matchlock in Sir Richard Steele's *The Funeral*, Cokes in Ben Jonson's *Bartholomew Fair* and Abel Drugger in his *The Alchemist*, Sir Joseph Wittol in Congreve's *The Old Bachelor*, Ben in his *Love for Love*, and Sir Wilfull in his *The Way of the World*. Miller inherited many parts played elsewhere by William Bowen, George Pack, and William Bullock, and he was noted for his version of Foigard in George Farquhar's *The Stratagem* and Clincher junior and later Beau Clincher in *The Constant Couple*, and for his Marplot in Susannah Centlivre's *The Busy Body* and Sir Philip Money Love in her *The Artifice*. He was also able to make use of his skill at singing and dancing in entr'acte entertainments, and later in his career he occasionally took roles in pantomimes, which included Pantaloon and Pierrot in *Apollo and Daphne* and the Squire in *The Comical Distresses of Pierot*. In addition he was well equipped for the developing form of ballad opera and played Brush in Charles Johnson's *The Village Opera* and Varole in William Chetwood's afterpiece *The Lover's Opera*.

However, Miller's work in the patent theatre was only half the story. Like many actors of the period, he found a valuable source of additional income performing in other venues during the summer. In July and August of 1718 he performed at William Pinkethman's Richmond Theatre in John Dryden's *The Spanish Fryar*, *The Busy Body*, and *The Committee*. He was there again in the summer of 1719, playing Somebody in the anonymous *Soldier's Stratagem*, and he was also well known as a manager of and a performer in the increasingly sophisticated theatrical offerings of the summer fairground booths. In 1719 he ran a booth at Bartholomew fair with Pinkethman and performed in the anonymous droll *Jane Shore* as Sir Anthony Noodle, a popular character he was to resurrect in various guises. The following summer the duo ran the booth at Bartholomew fair with Henry Norris, where Miller played Roger in *Maudlin, the Merchant's Daughter of Bristol*. In August 1721 Miller played Sousecrown in *The Injured General* at Bartholomew and Southwark fairs with Pinkethman and Norris. The following summer was particularly busy and saw him acting at Richmond, performing in *Richmond Wells* and *Distressed Beauty* in a booth he managed with Pinkethman and Anthony Boheme, and running his own booth at Southwark fair: 'Miller is not with Pinkethman, but with himself' (*London Stage*, 5 Sept 1722). With occasional interruptions, Miller continued summer performances at Richmond and at the fairs until his death.

The season 1730–31 was a dry one for Miller, who did not act that year at Drury Lane; his only known source of income was his summer booth work. Thomas Davies recalled that he had 'by some mean economy of the managers, been driven from Drury-lane to Goodman's Fields' (Davies, 3.220). In a later pamphlet Theophilus Cibber took up Miller's cause and complained that he 'was kept out of any Business upwards of Two Years, and was a Sufferer above 300l' because of the patentees (BL, Add. MS 1889.d.1 (32)). Miller spent the 1731–2 season at the new

Goodman's Fields, where he opened as Teague in *The Committee*, 'being the first time of his appearing on any Stage these two Years' (*London Stage*, 3 Jan 1732). He reprised a few favourites before returning to Drury Lane on 22 November 1732 with, of course, Teague. However, his time at Drury Lane was not a happy one, and in the summer of 1733 he made up one of the 'stage mutineers' (*Daily Advertiser*, 30 May 1733) who, guided by Theophilus Cibber, argued with the new patentee, John Highmore, and left to set up at the New Haymarket. The patentees issued a stinging defence, claiming that Miller had received a salary of £5 a week on rejoining the company and an *ex gratia* payment of £40 for the period September to December, when he had not been acting. At the Haymarket, Miller opened as Ben in *Love for Love* and played several of his favourite roles until the dispute was resolved, and in March the actors returned, triumphant, to Drury Lane. Miller held a respected place in the company, and in 1735 he was one of the actors who attempted to rent the theatre from the patentees, for £900 per annum, and manage it themselves. He was also one of many actors who petitioned against the new Licensing Act of 1737.

There is surprisingly little commentary on Miller's acting. Davies thought him 'a lively comic actor, and a favourite of the town in Ben, and many other diverting characters' (Davies, 3.220). Benjamin Victor thought him 'a natural, spirited Comedian; he was the famous Teague', and even conceded that he produced a passable Irish brogue suitable for 'an English audience'. Victor also admiringly noted 'as a full Proof of the Force of his Abilities, he died in the Receipt of a good Salary, which he had long enjoy'd' (Victor, 2.66–7). He was said to be a heavy drinker and a frequenter of the Bull's Head in Spring Gardens and the Black Jack in Portsmouth Street. His reputation as a comedian off-stage was enhanced by the posthumous publication of *Joe Miller's Jests* in 1739. In the main these witticisms, short stories, and jokes were drawn from earlier sources by the editor, John Mottley, and had little to do with Miller; he features in only three tales.

Miller's last appearance was on 30 May 1738 as Clodpole in Thomas Betterton's *The Amorous Widow* and as the Miller in the afterpiece *The King and the Miller of Mansfield*. At some point he retired from his usual lodgings in Clare Street, Clare Market, to the Strand on the Green, Chiswick, where he died, aged fifty-four, on 16 August 1738 'of pleurisy' (*London Daily Post and General Advertiser*, 17 Aug 1738). The *Daily Post* of 17 August fondly recalled the 'comedian, of merry memory. Very few of his profession have gained more applause on the stage.' The poet Stephen Duck composed an epitaph and some very poor poetry for the tombstone of:

Honest JOE MILLER
who was
A tender Husband
A sincere Friend
A facetious Companion
And an excellent Comedian.
(Esar, 10)

His wife, Henrietta Maria (1683–1766), received the income from a packed benefit performance on 14 December 1738 and survived him by many years. She was buried alongside her husband at St Clement Danes, London in 1766.   J. MILLING

Sources Highfill, Burnim & Langhans, *BDA* · B. Victor, *The history of the theatres of London and Dublin*, 2 vols. (1761) · T. Davies, *Dramatic miscellanies: consisting of critical observations on several plays of Shakespeare*, 3 vols. (1783–4) · E. Esar, 'The legend of Joe Miller', ed. N. Schmulowitz, *Anecdota Scowah*, 2 (1 April 1957) · E. L. Avery, ed., *The London stage, 1660–1800*, pt 2: *1700–1729* (1960) · J. Milhous and R. Hume, eds., *The London stage, 1660–1800*, new edn, pt 2: *1700–1729* (1996), vol. 1 · J. Milhous and R. D. Hume, eds., *A register of English theatrical documents, 1660–1737*, 2 vols. (1991) · *Joe Miller's jests*, ed. J. Mottley (1739) · PRO, C 11/83/17 · A. H. Scouten, ed., *The London stage, 1660–1800*, pt 3: *1729–1747* (1961)
Likenesses J. Sympson, junior, engraving on benefit ticket, 25 April 1717?, priv. coll. · J. Laguerre, engraving, 1733, Harvard TC · C. Stoppelaer, engraving, 1738 (as Teague), Harvard TC · A. Miller, mezzotint, 1739 (after C. Stoppelaer), BM, NG Ire. · C. Mosley, engraving, 1739, Harvard TC; repro. in Mottley, ed., *Joe Miller's jests* · G. P. Harding, pencil drawing (as Teague), NPG

Miller [*née* Fraser], **Lydia Mackenzie Falconer** [*pseud.* Mrs Harriet Myrtle] (*bap.* 1812, *d.* 1876), children's writer, was the daughter of Elizabeth Lydia McLeod (*d.* 1865), a schoolteacher, and her husband, an Inverness merchant, William Fraser (1789–1828), whose business failed. With financial help from her mother's Mackenzie relatives, Lydia was educated first at Inverness Academy, then in Edinburgh, boarding at the house of George Thomson, the friend and correspondent of Robert Burns. Having stayed for a time at Egham Lodge, Surrey, the home of her mother's cousins, she returned to her mother, now in Cromarty, and set up a small school in 1830. Here she met Hugh *Miller (1802–1856), the stonemason journalist. Intelligent and well-read herself, she was attracted by his personality and talents. In spite of initial opposition from her mother, Lydia and Hugh became engaged. In 1834 Hugh was appointed accountant of the Commercial Bank in Cromarty, which enabled them to marry on 7 January 1837, Lydia continuing to take pupils. In 1840, when Hugh became editor of *The Witness* in Edinburgh, Lydia at first assisted him in the management of the paper, occasionally writing articles and reviews. While bringing up their four surviving children, among them Harriet Miller *Davidson, and keeping abreast of Hugh's theological, geological, political, and social theories, she wrote, under the pen-name Mrs Harriet Myrtle, about twenty educational and moral, but often adventurous and lighthearted, stories for children. Her only adult novel, *Passages in the Life of an English Heiress, or, Recollections of Disruption Times in Scotland*, published anonymously in 1847, has a background drawn from her own and Hugh's upbringing and arguments from their discussions. On 23 December 1856, after completing the proof-reading of his fifth book, but unwell, dispirited, and fearful for his sanity, Hugh suddenly shot himself. Despite this shock and long periods of ill health, and with the assistance of friends and colleagues such as the Revd W. S. Symonds and Peter Bayne, Lydia realized her husband's intentions, editing and writing scholarly prefaces for four more of his books which had appeared in article form in *The Witness*, and selecting articles for another two. She also assisted Bayne in his biography of Hugh and continued writing her books for children until 1872. From 1863 Lydia lived at Old Drummond House in Inverness. She died on 11 March 1876 at her son-in-law's manse at Lochinver, Lairg, Sutherland, and was buried on the 20th beside her husband in the Grange cemetery in Edinburgh.

MARIAN MCKENZIE JOHNSTON

Sources P. Bayne, *The life and letters of Hugh Miller* (1871) · H. Miller, *My schools and schoolmasters* (1854) · L. M. Mackay, ed., 'Mrs Hugh Miller's journal', *Chambers's Journal*, 6th ser. (1902), 305–8, 369–72, 461–4, 513–16 · H. M. Taylor (*née* Ross), 'My recollections of Hugh Miller', unpublished MSS · NL Scot., Miller MSS · Old Parish Records Inverness, Cromarty, and Egham · priv. coll., Miller MSS · will dated 1863, with codicils, NA Scot. · will of Thomas Mackenzie, 1821, PRO [great-great-uncle] · records of Egham Lodge, Egham Public Library, Surrey · *The Times* (22 March 1876) · *The Scotsman* (16 March 1876) · *The Scotsman* (20 March 1876) · review, *The Witness* (1 Jan 1848) · tombstone of Lydia Falconer Miller in Grange cemetery, Edinburgh · tombstone of Revd Murdoch Mackenzie in Chapel graveyard, Inverness · bap. reg. Scot., 1789 · m. reg. Scot., 1809

Archives NL Scot., family corresp.

Likenesses G. Urquhart, *c*.1835, priv. coll.

Wealth at death £793 15s. 6d.: confirmation, 1877, *CCI* · £569 6s. 1d.: corrective inventory, 1877, *CCI*

Max Miller (1894–1963), by Russell Westwood, 1930s?

Miller, Max [*real name* Thomas Henry Sargent] (1894–1963), comedian, was born on 21 November 1894 at 43 Hereford Street, Brighton, the second of five children of James Sargent, builder's labourer, and his wife, Alice, *née* West. After a childhood marked by considerable poverty and a much disrupted education he left school at twelve, barely literate. He worked in Brighton as milk roundsman, tailor, and golf caddy and spent a short period in London as a motor mechanic. Inspired by the song-and-dance routines of black-face music-hall act G. H. Elliott, he began singing in local public houses, accompanied by his father on the piano, and joined an amateur concert party in 1913. After volunteering for the army in 1914 he was posted first to India, once again joining a concert party, and then in 1915 to Mesopotamia, where he was temporarily blinded by shellfire. After being discharged in 1918 he returned to Brighton and, as Harry Sargent, turned professional with Jack Sheppard's Concert Party as a light comedian. Here he met (Frances) Kathleen Marsh (*b*. 1897/8), a contralto and child impersonator, and they married on 17 February 1921: in the same year, and at her suggestion, he assumed the stage name Max Miller. As well as working in revue he increasingly concentrated on stand-up comedy, appearing as a solo music-hall turn and adding the distinctive Cheeky Chappie to his billing matter. Miller's rise was steady rather than dramatic, but a first booking at the London Palladium in 1929 boosted his career significantly and his appearance at the 1931 royal variety performance symbolized his arrival at the top of his profession.

Six feet tall with very blue eyes and a good physique, Miller embellished his natural advantages with an outrageously eye-catching costume consisting of multicoloured plus-fours—most famously he wore red, white, and blue at the 1937 royal variety performance—set off by white shoes and white trilby. He also exuded a boastful self-confidence on stage, exemplified by such catchphrases as 'This is clever stuff I am giving you lady'. However, his greatest gifts were his sense of timing, use of silences, winks, and gesture, and above all what *The Times* referred to as 'his engaging intimacy' (*The Times*). Often working from very close to the edge of the stage and drawing audiences in through continual asides and direct address, he created a rapport, almost a comic conspiracy, between performer and audience that has rarely been equalled.

By the 1930s, sexual innuendo had become Miller's stock-in-trade. It was delivered both through jokes (supposedly selected from his 'white' or 'blue' books, according to the level of indelicacy) and short comic songs which he accompanied on the guitar, a feature originally developed during a South African tour in 1932. Many commentators spoke of a sense of danger when Miller performed, an almost tangible testing of boundaries. This was heightened by a certain sexual ambiguity, with audience howls at his stage garb and rather feminine make-up being met with the challenging cry 'Well, what if I am?'. His act offended some managements, with the Finsbury Park Empire fining him for a quintessentially 'blue book' Millerism concerning 'the girl of eighteen who swallowed a pin but didn't feel the prick until she was twenty-one' (East, 105). However, Miller's popularity and the fact that he was deemed acceptable enough to play royal variety shows in 1931, 1937, and 1950 (his act suitably, although not totally, toned down), suggests that he articulated a strong strain of sexual knowingness within British culture. Although he played throughout Britain and made several foreign tours, he was most frequently seen and most popular in London and the south-east, his speech apparently too fast for some provincial audiences. Despite his Brighton roots (and, initially, accent) he was often seen as the embodiment of 'a real Cockney' (*Performer*, 18 Nov 1937), and in this context he perhaps helped construct certain notions of popular metropolitan style and attitude.

Miller continued to play in revue virtually throughout

his career, with *Apple Sauce* (1940), also featuring Vera Lynn, a particular success. However, his tendency to dominate the stage and a penchant for extended ad libs sometimes limited his effectiveness and tried the patience of fellow actors. He made his screen début with a much praised cameo portrayal of a song-plugger in the 1933 version of J. B. Priestley's *The Good Companions*. Although he was to make another thirteen feature films up to 1943, with the exception of *Educated Evans* (1936) his output was generally commercially and critically disappointing. He played too much to the camera (his success in the *Good Companions* owed something to director Victor Saville's distracting him with a dummy camera) and tended to reproduce his stage persona rather than developing character. Miller was a regular broadcaster on Radio Luxemburg and on the BBC, although his humour was a constant source of worry. He was 'faded' and subsequently banned for five years by the BBC in 1944 after fears that he was about to repeat a joke for which he had already been severely chastised.

Miller's career declined gradually from the late 1940s. In the immediate post-war period American comedians dominated the major London variety theatres—Miller deliberately over-ran in the 1950s royal variety performance in protest at the length of time allotted to Jack Benny—and in the 1950s the advent of television, which Miller never mastered, proved virtually terminal to the industry. His 1957 live long-playing recording *Max at the Met* showed a man still capable of outstanding performances but in September 1959 he suffered a heart attack; he performed only infrequently from then on—his final stage appearance was at Folkestone in December the following year. Apart from a few recording sessions he spent a rather solitary retirement in Brighton.

A talented golfer, Miller also enjoyed keeping parrots, gardening, and riding. He was not notably popular with his fellow performers. Alongside his dominating personality on stage, he was deemed to be excessively mean, although friends and family claimed that he was quietly generous to various individuals and favourite causes. His wife, Kathleen, was hugely influential in organizing and managing his career (she answered fan mail and even signed his autographs, partly to disguise his poor educational levels) but he felt dominated by her and enjoyed a close relationship with Ann Graham, usually described as his 'organizational secretary', from the 1930s. He died on 7 May 1963 at his home, 25 Burlington Street, Brighton, from complications following influenza, and was cremated at the Downs crematorium, Brighton, on 11 May. Although an increasingly marginal figure at the time of his death, subsequent critical reassessment has secured Miller's reputation as probably the greatest stand-up comedian of his generation. DAVE RUSSELL

Sources J. East, *Max Miller: the Cheeky Chappie* (1993) · J. Fisher, *Funny way to be a hero* (1976) · *The Times* (9 May 1963) · *Brighton and Hove Herald* (11 May 1963) · *Performer* (18 Nov 1937) · *Stage and Television Today* (16 May 1963) · b. cert. · m. cert. · *CGPLA Eng. & Wales* (1963)

Archives FILM BFI NFTVA, *40 minutes*, BBC2, 16 Feb 1989 · BFI NFTVA, *Heroes of comedy*, Channel 4, 27 Oct 1995 · BFI NFTVA, performance footage | SOUND BL NSA, 'There will never be another', 1994, H4287/1 · BL NSA, performance recordings

Likenesses R. Westwood, photograph, 1930–1939?, NPG [*see illus.*] · photographs, repro. in East, *Max Miller*

Wealth at death £28,091 10s. 0d.: probate, 19 Aug 1963, *CGPLA Eng. & Wales*

Miller, Patrick (1731–1815), banker and inventor, was born at Glasgow, the third son of William Miller of Glenlee, and his wife, Janet Hamilton. He was a younger brother of Sir Thomas *Miller, the lord president of the court of session. Although he was to claim that he began life 'without a sixpence', he and his brothers attended the University of Glasgow where he matriculated at the age of twelve in 1743. None of the brothers graduated; but that was not unusual at the time. During the mid-eighteenth century the Scottish economy was growing, and Patrick Miller seems to have decided to go into trade. His family was well connected with the Glasgow merchant community. They were related to the Yuilles (Zuille) of Darleith, partners of the Murdochs in the American trades. In 1753 his brother, Thomas, married the daughter of John Murdoch, a tobacco merchant, and one of the founders in 1750 of the Glasgow Arms Bank. Like other Scottish merchants, the Yuilles had shipping interests in Liverpool. Patrick Miller went to sea himself, and reputedly visited ports in Europe and North America. His experience of the dangers of piracy stimulated an interest in naval guns and gunnery. He gave up seafaring to become a merchant and a banker, possibly learning financial skills with the Glasgow Arms Bank.

By November 1760 Miller was in partnership with William Ramsay of Barnton, merchants and bankers, in Edinburgh. The partners had a substantial interest in the British Linen Company, which they used to finance their merchant adventures in finished textiles. In 1761 Miller built at Leith a ship, the *Wolfe*, named after General Wolfe, to trade with Quebec. On her first voyage—with a cargo of striped lawns, hollands, and thread lace valued at £536—she was taken by a French privateer. When she was discovered also to be carrying supplies for the British army her crew were taken prisoner, and the goods, for which Miller received a salvage value of only £19, returned to Orkney. The Linen Company was precarious as its notes were redeemable in cash on demand, or at six months plus interest. Consequently there were frequent runs on its resources, sparked in part by the Bank of Scotland, which collected notes, and presented them for payment in large parcels. Ramsay and Miller seem to have been behind the efforts to put the Linen Company's house in order and turn it round, after the 1765 Bank Act, into a fully-fledged bank.

Miller was elected in 1767 to the court of the Bank of Scotland, as part of an effort to reform the management. Over the next three years he was instrumental in making many improvements, particularly the introduction of note exchange, whereby the bank agreed to accept notes of its competitors, and negotiating guarantees to support the note issue from London private banks with Scottish

Patrick Miller (1731–1815), attrib. Sir George Chalmers, *c*.1770

connections. He also actively promoted the development of a branch network. As a result of these changes the bank was well equipped to weather the storm of the banking crisis, which brought down Douglas and Heron's Ayr Bank in 1772. In his efforts to reconstruct the bank, Miller found ready support from Henry Dundas, who was elected a director in 1768. In the early 1770s, with Miller's backing, Dundas began to build up a powerful political base in Scotland, entering parliament in 1774 and becoming lord advocate in 1775.

Part of Dundas's strategy to gain a stranglehold of Scottish patronage and politics was to win control of the banking system. An opportunity to extend his influence came in 1776, when the banking firm of Mansfield and Ramsay, of which Miller was a partner, built up with considerable discretion a large stake in the Royal Bank of Scotland, whose governor was Sir Lawrence Dundas. The market in shares, usually dull, became active. There is some disagreement about Miller's role in the subsequent events. Some claim he acted directly as Dundas's agent, others state that he was only a reluctant ally. Whatever the truth, he was the go-between who persuaded Ramsay to sell all his shares in December 1776 to a consortium controlled by Henry Dundas and Henry Scott, third duke of Buccleuch, both directors of the Bank of Scotland. As a result Lawrence Dundas was overthrown, and Buccleuch replaced him as governor.

Miller's position as a leading banker in Edinburgh did not deter him from maintaining his interest in artillery. He claimed later that he was responsible for the development of the carronade gun manufactured by Carron & Co. There are considerable doubts about the veracity of this claim; but he was involved with his Yuille relations in fitting out the privateer *Spitfire*, a ship of 200 tons, with sixteen light 18-pounder carronades, in November 1778, to operate out of Liverpool. It was almost certainly Miller's influence as banker to Carron that secured the guns for the vessel. As this was the first sale of the new gun, Charles Gascoigne of the company warned Yuille to 'prevent any person whatsoever from taking a pattern, model, drawing or dimensions …' (Campbell, 90–91). The *Spitfire* quickly demonstrated the effectiveness of the carronade in action; there was concern when she was subsequently captured by the French. Orders flooded into the Carron Company for the new gun. Miller's interest appears to have been in the development of a much heavier gun. During 1781 he took a half share in an experimental 100-pound carronade that was tested in August at Greenbrae, in Dumfriesshire, in the presence of General Robert Melville. In the following year Miller was invoiced by Carron for a 132-pound weapon. Professor R. H. Campbell, the historian of the Carron Company, concluded 'Miller undoubtedly had an interest, but probably that of a wealthy amateur willing to encourage the work, but with little independent contribution to make to it' (Campbell, 102). The real credit belonged to Charles Gascoigne and Melville.

By 1785 Patrick Miller was a rich man, buying the Dalswinton estate, not far from Dumfries. He immediately embarked on a massive programme of improvements, draining the land on the banks of the River Nith and preventing seasonal flooding by re-directing its course. He is reputed to have introduced iron ploughs, bone meal, the cultivation of the swede, and the threshing mill into the county. He also planted extensive woodlands. In 1788 the old castle of the Comyns was demolished, and a handsome new classical house was constructed over the next fourteen years. He became an admirer and patron of the poet Robert Burns in 1786, making an anonymous donation of 10 guineas. In January of the following year he approached him with the offer of a tenancy at Dalswinton. Privately Burns was suspicious, commenting in a letter to John Ballantine that Miller was 'no judge of land', and that the offer might be 'an advantageous bargain that may ruin me' (Roy, 1.82–4). However, he happily wrote to Miller thanking him for his 'beneficence' (Roy, 1.86–7). On 3 March 1788 Burns commented to Robert Ainslie that Ellisland was a 'bargain' (Roy, 1.250–51); but told Miller on the same day that the 'lands are so exhausted that to enter to the full rent would throw me under a disheartening load of debt' (Roy, 1.249–50). He eventually accepted the tenancy of Ellisland in the summer of 1788. In the event Burns found farming harder work than he had bargained for and within a year he had doubts about the wisdom of his decision and in 1791 negotiated for the termination of the lease. This was made possible by the sale of the farm to a neighbouring landowner, John Morin of Loggin, suggesting that at this time Miller was financially overstretched. Relations between Miller and Burns deteriorated; but improved subsequently.

If Dalswinton was not enough to engage his interests,

Miller had become deeply engaged with the possibility of the mechanical propulsion of boats. With the help of James Taylor, tutor to his sons, Miller experimented in the summer of 1786 on the Forth with hand-cranked paddles mounted in a double-hulled (catamaran) shallow-draught vessel. In the summer of the following year he built a larger catamaran—some 60 feet long—to conduct more rigorous trials. This was followed by another vessel reputed to have cost £3000; an enormous sum for the period. He later used three hulls (a trimaran), and worked the paddles using capstans mounted on the deck. At first Taylor assumed these trials to be as much for amusement as for serious scientific research until in the following spring he discovered Miller had laid a wager with the crew of the Leith Custom House wherry. Four men including Taylor manned the paddles, which he 'found very severe exercise' (Woodcroft, 32–3). Taylor later claimed that he suggested to Miller that a steam engine might be more effective than muscle power, and introduced him to William Symington, who had just developed his own rotary engine. Miller, however, almost certainly knew Symington already as the Carron Company had supplied him with his machinery, and were impressed with his work at the Wanlockhead mines in Lanarkshire. However the contact was made, Symington came to see for himself, and agreed to design suitable engines. The results of these early investigations were published in the summer of 1787, when the possibility of steam propulsion was mentioned in print for the first time.

Symington agreed to co-operate in Miller's work, and the first trials of a steam-propelled vessel took place on Dalswinton Loch in October 1788, using a small engine made by an Edinburgh brassfounder. The 25 foot long, double-hulled boat—made of tinned iron plate—achieved a speed of 5 miles an hour. Encouraged, Symington took up the project with the Carron Company, who undertook in June 1789 to let him have as much money as he needed. He immediately started making a much larger set of engines, which dominated work at Carron during the autumn. They took much longer to build, and were much more costly than Symington estimated, exasperating Miller. When finally completed they were mounted in a much bigger hull, and trials, in the presence of the partners in the Carron Company, were carried out on the Forth and Clyde Canal on 2 and 3 December 1789. To Miller's annoyance the paddlewheels broke, and Miller, infuriated, and less than satisfied, consulted James Watt, who considered that too much power was being lost in Symington's engines because of friction. Having seen Watt's rotary engine, Miller was convinced and withdrew from further development, describing Symington as 'a vain extravagent fool' (*James Taylor Memorial* and original correspondence, 1857, p. 5). It may well be that he could no longer afford to fund any more prototypes even with the backing of the Carron Company. He did not entirely lose interest in ship construction, patenting in 1796 a design of a flat-bottomed vessel with a shallow draught and large carrying capacity.

Miller transferred much of his enthusiasm to Dalswinton, and his interest to the Bank of Scotland, where he became deputy governor on Henry Dundas's promotion to governor in 1790. Over the next three years together they virtually controlled the bank. From 1790 to 1796 his eldest son, Captain Patrick Miller, was MP for Dumfries, supporting Dundas, who was then home secretary. Although Patrick Miller served as deputy governor of the bank until his death, as he became older he spent more time in Dumfries, engaged in further estate improvements. He introduced fiorin grass from Ireland, which he described in a pamphlet published in 1810, and was so pleased with the result that he constructed Clonfeckle Tower (rudely nicknamed Miller's Worm by local people) to celebrate the event.

Miller married a Miss Lindsay (*d.* 1798) and the couple had three sons and two daughters. He entailed the Dalswinton estate to his eldest son, Captain Patrick Miller, on his son's marriage in 1804. Miller died at Dalswinton on 9 December 1815. After his death the terms of the entail were contested in the courts by the other children, reaching the House of Lords in 1818 before being returned for settlement to the court of session four years later. By this time his executors had sold up the Dalswinton estate for £140,000 to meet legal costs and the claims against his estate.

In eighteenth-century Scotland there were many men from gentry families who made fortunes in the rapidly expanding economy following the union of the parliaments and inspired by the ideas of the Enlightenment dabbled in the arts and sciences. Most purchased landed property, which they improved in the fashion of the time. Miller stood out, partly because of his close association with Dundas, and, more importantly, because of his connection with two significant innovations: the carronade and the steam boat.   MICHAEL S. MOSS

Sources D. D. Napier, *David Napier, engineer, 1790–1869: an autobiographical sketch with notes*, ed. D. Bell (1912), 90–93 [note by D. Bell entitled 'Patrick Miller'] · R. H. Campbell, *Carron Company* (1961) · S. G. Checkland, *Scottish banking: a history, 1695–1973* (1975) · A. Cameron, *Bank of Scotland, 1695–1995: a very singular institution* (1995) · Royal Bank of Scotland, Edinburgh · *The letters of Robert Burns*, ed. J. de Lancey Ferguson, 2nd edn, ed. G. Ross Roy, 2 vols. (1985) · J. A. Mackay, *R. B.: a biography of Robert Burns* (1992) · *The Engineer* (Nov 1893) · B. Woodcroft, *A sketch of the origins and progress of steam navigation from authentic documents* (1848) · M. Fry, *The Dundas despotism* (1992) · C. A. Malcolm, *The history of the British Linen Bank* (privately printed, Edinburgh, 1950) · W. Singer, *General view of the agriculture, state of the property and improvements in the county of Dumfries* (1812), 249–56 · *JHL* (1818), Li 5421822, Lv. 465

Archives Birm. CA, letters to James Watt jun.

Likenesses G. Chalmers, oils, *c.*1770, NPG [*see illus.*] · plaster medallion, 1789 (after J. Tassie), Scot. NPG · J. F. Skill, J. Gilbert, W. Walker and E. Walker, group portrait, pencil and wash (*Men of science living in 1807–8*), NPG

Miller, Philip (1691–1771), horticulturist and writer, was the most distinguished and influential British gardener of the eighteenth century. Little is known about his origins or early life, except that his father, a Scot, was a market gardener at Deptford, near London, and gave young Philip both a good education and training. Pehr Kalm, a student of Linnaeus at Uppsala, on his way from Sweden to America in 1748 visited Miller at Chelsea and from him, as well as from his friends, recorded useful information on his early career in his diary.

Miller established a nursery of ornamental trees and shrubs in St George's Fields, Southwark, and when the Society of Apothecaries needed a new gardener for their Physic Garden at Chelsea, Patrick Blair, a Scottish doctor and author of *Botanik Essays* (1720), wrote to Sir Hans Sloane, the garden's benefactor, recommending Philip Miller for the post as one 'to go forward with a curiosity and genious superior to most of his profession' (BL, Sloane MS 4046, fol. 168). Miller was appointed in 1722. In the same year a condition of Sloane's deed of conveyance of the garden to the apothecaries was that they present annually to the Royal Society fifty dried specimens grown in the garden in the previous year. This necessitated the continuous introduction of new plants, achieved by Miller's wide correspondence and through which horticulture benefited generally.

Miller married Mary Kennet of Southwark, whose sister, Susanne, in 1738 became wife of the distinguished botanical artist Georg Dionysius Ehret. Three Miller children, Mary, Philip, and Charles, were baptized at Chelsea Old Church in 1732, 1734, and 1739 respectively. Both boys worked in the garden before the younger Philip went to the East Indies, where he died; and in 1763 Charles became first curator of Cambridge Botanic Garden under Thomas Martyn, professor of botany. Charles held this post for seven years, before travelling to Sumatra and India; he died in London and was buried beside his father in Chelsea. Accommodation for the Society of Apothecaries' gardener was first provided in the upper storey of the substantial brick greenhouse, a building used to house evergreens (orange, lemon, and myrtle) in winter. By 1734 Philip Miller occupied a small house in Swan Walk, adjoining the garden. Notes in the garden committee minutes of the society show that he returned to the greenhouse in later life, and nearby accommodation in Chelsea was provided when his appointment terminated.

The garden committee gives Miller little praise in these records, but in 1750 an entry indicates satisfaction with his diligent correspondence resulting in acquisition of a very large number of rare plants and seeds from various parts of the world. Exchange with John Bartram of Philadelphia, a collector of plants in Pennsylvania, Virginia, Delaware, and elsewhere, was particularly fruitful. Kalm observed that 'the principal people in the land set a particular value on this man' (Kalm, 111). The fourth duke of Bedford employed him on a regular basis to visit Woburn and inspect gardens and hothouses and to prune the trees. These included many American conifers, and Miller approved introductions of alternative timber owing to the great quantity of oak needed by the Royal Navy. He also catalogued numerous American plants grown by the young Lord Petre at Thorndon, Essex. His advice was sought by the dukes of Richmond at Goodwood, where his suggestions for a flower border remain. The Society of Arts consulted Miller on agricultural matters, from winter feed for domestic animals in England to grapes suitable for the climate of South Carolina. On the latter Miller often consulted growers in both France and Italy, and he was a member of the Botanic Academy of Florence; from both countries he received seeds.

Miller's writing on the theory of gardening matched his expertise in its practice. As a member of a society of leading London gardeners, he helped to produce a quarto *Dictionary of Gardening* in 1724, and an illustrated *Catalogus plantarum* of trees and shrubs flourishing in the London area in 1730. In that year he drew up a list of medicinal plants grown in the garden, and forty years later he made a much longer one. In compliance with Sir Hans Sloane's original deed of conveyance to the Society of Apothecaries, Miller named the dried specimens of new species sent yearly to the Royal Society, of which he became a fellow in 1729. These were all listed in the society's *Philosophical Transactions* and Miller himself contributed papers, one on growing exotic seeds, including the coconut, in this country (*PTRS*, 135, 1728, 435–88). Miller was responsible for the botanical entries in Nathan Bailey's *Dictionarum Britannicum* (1830). When in Holland he studied the production of dye from *Rubia tinctorum* (madder) and, roused by its enormous price in Britain, produced a lengthy pamphlet in 1758 encouraging farmers to provide employment in winter and thus ease the poor rate. In such suggestions Miller's observance of economy was meticulous.

Miller's outstanding work was *The Gardeners Dictionary*, produced in eight editions (1732–68) during his lifetime. Besides horticulture, it covered agriculture, arboriculture, and wine making. He also produced an *Abridgement* in eight editions (1735–71) and a practical, cheaper, *Gardeners Kalendar* in fifteen editions (1731–69). He supervised the publication, in parts, from March 1755 to June 1760 of *The figures of plants, being the most beautiful, useful and uncommon plants described in The gardeners dictionary on 300 copper plates*. Executed by leading botanical artists, including Georg Ehret, and with practical text, these made two handsome folio volumes, commended at the time for being drawn from nature in the best state of flowering, and for including illustrations of fruit and seed as they ripened.

Two editions of Miller's works remain nomenclaturally important: *The Gardeners Dictionary Abridged* (4th edn, 1754) for generic names; *The Gardeners Dictionary* (8th edn, 1768) for binomial specific names. Up to the seventh edition (1756–9), Miller adopted the classification and generic nomenclature of J. P. de Tournefort's *Institutiones* (1700). Tournefort had genera of first rank defined by the form of flower alone: *Rosa*, *Viola*, and genera at second rank defined only by vegetative characters, such as *Pinus*, *Abies*, and *Larix*. Linnaeus accepted only genera of Tournefort's first rank: he rejected the second rank genera by including them within first rank genera in 1753, the internationally accepted starting point for modern botanical nomenclature. Miller's conservatism in retaining in 1754 Tournefort's second rank genera, suppressed by Linnaeus nomenclaturally, re-established these genera and he is accordingly cited as the authority for *Abies*, *Larix* and suchlike. Moreover, Linnaeus had changed many generic names to make them shorter and easier to remember, altering *Anapodophyllum* to *Podophyllum*, for example. Miller disagreed with this in 1752, 'being unwilling to introduce any new Names, where the old established names were suitable, lest, by this, he should rather puzzle, than interest, the Lovers of Gardens' (Miller, iv–v). He was likewise reluctant to accept Linnaean two-word names for species but, at the age of seventy-seven, he at last used them in the eighth edition of *The Gardeners Dictionary* (published in 1768) and gave names of his own to species not recorded by Linnaeus. The several hundred new botanical names published there by Miller gave this monumental eighth edition lasting botanical importance (Stearn).

Miller was judged to be 'a benefactor to mankind: medicine, botany, agriculture and manufactures are all indebted to him' (Rogers, 342). Under his charge for almost half a century, the Chelsea Physic Garden of the Society of Apothecaries of London came to excel above all others in Europe, the number of its plants increasing fivefold in that time. Visitors from abroad apparently referred to him as 'Hortulanorum Princeps' (*DNB*).

Unfortunately, by 1769 relations between Miller, the garden committee, and the Court of Apothecaries had become strained and are fully recorded in the minute books. The main altercations were generally over Miller's assumed authority (though his terms of appointment had never been clearly defined), and in particular his obstructive stand over marking plants with index sticks. However, his employers' policy of *laissez-faire* had resulted in an increase of the garden's prestige, through Miller's exceptional achievement not only as the gardener but also as an acclaimed author, and he did warrant consideration. Miller agreed to resign on 29 November 1770 and was granted a pension of £60, much deserved.

Miller died in Chelsea on 18 December 1771; his grave in the churchyard of Chelsea Old Church remained unmarked until an obelisk was erected by fellows of the Linnean and Horticultural societies in 1810. There is no recognized likeness of Miller: one purported to be his in a French translation of *The Gardeners Dictionary* (Paris, 1785) is now considered to be of John Miller (Johann S. Müller), a German-born botanical artist who contributed illustrations to Miller's *The Figures of Plants*. However, Thomas Martyn, who knew Miller well, did not query the likeness in his preface to his own compilation, *The Gardener's and Botanist's Dictionary*, which he published under Miller's name in four volumes (1803–7), though he was critical of the unlikely dress; possibly both Millers had similar chubby features. In this preface Martyn commended Miller's attitude of 'more attention to integrity and to honest fame than to any pecuniary advantage', countering adverse criticism in this respect from contemporaries, who may have been motivated by jealousy. The Chelsea memorial records for posterity Miller's great achievements as curator at the Chelsea Physic Garden and author of *The Gardeners Dictionary*, ensuring him a prominent place in the history of gardening.

HAZEL LE ROUGETEL

Sources W. T. Stearn, 'Miller's "Gardeners' dictionary"', *Journal of the Society of the Bibliography of Natural History*, 7 (1974–6), 125–41 • H. Le Rougetel, *The Chelsea gardener, Philip Miller, 1691–1771* (1990) • H. Le Rougetel, 'Philip Miller / John Bartram botanical exchange', *Garden History*, 14/1 (1986), 32–9 • R. Pulteney, *Historical and biographical sketches of the progress of botany in England*, 2 vols. (1790) • J. Rogers, *The vegetable cultivator* (1839) • P. Kalm, *Kalm's account of his visit to England on his way to America in 1748*, trans. J. Lucas (1892) • F. D. Drewitt, *The romance of the apothecaries' garden at Chelsea* (1922) • H. Field, *Memoirs of the botanic garden at Chelsea belonging to the Society of Apothecaries of London*, rev. R. H. Semple (1878) • G. Meynell, 'Philip Miller's resignation from the Chelsea Physic Garden', *Archives of Natural History*, 14 (1987), 77–84 • P. Miller, preface, *The gardeners dictionary*, 6th edn (1752), iv–v • BL, Sloane MS 4646, fol. 168 • Society of Apothecaries' Garden, committee minutes, GL, MS 9223, 1–4 • Essex RO, T/A 5671 [microfilm] • Goodwood estate office, West Sussex, Goodwood MS 134 • T. Martyn, preface, in P. Miller, *The gardener's and botanist's dictionary*, rev. T. Martyn, 2 vols. in 4 (1803–7) • *DNB*

Archives MHS Oxf., corresp. • Royal Horticultural Society, London, papers | Essex RO, Chelmsford, catalogue of the plants in Lord Petre's garden at Thorndon Hall • Goodwood estate office, West Sussex, Goodwood MSS • LMA, Chelsea parish records • RSA, manufactures and commerce, guard books 4 and 5 • Woburn House, London, Woburn MS

Wealth at death 'no accrued wealth': Martyn, preface in Miller, *Gardener's and botanist's dictionary*

Miller, Ralph Willett (1762–1799), naval officer, was born on 24 January 1762 in New York, the son of a loyalist who later lost all his property in the War of American Independence. Willett was his mother's maiden name. He had two sisters, Martha and Mary, and as the only son he was sent to England to be educated at the Royal Naval Academy in Portsmouth. He went to sea in 1778, serving in the *Ardent* under James Gambier, then a rear-admiral of the blue and subsequently a vice-admiral of the red.

Miller's naval life was short, energetic, and much connected with fire. The *Ardent* took part in the War of American Independence, and it is said that he was 'in all the actions fought by Admirals Barrington, Rodney, Hood, and Graves, and was three times wounded' (Nicolas, 465). He was promoted lieutenant by Rodney on 25 May 1781 and transferred to the *Terrible*, which took part in the disappointing action off Cape Henry on 5 September. The ship was so badly damaged that she had to be abandoned and burnt. Miller returned to England and was appointed to the *Fortitude* on 20 December 1782; it may have been at this time that he married Anne Witchell (always known as Nancy), daughter of George Witchell, his former headmaster at the Royal Academy. The Millers had two daughters, Charlotte Sophia (*b.* 1791) and Maria Elizabeth (*b.* 1792).

Young officers were taught to sketch—a valuable skill when surveying or recording a strange or hostile coastline—and Miller would send such sketches to his wife. He also wrote long vivid letters home, meticulously describing the actions in which he took part: it has been said that if his letter on the battle of the Nile (1–2 August 1798) were the only surviving account, all the battle's main events would be accurately known.

When war against France began in 1793 Miller was in the *Windsor Castle* and was present at the evacuation of

Toulon (18 December), occupied since 27 August. Under the personal command of Captain Sir Sidney Smith, whom he described as 'a glorious fellow, cool, vigilant, and intrepid, humane, with a mind whose compass took objects in every point of view at once' (*Miller Papers*, 6), he was ordered to commit as much destruction as possible. During the operation he twice came close to drowning, but left with

> the Arsenal seriously in flames in many different parts, ten Sail of the Line, a heaving-down vessel and two frigates completely on fire, and four others so situated it was hardly possible they could escape, besides two blown up. (ibid.)

After being transferred into the *Victory* as third lieutenant, Miller was actively employed in the boats and on shore at the reductions of San Fiorenzo, Bastia, and Calvi where he first met Nelson. Having volunteered to take a fireship (the frigate *Poulette*, captured at Toulon) in among a moored French squadron, he was promoted commander on 1 July 1794, but he was frustrated in five attempts by light and contrary winds. In 1795 he was dismayed to hear his name was on a confidential list of officers not recommended for promotion. However, a request for intercession and the arrival of a new commander-in-chief, Admiral Sir John Jervis (later earl of St Vincent), changed his prospects for the better: on 12 January 1796 he was made post captain, and he commanded firstly the *Mignonne* and then the *Unité*, both frigates, taking the latter into the Adriatic to bolster Austrian resistance to the French. Captain Jahleel Brenton described him as 'a man of rare talents and amiable manners'; Nelson called him 'in my opinion a most exceeding good officer and worthy man', and (twice) 'the only truly virtuous man I ever knew' (Kennedy, *Nelson*, 40–41). Jervis wrote to the first sea lord saying Miller fully met all the positive descriptions, having 'raised the minds of the people at Trieste from abject despair to perfect confidence' (ibid., 41).

Miller's reputation was now such that in August 1796 Commodore Nelson selected him as his flag captain; he thus commanded the *Captain* in the battle of Cape St Vincent (14 February 1797). In May the two officers moved to the *Theseus*, the ship in which Miller met his premature death two years later. When they took her over she was a notoriously mutinous vessel, yet their leadership was so eminently fair and humane that before the middle of June the entire ship's company had pledged them their personal devotion.

The *Theseus* remained in command of the inshore squadron off Cadiz through June; then on 20 July came the disastrous attack on Santa Cruz de Tenerife, in which Nelson lost his right arm. Miller wrote long letters on both these actions to his 'dear, dear Girl', revealing his penchant for deceptive tactics—in the instance of Tenerife, having a dummy 18-pounder cannon made to give a greater appearance of strength to the boat in which he led the small-arms men ashore. 'When finished it could not be known from a real gun, [even from as close as] a pistol's shot distance' (*Miller Papers*, 22).

Miller and the *Theseus* returned to the blockade of Cadiz,

and in 1798 joined the recovered Nelson in the Mediterranean, playing a highly effective part in the battle of the Nile. His liking for disguise showed again: he had the outsides of hammocks (defensively placed as usual in netting on the upper deck) painted with gun-ports, giving the impression of a three-decker warship. Towards the end of the battle he was outraged by a notable breach of the etiquette of war: an enemy captain, having surrendered, set his ship—the frigate *Artemise*—on fire before it could be claimed as a prize. Miller, disgusted, wrote to his wife, 'This dishonourable action is not out of character for a modern Frenchman: the devil is beyond blackening' (Lavery, 207).

After the Nile, where he had been wounded in the face (Nicolas, 466), Miller accompanied Captain Sir James Saumarez and others to Gibraltar with the prizes, and in December 1798, at the particular request of Sir Sidney Smith, he was sent to the Levant, joining Smith in operations against the stranded French army on the Egyptian and Syrian coasts.

On 13 May 1799, as the prolonged and heroic defence of the besieged city of Acre was coming to its successful end, Smith received information that a small French squadron was approaching from the south. The *Theseus* was sent to intercept, and the following day was lying at anchor off Caesarea. The ship was carrying on deck a large quantity of unspent enemy shells, collected in order to be 'sent back to the enemy better prepared' (Nicolas, 466). One of these, hit by a seaman's hammer, exploded and set off a chain reaction. Twenty-six men were killed, nearly fifty more were wounded, much of the vessel's upperworks were wrecked, and a fire was started. Miller was among the dead.

By his will Miller divided his estate between 'my most tenderly beloved wife', 'the dear first born daughter of our mutual love' and 'her no less Beloved sister'. He added a most touching note to his widow:

> For that affectionate return of my love, that exquisite tenderness which rendered the part of my life spent in her society more uniformly delightful than is generally supposed possible in this world; I now solemnly render her the warmest thanks of a heart beating with every good wish for her, and which ventures to look forward with humble hope, as the greatest imaginable happiness to the meeting her in that world where bliss eternal reigns. (*Miller Papers*, 34)

Later his sister Mrs Martha Willett Dalrymple sent a copy to their uncle, writing, 'What a man he was! What a memento of love and confidence. The copying of it has been a painful task' (*Miller Papers*, 35).

The government granted annual pensions of £100 for life to his widow, and £25 each to his daughters until such time as they should marry. His loss was deeply lamented by his colleagues, who jointly subscribed the sum of £500 for a memorial sculpted by Flaxman and erected in St Paul's Cathedral; Nelson said that if subscriptions were not forthcoming he would pay the whole himself. Liaising with Flaxman on the design, Captain Edward Berry said,

'Of course our aim *must be* simplicity. Truth needs no ornaments: Miller requires none, himself was all' (Kennedy, *Nelson*, 220).   STEPHEN HOWARTH

Sources DNB · *The Miller papers*, ed. K. Buckland and S. Howarth (1990) · L. Kennedy, 'Introduction', in *The Miller papers*, ed. K. Buckland and S. Howarth (1990) · L. Kennedy, *Nelson and his captains* (1976) · D. Syrett and R. L. DiNardo, *The commissioned sea officers of the Royal Navy, 1660–1815*, rev. edn, Occasional Publications of the Navy RS, 1 (1994) · C. White, *1797: Nelson's year of destiny* (1998) · *Naval Chronicle*, 3rd edn, 2 (1799), 580–83 · *Naval Chronicle*, 3rd edn, 4 (1801), 469–70nn. · B. Lavery, *Nelson and the Nile: the naval war against Bonaparte, 1798* (1998) · T. Pocock, *A thirst for glory: the life of Admiral Sir Sidney Smith* (1996) · *The dispatches and letters of Vice-Admiral Lord Viscount Nelson*, ed. N. H. Nicolas, 7 vols. (1844–6), vol. 2

Likenesses engraving, *c.*1798, Royal Naval Museum, Portsmouth · W. Bromley, J. Landseer & Leney, line engraving, pubd 1803 (after *Victors of the Nile* by R. Smirke), BM, NPG · Worthington & Parker, line engraving, pubd 1803 (after *Commemoration of the 14th February 1797; Naval victories* by R. Smirke), BM, NPG · J. Flaxman, medallion on portrait, St Paul's Cathedral, London

Miller, Ruby Laura Rose (1889–1976), actress, was born on 14 July 1889 at 64 Water Lane, Brixton, London, the daughter of Arthur Miller, a commercial traveller in the leather trade, and his wife, Augusta Catherine Leon. She was educated in London and at a convent in Amiens. Her first marriage, to Lieutenant Phillip Samson, ended when he was killed in action in 1918. Her second marriage in 1929, to her long-time sweetheart, the composer, conductor, and concert pianist Max Darewski, ended with his early death some five months later.

Miller later claimed that her first professional stage appearance was in J. T. Tanner's musical play *The Orchid* (music by I. Caryll and L. Monckton) alongside Gertie Millar and George Grossmith jun., at the Gaiety Theatre in 1903 at the age of thirteen, though she told those auditioning her that she was eighteen. When her parents found out about her lie some three months later, George Edwardes, the musical comedy impresario who produced the show, withdrew her from the production and told her to come back when she was eighteen. Other sources suggest that her début was in 1906 as a dancer in *Nero* by Stephen Philips at His Majesty's Theatre, which would have been after her time at the Academy of Dramatic Art. Miller spent a number of years as a Gaiety girl under the management of George Edwardes, but much of her early work was with Herbert Tree's company, taking small parts and understudying in Shakespearian and costume dramas. She also toured with Herbert Tree in Berlin in 1907.

At nineteen Miller returned to the Gaiety and understudied both Gladys Cooper and Gertie Millar in J. T. Tanner's *Our Miss Gibbs* (music again by Caryll and Monckton). The Gaiety girls were the toast of Edwardian London, courting the many aristocrats who frequented the shows. They led fashion trends and often ended up marrying into the aristocracy. Miller's time as a Gaiety girl provided the basis for one of the most long-lasting myths about her career—that a Russian duke was so enamoured of her that he drank champagne out of her shoe; when she noted that the shoe was now ruined, he ordered numerous pairs of new shoes to be delivered to her rooms the next day. Such

Ruby Laura Rose Miller (1889–1976), by Bassano, 1911

romantic stories abound in her autobiographical volumes, *Believe me or not* (1934) and *Champagne from my Slipper* (1962). However, Miller was more interested in her professional career than in marrying into the social élite. In 1910 she went to work with Charles Hawtrey at His Majesty's Theatre and in 1913 she was given a cameo role in the touring and London production of a farce, *Oh! I Say!* by S. Blowe and D. Hoare. She then went on to one of her most famous roles, as Maimie Scott in the 1915 farce, *A Little Bit of Fluff* by W. W. Ellis, in which she apparently shocked a generation by revealing glimpses of her knee; she played the role for a year.

Miller also appeared in many early films, among them Bertie Samuelson's *Little Women and Good Wives* and *The Edge of Beyond* (1919), and Maurice Elvey's *The Mystery of Bernard Brown*. She later produced a stage adaptation of *The Edge of beyond* (1921) which she had co-written with with Roy Horniman. (Other co-authorships included her *Big Ben* with Evadne Price in 1939.) At this point she went into management as well as playing the lead in the show. The mid-1920s took Miller to America in the hope of an extended contract with Cecil B. De Mille, but she was usurped by Pola Negri, also known for her portrayal of what Miller called 'lurid vamp parts'. On her return to England, Miller performed in the pre-London run of Arnold Ridley's long-running *The Ghost Train* (1925) alongside a very young Laurence Olivier. During the 1930s and 1940s Miller worked on more British films, including *Power of Attorney* (1942), *Flying Fortress* (1942), and *The Hundred Pound Widow* (1943), and during the Second World War she took part in concerts for the troops. In the 1950s she did a lot of radio and television work, also giving national and international lecture tours in which she talked about her days as a Gaiety girl and about her professional acquaintance with the leading performers of a bygone age, such as Marie Lloyd, Evelyn Laye, and Gladys Cooper. It was on these tours that she used to make such statements as, 'Women have lost the power to excite romance and mystery', or 'Remember, girls, men are the hunters. Don't try to compete with them'. Miller came from an age of heightened femininity, but chose to work rather than get remarried in the early 1920s. She sought a career which marked her out as a modern, liberated woman during an age when marriage and family was the destiny for most women.

Ruby Miller died on 2 April 1976 at 8 Cawley Road, Chichester, Sussex.   MAGGIE B. GALE

Sources obituary cuttings file, Theatre Museum, London · obituary file, Mander and Mitchenson Theatre Collection, London · R. Miller, *Champagne from my slipper* (1962) · b. cert. · d. cert.
Archives Theatre Museum, London, MS autobiography, ephemera, and papers
Likenesses Bassano, photograph, 1911, NPG [*see illus.*] · Sasha, photograph, 1928, Hult. Arch. · photograph, 1928, Hult. Arch. · Sasha, photograph, 1931 (with Gerald Pring), Hult. Arch. · Sasha, photograph, 1933, Hult. Arch. · photograph, 1948 (with Vivien Leigh and Kieron Moore), Hult. Arch.

Miller, Sanderson (1716–1780), architect, was born at Radway Grange, Warwickshire, the son of Sanderson Miller (d. 1737), a wealthy wool merchant of Banbury, and his wife, Maria, daughter of the Revd John Welchman. For two or three years from 1734 he was an undergraduate at St Mary Hall, Oxford, where, under the influence of the principal of the college, the Jacobite Dr William King, he developed an interest in antiquarianism and a romantic attitude to the English past. Then, on the death of his father in 1737, he succeeded at the age of twenty-one to the Radway estate, which the latter had bought in 1712, and to the life of a cultured country gentleman.

A few years later, between 1743 and 1747, Miller carried out some improvements to his property, partly remodelling the modest Elizabethan house in the Gothic style and building a picturesque thatched cottage and an octagonal Gothic tower on the nearby escarpment of Edgehill: these works at once established Miller as an important figure in the early history of the Gothic revival. Advancing beyond the purely decorative rococo Gothic of William Kent, his designs reflected both the beginnings of a more scholarly approach to Gothic detail and the sentimental appeal of medieval buildings. The tower at Radway was based on the medieval Guy's tower at Warwick Castle, but it was also intended to underline the historical and political associations of the place: standing on the spot where King Charles I is supposed to have raised his standard before the battle of Edgehill, it was designed to house a statue of the British hero Caractacus and was decorated with emblems of the Saxon heptarchy, and its ceremonial opening took place on the anniversary of the death of Oliver Cromwell.

The impact of the Radway buildings was immediate, and from the mid-1740s onward Miller was in much demand among a wide circle of aristocratic friends and acquaintances for architectural advice and designs. The period of this activity was relatively short, and virtually came to an end about 1760, but during it he produced a significant body of work both in his own region of Warwickshire and Oxfordshire and further afield as well. The two most ambitious of these projects, the shire hall in Warwick (1754–8) and Hagley Hall, Worcestershire (1754–60), are in a competent if conventional classical manner, the latter being based on the Palladian Houghton Hall, Norfolk. However, most of his work continued to be in the Gothic style with which he had made his reputation. His first proposals for Hagley were Gothic, while other projects included some designs for Arbury Hall, Warwickshire (c.1750–52), one of the best Gothic houses of the mid-eighteenth century, and his well-known work at Lacock Abbey, Wiltshire (1754–5). But Miller's most characteristic products were his half-ruined mock castles—at Hagley (1747–8), Wimpole Hall, Cambridgeshire (designed 1749–51; built 1772), and Ingestre Hall, Staffordshire (c.1750; dem.)—which, developing the theme of the Radway tower, constituted pictorial embodiments of historical memory. Of the Hagley castle, even Horace Walpole—who as a fellow pioneer in the same field was in general highly critical of Miller's performances—was obliged to concede, in an oft-quoted aphorism, that it had 'the true rust of the Barons' wars' (H. Walpole, *Correspondence*, ed. W. S. Lewis, 35, 1973, 148).

Miller's excursions into architecture were in essence a facet of his active social life—which through his patron at Hagley, George, first Baron Lyttelton, included contact with the interlocking family 'cousinage' of the Lytteltons, Pitts, and Grenvilles. Like other amateur architects he made use of the assistance of professionals. His designs for Hagley Hall were drawn out by the architect John Sanderson, the Warwick shire hall was executed by the well-known mason–architects William and David Hiorne, who described themselves as its 'surveyors' as well as its 'builders', and he had as his regular assistant a mason called William Hitchcox. This regime, however, did not always guarantee a satisfactory result, as in the case of the tower he added to Wroxton church, Oxfordshire (1747–8), the top stage of which rapidly collapsed—as Walpole pointedly reported: 'Mr. Miller … unluckily once in this life happened to think rather of beauty than of the water-tables, and so it fell down the first winter' (H. Walpole, *Correspondence*, ed. W. S. Lewis, 35, 1973, 74)—but that does not seem to have affected his popularity.

In 1746 Miller married Susanna, daughter of Edward Trotman, gentleman, of Shelswell, Oxfordshire; they had two sons and four daughters. In his later years he suffered from occasional bouts of insanity. He died on 23 April 1780 and was buried at Radway church.   PETER LEACH

Sources Colvin, *Archs.* · L. Dickins and M. Stanton, *An eighteenth century correspondence being the letters … to Sanderson Miller* (1910) · A. C. Wood and W. Hawkes, *Sanderson Miller of Radway* (1969) · W. Hawkes, 'The Gothic architectural work of Sanderson Miller', *A gothick symposium*, Georgian Group (1983)

Archives Warks. CRO, corresp., diaries, etc.

Miller, Sir Thomas, first baronet, Lord Glenlee (1717–1789), judge and politician, was baptized in Glasgow on 3 November 1717, which was possibly also the day of his birth, the second son of William Miller (d. 1753) of Glenlee, Kirkcudbrightshire, and of Barskimming, Ayrshire, writer to the signet, and his wife, Janet, eldest daughter of Thomas Hamilton of Shield Hall. Patrick *Miller (1731–1815), banker and inventor, was his younger brother. He matriculated (November 1730) at Glasgow University, where he acquired a love of Greek and Latin classical texts, but did not graduate. He studied law at Edinburgh, and on 21 February 1742 was admitted a member of the Faculty of Advocates. Miller enjoyed the patronage of the earl of Selkirk, who recommended him for the post of sheriff-depute for Kirkcudbrightshire, on the grounds of ability and of his loyalty to the king and to the whig cause. He secured the appointment in 1748, and was also elected joint town clerk of the city of Glasgow. In 1755 he resigned the former office and became solicitor of the excise in Scotland. He rose to be made solicitor-general on 17 March 1759, and within a year was appointed lord advocate in succession to Robert Dundas the younger of Arniston.

Miller's first marriage, which took place on 16 April 1752, was to Margaret (d. 1767), eldest daughter of John Murdoch, provost of Glasgow; they had an only son, Sir William *Miller (1755–1846), also a judge, and a daughter, Jessie, who married John Dunlop. On 7 June 1768 he married Anne, daughter of John Lockhart of Castlehill, Lanarkshire; there were no children of this second marriage. His second wife died at Clifton on 12 January 1817.

At the general election of April 1761 Miller was returned to parliament for the Dumfries burghs. He opposed with some force the bill to repeal the American Stamp Act, creating the exceptional situation whereby as lord advocate he was confronting the cabinet on a major issue. He was elected rector of Glasgow University in November 1762, and was made lord justice clerk on 14 June 1766, taking the title Lord Barskimming, which he afterwards changed to that of Lord Glenlee. As lord advocate, Miller ruled on the right to appeal, raised in the case of the killing in 1765 of Lieutenant Thomas Ogilvie by his wife Katherine Nairne together with her brother-in-law Patrick Ogilvie. Miller contributed to Scots criminal law by clarifying the distinction between culpable homicide and murder and, in this particular case, finding no grounds for an appeal from the court of judiciary to the House of Lords.

Miller enjoyed a high reputation as a lawyer, and was an industrious and conscientious judge. With five other advocates he compiled *Decisions of the court of session from the beginning of February 1752 to the end of the year 1756* (1760). In 1781, suffering from consumption, he was permitted to go abroad, and he returned from a tour of France and Italy with a new lease of life. In 1783 he was one of the lawyers elected fellow of the new Royal Society of Edinburgh. Giving an account of his contribution to the society, the philosopher David Hume noted that Miller had chaired its first meeting and served as vice-president. Miller again succeeded Robert Dundas, this time as lord president of the college of justice on 15 January 1788. He was created a baronet on 3 March the same year. But his health was again failing, and he died at Barskimming on 27 September 1789, and was buried in the family vault at Stair, Ayrshire.   G. F. R. BARKER, rev. ANITA McCONNELL

Sources J. Foster, *Members of parliament, Scotland … 1357–1882*, 2nd edn (privately printed, London, 1882), 251 · *Scotland and Scotsmen in the eighteenth century: from the MSS of John Ramsay, esq., of Ochtertyre*, ed. A. Allardyce, 1 (1888), 342–50 · G. W. T. Omond, *The lord advocates of Scotland from the close of the fifteenth century to the passing of the Reform Bill*, 2 (1883), 68–72 · D. Hume, 'Account of the Right Honorable Sir Thomas Miller of Glenlee, bart., lord provost of the court of session, and FRS Edin.', *Transactions of the Royal Society of Edinburgh*, 2/1 (1790), 63–75 · N. Campbell and R. M. S. Smellie, *The Royal Society of Edinburgh, 1783–1983* (1983), 5, 125 · [F. J. Grant], *A history of the Society of Writers to Her Majesty's Signet* (1890), 145 · *Scots Magazine*, 10 (1748), 155, 207 · *Scots Magazine*, 14 (1752), 213 · *Scots Magazine*, 17 (1755), 269 · *Scots Magazine*, 51 (1789), 467 · IGI

Likenesses D. Blackmore, line engraving (after J. Reynolds), NPG; repro. in *Edinburgh Magazine* (1793) · James Tassie, paste medallion, Scot. NPG

Miller, Thomas (1731–1804), bookseller and antiquary, was born at Norwich on 14 August 1731, and was baptized on 5 September in St Peter Mancroft Church, the elder son of Thomas Miller (d. 1764) and his first wife, Elizabeth Bacon (d. 1756); his brother was Edward *Miller, the musician and historian of Doncaster. There were five sisters. His father, of Yorkshire origins, paved the city of Norwich, much of Bury St Edmunds, and Bungay after the great fire there in 1688. Thomas junior was apprenticed to a Norwich grocer, and spent a brief time in Swaffham, where he met Ann (1731/2–1763), daughter of Edward and Isabella Scarlett of Necton. They were married at Swaffham church on 12 July 1756. His father purchased him a house large enough to live and trade from at the back of the Market Place in Bungay, where fondness for reading led him to combine bookselling with grocery. His stock was large enough to attract custom from all over England.

For the next twenty years Miller was a prominent member of the Bungay Gentlemen's Club, where in 1760 he was paid 7s. 'for the first book of his [own] binding' (Mann, 167). His wife died on 9 October 1763 after giving birth to their only daughter, who did not long survive her mother. On 28 May 1764 at Holy Trinity Church, Bungay, he married Sarah (known as Sally; 1741–1773), daughter of William Kingsbury, maltster, and his wife, Sarah, of Waveney House, Bungay, with whom he had one son, William Richard Beckford *Miller (1769–1844), and three daughters. At the club Miller paid the customary 5s. on his marriage and presented a bottle of wine when their first child, a daughter, was born.

Sally Miller died on 14 May 1773. An advertisement which appeared that year shows that Miller was now an auctioneer with a greatly expanded business: men's clothing, hats and caps, haberdashery, furniture and carpets, china and glass, silver, buttery and ironmongery, spirits, wallcoverings, and, of course, grocery, books, and stationery. In the same year, he published a reissue of Thomas Bardwell's *The Practice of Painting* and a collection of Norwich sermons; he published a further collection in 1776.

Thomas Miller (1731–1804), by Edward Scriven (after Henry Edridge)

Noted for his eccentricity, he never stooped to curry favour, and was a noted collector in his own right of books, engraved portraits, and coins, of which collections he published catalogues in 1782 and 1790. His promised history of Suffolk proceeded no further than the printed prospectus. He had an almost complete series of Roman and English silver and brass coins. In 1795, when it was fashionable for provincial tradesmen to issue halfpenny tokens, he had finely engraved dies cast, but they failed after about twenty pieces had been struck off. It appealed to the antiquary in Miller to allow his halfpennies to remain rare. The obverse bears a strong profile likeness of Miller, the reverse a rayed beehive above books and manuscripts and laurel branches. He wrote articles on political subjects for the *Ipswich Journal* and *Norfolk Chronicle*, and as churchwarden of St Mary's in 1787 he used the accounts to record his thoughts on education and his pride that £26 had been raised in 1785 to found a Sunday school for 100 children. In 1799 he became quite blind, but continued in business until his death at Bungay on 25 June 1804. He was buried two days later in St Mary's Church beside his wives, where a mural monument was placed in the north aisle.

J. M. BLATCHLY

Sources E. Mann, *Old Bungay* (1934) · J. Atkins, *Eighteenth-century tokens* (1892) · *IGI* · D. E. Davy, 'MS collections for Suffolk Wangford Hundred', BL, Add. MS 19111 · *ESTC* · will, Suffolk RO, Ipswich, IC/AAI/224/48 · mural monument, Suffolk, Bungay, St Mary's · Norfolk RO, NCC Will, 47 Bird 1763

Likenesses Miller halfpenny token, 1795, repro. in Atkins, *Eighteenth-century tokens* · E. Scriven, stipple (after miniature by H. Edridge), BM, NPG [*see illus.*]

Wealth at death £600–£1000; incl. houses, shop, public houses: will, Suffolk RO, Ipswich, IC/AA1/224/48

Miller, Thomas (1807–1874), poet and writer, known as the Basket Maker, was born on 31 August 1807 in Sailor's Alley, Gainsborough, Lincolnshire, the son of George Miller, a wharf manager. In 1810 his father disappeared while on a visit to London, leaving Thomas to be brought up by his mother, who sewed sacks for a living, and a stepfather, who taught him basket making. Thomas attended the White Hart Charity School, and with his friend and neighbour Thomas Cooper, the future Chartist poet, voraciously read through the tattered library in the shop of a Mrs Trevor. Miller also found books in his grandfather's farm, where he spent his summers, socializing with Gypsies and gaining the love of country life that underlies his best writing.

Miller left school aged nine and became an itinerant basket maker before settling in Nottingham, where, on 22 September 1827, he married Mary Anne Potter (*d.* 1851). After working for a Mr Watts, he began business on his own, selling baskets and reciting poetry in Nottingham market. He became an active member of the Foresters, a local literary society presided over by Spencer T. Hall, and encouraged by Thomas Bailey in 1832 published *Songs of the Sea Nymphs*, dedicated to the countess of Blessington.

Perhaps prompted by favourable reviews, in 1835 Miller moved to London, where he lodged at 33 Elliott's Row, Southwark. He was noticed, impoverished, selling baskets in Whitechapel, and received a small grant from the Royal Literary Fund. In that year he sent poems in an ornate basket to the countess of Blessington, who invited him to her soirées at Gore House, showing him off as a working-class poet. Here he met, among others, Disraeli and Bulwer Lytton, and moved onto the fringes of literary London. He contributed poems to the annual *Friendship's Offering* in 1838 and 1839, and articles for *The Athenaeum*, the *Literary Gazette*, and other periodicals. Two volumes, *A Day in the Woods* (1836) and *Beauties of the Country* (1837), were well received, and Henry Colburn commissioned three historical novels, *Royston Gower* (1838), *Fair Rosamond* (1839), and *Lady Jane Grey* (1840). In 1841 Samuel Rogers gave Miller £300 to recover his copyrights and set himself up as publisher, stationer, and bookseller at 9 Newgate Street. Miller there wrote *Gideon Giles the Roper* (1842) and *Godfrey Malvern* (1843), novels that made his name.

But Miller's *Godfrey Malvern* contains, thinly disguised, his bitter resentment at the countess of Blessington's hollow patronage. Publishers and editors exploited Miller's inexperience, paying him a moiety of rates paid to middle-class authors. He tried to support a wife and four children—Henry, George, Emma, and Ellen—with a shop in an area more notable for butchers than for book buyers. A move to 17 Ludgate Hill only compounded disaster. In 1845 bailiffs stripped him of everything but a bed and chair, and only £20 from the Royal Literary Fund saved the family from the workhouse. In 1851, prostrated by the sudden death of his beloved wife, and unable to write, he was again rescued from destitution by the fund. A public petition, although backed by Bulwer Lytton, failed to gain him a public pension. Disraeli secured him £100 from the Royal Bounty Fund in 1874 but that year Miller died of a stroke on 5 October, at 23 New Street, Kensington, leaving one son and two spinster daughters.

Although much of his life was a struggle against poverty, fatigue, and, later, illness and spells of blindness, Miller produced more than any other Victorian working-class author, publishing over forty-five titles besides numerous contributions to periodicals. He showed great versatility. *Rural Sketches* (1839) and *Our Old Town* (1847) are vivid accounts of his childhood Lincolnshire; his continuation of G. W. M. Reynolds's *The Mysteries of London* (volume 5, 1949) dramatized urban crime. His miscellaneous writing includes *A History of the Anglo-Saxons* (1856), books for boys, and collections of poems and essays.

Miller's best writing of the countryside has genuine charm, and though non-political does record its sufferings. Miller attracted a large popular readership, and Spencer T. Hall records meeting a shepherd whose eyes were opened to rural beauty by *Gideon Giles* (Hall, 321–2). Although Miller's life was a tragic example of aspirations crushed by Victorian Grub Street, he merits a minor but significant place in literary history. LOUIS JAMES

Sources N. Cross, ed., *Archives of the Royal Literary Fund: 1790–1918* (1984), file 816 [microfilm] · T. Miller, *Rural sketches* (1839), 1–24, 18–22, 357 · T. Cooper, *The life of Thomas Cooper, written by himself*, [new edn] (1872) · S. T. Hall, *Biographical sketches of remarkable people* (1873), 168, 201–10, 321–2 · O. Ashton and S. Roberts, *The Victorian working-class writer* (1999) · N. Cross, *The common writer: life in nineteenth-century Grub Street* (1985) · H. Vizetelly, *Glances back through seventy years* (1893), vol. 1, pp. 308–9 · W. Wylie, *Old and new Nottingham* (1883), 207–9 · G. A. Sala, *Life and adventures* (1891), vol. 1, p. 226 · IGI
Archives Royal Literary Fund, London, archives · Wigan Archives Service, diary | BL, letters to Royal Literary Fund, loan 96
Wealth at death died in debt?

Miller, Walter Richard Samuel (1872–1952), missionary, was born on 22 March 1872 at Brook Hill, Honiton, Devon, the only son in the family of eight children of a respected merchant, Walter John Miller, and his wife, Jane Walker Sellers. His parents moved to Bristol in 1881 and after attending several private schools, Miller went to St Bartholomew's Hospital medical school in 1890, graduating MRCS and LRCP in 1896. Although a devoted Christian, he was not a mainstream Anglican. In childhood he was influenced by the Plymouth Brethren and later in life he inclined towards the Society of Friends and Moral Re-Armament. At medical school he played an active role in the Student Christian Movement. After qualifying he became travelling secretary for the Student Volunteer Missionary Union for a year. He worked in the Princess Christian Hospital at Freetown, Sierra Leone, for a short time before studying Hausa at Tripoli in Libya. He sailed to Nigeria as a Church Missionary Society missionary at the end of 1899.

From Lagos, along with Bishop Herbert Tugwell and three other missionaries, Miller began a long journey to Kano while Frederick Lugard was preparing to subdue the unsettled protectorate of Northern Nigeria. In the event, the emir of Kano would not allow them to stay there, and Lugard was reluctant to let them establish a base until the country was pacified. Miller had several temporary camps

until in 1905 he was allowed to settle in Zaria city, where he lived until 1929. This was the only mission allowed within a Muslim town in Northern Nigeria. Miller gave priority to developing a school rather than a hospital. For many years it was the best in Northern Nigeria and its pupils included the first two Hausa doctors, one of whom, Dr R. A. B. Dikko, became minister of health in the 1960s. Miller's sister Ethel came out in 1907 and together with other female missionaries started to provide education for Nigerian girls. A Hausa scholar in her own right, Ethel was unorthodox and individualistic and left to become a freelance evangelist. One significant event for Miller was the visit of some Isawa. These were scattered groups of Hausa who lived by Islamic standards, but gave primacy to Isa (Jesus). The emir gave some land where Miller organized a settlement for them. Unfortunately sleeping sickness caused many deaths, but those children who had come to Miller's school survived. The leader, Malam Audu, started a sugar crushing business and his son Dr Ishaya Audu became the first Nigerian vice-chancellor of Ahmadu Bello University, Zaria.

Miller's greatest achievement was the translation of the Bible into Hausa with the help of Hausa and other missionaries. It was completed in 1935. Though the Hausa readership was small, it increasingly influenced many groups where Hausa was becoming the lingua franca. In the mid-1920s younger missionaries were dissatisfied with the cramped quarters and constant friction with the authorities in Zaria. The mission was subsequently transferred to Wusasa, a site outside the city, where there was more space for a school and hospital. Miller himself moved to Kano in 1929 where he concentrated on completing his translation. He retired in 1935 to England, where he married, but could not settle down and in 1939, after the death of his wife, he returned to Nigeria, eventually settling near Jos.

As well as articles in periodicals, Miller wrote *Reflections of a Pioneer* (1936), *Yesterday and tomorrow in Northern Nigeria* (1938), *Have we Failed in Nigeria?* (1947), *Success in Nigeria* (1948), *For Africans Only* (1950), and *Walter Miller, 1872–1952: an Autobiography* which he completed in 1949 but which was published posthumously. He criticized the conservatism of the local administration, many Northern Nigerian Muslim customs, and some missionary practices, calling in 1938 for a moratorium on missions long before this became fashionable. Upright, autocratic, and uncompromising in his standards of integrity, Miller had many friends, but was difficult to live with. As his contemporaries died or retired he became a solitary figure, but one respected and admired by his former students. He died on 17 August 1952 at Plateau Hospital, Jos, Nigeria, and was buried at St Piran's Church, Jos. E. P. T. CRAMPTON

Sources U. Birm. L., special collections department, Church Missionary Society archives, Walter R. S. Miller MSS, Acc. 237 · U. Birm. L., special collections department, Church Missionary Society archive, G3/A9/o series · CUL, Bible Society Archives · Hausa translation files, CUL · SOAS, Conference of British Missionary Society Archives, West Africa boxes · W. R. S. Miller, *Reflections of a pioneer* (1936) · W. Miller, *Walter Miller, 1872–1952: an autobiography* (Zaria, Nigeria, [1953]) · E. P. Miller, *Likita Miller* (Zaria, 1954) ·

E. D. A. Hulmes, 'Christian attitudes to Islam: a comparative study of the work of S. A. Crowther, E. W. Blyden and W. R. S. Miller in West Africa', DPhil diss., U. Oxf., 1980 • 'Walter Miller and the Isawa: an experiment on Christian–Muslim relationships', *Scottish Journal of Theology*, 41/2 (1988), 233–46 • J. M. Garba, *The time has come* (1989) • I. Linden, 'The children of the Israelites in northern Nigeria: Islamic change in Kano, 1850–1918', *Religion and change in African societies* [seminar proceedings, Edinburgh 1979], ed. [R. Willis] (1979), 75–93 • 'Between two societies of the Book: the children of the Israelites', E. Isichei, *Varieties of Christian experience in Nigeria* (1982), 79–98 • *The Times* (27 Aug 1952) • b. cert. • CGPLA Eng. & Wales (1954)

Archives U. Birm. L., Church Missionary Society archives, diaries, notes, and corresp., private papers, Acc. 237 | CUL, Bible Society Archives

Likenesses line art portrait (of head and shoulders), repro. in Miller, *Walter Miller*, cover

Wealth at death £557 1s. 0d.: probate, 8 Jan 1954, CGPLA Eng. & Wales

Miller, William (c.1740–c.1810), painter, worked in London at the end of the eighteenth century. He exhibited portraits with the Free Society of Artists in 1768, and in 1769 he showed a battle piece before travelling to Rome. In 1780 and 1783 Miller exhibited at the Society of Artists, and from 1788 to 1803 he sent paintings to the Royal Academy. He specialized in history paintings but also exhibited portraits, landscapes, and genre subjects. Two of the plates in John Boydell's *Shakespeare*, *Romeo and Juliet, Act one, Scene Five* and *Henry the Sixth Part III, Act Four, Scene Five*, are from pictures by Miller. Many of his other works were engraved, including three subjects from the story *Werther*, by J. Cary and W. Sedgwick; *Alexander Presenting Campaspe to Apelles*, by J. B. Michel; *The Distracted Damsel*, by V. Picot (1785); *The Memorable Address of Louis XVI at the Bar of the National Convention* and *The Last Moments of Louis XVI*, both by Schiavonetti (1796); *Innocent Recreation* and *Animal Affection*, by J. Godby (1799); *Ceremony of Administering the Mayoralty Oath to Nathaniel Newnham, November 8, 1782*, by B. Smith (1801); and a portrait of the comte de Grasse, by J. Walker (1782). Miller is said to have died about 1810. His *Ceremony of Administering the Mayoralty Oath to Nathanial Newnham, November 8, 1782* is in the art gallery of the corporation of London.

F. M. O'DONOGHUE, *rev.* MATTHEW HARGRAVES

Sources G. Meissner, ed., *Allgemeines Künstlerlexikon: die bildenden Künstler aller Zeiten und Völker*, [new edn, 34 vols.] (Leipzig and Munich, 1983–) • Redgrave, *Artists* • Waterhouse, *18c painters* • B. Stewart and M. Cutten, *The dictionary of portrait painters in Britain up to 1920* (1997) • F. Lewis, *A dictionary of British historical painters* (1979)

Miller, Sir William, second baronet, Lord Glenlee (1755–1846), judge, was born on 12 August 1755, the only son of Sir Thomas *Miller, first baronet (1717–1789), lord president of the college of justice, and his first wife, Margaret (d. 1767), eldest daughter of John Murdoch, provost of Glasgow. Educated at Edinburgh high school, he was admitted a member of the Faculty of Advocates on 9 August 1777, and was subsequently appointed principal clerk in the high court of justiciary. At the general election in September 1780 Miller successfully contested Edinburgh on the government interest against Sir Lawrence Dundas. He spoke only once in the House of Commons, in

February, to defend Sir Hugh Palliser's appointment to Greenwich Hospital, before he was unseated on petition in March 1781. He was one of the lawyers elected to the Royal Society of Edinburgh on its foundation in 1783, holding the post of senior vice-president in 1837, and was also a member of the Society of Antiquaries of Scotland. He succeeded to the baronetcy on the death of his father in September 1789. He married on 5 November 1778 his cousin Grizel (d. 1817), daughter of George Chalmers, an Edinburgh grain merchant; they had six sons and three daughters.

On his appointment as a lord of session, Miller took his seat on the bench on 23 May 1795, with the title Lord Glenlee, resigning this post in January 1840. Glenlee was considered a very able man, with a profound knowledge of mathematics, his favourite subject. He also took pleasure in classical learning, and was acquainted with the language and literature of France, Spain, and Italy, to which, in extreme old age, he added that of Germany. He was notable for his striking appearance: Henry Cockburn wrote of him:

> the figure was slender, the countenance pale, but with a full dark eye; the features regular, unless, when disturbed, as his whole frame often was, by little jerks and gesticulations, as if he was under frequent galvanism; his air and manner polite

but also that 'he never used an English word when a Scots one could be got' (Cockburn, *Jeffrey*, 119–20). Glenlee was the last Scottish judge who made his way to court through the streets of Edinburgh clad in his wig and long cravat, silk stockings, and silver buckles, with his cocked hat in his hand. He died at Barskimming, Ayrshire, on 9 May 1846 and was buried in the family vault at Stair, Ayrshire. His son Thomas having predeceased him, his grandson William Miller succeeded as third baronet.

Glenlee's second son, **William Miller** (1785–1815), army officer, served as lieutenant-colonel of the 1st foot guards, was mortally wounded at Quatre Bras on 16 June 1815, and died the following day at Brussels, where a monument was erected in the cemetery to his memory. In his poem 'Field of Waterloo' Walter Scott referred to 'the gallant Miller's failing eye, still bent where Albion's banners fly' (*Poetical Works*, 625).

G. F. R. BARKER, *rev.* ANITA MCCONNELL

Sources J. Kay, *A series of original portraits and caricature etchings … with biographical sketches and illustrative anecdotes*, ed. [H. Paton and others], new edn [3rd edn], 2 vols. in 4 (1877) • G. Brunton and D. Haig, *An historical account of the senators of the college of justice, from its institution in MDXXXII* (1832), 542 • J. Foster, *Members of parliament, Scotland … 1357–1882*, 2nd edn (privately printed, London, 1882), 251 • *Journal of Henry Cockburn: being a continuation of the 'Memorials of his time', 1831–1854*, 2 vols. (1874) • H. Cockburn, *Life of Francis Jeffrey* (1872), 117–20 • Anderson, *Scot. nat.* • *GM*, 2nd ser., 25 (1846), 643 • *Scots Magazine*, 40 (1777), 469 • *Scots Magazine and Edinburgh Literary Miscellany*, 79 (1817), 239 • E. Haden-Guest, 'Miller, William', *HoP, Commons, 1754–90* • *The poetical works of Sir Walter Scott*, ed. J. L. Robertson (1904); repr. (1951) • IGI

Likenesses J. Kay, etching, 1799, NPG • H. Raeburn, oils, Parliament Hall, Edinburgh, Faculty of Advocates • H. Raeburn, oils, Hunt. L.

Miller, William (1785–1815). *See under* Miller, Sir William, second baronet, Lord Glenlee (1755–1846).

Miller, William (1795–1861), army officer, was born at Wingham, Kent, on 2 December 1795. Like his brother and biographer, John Miller, William served in the field train of the Royal Artillery, in which he was appointed assistant commissary on 1 January 1811. He landed in the Iberian peninsula in August that year, and served in the campaigns of 1811–14, including the sieges of Ciudad Rodrigo, Badajoz, San Sebastian, and Bayonne. He afterwards served in North America, in the operations in the Chesapeake and the expedition to New Orleans, and was shipwrecked off Mobile. Returning home at the peace he travelled for two years on the continent, and then went out to La Plata. He travelled towards Patagonia, and afterwards crossed the pampas and the Andes to Chile, where, as an officer in the Buenos Aires artillery, he repeatedly distinguished himself in the struggle for Chilean independence.

Miller served as major commanding the marines on board the *O'Higgins*, fifty guns, in which Thomas, Lord Cochrane, hoisted his flag on 22 December 1818. In August 1821 he landed at Pisco, defeated and pursued the Spanish garrison, and assumed the government of Yça. Hearing that Cantereau, a French royalist and one of the ablest of the Spanish generals, was threatening Lima, Miller marched to reinforce General San Martín, and was made a general of brigade there in 1823. He became the close friend of Simón Bolívar, who was invested with the chief authority in Peru on 1 September 1823, and under him he attained the rank of general of division and commander-in-chief of the cavalry. To commemorate Miller's services at the battle of Juria on 6 August 1824, Bolívar conferred on his regiment the title of *húsares de Juria*. The most conspicuous of his many gallant exploits was his charge at the head of these hussars at the decisive battle of Ayacucho, which secured the liberties of Chile and Peru, on 9 July 1824. He was many times wounded, and at the battle of Pisco nearly lost his life. At the attack on Chiloe a grape-shot passed through one of his thighs, and his right instep was crushed by a cannon ball. In 1825 he was appointed governor of Potosí, but in 1826 returned to Europe.

Miller received the freedom of the city of Canterbury and many marks of attention in Europe, notably from Austrian officers in garrison at Milan. He returned to Peru, and as commander-in-chief put down an insurrection under General Gamarra in 1834. However, changing political circumstances banished him from the republic, in which he was then holding the rank of grand-marshal. With Santa Cruz and some other officers he embarked in HMS *Samarang*, commanded by Captain William Broughton RN, in February 1839, thus closing a military career of twenty years, during which he had taken part in every major battle fought in Chile and Peru in the cause of South American independence. In 1843 he was made British consul-general in the Pacific, a post he held for some years. In 1859 he went to Callao to prefer some unsettled claims against the Peruvian government, which

the Peruvian congress unanimously agreed should be paid. But the president, General Castillo, stopped the payment, to Miller's great disappointment.

Miller became dangerously ill, and expressed a wish to die under the British flag. He was carried on board HMS *Naiad*, then in Callao harbour, and there died on 31 October 1861. He was buried in the English cemetery at Bella Vista, all the church bells in Callao tolling, an honour never before paid to any protestant in Peru. Miller was described as very tall and handsome, with a winning manner. He was an able officer, and distinguished alike by his conspicuous personal gallantry, solicitude for his soldiers, and humanity towards his prisoners.

H. M. CHICHESTER, *rev.* JAMES FALKNER

Sources J. Miller, *Memoirs of General Miller, in the service of the republic of Peru*, 2nd edn, 2 vols. (1829) · *GM*, 3rd ser., 12 (1862), 236 · *Army List* · Boase, *Mod. Eng. biog.*
Archives Hawaii archives division, Honolulu, papers
Likenesses C. Turner, mezzotint (after Sharpe), AM Oxf., BM, NPG; repro. in Miller, *Memoirs*

Miller, William (1796–1882), engraver, was born on 28 May 1796 at 2 Drummond Street, Edinburgh, the youngest son of George Miller, a shawl manufacturer descended from a Quaker family who had settled in Edinburgh in 1688, and his wife, Anne. He attended day school in Edinburgh and at the age of nine went to a Friends' boarding-school in Leeds with two elder brothers, returning home in 1807 for private tuition. His father intended him to enter the family business, but he expressed a strong desire to become an engraver and in 1811 was apprenticed to William Archibald, an Edinburgh engraver with Quaker connections. After four years he set up his own practice: one of his first commissions was to provide illustrations for an encyclopaedia, possibly the 1817 edition of the *Encyclopaedia Britannica*. The proceeds from this, together with financial support from his father, enabled him to go to London in 1819 to study with the landscape engraver George Cooke in Hackney.

Miller returned to the former family home, Hope Park in Edinburgh, in 1821 and established a successful business as a landscape engraver. In 1831 he set up his studio there. It was renamed Millerfield in 1863, and he resided there for the rest of his life. One hundred and twelve works are known to contain his illustrations. Two hundred of his engravings are listed in *A Catalogue of Engravings* by his son William Frederick Miller, appended to *Memorials of Hope Park* (privately printed, 1886); this provides an extraordinarily complete record of an engraver's work. He first used a steel plate for the title-page to volume 2 of *Constable's Miscellany* (1825). This was followed by *On the Thames Near Windsor* after W. Havall (1828) for *The Winter's Wreath* (1829), after which Miller employed steel continuously for books. He became best known for his engravings after J. M. W. Turner, which were greatly admired for their atmospheric effects. His large plates after Turner include *The Grand Canal, Venice* (1837), *Modern Italy* (1842), issued by the Art Union, *The Bell Rock Lighthouse* (1864), and *St Michael's Mount* (1866); those after other artists include *The Battle of Trafalgar* (1839) after Clarkson Stanfield, *A Sunset at Sea after a Storm* (1849) after Francis Danby, and engravings after Gainsborough and William Howison. Other illustrations include plates for Scott's Waverley novels (1842–7), the *Picturesque Annual* (1832–4), *Literary Souvenir* (1833), Hall's *Book of Gems* (1836–8), the *Imperial Family Bible* (1844), *Imperial Bible Dictionary* (1866), and *Hood's Poems* (1871–2). One work not included in *A Catalogue of Engravings* but attributed to Miller is a bookplate for Hugh Bransby after A. Nasmyth (1820). Slater (5th edn, 1921) indicated that some of Miller's plates were still in existence and printed from occasionally: their subsequent history is unknown.

Miller married twice: his first wife died young, leaving several children. His second wife, Jane, survived him, together with a son and three daughters. In 1826 he was elected a founder member (associate engraver) of the Royal Scottish Academy, where he occasionally exhibited watercolours, but he withdrew after the first meeting, together with eight others who felt the enterprise was too ambitious. In 1862 he was elected an honorary member, and in 1866 he made an unsuccessful bid to be elected to the Royal Academy in London. He had two assistants and six pupils at different times, but none attained his own eminence. Always active in Quaker and social affairs, during the last ten years of his life Miller retired from engraving and occupied himself with watercolour painting and philanthropic work. He died on 20 January 1882 at 1 Victoria Road, Ecclesall Bierlow, Sheffield, while visiting his daughter, and was buried in the cemetery of the meetinghouse of the Society of Friends in Plesaunce, Edinburgh. The Victoria and Albert Museum holds a collection of his work.   LOIS OLIVER

Sources B. Hunnisett, *An illustrated dictionary of British steel engravers*, new edn (1989) · R. K. Engen, *Dictionary of Victorian engravers, print publishers and their works* (1979) · E. Kilmurray, *Dictionary of British portraiture*, 2 (1979) · Thieme & Becker, *Allgemeines Lexikon* · I. Mackenzie, *British prints: dictionary and price guide* (1987) · *Engraved Brit. ports.*, vol. 2 · J. H. Slater, *Engravings and their value*, 5th edn (1921) · A. Lyles and D. Perkins, *Colour into line: Turner and the art of engraving* (1989) · d. cert.
Archives NA Scot., documents relating to legal matters · NL Scot., letters · V&A, collection of letters
Likenesses photograph (in old age), BM · woodcut (after photograph), BM, NPG
Wealth at death £1729 15s. 1d.: confirmation, 24 March 1882, *CCI*

Miller, Sir William, first baronet (1809–1887), merchant and politician, was born on 25 March 1809 at Leith, near Edinburgh, the third son of James Miller (1775–1855) and his wife, Elizabeth (d. 1862), the daughter of the Revd William Sutherland of Wick. He was educated at Edinburgh high school and Edinburgh University. In 1858 he married Mary Anne (1835–1912), the daughter of the MP John Farley Leith QC; they had three sons and two daughters.

Miller was born into a prosperous family, which is believed to have had a fleet of fishing smacks operating out of Wick. He was sent to Russia by his father to develop an export trade in herrings, and from 1832 until 1854 he was resident in St Petersburg, where the trading company he established, William Miller & Co., became a flourishing concern. It handled annually around 1.5 to 2 million roubles' worth of trade, importing from Leith mainly herrings and coal and exporting hemp, grain, and timber in return. His company also set up a tallow-processing factory near St Petersburg, which in 1851 was merged with the city's Neva Stearin and Soap Works Company.

Miller's status in the St Petersburg British community resulted in his serving as honorary British vice-consul there for sixteen years. His term ended with the outbreak of the Crimean War. He then returned to Britain, where he continued his commercial activities. He became a director of several companies, including the Shotts Iron Company, the London and North Eastern Railway Company, and the Northern Assurance Company.

In 1874 Miller was made an extraordinary director of the British Linen Bank, a politically significant appointment, coinciding with attempts by Scottish banks to extend their branch networks to England and political pressure by English banks to have their Scottish counterparts deprived of their Scottish note issue. A gentleman's agreement was reached confirming the status quo but allowing Scottish banks to establish a main London office. This held good until 1971.

In 1860 Miller had extended his manufacturing interests in Russia through exchanging a share in his St Petersburg trading company for a share in the Russian manufacturing concerns of the Cazalet family, who had been involved in Russian commerce since the 1790s. Miller effectively became a sleeping partner in the company which bore his name. Although his nephew James Marshall was by this time involved in the company, effective control passed to Edward Cazalet, who married Miller's niece Elizabeth Marshall in 1860. Through this asset exchange Miller extended his interests in tallow processing when, in 1867, the Neva Stearin and Soap Works Company was merged with the Moscow Stearin Works, the largest tallow-processing concern in the Russian empire. Miller also acquired a share in the Kalinkin brewery, the largest in the Russian empire. In addition, William Miller & Co. owned a mineral water plant and the Russian Steam Oil Mill Company. It moved into finance, and in 1864 participated in the establishment of the St Petersburg Private Commercial Bank and in the promotion of the Dünaberg–Vitebsk Railway Company.

In 1864, with his financial position secure, Miller purchased a large country house, Manderston, near Duns in Berwickshire, and entered public life. In March 1857 he stood for parliament in the Leith district, a seat to which he was elected in May 1859. He represented it as a Liberal 'independent of party' until November 1868. His most noteworthy contribution on behalf of his constituents was alleviating the financial burden on the port of Leith through his piloting the passage through parliament of the 1860 Leith Harbour and Docks Act. Under this act the Treasury agreed to write down the port's debt from £230,000 to £50,000. Miller was returned to the House of Commons in 1873 in a by-election for Berwickshire, only to be defeated at the 1874 general election. However, his silent but steadfast support for W. E. Gladstone in the house, allegedly aided by cleverly orchestrated political dinners, earned him a baronetcy in March 1874.

With a country seat in the Scottish borders and a town house in London on the corner of Park Lane and Piccadilly, Miller numbered among Britain's social élite. In 1871 he made Manderston's Georgian structure more grand by adding a pillared portico and creating additional servants' quarters under a new French Renaissance-style roof. He died in Manchester of heart disease on 10 October 1887, and was buried at Christ Church, Station Road, Duns. His eldest son, William, having choked to death at Eton in 1874, the baronetcy passed to his second son, James Percy (1864–1906), who married Eveline Mary Curzon, the third daughter of the fourth Baron Scarsdale. Sir James owned the winners of the Derby in both 1890 and 1903.

STUART THOMPSTONE

Sources The Times (11 Oct 1887) · J. C. Irons, Leith and its antiquities, 2 vols. [1898] · Boase, Mod. Eng. biog. · S. R. Thompstone, 'The organisation and financing of Russian foreign trade before 1914', PhD diss., U. Lond., 1991 · WWBMP, vol. 1 · Manderston guidebook · C. Aslet, 'Manderston, Berwickshire, I', Country Life, 165 (1979), 390–93 · E. Amburger, Deutsche in Staat, Wirtschaft und Gesellschaft Russlands: die Familie Amburger in St Petersburg, 1770–1920 (Wiesbaden, 1986) · private information (2004)
Archives Manderston, Berwickshire, inscribed silverware; sundry Russian artefacts · NRA, priv. coll., election accounts and draft speeches | Bank of Scotland, Edinburgh, British Linen Bank records · NA Scot., Shotts Iron Company Records · priv. coll., Cazalet MSS
Likenesses marble bust; formerly Leith Public Institute · oils, Manderston, Duns, Berwickshire
Wealth at death £1,029,389 19s. 5d.: confirmation, 10 Jan 1888, CCI · 'several million pounds': Country Life (15 Feb 1979)

Miller, William (1810–1872), poet, was born in August 1810 at Bridgegate, Glasgow, the son of Stephen Miller, a coppersmith master, and his wife, Margaret Roy. He spent his childhood in Parkhead, Glasgow. A severe illness led him to abandon an early ambition to become a surgeon, and he took up the trade of wood-turning in Glasgow.

From an early age Miller contributed to periodicals, and established his poetic reputation with songs published in *Whistle-Binkie* (1832–53). 'Wee Willie Winkie' and other nursery rhymes and miscellaneous lyrics became widely popular; Robert Buchanan called him the 'Laureate of the Nursery' (*St Paul's Magazine*, July 1872). The appeal of Miller's lyrics lay in his ease with the Scots dialect, and the directness and simplicity of his style. His *Scottish Nursery Songs and other Poems* appeared in 1863. 'Wee Willie Winkie', however, first published in 1841, was so popular that it was Anglicized soon after, and published in *Nursery Rhymes, Tales and Jingles* (1844).

Miller continued to work at his trade until 1871, when his health failed. He died at 21 Windsor Street, Glasgow, on 20 August 1872, survived by his wife, Isabella MacKay. He was buried in Tollcross graveyard, Glasgow; a monument was erected in the city necropolis.

T. W. BAYNE, rev. DOUGLAS BROWN

Sources Irving, Scots. · Boase, Mod. Eng. biog. · Whistle-binkie, or, The piper of the party: being a collection of songs for the social circle, new edn, 2 (1878) · Glasgow Herald (22 Aug 1872) · J. G. Wilson, ed., The poets and poetry of Scotland, 2 vols. (1876–7) · W. Miller, Willie Winkie and other songs and poems, ed. R. Ford (1902) [incl. an introduction by R. Ford] · H. Carpenter and M. Prichard, The Oxford companion to children's literature (1984) · d. cert.
Archives Mitchell L., Glas., Glasgow City Archives, autograph verses; literary MSS and papers

Miller, William (1838–1923), college head and Free Church of Scotland minister, was born in Thurso, Caithness, on 13 January 1838, the son of William Miller (d. 1883), merchant and shipowner, and his wife, Elizabeth (1802–1891), daughter of J. S. Gunn, landowner on the Latheron Road. The Miller family built the pier at Scrabster and the Thurso Educational Institute. Both families, and notably the younger of his two brothers, the Revd Alexander Miller, supported the college with prizes, endowments, and studentships. Two cousins joined its staff.

A precocious boarder at Bellevue Academy, Aberdeen, Miller led his class at Marischal College, Aberdeen, from 1852, graduating as gold medallist with a general degree in 1856. He studied theology at New College, Edinburgh, the post-Disruption (1843) Free Church seminary, and was ordained by the presbytery in 1861.

Miller's landfall at Madras in December 1862 followed an unpremeditated response to a missionary appeal, while briefly assistant minister at St George's, Edinburgh. By 1867 he had transformed the Free Church John Anderson Institution into a first grade college, and was himself a fellow and, shortly, syndicate member of Madras University. Principal from 1877, he finally left Madras in 1907, in poor health and with failing eyesight, having established, in collaboration with Wesleyan Methodists and the Church Missionary Society, the outstanding Indian Christian college.

Frequently at loggerheads with evangelical missionaries, theosophists, education department civil servants, Bishop Gell of Madras, and others, Miller fought with the determination of boasted Norse ancestry, an inheritance endorsed by formidable physical presence and a viking moustache. Like many leading Free Churchmen of his generation he was suspicious of doctrinal preoccupations. Increasingly respecting religious and social insights in Islam and Hinduism, he refused to pursue conversions, and never questioned Alexander Duff's strategy of patiently transmitting to Indian élites the illuminations of Western knowledge emerging from a Christian civilization.

Government economies regularly threatened the promises of the 1854 education dispatch. Miller led the national campaigning of non-governmental colleges. He demanded parity of financial support for Hindu and Muslim institutions too, on the grounds that the moral core of education was beyond the reach of government colleges and could be validly taught only in institutions with culturally focused religious commitments. He worked closely with the chairman, Sir W. W. Hunter, on Lord Ripon's education commission (1882), and was a leading witness before Lord Curzon's universities' commission (1902). National reputation underwrote his independence as an occasional critic of official India, most often in the *Madras Christian College Magazine*, the prestigious monthly he started in 1883. Locally he defended college interests as an unobtrusive member of the legislative assembly (1893–7; 1899–1902) and served as vice-chancellor of Madras University (1901–4).

Higher education offered good prospects, and rich pickings in the presidency's patronage-driven factional politics. While Presidency College spawned dissident activists, Christian College attracted students from families opting for co-operation with the raj and often resentful of a supposed Brahman domination of opportunities. Their subsequent loyalty to the college was understandable. In the 1920s Miller's students, brilliant or adroit 'justicites' like A. P. Patro and P. Subbaroyan, virtually monopolized the presidency ministerial posts open to Indians.

Appointed CIE (1884) and kaisar-i-Hind gold medallist (1907), Miller declined the chair of evangelical theology at the Free Church college in 1893, but was appointed moderator of the general assembly of the Free Church of Scotland for 1896. Edinburgh conferred honorary doctorates of laws and of divinity.

As a Gladstonian imperialist Miller sympathized with a 'natural' evolution of Indian nationalism, but drew solemn warnings in his teaching from episodes in Scotland's past, against ill-judged short cuts to 'freedom'. His memorable if eccentric lectures on Shakespeare dwelt on the same lesson of selfless commitment to an organic, morally informed social evolution (*Shakespeare's Chart of Life*, 1903). From his retirement he sent extended messages to former pupils through the *Madras Christian College Magazine*. While betraying anxieties about India's political maturity, he roundly taxed government with failing to prepare the country 'for that self-direction which is … the real aim of those to whom its destinies have providentially been entrusted' (Miller, 141). He died at his home at Burgo Park, Bridge of Allan, Stirlingshire, on 15 July 1923.

GERALD STUDDERT-KENNEDY

Sources G. Studdert-Kennedy, *Providence and the raj: imperial mission and missionary imperialism* (1998), 59–124 · O. K. Chetty, *Dr William Miller* (1924) · *Madras Christian College Magazine* (1883–1930) [at Madras Christian College, Madras, and BL only] · W. Miller, *The voice from Burgo Park* (1922) [autobiog] · Madras Christian College, Madras, William Miller collection [uncatalogued] · *CCI* (1923)
Archives Madras Christian College, notebooks and books
Likenesses J. H. M. Furse, statue, 1901, Madras Christian College Higher Secondary School, Chepat, India · cast-metal bust, Madras Christian College, India · photograph, U. Edin., New Coll. L.
Wealth at death £65,020 4s. 7d.: confirmation, 25 Sept 1923, *CCI*

Miller, William (1864–1945), historian and journalist, was born at Wigton, Cumberland, on 8 December 1864, the eldest son of William Miller, a mine owner, and his wife, Fanny Perry. He was educated at Rugby School and, as a scholar, at Hertford College, Oxford, where he was awarded a first class in classical moderations (1884) and in *literae humaniores* (1887). On leaving Oxford he read for the bar and was called by the Inner Temple in 1889; he never practised but turned instead to journalism. In 1895 he married Ada Mary, daughter of Colonel Thomas Parker Wright; there were no children.

From 1890 onwards Miller made frequent journeys to the Balkans, particularly to Serbia, Bosnia, and Montenegro, and soon became known as an authority on Balkan affairs, on which he contributed several articles to the leading political reviews. At the same time he began to interest himself in the medieval history of the Near East. His first signed historical article, a review of recent books on Montenegrin history, appeared in the *English Historical Review* in July 1896; and thenceforward he was one of its regular contributors and reviewers. During the next forty years his articles and reviews appeared in all the important historical journals in Britain; and up to the year of his death he contributed regularly to the *American Historical Review* and to several learned periodicals in Greece. His most important medieval work, *The Latins in the Levant*, was published in 1908, and his most important work on modern history, *The Ottoman Empire, 1801–1913*, was first published in 1913, and reissued in a fourth edition with supplementary chapters in 1934 as *The Ottoman Empire and its Successors, 1801–1934*.

From 1903 to 1937 Miller was correspondent of the *Morning Post* for Italy and the Balkans, and for the first twenty years established himself at Rome. But in 1923, disliking the atmosphere there after Mussolini's attainment of power, he moved his headquarters to Athens; there he remained until the German invasion of 1941 forced him at short notice to leave his flat and almost all his possessions. He retired to South Africa and spent the remainder of his life at Durban. His wife shared his interests and collaborated in the hospitality which he showed to all scholars and students who visited Rome and Athens while he lived there.

As a journalist Miller was very well informed, reliable, and objective. Unlike his contemporary J. D. Bourchier, he made no attempt to direct international politics; but he was frequently consulted by Balkan statesmen and his opinion was particularly valued by Eleutherios Venizelos. His sympathies were always with the liberal movements in the countries with which he dealt, but they never clouded his judgement. In international politics he became strongly but not uncritically philhellene. The same qualities are apparent in his works on nineteenth- and twentieth-century history, such as his *Ottoman Empire* and his *Greece* (1928), which are admirable and clearly written accounts by one who knew intimately the lands which he described. But his main interest and his chief contribution to historical studies lay in the medieval field. He first concentrated on the history of the Slavs in the Balkans; and his chapters on Serbia and Bulgaria, published in volume 4 of the *Cambridge Medieval History*, were derived from his earlier researches. They show wide erudition and a remarkable ability to bring together a vast assembly of facts into a coherent story.

Later Miller turned his attention to Byzantine history and in particular to the period of the Frankish and Italian establishments in the East after the fourth crusade. It was a period which delighted him for its romance and for which his knowledge of Greece and Italy especially suited him. He brought to it still greater detailed scholarship than he showed in his Balkan work and an enthusiasm and sympathy which are reflected in such books as *The Latins in the Levant* (1908) and *Essays on the Latin Orient* (1921). He was not a historian on the grand scale; but his power to present detailed and accurate scholarship in a clear and significant manner, the charm of his style, and the humanity of his outlook make him one of the most readable and most valuable writers on Near Eastern history.

Among his other main works were *The Balkans* (1896), *Travel and Politics in the Near East* (1898), *Mediaeval Rome* (1901), *Greek Life in Town and Country* (1905), *History of the Greek People, 1821–1921* (1922), and *Trebizond* (1926).

Miller was elected fellow of the British Academy in 1932. He received the honorary degree of LLD from the National University of Athens, and was an honorary student of the British School at Athens and a corresponding member of the Historical and Ethnological Society of Greece and of the Academy of Athens. He died at the Ocean View Hotel, Durban, South Africa on 23 October 1945.

STEVEN RUNCIMAN, *rev.*

Sources personal knowledge (1959) · private information (1959) · S. Runciman, 'William Miller', *PBA*, 62 (1976), 513–18 · *The Times* (10 Nov 1945) · *Wellesley index* · *WWW*

Wealth at death £28,849 14s. 2d.—in England: probate, 21 Nov 1946, *CGPLA Eng. & Wales*

William Allen Miller (1817–1870), by Ernest Edwards, pubd 1864

Miller, William Allen (1817–1870), chemist, was born on 17 December 1817 at Ipswich, one of at least two sons of William Miller and his wife, Frances Bowyer. William Miller was for nearly twenty years secretary to the Birmingham General Hospital, then became a brewer in the Borough, London, and married an intelligent lady of forceful character, traits which their son inherited. Miller spent one year at Merchant Taylors' School, London, then two at the York Friends' Boys' School, Ackworth, Yorkshire, until 1830. There he met his namesake, the Quaker scientist William Allen (1770–1843), and the lectures on chemistry and the occasional use of a telescope sowed the seeds of his later interest in stellar chemistry.

At fifteen Miller was apprenticed to his uncle, Bowyer Vaux, a surgeon in the Birmingham General Hospital, and five years later he entered the medical department of King's College, London. Having obtained in 1839 the Warneford prize in theology, he went to Germany in 1840, to work for some months in Professor Liebig's laboratory in the University of Giessen. On his return he was appointed demonstrator of chemistry in King's College; the following year he became assistant lecturer under John Frederic Daniell (1790–1845), and in 1841–2 took degrees of MB and MD in the University of London. He married in 1842 Eliza (*d.* 1869), eldest daughter of Edward Forrest of Birmingham, with whom he had two daughters and a son.

Miller collaborated with Daniell on his investigations, and was co-author of a paper on the electrolysis of secondary compounds, published in *Philosophical Transactions* in 1844. On Daniell's death he succeeded to the chair of chemistry at King's, and was elected a fellow of the Royal Society. His lecture notes were expanded into his *Elements of Chemistry, Theoretical and Practical*, of which the first part,

Chemical Physics, was published in 1855, the second, *Inorganic Chemistry*, in 1856, the third, *Organic Chemistry*, in 1857. This popular textbook ran into several editions and was also reprinted in the United States.

Miller's first experiments in spectrum analysis, a method of analysing complex salts more accurately than chemical methods then allowed, were made in a lumber room under the lecture theatre at King's College. His observations of both absorption and flame spectra, including the effects of atmospheric water vapour on the solar spectrum, were presented at the Cambridge meeting of the British Association for the Advancement of Science (BAAS) in 1845, and printed, with the first diagrams of flame spectra, in the *Philosophical Magazine*. His involvement in spectroscopy is the more remarkable as he was slightly colour-blind and had difficulty in distinguishing between green and grey. In later years Miller progressed to the study of spectra generated when metal alloys were strongly heated by electrical sparks. The use of quartz prisms enabled him to obtain collodion-negatives of the spectra of twenty-five metals, showing marked characteristics.

In 1862 Miller and his neighbour at Tulse Hill, the astronomer William Huggins, began investigating the spectra of celestial bodies. Having constructed special apparatus, they obtained the most accurate analyses thus far of the light of the moon, Jupiter, Mars, and many of the fixed stars. These yielded the first detailed and reliable information on stellar chemistry. Their preliminary findings were sent to the Royal Society in February 1863; fuller results followed in May 1864. The gold medal of the Royal Astronomical Society was conferred jointly on Miller and Huggins in 1867 for their discoveries. Miller exhibited their photograph of the spectrum of Sirius, the earliest such specimen, during a lecture at the Royal Institution on 6 March 1863. In later years he spent fewer hours on this night-time work, as he was fully occupied during the day, but he gave four lectures on spectrum analysis at the Royal Institution in 1867, and explained its value to astronomy in a lecture to the working men of Exeter during the BAAS meeting there in 1869.

Miller was recruited onto numerous official committees; in relation to potable water, he prepared, with professors Graham and Hofmann in 1851, a report on the Metropolitan Water Board. He also investigated the combined action of air and water on the lead of which most pipes were then made, and lectured on the analysis of drinking water. He reported to the BAAS in 1857 on recent progress of electrochemical research and served on committees set up by the BAAS to superintend Kew observatory, to provide standards of weight and measure, and to determine standards of electrical resistance. In addition, he presided over the chemistry section at the BAAS meeting at Birmingham in 1865.

From 1866 Miller served on the meteorological committee of the Board of Trade. His involvement with the scientific preparations for the 1869 research voyage of HMS *Porcupine* led him to devise, with the assistance of the instrument maker L. P. Casella, the Miller–Casella thermometer, a pressure-resistant version of Six's self-registering thermometer, for use in the depths of the sea. He became a member of the senate of the University of London in 1865, sat on the royal commission on scientific instruction in 1870, aided in the chemical testing of the stone employed to build the houses of parliament, and was assayer to the Royal Mint and the Bank of England. He served the Royal Society as a member of council (1848–50, 1855–7), and as treasurer from 1861 until his death. He took a prominent part in the foundation of the Chemical Society in 1841 and was twice its president. The University of Edinburgh conferred the degree of LLD on him in 1860, he was made DCL of Oxford in 1868, and LLD of Cambridge in 1869, when he gave the Rede lecture, entitled 'Coal-tar colours'.

Miller was a man of sound and penetrating judgement. His ideas were slow to form, but tenaciously held, and he combined unswerving integrity with a refined and sensitive nature. The religious convictions which were the mainspring of his life, and became more entrenched towards the end, were voiced in his address, 'The Bible and science' to the church congress at Wolverhampton on 3 October 1867, and in an introductory lecture at King's College on 1 October 1859. His religious passion overcame his scientific detachment, however, at the British Association meeting held at Liverpool in September 1870. According to the mathematician T. A. Hirst, after Huxley's address on 14 September, Miller, whose demeanour had been somewhat wild, announced that 'he had been ordained to combat the Heresy of Huxley and Tyndall. He grew wilder and wilder and Dr Inman, his physician, found it necessary to have him put under restraint (at an Asylum I believe)' (*Journals*). Miller died on 30 September

1870 at the Brook Villa, Green Lane, West Derby, Lancashire, of apoplexy following 'acute mania 16 days' (d. cert.). He was buried in Norwood cemetery, Surrey, beside his wife who had died a year previously.

A. M. Clerke, rev. Anita McConnell

Sources C. T., *PRS*, 19 (1870–71), xix–xxvi · *JCS*, 24 (1871), 617 · *Nature*, 2 (1870), 517 · C. J. Robinson, ed., *A register of the scholars admitted into Merchant Taylors' School, from AD 1562 to 1874*, 2 vols. (1882–3) · Ward, *Men of the reign* · A. McConnell, *No sea too deep* (1982), 97–8 · E. B. Collinson, *Bootham School register* (1935) · C. T., *Chemical News* (7 Oct 1870), 177–8 · *The Times* (6 Oct 1870), 12b · *Journals of T. A. Hirst*, ed. W. H. Brock and R. MacLeod [microfiche], fol. 1884 · d. cert.

Archives King's Lond., letter-book | CUL, letters to Sir George Stokes

Likenesses Shappen, group portrait, lithograph, pubd 1850 (after daguerreotypes by Mayall, *Celebrated English chemists*), BM · T. Butler, marble bust, exh. RA 1875, King's Lond. · E. Edwards, photograph, NPG; repro. in L. Reeve, ed., *Portraits of men of eminence*, 2 (1864) [*see illus.*] · H. J. Whitlock, carte-de-visite, NPG · photographs, RS

Wealth at death under £25,000: probate, 25 Feb 1871, *CGPLA Eng. & Wales*

Miller, William Galbraith (1848–1904), jurist, was born on 3 June 1848 in Glasgow, eldest of the three sons of Thomas Miller, warehouseman and pawnbroker, and his wife, Isabella, *née* Galbraith. Initially privately educated, he attended Glasgow high school for three years before matriculating at Glasgow University in 1864. He followed various arts courses, gaining distinctions in his classical subjects. He graduated with second-class honours in mathematics in 1872. In 1869 he had begun a legal apprenticeship, adding law courses to his studies. To fulfil the requirements for the Glasgow LLB degree, he needed to take further courses in Edinburgh. These included lectures by James Lorimer, to whom his first book was dedicated. He graduated again in 1875, the first to do so under the thirteen-year-old regulations. After setting a precedent by convincing the Court of Session that his LLB warranted direct admission as a law agent, he entered a local firm and became a partner there two years later. In 1884 he left to join the Faculty of Advocates, and moved to Edinburgh, though he continued to teach a course at Glasgow University as he had since 1876. Although his practice at the bar was not extensive, he was well respected and regularly consulted by colleagues.

Miller was most remembered for his teaching, for his efforts to improve legal education, and for his academic work. For more than fifteen years he gave a course in public and international law at Glasgow in return only for the fees paid by his students. During this period he was passed over for two chairs, one in Glasgow and one in Edinburgh, despite strong support from distinguished lawyers and his own students. It was not until 1894 that he was awarded an annual salary of £300 as a lecturer. This was insufficient to allow him to give up his practice and he continued to travel from Edinburgh. Throughout these years Miller corresponded with university authorities, legal practitioners, and the press in attempts to improve the content and funding of law teaching. He also published various articles, the most substantial being a pamphlet of forty-eight pages, *The Faculty of Law in the University of Glasgow* (1889). He met with little success in these campaigns and in an allied scheme for the LLD degree. This is reflected in his will, with his book collection being left away from the university. His friends were also forbidden to set up any memorial to him there, in the belief that, when the changes he sought did come about, his reputation and memory would 'take care of itself'. His brother Harry was, none the less, moved to publish a pamphlet within months of his death, 'to put on record the main facts of his connection with Glasgow University, and what he tried to do for the Faculty of Law' (Miller, preface).

Miller's academic writings are marked by intellectual acumen, humour, and a scholarship extending beyond law, philosophy, and history into philology, art, and poetry. They include fourteen articles in law journals, and in 1887 two papers in the *Journal of Jurisprudence* on various analogies between the development of language and law which foreshadowed later research. His main contributions to legal theory are found in three books: *Lectures in the Philosophy of Law* (1884); *The Law of Nature and Nations in Scotland* (1896); and *The Data of Jurisprudence* (1903). Like many Scottish and Glaswegian contemporaries, he wrote in the Kantian and Hegelian traditions, though the *Data* is of more sociological bent. The second volume, which he died before producing, was intended to return to the abstract. Miller's ideas were clearly influential on other scholars, with whom he corresponded extensively, and are, for example, recorded in the works of Roscoe Pound, the renowned American legal theorist. Miller travelled widely within Europe. In 1895 he was invited to become a member of the *Internationale Vereinigung für vergleichende Rechtswissenschaft und Volkswirthschaftslehre*, and in 1903 he was elected to the council of the International Law Association.

Miller was, as an illustrated appreciation in the *Scots Law Times* of 1898 put it, 'a capital cellist, as his many years as a prominent member and President of Glasgow University Orchestral Society bear witness' and a man of many friends. He died on 6 February 1904, at 13 Albany Street, Edinburgh, of congestion of the lungs. Belated acknowledgement by the university authorities came in a motion by the general council, encapsulating him 'as a pioneer in the systematic study of Jurisprudence on its scientific side, to which he devoted his life and made contributions of lasting value, as an able and successful teacher and as a man of gracious and attractive personality'.

ELSPETH ATTWOOLL

Sources H. C. Miller, *William Galbraith Miller, advocate* (1904) · 'W. Galbraith Miller esq., advocate', *Scots Law Times* (5 Feb 1898), 197–8 · *Scottish Law Review*, 20 (1904), 61–2 · volume of newspaper cuttings, Feb–May 1904, U. Glas., Archives and Business Records Centre, No. 31,336 · senate minutes, U. Glas., Archives and Business Records Centre, vols. 95, 98, 101–03 · *The Scotsman* (8 Feb 1904) · d. cert.
Likenesses photograph, repro. in 'W. Galbraith Miller', 197
Wealth at death £1461 15s. 6d.: confirmation, 1904, CU

Miller, William Hallowes (1801–1880), mineralogist, born on 6 April 1801, at Felindre, near Llandovery, was the son of Captain Francis Miller and his second wife, Ann, *née* Davies, who was Welsh. She died a few days after his birth. His father had served in the American war, and his family had military associations. Miller was educated at private schools, then proceeded to St John's College, Cambridge, where he graduated as fifth wrangler in 1826. He was elected to a college fellowship in 1829, and to the professorship of mineralogy in 1832. He proceeded in 1841 to the degree of MD in order to retain his fellowship, which, however, he vacated by marriage with Harriet Susan Minty in 1844. They had two sons and four daughters; one son and two daughters died before their father.

Miller's daily work in the university was interrupted only by occasional visits to the continent, often more or less on scientific business, but sometimes extended to a holiday trip in the eastern Alps. A diligent student and lover of science, with a singularly accurate and retentive memory, he possessed an exceptionally wide knowledge of natural philosophy, but it was in crystallography that his great reputation was won. Starting from the groundwork already laid by William Whewell and Franz Ernst Neumann, Miller developed a system of crystallography which was far more simple, symmetrical, and adapted to mathematical calculations than any which had yet been devised. His system

> gave expressions adapted for working all the problems that a crystal can present, and it gave them in a form that appealed at once to the sense of symmetry and appropriateness of the mathematician ... he thus placed the keystone into the arch of the science of crystallography. (Maskelyne, 248)

Miller's system was published in 1838 and quickly found favour with mineralogists.

Another important work in which Miller had a large share was the reconstruction of the standards of length and weight which had been destroyed in 1834 when the houses of parliament were burnt. He took part in more than one royal commission for this purpose, and gave an account of the operations for restoring the value of the old standard of weight in the *Philosophical Transactions* for 1856. He was also of great service on the Commission Internationale du Mètre, to which he was appointed in 1870. He received the honorary degrees of LLD from Dublin in 1865 and of DCL from Oxford in 1876, and was re-elected a fellow of his old college in 1874. He was elected a fellow of the Royal Society in 1838, was its foreign secretary from 1856 to 1873, and was awarded a royal medal in 1870. He was a knight of the order of Sts Maurizio e Lazzaro in Italy and of the order of Leopold in Belgium, and a corresponding member of many foreign societies, including the Académie Française.

Before his work on crystallography Miller had published brief but valuable textbooks on hydrostatics and hydrodynamics. He wrote at least forty-five scientific papers and contributed very largely to a new edition of William Phillips's *Elementary Introduction of Mineralogy* (1852) while limiting his name to that of associate.

Miller was a short, rather square-set man, with a roundish face, placid expression, and well-developed forehead. Though retiring, he was respected and even beloved by his friends. His knowledge, his vigour and grasp of mind, and his inventiveness were all remarkable, and he accomplished much with very simple means, some of his laboratory fittings being of the homeliest kind. In 1876 his health began to fail; he had a slight stroke of paralysis in the autumn, and after a slow decline of the vital powers he died in Cambridge on 20 May 1880. His wife survived him.

T. G. BONNEY, rev. ANITA MCCONNELL

Sources PRS, 31 (1880–81), ii–vii · T. G. B., PRS, 31 (1880–81), 2–7 · N. S. Maskelyne, Nature, 22 (1880), 247–9 · DWB · The Times (24 May 1880), 13a · CGPLA Eng. & Wales (1880)
Archives U. Cam., department of earth sciences, corresp. and notebooks | CUL, letters to Sir George Stokes
Likenesses photograph, RS
Wealth at death under £18,000: probate, 14 June 1880, CGPLA Eng. & Wales

Miller, William Henry (1789–1848), book collector, was born on 13 February 1789 in Upper Marylebone Street, Marylebone, Middlesex, the only child of William Miller, an affluent Edinburgh nurseryman of Quaker descent, and his third wife, Martha, daughter of Henry Rawson of Yorkshire. Privately educated, Miller entered parliament in 1830 as a member for Newcastle under Lyme, defeating John Evelyn Denison, afterwards speaker; he was re-elected in 1831, 1832, 1835, and 1837. As a staunch tory and a supporter of Wellington and Peel, Miller voted against the Reform Bill in 1832, and the following year opposed the admission of dissenters to the universities and the abolition of flogging in the navy. In the election of 1841 he was unseated, and he was resoundingly beaten in his last contest, when he stood for Berwick upon Tweed in 1847.

At Britwell Court, his residence near Burnham, Buckinghamshire, Miller formed a library particularly rich in early English and Scottish literature, and strong also in social history, science, music, travel, and Americana. He began collecting as early as 1816, when he made several purchases at the auction of the seventeenth-century library of Sir Robert Gordon of Gordonstoun; he was also active at the Sir Mark Masterman Sykes sale in 1824 and those of Thomas Caldecott and Joseph Haslewood in 1833, but it was at the dispersal of Richard Heber's unparalleled library in 1834–7 that Miller emerged as one of the premier bibliophiles of his time. Acting through the bookseller Thomas Thorpe, he consistently came away with the great literary rarities of the sixteenth and seventeenth centuries, although until late in life he chose not to pursue costly Tudor and Stuart drama as assiduously as he did poetry, romance, and ephemeral prose. In the 1840s he continued to buy heavily at auction, at the sales of Baron William Bolland, Edward Skegg, Thomas Jolley, Sir Francis Freeling, Benjamin Heywood Bright, and William Holgate, assimilating the cream of his rivals' collections as one by one they predeceased him; only Thomas Grenville's eluded him when it passed in its entirety to the British Museum in 1846.

Miller was a constant presence in antiquarian bookshops as well, and was famous for his attention to the size and condition of his books. He habitually carried a foot-rule about with him to measure potential acquisitions and compare them with his own copies, from which he became known as Measure Miller: his own set of the Heber catalogues is annotated throughout with height and width for every book that interested him. Although a member of the Roxburghe, Bannatyne, and Maitland clubs, he does not appear to have socialized freely with other collectors, and he was reluctant to permit access to his books, to the frustration of contemporary scholars. Sir Frederic Madden noted in his private diary (24 October 1836) that Miller was 'known to be a very strange sort of person', and he is undoubtedly the 'literary dog-in-the-manger' vilified by John Payne Collier in 1843 (The Harmony of Birds, Percy Society Publications, no. 32, vii). He is caricatured as Inchrule Brewer in John Hill Burton's The Book-Hunter (1862). Miller died, unmarried, at his family estate of Craigentinny, outside Edinburgh, on 31 October 1848. He had left instructions for his burial there in a 20-foot-deep pit, above which a costly monument was to be raised; designed by David Rhind and completed in 1866, this takes the form of a massive Roman mausoleum decorated with marble panels by Alfred Gatley.

Miller's collection was reported to have been left to the Advocates' Library at Edinburgh, but in fact descended with the Craigentinny and Britwell estates to his cousin Samuel Christy (1810–1889). The latter took the name Christie-Miller, and also represented Newcastle under Lyme, and he added considerably to the Britwell Court library, particularly at the sales of Thomas Corser's library in 1868–76. In 1852 he printed thirty copies of a specimen catalogue of William Henry Miller's collection, compiled by David Laing, and in 1873–6 issued a small edition of a fuller catalogue, covering in three volumes the areas of divinity, voyages and travel, and British history. On Samuel Christie-Miller's death, his nephew Wakefield Christy succeeded to the estates, again taking the Christie-Miller name and adding further to the collection, notably from the Isham rarities discovered at Lamport Hall in 1867. He also commissioned a good deal of elegant rebinding in morocco and vellum by Pratt and Rivière, some of it regrettable, although he was comparatively careful to avoid sophisticating his copies. His son Sydney Richardson Christie-Miller inherited in 1898, but no further purchases were made after the acquisition of three Caxtons in that year. Having already disposed of a few duplicates in 1908 and 1910, Christie-Miller determined in 1916 to sell the fashionable and pricey Americana; this segment of the library was catalogued by Sothebys for public auction, but was pre-empted in a private transaction by the Californian magnate Henry E. Huntington. In 1917–27 the main library, by now the greatest of its kind in private hands, was auctioned in twenty portions, much of it following the Americana to Huntington's vaults, at prices then considered phenomenally high. A small but distinguished remainder, including eighteenth- and nineteenth-century literature and bibliography, was finally dispersed in 1970, and today 'Britwell' books are preserved in institutional libraries and private collections worldwide.

JANET ING FREEMAN

Sources J. Smith, 'The story of Craigentinny', *Book of the Old Edinburgh Club*, 22 (1938), 201–60 • S. De Ricci, *English collectors of books and manuscripts* (1930) • S. R. Christie-Miller, *The Britwell handlist, or, Short-title catalogue of the principal volumes from the time of Caxton to the year 1800 formerly in the library of Britwell Court, Buckinghamshire*, ed. H. L. Collmann and G. A. P. Brown, 2 vols. (1933) • *GM*, 2nd ser., 31 (1849), 98–9 • J. Skelton, *The harmony of birds: a poem* (1843), vol. 7, no. 1 of *Early English poetry, ballads, and popular literature of the middle ages*, ed. J. P. Collier

Likenesses G. Hayter, group portrait, oils (*The House of Commons, 1833*) • T. Lawrence, portrait • engraving (after T. Lawrence)

Wealth at death approx. £300,000: *GM*

Miller, William John Clarke (1832–1903), mathematician and medical administrator, was born on 31 August 1832 at Beer, south Devon, the son of Reuben Miller, a dissenting minister, and his wife, Ann. During his childhood he was educated at the village school, where he is said to have developed a love of books and of nature. His dissenting parents would not allow him to be educated at a conforming establishment, and at the age of fifteen, in August 1847, he entered the newly created West of England Dissenters' Proprietary School, Taunton. There mathematics and classics were held in equal esteem and Miller became proficient in both, though mathematics became his passion. Years later a fellow pupil remembered his characteristic posture as 'book in hand, probably Euclid's *Elements*' (Record, 39).

Miller became a mathematics master at the Taunton school about 1850. During his first year as a student there the school had formed a connection with the University of London which enabled it to award University of London degrees, and he graduated with mathematical honours in 1854. He then taught at several institutions before becoming vice-principal at the Congregational Huddersfield College in 1861. He was married; his wife, who outlived him, was called Harriette Emma.

During the early 1850s a group of students and masters from the Taunton school started sending questions and solutions to the mathematical department of the *Educational Times*, a monthly journal of education, science, and literature (founded 1847); Miller's first contribution appeared in September 1850. The journal had a strong educational focus, and the editors wanted to see model solutions given to problems that juniors would encounter during their studies. However, Miller, who had greatly wanted to study at Cambridge but been prevented from doing so by his parents' religious stance, valued the journal more for the access it might give him, and others like him, to higher-level mathematics. In 1857 he wrote to the editors to express his desire to see original research flourishing in their journal via the publication of genuine unanswered questions. The editors published his letter and expressed approval of his sentiments, but professed themselves unable to fulfil its aims. In 1862 Miller, by now a major contributor to the journal, himself became its mathematical editor and was able put into practice the policy that he had first called for five years earlier.

One of Miller's early decisions as new editor of the mathematical department (which comprised a substantial portion of the journal) was to issue, as a separate reprint, *Mathematical Questions with their Solutions from the 'Educational Times'*. For the first volume (June 1864) he put together a formidable list of subscribers, including George Boole, Arthur Cayley, Augustus De Morgan, and James Joseph Sylvester. In subsequent volumes, which appeared regularly at biannual intervals, the range of contributors grew rapidly, including a substantial number of fellows from the Oxford, Cambridge, and Dublin colleges, and many of the questions posed were of an original nature. By the tenth volume Miller's publication had developed a genuinely international reputation, and included contributions from several eminent continental mathematicians; later it also drew contributors from the United States.

Though he held the editorship concurrently with his vice-presidency of Huddersfield College, Miller was assiduous and painstaking in his approach to the editorial task, sending out solutions to be scrutinized before publication, and correcting some of them himself (notably including those of such distinguished mathematicians as Sylvester and W. K. Clifford). The problems that he himself put forward were highly regarded by leading contemporaries. His journal was innovative and sometimes at the frontier of research; thus, many problems on probability theory occurred in the earlier volumes. In 1875 a separate volume was issued, exclusively devoted to geometrical problems and edited by Thomas Archer Hirst. By 1889 Miller could count 500 contributors drawn from four continents.

Miller remained mathematical editor of the *Educational Times* for thirty-five years. This occupation was by nature of a hobby, for professionally he made his living first as a teacher, and later as a medical administrator. He was appointed general secretary and registrar of the General Medical Council in 1876, whereupon he left Huddersfield; he remained in post until ill health forced his resignation in 1897, the same year as he gave up his editorship. His administrative abilities were greatly appreciated by the medical community, and the General Medical Council gave him a gratuity of £1000 on his retirement.

During his editorship Miller collected likenesses of several hundreds of his mathematical contributors, forming a unique visual record of nineteenth-century mathematical life. He sold his collection in the late 1890s to the American David Eugene Smith, with the hope that it would not be dispersed. (The collection is now in Columbia University, New York, to whom it was bequeathed by Smith.) An indefatigable correspondent, in conjunction with his editorial work Miller also acted as a mathematical intelligencer at large, regularly receiving and passing on much mathematical news. His focus on editorial work was not his preferred choice. At a number of points in his career he attempted, without success, to break into the higher echelons of the mathematical professoriate, notably in the 1860s when he sought to become professor of mathematics at Owens College, Manchester. In later life he expressed regret that he had not forsaken editing for a more auspicious career. His services to mathematics were none the less remarkable for that.

In 1896 Miller had been struck with aphasia, due to pressure of work, and he continued to suffer from this condition until his death. He died on 11 February 1903 at Castle Nursing Home, Kingswood, near Bristol, after a bout of influenza and bronchitis.   JANET DELVE

Sources B. F. Finkel, *American Mathematical Monthly*, 3 (1896), 159–63 • *BMJ* (28 Feb 1903), 525 • S. P. Record, *Proud century: the first 100 years of Taunton School* (1948) • I. Grattan-Guinness, 'A note on the *Educational Times* and *Mathematical Questions*', *Historia Mathematica*, 19 (1992), 76–8 • I. Grattan-Guinness, 'Contributing to the *Educational Times*: letters to W. J. C. Miller', *Historia Mathematica*, 21 (1994), 204–5 • *CGPLA Eng. & Wales* (1903)
Archives Col. U., Butler Library, David Eugene Smith historical MSS
Likenesses photograph, *c*.1890, Col. U., Butler Library, David Eugene Smith Historical MSS
Wealth at death £5529 19*s*. 11*d*.: probate, 20 April 1903, *CGPLA Eng. & Wales*

Miller, William Richard Beckford (1769–1844), publisher, was born on 25 March 1769 at Bungay, Suffolk, the only son of Thomas *Miller (1731–1804), bookseller, and his wife, Sarah (Sally; 1741–1773), daughter of William Kingsbury, maltster. He was educated at Bungay grammar school as a foundation scholar before joining his father's business at fourteen. At eighteen he left for London when his considerable promise as an artist was recognized by Sir Joshua Reynolds who advised him to enrol as a student at the Royal Academy. His stay at the academy was short-lived, however, for in 1787, presumably after family pressure, Miller was placed in Hookham's publishing house. He soon mastered the trade and started his own publishing business at 5 Old Bond Street, London, in 1790. Here he built up both his business and his reputation as a publisher of high quality books. On 31 July 1790 he married at Doncaster his cousin Mary (1769–1791), daughter of his uncle Dr Edward Miller.

Miller's first publication was his father-in-law's *The Psalms of David for the Use of Parish Churches* (1790). This was soon followed by a series of publications in large quarto, illustrating the costumes of various countries, with descriptions in French and English. The books made a considerable profit. Other works followed with equal success, including Sir John Stoddart's *Remarks on Local Scenery and Manners in Scotland* and the Revd Edward Forster's edition of the *Arabian Nights Entertainments*, illustrated by Robert Smirke.

Mary Miller died in 1791 and in 1799 William Miller married the daughter of the Revd Richard Chapman. They had five children. In 1804 Miller moved to larger premises at 50 Albemarle Street in the fashionable West End and soon became one of the most popular publishers in the capital. Between 1790 and 1805 he was the official bookseller to the duke of Clarence, and his music imprints of this period were especially well received. By 1807 it appears that it became necessary to expand his business premises: between 1807 and 1809 he was using the next door property at 49 Albemarle Street. He took shares in the poems of Sir Walter Scott and was the sole publisher of Scott's edition of Dryden (1808), which covered eighteen volumes. Among the new titles he published was *Voyages and Travels to India, Ceylon, the Red Sea, Abyssinia and Egypt* (1809) by George, Viscount Valentia. He also reprinted a collection of plays entitled *Ancient British Drama* in 1810 and nineteen volumes of the works of Samuel Richardson in 1811.

The vast majority of Miller's publishing ventures were successful, as he had a particular gift for being able to gauge public taste accurately. Failures were rare but did occur. For the copyright of Charles James Fox's *History of the Early Part of the Reign of James II* (1808) Miller paid the largest sum ever given until then for literary property: £4500. Production was soon under way. 5000 copies were printed in demy quarto at £1 16*s*. by Savage and 250 copies in lavish royal quarto at £2 12*s*. 6*d*., with 50 on elephant size quarto at £5 5*s*. by Bulmer. Fox was unpopular as a political figure at the time and this was reflected in the sales, with Miller barely covering his expenses. Perhaps his most unfortunate decision was to reject Byron's *Childe Harold's Pilgrimage* in 1810. John Murray II published it instead in 1811 and by 1812 had also acquired Miller's premises, copyrights and business for the considerable sum of £3822 12*s*. 6*d*.

With some of this money Miller bought a farm in Hertfordshire with the intention of retiring. After a short period in the country he decided to return to the activity of the city and settled in Duchess Street, Portland Place, London. One of his most famous works was produced during his retirement, his *Biographical sketches of British characters recently deceased, commencing with the accession of George the Fourth … with a list of their engraved portraits* (1826). This work included the first brief biographies of a number of influential figures. The engravings were of an extremely high quality and the two volumes sold well. A continuation was announced and planned but failed to materialize.

William Miller died on 25 October 1844 at the home of his son, the Revd Stanley Miller, at Dennington, Suffolk.
                                                                    J.-M. ALTER

Sources *GM*, 2nd ser., 23 (1845), 102–3 • J. Ames, T. F. Dibdin, and W. Herbert, eds., *Typographical antiquities, or, The history of printing in England, Scotland and Ireland*, 4 vols. (1810–19) • T. F. Dibdin, *The bibliographical decameron*, 3 vols. (1817) • P. A. H. Brown, *London publishers and printers, c.1800–1870* (1982) • I. Maxted, *The London book trades, 1775–1800: a preliminary checklist of members* (1977) • J. C. Smith, *British mezzotinto portraits*, 4 vols. in 5 (1878–84) • F. A. Mumby, *Publishing and bookselling* (1956) • T. Copsey, *Book distribution and printing in Suffolk, 1534–1850* (1994) • *IGI*
Archives NL Scot., letters to Sir Walter Scott
Likenesses J. D. Engleheart, lithograph (aged fifty-seven), repro. in W. Miller, *Biographical sketches of British characters recently deceased, commencing with the accession of George the Fourth … with a list of their engraved portraits* (1826) • E. Scriven, stipple (after T. Phillips), BM, NPG; repro. in Dibdin, *Bibliographical decameron* • Mrs D. Turner, etching (after T. Phillips), BM, NPG
Wealth at death sold business in 1812 for £3822 12*s*. 6*d*.: Maxted, *London book trades*, 154

Milles, Isaac (1638–1720), Church of England clergyman and schoolmaster, was born on 19 September 1638 at Cockfield, near Bury St Edmunds, Suffolk, the youngest of eleven children of Thomas Milles, 'a plain Country Gentleman' of Carrington's Farm, Cockfield. He was baptized at Cockfield on 30 September. Of his elder brothers, Samuel, of Queens' College, Cambridge, became vicar of Royston, Hertfordshire, and John 'a very considerable Tradesman' at Dedham, Essex (*Account*, 5–7). Isaac spent seven years at King Edward VI's School, Bury, under Dr Stephens, the editor of *Statius*, where he absorbed 'worthy Principles of Loyalty to his Prince', and numbered the future lord keeper Francis North among his peers (ibid., 10). In 1656 he was admitted to St John's College, Cambridge, where his tutors were Lawrence Fogge, later dean of Chester, and Francis Turner, the future bishop of Ely and leading nonjuror. Among Milles's contemporaries at St John's was its future master Humphrey Gower, whom he characterized as erudite, proud, and obstinate. Milles graduated BA in 1660.

After proceeding MA in 1663 Milles took holy orders. In his first appointment as sole curate of Barley, Hertfordshire, he was a beneficiary of university patronage; its non-resident rector was Joseph Beaumont, master of Peterhouse, Cambridge. Despite the modesty of his position, Milles distinguished himself by his charitable exertions, 'giving away large sums' (*Account*, 38). In so doing he earned a reputation he would preserve throughout his ministry. Beaumont's failure to secure Milles a living in Ely during this time established a more unfortunate pattern.

In 1670 Milles married Elizabeth Luckson or Luckin (*d.* 1708), a clergyman's daughter. The first of their sons, Thomas *Milles, was born the following year. In 1674, through the patronage of Chief Baron Sir Robert Atkyns, Milles became vicar of Chipping (High) Wycombe, Buckinghamshire, a move that brought him to 'the Eye of the World' (*Account*, 38). He made friends with the ecclesiastical historian Henry Dodwell, and Dr Martin Lluelyn, poet and physician, whose epitaph he later composed. During this time the prospect of a more illustrious career was suggested by his preaching before Archbishop Sancroft at Lincoln's Inn. Much of Milles's energy as a parish priest was devoted to combating nonconformity, albeit initially with mixed success. During the exclusion crisis his churchmanship led him to espouse the tory cause. Being on familiar terms with Edward Coleman, the Catholic courtier who fell victim to the accusations of Titus Oates, Milles regularly advertised his scepticism regarding Oates's reports, urging 'it was not *Popery* and *Slavery*, but *Presbytery* and *Republic*' that posed the greatest dangers (ibid., 102). Since Oates enjoyed the support of many leading politicians, and the authenticity of his testimony was, at the height of his power, approved by parliament, Milles's conduct was especially courageous. Only the intervention of well-disposed local magnates and a succession of personal suits during a feverish trip to the capital appear to have averted his prosecution.

The crisis did no harm to his stock with influential tories: in April 1681 Sir Robert Sawyer presented Milles to the rectory of Highclere, Hampshire, where he served until his death. Milles was perhaps disappointed in his promotion, since its previous patron had promised him the far richer living of neighbouring Burghclere when it should fall vacant. The modest nature of his income and a desire to educate his sons properly led Milles, himself reckoned 'a good textuary', to open a school which, by 1694, had expanded to accommodate boarders (*Account*, 75). Among his pupils Milles counted the sons of Thomas Herbert, eighth earl of Pembroke, the latest proprietor of Highclere. The school regime combined a humane ethos with high-church piety: averse to corporal punishment, Milles preferred to reason with his pupils, whose morning prayers began with a selection from the *Catechism* of the nonjuror John Kettlewell. These exertions allowed Milles to live comfortably so that 'he did not stand in much need of more Preferment' (ibid., 147). His energies were no less apparent in fulfilling his parish duties where, predictably, much of his labour was devoted to eliminating nonconformity, an endeavour given fulsome acknowledgement in his biographer's approving claim that 'for the last five and thirty Years' of his ministry, Milles 'had not one *Dissenter* … in his parish' (ibid., 81–2). Milles also funded at his own expense repairs and rebuilding of the church and parsonage to the tune of £500, conducting services in a barn at the first encroachment of an opportunistic dissenting minister.

In his politics Milles was a tory and the revolution exercised his conscience acutely. Like many high-churchmen he combined a profound distaste for the conduct of King James with a sense of revulsion and horror at the constitutional events of 1688–9, his own preferred solution being a protestant-dominated regency. Nevertheless, his friend Thomas Smoult, the casuist, convinced him that 'it was not only lawful, but his Duty to submit and swear to the Government then in being' (*Account*, 106). His acquaintance with John Herne, a canon of Windsor and a former chaplain of Princess Mary, also helped to reconcile him to the new regime. Nevertheless, the suspicion that Milles's doubts were far from entirely settled is suggested by the scruples of his son Jeremiah at abjuring James's son in 1704, while a fellow of Balliol College, Oxford. Isaac Milles felt happier with the accession of Queen Anne, whom he compared reverently with her grandfather.

Elizabeth Milles died of smallpox in 1708. The patronage of Pembroke extended to Isaac's son Thomas Milles, whom he took with him to Ireland when he became lord chancellor and later recommended to Queen Anne for the see of Waterford. The relative obscurity of a talented and well-connected clergyman requires some explanation; Milles's modest advancement may be ascribed to a combination of bad luck and, more tellingly, a retiring, even diffident, temperament. Milles was naturally modest and, his biographer concedes, apparently easily underestimated, his humility hiding 'some of his Excellencies from superficial Observers' (*Account*, 168). His aversion to preferment seeking left him 'disengaged, and sitting loose from world', thereby free to exercise the ministry for which he would be remembered. In his later years Milles increased his already remarkable charitable donations.

The *raison d'être* of Milles's anonymous biographer was no doubt to recommend to clergy and layman alike at a time of low morale the exemplary Christian life of the priest most eloquently recorded in Highclere's parish register: 'He never refused any of his Neighbours, that desired to borrow any money of him, leaving it to them to take their *own time* to repay it, *without Usury*', nor ever exacting 'the utmost of his Tithes'. Of his other priestly virtues his biographer distinguishes that of 'administering Comfort and the Holy *Eucharist* to sick and dying Persons'. The remarkable vignette of the ageing and infirm Milles meditating on last things while measuring out his burial plot suggests a mindset that owed more to the age of George Herbert than that of Gilbert Burnet.

In 1718 Milles suffered the first of a series of paralytical strokes, precipitated according to his biographer by the disagreeable task of reading the *Remarks* of the dissenter Edmund Calamy on the tory Laurence Echard's *History of England*. In June 1720 a further stroke 'took away from him the use of his left Side'; nevertheless, during his last days, while tended by his daughter, he still managed to satisfy his inclination to 'smoke a Pipe of Tobacco' (*Account*, 154–5). He died on 6 July 1720 and was buried three days later in the chancel of Highclere church, where a black slab with a Latin inscription was put up to his memory by his children. A white marble monument with inscription was also placed by his eldest son on the north wall of the chancel. An engraved half-length portrait of Milles in clerical attire by Vertue appeared posthumously; its Greek legend, *alethenein en agape* ('telling the truth in the love of God'), a fitting tribute to his ministry.

Finally, a word should be said about the authorship and wider purpose of Milles's biography. Traditionally the pamphlet has been attributed to Thomas Milles or one of his circle but a number of vagaries concerning family history render this improbable. A likelier candidate is the author of the pamphlet's accompanying funeral sermon, J. W. (Joseph Wood), a neighbouring clergyman. While the principal motive of its author was no doubt to extol an exemplary and remarkable ministry, other more narrowly political ends should not be disregarded. The anxious endeavour to emphasize Milles's reconciliation with the revolution settlement and the disparagement of dissenters are the familiar hallmarks of high-church polemics in the first years of the Hanoverian regime. More than a century later, the account of his piety, toryism, and fruitful obscurity courted new admirers when, in the anonymous preface of an edition of 1842, Milles was compared with another priest 'in the shade'—the young John Keble, founder of the Oxford Movement.

Of Isaac Milles's sons, his eldest, Thomas Milles (1671–1740) was bishop of Waterford and Lismore from 1708 until his death. **Jeremiah Milles** (*bap.* 1672, *d.* 1746), Church of England clergyman, was baptized at Barley on 8 October 1672. He matriculated from Balliol College, Oxford, on 2 May 1690, graduated BA on 17 February 1694, and proceeded MA in 1697. He was a fellow of his college from 1696, and a tutor, until 1704. The diary that he kept between 1701 and 1703 provides insights into both his spirituality and piety and his activities as tutor and proproctor. Every day he went to early morning chapel and 'read lectures' to his students. He received communion at least once a week and kept Lent rigorously with fasting

and prayer. He attended the university church of St Mary twice on Sundays and saints' days, noting his thoughts on the sermons he heard and taking great pains with the sermons he himself composed. As pro-proctor he was active in his attempts to discipline the behaviour of the students, breaking up their gatherings in ale houses, trying to drive them away from the bull-baiting at Gloucester Green, and keeping up a constant campaign against the town's streetwalkers. In 1704, as noted, he had scruples about abjuring James II's son, James Francis Edward. Shortly afterwards he left the college. He was rector of Riseholme, Lincolnshire, in 1704, and vicar of Duloe, Cornwall, from 1704 until his death there on 21 January 1746. He married Mary Harris (1678/9–1756), daughter of Humphrey Harris of St Issey, Cornwall, with whom he had at least six sons and six daughters, among them Jeremiah *Milles (1714–1784), antiquary and dean of Exeter.

Another son of Isaac Milles the elder, **Isaac Milles** (1676/7–1741), Church of England clergyman and schoolmaster, matriculated from Balliol College, Oxford, on 7 July 1692, aged fifteen, and graduated BA in 1696. He proceeded MA from Sidney Sussex College, Cambridge, in 1701. Through the influence of his eldest brother he was appointed treasurer of the diocese of Waterford on 21 May 1714 and prebendary of Lismore on 6 September 1716. He was a non-resident in both posts; after taking orders he carried on his father's school at Highclere. In 1727 he resigned both positions to become rector of Litchfield, Hampshire, a living that he held until his death in 1741.

D. A. BRUNTON

Sources [J. Wood (?)], *An account of the life and conversation of the reverend and worthy Mr Isaac Milles* (1721) · *The life of the Reverend Isaac Milles* (1842) · J. C. Findon, 'The nonjurors and the Church of England, 1689–1716', DPhil diss., U. Oxf., 1978 · *DNB* · Venn, *Alum. Cant.* · Foster, *Alum. Oxon.* · J. Jones, *Balliol College: a history*, 2nd edn (1997) · *Hist. U. Oxf.* 5: *18th-cent. Oxf.* · *GM*, 1st ser., 93/1 (1823), 516–17
Archives Balliol Oxf., diary [Jeremiah Milles]
Likenesses G. Vertue, engraving, AM Oxf., Hope collection

Milles, Isaac (1676/7–1741). *See under* Milles, Isaac (1638–1720).

Milles, Jeremiah (*bap.* 1672, *d.* 1746). *See under* Milles, Isaac (1638–1720).

Milles, Jeremiah (1714–1784), antiquary and dean of Exeter, was born on 29 January 1714 at Highclere, Hampshire, the third son of Jeremiah *Milles (*bap.* 1672, *d.* 1746) [*see under* Milles, Isaac (1638–1720)], vicar of Duloe, Cornwall, and his wife, Mary (1678/9–1756), daughter of Humphrey Harris of St Issey, Cornwall. There were at least six sons and six daughters of this marriage (though not all reached maturity), of whom Jeremiah was the fourth or fifth child. According to one account, both his father and his uncle Thomas *Milles, later bishop of Waterford and Lismore, had admired the same woman, and when the younger man was preferred, Thomas resolved never to marry and to sponsor the first of his brother's sons to be born at the house of their father, Isaac *Milles the elder, rector of Highclere (Cussans, 1.81).

Thomas Milles certainly acted as his nephew's patron,

Jeremiah Milles (1714–1784), by Nathaniel Dance

meeting the expenses of his education as an oppidan at Eton College (1725–1728?) and as a gentleman-commoner at Corpus Christi College, Oxford, where he matriculated on 9 July 1729, gaining his BA in 1733, MA in 1735, and BD and DD in 1747. He was ordained in the established church by his uncle, as deacon on 28 July 1734, priest on 11 August, and received preferment from him within his Irish diocese. He was treasurer of Lismore Cathedral from 1735 to 1745, precentor of Waterford Cathedral from 31 December 1737 to 12 November 1744 (as well as a notable contributor to its adornment), vicar of Reisk until c.1744, and vicar of Kilrossanty in 1736. Following Thomas Milles's death in 1740, Jeremiah Milles became the bishop's heir and centred his activities in England.

Milles's prospects for advancement in the church were further enhanced by the patronage of John *Potter, archbishop of Canterbury, whose daughter Edith (*bap.* 1725, *d.* 1761) he married in Lambeth Palace chapel on 29 May 1745. They had at least six children, of whom three sons and two daughters reached adulthood, and their family life was happy and affectionate, though Edith Milles was only thirty-five at her death on 9 June 1761. Frances Burney wrote in 1773 that the sons were 'very agreeable and amiable young men … [who] appear to regard their father only as an elder brother, to whom they owe more respect but not less openness' (*Early Diary*, 1.253), but in 1775 Samuel Pegge the elder criticized Milles's inappropriate indulgence to his children. Milles was rector of Saltwood with Hythe, Kent, from 11 December 1744 until early in 1746; of Merstham, Surrey, from 24 October 1745 (when he was also constituted archbishop's chaplain) until his death; of St Edmund the King with St Nicholas Acons, Lombard Street, City of London, from 1 November 1745 until his

death; and of West Tarring, Sussex, from 7 February 1747 to 6 January 1779. On 11 May 1747 he became a prebendary of Exeter Cathedral and its precentor, and on 30 May a canon residentiary. On 28 April 1762 he was elected dean (having resigned the precentorship), succeeding his great friend Charles Lyttelton. He was confirmed in office on 8 June. Frances Burney recorded in 1773 how impressed she was by his fine qualities as a preacher. He was also president of Sion College, London, for 1762/3 and, as prolocutor of the lower house of the convocation of Canterbury, he was presented to the upper house on 23 January 1775.

It is for his antiquarian activities, however, that Jeremiah Milles is chiefly remembered. As a young man he travelled extensively, often with his cousin Richard Pococke. The manuscripts constituting his 'Travels on the continent and through England and Wales' (1733–43) are in the British Library. He was elected fellow of the Society of Antiquaries of London on 24 December 1741 and fellow of the Royal Society on 1 April 1742. On 10 January 1769 he was council's unanimous choice as president of the Society of Antiquaries (again succeeding Lyttelton), a post he retained for life. For the next twelve years he was very active in this role, ably supported by Richard Gough, who wrote of Milles that 'If Ambition prompted him to take the Antiquarian Chair, he filled it with becoming dignity' but that perhaps 'he did not enough keep up his authority in the Society' (Nichols, *Lit. anecdotes*, 6.621). Together they extended the society's public activity and were largely responsible for the founding of its journal *Archaeologia*. The first volume (1770) included Milles's piece on the wardrobe account for 1483, in which he argued against Horace Walpole's views on Richard III. The convivial side of the society's life also flourished under Milles's presidency, and he instituted its first dining club in 1774. Despite his amiability and his attempts at reconciliation, he encountered many quarrels and difficulties, with the secretary William Norris among others but most notably with Walpole, and the antiquaries met with a degree of both criticism and ridicule, for example in Samuel Foote's *The Nabob*, first performed in 1772.

Milles also pursued his antiquarian interests at Exeter. From at least 1753 he was collecting information on Devon history. Notable among his many Devon manuscripts are the 'Parochial returns', comprising replies to a long and varied list of printed questions which he circulated among Devon parishes, and 'Parochial collections', which deal more fully with ecclesiastical details. This material is still a basic resource for local historians. (It was sold to the Bodleian Library in 1843 as part of Milles's impressive collection of printed books and manuscripts.) At the cathedral, initially in collaboration with Lyttelton, he vigorously pursued the dean and chapter's extensive programme of interior renovation and embellishment in line with the exuberant antiquarianism of the first period of the Gothic revival. Major glazing operations comprised part of the programme, most notably the reglazing of the great west window with glass by William Peckitt between 1764 and 1767, when Milles issued a printed description of the new window. (This glass was displaced in 1904, though some can still be seen at the cathedral.) In 1772, 'with what may be thought to have been excess of zeal' (Hope and Lloyd, 75), Milles had most of the church plate remade and modernized. In the early 1780s the final touch to this many-faceted scheme was the application of a brown and yellow colour wash to the cathedral interior. Milles was an enthusiastic fund-raiser and the driving force of the scheme, though little enough of his work remains to be seen in the cathedral.

Milles actively promoted the idea of moving the headquarters of the Society of Antiquaries from Chancery Lane to Somerset House, but once the grant of rooms had been secured he did little to direct policy, and in November 1780 he suffered a stroke. He recovered reasonably well, though he lost the use of his right hand, and his speech to the society on 11 January 1781 'upon their removal into the apartments assigned to them in Somerset House' was printed that year. High blood pressure seems to have affected his judgement, however, and his last years were marred by the sometimes virulent attacks he incurred for taking the wrong side in the Chatterton controversy. In 1782 he had issued his edition of *Poems, Supposed to have been Written at Bristol, in the Fifteenth Century, by Thomas Rowley*, in which he argued against their being modern compositions by Thomas Chatterton. S. T. Coleridge wrote that 'Milles ... (a priest; who, though only a Dean, in dulness and malignity, was most episcopally eminent) foully calumniated [Chatterton]—An Owl mangling a poor dead Nightingale!' (Cottle, 1.36).

Milles's other publications include *Inscriptionum antiquarum liber alter*, co-edited with Pococke and included as a supplement in the latter's *Inscriptionum antiquarum Graec. et Latin. liber* (1752), and several wide-ranging articles in *Philosophical Transactions of the Royal Society* and *Archaeologia*. His *Topographical Notes* on Bath, Wells, and other places were printed from his manuscript in 1851 and some of his correspondence is reproduced in Nichols's *Literary Anecdotes*, Evans, and elsewhere. Extensive collections of his manuscripts survive, including letters, travel writing, and a broad range of antiquarian studies, some illustrated.

Milles's privileged circumstances allowed his generous spirit to flourish. He 'liked doing a gracious thing' and was 'the most easy-going of men' (Evans, 163). His portraits show that he was brown-eyed, of ample figure and high colouring, and his marble bust depicts his 'epicurean countenance' (ibid., 134). On 13 February 1784, following 'a dangerous illness' (Nichols, *Illustrations*, 7.460), he died at Harley Street, St Marylebone, Middlesex, where he had maintained his London household. He was buried on 19 February 1784 near his wife, in the church of St Edmund, King and Martyr, Lombard Street, where a monument by John Bacon commemorates them.

PETER W. THOMAS

Sources A. W. B. Messenger, 'An eighteenth century dean of Exeter and his family', *Report and Transactions of the Devonshire Association*, 83 (1951), 22–33 · DNB · J. Evans, *A history of the Society of Antiquaries* (1956) · Nichols, *Lit. anecdotes* · Nichols, *Illustrations* · A. Erskine, 'Dean Jeremiah Milles', *Annual Report* [Friends of Exeter Cathedral], 66 (1996), 18–22 · V. Hope and J. Lloyd, *Exeter Cathedral: a short history and description*, rev. A. Erskine (1988) · *The early diary of Frances Burney, 1768–1778*, ed. A. R. Ellis, rev. edn, 1 (1907) · Act Book of the Vicar General, LPL, VB 1/VIII · Cornwall RO, Duloe registers, FP 51/1/2 [microfiche] · J. Cottle, *Early recollections; chiefly relating to the late Samuel Taylor Coleridge, during his long residence in Bristol*, 2 vols. (1837) · J. E. Cussans, *History of Hertfordshire*, 1 (1870) · parish register, Hants. RO, 91M70/PR [baptism] · GM, 1st ser., 93/1 (1823), 516–17 · parish register, Herts. ALS, D/P 14/1/1 [baptism]
Archives BL, travel journals, corresp., sketches, etc., Add. MSS 14263–14264, 14266, 15762–15778, 19941–19942, 32123 · Bodl. Oxf., Devonshire MS, collection and working papers, b1–7, c6, c8–17, c19, e7–8 · S. Antiquaries, Lond. | BL, letters to Thomas Birch, Add. MS 4314 · BL, letters to Charles Lyttelton, Stowe MSS 753–754 · BL, letters to Thomas Milles, Add. MS 22977 · S. Antiquaries, Lond., letters to Richard Gough, MS 447
Likenesses oils, c.1760–1780 (after N. Dance-Holland?), S. Antiquaries, Lond. · T. Rowlandson, watercolour cartoon, 1782, S. Antiquaries, Lond. · J. Bacon, marble bust, 1785, S. Antiquaries, Lond. · M. Black, oils, 1785? (after N. Dance-Holland?), S. Antiquaries, Lond. · J. Downman, watercolour drawing, 1785, NPG · N. Dance, oils, S. Antiquaries, Lond. [see illus.]
Wealth at death approx. £22,000 between family members and others; other specific items; remainder of estate to eldest son: will, PRO, PROB 11/1113, sig. 93

Milles, Thomas (c.1550–1626?), customs official and antiquary, was born in Ashford, Kent, the son of Richard Milles of Ashford and his first wife, Johanna, daughter of Thomas Glover of Ashford and sister of Robert *Glover (1543/4–1588), Somerset herald. Having received a 'free school' education (*Customer's Alphabet*, Bodl. Oxf., MS Bod. 913, manuscript note by Milles), he entered public service about 1570, which during the next sixteen years took him frequently to Flanders, France, and Scotland. He augmented his armorial bearings following a visit to Henri IV of France as an envoy of Queen Elizabeth. In 1579 he was appointed the queen's land and water bailiff and verger of Sandwich. He was employed by Walsingham as an agent between England and Scotland in 1585, and in 1586 he accompanied Randolph to Edinburgh where he assisted greatly in negotiations on the treaty of Berwick. On the conclusion of that treaty, 'desirous to betake himself to some staid course of life', he secured the lucrative post of customer of Sandwich, with powers to intercept foreign agents and correspondence, the government employing him in unravelling the numerous plots of the period.

In 1591 Milles was sent to Rye to receive four prisoners sent from Dieppe; he conveyed a secret communication to the queen from the king of Spain and was recommended as an 'honest person' to be sent to Brittany 'to view and report on the forces there' (CSP dom., 1591–4, 82–3, 89, 117). Early in April 1596 he and Sir Conyers Clifford travelled from Dover in a small man-of-war to explore 'how Calais is to be succoured' (ibid., 1595–7, 196–7). In August the same year, after the expedition to Cadiz, he was appointed at the queen's command a prize commissioner at Plymouth, 'to recover all prize goods brought in', to 'see that the goods are well preserved, locked up, and inventoried', and to 'see whether the bulky goods had not better be sent by ship to London, the rest coming by land', sending 'by the Queen's ordinary posts, accounts of your proceedings' (ibid., 264–5). In 1598 he acted as secretary to Lord Cobham, lord warden of the Cinque Ports, and on 15 June that year he obtained, in reversion after Sir Ralph Bourchier, the keepership of Rochester Castle. After the death of George Gilpin in 1602 he applied, without success, for the post of councillor to the council of estate in the Low Countries. In May 1603 James I renewed 'the dispensation granted by the late Queen to Thos. Mills, collector of the customs at Sandwich, for non-residence in that town' (ibid., 1603–10, 12). On 17 December 1611 Milles 'attended M. de Vitry's corpse to Dover, fearing the clamorousness of some of his creditors', since 'he never came to England with money sufficient for his expenses' (ibid., 1611–18, 100). On his resignation in 1623 of the post of bailiff of Sandwich he was succeeded on 10 July by John Philipot, pursuivant-at-arms and Somerset herald (1624–45), whose wife, Susanna, was daughter and sole heir of William Glover of Sandwich, one of the gentlemen ushers, daily waiters at the court of James I, and brother of Robert Glover, Somerset herald (1571–88). William and Robert Glover were respectively Milles's cousin and uncle. The post was evidently lucrative, there being a number of other candidates, some of whom had to be bought off before Philipot could secure the office.

During the latter part of Elizabeth's reign Milles purchased Norton Court, near Faversham, from Sir Michael Sonds, where he resided for some time, before moving to Davington Hall or Court, on a hill overlooking Faversham, early in the reign of James I. On 17 May 1608 he married Anne Nutt, daughter of John Polhill of Otford, Kent, and widow of William Nutt of St George's, Canterbury, counsellor-at-law, with whom he had two daughters: Anne (b. 1615), and a second (b. 1618) who died young. His wife died in 1624 at Davington Hall, and was buried beside her younger daughter in St George's Church, Canterbury, where a monument was erected to her memory.

Milles devoted his later years to the writing of influential treatises relating to early mercantilist ideas, the political and economic dominance of London, regulated trading companies, and customs farming, in which he expressed strong views, and to heraldry. As an early mercantilist he protested against the abolition of the ancient monopoly of the 'staples', defending and being an uncompromising advocate of the system, believing that while it made possible exchange without usury, it favoured freedom of enterprise and the development of commerce. He was among the most violent critics of the Merchant Adventurers, condemning the trade monopoly which that company exercised in exporting undressed cloth. He associated their monopoly with London's growth at the expense of outports, depriving merchants of 'their generall inheritance' of free traffic, and diminishing the revenue. Drawing on his experience as customer of Sandwich—a port which never won complete autonomy, the monarch reserving a right to appoint bailiffs to collect farmed customs—and having failed to influence the government, Milles made his views known in *The Customer's Apology: that is to Say, a Generall Aunswere to Informers of All*

Sortes (1601), in which he defended 'the honest reputation of Her Majesty's Customs, especially in the outports of this realm'. Only fifty copies were printed, and these were circulated among members of the privy council. Three abridgements were published, in 1602, 1609, and 1619. Attacked by the Adventurers, Milles issued *The replie, or, Second apologie: that is to say, an answer to a confused treatise of publicke commerce … in favour of the … Merchant Adventurers* (1604).

A Caution Against Extreamity by Farmers (1606) argued against the practice of farming out the customs, whereby purchasers guaranteed capital sums or incomes in return for a free hand in securing such profits as were possible. This was followed by *The True Use of Port Bandes* (1606). In 1608, in *The Custumer's Alphabet and Primer*, Milles objected on principle to the privileges of regulated companies, arguing that sufficient 'order' in trade could be secured through treaties with foreign powers and general rules imposed on subjects, and expressing a widespread provincial outcry against the supremacy and stranglehold of London:

> all our Creekes seek to one River, all our Rivers run to one Port, all our ports joyne to one Town, all our Townes make but one Citty, and all our Cities and suburbes to one vast, unweldy and disorderlie Babell of buildings which the worlde calls London.   (sig. L v)

This represented an exceptional view at the beginning of James I's reign but after the 1689 revolution it grew in popularity to become the dominant opinion in parliament, leading to the privileges of regulated companies being opened up very considerably. Other publications rehearsed and extended his ideas.

In the sixteenth century a knowledge of heraldry was considered a necessary part of a gentleman's education. Milles's *The Catalogue of Honor, or, Treasury of True Nobility, Peculiar and Proper to the Isle of Great Britaine, etc. … Translated out of Latyne* (1610) represented an important treatise in a burgeoning heraldic literature. It had been preceded by *Nobilitas politica et civilis* (1608), edited, with his own copious notes, from his uncle's manuscripts. Glover had begun work on *The Catalogue of Honor* and left it with Milles 'to foster' and complete, assisted by Lord William Howard, Sir Robert Cotton, William Camden, Nicholas Charles, and others: 'to what end … will your Cares and Labours be found at last to tend, if together with your Deaths they become forgotten?', or 'either to forget or to be forgotten is alike injurious to the dead as to the living' (dedication, sig. A3). Milles also authored *The Treasurie of Auncient and Moderne Times, etc.* in two volumes (1613–19), and worked on a manuscript catalogue of the knights of the Garter, in chronological order, now in the Bodleian Library, Oxford (MS Ashmole 1119x).

The date and place of Milles's death are uncertain but it is likely that he died at Davington, early in 1626. His will was proved before the commissary court of Canterbury on 31 July 1626, the properties at Norton and Davington being bequeathed to his daughter Anne. She conveyed them in marriage in 1627, when only twelve years of age, to John

Milles of Hampshire who, then only twenty, was subsequently knighted. Thomas Milles also left £200 to support the employment of the poor in Ashford, where he was born.   JOHN WHYMAN

Sources A. Winnifrith, *Men of Kent and Kentish Men: biographical notices of 680 worthies of Kent* (1913), 343–4 · A. J. Pearman, *History of Ashford* (1868), 117, 119 · J. Hutchinson, *Men of Kent and Kentish men: a manual of Kentish biography* (1892), 103 · W. Boys, *Collections for an history of Sandwich in Kent* (1792, [1892]), 424 · E. Hasted, *The history and topographical survey of the county of Kent*, 2nd edn, 6 (1798), 378–9, 403–4 · E. Hasted, *The history and topographical survey of the county of Kent*, 2nd edn, 7 (1798), 537–8 · R. Furley, *A history of the Weald of Kent*, 2/1 (1874), 227 · *CSP dom.*, 1591–4, 82–3, 89, 117; 1595–7, 196–7, 264–5; 1603–10, 12; 1611–18, 100 · W. K. Jordan, 'Social institutions in Kent, 1480–1660: a study of the changing patterns of social aspirations', *Archaeologia Cantiana*, 75 (1961) [whole issue], esp. 59–60 · H. Stanford London, 'John Philipot, MP, Somerset herald, 1624–1645', *Archaeologia Cantiana*, 60 (1947), 24–53 · A. Ruderman, *A history of Ashford* (1994), 34, 46 · W. Cunningham, *The growth of English industry and commerce in modern times: the mercantile system* (1925), 223 · O. Barron, 'Heraldry', *Shakespeare's England: an account of the life and manners of his age* (1932), 2.77 · K. M. E. Murray, *The constitutional history of the Cinque Ports* (1935), 5 · E. M. Tenison, *Elizabethan England: being the history of this country 'an relation to all foreign princes'* …, 13 vols. (1933–60), 9.xv; 12a.745 · E. A. J. Johnson, *Predecessors of Adam Smith: the growth of British economic thought* (1965), 330 n. 5 · J. Hurstfield, *Freedom, corruption and government in Elizabethan England* (1973), 231, 314 · I. I. Rubin, *A history of economic thought* (1979), 46–7
Archives Bodl. Oxf., Customer's Alphabet, MS Bod. 913 | Bodl. Oxf., MS Ashmole 1119x

Milles, Thomas (1671–1740), Church of Ireland bishop of Waterford and Lismore, was born at Barley, Hertfordshire, on 19 June 1671, the eldest son of the Revd Isaac *Milles (1638–1720) and Elizabeth Luckin (d. 1708). He matriculated from Wadham College, Oxford, on 12 March 1689 and was exhibitioner of the college in 1691–2; he graduated BA in 1692, MA in 1695, and BD in 1704.

Having been ordained by Bishop Hough, Milles became chaplain of Christ Church, Oxford, in 1694 and from 1695 to 1707 was vice-principal of St Edmund Hall. In either 1705 or 1707 he was appointed regius professor of Greek. A scholar of ability, he published (in addition to some controversial tracts and a memoir of his father) a valuable folio edition of the works of St Cyril of Jerusalem, with Greek and Latin notes (1703).

On becoming chaplain to his father's former pupil Thomas Herbert, earl of Pembroke, Milles accompanied his patron to Ireland on his appointment as lord lieutenant in April 1707. Through Pembroke's influence he was appointed bishop of Waterford and Lismore on 11 March 1708; he was consecrated in St Patrick's Cathedral, Dublin, on 18 April following.

Milles's long episcopate was marked by controversy. His appointment was unpopular in Ireland, drawing a letter of protest from Archbishop King. Dean Swift mocked his high-church pretensions: 'I do not hear that he showed his crucifix that he wears continually at his breast' (Mant, 2.198). King also criticized Milles for his nepotism and accused him of giving not only 'all livings of value in his gift to brothers and relations, but likewise his vicar-generalship and registry, tho' none of them reside in the

kingdom' (ibid., 2.445). He was at loggerheads with Waterford corporation, whom he accused of ruining the city by demolishing the old walls and mismanaging the hospitals. The corporation for its part denounced him to the government for employing popish servants and corresponding with papists. However, if Milles was surprisingly tolerant towards Roman Catholics, he was severe towards dissenting protestants. He forbade his clergy to have any dealings with them and requested the city recorder to have their new meeting-house demolished: 'I must confess that it grieves me that they should enjoy so fine a place when poor Father John, the titular [Roman Catholic] dean of Waterford, has no better than a thatched cabin without gates' (Dunlop, 15).

Milles's principal legacy to his diocese was the rebuilding of a number of ruined medieval churches, in particular St Olaf's beside his cathedral, which he furnished and appropriated to his own use, allegedly in order to escape the bullying of his eccentric dean, Hugh Bolton. In the pediment is an inscription listing these churches and concluding with the quotation:'Accepi lateritiam, reliqui marmoream' ('I received brick—I left marble'). Milles also intended to rebuild the cathedral and bishop's palace, and commissioned designs from the Bristol architect William Halfpenny, but death intervened and the task was left to his successors.

Milles died of a stone in the bladder at Waterford on 13 May 1740 and was buried in the cathedral. He was unmarried and left his property to his nephew Jeremiah Milles (1714–1784), antiquary and afterwards dean of Exeter. There is a monument to Milles's memory in his father's old church at Highclere in Hampshire.

G. LE G. NORGATE, *rev.* JULIAN C. WALTON

Sources *The whole works of Sir James Ware concerning Ireland*, ed. and trans. W. Harris, 1 (1739), 545 · *The whole works of Sir James Ware concerning Ireland*, ed. and trans. W. Harris, 2/2 (1746), 362–3 · H. Cotton, *Fasti ecclesiae Hibernicae*, 2nd edn, 1 (1851), 131 · J. J. Falvey, 'The Church of Ireland episcopate in the eighteenth century', MA diss., University College, Cork, 1995, 216–17 · Waterford corporation, minute books, 1700–70, City Hall, Waterford · J. Cook, diaries, 1677–1734, Genealogical Office, Dublin, MS 544 · M. Dunlop, *Waterford Presbyterian Church, 1673–1973* (1973) · J. C. Walton, 'The Boltons of co. Waterford', *Irish Genealogist*, 7 (1986–9), 197–8 · T. Friedman, 'William Halfpenny's designs for an "Early Christian" cathedral at Waterford', *Journal of the Irish Georgian Society*, 1 (1998), 8–33 · R. Mant, *History of the Church of Ireland*, 2 (1840), 197–9, 445, 559–60 · T. Gimlette, 'The annals of St Olaf's Church', *The history of the Huguenot settlers in Ireland, and other literary remains* (privately printed, Dublin, 1888) · parish register (death), 1740, Holy Trinity, Waterford

Millhouse, Robert (1788–1839), weaver and poet, was born on 14 (or 17) October 1788, at Nottingham, the second of ten children of John Millhouse and his wife, Ann, *née* Burbage. His only education was obtained at a Sunday school, and by the age of ten he worked at a stocking loom and sang in the choir of St Peter's Church. Nevertheless, during 1804 he read poetry, including the works of Shakespeare, Milton, Pope, and Gray, with his elder brother, John. In 1810 he joined the Nottinghamshire militia, and it was while with his regiment at Plymouth that his first verses were written and sent to the *Nottingham Review*. His poems attracted favourable notice (see 'Appendix' to *The Song of the Patriot*), and he found friends who in 1822 obtained for him a grant from the Royal Literary Fund. Ten years afterwards he became assistant at a savings bank, and was thus able to devote more of his time to literary pursuits.

Millhouse married first, on 25 August 1818, Eliza Saxby (*d. c.*1832), with whom he had eight children; and second, on 5 November 1836, Marian Muir, with whom he had two children. He published five books of poetry, including *The Song of the Patriot: Sonnets and Songs* (1826), *Sherwood Forest, and other Poems* (1827), and *The Destinies of Man* (1832), which brought him a degree of literary recognition, but little financial return. Despite their acknowledged, if modest reputation, Millhouse's poems tend to be cliché-ridden and overly mannered. Their tone is predominantly Christian and moral: *The Destinies of Man*, which attempts a kind of sequel to Milton, locates in the fall of man the origins of the social ills of the day. His forte was the sonnet, which he handles with some skill. His poetry combines a feeling for nature with a patriotic fervour, both grounded in a strong sentimental attachment to his own locality. Millhouse was very much a poet of his place, celebrated by a contemporary coterie of self-styled 'Nottingham' writers as a 'Nottingham' poet proving the locality's claims to independent distinction. The label 'the Burns of Sherwood Forest' given him by the Nottingham historian W. H. Wylie was quickly adopted; biographical accounts also refer to a 'Sherwood School' of poetry with Millhouse as its founder. His humble origins, his lack of education, the lowliness of his occupation as a weaver, the physical strain it entailed, and his continuing poverty and ill health, all contributed to the image of an 'artizan poet' (a tag that appears in the subtitle of Briscoe's edition), whose literary achievement defied the odds stacked against him. In his later years especially, he became reliant on financial assistance from friends, such as Thomas Wakefield, Colonel Gardiner, and Mrs Howitt Watts, daughter of William and Mary Howitt, and among those who helped him in his last illness was Ebenezer Elliot, the corn-law rhymer. Millhouse died in Nottingham on 13 April 1839, leaving his widow in indigent circumstances. He was buried on 18 April on the eastern side of the Nottingham cemetery, some lines being inscribed on the tomb a few years later by his friend Dr Spencer T. Hall. An oak in Sherwood Forest, under which Millhouse and Spencer Hall took refuge during a storm, bears the name of the poet.

G. Le G. Norgate, rev. U. Natarajan

Sources J. Millhouse, preface, in R. Millhouse, *The song of the patriot: sonnets and songs* (1826) · *The sonnets and songs of Robert Millhouse*, ed. J. P. Briscoe (1881) · *Annual Register* (1839), appx to 'Chronicle', 333 · *Literary Gazette* (27 April 1839), 267 · S. T. Hall, *Biographical sketches of remarkable people* (1873) · *GM*, 2nd ser., 11 (1839), 662–3 · A. Stapleton, *In the footsteps of Robert Millhouse* (1908) · W. H. Wylie, *Old and new Nottingham* (1853) · C. Bonnell, *Robert Millhouse: artisan-poet of Sneinton* (1903) · *IGI* · d. cert.

Archives BL, letters to Royal Literary Fund, loan 96

Milligan, Alice Letitia [*pseud.* Iris Olkyrn] (**1866–1953**), author and Irish nationalist, was born on 14 September 1866 at Gortmore, Omagh, co. Tyrone, the third of the thirteen children of Seaton Forest Milligan (1836–1916), managing director, and his wife, Charlotte, *née* Burns (*d.* 1916). Her parents were both Irish Methodists, and she had distant Scottish connections on her mother's side.

Alice Milligan's early education at home, followed by secondary instruction at Methodist College, Belfast (1879–86), and a year at the ladies' department of King's College, London, revealed an enquiring mind. Her first published work, *Glimpses of Erin* (1888) was written in collaboration with her father, who was a fellow of both the Royal Irish Academy and the Royal Society of Antiquaries of Ireland. Part travelogue, part philosophical reflection on Ireland and the Irish, *Glimpses* was well received, and marked the beginning of her lifelong preoccupation with Irish politics and literature. While in Dublin in 1888 to learn Irish she began to take an active interest in politics and was deeply impressed by Charles Stewart Parnell. Parnell's denunciation by the Catholic church following the O'Shea divorce scandal caused Milligan to champion the right of protestants to participate in the national movement, a concern reflected in her novel *A Royal Democrat* (1892).

In 1893 Milligan joined the Irish Literary Society and came into contact with key figures of the Gaelic revival. William Butler Yeats encouraged her to write plays and poetry, although he was more enthusiastic of her efforts as a dramatist than as a poet. The years between 1893 and 1916 were Milligan's most productive, in a political and literary sense. In 1895 she and Anna Johnston (whose pseudonym was Ethna Carbery) became founding editors first of the *Northern Patriot*, and in 1896 of the *Shan Van Vocht*, a seminal newspaper which provided a forum for the varied strands within the Irish nationalist movement. Ostensibly a literary publication, it addressed issues such as the morality of armed resistance, organized socialism, and the use of literature in politics. The final issue appeared in March 1899, when she and Johnston voluntarily halted publication in order to make way for Arthur Griffith's new journal, the *United Irishman*. Although she was not enthusiastic about the decision, her growing political commitments filled the void.

From 1895 Milligan had been involved in the establishment of the Henry Joy McCracken Literary Society in Belfast, being elected vice-president in August of that year. She was appointed organizing secretary for the 1798 centenary celebrations, and became a member of the Gaelic League, for whom she travelled the country, lecturing and recruiting. 1898 saw the publication of her *Life of Theobald Wolfe Tone*. In 1900 her play *The Last Feast of Fianna* was produced at the Abbey Theatre, although Yeats rated her *Red Hugh* more highly, citing it as the model for his own *Cathleen ni Houlihan* in terms of literary propaganda. Her collection of poetry, *Hero Lays*, appeared in 1908, and in the years leading up to the war she continued her work for the Gaelic League, despite increasing family disapproval of her political activities, and the family's pressure on her, as the unmarried daughter, to care for her elderly parents. The year 1916 marked a turning point, bringing the death of both her parents and her elder sister, and the trial and execution of Sir Roger Casement, the friend for whom she wrote the eulogistic poem 'The Ash Tree of Uisneach'.

Milligan's life after 1916 was one of increasing financial dependence upon her brothers Ernest and William, and she moved between England and Ireland, acting as governess and housekeeper in their homes. In 1932 she returned permanently to Ireland, where she lived in increasing poverty. Despite being awarded an honorary doctorate by the National University of Ireland in 1941, she remained in precarious circumstances. The intervention of friends and family, however, eased the final two years of her life, and she died at Tyrcur, Omagh, co. Tyrone, close to her birthplace, on 13 April 1953. She was buried in Drumragh, Omagh, two days later.

OONAGH WALSH

Sources S. T. Johnston, *Alice: a life of Alice Milligan* (1994) · *Shan Van Vocht* (1896–9) · M. Ward, *Unmanageable revolutionaries: women and Irish nationalism*, pbk edn (1983) · S. T. Johnston, *The harper of the only God* (1993) · *Irish Volunteer* (1914–16) · *Belfast News-Letter* (14 April 1953) · R. F. Foster, *Modern Ireland, 1600–1972* (1988) · archival sources, NL Ire. · T. Brown, *Ireland: a social and cultural history* (1985) · *Irish Times* (14 April 1953)
Archives NL Ire., Eoin Mac Neill MSS · NL Ire., Sheehy-Skeffington MSS · NL Ire., letters to Sinead de Valera and others, MS 18311 | SOUND BBC WAC · Radio Teleféis Éireann, Dublin, sound archive
Likenesses S. O'Sullivan, pencil drawing, 1942, NG Ire. · pencil sketch, repro. in Johnston, *Alice*, frontispiece · photograph, repro. in Johnston, *Alice*, 28, 144
Wealth at death very little: S. T. Johnston, *Belfast News-Letter*

Milligan, Francis Sydney (1894–1965), adult educationist, was born on 18 September 1894 at 5 Grosvenor Square, Poulton-cum-Seacombe, Birkenhead, the son of Alexander M'Call Milligan, a commercial clerk, and his wife, Emily Cummine. Educated at Wallasey grammar school in Cheshire, he won a scholarship to Liverpool University in 1914 but his studies were interrupted by the outbreak of the First World War. As a pacifist Frank Milligan initially joined the ambulance corps as a stretcher-bearer but, after a few weeks in France, he enlisted in the 7th King's regiment (Liverpool). Awarded the Military Medal as an NCO he was subsequently commissioned, won the Military Cross, and finished the war with the rank of major.

In 1918 Milligan resumed his education at the University of Birmingham, where he was awarded an MA degree for a thesis entitled 'Politics and industry within the state: a plea for evolution in place of revolution'. As president of the university's guild of students he was a member of the small group which established the National Union of Students in 1920. On graduation he spent four years teaching for the Workers' Educational Association, where he forged a lifelong commitment to adult education and local voluntary action. In 1924 he was headhunted to become warden of Beechcroft educational settlement in Birkenhead, where he relished the multifaceted role of warden which ranged from 'defining a common purpose' for the settlement's disparate user groups to 'acting as an odd-job man' (Milligan, 'The years between', 87).

On 14 June 1922 he married Gwendoline Mary (b.

1899/1900), daughter of James Henry Spencer, a schoolmaster; they had two sons. Increasingly preoccupied by the needs of the unemployed, Milligan resigned as warden in 1933 to launch a bold and imaginative experiment in residential adult education. At Wincham Hall, a country house near Northwich in Cheshire, he ran six-week courses for groups of men from the unemployed clubs of south-west Lancashire and Cheshire. The programme combined practical instruction and technical education with discussion groups on social affairs and cultural activities. This successful experiment was based on Milligan's distinctive educational philosophy that 'individuals must be free to choose their own way of education' and that 'no-one shall nourish his own interests in isolation but shall put them increasingly to the service of the community' (Milligan, 'Wire in the blood', 25).

The Wincham Hall experiment was brought to a premature end by the outbreak of war in 1939, when Milligan found himself unexpectedly running a hostel for evacuated women and children. The following year he rejoined the army as a welfare officer before becoming, in 1942, a full-time lecturer for Liverpool University's regional committee for forces education. In 1944 Milligan was appointed the first secretary of the National Council of Social Service's newly established community centres department which became the secretariat for the National Federation of Community Associations in 1945. The war had given a new impetus to the development of neighbourhood community associations and the educational value of community centres had been recognized by the Ministry of Education. But the high hopes of 1945 rapidly gave way to the harsh reality of post-war Britain; restrictions on the use of skilled labour for construction and constraints on educational expenditure meant slow progress in building new community centres and developing a professional cadre of centre wardens.

Despite these problems the community associations movement grew to maturity during the fifteen years of Milligan's leadership of the federation. In 1945 the federation had eighty-five members and was in contact with a total of 400 local groups. By 1958 the membership was nearing 400 and the total number of groups with which it worked exceeded 1650. These achievements owed much to Milligan's 'imaginative, patient efforts to translate ideals into practical achievement … his grasp of principle and his understanding of human diversity' (Brasnett, 113) and his 'tolerance, tenacity and humanity' (Hutchinson, 16). Milligan was appointed OBE in 1958, and he retired in 1959, but he retained an active interest in adult education until his death at Cheriton, Alexandra Road, St Ives, Cornwall, of lung cancer, on 18 August 1965. His wife survived him.

COLIN ROCHESTER

Sources F. S. Milligan, 'The years between: a pilgrimage in democratic education', 1944?, LUL, F. S. Milligan archive · F. S. Milligan, 'Wire in the blood', ed. G. Milligan, 1965, LUL, F. S. Milligan archive · M. Brasnett, *Voluntary social action: a history of the National Council of Social Service, 1919–1969* (1969) · R. Clarke, ed., *Enterprising neighbours: the development of the community association movement in Britain* (1990) · E. M. Hutchinson, 'Frank Milligan, 1894–1965', *Social Service*

Quarterly, 40/1 (June–Aug 1966) · letters and papers, LUL, F. S. Milligan archive · *Annual Report* [National Council of Social Service] (1944–59) · B. Jones, ed., *Serving the community: three lives* (1983) · b. cert. · m. cert. · d. cert.
Archives LUL, archive

Milligan, George (1860–1934), Church of Scotland minister and biblical scholar, was born at Kilconquhar, Fife, on 2 April 1860, the eldest son of the parish minister, William *Milligan (1821–1893), who later in the same year became professor of biblical criticism in the University of Aberdeen. His mother was Anne Mary, daughter of the physician and essayist David Macbeth *Moir (1798–1851), a physician and author, known as Delta. He was elder brother of Sir William *Milligan (1864–1929), a laryngologist and otologist.

After attending the Gymnasium at Aberdeen he graduated at Aberdeen University in arts (1879) and divinity (1883), studying also at the universities of Edinburgh, Göttingen, and Bonn. He superintended the early development of St Matthew's Church, Edinburgh (1883–94), becoming in 1887 its first ordained minister. In the country charge of Caputh, Perthshire (1894–1910), he added to the faithful performance of his parochial duties an assiduous devotion to biblical scholarship, and stirred by a lecture of Marcus Dods he took up zealously the study of the accumulating stores of non-literary Greek papyri, lecturing on the subject at Oxford (1899), Cambridge (1904), and in the USA (1909). As regius professor of biblical criticism in Glasgow University (1910–32) and clerk to the senate (1911–30), he won the confidence, honour, and affection of all with whom he had to do. He received honorary degrees from the universities of Aberdeen (1904), Durham (1919), Glasgow (1932), and Edinburgh (1933). Milligan was twice married. In 1891 he married Janet Simpson (d. 1898), daughter of John Rankine DD, minister of Sorn, Ayrshire; then in 1902 he married Margaret Catherine, daughter of William Ellis Gloag, Lord Kincairney, senator of the college of justice. One son was born of each marriage.

It was a notable pioneering achievement for Milligan to issue, while still at Caputh, a standard commentary on St Paul's epistles to the Thessalonians (1908), in which among other things he applied the new papyrological evidence to a re-examination of the Pauline grammar and vocabulary. He began his great work, *The Vocabulary of the Greek Testament* (1914–29), in collaboration with J. H. Moulton, and after the issue of part two in 1915 completed it single-handedly. Its comprehensiveness and accuracy provided a foundation for successors to build upon, while remaining readable and full of human interest.

Milligan served the Church of Scotland with spontaneous and conscientious loyalty, more particularly in the field of religious education, and, like his father and his father-in-law Dr John Rankine, he became moderator of the general assembly (1923). His simplicity and sympathy, which made him in private life so courteous and approachable, found early expression in his pastoral ministry and in collections of children's addresses, and later led him to make the results of scholarship more generally available in many courses of lectures and published volumes. By nature placid, receptive, and fair-minded, he wrote and taught with admirable balance and lucidity. Milligan died in Glasgow on 25 November 1934. He was survived by his second wife.   G. S. DUNCAN, rev.

Sources *Glasgow Herald* (26 Nov 1934) · personal knowledge (1949) · *DSCHT* · *CGPLA Eng. & Wales* (1935)
Archives NL Scot., corresp. with publishers | BL, corresp. with Arthur James Balfour, Add. MSS 49799
Wealth at death £27,265 0s. 3d.: confirmation, 1935, *CCI*

Milligan, George Jardine (1868–1925), trade unionist, was born on 11 December 1868 in Liverpool, the son of Samuel Milligan, an employee of the *Liverpool Mercury* for over forty years, and his wife, Mary (*née* Jardine). He was educated at the Liverpool Collegiate high school but little else is known of his early life. By 1890 he was employed as a barman but subsequently worked at the docks as a quay porter, becoming a specialist checker for the White Star Line.

In 1908 Milligan founded, edited, and largely wrote the *Mersey Magazine*. This consisted of articles, poems, and 'letters' of interest to dock labourers, and was published for some seventeen months. No copies of the magazine have been located but in 1911 Milligan published extracts from it in a book entitled *Life through Labour's Eyes*, which reveals his commitment to the cause of labour and his deep religious conviction. He was a devout Catholic who encouraged his fellow workers to accept the Christian faith. He was active in Catholic circles, contributed articles to Catholic journals, and joined a local group which studied the encyclicals of Pope Leo XII and which developed into the Catholic Social League.

Milligan was an active member of the National Union of Dock Labourers (NUDL), a regional union based on Merseyside with branches in northern England, Scotland, and Ireland. The union was a major participant in the 1911 Liverpool general transport strike which lasted for ten weeks, involving all transport workers and bringing the city to a virtual standstill. The dispute proved to be successful for most of the workers. The waterfront unions were recognized by the employers, concessions were granted, and the nature of industrial relations at the docks was fundamentally changed. Milligan played a vital role by organizing non-union dockers and rapidly became *de facto* deputy to James Sexton, the general secretary of the NUDL. During the First World War he undertook an increasing burden of work at local level as Sexton was involved in national affairs. Although Milligan deprecated strikes and favoured conciliation in industrial disputes he was a tough negotiator, respected by employers and the union membership. He was appointed OBE in 1917 in recognition of his contribution to the war effort. In 1919 he was appointed to the new post of assistant secretary of the NUDL and was elected vice-president of the Mersey district of the National Transport Workers' Federation.

Although never a socialist, Milligan was a strong supporter of the Labour Party and was an advocate of industrial trade unionism. In 1917 he was approached by the

British Empire Workers' League to stand as a party candidate and in 1920 he was offered the Labour candidature at Warrington. He declined both offers, commenting that his chief interests were with the dockers and transport workers of Liverpool and not with any particular political body.

Milligan was a strong supporter of the amalgamation that led the NUDL to become part of the Transport and General Workers' Union in 1922. Ernest Bevin, the secretary of the new union, sought to make Milligan a national officer of the Docks Group in recognition of his experience and popularity on Merseyside but he declined as his wife was reluctant to leave Liverpool. Instead he was appointed secretary of the Mersey area of the union, a position he held until his death in 1925. He was made a JP in 1924.

One of the problems facing early unskilled unions was to find officials of talent, integrity, and dedication. Milligan was a man who possessed these qualities, who served his union with unswerving loyalty and dedication, and who retained the respect and affection of the rank and file. He died of pneumonia on 30 May 1925, aged fifty-six, at his home at 94 Makin Street, Liverpool, where he had lived for many years. A requiem mass was held at St Francis de Sales Church, Walton, Liverpool, on 3 June and he was buried in Anfield cemetery. The route was lined with a large number of union members and of the public. He was survived by his wife and the list of chief mourners suggests that he had at least one brother and two children.

ERIC TAPLIN

Sources DLB · E. L. Taplin, *The dockers' union: a study of the National Union of Dock Labourers, 1889–1922* (1985) · G. J. Milligan, *Life through labour's eyes: essays, letters and lyrics from the workers' point of view* (1911) · E. Taplin, *Near to revolution: the Liverpool general transport strike, 1911* (1994) · d. cert.

Milligan, William (1821–1893), Church of Scotland minister and biblical scholar, was born on 15 March 1821 at Edinburgh, the eldest of seven children of the Revd George Milligan (1792–1858), a licentiate of the Church of Scotland, and his wife, Janet Fraser (d. 1873). He was educated at the high school in Edinburgh, where he was dux of his class, and when his father became minister at Elie in Fife in 1832 he attended the parish school at Kilconquhar. He went to St Andrews University at the age of fourteen, and graduated MA in 1839. Having decided to enter the ministry of the kirk, he spent two years of his divinity course at St Andrews and then two years at Edinburgh. In 1845, during an absence from parish duties because of ill health, he studied in Germany at Halle under F. A. G. Tholuck and J. A. W. Neander. Following the Disruption of 1843 Milligan decided to remain within the Church of Scotland rather than join the Free Church. He was licensed to preach by the presbytery of St Andrews in 1843 and was ordained on becoming minister of Cameron in Fife in 1844. He was translated to the parish of Kilconquhar in 1850. On 15 December 1859 he married Anne Mary Moir (1840–1914), daughter of David Macbeth *Moir; they had six sons and five daughters. Two sons followed him into the ministry of the kirk; the eldest, George *Milligan

(1860–1934), also became a biblical scholar and the youngest, Oswald, was a noted liturgist. Another son, Sir William *Milligan (1864–1929), became a notable laryngologist and otologist. Milligan was prominent in the work of the general assembly, becoming depute clerk in 1875 and principal clerk in 1886. In 1882 he was elected moderator.

Milligan was the first to hold the chair of biblical criticism at the University of Aberdeen; his tenure ran from 1860 until his retirement in 1893. He was awarded the degree of DD by the University of St Andrews in 1862, and his growing reputation as a scholar was recognized when he was invited to join the New Testament Revision Company in 1870. He joined forces with the more progressive elements among the revisers and formed a lifelong friendship with the English Methodist scholar William Fiddian Moulton. His chief interest lay in the Johannine literature, and the epistle to the Hebrews. With Moulton he published *A Popular Commentary on the Gospel of St John* in 1880, and he later brought out several studies on the Revelation of St John. A commentary on Hebrews remained unpublished at his death. His two most important works were the Croall lectures of 1879–80, published as *The Resurrection of Our Lord* (1881), which ran to several editions in Britain and in America, and the Baird lectures of 1891, which went into print as *The Ascension and Heavenly Priesthood of Our Lord* (1892).

Milligan welcomed the emphasis of much nineteenth-century theology upon the incarnation, but thought that attention should also be given to the resurrection and the ascension which he saw as completing the work of Christ. In Milligan's view, the present life and offering of Christ in heaven were at the centre of the life of the church on earth, the basis of her worship and the source of her power. In heaven Christ continues to exercise his threefold office as prophet, priest, and king. Milligan felt that the priestly office of Christ had been neglected in Scotland, perhaps because of a fear of sacerdotalism, although the reformers had stressed the 'priesthood of all believers'. The church is called to share in Christ's priestly work in the world, and to take on the characteristics of his life. The church should be visibly one, and Milligan made a plea in his 1882 address as moderator for reunion in Scotland to include Episcopalians as well as Presbyterians. Milligan was also active in social and educational issues. In the controversy over the Sabbath, he supported the Sunday opening of the Royal Botanic Garden in Edinburgh. He was elected to the Aberdeen school board, visited Germany in 1888 to investigate provision for secondary education, and sought to further the education of working women through the provision of evening classes. He was also concerned with temperance, and in 1889 visited Sweden to study the operation of the Göteborg licensing system.

It was in worship above all that Milligan saw the church as sharing in the priesthood of Christ. The eucharist was of the utmost importance for him, since in its celebration the church is joined to the one offering of Christ to the Father. Thus the eucharist is the meeting place of heaven and earth, and he thought that one of the greatest needs of the kirk was the restoration of a weekly celebration of communion. He became a member of the Church Service Society, which sought to promote the better ordering of worship, and argued for a greater place to be given to doctrine in the services of the church. Although Milligan's wide sympathies and active social involvement had allied him with broad churchmen, his study of the New Testament led him to identify himself more with high-churchmen in their stress upon the fundamental doctrines of the faith. He thus became closely associated with the formation in 1892 of the Scottish Church Society which sought to 'defend and advance Catholic Doctrine' ('Constitution of the Scottish Church Society, 3', *Scottish Church Society Conferences*, 1st ser., 1894, 198) in the kirk. Milligan was made first president of the society and provided the theological inspiration for such leading members as George Washington Sprott, James Cooper, and John Macleod. When he became terminally ill with kidney disease in September 1893 it was a trial to him that he would not be spared for his work with the society. On his retirement from the chair in Aberdeen he moved with his family to Edinburgh, but he died there shortly afterwards at his home, 39 Royal Terrace, on 11 December 1893, and was buried in Grange cemetery on the 15th. In 1898 a communion table, along with communion plate and a lectern, were dedicated to his memory in the college chapel. One of the foremost British theologians of his day, Milligan's emphasis upon the self offering of Christ in relation to the life and worship of the church has been influential in more recent ecumenical discussions on the nature of the eucharistic offering.

D. M. MURRAY

Sources A. M. Milligan, *In memoriam, William Milligan, D.D.* (1894) · J. Cooper, 'William Milligan', *Aurora borealis academica: Aberdeen University appreciations, 1860–1889*, ed. P. J. A. [P. J. Anderson] (1899), 181–8 · *DNB* · *Fasti Scot.* · W. F. Moulton, 'In memoriam: the Rev. William Milligan, DD', *Expository Times*, 5 (1893–4), 247–51 · A. M. Fairbairn, *The beloved disciple* (1893) · H. L. Yancey, 'The development of the theology of William Milligan (1821–1893)', PhD diss., U. Edin., 1970 · D. M. Murray, 'Doctrine and worship', *Liturgical Review*, 7/2 (1977), 25–34 · J. Macleod, *Judge nothing before the time* (1894) · H. J. Wotherspoon, *James Cooper: a memoir* (1926) · W. S. Bruce, *Reminiscences of men and manners during the past seventy years* (1929) · D. M. Murray, 'Disruption to Union', *Studies in the history of worship in Scotland*, ed. D. B. Forrester and D. M. Murray, rev. 2nd edn (1996), 87–106 · *CCI* (1894)
Archives U. St Andr. L., undergraduate essays
Likenesses G. Reid, oils, U. Aberdeen
Wealth at death £13,733 4s. 2d.: confirmation, 12 Feb 1894, *CCI* · £283 7s. 11d.: additional estate, 8 Feb 1895, *CCI*

Milligan, Sir William (1864–1929), laryngologist and otologist, was born at Aberdeen on 24 August 1864, the son of the Very Revd William *Milligan (1821–1893), professor of biblical criticism at Aberdeen University from 1860 to 1893, and his wife, Anne Mary, daughter of David Macbeth *Moir, physician and author. His elder brother was George *Milligan (1860–1934), Church of Scotland minister and biblical scholar. He was educated at Aberdeen University, graduating MB CM in 1886 and MD with the highest honours in 1892. He married on 17 June 1890 Bertha Warden (b.

1861/2), daughter of James Anderson, shipowner, of Frognal Park, Hampstead, London, and Hilton House, Aberdeenshire; they had one son and one daughter.

Milligan was demonstrator of anatomy in the Aberdeen medical school, and subsequently served for a time as house surgeon at the Northern Hospital, Liverpool. He then proceeded to study otolaryngology at Göttingen and Vienna, and finally settled in Manchester, then at the zenith of its prosperity.

Milligan had the opportunity of introducing more scientific methods, especially those of pathology, into a subject which was then in the stage of primitive empiricism. He became aural surgeon to the Manchester Ear Hospital, aurist and laryngologist to the Royal Infirmary and Christie Hospital, Manchester, and lecturer on diseases of the ear and throat to the nearby Victoria University. He extended his interest to the treatment of laryngeal and oral cancer with radium, and designed an applicator that could be fixed to a tracheotomy tube to hold radium between the vocal folds. He was president of the laryngological and otological sections of the Royal Society of Medicine (1911 and 1921) and with Sir Edward Holt founded the Radium Institute, in Manchester.

Milligan possessed all the attributes of the successful surgeon—impressive personality, sound judgement born of ripe experience, and the power of putting his opinion into action with his hands. He was eager in trying new methods, and was a firm believer in the employment of radium. He delighted in his carpentry workshop, but cared little for sport. His interests were wide and were justified by his ability. They extended from the Radium Institute to a financial trust which he founded in Edinburgh and of which he was chairman. Milligan had distinguished looks and was well built, with slightly aquiline features and fair hair. Well dressed, with charming and dignified manners, he was as successful in the financial world as in medicine. A lifelong Liberal, he (unsuccessfully) contested the west division of Salford in 1922.

During the First World War, Milligan was appointed consulting surgeon for the throat and ear in the north-western area, serving with the rank of major in the Royal Army Medical Corps (Territorial Force). In 1914 he was knighted for his work in the investigation of cancer. His publications include *A Practical Handbook of the Diseases of the Ear* (1911). Milligan died of pneumonia at High Elms Nursing Home, Victoria Park, Rusholme, Manchester, on 19 December 1929; he was survived by his wife.

E. A. PETERS, *rev.* ANITA MCCONNELL

Sources personal knowledge (1937) · N. Weir, *Otolaryngology: an illustrated history* (1990) · m. cert. · d. cert. · *CGPLA Eng. & Wales* (1930)
Likenesses W. Weatherby, watercolour drawing, Man. City Gall.
Wealth at death £293,470 0s. 8d.: probate, 25 April 1930, *CGPLA Eng. & Wales*

Milliken [Millikin], **Richard Alfred** (1767–1815), poet, was born at Castlemartyr, co. Cork, on 8 September 1767, the son of Robert Milliken, a Quaker of Scottish origin, who converted to the established church on arrival in Cork. Initially intended for a commercial profession, Milliken, encouraged by Henry Boyle, later earl of Shannon, was finally apprenticed to an attorney, and, having been admitted and sworn in, began business for himself in Cork. His heart was, however, never really in the law, and having little business he happily devoted his time to painting, music, and the translation of Greek poetry.

Having successfully contributed some of his poems to the Cork *Monthly Miscellany*, Milliken decided to begin his own periodical and in April 1797 started, jointly with his sister, who was herself a historical novelist, a magazine entitled *The Casket* which appeared monthly until the following February. At the time of the uprising in Ireland in 1798, Milliken temporarily abandoned his literary career to join the Royal Cork volunteers, and subsequently became notorious for his zeal and efficiency.

After the uprising had been put down Milliken returned to literature, publishing a wide variety of short fiction, blank verse, and comic ballads, which were often anthologized in the nineteenth and early twentieth centuries and which were particularly popular on the London stage, forming a part of the repertoire of the popular theatre entertainer Charles Matthews. Milliken also wrote several dramas and farces which, although never published, were frequently played with success at theatres including Sadler's Wells.

Milliken was also a keen artist determined to promote the fine arts in his native Cork. In 1815 he founded the Apollo Society for that purpose, whose many endeavours included an exhibition of drawings by local artists including his own, and a popular puppet show comprising farcical operatic scenes. Such aesthetic and philanthropic endeavours ensured that when Honest Dick developed water on the chest and died on 16 December 1815, he was buried with a public funeral at Douglas near Cork.

Milliken's name lived on for many years after his death. In 1816 a posthumous exhibition of his artworks was organized; in 1823 a volume of his poems, with a portrait and a short memoir of his life written by his sister, was published by subscription in London. Milliken is mostly remembered for 'The Groves of Blarney', a mock paean to a country estate overrun with bastard heirs, which made satiric reference to the Munster political scene in the 1780s, and which combined a characteristic use of chiming rhymes with occasionally arresting visual images. The poem was fondly remembered by the characters of Sydney Owenson's popular Gothic novel of 1829 *The O'Briens and the O'Flaherty's* and also finds a place in *The Field Day Anthology of Irish Writing* (1991, 1.1101–2, 2.871).

JASON EDWARDS

Sources R. A. Milliken, *Poetical fragments* (1823) • T. C. Croker, ed., *The popular songs of Ireland* (1839) • D. J. O'Donoghue, *The poets of Ireland: a biographical dictionary with bibliographical particulars*, 1 vol. in 3 pts (1892–3), pt 3, p. 163 • H. H. Spauling, ed., *Irish minstrelsy* (1887) • *N&Q*, 2nd ser., 11 (1861), 452 • *DNB*
Likenesses portrait, repro. in Milliken, *Poetical fragments*

Millin, Terence John (1903–1980), urological surgeon, was born at Helen's Bay, Belfast, on 9 January 1903, the elder of the two children of Samuel Shannon Millin, a Belfast barrister, and his wife, Ella Morton, who was of Scottish origin. He lived at Helen's Bay for only three years and then moved with the family to Rathgar, Dublin. His father became deaf, with a reduction in the family circumstances, and Millin was sent to boarding-school in Tipperary town, and to St Andrew's College, Dublin. Here he won a gold medal for sportsmanship as well as many scholarships, including an entrance award to Trinity College, Dublin, in mathematics. At university he switched to medicine, winning major distinctions and a travelling scholarship that eventually took him to London. After qualifying he took the FRCSI in 1928, the FRCS in 1930, and the MChir (Trinity College, Dublin) in 1931. He worked briefly in Dublin and then went to Britain for a series of training posts. He married, on 16 December 1939, Alice (Molly) Neville Street (1907–1996), a divorcée, and daughter of Herbert Guernsey. They had two daughters.

At All Saint's Hospital, Pimlico, Millin worked with a colourful urologist, Canny Ryall, a valuable apprenticeship that enabled him to develop skills in removing the enlarged prostate via an instrument passed through the urethra. Nevertheless, he recognized the procedure as unsatisfactory: it often caused serious bleeding and frequently had to be repeated. This dissatisfaction led eventually to Millin's developing a radical alternative. He had noted that the prostate was most accessible just behind the pubis, and set about devising an operation using this unique approach. Described in an article in *The Lancet* in December 1945 this technique immediately bore Millin's name, though he had wished to avoid the eponym and simply call it the retropubic procedure. It made him world famous overnight, and he was in demand not only to operate on prominent figures but also to give lectures and demonstrations all over the world. Nevertheless, the publicity did not endear him to the London urological establishment, which for some time was sceptical of the new procedure's superiority over the old operations.

Millin, who had been in charge of the Emergency Medical Service hospital at Putney, London, during the war, operating throughout the blitz, had made little money in this period. He disagreed with the concept of the National Health Service, and after its introduction set up a highly successful private clinic in Queen's Gate, London. In 1950 he bought a farm in Doneraile, co. Cork, determining to work in London only part time and gradually to diminish his practice, stopping altogether in 1963.

He moved near Dublin in 1957 and rapidly became involved in the affairs of the Royal College of Surgeons in Ireland, being appointed president in 1963 and serving for an unprecedented third year as well as raising large sums of money and having buildings named in his honour. Deliberately eschewing private practice, so as not to compete with the local consultants, he nevertheless gave demonstrations on difficult cases and continued to lecture. He moved to a smaller house outside Dublin, and thence further into co. Wicklow.

Millin may be judged as the most distinguished Irish surgeon of the twentieth century. Not only was his operation safer and more satisfactory than any existing procedure, but for twenty-five years it was the most widely used technique for an enlarged prostate. But this invention was only the most visible aspect of somebody who had earlier captained the Trinity rugby team (beating the Oxford fifteen) and scored for Ireland, and who had subsequently, as a speedy, facile surgeon, invented other operations and instruments, as well as being in demand as an after-dinner speaker and raconteur. Handsome, warm, and tall, he was also a non-stop smoker of cigarettes, even when operating. He developed cancer of the larynx and had radiotherapy, but refused radical surgery and endured some distressing last months of life. He died at his home, Wayside, Kilcoole, co. Wicklow, on 3 July 1980, in reduced circumstances.   BARRY O'DONNELL

Sources J. A. Miller and M. D. Staunton, 'The birth of retropubic prostatectomy: Millin', *Journal of the Royal Society of Medicine*, 82 (1989), 494–5 · S. C. Lewsen, 'Terence Millin', *Journal of the Royal Society of Medicine*, 83 (1990), 200 · J. D. H. Widdess, *The Royal College of Surgeons in Ireland and its medical school, 1784–1984*, 3rd edn (1984) · J. B. Lyons and others, *The irresistible rise of the RCSI* (1984) · *CGPLA Eng. & Wales* (1980) · private information (2004) · B. O'Donnell, *Terence Millin: a remarkable Irish surgeon* (2002)

Likenesses photograph, repro. in Lewsen, 'Terence Millin', 200

Wealth at death £62,033: probate, 18 Nov 1980, *CGPLA Éire* · £24,119—in England and Wales: probate, 18 June 1981, *CGPLA Eng. & Wales*

Millingen, James (1774–1845), archaeologist, was the second son of Michael Millingen, a Dutch merchant who had emigrated from Rotterdam to Batavia (in the Dutch East Indies) and had married there Elizabeth Westflaten Coole, daughter of the Dutch governor of the island. The family came from the town of Millingen in the north-west of the Netherlands. After leaving Batavia, the elder Millingen settled at 9 Queen Square, Westminster, where James Millingen was born on 18 January 1774. His brother was John Gideon *Millingen.

James Millingen was educated at Westminster School, and was encouraged by his father's friend and neighbour, the bibliophile Clayton Mordaunt Cracherode (1730–1799), to study numismatics. Poor health prevented him from entering the engineer corps. The father's business seriously declined while James was still young and when the family migrated to Paris in 1790, in the vague hope of prospering there, Millingen reluctantly became a clerk in the banking house of M. Van de Nyver, a connection of his mother. He subsequently obtained a post in the French mint, and came to know a wide circle of scholars.

Late in 1792 Millingen was arrested as a British subject by a decree of the National Convention, and was imprisoned in the Madelonettes prison, then in that of the Luxembourg, and finally in the Collège des Ecossais, where he remained until July 1794. On his release he settled in Calais. He married, about 1797, Elizabeth Penny, daughter of Christopher White of Calais, and had one daughter and three sons: Horace, a captain in the Madras army; Julius Michael *Millingen; and Augustus, assistant surgeon in the East India Company's service at Madras. He was a staunch member of the Church of England, and when his wife and daughter became Roman Catholics a

separation between him and them followed. In his later years he was much distressed by the detention, owing to his wife's machinations, of his son Julius in a school of the inquisition.

Millingen left Calais to become a partner in the banking house of Sir Robert Smith & Co. in the rue Céruti, Paris, but the concern failed and he went to live in Italy, where the climate eased his asthma. There he wrote and compiled valuable works in French and Italian on coins, medals, Etruscan vases, and related subjects, and also contributed articles to learned journals in Britain and on the continent. He bought antiquities with considerable discernment, and supplied private collections and most of the important museums of Europe, including the British Museum, with fine examples of ancient art. For some time he lived at Rome and at Naples, where he met Lady Blessington, but later he settled at Florence, paying occasional visits to Paris and London. A civil-list pension of £100 a year was granted him, and he was a royal associate and later an honorary member of the Royal Society of Literature, a fellow of the societies of antiquaries of London and of France, a correspondent of the Institut de France (18 January 1833), and a member of many other European learned societies.

When on the eve of moving from Florence to London, Millingen died of a catarrhal infection on 1 October 1845. His library was sold in London by Sotheby on 25 June 1849.   GORDON GOODWIN, rev. ELIZABETH BAIGENT

Sources *GM*, 2nd ser., 25 (1846), 98–9 · *The Athenaeum* (1 Nov 1845), 1058 · BM, Add. MS 22891, fol. 339 · private information (1894) · J. G. Millingen, *Recollections of republican France* (1848) · S. H. Reinach, *Peintures de vases antiques recueillies par Millin, 1808, et Millingen, 1813* (1891)

Wealth at death valuable library sold after death

Millingen, John Gideon (1782–1862), army surgeon and writer, born at 9 Queen Square, Westminster, on 8 September 1782, was the son of Michael Millingen, a Dutch merchant, and his wife, Elizabeth Westflaten (née Coole), and was the younger brother of James *Millingen. In 1790, at the age of eight, he was taken by his father to Paris, and lived through the horrors of the revolution. During the imprisonment of his brother, whose liberation he claimed to have attempted, he frequently met Robespierre, Danton, Barère, and other Jacobin leaders, according to his *Recollections*. He matriculated at the École de Médecine, and after studying under Boyer obtained a medical degree. On 26 January 1802 he joined the British army as assistant surgeon in the 97th regiment (Queen's Own), and was ordered to Egypt on campaign. On 16 November 1809 he was appointed surgeon in the 31st (Huntingdonshire) regiment, and full surgeon to the army on 26 May 1814. He served in all the Peninsular campaigns under Wellington and Lord Hill, and was present at Waterloo as principal surgeon of cavalry and at the subsequent surrender of Paris. He was afterwards sent to the West Indies, but loss of health compelled him to retire on half pay in 1823.

Millingen lived for some time in Boulogne, where he published in 1826 his *Sketches of Ancient and Modern Boulogne*. He was connected in a medical capacity with the military lunatic asylum at Chatham, and in 1837 was appointed, on the resignation of Sir William Ellis, resident physician to the Middlesex Pauper Lunatic Asylum at Hanwell. On resigning this post early in 1839, he reportedly opened a private lunatic asylum in Kensington. He wrote farces, a novel entitled *Adventures of an Irish Gentleman* (1830), works on various subjects including duelling and lunatic asylums, and his 'somewhat highly coloured' memoirs, *Recollections of Republican France from 1790 to 1801* (1848). He died in London in 1862.

T. B. SAUNDERS, rev. JAMES FALKNER

Sources *Army List* · J. G. Millingen, *Recollections of Republican France from 1790 to 1801* (1848) · Boase, *Mod. Eng. biog.*
Likenesses portrait, repro. in Millingen, *Recollections of Republican France*

Millingen, Julius Michael (1800–1878), physician and archaeologist, was born in London on 19 July 1800, the son of archaeologist James *Millingen (1774–1845) and his wife, Elizabeth Penny, daughter of Christopher White of Calais. His early years were divided between Calais and Paris. He was schooled in Rome; a visit to Goethe in Weimar indicates an early interest in literature. In 1817 he entered the University of Edinburgh, attending medical classes each winter until 1821, when he received his diploma from the Royal College of Surgeons.

Soon after Greece declared independence from the Ottoman empire, Millingen, whose observations on Greeks suggest that he was philhellenic in deed rather than thought, was recommended to the notice of the Greek Committee in London by William Smith, MP for Norwich. On 27 August 1823 Millingen left England for Corfu, with letters of introduction to the Greek government and to Lord Byron. Arriving in Cephalonia in November of that year, he found Byron at Metaxata, and immediately noted that the poet's health—already suffering under the strain of commanding the Greeks—was being further undermined by a strict diet which vanity was compelling him to follow. It was probably Millingen's refreshing lack of romanticism that prompted the disillusioned Byron to suggest that the doctor accompany him to Missolonghi and act as physician to his Suliote forces. As Byron's health deteriorated, Millingen, together with Dr Francesco Bruno, tended him until his death on 19 April 1824. Controversy over Byron's death was inevitable: none of those attending or visiting him was present in his room throughout; their personal enmities influenced their subsequent accounts. Byron told each one different things as his mood or his madness dictated and it was a condition of his charm to make each one believe himself the true confidant. At the autopsy, Millingen identified the cause of death as purulent meningitis. Bruno later accused Millingen of causing that death by delaying phlebotomy, an accusation to which Millingen replied at length in his *Memoirs*. But the controversy has overshadowed the fact that while Byron was still living, both doctors agreed that bleeding was the appropriate treatment, disagreeing only about where to apply the leeches. As repeated bleeding fatally weakened the poet, Millingen and Bruno share a

large measure of responsibility for his death. To Byron, both were 'butchers'.

After Byron's death, Millingen had a severe attack of typhoid fever. On recovering, he was appointed surgeon in the Greek army, in which he served until its surrender to the Turks. He was taken prisoner by Ibrahim Pasha, and released only on the urgent representations of Stratford Canning, then British ambassador to the Porte. In November 1826 Millingen went to Smyrna and, after a short stay in Kutaya and Broussa, settled in 1827 in Constantinople. There he attained considerable reputation as a physician. He was attached in that capacity to the Dutch legation, becoming Dutch delegate to the International Board of Health sitting at Galata. Millingen was also court physician to five successive sultans and was one of the commission appointed to inquire into the death of the second of these, Abdul Aziz. He was also a member of the International Medical Congress on Cholera held in Constantinople in 1866, and an original member and afterwards president of the General Society of Medicine. He did something to introduce the use of the Turkish bath in England in 1860 and contributed an article in French on oriental baths to the *Gazette Médicale d'Orient* (1 January 1858). Millingen published occasional pieces throughout his life, as particular subjects or events captured his interest, for example *Arbitrary detention by the inquisition at Rome of three protestant children, in defiance of the claim of their father* (1842).

The publication of Millingen's *Memoirs* in 1831 elicited a furious response from Edward John Trelawny, one of his acquaintances in Greece, which was published in the *Literary Gazette*. Trelawny wrote that Millingen was 'a tall delicately-complexioned, rosy-cheeked, dandy boy, of simpering and affected manners', who whined and cried 'like a sick girl' (Moore, 433). Trelawny was responding in kind to doubts about his own manliness hinted at by Millingen in his *Memoirs*.

Like his father, Millingen was an archaeologist. For many years he was president of the Greek *syllogos* or literary society of Constantinople, where he lectured in Greek on archaeological subjects. He discovered the ruins of Aczani in Phrygia, an account of which was published by George Thomas Keppel, and excavated the site of the temple of Jupiter Urius on the Bosphorus. Several of his manuscripts, including a life of Byron, were destroyed in the great fire at Pera in 1870, in which he lost nearly all his personal effects. Millingen died in Constantinople on 30 November 1878.

DAVID CAMERON HALL

Sources J. Millingen, *Memoirs of the affairs of Greece, … with anecdotes relating to Lord Byron, and an account of his last illness and death* (1831) · *DNB* · private information (1894) [sons; registrar of Edinburgh University] · D. L. Moore, *The late Lord Byron: posthumous dramas* (1961) · *Byron's letters and journals*, ed. L. A. Marchand, 11 (1981) · *The works of Lord Byron: letters and journals*, [rev. edn], ed. E. H. Coleridge and R. E. Prothero, 6 (1901); repr. (1904)

Millington, Gilbert (*c.*1598–1666), regicide, was probably born at Felley Abbey, Nottinghamshire, the eldest son of Anthony Millington (*d.* 1620), gentleman, and his wife, Prudence, daughter of William Gilbert of Colchester and his wife, Jane. Millington studied at Peterhouse, Cambridge, matriculating in 1612, graduating BA in 1616, and at Lincoln's Inn, where he had been admitted in October 1614; he became a barrister at Lincoln's Inn in 1621. About 1618 he married Alatheie (d. 1644x58), who may have been a member of the Lawley family of Shropshire. When his father died in 1620 Millington inherited Felley Abbey, an estate of 800 acres that was undoubtedly worth more than the £200 per annum assessment of its value made the following year, judging in part from the £50 that Millington pledged to defend parliament in June 1642. Throughout the mid- and late 1620s Millington followed the capital's political affairs in letters from his younger brother John, who held a minor position at court as purveyor of the king's wine cellar. Millington began a lengthy period of public service in Nottinghamshire as sewers commissioner in 1629; he was justice of the peace by 1631, and deputy lieutenant in 1638 and again in July 1642. He also maintained his contacts in London, for by May 1639 he had been appointed master of chancery.

Elected to parliament for Nottinghamshire in October 1640 Millington was closely involved in matters affecting his county. When Colonel John Hutchinson, governor of Nottingham Castle, needed funds, he appealed to Millington, whose concern for Nottingham Hutchinson commended in January 1643. The commissions on which Millington served attest to his stature in the county, beginning with the assessment commission in February 1643, and including the commissions to sequester delinquents' estates (March 1643), preserve documents seized by sequestrators (November 1643), administer the shrieval oath (September 1644), regulate the excise (June 1645), raise troops for the north (June 1645), and settle the militia (December 1648). In 1643 the earl of Clare designated Millington his deputy for Nottingham's recordership. The committee of both kingdoms dispatched Millington to Nottingham in July 1644 to serve on the committees and to resolve differences between the town and Governor Hutchinson. As late as December 1643 relations between Millington and Hutchinson were cordial, but by October 1644 they had degenerated. The colonel's wife, Lucy, bitterly complained that Millington had endeavoured 'to foment and rayse up the factions in the Towne against the Governor' (Hutchinson, 139). Millington, she charged, had maliciously written to each member of the committee of both kingdoms, creating false impressions of her husband. Colonel Hutchinson and his brother, alleged Millington, were planning to betray Nottingham Castle to the royalists. Dismayed at this rupture, on 11 November the committee of both kingdoms ordered the principal in the dispute to desist, and it appointed a seven-man committee, including Millington and Hutchinson, to oversee the latter's activities. Subsequent reports from Hutchinson to Millington were businesslike. For his services, in June 1645 the Commons voted Millington a weekly allowance of £4 until 20 August 1646. He served as clerk of the committee for plundered ministers in 1645 and on the joint parliamentary committee that discussed ways to preserve

the peace between England and Scotland in the following year.

Millington's concern with Nottinghamshire continued during the second civil war. Although he made few recorded appearances in the House of Commons before Pride's Purge, afterwards he became one of the Rump Parliament's leading members. Two days after the Commons declared its supremacy on 4 January 1649, it appointed Millington to the committee charged with designing a new great seal. Of greater consequence was his selection the same day to the court appointed to try Charles. He was one of the few barristers on the tribunal—which he attended assiduously—and he voted for the king's execution and signed the death warrant [see also Regicides]. During the ensuing two years he was active in parliament, supporting a presbyterian church settlement and sitting on such committees as those for the excise, the Royal Navy, the universities, soldiers' arrears, plundered ministers, and the renewed war against Scotland. During this period he also served as assessment commissioner for Nottingham town and county and as governor of the school and almshouses at Westminster. When he petitioned the Rump Parliament for compensation owing to losses sustained when Newcastle's troops plundered his estate, inflicting damages totalling £1713, parliament in 1651 granted him revenues of £135 3s. 4d. per annum from Ansley Woodhouse and Kirkby Woodhouse in Nottinghamshire; both properties had been part of Newcastle's estate. During the spring of 1652 Millington served on the committee to condemn the Racovian catechism of the Socinians, though he apparently avoided parliament later in the year, probably in opposition to Cromwell. After returning in November, the following month he was again named assessment commissioner for the town and county of Nottingham, an appointment repeated (for the county only) in June 1657 and July 1659. He was the target of a complaint in September 1654 from Margaret, widow of the minister Edward Rood, for refusing to forward an order to parliament from the committee for plundered ministers that ordered compensation of £100.

On the eve of the Restoration, Millington was named assessment commissioner for Middlesex and Westminster in January 1660 and for Nottingham county and town the same month and again in March. Two months later the government issued a proclamation ordering the regicides to surrender themselves. Although Millington complied he was excepted from the Act of Indemnity and was arraigned on 16 October, convicted of high treason, and sentenced to death on 17 October. From the Tower he petitioned Charles to pardon his 'prodigious' treason, and his life was spared; the crown, however, confiscated his estate. He again petitioned, this time to the House of Lords on 7 February 1662, claiming he had been overawed by those in power in 1648–9. For security reasons the government transferred him to Mont Orgueil Castle on the island of Jersey, where he died by 19 September 1666; he was interred in common ground. Lucy Hutchinson harshly depicted Millington as a hard drinker who spent considerable time in taverns and brothels, finally marrying a sixteen-year-old 'Alehouse wench' shortly after his first wife died (Hutchinson, 146). Whatever Millington's personal shortcomings, his record of government service suggests that he was reasonably diligent and capable, though certainly no leader.   RICHARD L. GREAVES

Sources *CSP dom.*, 1623–6; 1628–9; 1635–6; 1639–40; 1644–5; 1648–50; 1652–4; 1660–61; 1666–7; 1660–70, addenda · *JHC*, 3–8 (1642–67) · W. C. Metcalfe, ed., *The visitations of Essex*, 1, Harleian Society, 13 (1878) · PRO, State Papers 29/95/106; 29/96/26 · L. Hutchinson, *Memoirs of the life of Colonel Hutchinson*, ed. J. Sutherland (1973) · Keeler, *Long Parliament* · Bodl. Oxf., MS Tanner 62, fols. 295, 467 · Bodl. Oxf., MS Tanner 66, fol. 224 · C. H. Firth and R. S. Rait, eds., *Acts and ordinances of the interregnum, 1642–1660*, 3 vols. (1911) · *Sixth report*, HMC, 5 (1877–8), 18–19, 80, 155 · *Seventh report*, HMC, 6 (1879), 157 · Thurloe, *State papers*, 1.77–9 · *The manuscripts of his grace the duke of Portland*, 10 vols., HMC, 29 (1891–1931), vol. 1, pp. 105, 293, 295–6, 477 · B. Worden, *The Rump Parliament, 1648–1653* (1974) · Venn, *Alum. Cant.*

Archives BL, Add. MS 25302, fol. 145 · Bodl. Oxf., MSS Tanner 62, fols. 295, 467; 66, fol. 224

Wealth at death estate confiscated by crown

Millington, James Heath (1799–1872), portrait and miniature painter, was born in Cork. The miniaturist Mary Mannin, *née* Millington, may have been his sister. After spending his early years in England, he returned to Cork in 1821, setting up as a miniaturist, but moved later that year to Dublin, where he exhibited an oil portrait at the Society of Artists. He was admitted to the Royal Academy Schools on 1 April 1826, winning a silver medal each year from 1826 to 1829. He first exhibited at the Royal Academy in 1831, sending a portrait of J. C. Bishop, and *Vulcan's Cave*. He exhibited twenty-six pictures there, mainly portraits, including two of the Hon. Thomas Murray (exh. 1837 and 1849), and a painting of the children of Sir John Hobhouse (exh. 1834). His oil paintings may have been influenced by the work of William Etty (1787–1849) and A. E. Chalon (1780–1860), his fellow pupils at the Royal Academy Schools. He also showed at the British Institution and the Suffolk Street Gallery. Millington lent several miniatures to the South Kensington Museum for the exhibition of portrait miniatures in 1865, and the museum (now the Victoria and Albert Museum) has three of his miniatures: *A Lady* (1820), *Mrs Maria Walsh* (1821), and *Miss Isabella Laing* (1836). He was curator of the school of painting at the Royal Academy for a short time.

Millington died on 11 August 1872 at his home, 5 Chepstow Place, Bayswater, London.   L. H. CUST, *rev.* ANNE PIMLOTT BAKER

Sources D. Foskett, *Miniatures: dictionary and guide* (1987) · W. G. Strickland, *A dictionary of Irish artists*, 2 (1913), 116–17 · B. S. Long, *British miniaturists* (1929), 298–9 · Graves, *RA exhibitors* · S. C. Hutchison, 'The Royal Academy Schools, 1768–1830', *Walpole Society*, 38 (1960–62), 123–91 · d. cert.

Millington, John (1779–1868), engineer and natural philosopher, was born on 11 May 1779 in Hammersmith, Middlesex, the third child of Thomas Charles Millington, attorney, and Ruth Hill. After school he went to Oxford University at an unknown date, but financial difficulties forced his withdrawal in 1798, when he turned to the study of law. Admitted to the bar in 1803, he practised for

two years, particularly in the area of patents, before studying engineering. For twenty-five years he worked intermittently as chief engineer of West Middlesex Water-Works and superintendent of the royal grounds in London; he was also the owner of Hammersmith Iron-Works. In 1816 he obtained a patent (no. 3977) for a ship's propeller. Thirteen years later, a select committee of the House of Commons examined him on patent laws.

Elected a fellow of the Society of Arts in 1805 Millington served as steward in 1821 but resigned in the same year. In 1815 the Royal Institution retained him to lecture on natural philosophy, naming him professor of mechanics in 1817. For the next sixteen years, he lectured on the application of scientific and mathematical principles to the practical problems of public works. He left the Royal Institution in 1829. Millington and the chemist William Thomas Brande jointly edited the *Quarterly Journal of Science*, in which Millington published on the hydraulic ram (1816) and on street illumination (1818). He also served as first editor of the Library of Useful Knowledge. He published *An Epitome of the Elementary Principles of Mechanical Philosophy* (1823; 2nd edn, 1830). He married Emily Hamilton, daughter of the artist William Hamilton, on 18 December 1802 at the parish church of St James. They had six children; three survived childhood. Millington was an original member of the Royal Astronomical Society. He served as secretary from 1823 to 1825 and ten years later he compounded for life membership. In 1823 he was elected a fellow of the Linnean Society, and he was instrumental in founding the London Mechanics' Institution, in which he served as vice-president and lecturer until 1829. Interest in medicine led him to studies in London with Sir Astley Cooper as well as to lecturing on chemistry at Guy's Hospital. In 1827 the new University of London named him to their first faculty as professor of engineering and the application of mechanical philosophy to the arts, but he resigned the chair in 1828 after the council refused to guarantee him a salary of £400 a year.

In early 1829 the Anglo-Mexican Mining Association of Vera Cruz engaged Millington as chief engineer of their silver mines and superintendent of the mint for a three-year period. He and his family sailed for Mexico in October. There he oversaw the association's mineral industries, ensuring a sufficient level of mined silver for regularized coin production. At the end of his contract he travelled with his eldest son to Philadelphia. His wife died in 1833 on her voyage to join them. While in Philadelphia Millington opened a scientific equipment store, which soon failed. On 20 July 1834 he married Sarah Ann Letts (b. 1800). They had three children.

In late 1834 the Geological Society of Pennsylvania employed Millington and Andres del Rio to investigate the Rappahannock goldmines, to the south-west of Fredericksburg, Virginia. In 1835 the Rappahannock Mining Company named him their chief engineer, a post he held for eleven months, during which time he applied for the chair of chemistry and natural philosophy at the College of William and Mary, Williamsburg, Virginia. Joseph

Henry and Robert Hare offered recommendations for the position. In February 1836 he began his twelve-year tenure at William and Mary. In 1839 he published his eight-volume *Elements of Civil Engineering*. During his stay in Virginia he assembled a collection of scientific apparatus which, along with his library, he valued at $10,000; he served as lay reader at Bruton Parish Episcopal Church; bought the Wythe House on the Palace Green; and on 9 March 1838 received a doctorate of medicine from Jefferson Medical College, Philadelphia.

Tension between the faculty and board of visitors resulted in a full faculty resignation in 1848. Millington applied for a professorship at the new University of Mississippi, Oxford, Mississippi, which he accepted on 28 September 1848, immediately leaving Williamsburg with his family and his instrument collection. In 1851 the university purchased the majority of Millington's instruments, several of which were deposited in the university museum, including a replica of Joseph Henry's electromagnet, a 2000 volt chemical battery originally housed at the Royal Institution, a camera ludica, a brachistochrone, acoustic tubes, an unusual sextant, and a large transit.

At Mississippi, Millington taught chemistry, natural philosophy, geology, and agriculture. He managed the first geological survey of Mississippi. In 1853 he resigned in order to accept the chair of chemistry and toxicology at the medical college in Memphis, Tennessee. In 1855 the Mississippi Central railroad retained him as an engineering consultant. In 1859 or 1860 he retired and moved to LaGrange, Tennessee. Shortly thereafter the town became the headquarters sequentially for the Confederates and the Union army, the latter converting Millington's house into a federal hospital and burning his papers. Millington and his family moved to Philadelphia in 1863, where they remained for two years.

In 1865 Millington and his wife moved to Richmond, Virginia, to live with their daughter Kate Blankenship. Millington died at Richmond on 10 July 1868 and was buried in Bruton parish church in Williamsburg. His tombstone describes him as 'the worthy friend and associate of men like Sir H. Davy, Brewster, Herschel, and Lord Brougham'. His combined pursuit of natural philosophy, chemistry, and civil engineering was rare, even in the non-disciplinary environment of the early nineteenth century. It is in the American south, however, where he made his more enduring mark, establishing an effective system of engineering education and innovative classroom lectures built around demonstrations and experimentation.

CHARLOTTE WEBB

Sources John Millington MSS, College of William and Mary, Williamsburg, Virginia, Earl Gregg Swem Library · William and Mary College MSS, College of William and Mary, Williamsburg, Virginia, Earl Gregg Swem Library, folders 61, 62, 63, 108 · G. F. Holmes, 'Professor John Millington, MD, 1779–1868', *William and Mary College Quarterly*, 2nd ser., 3 (1923), 23–5 · S. C. Gladden, 'John Millington', *William and Mary College Quarterly*, 2nd ser., 13 (1933), 155–61 · L. O. Tarleton, 'John Millington, civil engineer and teacher, 1779–1868', MA diss., College of William and Mary, 1966 · H. H. Bellot, *University College, London, 1826–1926* (1929)

Archives College of William and Mary, Williamsburg, Virginia, Earl Gregg Swem Library, John Millington MSS | College of William and Mary, Williamsburg, Virginia, Earl Gregg Swem Library, William and Mary College MSS, folders 61, 62, 63, 108
Likenesses A. Kaufman, oils, 1780, Valentine Museum, Richmond, Virginia
Wealth at death Wythe House, Palace Green, Williamsburg, Virginia

Millington, Mary [*real name* Mary Ruth Quilter; *married name* Mary Ruth Maxted] (1945–1979), sex worker and actress, was born on 30 November 1945 at Willesden Maternity Hospital, London, the only child of (Ivy) Joan Quilter (1914–1976), a clerical assistant at the Foreign Office and in the reading room of the British Museum. It was in the museum library that Joan Quilter met her lover, John William Klein (1899–1973), opera critic, who also had two sons and three daughters with his wife. Klein's occasional visits to his second family were sometimes disturbing. Mary Quilter was sexually precocious, and from 1959 had many experiences with boys from the Dorking area who were grateful for the gusto and versatility of her performances. She was a kind, warm-hearted, and sensual woman who found it easiest to relate to men and other women physically. After a secretarial course in Cricklewood she enrolled at Reigate School of Art in 1962. On 4 April 1964 she married Robert Norman Maxted (*b.* 1941), a butcher's boy.

Mary Maxted was deputy manager of a boutique in Dorking when she was first approached, about 1968, by the pornographer John Lindsay to pose for magazines. She felt no shyness at nude modelling, looked stunningly attractive, and was a highly amenable worker. Money was always important to her sense of well-being, and in this period was urgently needed: she was supporting her mother, who was chronically ill through chain-smoking. In her first hardcore pornographic film, filmed in Germany and entitled *Miss Bohrloch* (1970), she played the part of an insatiable prostitute who in the course of fourteen minutes exhausts two young men. Among devotees of hardcore pornography, this film is always remembered as 'the one with the ping-pong ball'. It was followed by *Oral Connection* (1971). During the early 1970s she began working as a prostitute with a select list of clients: rich businessmen, well-known family entertainers, famous sportsmen, and the like. Her magazine fans, unlike these clients, were overwhelmingly working class. In 1974, still under the name of Maxted, she played the part of a traffic warden stripper in her first mainstream sex film, *Eskimo Nell*, a bawdy comedy about the sex film industry.

Mary Maxted's performances in 1975, as a lesbian stablehand in *Erotic Inferno* and having sex with a street hole-digger in a workman's tent in *I'm Not Feeling Myself Tonight*, were her last under her married name. Later in 1975 her career was relaunched under the name Mary Millington by the energetic young pornographer David Sullivan, who became her lover. She was a phenomenal success in Sullivan's magazines—*Private 21*, *Whitehouse 7*, and *Playbirds*—and managed his sex shop at 1539 London Road, Norbury. She relished this job, and energetically promoted the sale of sex toys. A series of police raids on the south London shop, and extortion demanded by corrupt Metropolitan officers, increased her loathing of puritanism, censorship, and the police. Sullivan strenuously promoted the film *Come Play with Me* (1977), which made him a fortune and secured Millington's fame. She revelled in the adulation, which some of her family believed was compensation for her father's neglect.

However, Millington's mother's death in 1976 affected her badly. She was so distressed that she began training as a mortician in order to be closer to her mother. The actress Diana Dors introduced her to cocaine in this period. Having become pregnant by Sullivan, she had an abortion. Her pleasure in bisexuality seems to have increased, although she was scared by police threats that they would put her in Holloway prison where she would be sexually abused. She was arrested on several occasions during 1977, although never charged, and understandably came to feel that the officers enjoyed humiliating or scaring her. She was an animal lover, active in the People's Dispensary for Sick Animals, and police threats to hurt her Alsatians affected her greatly. She reacted to this duress by campaigning against censorship laws, sexual repression, and the National Viewers and Listeners' Association headed by Mary Whitehouse. However, she was exceedingly deficient in self-confidence when not behaving sexually, and her high profile added to the strains on her. She was director of a Sullivan company that was prosecuted in 1977 under the Obscene Publications Act; she was acquitted, but the trial caused her great anxiety.

Mary Millington's last hardcore film was the Swedish *Private Pleasures* (1975), although she continued to appear in such softcore Sullivan films as *The Playbirds* (1978) and *Confessions from the David Galaxy Affair* (1979). By 1978 the British sex film industry was declining as home video machines became available. For years Millington had dealt entirely in cash. When pursued by the Inland Revenue with tax claims dating back to 1969, she refused to co-operate, and was eventually served with a tax demand totalling about £1 million. She did not understand that the figure was a negotiating ploy, and this combined with continuing police bullying made her very stressed. She had always been light-fingered, and now developed kleptomania. In June 1979, after taking a dress and brass lamp from a department store, she was arrested and roughly handled by the police. Her trial, which she dreaded, was scheduled for 21 August. On 18 August, sedated and after visiting her mother's grave, she was arrested in Banstead for shoplifting a bracelet. The police treated her with great verbal aggression. Dreading imprisonment, on 19 August 1979 she killed herself at her Surrey home with a mixture of paracetamol and gin. She was buried on 24 August beside her mother in St Mary Magdalene's churchyard, South Holmwood. All the sex shops and porno cinemas in Soho closed on the day of her funeral.

RICHARD DAVENPORT-HINES

Sources S. Sheridan, *Come play with me* (1999) · J. Adamson, *Sex and fame: the Mary Millington story*, documentary, 1996 [Channel 4] · M. Millington and D. Weldon, *The amazing Mary Millington* (1978) · A. Bennett, *Writing home* (1994), 105 · *CGPLA Eng. & Wales* (1981) · *The Times* (6 Sept 1973)
Archives FILM BFI NFTVA, J. Adamson, *Sex and fame: the Mary Millington story*, Channel 4, 1996
Likenesses photographs, repro. in Sheridan, *Come play with me*
Wealth at death £23,521: administration with will, 7 Sept 1981, *CGPLA Eng. & Wales*

Millington, Sir Thomas (1628–1704), physician, was born at Newbury, Berkshire, son of Thomas Millington. He was educated at Westminster School under Richard Busby, and at Trinity College, Cambridge, where he was admitted as pensioner on 31 May 1645, becoming scholar the following year, matriculated at Easter 1646, and took his BA in 1649. His tutor at Trinity was James Duport. In 1659 Millington was intruded fellow of All Souls, Oxford, where he took his MA on 30 May 1651 (incorporated at Cambridge 1657) and in 1659 the BD and DM degrees. On 30 September in that same year he deposed his candidature at the College of Physicians, London.

A college tradition at All Souls claims that Millington was chamber fellow there with Thomas Sydenham, who indeed spoke favourably of him in later years. Millington's medical studies led to his involvement with Ralph Bathurst, Jonathan Goddard, Thomas Willis, Richard Lower, Christopher Wren, Nathanael Hodges, George Castle, and others who, centred first on Thomas Willis, and later (after 1664–5) on Robert Boyle, were extending and completing the anatomical and physiological researches of William Harvey, particularly in the areas of respiration and study of the brain. Millington was an active participant in these researches, valued for his reflections and commentaries on the activities of the group. Millington was particularly close to Willis, who acknowledged him in the dedicatory epistle of his *Cerebri anatomiae* (1664), and with Richard Lower, who dedicated his *Tractatus de corde* (1669) to him, and maintained relations even after they had both departed to London, where the two physicians would consult together when needful.

On 2 April 1672 Millington became a fellow of the College of Physicians and in 1675, thanks to the intervention of Bathurst, succeeded Willis as Sedleian professor of natural philosophy at Oxford. Although Wood noted that the inaugural lecture the following year was 'much commended', Millington may already have been living in London. Although he retained the chair until his death, he generally discharged its duties by deputy. In 1676 Millington had a conversation with Nehemiah Grew which, as subsequently reported by the latter, has led to Millington being credited with the discovery of the sexuality of plants. Millington, as Grew's report shows, had an intuition of this, but full development of the idea was effected by Grew, whose understanding of the phenomenon was independent of Millington.

Censor of the Royal College of Physicians in 1678, 1680, 1681, and 1684, and Harveian orator in 1679, Millington was knighted on 6 March 1680. Shortly before, on 23 February, he had been licensed to marry Anne Hannah King, daughter of Sir William Russell of Worcestershire, and widow of Major John King; the couple had two children,

Sir Thomas Millington (1628–1704), by unknown artist, c.1690–1700

Thomas and Anne. In 1680 Fell proposed Millington to Sancroft for the vacant chair of medicine at Oxford; however, Millington's practice in London was extensive, fashionable, and lucrative. In 1685 he attended at the final illness of Charles II. From 1686 to 1689 he was treasurer of the Royal College of Physicians and president from 1696 until his death. He was first physician-in-ordinary to William III and then to Queen Anne. Millington's only published work was the *Report of the physicians and surgeons commanded to assist at the dissecting the body of his late majesty at Kensington March the tenth MDCCII* (1702), which he co-signed with Sir Richard Blackmore and Sir Edward Hannes. Sociable and of a pleasant disposition, Millington seems to have been esteemed for his learning and probity. Praised under the name of Machaon in Garth's *Dispensary* as of 'matchless merit', he is eulogized in the annals of the Royal College of Physicians as 'affable in his conversation, firm in his friendships, diligent, and happy in his practice, cordial and open in consultations, eloquent to an extraordinary degree' (Munk, 1.365). During his tenure as president of the college Millington succeeded in reducing its debt to the executors of Sir John Cutler from £7000 to £2000, which he then paid himself. If Millington's personal qualities were probably responsible for the success of his practice, which warranted him a fortune of £60,000 according to Carter, his career should be seen as exemplary of the success that a modest talent could attain through the support of privileged circles—in Millington's case, those of Busby's pupils and the Oxford experimental physiologists. Debilitated by recurrent fevers, Millington died of asthma in London on 5 January 1704, being buried

on 28 January in the Wentworth chapel of Gosfield church, Essex, of which he was patron as owner of the Gosfield estate and where there was a monumental brass to his memory, until it was stolen at the beginning of the nineteenth century. He was commemorated by the younger Linnaeus in the genus Millingtonia of the trumpet-shaped flowers *Bignonciae* native to hot climates.

A. J. TURNER

Sources Munk, *Roll* · *The life and times of Anthony Wood*, ed. A. Clark, 5 vols., OHS, 19, 21, 26, 30, 40 (1891–1900) · *Old Westminsters*, 2.647 · R. T. Gunther, *Early science in Oxford*, 3: *The biological sciences* (1925), 53, 132, 209, 266 · R. G. Frank, *Harvey and the Oxford physiologists* (1980) · *The works of Symon Patrick, including his autobiography*, ed. A. Taylor, 9 vols. (1858) · R. Plot, *The natural history of Oxford-shire* (1677) · E. Carter, *The history of the University of Cambridge* (1753), 329, 350 · W. Musgrave, *Obituary prior to 1800*, ed. G. J. Armytage, 5, Harleian Society, 48 (1901), 201–2 · Bodl. Oxf., MS Rawl. D. 1160, fol. 34a · Bodl. Oxf., MS Tanner 36*, fol. 51 · N. Grew, *The anatomy of plants…* (1682), 171 · DNB

Archives BL, Sloane MSS, Add. MSS 2148, 3565 · Bodl. Oxf., Rawl. MSS

Likenesses oils, c.1690–1700, RCP Lond. [*see illus.*] · T. Woolnoth, stipple, 1807 (after G. Kneller), Wellcome L.

Wealth at death £60,000: Carter, *History*, 350

Millington, William (d. 1466), college head, was probably born at Pocklington, Yorkshire. His family background and early education are unknown, but there is a strong presumption that he received his training in arts at Cambridge. After he had acquired the degree of MA, he went on to study theology and had attained the degree of DTh by 1441. Millington may have been a fellow of Clare College, Cambridge, before 1443, although this point has not been firmly established. A problem has arisen because William has often been confused with his brother, John Millington, who became master of Clare College in 1455 and for whom William acted as an executor. William Millington came to enjoy a high reputation for scholarship. The contemporary writer John Capgrave speaks of him, from personal knowledge, as surpassing his predecessors in 'scholastic questions, literary depth and ripeness of character' (*Liber de illustribus Henricis*, 133). This eminence brought him to the attention of Henry VI, and he was selected as the first rector of the royal college of St Nicholas in Cambridge, a college established by Henry VI in 1441. As first designed, the college was not specially privileged, and it was not specifically connected with Eton College, which had been founded by Henry VI on 11 October 1440.

The second and more elaborate version of what would become known as King's College was inaugurated in 1443. The name of the college was changed to the royal college of the Blessed Mary and St Nicholas in Cambridge, and Millington was retained as head of the reconstituted college with the new title of provost. During Millington's provostship the agreement known as the *Amicabilis concordia* was drawn up in 1444. This compact bound together the provosts of King's and Eton, and the wardens of New College and Winchester College, for their mutual defence in law before secular or ecclesiastical judges, and for their mutual aid against hostile outsiders. In the event, the *Amicabilis concordia* proved of little benefit to King's and

Eton when the colleges came under attack from the Yorkist government after the deposition of Henry VI.

By 1446 Henry VI's plans for King's College had reached maturity, and in 1447 a commission, which included Thomas Beckington, bishop of Bath and Wells (d. 1465), and William Alnwick, bishop of Lincoln (d. 1449), delivered new statutes for the royal foundation. Millington refused to swear obedience to these statutes, and for this he was deprived of the provostship. The reasons for his rejection of the new statutes are not entirely clear. It is unfortunate that the text of these statutes has not been found, and the earliest surviving statutes are those given to the college in 1453. Millington may have objected to a provision, present in the statutes of 1453 and perhaps in those of 1447, restricting elections to the college to scholars from Eton. However this may be, he was certainly concerned about his own situation after the statutes of 1447 had granted the college exemption from the jurisdiction of the university chancellor. Since Millington had sworn an oath to the chancellor before the issue of these statutes, he was adamant that he had to abide by his oath unless a dispensation was obtained. In a subsequent acrimonious exchange of letters between Millington and Beckington, the former attacked the bishop in threatening language for the part that he had played in his deprivation.

Between 1447 and 1450 Millington actively campaigned against the opinions of Reginald Pecock, bishop of Chichester (d. c.1460), who was tried for heresy in 1457. Millington preached at Paul's Cross, London, and declared that those who patronized Pecock would surely never prosper. It is noteworthy that Millington's successor as provost of King's, John Chedworth (d. 1471), was also antagonistic to Pecock and was one of the assessors at his trial. After being deprived of the provostship of King's, Millington seemingly remained in Cambridge and may have been associated with Clare College. He was one of a committee of seven that was authorized to frame statutes for Queens' College, Cambridge, in 1448, although no statutes were issued during Henry VI's reign. In 1457 Millington was appointed one of a team of six masters who were deputed to supervise the building of the new schools of philosophy and civil law, and he was still engaged in that capacity in 1459. As the executor of his brother, John Millington, master of Clare College, he gave four books of theology to the library of that college. He died in 1466 and was buried in the south chancel aisle of St Edward's Church, Cambridge. ALAN B. COBBAN

Sources Emden, *Cam.* · G. Williams, 'Notices of William Millington, first provost of King's College', *Cambridge Antiquarian Society Communications*, 1 (1858), 287–328 · *Memorials of the reign of Henry VI: official correspondence of Thomas Bekynton, secretary to King Henry VI and bishop of Bath and Wells*, ed. G. Williams, 2 vols., Rolls Series, 56 (1872), vol. 2, pp. 157–74 · *Johannis Capgrave Liber de illustribus Henricis*, ed. F. C. Hingeston, Rolls Series, 7 (1858), 133 · T. Gascoigne, *Loci e libro veritatum*, ed. J. E. Thorold Rogers (1881) · V. H. H. Green, *Bishop Reginald Pecock* (1945) · J. Saltmarsh, 'The founder's statutes of King's College, Cambridge', *Studies presented to Sir Hilary Jenkinson*, ed. J. C. Davies (1957), 337–60 · J. Saltmarsh, 'King's College', *VCH Cambridgeshire and the Isle of Ely*, 3.376–407 · T. Fuller, *The history of the University of Cambridge from the conquest to the year 1634*, ed. M. Prickett and T. Wright (1840), 85, 152 · V. Davis, *William Waynflete: bishop and educationalist* (1993) · R. W. Hunt, 'Medieval inventories of Clare College Library', *Transactions of the Cambridge Bibliographical Society*, 1 (1949–53), 105–25 · J. Twigg, *A history of Queens' College, Cambridge, 1448–1986* (1987), 6–7 · J. R. Wardale, *Clare College* (1899), 26

Millner, John (*fl.* **1701–1736**), soldier and military writer, served throughout Marlborough's campaigns of 1701–12 with the Royal regiment of Ireland (18th foot) in which he attained the rank of orderly room sergeant. He was the author of a *Compendious journal of all the marches, battles, sieges … and other actions of the … allies in their … war against … France in … Holland, Germany and Flanders … under the … duke of Marlborough*, which was completed in 1712 and published together with an introduction in 1733, and is chiefly noticeable for its very precise itinerary of all the marches, sieges, and battles of the army from 1702 to 1712. In 1736 he was still serving with his regiment, as a sergeant, in Minorca, when Major Gillman, then in command, wrote home to the colonel, Major-General Armstrong, recommending a commission be granted him as adjutant. A list of officers was attached to the letter pledging subscriptions totalling £80 for the purchase of a commission, yet nothing seems to have come of it. The army list of 1740 shows no Millner holding a commission at that date. The exact date of his death has not been discovered.

JONATHAN SPAIN

Sources J. Millner, *A compendious journal of all the marches, battles, sieges … and other actions* (1733) · H. W. Pearse, 'Marlborough's men', *Cornhill Magazine*, [3rd] ser., 30 (1911), 67–75 · D. Chandler, *Marlborough as military commander* (1973) · G. Le Mesurier-Gretton, *The campaigns and history of the royal Irish regiment*, 1 (1911), 71–2 · *The army list of 1740*, Society for Army Historical Research (1931)

Mills family (*per.* **1773–1939**), bankers, was one of the most distinguished families in English banking and came to prominence with **William Mills** (1714–1782). Five generations of Millses were partners in Glyn's, England's foremost private banking house, from its foundation in 1753 to its take-over by the Royal Bank of Scotland in 1939, the name of Mills appearing in the bank's various names from 1773 onwards. Moreover, in the second half of the nineteenth century, the Mills family was at the very core of the network of relationships linking landed aristocracy and City aristocracy.

Glyn's held a unique position in English banking, offering a combination of deposit, investment, and merchant banking. On the one hand it acted as the London correspondent for a large number of country banks, on the other hand, it behaved almost as a continental *banque d'affaires* (Cottrell, 229). The bank's partners, in the first place George Carr Glyn, later first Baron Wolverton, had played a leading role in railway finance in the 1840s; for many years Glyn's was known as the 'railway bank'. They had also handled Canadian loans in the 1850s and, with a group of business associates and family relatives, had promoted several overseas banks: in Australasia, with the Bank of Australasia in 1837; in the Middle East, with the Bank of Egypt and the Ottoman Bank in 1856, the latter becoming the Imperial Ottoman Bank in 1863; in central

Europe with the Anglo-Austrian Bank in 1863; and in Latin America with the London and Brazilian Bank in 1863 and later with the English Bank of the River Plate in the 1880s. Glyn's also had a large number of major provincial industrial customers, including John Brown, Vickers, Stavely Coal and Iron, and British Westinghouse, and its involvement in industrial finance extended to acting as an issuing house on behalf of customers.

These business activities were reflected in the size of the company. By 1850 Glyn's had probably become the largest London bank, though precise data are not available as private banks did not then publish their balance sheets. From the 1860s onwards, however, private banks could no longer compete in terms of size with the ever expanding joint-stock banks. Nevertheless, Glyn's remained a large bank until the last decade of the nineteenth century and maintained its pre-eminence among private banks, with total assets twice as large as those of its immediate follower, Barclays, in 1891. This partly explains the decision not to enter the amalgamation movement in the 1890s and to preserve, as Algernon Mills put it, 'a characteristic which we alone of all large and serious banks possess, namely of having only one door' (Fulford, 226–7).

Members of the Mills family took an active part in the bank's development, though none of them played the leading role until the twentieth century. As a banking family, however, it was among the most successful in the country, with a remarkable longevity due to the maintenance of the bank's independence until the eve of the Second World War. The first connection was established in 1773, when William Mills, a linen draper, became a partner in Glyn and Hallifax. The bank was forced to suspend payment for a few weeks following a temporary shortage of cash during the crisis of the summer of 1772. William Mills came forward with the sum of £10,000, another £20,000 being advanced by the third Lord Middleton. The name of the bank was then changed to Hallifax, Glyn, Mills, and Mitton. William Mills was the son of John Mills (1676/7–1717), a clerk in the six clerks office of the court of chancery, and his wife, Sarah Best, who also had one daughter, who died in infancy. He inherited £1500 from his father on coming of age and in 1739, married Selina, the only child of Sir John Salter of Warden's Hall, Essex, lord mayor of London, and became prominent in trade with the Orient through his father-in-law. William Mills was almost sixty by the time he joined Glyn's and, with no training or experience in banking, he played little role in the affairs of the bank which was mainly run by Thomas Hallifax. He died at his house, Warden's Hall, Essex, on 1 December 1782.

William Mills had no surviving children and was succeeded in the bank by his nephew **Charles Mills** (1755–1826), second son of the Revd John Mills, rector of Barford, near Warwick, and his wife, Sarah Wheler. Born on 13 July 1755, he was educated at Rugby School, and was a partner in the bank from 1777 to 1826. The business of the bank expanded considerably during this period, with the number of staff increasing from seven in 1790 to fifty-one in 1830, and the number of country bank agencies from four

to forty-nine. The outstanding personality of the period, however, was Richard Carr *Glyn, the other members of the partnerships being of far less consequence. The Mills, however, were important providers of business, especially through their connections with Indian trade. Charles Mills succeeded his older brother William Mills (1750–1820) as director of the East India Company in 1785 and was deputy chairman in 1801. He was MP for Warwick between 1802 and 1826. On 21 March 1810, at the age of fifty-five, he married Jane, daughter of the Hon. Wriothesley Digby of Meriden, Warwickshire, and the sister of his older brother's wife. They had no children. Charles Mills died on 29 January 1826.

Charles Mills was in his turn succeeded at the bank by his nephew **Sir Charles Mills**, first baronet (1792–1872), third son of William Mills (1750–1820), and his wife, Elizabeth Digby. After his retirement from the East India Company in the 1780s, William Mills bought the estate of Bisterne, near Southampton, and was MP for Coventry from 1805 to 1812. Born at Popes, Hatfield, on 23 January 1792, Charles Mills was educated at Harrow School and Christ Church, Oxford, and became partner in 1821. In 1825 he married Emily, a daughter of Richard Cox, one of the partners in Cox's Bank. He was created a baronet in 1868. Charles Mills was a senior partner at the time of his death on 4 October 1872 at Hillingdon Court, near Uxbridge, Middlesex. He ensured his family's entitlement to four-tenths of the bank's profits after the amalgamation in 1864 with Currie & Co., under the name of Glyn, Mills, Currie & Co., John Wheler Mills (1801–1865), Charles's younger brother, had become a partner in 1835, retiring in 1864 owing to ill health. The bank continued to expand during Charles Mills's years as partner. However, as in the previous generation, the bank's leading figure was a Glyn: George Carr *Glyn, first Baron Wolverton (1797–1873), was the driving force behind the bank's involvement in railway finance and in overseas issues.

Charles Henry Mills, first Baron Hillingdon (1830–1898), Sir Charles Mills's only son, was born on 26 April 1830 at Camelford House, Park Lane, London. He entered the bank in 1852 after Eton College and Christ Church, Oxford. He became senior partner in 1872 on his father's death, and succeeded to the baronetcy. However, the bank's guiding spirit from the mid-1860s to the mid-1890s was Bertram Woodehouse *Currie (1827–1896). In 1853 Charles Henry Mills married Louisa Isabella Lascelles (d. 1918), daughter of the third earl of Harewood; they had five sons and three daughters. This alliance with an old aristocratic family reflected the Mills's new social status and their increasing integration into the upper classes. But this marriage also took place within a network of relationships linking the old families of the banking aristocracy (Barings, Glyns, Grenfells, Mills, Smiths) with a few families of the landed aristocracy (Cassis, 221–43). Charles Henry Mills was the archetypal London private banker of the Victorian age, dividing his life between his bank, his outside City interests, politics, and society. His City directorships included the chairmanships of the London committee of the Imperial Ottoman Bank and of the Union

Bank of Australia, two overseas banks in the promotion of which Glyn's had played a major role, and of the North British and Mercantile Insurance Company. In politics he was conservative MP for West Kent from 1868 to 1886 when he was raised to the peerage as Baron Hillingdon. He died suddenly in Wilton Church, Wiltshire on 3 April 1898. One of the wealthiest private bankers of his day, Lord Hillingdon left £1,479,000.

Lord Hillingdon was succeeded to most of his offices by his eldest son, **Charles William Mills**, second Baron Hillingdon (1855–1919). Educated at Eton and Magdalen College, Oxford, he became a partner in Glyn's in 1879 and was conservative MP for the Sevenoaks division of Kent from 1885 to 1892. His directorates also included the Imperial Ottoman Bank, the Union Bank of Australia, and the North British and Mercantile Insurance Company, as well as the Anglo-Austrian Bank, another overseas bank originally linked to the Glyn's. In 1886 Charles William Mills followed the trend of aristocratic marriages by London private bankers by marrying Alice Marion Harbord, daughter of the fifth Baron Suffield who had himself married Cecilia Baring, sister of Edward Charles Baring, first Baron Revelstoke (1828–1897). Charles William Mills and his wife had three sons. He left about £1 million on his death on 6 April 1919, at 6 Park Place, Mayfair, London. Lord Hillingdon retired from active business life in 1907, owing to ill health, leaving the conduct of the bank to other partners, including his younger brother Algernon Henry Mills (1856–1922), one of the members of the Mills family most directly engaged in daily banking activities, in particular during the war years. The dominant force in the bank during the inter-war years was a Mills by marriage, General Sir Herbert Alexander *Lawrence (1861–1943), who in 1892 married Isabel Mary, eldest surviving daughter of the first Lord Hillingdon. He joined the bank in 1919, bringing to it much needed enterprise and energy, presiding in particular over the merger in 1922 with Holt & Co., bankers and army agents, and with the West End bank Child & Co. the following year. Lawrence was also chairman of Vickers, Glyn's long-standing customer and one of Britain's largest companies.

The bank's capital was sold to the Royal Bank of Scotland in the summer of 1939. The partners were mostly young men and with the approach of war it was feared that if some of them were to be killed, the payment of death duties on their family holdings would cause formidable difficulties. Although the days of the private banks had long gone, this state of affairs was partly due to the premature death of a promising member of the sixth generation. Charles Thomas Mills (1887–1915), the elder son of Charles William Mills, second Lord Hillingdon, had become a partner in the bank, as well as conservative MP for the Uxbridge division of Middlesex, in 1910. He was killed on the western front in October 1915.

YOUSSEF CASSIS

Sources R. Fulford, *Glyn's, 1753–1953: six generations in Lombard Street* (1953) • P. L. Cottrell, *Industrial finance, 1830–1914: the finance and organization of English manufacturing industry* (1980) • Y. Cassis, *City bankers, 1890–1914* (1994) • Boase, *Mod. Eng. biog.* • Burke, *Peerage* • *WWBMP* • *The Times* (4 April 1898) [obit. of C. H. Mills, first Baron Hillingdon] • Foster, *Alum. Oxon.* • HoP, *Commons, 1790–1820* • d. cert. [Charles William Mills] • b. cert. [Charles William Mills] • IGI • CGPLA Eng. & Wales (1872)

Wealth at death £1,479,000—Charles Henry Mills • approx. £1,000,000—Charles William Mills • under £600,000—Sir Charles Mills: resworn probate, July 1873, CGPLA Eng. & Wales (1872)

Mills, Alfred (1776–1833), draughtsman, of whose parents nothing is known, was a skilful designer of illustrations to small books of juvenile instruction, such as his *Pictures of Roman History in Miniature* (1809), *Pictures of Grecian History* (1810), *Pictures of English History in Miniature* (1811), *Portraits of the Sovereigns of England* (1817), and *A Short History of the Bible and New Testament* (1810). He worked in this line for about forty years for publishers including Messrs Darton and Harvey of Gracechurch Street, and J. Harris of St Paul's Churchyard. He also frequently drew designs on blocks for the leading wood-engravers. In 1807 he exhibited three figure drawings at the Royal Academy. After an industrious life he died at Walworth, London, on 7 December 1833, leaving a wife and six children.

L. H. CUST, rev. ANNETTE PEACH

Sources GM, 2nd ser., 1 (1834), 116 • R. K. Engen, *Dictionary of Victorian wood engravers* (1985)

Mills, Annette [real name Edith Mabel Mills] (1894–1955), entertainer, was born in Chelsea, London, the elder of the two children of Lewis Mills (b. 1867), schoolmaster, and his wife, Edith (d. c.1935). Her brother was the actor Sir John Mills (b. 1908). She changed her name to Annette when she became a professional dancer. The family moved to Suffolk when her father became head of the local school in Belton, near Great Yarmouth, and she was educated at King's Lynn high school, and the Convent of Notre Dame in Norwich. She studied the piano and the organ at the Royal Academy of Music, but after her fiancé was killed in action in France she married Captain McKlenaghan, and had one daughter, before training as a dancing teacher and taking a job teaching at a dancing academy in Notting Hill Gate, London.

Annette Mills became known as an exhibition dancer; she and her dancing partner, Robert Sielle (real name Cecil Leon Roberts), an American and later her second husband, gained an international reputation as the 'English Astaires'. They were engaged for a season at Ciro's Club in London, where they danced some comedy numbers, and appeared at the Ambassadors Club in New York, introducing the Charleston to London after they had seen it danced in New York. A few years later, after a tour of South Africa, they brought the Moochi, based on Zulu rhythms, to London. But her dancing career ended in 1930 when she broke a leg leaping through a window on stage in Cape Town, and she turned to writing popular songs and revue numbers. Her first hit was the song and dance 'Hands, knees, and boomps-a-daisy', and many of her songs from the 1930s, including 'With a Feather in her Tyrolean Hat', were published and became popular. She appeared in cabaret and revues, and for four years wrote the words and music for C. B. Cochran's Trocadero supper shows.

Annette Mills appeared on the first *In Town Tonight* programme on the BBC on 18 November 1933, and went on to broadcast frequently, playing and singing her own light comedy songs and accompanying others. Her full-length radio shows included the musicals *The Golden Rose* (1936), *Hawaiian Rhapsody* (1936), and *The Talking Horse* (1937), and in 1936 she wrote the lyrics and the script for an all-black variety programme, *Molasses Club*. A talented mimic, she devised a programme, *People who have Sung my Songs* (1938), in which she appeared as a songwriter doing impersonations of stars such as Douglas Byng singing her songs. She appeared in the series *Airs and Disgraces* in 1939. She also had some contracts with Radio Luxembourg as an announcer on the Pond's Cold Cream programme, and wrote signature tunes such as 'The Phillips' Tonic Yeast March'.

At the beginning of the Second World War, during the first air-raid warning, Annette Mills wrote the song 'Adolf', which became a great hit. In spring 1940 she went to Paris, where she spent three months as a cabaret artist at Lucienne Boyer's club Chez Elle: while there, she broadcast regularly to Britain, and also toured the Maginot line entertaining French troops. Although she wanted a job as a BBC announcer or producer, this did not materialize, and she spent the next two years entertaining the troops and broadcasting on the Home Service and the Forces' Programme. Her most famous wartime songs were 'When we're home, sweet home again' and 'Un jour' (1940), written at the request of the BBC French section. In November 1942, on her way back from a troop concert, she was seriously injured in a car accident, breaking both legs, and spent nearly two years in hospital, undergoing a series of operations. She came out briefly to be carried on stage for *Variety Bandbox* in June 1944, but spent most of her convalescence writing short stories, some of which were broadcast by the BBC, including *Mum* (1943), which was repeated

several times and translated into Afrikaans and Spanish for overseas transmission. She also wrote plays, and *Rotten Row Speaking*, a hospital play, was adapted for television in 1947.

In August 1946 Annette Mills made her first television appearance, in *Composer at the Piano*. By then she had been introduced to the puppeteer Ann Hogarth, who invited her to see the Hogarth puppet collection, and she chose the marionette Muffin the Mule, carved for the Hogarth Puppet Circus in 1934, for a new show on the *For the Children* programme in November 1946. She sat at the grand piano, singing songs such as:

Here comes Muffin, Muffin the Mule,
Dear old Muffin, playing the fool

and repeated what Muffin whispered in her ear, while Muffin danced on the lid, with Ann Hogarth pulling the strings. Muffin quickly became a television personality, and was joined by other Hogarth puppets, including Sally the Seal, Oswald the Ostrich, Peregrine the Penguin, and Louise the Lamb. She wrote the songs and the music, and Ann Hogarth wrote the scripts. When the television *Children's Hour* began in January 1948, the first programme was compered by Annette Mills and Muffin. Two Muffin films were made for the Rank Children's Clubs in 1948, the first Muffin songbook was published in 1948, illustrated by Annette Mills's daughter, Molly Blake, and these were followed by a Decca album of songs. *The Muffin Show* opened in the West End at the Vaudeville Theatre at Christmas 1952. Through the Muffin Club she received thousands of letters from children who read her Muffin books, which included *Muffin the Mule* (1949), *Here Comes Muffin* (1952), and *Muffin at the Seaside* (1953), while Ann Hogarth wrote stories for the Muffin annuals from 1951 to 1954. Despite personality clashes between the two partners, which threatened the breakup of the team in 1950, they stayed together. Annette Mills, however, devised a new glove

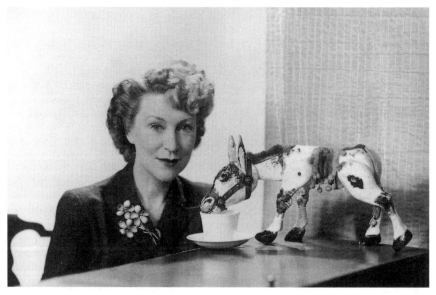

Annette Mills (1894–1955), by Elliott & Fry, 1949 [with Muffin the Mule]

puppet kitten for very young children, and Prudence Kitten made her first television appearance on 7 June 1950 on *For the Children*.

A supporter of animal causes, Annette Mills became vice-president of the Anti-Vivisection Society. At the end of 1954, at the height of her success, she developed a brain tumour, and died in the London Clinic on 10 January 1955. Her second marriage had ended in divorce. At the memorial service at St Martin-in-the-Fields on 14 January 1955 there was a replica of Muffin the Mule in red and white flowers on the altar, and wreaths 'To darling Muffin and his lovely Auntie Annette'. ANNE PIMLOTT BAKER

Sources J. Mills, *Up in the clouds, gentlemen please* (1980) • A. R. Philpott, *Dictionary of puppetry* (1969), 108–9, 163 • *The Times* (11 Jan 1955) • *Daily Telegraph* (11 Jan 1955) • BBC WAC • d. cert. • *CGPLA Eng. & Wales* (1955)

Archives FILM BFI NFTVA, documentary footage

Likenesses Elliott & Fry, photograph, 1949, NPG [*see illus.*] • double portrait, photograph (with John Mills), repro. in Mills, *Up in the clouds*, 84–5 • photograph (with Muffin the Mule), repro. in *Daily Telegraph*

Wealth at death £20,916 9s. 7d.: probate, 16 Feb 1955, *CGPLA Eng. & Wales*

Mills, Bertram Wagstaff (1873–1938), circus proprietor, was born on 11 August 1873 at 53 City Road, London, the eldest son of Lewis Halford Lupton Mills, secretary to a joint-stock company, and his wife, Mary Fenn Mills (*née* Wagstaff). He left school by the age of fifteen, and began to work with his father, who had since become a proprietor of a coach-building works and owned two small farms in Harefield, near Ricksmansworth, and Chalfont St Giles. While living in Chalfont, Bert, as he was familiarly known to his more intimate friends, learned how to drive four-horses-in-hand. On 23 March 1901 he married Ethel Kate, daughter of William Notley, a Suffolk farmer; they had two sons, Cyril Bertram *Mills (1902–1991) and Bernard.

Before the First World War, when he was in the carriage-building and harness business, Mills exhibited his carriages and horses on the continent at the Concours Hep-frique at Paris and similar shows at Brussels and The Hague. In Britain, he attended the first International Horse Show at Olympia in 1907, and was regularly in the ring at the Dublin and Richmond horse shows. When the war broke out, he was in charge of the purchase of horses for the English army, eventually becoming a captain in the Royal Army Service Corps. It was his love for horse exhibitions that sparked his interest in the circus, which in Britain was closely allied to equestrianism.

Mills's circus at Olympia became a renowned part of the London Christmas season from 1921, when it was first exhibited, until the 1960s, long after his death. One contemporary, assessing Mills's importance, observed: 'It is not an exaggeration to say that he brought back the circus to England at a time when it seemed that it was about to quietly expire, killed by the War and mechanical entertainment' ('Death of Bertram Mills', 18). Certainly the burgeoning film industry posed a threat—at least in the minds of contemporary impresarios—to the popularity of the circus in British society. Whatever negative forces may have affected the market for circus entertainment, Mills,

Bertram Wagstaff Mills (1873–1938), by Howard Coster, 1936

nevertheless, expanded his enterprise. After approximately nine years of exhibiting in London, he created a tenting show which was said to have cost £40,000 to launch and £2500 to run weekly.

From 1928 Mills involved himself in municipal affairs, acting as member of the London county council until his death in 1938. He was the chairman of three LCC committees—entertainment, licensing and inspection of films, and Sunday entertainment. He also occupied the esteemed role of president of the Showmen's Guild, founded by the circus showman, George Sanger. As a protector of the interests of showmen and also member of the LCC, Mills sometimes had conflicting interests. 'My last memory of him', said one observer, 'was of his protecting at the L.C.C. the interests of a small showman who had a performing lion, and who he thought was being victimized', a casualty of the LCC's concern for wild animal welfare ('The man we knew', 18). In addition, Mills was registered as prospective Conservative parliamentary candidate for the Isle of Ely less than a year before his death.

Mills's main passion in life, however, was coaching. As such, he published numerous articles on the subject and served as president of the Hackney Horse Society publications. Towards the end of his life, the Coaching Club elected him as a member, 'an honour which was unsolicited by him … and for that reason [was] a recognition that gave him very great personal pleasure' ('England's circus king', 5).

Mills died at the age of sixty-four of cardiac syncope and bronchial pneumonia on 16 April 1938 at his home, Pollards Wood, Chalfont St Giles. Reflecting on the day of Mills's funeral, one observer in Chalfont said, 'it was a general day of mourning. Shops were closed and cottages drew their blinds' ('England's circus king', 5). He was buried in Chalfont on 19 April. BRENDA ASSAEL

Sources 'England's circus king: death of Capt. Bertram Mills', *Buckinghamshire Advertiser* (22 April 1938), 5 • *WWW* • C. B. Mills, *Bertram Mills circus: its story* (1967) • 'The man we knew', *World's Fair* (23 April 1938), 1 • 'Death of Bertram Mills', *World's Fair* (23 April 1938), 18 • *DNB* • b. cert. • m. cert. • d. cert. • *CGPLA Eng. & Wales* (1938)

Archives Circus Friends Association, Liverpool • Theatre Museum, London, files relating to circus | FILM BFI, London, 'On tour with the circus', BBC Newsreel (2 July 1948) · BFI, London, 'Television is here again', Marcus Cooper (1946) · BFI, London, British Movietone News, vol. 20, no. 1020, 17 Dec 1948 · BFI, London, 'Bertram Mills Circus', BBC (17 Dec 1959) · BFI, London, 'Big top farewell', British Movietone (2 Jan 1967) | SOUND BL NSA [call nos. 1625, 9944, LP 27127]

Likenesses H. Coster, photograph, 1936, NPG [*see illus.*] · photograph, 1938, repro. in 'The man we knew', 1 · H. Coster, photographs, NPG

Wealth at death £146,574 15s. 1d.: probate, 4 July 1938, *CGPLA Eng. & Wales*

Mills, Charles (1755–1826). *See under* Mills family (*per.* 1773–1939).

Mills, Charles (1788–1826), historian, born on 29 July 1788 at Croom's Hill, Greenwich, was the youngest son of Samuel Gillam Mills, surgeon. He was educated privately, and, after a brief experience in a merchant's counting-house, was articled in 1804 to Messrs Williams and Brookes of Lincoln's Inn. In 1810 he placed himself for a year's study in conveyancing under James Humphreys. From boyhood he had always been an avid reader, and he now permanently injured his health by studying through the night. An attack of lung disease compelled him to spend the winter in Nice in 1814–15. He did not enjoy the law, and, on inheriting a moderate fortune, abandoned it for literature.

Mills was considered to be a man of learning, but as a historian was a very humble follower of Gibbon. His first work, *An History of Muhammedanism* (1817; 2nd edn, 1818), was accidentally seen in manuscript by Sir John Malcolm, who not only warmly recommended its publication, but helped in the revision by the loan of many valuable oriental treatises from his own library. The *History* received a good measure of critical commendation, which led to the publication of the amended second edition. At the time of its publication it was proclaimed to be the only complete authority on 'Muhammadanism' in any language. It was translated into French by G. Buisson in Guernsey in 1826, and was circulated in British India. His next book, *The History of the Crusades* (2 vols., 1820; 4th edn, 1828), bears fewer traces of the influence of Gibbon, and established for Mills a sound literary reputation, bringing him to the attention of Sir Walter Scott. His last and most popular work was *The History of Chivalry, or, Knighthood and its Times* (1825) which ran to a second edition within a year, its success reflecting the popularity of the growing Gothic revival and interest in medievalism. It led to a correspondence between Mills and Sir Walter Scott, conveyed in the preface to the second edition of the book and, on Scott's part, through his publisher Archibald Constable of Edinburgh. The correspondence concerned the nature of Scott's fictitious historical authorities in *The Talisman* (1825). *The History of Chivalry* led Scott to declare his great respect for the talents and industry of the author. Mills's collected works were translated into French by P. Tiby (7 vols., 1825).

Mills died of a recurrence of his old complaint, brought on by his exertions in his literary pursuits, at Southampton on 9 October 1826. He was a bachelor. A few months before his death he was elected one of the knights of Malta, in recognition of his allusions to that fraternity in his *History of the Crusades*. Despite the success of his last work and a good contemporary reputation, Mills's work soon fell into obscurity and was little known by the mid-century.   GORDON GOODWIN, rev. MYFANWY LLOYD

Sources A. Skottowe, *A memoir of the life and writings of Charles Mills* (1828) · *GM*, 1st ser., 96/2 (1826), 559–60 · *The letters of Sir Walter Scott*, ed. H. J. C. Grierson and others, centenary edn, 12 vols. (1932–79), vol. 8, pp. 271–2 · Allibone, *Dict.*

Likenesses R. W. Sievier, bust, 1824 · sketch, repro. in Skottowe, *Memoir of … Charles Mills*, frontispiece

Mills, Sir Charles, first baronet (1792–1872). *See under* Mills family (*per.* 1773–1939).

Mills, Sir Charles (1825–1895), colonial administrator, was born at Ischl, Austria, and educated chiefly at Bonn. He lived in Yorkshire with his stepfather, whose surname he bore. On 1 February 1843 he enlisted as a private in the 98th regiment, and went to China, where he was made staff clerk in the adjutant-general's office, and excused ordinary duty. He seems to have become well known in the general society of the station, though nominally only Corporal Mills. When his regiment was ordered to India in 1848, he was offered a clerkship in the consular service, but preferred to go into active military service. He was therefore with his regiment through the Punjab campaign, and was present in 1849 at Chilianwala, where he was wounded. On 6 June 1851 he received a commission as ensign in the 98th regiment, became adjutant on 17 June 1851, and on 22 November 1854 was promoted lieutenant in the 50th foot.

Mills, having returned home with his regiment, became, in 1855, brigade major of the 1st brigade of the British German Legion under General Woolridge. He went to the Crimea with the legion under Sir Henry Storks. During this war he gained special credit for his share in suppressing an attempt at mutiny among some of the Turkish troops. He received the order of the Mejidiye.

At the close of the Crimean War, when the German legion was disbanded, it was proposed to make a military settlement of Germans on the eastern border of British Kaffraria. Mills left the army, and was selected as officer in charge of the settlement; he arrived at Cape Town in January 1858, and became successively sheriff of King William's Town and secretary to the government of Kaffraria. He had brought out 3000 men, most of whom prospered; he himself stated that for seven years he was their 'guide, philosopher; and friend', and looked upon this as the most successful work of his life. He intended writing an account of the settlement, but never did so.

In 1865, when Kaffraria was incorporated with Cape Colony, Mills retired on a pension. In 1866 he was elected to represent King William's Town in the Cape parliament where he supported the government, opposing the party which at that time demanded responsible government. Sir Philip Wodehouse, who was then governor, eventually persuaded him to resign political life and enter the colonial service of the Cape, and in 1867 appointed him chief clerk for finance in the colonial secretary's office. In 1872 he became permanent under-secretary in the same office when self-government was conferred on the colony; in this capacity he rendered considerable service in organizing the Cape civil service. In 1880 he was sent to London to arrange as to the adjustment of expenditure on the Anglo-Zulu War. When in 1882 the Cape government decided to have an agent-general of their own in London, Mills was at once selected for the position, which he took up in October 1882.

As agent-general Mills was a familiar and popular figure at all functions in which the colonies were interested. In 1886 he was executive commissioner for the Cape at the Indian and Colonial Exhibition; in 1887 he was delegate for the Cape at the colonial conference; and in 1894 he was one of the delegates of the Cape at the intercolonial conference at Ottawa: this was his last special service. He died, unmarried, at his residence, 110 Victoria Street, Westminster, London, on 31 March 1895, and was buried at Highgate cemetery. He had been made CMG in 1878, KCMG in 1885, and CB in 1886. He was a governor of the Imperial Institute.

Mills was in later years stout and florid, very cheery in manner, and fond of society. He was always reckoned businesslike and capable; at times working exceedingly hard, as when he stayed almost continuously in the colonial secretary's office for over three months in 1872.

C. A. Harris, rev. Lynn Milne

Sources *The Times* (1 April 1895) · *Cape Times* (2 April 1895) · *Cape Argus* [weekly edn] (3 April 1895) · *Cape Illustrated Magazine* (April 1895) · *DSAB* · Boase, *Mod. Eng. biog.* · *CGPLA Eng. & Wales* (1895)
Archives Rhodes University, Grahamstown, South Africa, Cory Library for Historical Research, corresp. | NA Scot., letters to first Baron Loch
Likenesses R. T., wood-engraving, NPG; repro. in *ILN* (31 July 1886) · photographs, Cape Archives and South Africa Library, Cape Town, South Africa · portrait, colonial secretary's office, Cape Town, South Africa · portrait, Civil Service Club, Cape Town, South Africa
Wealth at death £1424 10s. 2d.: probate, 25 May 1895, *CGPLA Eng. & Wales*

Mills, Charles Henry, first Baron Hillingdon (1830–1898). *See under* Mills family (*per.* 1773–1939).

Mills, Charles William, second Baron Hillingdon (1855–1919). *See under* Mills family (*per.* 1773–1939).

Mills, Cyril Bertram (1902–1991), circus proprietor, was born on 27 February 1902 at 56 Norfolk Square, London, the elder son of Bertram Wagstaff *Mills (1873–1938), circus proprietor, and his wife, Ethel Kate, *née* Notley. Educated at Harrow School and Cambridge, where he studied engineering at master's level, Mills began his professional life by working in the oil industry between 1923 and 1925, a job that took him to Rangoon, where he worked in a mosquito- and snake-infested swamp.

Having previously only dabbled in their father's business, Mills and his brother, Bernard, took on the management of the Bertram Mills circus in 1925. The task was daunting for Mills, who commented that 'to accept [this post] meant taking a gamble of going into something for which I had no training and to which I might be totally unsuited' (Mills, 32). His first challenge was to arrange the

Cyril Bertram Mills (1902–1991), by unknown photographer, 1948 [right, with his brother, Bernard Mills]

transport of Alfred Schneider's seventy lions to the London Olympia from Paris. He also searched for talented artists and often flew his own plane to showground sites on the continent in order to audition them. One obituarist noted that:

> his arrival [at such places] was signalled round every caravan within minutes and artists changed into their Sunday-best costumes and resolved to attempt the latest death-defying addition to their acts in the hop[e] of catching his eye and winning a contract for Olympia. (*The Times*, 22 July 1991)

Although Bertram Mills's circus tented in virtually every major British town, it was the Christmas show at Olympia which gave the concern its spectacular reputation. Generations of children in Britain, including the royals, saw the Bertram Mills circus perform there. One member of the royal family told Mills during the circus's last show at Olympia that 'we *had* to bring the children to the last performance. We wanted them to be able to say in later years that they had actually seen the Bertram Mills circus' (ibid.).

In addition to being an engineer cum circus manager, Mills was a secret agent for MI5. Code-named Mr Grey, he was attached to the War Office during the Second World War. The famous British double agent Juan Pujol (code-named Garbo), whose autobiography was published in 1984, claimed that he was recruited into MI5 by Mr Grey, who served as his first case officer, directing his activities which changed the course of the war. A press photograph showed the two of them together in 1984 for the first time since 1940. Friends of Mills felt sure they recognized him standing with Garbo. Mills's wartime activities extended to his head offices in Dorset Square, London, which became the headquarters for the Free French forces of the French resistance. Even after the war he continued his work in intelligence. According to Peter Wright's *Spycatcher*, he was recruited to carry out surveillance activities on the Russians during the Suez Canal crisis, using his circus business as a cover. As a tenant in a flat sandwiched between a cluster of soviet diplomatic buildings in Kensington Palace Gardens, he intercepted signals between these buildings in London and Moscow. At the same time he operated his circus business from the house. 'Every time we needed to deliver staff or equipment to the house', said Wright, 'we used a garishly painted Mills circus van. It was a perfect cover, and the Russians never suspected a thing' (Wright, 104–5).

Spurred by the post-war boom in the circus business, Mills became both successful and rich. In 1947 he launched the circus as a public company on the London stock exchange. This was the first circus in Britain to go public. Two years later Mills became an underwriting member of Lloyd's. The success of the Bertram Mills circus began to ebb, however, with the advent of television, as well as with Mills's unwillingness to cater to the latest trends; he was said to prefer the traditional sawdust performances to New Age costumes, floats, and showgirls. Declining profits led to the closure of Mills's tenting show in 1964, and, as a consequence, its tents, wagons, and animals were sold. The company was later taken over by Maxwell Joseph, head of the Grand Metropolitan hotel chain, although this arrangement proved unprofitable and ended. The name of the company was transferred in 1978 to the new Brighton Centre, although the heyday of the Bertram Mills circus had clearly ended.

Even in his retirement Mills was the subject of popular interest, and in 1989 he was celebrated on *This is your Life*. Suffering from emphysema and a heart condition, he nevertheless made a guest appearance on the same programme in 1990 in order to pay tribute to his last ringmaster, Norman Barrett. He died at his home, 51 Cumberland Terrace, Camden, London, on 20 July 1991, of bronchopneumonia. He was survived by his wife, Mimi, two sons, and two daughters.   BRENDA ASSAEL

Sources C. B. Mills, *Bertram Mills circus: its story* (1967) · *The Times* (22 July 1991) · *The Independent* (23 July 1991) · 'Cyril Mills, British circus director', *Annual Obituary* (1991), 423–4 · J. Pujol and N. West, *Garbo* (1986) · P. Wright, *Spycatcher* (1987) · E. T. Macmichael, *Murder at the circus* (1951) · b. cert. · d. cert.
Archives Circus Friends Association, Liverpool · Theatre Museum, London | FILM BFI, London, 'On tour with the circus', BBC Newsreel (2 July 1948) · BFI, London, 'Television is here again', Marcus Cooper (pc) (1946) · BFI, London, British Movietone News (17 Dec 1948), 20/1020 · BFI, London, 'Bertram Mills Circus', BBC (17 Dec 1959) · BFI, London, 'Big top farewell', British Movietone pc (2 Jan 1967)
Likenesses photograph, 1948, Hult. Arch. [*see illus.*] · photograph, 1965, repro. in *The Independent* · photograph, repro. in *The Times*
Wealth at death £743,617: probate, 12 Feb 1992, CGPLA Eng. & Wales

Mills [*née* Walpole], **Lady Dorothy Rachel Melissa** (1889–1959), traveller and novelist, was born on 11 March 1889 at 4 Queen's Gate Terrace, Kensington, London, the daughter of Robert Horace Walpole (1854–1931), who succeeded as fifth earl of Orford in 1894, and his first wife, Louise Melissa (d. 1909), daughter of D. C. Corbin of New York. The death in infancy of her brother, Horatio Corbin Walpole (1891–1893), left her a solitary child, daydreaming of far-flung adventures. Before his marriage Robert Walpole had served on three overseas diplomatic missions; an enthusiastic antiquary and genealogist, he was a good sportsman whose fine physique was somewhat marred by

his deafness. After the death of his first wife he married in 1917 Emily Gladys, daughter of the Revd Thomas Oakes. He died in New Zealand, having gone there in 1928 for the benefit of his health.

Lady Dorothy Walpole was educated in Paris; she travelled a good deal, principally in the United States, spending time with her mother's family in New England and joining her father on west coast hunting and fishing expeditions. She was proud of her ancestry and her Norfolk home, and a brilliant conversationalist on 'Walpoliana'. Otherwise she led a conventional society life before her marriage on 22 June 1916 to her cousin Arthur Hobart Mills (1887–1955), a nephew of the earl of Buckingham, and the son of Barton Reginald Vaughan Mills, assistant chaplain at the Chapel Royal, St James's Palace. Arthur Mills had already done military service in China and France, and after their marriage he was posted to Palestine. Although handsome and well connected, he had little money. Lady Dorothy Mills, as she was now styled, had to learn about housekeeping, and in his absence undertook typing and voluntary work. After the war her husband embarked on a career as a short-story writer, and Dorothy supplemented their income by magazine journalism and the occasional novel. After three years ill health drove her to convalesce in the warmer climate of Algiers, and beyond into the Sahara. She fell in love with Africa and the Africans, and from their homeland pursued 'black humanity' to its dispersals in Haiti and the West Indies, 'where I shed a good many preconceived prejudices' (Mills, 18). As an adult she seems to have travelled alone; her childless marriage ended in divorce in 1933, after which Arthur Mills remarried.

In 1923 Dorothy Mills ventured into the heart of north Africa from a different direction, a story she published as *The Road to Timbuktu* (1924). Once an important trading post on the Niger River, Timbuktu (now in Mali) had by this time begun to crumble into the encroaching sands, having no commercial purpose and accessible only by river. Only the myth of its former glory remained to draw the occasional foreign traveller. Dorothy was the first white woman to make the journey. She was told that Timbuktu could be reached only from the west African coast in November or early December but, delayed by other business, she had landed in January, when the river levels were not conducive to travel and inland temperatures reached 130 °F in the shade. The river journey was trying, costly, and comfortless, made in a succession of dilapidated boats. For day-to-day living she hired a local man as a servant, cook, and interpreter, and relied on porters to handle her various trunks. At Timbuktu in February she was laid low by dysentery and fever, and plagued with mosquitoes.

Despite the discomforts of travel in west Africa, Dorothy found the region and its peoples, widely varying in their appearance, customs, and religions, quite irresistible. In 1926 she travelled in Liberia; in 1929 she made a coastwise journey by a zigzag succession of river boats and ancient lorries from Conakry, in French Guinea, through Portuguese Guinea, to Dakar, in Senegal, described in *The Golden*

Land (1929). Her luggage included suitable frocks for the rare occasion that she encountered a European house, occupied by some diplomat or commercial agent, with whom she enjoyed the comforts of hot baths and European cuisine. The intervening hardships did not trouble her; she was, as she remarked:

> blessed with a digestion that an ostrich might envy … most of the vicissitudes of travel leave me unmoved. I can wrestle cheerfully with a ton of baggage; I have the natural aptitude of a sergeant major for dealing with an awkward squad of porters; I can sleep in anything from a tree to a swamp; if needs be, I can footslog for twelve hours a day without lament. (p. 37)

In 1925 Dorothy headed east of the Mediterranean, going by rail to Istanbul, then across Turkey, Syria, Palestine (where she arrived in April during the celebrations surrounding Lord Balfour's opening of the Hebrew University), Transjordan, and Iraq. As usual on her travels, the account was written as she went; it was published in *Beyond the Bosphorus* (1926). In 1929, returning from Ascot in a London taxi, she was involved in a serious accident which injured her head and left her with a scarred face. This caused her prolonged ill health in later years, but did not immediately stop her heading once more to a remote part of South America.

In 1931, hearing of a forthcoming American expedition under Herbert Spencer Dickie to the headwaters of the Orinoco River in Venezuela, Dorothy decided to get there first, with the intention of studying Indian life and customs. She started out from Curaçao and visited Maracaibo and its oilfields as a guest of the Caribbean Petroleum Company. After a few weeks learning the language she set out on 13 February with a tent and supplies: 'I have no fear of hostility … Venezuela is a civilized country, and I am used to uncivilized West Africa … I shall use all native forms of transport' (*New York Times*, 15 Feb 1931). Thereafter the trials and tribulations were familiar: travel in small canoes along alligator-infested rivers, overland journeys in rickety lorries. Lost for several weeks in the backwaters of the Orinoco somewhere near the Colombian border, she faced down some escaped convicts from Devil's Island, shot one of them in the leg when he tried to rob her, then bandaged the wound and let him go. She reappeared at Port of Spain, Trinidad, in mid-April. No time was lost in getting her story into print. In *The Country of the Orinoco* (1932) she declared, 'I have travelled in most of the world's countries, and can only talk three languages with any fluency, but at long last I have come to the conclusion that the spoken word is one of the least essential of human needs' (pp. 26–7).

This seems to have been Dorothy's last expedition. During the 1930s she lived at 17 Burnsall Street, Chelsea, London, with a small collection of African carved figures. The *Biographical Quarterly* gives her interests as literature, art, exploration, music, and primitive theology. She was fond of entertaining, travelling, theatre-going, and dancing. She was a fellow of the Royal Geographical Society, the Portuguese Geographical Society, the Ladies' Empire Club, the Society of Authors, and the Soroptimists. She

was also a keen photographer, and illustrated her own books. According to her obituary, illness caused her to retire into seclusion, not wishing to be a burden to her friends (*The Times*, 16 Dec 1959, 13c). She died at 66 Montpelier Road, Brighton, on 4 December 1959.

ANITA McCONNELL

Sources *The Times* (16 Dec 1959), 13c · D. Mills, *A different drummer: chapters in autobiography* (1930) · *New York Times* (15 Feb 1931), 27, col. 6 · *New York Times* (22 March 1931), sect. 3, p. 8, col. 6 · *New York Times* (15 April 1931), 11, cols. 1–2 · W. Rye, *Later history of the family of Walpole of Norfolk* (1920) · *Biographical Quarterly* (1935), 262 · Burke, *Peerage* · *WWW* · *The women's who's who, 1934–5: an annual record of the careers and activities of the leading women of the day* (1934) · *Ladies' who's who* (1930) · b. cert. · m. cert. · d. cert.

Mills, Florence [*real name* Florence Winfrey; *married name* Florence Thompson] (1895–1927), singer and dancer, was born in Washington, DC, on 25 January 1895, the daughter of John Winfrey, carpenter, and his wife, Nellie, formerly Symonds, laundrywoman. Her parents had been born in slavery in Amherst county, Virginia. By the age of three Florence was already showing a talent for singing and dancing and by the age of six she had won medals in amateur cakewalking and buck dancing contests. She began her professional career in show business in 1902, as Baby Florence Mills, later joining her two sisters, Olivia and Maude, in a singing and dancing act called the Mills Sisters. By the 1920s she was working in vaudeville with her husband, comedian and tap-dancer Ulysses S. (Slow Kid) Thompson.

Mills's big break came in 1921 when Noble Sissle, composer of the smash hit musical *Shuffle Along*, heard her singing in a nightclub. 'She was Dresden china, and she turned into a stick of dynamite', he recalled in 1973 (Kimball and Bolcom, 118). *Shuffle Along* was the most successful musical yet created by African-Americans, and it demonstrated that there was a place for them in commercial musical theatre. Sissle invited Mills to replace Gertrude Saunders, the star of the show, and she went on to become an international celebrity. In an interview, singer Elisabeth Welch recalled seeing Mills on stage at that time:

> Florence was a gentle child who had beautiful eyes and a joyful smile. We adored her. There wasn't a sign of theatre about her. She wasn't flamboyant in dress, character, or humour. We were noisy in those days but she was a gentle creature. If you saw her at a party you'd ask 'Who's that over there?' (*The Stage*, 26 Jan 1995)

In 1922 Mills starred in Lew Leslie's *Plantation Revue* at New York's Plantation Club. The following year impresario C. B. Cochran launched her in London in the same show, which formed the second half of *From Dover Street to Dixie*. In 1925 Cochran described her in his autobiography:

> She controlled the emotions of the audience as only a true artist can. There was not a false note in any part of her performance. That night, and every night she appeared, Florence Mills received an ovation each time she came on the stage—*before* every song she sang. That is a tribute which in my experience I have never known to be offered to any other artist. (Cochran, 415)

Returning to New York, she triumphed again at the Plantation Club, this time in *Dixie to Broadway*. It was in this show

Florence Mills (1895–1927), by unknown photographer, c.1925

star's funeral. The cortège moved through Harlem with the drums beating at that slow funeral pace, and the sidewalks were jammed with people. Then an aeroplane appeared and released flocks of blackbirds overhead. A few years later, when I came to London in 1933, C. B. Cochran asked me to record her theme song, 'Silver Rose'. I was very proud to do so. Florence should not be forgotten. (*The Stage*, 26 Jan 1995)

During her brief career Florence Mills captivated audiences in America and Britain, but sadly she did not make any films or records for future generations to see or hear. However, photographs of her reveal her playfulness and vulnerability.   STEPHEN BOURNE

Sources B. Egan, 'Florence Mills: remembering "The Little Blackbird", part 1', *Brolga*, 5 (Dec 1996) · B. Egan, 'Florence Mills: remembering "The Little Blackbird", part 2', *Brolga*, 6 (June 1997) · D. Bogle, *Brown sugar: eighty years of America's black female superstars* (1980) · S. Bourne, 'Silver voice of stardom', *The Stage* (26 Jan 1995) · R. Kimball and W. Bolcom, *Reminiscing with Sissle and Blake* (1973) · C. B. Cochran, *The secrets of a showman* (1925) · J. Weldon Johnson, *Black Manhattan* (1930) · J. Ross Moore, 'Mills, Florence', *ANB* · b. cert.

Archives NYPL, Schomburg Center for Research in Black Culture | NYPL for the Performing Arts, Billy Rose Theatre collection

Likenesses two photographs, c.1925, Hult. Arch. [*see illus.*]

that she introduced one of her most popular hits, 'I'm a little blackbird, looking for a bluebird', dressed like a little boy in a shirt and overalls, carrying a bandanna-wrapped bundle suspended at the end of a stick.

In 1926 Mills returned (via Harlem and Paris) to London at Cochran's invitation to star in Lew Leslie's *Blackbirds* revue. It was one of her biggest successes and among the songs she popularized was 'Silver Rose'. Within a few months newspapers reported that the show had been seen twenty-two times by the prince of Wales (the future King Edward VIII). These reports started rumours that Florence and the future king were having an affair. But, as Elisabeth Welch insisted, 'Florence wouldn't have an affair with anybody but Ulysses' (*The Stage*, 26 Jan 1995).

In 1927 Lew Leslie planned to give Mills the starring role in a lavish Broadway revue called *Blackbirds of 1928*, but on 24 October she underwent an operation for appendicitis that proved to be fatal. She died at the Hospital for Joint Diseases, New York, on 1 November 1927, at the peak of her fame and aged just thirty-one. Over 250,000 people were said to have lined the streets of Harlem for her funeral on 6 November, one of the greatest tributes the city had ever given a performer. 5000 people were packed to suffocation in Harlem's Mother Zion Church for the service, which included a 200-piece orchestra and a 600-voice choir. She was buried at Woodlawn cemetery. Elisabeth Welch remembered:

Florence's death was a shock to everybody and when she died she was treated with great respect. They gave her a

Mills, Frederick Percival [Freddie] (1919–1965), boxer, was born on 26 June 1919 at 7 Terrace Road, the poorest street in Bournemouth, the youngest of the four children of Thomas James Mills, totter and marine store dealer, and his wife, Lottie Hilda (*née* Gray). At the age of eleven he received a pair of boxing gloves and would regularly spar with his brother Charlie. He left St Michael's School, Poole Hill, Bournemouth, at the age of fourteen and began work as an apprentice milkman. On 26 February 1936 he had his first match at Bournemouth's Westover ice rink. He won by a knockout in the first round. Shortly afterwards he was signed up by Bob Turner and began boxing full-time in fairground booths and at south coast venues.

By the end of 1940 (excluding fairground matches) Mills had fought fifty-eight professional fights, of which forty-six were wins. Although he never developed a great boxing style in these early fights, his two-fisted aggression, powerful left hooks, ability to take punishment, tenacity in pressing forward, and an exceptional courage became his well-established fistic characteristics. He was called up to the Royal Air Force in 1939 and spent the majority of his war years at various camps in England, first as a corporal and then as a sergeant instructor (physical training). He was allowed some time during his service to box professionally and on 7 August 1940 hitch-hiked to Liverpool (from Netheravon camp, Wiltshire) to fight, on the next day, the British middleweight champion, Jack McAvoy (1908–1971). The match went its full ten rounds and, although McAvoy was not at his best, Mills boxed fluently and achieved a clear victory. The fight was not a title bout but its significance lay in its putting Mills firmly into the big league. Shortly afterwards Ted Broadribb, an ex-boxer and well-known boxing promoter, became his manager.

After important victories over Jack London (*b.* 1913) and again McAvoy, Mills was matched for a British and empire

Frederick Percival [Freddie] **Mills** (1919–1965), by George Konig, 1948

light heavyweight match against Len Harvey (1907–1976) at White Hart Lane, Tottenham, on 20 June 1942. Although wartime restrictions were in force, a crowd of 40,000 assembled in north London for the afternoon fight. It proved, however, a short affair. During the second round Mills, with a withering left hook, floored Harvey for a count of nine, which he then followed with a left upper-cut and a knockout. Throughout his career it was as a light heavyweight boxer that Mills proved his excellence. On the important occasions that he fought above his weight for major titles he either lost bravely or achieved unsatis-factory victories.

Towards the end of 1944 Mills was posted to India as part of the Inter-Services Sports and Entertainments Control Committee (ISSECC). Here he proved a popular light entertainer—a career he subsequently continued, most notably, with BBC television. When he returned to Brit-ain, he was not in condition to take on the world light heavyweight champion, the American Gus Lesnevich (1915–1964), but Broadribb and the promoter Jack Solo-mons none the less arranged a match for 14 May 1946 at the Harringay arena. The beating Mills took was the worst he was ever to suffer and, although he went on to win the light heavyweight crown, he never fully recovered from it. In the second round, Lesnevich, with a right to the chin, knocked the contender down for a count of six. To general astonishment Mills came back in the third and punch for punch could claim the round. There ensued a fierce battle for the next six rounds with Mills probably ahead on points. However, in the tenth round the punishment of the second and Mills's unpreparedness for the fight

showed. Lesnevich, brought down Mills twice with flur-ries of powerful blows to the head and body and the ref-eree was forced to stop the fight. (In the September of the following year Mills beat the Belgian Pol Goffaux in four rounds for the vacant European light heavyweight title.)

If the first Lesnevich fight was the worst night of Mills's boxing career, the return bout was to be the best. When he stepped in the ring at the White City stadium on 26 July 1948 after a regime of hard training he looked in excellent physical shape. The fight went the full fifteen rounds and Mills, his chin often (characteristically) tucked in well behind his left shoulder, fought and won the coolest and best-judged fight of his career. Later that year, on 30 Sep-tember 1948, he married Chrissie Marie McCorkindale (1914–1994), daughter of his manager, Ted Broadribb, and the ex-wife of the boxer Donald McCorkindale. Mills had two natural children (daughters) with Chrissie, and a step-son from her previous marriage.

Mills defended his world light heavyweight title against the American Joey Maxim (b. 1922) at Earls Court on 24 January 1950. He dominated Maxim during the first three rounds, but during the next six the contender began to take the measure of the champion, and in the tenth floored Mills with a quick-fire round of blows to the head. Some weeks later, at the prompting of his wife, he retired from the ring.

In retirement Freddie Mills occupied himself with busi-ness interests, some boxing promotion, charity work, and frequent BBC television appearances as a light entertainer and celebrity guest (for which his craggy good looks well suited him). He was a keen family man and enjoyed spend-ing time at the family home, Joggi Villa, 186 Denmark Hill, Camberwell, London. His business ventures, most notably a Charing Cross Road Chinese restaurant which later became a nightclub, after initial success began to fail. Mills was not the first boxer, nor has he been the last, to be taken advantage of by the unscrupulous fraternity that can sometimes be found close to the fight game. He died in the Middlesex Hospital, London, on 25 July 1965 after sus-taining a gunshot wound to the head in Goslett Yard, behind his nightclub, the previous night. He was buried in St Giles's churchyard, Camberwell. The inquest verdict on his death was suicide, a finding that has been strongly con-tested. Whether he committed suicide or was murdered cannot be established, but what can be averred is that police corruption and gangland protection rackets were rife in the West End of the time.   MICHAEL ERBEN

Sources P. McInnes, *Freddie my friend* (1995) · F. Mills, *Battling for a title* (1954) · private information (2004) · b. cert. · m. cert. · d. cert. **Archives** FILM BBC WAC · BFI NFTVA, 'In suspicious circum-stances', ITV, 6 April 1992 · BFI NFTVA, documentary footage · BFI NFTVA, news footage · BFI NFTVA, performance footage · BFI NFTVA, sports footage | SOUND BBC WAC

Likenesses photographs, 1944–64, Hult. Arch. · G. Davien, plas-ter sculptoon, 1947, NPG · G. Konig, photograph, 1948, Hult. Arch. [*see illus.*] · black marble carving on headstone, St Giles's church-yard, Camberwell, London

Wealth at death £3767: probate, 16 Feb 1966, *CGPLA Eng. & Wales*

Mills, George (1792/3–1824), medallist, was born in 1792 or before 28 January 1793. Although his work is known and published, little is recorded of his life and career. His first patron was Benjamin West, who pronounced him the first medallist in England, and to whose memory Mills dedicated a portrait medal in or after 1820. He is known to have been employed by Matthew Boulton at the Soho Mint in Birmingham, probably after 1806. He never worked for the Royal Mint, but engraved for James Mudie a silver pattern-crown of George III and a pattern-crown (in gold and silver) of George IV, published by Whiteave. Mills also contributed to Mudie's series National Medals issued about 1820, including the battle of Talavera and portraits of Sir John Moore, Viscount Hill, Sir Thomas Picton, and Lord Lynedoch. Details of thirty-one further medals are included in Brown's *British Historical Medals* and several coins are also listed by Forrer. His works are usually signed 'MILLS F.', sometimes 'G. MILLS F.'

Mills was awarded gold medals by the Royal Society of Arts in 1817 and 1818 for his medal dies, and in 1823 for presenting the society with a new die for its vulcan medal. He also exhibited at the Royal Academy from 1816 to 1823. He died at Birmingham on 28 January 1824, aged thirty-one.

CHRISTOPHER MARSDEN

Sources L. Forrer, ed., *Biographical dictionary of medallists*, 4 (1909), 79–82; 8 (1930), 59–61 · *GM*, 1st ser., 94/1 (1824), 186 · L. Brown, *A catalogue of British historical medals, 1760–1960*, 1 (1980)

Mills, George (1808–1881), shipbuilder and newspaper proprietor, was the son of William Mills, a Glasgow merchant and steamboat pioneer who served as lord provost of Glasgow in 1834–7. William Mills, who was engaged in the cotton trade, started a steamer service between the Clyde and the Mersey in 1819 using the *Robert Bruce*, one of the first ocean-going steamers. The success of this venture encouraged him to buy four more ships and in 1826 to compete on the route from the Forth to the Thames. George Mills spent three years at the University of Glasgow (1822–5), where he studied Latin, Greek, and logic, and then joined his father in business, managing the east coast service. He left in 1834 to open a new shipyard in partnership with Charles Wood, one of the best naval architects of the period, at Littlemill near Bowling on the north bank of the Clyde. By 1836 they were employing thirty-one journeymen and forty-one apprentices, constructing some large steamships including in 1835 the *Arab* of 150 tons for the Dublin and Glasgow Sailing and Steam Packet Company and in 1836 the *Rover* for the Glasgow and Londonderry Steam Packet Company. Although it was formerly believed that Mills and Wood introduced iron shipbuilding on the Clyde in 1838, Tod and M'Gregor of Glasgow are now credited with this achievement a year earlier. In any event Mills and Wood seems to have closed at about that time. Wood, a mercurial character, moved to Dumbarton and started another yard, which became bankrupt in 1844. Mills returned to Glasgow, where he had political ambitions, and made his living as a broker of stocks and shares.

Mills was already well known in Glasgow as a radical and leading dissenter. He stood against the successful Liberal candidate, Lord William Bentinck, in the 1837 general election. The following year he warned Bentinck of the damage that would result if the Liberals lost nonconformist support. When he received no assurances that Melbourne's government would stop supporting the Church of Scotland he sided with the Chartists, standing as their candidate in the 1841 election. Never a committed Chartist, he lost badly, attracting most of his support from the tories. The following year he joined the complete suffrage movement earning the opprobrium of Fergus O'Connor. Thereafter he ceased to play a direct part in politics, but became an active publicist. In 1848 he gave up share dealing, becoming manager of the new Bowling and Balloch Railway Company and the reformed Loch Lomond Steamboat Company, and founded the *North British Railway and Shipping Journal*—a tabloid-sized newspaper designed to provide reading for passengers. Two years later the name was changed to the *Glasgow Advertiser and Railway and Shipping Journal*, reduced in 1853 to the *Glasgow Advertiser* and changed again in 1855 to *Glasgow Advertiser and Property Circular*. Reputedly this was the first penny paper published in Glasgow and competition from other newspaper proprietors who cut their prices to a penny drove him out of the trade, but this cannot be corroborated.

Mills dallied in shipbuilding once more in 1856 when he formed the Clyde Improved Steamboat Company and commissioned Tod and M'Gregor to build the steamer *Alliance* to his novel designs; these aimed to provide comfort rather than speed, and included the first through-deck saloon. Although considered to be luxurious, *Alliance* was too slow to be popular. One of his obituaries commented wryly of the ship: 'but for lack of power and speed [it] would have been an undoubted success' (Mills family press cuttings). He also turned to writing, reprinting a story from the newspaper, *Craigclutha: a Tale of the West of Scotland*, in 1857 and a more substantial novel based on the collapse of the Western Bank, *The Beggar's Benison, or, A Hero without a Name, but with an Aim: a Clydesdale Story*, in 1866. Neither publication has much to recommend it. He made another foray into newspapers in 1870 by launching the halfpenny *North Star and General Advertiser for Aberdeen and the Vicinity*—the first evening paper in that city. It closed after eighty issues in May of the following year. Much of his time in the 1860s seems to have been devoted to the textile trades, particularly calico printing in the Vale of Leven in Dunbartonshire. In 1866 he set up the Milton Chemical Works, Glasgow, to manufacture dyestuffs and bleaches for the industry. He remained a proprietor until his death, at 6 India Street, Glasgow, on 12 May 1881. His wife, who is named on his death certificate as Margaret Edwards or Pratt, died in 1875 leaving him a son and two daughters. Men with occasional flourishes of distinction in otherwise prosaic lives were common enough in nineteenth-century Glasgow, but when Mills was selected for inclusion in the *Dictionary of National Biography*, probably because he was thought to be the first iron shipbuilder on the Clyde, shipbuilders as distinguished as Peter Denny could barely recall who he was.

J. K. LAUGHTON, *rev.* MICHAEL S. MOSS

Sources Mills family press cuttings, Mitchell L., Glas., Glasgow City Archives · *Biographical sketches of the lord provosts of Glasgow*

(1863) • I. G. C. Hutchison, *A political history of Scotland, 1832–1924* (1986) • L. C. Wright, *Scottish chartism* (1953) • A. McQueen, *Echoes of old Clyde paddle-wheels* (1924) • J. Bruce, *History of the parish of West or Old Kilpatrick and of the church and certain lands in the parish of East or New Kilpatrick* (1893) • d. cert. • CCI (1881)

Archives Mitchell L., Glas., Glasgow City Archives, family press cuttings

Wealth at death £2298 0s. 2d.: confirmation, 6 July 1881, CCI

Mills, Gerald Rusgrove (1877–1928), publisher, was born on 3 January 1877 at High Park, Wollaston, Stourbridge, the eldest among the four children of Harry Mills (1848–1897), solicitor, and Jane Elizabeth Nash. His childhood was comfortable and privileged: his father was a partner of a Stourbridge law firm, had ties to the local glass-making industry (he was director of Mills, Walker & Co., glass manufacturers), and was clerk of the Stourbridge urban district council. Gerald Mills attended King Edward VI Grammar School in Stourbridge; Mason College, Birmingham; and Caius College, Cambridge (1895–8), where he took a third in natural sciences. He then worked as a teacher before entering Whitaker & Co., educational publishers, in London.

In 1903 Mills joined the publisher Methuen & Co. as educational manager (as well as having a strong fiction list, Methuen was a successful educational publisher). Here he met Charles *Boon (1877–1943), who was sales manager. Although their personalities and backgrounds were very different, both were experienced publishing men who knew how to edit and sell books, and shared an ambition to strike out on their own. Having watched Methuen expand and having contributed to its success, they felt they had not been fairly rewarded.

After ten years' service Gerald Mills and Charles Boon established their own firm in Covent Garden in 1908. Mills put up the bulk of the £1000 initial investment, which meant that the new company was named Mills and Boon, rather than Boon and Mills. The pair made a good team: Mills was refined and intellectual, interested in non-fiction and book production, and had financial resources; Boon was a scrapper and a charmer, an indefatigable man who took charge of sales and advertising, as well as the development of the fiction list, attracting established and first-time authors. Methuen had provided valuable grounding in publishing and indeed many of its authors of both fiction and educational textbooks were later published by Mills and Boon.

The firm, known later for romantic fiction, was in its early days a small, diversified publisher of high-quality fiction and non-fiction. Boon spared no expense in signing up established authors such as Cosmo Hamilton, Maurice Baring, Max Pemberton, and Oliver Onions. Mills, in charge of the educational and non-fiction lists, pursued a similar policy, commissioning professors to write textbooks on mathematics or chemistry, thereby ensuring that the published works would become set texts and reach large markets. An early advertisement named Eton, Harrow, and Sandhurst in a 'List of Schools and Colleges in which Mills & Boon's books are used'. Mills purchased the rights to educational books from his old employer, Whitaker & Co. Some were very successful, including Edwin

L. Ash's *Nerves and the Nervous*, which the *Daily Express* described as 'One of the most refreshing books published for some time. Dr Ash not only probes into exactly what one feels when one is nervous or worried, but the treatment is so free from fads that it does even an unnervy person good.' The book sold out its first edition of 1000 copies in 1911, and was still in print and selling in 1921.

The early years of Mills and Boon were successful and prosperous. Turnover in the first full year, 1909–10, amounted to £16,650, which generated a mild profit of £125. At Mills and Boon's annual general meeting in 1910, the board approved salary increases for all employees, and a dividend of 2.5 per cent paid to all shareholders. The firm expressed its pleasure in a press statement in 1910:

> It was an adventure, this starting a new firm of publishers, eighteen months ago, when trade was bad and political controversy the order of the day. Everybody whom we met was full of doubts and warnings. Yes, it was an adventure, but it has been so far successful beyond expectation. We have not only enjoyed the excitement of it, but we have found the results financially excellent.

By the following year Mills and Boon had gained a reputation; the *Publishers' Circular* (1911) declared that they were:

> rapidly coming to the front as the publishers of much of the best fiction of the day. It is a great thing for the publisher's imprint to come to mean 'first-class'; it has happened for some periods in the histories of some publishing houses. What a fortune if it could last!

On 3 September 1912 Gerald Mills married Rose Shawood Anderson (1877/8–1950), daughter of John Graham Anderson, stockbroker, in Bromley, Kent. They had no children. In 1916 war service called away both Mills and Boon. Boon enlisted in the Royal Navy, while Mills, physically less fit, undertook his national service in the Ministry of Munitions. While both Mills and Boon retained their positions on the board, they were not involved in the day-to-day transactions such as sales, distribution, and the all-important nurturing of authors and new titles. The business was directed by Boon's sister, Margaret.

The 1920s were difficult for Mills and Boon: it faced competition from Methuen, Macmillan, Collins, and Hodder and Stoughton, who were all expanding their fiction lists. Because of the firm's limited resources, it could not compete with the larger houses, nor afford to hold on to its 'star' authors. Industrial action, culminating in the general strike, depressed profits. At the lowest point, according to the minutes:

> Mr. Mills pointed out that the Managing Directors had owing to bad trade in the early part of 1926 decided not to draw their full salaries during July to December but that they would do so in the event of 1927 being a satisfactory year. (Harlequin–Mills and Boon archives)

Mills's unexpected death on 23 September 1928 at 7 Knaresborough Place, Kensington, London, was a devastating blow for the firm. His will, witnessed just nine days before he died, dictated that upon his death all his shares in the firm were to be offered for sale or converted into preference shares and held for one year by the public trustee. Boon regarded a merger with or take-over by another publishing house as unpalatable, and worked quickly to find a new partner, Joseph W. Henley, a former office boy from Methuen who had been employed in book production. Boon became the dominant shareholder, and shaped the direction of Mills and Boon without Mills. Determined not to run a risk of failure, Boon remade his company in the 1930s, setting it on a new and irreversible course as a single-genre publishing house, concentrating on romantic fiction.

It is ironic that the firm which is synonymous with romantic fiction, and is listed in the *Oxford English Dictionary* as 'romantic, story-book', has little to do with its co-founder, who would barely have recognized the turn of events. Mills was a simple, unassuming man who worked hard to promote quality in an industry that was changing fast. Some insight into his character can be gleaned from an obituary notice: 'As the business which he founded with Mr. Boon gradually matured, it was his increasing joy to father a good book, especially if it were one of the educational works which were his particular care' (Harlequin–Mills and Boon archives). JOSEPH McALEER

Sources J. McAleer, *Passion's fortune: the story of Mills & Boon* (1999) · J. McAleer, *Popular reading and publishing in Britain, 1914–1950* (1992) · Venn, *Alum. Cant.* · Harlequin–Mills and Boon Ltd, Richmond, Surrey, archives · b. cert. · m. cert. · d. cert.

Archives Harlequin–Mills and Boon Ltd, Richmond, Surrey, archives

Wealth at death £7510 18s. 11d.: resworn probate, 14 Nov 1928, CGPLA Eng. & Wales

Mills [*née* Jordan], **Gladys** [*performing name* Mrs Mills] (1918–1978), pianist and popular entertainer, was born on 29 August 1918 at 154 Beckton Road, Silvertown, Newham, Essex. She was the daughter of a Metropolitan police officer, Samuel Jordan, and his wife, Minnie Dixon. She took her first piano lesson when she was three and a half, but these came to an abrupt end when she was twelve. Gladys later explained that her piano teacher objected to her putting 'twiddly bits' into the classics, and the young girl tired of being rapped over the knuckles with a knitting needle. During the war, while working as a civil servant, she formed her own amateur concert party and toured Essex, entertaining the troops. After the war she often played at club dances, but never once considered becoming a professional.

On 24 February 1947 Gladys Jordan married Gilbert (Bert) Mills (*b*. 1902/3), a maintenance man with London Transport. At the age of forty-three she was supervising a civil service typing pool at the Treasury and earning a little extra in the evenings by playing for dances. When he heard her honky-tonk piano playing at a golf-club social event the manager of Frankie Vaughan, the popular singer, persuaded her to turn professional. Teamed with the record producer Norman Newell, who had helped launch the career of Russ Conway a few years earlier, Glad—as she was known to her family and friends—shot into the pop charts with the release of her début single, 'Mrs Mills' Medley', in December 1961. Overnight the world of the housewife and civil servant was turned upside down.

At first Gladys had no intention of leaving her job in the civil service. Determined to keep her feet firmly on the ground, she continued living with her husband in their modest maisonette in Loughton. But within a month of her first record's entering the charts offers of work piled in. She began making regular appearances on radio and television, and even took part in a concert at Buckingham Palace. But Gladys refused to be spoiled by her celebrity status. In 1962 she told Ramsden Greig in an interview in the *Evening Standard* (7 April) that she had been to the Dorchester Hotel to play the piano for the 'nobs', but would not feel right eating there. On another occasion she arrived at a recording studio, only to discover she was to play with a full orchestra. 'I nearly died', she told Patrick Doncaster of the *Daily Mirror* (4 January 1962).

> I thought there would be only me at the piano and maybe a drummer and bass. A whole crowd arrived first. I thought they'd come to the wrong studio. They were only the string section, they said. Then another lot came in. They were the choir. Then more musicians arrived. I didn't know what to do. I told the recording manager: 'You don't need me, do you? I'd rather sit back and listen to this lot!'

The piano has often been associated with good-time party fun—other successful entertainers at the piano from this time included Winifred Atwell, Russ Conway, and Joe 'Mr Piano' Henderson, but it was jolly Mrs Mills, a large middle-aged lady with a beaming smile, who had the 'common touch'. By the mid-1960s she was one of Britain's most popular entertainers, and something of a working-class folk hero with her singalong medleys. She made regular appearances in television programmes such as *The Billy Cotton Band Show*, as well as in variety shows all over the country. Her down-to-earth personality appealed to audiences, and for many fans she personified the home-loving cockney mum. Tours of Canada, South Africa, and Germany took Gladys far away from her new home in the rural peace of Penn in the Buckinghamshire Chilterns.

In the early 1970s Gladys was still to be seen on television and did not object to having jokes made at her expense. After her memorable appearance in *The Morecambe and Wise Show* Eric Morecambe informed another guest, actor John Mills, 'We've just had your grandmother on the show!' In 1975 Eamonn Andrews surprised her with his famous red book for a well-deserved tribute in Thames Television's *This is your Life*.

In addition to her show business work, Gladys and her husband ran a sixteenth-century pub called the King's Arms in the village of Hathern just outside Leicester. She often pulled beer for the locals in her spare time, but they sold the pub after four years. 'It got out of hand,' she explained in an interview in *The Sun* (10 March 1971). 'Too many people kept coming in and they made me feel like exhibit A.'

Ill health forced Gladys Mills to cut down her workload and on 24 February 1978 she died in St Joseph's Nursing Home in Beaconsfield after a prolonged illness. In the late 1990s renewed interest in 'easy listening' music—an interest often overlaid with irony—saw the re-release of her recordings on compact disc. STEPHEN BOURNE

Sources S. Bourne, 'Working class hero', *The Stage* (2 Nov 2000) · R. Greig, *Evening Standard* (7 April 1962) · P. Doncaster, *Daily Mirror* (4 Jan 1962) · *The Times* (1 March 1978) · *The Times* (5 July 1978) · *The Sun* (10 March 1971) · b. cert. · m. cert. · d. cert.

Wealth at death £105,364: *The Times* (5 July 1978)

Mills, (William) Haslam (1873–1930), journalist and author, was born on 20 September 1873 in Queen Street, Ashton under Lyne, Lancashire, the last of the five children of James Mills (1828–1897), musician and music critic, and his wife, Martha Saxon. He was brought up within the strong local tradition of dissent in its Congregational form and educated at Manchester grammar school. In 1895 he joined the staff of the *Manchester Guardian*, which since the 1860s had become less of a local paper and more the voice of a universal liberal philosophy.

Haslam Mills proved to be a born journalist, like his elder brother John Saxon Mills (1864–1929). For some years he served in the press gallery of the House of Commons but left the *Manchester Guardian* as its sales slumped in harmony with its pro-Boer stance. He moved to London, spent four years (1901–4) on the editorial staff of *The Times*, and in 1904 married Evelyn Travers, daughter of Colonel J. O. Travers. He rejoined the staff of the *Guardian* in 1904 and was called to the bar at Gray's Inn in 1907. In Manchester he served as special correspondent and as theatre critic, developing an aesthetic interest in music as well as in drama. He invented the style which made the paper's music-hall notices so famous that Arnold Bennett confessed he bought the *Guardian* specially to read them (Cardus, 'Fifty years', 12–13). He proved unexcelled as the reporter of a great occasion such as the packed political meetings in the Free Trade Hall which foreshadowed the Liberal landslide of 1906.

As chief reporter (1914–19) Haslam Mills made the 'MG' into his religion and the editor, C. P. Scott, 'righteousness incarnate', into its prophet (Spring, 94, 98). Into the solemn atmosphere of the *Guardian* office he blew 'like a combination of d'Artagnan and Villon' (Ayerst, 331). He transformed the reporters' room into 'the most gifted and resourceful in the world' (Cardus, *Autobiography*, 98) by serving as a tutor to younger writers, as the introspective C. E. Montague signally failed to do. He impressed upon his writers that the *MG* was less a newspaper office than 'an Academy almost in an Athenian sense' (ibid., 93). As he made the *MG* into a model of literary style, he himself became the great pattern for emulation by members of his staff. Circulation rose by 80 per cent (1904–19). The *MG* became 'the voice of the tabernacle' for Liberal England as well as an integral part of the life of Manchester.

In 1919 Haslam Mills left the staff of the *MG*, profoundly dismayed by the failure of C. P. Scott to utter a single word of appreciation for his sterling services (Spring, 95, 102–3). He was recruited as a copy-writer by C. W. Hobson, advertising agent and founder of the Cloister Press in Heaton Mersey, Stockport. Then for a year in 1919–20 he served as director of public information at the Ministry of Health. Thereafter he turned to the writing of copy in London, the hub of the advertising world. The capital remained free from those moral constraints which had led the *MG* since

(William) Haslam Mills (1873–1930), by unknown photographer, 1916 [second from left, front row, with *Guardian* reporters]

1873 to ban the advertisement of racing tips, while his transition from journalism to advertising proved smooth, because the revenues of the press had for long been generated by advertisements. In his new domain Haslam Mills gained 'the reputation of being the paramount practitioner of his new craft' (*Manchester Guardian*, 23 June 1930, 18iv).

Mills was 'a great and curious person' (Brighouse, 41), spectacularly handsome and attractive, like his writing. He had few equals in conversation and was also a brilliant lecturer. 'He talked as he wrote, and as he dressed, with a slightly theatrical affectation' (Spring, 92). In writing he became a master of style. He took pride in every turn of phrase and especially in the opening sentence of any essay. He loved words and was ever fastidious in their use. His calligraphy was beautiful and his copy was always written in green ink.

Mills's favourite themes stemmed from Lancashire, with which he possessed an inherent affinity. From 1911 he began to publish long essays devoted to the history of Manchester. In 1917 he published his first book, *Sir Charles W. Macara Bart.: A Study of Modern Lancashire*, setting its subject in the perspective of the golden age of the region's history. Then followed a centenary history, *The Manchester Guardian* (1921), and a jubilee history, *The Manchester Reform Club* (1922). He portrayed 'Cottonia' and its capital city in a perspective and a language unknown before, seeking always to correct entrenched and misleading stereotypes. His achievement was to associate the prosaic function of selling calico with the broad sweep of human progress. Victorian Manchester to Haslam Mills remained 'the powerful provincial city which laid down the law for England' (*Manchester Guardian*, 2 Oct 1926, 19) and which deemed itself 'the Hub of the Universe'. That city was unusual in so far as it remained 'almost totally destitute of the Greek conception of the State' (Mills, *Macara*, 131) and never became a whig city. It did, however, become 'an active manufactory of agitation and thought' (W. H. Mills,

'Manchester of today', *Manchester in 1915*, ed. H. M. McKechnie, 1915, 9), a 'Mecca for manufacturing and Dissenting England' (*Manchester Guardian*, 5 May 1921, 45), and 'a city with a soul. It stood for an idea' (Mills, *Macara*, 28). Mills emphasized the metropolitan functions of Manchester and the integrating role of commerce, typified by the warehouses of Portland Street, through which 'the history of the human race ran for a time'. Lancashire itself remained 'the messianic corner of earth in which the new world was announced' (ibid., 130) and the county which 'has always given itself the airs of a continent' (W. H. Mills, *Grey Pastures*, 1924, 125).

Haslam Mills's finest book was *Grey Pastures* (1924), written as homage to the central role played by Albion Congregational Church in the life of Ashton under Lyne. He portrayed with a deep nostalgia the great occasions in the chapel year (the Whit walks, the annual sermons, the bazaar, and the Christmas tea party) and the dominating personalities in its affairs, such as Hugh Mason. He reproduced 'the atmosphere of provincial Liberalism and Nonconformity with a tender and whimsical appreciation that I have not known equalled' (Spring, 94). Above all, he stressed the affinity between dissent and Liberalism. 'It was understood that God had read the *Manchester Guardian* that morning' (Mills, *Grey Pastures*, 17). Throughout his life he never wavered in his Liberal faith. He did, however, break free from the sabbatarian constraints of the dissenting fold and crossed the great divide in order to enter the Anglican communion. His departure from the *Manchester Guardian* marked the end of an era in its history, whereafter circulation declined by 28 per cent between 1920 and 1930 (Ayerst, 400). He became the first and the best historian of the paper. Among the *Guardian's* five historians he alone 'could have made himself at home … and written for the paper of the 1990's' (Taylor, ix).

After the death of his first wife in 1914 Haslam Mills married, on 22 July 1916, Doris Hague Phillips (*b.* 1881/2), the daughter of Alfred Phillips, commercial clerk. Mills died on 22 June 1930 at the Empire Nursing Home, Vincent Square, London, after an operation for a cerebral abscess. He was survived by his widow and by three children. His two sons inherited their father's talents. Hugh Mortimer Travers Mills (1906–1971) became a skilful screen writer, while Michael Haslam Mills (1919–1988) became the head of comedy at the BBC.   D. A. FARNIE

Sources N. Cardus, *Autobiography* (1947) • N. Cardus, 'Fifty years with the *Guardian*', *The bedside 'Guardian'*, ed. G. Fay, 15 (1966), 5–13 • H. Spring, *In the meantime* (1942) • *Manchester Guardian* (23 June 1930), 18iv • *Ashton-under-Lyne Reporter* (28 June 1930) • *The Times* (23 June 1930), 19b • *The Times* (24 June 1930), 21 • *The Times* (27 June 1930), 17d • *The Times* (11 Jan 1988) • H. Brighouse, *What I have had: chapters in autobiography* (1953) • D. Ayerst, *Guardian: biography of a newspaper* (1971) • G. Taylor, *Changing faces: a history of The Guardian, 1956–1988* (1993) • J. C. G. Binfield, 'The dynamic of grandeur: Albion Church, Ashton under Lyne', *Transactions of the Lancashire and Cheshire Antiquarian Society*, 85 (1988), 173–92 • b. cert. • d. cert. • *CGPLA Eng. & Wales* (1930) • m. cert., 1916

Archives JRL, *Manchester Guardian* archives • Man. CL, MS index to the *Manchester Guardian*

Likenesses group photograph, 1916, *Manchester Guardian* archives [*see illus.*] • photograph, 1916, repro. in Ayerst, *Guardian*, 504 • Cracowski, pencil sketch, JRL, *Manchester Guardian* archives, 223/49/6 • J. W. Schmidt, photograph, repro. in Cardus, *Autobiography*, 112 • J. W. Schmidt, photograph, repro. in Spring, *In the meantime*, 92

Wealth at death £6735: probate, 9 Aug 1930, *CGPLA Eng. & Wales*

Mills, James Philip (1890–1960), anthropologist, was born on 18 February 1890 at Oak Lea, Norbury Moor, Norbury, Cheshire, the younger son of James Edward Mills, hat manufacturer and later owner of Mills steelworks and Bredbury Hall, near Stockport, and his wife, Ada Smith, who was fatally injured in a carriage accident and died the day after giving birth to her son. He was educated at Winchester College (1903–8) and at Corpus Christi College, Oxford (1909–12), and entered the Indian Civil Service in 1913. He served as a trooper in the Jumna valley light horse throughout the First World War. By 1916, however, he was working in the Naga hills in Assam, where he later became deputy commissioner. Inspired by his colleague John Henry Hutton, by his friendship with the curator of the Pitt Rivers Museum at Oxford, Henry Balfour, and by the practical necessity of advising and arbitrating issues on the borders of the British empire, he soon became interested in anthropology.

During his numerous trips through administered and unadministered areas of the Naga hills, Mills was in a unique position to examine a vanishing world, full of extraordinary beauty and violence, among forest-dwelling groups of enormous diversity. The first of his classic monographs, *The Lhota Nagas*, was published in 1922, and was followed by *The Ao Nagas* in 1926. In 1926 he advised the government on the administration of the Chittagong Hill Tracts. He became acting deputy commissioner of Cachar (1927–8), and was made honorary director of ethnography for Assam in 1930, when he returned to the Naga hills and worked on his monograph *The Rengma Nagas* (1937). On 2 November 1930 he married Pamela Moira (1903–1992), daughter of John Foster-Vesey-Fitzgerald, of Moyrhea, co. Clare. They had three daughters, one of whom died at the age of fifteen. He became secretary to the government of Assam in 1932. He was made CIE (1941) and CSI (1947), and in 1942 was awarded the Rivers medal of the Royal Anthropological Institute. In 1943 he was appointed adviser to the governor of Assam for tribal areas and states. He was in Assam during the Second World War, an area engaged in some of the heaviest fighting of the war. He retired from India in 1947 and became a lecturer (1948) and then a reader (1950) in anthropology at the School of Oriental and African Studies in London. He was president of the Royal Anthropological Institute from 1951 to 1953. In 1954 he retired to Dorset, where he spent time on the gardening and fishing which had always been his hobbies. He died at his home, East House, Sydling St Nicholas, near Dorchester, on 12 May 1960, and was cremated in Weymouth.

Mills's closest associate in Assam, J. H. Hutton, wrote of him: 'Mills made an admirable colleague in administration. Apart from his practical and intellectual ability, his never failing sense of humour, his wit and his good temper in trying circumstances made him an invaluable companion' (Hutton). His three great Naga monographs are superb examples of ethnographic writing: clear, learned, a mine of facts and interpretations. Along with his numerous articles, they constitute over 2000 pages of careful documentation of the various groups living on the borders of India and Burma. They remain an invaluable source. They are supplemented by the valuable collections of Naga objects which he gave to the Pitt Rivers Museum in Oxford, which, with those given by Hutton, make this perhaps the widest and deepest collection of objects on any particular people in any anthropology museum in Britain. Mills, like Hutton, was a keen amateur photographer; several hundred photographs (now at the School of Oriental and African Studies, London), which complement the collections of Hutton, Christoph von Fürer-Haimendorf (whom he helped and inspired), Ursula Graham Bower, and W. G. Archer, again provide invaluable documentation of the first encounters with the Nagas.   ALAN MACFARLANE

Sources J. H. Hutton, *Man*, 60 (1960), 89–90 · private information (2004) [Christoph von Fürer-Haimendorf; Mildred Archer; Ursula Graham Bower; Mills family] · b. cert. · Burke, *Gen. Ire.* · P. A. Hunt, *Corpus Christi College biographical register*, ed. N. A. Flanagan (1988) **Archives** NRA, priv. coll., MSS · Royal Anthropological Institute, London, Mongsen Ao word list · SOAS, diaries and papers relating to Assam; photographic collection · U. Cam., Centre of South Asian Studies, papers · U. Oxf., Pitt Rivers Museum, artefacts **Wealth at death** £25,667 2s. 3d.: probate, 19 July 1960, *CGPLA Eng. & Wales*

Mills, John (d. 1736), actor and theatre manager, appears to have joined Christopher Rich's company at the Drury Lane and Dorset Garden theatres in the spring of 1695, following the secession of a number of actors, including Thomas Betterton and Mrs Barry, to Lincoln's Inn Fields. He is known to have taken the part of the Ynca of Peru in Dryden and Howard's *The Indian Queen* at Dorset Garden in 1695, and, judging by other parts he is reported to have taken on in the 1695–6 season, he must have come to the company with an established reputation and certainly a good measure of experience. He took the part of Nennius in John Fletcher's *Bonduca* in September 1695, was the original Jack Stanmore in Thomas Southerne's *Oroonoko* in November, and created the original Lawyer in Colley Cibber's *Love's Last Shift* in January 1696. He played Castillo in *Neglected Virtue, or, The Unhappy Conquerer* in February of that year, Mustapha in Mary Pix's *Ibrahim* in May, and Pisano in Thomas Scott's *The Unhappy Kindness* in July. At Dorset Garden in June he was Peregrine in *The Cornish Comedy*, with his wife, Margaret (d. 1717), in a supporting role. It is unknown when the couple married, though it may not have been much earlier than February 1696. Their son, William, was born on 14 June 1701 and was to follow his father into the theatre. Little is known about their daughter other than her receiving a benefit performance in 1737 following her father's death.

Mills was to stay at Drury Lane, with the occasional migration to the Haymarket, for forty years. That he quickly adopted a significant position in the troupe is

John Mills (d. 1736), attrib. Pieter van Bleeck [probably as Pierre in *Venice Preserv'd* by Thomas Otway]

testified by his being one of six named actors in a contract drawn up towards the end of the 1690s for the scene-painter Robert Robertson. Though rated principally by John Downes in his *Roscius Anglicanus* as having a talent to 'excel in Tragedy' (Downes, 109), Mills's main contribution to Rich's company in his first few years at Drury Lane seems to have been his comic performances. In 1697 he played the first Sir John Friendly in John Vanbrugh's *The Relapse, or, Virtue in Danger*, Ned Stanmore in Elkanah Settle's *The World in the Moon*, and Leontius in Fletcher's *The Humorous Lieutenant*.

By 1703 Mills was earning as much as £60 a year. He took a break from the Drury Lane theatre after the 1705–6 season, perhaps as a result of, or in response to, a change in theatre management. Owen Swiny attracted him and other actors over to his company at the Queen's Theatre, where he appeared for the first time on 26 October 1706 as Douglas in 1 *Henry IV*. Shortly before this, on 27 August 1706, he made his first appearance at Bartholomew fair, playing Colonel Lovewell in *The Siege of Barcelona*. During the 1706–7 season at the Haymarket he found himself much in demand. On 30 October 1706 he appeared as Edmund in *King Lear*. This was followed by a succession of significant roles, including Volpone, Timon of Athens, the King in Beaumont and Fletcher's *The Maid's Tragedy*, Morelove in Cibber's *The Careless Husband*, Bertram in Dryden's *The Spanish Fryar*, Octavius Caesar in *Julius Caesar*, the Ghost in *Hamlet*, Banquo in *Macbeth*, Petruchio in *Sauny the Scot*, John Lacy's adaptation of *The Taming of the Shrew*, Bosola in John Webster's *The Duchess of Malfi*, and the original Aimwell in George Farquhar's *The Beaux' Stratagem*.

Mills returned to Drury Lane as Horatio in *Hamlet* on 15

January 1708 and played Cassander in Nathaniel Lee's *The Rival Queens* on 31 January. During the ensuing season he added the parts of Corvino in Ben Jonson's *Volpone*, Prospero in *The Tempest*, Creon in Dryden and Lee's *Oedipus*, Surly in Jonson's *The Alchemist*, and Agamemnon in Dryden's *Troilus and Cressida* to his repertory. A published report of actors' salaries in July 1709 indicated that, including benefit receipts, Mills took home the substantial annual sum of £170. His weekly wage of £4 matched Betterton's and caused Colley Cibber to comment that in his lifetime no actor had ever earned so much. Such remuneration for a second player was clearly indicative of Mills's increasing worth to the company.

Tempted back to the Queen's by Owen Swiny in September 1709 by an annual salary of £100 and a March benefit, Mills broke once more with Drury Lane, only to return again in November 1710 to play Southampton in John Banks's *The Unhappy Favourite* and to resume his usual repertory of roles for the company, including now Melantius in *The Maid's Tragedy*, Pierre in Thomas Otway's *Venice Preserv'd*, Bellmour in Nicholas Rowe's *Jane Shore*, Buckingham in *Richard III*, Bajazet in Rowe's *Tamerlane*, Face in *The Alchemist*, Balance in Farquhar's *The Recruiting Officer*, and Jupiter in Dryden's *Amphitryon*.

In 1714 Mills petitioned the lord chamberlain's office for a managerial position at Drury Lane, claiming the co-manager Thomas Doggett was ineffectual, and highlighting his own experience over the course of his career at the theatre in assisting the management. He was eventually rewarded with the responsibility of managing the theatre's summer company, a post he held until 1727.

During his final two decades at Drury Lane, Mills interpreted a number of lead roles in addition to his usual position as support actor. These included the lead in Susannah Centlivre's *The Gamester*, Macbeth (on 20 October 1711), Julius Caesar, Titus Andronicus, and Hamlet (on 11 November 1732, with his son, William, in the notably paradoxical role of Claudius). By 1733 he was reported as earning £1 daily for 200 days certain and a benefit free of house charges. At the end of the 1734–5 season he was listed among a committee of actors who submitted an unsuccessful proposal to rent the theatre from its new patentee, Charles Fleetwood.

Mills died on the morning of 17 December 1736 at his home in Martlett Court, Bow Street, after an illness of ten to twelve days. On 20 December he was carried to St Martin-in-the-Fields, where he was buried. A collection of his theatre colleagues, including Cibber, Fleetwood, Benjamin Johnson, James Quin, and Benjamin Griffin, bore his pall. His last stage appearance had been on 4 December as the King in *2 Henry IV*, and he had been scheduled to follow this with the role of Macbeth, in which he was replaced by Quin.

The obituary in the *London Evening-Post* on 18 December 1736 described Mills as an actor who had 'deservedly acquir'd a very great reputation; not only for his capacity, but also for his application and diligence in his profession'. Victor, in his *History of the Theatres*, referred to him as 'the most useful actor that ever served a theatre', then described him as 'nearly approaching to the graceful; and his voice a full deep melodious tenor, which suited the characters of rage' (*BDA*). Thomas Davies, in his *Dramatic Miscellanies*, described Mills as having large features, 'though not expressive', and possessing a powerful 'but not flexible' voice (Davies, 2.132). Colley Cibber, in his *Apology*, wrote that Robert Wilks, the leading actor at Drury Lane, 'rather chose him for his second in many Plays, than an Actor of perhaps greater Skill that was not so laboriously diligent' (Cibber, 151), and inferred that his friendship with Wilks explained his advancement at the theatre more than any inherent talent. MARK BATTY

Sources Genest, *Eng. stage* · T. Davies, *Dramatic miscellanies*, 3 vols. (1784) · C. Cibber, *An apology for the life of Mr. Colley Cibber* (1740) · Highfill, Burnim & Langhans, *BDA* · J. Downes, *Roscius Anglicanus*, ed. J. Milhous and R. D. Hume, new edn (1987) · B. Victor, *The history of the theatres of London and Dublin*, 3 vols. (1761–71)
Likenesses attrib. P. van Bleeck, oils (probably as Pierre in *Venice preserv'd*), Garr. Club. [*see illus.*] · R. Clamp, stipple (after P. van Bleeck), BM, NPG; repro. in F. G. Waldron, *The biographical mirror*, 2 (1798)

Mills, John (*c*.1717–1786×96), writer on agriculture, is a figure about whom little definite is known, other than through his publications. He was apparently in Paris in 1743 in order to bring out a French edition of Ephraim Chambers's *Cyclopaedia*, in collaboration with Sellius, a German historian. However, Lebreton, the printer commissioned by Mills, cheated him out of the subscription money, attacked him, and managed to get a licence in his own name. This incident forms part of the origin of the *Encyclopédie*. Mills returned to England, and Sellius died at Charenton Lunatic Asylum in 1787.

In 1763 Mills completed, and dedicated to the earl of Bute, the third volume of *Memoirs of the Court of Augustus*, by Thomas Blackwell the younger, which had been left uncompleted at Blackwell's death in 1757. His first agricultural publication was his translation of Duhamel du Monceau's *Practical Treatise of Husbandry*, which he published in 1759. His subsequent works included an *Essay on the Management of Bees* (1766), a translation from the Latin of G. A. Gyllenberg's *Natural and Chemical Elements of Agriculture* (1770), an *Essay on the Weather* (1770, translated into Dutch in 1772), *Essays, Moral, Philosophical, and Political* (anonymous, but advertised under his name), and a *Treatise on Cattle* (1776). His most important work, *A New and Complete System of Practical Husbandry*, in five volumes (1762–5), was a compilation of the works of earlier authors, including John Evelyn, Duhamel, John Worlidge, and Jethro Tull. It was the earliest complete treatise on all branches of agriculture, and contains the first mention of the potato as grown in fields.

In 1766 Mills was elected FRS, and he was the first foreign associate of the French Agricultural Society. His name appears on its list, with London as his residence, from 1767 to 1784. Mills died between 17 July 1786 (the date on which he wrote a letter, now in the Royal Society) and 1796, after which the name John Mills ceases to appear in the list of Royal Society fellows.

J. G. ALGER, *rev.* ANNE PIMLOTT BAKER

Sources J. Donaldson, *Agricultural biography* (1854) · J. Thirsk, ed., *The agrarian history of England and Wales*, 6, ed. G. E. Mingay (1989) · Royal Society certificates

Mills, John [*pseud.* Ieuan Glan Alarch] (1812–1873), Calvinistic Methodist minister and writer, was born on 19 December 1812 at Mount Street, Llanidloes, Montgomeryshire, the fourth son of Edward Mills (1785–1849), a wool weaver and manufacturer, and his wife, Mary Evans (*d.* 1856); his grandfather was Henry Mills. He received his early education at the schools of the Independent and Methodist preachers of Llanidloes, both named D. Williams (1818–25); then, at the age of thirteen, he went to work in his father's woollen factory. He took a keen interest in music, reading widely on the subject in his spare time, and gave lessons on the rudiments of music to the musical society at Llanidloes, which was run by his uncle, James Mills. He was also involved in the literary and theological society at Bethel Calvinistic Methodist chapel at Llanidloes, where he was a member. By the age of seventeen, he was accomplished in English and Welsh grammar and had started writing poetry and essays under the name Ieuan Glan Alarch. In 1838 he travelled through Glamorgan, Carmarthenshire, and Cardiganshire, delivering lectures on music and temperance, and was instrumental in establishing musical societies in these areas. His musical grammar, *Gramadeg cerddoriaeth* (1838), proved extremely popular and ran into several editions.

In October 1838 Mills began preaching and, in 1841, he became minister at Ruthin. In 1846 he moved to London and undertook missionary work among the Jews. He visited Palestine twice, in 1855 and 1859, and published several books and articles on Jewish life. His history of the Jews in Britain, *Iddewon Prydain* (1852), which was published in English as *British Jews* (1853), made him a recognized authority on the subject. In 1863 he became minister of the Welsh chapel at Nassau Street, London. Mills continued to write on musical subjects and his publications did much to promote a knowledge of the rudiments of music in Wales. These works included: *Y cerddor eglwysig* (1846); *Y salmydd eglwysig* (1847); *Elfennau cerddoriaeth* (1848); *Y canor* (1851); *Yr athraw cerddorol* (1854); *Y cerddor dirwestol* (1855). Mills also contributed widely to Welsh periodicals such as *Y Traethodydd* and *Y Gwyddoniadur*, and wrote several English articles for Cassell's *Imperial Bible Dictionary*, and the *Journal of Sacred Literature*. He was a fellow of the Royal Asiatic and the Royal Geographical societies and was honorary secretary of the Anglo-Biblical Institute. Mills had five children with his first wife, Elizabeth Lewis (*d.* October 1849) of Llanidloes, whom he married on 8 May 1838, and three with his second wife, Sarah, daughter of William Hopkins, whom he married on 15 May 1851. He died on 28 July 1873 at 13 Brook Street, Hanover Square, London, and was buried at Abney Park cemetery, London. His second wife survived him. MARI A. WILLIAMS

Sources N. Cynhafal Jones and R. Mills, *Buchdraeth y parch John Mills* (1881) · M. O. Jones, *Bywgraffiaeth cerddorion Cymreig* (1890), 73–5 · R. Williams, *Montgomeryshire worthies* (1884) · *DWB*, 634 · T. Mordaf Pierce, 'Millsiaid Llanidloes III', *Y Traethodydd*, 58 (1903),

342–52 · T. R. Roberts, *Eminent Welshmen: a short biographical dictionary* (1908), 346 · D. Emlyn Evans, 'James, Richard, a John Mills, 1790–1873', *Y Cerddor*, 3/25 (1891), 3–4 · D. Jones, 'Hen gerddorion Llanidloes', *Y Cerddor*, 26/311 (1914), 117–19 · D. Emlyn Evans, 'Cerddorion Sir Drefaldwyn', *Cymru*, 30 (1906), 37–43 · *The Times* (31 July 1873) · *Y Drysorfa*, 43 (1873), 469–70 · *Y Goleuad* (9 Aug 1873) · *CGPLA Eng. & Wales* (1873) · m. cert.
Archives NL Wales, letters to Lewis Edwards
Likenesses W. Dickes, line engraving, repro. in Cynhafal Jones and Mills, *Buchdraeth y parch John Mills*
Wealth at death under £600: administration with will, 21 Oct 1873, *CGPLA Eng. & Wales*

Mills, Percy Herbert, first Viscount Mills (1890–1968), politician and industrialist, was born on 4 January 1890 at Thornaby-on-Tees, the fourth child of Daniel Mills, wholesale confectioner, of Stockton-on-Tees, and his wife, Emma Brown. A self-made man, he rose by intelligence and character from a comparatively humble origin to become one of the most respected cabinet ministers in the governments in which he served. He was educated at the North Eastern county school, Barnard Castle, co. Durham, but at fifteen in 1905 he left the north for London, where he served his articles with W. B. Peat & Co., chartered accountants.

After completing his training Mills married on 7 August 1915 Winifred Mary (*d.* 1974), daughter of George Conaty, engineer and manager of Birmingham Tramways, with whom he had a daughter and a son. In 1919 Mills entered the firm of W. and T. Avery Ltd (later also Averys Ltd), weighing machine manufacturers of Birmingham; he stayed with them for thirty-eight years until he retired in 1957. His original position was that of financial assistant to Gilbert Vyle, managing director, under whom he became general manager in 1924. In 1927 he was appointed to the board and, following Vyle's death in 1933, became managing director of the firm which was to be his industrial base in years to come.

On the outbreak of war Mills was appointed, first, deputy director of ordnance factories in the Ministry of Supply and later in the dual capacity of controller-general of machine tools (1940–44) and head of the production division in the Ministry of Production (1943–4). He was knighted in 1942. It was during this period that he made friends with and gained the confidence of many senior civil servants who became his collaborators in years to come: and, more importantly, of Harold Macmillan, parliamentary secretary to the Ministry of Supply, 1940–42. They were close friends thereafter and, to the end of his life, he and Winifred used to dine *en famille* with Macmillan once a week.

In his memoirs Macmillan recorded of the machine tool control: 'Here, one man emerged as the supreme figure, trusted by all—even, after considerable struggles, by the Ministry of Aircraft Production. This was Percy Mills' (Macmillan, *The Blast of War*, 95). The war being concluded, Mills became head of the economic subcommission of the British element of the control commission for defeated Germany. During this time he obtained a reputation for toughness with Russian and French chauvinism which not only earned him the respect of the representatives of those countries, but the admiration of his British colleagues. While determined to reduce Germany's war potential he insisted that its civilian industries must be maintained and assisted towards recovery.

To this period belongs an incident with a touch of the Nelsonian blind eye to it. The submarine yards of Blöhm und Voss were to be blown up according to instructions, but as their implementation approached Whitehall started to waver. On the arrival of a telegram which Mills suspected might contain orders countermanding the operation, he left it unopened and departed to ensure that existing orders were carried out. On returning with the mission accomplished, he opened the telegram, the contents of which were as he had supposed. After dictating his regrets that it had arrived too late to be implemented, he commented: 'They've nearly brought us to our knees in two wars running. We can well do without them.'

Following completion of his work on the control commission and his appointment as KBE in 1946, Mills became president of the Birmingham chamber of commerce in 1947, and in 1949 became chairman of the newly established National Research Development Corporation, a post which he held until 1955. In 1951 he became honorary adviser on housing to Harold Macmillan, by this time minister of housing and very senior in the cabinet, who had been asked to take over the relevant ministry. Many thought that the recently elected Conservative Party would be unable to keep its promises. The problem was to mobilize production, for example brickmaking facilities. Mills set up regional housing boards to do this; thus the government implemented its promises and Macmillan's trust in and admiration of his colleague grew correspondingly. His memoirs give a picture of how he saw his friend: 'what we should do without him, I shudder to think. He approaches every problem with realism and precision; his suggestions are at once bold and ingenious; and he has a quiet persistence which enables him to get his way' (Macmillan, *Tides of Fortune*, 399). Macmillan continued, 'With his quiet but inflexible will [he] has really moulded the whole Ministry to our purpose. I could have done nothing without him' (ibid., 410).

In July 1953 Mills was made a baronet and in 1955 reached the retiring age for executives at Averys, becoming non-executive chairman of the board and accepting appointments to other industrial boards coterminously. Two years later Macmillan became prime minister, and in January 1957 Mills was created Baron Mills in order to take his seat in the House of Lords as minister of power, a position which he held for two years until 1959, when he became paymaster-general until 1961. There followed a further period in the cabinet as minister without portfolio and deputy leader of the House of Lords in 1961–2 until Macmillan's reconstruction of the cabinet in July 1962 (the 'night of the long knives'). Mills, who was over seventy, accepted Macmillan's invitation to resign, and was created a viscount in August 1962, stepping out of political life to rejoin the board of Electric and Musical Industries. He became chairman of, and later special adviser to, their

electronic subsidiary, a post which he held until his sudden and unexpected death on 10 September 1968. He had left his Kensington home to post the morning mail and fell dead beside the postbox in Hornton Street. His widow survived him until 1974. He was succeeded in the peerage by his son, Roger Clinton (1919–1988).

Mills's character was a blend of toughness and friendliness, bluntness and courtesy, seriousness of purpose and gaiety, combined with a formidable intelligence, power of decision, and intuitive insight. To his prime minister he was 'wise old Percy'. To an industrial colleague he was 'a tough driving chief executive'. To civil service colleagues he was remembered as a fount of gaiety and much recalled laughter. No one enjoyed a bachelor dinner party, good food, and good wine more than Percy Mills. Notwithstanding his toughness and drive, it was recorded at Averys that 'his instinctive sense of management and the handling of men were always ahead of their time'. As president of the Birmingham, Wolverhampton, and Stafford district of the Engineering and Allied Employers' Federation, he once allowed a union representative to overreach himself. Suddenly and quietly Mills cut in: 'That is an impertinence'. After a painful interval the culprit, unable to improvise an escape route, apologized. 'Thank you', said Mills, smiling instantly and passing to the next business. The urbanity of his later years was learnt. 'When I was young', he once remarked, 'I had a pretty fiendish temper. But I have learnt to control it. It isn't the right way to treat people and it achieves nothing.' That in the achievement of power he learnt humility could be a fitting epitaph for one of the most politically influential industrialists of his time.   HALSBURY, *rev.*

Sources H. Macmillan, *The blast of war, 1939–1945* (1967) [vol. 2 of autobiography] · H. Macmillan, *Tides of fortune, 1945–1955* (1969) [vol. 3 of autobiography] · H. Macmillan, *At the end of the day, 1961–1963* (1973) [vol. 6 of autobiography] · personal knowledge (1981) · private information (1981) · *The Times* (11 Sept 1968) · Burke, *Peerage* (2000) · *CGPLA Eng. & Wales* (1968)
Archives NRA, corresp. and papers
Likenesses W. Stoneman, photograph, 1950, NPG · W. Bird, photograph, 1961, NPG
Wealth at death £107,781: probate, 12 Dec 1968, *CGPLA Eng. & Wales*

Mills, Peter (*bap.* 1598, *d.* 1670), surveyor and architect, was baptized on 12 February 1598, the son of John Mills, tailor, in East Dean, Sussex. He was apprenticed in 1613 to John Williams, a London bricklayer. From 1643 until about 1660, Mills was bricklayer to the City of London and from 1649 until 1660 was master of the Tylers' and Bricklayers' Company. From 1644 he was a governor of St Bartholomew's Hospital, his landlord at the time of his death, and he played an active part in rebuilding its property.

Mills's standing in the City at the Restoration was such that he was invited, with Sir Balthazar Gerbier, to design the four triumphal arches erected for Charles II's coronation progress and to organize the celebrations on the Thames for Charles and Queen Catherine in 1662. After the great fire, he was appointed as one of the supervisors of the rebuilding of the City, for which he produced a plan himself which does not survive; together with Robert

Hooke and John Oliver (*d.* 1701) he surveyed the destroyed areas and made directions for laying out the new streets.

Mills's activity as a surveyor and architect has been traced back to 1638, but his claim to architectural celebrity was his building in 1654–6 of Thorpe Hall, near Peterborough, for Oliver St John, Oliver Cromwell's lord chief justice. He may also, four years later, have been responsible for the designing of the stylistically similar Wisbech Castle, now demolished, for St John's parliamentary colleague, the secretary of state John Thurloe. Thorpe, a building of considerable power, is one of the most important houses of the interregnum. Built in the hybrid style which has been dubbed 'artisan mannerism', the house is exuberantly detailed and entirely lacking in the Italianate sophistication of the court style of Inigo Jones. Its plan is both innovative, in being an early example of the three rooms deep triple-pile, and *retardataire* in retaining the off-centre hall, entered at one end. By the time of his remodelling of the central block of Cobham Hall, Kent, in 1661–3, for the royalist Charles Stuart, sixth duke of Lennox and Richmond, Mills had modified his style to one more in keeping with the sober classicism of the court.

Among his works, Mills was responsible for building a handsome, pilastered terrace of houses in Great Queen Street, London (*c.*1640), houses in Holborn in 1641 and in Budge Row in 1668–9, and extensive works at Christ's Hospital in 1667–8. In his will (PRO, PROB 11/334/147), dated July 1670, Mills made bequests to his wife Elizabeth, his son Peter, and also to the nine children of his four daughters. He also bequeathed 10s. each to the governors of St Bartholomew's Hospital, in whose neighbouring church of St Bartholomew-the-Less he was buried on 25 August 1670. JOHN BOLD, *rev.*

Sources Colvin, *Archs.* · H. M. Colvin, 'Peter Mills and Cobham Hall', *The country seat*, ed. H. M. Colvin and J. Harris (1970) · O. Hill and J. Cornforth, *English country houses: Caroline, 1625–1685* (1966) · J. Summerson, *Architecture in Britain, 1530–1830*, 7th edn (1983) · will, PRO, PROB 11/334, sig. 147 · G. Worsley, 'Thorpe Hall in context', *Georgian Group Journal*, [3] (1993)

Mills, Richard [*pseud.* Rhydderch Hael] (1809–1844), composer, was the son by his second marriage of Henry Mills (1757–1820), an important pioneer of Welsh congregational singing. He was born at Tŷ newydd, Llanidloes, in March 1809. He showed musical talent at an early age, and competed successfully at eisteddfods on both musical and literary subjects. He left school at the age of eleven and established his identity as a musician when he was fifteen, when his hymn tune 'Maes-y-llan' was published in *Seren Gomer*, the first Welsh-language newspaper. In 1838 he published some of his literary compositions; however, his musical publications were more influential. *Caniadau Seion*, a collection of congregational tunes, was published in 1840 and supplemented in 1842; *Yr arweinydd cerddorol* was published in three parts (1842–45), and consisted chiefly of musical instruction. Mills and his son Richard (1840–1903) and nephew John (1812–1873), who carried on his work, did much to improve the character of Welsh religious music and to popularize musical knowledge in Wales. They were pioneers of the modern musical movement in that country. Mills died on 24 December 1844. His brother James (1790–1844) was also a musician of talent.

J. E. LLOYD, *rev.* TREVOR HERBERT

Sources *DWB* · J. E. Lloyd, R. T. Jenkins, and W. L. Davies, eds., *Y bywgraffiadur Cymreig hyd 1940*, 2nd edn (1954) · private information (2004)
Archives priv. coll.

Mills, William (1714–1782). *See under* Mills family (*per.* 1773–1939).

Mills, Sir William (1856–1932), engineer, was born in Wear Street, Southwick, Sunderland, on 24 April 1856, the son of David Mills, foreman joiner, of Sunderland, and his wife, Sarah Ann Kirkaldy. The earlier part of his working life was occupied with marine engineering. On leaving school at the age of fourteen he began a seven years' apprenticeship with Messrs George Clark, marine engineers, of Sunderland, and then spent a number of years at sea, obtaining a first class certificate as a marine engineer (1884), and gaining experience in the repair of submarine telegraph cables. For a short time he was a draughtsman with the Central Marine Engine Works at West Hartlepool and assistant outdoor manager with Messrs J. Dickinson, of Sunderland. In the 1880s he designed lifeboat-disengaging gear, which came into use in both naval and merchant ships.

Turning from marine engineering to metal manufacturing Mills began business on his own account as a general engineer in Sunderland in 1885, and established an aluminium foundry. There, and also at works which he set up in Birmingham soon afterwards (both later became limited companies under the style of William Mills Limited), he turned out castings for the motor-car and aircraft industries, taking out several patents for improvements in foundry technique. Early in 1915 he introduced and opened works in Birmingham (Mills Munitions Limited) for making the hand grenade for which his name is chiefly known and which was used in enormous quantities by the British and their allies during the First World War. This bomb had been invented by Captain Leon Roland and developed in Belgium, but its firing mechanism left much to be desired. Mills and Albert Dewandre, a colleague of Roland, later assisted by F. J. Gibbons, a lock manufacturer, worked to improve the bomb, and make it more reliable. Mills also prepared an instructional film demonstrating its use, and delivered lectures on the subject. His services were rewarded by a knighthood in 1922, and he received £27,750 from the government, but he failed in his contention that he was not liable to pay income tax on that sum, and was wont to declare that he had lost money by the grenade. He was chairman of the James Watt Memorial Trust. He was a collector of pictures, china, and antiques. On 10 November 1891 he married Eliza (*d.* 1930), daughter of William Vincent Hodgson, cotton spinner, of Manchester, and widow of John R. Gandy, of Warrington; there were no children of the marriage. He died at Edgefield, Broadoak Road, Weston-super-Mare, on 7 January 1932. H. M. ROSS, *rev.* ANITA MCCONNELL

Sources *The Times* (8 Jan 1932) · *The Engineer* (15 Jan 1932), 61 · *Engineering* (15 Jan 1932), 71 · G. Hartcup, *The war of invention: scientific developments, 1914–18* (1988), 62–3 · *CGPLA Eng. & Wales* (1932) · b. cert. · m. cert. · d. cert.
Wealth at death £37,829 11s. 9d.: probate, 18 April 1932, *CGPLA Eng. & Wales*

Mills, William Hobson (1873–1959), organic chemist, was born in London on 6 July 1873, the eldest of the five children of William Henry Mills, a Lincolnshire architect, and his wife, Emily Wiles Quincey, daughter of William Hobson, of Spalding, Lincolnshire. Mills's parents returned to Spalding in the autumn of 1873. He was educated at Spalding grammar school and Uppingham School, and entered Jesus College, Cambridge, in October 1892, but spent the academic year 1893–4 at home recovering from a foot injury received at school. He obtained a first class in part one of the natural sciences tripos in 1896 and in part two (chemistry) in 1897. In 1899 he was elected to a prize fellowship of his college and went to work for two years under Hans von Pechmann at Tübingen, where he was awarded his doctorate. In the Tübingen laboratory he met N. V. Sidgwick of Oxford, who became his lifelong friend. They shared a deep interest in both chemistry and natural history.

In 1902 Mills became head of the chemical department of the Northern Polytechnic Institute in London. On 11 August 1903 he married Mildred May Gostling [*see below*], chemist; they had one son and three daughters. In 1912 he returned to Cambridge to become demonstrator to the Jacksonian professor of natural philosophy, Sir James Dewar. (He succeeded H. O. Jones, who had been killed while climbing in the Alps.) Mills was also elected a fellow and lecturer of Jesus College. He was appointed a university lecturer in organic chemistry in 1919, and reader in stereochemistry in 1931, an appointment from which he retired in 1938. In 1940–48 he was president of Jesus College.

Mills's researches can be classified as relating almost entirely to two main topics, stereochemistry and the cyanine dyes, in each of which he attained an outstanding position. The Cambridge school of stereochemistry had been founded by H. O. Jones and greatly developed by W. J. Pope, but its greatest achievements were due to Mills and his co-workers, whose most important investigations were as follows: the first experimental confirmation of the Hantzsch–Werner theory of the isomerism of oximes; the first optical resolution of a spirocyclic compound and of an allene compound; the confirmation of the tetrahedral configuration of quaternary ammonium ions and of the planar configuration of platinous complexes; and the development of the 'obstacle' theory, involving restricted rotation, to explain the optical isomerism of certain substituted diphenic acids. Mills synthesized and resolved several novel types of compounds, the optical activity of which was dependent on restricted rotation.

Mills's work on cyanine dyes began early in the First World War. German photographic reconnaissance was carried out using plates which, by the addition of minute quantities of certain highly coloured compounds, had been 'sensitized' throughout the violet-blue-red regions, whereas the allies were initially using plates which were not sensitive in the red region and thus gave particularly poor results in early morning light. Pope and Mills investigated the preparation and chemistry of these 'photographic sensitizers', with the result that nearly all the dye-stuffs used by the allies in the manufacture of panchromatic plates were produced in the Cambridge laboratory. Mills later greatly extended the knowledge of cyanine dyes.

Mills was elected FRS in 1923 and received the Davy medal in 1933. He received the Longstaff medal of the Chemical Society in 1930, and was president of the society in 1941–4. He was president of the chemistry section at the British Association meeting in 1932. In 1937 he was George Fisher Baker lecturer at Cornell University, but contrary to tradition he did not publish the lectures.

Mills was an accomplished field botanist and ornithologist. After his retirement he spent much time studying the sub-species of British bramble, which he collected, classified, and finally preserved in the botany department at Cambridge.

Mildred May Gostling (1873–1962), chemist, was born at Stowmarket, Suffolk, on 15 December 1873, the daughter of George James Gostling, a dental surgeon and pharmaceutical chemist, and his wife, Sarah Abicail Aldrich. She was educated at Bedford College and Royal Holloway College, London, and was Bathurst student and assistant in the chemistry laboratory at Newnham College, Cambridge, in 1898–1900. Later (1901–2) she was demonstrator in chemistry at Royal Holloway College. At Cambridge she carried out research in organic chemistry in association with H. J. H. Fenton in the university laboratories. She published five papers, four of them in association with Fenton. Most of her research work was carried out before her marriage to Mills.

Mills died at his home, 23 Storeys Way, Cambridge, on 22 February 1959; his wife died on 19 February 1962.

F. G. MANN, *rev.* JOHN SHORTER

Sources F. G. Mann, *Memoirs FRS*, 6 (1960), 201–25 · D. H. Peacock, *Proceedings of the Chemical Society* (1960), 371–83 · *The Times* (23 Feb 1959) · Newnham College, Cambridge, register · *Cambridge Letter* [Newnham College Club] (1898–9) · M. R. S. Creese, 'British women of the nineteenth and early twentieth centuries who contributed to research in the chemical sciences', *British Journal for the History of Science*, 24 (1991), 275–305
Likenesses W. Stoneman, two photographs, 1924–43, RS, NPG · R. Schwabe, pencil sketch, 1945, Jesus College, Cambridge · photograph, Royal Society of Chemistry, Burlington House, London
Wealth at death £18,617 2s. 9d.: probate, 22 July 1959, *CGPLA Eng. & Wales*

Millyng, Thomas (*d.* 1492), abbot of Westminster and bishop of Hereford, was of unknown parentage, although it is recorded that he had at least one brother, John, to whom he granted land, and that he collated his nephew Thomas Millyng to the prebend of Overhall in Hereford Cathedral. He entered Westminster Abbey as a novice in 1445–6, was ordained acolyte on 4 March 1447, and celebrated his first mass in 1450–51. In 1456 he entered Gloucester College, Oxford, where he studied until 1465–

6, obtaining the degree of DTh. He preached before Edward IV on Passion Sunday (27 March) 1463. On the resignation of John Flete he was elected prior of Westminster in March 1466, and assumed additional responsibilities thereafter: as domestic treasurer (1466–70), warden of the new work (1467–70), and as one of the three commissioners to run the abbey after the enforced retirement of Abbot George Norwych who had run the abbey into debt. Millyng was elected abbot in November 1469. On 14 November 1469 a grant of £200 was made by the crown to Millyng and the convent out of the temporalities *sede vacante* of the abbey 'in consideration of their losses by fire, their expenses in the building of the nave of the church and their great indebtedness' (*CPR, 1466–7*, 179).

Queen Elizabeth took sanctuary in Westminster Abbey in October 1470 after her husband, Edward IV, fled the realm. There, on 2 November, their elder son, the future Edward V, was born: Abbot Millyng and his prior stood as godfathers. When Edward IV returned to England in April 1471, he showed his gratitude by a further contribution to the building of the nave, and by the appointment of Millyng as a king's councillor and chancellor to Prince Edward in 1471, with subsequent membership of the infant prince's council for the administration of his principality of Wales, duchy of Cornwall, and earldom of Chester.

On 22 June 1474 Millyng was papally provided to the see of Hereford, clearly by royal nomination. He was one of only two religious to be provided to an English see in Edward IV's reign. The see of Hereford was not wealthy or prestigious, but perhaps Millyng could not combine his abbatial duties with his services to the prince, and required a prelacy closer to the council based at Ludlow, where he now spent much time. In January and February 1480 he was a member of an embassy to Louis XI, and in May 1487 an envoy to the Roman curia. He delegated much of his diocesan work to others, and in 1482 secured a permanent suffragan, Richard Wycherley (Olensis). His register does show attempts to deal with abuses in the diocese. He was pardoned on 13 November 1481 for the escape of felons from custody in his prison. He died at Hereford in January 1492. He was not buried in the cathedral as was customary, but in the chapel of St John the Baptist, Westminster Abbey—an indication of his real sense of home. Whether the stone coffin placed on Abbot Fascet's tomb was that of Millyng is debatable.   ANN RHYDDERCH

Sources A. T. Bannister, ed., *Registrum Thome Myllyng … AD 1474–1492*, CYS, 26 (1920) · *CPR, 1467–94* · *CEPR letters*, vol. 12 · Emden, *Oxf.* · E. H. Pearce, *The monks of Westminster* (1916) · T. D. Hardy, *Syllabus, in English, of the documents relating to England and other kingdoms contained in the collection known as 'Rymer's Foedera'*, 3 vols., PRO, 76 (1869–85) · J. Duncumb and others, *Collections towards the history and antiquities of the county of Hereford*, 1 (1804) · F. T. Havergal, *Fasti Herefordenses and other antiquarian memorials of Hereford* (1869) · C. L. Scofield, *The life and reign of Edward the Fourth*, 2 vols. (1923) · C. Ross, *Edward IV* (1974)

Milman, Sir Francis, first baronet (1746–1821), physician, was born on 31 August 1746 at East Ogwell, Devon, the son of Francis Milman (d. 1773), rector of that parish, and vicar of Abbots Kerswell in the same county. His grandfather, also named Francis Milman, was rector of Marldon and vicar of Paignton, Devon. On 30 June 1760 Milman matriculated at Exeter College, Oxford, where he graduated BA on 9 May 1764, MA on 14 January 1767, MB on 7 July 1770, and MD on 23 November 1776. He was elected to a college fellowship in 1765 and to a Radcliffe travelling fellowship in May 1771. He became a fellow of the Royal Society in 1772. He was elected physician to the Middlesex Hospital (1777–9) and a fellow of the Royal College of Physicians on 30 September 1778. During the same year he took the degree of bachelor of divinity at Oxford.

Milman made the acquaintance of the duke of Gloucester while travelling in Rome, and through his influence obtained a practice in London. In 1785 he was made physician-extraordinary to the king's household, and in 1796 joint physician to the household. In 1800 he was created a baronet, a reward for attending Princess Sophia at Weymouth, and in 1806 became physician-in-ordinary to George III. At the College of Physicians he delivered the Goulstonian lectures on scurvy in 1780, was five times censor between 1779 and 1799, delivered the Croonian lectures in 1781, and the Harveian oration, which was not printed, in 1782. He was elected president in 1811 and 1812, and resigned on 6 October 1813.

Milman married Frances (1754/5–1836), daughter of William Hart of Stapleton, Gloucestershire on 20 July 1779: they had three sons. The eldest, William George (1781–1857), succeeded him in the baronetcy, and was father of Robert *Milman (1816–1876), bishop of Calcutta; his youngest son, Henry Hart *Milman (1791–1868) was dean of St Paul's.

Milman published two undistinguished works: *Animadversiones de natura hydropis ejusque curatione* (1782), which is dedicated to the Radcliffe trustees, and is in part based on his observations while travelling abroad, and *An Enquiry into the Source from whence the Symptoms of the Scurvy and of Putrid Fevers Arise* (1799), which is dedicated to Lord Southampton.

Milman died at Pinner Grove, Middlesex, on 24 June 1821, and was buried in the church of St Luke at Chelsea.

NORMAN MOORE, *rev.* CATHERINE BERGIN

Sources Munk, *Roll* · Foster, *Alum. Oxon.* · S. C. Lawrence, *Charitable knowledge: hospital pupils and practitioners in eighteenth-century London* (1996) · *The record of the Royal Society of London*, 4th edn (1940) · Burke, *Peerage* · *The later correspondence of George III*, ed. A. Aspinall, 5 vols. (1962–70), vol. 3

Milman, Henry Hart (1791–1868), historian and dean of St Paul's, born in London on 10 February 1791, was the third son of Sir Francis *Milman, first baronet (1746–1821), physician to George III, and his wife, Frances (1754/5–1836), daughter of William Hart of Stapleton, Gloucestershire. He was educated under Dr Burney at Greenwich, and subsequently at Eton College and at Brasenose College, Oxford, where his career was remarkably brilliant. He matriculated on 25 May 1810, and graduated BA (1814), MA (1816), and BD and DD (1849). In 1812 he won the Newdigate prize with an English poem on the 'Apollo Belvidere', which was considered by A. P. Stanley the most perfect of Oxford prize poems. In 1814 Milman was elected fellow of Brasenose, and in 1816 was awarded the chancellor's prize

Henry Hart Milman (1791–1868), by George Frederic Watts, c.1863

for an English essay, 'A comparative estimate of sculpture and painting'. He was an early and intimate friend of Reginald Heber, for whose *Hymnal* he wrote a number of hymns popular in their time. In 1821 he was elected professor of poetry at Oxford, but did not make the mark of John Keble, who succeeded him in 1831. He had meanwhile taken orders (1816), and was in 1818 presented to the important living of St Mary's, Reading.

Though attentive to his clerical duties, Milman continued for some time to be known principally as a poet, writing in the tradition of Scott and Byron. His first poetical publication was a verse drama, *Fazio*, written for the stage but published in book form in 1815. It was first acted at the Surrey Theatre, without the author's knowledge, under the title of *The Italian Wife*. Having succeeded there and at Bath, it was appropriated by the managers of Covent Garden, who astonished Milman by the request that Charles Kemble might be allowed to read the part of Fazio to him. Milman was flattered by the compliment, and the play was performed for the first time in London on 5 February 1818, with triumphant effect, mainly owing to the acting of Miss O'Neill, who had seen the piece before publication and had then discouraged Milman from anticipating for it any success on the stage. Fanny Kemble subsequently played the part of Bianca with great effect, both in England and America, while Adelaide Ristori had it translated into Italian in 1856 and appeared with much success as Bianca both in London and abroad. Milman had started writing his next publication, *Samor, the Lord of the Bright City* (1818), an epic of the class of Southey's *Madoc* and Landor's *Gebir*, at Eton, and nearly finished it at Oxford.

The subject is the Saxon invasion of Britain and the 'bright city' is Gloucester. The poem contains much fine writing in both senses of the term, and the author in later life subjected it to a severe revision. Southey, in criticizing the poem, suggested that Milman's powers were 'better fitted for the drama than for narration' (R. Southey, *The Life and Correspondence of Robert Southey*, 4, 1850, 301–2). Milman also published *The Fall of Jerusalem* (1820), *The Martyr of Antioch* (1822), and *Belshazzar* (1822), all dramatic poems showing a more authoritative touch. But *Anne Boleyn* (1826) ended his career as a dramatist. Seeking further subjects for his Oxford poetry lectures, Milman became interested in Indian poetry, learned some Sanskrit, and, with H. H. Wilson, was the first translator of parts of Indian epics, particularly of the *Mahabharata* (1835). He also edited Horace (1849). His translation of Euripides (1865) was still in print in the 1940s.

On 11 March 1824 Milman married Mary Ann, daughter of Lieutenant-General William Cockell. They had four sons and two daughters. The home was lively, with Milman's many friends, including Macaulay and Sydney Smith, regular callers. Milman maintained his literary output by writing for an hour each day before breakfast. He was a prolific contributor to the *Quarterly Review*, writing at least sixty-five articles between 1824 and 1865. His Bampton Lectures (1827) were unexceptional, but he then embarked on a remarkable enterprise, a history of Christianity which was not based on a literal interpretation of scripture and which reflected the theory of 'accommodation'—the ability of religion to adapt itself to progress. Milman's *The History of the Jews* (3 vols., 1830) shocked contemporaries by its depiction of the Jews as an oriental people, 'more or less barbarians, alternately retrograding and improving', little different from their contemporaries, with 'Abraham … a nomad Sheik'. *The history of Christianity from the birth of Christ to the abolition of paganism in the Roman empire* (3 vols., 1840) widened from national to epochal history: 'the story of the Jews was that of a nation, the history of Christianity is that of a Religion'. *The History of Latin Christianity* (6 vols., 1854–5) showed development during a 'mythic period, when poetry and history are inseparable' (Forbes, 81). The fourth part of this remarkable contribution to a broad-church understanding of historical development—a history of Teutonic Christianity—was never written. Milman's work produced predictable protests from high-churchmen and Tractarians. It stands with Thomas Arnold's *History of Rome* as the most formidable attempt at a history of Europe which was Christian in interpretation but which met the highest standards of contemporary historical evidence. His review in the *Quarterly Review* (March 1846) of J. H. Newman's *Essay on the Development of Christian Doctrine* (1845) was a devastating exposition of that work's historical deficiencies.

Side by side with his own interpretation of history, Milman became the best British nineteenth-century editor of Gibbon, though his edition of *The Decline and Fall* (12 vols., 1838) to a great extent incorporated a translation of Guizot's notes (which he reviewed in an influential article in the *Quarterly Review* in January 1854). He intended it 'for a scholarlike as well as a Christianised work' (Milman, 101), and it held the field until J. B. Bury's edition of 1896–1900. In 1839 he published the *Life of E. Gibbon, Esq., with Selections from his Correspondence and Illustrations*.

Milman's publications, caricatured as in thrall to German liberal theology and attacked by critics as diverse as Godfrey Faussett and J. H. Newman, made his preferment controversial. But Peel made him canon of Westminster and rector of St Margaret's, Westminster, in 1835, during which incumbency he lived in Ashburnham House (now part of Westminster School) with his growing family. In November 1849 Lord John Russell appointed him dean of St Paul's (the first dean for a century who was not also a diocesan bishop). Milman set the business of the cathedral on a sound footing, introduced evening services under the dome in 1858, and wrote its history, edited posthumously as *Annals of St. Paul's Cathedral* (1868). He died on 24 September 1868 at Queen's Hill Lodge, Sunninghill, Ascot, which he had taken for the summer. He was buried in St Paul's and a monument by F. J. Williamson, publicly subscribed, was erected in the south aisle of the choir in 1876.

Milman was, like the Oriel Noetics, among those who strove to make Christianity acceptable in nineteenth-century intellectual circles. His energy allowed him to continue the dual roles of prolific historian and reforming clergyman. His liberalism was sometimes taken for scepticism or secularism, but this reflected a profound misreading of his character and his intentions. His significance is brilliantly captured in Duncan Forbes, *The Liberal Anglican Idea of History* (1952).   H. C. G. Matthew

Sources C. Smyth, *Dean Milman* (1949) • D. Forbes, *The liberal Anglican idea of history* (1952) • W. E. H. Lecky, 'Dean Milman', *Historical and political essays* (1908) • A. P. S. [A. P. Stanley], 'The late dean of St Paul's', *Macmillan's Magazine*, 19 (1868–9), 177–87 • A. Milman, *Henry Hart Milman* (1900)
Archives Bodl. Oxf., corresp. • Westminster Abbey, account books | BL, letters to W. E. Gladstone, Add. MSS 44369–44414 • BL, corresp. with Sir Robert Peel, Add. MSS 40396–40537 • BL OIOC, letters to H. H. Wilson, MS Eur. E 301 • Bodl. Oxf., letters to Sir Thomas Phillipps • LPL, letters to A. C. Tait • NL Scot., letters to J. G. Lockhart • NL Scot., letters to third earl and countess of Minto • Trinity Cam., letters to Lord Houghton and I. M. Higgins
Likenesses T. Uwins, pencil drawing, 1813, BM • W. Walker, mezzotint, pubd 1852 (after T. A. Woolnoth), BM, NPG • G. F. Watts, oils, *c*.1863, NPG [*see illus.*] • F. J. Williamson, figure on monument, 1876, St Paul's Cathedral, London
Wealth at death under £20,000: probate, 28 Oct 1868, *CGPLA Eng. & Wales*

Milman, Robert (1816–1876), bishop of Calcutta, was born at Easton in Gordano, Somerset, on 25 January 1816, the third son of Sir William George Milman, second baronet (1781–1857), of Levaton in Devon, and his wife, Elizabeth Hurry (*d*. 1853), daughter of Robert Alderson, recorder of Ipswich. Henry Hart Milman (1791–1868), dean of St Paul's, was an influential and affectionate uncle. Robert Milman attended Westminster School as a day scholar from an early age, before going in 1833 to Exeter College, Oxford, where he graduated BA in 1837. After wintering in Rome with his family in 1838, he was ordained by the bishop of

Peterborough, in 1839, and presented to the curacy of Winwick in Northamptonshire. In 1840, through Henry Hart Milman, then a canon of Westminster, he was nominated to the comfortable living of Chaddleworth in Berkshire. Thereafter his skills as an extempore preacher (considerably aided by an exceptional memory and linguistic ability) and his reputation as an indefatigable parish priest ensured that he was presented to more neglected parishes: Lambourn in Berkshire in 1851, and Great Marlow in Buckinghamshire in 1862.

Both Lambourn and Marlow were in Bishop Samuel Wilberforce's Oxford diocese and Milman was a frequent lecturer at Wilberforce's newly founded diocesan divinity college at Cuddesdon. He was a moderate high-churchman who commanded respect by working himself as hard as his subordinates and by pouring his own funds into good causes. Endlessly energetic, he loved athletics and horse-riding, and brooked no nonsense from his parishioners. At Lambourn he was regarded as policeman and parson rolled into one and at Marlow he so galvanized the ailing parish that outside curates volunteered their services for the chance of training under him. Requiring little sleep, he read and wrote late into the night and, in addition to religious works such as *Meditations on Confirmation* (1849) and *Love of the Atonement* (1853), he published a *Life of Torquato Tasso* (2 vols., 1850), including verse translations of some of Tasso's poems, and a historical sketch of the twelfth century, *Mitslav, or, The Conversion of Pomerania* (1854), which for a time graced the reading lists of Oxford schools.

In January 1867 Milman was appointed bishop of Calcutta and metropolitan of all India and Ceylon, probably at the recommendation of Samuel Wilberforce. He was consecrated at Canterbury Cathedral on 2 February 1867, sailed almost immediately for Calcutta, and arrived there on 31 March. His sister, Frances Maria Milman, accompanied him. Neither had married and she had lived with him as his companion and housekeeper since their father's death in 1857. She was his devoted admirer and eventually biographer, but even she was unable to keep pace with the fury of his new life in India and abstained from some of his more exhausting tours.

The see of Calcutta was enormous, stretching from Burma and Assam in the east across to the Punjab in the far west, an area of nearly a million square miles ministered to by 180 clerics. Milman was an inspired choice for bishop. Within weeks he had worked out the details for spending most of the winter in Calcutta and then about nine months on the road during the hot weather. In the year of his arrival he visited both Burma and the North-Western Provinces; in a later year he covered some 10,000 miles. The expanding rail network throughout north India made the travel easier, though paradoxically it increased his workload; his standard procedure was to travel by night and then conduct services during the day—often five or six at each place—moving on again each night. Where railway lines were only partly completed, as in central India, Milman often travelled by trolley, halting in the isolated camps of the railway workers to conduct long-delayed marriages and baptisms. Back in Calcutta, he hosted regular receptions for Indian and European scholars, merchants, royalty, and civil servants, taking care to greet all with equal courtesy. It was an attempt to mute the bitter edge of racial estrangement that had sprung up in the wake of the mutiny of 1857.

Milman was the first non-evangelical bishop of India, but he was at heart a missionary. He could make sense of the British conquest of India only in terms of God's plan for the eventual conversion of all Indians. He therefore refused to see his chaplains as army chaplains whose only duty was to serve the occupying army, and he quashed any attempts by the army's chaplain-general in Britain to exert authority over the Indian chaplains. He also forced himself at an advanced age to learn Bengali and Hindustani so that he could preach directly to Indian Christians.

Milman's missionary objectives were aided by his high-church beliefs: he was prepared to accept help from anyone and he took a liberal attitude on doctrinal issues such as the baptism of polygamists. Ritualism did not pose an enormous threat to him. He disapproved of the use of eucharistic vestments and incense, but in 1872 he refused to sign a memorial against ritualistic practices and, indeed, with his services beset by squalling babies, irrepressible sparrows, and screeching hymn-singing, he often wondered how anyone could fear an excess of ritual and ceremony in the Indian church. He encouraged Anglican brotherhoods and sisterhoods to come to India and also welcomed missionaries who worked outside the established societies. In part he had the confidence to make use of irregular workers because he was so sure of the authority of the national church. In 1873 he arranged a formal conference between the three bishops of Calcutta, Madras, and Bombay (the first of its kind), expressly to put a halt to Canterbury's plans to send out coadjutor bishops or 'episcopal commissaries' for the Church Missionary Society and the Society for the Propagation of the Gospel. Alfred Gell, bishop of Madras, had been particularly keen that the Tinnevelly branches of these societies should have their own bishops, but to Milman this was a dilution of the national church's authority. He stressed, however, that he was happy to see an extension of the Indian episcopate by normal canonical division and in particular begged for his own see to be broken up and a new bishopric of Lahore established. He also established a lay diaconate and sub-diaconate to ease the pressure on his overstretched clergy.

Milman took an equally authoritative line with converts from other denominations. In 1869, in one of his most controversial decisions, he received three German pastors and over 650 of their Kol converts from Chota Nagpur into the Anglican communion. They were Lutherans who had broken away from Pastor Gossner's old Berlin mission. Milman was heavily criticized for taking on the Chota Nagpur mission; advocates of church union in India feared that he had irreparably damaged relations with the Lutherans. Milman, however, was unrepentant. Theoretically in favour of unity between Christians, he was never prepared to compromise the position of his own church. He insisted on a formal act of renunciation and profession from converts from Roman Catholicism and refused to allow his clergy to minister in dissenting chapels.

In February 1876, while on a typically frenetic visitation of the Punjab, Milman was laid up with exhaustion at the house of Sir Richard Pollock at Peshawar in Afghanistan. In early March he was shifted to Rawalpindi where the climate was said to be healthier, but he died of dysentery on 15 March and was buried in the new cemetery at Rawalpindi the next day. In Calcutta the government took the unusual step of erecting a monument to Milman in the cathedral, an honour not accorded to any previous bishop. Ironically, Milman's death achieved what he had been unable to win by argument and within months a new bishopric of Lahore was carved out from the Calcutta diocese. In 1879 Milman's bereaved sister published a lengthy *Memoir of the Right Rev. Robert Milman, D.D.*, minutely detailing his numerous episcopal tours and visitations.

KATHERINE PRIOR

Sources DNB · F. M. Milman, *Memoir of the Right Rev. Robert Milman, D.D.* (1879) · M. E. Gibbs, *The Anglican church in India, 1600–1970* (1972) · E. Chatterton, *A history of the Church of England in India* (1924) · E. Stock, *The history of the Church Missionary Society: its environment, its men and its work*, 4 vols. (1899–1916) · *The Times* (20 March 1876), 5 · ecclesiastical records, BL OIOC, N/1/155, fol. 299 · Burke, *Peerage* (1959) · *ILN* (30 March 1867)

Archives LPL, corresp. with A. C. Tait · U. Birm. L., Church Missionary Society archive

Likenesses wood-engraving, NPG; repro. in *ILN*

Wealth at death under £3000: probate, 21 June 1876, *CGPLA Eng. & Wales*

Miln, James (1819–1881), archaeologist, was the son of James Maud Miln of Woodhill, Barry, Forfarshire. He entered the navy and served in the First Opium War (1839–42) before becoming a merchant in China and India. He then returned to Scotland, where he inherited Murie, Perthshire, from his father, and Woodhill from his brother, and interested himself in small arms, astronomy, archaeology, and photography, designed rifles, and made telescopic lenses. Over the years Miln's antiquarian interests grew and he became a fellow of the Society of Antiquaries of Scotland, and was vice-president of both the Société Philomatique de Morbihan and the Société Française d'Archéologie.

In order to compare Scottish with Breton antiquities, Miln went in 1873 to Carnac, intending to stay only a few days, but he remained, with short intermissions, for seven years. In 1874–6 he excavated the hillocks of the Bossenno, discovering a Gallo-Roman villa of eleven rooms, the upper storey of which had evidently been destroyed by fire, probably in the third century. He also found traces of a villa on the flank of the adjoining Mont-St Michel. He published these discoveries in *Excavations at Carnac, Brittany* in both French and English versions, in Paris and Edinburgh, in 1877. He next explored three circular sepultures at Kermario, where he found pre-Roman buildings and defences.

In November 1880 Miln left for Paris and Edinburgh, to arrange for the publication of a second volume, but he was attacked at Edinburgh by typhoid fever and died there at 19 Rutland Street on 28 January 1881. The second volume of *Excavations at Carnac, Brittany* was finally issued later that year, in English and French, by his brother Robert Miln. Miln's manuscripts were passed by his brother to the Abbé Luco of Vannes, who subsequently published *J. Miln et les trois sépultures circulaires* at Tours in 1881. Miln's practical work was continued by his Breton assistant Zacharie Le Rouzic, and the museum at Carnac containing his collections of antiquities now bears both their names. The *Catalogue du Musée d' Archéologie James Miln–Zacharie Le Rouzic* was published in 1940.

J. G. Alger, *rev.* Joanne Potier

Sources Boase, *Mod. Eng. biog.* · R. Goring, ed., *Chambers Scottish biographical dictionary* (1992), 315 · *N&Q*, 8th ser., 2 (1892), 232 · Allibone, *Dict.* · *Proceedings of the Society of Antiquaries of Scotland*, 16 (1881–2), 7 · private information (2004) [Andrew Sherratt] · private information (1894) [George Hay] · d. cert.

Wealth at death £37,063 1*s.* 6*d.*: confirmation, 2 April 1881, *CCI*

Milne, Alan Alexander (1882–1956), writer, was born on 18 January 1882 at Henley House, Mortimer Road, Kilburn, in north London, the third son of John Vine Milne (1845–1932) and his wife, (Sarah) Maria (1840–1922), the daughter of Peter Heginbotham. J. V. Milne, who had been born in Jamaica, ran a private school, remarkable for having (briefly) H. G. Wells as a science master and Alfred Harmsworth, later Lord Northcliffe, as a pupil. Both were to have some influence on young Milne, but his father was his most important influence. Much praised and cherished as a child, A. A. Milne grew no protective coating and always found it hard to accept any form of criticism. At Henley House School, he said, 'it was natural to be interested; it was easy to be clever' (A. A. Milne, 43). The clever boy won a scholarship at the early age of eleven and joined his devoted brother, Kenneth, at Westminster School.

Milne became a public-school man and had the sort of life readers might assume from his books and plays, but his background was neither upper-class, Anglican, nor entirely English, and certainly not conventional. It is ironic that A. A. Milne should have been described by a fierce critic as 'metaphorically locked in the nursery'. His own ideal of childhood had little to do with nannies and nursery tea and much to do with adventuring. As small boys he and his brothers were given an unusual degree of freedom for Victorian children. 'Almost as babies', Milne recalled, 'we were allowed to go walks', and, later, bicycle rides, 'by ourselves anywhere, in London or in the country' (A. A. Milne, 39). His father encouraged sympathy for the underdog, the idea that brains count more than money, the value of fresh air and manual work, and the distrust of class distinctions. The son was always an 'incurable dissident' (P. Fitzgerald, *The Knox Brothers*, 1977, 182), but also, as Frank Swinnerton would put it, someone who 'stands for virtue', not 'the prevailing social codes', but for real goodness (F. Swinnerton, *Swinnerton: an Autobiography*, 1937, 323).

It was while at Westminster School that A. A. Milne developed his lifelong love of cricket, of Jane Austen, and of writing light verse, but it was his mathematics that won

Alan Alexander Milne (1882–1956), by Howard Coster, 1926 [with his son, Christopher Robin Milne, and Winnie-the-Pooh]

him a minor scholarship to Trinity College, Cambridge, in 1900. It was at Trinity that Milne stopped being a mathematician and became a writer. He edited *Granta* and wrote a great deal of it himself. J. V. Milne wanted his son to become a schoolmaster, and eventually to take over his school. Milne was determined to earn his living as a writer. He was both modest and ambitious. It was *Granta*'s well-established links with *Punch* that encouraged him. No art is so difficult as that of being funny, but it was an art that came naturally to A. A. Milne. His first piece was published in *Punch* in 1904. In February 1906, he started work as assistant editor, and in 1910 the *Daily Graphic* painted a vivid picture of families up and down the land tearing *Punch* apart in eagerness 'to read of Dahlia and Simpson and the captivating Myra … very up-to-date young men and women', known as the Rabbits (Thwaite, 142). 'Everyone loves A.A.M.', *The Observer* said. The *Times Literary Supplement* commented that with Milne it was 'more than usually futile to try to explain what makes him so funny' (Thwaite, 158).

In 1913 the *Daily Citizen* described Milne, accurately according to his niece:

> He is shy but confident, nervous but by no means silent … He is tall, lean, and athletic. His face is brown, his hair light, his eyes blue. Like nearly all men of great humorous gifts, he is exceedingly sensitive and intuitive … Few men know their limitations better than he does. He knows precisely what is within his powers … conversing with him it is necessary to keep one's wits extremely active. (Thwaite, 142)

On 4 June 1913 Milne married Dorothy (always known as Daphne; 1889–1971), the daughter of Martin de Sélincourt, who became chairman of both Swan and Edgar and the *Geographical Magazine*. It was an interesting, clever family, but she herself was characterized by more brightness than depth. The marriage survived, but for long periods they led rather separate lives.

In 1915 Milne, in spite of strong pacifist convictions, eventually volunteered and was commissioned into the

Warwickshire regiment. He became a signals officer and years later wrote: 'I never, as they say, fired a shot in anger' (A. A. Milne, *Behind the Lines*, 1940, 90). It was when he was stationed on the Isle of Wight that he wrote his first play, *The Two Wishes*, which was the germ of his first children's book, *Once on a Time* (1917). In July 1916 he was in France, on the Somme, in a 'nightmare of mental and moral degradation' (A. A. Milne, 211), about which he wrote very little. In November he left the front line, invalided out with trench fever. He spent the last part of the war in intelligence, but was glad he had known the real horror, as it gave him so much more right to speak out against it. His *Peace with Honour* was a best-seller when it was published in 1934, but in 1940 he realized Hitler had to be opposed, and *War with Honour* was the result.

In the course of a long writing life, A. A. Milne established three distinct reputations: as an essayist and light verse writer, as a playwright, and as the author of four famous children's books. His *Punch* pieces sold in huge quantities when they were collected and appeared between hard covers. His plays were extremely successful—in 1924 he was earning £2000 a year from the amateur rights alone. Some of the titles survive: *Mr Pim Passes by* (1919), *The Dover Road* (1921), *The Truth about Blayds* (1921). But even his most consistently popular play, *Toad of Toad Hall* (1929, his version of a book he loved, *The Wind in the Willows* by Kenneth Grahame), is now rarely performed.

Although Milne found in plays the most exciting form of writing, books were more straightforward. Milne's most successful piece of adult fiction was a detective story, *The Red House Mystery* (1922). It was much admired and much translated. His other novels were *Two People* (1931), *Four Days' Wonder* (1933), and *Chloe Marr* (1946). His American publisher hoped for another detective story after the first, but Milne had other things on his mind. In the summer of 1920 his son, Christopher Robin, known as Billy [*see below*], was born and a year later a teddy bear from Harrods joined the family. It was natural that he would write about them. A great many of the poems which made up the first of Milne's four famous children's books were written on a wet holiday in Wales in 1923. *When we were Very Young* was published in 1924. It was a huge success and was acclaimed in *The Times* as 'the greatest children's book since *Alice*' (Thwaite, 286). In 1933 Compton Mackenzie saw it above all as a social document. 'It is not extravagant to surmise that a distant posterity may find in that volume of children's verse a key with which to unlock the present more easily than with any contemporary novel, poem or play' (Thwaite, 266). Yet without E. H. Shepard's illustrations, which contribute so much to the charm of the book, most of the poems have not dated. Many of them appeal as much to children today as they did when they were written. Milne's technical skill is both admirable and delightful in poems such as 'The Dormouse and the Doctor', 'The King's Breakfast', and 'Disobedience' ('James James Morrison Morrison').

At Christmas 1925 Milne was asked to write a story for the London *Evening News*. He decided to write down a bedtime story he had told his son about his bear, which had now acquired the name Winnie-the-Pooh, Winnie after a black Canadian bear in the zoo and Pooh for more mysterious reasons. The story became the first chapter of *Winnie-the-Pooh* (1926). Christopher Robin himself was at the centre of the stories and most of the other characters (Piglet, Eeyore, Kanga, and Roo) came from his toy cupboard. Tigger would join them in the second book. Only Owl and Rabbit (and his friends and relations) were not toys.

The Milnes had bought Cotchford Farm, near Hartfield, Sussex, on the edge of Ashdown Forest, in 1925 and the combination of toy animals and real forest was irresistible. A second book of children's poems, *Now we are Six*, followed in 1927 and further adventures in the forest, *The House at Pooh Corner*, in 1928. They sold and continue to sell in millions, their popularity apparently increased, not diminished, by Walt Disney's films, videos, and marketing. The Pooh books have now been translated into more than thirty languages, including Latin, Japanese, Catalan, Serbo-Croat, and Russian. Oslo and Warsaw both have streets named after Pooh.

In 1952 Milne wrote the following rather sad lines:

If a writer, why not write
On whatever comes in sight?
So—the Children's Books: a short
Intermezzo of a sort:
When I wrote them little thinking
All my years of pen-and-inking
Would be almost lost among
Those four trifles for the young.

In *It's Too Late Now*, his autobiography (1939), Milne gives only a few pages to the children's books. But when his last book, *Year in, Year out*, appeared in 1952, a fan letter from a young journalist prompted him to show that he had come round to accepting Pooh almost as if he were 'the creation of one of my own favourite authors' (Thwaite, 479). A. A. Milne died, after a long illness, at his home, Cotchford Farm, on 31 January 1956, and was cremated at Tunbridge Wells; he was survived by his wife and son. His characters survive not only in the books and films, on greetings cards, mugs, and so on, but also in the English language. It is taken for granted that people know what is meant by 'an Eeyore-like tone' or 'behaving exactly like Tigger'.

Christopher Robin Milne (1920–1996), writer and bookseller, the son of A. A. Milne and his wife, Dorothy de Sélincourt, was born on 21 August 1920 at 11 Mallord Street, Chelsea, London. At the time of his birth J. M. Barrie, mentor and friend, had written, 'May Billy be an everlasting joy to you' (Thwaite, 215). As it turned out he was not, but the fault was hardly his own. As a child he was extremely close to his father and 'quite liked … being famous', as he wrote himself in 1973 (C. Milne, *Enchanted Places*, 92). In 1931 he had been named by the American *Parents' Magazine* as one of the most famous children in the world. But the pleasure of it turned sour. A columnist in *The Observer* suggested that Christopher Milne had spent 'over forty years trying to get off his knees from saying his prayers'. Certainly he had been teased during his time at Stowe School (1934–9), and as a young man it had seemed to him that his father had got where he was 'by climbing upon my infant shoulders, that he had filched from me my good name and had left me with nothing but the empty fame of being his son' (C. Milne, *Enchanted Places*, 165). But the impression the papers gave at his death that the father had ruined the son's life was far from true. In *The Path through the Trees* (1979) he summed up his own life as a happy one.

Christopher Milne went up to Trinity College, Cambridge, in 1939. His course of study was interrupted by his war service with the Royal Engineers, but he returned in 1946, and in 1947 took a degree in English. On 24 July 1948 he married his cousin, Lesley de Sélincourt, and the wedding represented the first meeting in more than twenty-five years between the parents of the bride and the groom, as a result of a long-standing estrangement between Dorothy Milne and her brother, Aubrey de Sélincourt. Christopher Milne's parents did not wholly approve of the match, but a courtship of shared walks and the 'discovery that though we were both solitaries, we liked being solitary in each other's company' (C. Milne, *Path*, 135) developed into a supportive and loving marriage. In 1951 they left London to start the Harbour Bookshop in Dartmouth, and Milne's determination to lead an independent life enabled him to come more fully to terms with his situation. The bookshop was a success, and in *The Path through the Trees* he wrote of the way in which he and his wife had learned the business as they worked.

Milne's autobiographical writing had begun, however, soon after his mother's death, with the best-selling *The Enchanted Places* (1974). He was in many ways very like his father; he was also an extremely good writer. Sadly he never found another subject as interesting to his readers as his own childhood. His only child, Clare, to whom he was devoted, was born severely disabled with cerebral palsy, and he set up a trust fund for her with his share of the Pooh money. Money had never interested him. He lived simply and gave much away. He died at Torbay Hospital, Devon, on 20 April 1996, survived by his wife and daughter; his cremation was followed by a service at the Quaker meeting-house, Totnes.   ANN THWAITE

Sources A. Thwaite, *A. A. Milne: his life* (1990) · A. A. Milne, *It's too late now* (1939) · C. Milne, *The enchanted places* (1974) · C. Milne, *The path through the trees* (1979) · *CGPLA Eng. & Wales* (1956) · b. cert. · m. cert. · d. cert. · b. cert. [Christopher Robin Milne] · m. cert. [Christopher Robin Milne] · private information (2004)
Archives Cheltenham College, letters · NRA, corresp. and literary papers · Ransom HRC, MSS and corresp. · Theatre Museum, London, letters · Trinity Cam. · U. Reading, Chatto and Windus archives · V&A, corresp. | BL, corresp. with Society of Authors, Add. MS 56757 · Cheltenham College, letters to Charles Turley · Col. U., Rare Book and Manuscript Library, letters to Curtis Brown · U. Leeds, Brotherton L., letters to Clement Shorter · U. Reading, Chatto and Windus archive · V&A NAL, corresp. and papers relating to Winnie the Pooh | FILM BFI NFTVA, four short comedies
Likenesses H. Furniss, pen-and-ink caricature, *c*.1910, NPG · H. Furniss, pen-and-ink drawing, *c*.1910, NPG · H. Coster, double portraits, photographs, 1926 (with Christopher Robin Milne), NPG [*see illus.*] · P. Evans, pen-and-ink drawing, *c*.1930, NPG · H. Earl, crayon and chalk drawing, 1952, U. Texas · D. Low, cartoon, repro. in *Lions and lambs* (1928) · Spy Junior [I. L. Uduardy], cartoon

Wealth at death £64,175 13s. 9d.: probate, 12 April 1956, *CGPLA Eng. & Wales* · £81,686—Christopher Robin Milne: probate, 3 Oct 1996, *CGPLA Eng. & Wales*

Milne, Sir Alexander, first baronet (1806–1896), naval officer, was the second son of Admiral Sir David *Milne (1763–1845) and his first wife, Grace (d. 4 Oct 1814), daughter of Sir Alexander Purves, bt. He was born at Inveresk, Musselburgh, near Edinburgh, on 10 November 1806.

Early career, 1817–1847 In February 1817 Milne entered the Royal Naval College at Portsmouth and first went afloat in 1819, on board the *Leander*, his father's flagship on the North American station. Subsequently he served aboard the *Conway* (Captain Basil Hall), the *Albion* (Captain Sir William Hoste), and in the *Ganges*, flagship of Sir Robert Waller Otway on the South American station. In June 1827 he was appointed acting lieutenant of the brig *Cadmus* on the Brazil station (rank confirmed 8 September). In 1830 the brig returned to Britain, and he was promoted commander on 25 November.

In December 1836 Milne commissioned the sloop *Snake* for the West Indies station, where in 1837 he captured two slaving ships, with 665 slaves aboard. On 30 January 1839 he was promoted captain of the *Crocodile*, and continued in her, and later in the *Cleopatra* in the West Indies and on the North American station, latterly in charge of the Newfoundland fisheries, returning home in November 1841. This last service, a combination of administration and diplomacy, he discharged with great care and considerable success, reflecting a high level of skill and application. Between April 1842 and April 1845 he served as flag-captain to his father at Devonport, and from October 1846 to December 1847 similarly served Sir Charles Ogle at Portsmouth.

Admiralty, 1847–1859 After a brief period of sea service with the western squadron, as Admiral Sir Charles Napier's flag-captain, Milne was appointed to the Board of Admiralty as the junior naval lord on 23 December 1847: he served there until June 1859. Despite being only a junior captain, Milne was selected on the basis of his proven administrative capacity. Although he was, by background at least, a Conservative, Milne was never politically active; as a result both Conservatives and Liberals would, at various times, consider him an opponent. Personally he was close to the first lord in 1849–52, Sir Francis Baring, while his relationship with the whig admiral Sir Maurice Berkeley, with whom he served almost a decade at the board, was reflected in the middle name of his only son. His appointment to the board and long continuation, under the whigs, twice under the Conservatives, and under two Liberal coalitions, reflected the lack of suitable alternatives, his outstanding administrative abilities, and the movement toward a professional naval administration begun by Lord Auckland between 1846 and 1848. While senior naval lords continued to be selected on political grounds into the 1860s Milne's appointment demonstrated that this did not apply to the entire board.

Milne's first task was to join Captain Sir Baldwin

Sir Alexander Milne, first baronet (1806–1896), by London
Stereoscopic Co.

Walker, the newly appointed surveyor, on an Admiralty
inquiry into the management of the royal dockyards. This
led to the reorganization of the yards, the introduction of
long-term construction programmes, and improved productivity. As the resident naval lord at Somerset House,
Milne oversaw the contracts branch, mastering and refining the arcane subject of naval stores contracts. He was
also responsible for the introduction of the good conduct
badge for seamen.

On 17 December 1850 Milne married Euphemia (d. 1 Oct
1889), youngest daughter of Archibald Cochran; they had
two daughters and one son. His administrative talents
were widely recognized, notably with his selection as one
of the commissioners for the Great Exhibition of 1851, a
task he repeated in 1867. His professional interests lay in
fields of strategy and tactics. His mastery of these subjects
was critical in bringing him to recognize the wider implications of an all-steam navy, for which he was an early and
effective proponent. During the Crimean War, Milne
supervised the victualling requirements of the navy, the
transport of the army to the Crimea, and its maintenance
there, an immense task which he discharged to the satisfaction of all, in contrast to the performance of other
departments.

In early 1858 Milne was selected by the first lord, Sir
Charles Wood, to respond to a memorandum from the
queen, expressing her concern following a visit to Cherbourg, at the growth of the French navy. In his memoranda Milne demonstrated the capacity to think strategically, and to meet the demands of a well-informed and anxious monarch with one of the first modern war plans ever
drafted at the Admiralty in peacetime. His recognition of
the vital role of coaling stations and colliers in the event of
war, both to facilitate the movement of fleets and for
defensive tasks, together with his mastery of the strategic
disposition of forces, make him the pioneer of modern
British naval strategic thought. On 2 January Milne had
been promoted to the rank of rear-admiral, and on 20
December 1858 he was gazetted a civil KCB, on the recommendation of Wood, the outgoing first lord.

In this phase of his Admiralty career Milne was primarily an administrator, with a limited role in the formation
of policy; however, his minutes and submissions were
often concerned with construction policy, coal supplies,
potential rivals, and strategy. His continuation under the
second Derby ministry (1858–9) reflected his expertise in
the field of stores and contracts.

North America, 1859–1866 After leaving office with the Conservatives in mid-1859, Milne was appointed to command
the North America and West Indies station in January
1860, a post that rapidly became central to British diplomacy and naval activity. The difficulties occasioned by the
American Civil War, notably the federal blockade of the
southern states, the *Trent* crisis of late 1861, concern for
the security of Canada, and French intervention in Mexico, ensured that his term, extended by one year until
1864, was peculiarly demanding. Although he had to
spend much of his time preparing for war, Milne revealed
considerable diplomatic talents. On 25 February 1864 he
was gazetted a military KCB, with authority to wear both
insignia. He was promoted vice-admiral on 13 April 1865,
and chaired a committee on naval medical officers in the
following year.

Admiralty, 1866–1869 Milne returned to the Admiralty as
senior naval lord, on Sir John Pakington's board in Derby's
third ministry, on 13 July 1866, and remained in this post
until the ministry fell in December 1868. In office Milne
worked to improve the efficiency of the board, setting out
the lines of authority and the relationship between the
first lord and the senior naval lord. Under his experienced
direction the 1832 Admiralty system reached a high level
of efficiency, although it was still primarily an administrative machine. He supported the junior naval lords in
their revolt against the reduced estimates of 1867,
although, as he had never taken a seat in parliament, his
voice had less obvious effect. This did not endear him to
Disraeli, who, for the third time, found the Admiralty
ruining his budget plans. Milne's major contribution was
to exploit the pressure for lower spending to ask fundamental questions about the role, strategy, and structure of
the navy. In this he continued his work on strategic planning. He left office with the ministry.

Mediterranean, 1869–1872 In April 1869 Milne took command of the Mediterranean Fleet for eighteen months. He

attended the opening of the Suez Canal. During the last two months the Channel Fleet was also under his orders for combined exercises off the coast of Portugal. He was particularly instructed to report on the performance of the masted turret ship *Captain*, designed by Captain Cowper Phipps Coles RN. On 6 September he inspected the ship, and expressed to her captain, Hugh Burgoyne VC, his concern that water was washing freely over the deck. He left the ship that afternoon. Early the following morning the *Captain* was caught by a squall and capsized with the loss of almost the entire crew. Milne was convinced that Coles, who was on board, had persuaded Burgoyne to carry too much sail. It was subsequently discovered that the ship had been fundamentally unstable. Milne had long been interested in ship design, and joined the Institution of Naval Architects. On 24 May 1871 he was awarded the GCB.

Admiralty, 1872–1876 Despite his close identification with the Conservative Party, the Liberal first lord, George Goschen, invited Milne to return to the board as senior naval lord in late 1872. After consulting naval and political friends he accepted, and served until 1876, under both Gladstone and Disraeli. In office Milne, perhaps uniquely, worked the system introduced by Hugh Childers. His experience and ability enabled him to function where lesser men failed. Convinced that there was a real threat to British seaborne trade, which he considered at least as serious as the threat of invasion, Milne stressed the need for trade protection, and stood out for cruisers as well as ironclads. He also continued the development of war plans, a process given added stimulus by the intellectual reaction to the dramatic Prussian victories in 1866 and 1870–71. He recognized the capability of naval forces to assault defended harbours and to destroy shipping that had taken shelter there, and supported the construction of suitable ships. His strategic appreciation was dominated by French domestic and overseas bases. In the event of war the former would have to be blockaded and assaulted, while cruisers were detached to patrol the main trade routes. He argued that the size of the British cruiser force should be calculated on the basis of the value of merchant shipping to be protected, not the scale of the enemy threat.

In his second term as senior naval lord Milne collected the evidence on which to base his plans: the number of arrivals and departures from British ports in a single year, the quantity of shipping passing various bases and choke points, the scale of naval force required, and the amount of coal necessary for effective trade defence from each of the various overseas cruiser bases. He concluded that the enemy would choose to attack at focal points, where there were more targets, rather than on the open seas, where evasion would be easier. This led him to favour patrols at choke points instead of convoy protection. This was entirely appropriate in the 1870s, when the French and Russians had few cruisers capable of oceanic steaming, and would be forced to operate as he predicted. Unfortunately his analysis remained unchallenged into the First World War, when the ocean-going submarine rendered

pre-war thinking obsolete. The construction programmes of his second term in office were distinguished more by a catholic taste than any clear theme. In the absence of a significant rival fleet this was only to be expected.

Carnarvon commission and retirement, 1876–1896 After leaving office, on 1 November 1876, Milne was created a baronet. In 1879 he served as chairman of Lord Carnarvon's royal commission on the defence of British possessions and commerce abroad. This had been set up in response to the public demands of Captain John Colomb for a unified imperial strategy based on naval supremacy. While Colomb is usually credited with providing the first impulse toward a modern British strategy, Milne, working inside the Admiralty, was at least a decade ahead of him, and rather more sophisticated. Unsurprisingly, the commission reported in favour of Colomb's analysis, seeing naval strength as a more effective guarantee of imperial security than large garrisons and fortifications. Following Milne's earlier work on trade statistics the report analysed in depth the various shipping routes, their necessary scale of defence, and the protection required for the relevant coaling bases.

Despite this clear case for naval expansion the Admiralty, represented by the incumbent senior naval lord, Astley Cooper Key, demonstrated no grasp of the issues, and no interest in grappling with the evidence. In the absence of a serious rival Gladstone's incoming government would not have been forthcoming. Milne submitted a minority report, complaining about the domination of the commission's proceedings by the army. On the commission Milne demonstrated his intellectual stature, proving himself the one flag officer of his generation with a fully developed concept of imperial strategy, and the ability to meet national needs with naval forces. His written contributions have been criticized for their lack of precision, but this should not obscure the unique value of his systematic and logical approach to the higher branches of his profession.

In 1881 Milne was gazetted admiral of the fleet. In 1887 he chaired a committee of naval officers who, on 22 November 1888, presented the queen with silver models of the *Britannia* of 1837, and the *Victoria* of 1887, to illustrate the progress in naval architecture during her reign. Late in life Milne, who was better qualified to render a judgement than anyone, reflected that the Admiralty system of 1832 had been superior to that of 1869. In retirement he lived principally at Inveresk House, Musselburgh. He died there, of a chill followed by pneumonia, on 29 December 1896, and was buried in Inveresk churchyard on 2 January 1897. He was succeeded in the baronetcy by his only son, Admiral of the Fleet Sir Archibald Berkeley *Milne (1855–1938). Sir Archibald lacked his father's professionalism; his inadequacies were cruelly revealed during his brief wartime command in the Mediterranean, which was marked by the escape of the German battle cruiser *Goeben*.

Milne's importance lay in his ability to work with the ideas of others, to improve upon them, and to integrate all their best features into his own system. These were precisely the qualities required as senior naval lord. If Milne lacked the charisma and fleet-handling skills of Geoffrey Phipps Hornby, or the technical expertise of Astley Cooper Key, he was without question the finest senior naval lord of the era. He had the professionalism and commitment to make effective use of the 1832 and 1869 Admiralty structures, demonstrating the critical role of the individual in the development of nineteenth-century naval policy. What distinguished his career from those of his contemporaries was that he was as professional about all aspects of the naval service as they were about the sea service or new technology.   ANDREW LAMBERT

Sources J. F. Beeler, *British naval policy in the Gladstone–Disraeli era, 1866–1880* (1997) · NMM, Milne MSS · B. M. Ranft, *Technical change and British naval policy, 1860–1939* (1977) · R. A. Courtemanche, *No need of glory: the British navy in American waters, 1860–1864* (1977) · C. I. Hamilton, *Anglo-French naval rivalry, 1840–1870* (1993) · D. M. Schurman, *The education of a navy: the development of British naval strategic thought, 1867–1914* (1965) · E. Rasor, *Reform in the Royal Navy* (1976) · N. A. M. Rodger, 'The dark ages of the admiralty, 1869–1885: business methods, 1869–1874', *Mariner's Mirror*, 61 (1975), 331–4 · N. A. M. Rodger, 'The dark ages of the admiralty, 1869–1885: peace, retrenchment and reform, 1880–1885', *Mariner's Mirror*, 62 (1976), 121–8 · N. A. M. Rodger, 'The dark ages of the admiralty, 1869–1885: change and decay, 1874–1880', *Mariner's Mirror*, 62 (1976), 33–46 · S. Sandler, *The emergence of the modern capital ship* (1979) · A. D. Lambert, *The Crimean War: British grand strategy, 1853–56* (1990) · K. Bourne, *Britain and the balance of power in North America, 1815–1908* (1967) · private information (2004) · Boase, *Mod. Eng. biog.* · Burke, *Peerage* (1924) · *ILN* (9 Jan 1897)

Archives NL Scot., corresp., diaries, and papers · NMM, corresp. and papers | BL, corresp. with Sir Charles Napier, Add. MSS 40024–40042 · BL, corresp. with Charles Wood, Add. MS 49532, *passim* · Bucks. RLSS, letters to duke of Somerset · U. Nott., letters to Sir James Graham and duke of Newcastle

Likenesses W. W. Ouless, oils, 1879, NMM · London Stereoscopic Co., cabinet photograph, NPG [*see illus.*] · T. [T. Chartran], chromolithograph caricature, NPG; repro. in *VF* (29 July 1882) · photographs, repro. in Courtemanche, *No need of glory* · portrait, repro. in *ILN*

Wealth at death £100,103 13s. 11d.: confirmation, 3 Feb 1897, CCI

Milne, Alvilde Lees- (1909–1994). *See under* Milne, (George) James Henry Lees- (1908–1997).

Milne, (Edward) Arthur (1896–1950), astrophysicist and cosmologist, was born in Hull on 14 February 1896, the eldest of three sons of Sidney Arthur Milne (1867–1921), a headmaster in Hull, and Edith Cockcroft (1870–1957), a teacher. Both of his brothers became scientists. Arthur Milne gained his education through a series of scholarships at Hymers College, Hull, which he attended from 1908 to 1913, and Trinity College, Cambridge, which he entered in 1914. Taught by S. Chapman and G. H. Hardy, he gained a first in part one of the mathematics tripos in 1915. A. V. Hill invited him to abandon his studies to analyse the behaviour of shells in the upper atmosphere. Commissioned into the Royal Naval Volunteer Reserve in 1916, by theory and experiment Milne's team refined binaural listening trumpets and produced a standard model for sound ranging. His outstanding mathematics for these projects relating to the earth's atmosphere led to a fellowship at Trinity College in 1919.

Slight in stature, modest and shy, yet quick of speech, Milne exuded vitality. He thrived on the cut and thrust of debate. He liked to build up a subject from a few basic premises, yet the fruitful stimulation he inspired, and his deductive methods were, eventually, of greater scientific value than the originality of his ideas. In 1919 he founded the Trinity Mathematical Society, and was prominent in other science clubs where he enjoyed the friendship of leading figures.

In 1920 H. F. Newall appointed him assistant director of the solar physics observatory. From 1925 to 1928 he was professor of applied mathematics in the University of Manchester. There Milne championed the use of vectors. Much as he enjoyed the informality and culture, he kept in close touch with Cambridge associates. Through constant journeys to the Royal Astronomical Society (he was a council member for nineteen years), and to his beloved Trinity, where he was always about the place, his work benefited from the scrutiny of C. G. Darwin, Newall, and R. H. Fowler, who restrained Milne's more outrageous suggestions. In January 1929, at the age of thirty-two, he took office as the first Rouse Ball professor of mathematics at Oxford and fellow of Wadham College, posts he held for the rest of his life.

It is by his original contributions that Milne's reputation may be judged. These fall into three stages. From 1920 to 1929 his researches centred on problems of radiative equilibrium and the theory of stellar atmospheres, from 1929 to 1935 on the theory of stellar structure, and from 1932 onward with relativity and cosmology. Milne's interest in stellar atmospheres was first aroused by Newall, who sensed his ability to work on theoretical problems concerning the outermost layers of stars, particularly those that deal with the transfer of radiation through an atmosphere and those relating to ionization of the material. These problems have to be combined and this leads to subtle considerations of the interaction of matter and radiation. Milne laid the foundations of stellar atmosphere theory, a subject in its infancy, by a prodigious output of thirty papers between 1920 and 1929, which brought him election to the Royal Society in 1926. Shortly after Darwin's and Fowler's development of statistical mechanics Fowler and Milne collaborated in developing M. Saha's earlier work, and established a theoretical stellar temperature scale for the Harvard sequence. In his 1929 Bakerian lecture 'The structure and opacity of a stellar atmosphere', Milne explained his method for calculating stellar magnitude from the intensity of a spectral line. Although his proposal for a calcium chromosphere proved incorrect it attracted enormous attention, prompting others to a better theory.

At Oxford in 1929–31 he devoted his main energies to developing a theory of stellar structure based on a constructive mathematical critique of the pioneer researches of Sir Arthur Eddington. With neither nuclear and atomic processes, nor the part played by radiation fully understood, Milne's four equations were inadequately defined. He and Jeans seemed to misinterpret Eddington's deductions, based on a perfect gas, and a famous controversy ensued, yet they remained friends. Although much of Milne's criticism was not generally accepted, by 1932 he had developed powerful analytical methods, but he did not apply them to degenerative cores which were discovered in 1930. His methods led to important developments, notably T. G. Cowling's fundamental study of the stability of gaseous stars and Chandrasekhar's standard theory of white dwarf stars.

In May 1932 Milne turned to cosmology. H. H. Plaskett found him less comfortable with quantum and wave mechanics, and missing the constant contact with Cambridge colleagues. But Milne had criticized applied mathematics as characterized by the abstraction of a problem from its physical surroundings (minutes of the Trinity College Mathematical Society, 22 May 1922). Hence in his inaugural Oxford lecture (1929) he declared his ambition to construct mathematical physics from general principles, and his cosmology, quite unlike that of others, stands alone for its deductive methods. Provoked by Jeans's remark that an explanation for the universe's expansion was 'forever beyond our reach' (*The Times*, 10 May 1932), which Milne dismissed as scientific pessimism, Milne developed a new analysis of time as the basis of his cosmology, and devised a new deductive approach to dynamics and gravitation, as well as to other areas of his studies. The resulting general cosmological theory was called kinematic relativity. The invention of radar showed that it foreshadowed later developments in metrology, including distance measurement by radio astronomy. From his cosmological hypotheses Milne sought to deduce the fundamental laws of physics such as the law of inertia and the law of gravitation. The three main achievements of his work on cosmology were: the discovery with W. H. McCrea of the Newtonian analogues of the various models of relativistic cosmology, the introduction of the uniformly expanding world model, and the systematic investigation of different uniform time scales which suggested secular variation in the gravitational constant, and gave rise to J. B. S. Haldane's biological inferences. Milne considered building up the laws of nature his life's work, but could not achieve this, and his theory was later abandoned. Nevertheless his ideas on time and the expanding universe became part of 'the cosmologist's toolbox' (Matravers, 17).

At Manchester, Milne had taught, and had completed, work started at Cambridge. At Oxford, free of undergraduate lecturing, he reoriented. Milne and his close friend Plaskett, whose appointment to the Savilian chair of astronomy he had largely brought about, built up a leading centre of astrophysics. Through service on many committees Milne improved facilities and gained rooms for a mathematical institute. Milne's weekly colloquia with speakers such as S. Chandrasekhar, E. Hubble, H. N. Russell and A. Einstein, drew graduates in physics, astronomy, and mathematics. These included R. V. Jones, D. G. Kendall, T. G. Cowling, A. G. Walker, and G. J. Whitrow as well as senior men like Lindemann and Hardy, at a time when DPhil students were usually left much to their own

devices. With two studentships available, in the mid-1930s Milne and Plaskett started the first graduate school of astrophysics in Britain.

Milne was married twice, first in 1928 to Margaret (Margot) Scott (1901–1938), a chemistry teacher. She was a daughter of Hugh Fraser Campbell (1857–1948), a Scots advocate, and Jessie Theresa Fiddes (1867–1910), the niece of Edward Fiddes, the pro-vice-chancellor of Manchester University, who brought her up. Margot died on 5 October 1938 leaving two daughters and an infant son. In 1940 Milne married Beatrice Brevoort Renwick (1912–1945), daughter of William W. Renwick (1864–1933), an ecclesiastical architect of New York, and his wife, Ilka Howells (*d.* 1941). Beatrice died on 28 August 1945 leaving a daughter. Milne weathered the loss of both his wives to suicide, and losing his father in 1921 and a brother in 1942, through his self-discipline and his Christian faith. Despite failing health, due to the after effects of encephalitis lethargica contracted in 1924, he maintained his pace to the end, dying of a heart attack on 21 September 1950 at the Princess Hospital, Dublin, at the age of fifty-four. He had been attending a meeting in Dublin of the Royal Astronomical Society. He was buried at Wolvercote cemetery, Oxford, on 25 September.

A founder of modern theoretical astrophysics, and awarded many honours, McCrea considered Milne a man of the highest genius who had played a 'tremendous role' (McCrea, 428). Oxford's twenty annual Milne lectures 1977–96 were held to honour him.   G. J. Whitrow

Sources W. H. McCrea, *Obits. FRS*, 7 (1950–51), 421–43 · personal knowledge (2004) · R. J. Tayler, 'E. A. Milne (1896–1950) and the structure of stellar atmospheres and stellar interiors', *Quarterly Journal of the Royal Astronomical Society*, 37 (1996), 355–63 · G. J. Whitrow, 'Milne, Edward Arthur', *DSB* · H. H. Plaskett, *Monthly Notices of the Royal Astronomical Society*, 111 (1951), 170–72 · S. Chandrasekhar, 'The 1979 Milne lecture: Edward Arthur Milne, his part in the development of modern astrophysics', *Quarterly Journal of the Royal Astronomical Society*, 21 (1980), 93–107 · D. R. Matravers, 'Of Milne and of mathematics: inaugural lecture', University of Portsmouth, 1993, 1–22 · W. McCrea, 'Cambridge physics 1925–1929: diamond jubilee of golden years', *Interdisciplinary Science Reviews*, 11/3 (1986), 269–84 · J. Morrell, *Science at Oxford, 1914–1939: transforming an arts university* (1997), 315–17 · private information (2004) · G. Gale and J. Urani, 'Philosophical midwifery and the birthpangs of modern cosmology', *American Journal of Physics*, 61 (1993), 66–73 · G. Gale and J. Urani, 'E. A. Milne and the origins of modern cosmology', *The attraction of gravitation*, ed. J. Earman, M. Janssen, and J. D. Norton (1994), 390–419 · A. J. Harder, 'E. A. Milne: scientific revolutions and the growth of knowledge', *Annals of Science*, 31 (1974), 351–63 · M. W. Smith, 'E. A. Milne and the creation of air defence: some letters from an unprincipled brigand, 1916–1919', *Notes and Records of the Royal Society*, 44 (1990), 241–55

Archives Bodl. Oxf., corresp. and papers · priv. coll., family letters | CAC Cam., corresp. with A. V. Hill · Institute of Theoretical Astrophysics, Oslo, Norway, S. Rosseland MSS, letters · Nuffield Oxf., corresp. with Lord Cherwell · Princeton University, New Jersey, H. N. Russell MSS · RS, J. Larmor MSS · Trinity Cam., corresp. with Harold Davenport · UCL, K. Pearson MSS | FILM American Institute of Physics, One Physics Ellipse, College Park, Maryland, Niels Bohr Library, opening of the McDonald Observatory, Texas

Likenesses photograph, *c.*1930, priv. coll. · S. Chandrasekhar, photograph, 1939, priv. coll. · W. Stoneman, two photographs,

1943–5, NPG · portrait, 1944 (Royal Astronomical Society, presidential)

Wealth at death £25,511 17s. 9d.: probate, 18 Dec 1950, CGPLA Eng. & Wales

Milne, Sir (Archibald) Berkeley, second baronet (1855–1938), naval officer, the younger but only surviving son of Admiral of the Fleet Sir Alexander *Milne, first baronet (d. 1896), and his wife, Euphemia, the youngest daughter of Archibald Cochran, of Ashkirk, Roxburgh, was born at his father's official residence at the Admiralty, London, on 2 June 1855. He was a grandson of Admiral Sir David *Milne. At the time of his birth his father was junior naval lord and his godfather Admiral Sir M. F. F. Berkeley was senior naval lord. After a short period at Wellington College he entered the training ship Britannia as a naval cadet in 1869 and passed out as midshipman in 1870. He served under Sir E. G. Fanshawe in the flagship Royal Alfred on the North America and West Indies station, and under Captain George Tryon in the Raleigh. He was promoted sublieutenant in 1875 and lieutenant in 1876, with three first-class certificates. He then joined Commodore Sullivan on the South Africa station, first in the corvette Tourmaline and then in the Active. He remained on that station for three years, being transferred to the Boadicea when Captain F. W. Richards succeeded Sullivan as commodore, but for most of the time he was lent for service on shore during the annexation of the Transkei in 1877–8 and later throughout the Anglo-Zulu War of 1879. He was naval aide-de-camp to Lord Chelmsford, was wounded at the battle of Ulundi, and was mentioned in dispatches. After returning to England later in the year he joined the Minotaur, the flagship of Vice-Admiral A. W. C. Hood, in the channel squadron. In June 1882 he was appointed to the Orion in the Mediterranean, and a month later, when Admiral Anthony Hoskins left the Board of Admiralty in order to bring reinforcements during the Egyptian campaign, he became his flag lieutenant in the Penelope and was at the battle of Tell al-Kebir.

On his appointment to the royal yacht Victoria and Albert in October 1882, Milne began a career as a sea courtier. He rapidly won the affection of the prince and princess of Wales, and spent eight of the next eighteen years in royal yachts, finishing as commodore and later (1903–5) rear-admiral in charge of HM yachts.

Milne was promoted commander in 1884 and captain in 1891, and in the intervals between turns of yacht duty he was commander in the channel squadron flagships Minotaur and Northumberland (1887–9) and captain of the flagship Trafalgar (1894–6), the Venus (1897–1900) in the Mediterranean, and the Jupiter (1900–04) in the channel squadron.

In his sea-going commands Milne had shown himself competent and popular, so that after reaching flag rank in April 1904, and leaving the command of HM yachts sixteen months later, he was selected to be second in command of the Atlantic Fleet (flag in the Victorious) under Admiral Sir William May (1905–6) and of the Channel Fleet (flag in the Hibernia) under Lord Charles Beresford (1908–9). Having been promoted vice-admiral in May 1908,

he was then transferred for another year to the command of the 2nd division of the Home Fleet (flag in the King Edward VII) under May.

Milne was promoted admiral in September 1911, and in November 1912 he hoisted his flag in the Good Hope, soon to be replaced by the battle cruiser Inflexible, as commander-in-chief in the Mediterranean. His appointment did not meet with universal approval and there were some who attributed it to court influence. This was particularly true of Lord Fisher, the former first sea lord. Milne had earned Fisher's enmity because of his association with Beresford and his opposition to some of Fisher's reforms. By July 1914, when war seemed imminent, his force had been much strengthened, and included three battle cruisers, four armoured cruisers, four light cruisers, and fourteen destroyers.

The naval situation in the Mediterranean was very obscure in those critical days. It was unknown whether Italy would join her allies of the triple alliance, or even whether Austria would come in at once. The fast new German battle cruiser Goeben was at large, and it was presumed it would try to get out into the Atlantic. Milne had somewhat ambiguous orders from the Admiralty directing him to give priority to assisting the French in the transport of their troops from north Africa to metropolitan France and, if possible, bringing the Goeben to action. However, he was warned to avoid engaging superior forces except in combination with the French as part of a general battle. After the situation was somewhat clarified by the Italian declaration of neutrality, Milne was ordered to respect rigidly the neutrality of Italian waters. This would have precluded his sending warships through the narrow Strait of Messina. Later Milne was diverted from his pursuit of the Goeben by an erroneous signal announcing the commencement of hostilities against Austria. The announcement was premature, but Milne wasted time by moving north towards the entrance of the Adriatic to join Rear-Admiral Ernest Troubridge's cruiser squadron. Troubridge might have engaged the Goeben, but turned away, believing his orders to avoid engagement with superior forces meant the Goeben. The Admiralty had intended it to mean the Austrian fleet. Troubridge was subsequently court martialled but exonerated. The Goeben and her consort, the light cruiser Breslau, succeeded in entering the Dardanelles and, despite a fictitious sale to the Turkish government, remained under German control. The presence of the German ships at Constantinople contributed to Turkey's entry into the war on the side of Germany.

Milne was criticized in the press and elsewhere, but he had carried out his instructions: he had no reason then to anticipate any understanding between Germany and Turkey; he had no communication from the French naval authorities about the transport of the African army; he knew that the Goeben was faster than any of his ships and much more powerful than all but his battle cruisers, two of which had been ordered by the Admiralty to Gibraltar to prevent the Goeben escaping westwards; and he was uncertain until too late whether Italy would be neutral and Austria an enemy. On 30 August 1914 the Admiralty issued a statement exonerating him. Nevertheless, there were many who thought he had demonstrated a lack of imagination in interpreting his orders by not discerning that the primary threat was the *Goeben* and failing to concentrate all available forces in the vicinity of Messina when the Germans were reported there.

As, by diplomatic agreement, the supreme command in the Mediterranean was to be assumed by the French, and Milne was senior to the French admiral, he returned home in his flagship on 18 August. He had been offered and had accepted the command of the Nore, but this post was later filled by Sir George Callaghan, who had been relieved in command of the Grand Fleet by Sir John Jellicoe. Milne's chance for immediate employment really ended with Turkey's entry into the war—widely assumed to be a consequence of the escape of the *Goeben*—and Fisher's recall as first sea lord. Fisher blamed Milne for the blunders in the Mediterranean and invariably referred to him as 'Sir Berkeley Goeben'. Milne was not employed again and was placed on the retired list at the end of the war.

In 1921 Milne published a small book, *The Flight of the Goeben and the Breslau*, in which he challenged Sir Julian Corbett's account in the (official) *History of the Great War: Naval Operations* and the implied censure of his conduct. Milne's book set forth clearly his own account and justified the official approbation which had been repeated in the Admiralty's announcement of his retirement in 1919.

Milne was an able officer, popular in the service and in London society, where his long association with King Edward VII and Queen Alexandra made him well known. He was a keen fisherman and deer stalker and a good shot, and devoted much of his half-pay time to horticulture at his ancestral residence, Inveresk Gate, Musselburgh, Midlothian. He bequeathed a collection of rare shrubs and orchids to the Edinburgh Botanical Gardens.

Milne's association with the court brought him several foreign orders, as well as the CVO (1903), KCVO (1904), KCB (1909), and GCVO (1912), and he was groom-in-waiting to Edward VII and extra equerry to his three successors. He died suddenly, unmarried, at Inveresk Gate on 5 July 1938, leaving no heir to the baronetcy. He was buried at Inveresk churchyard, Musselburgh, on 8 July.

V. W. BADDELEY, *rev.* PAUL G. HALPERN

Sources *The Times* (6 July 1938) · A. J. Marder, *From the Dreadnought to Scapa Flow: the Royal Navy in the Fisher era, 1904–1919*, 5 vols. (1961–70), vol. 2 · E. W. R. Lumby, ed., *Policy and operations in the Mediterranean, 1912–1914* (1970) · P. G. Halpern, *The naval war in the Mediterranean, 1914–1918* (1987) · G. Miller, *Superior force: the conspiracy behind the escape of Goeben and Breslau* (1996) · *Fear God and dread nought: the correspondence of Admiral of the Fleet Lord Fisher of Kilverstone*, ed. A. J. Marder, 3 vols. (1952–9) · Burke, *Peerage* · *Navy List* · *WWW*, 1929–40 · J. S. Corbett, *Naval operations*, 1 (1920) · Naval Staff (Training and Staff Duties Division), *The Mediterranean, 1914–1915* (1923), vol. 8 of *Naval staff monographs (historical)* · personal knowledge (1949) · Admiralty records, 1949

Archives NL Scot., corresp. · NMM, corresp. and papers | NMM, corresp. with Sir Julian S. Corbett

Likenesses W. Stoneman, photograph, 1917, NPG · photograph, repro. in R. Wright, '*Goeben* and *Breslau*: the ones that got away', *History of the First World War*, 1/13, 345

Wealth at death £30,806 0s. 1d.: confirmation, 22 Sept 1938, *CCI*

Milne [*née* Ross], **Christian** (*bap.* 1772, *d.* in or after 1816), poet, was baptized on 19 May 1772 in Inverness, the daughter of Thomas Ross (*d.* in or before 1797), a cartwright, and his first wife, Mary Gordon, the daughter of a schoolmaster in Forres. Mary Gordon died while her daughter was very young, and about a year later, Ross married Mary Denton, formerly a gentleman's housekeeper, and moved with his family to Auchentaul, to be near his new wife's relatives. Christian Ross learned to read and write during the six months she was able to attend a dame-school in Auchentaul; she quickly developed a love for writing and read whatever literature she could find in her father's house, including *The Spectator*, *The Gentle Shepherd*, and *Paradise Lost*. At fourteen, she went out to service and began writing poetry, destroying most of it; a later mistress, the wife of Dr Jack of King's College, Aberdeen, accidentally found one of the poems and encouraged her to begin saving her work. On 16 August 1797 Christian married Peter Milne, then a journeyman ship-carpenter, but she continued to engage the interest of Aberdeen intellectuals, and, with their patronage and encouragement, she published a volume of poetry in 1805, which included an autobiographical sketch followed by a list of clergymen and academics prepared to testify to the truth of her story. Prefatory verses (not by Milne) describe her as 'the mean/ Unletter'd—female Bard of Aberdeen' who has, quite extraordinarily, managed to write poetry even though she lives 'quite estranged from Nature's "witching smile"' (Milne, 8). She earned £100 from the volume, which she used, years later, to purchase a sixteenth share in a boat built by her husband's employer. The subjects of the poems vary widely, from an affectionate anniversary poem addressed to her husband to patriotic exhortations to ship-carpenters to join the militia. Her political poems are topical and vehemently anti-Napoleonic; in one, she calls for the French to 'Set virtuous LOUIS on his throne' in place of 'the vile Corsican' (ibid., 117). In both her autobiographical statement and her poetry, Milne presents herself as accepting the existing social order, but nevertheless she makes some sharp comments about the miseries suffered by her father during his attempts to escape poverty by honest labour; she is even sharper in her dismissal of allegations that she plagiarized her poems or that she neglected her household duties to write them. 'Spite and Ignorance', she proclaimed, are 'quite unfit to judge ... the gift that Nature only can bestow' (ibid., 35). Milne's reputation seems to have been short-lived and mainly local, but her work was still well enough known in 1816 for the travel writer Elizabeth Isabella Spence to visit her during a trip to Aberdeen. Spence printed another autobiographical sketch of Milne's life, in which Milne describes years of ill health and the financial difficulties she has encountered in supporting eight children. While Spence describes Milne as being 'gentle in adversity' (1.56), Milne herself complains bitterly about 'the ridicule and contempt' she has encountered from her peers (ibid., 1.62) and strongly defends her decision to invest her literary income in a business venture rather than using it for day-to-day expenses. According to Milne, illness had prevented her from doing much writing since 1810, and apparently none of her work except the 1805 volume survives. Nor does she seem to have received much critical attention. *Blackwood's*, with a casual disregard for accuracy, dismissed her as 'a fisherman's wife, who writes poetry and sells oysters' (ibid., 3.429) in its mocking review of Spence's travelogue—the closest it came to noticing Milne's work.   PAM PERKINS

Sources C. Milne, *Simple poems on simple subjects* (1805) • E. I. Spence, *Letters from the north highlands* (1817) • 'Miss Spence and the bagman', *Blackwood*, 3 (1818), 428–38 • bap. reg. Scot. • m. reg. Scot.

Milne, Christopher Robin (1920–1996). *See under* Milne, Alan Alexander (1882–1956).

Milne, Colin (*c.*1743–1815), Church of England clergyman and botanist, was born at Aberdeen. He was educated at the Marischal College under his uncle Dr Campbell, and afterwards received the degree of LLD from the university. He then moved to Edinburgh and became tutor to Lord Algernon Percy, second son of Hugh Smithson (who was afterwards Percy, first duke of Northumberland of the third creation).

Ordained as an Anglican priest, Milne soon made his mark as a preacher. He was appointed evening preacher to the City of London Lying-in Hospital, lecturer to both the old and the new church at Deptford, and subsequently rector of North Chapel, near Petworth, Sussex. He continued, however, to reside at Deptford, where in 1783 he founded the Kent Dispensary, subsequently known as the Miller Hospital, Greenwich. He was a prominent promoter of the Royal Humane Society, and several times preached the anniversary sermon for the society. A volume of his sermons was published in 1780.

As a botanist, Milne was chosen to preach the Fairchild sermon, and the sermons which he delivered before the grand lodge of freemasons and at the Maidstone assizes were also printed. His botanical works included *A Botanical Dictionary, or, Elements of Systematic and Philosophical Botany* (1770), which was dedicated to the duke of Northumberland. A third edition appeared in 1805. Another work by Milne, *The Institutes of Botany* (1771–2), was a translation of the *Genera plantarum* of Linnaeus. In conjunction with Alexander Gordon MD of Aberdeen ('reader in botany in London', son of James Gordon, the nurseryman of Mile End, who corresponded with Linnaeus), Milne produced *Indigenous Botany* (1793), which was described as 'the result of several Botanical Excursions chiefly in Kent, Middlesex, and the adjacent Counties in 1790, 1791, and 1793'. Milne died at Deptford on 2 October 1815.

G. S. BOULGER, *rev.* ROBERT BROWN

Sources Desmond, *Botanists*, rev. edn • *Cottage Gardener*, 8 (1852), 185 • *N&Q*, 6th ser., 4 (1881), 334 • Nichols, *Illustrations* • Nichols, *Lit. anecdotes* • G. W. Johnson, *A history of English gardening* (1829) • J. Poland, *Records of the Miller hospital and Royal Kent dispensary* (1893) •

J. Britten and G. S. Boulger, eds., *A biographical index of British and Irish botanists* (1893)

Archives NRA, priv. coll., corresp. with Petworth estate relating to Northchapel

Likenesses J. Russell, pastel drawing, 1803, NPG

Milne, Sir David (1763–1845), naval officer, the son of David Milne, a merchant of Edinburgh, and his wife, Susan, the daughter of Mr Vernor of Musselburgh, near Edinburgh, was born at Musselburgh on 25 May 1763. He entered the navy in May 1779 on board the *Canada*, with Captain Hugh Dalrymple, and, continuing in the same ship with Sir George Collier and Captain William Cornwallis, was present at the second relief of Gibraltar, at the capture of the Spanish frigate *Leocadia*, at the operations at St Kitts in January 1782, in the actions off Dominica on 9 and 12 April 1782, and in the disastrous hurricane of 16–17 September 1782. On arriving back in England he was appointed to the *Elizabeth* (74 guns), but she was paid off at the peace. Having no prospect of further employment, Milne entered the merchant service, and continued in it until the outbreak of the war in 1793, when he joined the *Boyne*, going out to the West Indies with the flag of Sir John Jervis. On 13 January 1794 Jervis promoted him lieutenant of the *Blanche*, in which, under the command of Captain Robert Faulknor, he repeatedly distinguished himself, and more especially in the celebrated capture of the *Pique* (5 January 1795). When, after a very severe action, the *Pique* surrendered, neither ship had a boat that could float, and the prize was taken possession of by Milne and ten seamen swimming to her. For his gallantry he was promoted commander of the sloop *Inspector* (26 April 1795). On 2 October 1795 he was made captain of the frigate *Matilda* in reward for his service as superintendent of transports, an office he continued to hold while the *Matilda* cruised under the command of her first lieutenant.

In January 1796 Milne was appointed, at his own request, to the *Pique* and was stationed at Demerara for the protection of trade. The governor forwarded to him on 16 July a memorial from the resident merchants saying that the admiral had promised them a convoy to St Kitts by 15 July; that, if their ships waited longer, they would miss the convoy to England; and that if they sailed without convoy they would forfeit their insurance. Milne consented to take them to St Kitts. As he arrived there too late for the convoy to England, on the further representation of the masters of the vessels he took charge of them for the voyage home, and anchored at Spithead on 10 October. On the 11th he wrote to the Admiralty explaining his reasons and enclosing copies of the correspondence with the governor and merchants of Demerara. His conduct, under the exceptional circumstances, was approved, and the *Pique* was attached to the Channel Fleet. She was thus involved in the mutinies at Spithead in 1797, and when these were suppressed was actively employed on the coast of France. On 29 June 1798, in company with the frigates *Jason* and *Mermaid* she fell in, near the Penmarks, on the south coast of Brittany, with the French frigate *Seine* (40 guns) and brought her to action, suffering severely before the *Jason* could come up. The three all went aground, and after an obstinate fight the *Seine* surrendered as the *Mermaid* also drew near. The *Jason* and *Seine* were afterwards floated off, but the *Pique*, being bilged, was abandoned and burnt. Milne, with her other officers and men, brought the *Seine* to England, and on her being bought into the British navy was appointed to command her.

In October 1799 Milne went on the west coast of Africa, whence, some months later, he convoyed the trade to the West Indies. In August 1800 he was cruising in the Mona passage, and on the morning of the 20th sighted the French frigate *Vengeance*, the same size and strength as the *Seine*. The *Vengeance* endeavoured to avoid her enemy, so it was nearly midnight before Milne succeeded in bringing her to action. Twice the combatants separated to repair damage; twice the fight was renewed; and it was not until nearly eleven o'clock the next morning (21 August) that the *Vengeance*—dismasted and sinking—surrendered. It was one of the very few frigate actions fought fairly to an end without any interruption from outside. But Milne received no reward. He continued to command the *Seine* in the West Indies and Gulf of Mexico until the peace, when he took her to England and paid her off (April 1802). He was reappointed to her in April 1803. However, three months later, on 21 July, she was wrecked on a sandbank near the Texel owing to the ignorance of the pilots, who were cashiered and sent to prison for two years by sentence of the court martial, which honourably acquitted Milne. However, for his conduct in attempting to protect the pilots, and for his offensive behaviour to the board, he was relegated to the command of the Forth district of sea fencibles. In 1804 Milne married Grace (*d.* 1814), the daughter of Sir Alexander Purves bt.; they had two sons. In 1811–12 he commanded the *Impétueux* off Cherbourg and on the Lisbon station. He was then appointed to the *Dublin*, from which he was moved into the *Venerable*. This ship was reported to be one of the dullest sailers in the service, but by a readjustment of her stowage she became, under his command, one of the fastest. Milne afterwards commanded the *Bulwark* on the coast of North America, but returned to England as a passenger on board the *Loire* frigate in November 1814 on the news of his promotion to flag rank on 4 June.

In May 1816 Milne was appointed commander-in-chief on the North American station, with his flag in the *Leander*, but his sailing was delayed to permit of his going as second in command under Lord Exmouth in the expedition against Algiers. For this purpose he hoisted his flag in the *Impregnable* (98 guns), in which he took a very prominent part in the action of 27 August 1816. As a result of his failing to follow the plan of action, and mooring too far out from the Algerian batteries, the *Impregnable* received 233 shot in her hull, many of them between wind and water, and sustained a loss in men of fifty killed and 160 wounded, by far the heaviest of any ship in the fleet. These losses reflected badly on Milne and his flag captain. For his services on this occasion Milne was nominated a KCB (19 September 1816) and was permitted to accept and wear the orders of Wilhelm of the Netherlands and St Januarius

of Naples. The City of London presented him with its freedom and a sword; and as a personal acknowledgement Lord Exmouth gave him a gold snuff-box.

In the following year Milne went out to his command in North American waters, but returned to England in the summer of 1819. Shortly before ending his commission he married, on 28 November 1819, Agnes, the daughter of George Stephen of the island of Grenada. In 1827 he stood for parliament at Berwick as a tory, but was defeated. He was made vice-admiral on 27 May 1825, GCB on 4 July 1840, and admiral on 23 November 1841. From April 1842 to April 1845 he was commander-in-chief at Plymouth, with his flag in the *Caledonia*. He accepted this service only in order to further his son Alexander's career. Within a year he was anxious to resign, finding his health unequal to the task, as his eyesight and hearing were failing fast. His last service was to raise seamen without any official sanction during the 1844 Morocco crisis. On his way to Scotland after completing this service he died, on 5 May 1845, on board the packet-steamer *Clarence*, which was on its way from London to Granton. In 1804 Lord Keith said of Milne, 'Lord St Vincent made him; he is a handy seaman' (Markham, 174): it will serve as an epitaph.

Milne's younger son was Admiral of the Fleet Sir Alexander *Milne, bt; his elder son, David Milne-*Home (1805–1890), was a founder of the Scottish Meteorological Society.   J. K. LAUGHTON, *rev.* ANDREW LAMBERT

Sources NMM, Milne MSS · private information (1894) · C. N. Parkinson, *Lord Exmouth* (1934) · C. Markham, ed., *Letters of Admiral Markham* (1904) · *The Keith papers*, 3, ed. C. Lloyd, Navy RS, 96 (1955) · W. P. Gossett, *The lost ships of the Royal Navy, 1793–1900* (1986) · O'Byrne, *Naval biog. dict.*

Archives NA Scot., corresp. · NL Scot., corresp. and papers · NMM, corresp. and papers · NRA, priv. coll., family corresp. and papers

Likenesses G. F. Clarke, oils, *c.*1818 (after H. Raeburn), NMM · H. Raeburn, portrait, 1819, NMM · stipple, BM, NPG; repro. in Brenton, *Naval history* (1837)

Milne, David. *See* Home, David Milne (1805–1890).

Milne, Sir David (1896–1972), civil servant, was born at 14 Comely Bank, Edinburgh, on 11 March 1896, the son of David Munro Milne, a Church of Scotland minister, and his wife, Jane Mackay. He attended Daniel Stewart's College, Edinburgh, where he excelled as a pupil, becoming dux and gold medallist. He then entered Edinburgh University, but when the First World War intervened he took a commission in the 9th Royal Scots, being wounded while serving with the 51st Highland division in France. On demobilization in 1919 he returned to Edinburgh, where he gained a first-class MA degree in classics and the John Welsh and Vans Dunlop scholarships. In 1921 he entered the Scottish Office, then based in London, as an assistant principal. He married on 23 August 1928 at the High Pavement Chapel, Nottingham, Maud Winifrede Mary Greg Kilroy (*b.* 1901/2), the daughter of Lancelot Kilroy, a surgeon-captain in the Royal Navy. They had a son and a daughter.

In 1928 Milne was appointed private secretary to the permanent under-secretary of state at the Scottish Office and in 1930 became private secretary to the Scottish secretary. It was in this office, during the minority Labour government, that he was first able to demonstrate his administrative talents, combining sympathy and tact with an ability to appreciate ministerial wishes and act as an interpreter between them and the civil servants' views on the nature of the Scottish interest. The hitherto devolutionary views of the ministerial team were rarely found in the memoranda submitted to the cabinet and in other correspondence. In 1935 he was promoted assistant secretary to head the newly established local government branch, based in Edinburgh. The branch was meant to signify an element of administrative devolution in Scottish affairs by ensuring that Scottish institutions could deal with a senior official in Scotland without travelling to London and paralleled the establishment of the Scottish special areas commissioner (who also reported to the Scottish secretary). His ability to deal with the commissioner with discretion (and prevent too ready an experimentation of state intervention in economic affairs) and generally ensure a better acquaintance between domestic institutions and the Scottish Office saw him promoted in September 1939 to deputy secretary of the Scottish home department. This department was newly created on the reorganization of the Scottish offices, and was based in Edinburgh. He became its secretary in 1942.

In 1945 Milne was appointed permanent undersecretary of state to the Scottish Office on the retirement of Sir Horace Perkins Hamilton. It was not an automatic succession. The Scottish secretary, Tom Johnston, had wanted a previous Scottish health department secretary, William Scott Douglas; there were also doubts whether Milne had the character to operate with authority as head of the four rather disparate Edinburgh departments (dealing with agriculture, education, health, and home affairs) and the reputation to check the growing centrifugal force of Scottish domestic opinion. However, Douglas had been earmarked for the Ministry of Health and the other Scottish alternatives appeared to have even more cogent administrative weaknesses to operate at that level. Milne remained in the post until he retired in autumn 1959.

During Milne's period as permanent under-secretary the Scottish Office was transformed from a rather minor Whitehall department that dealt mainly with re-drafting English bills and generally adapting English departmental deliberation to meet the exigencies of Scots law into a major department that often as not insisted that Scottish conditions demanded special consideration. Much of this was due to Milne's desire to deal effectively with the forces of Scottish centrifugalism, particularly the nationalists, who argued that unemployment and social deprivation could be more effectively reduced by home rule. In the late 1940s, using his contacts with Scottish institutions (then anti-nationalist, although somewhat reluctant to state their views in public) and the press, he carefully co-ordinated a ministerial campaign to deflate the Scottish covenant movement (which had gathered over 1 million signatures in favour of a Scottish parliament) with minor political concessions. The corollary of this was an official policy that sought to maximize government subvention of Scottish provision. During the 1950s, under Milne's guidance, Scottish officials were able to ensure government acceptance of the idea that Scottish provision should equal that in England, despite an increasingly lower rate (and tax) base. Milne even argued that to satisfy Scottish opinion of the benefits of the union, such provision ought, on occasion, to demonstrate that it exceeded that in England.

In administrative affairs Milne was essentially a club man, preferring to meet, talk, and agree a matter with others rather than resort to lengthy minutes and correspondence. His unobtrusiveness and unassuming manner might have suggested lack of authority and unwillingness to deal with matters directly, but his brand of comfortable unionism had successfully managed Scottish affairs since the nineteenth century. In a period of increased government intervention in social and economic affairs and when Scottish institutions were more likely to be affected by that intervention, his administrative style and ability to select deputies of similar mind did much to ensure that Scottish opinion felt able to work and prosper with the United Kingdom government.

In 1958 Milne published *The Scottish Office*, one of the series of books published on Whitehall departments by the Institute of Public Administration. He was knighted in 1947 and became a knight grand cross on retirement in 1959. In private life Milne liked to listen to music and generally appreciate the arts. He was chairman of the Scottish National Orchestra Society, 1961–70, as well as a governor of the BBC in Scotland, 1960–65. He died at the Royal Infirmary, Edinburgh, on 4 February 1972; his wife had predeceased him.   IAN LEVITT

Sources WW · *Glasgow Herald* (5 Feb 1972) · *The Scotsman* (5 Feb 1972) · *The Times* (8 Feb 1972) · D. Milne, *The Scottish office* (1957) · I. Levitt, ed., *The Scottish office: depression and reconstruction, 1919–59*, Scottish History Society, 5th ser., 5 (1992) · I. Levitt, 'Britain, the Scottish covenant movement and devolution, 1946–50', *Scottish Affairs*, 22 (1998) · I. Levitt, 'The Scottish secretary, the treasury and the Scottish grant equivalent, 1888–1970', *Scottish Affairs*, 28 (1999) · I. Levitt, 'Scottish papers submitted to the cabinet, 1917–45: a guide to records held at the Public Record Office and National Archives of Scotland', *Scottish Economic and Social History*, 19/1 (1999) · I. Levitt, 'Scottish papers submitted to the cabinet, 1945–66: a guide to records held at the Public Record Office and National Archives of Scotland', *Scottish Economic and Social History*, 20/1 (2000) · PRO, T 273/124 · NA Scot., SOE 2/25 · private information (2004) · b. cert. · m. cert. · d. cert.

Wealth at death £30,998.55: confirmation, 4 Aug 1972, *CCI*

Milne, George Francis, first Baron Milne (1866–1948), army officer, was born at Westwood, Queen Cross, Aberdeen, on 5 November 1866. He was the youngest child of George Milne (d. 1890), and his wife, Williamina, daughter of John Panton of Knonkiemill, Aberdeenshire. He had two elder sisters, Edith and Priscilla (always known as Edie and Sissy). His father was a leading member of prosperous Aberdonian business circles, as manager of the local branch of the Commercial Bank of Scotland, bequeathing to his son a certain frugality and circumspection. The Milnes lived comfortably at Westwood, Queen Cross, and

George Francis Milne, first Baron Milne (1866–1948), by Walter Stoneman, 1920

their son was educated locally as a day boy at the Chanonry School (c.1871–1876) and MacMillan's School (c.1876–1881), both in Old Aberdeen, before spending two years at the University of Aberdeen (1881–3), though he did not graduate. He then decided on a military career and entered the Royal Military Academy, Woolwich, as a gentleman cadet on 14 March 1884 and was gazetted to the Royal Artillery in September 1885. Much of his early career was spent in India, except for two spells, one in 1890–91 with the Royal Horse Artillery at Aldershot, and the other in 1895–6 when he transferred to no. 2 company, Royal Garrison Artillery, in Malta. Milne was promoted captain in 1895 having seen no active service, but he lived the not over-taxing life of a young officer, shooting and pigsticking, and attempting to match his limited income to expanding social horizons.

Milne saw his first action in 1898, when, having passed into the Staff College, Camberley, he was recalled to his battery serving in the Sudan. He took part in the battle of Omdurman, and returned to Camberley on 12 September. After graduating in October 1899 he was posted to serve as deputy assistant adjutant-general on the intelligence branch of Kitchener's staff during the Second South African War. He was promoted brevet lieutenant-colonel and in June 1902 made DSO. After the excitement of battle the following years were rather anticlimactic. On returning from South Africa he served as deputy assistant quartermaster, intelligence division, specializing in the Balkans and the Levant. Perhaps the most notable event of these

years was Milne's decision (aged thirty-nine) to marry Claire Marjoriebanks Maitland (d. 1970), the only daughter of Sir John Maitland, baronet, on 9 June 1905 at Holy Trinity Church, Brompton. Socially, Milne had married well, but his bride was much younger than he; though the marriage was happy, the years 1914–20 would bring much strain to the relationship, as the Milnes grew apart and the age difference made its mark. However, these tensions were overcome once Milne returned to England. The Milnes had two children, George Douglass and Joan.

From April 1908 Milne served in a series of formation staff appointments—GSO2, 46th north-midland division, Territorial Army; GSO1, 6th division in Ireland; and brigadier-general, Royal Artillery, 4th division Woolwich—which indicated that he was destined for high rank. Milne built up a record of efficiency, determination, and common sense. Although he was a stern disciplinarian, and sometimes hot-tempered, Milne had a strong vibrant personality, and lacking a public school reserve because of his Aberdonian background, he had a way with subordinates and his soldiers; he took an interest in them and developed an avuncular manner; hence his nickname Uncle George.

First World War service In the opening battles of the First World War, Milne distinguished himself during the retreat from Mons and was quickly promoted brigadier, general staff, 3rd corps, then major-general, general staff, Second Army. At the end of 1915 he received the command of 27th division and was ordered to the allied lodgement at Salonika. On arrival he was given command of 16th corps with the temporary rank of lieutenant-general. The Salonika front was a military cul-de-sac, dull and quiet. Much time was spent on coalition social activities which strained Milne's patience: long French lunches and interminable banquets, Greek festivals and Serbian *slavas* where copious drink was consumed. On 5 May 1916 Milne succeeded to command the British forces at Salonika under the overall command of the redoubtable but irascible French commander-in-chief, General Maurice Sarrail.

Milne distrusted Sarrail's judgement and argued consistently against his plans for an offensive. A further difficulty was not just the appalling weather but disease: between 6 August and 11 November 1916 there were 29,594 cases of malaria among British troops, and Milne himself was frequently ill at this time with minor ailments. Milne was instructed that his task was to distract as many Bulgarian troops to his front as possible consistent with his defensive stance. In December 1917 Sarrail was replaced by General M. L. A. Guillaumat, whom Milne praised for his belief 'in thorough organisation' (Nicol, 149). In June 1918 Guillaumat, in his turn, was replaced as commander-in-chief by the dynamic and charismatic General Franchet D'Esperey. A series of withdrawals of both British and French troops from Salonika during the summer had left Milne gloomy, bad-tempered, and pessimistic. He wrote to the chief of the Imperial General Staff (CIGS), General Sir Henry Wilson, 'I do trust that the British Government will not acquiesce in any mad hairbrained scheme of attacking fortified positions in this country' without greater resources (Nicol, 170). D'Esperey revived Milne's confidence and planned to launch an offensive in September 1918. Milne was permitted to take part so long as the operations of his French and Serbian allies were successful. On 18–19 September Milne launched an attack on the Vardar–Doiran position, but was initially repulsed; however, the Franco-Serbian attack west of the Vardar River was successful, and Milne's troops advanced through the Belasitza Mountains into Bulgaria, and thence after 10 October veered southeastwards towards the Turkish capital at Constantinople. Despite the many difficulties Milne had played a significant part in the forcing of an armistice on Bulgaria (29 September) and Turkey (30 October).

Milne had always believed that Salonika was a secondary theatre, but the experience gained here was of considerable benefit to his future career. He had learned the constraints of coalition operations and strategy, and whatever his personal feelings had managed to achieve good working relations with all three of his French commanders-in-chief. Moreover, his political skills had been honed. Although appointed KCB in 1918, Milne was alone among the British army commanders of the First World War in receiving no financial reward for his services. His tour of duty, even in a secondary theatre such as Salonika, had provided him with an essential qualification that was demanded of all the professional heads of the British army after 1918: command experience. In 1918–19 Milne was a dark horse but he bore the requisite qualifications to reach the pinnacle of his profession.

Yet Milne had still to face some of the most arduous challenges of his career. Feeling tired, dispirited, and in indifferent health, he was given the task of defending British strategic interests over a large area stretching from the Dardanelles via Anatolia to the Trans-Caucasus and the Caspian Sea. The forces available were insufficient (though allotted the grandiloquent title of the army of the Black Sea) for the range of tasks he was given. Milne was instructed to enforce the terms of the armistice on Turkey (while supporting the government of the Sultan against the nationalists); to protect the lines of communication between Batumi on the Black Sea and Baku on the Caspian; preserve law and order in the Trans-Caucasus (while supporting the White Russians against the Bolsheviks); and reduce German influence. Milne travelled tirelessly around his huge command and soon acquired a local knowledge that was superior to that of his political masters. He was constantly troubled by a 'lack of a clearly defined policy' (Nicol, 204). Let alone a less than wholehearted commitment to the military operations in which Milne soon became entangled. Among these were the chaotic efforts to support General A. Denikin's White Russian forces, assisted by a British military mission led by Lieutenant-General C. J. Briggs.

In September 1919 Milne was ordered to evacuate his forces from the Trans-Caucasus (except Batumi, which was not evacuated until July 1920). However, he had simultaneously become embroiled in the confused politics of post-war Turkey. In March 1920 the British Government ordered Milne to occupy Constantinople with military forces and take over the chaotic administration of the city. This policy was opposed by the French, and his old comrade-in-arms, Franchet D'Esperey, was once more his commander-in-chief, and their relations became very tense. Milne also had to cope with the repercussions of the Greek invasion of Anatolia, but he handed over to his successor, Tim Harington, before the Turkish revival led to the confrontation with the British at Chanak.

Chief of the Imperial General Staff On returning to England in October 1920, Milne was promoted general and then placed on half pay until a suitable appointment could be found for him. On 1 June 1923 he took over as general officer commanding, eastern command. Among the welter of inspections that formed part of his peacetime duties, the most important was his attendance in November 1924 at a Royal Tank Corps demonstration at Wool, Dorset, which opened his eyes to the potential of mechanization. On 25 July 1925, after the sudden death of General Lord Rawlinson, commander-in-chief in India, Lord Cavan, the CIGS, confided to Milne that he (Milne) had been nominated as his successor. Milne's experience by comparison with that of Rawlinson was rather narrow, but he had become accustomed to coping with variegated problems with inadequate resources, and this was to prove an inestimable advantage.

Milne's seven years as CIGS (19 February 1926 to 18 February 1933), were the most significant of his career. Milne began his tenure with some unexpectedly bold moves. He encouraged the radical reformers to expect much from him on the controversial issue of mechanization. Even before he had taken up his post, in August 1925, Milne had met Captain B. H. Liddell Hart at the Norfolk Arms Hotel, Arundel, and seems to have raised the latter's expectations unrealistically. Several months later, Colonel J. F. C. Fuller was named military assistant to the new CIGS (an appointment normally requiring punctilious administrative skills rather than imaginative intellect). The choice seemed to indicate that Milne intended to create a personal think-tank attached to his office. Milne produced a progressive paper on army reorganisation which had been written for him by Fuller. However, after he entered the War Office, he seems to have realized the enormity of the task set before him. Liddell Hart observed in his diary, 'My impression is that he is a little afraid of the war office machine, though quite sure what he wants' (Liddell Hart, *Memoirs*, 1.107). These early gestures reveal a sense of intellectual adventurousness in Milne quite at odds with his later reputation as a reactionary; they hint at what he might have achieved if he had become CIGS under more favourable circumstances.

Although Milne declined to lay down a clear-cut policy on mechanization, he did deliver a striking, radical address to the experimental brigade at Tidworth on 8 September 1927. This force, established to test new tactical theories, was informed that the CIGS was aiming at nothing less than 'a mobile armoured force that can go long distances and carry out big operations and big turning movements' (Liddell Hart, *The Tanks*, 1.204). Extracts from this address were published in the *Daily Telegraph*. Milne soon grasped, however, that such a change in conceptual thinking could not be completed overnight. Further, this radical experiment had revealed to Milne the dangers of relying on highly strung intellectuals like Fuller, who made importune demands and then after he had been appointed to command the experimental brigade, resigned his commission (later retracted) after a squabble over administrative duties with his divisional commander, Major-General J. T. Burnett-Stuart. Thereafter Milne trusted the radicals less, and Liddell Hart rapidly lost influence.

In any case Milne, who was promoted field marshal in 1928 (KCMG, GCMG, 1929), saw it as one of his prime duties to conserve the army's existing strengths and he was beset with problems all around. Politically he was not in a position to sanction a series of wild upheavals. He had no intention of allowing conceptual innovation to overturn the traditional structure of the army or tamper with the regimental system. The logic of those who favoured complete mechanization would result in a substantial reduction of the army's manpower and its replacement by machines (that is, armoured fighting vehicles). Milne rejected this sweeping argument. It was far from proven that numbers did not count in modern warfare. Besides, Milne had other and broader responsibilities, and he should not be judged solely on one (rather narrow) issue. The regimental system was central to the defence of the British empire, much of which was in turmoil during the 1920s, particularly in India and the Middle East. Imperial policing required infantry battalions, not tanks. Milne's time as CIGS during the Locarno era witnessed little discernible military threat in Europe. There was no need to deploy large-scale armoured forces. Moreover, the Royal Air Force was challenging the army's primacy in imperial defence by emphasizing its successful use of aircraft in colonial control, which dispensed with large numbers of men. The RAF's arguments posed a major political threat, and offered to the government an opportunity to reduce the size of the army still further. The RAF might also outflank the good working relations that Milne had cultivated with the second Labour government after 1929. This danger receded when Milne succeeded Air Chief Marshal Sir Hugh Trenchard as chairman of the chiefs of staff committee that year. Nevertheless he was sceptical about the disarmament conference of 1931–2, believing that reductions forced on him had 'already gone beyond the limit of security' (Nicol, 273). Milne's plans were also compromised by the deteriorating financial position during the great depression. The army estimates fell from £39,930,000 in 1931 to £36,488,000 the following year, not rising to about the 1931 level again until after Milne had left office in 1934. Indeed the cuts in pay that were enforced were administered sensibly, 'loyally accepted' (ibid., 332), and did not provoke a traumatic crisis like that faced by the Royal Navy during the Invergordon mutiny of 1931. Thus Milne's problems were more complex than some of the mechanization radicals appreciated.

Assessment as CIGS Yet the zealots were unforgiving, and Fuller and Liddell Hart took their revenge by depicting Milne as a prudent Scot, miserly in dispensing vision and courage, who had missed a historic opportunity to reform the army. Their unfavourable view of Milne's policies was imposed on posterity virtually from the day he stepped down as CIGS. Liddell Hart wrote a savage indictment of his record in the *English Review*. He argued that 'Scarcely any progress has been made in changing the structure of the army' (Liddell Hart, 'Seven years', 381). But this had never been one of Milne's priorities. He had made some progress—but nothing like that expected of him by Liddell Hart. The tank corps had been permitted to expand, and, in line with his Tidworth address, Milne encouraged thought about future warfare, so that the army could adapt when funding improved. In 1927 the Imperial Defence College was founded to train officers in higher strategy. He supported the publication of the 'purple primer', *Mechanised and Armoured Formations* (1929), a narrow but important doctrinal first step. The provisional tank brigade exercises continued in 1931 despite the deteriorating financial position. In short, considering the adverse circumstances, Milne's tenure as CIGS was a respectable one. He had shown a canny political awareness, a harsh sense of reality, and brought formidable diligence to the conduct of his duties. He was successful in conserving the army as an institution, had prevented serious regimental infighting, and had made some preliminary doctrinal progress. The great weakness of Milne's term was what Liddell Hart described as 'Buggins's Turn'. When the army shrinks, generals at the top tend to monopolize the senior posts and block the promotion of their juniors. Milne himself had offered a bad example, allowing his term as CIGS to be extended twice (in 1929 and 1931). However, he had been left exhausted; as early as 1929 he was described as 'an old man—mentally and physically' (Bond, 159).

Retirement Milne was sixty-seven years old when he finally left the War Office. He was created Baron Milne of Salonika and Rubislaw, county of Aberdeen, in January 1933. He sat as a cross-bencher in the House of Lords, though he disliked public speaking and used this platform sparingly. In 1933 he was also appointed governor and constable of the Tower of London (he had been lieutenant since 1920). In 1936 he became president of the Army Cadet Force Association. In 1939 he joined the ARP and became an air-raid warden in Westminster. From 1940 to 1945 he was a highly energetic colonel-commandant of the Pioneer Corps. Frustrated by not being able to take a larger part in the Second World War, he wrote a weekly column for the *Sunday Chronicle*. Through the Royal Artillery network (Milne was colonel-commandant, Royal Artillery, after 1918, and master gunner, St James's Park, 1929–46) he had periodic meetings with the CIGS, General Sir Alan Brooke, and offered shrewd advice for which Brooke was grateful. By 1946–7 Milne's health was failing, and he died in London on 23 March 1948. He was cremated at Woking on 27 March and his ashes were interred in the garden of remembrance, Rainhill crematorium.

In many ways an able and attractive figure, Milne was a man whose career is difficult to assess. For though luck certainly contributed to his rapid and rather unexpected rise to CIGS, circumstances often conspired to prevent him realizing his full potential, either as field commander or as professional head of the British army.

BRIAN HOLDEN REID

Sources G. Nicol, *Uncle George: Field Marshal Lord Milne of Salonika and Rubislaw* (1976) · B. H. Liddell Hart, *The memoirs of Captain Liddell Hart*, 1 (1965) · B. H. Liddell Hart, *The tanks: the history of the royal tank regiment and its predecessors*, 1 (1959) · H. R. Winton, *To change an army: General Sir John Burnett-Stuart and British armoured doctrine, 1927–1938* (1988) · B. Bond, *British military policy between the two world wars* (1980) · G. C. Peden, *British rearmament and the treasury, 1932–1939* (1979) · J. F. C. Fuller, *Memoirs of an unconventional soldier* (1936) · B. H. Liddell Hart, 'Seven years: the regime of Field Marshal Lord Milne', *The English Review*, 71 (April 1933), 376–86 · Burke, *Peerage* (1999) · *CGPLA Eng. & Wales* (1948)

Archives King's Lond., Liddell Hart C., papers | IWM, corresp. with Sir Henry Wilson · King's Lond., Liddell Hart C., letters to Sir J. E. Edmonds · King's Lond., Liddell Hart C., corresp. with Sir B. H. Liddell Hart · priv. coll., MSS · PRO, War Office MSS · Royal Artillery Institution, Woolwich, London, Webb-Gillman MSS | FILM BFI NFTVA, 'New Field Marshal', Topical Budget, 27 Feb 1928 · BFI NFTVA, news footage · IWM FVA, actuality footage

Likenesses O. Edis, photograph, 1920, NPG · W. Stoneman, photograph, 1920, NPG [*see illus.*] · J. S. Sargent, group portrait, oils, 1922 (*General officers of World War I*), NPG · J. S. Sargent, oils, *c*.1922, Scot. NPG · O. Edis, photograph, *c*.1926, NPG · W. Stoneman, photograph, 1931, NPG · M. Codner, oils, 1936, IWM · O. Birley, oils, School of Gunnery, Larkhill, Salisbury Plain · L. Boden, oils, officers' mess, Woolwich

Wealth at death £15,645 14*s*. 7*d*.: probate, 1948, *CGPLA Eng. & Wales*

(George) James Henry Lees-Milne (1908–1997), by unknown photographer

---

Milne, (George) James Henry Lees- (1908–1997), architectural historian and conservationist, was born at Wickhamford Manor, Worcestershire, on 6 August 1908, the second of three children and elder son of George Crompton Lees-Milne (1880–1949) and his wife, Helen Christina (1884–1962), daughter of Henry Bailey, of Coates, Gloucestershire. His early life is recounted in his minor masterpiece of an autobiography, *Another Self* (1970), which, artful as it is, is in strict detail unreliable. The portrait of his father, a Worcestershire squire of Lancashire mill-owning stock, is a comic *tour de force*; the author later regretted it.

After Lockers Park and Eton College, Lees-Milne was enrolled by his father at a 'stenography school for young ladies' in Chelsea, where he learnt shorthand and typing for twelve months before his mother rescued him and shooed him into Magdalen College, Oxford. There, without much enjoyment, he read modern history, taking a third in 1931; but, he recorded, on an outing to Rousham, the rare William Kent survival north of Oxford, he found his vocation. When Maurice Hastings, a friend of Maurice Bowra who was renting the house, took a whip to the Knellers and started shooting at a statue of Apollo, Lees-Milne 'made a vow … that I would devote my energies and abilities, such as they were, to preserving the country houses of England' (Lees-Milne, 95).

First, however, Lees-Milne pursued a career as a secretary, for three and a half years to Lord Lloyd and then, briefly, to Sir Roderick Jones of Reuters. In 1936 he was recommended by his friend Vita Sackville-West for the new job of secretary (not of the stenographical sort) to the country houses (later historic buildings) committee of the National Trust. He took up the post in March 1936 and worked for the trust, with only a gap for war service (he was in the Irish Guards, 1940–41, until invalided out) for thirty years, latterly (1951–66) as part-time adviser on historic buildings. For a further seventeen years after that he served on the trust's properties (formerly historic buildings) committee.

Until an initiative by the marquess of Lothian in 1934, buildings had played only a small part in the work of the National Trust for Places of Historic Interest or Natural Beauty, founded in 1895. The survival of the traditional estates, with their houses, artworks, and acres, was now imperilled by the depression and penal taxation. The applied efficiency of Lees-Milne, combined with the political clout of grandees such as Lothian, brought about changes in the law (the National Trust Acts 1937 and 1939) so that families could hand over their houses to the trust, break entail, and even, conditionally, remain *in situ*. In 1946 the incoming Labour government established the National Land Fund, and in 1953 the Conservative government established the historic buildings councils. The National Trust became an independent but government-sanctioned saviour of the country house. In 1934 it had owned only two significant houses, Montacute and Barrington Court. By 1945 it owned seventeen and by its centenary, 1995, it had 230 in its care.

Lees-Milne's one-man mission, by train and bicycle or on National Trust petrol rations, exercising his ruthless charm in pursuit of such houses as Ham, Cliveden, Polesden Lacey, Knole, Petworth, Stourhead, and Osterley, not to mention writers' houses such as Thomas Carlyle's in Chelsea, Rudyard Kipling's and Henry James's in Sussex, and Bernard Shaw's in Hertfordshire, is limpidly recorded in his volumes of wartime diaries, *Ancestral Voices* (1975) and *Prophesying Peace* (1977), his two volumes of diaries to 1950, *Caves of Ice* (1983) and *Midway on the Waves* (1985), and in *People and Places: Country House Donors and the National Trust* (1992). He hardly kept diaries in the fifties and sixties, but resumed them in the seventies and began publishing these in the nineties. He expressed surprise at the commotion they caused; but it is a mark of their distinction as diaries—an ability to stand quite apart, a recklessness about disclosure, not only about others but about himself—that some of his friends (and the families of National Trust donors) were so shocked. Lees-Milne was polite, but little concerned. He flaunted antique politics and defied the modern age, expressing himself with steely elegance and disarming (most) critics by his own habitual self-disparagement. He seemed to know everybody. His eye for small detail could be hilarious and devastating.

Lees-Milne's writing career had begun with *The Age of Adam* (1947), the first of several architectural history titles for Batsford. *Roman Mornings* (1956) won the Heinemann award, while his books on the baroque won him a specialist reputation. He would have liked to have been a novelist (he published three novels) or a poet, but it is as a historian of his own time that he will be remembered—for his diaries and his biographies, especially his two-volume *Harold Nicolson* (1980–81) and *Fourteen Friends* (1996), the friends including Sacheverell Sitwell, Rosamond Lehmann, Henry Green, Osbert Lancaster, and Robert Byron.

Jim Lees-Milne was careful of his carapace. He said he preferred buildings to people, yet his appetite for social activity was indefatigable. He believed himself a failure at everything he did, yet he almost single-handedly saved many of England's finest buildings and his industry was remarkable (his typewriter chattering away in William Beckford's splendid library at 19 Lansdown Crescent, Bath), and his output prodigious. He was attacked as a snob but was eloquently aware of his status as an 'outsider', he said, 'in every circle'; he was an élitist sharply critical of the governing class, devoted to its artefacts and architecture but abhorring its philistinism. Lean and handsome into old age, he decried himself as 'hideous'. An Anglican who converted in 1934 to Catholicism, he reverted to high Anglicanism; he thought himself 'odious' but longed to be 'good' (personal knowledge).

While by first instinct homosexual (a tendency made increasingly explicit in his posthumously published diaries), Lees-Milne was for more than forty years devotedly married to the gardener **Alvilde Lees-Milne** (1909–1994). The only child of Lieutenant-General Sir (George) Tom Molesworth *Bridges (1871–1939), and his wife, Janet Florence Marshall, *née* Menzies (1867/8–1937), she was born in

London on 13 August 1909, and married first, on 9 January 1933, Anthony Freskin Charles Hamby Chaplin (1906–1981), a zoologist, who succeeded in 1949 as third Viscount Chaplin, and with whom she had a daughter; their marriage was dissolved in 1950. She was living in France in a house left to her by Princesse Edmond de Polignac when she met James Lees-Milne; they married on 19 November 1951. She made one of her first gardens at the house they moved to together, La Meridienne, at Roquebrune in the Alpes Maritimes. Inspired by Vita Sackville-West, she made widely admired gardens at Alderley Grange, near Wotton under Edge, Gloucestershire, the house to which they moved on returning to England in 1961, and at Essex House, Badminton, where they lived from 1975, as well as fulfilling commissions in France for Mick Jagger and President Valéry Giscard d'Estaing. With Rosemary Verey, she edited *The Englishwoman's Garden* (1980) and *The Englishman's Garden* (1982); *The Englishwoman's House* (1984) and *The Englishman's Room* (1986) followed.

Alvilde, a formidable presence, died of a stroke at Essex House on 18 March 1994, Jim of cancer at Tetbury and District Hospital, Tetbury, on 28 December 1997. Their funerals were at St Michael and All Angels, Little Badminton, on 25 March 1994 and 3 January 1998, and their ashes were scattered together in the garden at Essex House. Portraits of James Lees-Milne by Peter Scott, Derek Hill, and Julian Barrow (one with Alvilde) hint at his elegance but none gets beneath his skin.   JAMES FERGUSSON

Sources *Daily Telegraph* (29 Dec 1997) · *The Guardian* (30 Dec 1997) · *The Independent* (29 Dec 1997) · *The Times* (30 Dec 1997) · *Daily Telegraph* (23 March 1994) · *The Independent* (22 March 1994) · *The Independent* (30 March 1994) · *The Times* (26 March 1994) · J. Lees-Milne, *Another self* (1970) · P. Mandler, *The fall and rise of the stately home* (1997) · J. Gaze, *Figures in a landscape: a history of the National Trust* (1988) · personal knowledge (2004) · private information (2004) · b. cert. · m. cert. · d. cert.
Archives Tate collection, corresp. with Lord Clark · Yale U., Beinecke L., literary MSS, corresp., and papers
Likenesses J. Barrow, portraits (one with Alvilde Lees-Milne), priv. coll. · D. Hill, portrait, priv. coll. · P. Scott, portrait, priv. coll. · photograph, repro. in *Daily Telegraph* · photograph, repro. in *The Guardian* · photograph, repro. in *The Independent* · photograph, repro. in *The Times* · photograph, NPG [*see illus.*]
Wealth at death £830,225, gross; £801,512, net: probate, 14 Dec 1998, *CGPLA Eng. & Wales*

Milne, John (1850–1913), geologist and seismologist, was born on 30 December 1850 in Mount Vernon, Liverpool. He was the only child of John Milne, wool-dealer, of 147 Drake Street, Rochdale, and his wife, Emma, daughter of James Twycross of Wokingham. As a boy, Milne was educated in Rochdale and at the Collegiate College, Liverpool. In 1867 he entered King's College, London, and, with a fine academic record, he moved on in 1870 to the Royal School of Mines to specialize in geology under Warrington Smyth. After gaining practical experience of mining engineering both in England and in Germany, he was selected to report on the mineral resources of Newfoundland and Labrador in 1873.

In 1875 Milne was appointed professor of geology and mining at the Imperial College of Engineering, Tokyo. He soon published papers on the geology of Japan and related

John Milne (1850–1913), by unknown photographer, 1900s

topics. However, his work in these subjects was eclipsed by his subsequent contributions to seismology. His interest in this subject was aroused forcibly on 22 February 1880, by the strong shock felt in Tokyo from the devastating Yokohama earthquake. Milne proceeded to investigate every aspect of this shock in great detail and realized the inadequacy of the methods then available. Together with his colleagues Thomas Gray and James Ewing, he began a course of research and instrumental development lasting sixteen years and culminating in the successful construction in 1896 of the first seismograph capable of recording major earthquakes occurring in any part of the world. Waves from a distant earthquake were detected by a horizontal pendulum which recorded on photographic paper rotated by a drum. This instrument was soon manufactured by the firm of R. W. Munro. Seismology thus acquired a sound scientific and mathematical basis. Distances from epicentres could be calculated and the complex nature of wave motion thoroughly investigated.

In 1895 Milne left his chair at the college with a generous pension and returned to England with his wife, Tone, daughter of Jokei Horikawa, abbot of the Buddhist temple of Ganjo-ji in Hakodate. The marriage was in 1881; they had no children. The couple settled at Shide Hill House in the village of Shide, Isle of Wight. By that time Milne had published a very considerable number of papers on his work in Japan together with a textbook on seismology, *Earthquakes and other Earth Movements* (1886). By now, the importance of his work had been recognized in the form of various awards and honours including honorary fellowship of King's College, London, the Lyell medal of the Geological Society (1894), fellowship of the Royal Society

(1887), which was later to present him with the Royal medal (1908), and conferment by the emperor of the order of the Rising Sun (third grade, 1895).

Milne now set up a seismological observatory at Shide; and did much to encourage the establishment of similar stations in many other countries. As joint secretary to the seismological committee of the British Association he co-ordinated reports of all the earthquakes recorded. He was also the author of two more books, *Seismology* (1898) and *Catalogue of destructive earthquakes, AD 7–AD 1899* (1912), and many more published papers on seismology.

Milne was a kindly man with a keen sense of humour. He enjoyed golf and had a great passion for travel. As a schoolboy he had visited Iceland in his holidays without parental leave; when he took up his position in Tokyo, he travelled there overland via Siberia, Mongolia, and China, arriving some six months after leaving Hull. He died at Shide Hill House on 31 July 1913 following a short illness and was buried on 5 August in the churchyard of St Paul's, Barton, Isle of Wight. JOHN WARTNABY

Sources L. K. Herbert-Gustar and P. A. Nott, *John Milne: father of modern seismology* (1980) · J. Wartnaby, 'The early work of John Milne', *Japanese Studies in the History of Science*, 8 (1969), 77–124 · 'Eminent living geologists: Professor John Milne', *Geological Magazine*, new ser., 5th decade, 9 (1912), 337–46 · L. W. Hoover, 'John Milne, seismologist', *Bulletin of the Seismological Society of America*, 2 (1912), 2–7 · J. P. [J. Perry], *PRS*, 89A (1913–14), xxii–xxv

Archives Isle of Wight RO, Newport, corresp., notebooks, and papers · Sci. Mus., library | ICL, letters to Sir Andrew Ramsay

Likenesses photograph, 1900–09, Sci. Mus. [*see illus.*] · photograph, repro. in 'Eminent living geologists' · photograph, repro. in Hoover, 'John Milne, seismologist'

Wealth at death £11,917 4s. 5d.: probate, 30 Aug 1913, *CGPLA Eng. & Wales*

Milne, Joshua (1776–1851), actuary, is of unknown parentage and origins. He received an education grounded in mathematics and languages, before being appointed the first actuary of the newly established Sun Life Assurance Society on 15 June 1810. The background to Milne's appointment was the decision 'that the Sun Fire office should grant Annuities on Lives, and Survivorships, and effect Insurance on Lives whereby the Interest of the said Proprietors might be greatly benefited' (Dickson, *Sun Life Assurance Society*, 8). Milne carried on the work of the office, with only two assistants, until 1843.

The premium rates and life tables which Sun Life adopted in 1810 were those recommended by Francis Baily, the well-known FRS and actuary. Milne soon found the former to be too low, and the latter (which were based on the table deduced by Dr Richard Price from the burial registers (1735–80) of All Saints' Church, Northampton) to depend on inadequate data. His knowledge of mathematics enabled him to reconstruct the life tables, taking as the basis of his calculations the Carlisle bills of mortality, which had been prepared by Dr John Heysham; after a long correspondence with Heysham (12 September 1812 to 14 June 1814), he published in 1815 his famous two-volume work, *A treatise on the valuation of annuities and assurances on lives and survivorships; on the construction of tables of mortality; and on the probabilities and expectations of life*. The result was a revolution in actuarial science. Milne's table was remarkably accurate, and was very generally adopted by insurance societies. The Sun retained for over a century some of the premium rates that Milne introduced in 1820, and his table of mortality was only finally superseded in 1870. Milne was the first to compute with accuracy the value of fines, and his notation for the expression of life contingencies suggested that afterwards adopted by Augustus De Morgan in his *Essay on Probabilities* (1838). He also gave evidence before the select committee on the laws respecting friendly societies (1825 and 1827).

Milne retired from Sun Life on 19 December 1843, having done much to establish the office on a secure financial footing. In later years he became interested in natural history, and is said to have possessed one of the best botanical libraries in London. 'I am far from taking an interest now', he wrote to Augustus De Morgan (May 1839), 'in investigations of the values of life contingencies. I have long since had too much of that, and been desirous of prosecuting inquiries into the phenomena of nature, which I have always regarded with intense interest.' Milne died at 2 Clapton Terrace, Upper Clapton, Hackney, Middlesex, on 4 January 1851. In *The English Cyclopaedia*, published five years after his death, he was fittingly described as 'one of the universally acknowledged authorities on the subject of life insurance' (p. 251).

W. A. S. HEWINS, rev. ROBERT BROWN

Sources P. G. M. Dickson, *The Sun Insurance office, 1710–1860* (1960), 105–8 · P. G. M. Dickson, *The Sun Life Assurance Society, 1810–1960* (privately printed, London, 1960) · C. Knight, ed., *The English cyclopaedia: biography*, 6 vols. (1856–8) · *The life of John Heysham … and his correspondence with Mr Joshua Milne relative to the Carlisle bills of mortality*, ed. H. Lonsdale (1870), 137–73 · *GM*, 2nd ser., 35 (1851), 215 · *Journal of the Institute of Actuaries and Assurance Magazine*, 14 (1869), 69 · 'Select committee on the laws respecting friendly societies', *Parl. papers* (1826–7), 3.93–112, no. 558 · A. De Morgan, *Essay on probabilities* (1838) · Boase, *Mod. Eng. biog.* · private information (1894) · J. F. Wilkinson, *The friendly society movement* (1886) · d. cert.

Likenesses photograph, repro. in Dickson, *Sun Life Assurance Society*

Milne, Mary Elizabeth Gordon

Milne, Mary Elizabeth Gordon (1891–1972), nurse, was born on 3 December 1891 at 22 Mornington Road, Bromley by Bow, London, the daughter of Robert Milne, a general practitioner in Bow and medical officer to Dr Barnardo's Homes, and his wife, Mary, formerly Thomson. After training as a shorthand typist and working as a governess, Milne entered the Nightingale School of Nursing at St Thomas's Hospital, London, in 1915. She was awarded the gold medal as most outstanding probationer on qualifying in 1918, and won a Nightingale scholarship to train as a sister tutor at King's College of Household and Social Science, Campden Hill, London.

After working as sister-in-charge of the St Thomas's Hospital midwifery district, in 1921 Milne took up a pioneering post as the first sister tutor in South Africa, and established a preliminary training school at Johannesburg General Hospital. In 1924 she became sister tutor and matron's assistant at Queen Mary's Hospital, Stratford, London, before returning to Johannesburg as sister tutor in 1926. On the reputation of her South African work, in 1928 she was appointed matron of St Mary's Hospital, Paddington, London, without formal interview. On taking up her new office, Milne was reminded of strict nursing hierarchies by her predecessor as matron, Dorothy Bannon, her senior when training at St Thomas's, who kept her waiting for over half an hour only to urge her to hide her modern short hairstyle with an artificial hair bun.

As matron of St Mary's from 1928 to 1933 Milne strove to improve conditions for the nursing staff, instituting an off-duty day every week and arguing for improved nurses' accommodation. She believed that a high standard of patient care was only possible with a happy and comfortable nursing staff, and from the first she made regular rounds of the wards to keep in touch with the problems faced by her staff. An imposing figure, Milne has been described as combining an autocratic efficiency with great humanity and kindliness. In 1933 she was appointed principal matron in the London county council nursing service, as senior assistant to Dorothy Bannon, matron-in-chief. She did not enjoy what was a predominantly administrative post and returned to hospital work as matron of Leeds General Infirmary in 1935.

In 1940 Milne was invited to return as matron of St Mary's, which she came to personify during the Second World War, invariably visiting each of the wards during air raids to raise the morale of staff and patients. She was also made sector matron of sector six of the Emergency Medical Service, and as such was responsible for nursing and nurse training in all hospitals in a sector stretching from Paddington to Amersham and Basingstoke. Wartime conditions enabled her to encourage previously prohibited social contact between her nurses and the students of St Mary's Hospital medical school; she overcame opposition with the argument that if her nurses had to work with the medical students, they should be allowed to play with them too. She instituted a matron's ball and supported joint musical and dramatic societies, and she encouraged romances and marriages between her nurses and the medical students; her own fiancé had died in action during the First World War. On finding male students in the nurses' home she is said to have commented, with a strategic blind eye, 'I suppose you are all busy fire-watching, gentlemen' (Parkes, 118).

Made an OBE in 1945, Milne was appointed by the minister of health to the Central Health Services Council in 1948, and she became chairman of the nursing services subcommittee. She was also appointed to the management committee of the Paddington group of hospitals and chaired its nursing subcommittee in 1949. Having retired from St Mary's in 1949 on grounds of ill health, she remained active in the Royal College of Nursing, on the council of Dr Barnardo's Homes, and on a committee to improve housing conditions in Paddington. She died on 14 October 1972 at her home, Howard House, Vicarage Way, Gerrards Cross, Buckinghamshire.

KEVIN BROWN

Sources M. Milne, letter and notes to Sir Zachary Cope, 28 Aug 1953, St Mary's Hospital Archives, London, DP 7/2 · W. Parkes, 'Miss Mary G. Milne', *St Mary's Hospital Gazette*, 50 (1949), 118–20 · *St Mary's Hospital Past and Present Nurses' League Journal*, 11 (1974), 8–20 ·

M. F. Gamble, 'Mary Milne: a personal tribute', *St Mary's Hospital Past and Present Nurses' League Journal*, 12 (1975), 32–3 · private information (2004) · *Nursing Mirror* (14 Feb 1949) · *Nursing Times* (9 April 1949) · 'Matron Milne praises South African nursing', *Johannesburg Star* (22 May 1947) · Z. Cope, *A hundred years of nursing* (1955) · matron's reports to the governors, 1922–49, St Mary's Hospital Archives, London, SM/NR1/1/9–12 · b. cert. · d. cert.
Likenesses photograph, *c.*1940, St Mary's Hospital Archives, London

Milne, William (1785–1822), missionary, was born in the parish of Kennethmont, Aberdeenshire, and was employed in his early years as a shepherd. His father died when he was six. At the age of twenty he decided to become a missionary, and after studying at the college of the London Missionary Society at Gosport in Hampshire he was ordained there in July 1812. In August he married Rachel (*d.* 1819), daughter of Charles Cowie of Aberdeen, and in September they sailed for the East. They landed at Malacca in June 1813, where Milne met Robert Morrison; all three went on to Macau (Macao) in July. Morrison stayed there but Milne was expelled (the Portuguese authorities only permitting one protestant missionary); he went to Canton (Guangzhou) and learned Chinese, and next went on a missionary tour of Java and Malacca, settling for a time at the latter before returning to Macau. Milne and Morrison decided to found a missionary college at Malacca. Building began in 1818, with Milne as principal. From the start daily instruction in Chinese was given. 'This is the only Institution that has yet proposed the cultivation of Chinese as its chief literary object', Milne declared (Harrison, 61). Unfortunately Milne, whose wife died in 1819, proved a dictatorial principal, some of his younger staff, such as Thomas Beighton, leaving Malacca with relief. But as a scholar his reputation was high. He edited and published the *Chinese Magazine* from 1815 to 1822, and the periodical *Indo-Chinese Gleaner* from 1817 to 1822, and he wrote several works in Chinese in theology and history. His monument is the Old Testament part of his translation with Robert Morrison of the Bible in Chinese (21 vols., 1823). His liver and his lungs both became diseased, and Milne died at Malacca on 2 June 1822 and was buried there in the Dutch cemetery of St Antony. The historian of Malacca College remarks that 'Morrison and Milne stand out as pioneers in the vital process of bringing the culture of the modern West to bear on the traditional culture of China' (Harrison, 160).

One of his sons, **William Charles Milne** (1815–1863), missionary in China, was ordained on 19 July 1837, and, appointed to Canton, sailed for the East on 28 July 1837; he arrived on 18 December at Macau, where he assisted until 1842 at the house of the Morrison Education Society. Proceeding via Chushan, Tinghai (Dinghai), Ningpo (Ningbo), and Canton, he arrived at Hong Kong in August 1843 and was given the task with Walter Medhurst of opening a station at Shanghai. In 1844 Milne visited England. He returned to China in 1846 and served on the translation committee, part of whose work he subsequently attacked. In 1852 he again visited England and ended his connection with the London Missionary Society. Despite the advice to the contrary of his permanent secretary, E. Hammond,

who distrusted missionaries, Lord Malmesbury, the foreign secretary, in 1858 appointed Milne as an interpreter and the latter returned to China. He became assistant Chinese secretary to the legation at Peking (Beijing). Milne was married to Frances Williamina, daughter of the Revd Dr Beaumont. Among his published works he wrote *Life in China* (1858) and 'Account of the political disturbances in China', *Edinburgh Review* (October 1855). Milne died at Peking on 15 May 1863.

A. F. POLLARD, *rev.* H. C. G. MATTHEW

Sources R. Morrison, *Memoirs of the Rev. William Milne* (1824) · R. Phillip, *The life and opinions of the Rev. William Milne* (1840) · *GM*, 1st ser., 92/2 (1822), 649 · *GM*, 3rd ser., 15 (1863), 381 · W. Milne, *A retrospect of the first ten years of the Protestant mission to China* (1820) · B. Harrison, *Waiting for China: the Anglo-Chinese college at Malacca, 1818–1843, and early nineteenth-century missions* (1979) · K. S. Latourette, *A history of Christian missions in China* (1929) · P. D. Coates, *The China consuls: British consular officers, 1843–1943* (1988)
Archives SOAS, journals of travel in Far East
Likenesses stipple, BM, NPG; repro. in *Evangelical Magazine* (1823)

Milne, William Charles (1815–1863). *See under* Milne, William (1785–1822).

Milner, Alfred, Viscount Milner (1854–1925), public servant and politician, was born on 23 March 1854 at Giessen, Hesse, the only son of Mary Ierne (*née* Ready) and Charles Milner MD, who descended from a Manchester merchant family with interests in the Rhineland trade. Charles Milner's father, James Richardson Milner, married Sophia von Rappard in Düsseldorf, became a German subject, and stayed in the Rhineland, where Charles was born about the time the business collapsed in 1830. Charles studied medicine at Bonn and was engaged as tutor at the age of twenty-three to the two children of Mary Ierne Cromie, a widow aged forty-two living in Bonn, and married her in Cologne on 9 December 1853, some four months before Alfred's birth. Mary Ierne, born in 1811, came from a military family: her father, Major-General John Ready, was sometime lieutenant-governor of Prince Edward Island and the Isle of Man. Her first husband, Captain St George Cromie, was from co. Mayo of Anglo-Irish stock and was shot dead, possibly in an agrarian uprising, in 1852.

Alfred was baptized by the British chaplain at Bonn on 21 December 1854, before the family moved to Tübingen, where Charles took his medical degree and Alfred passed his early childhood. In 1860 the family moved to Chelsea, London, living in modest circumstances, while Alfred attended St Peter's church school, Eaton Square. In 1866 his father found a post back at Tübingen University as a tutor in English literature, and Alfred had three years' sound education in classics at a *Gymnasium*. Mary Milner died in 1869, when Alfred was fifteen, and he returned to England, as she had wished, under the charge of his maternal uncle, Colonel Charles Ready. Advised by his cousin, Marianne Malcolm, with whom Milner had a lasting and close friendship, he enrolled as a student at King's College, living with his mother's relatives but keeping in close touch with his father. There Milner showed every sign of scholastic excellence, and was coached for Balliol

Alfred Milner, Viscount Milner (1854–1925), by H. Walter Barnett, *c.*1900

by Evelyn Abbott, assistant master at Clifton College, winning a first classical scholarship in 1872.

Oxford, politics, and the civil service At Oxford, Milner was a serious and talented student who thrived on the doctrine of hard work encouraged in the Balliol of Benjamin Jowett, who took a close interest in him and founded a lifelong friendship. Milner also owed much to his special tutor, Francis de Paravaccini, and to the philosopher T. H. Green. He took a first class in classical moderations (1874) and won a series of scholarships, including the prestigious Hertford, which eased his precarious financial position and gave him the leisure to share the interests and friendship of H. H. Asquith, Leonard Montefiore, Ernest Iwan-Müller, and others who penetrated his reserved and austere personality. He joined the Union Society in 1873 and spoke occasionally on imperial themes as one of a 'liberal' minority, though he made his mark not as a debater but as union treasurer and president in 1875. Milner rounded off a distinguished undergraduate career the following year with a first-class degree in *literae humaniores* and election to a New College open fellowship, which gave him a measure of security and a permanent association with Oxford. It was at this period that he fell under the influence of Arnold Toynbee, tutor in Balliol from 1878, who recognized Milner's potential for leadership and offered in return an ideal of social reform through education lofty enough to meet Milner's ambition for a life of 'public usefulness'.

Milner went down from Oxford in 1879 imbued with notions of public service, but with no very clear intentions. He lived with Marianne in London, read law, was elected a fellow of King's College, and lectured for the London Society for the Extension of University Teaching, the first president of which was the Liberal politician G. J. Goschen. Although called to the bar in 1881 Milner preferred freelance journalism on political and foreign affairs. Undecided on a career he temporized under the patronage of Goschen, for whom he became an occasional research assistant, and he joined the staff of the *Pall Mall Gazette* in 1882 under the editorship of John Morley and the imperial propagandist and social reformer William Thomas Stead. These were formative years, as Milner absorbed a good deal of economic and political theory which called in question mid-century liberalism, and as he continued to lecture on socialist theories and cultivate a circle of Oxford friends centred around Arnold Toynbee. After Toynbee's death in 1883 he joined with S. A. Barnett and others to help found Toynbee Hall in Whitechapel to bring university men into touch with the working poor, a movement which he supported for the rest of his life. In 1884 he became private secretary to Goschen, whose independent views and deep knowledge of public finance advanced Milner's grasp of political economy as much as his ideas on 'race and empire' were influenced by the more chauvinistic enthusiasms of Stead. Close to the mainstream Liberals on domestic issues, Milner was already (like Goschen) at odds with the party over foreign policy, especially Egypt. At this period Milner's view of empire, however, centred on consolidation around the colonies of British settlement led by a Britain 'vigorous, resolute and courageous'. Angered by the failure to save General Gordon in the Sudan and aware of the pressures of international rivalry, Milner was an outspoken 'imperial patriot', rather than an imperial expansionist in Africa or Asia. On domestic issues his views could be described as high-minded socialism with a strong welfare content, but little influenced by continental socialism or Marxism. Milner had read the work of Henry George and stood for class reconciliation, not division, through enlightened leadership, productive efficiency, enlarged taxation, and a mild measure of state intervention. As a patriotic and high-minded improver he stood as a Liberal candidate for Harrow in 1885, campaigning on a programme for free elementary education, reform of local government, and opposition to disestablishment, though he was curiously vague on home rule, and went so far as to defend Gladstone's record in South Africa and Egypt.

Although he failed to win a seat, this foray into active politics enabled Milner to move up the social ladder and into the organizing centre of the Liberal Unionist Association, formed by Goschen in 1886. To help define Unionist policies and rejection of home rule he toured the west of Ireland, gathering information on the need to reform the tenancy system. When Goschen (with some persuasion from Milner) joined Salisbury's cabinet as chancellor of the exchequer in December 1886, he followed his patron to the post of principal private secretary in the Treasury.

This invaluable training in public finance, and Milner's growing efficiency in handling complex economic issues, enabled him to assist in Goschen's conversion of the national debt in 1888 and to resolve the financial consequences of the County Councils Act of 1888. Outside the Treasury his active social and political life flourished, and the esteem in which he was already held led to the offer of a private secretaryship to Lord Lansdowne, as viceroy of India, which he turned down. Privately, he was still in training for 'a *big work*'.

This patience was rewarded by Goschen in 1889, when he secured for Milner a post as director-general of accounts in Egypt, responsible to Elwin Pasha, the financial adviser, and to Sir Evelyn Baring (Lord Cromer) in the government of the Khedive Tawfiq. He learned much from Baring's 'management' of the quasi-protectorate, and as acting financial adviser he participated in the work of the council of ministers. Milner's views about British responsibility were further strengthened by these insights and by his succession to the post of under-secretary of finance in 1890, when he had to deal directly with the Egyptian premier. This experience of control and power without legislative responsibility was one of the most congenial periods of Milner's career as a public servant. Opportunities to tour Upper Egypt, and detailed knowledge of agricultural and irrigation development, put him in a unique position to justify the British occupation as in the interests of the Egyptian people and international peace. The essence of his views and a detailed exposition of the government and economy were published on his return in 1892 as *England in Egypt*. His Egyptian experience also fed his tendency to rationalize the application of British power abroad as an imperial duty— in this case to save the Egyptians from the destructive forces of 'Arabist' nationalism by reconstruction of 'the whole administrative machine' and by elimination of poverty and 'corruption' (*England in Egypt*, 15–17).

Recalled to take over the post of chairman of the Board of Inland Revenue under the chancellorship of Sir William Harcourt in 1894, Milner continued to be consulted on Egyptian affairs, to the extent of correcting and moderating the style of Cromer's *Modern Egypt* in 1896. Like Harcourt, he did not support the reconquest of the Sudan, begun that year, though he advocated British financial support on the grounds that new provinces would produce revenue independent of the hold of international financiers on the country's debt repayments. He was offered (and rejected) the post of permanent under-secretary in the Home Office. But in recognition of his services he was created CB in 1894 and KCB in 1895. In the meantime, while awaiting another imperial post, Milner worked assiduously on death duties, taxation in Ireland (where his error of calculations for the 1893 Home Rule Bill led to considerable embarrassment), and the formulation of the new estate duty of 1894, earning the commendation of both Harcourt and Sir Michael Hicks Beach. In 1895 he first met Cecil Rhodes, Dr Leander Starr Jameson, and Albert Grey, who were important in his later career. It was at this period, too, as he digested the lessons of British

administration abroad in Africa, that Milner also absorbed the neo-Darwinist ideas of Benjamin Kidd, whose writings on 'social evolution' he commended for publication in keeping with his own view of natural selection and competition between nation states.

In 1897 Chamberlain (whom he had first met in Egypt) asked him to become permanent under-secretary in the Colonial Office. He refused and was offered the governorship of Cape Colony and high commissionership of South Africa, which he immediately accepted, to press approval.

South Africa Before he left for South Africa in April 1897 Milner informed himself on British colonial views by talking with Rhodes, the former governor, Henry Brougham Loch, Baron Loch, and with mining-house representatives. Convinced that President Kruger's Transvaal would disintegrate, he did not press at once for the settlement of outstanding issues over Uitlander (foreign residents) rights or mining company grievances but toured the country and Rhodesia instead. In the course of this tour he agreed to a revision of the Rhodesian constitution, with Rhodes giving representation to the settlers under a resident commissioner responsible to the high commissioner with nominal control of the police. In practice the British South Africa Company gained all Rhodes had intended in autonomous administration of land and population. He visited Beira in Mozambique, but not the Transvaal, where he had few direct sources of information. He began the study of Afrikaans, but talked to no Afrikaners.

By 1898 it was clear Kruger's state would not disintegrate. In February the president was overwhelmingly re-elected. In a private letter to Chamberlain, Milner spelt out the alternatives as reform of the Transvaal administration or war, and in a speech at Graaff-Reinet in March 1898 he emphasized his determination to defend British interests at the Cape against the 'disloyalty' of the Afrikaner-Bond Party. In his anxiety about the politics of Cape ministries in a self-governing colony, Milner managed to antagonize both the Bond and the pro-British Progressives with thinly veiled political speeches prior to an election in October 1898 in which the Progressives took the upper house and W. P. Schreiner's South African Party (linked with the Bond) commanded the lower house. Milner, moreover, would countenance no moves for international arbitration of outstanding issues with the Transvaal and, like Chamberlain, maintained the British claim to 'suzerainty' made at the end of 1897 under the London convention (1884). On the two outstanding differences over the Uitlander franchise and a state dynamite monopoly which raised costs for the mining companies no compromise seemed possible.

On leave in November 1898 Milner felt able to press his case for challenging Kruger, even at the risk of war, in the belief the Afrikaners would back down. Although it has been argued that he 'dominated' Chamberlain on this issue, it would be safer to conclude that Milner was still playing a long game and had certainly not committed

Chamberlain or the cabinet to his views. He returned in January 1899, as Pretoria initiated negotiations over Uitlanders' rights and other issues of concern to the mining houses. These collapsed, because Kruger would not be hurried and because Milner's appreciation of the issues was limited by his use of James Percy Fitzpatrick (prominent in H. Eckstein & Co.) as an intermediary. From then on Milner was able to work up the case for firm measures as minor incidents, such as the shooting of a British subject by a Boer policeman, were confounded with the wider issues of municipal taxation and representation in Johannesburg, summed up in the Uitlander petition to the crown on 24 March 1899. Milner expanded on this petition in a cable of 4 May, arguing for equality of treatment for Dutch and British (characterized as 'helots' under Transvaal rule). Though intended for public consumption, the dispatch was withheld from publication for a month by Chamberlain, who urged further discussions. Cape politicians, too, were not eager for a war, and Schreiner offered, without success, to accompany Milner to a conference with Kruger at Bloemfontein on 31 May–5 June 1899, where they met for the first and last time. Intractable and unsubtle, Milner made no progress on the issue of the full franchise for British subjects and the meeting broke up, to Chamberlain's disapproval. In any case, the prospect of loss of power to an immigrant constituency was more than Kruger could swallow, while Milner was too hard-headed to take the time to compromise over other issues. From this date Milner and Chamberlain moved at different speeds, but in the same direction: public opinion was prepared by the publication of selected correspondence; in August Milner secured the appointment to the Cape command of Lieutenant-General F. W. E. F. Forestier-Walker, who agreed with the policy of sending British troops; attempts at further compromises by the Transvaal state attorney, J. C. Smuts, were played down by Milner, with the effect that by September Salisbury and most of the cabinet thought war likely; and as Chamberlain issued a final demand for reform of grievances, Kruger sent a final ultimatum on 9 October which opened the way for Boer military action before the arrival of British reinforcements.

Remarkably, Milner as high commissioner had rested his case for control of the Boer republics on the vague political suzerainty over the affairs of southern Africa thought to be implicit in his office, and not on the military capabilities of the British colonies now at risk. This lack of military planning, and the disasters following the arrival of General Sir Redvers Buller with an army corps in October and November, left Milner immersed in the administration of two colonies under siege, and at odds with Schreiner and his ministers over the organization of volunteers and the application of martial law. The threat of Dutch rebellion at the Cape and measures taken to relieve the plight of thousands of British and foreign refugees kept him fully occupied until Lord Frederick Roberts and Lord Kitchener remodelled the army to deal with the Boer threat and regain the initiative in the Free State and

Natal. His proposals to blockade Delagoa Bay and to suspend the Cape constitution were rejected. The war situation improved with the capture of Pretoria on 5 June 1900, and the resignation of Schreiner's ministry removed a source of advice and criticism which clashed with Milner's more autocratic instincts concerning the trial of rebels. The return of Sir John Sprigg as premier ensured a less volatile ministry and left Milner free to consider the consequences of the military occupation of the two republics, which were annexed on 8 October 1900.

Milner was immediately appointed civil administrator of the Orange River and Transvaal colonies, 'taking my High Commissionership with me', as he noted when he moved to Johannesburg in March 1901. The governorship of the Cape passed to W. F. Hely-Hutchinson. Plans had already been laid for a period of 'paternal despotism', with British immigration and reconstruction to incorporate the two colonies within the imperial structure of South Africa, while keeping Cape disloyalty under control and furthering the economic integration of all the British territories. Little was done while the war dragged on through its lingering phase of guerrilla action, farm burning (which Milner condemned), and concentration camps (which he approved). Installed in Park Town, Johannesburg, Milner began the first stage of civil administration by creating a South African constabulary, by reorganizing Transvaal departments and municipal government, and by facilitating the reopening of the mines.

Significantly, Milner recruited few local officials from the Uitlander or Afrikaner communities, the Cape, or Natal. The nucleus of the dozen or so key officials was formed through Oxford and Colonial Office contacts, and the formation of 'Milner's kindergarten' reflected both his belief in loyalty through official and unofficial patronage and the abilities of an Oxford-trained elite. This group of 'guardians', which included J. F. Perry, Lionel Curtis, Basil Williams, Patrick Duncan, John Buchan, Hugh Wyndham, Geoffrey Robinson, Lionel Hichens, the Hon. Robert Brand, Philip Kerr, and D. Malcolm, bent their energies towards the solution of three major problems: reforming the finances and administration of Johannesburg and the two Boer states; ensuring an adequate labour supply for the mines; and laying the foundations for political unity through common services. In all this they were backed by Milner, who went on leave in May 1901 to receive new honours as a GCB, and who convinced the Liberal Imperialists and the government of the need for lands for immigrants, grants for railway extension, a tax on the profits of the goldmines, and a Transvaal war contribution (which was not, however, enforced).

On his return to South Africa in August 1901 Milner still hankered after suspension of the Cape constitution in order to build up a 'loyal majority' at the Cape, a proposition rejected by the British cabinet and by local politicians. He also took a harder line than Kitchener in the negotiations which led to peace in the treaty of Vereeniging on 31 May 1902. Thereafter, as governor of the Transvaal and the Orange River Colony, Milner was tireless in establishing a new administration with financial viability, a reformed magistracy, improved agriculture and forestry, and an expanded education system, in which English was made a medium of instruction. For the first time he talked to the rural Afrikaners. A Johannesburg commission under Lionel Curtis expanded local government into the mining areas, undertaking new responsibilities for roads, water, and housing. An inter-colonial council was set up from May 1903 under Milner's presidency to supervise a central railway system and other common services. A South African native commission was appointed to co-ordinate policies throughout the colonies. A loan of £38 million provided the financial basis for resettlement. Negotiations were begun for a customs conference with the Cape and Natal. On Chamberlain's visit in 1902 the final details of the funding of reconstruction were settled, though Milner did not get his way on the question of a permanent and enlarged garrison. He agreed with Chamberlain to invite leading Afrikaners to sit on the Transvaal legislative council (which they refused to do). By March 1903 repatriation of displaced Afrikaners and immigrant workers was completed. But the planned immigration scheme for settlements on lands confiscated by government or purchased by De Beers, Wernher, Beit, and Rhodes to the sum of £250,000 failed to attract empire settlers. More usefully, Milner persuaded the new colonial secretary, Alfred Lyttelton, to agree to the importation of cheaper sources of labour for the mines through the Rand Native Labour Association under an ordinance of 10 February 1904 that allowed the recruitment of Chinese. As gold output increased and a measure of stability returned, Milner turned his attention to the census of the two colonies and a calculation of the chances for a shift in power to the English-speaking section of an electorate. The first census of May 1904 revealed his failure to outnumber the Afrikaners. Milner conceded defeat by recommending that elections should replace nomination to the Transvaal legislative council, and he left South Africa in April 1905 pessimistic over the outcome of any representative system, even if it excluded Africans and landless Boers. He returned to a decline in his popularity in Britain as the storm over Chinese 'slavery' broke, culminating in a Commons censure motion on Milner, on 21 May 1906, for having sanctioned flogging. In fact he had made the mistake of delegating too much power to compound managers to inflict corporal punishment for minor offences, though he took full responsibility for the abuse. It was the last and least of a series of disasters that marked the most turbulent pro-consulship in the history of South Africa.

Philanthropy, politics, war This outcome to his exhausting years abroad discouraged Milner from an immediate return to public office. He refused the viceroyalty of India, kept a low political profile, and returned to his work in City chairmanships, the Rhodes Trust, and the council of Toynbee Hall. Unreconciled by the trend of events in South Africa, he moved out of London to a farm at Sturry Court near Canterbury in 1907, leaving much of the business of promoting the empire to the 'kindergarten', though he approved of the South African constitution of 1909.

The Rhodes Trust provided a continuity which imperial administration and politics did not. Nominated in Rhodes's last will of 1899 as a trustee, Milner could not participate openly while high commissioner, although both the educational and the political aims of the 'founder' were congenial to him. From 1903 Milner was a key residuary legatee with Sir Lewis Michell and Sir George Parkin in making arrangements with Oxford University for reception of Rhodes scholars. He protected the funding of the scholarships by securing them to income from De Beers shares, though he made less secure investments for the trust in government and American stocks. Milner helped elect the first Beit professor (H. E. Egerton) in 1905; and he utilized from within the trust a 'shares fund' from the Rhodes–Beit estates for various political purposes in South Africa and elsewhere consistent with the founder's beliefs, including financial assistance to the *Round Table*, founded by Lionel Curtis, and to the 'movement' which brought it into being. He successfully opposed handing over the management of the trust to Oxford dons and brought in new trustees, agreeing to restructure the legacy as a charitable trust to avoid death duties. In 1916 he reluctantly approved the redistribution of the German scholarships by a parliamentary act. Milner's last visit to South Africa, in 1924, when he still had the affairs of the trust in mind, actively encouraged the shift away from investments in loss-making fruit farms and political propaganda to educational purposes.

Milner also visited Egypt again in 1909 as chairman of the Bank of Egypt, and before and after the First World War he was closely concerned with the affairs of the Rio Tinto Company and its Spanish copper mines. In domestic political issues he argued against Lloyd George's 1909 budget for its supertax and duties on land values, and he backed army reform, national service, and tariff reform. In these years he served on the Port of London Authority and toured Canada, advocating imperial co-operation (rather than imperial union). Often appearing in the House of Lords, he seldom spoke. Behind the scenes Milner still worked through small coteries, and he was master of the Anglo-Colonial masonic lodge.

Events in Ireland drew him back into politics, as the war approached. He was influential with the Unionists through his report on land and owner-occupancy in Ireland. The Government of Ireland Bill of 1912 found him in strenuous opposition to home rule, in alliance with Edward Carson, and organizing a British covenant in parallel with Ulster's in order to force a general election. Milner may have been prepared to go quite far in supporting open rebellion (and was warned of the dangers of treason by A. V. Dicey). In public he encouraged the suspension of army supply in the Lords, and in private he continued to conspire with Carson to encourage resignation of officers in the event of an army revolt. Few Conservatives or Unionists backed such extreme measures, and when the bill was dropped in July 1914 Milner's political isolation left him without real influence or position as the nation faced a greater crisis.

From the sidelines Milner pressed for conscription and

criticized the government's Balkan policy and general mismanagement of the war. In 1915 he was appointed by Lord Selborne, as president of the Board of Agriculture and Fisheries, to chair a food supply committee, which recommended minimum price guarantees to farmers ('reasonable socialism') and increased agricultural wages, a scheme not adopted until 1917.

Lacking a firm political base for opposition to Asquith's coalition of May 1915, Milner campaigned through the press and coteries of 'Milnerites' and informants for central control of planning and production and for national service by conscription. He attracted disaffected acolytes such as Leo Amery and F. S. Oliver, some press barons (Dawson of *The Times*, J. L. Garvin and Waldorf Astor of *The Observer*, and, less reliably, Lord Northcliffe), as well as a useful military informant, Sir Henry Wilson, united only by loyalty or by common hatred of Asquith. As chairman of the National Service League he won over Curzon, Churchill, and Lloyd George within the cabinet, though he could not convince Kitchener at the War Office. In any case, the issue of manpower direction was, for Milner, larger than military conscription in wartime and arose from a deep-seated belief in compulsory education and employment in peacetime to improve the efficiency of the state. In other ways Milner contributed to the war effort as chairman of the British section of the Empire Producers' Association and as supervisor of coal committees. In the Lords he sponsored a municipal savings bank bill and steered it through.

Behind the scenes Milner moved closer to Lloyd George on the conscription issue and much closer to Carson when he resigned from the coalition over the Gallipoli campaign. At the death of Kitchener intrigue intensified to have Milner brought into the War Office. When Asquith resigned, Lloyd George brought Milner into his war council in December 1916 as minister without portfolio. The reasons were political—to appease sections of the Conservatives—and, at the same time, the move was a recognition of Milner's undeniable administrative gifts; his views on the overriding need for central control of wartime planning brought him to the attention of a national leader who quickly won Milner's loyalty at the heart of a dictatorial system of government.

From this vantage point Milner operated as co-ordinator of committees and departments within the 'committee of public safety' that ran Britain outside the cabinet. He successfully associated dominion and Indian representatives with the work of the imperial war cabinets and the imperial war conferences. He led the British delegation of the allied mission to Russia in 1917, which failed to solve the problems of supply on the eve of the Bolshevik Revolution (which he did not foresee). By mastering issues and reconciling ministerial actions with the facts, Milner made his greatest contribution to his country. His timely reconciliation with Smuts, moreover, was fruitful in decision making at the highest levels. Thus, he formed Lloyd George's war policy committee, including himself, Curzon, and Smuts, and with Smuts he framed the report on the necessity for an Air Ministry. He drafted the cabinet minute in favour of a Jewish national home, known as the Balfour Declaration. At the same time in 1917 he defined the functions of the department of national service and rationalized the allocation of manpower and essential supplies. Following his earlier recommendations, Milner assured grain production by conserving agricultural labour and by guaranteeing a minimum price for wheat and oats and a minimum agricultural wage in the Corn Production Bill of 1917. Together with Lloyd George he insisted on the implementation of a convoy system. Sent to Paris by Lloyd George to help set up the supreme war council created at Rapallo in November 1917, Milner found himself in the unaccustomed role of diplomat and broker between governments and generals. He chaired the Russian information committee and agreed to allied intervention in the internal conflict and kept closely in touch with Bruce Lockhart on his mission to the Bolsheviks. In the battle to create an allied reserve army under the war council he worked for the replacement of Field Marshal Sir William Robertson by General Sir Henry Wilson as chief of the Imperial General Staff, and in Paris during the crisis of the German offensive in March 1917 he was instrumental in the Anglo-French appointment of Marshal Foch to the strategic direction of the war as co-ordinator of allied armies in the west. For this he replaced Lord Derby as secretary of state for war on 20 April 1918, which took him out of the war cabinet.

Milner immediately found himself at the centre of a wrangle with Lloyd George over estimates of the relative strengths of German and allied forces. Although Milner was not deflected from rigorous prosecution of the war into 'peace-mongering' by the German–Russian treaty of March 1918, by the end of the year, following German reverses and peace feelers to Woodrow Wilson, he was in favour of a negotiated armistice to end German militarism and forestall chaos in central Europe and the possible spread of Bolshevism. Criticized for not taking a harder line on unconditional surrender, Milner's relations with Lloyd George deteriorated. Tired and disheartened, he took no part in the 1918 elections. He was replaced by Winston Churchill and went to head the Colonial Office in December 1918.

As colonial secretary Milner warmly supported the representation of the dominions at the peace conference. But, unlike a number of them, he argued for disarmament without heavy reparations, and he did not agree with the practicality of President Wilson's 'fourteen points'. He favoured the retention of occupied German colonies and submitted a memorandum to the peace conference defining the terms of continued allied administration under a mandates commission, but found it impossible to prescribe for 'A class' mandates in the Middle East. As chairman of the mandates commission he arranged boundary adjustments in Togo and the Cameroons and firmly limited Belgian claims in German East Africa to Ruanda-Urundi. To safeguard the Nile headwaters Milner supported Italian claims to Libya and Somaliland. With other representatives he settled the labour conditions to be complied with for 'C class' mandates, though he opposed commercial equality or an 'open-door' clause, in line with the dominions' views. With less success he supervised the partition of Syria and supported Zionist proposals for Palestine.

At the Colonial Office, Milner had little time to make much of a mark, though his views on empire moved towards acceptance of the concept of 'trusteeship' and the economic development of the tropical dependencies as a major responsibility. With Amery as his under-secretary he set up the Colonial Economic and Development Council and helped to found the London School of Tropical Medicine. To consolidate Britain with the dominions he still argued in vain for a 'council of empire', but successfully encouraged overseas migration schemes to strengthen imperial ties. He was surprisingly effective in negotiations with Egyptian nationalists, following a mission to Egypt in 1919 and 1920, and reported in favour of a treaty granting independence with safeguards for British control of foreign affairs and a military base. Although rejected by the government, the report was published and became the basis of the Anglo-Egyptian treaty of alliance in 1936.

After preparing for the Imperial Conference of 1921 Milner retired in early February and was created a KG. He maintained his links with business and especially the mining business of the Rio Tinto Company. On 26 February 1921 he married Violet, Lady Edward Cecil (1872–1958) [see Milner, Violet Georgina, Viscountess Milner]. Although still consulted on imperial matters, he refused important public offices and began a work on economics which became a book of essays, *Questions of the Hour*, containing a summary of his views on state intervention in agriculture and industry and the need for wages councils to end industrial disputes. He still hoped for a unified imperial economic policy and became chairman of Baldwin's protectionist tariff advisory committee. Above all, in retirement, he never missed a New College or Rhodes Trust occasion. On his final visit to South Africa he was fêted by pro-British politicians and was well received by Smuts; he supported the 1920 Memorial Settlers' Association and the future Rhodes University College. On his return he agreed to stand for the chancellorship of Oxford University; he was nominated and elected, as from 25 May, during a final illness (encephalitis lethargica), which brought about his death on 13 May 1925 at Sturry Court.

Milner was honoured with a service in Canterbury Cathedral and a private service in the parish of Salehurst, near Robertsbridge, Sussex, where he was buried; memorial services were held in New College and in Cape Town Cathedral. He left an estate of £46,000. There are memorials in the chapel of St Martin of Tours in Chichester Cathedral, and in Westminster Abbey. Milner scholarships were founded for King's School, Canterbury, and Sturry Court (Milner Court) was gifted to the school. Milner had wanted his papers selectively published, and Lady Milner engaged Cecil Headlam to edit two volumes. His official papers were left to New College in 1931 with other gifts and have become available in the Bodleian Library.

Reputation Milner remains a controversial figure, whose reputation has suffered from the South African phase of his career as much as his masterly performance in Lloyd George's wartime administration has been confirmed by later studies. Seen as the archetype of a rigorous late nineteenth-century imperialism, Milner the person has been confounded with 'Milnerism'—already a term of Liberal abuse by 1899. To Lord Ripon it meant a conspiracy of Oxford men influencing Chamberlain's South African policy, while to the South African it has always meant 'anglicization' with overtones of imperial autocracy. Occasionally, in the hands of enemies, the reputation for single-mindedness and efficiency was attributed to 'Germanic' origins.

The charge of a 'Teutonic' sympathy need not be seriously entertained. Milner had an unusual education abroad and at home in the classics which made him one of Plato's 'guardians', more comfortable within a small group of high-minded public servants devoted to a cause than exposed to the debates and compromises of political office. In an age of expanding democracy, Milner remained profoundly distrustful of the enfranchised.

In politics Milner moved from Liberal Imperialist to Liberal Unionist, very much under the influence of Goschen. His 'socialism' was that of the municipal reformer and educationist, though he did, under the stress of wartime conditions, advocate greater state intervention in agriculture and industry. Milner's sense of hierarchy and order, however, sat uneasily with any egalitarian principle. Of more importance than his early ideas about socialism was his experience of public finance in the Treasury, in Egypt, and in the Inland Revenue, which gave him (as Oxford did not) an appreciation of the management of resources in an economy. This experience, together with his lifelong belief in the value of imperial consolidation and unification, guided much of his policy in South Africa, where the failure of federation, the difficulty of changing the Transvaal from a pastoral to an industrial state, and the waywardness of Cape politicians presented to Milner a scene of disorder and made the region 'the weakest link in the Imperial chain'.

Milner's imperialism, therefore, has been central to the historiography of the Second South African War—or 'Milner's war', as it has been termed. In so far as he was an imperial consolidationist and a race patriot there is a measure of truth in this assertion, though it needs to be remembered that Milner had not made up his own mind on the inevitability of conflict until about May 1899. For an important length of time Milner was isolated. This isolation and lack of understanding for the situation in Johannesburg and his failure to analyse the volatile and shifting community of Uitlanders, whose demands became his political excuse for rapid reform, left him a prey to a facile 'racialist' interpretation of the issues between Boer and Briton in the Transvaal. For the failure to appreciate the strength of Afrikaner resistance and the military weakness of the British position, Milner must bear a large responsibility.

Until he was called into Lloyd George's war council,

Milner was an unpopular figure, whose outward austerity belied much of the personality that attracted admiration and loyalty among younger followers. For most of his life Milner's public face hid a man capable of great warmth and charm. The prodigality of his personal correspondence, his generosity towards friends and colleagues, and his endless and tactful provision for relatives and friends demonstrate an empathy noticeably absent in his relationship with Egyptians and Afrikaners. Although postponing marriage for much of his life Milner was attractive to women, and took a mistress in 1891 with whom he remained on good terms and to whom he left an annuity. His religious views remain obscure. Termed (doubtfully) an 'atheist' by Beatrice Webb, he was one of the founders of the Church Reform League for a decrease in dogma. But Milner's real enthusiasm was reserved for the idea of empire.

Milner's view of empire owed as much to the visions of Parkin and Rhodes as it did to the disillusionment of events at the Cape. The early ambition to foster 'a group of self-governing nations firmly united against the world' was toned down as Milner gained a better knowledge of dominion politicians. He never abandoned the idea that the British empire was a world power, or that imperialism was 'the highest development of patriotism'; but he was less sanguine that this entity could be given a constitutional form entailing representation at the centre, even after the experience of imperial co-operation in wartime.

That period saw Milner at the height of his powers—a resourceful organizer, a conciliator wiser in the need to placate and cajole, more understanding of the strengths and weaknesses of military men and politicians, and with a sound strategic sense of the need for an eastern as well as a western front. His opinions on peacemaking in Europe have also stood the test of time better than his earlier opinions on the need for war in South Africa, while the maturity of his liberal view of Egypt in the 1920s contrasts with his imperial view of Egypt in the 1890s. In many ways he outgrew 'Milnerism' towards the end of his career and reformed his imperial statecraft, just as he reformed the affairs of the Rhodes Trust away from political conspiracy and towards the investment in the higher education that shaped his own upbringing.   COLIN NEWBURY

Sources E. Crankshaw, *The forsaken idea: a study of Viscount Milner* (1952) · L. Curtis, *With Milner in South Africa* (1951) · A. M. Gallin, *Proconsul in politics: a study of Lord Milner in opposition and in power* (1964) · *The Milner papers*, ed. C. Headlam, 2 vols. (1931–3) · G. H. L. Le May, *British supremacy in South Africa, 1899–1907* (1965) · S. Marks and S. Trapido, 'Lord Milner and the South African state', *History Workshop Journal*, 8 (1979), 50–80 · A. Milner, *England in Egypt*, 9th edn (1902) · A. Milner, *Constructive imperialism* (1908) · W. Nimocks, *Milner's young men: the kindergarten in Edwardian imperial affairs* (1968) · T. H. O'Brien, *Viscount Milner of St James's and Cape Town, 1854–1925* (1979) · A. N. Porter, *The origins of the South African war: Joseph Chamberlain and the diplomacy of imperialism, 1895–99* (1980) · E. Stokes, 'Milnerism', *HJ*, 5 (1962), 47–60 · *DNB* · GEC, *Peerage*
Archives Bodl. Oxf., corresp. and papers · CKS · Duke U., Perkins L., letters · PRO, papers relating to Egypt; corresp. and papers, FO 848, 30/30 | Bishopsgate Institute, London, letters to George Howell · BL, corresp. with Emrys Evans, Add. MS 60329 · BL, letters to F. E. Garrett, Add. MS 45929 · BL, letters to J. A. Spender, Add. MS 46393 · BLPES, letters to Violet Markham · Bodl. Oxf., letters to Margot Asquith; letters to Herbert Asquith · Bodl. Oxf., corresp. with Sir Henry Burdett · Bodl. Oxf., corresp. with L. G. Curtis · Bodl. Oxf., corresp. with Geoffrey Dawson · Bodl. Oxf., corresp. with Sir William Harcourt and Sir Lewis Harcourt · Bodl. Oxf., letters to Violet Milner and corresp. · Bodl. Oxf., corresp. with Lord Selborne · Bodl. RH, corresp. with Sir Godfrey Lagden · Bodl. RH, corresp. with Lord Lugard · Bodl. RH, corresp. with W. B. Worsfield · Bodl. RH, corresp. with Sir Francis Wylie · CAC Cam., corresp. with Alfred Lyttelton · CAC Cam., letters to W. T. Stead · Cumbria AS, Carlisle, letters to Lord Howard of Penrith · Derbys. RO, corresp. with P. L. and Mrs P. L. Gell · Glos. RO, corresp. with Sir Michael Hicks Beach · Herts. ALS, letters to Lady Desborough · HLRO, corresp. with Lloyd George · HLRO, corresp. with Andrew Bonar Law · HLRO, corresp. with J. S. L. Strachey · IWM, corresp. with H. A. Gwynne · IWM, corresp. with Sir Henry Wilson · LMA, corresp. relating to Toynbee Hall · NA Scot., corresp. with G. W. Balfour · NAM, letters to Earl Roberts · NAM, letters to Spencer Wilkinson · National Archives of South Africa, Pretoria, Transvaal archives depot · National Archives of Zimbabwe, Harare, corresp. with Francis Chaplin · NL Aus., corresp. with Alfred Deakin · NL Aus., corresp. with Lord Novar · NL Scot., letters to John Buchan; letters to Susan Buchan · NL Scot., corresp. with Lord Haldane · NL Scot., letters to F. S. Oliver · NL Scot., corresp. mainly with Lord Rosebery · PRO, Colonial Office MSS, CO 291, 417 · PRO, corresp. with Lord Midleton, 30/67 · PRO NIre., corresp. with Asquith, Curtis, Dawson, Harcourt, Lugard, Selborne, W. B. Worsfield, A. J. Balfour, E. Evans, F. E. Garnett, Bonar Law, Lloyd George · PRO NIre., corresp. with Edward Carson · Rhodes University, Grahamstown, South Africa, Cory Library for Historical Research, letters to Sir John Sprigg · U. Birm. L., corresp. with Joseph Chamberlain · U. Durham L., corresp. with Sir Reginald Wingate · U. Lond., Institute of Commonwealth Studies, corresp. with Richard Jebb · University of Bristol Library, letters to Alfred Austin · University of Cape Town Library, corresp. with W. P. Schreiner · University of Sheffield, letters to W. A. S. Hewins
Likenesses H. W. Barnett, photograph, *c.*1900, NPG [*see illus.*] · Elliott & Fry, photograph, 1901, NPG · H. de T. Glazebrook, oils, 1902, NPG · M. Balfour, oils, 1905, New College, Oxford · J. S. Sargent, pencil drawing, 1909, Municipal Gallery of Modern Art, Johannesburg, South Africa · M. Beerbohm, caricature, drawing, 1913, New College, Oxford · H. Olivier, oils, 1919, Gov. Art Coll. · J. Guthrie, oils, *c.*1919–1921, Scot. NPG · W. Orpen, oils, 1923, South African National Gallery, Cape Town, South Africa · J. Guthrie, group portrait, oils, 1924–30 (*Statesmen of World War I*), NPG · J. Guthrie, oils, Bodl. RH · Lady Kennet, marble bust (posthumous), Bodl. RH · London Stereoscopic Co., photograph, NPG · T. Roussel?, portrait, Johannesburg, South Africa · J. Russell & Sons, photograph, NPG · F. Sicard, bronze bust, Doullens, France · F. Sicard, bust, Examination Schools, Oxford · Spy [L. Ward], chromolithograph caricature, NPG; repro. in *VF* (15 April 1897) · H. Young, bust, Bodl. RH · oils, Balliol Oxf. · plaque, Westminster Abbey; replica, Toynbee Hall, Whitechapel, London
Wealth at death £45,868 12s. 4d.: probate, 10 July 1925, CGPLA Eng. & Wales

Milner, Edward (1819–1884), gardener, was born on 20 January 1819 in Darley, Derbyshire, the eldest of the two sons and six children of Henry Milner, sawyer and later gardener, and his wife, Mary Scales. By 1826 Henry Milner was in the employ of William Cavendish, sixth duke of Devonshire, at Chatsworth, where he served in a variety of posts, including gardener and porter. Edward Milner was educated at Bakewell grammar school and then apprenticed to the duke's head gardener, Joseph Paxton. In 1841 he went to Paris, where he studied at the Jardin des Plantes, before returning to Britain to become Paxton's assistant. Paxton made him foreman of works at Prince's

Park, Liverpool, in 1844, and after completion he remained as superintendent. While there he assisted Paxton in works at Osmaston Manor, Derbyshire (1846–9). On 10 July 1844 he married Elizabeth Mary Kelly of Liverpool. They had five sons and six daughters.

In 1852 Paxton began work on re-erecting the Crystal Palace at Penge Park, Sydenham, and once again he hired Milner as superintendent of works. Milner moved to Oak Lodge, Norwood, and later to Hillside, Dulwich Wood Park. These works continued until 1856, when he again worked with Paxton in creating People's Park, Halifax, for Francis Crossley, carpet manufacturer and philanthropist.

From the mid-1850s Milner worked as an independent landscape gardener. Among his commissions were: Bryn-y-Neuadd, Llanfairfechan; Hartsholme Hall, Lincolnshire, for Joseph Shuttleworth; Stancliffe Hall, Derbyshire, for Joseph Whitworth; the initial garden at Bodnant, Tal-y-Cafn, for H. D. Pochin; Rangemore Hall, Staffordshire, for M. T. Bass; Iwerne Minster, Dorset, for G. G. Glyn, second Baron Wolverton; Highbury, Birmingham, for Joseph Chamberlain; and Locksbrook cemetery, Bath. In 1862 he received a commission from the town of Preston to design a series of parks, to be laid out as a scheme for relieving unemployment caused by the cotton famine; Moor Park, Miller Park, and Avenham Park were eventually opened in 1867. He landscaped the Lincoln arboretum (opened 1872), and the grounds of the Buxton Pavilion (1871), as well as Stoney Royd cemetery, Halifax. Among his works abroad were Schloss Anholt in Westphalia for Prince Salm-Salm, and Knutenborg Park, Denmark, for Count E. C. Knuth.

In 1881 the Crystal Palace Company set up the Crystal Palace School of Gardening, and Milner became its principal. He now took his son Henry Ernest *Milner (1845–1906), for several years his principal assistant, into partnership. Milner never published a treatise on landscaping, but Henry Ernest's book *The Art and Practice of Landscape Gardening* (1890) was based to a great extent on his practice. Milner died on 26 March 1884 at home at Hillside, Fountain Road, Dulwich Wood Park.

BRENT ELLIOTT, rev.

Sources *Gardeners' Chronicle*, new ser., 21 (1884), 459 · *The Garden* (12 April 1884) · H. E. Milner, *The art and practice of landscape gardening* (1890) · A. Hodges, 'A Victorian gardener: Edward Milner (1819–1884)', *Garden History*, 5/3 (1977), 67–77 · private information (1993) [Mrs Alison Hodges] · m. cert. · d. cert.
Wealth at death £8191 3s. 7d.: probate, 1884, CGPLA Eng. & Wales

Milner, Henry Ernest (1845–1906), landscape gardener, was born on 18 April 1845 in Liverpool, the eldest of five sons and eleven children of Edward *Milner (1819–1884), landscape gardener, and his wife, Elizabeth Mary Kelly. He was educated by a private tutor in France and Germany, and in 1862–4 worked in the London office of the builder Sir Samuel Morton Peto, who then sent him to Russia as an assistant engineer on railway works. In 1868 he was appointed a resident engineer on the Windsor and Annapolis Railway in Nova Scotia. There he met Mary, daughter of Senator Robert Barry Dickey of Amherst, whom he married in 1869. They had a son and a daughter.

On his return to England, Milner joined his father's practice as a landscape gardener, and in 1878 was made a member of the Institution of Civil Engineers. Among his commissions after his father's death were Victoria Park, Glossop (1887–8), Yeaton Peverey, Shropshire (1890), and Keszthely, Hungary (1885), for Count Festetics.

In 1890 Milner published *The Art and Practice of Landscape Gardening*, with most of the examples drawn from his father's work. It was well received in the horticultural press but drew fire from the advocates of formal gardening, especially Reginald Blomfield in his *The Formal Garden in England* (1892). In the wake of his book Milner received several of his most important commissions: the grounds of Wembley Park, for the tower proposed by Sir Edward Watkin in 1891; the enlargement of Princes Street Gardens, Edinburgh (1891); Gatton Park, Surrey, for Jeremiah Colman; Friar Park, Oxfordshire, for Sir Frank Crisp; Gisselfeld, Denmark (1896–8); and various works on the Swedish royal gardens, for which he was invested with the award of the North Star in 1899. In 1892 he began an involvement with Earls Court, by laying out the grounds for the international horticultural exhibition, but the industrial exhibition of 1894, of which he was a director, was a financial failure, and Milner made himself responsible for some of the debts. In 1897 he was one of the original recipients of the Victoria medal of honour in horticulture, presented by the Royal Horticultural Society.

Milner was known for his charm and the ease with which he made friends. He died on 10 March 1906 at his home at 119 Gipsy Hill, Norwood, and was buried in Darley; his wife survived him. His son, Barry Ernest Milner, entered his firm, but Edward White, who married his daughter, Winifred, became the dominant force in Milner, White & Partners.

BRENT ELLIOTT, rev.

Sources *Figaro* (22 June 1892) · *Gardeners' Chronicle*, 3rd ser., 39 (17 March 1906) · I. W. Leigh, 'Milner White and Partners', *Landscape Design*, 156 (Aug 1985), 9–13 · press cuttings book, Royal Horticultural Society, London · private information (1993) · CGPLA Eng. & Wales (1906)
Wealth at death £3693 2s.: probate, 30 March 1906, CGPLA Eng. & Wales

Milner, Isaac (1750–1820), natural philosopher and dean of Carlisle, was born on 11 January 1750 in Mabgate, Leeds, the third son of a pious mother (c.1715–1796) and an unlucky businessman (c.1715–1760) who had suffered greatly after the Jacobite rising of 1745. He began his education at a grammar school in Leeds in 1756 and enjoyed his studies, but these were terminated in 1760 with the death of his father. He was apprenticed as a weaver and toiled at the loom for a number of years, reading the classics when time permitted, until his elder brother Joseph *Milner provided him with the opportunity to escape his 'mechanick' life. Joseph was offered the mastership at Hull's grammar school and invited Isaac to become the institution's usher. Here the latter became 'a tolerably good classic, and acquainted with the first six books of Euclid' (Milner, 523).

Cambridge work from 1770 Through the patronage of his brother, Milner was subsequently freed from his duties in

Hull and entered Queens' College, Cambridge, as a sizar in 1770. Although he knew fortune had smiled upon him, he was not always happy as an undergraduate: he detested the menial duties that were foisted upon him as a sizar, and he was teased for his broad northern accent. In addition, he received abuse for his refusal to sign the Feathers tavern petition of 1772. Nevertheless, he was a particularly hard reader and excelled on the university's Senate House examination; he became the year's senior wrangler with the further distinctions of being designated *incomparabilis* and taking the Smith's first prize. As his biographer and niece recalled, it was at this moment that he was 'tempted to commit his first act of extravagance. In the pride of his heart, he ordered from a jeweller a rather splendid seal, bearing a finely-executed head of Sir Isaac Newton' (Milner, 12).

With the combination of his credentials, sagacity, and imperious demeanour, Milner was able to advance his career rapidly. Shortly after he took his bachelor's degree in 1774 he was ordained as deacon; in 1776 Queens' offered him a fellowship; in the following year he became a priest and college tutor; and in 1778 he was presented with the rectory of St Botolph. During these years his career as a natural philosopher began to take off. In 1776 Nevil Maskelyne hired him as a computer for the board of longitude, and two of his mathematical papers were presented to the Royal Society, of which he was elected fellow in 1780. In these papers Milner displayed three things—proficiency in mathematics, suspicion of French philosophy, and adherence to English Newtonian mechanics.

It was precisely these philosophical sentiments that Milner emphasized throughout his life, and in doing so he helped to define the role of the University of Cambridge in late Georgian times. In the opinion of Milner and other Cantabrigians, such as Samuel Vince, George Atwood, Edward Waring, and James Wood, Newton's rational mechanics, fluxions, and experimental philosophy were an excellent antidote against materialism and atheism. In Milner's mind the Anglican and Newtonian philosophy of Cambridge protected the interests of the ancient institution, true religion, and the country, since it gave Britons reason to believe in the central doctrines of the church, such as the immateriality of the soul. In particular Milner stressed that the 'established principles of Experimental Philosophy' showed that an incorporeal and free mind was needed to govern inert matter (*Essay on Human Liberty*, 1824, 5–6). Moreover, he contended that a strict regime of mathematics forced undergraduates to think soundly:

> I have often contended, the best answer that we could give to persons who sometimes accuse resident members of the University of Cambridge of employing their time too much in mathematics and natural philosophy was to inform them, that our lectures on these subjects were subservient to the cause of religion; for that we endeavoured, not only to fix in the minds of young students the most important truths, but also to habituate them to reason. (Milner, *Strictures on some of the Publications of the Reverend Herbert Marsh, D.D.*, 1813, 230)

He placed great emphasis on Cambridge's mathematical tripos, expertly examining students through the course of five decades.

Throughout his life Milner devoted much attention to chemistry and was remembered as 'a great dabbler in air-pumps' (Milner, 70). As a chemical philosopher he worked hard to ensure that the discipline remained within the Newtonian framework and that chemical speculation would not infringe upon politico-theology. His interest in chemistry was sparked in the early 1770s by Richard Watson, who was then the incumbent professor of that discipline at Cambridge. From Watson he received tuition, and by the end of the decade he was acting as deputy to Isaac Pennington, Watson's successor. During these years he also received permission to set up a laboratory in the stable yard at Queens'.

In 1782 the Jacksonian professorship of natural philosophy was established and the syndicate selected Milner as the inaugural professor, a position he retained until 1792. Richard Jackson stipulated that the holder of his eponymous professorship should make 'further discoveries' in natural philosophy that would 'tend to set forth the Glory of the Almighty God, and promote the welfare of mankind'. To fulfil these requests Milner presented lectures each year, alternating between mechanics and chemistry. As a lecturer he was remembered as a 'first-rate showman' (Milner, 29) who always held his audience in 'a high state of interest and excitement' (ibid., 31). He considered his lectures in these subjects to be important pedagogical tools that helped teach undergraduates to reason effectively in other modes of life, but he also warned that chemical phenomena should not be exploited to convey simple moral lessons, and he admonished fellow chemists for committing this blunder. Thus he wrote: 'the Subject is intricate & mysterious & … whenever we meddle in it without the utmost care and circumspection, we are likely to involve ourselves in Error & Absurdity' (*Essay*, 14). He had a strong distaste for comprehensive theories, and remained noncommittal to either the 'phlogistonists' or 'anti-phlogistonists'.

Besides lecturing, Milner also developed an important process to fabricate nitrous acid, a key ingredient in the production of gunpowder. His paper describing this process was published in the Royal Society's *Philosophical Transactions* in 1789 alongside an article of Joseph Priestley's, and the two corresponded on the subject. Ironically, however, it was the Jacobins who first availed themselves of his ingenuity on a grand scale. In later years Milner transferred his elaborate collection of chemical apparatus into the president's lodge at Queens' and performed experiments with E. D. Clarke, William Whewell, and the Wollaston brothers; he also collaborated with Humphrey Davy and Joseph Banks in the quest to cure gout.

Evangelical commitments Over the span of his forty-five-year career, Milner's scientific sentiments came to reflect his religious sentiments strongly. Although he never parted from the Anglican fold, he came to embrace the central evangelical doctrines of the late eighteenth century. Indeed, near the end of his life he could proclaim: 'I may safely defy anyone to produce an instance where I have failed to stand forward with every grain of weight with which I could load the scale of evangelical religion'

(Milner, 469). In particular, Milner placed great emphasis upon the personal search for redemption and justification through faith alone, while de-emphasizing the church's Thirty-Nine Articles and Paleyite natural theology; none the less, he remained great friends with many high-churchmen. This amalgam of beliefs and actions led Gilbert Wakefield to state

> I ever esteemed this gentleman to be endowed with one of the most vigorous and penetrating minds I know, but his theological conceptions were always, I confess, one of the inscrutabilities of mystery; a *heterogeneous* composition of *deistical* levity and *methodistical* superstition: disparaging the ceremonies of religion, and performing them with slovenly precipitation.   (Wakefield, 130)

Despite Wakefield's comments, Milner, with Charles Simeon, was largely responsible for the evangelical revival at Cambridge. Indeed, through the years of his tenure at Queens' he dramatically changed the entire complexion of the college. He was also responsible for the conversion of William Wilberforce, which occurred during their long continental tour of 1784–5. While the parliamentary act of 1807 to abolish slavery owed much to their partnership, Milner's co-authorship of the seven-volume *Ecclesiastical History of the Church of Christ* (1818) with his brother Joseph also earned him nationwide renown.

Although his evangelical sentiments probably prevented Milner from being presented with a profitable see, he was nevertheless rewarded with several lucrative posts throughout his career. In 1788 no one contested his bid for the presidency of Queens', a post he retained until his death. In 1791, through his connections with Bishop Pretyman-Tomline and William Pitt, he was able to secure the deanship of Carlisle. In 1793 and again in 1810 he was appointed vice-chancellor of the university, and in 1798 he finally managed to secure for himself the Lucasian professorship of mathematics, a chair he had coveted for decades. As holder of that post he sat on the committee that oversaw Telford's project to span the Thames with an iron bridge. From 1787 he also served on the board of longitude and was involved in settling the fierce disputes concerning accurate chronometers.

Disputes and controversies, 1793 and 1813 Not everyone agreed with Milner's convictions, policies, and practices, and he was frequently embroiled in disputes. Of these controversies the trial of William Frend and the furore surrounding the formation of the Cambridge branch of the British and Foreign Bible Society are the best remembered. Milner put an end to the university career of Frend, a fellow of Jesus College and disciple of Theophilus Lindsey and Joseph Priestley. In the late 1780s and early 1790s Frend had vexed the conservative element of Cambridge with his radical pamphlets, which urged wholesale religious, legal, and philosophical changes in Britain. In a series of increasingly inflammatory publications, he mocked the established theology and its exponents in Cambridge. Frend's derision of state and university policy culminated with his publication of *Peace and Union* (1793), in which he condemned the dualistic ontology adhered to by the Church of England and labelled the church a political outfit. After reading this pamphlet, twenty-seven senior members of the university approached Milner at the president's lodge at Queens'. As vice-chancellor, Milner decided to try Frend in the Cambridge Senate House for breaking the statute *De concionibus*. According to Henry Gunning, Milner hoped to make it evident to the government that he detested Jacobinical principles. However, his scheme nearly backfired, for Frend came to the courtroom prepared for battle. He denounced the 'immaterialist' natural philosophy of the university and derided Milner as a 'mechanick' and disadvantaged plebeian. Yet, as Gunning noted, 'it was apparent from the first that the vice-chancellor was determined to convict' (Gunning, 1.272). Milner rusticated the Jesus fellow, claiming that Frend had destroyed many 'unsuspecting minds' (Beverley, 77), and in later life proudly proclaimed that the trial 'was the ruin of the Jacobinal party as a university thing' (BL, MS 35657).

The other great controversy in which Milner was immersed concerned the formation of an auxiliary branch of the British and Foreign Bible Society in Cambridge. Several junior members of the university, mostly of evangelical bent, attempted to establish the society in 1811, considering it their Christian duty to disperse cheap Bibles. Despite the robust misgivings of the high church, the undergraduates enlisted the aid of Charles Simeon, E. D. Clarke, and William Farish in order to set their scheme into motion. Although at first ambivalent towards the fledgeling society, Milner was finally persuaded to enter the fray after a number of eminent and influential aristocrats pledged their allegiance. However, he needed to contend with the vehement denunciations of the society by Herbert Marsh—Lady Margaret professor of divinity and cousin of William Frend—who published a series of vituperative sermons that claimed that such societies would be the ruin of the state. Milner counter-attacked with his *Strictures on some of the Publications of … Marsh* (1813). This curious work marshalled the might of Newton and rational philosophy against his fellow professor. He equated his own arguments for the establishment of the society with the 'sound principles of the Newtonian philosophy' and the reasoning of Marsh with the 'dangerous and fanciful levities of Des Cartes' (*Strictures*, 212). Although he remained intellectually and socially active until his death, his controversy with Herbert Marsh in 1813 was Milner's last great battle. He died on 1 April 1820 and was buried in Queens' College chapel.

Reputation After his death Milner was remembered for his astonishing intellect, his peculiar lifestyle, his tremendous physical bulk and his part in the rise in evangelicalism. Even Henry Gunning, a devoted whig, admitted that 'the University, perhaps, never produced a man of more eminent ability'. Gunning also remembered Milner's social skills: 'the public dinners were very merry, but the private ones were quite uproarious' (Gunning, 1.234–5). Thomas De Quincey, in his preface to the *Confessions*, deemed Milner an 'eloquent and benevolent' opium user.

Others recalled Milner's nude romps through the president's garden at Queens' and his love for feats of legerdemain. James Stephen acknowledged Milner's tremendous acumen but ultimately ridiculed his lifestyle:

> He had looked into innumerable books, had dipped into most subjects, and talked with shrewdness, animation, and intrepidity on them all. Whatever the company or whatever the theme, his sonorous voice predominated over other voices, even as his lofty stature, vast girth, and superincumbent wig, defied all competitors. … The keen sarcasm, that science [was] his forte—omniscience his foible, could never have been aimed at any of the giants of Cambridge than at the former president of Queens'.
> (Stephen, 233)

Augustus De Morgan, son-in-law of William Frend, simply designated Milner a 'rational paradoxer', relating the anecdote of Milner's attempt to create a comfortable chair for his hulking frame by making a plaster copy of his posterior to enable a craftsman to imitate it in wood. However, it was with his working friendships with people such as William Wilberforce, Hannah More, and his brother Joseph that his historical impact was greatest.

KEVIN C. KNOX

Sources M. Milner, *Life of Isaac Milner* (1842) • J. Stephen, *Ecclesiastical studies* (1849) • H. Gunning, *Reminiscences of the university, town, and county of Cambridge, from the year 1780*, 2 vols. (1854) • D. A. Winstanley, *Early Victorian Cambridge* (1940) • J. Gascoigne, *Cambridge in the age of the Enlightenment* (1989) • J. Beverley, *The trial of William Frend* (1793) • R. I. Wilberforce and S. Wilberforce, *Life of William Wilberforce*, 5 vols. (1838) • L. J. M. Coleby, 'Isaac Milner and the Jacksonian chair of natural philosophy', *Annals of Science*, 10 (1954), 234–57 • G. Wakefield, *Memoirs of the life of Gilbert Wakefield* (1792) • C. Wordsworth, *Scholae academicae: some account of the studies at the English universities in the eighteenth century* (1877); repr. (1968) • W. W. R. Ball, *A history of the study of mathematics at Cambridge* (1889) • F. K. Brown, *Fathers of the Victorians: the age of Wilberforce* (1961) • J. W. Clark, *Endowments of the University of Cambridge* (1904) • A. De Morgan, *Budget of paradoxes*, 2 vols. (1885) • T. De Quincey, *Confessions of an English opium eater* [n.d.] • R. H. Martin, *Evangelicals united* (1983) • Queens' College conclusion book, Queens' College, Cambridge, 1784–1820 • BL, MS 35657

Archives BL, Add. MSS 35657–35658 • CUL, lectures • Queens' College, Cambridge • RS, papers • Trinity Cam. | BL, letters to A. Young and Lord Hardwicke, Add. MSS 35126, 35129, 35132, 35658, 35686–35687 • Bodl. Oxf., letters to William Wilberforce • CUL, Pitt corresp. • Hunt. L., Z. Macaulay corresp.

Likenesses J. Opie, oils, *c*.1790, Queens' College, Cambridge • oils, *c*.1805, Queens' College, Cambridge • T. Kerrich, chalk drawing, 1810 • Facius, stipple, pubd 1811 (after T. Kerrich), BM, NPG • H. Meyer, stipple, 1815 (after J. Jackson), BM, NPG; repro. in *Contemporary portraits* (1815) • T. Uwins, pencil drawing, BM • engraving (after portrait by J. Opie, *c*.1790), repro. in Milner, *Life* • engraving, RS

Wealth at death £10,000

Milner, James (*b*. after **1653**, *d*. **1721**), merchant and financier, was the son of the London alderman Tempest Milner (*d*. 1673) and his wife, Anne (*b*. 1624), the daughter of James Houblon, a City merchant. Of Yorkshire stock, Milner's father presided as alderman from 1653 to 1657 and from 1660 to 1662, and was also elected master of the Merchant Taylors' Company in 1655. Although details of Milner's own business career are frustratingly sparse, he spent some time in Lisbon and his brother John served as consul in Portugal under Queen Anne. Milner's commercial transactions with that country enabled him to render great service to the government in the remittance of money abroad. He acted as a government financier as partner with Sir Henry Furnese in 1702–3, but by 1708 he had struck out on his own, and played an increasingly important role until the end of the war. As one observer commented in September 1710: 'James Milner understands the Portuguese exchange best and he has a cabal under him who are concerned in whatever he undertakes, and they are men of substance' (*Portland MSS*, 4.573).

Further proof of Milner's eminence in City circles came during the controversy on the bill to satisfy the eighth and ninth clauses of the commercial treaty with France. On 2 June 1713 he went before the House of Lords to warn of the danger which the bill posed to England's trade, and was later celebrated for having 'plainly made appear before Parliament the great importance of our trade to Portugal, and of the [Methuen] treaty which supports it' (King, 1.xiv). Such arguments helped bring about the bill's defeat in the Commons, and in the course of 1713–14 Milner contributed to the twice-weekly *British Merchant* several articles on the 'Methuen treaty and the trade with Portugal', in which he combated the arguments advanced by the government agent Defoe in *The Mercator*.

Having established himself as a prominent spokesman on trade, in 1715 Milner sought a parliamentary seat at Minehead. After a bitter struggle he was eventually returned on petition on 23 May 1717, and subsequently betrayed whig principles by voting in January 1719 for the repeal of the acts to prevent occasional conformity. The following year he emerged an obdurate opponent of the South Sea scheme, and published a series of 'Three letters relating to the South Sea Company and the bank' in order to expose the disastrous course on which the company was set. Following the great crash, in the session of 1720–21 he was a vociferous critic of the company's directors. Although he had wisely avoided investment in the Bubble, his will of September 1721 suggests that his finances were in some disarray. A subsequent (undated) codicil made ominous directions for his funeral, and on 23 November 1721 he 'shot himself in the head, and died the next day' (Historical Reg: Diary, 44). Having remained a bachelor, he left his estate to the offspring of his brother John. In that same year tribute was paid to his commercial acumen by Charles King, who republished *The British Merchant* as a three-volume work.

PERRY GAUCI

Sources W. A. Shaw, ed., *Calendar of treasury books*, 18, PRO (1936); 22–9 (1950–59); 32 (1958–62) • R. Thoresby, *Ducatus Leodiensis, or, The topography of … Leedes*, ed. T. D. Whitaker, 2nd edn (1816), 176–7 • *The manuscripts of his grace the duke of Portland*, 10 vols., HMC, 29 (1891–1931), vol. 4, pp. 559, 573; vol. 5, p. 609 • J. R. Woodhead, *The rulers of London, 1660–1689* (1965), 116 • will, PRO, PROB 11/583, sig. 11 • will, PRO, PROB 11/531, sig. 16 • A. A. Houblon, *The Houblon family: its story and times*, 1 (1907), 358 • *IGI* • D. Pam, *A history of Enfield* (1990), 1.267 • J. Redington, ed., *Calendar of Treasury papers*, 3–4, PRO (1874–9) • *The historical register*, 5 (1721), 44 [incl. 'The chronological diary'] • C. King, ed., *The British merchant*, 3 vols. (1721) • PRO, HCA 13/79, deposition of 21 Oct 1689

Milner, James, first Baron Milner of Leeds (1889–1967), politician and lawyer, was born on 12 August 1889 at Scholes, near Leeds, the eldest son in the family of three sons and one daughter of James Henry Milner (1863–1948), solicitor, and for some years city coroner, and his wife, Elizabeth (d. 1939), daughter of Robert Tate of Leeds. He was educated at Easingwold grammar school, Leeds modern school, and the university, where he obtained his LLB in 1911. He joined the family firm, J. H. Milner & Son, of Leeds and London, and eventually succeeded his father as senior partner.

At university Milner was an active member of the Officers' Training Corps; he became an officer in the Territorial Army and went as adjutant with his regiment to France after the outbreak of war in 1914. He served with great distinction, ending the war with the rank of major, the MC with bar, and a mention in dispatches. Wounded and taken prisoner, he twice attempted to escape but was recaptured. His wounds left him with a permanent limp and long afterwards, at the age of seventy-one, he had to have a leg amputated. On 10 February 1917 he married Lois Tinsdale (1886/7–1982), daughter of Thomas Brown of Leeds. They had two daughters and a son.

Milner joined the Labour Party in 1916, having already concluded that it offered more scope for advancement than the Conservative Party. On returning to Leeds to resume his lawyer's life, he became an active member of the local party and served on the city council in 1923–9. At different times he was either chairman or deputy chairman of the improvements committee when there was considerable replanning of the centre of the city. The Headrow of Leeds became one of the best-known streets in the country: Milner was responsible for the choice of the name and active in the negotiations which brought Lewis's to the city and to the Headrow. In 1928–9 Milner was both deputy lord mayor of Leeds and president of the Leeds Labour Party.

Milner was prominent and active in many important institutions of Leeds life: a founder of the Leeds Civic Trust, president of the Leeds Law Society, vice-president of the Leeds Thoresby Society and of the Leeds National Savings Committee, an honorary member of the Leeds chamber of commerce, and a patron of the Leeds Trustee Savings Bank. His valued help and advice were in constant demand and never refused; for he was abundantly blessed with the gifts of compassion and kindness.

In 1929 Milner became member of parliament for South East Leeds and held the seat until 1951. He was quickly a noticeable figure in the house and had a fine record of active and responsible work. He became parliamentary private secretary to Christopher Addison, served on the select committee on capital punishment (1931), and went to India in 1932 as a member of the Indian franchise committee. His speeches in the house were rarely substantial, and he increasingly pursued his career within the procedural system of the house, rather than through the conflicts of party debates. He enjoyed some success at this,

but the ultimate prize of becoming speaker eluded him. From 1935 he was on the chairmen's panel of the House of Commons, in 1936 and 1937 he sat on committees dealing with Commons' procedures, and in 1943–5 he was chairman of the fire committee in charge of civil defence of the houses of parliament. In 1943 he became chairman of the committee of ways and means, and thus deputy speaker; he was sworn of the privy council in 1945. As chairman of the British group of the Inter-Parliamentary Union he went frequently abroad—he was especially fond of travel—and in 1949 he was leader of the parliamentary delegation to Ceylon to present a speaker's chair and mace to its new parliament. He led parliamentary delegations to Austria in 1948 and Turkey in 1953.

This record of energy and achievement was marred by Milner's failure to become speaker in 1951, when the Conservatives had returned to office, which suggested a lack of regard and trust within his own party. Had he not been defeated by W. S. Morrison, he would have been Labour's first speaker. He might reasonably have expected to succeed to the speakership from his chairmanship of ways and means, a route followed by his predecessors. The division on the speakership was the first since 1895, and certain Labour MPs felt that Attlee and the whips had not pressed his claims forcefully enough in their negotiations with Churchill. But the decision to put him forward against Morrison was only narrowly won within the parliamentary party (108 to 86), and as Richard Crossman recorded, 'Milner is certainly unpopular in the Party and I doubt whether many people thought he would be a better Speaker than Morrison' (Crossman, 29). His path to the deputy speakership during the war had been complicated by rumours of his minor involvement in a scandal in 1940, which damaged Robert Boothby's career, over the financial claims of Czech émigrés on assets held by the British government (*War Diary of Hugh Dalton*, 528). He was cleared of partiality by a select committee when, as deputy speaker in 1948, he had represented Emanuel Shinwell against another MP, Emrys Hughes, who made uncomplimentary remarks about Shinwell on the BBC. Although Milner was exonerated, a rule was drawn up as a result of the incident that the speaker should not act in a professional capacity (in Milner's case as a solicitor) on behalf of, or against, another MP. Hugh Dalton, one of the key political patrons within the party, had little regard for Milner, was suspicious of his masonic links with a number of other Labour MPs, and recommended to Attlee Milner's elevation to the Lords as Baron Milner of Leeds in December 1951, where he served as deputy speaker.

Milner, always affectionately known as Jim, was a distinguished and imposing figure. He was made a freeman of the city of Leeds in October 1966 and was the crown representative on the court and council of Leeds University, which conferred on him an honorary LLD in 1953. He was a deputy lieutenant of the West Riding of Yorkshire, a vice-president of the Association of Municipal Corporations and of the Building Societies' Association, and a past president of the Society of Yorkshiremen in London. Milner died at The Grove, North Lane, Roundhay, his home in Leeds, on 16 July 1967, and was buried at St John's Church, Moor Allerton, Leeds.   S. PEARCE, *rev.* R. C. WHITING

Sources *The Times* (17 July 1967) · *Yorkshire Post* (17 July 1967) · 'Lady Milner', *Yorkshire Post* (21 April 1982) · T. Driberg, 'James Milner, M.P.', *Yorkshire Illustrated* (Feb 1947) · R. Abbiss, 'Major, the Rt. Hon. Lord Milner', *Leeds Graphic* (Aug 1958) · personal knowledge (1981) · private information (1981) · private information (2004) · Burke, *Peerage* (1959) · *The political diary of Hugh Dalton, 1918–1940, 1945–1960*, ed. B. Pimlott (1986) · *The Second World War diary of Hugh Dalton, 1940–1945*, ed. B. Pimlott (1986) · *The backbench diaries of Richard Crossman*, ed. J. Morgan (1981) · 'Report from the select committee', *Parl. papers* (1947–8), 6.615, no. 104 [chairman of ways and means]
Likenesses W. Stoneman, photograph, 1949, NPG · photographs, repro. in *Yorkshire Illustrated*
Wealth at death £61,030: probate, 9 Nov 1967, *CGPLA Eng. & Wales*

Milner, John (1628–1703), nonjuring Church of England clergyman, was born at Skircoate, in the parish of Halifax, on 9 February 1628 and baptized the following day, the second son of John Milner (*d.* 1660) and Mary Ramsden (*d.* 1667), daughter of Gilbert Ramsden. He was educated at the free grammar school of Halifax under Mr Halstead, entered Christ's College, Cambridge, as a sizar on 21 June 1642 under Mr Wilding, and was probably admitted BA in 1645.

On his return to Halifax, Milner met John Lake, a minister at the parish church, and married his sister Sara Lake (1627–1667?). Milner received clandestine ordination from Henry Tilson, bishop of Elphin, on 7 June 1649, and in the following year he was the minister at Sowerby Bridge. His only son, Thomas, was born in 1652, and about that time he joined his brother-in-law at Chadderton, in Lancashire, where they tried to retain control of the church at Oldham. Although they were both disaffected royalists, they were permitted to preach at exercises there in 1654. Nevertheless, by the end of that year they surrendered Oldham to a popular presbyterian and returned to Halifax, where each was heard preaching in 1655. Perhaps Milner returned to Lancashire, as Thoresby says he was 'curate at Middleton but was forced thence upon Sir George Booth's unsuccessful attempt to restore the Royal Family' (Thoresby, *Vicaria*, 113). Middleton's patron participated in Booth's rising in August 1659 and drew in those around him. Also, the Middleton register lists an 'Edmund son of Mr. John Millnor, baptised 16 Feb. 1659'. Milner's father was buried on 25 February 1660, in Halifax, and Lake conducted the funeral.

During the Restoration, Lake became vicar of Leeds and gave Milner the curacy of Beeston, in that parish, in October 1661. At the same time Lake, Milner, and Samuel Drake, the vicar of Pontefract, petitioned the king for Cambridge degrees by royal mandate. In their petition they claim that all three had 'been deprived of very good benefices by reason of their loyalty' (SP 29/43/95). Being unable to travel to Whitehall with his friends, because his wife needed his care in Leeds, Milner was admitted BD later, in Cambridge, on 12 December. Their daughter Mary was born two days after Christmas. In August 1662 Milner was one of the first to subscribe the Act of Uniformity at

York. When the incumbent curate of St John the Evangelist in Leeds refused to subscribe and was deprived, Lake moved Milner into that new, and well-endowed, church. They subsequently erected the memorial there to its founder. Sara Milner seems to have died in 1667, and a second wife, Elizabeth, was buried at St John's in 1676.

Meanwhile, Milner taught Hebrew to his son, Thomas, before sending him to Magdalene College, Cambridge, as a pensioner in 1669. Milner also had an influence upon the young Ralph Thoresby, who said Milner had excited him, when a schoolboy, to be interested in the antiquities of Leeds. In 1673 Milner published a learned pamphlet, *Conjectanea in Isaiam ix, I, II. Item in parallela quaedam veteris ac novi testamenti, in quibus versionis 70. Interpretum … cum textu Hebraeo conciliationem*, and dedicated it to his friend Dr Duport, master of his son's college. Dr Castell, professor of Arabic, said 'it showed incredible reading and diligence', but was probably too learned to be popular, even in the university (MS Birch 4275/95). At the same time, Thomas proceeded BA and was elected a fellow of Magdalene. On the resignation of the incumbent vicar of Leeds in 1677, John Milner was instituted on 2 August to that vicarage, where he lived as a widower with his daughter Mary for the next twelve years. He was elected a prebendary of Ripon on 29 March 1681. After his brother-in-law became bishop of Chichester in 1685, the two clerics continued to correspond about ecclesiastical matters, and within a year the bishop gave his nephew, Thomas, the vicarage of Bexhill on the coast of Sussex. When Thomas died there in 1722 his will and codicil provided scholarships for Magdalene College, and his sister Mary's will increased the bequest in 1736.

John Milner published *A collection of the church history of Palestine from the birth of Christ to the beginning of the empire of Diocletian* (1688) and *A Short Dissertation Concerning the Four Last Kings of Judah* (1689), the latter supporting the principle of strict hereditary succession. After the revolution of 1688 he became a nonjuror, was deprived of all preferments, and sought refuge in Cambridge, where St John's College offered him hospitality and a satisfying retirement. Although unable to take the new oaths, he never separated from the established church, but continued to attend its services. He published *De Nethinium sive Nethinaeis* (1690), *A Defence of Archbishop Usher* (1694), *A Discourse of Conscience* (1697), and five more examinations of theological books by Richard Bentley (1698), William Sherlock (n.d.), John Locke (1700), and Jean le Clerc (1702), defending the traditional Anglican orthodoxy against Socinian and novel Platonist views. He was particularly eager to discourage revisionist studies of biblical chronology. St John's College Library received his unpublished manuscripts, including an annotated translation in Latin of the targum on the first and second books of Chronicles, and eleven other works on scriptural history and current ecclesiastical controversies. Milner died at St John's on 16 February 1703, and was buried in the old college chapel on 19 February with great state. Dr Gower, then the master of his college, said he was truly a learned and pious man, who set a good example of modesty and moderation. 'I had the hapiness of much of his conversation, but still desired more' (Hunter, *Letters of Eminent Men*, 2.18).

H. H. POOLE

Sources [J. Hunter], ed., *Letters of eminent men, addressed to Ralph Thoresby*, 2 vols. (1832) · *The diary of Ralph Thoresby*, ed. J. Hunter, 2 vols. (1830) · R. Thoresby, *Vicaria Leodiensis, or, The history of the church of Leedes in Yorkshire* (1724), 12, 113–20 · *DNB* · W. A. Shaw, ed., *Minutes of the Manchester presbyterian classis*, 3, Chetham Society, new ser., 24 (1891), appx, pp. 390, 393, 395 · J. Peile, *Biographical register of Christ's College, 1505–1905, and of the earlier foundation, God's House, 1448–1505*, ed. [J. A. Venn], 1 (1910), 482 · *Halifax Parish Register, III*, Wakefield RO, Yorkshire · G. Shaw, ed., *Registers of the parish church of Middleton* (1904) [bap. 16 Feb 1659, E. Milner] · G. D. Lumb, ed., *The registers of the parish church of Leeds, from 1639 to 1667*, Thoresby Society, 7 (1897), 293, 301 · will, CUL, department of manuscripts and university archives, vice-chancellor's court, 4.417 · will of T. Lake, proved 29 June 1649, 2 Feb 1649, Borth. Inst. · admissions 21 June 1642, Christ's College, Cambridge · Borth. Inst., York Archiepiscopal V.1667/Exh.Bk, fol. 59r · 1650, LPL, MS Comm XIIa/18,178 [1650 church surveys] · T. Hanson, 'Halifax parish church, 1640–60', *Transactions of the Halifax Antiquarian Society* (1916), 310 · T. Hanson, 'Halifax parish church, 1640–60', *Transactions of the Halifax Antiquarian Society* (1917), 49 · State Papers, Domestic, PRO, SP 29/43/95 · mandates and subscriptions, 12 Dec 1661, CUL · Milner correspondence, BL, Add. MSS Birch 4275, fols. 95, 106–8, 113–17, 201 · [J. T. Fowler], ed., *Memorials of the church of SS Peter and Wilfrid, Ripon*, 2, SurtS, 78 (1886), 314 · W. Sussex RO, MS EPI/1/10 (Bexhill, 29 Jan 1686) · Venn, *Alum. Cant.* · B. G. Blackwood, *The Lancashire gentry and the great rebellion, 1640–60*, Chetham Society, 3rd ser., 25 (1978), 75–6, 359–60, 10.160 · T. Cox, *A popular history of the grammar school of Queen Elizabeth, at Heath, near Halifax* (1879)

Archives BL, corresp., Add. MSS Birch 4275, fols. 95, 106–8, 113–17, 201 | W. Yorks. AS, Leeds, Yorkshire Archaeological Society, letters to R. Thoresby

Wealth at death lands, tenements, hereditaments in Norland, York, plus £100 and all books to Thomas Milner; residue, incl. credits and lands, tenements, and hereditaments in Skircote, York, to Mary Milner: will, CUL, department of manuscripts and university archives, vice-chancellor's court wills, 4.417

Milner, John (1752–1826), vicar apostolic of the midland district and religious controversialist, was born on 14 October 1752 in London, the son of Joseph Miller, tailor, and his wife, Helen Marsland; both were Catholics from Lancashire.

Education and mission in Winchester Milner was baptized by Bishop Richard Challoner's chaplain, William Errington, and at the age of seven was sent to the Franciscan school at Edgbaston, near Birmingham. Challoner took a close interest in the family and ensured that John was transferred to Sedgley Park School in Wolverhampton at the age of thirteen, in 1765, by which time it appears that his father had died and that the family had changed their name to Milner (Husenbeth, 4–5). Like most of the pupils Milner remained at the school for little more than a year and then left for the English College at Douai, in northern France, for his clerical training. He spent eleven years there and returned to London in 1777, following his ordination to the priesthood in Douai. If the long years at Douai blurred his recollection of English Catholic life Milner was soon plunged back into its hardships. The only patronage on which he could depend was that of Bishop

John Milner (1752–1826), by Georges Antoine Keman

Richard Challoner, who had few material goods to share but who initiated Milner into the life of a travelling missioner by employing him for two years around London.

Eventually, on 15 October 1779, Bishop Challoner placed Milner at the mission in Winchester, which became the base for his opposition to the liberal Catholics known as Cisalpines, and for his literary and artistic activities. While in Winchester he published a large number of controversial and polemical essays and pamphlets to counter the liberal Cisalpine viewpoint espoused by the Catholic Committee and their leading spokesman, Joseph Berington. Milner was an equally ferocious critic of protestant dissenters and their low-church allies, who were being courted by Berington's party. From Winchester he published an early study of Gothic architecture (*The History, Civil and Ecclesiastical, and Survey of the Antiquities of Winchester*, 2 vols., 1798–1801), which gained him a fellowship of the Society of Antiquaries but which was equally controversial in that it contained a trenchant attack on the latitudinarian and deeply anti-Catholic late bishop of Winchester, Benjamin Hoadly. He also built a new Catholic church in Winchester (1792) in the Strawberry Hill Gothic style, which he included in his study of Gothic architecture as an example of the continuity of Gothic between the nearby cathedral and modern Catholicism.

Milner made enemies not only among the low-church Anglicans of Winchester but also among his fellow Catholics for his fierce attack on the inclusion in the second Catholic Relief Bill of the phrase 'Protesting Catholic Dissenters'. Milner was the chief protagonist of those who opposed this form of words in the bill, and with bishops Douglass and Walmesley he sought the aid of high-church Anglican bishops in the House of Lords to defeat it. The bill was passed in March 1791 without the offending phrase. His uncompromising Catholic orthodoxy and political authoritarianism was in tune with high-church Anglican anxieties of the 1790s, and Milner threw in his lot with the likes of Bishop Samuel Horsley of Bangor, who helped the relief act through the Lords. However, Milner was 'merely engaged in a tactical ploy' (Nockles, 207); his apparent sympathy with high-church Anglicanism was a short-lived product of the political and religious circumstances of the 1790s.

Milner's consistent and fierce opposition to the liberals shaped his attitude to clergy and laity alike within the Catholic community. Throughout the controversies that divided English Catholicism during his lifetime he stood firm for his interpretation of orthodoxy—a bolder view than that to which the eighteenth century was accustomed and one in which ecclesiastical authority was a reality. Yet recent scholarship suggests that these differences were more of style and emphasis than of real theological substance (Nockles, 223). Milner spoke in 1790 at Bishop William Gibson's consecration of the 'epidemical phrenzy … for establishing certain chimerical rights of man in a business in which man has no right at all … I mean the principle of vesting in the people at large the authority of appointing their own prelates' (Duffy, 309). He opposed the concessions that the liberals were prepared to make to secular government in order to make further progress towards political and social freedom and to be ranked alongside protestant nonconformity in the public mind. The authority of pope and bishops must, he believed, be maintained against the powerful laity and even against fellow clerics who were prepared to go along with them.

The end of religious controversy Milner's most famous controversial work was *The End of Religious Controversy* (1818), which took the form of a catechetical preamble and a dialogue of letters between Christian ministers of different denominations. Its publication was delayed from 1802, specifically at the request of Bishop Horsley. It was widely read and translated into French and Italian, and was credited with producing a number of converts to Catholicism. By 1818 Milner had abandoned his tactic of flirting with high-churchmanship to discredit the low-church and dissenting radical friends of Catholic liberalism, and portrayed latitudinarianism as normative within the Church of England, thus making it an intolerable ally. *The End of Religious Controversy* was the culmination of his controversial writings, but marked a distinct change of approach to the more uncompromising antagonism between Christian bodies of the next generation.

The midland district was the heartland of Cisalpinism, so Milner's appointment as vicar apostolic of the district in 1803, with the title of bishop of Castabala *in partibus*, was not greeted with overwhelming enthusiasm, although much of the heat had gone out of the antagonism by then. Milner himself was reluctant to leave the London district but the balance was finally swung by the advice of the Vatican diplomatic representative in England, Cardinal Charles Erskine. Setting aside his own personal antipathy to Milner he advised that Milner's strength of personality would be invaluable to the midland district; the men of peace had had their day and the time was ripe for a man of power and discipline (Ward, 2.254). Milner was certainly the most powerful and distinctive of the vicars apostolic of the early nineteenth century. He was a dominant and vigorous character, who refused any kind of concession to the civil government. His attitudes were dominated by opposition to government interference and to lay usurpation of clerical authority (Duffy, 308). He resisted proposals for a government veto over Catholic episcopal appointments and became much involved in Irish affairs, acting as agent for the Irish Catholic bishops in London. Urged on by the Irish bishops he resisted the willingness of his fellow vicars apostolic to exchange the right of veto in return for Catholic emancipation, believing that it would compromise the independence of the church. On this issue, not for the first time, Milner stood almost alone against the prevailing mood of English Catholic opinion. Thus a bill for Catholic emancipation on those terms was lost in 1813 and political liberty for Catholics was not achieved until after Milner's death, but the veto plan was abandoned.

It was not just as an ecclesiastical politician that Milner was of the greatest significance but as a local bishop who reshaped the traditional pastoral tasks to meet the demands of the new century, asserting the rights and duties of episcopal leadership in a new way. The tasks of organization, distribution of manpower, encouragement of education, and husbandry of resources remained basically the same as in earlier generations; conduct and strategy, however, were pursued in a different environment and by a different type of bishop. Milner was cast in a wholly different mould from his predecessors as vicar apostolic, all of whom were members of recusant landowning families. None of his successors in the midland district would ever again be sons of aristocratic or gentry families. This was a result partly of social forces but also of deliberate policy on the part of men such as Milner. He consciously set out to curb what he regarded as the overweening arrogance of the leading laymen in church affairs. His freedom from social and family ties enabled him to curtail their influence and helped in his assertion of clerical authority.

Thus Milner took firm control of a district shaken by dissension and discord. His task was to control and channel the obvious possibilities there in the direction of orthodoxy. The area of greatest opportunity, and of immense significance to Milner, was that of clerical education. His battles with the Cisalpine clergy had impressed upon him the need for strict and careful clergy training. His appointment spread dismay among his old liberal opponents involved in the running of the joint school and seminary at Joseph Berington's old home at Oscott, near Birmingham. The mainly Cisalpine governors of the college, founded in the wake of the French Revolution, feared that Oscott's days were numbered. John Bew, the superior, had the wisdom to realize that he had to gain the support and understanding of the bishop. Most importantly this had to be achieved before the enemies of Oscott had the chance to sow further seeds of suspicion. Within a month of Milner's consecration as bishop, Bew invited him to Oscott to 'submit to [his] judgment, the plan they are going to pursue at that place, and everything else relative to the place' (Milner to Poynter, 17 June 1803, Milner letters, Westminster Archdiocesan Archives). Milner was dubious about the whole thing and confided to Bishop Poynter of London his fear of being 'drawn in to sanction any bad or defective plan for forming Catholics and still more, priests, by corrupt ceremonies' (ibid.). In the light of long battles waged with its supporters Milner's first instinct was to move against Oscott but he realized the overwhelming need for clerical education and was determined to exert his influence to ensure proper orthodox training.

The horrors of the Cisalpine school were far less in practice than in rumour; the effective influence of Cisalpinism in either the school or seminary was negligible. Milner found much more good than bad, and great possibilities in the place, taking in hand the clerical education himself. Changes in liturgical and religious practice more fitted to clerical students were introduced in order to enhance the correct spiritual education of the students. To this end he made a clear distinction between lay and clerical education and separated the church students from the school. Meanwhile the college continued its unequal struggle against financial ruin, while an uncomfortable peace survived between Milner and the lay governors. In 1808 the laity finally had to admit defeat. They offered the bishop the entire control of Oscott if he would also relieve them of the running debt of £600. Milner accepted with alacrity and at once set about remodelling the college, which contained thirty lay students and seven clerical students.

The 'new government' Milner's 'new government' was inaugurated on 15 August 1808. The clergy were set apart in their training and education, and were never allowed to forget it for a moment; different, and higher, standards of morality and behaviour were expected of them. The clergy were placed on a pedestal from which they were expected to teach and instruct the laity by word and example. If the clergy conformed to Milner's code of behaviour they could expect total support from him, especially if the question of lay interference arose. Milner delayed the issue of his first *ad clerum* until the new *Rules for the English Clergy* were in print at the end of 1813, a copy of which was sent out with the *ad clerum*. His letter delighted in the end of all dissension, and encouraged his clergy to learn from past mistakes and to submit dutifully to their proper superiors. He emphasized the tradition of clerical discipline in the church, and the duties and responsibilities of the clergy. Finally he drew their attention to the need for good standards of clerical education: 'O let not that sacred cause fail in our hands, through irreligious indifference, which our Catholic ancestors and predecessors supported for so long a time at the expense of their blood' (Husenbeth, 104–5). His relationship with his clergy was characterized by a stern, orthodox paternalism. He expected of them piety and learning, and constantly emphasized the need for preaching and teaching.

Milner was strict on all issues of morality and abhorred any whiff of scandal, furiously attacking any suggestion that 'celibacy was a burden which ought to be removed' (Milner to Douglas, Oct 1799, Westminster Archdiocesan Archives). His diary, which otherwise was a bald record of confirmations and ordinations, reveals an obsession with stories of the untimely deaths of apostate and immoral priests. Many of the entries were later scribbled out. The connection in his mind between the abandonment of priestly vows and divine retribution was quite clear. Scrupulous standards were expected of all priests, to the extent of forbidding all forms of public entertainment. This strongly sacerdotal attitude to the priesthood began the creation of a new kind of clerical caste.

Milner's authoritarian view of the clergy and his experience of vocal liberal laity in the 1790s meant that his view of the role of the laity was subservience to the priest. Financial dependence on the laity for chapels, schools, and charities did not mean that he was prepared to concede control to them; he was touchy where there was any suggestion of laymen controlling clergy. Just as he opposed the arrogation of powers by the Catholic Committee and its successor, the Catholic Board, to speak on behalf of the Catholic church in England, so he denied any rights locally to laity who tried to take control. Thus, when between 1804 and 1807 the wealthy Catholic businessmen of Birmingham endeavoured to drive out the resident Franciscan missioners and to control the building, staffing, and running of the mission there through a body of trustees Milner kept them firmly in check. A trustee-run chapel was set up, but very clearly on Milner's terms.

Later years From 1824 Milner was subject to paralytic attacks, and his deteriorating health forced him to accept the appointment of a coadjutor bishop, Thomas Walsh, who had been his closest colleague and ally at Oscott. Despite a year as Milner's coadjutor and twenty-three years of working in his shadow Walsh was ill-equipped to succeed. He wrote pitifully after Milner's death, 'I have been taught to love and esteem those as my best friends who have the courage to point out to me my faults. Dr Milner did not spare me' (Walsh to Poynter, 16 July 1826, Westminster Archdiocesan Archives). It is clear from that relationship that Milner had little capacity for deep warmth and friendship and could be a bully. Much of existing knowledge and familiarity with him comes from Husenbeth's biography, written less than forty years after the subject's death, not as an attempt to rescue the reputation of a maligned and unpopular superior but as a celebration of a much respected figure. It was the work of a devoted student and disciple but in general terms it seems to reflect the attitude of many of the clergy: 'He was a man of great abilities, of powerful mind and energetic action; he was a prelate of great zeal, extensive learning, undaunted courage and noble independence … a holy and exemplary Bishop of God's Church' (Husenbeth, 2).

Milner died at his residence, Giffard House, Wolverhampton, on 19 April 1826, at the age of seventy-three, and was buried on 27 April in the adjoining church of Sts Peter and Paul.   JUDITH F. CHAMP

Sources J. Milner, diary, Birmingham Archdiocesan Archives · Westm. DA, Milner letters · Oscott College archives · P. B. Nockles, '"The difficulties of protestantism": Bishop Milner, John Fletcher, and Catholic apologetic against the Church of England', Recusant History, 24 (1998–9), 193–236 · F. C. Husenbeth, The life of … John Milner (1862) · Gillow, Lit. biog. hist., vol. 5 · E. Duffy, 'Joseph Berington and the English Catholic Cisalpine movement, 1772–1803', PhD diss., U. Cam., 1973 · J. Champ, 'The Catholic revival in Birmingham, c.1650–1850', PhD diss., U. Birm., 1985 · B. Ward, The dawn of the Catholic revival in England, 1781–1803, 2 vols. (1909) · C. Buscot, History of Cotton College (1942) · J. Champ, Oscott (1984) · M. N. L. Couve de Murville, John Milner (1986)

Archives Birmingham Archdiocesan Archives, corresp. and papers; diary · Oscott College, Birmingham, archives · St Peter's Church, Winchester, corresp. and papers · Westm. DA, letters | Archives of the British Province of the Society of Jesus, London, letters to Charles Plowden, Robert Plowden, and others · NL Ire., letters to Denis Scully · PRO, corresp. with James Wheeler, J90/465–6 · Ushaw College, Durham, letters relating to Ushaw College

Likenesses portrait, c.1797, Oulton Abbey, Stone, Staffordshire · J. V. Barber, portrait, 1816, Oscott College, Birmingham · W. Radclyffe, line engraving, pubd 1819 (after J. V. Barber), BM, NPG · G. Clarke, bust, 1822, Oulton Abbey, Stone, Staffordshire · C. B. Fox, line engraving, pubd 1822 (after G. A. Keman), BM · T. Wyatt, lithograph, pubd 1826 (after bust by G. Clarke), NPG · J. R. Herbert, portrait (posthumous), Oscott College, Birmingham · G. A. Keman, miniature, Oscott College, Birmingham [see illus.] · W. Roffe, stipple, NPG · pencil miniature, Oscott College, Birmingham

Milner, Joseph (1745–1797), Church of England clergyman and ecclesiastical historian, was born on 2 January 1745 at Quarry Hill, near Leeds, and baptized on 30 January at St Peter's, Leeds, the elder son of Joseph Milner (c.1715–1760), a poor weaver. An attack of measles at three left him permanently weakened, and throughout his boyhood his health was precarious. Spending much time indoors, he was attracted to books and learning from an early age. His father recognized his son's intellectual precocity but it was John Moore, headmaster of Leeds grammar school, who took an interest in him and gave him the rudiments of a classical education. A close student of Greek and Latin, Milner soon assisted at the school, and then began privately to tutor the adult children of well-to-do families. Notwithstanding the sudden death of his father, Milner was able to attend university because of help from Moore and others, and because of the offer of a position of chapel clerk at St Catharine's College, Cambridge. Milner proved himself a competent classical and mathematical scholar and took his BA in 1766, achieving the rank of third senior optime and winning a chancellor's medal. He went on to become an assistant to Christopher Atkinson at a school at Thorp Arch near Tadcaster in Yorkshire, and soon after entered deacon's orders and became a curate to Atkinson in the parish church. He also began a lasting friendship with the vicar's son, Myles Atkinson, later a leading evangelical as vicar of St Paul's in Leeds.

Milner secured a post at the grammar school at Hull early in 1767, and in 1768 he was elected afternoon lecturer at Holy Trinity, or the High Church. In 1768 he also began serving as curate of North Ferriby, a village on the Humber about 9 miles from Hull. As headmaster at Hull he restored the fortunes of the school, which had languished prior to his arrival. Earning upwards of £200 per annum, he took on his younger brother Isaac *Milner (1750–1820) as assistant at the school and then supported him at Queens' College, Cambridge, in 1770. About this same time, Milner experienced an evangelical conversion. Some of Lady Huntingdon's Methodist students were in Hull in 1769 and Milner attended their services frequently. A bookish soul, he was also influenced by reading Richard Hooker's On Justification, and by a close study of Galatians. It was two years until his judgement was 'settled and confirmed'. A letter from the evangelical clergyman John Newton helped him over some of his objections to predestination, and he soon joined the growing number of moderate Calvinists in the Church of England. He described himself as 'partly siding with Methodists in opinion, and partly with those called Calvinists'. Ever the loyal churchman, he added, 'This was exactly the medium, I think, upon which the Church of England was constructed' (Evangelical Magazine, 1823, 232). His closest friends were two evangelical ministers, James Stillingfleet of Hotham and William Richardson of York.

Milner soon fell out of favour among the leading citizens of Hull, including many of the city merchants who had their country seats at North Ferriby. What evangelicals would have described as a new 'seriousness' appeared to his fashionable parishioners as an unsociable severity, as he gave up cards, plays, and the assembly house, and eschewed even polite civilities. Popular with the poor, he held weekday religious meetings after the pattern of many evangelical societies. When his enemies accused him under the Conventicle Act of holding illegal meetings, the mayor dismissed the charges as frivolous. After about seven or eight years the opposition died out, and Milner's authority grew in Hull, making it a significant centre of evangelicalism by the end of the century. He accomplished a remarkable religious reform among the poor and middle classes, and eventually regained the respect of the town élite. Typically, he preached at North Ferriby in the morning and then at Hull in the afternoon; for many years he also preached midweek at Holy Trinity and led prayers at Lister's hospital. He also became vicar of North Ferriby in 1786. After a debilitating fever in 1792, the mayor and corporation of Hull voted him £40 per annum to support an assistant at the school. They were also persuaded by William Wilberforce to offer him the living of Holy Trinity in 1797. His health did not last, however, and a cold caught on his way to York for institution in September led to his death in Hull on 15 November 1797. He was buried in Holy Trinity Church, and a monument was erected to his memory.

Milner's influence as a headmaster was significant and numbers of his pupils went on to Cambridge. Moreover, there is a long list of evangelical clergymen and missionaries who received their early schooling from him. It is as the author of *The History of the Church of Christ* (1794–1809) that Milner is chiefly remembered, however. He had been unhappy with available accounts of church history, such as the standard work by J. L. Mosheim, which seemed to be preoccupied with error and schism. To Milner this was as absurd as thinking that the history of English highwaymen were a history of England. In contrast, Milner set out to trace a silent stream of godliness in the church, and by so doing he created a distinctively evangelical narrative of Christianity. He began work on the project in the early 1770s but died before the whole could be finished. His brother Isaac had assisted with volumes 1 (1794), 2 (1795), and 3 (1797), and after Milner's death drew on his extensive papers to complete volumes 4 (1803) and 5 (1809).

Milner's history essentially transferred the art of evangelical biography onto a large canvas. In the early church he celebrated Cyprian, Ambrose, and Augustine. In the early medieval period he eulogized Gregory the Great and traced the lives of several missionaries. Anselm and Bernard were the focus of the twelfth century, but Aquinas he passed over in the thirteenth as a semi-Pelagian. The Cathari, Waldenses, and Lollards helped preserve the doctrine of grace. A few other figures are notable for their inclusion (Grosseteste), for their only qualified approval (Wyclif and Hus), or for their absence (Calvin). It was appropriately with Luther that the history ended, though John Scott later published a three-volume continuation (1826, 1829, and 1831). Milner's history did more than inform evangelicals: it gave them a pedigree and helped to forge their identity. It was their issues which he took with him back through the centuries, finding evangelicals, Socinians, and dissenters in surprising places, and advancing a none-too-subtle apology for distinctive tenets such as justification by faith, regeneration by the Holy Spirit, the propriety of a religious establishment, and the dangers of philosophy. There were other examples of evangelical church history, but Milner's was the most ambitious and influential. Indeed, it was from Milner that the young John Henry Newman first discovered a love for the fathers. The work was in print for some fifty years until it was eclipsed by the critical church historiography of liberals such as H. H. Milman and high-churchmen such as Samuel Roffey Maitland. Milner's scholarship could not stand up to their more rigorous standards of historical research, and his interpretation appeared procrustean in comparison with the newer historical consciousness of cultural change.

Milner's aim may have been in part to redress the critical account of Christianity in Edward Gibbon's *Decline and Fall of the Roman Empire* (1776–88). His direct response was *Gibbon's Account of Christianity Considered* (1781). He also published *Essays on Several Religious Subjects* (1789) which treated key evangelical doctrines. With William Richardson, he edited Thomas Adam's posthumous *Works* (1786). After his own death, four volumes of sermons were published (more than 800 sermons were left in manuscript) along with his *Essentials of Christianity* (1855).

D. BRUCE HINDMARSH

Sources J. Milner, *Practical sermons … to which is prefixed an account of the life and character of the author*, 3 vols. (1804–23) [by Isaac

Milner] · J. D. Walsh, 'Joseph Milner's evangelical church history', *Journal of Ecclesiastical History*, 10 (1959), 174–87 · J. D. Walsh, 'The Yorkshire evangelicals in the eighteenth century', PhD diss., U. Cam., 1956 · C. J. Abbey and J. H. Overton, *The English church in the eighteenth century*, 2 (1878), 209–13 · letter, *Evangelical Magazine and Missionary Chronicle*, new ser., 1 (1823), 232 · A. Pollard, 'Milner, Joseph', *The Blackwell dictionary of evangelical biography, 1730–1860*, ed. D. M. Lewis (1995) · D. B. Hindmarsh, *John Newton and the English evangelical tradition* (1996), 159–61 · L. E. Elliott-Binns, *The early evangelicals: a religious and social study* (1953) · J. H. Newman, *Apologia pro vita sua* (1864) · J. Bradley and R. Muller, 'The emergence of critical church historiography', *Church history: an introduction* (1995), 11–25 · P. Schaff, 'Literature of church history', *History of the Christian church*, 1 (1890), 27–53 · IGI · Venn, *Alum. Cant.* · DNB

Likenesses silhouette engraving, pubd 1809, BM, NPG · line engraving, pubd 1819, BM, NPG · J. Cochran, stipple (after W. Gush), BM, NPG

Milner [*née* Compton], **Mary** (1797–1863), author, was born on 12 November 1797, the daughter of Thomas Wilberforce Compton and his wife, Sarah. Her birth coincided with the death of her great-uncle Joseph *Milner, vicar-elect of Kingston upon Hull, with whom her mother, his niece and legatee, was living. After the death of her mother in August 1812, Mary Compton found a permanent home with her great-uncle Isaac *Milner, president of Queens' College, Cambridge, and dean of Carlisle. Her education gained greatly from her conversations with him on religion, mathematics, natural science, and history. Shortly before the death of Dean Milner, Mary Compton married a distant cousin, Joseph Milner (1797?–1864), in 1820. He became vicar of St Lawrence, Appleby, near Penrith, in Westmorland, and they had at least six children, three sons and three daughters.

By 1840 Mary Milner had returned from domestic to literary pursuits with *The Christian Mother, or, Maternal Duties Exemplified*, a popular work of evangelical piety which stressed the value of the individual child in the sight of God. Some were shocked that she advocated a permissive attitude to mischievous children, although she emphasized that defects of character were to be punished. At the same time she was also at work on *The Life of Dean Milner, DD, FRS* (2 vols., 1842). This demonstrated an incisive style, attacking those 'who secretly if not avowedly, associate the ideas of piety and imbecility' ('Preface', iv). Aiming at impartiality towards the subject, she handled historical evidence ably and generally avoided personal reminiscence in an impressive biography. Dean Milner's influence can be seen in *The Garland of the Months* (1852), in which natural history and sciences were used to exemplify 'the first great cause of all things' (*The Garland of the Months*, 240), as a stimulus to observations by the growing child. In her *Sketches Illustrative of Important Periods in the History of the World* (1843) Mary Milner showed a grasp of historical change from an evangelical point of view; she was asked to continue Sarah Trimmer's popular textbook *History of England* to the marriage of Queen Victoria (1849).

As an editor, Mrs Milner was probably able to count for support on William Wilberforce and Clapham Sect contacts among publishers in London and elsewhere. Her lively intellect can be seen in the *Christian Mother's Magazine* (1844). Apart from articles on religion and the truth of scripture, this periodical contained series on astronomy, mathematics, history, archaeology, and natural history, as well as poetry and other arts which reflected Mary Milner's broad interests. It soon became the *Englishwomen's Magazine* (9 vols., 1845–55), in which Thomas Arnold's call for articles 'written with a decidedly religious tone' (1846, frontispiece) was answered. There was a feminist edge to the contents, which included a series on celebrated women such as Hannah More, Felicia Hemans, and Maria Edgeworth, and female influence on literature and society. Reviews kept readers in touch with the latest ideas and covered such social issues as the poor laws, infanticide in India and the potato famine in Ireland. As the editor of a popular periodical series of engravings, *The People's Gallery* (1848–9), Mrs Milner encountered redoubtable women contributors such as Caroline Norton. In 1855–6 she returned to 'scriptural christianity' with the *Christian Lady's Magazine*. Series on the human body and the training and development of children were short-lived, possibly owing to religious opposition. She also edited a new edition of *The Essentials of Christianity* (1855), by her great-uncle Joseph Milner.

Mary Milner died at the vicarage, Appleby, on 10 May 1863, and was buried in St Lawrence's churchyard there. As a scholar, she demonstrated the versatility of the mid-nineteenth-century woman writer, and her editorial skill gave women a voice in Christian and wider circles.

V. E. CHANCELLOR

Sources I. Milner, *An account of the life and character of the late Rev. Joseph Milner* (1804) · H. G. Adams, ed., *A cyclopaedia of female biography* (1857) · Boase, *Mod. Eng. biog.* · V. E. Chancellor, *History for their masters* (1970) · M. Milner, *The life of Isaac Milner*, 2 vols. (1842) · IGI · I. Milner, letters to William Wilberforce, 1788–1819, Bodl. Oxf. · d. cert.
Archives County Reference Library, Carlisle, letters to Sir Robert Peel, Add. MSS 40513, fol. 252

Milner, Thomas (1719–1797), physician, son of John Milner, a Presbyterian minister, was born at Peckham, near London, where his father preached and kept a school famous because Oliver Goldsmith became one of its ushers in 1757. Milner graduated MD at St Andrews in 1740, and in 1759 was elected physician to St Thomas's Hospital, London. He became a licentiate of the Royal College of Physicians in 1760, but in 1762 resigned from St Thomas's, and settled in Maidstone, Kent, where he achieved a large practice; he was noted for walking to the parish church every Sunday, bearing a gold-headed cane, and being followed in linear succession by his three unmarried sisters who lived with him. In 1783 he published in London *Experiments and Observations on Electricity*, a work in which he described some of the effects which an electrical power is capable of producing on conducting substances, and the similar effects of the same power on electric bodies themselves; he also made observations on the air, electric repulsion, the electrified cup, and the analogy between electricity and magnetism. He died at Maidstone on 13 September 1797, and was buried on 20 September in All Saints' Church there.

NORMAN MOORE, rev. CLAIRE L. NUTT

Sources Munk, *Roll* · J. Forster, *The life and adventures of Oliver Goldsmith* (1848)

Milner [*née* Maxse], **Violet Georgina**, Viscountess Milner (1872–1958), imperial activist, was born on 1 February 1872 at 38 Rutland Gate, Brompton, London, the youngest surviving child of Admiral Frederick Augustus *Maxse (1833–1900), a Crimean War hero, landowner, and maverick politician, and his wife, Cecilia Steel (1842–1918), an art-loving society beauty. When Violet was five, her parents separated. She lived mainly with her father, brothers, and sister: of these, (Frederick) Ivor *Maxse became a leading First World War general and Leopold James *Maxse a prominent journalist. She was educated by a succession of governesses organized by her father.

Violet Maxse was short and slender with an attractive, delicate-featured face and a challenging expression. Painting classes in Paris failed to make an artist of her, but there she acquired a passion for French culture and couture, and the lifelong friendship of the writer-statesman Georges Clemenceau.

Lord Edward Herbert Gascoyne-*Cecil (1867–1918), whom she married on 18 June 1894, was the fourth, soldier, son of the prime minister, Lord Salisbury. Their first child, George, was born in the following year. They spent much of their early married life with the Salisburys at Hatfield House; this she found enthralling but oppressive—the incessant talk about the Anglican church dividing her, an atheist, from the religious Cecils. Her relationship with Edward, able but a late developer, deteriorated; his military service separated them for long periods. Accompanying him in July 1899 to South Africa, where he was Baden-Powell's chief staff officer and was besieged in Mafeking, she became a friend of such colonial heroes as Cecil Rhodes and Dr Jameson, and fell in love with Sir Alfred *Milner (1854–1925), then high commissioner.

Violet and Edward Cecil returned home late in 1900. Their daughter Helen was born in May 1901. By then Edward was in Sudan, before entering Egyptian government service. Concerned for the children's health and disliking Egyptian life, Violet chose to live in England, seeing her husband only on his annual leaves. In 1906 she bought a derelict Jacobean manor, Great Wigsell, on the Kent–Sussex border, which she restored lovingly. She became a close friend of her neighbours Rudyard and Carrie Kipling and worked for the Victoria League, the National Service League, and other imperial causes. After Milner returned to England in 1905, such was their discretion, involving her later systematic destruction of compromising letters, that no hint of scandal attached to their friendship.

In August 1914, eighteen-year-old George Cecil, now a grenadier officer, went out to France and was killed two weeks later at Villers-Cotterêts. Edward was unable to return from Egypt for two years. His Christian words of consolation about an afterlife in which Violet could not believe drove them further apart. For the rest of her life she mourned George, visiting his grave yearly from 1918 to 1940 and after the Second World War, until she was too old to travel.

In 1917 Edward contracted tuberculosis. Violet was at his

Violet Georgina Milner, Viscountess Milner (1872–1958), by unknown photographer, c.1921

deathbed in a Swiss sanatorium the following December. In 1921 she published, without judicious editing, sketches of Egyptian life he had sent home, as *The Leisure of an Egyptian Official*. These amused her and many readers but struck others as patronizing.

On 26 February 1921 Violet and Milner married. They divided their time between his home, Sturry Court, near Canterbury, and 14 Manchester Square, London. In May 1925 he died, on return from South Africa, from a tsetse fly bite. When her brother Leo fell ill in 1929, the still grief-stricken Violet took over his editorship of the *National Review*, owned by their family since 1893. A controversial radical right-wing paper, the '*Nat*' had recently lost money, but she restored its finances. For fifteen years after Leo's death in 1932 she travelled from Wigsell to London, even during the blitz and V1 raids, to see every issue into print. The American broadcaster Ed Murrow later declared that even more than Winston Churchill she represented the spirit of British wartime resistance. The '*Nat*' had always been anti-German and under Violet it uncompromisingly opposed the appeasement of Hitler, attacking even Milner's old friends Lord Lothian and Geoffrey Dawson. She dismissed as futile the 'internationalism' of the League of Nations—'this huge unwieldy affair'—to the annoyance of its champion, Lord Robert Cecil, her erstwhile brother-in-law. Milner's chief enemy had been Boer nationalism, so the '*Nat*' took the black South Africans' part against racial discrimination.

After the Second World War, Violet Milner was renowned for maintaining at Wigsell the aristocratic standards of the bygone Edwardian era, at minimal cost. In her last years she broadcast recollections of her past including those of Milner, whose memory she sought to keep ever fresh. Her lively memoir *My Picture Gallery* (1951) told her story up to 1900. The fragmentary manuscript of a second volume is among her papers in the Bodleian Library, Oxford.

Tough and strong-willed, articulate and argumentative, Violet Milner cared little about antagonizing those with whom she disagreed. Lord Edward's family were not fond of her, feeling she had treated him badly. Although her views on Britain's imperial destiny belonged to a vanished age, her zest, intelligence, courage, and sense of humour, which had attracted both her husbands, always drew friends, particularly writers and politicians, of every generation, to the end of her life. Her lunches at the Ladies' Empire Club and the Connaught Hotel, London, were stimulating, if alarming, for she expected informed, sparkling discussion. She died at Wigsell on 10 October 1958 and was buried beside Milner, her mother, and her sister in a monumental tomb, designed by Edwin Lutyens, at Salehurst churchyard nearby. HUGH CECIL

Sources *The Times* (11 Oct 1958) · *The Times* (15 Oct 1958) · V. Milner, *My picture gallery* (1951) · *DNB* · H. Cecil and M. Cecil, *Imperial marriage: an Edwardian war and peace* (2002)

Archives Bodl. Oxf., corresp. and papers, incl. print-outs of four BBC broadcasts · Bodl. Oxf., further corresp. and papers · NRA, priv. coll., corresp. and sketchbooks | Hatfield House Muniments, letters to third marquess of Salisbury and family · Herts. ALS, letters to Lady Desborough · King's School, Canterbury, corresp. relating to gift of Sturry Court to King's School, Canterbury

Likenesses photograph, c.1921, priv. coll. [*see illus.*] · M. Menpes, watercolour, priv. coll.; repro. in Cecil and Cecil, *Imperial marriage* · W. Sickert, sketch, repro. in Milner, *My picture gallery* · photograph, repro. in A. S. Williams, *Ladies of influence: women of the elite in inter-war Britain* (2000)

Wealth at death £26,268 12s. 3d.: probate, 1959

Milner, William (1662–1740), woollen cloth merchant, was born on 29 November 1662 at Leeds, the third and youngest son of William Milner of Leeds, a merchant. Of dissenting stock, he recalled towards the end of his long life that he had enjoyed a 'pious upbringing' and 'tolerable schole learning'. In the late 1670s and early 1680s he spent five years in the Netherlands gaining a thorough knowledge of business and accounts. On his return he married, in 1685, Mary (d. 1745), the daughter of Joshua Ibbetson, a merchant, and mayor of the town in that same year, and his wife, Mary, the daughter of Christopher Breary, lord mayor of York in 1666.

Milner maintained that he started life as a cloth merchant in Leeds from 'no very great beginnings', although it is clear that his expensive training abroad and marriage into one of the leading merchant dynasties in Leeds thrust him into the front ranks of the town's merchant élite. Certainly he was a man of enormous drive and shrewdness. In 1707 he recounted his success in exporting cloth to Hamburg to a cousin, the diarist and antiquary Ralph Thoresby, who noted:

> [I] was mightily pleased with some remarkable providences that have attended this worthy magistrate who is of good

family ... yet began the world with little, being the youngest son ... [he], with a thankful heart to God recounted to me the various stages of his growth, the first year he had commissions for £5000; the second for £10,000; the third for £15,000; the fourth for £20 or 25,000 pounds; and has now dealt for £80,000 per annum.   (*Diary of Ralph Thoresby*, 1.429–30)

There is an implausibility about this mathematical progression, but there is no doubt that Milner enjoyed more than fifty years of profitable foreign trading in cloth from the West Riding. It was, he maintained in 1736, 'such success as few ever had'. Thoresby and the coterie of antiquarians who surrounded him knew Milner as 'Alderman Million, the Bashaw of Pannopolis'.

The most tangible evidence of Milner's claim to be one of the most successful provincial merchants of the period 1680–1740 was his purchase for £17,000 in 1707 of the 2800-acre Nun Appleton estate, some 17 miles east of Leeds, from the impoverished Fairfax family. He immediately set about rebuilding the great ramshackle house in which Lord Fairfax and General Monck had planned Charles II's return. In 1716 he gave the property to his son William (created a baronet the following year) on his marriage to a daughter of the archbishop of York, Sir William Dawes.

Milner himself always lived in Simpson's Fold, Leeds, close by the River Aire, and traded to the end. He was mayor of Leeds in 1697–8 and was instrumental in securing an act of parliament (1699) to improve the rivers Aire and Calder, opening up to water carriage the great inland cloth markets of Leeds and Wakefield to Hull. It was perhaps the most notable river navigation improvement of the eighteenth century. Milner was the driving force in the first three decades of its history and largely responsible for raising the capital stock of £26,700 to effect improvement in the difficult first twenty-five years of the venture. It was a superb investment for his family, providing his great-great-grandson with an income of £9494 per annum by 1817.

Milner was also prominent in financial matters. He was deputy receiver of the land tax in Yorkshire, Northumberland, and Durham from 1697 to 1717. By the 1720s he was lending large sums of money to the Irwins of Temple Newsham, who were placed in considerable financial difficulties by the deaths, in quick succession, of the third, fourth, and fifth viscounts. He was a justice of the peace and deputy lieutenant of the West Riding of Yorkshire. In 1713, to establish the questionable patriotism of the low-church party in Leeds, he commissioned a white marble statue of Queen Anne (still to be seen in the City Art Gallery), which was erected in front of the town's Moot Hall. A convert to the established church, he was a noted benefactor in Leeds. 'What should I render to the Lord for all his benefitts?' asked Milner shortly before his death . His will revealed that he had left £20 per annum to the poor, £10 yearly for repairs to Holy Trinity Church (built in the 1720s), and £20 a year for a clergyman to read prayers each evening in the parish church. Few provincial merchants were more pious or prosperous than Milner; none straddled more easily the worlds of trade and landownership in

the early eighteenth century. He died at his home on 23 December 1740, leaving a widow, his son, Sir William Milner, bt, MP for York (1722–34), and four daughters. He was buried in Leeds parish church.   R. G. WILSON

Sources R. G. Wilson, *Gentleman merchants: the merchant community in Leeds, 1700–1830* (1971) · R. V. Taylor, ed., *The biographia Leodiensis, or, Biographical sketches of the worthies of Leeds* (1865), 150–51 · *The diary of Ralph Thoresby*, ed. J. Hunter, 2 vols. (1830) · R. Thoresby, *Ducatus Leodiensis, or, The topography of ... Leedes*, ed. T. D. Whitaker, 2nd edn (1816) · J. Risby, ed., 'Pedigrees and arms of Leeds families', 1892, Leeds Reference Library · J. Hunter, *Familiae minorum gentium*, ed. J. W. Clay, 4 vols., Harleian Society, 37–40 (1894–6) · J. Mawman, *An excursion to the highlands of Scotland and the English lakes* (1805), 33 · private information (2004)
Archives W. Yorks. AS, Leeds, DB/65
Wealth at death wealthy; £20 p.a. to the poor; £10 p.a. to Holy Trinity Church, for repairs; £20 p.a. for a clergyman to read prayers

Milnes, Richard Monckton, first Baron Houghton (1809–1885), author and politician, was born on 19 June 1809, in Bolton Street, Mayfair, Westminster, the only son of Robert Pemberton Milnes. His grandfather Richard Slater Milnes (1759–1804), MP for York 1784–1802, was the elder son of a cloth merchant of Wakefield; he bought the Fryston Hall estate outside Wakefield after 1771 and took Effingham House in Piccadilly during the 1790s.

His father Robert Pemberton Milnes (1784–1858) was born on 20 or 28 May 1784, and educated privately in Liverpool and Hackney, and at Trinity College, Cambridge (BA 1804). He was elected tory MP for Pontefract in 1806. A brilliant Commons maiden speech (15 April 1807) resulted in Spencer Perceval offering Milnes the post of chancellor of the exchequer or secretary of war in 1809. He refused, and sank into parliamentary obscurity. Unable to support the tories after they refused enfranchisement to large towns, he retired from the Commons in 1818. Milnes maintained his ancestors' dissenting views, disliked London society, and had the whimsies of a squire in *Tristram Shandy*. In 1817 he rented Thorne Hall near Doncaster and experimented in reclaiming waste land for agriculture. For many years his life was disturbed by the gambling of his brother Rodes, and he was obliged to retrench by living on the continent in 1829–35. In 1835 he inherited the Bawtry estate near Doncaster and £11,000 from the Dowager Viscountess Galway (who was both his cousin and stepmother-in-law), took possession of the Fryston estate on his mother's death, and was liberated from further troubles by the death of Rodes Milnes. Railway building on his property further revived his fortunes. He declined the offer of a barony in 1856. Milnes had married in 1808 Henrietta Maria Monckton (d. 1847), daughter of the fourth Viscount Galway, with whom he had a son, Richard Monckton, and daughter, Henrietta, who married the sixth Viscount Galway. His friend James Spencer Stanhope wrote:

> Milnes was a wild, unstable creature, at one time devoting his days and nights to reading; at another giving them up to play; at another engrossed entirely with shooting; always agreeable, clever, sarcastic, he was everything by fits and nothing long, yet always dearly loved by his friends and companions, always a straightforward man, full of high feeling and honour.   (Stirling, 1.119)

Richard Monckton Milnes, first Baron Houghton (1809–1885), by London Stereoscopic Co.

Milnes died after a gentle decline on 9 November 1858 at Fryston Hall, and was buried at Ferry Fryston.

Youth and education Richard Monckton Milnes was a delicate child. He was educated at home and at Hundhill Hall near Doncaster before matriculating from Trinity College, Cambridge, in 1827. His undergraduate friendships and literary avocations showed his pleasure in the influence of great minds. He had an early interest in Keats and Shelley. After leaving Cambridge in 1830, he enrolled at the newly formed London University. He next studied at Bonn. Though he claimed a well-informed sympathy with German culture and political aspirations throughout his life, A. W. Kinglake mocked 'the half-German school of philosophy to which Mr Milnes, for the sake of variety, will now and then give his adhesion' (Kinglake, 101). Having been raised as a Unitarian, he was attracted by turns to the Irvingites and Roman Catholicism before evolving into a self-styled 'Puseyite sceptic'. Like his father, Milnes was spry, quirky, and versatile, but far more purposive. His provocative, paradoxical chatter was developed as a subtle armour against his father's biting wit and harsh logic. In his own self-description, he was:

a man of no common imaginative perceptions, who never gave his full conviction to anything but the closest reasoning; of acute sensibilities, who always distrusted the

affections; of ideal aspirations and sensual habits; of the most cheerful manners and of the gloomiest philosophy. He hoped little and believed little, but he rarely despaired and never valued unbelief, except as leading to some larger truth. (Reid, 2.491)

Solitude had 'at once an irreligious and an immoral effect' on him: 'it makes me set great store by sensual pleasures, and in exciting my critical faculty checks the sentimental instincts, and drives me to the acutest logical distinctions' (ibid.). Despite a dilettante manner—'a most bland-smiling, semi-quizzical, affectionate, high-bred, Italianized little man, who has long olive-blonde hair, a dimple, next to no chin, and flings his arm around your neck', according to Carlyle in 1840 (*Collected Letters*, 12.9–10)—he was never a lounger. His energies were deployed as a traveller, poet, politician, patron, and host.

Poetry and prose In the early 1830s Milnes travelled extensively. The opening line of a poem written at Rome in 1834: 'To search for lore in ancient libraries', alludes to one of his abiding delights. After visiting Italy and Greece he published *Memorials of a Tour in some Parts of Greece, Chiefly Poetical* (1834), *Memorials of a Residence on the Continent, and Historical Poems* (1838), and *Memorials of many Scenes* (1840). The poems in these volumes were mixed with prose narratives and antiquarian researches; they celebrated the historic sympathies and local associations aroused on his journeys. Having in 1842–3 revisited Greece and the Ottoman empire, he published *Palm Leaves* (1844). This ambitious attempt to write poetry in an oriental tone idealizing 'Muhammadanism' was not acclaimed. 'His poems want those flashing, cleaving, bolt-like passages, that earnestness and heart … with which only these Oriental notions would become living' judged one reviewer. 'All here is calm, equable and placid … it is all a dreamy vision' (*The Athenaeum*, 30 March 1844, 292–3). His friend A. W. Kinglake challenged Milnes's version of the harem system and teased the pretensions of *Palm Leaves*: 'he loses no opportunity for showing his omnicredulity. Like the Romans of old, he opens his facile Pantheon to all the stray gods he can catch' (Kinglake, 103). Overall, Milnes's poetry was thoughtful, cultivated, but uninspired; his minor poems and lyrics are usually more successful. His few late verses, such as the elegy on David Livingstone (1873), are poor.

The cleverest of Milnes's prose writings was *One Tract More* (1841); this calm, adroit plea for toleration of Anglo-Catholicism vexed his dissenting constituents, but was praised by J. H. Newman and W. E. Gladstone. He advocated the concurrent endowment of the protestant and Roman Catholic churches in *The Real Union of England and Ireland* (1845). Milnes's letter to Lord Lansdowne, *The Events of 1848, Especially in their Relation to Great Britain* offended tories by its zealous defence of Italy against Austria. The attack on this pamphlet by George Smythe, afterwards Viscount Strangford, as the work of a 'pantaloon' provoked Milnes to challenge him to a duel: fortunately their seconds arranged the matter without a fight. Milnes's most significant publication was the *Life, Letters and Literary Remains of John Keats* (2 vols., 1848). The belated rescue of Keats from obscurity and from disparagement as a weak and unhealthy sensualist was chiefly due to Milnes. He was also a prolific contributor to reviews and magazines; his essays on Disraeli in *Hood's Magazine* (1844) and the *Edinburgh Review* (1847), and his account of Heine in the *Edinburgh Review* (1856), are representative of his critical faculties. In 1853 he was a founder of the Philobiblon Society. He wrote on Boswelliana for the society (1855) as also for the Grampian Club in 1874: Disraeli in 1869 called him 'another Boswell, but without a Johnson' (Vincent, 340). In a moderate way he served as the Boswell of such of his friends as Walter Savage Landor, Sydney Smith, and Cardinal Wiseman, all of whom he celebrated in *Monographs, Personal and Social* (1873).

Political career Milnes was elected MP for Pontefract in 1837, holding this seat until his elevation to the peerage in 1863. He hoped to figure as more than a littérateur, and was encouraged by distinguished friends who expected great things of him. Initially he was a tory follower of Peel, with whom he voted to repeal the corn laws in 1846, but he developed an antipathy for the premier even deeper than for his policy. Soon afterwards he severed his old political connections, moving, like many of Peel's followers, but more ardently than most, into the Liberal Party. He had sought the under-secretaryship for foreign affairs as early as 1841, and was several times rebuffed; Peel's lofty rejection of his application in December 1845 confirmed his disaffection. Milnes supported the administration of Lord John Russell which took office in June 1846, and henceforth voted with the Liberals. In politics he was always the friend of religious and civil liberty. He supported factory education, mechanics' institutes, penny savings banks, public readings, and other progressive causes. In 1842 he was instrumental in the passage of the Copyright Act. He moved the Deceased Wife's Sister Marriage Bill in 1862 and worked for the repeal of the Contagious Diseases Acts. Few other landed gentlemen in the Commons supported, as he did, the North against the Confederacy, or shared his sympathies with republicanism. He was the most attractive type of ameliorative reformer who knew the corruption of humankind and had no zeal for purifying humanity or purging error; no one could have been less like De Maistre. His compassion was the counter-side to his candid interest in punishment and venality. He voted for the abolition of capital punishment in 1840 and yet collected the autographs of hangmen; his visit to the public execution of François Courvoisier is described in Thackeray's essay 'Going to See a Man Hanged'. Though he supported franchise extension to the working class and women's suffrage, his pamphlet *Thoughts on Purity of Election* (1842) argued that bribery was not only essential but beneficial in politics. In 1846 he introduced the bill establishing reformatory schools for juvenile criminals, and was afterwards president of Redhill Reformatory; yet he was fascinated by flogging and collected books on flagellation, which constituted part of his extensive collection of pornography.

Milnes's parliamentary speeches were 'a signal for emptying the House', Emerson noted in 1848. 'He makes bad speeches of exquisite infelicity, & joins in the laugh against himself' (*Journals*, 10.530–31). Milnes's elaborate oratory, however, suited formal parliamentary occasions such as the death of Cavour (7 June 1861). Politically he was cautious and disliked extremes. With friends in all camps he was incapable of acrimonious party feeling, which was one reason for his political failure. Abstract ideas and intellectual movements had little influence on him, but personal factors and emotional reactions counted for too much. He desired reconciliation of the church and the mundane, idealism and materialism, conservatism and liberalism, mystic contemplation and sensuality. Visiting Paris during the revolution of 1848 he characteristically fraternized with both sides. His poem 'Pleasure and Pain' shows his sense of the contradictoriness of things:

> Vain the distinction our senses are teaching,
> For Pain has its Heaven, and Pleasure its Hell!
> (lines 19–20)

When Peel ignored Milnes's claims to an under-secretaryship, Carlyle consoled him: 'there is only one post fit for you, and that is the office of perpetual president of the Heaven and Hell Amalgamation Society' (Reid, 1.187).

Milnes, who was himself a sweet and graceful singer, reverenced creativity. He had an affinity with madly ungovernable men like Landor and Charles Algernon Swinburne. Harsh, refractory, or difficult individuals like Carlyle never deterred him. He was singularly free of literary resentment or envy, and had a generous respect for intelligence and genius. He was quick to appreciate young talent. He sympathized with literary rebels, and encouraged or financed struggling poets. For Alfred Tennyson he obtained a pension (1845), and for Coventry Patmore a job in the British Museum (1846). In 1860–61 he eased the circumstances of the dying consumptive poet David Gray, and afterwards fostered his reputation. He was a benevolent patron who enjoyed flattery. Milnes never pretended to be heroic, profound, or original, but had a versatile, graceful, and useful life. He was both self-indulgent and idealistic; he aspired to noble thoughts and constructive deeds.

Society host In emulation of Samuel Rogers, Milnes was famous for holding breakfast parties in London at which all the geniuses and celebrities of the day assembled. These breakfasts, Connop Thirlwall wrote in 1867, 'were always among the pleasantest, partly from his knowing everybody, and partly from his fancy for bringing the apparently most incongruous people together' (*Letters to a Friend*, 97). Typically, when William Macready breakfasted with Milnes (1 July 1843) he 'met a captain from China, a Mr Rowley, from the borders of Abyssinia, Carlyle, Chevalier Bunsen, Lord Morpeth, and several other agreeable people' (*Diaries*, 2.215). Breakfast (12 June 1846) with Richard Cobden, Disraeli, Count d'Orsay, Kinglake, Louis Napoleon, and Suleiman Pasha, however, turned into a feast of antipathies. George Eliot's fellow breakfast guests (13 June 1865) included the bishop of Minnesota, Leopold von Ranke, Sir James Lacaita, and the Polish-born Louis Wolowski, a French economist and politician.

After 1836 Milnes entertained generously at Fryston

Hall, which was easily accessible from London by coach and later railway. Fryston was described by Carlyle in 1841 as 'a large irregular pile, of various ages, rising up among ragged old wood, in a rough large park … chiefly beautiful because it does not set up for beauty' (*Collected Letters*, 13.80). The house is depicted as Dickiefield in Laurence Oliphant's satire *Piccadilly* (1870), with Milnes figuring as Lord Dickiefield. Fryston's eighteenth-century front, containing the drawing-room and long library, was gutted by fire in 1876. This ruined many of Milnes's books, which were a special feature of the place. There were many autograph letters, manuscripts, presentation volumes, rare editions, and fine bindings. He collected books on spiritual research, religious eccentricity, genealogies, criminology, and gastronomy, as well as French novels, German treatises, and Italian classics. He had a choice collection of erotica and other curiosities, including a lock of Keats's hair and the skin of a murderer inserted in the pages of a volume of criminal trials.

Emerson summarized Milnes in 1848: 'fat, easy, affable and obliging; a little careless and slovenly in his dress' (*Journals*, 10.530). John Lothrop Motley described him in 1867 as voracious for conversation and life: 'Hearty, jolly, paradoxical, genial' (*Correspondence*, 1.271). Milnes is brilliantly represented by Disraeli as Mr Vavasour in *Tancred* (1847):

a real poet, and a troubadour, as well as a member of Parliament; travelled, sweet-tempered, and good-hearted; amusing and clever. With catholic sympathies and an eclectic turn of mind, Mr Vavasour saw something good in everybody and everything, which is certainly amiable, and perhaps just, but disqualifies a man in some degree for the business of life, which requires for its conduct a certain degree of prejudice.

Disraeli, though, was one of his less grateful guests:

Individuals met at his hospitable house who had never met before, but who for years had been cherishing in solitude mutual detestation, with all the irritable exaggeration of the literary character. … He prided himself on figuring as the social medium by which rival reputations became acquainted, and paid each other in his presence the compliments which veiled their ineffable disgust.

Yet Disraeli admired his versatility and ubiquity: 'He was everywhere, and at everything; he had gone down in a diving-bell and up in a balloon. As for his acquaintances, he was welcomed in every land … emperor and king, jacobin and carbonaro, alike cherished him.' One sentence of Disraeli's encapsulated Milnes: 'His life was a gyration of energetic curiosity; an insatiable whirl of social celebrity' (Disraeli, chap. 14). Henry James met Milnes later in life. 'A battered and world-wrinkled old mortal, with a restless and fidgety vanity, but with an immense fund of real kindness and humane feeling', James reported in 1879. 'He is not personally fascinating, though as a general thing he talks very well, but I like his sociable, democratic, sympathetic, inquisitive old temperament' (*Henry James: Letters*, 2.208).

Family and finale His friend Alexis de Tocqueville believed that Milnes in 1848 was infatuated with George Sand, for whom he gave a disastrous dinner to which he invited her

former lover, Prosper Merimée. Milnes courted Florence Nightingale in 1849. He married in 1851, the Hon. Annabella Hungerford Crewe (1814–1874), daughter of the second Baron Crewe. They had two daughters and two sons, of whom the elder was stillborn and the younger, Robert Offley Ashburton *Milnes, was later created marquess of Crewe. Milnes was supposedly called 'a Miss Nancy' by Thackeray (Pope-Hennessy, 1.133), but twentieth-century suppositions of his bisexuality are unproven. Suspicions of his libertinism originated during his travels in Muslim lands in the 1840s, and were more eloquent of British prurience and insularity than of the facts of his life; his responsibility for corrupting Swinburne has certainly been exaggerated.

Milnes was created Baron Houghton on 20 August 1863. He became DCL of Oxford (1855) and LLD of Edinburgh (1877). He was president of the Statistical Society (1865–7), FRS (1868), FSA (1876), secretary for foreign correspondence of the Royal Academy from 1878 until his death, trustee of the British Museum and of the Royal Geographic Society, and one of the earliest vice-presidents of the Society of Authors. He succeeded Carlyle as president of the London Library in 1881.

Lord Houghton died of angina pectoris on 10 August 1885 at a hotel in Vichy, France, and was buried on 20 August at St Andrew's Church, Ferry Fryston. 'Monckton Milnes was a social power in London, possibly greater than Londoners themselves quite understood, for in London society as elsewhere, the dull and the ignorant made a large majority, and dull men always laughed at Monckton Milnes', wrote Henry Adams.

Every bore was used to talk familiarly about 'Dicky Milnes' or the 'cool of the evening'; and of course he himself affected social eccentricity, challenging ridicule with the indifference of one who knew himself to be the first wit in London, and a maker of men. … Behind his almost Falstaffian mask and laugh of Silenus, he carried a fine, broad and high intelligence which no one questioned … he was one of two or three men who went everywhere, knew everybody, talked of everything, and had the ear of Ministers. … He was a voracious reader, a strong critic, an art connoisseur in certain directions, a collector of books, but above all he was a man of the world by profession, and loved the contacts—perhaps the collisions—of society … Milnes was the good-nature of London; the Gargantuan type of its refinement and coarseness; the most universal figure of May Fair. (Adams, chap. 6)

RICHARD DAVENPORT-HINES

Sources *The Times* (12 Aug 1885) · *The Spectator* (15 Aug 1885) · *The Athenaeum* (15 Aug 1885), 209 · J. Pope-Hennessy, *Monckton Milnes*, 2 vols. (1949–51) · T. W. Reid, *The life, letters, and friendships of Richard Monckton Milnes, first Lord Houghton*, 2 vols. (1890) · Lord Quinton, 'Richard Monckton Milnes', *Founders and followers* (1992), 23–46 · A. M. W. Stirling, *The letter-bag of Lady Elizabeth Spencer-Stanhope*, 2 vols. (1913) · *The collected letters of Thomas and Jane Welsh Carlyle*, ed. K. J. Fielding, 12–13 (1985–7) · *Disraeli, Derby and the conservative party: journals and memoirs of Edward Henry, Lord Stanley, 1849–1869*, ed. J. R. Vincent (1978) · *Letters to a friend by Connop Thirlwall*, ed. A. P. Stanley (1881) · *The diaries of William Charles Macready, 1833–1851*, ed. W. Toynbee, 2 vols. (1912) · H. Adams, *The education of Henry Adams* (1907), chap. 6 · B. Disraeli, *Tancred* (1847), chap. 14 · *The journals and miscellaneous notebooks of Ralph Waldo Emerson*, ed. M. Sealts (1973), 10.530–33 · *The correspondence of John Lothrop Motley*, ed. G. W. Curtis,

2 vols. (1889) • [A. W. Kinglake], review, *QR*, 75 (1844–5), 94–125 • *Henry James: letters*, ed. L. Edel, 2: *1875–1883* (1978) • GEC, *Peerage*, new edn

Archives Duke U., Perkins L., corresp. and papers • Harvard U., Houghton L., papers • Hunt. L., letters • NL Scot., letters • NRA, priv. coll., papers • Ransom HRC, papers • Sheff. Arch., corresp. and papers • Trinity Cam., corresp. and papers • U. Nott. L., corresp. • U. Reading L., letters | BL, corresp. with Sir Charles Dilke, Add. MSS 43898 • BL, corresp. with W. E. Gladstone, Add. MSS 44215–44786 • BL, letters to Lord Holland and Lady Holland, Add. MSS 52064, 52126 • BL, corresp. with Florence Nightingale, Add. MSS 45796–45805 • BL, corresp. with Sir Robert Peel, Add. MSS 40426–40602 • BL, letters to Royal Literary Fund, loan 96 • Bodl. Oxf., letters to W. D. Christie • Bodl. Oxf., letters to Arthur Clough • Bodl. Oxf., letters to Benjamin Disraeli • Bodl. Oxf., letters to Sir William Harcourt • Bodl. Oxf., letters to Sir William Harcourt, and typescripts of corresp. • Camden Public Library, London, corresp. with Dilke • CUL, letters to Lord Acton • CUL, letters to his son, Robert Milnes • Keats House, Hampstead, London, corresp. with Sir Charles Dilke relating to a biography of Keats • King's AC Cam., letters to Oscar Browning • Lincoln Central Library, letters to Hallam Tennyson • Mitchell L., Glas., Glasgow City Archives, letters to Sir William Stirling-Maxwell • NL Scot., letters to William Blackwood & Sons • NL Wales, letters to George Stovin Venables • NRA, priv. coll., corresp. with fourth earl of Harrowby • Sandon Hall, Staffordshire, Harrowby Manuscript Trust, corresp. with fourth earl of Harrowby • Trinity Cam., letters to William Whewell • U. Southampton L., letters to Lord Palmerston • W. Yorks. AS, Leeds, corresp. with Lord Canning • Yale U., Beinecke L., corresp. with Frederick Locker and his wife

Likenesses Count D'Orsay, pencil and crayon drawing, 1839 • R. J. Lane, lithograph, pubd 1839 (after Count D'Orsay), BM, NPG • G. Richmond, chalk drawing, *c*.1844, NPG • J. Severn, oils, 1847 • G. Richmond, pastel drawing, *c*.1851, NPG • J. & C. Watkins, carte-de-visite, *c*.1870, NPG • R. Lehmann, drawing, 1871, BM • R. Lehmann, oils, 1883 • W. W. Story, marble bust, *c*.1886, Trinity Cam. • Ape [C. Pellegrini], watercolour study, NPG; repro. in *VF* (3 Sept 1870) • W. Holl, stipple (after G. Richmond), BM • London Stereoscopic Co., carte-de-visite, NPG [*see illus.*] • lithograph, NPG

Wealth at death £27,422 9*s*. 7*d*.: probate, 19 Dec 1885, *CGPLA Eng. & Wales* • under £35,000—Robert Milnes: probate, 9 Nov 1859, *CGPLA Eng. & Wales*

Milnes, Robert Offley Ashburton Crewe-, marquess of Crewe

(1858–1945), politician, was born at 16 Upper Brook Street, London, on 12 January 1858, the only son of Richard Monckton-*Milnes, first Baron Houghton (1809–1885), and Annabella Hungerford (*d*. 1874), daughter of the second Baron Crewe. He was educated at Winton House, near Winchester, Harrow School, and Trinity College, Cambridge, where he graduated in 1880. In that year he was engaged to Sybil Marcia (1857–1887), daughter of Sir Frederick Graham, third baronet, of Netherby, and they married on 3 June. Milnes shared his father's Liberalism and was appointed assistant private secretary to Lord Granville, foreign secretary in Gladstone's second ministry, in April 1883. In 1884 he was adopted as Liberal candidate for Barnsley, but he never contested the seat, as the death of his father in August 1885 consigned him to the House of Lords as Baron Houghton. He was made a Liberal whip in the Lords and lord-in-waiting to Queen Victoria when Gladstone formed his third ministry in January 1886. He apparently inherited his father's view that England was responsible for Ireland's misfortune, and his loyalty to his party during the Irish home-rule crisis left him one of the few Gladstonian peers after 1886, ensuring his

Robert Offley Ashburton Crewe-Milnes, marquess of Crewe (1858–1945), by Walter Frederick Osborne

subsequent political influence. The death of his wife in September 1887, though, led him to seek to leave politics. He resigned as Liberal whip in order to study agriculture at the Royal Agricultural College, Cirencester, only to be prevented by illness from taking up the course. Instead he devoted himself to travel (he visited Egypt in 1889) and to his literary interests: a volume of poems entitled *Stray Verses, 1889–90* was written on the journey to Egypt and he produced a translation, *The Songs of Béranger*, in 1889. Further family tragedy struck in March 1890, with the death of Houghton's eight-year-old son Richard Charles Rodes (1882–1890).

On the Liberals' return to office in 1892 Houghton, who had emphasized in print his commitment to home rule since the 1886 crisis, was appointed lord lieutenant of Ireland and given the difficult task of conveying Gladstonian Irish policy to the unsympathetic Queen Victoria. He remained in office after Rosebery succeeded Gladstone in 1894. In that year Houghton's uncle the third Baron Crewe died; Houghton succeeded to the Crewe estates and, by royal licence, took the name of Crewe as a prefix to that of Milnes (8 June 1894). When the Liberals fell from power in 1895, he was created earl of Crewe (17 July).

On 20 April 1899 Crewe married the eighteen-year-old Lady Margaret Etienne Hannah (Peggy) Primrose, daughter of the fifth earl of Rosebery. He was less critical than his father-in-law, though, of radical opposition to British involvement in the Second South African War: he acted as conciliator and healer of Liberal divisions and never joined Rosebery's Liberal League. As Rosebery distanced himself from the Liberals during the last months of the long Unionist ascendancy in 1905, Crewe was credited with devising the 'step-by-step' Irish policy which would limit the liability represented by the Liberals' commitment to home rule, and he became lord president of the council in the government formed by Campbell-Bannerman in December 1905. This appointment launched a long period of continuous cabinet office during which Crewe became a pivotal figure in the Liberal governments from 1905 to 1916, less because of his skills in policy making or public oratory, which were minimal, than because he won the trust of those who did lead. Campbell-Bannerman thought none of his cabinet colleagues straighter, wiser, or more helpful than Crewe, while Asquith considered him to have the best political judgement in the cabinet. Crewe would become the principal political aide and confidant to Asquith during the eight years of his premiership and a virtually automatic appointee to the many *ad hoc* committees set up to handle specific crises before and during the First World War.

When Asquith became prime minister in 1908 Crewe succeeded Lord Elgin at the Colonial Office, but his appointment in succession to Lord Ripon as Liberal leader in the House of Lords in the same year did more to secure his public prominence, by making him the principal defender of Liberal policy in a Unionist upper house which was becoming feverishly hostile to the Liberal government and increasingly ready to sabotage its measures. Crewe had resented the peers' wrecking of the 1906 Education Bill, in which he took a strong personal interest, and which he had attempted to save by convening a cross-party conference of peers. He had been unable to prevent the damage done to subsequent education, licensing, and land bills by the Unionist majority in the Lords. The naturally conciliatory Crewe was thrust into the front line of constitutional conflict during the crisis prompted by Lloyd George's radical budget of 1909. Crewe was generally unsympathetic to the budget itself and privately resented the chancellor's demagogic language in his Limehouse speech of 1909, but he had no time for the nihilism of the Unionist peers. When the Liberals' qualified victory in the election of January 1910 led to the passage of the budget and shifted attention to the blocking powers of the Lords themselves, Crewe participated in the constitutional conference which sat for five months in 1910; characteristically, he was said to have sympathized with Lloyd George's proposals for a cross-party government to handle the crisis. When the conference collapsed, however, Crewe (who had earlier in the year been one of those on the right wing of the cabinet arguing for reform of the Lords' composition) participated, with Asquith, in the controversial meeting with the new king, George V, at which the monarch was persuaded to promise the creation of new Liberal peers, if necessary, to approve the curtailment of the Lords' right of veto should the Liberals win a second election. George V remained suspicious of Crewe thereafter, believing that advantage had been taken of his inexperience. Crewe none the less led the negotiations with Lord Cromer and the archbishop of

Canterbury to secure sufficient Unionist support to pass the 1911 Parliament Bill, which limited the Lords' veto powers.

Amid the constitutional crisis, in September 1910, Crewe was appointed secretary of state for India; he was thus responsible for the Delhi durbar of 1911, when George V became the first reigning monarch actually to visit India and Crewe the first India secretary to travel through the country. In recognition of his work in preparing this masterpiece of imperial pageantry Crewe was made a marquess in 1911, with the additional title of earl of Madeley. This became the courtesy title of his short-lived second son, Richard George Archibald John Lucian Hungerford, known as Jack (1911–1922). Crewe also presided over the transfer of the raj capital from Calcutta to Delhi, and was responsible for the successful appointment of Lutyens to design New Delhi.

In 1914 Crewe worked with Lloyd George in the negotiations with the Bank of England over currency and exchange arrangements in wartime which calmed the financial panic stimulated by the outbreak of war. He placed his London home, Crewe House, in Curzon Street, at the disposal of the government, and it became the centre for the production of war propaganda. On the formation of the Asquith coalition in May 1915 he became lord president of the council once again, before moving to become president of the Board of Education in 1916. Education interested him, and it is interesting to speculate what role he would have played in post-war educational reconstruction, but the break-up of the coalition and the Liberal split in December 1916 denied him the chance. Crewe, who had been loyal to his party leadership over Irish home rule, the Second South African War, and the constitutional crisis, remained loyal to Asquith when the prime minister fell victim to the coup promoted by Lloyd George and Bonar Law. Asquith's departure from office ended eleven years of continuous cabinet office for Crewe, and virtually ended his career as a national politician. His decision in 1917 to become chairman of the London county council (LCC)—far more of an honorific post than when his father-in-law had held it in 1889—amounted to a recognition of the fact. So, more strikingly, did his acceptance of the post of ambassador to France in October 1922; he served for almost six years. He could not, of course, have anticipated the circumstances which led to his return to cabinet office for a ten-week stint as secretary for war in Ramsay MacDonald's first National Government in August 1931. Without a parliamentary constituency to defend, he did not, unlike his Liberal colleagues, feel trapped in the national coalition, and held no government post after the general election of November 1931. He supported the decision of the Samuelite Liberals to withdraw from the National Government over the issue of free trade in 1932, and from 1936 to the end of 1944 he led the independent Liberals in the House of Lords.

The fourth marquess of Salisbury described Crewe in 1945 as 'perhaps the last of the Whig statesmen'; his biographer considered him more radical than whig (Pope-

Hennessy, 54). Crewe's whiggishness was more temperamental than ideological. Disposed by nature and training to conceal all emotion, he recoiled from the fanaticism of Edwardian politics, involving himself in the attempts to resolve both the 1906 Education Bill dispute and the crisis over the House of Lords by mediation. In 1912 he sought to resolve the embittered party dispute over the future of Ulster over a round of golf at Deeside with the Unionist leader Bonar Law. He despised the platform demagogy of Lloyd George, whom he neither liked nor admired—an attitude which perhaps reflected his own unease as a public speaker (Pope-Hennessy, 150). 'Slow of thought and slower of speech' (David, 120–21), according to Charles Hobhouse, Crewe was an uncomfortable orator, whose speeches were punctuated, as his biographer recalled, by 'prolonged moments—almost minutes—of hesitation while he fastidiously chose the correct word' (Pope-Hennessy, x). His cabinet colleague Edwin Montagu claimed to have a constituent whose wife had lost her sanity listening to Crewe speak for an hour and a half on the land question. It is questionable whether his radicalism amounted to much more than a loyalty to the touchstone policy of Irish home rule, though Hobhouse considered him, like Sir Edward Grey, to be more radical than was widely believed. But he was not whig enough to contemplate crossing the floor. In fact he remained a partisan, loyal to the Liberal Party in its moments of tension and division—in 1886, in 1900–01, in 1909–11, and in 1916. Before 1914 his position as a patient and clear-sighted Liberal in a hostile House of Lords gave him political significance and influence, but the collapse of the Liberal Party as a party of government during the First World War made his supple skills otiose. 'War smothers all the aspirations of Liberalism', he wrote in 1940, and war certainly smothered his active political career (Crewe-Milnes, 481). After 1916 his public role became that of the elder statesman and 'safe pair of hands': he guided the London county council, filled the Paris embassy during a tense period in Anglo-French relations (without apparently doing much to shape policy), served in the first National Government during the emergency of 1931, and joined a group of 'half a dozen old stagers', in Austen Chamberlain's words (*Austen Chamberlain Diary*, 518), to advise Baldwin on the handling of the abdication crisis in 1936.

Crewe's hands were less safe in private than in public affairs. 'Both extravagant and poorly advised' (Crewe, 34), according to his grandson, he inherited 30,000 acres and died with 6000, having sold Crewe Hall in Cheshire and a family home in Yorkshire. He regarded money and business as 'unmentionable topics', and preferred reading (he inherited his father's library of 24,000 books, but disposed of the collection of 'pornographic and sadic literature and manuscripts' included in it), writing poetry—his *A Harrow Grave in Flanders* would find a place in several anthologies—and country pursuits, including racing and the breeding of shorthorn cattle (Crewe, 34; Pope-Hennessy, 24). He published a leaden official biography of his father-in-law Rosebery in 1931. He was lord lieutenant of the county of London (1912–44), an elder brother of

Trinity House, and chancellor of Sheffield University (1918–44).

The tight self-control that made Crewe unfailingly courteous to strangers could also make him appear, according to his second wife, 'rather formal and aloof'. Asquith considered dining at Crewe's 'a great bore' (*Letters to Venetia Stanley*, 51), while playing golf with him became a trial on account of 'the extraordinary deliberation of his methods' (ibid., 549). Conduct trying to his friends shaded into callousness towards his family: he embarked on a lengthy foreign tour in 1890, when his eight-year-old son, already motherless, was dying, and upstaged his first daughter on her 'coming out' by announcing his engagement to a woman a year her senior. His grandson remembered Crewe as 'a man of few feelings' (Crewe, 24).

Crewe died at West Horsley Place, the house near Leatherhead which he had acquired in 1931, on 20 June 1945. As his two sons had died before him, his peerages became extinct. He was survived by his second wife and four daughters, Annabel Hungerford (*b.* 1881), Celia Hermione (*b.* 1884), and (Helen) Cynthia [*see* Colville, Lady (Helen) Cynthia] by his first marriage and Mary Evelyn Hungerford (*b.* 1915) by his second.   JOHN DAVIS

Sources J. Pope-Hennessy, *Lord Crewe, 1858–1945: the likeness of a liberal* (1955) · R. O. A. Crewe-Milnes, 'The eclipse of liberalism', *The Fortnightly*, 153 (1940) · Q. Crewe, *Well I forget the rest* (1991) · *DNB* · B. K. Murray, *The people's budget, 1909/10: Lloyd George and liberal politics* (1980) · N. Blewett, *The peers, the parties and the people* (1972) · E. O'Halpin, *The decline of the union: British government in Ireland, 1892–1920* (1987) · *The Austen Chamberlain diary letters: the correspondence of Sir Austen Chamberlain with his sisters Hilda and Ida, 1916–1937*, ed. R. C. Self, CS, 5th ser., 5 (1995) · *Inside Asquith's cabinet: from the diaries of Charles Hobhouse*, ed. E. David (1977) · J. O. Fair, *British inter party conferences: a study of the procedure of conciliation in British politics* (1980) · GEC, *Peerage* · H. H. Asquith: letters to Venetia Stanley, ed. M. Brock and E. Brock (1982) · J. A. Spender, *The life of the Right Hon. Sir Henry Campbell-Bannerman*, 2 vols. (1923) · Burke, *Peerage* · *WWW*, 1941–50 · *CGPLA Eng. & Wales* (1947)

Archives CUL, corresp. and papers · CUL, corresp. and MSS relating to India · ICL, corresp. and papers relating to Imperial College · NL Scot., corresp. and MSS relating to Rosebery biography | BL, corresp. with Arthur James Balfour, Add. MS 49739 · BL, corresp. with Sir Henry Campbell-Bannerman, Add. MS 41213 · BL, corresp. with Lord Gladstone, Add. MS 45996 · BL, letters to W. E. Gladstone, Add. MSS 44499–44522 · BL, corresp. with Lord Ripon, Add. MS 43552 · BL OIOC, corresp. with Lord Curzon, Eur. MSS F 111–112 · BL OIOC, corresp. with Sir G. Fleetwood Wilson, MS Eur. E 224 · Bodl. Oxf., corresp. with Herbert Asquith · Bodl. Oxf., letters to William Montgomery Cook · Bodl. Oxf., corresp. with H. A. L. Fisher · Bodl. Oxf., letters to Lewis Harcourt · Bodl. Oxf., corresp. with Lord Kimberley · Bodl. Oxf., corresp. with Lord Selborne · CAC Cam., letters to Austen Chamberlain · CAC Cam., letters to Lord Curzon · CAC Cam., letters to J. Ramsay MacDonald · CAC Cam., corresp. with Sir Eric Phipps · CUL, letters to Lord Hardinge · HLRO, corresp. with Andrew Bonar Law · HLRO, corresp. with Herbert Samuel · JRL, letters to *The Guardian* · Lpool RO, corresp. with seventeenth earl of Derby · NA Scot., corresp. with Lord Lothian · NL Aus., corresp. with Alfred Deakin · NL Scot., corresp. with Lord Haldane · NL Scot., corresp. with earl of Minto · NRA, priv. coll., letters to Lord Aberdeen relating to Ireland · Nuffield Oxf., corresp. with Lord Emmott · Nuffield Oxf., corresp. with Mottistone · PRO, corresp. with Lord Cromer, FO633 · PRO, corresp. with Lord Kitchener, 30/57; WO159 · Royal Society of Literature, London, letters to Royal Society of Literature · Surrey HC, letters to earl of Onslow · U. Birm. L., corresp. with Austen Chamberlain · U. Leeds, Brotherton L., letters to Sir Edmund Gosse · U. Newcastle, Robinson L., corresp. with Walter Runciman · U. Nott. L., corresp. with Lady Galway

Likenesses W. Carter, oils, exh. RA 1893, University of Sheffield · Bassano, five photographs, 1895, NPG · A. McEvoy, oils, 1918, Great London Council · W. Rothenstein, pastel drawing, 1918, University of Sheffield · W. Rothenstein, pencil drawing, 1918, NPG · M. Beerbohm, caricature, 1919, Savile Club, London · M. Beerbohm, caricature, 1924, AM Oxf. · W. Stoneman, photograph, 1925, NPG · W. Stoneman, photograph, 1938, NPG · H. Furniss, pen-and-ink caricature, NPG · W. F. Osborne, oils, NPG [*see illus.*] · J. Russell & Sons, photograph, NPG · Spy [L. Ward], caricature, chromolithograph, NPG; repro. in *VF* (10 Dec 1892) · portraits, repro. in Pope-Hennessy, *Lord Crewe*

Wealth at death £122,494 14s. 8d.: probate, 8 Feb 1947, *CGPLA Eng. & Wales*

Milnes, Robert Pemberton (1784–1858). *See under* Milnes, Richard Monckton, first Baron Houghton (1809–1885).

Milred [Mildred] (*d.* 774/5), bishop of Worcester, was one of the most important literary figures in eighth-century England. His name is Anglo-Saxon (the form with elided *d* is now generally preferred to that of Mildred), but his origins are unknown. He became bishop of Worcester in 743 according to John of Worcester and was certainly bishop by 745. He must have been appointed to succeed his ageing predecessor, Wilfrith (*d.* 744/5?), during the latter's lifetime, since they both attest a charter (*AS chart.*, S 98) by which Milred obtained exemption from King Æthelbald (*d.* 757) from tolls on two ships at London. This suggests that Milred was engaged in trade. He must have played a part in building up his see's control over the originally independent monasteries (or 'minsters') of his diocese. For instance, Milred granted Old Sodbury to a certain Eanbald for so long as someone in his family was willing to take orders; otherwise it was to revert to the see. Similarly, in 774 he received the monastery of Withington and made it over to the abbess of Twyning on condition that both monasteries reverted to Worcester after her death. Thegn-abbots, previously characteristic of the diocese, disappear during Milred's episcopate, perhaps because he succeeded in enforcing the opposition to lay control voiced at the council of 'Clofesho' in 747, which he attended.

In 753 Milred visited the English missionaries in Germany, Boniface and Lull; perhaps he took with him a manuscript of Jerome (Würzburg, Universitätsbibliothek, MS M.p.th.q.2), which bears the ex-libris of Cuthswith, who had been an abbess in his diocese in the seventh century. On his return Milred heard about Boniface's martyrdom (754), and wrote an eloquent letter to Bishop Lull, with whom he had formed a bond of friendship. The letter, which is preserved in the Vienna manuscript of Lull's correspondence (Tangl, no. 112), shows familiarity with ancient and Christian commonplaces of consolation, in particular those in Sulpicius Severus's second epistle, and draws additional comfort from Boniface's status as a national martyr. A similar note is struck by Archbishop Cuthbert's letter on the same occasion (Tangl, no. 111). Milred's letter shows his familiarity with Virgil and a postscript further reveals his literary interests: he apologizes

for not sending 'liber pyrpyri metri', that is, a manuscript of Optatianus Porfyrius's 'picture poems', because [Arch]bishop Cuthbert had not returned it. Other evidence for Milred's interest in poetry is provided by verses naming him (as author or recipient) in a tenth-century manuscript from St Augustine's Abbey, Canterbury (BL, Cotton MS Vitellius A.xix). Moreover, a copy of a book of epigrams compiled by or for Milred was seen and excerpted at Malmesbury by John Leland in the sixteenth century. A fragment of this manuscript, datable to the tenth century, survives as Urbana–Champaign, University of Illinois Library, MS 128, and further excerpts survive in the works of William of Malmesbury. Milred was evidently interested not only in inscriptional verse from the continent, and especially Rome, but also in the Latin poetry of Bede and of more local writers, such as the verses composed by Archbishop Cuthbert while bishop of the Magonsæte. Milred died in either 774 (so the Anglo-Saxon Chronicle) or 775 (so John of Worcester). In the sixteenth century the poet and antiquary John Leland reported that 'S. Mildredus' was said to be buried at Berkswell, Warwickshire.   PATRICK SIMS-WILLIAMS

Sources M. Tangl, ed., *Die Briefe des heiligen Bonifatius und Lullus*, MGH Epistolae Selectae, 1 (Berlin, 1916) · P. Sims-Williams, *Religion and literature in western England, 600–800* (1990) · P. Sims-Williams, *Britain and early Christian Europe: studies in early medieval history and culture* (1995) · *AS chart.*, S 98 · D. J. Sheerin, 'John Leland and Milred of Worcester', *Manuscripta*, 21 (1977), 172–80 · M. Lapidge, 'Some remnants of Bede's lost *Liber epigrammatum*', *EngHR*, 90 (1975), 798–820 · L. Wallach, 'The Urbana Anglo-Saxon sylloge of Latin inscriptions', *Poetry and poetics from Ancient Greece to the Renaissance*, ed. G. M. Kirkwood (1975), 134–51 · R. M. Thomson, *William of Malmesbury* (1987) · John of Worcester, *Chron.*, s.a. 775 · BL, Cotton MS Vitellius A.xix · J. Blair, 'A handlist of Anglo-Saxon saints', *Local saints and local churches in the early medieval West*, ed. A. Thacker and R. Sharpe (2002), 495–565

Archives BL, Cotton MS Vitellius A.xix · Nationalbibliothek, Vienna, MS Vindobensis 751 · University of Illinois, Urbana-Champaign, MS 128

Milroy, Gavin (1805–1886), physician and epidemiologist, was born in Edinburgh, the son of Andrew Milroy, jeweller. Educated locally at the high school and then at Edinburgh University, Milroy distinguished himself in the study of medicine and became MRCS (Edin.) in 1824; he graduated MD in 1828. He was an enormously popular student, renowned for both his kindness and his intellectual ability. He was known among his fellow students as 'Little Milroy'—a term of endearment as much as a reflection on his diminutive stature. Milroy also played an important part in the foundation of the Hunterian medical society, established to commemorate John Hunter.

After graduating Milroy left Edinburgh to take up a post as assistant to a physician in London, but he remained there for only a short time as he had a strong inclination to visit foreign lands. To this end he found a position as medical officer with the government's mail packet service, which took him to the Mediterranean and to the West Indies. It was in the Mediterranean that Milroy first encountered the system of quarantine, which was imposed as a precaution against plague on vessels sailing from the Levant. He believed quarantine to be an unnecessary restriction on trade and liberty, and was to devote much of his professional life to its abolition.

Milroy's first opportunity to attack the system of quarantine came when he was offered a post on the influential periodical, the *Medico-Chirurgical Review* (later the *British and Foreign Medical Chirurgical Review*). After the death of its founder and editor—the Anglo-Indian physician James Johnson—in 1845, Milroy came to edit the journal jointly with Richard Grainger. On 4 January 1844 he had married Sophia Chapman, daughter of William Francis Chapman; there were no children. Milroy made his mark as a medical writer when, in 1846, it fell to him to review a report, *La peste et les quarantines* (1845), presented by René Prus to the Paris Academy. After translating the report for the benefit of his readers, Milroy embarked on what was to become a famous critique of the quarantine system, *Quarantine and the Plague* (1846). He attacked it not only for its effects on commerce but claimed that the contagionist theories on which it was based were not sufficient to account for the spread of diseases such as the plague and cholera. With many contemporaries, such as Edwin Chadwick and Thomas Southwood Smith, he believed that the incidence of these diseases depended on local conditions, and he advocated sanitary reform as the only sure way of preventing their occurrence. He was admitted a licentiate of the Royal College of Physicians in 1847, and elected a fellow in 1853.

Milroy's robust critique of quarantine soon brought him to the attention of government, which was equally anxious to be rid of quarantine for commercial reasons. It is interesting that his diatribe against quarantine came in the same year that the protectionist corn laws had been repealed. The congruence between Milroy's views and the prevailing ethos of free trade led to his employment as a superintendent medical inspector of the General Board of Health during the cholera epidemic of 1849–50 and again in 1853–5. When cholera broke out in Jamaica in 1850, Milroy was also seconded to the Colonial Office, which dispatched him to report on the sanitary condition of the island. Having impressed the government by his efficiency, he seemed the natural choice to replace the recently deceased Hector Gavin as one of the commissioners investigating the health of the British army in the Crimea, in the spring of 1854. The ranks of the army had been severely depleted by disease and malnutrition, but working closely with the army medical department Milroy and his fellow commissioners transformed the health and morale of the army by improving sanitary and other conditions. After the cessation of hostilities he and another commissioner, John Sutherland, recounted their transactions in the 'Report on the sanitary condition of the army of the East', which was to provide valuable ammunition for Florence Nightingale and others campaigning for sanitary reform in the army after the Crimean War.

With the war behind him Milroy returned to the subject in which he had made his name. Serving as honorary secretary of the quarantine committee of the National Association of Social Science, Milroy gathered a mass of information on the systems of quarantine in place throughout the world. The reports based on these observations were submitted to government and published as a series of parliamentary papers in the early 1860s. Here and elsewhere Milroy continued to express his opposition to the system of quarantine, which had been abandoned in Britain but which continued to cause great inconvenience to British shipping in the Mediterranean and the Red Sea. He was supported in these views by the majority of the British medical profession and particularly by the Epidemiological Society of London, of which he was secretary from 1864 to 1866. The society's *Transactions* contain several notable articles on quarantine by Milroy, as well as his reflections on diseases among the poor and among the inhabitants of British India.

Milroy's last government appointment was as medical commissioner to the West Indies in 1871–2. After returning to England, he retired from official duties on a pension of £100 per annum, but continued to take an active interest in epidemiology, serving the Royal College of Physicians on its committee on leprosy and yaws. Renowned for his abstemiousness but also for his generosity, Milroy presented the college with £2000 for the endowment of a lectureship on public health. An annual lecture on the subject—the 'Milroy lecture'—was subsequently held in his honour.

Milroy died at his home, 21 Church Road, Richmond, Surrey, on 11 January 1886, and was buried on 15 January in Kensal Green cemetery.   MARK HARRISON

Sources W. R. E. S., *The Lancet* (27 Feb 1886), 425 · *BMJ* (27 Feb 1886), 425–6 · *Transactions of the Epidemiological Society of London*, new ser., 5, 169–70 · m. cert. · *CGPLA Eng. & Wales* (1886)
Wealth at death £10,491 10s. 9d.: probate, 23 Jan 1886, *CGPLA Eng. & Wales*

Milton. For this title name see Fletcher, Andrew, Lord Milton (1691/2–1766).

Milton, Sir Christopher (1615–1693), judge, was the younger son of the composer and scrivener John *Milton (1562–1647) and his wife, Sara, *née* Jeffrey (c.1572–1637), and brother of the poet John *Milton. In the flyleaf of his family Bible (BL, Add. MS 32310) the poet John Milton recorded that his brother Christopher was born in 1615 'on Friday about a month before Christmas'. Like his brother, Christopher was educated at St Paul's School and on 15 February 1631 he joined his brother at Christ's College, Cambridge, where he was assigned to his brother's tutor, Nathaniel Tovey. Christopher stayed in residence for five terms (until his brother had proceeded MA) and he then left to join the Inner Temple, to which he was admitted on 22 September 1632. About 1637 Milton married Thomasine (*bap.* 1618), the daughter of John Webber, a prosperous tailor, and his wife, Isabel. After her marriage Thomasine moved to Horton in Buckinghamshire to live with her widowed father-in-law and, until Milton completed his legal studies, he divided his time between Horton and the Inner Temple, where he was 'restored into commons' (took up residence) on 26 November 1637. He was called to the bar on 26 January 1640.

In 1640 or 1641 Milton moved with his wife and father to Reading, where they stayed until after the siege of April 1643. Milton's sympathies lay with the royalist side, and on 21 October 1642 he was added to the muster roll of Reading. After the fall of Reading on 27 April Milton's family moved to London and his father moved to his elder son's house in Aldersgate. For the next few years Milton lived an itinerant life as royal commissioner of sequestrations with responsibility for three counties; in this capacity he lived for a time in Wells (1644) and spent seven months in Exeter in the winter of 1645-6. He left Exeter before it surrendered to Fairfax on 13 April 1646 and he returned to his family in London. He secured the return of the sequestered house called the Cross Keys in Ludgate Hill which he had inherited from his father, and he lived there with his family until 1652. From 1652 until Milton's retirement in 1688 his family lived in Ipswich, and Milton worked both there and in London; the surviving legal documents suggest that during the Commonwealth and protectorate his legal practice was largely concerned with composition cases. After the Restoration the new political climate facilitated an improvement in Milton's fortunes. On 25 November 1660 he was called to the bench of the Inner Temple and so became a senior member of his inn of court. As a master of the bench he was called upon to serve his inn in various capacities, including that of reader and member of the parliament; in Suffolk he became a justice of the peace and a deputy recorder. On the death of his brother he became involved in the legal proceedings arising out of John Milton's nuncupative will, and he later supplied John Aubrey with biographical information about his brother and their family.

It is possible (but not certain) that Milton converted to Roman Catholicism; if so, that might explain why his daughter Anne described him as 'deceased' on her marriage to a protestant minister. Such a conversion might also explain why in April 1686 James II appointed him serjeant-at-law (21 April) and baron of the exchequer (24 April) and knighted him (25 April); the following year, on 14 April 1687, Milton was appointed justice of the common pleas with an annual salary of £1000. This eminence was to be short-lived because Milton retired, perhaps involuntarily, on 6 July 1688. He had acquired a country home at Rushmere St Andrew, about 2 miles from Ipswich, and he lived there for the rest of his life. He was buried in the church of St Nicholas, Ipswich, on 22 March 1693. Milton is sometimes said to have written *The State of Church Affairs* (1687), which is in part a Roman Catholic riposte to John Milton's *History of Britain*, but the attribution is simply a surmise that has been hardened into fact by constant repetition.

Christopher and Thomasine Milton had ten children. Christopher (c.1637–1668) was admitted to the Inner Temple on 30 June 1661 and called to the bar on 9 February 1668; the second son was an unnamed infant who was buried in Horton on 26 March 1639. The eldest daughter was Sarah (*bap.* 1639); the second daughter was Anne (*bap.* 1641). The next three children were sons: John (*bap.* 1643, *d.* 1664); Thomas (*bap.* 1647, *d.* 1694), who was admitted to the Inner Temple on 27 November 1670 and called to the bar on 29 November 1677—in 1673 he succeeded his uncle Thomas Agar as deputy clerk of crown in chancery; and Richard, the youngest son, who was probably born between 1648 and 1652—he was admitted to the Inner Temple on 24 November 1667 and called to the bar on 26 November 1676. As a lawyer Richard worked with his father and he assumed responsibility for the posthumous affairs of his uncle the poet. He lived in Suffolk (in the village of Cockfield, and in Ipswich), and on his father's death he migrated to Ireland; he died before 1713. The three youngest Milton children were daughters; Thomasine was born about 1648, and was buried in Ipswich on 6 July 1675; Mary was baptized in Ipswich on 29 March 1656; and Catherine was approximately the same age—the two unmarried sisters lived together in Highgate, Middlesex. Mary was buried in Farningham, Kent, on 26 April 1742; Catherine was buried beside her in April 1746, when she was said to be about ninety years of age.

GORDON CAMPBELL

Sources W. R. Parker, *Milton: a biography*, ed. G. Campbell, 2nd edn, 2 vols. (1996) · J. M. French, *The life records of John Milton*, 5 vols. (1949–58) · G. Campbell, *A Milton chronology* (1997) · admissions book, Christ's College, Cambridge [MS in college archive] · admissions book, 1571–1640, Inner Temple, London, 593 · F. A. Inderwick and R. A. Roberts, eds., *A calendar of the Inner Temple records*, 5 vols. (1896–1936) · parish register, St Nicholas Ipswich, Suffolk RO, Ipswich

Milton, John (1562–1647), composer, was born late in 1562, the son of Richard Milton (*fl. c*.1560–*c*.1601), a forest underranger from Stanton St John, Oxfordshire; he was the grandson of Henry Milton (*d.* 1559), of the same village, and his wife, Agnes. According to one family tradition, recorded by his descendant Elizabeth Foster, he was born in France. His mother's name is unknown, but his father was a recusant who was excommunicated on 11 May 1582 and twice fined for non-attendance at the parish church in 1601. Aubrey reported that Milton was educated at Christ Church in Oxford, but there is no other evidence for the contention that he was a chorister or undergraduate there. As a young man he became a protestant and was disinherited by his father. About 1583 he moved to London and became an apprentice scrivener; he was admitted to the Company of Scriveners on 27 February 1599, and shortly thereafter married Sara Jeffrey (*c*.1572–1637), the elder daughter of Paul Jeffrey (*d.* 1583), a merchant tailor, and his wife, Ellen (*d.* 1611), who lived with John and Sara at the Spread Eagle in Bread Street, until her death.

John and Sara Milton are known to have had six children, of whom three survived to adulthood. The eldest was Anne (*d.* *c*.1640), who married Edward Phillips on 22 November 1623 at a service conducted by the rector of St Stephen Walbrook, Thomas Myriell, apparently her father's musical friend of that name; her children were Edward Phillips (1630–1696) and John Phillips (1631–1706). The second surviving child was John *Milton (1608–1674), who was later to write a Latin poem, 'Ad patrem', in honour of his father; the third child was Christopher *Milton (1615–1693).

Milton's profession of scrivener meant in practice that he worked as a financial broker, moneylender, and notary. His work often involved him in legal proceedings, and substantial documentary evidence has enabled scholars to reconstruct his business dealings in considerable detail. Two of these documents name Milton as a trustee of the Blackfriars Playhouse in 1620.

Milton is known to have written two poems (a sonnet and a commendatory poem for John Lane, the verse writer, both unpublished) and twenty musical compositions. The music was all written for domestic use and is almost all sacred, though none of the texts derives from a liturgical source. Milton's earliest surviving composition, which is also his only known secular work, is a six-part madrigal called 'Fair Oriana in the morn', which was published in Thomas Morley's *Triumphs of Oriana* (1601). In 1614 Milton published four anthems in William Leighton's *The Tears or Lamentations of a Sorrowful Soul*. Three of his harmonizations of the York and Norwich psalm tunes are included in Thomas Ravenscroft's metrical psalter, *The Whole Book of Psalms* (1621). Milton's other surviving music was unpublished; these compositions survive in manuscripts associated with John Browne, clerk of the parliaments, and with Milton's friend Thomas Myriell. The partbooks from the library of John Browne (Christ Church, Oxford), written in Myriell's hand, consist of three five-part fantasias and one six-part fantasia, all for consorts of viols, and a fantasia on 'In nomine' for voice and five viols; the collection also includes an anthem for four voices, 'If ye love me' (John 14: 15–16). Myriell's unpublished 'Tristitiae remedium' (BL) contains settings of five English biblical texts and of two verses (*incipit Precamur sancte domine*) of *Christe qui lux es*, a Latin hymn for compline. The passionate idiom of the *seconda practica* had advocates in England, and some English composers were writing light-hearted pieces, but the music of Milton and of the Myriell circle with which he was associated drew on a more conservative tradition and articulated the traditional values of the *prima practica* in its seriousness, abstraction, deployment of counterpoint, and even choice of instrument. These values seem to have been transmitted by Milton to his son the poet, whose preferences for part-singing, the organ, and the viol (as opposed to solo singing, the harpsichord, and the violin) place him in the same conservative musical tradition as his father.

In 1631 Milton moved with his family from Bread Street to Hammersmith, where they stayed until he retired from business in 1636 and moved with Sara to Horton, Buckinghamshire. On 3 April 1637 Sara died in Horton, and was buried in the aisle of the parish church. John's son Christopher was also living in Horton with his family, and the scrivener followed them to Reading in 1641; he remained there until Reading fell to parliament in 1643, and then moved to live with his son John, who was separated from his wife, in Aldersgate Street in London. In 1645 the younger John Milton was reconciled with his wife, and the elder Milton moved with them into a large house in Barbican, where he remained until his death; he was buried in St Giles Cripplegate on 15 March 1647.

GORDON CAMPBELL

Sources E. Brennecke jun., *John Milton the elder and his music* (1938) · W. R. Parker, *Milton: a biography*, ed. G. Campbell, 2nd edn, 2 vols. (1996), vol. 2, pp. 684–95, 788–9, 815–16, 929–31 · J. M. French, *The life records of John Milton*, 5 vols. (1949–58) · G. Campbell, *A Milton chronology* (1997) · parish register, Horton, Bucks. RLSS, PR 107/1/1 · common paper of the Company of Scriveners, GL, MS 5370, p. 162 · parish register, All Hallows, Bread Street, GL, MS 5031 · parish register, St Giles Cripplegate, GL, MS 6419 · parish register, St Stephen Walbrook, GL, MS 8319 · poor relief assessments, Hammersmith and Fulham RO, London, PAF/1/21, fols. 68, 85, 92*v* · PRO, E112/221/1215; E125/27/199–200; E377/29d/10 (exchequer recusant rolls for Oxfordshire · Bodl. Oxf., MS Aubrey 8, fols. 63–8 · Bodl. Oxf., MS OAP Oxon.e.11, fol. 182*v* · Oxfordshire Archives, wills 182/236 [Henry Milton's will] · Oxfordshire Archives, wills 184/2 [Agnes Milton's will]

Milton, John (1608–1674), poet and polemicist, was born at 6.30 a.m. on Friday 9 December 1608 in the house at the sign of the Spread Eagle, Bread Street, London, and baptized in nearby All Hallows Church on 20 December, the third child of John *Milton (1562–1647), and his wife, Sara, *née* Jeffrey (*c*.1572–1637). The house in Bread Street accommodated the scrivener's business of Milton's father, and was also the family home. The most remarkable feature of the domestic life of Milton's childhood was music: Milton's father was a composer, and the music that he wrote was designed for performance in private houses, without an audience. Milton grew up in a household in which music was performed, and his skills as a singer in consorts and as a player of the organ and the bass viol were acquired as a child in Bread Street.

Education Milton was initially educated at home by private tutors, including Thomas Young, a Scottish schoolmaster who eventually became master of Jesus College, Cambridge. In *Ad patrem* ('To my Father') Milton was later to express his gratitude that his father had paid for lessons in Latin, Greek, Hebrew, French, and Italian. It is likely that instruction in these languages began with private tutors; although Milton went on to study the ancient languages at school, modern languages were not taught in schools, and all of Milton's instruction in French and Italian (and possibly Spanish) was given by private tutors. At an unknown date between 1615 and 1621 Milton became a pupil at nearby St Paul's School; the most likely date is 1620, when the departure of Thomas Young for a pulpit in Hamburg may have prompted the decision to send Milton to school. At St Paul's, Milton was taught by Alexander Gil the elder and became a friend of Alexander Gil the younger and of Charles Diodati. A lifetime later, Milton's widow told John Aubrey that Milton was a poet at the age of ten. None of Milton's extant poems can be assigned to this date, but a few of his schoolboy juvenilia survive, including an imitation of Mantuan entitled *Apologus de rustico et hero* ('The Fable of a Peasant and his Master') and a Greek epigram, *Philosophus ad regem quendam* ('A philosopher to a certain king'). About 1874 a page (now in Austin, Texas) apparently in Milton's youthful hand came to

John Milton (1608–1674), by William Faithorne the elder, 1670

light, and it contains a prose theme on early rising and two Latin poems. Milton's earliest datable poems are English paraphrases of psalms 114 and 136; when Milton printed them in 1645 he said that they 'were done by the Author at fifteen years old', which was in 1624.

Early in 1625 Milton arrived in Cambridge, perhaps in time for the start of the Lent term on 13 January. On 12 February, on payment of 10s., he was admitted to Christ's College as a minor pensioner, a status below that of fellow-commoner but above that of sizar. The tutor to whom he was assigned was William Chappell, who was later to become provost of Trinity College, Dublin. On 9 April 1625 Milton presented himself to John Tabor, the university registrary, and formally matriculated at the university. Undergraduates did not necessarily return home during the university vacations, and it is likely that Milton stayed in college after term ended on 8 July, because a plague epidemic had broken out in London; when plague arrived in Cambridge at the beginning of August, Milton presumably left Cambridge to join his family at a retreat in the country. This outbreak of plague may be the 'slaughtering pestilence' to which Milton refers in his poem 'On the Death of a Fair Infant Dying of the Cough'; if so, the poem would seem to have been written in the winter of 1625–6. Alternatively, the subject of the poem may, as Edward Phillips recalled many years later, be Milton's niece (and Edward's sister) Anne, who died in January 1628, aged two.

Milton's earliest Latin poem from this period is a verse letter (later *Elegia prima*) addressed to his friend Charles Diodati, which seems to have been written from London early in April 1626, shortly before Milton returned to Cambridge. The deaths of four dignitaries in the autumn of 1626 offered occasions for Milton to venture into Latin memorial verse. Lancelot Andrewes, the distinguished scholar and divine, died on 25 September; Milton's commemorative poem (later *Elegia tertia*) for the celibate Andrewes ends with a startling adaptation of a line from Ovid (*Amores*, i.5) in which Ovid recalls an assignation with Corinna. On 26 September Richard Ridding, one of the university's esquire bedells, died, and Milton joined in the academic mourning with a memorial poem which he subsequently printed as *Elegia secunda*; 5 October brought the death of Nicholas Felton, who had succeeded Andrewes as bishop of Ely, and Milton once again used the occasion to compose a Latin poem. On 21 October Cambridge lost its vice-chancellor, John Gostlin, master of Gonville and Caius College and regius professor of medicine ('physic'), and once again Milton marked the occasion with a poem. It may have been in the same term that Milton turned his pen to vindictive anti-Catholic polemic in a series of Latin poems on the occasion of the Gunpowder Plot. Milton's contributions to the university celebrations of the defeat of the conspirators were the tiny verse-epic *In quintum Novembris* ('On the fifth of November'), four epigrams *In Proditionem Bombardicam* ('On the Gunpowder Plot'), and a fifth, *In inventorem bombardae* ('On the inventor of gunpowder'); the verse epic contains Milton's first portrayal of Satan.

The only remnants of Milton's prose to survive from this period are a Latin letter to Thomas Young and a collection of Latin academic exercises known as prolusions. The letter to Young was written on 26 March 1627; it was later printed as the first letter in Milton's *Epistolares familiares* ('Private letters'), but misdated as 26 March 1625. In this letter Milton alludes to a companion poem, which must be his verse letter to Young (later *Elegia quarta*). Six of Milton's seven Latin prolusions are speeches that he delivered to meet the academic requirements of the university and his college; four (1, 2, 3, and 7) are orations (*declamationes*) and two (4 and 5) are Milton's half of formal debates (*disputationes*). Prolusions 2, 3, and 5 were read in the 'Public Schools' (university lecture rooms, now known as 'Old Schools'), and prolusions 1, 4, and 7 were read in Christ's College. Prolusion 6 is not part of the statutory exercises, but is rather an address to Milton's fellow students at an entertainment (known as a 'salting') on the eve of the long vacation; this prolusion, which Milton delivered on or shortly before 4 July 1628, is preceded by a Latin oration addressed to his fellow students and followed by an English poem, 'On the Vacation Exercise'. This prolusion also contains the first reference to Milton's nickname, 'the Lady': just as the young Virgil *parthenias vulgo appellatus sit* ('was usually called the Lady'), so Milton became known as 'the Lady of Christ's'.

On 25 May and 11 June 1627 Milton was in London, where he signed two legal documents. These absences from Cambridge during term time suggest that this may be the term when he fell out with Chappell and was consequently sent down from the university. This period of suspension (or rustication) in London may have been the time when Milton wrote his mildly erotic *Elegia septima*, though it is possible that the poem was written as late as 1630. On returning to Cambridge, probably in the autumn of 1627, Milton was assigned to a new tutor, Nathaniel Tovey. When Milton's younger brother Christopher [*see* Milton, Sir Christopher] was admitted to Christ's College in February 1631, he too was assigned to Tovey, which may imply that Milton had established a better relationship with Tovey than he had managed with Chappell.

Milton's final year as an undergraduate began badly when his friend Alexander Gil the younger was imprisoned for toasting the assassin of Buckingham, but Milton continued to study and occasionally to compose verse. He supplicated for his BA early in 1629 and later signed (apparently without scruple) the three articles of religion in the university subscription book. The spring of 1629 is the most likely date of composition for Milton's sonnet 'O nightingale' (later Sonnet 1), his 'Song. On May Morning', and his sensuous Latin poem *In adventum veris* ('On the coming of spring'), later *Elegia quinta*.

The Cambridge MA is now taken without residence, but such was not the case in the seventeenth century, and Milton returned to Cambridge in October 1629. It may have been during this term that he wrote five Italian sonnets (later sonnets 2–6) and a *stanza di canzone*. The native-speaker fluency of these youthful love poems is an earnest of the formidable linguistic ability that was later to be associated with Milton. One of the sonnets is addressed to Diodati; another seems furtively to address a lady called Emilia, who may have been a member of the Italian protestant community in London or a product of Milton's enamoured imagination. Early on Christmas day 1629 Milton completed 'On the Morning of Christ's Nativity'; shortly thereafter he sent a copy of the poem to Diodati, describing it in his accompanying Latin verse letter (later *Elegia sexta*) as a birthday gift to Christ, composed by the first light of dawn. In one of the introductory stanzas to the poem, Milton describes his 'hymn' as a 'humble ode', so aligning his Christian hymn with the pagan traditions of the ode; the poem is now known as the 'Nativity Ode'. It was Milton's first English poem on a religious theme, and he later indicated its importance in his spiritual and poetic development by placing it first in his 1645 and 1673 *Poems*. The 'Nativity Ode' inaugurated a triptych of poems based on the church calendar: Milton's unfinished poem in the metaphysical style, 'The Passion', was composed for Good Friday, probably in 1630, and 'Upon the Circumcision' marks new year's day, possibly in 1633.

In the autumn of 1630 the booksellers who had published the first folio of Shakespeare's plays began to make arrangements to produce a second folio, which was eventually published in 1632. For reasons that are not clear, Milton was asked (or volunteered) to contribute a commendatory poem; this was to be Milton's first published poem, and he later collected it as 'On Shakespeare' and dated it 1630. On new year's day 1631 Thomas Hobson, the

octogenarian driver of the Cambridge to London coach, died in Cambridge, and university wits who had endured his reckless driving were quick to mourn his passing. Milton joined in the affectionate commemorations with two (or possibly three) poems 'On the University Carrier'; the tone of the poems is light-hearted, but the closing lines of the first poem, in which Death is personified as the bedroom attendant in an inn, constitute one of the most graceful descriptions of mortality in English poetry. A more serious memorial poem followed a few months later: Jane Savage, the marchioness of Winchester, died on 15 April 1631, and although Milton seems not to have known her, he joined in the public mourning with an 'Epitaph on the Marchioness of Winchester', which he wrote on 'the banks of Cam'.

Hammersmith and Horton, 1631–1638 Early in 1631 the Milton family moved to Hammersmith, which was then a hamlet in the parish of Fulham, some 6 miles west of London on the north bank of the Thames. Milton's father was certainly in residence in April 1631, when he was assessed for poor relief. Two months later, on 7 June 1631, a newly established chapel of ease was consecrated by Bishop Laud; Milton's father became a churchwarden, and, on coming down from Cambridge, Milton became a parishioner. He had sworn on supplicating for his MA to continue his studies for an additional five years; two years later (in 1639) he would have been eligible to apply for the degree of bachelor of divinity (Latin *sanctae theologiae baccalaureus*). This oath was merely the vestige of an earlier custom, but Milton seems to have taken it seriously, because he chose to spend the next five years in private study; he was later to claim that he was making good the deficiencies of his Cambridge education. In signing the subscription book to take his MA, Milton once again acknowledged the liturgy and doctrine of the Church of England and the supremacy of the king; he was eventually to ignore the liturgy, repudiate several key aspects of the doctrine, and applaud the execution of the king to whom he had sworn allegiance.

From time to time Milton interrupted his private studies in order to compose verse, but there is no evidence for the dates of several important works that seem to be products of the early 1630s. The Latin poem addressed to his father, *Ad patrem*, may be a product of this period, as may Milton's English translation of Horace's fifth ode, *Ad Pyrrham*. His pastoral entertainment, *Arcades*, was performed in the garden of Harefield, the estate of the dowager countess of Derby near Uxbridge. The poised and sprightly twin poems 'L'Allegro' and 'Il Penseroso' may date from this period, if indeed they were written at the same time, but the countryside described in 'L'Allegro' contains no features that enable it to be tied to a specific place and time. Similarly, 'At a Solemn Music' and 'On Time' are likely to have been written during this period, but cannot be dated with any precision. His sonnet 'How soon hath time' (later Sonnet 7), however, can be assigned with some confidence to December 1632, close to Milton's twenty-fourth birthday.

In 1634 Milton was asked to compose the text of a

masque which was to be mounted in Ludlow in honour of the inauguration of John Egerton, earl of Bridgewater, as lord president of Wales; Ludlow is in England rather than Wales, but it is in the Welsh marches and was the seat of the court of marches, over which the earl of Bridgewater was to preside. The music for the masque was written by Henry Lawes, who had probably commissioned Milton to compose the text. The masque was performed at Ludlow Castle on Monday 29 September 1634. Three of the earl's children (all of whom had acted before) played the central roles, and Henry Lawes acted the part of the Attendant Spirit. The idea that Milton travelled to Ludlow and acted the part of Comus is a scholarly fantasy without foundation. In 1637 or early in 1638 Lawes published Milton's text (without any indication of its authorship) as *A Maske Presented at Ludlow Castle*, and Milton reprinted it in his *Poems* of 1645. Since the late seventeenth century the masque has been known as *Comus*; to call the masque after the tempter is rather like referring to *Paradise Lost* as *Satan*, but the title is now firmly established. Later in the year, Alexander Gil wrote a Latin epithalamium, and sent a copy to Milton; on 4 December Milton replied, enclosing a recently composed translation of Psalm 114 into Greek verse.

On 12 May 1636 Milton's father resigned as assistant to the Company of Scriveners on the grounds of his 'removal to inhabit in the country'. This phrase (in a manuscript that is now lost) indicates the retirement of Milton's family to Horton, Buckinghamshire (later Berkshire). Milton may have used the nearby libraries at Eton College and Langley (the Kedermister Library) to support his programme of private study, but London was much less accessible than it had been in Hammersmith. It was about this time that Milton started to record titbits from his voluminous reading in a commonplace book (now in the British Library), which he continued to use until after the Restoration.

Less than a year after Milton had settled with his parents into the rural seclusion of Horton, his mother, Sara, died, on 3 April 1637. Milton and his father buried her in the aisle of the chancel of Horton church; the inscribed blue stone still bears her name. Milton seems not to have written a poem in her memory, but soon occasion arose for him to write his greatest memorial poem, one that is arguably the finest short poem in the English language. The occasion of 'Lycidas' was the death of Edward King, a fellow of Christ's College who had drowned off the coast of Anglesey on 10 August 1637. King had been a younger contemporary of Milton at Christ's College, and had been awarded a fellowship by royal mandate. The myth that Milton was aggrieved because he had been robbed of the fellowship for which he was destined was invented in the eighteenth century, and is based on the groundless assumption that an academic post, with its attendant obligations of celibacy and ordination in the Church of England, would have been the highest calling to which Milton might have aspired. In fact Milton was contemptuous of Cambridge, and in any case he was ineligible for election, because the statutes of the college prohibited the election

of more than one fellow from any county; Michael Honywood was, like Milton, a native of Middlesex, and so Milton could not have been elected to a fellowship as long as Honywood was in post.

The death of Ben Jonson on 16 August, six days after the death of Edward King, was marked in Oxford by a collection of memorial poems entitled *Jonsonus virbius*. It is possible that this volume provided a stimulus for the poets of Cambridge to assemble a rival volume in memory of King, who had lacked Jonson's great gifts as a poet, but had none the less published ten competent Latin poems. Milton was asked to contribute a poem, and in November 1637 copied a draft of 'Lycidas' into his poetical notebook (now in Trinity College, Cambridge, and so known as the Trinity manuscript). The poem was published in *Justa Edouardo King naufrago ab amicis moerentibus, amoris et mneias charin* ('Obsequies to Edward King, drowned by shipwreck, in token of love and remembrance, by his grieving friends') late in 1638. Milton had chosen to write in English, and his poem was placed at the end of the English section of the volume, which had a separate title-page (*Obsequies to the Memory of Mr Edward King*). Most of the poems in the volume were written in the fashionable idiom of the metaphysical poem, often in imitation of Donne. Milton chose to ignore this contemporary enthusiasm for wittily expressed grief in favour of the traditional genre of the pastoral elegy. His poem originated in a desire to commemorate King, but in the act of composition Milton transcended his ostensible subject and produced a meditation on human mortality that retains the power to move readers centuries after the death of King and those who mourned him.

The origins of Milton's disenchantment with the Caroline church are not clear, but the earliest unambiguous evidence would seem to be enshrined in 'Lycidas', in which the apostle Peter censures the English church. Satire directed against the church had been a part of pastoral elegy since Petrarch, and Milton took advantage of this convention to mount an attack on the greed of the clergy, whom he stigmatizes as 'blind mouths'; he does, however, furnish Peter with a bishop's mitre, because in 1637 Milton was still content with the notion that it was Peter who had inaugurated the succession of bishops.

'Lycidas' concludes with an affirmation that when grieving has finished, life must go on: 'Tomorrow to fresh woods and pastures new'. Milton had grieved privately for his mother and publicly for Edward King, and he then turned to his plans to travel to the woods and pastures of Italy. He sought advice from Sir Henry Wotton, who had retired from his diplomatic career to become provost of Eton, which was within a few miles of Horton. On 6 April 1638 Milton wrote to Wotton, enclosing a copy of *Comus* and mentioning his intention to travel to Italy in the next few weeks. Wotton's reply, which Milton printed in the edition of *Comus* in his 1645 *Poems*, contained advice about the best route and about deportment, together with an introduction to the English ambassador in Paris.

Italy, 1638–1639 In May 1638 Milton left England for a tour of the continent that was to last approximately fifteen months. He first travelled from London to Paris, where he met the ambassador of King Charles, Viscount Scudamore of Sligo. Lord Scudamore arranged for Milton to meet Hugo Grotius, the learned Dutch jurist who was living in Paris as the ambassador of Queen Kristina of Sweden. On leaving Paris, Milton travelled south to Nice, along the coast to Genoa, thence to Leghorn by ship, and then inland via Pisa to Florence, where he arrived in June 1638 for a visit of about five months. During this first visit to Florence, Milton participated in the meetings of at least two Florentine academies (the Svogliati and the Apatisti) and so became acquainted with the learned men of the city, several of whom composed tributes to Milton which he was later to print in his 1645 *Poemata*. Milton's attendance at the weekly meetings of the Svogliati in the new *palazzo* of the Gaddi family (later the Hotel Astoria) enabled him to meet the poet Antonio Malatesti, who subsequently dedicated *La Tina*, an erotic sonnet sequence, 'al grande poeta inghilese Giovanni Milton Londra' ('to the great English poet John Milton of London'). At these meetings Milton also met the scholar Benedetto Buonmattei, to whom Milton subsequently wrote proposing additions to his *Della lingua Toscana* (the suggestions were ignored) and Vincenzo Galilei, the illegitimate son of Galileo. It may have been Vincenzo who arranged for Milton to visit Galileo, either in the astronomer's house at Arcetri or in Vincenzo's house on the Costa San Giorgio, where Galileo was staying for medical treatment; Milton was later to recall the visit in *Areopagitica* (1644). On 6/16 September 1638 Milton read one of his own Latin poems to the academicians, who judged it to be 'molto erudita'. There is a late tradition to the effect that Milton visited Vallombrosa while staying in Florence, but there is no evidence and little likelihood that such a visit took place; Milton's allusion to the 'autumnal leaves that strew the brook / In Vallombrosa' (*Paradise Lost*, book 1, ll. 302–3) derives from Ariosto, not from a recollection of an excursion to the monastery at Vallombrosa.

In October 1638 Milton travelled south to Siena and thence to Rome, where he stayed for about two months. On 20/30 October he dined in the English College, where the pilgrim book records the presence of Milton and his unnamed servant as well as three other English guests. In December Milton journeyed on to Naples in the company of an unidentified traveller whom Milton later described as a hermit; he was presumably a Carmelite friar. This well-connected hermit introduced Milton to his Neapolitan host, Giovanni Battista Manso, marchese di Villa, to whom Milton later addressed *Mansus*, a poem that sought to demonstrate in its elegant Latin hexameters that Manso, who had been the patron of Torquato Tasso and Giambattista Marino, had once again offered hospitality to a poet. Milton had originally planned to go on from Naples to Sicily and Greece, but he decided to abandon these plans and travel slowly home; he later attributed this decision (in the *Defensio secunda*) to 'the sad tidings of civil war from England … For I thought it base that I should travel abroad at my ease for the cultivation of my mind while my fellow citizens at home were fighting for liberty'.

In January 1639 Milton returned to Rome, where he met (or renewed his acquaintance with) the poet Giovanni Salzilli (to whom he later addressed his Latin poem *Ad Salsillum*), the German scholar and Catholic convert Lukas Holste, and Cardinal Francesco Barberini. Holste, who was secretary and librarian to Cardinal Barberini, showed Milton around the Barberini Library and presented him with a copy of his recently published bilingual edition of the axioms of the later Pythagoreans; on learning that Milton was returning to Florence, Holste asked him to visit the Laurentian Library to copy parts of a Medicean codex for him. During this visit to Rome, Milton attended at least two musical events. He was present at a recital given by the singer Leonora Baroni and subsequently wrote three conventionally enraptured epigrams in her honour, *Ad Leonoram Romae canentem* ('To Leonora, Singing in Rome'). On 17/27 February he attended a comic opera (Rospigliosi's *Chi soffre, speri*) mounted by Cardinal Francesco Barberini in the vast theatre of the newly completed Palazzo Barberini; the audience of 3500 included Cardinal Mazarin. Milton later recalled that he was greeted at the door by Cardinal Barberini, who granted him a private audience the next day; Barberini was prime minister of Rome and chief adviser to his uncle Pope Urban VIII, but he was also protector of the English, and in that capacity regularly offered hospitality and assistance to travellers such as Milton.

In March 1639 Milton returned to Florence, where he tried unsuccessfully to obtain permission to copy the manuscript for Holste. He again attended the Thursday meetings of the Svogliati, reading his Latin poems on 7/17 and 14/24 March. In April Milton travelled to Bologna and Ferrara and thence to Venice, where he stayed for at least a month. He shipped home the collection of books that he had amassed in his travels, including at least one case of music books containing works by Claudio Monteverdi (who was still living in Venice), Luca Marenzio, Orazio Vecchi, and Don Carlo Gesualdo. He then proceeded from Venice to Verona and Milan, through Lombardy and the Apennine Alps to Lake Geneva and on to Geneva, where he visited the theologian Giovanni (or Jean) Diodati, uncle of his friend Charles Diodati; if he had not heard the news of Charles's death earlier, Milton may have been told in Geneva. In July he returned to England through France, and shortly thereafter published a Latin poem in memory of Diodati; the only known copy of this edition of the *Epitaphium Damonis* ('Epitaph for Damon'), the greatest of Milton's Latin poems, survives in the British Library.

Schoolmaster and polemicist, 1639–1642 On returning to London, Milton took lodgings at the house of a tailor called Russell in St Bride's Churchyard (near Fleet Street), where he inaugurated his career as a schoolmaster by assuming responsibility for the education of his nephews Edward and John Phillips. He soon moved to a large house in Aldersgate Street, where he was able to take on additional pupils. Milton's life in the 1640s was divided between his duties as a teacher and his avocation as a polemicist involved in the controversy about church government and initiating a debate about divorce.

In 'Lycidas', Milton's attack on the Caroline church had centred on what he saw as ecclesiastical cupidity; when he renewed his attack four years later his censure was directed towards episcopacy, the system whereby churches are governed by bishops. Episcopacy had been enshrined in the Elizabethan settlement, but throughout the late sixteenth and early seventeenth centuries, vigorous opposition had been voiced by reformers who felt that episcopacy was a vestige of Roman Catholicism and an impediment to the realization of a full reformation. Under Elizabeth the crown had assumed the title of 'supreme governor' of the English church, and so the monarch stood at the head of the episcopate. The crown became associated with the episcopal cause, and so it seems likely that Milton's anti-monarchical sentiments of the 1650s had their origins in his anti-episcopal stance of the early 1640s. The debate about episcopacy had rumbled on for decades, but in 1637 had erupted because of the indictment of three prominent puritans (Henry Burton, John Bastwick, and William Prynne) for publishing tracts which attacked episcopacy; the court of Star Chamber sentenced the three defendants to torture and mutilation on the scaffold and subsequent incarceration. By 1641 the combatants in the debate had begun to write polemical treatises: Joseph Hall, bishop of Norwich, had published a defence of episcopacy called *An Humble Remonstrance to the High Court of Parliament*, and a few months later, in March 1641, a group of puritan ministers known collectively by their initials as Smectymnuus (Stephen Marshall, Edward Calamy, Milton's former tutor Thomas Young, Matthew Newcomen, and William Spurstow), responded to Hall with *An Answer to a Book Entitled 'An Humble Remonstrance'*. In April Hall hit back with *A Defence of the Humble Remonstrance*, to which Smectymnuus replied in June with *A Vindication of the Answer of the Humble Remonstrance*; the following month Hall responded yet again with his *Short Answer to the Tedious Vindication of Smectymnuus*.

At this point Milton entered the lists with the first of his five anti-prelatical pamphlets, *Of reformation touching church discipline in England and the causes that hitherto have hindered it*, which was published between 12 and 31 May 1641. This anonymous tract outlines the pernicious effects of episcopacy, but sets aside the theoretical arguments about church government in favour of fulminations against the episcopate which culminate in a call for the execution of bishops and a prophecy that they will spend eternity being tortured in Hell. In the same month that Milton's first tract was published, the patristic scholar James Ussher, archbishop of Armagh, published *The Judgement of Dr Rainolds Touching the Original of Episcopacy*, in which he sought to confirm the views of the Elizabethan churchman John Rainolds by recourse to patristic authority. Milton responded with *Of prelatical episcopacy, and whether it may be deduced from the apostolical times by virtue of those testimonies which are alleged to that purpose in some late treatises, one whereof goes under the name of James, archbishop of Armagh*. In this short tract Milton contended that to support episcopacy by resort to the church fathers was tantamount to denying the sufficiency of scripture, and also

lent hostages to fortune in providing arguments that could be used to defend Roman Catholicism; throughout the tract Milton maintains a civil tone with his learned opponent, but he none the less declares Ussher's scholarship to be wanting in several important particulars.

Milton's third anti-prelatical tract was a response to Hall's *Defence of the Humble Remonstrance*, which had been published in April 1641; Milton replied in July with *Animadversions upon the Remonstrant's Defence Against Smectymnuus*. The qualified deference that Milton had shown to Archbishop Ussher is nowhere in evidence; instead Milton mounts an excoriating personal attack on Bishop Hall. He returns to the attack on the greed of the clergy first articulated in 'Lycidas'; the reticence of pastoral elegy has given way to the savagery of seventeenth-century polemic, and Milton pours vitriol on those who would use the church to amass personal fortunes.

In 1641 episcopalian apologists assembled a tract (possibly edited by Archbishop Ussher) entitled *Certain brief treatises written by learned men concerning the ancient and modern government of the church*. At the end of January 1642 Milton published his reply, *The Reason of Church Government Urged Against Prelaty*; the title-page (which is dated 1641) reveals the identity of this tireless polemicist as 'Mr John Milton'. The decision to shed the cloak of anonymity is reflected in the body of the tract by the emergence of a newly radical Milton who is willing to 'divulge unusual things of myself' in an autobiographical digression. Whereas in *Of Prelatical Episcopacy* and *Animadversions* Milton had argued as a presbyterian within the national church of England, in *The Reason of Church Government* he moves away from state presbyterianism towards independent congregationalism, which had taken root in the puritan colonies of America and had been re-exported to England as radical tolerationism: Milton had not become a sectarian, but he now differed from the presbyterians in arguing for a measure of toleration, so adumbrating the explicitly tolerationist position that he was to take up in his later years.

Milton's fifth and final anti-prelatical tract, published in April 1642, is entitled *An apology against a pamphlet called 'A modest confutation of a scandalous and scurrilous libel entitled Animadversions'*. The anonymous *Modest Confutation* to which Milton replies had been published the previous month; its authorship is uncertain, but it may be the joint work of Joseph Hall and his son Robert. The attack that Milton had directed against Bishop Hall in *Animadversions* is heartily reciprocated in the *Modest Confutation*, which accuses Milton of personal immorality. Milton was always sensitive to personal attacks, and although this sensitivity did not inhibit him in the return of fire in these polemical skirmishes, he always insisted on defending his personal purity: on this occasion he testily insisted that he had never visited brothels as an undergraduate, but that he had observed the irresponsible behaviour of fellow undergraduates who were in due course to rise to senior positions in the church while never managing to shed their adolescent irresponsibility. In the course of the five years between mid-1637 and mid-1642 Milton had moved from being a constructively critical member of the national church to taking up the cause of ecclesiastical reform, and eventually becoming an impassioned opponent of ecclesiastical abuses: he had become an Independent.

Marriage and prose tracts, 1642–1648 In June 1642 Milton embarked on a journey to Forest Hill, in Oxfordshire, with a view to collecting an interest payment of £12 from Richard Powell, an improvident landowner and magistrate to whom Milton's father had lent £300 in 1627. Edward Phillips was later to record that 'after a month's stay, home he returns a married man, that went out a bachelor, his wife being Mary the eldest daughter of Mr Richard Powell'. After the wedding Milton took his seventeen-year-old bride home to his house on Aldersgate Street. A few weeks later Mary returned to her parental home. The initial extension of what was intended as a short separation may have been occasioned by the outbreak of civil war on 22 August, when King Charles raised his standard at Nottingham, but it eventually became clear that the newly wedded couple were estranged.

The reasons for the almost instantaneous collapse of Milton's marriage are not known, but the seriousness of the rift is attested by the fact that Milton redirected his scholarly energies from episcopacy to divorce. In seventeenth-century England a divorce that permitted remarriage could be granted only by parliament; ordinary citizens without access to parliament had to turn to the ecclesiastical courts, which had the power only to grant a form of judicial separation called divorce *a mensa et thoro* ('from table and bed'). For centuries canon law had stipulated six grounds for divorce: sexual offences (adultery, sodomy, and bestiality), impotence, physical cruelty, infidelity (that is, apostasy), entry into holy orders, and consanguinity; Milton's wife may have deserted him, but in England desertion did not constitute grounds for divorce until 1857. On 1 August 1643 Milton published *The doctrine and discipline of divorce, restored to the good of both sexes from the bondage of canon law and other mistakes to Christian freedom*, in which he argued that the traditional grounds for divorce were insufficient, and that a man should be able to divorce his wife if the marriage had become spiritually and emotionally barren. Milton does not argue for equal rights for the woman in marriage, but his views none the less anticipate in several respects the position that English law reached in 1977, when it was decreed that the sole ground for divorce was the irretrievable breakdown of a marriage.

On 2 February 1644 Milton published a heavily revised second edition of *Doctrine and Discipline of Divorce* which he addressed to the English parliament and the Westminster assembly; the reason for the twofold audience was that if the assembly approved of Milton's suggestions, parliament would probably have enshrined new divorce rules in law.

Milton's practical experience of a domestic classroom had led him to reflect on the education appropriate to young members of the governing class. The educational reformer Samuel Hartlib asked Milton to set out his views on the education of children. Milton replied with *Of Education*, a public letter to Hartlib which was published on 5 June 1644. The pamphlet sets out the daunting programme of a Miltonic education, which encompasses ancient languages (Latin, Greek, Hebrew, Aramaic, Syriac) and a huge range of academic and practical subjects; the only modern language mentioned is Italian, which Milton magisterially claims can be 'easily learned at any odd hour'. The boys in this academy would be prepared to govern a nation, but also to fight for it and oversee its agriculture. To teach in such an academy would not, Milton concedes, be a task for anyone 'that counts himself a teacher, but will require sinews almost equal to those which Homer gave Ulysses'. Milton's educational aspirations were heroic, but his practical efforts as a teacher failed to produce highly educated warrior princes: the Miltonic education of his two nephews equipped them for only the modest profession of hack writing.

On 6 August 1644 Milton published his second divorce tract, again addressed to parliament; this tract is a translation and condensation of chapters 15 to 47 of the second book of *De regno Christi* ('On the kingdom of Christ') by Martin Butzer (or Bucer), which Milton called *The Judgement of Martin Bucer Concerning Divorce*. A week later, on 13 August, Herbert Palmer condemned Milton's divorce tracts in a sermon to parliament, and eleven days later parliament was asked by the Company of Stationers to control unlicensed and unregistered books, including Milton's *Doctrine and Discipline of Divorce*.

This attempt to stifle Milton's tract may have been the spark that ignited his wrath against those who would censor books before publication. *Areopagitica* was Milton's belated response to the licensing order of June 1643, which stipulated that all books had to be examined by a censor prior to publication. His tract, published on 23 November 1644, takes the form of an oration addressed to parliament, which Milton accused of reviving the oppressive measures of a Star Chamber decree of July 1637. Milton's Greek title proposes an analogy between the English parliament and the ancient council of Athens which met on the Areopagus (the 'Hill of Ares' north-west of the Acropolis), and also recalls the *Areopagiticus*, an oration by the ancient orator Isocrates. In the short term Milton was unsuccessful, because parliament ignored his plea; in subsequent centuries, however, *Areopagitica* came to be valued as the most eloquent defence in English of the right to publish without prior censorship. It has also been invoked as a defence of free speech, but in fact the limits of Miltonic toleration were strictly circumscribed, and include a denial of the rights of Roman Catholics to publish works in defence of their religion.

On 4 March 1645 Milton published his third and fourth divorce tracts, *Tetrachordon* and *Colasterion*. Both titles are taken from ancient Greek. *Tetrachordon* is an adjective meaning 'four-stringed', and the neuter suffix links it to the word for musical instrument; Milton is straining to suggest that in the tract he is harmonizing the four main biblical treatments of marriage and divorce. *Colasterion* is a noun which refers to a place or instrument of torture;

Edward Phillips translated the term as 'rod of correction', which may imply that he understood his uncle to be alluding to the beating that he had inflicted on his opponent, who in this instance was the anonymous author of *An Answer to a Book Entitled 'The Doctrine and Discipline of Divorce'*, which had been published on 19 November 1644. Milton's reputation as an advocate of divorce had incurred the obloquy of the ecclesiastical establishment, but at least one person seems to have invoked Milton to justify an otherwise unsanctioned divorce: Mrs Attaway, the lacewoman turned radical preacher, spoke approvingly of Milton's tract, and deserted her ungodly husband for William Jenny, the godly husband of another woman. It was about this time that news reached the Powell family to the effect that Milton was planning to divorce Mary and marry the daughter of one Dr Davies. Phillips reports that this prospect 'caused them to set all engines on work to restore the late married woman' (Masson, 3.437); a reconciliation was effected, probably in mid-1645, and when Milton moved into a large house in Barbican in the autumn of 1645, he was joined by Mary. Their daughter Anne was born on 7 July 1646; Milton entered the details on the flyleaf of his family Bible (now in the British Library), where he had recently begun to record his family's births and deaths.

Milton's father died in March 1647, and that autumn Milton moved with his young family to a smaller house in High Holborn, backing onto Lincoln's Inn Fields. In the following year, on 25 October, his daughter Mary was born. The move to a smaller house may reflect a diminution of (or even a conclusion to) Milton's career as a teacher. In this period of relative calm between the end of teaching and the onset of his career as a public servant, Milton turned to private study and writing. It may have been in 1648 that he wrote his *Brief History of Moscovia*, published posthumously in 1683. At the same time it seems likely that Milton was gathering materials for his *History of Britain*, the first four books of which he drafted, according to his own account, in the six weeks between the execution of the king on 30 January 1649 and his own appointment as Latin secretary on 13 March.

Poetry, 1641–1648 The poems that Milton wrote in the 1640s were all short occasional pieces, and for the most part consisted of sonnets. After the battle of Edgehill on 23 October 1642, the army of Charles I advanced towards London, causing widespread panic in the capital. Milton's 'Captain or Colonel' (later Sonnet 8), which is entitled 'When the assault was intended to the City' in the Trinity manuscript, may have been occasioned by the prospect of the fall of London. The next poem in the Trinity manuscript is 'Lady, that in the prime of earliest youth' (later Sonnet 9), which uses the parable of the wise and foolish virgins to praise an unidentified lady. This poem may have been followed by 'To the Lady Margaret Ley' (later Sonnet 10). Lady Margaret was the daughter of James Ley, the first earl of Marlborough, and the second wife of Captain John Hobson, who had fought on the side of parliament; the

Hobsons lived near Milton on Aldersgate Street, and Milton was a regular visitor to their home during the years when he was separated from Mary.

In 1645 Milton decided to collect his youthful poems. The edition was published as *Poems of Mr John Milton, both English and Latin*; the edition is dated 1645, but may have been published on 2 January 1646, which is the date that George Thomason inscribed on his copy, which is now in the British Library. The English section was a miscellany consisting of early poems and translations, Milton's first ten sonnets (including the Italian sonnets), and *Comus*, which Milton had revised since its last publication. The Latin section (which included a few Greek poems) had a separate title-page, *Joannis Miltoni Londoniensis poemata. Quorum pleraque intra annum aetatis vigesimum conscripsit* ('Poems by John Milton of London, most of which were Written before he was Twenty'); this section was paginated separately, and was divided into a book of poems in elegiac couplets (*Elegiarum liber*) and a collection of poems in various metres (*Sylvarum liber*). The publisher, Humphrey Moseley, commissioned a portrait of Milton from the engraver William Marshall. The portrait is unflattering, and when Milton was shown it, he sought a cruel revenge by composing a few lines of Greek verse, which the hapless (and Greekless) Marshall engraved beneath the portrait; the verses invite the reader to laugh at the portrait, which Milton says is not a picture of him but of the incompetence of the engraver. It seems possible that the cruel humour of the God of *Paradise Lost* has its origins in the personality of his creator.

Milton felt that his *Tetrachordon* had been ignored, and lamented this injustice in 'A book was writ of late called *Tetrachordon*' (later Sonnet 11), the precise date of which is unknown: it seems to have been written too late for inclusion in the 1645 *Poems*, and its position in the Trinity manuscript may imply a date of composition in 1647. This sense of injured merit is extended to all four of Milton's divorce tracts in 'On the Detraction which Followed upon my Writing Certain Treatises' (later Sonnet 12); again the date of composition is uncertain, but the winter of 1645–6 is not unlikely, and so the numbering of sonnets 11 and 12 is normally reversed in modern editions. The sonnet in praise of the music of Henry Lawes ('To Mr Henry Lawes, on his Airs', later Sonnet 13) can be dated more precisely, because the first of the three drafts in the Trinity manuscript is dated 9 February '1645' (that is, 1646). In 1646 or early 1647 Milton wrote a twenty-line poem 'On the new forcers of conscience under the Long Parliament', which concludes with the etymological epigram 'new *Presbyter* is but old *Priest* writ large'.

On 16 December 1646 Katharine Thomason, the wife of Milton's friend George Thomason, was buried in the south aisle of St Dunstan-in-the-West; shortly thereafter Milton wrote a sonnet in her memory (later Sonnet 14). A few weeks later, on 23 January 1647, he returned to Latin poetry with an ode to John Rouse, Bodley's librarian, to accompany a presentation copy of his 1645 *Poems* intended to replace a copy that had gone astray. In April 1648, on the eve of the second civil war, Milton translated psalms 80–88 from the Hebrew. His next poem is a direct reaction to one event in that war: General Lord Fairfax besieged Colchester on 14 June, and the town fell on 27 August; during the siege Milton wrote a sonnet in praise of Fairfax (later Sonnet 15). By the end of the year the Rump Parliament had decided to indict the king, which set England on a course that was to carry Milton into a public role as a writer and translator in the service of the English republic.

Public service and the three defences, 1649–1655 Between 15 and 29 January 1649, during the trial of Charles I, Milton wrote his *Tenure of Kings and Magistrates*, which argued on its title-page that 'it is lawful … for any who have the power, to call to account a Tyrant or wicked King and after due conviction, to depose, and put him to death'. Charles was executed on 30 January 1649, and a fortnight later, on 13 February, Milton's tract was published. At noon on 13 March the council of state decided to invite Milton to be secretary for foreign tongues. He was appointed two days later, on Thursday 15 February, at an annual salary of £288 13s. 6½d. Before he could take up his post on the following Tuesday, parliament abolished the House of Lords (17 February) and the monarchy (19 February), so Milton entered the service of a nascent republic. The post included accommodation in Whitehall, but as an interim measure Milton lodged next to the Bull-head tavern in Charing Cross, opening on to Spring Garden. In November Milton moved with his household into an apartment formerly occupied by Sir John Hippesley at the Scotland Yard end of Whitehall; when the art collection of Charles I was put on sale in nearby Somerset House, Milton was given a warrant (dated 18 June 1650) to choose some hangings from the royal collection 'for the furnishing of his lodging in Whitehall'.

In the first instance Milton's duties in the service of the council of state consisted for the most part in translating international correspondence into the Latin of diplomacy; this was a task which Milton discharged throughout his period as a civil servant, but he quickly assumed more important tasks alongside these routine duties. On 28 March the council ordered:

> that Mr. Milton be appointed to make some observations upon the complication of interests which is now amongst the several designers against the peace of the Commonwealth; And that it be ready to be printed with the Papers out of Ireland which the House hath ordered to be printed. (Masson, 4.87)

The *Articles of Peace* were published on 16 May, and Milton's *Observations* were printed as an appendix. From Milton's English perspective the native Irish were barbarians who massacred civilized English settlers and soldiers; the anachronistic condemnation of Milton's hostile attitude does not facilitate historical understanding, but it is undeniably the case that the consequences of such hostility were immediately felt in the massacres at Drogheda and Wexford, and still reverberate in Anglo-Irish politics.

On 9 February 1649, ten days after the execution of King Charles, *Eikōn Basilikē* had been published; the Greek title means 'image of the king'. This book, which purported to have been written by the king (and was in fact written by his chaplain John Gauden), achieved an instant popularity, and within a year had been published in some fifty editions in various languages. The council of state was concerned that sympathy for the king could subvert the Commonwealth, and so commissioned an official reply. Initially John Selden had been asked to respond, but when he declined the council turned to Milton. In October Milton published his reply, which he entitled *Eikonoklastēs*; the literal meaning of the Greek title is 'image-breaker', but the term was meant to evoke the surname adopted by Greek emperors 'who in their zeal to the command of God, after long tradition of idolatry in the church, took courage and broke all superstitious images to pieces'. The regicide had alarmed continental Europe, and one of the first scholarly defences of Charles I, the *Defensio regia pro Carolo I* ('The royal defence of Charles I') written by the learned French protestant Claude de Saumaise (Claudius Salmasius), reached England in May 1649. On 8 January 1650 the council of state ordered Milton to prepare a reply to this damaging book, which threatened to delay the resumption of normal trade relations with the continent. Milton's reply, *Joannis Miltonii Angli defensio pro populo Anglicano contra Claudii Anonymi, aliàs Salmasii, defensionem regiam* ('The defence of John Milton, Englishman, on behalf of the people of England against the royal defence of Claudius the Anonymous, otherwise Salmasius') was not published until 24 February 1651; it is now known by the non-Miltonic title *Defensio prima* or *First Defence*. In the text Milton excuses his delay on grounds both of a lack of time to write and of insufficient health for the labour of writing; even now, he explains in his preface, his health is so poor and precarious that he has to take a break virtually every hour. Among the purchasers of this volume were the second earl of Bridgewater, who as a child had acted the part of the Elder Brother in Milton's *Comus*; he inscribed his copy (which is now in the Huntington Library) with the words (in Latin) 'this book is most deserving of burning, its author of the gallows'. This judgement, which was typical of English royalist reactions, was echoed in the chancellaries of Europe, and it was to the educated citizens of Europe (especially those of the United Provinces) that Milton addressed his defence of the regicide.

The first response to Milton's tract, *Pro rege et populo Anglicano apologia, contra Johannis Polypragmatici* (*alias Miltoni Angli*) *defensionem destructivam regis et populi Anglicani* ('An apology for the king and people of England against the defence, destructive of the king and people of England, by John the Multifarious, alias Milton the Englishman') was a plodding refutation in inept Latin (and subsequently in competent Dutch) published anonymously in Antwerp; it was popularly attributed to John Bramhall, but actually written by John Rowland. Milton decided, possibly for reasons of health, not to respond to this tract; the *Responsio* was instead written by his nephew John Phillips.

Milton had realized before Mary's return in 1645 that he was losing the sight in his left eye, and by 1648 the eye had ceased to function. Early in 1652 his right eye collapsed, and Milton became permanently blind; he never saw his son, John, who was born on 16 March 1651. In the following year, early in May 1652, Mary Milton died shortly after giving birth to their daughter Deborah, and Milton was left, alone and blind, to care for four young children; six weeks later, his only son, John, died. Later that year Milton was evicted from his Whitehall apartment, and on 17 December he moved with his three surviving children into a house in Petty France opening on to St James's Park; he stayed in this house until the Restoration.

In August 1652 an anonymous tract called *Regii sanguinis clamor ad coelum adversus parricidas Anglicanos* ('A cry to heaven of the king's blood against the English parricides') was published in The Hague. The *Clamor* contains a brutal personal attack on Milton in its opening pages, and concludes with a 245-line poem that renews the attack. The author of this work was almost certainly the Anglican divine Peter Du Moulin, who sent it to Salmasius in order that it could be published in the Netherlands; Salmasius passed the manuscript to Alexander More, a minister of the Reformed church. More (Latin Morus) contributed a preface to Du Moulin's treatise, and sent it to Adriaan Vlacq, who published it in The Hague. Milton mistakenly assumed that More was the author of the treatise, and although he was apprised of his error by John Durie and Samuel Hartlib, he stood by his mistake and flatly refused to be dissuaded. In May 1654 Milton replied to the *Clamor* with *Joannis Miltonii Angli pro populo Anglicano defensio secunda, contra infamem libellum anonymum cui titulus 'Regii sanguinis clamor ad coelum adversus parricidas Anglicanos'* ('The second defence of John Milton, Englishman, on behalf of the English people, against an infamous anonymous libel entitled A cry to heaven of the king's blood against the English parricides'). This tract, which is usually known as the *Defensio secunda* or the *Second Defence*, is for two important reasons less republican than its predecessor: first, Cromwell had assumed the quasi-regal title lord protector in December 1653, and so Milton praises him in terms that befit a monarch; second, the need to restore relations with Sweden leads Milton to formulate a paean of praise for Queen Kristina.

The *Clamor* had alleged that Milton had been expelled from Cambridge and had fled in shame to Italy. Milton decided to combat this calumny by defending himself and attacking More. Milton's self-defence is a long account of his youth in which he presents himself as the epitome of moral probity in Cambridge and as a courageous protestant champion in Italy. His attack on More centres on sexual indiscretions, particularly More's seduction of a servant in the household of Salmasius. Milton seizes on this violation of Christian morality and of the hospitality of his host to pummel More, constantly playing on More's name in Latin and Greek (in which it can mean 'mulberry tree' and 'fool'), and proposing an analogy between an immoral sexual act and an immoral book; in this unnatural coupling of minister and servant, Milton alleges, both sinners became pregnant: the servant gave birth to a bastard child and the minister of the gospel gave birth to an evil book, the *Clamor*.

In October 1654 the deeply wounded Alexander More hit back at Milton with *Alexandri Mori ecclesiasticae et sacrarum litterarum professoris fides publica, contra calumnias Ioannis Miltoni* ('The public faith of Alexander More, minister and professor of sacred literature, against the misrepresentations of John Milton'); in the following spring he published a *Supplementum* which consists for the most part of additional evidence. These two tracts are largely concerned with personal morality (Milton's is attacked, More's defended) and with Milton's doggedly mistaken insistence that More was the author of the *Clamor*. Milton replied in August 1655 with his third and final defence, *Joannis Miltonii Angli pro se defensio contra Alexander Morum, ecclesiasten, libelli famosi, cui titulus, 'Regii sanguinis clamor'* ... *authorem recte dictum* ('The defence of himself of John Milton, Englishman, against the minister Alexander More, who is rightly said to be the author of a famous libel entitled Cry of the royal blood'), in which Milton defends his own morality, attacks More's, and defends his indefensible attribution of the *Clamor* to More.

Poetry, 1652–1659 Milton's public voice may have echoed around Europe during the 1650s, but most of the poems that he was writing remained unpublished until 1673. In August 1653 Milton had returned to the Psalms, producing verse translations of psalms 1–8. His other poetical works of the 1650s were all sonnets. The sonnet had hitherto been a form used primarily to express the love of a man for a woman or (in the case of John Donne) for God. Milton chose instead to use the sonnet as a vehicle for principled statements on public affairs. The earliest sonnet from this period is 'To the Lord General Cromwell' (later Sonnet 16), which Milton dated 'May 1652'. Two months later, on 3 July, he composed a sonnet (later Sonnet 17) to Sir Henry Vane the younger and sent it to him. The next five sonnets seem to have been composed in 1655. The powerful 'On the late massacre in Piedmont' (later Sonnet 18), which articulates Milton's horror at the barbarous massacre of some 1700 Vaudois in April 1655, was probably composed two months later, in the last week of June. The date of 'On his Blindness' (Sonnet 19), a title first used in 1752, is unknown; several strands of evidence point to the second half of 1655, but it could have been written as early as 1651, when Milton was enduring the final stages of encroaching blindness. The sonnet 'Lawrence of virtuous father' (later Sonnet 20) was probably composed late in 1655, as were the two sonnets addressed to Cyriack Skinner (later sonnets 21 and 22).

On 12 November 1656 Milton married Katherine Woodcock (*bap.* 1628, *d.* 1658) and in the following October Katherine gave birth to a daughter, who was named after her mother. Four months later Katherine died, and a month later their infant daughter was buried beside her. If, as seems likely but not certain, Milton's wife Katherine is the subject of 'Methought I Saw my Late Espoused Saint' (later Sonnet 23), Milton must have composed the poem in the wake of her death on 3 February 1658. Shortly thereafter he began to dictate *Paradise Lost*, though he regularly interrupted his work on the epic to attend to ecclesiastical and political issues in a final flurry of political tracts, the last of which appeared on the eve of the Restoration.

Prose, 1659–1660 One of the debates that had persisted throughout the Commonwealth and protectorate republic concerned Erastianism. In 1659 Thomas Erastus's *Explicatio gravissimae quaestionis* (1589) appeared in English translation as *The Nullity of Church Censures*, so giving a wide audience to Erastus's view that in a state with one religion, the jurisdiction of the state should extend to ecclesiastical as well as civil matters. Milton was resolutely opposed to Erastianism, and in February 1659 published *A treatise of civil power in ecclesiastical causes, showing that it is not lawful for any power on earth to compel in matters of religion*. Once again the tract is addressed to parliament, this time to the parliament of Richard Cromwell, which had been convened on 27 January. Milton's short book is a polemic directed 'against Erastus and state-tyranny over the church'.

The argument about Erastian principles was closely related to the argument about tithes, which were compulsory ecclesiastical taxes levied by local churches. Radical Independents opposed tithes on theological grounds (they were said to have emerged from the law of the Old Testament rather than the new dispensation heralded by Jesus), but also because tithes were used to support either the state church from which they wished to dissociate themselves or the secular impropriators into whose families had passed the rectorial tithes that had formerly gone to the monasteries. Milton set out his position on tithes in *Considerations touching the likeliest means to remove hirelings out of the church, wherein is also discoursed of tithes, church-fees, church revenues, and whether any maintenance of ministers can be settled by law*, which was published in August 1659. This tract is again addressed to parliament, but to a different parliament: Richard Cromwell had abdicated on 25 May, and the Rump Parliament had re-established the Commonwealth. In this tract Milton praises the Rump as 'the best patrons of religious and civil liberty that ever these islands brought forth', and asks them to deliver England 'from the oppressions of a simonious decimating clergy'. The phrase recalls Milton's denunciation of the 'blind mouths' of the greedy clergy in 'Lycidas'.

On 13 October 1659 General John Lambert dissolved the Rump Parliament, and on 29 October Milton expressed his dismay about this *coup d'état* in *A Letter to a Friend, Concerning the Ruptures of the Commonwealth*. The identity of the friend is not known, but it is clearly a senior political figure, perhaps the dying John Bradshaw, who may have been related to Milton and who bequeathed £10 to Milton when he died a few weeks later. In this letter, first published by John Toland in 1698, Milton explains to his influential friend that he deplores the 'backsliding' action of the army in deposing the parliament that they had recently restored, and waxes indignant that a state army could 'subdue the supreme power that set them up'. In Milton's view, the civil power, be it parliament or council of state, must always be the supreme power.

In the first fortnight of November 1659 Milton dictated *Proposals of certain expedients for the preventing of a civil war now feared, and the settling of a firm government*, a short tract not published until 1938; the surviving text seems to be a draft or a briefing document rather than a completed work. The tone of the pamphlet is much less combative than that of *A Letter to a Friend*; parliament is defended, but the army is not attacked. Milton proposes that England be governed by a 'Grand or Supreme Council' in which members 'sit indissolubly' for the rest of their lives; he rejects the term 'parliament' for this body on the grounds that it is a 'Norman or French word, a monument of our ancient servitude'.

From 18 to 21 February 1660, when the Commonwealth was on the verge of collapse, Milton dictated a passionate pamphlet entitled *The ready and easy way to establishing a free commonwealth, and the excellence thereof compared with the inconveniences and dangers of re-admitting kingship in this nation*, which was published before the end of the month. In the face of a Restoration that looked increasingly inevitable, Milton chose defiantly to set the bondage of monarchy against the freedom of a Christian commonwealth ruled by a grand council. This council would be both permanent and self-perpetuating; Milton was not an instinctive democrat, and did not think that popular elections were an appropriate mechanism for filling vacancies in the council.

Early in March Milton dictated *The present means and brief delineation of a free commonwealth, easy to be put in practice, and without delay*, the manuscript of which has disappeared; when John Toland published it in 1698 he added the words *In a Letter to General Monck*, a reasonable inference from the content of what seems to be the draft of a letter. The formal title, more likely to be Milton's than Toland's, implies that Milton had intended to write a pamphlet in the form of an open letter rather than a private letter to George Monck. The letter summarizes the proposals of *The Ready and Easy Way*, but with two important differences: the authority of the grand council would be limited so that it would not have the 'power to endanger our liberty', and the establishment of the council should be implemented even if there were opposition, if necessary by military force.

Milton soon set to work on the second edition of *The Ready and Easy Way*, revised at the end of March to accommodate the headlong rush of political change in the last days of the English republic; the tract was published in the first week of April, a month before the restoration of Charles II was proclaimed on 8 May. Milton's eloquent defence of the nobility of republican values and his horrific vision of the degeneracy and servitude that would follow in the wake of a restored monarchy make this pamphlet England's greatest monument to a lost political cause. The government that he proposes is not a direct democracy: Milton opposes 'committing all to the noise and shouting of a rude multitude', a phrase that anticipates the contempt of the Jesus of *Paradise Regained* for the 'miscellaneous rabble'. Instead he envisages an aristocracy of godly men, an ideal that recalls the assumption in *Comus* and *Of Education* that rulers should be an aristocracy of virtue. This argument leads Milton to the conclusion that the enlightened minority should be able to impose liberty on the ignorant majority, if necessary by force.

On 25 March Matthew Griffith, a former chaplain of Charles I, preached a royalist sermon which he published at the beginning of April as *The Fear of God and the King*. Milton replied, probably in the second week of April, with *Brief Notes upon a Late Sermon*—his last publication before the Restoration cut off his access to the medium of print. Milton expresses his satisfaction that the council of state had been quick to incarcerate Griffith, and goes on to denounce him for advocating episcopacy and for dedicating the sermon to Monck. Milton concludes that if England is about to submit to the thraldom of monarchy, it should at least choose its own monarch: Milton thought that Monck would be a better choice than Charles Stuart. Milton's last republican tract thus advocated the second-best choice of an elected monarch. Milton was not a constitutional theorist, but it is in these tracts written in the final years of the interregnum that he articulates a shifting compromise in which he adapts the republican values that he had celebrated for more than a decade to an unstable and uncertain political situation.

One of Milton's private projects during his years as a servant of the Commonwealth and protectorate was the composition of a systematic theology. This ordonnance began as a compilation of theological writings in the 1640s, and was successively described as a 'System of Divinity', a 'Body of Divinity', and '*Idea Theologiae*'. The preparation of this treatise was broken off by the Restoration; it survives as a working document, frozen in time by the cataclysm of the Restoration. How far the raw materials of the treatise have been assimilated into Milton's own thinking is unclear, and the arrangement of some chapters may not reflect Milton's final judgement. There was an abortive attempt to publish the treatise in the Netherlands shortly after Milton's death, but the manuscript was impounded by the English government, together with a collection of Milton's state papers, and was locked in a cupboard in Whitehall and forgotten until rediscovered in November 1823. By that time (or possibly at that time) the manuscript had acquired the Augustinian title *De doctrina Christiana*, and it was published in Latin and in English translation in 1825.

Milton's theology evolved throughout his adult life, and *De doctrina* and *Paradise Lost* represent his thinking in the 1650s and 1660s. Many of his theological ideas would have been regarded as unsound or even heretical by his contemporaries. He rejected the doctrine of the Trinity in favour of a modified Arianism, insisted on the materiality of angels and denied that the world had been created out of nothing; his understanding of divine grace and of soteriology aligned him with the Arminians rather than the Calvinists, and so the Adam and Eve of *Paradise Lost* exercise free choice.

The Restoration years, 1660–1674 The restoration of Charles II was proclaimed on 8 May 1660, and Milton went into hiding at the house of an unidentified friend in Bartholomew Close (West Smithfield). On 16 June an order for Milton's arrest was issued, and on 13 August a proclamation ordering books by Milton to be called in for burning was published; on 27 August copies of his books were duly burnt by the public executioner at the Old Bailey. Milton's life hung in the balance until 29 August, when the Act of Free and General Pardon, Indemnity and Oblivion was given the royal assent; Milton was not named as an exception to the general pardon, so he escaped the death penalty, while none the less remaining liable to arrest and assassination. Milton emerged from hiding and took a house in Holborn (in the parish of St Giles-in-the-Fields), where he lived until the autumn, when he was arrested and imprisoned in the Tower. On 15 December he was ordered to be released from the Tower and to pay the cost of his imprisonment, which was set at £150. Milton had been pardoned, but no copy of the pardon has survived (even though two copies survived long enough to be entered into indices in the Public Record Office), so the precise reason for his release is not known. One effect of the Restoration had been the collapse of the Excise Office, which took with it Milton's savings of £2000. He emerged from prison in financial difficulty, and promptly protested against what he saw as the excessive fee for his imprisonment. On 17 December Andrew Marvell raised the matter in parliament, which referred it to the committee of privileges; the eventual outcome is not known. On his release from prison Milton moved to a house on Jewin Street, where he lived until about 1669.

On 24 February 1663 Milton married for the third time. He was fifty-four and his red-haired bride, Elizabeth Minshull (1638–1727), was twenty-four; she outlived her husband by more than half a century. By this stage Milton seems to have been estranged from his daughters: on being informed of her father's impending wedding, Mary replied (according to Milton's servant) 'that it was no news, to hear of his wedding, but, if she could hear of his death, *that* was something' (Masson, 4.476). The visitation of plague in 1665 was unusually virulent, and in July the Miltons moved to a cottage in Chalfont St Giles, a Quaker village in Buckinghamshire. The cottage belonged to Anne Fleetwood, daughter of the regicide George Fleetwood, and had been rented on Milton's behalf by the Quaker Thomas Ellwood; the cottage is the only residence of Milton still standing, and is now a museum. Milton returned to London when the plague had abated, probably in February 1666. On 2 September 1666 the conflagration later known as the great fire of London began to spread through the city, and three days later two-thirds of London had been consumed. Milton's home in Jewin Street was just north of the city wall, but in the event the fire was successfully contained on its northern flank by the wall and the ditch. Milton's house was safe, but most of his London had disappeared, including his childhood home on Bread Street, his school, and St Paul's Cathedral. In 1670 Milton lodged for a time in Duck Lane, Little Britain. The reason for this temporary accommodation is not known, but it may have been occasioned by the move from Jewin Street to Milton's last home, in Artillery Walk (now Bunhill Row).

Paradise Lost The Restoration interrupted Milton's composition of *Paradise Lost*, which assumed its final form in the years 1658–63. The remote beginnings of his epic can be seen in four drafts of a tragedy called 'Paradise Lost' (in the third draft) or 'Adam Unparadised' (in the fourth draft) which survive in the Trinity manuscript; these drafts seem to have been written about 1640. Edward Phillips claimed that he had been shown part of Satan's first soliloquy (*Paradise Lost*, book 5, ll. 32–41) 'several years before the poem was begun', when Milton still intended it to be a tragedy rather than an epic. The difficulties of composing such a long and complex work were exacerbated by Milton's difficult personal circumstances and by his blindness. He seems to have composed during the winter months, usually at night or in the early morning; when an amanuensis arrived he would dictate the lines that he had composed (usually about forty), and then 'reduce them to half the number'. Edward Phillips would then correct the spelling and punctuation of 'ten, twenty or thirty verses at a time'. Composition of the poem was inevitably interrupted by Milton's months in hiding and in prison, and when he eventually resumed his dictation, his world had changed irrevocably; at the beginning of book 7 the narrator's voice acknowledges that:

> More safe I sing with mortal voice, unchanged
> To hoarse or mute, though fallen on evil days,
> On evil days though fallen, and evil tongues;
> In darkness, and with dangers compassed round,
> And solitude.

This is the voice of a blind poet whose life was in danger after the calamity of the Restoration. Milton had aspired in the opening invocation of the poem 'to justify the ways of God to men', and the collapse of the godly republic had certainly left God's ways in need of justification. Milton's view was that the Commonwealth had failed not because God had caused it to fail, but rather because the frailty of humankind can be successfully exploited by the forces of evil. The Satan whom Milton created in *Paradise Lost* is not a king in exile who conquers Eden by force, but rather a traitor who speaks the language of radical republicanism in order to advance his own interests; in this respect *Paradise Lost* reflects Milton's contention that the reign of the godly was betrayed from within. Despite this reflection of the time of crisis during which the poem was composed, *Paradise Lost* is neither a political allegory nor a *roman-à-clef*; it is rather an epic which aspires to achieve in English what Homer, Virgil, and Dante had achieved in their languages, and its avowed purpose is theological rather than political. He aspired in his epic, as he had many years earlier in *Of Education*, 'to repair the ruins of our first parents by regaining to know God aright'. He saw himself as a latter-day prophet chosen by God to explain the divine ways to those who would know God aright, and he hoped that *Paradise Lost* would 'fit audience find, though few' (book 31); the godly survivors of the republic had the requisite fitness, and it is to them that Milton addressed his poem. The godly government of the interregnum had been displaced by the profligate court of Charles II, and for those who had laboured for the good old cause, God's ways stood in need of justification.

Paradise Lost is an epic which accommodates within that genre several other genres: the account of Sin and Death is an allegory, the description of Eden is pastoral, the gardening labours of Adam and Eve are georgic and, most important of all, the fall of Adam and Eve is presented as a tragedy. Milton describes the fall in book 9, at the outset of which he declares that he 'now must change / Those notes to tragic', so signalling that he proposes to transform the crime and punishment narrative of the biblical account of the fall into a tragedy. It is this shift of genre that has necessitated the endowment of Adam and Eve with dramatic characters and with motives for their actions. The sympathetic presentation of these motives, together with the detailed account of the role of Satan in the fall of Eve, constitutes a plea in mitigation for the fall. Milton's version of the fall is thus an affirmation of the dignity of humankind, a sentiment rooted in the Renaissance rather than the Reformation and one which, on a political level, explains to God the human failings that led to the fall of the godly republic. In this respect, Milton was attempting to justify the ways of men to God.

The focus of *Paradise Lost* is the fall of Adam and Eve, but the action is also played out on a cosmic stage in which the principal characters are God, the Son, and Satan. Milton's seventeenth-century God is much more anthropomorphic than his twenty-first century descendant in which Milton's readers believe or disbelieve. The God of *Paradise Lost* can be ill-tempered and irrational, and to a modern reader can seem shockingly immodest in his insistence that the purpose of creation is to praise him. Milton's Son is also rooted in the century in which he was conceived. He does not have a pre-incarnate name, and is simply called the Son: in *Paradise Regained* Milton was to deploy his earthly name of Jesus, but he never used the term Christ to denote his character; indeed, he eschewed the term in all poems after 1646, when he used it in 'On the new forcers of conscience'. Milton's Son, like his New Testament original, 'came not to send peace, but a sword' and in *Paradise Lost*, he is, like the angels, primarily a warrior. The accounts of the war in heaven in book 6 and of the creation in book 7 both culminate in a celebration of the Son, whose achievements occlude the work of God the Father. In Puritan soteriology it was the Son rather than the Father who effected salvation, and so the Son is the central figure in the puritan godhead.

In the minds of many of its readers, the most important character in *Paradise Lost* is Milton's Satan, who dominates the first two books of the poem and in a magnificent soliloquy at the beginning of book 4 tries to establish himself as a tragic figure. Seventeenth-century readers shared with Milton an unshakeable conviction of the total and irredeemable depravity of Satan and so regarded him as a falsely heroic figure, but in succeeding centuries, as Enlightenment ideas eroded Christian belief, Satan gradually came to be seen as the truly heroic figure at the imaginative heart of the poem. In the nineteenth century

Romantic Satanism spread through Germany as far as Russia, and in the twentieth century Milton was often said to have had an unconscious sympathy with the Satan of *Paradise Lost*.

Paradise Lost was finally completed by 1663, but Milton's reputation as a champion of the republic meant that he could not publish the poem immediately. The politically opportune moment for the publication of *Paradise Lost* finally arose in the spring of 1667. On 27 April Milton sealed a contract (now in the British Library) with the printer Samuel Simmons; Milton received £5 immediately, with the promise of another £5 when the first edition of 1300 copies had been sold; the second and third editions, neither of which would exceed 1500 copies, would each generate an additional £5. Had the poem proved to be particularly popular, Milton stood to make £20. The first edition was exhausted in the spring of 1669, and on 26 April Simmons paid Milton another £5; the price seems to have been 3s. a copy, and so Simmons would have received £195. Milton died shortly after the second edition was published, and so he received only £10 for *Paradise Lost*; after his death his widow sold the rights to the poem to Simmons for £8. The sums involved are modest but quite normal, and certainly no more derisory than the royalties paid by publishers in succeeding centuries.

Milton's epic was registered as 'Paradise Lost: a Poem in Ten Books' on 20 August 1667, and was published late in October or early in November. Sir John Denham is said (by Jonathan Richardson the elder) to have come into the House of Commons (which had reconvened on 10 October) carrying a sheet of *Paradise Lost* 'wet from the press' and proclaiming it 'part of the noblest poem that ever was wrote in any language or any age' (Masson, 6.628); by mid-November the poem was the subject of correspondence between John Beale and John Evelyn. The poem did not sell particularly quickly: between 1667 and 1669 six successive title-pages, each for a different issue, were required to sell the first edition of 1300 copies. The first three editions of *Paradise Lost* sold in modest numbers, but the fourth edition, a sumptuous gilt-edged folio published in 1688, was bought by subscription by many of the most influential readers in England, and thereafter the poem came to be widely regarded as England's national epic.

Paradise Regained and Samson Agonistes In August 1665 Milton had shown the unpublished manuscript of *Paradise Lost* to Thomas Ellwood, who read it and told Milton that 'thou hast said much here of *Paradise Lost*, but what hast thou to say of *Paradise Found?*' (Masson, 6.496). In the following year Ellwood visited Milton in London, and Milton showed him the manuscript of *Paradise Regained*, graciously telling Ellwood that 'this is owing to you; for you put it into my head by the question you put to me at Chalfont' (ibid., 6.654). It is possible that *Paradise Regained*, which depicts the temptations of Jesus in the desert, owes its pacific tone to the influence of the values of the Quaker community at Chalfont St Giles. The Jesus of *Paradise Regained* is not a warrior like the Son in book 6 of *Paradise Lost*, but rather a man who outwits his opponent. Milton's fictional Jesus is not, however, a sentimentalized figure:

he denounces ordinary citizens as 'a herd confused, a miscellaneous rabble', so reflecting Milton's disdain for popular democracy, and he denounces the cultural accomplishments of ancient Greece, so reflecting the opinion of Milton in his late years that worldly learning was a vain pursuit; in taking this position he approaches the radical view that education, like riches, constituted an impediment to salvation.

In the autumn of 1671 Milton published *Paradise Regained, a Poem in IV Books, to which is Added Samson Agonistes*. The date of *Paradise Regained* can be ascertained by the testimony of Thomas Ellwood, but there can be no certainty about the date of *Samson Agonistes*. Topical references and stylistic markers show that *Samson* is substantially a post-Restoration work, though scholars debate whether it was written immediately after the Restoration or shortly before publication; on the other hand, echoes of the divorce tracts of the 1640s make an early stage of composition distinctly possible. It is difficult to gainsay the authoritative opinion of Edward Phillips, who noted that its date of composition 'cannot certainly be concluded'; as Henry Todd pointed out in his edition of 1801, *Samson Agonistes* 'furnishes some internal proofs of its having been composed at different periods'.

Samson Agonistes is a closet drama intended to be read rather than performed; it is therefore a literary rather than a dramatic work, and so claimed affinity with the plays of classical antiquity, which in seventeenth-century England were read rather than performed. The structure of the play is modelled on that of ancient Greek drama, but the characterization of Samson is resolutely modern. Like Racine, who was at the height of his powers when Milton published *Samson Agonistes*, Milton created a protagonist who was much more self-conscious than were the dramatic characters of antiquity; in this respect Milton's Samson has more in common with Hamlet than with Oedipus. Indeed, Samson is in some respects a Restoration nonconformist struggling to discern a pattern of divine intervention in his life. God is absent from *Samson Agonistes*, as he is in similar works such as Bunyan's *Pilgrim's Progress*: for late seventeenth-century nonconformists, spiritual growth was not assisted by any vision of God. Samson's massacre of the Philistines at the end of the play also has a contemporary agenda: in Milton's version of the massacre it is only the Philistian lords that are killed, because 'the vulgar only scaped who stood without'. In Milton's view, retribution should be directed at political leaders rather than at those whom they lead.

Prose, 1669–1674 In 1669 Milton published his *Accidence commenced grammar, supplied with sufficient rules for the use of such (younger or elder) as are desirous without more trouble than need to attain the Latin tongue, the elder sort especially, with little teaching and their own industry*; it is not clear when Milton had written this primer of Latin accidence (that is, the variable forms of words) and grammar, but it is possible that it was a product of his years as a teacher in the 1640s.

In 1671 Milton published his *History of Britain*. The first four books had been drafted in February and March 1649, and the last two books seem to have been written in the mid-1650s, possibly in 1655. The most problematical element in the *History* is the digression, a passage in book 3 which was omitted from all editions until 1738, but published separately in 1681 as *Character of the Long Parliament*; this comparison of the ancient Britons at the time of the Roman withdrawal with the English in Milton's own time was probably written in 1648, but a case for composition in 1660 has been advanced.

In May 1672 Milton published his *Joannis Milton Angli artis logicae plenior institutio ad Petri Rami methodum concinnata, adjucta est praxis analytica & Petri Rami vita* ('A fuller course in the art of logic, arranged according to the method of Pierre de la Ramée; an analytical exercise and a life of La Ramée are appended'). The *Ars logicae* is a derivative Ramist treatise on logic drawn for the most part from a Latin commentary on Petrus Ramus by George Downham, as is the analytical exercise; the biography is a condensed version of the life of Ramus by Johann Freige. In the following year Milton published a revised edition of his minor poems and his first polemical tract since the Restoration, *Of true religion, heresy, schism, toleration and what best means may be used against the growth of popery*, which appeared early in May 1673. Charles II had promulgated the declaration of indulgence (which had suspended the penalties for Catholicism and nonconformity) in March 1672, but had been forced to rescind it in March 1673. Milton's tract is tolerant of the sectarians, who 'may have some errors, but are not heretics', but mounts a coruscating attack on Roman Catholicism, which he denounces as politically dangerous and theologically idolatrous.

In 1674 Milton published a volume containing a collection of thirty-one private letters (*Epistolae familiares*) and the Latin prolusions that he had delivered while a student in Cambridge. He had also saved many of his state papers, most of which were his translations into Latin of letters from the English government to the chancelleries of Europe, but these were not published until after his death. The first edition, *Literae pseudo-senatûs Anglicani Cromwellii reliquorumque perduellium nomine ac jussu conscriptae a Joanne Miltono* ('Letters written by John Milton in the name and by the order of the so-called English parliament of Cromwell and other traitors'), was printed by two different printers (in Amsterdam and Brussels) in October 1676; a preface carefully distances the edition from the politics of the reviled interregnum government by insisting disingenuously that the sole interest of the letters lies in their exemplary Latin style.

Milton's final political work was a translation of the Latin version of *A Declaration, or, Letters Patent*, a Polish tract advocating an elective monarchy; this pamphlet was a contribution to the Exclusion debate, in that it contests the Catholic succession, but its advocacy of a form of monarchy also implies that Milton may not have espoused unequivocally the republicanism with which he came to be associated after his death.

Last days Milton's final publication, early in July 1674, was the second edition of *Paradise Lost*, which he had reorganized into twelve books, so making explicit the parallel with the epics of classical antiquity; this edition also contained two prefatory poems, one in Latin by 'S. B.' (probably Milton's physician friend Samuel Barrow) and one in English by Andrew Marvell. A few weeks after the publication of this edition, Milton prepared a nuncupative (that is, orally declared) will with the help of his brother Christopher. In his will Milton chose to recall with smouldering resentment that his first father-in-law, Richard Powell, had never paid the dowry of £1000 that was due to Milton on his marriage to Mary Powell. According to Christopher's testimony on 23 November, the will stated that 'the portion due to me from Mr Powell, my former wife's father, I leave to the unkind children I had by her, having received no part of it'. This worthless legacy of an unpaid dowry testifies to the bitterness of Milton's estrangement from his daughters; he left everything to Elizabeth, 'my loving wife'. Milton died, probably of renal failure associated with gout, on the night of 9–10 November 1674, at his home in Artillery Walk, and was buried beside his father near the altar in St Giles Cripplegate on 12 November.

Posthumous reputation After his death Milton became associated with the whig cause. His enthusiastic praise of Queen Kristina was forgotten, as was his insistence in the *Defensio secunda* that he had written not against kings, but only against tyrants; instead, Milton came to be regarded as an unambiguous republican. Milton's republican ideas and ideals were eventually taken up in France and America. An anonymous pamphlet called *Théorie de la royauté, d'après la doctrine de Milton* (Paris, 1789) appropriated Milton to the revolutionary cause in France, and in 1792 Jacobin regicides reissued the French translation of Milton's *Defensio prima*. In the United States, Benjamin Franklin, Thomas Jefferson, and John Adams drew on their wide reading in Milton's poetry and prose to articulate their republicanism: Franklin evoked the Chaos of *Paradise Lost* in his diatribe against British taxes in America, Jefferson deployed the arguments of Milton's anti-prelatical tracts to support the case for ecclesiastical disestablishment in Virginia, and Adams excoriated British rulers as embodiments of the arrogance and futile rebellion of Milton's Satan. Milton may rightly be regarded as one of the founding fathers of American and French republicanism, but in England he had no political progeny; English republicanism died on the scaffold with Algernon Sidney, and has never been successfully revived.

The 1695 edition of *Paradise Lost* included learned annotations by 'P. H.' (probably Patrick Hume), and so Milton's epic became the first English poem to be edited as if it were a classical text. Thereafter the poem attracted serious critical attention. In 1712 Joseph Addison published a series of 'Notes' on *Paradise Lost* in *The Spectator*, and these notes were soon translated into French (1727), German (1740), and Italian (1742). In 1732 Richard Bentley published an emended edition of *Paradise Lost* in which he 'corrected' hundreds of imagined errors in what he thought was a corrupt text; Bentley's misconceived erudition was soon discredited by scholars and mocked by satirists (including Pope, who included him in his *Dunciad*), but his edition and the analyses of his detractors demonstrate the care with which educated eighteenth-century readers attended to the text of Milton's poem. Later in the century Samuel Johnson included an insightful and opinionated critical biography of Milton in his *Lives of the Poets* (1779–81).

Paradise Lost was written in blank verse, but in the late seventeenth century portions of the poem were twice published in rhymed versions: John Dryden secured the permission of Milton to 'tag' (that is, rhyme) *Paradise Lost* for his operatic adaptation, *The State of Innocence and Fall of Man* (1677), and John Hopkins gallantly tried to offer assistance to ladies who found the poem too difficult by publishing a rhymed paraphrase of books 4 and 9 (1699). During this period translations into German (1682) and Latin (1686) rendered the poem accessible to European audiences.

In the eighteenth century Milton's epic was responsible for the shift from rhyme to blank verse, and also for many features of poetic diction and syntax. The style of *Paradise Lost* was imitated by classical translators such as Alexander Pope and Joseph Trapp and by poets such as Sir Richard Blackmore, John Dennis, Matthew Smith, and William Thompson; it was also parodied, most notably by John Philips (*The Splendid Shilling*, 1701) and John Gay (*Wine*, 1709). The taste for the picturesque that became an important factor in the gardens, paintings, and nature poetry of the eighteenth century took as its starting point Milton's Eden, a 'happy rural seat of various view'. What was perceived as the awesome seriousness of *Paradise Lost* became the corner-stone of the sublime, a concept so all-pervasive that Mary Wollstonecraft could complain in 1787 that she was 'sick of hearing of the sublimity of Milton'; this was not a complaint about Milton, but rather a protest about the invoking of the sublime as a substitute for a proper critical understanding of Milton's poetry. The process of translation continued apace throughout the eighteenth century, including versions of *Paradise Lost* in Dutch (1728), French (1729), Italian (1729), Greek (1735), Russian (1777), Norwegian (1787), Portuguese (1791), Polish (1791), Hungarian (1796), and Manx (1796).

The appropriation of Milton by the Romantic poets included both critical comment—Shelley and Blake championed Milton's Satan—and creative imitation, most notably *The Prelude*, in which Wordsworth aspires to establish himself as the successor to Milton. Blake illustrated all of Milton's major poems (except *Samson Agonistes*) and wrote two Miltonic poems, *The Four Zoas* (a rewriting of *Paradise Lost*) and *Milton, a Poem in Two Books*. The political Milton was also taken up as an early radical: as Wordsworth ringingly proclaims in 'London, 1802':

Milton! thou should'st be living at this hour:
England hath need of thee.

In the course of the nineteenth century this idolatry led to Milton's enthronement as the national poet; the greatest monument to the national reverence for Milton was David Masson's vast seven-volume biography of Milton. At the same time the tide of faith in Milton's anthropomorphic God and his historical Adam and Eve was beginning to retreat, and the study of Milton seemed to some to be an exhausted endeavour; Sir Walter Raleigh memorably formulated this position when he conceded that '*Paradise Lost* is a monument to dead ideas' (W. Raleigh, *Milton*, 1922, 88). Throughout the century new translations of Milton's poems continued to be published, including versions of *Paradise Lost* in Czech (1811), Spanish (1812), Swedish (1815), Armenian (1819), Welsh (1819), Icelandic (1818), Hebrew (1871), and Tongan (1892).

In the early twentieth century Milton fell 'on evil days and evil tongues' in his native England. The bitterest of those tongues was that of F. R. Leavis, who complacently announced in 1933 that 'Milton's dislodgement, in the past decade, after two centuries of predominance, was effected with remarkably little fuss'. This dislodgement, which Leavis attributed to the strictures of T. S. Eliot and J. Middleton Murry, proved to be an illusion beyond the narrow confines of the Cambridge of Leavis's day, though the popular idea of Milton as a grim misogynist has persisted; the most influential embodiment of this image is Robert Graves's *Wife to Mr Milton* (1943).

In the early twenty-first century Milton continues to be widely read. Schoolchildren in many countries still study Milton's poems (especially the sonnet on his blindness), *Paradise Lost* is studied in universities, and there is a substantial scholarly industry devoted to the study of Milton's works. There are large Milton societies in America and in Japan, and the learned presses continue to issue huge numbers of books and articles on Milton; there are even two journals wholly given over to Milton, *Milton Quarterly* and *Milton Studies*. For literary scholars and educated general readers alike, the poetry of Milton retains a central place in the canon of English literature. *Paradise Lost* is widely and rightly regarded as the supreme poetic achievement in the English language, fit to sit alongside the poems of Homer, Virgil, and Dante. In America, where Christianity is still a vital force, *Paradise Lost* is valued as the supreme epic of Christendom. In post-Christian Europe and in secular American circles, *Paradise Lost* has become a cultural battlefield for feminists and Freudians, cultural materialists and new historicists. These ephemeral ideologies have replaced earlier concerns with humanistic values and Christian ideas, and will in turn be supplanted by new critical fashions, but *Paradise Lost* will retain its importance as one of the greatest works of the human imagination.

GORDON CAMPBELL

Sources D. Masson, *The life of John Milton*, 7 vols. (1859–94) • W. R. Parker, *Milton: a biography*, 2nd edn, ed. G. Campbell, 2 vols. (1996) • J. M. French, *The life records of John Milton*, 5 vols. (1949–58) • G. Campbell, *A Milton chronology* (1997) • J. Shawcross, *Milton: a bibliography for the years 1624–1700* (1984); *Addenda and corrigenda* (1990) • P. Beal, 'Milton', *Index of English literary manuscripts*, ed. P. J. Croft and others, 2/2 (1993), 69–104 • *The works of John Milton*, ed. F. A. Patterson, 18 vols. (1931–8) • H. Darbishire, ed., *The early lives of Milton* (1932) • A. Stern, *Milton und seine Zeit*, 4 vols. in 2 (Leipzig, 1877–9) • D. L. Clark, *Milton at St Paul's School* (1948) • M. Di Cesare, ed., *Milton in Italy* (1991) • C. Hill, *Milton and the English revolution* (1977) • R. Fallon, *Milton in government* (1993) • B. Lewalski, *The life of John Milton*, rev. edn (2003)

Archives BL, Bible with autograph memoranda, Add. MS 32310 • BL, family Bible, Add. MS 32310 • BL, commonplace book, Add. MS 36354 • BL, presentation copy of *Comus*, loan 76 • Col. U., letter-

book · Morgan L., MSS · NYPL, family MSS · Trinity Cam., poetical MSS, MS R. 3. 4
Likenesses attrib. C. Johnson, oils, 1618, Morgan L. · oils, c.1629, NPG · W. Marshall, line engraving, 1645, BM, NPG; repro. in J. Milton, *Poems of Mr. John Milton* (1645) · attrib. E. Pierce, clay bust, c.1660, Christ's College, Cambridge; plaster cast, NPG · W. Faithorne the elder, line engraving, 1670, BM, NPG [*see illus.*] · J. Faber junior, mezzotint, pubd 1740, BM, NPG · L. F. Roubiliac, terracotta bust, c.1759, Scot. NPG · H. Cousins, mezzotint (after F. Newenham), NPG · Deis, mezzotint (after F. Newenham), NPG

Milton, John (*fl.* 1743–1776), painter, was a descendant of the judge Sir Christopher *Milton, brother of the poet John Milton. He worked in the neighbourhood of London, first at Southwark and later at Charlton in Kent, Soho, and Peckham, exhibiting with the Free Society from 1767 to 1776 and with the Society of Artists in 1773 and 1774. He chiefly painted seapieces, with an occasional landscape, and some animal subjects, such as sporting dogs. His *Strong Gale* was mezzotinted by R. Laurie, and his *English Setter* was engraved by J. Cook and S. Smith as a companion plate to William Woollett's *Spanish Pointer*, after Stubbs. His *Six Views of Dockyards*, engraved by P. C. Canot, was published by Boydell. His untraced painting *A Tropical Rice Field* suggests he may have travelled abroad.

John Milton was the father of Thomas *Milton, the landscape engraver.　　F. M. O'DONOGHUE, *rev.* PAUL A. COX

Sources Graves, *Artists* · Graves, *Soc. Artists* · M. H. Grant, *A chronological history of the old English landscape painters*, rev. edn, 4 (1959), 267 · Redgrave, *Artists* · Waterhouse, *18c painters*

Milton, John (1759–1805), seal engraver and medallist, was born on 19 July 1759. In 1785 he married Sarah (*d.* 1796), the daughter of Henry Gretton, a seal engraver of Fenchurch Street, London; they had a son, Henry, and two daughters, Emma and Sarah.

Milton exhibited at the Royal Academy between 1785 and 1802. In March 1787 he was recruited by the Royal Mint as an assistant engraver at a salary of £80 and free lodgings. He engraved a seal for America which was not adopted and produced a number of medals, a pattern penny for Anglesey in 1786, and copper coins for Barbados in 1788 and 1792. While he supplemented his income by executing private commissions for medals and tokens, he made the mistake of preparing dies imitative of French and Portuguese gold coins which were used by counterfeiters, and he was dismissed from the mint in March 1797. Thereafter, working privately, his productions included a pattern shilling in 1798 and a series of Scottish pattern coins in 1799 in the name of the prince regent for Colonel Fullerton, later governor of Trinidad.

While at the mint, Milton took George Valentin Bauert of Altona as his pupil, and they engraved dies for several medals, including one dated 1744 to commemorate Robert Walpole, earl of Oxford. The obverse die, which quickly cracked, was by Bauert, the reverse by Milton. Milton's signature was normally J. MILTON, but IM, IMF.M-INT, I.M.F. TOWER, and MILTON are also known.

Milton was elected a fellow of the Society of Antiquaries on 24 May 1792. He died on 11 February 1805, and his body was interred at St Dunstan-in-the-West, Fleet Street. He was survived by his three children. His son, Henry, followed in his footsteps by becoming a seal engraver.　　MICHAEL SHARP

Sources T. Stainton, 'John Milton, medallist, 1759–1805', *British Numismatic Journal*, 53 (1983), 133–59 · L. Forrer, *Biographical dictionary of medallists*, 8 vols. (1904–30) · E. Hawkins, *Medallic illustrations of the history of Great Britain and Ireland to the death of George II*, ed. A. W. Franks and H. A. Grueber, 2 vols. (1885) · J. Craig, *The mint* (1953)
Likenesses J. Boyle, miniature, 1788, V&A

Milton, Thomas (1742/3–1827), printmaker and topographical draughtsman, was probably born in London in either 1742 or 1743. He was the great-nephew of the poet John Milton and the son of another John Milton (*fl.* 1770), a minor marine artist who sometimes produced landscape and animal subjects for engraving. Little is known of his early life in London, but he obviously received some architectural training, as his name first appears on engravings in a design manual entitled *The Chimney-Piece Maker's Daily Assistant* (1766). By 1782 he had moved to Great George's Street in Dublin, where he published a prospectus for his best-known work, *The Seats and Demesnes of the Nobility and Gentry in Ireland* (1782–7), a planned series of fifty engravings after the views of artists such as J. H. Barralet and Francis Wheatley. The first four plates of this series of gentlemen's seats was published in 1783, in collaboration with J. Walter in London, and later parts were issued sporadically over the next four years. The final instalments were issued, solely by Milton, between 1786 and 1793 after his return to London. Despite his original intentions, and some favourable reviews, publication terminated after only twenty-four plates, suggesting that the project was no longer commercially viable.

After this enterprise Milton relied on publisher's commissions, and he engraved plates for such lavish illustrated books as Thomas Macklin's edition of the *Holy Bible* (1800) or W. Y. Ottley's *The Marquis of Stafford's Collection* (1818). Most of his work was line engraving, but he also produced forty-eight colour aquatints, after designs by Luigi Meyer, to illustrate his *Views in Egypt* (1801). Perhaps as a result of this later reliance on publishers, Milton was committed to improving the status and rights of engravers; in 1803 he was one of the founder members of the short-lived Society of Engravers. He died in Bristol on 27 February 1827.　　LUCY PELTZ

Sources Anderton catalogues [exhibition catalogues, Society of Artists, BM, print room] · T. Dodd, 'Memoirs of English engravers, 1550–1800', BL, Add. MS 33403 · *GM*, 1st ser., 97/1 (1827), 379 · J. Pye, *Patronage of British art: an historical sketch* (1845) · W. G. Strickland, *A dictionary of Irish artists*, 2 vols. (1913) · Bryan, *Painters* (1903–5) · J. C. Smith, *British mezzotinto portraits*, 4 vols. in 5 (1878–84)

Milton [Meliton, Middleton, Milditone, Militon], **William of** (*d.* 1257×60), Franciscan friar and theologian, is listed as 'Fr. W. de Milton', the fifth Franciscan 'master' at Cambridge, on a leaf inserted in the oldest manuscript of the chronicle by the author known as Thomas of Eccleston. Historians have identified him with a William de Middletoun (or Melitona, and so on) who was a Franciscan regent master at Paris, and whom Pope Alexander IV put in charge of the task of completing the *Summa* associated with Alexander of Hales (*d.* 1245). If so, Milton was a major intellectual figure among the early Cambridge men (not a great distinction, it is true). The identification is not certain. The dates given by Moorman for the Cambridge master are hardly to be reconciled with what is known of the Paris master. But if his unreliable chronology is abandoned, it is possible to avoid multiplying Franciscan Master W.s beyond necessity.

Even the most scanty and tentative reconstruction of Milton's curriculum vitae is beset with difficulties. He seems to have been a regent master in theology at Paris in 1248, and may have kept that position until as late as 1253. He would have been a master at Cambridge for a period in the mid-1250s. According to Doucet it was in 1255 that Alexander IV made him head of a commission to finish the *Summa Fratris Alexandri*, by the bull *De fontibus paradisi*. This appears correct—Doucet cites his source. An alternative version, that the bull was issued in 1256, seems to be a misunderstanding. A. G. Little's statement, that Milton was appointed by Innocent IV in 1252 to finish the *Summa*, may have been derived from the *Histoire littéraire de la France*, which in turn seems to be following the early modern scholar J. A. Fabricius, who gives no medieval source. Consequently this dating to 1252 should probably be disregarded. There is also a problem about the date of Milton's death. Callebaut (followed by Smalley) argues that he died in 1257. Doucet leaves open the possibility that Milton died as late as 1260. He was one of the Franciscans who helped Isabelle, sister of Louis IX of France, with her rule for her nunnery at Longchamp; but if the 1257 date is right, Milton did not live to see the end of these preparations.

A range of commentaries or postills on books of the Bible have been attributed to Milton, but it is at present impossible to be certain of his authorship of all of these. The Apocalypse commentary has been studied by Burr, and there seems no reason to doubt Milton's authorship. In a Paris university stationer's *pecia* list of 1275 Guillermus de Milditone appears as author of commentaries on Psalms, the twelve prophets, St Mark's gospel, Ecclesiasticus, and Job. The commentary on the twelve lesser prophets, whose authenticity is assured, and which was popular in Milton's lifetime and/or within a few decades of his death, gives an idea of what his biblical lecturing was like. It shows originality of a kind in returning to Benedictine spirituality by drawing on a work written in the early twelfth century by Guibert de Nogent. Apart from biblical commentaries, his authorship of *Quaestiones de sacramentis* and *Quaestiones disputatae xxiv* seems accepted, but not of the twelve *quaestiones disputatae* in MS Padua, Biblioteca Antoniana MS 152, which were once attributed to him.

The history of Milton's *Quaestiones de sacramentis*, as reconstructed by Doucet, is a good example of how thirteenth-century Franciscan scholars worked. Milton drew heavily on the *quaestiones* of Alexander of Hales, but Milton's *quaestiones* were in turn incorporated to a great extent word for word into the fourth part of the *Summa* 'of

brother Alexander', probably when Milton was working to complete it. Milton and his collaborators apparently made additions to the earlier parts of the synthesis too, but the task was not completed when Milton died, after which the commission under his charge seems to have given up the task. Doucet is probably right to think that Milton had been working on Alexander's unfinished *opus* even before the papacy came to his aid by asking the order to find him collaborators. William of Milton seems to have played a tenacious if unostentatious part in the formation of the powerful Franciscan intellectual tradition.

D. L. D'AVRAY

Sources *Guillelmi de Militona Quaestiones de sacramentis*, ed. C. Piana and G. Gál, 2 vols. (Florence, 1961) · *Fratris Thomae vulgo dicti de Eccleston tractatus de adventu Fratrum Minorum in Angliam*, ed. A. G. Little (1951), 58 and n. 3 · A. G. Little, *Franciscan papers, lists, and documents* (1943), 48–9, 133–4 · H. Denifle and A. Chatelain, eds., *Chartularium universitatis Parisiensis*, 4 vols. (Paris, 1891–9); repr. (Brussels, 1964) [index, S.V. Guillelmus de Melitona] · B. Smalley, 'William of Middleton and Guibert of Nogent', *Recherches de Théologie Ancienne et Médiévale*, 16 (1949), 281–91 · *Doctoris irrefragibilis Alexandri de Hales Ordinis Minorum 'Summa theologica'*, ed. Fathers of the College of St Bonaventure, 4 (1948) [Prolegomena] · V. Doucet, 'Maîtres franciscains de Paris: supplément au *Repertoire de maîtres en théologie de Paris au XIIIe siècle de M. le Chan. P. Glorieux*', *Archivum Franciscanum Historicum*, 27 (1934), 531–64, esp. 542–5 · A. Callebaut, 'L'année de la mort de Fr. Guillaume de Melitona', *Archivum Franciscanum Historicum*, 19 (1926), 431–4 · A. G. Little, 'The friars and the foundation of the faculty of theology in the University of Cambridge', *Mélanges Mandonnet: Études d'histoire littéraire et doctrinale du moyen âge*, 2 (1930), 389–401, esp. 398 and 400 · J. R. H. Moorman, *The Grey friars in Cambridge, 1225–1538*, The Birkbeck Lectures (1952), 31, 144, 195 · D. Burr, *Olivi's peaceable kingdom: a reading of the Apocalypse commentary* (1993) · A. Rivet de la Grange and others, eds., *Histoire littéraire de la France*, 19 (Paris, 1838), 416; 26 (Paris, 1873), 403

Milverley, William (*fl.* 1400), logician, is known only as the author of several treatises that survive in manuscript. According to Leland, he lived in the middle of the fourteenth century but, as his works are usually found in association with those of a somewhat later period, it is more probable that he was active at the end of that century. He is noted as holding the degree of MA almost certainly from Oxford University. Milverley has been linked with a 'Martilis', perhaps John Martel, fellow of Oriel College, Oxford (*c.*1410–*c.*1426). He wrote several commentaries and treatises examining logical material used in the faculty of arts. The variety of these works, the number of manuscripts that survive, and their scattered provenance suggest that Milverley was a significant figure among contemporary Oxford teachers. His influence also spread to the continent, and there is evidence that his writings were still being used in early sixteenth-century Oxford.

JOHN M. FLETCHER

Sources Emden, *Oxf.*, 2.1284 · P. V. Spade and E. J. Ashworth, 'Logic in late medieval Oxford', *Hist. U. Oxf.* 2: *Late med. Oxf.*, 35–64

Milverton. For this title name *see* Richards, Arthur Frederick, first Baron Milverton (1885–1978).

Milverton, John (*d.* 1487), Carmelite friar, theologian, and religious controversialist, was probably born near Bristol, where he joined the Carmelite order. His early studies were in Stamford, where he was ordained subdeacon on 30 April and deacon on 20 September 1432. He continued at Oxford and incepted as DTh in 1452. He was possibly the unnamed prior of Oxford who represented the Oxford distinction (region) in 1446 at a meeting called to discuss reform in the province, and in 1451 he was present at the general chapter in Avignon. He was elected provincial in 1456 at the request, it was said, of the reforming prior-general, John Soreth, and a year later Soreth appointed Milverton his vicar-general for Scotland and Ireland. In 1458, after Reginald Pecock, bishop of Chichester, had attacked the friars, Milverton debated against him before parliament and wrote to Pope Pius II (r. 1458–64) supporting Pecock's condemnation by Thomas Bourchier, archbishop of Canterbury (d. 1486).

It is claimed that at this period Milverton was being considered for a bishopric. However, on 16 September 1464, a fellow Carmelite, Henry Parker, preached at Paul's Cross arguing that Christ was a mendicant like the friars, which provoked a fierce debate between the friars and the secular clergy. Milverton was drawn into the controversy and, on 23 December 1464, he preached in the Carmelite church, London, supporting Parker's views. As a result, Milverton and Thomas Holden, the prior of the London house, were cited for heresy by the bishop of London. They claimed papal immunity but were ordered to answer the charges of heresy. Instead, fleeing to Rome, they appealed to Pope Paul II (r. 1464–71). Under questioning, Milverton was evasive and the pope ordered him to be detained in the Castel Sant' Angelo. The arrival of a letter from the archbishop of Canterbury led to Milverton's being examined by a commission of cardinals, who found him guilty of a number of errors. He remained in prison until 1468 when, lacking funds and influence, he was forced to recant. He returned to England with a letter from the pope to the archbishop of Canterbury, dated 22 December 1468, authorizing his reinstatement in all his former offices. He was re-elected provincial, and in 1472 was appointed vicar-general for the English, Scottish, and Irish provinces. On 16 November 1479 he was admitted as rector of Enborne, Berkshire. About this time an unknown English Carmelite wrote to the prior-general complaining that, although Milverton lived a blameless life, he was old and unable to cope with the affairs of the province. In 1482 Milverton resigned from office, and he died at the Carmelite house in London on 30 January 1487, and was buried there.

Leaving aside his clash with authority, Milverton was a memorable provincial, intellectually gifted and popular with his fellow Carmelites. Bale records that he was an outstanding preacher with a wonderful memory and great clarity of thought. None of his works survives although thirteen titles are known, many being responses to contemporary events, such as 'On the poverty of Christ', 'Against Reginald Pecock', as well as sermons, scholastic lectures, determinations, a treatise on St Augustine's *City of God*, and sixty-four letters written while Milverton was provincial. Others, dating from his Roman imprisonment, include an account of his captivity, letters to various cardinals, a letter to an unnamed Roman doctor on Christ's mendicancy dated 1469, and a statement of his beliefs which may have been his formal recantation.

RICHARD COPSEY

Sources J. Bale, Bodl. Oxf., MS Bodley 73 (SC 27635), fols. 12, 29, 50v, 51, 81v–82, 109, 115v, 120v, 133v, 197, 217v · J. Bale, BL, Harley MS 1819, fols. 67v, 87v, 197, 197v · J. Bale, BL, Harley MS 3838, fols. 38v–39v, 43v, 107–107v, 216v · F. R. H. Du Boulay, 'The quarrel between the Carmelite friars and the secular clergy of London, 1464–1468', *Journal of Ecclesiastical History*, 6 (1955), 156–74 · Emden, *Oxf.*, 2.1285–6 · Bale, *Cat.*, 1.618–20 · J. Bale, BL, Cotton MS Titus D.X., fols. 182–187v · 'William Gregory's chronicle of London', *The historical collections of a citizen of London in the fifteenth century*, ed. J. Gairdner, CS, new ser., 17 (1876), 55–239 · J. Bale, Bodl. Oxf., MS Selden supra 41, fols. 181v, 182v · *Commentarii de scriptoribus Britannicis, auctore Joanne Lelando*, ed. A. Hall, 2 (1709), 465–6 · J. Pits, *Relationum historicarum de rebus Anglicis*, ed. [W. Bishop] (Paris, 1619), 673–4 · Tanner, *Bibl. Brit.-Hib.*, 528–9

Milward, Sir Anthony Horace (1905–1981), airline executive, was born in Feckenham, near Worcester, on 2 March 1905, the son of Henry Tomson Milward, a needle manufacturer, and his wife, Elsie Newton. He was educated at Rugby School and at Clare College, Cambridge.

After leaving university, Milward joined the Manchester textile merchants Glazebrook Steel & Co. in 1926, instead of entering the family firm, Milward Needles of Redditch. In 1927 he was sent to India and worked for a year in Calcutta, with shorter spells in Madras, Bombay, and Karachi. In 1929 he returned to Manchester, and became a director of Glazebrook Steel in 1930. He married Frieda Elizabeth Anne (d. 1984), daughter of the merchant Gustav Adolf von der Becke in 1931. They had a son and a daughter.

Milward learned to fly under the Civil Air Guard scheme and acquired his 'A' pilot's licence in 1939. In 1940, at the age of thirty-five, he joined the Fleet Air Arm. He remained on flying duties throughout the Second World War, serving in Trinidad on anti-submarine and convoy protection sorties. In 1943 he was made lieutenant-commander, and was given command of the naval section of the radar experimental airfield at Defford in Worcestershire, testing airborne radar and night-flying equipment. In 1945 he was made an OBE.

At the end of the war, with a successful business career and wartime flying experience behind him, Milward relinquished his interests in the textile industry, and began a new career in civil aviation. After a brief period at the British Overseas Airways Corporation (BOAC), in April 1946 he joined the state-owned British European Airways (BEA), as general services manager, and became general manager of continental services shortly afterwards. In 1952 he became controller of operations at BEA, and in 1956 was appointed chief executive by the chairman, Lord Douglas of Kirtleside. Finally, in 1964 he succeeded Lord Douglas as BEA's chairman, a position he held until his retirement in 1970. He was made a CBE in 1960 and knighted in 1966.

Milward devoted twenty-five years' service to BEA, and although he was not as well known as his predecessor, Lord Douglas, he must be credited with a large share of the responsibility for BEA's success as an effective, and largely profitable, European flag-carrier. His business experience, combined with his technical background, was of great value in the management of the corporation, as was his quiet determination, and sense of leadership.

Convinced that BEA should make profits, and that nationalized industries should be commercial enterprises in public ownership, Milward spent a considerable amount of time battling with ministers and officials in the 1960s, a period when the nationalized industries were experiencing a high degree of government involvement. He was less inclined to continue Lord Douglas's rigid preference for British-built aircraft, and showed greater concern for the operating economics of new types acquired by BEA. A notable instance occurred in 1966 when BEA sought to abandon its British-only procurement policy, and buy the American Boeing 727 aircraft. The government refused to allow this purchase, and its insistence that BEA use the inferior Hawker Siddeley Trident Three instead, led to the payment of substantial compensation to the airline. On other occasions, however, Milward did seek to encourage the British aircraft industry. With the move to wide-bodied aircraft, he pleaded unsuccessfully for the development of the British Aircraft Corporation Three-Eleven jet, warning in 1969 that failure to do so would mean the demise of a major civil aircraft manufacturing industry in Britain; it is ironic that a very similar project to the Three-Eleven later reached fruition as the European Airbus A-300.

After his retirement from BEA, Milward was chairman of the London Tourist Board from 1971 until 1976, and thereafter its president. He died at Moore Cottage Hospital, Bourton on the Water, on 12 May 1981.

PETER J. LYTH

Sources A. H. Milward, 'Wasted seats in air transport', *Journal of the Institute of Transport* (May 1966) • *Flight International* (29 Sept 1966) • *Flight International* (4 Sept 1969) • BEA Annual Reports and Accounts, 1964–70, British Airways archive, Hatton Cross • P. J. Lyth, 'Aircraft procurement and operating costs at BEA, 1946–1964', *Accounting, Business and Financial History*, 3/1 (March 1993) • R. Wilson, 'Milward, Sir Anthony Horace', *DBB* • *CGPLA Eng. & Wales* (1981) • *The Times* (13 May 1981) • *The Times* (26 May 1981) • *The Times* (17 July 1981) • *The Times* (8 Aug 1984) • d. cert.
Wealth at death £100,765: probate, 15 Sept 1981, *CGPLA Eng. & Wales*

Milward, Edward (1711/12–1757), physician and writer, was probably born at Lindridge, Worcestershire, an area with which his family had a long connection. He was entered at Trinity College, Cambridge, but left without graduating, and acquired the degree of doctor of medicine from a European university, probably Leiden, although his name does not appear in the records of that university. According to the date of his first book, *The Essay on Trallianus*, he was a doctor of medicine, living in London at Queen Square, Ormond Street, in 1733. He later moved to Hammersmith, where he was living in 1743. On 7 July 1741 he was created by royal mandate MD of Cambridge as a member of Trinity College. He was admitted as a licentiate of the Royal College of Physicians on 30 September 1747, as a fellow exactly one year later, and was censor in 1752 and 1758. He delivered the Harveian oration in 1752.

He became a fellow of the Royal Society on 21 January 1742.

Milward's chief scholarly interest was the medical writers of antiquity, about whom he seems to have known a good deal. His principal published work was his 1733 study on Alexander Trallianus, a Greek physician of the sixth century, whom he sought to rescue from obscurity. Milward intended this essay to be the prelude to a new edition of the text of Alexander, for which he had made, he says, elaborate preparations, but this never appeared. Another ambitious scheme was that which occasioned his *Circular Invitatory Letter to Learned Men* (1740), namely, the plan of a complete history of British writers on medicine and surgery together with a history of medicine in Britain dating back to the time of the druids. For this he desired to obtain the assistance of other scholars, and had himself made large collections. Among these were the papers of the surgeon William Becket (1684–1738), who had for thirty years been collecting materials for such a purpose, but had died without carrying out his intention. The acquisition of these papers from the bookseller Edmund Curll was the starting point of Milward's scheme; he again refers to it in the preface to James Drake's *Orationes* (1742), but the projected work was never published. Another projected but unrealized work is advertised at the close of the *Circular Invitatory Letter* as in preparation for the press. This was *Gangraenologia, sive, De gangraena et sphacelo liber*, intended to be an elaborate treatise on gangrene. The important materials collected by the author with a view to these works seem to have disappeared. At some time after 1743 Milward moved to Worcester, where he died on 26 August 1757, aged forty-five, and was buried in the Knighton Chapel, Lindridge, with other members of his family. Milward's will includes a reference to his wife, Elizabeth, though no further details are known.

ALEXANDER DU TOIT

Sources *DNB* • Munk, *Roll* • T. Nash, *Collections for the history of Worcestershire*, 2 (1782), 97–8 • *GM*, 1st ser., 27 (1757), 435 • will, PRO, PROB 11/848
Archives BL, Sloane Birch MSS

Milward, John (1556–1609), Church of England clergyman, was born into a Cambridgeshire family, possibly at Ely. He matriculated as a sizar of Queens' College, Cambridge, in Lent term 1578, but migrated to St John's College in 1579. Having graduated BA in 1582 he was licensed to teach at Sutton, a few miles west of Ely, in 1584 and proceeded MA a year later. (He has been confused with another John Milward, a Derbyshire man who was educated entirely at Oxford.) He was ordained priest at Peterborough on 3 October 1585, and presented to the vicarage of Dullingham, Cambridgeshire, on 17 January 1591, holding the living until 1598. He lived in Cambridge, visiting Dullingham to hold hasty services, sometimes reading unsurpliced and in his riding boots. On 28 December 1596 he was presented to the vicarage of Bovey Tracy, Devon, by the second Baron North. Presumably he was the John Milward who in early summer 1604 became involved in litigation, for unknown reasons, over his marriage to Agnes How; the nuptials appear to have taken place. About 1605 he was defeated in a contest for the office of lecturer at Christchurch, Newgate Street, London, by William Bradshaw, but Bishop Richard Vaughan refused Bradshaw a licence, so Milward was appointed after all. On 8 November 1608 he was presented by the mayor and commonalty of London to the rectory of St Margaret Pattens, Billingsgate Ward.

Soon after the accession of James I, Milward was appointed one of his chaplains, and on 5 August 1607, by royal command, he preached a thanksgiving anniversary sermon at St Paul's for the king's deliverance from the Gowrie conspiracy seven years earlier. The sermon, on Jeremiah 30: 7, was printed in 1610 as *Jacob's Great Day of Trouble and Deliverance*. A learned and earnest address, showing much biblical and patristic learning, it repeatedly compares the patriarch Jacob with King James, not least with regard to the trials each had been forced to endure. Gowrie and his brother are denounced as traitors, as are Jesuits and Catholic priests, and the sermon ends with acclamation of Queen Elizabeth and of her successor, 'a king of Justice, a king of peace' (*Great Day*, sig. K3r).

Milward's sermon was published posthumously by his brother Matthias [*see below*], who in the 'Epistle dedicatorie' refers to his brother's life as having been 'fraught with crosses', but alleviated by the support of the king, who 'did rescue him from the jawes of conspiring perjurie'. The 'crosses' remain obscure, but James trusted Milward sufficiently to send him and another royal chaplain (probably William Goodwin) to Scotland in 1609, to attend the parliament that met in June and endeavour to promote the cause of episcopacy. Before he left, Milward made his will and was given 100 marks by the crown. Scottish sources noted how the king's ecclesiastical representatives 'taught in tyme of parliament' (Calderwood, 7.38), and on 5 July the Scottish treasurer, the earl of Dunfermline, wrote to James testifying to the great contentment and satisfaction which 'your highnes twa chaplaynes, Doctor Goodwin and Doctor Milwaird, hes given to all in this cuntrie in their doctrine, boithe in learning, eloquence and godlines' (Maidment, 169). But Milward did not profit from his good service, for he died in the earl of Dunbar's house in Edinburgh on 1 August, and was buried in the town's Canongate church. The king gave an annuity of £100 to his widow and children. On 27 October 1610 his widow, Agnes, was licensed to marry Thomas Proud, vicar of Enfield. Milward had a son, James, and two daughters, Mary and Margaret. When he died he owned houses in Warwick Lane, London, and at Hertford, as well as land at Sutton.

John's younger brother **Matthias Milward** (*d.* 1645/6) was a scholar of St John's College, Cambridge. Having graduated BA there, perhaps in 1595, he proceeded MA in 1598 and BD in 1605. He was ordained deacon in London on 20 April 1600 and priest five days later. In the same year he became curate of Wentworth, Cambridgeshire. He was presented by the crown to the rectory of East Barnet, Hertfordshire, on 18 May 1603, and held the living until 1639. On 28 March 1605 he was licensed to marry Anne Evans,

late of St Giles Cripplegate, and married her at Clerkenwell on 25 April. In 1610 he published his brother's *Jacob's Great Day of Trouble*, with a dedication to the earl of Dunbar, at whose expense John Milward had been buried. Admitted a member of Gray's Inn on 1 November 1624, Matthias Milward became vicar of Aldenham in 1626 and was rector of St Helen, Bishopgate, London, from 1639 to 1642. A sermon on Romans 13: 4 was published in 1639 as *The Sword-Bearer, or, Magistrates Charge*. On 31 August 1641 he preached at St Michael Cornhill to the Company of Artillery, under Colonel Thomas Soame; his sermon was printed later that year as *The Souldiers Triumph and the Preachers Glory*, with a dedication to Prince Charles. On 25 August 1645 he was vicar of Plumstead, Kent, but he had died by 17 September 1646, when letters of administration were granted to his son John. Another son, Joseph, born at Barnet in 1621, graduated at Cambridge in 1642 but died later that year.   MARGOT JOHNSON

Sources Venn, *Alum. Cant.*, 1/3.194 · R. Newcourt, *Repertorium ecclesiasticum parochiale Londinense*, 1 (1708) · *VCH Cambridgeshire and the Isle of Ely*, vol. 6 · *CSP dom.*, 1603–10 · A. Gibbons, ed., *Ely episcopal records: a calendar and concise view of the episcopal records preserved in the muniment room of the palace of Ely* (privately printed, Lincoln, 1891) · J. Milwarde [J. Milward], *Jacob's great day of trouble and deliverance* (1610) · *Reg. Oxf.*, vols. 1–2 · J. Nichols, *The progresses, processions, and magnificent festivities of King James I, his royal consort, family and court*, 1 (1828) · J. Bridges, *The history and antiquities of Northamptonshire*, ed. P. Whalley, 1 (1791) · S. Clarke, *The lives of thirty two English divines*, in *A general martyrologie*, 3rd edn (1677) · J. Foster, *The register of admissions to Gray's Inn, 1521–1889, together with the register of marriages in Gray's Inn chapel, 1695–1754* (privately printed, London, 1889) · J. Maidment, ed., *Letters and state papers during the reign of King James the Sixth*, Abbotsford Club, 13 (1838) · J. H. Burton and D. Masson, eds., *The register of the privy council of Scotland*, 1st ser., 14 vols. (1877–98) · D. Calderwood, *The history of the Kirk of Scotland*, ed. T. Thomson and D. Laing, 8 vols., Wodrow Society, 7 (1842–9), vol. 7 · J. L. Chester and J. Foster, eds., *London marriage licences, 1521–1869* (1887) · Wood, *Ath. Oxon.: Fasti* (1815), 226 · *DNB*

Milward, John (1599–1670), parliamentary diarist, was born on 28 October 1599 and baptized at Thorpe, Derbyshire, the second son of John Milward (1551–1633) of Bradley Ash and Mary (*d.* 1651), daughter of William Blount of Osbaldeston, Lancashire. Milward served as a captain in the Derbyshire militia in the late 1630s and as sheriff of Derbyshire in 1635–7. During the civil war he commanded a foot regiment in the marquess of Newcastle's royalist army and in early 1644 he, with other Derbyshire gentlemen, was left in the county to confront troops under the command of Sir John Gell (another Derbyshire gentleman, and Milward's predecessor as sheriff) when Newcastle was called north to fight the Scots. Subsequently his regiment was called away by Goring, and may have fought at Marston Moor. Milward submitted to parliament after July 1644. His application to compound came with the recommendation of the county committee because he had restrained his soldiers from plundering, but he was, nevertheless, fined £1000 in December 1645. After the war he was engaged in some business interests with his former adversary, Gell: Gell demised land to him in 1649, and Gell's son and Milward appear to have been sold a lease of lead mines at Wirksworth in 1648. Milward's wife, Anne, daughter of James Whitehalgh of Whitehalgh, Ipstones, Staffordshire, with whom he had three sons and eight daughters, died on 20 June 1658.

After the Restoration Milward was regarded locally as one of the most deserving of cavaliers. He was praised for his initial refusal to join with Derbyshire presbyterians (including Gell) in the commission of the peace; indeed their continuance in office appears to have been a particular grievance of his, as he raised it in the Commons in 1668. He was appointed a deputy lieutenant for Derbyshire in August 1660: his letter-book on militia business survives and suggests that he was among the most active of the Derbyshire deputies, and closely consulted by the lord lieutenant, the third earl of Devonshire.

After the conferral of a peerage on John Frescheville in 1665 Milward replaced him as one of the knights of the shire for Derbyshire. From the time he took his seat at the beginning of the 1666–7 session of parliament to the adjournment of the 1667–9 session in August 1668, he kept a detailed diary of its proceedings, providing a daily account of business in the House of Commons. His diary, which exists in a scribal copy in the British Library, gives reasonably full coverage of the major debates, including those on supply and Irish cattle in the 1667 session and the impeachment of Clarendon in late 1667. It also includes fairly detailed accounts of sermons delivered to the Commons and elsewhere. It is the only complete informal record of the first of the sessions, and for the second of them it complements the diary taken by his countryman Anchitell Grey, who was elected as burgess for Derby a few months before Milward's own return. The fact that two Derbyshire men should be engaged in compiling the only extant Commons diaries of this period, combined with Milward's connections with the earl of Devonshire as revealed in the militia business letter-book, has led to the suggestion that both diaries may have been produced for Devonshire's benefit (*Diary*, xv).

The diary shows that Milward was a loyalist and suspicious of the intentions of the government's principal parliamentary critics. He regarded Sir Richard Temple's Triennial Bill of 1668 as abhorrent, and noted how it was seconded and supported by Sir Thomas Littleton, Sir Robert Howard, and Sir Robert Carr 'and all that gang' (*Diary*, 190). He was no courtier, however. He was keen on the banning of the Irish cattle trade, against the court's wishes, and on popular solutions to the government's financial crises such as the replacement of the hearth tax and the excise. He may have been identified by 'country' politicians and by the duke of Buckingham as a possible ally: he records himself as accepting dinner from Sir Robert Carr on one occasion and Sir Thomas Osborne in 1670 assumed that he would be susceptible to an approach from the duke on behalf of the court. What most concerned Milward, though, was the state of the church and the defence of its supporters. The diary gives particularly detailed coverage of ecclesiastical business, especially of the debates on toleration and the Conventicle Act in March and April 1668, and indicates his own strong objections to the proposals. He was close to Gilbert Sheldon, the archbishop of

Canterbury and a fellow countryman from Derbyshire. The diary records twelve occasions on which he met Sheldon or was invited by him to dine at Lambeth, and Sheldon, who referred to Milward as his 'ancient acquaintance countryman and my good friend' helped to get his son into Trinity College, Oxford (Bodl. Oxf., MS Add. C. 308, fol. 378).

Milward died at Snitterton, Darley Dale, Derbyshire, on 14 September 1670 and was buried a week later at Darley Dale church, as his wife had been. Despite a reputation as one of the strongest of cavaliers, Milward was apparently a popular figure, noted as even-handed and public-spirited; a local poet marked his death with lines which celebrate him as an old-fashioned type of the good landlord, neighbour, and father.   PAUL SEAWARD

Sources *The diary of John Milward*, ed. C. Robbins (1938) · 'Parliament observations', BL, Add. MS 33413 · letter-book on militia business, BL, Add. MS 34306 · A list of gentlemen in Derbyshire and how they stand affected, PRO, SP 29/66/35 · BL, Harleian MS 2043 · M. A. E. Green, ed., *Calendar of the proceedings of the committee for compounding … 1643–1660*, 2, PRO (1890), 1025; 3 (1891), 1847–8; 4 (1892), 2750 · *CSP dom.*, 1644, 191 · C. Kerry, 'Leonard Wheatcroft, of Ashover', *Journal of the Derbyshire Archaeological and Natural History Society*, 18 (1896), 29–80, esp. 73–4 · Archbishop Sheldon's letter-book, Bodl. Oxf., MS Add. C. 308, fol. 378 · A. Browning, *Thomas Osborne, earl of Danby and duke of Leeds, 1632–1712*, 3 vols. (1944–51) · E. R. Edwards, 'Milward, John', HoP, Commons, 1660–90 · BL, Add. MS 6675, fol. 397

Archives BL, letter-book and parliamentary diary, Add. MSS 34306, 33413

Wealth at death over £5000 in legacies; two houses; residue to eldest son: will, PRO; summarized in *Diary*, ed. Robbins, xxvi

Milward, John (1619/20–1680x83), clergyman and ejected minister, was the son of a Somerset gentleman, George Milward of Shepton Mallet. On 16 March 1638, aged eighteen, he matriculated at New Inn Hall, Oxford, graduating BA on 1 July 1641. He appears to have left Oxford during the civil war, but returned soon after to academic life. He was created MA on 14 April 1648 and that year was admitted a fellow of Corpus Christi College, Oxford. He acted as a delegate to the parliamentary visitors in 1649 and served as college vice-president from that year until his resignation from the fellowship on 8 February 1657.

Before leaving Oxford, Milward acquired the rectory of Darfield, Yorkshire, having been admitted on 21 December 1655 to the first portion of the rectory following the death in July of Walter Stonehouse. Milward perhaps owed his appointment to the living, valued by Edmund Calamy at £300 per annum, to the influence of the puritan Sir Edward Rodes, of Great Houghton in that parish. He was named as an assistant to the commission for the ministry of the West Riding on 10 December 1657. In May 1660, it was reported, he warned his congregation that Charles II would introduce popery, urging them to:

> shew ourselves men, and gird every man his sword upon his thigh and sheathe it in his neighbour's bowell, for I doe believe too many of us have popes in our bellies. Let us fear the king of heaven and worship him, and bee not so desirous of an earthly King, which will tend to the imbroiling of us again in blood. (Greaves, 25)

Robert Rogers was instituted to Darfield on 9 November

1660, but was unable to gain possession of the rectory; Milward returned with the support of the patron, Henry Pierpoint, marquess of Dorchester.

However, by 22 November 1661 Milward had been ejected, and this time he accepted the situation: in a sermon given at St Giles Cripplegate, London, he argued that to take revenge for injuries and insults committed by others was sinful: 'for this were to take upon you to be judge in your own cause. God hath set up the ordinance of magistracy for this purpose' (S. Annesley, ed., *The Morning Exercises at Cripplegate*, 6 vols., 5th edn, 1844, 3.467). On 2 May 1672 he was granted a licence as a presbyterian at the house of George Millward (probably a kinsman) in Farncombe, Somerset. Milward died between the signing of his will on 13 October 1680 and the grant of probate on 24 October 1683. He seems to have been unmarried: among the beneficiaries were his brother Daniel (a London merchant), his sisters Katherine Stephens and Anne Burnell, ten ejected Somerset and Yorkshire ministers, the poor of Shepton Mallet and Darfield, and the libraries of Corpus Christi and Bodley in Oxford. STEPHEN WRIGHT

Sources *Calamy rev.*, 351 · Foster, *Alum. Oxon.* · Wood, *Ath. Oxon.: Fasti* (1820), 111 · R. L. Greaves, *Deliver us from evil: the radical underground in Britain, 1660–1663* (1986) · will, PRO, PROB 11/374, sig. 115
Wealth at death see will, PRO, PROB 11/374, sig. 115

Milward, John. *See* Holloway, James (d. 1684).

Milward, Matthias (d. 1645/6). *See under* Milward, John (1556–1609).

Milward, Richard (*bap.* 1609, d. 1680), amanuensis to John Selden, was baptized on 25 April 1609 at Flitton in Bedfordshire, son of Richard Milward, a yeoman. He matriculated from Trinity College, Cambridge, as a sizar on 7 July 1625 and was elected a scholar of his college on 13 April 1627. He received his BA in 1625 and his MA in 1632.

Milward became associated with the jurist Selden some time during the mid-1630s, and was his amanuensis for twenty years before Selden's death in 1654. During this time 'least all those excellent things that usually fell from him might be lost' Milward had 'from time to time ... faithfully committed to writing' Selden's thoughts and sayings (Selden, preface). He then compiled them into a book, *Table Talk*. The book was published for the first time in 1689 by the publisher John Smith and again in 1696 by Smith's associates, the brothers John and Awnsham Churchill. It is unclear who had the manuscript between the time of Milward's death in 1680 and its publication in 1689.

Milward married Mary, daughter of Sir Anthony Thomas of Cobham, Surrey, and they had just one child, also Mary, who later married Sir Anthony Abdy. Milward became rector of Great Braxted in Essex on 12 December 1643. His patron was Mary, countess of Pembroke. He retained this living until his death. He became a canon of the Chapel Royal, Windsor, in June 1666, and the vicar of Isleworth in Middlesex on 3 July 1678 after a warrant was issued from Whitehall to William Sancroft, archbishop of Canterbury, on 15 June 1678.

Milward received his DD in May 1662 by recommendation of King Charles because he had 'suffered from the rigour of the late times, and was discouraged from taking his degree'. He seems to have retained the good graces of the king despite his connection with John Selden. Although Selden was associated with parliament during the interregnum, perhaps his refusal to write the answer to the *Eikon basilike* when asked by Cromwell in 1650 redeemed him, and by association his amanuensis, in the eyes of Charles II. Milward died on 20 December 1680. In his will he left his land in Flitton to his widow and then his daughter. ANNE MCGOWAN

Sources J. Selden, *Table talk*, ed. R. Milward (1689) · parish register, Flitton, Beds. & Luton ARS, 25 April 1609 [baptism] · R. Newcourt, *Repertorium, etc., or, An ecclesiastical parochial history of the diocese of London*, 2 (1710), 92; 1 (1710), 676 · W. C. Metcalfe, ed., *The visitations of Essex* (1878), vol. 2, appx · R. C. Harold, *Index to the wills proved in the prerogative court of Canterbury*, 10: 1676–1685 (1948), 234 · land deeds, Beds. & Luton ARS, BS 40–146 · *CSP dom.*, 1661–2, 371; 1680–81, 110; 1678, 225 · J. Aiken, *The lives of John Selden esq and Archbishop Usher* (1812), 145, 167 · admissions registers, Trinity Cam.

Mimpriss, Robert (1797–1875), Sunday school worker, was born at Deptford, Kent, on 14 January 1797, into a devout home of Welsh origin. His father was an official in Deptford Dockyard, and had nine sons, of whom Robert and Thomas, afterwards a surgeon, alone survived infancy. After education at a Blackheath boarding-school, Robert, at the age of sixteen, went to sea as purser on a foreign merchantman. But after the first voyage he abandoned the occupation, and after a brief trial of a clerkship in a London merchant's office, and subsequently of a desultory study of art, he married a woman with private money in 1821. Her wealth made possible his lifelong work for Sunday schools, which he began at this time, after a gradual conversion to evangelical Christianity. Shocked by the ignorance of scriptural knowledge he witnessed among children of all classes, he devised what was known as the 'Mimpriss system of graduated simultaneous instruction', based on Edward Greswell's *Harmony of the Gospels* (1830). He moulded the gospel history into a continuous narrative, and divided it into one hundred lessons. The course was illustrated by pictorial maps, charts, and tables, in the preparation of which he was assisted by John Wilson, author of several millenarian works. From 1830 to 1850 Mimpriss was chiefly engaged in writing books in connection with his system, but he repeatedly travelled round the country setting forth its merits or advocating millenarian and teetotal principles. He was also a supporter of sabbatarianism, an active member of the Society for the Prevention of Cruelty to Animals, and a promoter of the education of deaf mute people.

In 1860 his wife suffered a stroke, and Mimpriss incurred increasingly heavy losses from his publishing efforts, which his biographer partly attributed to the hostility of the organized societies, the Sunday School Union and the Church of England Sunday School Institute, towards Mimpriss's disinterested private enterprise.

There was also a suggestion that he was too much of a perfectionist and perhaps too headstrong to make his ventures a commercial success. Impulsive and generous, he had a simple and unconventional manner, and made many friends among the Quakers, though he was himself an Anglican. Mimpriss died at his home, 18 Rectory Grove, Clapham, London, on 20 December 1875, and was survived by his wife. He left a small estate which was administered by a creditor, the textile manufacturer who had collaborated with him in his last, impractical, venture: to mass produce the scripture patchwork quilt.

E. G. HAWKE, *rev.* M. C. CURTHOYS

Sources *Robert Mimpriss: a memoir of his life and work* (1876) · *Record* (Dec 1875) · *Rock* (Dec 1875) · private information (1894) · *CGPLA Eng. & Wales* (1876)
Likenesses photograph, repro. in *Robert Mimpriss*, frontispiece
Wealth at death under £300: administration, 31 Jan 1876, *CGPLA Eng. & Wales*

Minett, Francis Colin (1890–1953), veterinary pathologist, was born in Acton Turville, Hawkesbury, Gloucestershire, on 16 September 1890, the son of Francis Minett, farmer, and his wife, Elizabeth Louisa Birch. He attended King Edward's School, Bath, and the Royal Veterinary College, London, qualifying MRCVS in 1911. In 1912 he obtained the degree of BSc (veterinary science) of the University of London, and from 1912 to 1914 he was a research scholar at the Ministry of Agriculture. He continued his studies in Paris at the Institut Pasteur, and after returning to the Royal Veterinary College came under the influence of Sir John McFadyean who, with A. L. Sheather, was studying contagious abortion, tuberculosis, and other diseases of the domesticated animals.

On the outbreak of the First World War, Minett joined the army veterinary corps (which became the Royal Army Veterinary Corps on 27 November 1918); he served for ten years in France and England. He embarked for Egypt on 31 August 1921 but was rejected by the Egyptian army on medical grounds. He attained the rank of captain, and was created MBE in 1916. During his period of service he studied and wrote on the pathology and control of equine infections, especially ulcerative lymphangitis, a disturbing disease among the horses in France during the war. Some of Minett's observations were of interest to comparative pathologists, for he demonstrated the presence of diphtheria bacilli, presumably of human origin, in some of the lesions on the limbs of horses. It became recognized that diphtheria bacilli might be involved in skin wounds in man, horses, and elephants.

On 15 July 1919 Minett married Iza, daughter of Robert Stitt, of Belfast; they had one son. Minett returned to civilian life in 1924 and worked on foot-and-mouth disease as a research officer at the Ministry of Agriculture's veterinary laboratory at Weybridge in Surrey. From 1927 until 1939 he was director of the research institute in animal pathology at the Royal Veterinary College; at that time its activities were separate from the teaching programme of the college. In 1927 he obtained the DSc degree of the University of London. During the years 1926–33, together with his colleagues A. W. Stableforth and S. J. Edwards, he made a survey of the bacterial causes of bovine mastitis, a disease which had not previously been studied extensively in Britain. Minett and his colleagues were responsible not only for drawing attention to the economic significance of this disease but for distinguishing the different bacteria which caused it in Britain—paying special attention to the types of streptococci involved. Minett also extended his investigations to include problems involving staphylococci, *Brucella*, and other organisms. Some of these bacteria are pathogenic for humans and conveyed by cows' milk, and Minett was therefore collaborating with many who were interested primarily in human health.

In 1933 there was some reorganization in the Royal Veterinary College and Minett combined his duties as director of the institute with those of professor of pathology. He himself undertook the teaching of the morbid-anatomical aspects of the pathology of animal diseases and of those diseases caused by viruses. He held this dual post until 1939, when he resigned to become director of the Imperial Veterinary Research Institute at Mukteswar and Izatnagar in India. He was appointed CIE in 1945, but in 1947 he left Mukteswar, which was within the Indian part of the subcontinent, and accepted the post of animal husbandry commissioner with the government of Pakistan. During this period he was made foreign corresponding member of the Royal Academy of Medicine in Belgium, and of the French Veterinary Academy. Minett remained in post until his retirement in 1949, and then returned to England.

In 1950 Minett joined the Animal Health Trust as director of their bovine research station in Huntingdonshire; shortly after accepting this post, however, he was released to advise the Turkish government on some of their difficulties connected with diseases of animals. He returned to England in 1952 to resume the direction of the station, where he continued his work on Johne's disease, in which he had been interested for many years, and also investigated the diseases of young pigs. From 1923 to 1952 Minett contributed more than fifty original research papers to several learned scientific journals. He also presented papers at many scientific meetings.

Minett was a curious individual, not easy to know. He was meticulous in everything he did; this was demonstrable in his technique at the laboratory bench and in his attention to detail in the writing of reports. These were his characteristics, but there were times when he was unable to see broader issues because he was surrounded with such a mass of detail. His energy and enthusiasm coloured his outlook, and those who met him found it took some time before they realized that a sensitive nature lay beneath a rather brusque exterior. Minett died at his home, Windy Bank, Gorse Way, Hartley Road, Hartley, near Dartford, Kent, on 26 December 1953.

REGINALD LOVELL, *rev.* LINDA WARDEN

Sources *Veterinary Record* (2 Jan 1954), 16–17 · E. Cotchin, *The Royal Veterinary College, London: a bicentenary history* (1990), 128, 133, 147, 168, 178, 191 · records, 3/30 Nov 1962, war office, WORC ENCL 2/26/DOCS 48 · *Veterinary Record* (26 Aug–2 Sept 1950), 513, 524 · minute books, Royal Veterinary College, London · student entry

book, 1873–1930, Royal Veterinary College, London, 86 · personal knowledge (1971) · d. cert. · b. cert. · *CGPLA Eng. & Wales* (1954)
Likenesses F. C. Minett, photograph, 1934, Royal Veterinary College, London, Research Institute in Animal Pathology · photograph, repro. in *Veterinary Record*, 108
Wealth at death £15,705 1s. 7d.: probate, 21 May 1954, *CGPLA Eng. & Wales*

Mingana, Alphonse [*formerly* Hurmiz Mingana] (1878?–1937), Syriac and Christian Arabic scholar, was born on 23 December probably in 1878 (not 1881 as usually stated) in Sharansh al-ʿUlya in the district of Zakho, vilayet of Mosul (now northern Iraq), the eldest of the eight children of Paôlôs Mingana, Chaldean Catholic priest, and his wife, Maryam Nânô, both of Burjan. He had an extraordinary facility with languages. Brought up speaking neo-Aramaic, he was sent in 1891 to the Syro-Chaldean Seminary of St Jean in Mosul where, in addition to the usual theological education, he studied Arabic and Syriac—taught by the great Yaʿqub Awgin Manna (1867–1928)—Turkish, Persian, Kurdish, biblical Hebrew, Latin, and French.

After being ordained priest in 1902, when he assumed the religious name Alphonse, Mingana taught Syriac in the seminary. From 1903 to 1910 he was also corrector of Syriac and Arabic books for the Dominican Press in Mosul. This period is remarkable, however, for two publications which established Mingana's controversial reputation. In 1905 he published an edition of the works of Narsai, an important fifth-century theologian, which included in its introduction a passage without any textual basis, despite Mingana's claims. In 1907 he published the Syriac chronicle of Mshiha-Zkha from a manuscript said to be of the tenth century but subsequently revealed to be an early twentieth-century work whose scribe admitted having 'aged' it on Mingana's instructions. Most scholars decided that Mingana had composed the chronicle himself, and repeated charges of forgery, though never substantiated, were to dog his career. Ironically one of his footnotes to the chronicle, in which he questioned the historicity of Mar Mari, one of the apostles credited with founding the Syrian churches, angered the Chaldean patriarch who in 1910 removed Mingana from his seminary position.

In March 1913, having severed his connections with the Chaldean church, Mingana left for England where he was welcomed and employed as a teacher of Arabic and Hebrew by J. Rendel Harris, the director of studies at Woodbrooke, a Quaker college in Selly Oak, Warwickshire. Mingana, who from 1914 assumed the title Doctor, collaborated with Harris to produce the celebrated edition of the *Odes and Psalms of Solomon* (1916; 1920). While at Woodbrooke, Mingana met Emma Sophie Floor (d. 1974), a Norwegian Lutheran from Stavanger, the daughter of a bookseller. They were married on 14 July 1915 at a Quaker meeting-house in King's Norton, and had two children: John, born in 1916, and Marie, born in 1918.

From 1915 until 1932 Mingana was employed by the John Rylands Library, Manchester, to produce a catalogue of its Arabic manuscripts (published in 1934). For a few years

(1916–23) he was a special lecturer in Arabic at the University of Manchester, although he never enjoyed public speaking. During the First World War, Mingana produced vocabularies for the use of the British armed forces in the Middle East and in 1920 he was naturalized as a British citizen.

The remainder of Mingana's life was to be dominated by his passion for manuscripts. Largely at the expense of Dr Edward Cadbury, Mingana travelled in 1924 and 1925 to Syria and Iraq and in 1929 to the Sinai and Upper Egypt where he acquired more than 2000 Syriac and Arabic manuscripts. The majority of these, constituting one of the largest such collections in the world, went to the college in Selly Oak where he himself catalogued them (1933–9). From 1932 he lived not far away, at 168 Middleton Hall Road, King's Norton, in a house named Manuscripta. Some Syriac manuscripts went to the John Rylands Library, although Mingana replaced ten of the most important of these with inferior texts from Selly Oak. He published many Syriac and Arabic texts in the series Woodbrooke Studies (1927–34), followed in 1935 by Job of Edessa's *Book of Treasures*. He died at his home on 5 December 1937.

D. G. K. TAYLOR

Sources S. K. Samir, *Alphonse Mingana, 1878–1937, and his contribution to early Christian–Muslim studies* (1990) · D. S. Margoliouth and G. Woledge, 'Alphonse Mingana 1881–1937', *Catalogue of the Mingana collection of manuscripts*, 3 (1939), v–xii · J.-M. Fiey, 'Auteur et date de la chronique d'Arbèles', *L'Orient Syrien*, 12 (1967), 265–302 · J.-M. Vosté, 'Alphonse Mingana', *Orientalia Christiana Periodica*, 7 (1941), 514–18 · J. F. Coakley, 'A catalogue of the Syriac manuscripts in the John Rylands Library', *Bulletin of the John Rylands University Library*, 75 (1993), 105–207 · *WWW, 1941–50* · *The Times* (6 Dec 1937) · m. cert. · d. cert.
Archives Selly Oak College, Birmingham
Likenesses photograph, 1902–10, repro. in A. Nouro, *My tour in the parishes of the Syrian church in Syria and Lebanon* (1967), 176 [Beirut] · photograph, 1915?, repro. in Samir, *Alphonse Mingana*, 20 · photographs, 1920–39, repro. in Samir, *Alphonse Mingana*
Wealth at death £11,310 18s. 7d.: resworn probate, 31 Jan 1938, *CGPLA Eng. & Wales*

Mingay, James (1752–1812), barrister, was born on 9 March 1752 in Thetford, Norfolk, the second child and elder son in the family of ten children of James Mingay (d. 1801), surgeon, of Thetford, and his second wife, Dorothy (d. 1783), the daughter of William Fuller of Caldecot, Huntingdonshire.

Mingay was educated at Thetford grammar school and at Trinity College, Cambridge (1768). He went down without taking a degree and was admitted to the Inner Temple in 1770. He read in the chambers of Charles Runnington. In 1775 Mingay was called to the bar (Inner Temple) and joined the Norfolk circuit. His practice quickly grew. He took silk on 26 November 1784 and became a bencher on 25 January 1785, reader in 1790, and treasurer in 1791. He retired from practice at the bar in the summer of 1802 at the age of fifty, after a long and painful illness, having made a fortune. Mingay married Eliza (d. 1817), daughter of Robert Corrall of Maidstone, gentleman. They had no children.

Both before and after his retirement Mingay was active in public affairs in his locality. He was chairman of the quarter sessions for Norfolk and Suffolk for many years, JP for Thetford in 1806, and mayor of Thetford three times (1798, 1800, and 1804). He also stood for parliament, unsuccessfully, in 1794 and 1806.

An accident when he was a boy resulted in the loss of his right hand, and throughout his adult life he wore a hook, hence the reference in *The Old Benchers of the Inner Temple* by Charles Lamb: 'Mingay with the iron hand. He had lost his right hand by some accident, and supplied it with a grappling hook, which he wielded with tolerable adroitness … He was a blustering loud talking person' (pp. xvi, 109). Henry Crabb Robinson, recording a case at Colchester spring assizes, describes him as 'loud and violent' (*Diary*, 1.9–10). His obituary in the *Gentleman's Magazine*, however, states that as an advocate he possessed 'a persuasive oratory, infinite wit, and most excellent fancy' and that he was 'distinguished as the powerful rival of his friend, Lord Erskine', who became lord chancellor in 1802 (*GM*). He was probably the most able lawyer among the benchers described by Lamb, and appeared in some important commercial cases long cited in later textbooks.

Mingay died on 9 July 1812 at Ashfield Lodge, Great Ashfield, Suffolk. He was buried on 17 July in a vault of St Mary's Church, Thetford. His wife survived him.

J. N. Adams, *rev.*

Sources *N&Q*, 11th ser., 8 (1913), 41 · *The old benchers of the Inner Temple*, ed. F. C. MacKinnon (1927) · Venn, *Alum. Cant.* · *GM*, 1st ser., 82/2 (1812), 187 · *Diary, reminiscences, and correspondence of Henry Crabb Robinson*, ed. T. Sadler, 3rd edn, 1 (1872), 9–10
Likenesses T. Romney, double portraits (with his wife)

Minnitt, Robert James (1889–1974), anaesthetist and general practitioner, was born in Preston on 25 October 1889, the son of Robert Minnitt (1852–1918), Church of England clergyman, and his wife, Isabella, *née* Cookson (1853–1922). He was educated privately, and went up to Trinity College, Cambridge, in 1908 intending to read for the church; his father and grandfather were both in holy orders. He left after a year to study medicine at Liverpool, qualifying in 1915. On 1 September 1916 he married Eileen Dooley (1897–1975).

Minnitt is chiefly remembered for the development of a machine for self-administration of nitrous oxide ('gas') and air to relieve pain in childbirth. Helped by Charles King, an engineer with a special interest in anaesthetic equipment, he modified an existing machine which started trials at the Liverpool Maternity Hospital in October 1933. By 1936, with his research assistant Dr Hilda Garry, he was able to demonstrate to the Royal Society of Medicine that the technique provided satisfactory pain relief in over 90 per cent of cases with no ill effects. Concurrently a report co-ordinated by the British College of Obstetricians and Gynaecologists confirmed these findings. Both these studies received funding from the National Birthday Trust Fund, one of whose members, Lucy Baldwin, the prime minister's wife, had a particular interest in analgesia in childbirth.

In 1936 the Central Midwives' Board accepted the machine for use by unsupervised midwives, who then managed 60 per cent of deliveries, subject to strict conditions. Minnitt devised a portable model which could fit in the carrier of a bicycle, thus extending the technique to the domiciliary setting where 80 per cent of deliveries took place. Gas and air remained the only form of pain relief available to millions of women until the early 1960s. Then defects were found in some Minnitt machines; nitrous oxide and oxygen (Entonox) from a single cylinder was developed and was recognized by the Royal College of Midwives.

Minnitt received many honours, including fellowships from the Royal College of Obstetricians and Gynaecologists (1950) and the Faculty of Anaesthetists (1953). The Royal Society of Medicine awarded him the Hickman medal (1950) for original work of outstanding merit. A commemorative plaque was mounted outside the labour ward at the Liverpool Maternity Hospital.

Minnitt's many other pioneering achievements should not be overshadowed. He obtained an MD degree in 1925, and in 1930 was a founder member of the Liverpool Society of Anaesthetists, the first provincial society of its kind in England. He acted as secretary for twenty years before becoming president. The university appointed him the first lecturer in anaesthesia (1933), and he was the first anaesthetist to sit on the board of the faculty of medicine. He thus strongly influenced the establishment of a full-time department of anaesthesia (1947). This was highlighted in the citation for his honorary MSc (1967). His publications included *Gas and Air Analgesia* and (with John Gillies) a re-editing of Ross and Fairlie's *Handbook of Anaesthesia*.

In 1948 Minnitt found himself unable to accept a contract in the National Health Service and spent the rest of his life in private general practice, probably at some financial cost. Nevertheless his reputation remained and he was still in demand as a lecturer. He was president of the section of general practice at the Royal Society of Medicine (1954–5) and was an honorary fellow on the foundation of the Royal College of General Practitioners. Locally he was president of the Liverpool Medical Institution (1957) and continued to attend meetings of the Liverpool Society of Anaesthetists. Minnitt is recalled as an inspiring teacher and a man of infinite courtesy whose devotion to his patients was legendary. It was said that he never took a holiday. He died on 21 February 1974 at Broadgreen Hospital, Broadgreen, Liverpool, and was buried that month at Christchurch, Healey, Rochdale. He was survived by his wife, son, and three daughters.

P. M. E. Drury

Sources U. Lpool L., special collections and archives, D160/5 · R. J. Minnitt, 'Self-administered analgesia for the midwifery of general practice', *Proceedings of the Royal Society of Medicine*, 27 (1933–4), 1313–18 · British College of Obstetricians and Gynaecologists, *An investigation into the use of analgesics suitable for administration by midwives* (1936) · R. J. Minnitt, 'The history and progress of gas and air analgesia for midwifery', *Proceedings of the Royal Society of Medicine*, 37 (1943–4), 45–8 · R. J. Minnitt, 'History of the method', *Gas and air analgesia* (1938), 1–10 · K. B. Thomas, 'The analgesia story', *The development of anaesthetic apparatus* (1975) · E. P. O'Sullivan, 'Dr Robert James Minnitt: a pioneer of inhalational analgesia', *Journal of the*

Royal Society of Medicine, 82 (1989), 221–2 • A. S. Williams, 'Pain relief for childbirth', *Women and childbirth in the twentieth century* (1997) • Liverpool Maternity Hospital medical board minutes, Lpool RO, 614 MAT 2/3; 614 MAT 3/3 • J. A. Shepherd, 'Problems and trends of the new century (1900–1939)', *A history of the Liverpool Medical Institution* (1979), 214 • *The Times* (25 Feb 1974) • b. cert. • m. cert. • d. cert.

Archives U. Lpool L., special collections and archives, corresp. and papers, D160/5 • Wellcome L., SA/NBT/H2/1

Likenesses photograph, repro. in O'Sullivan, 'Dr Robert James Minnitt', 221

Wealth at death £20,689: probate, 18 April 1974, *CGPLA Eng. & Wales*

Minns, Sir Ellis Hovell (1874–1953), archaeologist and palaeographer, was born in Weston, Hampshire, on 16 July 1874, the third in the family of two sons and a daughter of the Revd George William Walter Minns (1837–1919), vicar of Weston, and his wife, Jane Porter Boggs. He was educated at Charterhouse School and Pembroke College, Cambridge, where he obtained first classes in each part of the classical tripos (1896 and 1897).

After mastering the language at the École des Langues Orientales Vivantes, Paris, Minns went to Russia where, between 1898 and 1901, he worked in Moscow, St Petersburg, Kiev, Odessa, and other centres, acquiring the detailed knowledge of the archaeology of the region on which his reputation was to be built. Returning to Pembroke, of which he had been elected a fellow in 1899, he became librarian and lecturer in Slavonic studies in 1901. In 1906 he became university lecturer in palaeography, in 1920 he was made LittD by Cambridge, in 1925 he served as Sandars reader in bibliography, and in 1927 he was elected as the first full-time Disney professor of archaeology. Before he retired in 1939 he had played a key role in the establishment of archaeology and anthropology at Cambridge.

Minns brought a broad range of expertise to bear on a field extending from eastern Europe to China, while at the same time paying close attention to the antiquities and books of his own college, where he occupied the same rooms over a period of fifty-five years as undergraduate, fellow, president (1928–49), and senior fellow. As a palaeographer he enjoyed reproducing ancient scripts using implements of his own devising, while as an archaeologist he sought a deeper insight into ornaments by drawing them or even carving them with his own hands. He was shrewd in personal assessments. For those whose scholarship he respected he was prepared to go to endless trouble, but to those whom he suspected of pretensions exceeding their knowledge or understanding he gave short shrift. On his sixtieth birthday he received a Festschrift edited from Helsinki with contributions from over thirty colleagues, covering a field ranging from Scandinavia and east Europe to China. He did not allow the revolution of 1917 to interfere with his contacts with Russian colleagues and it was appropriate that he should have been asked to supply the inscription for the sword presented by George VI to the people of Stalingrad.

In his *Scythians and Greeks* (1913), Minns presented a survey of the ancient history and archaeology of the territory north of the Euxine from the Danube to the Caucasus. The greater part dealt with the Greek colonies but his heart lay with the Scyths and their affinities, a topic which he addressed in his 1942 British Academy lecture, *The Art of the Northern Nomads* (1944).

Minns was elected a fellow of the British Academy in 1925, received the gold medal of the Society of Antiquaries in 1943, and was knighted in 1945. In 1907 he married Violet (*d.* 1949), daughter of Frederick Nalder, solicitor, of Falmouth. They had a son and a daughter, (Lydia) Marian, who married Humphrey Mynors, later first baronet, deputy governor of the Bank of England. Minns died at his home, 2 Wordsworth Grove, Cambridge, on 13 June 1953.

GRAHAME CLARK, rev.

Sources personal knowledge (1993) • private information (1993) [Marian Mynors, daughter] • G. Clarke, 'Ellis Hovell Minns, 1874–1953', *PBA*, 71 (1985), 597–602 • M. C. Burkitt, *Cambridge Review* (10 Oct 1953), 6–8 • E. Hill, *Slavonic and East European Review*, 32 (1953–4), 236–8 • E. D. Phillips, *Artibus Asiae* (1954), 168–73 • Venn, *Alum. Cant.* • *CGPLA Eng. & Wales* (1953) • d. cert.

Archives BL, lecture notes, Add. MS 41320 • CUL, corresp.; corresp. and MSS; notebook of Russian grammar and vocabulary | BL, corresp. with Sir Idris Bell, Add. MS 59516 • Bodl. Oxf., letters to O. G. S. Crawford

Likenesses photograph, repro. in *PBA*

Wealth at death £22,630 18s.: probate, 26 Oct 1953, *CGPLA Eng. & Wales*

Minor, William Chester (1834–1920), military surgeon, asylum inmate, and contributor to the *Oxford English Dictionary*, was born on 21 June 1834 at Manepay, Ceylon, the elder child of Eastman Strong Minor (1809–1867), printer and Congregational missionary of Milford, Connecticut, and his first wife, Lucy Bailey (1809–1837), also a missionary, of Boston, Massachusetts. The chronic insanity—almost certainly a paranoid form of schizophrenia—which was to dog and define William Minor's long life, became apparent only in his early adulthood, and his formative years seem to have been troubled solely by an excessive interest in the opposite sex. It was what his extremely pious parents regarded as his unhealthy fascination with young Indian girls that prompted them to send him away from Ceylon, where he had attended the mission school at Manepay, to school in New Haven, Connecticut, when he was thirteen. He then entered Yale University (1852) and attended the medical school, and in due course graduated as a surgeon.

In 1863 Minor joined the Union army as an assistant surgeon, and held the rank of lieutenant. He spent an initial six months attending to civil war casualties at hospitals in New England before being sent to the front line in May 1864. It then appears that the trauma of the battlefield—particularly the notoriously ferocious battle of the Wilderness in Orange county, Virginia, at which he was present—triggered his mental deterioration and subsequent illness. Some accounts say that his insanity may have been precipitated by his being ordered to brand an Irish deserter on the cheek as a punishment.

Minor was compelled by his breakdown to leave the American army in 1871, though he was permitted to keep his pension, and was sent by his distressed family to convalesce in London. He settled in an insalubrious part of

Lambeth, and, though trying gamely to rehabilitate himself by painting watercolours and playing the flute, was overwhelmed by his illness to the extent that, on 17 February 1872, he shot and killed a brewery stoker named George Merrett, in the mistaken belief that Merrett was an Irishman bent on vengeance for the branding incident. He gave himself up to the police, and was tried at Surrey assizes and sentenced to be confined in the newly opened Broadmoor Asylum 'Until Her Majesty's Pleasure Be Known'.

Some time about 1880, and thus while at Broadmoor—where he had two cells, a manservant, a prodigious collection of books, and, incredibly, regular visits from Eliza Merrett, the widow of the man he had murdered—Minor came across the famous 'Appeal for volunteer readers' sent out by James Murray, editor of the *Oxford English Dictionary (OED)*, in which Murray asked interested members of the reading public to scour published literature for quotations to illustrate the use of English words. Minor, who was described by various sources, including the Broadmoor administrators, as highly learned, despite his often florid displays of madness, set to work assembling lists of quotations, and by the mid-1880s was sending hundreds, and later thousands, of slips of paper to Murray and his team at the famous *scriptorium* at 79 Banbury Road, Oxford. He signed his letters simply 'W. C. Minor, Crowthorne, Berkshire', and for very many years Murray had no idea that his energetic and assiduous correspondent was an American murderer and an inmate at one of Britain's most secure and infamous lunatic asylums.

When Murray, through the good offices of a visiting American librarian, did learn of the curious circumstances of Minor's life, he decided he should visit him at the asylum. From the early 1890s the two men became firm friends, divided in so many ways and yet united by their evident passion for the rich complexity of the English language. Despite the supportive warmth of the friendship, and the undoubted therapeutic benefits of his dictionary work, Minor became ever more unwell with age, and in 1902, in a fit of delusional guilt, amputated his own penis in the belief it might curb his troublesome sexual appetite. This the autopeotomy may well have done, but it also severely debilitated him, prompting the home secretary, Winston Churchill, at Murray's urging, to allow the American's release and deportation, in 1910.

After an emotional farewell from Sir James and Lady Murray, Minor—together with the first six completed volumes of the *OED*—sailed back to New York, to be committed promptly to St Elizabeth's Hospital in Washington, DC. He deteriorated steadily, and was eventually moved to the Retreat for the Elderly Insane in Hartford, Connecticut, in 1919, and there died of a respiratory infection on 26 March 1920. He was buried three days later in the family plot in Evergreen cemetery, New Haven. Aside from two lines in the *New Haven Register*, and a year later a brief notice in a publication for Yale alumni, there was no obituary. His legacy as a volunteer reader can be found scattered among the pages of the twenty-volume *Oxford English Dictionary*. James Murray said of him at the time that 'so

enormous have been Dr. Minor's contributions … that we could easily illustrate the last four centuries from his quotations alone' (Winchester, 160). Physically William Minor was of military bearing, bald and with a striking long white beard—uncannily similar, in fact, to James Murray, such that when they first met observers said it was, for each of them, like walking towards a mirror.

SIMON WINCHESTER

Sources S. Winchester, *The surgeon of Crowthorne* (1998) · J. Green, *Chasing the sun: dictionary-makers and the dictionaries they made* (1996) · K. M. E. Murray, *Caught in the web of words: James A. H. Murray and the 'Oxford English dictionary'* (1977) · medical records, patient no. 742, 1872–1910, Broadmoor Special Hospital, Crowthorne, Berkshire · records, Yale U., divinity school · burial records, Evergreen cemetery, New Haven, Connecticut
Archives Broadmoor Special Hospital, Crowthorne, Berkshire · National Archives and Records Administration, Washington, DC · Oxford University Press, archive · US Army archives
Likenesses J. Russell & Sons, photograph, 1910, Broadmoor Special Hospital, Crowthorne, Berkshire
Wealth at death $74,000: New Haven probate court, July 1915

Minorsky, Vladimir Fyodorovich (1877–1966), orientalist and Persian scholar, the son of Fyodor M. Minorsky and his wife, Olga, *née* Golubitskaya, was born on 5 February 1877 at Korcheva, on the upper Volga to the north-west of Moscow. He was educated at Moscow University from 1896 to 1903, studying law and oriental languages. In 1903 he entered the imperial Russian ministry of foreign affairs, serving in Persia, St Petersburg, central Asia, and Turkey. He represented Russia on the Turco-Persian Frontier Commission, and eventually became chargé d'affaires at the Russian legation in Tehran. In 1913 he married Tatyana Shebunina (d. 27 Dec 1987); their only son died in 1950. With the Russian Revolution, Minorsky and his wife settled in Paris. Moving from an official and diplomatic career to an academic one, in 1923 he became lecturer in Persian at the École des Langues Orientales Vivantes in Paris. In 1932 he began teaching at the School of Oriental Studies, London, where in 1937 he became professor of Persian. The school was evacuated to Cambridge during the first part of the Second World War, and the Minorskys settled there permanently after he retired in 1944. He died at Cambridge on 25 March 1966 at the age of eighty-nine, still in the plenitude of his intellectual powers, and in 1969 his ashes were interred in the cemetery of the Novodevichye monastery at Moscow. He had by the time of his death received many honours from academies and universities of Europe and Asia, including the triennial gold medal of the Royal Asiatic Society, London.

Minorsky was a scholar of outstanding calibre, who dominated historical, topographical, and ethnological studies in the Turco-Persian regions of western Asia and beyond as the worthy successor of his compatriot V. V. Bartold and the German Josef Markwart. The focus of his interests was Persia and the Iranian cultural world in general, including component peoples such as the Kurds, Armenians, and Afghans. But he was also interested in adjacent regions such as the Caucasus and Turkish central Asia. Much of his work, and especially that in the fields of historical geography and ethnography, was informed by personal experience; thus he had surveyed on horseback the whole 700 miles of the Turco-Persian frontier from the Persian Gulf to Mount Ararat as part of his delimitation duties of 1913–14. His *magnum opus* was the *Hudūd al-ʿālam. 'The Regions of the World'* (1936), a medieval Persian geography which he translated with a commentary of amazing complexity and insight. Other works included a translation and edition of an Arabic work, *Sharaf al-Zamān Tāhir Marvazī on China, the Turks and India* (1942), dealing with the ethnography and history of inner, south, and east Asia; a facsimile edition of and commentary on a Safavid Persian manual of administration (1944); two books on the history of the Caucasus (1953, 1958); an edition and translation of a work by a tenth-century Arab traveller in Persia (1955); and an abridged translation of a history of the Turkmen dynasties of Persia in the fifteenth century. His aesthetic sensibilities (he had, among other interests, a great love of music and was himself a pianist) showed themselves in works on Persian art. He had been oriental secretary for the Persian Art Exhibition of 1930–31 in London, and contributed to the exhibition catalogue; later he produced two books on Turkish and Persian miniature painters and calligraphers (1958, 1959). All this was in addition to hundreds of articles, many of them studies of major significance; some of these were in the further field of Persian literature.

Minorsky was a kindly and hospitable person, ever ready to encourage younger scholars; in his later years, his stocky figure gave him something of the appearance of a genial teddy bear. As a teacher he was better with individuals than with larger groups. He saw his own scholarly task as the recovery and elucidation of information about regions whose history, topography, and ethnology were often profoundly obscure. He did not think that the groundwork had yet been done for more general works of synthesis, as was possible for historians of Europe. Noteworthy, too, was his firm Russian patriotism, even though events had compelled him to spend the second half of his life outside his native country.

C. EDMUND BOSWORTH

Sources D. M. Lang, *Bulletin of the School of Oriental and African Studies*, 29 (1966), 694–9 · I. Gershevitch, 'Professor Vladimir Minorsky', *Journal of the Royal Asiatic Society of Great Britain and Ireland* (1967), 53–7 · C. E. Bosworth, preface, *Iran and Islam: in memory of the late Vladimir Minorsky*, ed. C. E. Bosworth (1971), v–ix
Archives St Petersburg University, faculty of oriental studies
Likenesses photograph, repro. in Bosworth, ed., *Iran and Islam*, frontispiece

Minot, Laurence (*fl.* **early 14th cent.**), poet, was the author of a number of English poems concerning military events in the earlier part of the reign of Edward III. Almost nothing is known about his life. He may well have been connected with the Minot or Miniot family found in the fourteenth century especially in Yorkshire and Norfolk. Its members included knights and merchants, and a Thomas Mynot, the king's notary, who was in Flanders at the time of the siege of Guînes, which is described in one of the poems. The name of a Laurence Minot (Laurence Mynotz, Loreng de Minguot) appears in a patent roll deed and an entry in the receiver of Ponthieu's account book recording a purchase of land in Cressy (Crécy) Forest in Ponthieu in 1329 and the remission by Edward III in 1331 of a part of the price still unpaid. It is usually assumed that this is the poet. He records his name twice in a series of eleven poems (which seem certainly to be by one author) found in BL, Cotton MS Galba E.ix (a manuscript of the early fifteenth century written in the northern dialect):

> Help me, God, my wit es thin,
> Now Laurence Minot will begin.
> (*Poems*, ed. Hall, no. 7, ll. 19–20)

and:

> Minot with mowth had menid to make
> Suth sawes and sad for sum mens sake.
> (ibid., no. 5, ll. 1–2)

The first poem opens with the threats from the French and the Scots 'when Edward founded [went] first to were' (*Poems*, ed. Hall, no. 1, l. 12) and describes the victory over the Scots at Halidon Hill (1333):

> þare was crakked many a crowne
> Of wilde Scottes and alls of tame.
> (ibid., ll. 59–60)

The second celebrates the victory as a triumphant revenge for Bannockburn. In poem 3 Edward goes to Flanders (1338), but Philippe de Valois and the deceitful French raid Southampton. Edward invades France from Flanders (1339)—'furth he fered into Fraunce' (ibid., no. 4, l. 19)—and Philippe fled at the battle of Flamengerie. The great victory in the sea battle at Sluys (1340) is the subject of the fifth poem. The sixth describes the siege of Tournai (1340). The seventh (and longest) celebrates Edward's march through Normandy and his victory at Crécy (1346). Just as poem 2 becomes a triumphant invective against the Scots, here three stanzas scornfully deride the defeated French:

> Franche man …
> Inglis men sall …
> Knok þi palet or þou pas,
> And mak þe polled like a frere
> (ibid., no. 2, ll. 118–31)

This poem leads on to the next, which deals with the siege of Calais ('Calais men, now may ye care'; ibid., no. 8, l. 1) and its fall (in August 1347). The ninth poem returns to the Scots and the defeat of David II at Nevilles Cross (1346)—though (urged on by Philippe) he boasted that he would ride through England, he was brought to the Tower of London. In the tenth, Edward defeats the Spanish fleet off Winchelsea (1350). The last celebrates the successful siege of Guînes (1352). It ends with a prayer:

> God save Sir Edward in euerilka nede …
> and len oure sir Edward his life wele to lede,
> þat he may at his ending haue heuin til his mede.
> (ibid., no. 11, ll. 37–40)

The poems vary in length (from 30 to 172 lines) and in metrical form (5 are in stanzas of 6 rhyming alliterative lines). They are a series unified by the central figure of Edward 'oure king', whose great deeds they celebrate, and by explicit links between individual poems. In one such linking remark, perhaps the word *romaunce* (if it does not simply and vaguely mean 'the story') may suggest that he thought of his works as constituting a kind of romance or verse chronicle:

Heres now how þe romaunce sais,
How sir Edward, oure king with croune,
Held his sege, bi nightes and dais,
With his men bifor Calays toune.
(*Poems*, ed. Hall, no. 7, ll. 170–72)

He certainly uses the stock phrases and tags found in popular romance. But often panegyric and invective seem as important as narrative, and the series does not fit easily into any accepted literary genre. Uncertainties and ambiguities also remain concerning the status of the author and the context and purpose of his poems. No other work can be confidently ascribed to him (though Joseph Hall thought him the author of a hymn to Christ and Mary). It is difficult to tell if he wrote his historical poems separately in an 'occasional' manner, and then put them together as a series. Nor is it clear from where he derived his information. There is no certain evidence that he was present at all or even some of the events he describes. There are errors—Edward III did not take part in the fight off Southampton for instance—but on the other hand he has access to some quite detailed information. Earlier scholars and editors described him as a minstrel, a status vehemently repudiated by his modern admirers. He seems unlikely to have been a simple minstrel following the English armies and his name does not seem to appear in the documents concerning the minstrels in Edward's court. That he does not remain anonymous, but claims authorship, and that there is some evidence for revision might suggest a certain poetic self-consciousness. There is, however, no evidence of familiarity with more learned or rhetorical writing, nor of any clerical training. His possible background in the landed gentry has given rise to the suggestion that he was 'one amongst the increasingly large retinue of minor functionaries who thronged the later medieval courts, and who decided to seek preferment through the production of laudatory poetry' (*Poems*, ed. James and Simons, 10). His possible patrons may have been Edward III, the giver of the remission of 1331, or perhaps Philippa of Hainault, or Queen Isabella, the owner of Crécy Forest in 1329 before it reverted to Edward III in 1331, but there is little hard evidence. Further attempts at biography—that he was, for instance, probably 'a soldierly minstrel, who wrote and sang mainly for the army, but was also favoured by the court' (*DNB*), or perhaps a younger son who had become a soldier of fortune—must remain speculative.

Few now would share the enthusiastic view of Joseph Ritson that Minot was 'perhaps equal, if not superior to any English poet before the sixteenth, or even, with very few exceptions, before the seventeenth, century' (Ritson, xiv). The style of popular satire that he exemplifies deliberately eschews literary graces and subtleties, and he uses its techniques with appropriate vigour. Ironies are grim, battle-scenes brief and violent. There is little pity for the defeated enemies of Edward: even the burghers of Calais, coming with ropes around their necks, lament that they have been betrayed by their rulers, who have:

left us ligand in þe mire
And broght us till þis doleful dance.
(*Poems*, ed. Hall, no. 8, ll. 71–2)

The driving passion is an enthusiastically patriotic—indeed, jingoistic—celebration of 'gude king Edward' and his loyal followers and their valiant deeds.

DOUGLAS GRAY

Sources *The poems of Laurence Minot*, ed. J. Hall (1887) · *The poems of Laurence Minot, 1333–1352*, ed. T. B. James and J. Simons (1989) · S. Moore, 'Laurence Minot', *Modern Language Notes*, 35 (1920), 78–81 · D. Savoia, 'Poesia e storia nei versi di Laurence Minot', *Studi Medievali*, 3rd ser., 19 (1978), 339–62 · J. Ritson, *Poems on interesting events in the reign of Edward III written in the year MCCCLII* (1795) [incl. preface, dissertations, notes, glossary] · *DNB*
Archives BL, Cotton MS Galba E.ix

Minsheu, John (1559/60–1627), lexicographer, is of unknown parentage. His family may have originated in Cheshire, where Minshull, of which Minsheu is a possible variant, was the name of a village. He refers to a cousin living in Oxfordshire, John Vesey, who was a self-made man of dubious probity. Minsheu may have resembled him in these two respects: he was educated by extensive travels rather than in a university, and he was described as a rogue by Ben Jonson. He was taken prisoner abroad, possibly by the Spaniards, and was brought home by the same helpful merchants who had previously assisted him in his travels, and to whom he expresses such warm gratitude.

Having settled in London as a language teacher, Minsheu compiled a *Dictionarie in Spanish and English* (1599), which was published together with a Spanish grammar and dialogues. They were all based on two textbooks of Spanish by Richard Percyvall, entitled *Bibliotheca Hispanica* (1591), the lexicon of which Minsheu considerably augmented. He refers to hostility towards his work in certain quarters, but ensured the grant of a licence to print by applying successfully to the archbishop of Canterbury. The printers set to work, so hurriedly that Minsheu, who had retired to the country 'upon necessitie' (*Dictionarie*), was given no opportunity to read the proofs; consequently he promised his readers to publish a corrected and augmented version. He records that he spent some time in Cambridge, where he both began and completed the revised Spanish dictionary; this was finally published in 1617 as *Vocabularium Hispanicolatinum et Anglicum*, an appendix to his *magnum opus, Ductor in linguas: the Guide into Tongues*.

The first part of *The Guide*, an etymological dictionary (*Glosson etymologicon*), was a huge undertaking, based on an examination of eleven languages. Minsheu employed native speakers of various languages to read through the best authors for material; he admitted that he found 'searching words for a dictionarie' (*Dictionarie in Spanish and English*, 1599, sig. A2r) an unprofitable and unpleasant study in which he lit a candle for others while his own light burnt out—one of a number of comments revealing the often distressing circumstances of his life.

At the end of July 1610 Minsheu moved with his assistants to Oxford, where he intended to complete the editing of the etymological dictionary. Anxious for recognition, he approached senior members of the university: they declared that the dictionary was a rare and excellent piece of work, which had already cost its author over 1000 marks, and that it fully deserved publication. Later in 1610 Minsheu returned to London with the university's testimonial, leaving the manuscript and his assistants in Oxford, while he took samples of his work with him, hoping to attract potential patrons. He obtained a royal patent which conferred on 'Minshon' the sole right of publication for twenty-one years; nevertheless the Stationers' Company refused to help him, on the ground that he was heavily in debt. Fortunately, distinguished scholars such as William Camden provided him with a second testimonial (8 December 1610), and two members of the inns of court offered financial assistance which enabled him to start printing. With the dictionary at press he was able to obtain credit, and in 1617 he finally saw his *Ductor in linguas* in print. Minsheu was also working on a 'topical' dictionary by 1617, but this was never published.

To dispose of his stock Minsheu visited several towns, some as far away as Winchester, with new promotional leaflets which included printed lists of those who had already bought the *Ductor*. As the number of purchasers grew, Minsheu had to revise the list, which eventually appeared in ten versions, recording more than 400 names of individuals and libraries, among them many distinguished authors.

Having disposed of the first edition, Minsheu and his printers reissued his Spanish dictionary (1599) in 1623. They now embarked on a second edition of the *Ductor* which, heavily revised and supported by a further promotional leaflet, appeared in 1625 as *Minshæi emendatio, vel a mendis expurgatio*. The second edition omitted the original appendix, the *Vocabularium*, presumably because the Spanish–English dictionary (1599) had been recently reprinted. The second edition was reissued in 1626 and 1627. In 1627 Minsheu, aged sixty-seven, 'decaied, and in debt' (as he admitted in his last leaflet) and suffering from deafness, died. He was buried at All Hallows, London Wall, on 12 April, leaving a young family whose mother, Margerie, had died in 1617. The Stationers' Company at last made amends for its earlier lack of co-operation by donating the profits of several publications, up to 1639, to Edward Minsheu, apparently the eldest of the orphan family.

Minsheu hoped to make foreign-language learning easier for English speakers; consequently, for the first time in a multilingual dictionary, the headword was in English. It is followed by any cognates which might exist, an arrangement designed by Minsheu to assist the memory, as were the generous citations and the etymological explanations. It is unlikely that Minsheu had much success with his teaching methods, and doubt is cast on his scholarship in the light of his frequent plagiarisms. Nevertheless, his achievement was, in the face of unremitting toil and adversity, to produce a magnificent dictionary, *The Guide into Tongues*, which was cited by many later lexicographers, in particular by Stephen Skinner in his *Etymologicon Linguae Anglicanae* (1671).

VIVIAN SALMON

Sources J. Schäfer, introduction, in J. Minsheu, *Ductor in linguas* (*Guide into the tongues*) and *Vocabularium Hispanicolatinum* (*A most copious Spanish dictionary*) (1617), facs. edn (1978), v–xx • F. B. Williams, 'Scholarly publication in Shakespeare's day', *J. Q. Adams memorial studies*, ed. J. G. MacManaway (1948), 755–73 • J. Rosier, 'The sources and methods of Minsheu's *Guide into the tongues*', *Philological Quarterly*, 40 (1961), 68–76 • R. Steiner, *Two centuries of Spanish and English bilingual lexicography, 1590–1800* (1970) • J. Minsheu, *A catalogue and true note of the names of such persons which … have receaved the etymological dictionarie of XI languages* [1617] • J. Warren, 'Reflections of an electronic scribe', *Early Modern Literary Studies* [Special Issue], 1 (1997) • parish register, 12 April 1627, All Hallows, London Wall [burial]

Minshull [Mynshul], **Geffray** (*bap.* 1594, *d.* 1668), debtor and author, was baptized at Nantwich on 25 October 1594, the son of a Cheshire gentleman, Edward Minshull of Stoke manor, Nantwich (*c.*1559–1628), and his wife, Margaret, daughter of Thomas Mainwaring. Geffray Minshull was admitted as a student at Gray's Inn in 1612. In 1617 he was imprisoned in the king's bench prison in Southwark for debts which may have been connected to a libel suit: his error, soon bitterly regretted, was 'so rashly to thrust my self into a printers press, though against my will … I undertook a war when I adventured to speak in print'; Minshull was consoled by visits from his student friends, greeting them and 'all the rest of my fellow students incorporated into your most worthy society' (Minshull, first preface). He warns his readers that 'usury and extortion bite deepe, and credit once crackt is not easily recovered, nor all creditors of one mind, for some will in pity forbeare, and others will shew the greatest severity'. While in prison Minshull produced the sketches of life there for which he is chiefly remembered, sending the manuscript to his uncle, Matthew *Mainwaring (later author of the romance *Vienna*), who had 'always been my anchor when I have been shipwracked, and many times saved my poor barque when it was ready to split' (ibid., second preface).

Minshull's book was published in 1618 as *Essayes and Characters of a Prison and Prisoners*, and reissued without alteration in 1638. In the frontispiece appears the image of a burly gaoler holding a spiked stave, with a thick chain and heavy keys attached to his waist. Minshull reported that the prisoner on arrival was conducted to his chamber where 'his chamberlain salutes him' and 'having no sooner fingered thy coyne, but sends thee a pair of sheets, fitter for a horse than a man' (Minshull, 24); other characters are 'cut throat the Steward' and 'Mistress Mutton Chops, the head cook', all of which are 'merciless bloodhounds' who drink 'the blood of thy purse' (ibid., 25). As for the keeper, 'his eye shoots at two whites, thy person and thy purse, the one is to guard thee, the other to feed him'; the author urges: 'protect thy carcase under his shelter as a sheep in a terrible storm under a briar' (ibid., 27). Minshull had some pithy observations about the value of prison: there, 'a man for half a years experience may learne more law, than he can at Westminster for an hundred pound'; it was a

little world of woe … a map of misery, it is a place that will learn a young man more villainy, if he be apt to take it, than he can learn at twenty dicing houses, bowling alleys, brothel houses or ordinaries; and an old man more policy than if he had been pupil to Machiavel. (ibid., 2–3)

'It is a little commonwealth, though little wealth be common there' (ibid.). And furthermore, 'A prison is nothing else but a great Alehouse, for every chamber is nothing else but a continuall drinking roome' (ibid., 44).

Little else is known of Minshull's life. At a Gray's Inn pension meeting of 30 June 1617 he was listed as one of the members who had not attended communion for the last year and fined £1; the first preface from the prison was dated 6 June 1618, but it seems that he soon regained his freedom and resumed his career, for on 23 November of that year he was called to the bar. At a date unknown Minshull married Mary, daughter of Sir Edward Fitton of Gawsworth, Cheshire; of their children, Edward, Richard, Thomas, Anne, Jane, Margaret, Mary, and Ellen were all living in 1668. Geffray Minshull died on 27 November 1668 at Nantwich and was buried there on 1 December. A memorial tablet to him was set up in the parish church, erroneously giving his age as 'aet. 76' (Hall, 315).

STEPHEN WRIGHT

Sources J. Hall, *A history of the town and parish of Nantwich* (1883) · A. Adams, *Cheshire visitation pedigrees, 1663*, Harleian Society, 93 (1941) · G. Armitage and J. Rylands, *Pedigrees made at the visitation of Cheshire, 1613*, Harleian Society, 59 (1909) · J. Foster, *The record of admissions to Gray's Inn, 1521–1889* (1889) · R. J. Fletcher, ed., *The pension book of Gray's Inn*, 1 (1901) · G. Minshull, *Essayes and characters of a prison and prisoners* (1618) · IGI

Minto. For this title name *see* Elliot, Sir Gilbert, first baronet, Lord Minto (1650/51–1718); Elliot, Sir Gilbert, second baronet, Lord Minto (*bap.* 1693, *d.* 1766); Kynynmound, Gilbert Elliot Murray, first earl of Minto (1751–1814); Kynynmound, Gilbert Elliot Murray, second earl of Minto (1782–1859); Kynynmound, Gilbert John Elliot Murray, fourth earl of Minto (1845–1914).

Minto, William (1845–1893), literary scholar, was born on 10 October 1845 at Nether Auchintoul, near Alford, Aberdeenshire, the son of James Minto, farmer, and his wife, Barbara Copland. As a child he was educated at various village and private schools, including the Gordon Schools, Huntly (1857–61). He gained a bursary and entered Aberdeen University in 1861, where he achieved great academic success. When graduating MA in 1865, he performed the unique feat of taking honours in three departments—classics, mathematics, and philosophy. He attended Divinity Hall in 1865–6. In 1866 he went to Merton College, Oxford, as an exhibitioner, but left next year without taking a degree.

Minto returned to Aberdeen to become, briefly, the assistant to the professor of natural philosophy, after which he was assistant to the professor of logic and English literature, Alexander Bain, from 1867 to 1873. It was while thus engaged that he began seriously to consider English literature, and planned his *Manual of English Prose Literature, Biographical and Critical*, an exhaustive and systematic work which he published in 1872.

In 1873 Minto moved to London and contributed literary and political articles to *The Examiner*, which he edited

between 1874 and 1878. Subsequently he was on the leader-writing staff of the *Daily News* and *Pall Mall Gazette*. In the *Daily News* he conducted his able and pungent criticism of Disraeli's imperial policy. His achievements as political writer allegedly also included giving currency to the word jingoism. In 1874 he published *Characteristics of English Poets from Chaucer to Shirley*, and in 1879 a monograph on Defoe for the English Men of Letters series. As a critic he wrote with great penetration and originality. Besides contributing to the leading reviews he wrote for the *Encyclopaedia Britannica* a number of important articles on literary subjects. As an editor he discovered and encouraged many new authors, including Edmund Gosse and Theodore Watts.

On 8 January 1880 Minto married Cornelia, daughter of the Revd Lewis Griffiths, rector of Swindon, Gloucestershire. In the same year, on the retirement of Professor Bain, he was elected to the chair of logic and English in Aberdeen University, a post he held until his death. During his professoriate he wrote three novels—*The Crack of Doom* (1886), *The Mediation of Ralph Hardelot* (1888), and *Was she good or bad?* (1889). He edited Walter Scott's *Lay of the Last Minstrel* (1886) and *Lady of the Lake* (1891), Scott's poetical works (1887), and *Autobiographical Notes of the Life of William Bell Scott* (1892).

Minto's health began to decline in 1891, and although a voyage to Greece helped somewhat, he succumbed to a complication of ailments on 1 March 1893 in Aberdeen, just when the separation of logic from English in his dual chair appeared to open up fresh opportunities of pursuing his favourite subject. His wife survived him. After his death there appeared *Logic Inductive and Deductive*, a university extension manual, and *Plain Principles of Prose Composition*, both in 1893, and a third volume, *English Literature under the Georges* (1894). His career 'reflects the Scottish intellectual's easy mobility between the academy and higher journalism' (Sutherland, 437).

ALEXANDER MACKIE, rev. SAYONI BASU

Sources W. Knight, introduction, in W. Minto, *Literature of the Georgian era*, ed. W. Knight (1894) · personal knowledge (1893) · J. Sutherland, *The Longman companion to Victorian fiction* (1988) · CCI (1893)
Archives U. Aberdeen L., diary and notebook | NL Scot., letters to Blackwoods · UCL, letters to G. C. Robertson
Likenesses wood-engraving, NPG; repro. in *ILN* (11 March 1893)
Wealth at death £2528 9s. 11d.: confirmation, 14 April 1893, CCI

Minton, Herbert (1793–1858), pottery manufacturer, was born on 4 February 1793 in Stoke-on-Trent, the second son of ten children of **Thomas Minton** (1765–1836), engraver and pottery manufacturer, and Sarah, *née* Webb (1772–1856). Thomas Minton was born at Wyle Cop, Shrewsbury, and on leaving school became an apprentice engraver at the Caughley Works, Broseley, Shropshire, where he worked on the engraving of the famous 'willow' pattern, among others, under the supervision of Thomas Turner. He soon established himself as an engraver in London, and during that time married Sarah Webb; their first child was baptized in 1791. Afterwards they moved to Stoke, where in 1793 Thomas Minton founded the Minton pottery and porcelain factory in London Road. Early productions at Minton concentrated on underglaze blue-printed earthenware tableware, and about 1799 bone china was introduced.

Herbert Minton was educated at Audlem grammar school, Cheshire, and at eighteen became involved with the Minton business as its representative. In 1817 he and Thomas Webb Minton, his elder brother, were taken into partnership. Thomas Webb was designated the clerical work, while Herbert, who arrived at work at five in the morning, approved design trials, undertook daily stock-taking in the warehouse, ordered bodies and glazes, and checked the factory accounts.

During the 1830s Minton and the Gothic architect and designer Augustus Welby Northmore Pugin found that they shared an interest in inlaid clay medieval floor tiles, and had a strong desire to reproduce them. One of the problems that Minton had to overcome was the irregular contraction of clays that caused the inlaid pattern to become easily dislodged from the main body of the tile. Repeated failures seemed only to strengthen his resolve. Matthew Digby Wyatt, architect and designer, commented:

> He set to work with a thorough English determination to succeed, and with untiring energy and perseverance, notwithstanding repeated failures and many difficulties and obstacles which presented themselves in his successive experiments, at length succeeded in producing tiles very far superior to those of the ancients.   (Minton archives, MS 31; *Journal of the Society of Arts*, 28 May 1858)

The combination of Pugin's designs and Minton's technical skill led to important commissions that included the houses of parliament; St Georges Hall, Liverpool; and Cheadle church, Staffordshire. Other important and ambitious tile schemes executed by the Minton factory were for the Capitol, Washington, DC; the Foreign Office, London; the royal dairy, Windsor; and the South Kensington Museum, London (now the Victoria and Albert Museum).

Thomas Webb Minton had entered the church twelve years before his father's death in 1836, and though Herbert Minton had made a major contribution towards the success of the factory, Thomas Webb was named chief beneficiary of his father's estate; Herbert was awarded only the interest on £3000 and a quarter of the profits. Thomas Kirkby, a Minton artist, recalled a devastated Herbert Minton saying 'If it had not have been for my mother and my sisters, I would have given up the potting business' (Minton archives, MS 115). Thomas Webb Minton, after family consultation, donated £23,000 to enable the executors of Thomas Minton's will to fund a new partnership between Herbert Minton and John Boyle, a local potter, who both contributed capital themselves; however, on 21 November 1841 the partnership ended.

Herbert Minton married Anne, the third daughter of John Hollins of Shelton, near Stoke-on-Trent, on 1 September 1819, and after her death, in 1841, he married Mary Brown. Isabella Stewart Fraser, *née* Leckie, became his third wife, following the death of Mary. Minton had no children, and in 1845 he was joined by two partners in the factory: Michael Daintry Hollins, his first wife's nephew, and Colin Minton Campbell, his own nephew.

By the 1840s the Minton factory was producing a range of figures, ornamental ware, and encaustic floor tiles. During the mid- to late 1840s Herbert Minton developed Parian body (named after the Greek island of Paros) for statuary, and low-temperature lead glazes that Minton named majolica. Both majolica and Parian were launched at the Great Exhibition of 1851 and contributed greatly to Minton's being awarded the bronze council medal—a most prestigious accolade—for 'beauty and originality of design', the only one of its kind bestowed on an English manufacturer.

The development of Parian led to Minton securing the services of the finest sculptors in England, France, and Italy, whose works created a new awareness among the workforce and the general public of classical and contemporary sculpture. The popularity of majolica, the most characteristic Victorian art form, with its vigorous modelling and vibrant glazes, remained constant until the 1880s, when there was a change in public taste and less demand for flamboyant ceramic pieces; however, its reputation is retained to this day as the most decorative pottery ever produced.

Herbert Minton was chosen as Queen Victoria's personal escort at the Great Exhibition, and she wrote in her journal on 30 April 1851: 'we walked the whole round of the galleries. We saw beautiful china from Minton's factory and beautiful designs' (Gibbs-Smith, 16). On 22 May she made a return visit to the Minton stand and recorded: 'this is upon the whole the finest, everything for the table, bedroom sets, flower vases, all in the best taste' (ibid., 20). A reviewer in the *Journal of the Society of Arts* (9 August 1858) commented:

> The verdicts of two international juries had assigned to Mr. Minton an European fame and the chief place among manufacturers of pottery since the first Wedgwood, no one has done so much to advance his art as Mr. Minton. Both at the London and Paris Exhibitions his works proved that individual enterprise was more than a match for state subsidies.   (Minton archives, MS 26)

In 1856 Herbert Minton, Michael Daintry Hollins, and Colin Minton Campbell were granted the royal warrant 'to be manufacturers of china, earthenware, encaustic and plain tiles and tesserae at Stoke-upon-Trent in ordinary to Her Majesty'.

Herbert Minton was well known for his philanthropic qualities. He lived for many years at Longfield Cottage, Hartshill, near Stoke, where in 1842 he built and endowed a church (one of Sir Gilbert Scott's early works) and schools for 1500 children, with houses for teachers, providing for their maintenance and for the education of the children. He built almshouses for the aged and infirm, and infirmaries for the sick. He donated £500 towards the erection of public baths; a future project was to build by public subscription a school of art and literature next to the public baths.

On 1 April 1858 Herbert Minton died at his retirement residence, Belmont, Middle Woodfield Road, Torquay. He had been a magistrate, a lieutenant of Stafford, a member of the Society of Antiquaries, and a knight of the imperial order of the Légion d'honneur. He was buried at Trinity Church, Hartshill. As a tribute to his memory the school of art in London Road, Stoke-on-Trent, was erected by public subscription, and at Torquay it was proposed to add a spire to St Mark's Church.

Probate records that Herbert Minton left under £70,000. On 22 March 1857 he wrote to his brother-in-law John Campbell stating that he had made his will and would show it to him soon. In that letter he encouraged Campbell to purchase 6½ acres of land that was on the market from Mr Spode (who owned a ceramic manufactory in close proximity). Minton wanted to buy the land himself, but in addition to the substantial bequests set out in his will he had gifted the church and the school, and made alterations to his house that cost £3000, and consequently could not afford to buy the land. He also mentioned that he had taken out life insurance for £7000. Colin Minton Campbell, Minton's nephew, inherited the factory after his uncle's death, and it was Minton's wish that the land purchased from Spode would be available for Colin's use.

At a discussion of the Society of Arts the interior decorator J. G. Crace (formerly A. W. N. Pugin's assistant) said of Minton:

> in fact, taking his productions altogether we had reason as Englishmen to be proud of our dearly departed friend. He had not only earned a reputation which would probably live as long as this country remained; but he had greatly aided in gaining for England the respectable position she had now attained in the arts. (Minton archives, MS 31; *Journal of the Society of Arts*, 28 May 1858)

JOAN JONES

Sources A. G. Jones, *Catalogue of the Minton manuscripts*, 2 vols. (1973–5) · Minton archives, Stoke-on-Trent, MSS 16, 17, 25, 31, 30, 33, 26, 10, 48, 151, 115 · P. Atterbury and M. Batkin, *The dictionary of Minton* (1990) · B. Ferry, *Recollections of A. N. Welby Pugin and his father Augustus Pugin* (1861) · C. H. Gibbs-Smith, *The Great Exhibition of 1851: a commemorative album* (1950) · G. A. Godden, *Minton pottery and porcelain of the first period, 1793–1850* (1968) · L. Jewitt, *The ceramic art of Great Britain* (1878) · J. Jones, *Two hundred years of design and production* (1993) · CGPLA Eng. & Wales (1858) · P. Atterbury, ed., *The parian phenomenon* (1989) · will, probate department of the Principal Registry of the Family Division, London

Archives Royal Doulton, Burslem, Stoke-on-Trent, Minton archives | Horace Barks Reference Library, Hanley, Stoke-on-Trent, Solon MSS

Likenesses H. Protât, Parian figure, 1860, Minton Museum, Stoke-on-Trent · H. W. Pickersgill, oils, Royal Doulton Headquarters, Stoke-on-Trent

Wealth at death under £70,000: probate, 23 June 1858, *CGPLA Eng. & Wales*

Minton, (Francis) John (1917–1957), painter and illustrator, was born on 25 December 1917 at Great Shelford, Cambridgeshire, the second of the three sons of Francis Minton (*c.*1876–1930), solicitor, then of East Sheen, London, and his wife, Kate Key, *née* Webb (*c.*1876–1952). He received his education between 1925 and 1935 at Northcliff House, Bognor Regis, Sussex, and at Reading School, where he opted for John as his principal forename. He then studied

under P. F. Millard at St John's Wood Art Schools, London. There he met Michael Ayrton who, though his junior by several years, greatly affected his development by introducing him to James Thrall Soby's book *After Picasso*. Minton's response to the Parisian neo-romantics described therein was increased by eight months, largely in the company of Ayrton, spent in Paris and—at that time remote and magical—Les Baux-de-Provence immediately prior to the outbreak of war. The influence of Eugène Berman, Pavel Tchelitchew, and the early work of Giorgio de Chirico was plainly evident in the crepuscular street scenes from London's war-torn docklands which he painted between 1940 and 1942. He collaborated with Ayrton on costumes and décor for John Gielgud's production of *Macbeth* (1942); in the same year he shared an exhibition with Ayrton at the Leicester Galleries in London.

Having withdrawn an earlier expressed conscientious objection to the war, Minton was called into the Pioneer Corps in the autumn of 1941, was commissioned in 1943, but was released on medical grounds later that year. On his return to London he shared a studio until 1946 with the Scottish painters Robert Colquhoun and Robert MacBryde, and thereafter for some years with Keith Vaughan. His mature style comprised a compound of urban romanticism learned from Berman and pastoral intricacy learned from Samuel Palmer, and the formalizations employed by Wyndham Lewis and the sonorous colour employed by Colquhoun and MacBryde. He quickly gained recognition among the young British romantics of those first post-war years.

Minton's activities were manifold, his capacity for work prodigious. He taught in turn at three distinguished London schools—Camberwell School of Arts and Crafts (now Camberwell College of Arts), briefly at the Central School of Arts and Crafts, and between 1948 and 1956 at the Royal College of Art. He undertook very many richly textured decorations and illustrations for books, magazines, and advertising—notably a travel book on Corsica (*Time was Away*, 1948) with Alan Ross, an English translation (1947) of Alain-Fournier's *Le grand Meaulnes*, and Elizabeth David's first cookbooks, *A Book of Mediterranean Food* (1950) and *French Country Cooking* (1951). *The Listener*, *Penguin New Writing*, *Lilliput*, and *Vogue* were only some of the publications to use his drawings, and he made sorties into almost every field of design, from posters (Ealing Studios, London Transport) to wallpaper (John Lines & Sons), the Chelsea Arts ball to settings for *Don Juan in Hell* at the Royal Court Theatre (1956).

Minton's paintings, drawings, and watercolours poured forth in a steady stream, many reflecting his travels in Spain (1948 and 1954), the West Indies (1950), and Morocco (1952). Between 1949 and 1956 he held five one-man shows at the Lefevre Gallery and contributed to many group exhibitions. His natural facility embraced an exceptional sense of decoration and colour combined with precision of draughtsmanship—seen clearly in his admirable portraits of students and friends, such as that of the critic Nevile Wallis (1952). From the late 1940s he embarked on large set-pieces; for example, *The Death of Nelson* (1952,

Royal College of Art, London). In 1949 he was elected to the London Group and, from that year, showed regularly at the Royal Academy's summer exhibitions. However, he could not respond to the new waves of abstraction sweeping in from the United States and he increasingly felt himself out of touch with current fashion.

From the mid-1940s Minton made no secret of his homosexuality, though he is thought to have remained ill at ease with it. He lived always in the moment, driven urgently by a need for company and change. These he found in the press of young students he took under his wing—'Johnny's circus'. An inheritance in 1949, stemming from his maternal grandfather, served further to lubricate a way of life that was already frenetic. As he oscillated between exuberance and black despair his days became increasingly disordered, and his dependence on alcohol, finally, self-destructive. In 1956 he took a year's leave of absence from the Royal College of Art. On 20 January 1957 at his home in Apollo Place, Cheyne Walk, Chelsea, London, he took an overdose of drugs and died while being taken to St Stephen's Hospital. He was cremated four days later at Golders Green.

In appearance Minton was striking, with a shock of jet-black hair surmounting a lantern face of extraordinary gravity in repose but totally transformed by enthusiasm or mirth. His hands were long and lean. From his gangling presence came a ceaseless crackle of nervous energy. He was an exuberant companion, beloved by his very many friends for the sweetness of his character, an infectious gaiety, and the intelligence which underlay his defensive clowning. In a letter to *The Times* after his death Robin Darwin wrote of 'a magical quality in him which will remain for us unique'.

Minton is often seen as an illustrator rather than a painter. He certainly extended and enriched the English graphic tradition. In all his varied output, however, may be sensed an elegiac awareness of the evanescence of physical beauty that is entirely personal. His work is to be found in the Tate collection, and many public and private collections at home and abroad. A retrospective exhibition of 1994, curated by his biographer, Frances Spalding, provided a convincing reminder of the range of his gifts. For the historian he must remain a potent symbol of his period.   MICHAEL MIDDLETON

Sources F. Spalding, *Dance till the stars come down* (1991) · *John Minton, 1917–1957: a selective retrospective* (1993) [exhibition catalogue, Davies Memorial Gallery, Newtown] · *CGPLA Eng. & Wales* (1957) · personal knowledge (2004) · private information (1971, 2004)
Archives Tate collection, letters to Michael Ayrton · Tate collection, letters to Beryl (Judith) Holman [photocopies] · Tate collection, corresp. with Edie and Newton Lamont
Likenesses P. F. Millard, oils, *c.*1937 · R. Moynihan, group portrait, oils, 1951, Tate collection · L. Freud, oils, 1952, Royal College of Art, London · F. J. Minton, self-portrait, oils, 1953, NPG
Wealth at death £13,518 17s. 2d.: probate, 26 March 1957, *CGPLA Eng. & Wales*

Minton, Thomas (1765–1836). *See under* Minton, Herbert (1793–1858).

Mir Jafar Ali Khan (*c.*1691–1765). *See under* Bengal, nawabs of (*act.* 1756–1793).

Mir Kasim Ali Khan (*d.* 1777). *See under* Bengal, nawabs of (*act.* 1756–1793).

Mirfield, John [Johannes de Mirfeld] (*d.* 1407), ecclesiastic and medical writer, became chaplain of the hospital of St Bartholomew, Smithfield, in London. His two massive Latin encyclopaedias, *Breviarium Bartholomei* and *Florarium Bartholomei*, are unusually rich sources for information about medical lore in late-medieval London. His family probably came from the Yorkshire town of Mirfield. One of several Londoners of that name who appear in fourteenth- and fifteenth-century records, he was the kinsman, possibly the son, of William Mirfield, a priest sometimes styled 'great clerk' in the household of John of Gaunt, for whom William acted as chief attorney. William died in 1375 and may have been buried in St Bartholomew's Priory.

John Mirfield seems to have lived in the environs of the priory for most, if not all, of his life. An entry on the patent rolls for 4 April 1390 confirms an indenture between him and the priory and convent of St Bartholomew, originally dated 9 May 1362, granting him an annual pension of £4 8s. for life, and leasing to him for a rent of 4s. a chamber in the church. A clerical subsidy roll for 1379 records Mirfield as a clerk of the priory of St Bartholomew paying 4d. in tax. This argues that he was not a full canon, who would have paid more. As clerk, he is reported in 1382 as receiving 40s. in return for executing the will of John Chishull, a chaplain lodging in St Bartholomew's close.

The register of Bishop Robert Braybrooke of London records that Mirfield was refused ordination as acolyte on 19 September 1394 (perhaps because of illegitimacy), but was ordained deacon on 27 March 1395 and priest on 10 April 1395, each time being named as of the confraternity of the hospital of St Bartholomew, Smithfield. Exactly what he did for either the hospital or the priory is not clear; however, given the legal technicalities that increasingly surrounded the transfer of properties owned by religious houses, it may have been a convenience for both institutions to have a resident agent who was not an Augustinian canon.

Mirfield wrote two Latin encyclopaedias toward the end of his life that reflect the dual nature of his association with the priory and with the hospital. The first, *Florarium Bartholomei*, is a religious encyclopaedia, covering the health of the spirit. The volume, which fills nearly 300 folios, is found in two manuscripts: London, Gray's Inn, MS 4 and BL, Royal MS 7 F.xi. Mirfield's remarks are principally aimed at priests like himself, who have to take care not to injure or kill a patient during surgery or medical treatment, and thus interfere with their principal duties to God. But abuse is also directed at the unlettered, the greedy, and women who presumptuously try to practise medicine in spite of their natural inability to do so. One chapter is devoted to the duties of the physician, especially to medical deontology or etiquette. But the *Florarium* presents medicine as only one among nearly 200 other topics, including chapters on the Holy Trinity, the sacraments, and the various Christian virtues.

The *Breviarium Bartholomei* devotes the same length to medicine alone, in a book intended for use at the hospital. Mirfield deals with diseases from the head downward. He also covers wounds and abscesses, fractures and dislocations, the compounding of drugs, and finishes with bloodletting and a regimen of health. He presents useful recipes, including one for a 'powder for that warlike or diabolic instrument that commonly is termed the gun' (Oxford, Pembroke College, MS 2, fol. 282). Mingled with more conventional medical advice, he suggests charms and prayers. Travellers are told to boil their drinking water or to distil it, and also to pray to the three wise men. The royal touch is recommended as a cure for scrofula (a skin disease), and if that fails, the sufferer is to float in a spring on the night of the feast of St John the Baptist. Finally, prayer is advised for things medicine is powerless to help, a practice Mirfield notes has fallen off of late. The entire text survives in two manuscripts from the late fourteenth century. The first, Oxford, Pembroke College, MS 2, was prepared for the Benedictine abbey of Abingdon, near Oxford. The second, BL, Harley MS 3, was purchased in 1573 by John Dee and was heavily annotated by Dee himself. Part of the text, on the signs of death, is found in a mid-fifteenth-century manuscript, London, Lambeth Palace, MS 444.

Mirfield had died in London by 5 May 1407, having asked to be buried in St Botolph, Aldersgate, and leaving unspecified property to his mother. FAYE GETZ

Sources P. H.-S. Hartley and H. R. Aldridge, *Johannes de Mirfeld of St Bartholomew's, Smithfield: his life and works* (1936) · C. Rawcliffe, 'The hospitals of later medieval London', *Medical History*, 28 (1984), 1–21 · J. L. G. Mowat, ed., *Sinonoma Bartholomei: a glossary from a fourteenth-century manuscript in the library of Pembroke College, Oxford* (1882) · Pembroke College, Oxford, MS 2

Archives BL, Royal MS 7 F.xi · BL, Harley MS 3 · Gray's Inn, London, MS 4 · LPL, MS 444 · Pembroke College, Oxford, MS 2

Mirk, John (*fl. c.*1382–*c.*1414), Augustinian author, was a canon and later prior of Lilleshall in Shropshire, a house of Augustinian canons. The three works attributed to him demonstrate that, in accordance with the vows of his order, he was intensely committed to pastoral work. Two, known today as the *Instructions for Parish Priests* and the *Manuale sacerdotis*, are priests' manuals, while the third, named by Mirk in his prologue as the *Festial* ('and for this treti speketh alle of festis I wolle and pray that it be called a festial'; BL, Cotton MS Claudius A.ii, fol. 3v), is a collection of sermons *de temporibus* and *de sanctis*. The preparatory material to all three works emphasizes the need to provide guidance for the ignorant or errant parish priest since, as the *Instructions* points out, 'whenne þe blynde ledeth þe blynde/Into þe dyche þey fallen boo' (Mirk, *Instructions*, 67).

It was assumed until recently that Mirk wrote in the early fifteenth century. In fact, though no extant manuscript of any work is earlier than the fifteenth century, recent research has shown that the *Festial* was most likely written in the later 1380s. But the *Manuale* probably dates

from later in Mirk's career, for in its *prefacio* Mirk refers to himself as prior of Lilleshall, whereas in colophons to the *Instructions* and the *Festial* he is merely a canon. If recent conjecture about the dedication is correct, the *Manuale* was written at least as late as 1414. Both the *Festial* and the *Manuale* contain hostile references to Lollardy, which emerged in Mirk's vicinity in the early 1380s. It may be that the *Instructions*, which does not mention the Lollard threat, was written earlier and that it was frequently issued together with the *Festial* (as in BL, Cotton MS Claudius A.ii, and Bodl. Oxf., MS Douce 60) in order to provide a comprehensive pastoral programme for the unlettered parish priest. Mirk's works are impeccably orthodox, and, though there is no indication that any of them was officially disseminated, it may be that the circulation of the *Festial* in the central midlands, which is well attested by extant manuscripts, was officially encouraged in opposition to the Lollard sermon cycle.

No list of the priors of Lilleshall exists, and no more is known of Mirk than is attested by the works themselves. On the basis of northern rhymes and lexis, the most recent editor of the *Instructions* suggests a northern provenance, and indeed the name Mirk may be Scandinavian in origin. It is tempting, but entirely speculative, to suggest that Mirk's strong pastoral interests might have been fostered in York province, where Archbishop John Thoresby (*d.* 1373) in 1357 had instituted an educational crusade against ignorant priests by the dissemination of what is now known as *The Lay Folks' Catechism*.

It has already been suggested that the *Instructions* was an early and the *Manuale* a late work of Mirk's. This is perhaps confirmed by the nature of the two manuals. The *Instructions* is composed in English rhyming couplets, whereas the *Manuale* is in Latin prose. Both appear to be loosely based on William Pagula's *Oculus sacerdotis* of the 1320s, but whereas the *Instructions* is an elementary handbook, presumably for a recently ordained priest, the Latin manual, as its medium suggests, is altogether more advanced and explores the spiritual more than the practical duties of the priesthood.

It was, however, with the practical duties of the priesthood that Mirk was concerned when he compiled his *Festial* out of the immensely popular *Legenda aurea* of Jacopo da Voragine: 'But for mony excuson ham by defaute of bokus and sympulnys of letture, therfor in helpe of suche mene clerkus as I am myselff, I haue drawe this treti sewyng owt of *Legend aurea* with more addyng to' (BL, Cotton MS Claudius A.ii, fol. 3v). As Mirk goes on to say, his aim was to provide a ready-made sermon for all the principal feasts of the year, and the sermons are notable for their popular appeal by virtue of the simplicity of their language and structure, and Mirk's frequent recourse to narrative and *exempla*.

Far fewer copies survive of the *Instructions* and the *Manuale* than of the *Festial*, though the nature of these handbooks (and Mirk's expressed wish in both works that their owners should consult them frequently) makes it inevitable that many should have been lost through overuse. At least seven manuscripts of the *Instructions* are known, and thirteen of the *Manuale*, two of them abridgements.

There are to date forty-three known manuscripts containing *Festial* material in various states of transmission. Only half of these can be said to approximate to Mirk's original text; of the rest, four contain texts of a substantial mid-fifteenth-century revision. Differences in content and arrangement between manuscripts reveal that a 'Group A' text, circulating from Lilleshall, underwent a 'Group B' recension which spread further eastwards. The transmission is complex but typical of a widely used text, the dissemination of which was accelerated by the advent of printing. Caxton's decision to print the *Festial* in 1483 must have depended on its appeal beyond the narrow market for which it had been originally written, and indeed a lay emphasis had already been introduced in certain recensions of the work. Between 1486 and 1532 a further twenty-two editions were produced at home and abroad. Not only was the *Festial* the most widely read English sermon cycle in the fifteenth century, it would also appear to have been the most frequently printed English text before the Reformation.   SUSAN POWELL

Sources *John Mirk's instructions for parish priests*, ed. G. Kristensson, Lund Studies in English, 49 (1974) · *Mirk's Festial: a collection of homilies*, ed. T. Erbe, EETS, extra ser., 96 (1905) · J. M. Girsch, ed., 'An edition with commentary of John Mirk's *Manuale sacerdotis*', PhD diss., University of Toronto, 1990 · S. Powell, 'John Mirk's *Festial* and the pastoral programme', *Leeds Studies in English*, new ser., 22 (1991), 85–102 · S. Powell, ed., *The Advent and Nativity sermons from a fifteenth-century revision of John Mirk's Festial*, Middle English Texts, 13 (1981) · *ESTC*, 17959–75 · S. Powell, 'A new dating of John Mirk's *Festial*', *N&Q*, 227 (1982), 487–9 · A. J. Fletcher, 'John Mirk and the Lollards', *Medium Aevum*, 56 (1987), 217–24 · M. F. Wakelin, 'The manuscripts of John Mirk's *Festial*', *Leeds Studies in English*, new ser., 1 (1967), 93–118 · A. J. Fletcher, 'Unnoticed sermons from John Mirk's *Festial*', *Speculum*, 55 (1980), 514–22 · A. J. Fletcher, 'The manuscripts of John Mirk's *Manuale sacerdotis*', *Leeds Studies in English*, new ser., 19 (1988), 105–39

Archives BL, Cotton MS Claudius A.ii · BL, Royal MSS 17 C.xvii, 18 B.xxiii, 18 B.xxv · BL, Harley MSS 5306, 2403, 2420, 2417, 2371, 2391, 2247, 2250, 1288 · BL, Lansdowne MSS 392, 379 · BL, Arundel MS 279 · Bodl. Oxf., MSS Douce 60, 103, 108 · Bodl. Oxf., MS Tanner 196 · Bodl. Oxf., Greaves MSS 57, 54 · Bodl. Oxf., Bodley MSS 632, 549 · Bodl. Oxf., MS Gough ecclesiastical topography 4 · Bodl. Oxf., MS Digby 75 · Bodl. Oxf., MS Jesus College 1 · Bodl. Oxf., MSS Hatton 97, 96 · Bodl. Oxf., MS Rawl. A.381 · Bodl. Oxf., MS University College Oxford D.102 · Bodl. Oxf., e Museo 180 · Borth. Inst., H C C P 1590/5 · Cardiff Public Library, MS Havod 22 · CUL, MSS Ff.5.48, Ff.1.14, Dd.10.50, Nn.3.10, Ee.2.15, Ff.2.38 · DWL, MS Anc. 11 (formerly New College London MS Z.c.19) · Gloucester Cathedral library, MS 22 · Gon. & Caius Cam., MS 168/89 · Hatfield House, Hertfordshire, Cecil MS 280 · Lincoln Cathedral, MSS 50, 133 · Peterhouse, Cambridge, MS 236 · Southwell Minster Library, MS 7 · St John Cam., MS G.19 · Stonyhurst College, Lancashire, MS A.II.8 · TCD, MSS 201, 428 · Trinity Cam., MSS B.11.23, B.11.24 · U. Durham, Cosin MSS V.iii.5, V.iv.3 · U. Leeds, Brotherton L., MS 502 · University of Chicago, Illinois, MS 697 · York Minster Library, MSS xvi.O.11, xvi.L.8

Mirrielees, Archibald (1797–1877). *See under* Muir, Andrew (1817–1899).

Mirrlees, (Helen) Hope (1887–1978), writer and poet, was born on 8 April 1887 at Erpingham, Chislehurst, Kent, the eldest child of William Julius Mirrlees (*d.* 1924) and Emily Lina Moncrieff (Mappy to her family) (*d.* 1948). Both her parents were Scots, and her father 'WJ' had trained in Glasgow as an engineer, though he later became an immensely successful businessman, with interests in various manufacturing firms, as well as in a large sugar plantation near Durban. Her grandfather had established the firm of Mirrlees–Blackstone, which made diesel engines for many years. Her mother's family were cultured Edinburgh lawyers. Although six children had been born, only three survived to adulthood: Hope (known as Hopy), William (Reay), who eventually became a major-general, and Margaret (Margot), who married an army officer. Hope grew up in Scotland and South Africa, which she loved—she learned to speak Zulu. She was educated first at home, then at the age of eleven attended the Besires School as a boarder, and later St Andrews preparatory school and St Leonard's School, St Andrews. As a young woman she was presented at court, and then, under the influence of Mrs Patrick Campbell, attended the Royal Academy of Dramatic Art, but soon found herself more interested in languages; above all, she wanted to learn Greek.

In 1910 Mirrlees went up to Newnham College, Cambridge, having already met the great classical scholar Jane Ellen *Harrison (1850–1928), who became her tutor. Hope became deeply attached to her and, in turn, became Jane's favourite pupil. After Hope went down in 1913 the two remained in close contact, writing to each other in a private language in different personae, sometimes as the elder and younger walrus, or else as the two wives of 'the Old One', Jane's ancient teddy bear. Late in 1913 Hope visited Paris with her friend Karin Costelloe (soon to marry Virginia Woolf's brother Adrian); she went back again in 1914, 1915, and 1919, staying at the Hotel de l'Elysée, 3 rue de Beaune, on the Left Bank. Paris provides the scene for her first novel, *Madeleine, one of Love's Jansenists* (1919), set in the seventeenth century among the circle of *précieuses* around Mme de Scudéry (who fancies herself as 'Sappho'). The novel seems to be a *roman à clef* recording Mirrlees's flirtation with Left Bank lesbianism (Mme de Scudéry may be an unflattering portrait of the writer and literary hostess Natalie Clifford Barney). As a young woman, Hope was striking, with dark hair, bright blue eyes, and a beautiful voice. Virginia Woolf described her as 'her own heroine—capricious, exacting, exquisite, very learned, and beautifully dressed' (*Letters of Virginia Woolf*, 3.200).

In 1919 Mirrlees was studying Russian at the École des Langues Orientales in Paris where she observed events in the city and read avant-garde poetry including that of Apollinaire, Pierre Reverdy's journal *Nord–sud*, and Jean Cocteau's sequence *Le Cap de Bonne-Espérance*, which she claimed 'liberated' her into writing her own experimental poem. Hope had met Virginia and Leonard Woolf the previous year, when they invited her to write for the Hogarth Press: *Paris* (1920) became their fifth publication (T. S. Eliot's *Poems* was the fourth). It was hand set by Virginia herself in an edition of 175 copies—only the smallness of the edition can explain the subsequent neglect of this extraordinarily daring and brilliant poem, which was arguably her greatest achievement. A 600-line modernist poem, it describes the city recovering from the First World War, haunted by its dead, yet springing back to life as it hosts President Wilson and the peace conference delegates. *Paris* is written partly in English, partly in French, citing or reciting Métro station names, posters, shop signs, and memorial plaques. Highly allusive and typographically original, it has claims to be the missing link between French avant-garde poetry and Eliot's *The Waste Land* (1923).

In 1922 Jane Harrison retired from Cambridge, and she and Hope moved to Paris, where they stayed at the American University Women's Club. Together they translated from Russian *The Life of the Archpriest Avvakum by himself* (1924), to which their friend Prince Mirsky contributed an introduction, and *The Book of the Bear* (1926), a collection of folk-tales. The bear was part of their private mythology, and the constellation of Ursa Major appears not only at the end of *Paris* but also as the tailpiece to Hope's three novels. Her second, *The Counterplot* (1924), is a contemporary story of family life (said to be based on her own), ending with a play set in a Spanish convent which reworks the family's relationships in fantasy mode. It numbered Christopher Isherwood among its admirers and in 1929 was translated into French as *Le choc en retour*, with an afterword by Charles Du Bos. Her third novel, the fantasy *Lud-in-the-Mist* (1926), is the story of Master Nathaniel Chanticleer, mayor of Lud, who struggles to save his town from an invasion by sinister fairy fruit that induce strange states of mind. In May 1925 Hope and Jane found they could no longer stay at the club, and returned to London, to 11 Mecklenburgh Street, where Jane died in 1928, leaving Hope bereft.

In the wake of Jane's death, probably at some time in 1929, Hope became a Roman Catholic convert, and during the 1930s she lived with her mother at Thurloe Close, next to the Brompton Oratory. Here she worked on her fanciful biography of the seventeenth-century antiquary Sir Robert Cotton (part of which was published as *A Fly in Amber* in 1962) and a projected but never completed biography of Jane Harrison. The material she collected for the latter and various drafts for it are deposited at Newnham. T. S. Eliot had become a close friend in the 1920s, and during the Second World War he stayed with Hope and her mother in their house at Shamley Green, near Guildford, where he wrote *Dry Salvages* and *Little Gidding*. In 1948 her mother died, and Hope moved to South Africa, to the Cape of Good Hope, where she wrote occasional elegant poems and continued working on her life of Cotton.

By now, Hope Mirrlees had grown heavy, with a booming contralto and a passion for dogs—at different times, she owned chows, pugs, and dachshunds. In 1963 she finally returned to England to live at Headington, Oxford. Here she was briefly rediscovered by Suzanne Henig, who in 1972 wrote an article about her for the short-lived *Virginia Woolf Quarterly*, which also reprinted a version of *Paris*, bowdlerized by its author, who now disapproved of its blasphemies. In 1970, in the wake of Tolkien, Lin Carter recommended *Lud-in-the Mist* to Ballantine Books, and

since then it has been reprinted several times in Britain and the United States. Joanna Russ wrote a pastiche of it as 'The Zanzibar Cat' (in her collection *The Zanzibar Cat*), and it remains very popular and influential as a 'fantasy novel of ideas' (Swanwick); Henig drew attention to its allusions to Plato's 'Allegory of the cave', and its philosophical enquiries into the nature of reality and the imagination. Forty of Mirrlees's poems were published in *Moods and Tensions* (1976), with a preface by an old friend, Raymond Mortimer.

Hope Mirrlees died at Thames Bank, Goring, on 1 August 1978. There were no obituaries, though the newspapers noticed the size of her estate. She had always had everything she needed in a material sense, and it has been suggested that she might have written more had she found it necessary to earn her own living. Yet what is most striking about her work is the way in which she never repeated herself: her achievements are of amazingly different kinds, united only by the continuous need to relate the inner life of fantasy and passion to a stubborn and unresponsive world of fact. JULIA BRIGGS

Sources private information (2004) · Newnham College, Cambridge, register · Newnham College, Cambridge, archive · S. Henig, 'Queen of Lud: Hope Mirrlees', *Virginia Woolf Quarterly*, 1/1 (autumn 1972) · *The letters of Virginia Woolf*, ed. N. Nicolson, 3 (1977) · M. Beard, *The invention of Jane Harrison* (2000) · M. Swanwick, 'The lady who wrote Lud-in-the mist', www.infinityplus.co.uk/introduces/mirrlees.htm, 23 Aug 2001 · b. cert. · d. cert. · *Diary of Virginia Woolf 1931–35*, ed. A. O. Bell and A. McNeillie, 4 (1982) · G. Stein, *The autobiography of Alice B. Toklas* (1933)
Archives Newnham College, Cambridge, Harrison papers
Likenesses photographs, Newnham College, Cambridge
Wealth at death £120,816: probate, 25 Jan 1979, *CGPLA Eng. & Wales* · £2188: further grant, 20 Sept 1979, *CGPLA Eng. & Wales*

Mirror Club (*act.* 1776–1787), a prominent group of Scottish literati who published the Edinburgh journals *The Mirror* (1779–80) and *The Lounger* (1785–7), evolved from a small Edinburgh literary debating society known as the Feast of Tabernacles (1770–77). The latter was a self-selected group of young writers, lawyers, preachers, and landed scions whose acknowledged leader was the politician Henry *Dundas. Many of these individuals had earlier belonged to the Belles Lettres Society (1759–63), the junior version of the *Select Society, a famous grouping of Scottish politicians, philosophers, preachers, and writers.

In its early evolution from the Feast of Tabernacles about 1776–7, the founding members of the Mirror Club included Henry *Mackenzie, William *Craig, Alexander *Abercromby, William Macleod *Bannatyne, and Robert *Cullen. Other members from this time were the lawyers **George Ogilvie** (*d.* 1785), **William Gordon of Newhall** (*d.* 1778), and **George Home of Wedderburn** (1734–1820). Later corresponding members, who contributed essays or correspondence, included James *Beattie, David *Dalrymple, William *Greenfield, Robert *Henry, David *Hume (*bap.* 1757, *d.* 1838), William *Richardson, William *Strahan, Alexander Fraser *Tytler, and his father, William *Tytler. The publisher and future lord provost of Edinburgh, William *Creech, whose idea it was to publish

The Mirror, should be considered an *ex officio* club member since he was the only contact for many of the correspondents. Any forced division between core and corresponding members is somewhat misleading, however, since Dalrymple, Richardson, and Alexander Fraser Tytler made a far greater contribution to the club's publications than certain full members. Tytler, in fact, became one of the club's principal essayists.

The Mirror Club's ethical essays—which copied the form and continued the function of *The Spectator* (1711–14) of Addison and Steele—appear to have been well received. Macleod Bannatyne reported that 400 copies of each issue were printed, the same number that was recorded in *Eminent Scotsmen* by William Chambers. This number significantly underestimates the number of actual readers in an age when paper periodicals were widely circulated. Many of the club's essays were printed elsewhere, with twenty-three papers and one poem appearing in the *Caledonian Mercury*, the *Scots Magazine*, and *The Bee*. The bound collection of *The Mirror* went through eleven editions prior to 1802 and *The Lounger* six editions before 1805. While no subscription lists have been found, acknowledged subscribers included James Beattie, William Strahan, Dugald *Stewart, John *Home, William Richardson, Hugh *Blair, and Jane *Gordon, duchess of Gordon.

The indisputable driving force of the Mirror Club was Henry Mackenzie, who, from his early years, had been groomed by the Edinburgh literati to succeed David Hume as their convivial leader and adjudicator of literary taste. Mackenzie composed 49 of the 110 issues of *The Mirror* and 62 of the 101 issues of *The Lounger*. Occasionally he composed several different drafts of a paper that he sent to friends, including Adam Smith, for comment. He also revised the majority of the essays for publication. Three of Mackenzie's closest friends, William Craig, Alexander Abercromby, and Alexander Fraser Tytler, accounted for 68 of the remaining 100 essays.

As a microcosm of the Scottish literati the publishing arm of the Mirror Club provides valuable insights into the socio-economic agenda, professional background, and inter-generational networks of landed and literary lowland society. All club members came from families well connected to Scotland's élite by status, interests, marriage, and profession. They viewed themselves as the legal and literary representatives of Scottish landed society, and they believed that a united and enlightened class of landowners could lead the country out of its economic backwater. Along with their teacher and, in the case of Mackenzie and Craig, their friend Adam Smith, the core members of the Mirror Club shared a vision of Scotland as an improving capitalist community where economic and social power was held by the owners of land and where the status quo was strengthened by a complicated system of patronage deployed by Henry Dundas. The agrarian nature of Scottish improvement was strongly endorsed by club members. The liberal Macleod Bannatyne and conservative Abercromby composed a series of essays on the corruption of rural values by urban fashion. Other issues

were thinly disguised warnings against the upward mobility of Scotland's urban merchant classes, and paeans to the independence and gentility of landowners. On landed estates gentlemen could continue to perform the roles of patriarchs over small leaseholders, while maintaining a happy and deferential retinue of servants. This gentrified world was personified by Home and Tytler, who preferred to live and write from their estates, as well as by Macleod Bannatyne's memorable character Umphraville.

A competing interest group within the membership came from the legal profession. Two young lawyer members were George Ogilvie and William Gordon of Newhall, though neither published an essay in *The Mirror*. Gordon died on 11 January 1778, a year before its appearance, while Ogilvie died shortly before the initial publication of *The Lounger* in 1785. George Home of Wedderburn was already establishing himself in Edinburgh's legal community when *The Mirror* first appeared. He served for more than thirty years as principal clerk of the court of session, where he was eventually succeeded by Sir Walter Scott. He was also elected a fellow of the Royal Society of Edinburgh. As befitted his status and seniority in legal circles, Home had the privilege of composing the first *Mirror* essay, and later contributed on staple club themes such as the value of social affection and personal cheerfulness (see no. 34). In the prominence given to the legal profession the club demonstrated a clear preference for law over the church. Nevertheless, clergymen such as John *Logan were prominent in the Feast of Tabernacles, and the connection between the 'moderate' party of the Church of Scotland and the revival of Scottish *belles-lettres* was retained in *Lounger* essays by William Greenfield and Robert Henry. Moreover, many *Mirror* papers, including Mackenzie's famous series 'The story of La Roche' (nos. 42–4), advocated religious belief and feeling.

In terms of form and style the Mirror Club's offerings were self-conscious imitations of *The Spectator*, Mackenzie proudly earning the epithet of the Scottish Addison. However, it is evident that the club also developed the essay genre and championed the new literary form of the novel as the moral preceptor of the modern age. At one level the club's thinking remained parochial and transitional, providing advice to a Scottish élite that was distinctly hierarchical and yet sufficiently poor to provide greater social and economic mobility than its English counterpart. But in its literary output the club also aimed to create a revolutionary new paradigm for ethical and cultural analysis by delineating the progress of individual character and passions through the structures of civilized manners, formal education, and custom. Nowhere was this more forcefully advanced than in the club's re-evaluation of Shakespeare as the creator of unique individuals with complex personalities. The club's attention to the philosophical analysis of Shakespeare was continued by Schlegel, Coleridge, and Hazlitt, to name a few. Improving, humane, and tolerant, the Mirror Club popularized Enlightenment values principally among the Scottish gentry. Yet, collaterally, the club and its publications provided a far wider readership with an innovative characterization of Scottish identity—one that affirmed the ethical and sociable community rather than the uniquely covenanted nation.   JOHN DWYER

Sources The Mirror (1779–80) · The Lounger (1785–7) · H. Mackenzie, Anecdotes and egotisms, 1745–1831 (1996) · D. McElroy, 'The literary clubs and societies of eighteenth-century Edinburgh', PhD diss., U. Edin., 1952 · H. W. Drescher, Themen und Formen des periodischen Essays im späten 18. Jahrhundert (Frankfurt am Main, [1971]) · J. Dwyer, Virtuous discourse: sensibility and community in late eighteenth-century Scotland (1987) · The correspondence of Adam Smith, ed. E. C. Mossner and I. S. Ross (1977), vol. 6 of The Glasgow edition of the works and correspondence of Adam Smith · R. B. Sher, Church and university in the Scottish Enlightenment: the moderate literati of Edinburgh (1985) · J. Dwyer and R. B. Sher, eds., Sociability and society in eighteenth-century Scotland (1993) · C. Knight, 'The created world of the Edinburgh periodicals', Scottish Literary Journal (1979), 20–36 · Burke, Gen. GB (1937)
Archives NL Scot., Belles Lettres Society MSS · NL Scot., Mackenzie MSS · NL Scot., Newhailes MSS | U. Edin. L., Dugald Stewart MSS · U. Edin. L., Laing MSS

Mirsky, Dmitry Svyatopolk (1890–1939), Russian scholar, was born on 9 September (28 August OS) 1890 on his father's country estate at Gievka, near Kharkov, Ukraine, the second of the four children and eldest son of Prince Pyotr Dmitryevich Svyatopolk-Mirsky (1857–1914), army officer and civil servant, and his wife, Countess Yekaterina Alekseyevna Bobrinskaya (1864–1926), the daughter of Count Aleksey Alekseyevich Bobrinsky of Tula. On the father's side the Svyatopolk-Mirskys claimed descent from Ryurik, the founder of the Russian state, and the mother's side was descended from the illegitimate son of Catherine the Great and Grigory Orlov. Prince P. D. Svyatopolk-Mirsky rose to become minister of the interior for five months in 1904–5; he stepped down after the events of 'bloody Sunday', 9 January 1905, and lived out his life in retirement. Dmitry was tutored at home until the age of fourteen, an especially valued mentor being his English nanny, Miss Trend, the sister of J. B. Trend, who became professor of Spanish at Cambridge University.

Mirsky then attended the imperial lycée in Moscow for two years, and for a further two years from 1906 the élite Tenishev Gymnasium in St Petersburg. From 1908 to 1911 he studied oriental languages at the University of St Petersburg, then served for two years as an officer in the imperial guards rifle regiment. He went back to the University of St Petersburg and graduated in classics in 1914. His poems and critical articles first appeared in a school publication in 1906, and he brought out a collection of poetry in 1911. He rejoined his regiment on the outbreak of the First World War and served on the German front for two years, and then in the Caucasus. He was wounded in 1916 and during convalescence married a nurse named Flevinova, but never saw her again after he left the hospital; the marriage ended in divorce. Just before the February revolution of 1917 Mirsky passed out from the Academy of the Imperial General Staff, and was posted to Armenia. In June 1918 Mirsky made his way back to Gievka, studied briefly at the University of Kharkov, and in December fled with his family to the Crimea. In March 1919 he joined the White Army of General Denikin, and served with the rank of captain as adjutant in various regiments, emigrating via Poland to Athens when this army was defeated in 1920.

In the autumn of 1921 Mirsky went to London at the invitation of Maurice Baring, who had known his family in Russia. Sir Bernard Pares, who also knew Mirsky's family, appointed him as lecturer in Russian at the School of Slavonic Studies, King's College, University of London, in May 1922. In emigration, Mirsky preferred not to use his title of prince, and simplified his name to D. S. Mirsky. People who knew him well in England remembered particularly his phenomenal verbal memory, his astonishingly fluent command of English, French, and German, and his imposing stature, with black beard, bald head, and oriental eyes. Besides carrying out his teaching duties in London, where his pupils included the future Professor Dame Elizabeth Hill, Mirsky was active in British and French literary circles, and was personally acquainted with, among others, T. S. Eliot, E. M. Forster, Jane Ellen Harrison, Leonard and Virginia Woolf, and André Gide. Among his closest associates in the Russian literary emigration was the poet Marina Tsvetaeva; he brought her to London to give a reading in March 1926.

Mirsky was the first critic in Russian or English to appreciate and write about the significance of all four of the great Russian poets of his generation: Akhmatova, Mandelshtam, Pasternak, and Tsvetaeva. He also pioneered the serious discussion of Babel, Pilnyak, and many other important Russian writers. His most important work, which he wrote in English, was published in two volumes, Contemporary Russian Literature (1926) and A History of Russian Literature from the Earliest Times to the Death of Dostoevsky, 1881 (1927). These volumes were condensed by Francis J. Whitfield into the standard A History of Russian Literature (1949). During his time in London, Mirsky published six books and about 150 articles in English on Russian literature, culture, and history.

Mirsky also played an important part in the intellectual and political life of the Russian emigration as a prominent figure in the Eurasian movement, which was subsidized by the English philanthropist H. N. Spalding. Mirsky's political evolution was shaped by his observing the social and political conditions in Britain, continental Europe, and the United States in the period beginning with the general strike of 1926, and was particularly influenced negatively by the rise of fascism, and positively by the five-year plans and collectivization of agriculture that began in the USSR under Stalin in 1929. The evolution of Mirsky's political views was attested in his Russia: a Social History (1931), Lenin (1931), and 'Why I became a Marxist' (Daily Worker, 30 June 1931). His actions were also affected by his relationship with Vera Suvchinskaya (née Guchkova; 1906–87), who in 1930 refused to marry him and live in London.

In June 1931 Mirsky joined the Communist Party of Great Britain. His work for the party included a celebrated speech on dialectical materialism to the Heretics at Cambridge University. In the autumn of 1931 he applied simultaneously for Soviet and British citizenship, taking the

Soviet because it arrived first. His relations with Sir Bernard Pares became acrimonious, and he resigned from his post at the School of Slavonic and East European Studies in March 1932. In September he went back to Russia. Often referred to privately as 'Comrade Prince' Mirsky, he then began a tumultuous career as a Soviet literary critic. In his first year in Moscow he was friendly with the *Manchester Guardian* correspondent, Malcolm Muggeridge, and in the summer of 1935 he came to know Edmund Wilson. Mirsky published a scathing valedictory book drawing on his *émigré* years, which was translated into English as *The Intelligentsia of Great Britain* (1935). He was arrested on 3 June 1937 during Stalin's great purge, found guilty of 'suspected espionage', and sentenced to eight years' correctional labour. He was transported to Siberia, put to work on tree felling, rapidly became ill with dysentery and frost-bite, and died in the labour camp Invalidnaya Hospital near Magadan on 6 June 1939. He was buried at Invalidnaya the following day.

An underlying logic and sense of purpose may be discerned beneath the vicissitudes of Mirsky's life and thought: he remained rooted in the aristocratic service mentality of his forebears, but was driven by a personal need for commitment to some force that would overcome the degeneration he eventually diagnosed in the social milieu into which he was born. As the author of *A History of Russian Literature* Mirsky can claim to be one of the most important single mediators between the Russian- and English-speaking literary worlds. His restless mind and impulsive temperament compelled him to deal with the fateful choices facing the Russian men of his generation in an extraordinarily dramatic and instructive way.

G. S. SMITH

Sources N. Lavroukine and L. Tchertkov, *D. S. Mirsky: profil critique et bibliographique* (1980) · G. S. Smith, *D. S. Mirsky: a Russian-English life, 1890–1939* (2000) · G. S. Smith, 'D. S. Mirsky, literary critic and historian', in D. S. Mirsky, *Uncollected writings on Russian literature* (1989), 19–43 · G. S. Smith, 'Introduction', in *The letters of D. S. Mirsky to P. P. Suvchinskii, 1922–31* (1995), 1–14 · V. V. Perkhin, 'K istorii aresta i reabilitatsii D. P. Svyatopolk-Mirskogo' [Towards a history of the arrest and rehabilitation of D. P. Svyatopolk-Mirsky], *Russkaya Literatura*, 1 (1997), 220–37 · V. V. Perkhin, 'Odinnadtsat' pisem (1920–1937) i avtobiografiya (1936) D. P. Svyatopolk-Mirskogo' [Eleven letters (1920–1937) and autobiography (1936) of D. P. Svyatopolk-Mirsky], *Russkaya Literatura*, 1 (1996), 235–62 · D. S. Mirsky, 'Histoire d'une émancipation', *La Nouvelle Revue Française*, 37 (1931), 384–97 · G. S. Smith, 'D. S. Mirsky to Dorothy Galton: thirty-nine letters from Moscow, 1932–1937', *Oxford Slavonic Papers*, new ser., 29 (1996), 93–131 · G. S. Smith, 'Jane Ellen Harrison: forty-seven letters to D. S. Mirsky, 1924–1926', *Oxford Slavonic Papers*, new ser., 28 (1995), 62–97 · R. Davies and G. S. Smith, 'D. S. Mirsky: twenty-two letters, 1926–34, to Salomeya Halpern; seven letters, 1930, to Vera Suvchinskaya (Traill)', *Oxford Slavonic Papers*, new ser., 30 (1997), 91–122 · O. Kaznina, *Russkie v Anglii: Russkaya emigratsiya v kontekste russko-angliiskikh literaturnykh svyazei v pervoi polovine XX veka* (1997) · E. Wilson, 'Comrade Prince', *Encounter* (Jan 1995), 10–20 · M. Muggeridge, *Winter in Moscow* (1933)
Archives BL, letters to Sir Bernard Pares, Add. MS 49604 · BL, letters to Dorothy Galton, Add. MS 49530
Likenesses photographs, 1922–5 (with staff of School of Slavonic Studies), UCL, School of Slavonic and East European Studies · V. Traill, photograph, *c.*1928 (with P. S. Arapov, south of France), priv. coll.; repro. in Mirsky, *Uncollected writings on Russian literature* (1989), facing p. 36 · Kukriniksy, caricature, 1936, repro. in D. S. Mirsky, *Uncollected writings on Russian literature* (1989), facing p. 37 · P. Evergood, oils, repro. in G. S. Smith, 'The correspondence of D. S. Mirsky and Michael Florinsky, 1925–1932', *Slavonic and East European Review*, 72/1 (1994), 116

Mirza Abu Talib Khan Isfahani (1752–1806). *See under* Indian visitors (*act. c.*1720–*c.*1810).

Mirza I'tizam al-Din (*fl.* 1765–1785). *See under* Indian visitors (*act. c.*1720–*c.*1810).

Misaubin, John (1673–1734), physician, was born in Mussidan, France, and is said to have graduated MD at the University of Cahors on 7 July 1687. He was in Canterbury in 1697 but later settled in London, and on 25 June 1719 became a licentiate of the Royal College of Physicians. Misaubin was naturalized in 1707, and in 1709 married Martha Augibaud, daughter of Charles Augibaud, apothecary to Louis XIV; they had a son, Edmund. His foreign manner and accent sometimes excited ridicule, and though he was a regular licentiate, his arrogance and method of practice caused him to be described and caricatured as a quack. In one contemporary print Misaubin is represented as saying 'Prenez des pilules, prenez des pilules', and Henry Fielding relates in *Tom Jones* (bk 13, chap. 2) that he 'used to say that the proper Direction to him was To Dr. Misaubin *in the World*; intimating, that there were few People in it to whom his great Reputation was not known'. He has left no writings, and his chief claims to fame are that he is one of the four medical practitioners mentioned in *Tom Jones*, the others being Thomas Sydenham, and the surgeons John Freke and John Ranby, and that he was the model for the doctor portrayed in Hogarth's *The Harlot's Progress*. Misaubin lived near Covent Garden, and died at his home, 96 St Martin's Lane, London, on 20 April 1734.

NORMAN MOORE, *rev.* MICHAEL BEVAN

Sources B. Hoffbrand, 'John Misaubin, Hogarth's Quack: a case for rehabilitation', *Journal of the Royal Society of Medicine*, 94 (2001), 143–7 · Munk, *Roll* · *GM*, 1st ser., 4 (1734), 218 · H. Fielding, *Tom Jones* (1749), bk 13, chap. 2
Likenesses A. Pond, coloured soft-ground etching, 1739 (after A. Watteau), BM, Wellcome L. · J. Goupy, group portrait, Wellcome L. [*see illus.*] · W. Hogarth, drawing, Royal Collection

Miskin, Sir James William (1925–1993), barrister and judge, was born in Hong Kong on 11 March 1925, the son of Geoffrey Miskin, general manager of the Hongkong and Shanghai Bank, and his wife, Joyce. The Miskins were of Huguenot origin, and had settled in Kent. He was educated at Haileybury College before seeing war service as a sub-lieutenant in the Royal Naval Volunteer Reserve. After demobilization in 1946 he went to Brasenose College, Oxford, where he was senior Heath Harrison exhibitioner, and from where he graduated with a second-class degree in jurisprudence in 1949. On 28 April 1951 he married Mollie Joan Milne (*b.* 1927/8), daughter of Eric Ivan Milne of Crowborough, Sussex. They had two sons and two daughters.

Called to the bar by the Inner Temple in 1951, Miskin joined the south-eastern circuit, and developed a good

John Misaubin (1673–1734), by Joseph Goupy [centre, with members of his household]

common law practice, mainly civil, principally in family and medical negligence work. He so impressed Desmond Ackner that he was invited to join the latter's chambers. He was led by Ackner in a number of important cases, and was given a red bag by Ackner in recognition of his outstanding contribution as an advocate, 'the like of which [Ackner] had not seen' (private information). Thereafter his career progressed well. From 1964 to 1967 and from 1970 to 1973 he served on the bar council, including service on a committee looking at the position of women at the bar. He was made a queen's counsel in 1967. From 1968 to 1971 he was deputy chairman of the Hertfordshire quarter sessions, in 1972 he became a crown court recorder (a part-time post entailing four weeks on the bench yearly), and from 1974 to 1975 he was leader of the south-eastern circuit. He succeeded Ackner as counsel for the children in the thalidomide tragedy. In the end the case against Distillers did not come to trial but was settled, those acting for the victims taking the view that there was no more than a 40 per cent chance of success in an action for negligence.

In 1975, on the recommendation of Mr Justice Melford Stevenson, Miskin was appointed recorder of London, the senior judge at the central criminal court (the Old Bailey), and second citizen to the lord mayor. The appointment was something of a surprise as he had not been common serjeant, the deputy, and his practice had not been principally criminal. At the time it was believed in the profession that he was appointed in order to get the Old Bailey moving and to deal with complacency among those who regularly sat and practised there. He disliked waste of time and insisted that all courts start promptly at 10.30

a.m. With a considerable sense of humour, he was an outstanding after-dinner speaker and made many such speeches; indeed he was a sort of court jester for the City of London.

The office of recorder of London is very arduous, involving the trial of many very serious cases, including murder, manslaughter, rape, grievous bodily harm, and robbery; it also involves considerable administrative responsibilities. Miskin enjoyed a reputation for fair summings-up ('straight down the middle') and was generally well thought of as a judge. Although he was outwardly tough in sentencing, it was said that his bark was worse than his bite; his sentencing, however, was often unpredictable and surprising. He was inconspicuously kind to young counsel.

Like many good lawyers, Miskin was not good at administering his own affairs. He ran into tax problems, and had to sell his house in Wimbledon, to the great disappointment of his wife, Mollie. Being so involved in all his various activities he neglected his wife and the first marriage broke up. He married second, on 6 December 1980, Sheila Joan Collett (b. 1927/8), a widow, and the daughter of Harold Radcliffe Scott, schoolmaster.

In his latter years on the bench Miskin's health declined, and he was reluctant to take medical advice; ill health converted his fine speaking voice to hoarseness, and he became known as 'Whispering Jim'. He became increasingly indiscreet and open to criticism. He was sometimes difficult with counsel, expressed himself unnecessarily forcefully, and told convicted criminals what he thought of them. Publicly he made a number of trenchant remarks and criticisms; these may have been justified but they were imprudent, indeed unwise, in a judge in office. He wanted the minimum age for jurors raised to twenty-five, and wanted capital punishment for premeditated murder. He cast doubt upon the innocence of the Guildford four after their conviction was quashed. He made unfortunate remarks about ethnic minorities, referring to a black man as a 'nig-nog', and to 'murderous Sikhs'. He wanted more money spent to increase the number of prison places. Some years previously he would have liked to move from the Old Bailey to the High Court, but consent from the lord chief justice was not forthcoming. The surprising deterioration in his personality and judicial performance was subsequently attributed to incipient, undiagnosed Alzheimer's disease, and a hitherto excellent reputation was spoilt.

Miskin was involved in many extra-judicial activities. A keen boxer in his youth, he was appeals steward for the British board of boxing control from 1972 to 1975. He was also chairman of the board of discipline of the London School of Economics (1972–5), chairman of the inner London probation committee (1979–88), a liveryman of the Worshipful Company of Furriers, an honorary liveryman of the Worshipful Company of Cutlers, and one of her majesty's lieutenants for the City of London (1976–93). He retired from the bench in 1990, having been knighted in 1983. He died of bronchopneumonia and senile dementia at his home, 25 Collingwood Road, Horsham, Sussex, on 21 November 1993, and was survived by his second wife, Sheila, and the four children of his first marriage.

ALEC SAMUELS

Sources *The Times* (24 Nov 1993) · *The Independent* (20 Dec 1993) · *WWW* · private information (2004) [Claire Miskin, Lord Ackner] · personal knowledge (2004) · m. certs. · d. cert.
Archives PRO, papers relating to central criminal court, J164
Likenesses photograph, repro. in *The Times* · photograph, repro. in *The Independent*

Misselden, Edward (*fl.* 1615–1654), merchant and writer on economics, whose parentage, date of birth, early years, and date of death are unknown, first comes to notice as an active member of the Merchant Adventurers' Company in 1615. In his published works he described himself as a merchant, born in England. When the company lost its charter Misselden signed a petition to the privy council on 8 January 1615 to wind up his business as a cloth exporter in the Netherlands. But he probably continued to trade, since he was accused by the new company of surreptitious exports and, when the old company was restored, he was listed as an exporter in the company's cloth book for 1618.

Having probably trained in the civil law, Misselden gravitated towards commercial diplomacy. In 1616 he was asked by the new Merchant Adventurers' Company to negotiate with the Dutch, who had reacted to Cokayne's project by prohibiting the import of dyed English cloth. In the early 1620s he lived at Hackney, where his daughter Lidia was baptized in St John's Church on 11 February 1620 and his son Samuel on 16 June 1622. In 1622 he was appointed to the committee of inquiry into the trade depression set up by the privy council and his analysis was largely accepted. In October 1623 the East India Company invited him to act as one of their commissioners at Amsterdam to negotiate a private treaty with the Dutch to settle conflicts in Asia, but the Amboyna massacre killed the chances of any agreement.

From 1623 until 1633 Misselden was deputy governor of the Merchant Adventurers' Company at Delft and he acted for both the merchant adventurers and the English crown. He sought a reduction in the duties on English cloth in the Netherlands and a syndicate which he headed furnished the royal financier, Philip Burlamachi, with large sums, of which £13,000 was still unpaid in May 1633. Misselden acknowledged the fiscal strength and religious tolerance of the Dutch and the importance of their fisheries and cloth-finishing industries. His recommended response to Dutch competition was to cut off their supply of English wool and fuller's earth and, more drastically, to occupy Brabant and move the merchant adventurers back to Antwerp.

While at Delft, Misselden also tried to impose the Laudian prayer book and liturgy on the English congregation. Many of the resident merchants were Presbyterian and under the spell of the implacable preacher John Forbes. When accused by Misselden of being schismatics they responded that they were loyal to the crown but had to conform to local standards while abroad. Misselden tried to discredit Forbes, but he failed to infiltrate the Presbyterian eldership or to prevent a conspiracy against himself, which ejected him from the sub-deputyship in July 1633. Misselden urged in retaliation that the company charter be examined in Star Chamber. The privy council did declare the election of Robert Edwards as his successor void, but the merchants then elected Samuel Avery, a Presbyterian.

During his time in Delft, Misselden returned to England, in November 1624, to report to the East India Company, which paid him £100 for his services and retained him for the next four years to press for reparations. By trying to act for both the crown (promising them an ambassador without the cost of an embassy) and the company, Misselden fell between two stools. When he was accused both by Carleton and the states general of acting for the other side, an aggrieved Misselden on 18 October 1628 discontinued his relationship with the East India Company, which, however, made reparation after intervention by the privy council.

In 1635 Misselden failed, despite royal support, to become deputy governor of the merchant adventurers at Rotterdam. He was resident in Hackney in the late 1640s and served as a churchwarden of St John, Hackney, in 1650. The merchant adventurers did, however, continue to employ him on missions, and there were rumours, in 1649, that he was to be appointed deputy at Hamburg, despite his royalist background. He was in Hamburg in 1650 and Richard Bradshaw recommended his employment. Misselden was certainly prepared to serve the Rump and Cromwell, to whom he wrote in 1654 listing his accomplishments. He furnished the council of state with information relating to the Netherlands and Brabant, but his enquiries were ignored.

Misselden is best known as an economic pamphleteer and for his debates with another such, Gerard Malynes, who continued to blame an exchange conspiracy for all of England's economic woes. An officially inspired clash of doctrine on bullion flows and exchange rates began in 1618 with complaints of scarcity of coin. In his *Free Trade, or, The Means to Make Trade Flourish* of 1622 Misselden emphasized real rather than monetary factors. Although he recognized the adverse effects of enhancement and debasement of European coin, Misselden blamed the depression on the excessive consumption of imported commodities, the export of bullion by the East India Company, and defective searching in the cloth trade. When Malynes immediately wrote a rejoinder, *The Centre of the Circle of Commerce*, Misselden countered with his *Circle of Commerce, or, The Ballance of Trade* (1623), which demoted the role of the exchanges and substituted the balance of trade as the universal, determining factor. The low exchange rate became a result and not a cause of the depression. In flat contradiction to his previous tract Misselden now defended the export of bullion on the ground that the loss was ultimately made good by the re-export of commodities so purchased.

Misselden emphasized the role of money as a measure of value rather than as a medium of exchange. Commerce was an exchange of wares for wares, not of money for wares. He distinguished between three kinds of money—permission, bank, and current—and argued that plenty of money would bring down the rate of interest. It was not the rate of exchange but the relative value of money (lower in England and higher abroad) which caused export of specie. Value was determined by plenty or scarcity of money. The price for sterling as expressed by foreign exchange rates was determined, like other prices, by supply and demand. The cause was extrinsic, not intrinsic.

Misselden dropped many names and indulged in long-winded and rhetorical philosophizing. Many of his proposals to remedy the depression were, however, practical and he accepted that it was private wealth which supported a commonwealth. He advocated compensating for tight credit by increasing the supply of money and by making bills of debt transferable. The Statute of Employments should be enforced to prevent loss of bullion. The high rate of interest, which took priority in his ten causes of the depression, could be remedied by establishing a bank and a court of conscience. More efficient regulation would improve the quality of English cloth and end the encroachment by foreigners on the English fisheries. Misselden proposed to raise the valuation of silver and silver coins and advocated debasement to bring in bullion and stop hoarding. He thought inflation was a lesser evil and argued that rents and contracts should be paid at the original intrinsic value. Misselden defended the regulated merchant adventurers, arguing that they had driven out the Hansards and helped with naval stores. At the same time he attempted to deflect criticism towards the joint stock East India Company, which he attacked as a monopoly for limiting access by investors.

Malynes was so out of date that he was an easy target, and Misselden's theory was applicable to a bimetallic outflow. But he confused causes with symptoms in his explanation of the depression and he underestimated the lack of foreign demand caused by the disruptions of war. In 1622 Misselden did not appreciate the impact of enhancement and debasement in Eastland and Germany on the profits of textile exports and the cost of imports. Nor had he an answer to the prospect of retaliatory enhancement. His theory of multilateral balances was essentially the same as that which Thomas Mun developed in the 1620s with greater depth and authority. It is possible that Missenden knew Mun personally either from the Amboyna negotiations or as a neighbour in Hackney.

RICHARD GRASSBY

Sources K. L. Sprunger, *Dutch puritanism: a history of English and Scottish churches of the Netherlands in the sixteenth and seventeenth centuries* (1982) · *CSP col.*, vol. 6 · L. Muchmore, 'Gerard de Malynes and mercantile economics', *History of Political Economy*, 1 (1969), 336–58 · B. E. Supple, *Commercial crisis and change in England, 1600–1642* (1970) · J. D. Gould, 'The trade crisis of the early 1620s', *Journal of Economic History*, 15 (1955), 121–33 · A. Friis, *Alderman Cockayne's project and the cloth trade: the commercial policy of England in its main aspects, 1603–1625*, trans. [A. Fausboll] (1927) · M. Bowley, *Studies in the history of economic theory before 1870* (1973) · R. de Roover, *Gresham on foreign exchange* (1949) · L. Gomez, *Foreign trade and the national economy* (1987) · Thurloe, *State papers* · R. Simpson, *Memorials of St John's at Hackney* (1880) · IGI · administration, PRO, PROB 6/37, fol. 17v

Archives BL, Add. MSS 6394–6395 · PRO, SP 84/144–6, SP 16/257

Misson, Francis Maximilian

Misson, Francis Maximilian [*formerly* François Maximilien] (*c.*1650–1722), traveller and author, was born in Lyons, France, the eldest of four children of Jacques Misson (*b.* 1619, *d.* in or after 1695), originally from Niort and later pastor at St Mère-Eglise in Normandy, and his wife, Judith, of whom nothing more is known. Initially he seems to have been destined for a clerical life and attended the academy at Geneva. Later he apparently became one of the protestant judges in the 'chamber of the edict' in the *parlement* of Paris (Agnew, 152). On the revocation of the edict of Nantes in 1685 he and his family crossed the channel to take refuge in England. They were listed in the denization entry book on 9 April 1687 and were naturalized by letters patent on 15 April. Jacques, or James, Misson became a minister within the Huguenot community of London.

Misson himself found employment when James, first duke of Ormond, chose him as tutor to his younger grandson, Charles Butler, afterwards earl of Arran. Misson made the grand tour with his pupil during 1687 and 1688, travelling to Italy by way of Rotterdam, Cologne, Munich, and Innsbruck, over the Brenner Pass, and then via Verona to Venice. He visited the Santa Casa at Loreto and places of interest in and near Naples and Rome, and returned by stages through Bologna, Milan, Genoa, Turin, Geneva, Strasbourg, and Brussels. As a consequence of this journey Misson published, at The Hague, a work which became the standard travel guide to Italy for at least the following fifty years, the much-quoted *Nouveau voyage d'Italie, avec un mémoire contenant des avis utiles à ceux qui voudront faire le mesme voyage* (1691). Based upon his travel journal it was presented in the form of a series of letters. The text is resoundingly modern, comprising the sequential exposition of first-hand factual observations, none the less augmented by the critical perspective of a protestant travelling through a Catholic country. An English translation first appeared in London in 1695, followed by a corrected second edition in 1699.

Misson's second work was *Mémoires et observations faites par un voyageur en Angleterre … avec une description particulière de ce qu'il y a de plus curieux dans Londres* (The Hague, 1698). A translation by Ozell appeared in London during 1719. Structured as an alphabetical series of commentaries the volume is in effect a highly original descriptive dictionary of facets of society and culture in London and other parts of the British Isles. The *Observations* has proved to be an important source of information for social historians of the later seventeenth century.

Misson continued to live in London, almost certainly in Westminster, where he participated in the activities of the conformist French churches of Le Carré and Berwick Street, and Swallow Street. It has also been suggested that Misson undertook military service, first as a trooper in the Life Guards, possibly during the early 1690s, and later holding a commission in the earl of Macclesfield's regiment of English horse during its posting to Ireland which commenced in 1700. Whether or not Misson undertook such military service he was notably active in the affairs of the London French church by 1707, when he published his third and most controversial work, *Thèâtre Sacré des Cévennes, ou, Recit des prodiges arrivés dans cette partie du Languedoc*. In order to report, and allegedly promote, the activities of the 'French prophets' of the Cévennes, several of whose leaders had arrived in London, Misson scoured the registers of the consistory court of London for the names of suitable refugees. He then took witness statements made under oath from each individual before publishing the same. Misson published in French but John Lacy, who accompanied Misson during his interviews, simultaneously issued an English version, *A cry from the desart, or, Testimonials of the miraculous things lately come to pass in the Cevennes, verified upon oath and by other proofs*. Misson soon found himself under attack from a united front of leading ministers from the conformist and nonconformist French churches in London. Fearful of being tarred by the brush of excessive religious and political enthusiasm, the ministers undertook their own investigations of the 'witnesses', and in a campaign spearheaded by Claude Groteste de la Mothe, presented the 'French prophets'' activities as fraud.

Misson's final work was that traditionally credited to the authorship of François Leguat, *A new voyage to the East-Indies by Francis Leguate and his companions containing their adventures on two desert islands* (1708). It is now clear that while Leguat was undoubtedly the subject of the work the text was written wholly by Misson. It is possible that this book was one of the models for Daniel Defoe's *Robinson Crusoe*, first published in 1719. This view is perhaps supported by the appearance of a fictional French pirate named Captain Misson in the second volume of *A History of the … Pyrates* (1726), a work also attributed to Defoe. Captain Misson is said to have gone to sea after being 'much affected with the Accounts he had read in Books of Travel'. Misson died in London on 12 January 1722 and was buried at St Anne, Westminster, on 19 January. He was unmarried and left most of his estate to his sister, with gifts to her son, who he anticipated would eventually inherit everything.   CRAIG SPENCE

Sources M. Misson, *A new voyage to Italy with a description of the chief towns, churches, tombs, libraries, palaces, statues, and antiquity of that country: together with useful instructions for those who shall travel thither* (1695) · M. Misson, *Memoirs and observations in his travels over England, with some account of Scotland and Ireland. Dispos'd in alphabetic order* (1719) · D. C. A. Agnew, *Protestant exiles from France, chiefly in the reign of Louis XIV, or, The Huguenot refugees and their descendants in Great Britain and Ireland*, 3rd edn, 2 vols. (1886) · W. A. Shaw, ed., *Letters of denization and acts of naturalization for aliens in England and Ireland, 1603–1700*, Huguenot Society of London, 18 (1911) · I. H. Van Eeghen, 'The voyage and adventures of Francois Leguat', *Proceedings of the Huguenot Society of London*, 18 (1950–51), 396–417 · G. Cosmos, 'Huguenot storytellers in London in the 18th century', *Proceedings of the Huguenot Society of Great Britain and Ireland*, 27 (2000), 403–17 · *Nouvelle biographie generale*, vols. 35–6 (1865) · W. Minet and S. Minet, eds., *Registers of the church of Le Carré and Berwick Street, 1690–1788*, Huguenot Society quarto series, 25 (1921) · W. Minet and S. Minet, eds., *Registers of the churches of Chapel Royal, St James and Swallow Street*, Huguenot Society quarto series, 28 (1924) · H. Schwartz, *Knaves, fools, madmen and that subtile effluvium: a study of the opposition to the French prophets in England, 1706–1710* (University of Florida, 1978) · C. E. Lart, 'The Huguenot regiments', *Proceedings of the Huguenot Society of London*, 25/3 (1910–11), 476–529 · *The royal bounty: petition of the French ministers to William III*, Publications of the Huguenot Society of London, 1 (1887) · D. Defoe (?), *A general history of … the pyrates*, ed. M. Schonhorn (1999) · will, PRO, PROB 11/584, sig. 78 · St Anne, Westminster, parish register, City Westm. AC

Mist, Nathaniel (*d.* 1737), newspaper printer and publisher, was possibly the son of James Mist of Easton, Wiltshire, and Martha Stagg of Kensington, London, who appear to have been married in 1666. In print Mist refers to his family as 'honest soaky Fellows' from Lincolnshire (*Fog's Weekly Journal*, 28 Sept 1728), although this was probably for propaganda purposes. He served in the Royal Navy, in the Spanish seas, as a common sailor. He does not seem to have had any formal education.

Jacobite journalist From 1716 until his flight to France in 1728 Mist ran a successful printing business at Great Carter Lane, London. He was responsible for the production of one of the most popular newspapers published in opposition to both the whig government and the Hanoverian dynasty. Throughout this period Mist was subject to constant investigation by government officials anxious to prevent the circulation of seditious views, and he was in trouble with the authorities on at least fourteen occasions.

Mist seems to have been involved in three short-lived journals: *The Citizen* (22 June–20 July 1716, nine issues), the *Wednesday's Journal* (25 September–23 October 1717, five issues), and *The Entertainer* (6 November 1717–23 July 1718, the first thirty-eight issues of forty-three printed by Mist). However, by far the most important part of his publications was the newspaper that he began to print on 15 December 1716 (taking over from Robert Mawson) as the *Weekly Journal, or, Saturday's Post* and that was relaunched on 1 May 1725 as *Mist's Weekly Journal*. After Mist's hurried departure to France in September 1728 this newspaper metamorphosed again into *Fog's Weekly Journal* in which form it continued until 22 October 1737. Although Mist employed a range of different writers and journeymen during the period of publication, the guiding hand as both proprietor and editor, as well as printer, was certainly his until 1728; thereafter he retained ownership but found it difficult to exert control from France, and he retired from ownership in May 1737.

Mist's name was famously preserved by a cutting reference in Alexander Pope's *Dunciad* (1728), where the poet disparagingly observed, 'To Dulness Ridpath is as dear as Mist' (i. 208). This was in revenge for several critical references to Pope in *Mist's Weekly Journal* during March 1728; the reference indicates Mist's status as a figure generally known by the eighteenth-century reading public.

Mist's relationship with Daniel Defoe was much more long-lasting, temporarily far more cordial, and ultimately perhaps even more bitter. With a short break between November 1718 and January 1719 Defoe wrote for Mist's newspaper from August 1717 until 24 October 1724. Defoe was paid by the government to moderate the anti-Hanoverian and anti-whig tone of the paper, and under the guise of friendship sometimes persuaded Mist to hold back from publishing objectionable articles. In June 1718 Defoe boasted to Charles Delafaye, the under-secretary of state responsible, that he had extended his influence over Mist so that Mist 'professes himself Convinc'd that he has been Wrong, that the Government has Treated him with Lenety and Forbearance and he sollemnly Engages to me to give no more offence' (*CSP dom.*, 35/12/38). Defoe wrote of 'many treasonable papers' in Mist's possession which often 'Dye in our hands' because Mist had refrained from printing them and other printers were prevented from getting hold of them. Defoe's claims to have moderated Mist's work at this time were clearly self-interested in that he was writing to his employer, but it is likely that he did have some influence in this direction for a while.

However, any attempt to curb Mist's Jacobite tendencies were unlikely to succeed for long and the extent to which Defoe himself was drawn into 'treasonable' articles in order to preserve his credibility with Mist remains in doubt. The temporary break-up between Mist and Defoe in November 1718 was the result of Mist's arrest for printing an article attacking the war against Spain. Defoe returned to Mist's employment in January 1719 on condition that Mist would eschew dangerous controversy, but this was very short-lived and in July 1720 Defoe ceased to play a major role in the direction of the paper and protested to the government his innocence of Mist's latest misconduct. By the end of 1724 Defoe had ceased even to supply Mist with items for printing and lamented (anonymously in the pages of *Applebee's Journal*) that one to whom he had provided repeated assistance, not least in securing his release from prison on three occasions, had insulted and fought him, displaying gross ingratitude. In 1730 it is likely that Defoe was again referring to Mist when he wrote of injury 'from a wicked, perjured, and contemptible enemy'. According to William Lee this injury involved Mist's denunciation of Defoe's duplicity to the government and to a wider public, including other printers who then refused to have any dealings with Defoe (Lee, 1.463).

Treason and popularity Mist's commitment to Jacobitism certainly transcended all attempts to suborn or divert it. In April 1717 he was arrested on suspicion of printing libels against the government and released after questioning. A week later he was tried for printing 'The case of Mr. Francis Francia, the reputed Jew' but was immediately discharged. In December messengers searched Mist's house, finding seditious articles. In October 1718 Mist was questioned again and bailed. Almost immediately the *Weekly Journal* for 25 October was seized along with members of Mist's workforce. His servants and print materials were ordered to be released on 1 November, but his newspaper

for 8 November was presented by the grand jury of Middlesex as 'a false scandalous seditious & profane Libell tending to the poysoning & corrupting of the Minds of his Majesties subjects & reflecting in a false scandalous Manner on his Majestie & his Governmt' (*CSP dom.*, 35/13/59).

In June 1720 the House of Lords ordered that Mist be prosecuted by the attorney-general and he was arrested and committed to the king's bench prison. Found guilty by Lord Justice Pratt at the Guildhall in 1721 he was pilloried at Charing Cross and the Royal Exchange, where he was reportedly well treated by the mob, fined £50, jailed for three months, and required to provide sureties of good behaviour for seven years. Despite all of this Mist was in trouble again in May 1721 for articles in his journal critical of George I, referring to 'a cruel ill-bred uneducated old Tyrant, and the driveling Fool his Son' (*Weekly Journal, or, Saturday's Post*, 27 May 1721). He was called to the bar of the House of Commons and was sent to Newgate when he refused to divulge the identity of his authors. Mist pleaded sickness and the trial was postponed from 9 October to 9 December when, in the absence of conclusive evidence, he was discharged.

In 1723 and 1724 Mist again fell foul of the authorities. On the latter occasion he was tried at the king's bench and sentenced in May to pay a fine of £100, to a year's imprisonment, and to find security for good behaviour for life. This did not prevent him from being tried again in 1727 for another libel on George I and receiving a similar fine and demand for sureties, with the stricture that he should be imprisoned until the sentence was fulfilled.

In January 1728 Mist fled to France but his newspaper continued to provoke the government, particularly with the notorious 'Persian letter', signed by 'Amos Drudge' but written by the exiled Jacobite the duke of Wharton. Published on 24 August it resulted in the arrest of more than twenty people. More arrests followed the publication of a joint issue of *Mist's Weekly Journal* for 7 and 14 September and Mist's press was destroyed. The newspaper of 21 September was the last to appear under the Mist title, but it was replaced on the 28th by *Fog's Weekly Journal* produced by Mist's friends with an introductory letter from 'N. Mist' to his 'Dear Cousin Fog' encouraging him to 'take up my Pen' (*Fog's Weekly Journal*, 28 Sept 1728). This successor continued to be published until 1737, for the most part under the direction of Charles Molloy; generally it showed more restraint than Mist, emphasizing a general 'country' opposition rather than Jacobitism.

One of the reasons that Mist survived so long as a newspaper printer was that he constantly trod very carefully the fine line between what could be proved to be treasonable and what could not. At difficult times he deliberately held back from political controversy, such as in the aftermath of the 1722 Atterbury plot: in his newspaper of 2 June 1722 he remarked coyly, 'why politics are not a subject seasonable to this Month; … my Reader has the Liberty of guessing at'. But even at his most outspoken his criticism of the Hanoverian kings and Robert Walpole's 'tyranny' was disguised in allegory and parallel history. In several cases Mist printed theoretical articles which sought to use whig arguments against themselves, citing for example John Locke to argue that 'one branch of the Legislative Power is as much to be resisted if it betrays its Trust, as the other' (*Mist's Weekly Journal*, 23 Sept 1727). More typically he would draw lessons by implication from parallel examples such as that of the government of pirates which, 'like all others', was 'founded on Covenant', giving them the right to elect a new leader if the present one betrayed them. Perhaps the most notorious example of such a tactic was the Persian letter. Here, after ironically commending the Hanoverian government 'as amiable at Home, as it is formidable Abroad', Wharton wrote as if from Persia detailing 'all the Miseries that Usurpation has introduced', contrasting the evil qualities of the avaricious Esreff with those of the true ruler, the young Sophi, 'the greatest Character that ever Eastern monarch bore'. Similar Jacobite messages were drawn from historical examples, particularly that of the restoration of Charles II and the 'heroism' of General Monck. Even a discussion on sword fencing was used to point a moral; it was 'that Art by which the Rights and Privileges of the Subject are to be maintained' (ibid., 13 April 1728). Mist's newspaper also discussed the value of tyrannicide and saw the evils of tyranny as 'Crimes which Ax and Gibbet claim' (ibid., 6 Jan 1728).

Government officials found Mist's perseverance and the difficulty of proving sedition against him frustrating. They also worried about the evident popularity of his wares which they found hard to counter. A government memorandum of 1722 complained that 'There never was a Mist or any other Person taken up or tryed but double the number of papers were sold upon it' (*CSP dom.*, 35/30/52). In 1741 the *Daily Gazetteer* recollected that 'Mist's treasonable Papers were sold sometimes for Half a Guinea a-piece', such was the demand for them (Harris, 105). Charles Delafaye noted that Mist's newspaper caused him especial concern as it was distributed in large numbers in both town and country, and did 'more mischief than any other libel, being wrote *ad captum* of the common people' (*CSP dom.*, 35/13/31).

Objective measures of the popularity of early eighteenth-century newspapers are scarce. The only exact figure noted for *Mist's Weekly Journal* is for the extraordinary issue of 24 August 1728, containing the Persian letter, of which 10,750 copies were printed by Mist's employee John Clarke. That two volumes of letters and essays from Mist's newspapers were reprinted in 1722 and a further two volumes in 1727 suggests an attempt to cash in on a perceived popularity. In later years Mist himself wrote nostalgically of his former prosperity while producing his journal. By a series of comparisons with other journals, using the few statistics available, it seems reasonable to conclude that, although it fluctuated, Mist's London circulation may have approached eight or ten thousand a week during much of the 1720s, one of the largest of its day (Chapman, 198–200; Harris, 115). Outside of London it was clearly harder to get hold of Mist's work, although the government found it expedient to impose a ban on sending his journals through the post in 1728, and in a few famous cases provincial printers were prosecuted for copying items from Mist's journal.

Exile in France, 1728–1736 When Mist fled to France in 1728 he joined the household of the duke of Wharton and at first seems to have been employed ostensibly as a coach driver at Rouen. In August the Old Pretender wrote personally in reply to a letter from Mist of 26 July, referring to him as 'one that has been so zealously useful to the good Cause' and commiserating on 'the sufferings you lye under' (Royal Stuart MSS, 119/42). By November 1728 Mist had parted company from the mercurial Wharton and had set up at Calais; by August 1729 he was established at Boulogne. Mist worked for the Pretender by establishing a line of secret correspondence between the exiled Stuart court and supporters in England, and he acted to have pieces of 'news' inserted in both sympathetic and hostile newspapers.

Mist's personal fortunes were clearly at a low ebb and he lamented his changed circumstances and the lack of support which he perceived from his supposed 'friends' in England: 'I now light my own Fire with the same satisfaction that I us'd to ride in my own Coach … my Servants are no more, my House is shut up, and I suppose by this Time the Goods sold' (Royal Stuart MSS, 121/165, 7 Nov 1728). Despite his own troubles Mist helped to support his former employees Edmund Bingley and James Wolf in their financial difficulties in exile, as also his former servants in England on whom he claimed to have expended £800 by 1730. He wrote to the Pretender on several occasions asking for further help for them.

Mist recommended Charles Molloy, who ran *Fog's Weekly Journal* and later *Common Sense*, another Jacobite newspaper, to the Pretender as a loyal and trustworthy agent who could act for him in London, and by December 1730 was trying to establish a business jointly with Molloy which would trade in fine wines but which would also act as a cover for a regular Jacobite correspondence. However their sloop was lost by March 1731 and again Mist was lamenting that 'I am exceedingly ill treated in England as to my private Affairs' (Royal Stuart MSS, 143/158). He continued to correspond regularly with the Pretender's representatives both in Paris and in Rome, sending them reports of parliamentary debates from London (although often complaining that his friends were being denied access), advising on fund raising in England, and reporting on the views of possible sympathizers. However, the fact that Mist was essentially viewed as a pawn in a much bigger game by James Stuart is demonstrated by the Pretender's suggestion (never implemented) that, to maintain secrecy, his agent in Paris might seize Mist by force, and confine him somewhere like the Bastille, in order to print the latest Jacobite Declaration in May 1732.

In 1734 Mist printed some 'Observations' attacking Charles Hamilton on behalf of the Jacobite earl of Dunbar, having been falsely assured by Dunbar that the Pretender approved of this. His name fades out of regular Jacobite correspondence at about this time; he seems to have suffered as a result of infighting among the Jacobite diaspora and to have become associated with one unpopular faction.

Personal life and final years, 1736–1737 By 1736, when he visited London, Mist had made and received special application for leave to return home. This seems to have been granted on condition that he refrained from politics, and it may account for a decline in the effectiveness of *Fog's Weekly Journal* which some contemporaries claimed to observe. However, Mist asserted in a letter to Cameron of Lochiel, 'I hope to live quietly, and that without coming to any sort of Terms, for I have had no Treaty wth them, nor ask'd any sort of Favour' (*CSP dom.*, 36/39/21). He ended his ownership of the journal in May 1737 and seems to have been engaged in the wine trade.

Little is known of Mist's private life beyond the fact that his wife, Anne, appears to have supported him throughout his years of adversity, acting for example as an emissary to England for him in 1731. Mist had earlier been concerned for her health and seems to have moved from Boulogne to Paris from December 1729 until mid-1730 partly because the sea air was bad for her, as well as in order to save money. A son, James Nathaniel Mist, was born to them in March 1731 who was subsequently admitted as an apprentice printer to William Bowyer. Mist died of asthma on 20 September 1737 at Boulogne. His family was left in a degree of hardship, and his wife was forced to pawn his effects in order to pay outstanding customs duty to secure the release of a shipment of wine.

Mist appears to have been a pugnacious and robust character; there are several accounts suggesting that he fought or threatened duels, and several stories of dramatic escapes from the clutches of the law. His personal integrity, as well as his loyalty to the Jacobite cause, are well evidenced by the testimony of contemporaries, not least by the notoriously irascible Francis Atterbury, exiled bishop of Rochester. Although he clearly made a good living by the production of newspapers which were highly critical of the government, his Jacobitism, unlike that of his contemporary Francis Clifton, was heartfelt and continued even after his fall and exile. Moreover, the success of his newspaper, alongside the careers of George Flint and Francis Clifton, demonstrates the considerable popular hostility to the newly established Hanoverian dynasty as well as the potential importance of a Jacobite press which both the exiled Jacobite court and Jacobite political leaders in England failed to exploit. PAUL CHAPMAN

Sources *DNB* · P. M. Chapman, 'Jacobite political argument in England, 1714–66', PhD diss., U. Cam., 1983 · M. Harris, *London newspapers in the age of Walpole* (1987) · state papers, domestic, George I, PRO, SP 35 · state papers, domestic, George II, PRO, SP 36 · Royal Arch., Stuart MSS · Bodl. Oxf., Nichols newspapers · A. S. Limouze, 'A study of Nathaniel Mist's weekly journals', PhD diss., Duke U., 1947 · P. K. Monod, *Jacobitism and the English people, 1688–1788* (1989) · J. Black, *The English press in the eighteenth century* (1987) · CUL, Cholmondley Houghton MSS · Nichols, *Lit. anecdotes* · [Marforio], *An historical view of the principles, characters, persons … of the political writers in Great Britain* (1740) · *Daniel Defoe: his life, and recently discovered writings*, ed. W. Lee, 3 vols. (1869) · J. Black, 'An underrated journalist: Nathaniel Mist and the opposition press during the whig ascendancy', *British Journal for Eighteenth-Century Studies*, 10 (1987), 27–41 · *GM*, 1st ser., 7 (1737), 574 **Archives** Bodl. Oxf., Nichols newspapers · Bodl. Oxf., Hope newspapers · PRO, state papers, domestic, series 35, 36, George I, George II · Royal Arch., Stuart MSS **Wealth at death** plate, watch, and trinkets pawned by wife to pay for shipment of wine held by customs

Mistahimaskwa. *See* Big Bear (*c*.1825–1888).

Misyn, Richard (*d.* 1462), bishop of Dromore, joined the Carmelites in Lincoln and commenced his studies at York, where he was ordained acolyte on 11 March 1419, subdeacon on 23 December 1419, and deacon on 17 May 1421. He attended a university, possibly Oxford, before returning to Lincoln, where he became a hermit. During this period he made translations into English of works by Richard Rolle, *De emendatione vitae* as *The Mendynge of Lyfe*, and *Incendium amoris* as *The Fyre of Love*. From the inscriptions in each book, the former was completed in 1434 'to informacioun of Cristyn sauls' (Rolle, ed. Harvey, 131), and the latter in 1435, at the request of an anchoress, Margaret Heslyngton. At the end of the first book of his translation of *Incendium amoris*, Misyn describes himself as a hermit, Carmelite friar, and bachelor of theology. However, having completed the translation of the second book, on 12 July 1435, he writes as prior of Lincoln.

Misyn became chaplain to Henry Percy, earl of Northumberland (*d.* 1455), for he is described as such on 15 November 1441, when he was given a dispensation to hold a benefice. On 18 November 1443 he was admitted as rector of Edlaston, Derbyshire, but resigned this benefice probably in 1446, for on 8 September that year he was admitted as perpetual rector of Colwich, Staffordshire. Some time between 1446 and 1456 Misyn was appointed 'inquisitor and prosecutor for apostate [friars]' (Bale, BL, Harley MS 1819, fol. 200v) by the Carmelite provincial, Nicholas Kenton (*d.* 1468).

On 29 July 1457 Misyn was provided to the see of Dromore in Ireland, with permission to retain the parish of Colwich 'on account of the insufficiency of the fruits of his diocese' (*CEPR letters*, 1455–1464, 172). However, he resigned Colwich before June 1460, having been admitted as rector of East Leake, Nottinghamshire, on 3 January 1459. Later that same year, on 20 July, he was collated as warden of St John's Hospital, Ripon. He had resigned from East Leake before October 1462, possibly to become vicar of Birstall, Yorkshire, a benefice he held until his death. There is no indication that Misyn ever visited his Irish see and, between 1458 and 1462 he acted as suffragan to Archbishop William Booth of York (*d.* 1464). An indulgence granted by Misyn is inscribed on a mazer bowl originally presented by Archbishop Richard Scrope (*d.* 1405) to York Minster, and probably indicates his support for Scrope's cult. Misyn was admitted as a member of the Corpus Christi Guild in York in 1461–2. He died on 29 September 1462 and was buried in the Carmelite house in York. Nothing further is known about Misyn and no other works by him are recorded. However, his two translations have been printed twice and are a lasting memorial to his deep spirituality and to his time spent as a hermit.

RICHARD COPSEY

Sources Emden, *Oxf.*, 2.1286 · J. Bale, Bodl. Oxf., MS Bodley 73 (SC 27635), fol. i · J. Bale, BL, Harley MS 1819, fols. 200, 200v (bis) · R. Rolle, *'The fire of love' and 'The mending of life, or, The rule of living'*, ed. R. Harvey, trans. R. Misyn, EETS, 106 (1896) · R. Rolle, *'The fire of love, or, Melody of love' and 'The mending of life, or, Rule of living'*, trans. R. Misyn, 2nd edn, ed. F. M. M. Comper (1920) · E. Schnell, 'Die Tractatus der Richard Rolle von Hampole *Incendium amoris* und *Emendatio vitae* und der Übersetzung durch Richard Misyn', diss., University of Erlangen, 1932 · Borth. Inst., reg. 18 Bowet, fols. 402, 404v, 408v · J. Bale, Bodl. Oxf., MS Selden supra 41, fol. 183 · J. Bale, BL, Harley MS 3838, fol. 40 · *Commentarii de scriptoribus Britannicis, auctore Joanne Lelando*, ed. A. Hall, 2 (1709), 473 · J. Pits, *Relationum historicarum de rebus Anglicis*, ed. [W. Bishop] (Paris, 1619), 897–8 · Tanner, *Bibl. Brit.-Hib.*, 529 · *The whole works of Sir James Ware concerning Ireland*, ed. and trans. W. Harris, rev. edn, 1 (1764), 260
Archives BL, Add. MS 37790 · CCC Oxf., MS 236 · Yale U., Beinecke L., MS 331, 1–167

Mitan, James (1776–1822), printmaker and architectural draughtsman, was born in London on 13 February 1776; his younger brother **Samuel Mitan** (1786–1843) was also an engraver. Nothing is known of their family background, although their father must also have been a printmaker, as it is known that James received his earliest training at home; it may be assumed that the same was true for Samuel. In 1786, at the age of ten, James continued his education at Mr King's academy in Soho. After leaving that establishment in 1788, he once again studied with his father until 1790, when he was apprenticed to a Mr Vincent who specialized in engraving calligraphy. Apparently finding this path too limiting, and encouraged by a fellow apprentice named William Sharp, he sought alternative instruction in drawing with John Samuel Agar (d. c.1820), in the hope of developing his skills as an engraver of history subjects. He obviously showed considerable talent as, at the age of seventeen, although still officially apprenticed to Vincent, he successfully entered himself as a student at the Royal Academy Schools, on 31 December 1792.

After his seven-year tenure with Vincent expired, on 7 June 1797, Mitan started working with some of the most influential and well-connected engravers of the day. Doubtless he must have contributed to numerous plates, but his position as an assistant means that there are relatively few prints from this period that bear his name; nevertheless he gained a reputation as an able line engraver, and after the early 1800s he produced a number of vignettes, signed 'J. Mitan', which were intended as luxury book illustrations. Nearly all of his engravings reproduced designs by popular artists such as Robert Smirke and William Westall. Thomas Stothard's neo-classical design for a frontispiece to *A selection of popular national airs, with symphonies and accompaniments by Sir John Stephenson* (1818) is typical of the plates Mitan executed, in a combination of stipple, engraving, and etching, to illustrate Shakespeare and a variety of literature and books of British history. Although he was prolific a few examples do stand out. In 1822 he designed and produced a set of fifty-six small yet elaborate plates of animal subjects which have more in common with still life than the natural history; these were published by H. Gibbs at 23 Newport Street. He also exhibited several pieces at the Royal Academy, including a large-scale design for a monument to commemorate the battle of Waterloo in 1818. The latter marks Mitan's later passion for architectural subjects, and in his final years he concentrated on compositions for the Admiralty and the Freemason's Society and in designing a chain bridge over the River Mersey.

Mitan's other important contribution was as a teacher; among others he trained his younger brother Samuel in draughtsmanship and landscape engraving, and the latter's work is characterized by its similarly small scale and fine precision. During his career Samuel Mitan worked for a number of publishers, including Rudolph Ackermann, for whom he produced plates to illustrate *The History of the Abbey Church of St Peter's Westminster* (1812) and *French Scenery* (1822), and for Charles Heath on *The Keepsake* annual (1823–38). However, the fact that Heath rarely allowed Mitan to sign his plates suggests that there are probably many more prints which should be ascribed to this engraver. He also exhibited several historical engravings at the Suffolk Street Gallery in 1840. Little else is known of Samuel Mitan except that, in 1810, he was a founder member of the Artists' Annuity Fund—a charitable organization for the support of the widows and children of fellow artists. He died on 3 June 1843, at The Polygon, Somers Town, London.

James Mitan died on 16 August 1822 of a paralysis, which is supposed to have been caused by overwork. His wife, Mary, survived him, and in 1823, from their home at 63 Warren Street, she published her husband's engraving of C. R. Leslie's *Anne Page and Slender*, which had been completed by F. Englehart, one of the many engravers with whom Mitan collaborated throughout his career.

LUCY PELTZ

Sources Bénézit, *Dict.* · Farington, *Diary* · Graves, *Artists* · S. C. Hutchison, 'The Royal Academy Schools, 1768–1830', *Walpole Society*, 38 (1960–62), 123–91 · Redgrave, *Artists* · B. Adams, *London illustrated, 1604–1851* (1983) · B. Hunnisett, *An illustrated dictionary of British steel engravers*, new edn (1989) · J. Pye, *Patronage of British art: an historical sketch* (1845); facs. edn [1970] · PRO, PROB 6/196, fol. 227 · *GM*, 1st ser., 93/2 (1823), 86–7
Archives BL, letter to A. Cooper, Add MS 2075, fol. 103
Wealth at death under £1000: administration, PRO, PROB 6/196, fol. 227

Mitan, Samuel (1786–1843). *See under* Mitan, James (1776–1822).

Mitch, Richard (*fl.* 1542–1576), civil lawyer, was from an Essex family, but the identity of his parents is not known. He graduated BA at the University of Cambridge in 1542, proceeded MA in 1544, and was admitted as a fellow of St John's College on 14 March 1543. He later moved to Trinity Hall, where he commenced LLD in 1557, and proceeded on 26 April 1559.

Mitch was actively opposed to reformers at Cambridge, being conservative in religion. His move to Trinity Hall may have been influenced by Stephen Gardiner, bishop of Winchester and master of Trinity Hall. Mitch was one of

Gardiner's proctors during the latter's trial in 1551. During Mary I's reign Mitch organized an attack on Dr Edwin Sandys, vice-chancellor of the University of Cambridge, who had shown sympathy towards Lady Jane Grey. He served on the commission appointed by Cardinal Reginald Pole, archbishop of Canterbury, to root out protestant books and heresy in 1556, along with Henry Harvey, also from Trinity Hall. In the same year Mitch was one of the examiners of John Hullier, preacher of King's Lynn, Norfolk, who was charged with heresy, found guilty, and burnt at the stake. He was among other lawyers who, in January 1557, gave evidence concerning the heresies of Martin Bucer and Paul Fagius before their bodies were exhumed and burnt.

Mitch became an advocate in Doctors' Commons on 26 April 1559 and began working in the court of arches. He was among five Trinity Hall members of Doctors' Commons listed in 1568. He was relatively inactive after the succession of Elizabeth I. At some point after 1568 he left England, being listed among Essex recusants who were fugitives abroad, and is listed in Doctors' Commons' records as living on the continent in 1576. What prompted his move is unknown. Mitch was probably among those at Cambridge who gave protestants reason to complain about Henry Harvey, master of Trinity Hall, who seems to have led the conservative opposition to reform. Mitch's prominence as well as enthusiasm as a conservative may explain his actions, as might his earlier conflict with Sandys, now archbishop of York. But Trinity Hall enjoyed relative peace and stability owing to Harvey's moderate approach, and the long tenure of Mitch as fellow there suggests that his earlier zeal had moderated to such a degree as to allow him to stay. It is quite likely that he left England to live abroad for other reasons than just his conservative religious beliefs.   JOHN F. JACKSON

Sources G. D. Squibb, *Doctors' Commons: a history of the College of Advocates and Doctors of Law* (1977), 59, 154 · D. MacCulloch, *Thomas Cranmer: a life* (1996) · J. Strype, *Annals of the Reformation and establishment of religion … during Queen Elizabeth's happy reign*, 2 vols. (1709–25); 2nd edn, 4 vols. (1725–31) · T. Baker, *History of the college of St John the Evangelist, Cambridge*, ed. J. E. B. Mayor, 2 vols. (1869) · C. H. Cooper and J. W. Cooper, *Annals of Cambridge*, 5 vols. (1842–1908) · Cooper, *Ath. Cantab.* · [C. Coote], *Sketches of the lives and characters of eminent English civilians, with an historical introduction relative to the College of Advocates* (1804) · *DNB*

Mitchel, Jane (1819/20–1899). *See under* Mitchel, John (1815–1875).

Mitchel, John (1815–1875), Irish nationalist, the first surviving son of John Mitchel (d. 1840), a Presbyterian minister, and his wife, Mary Haslett (1786–1865), was born at the manse, Camnish, near Dungiven, co. Londonderry, on 3 November 1815. His father was appointed minister of Newry Presbyterian Church in 1823, and the family moved to Dromalane House. John Mitchel was educated at Dr Henderson's classical school at Newry, where he met his lifelong friend John Martin (1812–1875). In 1830 he matriculated at Trinity College, Dublin, and graduated in 1834. His father was deeply disappointed that Mitchel felt he

John Mitchel (1815–1875), by unknown engraver, pubd 1848 (after Leon Gluckman)

had no vocation for the ministry. After an attempt at working as a bank clerk he entered the office of John Henry Quinn, a solicitor at Newry. At the close of 1836 he eloped with Jane Verner, a sixteen-year-old schoolgirl. The fugitives were captured at Chester, and Mitchel was taken back in custody to Ireland, where he was kept a few days in prison before being released on bail. Their second attempt was, however, more successful, and on 3 February 1837 they were married at Drumcree church. The marriage was said to have been extremely happy, and the couple had six children. In 1840, after being admitted a solicitor, Mitchel entered into partnership with Samuel Livingstone Fraser, a successful attorney, and ran the branch office at Banbridge, often defending Catholics against local Orangemen. In 1839 he helped organize a public dinner for Daniel O'Connell in Newry. In the same year he began suffering from asthma, an illness that haunted him for the rest of his life.

In 1842 Mitchel became acquainted with Thomas Davis, the friend who, in Mitchel's own words, 'first filled his soul with the passion of a great ambition and a lofty purpose' (Dillon, 1.70). The following year Mitchel and Martin joined Daniel O'Connell's Repeal Association, but only after the death of Davis in September 1845 did he totally commit himself to politics, and accept a place on the staff of *The Nation*. Sir Charles Gavan Duffy, the paper's proprietor and editor, described him as follows:

> He was rather above the middle size, well made, and with a face which was thoughtful and comely, though pensive blue eyes and masses of soft brown hair, a stray ringlet of which he had the habit of twining round his finger while he spoke, gave it, perhaps, too feminine a cast … (Duffy, bk 3, 191)

As early as on 22 November 1845 his *Nation* article 'Threats of coercion' caused great controversy, as Mitchel suggested that railways could be sabotaged in an Irish uprising. In June 1846 Duffy was prosecuted for publishing it, but the jury could not reach a verdict. In the same year Mitchel published *The life and times of Aodh O'Neill, prince of Ulster; called by the English, Hugh, earl, of Tyrone*, and edited the poems of Thomas Davis.

Mitchel seceded from the Repeal Association with the rest of the Young Ireland party on 28 July 1846. Under the influence of James Fintan Lalor, Mitchel's political views became more radical, and he began to proclaim that peasants should withhold rent to survive the famine. Finding himself unable any longer to agree with Duffy's more moderate policy, he left *The Nation* in December 1847. After the council of the Irish confederation voted against his radical ideas, he withdrew from that also.

On 12 February 1848 Mitchel issued the first number of the *United Irishman*, a weekly newspaper published in Dublin, which included his well-known letters to Lord Clarendon, and to the protestant farmers in the north. With the onset of revolutions in Europe, Mitchel openly advocated a 'spontaneous revolution' in Ireland. A charismatic figure and excellent writer, Mitchel came to epitomize revolutionary nationalism and Irish hatred of British rule in Ireland.

On 13 May Mitchel was arrested under the new Treason Felony Act, which he claimed was passed because of him. He was tried at the commission court in Green Street, Dublin, before Baron Lefroy and Justice Moore, on 25 and 26 May 1848, and was sentenced on the following day to fourteen years' transportation. His paper was suppressed. Immediately after the verdict, he was taken by the *Shearwater* to Spike Island, co. Cork, as the authorities feared a rescue operation in Dublin. The court case had attracted enormous interest in Ireland and abroad, and copies of Mitchel's speech from the dock and a photograph of him taken in prison were sold all over Ireland. The press heavily questioned the legality of the verdict, since the jury had been packed.

In June Mitchel was conveyed in the *Scourge* to Bermuda, where he was confined to the hulks. Because of his bad asthma, he was removed in the *Neptune* to the Cape of Good Hope. Owing to the colonists' refusal to permit the convicts to land, a stance that Mitchel wholeheartedly supported, the *Neptune* remained at anchor in Simon's Bay from 19 September 1849 to 19 February 1850. In April 1850, Mitchel arrived in Van Diemen's Land, where he was allowed to reside with John Martin in one of the police districts on a ticket-of-leave. In June 1851 he was joined by his wife and family. On 9 June 1853 Mitchel resigned his ticket-of-leave, and escaped from Van Diemen's Land with the aid of Patrick James Smyth and his wife, hiding for over a month until sailing on 2 August to Tahiti, and from there on the *Julia Ann* to San Francisco, where he met with an enthusiastic welcome. After moving to New York in the hope that he could achieve something for Ireland there, he started a newspaper, *The Citizen*, on 7 January 1854. It became known for its strong opposition to the abolition

movement, and for serializing Mitchel's *Jail Journal*, a detailed personal account of his transportation, published as a book in 1854; it became a classic of Irish revolutionary writing. His criticism in the *Journal* about Duffy's conduct during his trials in 1848–9 led to a bitter and acrimonious quarrel between the two men.

At the close of the year Mitchel moved to East Tennessee, and took to farming and lecturing. This was the first of many moves, reflecting his restlessness caused by the feeling that his real Irish home was barred to him. From October 1857 to August 1859—together with the major of Knoxville, William G. Swan—he conducted the *Southern Citizen*, a weekly journal advocating the interests of the southern states, which was first published at Knoxville, and subsequently at Washington. His pro-slavery stance has been widely criticized, being regarded as contradictory to his revolutionary ideas. It was based on the belief that slavery was a better system than the wage slavery of industrialization. He was highly influenced by the ideas on slavery of Thomas Carlyle. Additionally, he felt that there were two nations in America, north and south, and he was strongly in sympathy with the agrarian lifestyle of the southern planters.

Although Mitchel was heavily involved in the debate over abolition his heart was in Irish rather than American affairs. In 1859 he edited the poems of James Clarence Mangan, and a year later *An Apology for the British Government in Ireland* and *The Last Conquest of Ireland (perhaps)* were published; in these he again emphasized that 'The Almighty, indeed, sent the potato blight. But the English created the Famine' (*Last Conquest*, 1860, 219).

In August 1859 Mitchel visited Paris, where he went to reside in the following year as correspondent for American newspapers, hoping that in the event of an Anglo-French war, Ireland would seize the opportunity. In Paris, his daughter Henrietta finally converted to Catholicism, a step that Mitchel accepted, being very tolerant in religious matters. Although his writings reflect his Presbyterian upbringing, he felt that his own beliefs were often 'almost pagan'.

Mitchel returned to New York in September 1862, after the outbreak of the civil war, and managed after much difficulty to get through the federal lines to Richmond. Finding that he was disqualified for military service by reason of his nearsightedness, he became editor of *The Enquirer*, the semi-official organ of the Confederate president Jefferson Davis. Owing to a divergence in their views Mitchel resigned this post in 1864, and began writing the leading articles for *The Examiner*. Additionally, he joined the Richmond city guard and the ambulance corps. The American Civil War cost Mitchel dearly. Fighting in the Confederate army, his sons John and William were killed, and another son, James, was severely wounded.

On the conclusion of the war Mitchel went to New York, where he became editor of the *Daily News*, a staunch southern paper. In consequence of his articles supportive of the southern cause Mitchel was arrested by the military authorities on 14 June 1865, and was confined in Fortress Monroe for nearly five months. Later he mused:

I suppose that I am the only person who has ever been a prisoner-of-state to the British and the American Government one after the other. ... I despise the civilization of the nineteenth century, and its two highest expressions and grandest hopes, most especially—so the said century sees nothing that can be done with me, except to tie me up. (Dillon, 2.218)

The treatment Mitchel received in prison was extremely harsh, and his health broke down irretrievably. Shortly after his release on 30 October 1865 he went to Paris as the financial agent of the Irish Republican Brotherhood, hoping that amid the mounting tensions between England and America, the Fenians could accomplish a revolution in Ireland. When he realized that this would not happen, he resigned that office in the following year, returning to America in October 1866. Here he began work on his *History of Ireland*, which was published in 1867. In February 1867 he refused the post of chief executive officer of the Fenians in America, and on 19 October following published at New York the first number of the *Irish Citizen*. In this paper, which was strongly democratic in American politics, he opposed both the Fenians and the home rulers, but spoke at a rally in New York in support of the families of the Manchester martyrs in the winter of 1869/70. In the same year he serialized a continuation of the *Jail Journal*, which embraced the years 1853–66. Increasing health problems caused him to discontinue his paper on 27 July 1872, which rendered his financial situation very insecure. In the same year he wrote letters against James Anthony Froude's anti-Irish prejudices in *The Irish-American*, which were published as a book, *The Crusade of the Period* (1873). In February 1874 Mitchel, despite his dislike of the home rule movement, allowed himself to be put forward *in absentia* as its candidate in Tipperary. He failed. In summer 1874 Mitchel returned to Ireland after twenty-six years of exile. On 16 February 1875 he was elected unopposed for Tipperary while he was on his way once again to Ireland, arriving the following day. On 18 February Mitchel was disqualified for being a convict, but was again returned by a majority of 2368 votes on 11 March, when he declared that he would not take his seat. Mitchel died at Dromalane House, Newry, on 20 March 1875. He was buried on the 23rd of the same month in the Unitarian cemetery, Old Meeting-House Green, High Street, Newry, where a monument was erected to his memory by his widow, who regretted that after following him all over the world, she had not accompanied him to Ireland. On 26 May 1875 the Irish court of common pleas posthumously issued another disqualification of Mitchel. Mitchel's ideas strongly influenced the Irish republican movement especially at the beginning of the twentieth century. However, since that time, no new biography has been written about him. A statue of him stands in John Mitchel Place, Newry.

Mitchel's wife, **Jane** [Jenny] **Mitchel** [*née* Verner] (1819/20–1899), was born Jane Verner, only daughter of Mary Ward (*d.* before 1847?). Her mother was the daughter of a coachman on the Verner estate in Loughgall, co. Armagh, and Captain James Verner was most likely her stepfather. There were rumours of illegitimacy, and the Verner family later denied that Captain James was ever married to Mary Ward.

Jenny Mitchel was gentle and petite in appearance, but strong-willed and independent-minded. Although she opposed John's desire to give up his profession to work on *The Nation*, she soon got involved in Young Ireland activities herself. When John started the *United Irishman*, she organized his newspaper files, edited contributions, and wrote anonymous letters to the editor. Her politics were as radical as her husband's. After his arrest she urged his friends to attempt a rescue operation, and was deeply disappointed when he was transported without resistance. Eager to follow her husband into exile, she would have immediately set out for Bermuda, but he urged her to wait until he was settled. With her five children she set out to Van Diemen's Land on 22 January 1851, and immediately after the birth of her sixth child, Isabel, she organized Mitchel's escape with Smyth.

In America and France Jenny Mitchel supported her husband's activities, and was able to organize the frequent moves of the household quickly and successfully. When John returned to America in 1862, she remained in Ireland with two of her daughters, Minnie and Isabel, but soon decided to bring food and clothing to blockaded states. However, the blockade runner, *Vesta*, ran aground and caught fire, which left them stranded on a sandy island near the coast of North Carolina. They made their way back to Richmond only with great difficulty. While she supported the southern states, she did not openly advocate slavery. During the war, she worked as a nurse in Richmond.

After her husband's death Mitchel established a partnership with her son James in a photolithographic firm, and was the manageress in his absence. Jenny Mitchel died on 31 December 1899 at her home in Briggs Avenue, Fordham, New York, and was buried in Woodlawn cemetery, Bronx, New York.

BRIGITTE ANTON

Sources W. Dillon, *Life of John Mitchel*, 2 vols. (1888) • R. O'Conner, *Jenny Mitchel: Young Irelander* (1988) • J. Mitchel, *Jail journal ... with a continuation of the journal in New York and Paris* (1913); facs. edn with introduction by T. Flanagan (1982) • B. Anton, 'Northern voices: Ulsterwomen in the Young Ireland movement', *Coming into the light: the work, politics and religion of women in Ulster*, ed. J. Holmes and D. Urquhart (1994), 60–92 • *Blackwood's pedigrees*, 16.82–6 [family trees of the Mitchels and the Martins] • T. F. O'Sullivan, *The Young Irelanders*, 2nd edn (1945) • L. J. Walsh, *John Mitchel* (1917) • P. S. O'Hegarty, *John Mitchel* (1917) • C. G. Duffy, *Young Ireland: a fragment of Irish history, 1840–1845*, rev. edn, 2 vols. (1896) • P. A. Sillard, *The life of John Mitchel* (1889) • R. J. Hayes, ed., *Manuscript sources for the history of Irish civilisation*, 3 (1965) • R. J. Hayes, ed., *Manuscript sources for the history of Irish civilisation: first supplement, 1965–1975*, 1 (1979) • B. Ó Cathaoir, *John Mitchel* (1978) • J. Mitchel, letters, 1849–54, PRO NIre., MIC 426 Reel 1/3 and 1/4 • *DNB*

Archives Col. U., Rare Book and Manuscript Library, corresp. and papers • NL Ire., corresp. • PRO NIre., letters to family • PRO NIre., letters by Jenny Mitchel, MIC 426 Reel 1/3 and 1/4 | Col. U., William Brown Meloney MSS, incl. letter by Jenny Mitchel • New York Historical Society, MSS of Charles O'Conner, Richard O'Gorman, James Adam Dix • NL Ire., journals of W. J. O'Neill Daunt • NL Ire., letters to Samuel Ferguson [copies] • NL Ire., Hobson MSS, comments on Mitchel • NL Ire., Larcom MSS, comments on 1845 • NL

Ire., Lennon MSS • NL Ire., corresp. with William Smith O'Brien • NL Ire., O'Conner Trust MSS • PRO NIre., Joseph Connellan MSS
Likenesses M. & N. Hanhart, two lithographs, 1848 (after daguerreotype by L. Gluckman), NG Ire. • daguerreotype, 1848 (Jenny Mitchel) • lithograph, pubd 1848 (after daguerreotype by L. Gluckman), NG Ire., NPG [*see illus.*] • photograph, 1848, repro. in J. Mitchel, *Jail journal*, cover • group portrait, 1866 • C. Baugniet, lithograph (after photograph), BM • C. Baugniet, lithograph (after daguerreotype by L. Gluckman), NPG • T. Farrell, plaster death mask, NG Ire. • H. A. Kernoff, ink and pencil on card, NG Ire. • drawing (Jenny Mitchel), repro. in O'Conner, *Jenny Mitchel* • group portrait, chromolithograph (*The illustrious sons of Ireland*), NPG • illustration (in Bermuda), repro. in *ILN* [n.d.] • statue, John Mitchel Place, Newry, Ireland
Wealth at death Dromalane House automatically went to eldest son; testimonial movement collected $10,000 in 1873

Mitchel, Jonathan (1624–1668), minister in America and author, was born in Halifax, Yorkshire, the fifth son of Matthew Mitchel (1590–1645) and Susan Butterfield. His parents dissented from the Laudian Church of England, and the family departed from Bristol for the New World and arrived in Boston on 17 August 1635. Mitchel was a sickly child, suffering at the age of ten from a fever that disabled one of his arms for life. As he grew his body changed from 'extream lean' to 'extream fat', in spite of an exercise regimen he adopted (Mather, *Magnalia Christi*, 4.184). When he was fifteen he was affected by the startling accident of a family servant who, refusing to attend the Sunday lecture, stayed at home instead to chop down a tree and was killed by a falling branch. 'This Amazing Stroke', he wrote, 'did much stir my Heart, and I spent some time in Endeavouring the work of my Repentance' (ibid., 4.167). From this time forward he felt called to the Christian ministry.

Mitchel was admitted 'upon a strict Examination' to Harvard College in 1645 (Sibley, 145). He graduated MA in 1647, was elected a fellow of Harvard in 1650, and also served the college as a tutor. At Harvard he was decisively influenced by Thomas Shepherd, pastor of the Cambridge, Massachusetts, Congregational Church, and with Shepherd's dying blessing he became the next pastor of the church in August 1650. He had been engaged to Sarah Cotton, but after her death in January 1650 he married Shepherd's young widow, Margaret, née Boradale, on 19 November of the same year. They had six children, including two sons, Samuel and Jonathan, who also graduated from Harvard College, and a daughter, Margaret, who married Major Stephen Sewall of Salem.

The main source for Mitchel's life is Cotton Mather's 'Ecclesiastes, or, The life of Mr. Jonathan Mitchel', printed in *Magnalia Christi Americana*. Mather based his account in part on the Latin diary, *Vitae hypomnemata*, that Mitchel kept for most of his adult life but that has not survived. Mather vividly describes Mitchel preaching from the pulpit: 'He would speak with such a Transcendent *Majesty* and *Liveliness*, that the People … would often Shake under his Dispensations, as if they had Heard the *Sound* of the *Trumpets* from the *Burning Mountain*' (Mather, *Magnalia Christi*, 4.174).

Of the published works of Mitchel, his popular *Mr. Mitchel's Letter to his Brother* (1649) and *A Discourse of the Glory*

(1677) went through multiple editions, but his sermon *Nehemiah on the Wall in Troublesom Times* (1671), and his treatises *Propositions Concerning the Subject of Baptism and Consociation of Churches* (1662) and (with Richard Mather) *A Defence of the Answer* (1664) are the texts most frequently cited by historians. In his 'election day' (1667) and *Nehemiah* sermons (1671) Mitchel coined the phrase 'Errand into the Wilderness' for the puritan mission to New England. The baptism treatises came about as a result of Mitchel's leadership of a synod of clergy at Boston in 1662. This took up the question of whether, due to the declining membership of the colonial churches, the children of church members should be baptized and recognized as members without an assurance of their conversion. In opposition to the Baptists, Mitchel successfully advocated the 'half-way covenant', which allowed the young children of church members to be baptized as a partial, or half-way, form of church membership.

Mitchel also performed many duties for the colony of Massachusetts. He and Daniel Gookin served as the first licensers of the press in the colony in 1662, and with Francis Willoughby and John Leverett he drew up a petition in 1664 asking Charles II to respect the colony's charter. Mitchel was also a writer of occasional verse, and his verses included elegies for Harvard president Henry Dunster and the Revd John Wilson of Boston, and 'On the Following Work and its Author', a commendatory verse for Michael Wigglesworth's *The Day of Doom*. Mitchel died of a fever on 9 July 1668 in Cambridge, Massachusetts. The inventory of his estate at his death was £786 17s. 9d. The Massachusetts Historical Society in Boston has preserved manuscripts of some of Mitchel's unpublished sermons and sermon notes.   JEFFREY POWERS-BECK

Sources C. Mather, 'Ecclesiastes, or, The life of Mr. Jonathan Mitchel', *Magnalia Christi Americana, or, The ecclesiastical history of New England*, 7 vols. (1702), vol. 4, pp. 166–85 • J. L. Sibley, *Biographical sketches of graduates of Harvard University*, 1 (1873), 141–57 • C. Mather, *Ecclesiastes, or, The life of the reverend and excellent Jonathan Mitchel* (Boston, 1697), 33–111 • N. Morton, *New-Englands memoriall* (Cambridge, MA, 1669), 191–6 • G. L. Walker, *History of the First Church in Hartford, 1633–1883* (Hartford, CT, 1884), 146–9, 173 • R. H. B., 'Mitchell, Jonathan', *DAB* • W. Cothren, *History of ancient Woodbury, Connecticut* (Waterbury, CT, 1854), 633–5 • H. T. Meserole, *American poetry of the seventeenth century* (University Park, PA, 1985), 412–13 • S. B. Caton, 'The compleat minister: the "De profundis" sermons of Jonathan Mitchel', PhD diss., University of Rochester, New York, 1998, 67–114 • M. R. McCarl, 'Mitchell, Jonathan', *ANB*
Archives Mass. Hist. Soc., MS sermons and sermon notes
Wealth at death £786 17s. 9d.: Sibley, *Biographical sketches*, vol. 1, p. 163

Mitchel, William (1670–1740?), tinsmith and pamphleteer, was born in Scotland but nothing is known of his early life. In or about 1696 he moved to Edinburgh and took up residence in the Bowhead. There he earned a living as a tinsmith and by superintending the lighting of the town lamps. Chambers describes him as 'an odd half-crazy varlet of a tinsmith' (Chambers, 53). He occasionally preached on the streets but was better known for writing over fifty pamphlets and broadsheets on diverse subjects but concerned mainly with church government and what he considered to be the religious derelictions of his time.

These barely literate writings were badly printed on shabby paper and were sold in his shop. They contain a 'strange mixture of fanaticism, humour and low cunning' (ibid., 53) and are full of characters, both real and fictitious, who speak in glowing terms of the author or, on occasions, are used to advertise his wares. Claiming 'to give light', a metaphor borrowed from his trade, he generally styled himself the Tinklarian Doctor and displayed the 'Mitchel coat of arms' above the title in these pamphlets.

Mitchel's first known publication, *The Tinklarian's Testament*, appeared in 1711 and was dedicated to Church of Scotland ministers. It touched upon what became one of his favourite themes, church government in Scotland. This he examined in more depth in *Descriptions of the Divisions of the Church of Scotland* (1713) and *The Tinklarian Doctor's Catechism where he Examines All the Ministers of the General Assembly* (1737). He was suspicious of Lutheranism and an opponent of episcopacy. The bishops of both England and Scotland were a constant target for his sarcasm, as in *Speech Against the Bishops and the Book of Common Prayer* and his second and third 'catechisms', examining the bishops in England (1736, 1737). Mitchel, however, reserved his most venomous attacks for the Catholic church, in his treatise of 1736 entitled *The Great Mystery of Babylon, Opened and Explained, where the Whore is Deeply Wounded*. The city fathers of Edinburgh were another target for his invective. In a pamphlet of 1719 addressed to the 'Lord Provost, Baillies and the whole council of Edinburgh' he showed his contempt for them by drawing up a list of a new set of officials whom he claimed would be more competent and conscientious in the performance of their duties. Mitchel also commented on the murder of Captain Porteous and the Porteous riots in *The Tinklarian Doctor's Twenty-First Epistle … Concerning Captain Porteous* (1737). His last known work, *Speech which Contains Pleasant and Dreadful Prophecies*, appeared in 1739.

Despite the derision and sarcasm in much of his writings Mitchel does not appear to have attracted any great enmity and, until his death in Edinburgh, probably in 1740, he was regarded as a harmless eccentric.

G. G. SMITH, rev. M. J. MERCER

Sources R. Chambers, *Traditions of Edinburgh*, new edn (1869), 53–5 · Irving, *Scots.*

Archives BL, letter, Stowe MS 750, fol. 292

Mitchelburne [Michelborne], **John** (1648–1721), army officer and military governor, was born on 2 January 1648 and baptized six days later in Horsted Keynes church, Sussex, the son of Abraham Michelborne (d. 1664) of Horsted Keynes, and his first wife, Penelope (d. 1648), daughter of John Wheeler of Droitwich, Worcestershire. Mitchelburne's mother died giving birth to him. At some point after Mitchelburne's birth his father settled at Kilcandra, co. Wicklow, where he died in 1664. Mitchelburne himself was married twice, first to Susan (d. 1689), daughter of Sir Tristram Beresford of Coleraine and widow of William Jackson of Coleraine, with whom he had seven children, and second to Elizabeth, who was believed to be the daughter of Captain Michael Cunningham of Prehen, co.

Londonderry. This second marriage remained childless. Mitchelburne's first wife and all seven children died during the siege of Londonderry in 1689.

Having probably joined the army in the late 1660s and served in the ranks during the 1670s before buying a lieutenant's commission in 1678, Mitchelburne served in the Tangier garrison in the early 1680s, during which time he got to know Percy Kirke and Robert Lundy, two senior officers who were to have significant roles in his later career. After his return from Africa he was placed on the Irish military establishment, serving under Lundy in Londonderry, Kinsale, and Dublin in Lord Mountjoy's regiment of foot. Being one of the few protestants left in the regiment at the time of the revolution of 1688, he made his escape from Dublin to Londonderry. He received a major's commission under William of Orange in February 1689, and was involved in several military actions in Ulster. By April he was at Londonderry, where the civil governor, the Revd George Walker, and the military governor, Major Henry Baker, chose him as one of eight colonels to command the forces defending the city against the Jacobites. He was given command of Colonel Clotworthy Skeffington's regiment, in which he had been serving since February. Before he was appointed military governor in late June following the death of Baker, Mitchelburne was placed under house arrest in May owing to a quarrel with Baker in which Mitchelburne was wounded. However, the two men made up their differences, and he was appointed governor on Baker's recommendation, and served as a pallbearer at Baker's funeral. He continued as military governor for the remainder of the siege, and after the relief of the city Major-General Kirke made him sole governor, and gave him command of a second regiment, which he amalgamated with that of Skeffington. Following the siege he placed the Jacobite flag captured at Windmill Hill in the chancel of the city cathedral. He remained at Londonderry for the next year, though his regiment served at the Boyne and first siege of Limerick. In 1691 he commanded the forces at the siege of Sligo, during which a quarrel with the militia forces over booty resulted in the withdrawal of the militia, thereby extending the siege. Another failure to take the city with the tenuous assistance of Hugh Baldearg O'Donnell's Irish forces resulted in Mitchelburne being removed from command of the siege, so that when Sligo surrendered in September 1691 it was to the earl of Granard, though Mitchelburne was made temporary governor of the town.

Having had a charge of corruption against him dismissed in November 1691, Mitchelburne spent most of the 1690s in Londonderry, where he had been elected alderman for life. In debt, and believing he had received scant reward for his services during the war, he may have been the author, or at least instigator, of three pamphlets, entitled *An Account of the Transactions in the North of Ireland, anno Domini 1691* (1692), *The Case of Col. John Mitchelburne, Late Governor of Londonderry* (1699), and *The case of the governor, officers and soldiers actually concerned in the defence of Londonderry in the kingdom of Ireland* (1699). The last two were produced at a time when Mitchelburne had gone to

London to petition for pay arrears for his regiment. Unlike Walker, Mitchelburne had received no reward for his role in the siege of Londonderry. The last pamphlet resulted in Mitchelburne's dismissal as an alderman of Londonderry, but he was soon restored by act of mandamus. Although the sacramental test of 1704 excluded his Presbyterian opponents from the Londonderry corporation, he still felt the need to write a play, entitled *Ireland Preserv'd, or, The Siege of Londonderry, together with the Troubles of the North* (1705), promoting his own role, and that of his fellow Episcopalians, in the siege. The play was regularly reprinted during the next 100 years, and from 1783 onwards, being bound with Robert Ashton's *The Battle of Aughrim* (1727), formed a staple of the pedlars' chapbooks.

Mitchelburne remained in Londonderry for the rest of his life, apart from intermittent visits to London to press for some form of reward, on one occasion being imprisoned for debt. In 1713 he placed a memorial inscription at the east window of Londonderry Cathedral, and the following year is said to have formed the first Apprentice Boys Club in 1714, when the siege was supposedly celebrated for the first time with a church service, a crimson flag raised on the cathedral steeple, the firing of cannon over the walls, and feasting and dancing in the evening. However, this account is suspect, and it is more likely that it was in 1718 that the traditional celebrations were initiated, with Bishop Nicolson officiating; he 'preached again in the cathedral two years later, and dined afterwards with Mitchelburne while bonfires burned in the town' (McBride, 36). Mitchelburne died at Londonderry on 1 October 1721, and was buried in Glendermot churchyard. In his will he left £50 for maintaining the crimson flag on the steeple. In 1775 the short-lived Independent Mitchelburne Club was founded as one of the siege commemorative clubs. In 1845 the Mitchelburne Club, one of the apprentice boys clubs, was founded, and revived in 1854.

C. I. McGrath

Sources W. Berry, *County genealogies: Sussex* (1830) · P. Wauchope, 'Colonel John Michelburne', *Irish Sword*, 20 (1996–7), 137–44 · I. McBride, *The siege of Derry in Ulster protestant mythology* (1997) · *Reprint of Walker's diary of the siege of Derry in 1688–89*, 4th edn (1907) · T. Witherow, ed., *Two diaries of Derry in 1689, being Richards' diary … and Ash's journal* (1888) · N. Luttrell, *A brief historical relation of state affairs from September 1678 to April 1714*, 2 (1857) · R. Welch, ed., *The Oxford companion to Irish literature* (1996)
Likenesses portrait, 1689?, repro. in J. Mitchelburne, *Ireland preserved, or, The siege of Londonderry, together with the troubles of the north* (1708), facing title-page · portrait, repro. in Wauchope, 'Colonel John Michelburne', facing p. 144

Mitchell. *See also* Michell, Mitchel.

Mitchell, Alexander (1780–1868), civil engineer, was born at William Street in Dublin on 13 April 1780. He was the eighth son of William Mitchell, inspector-general of barracks in Ireland, and Jane, daughter of George Ferguson of Belfast. He lived at Clontarf in Dublin until 1787, when his family moved to Pine Hill near Belfast. Following the death of his father in 1790, the family moved to more modest accommodation nearer the city and Mitchell studied at the Royal Belfast Academy under Dr William Bruce, a classical scholar. He had a natural aptitude for mathematics and a very retentive memory. In 1800, he started business in Belfast as a brick manufacturer and builder. In the following year he married a local girl, Mary Banks, with whom he had two sons and three daughters, and went to live at Ballymacarrett, a suburb of Belfast. He was a strong and active man, over 6 feet in height, upright with broad shoulders. He became totally blind at the age of twenty-three, having as a child contracted smallpox, which led to amaurosis, a disease of the optic nerve. He retired from the business in 1832, having invented a number of machines to improve the manufacturing processes.

In 1833, Mitchell took out a patent for the screw-pile and screw-mooring systems, simple yet effective means of providing foundation for lighthouses and beacons on mud or sandbanks and for mooring ships. The screw-pile consisted of an iron rod at the end of which was a helical shaped disc or screw, which resisted upwards force in the mooring application and downwards force when supporting a structure. For this invention he was made an associate of the Institution of Civil Engineers, and in 1848 was elected a member, receiving a Telford silver medal for a paper on submarine foundations, particularly the screw-pile and moorings (*Minutes of Proceedings of the Institution of Civil Engineers*, 7, 1848, 108–58), read to the institution on 22 February 1848. His system was generally approved of by the leading engineers of the time. At the expiration of his patent in 1847 the privy council, in consideration of its merit, granted Mitchell a renewal for fourteen years, an unusual procedure at the time. In order to exploit his invention, Mitchell had established himself at Belfast, and at 17 Great George Street, Westminster, as Mitchell's Screw-Pile and Mooring Company. The business was initially carried on with one of his sons, and then with a grandson.

The screw-pile was first used in the foundations of the Maplin Sands lighthouse at the mouth of the Thames in 1838. In 1839 Mitchell designed and constructed, with the aid of his son John (also a civil engineer), the lighthouse at Fleetwood, on the Wyre in Morecambe Bay. In the summer of 1844 a screw-pile lighthouse, serving also as a pilot station, was successfully placed by him in Carrickfergus Bay in Belfast Lough, but his attempt to construct a similar lighthouse on the Kish Bank, between Dublin Bay and Wicklow, proved unsuccessful. He also constructed, in the summer of 1847, a substantial screw-pile jetty at Courtown harbour on the coast of co. Wexford. This was followed by lighthouses in Dundalk Bay (1849) and near Cobh in Cork harbour (1852). After the success of screw-piles had been established, they were applied to more extensive undertakings, such as the government breakwater at Portland, the long viaduct and bridges on the Bombay and Baroda Railway, the Indian telegraph system, and a pier at Madras. Their most typical application, however, was as foundations for the increasingly fashionable seaside piers which began to be erected at British coastal resorts in the second half of the nineteenth century. The first to utilize Mitchell's system was that at Margate (1853–6).

Mitchell's improved method of mooring ships using screw-piles was also generally adopted and Newcastle upon Tyne corporation paid for the right to put down screw moorings in the Tyne. Mitchell also patented some improvements in ship propellers. Mitchell was an accomplished musician with a fine singing voice. His great friends were Dr James MacDonnell and Edward Bunting.

Following the death of his daughter Mary, Mitchell lived for a while at Farm Hill, Holywood, before ending his days at Glen Divis, near Belfast. He died on 25 June 1868 at Glen Divis and was buried in Clifton Street cemetery in the city.   GORDON GOODWIN, rev. R. C. COX

Sources F. J. Bigger, 'Alexander Mitchell, the famous blind engineer of Belfast', *Report and Proceedings of the Belfast Natural History and Philosophy Society* (1906–7), 19–29 · *Belfast News-Letter* (29 June 1868) · J. B. Redman, 'Description of the Maplin sands lighthouse at the mouth of the River Thames', *PICE*, 2 (1842), 150–54, esp. 150 · A. Mitchell, 'On submarine foundations: particularly the screw pile and moorings', *PICE*, 7 (1848), 108–46 · C. J. Robb, 'The sightless lighthouse engineer', *Irish News and Belfast Morning News* (24 Nov 1961) · 'The pile lighthouse', *Belfast News-Letter* (25 Aug 1958) · *Men of the time* (1862)
Archives NA Scot., letters and reports to Samuel Brown
Likenesses S. Wood, marble bust, *c.*1860, possibly Belfast · S. F. Lynn, marble bust, 1868, Belfast · oils, Belfast Harbour Commissioners

Mitchell, Alexander Ferrier (1822–1899), ecclesiastical historian, was born at Brechin, Forfarshire, Scotland, on 10 September 1822, the son of David Mitchell, convener of local guilds, and his wife, Elizabeth, daughter of James Ferrier of Broadmyre. After receiving his early education at Brechin grammar school, he proceeded to the University of St Andrews in the autumn of 1837 where at the age of fifteen years he won first place in the open bursary competition. He enrolled as a student in the faculty of arts in the United College of St Salvator and St Leonard and matriculated in the university on 23 February 1838. On completion of the four-year course in 1841 he graduated MA and in the following session entered St Mary's College (the divinity college of the university) to prepare himself for entering the ministry of the Church of Scotland. In St Mary's College he was presented to an exchequer bursary by the crown, and won distinction as a student of Hebrew and oriental languages. On completing his studies, Mitchell was licensed as a probationer for the ministry by the presbytery of Brechin and served first as assistant to the minister at Meigle, and subsequently to the minister in Dundee. In December 1847 he was presented to the parish of Dunnichen, ordained to the Christian ministry, and inducted to the pastoral charge. Mitchell's years as a student had for the most part coincided with the momentous events that had led to the Disruption of the church in 1843 and the subsequent setting up of the Free Church of Scotland. Those events within the national church and especially the crucial general assembly of 1843, which he witnessed from the public gallery, had a profound and lasting effect upon him. Along with his distinguished fellow student and subsequent colleague in St Mary's College, John Tulloch (1823–1886), Mitchell adhered to the established church.

On 8 December 1852, Mitchell married Margaret Tweedie (*d.* 1900), eldest daughter of Michael Johnstone of Bodsbeck. They had three sons and four daughters.

Already marked out at his university as a student of considerable promise, Mitchell was not permitted to remain long in his parish. Within a year of ordination and induction he was appointed to the chair of Hebrew and oriental languages at St Andrews, which he held until his appointment on 30 October 1868 by Queen Victoria to the chair of ecclesiastical history. During his twenty years as Hebrew professor, considerable advances were being made in the study and teaching of Hebrew and allied languages, and Mitchell has been credited as being 'one of the first in Scotland to introduce a scientific method in the teaching of Hebrew' (Christie, xx). He did not publish in the subject, but could count among his students the orientalist William Wright (1830–1889) and two others who went on to hold Hebrew chairs at Scottish universities.

The nineteenth century had seen in Scotland, both in the Church of Scotland and in the Free Church, an interest in missions to the Jews in Europe and the Middle East, and in 1856 Mitchell was appointed convener of the Church of Scotland's committee entrusted with this work. From then until his retirement from this post in 1875, he threw himself wholeheartedly into it. In 1857 he undertook on behalf of the church extensive travels to Turkey, Palestine, and Syria.

Before his appointment to the chair of ecclesiastical history, Mitchell had given evidence of a keen and active interest in that discipline. In two short publications, in 1866 and 1867, he indicated those areas of study within church history which were to become the dominant areas of his research and in which he was to make a significant and permanent contribution: the early history of the Scottish Reformation, in particular in its Lutheran phase; and the history of the Westminster assembly of divines, its theological standards, and their significance for Presbyterians. In the former of these studies (in particular in his research into the work of the Wedderburn brothers, to whom he probably felt drawn by his family background in Forfarshire) he evinced a detailed knowledge of early Lutheran literature, particularly in hymnology. This publication, *The Wedderburns and their Work* (1867), subtitled 'The sacred poetry of the Scottish Reformation in its historical relation to that of Germany', marks a significant development in the understanding of the early stages of the Reformation in Scotland—a subject of which Mitchell never tired and of which he gave the mature results in his edition for the Scottish Text Society of *A compendious book of godly and spiritual songs, commonly known as the gude and godlie ballatis* (1897). Some nine years earlier he had edited for the same society, from a unique surviving copy, John Gau's *The Richt Vay to the Kingdom of Heuine* (1888). Mitchell showed conclusively that this work by a Scottish exile in Malmö, extensively drawn from Lutheran sources, was probably one of the publications which the Scottish parliament had targeted by its acts that sought to exclude heresy from the country.

In the general area of the Scottish Reformation (in

which, through the important contributions of such eminent contemporary scholars as David Laing, Peter Lorimer, Thomas McCrie, and David Hay Flemming, significant development was taking place), Mitchell planned towards the end of his life to provide an overview of his research in his second series of Baird lectures; but he did not live to put his material into final form. Nevertheless, under the careful editorship of Flemming, *The Scottish Reformation* (1900) embodies, as the editor commented, the fruit of the author's lifelong study 'on many obscure and important points' and represents 'the matured views of one of the most competent and cautious of historical students'.

In the first of the two early short essays mentioned above, published in 1866 and entitled *The Westminster confession of faith: a contribution to the study of its historical relations and to the defence of its teaching*, Mitchell indicated his particular conservative theological stance, and the area of much of his future contribution to the history of presbyterian protestantism. In 1874 he edited, with John Struthers, *The minutes of the sessions of the Westminster assembly of divines: while engaged in preparing their directory for church government, confession of faith and catechisms (November 1644 to March 1649)*. From those sessions emerged the primary standards of presbyterianism that have continued to have a prominent and definitive role in the history of all presbyterian churches originating from the presbyterian churches of the British Isles. In the introduction to this work and in his Baird lectures for 1882, *The Westminster Assembly and its Standards*, Mitchell not only surveyed the chequered history of the assembly itself, but also placed it against its wider background in English puritanism. Other publications of these years reveal his extensive study in catechetical literature generally and especially in that of protestantism.

In addition, Mitchell contributed historical and theological articles to various periodicals and encyclopaedias. He was a founder member of the Scottish History Society (for which he edited in two volumes *The Records of the Commissions of the General Assembly 1646–1650*, in 1892 and 1896), and of the Scottish Text Society. He was one of the representatives of the Church of Scotland at the formation of the Presbyterian Alliance, which was later to become the World Presbyterian Alliance, and played an important part in its early development; he also attended meetings in the United States of America. In 1885 he was elected moderator of the general assembly of the Church of Scotland.

During his forty-six years as a professor in St Andrews, Mitchell gave devoted service to his colleagues and students in St Mary's College and to the university as a member of the senate and, for a time, as one of its assessors on the university court. He was convener of the committee entrusted by the senate with bringing in the report in 1868 which led to the adoption by the university of its much-admired system of academic dress, based on detailed research into the medieval practice at the University of Paris. His alma mater conferred upon him in 1862 the DD degree *honoris causa*, and the University of Glasgow the

honorary degree of LLD in 1892. At the age of seventy-two, under pressure and reluctantly, Mitchell, whose health had never been robust, retired from his chair. He was presented with his portrait by Sir George Reid, president of the Royal Scottish Academy, in 1895.

Mitchell was highly regarded by his contemporaries for his judgement and, although somewhat reserved in expressing his views on contemporary issues and 'rarely a fighter', when some great interest was endangered he was not slow to present himself as its champion, as he did with effect in the disestablishment debate in 1885. In his retirement he divided his time between his house in Brechin and his home in St Andrews, 56 South Street, where he died on 22 March 1899. He was buried in Brechin Cathedral churchyard.   JAMES K. CAMERON

Sources *St Andrews Citizen* (25 March 1899) · *The Scotsman* (23 March 1899) · *The Times* (23 March 1899) · minutes of the Senatus Academicus, 1841–98, U. St Andr., vols. 16, 18–20, 22–3 · J. M. Anderson, ed., *The matriculation roll of the University of St Andrews, 1747–1897* (1905) · J. Christie, Biographical sketch, in A. F. Mitchell, *The Scottish Reformation* (1900), xiii–xliv, 13–44 · *Fasti Scot.*, 427, 433, 446 · *CGPLA Eng. & Wales* (1899)
Archives U. Edin., New Coll. L., corresp. | U. Edin. L., letters to David Lang
Likenesses G. Reid, oils, 1895, U. St Andr., St Mary's College
Wealth at death £2439 13s. 1d.: confirmation, 19 July 1899, *CCI*

Mitchell, Sir Andrew (1708–1771), diplomatist, born in Edinburgh on 15 April 1708, was one of three children and the only surviving son of William Mitchell (1670–1727) and his first wife, Margaret Stewart, *née* Cunningham (d. in or before 1723), the daughter of Sir Hew Cunningham, lord provost of Edinburgh, and the widow of an advocate, James Stewart. His father came from a prominent and wealthy Aberdeenshire family of lairds and was a leading figure in the Church of Scotland: successively minister of the Canongate and St Giles's in Edinburgh, he was one of the king's chaplains for Scotland and moderator of the general assembly on five occasions. A desire to consolidate the family's landed power base was apparent in 1722, when Andrew, then fourteen, was betrothed to his twelve-year-old second cousin, Barbara Mitchell (1710–1726), the only daughter of Thomas Mitchell and his wife, Barbara Forbes, and heir of the family estate of Thainston in Aberdeenshire. Their marriage on 22 July 1722 was short-lived: Barbara died in 1726, soon after giving birth to a daughter who herself did not survive infancy. Andrew Mitchell, widowed at eighteen, never remarried. His father died in September 1727, and from his inheritance and that of his wife he enjoyed an annual income of some £700 sterling. Membership of Aberdeenshire landed society and particularly the links established with the important Forbes family network were to be vital in his career.

Mitchell had begun the study of law at Edinburgh University in 1723, and in 1725 had been articled to an advocate. But in the summer of 1729 he left Scotland and, following a stay of several months in London, in December of that year set out on the grand tour. This took him first to the Dutch Republic and Germany, with two semesters studying law at Leiden University, and then on to Paris, which he reached by July 1731. After leaving the French capital in early 1732 he made leisurely progress south through France and into the Italian peninsula, spending eighteen months in Rome. Following a further stay in Paris he returned to London in December 1735. The six years during which Mitchell was travelling on the continent, apart from the conventional visits to churches, art collections, and sites of historical and cultural interest prescribed by the grand tour, were notable for the time he spent in the company of philosophers and writers and for the knowledge he acquired of French and Italian. His enduring friendship with the philosopher Montesquieu, whom he had first met in London in 1729, was especially significant. For the remainder of his life Mitchell would retain strong literary and scientific interests; he was elected to the Royal Society in 1736 and became a member of its council four years later. On his return to England at the end of 1735 he resumed his legal studies, and was admitted to the Faculty of Advocates in Edinburgh in 1736 and called to the English bar two years later.

In 1741 Mitchell turned his back on the law and took the first overt step towards a career in public life by becoming the private secretary of John Hay, fourth marquess of Tweeddale. When Tweeddale (for whom the post was revived) became secretary of state for Scotland in the following year he appointed Mitchell as his under-secretary. Although the burdens of the post were not at first especially onerous, the outbreak of the Jacobite rising in 1745 increased his duties. Mitchell left office when Tweeddale was dismissed in January 1746, but continued to be consulted by the government about the pacification of Scotland after the rising had been suppressed. Duncan Forbes of Culloden, then lord president of the court of session, was a relative and sought his advice. In 1747 another relative, Sir Arthur Forbes, stood down from the Aberdeenshire constituency in his favour, and Mitchell served as its MP until 1754. In the following year he was elected for Elgin burghs, within which his own estate of Thainston was located, which he continued to represent until his death in 1771.

For most of the time that Mitchell was an MP he was abroad serving as a diplomat. Indeed, he had viewed his original election as a step towards employment in government service. Like many able and ambitious Scotsmen of his generation, he found it difficult to secure advancement in England during a period when anti-Scottish prejudice was rife. He was instead to make his career in diplomacy, for which his knowledge of languages and of Europe in any case fitted him. In 1752 he was sent to Brussels as a trade commissioner, to take part in some complex and inconclusive commercial negotiations, which dragged on intermittently until late 1755, over the modification of the 1715 barrier treaty. He was by now firmly attached to the duke of Newcastle, but his continuing hopes of employment at home were unrealized. In April 1756, through the intermediacy of another patron, Lord Holdernesse, then secretary of state for the northern department, he was offered and accepted the post of minister to Prussia. He was to remain there until his death: in 1760 he was promoted to the rank of minister-plenipotentiary and in 1766 he returned to Berlin as envoy-extraordinary and -plenipotentiary.

Mitchell was the most successful British representative in Berlin during the entire eighteenth century. Britain's relations with Prussia were traditionally distant and complicated by the position of Hanover, and the Berlin legation was far from a prized posting at this period. Events, however, were about to make it quite central to British foreign policy. In January 1756 the two states had signed a vague agreement to uphold the neutrality of Germany, should the Anglo-French war under way in the colonies spread to Europe and threaten the Electorate, the so-called convention of Westminster. This triggered the celebrated diplomatic revolution of that year, by which Britain and Prussia found themselves on the same side in the Seven Years' War of 1756–63. Prussia's king, Frederick the Great (r. 1740–86), was anxious for good relations with London and, in particular, for British financial and naval support in his struggle for survival against a coalition headed by Austria, France, and Russia. From his very first audiences in mid-May 1756, Frederick took a liking to the bluff, straightforward, and humorous Scot, who shared his literary interests and, more important, spoke his mind and debated with the king as an equal—rather than being subservient, as many diplomats were wont to be.

Mitchell's contribution to the smooth operation of the Anglo-Prussian partnership during the early years of the Seven Years' War was considerable. He quickly became a close friend of Frederick's and was admitted to his private society, while his lively conversation won him an ever-widening circle of friends in Berlin. Exceptionally, he was allowed to accompany Frederick on campaign, which he did throughout much of the war, until his own health failed. The coming to power in 1757 of William Pitt for a time imparted considerable warmth to the relationship. An annual treaty, concluded for the first time in the spring of 1758 and renewed each year until the earl of Bute refused to do so in 1762, gave Frederick a subsidy of £670,000 per annum and more substantial support in the shape of a British-financed 'army of observation' which fought in Westphalia for the rest of the war and protected Prussia's vulnerable western flank. The Anglo-Prussian partnership, however, had a largely accidental origin and was increasingly marked by strain and mutual distrust. At first Mitchell sought and, to some extent, succeeded in papering over the cracks, and in so doing came to be suspected of being more Prussian than British in his sympathies, a common fate of effective diplomats at this period. This was one reason for his reduced role in Anglo-Prussian diplomacy, which after 1758 came to be transacted primarily in London rather than Berlin.

As the years passed Mitchell grew more critical of the king, whose increasing harshness was more and more evident. Frederick's brutal treatment of occupied Saxony, despoiled to finance Prussia's war, was especially important in this alienation. Mitchell's unique relationship with him, however, was weakened, not destroyed, and this enabled him to survive the acrimonious breach in relations in 1762 and the bitter and distant diplomacy which followed. Frederick believed that he had been 'deserted' by his perfidious British ally, and this poisoned relations with London throughout the second half of his reign. Although Mitchell remained in Berlin for the rest of his life, returning to Britain only in 1764–6 when relations were particularly acrimonious and the level of representation was temporarily downgraded, his political importance was at an end. He remained at his post and discharged such official business as he was called upon to transact, which was little enough. His hopes of preferment at home continued to be disappointed, though he finally became a knight of the Bath and was granted a pension of £500 for life in December 1765. Like many Scotsmen during the eighteenth century, he found that a diplomatic career, originally undertaken as a route to eventual advancement at home, instead became a permanent vocation. This diaspora imparted a strongly professional element to Britain's eighteenth-century diplomatic service. During the final decade of his life, Mitchell enjoyed the company of the wide circle of academic and literary friends he had built up in Berlin, retained the respect and grudging friendship of the king, and lived out what amounted to an honourable semi-retirement. He died of pleurisy in the Prussian capital on 28 January 1771 and was buried in Berlin's Dorotheenstädtische Kirche on 1 February. A marble memorial was put up by the king's brother, Prince Henry of Prussia, and by his other friends in the Hohenzollern capital, testifying to the strong friendships which had been so central to Mitchell's life and which had survived the vicissitudes of Anglo-Prussian diplomacy.

H. M. SCOTT

Sources P. F. Doran, *Andrew Mitchell and Anglo-Prussian diplomatic relations during the Seven Years War* (1986) · *Memoirs and papers of Sir Andrew Mitchell, K.B.*, ed. A. Bisset, 2 vols. (1850) · E. Haden-Guest, 'Mitchell, Sir Andrew', HoP, *Commons, 1754–90* · *DNB* · IGI
Archives BL, Add. MSS 58283–58367, corresp. and papers · BL, corresp., dispatches, etc., Add. MSS 6804–6871 · Craigievar Castle, Aberdeenshire · NA Scot., papers · NRA Scotland, priv. coll., diplomatic papers · PRO, state papers, foreign, official dispatches | BL, corresp. with Lord Holdernesse, Egerton MSS 3455, 3460–3461 · BL, letters to Robert Keith, Add. MSS 35474–35485 *passim* · BL, corresp. with duke of Newcastle, Add. MSS 32711–33055 *passim* · BL, corresp. with Lord Sandwich and Richard Phelps, Stowe MSS 257–259 *passim* · NA Scot., letters to Robert Craigie · NA Scot., letters to Sir Archibald Grant · NA Scot., letters to George Warrender · NL Scot., corresp. with Duncan Forbes · NL Scot., corresp. with the fourth marquess of Tweeddale · NRA Scotland, priv. coll., corresp. with Lord Stormont · Yale U., Farmington, Lewis Walpole Library, letters to Edward Weston
Likenesses portrait, 1766 (after A. Ramsay), NPG
Wealth at death heir was relative, Sir Arthur Forbes

Mitchell, Sir Andrew (1757–1806), naval officer, was the second son of Charles Mitchell of Baldridge, near Dunfermline, Fife. Educated at the Edinburgh high school, he entered the navy in 1771 on the *Deal Castle*. After serving in different ships on the home station, in 1776 he went out to the East Indies in the *Ripon* with Sir Edward Vernon who promoted him lieutenant of the frigate *Coventry* (11 October 1777), and captain of that ship after the skirmish off Pondicherry on 10 August 1778. His post rank was confirmed by the Admiralty as of 25 October 1778.

Mitchell continued in the *Coventry* after Sir Edward Hughes took command of the station, and on 12 August 1782 he fought a severe but indecisive action with the French frigate *Bellona* (40 guns) off Friar's Hood in Ceylon. In September Hughes appointed him to the *Sultan*, in which he took part in the fight off Cuddalore on 20 June 1783. After the peace Mitchell remained on the station as commodore of a small squadron, with his broad pennant in the *Defence*. He returned to England in 1786, having acquired in ten years' service a very considerable sum in prize money, which was lost by the bankruptcy of his agent. In the Spanish armament of 1790 he commanded the *Asia* (74 guns), which was paid off on the settlement of the dispute. He was unemployed until February 1795 when he was appointed to the *Impregnable* (90 guns), in the Channel Fleet. Promotion to rear-admiral of the blue followed on 1 June 1795.

On 14 February 1799 Mitchell was advanced to vice-admiral, and in April he was appointed to a command in the North Sea under Lord Duncan. In August he had charge of the transports for the expedition to the Netherlands and though Duncan himself convoyed them across and superintended the disembarkation of the troops, he left further operations to Mitchell. On 30 August he received the surrender of the Dutch ships, following the mutiny of the Dutch seamen, who refused to fight against allies of the prince of Orange. Dutch forces on shore took a different view of the situation, and in conjunction with the French repulsed the British and Russian army. The duke of York, who was in command, had no option but to ask for an armistice. In the meantime Mitchell, with a squadron of small vessels, had gained control of the Zuyder Zee, but bound by the same treaty, he too withdrew his ships. Subsequently neither he nor Sir Ralph Abercromby, who had commanded the army at its first landing, received any blame for the ignominious termination of the campaign. In fact the thanks of parliament were given to both, as well as to the officers and men, and Mitchell was nominated a KB on 9 January 1800. The City of London also presented him with a sword valued at 100 guineas.

During 1800 and 1801 Mitchell served in the Channel Fleet under Lord St Vincent and Admiral William Cornwallis, and in November 1801 he commanded a detached squadron to the coast of Ireland and to Bantry Bay. In December, on some of the ships being ordered to the West Indies, a mutiny broke out, especially on the *Téméraire*, the flagship of Rear-Admiral George Campbell. The mutiny was suppressed, and some twenty of the ringleaders were brought to Spithead, to be tried by court martial. Mitchell presided at the trial, in which the greater number were found guilty and executed. In spring 1802 Mitchell was appointed commander-in-chief on the North American station. On 9 November 1805 he was made a full admiral, but after a short illness he died at Bermuda on 26 February 1806, and was buried there with military honours.

Mitchell was survived by his second wife, a native of Halifax, Nova Scotia (of whom further details are unknown), and his three sons from his first marriage—Charles, Nathaniel, and Andrew—who all achieved the rank of captain in the navy.

J. K. LAUGHTON, rev. P. L. C. WEBB

Sources J. Ralfe, *The naval biography of Great Britain*, 4 vols. (1828) • W. James, *The naval history of Great Britain, from the declaration of war by France in 1793, to the accession of George IV*, [5th edn], 6 vols. (1859–60), vol. 2 • *Naval Chronicle*, 16 (1806), 89–107 • J. Marshall, *Royal naval biography*, 1 (1823) • D. Syrett and R. L. DiNardo, *The commissioned sea officers of the Royal Navy, 1660–1815*, rev. edn, Occasional Publications of the Navy RS, 1 (1994) • R. Beatson, *Naval and military memoirs of Great Britain*, 2nd edn, 6 (1804), 360
Archives Morgan L., list of Dutch vessels taken in the expedition against Holland | PRO, Admiralty 'In Letters'
Likenesses mezzotint, pubd 1799 (after unknown artist), NPG • J. Chapman, stipple, pubd 1800, NPG • L. F. Abbott, oils, Dunfermline Town Council; copy, NMM • Bowyer, engraving, repro. in *Catalogue of the naval exhibition, 1891* • H. R. Cook, stipple (after R. Bowyer), BM, NPG; repro. in *Naval Chronicle*, 89 • engraving, NMM • print, NMM

Mitchell, Sir Arthur (1826–1909), commissioner in lunacy for Scotland and antiquary, born at Elgin, Moray, on 19 January 1826, was the son of George Mitchell, CE, and his wife, Elizabeth Cant. He was educated at Elgin Academy and graduated MA at Aberdeen University in 1845, before pursuing the study of medicine at Paris, Berlin, and Vienna, and gaining his MD at Aberdeen in 1850. He married Margaret (d. 1904), daughter of James Houston of Tullochgriban, Strathspey, in 1855; they had one son.

Devoting himself to mental illness, Mitchell quickly showed an aptitude for this area of medicine. When the Lunacy Act of 1857 was passed, he was chosen as one of the deputy commissioners for Scotland, and was commissioner from May 1870 to September 1895. He was an enthusiastic proponent of the Scottish system of boarding out the insane, which he described and advocated in his book *The Insane in Private Dwellings* (1864). Considerable support was found for his views in Scotland and abroad, although the profession remained rather dubious towards the adaptability of the system to England. From 1880 to 1881 he was a member of the English commission on criminal lunacy, and his experience considerably influenced the report upon which the act of 1880 was founded. In 1885 he served on the departmental committee on criminal lunatics in Ireland and was chairman of the Irish commission on lunacy administration from 1888 to 1891.

From May 1869 until March 1872 Mitchell was Morison lecturer on insanity to the Royal College of Physicians of Edinburgh. Among the subjects he dealt with were the medico-legal relations and the curability of insanity and the extent and effects of consanguineous marriages. He published much of this and other research in numerous articles in the medical journals.

Mitchell also had a keen interest in antiquarian studies. In 1861 he was appointed a corresponding member, and in 1867 he was elected a fellow, of the Society of Antiquaries of Scotland, and he continued an active member until his death, serving as secretary and vice-president. His researches dealt largely with existing superstitions in the Scottish highlands, especially in their bearing on problems of insanity. He contributed many papers to the *Proceedings*, culminating in a series on Scottish topographers (1901–9). In 1876 Mitchell was the first Rhind lecturer in archaeology, and delivered three courses of six lectures each which were published under the title *The Past in the Present: what is Civilisation?* (1880). Mitchell was one of the founders of the Scottish History Society, and was a member of council and vice-president. He edited for the society *Macfarlane's Topographical Collections* (3 vols., 1906–8). He was also president of the Scottish Text Society and professor of ancient history to the Royal Scottish Academy from 1878. He was a member of the royal commission on Scottish universities in 1889, and served until 1900. He was also president (1908) of the Royal Meteorology Society and a council member of the Scottish Meteorology Society.

In 1886 Mitchell was made CB and in 1887 KCB. He received the honorary degree of LLD from Aberdeen in 1875, and became honorary fellow of the Royal College of Physicians of Ireland in 1891. He died at his home, 34 Drummond Place, Edinburgh, on 12 October 1909, and was buried in Rosebank cemetery, Edinburgh.

Besides the works mentioned and editions of Andrew Combe's *Observations on Mental Derangement* (1887) and *Management of Infancy* (1896), Mitchell published, in 1905, *About Dreaming, Laughing, and Blushing*.

A. H. MILLAR, rev. JONATHAN ANDREWS

Sources *The Scotsman* (13 Oct 1909) • *Dundee Advertiser* (13 Oct 1909) • *The Lancet* (23 Oct 1909) • *Journal of Mental Science*, 56 (1910), 378–80 • private information (1912) • A. S. Bell, ed., *The Scottish antiquarian tradition* (1981) • *DNB* • *Journal of Psychological Medicine* (1909) • CGPLA Eng. & Wales (1910)
Likenesses N. Macbeth, oils, 1880 • J. H. Lorimer, pencil drawing, 1891, Scot. NPG • G. Reid, oils, 1896, Scot. NPG • W. G. Boss, pencil drawing, Scot. NPG • J. Faed, mezzotint (after G. Reid), Wellcome L.
Wealth at death £29,931 12s. 2d.: confirmation, 18 Feb 1910, CCI • £1106 15s. 9d.: eik additional estate, 5 April 1911, CCI

Mitchell, Charles (1807–1859), advertising agent and publisher of the first British press directory, was born in Norwich and baptized on 22 March 1807 at St Giles's Church, Norwich. He was the son of Robert Mitchell, a fruiterer, and his wife, Letitia, née Moore. Of his first marriage nothing is known, but on 27 May 1839 he married, as a widower, Eliza Wellsman (née Rogers), an innkeeper's widowed daughter, at the parish church of St Benedict, Norwich.

Fresh from an apprenticeship under Thomas Sowler, founder in 1825 of the *Manchester Courier*, a conservative paper in opposition to the *Manchester Guardian*, he founded in 1837 C. Mitchell & Co., one of the earliest advertising agencies, there being at the time probably no more than two or three others in the British Isles and none in Europe and America. In the quaint little offices at 12–13 Red Lion Court, Fleet Street (demolished by 1912), he became acquainted with or had business dealings with the great journalists of the day, including Charles Dickens, Mark Lemon, Shirley Brooks of *Punch*, and Stirling Coyne, drama critic of the *Sunday Times* and a co-signatory of the foundation document of *Punch*. The exact circumstances of *Punch's* establishment remain unclear, but according to the *City Press* of 27 June 1892 Mitchell frequently asserted that the comic journal originated with him, Brooks, Henry Mayhew, and Ebenezer Landells. In his magisterial *History of 'Punch'* (p. 32) M. H. Spielmann merely notes that the printing was executed by Mitchell.

As a publisher Mitchell issued the dramatic works of John Westland Marston (1819–1890), notably his heroic blank verse poem 'The Patrician's Daughter' (1842–3), and in 1853 he acted as agent and publisher for a prospectus for the Athenaeum Institute in Sackville Street.

Mitchell's place in newspaper history stems directly from his chosen role of advertising agent for town and country newspapers. Awareness of a gap in the market prompted his decision in March 1846 to issue the first edition of the *Newspaper Press Directory*. Preceded by the intermittent *Advertisers' Guide to the Newspaper Press of the United Kingdom* (1844) and *S. Deacon's Correct List of All the English, Scotch and Irish Newspapers* (1846), the latter 'distinguishing those of Conservative Principles', Mitchell's directory promised to offer a regular and 'more dignified and permanent record' replacing the more fugitive handbooks which he claimed inadequately promoted the 'interests of the proprietors' and failed to guide advertisers in the choice of media best suited to their needs. Numerically slim as was the newspaper press at the time, the enterprise demanded great ability, tact, and judgement. Published initially in 1846, 1847, 1851, and 1854, and annually after 1856, this, among the eldest of all trade directories, offered generally impartial coverage of the national press. The earlier octavo volumes are primarily geographical indexes covering London, the provinces, the Channel Islands and Isle of Man, Scotland, Ireland, and Wales, with alphabetical cross-indexes. While reserving judgement on aims and characteristics, the directory's pen portraits of individual newspapers were generally friendly though naturally governed by self-interested commercialism and the wish for future generous treatment and advertisement allocation. There was surprisingly little early information on rates or circulation figures. Religious 'advocacy' was given as much prominence as political affiliation. Entries varied in length and it is salutary to observe the warm welcome given to the closely coincidental arrival of the *Daily News*, in January 1846. Edited for twenty days by Dickens, with the assistance of John Forster and George Hogarth, the new paper was described in the directory as 'an organ which includes so eminently the men who at once guide and represent the public mind', lauding those leading minds who had not 'received their principles from tradition, but evolved them from a vivid and primary experience of life'. The post-Dickens entry was significantly perfunctory. Due deference was paid in the first issue to *The Times*, whose influence Mitchell felt to be 'co-extensive with civilization'. Uniquely featured in the 1846 issue was the topical theme of 'railway papers' (eighteen titles). A year later the railway mania bubble had evidently burst, the list having completely disappeared.

Editorship passed in 1859 to Mitchell's adopted stepson Walter Wellsman (1834–1911), then in his mid-twenties but well versed since schooldays in proof-reading and editorial duties and destined to become a most durable editor and a significant press historian. A notable collector also of Dickens memorabilia, Wellsman expanded the directory's scope by adding in 1860 an index of magazines and periodicals and a national newspaper map. Subsequent additions included an index of continental newspapers (1878), an index of American papers (1879), and a colonial supplement in 1885/6. Mitchell was strongly opposed to the abolition of stamp duty in 1855, which he feared would reduce press respectability to the level of American papers. But with the first change of format to 'extra imperial' in 1854 (at the reduced price of a florin), due coverage was accorded to the highly contentious issue of press emancipation. Mitchell's death on 8 February 1859 at his home at 1 Edith Villas, Edith Grove, Chelsea, London, was reportedly as the result of a serious railway accident the previous year. The indispensable reference work he founded continues to this day in three volumes as *Benn's Media*.   GORDON PHILLIPS

Sources *Newspaper Press Directory* (1891) · *Newspaper Press Directory* (1912) · D. Linton, 'A classic among dictionaries', *Media Reporter*, 1/3 (1977), 14–15 · D. Linton, 'Mr Mitchell's national work', *Journal of Advertising History*, 2 (1979) · S. Gliserman, 'Mitchell's *Newspaper Press Directory*: 1846–1907', *Victorian Periodicals Newsletter*, 2/1 (1969), 10–29 · D. Griffiths, ed., *The encyclopedia of the British press, 1422–1992* (1992) · W. Wellsman, 'Fleet Street 1846–1890', *Newspaper Press Directory* (1891) · Boase, *Mod. Eng. biog.* · M. H. Spielmann, *The history of 'Punch'* (1895) · *N&Q*, 3rd ser., 1 (1862), 479 · *N&Q*, 3rd ser., 2 (1862), 38 · IGI · m. cert. · d. cert.
Likenesses oils, repro. in Linton, 'Mr Mitchell's national work', 31
Wealth at death under £5000: probate, 17 March 1859, *CGPLA Eng. & Wales*

Mitchell, Charles Watson [Charlie] (1861–1918), pugilist, the youngest of nine children of James Lackerman Mitchell and his wife, Sarah Watson, was born on 20 November 1861 at Sydenham medical college, Summer Lane, Birmingham, where his father was lodge porter (although subsequently described as 'surgeon' and 'medical curator'). He was educated at Christ Church School, Birmingham, and King Edward's Grammar School, also in Birmingham. At the time the prize-ring was not yet extinct and Mitchell's career coincided with boxing's transitional period from the bare-knuckle era to the sport known today.

Mitchell's first fight was in the old style on 11 January 1878, at Birmingham, against Bob Cunningham, a local man. Mitchell won, following a hard battle of fifty minutes. Thereafter, in a period spanning some three years, he fought in Wolverhampton, London, Manchester, and Antwerp, sometimes with bare knuckles, at other times with gloves. In his first real test, in May 1881, he defeated Tom Tully in a glove bout lasting six rounds. The performance encouraged supporters to back him against the Irish Lad, Jack Burke, and on 16 June the two men participated in a 25 round, drawn contest at Ascot, under prize-ring rules.

For this Mitchell was sentenced to six weeks' hard labour and he did not appear in the ring again until spring the following year, when he won a 10 stone 7 lb competition at Chelsea. His next engagement was in December 1882 in William Madden's open championship competition. The youngest and lightest competitor, he beat Dick Roberts in the final to be proclaimed champion of England.

After a tour of the country Madden took Mitchell to America, where on 9 April 1883 he outclassed Mike Cleary. The match, under Queensberry rules, was stopped by police in the third round. This led to a four-round glove contest with John L. Sullivan on 14 May in which Mitchell, much the smaller man, floored the redoubtable American champion for the first time in his career. However, weight told and in the third round, with the Bostonian dominating, police intervened and Sullivan was declared winner.

Mitchell spent virtually all of the next four years in America, where he toured with great success. Among the better-class men he encountered, in glove bouts of varying lengths, were William Sheriff, Jake Kilrain, Billy Edwards, Dominick McCaffrey, Jack Burke (four more times), Mike Cleary again, and Patsy Cardiff. He lost but once, a surprise decision, to McCaffrey on 13 October 1884, although Kilrain did succeed in winning the $100 on offer for standing up to Mitchell for four rounds.

During this time abortive efforts were again made to match Mitchell with his great rival Sullivan. On the first occasion (30 June 1884) the American arrived drunk and refused to set to, claiming illness. In the summer of 1886 another attempt was prohibited by the authorities in both Chicago and New York. The two men eventually met on 10 March 1888 in a bare-knuckle encounter near Chantilly, France. Mitchell fought a clever, cautious fight in atrocious conditions and was the fresher of the two when, after 39 rounds occupying nearly 3 hours 11 minutes, both men assented to a draw. The veteran Jem Mace was defeated next, in Glasgow on 7 February 1890, in a four-round glove match for £1000. Mitchell's final contest occurred at Jacksonville, Florida, on 25 January 1894; past his best, he succumbed in three rounds to Sullivan's conqueror, James J. Corbett.

Mitchell's height was fractionally over 5ft 9in and, in his prime, he weighed little more than a middleweight. His motto inside the ring was 'brain will beat brawn' but outside he could be quick to take offence. However, he was not always at fault, for when in October 1892 Mitchell was sentenced to two months' imprisonment for assault, it would appear that he took the blame for a fellow pugilist. He was utterly fearless and anecdotes abound of his courage when faced with violent gangs and bullies. He was also highly intelligent, and the sporting journalist R. P. Watson paid tribute to his 'mental qualifications' as being unsurpassed by other fighting men of the time (Watson, 248). On 4 November 1886 Mitchell married Victoria Alexandra, daughter of George Washington Moore of the Moore and Burgess Minstrels, and for a time he managed the Washington Music Hall, Battersea, London, for his father-in-

law. Mitchell died on 2 April 1918 at his home, 34 Goldstone Villas, Hove, Sussex, and was buried four days later in Hove cemetery. TONY GEE

Sources A. G. Hales, 'The life of Charlie Mitchell', *Sporting Chronicle* [Manchester] (9 April–23 July 1918) · 'The life and battles of Charlie Mitchell', *Health and Strength* (1909) · *Sporting Life* (4 April 1918) · *Evening Despatch* [Birmingham] (4 April 1918) · *Sporting Chronicle* [Manchester] (4 April 1918) · *The Sportsman* (4 April 1918) · *The Times* (4 April 1918) · fight reports, etc., *New York Times*, *Sporting Life*, *New York Tribune*, *Chicago Tribune*, *Bell's Life In London*, *Sporting Chronicle* [Manchester], *The Sportsman*, *Daily Picayune* [New Orleans], *Boston Post*, *Daily Examiner* [San Francisco], *Minneapolis Tribune*, *Evening Citizen* [Glasgow], *The World* [New York] · b. cert. · m. cert. · d. cert. · R. P. Watson, *Memoirs of Robert Patrick Watson: a journalist's experience of mixed society* (1899), 62–5, 248 · *The Times* (8 Oct 1892) · 'Performances of Charlie Mitchell (the English boxing champion)', *Sporting Life* (10 March 1883) · W. E. Harding, 'Charley Mitchell', *The champions of the American prize ring* (New York, 1881); repr. (1993), 46–9 · E. Van Every, 'Mr Sullivan and Mr Fox', *Sins of New York as 'exposed' by the Police Gazette* (1972), 266, 268–9 · H. Preston, *Memories* (1928), 100–101 · CGPLA Eng. & Wales (1918) · private information (1946)
Likenesses cigarette card, 1908 (*Ogden's pugilists and wrestlers*), repro. in T. Gee, *John L. Sullivan, cradle to grave*, booklet (1998)
Wealth at death £5437 16s. 10d.: resworn probate, 10 May 1918, CGPLA Eng. & Wales

Mitchell, Colin Campbell (1925–1996), army officer and politician, was born on 17 November 1925 at 44 Brigstock Road, West Croydon, London, the younger child and only son of Colin Mitchell, solicitor's managing clerk, of Thornton Heath, Surrey, and his wife, Janet Bowie, *née* Gilmour. Both parents were Scottish, and Campbell and his sister, Hettie, felt that they were very much Scots living among English people. Their father had enlisted as a private in the Highland light infantry in August 1914, but was soon commissioned into the 10th battalion of the Argyll and Sutherland Highlanders and won a Military Cross at the second battle of Ypres, before being badly gassed. After the war he returned to his work in a solicitors' office, and later as an arbitrator. Mitchell's maternal grandfather, John Gilmour, was the carting superintendent of the old London, Midland, and Scottish Railway. One of Mitchell's earliest thrills was being taken round the large stables of Clydesdale horses, which in those days plodded majestically through the cobbled streets of Glasgow pulling the freight and merchandise to and from railway yards, docks, and warehouses. He was educated at Streatham grammar school and the Whitgift School, Croydon.

In May 1943 Mitchell walked out of the Whitgift School into the Croydon recruiting office and enlisted in the army as 14432057 Private Mitchell in the General Service Corps. Soon he became a lance-corporal, and instructed newcomers in physical training, in the old barracks beside Maidstone prison. The staff sergeant instructor was none other than Stanley Cullis, who had been captain of the cup-winning Wolverhampton Wanderers side at Wembley in 1939, and was the captain of England at the time. Mitchell later recalled, 'I felt like a fly on the wall of Olympus to be living so close to the great man' (personal knowledge). From Cullis, Mitchell learned to engender loyalty. He was superb at handling those below him: with his superiors, his relations were altogether less satisfactory.

Colin Campbell Mitchell (1925–1996), by unknown
photographer

Commissioned into the 8th battalion of the Argyll and
Sutherland Highlanders in 1944, he fought up the spine of
Italy, and was wounded in the battle for the Argenta Gap.

Having recovered, Mitchell, who had decided to make a
career in the army, joined the 1st Argylls in Palestine,
where he served in the difficult years (1945–8), when the
Jewish Irgunzwai Leumi made the lives of soldiers in the
British army extremely dangerous. Brother officers
thought that it was in Palestine that Mitchell developed
his perceptive military mind in dealing with insurgency.
In Palestine he was again wounded, this time by one of his
own bren-gunners. After a brief spell as aide-de-camp to
General Sir Gordon Macmillan he joined his regiment in
Korea, where he took part in the advance to Taechon, and
the subsequent retreat following the intervention of Chinese forces. Over the winter of 1950–51 Mitchell's Argylls
held 'Frostbite Ridge' where, as he recalled, even anti-
freeze froze. Various staff appointments followed, and in
1955 he qualified at Staff College, Camberley. On 31 March
1956 he married Jean Hamilton (Susan) Phillips (b.
1930/31), secretary, and daughter of Stephen Phillips, of
independent means. They had two sons and a daughter.

At the end of 1957 Mitchell returned to the 1st battalion
of the Argylls as company commander, and he went on to
serve with them in Cyprus in 1958–9 at the height of the
Eoka campaign. Following his regiment's posting to the
British army of the Rhine, he applied successfully for service with the King's African rifles in Kenya. There he took
part in the restoration of order in Zanzibar and in various
operations on the northern frontier. From Kenya he
rejoined the Argylls in Borneo, where for six months in
1964 they engaged in undeclared jungle warfare with

Indonesian forces. Mitchell was promoted brevet
lieutenant-colonel in recognition of his leadership qualities. He was then posted home as GSO1 to the chief of
defence staff, Earl Mountbatten of Burma, whom he
found an exacting superior.

In 1967 Mitchell was posted in command of the 1st
Argylls in Aden, where the British occupation was being
strongly challenged by a nationalist insurgency. On 20
June police mutineers joined the anti-colonialists to seize
control of the Crater district of the city, with the loss of
twenty-two British soldiers, including several Argylls, several others being unaccounted for. Ignoring the express
intentions of his commanding officer, General Philip
Tower, on the night of 3–4 July Mitchell led the Argylls,
with bayonets fixed and their pipers playing the regimental charge, 'Monymusk', in reoccupying the district, with
the loss of one (Arab) life. Mitchell and the Argylls held the
district until the British withdrawal five months later.
'They know if they start trouble we'll blow their bloody
heads off', he was reported as saying (*Daily Telegraph*).
Mitchell's actions brought him immediate acclaim from
wide sections of the British media, who dubbed him 'Mad
Mitch' (not a sobriquet that he relished later in life). One of
the last popular heroes produced by the British empire, he
was also one of the first heroes created by television.
Nevertheless his actions did not endear him to his superiors, the Ministry of Defence, or the Labour government,
which was intent on withdrawing from southern Arabia
and other outposts of empire. The rights and wrongs of
the 'Crater Affair' were the subject of books and numerous television programmes. But the flavour of Mitchell's
difficulty with those above him was encapsulated in his
autobiography, *Having been a Soldier* (1969):

> General Tower was an Artillery Officer, and as far as I was
> aware he had not taken part in any operations since the end
> of the war in 1945. This gave him little common ground with
> the Argylls. Like the Commander-in-Chief, General Tower
> worked in the massive headquarters complex on Barrack
> Hill, Steamer Point, overlooking the Arabian Sea. Its view of
> blue sea and golden beaches was very different from the
> squalid alleys and bazaars of Crater cut off as if in a different
> world by the thousand-foot peaks and ridges dividing them.
> (*The Independent*)

Mitchell was mentioned in dispatches for his actions in
Aden but, pointedly, was not awarded the DSO or MC,
unlike other officers of the same rank who served in Aden.
It was also made clear to him that he could not expect to
rise further in the army. To personal pique was added
indignation in 1968, when Mitchell learned that the Ministry of Defence intended to disband the Argylls, as the 'junior' Highland regiment. He retired at his own request the
same year. He immediately threw himself into the 'Save
the Argylls' campaign, which achieved partial success:
though reduced to a single company, the Argylls were
saved from disbandment or amalgamation. Mitchell also
served as Vietnam correspondent for the *Daily Express*, and
was adopted as Conservative candidate for West Aberdeenshire.

In the general election of 1970 Mitchell was elected to
parliament by 18,396 to the 12,847 of Laura Grimond, wife

of the Liberal Party leader. His maiden speech amounted to a ferocious criticism of recent defence cuts. He supported a continued British presence east of Suez, and warned of the dangers of Soviet expansionism. At home, he foresaw 'a weak and ideologically subverted Britain offering a temptation to communism … I believe that the day will come when the British Army, particularly, will be concerned with counter-subversion on the ground in this country' (*The Guardian*). He spoke in several defence debates and was, briefly, a member of the select committee on the armed services. He was also, briefly, a parliamentary private secretary to the secretary of state for Scotland, but he was too independent-minded to hold the position for long. He voted against the government on a number of occasions, including a debate on membership of the Common Market in 1971. He was by no means a conventional right-winger: he was vehemently opposed to apartheid, and was a strong supporter of devolution for Scotland.

Mitchell decided not to contest his seat at the February 1974 election. When he left the House of Commons he hoped to be involved in promoting sporting estates, but the opportunity fell through. He then, for a number of years, engaged in consultancy work based on his military experience: he advised Ian Smith in Rhodesia, the mujahhedin in Afghanistan, and the Contras in Nicaragua. His experiences in Afghanistan led him to establish, in 1987, with other former military personnel, the Halo Trust (Hazardous Areas Life-Support Organisation), dedicated to clearing landmines and unexploded shells from areas of former conflict. Mitchell served as an active first chairman of the trust until his death, travelling frequently to Afghanistan, Cambodia, Mozambique, Angola, and other countries to establish and supervise the work of Halo teams.

Mitchell died of cancer at Beaumont House, Beaumont Street, Westminster, on 20 July 1996. He was survived by his ever-supportive wife of forty years, Susan, and by their three children.   Tam Dalyell

Sources C. Mitchell, *Having been a soldier* (1969) · *The Independent* (24 July 1996) · *The Guardian* (24 July 1996) · *The Times* (24 July 1996) · *Daily Telegraph* (24 July 1996) · *WWW* · personal knowledge (2004) · private information (2004) · b. cert. · m. cert. · d. cert.
Likenesses photograph, 1967, repro. in *Daily Telegraph* · two photographs, 1967–*c*.1970, repro. in *The Guardian* · photograph, repro. in *The Independent* · photograph, repro. in *The Times* [*see illus.*]
Wealth at death under £180,000: probate, 6 Jan 1997, *CGPLA Eng. & Wales*

Mitchell, Cornelius (*fl.* 1709–1748), naval officer, entered the navy in 1709 on the *Ranelagh*, then carrying the flag of Sir John Norris in the channel. On 22 December 1720 Commodore Charles Stewart, in the Mediterranean, promoted him lieutenant of the *Dover*, an appointment which was confirmed on 2 December 1721. On 25 January 1726 Mitchell was second lieutenant of the *Weymouth*, and in June 1729 he was appointed third lieutenant to the *Lion* going out to the West Indies with the flag of his old patron Rear-Admiral Charles Stewart. On 14 June 1731 Stewart appointed Mitchell captain of the *Lark*, which he took to England

and paid off in the following February. From that time he had no service until August 1739, when he was appointed to the *Rochester*. In September of the following year he was moved into the *Buckingham*, in which he sailed for the West Indies in the fleet under Sir Chaloner Ogle. However, the *Buckingham* was disabled in a storm on the way out, and returned home. Mitchell, appointed to the *Kent*, went out later. In July 1745 he was moved into the *Strafford*, and in December of that year, with the *Plymouth* and *Lyme* frigates in company, he convoyed a fleet of merchant ships through the Windward Passage. On 15 December he fell in with three French ships of war off Cape Nicolas. A slight engagement ensued, and, content with having beaten off the enemy, Mitchell pursued his voyage. A court martial afterwards decided that he was justified in so doing, as the French force was superior, and the safety of the convoy his first consideration.

In August 1746 Mitchell was again in command of a squadron, and again met a French squadron off Cape Nicolas, but this time the circumstances were reversed. The French had the convoy and Mitchell the superior force, consisting of four ships of the line, and a small frigate. Mitchell hesitated to attack, and when the French, encouraged by his apparent timidity, chased, he fled under a press of sail. At night he gave orders to show no lights, but did not part company with the enemy; day after day the experience was repeated. Once only did the squadrons engage, and after a few broadsides Mitchell drew off. On the tenth day, 13 August, the French entered the harbour of Cape François.

With Ogle sick and incapable, Mitchell was the next senior officer on the station and, although his conduct was criticized, no further action was taken. It was only when the affair was reported to the Admiralty that special orders were sent out to try him by court martial. Even then there was some difficulty about forming a court, and it was thus 27 October 1747 before he was put on trial. The evidence against him was persuasive and the hearing lasted for nearly three months. On 28 January 1748 the court determined that Mitchell 'fell under part of the 12th and 14th articles of war', and sentenced him 'to be cashiered and rendered incapable of ever being employed in his Majesty's service'. Mitchell's case was one of a number of courts martial which enquired into the inadequate performance of naval officers in action against the enemy. There was growing political disquiet that neither the professional discipline of the sea officers nor the results of courts martial were adequate to restore confidence in the navy. As a result, in 1749 parliament undertook to revise the code of naval discipline, removing the discretionary power of courts martial in cases such as Mitchell's. Under the altered regulations Admiral John Byng was executed in 1757.

Despite John Charnock's claim that Mitchell was restored to half pay, his name does not appear on the half pay lists; and though it is possible that an equivalent pension was given him in some irregular manner, no minutes of such can be found. There is no official record of his death.   J. K. Laughton, *rev.* Richard Harding

Sources PRO, ADM 1/2098; ADM 1/2099; ADM 1/2100; ADM 1/2101; ADM 6/13, fols. 22v, 96v; ADM 6/14, fols. 31, 99; ADM 6/15, fols. 335, 336, 358, ADM 8/20 (ship's disposition) · J. Charnock, ed., *Biographia navalis*, 4 (1796), 230–32 · A. T. Mahan, *The influence of sea power upon history, 1660–1783* (1890)
Archives PRO, ADM MSS

Mitchell, Sir David (*c.*1650–1710), admiral and parliamentary official, whose parents and birthplace are not known, was reportedly 'a poor boy from Scotland' (Marshall, 461), who was apprenticed to a Leith shipmaster, and later served as mate of a vessel in the Baltic trade. He is reputed to have been impressed into the navy about 1672 and, showing promise, became a prominent 'tarpaulin' naval officer, rising from the ranks to be an admiral.

The first documented evidence of Mitchell's naval service, in ships' pay books, shows him serving from 31 October 1673 to 15 October 1674 in the Mediterranean as midshipman in the *Swallow* (46 guns, Captain Edward Russell). He is revealed to have followed Russell to several further ships: the *Reserve* (48 guns) from 21 May 1676 to 19 June 1677, participating in Russell's voyage to Newfoundland; the *Defiance* (56 guns) as second lieutenant (16 January 1678–23 March 1678), and the *Swiftsure* (70 guns) on station in the channel, in which he remained until November 1679. During this period he was recommended for promotion, but not selected. With Russell's appointment to command the *Newcastle* Mitchell remained his lieutenant, and during this period saw service in the Mediterranean from May 1680 until May 1682. Upon Russell's withdrawal from service Mitchell joined the *Tiger* (46 guns). Serving under Vice-Admiral Arthur Herbert he participated in the capture of the Algerine corsair *Two Lions* in July 1682. Mitchell returned to England with Herbert in July 1683, remaining in the *Tiger* until August 1683.

On 5 February 1684 Mitchell was promoted captain and appointed to command the *Ruby* (48 guns), serving in the West Indies convoying ships in the slave trade and pursuing pirates. When the *Ruby*'s channel wale broke while heaving her down in November 1685 the governor of Jamaica ordered him to command two local sloops in pursuit of the pirate Bannister until the repairs were completed. Mitchell was discharged from the *Ruby* in October 1686, but received no new orders. Having a facility with the Dutch language he eventually went to the Netherlands, where he became one of the prominent naval defectors to William III's cause. Mitchell was quoted in September 1688 as saying, 'divers others will come over before the fleet will set sayle' (Davies, 206), suggesting that he was at least aware of a naval conspiracy. In March 1689 Mitchell was appointed to command the *Elizabeth* (2 decks, 70 guns), Admiral Herbert's flagship at the battle of Bantry Bay on 1 May 1689, and he commanded her at the battle of Beachy Head in June 1690.

In August the Admiralty proposed to the queen four candidates for promotion to flag rank: Mitchell, George Churchill, Matthew Aylmer, and Francis Wheeler. Not among the two selected, Mitchell remained in command of the *Elizabeth* until January 1691 when he became first captain of the *Britannia* (100 guns), Admiral Russell's flagship, a position he held until 7 October 1691. On 26 October Mitchell was appointed major of the 1st marine regiment, and after a four-month gap in sea pay, he was reappointed first captain in the *Britannia* (7 February 1692–26 January 1693). As first captain he was present at all meetings of flag officers and signed the war council reports in which they gave their collective judgement. After the initial stage of the battle of Barfleur Mitchell is reputed to have initiated the order for the general chase of the French fleet.

Proposed and again passed over for a flag in 1692, Mitchell finally received his commission as rear-admiral of the blue on 7 February 1693 under the joint admirals Henry Killigrew, Sir Ralph Delaval, and Sir Cloudesley Shovell, and he was simultaneously appointed to his flagship, the *Duke* (90 guns). In March 1693 he commanded the squadron that convoyed King William to the Netherlands. He returned to the main fleet for the remainder of the summer, was promoted rear-admiral of the red in July, and in October returned to the Netherlands to escort the king back to England. In February 1694 he commanded a squadron for the protection of trade entering the channel from the west, then joined Russell's fleet for service in the Mediterranean. While serving abroad Mitchell was promoted vice-admiral of the blue on 19 August 1695 and then, on 14 October 1695, became lieutenant-colonel of the 1st marine regiment.

On Russell's return to England in October Mitchell served briefly as temporary commander-in-chief with a squadron of third and fourth rates and seven Dutch warships until the arrival of Admiral Sir George Rooke. Mitchell remained as Rooke's second in command in the Mediterranean until the fleet returned to England in the spring of 1696. For the remainder of the year he served in the channel with Rooke, flying his flag in the *Royal William*. In May 1697 Mitchell returned to sea, serving under Rooke, and commanded a squadron protecting trade in the western approaches to the channel.

In January 1698 Mitchell sailed for the Netherlands with a squadron to bring Tsar Peter of Russia to England. During the crossing Peter came to admire the bluff seaman and with Mitchell's facility to translate the tsar's Dutch into English, Peter requested William III to appoint Mitchell as his official escort and translator during his stay in England. Mitchell was present during the tsar's audience with William on 23 January 1698, commanded the fleet review for Peter off Spithead, and escorted him back to the Netherlands. For these services, on 11 March 1698 William III appointed him to the post of gentleman usher daily waiter in the royal household, with a salary of £150.

On 28 September 1698, at Christ Church, Newgate, London, Mitchell married Mary (1660–1722), daughter of Robert Dodd of Chorley, Shropshire. They had one son, who died in infancy. On 5 December 1698 the king knighted Mitchell at Kensington and selected him from the existing gentlemen ushers to be gentleman usher of the black rod. He was first appointed an Admiralty commissioner on 31 May 1699 and reappointed in a new commission on 28

October 1699. On 28 January 1701 he was promoted vice-admiral of the white and in April 1701 he was reappointed an Admiralty commissioner, remaining until the commission was dissolved when Lord Pembroke became lord high admiral on 26 January 1702. He was unemployed until the appointment of Prince George as lord high admiral on 22 May 1702, when he was made a member of the prince's council. On joining it, Mitchell became involved in a dispute over seniority with Admiral George Churchill that was quickly resolved in Mitchell's favour. Mitchell served at the Admiralty until the prince's death on 19 April 1708.

As black rod from 1698 to 1710 Mitchell played a prominent role on ceremonial occasions for both the House of Lords and for the Order of the Garter, though as a serving naval officer he was granted the right by William III and Anne to have a deputy when naval duties required his presence elsewhere. In the House of Lords he was prominent in leading the procession that installed the new duke of Marlborough on 18 December 1702, and regularly drew 6s. 8d. a day for attending the house. As the first member of the armed services to be black rod, he established a precedent for the following centuries.

During the first half of the War of the Spanish Succession, Mitchell played an extremely important role as the Admiralty's representative in negotiations with the Dutch admiralties over the politically contentious matter of the annual Dutch naval contribution to the war. For this purpose he travelled to the Netherlands regularly between 1702 and 1706. For each of these journeys he was allowed £500.

Towards the end of Mitchell's life John Macky described him as 'a fat sanguine complexioned Man' and wrote of him that

> without any recommendations, but his own merits, [he] hath raised himself to the honourable Post he now enjoys, and had risen faster had he been an Englishman … His is a just worthy man of good solid sense, but extremely afflicted with the spleen, which makes him troublesome to others as well as himself   ([John Macky], *Memoirs of the Secret Services of John Macky, Esq.*, 1733, 168–9)

Mitchell died on 1 June 1710 at his home, the manor house at Popes, near Hatfield, Hertfordshire, which he had purchased at some time between 1696 and 1705. He was buried in Hatfield parish church, under an inscribed stone that briefly described his services (J. Le Neve, *Monumenta Anglicana*, 188). On the condition that his heir took the sole surname of Mitchell, he left the bulk of his property to a nephew, his sister's son David Cooke, who had married a daughter of Bishop Gilbert Burnet.

JOHN B. HATTENDORF

Sources ships' pay books, PRO, ADM 33/121, 111, 95 · applications, PRO, ADM 6/428 · register of commission officers, 1660–85, PRO, ADM 10/15 · commissions and warrants, PRO, ADM 6/3 · commissions and warrants, PRO, ADM 6/425 · general list of captains, PRO, ADM 7/549 · succession books, 1688–1725, PRO, ADM 7/655 · list of captains, 1688–1715, NMM, Sergison MS SER/136 · Pitcairn-Jones, 'Ship histories', NMM [card file] · *CSP dom., 1693; 1696–1704* · *JHL*, 16–17 (1696–1704) · M. Bond and D. Beamish, *The gentleman usher of the black rod* (1976) · *VCH Hertfordshire*, 3.104 · *Le Neve's Pedigrees of the knights*, ed. G. W. Marshall, Harleian Society, 8 (1873), 461–2 · J. D. Davies, *Gentlemen and tarpaulins: the officers and men of the Restoration navy* (1991), 206 · *Report on the manuscripts of Allan George Finch*, 5 vols., HMC, 71 (1913–2003), vol. 2, pp. 66, 386

Archives Northants. RO, corresp. | CKS, corresp. with Alexander Stanhope

Likenesses oils, NMM · two portraits; bequeathed to David Cook Mitchell, 1710

Wealth at death £1000 to wife; two portraits to nephew; £500 for funeral; stables in Bond Street, London; owned Manor House at Popes, Hertfordshire: will, PRO, PROB 11/515, sig. 125

Mitchell, Denis Holden (1911–1990), television and radio producer, was born on 1 August 1911 in Cheadle, Cheshire, the younger child and only son of Ernest George Mitchell, Congregational minister, and his wife, Ethel, *née* Alderson. The family went to South Africa when he was six but returned to England when he was ten, his father having been appointed minister of a church at Redhill, Surrey. Mitchell attended Caterham School, Surrey, where he twice failed his matriculation examination.

Mitchell shared his mother's enthusiasm for drama, and as a teenager his temporary work included the carrying of spears at the Old Vic theatre. At the age of eighteen he returned to South Africa, where he stayed until 1949. His first work was as a bank clerk, and during his holidays he appeared as an actor in local stage productions, as well as acting and writing radio scripts for the South African Broadcasting Corporation.

On the outbreak of the Second World War, Mitchell volunteered for service in the South African artillery, but because of his knowledge of drama and radio he was soon transferred to the entertainment unit of the Union Defence Force, being promoted to the rank of captain and placed in command of its operation in the Middle East and Italy. One of the members of his unit was Sid James, the actor.

At the end of the war Mitchell worked briefly for a local newspaper, and then joined the staff of the South African Broadcasting Corporation. His programme work covered a wide range, but his main concern, he insisted, was with 'real people and real voices', and his own personality, quiet and sympathetic, explains why no interviewer has extracted more by saying less. His passion for drama had already vanished, never to return.

On the advice of the BBC features producer D. G. Bridson, who had visited South Africa, Mitchell returned to Britain in 1949 and in 1950 became the BBC's features producer in Manchester, near to his birthplace. Most of his programmes were based on interviews with people whose voices were rarely heard: the homeless, nurses, the unemployed, and criminals. He always walked alone, often at night, usually finding people by chance. At a time when cameras and microphones were mainly studio-based, he worked out in the streets, recording people in their own surroundings.

In 1955 Mitchell was briefly attached to the BBC television service in London, where he made his first documentary film, about teenagers, which gained an award at the

Brussels Experimental Film Festival. On his return to Manchester in 1956 he continued to make television documentaries, notably *Morning in the Streets* (1959), which won both the Prix Italia and an award of the Society of Film and Television Arts. He joined the Television Service at Shepherd's Bush in 1959, continuing his own style with *Soho Story*, about a London busker, but he also returned to Africa to make a series, *The Wind of Change*, and in 1961 he produced *Chicago*, the story of a city 'seen through the eyes of the people who live there, from the very poor to the extremely rich' (Denis Mitchell's notes proposing the film).

Mitchell left the BBC in 1962, and the following year formed Denis Mitchell Films Ltd, a small company which survived until his death. It made documentaries for many organizations, including ATV, the BBC, Rediffusion, Southern Television, and Channel 4. Much of his most personal work was made for Granada Television, based again in Manchester, and his subjects (especially in the series *This England*, 1964–7) were usually 'ordinary folk'; but his interviewing technique was equally effective in *Private Lives* (1972–3), in which the subjects came from many classes of society. A programme which he always regarded as one of his best was a portrait of Quentin Crisp. Towards the end of his life he became increasingly keen on making very short programmes, lasting between five and ten minutes, whose subjects were inevitably men and women in various walks of life. He made over 100 documentaries, and in 1975 received the SFTA's Desmond Davis award for his outstanding talent.

Mitchell was of medium height, with hazel eyes and brown hair; he was gentle and softly spoken, and frequently smiling. In 1938 in Durban he married Dorothea (Sally), daughter of William Arthur Bates, telegraphic engineer in the Post Office. They had two daughters, the younger of whom died in 1970. His first marriage was dissolved in South Africa in 1948, and in 1951 he married Betty Annie, a BBC secretary and the daughter of a transport inspector, Albert Elmer Horne. They had one son. His second marriage was dissolved in 1965, and in the same year he married (Norah) Linda, who had been his secretary in the BBC, the daughter of John Hastings Webster, chartered accountant. They lived in the Norfolk countryside, the location of his film *Never and always* (1977), which expressed its social history as seen by the local people. Mitchell died on 30 September 1990 at his home, Avondale, 42 Station Road, Great Massingham, Norfolk (although his death certificate gives 1 October as the day of death).   NORMAN SWALLOW, *rev.*

Sources *The Times* (4 Oct 1990) · *The Independent* (4 Oct 1990) · BFI NFTVA · *CGPLA Eng. & Wales* (1991) · private information (1996) · personal knowledge (1996)
Archives Tate collection, transcript of interview for TV South West | BFI NFTVA, Broadcasting, Entertainment, Cinematograph, and Theatre Union History project
Wealth at death £135,181: probate, 26 June 1991, *CGPLA Eng. & Wales*

Mitchell, Gladys Maude Winifred (1901–1983), novelist, was born on 19 April 1901 in Crescent Road, Cowley,

Oxford, the eldest daughter of James Mitchell, of Scottish ancestry, and Annie Julia Maude, *née* Simmonds. She moved with her family in 1909 to the Brentford and Isleworth area of Middlesex, where she received her early education at the Rothschild School in Brentford, and the Green School in Isleworth. She studied at Goldsmiths' College, London (1919–21), and later attended University College, London, where she gained an external diploma in European history in 1926 and qualified as a teacher.

Gladys Mitchell became a distinguished writer of detective novels, a survivor of the 'golden age' of detective fiction of the 1920s and 1930s which included such writers as Dorothy Sayers, Agatha Christie, and G. K. Chesterton. Like them, she was a member of the Detection Club. In 1976 she won the Crime Writers' Association silver dagger award. During much of her writing career she was also a dedicated teacher of history, athletics, English, and Spanish at several girls' schools in Middlesex. She taught at St Paul's School, Brentford (1921–5), and at St Ann's Senior Girls' School, Ealing (1925–39). After a period of ill health she took up a post at Brentford Senior Girls' School in 1941 and resigned in 1950 with the intention of retiring. Three years later, having devoted herself to writing, she returned to teaching, this time at the Matthew Arnold School, Staines, where she remained until 1961 when she finally retired.

Mitchell, who also wrote under the pseudonyms Stephen Hockaby and Malcolm Torrie, began writing early. Undeterred by the rejection of her first four novels, she launched her long and prolific literary career with *Speedy Death* (1929) and continued to produce at least one book a year for the rest of her life. This first book introduced her famous character Mrs Beatrice Adela Lestrange Bradley (later Dame Beatrice), a sleuth and 'psychiatric consultant to the Home Office'. The formidable Mrs Bradley, with her unattractive physical features, claw-like hands, yellow skin, and cackling laugh, was sometimes nicknamed Mrs Croc. She appears in all the crime novels written under Gladys Mitchell's name. Like her creator, Bradley possessed a strong sense of justice, socially progressive views, and a warm understanding of humanity. Characteristic features of Mitchell's novels include sustained tension, improbable plots, black humour, and eccentric themes with frequent use of folklore and the supernatural. In *Speedy Death*, a double murder story, Bradley commits the second murder herself but is acquitted with the assistance of her defence counsel, who is also her son; the victim of the first murder, known as a male explorer, turns out to be a woman.

Mitchell's settings varied enormously but she frequently used the enclosed atmosphere of schools, as in *Death at the Opera* (1934), *St Peter's Finger* (1938), *Laurels are Poison* (1942), and *Faintley Speaking* (1954), while *Spotted Hemlock* (1958) is set in two adjacent agricultural colleges, one male and one female. *The Rising of the Moon* (1945) recalls Mitchell's childhood in Brentford. As the novels progress, various members of Bradley's family and associates begin to appear, and reappear, such as her son Ferdinand Lestrange, a barrister, and Carey Lestrange, her pig farmer nephew. Sally Lestrange, Bradley's granddaughter, is the key figure in *Winking at the Brim* (1974), a comic work in which the Loch Ness monster eliminates the culprit. A grand-niece, Hermione Lestrange, appears in *The Death-Cap Dancers* (1981), where the suspect is killed by a boar on her father's pig farm. George, the faithful chauffeur, is in frequent attendance, as is Laura, Bradley's secretary, whose investigative skills are put to good use in the Holmesian satire *Watson's Choice* (1955). While Mitchell's novels are firmly rooted in the golden age tradition of detective fiction, she was equally capable of turning the genre on its head. Such was the confidence of her narrative style, it is often impossible to distinguish serious crime from parody, or tragedy from comedy. While some readers found her implausible plots taxing, her numerous loyal followers, not least Philip Larkin, enjoyed her inimitable mixture of horror and jollity. Other notable Bradley novels include *Lament for Leto* (1971), which centres on an archaeological expedition, *The Saltmarsh Murders* (1932), and *Here Lies Gloria Mundy* (1982).

In the Stephen Hockaby novels, written during the 1930s, Mitchell moved from crime detection to historical fiction with works such as *Marsh Hay* (1933), set in Edwardian rural England, and *Grand Master* (1939), a Mediterranean adventure story about the knights of Malta.

Mitchell had a lifelong fascination with the legends and folklore of the British Isles and a serious interest in archaeology and ancient buildings. These interests are reflected throughout her work, but are particularly evident in the six crime novels she published as Malcolm Torrie. They all feature the male detective Timothy Herring, who is also the secretary of the Society for the Preservation of Historic Buildings, a role which frequently leads him to corpses in bizarre situations, as in *Heavy as Lead* (1966). In *Your Secret Friend* (1968), Timothy becomes engaged to Alison Marchmont Pallis, an embittered schoolteacher whose knowledge of history makes her a useful sidekick in subsequent Torrie novels.

Gladys Mitchell also wrote several mystery stories for children. She never married and spent the latter part of her life at 1 Cecil Close, Corfe Mullen, Dorset, where she died of cancer on 27 July 1983.   J. STRINGER

Sources J. M. Reilly, ed., *Twentieth century crime and mystery writers* (1983) · *Contemporary Authors: New Revision Series*, 9 (1983), 369–70 · *Contemporary Authors: New Revision Series*, 63 (1998), 302–5 · M. J. DeMarr, 'Gladys Mitchell', *British mystery writers, 1920–1939*, ed. B. Benstock and T. F. Staley, DLitB, 77 (1989), 232–8 · *TLS* (26 Oct 1984) · *The Times* (29 July 1983) · b. cert. · CGPLA Eng. & Wales (1983)
Wealth at death £48,082: probate, 14 Nov 1983, CGPLA Eng. & Wales

Mitchell, Sir Godfrey Way (1891–1982), construction engineer and entrepreneur, was born at 54 Scylla Road, Peckham, London, on 31 October 1891, the younger son (there were no daughters) of Christopher Mitchell, stonemason and quarry owner, and his wife, Margaret, *née* Way, of Weymouth, Dorset. He was educated at the nearby Haberdashers' Aske's School, Hatcham. From 1908 he worked for Rowe and Mitchell, his father's quarry business in Alderney, Channel Islands, from which stone was exported to Britain. He joined the forces on the outbreak of war and received a temporary commission in the Royal Engineers in December 1916. He later commanded a quarry company in Pas-de-Calais, France, with a labour force of prisoners of war, sending aggregate to the trenches. He was demobilized in January 1919 with the rank of captain but, with business conditions having adversely changed, he sought an opportunity in which to invest a decade of experience. With his war gratuity and a £3000 loan from his father, in 1919 he bought a small insolvent masonry and stone-laying contracting business in Hammersmith, London, founded by George Wimpey in 1880.

Mitchell proceeded to build up the civil engineering side of the new limited liability company he created, George Wimpey & Co. Ltd. From being a small, local subcontractor he enlarged the business to that of a main contractor, seeking building contracts with local authorities in the home counties. In 1928 he started private house building, quickly becoming one of the largest London-based house builders. In time Wimpey became the largest home builder in the world. Growth was particularly achieved by retaining and reinvesting profits rather than taking them as dividends, a policy continued after the company became public in 1934. By the late 1930s, especially with the advent of rearmament, the Wimpey organization was at the forefront of British contractors. On 31 August 1929 Mitchell married Doreen Lilian (1901/2–1953), daughter of Ernest Mitchell, a civil servant of Melbourne, Australia. They had two daughters.

During the Second World War the company's headquarters was evacuated from Hammersmith to Denham in Buckinghamshire, from where it successfully carried out some of the largest building and civil engineering projects. It built ninety-eight airfields throughout Britain, as well as factories, barrage balloon stations, docks, and army camps, and the largest underground oil storage facility then capable of being constructed. It was chiefly for his skill in organizing and administrating this diversified work of national importance that Mitchell was knighted in 1948. During the war he had also served on several ministry committees, including the advisory committee of the Ministry of Defence on scientific research, the advisory council to the Ministry of Works, the Economic Planning Board, and the Ministry of Labour's Hankey committee assessing the likely staffing requirements at higher levels in industry after the war and how to meet them. For a time he was controller of building materials at the Ministry of Works.

After the war Mitchell served for over two years on the National Coal Board's advisory committee on the structure of the coalmining industry, as well as on the restrictive practices court, the Civil Engineering Scholarship Trust, and the 1954 court of inquiry into the docks dispute. Keenly aware of the problems left by the war, he was also concerned how to re-employ several thousand demobilized former service employees. This was to be a major consideration in both setting up regional offices, thereby spreading work opportunities throughout the provinces, and creating a highly efficient overseas contracting organization which also embraced electrical and mechanical engineering and plant erection. At its peak, overseas work accounted for over one-third of total turnover.

Overseas expansion began in Kuwait in 1947 and by the 1950s very large projects were being carried out in various parts of the world, particularly in the Middle East. Perhaps the most notable was the BP/IPC pipeline and oil refinery in Aden, built in partnership with Bechtel of California, and there followed the construction of Brazil's largest hydroelectric dam at Furnas, Salaverry harbour in Peru, Hong Kong power-station, and many others. Permanent offices were also set up in Canada, Australia, and elsewhere. Eventually, in recognition of such tremendous overseas efforts, the company received the queen's award to industry for export achievement in 1977.

Concurrently, the regionalization of the home-based construction activity proved highly successful. The company developed the 'no fines' system of house building for local authorities and built more than 350,000 homes throughout Britain. Additionally, its road surfacing activity became Wimpey Asphalt and grew rapidly. The problem now was not how to re-employ former service personnel but how to obtain a sufficiently able and mobile labour force. Sophisticated but highly practical training at all levels up to graduate engineering was undertaken and thousands of people in the construction industry became 'Wimpey-trained'. Mitchell constantly ensured that he had around him a strong team of management and operatives. As the demand for local authority housing dropped the company increased its private housing activities and, by the time of Mitchell's death, it was the major private house builder in Britain. And overseas the company was engaged in over thirty countries with a wide range of subsidiaries covering every field of the construction industry.

Mitchell was chairman of his company from 1930 to 1973, executive director from 1973 to 1979, and life president from 1979. He was a member of the Worshipful Company of Paviors from 1924 to 1973, a livery company he had done much to revive after the Second World War, and was its master in 1948. He was chairman of the Federation of Civil Engineering Contractors (FCEC) in 1948–9 and of the Export Group for the Construction Industries in 1949–51. For almost thirty years he was a member of the joint ICE/FCEC standing joint committee for the practical training of young engineers with contracts. He became an honorary fellow of both the Institution of Civil Engineers, in 1968, and the Institute of Building, in 1971. In 1955 he established a charitable trust, the Tudor Trust, to which he transferred almost the whole of his personal company shareholding and private estate and since when it has continued to make substantial payments to charities, particularly to those concerned with education, old age, and mental and physical disabilities.

Mitchell was very well read, particularly in philosophy. He had a particular interest in ancient civilizations and archaeology and enjoyed foreign travel. He died at his home, Copper Beech, 2 Curzon Avenue, Beaconsfield, Buckinghamshire, on 9 December 1982.

ROBERT SHARP

Sources *The Times* (10 Dec 1982), 14g · personal knowledge (1990) [*DNB*] · private information (1990) · *WWW* · obituary, 1982, Inst. CE · b. cert. · m. cert. · d. cert. · *CGPLA Eng. & Wales* (1983)
Wealth at death £693,822: probate, 28 Feb 1983, *CGPLA Eng. & Wales*

Mitchell, Graham Russell (1905–1984), intelligence officer, was born on 4 November 1905 in Broom House, Warwick Road, Kenilworth, the only son and elder child of Alfred Sherrington Mitchell, a captain in the Royal Warwickshire regiment, and his wife, Sibyl Gemma Heathcote. He was educated at Winchester College, of which he was an exhibitioner, and at Magdalen College, Oxford, where he read politics, philosophy, and economics. In spite of suffering from poliomyelitis while still at school he excelled at golf and sailed for his university. He was also a very good lawn tennis player, and won the Queen's Club men's doubles championship in 1930. He played chess for Oxford, and was later to represent Great Britain at correspondence chess, a game at which he was once ranked fifth in the world. He obtained a second class honours degree in 1927. In 1934 he married Eleonora Patricia, daughter of James Marshall Robertson; they had a son and a daughter.

Mitchell's first job was as a journalist on the *Illustrated London News* but his only credited article, which appeared in the 12 October 1935 edition, was entitled 'What was known about Abyssinia in the seventeenth century—a detailed account in a geography of 1670'. Thereafter he joined the research department of Conservative central office which was then headed by Sir G. Joseph Ball.

Mitchell's bout of polio had left him with a pronounced limp and when war broke out in September 1939 he was considered unfit for military service. Instead he joined the Security Service, MI5, in November. Exactly who sponsored his recruitment is unknown although Sir Joseph Ball, who was later to be appointed deputy to Lord Swinton on the top secret home defence security executive, was sufficiently influential and well connected in security circles to have assisted his entry into the organization.

Mitchell's first post in MI5 was in the F3 sub-section of F division, the department headed by Roger Hollis responsible for monitoring subversion. F3's role was to maintain surveillance on right-wing nationalist movements, the British union, German and Austrian political organizations, and individuals suspected of pro-Nazi sympathies. One of Mitchell's first tasks was to assist his immediate superior, Francis Aiken-Sneath, to investigate the activities of Sir Oswald Mosley and collate the evidence used to support his subsequent detention.

At the end of the war Mitchell was offered a permanent position in the Security Service and was promoted to the post of director of F division, where he remained until 1952 when he was switched to the counter-espionage branch. While in charge of D branch Mitchell led the team of case officers pursuing the clues of Soviet penetration left by Guy Burgess and Donald Maclean, the two diplomatists who defected to Moscow in May 1951. At the same time he was one of the chief architects of positive vetting, the screening procedure introduced in Whitehall to prevent 'moles' from penetrating the higher echelons of the civil service. In addition Mitchell was the principal author of the notorious 1955 white paper (*Parl. papers*, 1955–6, 41, Cmd 9577) on the Burgess and Maclean defection.

In 1956 Roger Hollis succeeded Sir Dick White as director-general of MI5 and selected Mitchell as his deputy. He remained in this post until September 1963 when he unexpectedly took early retirement. It was later revealed that at the time of his departure Mitchell was himself under investigation as a suspected Soviet spy. The evidence accumulated against Mitchell was all very circumstantial, and centred on the poor performance of MI5's counter-espionage branch during the 1950s. During this period MI5 experienced a number of set-backs, failed to attract a single Soviet defector, and only caught one spy on its own initiative.

During the last five months of his career Mitchell was the subject of a highly secret and inconclusive 'molehunt' which was eventually terminated when he was brought back from retirement to face interrogation. This gave him the opportunity to answer his accusers, but did little to end the debilitating atmosphere of suspicion that at one point threatened to paralyse the entire organization, and resulted in Roger Hollis himself being accused of having spied for the Russians. Both Mitchell and Hollis strenuously denied having been traitors, leaving the whole question of the identity of the KGB's master spy, if indeed there was one, unresolved.

Tall, stooped, and habitually wearing tinted glasses, Mitchell cut a lonely figure with solitary interests, like chess puzzles and the *Times* crossword. He died at his home, 3 Field Close, Sherington, Buckinghamshire, on 19 November 1984. NIGEL WEST, *rev.*

Sources *The Times* (3 Jan 1985) · N. West, *Molehunt: the full story of the Soviet spy in MI5* (1987) · *CGPLA Eng. & Wales* (1985)

Wealth at death £226,226: probate, 22 Feb 1985, *CGPLA Eng. & Wales*

Mitchell [*née* Webster], **Hannah Maria** (1872–1956), socialist and suffragette, was born on 11 February 1872 at Alport Farm in the parish of Hope Woodlands, Derbyshire, a remote area of the Peak District. The fourth of six children of poor farming parents, Hannah had a harsh childhood that involved long hours of farm and domestic work. All of the children lived in fear of their mother's rages, but it was Hannah in particular who was Mrs Webster's scapegoat and who was subjected to frequent scoldings and beatings. Although her father and uncle had taught the unhappy and shy child how to read, her mother had no sympathy with her daughter's desire for education and forced her to darn her brothers' stockings in the evenings while they read or played cards or dominoes. Even the promised year at school, enjoyed by her sister Lizzie, was denied to Hannah who attended school for just one fortnight. The antipathy between Mrs Webster and her daughter (which lasted all their lives) came to a crisis in 1885

Hannah Maria Mitchell (1872–1956), by unknown photographer

when Hannah snatched from her mother the stick with which she was being beaten and dared her to strike again. Realizing that it was best to leave home, Hannah went to live with a brother and his wife, and then later took lodgings.

During the years before she married Hannah Webster earned her living in a variety of low-paid jobs that young working-class women traditionally entered, such as domestic service and dressmaking. Involvement in the growing socialist movement introduced her to (Frank) Gibbon Mitchell, a shop assistant, whom she married in 1895. After the difficult birth of a son, both parents resolved to have no more children and Hannah, like most working-class wives and mothers, supplemented the meagre family income by taking in home-based jobs that could be fitted around a domestic routine. She disliked intensely, however, the ways in which domesticity intruded on her need for solitude, time for study, and opportunities for a wider life. Furthermore, she found a wide discrepancy between socialist ideals and practice, especially in regard to freedom for women, and deeply resented the hours her husband expected her to spend cooking dinners and baking home-made cakes, potted meat, and pies.

Hannah Mitchell nevertheless began to be drawn into political life through speaking at meetings of the Independent Labour Party (ILP) and through campaigning for the enfranchisement of her sex. She joined the militant Women's Social and Political Union (WSPU) founded in 1903 by Mrs Emmeline Pankhurst and her eldest daughter, Christabel, and became a part-time paid organizer. Overwork for the women's cause contributed to a nervous breakdown. Hurt by the fact that none of the Pankhursts made contact with her during her illness, Hannah resigned from the WSPU and joined a breakaway group, the Women's Freedom League, headed by Mrs Charlotte Despard. After the First World War, during which she became a pacifist supporting such anti-war organizations as the ILP No Conscription Fellowship and the Women's

International League, Hannah devoted many years to public service, especially to the needs of the poor. In 1924 she was elected to Manchester city council and was appointed as a magistrate two years later. While she retired from council work in 1935, she continued on the bench for another eleven years.

Hannah Mitchell did not lose sight of the pioneering days of the suffrage movement during these years: she was one of the organizers for a meeting of forty ex-suffragettes held in Manchester on 9 May 1939 to honour the twenty-first year of women's full enfranchisement. Correspondence in the 1950s with Edith How Martyn, founder of the Suffragette Fellowship, also reveals that she was active in trying to bring suffrage mementoes to museums in Manchester. Her childhood ambition to be a writer also came to fruition during the inter-war years, when, using the pseudonym Daisy Nook, she began to write sketches in the Lancashire dialect for the *Northern Voice*, a small paper run by the ILP. Articles under her own name also appeared in other local papers, such as the *Manchester Guardian*. During the last years of the Second World War and immediately after, Hannah worked at writing her autobiography. She failed, however, to find a publisher and had to be content with seeing instalments of her life printed in the *Northern Voice* in the 1950s.

Hannah Mitchell died on 22 October 1956 at her home, 18 Ingham Street, Newton Heath, Manchester. Her husband had predeceased her. Her full autobiography, edited by her grandson Geoffrey Mitchell, appeared posthumously in 1968 and has been much cited by historians, especially as more attention has been given to the involvement of working-class women in the suffrage movement. Its importance lies mainly in the fact that she was a working-class political activist who wrote about her experiences in both the labour and feminist movements, especially her struggle to integrate her socialist and feminist beliefs.

JUNE PURVIS

Sources *The hard way up, the autobiography of Hannah Mitchell, suffragette and rebel*, ed. G. Mitchell (1968) · S. Rowbotham, introduction, in H. M. W. Mitchell, *The hard way up: the autobiography of Hannah Mitchell, suffragette and rebel*, ed. G. Mitchell (1977) · autobiographical note, Suffragette Fellowship Collection, Museum of London, REEL 1, group C 60·15/21 · J. Liddington and J. Norris, *One hand tied behind us: the rise of the women's suffrage movement* (1978) · *CGPLA Eng. & Wales* (1956)
Archives Man. CL, Manchester Archives and Local Studies, corresp. and papers
Likenesses photograph, Man. CL, Manchester Archives and Local Studies [*see illus.*]
Wealth at death £1232 18s. 11d.: administration, 6 Nov 1956, *CGPLA Eng. & Wales*

Mitchell, Sir Henry (1824–1898), textile merchant and philanthropist, was born in November 1824 at Esholt, near Bradford, Yorkshire, the son of Matthew Harper Mitchell, a small local textile manufacturer, and his wife, Ann. He went to a local elementary school, and at the age of fourteen entered his father's worsted mill to learn the principles of textile manufacture. In 1841 he was taken on by the worsted firm of William Fison & Co. Seven years later he moved as a buyer to the Bradford firm of A. and S. Henry & Co., of which he was made a partner in 1852, and with which he was associated for the rest of his life, gaining a reputation, with Jacob Behrens, as one of the chief authorities on the worsted trade, and achieving a very influential position within that trade. Mitchell married, in 1851, Annie, daughter of the Revd D. W. Gordon of Earlston in Scotland. They had three sons: Gordon, who became a successful merchant in South Africa; Henry, who became a sergeant-major in the guards; and Samuel. Annie died in 1886 following a long period of mental illness.

The firm of A. and S. Henry was one of the major mercantile houses in the transatlantic textile trade, having been founded in Manchester in 1804 by the brothers Alexander and Samuel Henry. The beginnings of the business perhaps lay in the emigration to America in 1783 of their uncle, Alexander Henry, who had been born in the north of Ireland in 1766. He became a clerk in Philadelphia, but soon developed a successful merchanting business, importing cloth from Britain. The firm retained strong commercial links with America and traded in all types of textiles. It established branch warehouses in Leeds, Huddersfield, Bradford, Belfast, and Glasgow, which by the 1840s were operating with a degree of autonomy. Samuel died on 13 January 1840 in a fire on the American steamer *Lexington* sailing from New York to Providence, Rhode Island. Alexander died in 1862. By 1848 the business was in the control of Alexander's two sons, John Snowden Henry and Mitchell Henry, but neither was very actively involved. The management of the Bradford branch of the business was in the hands of Henry Mitchell from the 1850s, at a time when the worsted trade was expanding very rapidly. He travelled regularly to America, and gained a widespread commercial reputation, expanding the business considerably as the main branch of A. and S. Henry. The company was converted to limited liability status in 1889, with a capital of about £1 million.

Although from an Anglican family, Henry Mitchell converted to Wesleyanism, staunchly supporting the church, and contributing financially to local Wesleyan chapels and schools. He also supported a variety of other local activities, and is reported to have donated over £100,000 to philanthropic causes in Bradford during his lifetime. He championed the promotion of technical education, believing that continental success in industry had benefited greatly from technical schools there. He helped found the Bradford Technical College between 1878 and 1882, providing substantial donations to it. He served as a governor of the Bradford school board and Bradford grammar school, and as vice-president of the Bradford Mechanics' Institute. He was knighted in 1887 for his services to education.

Mitchell was a strong supporter of the interests of the worsted trade, not least through his service to Bradford chamber of commerce, of which he was president for six years. He was one of the main witnesses, on behalf of Bradford, to the royal commission on depression in trade and industry in 1886, providing detailed evidence on the state of the Bradford worsted trade. He was critical of the services provided by British consuls; campaigned for improvements in rail transport; and supported 'fair trade', rather than free trade, arguing for reciprocal arrangements in trading relations and, at times, advocating commercial retaliation, as for example, to the proposed new French tariff in 1890. He served as a judge at the important Philadelphia Centennial Exhibition in 1876; an exhibition that many Bradford manufacturers boycotted in protest at United States protectionist policy. In 1878 he was vice-president of the jurors for worsted yarn and fabrics at the Paris Universal Exhibition, and wrote a perceptive report about it.

Sir Henry Mitchell died at his home, Parkfield House, Manningham, Bradford, on 27 April 1898, after a long illness, a few days after he had been made a freeman of the city of Bradford. He was buried at Undercliffe cemetery, Bradford, on 30 April.   D. T. JENKINS

Sources *Bradford Observer* (28 April 1898) • D. T. Jenkins, 'Mitchell, Sir Henry', *DBB* • J. R. Beckett, ed., *Bradford portraits of influential citizens* (1892) • [J. Hogg], ed., *Fortunes made in business: a series of original sketches*, 3 (1887) • W. J. Heaton, *Bradford's first freeman: Sir Henry Mitchell* (1913) • *Report of Henry Mitchell upon the Paris exhibition, together with the report of the artisans* (1878) • A. H. Robinson, 'Bradford's first freeman: Sir Henry Mitchell', *Bradford Bystander*, 2/81 (May 1971) • IGI
Likenesses Spy [L. Ward], caricature, watercolour study, NPG; repro. in *VF* (5 July 1890)
Wealth at death £139,803 14s. 5d.: probate, 1898, *CGPLA Eng. & Wales*

Mitchell, Hugh Henry (1770–1817), army officer, was born on 9 June 1770. Appointed ensign in the 101st regiment in January 1782, and lieutenant in June 1783, he served with the 101st in India and until it was disbanded in 1784. In May 1786 he was gazetted to the 26th, and served with it in the latter part of the 1801 campaign in Egypt. He rose to the rank of lieutenant-colonel in December 1805. In June 1811 he exchanged into the 51st light infantry, which he commanded in the Peninsular War until its conclusion in 1814. He obtained the rank of colonel in June 1813, and the CB on 4 June 1815.

In the Waterloo campaign Mitchell commanded a brigade consisting of the 3rd battalion of the 14th, the 23rd fusiliers, and the 51st light infantry. He was the only brigade commander at Waterloo under the rank of general officer who was mentioned in dispatches. For his services in the campaign he received from the tsar the order of St Vladimir of the third class, and also the Russian order of St Ann. He died on 20 April 1817, in Queen Anne Street, London.   EDWARD O'CALLAGHAN, rev. DAVID GATES

Sources *Army List* • *GM*, 1st ser., 87/1 (1817), 473 • W. Siborne, *History of the war in France and Belgium in 1815*, 2 vols. (1844) • *The dispatches of … the duke of Wellington … from 1799 to 1818*, ed. J. Gurwood, 13 vols. in 12 (1834–9)

Mitchell, James (d. 1678), presbyterian preacher and insurgent, was born and raised in Edinburghshire. He studied

at Edinburgh University under the theologian David Dickson and graduated on 9 July 1656. During the 1650s he adhered to the militant wing of the Scottish covenanters, the remonstrants, but his clerical career was less than distinguished, perhaps because he was 'a weak scholar' (Kirkton, 277). According to Robert Wodrow he was 'a preacher of the gospel, and a youth of much zeal and piety; but perhaps had not these opportunities for learning and conversation, which would have been useful to him' (Wodrow, 2.115). The presbytery of Dalkeith rejected him as insufficiently qualified for the ministry, and Mitchell seems to have become a freelance preacher. In 1661 the presbyterian divine Robert Traill recommended him to ministers in Galloway as someone who was 'fit for a school, or teaching gentlemen's children' (ibid.). Soon afterwards the laird of Dundas made Mitchell his private chaplain and his children's tutor. According to the tory propagandist George Hickes, Mitchell was expelled from this post in disgrace after an affair with a young woman, and returned to Edinburgh where he stayed in the same house as the covenanter Major Thomas Weir. He then found a post as chaplain to the niece of Sir Archibald Johnston of Wariston and her family.

In November 1666 Mitchell heard of the covenanter rising in south-west Scotland and rode directly to Ayr to join it. On the night before the covenanters' defeat at Pentland he was sent back to Edinburgh by one of his officers to promote the rebellion in the capital. In a royal proclamation following the Pentland rising Mitchell was named as one of those guilty of treason, and in a later proclamation he was excluded from the pardon granted to the rebels. About a month after Pentland, Mitchell fled to the Netherlands, where he joined a cousin working in Rotterdam, and conversed with exiled covenanters like John Livingstone. After nine months in exile, he returned to Edinburgh.

It was at this point that Mitchell resolved to assassinate the archbishop of St Andrews, James Sharp, who had betrayed his fellow covenanters at the Restoration and engineered the suppression of dissenters thereafter. Mitchell acquired 'a pair of long Scots iron pistols, near musket bore' (*Justiciary Records*, 2.308) and awaited his moment. On 11 July 1668 he shot at Sharp as the archbishop sat in his coach in the High Street in Edinburgh, but only succeeded in wounding the bishop of Orkney, Andrew Honyman. In the confusion that ensued Mitchell escaped. A reward of 5000 marks was offered for his apprehension, and Mitchell was quickly identified as the would-be assassin, but once again he took flight. According to the record of his later trial he 'did rove and go abroad several times to Holland, England, and Ireland' (ibid., 2.310) before finally settling in Edinburgh in late 1673. Some time afterwards he was married there to Elizabeth Sommerville (d. in or after 1678) by the outlawed covenanter preacher John Welsh. Mitchell and his wife kept a shop selling tobacco close to Archbishop Sharp's Edinburgh residence.

In February 1674 Mitchell was recognized in the street

by Archbishop Sharp himself and arrested. When examined by a committee of the privy council he only confessed to the assassination attempt after he had received a promise from the council that his life would be spared. However, he refused to repeat his confession before the justiciary court on 2 March, and in frustration the council declared that its promise was now invalid. Mitchell was imprisoned in the Tolbooth awaiting trial, and may have been kept there indefinitely had he not attempted to escape in December 1675. In January 1676 the council ordered that Mitchell be interrogated under torture in order to wring a confession from him. Mitchell stubbornly refused to confess, and was returned to the Tolbooth before being transferred to the notorious Bass Rock in January 1677. In October 1677 it was decided to bring him to trial, and on 6 December he was brought from the Bass to Edinburgh.

The trial took place in January 1678. Mitchell was ably defended by Sir George Lockhart and John Elies, who argued that he had given his confession upon assurance of his life. This was denied by the prosecution, and by leading figures from the privy council, including Sharp himself, Rothes, Lauderdale, and Halton. The defence requested that the entry in the privy council's register for 12 March 1674 be read to the court, since this seemed to confirm that Mitchell had been promised his life. Faced with the prospect of finding four members of the council guilty of perjury, the commissioners ruled the extract from the register to be inadmissible evidence. The next day, 10 January, the court found Mitchell guilty of a capital crime on his own confession, and declared that the promise of life was not proven. He was executed on 18 January 1678 in the Grassmarket in Edinburgh. He left behind his wife, who was suffering from fever and had just given birth to a child. Their son, also called James, graduated from Edinburgh University in 1698 and later became a Church of Scotland minister.

Mitchell's trial did considerable damage to the reputation of a government that was now associated with torture and perjury. In the words of Sharp's biographer, 'Not only had he perjured himself, he had been seen to do so' (Buckroyd, 103). On 3 May 1679 a gang of covenanter militants succeeded where Mitchell had failed and assassinated Sharp on Magus Moor outside St Andrews; before they killed him, they declared that they were avenging the death of James Mitchell. In 1681, Halton was indicted for perjury on the evidence of letters he had written in 1674 reporting Mitchell's confession, 'upon assurance of his life' (State trials, 6.1263–4). However, Mitchell's religious terrorism was exploited by tory propagandists to blacken the reputation of whigs and dissenters. In Ravillac redivivus (1678) George Hickes linked Mitchell's story to that of the notorious covenanter Major Thomas Weir (who had been executed for bestiality and incest in 1670), in order to demonstrate that fanatical dissenters considered themselves to be above the moral law, and were capable of committing the most outrageous crimes in the name of religion.

Mitchell himself left behind a significant set of papers (reprinted in Naphtali, ed. W. Wilson, 1845), which reveal his own ideology. Steeped in radical covenanter works like Lex rex, The Causes of God's Wrath, and Naphtali, he viewed himself as an Old Testament saint appointed to destroy idolatrous tyrants. In the year 2000 he re-emerged as the protagonist of James Robertson's powerful historical novel The Fanatic.　　　　　　JOHN COFFEY

Sources R. Wodrow, The history of the sufferings of the Church of Scotland from the Restoration to the revolution, ed. R. Burns, 4 vols. (1828–30) · J. Kirkton, The secret and true history of the Church of Scotland, ed. C. K. Sharpe (1817) · G. Hickes, Ravillac redivivus (1678) · W. G. Scott-Moncrieff, ed., The records of the proceedings of the justiciary court, Edinburgh, 1661–1678, 2 vols., Scottish History Society, 48–9 (1905) · Burnet's History of my own time, ed. O. Airy, new edn, 2 vols. (1897–1900) · W. Wilson, ed., Naphtali, or, The wrestlings of the Church of Scotland for the kingdom of Christ (1845) · State trials · D. Laing, ed., A catalogue of the graduates … of the University of Edinburgh, Bannatyne Club, 106 (1858) · G. Mackenzie, Memoirs of the affairs of Scotland (1821) · Historical notices of Scotish affairs, selected from the manuscripts of Sir John Lauder of Fountainhall, ed. D. Laing, 2 vols., Bannatyne Club, 87 (1848) · J. Buckroyd, The life of James Sharp, archbishop of St Andrews, 1618–1679 (1987)

Mitchell, James (bap. 1785?, d. 1844), scientific writer, was probably the son of James Mitchell and Elizabeth Cumming baptized at Longside, Aberdeenshire, on 28 October 1785. Nothing is known of his early schooling, but he graduated MA from King's College, Aberdeen, in 1804. He may then have made a tour through France and Italy before arriving in London in 1805. After some years spent as a schoolmaster and a private tutor, he gained a position at the Star Assurance Company, subsequently becoming company secretary. He was still with the firm in March 1820, and probably remained there until its dissolution in 1822. Later (possibly after a brief return to teaching) he was appointed to a similar position at the British Annuity Company.

Mitchell had strong scientific interests. A lecture he read to the Mathematical Society of London on proof of the universe's being inhabited was published in 1813 as On the Plurality of Worlds. Other scientific works included The Elements of Natural History (1819), The Elements of Astronomy (1820), and an introduction to the Newtonian system for children (written under the pseudonym Tom Telescope). He also produced three dictionaries: on chemistry, mineralogy, and geology (1823); on mathematical and physical sciences (1823); and on universal history, chronology, and historical biography (1827). The last of these followed The Scotsman's Library (1825), which included biographies of some eminent Scotsmen. Among his more general works were An Easy System of Short Hand (1815) and A tour through Belgium, Holland, along the Rhine and through northern France, in the summer of 1816 (1816). He was a corresponding member of the Society of Scottish Antiquaries, to which he presented some of his large collection of material relating to Scottish antiquities. In 1823 he was made LLD of King's College, Aberdeen.

Mitchell's greatest interest however, appears to have been in the geology and botany of London and the southeast. He was elected a fellow of the Geological Society in 1832, and published several notes in their Proceedings. That he did not publish more seems to have been a matter of politics rather than science. He wrote to a friend that it was:

> not sufficient to be a Fellow; if you be not also in high office you do not get justice. There is a certain set of brethren ... who monopolise as much as they can ... and a new man has to fight his way through them. (Woodward, 135)

Thus the majority of Mitchell's work remained in manuscript. Between 1832 and 1840 he wrote some 1370 pages on the geology and botany of the London area and on the current state of industrial technology (including tunnelling, water well sinking, and brickmaking). His observations were generally very accurate, indeed 'no one was clearer and more minute in detailed description of what he had actually seen' (GM, 432).

Mitchell served as actuary to the parliamentary commission on factories, and as a sub-commissioner on the royal commissions of inquiry into handloom weavers (1838–41) and children's employment (1840–43). In undertaking the last of these he was severely overworked and he suffered a stroke in June 1843. He never recovered fully, and died of apoplexy at the home of his nephew, Mr Templeton, at 3 Bedford Circus, Exeter, on 3 September 1844. His folio volumes of manuscript on the geology of the London area were given to the Geological Society of London by Joseph Prestwich in 1889 (much of the material in them had already contributed to a Geological Survey memoir). His material relating to Scottish antiquities was bequeathed to the University of Aberdeen.

PETER OSBORNE

Sources GM, 2nd ser., 22 (1844), 432–3 · A new biographical dictionary of 3000 cotemporary [sic] public characters, British and foreign, of all ranks and professions, 2nd edn, 3 vols. in 6 pts (1825) · IGI · DNB · J. Mitchell, The elements of astronomy (1820) · W. A. Cawthorne and J. C. G. M. Fuller, 'James Mitchell's "Brickmaking": an early nineteenth-century study in economic geology', London Naturalist, 73 (1994), 31–5 · W. A. Cawthorne and J. C. G. M. Fuller, 'James Mitchell's "The Thames Tunnel": unpublished notes by an amateur geologist, August 1839', London Naturalist, 73 (1994), 27–9 · H. B. Woodward, The history of the Geological Society of London (1907) · d. cert.
Archives GS Lond., notes on geology of the London area · NHM, geological notes · NL Scot., notes on the antiquities of Buchan | UCL, corresp. with Edwin Chadwick

Mitchell, James (1791–1852), engraver, was probably born in Edinburgh. His earliest works, on steel, were for the annuals: he engraved The Contadina, after Sir Charles L. Eastlake (president of the Royal Academy), and Lady Jane Grey, after James Northcote RA, for the Literary Souvenir of 1827 and 1832; The Farewell, after Abraham Cooper RA; and Saturday Night and The Dorty Bairn, after Sir David Wilkie RA, and The Corsair, after Henry P. Briggs RA, for The Gem of 1829, 1830, and 1832. His most important works were Alfred in the Neatherd's Cottage (1829) and Rat Hunters (1830), both after Wilkie. Besides these he produced Edie Ochiltree, after Sir Edwin Landseer, and five other illustrations, after William Kidd, Clarkson Stanfield, John William Wright, and Alexander Fraser, for the author's edition of the Waverley Novels between 1829 and 1833. He engraved several

plates for the Raphael Bible as well as Rubens's picture Daniel in the Den of Lions. Mitchell exhibited at the Society (later Royal Society) of British Artists between 1824 and 1831. He joined the Artists' Annuity Fund in 1822, and was a signatory in the 1837 petition. He died in London on 29 November 1852, aged sixty-one.

Robert Mitchell (1820–1873), his son, was born on 19 May 1820. He produced mezzotints after Sir Edwin Landseer, notably Tapageur, a Fashionable Member of the Canine Society (1852), and The Parish Beauty and The Pastor's Pet, a pair after Alfred Rankley (1853, 1854). Mitchell also worked in the mixed style and engraved The Happy Mothers and The Startled Twins, a pair after Richard Ansdell RA (1850), and Christ Walking on the Sea, after Robert Scott Lauder RSA (1854). In addition he etched several plates, which were completed in mezzotint by other engravers. He died at his home, Rochester Place, Bromley, Kent, on 16 May 1873, leaving two sons, Harry Edward and Richard Edwin Mitchell. R. E. GRAVES, rev. GREG SMITH

Sources B. Hunnisett, A dictionary of British steel engravers (1980), 93 · P. J. M. McEwan, Dictionary of Scottish art and architecture (1994) · B. Hunnisett, An illustrated dictionary of British steel engravers, new edn (1989) · CGPLA Eng. & Wales (1874)
Archives BM, department of prints and drawings · V&A, department of prints and drawings
Wealth at death under £450—Robert Mitchell: probate, 18 Feb 1874, CGPLA Eng. & Wales

Mitchell, James Alexander Hugh (1939–1985), publisher, was born on 20 July 1939 at Great Hallingbury in Essex, the youngest of the three sons of William Moncur Mitchell, a solicitor, and his wife, Christine Mary Browne. The family subsequently moved to Cirencester, Gloucestershire, from where Mitchell and his brothers Julian (subsequently a novelist and playwright) and Anthony went to Winchester College. At Winchester, James's principal achievement, as he recalled, was to found the Winchester College Astronomical Society and to persuade no fewer than 400 of the 480 boys to join.

Mitchell went to Trinity College, Cambridge, and obtained a third class in both part one of the economics tripos (1958) and part one (A) of the theological tripos (1960). At that time, influenced by the Revd Harry Williams and the Revd Mervyn Stockwood, later bishop of Southwark, and subsequently he considered taking holy orders. But he was dissuaded by an entrepreneurial instinct that led him, via a short spell as a sales assistant at Hatchards bookshop in Piccadilly, into publishing, becoming editor at Constable & Co. in 1961. On 23 June 1962 he married Janice Page (b. 1939/40), a teacher, and daughter of Jack Gunn Davison, a Lloyd's broker; they had three sons. In 1967 he was appointed editorial director of Thomas Nelson & Sons in Park Street, London where he met his future business partner, the production director John Beazley, who had been experimenting with new printing techniques.

In 1969 Mitchell and Beazley opened a tiny office in Goodwin's Court off St Martin's Lane, London, with the notion that they would publish only best-sellers. One a year, they reckoned, would do. The press was full of excitement about the imminent American moon flight programme and so Mitchell asked the astronomer Patrick Moore (whom he had met at Winchester) to write what became the *Moon Flight Atlas* (1969). Moore's text combined with the United States Space Agency pictures to make a historic and authoritative account which was ready for the printer by the time the astronauts returned to earth. It sold 800,000 copies and revolutionized the publishing in Britain of high-quality illustrated reference books. Moore's *The Atlas of the Universe* (1970), and Hugh Johnson's *The World Atlas of Wine* (1971) followed. By the end of the decade the latter had sold one million copies. (The firm's bias towards atlases was partly due to the financial backing of George Philip & Son, the cartographers and educational publishers.)

The design principle of these books was largely the work of Peter Kindersley (who had also worked at Thomas Nelson & Sons and who left Mitchell Beazley in 1974 to found his own firm). Their inspiration, and the sales technique that made them possible, were Mitchell's own. He offered each book as a completely designed package intended for international consumption. A foreign publisher had only to translate the text; all the colour printing was done together, at considerable saving. Such was Mitchell's persuasiveness and Beazley's organization that initial international orders for apparently specialist reference books made them best-sellers before publication. In 1975 Mitchell Beazley Ltd was given a queen's award to industry for success in exporting, despite the near-collapse of the firm when it made a financial disaster of two magazine launches. In the mid-1970s Mitchell and Beazley capitalized on more frank public discussions of sexual matters with Alex Comfort's *The Joy of Sex* (1972). The 'joy of' label was seized on by Mitchell for *The Joy of Knowledge*, a vastly ambitious project, inspired as Mitchell put it by 'Diderot's great 18th-century *L'Encyclopédie*, *The Guinness Book of Records*, and *The Whole Earth Catalog*' (*Sunday Times Magazine*), for which he assembled a formidable team of experts and commissioned an 'art-bank' of illustrations. The main innovation was a double-page spread designed to deliver information compactly. It was published, in eight thematic volumes, in 1977–8, with Mitchell as principal editor. Its format was at first criticized but Mitchell sold the rights for translation into twenty-three languages, among them Chinese and Arabic.

For this huge undertaking Mitchell had to expand Mitchell Beazley to employ nearly 200 people. It was an unsustainable effort, and Mitchell's vision faltered. He saw the possibilities of video but was not able to realize the potential. John Beazley died of cancer in 1977 and in 1980 Mitchell sold the firm to American Express Publishing, retaining the chairmanship. The experience was not a happy one and in 1983 he bought it back again.

Throughout his career Mitchell remained an essentially boyish character, given to fits of boisterous, even irresponsible, enthusiasm. He became bald in his thirties, and his plump and shiny face exuded a charm that was sometimes wily, but always high-spirited. His best friends,

among them the Revd Harry Williams, whose devotional books he published, knew him to be far more introspective than he appeared. His favourite recreation was fly fishing on the Avon near his greatly enlarged 'cottage' at Wilsford. Mitchell died on 12 March 1985 at his home, 110 Regent's Park Road, London NW1, after a long illness.

HUGH JOHNSON, *rev.* CLARE L. TAYLOR

Sources *The Times* (15 March 1985) · *Sunday Times Magazine* (20 March 1977) · m. cert. · d. cert. · *CGPLA Eng. & Wales* (1985) **Archives** Bodl. Oxf., corresp. with William Clark **Wealth at death** £1,134,686: probate, 4 June 1985, *CGPLA Eng. & Wales*

Mitchell, Jean Brown (1904–1990), geographer, was born on 26 July 1904 at 396 Lower Broughton Road, Manchester, the elder of the two daughters (a son died in infancy) of James Mitchell (1866–1908), a veterinary surgeon, and his wife, Margaret Brodie Cowan (1877–1911). After six years at Macclesfield high school, she went to Cambridge in 1923 as an outstandingly able undergraduate to read for the newly established geographical tripos and graduated with first-class honours. She then lectured at Bedford College, London, before returning in 1931 to her undergraduate college, Newnham, as a research fellow. Later she became a fellow and college lecturer, and from 1945 until her retirement in 1968 she was a university lecturer in geography.

Jean Mitchell's intellectual inclinations were those of the eighteenth- and nineteenth-century naturalists. Endowed with a thirst for knowledge, she allied a sharp eye with a rigorously logical and precise mind. She saw geography as a discipline in which observation and analytic comparison could yield a description and understanding of variation in the earth's features. For her, geographical practice was grounded in observation: 'Let one thing be said at the outset and borne in mind throughout, it [geography] must be studied at first hand, on the ground itself' (Mitchell, 3). Physical geography was her first love, but when constraints of serious illness redirected her research into historical geography her talents found full expression. In unravelling the human geographies of the past her quick eye sought out both natural and man-made features. Her 'ground' included old maps and records. She would explore England by car—and had travelled most of the roads, even tracks, from England to Scotland. She developed a shrewd knowledge of English architecture and of atlases and rare prints. For recording her observations she became an adept photographer.

Jean Mitchell set out her creed in her influential *Historical Geography* (1954), a volume in the Teach Yourself Geography series. The book follows themes in the human geography of England and Wales, showing why topics repay historico-geographical attention and indicating sources and their use. Apart from this, she mainly contributed to compilations, including the 1938 and 1965 volumes prepared for the Cambridge meetings of the British Association. As one of the geographers in Cambridge during the Second World War she wrote part of the volumes of the naval intelligence division geographical handbooks covering Greece (1944–5). But it was rather by the superb quality of her teaching and by sharing her geographical insights in the field that Jean Mitchell influenced generations of geographers. True to her own precept that 'geography like charity should begin at home', she concerned herself much with East Anglian landscapes. Excursions became legendary for the variety of information conveyed, the vividness of the interpretation, the stamina displayed and demanded. Small in physique, Jean Mitchell could outlast most of her audience and outface them too if need be: 'Out of the bus. The rain won't hurt you. Skin is waterproof.' Through these excursions she passed on her message not only to undergraduates (to whom she was strongly committed) but also to lecturers from the colleges of education and her academic peers.

Jean Mitchell helped to establish the reputation of geography as an academic discipline in Cambridge University and also formed part of the national geographical scene; she served as a member of the council of the Royal Geographical Society from 1951 to 1952 and 1958 to 1961, but Cambridge was her centre. Unmarried, and valiantly combating frequent bouts of severe ill health, she lived in college, unstintingly giving it, and also the department of geography, her loyalty and her time. In this she was a characteristic daughter of her generation. She was not a natural committee woman but was enthusiastically devoted to her students and to caring for and enhancing Newnham's fabric and its artistic contents. She was a generous benefactor to the college. Her interest in antique silver gave opportunities to exercise her discerning eye and taste, and she built for herself a small but fine collection of Scottish silver. Her working life was spent in England, but Scotland, where her parents had come from, remained her spiritual home. She retired to Edinburgh, and died at the Royal Victoria Hospital there on 5 January 1990. She was buried in Mortonhall cemetery, on 10 January.

As memories of her teaching fade, *Historical Geography* stands as a lasting testament to Jean Mitchell's qualities. It embodies many of the characteristics of its author: small in size, vigorous, erudite, exemplarily clear in argument, and imbued with enthusiasm, honesty, and humanity.

LUCY ADRIAN

Sources J. B. Mitchell, *Historical geography* (1954) · private information (2004) · private information (2004) · M. Sweeting, 'Memorial address', *Newnham College Roll Letter* (1991), 120–24 · L. Adrian, 'Jean Brown Mitchell, 1904–1990', *GJ*, 156 (1990), 242–3
Likenesses D. Hahn, photograph, Newnham College, Cambridge · photograph, Newnham College, Cambridge
Wealth at death £197,380.70: confirmation, 1990, Scotland

Mitchell [Mychell], **John** (d. 1556), printer, was active both in London and at Canterbury, but few details are known of his career in either city. Most of his books are undated, many lack imprints, and several are preserved only as fragments, making any attempted chronology of his work dependent largely on changes in his typographic stock and practice. He undoubtedly learned to print in London, and may have been in business there by 1530. Among the books thought to be his earliest and tentatively assigned to the early 1530s are a fragmentary *Life of St. Margaret* with an imprint giving Mitchell's address as the Long Shop by

the church of St Mildred Poultry. A *Life of St. Gregory's Mother* also naming Mitchell but specifying only 'London' probably dates from the same period, when Mitchell also appears to have been printing for at least one other publisher, John Butler. He may have been involved as well with Thomas Godfray in the printing of a verse *History of King Boccus* (c.1530) edited by John Twyne, master of the Canterbury grammar school. The colophon of the book states that it was printed 'at the cost and charge' of Robert Saltwood, a monk of St Augustine's, Canterbury, and both the type and initials used in *King Boccus* later appear in some of the books printed by Mitchell at Canterbury, including an edition of Saltwood's *Comparison between Four Birds*.

It is likely that Mitchell's connection with Canterbury predates his appearance as a London printer. He may be the John Mychell who witnessed a will in St Paul's parish in 1525, and he was definitely resident in the city by 1533, when he paid 8d. for permission to carry on the trade of bookbinder. In June 1536 John Twyne was one of thirteen citizens presented at the Canterbury municipal quarter sessions, charged with having 'mayntenyd procured and abetited' an unnamed printer dwelling in St Paul's parish, who was accused of having printed and sold books 'demed to be … clerely agense the fayth of true Cristen men'. The case never came to trial, but the man involved was almost certainly John Mitchell, who can be associated both with Twyne and with St Paul's. The imprints of a dozen extant books locate Mitchell's press in that parish (only three provide dates of printing, 1549 to 1553), and he is undoubtedly the John Mychell recorded as living in the parish in 1538 and the John Michell who in 1543 rented another property there, next door to Twyne. In 1541 'John Michell buke prynter of Canterbury' was sued for non-payment of a bill for 20 reams of paper, and an inventory of St Paul's taken in autumn 1552 notes among the debts to the church one in the hands of John Michell.

A few books with imprints naming Mitchell and Canterbury may date from about 1533–4, including an edition of John Lydgate's *The Churl and the Bird* that specifies St Paul's parish. Four other works lacking an imprint but assigned to Mitchell on typographic grounds can plausibly be proposed as the objectionable books of 1536: William Tyndale's *Obedience of a Christian Man* and *Parable of the Wicked Mammon*, and John Frith's *Disputation of Purgatory* and his corollary attack on John Rastell, *The Subsidy or Bulwark to his First Book*. Later than these are Randall Hurlestone's antimass *News from Rome*, an edition of two dialogues by Erasmus, and Lancelot Ridley's commentary on Paul's epistles to the Philippians. All three name Mitchell and Canterbury, with the last adding that the book was printed in St Paul's parish for Edward Whitchurch of London. In 1548 Mitchell printed at least two Reformation texts for the London publisher Hugh Singleton, and part of Edward Halle's *Union of the … Families of Lancaster and York* for Richard Grafton, but there is no evidence that he himself was resident in London at the time

From 1549 onward Mitchell occasionally dated his books. In that year he printed a quarto psalter, re-issued the following year, and in 1552 he published the first of three editions of a *Breviat Chronicle* of English history, his own reworking of earlier compilations. He continued to print after the accession of Mary in 1553, his last dated work being a list of articles to be inquired into during the visitation of Archbishop Reginald Pole (1556). Mitchell died later that same year, leaving numerous creditors including an Oxford bookseller; after his death Canterbury was without a printer until 1717.

JANET ING FREEMAN

Sources STC, 1475–1640 · H. R. Plomer, 'The libraries and book shops of Canterbury', *Book Auction Records*, 14 (1917), i–vii · M. L. Zell, 'An early press in Canterbury?', *The Library*, 5th ser., 32 (1977), 155–6 · J. E. Hobbs, 'An early press in Canterbury', *The Library*, 5th ser., 33 (1978), 172 · P. Clark, *English provincial society from the Reformation to the revolution: religion, politics and society in Kent, 1500–1640* (1977) · M. E. C. Walcott and others, 'Inventories of parish goods in Kent, AD 1552', *Archaeologia Cantiana*, 8 (1872), 74–163

Mitchell, John (1711–1768), botanist and cartographer, was born in White Chapel parish, Lancaster county, Virginia, on 13 April 1711, the son of Robert Mitchell (1684–1748), tobacco farmer and shopkeeper, and Mary, *née* Chilton (*d. c.*1711), widow of John Sharpe. His mother died when he was an infant and he was brought up with numerous half-siblings after his father's remarriage. He was educated at Edinburgh University, graduating MA on 6 June 1729 after having studied natural philosophy and having particularly enjoyed instruction in botany by Charles Alston and mathematics by Colin Mac Laurin. He then enrolled in the Edinburgh University medical school as a student of Alexander Monro Primus. It is likely that he went to Europe in 1731 and graduated MD of a continental university. Mitchell returned to his now much more prosperous family and practised in Lancaster county before buying land in Urbanna in the adjoining county in 1734. There he established a medical practice, an apothecary's business, and a physic garden, and married Helen (*d. c.*1748); no more is known of her. He spent his spare time botanizing and, through Virginia botanist John Clayton, making scientific contacts in the United States and Europe including those with Linnaeus. His discovery of several plants was recorded in the *Flora Virginica* (vol. 1, 1739; vol. 2, 1743; vol. 3 not published; 2nd edn, 1762) of Clayton and Gronovius, and he was soon sending botanical specimens to Johan Jakob Dillenius at Oxford and Charles Alston at Edinburgh, and corresponding with Peter Collinson. In the 1730s Mitchell came to the conclusion that plants, like animals, have male and female reproductive organs, that plants of the same species mutually fertilize and produce fertile offspring, and that plants of different species may cross-fertilize but their offspring will be sterile. Mitchell thereby established an experimental basis for determining the generic relationships of plants. He had also been identifying new, and reclassifying known, plants and described ten new genera, although delayed publication meant that many were attributed to Linnaeus in whose *Species plantarum* they first appeared. Mitchell's botanical work was published as 'Dissertatio brevis de principiis botanicorum et zoologorum' (*Acta Physico-Medica Academae*

Caesarae … Ephemerides, 8, 1748, 188–224; republished in Nuremberg, 1769). Interested in zoology, Mitchell's pioneering paper on the reproduction of the opossum occasioned considerable interest at the Royal Society, since marsupials were then virtually unknown. The society was further interested by his paper on the origin of different human skin colour (*PTRS*, 43, 1744), Mitchell's first essay in print. He deduced that both black and white races were descended from common ancestors and that their skin colour had diverged in response to different environments. He showed empirically that differences between the two were merely superficial. Bringing to his medicine the same systematic observation and logical deduction, Mitchell increased his practice and enhanced his reputation when he reported medical phenomena such as a particularly severe outbreak of 'yellow fever' (possibly Weil's disease), an account of which was published posthumously in 1804. In 1744 he was invited to join Benjamin Franklin's American Philosophical Society and met Franklin and other Philadelphia scientists in the city that year. By 1745 Mitchell was so ill from recurrent malaria that he sold his property in Urbanna and left with his wife for London.

The Mitchells' ship was intercepted by pirates off Brittany and he lost all his goods, including his herbarium and his botanical notes, the fruit of many years' study. He arrived in London in 1747 in want, and with his wife very ill. Welcomed by scientific contacts he was soon immersed in London scientific circles, especially that surrounding the duke of Argyll where he met many people of social and political influence; his involvement increased after the death of his childless wife about 1748. He may have been employed as a physician by Argyll and certainly obtained seeds and executed other commissions for him, often living in his household and working in his laboratory. He was an important guide to the Swedish traveller and scientist Pehr Kalm on his visit to England in 1747–8, and was elected fellow of the Royal Society on 15 December 1748. He worked on potash (*PTRS*, 48, 1749) and a natural and medical history of North America, which was never published. Mitchell was increasingly drawn to cartography, as his worries over French territorial claims in North America increased. His preliminary map of the continent of 1750 so impressed the lords commissioners of trade and plantations that they commissioned him to make a second. He gathered information from Kalm and the governors of each North American colony, who were required by the lords commissioners to provide Mitchell with a map, published maps and texts, and travellers' reports. In 1755 Mitchell published his map in eight sheets, engraved by Thomas Kitchin. It was acclaimed by Europeans and Americans as a significant geographical achievement, but its design was avowedly political. He represented British trading posts which were occupied for only part of the year as established settlements to bolster British claims that huge tracts of land had already peacefully come under British control. It was used in boundary negotiations from 1783 until as late as 1932. Most famously the copy in the possession of George III known as the 'Red-lined' map, which was used at the Peace of Paris in 1783, showed extensive tracts of Canada which the British were prepared to cede, although they did not in the end have to. It appeared in twenty-one variations (editions and impressions) and on later versions Mitchell answered his critics and elaborated his sources. His complementary *Contest in North America between Great Britain and France with its Consequences and Importance* was published in 1757. This marked the peak of Mitchell's career and influence. He had the previous year been beaten in the contest for appointment as first librarian to the British Museum, and although in 1759 he performed invaluable service in the establishment of the botanical gardens at Kew, ill health drove him to resign from his work there and leave London in 1761. Between 1762 and 1767 he worked on *The Present State of Great Britain and North America* (1767) which, although prolix, was quite well received. He died on 29 February 1768, although it is not known where. He was best known immediately after his death as a cartographer, but his contribution to natural history and his role in early American scientific circles have more recently been the subject of investigation, leading Theodore Hornberger to describe him as 'the ablest scientific investigator in North America' ('Scientific ideas', 277).

ELIZABETH BAIGENT

Sources E. Berkeley and D. S. Berkeley, *Dr. John Mitchell: the man who made the map of North America* (1974) · T. Hornberger, 'The scientific ideas of John Mitchell', *Huntington Library Quarterly*, 10 (1946–7), 277–96 · R. W. Stephenson, 'Table for identifying variant editions and impressions of John Mitchell's map of the British and French dominions in N. America', *A la Carte*, ed. W. R. Ristow (1972), 109–13 · C. O. Paullin, *The atlas of historical geography of the United States* (1972) · L. Martin, 'Mitchell, John', *DAB* · W. Klinefelter, *Lewis Evans and his maps* (1971) · A. Carlucci and P. Barber, eds., *Lie of the land: the secret life of maps* (2001)

Mitchell, John (1785–1859), army officer and writer, born on 11 June 1785 in Stirlingshire, was the son of John Mitchell (*d.* 1826) of the diplomatic service, sometime consul-general for Norway and afterwards engaged on missions to the courts of Stockholm and Copenhagen. In 1797 Mitchell went to Berlin with his father, who was dispatched on a mission to the court of the new Prussian king, Frederick William III. He was placed at the Ritter Academy at Lüneburg, where he acquired a knowledge of languages and a love of literature. In 1801 he was sent to a mathematical school in London taught by a Mr Nicholson, and on 9 July 1803 was commissioned as ensign in the 57th West Middlesex regiment. On 5 December 1804 he was promoted to a lieutenancy in the 1st (Royal Scots), and went with the 1st battalion of his regiment to the West Indies. On 1 October 1807 he was promoted captain in the regiment. In 1809 he joined the 3rd battalion of his regiment at Walcheren, and was present at the siege of Flushing. He served with the same battalion in the Peninsula from 1810 to 1812, and was present at the battles of Busaco and Fuentes d'Oñoro, in the action of Sabugal, and in the pursuit of Masséna. He accompanied the 4th battalion on the expedition under Major-General Gibbs to Stralsund in 1813, and served on the staff as a deputy assistant quartermaster-general. He also served in this capacity in

the campaign of 1814 in the Netherlands and Flanders, and with the army of occupation in Paris. His knowledge of languages made him of particular use to Wellington in correspondence and negotiations with the allied powers. He was promoted major on 19 July 1821, and placed on the unattached half-pay list on 1 June 1826. His father died in Edinburgh on 17 October the same year.

Mitchell did not return to military duty from half pay, but wrote articles and books, passing a part of each year on the continent up to 1848, after which he spent the remainder of his life living with his sisters in Edinburgh. In 1833–4 he contributed a series of articles to *Fraser's Magazine* under the name of Bombardino or Captain Orlando Sabretache. In 1837 he published a life of Wallenstein, in the preparation of which he travelled extensively in Hungary and Bohemia. Between 1841 and 1855 he contributed to the *United Service Journal*, and in 1841–2 wrote seven letters to *The Times* on the defects of the British army. In 1845 he published *The Fall of Napoleon* (3 vols.), and received in appreciation a diamond brooch from King Augustus of Hanover and a complimentary letter from Sir Robert Peel. In 1846 he contributed to *Fraser's Magazine* a series of articles on Napoleon's early campaigns. He also published other works, such as a book on tactics (1837), another on conversation (1842), and a volume of biographies of eminent soldiers (1865). He was promoted lieutenant-colonel unattached on 10 January 1837, colonel on 11 November 1851, and major-general on 31 August 1855. Mitchell was noted as a man of handsome appearance and pleasing manner. He died in Edinburgh on 9 July 1859, and was buried in the family vault in the Canongate churchyard.   R. H. VETCH, rev. JAMES FALKNER

Sources J. Mitchell, *Biographies of eminent soldiers …: with a memoir of the author by Leonhard Schmitz* (1865) · *Army List* · *Hart's Army List* · Boase, *Mod. Eng. biog.* · Allibone, *Dict.*

Mitchell, John (1806–1874), theatre manager, was born in London on 21 April 1806. Early in life he was employed by William Sams of St James's Street, London, who started the system of theatrical agency. In 1834 Mitchell opened a library in Old Bond Street, which became the headquarters of his extensive business for the next forty years. He made a practice of engaging a large number of the best seats in every theatre and public hall, which he sold through his library.

In 1836 and the two following seasons Mitchell opened the Lyceum Theatre for Italian comic opera, giving it the name of 'Opera Buffa'. Donizetti's *L'elisir d'amore*, on 10 December 1836, was the first of a series of light operas, which, together with Rossini's *Stabat mater* in 1842, were thus produced in England for the first time. In 1842 Mitchell brought to London French plays and players, including Rachel, Regnier, Plessy, Déjazet, and several others, who for a number of years performed at St James's Theatre, of which he was the manager for fifteen years. For the same theatre he engaged a French comic opera company, which opened in January 1849 with *Le domino noir*, which in turn was followed by *L'ambassadrice*, *La dame blanche*, *Richard Coeur de Lion*, *Le chalet*, and many other popular French works. In 1853 Mitchell brought the Cologne Choir to London. He also arranged royal visits to various theatres, organized command performances at Windsor Castle, and made a fortune publishing portraits of the royal family.

Mitchell was held in great esteem by the leaders of the stage and concert room. He died, after two days of illness from bronchitis, on 11 December 1874 at his residence, 10 Bolton Street in London, leaving a son and daughter. He was buried in Brompton cemetery on 18 December.

L. M. MIDDLETON, rev. NILANJANA BANERJI

Sources *The Era* (20 Dec 1874) · Grove, *Dict. mus.* · *Musical World* (19 Dec 1874), 842 · *The Choir*, 23, 400 · review of 'Lyceum–Opera Buffa', *The Athenaeum* (24 Dec 1836), 907 · *CGPLA Eng. & Wales* (1875)
Wealth at death under £70,000: probate, 2 Feb 1875, *CGPLA Eng. & Wales*

Mitchell, John Mitchell (1789–1865), merchant and writer, was the second son of John Mitchell of Craigend, Stirlingshire, and Janet Wilson. Sir Thomas Livingston *Mitchell was his younger brother. John was born at Craigend and educated at the Polmont School in Falkirk, and subsequently at the University of Edinburgh. For nearly fifty years he was engaged in business as a merchant at Leith, and for some time acted as consul-general for Belgium. Nevertheless he found time to study archaeology, natural history, mineralogy, and Scandinavian languages and literature. He was an active fellow (and joint secretary for its foreign correspondence) of the Society of Antiquaries of Scotland. He took a share of the administrative work of the society at a time of considerable upheaval and was one of several fellows to form links with Scandinavia. He visited Denmark and Sweden in 1846 and on his return gave two papers at the society on Scandinavian archaeology, inspired not only by intellectual progress in Scandinavian prehistory, but particularly by the prominent place it held in the mind of the general public and the financial support it received from public funds. It was a model he hoped to emulate in Scotland, to capture and build on the current wave of patriotic interest in the Scottish past. He was also a fellow of the Royal Physical Society and of the Royal Society of Northern Antiquaries of Denmark, and he contributed to the *Transactions* of each many valuable papers. He was on friendly terms with the king of Denmark and the king of the Belgians, and received from the latter the gold medal of the order of Leopold.

Mitchell's chief antiquarian work was *Mesehowe: Illustrations of the Runic Literature of Scandinavia* (1863), which included translations in Danish and English of the eleventh-century inscriptions found in the mound of Maeshowe in Orkney, opened in 1861. His work on *The Herring: its Natural History and National Importance* (1864) was an expansion of a paper which gained the medal offered by the Royal Scottish Society of Arts. It remained an authority for many years and showed both Mitchell's knowledge of natural history and his interest in his native land and in Scandinavia, in whose household and trading economies the herring is of great significance. He also wrote a

pamphlet *On British Commercial Legislation in Reference to the Tariff on Import Duties … (1849). Mitchell died unmarried at his home, Mayville, Trinity, near Edinburgh, on 24 April 1865.

W. C. SYDNEY, rev. ELIZABETH BAIGENT

Sources *GM*, 3rd ser., 18 (1865), 796–7 · A. S. Bell, ed., *The Scottish antiquarian tradition* (1981) · J. H. L. Cumpston, *Thomas Mitchell* (1954) · Boase, *Mod. Eng. biog.*
Wealth at death £3558 9s. 10d.: inventory, 20 Jan 1865, NA Scot., SC70/1/128, 716

Mitchell, John Murray (1815–1904), missionary and orientalist, was born in Aberdeen on 19 August 1815, the fourth of five sons and three daughters of James Mitchell, burgess of Aberdeen, and his wife, Margaret, *née* Gordon. His brothers James (1808–1884), Gordon (1809–1893), and Alexander (1822–1901) also became ministers of the Church of Scotland. He was educated at the parish school of Kinneff, Kincardineshire, and entered Aberdeen grammar school for a final year before going on to Marischal College, Aberdeen, in 1829; he secured the second highest bursary on the strength of his Latin prose. On the completion of his MA in 1833 he began to study for the ministry, first at Aberdeen and then for the 1837–8 session at Edinburgh, where he gained a gold medal offered by Professor Welsh for the best essay on Eusebius. He also returned for a time to Aberdeen grammar school as a teacher at the request of the rector, the Latin scholar James Melvin.

Much influenced by Alexander Duff, Murray Mitchell would gladly have joined Duff in Calcutta but, after being ordained in Aberdeen in July 1838, he was sent instead to Bombay, where he joined fellow missionaries John Wilson and Robert Nesbit in November of that year. His facility with languages enabled him quickly to master Marathi and he also studied Sanskrit and Zend. He was greatly interested in Marathi literature and in particular the poet Tukaram. At the end of 1842 he was joined by his fiancée Maria Hay Mackenzie Flyter [see below], and they were married in Bombay on 22 December. There were no children of the marriage.

On the Disruption of the Church of Scotland in 1843 Murray Mitchell was one of the many missionaries who opted to join the Free Church of Scotland. In 1844 he accompanied Stephen Hislop on the long and arduous journey to Nagpur in order to establish a new mission station there. He made frequent tours in inland districts, usually in the cool season, and often spoke to his audiences in Marathi from the back of his pony. His wife's illness prompted a return to Scotland and he addressed the church general assembly in 1846, before returning to India alone at the end of the year. His wife did not rejoin him until October 1849 and her health was to remain a source of concern. In 1854 he moved to Poona to relieve another missionary, James Mitchell, and he remained there until Mitchell's return in 1856. His wife's health again took her back to Europe and Murray Mitchell followed in January 1857. He was thus away from India during the time of the mutiny and did not return until November 1859. While in Scotland he was awarded an LLD degree from Marischal

College, in December 1858. On his return to India he once again deputized at Poona for James Mitchell until the latter was restored to health. His wife left India in October 1862 and he finally followed from Bombay in April 1863.

From 1863 to 1867 Murray Mitchell ministered to a Free Church congregation at Broughty Ferry, near Dundee. A crisis in the mission at Calcutta led to his leaving this charge and going out to Bengal in January 1868, where he became principal of Duff College. During his time there he was instrumental in setting up a European congregation, the Simla Union Church, and he also assisted Andrew Campbell in establishing a mission among the Santals, reflecting his interest in aboriginal peoples. In 1873 he returned to Scotland and acted as secretary of his church's foreign mission committee. In 1880, as part of a wider tour, he returned to India for a further two years. He reached his ministerial jubilee in 1888, and thereafter undertook a further ten years in the service of the Scotch Church at Nice in France, thus achieving the unusual distinction of serving his church at home, in the mission field, and on the continent. As the oldest minister of the Free Church, it fell to him to move the adoption of the Uniting Act of 1900 which brought about the union of the Free Church of Scotland with the United Presbyterian church. In spite of his advancing years he gave the Duff lectures in 1903, published posthumously as *The Great Religions of India* (1905). He died, at his home, 44 Heriot Row, Edinburgh on 14 November 1904 and was buried there, in the Dean cemetery, four days later.

Murray Mitchell was thoughtful, scholarly, gentle, and guileless, with a gift for languages and exposition which fitted him for his long missionary career. His *Letters to Indian Youth* passed through many editions, and he published a *Memoir* (1858) of his missionary colleague Robert Nesbit. His other works included *Hinduism, Past and Present* (1885), as well as a partial autobiography, *In Western India* (1899).

His wife, **Maria Hay Mackenzie Mitchell** [*née* Flyter] (1820–1907), was born on 5 December 1820, daughter of Alexander Flyter (1782–1866), minister of Alness in Rossshire, and his wife, Elizabeth Bayne (d. 1863). She was naturally obliged to share her husband's calling to an unusual degree but their marriage was recognized as being a true missionary partnership. Repeated and serious ill health did not deter her and she set down her own and their shared experiences in *A Missionary's Wife among the Wild Tribes of South Bengal* (1871); *In India* (1876); *In Southern India* (1885); and *Sixty Years Ago* (1905). She died on 31 March 1907.   LIONEL ALEXANDER RITCHIE

Sources J. M. Mitchell, *In western India* (1899) · *The Scotsman* (16 Nov 1904) · *Fasti Scot.* · Mrs J. M. Mitchell [M. H. M. F. Mitchell], *Sixty years ago* (1905) · Mrs J. M. Mitchell [M. H. M. F. Mitchell], *In India* (1876) · *Jubilee of the Rev. Dr Murray Mitchell* (privately printed, 1889) · R. Hunter, *History of the missions of the Free Church of Scotland in India and Africa* (1873) · W. Ewing, ed., *Annals of the Free Church of Scotland, 1843–1900*, 1 (1914), 272 · private information (1912) · CCI (1905) · DNB
Likenesses W. E. Lockhart, oils, 1898; Assembly Hall, Edinburgh, 1912

Wealth at death £4388 14s. 6d.: Scottish confirmation sealed in London, 3 March 1905, CCI · £198 15s. 5d.: additional estate, 1 Dec 1905, CCI

Mitchell, John Thomas Whitehead (1828–1895), co-operative society administrator, was born on 18 October 1828 in Rochdale, with no recognized father. His mother was a beerhouse keeper in Red Cross Street, where Mitchell attended the national school. His mother's forebears were in the hat trade, which became extinct in Rochdale during the early 1850s. His father was almost certainly a man by the name of Whitehead, alleged by Beatrice Webb to be 'a man in good position but of ungoverned character' (Webb, *My Apprenticeship*, 307). Although Mitchell's mother was poor, she kept him out of the factories for as long as she could, until he was ten or eleven, when he went to work as a piecer in Townshead mill for 1s. 6d. per week. However, he was sent to learn reading and writing at a Sunday school run by a clerk in the foundry.

One day in 1846 two men were canvassing the streets round Hope Street in Rochdale for Providence Chapel Sunday school. In the Mitchell house they found the boy reading and his mother making the dinner. 'They seemed to live on the most affectionate terms' (Maxwell, 395). They asked John to join, and secured his mother's agreement. The next Sunday, one of the men, Mr Pagan, a flannel weaver (and later twice mayor of Rochdale), called for Mitchell and enrolled him in his own class. This led Mitchell to accept radical and puritan ideals and to sign the pledge. This must have been a big decision, as it meant breaking with his mother's only visible means of support.

Mitchell subsequently used the library at Providence Sunday school, and joined its juvenile temperance society, which led him into the Rochdale Temperance Society, of which he became a committee member. He also became a member of the local Rechabite Tent which became the 'love and truth' division of the Sons of Temperance. He remained a member and an official until he died. The subcommittee of the temperance society held meetings in Mitchell's room at the top of his mother's house.

Then, about 1850, Mitchell personally experienced secession, a characteristic event in the associational culture of the day. There was disagreement at Providence about the appointment of a new pastor. A number of members split to form the New Milton Congregational Church in Bailie Street. Mitchell went with them. By 1854 he was a Milton Sunday school teacher. Mr Pagan did more than recruit and teach his young clients. He offered Mitchell a situation in the warehouse at 16s. a week. The firm changed hands several times. Mitchell stayed for eighteen years until 1867, and was promoted from wool sorter to manager of the wool department. By June 1871 he was a 'manufacturer', having set himself up in trade as a flannel dealer. He did this on his own account for some years until he gradually let it go, as his work in the co-operative movement became too demanding.

Mitchell was clearly a man who longed for organizational work and the chance to do business. This was his lifetime affair. His contacts in the flannel trade later led to his appointment as liquidator of the Lancashire and Yorkshire Productive Society, a co-operative concern at Littleborough which hit bad times. From 1878 until the end of his life he nursed that company round, incurring attacks on his probity partly as a result. No one else had hope for the society. But for much of his working life Mitchell worked every day between 7.30 a.m. and 9.30 a.m. to try to make it viable. Finally he managed to free it from creditors and prepare it for take-over by the Co-operative Wholesale Society. Meanwhile, Mitchell had established a London agency to run his own business, getting cotton goods made by the Rochdale Manufacturing Society dyed and finished at Middleton which he then sold through his agency. He used his home as a warehouse, adding an adjoining cottage as the business grew.

Mitchell joined the Rochdale Equitable Pioneers' Society in 1853, and in 1856 became a member of its committee [see Rochdale Pioneers]. About 1857 he moved in with Abraham Howard, and they remained close friends. Mitchell's other very close friend was Thomas Butterworth (their deaths occurring within a few days of each other). At one time Butterworth had been in disgrace in Rochdale, imprisoned for stealing from a co-op. When he was released about 1872, Mitchell held out his hand in friendship. They became inseparable.

It was through the Rochdale Pioneers that Mitchell was elected to the board of the Co-operative Wholesale Society (CWS) in 1869 and, in June 1874, became its chairman. This was the most important step in his life. It was an immensely demanding and influential post; and Mitchell remained chairman until his death. He nevertheless remained as a Sunday school teacher at Milton School, always returning from national or international meetings on every possible Sunday. Apart from his secretaryship to the government-financed science and art classes for many years in Rochdale and running for office as a radical Liberal in local election campaigns in Rochdale in 1893 and 1894, it was to the co-operative movement that he devoted his formidable energies. Beatrice Webb saw him as a business genius. In her *Diaries*, she described him as 'corpulent' with a 'shiny bald head, clean shaven face, exhibiting a full, good-tempered mouth, largely developed jaw and determined chin' (Webb, *My Apprenticeship*, 315). Webb received considerable help from Mitchell with her book about the co-operative movement. Published in 1891, this 'revealed a sympathy with Mitchell's view of the role of the CWS in industrial production' (Bellamy and Saville, 242).

By the late 1880s the annual turnover of the CWS exceeded £6 million, its warehouse at Manchester was a small town, and it was administering nearly £1 million of funds in shares, loan capital, and reserve. By the late 1890s there were 8407 people employed by the society, working in the distributive departments and in the bank as well as in the productive works and services. It remains an extraordinary fact about Mitchell, however, that as chairman of what Beatrice Webb saw as 'the most varied if not the largest business enterprise in the world at that time' (Webb, *My Apprenticeship*, 307), he received only something like £150 a year in fees—and this at a time when (to use a Mitchell phrase) in 'the Barnum wickedness of the competitive world' (*Co-operative News*, 11 Dec 1880) conspicuous consumption by capitalists on the one hand, and self-regarding professional managers as a separate social group on the other, were busy establishing themselves. 'Perhaps no man in Europe presided over so large a business, and certainly no man ever presided over so vast a concern who took such slender remuneration for so doing' (*Rochdale Observer*, 3 April 1895).

For Mitchell, means were united with ends through the movement, with all its constitutional inventions and disciplines. If, like idealistic Christian socialists, despising the store, you did not take the movement seriously, the movement as a way of life rather than as an idea, and as a real life association of large numbers of disagreeing, and sometimes disagreeable, working people, then you did not take Mitchell seriously. Mitchell's strong views were at the heart of a strategic argument about co-operative production which took place within the movement during his lifetime. The Christian socialists, on one side, advocated self-governing workshops (with bonus to labour, profit sharing, and other such measures), while the CWS, on the other, held that all production should be carried on in large-scale factories governed by the CWS general committee, with the CWS itself being owned and controlled as a federation of local retail co-operative societies. In the CWS system, advocated by Mitchell, the benefits of co-operation were to be realized by the worker as member (along with all other members) rather than by the worker as producer in his own, self-governing workshop. This was a serious debate, both sides of which are still relevant to anyone interested in the connections which complex co-operation in an era of large-scale industry requires.

Concentration of trade in a single channel was Mitchell's dream and that of the CWS:

> My desire is that the profits of all trade, all industry, all distribution, all commerce, all importation, all banking and money dealing, should fall back again into the hands of the whole people. If co-operators will manage their enterprises in such a way as to concentrate all their trade in one channel, I am certain that this can be accomplished. (Redfern, 'The Mitchell centenary', 15–16)

Sharing a platform with Tom Mann in Bristol in 1893, Mitchell expressed his vision thus:

> we want to put the profits of trade into the pockets of the people, not a section of them, but the entire community. Until the people get hold of trade profits they will never be able to undertake the productive business of the world. Mr Carnegie of America said that £1,000 in the hands of one person would do more good to the community than 1,000 persons owning £1 apiece. That was absolutely untrue. It would be better still if the seven hundred million pounds of the British Debt were owned by the forty millions of British people, than to belong to a small section of the community. Co-operators want to use the best means to get the entire wealth of this country, land and everything else, into the

possession of the entire body politic. (Co-operative Congress, 132)

The difference between this form of late nineteenth-century Owenism, with strong early nineteenth-century plebeian-radical connections and earlier forms of communitarianism, is that it was practical rather than rhetorical and led to very large-scale voluntary association among people arranging the means of life for themselves, rather than to demands for political concessions from Britain's government. In party political terms, it was non-political.

Mitchell believed in singular, complete solutions to society's problems. He was wary of theory and theorists. In terms of conventional nineteenth-century political categories, he was a radical or an advanced Liberal. He very occasionally referred to himself as a 'collectivist', but this was not a label he favoured and in 1894 he qualified the remark, adding but 'not by Act of Parliament' (Co-operative News, 20 Oct 1894). Strongly anti-individualist, even anti-individual, Mitchell espoused only an individuality for the good of all. To use an early nineteenth-century word with which he was familiar, he was an associationist. 'Co-operation ought to be based on the principle of united interest with the societies and not individuals. Some persons thought that individuals should be the basis' (Haslam, 76). Mitchell's main belief was in association, with very large numbers of working people choosing to do their own business instead of allowing other people to do it for them.

Mitchell died at his home, 15 John Street, Rochdale, on 16 March 1895 from chronic bronchitis and pneumonia. He left effects worth only £350 and his bedroom was described as humble in the extreme. It contained reports and balance sheets, portraits of a few friends, his Bible and hymnbook, and that was all. He was buried on 20 March in Rochdale cemetery. The CWS erected a granite monument there in his memory, engraved with a key sentence from his presidential address at the 1892 Co-operative Congress:

> The three great forces for the improvement of mankind are religion, temperance and co-operation; and, as a commercial force, supported and sustained by the other two, co-operation is the greatest, noblest and most likely to be successful in the redemption of the industrial classes. (Bellamy and Saville, 242)

STEPHEN YEO

Sources P. Redfern, John T. W. Mitchell (1923) · W. Maxwell, 'The late John Thomas Whitehead Mitchell', CWS Annual (1896), 392–414 · B. Webb, My apprenticeship, 2nd edn (1946) · B. Webb, The co-operative movement in Great Britain (1891) · Co-operative News (11 Dec 1880) · Co-operative News (20 Oct 1894) · Co-operative News (23 March 1897) · J. Haslam, 'Pioneers and leaders', The Wheatsheaf (May 1923), 76 · Rochdale Observer (3 April 1895) · 'Minutes of evidence taken before the royal commission on labour', Parl. papers (1893–4), 39/1.1–33, C. 7063-I · P. Redfern, 'The Mitchell centenary and its significance', The People's Year Book (1929), 15–16 · d. cert. · CGPLA Eng. & Wales (1895) · J. Bellamy and J. Saville, 'Mitchell, John Thomas Whitehead', DLB, vol. 1 · Co-operative Congress, Addresses at the 26th Annual Co-operative Congress, held at Bristol ... 1893 (1893)

Likenesses bust, Co-operative Wholesale Society offices, Manchester · photograph, repro. in Redfern, John T. W. Mitchell
Wealth at death £350 17s. 8d.: administration with will, 18 May 1895, CGPLA Eng. & Wales

Mitchell, Joseph (c.1684–1738), playwright and poet, was born in Ratho, near Edinburgh, the son of a stonemason, according to Cibber's Lives of the Poets. He studied at Edinburgh University with the intention of entering the kirk, but the presbytery of Edinburgh 'refus'd him their Testimony and Licence because he had read and recommended Dramatick Poetry', or so he later asserted (J. Mitchell, The Shoe-Heel, 1727, 15 n.). He was by 1719 enjoying some celebrity as an author in Scotland, a leading member of the literary fellowship known as the Athenian Society (Scott, 56). The poetry miscellany Lugubres cantus, largely written by himself and John Callender, was sponsored by the Athenian and published that year in London and Edinburgh. It included dedicatory poems by Ambrose Philips and Edward Young. In 1720 Mitchell was in London, publishing the religious narrative poem Jonah, dedicated to Isaac Watts and borrowing liberally in phrase and motif from Young's A Poem on the Last Day (1713).

In 1721 Aaron Hill, according to Benjamin Victor, gave Mitchell a two-scene domestic tragedy which he had written, The Fatal Extravagance, and saw to its production at Lincoln's Inn Fields as the work of Mitchell. Extravagance achieved critical and popular success and Mitchell attempted to capitalize on this success. He wrote and published a five-act version (1726), which was never produced, and he published occasional poems such as The Totness Address, Versified and The Shoe-Heel (both 1727), the latter dedicated to Viscount Killmorey. Here and always he pursued patrons.

It was this unceasing quest for patronage, no doubt, as in Two Poetical Petitions to ... Walpole (1725), which brought him the title Walpole's Poet. In the first, entitled The Sinecure, he petitioned Walpole to appoint him warden of Duck Island in St James's Park, the second begged the office of poet laureate of Scotland. Mitchell continued to address Walpole annually until as late as 1735, and apparently received as much as £500 over the years, but he was not, in fact, active politically. His lavish two-volume Poems on Several Occasions was published in 1729 by Lawton Gilliver, who published the Dunciad that year. Mitchell's Poems carried a list of subscribers including the archbishop of Canterbury and twenty-three dukes but also Swift and Pope, who would scarcely have bought books from a court whig.

By this time, however, Mitchell's fame had been decisively overshadowed by that of his younger fellow Athenian, James Thomson, who referred to Mitchell in correspondence as a 'Blockhead' (Thomson, Letters and Documents, 50). Mitchell's principal, indeed only, contribution to the London stage emphasized his Scottish roots. His ballad opera The Highland Fair, or, Union of the Clans, opened at Drury Lane in March 1731, and closed after four performances including two author's benefits. In an opening framing scene borrowed obviously from The Beggar's Opera, a poet and a critic discuss the nature of a 'Scotch opera'. The poet explains that he wanted 'to show the ancient Temper, Spirit, Customs, Manners, and Dresses of my Countrymen'. The ballad opera portrays the reconciliation of two quarrelling highland clans, by the vehicle of two pairs of young lovers, and culminates in a wedding of the lovers and, to the accompaniment of pipers, 'A dance in the *highland manner*'. Mitchell's prompt book, as reflected in the printed version (1731), is very long and must have been cut drastically for production: it includes fifty-one airs. The airs, Scottish folk tunes for the most part, had been used earlier by Allan Ramsey, and Mitchell's lyrics display a fatal lack of originality and verbal wit. *Highland Fair* was never revived.

Perhaps the most interesting aspect of Mitchell's only ballad opera is the frontispiece of the printed version, which is an engraving of the assembled clans by William Hogarth. In 1731 Mitchell published *Three poetical epistles: to Mr. Hogarth, Mr. Dandridge, and Mr. Lambert, masters in the art of painting*. These three poems demonstrate that Mitchell had been meditating on the nature of visual art. Paulson points out that Mitchell's description of Hogarth as a history painter anticipates by a number of years Fielding's better-known formulation of the concept in the preface to *Joseph Andrews* (Paulson, 235).

Mitchell's creative powers, never very strong, were ebbing. His supplicatory poem, *A Sickbed Soliloquy to an Empty Purse* (1735), was published in both Latin and English, at Mitchell's expense. A Joseph Mitchell was imprisoned in the Fleet in 1737, and it is possible that this was the author (P. Rogers, *Grub Street*, 1972, 303). When Mitchell died on 6 February 1738 at Islington the *London Evening-Post* recalled him as an author 'who had been for a long Time *Heir-Expectant* of several considerable Places'.

CALHOUN WINTON

Sources M. J. W. Scott, *James Thomson, Anglo-Scot* (1988) · R. Shiels, *The lives of the poets of Great Britain and Ireland*, ed. T. Cibber, 5 vols. (1753) · B. Victor, *The history of the theatres of London and Dublin*, 2 vols. (1761) · D. F. Foxon, ed., *English verse, 1701–1750: a catalogue of separately printed poems with notes on contemporary collected editions*, 2 vols. (1975) · *Letters and documents*, ed. A. D. McKillop (1958) · R. Paulson, *Hogarth: his life, art and times*, 2 vols. (1971) · J. Sambrook, *James Thomson, 1700–1748: a life* (1991) · J. May, 'Extensive borrowings from Edward Young in Joseph Mitchell's *Jonah*', *N&Q*, 235 (1990), 302–5 · C. Winton, 'Authorship of *The fatal extravagance*, once again', *Theatre Survey*, 24 (1983), 130–33 · J. Mitchell, *Ratho: a poem to the king* (1728) · A. H. Scouten, ed., *The London stage, 1660–1800*, pt 3: *1729–1747* (1961) · D. Griffin, *Literary patronage in England, 1650–1800* (1996)

Mitchell, Joseph (1803–1883), civil engineer, was born in Forres, Morayshire, on 3 November 1803, the eldest of the eight children of John Mitchell (d. 1824), a stonemason, and his wife, Margaret, *née* Philip. John Mitchell was employed on the building of the Caledonian Canal; his diligence and skill were noticed by Thomas Telford and for the last eighteen years of his life he was principal inspector for the commissioners for highland roads and bridges in Scotland. The family moved to Inverness about 1810 and Joseph attended the academy there for three and a half years. His education was completed by a year of

studies in Aberdeen, and it was determined that engineering should be his profession, after an apprenticeship as a mason.

In 1820 Mitchell was sent to Fort Augustus, where the locks of the Caledonian Canal were under construction, and, as his father was well known to everyone there, he was given the opportunity of learning not only masonry but all the branches of civil and mechanical engineering that were being practised at that time. Within a year he had so impressed Telford that he was invited to become his assistant in London, where he spent the next three years, until his father's illness in the summer of 1824 prompted Telford to send him back to Inverness; two months later his father died. For many years after his father's death Mitchell supported his mother and her seven younger children. In 1841 he married Christian (d. c.1880), daughter of James Dunsmure, secretary to the board of fisheries in Edinburgh. They were happily married for nearly forty years and had two daughters and one son, who became a minister in the Church of Scotland.

After six months' trial the commissioners appointed Mitchell general inspector and superintendent of the highland roads and bridges, a post he held for almost forty years. In addition to his responsibilities for roads and bridges, the commissioners employed him to plan and erect forty new churches, mostly in outlying districts and on the islands of the Hebrides. From 1828 to 1850 he acted as engineer to the Scottish fisheries board. In this capacity and through private consultancy work, he reported on, and in many cases either improved or built, most of the harbours around the north coast of Scotland, the Hebrides, and the Orkneys, including Dunbar, Fraserburgh, Inverness, and Wick.

To Mitchell belongs much of the credit for the creation of the railway system in the highlands and for overcoming the formidable engineering problems of mountainous terrain, fast-flowing rivers, and treacherous peatbogs. He began in the central lowlands by surveying the lines for a railway from Edinburgh to Glasgow (1838), and for the Scottish Central Railway (1844). As early as 1845 he surveyed a line for a railway crossing the Grampian mountains between Perth and Inverness; the bill presented to parliament was defeated in 1846 on the grounds of impracticality, yet the Highland Railway, which linked these two cities in 1863, followed Mitchell's line almost exactly. Other main railway lines which he surveyed and supervised included Inverness to Keith (1853–8), Inverness to Wick and Thurso (1859–74) which, because of exceptional difficulties, was not completed until after his retirement in 1867, and the Skye line from Dingwall to Strome Ferry (1868–70). For much of the construction work on these lines he had the assistance of William and Murdoch Paterson, whom he took into partnership in 1862. In the same year he suffered a stroke, from which he slowly recovered; he was able to resume work until he retired in 1867.

Mitchell was one of the first members of the Institution of Civil Engineers, joining in 1824 and attending some of the earliest meetings. He was elected a fellow of the Royal

Society of Edinburgh in 1843, a member of the Smeatonian Society of Civil Engineers in 1870, and a fellow of the Geological Society (1825). He was a prominent freemason, and helped to establish a local masonic friendly society. He was a supporter of the Inverness public library and involved in the establishment of the Inverness-based Caledonian Bank. He wrote a succession of pamphlets on railway administration and finance, road pavement design, and road and rail improvement in London. He dominated civil engineering in the highlands for half a century, and vigorously defended his position against professional competition in the press and elsewhere. The first volume of his *Reminiscences of my Life in the Highlands* was printed privately in 1883 and caused offence in some quarters by its frankness; the second volume was still in the press when he died, and although printed, was not widely distributed, to avoid threatened lawsuits. Mitchell died at his London home, 66 Wimpole Street, on 26 November 1883.

RONALD M. BIRSE, *rev.* MIKE CHRIMES

Sources J. Mitchell, *Reminiscences of my life in the highlands*, 2 vols. (1883–4); facs. edn (1971) · *PICE*, 76 (1883–4), 362–8 · *Engineering* (7 Dec 1883), 523–4
Archives Inst. CE, letter-books, notebook | Inst. CE, membership records, etc. · Inst. CE, Telford collection · NA Scot., Highland railway co. · NA Scot., commissioners of highland roads and bridges records, etc.
Wealth at death £97,316 13s. 8d.: corrective inventory, 28 June 1886, CCI (1884)

Mitchell, Joseph Harger (1859–1936), banker, was born on 21 January 1859 at Cross Hill, Greetland, near Halifax, Yorkshire, the youngest child of George Mitchell (1818–1886), grocer and joiner, and his wife, Mary Harger, *née* Holroyd. Both his paternal and his maternal ancestors hailed from Greetland, an industrial village, where Mitchell lived throughout his life. His family had strong Methodist roots and he attended the Greetland Wesleyan Chapel and Sunday school from an early age. He was educated at the Greetland Wesleyan day school before proceeding in 1871 to Heath grammar school, Halifax, where he gained many prizes and was appointed head boy in his final year. He inclined towards a legal career and passed the preliminary examination of the Incorporated Law Society, but then accepted a post on the staff of the Halifax Equitable Building Society in 1876, rising from junior clerk to managing director of the society. On 24 July 1884 at Greetland Wesleyan Chapel he married Harriet Shaw (*b.* 1859), the youngest daughter of Jacob Shaw, woollen weaver and mason, and Elizabeth (*née* Parr). They had two daughters and two sons, one of whom, George, a promising Halifax solicitor, was one of eleven young men from the chapel killed on active service in the First World War. His parents established an institute at the chapel in his memory in 1920.

Under Mitchell's leadership the Halifax Equitable Building Society, founded in 1871, expanded rapidly to become one of the largest building societies in the United Kingdom, second only in size and status to the Halifax Permanent Benefit Building Society, with which it merged in 1927. Mitchell worked at the head office of the society in Halifax and then managed branches at Elland, Greetland, and Stainland, before his appointment as secretary of the society in 1897. For the next twenty-five years 'his driving power, enthusiasm and untiring efforts' as secretary led to an enormous expansion in business (Alderson and Ogden, 24). At the end of his first year as secretary he was specially commended by the board of directors. In the five years following his appointment the society doubled the number of its customers to 3600. By 1914 the number of open accounts had more than trebled to 12,031. By 1921 it had nearly doubled again to 23,445, when the society's assets, which had stood at £163,780 when Mitchell was appointed secretary, had reached £3,126,302. Mitchell also established a reserve fund, which by 1921 amounted to £50,000.

In 1898 Mitchell proposed the establishment of a bank to extend the financial services provided by the society to customers who wished to start small businesses or needed private banking accounts. The directors were initially sceptical and asked Mitchell if he could quote a precedent for his proposal. His reply was that 'it was for them to make precedents not simply to follow them' (Alderson and Ogden, 74). They eventually agreed to his proposal and the Halifax Equitable Bank commenced business on 1 January 1900, with an issue of 2000 £1 shares. However, applications for shares exceeded the number issued by ten times and the initial allocation was raised to 2395. At the end of the first year the bank had accumulated assets of £7921 and a dividend of 4 per cent was declared; by 1911 the assets totalled £148,185 and the dividend was 10 per cent, and by the end of 1920 the assets had reached £1,176,092 and the dividend was 16 per cent. Despite the misgivings of some directors that the bank, which was under the same management as the building society, might detract from the strength of the latter, by 1921 the Halifax Equitable Building Society was fourteen times as large as it was when the bank was founded. It had also acquired a network of fifty-five branches, forty of which were within a radius of 12 miles of Halifax. In 1908, in a speech to the Building Societies Association meeting in Halifax, Mitchell claimed that the amount invested in building societies in his district was forty times as great in proportion to population as the average for the whole country.

Mitchell was elected to the board of the society in 1920 and appointed managing director in 1921. His retirement from ill health in 1921 after over fifty years' 'devoted and distinguished service to the society' (Hobson, 83) provided the opportunity for the amalgamation of the Halifax Equitable with the Halifax Permanent Benefit Building Society, to become the largest building society in the world. On his retirement the combined assets of the Halifax Equitable Building Society and the Halifax Equitable Bank totalled nearly £14 million, and the staff had increased from an assistant manager and a clerk to a workforce of a hundred.

Outside the business world Mitchell was well-known for his work as a Methodist local preacher, temperance leader, politician, and educationist. The Greetland Wesleyan Sunday school and Young Men's Improvement Society had a formative influence on his youth and he subsequently taught in the Sunday school for nearly sixty years; preached in every nonconformist chapel pulpit in the district; and held every office open to a layman in his local Methodist circuit. A lifelong teetotaller, he was honorary secretary of the Halifax and District Band of Hope Union. He was also an advocate of a progressive educational system 'with well-staffed and well-equipped schools' (*Halifax Daily Courier*, 5 March 1936) and served on the Halifax district technical instruction committee for eleven years; the Elland-cum-Greetland school board for eighteen years, including six years as chairman; and as the first chairman of the Greetland and Stainland education committee. In 1887 he was unanimously elected a member of the Greetland local board and held the seat until 1892. On the formation of the Greetland urban district council in 1894 he was elected at the head of the poll of twenty-one candidates and was subsequently appointed chairman of the council. Liberal in politics, he served as secretary of both the Greetland and West Vale Liberal Association from its formation in 1885 and the parliamentary division of Elland Liberal Association. He was also a founder member of the 1899 Club, a pioneering Yorkshire young Liberal association. He served as deputy registrar of marriages for the district and was chairman of the Greetland military service tribunal during the First World War. Finally, in 1923, he was appointed to the commission of the peace for the West Riding.

Photographs of Mitchell in 1921 reveal a smart-suited businessman with a strikingly healthy complexion, receding silvery hair, and a neatly trimmed beard and moustache. He died in the Duke of York Nursing Home, Duckworth Lane, Bradford, on 5 March 1936, of hypostatic pneumonia and a subacute intestinal obstruction. He was survived by his wife. His funeral service was held at Greetland Wesleyan Methodist Church on 9 March, followed by burial in the adjoining graveyard, where his maternal great-great-grandfather had been the first interment. The Revd Donald G. Brook in his eulogy observed that while Mitchell had 'made his way in the business world' and had 'reached the heights' by 'hard work and tenacity of purpose', he had 'ever kept in touch' with the local community, and 'many people in lowly dwellings had reason to be grateful to him' (*Halifax Daily Courier*, 9 March 1936).

JOHN A. HARGREAVES

Sources J. W. Alderson and A. E. Ogden, *The Halifax Equitable Benefit Building Society, 1871–1921* (1921) · J. A. Hargreaves, *Halifax* (1999) · O. R. Hobson, *A hundred years of the Halifax* (1953) · P. Pugh, *The strength to change* (1998) · *The Home Owner* [Halifax Building Society] (1953) [centenary number, 1853–1953] · D. W. Watson and H. Howe, *In the beginning: a history of Methodism in Greetland* (1973) · E. Perry, *Greetland Wesley Methodist Sunday school, 1811–1961* (1961) · *Halifax Courier* (7 March 1936) · *Halifax Courier* (14 March 1936) · *Halifax Daily Courier* (5 March 1936) · *Halifax Daily Courier* (9 March 1936) · b. cert. · m. cert. · d. cert.
Archives W. Yorks. AS, Calderdale, Halifax Equitable Bank, records, FW: 119/173–178; ME: 25, 31 · W. Yorks. AS, Calderdale, Halifax Equitable Benefit Building Society, records, MAC: 71; MAC: 102/24 · W. Yorks. AS, Calderdale, Halifax Equitable Building Society, records, MAC: 142; MAC: 144; ME: 22
Likenesses H. Sommerville, portrait, 1921 · photograph, c.1921, repro. in Alderson and Ogden, *Halifax Equitable Benefit Building Society*, p. 87 · photograph, c.1936, repro. in *Halifax Courier* (7 March 1936)

Mitchell, Joseph Stanley (1909–1987), radiotherapist and physicist, was born in Birmingham on 22 July 1909, the eldest of the three children and only son of Joseph Brown Mitchell, schoolteacher, and his wife, Ethel Maud Mary Arnold, also a schoolteacher. He won an open scholarship to King Edward VI High School, Birmingham, where he won a state scholarship, which he took up at Birmingham University in 1926, studying preclinical subjects. Two years later he won a scholarship to St John's College, Cambridge, where he read natural sciences and obtained first classes in both parts of the tripos (1930 and 1931).

Mitchell completed his clinical training in Birmingham, qualifying MB, BChir. (Cambridge) in 1934, and served as a house officer at Birmingham General Hospital. In that year he married Lilian Mary Buxton MB ChB, and he later helped her direct the outfitting business she inherited from her father, George Buxton. She devoted her life to supporting him and his research until she died in 1983. They had a son and a daughter.

Mitchell returned to Cambridge to study for his PhD (1937) on the physics of radiation. He held first an Elmore research studentship and then a Beit memorial fellowship. In 1936 he was elected to a fellowship of St John's College, which he held until his death. He took up the post of radiological officer at the Christie Hospital and Holt Radium Institute in Manchester (1937–8) and in 1938 was appointed assistant in research to the regius professor of physic at Cambridge, J. A. Ryle.

In 1939 Mitchell became radiotherapist to the Emergency Medical Service in Cambridge and in 1944 was selected to go to Chalk River, Montreal, Canada, to take charge of medical investigations at the National Research Council laboratory, where the joint British and Canadian atomic energy project was installed. He later described demanding a foot of concrete to be laid over the entire floor of the laboratory to protect the workers from the spilled radiation. He continued studies on the biological effects of radiation and was the first to realize the potential value of the gamma-emitting radiation of the isotope 60 Cobalt in the treatment of cancer.

After the Second World War, Mitchell was elected to the new Cambridge chair of radiotherapeutics in 1946 and became the director of the radiotherapeutic centre at Addenbrooke's Hospital, Cambridge. He became internationally known for his work on the treatment of cancer by irradiation. He also tried to improve cancer treatment with a cancer-seeking drug (Synkavit) to carry radioactivity to cancer cells, but had limited success. The acme of his academic career came with his appointment as regius professor of physic at Cambridge in 1957. He set about establishing a postgraduate medical school. The first of the clinical chairs (medicine) was set up in 1963 and surgery in 1965. When the new professor of medicine initiated steps towards a clinical school (opened in 1976), Mitchell gave it his wholehearted support from the outset, and in 1974 he made a generous offer to vacate the regius chair in 1975, so that a new regius professor of physic could be in post before the clinical school was due to open. He reverted to his previous chair of radiotherapeutics, retiring in 1976 but continuing his research and training of PhD students. He wrote numerous articles and a few books, including *Studies in Radiotherapeutics* (1960).

Mitchell's skills were recognized in 1952 by the Royal Society electing him to their fellowship. He was appointed CBE (1951) and MD (1957), and a fellow of the Faculty (later Royal College) of Radiologists (1954) and the Royal College of Physicians (1958). He became Dunham lecturer at Harvard (1958), Withering lecturer at Birmingham University (1958), and honorary DSc. of Birmingham (1958). He was also Pirogoff medallist of the USSR Academy of Sciences (1967), an honorary member of the German Roentgen Society (1967), Silvanus Thompson lecturer of the British Institute of Radiologists (1968), and a foreign fellow of the Indian National Academy of Sciences. In 1970 he was Linacre lecturer of St John's College, Cambridge, and was appointed honorary consultant to the Atomic Energy Authority.

Mitchell was a well-built man, a little portly in later years, and with a well developed moustache. Although in public he appeared somewhat dour, in private he had a ready sense of humour. Even in the heat of summer he always wore the waistcoat of his three-piece suit. He was kind and gentle, and showed immense compassion when treating his cancer patients. He had a German grandfather and spoke fluent German. He showed a great interest in the Anglo-German Medical Society and was president of the British section from 1959 to 1968. Mitchell died in Cambridge where his home was Thorndyke, Huntingdon Road, on 22 February 1987.   IVOR H. MILLS, *rev.*

Sources D. H. Marrian, *Memoirs FRS*, 34 (1988), 581–607 · *CGPLA Eng. & Wales* (1987) · personal knowledge (1996)

Archives CUL, notebooks, lecture notes, papers, and corresp.

Wealth at death £209,687: probate, 11 Aug 1987, *CGPLA Eng. & Wales*

Mitchell, (James) Leslie [*pseud.* Lewis Grassic Gibbon] (**1901–1935**), writer, was born on 13 February 1901 at Hillhead of Seggat, Auchterless, Aberdeenshire, the third son and last child of James McIntosh Mitchell (1862–1936), farmer, and his wife, Lilias Grant Gibbon (1873–1953), daughter of George Gibbon, a farm servant, and his wife, Lilias Grassick. Those who knew James McIntosh Mitchell remember him as a hard-working but rather strict and severe man who was already nearly forty when Leslie was born; Lilias Mitchell appears to have been more lively and spontaneous. Both sides of Mitchell's family could be traced back to Scots peasant stock for several generations.

Early life The lease of their farm having not been renewed, after a brief spell in Aberdeen the Mitchell family moved in 1909 to Bloomfield, in the Kincardineshire parish of Arbuthnott, in the district known as the Howe of the Mearns, close to where Robert Burns's father had been

(James) **Leslie Mitchell** (1901–1935), by unknown photographer

born and brought up. It was there that Leslie spent his formative years. Bloomfield was a smaller and poorer holding than Seggat and the struggle to scrape a living from it even harder, so that quite naturally James Mitchell expected that as his son grew up he would lend a hand with the endless work. Leslie had different ideas. He was an intelligent boy with very much a mind of his own, which did not accept that he should waste time on the mindless routine of farm work. Resentments built up on both sides. As often as not, to escape the unhappiness and drudgery of home he would simply go off on his own and wander in the nearby hills and moorland. There he came across relics of ancient history, the standing stones and flints, which stimulated an interest in prehistoric times that remained with him all his life.

But books were Mitchell's abiding interest during these difficult adolescent years, for through them he could enter into magic worlds far from the grey routine of Bloomfield. He loved the romantic fiction of Rider Haggard and Conan Doyle, and this inspired not only his determination to be a writer but also the belief, which took him some time to get beyond, that fiction was about the remote and the exotic, not about the immediate world in which he was living, and that it was written in English, not the vulgar Scots that his community spoke.

Books also introduced Mitchell to ideas that seemed alien in Arbuthnott. At an early age he was reading Darwin, Huxley, and Haeckel. H. G. Wells, however, was his particular favourite, for he brought not only the delight of science fiction but also an exciting radicalism. Later Mitchell was to turn from Wells 'the inspirer and bamboozler of youth' (Gibbon) but at this stage Wells had a huge formative influence on him. He taught Mitchell, among other things, to despise traditional religion and to place his faith instead in science, to have contempt for conventional education and schoolmasters, to call himself a socialist, and to question the stereotype of women's role in society. All these concerns, in more or less modified form, can be seen in Mitchell's later writing.

These controversial notions, and the outspoken way in which he made them public, did not help to reconcile Mitchell to his parents and the rather traditional community in which he lived. He was looked upon as an eccentric—some would say without all his wits—and it was fortunate that he had at Arbuthnott village school a teacher, Alexander Gray, who recognized that in this oddity lay real talent. They remained friends for the rest of Mitchell's life. When he moved to secondary school, however—Mackie Academy, in Stonehaven—he did not receive such understanding. There he was looked upon as a difficult and opinionated young man who refused to conform. His time there was not happy, and at the age of sixteen he left school as an academic failure.

The expectation now was that Mitchell would get a job as a farm labourer, like most other boys, but he was determined not to be caught up in that narrow and restrictive existence. In 1917, through his own efforts, he got himself a post in Aberdeen, as a junior reporter on the *Aberdeen Journal*. And so at the age of sixteen he left the Mearns, never to return except on holidays and, of course, in his imagination. The move to Aberdeen brought him into a whole new world, the life of a modern city, and his first acquaintanceship with the urban proletariat. Observation of their conditions, particularly when he was assigned to 'the harbour run', hardened his political beliefs, and by this time he was calling himself a communist. This was the year of the Russian revolution, and in a way that he was later to realize was naïve and idealistic he saw this as the beginning of a whole new era. When in 1919 he was appointed to a better-paid post in Glasgow, with the *Scottish Farmer*, his impressions of the horror of capitalist industrialism were strengthened. His essay on Glasgow in *Scottish Scene* (1934) is a virulent attack on the whole system, and describes the 'life that festers in the courts and wynds and alleys of … the Gorbals' (L. G. Gibbon and H. MacDiarmid, *Scottish Scene*, 1934, 137) in a way that shows how deep an impression had been made on him. This was the time of the 'red Clydeside' movement, and he became politically active to such a degree that he lost his job as a journalist, apparently for fiddling his expenses to fund his politics.

Mitchell's response to the horror of Glasgow and to his dismissal left him deeply despondent, and there was even an attempted suicide at this time. The future looked bleak. His prospects in journalism were now gone and yet he was determined not to end up in farming. Like many before him in a similar situation, joining the army seemed the only way to survive, and on 26 August 1919 he joined the Royal Army Service Corps, to spend the next ten years in the services.

As a rather opinionated and sensitive young man Mitchell was clearly not one to take easily to army life, and he hated it with an intensity that comes out in nearly everything that he wrote. The mindless discipline that was demanded and the squalid conditions of the barrack-room appeared to him to have a brutalizing effect upon the men, and in his fiction there are a number of examples of characters who have their souls, as well as their bodies, destroyed by the experience. The army did, however, have some compensations. It allowed him to travel in a way that he would not otherwise have been able to do. In the next four years he was stationed in various countries in the Middle East and central Asia, such as Persia, Palestine, and Egypt, and this provided him with some local colour, which he was later to exploit, sometimes over-zealously, in stories; even at the time, in letters home, he was cultivating the romance of it, describing himself riding across the desert on a camel to Hebron and exploring the bazaars of Alexandria and Cairo. Another advantage was that he was able to visit at first hand many of the great sites of antiquity, and this encouraged him to build on that interest in ancient history which he had had since childhood.

Religion and politics Mitchell's travels in the Middle East and his interest in Egyptology led him to a particular approach to prehistory called the diffusionist theory—associated with Professor Elliot Smith, of London University—that became central to his world view and a preoccupation in his writing. The diffusionists believed that primitive man had lived in a kind of golden age. He was a hunter and food gatherer rather than food producer, a nomad roaming the world in innocent contentment. He had no laws to curb and confine him, and there was no need for them; in his pristine state man was kind and generous and sociable. There was no governmental authority, for no such thing as a state existed prior to the emergence of civilization. There was no religion and no externally imposed moral code, no taboo, no sense of sin. And there was peace in the world. The theory goes on to assert that man lived in this natural state for many thousands of years until, quite by accident, there occurred on the banks of the Nile an event that changed the whole course of the world. This was the emergence of what we now call civilization. It began with the chance discovery of agriculture, due to the peculiar circumstances of the annual flooding of the river. From that developed a settled community and with it a governmental system, a class structure, religious beliefs, and, as this civilization was diffused around the world, the inevitability of war.

Mitchell adopted and propagated this theory enthusiastically, and it shaped his thinking—not so much by changing his convictions as by giving him a theoretical underpinning to what was already there. Thus the religious scepticism that had been his since his youth now became a firm conviction that religion was a disease by which man had been stricken rather than a natural part of a healthy human life, 'no more fundamental to the human character than cancer is fundamental to the human brain' (Gibbon and MacDiarmid, *Scottish Scene*, 313). This disease called religion had had a particularly virulent form in Scotland, where Calvinism was a withering and distorting influence on the human spirit, particularly in matters sexual.

Similarly Mitchell's theory of history was used to underpin his existing political radicalism. It is not possible to say whether he ever belonged to a particular political party. Different friends have made differing claims as to his position, usually to imply that he shared their own stance. Orthodox Marxists in particular have regretted that his views on primitive society got in the way of the true faith. From his youth until his death Mitchell would always have called himself a socialist. At other times he used the term communist, and also anarchist, and this latter term probably best describes his position. There was never any doubt in his mind about the kind of free and egalitarian society to which he aspired; what was less certain was the process by which to get there.

Writings and later life Mitchell left the army on 22 March 1923, and again the question arose of how he was going to make a living. He later told a newspaper feature-writer that for six months he nearly starved in London. Once again the services beckoned, and on 31 August 1923 he enlisted as a clerk in the Royal Air Force, spending the next six years at various bases in the south of England. His duties do not appear to have been too onerous, for it was at this time that he began seriously with his own writing. Nevertheless he seems to have been an efficient clerk, for in April 1924 he was promoted leading aircraftman, and in September 1927 corporal.

One advantage of being back in Britain was that Mitchell was able to develop his relationship with a young woman called Rebecca Middleton (*b*. 1901/2), usually called Ray. They had known each other since childhood in Arbuthnott. Her father, Robert Middleton, was tenant of the farm of Hareden, just across the road from Bloomfield. While Mitchell was abroad he had written regular letters to Ray, and even a few poems; now she was working as a civil servant in London. She and Mitchell formed a strong attachment, and were married at Fulham register office on 15 August 1925.

On marrying Ray was obliged to leave the civil service, and on Mitchell's RAF allowance alone they were desperately poor. They rented rooms in various of the cheaper parts of London, which Mitchell of course was only able to visit when he had leave. The precariousness of their lives became even greater when incredibly he decided to give up the only income that they had. On 31 August 1929 he left the RAF. The foolhardiness of this was even more apparent when a daughter, Rhea, was born, and later a son, Daryll. But Mitchell was now determined that he was going to try to make it as a full-time writer. The omens were not good. To date he had published one slim volume of non-fiction, *Hanno, or, The Future of Exploration* (1928), and a short story or two, but the combined income from this would not have kept them going for long. Gradually

he did establish himself as a writer, and although income was never great he was able to move at Christmas 1931 to a more comfortable home in the new town of Welwyn Garden City, in Hertfordshire. Now with his own study, he was able to see himself as the real writer that Arbuthnott sceptics had always doubted.

The Mitchell fiction Mitchell's breakthrough as a writer came with a series of short stories in *Cornhill Magazine*, starting in January 1929 and drawing heavily on his Middle Eastern experiences. Getting his first novel published proved more difficult, and *Stained Radiance* had been revised again and again, and rejected by twenty publishers, before it appeared in September 1930. A deeply ironic and sardonic anatomy of life in the modern city, it has as its hero an airman who aspires to be a writer. Mitchell's second novel, *The Thirteenth Disciple* (1931), was even more autobiographical. The story takes the hero through his childhood in the north-east of Scotland, journalism in Glasgow, and service in the army before he sets off on an expedition to Yucatan, in search of a lost city.

From his boyhood reading in Haggard and Wells, Mitchell was steeped in romance, and this is evident in much of his fiction. *The Lost Trumpet* (1932) follows an archaeological expedition by a group of characters, all of whom display sterility of some kind in their lives, so that it becomes a quest for fertility in the desert, while in *Image and Superscription* (1933) the hero, who has been damaged by a religious upbringing, follows a quest for meaning and enlightenment that takes him to a commune of naturists in Minnesota. *Three Go Back* (1932) and *Gay Hunter* (1934) adopt Wellsian time travel to compare modern civilization with the values of the primitive past.

There is a consensus that *Spartacus* (1933) is the best of the Mitchell novels, and in it he takes the story of the slave revolt in ancient Rome and makes of it a political paradigm of the revolutionary process itself. Making this link was not original to him. Spartacus was a recurring figure in socialist iconography, and Mitchell was familiar with the Spartacist movement in Germany led by the Marxists Karl Liebknecht and Rosa Luxemburg. In *Spartacus* is to be found Mitchell's most acute analysis of the nature and the demands of revolution, of the tension between idealism and ruthless practicality. It is presented as a problem of means and ends, the paradox of the cruel inhumanity required to bring about a humane society, which he confronts later in *Grey Granite*, but less convincingly. Mitchell's absorption in primitive history had led him to a vision of the true society that emphasized freedom and anarchy, but on the other hand the harsh experience of the general strike of 1926 had taught him that political effectiveness depended on the antithesis of these, on the kind of discipline that he had hated in the army: strict mass organization, the suppression of self.

In the novel this issue is explored through the juxtaposed characters of Elpinice and Kleon, with Spartacus trying to find his way between them. The whole venture begins in his love for Elpinice and their vision of the free life that they will live together; it is she who releases him from the chains that the masters have placed upon him.

But he soon learns the necessity of Kleon's political authoritarianism, and one of the most admirable features of *Spartacus* is the way in which the character of the hero develops as he gradually apprehends the significance of what he is engaged in. He abandons the open, democratic organization of the army in favour of a kind of dictatorship, and reaches his own sacrificial crisis point when he is prepared to abandon Elpinice in childbirth. But Kleon himself can only be a temporary guide. He has been distorted by his experience of oppression; he is a eunuch, essentially sterile. Even to the end Spartacus retains his vision of the future, when there will be neither master nor slave, which is quite alien to Kleon's idea of the totalitarian state.

The Gibbon fiction On 2 September 1932 Mitchell published a novel, *Sunset Song*, that was so different from what he had written so far that he felt the need to adopt a pseudonym, Lewis Grassic Gibbon, derived from his mother's family names. It had been written at great speed—it is said in a mere six weeks—but then he was working through matter that had been simmering in his mind for years.

The difference lies not so much in theme or location as in language and style. Mitchell had always been aware of his uncertainty in standard English. He claimed that for someone brought up speaking Scots that voice always remained a real and haunting thing, no matter how hard he tried to Anglicize himself. But to write in broad dialect was not a commercial possibility. His solution is highly personal and ingenious, and confirms him as one of the great experimental writers of modernist literature. What he does in effect is to invent his own language, in which he tries to capture the rhythm and intonation—the voice, as it were—of north-east Scots without a lot of dialect words. The result is essentially a spoken novel. The voice changes, the point of view fluctuates, but there is always a distinctive spoken voice behind the prose. And with this return to his linguistic roots comes naturally a sharper focus in what he is writing about, a return to the world of his mother tongue that makes *Sunset Song* the greatest evocation of that particular community and culture.

It is the emergence of this authentically Scots voice of Lewis Grassic Gibbon that creates the great writer, for with that voice comes the ability to present Scottish rural life from the inside in a way that had never been done before and not from the point of view of some alien external narrator. For the first time ordinary Scots folk are given their own voice to present themselves, warts and all.

The central character, Chris Guthrie, is in many ways clearly based on the author himself. She grows up in the same kind of place, in the same social situation, and goes through many of the conflicts with parents and the community at large that Mitchell himself experienced. But equally obviously Chris is not Mitchell himself. She is female through and through, so much so that when the book first came out one female critic insisted that the author must be a woman, for no man could have made such an imaginative leap into essential femininity. The author both identifies with the character and is detached from her, and it is this combination of subjective introspection and objective distancing that helps to make the characterization so effective. And she is not a fixed or flat character but one who changes and matures, so that in the story of Chris's development from childhood, through the confusions and uncertainties to the full flower of womanhood, Gibbon is able to explore and open up areas of human experience in which we can all share.

Chris is more intelligent than her parents and others in the community around her, more alive to things of the imagination, more reflective, and with a spirit that can look beyond the narrowness of farm life. When she goes to school this spirit is released and she discovers that books can carry her into another world, where life is more refined and exciting. And yet she is a peasant girl with generations of peasant blood in her veins, with a strong emotional attachment to the land itself and the folk who live on it. That is the inheritance from her mother, who could 'never forget the singing of the winds in those fields when she was young … or the feel of the earth below her toes' (L. G. Gibbon, *Sunset Song*, 1959, 33). While her father encourages her education as a means of getting on, her mother insists that 'there are better things than your books or studies … there's the countryside your own, you its, in the days when you're neither bairn nor woman' (ibid.). For a time these conflicts are laid to rest when, with the death of her mother, Chris's chance of education and a career disappears, and she has to fulfil a more traditional female role, staying at home to look after the house. But with the death of her father comes the opportunity once more to move into an educated, professional, middle-class way of life. And it is then, when she is all set to leave behind this life of the land and go off to college, that she realizes that to do so would be a fundamental betrayal of her real self. In a profound moment of self-awareness it becomes clear to her that her attachment to the land is basic to her being, for the land is the one thing that is permanent in a world of change. She marries Ewan Tavendale, a young farmer who 'had fair the land in his bones' (ibid., 29). Their relationship is evoked with such lyricism that when the First World War comes along and destroys it the novel takes on a tragic force.

This personal story of the conflicts and self-discovery of a girl growing up in rural Scotland at the beginning of the twentieth century is at the heart of *Sunset Song*. But equally important is the fact that this drama all takes place at a time of enormous change in farming life. At the start of the book Kinraddie is a community of small farms, each sustaining its own family. By the end it is very different; mechanization and economic change have turned farming into a large-scale capitalist industry. And with the changes in farming come changes in the whole way of life. The old language, the old songs, the old neighbourly ways have all disappeared. This is the sunset of which we are singing, and again the First World War provides the climax, the final setting of the sun. The new young minister of Kinraddie, Robert Colquohoun, makes this point at the unveiling of the war memorial when he says of the dead of the parish 'With them we may say there died a thing older than themselves, these were the Last of the Peasants, the last of the Old Scots folk' (p. 193).

When published in 1932 *Sunset Song* was received rapturously both in Britain and in America. Compton Mackenzie, for instance, declared, 'I have no hesitation in saying that *Sunset Song*, by Lewis Grassic Gibbon, is the richest novel about Scottish life written for many years' (*Daily Mail*, 13 Sept 1932). Only back home in the Mearns was the response more grudging, where some felt that he had presented the folk and their way of life less than flatteringly. Buoyed up by his success, Gibbon went on quickly to produce the second novel, *Cloud Howe* (1933), in what was always intended as a trilogy, to be called *A Scots Quair*. In this book Chris has married the Revd Robert Colquohoun, and soon after their marriage they move from Kinraddie to Segget, where Robert becomes the minister. Segget is a creation of the author's imagination, a small manufacturing town in the Mearns depending upon its jute mills—very different from Kinraddie, which is based directly on what Gibbon had known at first hand since childhood.

Cloud Howe is set in the 1920s—a period of severe economic depression—and Gibbon gives a vivid picture of the hardship and injustice that he sees as an inevitable part of the capitalist structure. Much of the novel is concerned with differing political views about how this terrible situation can be remedied. Fascism, Scottish nationalism, labour socialism are all examined and dismissed. The main interest lies with Robert Colquohoun and his struggle to find his own solution to the ills of the time. When he first comes to Segget he naïvely thinks that he can turn to the so-called Christian community of the kirk and that merely by exhorting them to put their principles into practice he can change the face of the town. He soon realizes that the respectable kirk folk have no interest in reform and social justice. Robert then aligns himself with the mill workers and their kind of socialism, only to be disillusioned by the collapse of the general strike, and eventually to fall into a vague kind of mysticism that relies on the second coming of Christ. Chris has very little sympathy for this 'madman's dream' of Robert's (L. G. Gibbon, *Cloud Howe*, 1959, 127), and this gives a sense of estrangement and failure to their marriage. Chris indeed is sceptical about all the schemes for putting the world to rights. To her they are all clouds that will pass, all illusions. Her role in the novel is to stand back from the main action and provide critical commentary. The most positive character is her son young Ewan Tavendale, whom we see growing up to be a very clear-headed and forceful figure who 'refused all clouds and all dreams' (ibid., 122). When Robert, aware that he is close to dying and at last realizing the seriousness of the situation, preaches one final sermon, in which he turns away from the soft old creeds, Christianity and socialism, and advocates 'a stark, sure creed that will cut like a knife, a surgeon's knife through the doubt and disease' (ibid., 156) it is Ewan who

picks up on this, and it is his role in the last novel of the trilogy to discover this creed in communism.

Grey Granite (1934) is set in the imagined industrial city of Duncairn and focuses on the differing responses of Chris and her son to its severe social problems. Now a widow again, she helps to run a boarding-house, while Ewan too is forced to earn a living and goes to work in the local ironworks. At first he feels alien from the working classes around him, dismissing them as mindless 'keelies'; he is more interested in books and in history. But gradually we see him develop into the kind of revolutionary leader that was foreshadowed in *Spartacus*—wholly committed and willing to sacrifice personal fulfilment to the necessary movement of history. Chris again stands back sceptically. Towards the end Ewan goes off on a hunger march, but the novel concludes not with him but with Chris, who returns to the land from which she came, 'concerning none and concerned with none' (p. 144). It was essential to the plan of the trilogy that it should move from a traditional farming community to a town, and then to an industrial city. Thus not only is the central theme of change maintained but *A Scots Quair* as a whole reflects the main pattern of development of the western world in our time.

The completion of *A Scots Quair* established Lewis Grassic Gibbon as perhaps the most important Scottish novelist of the twentieth century. Growing success as a writer, however, also had its downside. There is no doubt that overwork played a part in Mitchell's tragically early death, at not quite thirty-four. Partly this was due to the need to prove himself to those doubters back home, partly it stemmed from the very precarious nature of his early finances. In the last year of his life he published no fewer than six books. At the time of his death he left a huge number of projects at various stages of preparation, and it has been estimated that by the summer of 1934 he was committed to an output of over a million words.

Mitchell suffered from gastric problems for most of his later life. He put this down to the damage wrought by years of services food, though the fact that he was a heavy cigarette smoker perhaps did not help. He was admitted to Queen Victoria Hospital, Welwyn Garden City, at the beginning of February 1935, and there he underwent an operation for a perforated gastric ulcer. He died, of peritonitis, on 7 February. There was a non-religious service for him at Golders Green crematorium on 11 February, and his ashes were interred on 23 February in Arbuthnott churchyard, where a handsome granite memorial now stands.

A Scots Quair was first issued as a single volume in 1946 and has remained in print ever since. The reissue in recent years of most of Mitchell's other work is a mark of his growing stature. *Sunset Song* has become perhaps the most widely taught novel in Scottish schools. The televising of *A Scots Quair* in the 1970s brought his work to an even wider audience, reflected in the founding in 1991 of the Grassic Gibbon Centre at Arbuthnott, with an archive of manuscripts and memorabilia. Academic interest in Mitchell, both in Scotland and throughout the world, has grown apace, and in 2001, to mark the centenary of his birth, the Association for Scottish Literary Studies devoted its annual conference to his life and work.

DOUGLAS F. YOUNG

Sources I. S. Munro, *Leslie Mitchell: Lewis Grassic Gibbon* (1966) · D. F. Young, *Beyond the sunset* (1973) · W. K. Malcolm, *A blasphemer and reformer* (1984) · b. cert. · m. cert. · d. cert. · L. G. Gibbon [J. L. Mitchell], 'Memoirs of a materialist', NL Scot. [typescript]
Archives NL Scot., corresp. and literary papers · NL Scot., corresp. and papers · NL Scot., further corresp. and papers | NL Scot., letters to Mr Alexander Gray and Mrs Alexander Gray · U. Aberdeen, letters to Jean Baxter · U. Edin. L., letters to Helen B. Cruickshank
Likenesses photograph, Grassic Gibbon Centre, Arbuthnott [*see illus.*]
Wealth at death £329 3s. 10d.: administration, 9 April 1935, CGPLA Eng. & Wales

Mitchell, Leslie Scott Falconer (1905–1985), actor and television broadcaster, was born on 4 October 1905 in Edinburgh, the only child of Charles Eric Mitchell (1881–1947), caterer, of Edinburgh, and his wife, Leslie Florence Whittington (1884–1956), *née* Lowe. He had a clouded childhood. His parents separated. His beautiful but wayward mother (whose three marriages were all to end unhappily and who twice attempted suicide) went on a holiday to the United States early in the First World War and found herself unable to return. He was told that his absent father had died in battle. He was left to be brought up by the novelist W. J. *Locke and his wife. Locke became a trusted mentor, and arranged for Mitchell to be educated at King's School, Canterbury. He was destined for the navy, but ill health, which dogged him for most of his life, thwarted that plan. He completed his education at Chillon College on Lake Geneva.

In 1923 the first of two unsympathetic stepfathers found Mitchell a job as a trainee stockbroker. However, after a short period he tried the stage. He had not had any professional dramatic training, but striking good looks and a strong, clear voice, aided by some useful introductions from a number of theatrical friends, secured him some small parts in which he rapidly demonstrated natural ability as an actor. Between 1923 and 1925 he toured Britain with the Arts League and for the next three years acted in various West End productions. In 1928, after a successful tour in *Flying Squad* by Edgar Wallace, he suffered a major motor cycle accident. His multiple injuries were treated by many operations. Plastic surgery to his face, a rebuilt jawline, a damaged eye, and the fitting of a brace to his leg kept him away from work for more than a year.

Eventually Mitchell returned successfully to the West End stage. He narrowly missed being the first to play Captain Stanhope, the leading part in *Journey's End* by R. C. Sherriff, but he later acted the part in London, in a BBC broadcast on armistice day, and on tour in South Africa. In Johannesburg he happened to meet the father he believed had been killed seventeen years earlier.

In 1934, after more than a decade of acting, Mitchell joined the BBC as a general announcer and soon transferred to compèring dance-band music. He was chosen from 600 applicants as the male announcer to launch the

Leslie Scott Falconer Mitchell (1905–1985), by Baron Studios, 1951

world's first public service of high definition television at Alexandra Palace on 2 November 1936. *The Times* referred to Mitchell's 'very successful transmissions'. He was charming and handsome, despite the injuries of the motor cycle accident, and always immaculately groomed, usually with a red carnation in his buttonhole. He soon became a favourite with the pre-war television audience.

Mitchell conducted some twenty interviews a week for *Picture Page*, a television magazine. Before the outbreak of the Second World War, which was to suspend television for the duration, he resigned from the BBC to become the British Movietone news commentator and a freelance broadcaster. He enlisted in the Home Guard and in addition to being the encouraging voice of the cinema newsreels he worked on the Allied Expeditionary Forces Radio. His innumerable wartime broadcasts ranged from the *March of the Movies* to *The Brains Trust*. After the war he visited the United States to study publicity methods, and on his return he was appointed publicity director to the film-maker Sir Alexander Korda.

In 1948 Mitchell returned to his freelance activities as a writer, commentator, and producer. He was a television commentator for the wedding of Princess Elizabeth and the duke of Edinburgh, and for the silver wedding of George VI and Queen Elizabeth. In 1951, when the political parties first tentatively used television for publicity, he interviewed Anthony Eden in the Conservatives' one general election programme. He was prominent in the launch of commercial television in London in 1955, and in Birmingham a year later. In 1981 he produced an entertaining autobiography *Leslie Mitchell Reporting …*. In 1983 he was made the first honorary member of the Royal Television Society and in 1984 a freeman of the City of London in recognition of his wartime contribution to the morale of Londoners.

On 2 June 1938 Mitchell married Phyllis Joan Constance (1913–1965), a young widow whose husband Anthony Wood had died after less than a year of marriage. She was the daughter of the London impresario Firth Shephard. In 1965 Phyllis died and on 29 October 1966 Mitchell married Inge Vibeke Asboe (b. 1927), daughter of Niels Andreas Jorgensen, a merchant of Aarhus, Denmark. There were no children of either marriage. Deteriorating health cast a shadow over Mitchell's last years but he continued to work, his last television programme about the newsreels, *Around the World in Seven Minutes and Four Times on Saturday*, being completed two months before his death. He died in Paddington Community Hospital, London, on 23 November 1985, after a brief final illness; he was survived by his second wife. His ashes were scattered in Scotland.

LEONARD MIALL

Sources L. Mitchell, *Leslie Mitchell reporting …* (1981) [autobiography] · private information (2004) [Inge Mitchell] · personal knowledge (2004) · *The Times* (25 Nov 1985) · *Daily Telegraph* (25 Nov 1985) · *Daily Mail* (22 May 1936) · A. Briggs, *The history of broadcasting in the United Kingdom*, 4 vols. (1961–79), vols. 2, 4 · B. Sendall, *Origin and foundation, 1946–62* (1982), vol. 1 of *Independent television in Britain* (1982–90) · R. Dougall, *In and out of the box* (1973) · B. Norman, *Here's looking at you* (1984) · m. certs.
Archives FILM BBC WAC · BFI NFTVA, *This is your life*, Thames, 1 Dec 1983 · BFI NFTVA, performance footage | SOUND BL NSA, documentary recordings
Likenesses Baron Studios, photographs, 1951, NPG, Hult. Arch. [*see illus.*]
Wealth at death £32,357: probate, 11 Feb 1986, *CGPLA Eng. & Wales*

Mitchell, Maria Hay Mackenzie (1820–1907). *See under* Mitchell, John Murray (1815–1904).

Mitchell, Peter (1824–1899), businessman and politician in Canada, was born at Newcastle, New Brunswick, on 4 January 1824, the son of Peter Mitchell (1795–1851), a hotel owner and tavern keeper, and his wife, Barbara, *née* Grant (1800–1869). Educated at the county grammar school, he studied law and was called to the bar in 1849. He married Isabella, *née* Carvell (d. 1889), the widow of James Gough, of Saint John, New Brunswick, on 9 March 1853. In the same year he entered into a partnership with his brother-in-law John Haws in the business of lumbering and ship-building.

Mitchell was elected to the legislative assembly in 1856 as a member for Northumberland county. He did not stand in the 1861 election but in the same year he was appointed to the legislative council, and was also named to the executive council as a member of Samuel Leonard Tilley's government. In September 1864 he attended, unofficially, the Charlottetown conference held to discuss the union of the maritime provinces. This project was dropped in favour of a larger union of British North America. Mitchell championed this scheme and, with Sir George Cartier, was a strong supporter of the federal principle, as opposed to Sir John A. Macdonald's preference for a legislative union. He was a New Brunswick delegate to the Quebec conference in October 1864, where he assisted in drawing up the Quebec resolutions, which became the basis for confederations.

Tilley's government faced a general election in 1865 and was soundly defeated by the anti-confederates led by Albert Smith. Members of Smith's government were united only in their opposition to the confederation scheme as proposed at Quebec. Shortly after they took power Lieutenant-Governor Arthur Hamilton Gordon received instructions to promote confederation. Mitchell, a member of the legislative council, and the only member of Tilley's government still in office, became Gordon's adviser and attempted, unsuccessfully, to manoeuvre Smith into supporting the Quebec resolutions, but Gordon's attempt to form a coalition government with Smith and Mitchell as leaders failed. In April 1866 Mitchell persuaded the legislative council to pass resolutions in favour of confederation which Gordon accepted. Smith's government then resigned in protest. The assembly was dissolved and a general election was called. Taking advantage of exaggerated fears of a Fenian invasion, the confederates led by Mitchell and Tilley won an easy victory. Mitchell attended the final confederation conference in London, where he played a part in obtaining concessions for the maritime provinces. His blunt manner and bullying tactics in the events of 1865–6 earned him the nickname of 'Bismarck' from his political opponents.

The dominion of Canada was proclaimed on 1 July 1867. Mitchell was appointed to the Canadian senate and became a member of Macdonald's first cabinet as minister of marine and fisheries. Enforcing the fishery regulations was the responsibility of British warships assisted by two small Canadian vessels, but Mitchell felt the British were not doing their job. In 1869 he therefore added six new cruisers and ordered the seizure of American vessels fishing illegally in Canadian waters. So many vessels were seized that it caused alarm in Britain and strained relations between Canada and the United States, with President Grant referring to Canada as 'a semi-independent but irresponsible agent' (Greaves, 62). In response, Mitchell, in 1870, published *A Review of President Grant's Message to the US Congress*. Because of Mitchell's actions the British agreed to the setting up of a joint commission to settle this and other disputes between Canada and the United States, which resulted in the treaty of Washington in 1871. Mitchell was influential in establishing acceptance by the United States of Canada's right to control the fisheries, and one of the articles in this treaty permitted the Americans to fish in Canadian waters for twelve years in exchange for a sum of money to be determined by arbitration. The British were happy with this treaty, which eased tense relations between Britain and the United States, but Mitchell, Macdonald, and many other Canadians felt that

Britain had failed to win other concessions for Canada or to defend Canadian interests.

In 1872 Mitchell resigned from the senate to stand for a seat in the House of Commons. He won the seat in his old constituency by acclamation and continued to hold it, from 1872 to 1878 and from 1882 to 1890, as an independent Liberal, having split from the official Liberal Party. At the time of the scandal over the Canadian Pacific Railway Mitchell had been the only member of the former government who would not support Macdonald as party leader. Since he also refused to follow Alexander Mackenzie as leader, he sat as an independent. He moved to Montreal in the 1870s and in 1885 became the owner of the *Montreal Herald*.

By the 1890s Mitchell was a forgotten man who felt his political role in confederation had not been properly acknowledged. He considered that he had been badly treated by Macdonald, and he expressed his views in 'The secret history of Canadian politics', published in the *Evening News* in 1894. He suffered defeat in the elections of 1891 and 1896, and his attempts to obtain a knighthood failed while the anti-confederate leader Smith was successful. His requests for an appointment as lieutenant-governor of New Brunswick were also unsuccessful. Instead, in 1897, he was appointed an inspector of fisheries for Quebec and the maritime provinces.

In July 1899 Mitchell suffered a stroke. He died on 24 October in his rooms at the Windsor Hotel, Montreal, where he had lived since his wife's death and his daughter's confinement to a psychiatric hospital. He was buried in the Presbyterian cemetery in Newcastle. His reputation rests chiefly on his strong support for confederation, his involvement in the organization of the first department of marine and fisheries, and his attempts to establish Canadian rights to the fisheries off the Atlantic coast.

W. A. SPRAY

Sources E. H. Greaves, 'Peter Mitchell, a father of confederation', MA diss., University of New Brunswick, 1958 · R. S. Longley, 'Peter Mitchell, guardian of the north Atlantic fisheries, 1867–1871', *Canadian Historical Review*, 22 (1941), 389–402 · R. Tallman, 'Peter Mitchell and the genesis of a national fisheries policy', *Acadiensis*, 2/2 (spring 1975), 66–78 · D. Creighton, *The road to confederation* (1964) · M. O. Hammond, *Confederation and its leaders* (1927), 213–23 · W. S. MacNutt, *New Brunswick: a history, 1784–1867* (1963) · P. B. Waite, *The life and times of confederation, 1864–1867* (1962), 229–62 · *Montreal Star* (26 Oct 1899) · *The Gleaner* (25 Oct 1899) · Graves MSS, public archives of New Brunswick, MC I/56/I · J. Hannay, *Wilmot and Tilley* (1907), 246–7, 262, 271 · W. A. Spray, 'Mitchell, Peter', *DCB*, vol. 12
Archives University of New Brunswick, Fredericton, Harriet Irving Library, MSS collection H6
Likenesses photographs, public archives of New Brunswick [P106/2, P37]

Mitchell, Sir Peter Chalmers (1864–1945), zoologist, was born at Dunfermline, Fife, on 23 November 1864, the third of the eleven children of the Revd Alexander Mitchell, and his wife, Marion Hay, daughter of the Revd Peter Chalmers. He was educated at Dunfermline high school and Aberdeen grammar school before passing on to King's College in the University of Aberdeen. Capped MA in 1884, he won an exhibition to Christ Church, Oxford, where he obtained a first-class degree in comparative anatomy in 1888. From 1888 to 1891 he was a university demonstrator in the subject, and assistant to the Linacre professor. It was during this period that Chalmers Mitchell started supplementing his income by journalism; over the following decade he translated several books, and in 1900 published a biography of T. H. Huxley.

In 1893 Chalmers Mitchell married Lilian Bessie Pritchard (*d.* 1965), youngest daughter of Charles *Pritchard (1808–1893). The marriage was childless and his relations with his wife seem to have been distant. He moved to London in the same year, and was appointed lecturer at Charing Cross Hospital medical school, and then in 1894 at the London Hospital. Chalmers Mitchell also worked in the prosectorium of the Zoological Society of London, where at the turn of the century there was widespread criticism of the management of London Zoo under Philip Lutley Sclater, the society's secretary since 1859. In 1902 Sclater retired and attempted to arrange for his son, William Lutley Sclater, to succeed him. Chalmers Mitchell was nominated as an alternative candidate and in April 1903 was elected by 530 votes to Sclater's 336. He immediately embarked on implementing the recommendations of the 1902 committee of inquiry. Chalmers Mitchell wholeheartedly subscribed to the view expressed by the German animal dealer Carl Hagenbeck that animals need fresh air, rather than heat, in order to remain healthy. As a result, he ensured that the animals had access to open air at will and were kept in well-ventilated accommodation. In 1907, Hagenbeck opened a zoo near Hamburg, where the animals were confined by moats instead of bars. Impressed, Chalmers Mitchell oversaw a similar development, at London Zoo; in 1914 the Mappin Terraces, a massive reinforced concrete structure for animals, including bears and wild goats, were opened.

During the First World War, Chalmers Mitchell was attached to the department of military intelligence at the War Office. He concentrated on propaganda for distribution on the German front lines, and developed the idea of dropping leaflets from hydrogen balloons. For his military work, he was mentioned in dispatches and appointed CBE in 1918.

After the war, Chalmers Mitchell felt unsettled and contemplated leaving the Zoological Society. He undertook much work for *The Times* and in 1920 was a passenger in the aeroplane which the paper commissioned to fly from Cairo to the Cape. This gallant attempt, which he called 'The golden journey' and regarded as the adventure in which he lived most, ended in failure when the aeroplane crashed 200 miles from Dar es Salaam. During the 1920s Chalmers Mitchell developed a close friendship with Joan Beauchamp Procter (1897–1931), curator of reptiles at London Zoo. Despite the distant relationship with his wife, and contemporary gossip, there is no evidence that she was his mistress—her poor health would probably have prevented the relationship from being other than platonic. In 1924 an aquarium, the most ambitious single project ever undertaken by the Zoological Society, was opened under the Mappin Terraces. A new reptile house was opened in 1927.

In 1907 Chalmers Mitchell had been very impressed by New York's Bronx Zoo, but plans for a similar park near London were delayed by the First World War. In 1928, however, the Zoological Society, acting on Chalmers Mitchell's advice, purchased Whipsnade Farm in Bedfordshire. The new zoological park opened to the public in 1931. It proved unexpectedly popular, and Chalmers Mitchell always regarded Whipsnade as his crowning achievement.

Although the Zoological Society's affairs had first call on his time, Chalmers Mitchell remained active in other areas. As early as 1912 his address to the British Association drew attention to the need to preserve wild life and he was president of the Society for the Preservation of the Fauna of the Empire from 1923 to 1927. In 1906 he was elected a fellow of the Royal Society and thereafter served on its council and many of its committees. He was knighted in 1929. He was responsible for editing most of the life-science articles in the eleventh edition of the *Encyclopaedia Britannica* (1910).

Chalmers Mitchell retired as secretary of the Zoological Society in 1935, a year in which London Zoo had 1,962,136 visitors (in 1903, there had been just 657,208). He had hoped to spend much of his retirement at Málaga in Spain, but the Spanish Civil War compelled his reluctant return to England. Much of this period was spent in writing—notably an autobiography, *My Fill of Days* (1937), and an account of his experiences in Spain, *My House in Málaga* (1938). He unsuccessfully contested the Scottish Universities' parliamentary seat in 1938. His political views were popularly regarded as communist, but his thoughtful writings on politics reveal that he had no affiliation to any party. During the Second World War, he served as honorary treasurer of the Joint Committee for Soviet Aid. He had an enthusiasm for motoring which dated from the turn of the century, and continued to drive a fast sports car into old age.

Chalmers Mitchell died in University College Hospital on 2 July 1945 as a result of being knocked down outside the north gate of London Zoo—an accident which he insisted was his fault. He was cremated and his ashes were interred at Whipsnade. J. C. EDWARDS

Sources P. C. Mitchell, *My fill of days* (1937) · E. Hindle, *Obits. FRS*, 5 (1945–8), 367–72 · *The Times* (3 July 1945) · P. Chalmers Mitchell, *Centenary history of the Zoological Society of London* (1929) · *WWW*, 1941–50 · P. C. Mitchell, *My house in Málaga* (1938) · L. Pendar, *Whipsnade, my Africa* (1991) · minute books of the Zoological Society of London, Zoological Society of London, Regent's Park, London · *CGPLA Eng. & Wales* (1945)

Archives News Int. RO, papers as contributor to *The Times* | JRL, letters to the *Manchester Guardian* · Rice University, Houston, Texas, Woodson Research Center, corresp. with Sir Julian Huxley

Likenesses photograph, *c*.1929, Zoological Society of London, Regent's Park, London · H. Coster, photographs, 1930–39, NPG · W. Nicholson, oils, 1935, Zoological Society of London, Regent's Park, London · W. Stoneman, photograph, 1935, NPG · A. Mandl, clay head, *c*.1958, Zoological Society of London · A. Mandl, bronze bas-relief, 1960, Whipsnade, Bedfordshire, Chalmers Mitchell Memorial

Wealth at death £13,249 2*s*. 11*d*.: probate, 15 Nov 1945, *CGPLA Eng. & Wales*

Mitchell, Peter Dennis (1920–1992), biochemist, was born on 29 September 1920 at 19 Rustic Avenue, Mitcham, Surrey, the younger son of Christopher Gibbs Mitchell (1889–1951), civil servant, and his wife, Kate Beatrice Dorothy, *née* Taplin (1892–1974), daughter of William George Taplin of Peckham and his wife, Rosetta. His father was the elder son of Christopher Mitchell, a stonemason and quarry owner who had moved to London towards the end of the nineteenth century, going into partnership in a business importing stone to London. His father's brother, Sir Godfrey Way *Mitchell, went into his father's business, but after the First World War he acquired and built up the firm of George Wimpey and was chairman from 1930 to 1973. Wimpey shares were passed to the family and Mitchell became one of the beneficiaries, particularly through his mother and his elder brother. His father was a successful civil servant and was made OBE. His mother, who probably had the greater influence on him, was a shy, gentle person, of very independent thought and action, with a strong artistic perceptiveness. Being a rationalist and an atheist, she taught him that he had to accept responsibility for his own destiny and especially for his failings in life.

Mitchell went initially to Streatham grammar school and transferred to Barrow Hedges School after the family moved to Carshalton, Surrey, in 1927. In 1931 he entered Queen's College, Taunton, a school with a Methodist foundation, though from the age of about fifteen he adopted an atheistic philosophy. He failed the Cambridge scholarship exam in 1939, but went to Jesus College on the recommendation of his headmaster at Taunton, C. L. Wiseman, an able mathematician who influenced Mitchell significantly. At Cambridge, Mitchell followed courses for the natural sciences tripos, studying physics, chemistry, physiology, mathematics, and biochemistry in part one (in which he obtained a second class), and specializing in biochemistry for part two (in which he obtained an upper second). After graduating in 1942, he continued in Cambridge, undertaking research with Jim Danielli as his supervisor while also working on aspects of British anti-Lewisite as part of the war effort. Danielli introduced him to David Keilin, the scientist whom he came to love and respect more than any other. It was during this time that he met Jennifer Moyle, also working in the biochemistry department at Cambridge. Moyle worked with Mitchell from about 1948 until her retirement in 1983. Mitchell's thesis for the PhD degree was referred because it was too speculative, Mitchell having incorporated many philosophical elements. The final thesis, on the action of penicillin, was accepted in December 1950. Meanwhile, on 11 December 1944, Mitchell married Eileen Margaret Forbes Rollo (*b*. 1917/18), a nurse, and daughter of William Forbes Rollo, a civil servant; they had twins, Jeremy and Julia. However, the marriage was not successful and they parted some years later.

During the 1950s Mitchell worked on aspects of the properties of bacterial membranes, especially the transport of phosphate. In 1955 he was persuaded by Michael Swann, then professor of zoology at Edinburgh, to leave

Cambridge in order to set up a new chemical biology unit in the zoology department at Edinburgh, where he would be a lecturer (later senior lecturer and ultimately reader) and director of the new unit. Moyle also transferred to Edinburgh and their collaboration continued. Mitchell bought the Old Manse at Carrington, south of Edinburgh, and renovated it for use as his home. His most significant intellectual development during this period was the formulation of ideas about vectorial metabolism. In essence this considered the directional aspect of the chemical processes taking place in cells. With membrane-bound enzymes, it implied that a reaction could be catalysed where the reactants came from one side of the membrane but the products were released on the other, thus bringing about both the reaction and the transfer of a substance across the membrane. Initially Mitchell applied his ideas to reactions such as those in which a phosphate group is added to or removed from a sugar. Mitchell himself considered this theoretical aspect of his work as his most fundamental and important contribution to biology, though he is remembered more for its specific application in the chemiosmotic theory where he considered the addition of a phosphate to the adenine nucleotide ADP, to form ATP as a vectorial process.

The means by which energy is drawn from oxidation of substances in cells and converted to the energy currency, ATP, is known as oxidative phosphorylation. Mitchell proposed his chemiosmotic theory in 1961 and revised it five years later to its final form. He suggested that the respiratory chain, the enzyme system which reduces oxygen to water in all aerobic cells, pumps protons across the membrane, creating both a gradient of protons from one side to the other and an electrical potential. The protons return across the membrane, encouraged by the potential via any route available. The major route is through the ATPase or ATP synthase enzyme driving the addition of a phosphate to adenosine diphosphate (ADP) to form adenosine triphosphate (ATP). Thus energy from oxidation is initially stored as a proton gradient and membrane potential, which is then used for ATP synthesis. These proposals were not easily accepted by the scientific community. Workers in the field of oxidative phosphorylation were almost all trained chemists and believed that energy from oxidation must initially be stored in a chemical substance, the search for which had occupied many workers for a long period without success. Moreover, Mitchell's proposals appeared with arguments sufficient enough to make them plausible but without any experimental evidence in their support. It was therefore some years before the theory was accepted.

On 1 November 1958 Mitchell married (Patricia) Helen Mary (b. 1924), formerly Robertson. An artist whom he had originally met in Cambridge, she was the daughter of Colonel Raymont Patrick Thomas ffrench, formerly of the Indian army. They brought up two more boys, Jason and Gideon, and enjoyed more than thirty years of a close and happy marriage.

During the early 1960s Mitchell's health deteriorated and he suffered from stomach ulcers. On medical advice he resigned his readership in 1963 and moved to a cottage outside Bodmin in Cornwall. He had earlier been attracted by a dilapidated, Regency-fronted mansion at Glynn, to the south-east of Bodmin, which he bought and with the co-operation of Moyle restored to form a research institute together with a home for his family and flats. The new Glynn Research Institute, which opened for research work in 1965, possessed laboratories, preparation rooms, a library, and ancillary facilities. It was initially staffed by Mitchell, Moyle, and as technician Roy Mitchell (no relation to Peter), together with the company secretary. Research was directed at testing the validity of the chemiosmotic theory. The isolation of Glynn gave Mitchell an ideal environment for his work, and it was compensated by his ability to discuss ideas prodigiously by letter.

In 1966 Mitchell published the first Grey Book from Glynn, a revised and much fuller version of the theory proposed in the 1961 paper in *Nature*. It was the Grey Book rather than other publications such as a major review in *Biological Reviews* (also in 1966) which enabled scientists around the world to begin to understand Mitchell's chemiosmotic theory. The theory itself, however, was still not acceptable to large numbers of workers in the field, a situation which persisted until the mid-1970s. Although the first clear support for the theory came from an American group led by Andre Jagendorf, working on chloroplast photosynthesis, research at Glynn revealed evidence for the theory, the first demonstration that protons were pumped by the respiratory chain being published in 1965. The Glynn group also provided evidence for the involvement of protons in ATP synthesis in the same year.

The question of *how* the respiratory chain pumped protons across the membrane occupied Mitchell from the outset. The 1966 Grey Book and its sequel, the second Grey Book (published in 1968), considered possible mechanisms for linking the process of oxidation-reduction to proton pumping based on the idea of the redox loop. In 1975 Mitchell put forward the 'Q-cycle', a version of his redox loop principle, as a mechanism for the transport of protons by the second of the three energy-conserving complexes of the respiratory chain. This provided not only a much needed, plausible mechanism for proton pumping but also explained hitherto puzzling experimental results obtained with the middle (second) complex of the respiratory chain; it also demonstrated how a single electron passing through the complex might pump two protons across the membrane. Initially the cycle was received with some scepticism, but progressively over the next ten to fifteen years sound evidence was accumulated in its support.

As the 1970s progressed, despite its unorthodox character the correctness of the basic postulates of the chemiosmotic theory was increasingly recognized. In 1974 Mitchell was elected a fellow of the Royal Society, and in 1981 he was awarded the society's Copley medal. In 1978 the Nobel committee decided to award Mitchell the prize for chemistry for his work in the field of bioenergetics and particularly the chemiosmotic theory. The ultimate acceptance of his initial proposals convinced Mitchell of the validity of his approach to oxidative phosphorylation. From the outset he had ascribed to the final complex of the respiratory chain, the cytochrome *c* oxidase, only an electron-transporting function, since this complex possessed nothing which Mitchell could identify as a proton carrier. This situation led to a major conflict with a Finnish biochemist, M. Wikström (and an increasing number of other biochemists worldwide), between 1977 and 1985, which concluded with Mitchell's acceptance of the argument that the oxidase pumped protons. This argument was one of several in which Mitchell engaged, including those on the total number of protons pumped by the respiratory chain, and the mechanism by which protons would drive the synthesis of ATP by the ATPase. Although in many (though not all) of these disputes on detailed aspects of the chemiosmotic theory he ultimately accepted the opposing viewpoint, he maintained his position and the respect of the opposition by virtue of the skill which he used to suggest valid alternative interpretations of the experimental results, thus undermining his opponents' positions. In his later years Mitchell was forced to give increasing amounts of time to fund-raising for the Glynn Research Institute, whose original endowment could no longer support all of its needs. In order to give more time to these activities and to provide a base for the future research of the institute, a new research director, Peter Rich, was appointed.

Mitchell remained an active scientist until his death. In the course of his career he published some 200 scientific papers and essays. His major contribution to biological science was to provide a new framework for bioenergetics, in which the process of energy conservation in oxidation was firmly linked to the transport of molecules across cell membranes. While physiologists developed an understanding of transport processes and while biochemists established the chemical reactions in metabolism, the failure of the two groups to interact inhibited the solution of major biological problems. Mitchell's achievement was to bring transport and metabolism together, providing a single unified conceptual framework, thus benefiting both fields.

Mitchell had considerable charm, which enabled him to communicate his ideas to others and which was also a necessary compensation for an aggressive tendency in argument. He was distinguished in appearance, with dark, wavy, receding hair worn down to his shoulders over much of his life. He also sported a gold earring in his left ear, imitating one of his sons. He had other serious interests. Philosophy, on which he published some essays, had fascinated him since his undergraduate years or earlier, though it was not a subject on which he received tuition at Cambridge. The philosophical system which he developed as the basis for the first rejected thesis was fully consistent with his theoretical approach to biology, and it no doubt influenced the development of most of his theoretical ideas. If Keilin had been the scientist he most admired, then Karl Popper was his other hero. Popper's philosophy greatly interested him.

Partly out of his concerns over inflation (which always threatened the financial security of the institute) Mitchell also became keenly interested in economics. For many years he was a member of a private think-tank, the Economic Research Council. Arising from the many controversies in which he had been engaged, Mitchell was concerned about the process of human communication, and occasionally wrote on this subject. At various times he considered redirecting the work of the Glynn Institute either towards economics or towards the study of human communication. However, friends persuaded him that his greatest contribution would be in the biological sciences, the area which retains his imprint. He died of cancer at Glynn House on 10 April 1992. He was survived by his second wife.

JOHN N. PREBBLE

Sources CUL, P. D. Mitchell MSS · private information (2004) · personal knowledge (2004) · E. C. Slater, *Memoirs FRS*, 40 (1994), 283–305 · J. Prebble and B. Weber, *Wandering in the gardens of the mind: a biography of Peter Mitchell and Glynn* (2003) · 'Mitchell, Godfrey Way', *DNB* · *The Times* (18 April 1992) · *The Times* (21 April 1992) · *The Independent* (16 April 1992) · *The Independent* (5 May 1992) · m. certs. · *WWW, 1991–5* · *WW* · d. cert. [Kate Mitchell]
Archives CUL, corresp. and papers
Likenesses photograph, repro. in *Memoirs FRS*, 282
Wealth at death £313,017: probate, 30 June 1992, *CGPLA Eng. & Wales*

Mitchell, Sir Philip Euen (1890–1964), colonial governor, was born on 1 May 1890 at 32 Spencer Hill, Wimbledon, London, the sixth of seven children of Hugh Mitchell, barrister, and his wife, Mary Catherine Edwards (Katie) Creswell (*d.* 1892). His mother was the sister of Colonel F. H. P. Creswell, the Transvaal goldmining engineer who was South African minister of labour and then minister of defence in J. B. M. Herzog's coalition governments from 1924 to 1933. Mitchell frequently visited South Africa throughout his career as a colonial administrator and was strongly influenced by his uncle. His mother died in childbirth shortly after Mitchell's second birthday. His father, who had been an officer in the Royal Engineers before being called to the bar, moved his practice to Tangier and Gibraltar, where his wife's family lived.

Education and early career Educated by a French tutor and his father, Mitchell won a scholarship first to St Paul's School and then to Trinity College, Oxford, where he read classics. Motherless and perhaps rather frightened of his dour father, Mitchell was a lonely boy and, as a youth, had a tendency to show off in order to attract attention and appear self-confident. His time at Oxford was not a success and, as a result of his escapades (culminating in painting the noses of the statues in Trinity red), he was sent down after two years without a degree and frittered away a year in London, visiting the opera and drinking to excess. With little chance of being admitted to the diplomatic or Indian Civil Services without a degree, Mitchell opted to apply for the colonial service where temperament was judged more important than formal qualifications. Interviewed by the soon to be legendary civil servant Ralph Furse, Mitchell in

Sir Philip Euen Mitchell (1890–1964), by Walter Stoneman, 1937

January 1913 found himself in Nyasaland as assistant resident in Zomba, administering 80,000 Africans in a district of nearly 1700 square miles.

Denied permission to enlist in the First World War, Mitchell disobeyed his superiors and joined the King's African rifles as a private. The death-rate among officers ensured that he soon received a commission. He spent the war fighting in German East Africa, mastering Swahili and Nyanja, and playing *bao* (a board game). Reluctant to return to a subordinate position in the Nyasaland administration after life in the army and a brief spell as private secretary to the governor, Mitchell successfully applied for a position in the temporary British military administration of Tanganyika. He quickly rose through the ranks, becoming in 1922 district commissioner in Tanga amid the north coast sisal plantations and three years later commissioner at Iringa in the southern highlands. Mitchell arrived at Iringa straight from leave in South Africa where he had married in 1925 the local golf champion Margery, the daughter of John D'Urban Tyrwhitt-Drake, of Port Alfred, Cape Province. There were no children of the marriage.

Mitchell's stint in Iringa was brief, because the new governor of Tanganyika, Sir Donald Cameron, who had arrived from Nigeria, appointed him assistant secretary for native affairs under Charles Dundas. Four years later Mitchell succeeded as secretary for native affairs and in February 1934 became chief secretary, the number two in the Tanganyika administration, while continuing to oversee native affairs. Mitchell was an active secretary for native affairs, masterminding the introduction of indirect rule and the creation of 'native courts' and treasuries, adapting Lord Lugard's system in Northern Nigeria to the very different requirements of Tanganyika. Regarded as the way to reconcile Africans' abilities and culture to British control, indirect rule soon became the official ideology of inter-war British colonialism. Cameron may have determined the grand strategy in Tanganyika, but its successful implementation was Mitchell's achievement, thereby confirming his reputation in the Colonial Office as one of Africa's coming pro-consuls.

Governor and political adviser In 1935, after sixteen months as chief secretary in Tanganyika, Mitchell, now aged forty-five, was rewarded with the governorship of Uganda. Mitchell's view of native administration, ironically, proved too democratic for the princelings of western Uganda; they disliked his attempts to end tribute, restrict their powers of taxation, and introduce courts and consultative councils. Relations with Kabaka Daudi Chwa of Buganda were fraught, as Mitchell sought to transform the nominal system of indirect rule, making Buganda a protected state, while enhancing the status of the *lukiko* or parliament. As part of this policy the provincial commissioner in 1938 became the resident, and geographical district officers were given functional responsibilities, supervising the work of the *kabaka*'s ministers. Attempts were started to reconcile African customary laws with the English common law and to develop a primarily African local civil service. Mitchell also sought to diversify the Ugandan economy, lessening its dependence on cotton, by promoting the peasant cultivation of coffee, tea, sugar, and pyrethrum. He was made KCMG in 1937. While governor of Uganda, Mitchell also played a crucial role in transforming Makerere College from a technical school for African mechanics and carpenters into the University College of East Africa, guiding the De La Warr commission on higher education.

The outbreak of the Second World War swiftly persuaded the Colonial Office that its campaign for increased production in Britain's east African colonies of Uganda and Kenya, its League of Nations' mandate in Tanganyika, and the protectorate of Zanzibar, needed reorganization. As a result, in July 1940 Mitchell was transferred to Nairobi as deputy chairman—and, in practice, chief executive—of the East African Governors' Conference. As such, it was his responsibility to co-ordinate war production and to liaise with the general-officer-commanding east Africa over the supply of material and men. Before much could be achieved, however, in January 1941 Mitchell was invited to become chief political adviser to Field Marshal Lord Wavell in Cairo with the rank of major-general. His new task was to prepare and oversee the establishment of British administration in Italian East Africa (that is Ethiopia, Eritrea, and Italian Somaliland) under the control of the War Office. Not surprisingly, Emperor Haile Selassie, who arrived in Alexandria from exile in Bath shortly before Mitchell's arrival in Egypt, had a rather different view and was eager to re-establish his authority in Ethiopia as quickly as possible.

When Addis Ababa fell to British forces advancing from Kenya and British Somaliland on 6 April 1941 the political branch of general headquarters, Middle East, had a total staff of only eighteen (including six secretaries) to oversee 119,400 Italian civilians and 40,000 soldiers and to administer the three territories. Mitchell's problems grew when the emperor entered Addis Ababa in May and, without consulting his British military advisers or Mitchell's deputy in Addis Ababa, appointed seven ministers. Supported by old Ethiopia hands in the Foreign Office, the emperor intrigued to undermine Mitchell's authority and re-establish his feudal regime. Now high commissioner for the Italian colonies and Somaliland and agent-general for Ethiopia, Mitchell struggled to implement the June 1941 cabinet agreement that the emperor was to administer under the 'guidance and control' of the civil arm of the Middle East command. Haile Selassie and the Foreign Office obstructed his efforts, delaying the recruitment of a trained police force with British officers at a time when law and order in the outlying regions were breaking down. Mitchell was so frustrated that in November 1941 he resigned, precipitating a crisis. The Foreign Office backed down, with Anthony Eden admitting in cabinet that he had become aware that his officials had thought nothing out and had neither knowledge nor plans. The foreign secretary was forced to ask Mitchell to withdraw his resignation and promised him full support. The emperor, however, remained obdurate, and an agreement was not concluded until 31 January 1942, after months of difficult negotiations. Ultimately, however, Mitchell's schema for military administration provided the basis for Britain's continuing presence in Ethiopia and wartime control of Eritrea, Italian and British Somaliland, Tripolitania, and Cyrenaica, and was later applied to the Dodecanese Islands, Burma, and Malaya.

Governor of Fiji In May 1942 Mitchell was appointed governor of Fiji and high commissioner for the Western Pacific. As head of the civil administration and governor of the British colony, he now had to work with an American supreme commander, and to oversee the re-establishment of British rule in Micronesia and Melanesia as American, Australian, and New Zealand forces under the command of Admiral Nimitz liberated the islands. The influx of American military personnel into Fiji with a spending power of $24 million a year had led to inflation, labour shortages in the docks and sugar plantations, and some racial incidents. Some American officials, both locally and in Washington, were hostile to Britain's imperial pretensions and disdainful of the New Zealand contingent's military contribution. Mitchell sought to improve relations, which had deteriorated under his predecessor Sir Harry Luke, and quickly established good relations with Admiral Nimitz at Pearl Harbor and the local commander, General Thompson. He formed a labour corps to control recruitment of dock workers and insisted that the Americans work through the colonial administration rather than deal directly with the shipping firms. He also encouraged Fijian notables to recruit men for a Fiji military force. More than 5000 enlisted out of a total male population of 55,000, operating as commandos in the Solomon Islands and at Bougainville and Guadalcanal.

Mitchell less successfully attempted to enlist the support of the islands' 92,000 Indian community, most of whom worked as sharecroppers on the sugar plantations of Fijian landowners and the Australian owned Colonial Sugar Refining Company. A long strike on the sugar plantations highlighted the racial tensions between the Fijians and Indians, whose loyalties lay with M. K. Gandhi's nationalist movement rather than the British empire. Although Mitchell became increasingly exasperated by the behaviour of the Indian leaders, he sympathized with the sharecroppers' refusal to sell their sugar cane to the Australian controlled Colonial Sugar Refining Company, and pressed the Colonial Office to secure a higher guaranteed price for the 1944 harvest. He also sought approval for reforms in the colony's secretariat, ending what he called 'the Chief Secretary bottleneck' by transforming the executive council into a quasi-ministerial system. Progress was slow and permission had not been granted for the reforms by the time Mitchell left Fiji in 1944.

While in some ways Suva was an improvement on Cairo—Lady Mitchell, for example, was able to join her husband—Mitchell became increasingly tired and depressed. Although aware that he was playing an important role in solidifying the alliance between Britain and the United States in the Western Pacific, Mitchell nevertheless felt that he was in a backwater, and yearned for east Africa. He requested an appointment as governor of Tanganyika or as executive council member for native affairs in a newly formed colony of the whole of east Africa; and in July 1944 he was offered the governorship of Kenya.

Governor of Kenya Despite his dislike of Kenya's European settler community, Mitchell eagerly accepted. Arriving in Nairobi in December 1944 the new governor embarked on a series of major reforms. As in Fiji, Mitchell considered it imperative to reform the colony's central administration, creating a semi-ministerial executive council instead of a centralized secretariat. He also soon concluded that the Kenya settlers' leaders during the war had become so integrated into policy making that the only way forward was to co-opt them into the fledgeling ministerial system. Thus, Ferdinand Cavendish-Bentinck, the settlers' leader on the legislative council, became member for agriculture and natural resources in 1946, and Charles Mortimer, member for health and local government. Mitchell also worked hard to secure advantageous terms for new immigrants from Britain in a post-war soldier settlement scheme: European settlers, he believed, would provide 'the scaffolding' for the colony's political and economic development, in the early stages providing the bulk of tax revenue and consumer demand for Kenya's economic diversification. His attempt to strengthen the common services organization, which controlled the railways, harbours, and currency, led to the formation of the east African high commission in 1948.

As 1945 progressed Mitchell became increasingly concerned about the problem of soil erosion, caused by overstocking and over-cultivation in the African 'reserves'.

African market production had soared during the latter part of the war, and in Kikuyuland, the home of the largest ethnic group, commercial farmers were already privatizing traditional communal grazing grounds. The agriculture department, fearful of the ecological and social consequences of increasing cash-crop production and differentiation, and prodded by Mitchell, devised a programme of compulsory contour terracing in the densely populated central highlands. At the same time the settler controlled district councils attempted to restrict cultivation and stock ownership among African squatters, turning them into low-paid wage-labourers instead of comparatively prosperous sharecroppers. Controls were most draconian in the dairy and stock farming zones of the eastern Rift Valley, where most of the squatters were Kikuyu. The exodus of landless from both the Kikuyu reserves and the 'white highlands', the settler farming zone in the Rift Valley, increased the flood of people into Nairobi, more than doubling its population during the 1940s and surrounding the town with a penumbra of shanty towns and slums. Inflation outpaced wage increases, and unskilled migrants found it increasingly difficult to find jobs. Crime escalated and government control over Nairobi's African population, already a weak link, declined.

Mitchell proved incapable of dealing with the colony's mounting problems. For the first twelve months he had undertaken a hectic series of tours, visiting all parts of the colony, and had bombarded the Colonial Office with dispatches, outlining Kenya's political, economic, and social problems and proposing remedial action. Already overworked and exhausted from Fiji and his duties in the Western Pacific, in December 1945 Mitchell suffered a serious collapse, and took leave in South Africa. He never fully recovered. On his return he became increasingly set in his ways, intolerant of criticism, and determined to push ahead with the programmes he had established, regardless of mounting African opposition. Dismissing the growing ranks of African politicians in Nairobi and the reserves as 'street corner boys' and unscrupulous agitators, Mitchell stressed the need to push ahead, and for 'a firm refusal to be rattled'. Now rarely leaving Nairobi and reluctant to listen to bad news, he became increasingly out of touch with the situation on the ground. Local reports of trouble in the Kikuyu regions were watered down as they passed up the chain of command to Government House, and little news of the deteriorating situation reached the Colonial Office. Mitchell was appointed GCMG in 1947.

Mau Mau and retirement Opposition first surfaced in 1947 with a general strike in Mombasa, mass protests among the squatters in Naivasha and Nakuru, and among women digging the compulsory terraces in Murang'a district in Central Province. The protests gradually died down, but the administration's policies remained in place. In 1950 a new round of more serious protests erupted. Armoured cars patrolled the streets of the capital, and in an attempt to break a general strike in Nairobi, tear gas was used for

the first time in the colony. Attacks on farm foremen, agricultural instructors, and local headmen increased; settler owned cattle were slaughtered and crops set on fire. The governor responded by outlawing the secret Mau Mau society, which was blamed for the increasing unrest, but failed to inform London of the deteriorating situation. Morale declined in the field administration in Central Province, which faced mounting opposition and violence. Mitchell, however, remained convinced that his policies would succeed and that the political agitators, led by Jomo Kenyatta, would be discredited. Kenya would emerge, next year, if not this, into a prosperous, multiracial stability.

Unaware of the impending eruption, the Colonial Office twice extended Mitchell's tour of duty, and shortly before his retirement in 1952 arranged a visit by the Princess Elizabeth and her husband. By then the situation had deteriorated so far that Mervyn Cowie, the head of the game parks, warned Mitchell not to permit the royal couple to visit Treetops in the Aberdare Forest for fear of a Mau Mau attack. When Mitchell overruled him, Cowie ordered the chief game warden to sit up all night under their tree house with his shotgun. The visit, however, passed without incident and the princess returned to Britain as queen, following the death of her father, George VI, on 6 February. Mitchell, evidently convinced of the colony's bright future, retired on 21 June 1952 to his farm in Kenya's 'white highlands', where he wrote his memoirs, *African afterthoughts* (1954). Long before they were published, his successor had declared a state of emergency to combat the Mau Mau disturbances.

On 20 October 1952, following the assassination of Senior Chief Waruhiu wa Kungu, Sir Evelyn Baring, who had been rushed to Kenya as the new governor, declared a state of emergency which lasted until January 1960. He ordered the arrest of Kenyatta and 184 other leaders of the Kenya African Union and the trade union movement. The Kikuyu reserves, Nairobi, and the Kikuyu-settled areas of the Rift Valley were placed under strict curfew and patrolled by the Lancashire Fusiliers and the Black Watch. Over the next two years the Mau Mau sought refuge in the Aberdare and Mount Kenya forests, from which they continued to launch operations until late in 1956. Mitchell came under strong criticism and his reputation plummeted.

Short of money, Mitchell found it impossible to make a success of farming and accepted various minor jobs, serving as a director of the Kenya Power Corporation and as chairman of the Kenya Girls' High School. A paternalist who believed that it would take centuries for Africans to advance to 'civilization', he could not adjust to the 'wind of change'. Mitchell never achieved his ambition of reaching the House of Lords. Instead, his retirement was embittered by the criticism of his settler neighbours and then by the rehabilitation of Jomo Kenyatta. An increasingly isolated and pathetic figure, suffering from gout and heart troubles, he ate and drank too much, and his health deteriorated. Rather than remain in an independent Kenya, Mitchell leased his farm to his manager and moved late in 1963 to Algeciras, Spain, close to Gibraltar. He died on 11 October 1964 in the Royal Naval Hospital, Gibraltar, and was buried in Gibraltar. Only four people attended the funeral: the security officer at Government House and his wife, the governor's aide, and Lady Mitchell, who then retired to South Africa.

D. W. THROUP

Sources P. E. Mitchell, *African afterthoughts* (1954) · R. Frost, *Enigmatic proconsul: Sir Philip Mitchell and the twilight of empire* (1992) · D. W. Throup, *Economic and social origins of Mau Mau* (1987) · *DNB* · *The Times* (13 Oct 1964) · *CGPLA Eng. & Wales* (1965) · b. cert. · *WWW*
Archives Bodl. RH, diaries relating to East Africa | Bodl. RH, letters to Arthur Creech Jones · Bodl. RH, corresp. with Lord Lugard · Bodl. RH, corresp. with J. H. Oldham · Bodl. RH, corresp. with Margery Perham and related papers · PRO, corresp. relating to East Africa, CO967/59, 62–63, 166–68
Likenesses W. Stoneman, photograph, 1937, NPG [*see illus.*]
Wealth at death £4734 in England: probate, resealed in Kenya, 24 Nov 1965, *CGPLA Eng. & Wales*

Mitchell, Reginald Joseph (1895–1937), aircraft designer, was born on 20 May 1895 at 115 Congleton Road, Butt Lane, near Stoke-on-Trent, the eldest of the three sons of Herbert Mitchell (1865–1933), a Yorkshireman who served as headmaster successively in three Staffordshire schools and later established a printing business in the Hanley district of Stoke. His mother was Eliza Jane Brain, the daughter of William Brain, a master cooper of Longton, to the south of Stoke. He spent his childhood in Normacot, near Longton, and attended the Queensberry Road higher elementary school before moving to Hanley high school. This was where he first became interested in aviation, designing, making, and flying model aeroplanes.

At the age of sixteen Mitchell began an apprenticeship with the locomotive engineering firm of Kerr, Stuart & Co. at Stoke. His practical training, starting in the engine workshops and progressing to the drawing office, was supplemented by evening classes at a local technical college, where he studied engineering drawing and mechanics and displayed a particular aptitude for higher mathematics. But his interest in aviation persisted, and in 1917 he joined the Supermarine Aviation Works at Woolston, Southampton, as assistant to the company's owner and designer, Hubert Scott-Paine. Within a year he had been promoted to the post of assistant to the works manager. Shortly afterwards, in 1918, he married a schoolteacher, Florence (d. 1946), the daughter of Henry James Dayson, a farmer. They had one son, Gordon (b. 1920).

In 1919, at the age of only twenty-four, Mitchell was appointed chief designer, and in the following year he was also made chief engineer. His short but illustrious career subsequently advanced along two parallel paths. It was founded, beyond all else, on the design and development of military flying boats for the Royal Air Force. From its formation in 1912 Supermarine had specialized in flying-boat manufacture, and Mitchell built on the company's tradition. Through designs such as the Sea Eagle, the Scarab, and the Swan, he progressed to an armed military flying boat called the Southampton, which first flew in 1925. Ordered not only by the RAF but also by Japan, Argentina, and Australia, the Southampton set new standards for range, reliability, and versatility, establishing

Reginald Joseph Mitchell (1895–1937), by unknown photographer, *c.*1933

Britain at the forefront of marine aviation and helping to transform Supermarine into one of the most profitable enterprises in the aircraft industry. It equipped six RAF squadrons and remained operational until 1936. The Southampton was eventually succeeded by such aircraft as the Walrus and the Stranraer, which both rendered sterling service in the Second World War.

Despite the success of Mitchell's flying boats, his name is more commonly associated with the design of high-speed aircraft for the Schneider trophy races between 1922 and 1931. The first such aircraft, a small biplane flying boat named Sea Lion II, won the 1922 race against French and Italian competition by achieving an average speed of 145.7 m.p.h. But Mitchell was profoundly influenced by the American Curtiss seaplanes, which dominated the race in 1923. He began developing a series of Supermarine float seaplanes soon afterwards and produced four beautifully streamlined racing monoplanes. The first, the S4, although unsuccessful, provided invaluable practical experience that was incorporated in its successor, the S5. In 1927 the S5 achieved an average speed of 281.7 m.p.h. in the Schneider race to recapture the trophy for Britain. The third aircraft, the S6, retained the trophy two years later (from 1928 the race was held every two years, instead of annually), while the fourth and most famous, the S6B, won the Schneider trophy outright in 1931, averaging 340 m.p.h. around the course. Soon afterwards the S6B set a new world speed record of 407.5 m.p.h.

The technical prowess of Mitchell's flying boats and seaplanes established him as the foremost aircraft designer in Britain. A ten-year contract, commencing in 1923, signified his indispensability to Supermarine, and a technical directorship followed in 1927. When Vickers acquired Supermarine in the following year, it was on the understanding that Mitchell was contractually obliged to remain with the company until 1933: he was their most valuable asset.

The aircraft for which Mitchell will always be remembered is the Spitfire single-seat fighter, designed between 1934 and 1936. In truth the Spitfire was a hybrid, the product of many diverse technical developments. Its thin, elliptical wing—the key to its exceptional performance and flying characteristics—was the brainchild of Supermarine's aerodynamicist, Beverley Shenstone, who was in turn influenced by the work of the German aircraft manufacturer, Junkers. Its deadly eight-gun armament was proposed by the Air Ministry's directorate of operational requirements. Its power source was the new Rolls-Royce Merlin engine. Its low-drag, ducted radiator, mounted under the starboard wing, drew directly on research undertaken by the Royal Aircraft Establishment at Farnborough. Configured as a cantilever monoplane, it embodied many of the latest features of American and German aircraft design, such as stressed-skin construction, a monocoque fuselage, and a retractable undercarriage. Mitchell's most direct personal contribution was an unparalleled expertise in high-speed flight, gained from the Schneider trophy racers, and a brilliant practical engineering ability, exemplified in this instance by the incorporation of vital lessons learned from Supermarine's unsuccessful type 224 fighter. Otherwise the essence of his achievement lay in the merger of all these influences into a single, outstanding design.

The Spitfire entered service in 1939 and was unquestionably better than any other interceptor fighter during the early stages of the Second World War. But it proved no less remarkable in its capacity for further development. Once it was slightly modified and equipped with more powerful engines, the Spitfire's top speed was raised from 346 m.p.h. in 1939 to 460 m.p.h. five years later. Hence it provided RAF squadrons with a fighter capable of matching the most formidable German aircraft for the duration of hostilities. Some 19,000 Spitfires were eventually built in Britain between 1939 and 1945.

Mitchell was a handsome man with striking blond hair and bright blue eyes. Quiet, reserved, and modest, he shunned fame and publicity; he was appointed CBE in 1932, but his name was not widely known beyond aviation circles during his lifetime. Although he was primarily a practical engineer and lacked any formal training in aeronautical science, he nevertheless consistently demonstrated an intuitive understanding of aerodynamic problems. An indefatigable worker, endowed with great intelligence and remarkable powers of concentration, he was often stern and irascible towards those less gifted than

himself. But he was also well known for his kindness and humanity, and he commanded the unerring respect, loyalty, and affection of his staff, to whom he was utterly devoted. In 1933 he was diagnosed with cancer, and a major operation left him with a serious physical disability in the form of a permanent colostomy. Yet he steadfastly refused to contemplate retirement or the life of an invalid. It is rarely appreciated that the designer of Britain's most famous fighter aircraft was engaged in a courageous struggle against acute physical and psychological discomfort during the four most productive years of his career. The Spitfire first flew in March 1936; a production order was placed in June. But Mitchell did not live to witness the spectacular wartime achievements of his finest creation. He died at his home, Hazeldene, 2 Russell Place, Portswood, Southampton, on 11 June 1937, aged only forty-two. His ashes were interred at South Stoneham cemetery, Eastleigh, Hampshire, four days later.

SEBASTIAN RITCHIE

Sources G. Mitchell, ed., *R. J. Mitchell, world-famous aircraft designer: schooldays to Spitfire* (1986); rev. edn (1997) · J. Quill, *Birth of a legend: the Spitfire* (1986) · S. Ritchie, *Industry and air power: the expansion of British aircraft production, 1935–1941* (1997) · C. F. Andrews and E. B. Morgan, *Supermarine aircraft since 1914* (1981) · A. Price, *The Spitfire story* (1982)
Archives Royal Air Force Museum, Hendon, papers | CUL, Vickers Ltd archive | SOUND IWM SA, oral history interview
Likenesses photograph, *c*.1930, Hult. Arch. · photograph, *c*.1933, Sci. Mus. [*see illus.*] · S. S. Miles, bust, Royal Air Force Museum, Hendon · E. Mitchell, portrait, priv. coll. · photograph, priv. coll.
Wealth at death £33,124 13*s.* 10*d.*: probate, 6 Aug 1937, *CGPLA Eng. & Wales*

Mitchell, Robert (*fl.* 1782–*c*.1809), architect, is thought to have been born in Aberdeen. He resided in London, first in Upper Marylebone Street, and afterwards in Newman Street. He may have had a son or younger relative called George Mitchell. According to Colvin, this 'was probably the George Mitchell who had been admitted to the Royal Academy Schools as an architectural student in 1795 at the age of 20' (Colvin, *Archs.*, 659). Robert Mitchell is known to have practised in London from 1782. From that date onwards he exhibited a number of schemes at the Royal Academy. His architectural designs were mainly in the style of James Wyatt, but he also freely mixed neoclassical designs with the characteristics of earlier Palladianism. His first known works were a number of bridges and entrance-lodges at Cottisbroke Hall, Northamptonshire (*c*.1770–80). Other works included the Rotunda, Leicester Square (1793–4), for Robert Barker (1737–1806), who exhibited there his panoramas. The building is now the Roman Catholic school of Notre Dame de France.

Mitchell published *Plans and views in perspective, with descriptions of buildings erected in England and Scotland; with an essay to elucidate the Grecian, Roman, and Gothic architecture, accompanied with designs* (1801), in English and French. This book is notable for including an early design for a country house in the form of a Greek Doric temple. He is also thought to have been the author of *Mitchell's Designs for*

Rural Villas on Economic Principles (1785). His last known work, according to Colvin, is the Nelson Column, Montreal, Canada, of *c*.1808–9 (Colvin, *Archs.*, 659).

JANE HARDING

Sources Colvin, *Archs.* · *GM*, 1st ser., 71 (1801), 639–41 · *DNB*

Mitchell, Robert (1820–1873). *See under* Mitchell, James (1791–1852).

Mitchell, Thomas (*d.* 1790), marine painter and naval official, became a freeman of the Shipwrights' Company on 25 February 1723. He held the posts of first assistant to master shipwright, Woolwich (1754); master caulker, Chatham (1763); second (1765) and first (1772) assistant to master shipwright, Chatham; first assistant to master shipwright, Deptford (1773), and first assistant surveyor of the navy, from 15 February 1775. He advocated preserving masts in storage from rot by leaving them standing, dispensing with woolings, and covering the tops of lower masts left standing in ships, and experimented with making masts by barking trees and allowing them to season before felling them.

Mitchell exhibited at the Free Society of Artists from 1763, when he was residing on Tower Hill, London, until 1780, and at the Royal Academy from 1774 to 1789. Besides a portrait, *Sir John and Lady Freke and a Friend in Ireland* (1757; ex Sothebys, 9 July 1980, Lot 36), and a drawing of a widow, Mrs Collins (referred to in his will), his known works, some of which were later engraved, were of marine subjects, particularly large battle pieces in oils, some of which are at the National Maritime Museum, such as *The Battle of La Hogue, 23 May 1692* (1779), and ships in locations ranging from Chatham to Plymouth. Some of his watercolours and drawings are in the print room at the British Museum, including a watercolour, *Westminster Bridge* (1755, previously believed to have been dated 1735).

The surname of Mitchell's wife, to whom he referred in his will as 'my patient wife Catherine', is unknown. His five surviving children were: Thomas, master shipwright at Sheerness; Grace, wife of Richard Hawkins; Margaret, wife of William Elton of Bristol, ancestors of the first Baron Elton; Dorothy, wife of Edward Trapp Pilgrim; and Elizabeth (1755–1813), wife of William Hammond of Camberwell, whose great-uncle William Bately, surveyor of the navy, had recommended Mitchell's promotion in 1772. Mitchell lived in London at Bethnal Green (1780–82) and then at 16 Canterbury Road, Newington (1783–9). He died on 18 January 1790 at Newington Butts, London. Examples of his paintings are held at the National Maritime Museum, London.

L. H. CUST, *rev.* ANTHONY R. J. S. ADOLPH

Sources PRO, indexes 9254, 9255 · dockyard officers index, NMM · will, PRO, pr. 28/1/1790 · E. H. H. Archibald, *Dictionary of sea painters* (1980) · notebooks of officers' appointments, NMM, Sandwich MSS, SAN 1, fols. 191, 230 · dockyard employees' index, NMM · Burke, *Peerage* [Elton, baron] · Worshipful Company of Shipwrights account book, 1691–1736, GL · T. Mitchell, letters to Admiral Middleton, NMM, MID/1/121 [9 May 1771, 4 May 1787, 12 April 1788] · *The exhibition of the Royal Academy* [exhibition catalogues] · sale catalogue (1980) [Sothebys, 9 July 1980] · Redgrave, *Artists* · Graves, *Artists* · priv. coll., Hammond family MSS · *GM*, 1st ser., 60 (1790), 90

Wealth at death over £3800 invested in annuities held at Bank of England, London: will, PRO

Mitchell, Thomas (1783–1845), classical scholar, was born in London on 30 May 1783, the son of Alexander Mitchell, riding master, successively of Hamilton Place and Grosvenor Place, London. In June 1790 he was admitted to Christ's Hospital, and in October 1802 went to Pembroke College, Cambridge, with one of the hospital exhibitions. In 1806 he graduated BA as eighth senior optime and was first chancellor's medallist. Because of a novel regulation, which enacted that not more than two students educated at the same school should be fellows of the college at one time, he was refused a fellowship at Pembroke, greatly to his disappointment, as he could have held it without taking orders. In 1809 he proceeded MA and was elected to an open fellowship at Sidney Sussex, which he had to vacate in 1812 on account of his refusal to be ordained. He supported himself by private tuition and literary work. From 1806 to 1816 he was tutor successively in the families of Sir George Henry Rose, Robert Smith (whose son, afterwards the Rt Hon. Vernon Smith, was his favourite pupil), and Thomas Hope. In 1810 he was introduced to William Gifford, and in 1813 he commenced a series of articles in the *Quarterly Review* on Aristophanes and Athenian manners, the success of which subsequently induced him to undertake his spirited and accurate verse translation of Aristophanes' comedies of the *Acharnians*, *Knights*, *Clouds*, and *Wasps*, (2 vols., 1820–22). He declined soon afterwards a vacant Greek chair in Scotland, on account of his objection to sign the confession of the Scotch kirk. In June 1813 Leigh Hunt invited him to dinner in Horsemonger Lane gaol, along with Byron and Moore. Byron afterwards spoke of his translation of Aristophanes as 'excellent'.

For the last twenty years of his life Mitchell resided with his relatives in Oxfordshire, occasionally superintending the publication of the Greek authors by the Clarendon Press. Between 1834 and 1838 he edited in separate volumes for John Murray five plays of Aristophanes, with English notes. This edition was adversely criticized by the Revd George John Kennedy, fellow of St John's College, Cambridge, and Mitchell published a reply to Kennedy in 1841. His 'Preliminary discourse' was republished in volume 13 of Philippus Invernizi's edition of Aristophanes (1826). Mitchell was the first English translator to do justice to Aristophanes' metrical variety, and his editions, articles, and translations did much to spread interest in the author among later generations of scholars. In 1839 he entered into an engagement with John Henry Parker, publisher, of Oxford, to edit Sophocles, but after the publication of three plays in 1842, Parker suspended the edition on the ground that schoolmasters objected to the diffuseness of English notes. Mitchell, left without regular employment, fell into straitened circumstances, but was granted by Sir Robert Peel £150 from the royal bounty. In 1843 Parker resumed his publication of Sophocles, and Mitchell edited the remaining four plays, with shorter notes than before, and in 1844 he began a school edition of a *Pentalogia Aristophanica*, with brief Latin notes. He had nearly completed this task when he died suddenly of 'apoplexy', on 4 May 1845, at his house at Steeple Aston, near Woodstock. He was unmarried.

Mitchell also published useful indexes to Reiske's edition of the *Oratores Attici* (1828), Isocrates (1828), and Plato (1832). The British Library holds Mitchell's copiously annotated copies of Aeschylus, Euripides, Aristophanes, and Bekker's edition of the *Oratores Attici*.

GORDON GOODWIN, rev. RICHARD SMAIL

Sources *GM*, 2nd ser., 24 (1845), 202–4 · Venn, *Alum. Cant.* · G. A. T. Allan, *Christ's Hospital exhibitioners to the universities of Oxford and Cambridge, 1566–1923* (1924) · M. L. Clarke, *Greek studies in England, 1700–1830* (1945), 156–7

Archives BL, corresp. with James Leigh Hunt, Add. MSS 38108, 38523–38524 · NL Scot., letters to J. G. Lockhart

Mitchell, Sir Thomas Livingston (1792–1855), surveyor and explorer in Australia, was born on 15 June 1792 in the parish of Falkirk, Stirlingshire, Scotland, the eldest of the four children of John Mitchell and his wife, Janet Wilson. He was educated at Grangemouth School and the University of Edinburgh, then at the age of nineteen, in July 1811, he joined the army in Spain and Portugal as a lieutenant in the 95th regiment. From time to time he was seconded to the department of the quartermaster-general under Quartermaster-General Sir George Murray for military surveying. He took part in the storming of Ciudad Rodrigo, Badajoz, and to a lesser extent Salamanca as well as being involved in the dangerous military surveying connected with the Pyrenees and San Sebastian battles. For this service over three years he received a silver medal with five clasps. After the war, then permanently on the quartermaster-general's staff, he was sent back to Spain and Portugal to survey the battlefields and record the positions of the armies. This work lasted from 1814 to 1819 and continued afterwards at Sandhurst.

On 10 June 1818 Mitchell married Mary Thomson Blunt (1800–1883), the eldest daughter of Lieutenant-General Richard Blunt. The couple had eleven children. Mitchell was promoted to captain on 3 October 1822 and to major on 29 August 1826, but was then put on half pay. In 1827 he published his *Outline of a System of Surveying for Geographical and Military Purposes*. Early the same year he was appointed deputy surveyor-general of New South Wales, and succeeded John Oxley as surveyor-general on 27 May 1828. This position he held until his death.

Mitchell arrived in Sydney on 27 September 1827. The great task that faced him was to apportion the colony into counties having regard to the natural features, and to put in order a survey so that land could be allocated to the graziers and farmers flooding into the country with their capital. He determined to produce a detailed topographical map of the colony. He and the greater part of the survey staff were engaged on this project for more than six years. The *Map of the Colony of New South Wales* (1834), otherwise known as the 'map of the nineteen counties', has scarcely been equalled anywhere. It was perhaps Mitchell's greatest achievement. He determined too to extend his surveys outside the nineteen counties, and though there are other

Sir Thomas Livingston Mitchell (1792–1855), by unknown artist

reasons for his exploratory expeditions this was a major factor. On all his four expeditions this chained survey was made, which singles him out from the other major explorers. His location and construction of great roads through the colony also were of much benefit.

Mitchell's first exploration was directed to the north-west. He left Sydney in November 1831, explored between the Nammoi and the Gwydir and crossed the latter to strike the Barwon, but there was no north-west river; all streams were clearly tributaries of the Darling. The murder by Aborigines of two of his party as they were bringing up provisions made a return to the settled colony imperative. The expedition arrived back in Sydney in February 1832. Mitchell's survey was a useful adjunct to the map, but he held on to it until he could publish it in 1838.

Mitchell's second exploration was undertaken to trace and record the course of the Darling. Leaving Sydney on 31 March 1835, he travelled down the Bogan River (the course of which was only partially known) to near where Sturt had discovered the Darling on 1 February 1828. Here he established Fort Bourke. On route, Richard Cunningham, the expedition's botanist, lost his way and was killed by the Aborigines. Mitchell succeeded in tracing the Darling to where it turns south, only a hundred miles from its junction with the Murray, generally confirming that it would join the Murray where Charles Sturt had discovered a major junction in January 1830. Not being able to proceed on account of the Aborigines' confrontation he returned the way he had come, reaching Sydney in September.

Mitchell's third and most significant journey was undertaken ostensibly to connect the Murray with the Darling, but also to explore the Murray and perhaps the country south of it. The expedition left Sydney in March 1836 and moved down the Lachlan. It was impossible to cross to the Darling so Mitchell proceeded to the Murrumbidgee and into the Murray, following it down to what was thought to be the Darling junction. He traced the Darling upstream only sufficiently far to satisfy himself that it was in fact that river. On his return up the Murray he had a serious encounter with his old enemies, the Darling tribe, of which several were killed. This 'dispersion of the natives' proved to be a serious embarrassment to his career. Travelling up the Murray was no straightforward matter, and with little promise of discovering good country Mitchell turned his attention south. Some 30 miles below the Goulburn river junction he turned off south-west. The region he then opened up he named Australia Felix (now the western district of Victoria), which certainly forms one of the richest tracts in Australia. The south-flowing river he struck he eventually named the Glenelg after the colonial secretary. He followed it to the sea and, at Portland Bay, found Edward Henty settled on the seaboard. Mitchell returned to Sydney in a generally direct line. From Mount Macedon he was able to see the tents of the new Port Phillip settlement. His route from the Goulburn River was parallel but west of Hamilton Hume and William Hovell's route. At the Murray he found the country on the eve of being taken up by graziers, and the deep tracks of his boat carriage quickly became their ribbon to follow to the south-west. This journey, which lasted over seven months, thus added greatly to the knowledge of a very fertile region of Australia.

Mitchell now took steps to return to England for a period, intending to publish his book with the maps to accompany it, and hoping to improve his status. He did both—his excellent two-volume *Three Expeditions into the Interior of Eastern Australia* was issued in 1838, and on 17 April 1839 a knighthood was conferred upon him. He spoke and wrote as a propagandist to attract migrants to the Port Phillip district, received the honorary degree of DCL at Oxford, and was promoted to the rank of lieutenant-colonel on 23 October 1841. He also completed the Peninsular War maps, which were published in 1841.

Mitchell resumed duty in Sydney on 15 February 1841. In 1844 he was elected one of Port Phillip's representatives in the legislative council, largely as an opponent of the governor, Sir George Gipps, but when the latter ordered him to choose between his position as surveyor-general and that of member of the legislative council, he resigned his seat after four months. In November 1845, with Edmund Kennedy as second in command, he set out for an exploration to the north which lasted a full year, when he almost solved the riddle of the drainage of north-eastern Australia—detailing the sources of the Belyando, Nogoa, Maranoa, Warrego, Bulloo, and Barcoo rivers. For a time he thought the Barcoo (his Victoria River) must be the great river that would flow into the Gulf of Carpentaria, along the banks of which the great road to the north would follow. He traced the Barcoo to within a few miles of where it turns south-west, thus finding nothing to shake his belief. He sent Kennedy out in March the following year only to be proved wrong. By the time Kennedy had returned in February 1848 Mitchell's new book—*Journal of an Expedition into the Interior of Tropical Australia* (1848)—was well under way. Despite Mitchell's mistaken supposition, this last expedition further confirmed his high reputation as an explorer. On all his expeditions important additions were made to Australian natural history as well as geography. These expeditions were always carefully planned and carried out meticulously. They consisted of a large number of men and much equipment. The rank and file always consisted entirely of convicts who, hoping for the granting of ticket-of-leave, if not a free pardon, almost invariably gave good service; that these men should have been led for such long periods in the wilds without any disturbance speaks well for Mitchell's discipline and fairness. With his officers he was not always seen to be fair, although in the carrying out of his surveying responsibilities his exceptional organizing ability was continually demonstrated. Politically, he made many enemies, mostly brought about by his unshakeable faith in his own decisions. He quarrelled with every governor of New South Wales under whom he served—Darling, Bourke, Gipps, FitzRoy, and Denison. Under the last, in 1855, commissioners of an inquiry into the surveyor-general's department severely condemned the administration of the department, criticizing Mitchell's long absences (on exploration and on leave) and accusing him of an inability to delegate. Notwithstanding such criticism, his contribution to the survey of the colony was immense, and unequalled by any before or after him. Professionally greatly accomplished, Mitchell was also a man of culture and wide interests; his publication of his translation of the *Lusiad* of Luis de Camoens (1854) and his patenting of a new 'Boomerang' screw propeller for steamships are just two examples. He died at his home, Carthona, Darling Point, Sydney, on 5 October 1855, and was buried on 9 October at St Stephen's Church, Camperdown.

ALAN E. J. ANDREWS

Sources W. C. Foster, *Sir Thomas Livingston Mitchell and his world, 1792–1855* (1985) • A. E. J. Andrews, *Major Mitchell's map. 1834* (1992) • A. E. J. Andrews, ed., *Stapylton: with Major Mitchell's Australia Felix expedition, 1836* (1986) • T. L. Mitchell, *Three expeditions into the interior of eastern Australia: with descriptions of the recently explored region of Australia Felix, and the present colony of New South Wales*, 2 vols. (1838) • T. L. Mitchell, *Journal of an expedition into the interior of tropical Australia in search of a route from Sydney to the Gulf of Carpentaria* (1848) • J. H. L. Cumpston, *Thomas Mitchell: surveyor general and explorer* (1954) • E. Beale, *Kennedy, the Barcoo and beyond, 1847* (1983) • D. W. A. Baker, 'Mitchell, Sir Thomas', *AusDB*, 2.238–42

Archives Mitchell L., NSW, corresp. and papers • RGS, papers relating to Australian exploration • State Library of New South Wales, Sydney, Dixson Library, letters, drawings, and papers | NL Aus., letters to James Wyld • NRA, priv. coll., letters to Edmund Kennedy

Likenesses oils, c.1839, Mitchell L., NSW • photograph, c.1847 (after oil painting), Royal Geographical Society of Queensland • W. P. McIntosh, statue, Lands Department Building, Bridge Street, Sydney, Australia • portrait, Dixson Gallery, Sydney, Australia;

repro. in *Illustrated Sydney News* (1853) · portrait, State Library of Victoria, Melbourne, La Trobe picture collection [*see illus.*]
Wealth at death very little: Foster, *Sir Thomas Livingston Mitchell*

Mitchell, Sir William (1745/6–1816), naval officer, had obscure origins: neither his place of birth nor his parents are mentioned in the *Naval Chronicle*'s report of his death, but it is probable that he went early to sea, since on joining the *Dolphin* on 8 July 1766 he was rated able. The *Dolphin* was commanded by Captain Samuel Wallis, who also had the *Prince Frederick* and the *Swallow* (Captain Carteret) under his orders, and she sailed round the world by way of the Strait of Magellan, Tahiti, Java, the Cape of Good Hope, and St Helena, leaving Plymouth on 19 August 1766 and anchoring in the Downs on 20 May 1768, paying off in June.

Among other ships of the Royal Navy which Mitchell listed in his record of service was the *Hector* (74 guns), which he joined, again as an able seaman, on 31 July 1777. On 1 November 1777 he was rated midshipman and master's mate, and on 26 August 1778 he left the ship to join the *Victory* (100 guns) the next day, again as master's mate. He served in her, with breaks of a few days, until 12 March 1781, when he moved to the *Foudroyant* (80 guns) as acting lieutenant, staying until the end of October. On 1 November 1781 he appeared before a board at the Navy Office, produced the necessary certificates and papers, answered the examining captains' questions satisfactorily, and passed for lieutenant, the board observing that 'he was more than 31 years old', which suggests the lack of a birth certificate. He was commissioned almost at once, was made post captain in 1790, and early in 1792 he returned to the *Foudroyant* as first lieutenant; in April of the same year he was promoted master and commander, being given the *Pigmy* (14 guns). In 1794 he was acting captain of the *Adamant* (50 guns) and then captain of the *Isis*, also of 50 guns. The *Isis* was not a line-of-battle ship, but like the *Adamant* she acted as one in the battle of Camperdown in October 1797, when she set about the much heavier *Gelijkheid* (64 guns), one of the eleven Dutch ships that were taken. In 1800 he was given the *Resolution* (74 guns) and in 1803 he was captain of the *Zealand*, the flagship of Sir James de Saumarez. It was in this connection that Sir John Ross wrote of Mitchell, thirty years later: 'Captain, afterwards Admiral, William Mitchell, an officer who had risen to the rank of rear-admiral by his good conduct, after having been flogged round the fleet for desertion' (Ross, 2.72). This is a startling remark, but it is delivered as a matter of course, and Ross, a naval officer and eventually an admiral himself, is unlikely to have been mistaken about something generally known in the service at the time. It is true that the record of service presented in 1781 shows no ship from which it is probable that Mitchell deserted when he was a seaman; but the years between 1768 and 1777 are passed over in silence.

However that may be, in 1807 Captain Mitchell was certainly commanding the sea fencibles at Shoreham by Sea, and the next year he was promoted rear-admiral of the blue, moving steadily up the grades by seniority until he became vice-admiral of the white in 1813. He was also

appointed KCB before his death, aged seventy, at his home in Camberwell Grove, Camberwell, Surrey, on 7 March 1816.   PATRICK O'BRIAN, *rev.*

Sources *Memoirs and correspondence of Admiral Lord de Saumarez*, ed. J. Ross, 2 vols. (1838) · *Naval Chronicle*, 35 (1816), 264

Mitchell, Sir William (1811–1878), maritime writer, the son of John Mitchell of Modbury, near Ivybridge, Devon, a turner in wood and ivory and then a farmer, was born at Modbury. He was apprenticed to a printer at Modbury, and at an early age went to London as a journalist. He was for some time on the *True Sun*, and from 1836 was chief proprietor and editor of the *Shipping and Mercantile Gazette*, a daily paper which he established in 1836 and which soon took the position of influence it for long maintained. In 1840 he began to urge the necessity of compulsory examinations for officers of merchant ships, and it was partly in consequence of his action that the Mercantile Marine Act of 1850 was passed (13 & 14 Vict. c. 93). In 1857 he was called on to advise with the registrar-general of seamen in the preparation of the measure for the Royal Naval Reserve, which eventually took form in the act of 1859 'for the Establishment of a Reserve Volunteer Force of Seamen, and for the Government of the same' (22 & 23 Vict. c. 40). Mitchell succeeded in introducing an international code of signals, which was gradually adopted by every maritime country, and in establishing signal stations round the British coast for reporting the movements of all ships using the international code. In reward for his public services he was knighted in 1867, and in 1869 was made by the king of Sweden a knight commander of the order of St Olaf. He edited for publication in 1869 *A Review of the Merchant Shipping Bill*, a series of leading articles from the *Shipping and Mercantile Gazette*, and in 1873–6 *Maritime Notes and Queries, a Record of Shipping Law and Usage*. He also played the cello, bassoon, viola, and flute. He married in 1835 Caroline, the eldest daughter of Richard Andrews of Modbury; she survived him. He died at Strode, Modbury, on 1 May 1878, and was buried in Modbury churchyard on 6 May.   J. K. LAUGHTON, *rev.* ROGER MORRISS

Sources Ward, *Men of the reign* · *The Times* (4 May 1878) · Boase, *Mod. Eng. biog.* · *CGPLA Eng. & Wales* (1878)
Wealth at death under £35,000: probate, 1 July 1878, *CGPLA Eng. & Wales*

Mitchell, William (1819/20–1908), print collector and connoisseur, had Scottish and German connections, although his place of birth and parentage remain unknown. Sidney Colvin, former keeper of the British Museum's print room, recorded that Mitchell was of 'education (and I believe origin) partly German' (Colvin, *Memories*, 207). The bibliophile and poet Frederick Locker-Lampson, who referred to Mitchell's 'countrymen, the Germans and the Scots' (Locker-Lampson, 115), wrote an intimate portrait of his friend which is all the more remarkable given the highly private and reserved nature of Mitchell's personality. Privately printed in 1884 for his closest friends in only twelve copies, Locker-Lampson's anonymous autobiography discloses that he had first met Mitchell twenty years earlier 'through the dim light of a Turkish bath … clad in the scantiest attire' at Malvern where they were both taking the waters for nervous dyspepsia (ibid., 111).

Mitchell first comes to notice as a collector with the sale of his collection of autograph letters on 17 December 1849 by Puttick and Simpson, the London literary auctioneers; it was particularly notable for autographs of German poets, literati, and musicians and of learned Scots and Scottish poets, confirming Mitchell's twin attachment to German and Scottish culture by his twenties. Locker-Lampson states that Mitchell lived for between twelve and fourteen years in Australia where he made a small fortune from sheep-farming; although no further details are known, this period in Australia was in all likelihood during the 1850s. Following his return to London by the early 1860s Mitchell henceforth led the life of a gentleman bachelor of independent means, residing for many years in his richly furnished chambers at 16 Grosvenor Street, Mayfair. His regular haunts were the salerooms of Christies and Sothebys, the National Gallery, and the British Museum's print room.

Mitchell's reputation rests on the formation of a comprehensive collection of early German woodcuts, unsurpassed in Britain and on the continent, which he donated to the British Museum in 1895. Of the collection of 1290 woodcuts, nearly 1150 were German, including almost 300 by Albrecht Dürer and over 270 by Hans Holbein the younger, as well as numerous examples by the other German Renaissance masters, including Lucas Cranach the elder, Hans Burgkmair, and Albrecht Altdorfer. Whereas most nineteenth-century British print connoisseurs formed their collections along the traditional lines of the masters of engraving and etching, Mitchell was unusual in specializing in woodcuts which lay outside the mainstream of print collecting. Within this area Mitchell focused on early German practitioners, including the rare anonymous artists predating Dürer and those identifiable only by a monogram, who were considered too obscure and difficult by other collectors. Mitchell assembled his collection from the 1860s and during the following decade was a frequent visitor to the salerooms on the continent, particularly in Germany, where he bought in person at the famous print sale of K. E. von Liphart at Leipzig in 1876. Mitchell's international stature as a collector was well established by this date when the *Times* sales correspondent George Redford referred to his collection of woodcuts as 'one of the most complete of any private cabinets' (Redford, 234). In 1895, when Mitchell presented his collection to the British Museum, Colvin in his keeper's report to the trustees described this gift as 'one of the most important which has been made to the Department of Prints and Drawings for many years' (Colvin, report). Mitchell's collection was the basis for Campbell Dodgson's *Catalogue of Early German and Flemish Woodcuts in the British Museum*, the department's first scholarly catalogue published in two volumes in 1903 and 1911. In 1904 Mitchell made an additional gift of his collection of early German illustrated books, which included at least eighteen volumes now known to have once belonged to Dürer's humanist friend Willibald Pirckheimer.

Mitchell's career as a collector was guided by his involvement with the Burlington Fine Arts Club (BFAC), based from 1870 at 17 Savile Row, London, which was a meeting place for like-minded connoisseurs that had been established in 1866 under the aegis of J. C. Robinson, then superintendent of the art collections at the South Kensington Museum (later the Victoria and Albert Museum). Mitchell was a founding member of the BFAC, as was his close friend John Malcolm of Poltalloch, the wealthy Scottish landowner and collector, who like Mitchell had made a fortune in Australia, from raising cattle. The two were introduced through Locker-Lampson and became inseparable companions. As Locker-Lampson described their friendship:

> They live under the same roof in Scotland, they tour in company on the Continent, and if you chance to see Malcolm at Christie and Manson's, or the Kensington Museum, you may make up your mind that M[itchell] is not very far off. (Locker-Lampson, 112)

Mitchell and Malcolm were prominent members of the BFAC during the 1870s and early 1880s, both serving on the general committee which decided upon the club's principal objectives of organizing exhibitions and publishing accompanying catalogues. To some extent their collecting interests influenced the choice of exhibitions during this period. In 1877 Mitchell organized his first exhibition devoted to the early sixteenth-century German little masters, Hans Sebald Beham and Barthel Beham, for which he prepared the catalogue, and in 1882 he lent heavily from his own collection to an exhibition of fifteenth- and sixteenth-century German woodcuts, where he was largely responsible for the catalogue entries. Mitchell was also a generous contributor to the major loan exhibition of wood engravings in Liverpool in 1878. Whereas Malcolm with his superior purchasing power concentrated in assembling an unrivalled collection of principally Italian Renaissance drawings, Mitchell also put together a smaller but choice collection of predominantly northern drawings, including twenty Dürer drawings, which was dispersed by sale in Frankfurt in 1890.

According to Locker-Lampson, Mitchell's habit of periodically dispersing his collections was due to an 'extreme fastidiousness' in his character; this saw him successively dispose of collections of Dresden china, blue and white oriental porcelain, sixteenth-century Italian maiolica and Renaissance engravings, before turning his attention to early German woodcuts. Writing in 1883 Locker-Lampson prophesied that even of this collection 'long before he is seventy years of age he will have entirely got rid of it', concluding that 'we shall some day find my fastidious friend seated in the emptiest of rooms, between four bare walls, perhaps twirling his thumbs and gazing on Malcolm, or on vacancy' (Locker-Lampson, 113). Apart from his books and fine furniture, little remained of Mitchell's collection after his gift in 1895 to the British Museum, with the residue, principally sixteen framed Dürer engravings, sent by his executors for sale at Christies on 24 February 1909.

Mitchell made his will on 19 June 1895, when he was

seventy-five, nominating his brother, John, then living in Paris, as residuary legatee, with the income from his estate to pass on the latter's death to Mitchell's four nieces, one of whom was married to Heinrich von Seckendorff, a German army major. In his 1902 codicil he remembered Malcolm's daughter, Isabella (wife of Mitchell's executor, the Hon. Alfred E. Gathorne-Hardy), and Malcolm's youngest son, William Rolle, also an executor. He died on 3 December 1908 in his rooms at 91 Jermyn Street, St James's, London. He was buried outside the Episcopalian chapel at Malcolm's Scottish seat of Poltalloch, near Lochgilphead, Argyllshire, where his epitaph reads: 'He was for many years the intimate friend and companion of John Malcolm Esq. of Poltalloch'. Perhaps in keeping with his intensely private character, no obituary was published. In the absence of any known portrait or photograph, Locker-Lampson's description of Mitchell's physical appearance must suffice:

> He is slight, considerably more than six feet high, and he has an air of refinement, not to say distinction. … [H]is ideas and habits, his likes and his dislikes, have all been considerably affected by an abnormal physical delicacy, shyness and reserve.   (Locker-Lampson, 111)

STEPHEN COPPEL

Sources S. Coppel, 'William Mitchell (1820–1908) and John Malcolm of Poltalloch (1805–93)', *Landmarks in print collecting: connoisseurs and donors at the British Museum since 1753*, ed. A. Griffiths (British Museum Press, 1996), 159–88 [exhibition catalogue, Museum of Fine Arts, Houston, TX, 1996, and elsewhere] · [F. Locker-Lampson], *An autobiography* (privately printed, 1884) [12 copies only; 'Rowfant, August 10, 1883' dated on first page of Bodl. Oxf. copy, Don. d. 161] · F. Lugt, *Les marques de collections* (1921) · S. Colvin, *Memories and notes of persons and places, 1852–1912* (1921) · G. Redford, *Arts sales: a history of sales of pictures and other works of art*, 1 (1888) · S. Colvin, report to the trustees, 4 Feb 1895, BM, department of prints and drawings · will, 19 June 1895, probate granted, 23 Jan 1909 · d. cert. · memorial, Episcopalian chapel, Poltalloch, near Lochgilphead, Argyllshire · D. Paisey, *Catalogue of German printed books to 1900: the British Museum, department of prints and drawings* (2002), 8
Archives BM, report to the trustees
Wealth at death £20,386 12s. 3d.: resworn probate, 23 Jan 1909, CGPLA Eng. & Wales

Mitchell, Sir William Gore Sutherland (1888–1944), air force officer, was born in Cumberland, New South Wales, Australia, on 8 March 1888, the son of William Broadfoot Mitchell, a brewery owner of Sydney, and his second wife, Edith Gore. He was educated in England at Wellington College (1902–6), where he captained the rugby fifteen. On leaving school he was commissioned into the special reserve battalion of the Devonshire regiment, and he transferred to the regular army in 1909, when he joined the Highland light infantry. 'In common with other enterprising and adventurous officers of the period, he was seized with a desire to fly' (*DNB*), and he obtained his Royal Aero Club pilot's certificate (no. 483) in May 1913. Having qualified at the Central Flying School at Upavon in December 1913, he was seconded to the Royal Flying Corps (RFC).

On the outbreak of the First World War, on 13 August 1914 Mitchell went to France with 4 squadron as part of the original RFC deployment in support of the British expeditionary force. Flying the B.E.2 and Farman S.7, he took part in the retreat from Mons. As a temporary captain he was sent home to command 10 squadron, which, equipped with B.E.2c aircraft, he took to France in July 1915, later taking part in the battle of Loos. After serving on the Somme, where he was awarded the MC and promotion to lieutenant-colonel, he commanded the twelfth wing at Arras from the spring of 1917. He was appointed to the DSO, mentioned four times in dispatches, and awarded the AFC. In 1918 he took over 20 group in northwest Africa, and the following year he was awarded a permanent commission in the Royal Air Force, with the rank of wing commander. Later in 1919 he went to India, where he commanded the RAF wing on operations in Waziristan (1922–23) and was twice mentioned in dispatches and awarded the CBE. On 31 October 1919 he married Essy Gordon Jane, the daughter of Lieutenant-Colonel William Plant, Indian army, and the widow of Captain F. L. Hingston of the Duke of Cornwall's light infantry. Their only child died in infancy. The popular couple were known to their many friends as the Mitches and he to his colleagues as Ginger Mitch.

Following his return to England in 1924, Mitchell commanded the Flying Training School at Netheravon, Wiltshire, then went to RAF Halton, Buckinghamshire, as second in command, in both posts demonstrating his capacity for and interest in training youth. In 1928 he went to Aden to command the station when the RAF took over responsibility for the protectorate from the army. He returned to the Air Ministry in October 1929 as director of training until 1933, when he was made commandant of the RAF College at Cranwell and was promoted air vice-marshal. At Halton he had hunted and at Cranwell he played polo, where, although critics found fault with his seat, his enthusiasm was boundless. He then spent two years, from 1935, as air officer commanding British forces in Iraq, returning, in 1937, to become air member for personnel at the Air Ministry. Knighted (KCB) in 1938 and promoted air chief marshal, he served in Egypt as air officer commanding, Middle East, from 1939 to 1940 and was inspector-general of the RAF from 1940 to 1941.

Mitchell's final responsibility in the RAF demanded his zeal, leadership, and organizational skills, as he was based in Glasgow to oversee the distribution, installation, and speedy completion of the chain of radio direction-finding (radar) stations on the highlands and islands of Scotland. Described by the air minister as 'temporary work of exceptional importance', his task was completed by September 1941, and he was placed on the retired list. This enabled him to take up his new post as gentleman usher of the black rod in the House of Lords—the first officer of the RAF to be appointed to that post.

Mitchell was commandant of the Air Training Corps in London and Essex and was at Lord's watching his cadets play the army at cricket on the day of his death. He died of a cerebral thrombosis at his home, 14 Eresby House, Rutland Gate, Westminster, London, on 15 August 1944, survived by his wife, and was buried at Putney Vale cemetery four days later.   ROBIN WOOLVEN

Sources *The Times* (17 Aug 1944) · *The Times* (18 Aug 1944) · *The Times* (21 Aug 1944) · *The Times* (26 Aug 1944) · PRO, file AIR 19/281 [appointment to office of black rod] · *DNB* · *Royal Air Force Lists* (1918–41) · *Wellington College Record* (1913) · *Wellington College Record* (1933) · *Wellington College Record* (1948) · d. cert. · Burke, *Peerage* (1939)
Likenesses W. Stoneman, photograph, 1938, NPG
Wealth at death £3461 4s. 8d.: probate, 1945, CGPLA Eng. & Wales

Mitchell, Sir William Henry Fancourt (1811–1884), politician in Australia, was born in Leicester, the second son of George Barkley Mitchell, vicar of St Mary's and later All Saints', in Leicester, and his wife, Penelope, the daughter of William Fancourt. He went to Van Diemen's Land in 1833 to take up the appointment of writer in the colonial secretary's office, and later held various other public positions. On 21 August 1841 he married Christina, the daughter of Andrew Templeton of Glasgow, and in 1842 he and his wife, with whom he had nine children, went over to the Port Phillip district (afterwards Victoria) and began life as squatters on Barfold Station, near Kyneton and Mount Macedon.

On 1 January 1853, when bushrangers and troubles on the goldfields were causing serious disorder, Mitchell, by then a territorial magistrate, was invited by Lieutenant-Governor La Trobe to take overall command of the police. In this capacity, having received almost unlimited powers, he reorganized and rebuilt the force, restored order in the gold districts, and stamped out bushranging.

In 1854–5 private affairs took Mitchell back to England. On his return to Victoria he served as honorary minister under William Haines in 1855, was elected to the legislative council as one of the five original members for the North-Western Province in 1856, and served as postmaster-general in the second Haines ministry from April 1857 to March 1858, when he carried out a complete reform of the post office. He was out of parliament in 1858–9, but after his re-election he was minister of railways and roads (1861–3) in John O'Shanassy's administration. In the sessions of 1866–8 he gave special attention to the bill respecting the constitution of the legislative council, which became law in September 1868. In 1869 he was elected chairman of committees in the legislative council, and in 1870 its president. Distinguishing himself by the vigour of his rulings, he served in this capacity until his death, through a period of considerable anxiety, leading the opposition of the legislative council to the assembly in the disputes with the government of Sir James McCulloch over the tariff and the Darling grant, and later respecting payment of members.

In 1875 Mitchell was appointed knight bachelor. He died of a heart attack at his residence at Barfold Station, near Kyneton, on 24 November 1884, and was buried on 27 November in the family grave at St Kilda cemetery, Melbourne, beside his wife and four of his children. At the time of his death he was a large landed proprietor near Kyneton and chairman of R. Goldsborough & Co. and the Australasian Agency and Banking Corporation.

C. A. HARRIS, *rev.* ELIZABETH BAIGENT

Sources AusDB · *The Argus* [Melbourne] (25 Nov 1884)

Mitchelson [Mitchel], **Margaret** (*fl.* 1638), prophetess, is said to have been the daughter of a parish minister, possibly James Mitchelson (1585–1625), minister of Yester. She achieved fame in September 1638 through having fits during which she prophesied success for the national covenant and denounced the rival king's covenant. Henry Rollock, an Edinburgh minister, proclaimed his belief that she spoke with the voice of God, and many flocked to hear her words. 'Great numbers of all rankes of people wer her dayly hearers; and many of the devouter sexe, the women, prayed, and wept with joy and wonder, to heare her speacke', while her words were taken down in 'brachgraphy' (shorthand) and distributed in manuscript. Opponents suggested that 'the Shee Prophetesse' was mad or an impostor (Gordon, 1.131–2), while Gilbert Burnet took her to be 'a devout person … troubled with Vapours' whose illness caused her to 'speak as one transported' (Burnet, 83). On 13 September Rollock took Archibald Johnston of Wariston to hear the 'poor damsel', and he was much impressed by 'the wonderful work' of one whose 'saule was full to the brim and to the overflouing of the most sensible conceptions and expressions'. On 2 October Johnston recorded that she was 'transported in heavinly raptures' to the astonishment of 'many thousand' including doubting nobles who were converted to the cause of the covenant (*Diary of Sir Archibald Johnston*, 385, 393). 'But this blazing starr quickly vanished, and her prophecyes wer never printed' (Gordon, 1.132). After the end of 1638 Mitchelson vanished back into obscurity, but her brief career as a prophetess had been influential in stirring up zeal for the covenanters.

DAVID STEVENSON

Sources *Diary of Sir Archibald Johnston of Wariston*, ed. G. M. Paul and others, 3 vols., Scottish History Society, 61, 2nd ser., 18, 3rd. ser., 34 (1911–40) · 'Fragment of the diary of Sir Archibald Johnston, Lord Wariston, 1639', ed. G. M. Paul, *Wariston's diary and other papers*, Scottish History Society, 26 (1896), 1–98 · J. Gordon, *History of Scots affairs from 1637–1641*, ed. J. Robertson and G. Grub, 3 vols., Spalding Club, 1, 3, 5 (1841) · *Fasti Scot.*, new edn, 1.399 · G. Burnet, *The memoires of the lives and actions of James and William, dukes of Hamilton and Castleherald* (1677)

Mitchenson, (Francis) Joseph Blackett (1911–1992). *See under* Mander, Raymond Josiah Gale (1911–1983).

Mitchinson, John (1833–1918), bishop of Barbados and headmaster, was born on 23 September 1833 in Durham, the only son of John Mitchinson (*c.*1799–1835), commander and part-owner of a merchant ship, and his wife, Louisa, whose maiden name was probably Hole. His father was a native of Stockton-on-Tees, and while the young Mitchinson's earliest months were spent in Liverpool, his earliest recollections were of a house in Allergate, Durham, where his widowed mother and her elder sister kept 'a girls' & tiny boys' school' (Mitchinson, autobiography). Here John Mitchinson received his earliest education, but he was later sent to Durham School, where he was a king's scholar from 1843 to 1851. In December 1850 he won a scholarship to Pembroke College, Oxford. At Oxford he won firsts in both moderations (1853) and Greats (1854) and in the new and unfashionable school of natural science (1855). Having graduated BA, he was elected fellow of Pembroke in July 1855, a position he retained until he resigned in 1882. Like many others he supplemented his fellowship income by coaching at Oxford, but by 1857 he had decided to pursue a career as a schoolmaster.

After the long vacation of 1857 Mitchinson took up duties as headmaster's assistant at Merchant Taylors' School, London, under James Hessey (headmaster, 1845–70). Ordained deacon on Trinity Sunday 1858, Mitchinson combined his school work with a curacy at St Philip's, Clerkenwell (1858–9). His own reputation as a scholar and some influential recommendations secured his appointment as headmaster of the King's School, Canterbury, in June 1859, at the age of twenty-five. He was ordained priest on 23 September 1860.

The King's School was an ancient foundation faced with declining numbers and increasing competition from other schools. Mitchinson, who soon won a reputation as a stern disciplinarian, was to raise the numbers from 70 to 137, and to see many of his pupils secure prestigious awards at the universities. When in 1869 there was an Endowed Schools Bill before parliament, which would have reduced the independence of headmasters and subjected them to a government bureaucracy, Mitchinson invited a number of heads to a meeting in London. About a score attended, including Edward Thring of Uppingham (a friend whose work Mitchinson admired). They agreed that a delegation headed by Mitchinson should call on the minister responsible, with the result that the bill as eventually passed was much more to their liking. Another result was that Thring invited those present to a conference at Uppingham. This was the origin of the Headmasters' Conference, for which Thring usually got the credit, though Mitchinson insisted that he himself 'laid the egg, Thring hatched it' (Mitchinson, autobiography).

Having been previously offered the sees of Mauritius and Hong Kong, Mitchinson was elected bishop of Barbados in February 1873 and consecrated in Canterbury Cathedral on 24 June 1873. He arrived in Barbados on 10 August that year. At this date his diocese consisted of the island of Barbados alone, where the Anglican church was supported almost entirely by the colonial government, as nearly all of the funds provided by the British government to the church in its Caribbean colonies had been withdrawn. Mitchinson successfully organized the other islands which had previously formed part of the diocese into a separate diocese of the Windward Islands, where the church was entirely dependent on voluntary contributions. He visited the diocese regularly, and started an endowment fund which eventually allowed it to have a bishop of its own. From 1879 to 1882 he was also coadjutor bishop of Antigua, taking over the duties of Bishop William Walrond Jackson, who had retired to England from ill health, but who remained as bishop so that his salary

from the old imperial grant would not lapse. Mitchinson undertook the duties in return for expenses only, so that nearly half of Jackson's salary could be put aside each year to endow his eventual successor.

In Barbados itself Mitchinson faced problems caused by political upheaval and racial tension. His outspokenness on many subjects brought him many enemies and earned him frequent unfavourable comment in the local press. He was chairman of important commissions on education (1874–5) and poor relief (1875–7). He submitted a minority report on poor relief which prophesied, correctly, that the oligarchical nature of local government in Barbados would ensure that there was little real change in this area. The education commission was more productive. Many of the changes it produced benefited the minority of pupils who went on to the higher forms in secondary schools; these included a new emphasis on the teaching of science as well as the classics, and the creation of a first-grade school for girls. Nevertheless, the commission persuaded the Barbados government to increase the amount it spent on the education of the masses by nearly 80 per cent, and it accepted the principle that 'education, if by education is meant sound training and discipline, is desirable for all' (*Report of Commission on Education*, 1875–6, 3). Mitchinson's influence on the commission's thinking was widely recognized, though it would appear that it was greatest in the aspects which dealt with secondary education. The bishop also secured the affiliation of Codrington College in Barbados, a long-established but sparsely attended theological college, to the University of Durham in 1875, an affiliation which lasted until 1955, making it possible for many Barbadian and other West Indian students to obtain a British university degree without the expense and danger of crossing the Atlantic. In addition, he supported at least one Barbadian student at Pembroke out of his fellowship income, and this led to the establishment of a government-funded Barbados scholarship for study at a British university. In 1880 he also acted for nine months as headmaster of the island's leading secondary school, Harrison College.

While in his sermons Mitchinson was not sparing of what he saw as the vices of the poor, he warned the upper classes that their position had obligations and that they should avoid the temptations of 'self-indulgence and prodigal luxury', 'oppression and injustice', 'covetousness and unscrupulousness' (Mitchinson, *Sermons*, 87–100). Although some accused him of racism, he later claimed that 'From the first, I championed the negro' (Rendall), and he did increase the number of black clergy in Barbados and the Windward Islands. In the cathedral in Barbados, he replaced a white choir which performed on its own in the gallery with a black one which led, rather than replaced, congregational singing. While these actions offended some of the white élite, they seem to have been generally popular, and Mitchinson should perhaps be credited with the beginning of the process which turned Anglicanism in Barbados into a church of, and not merely for, the people, securing its enduring hold on the island's religious life.

Nevertheless, Mitchinson felt worn down by constant criticism, and he retired to England, leaving Barbados on 29 June 1881. Pembroke had offered him the college living of Sibstone, Leicestershire, and he was rector there from 1881 to 1899. He was also archdeacon of Leicester (1886–99), assistant bishop of Peterborough (1881–1913), and assistant bishop of Gloucester (1904–5), and his willingness to perform episcopal duties for colleagues who needed assistance earned him the nickname the Toiler of the Sees. While as a child Mitchinson had been influenced by his mother's evangelicalism and, as an undergraduate, by Tractarianism, in later life he adopted a moderately high-church position of a somewhat idiosyncratic kind, as shown by his support for both the Woodard Schools and the British and Foreign Bible Society. He was proud of the fact that he had preached in every cathedral in England, and believed that no one else could pack a set of episcopal robes into so small a suitcase without crumpling them.

Elected master of Pembroke on 8 February 1899, Mitchinson held the position until his death. As master, he was also a canon of Gloucester Cathedral, and ran a sort of summer school for boys in his house in the Cathedral gardens during his annual residence there. A former King's School pupil, whose main recollection of his old headmaster was one of overwhelming awe, visited the octogenarian Mitchinson in Gloucester and was surprised to see how well he got on with the boys. Mitchinson died suddenly of angina pectoris at his Gloucester residence on 25 September 1918, two days after his eighty-fifth birthday. His remains were cremated in Birmingham and taken to Oxford; after a funeral service in Pembroke chapel on 1 October 1918 they were interred in Wolvercote cemetery.

JOHN GILMORE

Sources J. Mitchinson, autobiography (to 1873), Pembroke College, Oxford, Mitchinson papers · J. Mitchinson, 'Liber vitae meae', Pembroke College, Oxford, Mitchinson papers [a series of chronological notes on the end-papers of a photograph album] · E. D. Rendall, typescript biography of Mitchinson, archives of the King's School, Canterbury [based on a version of Mitchinson's autobiography; also includes material communicated orally by Mitchinson to Rendall, n. d.] · J. Mitchinson, *Sermons preached on special occasions* (1879) · J. Gilmore, *The toiler of the sees: a life of John Mitchinson, bishop of Barbados* (1987) [includes detailed notes and bibliography] · *The Times* (26 Sept 1918) · *Morning Post* (26 Sept 1918) · *Oxford Chronicle* (4 Oct 1918) · newspaper clipping, Pembroke College, Oxford, Mitchinson papers

Archives Bodl. Oxf., notes and photographs · King's School, Canterbury · Pembroke College, Oxford, corresp., memoirs, and MSS | LPL, corresp. with A. C. Tait

Likenesses S. A. Walker, photograph, carte-de-visite, c.1878, John Gilmore collection, London · portrait, 1904, Pembroke College, Oxford

Wealth at death £4800: unidentified newspaper clipping, Mitchinson papers, Pembroke College, Oxford

Mitchison [*née* Haldane], **Naomi Mary Margaret**, Lady **Mitchison** (1897–1999), writer and social activist, was born on 1 November 1897 at 10 Randolph Crescent, Edinburgh, the younger child of John Scott *Haldane (1860–1936), physiologist, and his wife, (Louisa) Kathleen (1863–1961), an active suffragist, daughter of Coutts Trotter of Dreghorn, Midlothian, and his wife, Harriet. Naomi's

Naomi Mary Margaret Mitchison, Lady Mitchison (1897–1999), by Wyndham Lewis, 1938

father was Scottish, his wife part Scottish, but with Irish and Jewish blood on her mother's side. When they married, John Haldane agreed not to refer to his Liberal views at home; his wife was passionately tory, and a lifelong supporter of empire. While Naomi and her brother Jack [*see* Haldane, John Burdon Sanderson (1892–1964)] began by abiding by her views, both rebelled later: Jack became a communist, Naomi a passionate, if often critical, member of the Labour Party.

Naomi Mitchison spent her early years in Oxford, where her father was a fellow of New College, specializing in the physiology of respiration. Her mother was a complex mixture of traditionalist and feminist: she allowed Naomi to follow her brother to the Oxford Preparatory (later the Dragon) School for Boys from 1904 to 1911, but whisked her away to be taught at home by a governess as soon as she reached puberty. Home was a complex blend of adherence to upper-class Edwardian notions of girlhood and exploration of scientific ideas with her brother: together they bred guinea-pigs to investigate genetics. The Haldanes entertained a constant stream of intellectuals, but Naomi felt frustrated that she was not given as much access to her father's laboratory as her brother. In 1914 she passed the Oxford higher local examination, entering the Society of Oxford Home Students (later St Anne's College), where she was able to indulge her love of biology, if sporadically, until 1918. However, she never took the final diploma. War and marriage intervened: having completed a course of first aid and home nursing in 1915, Naomi was allowed to join a voluntary aid detachment at St Thomas's Hospital, London, although her time there was curtailed by scarlet fever. On 11 February 1916 she married a close friend of Jack's, Gilbert Richard (Dick) Mitchison (1890–1970), later QC, Labour MP (1945–64), and life peer (1964–70). They had seven children. Geoff, the eldest, died in 1927 from meningitis, causing a major rift with Naomi's much-loved brother and his first wife, Charlotte, as they felt she did not put her children first; the youngest, Clemency, died a day after birth in 1940. Both deaths severely affected their mother. After some years Naomi and Dick agreed to an open marriage; both had a number of lovers, but despite several emotional crises their relationship remained secure until Dick's death on 14 February 1970.

As a young woman Naomi was often described as beautiful; all her life she had charm, and there are portraits of her in both the National Portrait Gallery, London, and the National Portrait Gallery of Scotland. As a person she appears to have been a mass of contradictions: imperious, sensitive, wholehearted about issues that fired her imagination, fond of real-life dramas, often yielding to an urge to outrage, yet easily hurt and desperately in need of love and reassurance. These qualities could be hard to live with, but were unstintingly offered in defence of people or issues she took to her heart. Her friendships were legion: a sample must include Aldous Huxley, Lewis Gielgud (with whom she wrote several plays), Wyndham Lewis (whose 1938 painting of her is on loan to the National Portrait Gallery of Scotland), W. H. Auden, Stella Benson, Storm Jameson, and Stevie Smith. At River Court, Hammersmith, the Mitchisons' main home in London from 1923 to 1939, their circle rivalled Bloomsbury as an intellectual centre.

Naomi Mitchison began her prolific career as a writer with historical novels set in classical or pre-classical times. Her first book, one of over seventy, was *The Conquered*, published in 1923, which explores the relationship between a first-century Celt and his Roman master, although the epigraphs to many of the chapters (drawn from poems by Yeats and from songs of the fight for independence), invite comparison with the situation in Ireland as Naomi perceived it at the time. This novel was an immediate success, and became recommended reading for students of classics at Oxford and Cambridge, while a school edition was printed in 1926. However, by far her best-known novel today is *The Corn King and the Spring Queen* (1931), which follows the fortunes of the young queen, Erif Der. The narrative shows a democratic movement replacing conservative capitalist tyranny in Sparta for a time, a decadent autocracy in Egypt, and Erif Der's own tribal society in Marob, where fertility rituals and magic are practised. The novel explores sex and sexuality (rape and homosexuality are frankly discussed), as well as very astutely probing differing political practices. Mitchison does not indulge in any false archaizing of the language, and she uses historical fiction to illuminate current social and political concerns debated by the intellectual left of her own time. Mitchison's great strength in historical fiction was to offer sensitive material to a wide audience under the guise of entertainment: she was already championing issues such as birth control and abortion—she was on the founding council of the North Kensington Women's Welfare Centre in 1924—but such topics were best accepted in fiction when cloaked in history. Her novel *We have been Warned* (1935) proved difficult to publish precisely because it was Mitchison's first attempt to fictionalize contemporary life in a contemporary setting; the explorations of sex and sexuality which were acceptable to a readership of the 1930s when placed in ancient Greece or ancient Rome became shocking when transplanted into the present. And while *The Corn King and the Spring Queen* had led Winifred Holtby to assert, in the *News Chronicle* (4 June 1931), that Mitchison was 'of the calibre of which Nobel prizewinners are made', Mitchison was often belittled personally in the 1930s, famously by Q. D. Leavis, who attacked her in her *Scrutiny* article 'Lady novelists and the lower orders' (September 1935) for what Leavis saw as her blinkered view of other classes. Mitchison's edition of a controversial book of essays, *An Outline for Boys and Girls and their Parents* (1932), which explored the views of leading liberal thinkers of the time, was savagely received. Mitchison was sensitive to such criticisms, and partially withdrew from the London scene when her novel *The Blood of the Martyrs* (1939), which attempted to draw parallels between Nero's treatment of early Christians and Hitler's persecution of the Jews, met with unkind reviews.

The thirties had nevertheless been a time of increasing political activity for both Mitchison and her husband. They joined the Fabian Society, although Mitchison herself was not passionately committed to its earnest debating style. However, she helped her husband with electioneering and with work in the constituency he hoped to represent, and she starred in *The Road to Hell* (1933), a film made by the Socialist Film Council in protest at the means test. She visited the Soviet Union in 1932, and in 1934 went to Austria to support those victimized for their socialist beliefs, as her *Vienna Diary* testifies. In 1935 she travelled to the United States, where she took up the cause of southern sharecroppers, and she also stood, unsuccessfully, as a Labour candidate for the Scottish Universities. From September 1939 she kept a diary for Mass-Observation. *Among you Taking Notes* (1985) concentrates on the entries covering the war years, and reveals what is both a vivid social document and a record of Mitchison's own reactions to the war she hated but knew must be fought.

In 1939 the family moved to Carradale on the Mull of Kintyre, the house which Mitchison and her husband had bought in 1937, and there they continued to entertain friends of all kinds, including the local fishermen. Mitchison drew great inspiration from the local community. She learned to farm the estate at Carradale, and actively participated in the fishing of the village's fleet of boats. Her fine poem 'The *Alban* goes out: 1939' (1939), reflects her delight in these fishing expeditions. After the move to Scotland many of her works are based there. *The Bull Calves* (1947) is one of her finest; much of what Mitchison felt for and against the war, about issues of femininity, and most of all about Scottish issues comes to life in this humane, wise novel. Interested in Scottish nationalism in the 1940s, she fought for many causes in Scotland, serving as a member of Argyll county council from 1945 to 1948 and from 1951 to 1964, of the Highland Panel from 1947 to 1965, and of the Highlands and Islands Development Consultative Council from 1966 to 1976. In her novel *Lobsters on the Agenda* (1952), she captures the vulnerability of a small west highland village, and the problems facing the panel as they try to persuade the people to accept some element of change. She also wrote a number of books for children, based on her growing understanding of highland life: *The Big House* (1950), *Little Boxes* (1956), and *The Far Harbour* (1957) are some of her finest works about Scotland.

In the 1950s and 1960s Mitchison wrote more excellent novels for children, always with a subtly didactic point which never spoils the tale: *Judy and Lakshmi* (1959), written while she was in India, was well received in the Madras press. She also wrote science-fiction novels, including the popular *Memoirs of a Spacewoman* (1962), dealing with genetic issues. Notably *Not by Bread Alone* (1983) draws on the expertise of both her brother and her sons, anticipating anxieties about the over-rapid commercializing of genetically modified plants before scientific tests have given the all-clear.

Mitchison travelled widely in India and the Middle East, and was particularly drawn to west Africa; in 1957 she covered the independence celebrations in Ghana for the *Manchester Guardian*. Then, from the sixties on, Mitchison's links with the Bakgatla people in Botswana inspired a steady stream of fiction and non-fiction on African issues. These links began in 1960, when Mitchison met the schoolboy paramount chief designate of the Bakgatla, Linchwe, who was one of a British Council group touring Scotland. A friendship sprang up which led Mitchison to make frequent visits over many years to the Bakgatla in southern Africa, helping the tribe in a number of practical ways, and becoming a tribal mother. Among the books she wrote about Africa was the political novel *When We Become Men* (1965)—about a South African resistance fighter who learns commitment to a tribe as well as to a cause. In one of her most important non-fictional works about Africa, *African Heroes* (1968), Mitchison argues that, crucially, African identity had its roots in tribal identity, a theme to which she returned in many publications. She also wrote stories for children; her book *The Family at Ditlabeng* (1969), about a girl who finds she is skilled at making pots, was included in the school syllabus in Botswana. Her passionate involvement made her for many years *persona non grata* in both the then Southern Rhodesia and South Africa.

Naomi Mitchison was for over seven decades a prolific writer of plays (her first love), fiction (including books for children and science fiction), poetry, and non-fictional works, essays, and articles covering a vast range of social and political issues. She had a lively awareness of an audience beyond her own class, a keen ear for idiom; in the bulk of her fiction it is as if she aims to reinvent the story-telling mode. She was always a woman of action as well as a writer—she fully participated in the many matters which laid claim to her

considerable talents. She made significant contributions to socialist debate, to women's issues, to protests against fascist oppression in Europe and beyond, to the people of Botswana, to Carradale, and to Scotland. She did not on the whole like to be called Lady Mitchison, but she did accept being appointed CBE in 1981, which she had more than earned. She died at Carradale on 11 January 1999 and was cremated at the Clydebank crematorium, Glasgow, on 16 January. The ashes were scattered at Carradale on the following day.   ELIZABETH MASLEN

Sources J. Benton, *Naomi Mitchison: a biography* (1990) · J. Calder, *The nine lives of Naomi Mitchison* (1997) · archive, Dragon School, Oxford · archive, St Anne's College, Oxford · private information (2004) [A. Blair, funeral director, Campbeltown, Argyll] · British Red Cross Museum and Archive · catalogue, NPG, Heinz Archive and Library · catalogue, Scot. NPG · L. K. Haldane, *Friends and kindred* (1961) · Q. D. Leavis, 'Lady novelists and the lower orders', *Scrutiny*, 4/2 (Sept 1935), 112–32 · W. Holtby, 'A new subject for fiction', *News Chronicle* (4 June 1931) · *DNB* [J. S. Haldane] · *WWW*, 1929–40 · *WW* (1966) · N. Mitchison, *Small talk: memoirs of an Edwardian childhood* (1973) · N. Mitchison, *All change here: girlhood and marriage* (1975) · N. Mitchison, *You may well ask: a memoir, 1920–1940* (1979) · N. Mitchison, *The corn king and the spring queen* (1931) · N. Mitchison, ed., *An outline for boys and girls and their parents* (1932) · *Naomi Mitchison's Vienna diary* (1934) · N. Mitchison, *We have been warned* (1935) · N. Mitchison, *The bull calves* (1947) · N. Mitchison, *Judy and Lakshmi* (1959) · N. Mitchison, *Not by bread alone* (1983) · private information (2004) [Amanda Mitchison, granddaughter]

Archives Borth Inst., papers and diaries relating to Botswana, CSAS MIT. L87 · Col. U., Rare Book and Manuscript Library, corresp. and literary MSS · IWM, corresp. and papers · Mitchell L., Glas., corresp. and literary MSS · NL Scot., corresp. and literary MSS · NL Scot., corresp. and MS drafts of autobiography · NRA, papers · Ransom HRC, corresp. and literary papers · SOAS, papers relating to Botswana · State University of New York, Buffalo, corresp. and literary papers · University of Melbourne, corresp. and papers relating to visit to Australia | Bodl. Oxf., corresp. with J. L. Myres · JRL, letters to Samuel Alexander · JRL, letters to the *Manchester Guardian* · NL Scot., letters to Niel Gunn · NL Scot., letters to Eric Simons · Rice University, Houston, Texas, Woodson Research Center, corresp. with Sir Julian Huxley · U. Lpool L., letters to O. Stapledon · U. Reading L., letters to the Bodley Head Ltd · U. Reading L., letters to the Hogarth Press · U. Sussex, Brighton, Mass-Observation archive · UCL, letters to Arnold Bennett | FILM BFI NFTVA, 'Spring queen', Channel 4, 5 April 1984 · BFI NFTVA, *Scotland's war*, 'Among you taking notes', Scottish TV, 13 Sept 1990 · BFI NFTVA, *Literature in the modern world*, 'Left and write: recalling the 30s', Open University (1991) · BFI NFTVA, *Highway*, Scottish TV, 6 Oct 1991 · BFI NFTVA, *Comment*, Channel 4, 29 July 1987 · BFI NFTVA, 'Women of our century', BBC 2, 6 July 1984 | SOUND BL NSA, recorded talks · BL NSA, 'Women of our century: Naomi Mitchison' · BL NSA, 'Friends' · BL NSA, *Desert island discs*

Likenesses photograph, *c*.1925, Hult. Arch. · W. Lewis, oils, 1938, Scot. NPG [*see illus.*] · J. Goldblatt, photograph, 1970, NPG · F. Mott, photograph, 1970, Hult. Arch. · E. Blackadder, oils, 1988, NPG; on loan to 10 Downing Street · C. Pugh, oils, Scot. NPG · photograph, NPG

Wealth at death £286,923.79: confirmation, 1 Sept 1999, *CCI*

Mitford, Algernon Bertram Freeman-, first Baron Redesdale (1837–1916), diplomatist and author, was born in South Audley Street, London, on 24 February 1837. He was the third son of Henry Revely Mitford (1804–1883) and his wife, Lady Georgiana Jemima Ashburnham (1805–1882), daughter of George, third earl of Ashburnham, and the great-grandson of William *Mitford, the historian. To

Algernon Bertram Freeman-Mitford, first Baron Redesdale (1837–1916), by unknown photographer

save money, the family left for the continent when he was three, and settled at Frankfurt am Main; then from 1842 to 1846 they lived principally in Paris and at Trouville. Mitford was educated at Eton College (1846–54), where he spent much time in the company of his cousin Algernon Swinburne, with whom he became close friends. Mitford went up to Christ Church, Oxford, in October 1855. As an undergraduate he read voluminously, but hated Greek philosophy, and left in 1858 with 'a dismal second-class' in moderations. He was immediately appointed to the Foreign Office, worked creditably, and secured by his breeding and good looks an entry into the most exclusive London society; he soon became one of the associates of the prince of Wales and was running the risk of becoming a brilliant but rather showy 'young man about town' when in 1863 he was sent to St Petersburg as second secretary of embassy.

Mitford's great energy was now turned into a political channel, and he made a close study of the conditions of life in Russia. Then, late in 1864, he travelled to Constantinople, by way of Wallachia, and from there to Ephesus. His linguistic gifts were developing, and in 1865 he volunteered for China, where he was welcomed in Peking (Beijing) by Thomas Wade. Of his adventures there he gave an entertaining account in *The Attaché at Peking* (1900). He was transferred to Japan in 1866, not expecting that this country, then seen as of little significance to Britain, would be

his home for nearly four years. When the British minister, Sir Harry Smith Parkes, decided that it was undignified for the legation to be excluded from the capital, and forced his way to Yedo (Tokyo), Mitford accompanied him, thus becoming a witness to the great struggle between the *daimios* and the *Shogun* (tycoon). In May 1867 Parkes and Mitford were received at Osaka by the Shogun in circumstances of extraordinary solemnity and romance.

When the civil war broke out, the British legation was in great danger. Mitford was left for five months alone at Kyoto, in order to preserve the prestige of Britain at the Japanese court, and his life was constantly threatened. He spent his leisure time thoroughly mastering the Japanese language, and he conducted difficult negotiations with the mikado to the complete satisfaction of the Foreign Office. At Kyoto he began to collect and to translate the *Tales of Old Japan* (1871). He returned unharmed to Tokyo, but the anxieties and fatigues of a strenuous and isolated existence had told upon his health, and in 1870, on being invalided home, he returned to the Foreign Office, and to London society.

Mitford was now a young man of some celebrity, and he dreamed of a more interesting existence than that of secretary of legation at a humdrum European capital. He was offered the embassy at St Petersburg by Lord Granville, but refused this post and at his own desire was placed on the unattached list in 1871. He did not definitely resign the diplomatic service until 1873. Before that, he had started for the East again; he was soon in Damascus with his old friend Richard Burton, at that time British consul there. Early in 1873 he visited Garibaldi in Caprera. He was received with much cordiality, and later preserved a precious record of the great Italian's habits on his 'storm-beaten island rock'. Mitford eventually returned to London, only to start immediately on a long visit to the United States, where out of curiosity he visited Brigham Young in Salt Lake City.

On his return to London, Mitford found the direction of his life changed through his appointment by Disraeli in May 1874 to be secretary to the board of works. In December of the same year he married Lady Clementine Gertrude Helen Ogilvy (d. 30 April 1932), second daughter of the seventh earl of Airlie; they had five sons and four daughters. They settled in Chelsea, having as a near neighbour James Whistler, who was a constant visitor at their house. Mitford was present on the famous occasion when the painter cut some of his own pictures to ribands in a frenzy of rage. He was also at this time friendly with Carlyle, Leighton, Joachim, and Millais. During his twelve years at the office of works he encountered great difficulties. Disraeli, when Mitford was appointed, described the office of works as 'an Augean stable, which must be swept clean'. Mitford carried out this labour satisfactorily, and gave a fine account of the restorations which he directed at the Tower of London in *A Tragedy in Stone* (1882).

In May 1886 Mitford's cousin John Thomas Freeman-*Mitford, first earl of Redesdale, died unmarried, leaving Mitford his very considerable fortune on condition that he added Freeman to his name (the titles became extinct). Mitford resigned his office, sold his house in Chelsea, and took possession of Batsford Park, his cousin's estate in Gloucestershire; but he decided he did not like the house and pulled it down to build another, of lordlier proportions. He also began to lay out a celebrated tropical garden with over forty species of bamboo. From 1892 to 1895 he was tory MP for Stratford upon Avon. During these years he wrote little, but in 1896 Mitford published *The Bamboo Garden*, a charming and fantastic work which he called an '*apologia pro Bambusis meis* at Batsford'. In 1898 he visited the East again, exploring Ceylon.

In 1902 Mitford was raised to the peerage, as Baron Redesdale, of Redesdale in Northumberland; this was a new creation of the title first granted to his great-great-uncle John Freeman-Mitford in 1802. He became a constant attendant at the House of Lords, where he took little part in the debates, but sometimes spoke effectively on subjects connected with the Far East. He began to suffer from deafness, which was very painful to a man of such gregarious habits. He was forced to rely more and more on his own inner resources, and he became an industrious writer. In 1906 he accompanied Prince Arthur of Connaught on the latter's visit to the emperor of Japan. On his return he published *The Garter Mission to Japan* (1906), the best pages of which deal with the disconcerting changes which had taken place since his previous visit to that country. He further elaborated the same theme in *A Tale of Old and New Japan* (1906).

In the last decade of his life Redesdale occupied himself by writing his autobiography, which appeared in 1915 as *Memories*. He was also busy with translations, addresses, and pamphlets to such an extent that he seemed, after the age of sixty-five, to have turned from an amateur into a professional man of letters, writing *Veluvana* (published posthumously, 1917) and working on Dante. He died at Batsford on 17 August 1916 and was buried there. He was succeeded by his second son, David (his first son, Clement, having been killed in action in 1914). Redesdale was an accomplished amateur who lacked concentration. He had the dandy's charm and his cosmopolitanism lingered long in the memory of his granddaughter Nancy *Mitford.

EDMUND GOSSE, rev. H. C. G. MATTHEW

Sources Lord Redesdale [A. B. Freeman-Mitford], *Memories*, 2 vols. (1915) · E. Gosse, 'The writings of Lord Redesdale', *EdinR*, 217 (1913), 314–33 · GEC, *Peerage*
Archives Glos. RO, corresp. and papers · NRA, corresp. and literary papers | BL, letters and memoranda to W. E. Gladstone, Add. MSS 44467–44498 · U. Leeds, Brotherton L., letters to Edmund Gosse
Likenesses Ape [C. Pellegrini], caricature, lithograph, NPG · Spy [L. Ward], caricature, watercolour study, NPG; repro. in *VF* (16 June 1904) · photograph, NPG [*see illus.*]
Wealth at death £33,031 7s. 10d.: probate, 13 Dec 1916, *CGPLA Eng. & Wales*

Mitford, Jessica Lucy Freeman- (1917–1996), writer and journalist, was born on 11 September 1917 at Asthall Manor, Oxfordshire, the fifth of six daughters and sixth of seven children of David Bertram Ogilvy Freeman-Mitford, second Baron Redesdale of the second creation (1878–

Jessica Lucy Freeman-Mitford (1917–1996), by Mayotte Magnus, 1976

1958), soldier and landowner, and his wife Sydney (1880–1963), daughter of Thomas Gibson *Bowles, magazine proprietor (the founder of *Vanity Fair* and *The Lady*) and MP. Although she lived for much of her adult life as a self-proclaimed communist in California, she never lost the voice and mannerisms of her privileged English background. Her sympathies were always with the outsider and the underdog, but she disliked earnestness and displays of emotion, preferring jokes and teasing. Her childhood was spent at Swinbrook, also in Oxfordshire, in a large and ugly house built by her father, with occasional visits to London where he kept an establishment in Rutland Gate. Her own memoir, *Hons and Rebels* (1960), and the novel by her elder sister Nancy *Mitford, *The Pursuit of Love* (1945), depicted the family life of the Mitfords as a series of comic but unnerving episodes, dominated by their father's frequent fits of rage and irrational prejudices, which led him to attack:

> not only Huns, Frogs, Americans, blacks, and all other foreigners, but also other people's children, the majority of my older sister's acquaintances, almost all young men—in fact the whole teeming population of the earth's surface, except for some, though not all, of our relations and a very few tweeded, redfaced country neighbours. (*Daily Telegraph*, 25 July 1996)

As a child, Jessica (or Decca, as she was usually called by friends and family) longed to go to school; but her parents, following upper-class conventions of the time, saw no need for girls to be educated outside the home.

The restrictions of her upbringing produced in Jessica Mitford unusual determination and independence of mind. By the time she was twelve she had opened a 'running away account' at Drummonds Bank; by the time she was eighteen she had decided she was a Marxist and had taken out a subscription to the communist newspaper the *Daily Worker*. While she was an admirer of Joseph Stalin, her sister Unity *Mitford had become a devotee of Adolf Hitler and the Nazis; their political posturings may have started as a game but soon grew deeply serious. Although her sister Nancy had socialist sympathies for a time, both their parents, their brother Tom, and their sister Diana (who in 1936 married Sir Oswald Mosley, the British fascist leader) as well as Unity supported fascism.

In 1937 Jessica Mitford met and fell in love with her second cousin Esmond Marcus David *Romilly (1918–1941), younger son of Colonel Bertram Henry Samuel Romilly, and a nephew of Winston Churchill. Romilly was also in open rebellion against his background. After running away from school and founding a subversive magazine he had joined the International Brigades and fought for the republicans against Franco in the Spanish Civil War. When he returned to Spain, Jessica Mitford laid a false trail for her parents and went with him, and despite every effort by her family to dissuade her they were married by the British consul in Bayonne, France, on 18 May 1937. She never saw her father again. On their return to England they joined the Labour Party and moved to Bermondsey in the East End of London; they had a daughter, Julia, who died of measles at the age of four months. At first, like many of their left-wing contemporaries, the Romillys regarded the prospect of war between Britain and Germany as irrelevant to the revolutionary struggle and left for the United States in February 1939. When the Second World War began in September, they were further confused by the fact that since the Nazi–Soviet pact the previous month Russia and Germany were allies; but Germany's attack on Russia in 1941, as Jessica Mitford put it, 'changed everything overnight' (*A Fine Old Conflict*, 29). Leaving his wife and baby daughter (Anne) Constancia (born in 1941 and named after a heroine of the Spanish Civil War) living in Virginia with friends, Esmond Romilly joined the Canadian air force. He was killed during a bombing raid on Hamburg in November 1941.

According to her own account of her political life, *A Fine Old Conflict* (1977), Jessica Mitford joined the Communist Party in America after her first husband's death. She moved to Washington, DC, and found work with the office of price administration, where she met Robert Edward Treuhaft (b. 1912), a Harvard-educated lawyer of Hungarian-Jewish extraction, son of Albin Treuhaft, of New York. They married on 8 June 1943, and Jessica Mitford took American citizenship in 1944. Despite their very different backgrounds, Bob Treuhaft and Decca Mitford had the same political opinions and the same subversive sense of humour. They settled in Oakland, California, near San Francisco and close to the Berkeley campus of the University of California, where their agreeable but modest suburban house became a haven for the next four decades for radicals and protesters and campaigners against racial and social injustice. They had two sons:

Nicholas, born in 1944, and Benjamin, born in 1947. In 1955 Nicholas was killed in a traffic accident. Jessica Mitford preferred never to mention the loss of two of her children.

Although she worked hard for the Communist Party during the 1940s and 1950s, attending meetings and study groups and campaigning with particular courage and conviction against racial discrimination, Jessica Mitford was too anarchic and individualistic by nature to take kindly to party discipline. She always liked breaking rules and had an instinctive distaste for jargon; in 1956, after her sister Nancy Mitford had invented U (for upper class) and non-U language, Jessica promptly produced a parallel investigation 'into current L (or Left Wing Usage)' (Mitford, *A Fine Old Conflict*, 254). In 1958 she and her husband both resigned from the party, feeling that they could pursue their ideals more effectively outside. Later, she admitted that the party had made mistakes but she would never attack it or the former Soviet Union directly, nor would she apologize for her own allegiance to it.

Jessica Mitford's book about her background and how she escaped from it, published in 1960 as *Hons and Rebels* in the UK and as *Daughters and Rebels* in the USA, began in 1957 as a short introduction to a proposed collection (never published) of her first husband's letters. It was written, she explained, as 'a thoroughly collective endeavour' (*A Fine Old Conflict*, 222): a group of friends, as well as Bob Treuhaft, formed a book committee to advise and encourage her. It was initially turned down by several American publishers, but it was widely praised when it came out in 1960 as an affectionate, if mocking, picture of her eccentric family, although her estranged sister Lady Mosley described it in print as 'supremely unpleasant' (ibid., 230). Jessica Mitford was more concerned about the reaction of her former Communist Party colleagues; to her slight surprise, they were in favour. Even so, she acknowledged that she would probably not have become a writer had she stayed in the party, 'since members were somewhat circumscribed by Party discipline in their choice of occupations' (ibid., 231). The good reception of this first book launched Jessica Mitford on her successful career as a writer and journalist. At Bob Treuhaft's instigation and with his collaboration, she wrote a macabre and satirical exposé of the funeral business, *The American Way of Death* (1963), which became a best-seller and established her as a witty and effective critic of her adopted society. Subsequent books included *The Trial of Dr Spock* (1969), *The American Prison Business* (1975), and a collection of her journalism, *Poison Penmanship: the Gentle Art of Muckraking* (1979).

From the late 1950s Jessica Mitford made regular visits to England, where she would rent a London base and entertain her left-wing friends and selected relations—the breach with her sister Lady Mosley was never healed—over martinis and Bob Treuhaft's speciality, Boston baked beans. She would then repair to Chatsworth to visit her sister Deborah (Debo), the duchess of Devonshire. But if she retained many ties with and much affection for England, there was never any doubt that California was her home. With her pretty round face, large, deceptively innocent blue eyes, and precise, slightly languid voice she continued to reveal her origins, but her tough professionalism and her unwavering support for radical causes set her apart from the society she had left behind. In 1984 she published *Faces of Philip*, a memoir of her old friend the writer and critic Philip Toynbee, followed in 1984 by a short life of Grace Darling and in 1992 by *The American Way of Birth*. She became much in demand as a lecturer at American colleges, where she would always encourage the young to stir up trouble, and she also turned out to be a natural television performer, with her quick wit and deadpan humour.

When she became ill, Jessica Mitford was working on a new edition of *The American Way of Death*, an irony that did not escape her. She died of cancer in Oakland, California, on 23 July 1996, and was cremated in San Francisco, her ashes being scattered at sea. She was survived by her husband Bob Treuhaft, her daughter Constancia, and her son Benjamin. Her new edition of *The American Way of Death* was completed by her husband and published in 1997.

ANNE CHISHOLM

Sources J. Mitford, *Hons and rebels* (1960) · J. Mitford, *A fine old conflict* (1977) · *The Guardian* (25 July 1996) · *Daily Telegraph* (25 July 1996) · *The Independent* (25 July 1996) · *The Times* (25 July 1996) · Burke, *Peerage* · *WWW* · personal knowledge (2004) · private information (2004)
Archives Ohio State University, Columbus, MSS · Ransom HRC, corresp. and papers |FILM priv. coll. |SOUND BL NSA, 'Jessica Mitford', T7121/01 TRI · BL NSA, performance recording · priv. coll.
Likenesses photograph, 1937, Hult. Arch. · M. Magnus, photograph, 1976, NPG [*see illus.*] · photograph, repro. in *The Guardian* · photograph, repro. in *Daily Telegraph* · photograph, repro. in *The Independent* · photograph, repro. in *The Times* · photograph, priv. coll.

Mitford, John (1781–1859), literary scholar and Church of England clergyman, was born at Richmond, Surrey, on 13 August 1781. He was the elder son of John Mitford (*d.* 1806), commander of a vessel engaged in the China trade of the East India Company, and his second wife, Mary, eldest daughter of J. Allen of Clifton, Bristol. He was descended from the Mitfords of Mitford Castle, Northumberland, and was closely related to John Freeman-Mitford, first Baron Redesdale (1748–1830), who patronized him, and to William Mitford (1744–1827), the historian of Greece. Early in life John Mitford went to school at Richmond, and for a time was at Tonbridge grammar school, under Vicesimus Knox, but most of his younger days were passed in the diocese of Winchester, where the Revd John Baynes of Exton, near Droxford, Hampshire, was his friend and tutor. After a brief experience as clerk in the army pay office, on 6 March 1801 he matriculated at Oriel College, Oxford, under the tutorship of Edward Copleston, with Reginald Heber as his 'intimate associate', and graduated BA on 17 December 1804. When Heber won the English verse prize with a poem entitled 'Palestine', his most prominent competitor was Mitford.

In the autumn of 1809 Mitford was ordained, and was licensed to the curacy of Kelsale in Suffolk. Within three months he obtained through Lord Redesdale's interest the vicarage of Benhall, near Saxmundham, Suffolk, to which he was instituted on 17 February 1810. On 21 October 1814 he married, at St George's, Hanover Square, London, Augusta, second daughter of Edward Boodle, of Brook Street, Grosvenor Square, London. Their only son, Robert Henry Mitford, was born on 24 July 1815; the marriage was unhappy. In August 1815 Mitford became domestic chaplain to Lord Redesdale. In the same month he was appointed to the rectory of a church in Weston, and a few years later he was nominated to the rectory of Stratford St Andrew, both in Suffolk, and then in crown patronage. The whole of these livings were united, during his incumbency, in 1824, when he was reinstituted, and he retained them all until his death. He had little interest in being a clergyman. Charles Lamb spoke of him as 'a pleasant layman spoiled' (*Letters of Charles Lamb*, 61), although Mrs Houstoun used severer language to condemn some of his errors of conduct. Lamb also reported that when a Yorkshire lad learned that Mitford was a clergyman he stared, evidently in disbelief. In 1828 Lamb wrote more scornfully to Barton about Mitford's 'Salamander God' (*Letters of Charles Lamb*, 179).

At Benhall, Mitford built a handsome parsonage, consolidated the glebe, and gratified his love of shrubs and books by planting a great variety of ornamental and foreign trees, and by forming an extensive library, mainly of English poetry. Barton in an 1823 letter to Letitia Landon commented that Mitford 'resides in one of the most elegant Vicarages I ever saw', and added that Mitford had 'the most valuable library to which I ever had access' (*Literary Correspondence*, 64). The care of his livings did not hinder Mitford from renting for many years permanent lodgings in Sloane Street, London, where he enjoyed a twenty-year friendship with Samuel Rogers. Along with Alexander Dyce, William Beattie, and Henry Luttrell, he frequented Rogers's famous breakfast parties, and Mitford was responsible for introducing Dyce to Wordsworth. In order to indulge his love of paintings and landscape gardening he travelled all over England, and in search of the picturesque he explored the scenery on all the chief rivers of Europe.

Mitford in early life was a great cricketer, and from the conversation of William Fennex, a cricket veteran whom he supported by charitable work in his garden at Benhall, he wrote many newspaper articles and compiled a manuscript volume; this he gave in 1836 to the Revd James Pycroft, and on it Pycroft later laid the structure of his work, entitled *The Cricket Field* (1851).

In 1833 Mitford began to contribute to the *Gentleman's Magazine* a series of articles on the old English poets and on sacred poetry, paying particular attention to the works of Prudentius. During that year William Pickering, a publisher, purchased a share in the magazine, and a new series was started in January 1834, when Mitford became editor. For seventeen years Mitford's contributions never failed for a single month, and he edited the magazine assiduously and successfully until the close of 1850. During these prosperous years of that periodical he varied this routine work with the composition of numerous poems signed J. M. His communications after 1850 were few. One of the last of his articles was a letter concerning Samuel Rogers (*GM*, 2nd ser., 45, 1856, 147–8).

Mitford was praised by Mrs Houstoun for his 'brilliant conversation, totally unmarred by any desire to shine'. This opinion was confirmed by Samuel Sharpe, who called Dyce and Mitford 'simple, unaffected men, learned, full of conversation and literature' (*Reminiscences of Alexander Dyce*, 12). Mitford was an indefatigable student of the Greek and Roman classics, and was well acquainted with the principal French, German, and Italian authors. He was well read in English literature, and was an ardent lover of painting, especially of the works of the Italian school. His interest in collecting *objets d'art* is reflected in a series of letters from Lamb to Barton in 1826. Lamb details his frustration over Mitford's delay in reimbursing him promptly for the purchase of Chinese pots and flower stands, which had been shipped from Canton (Guangzhou).

As early in his life as 1811 Mitford contemplated an edition of Gray's works. In 1814 he produced the first accurate edition: *The poems of Thomas Gray, with critical notes, a life of the author, and an essay on his poetry*. This was followed in 1816 by *The Works of Thomas Gray* in two quarto volumes, which contained very large additions to the published letters of the poet, and for which the publisher paid him £500. Much of Mitford's contribution reappeared in the Aldine edition of Gray's *Works*, in five volumes (2 vols. 1835, 2 vols. 1836, 1 vol. 1843). The last volume consisted mainly of the poet's correspondence with the Revd Norton Nicholls, and this was also issued in a separate volume, with a distinct title-page. The first volume of the Aldine edition, comprising the poems, was reprinted in 1853, and reissued at Boston, Massachusetts, in 1857, and in the reprint of the Aldine Poets in 1866. The Eton edition in 1847 of the poems contained 'An Original Life of Gray' by Mitford, which was inserted in the subsequent impressions of 1852 and 1863. In 1853 he edited the *Correspondence of Gray and Mason, with some letters addressed by Gray to the Rev. James Brown, D.D.*, and some pages of 'Additional notes thereto' were printed in 1855. Many of Mitford's comments are reproduced in Edmund Gosse's edition of Gray, and much of the information in Tovey's *Gray and his Friends* is drawn from Mitford's manuscripts in the British Library.

When Pickering began the Aldine edition of the British poets he enlisted the services of Mitford. For it he edited, with memoirs, in addition to the poems of Gray, those of Cowper (1830); Goldsmith (1831); Milton (1832); Dryden (1832–3); Parnell (1833); Swift (1833–4); Young (1834); Prior (1835); Butler (1835); Falconer (1836); and Spenser (1839). The text and lives by Mitford in the original Aldine edition were reprinted at Boston, Massachusetts, in 1854–6, and his notes to Milton's poems were reprinted, after considerable correction, in an edition of the *Poetical Works of Milton and Marvell*, in Boston in 1878. In 1851 Mitford edited in eight volumes *The Works of Milton in Verse and Prose*, and wrote for it a memoir, expanded from that in the 1832 edition of Milton's poems.

In addition to Mitford's major work on Gray, and his volumes in the Aldine editions, he published some original work, including *Agnes, the Indian Captive, a Poem in Four Cantos, with other Poems* (1811). Other poetry appeared in his 1858 *Miscellaneous Poems*. His edition of the *Correspondence of Horace Walpole and Rev. W. Mason* (1851) reveals his considerable knowledge of the eighteenth century, but does not meet modern scholarly standards. A letter from him on his notice of the early works of Mary Russell Mitford in the *Quarterly Review*, which was much mutilated by Gifford, is in *Friendships of Miss Mitford* (1.53–4). He recommended to J. B. Nichols the publication of Bishop Percy's correspondence, which forms the staple of the seventh and eighth volumes of the *Illustrations of the Literary History of the Eighteenth Century*; the seventh volume was dedicated to Mitford.

Following an attack of paralysis on a London street, Mitford was confined to his rooms in Sloane Street for some time before he moved to his Benhall vicarage; he died there on 26 April 1859, and was buried at Stratford St Andrew. His son had married at Wellow, Somerset, on 12 August 1847, Anne, youngest daughter of Lieutenant-Colonel William Henry Wilby, and their eldest son was Robert Sidney Mitford of the Home Office. Augusta Mitford died at her son's home, Weston Lodge, Hampstead, London, on 25 December 1886, and was buried at Hampstead cemetery.

Mitford's collections were dispersed after his death by Sotheby and Wilkinson. They included his fine-art collection of silver Greek coins, cameos, and miniatures, engravings, and drawings, and his Greek and Latin classics, the sale producing £1029 19s. The library of English history, plays, and poetry was sold for £2999 2s.; and his manuscripts for £817 3s. The manuscripts contained three volumes of autograph letters, papers relating to Gray, Mitford's own recollections in fifty-five volumes, and the correspondence of Jonathan Toup. On Mitford's letters was based Mrs Houstoun's *Sylvanus redivivus (the Rev. John Mitford): with a Short Memoir of Edward Jesse* (1889) reissued in 1891, with new title-page and slip of errata as *Letters and Reminiscences of the Rev. John Mitford: with a Sketch of Edward Jesse. By C. M.* Mitford wrote many letters to Bernard Barton, and Charles Lamb frequently refers to him in his correspondence with Barton. Many of Mitford's letters afterwards passed to Barton's friend and later son-in-law, Edward Fitzgerald, who collected and bound together Mitford's papers in the *Gentleman's Magazine*.

W. P. COURTNEY, *rev.* JAMES EDGAR BARCUS, JR.

Sources Allibone, *Dict.* · Boase, *Mod. Eng. biog.* · *GM*, 2nd ser., 28 (1847), 534 · *GM*, 3rd ser., 6 (1859), 652 · *GM*, 3rd ser., 7 (1859), 84–6, 206 · Foster, *Alum. Oxon.* · J. Foster, ed., *Index ecclesiasticus, or, Alphabetical lists of all ecclesiastical dignitaries in England and Wales since the Reformation* (1890) · J. Foster, 'Redesdale', *The peerage, baronetage, and knightage of the British empire for 1880*, [pt 1] [1880] · Mrs Houstoun, *A woman's memories of world-known men*, 1 (1883), 122–5, 178–204 · M. C. Houstoun, *Sylvanus redivivus: the Rev. J. Mitford* (1889) · *The reminiscences of Alexander Dyce*, ed. R. Schrader (1972) · *The letters of Charles Lamb: to which are added those of his sister Mary Lamb*, ed. E. V. Lucas, 3–4 (1968) · *The literary correspondence of Bernard Barton*, ed. J. E. Barcus (1966) · private information (1894) · J. A. Davies, *John*

Forster: a literary life (1983) • M. Magnusson, ed., *Cambridge biographical dictionary*, rev. edn (1990) • C. A. Prance, *Companion to Charles Lamb: a guide to people and places, 1760–1847* (1983) • d. cert.

Archives BL, commonplace books and recollections, Add. MSS 32559–32575 • BL, various printed works with copious MS notes and additions • CUL, literary and family corresp. and papers • CUL, travel journals, poems, and papers • V&A NAL, Dyce Library • V&A NAL, Forster Library • Yale U., Beinecke L., corresp. and autograph collection | BL, business transactions with Richard Bentley, Add. MSS 46615–46616, 46651–46652 • BL, letters to Joseph Hunter, Add. MS 24871 • BL, letters to Royal Literary Fund, loan 96 • Bodl. Oxf., letters to Isaac Disraeli • Bodl. Oxf., letters to Richard Heber • Suffolk RO, Ipswich, letters to John Lorraine • V&A NAL, corresp. with Alexander Dyce

Wealth at death under £5000: probate, 23 Aug 1859, *CGPLA Eng. & Wales*

Mitford, John (1782–1831), writer, was born on 22 January 1782 at Newton Red House at Mitford, son of John Mitford and his wife, Dorothy Young, and baptized at the parish church there. He was a member of the elder branch of the family of Mitford of Mitford Castle and a remote cousin of the Revd John Mitford and John Freeman-Mitford, Lord Redesdale. Lord Redesdale acted as his sponsor for entry into the navy, and indeed supported him and his family throughout their lives. In the navy he joined the *Victory* as a midshipman, in which he went to the Mediterranean, and was present at the battle of Toulon on 13 July 1795 and later commanded the *Buckingham*. He took part in the attack on Santa Cruz in July 1797 and was at the battle of the Nile on 1–2 August 1798. In 1801 he was in the *Venerable* with Samuel Hood, although he said he 'deserted' after insulting his captain on Christmas day 1800 after a drinking bout. His accounts of his exploits have, however, always been viewed with suspicion. From 1804 to 1806 he commanded a revenue cutter on the coast of Ireland. He married in 1808 Emily, daughter of Charles Street of Dulintabor, with whom he had two sons and two daughters. From 1809 to 1811 he was acting master of the *Philomel*, a brig, in the Mediterranean.

Mitford states that he received a letter from his wife in September 1811 while at Port Mahon telling him that Lady Perceval, a connection of Lady Redesdale, offered to secure him a lucrative appointment in the civil service, and in order to accept this he took passage in the *Canopus* for England. Lady Perceval had, in fact, another type of work in mind for him, and employed him to copy and publish letters in support of the princess of Wales, to whose cause she was devoted. Mitford relates in his *Description of the crimes & horrors in the interior of Warburton's private madhouse at Hoxton*, published as a pamphlet about 1825, that he was hidden away in this asylum to deal with these letters for Lady Perceval in secret. Warburton told T. A. Phipps on 8 April 1813 that Mitford had been confined in his house from May 1812 to March 1813, giving the impression that he was an inmate of the madhouse on grounds of health. The letters, which dealt with requests for improvement in the arrangements for the estranged princess's establishment, appeared in the *Star*, edited by John Mayne, and *The News*, edited by Phipps. When the letters seemed likely to become seriously troublesome for Lady Perceval, she brought an action against Mitford on the grounds that he had falsely sworn that the letters were provided by her. The case was held before Lord Ellenborough on 24 February 1814 and lasted from 9 a.m. to 6.30 p.m., Mitford's expenses being paid by Lord Redesdale. The main claim for the defence was that Lady Perceval must have given the letters to Mitford, as there was evidence that they had been taken back to her house, so that it could be assumed that they must have originated from there. While Lord Ellenborough was summing up, showing the untruth of statements made by Lady Perceval (some say he said she was 'as false as Hell'), the foreman of the jury intervened to say that they were all satisfied and found the defendant not guilty.

It seems likely that Mitford was, however, at this time showing signs of mental illness. He was discharged from the navy as insane, and took to journalism and poetry. He was unable to make a living and became poverty-stricken, leaving his wife and children to be cared for by Lord Redesdale. He was associated with *The Scourge* and contributed to the *Bon Ton Magazine*, publications of little repute, though the former contained splendid political caricatures or cartoons by G. Cruickshank. In 1818 he wrote, under the pseudonym of Alfred Burton, *The Adventures of Johnny Newcome in the Navy, a Poem in Four Cantos*, of which there was another edition in 1819. *The Poems of a British Sailor* also appeared in 1818. A tale entitled 'The Vampyre' appeared in the *New Monthly Magazine* of April 1819, supposedly by Byron, Polidori, and Mitford, but this was repudiated by Byron. The publisher who employed Mitford realized that he had become an alcoholic, and in order to ensure the flow of work paid him only 1s. each day, which he spent on bread, cheese, an onion, and gin. Mitford, unkempt, ragged, and filthy, lived and worked for forty-three days in the open in an old gravel pit in Battersea Fields, with a bed of grass and nettles, as described by Sir N. H. Nicolas in *Despatches of Lord Nelson* (1844) in the course of rebutting Mitford's claim to have seen Lady Hamilton being rowed round the *Minerva* to view a corpse swinging from the ropes. Mitford was said at this time to be unable to tell truth from fiction and wrote a libellous *Life of Sir John Sylvester*, recorder of the city of London. He also wrote a memoir of the historian William Mitford for the *Literary Gazette* in 1827 which was critical and was refuted by the family, leading to an apology from the editor. He edited the *Quizzical Gazette* until the time of his death, which took place in St Giles's workhouse, London, on 24 December 1831. He was buried in St Dunstan's graveyard, Fleet Street.

Mitford's list of publications includes, as well as those mentioned above, a song entitled 'The king is a true British sailor', 'A Peep into W..r Castle after a Lost Mutton—Poem' (1820), and 'My Cousin in the Army' (*c*.1825). He probably wrote *The Private Life of Lord Byron, Comprising his Voluptuous Amours* (1836?), the author of which claimed to be 'long a companion of the noble Lord', and was said also to have written about Byron's travels.

J. GILLILAND

Sources J. Mitford, *A description of the crimes and horrors in … Warburton's private mad-house at Hoxton, commonly called Whitmore House*,

2 vols. in 1 (c.1825) · *A correct report of the interesting and extraordinary trial of John Mitford* (1814) · T. A. Phipps, *The important trial of John Mitford* (1814) · J. Foster, 'Redesdale', *The peerage, baronetage, and knightage of the British empire for 1880*, [pt 1] [1880] · *GM*, 1st ser., 101/2 (1831), 647 · *Sketches of obscure poets* (1833), 91 · W. Beckett, *A universal biography*, 3 vols. (1835–6) · J. Gorton, *A general biographical dictionary*, 3 vols. (1841) · W. D. Adams, *Dictionary of English literature*, rev. edn [1879–80] · Allibone, *Dict.* · *DNB*

Wealth at death none; died in workhouse

Mitford, John Freeman-, first Baron Redesdale (1748–1830)

Mitford, John Freeman-, first Baron Redesdale (1748–1830), lord chancellor of Ireland and speaker of the House of Commons, was born on 18 August 1748 in the parish of St Andrew, Holborn, London, the younger son of John Mitford (*d.* 1761), barrister, of Exbury Park, Hampshire, and Philadelphia (*d.* 1797), daughter of Willey Reveley of Newby Wiske, Yorkshire.

Having been educated at Cheam School, Surrey, under William Gilpin he entered the six clerks' office. In 1772 he was admitted a student of the Inner Temple and he was called to the bar on 9 May 1777. To advance his prospects he wrote *A Treatise on the Pleadings in Suits in the Court of Chancery by English Bill*; first published in 1780 this was, according to John Scott, earl of Eldon, 'a wonderful effort to collect what is to be deduced from authorities speaking so little that is clear' (*Lloyd v. Johnes*, 1804; Vesey, 9.54). The book ran to a fifth edition (edited by Josiah Smith) in 1847 and was acknowledged by Story as the 'essential foundation' for his *Commentaries on Equity Pleadings*, first published in America in 1838 (*Commentaries on Equity Pleadings*, xiv). Mitford rapidly acquired a large chancery practice and took silk in July 1789. Having been elected a bencher of Inner Temple in November 1789 he was appointed second justice of the Carmarthen circuit and chancellor of Durham. Other honours came his way and his success in practice enabled him to purchase the Redesdale estate in Northumberland, the ancestral lands of the Anglo-Norman Mitford family.

Through the influence of his kinsman Hugh Percy, second duke of Northumberland, Mitford entered parliament in December 1788 as member for the borough of Bere Alston, Devon, which he represented until 1799. Ultra-conservative, he believed that the principle of equality was inconsistent with well-constituted government. A devout Anglican, he nevertheless introduced in February 1791 a bill to provide some relief for 'persons called protesting Catholic dissenters', which, after amendment, became law, but in May 1792 he opposed Fox's motion for the repeal of the penal statutes respecting religious opinions. Although he spoke in many other debates 'he was not a great orator … [but] he made his points clearly and drove them home with force' (Mitford, 9).

When his lifelong friend Sir John Scott (later Lord Eldon) became attorney-general Mitford replaced him as solicitor-general, on 13 February 1793, and was knighted two days later. The following year Scott and Mitford unsuccessfully prosecuted Thomas Hardy, John Horne Tooke, and other Jacobin Corresponding Society leaders. On Scott's elevation to the judiciary Mitford was appointed attorney-general, on 17 July 1799. Having resigned his

John Freeman-Mitford, first Baron Redesdale (1748–1830), by Sir Martin Archer Shee, *c*.1802

seat at Bere Alston he was returned in the same year for the borough of East Looe, Cornwall.

On 11 February 1801 Mitford succeeded Addington as speaker of the House of Commons and was admitted to the privy council one week later. Within a year, however, the lord chancellor of Ireland, John Fitzgibbon, first earl of Clare, died and the government determined to appoint an Englishman in his place. In the words of the then chief secretary for Ireland, Charles Abbot, Mitford was considered to be 'super-eminently' qualified both to assimilate the principles of equity in the two jurisdictions and to 'cement the Union' (Mitford, 44). Reluctant to leave the English political scene he allowed himself to be persuaded to accept, possibly as much in the hope of financial gain—his salary was set at £10,000 per annum by parliament in 1802 (42 Geo III c.105)—as from a sense of public duty. He took up office on 9 February 1802, and on 15 February 1802 he was created a peer of the United Kingdom with the title of Baron Redesdale of Redesdale in the county of Northumberland. For his Dublin residence he bought 6 Ely Place (the former home of Lord Clare) but he preferred to stay in his 'country' house at Kilmacud, away from 'the stew and dust of Dublin' (Mitford, 54).

Redesdale's appointment as lord chancellor was 'the dominating and tragic event of his political life' (Mitford, 49). He was highly regarded as a judge. R. L. Sheil, in his *Sketches of the Irish Bar* (1854), credited him with 'substituting great learning, unwearied diligence, and a spirit of scientific discussion, for the flippant apothegms and irritable self-sufficiency of Lord Clare' (1.228). His stiff manner and lack of a sense of humour, however, often made Redesdale an easy prey for the wits of the Irish bar. His integrity (and that of the lord lieutenant and others) was impugned by Robert Johnson, a judge of the Irish court of common pleas, in the Juverna letters published in Cobbett's *Political Register* on 11 November 1803; Johnson was tried at the bar for criminal libel in the king's bench at Westminster on 23 November 1805 and found guilty (*State trials*, 29). Redesdale's legal knowledge and learning prompted the compilation of the first series of equity law reports in Ireland, J. Schoales's and T. Lefroy's *Reports of Cases Argued and Determined in the High Court of Chancery in Ireland*, published (in New York, Dublin, and London) in two volumes between 1806 and 1811. Many of Redesdale's judgments are still regarded as good authority on principles of equity.

Redesdale was much less successful in his more general role as a member of the Irish privy council. A bitter opponent of Catholic emancipation, he was deeply distrustful of the Catholic priesthood in Ireland, whom he regarded as intolerant agitators constantly plotting to weaken the union. These views, apparently exacerbated by Robert Emmet's rising in July 1803, led him from one controversy to another. When Arthur James Plunkett, eighth earl of Fingall and a leading Roman Catholic, sought magisterial office in August 1803 Redesdale made the appointment but in a series of letters he lectured Fingall on the need for vigilance in the face of Catholic priests who 'do not teach Christ's doctrine of allegiance to their flocks'. The letters quickly became public and provoked severe criticism, not only in Ireland but also in the House of Commons in March 1804. When parliament debated a petition for Catholic emancipation in May 1805, however, an unrepentant Redesdale made a lengthy speech, strongly condemning the Irish clergy and arguing for the abolition of the Roman Catholic hierarchy.

Redesdale worked closely with Philip Yorke, third earl of Hardwicke, the lord lieutenant, to establish a degree of independence for the Irish government under the new constitutional arrangements. At the same time he clearly felt that they were not getting the support from London that was necessary and he was often angered by the government's dilatoriness and indifference with regard to Irish affairs. But it was his views on Catholic emancipation and the Irish Catholic church, underlined by the controversy in the early months of 1806 surrounding the application of Valentine Lawless, second Baron Cloncurry, for magisterial appointment, that led to his recall. The 'ministry of all the talents', which took office in February 1806, was intent on conciliating Catholic opinion in Ireland and one of their first actions was to replace Redesdale. He took leave of the Irish bar on 4 March 1806 'with a firm conviction that you will do me the justice to say that I discharged my duty with honest and conscientious zeal' (O'Flanagan, 2.309). But he realized how unpopular he was in Ireland and, when offered reappointment in 1807, he firmly declined.

Redesdale never held office again. He took an active, if largely ineffective, part in parliamentary debates and sat frequently to hear appeals and peerage claims. His principal achievement was to obtain some relief for insolvent debtors through legislation enacted in 1813 and 1814, later characterized in *The Times's* obituary of him (20 January 1830) as 'a lasting monument to the philanthropy of Lord Redesdale'. He introduced the bill to create the office of vice-chancellor and was a member of the committee appointed in 1824 to consider delays in the court of chancery. But reform was opposed by Eldon, whom Redesdale defended by attributing the inordinate delay and expense in chancery litigation mainly to the actions of solicitors and barristers. Redesdale continued to take an interest in Irish affairs and in particular denigrated attempts to abolish the office of lord lieutenant. He opposed to the last the repeal of the Test and Corporation Acts and Catholic emancipation. But his last speech in the House of Lords, on 21 May 1829, was appropriately on the Suitors in Equity Bill which, typically, he wished to see withdrawn for further consideration.

Redesdale had married Lady Frances Perceval (1767–1817) at St George's, Hanover Square, London, on 6 June 1803. She was the seventh daughter of John *Perceval, second earl of Egmont, and sister of Spencer Perceval, prime minister from 1809 to 1812. Lady Redesdale was a relative of Thomas Edwards Freeman of Batsford Park in Gloucestershire; when Freeman died in February 1808 Redesdale inherited the estate and he took the additional name and arms of Freeman by royal licence on 28 January 1809. The Redesdales had three children: John Thomas Freeman-*Mitford, first earl of Redesdale (1805–1886), Frances Elizabeth (1804–1866), and Catherine (1807–1811). Lady Redesdale died on 22 August 1817 at the Redesdale's London residence on Harley Street. Redesdale—described by Sir Egerton Brydges as 'a sallow man, with round face and blunt features, of a middle height, thickly and heavily built … [with] a heavy, drawling, tedious manner of speech' (Brydges, 1.159)—survived his wife by over twelve years. He died at Batsford Park, Gloucestershire, on 16 January 1830 and was buried in Batsford church.

D. S. GREER

Sources E. B. Mitford, *Life of Lord Redesdale* (1939) • W. C. Townsend, *The lives of twelve eminent judges*, 2 (1846), 145–90 • F. E. Ball, *The judges in Ireland, 1221–1921*, 1 (1926), 241–55, 334–5 • J. R. O'Flanagan, *The lives of the lord chancellors and keepers of the great seals of Ireland*, 2 (1870), 284–322 • O. J. Burke, *The history of the lord chancellors of Ireland from AD 1186 to AD 1874* (1879), 181–92 • *The diary and correspondence of Charles Abbot, Lord Colchester*, ed. Charles, Lord Colchester, 3 vols. (1861) • Holdsworth, *Eng. law*, 9.335ff.; 12.183–5 • E. Brydges, *The autobiography, times, opinions, and contemporaries of Sir Egerton Brydges*, 1 (1834), 157–9, 250–51, 260–65, 268–9, 298–9, 306–9, 357–60 • S. Walpole, *A history of England from the conclusion of the great war in 1815*, 5 vols. (1878–86), vol. 1, pp. 318, 509; vol. 2, pp. 77, 217–18, 221, 245, 474; vol. 3, pp. 46, 60 • Lord Redesdale [A. B. Freeman-Mitford], *Memories*, 2 vols. (1915), vol. 1, pp. 1–23 • V. B. L. Cloncurry, *Personal recollections of the life and times: with extracts from the correspondence of Valentine, Lord Cloncurry* (1849), 221–30 • F. Vesey, *Reports of cases argued and determined in the high court of chancery*, 20 vols. (1795–1822), 9.54 • *Law Magazine*, 3 (1830), 297–9 • *Annual Register* (1830), pt 2, 473–9 • Cobbett, *Parl. hist.*, 28.1262–4, 1364–5; 29.1398; 35.948–55 • *State trials*, vols. 22, 24–7, 29 • *Hansard 1* (1804), 1.760–62, 787–8; (1805), 4.1061–82; (1813), 24.182 • *Hansard 2* (1829), 21.1507

Archives BL, letters, estate and family papers, Add. MSS 36639–36651 · Glos. RO, corresp. and papers · Inner Temple, London, legal papers, notebooks as lord chancellor, etc. · NL Wales, letters | BL, corresp. of Jeremy Bentham · BL, corresp. with John Caley, Add. MS 36650 · BL, corresp. with Lord Hardwicke, Add. MSS 35645–35765 · BL, corresp. with second earl of Liverpool, Add. MSS 38241–38269, 38571–38574 · BL, corresp. with Sir Robert Peel, Add. MSS 40239–40393 · BL, letters to Spencer Perceval, Add. MS 49188 · BL, letters to Charles Philip Yorke, Add. MS 45037 · Bodl. Oxf., letters to William Gilpin · Bodl. Oxf., corresp. with Sir Thomas Phillipps · CKS, letters to William Pitt · Devon RO, corresp. with Lord Sidmouth · NRA, priv. coll., letters to William Adam · NRA, priv. coll., letters to Lord Eldon · NRA, priv. coll., corresp. with Spencer Perceval · PRO, letters to William Pitt, PRO 30/8 · Sandon Hall, Staffordshire, Harrowby Manuscript Trust, letters to Lord Harrowby

Likenesses M. A. Shee, oils, *c*.1802, NPG [*see illus.*] · T. Lawrence, oils, 1803–4, Palace of Westminster · J. Doyle, caricature, pen over pencil, 1829, BM · J. Doyle, pencil caricature, 1829, BM · G. Clint, engraving (after Sir T. Lawrence) · K. A. Hickel, group portrait, oils (*The House of Commons, 1793*), NPG · M. A. Shee, oils, Palace of Westminster

Wealth at death approx. £20,000: will, PRO, PROB 11/1767, sig. 118

Mitford, John Thomas Freeman-, first earl of Redesdale (1805–1886), politician, son of John Freeman-*Mitford, first Baron Redesdale (1748–1830), and his wife, Lady Frances Perceval (1767–1817), was born at Port Rush, co. Antrim, on 9 September 1805. He was educated at Eton College (1818–23) and New College, Oxford (BA 1825, MA 1828, DCL 1853). On the death of his father in 1830 he succeeded as second baron, but took little part in the debates of the House of Lords until 1837, when he began to interest himself in the wording and detail of parliamentary bills. Wellington recommended him to study the private business of the house, so as to qualify himself for the chairmanship of committees, and in 1851 he succeeded Lord Shaftesbury as lord chairman, with inter-party support. He was chairman until his death, becoming especially known for his domination of private bill legislation. His handling of this did much to assert the Lords' prominence over the Commons with respect to the large volume of private bills. His shrewdness and independence of judgement enabled him to detect the artifices of attorneys and agents, while his dictatorial manner was proverbial. Although he regarded all things, great and small, with a genuine conservatism, yet he never allowed his peculiar views to warp his decisions (Lord Granville and Lord Salisbury in the House of Lords, 6 May 1886, *Hansard 3*). Redesdale was especially severe on the drafting of railway bills, and in 1867 threatened to bring a contractor named France to the bar of the house for expressions reflecting on him as chairman. The correspondence showed that he was acting under a misapprehension (*Lord Redesdale and the New Railways: Correspondence between his Lordship and Mr France*, 1867). Nevertheless his firm and honest management increased the authority of the House of Lords in connection with private business.

Redesdale was also a frequent speaker on general topics, especially when innovation was suggested. He passionately opposed repeal of the corn laws in 1846 and, during

John Thomas Freeman-Mitford, first earl of Redesdale (1805–1886), by Lock & Whitfield, pubd 1876

the debates on reform in 1867, he opposed Earl Grey's amendment for the disfranchisement of certain boroughs, on the ground that the matter was beyond the proper jurisdiction of the peers, and that it was a mistake to make the franchise a party question. On the Alabama affair he maintained in 1872 that the United States had no claims to compensation because the Southerners had re-entered the Union at the close of the war.

But Redesdale's interests lay chiefly in religious topics, on which he assumed a pronouncedly protestant and orthodox attitude. He published in 1849 some *Reflections on the Doctrine of Regeneration and its Connection with both Sacraments*, and in 1850 some *Observations on the Gorham Judgment*. In 1853 he was one of the revivers of convocation. He refused to sign the report of the royal commission on the law of divorce, of which he was a member, on the ground that the dissolution of the marriage tie was contrary to scripture; besides vindicating his views in a pamphlet entitled *The Law of Scripture Against Divorce* (1856), he offered vigorous opposition to the measure of the following year in the Lords. Equally outspoken was his resistance to the disestablishment of the Irish church, which he maintained to be a violation of the coronation oath. On 17 July 1868 he moved in the Lords for a copy of the oath, and in that year and the next published pamphlets on the subject. In 1874 appeared *Reasoning on some Points of Doctrine*, and in 1875 Redesdale entered into a controversy with Cardinal Manning in the *Daily Telegraph* on the subject of communion in both kinds, republished as *The Infallible Church and the Holy Communion*.

On 3 January 1877 he was, on Beaconsfield's recommendation, created earl of Redesdale (this despite Beaconsfield's view that he was 'narrow-minded, prejudiced, and utterly unconscious of what is going on in the country' (Monypenny and Buckle, 6.589)). On 14 June he called attention in the Lords to a manual entitled *The Priest in Absolution*, published privately for the use of the clergy by the Society of the Holy Cross, and elicited a strong condemnation of its doctrines from Archbishop Tait. Further pamphlets, on the real presence, appeared in 1877 and 1879. He also published *Thoughts on English Prosody and Translations from Horace* and *Further Thoughts on English Prosody* (1859), odd attempts to formulate rules of quantity for the English language on Latin models. His last pamphlet was *The Earldom of Mar: a Letter to the Lord Register of Scotland, the Earl of Glasgow*, a reply to the earl of Crawford's criticisms on Glasgow's judgment.

Redesdale died unmarried on 2 May 1886 at Vernon House, St James's, London, and was buried at Batsford Park, near Moreton in Marsh, Gloucestershire. His peerage became extinct, but Algernon Bertram Mitford was created Baron Redesdale in 1902. To the end of his days the earl wore the old-fashioned tailcoat and brass buttons of the previous generation.

L. C. SANDERS, *rev.* H. C. G. MATTHEW

Sources *The Times* (3 May 1886) · GEC, *Peerage* · A. Adonis, *Making aristocracy work: the peerage and the political system in Britain, 1884–1914* (1993) · W. F. Monypenny and G. E. Buckle, *The life of Benjamin Disraeli*, 6 (1920)

Archives Glos. RO, corresp. and accounts | BL, corresp. with Sir Robert Peel, Add. MSS 40487–40577 · Bodl. Oxf., corresp. with Lord Kimberley · Bodl. Oxf., corresp. with Sir Thomas Phillipps · Bucks. RLSS, letters to first Baron Cottesloe · Lpool RO, letters to fourteenth earl of Derby · NRA, priv. coll., corresp. with Drummond family · NRA, priv. coll., letters to S. H. Walpole · U. Southampton L., letters to first duke of Wellington · W. Sussex RO, letters to duke of Richmond

Likenesses Ape [C. Pellegrini], chromolithograph caricature, NPG; repro. in *VF* (27 Feb 1875) · Lock & Whitfield, woodburytype photograph, NPG; repro. in T. Cooper, *Men of mark: a gallery of contemporary portraits* (1876) [*see illus.*]

Wealth at death £194,530 18s.: resworn probate, Nov 1886, CGPLA Eng. & Wales

---

Mitford, Mary Russell (1787–1855), playwright and writer, was born on 16 December 1787 at 37 Broad Street, Alresford, Hampshire, the only surviving child of George Mitford or Midford (1760–1842), who practised for a short time as a surgeon, and Mary Russell (1750–1830), a wealthy distant relation of the dukes of Bedford.

Early years In 1792 the family moved to Reading and in 1796, amid growing financial problems, to Lyme Regis. Dr Mitford (he assumed the title although not technically qualified to do so) rapidly ran through much of the £28,000 of his wife's inheritance and continued to spend hard on gambling, speculation, greyhounds, entertaining, and whig electioneering. Later his daughter would have to write to support him. More immediately, reduced circumstances forced the Mitfords to auction the fine house at Lyme and move into London lodgings in 1797. But at last a gamble paid off: Mary won £20,000 on a lottery

Mary Russell Mitford (1787–1855), by John Lucas, 1852

ticket given to her for her tenth birthday. She saw very little of the money, however; in 1798 Dr Mitford had the dilapidated Grazeley Court, Reading, rebuilt as the large and comfortable Bertram House.

From 1798 to 1802 Mitford attended M. de St Quintin's school in Chelsea (this was the successor to the Abbey School which Jane Austen had attended). Here she was particularly good at French (she encountered a number of émigré friends of the St Quintins and remained a lifelong enthusiast for French literature) and also insisted, against her parents' advice, on studying Latin. She settled at home in 1802 and continued to read widely, particularly novels and drama. In her late teens she began to publish poetry—not, at this stage of relative prosperity, with financial gain in mind. Her first collection, *Poems*, was published in 1810 (enlarged second edition 1811). Longer poems followed including *Christina, or, The Maid of the South Seas* (1811), inspired by the mutiny on the *Bounty*, *Watlington Hill* (1812), a poem about greyhound-racing, and *Narrative Poems on the Female Character in the Various Relations of Human Life* (1813). They were criticized in the *Quarterly Review* but sold well. Coleridge, who had read *Christina*, suggested she turn her hand to drama.

George Mitford's continuing extravagance forced him, after a spell in debtors' prison in 1811 and protracted legal difficulties, to sell Bertram House and move in 1820 to a labourer's cottage at Three Mile Cross, south of Reading. His daughter made the village and the cottage well known. Following Coleridge's advice, it was as a writer of historical tragedies that she began to earn enough to support her parents. Since childhood she had been a keen theatregoer and now her friend Thomas Noon Talfourd also encouraged her to write her own plays. *Fiesco* was rejected by actor and theatre manager William Macready in 1821, as was *Foscari*, after many alterations, in 1823. The same year, however, Macready played the eponymous hero of Mitford's *Julian* (submitted 1822, published 1823), which ran for eight performances and brought the author £200. Initially Macready responded favourably to *Rienzi* also, but rejected it at the end of 1824 after demanding immediate and extensive alterations. In June 1825 the coolness between Macready and Mitford increased when an article in *Blackwood's Magazine* cited his recent treatment of her play as an example of his arrogance. The author or part-author was almost certainly her close friend the Revd William Harness, although in 1839 Harness persuaded Macready that he was guilty only of passing on information. Charles Kemble wanted to put on Mitford's *Charles the First* (published 1834) at Covent Garden but it was refused a licence on grounds of political sensitivity, even though the king was shown in a favourable light. (The play was finally produced at the Royal Victoria Theatre, outside the lord chamberlain's jurisdiction, in 1834.) Instead, in 1826, Kemble appeared at Covent Garden as Francesco in *Foscari*, which ran for fifteen nights, made Mitford £200, and sold well when printed the same year.

Fame From the beginning of her chequered career as a playwright Mitford had continued, less stressfully, to contribute verse and prose to magazines and annuals. Financial necessity and 'the uncertainties and delays of the drama … made it a duty to turn away from the lofty steps of Tragic Poets to the every-day path of Village Stories' (Mitford, *Dramatic Works*, 1.xxxii). The first of the stories, some of which had been rejected by Thomas Campbell's *New Monthly Magazine*, appeared in the less prestigious *Lady's Magazine* between 1822 and 1824, sales of the magazine increasing dramatically as a result. They were included in the first volume of *Our Village: Sketches of Rural Character and Scenery* (1824). This sold well (going into a second edition after four months) and gained the good word of such influential readers as Charles Lamb, whom Mitford knew through Talfourd. Further volumes followed in 1826, 1828, 1830, and 1832. *Our Village* is 'an attempt to delineate country scenery and country manners, as they exist in a small village in the south of England'; if the author 'be accused of having given a brighter aspect to her villagers than is usually met with in books, she cannot help it, and would not if she could', for 'in every condition of life goodness and happiness may be found by those who seek them' (Mitford, *Our Village*, v). A few reviewers disapproved of Mitford's close engagement with 'low' stories and scenes unsuitable for a lady. To most readers, however, the work seemed neither unrefined nor unfeminine. The 'low life' was represented 'in a style vivid and particular enough to pass for realistic, but selective and aesthetically appealing enough not to grate on middle-class sensibilities' (Edwards, 9). *Our Village* established her as a well-known figure; and as a woman she could more easily be accepted and exalted as author of country sketches than as tragic dramatist. Mitford initiated a new genre which

Harriet Martineau called 'graphic description' and Peter David Edwards has termed 'idyllic realism'.

The critical and commercial success of *Our Village* briefly ignited Mitford's dramatic career. *Rienzi* was performed to considerable acclaim at Drury Lane in 1828 with Charles Young in the title-role. It ran for thirty-four performances, making Mitford £400, and sold 8000 copies by December. (Unfortunately, however, she had sold the copyright of several plays and of *Dramatic Scenes, Sketches, and other Poems* (1827) to her publisher George Whittaker.) Praise for *Rienzi* was general; Mitford was particularly gratified by the acclaim of some of the best-known women writers of the day, including Maria Edgeworth, Joanna Baillie, and Felicia Hemans. In America, Charlotte Cushman played Claudia in successful performances in the 1830s, and there was a production at Sadler's Wells in 1839. *Rienzi*, however, was effectively the end of Mitford's dramatic career. She wrote *Gaston de Blondeville* and *Inez de Castro* in 1826–7. *Gaston* remained unperformed. *Inez* got as far as rehearsals with Fanny Kemble in the title-role in 1830 and was eventually put on at the Royal City of London Theatre in 1841. Edwin Forrest wanted to put on *Otto of Wittelsbach* but the scheme foundered as a result of a financial disagreement with Macready, who besides judged the play 'too heavy and gloomy to be worth acting' (*Diaries*, 1.429). *Sadak and Kalasrade*, an opera with words by Mitford and music by Charles Parker, achieved only one performance at the English Opera House in 1835.

Following the success of *Our Village* Mitford returned to prose and extended similar treatment to Reading in *Belford Regis, or, Sketches of a Country Town* (1835, republished 1846 and 1849). She also published *Country Stories* in 1837. She was asked, partly because of the popularity of her work in America, to edit (with the assistance of James A. Jones) such volumes as *Stories of American Life, by American Authors* (3 vols., 1830) and *Lights and Shadows of American Life* (3 vols., 1832). But for her father, she would have been rich. In 1837 she was granted a civil-list pension of £100 a year. She still needed, however, to work hard both to support her father financially and, especially after her mother's death on 1 January 1830 (preceded by a period of senility), to look after and entertain him. Much of her writing was done after midnight. She often faced

> eight or ten letters to read and answer in a day, almost as many notes, often more sets of visitors, the care of my small household, the necessity of seeing everything done, and generally of doing that which my poor father … is sure to leave undone! (*Brownings' Correspondence*, 3.299)

While shouldering these burdens she edited and contributed to the four annual *Findens' Tableaux* of 1838–41 and, under great strain at the time of her father's last illness in 1842, the miniature *Schloss's English Bijou Almanack* for 1843.

Final years George Mitford, nursed by his remarkably devoted daughter, died on 11 December 1842. He left debts of up to £1000, but her many friends organized a subscription to enable her to pay them off, raising more than £1500. Mitford now wrote much less than when the need was pressing; her most substantial work in the 1840s was *Fragments des œuvres d'Alexandre Dumas choisis à l'usage de la jeunesse* (1846) and a series of Christmas tales. She continued to take a great interest in children, dogs, and gardening; she and her gardeners were successful at local horticultural shows, particularly with geraniums. Her plans for a local school came to nothing, but she was able to fulfil her love of children by, for instance, organizing 290 of them and their teachers on a trip to see the queen and Prince Albert pass by after a visit to Stratfield Saye on 23 January 1845.

Mitford kept up a voluminous correspondence with her many friends and acquaintances, including Harness, Talfourd, Henry Chorley, Harriet Martineau, Ruskin (from 1847), and, above all, Elizabeth Barrett, whom she had first met in 1836 and with whom she had much in common including a passion for French books and a difficult father. Barrett called Mitford 'a sort of prose Crabbe in the sun' (*DNB*). Their friendship cooled a little after Barrett's marriage, which Mitford told other correspondents she thought was quite unsuitable. (Mitford had disliked Browning when she met him, also in 1836. On the whole she disliked his poems, and increasingly Barrett's too; she often expressed a preference for lucid, musical verse.) But the friendship survived even the considerable (if unintentional) offence caused by Mitford when she referred in print to the grief and trauma following the drowning of Barrett's favourite brother 'Bro' in 1840 (Mitford, *Recollections*, 1.268–71). It was to help her though her grief that Mitford had given Barrett the spaniel Flush, son of her own Flush, in January 1841.

At the end of her life Mitford wrote or published three of her most substantial works. Her *Recollections of a Literary Life* (1852), substantially based on pieces published in the *Lady's Companion* in 1850–51 and on earlier letters, is 'an attempt to make others relish a few favourite writers as heartily as I have relished them myself' (p. vii). Extracts from a wide range of British and American literature are interspersed with reminiscence and further sketches of life at Three Mile Cross. *Atherton, and other Tales* (1854) included the novel she had first worked on in the late 1830s, generally regarded as less readable than her earlier tales. Her *Dramatic Works* (2 vols., 1854) gathered both the rejected pieces and the commercially successful ones.

In 1851 Mitford moved from her increasingly damp and uncomfortable home to a cottage 3 miles further south at Swallowfield. She had long suffered from rheumatism and the after-effects of years of overworking. In December 1852 she was thrown from her pony-chaise and left partly paralysed. In spite of this she continued, as much as possible, to work and write letters. She died on 10 January 1855 and was buried in Swallowfield churchyard eight days later.

In person Mitford was, from childhood onwards, short and 'in sincere truth and very plain English, decidedly fat'; she was generally liked for her pleasant voice, 'sweet smile, her gentle temper, her animated conversation [and] her keen enjoyment of life' (L'Estrange, 1.13–14).

Financial worries never for long suppressed this keenness. One quality less often mentioned by her contemporaries, evident particularly in *Our Village* and her letters, is her wit (often quiet, sometimes acerbic). Although an early admirer of Jane Austen, Mitford is infamous for relaying a malicious observation about Austen who was thought to have 'stiffened' into 'a perpendicular, precise, taciturn piece of single blessedness … no more regarded in society than a poker or a fire screen or any other thin, upright piece of wood or iron that fills its corner in peace and quiet' (letter to Sir William Elford, December 1814, quoted in Tomalin, 312). Most of her work was reprinted in the later nineteenth century but only *Our Village* remained relatively popular into the twentieth, often in the form of selections which give special prominence to the 'Walks in the country' sections. MARTIN GARRETT

Sources M. R. Mitford, *Recollections of a literary life*, 3 vols. (1852) · P. Horn, *Life in a country town: Reading and Mary Russell Mitford (1787–1855)* (1984) · V. Watson, *Mary Russell Mitford* (1949) · M. R. Mitford, *The dramatic works of Mary Russell Mitford*, 2 vols. (1854) · *The life of Mary Russell Mitford, related in a selection from her letters to her friends*, ed. A. G. K. L'Estrange, 2 vols. (1870) · *Letters of Mary Russell Mitford*, ed. H. Chorley, [2nd edn], 2 vols. (1872) · M. R. Sullivan, 'Mary Russell Mitford', *British Romantic novelists, 1789–1832*, ed. B. K. Mudge, DLitB, 116 (1992), 192–201 · N. R. Jones, 'Mary Russell Mitford', *British Romantic prose writers, 1789–1832: second series*, ed. J. R. Greenfield, DLitB, 110 (1991), 198–208 · *The Brownings' correspondence*, ed. P. Kelley, R. Hudson, and S. Lewis, [14 vols.] (1984–) · *The letters of Elizabeth Barrett Browning to Mary Russell Mitford*, ed. M. B. Raymond and M. R. Sullivan, 3 vols. (1983) · *The diaries of William Charles Macready, 1833–1851*, ed. W. Toynbee, 2 vols. (1912) · P. Horn, 'Alresford and Mary Russell Mitford', *Hatcher Review*, 3/22 (1986), 86–94 · W. A. Coles, 'Mary Russell Mitford: the inauguration of a literary career', *Bulletin of the John Rylands Library*, 40 (1957–8), 33–46 · P. D. Edwards, *Idyllic realism from Mary Russell Mitford to Hardy* (1988) · M. R. Mitford, *Our village: sketches of rural character and scenery* (1824) · C. Tomalin, *Jane Austen: a life* (1997)

Archives BL, corresp., Add. MS 54973 · BL, MS diary, GK iii c60 b7 · Boston PL, letters and papers · Duke U., Perkins L., papers · Harvard U., Houghton L., corresp., papers, and literary MSS · Hunt. L., letters · Ransom HRC, papers · Reading Central Library, corresp. and literary papers · Reading Museum and Art Gallery · U. Reading L., commonplace book · University of Iowa, Iowa City, papers · Yale U., papers | Berks. RO, letters, mainly to William Coxe Bennett · BL, letters to William Coxe Bennett, etc., Eg MS 3774 · BL, letters to Francis Bennoch, M/505 [copies] · BL, letters to R. A. Davenport, Add. MS 35341 · BL, letters to Macmillans, Add. MS 54973 · BL, letters to Thomas James Serle, Add. MS 52476 · Bodl. Oxf., corresp. with Sir Thomas Noon Talfourd · Harvard U., Houghton L., letters to William Cox Bennett and J. T. Fields · JRL, corresp. with Sir Thomas Noon Talfourd · NL Scot., letters to *Blackwood's* · NRA, letters to William Harness · Reading Central Library, corresp. with Sir Thomas Noon Talfourd, Anne Parry, and others · U. Reading L., letters to Sir William Elford, etc. · Wordsworth Trust, Dove Cottage, Grasmere, letters to Francis Wrangham and Captain Osbaldeston

Likenesses B. R. Haydon, oils, 1824, Reading Museum and Art Gallery · J. Bromley, mezzotint, pubd 1830 (after J. Lucas, 1828), BM · D. Maclise, pencil drawing, 1831, V&A · A. R. Burt, watercolour drawing, 1832, Folger · A. Collas, engraving, 1838, repro. in H. F. Chorley, *The authors of England* (1838) · J. B. Hunt, stipple, pubd 1852 (after miniature by J. Plott, *c.*1790), repro. in Watson, *Mary Russell Mitford*, facing p. 177 · J. Lucas, chalk, 1852 (sketch for his oil painting, 1852), NPG [*see illus.*] · J. Lucas, oils, 1852, priv. coll. · J. Lucas, oils, *c.*1853 (after B. R. Haydon, 1824), NPG · G. Baxter, print, repro. in M. R. Mitford, *Our village* (1835) · W. Read, stipple (after Miss Drummond), repro. in *La belle assemblée* (1823) · I. Slater, lithograph (after J. Slater), BM · J. Thomson, engraving (after F. Say), repro. in *New Monthly Magazine* (1831) · R. Woodman, lithograph (after Branwhite), NPG · lithograph (after D. Maclise, 1831), BM, NPG; repro. in *Fraser's Magazine*, 3 (May 1831)

Wealth at death maid and residuary legatee received £2212 4s. 6d. (less duties of £221 4s. 6d.); £500 in trust to son: Horn, *Life*, 12

Mitford, Nancy Freeman- [*married name* Nancy Rodd] (1904–1973), novelist and biographer, was born on 28 November 1904 at 1 Graham Street (now Terrace), London, the eldest of the seven children of David Bertram Ogilvy Freeman-Mitford, second Baron Redesdale (1878–1958), and his wife, Sydney, *née* Bowles (1880–1963). Both parents were the children of remarkable men. David was the second son of Algernon Bertram Freeman-*Mitford (1837–1916), created Baron Redesdale in 1902. 'Bertie' Mitford, traveller, horticulturist, and close friend of Edward VII, had a distinguished career as a diplomat, first in Russia, then in China and Japan, where he was awarded the grand cordon of the Rising Sun. Sydney's father, Thomas Gibson *Bowles MP (1842–1922), was the illegitimate son of a Liberal politician, Thomas Milner-Gibson. Educated in France, he became well known as an outspoken backbencher and as a journalist, the founder of two magazines, *Vanity Fair* and *The Lady*. In 1910, at the age of five, Nancy was sent briefly to the Francis Holland School, conveniently situated at the other end of Graham Street, but when later that year the family moved to a larger house in Victoria Road, Kensington, her education was continued by governesses in the schoolroom, a never-failing source of complaint in later years. Summers were spent in a rented cottage in High Wycombe, Buckinghamshire; with the Redesdale grandparents at their large house, Batsford Park in Gloucestershire; and with Bowles in a small *cottage orné* overlooking the Solent in Hampshire.

On his father's death in 1916, David Mitford inherited the title (his elder brother having been killed in the war) and the family moved first to Batsford, then, as a measure of economy, to the smaller Asthall Manor in Oxfordshire, before finally settling into a house built by Lord Redesdale in the nearby village of Swinbrook. (Nancy used to tease her father with their descent in the world which these moves marked, from Batsford *Park* to Asthall *Manor* to Swinbrook *House*.) It was her Cotswold childhood with her brother Tom and five sisters, Pamela, Unity Valkyrie Freeman-*Mitford (1914–1948), Diana, Jessica Lucy Freeman-*Mitford (1917–1996), and Deborah, that she later portrayed so vividly in her novel *The Pursuit of Love*. In this she famously caricatured her father (known as 'Farve' to his children) as the notoriously eccentric and irascible Uncle Matthew: like Farve, Uncle Matthew 'knew no middle course, he either loved or he hated, and generally, it must be said, he hated' (*Pursuit of Love*, 1945, ch. 2, p. 13).

In 1923, at the age of eighteen, Nancy 'came out' as a débutante, and as a consequence was granted some extremely limited independence; she was allowed, heavily chaperoned, to attend dances and weekend house parties, and, after some stupendous rows with her father, to enrol for a short period as a student at the Slade School of

Nancy Freeman-Mitford (1904–1973), by Bassano, 1935

Fine Art. Unlike her blond and blue-eyed siblings, Nancy had green eyes and dark hair; tall and slim, she dressed with notable chic, and was popular with her contemporaries for her wit and high spirits, as well as dreaded for her malicious tongue, never able to resist what the Mitfords called 'a tease', however hurtful to the victim. In her twenties Nancy remained emotionally immature, mocking the suitable young men who came to pay court, preferring instead the company of such dandified aesthetes as Robert Byron, Mark Ogilvie-Grant, Stephen Tennant, Brian Howard, and Harold Acton. In 1928 she convinced herself she had fallen in love with the charming and effeminate Hamish (James Alexander) St Clair Erskine, second son of the earl of Rosslyn. Although for five years they skipped about together pursuing an energetic social life, predictably the affair came to nothing, and Nancy, on the rebound, accepted a proposal from Peter Murray Rennell Rodd (1904–1968), son of Sir Rennell Rodd (later Lord Rennell). During this time Nancy was supplementing her tiny allowance by writing articles for *Vogue* and *The Lady*. In 1931 she published her first novel, *Highland Fling*, a comic depiction of the war between the generations as epitomized in an ill-matched house party of fierce old philistines and Bright Young Things. It was followed the next year by *Christmas Pudding*, another high-spirited story of love and larks among the young and fashionable, with Hamish appearing thinly disguised as the young exquisite Bobby Bobbin.

Nancy and Peter Rodd were married in London on 4

December 1933 at St John's, Smith Square, after which they moved into Rose Cottage, a tiny house by the Thames at Strand on the Green. The marriage was not a success. Peter, handsome and clever, was an irresponsible husband and a bore. A buccaneer by nature and incurably unfaithful, he was unable to hold down a job for more than a few weeks at a time, so that the couple were forced largely to depend on Nancy's allowance and the small income brought in by her writing. In 1935 she published her third novel, *Wigs on the Green*, a facetious parody of the British Union of Fascists, which attracted little critical attention but a considerable amount of bad feeling within her own family: one sister, Diana, had left her first husband to marry the Fascist leader, Sir Oswald Mosley, and another, Unity, was spending most of her time in Germany, an ecstatic follower of Hitler. Neither was amused by their older sister's book.

By the outbreak of war the Rodds' marriage had effectively broken down, although they were not divorced until 1958. It was a relief when Peter obtained a commission in the Welsh Guards, and Nancy could return to a single life, working at a first-aid post in Paddington, then as an assistant at Heywood Hill's bookshop in Curzon Street, of which she later become a partner. In May 1940 her fourth novel, *Pigeon Pie*, a cheerful comedy about the 'phoney war', was brought out by Hamish Hamilton, who from then on was to remain her publisher. This was in spite of the fact that *Pigeon Pie* sank almost without trace, 'an early and unimportant casualty of the real war which was then beginning', as Nancy wrote in her introduction to the second edition in 1951.

In September 1942 Nancy met Colonel Gaston Palewski, a close associate of de Gaulle, recently arrived in London to work for the Free French as the general's *directeur de cabinet*. She fell deeply in love with him, and he quickly became the centre of her life and the most important source of inspiration for her writing. Although for his part he was never able to reciprocate her feelings, he remained fond of her as a friend and enormously entertained by her sense of humour and skill as a raconteur. Charming, sophisticated, a connoisseur of art and an incorrigible womanizer, Palewski provided not only the pattern for the fascinating French heroes of her novels (Fabrice in *The Pursuit of Love*, Charles-Edouard in *The Blessing* and *Don't Tell Alfred*) but also in her biographies for the characters of Louis XIV, Louis XV, and (to a lesser extent) Voltaire. In April 1946 Nancy moved permanently to Paris to be near 'Colonel', as she called him, and with the proceeds of her fifth novel, *The Pursuit of Love* (1945), she was able to rent a ground-floor flat in an eighteenth-century house in the rue Monsieur, only a few minutes' walk from Palewski's apartment in the rue Bonaparte.

The Pursuit of Love, funny, frivolous, and sweepingly romantic, was Nancy's first major success, intensely autobiographical in its depiction of her childhood under the iron rule of her eccentric father, of her marriage to Peter Rodd, and her falling in love with Palewski. Four years later she followed it with the even more successful *Love in a Cold Climate*, which was chosen as book of the month

three times over, topping the best-seller lists on both sides of the Atlantic. The novel is dominated by two great comic characters, Cedric and Lady Montdore. Cedric, partly modelled on Stephen Tennant, is also a distillation of the most precious and affected among the aesthete set, while Lady Montdore owes her origins mainly to Nancy's terrifying mother-in-law, Lady Rennell.

In spite of substantial royalties Nancy always worried that she would not be able to earn enough to pay for her expensive life in Paris: Paris and the Colonel meant everything to her. 'The day one sets foot in France', she wrote to Evelyn Waugh, 'PURE happiness begins … every minute of every day here is bliss & when I wake up in the morning, I feel as excited as if it were my birthday' (Mosley, 261). And apart from her constant anxiety over Palewski's roving eye, she enjoyed her life immensely: she was well known, surrounded by a large circle of sophisticated friends, and living in the centre of what she regarded as the most civilized city on earth. Now she had enough money to indulge her passion for pictures and furniture, and, more importantly, for French clothes. Good clothes were a necessity of life to Nancy, and her narrow English figure was much admired by the *vendeuses* at Dior, Grès, Lanvin, and Patou. She was painted by Mogens Tvede in 1947 in characteristic poise dressed elegantly in black sitting surrounded by her pretty French furniture in the rue Monsieur.

There was little reason to miss England. Nancy returned nearly every year for brief visits, nearly all her English friends came regularly to Paris, and in between she kept in touch by letter. She was an inimitable correspondent. Among her regular recipients, apart from her sisters and the Colonel, were her old employer Heywood Hill and Evelyn Waugh, who had been a friend since Nancy as a young woman had shared a flat with his first wife. Nancy saw past Waugh's persona of irascible old buffer, 'knowing as I do the real bonhomie behind that mask of iron' (Mosley, 250). Both were mischievous, revelled in gossip, and found the same jokes funny, and Nancy very much relied on Waugh as literary mentor, sending him the manuscripts of her novels for comment and correction. 'You are cher maître to me' she told him (ibid., 138).

In 1951 Nancy published *The Blessing*, the story of a naïve English woman's marriage to a charismatic but compulsively unfaithful Frenchman, which was followed by two biographical works, *Madame de Pompadour* (1954) and *Voltaire in Love* (1957). These were interspersed with some highly-paid journalism, mainly for the *Sunday Times*, but most famously for *Encounter*, for which she wrote her notorious article entitled *The English Aristocracy* on 'U' and 'Non-U', which was later expanded and published in book form, with other contributions, as *Noblesse Oblige* (1956). Nancy's inspiration came from an article in a Finnish philological journal on class indicators in speech, a subject which she seized on and made entirely her own, enjoying herself immensely by laying down the law on what was acceptable in upper-class usage: 'looking-glass' not 'mirror', 'house' not 'home', 'pudding' not 'sweet'. Both the book and the article became immediate best-sellers, and

Nancy found to her delight she had touched on a raw nerve and unsettled thousands of her countrymen, as well as ensuring the words 'U' and 'non-U' a permanent place in the language.

In 1960 Nancy published *Don't Tell Alfred*, a novel whose tepid critical reception persuaded her that it should be her last. She did, however, win great acclaim with *The Sun King* (1966), a lavishly illustrated life of Louis XIV, although her final book, *Frederick the Great* (1970), in the same format, proved less popular. To her great joy in 1972 she was admitted to the Légion d'honneur, and in the same year appointed CBE.

Nancy Mitford died on 30 June 1973 at home at 4 rue d'Artois, Versailles, where she had moved from rue Monsieur in 1967. The cause of her death was Hodgkin's disease, from which she suffered in excruciating pain for nearly four years. She was cremated at Père Lachaise in Paris, and her ashes were buried on 7 July in the churchyard at Swinbrook in Oxfordshire.   SELINA HASTINGS

Sources S. Hastings, *Nancy Mitford* (1985) · *Love from Nancy: the letters of Nancy Mitford*, ed. C. Mosley (1993) · *The letters of Nancy Mitford and Evelyn Waugh*, ed. C. Mosley (1996) · J. Guinness and C. Guinness, *The house of Mitford* (1984) · b. cert. · private information (2004)
Archives Chatsworth House, Derbyshire, corresp. and literary papers | Georgetown University, Washington, DC, letters to Christopher Sykes · U. Oxf., Taylor Institution, letters to T. D. N. Besterman | FILM BBC
Likenesses photographs, 1932–70, Hult. Arch. · Bassano, photograph, 1935, NPG [*see illus.*] · photographs, priv. coll.; repro. in Hastings, *Nancy Mitford*
Wealth at death £4546: administration with will, 1974, *CGPLA Eng. & Wales*

Mitford, Rupert Leo Scott Bruce- (1914–1994), archaeologist and art historian, was born on 14 June 1914 at 1 Deerhurst Road, Streatham, the youngest of the four sons of Charles Eustace Bruce-Mitford (1875–1919), journalist, geographer, and vulcanologist, and his wife, Beatrice Jean (1873–1956), elder daughter of John Fall Allison, goldminer and pioneer cattle-rancher, of British Columbia. Terence Bruce Mitford (1905–1978), archaeologist, was his eldest brother. By 1912 the family had returned to England from Yokohama, where Bruce-Mitford's father had been founder of the Yokohama Modern School and assistant editor of the *Japan Mail*, but his mother continued their love of Japan and its people by teaching the young Bruce-Mitford the Japanese style of flower arrangement.

Bruce-Mitford went to Christ's Hospital, Horsham, Sussex, and from there to Hertford College, Oxford, as a Baring scholar in history. In 1936 he graduated with a second-class degree and began a BLitt on the development of English narrative art in the fourteenth century, supervised by Robin Flower of the British Museum, but the next year he was appointed a temporary assistant keeper at the Ashmolean Museum and in March 1938 withdrew from the BLitt. From reading Samuel Gardner's *English Gothic Foliage Sculpture* (1927) in the sixth form at Christ's Hospital, and from being allowed in his first year at Oxford to handle and look at the 'Ashmole bestiary', he had already found

his love of things concrete and visual, and began to discover that art of seeing, that 'intense eye' (Cherry, 179) for the analytical examination of objects, which—combined with great breadth of scholarship—distinguished all his subsequent work. One of his duties at the Ashmolean was, with his lifelong friend Martyn Jope, to record the buried evidence of medieval Oxford as it was carted away from the huge hole being excavated for the basement of the New Bodleian. His job was 'to jump on the lorry and sitting on the pile … pick out all the bits of medieval pottery I could find. … It was a taste of rescue archaeology before that term was invented' (Bruce-Mitford, 'The archaeologist', 68). It was also the real beginning of medieval archaeology in Britain, as the report published in *Oxoniensia* (vol. 4, 1939) showed.

In 1938 Bruce-Mitford went to the British Museum (an institution he served for thirty-nine years) as assistant keeper in the department of British and medieval antiquities under T. D. Kendrick. His time there was interrupted by war service in a territorial unit of the Royal Signals in Essex, London, and Yorkshire. On 7 November 1941 he married Kathleen Dent (*b.* 1916), with whom he had a son and two daughters. After he returned to the museum in 1945, his responsibility as assistant keeper was for 'dark age' antiquities, the post-Roman Celtic, Anglo-Saxon, Viking, Germanic, and Slavonic collections. Staff was lacking, accommodation was inadequate and unsuitable, and an appreciable portion of the collections was wrapped and stored in boxes, which meant that he was unable to see much of the material. These problems persisted. Nevertheless, appointed keeper in 1954, by 1969 Bruce-Mitford had brought about the birth of the department of prehistoric and Romano-British antiquities while remaining (until 1975) keeper of the now renamed parent department of medieval and later antiquities. Among his outstanding acquisitions during twenty-one years of keepership were the Rothschild Lycurgus cup and the Ilbert collection of clocks and watches, his greatest coup. He also made every attempt to secure one of the great treasures of English medieval art, the twelfth-century 'Bury St Edmunds' ivory cross, but was thwarted by the vendor's refusal to reveal where he had acquired the cross.

In 1938, in his first year as assistant keeper, the museum sent Bruce-Mitford to gain digging experience with Gerhard Bersu, at Little Woodbury, near Salisbury. In the following year he began the first scientific excavation of a deserted medieval village at Seacourt, west of Oxford. In 1949–52, 1954, and 1974 he excavated a settlement of the late Saxon period at Mawgan Porth on the north Cornish coast, and in 1955 he investigated the chapter house graves at Lincoln Cathedral. These were also the years of his principal works on two early medieval manuscripts, the Codex Lindisfarnensis and the Codex Amiatinus.

As early as 1940 T. D. Kendrick had written to say that when Bruce-Mitford returned from the forces he would in addition to his other duties 'be responsible for Sutton Hoo. Brace yourself for this task' (Bruce-Mitford, 'Forty years with Sutton Hoo', first page). The finds from the

Anglo-Saxon ship-burial excavated at Sutton Hoo in 1939 had spent the war in a disused tunnel of the London underground railway. In 1944 they returned to the museum, and early in 1946 Bruce-Mitford took charge of them and prepared a full catalogue. Sutton Hoo was his greatest challenge, the source of almost insuperable difficulties, and his greatest achievement. By 1947, the year after he was elected a fellow of the Society of Antiquaries, some of the objects had been restored and put on display and the first edition of *The Sutton Hoo Ship-Burial: a Provisional Guide* was published. Nevertheless it was not until 1960 that two floors of a house in Montague Street were at last made available, and into this he moved the whole Sutton Hoo operation. He was determined to publish 'the most significant, as it is certainly the most splendid, archaeological discovery ever made in the British Isles' (T. D. Kendrick, 'Sutton Hoo and Anglo-Saxon archaeology', *British Museum Quarterly*, 13, 1939, 136) to what he saw as the necessary standard and in appropriate detail, recognizing 'the responsibility for faultless and complete publication resting upon us all' (Bruce-Mitford, 'Forty years with Sutton Hoo', fifth page). The first volume of *The Sutton Hoo Ship-Burial* appeared in 1975, fifteen years after the birth of the unit, the second in 1978, and the third in 1983. In welcoming the first volume the president of the Society of Antiquaries described it as 'one of the great books of the century' (A. J. Taylor, 'Anniversary address', *Antiquaries Journal*, 56, 1976, 4), a verdict echoed in different ways by a long series of reviewers.

By this time Bruce-Mitford's marriage had long been in trouble. He had left home in the later 1950s, formed a series of relationships, some of long standing, within the Sutton Hoo unit itself, and was often in poor health and financial difficulty. His first marriage was finally dissolved in 1972, and on 11 July 1975 he married Marilyn Roberta Luscombe (*b.* 1945), formerly his research assistant in the unit, with whose help he had published a collection of his papers, *Aspects of Anglo-Saxon Archaeology: Sutton Hoo and other Discoveries* (1974). He was elected a fellow of the British Academy in 1976 and retired from the British Museum (having been appointed research keeper in 1975) in 1977. He was Slade professor of fine art at Cambridge and professorial fellow of Emmanuel College in 1978–9, and visiting fellow of All Souls College, Oxford, in the same year. His last post was as faculty visitor in the department of English at the Australian National University, Canberra, in 1981.

Despite continuing ill health and financial problems, Bruce-Mitford spent his retirement working steadily to bring earlier work to publication. He completed his report on the excavations at Mawgan Porth (published posthumously in 1997) and again took up his major project, *A corpus of late Celtic hanging bowls*, AD *400–800*, begun in the 1940s, and also published posthumously. Following the end of his second marriage in 1984 he found it necessary to sell his great library, which went to Okinawa Christian Junior College in Japan. He lived in Woodstock in 1984–6 by courtesy of Marc Fitch and then in Cheltenham. On 14 June 1988 he married Margaret Edna Adams (1916–2002), a

retired social worker whom he had first met at Oxford fifty years before, and went to live with her at Bampton in Oxfordshire. He died of a heart attack following many years of inherited heart disease on 10 March 1994 at the John Radcliffe Hospital, Oxford, to which characteristically he had driven himself two days before. He was buried on 18 March in the burial-ground by the church of St Mary the Virgin, Bampton. A memorial service was held at St George's, Bloomsbury, on 14 June.

Bruce-Mitford was an energetic, romantic man, who often got into difficulties, some of them avoidable. He was not detached. He drove cars in a somewhat perplexing way. But his passionate commitment to precise and accurate scholarship and his intense eye allowed him in curatorship and research to bring all his greatest projects to their full conclusion. He had a genius for friendship and throughout his life inspired and instructed the young. He was a man of warmth, wit, courtesy, and courtliness.

MARTIN BIDDLE

Sources M. Biddle, 'Rupert Leo Scott Bruce-Mitford', *PBA* [forthcoming] · J. Cherry, 'Rupert Bruce-Mitford, 1914–1994', *Medieval Archaeology*, 39 (1995), 178–9 · R. Bruce-Mitford, 'The archaeologist', *Antique Collector*, 1 (1978), 68–9 · R. Bruce-Mitford, 'Forty years with Sutton Hoo', introductory note to 'Anglo-Saxon and Medieval Archaeology, History and Art with special reference to Sutton Hoo: the highly important working library and archive of more than 6000 titles formed by Dr Rupert L. S. Bruce-Mitford' (typescript catalogue, Merrion Book Co., Wickmere House, Wickmere, Norfolk, 1989) [unpaginated] · *The Times* (23 March 1994) · *The Independent* (23 March 1994) · *WWW* · personal knowledge (2004) · private information (2004) · b. cert. · m. cert. [Kathleen Dent] · m. cert. [Marilyn Roberta Luscombe] · m. cert. [Margaret Edna Adams] · d. cert.

Archives S. Antiquaries, Lond., corresp. relating to Scripta Minora | Bodl. Oxf., letters to O. G. S. Crawford

Likenesses photograph, repro. in *The Times* · photograph, repro. in *The Independent*

Wealth at death under £125,000: probate, 10 Oct 1994, *CGPLA Eng. & Wales*

Mitford, Unity Valkyrie Freeman- (1914–1948), Nazi sympathizer, was born on 8 August 1914 at 49 Victoria Road, Kensington, London, the fourth of six exceptionally spirited daughters of David Bertram Ogilvy Freeman-Mitford (1878–1958), who succeeded as second Baron Redesdale of the second creation in 1916. Her mother was Sydney (1880–1963), eldest daughter of Thomas Gibson *Bowles. She was chiefly educated at home by governesses. 'Her immense, baleful eyes, large, clumsy limbs, dead straight tow-coloured hair, sometimes in neat pigtails but more often flowing loose, gave her the appearance of a shaggy Viking or Little John', according to her sister Jessica *Mitford (Mitford, *Hons*, 16). This *farouche* child, however, matured into a bold, generous, quick-witted, and amusing young woman. She was incapable of deviousness or dissimulation: her preferred occupation, she averred, would be gangster or airman; her besetting sin was boastfulness. She was an avid but discriminating reader, who memorized reams of esoteric poetry and created intricate collages.

In June 1933 Unity Mitford joined the British Union of Fascists, which had been organized in the previous year by

Unity Valkyrie Freeman-Mitford (1914–1948), by Bassano, 1937

Sir Oswald Mosley, who later married her sister Diana. Following Hitler's accession to power in 1933 she toured Germany in the company of Diana and the young tory politicians Nigel Birch (afterwards Lord Rhyl) and Victor Montagu, Viscount Hinchingbrooke. She settled in Munich in May 1934 in order to learn the German language. By reserving a nightly table in the Osteria Bavaria inn, where the Führer often dined, and staring at him, she contrived a meeting on 9 February 1935: 'the most wonderful and beautiful day of my life' (Moyne and Guinness, 368). Thereafter she met Hitler on 140 occasions before the outbreak of war in 1939—finding him always sweet and unaffected. Her veneration of him was so absolute that she became a blindly fervent devotee of his political creed.

On 22–23 June 1935 Mitford was guest of honour at the Nazi summer solstice celebrations where she addressed 200,000 people. Soon afterwards her short personal manifesto of antisemitism was published in *Der Stürmer*. Thereafter, as a British peer's daughter, she was often photographed accompanying Nazi leaders at rallies, Bayreuth festivals, and the Olympic games of 1936. She and her father joined the Anglo-German Fellowship, and attended the Nuremberg rally of 1938 together with Robert Byron: Lord Redesdale, said Byron, 'treated the Nazi Party Conference as though it were a house party to which five hundred thousand rather odd and unexpected guests had turned up' (Ritchie, 38). Mosley described her as 'young, ingenuous, full of enthusiasm, in a way stage-struck by the glamour and panoply of the national socialist movement and the mass admiration of Hitler' (O. Mosley, 368). The fixity of her admiration for Nazidom was unreasonable: her conduct and conversation became exaggerated. She saluted the postmistress of Swinbrook, Oxfordshire, with raised hand, '*Heil Hitler!*', collected Nazi trophies, chanted Blackshirt rhymes about Jews, and agreed with her friend Julius Streicher that Jews should be made to eat grass. However, she had no influence on the Nazi inner circle, and stories that she was Hitler's mistress, or that she aspired to marry him, were untrue. She had love affairs with Erik Widemann, a member of the SS, and with Janos Almasy.

In Britain, Mitford's antics were reported in popular newspapers. Her influence, though, was negligible. Her ardent defence of the Austrian *Anschluss* sent on 5 March 1938 to Winston Churchill did not sway him; but after she reached Vienna on the same day as the Führer (14 March), Hitler declared: 'They said England would be there to stop me, but the only English person I saw was on my side' (Moyne, 410). In May 1938 she provoked arrest in Czechoslovakia by wearing her swastika badge.

Having often threatened suicide if Britain and Germany went to war, Unity Mitford shot herself with a pistol in the English Garden at Munich on 3 September 1939. She was unconscious for two months. German surgeons saved her life but were unable to extract the bullet from her brain. On Hitler's instructions she was moved to Switzerland, and then returned to England on 3 January 1940. Her mental and physical powers were impaired, and she lived under the unwavering protection of her mother. James Lees-Milne visited her in 1944 and reported that she: 'has become rather plain and fat, and says that she weighs 13½ stone. Her mind is that of a sophisticated child, and she is still very amusing in that Mitford manner' (Lees-Milne, 146–7). She was saved from the dismal wreckage of her fantasies when the bullet wound in her brain became inflamed: she died unmarried, of meningitis, on 28 May 1948, at the West Highland Cottage Hospital, Oban. Her burial on 1 June was at Swinbrook, Oxfordshire. She is satirized as Eugenia Malmains in the novel *Wigs on the Green* (1935) by her sister Nancy *Mitford.

RICHARD DAVENPORT-HINES

Sources D. Pryce-Jones, *Unity Mitford: a quest* (1976) · Lord Moyne and C. Guinness, *The house of Mitford* (1984) · *Love from Nancy: the letters of Nancy Mitford*, ed. C. Mosley (1993) · D. Mosley, *A life of contrasts* (1977) · J. Mitford, *Hons and rebels* (1960) · J. Mitford, *A fine old conflict* (1977) · O. Mosley, *My life* (1968) · J. Lees-Milne, *Prophesying peace* (1977) · C. Ritchie, *The siren years* (1974) · M. Gilbert, ed., *Winston S. Churchill*, companion vol. 5/3 (1982), 924–6, 927–9 · *CGPLA Eng. & Wales* (1948)

Archives CAC Cam., Sir Winston Churchill MSS · priv. coll., Lady Mosley MSS

Likenesses photographs, 1923–40, Hult. Arch. · W. Acton, pencil drawing, *c*.1934, repro. in Mosley, ed., *Letters of Nancy Mitford* · photographs, *c*.1934–1938, repro. in Moyne and Guinness, *House of Mitford*, following p. 384 · photograph, *c*.1936, repro. in Mosley, ed., *Letters of Nancy Mitford*, facing p. 90 · Bassano, photograph, 1937, NPG [*see illus.*]

Wealth at death £850: administration, 2 Sept 1948, *CGPLA Eng. & Wales*

Mitford, William (1744–1827), historian of ancient Greece, born in London on 10 February 1744, was the elder son of John Mitford (d. 1761), barrister, of Exbury House, Hampshire, and his wife, Philadelphia, daughter of Willey Reveley of Newton Underwood and Throphill, Northumberland. John Freeman-*Mitford, Baron Redesdale, lord chancellor of Ireland, was the younger son. William Mitford was educated at Cheam School, Surrey, under William Gilpin before matriculating from Queen's College, Oxford, on 16 July 1761, as a gentleman commoner. Distinguished by his physical strength and good looks, he belonged to the same breakfast and cricket clubs as Jeremy Bentham, who 'thought his conversation commonplace' (*Works of Jeremy Bentham*, 10.40). He attended the Vinerian lectures of Sir William Blackstone, and in the vacations read some Greek. He left Oxford without a degree in 1763 and was admitted a student of the Middle Temple in January 1763 but never practised. He had succeeded to the property at Exbury on his father's death in 1761, and on 18 May 1766 he married Frances (d. 1776), daughter of James Molloy of Dublin, and his wife, Anne, daughter of Henry Pye, MP for Faringdon, Berkshire. They had five sons and one daughter.

In 1769 Mitford accepted a commission in the South Hampshire militia. He was briefly the brother officer of Edward Gibbon. The extent to which the future historian of Rome influenced the future historian of Greece is a matter for speculation. In 1774 Mitford published *An Essay on the Harmony of Language*, dealing with English prosody. Following the death of his wife in 1776 he travelled to France, where he met the Greek scholars J. B. G. d'Ansse de Villoison and the baron de Sainte-Croix. In 1784 he published the first volume of his principal work, the *History of Greece*. This was on an unprecedentedly large scale. Previous treatments (the Grecian histories of Temple Stanyan and Oliver Goldsmith) had been moralistic compilations. Mitford's first volume covered events from early times to the end of the Persian wars (479 BC). A magistrate, and from 1778 verderer of the New Forest, in 1785 he was elected MP for Newport, Cornwall, on the interest of his cousin, the first duke of Northumberland. He made two speeches, both on the militia, during his first five years in the Commons, and published a *Treatise on the Military Force, and Particularly the Militia, of this Kingdom* (undated). In 1787 he was elected to the council of the Society of Antiquaries; in 1788 he travelled to Italy and into the orbit of the Society of Dilettanti. He never, however, visited Greece.

The outbreak of the French Revolution in 1789 had a great impact on Mitford. The second volume of his *History*, which appeared in 1790, took the story of events in Greece down to 404 BC and gave ample scope for an analogy between the radical democrats of fifth-century Athens and the revolutionaries in France. In 1791 he published *Considerations on the Corn Laws*, in which he contended that England could grow enough for its own supply. After Gibbon's death in 1794 there ensued a lively contest between Mitford and John Gillies, author of a complete *History of Greece* (2 vols., 1786), to succeed him as professor of ancient history at the Royal Academy. In the event the post was

left unfilled, Mitford finally taking it up in 1818. In 1797 he published the third volume of his *History*, covering the period from the oligarchic coup of the Thirty Tyrants in Athens at the end of the Peloponnesian War in 404 BC to the peace of Antalcidas (between Sparta and Persia) in 386. This volume covers the rise of Mitford's hero, Philip of Macedon; but it is prefaced by a résumé of the late fifth century, in order to re-emphasize what is repeatedly called 'a tyranny in the hands of the people' at Athens. Such was now the climate of opinion in England that, whereas in 1790 Mitford had incurred liberal criticism, his more extreme comments in 1797 won wide acclaim.

Denied the political backing of the second duke of Northumberland, Mitford remained outside parliament from 1790 to 1796 when he was returned for Bere Alston, Devon, by the duke's younger brother, the earl of Beverley. He generally voted with the ministry but was outspoken in his criticism of the measures to reform the militia in 1797–8 and 1803–4. In 1802 he inherited the Reveley estates in Yorkshire but continued to live at Exbury, where he rebuilt the house at about this time. In 1806 he gave up his parliamentary seat to one of Beverley's sons, and did not return to the Commons until 1812 when elected MP for New Romsey, Hampshire. In 1808 appeared the fourth volume of the *History*, covering events from 386 to the battle of Chaeronea in 338 (when Philip established his supremacy in Greece). In 1816 a *History of the Mahometan Empire in Spain* by John Shakespear and T. H. Horne was published with an introductory *Review of the Early History of the Arabs* that was attributed to 'the Historian of Greece': this was probably Mitford rather than Gillies. The fifth and final volume of his *History* was published in 1818, ending with the death of Alexander the Great in 322 BC. In the fourth and fifth volumes he praised the monarchy of Macedon, as in the first he had praised the kingdoms of early Greece: in both he saw (with some straining of the evidence) parallels to the balanced constitution of Britain in his own day. But his views no longer commanded wide agreement. In 1808 Henry Brougham in the *Edinburgh Review* (12.478 ff.) already distanced himself from Mitford's political bias while commending his overall achievement. By the 1820s liberal hostility had increased, and was now accompanied by criticism of Mitford's accuracy and handling of sources. William Haygarth in the *Quarterly Review* for 1821 (25.154 ff.) argued that a replacement for Mitford's work, a more adequate and just history of Greece, was wanted. This call was taken up by Macaulay (*Knight's Quarterly Magazine*, November 1824, reprinted in T. B. Macaulay, *Miscellaneous Writings*, ed. T. F. Ellis, 1860) and by George Grote (*Westminster Review*, 1826, 5.269 ff.). In due course new histories of Greece that were wider in scope, technically more sophisticated (incorporating the fruits of German scholarship), and more liberal in outlook, were written: by Connop Thirlwall (1835–44), and more influentially by Grote himself (1846–56), who rehabilitated Athenian democracy from the standpoint of Benthamite utilitarianism.

After completing his major work, Mitford published in 1823 *Observations on the history and doctrine of Christianity, and on the primeval religion, on the Judaic and the heathen … as an appendix to the military and political history of ancient Greece*, and in 1824 *Principles of Design in Architecture … in a Series of Letters to a Friend*. He died on 10 February 1827 (his eighty-third birthday) and was buried at Exbury; a memorial to him was set up in the church.

W. W. WROTH, *rev.* J. S. TAYLOR

Sources Lord Redesdale [J. F. Mitford], 'Memoir of the author', in W. Mitford, *History of Greece*, new edn, 1 (1829) · J. S. Taylor, 'William Mitford and Greek history', DPhil diss., U. Oxf., 1984 · F. M. Turner, *The Greek heritage in Victorian Britain* (1981) · K. N. Demetriou, *George Grote on Plato and Athenian democracy* (1999) · H. Brougham, 'Mitford's *History of Greece*', *EdinR*, 12 (1808), 478ff. · [W. Haygarth], review of William Mitford's *History of Greece*, *QR*, 25 (1821), 154–74 · G. Grote, 'Institutions of ancient Greece', *Westminster Review*, 5 (1826), 269ff. · Lord Redesdale [A. B. Freeman-Mitford], *Memories*, 2 vols. (1915) · Farington, *Diary*, vol. 1 · J. Shakespear and T. H. Horne, *History of the Mahometan empire in Spain* (1816) · *The works of Jeremy Bentham*, ed. J. Bowring, [new edn], 11 vols. (1843–59) · M. M. Drummond, 'Mitford, William', HoP, *Commons, 1754–90* · J. M. Collinge, 'Mitford, William', HoP, *Commons, 1790–1820*

Archives Glos. RO, MSS D 2002 C2 and C4 | Bodl. Oxf., letters to William Gilpin · Devon RO, corresp. with first Viscount Sidmouth · Norfolk RO, Walsingham MSS, incl. memoir 'How I came to write Grecian history', LXX.4

Likenesses J. Jackson, oils, repro. in Redesdale, *Memories*, 1 · C. Picart, stipple (after H. Edridge), BM, NPG; repro. in *The British gallery of contemporary portraits* (1811) · drawing, repro. in Turner, *Greek heritage* · pencil drawing (after H. Edridge), NPG

Mitrany, David (1888–1975), political scientist, was born on 1 January 1888 in Bucharest, the son of Moscu and Jeannette Mitrany. He left Romania in 1908 in search of further education, for in that country opportunities in higher education and in the professions were limited for Jews. He spent three years in Hamburg, working and studying at the Kolonial Institut, University of Hamburg, becoming interested in social projects, before moving to London, where he intended to continue his studies in such work. In 1912 he enrolled at the London School of Economics and Political Science (LSE) to study sociology and economics. The outbreak of the First World War changed Mitrany's outlook and the purpose of his career. From 1914 to 1918 he was involved in diplomatic work with the Romanian legation and in intelligence work for the British Foreign and War offices. He contributed to the series of Peace Handbooks prepared under the direction of the historical section of the Foreign Office, and became an active member of the first League of Nations Society.

A fortuitous encounter with C. P. Scott, editor of the *Manchester Guardian*, led to a position on its editorial board, with a special responsibility for foreign affairs, which lasted from May 1919 to 1922. Mitrany's relationship with Scott was particularly cordial: Scott had confidence in the accuracy of Mitrany's facts and approved of his political views, which were akin to his own. In 1922 Mitrany became assistant European editor for the publications on the economic and social history of the war that were financed by the Carnegie Endowment for International Peace. This experience was to form the basis for the development of his ideas, through working with authors from many countries and acquiring a detailed knowledge of

post-war problems, such as sanctions, minorities, nationalism, and land disputes. On 9 June 1923 he married Ena Victoria Limebeer (1897/8–1986), writer and artist, and they moved to Kingston Blount, Oxfordshire, which was to be Mitrany's home for the rest of his life.

During this period Mitrany determined his role in the international political scene. His purpose was to work towards the development of effective peace organizations, and in so doing he was resolute in maintaining a personal neutrality. He would not accept membership of any political party, nor would he participate in any organization which was nationalist or religious. This was his strength, but it was to isolate him from the main stream of political scientists. He also found time to conclude his academic studies at LSE: he became BSc (Econ) (war) (1918), followed by PhD (1929), and DSc in economics (1931).

Through Mitrany's work for the Carnegie Endowment came invitations during 1931–3 to Harvard University and to present the Dodge lectures at Yale University. In these lectures, published as *The Progress of International Government* (1933), he first outlined his functional ideas. Recognition of his academic standing and of his knowledge of European affairs followed, with the appointment in 1933 as professor in the School of Economics and Politics at the prestigious Institute for Advanced Study, Princeton University. His was the first appointment in the school and the only non-American, and gave him a status in American academic life which he was to lack in the UK. Working in the USA during the depression studying Roosevelt's new deal strengthened his belief in functional solutions.

At the outbreak of the Second World War, Mitrany became a member of the Foreign Office's academic intelligence unit, the foreign research and press service, based at Balliol College, Oxford. Mitrany produced a series of innovative documents, and as early as June 1941 was setting out an 'Agenda of peace making'. In another paper, 'Territorial, ideological, or functional organization?', he expanded his own ideas, and at the end of 1942 he resigned to pursue these further. The results appeared in a pamphlet, *A Working Peace System* (1943), which had an immediate public appeal and was translated into various languages. Mitrany embarked on an extensive programme of lecturing, broadcasting, and writing, with the aim of ensuring that a new peace organization would not be handicapped by a rigid constitution (as had the League of Nations) but would be given the capacity to develop on functional and sociological lines. The validity of the functional approach was accepted and incorporated in the founding documents of the specialized agencies of the new United Nations. Mitrany, in a new edition of his pamphlet in 1946, in analysing the new organization, stressed the importance of its functions in social and economic spheres.

In 1945 Mitrany was invited by the multinational company Unilever to act as its adviser on international affairs. He accepted the position, as an experiment and a challenge, acknowledging that, with an invalid wife, he was thus given the freedom to stay in the UK and to continue with his academic role at Princeton. The experiment was to continue to his retirement in 1960. His next substantial work was very different, and was based on his experiences with the Carnegie Endowment, on his knowledge of eastern Europe, and his accumulated research material: *Marx Against the Peasant: a Study in Social Dogmatism* was published in 1951. The book was examined worldwide, translated into European and Asian languages, and received much praise and abuse, though even left-wing critics acknowledged the depth and accuracy of its scholarship.

Mitrany continued to write and lecture on international politics and functionalism and to probe new ideas in a society where economics and politics were increasingly entwined. He gave up his professorship at Princeton and became a permanent member, with access to the institute, while undertaking extensive university lectures in the USA. In the 1960s there was new interest in functionalism as the organizations of the European Union came into being. Mitrany, although not an advocate of regionalism, which he believed stifled true internationalism, welcomed the functional solutions put forward. The increased interest resulted in the publication of a collection of his writings in 1966, including the text of the original pamphlet. At a conference devoted to functionalism in 1969 he presented the introductory paper, which was published, with a further collection of his writings, in 1975 as *The Functional Theory of Politics*. This included an autobiographical account of how his functional approach to international government had developed. David Mitrany died in London on 25 July 1975, and was cremated at Golders Green on 29 July.

In its essence the 'Mitranian' approach is simple and pragmatic: to work with and for people; to co-operate on issues that unite not divide; to allow the 'form' of a solution to follow its 'functions'. Functionalism is the reflection of David Mitrany himself, a man of vision and simplicity, compassion and tolerance, a scholar who, aware of the past, looked to develop a future world community.

DOROTHY ANDERSON

Sources D. Mitrany, *The functional theory of politics* (1975) • D. Mitrany, *A working peace system* (1966) • personal knowledge (2004) • *WW* (1971) • *London School of Economics register, 1895–1932* (1934) • m. cert. • *CGPLA Eng. & Wales* (1975) • *The Times* (28 July 1975)
Archives BLPES, papers | SOUND BL NSA, performance recording
Likenesses portrait, c.1960–1969
Wealth at death £5656: probate, 10 Sept 1975, *CGPLA Eng. & Wales*

Mittelholzer, Edgar Austin (1909–1965), novelist and short-story writer, was born on 16 December 1909 in New Amsterdam, British Guiana, the second child of William Austin Mittelholzer (1865–c.1960), commercial clerk, and his wife, Rosamond Mabel Leblanc (1889–c.1960), a spinner. Of Swiss-German, French, British, and African blood, he was a 'swarthy' child, to the horror of his light-skinned, negrophobe father. Some relief from his repressive puritanical upbringing came when a church grant enabled him to enter Berbice high school in 1922. At eleven he began writing, inspired by a Buffalo Bill story, and at nineteen

decided to become an author, and never swerved from this vocation. After leaving school in 1927 he took a succession of casual jobs so that he could ply editors in England and America with manuscripts, though with little success. In 1937 he privately published a series of local sketches, *Creole Chips*, and sold them from door to door. In 1941 he moved to Trinidad, where he served briefly (and unhappily) in the Trinidad Royal Naval Volunteer Reserve, and married Roma Halfhide, a Trinidadian, in March 1942.

In 1941 the London firm Eyre and Spottiswood had published Mittelholzer's novel *Corentyne Thunder*, an atmospheric evocation of West Indian peasant life based on childhood memories of visits to coastal Guiana. Although most copies were destroyed in an air raid, this encouraged him to move to England in 1948 with his wife and daughter Anna. Living in Bagshot, Surrey, he worked as copytypist for the books department of the British Council, and contributed to, and briefly produced, the seminal BBC literary programme *Caribbean Voices*, generously encouraging younger writers. In 1950 the Hogarth Press published *A Morning at the Office*, Doubleday taking the American rights. A detailed evocation of Trinidad society within the five hours' traffic of an importing company, it established Mittelholzer's literary reputation. In 1951 Peter Nevill published *Shadows Move among them*, an eldritch fantasy of life in a jungle commune, and with a second Guianese novel, *The Children of Kaywana* (1952), Mittelholzer entered a long-standing engagement with Secker and Warburg.

Mittelholzer now felt able to live entirely by his pen. He visited Montreal on a Guggenheim fellowship in 1952–3, and Barbados in 1953–6. Over fifteen years he published twenty-two novels, besides *A Swarthy Boy* (autobiography) and *With a Carib Eye* (travel book). His novels were variously set in Guiana, Barbados, and England, and constantly experimented with new styles and forms. They reflect his passionate interest in the interaction of character, place, and weather; and in music, particularly Wagner. Rejecting Christianity, he adopted yoga and occultism, and was fascinated with psychic phenomena. This melded in his novels with a preoccupation with violence, mental abormality, and sexual perversion. Mittelholzer himself paradoxically combined a belief in absolute discipline with gentle kindness to individuals. He wrote out of passionate conviction and with meticulous concern for literary craft. However, his bizarre subjects and extreme right-wing politics, influenced by Clive Bell's *Civilization* (1947), generated increasing friction with his publishers, and brought rejection by literary critics. He separated from Roma in 1956, and moved alone to Maida Vale, London.

In 1959 Mittelholzer was granted a divorce, losing custody of his children Anna, Stephan, Griselda, and Hermann. In April 1960 he married the writer Jacqueline Pointer, and moved to Dippenhall, Farnham, Surrey. In 1961 he broke with Secker and Warburg over the subject of *The Piling of Clouds*—child rape and murder set in English suburbia—and his bleak last novels reflect deepening financial difficulties and increasing isolation. He had twice earlier attempted suicide, and on 5 May 1965, he poured a gallon of petrol over himself and ignited it. He died at Farnham Hospital, Farnham, Surrey, on 6 May, leaving a two-year-old son, Leodgar Edward.

Mittelholzer was the first British West Indian writer to live entirely by novel-writing. His most popular work—the historical trilogy *The Children of Kaywana* (1952), *The Harrowing of Hubertus* (1954), and *Kaywana Blood* (1958)—reflected a personal interest in Guianese history originating with his Swiss ancestor, Constanz Mittelholzer, a Berbice plantation manager in 1760. It was carefully researched, and broke the taboo against writing of the Caribbean slave past. A prolific writer of great integrity, who breached the fortress of London publishing for Third World writers, he may be considered the 'father' of modern Caribbean writing in English.   LOUIS JAMES

Sources E. Mittelholzer, *A swarthy boy* (1913) · J. Mittelholzer, 'The idyll–and the warrior (recollections of Edgar Mittelholzer)', *BIM: the Literary Magazine of Barbados*, 17 (1983), 39–89 · F. Colleymore, 'Edgar Mittelholzer: a brief biographical sketch', *BIM: the Literary Magazine of Barbados*, 10 (1965), 23–6 · A. J. Seymour, *Edgar Mittelholzer: the man and his work* (Georgetown, Guyana, 1968) [1967 Edgar Mittelholzer Lecture] · J. Mittelholzer, 'My husband Edgar Mittelholzer', *BIM: the Literary Magazine of Barbados*, 15 (1976), 303–9 · C. Richards, 'A tribute to Edgar Mittelholzer', *BIM: the Literary Magazine of Barbados*, 11 (1966), 98–105 · E. Mittelholzer, *With a Carib eye* (1958) · d. cert.
Archives U. Reading L., letters to the Bodley Head Ltd · U. Reading L., letters to the Hogarth Press
Likenesses M. Gerson, photograph · photographs, repro. in Mittelholzer, *A swarthy boy*
Wealth at death £82: administration, 4 June 1965, *CGPLA Eng. & Wales*

Mivart, St George Jackson (1827–1900), zoologist and Roman Catholic polemicist, was born on 30 November 1827, at the family hotel in Brook Street, Grosvenor Square, London, the fourth child of James Edward Mivart (1781–1856), hotelier, and Caroline Georgina Cunningham. His education at Clapham grammar school, Harrow School, and King's College, was designed to lift him out of the tradesman class and to prepare him for entrance to Oxford. In an England whose industrial successes were creating a society drab in appearance and spirit, a romanticized medieval past (evoked in Pugin's Gothic revival architecture) and a popular medievalized literature glorified an age when an unreformed Catholicism was the guarantor of social, intellectual, and spiritual harmony. The vision of that past appealed to Mivart as an adolescent as it did to many others who sought a return to that harmony in a reviving Roman Catholicism. Exercising his own judgement, as he was to do in analogous situations throughout his life, and despite the initial opposition of his father, Mivart pledged his faith in and to the Roman Catholic church at a public ceremony on 2 June 1844 in Birmingham's St Chad's Church, one of the most magnificent of Pugin's Gothic reconstructions.

Mivart's conversion blocked his anticipated entry to Oxford, and he entered the then recently established Roman Catholic St Mary's College at Oscott. Leaving after only a year, he began a five-year programme at Lincoln's

St George Jackson Mivart (1827–1900), by Ernest Lintz

Inn to prepare for a career as barrister-at-law. For Mivart the title was principally a badge of class affiliation in lieu of the university degree, for, whatever his original intentions, he never practised law. His primary interest, fostered early by his father and his friends within the Zoological Society, was in natural history.

Mivart was married; his wife's name was Mary Anne. Their son, Frederick St George Mivart, was a distinguished medical man.

Scientific career, 1850s–1869 With the formalities of position established and the financial support of his father assured, Mivart was free to build and to pursue a scientific career. He became a self-made natural scientist, with Richard Owen as his most important initial patron and guide. The elaboration of Owen's ideas of homology, and subsequently of the 'archetype', provided the underlying conceptual base for most of Mivart's work in descriptive comparative anatomy. Their philosophical implications satisfied his deeply felt need for some unifying principle that would make sense of the visible diversity within the natural world, such as his religious faith provided for the complexities of the spiritual world.

As an aspiring naturalist Mivart probably attended Owen's annual series of Hunterian lectures at the Royal College of Surgeons. As a member of the Royal Institution from 1849, he also attended its popular Friday evening discourses as well as occasional courses of instructional lectures given there in the natural sciences. It was at one such Royal Institution course, 'The principles of biology', given by T. H. Huxley early in 1858, that he encountered for the first time both the principles of the new biology and its principal spokesman.

Two years older than Mivart, Huxley was already challenging Owen for leadership of the still small community of natural scientists. Huxley's revisionism promised a new biology, with new goals and new methods. A year after the lecture, Mivart was personally introduced to Huxley and, 'impressed with the lucidity of his thought and the admirable clearness with which he gave expression to it' (Mivart, 'Some reminiscences', 996), began a personal, tuitional, and professional relationship that, despite later difficulties, was the most important of his scientific career. Although his philosophical outlook in regard to biology would continue to have its source in Owen's teleology, the publications which embodied the most important results of his own research followed the pattern being set by Huxley's advocacy of an inductive science separate from extraneous philosophical assumptions.

The decade of Mivart's studentship and close personal relationship with Huxley was his most productive period as a natural scientist. From 1864, when his first professional paper appeared, until 1870, Mivart published, alone or as a collaborator, twenty-three technical articles, most of which appeared in the *Proceedings* or *Transactions* of the Zoological Society of London to which he had been elected a fellow in 1858. The core of this oeuvre, each item of which displayed Mivart's skill as a comparative anatomist or as a systematist, dealt with the primates.

The first of Mivart's scientific memoirs, 'Notes on the crania and the dentition of the *Lemuridae*', appeared in 1864 (*Proceedings of the Zoological Society*, 32, 1864, 611–48). A descriptive analysis of the skeletal structure of the then hardly known and most 'primitive' family of the primates, it was indicative of what were to be his major interests in and contributions to comparative anatomy: namely vertebrate osteology in general and, more particularly, the demonstrable affinities within the primate order. The second was then a subject of great importance and controversy as a result of the implications drawn from Darwinian evolution theory for questions of human origins, and mankind's place in nature. From these investigations of the exotic and varied 'half apes' of Africa, Mivart was able to provide an acceptable classification and to establish a taxonomic sub-order, the *Lemuroidea*.

From his initial interest in the *Lemuroidea*, Mivart moved on to the comparative osteology and the systematics of the primate order as a whole. This series of papers was his most important contribution to the field of inductive zoology; they represented the most complete and comprehensive study of the osteology of the order for most of the century, and established his reputation as one of the few authorities on its structural relations. At their end, demonstrating the essential unity of the order, he established its formal classification.

In these works Mivart sought with some success to accommodate the views derived from both Owen and Huxley, a position he was unable to maintain as their divisions widened. In these years, too, though differing in details, he thought himself 'a hearty and thoroughgoing disciple of Mr. Darwin' (Mivart, 'Specific genesis', *North American Review*, 114, 1872, 451–68). Owen's homology-based system was, in Mivart's eyes, complementary rather than opposed to the implicit progressionism of Darwin's theory; and Mivart's own work demonstrated the varying degrees of affinity that testified to the unity which underlay the diversity of at least the large class of vertebrates.

By the end of the 1860s Mivart had made his reputation as a professional natural scientist and a respected member of a generation that was in the process of revising the concepts and methods of scientific enquiry. He was a lecturer in comparative anatomy at St Mary's Hospital medical school from 1862, and was elected a fellow of the Linnean Society in the same year. In 1869 his detailed memoir 'On the appendicular skeleton of the primates' (*PTRS*, 157, 1867, 299–429) earned him election as a fellow of the Royal Society.

Mivart, however, was not only a faithful practising scientist but also a faithful practising Roman Catholic. He was the only English natural scientist of any reputation within a renascent English Catholic community seeking to define its role in a still hostile society, and fearful of the threats of the new science to its fundamental beliefs. Just as the community of scientists was divided in sometimes personally hostile divisions over the new biology during the 1860s, so was the Catholic establishment divided (between its 'liberals' and its 'conservatives') over the new learning and its effect on traditional doctrine. As Mivart's reputation rose among the new scientists so did his responsibilities increase as the scientist-spokesman for a resistant Catholicism. In the end, his earlier enthusiasm for Darwinism, tempered as it may have been, waned as by the end of the decade, pressured by the anxieties of increasingly conservative churchmen and counselled by clerical friends, his sense of its weaknesses increased.

Mivart's critique of Darwin's evolutionary theory What doubts he had of the merits of the Darwinian case Mivart first raised anonymously in a series of three articles entitled 'Difficulties of the theory of natural selection' in the liberal Catholic journal *The Month* in 1869. A year later he revised them, for what was to be his then most serious criticism of the Darwinian theory, in the extended essay that he published under his own name as *On the Genesis of Species* (1871), to be followed two years later with *Man and Apes* (1873) and the last of his technical articles on the *Lemuroidea*. Together they constitute his case against the sufficiency of the Darwinian answer to the question of organic diversity. It was his public break with Darwin and his friends.

Mivart's criticisms of Darwin were in many cases perceptive, if not always to the point. Where they did not misinterpret what Darwin had written, they ignored his own confession of the gaps which could only be filled through further research. His view was that whatever the role played by the 'chance' mechanism of natural selection, and he considered it to be an important though relatively minor one, the unanswered questions in evolutionary theory tended to support the existence of some ultimate planning agent, manifested as a creative universally oper-ating 'innate force' which guided the evolution of the spe-cies. This overarching intelligence was, in fact, the ultim-ate source of all, a creative and creating divinity.

Although under the tutelage of Huxley he had flirted with Darwinian evolution, Mivart was much more a developmentalist of an earlier generation, of which Owen was a leader, accepting the naturalness of organic change but ultimately referring the process as a whole to the con-tinuing plan of a creator, the primary cause of it all.

Increasingly, the real question at issue for Mivart as both Catholic and scientist was that of human origins, of the genesis of that single species, the divine nature of which had always been central to Christian belief. Whatever the similarities in bodily structure between the human spe-cies and those of the higher primates, there existed an unbridgeable gulf separating them. 'There is far more dif-ference between the lowest savage and the highest ape', he wrote, 'than there is between the highest ape and a lump of granite' (The Tablet, 11 March 1871). The difference lay in the human capacity to reason, which was itself a function of mind and the divinely inspired soul that was its source. Impossible as a product of the gradual work-ings of natural selection over long periods of time, that power could only have been the product of an immediate act of a divine creation, the reality of which, explicitly recorded in the revelatory words of scripture, lay at the core of Catholic faith. Mind, unlike body, could not be accounted for by any evolutionary process, even a goal-directed, God-driven, one.

Mivart expanded on his position in an anonymous and bitterly argued review of Darwin's Descent of Man (1871), published in the Quarterly Review a few months after the appearance of the Genesis. Stung by the full extension of Darwinian theory to the 'man question', and what now seemed to him the translation of Darwinian theory into a too comprehensive scientific dogma, he struck out against both. In addition to the apparent treason of attack-ing Darwin and his circle in a tory journal, the argument and its tone were personally offensive and considered insulting by Darwin and his friends. Huxley's sharp and satirical reply matched the tone of Mivart's attack. He who had been loyal student, friend, and follower had now become an apostate, a 'slavery humbug' (Huxley corres-pondence, Imperial College, London) whose mind, chained by a restrictive theology, was unfit to pursue true science. The break between Mivart and the Darwinians had begun; a year later, further injudicious remarks by Mivart in an anonymous review were to make it formal and specific. Huxley had predicted as much when he had warned Mivart early on that 'one cannot go on running with the hare and hunting with the hounds' (St G. Mivart, 996).

Mivart's subsequent work in science, although useful, was marginal to the changing biological sciences led by Huxley, his friends, and students. He continued his scien-tific associations, particularly in the Linnean Society of which he was secretary from 1874 to 1880 and vice-president in 1892; and with the British Association for the Advancement of Science, in which he served as the presi-dent of the biological section in 1879. In the main, how-ever, he concentrated his facile literary ability on the edu-cation in and the popularization of biological science. His use of the cat (1881) as a laboratory model for the teaching of vertebrate anatomy was inventive, and served as a teaching model for generations of teachers and students. At the same time, his concerns were shifting to the philo-sophy of mind, as he sought to sharpen the definition of that most important and distinctive of human attributes.

His quarrel with the Darwinians gave Mivart a name, a reputation, and a notoriety which served him in what had become his major goal as both scientist and Catholic, namely, the demonstration through reason (rather than faith) of the 'essential harmony which exists between the truths of science and the dictates of religion' (St G. Mivart, 'Modern Catholics and scientific freedom', Nineteenth Cen-tury, 18, 1885, 47), between those of nature and those of revelation. His double-barrelled approach to Darwinian theory, namely to argue that natural selection was only a part of what was generally a more teleological evolution-ary process, and that this evolutionary process as a whole explained only the physical body of man but not his moral and intellectual capacities, remained for long a key resource among liberal theologians, both inside and out-side the Roman Catholic church. Although there were those who were highly critical of his acceptance of an evo-lutionary process for the origins of physical man, Mivart received from leaders within the laity and the clerical hierarchy acceptance and some praise for the dualism of mind and body through which he was able to accommo-date the apparent materialism of science to the trad-itional teachings of the church. There was little awareness that his next step would be to accommodate the long held doctrines of the church to the responsible teachings of science.

Intra-Catholic polemics, 1876–death In his Contemporary Evo-lution (1876), essentially a compilation of recently pub-lished essays, Mivart described his vision of a future in which, after long continued changes of outmoded and vestigial church teachings, science and theology, each with its own truths, would occupy together the throne of St Peter in a universal Catholic Christianity. This would be an evolutionary process, guided by human reason, analo-gous to that which had occurred in organic nature. The revitalized church would stand as the rationally selected victorious survivor over its failed competitors. As it had emerged strengthened from its errors of the past, notably that of its opposition to Galileo and his science, so the church would gain strength by the criticism of present errors and those to come. Over the next twenty years Mivart pressed his claims for doctrinal change on the evo-lutionary model in a series of articles in popular journals. There he criticized a growing list of particular errors in church doctrine and dogma, both past and present, to illustrate the historical changes needed for the church continually to accommodate itself to changing social, moral, and intellectual conditions.

The clerical hierarchy, under increasing conservative

pressure, had heard enough. To suggest that science was for scientists and religion was for theologians was marginally acceptable; but when Mivart went on to support the aims of the new biblical criticism, he was close to questioning the central beliefs of Catholics and the sacred text which was their divine source. Again he narrowly escaped formal sanction against his aggressive modernism, although he was persuaded by clerical friends to tone down his criticism.

It is one of the ironies of Mivart's life that, despite the continuation unchecked of his strongly worded challenges to church authority on the border and between faith and science, it was a less consequential article, on hell, in which he argued that there was even hope for those condemned to the vividly expressive Catholic hell, that finally brought down on his head the formal wrath of the church. His articles on hell in 1893 were placed on the Index; Catholics were forbidden to read them, to publish them, and to possess them; and he himself was forcefully persuaded by his friends to submit and to admit his errors. At the same time, he was appalled and felt betrayed by the papal encyclical *Providentissimus Deus* (1895), which, responding to the modernists in general, upheld as true the whole of the scriptural text and stated, among other things, that those who sought to accommodate part of it to present-day knowledge 'either pervert the Catholic notion of inspiration, or make God the author of such error' (*The Times*, 28 Jan 1900). Though a number of modernists took encouragement from the ambiguity and caution of this encyclical, it was Mivart's view that under such instructions to the faithful, there was no hope for his kind of continuous reform.

Mivart continued to write, producing the occasional technical memoir, reviews on various subjects, and several book-length attempts to examine the nature of science. In 1899, however, weakened by a serious diabetic condition and an occasional heart attack, knowing that he was dying, he entered the lists again for the last time.

Mivart's old condemnation of Catholic-inspired injustice was raised again by the explicit antisemitism of the French Catholic press during the second Dreyfus trial, and he published a long letter in which he strongly condemned the whole of the church hierarchy, from priest to pope, for its implicit support of the antisemites. He described Dreyfus as 'the Galileo of the nineteenth century', and went on to write that 'through him [papal] authority has now misled the world with respect to morals, with the probable result that other millions of Catholics will, one by one, abandon Catholicity' (*The Times*, 17 Oct 1899). Almost immediately afterwards he published simultaneously two articles in the *Nineteenth Century* and the *Fortnightly Review* that constituted his public farewell to the church in whose cause he had so long and valiantly laboured. They summed up his unrealized hopes for an evolving faith in conformity to knowledge and reason, instead of stultifying dogma.

This time Mivart had, as he intended, gone too far. There was no room for manoeuvre on either side. Cardinal Vaughan, the head of the English Catholic congregations,

a conservative himself, required that Mivart sign a profession of faith which both knew would have required him to give up and abjure the positions which he had maintained and for which he had fought for the better part of his life. He rejected the demand, concluding that 'Happily I can now speak with entire frankness as to all my convictions. *Liberavi meam animam.* I can sing my *Nunc dimittis* and calmly await the future' (*The Times*, 25 Jan 1900). Deprived of the sacraments, he was in effect, excommunicated.

Six weeks later, on 1 April 1900, at his home, 77 Inverness Terrace, London, shortly before he was to give a speech at the Author's Club, Mivart died of a final heart attack. He was buried on 7 April at Kensal Green cemetery. Friends and family excused his latest and strongest arguments on the grounds that in these last months his mind was diseased or he suffered from a hubris-induced madness. It was the final insult to his life as a constant protestant. JACOB W. GRUBER

Sources J. W. Gruber, *A conscience in conflict: the life of St. George Mivart* (1960) [incl. complete list of works and major pubd and unpubd biographical sources] · J. W. Gruber, 'St. George Mivart, F.R.S.', PhD diss., University of Pennsylvania, 1952 · F. St G. Mivart, 'Early memories of St. George Mivart', *Dublin Review*, 174 (1924), 1–20 · St G. Mivart, 'Some reminiscences of Thomas Henry Huxley', *Nineteenth Century*, 42 (1897), 985–98 · *Nature*, 61 (1899–1900), 569–70 · *PRS*, 75 (1905), 95–100, esp. 97 · *WWW*, 1916–28 [for son]

Archives Birmingham Oratory, Newman MSS · CUL, letters to Lord Acton · Downside Abbey, near Bath, Bishop corresp. · DWL, letters to Henry Allon · ICL, corresp. with Thomas Huxley · NHM, letters to Charles Darwin [photocopies; originals in CUL] · NHM, letters to Albert Gunther and R. W. T. Gunther · NHM, letters to members of the Sowerby family · Oxf. U. Mus. NH, letters and postcards to Sir E. B. Poulton · University of Strathclyde, letters to Sir Patrick Geddes

Likenesses E. Lintz, portrait, Linn. Soc. [*see illus.*] · Maull & Fox, photograph, RS · Soloman, oils, Linn. Soc. · oils (as older man), Linn. Soc.

Wealth at death £28,308 3s. 5d.: probate, 11 June 1900, *CGPLA Eng. & Wales*

Mo Chóe mac Luacháin (d. 497). *See under* Ulster, saints of (*act. c.*400–*c.*650).

Mo Chóemóc mac Béoáin (d. 656). *See under* Munster, saints of (*act. c.*450–*c.*700).

Mo Chommóc. *See* Commán mac Fáelchon (d. 747) *under* Connacht, saints of (*act. c.*400–*c.*800).

Mo Chua mac Bécáin (d. 694). *See under* Connacht, saints of (*act. c.*400–*c.*800).

Mo Chutu mac Fínaill (d. 637). *See under* Munster, saints of (*act. c.*450–*c.*700).

Mo Fhéccu mac Caílcharna. *See* Féchín moccu Cháe (d. 665) *under* Meath, saints of (*act. c.*400–*c.*900).

Mo Genóc (*fl.* 5th cent.?). *See under* Meath, saints of (*act. c.*400–*c.*900).

Mo Laga mac Duib Dligid (*fl.* late 6th cent.?). *See under* Munster, saints of (*act. c.*450–*c.*700).

Mo Laisse mac Nad Froích (d. 564). *See under* Ulster, saints of (*act. c.*400–*c.*650).

Mo Ling [St Mo Ling, Mo Ling Lúachra, Tairchell, Daircell] (*d.* 697), abbot of St Mullins, was the founder abbot of St Mullins (Tech Moling), situated in southern Leinster on the River Barrow. His feast day is commemorated on 17 June in the martyrology of Tallaght and *Féilire Óengusso*. Genealogically he was affiliated to the Uí Dego of south Leinster through his reputed father, Fáelán (Oílán). He is often called Mo Ling Lúachra, denoting an association with the uplands of Lúachair in Munster. The origin of this epithet is uncertain, though the Irish life of the saint, which is not earlier than the twelfth century, claims by way of explanation that he was born in Lúachair. Dedications to Mo Ling are found throughout Leinster.

Very little is known about the historical Mo Ling. He was one of the guarantors of Adomnán's *Lex innocentium* in 697, which was also the year of his death. As such, he was one of the more important churchmen of his day. His church, St Mullins, was a major religious foundation that benefited from its location on the Barrow between Osraige and Leinster; it was here that Mo Ling died and was buried. The Book of Mulling, a collection of the four gospels influenced by the *Vetus Latina*, dates from the earlier years of the monastery. Other miscellaneous materials, including liturgical notes, were bound into the original at some later date. During the eleventh and twelfth centuries the resurgence of the Uí Chennselaig, in whose territory St Mullins lay, gave that church an added boost. A great deal of the Mo Ling dossier dates from this period.

In Irish hagiographical literature Mo Ling is imagined as the younger associate of Máedóc (*d.* 625), the founder of Ferns, and is supposed to have succeeded him as bishop of Ferns. However, this detail may owe more to the ambitions of the Uí Chennselaig kings in the eleventh century than to any factual basis. Ferns was one of the chief churches within the Uí Chennselaig sphere of influence. The creation of a pseudo-historical link between the two was a natural political move. A similar cause may lie behind the connection of both Mo Ling and Máedóc with the legendary builder of churches known as **Gobbán Sáer** (*supp. fl.* 7th cent.). Gobbán Sáer (Gobbán the Wright), a figure with magical associations who still features in modern folk traditions, appears in the company of Mo Ling in the Irish life of the saint.

Mo Ling is also associated with the monastery of Glendalough, which lay within the ambit of Uí Dúnlainge power. The Uí Dúnlainge were the main rivals to the Uí Chennselaig in Leinster. Mo Ling is imagined as becoming a bishop at Glendalough, which reflects the tensions and divisions between the two major Leinster dynasties rather than his actual biography.

While the historical person is indistinct, there is a great deal of material concerning the imaginary Mo Ling. He is celebrated in several anecdotes, poems, and lives. He is a central character in the *Bóroma Laigen* tract and in the Suibne traditions that culminated in the twelfth-century *Buile Shuibhne*. The oldest of the Latin lives, that in the Dublin collection, probably dates from the twelfth century. Another life, preserved in the Codex Salmanticensis, is both derivative of and later than the Dublin life. The same is true of the life in the Oxford collection. The Dublin life of the saint incorporates material from the *Bóroma*, and refers to the *Baile Moling*, a prophecy which Mo Ling is said to have made (but which dates to the middle of the twelfth century), predicting various disasters that will befall Leinster. The entire tenor of the life is aimed at glorifying the saint and his monastery. Much of Mo Ling's career and his death take place in St Mullins. The political ambience throughout points to the milieu of the ambitious Uí Chennselaig and St Mullins was very much part of their establishment.

The Middle-Irish life, *Geinemain Mo Ling ocus a Bhetha* ('The Birth and Life of Mo Ling'), seems to be later than the Dublin life. It is compilatory in nature and incorporates material from the *Bóroma*. It also clumsily includes some of the traditions that linked Mo Ling with Suibne Geilt. This life is very different from its earlier Latin counterpart. While both agree that Mo Ling was of the Uí Dego, the Latin life does not name his mother, but simply states that God appeared in the form of a man and blessed the future saint while he lay in his mother's arms. In the *Geinemain Mo Ling* the saint's mother is identified as Emnait of the Cenél Sédna from Bréifne, and sister of Fáelán's wife. Fáelán has an extra-marital affair with Emnait, who becomes pregnant. She gives birth to Mo Ling and desperately attempts to kill the newborn child. She fails, due to divine intervention: Brendan of Clonfert, who is passing through the region, recognizes the child's holiness and gives him to one of his priests, Collanach, to foster. Mo Ling comes into contact with several saints during his career in the *Geinemain Mo Ling*, including Máedóc and Mo Laisse, and is visited by Patrick's angel, Victor. In addition, the Irish life attempts to explain Mo Ling's unusual hypocoristic name by fastening on its similarity to the verb *lingid*, to jump. It suggests that the saint was originally known as Tairchell and was named Mo Ling after making three prodigious leaps to escape a band of spectres. The scholia to *Féilire Óengusso* explain the name by reference to a great leap of Mo Ling's over water in Lúachair. The aim of *Geinemain Mo Ling* is less clear than that of the Dublin life; unlike the latter, it does not seem to have an overt political agenda. Rather, it is a collection of various anecdotes celebrating the saint.

The oldest of these anecdotes date back to the ninth century. Of particular interest is the incident involving Mo Ling's 'bad neighbour', Grác, and his wife, Crón, preserved in the Book of Leinster. Grác incites his wife to attempt a seduction of the saint. She fails, but Mo Ling curses her and prophesies that she will be raped by bandits. This happens and Crón becomes pregnant. Grác suggests that Crón identify Mo Ling as the father of the child. The scheme goes awry: Grác is killed by Mo Ling's vengeful Uí Dego kinsmen and Crón is left with the child. This episode is notable for its extreme misogyny. Moreover, a version of it found its way into the complex of stories surrounding the figure of Suibne Geilt, a prince who reputedly went mad at the battle of Mag Roth in 637. Suibne's association with Mo Ling may date back to the ninth century and it is fully developed in an eleventh-century set of poems ascribed to Mo Ling. Here, Grác is transmuted from a bad neighbour into the killer of Suibhne, Crón is not named, and the role of the child seems redundant.

In the twelfth-century *Buile Shuibhne* the relationship of saint and hero is further expanded. Suibhne, who is a Scot in the poems, becomes an Irish prince of Dál nAraidi. His madness, precipitated by the battle, is a punishment for insulting St Rónán. After wandering throughout Ireland and beyond, Suibhne finds a form of salvation with Mo Ling. However, he is killed by the cowherd Mongán, who wrongly believes that Suibhne has been sleeping with his wife, Muirghil. Mongán is clearly based on the earlier figure of Grác. The link between Mo Ling and Suibhne is interesting. It has been argued that the holy wildman Suibhne, who can leap from tree to tree, bears a close resemblance to the saint whose name was imagined as reflecting his ability to make prodigious leaps. Moreover, both saint and wildman were regarded as inspired poets.

The nature-loving saint of the Suibhne traditions is very different from the saint-hero of the *Bóroma*. The poems and tales that make up the *Bóroma* vary in date and the material is heterogeneous. Several of the poems praise St Mullins and its locale. The tract, as it stands, seems to be a product of the eleventh century. In the *Bóroma*, Mo Ling aids the Leinstermen against the Uí Néill, who demand a tribute known as the *bóruma* from Leinster. Mo Ling, dodging plots and murder attempts, makes his way to the fair of Tailtiu, the political gathering of the Uí Néill king of Tara. He tricks the king, Fínsnechtae Fledach mac Dúnchada (*d.* 695), into remitting the tribute until Monday. The Monday in question turns out to be the Monday of doomsday, and so the tribute is remitted for ever.

Thus we are presented with two images of Mo Ling. One is that of the ascetic saint who befriends a holy man from the wilderness. The other is the Leinster patriot who takes on kings and fellow saints to protect his people. Both have very little to do with the man who was a guarantor of the *Lex innocentium* in 697.   ELVA JOHNSTON

Sources W. W. Heist, ed., *Vitae sanctorum Hiberniae ex codice olim Salmanticensi nunc Bruxellensi*, Subsidia Hagiographica, 28 (Brussels, 1965), 353–6 · C. Plummer, ed., *Vitae sanctorum Hiberniae*, 2 (1910), 190–205 [incl. the Dublin life] · W. Stokes, ed. and trans., 'The birth and life of St Moling', *Revue Celtique*, 27 (1906), 257–312 · W. Stokes, ed., 'Poems ascribed to S. Moling', *Anecdota from Irish manuscripts*, ed. O. J. Bergin and others, 2 (1908), 20–41 · R. I. Best and others, eds., *The Book of Leinster, formerly Lebar na Núachongbála*, 6 vols. (1954–83), vol. 5, pp. 1236–42 · V. Hull, 'Two anecdotes concerning St Moling', *Zeitschrift für Celtische Philologie*, 18 (1929–30), 90–99 · K. Meyer, 'Anecdotes of St. Moling', *Revue Celtique*, 14 (1893), 188–94 · *Félire Óengusso Céli Dé / The martyrology of Oengus the Culdee*, ed. and trans. W. Stokes, HBS, 29 (1905), 151–7 · J. G. O'Keefe, ed., *Buile Suibhne (The frenzy of Suibhne)*, Irish Texts Society, 12 (1913) · W. Stokes, ed. and trans., 'The Bóroma', *Revue Celtique*, 13 (1892), 32–124, see also 299–300 · J. Carney, 'Suibne Gelt and the children of Lir', *Studies in Irish literature and history* (1955), 129–64 · F. J. Byrne, *Irish kings and high-kings* (1973), 144–6 · M. Ní Dhonnchadha, 'The guarantor list of Cáin Adomnáin, 697', *Peritia*, 1 (1982), 178–215, esp. 189–90 · *Ann. Ulster*, s.a. 697

Mo Lua moccu Óche (554–609). *See under* Munster, saints of (*act. c.*450–*c.*700).

Mo Nennus [St Mo Nennus, Maucennus, Mugint, Mo-Nennius] (*fl.* **5th–early 6th cent.**), ascetic and teacher, is, in fact, substantially identical with St *Ninian, a bishop and the reputed founder of Candida Casa (Whithorn) in Galloway. Ninian himself is mentioned in Bede's *Historia ecclesiastica* and seems to have flourished during the fifth or early sixth centuries. However, as is the case with many insular saints, chronology is uncertain.

The various name-forms, Mo Nennus, Maucennus, and Mugint, have led to confusion. Mo Nennus is an Irish hypocorism literally meaning 'my Nennus', in other words 'my Ninian'. It is clearly a latinization of something like the Irish Mo Ninn or Mo Nend. The latter form occurs in the Latin life of Énda which is of twelfth- or thirteenth-century provenance but contains earlier materials. On the other hand, Maucennus, and the related Irish form Mugint have a different origin. The former occurs interchangeably with Mo Nennus in the life of Énda and is the form used in the life of Eógan of Ard Sratha (Ardstraw), another twelfth- or thirteenth-century Latin production. The actual name Mugint or Maucennus originates, in all likelihood, with the Welsh saint, Meugan or Meigant [*see* Mawgan]. Moreover, Irish sources compound Ninian/Mo Nennus with a Welsh saint, Meugan, who has associations with an Eglwys Wen, or White Church, which may have become confused with Ninian's 'white house' of Candida Casa. Meugan is probably identifiable with the Cornish Mawgan and is imagined as a contemporary of the sixth-century St David in the late eleventh-century life of David.

In his guise as Mo Nennus and Maucennus, the saint is, according to their lives, the reputed teacher of the Irish saints Tigernach of Cluain Eois (Clones) and the associated Eógan of Ard Sratha. Eógan's life is closely related to that of Tigernach and may originate from the same source and date. Eógan died in 549 according to the annals of Ulster. Mo Nennus, supposedly, also taught St Finnian of Mag Bile (Moville), whose death notice is given under 579 in the annals of Ulster, and St Énda of Aran. The latter seems to have flourished in the sixth century, although this is uncertain. The same could be said of Finnian; his Latin life was abridged from Welsh sources in the fourteenth century by John of Tynemouth.

In a further convolution of the identities of Mo Nennus and Ninian, the lives of Eógan, Énda, and Tigernach imagine Mo Nennus as teaching at the monastery of 'Rosnat', which has often been identified with Whithorn. Charles Thomas's speculation that a Cornish monastery, perhaps associated with Mawgan, existed at a site which he has tentatively identified as a 'Rosnant', at Tintagel, offers an alternative for the place in question, although it must be noted that no convincing archaeological evidence that would suggest the presence of an early monastery has turned up at this site. There is some supporting evidence that 'Rosnat' could have been south-east rather than north-east of Ireland. However, it is probable that the later medieval Irish themselves were no longer aware of the separate existence of 'Rosnat', and identified it with Whithorn. It is also possible to link Meugan with a place called Rosnat, but, for whatever reason, he failed to maintain an individual identity in Irish writing and became subsumed into the much more famous figure of Ninian. The twelfth- or thirteenth-century life of Eógan describes: 'vir sanctus ac sapiens Nennyo, qui Maucennus dicitur, de Rosnatensi monasterio' (Heist, 'Vita sancti Eogani', 400), which may be translated as 'a holy and wise man, Nennyo, who is called Maucennus, of the monastery of Rosnat'. Meugan had lost his separate identity in that of Ninian.

Called Mugint, the saint appears in an anecdote which prefaces the *Liber hymnorum* hymn 'Parce domine'—a hymn that is also ascribed to him. Although the *Liber hymnorum* was compiled in the late eleventh or early twelfth century from earlier sources, the material in the preface probably dates to the time of compilation. The same anecdote occurs in an abbreviated version in the Middle Irish scholia to *Félire Óengusso*. In this story Futerna (Whithorn) is the scene for the love of Drustic, the daughter of the king of Britain, for Rióc, an Irish pupil of Mugint. Drustic asks Finnian, who is also studying with Mugint, to marry her to Rióc in return for Mugint's books. Finnian agrees but sends his friend Talmach to her in the place and form of Rióc. She becomes pregnant; Mugint blames Finnian and plans to kill him; but he himself suffers the mortal blow intended for Finnian. This story shows how, effectively, Mo Nennus (or Maucennus or Mugint) had taken on a life almost independent both of Ninian and of Meugan, a process which appears to have happened during the eleventh century.

ELVA JOHNSTON

Sources C. Plummer, ed., 'Vita sancti Endei abbatis de Arann', *Vitae sanctorum Hiberniae*, 2 (1910), 60–75 · C. Plummer, ed., 'Vita sancti Tigernaci episcopi de Cluain Eois', *Vitae sanctorum Hiberniae*, 2 (1910), 262–9 · W. W. Heist, ed., 'Vita sancti Eogani episcopi Ardsratensis', *Vitae sanctorum Hiberniae ex codice olim Salmanticensi nunc Bruxellensi*, Subsidia Hagiographica, 28 (Brussels, 1965), 400–04 · W. W. Heist, ed., 'Vita sancti Tigernachi episcopi in Cluain Eois', *Vitae sanctorum Hiberniae ex codice olim Salmanticensi nunc Bruxellensi*, Subsidia Hagiographica, 28 (Brussels, 1965), 107–11 · *Rhigyfarch's Life of St David*, ed. J. W. James (1967), 82 · J. H. Bernard and R. Atkinson, eds. and trans., *The Irish Liber hymnorum*, 2 vols., HBS, 13–14 (1898), vol. 2, p. 112 · *Félire Óengusso Céli Dé / The martyrology of Oengus the Culdee*, ed. and trans. W. Stokes, HBS, 29 (1905), 238 · C. Thomas, 'Rosnat, Rostat, and the early Irish church', *Ériu*, 22 (1971), 100–06 · P. C. Bartrum, *A Welsh classical dictionary: people in history and legend up to about AD 1000* (1993), 476–7 · C. Horstman, ed., *Nova legenda Anglie, as collected by John of Tynemouth, J. Capgrave, and others*, 1 (1901), 444–7

Mo Sinu. *See* Sillán moccu Mind (*d.* 610) *under* Ulster, saints of (*act. c.*400–*c.*650).

Mobbs, Edgar Roberts (1882–1917), rugby player, was born on 29 June 1882 at Billing Road, Northampton, the third of six children of Oliver Linnell Mobbs (1851–1924), engineer, and his wife, Elizabeth Anne Hollis (1854–1903). His father sold cars, as did his brother Herbert (Bertie), the inventor of sliding roofs for cars.

Mobbs learned to play rugby at Bedford modern school,

although a knee injury, when aged sixteen, interrupted his rugby career; he did not obtain his 'colours' and gave little indication that he would become an international player. After leaving school, he played centre forward in Olney mixed hockey eleven, and from 1903 he played rugby for Olney, the Weston Turks, and Northampton Heathens.

Mobbs went on to captain the Northampton rugby union side (1907–13), and became a 'living legend' by scoring 177 tries. He also captained the Barbarians, the East Midlands (1906–13), and led the joint Midlands/East Midlands side which, on 2 December 1908, beat the Australians 16–5 at Leicester, their only defeat in England. He captained London and the Midlands against the West; the South against the North at Twickenham; and England against France in Paris. He was capped seven times for his country, playing at left wing three-quarter. He also played for Toulouse, where he became a great favourite, and played cricket for Buckinghamshire.

Mobbs was a big man physically, standing well over 6 feet, and his pace, strength, and tremendous hand-off made him one of the most dangerous attacking three-quarters of his time. A 'curious custom' existed at Toulouse, where the man playing opposite him always wore a cap, 'the reason being that the Frenchmen have the idea that Mobbs hands off on the top of the head, and the cap is therefore worn as a protector' (Barron, 50).

Mobbs represented the east midlands on the Rugby Football Union (RFU) committee. An outspoken man, he had several clashes with the RFU and, as Northampton captain, was called before the RFU's professional inquiry committee, together with club officials, to answer 'general charges' that veiled professionalism was rampant in midland clubs. Northampton were criticized for providing tea and cigarettes for players after matches; tea was allowed, but not cigarettes. The RFU eventually agreed to issue a statement exonerating 'the Saints' from charges of professionalism, thus establishing Mobbs 'as a forthright spokesman for the club who would not be pushed around by petty officialdom' (Barron, 41). During the 1912–13 season, Mobbs—by now an elder statesman of thirty—criticized the shabby treatment accorded the touring South Africans by the RFU. After landing in Southampton the South Africans had their taxis dismissed and were put on the midnight train to London, where they arrived at 3 a.m.; tea and coffee after dinner were forbidden. A grateful touring party sent Mobbs a signed team picture.

When war broke out, Mobbs was running the Market Harborough branch of the Pytchley Auto Car Company and contemplating emigration to Canada. He was refused a commission in August 1914 on age grounds—he was thirty-two—but raised his own company of over 250 men, the sportsmen's battalion, which formed a large part of the 7th battalion, the Northamptonshire regiment. Many members were personal friends who had refused commissions to fight alongside him, also as privates. Mobbs, with no previous military experience, by 23 April 1916 had become battalion commander, with the rank of lieutenant-colonel. Wounded three times, he played his last game in an England–Scotland international in 1915 while recovering. He was gazetted DSO on 1 January 1917. He returned to his battalion for the third battle of Ypres, Passchendaele, and was killed in action at Zillebeke, Belgium, on 31 July 1917. It is said that a machine-gun post, holding up the infantry, was charged single-handedly and that he was only 30 yards from the guns when hit. As he lay dying he scribbled the gun's map reference for his brigadier. His body was never found. An old schoolfriend, Lieutenant Spencer, said later: 'I saw the old three-quarter in his own 25, get the ball from a scrum and go. Thank God for such men' (Barron, 53). Whether this story is true or apocryphal is hard to say—one report says Mobbs was rallying his men for a charge on the trench containing the machine-gun when he was cut down in a hail of bullets— but it is part of his legend that he would lead an attack 'over the top' into no man's land by punting a rugby ball ahead of him and following it up. Wartime cartoons depicted him charging 'the Hun' and handing them off in typically robust fashion. He was unmarried.

Mobbs is commemorated by the annual Edgar Mobbs memorial match at Northampton between East Midlands and the Barbarians. A memorial statue costing approximately £1500, raised by subscriptions from around the world, was also erected in Northampton market square, and now stands in Abington Square.   K. G. SHEARD

Sources B. Barron, *Oh when the saints* (1993) · U. A. Titley and R. McWhirter, *Centenary history of the Rugby Football Union* (1970) · R. Maule, *The complete who's who of England rugby union internationals* (1992) · *The Times* (6 Aug 1917) · *The Times* (18 Aug 1917) · *The Times* (9 Feb 1918) · *The Times* (7 Oct 1920) · *The Times* (18 July 1921) · *CGPLA Eng. & Wales* (1917) · private information

Likenesses caricature (charging the 'Hun'), repro. in Barron, *Oh when the saints*, 53 · photographs, repro. in Barron, *Oh when the saints*

Wealth at death £961 14s. 3d.: probate, 25 Oct 1917, *CGPLA Eng. & Wales*

Moberly, Charlotte Anne Elizabeth [Annie] (1846–1937), college head, was born on 16 September 1846 at Winchester. She was the tenth child and seventh daughter of George *Moberly (1803–1885), headmaster of Winchester College, and his wife, Mary Anne (1812–1890), daughter of Thomas Crokat, a Scottish merchant who traded at Leghorn. This family of eight girls and seven boys, with their awe-inspiring but much admired father and beautiful, Italian-educated mother, spent their childhood at Winchester and, in the summer holidays, in a rented farmhouse at Hursley, Hampshire, John Keble's parish. It was a devout, though liberal, high-Anglican upbringing. Mrs Keble was Annie's godmother. All five boys who survived into adulthood made their careers in the church; the most eminent, Robert Campbell *Moberly, became regius professor of pastoral theology at Oxford. But their Hampshire neighbour and friend, the novelist Charlotte M. Yonge, recalled the Moberlys' 'habits of fun, games, and habitual merriment, animation, and playfulness' (Olivier, *Victorian Ladies*, 27). The May family in Yonge's *The Daisy Chain* was named after the youngest daughter, her godchild May Moberly.

Charlotte Anne Elizabeth [Annie] **Moberly** (1846–1937), by Sir William Llewellyn, 1899

The girls were educated at home by their mother and a governess, but within the ambience of a big public school. They attended the college chapel and were taught music by its organist. A bookish child, Annie acquired the rudiments of Latin, New Testament Greek, and Hebrew by attending her brothers' lessons and by private study. Until her fortieth year she remained a contented 'home daughter'. When George Moberly became bishop of Salisbury in 1869 (after a brief period as vicar of Brighstone in the Isle of Wight, following his retirement from Winchester in 1866), she acted as his personal secretary and, in his last years of failing health, his chief nurse-companion. This phase of her life ended with his death in 1885. Annie and two older unmarried sisters now moved with their mother to a dull street in Salisbury and faced a future of genteel poverty. But within the year she was invited by Elizabeth *Wordsworth, sister of the new bishop of Salisbury and principal of Lady Margaret Hall, to take charge of a new Anglican hall for women students at Oxford. This was, she felt, a 'call' in answer to her prayers—yet she left the family circle for the unfamiliar atmosphere of a university 'most unwillingly' (Moberly to Johnson, 28 Oct [1894], Bertha Johnson MSS).

Annie Moberly was to preside, however, over an embryonic women's college that established itself against considerable odds. Founded by Elizabeth Wordsworth for students who could not afford the fees at Lady Margaret Hall, St Hugh's Hall opened in 1886 with four students in a semidetached north Oxford house, 25 Norham Road, run by Miss Moberly, on a nominal salary of £40 a year, assisted by two servants. To her chagrin, seven years later Miss

Wordsworth proposed that the hall, now with about twenty students and housed in larger premises at 17 Norham Gardens, should be absorbed by Lady Margaret Hall as a hostel. This plan was rejected by the Lady Margaret Hall council, but relations with the hall's founder remained touchy and its finances precarious. Yet by the time of Miss Moberly's retirement in March 1915 St Hugh's College (as it was named from 1911) had over sixty students and its own staff of tutors, and it was on the point of moving to purpose-built premises on the spacious site in St Margaret's Road it occupies today.

Like other women's colleges, St Hugh's throve in a buoyant market for higher education, and many women and university men had a hand in its success. Annie Moberly's part in it was, however, important. A bishop's daughter of impeccable orthodoxy and gentility, she won the confidence of Anglican parents with conservative views on women's education. Even after fees were raised to allow for collegiate development, St Hugh's was particularly attractive to clergy daughters. At the same time, although never an activist herself, Miss Moberly had progressive sympathies on women's questions, including the opening to women of Oxford degrees and women's suffrage. In shaping corporate life at St Hugh's, she drew on memories of her father's regime at Winchester. Students were expected to work hard and develop an *esprit de corps*. Sport was encouraged, as were sociability and music-making—Miss Moberly played the piano at dances and conducted an intercollegiate women's orchestra as well as St Hugh's instrumental and choral groups. It was she who planned the transition from a domestic hall to a college with appropriate new buildings, and the benefactor who made that possible, the suffragette Clara Evelyn Mordan, was cultivated by her as a personal friend.

Dark, square-set, and with striking eyes and strong features, Annie Moberly inherited from her father a Slavonic appearance that lent support to a cherished family myth that they were descended from an illegitimate son of Peter the Great. Her Sunday evening addresses, delivered in a study furnished with family portraits, books, and furniture from the bishop's palace, were remembered as inspiring. Versions that were later published are *Five Visions of the Revelations* (1914; 2nd edn, 1939) and *The Faith of the Prophets* (1916). Students read Dante with her too. They recalled the allure of her deep, distinctive voice. In the words of one admirer, 'she was a very exciting head of a college' (Olivier, *Without Knowing*, 175). On the other hand, she was by common consent a very poor housekeeper—the food and domestic discomforts at St Hugh's were notorious. Early students remembered her keen sense of humour, but in later years some found her remote, brusque, and arrogant. A naturally shy woman and lacking in professional background, she was never really at ease in Oxford.

Eleanor Jourdain, the Lady Margaret Hall trained headmistress whom she appointed in 1902 as vice-principal, provided much needed support and also, perhaps, the stimulus to develop her literary talents, displayed in two books published in 1911. One was a well-received family memoir, dedicated to her forty-one nephews and nieces—*Dulce domum* (the title recalled the Winchester College song). Despite its reticence (the product, in part at least, of censorship imposed by the family), this is an intimate, charming account of the world in which she grew up. The other was a collaborative work with Miss Jourdain, *An Adventure*. Published under the pseudonyms Elizabeth Morison and Frances Lamont, this classic ghost story was based on an experience they had shared at Versailles; it was a best-seller and there have been several later editions (1913, 1924, 1931, 1955, 1988). Visiting the Petit Trianon as sightseers on 10 August 1901, the anniversary of the capture of the Tuileries in the French Revolution, they had seen figures in eighteenth-century dress. Their later researches suggested to them that these were Marie Antoinette and members of her court, and that the landscape and buildings they had seen were also as they had been at that time. They believed that they had travelled back in time, in telepathic rapport with an 'act of memory' emanating from the queen in captivity. Even sceptics (among them Eleanor Sidgwick, who reviewed the book for the Society for Psychical Research) acknowledged that this was a well-written story. Less scientifically minded readers, high-church Oxford academics among them, gave it credence as an account of a brush with the supernatural.

Annie Moberly, it seems, took the lead in publicizing the 'adventure'. For her this was not the first experience of 'visions', and she left records of later experiences of 'time-travel', published for the first time in Edith Olivier's sympathetic portrait of her in 1945. A plausible explanation for the Versailles adventure emerged some decades later: the 'ghosts' may have been taking part in a rehearsal for one of the fancy-dress parties given at Versailles by Comte Robert de Montesquiou (Evans, 'An end to *An Adventure*'). But speculation has persisted about the significance for these two women of their preoccupation with this uncanny experience. Did it become the vehicle for a repressed lesbian affinity, as Terry Castle has suggested ('Contagious folly: an adventure and its skeptics')? For Miss Moberly, at least, it was more obviously a vehicle for nostalgia. As children the Moberlys devoured historical romances and heard tales of second sight associated with their Scottish maternal ancestors. Their father did not rule out the possibility of ghostly encounters, while making it clear that occultism and spiritualism were heterodox.

Miss Moberly's retirement at the age of sixty-nine appears to have been delayed by fears that she could not afford to rent a house in Oxford. Doubtless Eleanor Jourdain, her successor as principal, shared the costs at 4 Norham Road, where until her death in 1924 she spent vacations with Annie Moberly. They became close friends, though always (in Joan Evans's view) somewhat distanced by differences in age and status and the habits of reserve ingrained by upbringing. In the 'row' over the sacking of a tutor that divided the college in 1923–4 Annie Moberly was fiercely loyal to Miss Jourdain. She was herself a member of the college's governing council until her death and became an honorary fellow. She was made an honorary MA in 1920 when Oxford degrees were opened to women. Under the name Elizabeth Morison she published in retirement a series of religious stories for children—*Signposts* (1–12, 1928)—and *Simple Meditations and Intercessions on the Stations of the Cross* (1931). She died at her home in Norham Road, at the age of ninety, on 5 May 1937, and was buried three days later in Wolvercote cemetery.

'Annie Moberly's intellect was of the vigorous rather than the critical order', wrote Barbara Gwyer (*Oxford Magazine*, 1937, 594). This is hard to deny, and it was seen as a reproach by later generations at St Hugh's. But the criticism is misplaced. For the role of academic woman she had neither training nor vocation. Yet her achievement in establishing the college is unquestioned. Both as principal and in her spiritual and imaginative life, she drew on a distinctively Victorian family inheritance.

JANET HOWARTH

Sources C. A. E. Moberly, *Dulce domum: George Moberly ... his family and friends* (1911) · E. Olivier, *Four Victorian ladies of Wiltshire* (1945) · E. Olivier, *Without knowing Mr Walkley* (1939) · E. Morison [C. Moberly] and F. Lamont [E. Jourdain], *An adventure*, ed. J. Evans (1955) · J. Evans, 'An end to *An adventure*: solving the mystery of the Trianon', *Encounter*, 47/4 (1976), 33–47 · J. Evans, *Prelude and fugue: an autobiography* (1964) · L. Iremonger, *The ghosts of Versailles: Miss Moberley and Miss Jourdain and their adventure, a critical study* (1957) · P. Griffin, ed., *St Hugh's: a centenary history* (1986) · T. Castle, 'Contagious folly: an adventure and its skeptics', *Questions of evidence: proof, practice and persuasion across the disciplines*, ed. J. Chandler, A. I. Davidson, and H. Harootunian (1994), 11–42 · G. [B. Gwyer], *Oxford Magazine* (13 May 1937), 593–4 · *The Times* (7 May 1937) · *St Hugh's Club Paper* (1899) · *St Hugh's Club Paper* (1900) · *St Hugh's Club Paper* (1915) · *St Hugh's Chronicle* (1938) · *DNB* · St Anne's College, Oxford, Bertha Johnson MSS · b. cert. · d. cert.

Archives Bodl. Oxf., diary, corresp. and papers, MSS Eng. misc. c. 257, c. 376, d. 249–56, c. 221–4, fols. 73–4, g. 12, 13 · St Hugh's College, Oxford, archive | St Anne's College, Oxford, Bertha Johnson MSS

Likenesses W. Llewellyn, portrait, 1899, St Hugh's College, Oxford [*see illus.*] · L. L. Brooke, portrait, 1912, St Hugh's College, Oxford

Wealth at death £3155 16*s.* 4*d.*: probate, 16 July 1937, *CGPLA Eng. & Wales*

Moberly, George (1803–1885), bishop of Salisbury, was born in St Petersburg on 10 October 1803, the seventh son of Edward Moberly, a Russia merchant, and his wife, Sarah, daughter of John Cayley, British consul-general in Russia. When his parents returned to Russia in 1813 he was left in the care of his eldest brother. He attended Mr Richards's school in Hyde Street, Winchester, before being nominated in 1816 by Lady Pembroke, a friend of his mother, to a scholarship at Winchester College. He matriculated at Balliol College, Oxford, with a scholarship in 1822. He graduated BA in 1825 with a first class in *literae humaniores*, gained the chancellor's prize for the English essay in 1826, on the subject 'Is a rude or a refined age more favourable to the production of works of fiction?', and proceeded MA in 1828 and DCL in 1836. In 1826 he was ordained by Charles Lloyd, bishop of Oxford, and in the same year was elected to a fellowship at Balliol College. For some years he was one of the most brilliant and successful of the tutors who helped Dr Jenkyns to make Balliol a leading college in Oxford. He was a public examiner in 1830, and again in 1833, 1834, and 1835. H. E. Manning was among his pupils, and also A. C. Tait, who succeeded him in his tutorship, and eventually consecrated him bishop of Salisbury. He vacated his fellowship on his marriage, on 22 December 1834, to Mary Anne (1812–1890), daughter of Thomas Crokat of Leghorn, a Scottish merchant and close cousin of the old high-churchman and judge James Alan Park.

In 1835 Moberly was appointed headmaster of Winchester College, a post which he held for thirty years. Leaving Oxford on the eve of the Oxford Movement, he took little, if any, active part in the various ecclesiastical controversies which were occasioned by it. His sympathies and opinions, however, were of the high-church school. Keble was his neighbour at Winchester and intimate friend, as was the novelist Charlotte Yonge. He formally protested against the sentence of degradation pronounced upon W. G. Ward for the opinions expressed in his *Ideal of a Christian Church Considered*. This protest, contained in a letter to Richard Jenkyns, master of Balliol, was published in 1845. He was select preacher before the university in 1833, 1858, and 1863, and Bampton lecturer in 1868.

As a schoolmaster Moberly exerted much personal influence over his boys. When examining Rugby School along with Christopher Wordsworth, he caught from Arnold much of his enthusiasm and some of his views. He attached paramount importance to making religious training in the school effective: he introduced sermons, many of which he preached himself, and published two series of them (1844, 1848), and he carefully prepared boys for confirmation. He approved the 'fagging' system (see the preface to his second series of *Winchester College Sermons*, 1848), supported all the school traditions, and was conservative in his modes of teaching. He reduced the number of floggings, but those which he administered were more severe than formerly. Although beloved by many pupils, he was only a cautious reformer. During his time as headmaster the first commoner boarding-houses were started, but the numbers of commoners did not increase greatly under his rule. The seventy scholars in 'college', previously appointed by patronage, were now chosen by competitive examination. He felt a hostility towards him among the governing body of the school on account of his not being a New College man and in consequence of his high-church leanings. In 1866 he resigned, being succeeded by his son-in-law, George *Ridding, and was presented to the rectory of Brighstone, Isle of Wight. In 1868 William Jacobson appointed him a canon of Chester Cathedral.

Moberly had been regarded as a possible bishop ever since 1850, and in 1857 an unsuccessful attempt had been made to induce the duke of Newcastle to appoint him bishop of Sydney. Newcastle dismissed him as an unsuccessful schoolmaster (pupil numbers at Winchester had slumped in 1856), lacking in parochial experience. His promotion was further delayed by a preference for low-churchmen in episcopal appointments. At length, in August 1869, he was appointed by Gladstone to succeed another high-churchman, Walter Kerr Hamilton, as bishop of Salisbury, the first high-church appointment for many years, and he was consecrated on 28 October.

In the administration of his diocese Moberly followed the lines of his predecessor. He avoided dissensions; he founded a 'diocesan synod' and escaped public attention. He was a diligent attendant in convocation and an infrequent one in the House of Lords, and, though a fairly impressive preacher, spoke rarely in either assembly. Though not unfavourable to the principle of the Public Worship Regulation Act of 1874, he voted for its withdrawal in deference to the public outcry which it occasioned, and refused to sign the bishops' pastoral, which was issued before the act came into operation. In 1872 he issued an appeal to churchmen, much to the indignation of the ritualists, to consent to the omission of the damnatory clauses from the Athanasian creed. In 1873 he was a member of the committee appointed by convocation to consider the attitude of the church towards auricular confession, and helped to draw up its report; in 1877 he spoke strongly in convocation against the use of the confessional, especially in schools (see *Chronicle of Convocation*, 6 July 1877, 331). The most concise indication of his general ecclesiastical position is to be found in the preface to the second edition of his university sermons, *Beatitudes* (1861). His publications were numerous, but apart from his 1868 Bampton lectures, *The Administration of the Holy Spirit in the Body of Christ*, consisted chiefly of sermons and episcopal charges.

For some time before his death Moberly's faculties had been decaying, and his episcopal duties were discharged by J. B. K. Kelly, formerly bishop of Newfoundland. In 1884 his resignation was determined upon, but the papers had not received his signature when he died at the bishop's palace in the close, Salisbury, on 6 July 1885. His widow, who was keenly interested in mission work and who helped to found the Salisbury diocesan association for friendless girls, survived him, together with five of their seven sons and seven of their eight daughters. Among their children were Robert Campbell *Moberly and Charlotte Anne Elizabeth *Moberly.

J. A. HAMILTON, rev. GEOFFREY ROWELL

Sources C. A. E. Moberly, *Dulce domum: George Moberly ... his family and friends* (1916) · *The Guardian* (8 July 1885) · *The Times* (7 July 1885) · *Saturday Review*, 60 (1885), 47–8 · F. D. How, *Six great schoolmasters* (1904) · W. Benham and R. T. Davidson, *Life of Archibald Campbell Tait*, 2 vols. (1891) · R. G. Wilberforce, *Life of the right reverend Samuel Wilberforce ... with selections from his diary and correspondence*, 2 (1881) · J. D'E. Firth, *Winchester College* (1949) · J. Bentley, *Ritualism and politics in Victorian Britain* (1978)
Archives BL, corresp. with W. E. Gladstone, Add. MSS 44208–44487 · LPL, letters to Lord Selborne · LPL, corresp. with A. C. Tait · Wilts. & Swindon RO, letter-book (with Bishop Wordsworth)
Likenesses F. Grant, oils, 1852, Winchester College, Hampshire · photograph, c.1860, repro. in F. D. How, *Six great schoolmasters* (1900), 38 · L. C. Dickinson, oils, 1876, Winchester College, Hampshire · T. L. Atkinson, engraving (after portrait by F. Grant), repro. in Moberly, *Dulce domum*, frontispiece · Elliott & Fry, photograph, repro. in Moberly, *Dulce domum*, 254 · Lock & Whitfield, woodburytype, NPG; repro. in T. Cooper, *Men of mark: a gallery of contemporary portraits* (1877) · L. Lowenstam, etching (after W. B. Richmond), Salisbury Corporation · wood-engraving (after photograph by J. Watkins), NPG; repro. in *ILN* (30 Oct 1809)
Wealth at death £29,953 2s. 11d.: probate, 14 Aug 1885, *CGPLA Eng. & Wales*

Moberly, Mary (1853–1940), headmistress, was born at Rugby, Warwickshire, daughter of the Revd Charles Edward Moberly (1821?–1893), clergyman, schoolmaster, and author, and Catherine Temple (b. 1812), elder sister of Frederick Temple, headmaster of Rugby School and archbishop of Canterbury. Most of her early life was spent in Rugby, where her father was assistant master at the school, and it is likely that she was educated at home. She passed five Cambridge higher local examinations before entering Newnham College, Cambridge, in 1878, where she had a distinguished career and was made Drapers' scholar in 1879. A pupil of Professor Sidgwick, she gained distinctions in logic and political economy, and a first class in the moral sciences tripos in 1881. She was an associate of Newnham from 1893 to 1903.

From Newnham Moberly followed many of her peers in becoming a teacher in one of the new girls' academic high schools. Her career began in 1882 as assistant mistress at Notting Hill high school, London, which had developed into a *de facto* training institution for future headmistresses. After only a year she was appointed by the Girls' Public Day School Company to open their new school at Tunbridge Wells as its first headmistress. Under her leadership the school grew from twenty-two pupils to a full range of years from kindergarten to sixth form. In 1891 she was transferred to Gateshead high school. There she had a particularly difficult task, facing falling rolls as a result of the economic situation at Gateshead and competition from other local schools. The company's response to the latter was to upgrade the Gateshead school's preparatory department in nearby Newcastle upon Tyne to a full high school, and within three years Moberly was entrusted with the headship of the new Central Newcastle high school, which opened in January 1895. When Gateshead was finally merged with the Newcastle school in 1907 she was appointed head of the new school, and remained there until her retirement.

In building up the Central Newcastle school Moberly gathered round her a number of excellent teachers, some of whom had been with her at Gateshead. She kept up good relations with her old school, and it was thanks to her statesmanship that the merger was implemented with so little friction. The new school lacked facilities and there was much making do in the early years. Despite the difficulty of having no laboratories science was on the curriculum from the beginning. The school developed as an all-round institution, with a concentration on games and drama; it was described as having an overall light-heartedness. Moberly was no autocrat but a strong supporter of self-government who believed in training the girls to be self-reliant for themselves and for the school. One of her main innovations, soon after the school's foundation, was the introduction of a prefect system, followed some years later by elected form captains. She stated that she wished to make the school more like a civic organization and genuinely alive. Her successor said that she had built into the school 'some share of her own integrity, tolerance and generosity' (Carter, 35).

Moberly was tall and slim, with a long narrow face and high forehead; she wore spectacles and was impeccably dressed. It was said of her that she was made up of 'the academic, the episcopal and the Liberal' (Carter, 33). She was a deep-thinking scholar, with a fine mind and a precision in her conversation that some found daunting. In many ways she seemed more suited to the libraries of Cambridge than to a girls' school in the north of England—yet she had a strong feeling for the north east, and after her retirement stayed in Newcastle for the rest of her life. She was a devoted churchwoman, with a genuine and profound Christian belief that permeated everything she did. Unlike many of her contemporaries she does not appear to have played any public role in education. A mix of many elements, she roused different emotions in those who knew her. To some she was austere and difficult to get to know or understand, a solemn woman who rarely smiled; to others she was a remarkable woman of vivid personality, warm-hearted, understanding, and gentle, inspiring love and gratitude in former pupils and staff. Her generosity to those in need was unstinted, and many girls were thus given chances that they would otherwise have lacked. She was broad-minded but at the same time had very high mental and moral standards. (These did not extend to remedying her own chronic lack of punctuality.)

Moberly retired in 1911, aged fifty-eight. She became totally blind and was cared for by her companion and former school secretary, Blanche Edith Dixon. She died of heart failure and a stroke at her home, 28 Lansdowne Gardens, Jesmond, Newcastle, on 4 August 1940; she was buried in St Andrew's cemetery, Newcastle, on 7 August.

SYLVIA HARROP

Sources O. Carter, *History of Gateshead high school, 1876–1907, and Central Newcastle High School, 1895–1955* (1956?) • Newnham Hall register, Oct 1878 • [A. B. White and others], eds., *Newnham College register, 1871–1971*, 2nd edn, 1 (1979), vol. 1 • *Newcastle Journal* (5 Aug 1940) • *Newcastle Journal* (8 Aug 1940) • *Newnham College Roll Letter* (1941), 27–8 • L. Magnus, *The jubilee book of the Girls' Public Day School Trust, 1873–1923* (1923) • E. G. Sandford, ed., *Memoirs of Archbishop Temple, by seven friends*, 2 vols. (1906) • Crockford (1890) • Foster, *Alum. Oxon.* • d. cert.

Likenesses photograph, Tyne and Wear Archives Office, 1329/28; repro. in Carter, *History*, 40

Wealth at death £2586 17s. 7d.: probate, 12 Oct 1940, CGPLA Eng. & Wales

Moberly, Robert Campbell (1845–1903), theologian, born at Winchester on 26 July 1845, was third son and tenth child of George *Moberly (1803–1885), headmaster of Winchester College and afterwards bishop of Salisbury, and Mary Anne Crokat (1812–1890), daughter of Thomas Crokat, a Scottish merchant at Leghorn. The family of seven sons and eight daughters was brought up in close personal friendship with their near neighbours at Winchester, John Keble and Charlotte Yonge: Robert's nearest

sister, Annie [see Moberly, Charlotte Anne Elizabeth], who became first principal of St Hugh's College, Oxford, recorded the background in which they grew up in C. A. E. Moberly, *Dulce domum: George Moberly, his Family and Friends* (1911). For thirty years (from the mid-1830s to the mid-1860s) the three representatives of the Oxford Movement, 'in differing degrees, centres of Church teaching and influence' (Moberly, 4), lived within walking distance of each other and met almost daily, a routine which the respective families 'absolutely shared' (ibid., 5). Charlotte Yonge was thought by many to have based her most famous family, the Mays in *The Daisy Chain*, on the Moberlys, though she and they denied it stoutly (ibid., 210–11).

After two years at a preparatory school at Twyford near Winchester, Moberly became a commoner of Winchester College in 1856, and a scholar in 1857. He then began his university education in 1863, at New College, Oxford, where he had won a Winchester scholarship. In Easter term 1865 he achieved a first in classical moderations, but in the final classical schools, in 1867, he was placed in the second class. He won the Newdigate prize in June 1867 for a poem on Marie Antoinette. He graduated BA in 1867, proceeding MA in 1870 and DD in 1892. He was ordained deacon in 1869 and priest in 1870. In December 1867 he was elected senior student of Christ Church, and held his studentship until his marriage in 1880. He was engaged in lecturing and teaching in classical subjects at the college during 1868–75. From 1871 to 1885 he was domestic chaplain to his father, the bishop of Salisbury.

One of the significant characteristics of the Oxford Movement was its commitment to foreign missions. In January 1876 Moberly accompanied his friend Reginald Stephen Copleston (Moberly, 254) to Colombo, where Copleston had been appointed bishop. The visit lasted six months, and on his return to Oxford Moberly published a pamphlet, *An Account of the Question between the Bishop and the CMS in the Diocese of Colombo*. His experience in Colombo proved a turning point in his life, where he found his identity, and he came back 'possessed by what he had seen' (Holland, 275). In 1876 he became principal of St Stephen's House, Oxford, then founded for the training of Anglican clergy for foreign mission work. In 1878, at his father's urgent request, he undertook the principalship of the Diocesan Theological College at Salisbury. In 1880, after his marriage to Alice Sidney, second daughter of Walter Kerr *Hamilton, bishop of Salisbury before his father, he became vicar of Great Budworth, Cheshire. Their marriage produced one son, Sir Walter Hamilton *Moberly, later vice-chancellor of Manchester University. In 1884 his diocesan, William Stubbs, bishop of Chester, brought him out of this retirement to act as his examining chaplain, a position he retained under Stubbs's successor, Francis John Jayne (1889–92), who nominated him honorary canon of Chester in 1890.

A later manifestation of the Oxford Movement was the collection of essays edited by Charles Gore in 1889, *Lux mundi*, and Moberly established a reputation as an exponent of philosophical theology by his paper entitled 'The incarnation as the basis of dogma'. His position was strengthened by his paper 'Belief in a personal God', read before the church congress at Rhyl in 1891. *Lux mundi* was something of a transformation of the Oxford Movement, its object being 'to put the Catholic faith into its right relation to modern intellectual and moral problems' (C. Grove, ed., *Lux mundi*, 1889 Preface): it embodied the testimonies of the younger school of Oxford theologians, and shook the religious world with its bold endorsement of contemporary views on science and criticism. Like his fellow contributors to *Lux mundi* Moberly was influenced by the theology of the Greek fathers, and shared their desire to maintain an Anglo-Catholic stance while rejecting Tractarian conservatism in favour of an open engagement with modern critical scholarship. In 1892 he was appointed regius professor of pastoral theology at Oxford and canon of Christ Church. In 1900 he became proctor for the dean and chapter of Christ Church in the lower house of convocation, and showed brilliant powers of advocacy. From 1893 he was examining chaplain to William Stubbs, bishop of Oxford, and he was honorary chaplain to Queen Victoria (1898–1901) and chaplain-in-ordinary to Edward VII (1901).

Moberly was widely regarded as 'one of the best thinkers alive' (Holland, 276), and his *Atonement and Personality* (1901) is a major contribution to dogmatic theology: one reviewer, William Sanday, declared that it put the writer in the same league as Butler and Hooker. Moberly wrote extensively on Anglican questions of the day, such as disestablishment and denominationalism. His *Ministerial Priesthood, with an Appendix upon Romanist Criticism of Anglican Orders* (1901) is a reply to Pope Leo XIII's dismissal of Anglican orders, and it urges, in the best Tractarian tradition, the doctrine of apostolic succession and the theology of the Christian priesthood. It moved well beyond the mechanical views of early Tractarianism and established a distinctive Catholic Anglican position. It has been widely recognized as the finest exposition of an Anglican theology of the ministry. He repudiates sacerdotalism in favour of a view of the priesthood of the ordained ministry as representative of the priesthood of the whole church, exercising pastoral leadership on behalf of all. The influence of Moberly's work on twentieth-century Anglican Catholicism is confirmed by the reissue in 1969 of *Ministerial Priesthood* with an important introduction by A. T. Hanson. *Atonement and Personality* rejects penal substitionary theories of atonement in favour of a new approach in terms of human personality. Christians are delivered from sin by the Holy Spirit who enables them to share in the penitence of Christ, the perfect penitent.

Moberly's whole life was passed in the deepest Tractarian tradition of discipline, reserve, and submission, and his early death cut him off from the fullest achievement of his potential. He died at Christ Church, Oxford, on 8 June 1903, and was buried at the east end of Christ Church Cathedral.　ANDREW CLARK, *rev.* BARBARA DENNIS

Sources C. A. E. Moberly, *Dulce domum: George Moberly … his family and friends* (1911) · H. S. Holland, *Personal studies* (1905) · *The Times* (9 June 1903) · *Oxford Times* (12 June 1903) · *Guardian* (1903), 817 · *Journal of Theological Studies*, 4 (1903), 499 · CGPLA *Eng. & Wales* (1903)

Wealth at death £5237 15s. 8d.: probate, 29 July 1903, CGPLA *Eng. & Wales*

Moberly, Sir Walter Hamilton (1881–1974), philosopher and university administrator, was born at the vicarage, Budworth, Cheshire, on 20 October 1881, the son of Robert Campbell *Moberly (1845–1903), vicar of Great Budworth, and his wife, Alice Sidney Hamilton. He was born into a distinguished clerical dynasty. Both his grandfathers had been bishops of Salisbury, his paternal grandfather, George Moberly, having succeeded his maternal grandfather, Walter Kerr Hamilton. Walter Moberly's father later became regius professor of pastoral theology at Oxford and in 1889 was a contributor to the celebrated collection of theological essays *Lux mundi*. Walter Moberly was educated at Winchester College before going as a scholar to New College, Oxford, where he took a first in Greats in 1903. He became a fellow in theology at Merton College in 1904, but moved to Aberdeen University as lecturer in philosophy in 1905. He returned to Oxford in 1906 as fellow and tutor in philosophy at Lincoln College. During the First World War he served in France and Belgium in the Oxford and Buckinghamshire light infantry. He was wounded three times, and was twice mentioned in dispatches, receiving the DSO (1917).

Along with his friend William Temple, Moberly was a contributor to *Foundations* (1912), a collection of essays edited by B. H. Streeter, which sought to justify Christianity in the light of modern thought. Moberly contributed two essays. The first was entitled 'The atonement', which had been the subject of his father's celebrated book *The Atonement and Personality* (1901). In his second essay, 'God and the absolute', Moberly argued that recent idealist philosophy could help illustrate the nature of God. Moberly was among those criticized by Ronald Knox in his rejoinder to *Foundations*, *Some Loose Stones* (1913), though this was more for the obscurity of his arguments than for his liberal theology.

In 1921 Moberly became professor of philosophy at the University of Birmingham, and later in the same year (29 December 1921) married Gwendolen Gardner (*b.* 1891/2), who had been one of his pupils in political philosophy at Oxford; she was the daughter of Walter Myers Gardner, a chemist and principal of Bradford Technical College. They had four sons. In 1924 he moved to be principal of University College, Exeter, but after only two years he became vice-chancellor of Manchester University. Here he worked to cement links between the university and the industrial city, promoting university extension classes. In 1934 Moberly became first full-time president of the University Grants Committee, serving in this role for fourteen years, though the Second World War prevented him from implementing many of his ideas about university funding.

Moberly was best-known as an active Anglican. From 1922 he was a member of the Church of England commission on Christian doctrine, and in 1949 he was asked by the church assembly to chair a committee on the relations between church and state which reported in 1952 and which strongly supported the continuance of establishment. His friend Archbishop William Temple recruited him as one of the committee which supervised the Pilgrim Trust report on long-term unemployment, *Men without Work*, which was published in 1938. Moberly was also heavily involved in the Oxford conference 'Church, community and state' in 1937, and was a member of the Council on the Christian Faith and the Common Life which emerged from it. In 1942 he joined a successor body, the Christian Frontier Council, contributing many articles to its journal, the *Christian News-Letter*. Moberly was also a leading light in the Moot, a discussion group mostly composed of Christian intellectuals, which also included T. S. Eliot, Karl Mannheim, and John Middleton Murry, which met throughout the Second World War to discuss social reconstruction.

Moberly developed his ideas on higher education through his work with the Student Christian Movement and the University Teachers' Group. These ideas were most fully expressed in his book *The Crisis in the University* (1949). The crisis diagnosed by Moberly was spiritual: he argued that academic neutrality was undermining the moral character of universities, and that the growth of academic specialization was robbing students of a broad cultural education. The solution was a return to Christian values (though not to narrowly confessional universities), and a broader curriculum. Moberly sought to implement his ideas on education as first principal (1949–55) of St Catharine's, Cumberland Lodge, a Christian training institute situated in Windsor Great Park, which sought to bring together students from Britain and the Commonwealth. He also supported the attempts of his friend A. D. Lindsay at developing a broad university curriculum at the University College of North Staffordshire at Keele.

Moberly's public career precluded extensive philosophical writing, but he had a long-standing interest in the question of punishment. He wanted to develop the arguments of his father's *The Atonement and Personality*, and he did so in his Riddell lectures entitled *Responsibility* (1951), and in *The Ethics of Punishment* (1968), published when he was eighty-seven. In these books Moberly argued that prisons should concentrate on reform rather than retribution.

Moberly received an honorary degree of LLD from Belfast, and honorary degrees of DLitt from Manchester, Nottingham, and Keele. He was an honorary fellow of three Oxford colleges: Lincoln (1930), Merton (1937), and New College (1942). He was knighted in 1934, and made KCB in 1944 and GCB in 1949. He died at his home, 9 Wyndham House, Plantation Road, Oxford, on 31 January 1974; he was cremated at Oxford on 9 February 1974.

MATTHEW GRIMLEY

Sources *The Times* (2 Feb 1974) · *The Guardian* (2 Feb 1974), 5 · *Church Times* (8 Feb 1974) · A. H. Halsey, *Decline of donnish dominion: the British academic professions in the twentieth century* (1992) · *Lincoln College Record* (1974) · *DNB* · b. cert. · m. cert. · d. cert. · F. A. Iremonger, *William Temple, archbishop of Canterbury* (1948) · M. Reeves, ed., *Christian thinking and social order: conviction politics from the 1930s to the present day* (1999) · E. R. Norman, *Church and society in England, 1770–1970* (1976) · Burke, *Peerage* (1967) · V. H. H. Green, *The commonwealth of Lincoln College* · B. Pullan and M. Abendstern, *A history of the University of Manchester* (2000) · H. B. Charlton, *Portrait of a university* (1951)
Likenesses W. Stoneman, photograph, 1933, NPG · S. Whittingham, double portrait, photograph, 1973 (with Lady Moberly), NPG
Wealth at death £23,529: probate, 11 March 1975, *CGPLA Eng. & Wales*

Moberly, Winifred Horsbrugh (1875–1928), college head, was born on 1 April 1875 in Calcutta, the ninth child and the fourth daughter of Charles Morris Moberly (1837–1897) and his wife, Eliza Augusta (1841–1909), daughter of James Dorward of Trichinopoly. Her father, an officer in the Madras staff corps, was cousin to Charlotte Anne Elizabeth Moberly (1846–1937), the first principal of St Hugh's Hall, Oxford. As a young woman, she visited her elder sister Ethel Charlotte and her husband, Frederick James Wishaw, in St Petersburg (where the Moberly family also had connections during the nineteenth century); she retained her delight in travel throughout her life, together with a love of pictures and flowers.

Winifred Moberly was educated at Winchester and Sydenham high schools before entering Lady Margaret Hall, Oxford, as Romanes scholar in English literature in 1894. In 1896 she gained a second in classical honour moderations but left Oxford a year later when her father died. Until her mother died in 1909, most of Winifred Moberly's time after Oxford was given to her family, but she was appointed briefly as a housekeeper at Lady Margaret Hall in 1906. In 1910 she returned from New Zealand to become bursar of the Hall for two years following an extension of its buildings; she was a great success both in her duties and with the students, who particularly appreciated the parts she played in their amateur dramatics as stage manager, scene-painter, and actress.

The outbreak of the First World War brought challenging opportunities for Winifred Moberly. For the first few months she organized training schemes for unemployed women on behalf of the Central Committee on Women's Employment; her responsibilities included the organization of Queen Mary workshops and the training of women for a home help scheme. Between 1915 and 1917 her management skills were fully employed when she became organizer, in Russia and Galicia, of five Millicent Fawcett hospitals. These were units of doctors, matrons, and nurses sent out to the eastern front by the National Union of Women's Suffrage Societies and partly financed by the Polish Fund in Britain. The hospitals were scattered over a very wide area with very little means of communication between them. In Petrograd, opposite the Warsaw station, she established a unit in a small maternity hospital for refugees who had fled from Poland, Estonia, and Latvia before the major advance of the German army. At the same time she was administering a fever hospital at Kazan on the Volga as well as two general hospitals and a convalescent home for mothers and children. In 1917 she moved to Galicia and organized a unit in an Austrian agricultural college which had been converted into a hospital for peasants with infectious diseases (but overflowing with military patients) in a region that had changed hands six times in the course of the war. Work in Galicia was followed, in 1917–18, by her appointment as area secretary in Calais for the Young Women's Christian Association with the task of setting up recreation huts and canteens for the Queen Mary's Army Auxiliary Corps. Finally, in 1918, she undertook a six weeks' tour in the USA, on behalf of the War Workers' Campaign, lecturing on women's work.

By the end of the war, Winifred Moberly had won a reputation for courage, determination, and persuasive leadership. In 1919 she was appointed principal of St Hilda's Hall for women in Oxford. When she arrived there it was small, short of money, and ultimately controlled by a committee in Cheltenham associated with the Ladies' College. She led the great changes in the early 1920s which provided a secure foundation for the subsequent development of the Hall. St Hilda's doubled in size by the acquisition and extensive modification of a neighbouring property; an appeal for funds was launched and, with the granting of a royal charter in 1926, the traditional link with Cheltenham was broken so that St Hilda's (as a college) could become firmly established within the university. In 1920, with the other women principals, she was awarded an honorary MA when the university admitted women for the first time.

Winifred Moberly had an extraordinary gift for making and retaining friends. Within St Hilda's she welcomed everyone with warmth and cheerfulness, and she never seemed to forget a name; even shy freshers found themselves talking easily to her. She generated good conversation and laughter on high table and in student gatherings. In appearance she was well built with dark hair; her round face, so readily covered with a smile, was dominated by blue eyes. By 1925 there were signs of the physical and mental illness which would cut short her career as principal. Winifred Moberly died, unmarried, at Laverstock House, Laverstock, near Salisbury, on 6 April 1928, and was buried five days later at St Andrew's in Laverstock.

MARGARET E. RAYNER

Sources W. H. Moberly, 'With the NUWSS hospitals in Russia', *Brown Book* (1916), 62–4 · W. H. Moberly, 'Galicia', *Brown Book* (1917), 45–8 · W. H. Moberly, 'YWCA work for the WAACs', *Brown Book* (1918), 40–42 · E. M. J. [E. M. Jamison], 'Winifred Horsbrugh Moberly', *Brown Book* (1928), 25–7 · *Brown Book* (1915), 18–19, 36 · *Brown Book* (1917), 10–12 · *Brown Book* (1918), 18 · M. E. Rayner, *The centenary history of St Hilda's College, Oxford* (1993) · *The Times* (10 April 1928) · *The Times* (13 April 1928) · *Oxford Mail* (13 April 1928) · *Oxford Chronicle and Berks and Bucks Gazette* (13 April 1928) · *Oxford Chronicle and Berks and Bucks Gazette* (4 May 1928) · baptismal register for Bengal, BL, 5 May 1875 · d. cert.
Archives Lady Margaret Hall, Oxford · St Hilda's College, Oxford
Likenesses photographs, 1919–28, St Hilda's College, Oxford · Bassano, photographs, 1920, NPG [*see illus.*] · Bassano, photographs, 1920, St Hilda's College, Oxford · C. Ouless, oils, 1929 (after photographs), St Hilda's College, Oxford · photograph, repro. in *The Times* (11 April 1928), 16
Wealth at death £4162 19s. 2d.: probate, 19 May 1928, CGPLA Eng. & Wales

Mocatta family (*per.* 1671–1957), bullion dealers and brokers, traces its origins in the City of London to **Moses Mocatta** (*d.* 1693), who came from Amsterdam where his forebears, of Portuguese origin, were leading diamond-traders. Active as a merchant and diamond dealer in London by 1671, he established a significant presence by regularly acquiring Indian diamonds, often through the East India Company, and paying for them with silver and gold, which the company then shipped to India. From the outset the Mocattas closely identified with London's Jewish

Winifred Horsbrugh Moberly (1875–1928), by Bassano, 1920

community and the Portuguese synagogue at Bevis Marks.

Moses Mocatta died at Amsterdam in 1693 leaving a widow, Rebecca (who was his niece), three daughters, and two sons; his business may have been in abeyance until his sons **Abraham** [i] **Mocatta** (d. 1751) and Isaac (d. 1729, unmarried) came of age. By 1701 Abraham [i] was working as a general merchant, and later he also became a stockbroker; in 1710 he acquired a much coveted broker's medal, which had eluded his father, licensing him as one of twelve 'Jew brokers' to do business on the royal exchange. Soon he emerged as London's premier silver broker.

Silver broking Abraham [i] Mocatta's transactions were of enormous extent; between 1713 and 1725 two-thirds of the Bank of England's loans against silver were made to him. Underpinning this was his work as exclusive bullion broker to the bank, the East India Company, and the Royal Mint. In 1717 he co-ordinated a gigantic but somewhat obscure transaction, probably for the bank's account, involving the purchase of 1 million ounces of silver against loans of £300,000, as a step to support silver prices and stem silver exports. His significance within London's merchant community was such that in 1744 he joined the group of merchants pledging loyalty to George II and the support of 'public credit' in the face of Charles Edward Stuart's claim to the throne. His commercial links with North America were important and in 1728 he offered to purchase land for a New York synagogue.

Abraham [i]'s marriage on 3 October 1712 to Grace (d. 1753), daughter of Abraham Levy Ximenes, produced no son but a daughter, Rebecca Sarah (d. 1737). Her second husband, whom she married in 1730, was **Moses Lumbrozo de Mattos** (d. 1759), a London broker since about 1740, and they had a daughter and two sons, **Abraham** [ii] **Mocatta** (1730–1800) and Jacob. Mattos joined Abraham [i] in partnership, though they shared neither premises nor a trading name, but on the latter's retirement from the royal exchange in 1749 Mattos did not receive the broker's licence. It went instead to Mattos's son Abraham [ii].

Abraham [i] died at Bevis Marks in 1751 and was succeeded as leader by Mattos, who died in 1759. Abraham [ii] succeeded as head of the business and his reputation as London's premier bullion broker came to rival that of his grandfather. By 1763 he styled himself Abraham de Mattos Mocatta; he changed his name to Mocatta in 1791, thereby keeping the surname alive. His marriage in 1759 to Esther (1737–1799), daughter of Isaac Lamego, resulted in a family of six sons and five daughters.

The role of exclusive broker in precious metals to the bank continued. Notably Abraham [ii] assisted with massive gold purchases required for the recoinage of gold guineas between 1773 and 1777 and was responsible for much of the daily management of the sterling exchange rate. His firm was known as Mocatta and Keyser from about 1777, when Alexander Isaks Keyser (d. 1779) was admitted a partner. However, it seems that Keyser took over the royal exchange licence in 1767.

Shortly after 1779 Asher Goldsmid, son of a London merchant of Dutch origin and son-in-law of Keyser, joined the partnership; his elder brothers, Abraham and Benjamin, were to be major government loan contractors during the French wars. Following his admission the business was restyled Mocatta and Goldsmid about 1782.

Abraham [ii] Mocatta died in London in January 1800 leaving estate of £150,000; seventeen mourning coaches attended his funeral and he directed that for one year three men should watch over his grave. His sons appear as unremarkable businessmen and Goldsmid succeeded as senior. Three of Abraham's sons, Isaac (1765–1801), Moses (1768–1857), and Jacob (1770–1825), had joined as partners; but Isaac was dismissed in 1793 for unauthorized speculation, and Moses chose to retire in mid-life to devote himself to social and philanthropic works and to study. David Alfred *Mocatta (1806–1882), son of Moses, was an architect noted for his work for the London, Brighton, and South Coast railway. Another son, Isaac Lindo (1818–1879), wrote tracts on Jewish moral teachings and social questions.

For the next forty years the Goldsmids dominated the business, especially Asher (d. 1822) and his sons Sir Isaac Lyon and Aron Asher. As though to underline the position, no Mocatta was called upon to give evidence to the 1810 select committee on the high price of bullion.

From 1840, when the bank ended its exclusive brokerage arrangements with Mocatta and Goldsmid thereby greatly diminishing the firm's significance (although such arrangements continued with the India Office), the firm once more came under the Mocattas' leadership. The senior was now **Abraham** [iii] **Mocatta** (1797–1880), grandson of Abraham [ii] through his third son, Jacob. Abraham [iii] had joined as a partner in 1826. On 27 May 1818 he had married Miriam, daughter of Gabriel Israel Brandon; they had two sons and two daughters: the elder son, Frederic David *Mocatta (1828–1905), joined the firm about 1843 and was admitted a partner in 1849. Frederic married Mary Ada (1836–1905), daughter of the politician Frederick David Goldsmid, in 1856; there were no children of the marriage.

Under their leadership the business was revitalized, and it now benefited from gold discoveries in California and Australia and the consequent shift of the world towards a gold standard. Abraham [iii] retired in 1859 and died at 35 Gloucester Place, Portman Square, in central London, on 21 April 1880. His son Frederic followed him into retirement in 1874 leaving an outsider, Sir Hector Hay, baronet (1821–1916), and two nephews, Benjamin and Abraham (c.1853–1891), to lead the business.

Contributions to Jewish social life More than any other member of his family, Frederic made his mark away from the City, largely through his promotion of philanthropy and Jewish religion and culture. Educated at home he excelled at history and became fluent in five or six languages. As a young man he supported Jewish schools in London's East End and later extended his interests:

the condition of the working classes of all creeds, the improvement of their dwellings, and the administration of charities—Jewish and gentile, public and private—with a view to promoting the independence of the poor, were amongst the principal objects which engaged his attention. (F. D. Mocatta, 17)

Frederic was a founding member of the Charity Organization Society, which sought to prevent duplication of effort and promote proper management. He favoured the amalgamation of institutions to create more effective and viable units; he was the architect of the Home for Aged Jews and of the Jewish Orphanage. He also promoted the Charity Voting Reform Association and gave generously to charitable institutions ranging from the Factory Girls' Country Home Fund to the Philanthropic Society for the Reformation of Criminal Children. But his philosophy was to render the poor independent of charity and thus cure the causes of poverty. For this reason he opposed the provision of state pensions in old age. As a member of the Jewish Board of Guardians he was concerned with the welfare of Jewish immigrants in London's East End. He worked also for the well-being of Jews persecuted in Russia and Romania.

In promoting Jewish religion and culture Frederic published modestly, his best-known works covering Jews in Spain and Portugal and the Inquisition, but his support of the publications of others had more impact. At his death in January 1905 his large library was bequeathed to the Mocatta Museum and Library which from 1906 was located in University College, London, where it came to form a foundation for Jewish studies.

Leading the bullion market The Mocattas returned to leadership of their firm in the twentieth century. In 1900 **Edgar Mocatta** (1879–1957), great-grandson of Abraham [iii] and son of Abraham [iv] (1853–1891), a partner who died tragically when young, and his wife, Florence Justina Cohen (1859–1920), was admitted a partner. For much of the next fifty-seven years Edgar Mocatta was the City's leading authority on the bullion market and was dubbed the 'silver king'. This reputation was won through transactions such as the 1913 rescue of the Indian Specie Bank, which was hopelessly over-extended through massive silver speculation, and through co-ordinating silver purchases of allied governments during the First World War. The British and Indian governments, together with the Bank of England, frequently sought his advice and confidential execution of sensitive transactions. He married in 1913 Mabel, daughter of Alfred Beddington of Cornwall Terrace, Regent's Park, London.

In 1957, after several difficult years for the London bullion market consequent to the effects of world war and changing patterns of demand and market procedures, the Mocattas sold their business to Hambros Bank ending almost 300 years of business as an independent entity. Edgar then joined Hambros' board but died at his London office, 7 Throgmorton Avenue, London Wall, on 30 September that year.

The Mocatta family, in particular Abraham [i] and his grandson Abraham [ii], dominated the London bullion market for most of the eighteenth century and thereafter played an influential part in it until the 1950s. Having accumulated wealth they were inevitably distracted into other areas of life and here their role, especially that of Frederic, in promoting Jewish culture was significant.

JOHN ORBELL

Sources T. Green, *Precious heritage: three hundred years of Mocatta and Goldsmid* (1984) • C. Wolton, 'Broker to the Bank of England: a short history of the Mocatta dynasty', *Goldsmiths' Review* (1988–9) • [F. D. Mocatta], *F. D. Mocatta: a brief memoir, lectures and extracts from letters* (1911) • A. Mocatta, 'Frederic David Mocatta, 1828–1905', *Jewish Historical Society of England Transactions*, 23 (1971) • P. H. Emden, *Jews of Britain: a series of biographies* (1944) • 'Mocatta', *Encyclopaedia Judaica*, ed. C. Roth, 12 (Jerusalem, 1971) • *Jewish Chronicle* (4 Jan 1901) • *Jewish Chronicle* (20 Jan 1905) • *CGPLA Eng. & Wales* (1880) • *CGPLA Eng. & Wales* (1958) • d. certs. [Edgar Lionel de Mattes Mocatta; Abraham Mocatta] • UCL, Wolf MSS • Gladstone, *Diaries*

Archives GL, Mocatta and Goldsmid Archives | King's AC Cam., letters to Oscar Browning [F. D. Mocatta]

Likenesses oils (Abraham de Mattos Mocatta), repro. in Green, *Precious heritage*; priv. coll.

Wealth at death under £100,000—Abraham Mocatta: probate, 20 May 1880, *CGPLA Eng. & Wales* • £155,706 15s. 4d.—F. D. Mocatta: resworn probate, *CGPLA Eng. & Wales* (1905)

Mocatta, Abraham (d. 1751). See under Mocatta family (per. 1671–1957).

Mocatta, Abraham (1730–1800). See under Mocatta family (per. 1671–1957).

Mocatta, Abraham (1797–1880). See under Mocatta family (per. 1671–1957).

Mocatta, David Alfred (1806–1882), architect, was born on 17 February 1806, the son of Moses Mocatta (1768–1857), bullion dealer, and Abigail Lindo (1775–1824). A pioneer of Jewish entry into the artistic professions, he was from February 1821 a pupil of Sir John Soane for a period of six years. He was awarded the medal of the Society of Arts in 1825, and afterwards travelled in Italy, exhibiting paintings of Rome at the Royal Academy in 1831–2. His training, influences, and artistic inclinations were classical. He worked on the drawings for the Bank of England (1826–7) and submitted designs in the competition in 1839 for the Royal Exchange, London. He designed several London synagogues: the Reform in Bruton Street (1841), the West London Synagogue in Great St Helen's Street (1851), which congregation he and his father helped to found, and the Montefiore in Ramsgate (1833). One of the first fellows of the Royal Institute of British Architects (RIBA), he was elected in 1837 and eventually became a vice-president of the institute. In 1835 he married Knendal (Ann) Susskind (1814–1896) at the Spanish and Portuguese Jews' synagogue in Bevis Marks, London.

It was perhaps in his designs for the railway that Mocatta made his most important contribution to British architecture. He designed Brighton Station and several others for the London and Brighton Railway. His drawings in 1840 and 1841 for stations at Croydon, Redhill and Reigate Road, Horley, Crawley, Haywards Heath, Hassocks, and Brighton survive in the drawings collection of the RIBA. The intermediate stations were all built with white Suffolk brick and Yorkshire stone cornices. The internal layout was practical and well designed, and the exterior style was usually single-storeyed, with an Italianate or Doric appearance, but Horley was a two-storey design with a Tudor feel. The Brighton station was designed in 1839–40 and housed the railway company's headquarters, offices, and board-room. The buildings were in a dignified Italianate style, three storeys high, with an arcaded entrance. The platforms were covered by a saw-toothed roof 250 feet long. This is the only one of his stations still in use at the end of the twentieth century, but extensions have since obscured the original building.

Mocatta worked with the engineer of the London and Brighton Railway, John Urpeth Rastrick (1780–1856), on his greatest work, the Ouse Valley Viaduct, north of Haywards Heath. This otherwise monotonous brick structure, 491 yards long and 96 feet high, and consisting of thirty-seven semicircular arches each spanning 30 feet, was ennobled by Mocatta's embellishments. He designed eight stone and brick pavilions, placing four at each end, two on each side of the line, and a stone balustrade which runs from end to end, punctuated every 30 feet with a safety refuge projecting beyond the balustrade. The design is simple yet exuberant and triumphant. Mocatta ceased to work for the railway in 1843, though in 1845 he made detailed drawings for a central London terminus in Farringdon Street (RIBA). He won the competition for the design of the London Fever Hospital, although his design was set aside in favour of a lesser one. He designed offices for Whiteknights Park, Reading (1844), Stowlangtoft Hall, Suffolk (1845), and the Imperial Insurance Company (1846).

On inheriting a fortune from his father in 1857 Mocatta retired from architectural practice and busied himself with philanthropic work, particularly for hospitals. He was a leader in the struggle for Jewish emancipation, a most active promoter of the Architects' Benevolent Society, a senior trustee of Sir John Soane's Museum, and a fellow of the Society of Antiquaries. He died on 1 May 1882 at his home, 32 Prince's Gate, South Kensington, London, and was buried at the Kingsbury Road Jewish cemetery on 5 May. ADRIAN VAUGHAN

Sources D. Cole, 'Mocatta's stations for the Brighton railway', *Journal of Transport History*, 3 (1957–8), 149–57 · D. Cardozo and P. Goodman, *Think and thank: The Montefiore Synagogue and College, 1833–1933* (1933), 25–6 · *The Builder*, 42 (1882), 577 · *Dir. Brit. archs.*, 626–7 · *CGPLA Eng. & Wales* (1882) · private information (2004) [Mocatta family] · C. F. D. Marshall, *A history of the southern railway*, 1936; new rev. edn (1968) · T. Carder, *The encyclopaedia of Brighton* (1990) · E. Jamilly, 'Anglo-Jewish architects, and architecture in the 18th and 19th centuries', *Transactions of the Jewish Historical Society of England*, 18 (1953–5), 127–41, esp. 134

Archives RIBA BAL, drawings catalogue; nomination papers; specifications and note and sketch book

Wealth at death £58,365 14s. 8d.: probate, 15 June 1882, *CGPLA Eng. & Wales*

Mocatta, Edgar (1879–1957). *See under* Mocatta family (*per.* 1671–1957).

Mocatta, Frederic David (1828–1905), philanthropist, born in London on 16 January 1828, was the elder son in a family of two sons and two daughters of Abraham *Mocatta (1797–1880) [*see under* Mocatta family], a banker.

Frederic David Mocatta (1828–1905), by Nadar

His father was an active member of the movement in England in 1840 for reform of Jewish worship; his mother, Miriam (*d.* 1878), was the daughter of Gabriel Israel Brandon. The Mocatta family were Jews driven from the Iberian peninsula in 1492; the family moved to England from the Netherlands about 1670. Mocatta's great-grandfather, Abraham *Mocatta (1730–1800) [*see under* Mocatta family] founded the firm of Mocatta and Goldsmid, bullion brokers to the Bank of England.

Mocatta was educated at home by private tutors, among them the Hebrew scholar Albert Löwy; he was also taught Hebrew and Latin by his father, and eventually spoke five or six languages. About 1843 he entered the family business, from which he retired in 1874. In 1856 he married Mary Ada (1836–1905), the daughter of Frederick David Goldsmid, MP for Honiton, and the sister of Sir Julian Goldsmid.

Childless and enjoying a large income, Mocatta was best known as a philanthropist. The charitable causes to which he devoted himself were numerous and wide-ranging in character. He was a leading supporter of the Royal Society for the Prevention of Cruelty to Animals. Among the questions that engaged his constant attention were better housing for the working classes and the administration of charity in such a way as not to demoralize the poor. He was an active promoter and vice-president from its formation in 1869 of the Charity Organization Society, and was chairman from 1901 of the Charity Voting Reform Association, with whose attempts to abolish electioneering in charity administration he was in fullest sympathy. He was also interested in hospital and nursing work, and he liberally supported many voluntary hospitals in London.

To Jewish charities Mocatta devoted the greater part of his wealth and leisure. He was active in organizing the Board of Guardians for the Relief of the Jewish Poor (founded in 1859), and was chairman of a Jewish workhouse started in 1871, and reorganized in 1897 at Stepney as the Home for Aged Jews with himself as president; he also helped to form the Jews' Deaf and Dumb Home at Notting Hill in 1865. The situation of the Jews in eastern Europe engaged his constant attention. He was vice-president of the Anglo-Jewish Association, a member of the Alliance Israélite in Paris, and a member of the Romanian committee which was founded in London in 1872 to watch over the affairs of the Romanian Jews. In 1882 he took active part in administering the Mansion House Fund for assisting Jews to leave Russia.

However, like many members of the Anglo-Jewish upper-middle classes at this time, Mocatta, though sympathizing with the plight of his persecuted co-religionists under tsarist rule, had no wish to encourage large numbers of them to settle in Britain. In April 1885, when vice-president of the Jewish Board of Guardians, he was instrumental in obtaining the closure of a makeshift 'home for the outcast poor' run by a Polish-Jewish refugee in London's East End, declaring that such a refuge would encourage the immigration of 'helpless Foreigners' and was therefore 'not a desirable institution'. Two years later, fearful at the spread of socialism among the Russian-Jewish proletariat in the capital, Mocatta joined Samuel Montagu in an attempt to suppress the production of the Yiddish socialist paper *Arbeter Fraint* by bribing the printer and compositor to sabotage its production.

Mocatta enthusiastically promoted education, especially that of the Jewish poor. He also encouraged Jewish literature and research, defraying some or all of the expenses of many important publications, including Leopold Zunz's two books *Zur Geschichte und Literatur* (1850) and *Literaturgeschichte der Synagogalen Poesie* (1855), Abraham Berliner's *Juden in Rom* (1893), and the English translation of Heinrich Graetz's *History of the Jews* (1891). A keen historian and antiquary, he was in 1887 president of the Anglo-Jewish Historical Exhibition at the Albert Hall, which led to the establishment of the Jewish Historical Society of England. He was president of the society in 1900. He published several works, notably *The Jews and the Inquisition* (1877), which was translated into German, Italian, and Hebrew, and *The Jews at the Present Time in their Various Habitations* (1888). He was elected FSA in 1889. From 1896 to 1904 he was chairman of the council of the West London Reform Synagogue. On 16 January 1898, his seventieth birthday, he was presented with a book containing signatures of the Empress Frederick and of 8000 other representatives of 250 public bodies to which he had given his support.

Mocatta died at 9 Connaught Place, Hyde Park, London,

on 16 January 1905, and was buried in the Dalston cemetery of the West London Synagogue. He was survived by his wife who died four months later. Mocatta left an unsettled estate of nearly £156,000, of which the Jewish Board of Guardians and the Charity Organization Society shared £110,000. His extensive book collection was bequeathed to the Mocatta Museum and Library, located from 1906 at University College, London, where it formed a foundation for Jewish studies.

M. EPSTEIN, *rev.* GEOFFREY ALDERMAN

Sources A. Mocatta, ed., *A memoir of F. D. Mocatta* (1911) · A. Mocatta, 'Frederic David Mocatta, 1828–1905', *Transactions of the Jewish Historical Society of England*, 23 (1969–70), 1–10 · G. Alderman, *Modern British Jewry* (1992) · *Jewish Chronicle* (20 Jan 1905) · *CGPLA Eng. & Wales* (1905)
Archives King's AC Cam., letters to Oscar Browning · UCL, Gaster MSS
Likenesses Nadar, cabinet photograph, NPG [*see illus.*] · photograph, UCL · photograph, repro. in *Jewish Chronicle*, 11
Wealth at death £155,706 15*s.* 4*d.*: probate, 14 Feb 1905, *CGPLA Eng. & Wales*

Mocatta, Moses (*d.* 1693). *See under* Mocatta family (*per.* 1671–1957).

Mochtae (*d.* 535). *See under* Meath, saints of (*act. c.*400–*c.*900).

Mocket, Richard (1577–1618), writer on religion and college head, was born at Dorchester in Dorset. He graduated BA from Brasenose College, Oxford, on 16 February 1596, and was elected fellow of All Souls in 1598, proceeding MA on 5 April 1600, BD on 23 April 1607, and DD on 26 July 1609. George Abbot, bishop of London and from April 1611 archbishop of Canterbury, presented Mocket to the London rectories of St Clement, Eastcheap, on 29 December 1610, and of St Michael, Crooked Lane, on 1 October 1611. He resigned St Clement's before 9 December 1611, and St Michael's before 17 June 1614. He held the rectories of Newington, Oxfordshire, and of West Tarring, Sussex, from 1614, and of Monks Risborough, Buckinghamshire, from 1615 until his death. He was for some time domestic chaplain to Abbot, and one of the king's commissioners concerning ecclesiastical affairs. From March 1610 to June 1614 he was actively employed in licensing books for entry at Stationers' Hall. On 12 April 1614, probably through the influence of Abbot, the college's visitor, he was elected warden of All Souls College, Oxford.

Mocket is generally taken to have been the author of a short tract, *Deus et rex* (1615), translated as *God and the King* (1615). The work was a dialogue in defence of the oath of allegiance, and remained an authoritative summary of the church's political theology into the eighteenth century. King James in a proclamation of 8 November 1615 ordered 'the universall dispersing, and teaching of all Youth in the Saide Booke'. The privy council of Scotland issued a similar command in June 1616, and the Aberdeen general assembly decreed in August 1616 that all children should learn this 'catechism' by heart. A special edition was printed for Scottish use. However, there is no firm evidence for Mocket's authorship. In 1616, in London, Mocket published *Doctrina et politia ecclesiae Anglicanae*, which contains Latin translations of John Jewel's *Apology*, Nowell's *Catechism*, the Thirty-Nine Articles (with summaries of the homilies), the prayer book, and the ordinal. To these he added a work of his own entitled *Disciplina et politia ecclesiae Anglicanae*, which was a general view of ecclesiastical jurisdiction in the English church, mainly prepared for the information of foreigners. The manuscript of the work, now in Lambeth Palace Library, was dedicated to Archbishop Abbot. The book offended the king, and by public edict was condemned and burned in 1617, earning Mocket a reputation as 'the roasted Warden' (C. G. Robertson, *All Souls College*, 1899, 97). There is no good contemporary evidence to indicate the reasons for the king's displeasure, but Fuller considered that Mocket suffered on account of his patron Abbot, 'against whom many bishops began then to combine' (Fuller, 5.444–6). Heylyn, while condemning the writer's 'little knowledge in the constitution of the church' and his bias 'towards those of Calvin's platform' (Heylyn, *Cyprianus*, 75–6), was of the opinion that the real offence was the omission of the first clause in the translation of the twentieth of the Thirty-Nine Articles, which runs: 'The Church hath power to decree rites or ceremonies, and authority in controversies of faith.' It is also said that Mocket's extracts from the homilies were made so as to support the views of Abbot, and that as a translator he had usurped the duties of a commentator, while James Montagu, bishop of Winchester, resented the order in which the bishoprics were enumerated. Recent research suggests that the work did introduce minor alterations into the texts translated, perhaps to avoid for an international audience the impression that the Church of England was dependent on the royal prerogative. The 1616 edition of the *Doctrina et politia ecclesiae Anglicanae* was reprinted in 1617.

Mocket died, probably at All Souls, on 6 July 1618, allegedly from disappointment at the reception of his book, and was buried in the chapel of All Souls College, where there remains a marble memorial tablet.

BERTHA PORTER, *rev.* GLENN BURGESS

Sources Wood, *Ath. Oxon.*, new edn, 2.232–3 · register of Archbishop Abbot, LPL, Lambeth Palace MS · BL, Lansdowne MS 983 · Foster, *Alum. Oxon.* · Arber, *Regs. Stationers*, vol. 3 · Whiteway's chronology, CUL, MS Dd. xi. 73 · T. Fuller, *The church history of Britain*, ed. J. S. Brewer, new edn, 6 vols. (1845), vol. 5, pp. 444–6 · P. Heylyn, *Cyprianus Anglicus* (1668), 75–6 · P. Heylyn, *Examen historicum* (1659), 185–7 · R. Mocket, *Doctrina et politia ecclesiae Anglicanae*, ed. M. A. Screech (1995) · J. F. Larkin and P. L. Hughes, eds., *Stuart royal proclamations*, 2 vols. (1973–80), vol. 1, pp. 355–6 · *Reg. PCS*, 1st ser., 10.521–2, 530–31, 534–8, 598–60
Archives All Souls Oxf. · LPL, MS 178

Mocket, Thomas (*c*.1602–1670?), ejected minister and religious controversialist, was born in Kent of unknown parents. He matriculated from Queens' College, Cambridge, in the Easter term of 1622, graduated BA early in 1626, and proceeded MA in 1631 (incorporated at Oxford in July 1639). From an unknown date he ministered to the people of Reigate, Surrey, until in 1633, in his first experience of what he later termed 'the hard dealings of the prelates',

he was compelled to move (Mocket, *Gospell Duty*, dedication). For a time he was chaplain to the earl of Bridgewater, lord president of the council of the marches, and, doubtless through Bridgewater's patronage, was preacher at Newport, Monmouthshire (until forced out in 1639), and vicar of Holt, Denbighshire (until removed, probably late in 1642).

While still at Holt, Mocket identified himself with the cause of parliament and with the presbyterians. His *The Churches Troubles and Deliverance*, printed by parliamentarian order dated 21 July 1642 and dedicated, among others, to Sir Richard Newport, Margaret, Lady Bromley, and Sir Edward Broughton, encouraged God's people to persevere in the context of the outbreak of 'the fire of civil dissension'. His *The national covenant … wherein … the severall parts of the late protestation are proved to be grounded in religion and reason* (1642) was dedicated to the House of Commons, which was exhorted to continue the work of reformation. It registered approval of all the key religious and political legislation of the previous two years and urged the ejection of 'dumb and scandalous ministers', the eradication of the church hierarchy, and the removal of the liturgy and unnecessary ceremonies.

On 5 April 1643 Mocket was admitted as rector of Gilston, Hertfordshire, following the sequestration of his predecessor. Further systematic apologies for religious and political innovation followed in *A View of the Solemn League and Covenant* and *The Covenanters Looking-Glasse*, both published in 1644. In 1646 he was a signatory to the petition of Hertfordshire ministers for the retention of tithes. His *A New Catechisme* (1647) included explanation of the new 'directions concerning suspension from the Lord's Supper'. By 17 April 1648, when he wrote the dedication to *Gospell Duty and Dignity: a Discourse of the Duty of Christians and their Privileges by Christ* (1648), he had become alarmed by threats to the new order. Addressing his 'Dearly Beloved Friends and Allies' in Kent, Surrey, Shropshire, Staffordshire, Cheshire, and Denbighshire, he declared his support for the recent 'Testimony' of the London ministers in favour of the covenant and for the Westminster assembly proposals on church government, and his 'detestation of the abominable mungrell toleration' (Mocket, *Gospell Duty*, A2). The text itself discussed all the things from which the Christian should distance himself 'for Christ'; all 'externall church privileges' were to be eschewed and the importance of baptism was downplayed. A similar austerity is evident in *Christmas, the Christians Grand Feast* (1651), which discussed the heathen roots of Christian holy days and the gluttony and profaneness that had accompanied them. Endorsing official policy in the matter, Mocket encouraged the 'truly conscientious Christian' (p. 24) to practise instead sanctification of the sabbath, obedience, godliness, and charity.

Little is known of Mocket's later career. In 1654 he served as an assistant to the Hertfordshire commission for settling the ministry. At the Restoration the sequestered vicar of Gilston, Christopher Webb, was reinstated. Mocket seems to have remained in some ministerial capacity in the same county for during an episcopal visitation of 1665, when he was described as 'of Sawbridgeworth', he was admonished 'to exercise his priestly office according to the laws established and to conform himself before Michaelmas next' (*Calamy rev.*, 351). His final work, *Christian Advice to Old and Young* (1671), dedicated to the countess of Exeter and calling to remembrance his early chaplaincy to her father, Bridgewater, is in the same vein as its predecessors. A very lengthy preface addressed to 'Relations, Friends and Acquaintance' from various counties laments that 'We live in an Age, in which the damning sin of unbelief and Atheism is much more frequent then (I think) in any Age heretofore amongst Christians' (Mocket, *Christian Advice*, A3) and sets out to prove that there is a God. The frontispiece has a portrait of the author in 1670, but it is probable that he died that year, and before publication; this is certainly the implication of the endorsement of the portrait by the publisher, Edward Brewster, who claims to have 'knowne him many yeares', and the 'sculptor', T. Cross.   VIVIENNE LARMINIE

Sources *Calamy rev.*, 351 · Venn, *Alum. Cant.* · *The nonconformist's memorial ... originally written by ... Edmund Calamy*, ed. S. Palmer, 2 (1775), 303 · T. Mocket, *Gospell duty and dignity: a discourse of the duty of Christians and their privileges by Christ* (1648) · T. Mocket, *Christian advice to old and young* (1671)
Likenesses T. Cross, line engraving, 1670?, BM, NPG; repro. in Mocket, *Christian advice* · pen-and-ink drawing, NPG

Model [*née* Sichel], **Alice Isabella** (1856–1943), philanthropist and family welfare worker, was born on 13 November 1856 at 27 Priory Road, Kilburn, London, the daughter of Gustavus Sichel, an Australian merchant, and his wife, Henriette Goldschmidt. A middle-class family, they resided in Hampstead. Alice married Louis Model when she was twenty-four; the couple had no children, and Model devoted her life to social work. One of Anglo-Jewry's most forward-thinking and respected women philanthropists, Model was one of the first two women appointed to the Jewish Board of Guardians in 1900. She was involved with Highbury Home for Friendless Children, the Babies' Hostel, and the Jewish Health Organisation, and was honorary secretary, president, and chair of the Union of Jewish Women.

Model founded the Sick Room Helps Society (SRHS) in 1895, a pioneer organization in home health care and the nucleus of the Jewish Maternity Hospital, later the Bearsted Memorial Hospital. Based on a plan from Frankfurt, the SRHS reduced the difficulties of sickness among poor Jews by providing a 'help' to assist with domestic and child-care duties. In most cases district nurses could not undertake these responsibilities, and often friends and relatives were unable to provide such assistance. In part a response to national concerns over infant mortality, the SRHS kept mothers from returning to work too quickly after childbirth. The 'helps' also prevented the burden of the household from falling on fathers, which often resulted in lost work time and complete destitution. The SRHS assisted confinement cases, hospital cases, and in ordinary sickness. They took over investigation of maternity cases from the Jewish Board of Guardians in 1900.

Numerous private and state agencies modelled their programme on the SRHS.

Model also established the Jewish Day Nursery (later the Alice Model Nursery) in 1897 at 35 Shepherd Street in Spitalfields. The facilities quickly proved too small; the day nursery leased new accommodations from the London Hospital in May 1900, at 23 New Road; the crèche took possession of the building in 1901 and remained there until 1943. The nursery largely served widows, enabling them to work and thus eliminating their total dependence on charity. Model believed that institutions such as the nursery were particularly important during the First World War, saved future generations of men, and developed the characters of the children. Model was proud of the nursery's commitment to the latest methods such as those promoted by the open-air school movement. During good weather, infants slept on the balcony. Model favoured the establishment of a school for Jewish mothers. Many poor Jewish mothers felt uncomfortable attending English schools and often faced language barriers.

Committed to scientific charity and training of philanthropic workers, Alice Model advanced this work through the Union of Jewish Women. Like many late nineteenth-century reformers she favoured self-help and the elimination of pauperizing gifts. She regularly recruited volunteers, believing that leisured Jews had an obligation to the state to assist co-religionists and create good Jews. She was pleased at the growing recognition of the value of women's work and believed that men and women each had distinct spheres of activity.

Model also gave time to numerous local and national causes. In 1912 the London county council (LCC) named Model to the provisional committees for London dealing with the National Health Insurance Act. In 1914 she and Otto Warburg represented the LCC on the London insurance committee. During the First World War she was one of the representatives from the Jewish Board of Guardians to the central committee, which administered the National Relief Fund. In the 1920s Model sat on the maternity and child welfare committee for Stepney and the London Federation of Infant Welfare Centres. On her seventieth birthday Alice Model's admirers celebrated her lifetime's achievement aiding women and children in a personal tribute. Recognized for her singleness of purpose and selflessness, she was open to new ideas. She was a leader in every effort to improve pre-natal and post-natal care.

In 1933 Alice Model, then in her seventies, joined the Jewish Refugees' Committee, and assisted refugees from Nazi Germany who needed housing, working until it became physically impossible. In 1935 Model was appointed MBE after forty years of involvement in maternal and infant welfare. She died at her home, 33 Belsize Park, London, on 26 April 1943. Her funeral took place at West London (Reform) Synagogue and a memorial service was held at the Liberal Jewish Synagogue, St John's Wood.

SUSAN L. TANANBAUM

Sources *Jewish Chronicle* (1897–1943) · *Jewish Chronicle* (30 April 1943) · L. Marks, *Model mothers: Jewish mothers and maternity provision in east London, 1870–1939* (1994) · E. C. Black, *The social politics of Anglo-Jewry, 1880–1920* (1988) · *The Times* (30 April 1943) · L. G. Kuzmack, *Woman's cause: the Jewish woman's movement in England and the United States, 1881–1933* (1990) · b. cert. · d. cert. · G. D. Black, 'Health and medical care of the Jewish poor in the East End of London, 1880–1939', PhD diss., University of Leicester, 1987
Likenesses portrait, repro. in *Jewish Chronicle* (19 March 1909)
Wealth at death £8212 6s. od.: probate, 28 July 1943, *CGPLA Eng. & Wales*

Modern Methuselah, the. *See* Jenkins, Henry (*d.* 1670).

Moders, Mary. *See* Carleton, Mary (1634x42–1673).

Modestus [St Modestus] (*d. c.*763), missionary, is, despite his name, believed to have been Irish since he was sent by the Irishman Virgilius (*d.* 784), bishop of Salzburg, to preach to the Slavs in Carinthia, where he stayed until his death. Other Irishmen in the circle of Virgilius are associated with the eighth-century Céli Dé reform movement, an ascetic movement in the Irish church. Modestus was accompanied on his mission by the priests Watto, Reginbert, Cozharius, and Latinus and the deacon Ekehard, according to the *Conversio Bagoariorum et Carantanorum*. He is believed to have been an archdeacon; that is, he assisted a bishop with a fixed see, although the *Conversio*, the *Vita Gebehardi*, and the late twelfth- or early thirteenth-century *Excerptum de Karentanis* call him a bishop, while the *Excerptum* states that he was consecrated by Virgilius under Pippin, king of the Franks (*d.* 768). The confraternity book of St Peter's, Salzburg, does not include his name. His mission probably began between 755, the date of Virgilius's consecration as bishop, and 757, the date of the death of Pope Stephen II. Modestus died *c.*763 and after his death the Slavs reverted to paganism.

According to the *Conversio Bagoariorum et Carantanorum*, Modestus was sent to ordain priests and consecrate churches. Three of the churches he founded are mentioned by name in the *Conversio*. The first was St Maria Saal; the second the *civitas Liburnia* (either Lurnfeld, near Spittal, on the Drau or St Peter in Holz), the third is described as *ad Undrimas* and its location is uncertain—either Ingering, near Knittelfeld, or Aichfeld, west of the Pölshalsplateau and east of St Margaret near Knittelfeld. A sarcophagus in St Maria Saal Church, regarded as Modestus's, and placed beneath a Carolingian altar, was opened in 1953 and a lead cup was found, as well as the remains of three different bodies. No life of Modestus is included in the *Acta sanctorum* but his feast day is believed to fall on 5 December. Modestus is revered in Carinthia as the local saint and current traditions about him indicate his continuing status in the religious life of the region. LUNED MAIR DAVIES

Sources H. Wolfram, ed., *Conversio Bagoariorum et Carantanorum* (Vienna, 1979) · 'Vita et miracula sanctorum Juvavensium Virgilii', ed. W. Wattenbach, [*Historiae aevi Salici*], ed. G. H. Pertz, MGH Scriptores [folio], 11 (Stuttgart, 1854), 84–103 · 'Gesta archiepiscoporum Salisburgensium', ed. W. Wattenbach, [*Historiae aevi Salici*], ed. G. H. Pertz, MGH Scriptores [folio], 11 (Hanover, 1854), 1–103 [esp. the anonymous life of St Gebehard] · J. Wodka, *Kirche in Österreich* (1959) · H. Wolfram, *Die Geburt Mitteleuropas* (1987) · H.-D. Kahl, 'Das Fürstentum Karantanien und die Anfänge seiner Christianierung', *Karantanien und der Alpe-Adria-Raum*, ed. G. Hodl and J. Grabmayer (1993) · H. Dopsch, *Das Erzbistum Salzburg und der Alpe-Adria-Raum im Frühmittelalter* (1992) · A. Maier, *Kärnter Kirchengeschichte* (1979) · H.-D. Kahl, 'Zur Rolle der Iren im östlichen Vorfeld des agilolfingischen und frühkarolingischen Baiern', *Die Iren und Europa im früheren Mittelalter*, ed. H. Löwe, 1 (Stuttgart, 1982), 375–98

Modwenna, St, of Burton (*fl.* before **12th cent.**). *See under* Moninne (*d.* 517).

Modyford, Sir James, baronet (1618–1673), merchant and colonial agent in Jamaica, was born in Exeter; he was the younger brother of Sir Thomas *Modyford. Having been apprenticed to a Levant company merchant, he spent part of his youth in Constantinople, where he learned Turkish. On his return to London he appears to have settled in Chelsea as a merchant. In 1657 he married Elizabeth Stanning (1630–1734), the daughter of Sir Nicholas Stanning of Maristow, Devon, with whom he had four children—Mary, Elizabeth, Grace, and Thomas.

Under the Commonwealth Modyford was employed in Ireland, presumably through the interest of his cousin George Monck, first duke of Albemarle. He was appointed 'Clerk of the first fruits in Ireland' on 18 October 1660, was knighted about the same time, and on 18 February 1661 was created a baronet in consideration of his having 'liberally and generously provided and sustained thirty men for three years for the care and defence of Ireland' (patent roll, 13 Chas. II, pt 1, no. 2).

After the Restoration Modyford became interested in Atlantic trade, perhaps partly because his brother became a successful sugar planter in the 1650s. In 1663 he was listed as a shareholder in the newly formed Company of Royal Adventurers trading in Africa, for which his brother was agent in Barbados. There is evidence that he visited Jamaica (captured in 1655), which was seen as both market and transhipment point for slaves to Spanish colonies, as he wrote a survey and description of the island. When his brother Thomas was appointed governor of Jamaica in 1664, Modyford became his agent and lobbyist in London and obtained a five-year licence to send convicted felons to Jamaica as indentured servants.

Meanwhile, Modyford was seeking office. In June 1666 Albemarle recommended him for the embassy in Constantinople without success, but in November he was appointed lieutenant-governor of Providence Island, or Santa Catalina, which had been seized by a group of Jamaican privateers. The precarious nature of the position may explain why he left his wife and family in London when he embarked for the Caribbean. In fact, when, after a long delay in Barbados, he arrived in Jamaica on 15 July 1667 he found that Providence had been recaptured by the Spaniards. His brother, the governor of Jamaica, did all he could to compensate. He appointed Modyford deputy governor of the island, with a salary of £1000 per annum, governor of Port Royal, and judge of the Admiralty, which must have given him ample opportunity for profit as, despite the treaty of Madrid between England and Spain in 1667, this was the period known as the heyday of the buccaneers and famous for the exploits of Henry Morgan and others. Modyford could complain only that he did not have more cash for purchasing prize goods, which enabled those with cash 'to double nay treble their money without any hazard' (Westminster Abbey Muniments, 11922).

Modyford acted as agent, or attorney, for a number of London merchants, including the owners of the privateer *Lilly*, which was engaged in Morgan's famous assault on Panama. His surviving correspondence with Sir Andrew King provides a vivid picture of business conditions in Port Royal, with detailed discussion of the prospects for peaceful trade with the Spanish colonies and a sharp insight into the difficulties faced by London merchants entrusting business to agents at long distances.

Modyford profited sufficiently from the fruits of office and trade to build up a valuable estate on the island. He bought a small cocoa plantation with seventeen slaves almost as soon as he arrived, and in 1670 he held 530 acres in St Andrews parish, 1000 acres in St John's, and 3500 acres in St Katherine's. After the second treaty of Madrid in 1670, promising peace and friendship in America between England and Spain, the king had high hopes that peaceful trade would follow if the terms were adhered to, and Thomas Modyford was replaced as governor, recalled to England, and placed in the Tower of London. Meanwhile, James Modyford was joined by his wife and, although his offices appear to have lapsed, continued to pursue his business activities on the island and remained on the elected ruling council. In 1672, when the Royal African Company was re-formed, he requested Andrew King to 'procure the new Royal Company's Negro ships to be consigned to our family here' (Westminster Abbey Muniments, 11348).

Modyford died in Port Royal, Jamaica, in January 1673, shortly before the birth of his son, Thomas, and was buried at Half-Way Tree, St Andrews, on 13 January. Thomas died in 1678, and the estate passed to James Modyford's three daughters. An indenture of 1684 records that Peter Heywood (later governor of Jamaica), who married Grace, purchased the shares of Elizabeth and Mary for £650 each.　　　　　　　J. K. LAUGHTON, *rev.* NUALA ZAHEDIEH

Sources A. P. Thornton, 'The Modyfords and Morgan: letters from Sir James Modyford on the affairs of Jamaica, 1667–1672, in the Muniments of Westminster Abbey', *Jamaica Historical Review*, 2 (1952), 36–60 · *CSP col.*, vols. 6–7 · V. L. Oliver, ed., *Caribbeana*, 1–6 (1909–19) · 'A journal kept by Coll. William Beeston from his 1st coming to Jamaica, 1655–80', BL, Add. MS 12430, fols. 41–75 · 'Articles of agreement had and made this 3rd day of October 1684', Institute of Jamaica, Kingston, Jamaica, MS 1316 · Deeds, Old Series I, Island RO, Spanish Town, Jamaica [fols. 44, 47, 78, 82] · Westminster Abbey Muniments, 11348, 11351, 11417, 11683, 11686, 11689, 11691, 11693, 11697–702, 11704, 11906–40 · 'Survey of Jamaica', 1670, PRO, CO 138/1, fol. 66 · BL, Long MSS, Genealogical and Heraldic, Add. MS 27968, fol. 30 · *IGI* · admon, PRO, PROB 6/48, fol. 98*r*

Archives Westminster Abbey Muniment Room and Library, letters from Jamaica | Westminster Abbey Muniments, 11348, 11351, 11417, 11683, 11686, 11689, 11691, 11693, 11697–702, 11704, 11906–40

Modyford, Sir Thomas, first baronet (*c.*1620–1679), planter and colonial governor, was the seventh child and

eldest son of John Modyford, alderman and mayor of Exeter, and his wife, Maria, daughter of Thomas Walker, alderman of Exeter. He trained at Lincoln's Inn and worked as a barrister until the outbreak of the civil war, in which he served as a colonel in the king's army. The opportunism which marked his entire career was soon apparent. Captured at Exeter, where some royalists claimed that his duplicity had led to the fall of the city, he volunteered to leave England for the West Indies.

Barbados planter and governor Modyford had married Elizabeth (*d.* 1668), daughter of Lewin Palmer of Devon, about 1640 and he left England with a wife and young family. They arrived in Barbados in 1647, soon after the introduction of sugar cultivation. Although the planters were still in the learning stage of this complex business, the potential for very high profits was apparent. Modyford's companion, Richard Ligon, remarked that sugar 'will make it [the island] one of the richest spots of earth under the sun' (Ligon, 85–6). Land prices had soared and labour was in short supply. Modyford was advised that, as he had goods and credit, he should buy into an existing enterprise rather than embark on the long and expensive task of building a plantation from scratch. He agreed to pay £7000 (£1000 down and the rest in instalments) for a half share in William Hilliard's plantation (which had been worth £400 in 1640) with his brother-in-law, Thomas Kendal, a London grocer, as a third partner. The estate, containing 500 acres (200 acres in sugar, ninety-six slaves, twenty-eight servants, livestock, and buildings), was among the largest on the island and, on Hilliard's return to England, the young and inexperienced Modyford took over the management of the complex business, which involved agricultural and industrial operations, as well as managing a large alien workforce. The difficulties were highlighted in the Modyford family's first year on the plantation when a slave rebellion was narrowly averted by information given by Modyford's favourite slave. Sugar planting required a large supply of capital, skill, and courage, and Ligon, who spent three years on the plantation with him, remarked that 'to do him right, I hold Colonel Modyford as able, to undertake and perform such a charge, as any I knew' (ibid., 23). Ligon also reported Modyford's ambitious resolution 'not to set his face for England, til he had made his voyage, and employment there, worth him an £100,000 sterling; and all by this sugar plant' (ibid., 82).

As a major landowner and trained lawyer Modyford was soon drawn into the business of governing Barbados. During the 1640s, when the English authorities were distracted by civil war, the island enjoyed considerable autonomy, but after the execution of Charles I in 1649 there were unwelcome signs that the home government would try to tighten control. In 1651 leading islanders, including Modyford, who was a member of the council, signed a declaration in support of Charles II. In response parliament dispatched Sir George Ayscue with a naval squadron to bring the colonists to heel and it was mainly through Modyford's defection, or treachery, that Lord Willoughby, the royal governor, was obliged to yield. In

January 1652 the new governor, Searle, dismissed Modyford from the council, perhaps because he was associated with the strong home rule sentiment in the assembly, but after petitioning Oliver Cromwell he was restored.

Modyford did all he could to obtain political preferment. Cromwell consulted him about attacking the Spanish Indies in 1654, and Modyford's desire to please may explain his optimistic assessment of English strength and Spanish weakness. Both contributed to Cromwell's unrealistic expectations and the poor planning and execution of the 'western design'. The English fleet met obstruction and hostility at Barbados, rather than the expected help, and went on to a sound defeat at Hispaniola before the capture of the smaller island of Jamaica in 1655. However, Modyford's lobbying secured his appointment as governor of Barbados in April 1660 and he made a triumphant speech announcing himself the first of a new order of 'planter governors' (minutes of council of Barbados, 31 July 1660, PRO, CO 31/1). He attempted to survive the Restoration by again changing his colours and proclaiming Charles as king. Although Modyford was widely denounced for his earlier treachery, his kinsman General George Monck, who had helped engineer the return of the king, was able to secure a full pardon for Modyford's betrayal of the royalist cause at Exeter, Barbados, and subsequent services to the Commonwealth. However, Modyford lost his place as governor and, after resigning, he was elected speaker of the assembly.

Modyford continued to build his fortune and, in addition to planting, he became involved in the slave trade. On the formation of the Royal African Company in 1663 he became its agent in Barbados and reported that high profits could be made by selling slaves to the Spaniards. The king and the duke of York, who were heavily involved in the African Company, were anxious to promote the commerce and Jamaica was well placed to serve as a base. When the king decided to keep Cromwell's prize he allowed the islanders to continue their policy of trading with the Spaniards 'by force', but behaviour which alienated potential customers was now seen as a liability. Modyford, with his experience of life in the Caribbean and the slave trade, seemed well suited to the task of putting the island economy on a new footing and, with support from Monck (now duke of Albemarle), in February 1664 he was appointed governor of Jamaica and made a baronet. After spending seventeen years in Barbados and playing a major role in shaping the infant settlement Modyford transferred his family to Jamaica, England's frontier colony, persuading about 800 planters to accompany him with promises of free passage, free land, and a bright future in the thinly populated infant settlement. The move was marked by a personal tragedy as Modyford's eldest son, John, was lost at sea when going back to fetch his mother from Barbados.

Governor of Jamaica Modyford acted quickly to secure the material rewards of office. The former champion of planter rights took tight control of government. The council was culled and packed with his own supporters.

The assembly, called after five months, was marked by bitter feuding between the governor's party and earlier settlers trying to protect their own interests. The session ended with a squabble in which a member was killed, shaping a lasting factionalism in the island. Apart from a brief meeting in 1665 the assembly was not convened again during Modyford's rule. Meanwhile, patent officers such as Thomas Lynch, the provost marshal, were turned out and the posts were divided between Modyford himself (who took the post of chief justice, 'for want of a better lawyer'), his family, and friends (including a number of fellow west country men). Lynch, who played a prominent part in the early settlement of Jamaica, left the island after complaining to Lord Arlington that Modyford 'would have none to shine in this hemisphere but himself and his son' (Lynch to Arlington, 12 Feb 1665, PRO, CO 1/19, fol. 31).

Following the king's instructions to promote better relations with the Spaniards, Modyford issued a proclamation against privateering on 11 June 1664, four days after his arrival in Jamaica, but by the end of the month his usual pragmatism prevailed and he revised his position. Jamaica was thinly settled, with a population of under 5000, and scarcely planted as the English conquerors had inherited little from the Spaniards. About 1500 privateers, of different nationalities, were based at the island, using Port Royal to fit their ships and sell their prize, and providing lucrative business for merchants and craftsmen. A suppression of plunder would have caused economic depression and exposed Jamaica's own infant trade to danger, as many of the marauders would have transferred operations elsewhere rather than abandon their careers. At the end of June Modyford wrote home that he 'thought it more prudent to do that by degrees and moderation which I once resolved to have executed suddenly and severely' (Modyford to Bennet, 30 June 1664, PRO, CO 1/18, fol. 177).

By August it was clear that Modyford was colluding with the privateers and had used his power as governor to purchase a share in one or more of their ships on very favourable terms. By 1665 the hopes of a peaceful slave trade with the Spaniards faded as the Dutch destroyed the Royal African Company's trading posts. War broke out, allowing Modyford to issue commissions against the Dutch, but the marauders were more interested in Spanish targets and, in February 1666, Modyford drew up a list of reasons for allowing war with Spain and began to issue letters of marque against her ships, putting a legal gloss on what was already happening in practice. Albemarle continued to defend the actions of his kinsman and Kendal, Modyford's brother-in-law and agent, lobbied the home authorities to authorize Modyford's privateering policy. The king did not go so far as to formally condone plunder, but as the promise of accessing Spanish colonial markets receded the arguments for force regained favour. In 1666, when news reached England that Mansfield, the admiral of the Jamaican privateers, had captured Providence Island, the king decided to appoint a governor, and dispatched Modyford's brother Sir James *Modyford to fill the post (although the Spaniards recaptured the island before Modyford's arrival and his older brother, always mindful of his family's interests, compensated by making him deputy governor of Jamaica and judge in the admiralty court). In 1668 the duke of York expressed further tacit approval of plunder when he sent the *Oxford* to take command of the privateers and ensure him a good share of the prize, although he was disappointed as the ship was blown up in an accident soon after arrival in the Caribbean. The royal brothers and various courtiers had investments in other ships although it proved difficult to extract a profit at a distance and most of the large prize money went to those on the spot.

With semi-official sanction Modyford pursued his pro-privateering policy with one short break until the end of his government in 1671, and the period, which witnessed the famous exploits of Henry Morgan at Portobello and Panama, is known as the heyday of the buccaneers. The governor showed skill in exerting firm control, and enforcing strict discipline, over a mob of 'wild, dissolute, tattered fellows' by instituting strict rules and imposing severe penalties for non-adherence ('Mr Worsley's discourse of the privateers of Jamaica', BL, Add. MS 11410, fol. 623). Modyford was positioned to take a large share of the profits of plunder, charging £20 for commissions, and extracting further dues on condemnation of prize, as well as securing favourable terms for investments in ships and adventures. But privateering provided a much wider circle with much needed cash, and armed protection, for the infant settlement's own commerce. According to the planter John Style, the island trade consisted almost entirely of 'plate, money, jewels and other things brought in [by the privateers] and sold cheap to the merchant' (Style to William Morrice, 14 Jan 1669, PRO, CO 1/24, fol. 19). The prize from Portobello alone amounted to £100,000, substantially more than the total value of Jamaica's annual agricultural output at the time. Port Royal's population grew threefold in the 1660s and trade flourished, and as governor and merchants prospered they invested surplus funds in the agricultural hinterland.

Ultimately the profits of planting Jamaica would far exceed those of plunder, but clearing and planting the land was a long, slow project, especially as the English inherited little from their Spanish predecessors. Many of the planters who went to Jamaica with Modyford took little capital and perished before they could establish themselves. Modyford eagerly patented and bought land, and by 1670 he had over 6000 acres (much in his son Thomas's name). In the early years he experimented with cocoa, grown by the earlier Spanish settlers and a new crop to the English, which promised to be highly profitable until it was destroyed by a mysterious blight in 1670–71. The governor reverted to sugar planting, with which he was thoroughly familiar, and by 1670 he had a fully operational sugar plantation in St Catherine's parish with 300 slaves and a watermill which he used to grind his neighbours' canes as well as his own. He was able to expand his labour supply on favourable terms as he continued to be involved in the slave trade and acted as agent for the African Company. Despite his patronage of plunder, he also managed to sell slaves in Spanish markets, a lucrative business, although in 1678 the Guinea Company complained that he retained most of the profits for himself and owed them almost £20,000.

Modyford's wealth and power allowed him a relatively luxurious lifestyle, although both comfort and entertaining diversions were in limited supply in an infant colony, and Modyford's wife died in 1668, leaving him to a bachelor life. Henry Morgan and other leading privateer commanders were friends as well as business partners, and their notorious drunkenness and debauchery drew disapproval from more puritanical observers. Nevil reported to the earl of Carlisle that apart from Modyford's 'avowed antimonarchical principles he is the openest atheist and most profest immoral liver in the world as your Lordship will soon discover if ever you have to do with him' ('The present state of Jamaica in a letter from Mr Nevil to the earl of Carlisle', 1677, BL, Add. MS 12429, fol. 152).

Imprisonment and last years In 1670 England and Spain signed the treaty of Madrid promising peace and friendship in the Indies. The Royal African Company, which had collapsed during the Dutch war, was reconstituted and again there were high hopes of securing Spanish custom. Modyford's policy of plunder and the news of Morgan's exploits at Panama in 1671 were an embarrassment. Furthermore, Modyford's kinsman Albemarle had died in 1669, depriving the governor of valuable protection at court. Thomas Lynch was dispatched to take over the government of Jamaica and promote peaceful relations with the Spaniards, and Modyford and Morgan were recalled to England, where they were imprisoned in the Tower of London until 1674. A lingering ambivalence towards the Spaniards was reflected in John Evelyn's reaction to Modyford's description of the exploit at Panama read in the council of trade and plantations: '[it] was very brave … Such an action had not been done since the famous Drake' (*The Diary of John Evelyn*, ed. G. de La Bédoyère, 1995, 184). Evelyn also records dining at Lord Berkeley's with the two men after their release and was impressed by their boastful stories. However, whereas Morgan found royal favour and was appointed deputy governor of Jamaica in 1674, Coventry reported that, perhaps on account of Modyford's earlier treachery, the king was very reluctant to receive Modyford in his presence or to allow him to return to Jamaica.

Modyford did return to Jamaica in 1675, although there are reports that he was not well received and failed in an attempt to gain election to the assembly, being widely hated for his earlier authoritarian style of government. However, Vaughan, the new governor, who was connected to Modyford by marriage, restored him to the position of chief justice and put his sons in other major positions of power, earning a reprimand from Coventry:

> If you manage not your kindness to that family with great discretion you will be far from doing them or yourself a kindness … this is a much readier way to offend the king than advance them and possibly treat such a jealousy as

may lessen that very good esteem the King hath of you, the king doth not intend the island shall be solely in the power of any one family or party and anyone to oppress the other or pursuing their private animosities to prejudice the publick … when you consider that by the places aforesaid you place almost all the power civil and military (but what you keep yourself) in one family you cannot think it unnatural for the King and council to make reflections. (Coventry to Vaughan, 30 July 1675, BL, Add. MS 25120, fol. 53)

Not only was Modyford able to regain much of the power he had in Jamaica but he also acted as agent for the African Company and the Dutch West India Company. It is unsurprising that in the 1670s Modyford continued to be known as the richest man in the island. He died in Jamaica on 1 September 1679 and was buried there the following day, beside his wife, in the church of St Catherine, Spanish Town. His son, Thomas, who had managed the family plantations while his father was in prison, survived his father by five weeks and his younger brother, Charles, succeeded to the baronetcy, which became extinct in the third generation. Modyford's daughter, Elizabeth, married Colonel Samuel Barry on 25 December 1676.

NUALA ZAHEDIEH

Sources state papers colonial, general series, PRO, CO 1/12–27 · state papers colonial, Jamaica, PRO, CO 138/1-2 · minutes of council of Barbados, PRO, CO 31/1 · *CSP col.*, vols. 5, 7 · F. Cundall, *Governors of Jamaica in the 17th century* (1936) · papers relating to the West Indies, 1654–82, BL, Add. MS 11410 · collection of tracts relating to Jamaica, 1603–95, BL, Add. MS 12429 · journal of William Beeston, BL, Add. MS 12430 · Coventry papers, vol. 4, BL, Add. MS 25120 · papers of the earl of Carlisle relating to Jamaica, BL, Sloane MS 2724 · R. Ligon, *A true and exact history of the island of Barbadoes* (1657) · G. A. Puckrein, *Little England: plantation society and Anglo-Barbadian politics, 1627–1700* (1984) · R. S. Dunn, *Sugar and slaves: the rise of the planter class in the English West Indies, 1624–1713* (Chapel Hill, 1972) · N. Zahedieh, 'Trade, plunder and economic development in early English Jamaica', *Economic History Review*, 2nd ser., 39 (1986), 205–22 · N. Zahedieh, 'A frugal, prudential, and hopeful trade', *Journal of Imperial and Commonwealth History*, 18 (1990), 145–68 · N. Zahedieh, 'The capture of the Blue Dove, 1664: policy, profits and protection in early English Jamaica', *West Indies accounts: essays on the history of the British Caribbean and the Atlantic economy*, ed. R. A. McDonald (Kingston, Jamaica, 1996) · DNB

Moels [Meulles, Molis], **Sir Nicholas de** (d. 1268/9), soldier and diplomat, was of uncertain origins. The fact that his landed interests came to be heavily concentrated in southwest England suggests an affiliation (albeit probably remote) with the Devon family of Molis or Mules, whose name derived from Meulles in Normandy (Calvados). Moels had entered the service of King John by 1215, probably as a soldier, and was rewarded with grants of rebels' lands; in 1217 he received the manor of Watlington, Oxfordshire, for his maintenance. He fought in Wales in 1223, and took part in the siege of Bedford Castle in 1224. But he also acted as a diplomat, going on embassies to Germany in 1225, and to France in 1228; by this time he was a knight of the king's household. In 1230 he accompanied Henry III to Brittany, and was sent to make contact with the king's mother and her husband, the count of La Marche. In 1232 he went to the Welsh marches, at first to negotiate with Llywelyn ab Iorwerth, and then to take command of St Briavel's Castle, Gloucestershire. In 1234 he was appointed sheriff of Devon, an office he exercised through a deputy, and also warden of the Channel Islands. But he held the latter post for only a few months, and went abroad again on embassy in October 1235. His standing at court is shown by his having been one of the sceptre-bearers at the coronation of Queen Eleanor on 20 January 1236. In 1239 he became sheriff of Yorkshire, and at about the same time had the custody of the vacant see of Durham, and of the lands of the earl of Lincoln and the Earl Warenne.

In 1241 Moels went abroad again, on an embassy to the count of Angoulême, and in the following year accompanied Henry III on his expedition to Gascony. He acted as one of the king's envoys to Louis IX of France, to deliver the charge of truce-breaking which justified the outbreak of hostilities. Then, as part of King Henry's arrangements for the government of Gascony, on 17 June 1243 he was appointed seneschal of the duchy, with a yearly salary of 1000 marks. Shortly afterwards there were serious outbreaks of disorder in the south of Gascony, and during his efforts to suppress them Moels appears to have suffered a sharp reverse before the castle of Gorro. His enthusiasm for his charge dwindled, so much so that on 8 September Henry promised that he could resign his office after a year if he chose. In the event his seneschalcy was reasonably successful. He made peace with the troublesome Arnaud Guillaume, lord of Gramont, and his rule was remembered as benevolent by the townsmen of Sault de Navailles. And when Thibault I, king of Navarre, invaded Gascony in November 1244, in pursuit of a claim to the *vicomté* of Béarn, Moels defeated him and drove him out of the duchy.

On 15 July 1245 Moels was relieved of the seneschalcy and returned to England; arrangements to pay the arrears of his salary went on being made for several years. On 17 August 1245 he was appointed to the custody of Carmarthen and Cardigan castles, and in the following year was responsible for one of the most notable feats of arms of Henry III's reign, when he led a force of predominantly Welsh troops from Carmarthen to Deganwy on Conwy Bay, forcing the surrender of the recalcitrant Maelgwn Fychan of Is Aeron, and in the process demonstrating that the uplands of north Wales were not impenetrable to English invaders. Moels remained in Wales until 1248, when he returned to Gascony, and from then until 1252 he was constantly involved in efforts first to support Simon de Montfort in Gascony, and later to mediate between Montfort and the Gascons. In January 1250, for instance, he was sent to arbitrate in the increasingly bitter dispute, and in June 1252 he was appointed a conservator of the truce to be made between the two sides. In 1253 he came back to Gascony with Henry III, and remained there throughout the king's sojourn; in February 1254 Henry ordered that Moels be paid £100, on the grounds that he had received nothing from the king during the past year.

In 1257 Moels was once more employed in Wales, but now as a diplomat rather than a soldier, negotiating a settlement with Maredudd ap Rhys Gryg of Deheubarth.

In the following year he became keeper of the Cinque Ports, and then sheriff of Kent, retaining the latter office until October 1259. Under the provisions of Oxford, drawn up in June and July 1258, he was entrusted with Rochester and Canterbury castles, but lost control of the Cinque Ports and Dover Castle. It seems clear that his loyalties remained with the king, but he was ageing by now, and when war once more threatened in the Welsh marches, in January 1263, Moels was instructed to send his son to the muster rather than attending himself. He was still alive in November 1268, when (about the 25th) he appeared before assize justices at Gloucester, but was dead by 24 June 1269, when his son Roger was given favourable terms for the payment of the relief due from his father's lands.

About 1230 Moels married Hawise, widow of John Boterel and coheir of James of Newmarket, and thereby became lord of half the barony of North Cadbury, Somerset. Also in 1230 he was given the royal demesne manors of Kingskerswell and Diptford in Devon, and with them the hundreds of Haytor and Stanborough. He received numerous other grants of lands from the king, in several counties, held a number of wardships, and was a regular recipient of gifts of wine, timber, and game. His eldest son, James, who as an infant was brought up with Prince Edward in Windsor Castle, predeceased Nicholas, who also had a daughter, Maud, who married Richard de Urtiaco, the heir to another Somerset barony, that of Stoke Trister. A loyal and able servant of Henry III, Nicholas de Moels enjoyed the rare accolade of a complimentary notice from Matthew Paris, who described him as 'a most energetic and circumspect knight' (Paris, *Chron.*, 4.255). HENRY SUMMERSON

Sources GEC, *Peerage*, new edn, 9.1–4 · Chancery records [PRO and RC] · F. Michel, C. Bémont, and Y. Renouard, eds., *Rôles Gascons*, 4 vols. (1885–1962), vol. 1 · Paris, *Chron.*, vols. 4–5 · W. W. Shirley, ed., *Royal and other historical letters illustrative of the reign of Henry III*, 2 vols., Rolls Series, 27 (1862–6) · H. C. M. Lyte, ed., *Liber feodorum: the book of fees*, 2 (1923) · C. E. H. Chadwyck-Healey and L. Landon, eds., *Somersetshire pleas*, 2, ed. L. Landon, Somerset RS, 36 (1923), 63 · A. Hughes, *List of sheriffs for England and Wales: from the earliest times to AD 1831*, PRO (1898); repr. (New York, 1963) · L. C. Loyd, *The origins of some Anglo-Norman families*, ed. C. T. Clay and D. C. Douglas, Harleian Society, 103 (1951), 65 · R. Studd, 'The marriage of Henry of Almain and Constance of Béarn', *Thirteenth century England: proceedings of the Newcastle upon Tyne conference* [Newcastle upon Tyne 1989], ed. P. R. Coss and S. D. Lloyd, 3 (1991), 161–77 · Y. Renouard, ed., *Bordeaux sous les rois d'Angleterre* (1965), 97 · J. Ellis, 'Gaston de Béarn: a study in Anglo-Gascon relations, 1229–1290', DPhil diss., U. Oxf., 1952 · R. F. Walker, 'The Anglo-Welsh wars, 1217–1267', DPhil diss., U. Oxf., 1954 · *Close rolls of the reign of Henry III*, 14, PRO (1938), 60

Möens, William John Charles (1833–1904), antiquary, born at Upper Clapton, London, on 12 August 1833, was second son and one of five children born to Jacob Bernelot Möens (*b.* 1796), a Dutch West Indies merchant who, born in Rotterdam, had settled in London, and who died at Tunbridge Wells on 19 July 1856. His mother was Susan Baker (*d.* 1876), daughter of William Wright of the City of London, solicitor. The family, of old standing in Flanders, derived its name from Mons in Hainault. A great-uncle, Adrian Möens (1757–1829), became a naturalized British

subject in 1809, and was from 1800 consul for the Netherlands in Bristol, where he died in 1829.

Möens, who was privately educated, began his career on the stock exchange, but soon retired to a house which he had bought at Boldre in Hampshire, devoting himself to travel, and later to antiquarian researches. In January 1865 he and his wife, Anne, sixth daughter of Thomas Warlters of Heathfield Park, Addington, whom he had married on 3 August 1863, went to Sicily and Naples. On 15 May, while returning from Paestum, he and another Englishman were suddenly captured near Battipaglia by a band of about thirty brigands. Möens, a pioneer of amateur photography, had been photographing the temples. Mrs Möens took refuge in the village, but Möens himself remained in the brigands' custody for over three months, during which time he was dragged over the mountains, ill clad and often hungry. Italian soldiers pursued the band, but it was only on 26 August that Möens was released, after paying a ransom of £5100. In 1866 he published a lively account of the episode in *English Travellers and Italian Brigands*. He devoted the profits from this popular book to building a school near his home at Boldre. In 1867 he bought the estate of Tweed in the same county. In 1869 he made a tour in his steam yacht *Cicada* and in 1876 he published *Through France and Belgium by River and Canal in the Steam Yacht Ytene* after a similar trip in 1875.

Möens was keenly interested in the New Forest. He made a study of forest law, and fought for the commoners' rights. By his support of the New Forest Pony Association he did much to improve the breed. He was a member of the Hampshire county council from its formation. He published pamphlets on the Allotment Acts in 1890 and Parish Councils Act in 1894.

Möens studied genealogy, especially that of Flemish families settled in England. In 1884 he edited *The Baptismal, Marriage, and Burial Registers of the Dutch Church, Austin Friars*. In 1885 he was one of twelve founders of the Huguenot Society of London, for which he read the first paper and edited the earliest publications. He edited volumes on French, Dutch, and Walloon churches in England for the Huguenot Society. He was vice-president in 1888, and president from 1899 to 1902. Elected FSA in 1886, he was appointed a local secretary, and was a member of the Hampshire Field Club and Archaeological Society. In 1893 he edited a volume on Hampshire allegations for marriage licences for the Harleian Society.

Möens died suddenly at his home at Tweed on 6 January 1904, and was buried at Boldre church. He left no children. By his will he divided his library between the Hampshire county council and the French Hospital, Victoria Park, London.

CHARLOTTE FELL-SMITH, *rev.* ELIZABETH BAIGENT

Sources Burke, *Gen. GB* · *The Athenaeum* (16 Jan 1904), 81 · *Proceedings of the Huguenot Society*, 7 (1901–4), 324–7

Likenesses portrait, repro. in *Proceedings of the Huguenot Society*

Wealth at death £6805 5*s.* 9*d.*: probate, 9 April 1904, CGPLA Eng. & Wales

Móenu (*d.* 572). See under Connacht, saints of (*act. c.*400–*c.*800).

Moeran, Ernest John Smeed (1894–1950), composer, was born on 31 December 1894 at the vicarage, Spring Grove, Heston, Brentford, Middlesex, the younger son of the Revd Joseph William Wright Moeran, vicar of St Mary's Church, Spring Grove, and his wife, Ada Esther Smeed Whall (*b.* 1866, *d.* in or after 1953). Joseph Moeran had been born in Dublin and was of partly Irish descent, while Esther came from King's Lynn, Norfolk.

Shortly after Moeran's birth the family moved to Bacton in Norfolk, and what was then a remote region of fen and reed cast its spell on the impressionable boy. In 1904 he was boarded at Suffield Park preparatory school, Cromer, in 1908 he was sent to Uppingham School, and in 1913 he enrolled at the Royal College of Music. His studies there were interrupted by the First World War. Having enlisted as a dispatch rider, he was soon commissioned second lieutenant, but in 1917 he received a severe head wound which required the insertion of a metal plate. To an extent his subsequent erratic behaviour and his wayward character were attributable to this wound. Following his discharge in 1919 he returned to the Royal College in 1920 to work under John Ireland. The main influences to be heard in his music were now in place: his teacher, his Irish and East Anglian heritages, and his love of rural England. Ever present behind these were his horrific war memories. In the early post-war years he found a balm in the folk-song movement, in which, as an enthusiastic collector, he joined—publishing sets of Norfolk, Suffolk, and Kerry folk-songs, arranged for voice and piano.

Moeran's earliest work was heavily influenced by John Ireland's compositions and included a number of attractive songs and some atmospheric piano pieces, such as *Stalham River* (1921) and *The Lake Island* (1919). A piano trio in D (1920; revised, 1925) and a sonata in E minor for violin and piano suggested a capacity for work on a larger canvas. Two orchestral works—*In the Mountain Country* (1921) and the rhapsody no. 1 (1922)—revealed responses to the work of Vaughan Williams and Delius, while the string quartet no. 1 in A minor showed that he was indebted, too, to that of Ravel. Despite these influences a pronounced individuality was nevertheless emerging, which occasionally made use of allusion to the work of others to reinforce—or underscore with irony—an emotional statement of its own. He received much encouragement from the Irish conductor Sir Hamilton Harty, who asked him for a symphony. In 1924 one was indeed almost completed, but Moeran, always ruthlessly self-critical, abandoned it.

From 1925 to 1928 Moeran shared a house at Eynsford, Kent, with his fellow composer Philip Heseltine (Peter Warlock). It was a comparatively barren period creatively, in which Moeran, who essentially needed prolonged quiet for his ruminative work to develop, was perhaps inhibited by his friend's rumbustious lifestyle and overpowering personality. Following the dissolution of the *ménage*, creativity returned with the composition of the *Seven Poems of James Joyce* (1929) for voice and piano. This was confirmed in 1930 by the *Songs of Springtime* for unaccompanied chorus—the work by which Moeran is still best known.

About 1930 Moeran was incapacitated in East Anglia with a knee injury, and the enforced inactivity enabled him to reappraise his compositional style. Subsequent works showed less reliance on lush harmony and a new, spare texture, to be heard most notably in the sonata for two violins (1930) and the string trio (1931). On his recovery he began to spend much time in south-west Ireland. Here, in Kenmare, co. Kerry, his friend Arnold Bax noted that he became personally so popular that, had there been a town mayor, Moeran would have been everyone's first choice. It was also here that he found the inspiration to rewrite the symphony in G minor (1937), first conceived in 1924. This work may well be Moeran's distillation of his wartime experience—an orchestral requiem, in fact. It was to be followed by the violin concerto (1937–41), to which it bears a loose relationship: 'sensitive, lyrical, it reflects the Southern Irish coast in full summer, with a scherzo representing a Kerry fair' (*DNB*). The set of six madrigal-style partsongs *Phyllida and Corydon* (1939) was a further fruit of the immediate pre-war years. They suggest a new influence, that of Bernard Van Dieren.

By the 1940s Moeran's music had achieved some recognition and he could respond to requests and commissions. For the pianist Harriet Cohen he produced the rhapsody in F♯ for piano and orchestra (1943), while the Entertainments National Service Association commissioned the *Overture for a Masque* (1944). His family had by now moved to Kington, Herefordshire, and his love of the nearby Welsh border country inspired the *Sinfonietta* (1944). On 26 July 1945 he married the cellist (Kathleen) Peers Coetmore, the daughter of Stanley Coetmore-Jones, an estate agent of Lincolnshire, for whom he wrote the cello concerto (1945) and the sonata for cello and piano (1947).

Moeran's last years were tragic. His marriage ultimately failed, and his chronic alcoholism led to a gradual disintegration. On 1 December 1950 he suffered a cerebral haemorrhage while walking on the pier at Kenmare and fell into the water. For his funeral Kenmare turned out in strength. He was buried there in the churchyard. There were no children from his marriage.

Moeran was a wanderer who owned little, held no positions, and lived chaotically. Nicknamed Raspberry on account of his rubicund complexion, he was a solidly built countryman. Often withdrawn and shy, he would nevertheless blossom in congenial company and had a notable capacity for staunch friendship. His music, always produced to the highest professional standards, is intense in harmony and lyrical in folk-song-influenced melody. He was one of the last representatives of the English/Celtic school of pastoral melancholy which flourished in the first half of the twentieth century.   GEOFFREY SELF

Sources G. R. Self, *The music of E. J. Moeran* (1986) · L. Hill, *Lonely waters: the diary of a friendship with E. J. Moeran* (1985) · S. Wild, *E. J. Moeran* (1974) · H. Foss, *Compositions of E. J. Moeran* (1948) · J. A. Westrup, 'E. J. Moeran', *British music of our time*, ed. A. L. Bacharach (1951) · *DNB* · b. cert. · *CGPLA Eng. & Wales* (1951)
Archives TCD, folk music notebook · University of Melbourne, Victorian College of Arts | SOUND BL NSA, documentary recording · BL NSA, 'Lonely waters', 1994, H4353/2 · BL NSA, performance recordings · BL NSA, *Richard Baker compares notes*, H4132/2

Likenesses photograph, *c*.1930, Hult. Arch. · H. Coster, photographs, 1930–39, NPG
Wealth at death £1441 4*s*. 6*d*.: probate, 24 Jan 1951, *CGPLA Eng. & Wales*

Moffat, Abraham [Abe] (1896–1975), trade unionist, was born in Main Street, Lumphinnans, in Fife, a mining village close to Cowdenbeath, on 24 September 1896. His father, also named Abraham Moffat, was a miner, a trade unionist, and a lay preacher for the Plymouth Brethren. His mother, Elizabeth, *née* Bennett, had worked on the pit top until her marriage. Abe (as he was generally known) was the second of fourteen children, three of whom died in infancy. Lumphinnans, dominated by the Fife Coal Company, was a typical Scottish mining community; the quality of its housing was low, and there was much overcrowding.

Inevitably on leaving school in 1910 Abe went into the pit. Although he took part in the British miners' strike of 1912 he showed no early signs of activism. He seemed a typical young miner—an athlete, a gambler for a brief period, a violinist in a dance band, physically tough, able when necessary to settle an argument with his fists. He supported British involvement in the First World War, joined the army in 1917, and briefly served in France as a guard for German prisoners of war. On 30 May 1917 he married Euphemia Dickson (*b*. 1897/8), who died shortly after the end of the war.

Moffat's radicalization came with the turbulence of the post-war coal industry. He was active in the lockout of 1921; the miners' defeat was followed by his first, and this time brief, experience of victimization. A limited pre-war and wartime revolutionary socialist tradition in the district had subsequently facilitated the establishment of a Communist Party presence; in January 1922 Abe Moffat became a party member. He married second, on 7 November 1924, Helen McNair (*b*. 1903/4), a pithead worker in Fife prior to their marriage and the daughter of a Glasgow carter. More gregarious than her rather reserved and serious husband, she joined the Communist Party, but did not take an active role.

Moffat remained very much the local militant for several years; election as a Communist to the Ballingry parish council in 1924 probably owed more to his reputation in his community than to the party label. Inevitably the plight of the coal industry was his dominant concern. Economic difficulties, and the consequences of falling coal prices for miners' wages and conditions, were given an additional twist in Fife by the Fife Coal Company's programme of mechanization, with its undercutting of traditional skills. In the long lockout during 1926 Abe Moffat was a disciplined and courageous militant. He was arrested and fined, and two of his brothers were gaoled; the Fife Coal Company took its revenge. No member of the Moffat family was re-employed.

The plight of Fife's miners was exacerbated by the state of the coalfield's trade-union organization. The established union had split in 1922 as radicals condemned the cautious policies and procedural manipulation of Willie Adamson, the leading official, and his allies. Reunification in 1927 brought more chaos as successes of the left in trade-union elections were largely blocked by the old guard. The Comintern demanded that the Communist Party show its commitment to the new line, 'class against class', and break with reformist political practices and trade unions. In April 1929 the party supported the formation of a professedly revolutionary trade union, the United Mineworkers of Scotland (UMS).

Abe Moffat's role in this drama had been secondary. After two years largely unemployed he and his communist brother, Alex, had been elected checkweighmen at their local pit in 1928. Their election was soon challenged by the Fife Coal Company, which secured a court order for their removal on the ground that they had led a strike. Abe in particular was developing a reputation as an effective organizer in difficult circumstances. By 1930 he was a paid organizer for the UMS; in September 1931 he became UMS general secretary.

The revolutionary union's grand vision had been supplanted by the recognition that organizational division, economic depression, and employer intransigence offered limited prospects for progress. Despite its title the UMS was essentially a Fife-based union. Abe Moffat built on his own success at Lumphinnans with a wider campaign to elect workmen's inspectors in the mines; such achievements gave the 'red' union a kind of recognition.

Moffat's position as UMS leader gave him an entry to the wider world of communist politics. A member of the Communist Party's Scottish district committee from 1931 and the central committee from November 1932, he became involved in the miners' section of the Profintern. In 1933 he visited the Soviet Union for the first of three visits. On his trip to Moscow for the Comintern's seventh congress in 1935 there was evidence of his status; he returned to Britain with 6000 Swiss francs, a subvention to the British party from the Comintern.

The seventh Comintern congress performed the last rites for 'class against class'. In fact the destruction of the left in Germany and the realities of political life in the diminishing number of places where Communist parties were still legal had already induced significant shifts away from its rigorous precepts. Now under the auspices of the United Front, the UMS was liquidated at the end of 1935. Old enmities died hard; right-wing leaders in the Scottish district unions and in the National Union of Scottish Mineworkers (NUSMW) were resistant to the readmission of UMS officials. Gradually, however, Abe Moffat established his position first with the Fife Union and then, by 1940, on the executive committee of the NUSMW. Ironically by then the communist emphasis on the united front and the popular front had been replaced by a shift back to a more polarized situation. When the Communist Party changed its position on the war in autumn 1939, as a result of the Nazi–Soviet pact, Abe Moffat faithfully followed the party line. A war against fascism had become an imperialist war. His commitment to the Soviet Union overrode any concern to protect trade-union influence. Indeed the Fife executive and the NUSMW conference both took broadly pro-communist positions on the war during the first half of 1940.

Hitler's invasion of the Soviet Union in June 1941 transformed Abe Moffat's position. He attacked unofficial strikes and demanded maximum output. In November 1942 he was elected president of the NUSMW, and was overwhelmingly re-elected against a left critic from the Independent Labour Party in 1944. This re-election resulted from the streamlining of Scottish mining unionism; on a wider canvas the Miners' Federation of Great Britain became the rather more centralized National Union of Mineworkers (NUM) and Moffat presided over what was now the Scottish area of the NUM. He served on the NUM national executive from 1945 until his retirement, and became the senior figure among the executive's left wing members. After the war he was thoroughly committed to the success of the nationalized coal industry. The one-time leader of a 'red' union refused to negotiate on behalf of unofficial strikers. He believed that, whatever the imperfections of the National Coal Board (NCB), the publicly owned industry represented a partnership. On this issue at least all political opinions within the NUM could agree. Within Scotland relationships between left NUM officials and coal board managers were harmonious.

Yet alongside this consensual element the politics of the cold war marked NUM discussions with a well-defined factionalism. The left, heavily influenced by the Communist Party and centred around Scotland and south Wales, was in a minority. Abe Moffat was a vocal opponent of the Attlee government's policy of wage restraint. Yet a belief in the achievements and potential of nationalization put limits on such wage-based militancy. Exchanges could be more robust within the NUM on international questions such as Korea, where anti-communist rhetoric could be particularly effective. Such sentiments surfaced when Moffat stood unsuccessfully for the NUM presidency in 1954. Despite polling over 162,000 votes, this vote was more than doubled by the successful candidate, the anti-communist Yorkshireman, Ernest Jones.

Whatever Moffat's frustrations within the NUM he and his political allies dominated the union's Scottish area. Senior officials were usually communists; so were many activists. The union sponsored a wide range of educational and cultural events. This dominance rested to a marked degree on the competence of Moffat and his senior colleagues. The president's concern with safety in the mines remained evident, and this communist leadership performed effectively within the framework of co-operation with the NCB. Moreover the Scottish coalfields contained some radical communities, not least in Fife where Abe had played a significant part in the campaigns that had returned Willie Gallacher as a Communist member of parliament in 1935 and 1945.

Yet this dominance had its oligarchic side, just as it did in those more numerous NUM areas controlled by the right. Senior officials, elected permanently, were masters of the rulebook. Abe Moffat was adept at its rigorous and creative interpretation. The leadership also controlled patronage; they could groom promising young miners for full-time positions, and such aspirants would know when to put their hands up at meetings. Such resources allowed the leadership to meet even the most serious challenges. The events of 1956—Khrushchov's criticism of Stalin at the Twentieth Congress of the Communist Party of the Soviet Union, and the Soviet invasion of Hungary—put Abe and his colleagues under unprecedented pressure. Criticism came not just from established opponents, but also from a talented rising man on the left, Lawrence Daly. Abe Moffat combined smart procedural footwork with impassioned defence of the Soviet Union. The leadership held the line, just.

Moffat and his colleagues defused widespread unofficial action against the increasing rate of pit closures early in 1959. The weakening demand for coal was eroding the vision of partnership between NUM and NCB. Yet this vision was at the root of Abe Moffat's policy and a basic element within this position was thorough opposition to unofficial stoppages. By the end of his career protection of the union's organization had become a prime value; it was difficult to detect a distinctive left policy on many industrial questions. He retired from the Scottish NUM in 1961. Active thereafter in the Scottish Old Age Pensioners' Association, he died on 28 March 1975.

Abe Moffat was above all a trade unionist; he was also a committed communist. A key feature of his communism was the defence of the Soviet Union. In the early 1940s this probably strengthened his position; otherwise, especially during the cold war, it proved damaging. His communist commitment involved only a slight sense of wider intellectual debates. He had little acquaintance with Marxist classics, but his organizational abilities and discipline allowed him an eminence beyond that of more flamboyant but less predictable comrades. All these characteristics—not least the sobriety and seriousness—are apparent in his autobiography, *My Life with the miners* (1965).

A product of a particular generation—he was twenty-one at the time of the October revolution—Moffat was also above all a miner from a coalfield with a distinctive experience: the power of the Fife Coal Company and the passivity of the older union leadership. As a response he sought to construct the Scottish NUM as a force for what he defined as progress. Yet the house that Abe built proved transient. Within fifteen years of his death its foundations—the Scottish coal industry and the Soviet Union—had been destroyed.   DAVID HOWELL

Sources A. Moffat, *My life with the miners* (1965) · S. Macintyre, *Little Moscows: communism and working-class militancy in inter-war Britain* (1980) · A. Campbell, *The Scottish miners, 1874–1939*, 1: *industry, work and community* (2000) · A. Campbell, *The Scottish miners, 1874–1939*, 2: *trade unions and politics* (2000) · A. Campbell and J. McIlroy, 'Miner heroes: three communist trade union leaders', *Party people, communist lives*, ed. J. McIlroy, K. Morgan, and A. Campbell (2001) · R. P. Arnot, *A history of Scottish miners from the earliest times* [1955] · R. P. Arnot, *The miners: a history of the Miners' Federation of Great Britain*, 3: *... from 1930 onwards* (1961) · I. MacDougall, ed., *Militant miners* (1981) · P. Long, 'Abe Moffat, the Fife miners and the United Mineworkers of Scotland', *Scottish Labour History Society Journal*, 17 (1982) · A. Campbell and J. McIlroy, 'Moffat, A.', *DLB*

Archives Methil Public Library, Fife, Proudfoot papers · National Union of Mineworkers (Lancashire area), Hilden Street, Leigh, National Union of Mineworkers national executive and conferences · NL Scot., observations by Abe Moffat on draft MS of Robin Page Arnot, *A history of the Scottish miners* · NL Scot., National Union of Scottish Mineworkers and National Union of Mineworkers (Scottish area), records · People's History Museum, Manchester, communist party of Great Britain archive · Russian State Archive of Socio-Political History, Moscow, Comintern and Communist Party of Great Britain archives | SOUND South Wales Miners' Library, Swansea, taped interview with Margot Heinneman
Likenesses photographs, repro. in Moffat, *My life with the miners* · two photographs, repro. in MacDougall, *Militant miners*

Moffat, Mary (1795–1871). *See under* Moffat, Robert (1795–1883).

Moffat, Robert (1795–1883), missionary in Africa and linguist, was born on 21 December 1795 in Ormiston, East Lothian, near Haddington, Scotland, the third of seven children of Robert Moffat (1768–1847), and his wife, Ann, *née* Gardiner (1767–1854). A pioneer of protestant missionary activity among the Tswana of southern Africa under the aegis of the London Missionary Society (LMS) and the first transcriber of seTswana, Robert Moffat had an important influence in Africa during his long sojourn there between 1817 and 1870. He helped to open the 'missionary road' from the Cape north-eastward, which was important in southern African imperial politics from the middle to the late nineteenth century. In later life he helped to shape British conceptions of southern Africa before the Second South African War, extolling British imperial rule, criticizing Afrikaners (Boers), and portraying Africans as in need of Christianity and civilization. His voluminous private and official papers are an important record of the southern African interior before colonial rule.

Early years Moffat's parents were stern Calvinists of modest means; his mother came from a poor Ormiston family and his father became a customs official in 1797 and moved his family to Portsoy, near Banff, to take up his first appointment. In 1806 the family moved to Carronshore, near Falkirk. Robert received a fairly sketchy education, particularly as he interrupted schooling to work on a coasting vessel. Giving up the sea, to his parents' relief, he was sent at the age of eleven with his elder brother Alexander for a final six months' education with a Mr Paton of Falkirk. About 1809 he was apprenticed as a gardener to the demanding John Robertson of Parkhill, Polmont. In 1811 his parents moved again, to Inverness, and in 1812 Moffat worked in the gardens of the earl of Moray, near Aberdour. The following year he became an undergardener to Mr Leigh of High Leigh, Cheshire, and left Scotland for good.

In High Leigh, Moffat alarmed his parents by worshipping with Wesleyan Methodists. In nearby Warrington in 1815 he saw an advertisement for a missionary meeting; although the meeting was over, Moffat travelled to Manchester to consult the meeting's chairman, the Revd William Roby, about becoming a missionary. Roby became Moffat's mentor and found him a job in a nursery garden in Dukinfield, Lancashire, in order to spend a year

Robert Moffat (1795–1883), by George Baxter, *c.*1842

instructing and observing him. Roby ultimately recommended Moffat to the directors of the interdenominational London Missionary Society (LMS), then in its early phase of accepting relatively uneducated candidates. After an initial refusal and some delay, the directors agreed to take on Moffat. In October 1816 he was ordained as an LMS missionary and set apart for Africa. He left the same month for the Cape of Good Hope and arrived on 13 January 1817.

The LMS directors then did not employ female missionaries, but they felt strongly that their missionaries ought to be accompanied by wives. Contrary to his employers' suggestions Moffat left for Africa alone, in love with Mary Smith, the daughter of his Dukinfield employer. In 1818 Mary was able to overcome her parents' objections to her marriage to Robert in distant Africa; she sailed in 1819 and the couple married in St George's Church, Cape Town, on 27 December 1819. They had ten children between 1821 and 1840; two died in early infancy and one aged seven. Mary Moffat [*see below*] also proved an indispensable partner in her husband's missionary endeavours.

Cape Town and Great Nama Land The British administration of Cape Colony viewed missionaries as troublemakers, thanks partly to LMS concern for the legal rights of non-Europeans. The British officials also worried about their seeming inability to control Khoi-Khoi (Hottentot) and coloured (mixed race) groups under missionary patronage to the north of the colony. So Governor Charles Somerset denied Moffat and three other recently arrived missionaries permission to leave Cape Colony. Moffat refused a position as government resident with a Xhosa chief and began to learn Dutch instead. Meanwhile he participated in a synod in 1817 run by a dissident faction of the LMS, which uncovered sexual scandals among its fellows. Among other things the synod revealed that the LMS southern African superintendent, the radical James Read, had an illegitimate child, having betrayed his Khoi-Khoi wife with the Khoi-Khoi daughter of a church deacon. A series of bitter quarrels split the LMS, presaging Moffat's lifelong opposition to the more politically radical wing of the LMS represented by Read and, later, John Philip.

In late 1817 Moffat was at last permitted to depart for Great Nama Land (in south-west Africa, later Namibia); he arrived in January 1818. He spent a year working with a Khoi-Khoi chief named Jaeger (Christian) Afrikaner in the vicinity of Warmbad. Like many others Afrikaner had fled Cape Colony, where he had been pressed into service; beyond the Cape boundaries he and his followers survived by raiding. He became a feared figure with a price on his head, though he had already fallen under missionary influence by the time Moffat was stationed with him, and had abandoned raiding. Moffat accompanied Afrikaner to Cape Town to meet Governor Somerset in a brilliant publicity coup which advertised the potential of missionaries for creating peaceful relations in the interior. During his time in south-west Africa Moffat also travelled extensively to the north with Afrikaner and to the east to visit Griquatown and Dithakong.

Back in Cape Town, Moffat met John Philip and John Campbell, sent out by the LMS to investigate the southern African mission's growing problems. The delegates persuaded Moffat to accompany them on a tour of inspection of the interior, which was truncated by frontier warfare.

The southern Tswana mission: early years Philip appointed Moffat to replace the disgraced Read as mission head at Dithakong in Transorangia, among the Tlhaping, a southern Tswana group headed by Mothibi. Read, Ann and Robert Hamilton, and a number of converts from Read's mission station Bethelsdorp had pioneered this mission in 1815; it was about a hundred miles from Griquatown, and within the ambit of the Griqua. A multi-ethnic group including many immigrants, especially coloureds from Cape Colony with Khoi-Khoi mothers and white fathers, the Griqua had formed new polities, were professing Christians in contact with the LMS, and were allowed to buy arms from the colony. Colonial Khoi-Khoi assistance and LMS links to the powerful Griqua were thus essential to the survival of the mission.

At the outset neither the colonial government nor the Tlhaping themselves evinced much enthusiasm for the mission. Indeed the Moffats returned from an expedition to westerly Tswana villages to discover that Somerset had rescinded permission to settle at Dithakong. The couple waited in Griquatown until Somerset permitted them to return for good to Dithakong, on 17 May 1821. They found the Tlhaping angry about Read's dismissal. Furthermore, Mothibi's acceptance of missionaries stemmed mostly from a hope for material and diplomatic benefit, including access to the colonial arms trade. Inhabitants were relatively uninterested in Christianity throughout the 1820s, and many worried that the missionary presence was deterring rain. Moffat quite quickly established white

control over the mission administration and undercut Read's influence by dismissing for moral turpitude certain Khoi-Khoi agents (by one of whom the Moffats' maid had become pregnant, for example) and establishing others firmly as servants rather than as the assistant missionaries James Read had designated them. Moffat also quarrelled with Mrs Hamilton, who was refusing to sleep with her husband, and encouraged her departure.

Throughout the 1820s regional conflict affected the Tswana mission. Late twentieth-century historians have debated this early nineteenth-century upheaval and the 'Cobbing thesis' proposed by Julian Cobbing and others, which maintained that the destabilization formerly attributed to Zulu expansion was in fact fostered by white colonialism and by slave trading carried out in the Delagoa region by the Portuguese and, covertly, further south by the British, the Boers, and the Griqua. Moffat's actions loomed large in these debates because Cobbing contended that Moffat himself was trading slaves and that a key confrontation, the 1823 battle of Dithakong, fought in defence of the Kuruman mission, was in fact a slave raid co-ordinated by Moffat and other missionaries. So consideration of Moffat necessarily involves reference to local warfare and the historians' debates.

The region around Dithakong suffered in the 1820s from drought, hunger, the destabilizing impact of imported guns, and the competition of small mobile groups for survival, which disrupted the more settled communities. Moffat's mission escaped direct attacks in the early 1820s probably only because it was protected by the powerful Griqua. This was exemplified by the battle of Dithakong in 1823. When a mixed group of fugitives that Moffat called the Mantatees drove the more northerly BaRolong Tswana from their homes and seemed to threaten the mission, Moffat hastily gathered an armed and mounted Griqua commando under the leadership of Andries Waterboer. The resulting rout left some 400–500 Mantatees dead. A number of women and children who had surrendered during this battle, and whom Moffat described as starving, were subsequently taken to Cape Town and to Griquatown and employed as labourers; Moffat himself added four servants to his household from among the women of the defeated group. There is no known evidence, however, that this battle was organized as a slave raid nor that Moffat was involved in slaving. By late 1823 his journals reported the Mantatees fleeing in all directions, apparently dying of hunger.

At the end of 1823 the Moffat family travelled to Cape Town to obtain medical advice for the ailing Mary and to consult with Dr Philip, now southern African superintendent. They took with them a local chief named Teysho, and Mothibi's heir Peclu; Moffat's hopes that Peclu would cement alliances between missionaries, the colony, and the Tlhaping were later to be dashed, on Peclu's death in 1825. On the group's return from the Cape in 1824, Moffat moved the mission to New Dithakong, later called Kuruman, by the Kuruman fountain. He began the arduous work of building houses, church, and gardens, and channelling the abundant waters of the Kuruman to irrigate the station. He saw this as a key step in 'civilizing' the African landscape.

Over the next five years internecine conflict affected both the southern Tswana and the Griqua, and new raiding groups emerged, such as the dissident Griqua faction known as the Bergenaars. Violent political struggle marked the period. In 1825, for example, the Bergenaars threatened to drive the missionaries from Kuruman, though they never made the attempt. Other roving forces made serious depredations on the outskirts of Kuruman, one capturing and raping young Tswana women. Mothibi moved away from the station in 1825, his place temporarily taken by his brother Mahura as the Tlhaping chieftaincy fractured; Mothibi was to return in 1826 after being attacked by San (bushmen). Meanwhile, the powerful Ndebele (Matabele) left the ambit of Shaka Zulu to conquer new territory in the region, thereby sparking new conflicts. In 1827, the year in which the Moffats' first son, Robert, was born, the Bergenaars assaulted Griquatown itself, leading the newly vulnerable Moffats to flee Kuruman for a time. Internecine Griqua conflict quietened down once Waterboer's Griqua had defeated the Bergenaars, bolstered by renewed colonial support. In 1828 the inhabitants of Kuruman drove off an attack by armed Kora bandits. In December Kuruman was targeted by another, larger force, which sought revenge against a group sheltering at the station; Moffat persuaded the leader, a Nama chief known to him from Nama Land, to abandon the attack.

By now Moffat suspected that the Tlhaping saw the missionaries as barriers to their participation in the extensive illicit colonial trade in guns and ammunition. Certainly, missionary preaching was unpopular and attendance at the school had dwindled severely by the late 1820s. Even relationships with Griquatown proved fragile. By the beginning of 1829 Moffat had still baptized no converts. In 1829, however, Mothibi left the station permanently. Kuruman then became a haven for a mixed group of refugees, many of whom turned to Christianity in an emotional atmosphere. Also in 1829 the Ndebele chief Mzilikazi sent two of his head people to investigate Kuruman. Moffat gave them an escort through dangerous territory, and was then persuaded to continue on to meet Mzilikazi, with whom he was to form a lifelong bond.

Another turning point was Moffat's departure in 1830 for Cape Town, to have printed his translation into seTswana of the gospel of St Luke. Moffat had first produced a seTswana spelling book, printed in London in 1826, but had not until now made steady progress in Bible translation—and indeed does not seem to have become fully fluent in seTswana until at best 1827. At Cape Town he was frustrated in his attempts to find a printer until the government lent its press, albeit without operating staff, to Moffat and his fellow missionary Rogers Edwards. The two colleagues printed their edition of St Luke themselves, under the supervision of B. J. Van der Sandt, though the effort so exhausted Moffat that he became ill and had to be carried on board ship for the return journey. When he and Mary returned to Kuruman in June 1831 they brought with them some tools to entrench Christianity and 'civilization': a hand printing-press which Moffat was now able to use, cloth from Manchester with which Mary began to fashion long dresses for Tswana women, and a mason, Mr Millen, who helped to build a permanent church.

The early 1830s were calmer than the 1820s, despite fighting between Griqua groups and the Ndebele, and the death in 1832 of the Moffats' infant daughter Elizabeth, who had been born in Cape Town. In 1835 an expedition led by the scientific explorer Dr Andrew Smith reached Kuruman. Smith cared for Mary Moffat, herself close to death after the birth of another son. Moffat then accompanied Smith on another visit to Mzilikazi's headquarters, during which he persuaded Mzilikazi to accept American protestant missionaries.

By the mid-1830s disaffected Afrikaner groups trekking away from British hegemony at the Cape had begun to disrupt the interior. In 1837 serious conflict broke out between Afrikaners and the Ndebele. When the American missionaries left with an Afrikaner raiding party, Mzilikazi's suspicion that they were spies deepened and the mission was doomed. Under a dual threat from the Zulu king Dingaan, Shaka's murderer and successor, and from trekking Afrikaners, the Ndebele migrated to the territory which became named after them, Matabeleland. The 1830s were also marked by bitter conflict between LMS missionaries and Christianized Griqua over who should spearhead missions in the region, as the Griqua sought to expand their political influence through Christianization of the Tswana.

Return to Britain In 1838 the Moffats left for Cape Town, where they hoped to recuperate their failing health and to print a seTswana New Testament. When printing there proved impossible they decided to go to England. Just after they boarded ship another daughter was born; three days later, their six-year-old son James died, a victim of a measles epidemic. After a three-month sea voyage the family arrived in Britain in June 1839 to find that Robert Moffat had become a public figure. He was lionized in evangelical circles, as he travelled the country proselytizing for missions, and he persuaded the young David Livingstone to undertake missionary work among the Tswana. In 1840 Livingstone and another young missionary, William Ross, left to reinforce the Tswana mission.

During this fruitful three-year sojourn Moffat printed his seTswana New Testament and Psalms. In 1842 his *Missionary Labours and Scenes in Southern Africa* appeared, to become a widely read Victorian missionary classic. Moffat also published several missionary sermons, including his *African Scenes* (1843).

The Moffats sailed again for South Africa on 30 January 1843, following valedictory services, addresses, and presentations, and accompanied by a further two young men going out as missionaries. They left some of their children in Britain for education. During a pause on their return journey, Moffat took a tour of the eastern Cape missions of the LMS. The party was met by David Livingstone at the Vaal River, and returned to Kuruman at last in December 1843.

The southern Tswana mission: later years By the time the Moffat party returned to Kuruman, it was home to several other white missionaries. Indeed, Livingstone would soon be complaining of poor relationships among the quarrelsome denizens of Kuruman. Once most of this group dispersed to work among the Tswana elsewhere, Kuruman became its members' base of operations, as well as the source of a wide range of religious material in seTswana as literacy grew in importance among the Tswana. Kuruman spearheaded the missionary, and ultimately imperial, expansion into Tswana territory.

In 1844 Livingstone was attacked by a lion and returned to Kuruman to convalesce. In January 1845 he married Moffat's eldest daughter, Mary. In 1846, after a bitter quarrel between Livingstone and Rogers Edwards, the Livingstones established a new station at Chonuane where David worked (and quarrelled) with the Tswana chief Sechele. Mary Livingstone soon fell seriously ill; her mother travelled to Chonuane to nurse her. In 1847 Moffat's elderly father died in Scotland.

Meanwhile the displacement and subjugation of Tswana groups by Afrikaner trekkers from the Cape accelerated, from the mid-1840s onward. In 1848 Sir Harry Smith proclaimed the Orange River Sovereignty, giving the British putative control over the region between the Orange and Vaal rivers; this lent impetus to Afrikaner migration to the Transvaal region, to land which had recently been vacated by the Ndebele. The Sand River Convention (1852) between the British government and the Transvaal settlers directly threatened LMS mission fields by guaranteeing settlers internal self-government (on condition that they did not participate in slaving nor move south of the Vaal), as well as by granting them an open market in gunpowder. Groups among whom the LMS were working, including Sechele's Kwena, were attacked and in some cases dispersed by the trekkers, while Livingstone's new station at Kolobeng was a casualty of conflict. Moffat argued passionately in letters to the LMS and to the press that the Transvaalers used the Sand River Convention to claim hegemony over a vast area of land, and that the convention permitted them to kill, dispossess, and rape with impunity. Conflict between the LMS and Afrikaner communities in the region was exacerbated by the attempt of nascent Afrikaner polities to enforce an embargo on the sale of arms and ammunition to non-European groups; both Livingstone and Moffat had provided guns, gunpowder, and gun repair to Africans in the past, albeit on a much smaller scale than Afrikaners alleged. Many Afrikaners accused missionaries of continuing a long LMS tradition of illegitimate interference in Afrikaner affairs; many black Africans attacked the missionaries as, at best, powerless pawns of a British government which tacitly acquiesced in the Afrikaner takeover, and, at worst, as having opened the door to white incursions.

By 1853 the British had decided to withdraw from the abortive Orange River Sovereignty. Moffat chaired an LMS committee which produced a memorial pleading with the newly arrived British representative, Sir George Clark, that the British not abandon the sovereignty and that Christian missions be permitted to continue their work. Moffat travelled to Bloemfontein to present this memorial to Clark, but predictably it had little effect. In 1854 the Bloemfontein Convention established the Afrikaner Orange Free State. Conflict shut down the possibility of LMS expansion in the Transvaal region and compelled missionaries to withdraw from some existing stations. By the mid-1850s Moffat was also reporting a falling away of converts and influence at Kuruman. The British were widely hated, he claimed, and the influence of British missionaries was declining.

Throughout these trials Moffat continued to translate the Bible. It was indeed with the partial aim of rectifying the health problems he attributed to excessive study that Moffat set out in May 1854 with Tswana attendants and two young British traders to visit Mzilikazi once again and to contact the peripatetic Livingstone. Once Moffat's party reached Mzilikazi, the Ndebele monarch gave further unusual displays of affection towards Moffat, who was able to spend much of his visit in the king's presence observing his management of the kingdom. Moffat also tried to cure Mzilikazi of a debilitating illness which the missionary diagnosed as dropsy. When Moffat tried to leave to deliver supplies to Livingstone, Mzilikazi at first sought to detain Moffat and then decided to accompany Moffat himself. On the verge of dangerous tsetse fly country, Mzilikazi dispatched a Ndebele team to transport Livingstone's effects to him and the larger group turned back.

In 1857 Moffat at last completed his translation of the Bible. Meanwhile the LMS had decided to establish new stations among two antagonistic groups, the Kololo and the Ndebele, and Moffat was asked to spend a year founding the Ndebele mission. Moffat made a further journey to Mzilikazi, obtaining grudging permission to establish a station. He also won from Mzilikazi the return of the putative heir to the Ngwato kingdom, Macheng, whom the Ndebele had captured in battle many years before; what Moffat did not know, however, was that the dispute over Macheng's chieftainship would lead to extensive factional conflict among the Ngwaketse.

In 1858 the Moffats travelled to Cape Town with Livingstone, about to leave on his Zambezi expedition. There they met three of their children returning from study in England, including John Smith Moffat, recently hired by the LMS as a missionary to the Ndebele, and his new wife, Emily. After a difficult and thirsty journey back, Robert Moffat found conflict raging between Tlhaping and Afrikaner groups. He petitioned Governor Grey on behalf of the Tlhaping, whose land he felt the Afrikaners were trying to steal. In return he was accused of gun-running by Afrikaner leaders, and threats were made against Kuruman. Intervention by Grey on Moffat's behalf forced settlers to permit Moffat to travel to the Ndebele, despite initial threats to stop the expedition.

In late 1858 missionaries designated for the Ndebele and the Kololo converged on Kuruman, to set out in 1859 with Tswana assistants. Once the Ndebele mission had reached

Mzilikazi, however, Moffat discovered that, as he had feared, the chief had not thought his earlier vague concessions to Moffat would amount to much in practice. Indeed, the intense conflict among the Ndebele (fuelled by recent contact with disaffected Tlhaping), over whether to accept the missionaries, indicates the contemporary controversy among the Africans over the costs and benefits of missions; it was argued that mission stations opened the way to Afrikaner incursions and compelled converts to abandon polygamy. None the less, Mzilikazi finally (though reluctantly) agreed to the establishment of the Inyati mission—a critical step in developing the relationships between the Ndebele and the British, and which eventually included the incorporation of the Ndebele into British Rhodesia. Moffat remained for some months, helping to build houses and to plant food for the mission. Meanwhile fever killed a young Tswana assistant, Marelole.

Shortly after Moffat's return in August 1860 to Kuruman, he heard that the Kololo mission had ended in disaster: three children and one missionary couple had died at the station, some said of fever and others said of poisoning at the hands of Chief Sekeletu. The surviving white missionary, Richard Price, who believed the poison story, had fled the station with his wife, the two children of the dead couple, and his Tswana assistants. Mrs Price had died on 5 July, before the survivors met their colleague John Mackenzie. Moffat rushed to escort the returning party back to Kuruman.

In 1861 Moffat's daughter Elizabeth married Price and went to work with him among the Kwena. Missions in the southern African interior were a Moffat family enterprise: in addition to Mary's marriage to Livingstone and John Smith Moffat's work at Inyati, another daughter, Ann, was married to the French missionary Jean Frédoux. However, in 1862 Mary Livingstone died of fever in the Zambezi, for which her mother blamed Livingstone; another Moffat child, Charles, died in the same year; and in 1866 Jean Frédoux was accidentally killed during an altercation with a white trader, and the Moffats became responsible for Ann and her seven children.

Retirement In 1870 Robert and Mary Moffat finally and reluctantly retired to Britain in the company of their youngest daughter, feeling unsure whether or not it was really their home. After a tour of friends and relations, they settled for six months in Brixton, London, at the home of Henry Vavasseur. In January 1871 Mary Moffat died, in Brixton, following a very brief illness.

Moffat then spent two and a half years without a permanent address, travelling around Britain with his daughter, preaching and raising money for the missionary cause, including the Moffat Institute, a Tswana seminary. In 1872 the University of Edinburgh made him an honorary doctor of divinity. In January 1873 he settled at last at 64 Knowle Road, Brixton, his residence for the next seven years. Despite advancing age he nevertheless continued to travel around Britain to popularize missions. He also continued to work on seTswana material, producing a hymn book.

In 1874 Moffat travelled to Southampton to meet the ship bearing David Livingstone's remains and to identify his body. In 1877 he went to Paris for three weeks, and spoke to four thousand French schoolchildren. In November 1879 he left London for the countryside, finding pleasure in his garden and in village life, at Leigh, near Tonbridge. He followed southern African affairs closely, and often longed to return; the British retrocession of the Transvaal to Afrikaners after the 1881 First South African War depressed him deeply. Moffat was much honoured throughout these final years. In 1873 a subscription for him raised some £5000. He had a brief meeting with Queen Victoria at the unveiling of a statue of David Livingstone in 1876, and he breakfasted with Gladstone in 1876 and 1878.

Robert Moffat died peacefully at Park Cottage, Leigh, on 8 August 1883. He was buried in Norwood cemetery, London, on 16 August, alongside his wife, Mary.

Robert Moffat's wife, **Mary Moffat** (1795–1871), was born in New Windsor, Lancashire, the eldest of the four children of James Smith (1763–1853), a Scottish gardener, and his English wife, Mary *née* Gray, from York. Mary, like her father, was an Independent (her mother was Anglican); her brother John became a pastor near Manchester and later a missionary at Madras. She was educated at a Moravian school at Fairfield, Lancashire, and fell in love with Robert Moffat when he was working as a gardener in her father's nursery garden at Dukinfield, Lancashire. Moffat was then under the tutelage of William Roby in anticipation of his future posting with the LMS. Mary Smith felt herself torn on the one hand between her family obligations as a dutiful only daughter and on the other her love for Robert and strong sense of religious obligation to work as a missionary. In this she confronted some of the contradictions of evangelical prescriptions for women, as well as the problem of whether evangelical marriage was primarily for love or duty. She had a painful two years during which she was her parents' companion but with the understanding with Robert that she would join him at some unspecified time. At one point she broke off the relationship, consumed by guilt towards her mother and worried by news of various sexual scandals among the southern African missionaries. Ultimately, however, the difficult decision to part with her parents was made and her marriage to Robert took place. She never saw her mother again, nor saw her father for some twenty years: being a woman missionary in the early nineteenth century demanded an abrogation of certain family duties as contemporaries perceived them.

Mary Moffat was indispensable to the family missionary enterprise and became well known in evangelical circles as the archetypal missionary wife, dispensing domesticity and 'civilization' to Africa. This image was later bolstered by John Smith Moffat's biography of his parents, *The Lives of Robert and Mary Moffat* (1886) and by Mary Moffat's status as David Livingstone's mother-in-law. She embodied some of the contradictions of certain evangelical ideas about women: she took a public role as a protestant evangelist in Africa, and yet was celebrated in Britain as an angel of the domestic sphere—as support to her husband, as a teacher of sewing and model of domestic virtue to Tswana girls and women, and as dispenser of food and home comforts to travelling male missionaries. However, it is unclear whether the Tswana so perceived her, and her long-term significance perhaps lay as much in her image among the Victorians as in her actual daily work. Nevertheless, Mary Moffat was important in fostering Christian proselytization in southern Africa. She led and taught women's groups, educated her own children when young, planted the garden, made food, took care of Robert when he was sick, and kept the mission station going when he was absent. She also corresponded extensively with people in England and Scotland, and with Robert during his frequent absences; moreover, her letters furnish an important source of information about the southern African interior in the mid-nineteenth century. From 1839 to 1842, when the family were in Britain, she not only took care of the children but also fostered female evangelical networks.

During the thirty years before the Moffats' final return to Britain, Mary remained based at Kuruman. She travelled extensively without Robert, mostly to visit her children. She had a cordial but vexed relationship with David Livingstone, who had married her eldest daughter, Mary, in 1845. John Smith Moffat later recalled that in 1858 his mother was convinced that Mary Livingstone would not return alive from the Zambezi expedition planned by Livingstone, and she had travelled to Cape Town to say goodbye to her. After Mary Livingstone died of fever in the Zambezi in 1862, her mother blamed Livingstone for having brought her there, just as she had many years earlier blamed Livingstone for the death of his six-week-old daughter Elizabeth. Despite internal tensions, however, Mary Moffat was a lynchpin of the Moffat and Livingstone family missionary enterprise, and several of her own children became missionaries in Africa, and many of their descendants became important figures in the white settler communities of Rhodesia and South Africa.

Mary Moffat's life also illustrates some of the difficulties of childbirth and child rearing then faced by women. Her first child, Mary, was born in 1821; her tenth, Jane Gardiner, in 1840, by which time she had suffered miscarriages and the deaths of three of her children. Shortly after the death of her first son, Robert, she adopted and nursed a Tswana baby girl abandoned near Kuruman, whom she and her husband named Sarah Roby, after Robert's mentor William Roby. Like other white missionary women of the period, Mary Moffat sent her children away for education for long periods—a particular irony, given her status as an iconic mother and proffered gender role-model for the Tswana. She was convinced that this was God's will, just as she herself had left her parents. Her eldest children, Mary and Ann, were sent to school in Grahamstown in 1830 aged nine and seven respectively, and they saw their parents only sporadically during their several-year sojourn there. Many years later, in 1847, the year of her father-in-law's death, Mary Moffat took her three youngest children, aged about thirteen, eight, and seven, by ox-wagon to Cape Colony in search of opportunities for education; one of them, John Smith Moffat, attested in his joint biography of his parents that this was an excruciating task for his mother, to which she was reluctantly persuaded by her husband and by David Livingstone; 'there was a pathetic tenderness', he claimed, 'in the interest which the mother took in the wild flowers and curious pebbles which the children gathered on the hill-sides and in the stoney river-beds' on the long journey to the Cape (J. S. Moffat, 261). Mary Moffat eventually put the children on a ship to England, and did not see her daughter Bessie again for eight years, nor John and Jane for eleven.

By the time Mary and Robert Moffat left Kuruman in 1870 to retire to Britain, Mary had become increasingly feeble; she had needed help in running the domestic side of the station for some time. She died shortly after arriving in Britain, at Brixton, London, on 9 January 1871, and was buried in Norwood cemetery, London.

ELIZABETH ELBOURNE

Sources South Africa: outgoing correspondence, SOAS, Archives of the Council for World Mission (incorporating the London Missionary Society) · J. S. Moffat, *The lives of Robert and Mary Moffat* (1886) · I. Schapera, ed., *Apprenticeship at Kuruman: being the journals and letters of Robert and Mary Moffat, 1820–1828* (1951) · J. P. R. Wallis, ed., *The Matebele journals of Robert Moffat, 1829–1860*, 2 vols. (1976) · C. Northcott, *Robert Moffat: pioneer in Africa* (1961) · R. Moffat, *Missionary labours and scenes in southern Africa* (1842); repr. (New York, 1969) · J. Comaroff and J. Comaroff, *Of revelation and revolution: Christianity, colonialism and consciousness in South Africa*, vol. 1 (1991) · J. Cobbing, 'The Mfecane as alibi: thoughts on Dithakong and Mbolompo', *Journal of African History*, 29 (1988), 487–519 · J. D. Omer-Cooper, 'Has the Mfecane a future? A reponse to the Cobbing critique', *Journal of Southern African Studies*, 19/2 (June 1993), 273–94 · E. A. Eldredge, 'Sources of conflict in South Africa, *c.*1800–30: the 'Mfecane' reconsidered', *Journal of African History*, 33 (1992), 1–35 · M. Legassick, 'The northern frontier to *c.* 1840: the rise and decline of the Griqua people', *The shaping of South African society, 1652–1840*, ed. R. Elphick and H. Giliomee, 2nd edn (1989), 358–420 · O. Ransford, *David Livingstone: the dark interior* (1978) · P. Landau, *The realm of the word: language, gender and Christianity in a southern African kingdom* (1995) · J. Wright, 'Political mythology and the making of Natal's Mfecane', *The Canadian Journal of African Studies*, 23/2 (1989), 272–91 · J. T. du Bruyn, 'James Read en die Tlhaping, 1816–1830', *Historia*, 35 (1990), 23–38 · C. Hamilton, ed., *The Mfecane aftermath* (1995) · CGPLA Eng. & Wales (1883) · I. Schapera, ed., *Apprenticeship at Kuruman: being the journals and letters of Robert and Mary Moffat, 1820–1828* (1951)

Archives British and Foreign Bible Society archives, London · National Archives of Zimbabwe, Harare, corresp. · SOAS, Council for World Mission Archives, corresp., journals, and sermon notes | NL Scot., corresp. with David Livingstone

Likenesses engraving, 1819, repro. in Northcott, *Robert Moffat*, 30 · C. Bell, sketch, 1835 (*Visit to Moselekatze*), University of Witwatersrand, South Africa; repro. in Northcott, *Robert Moffat*, 160 · portrait, *c.*1839 (after print by G. Baxter), repro. in Wallis, ed., *Matebele journals*, vol. 1 · J. C. Armytage, stipple, pubd 1842 (after E. Heaphy), NPG · G. Baxter, watercolour, *c.*1842, NPG [see illus.] · W. Scott, group portrait, oils, 1842, Scot. NPG · W. Scott, oils, 1842, NPG · G. Baxter, colour print, pubd 1843 (after his earlier work), NPG; repro. in Northcott, *Robert Moffat* · G. Baxter, print, 1843 (after his earlier work), NPG · engraving, *c.*1843 (*Robert Moffat waving goodbye to London, January 30, 1843*; after a drawing by H. Anelay), repro. in Northcott, *Robert Moffat*, frontispiece · photograph, 1870, repro. in Northcott, *Robert Moffat*, 177 · J. Cochran, stipple (after H. Room), NPG · Elliott & Fry, photograph (in old age), repro. in Moffat, *Lives*, frontispiece · Elliott & Fry, photograph, carte, NPG ·

portrait (Mary Moffat; in youth), repro. in Moffat, *Lives*, 47 • portrait (Mary Moffat; in old age), repro. in Moffat, *Lives*, 356 • portrait (Mary Moffat), repro. in Northcott, *Robert Moffat*

Wealth at death £3796 7s. 3d.: probate, 19 Oct 1883, CGPLA *Eng. & Wales*

Moffatt, George (1806–1878), tea broker and politician, was born on 11 May 1806, sixth of the seven children of William Moffatt (1767–1815), tea agent and broker at 4 Fenchurch Buildings, London, and his wife, Alice (d. 1847x9). He entered the family tea business, known as Moffatt & Co., early in life. From 1834 he enjoyed a cordial business relationship with Jardine, Matheson & Co., the China traders. In a precarious business Moffatt succeeded by giving his suppliers clear indications of market requirements and by selling on tea at the average daily market price plus ½d. per pound.

Moffatt served his political apprenticeship negotiating with successive governments over the scale of tea duties, and he served as treasurer and chief mover of the Mercantile Committee of radical city businessmen, formed in 1838, to promote Sir Rowland Hill's uniform penny postage proposals. He unsuccessfully contested by-elections at Ipswich in June 1842 and at Dartmouth in December 1844, before winning Dartmouth in a by-election in July 1845. At the 1852 election he was elected MP for Ashburton, where Jardine Matheson had a strong electoral interest, because of the town's manufacture and export of woollens to China. In parliament Moffatt was a free-trader; he also advocated the total abolition of church rates and was in favour of the ballot and a large extension of the suffrage. He was a close political associate of Richard Cobden and his financial adviser and friend, but he disagreed with the latter's pacifism in the early 1850s.

Moffatt's extensive foreign travels, which were to include visits to Russia and the United States, started in the mid-1840s. In 1845 Moffatt acquired 103 Eaton Square as a London home, and from the 1850s he had another residence in St Leonard's Hill, Windsor. Expanding and diversifying his interests, he became chairman of the Lhynvi Iron and Coal Company and invested in United States railway stocks. By this time his tea company had offices in Mincing Lane, Fenchurch Street, and in Liverpool. In 1856 he married Lucy (1825–1876), the eldest daughter of another merchant prince, James Morrison, and they had a son and three daughters.

Moffatt lost his Ashburton parliamentary seat in 1859, perhaps from insufficient largesse with a small electorate but more probably from his inability to halt the town's continuing economic decline. Moffatt then sat as MP for Honiton from 1860 to 1865, when he won a seat at Southampton. In the latter year he sat on the Commons committee on trade marks and published a pamphlet on bankruptcy law reform.

In the 1868 election Moffatt lost his seat in a contest portrayed by George Meredith in *Beauchamp's Career* (1876), in which he figures as the long-winded and non-radical Mr Cougham. In 1869 he was appointed to the royal judicature commission, but he failed to be nominated to defend a parliamentary vacancy at Hastings. In June 1870 he

unsuccessfully defended a vacancy at the Isle of Wight and again failed at Southampton in 1874.

In 1871 Moffatt purchased Goodrich Court, near Ross-on-Wye, Herefordshire, a Gothic mansion, together with its remaining collections of armour, to which he added. He became a JP and deputy lieutenant for Herefordshire, settled down as a country gentleman, and was still purchasing property locally at the time of his death at the Imperial Hotel, Torquay, on 20 February 1878. He was buried in the churchyard at Goodrich on 27 February.

Moffatt was very much the sound and enterprising Victorian businessman who turned his skills to the public good. A descendant, pitching his judgement on the size of Moffatt's waistcoat, pictured him as a small man of domineering temperament.   THOMAS BEAN

Sources Burke, *Gen. GB* • *WWBMP*, vol. 1 • Boase, *Mod. Eng. biog.* • *Exeter and Plymouth Gazette* (1 March 1878) • *The Times* (25 Feb 1878) • *The Times* (28 Feb 1878) • *Hereford Times* (2 March 1878) • *Ross Gazette* (28 Feb 1878) • H. J. Hanham, 'Ashburton as a parliamentary borough, 1640–1868', *Report and Transactions of the Devonshire Association*, 98 (1966), 206–56 • *Fifty years of public work of Sir Henry Cole*, ed. A. S. Cole and H. Cole, 2 vols. (1884) • S. Graveson, 'The mercantile committee on postage – 1838', *The philatelist*, 10 (1945–6), 226–9 • M. Greenberg, *British trade and the opening of China, 1800–42* (1951) • parish register, London, St Katherine Coleman, 15 June 1806, GL [baptism]

Archives Herefs. RO, political corresp. • priv. coll. | BL, corresp. with W. E. Gladstone, Add. MSS 44373–44782 • BL, corresp. with Peel, Add. MS 31978 • BL, corresp. with Rowland Hill, Add. MSS 40426–40460 • CUL, Jardine Matheson MSS • GL, Jewers MSS, 2480/2 • Mitchell L., Glas., Strathclyde Regional Archive, Stirling (Keir) MSS • W. Sussex RO, Cobden MSS, Moffatt family MSS

Likenesses H. von Herkomer, etching (after photograph, 1870–79), priv. coll.

Wealth at death £439,049 13s. 2d.: CRO, Chichester, Cobden MSS, Moffatt family MSS • under £350,000: probate, 10 April 1878, CGPLA *Eng. & Wales*

Moffatt, James (1870–1944), biblical scholar, was born at Glasgow on 4 July 1870, the eldest son of George Moffatt, chartered accountant, and his wife, Isabella Simpson, daughter of Robert Starret Morton, general merchant, of Edinburgh. He was educated at Glasgow Academy and Glasgow University, where he graduated with honours in classics in 1890. He studied theology in the Glasgow College of the Free Church of Scotland, and became deeply interested in New Testament criticism under the influence of Alexander Balmain Bruce. In 1896 he was ordained minister of the Free Church in Dundonald, Ayrshire, and in the same year married Mary, daughter of Archibald Reith MD of Aberdeen.

In 1901 Moffatt published *The Historical New Testament*, a work of remarkable learning, in which the New Testament writings were examined in the light of their chronology and mutual relations. The book was so obviously important that in 1902 he received from the University of St Andrews the degree of DD, although it had never previously in Scotland been conferred upon so young a man. From 1907 to 1911 he was minister of the United Free Church at Broughty Ferry, and while there published his *Introduction to the Literature of the New Testament* (1911), for

James Moffatt (1870–1944), by Olive Edis

long a standard work. In this period, too, he was Jowett lecturer in London, wrote numerous articles on theological and literary subjects, and began his quarterly survey in the *Hibbert Journal* of current religious books, which he continued for the next thirty years.

From 1911 to 1915 Moffatt was professor of Greek and New Testament exegesis at Mansfield College, Oxford, and in 1913 published his translation of the New Testament, which was followed in 1924 by a translation of the Old Testament on similar lines. This is the work by which he is most widely known, and by means of which he placed the results of biblical scholarship in the hands of the general public throughout the English-speaking world. Although the style of these translations has been criticized by some, they 'undoubtedly illumined the meaning of scripture for many' (Anderson, 597). In 1915 he returned as professor of church history to his college at Glasgow, receiving the degree of DD from the University of Oxford on his departure.

The twelve years during which Moffatt now worked in Glasgow were filled with incessant literary production and also with preaching, lecturing, and varied activities on behalf of the great church in which all the main branches of Scottish presbyterianism had recently been united. At this time he felt that he had made his contribution to New Testament study, and was anxious to carry his inquiries into later phases of Christian development. He wished to make a new start, in different surroundings. So in 1927 he accepted the Washburn chair of church history in the Union Theological Seminary, New York, remaining

there until he retired in 1939. His plan of devoting himself entirely to his new subject was not fulfilled, for he was now so much identified with New Testament criticism that he was not allowed to break away from it. His published work in church history was confined to a masterly sketch, *The First Five Centuries of the Church* (1938); a book on Tertullian, for which he had gathered much material, was never finished.

Moffatt quickly adapted to American conditions, and made himself a force in the cultural and religious life of the country. Most notably, he served as executive secretary of the translation committee of the Revised Standard Version of the Bible in his later years. In the last year or two of his life his health broke down, but he held resolutely to his work almost to the day of his death, in New York on 27 June 1944. He was survived by his wife (who died two years later) and by two sons and one daughter. His eldest son had died in boyhood.

James Moffatt was a man of simple and beautiful character, who endeared himself to a multitude of friends. Although a tireless student he had a great variety of interests. In his youth he had been an athlete, and he never lost his enthusiasm for football and golf. He was a musician and at least one tune of his composition, 'Ultima', has found its way into hymnbooks. He was not only a theological writer but a man of letters in the widest sense. He wrote the introductions for an edition of Shakespeare, and also a book on George Meredith. He was the author of a detective novel, *A Tangled Web* (1929).

The most notable of Moffatt's forty or so theological works were his *Introduction to the Literature of the New Testament* and his single-handed translation of the whole of the Bible. Hardly less noteworthy were the commentaries which he wrote for the series entitled The Moffatt New Testament Commentary, which he edited. His significance for the religious life of his time cannot be doubted. A new attitude to the Bible had become imperative, and Moffatt showed that nothing essential was lost when it was frankly adopted. To his interpretation of the ancient writings he brought a profound scholarship, a rare power of judgement, and a genuine religious sympathy. He rendered them in a language which enabled the common reader to study them intelligently, in the best light of modern knowledge. E. F. SCOTT, *rev.*

Sources personal knowledge (1959) · private information (1959) · *The Times* (29 June 1944) · *WWW* · D. C. Browning, ed., *Everyman's dictionary of literary biography*, 3rd edn (1962) · G. W. Anderson, 'Moffat, James', *DSCHT*, 597

Archives U. Glas. L., papers incl. notes, sermons and lectures

Likenesses O. Edis, photographs, NPG [*see illus.*]

Moffatt, John Marks (*d.* 1802), antiquary, was the minister of nonconformist congregations at Forest Green, Avening, Gloucestershire, at Nailsworth in the same county, and lastly at Malmesbury, Wiltshire. He published two religious works which expounded his nonconformist principles; one was a collection of prayers and hymns. He died, however, before his major work, *The History of the Town of Malmesbury and of its Ancient Abbey*, was printed; it was published posthumously in Tetbury in 1805 for the benefit of his family. Moffatt died at Malmesbury on 25 December 1802, leaving a widow and seven children.

GORDON GOODWIN, *rev.* J. A. MARCHAND

Sources *GM*, 1st ser., 73 (1803), 193 · *Monthly Magazine*, 15 (1803), 96, 197 · Watt, *Bibl. Brit.* · J. D. Reuss, *Alphabetical register of all the authors actually living in Great-Britain, Ireland, and in the United Provinces of North-America*, 3 vols. (1791–1804)

Moffet, Peter (*d.* 1617). *See under* Moffet, Thomas (1553–1604).

Moffet [Moufet, Muffet], **Thomas** [T. M.] **(1553–1604)**, physician and naturalist, born probably in the parish of St Leonard, Shoreditch, London, was of Scottish descent, and the second son of Thomas Moffet (*d.* 1583), citizen and haberdasher of London, who was also free of the Girdlers' Company. His mother was Alice Ashley, or Asheley, of Kent. Both the physician and his father should, it seems, be distinguished from a third Thomas Moffett, who was employed as a government agent in Antwerp in 1575 and who claimed to have served Edward VI and Queen Mary in many countries. An elder brother of the physician, William Moffet, lived at Aldham Hall, Essex.

Peter Moffet (*d.* 1617), a younger brother, was rector of Fobbing, Essex, from 1592 until his death in the autumn of 1617. He wrote two works of protestant divinity. He was married to Jane Parry.

Thomas Moffet appears to have spent five years at Merchant Taylors' School before matriculating as a pensioner of Trinity College, Cambridge, in May 1569. He migrated on 6 October 1572 to Gonville Hall, where he graduated BA in 1573. While becoming proficient in classics, he studied medicine under Thomas Lorkin and John Caius. His fellow students and friends included Peter Turner, Timothy Bright, and Thomas Penny, who all distinguished themselves in medicine. During his undergraduate days Moffet was nearly poisoned by eating mussels. Choosing to proceed MA from Trinity College in 1576, he was expelled from Gonville Hall by Thomas Legge, the master. In 1581 Legge was charged, among other offences, with having expelled Moffet without the fellows' consent. There is no evidence that he was ever educated at Oxford.

On leaving Cambridge Moffet went abroad, equipped with a letter of introduction from Penny to Theodore Zwinger, professor of medicine at Basel. He boarded with Felix Platter, chief physician of Basel, from spring 1578 and soon adopted with enthusiasm the Paracelsian system of medicine. After publicly defending one medical thesis, *De venis mesaraicis obstructis* (1578), he encountered opposition from the Basel University authorities over his doctoral thesis, *De anodinis medicamentis* (1578), which contained attacks on Thomas Erastus, the influential opponent of Paracelsian medicine. On the basis of a censored version of his thesis he was awarded the degree of MD in February 1579. After visiting Johann Sturm in Strasbourg, where he befriended Robert Sidney, Moffet established a successful medical practice in Frankfurt. In 1580 he visited Italy, where he studied the culture of the silkworm (which he later made the subject of a poem), and developed an absorbing interest in entomology. On the same tour he visited Petrus Monavius at the court of Rudolf II in Prague, and Joachim Camerarius sen. in Nuremberg.

Moffet returned to England before the end of 1580, and took a great interest in specimens such as the flying fish, brought back by Sir Francis Drake from his circumnavigation. Moffet's active promotion of the principles of Paracelsian medicine brought him into conflict with the College of Physicians in London, which recognized him as a qualified physician only in December 1582. In July 1582 he accompanied Peregrine Bertie, Lord Willoughby, to Elsinore, to invest King Frederick of Denmark with the Order of the Garter. He noted that the court dinners lasted from seven to eight hours, and made the acquaintance of Tycho Brahe and Petrus Severinus. At the end of 1583 he completed in London, with a dedication to Severinus, his most elaborate exposition of his medical principles, *De jure et praestantia chemicorum medicamentorum* (1584), a dialogue modelled on Erasmus's *Colloquys*. The work 'is dominated by a sustained emphasis on evidence, reason, education, and objective re-evaluation of authority. In many respects the language, feeling, and argument anticipate Bacon's more famous appeal for the advancement of learning' (Houliston, 239). One of five fictional letters appended to the dialogue was addressed to *Endymion Luddipolensis* ('the sleeping Londoner') and challenged the College of Physicians to be more open to Paracelsian practices: *neque unquam sera nimis est ad bonos mores via* ('nor is it ever too late to change to better ways'; p. 110). The work attracted attention abroad and was reprinted in Lazarus Zetzner's *Theatrum chemicum*, vol. 1 (1602). Moffet subsequently reinforced his criticism of the predominantly Galenist medical establishment by publishing his *Nosomantica Hippocratea* (1588), a digest of Hippocrates, whose merits were advocated by many of the newer school of medicine to which Moffet belonged.

By 1588 Moffet had secured a good practice, at first in Ipswich and afterwards in London. On 22 December 1585 he was admitted a candidate of the College of Physicians, and on the last day of February 1588 a fellow, becoming censor in the same year. His success in influencing attitudes towards chemical medicine was reflected in his appointment, in December 1589, to a committee responsible for compiling the *Pharmacopoeia Londinensis* (1618) for the College of Physicians. As a leading London physician he made many connections at court. Among his early patients were Lady Penruddock and Sir Thomas and Edmund Knyvet of Norfolk. Sir Philip Sidney consulted him soon after his marriage in 1583 about his wife's apparent infertility. In July 1586 Moffet and Penny attended during her last illness at Hansworth Anne Seymour, duchess of Somerset, widow of the protector, and they attested her will. In 1590 Moffet was in attendance on Sir Francis Walsingham at Barn Elms, Surrey. Next year he was appointed physician to the forces serving in Normandy under the earl of Essex; and on 6 January 1592 he sent a note to the earl from Dieppe advising him to return to England. Soon after Moffet's return to London, Henry Herbert, second earl of Pembroke, replaced Essex as his chief patron. Mary

Herbert, the earl's wife, and sister of Moffet's former patient Philip Sidney, induced him to leave London for her own home in Wiltshire, and the latter part of his life was spent at or near Wilton as a pensioner of her husband. By the earl's influence he was elected MP for Wilton on 24 October 1597. His patron gave him the neighbouring manor house of Bulbridge for his residence.

Moffet combined real literary aptitude with his interests in natural philosophy. In 1599 he published a lengthy and interesting poem entitled *The Silkewormes and their Flies* and somewhat mischievously attributed to 'T. M. a Countrie Farmar, and an Apprentice in Physicke'. This was the first Virgilian georgic poem in English, and contributed to the attempt, later encouraged by James I, to establish sericulture in England. It was dedicated to the countess of Pembroke, whom he described as 'the most renowned patroness and noble nurse of learning', referring in detail to her various literary projects. John Chamberlain wrote to Dudley Carleton on 1 March 1599, 'The Silkworme is thought to be Dr. Muffetts, and in mine opinion is no bad piece of poetrie' (*Letters of John Chamberlain*, 1.70).

Two professional works by Moffet appeared posthumously. He had completed in 1590 a compendious work on the natural history of insects, partly compiled from the unpublished writings of Edward Wotton and Conrad Gesner, and from papers left to him by his friend Penny. He obtained permission to print it at The Hague on 24 May 1590, and wrote an elaborate dedication to the queen, but continued to add further material. Among those who sent him specimens or illustrations was John White, the Virginian pioneer. After the accession of James I, Moffet readdressed the dedication to him. At Moffet's death the manuscript (BL, Sloane MS 4014), still unprinted, came into the hands of Darnell, his apothecary, who sold it to Sir Theodore Mayerne, and in 1634 Mayerne published it as *Insectorum, sive, Minimorum animalium theatrum*, dedicating it to Sir William Paddy, and describing Moffet as 'an eminent ornament of the Society of Physicians, a man of the more polite and solid learning, and renowned in most branches of science'. Translated into English by J. Rowland as *The Theater of Insects, or Lesser Living Creatures*, it was appended with the plates to Edward Topsell's *History of Four-Footed Beasts and Serpents* (1658). Haller praised the copiousness of the species described and the character of the engravings, and, while admitting that Moffet gave credence to too many fabulous reports, acknowledged him to be 'the prince of entomologists' before John Swammerdam (Haller, 1.110). The work gives a systematic account of the habits, habitat, breeding, and economic importance of insects. Special emphasis was given to bees, and the larvae and adult forms of various insects were discussed.

Moffet's second posthumously issued book was *Healths improvement, or, Rules comprizing and discovering the nature, method, and manner of preparing all sorts of food used in this nation* (1655), edited by Christopher Bennet. This is a gossipy treatise on various aspects of diet and eating habits which Moffet intended to supplement by a similar work on drinks. It was probably compiled about 1595 and contains, *inter alia*, descriptions of an unusually wide range of birds and fish. As a new year's gift for 1594 to William Herbert, later third earl of Pembroke, Moffet wrote a laudatory biography of the boy's uncle on his mother's side, Sir Philip Sidney. This work, entitled *Nobilis, sive, Vitae mortisque Sydniadis synopsis*, and accompanied by an elegiac poem, *Lessus lugubris*, remained in manuscript (Hunt. L., MS HM 1337) until 1941. It appears to be the earliest biography of Sidney.

By licence dated 23 December 1580 Moffet married, at St Mary Colechurch, London, his first wife, Jane, daughter of Richard Wheeler of a Worcestershire family, though she was described at the time of her marriage as a spinster of St Ethelburgh's parish. She was buried at Wilton on 18 April 1600. Moffet's second wife, whom he married about the same year, was Catherine Brown, widow of Richard Brown and daughter of Robert Sadler of Salthorpe, Wiltshire. Moffet died at Bulbridge Farm, Wilton, Wiltshire, on 5 June 1604, and was buried the same day. He was survived by his wife. To her children with her first husband—two sons, Richard and Benedict, and two daughters, Susan and Martha—Moffet left, with other bequests, his musical instruments, including a pair of virginals. Of his will (proved 20 November 1604 and printed by Oldys) his brothers William and Thomas were overseers, and mention is made in it of his own daughter Patience and his 'dear friend and father in Christe', the clergyman Robert Parker. His widow appears to have died at Calne, Wiltshire, in 1626. By her will, proved 26 June in that year, she left a portrait of Moffet and a book in his writing, probably *Healths Improvement*, to his daughter Patience. It has been supposed, on the basis of Moffet's interest in spiders, that Patience was the 'little Miss Muffet' of the nursery rhyme.

VICTOR HOULISTON

Sources W. Oldys, introduction, in T. Moffet, *Healths improvement* (1746) · pedigree of William Moffet, Bodl. Oxf., MS Ashmole 799, fol. 130 · annals, RCP Lond., vol. 2 · J. Aikin, *Biographical memoirs of medicine in Great Britain: from the revival of literature to the time of Harvey* (1780) · G. Clark and A. M. Cooke, *A history of the Royal College of Physicians of London*, 1 (1964) · *The letters of John Chamberlain*, ed. N. E. McClure, 1 (1939) · A. Haller, introduction, in H. Boerhaave, *Methodus studii medici*, 2 vols. (1751) · L. Scholz, ed., *Epistolarum philosophicarum, medicinalium, ac chymicarum* (1598) · R. Newcourt, *Repertorium ecclesiasticum parochiale Londinense*, 2 vols. (1708–10) · C. J. Robinson, ed., *A register of the scholars admitted into Merchant Taylors' School, from AD 1562 to 1874*, 2 vols. (1882–3) · J. R. Tanner, ed., *Historical register of the University of Cambridge … to the year 1910* (1917) · D. Simpkins, 'Moffett, Thomas', *DSB* · V. Houliston, 'Sleepers awake: Thomas Moffet's challenge to the College of Physicians of London, 1584', *Medical History*, 33 (1989), 235–46 · Venn, *Alum. Cant.* · HoP, *Commons, 1558–1603* · J. L. Chester and J. Foster, eds., *London marriage licences, 1521–1869* (1887), 931

Archives Hunt. L. | BL, Sloane MSS · University of Basel, Zwingler MSS

Likenesses W. Rogers, line engraving, NPG; *see illus. in* Penny, Thomas (c.1530–1589)

Wealth at death bequeathed musical instruments and books; substantial inventory of household effects in wife's will: Oldys, introduction, in T. Moffet, *Healths improvement*; wife's will: Oldys, 'Will of Katherine Moffett, 1626 (abridged)', Wiltshire Notes and Queries, 5 (1905–7), 541–4

Mogford, Thomas (1809–1868), landscape painter, was born at Exeter on 1 May 1809, the son of William Mogford, a veterinary surgeon at Northlew, Devon, and his wife Marguerite. He showed an early talent for drawing, as well as for mechanics and chemistry, but eventually decided on painting in preference to engineering. He studied in Exeter under the landscape painter John Gendall, and was articled for some years to him and to Mr Cole. At the end of his apprenticeship, on 1 May 1833, he married Cole's eldest daughter, Ann, and settled in Northernhay Place, Exeter.

Mogford sent three pictures to the Royal Academy in 1838, and three in 1839, including a full-length portrait of Sir Thomas Lethbridge. About 1843 he moved to London, and subsequently exhibited several portraits at the Royal Academy; among his sitters were Samuel Cousins, the engraver; Professor J. C. Adams, the astronomer, for Cambridge University (engraved by S. Cousins); and Colonel Napier, the historian. He also painted and exhibited *The Sacrifice of Noah* and *The Loves of the Angels* (exh. RA, 1846), the latter regarded by contemporaries as a very original work. Subsequently he moved to Guernsey, where he founded a school of painting, and practised almost entirely as a landscape painter, occasionally revisiting England to paint portraits. Though for some years disabled through the effects of lead poisoning, he continued to paint up to the day of his death, at rue Poudreuse, St Martin's, Guernsey, on 13 June 1868.

L. H. CUST, rev. PATRICIA MORALES

Sources G. Pycroft, *Art in Devonshire: with the biographies of artists born in that county* (1883) · *Art Journal*, 30 (1868), 158 · Redgrave, *Artists* · Bénézit, *Dict.*, 3rd edn · d. cert.

Mogg, Mary [Molly] (1698/9–1766), celebrated beauty, was one of two daughters born to John Mogg (d. 1736), landlord of The Rose inn at Wokingham in Berkshire. Little is known of Molly other than that she worked in her father's tavern and that her exceptional beauty inspired John Gay, in company with Alexander Pope and Jonathan Swift, to write a poem about her entitled 'Molly Mogg, or, The Fair Maid of the Inn', which quickly became a popular song. However, even these bare details have been the subject of disagreement.

Notes and Queries, in quoting from the *Quarterly Review* for 1859, claims that Molly's sister Sally was in fact the great beauty and the subject of the song. It suggests that Gay and his friends had been too drunk to distinguish between the sisters and that thus the tributes had been paid to Molly erroneously (*N&Q*, 84–5). This version of events is denied in the *Gentleman's Magazine*: listing Molly among the deaths for 1766 aged sixty-seven (she died a spinster at Wokingham on 7 March), the entry states unequivocally that she was the person about whom Gay had written the song 'Molly Mogg' (*GM*, 36.151). Similarly in the *London Daily Post* for 21 October 1736 notice was given that Mr Mogg, who was confirmed as having kept The Rose inn for several years, had died a few days previously. He was described as 'Father of Molly Mogg on whom the famous song was made' (*N&Q*, 175).

The other area of disagreement concerns authorship and whether the poem was the result of the collaborative efforts of Swift, Gay, and Pope, or written solely by Gay or by Pope. What is not contested is that the poem was probably written in the summer of 1726, a couple of months after Swift had arrived in England to arrange publication of *Gulliver's Travels*. It is generally accepted that about this time Pope, Swift, and Gay had gone together to Wokingham and to nearby Binfield, where Pope had lived ten years earlier. It has been suggested that Pope was taking his fellow wits on a nostalgic journey into his past and possibly to meet his old Binfield friends the Doncastles (*N&Q*, 172).

AAA, a contributor to the *Gentleman's Magazine* for June 1755, claims that Pope had written the original poem, the eleven stanzas of which were reprinted in the issue in French, at the age of seventeen. However, as J. Yeowell notes, when Pope was seventeen, in 1705, Molly Mogg would have been only about six years old (*N&Q*, 173). Other evidence points to Gay as the author, and the poem is generally attributed to him. Vinton Dearing says that Swift referred to 'Molly Mogg' as Gay's, and that Gay authorized the printing of the full fifteen stanzas under his own name in the fifth edition of Lintot's *Miscellany* (2, 1727, 617). However, Dearing also makes the valuable point that since 'Molly Mogg' is a 'crambo' poem (one designed to exhaust all possible rhymes on a given name) it was likely to have been a collaborative effort. Indeed when the poem was first published, in *Mist's Weekly Journal* on 27 August 1726, authorship was attributed to 'Two or Three Men of Wit'. Furthermore the inclusion of stanzas 8 and 13 in the full version of the poem was the result of a challenge thrown down by Incog, in *Mist's Weekly Journal* for 20 August 1726, to 'furnish another Rhime' on Molly Mogg.

The poem, which had probably been handed about privately before appearing in *Mist's Weekly Journal*, enjoyed immense success and soon acquired a couple of tunes to add to its popularity. The full text of fifteen four-line stanzas was printed in Dublin in two broadsides; another version, without stanzas 8 and 13, was reprinted in *The Choice* in 1729 and 1732. Another broadside appeared in *Musical Miscellany*, *Read's Weekly Journal*, and *The Hive*. In addition four other broadsides were published between 1726 and 1732 which omitted stanza 13 and arranged the remaining fourteen stanzas into pairs to make seven verses in order to fit them beneath the musical scores of different tunes.

BARBARA WHITE

Sources 'The famous poem of Molly Mogg, or, The fair maid of the inn by Mr Gay' (1726) · *N&Q*, 2nd ser., 8 (1859), 84–5, 129, 145, 172–5 · *John Gay: poetry and prose*, ed. V. A. Dearing and C. E. Beckwith, 2 vols. (1974) · *GM*, 1st ser., 25 (1755), 278 · *GM*, 1st ser., 36 (1766), 151 · *Mist's Weekly Journal*, 70 (27 Aug 1726)

Mogridge, George (1787–1854), children's writer and religious author, was born on 17 February 1787, at Ashted, a suburb of Birmingham. His father, Matthias, a successful canal agent, was brother of the Revd John Mogridge and grandson of the Revd Anthony Mogridge of Martley, Worcestershire, author of the manuscript volume 'The conscience's recorder', and descendant of John Mogridge, who in 1530 had founded an almshouse at Exeter. After attending a village school, George Mogridge boarded at Boarscote Boys' School, near Bromsgrove, from the age of five to fourteen, when he was apprenticed to a japanner in Birmingham. In his leisure time he read Chaucer, Spenser, and Ossian and attempted imitations of Gray and the English ballads; his first appearance in print was in a local newspaper with verse commemorating the raising of a statue to Nelson after Trafalgar, and Mogridge and his sister Mary also contributed to Ackermann's *Poetical Magazine*. For three years he single-handedly produced a manuscript serial, 'The Local Miscellany', a collection of secular and sacred poetry and prose for his friends.

At twenty-four Mogridge entered into partnership with his elder brother in the japan trade in Birmingham, and began writing a series of articles in the *Birmingham and Lichfield Chronicle*, under the pseudonym Jeremy Jaunt and under the heading 'Local perambulations', on pollution, poor road conditions, smallpox vaccination, and the anti-slavery cause. In 1812 Mogridge married Elizabeth Bloomer (d. 1822), with whom he had two sons, George and Matthias, and one daughter, Eliza. About 1825 he married Mary Ridsdale, with whom he had one son, Charles. Mogridge had little head for business, and by 1826, after the retirement of his brother, he was bankrupt; his pregnant second wife returned to Ashted with his three children, while he wandered alone, spending time in Herefordshire, as the guest of his uncle, the Revd J. W. Phillips, then tramping for two months in France, and arriving in London in July 1827 to take lodgings at Kingsland Road. The family, with the exception of the two older boys, was finally reunited at 3 Enfield Road, Kingsland Road.

Diffidently and under the signature X.Y.Z., Mogridge submitted four metrical tracts to the Religious Tract Society, two of which ('Two Widows' and 'Honest Jack') were approved and effectively launched his writing career. He had had an earlier success with the Houlston tract *Thomas Brown* (1820?), a sentimental, anonymous ballad about reforming the sabbath. Another anonymous Houlston success was *The Juvenile Culprits* (1829), a play teaching children the consequences of cruelty to insects and animals. The first Houlston publication to bear his name was *The Churchyard Lyrist* (1832), a volume of epitaphs. In 1833 Mogridge began writing as Old Humphrey for the Tract Society's new magazine the *Weekly Visitor*, contributing a regular 'Observations' column to this periodical and, after 1837, to its monthly sequel, *The Visitor*. As Ephraim Holding he wrote for Sunday school teachers and working men; as Old Father Thames he supported the ragged schools. Although he wrote 226 works (stories, collections, verses) for a range of publishers (RTS, Houlston & Son, Tegg, Grant, and Griffiths, Nesbit & Co., Sunday School Union, Working Men's Educational Union), Mogridge was never rich or even financially secure. Harvey Darton called him 'a Proteus of the Early Victorian Juvenile Library' (Darton, 230), as Mogridge used over twenty pseudonyms. In addition to Old Humphrey and Ephraim Holding, he also wrote as Peter Parley (for seven titles from Tegg, and over the objections of the American Samuel Griswold Goodrich, who claimed ownership), Grandfather Gregory, Amos Armfield, Grandmamma Gilbert, and Aunt Upton. His successful, widely marketed work was well suited to the tastes and capacities of the labouring classes.

George Mogridge died on 2 November 1854 at 4 High Wickham, East Hill, in Hastings, Sussex, where, emaciated by disease originating from a sprained ankle, he had travelled four times in the hope of a cure. He was buried there in All Saints' graveyard. His second wife transcribed all his works for the printers, edited several, and wrote *Domestic Addresses* (1863).   PATRICIA DEMERS

Sources C. Williams, *George Mogridge: his life, character and writings* (1856) · *Memoir of Old Humphrey: with gleanings from his portfolio, in prose and verse*, new edn (1860) · BL cat. · WorldCat · J. St John, *The Osborne collection of early children's books, 1476–1910: a catalogue*, 2 vols. (1958–75) · F. J. Harvey Darton, *Children's books in England: five centuries of social life*, rev. B. Alderson, 3rd edn (1982) · H. Carpenter and M. Prichard, *The Oxford companion to children's literature* (1984)
Likenesses R. Gover, engraving, repro. in *Memoir of Old Humphrey*, ed. Religious Tract Society · D. J. Pound, engraving (after A. Stanesby), repro. in Williams, *George Mogridge*
Wealth at death almost destitute: Williams, *George Mogridge*, 350–51

Mohl [*née* Clarke], **Mary Elizabeth** (1793–1883), salon hostess and author, was born on 22 February 1793 in Millbank Row, Westminster, London, youngest child of an Anglo-Irish builder, Charles Clarke (d. 1809), and his Scottish wife, Elizabeth Hay (d. 1846). A brother died in infancy; a sister, Eleanor (1786–1879), married John Frewen Turner MP (1755–1829), had children, and resided at Cold Overton in Leicestershire, where Mary would frequently stay. The ailing Elizabeth Clarke brought up her daughter mostly in the south of France, and, when widowed, lived with her at various addresses in Paris. Although Mary Clarke always loved England, and met famous people there including Wordsworth, she preferred France where she could speak her mind more openly. The Clarkes' meagre income derived partly from an unsatisfactory investment in the Sirey law firm, which gave rise to litigation. For a time Mary Clarke undertook portrait work, at which she was greatly gifted. The women lived frugally, but entertained, if only with tea and biscuits; thanks to Mary's vivacity and wit, their hearth became a rendezvous for intellectuals. Not exactly gentle, not always coherent, often opinionated, Mary Clarke was consistently intriguing and above all unconventional in conversation and philosophy. Although Stendhal affected to dislike her, she was widely admired. Among her suitors were Quinet, Thiers, Thierry, and Cousin; those who just enjoyed her company included Mérimée, Hugo, Constant, Sainte-Beuve, Guizot, Tocqueville, and (later) Renan.

In 1831 mother and daughter subleased rooms from Mme Récamier at the Abbaye-aux-Bois (rue de Sèvres). Mary Clarke thus also came close to Chateaubriand, and in 1838 moved to the floor above his at 120 rue du Bac, where she remained for the rest of her life. Her longest early love relationship was with the polyglot scholar during the Second Empire, Mary Mohl, who by way of independent writing had earlier done only a little magazine work on social questions, wrote first an important article on Turgenev ('Peasant life in Russia', *National Review*, 8, 1859, 469–87), then 'Mme Récamier' (*National Review*, 10, 1860, 347–91) which she subsequently developed as *Madame Récamier: with a Sketch of the History of Society in France* (1862); here she aired a lifetime project for a history of women and their rights.

The Franco-Prussian War of 1870–71 was a setback; Mary Mohl spent it in London 'on the parish' (as she said) with friends, 'small and shrunk'. She returned to Paris weak and weary; she had a heart condition, suffered from so-called 'catarrh of the stomach' and fainting fits, and her thoughts were 'like jellyfish'. 'My memory is so bad', she once confessed, 'that I often invent quotations, and am ready to die for their exactness' (Lesser, 161). Conspicuously antiquated in her Louis Philippe-style dress, a frizzy white mop of hair about her face, little old 'Clarky' rather resembled a terrier; yet her piquant conversation continued to attract discerning minds like Henry James. However, when her husband died (4 January 1876), she could no longer profess to be 'ridiculously fond of living'; she busied herself with his papers, publishing *Le livre des rois* (a translation and commentary on Firdausi, 7 vols., 1876–8) and *Vingt-sept ans d'histoire des études orientales* (addresses to the Société Asiatique, 2 vols., 1879–80), but further declined and gave up receptions. She died in Paris on 15 May 1883 and was buried three days later beside Jules at Père Lachaise cemetery. To the end, she had read avidly. 'If there were no more books', she contended, 'the best thing would be to hang oneself, for life would not be worth having' (Simpson, *Letters*, 15).   PATRICK WADDINGTON

Mary Elizabeth Mohl (1793–1883), by unknown artist

Claude Fauriel, who introduced her to distinguished figures like Manzoni, but frustrated her emotionally. She tried fostering children, disastrously, then cats, which prevented life from becoming 'a dreary waste'. When Fauriel died in 1844 she edited his lectures, *Histoire de la poésie provençale* (3 vols., 1846), and after her mother's death in 1846 married, on 11 August 1847, the German orientalist Julius Mohl (naturalized French as Jules; 1800–1876), for long an intimate friend. Always coy about how old she was, she thought that women should appear younger than their husbands; a witness loudly blew his nose when the mayor announced her age, and thirty-nine (instead of fifty-four) crept into the marriage certificate. By religion nominally Anglican, she became a Lutheran to please her husband. He was a sober bookman, not keen on parties, but his numerous colleagues helped revitalize her salon.

Despite the 1848 revolution and the rise of her despised Louis-Napoléon, Mary Mohl's at-homes and invitation dinners became internationally famous. Her guests included Turgenev, George Eliot, and Mrs Gaskell, who stayed more than once in the rue du Bac and wrote part of *Wives and Daughters* there. Other British associates numbered Thackeray, Bagehot, Monckton Milnes (Lord Houghton), Holman Hunt, and A. P. and Lady Augusta Stanley, who first met at her table. But her most rewarding friendship was with Florence Nightingale, whom she had long encouraged; the Mohls facilitated Nightingale's study with the Sœurs de la Charité, and in 1854 assisted her in Paris on her way to the Crimea with a party of nurses. Also

Sources M. Lesser, *Clarkey: a portrait in letters of Mary Clarke Mohl, 1793–1883* (1984) · M. C. M. Simpson, 'Some personal recollections of Madame Mohl', *Macmillan's Magazine*, 48 (1883), 424–36 · M. C. M. Simpson, *Letters and recollections of Julius and Mary Mohl* (1887) · M. C. M. Simpson, *Many memories of many people* (1898) · K. O'Meara, *Madame Mohl: her salon and her friends* (1885) · M. E. Smith, *Une Anglaise intellectuelle en France sous la Restauration: Miss Mary Clarke* (Paris, 1927) · 'Le roman de Claude Fauriel et de Mary Clarke: lettres d'amour de 1822 à 1844', *La Revue des deux mondes*, 48 (1908–9), 551–87, 832–62 · 'Le roman de Claude Fauriel et de Mary Clarke: lettres d'amour de 1822 à 1844', *La Revue des deux mondes*, 49 (1908–9), 131–61 · O. de Mohl, ed., *Correspondance de Fauriel et Mary Clarke* (1911) · Mrs H. Ward, *A writer's recollections* (1918), 158–60 · d. cert.
Archives BL, corresp., Add. MSS 70611–70624 · Institut de France, Paris · U. Leeds, Brotherton L. | BL, corresp. with Florence Nightingale, Add. MS 43397 · Leics. RO, corresp. with Clarke and Martin families · Royal Holloway College, Egham, Surrey, letters to Mrs Reid · Trinity Cam., Houghton MSS
Likenesses M. E. Mohl, self-portrait, 1831, priv. coll.; repro. in Lesser, *Clarkey* · H. Bonham-Carter, portrait, *c*.1842, priv. coll.; repro. in Lesser, *Clarkey* · W. W. Story, portrait, 1870–79, priv. coll.; repro. in Lesser, *Clarkey* · photogravure, NPG [*see illus.*]

Mohun, Charles, fourth Baron Mohun (1675?–1712), duellist and politician, was born in London, the second child and only son of Charles, third Baron Mohun of Okehampton (d. 1677), and his wife, Lady Philippa, daughter of Arthur *Annesley, earl of Anglesey. The story of Mohun would scarcely be worth telling, except as a sidelight on the decay of one section of the aristocracy. He belonged to the licentious era of the Restoration, and grew up all the more unchecked because about the time of his birth his father was mortally wounded in a duel of the old-fashioned sort, in which, though only a second, he took part in the fighting. Mohun's mother, Philippa, was a self-assertive young woman whose married life had been brief, and early interrupted by an estrangement that had to be smoothed over by her father.

Charles Mohun seems to have had no formal education. Considerable land remained to the family in Cornwall and Devon, but it was heavily mortgaged. His father left him heavy debts, and he may have come to depend too much on cards and dice to support his style of living. In 1691 he married Charlotte Orby, a granddaughter of Charles Gerard, first earl of Macclesfield. This ambitious and grasping family had been royalist in the civil war, but like many others turned against James II and became staunchly whig. Apparently Mohun was cheated by being paid no dowry, to which his rank entitled him. His marriage ended soon after in a permanent separation, its only legacy a daughter whom Mohun repudiated. Charlotte was left to sink or swim as best she might; Mohun drifted into bad company, particularly that of Edward Rich, the roistering young earl of Warwick, and got into pranks and quarrels where he displayed a boorish disposition and the arrogance of rank.

In December 1692 a gambling dispute with a Scottish fledgeling, Lord Kennedy, led to Mohun's first duel. Any injuries must have been light, because within a day or two the most outrageous of all Mohun's affrays took place. A juvenile crony, Captain Richard Hill, had designs on a much admired actress, Anne Bracegirdle, and according to the diarist Narcissus Luttrell the two of them were planning to 'trepan' or carry her off (Luttrell, 2.637). A fellow actor, William Mountfort, stood in their way. Mohun and Hill ambushed him, and then while Mohun embraced him—with drunken cordiality, or to prevent him from defending himself—Hill stabbed him. Mountfort died next day. Hill escaped; Mohun was charged with murder. His trial before the House of Lords opened on 1 January 1693. Much excitement had been aroused, and the affair was indeed, as Macaulay was to write, 'a striking illustration of the state of manners and morals in that age' (Macaulay, 2266). Proceedings dragged on until 4 February, when the defendant was acquitted by 69 votes to 14. His extreme youth has sometimes been pleaded in extenuation; and Colley Cibber's 1822 editor, Edmund Bellchambers, made the most of some circumstances in his and Hill's favour, as against the actor's. At the time, however, the verdict was widely condemned as an abuse of class privilege.

In 1694 Mohun accompanied his new patron, Charles Gerard, second earl of Macclesfield, to Flanders, where he participated in the unsuccessful attack on Brest. Army discipline had no curative effect; officers were often the most persistent duellists. In October 1694 he was back in London and attacked a coachman in Pall Mall. A journalist, Dyer, was the next victim of Mohun's wrath. In April 1697

there was an encounter with a Captain Bingham in St James's Park, which was stopped by the custodians. On 14 September Mohun was in a tavern row with Captain William Hill, who was left fatally wounded.

Before the Lords could take this up, a tipsy brawl gave rise to a duel or scrimmage in Leicester Square, with Mohun and Warwick involved as seconds. This time it was a Captain Richard Coote who fell. Both Mohun and Warwick were accused of murder, but their cases were not decided by the Lords until the spring of 1699. Warwick was then convicted of manslaughter, a trivial offence when committed by a peer; Mohun, who claimed to have tried to avert the contest, was acquitted. Both pleaded royal pardons, which were accepted by a government in need of supporters. Mohun certainly seems to have felt it was time to show his discretion, and took his seat in the Lords. By the summer of 1701 he had grown respectable enough to be chosen as aide to his patron Macclesfield on a special mission to the Electress Sophia of Hanover, concerning the succession.

In November 1701 Macclesfield died, still little over forty and childless. He bequeathed the greater part of his property to Mohun, though James Douglas, fourth duke of Hamilton, whose second wife was another Gerard connection, also had claims. Macclesfield clearly favoured Mohun: the pair had found one another congenial company and Macclesfield had borne grudges against Hamilton for his tory sympathies. Eleven years of doubtless expensive litigation ensued, principally over ownership of the valuable estate of Gawsworth, in Cheshire.

Mohun was in the enjoyment of a good income, and had already gained a substantial sum, including Macclesfield House, London, from his former patron's will. In 1701 he also received the colonelcy of a newly enrolled regiment, though Mohun showed little enthusiasm when it was posted to Ireland. He continued to make a point of showing himself at parliamentary sessions, and even if his performances there were 'in no way brilliant' he would, in R. S. Forsythe's opinion, 'very certainly … have held office' if he had outlived Queen Anne (Forsythe, 146, 170). He was sufficiently in the limelight to be admitted in 1707 to the whig Kit-Cat Club, and had his portrait painted by Godfrey Kneller. In 1711 he married his mistress, Elizabeth Griffin (née Lawrence), daughter of Thomas Lawrence, one of the queen's physicians, and the recent widow of Colonel Griffin. The marriage brought helpful connections with the Marlborough clique. By now the political atmosphere was growing tense. In August 1710 the tories had won a crushing election victory. In the following year they sought peace with France and secured the dismissal of Marlborough, the British military leader. On 28 May 1712, in a debate on the conduct of the war, Marlborough was grossly insulted by Earl Poulett, and sent him a challenge: its bearer was Mohun, who warned Poulett that he meant to take part on his principal's side. A fight was averted, and the rash Poulett saved, only following government intervention.

Meanwhile the fortunes of law seemed to be turning against Mohun; the Gawsworth estate, and with it his whole financial position, was in jeopardy. Hamilton's influence was growing; later in 1712 the government appointed him special envoy to Paris, amid mounting whig fears that Anne and the tories were moving towards the Jacobite camp. On 13 November, shortly before his intended departure, Hamilton attended a meeting with Mohun in the chambers of a Mr Olebar. Accounts of what passed there vary, but the discussion broke up in ill humour, and was followed by a challenge from Mohun; this was not couched in over-aggressive terms, it would seem, but it was accepted at once. Very early on the 15 November the old grudge was fought out in Hyde Park. A second took part on each side, though Mohun is said to have wanted a single fight: he was heavier than he had been, but nearly twenty years younger than his opponent. There were no seconds in the later sense, of referees; servants and a surgeon were the only witnesses. Mohun's partner was General George Macartney, a supporter of Marlborough lately dismissed on political grounds and smarting under his treatment. He was a good soldier, but a poor gambler and a worse character. It was the principals who did most of the fighting, while the others skirmished. Hamilton may well have felt that he must win quickly, if at all. No fencing skills were displayed: blind ferocity ruled. Hamilton was killed at the site of the duel, while Mohun died at Macclesfield House later that day from his injuries. Mohun was buried on 25 November in the church of St Martin-in-the-Fields, like his father before him, but without monument or tablet. As if by way of epitaph, a pamphleteer looked back at his vicious youth, and its 'breaking of windows, beating of Constables and Watchmen', and the like (Forsythe, 12–13). Both Hamilton's and Mohun's seconds were indicted, but eventually escaped punishment.

Keen political writers like Jonathan Swift, then in London and at the height of his toryism, easily believed that Mohun had been instigated by the whigs to kill a man of tory, maybe Jacobite, sympathies. The impression left by the fight was certainly strong. Daniel Defoe saw in it a symptom of England's 'Outrageous party-quarrelling', and as 'Illegal and UnChristian' (Defoe, 67–8), while the episode 'sharpened and focused public opinion towards an examination of the value of the duel' (Andrew, 410). A bill for its suppression was brought into the House of Commons, but rejected.

Mohun's last combat may, however, have helped to put an end to the practice of group-duelling. This in turn helped to replace the sword, much earlier in England than in France, with the pistol, which could kill, but did not butcher. In this dubious sense Mohun might be called a martyr to progress. All of his property was bequeathed to his second wife, who defended it against the Hamiltons tenaciously, and in the end successfully. However, Mohun's life and his ill-starred peerage came to an end together. He was given a new lease of life by Thackeray, in his novel *Henry Esmond* (1852), which altered the events of his career, but depicted faithfully the morbid social existence which fettered and at last destroyed him.

V. G. KIERNAN

Sources DNB · V. L. Stater, *Duke Hamilton is dead! A story of aristocratic life and death in Stuart Britain* (1999) · R. S. Forsythe, *A noble rake: the life of Charles, fourth Lord Mohun* (1928) · N. Luttrell, *A brief historical relation of state affairs from September 1678 to April 1714*, 6 vols. (1857) · H. T. Dickinson, 'The Mohun–Hamilton duel: personal feud or whig plot?', *Durham University Journal*, 57 (1964–5), 159–65 · C. Cibber, *An apology for the life of Mr Colley Cibber*, new edn, ed. E. Bellchambers (1822) · W. Coxe, *Memoirs of the duke of Marlborough, with his original correspondence*, rev. J. Wade, 3rd edn, 3 vols. (1847–8); repr. (1905–8) · T. B. Macaulay, *The history of England from the accession of James II*, new edn, ed. C. H. Firth, 6 vols. (1913–15) · G. M. Trevelyan, *England under Queen Anne*, 3 vols. (1930–34) · V. G. Kiernan, *The duel in European history* (1988) · D. T. Andrew, 'The code of honour and its critics … in England, 1700–1850', *Social History*, 5/3 (1980), 409–34 · D. Defoe, *The Review* (29 Nov 1712); repr. in *Defoe's Review*, ed. A. W. Secord (1938), 67–8 · J. Cockburn, *The history and examination of duels* (1720)

Likenesses G. Kneller, oils, 1707, NPG; repro. in Forsythe, *A noble name*, frontispiece [*for Kit-Cat Club*] · J. Faber junior, engraving, 1732 (after G. Kneller), BM, NPG

Wealth at death valuable estate of Gawsworth, near Macclesfield, Cheshire; patrimonial lands, chiefly in Cornwall, loaded with debts by two predecessors; some sold by widow: Forsythe, *Noble rake*; Stater, *Duke Hamilton is dead!*

Mohun [Mone], **Guy** (d. 1407), administrator and bishop of St David's, has been claimed as a member of the baronial family of Mohun of Dunster, Somerset, on the basis of nothing less flimsy than a common enough surname, his being priested in the neighbouring Exeter diocese, and Lady Joan Mohun's move to Kent, where the bishop himself chose to live. There was a contemporary king's esquire called Simon Mohun, and, perhaps the likeliest morsel of evidence, a William Mohun who twice gained preferment from the bishop.

Mohun was in the service of Bishop William Courtenay of London (himself a Devonian, of course) by 12 February 1381, and probably in fact by the preceding September. Courtenay became archbishop of Canterbury that year and kept with him his *clericus familiaris* (August 1384), promoting him to be his domestic steward by 1390 and naming him as an executor in 1395. The future Innocent VII, coming to England as a papal tax collector, was impressed. This dedicated talent for financial administration led to his appointment as receiver of Richard II's chamber on 13 June 1391, a post he kept until 1 February 1398. He took custody of the privy seal on 18 February 1396 and was paid as keeper (apparently without formal appointment) from 18 June 1396 to 14 November 1397.

Mohun was well paid, but his ecclesiastical preferments were thin. It was appropriate that, after some difficulty, the treasurership of St Paul's was obtained for him in May 1394. The king's attempt to secure him the deanship of Wells failed in 1396. His papal provision to the see of St David's on 30 August 1397 implies some urgency on the king's part to have him made a bishop, for it was a modest preferment for one of his standing in the government. It was, though, the time when the king was delivering his coup against his many political enemies. Mohun was consecrated at Abingdon, Berkshire, on 11 November. On 8 September 1398 he was enthroned in his remote cathedral during a twelve-day introduction to his new diocese.

Mohun became treasurer of the realm on 22 January

1398. He resigned as soon as 17 September, but was reappointed to the king's council at the same salary just eleven days later, to play a part in governing the country while Richard led an expedition to Ireland. Mohun wrote to the king there in 1399 that he had suppressed an attempted rising in Oxfordshire and made his own way out to Dublin by 8 July, via his diocese. He was in the diocese again by 30 July and on 2 and 21 August, presumably liaising with the king when Richard returned by that route to face Henry Bolingbroke's invasion. Mohun seems, in the event, to have accepted the king's deposition without demur. He was not personally discredited, but neither was he reappointed to the council. Archbishop Arundel, restored from exile, required his oath of fealty as a suffragan on 9 January 1400.

Mohun chose to live at a manor he owned in Charlton, Kent, and made no attempt to go to his diocese until Owain Glyn Dŵr's revolt became dangerous. Then on 12 October 1401 he is to be found moving through Oxford, on 8–10 November in Brecon, and on 14 November in Carmarthen, when he was appointed as a surveyor of garrisons in Wales. For ten months he worked in his diocese to repel the rebel tide, but also, it should be noted, to implement his triennial episcopal visitation at the right time. He returned to London in late September 1402 and, remarkably, was recalled as treasurer of the realm on 25 October 1402, not the first Ricardian officer of state to whom Henry IV was obliged to turn back. Mohun's especial suitability in the hour of crisis rested on an unblemished background in both royal household and public financial administration, and on a first hand awareness of the enormous logistical problems involved in subduing Wales. He resigned the office, a thankless one at this time, on 9 September 1403, but stayed in London. Adam Usk asserts that Innocent VII was pressed in the curia to translate Mohun out of Wales to London in 1404, to make room for the chronicler himself. Usk's explanation why this proposal failed—that it was made known that Henry IV would be enraged to the point of violent sanctions against cardinals and Italian merchants—is the most plausible part of his whole story.

Mohun, for his part, showed no lack of spirit by making for his diocese once more in April and May 1405, perhaps even longer, to assert the next triennial visitation at the due time in so far as he could. He then returned to live in Kent, mainly in Charlton, sometimes in Ulcombe. He died at Charlton on 31 August 1407, a fortnight after making his will. He requested burial on the north side of the altar in the Augustinian priory at Leeds, Kent, 10,000 masses in all haste, and 24 paupers round his cortège. There were bequests to Maidstone church (the favourite of his first patron, Archbishop Courtenay), including a large missal he had commissioned himself, to Archbishop Arundel, to Canterbury Cathedral, and to his chaplains; there was no mention of family or of Wales. R. G. DAVIES

Sources R. F. Isaacson, ed. and trans., *The episcopal registers of the diocese of St David's, 1397-1518*, 2 vols. in 3, Honourable Society of Cymmrodorion, Cymmrodorion Record Series (1917-20) · R. G. Davies, 'The episcopate in England and Wales, 1375-1443', PhD diss., University of Manchester, 1974, 3.cxcix–cc · *The chronicle of Adam Usk, 1377-1421*, ed. and trans. C. Given-Wilson, OMT (1997), 188-91

Mohun, John, first Lord Mohun (1269?–1330), landowner and soldier, son and heir of John de Mohun of Dunster, Somerset, and Eleanor Fitzpiers, and great-grandson of Reginald de Mohun, was a minor at his father's death in 1279 and was a ward of *Edward I until 1290 under the charge of a tutor named John Launcelewe. He was heir to a considerable estate concentrated around Dunster Castle, Somerset, but he also owned land in Devon, Berkshire, Warwickshire, and Ireland which, after attaining his majority, he partially rationalized by exchanges. John de Mohun married first Ada, daughter of Robert Tibetot, to whom his marriage had been granted in 1279. With her he had seven or eight sons and a daughter. He had no children with his second wife, Sybil, widow of Sir Henry de Lorty, whom he had married by 1325.

By 1296 Mohun was serving with the army in Gascony and between 1297 and 1323 he regularly received summonses for military service once in Flanders, again in Gascony, but principally against the Scots. He was present at the siege of Caerlaverock in 1300. From 1299 until 1329 he was summoned to parliament; in 1299 and 1311 he was addressed as a baron, and in 1318 as one of the *majores barones* when parliament was postponed in the face of a Scottish invasion. In 1308 he was required to attend the coronation of Edward II. His military exploits overshadowed his local activities: in 1307 he was appointed conservator of the peace in Somerset and in 1320 was on the commission of the peace in the county. For a short time in 1326 he was one of the chief inspectors of array in Somerset and Dorset.

John Mohun was evidently an adherent of Thomas, earl of Lancaster, and in October 1313 was pardoned for his role in the death of Piers Gaveston. He seems to have retained some of his sympathies and in 1321 he was warned not to attend meetings of Lancaster's supporters but instead to muster at Coventry against the earl. In 1329 he was exempted from personal attendance in parliament or at musters so long as his second son, Robert, took his place. He died on 25 August 1330 and was buried in the priory church at Dunster. His eldest son John, a knight-banneret, was summoned to fight for the king in 1322 and died soon afterwards in the north, leaving a young son, John *Mohun. The second son of John (d. 1330), Robert, from whom the Mohuns of Fleet claim descent, was murdered about 1331; his fourth son, Payn, served in the retinue of Henry of Lancaster, earl of Derby; and the fifth, Reynold, was the ancestor of the Mohuns of Cornwall.

ROBERT W. DUNNING

Sources H. C. Maxwell Lyte, *A history of Dunster* (1909) · Chancery records · F. Palgrave, ed., *The parliamentary writs and writs of military summons*, 1 (1827) · W. Hunt, ed., *Two chartularies of the priory of St Peter at Bath*, Somerset RS, 7 (1893), 182

Mohun, John, second Lord Mohun (1320?–1375), landowner and soldier, was grandson and heir of John *Mohun (1269?–1330) and son of John Mohun (d. 1322) and his wife, Christian, daughter of Sir John Seagrave. He succeeded his grandfather at the age of ten years, the second successive minor heir in the family. His lands and marriage were acquired by Henry Burghersh (d. 1340), bishop of Lincoln and lord chancellor. The bishop's control of the land was short-lived but his half-brother Bartholomew Burghersh the elder (d. 1355) retained control of his marriage, and the young heir, perhaps already married to Burghersh's daughter Joan, was given livery of his lands without proof of age in 1341.

As a youth Mohun was summoned in 1332 to attend the young Edward III and was knighted in 1340. In 1342 he was summoned to a council and from 1348 to every parliament during his lifetime, being addressed in writs of summons as John Mohun of Dunster. In 1341 he was summoned to do service in Scotland and from 1342 he served regularly in France: in that year in Brittany under Lord Burghersh; in 1344 in Gascony under the earl of Derby. In 1346 he fought under Edward, the Black Prince, at Crécy, in 1350 in a naval battle against the Spanish off Winchelsea. He was in the prince's retinue at Poitiers in 1356, in Brittany under John of Gaunt, duke of Lancaster, in 1357, under the prince again in 1359, and finally in 1373 with Gaunt. He owned a horse called Grisel Gris, which was a gift from the Black Prince, and in 1348 he was nominated one of the original knights of the Garter. His Garter plate remains in St George's Chapel, Windsor.

At home Mohun was appointed to the commission of the peace for Somerset in 1345, a year after being committed to prison for kidnapping one of his own tenants for bringing a case against him. In the following year he was on a local commission of array. From 1348 he was involved in various legal manoeuvres occasioned by the absence of a male heir and perhaps financial difficulties. In 1369 his main estates including Dunster Castle and manor, nearby Minehead manor, and the surrounding hundred of Carhampton were conveyed to trustees for the benefit of his wife.

John Mohun died on 15 September 1375 and was buried in the conventual church of Bruton, a religious house of which his family were patrons. With his wife Joan he had three daughters: Elizabeth, who married William Montagu, earl of Salisbury (d. 1397); Philippa, who was successively wife of Walter *Fitzwalter, Lord Fitzwalter (d. 1386) [see under Fitzwalter family (per. c.1200–c.1500)], Sir John Golafre (d. 1396), and Edward, duke of York (d. 1415); and Maud, who married John, Lord Strange of Knockin (d. 1397). Richard, son of the last, is held to have inherited the barony of Mohun on the death of his aunt Philippa in 1431.   ROBERT W. DUNNING

Sources H. C. Maxwell Lyte, *A history of Dunster* (1909) · *Chancery records* · F. Palgrave, ed., *The parliamentary writs and writs of military summons*, 2 (1830–34)

Mohun, John, first Baron Mohun (c.1592–1641), local politician, was probably born in Boconnoc, Cornwall, the only son of Sir Reginald Mohun, baronet (d. 1639), of Boconnoc, and his second wife, Philippa (fl. 1580–1620), daughter of Sir John Hele of Wembury, Devon. He was educated from 1605 at Exeter College, Oxford, where he graduated BA on

7 July 1608, and then was admitted as a student at the Middle Temple on 5 January 1611. He was appointed a justice of the peace for Cornwall in May 1625 and a deputy lieutenant in the summer of the following year. He also served as MP for Grampound, Cornwall, in the parliaments of 1624 and 1625.

Mohun made his mark chiefly in local politics in which he was one of the leaders of a faction among the Cornish gentry which used its connections with the duke of Buckingham to dominate the county in the late 1620s. To contemporaries he represented the worst type of court-backed local tyrant. His ambition to make an impact in the county was apparent from 1620 when he was talked about as a candidate for the knightship of the shire; however, he was held back by his father's reluctance to support him. This was symptomatic of a bitter quarrel between father and son over the descent of the family estates. Sir Reginald did not die until 1639 which impeded his son's early advancement and made it difficult for him to command the authority to which he aspired. His prospects improved when he patched up his relationship with his father and worked out a favourable land settlement confirmed by private bill in the parliament of 1624. However, the most significant factor in advancing his career was the alliance he formed with Sir James Bagg, Buckingham's principal agent in the south-west.

Bagg recommended Mohun to the royal favourite as someone who 'studies nothing more than to honour your grace and to advantage his Majesty's commands' (PRO, SP 16/37/91) and Mohun showed himself to be a zealous and effective servant of the court. When Buckingham sought to deprive Sir John Eliot of his local admiralty offices after the 1626 parliament, Mohun, with Bagg and Sir Bernard Grenville, headed the commission to investigate his activities, and when the crown was seeking loyal commissioners to collect the forced loan of 1626–7 Mohun again came to the fore. He also took a leading role in sorting out the problems associated with billeting soldiers in the shire in 1627–8. As a reward Buckingham pressurized the earl of Pembroke into appointing Mohun in 1626 to replace Eliot's ally William Coryton as vice-warden of the stannaries and later secured his grant of a peerage—he was created Baron Mohun of Okehampton on 15 April 1628 and took his seat in the Lords on 12 May.

Factional conflict among the Cornish gentry reached a peak in these years. There was a particularly bitter struggle during the county election in February 1628 when Mohun and his allies attempted to stop the return of Eliot and Coryton by warning local gentry that this would incur the king's displeasure. When parliament met, Eliot took revenge by initiating an inquiry into affairs in Cornwall which exposed Mohun's abuse of his authority as vice-warden of the stannaries. Among other things, he was accused of extorting money by forcing local inhabitants to buy privileges as tin miners, falsely imprisoning those, such as the mayor of Looe, who stood up to him, and sending out warrants in which he simply declared 'To this submit or you will provoke me'. Eliot also took notes of an after-dinner conversation in which Mohun argued that while parliaments were allowed to continue 'no state could be well ordered'. Instead Mohun proposed that the privy council entrust power in each county 'to a certain number of men selected for the purpose' (Forster, *Eliot*, 2.112–13). Proceedings against Mohun continued through the 1628 parliament and were revived again in 1629. He lost his vice-wardenship but otherwise appears to have escaped punishment; however, the assassination of Buckingham in August 1628 deprived him and his allies of much of their support at court and fatally undermined their position in the shire.

During the 1630s Mohun took a much less active role in local politics. He served as one of the commissioners collecting knighthood compositions in 1630 but otherwise kept a low profile. By 1632 he had had a definitive falling out with Bagg, accusing him of embezzling funds intended to support the 1627 expedition to the Île de Ré off La Rochelle. Bagg sued Mohun in Star Chamber and the case was heard at various times between 1634 and 1637, resulting in a £500 fine for Mohun. He became resident at Westminster and was more in evidence at court, in 1633 nearly coming to blows after an altercation with Lord Newport at the baptism of the duke of York. Mohun was married once, to Cordelia (*d.* 1639), daughter of Sir John Stanhope and widow of Sir Roger Aston. He died on 28 March 1641.   RICHARD CUST

Sources P. Hunneyball, 'Mohun, John', HoP, *Commons* [draft] · J. Forster, *Sir John Eliot: a biography*, 2 vols. (1864) · G. Radcliffe, *The earl of Strafforde's letters and dispatches, with an essay towards his life*, ed. W. Knowler, 2 vols. (1739) · PRO, SP16 · R. P. Cust, *The forced loan and English politics, 1626–1628* (1987) · A. Duffin, *Faction and faith: politics and religion of the Cornish gentry before the civil war* (1996) · Foster, *Alum. Oxon.* · H. A. C. Sturgess, ed., *Register of admissions to the Honourable Society of the Middle Temple, from the fifteenth century to the year 1944*, 3 vols. (1949)
Likenesses portrait, priv. coll.; repro. in Duffin, *Faction and faith*, 11

Mohun [Moone], **Michael** (*c.*1616–1684), actor and army officer, has an obscure family background. The variant form of his name, Moone, indicates that it was pronounced as a monosyllable: the written name Mohun scans so in verses of 1703. By his own account, written late in life, he became an actor in royal service in 1634, probably as a member of Queen Henrietta's company, joining Christopher Beeston's company in 1636, and performing at the Cockpit playhouse in Drury Lane. By 1637 he was a prominent actor, though only one of his roles from this period is known: that of Bellamente in Shirley's *Love's Cruelty*, which he was performing by 1639, and which he revived after the Restoration. Among his colleagues during this part of his career was the actor Theophilus *Bird (*bap.* 1608, *d.* 1663), who rejoined Mohun as a fellow player after the Restoration, and whose daughter Anne (*d.* 1701/2) became Mohun's wife.

From 1642 Mohun devoted himself to the royal cause as a soldier, with the rank of captain and later of major, a title he retained during his second career on the stage. He claimed to have fought in the principal English campaigns until 1646, and thereafter in Ireland: he was 'desperately wounded' and captured at the siege of Dublin in

Michael Mohun (*c.*1616–1684), by unknown artist, *c.*1660

1649, and spent a year as a prisoner. After his release he joined the English forces in Flanders, and began to revive his skills as a performer. At Antwerp in 1658 he delivered a prologue and epilogue to an entertainment put on for the future Charles II, written by William Cavendish, earl of Newcastle. Mohun had returned to London by 1660, and organized a group of players who began to perform at the Red Bull playhouse, and in later 1660 at the Cockpit.

Mohun and his fellows formed the nucleus of the King's Company, one of the two chief Restoration troupes, and with which Mohun remained as a leading player—notably in partnership with the actor Charles Hart—until the foundation of the United Company in 1682. His fame as an actor is well attested throughout this period for rather more than twenty years: Pepys, who saw him for the first time on stage in Fletcher's *Beggars' Bush* in November 1660, noted in his diary that he had already heard him spoken of as 'the best actor in the world', while in the late 1670s the dramatist Nathaniel Lee is supposed to have exclaimed in praise of Mohun's physical and vocal skills. Mohun's range was wide: he acted in both comedy and tragedy from the old repertory and the new. In the years immediately following the Restoration he had a line in dynamic, witty deceivers, with chief roles in Jonson's famous comedies: the title role in *Volpone*, Face in *The Alchemist*, and Truewit in *Epicoene*. In the same vein he took over Iago in *Othello* after Walter Clun's murder in 1664; his only other accredited Shakespearian part is Cassius in *Julius Caesar*, which he was acting by 1672. The older repertory in the decade after the Restoration included several plays by Fletcher and his collaborators: Mohun played Aubrey in *Rollo*, Melantius in *The Maid's Tragedy* (a part he continued to play, opposite Charles Hart as Amintor, in scenes for which they were jointly renowned), Leontius in *The Humorous Lieutenant*, Don Leon in *Rule a Wife and have a Wife*, Ruy Dias in *The Island Princess*, Valentine in *Wit without Money*, and Mardonius in *A King and No King*. Several plays by Shirley were also produced, in addition to *Love's Cruelty*: Mohun played both Bertoldi and the Friar in *The Imposture*, Columbo in *The Cardinal*, Carlo in *The Court Secret*, and Sebastiano in *The Maid's Revenge*. In other older plays Mohun played Cethegus in *Catiline* (Jonson), Ziriff in *Aglaura* (Suckling), the title role in *Brennoralt* (Suckling), and both Caraffa and Fernando in *Love's Sacrifice* (Ford). In new and adapted plays Mohun is known to have played the following roles, chronologically listed: Mopus in *The Cheats* (Wilson), Fernando in *The Siege of Urbin* (Killigrew), Montezuma in *The Indian Emperor* (Dryden), Mascarillo in *The Damoiselles à la Mode* (Flecknoe), Alberto in *Flora's Vagaries* (Rhodes), Philocles in *Secret Love* (Dryden), King Edward in *The Black Prince* (Orrery), Bellamy in *An Evening's Love* (Dryden), Maximin in *Tyrannic Love* (Dryden), Abdelmelech in *The Conquest of Granada* (2 parts, Dryden), Valentius in *The Roman Empress* (Joyner), Dapperwit in *Love in a Wood* (Wycherley), Don Alvarez in *The Generous Enemies* (Corey), Rodophil in *Marriage à la mode* (Dryden), the duke of Mantua in *The Assignation* (Dryden), Mr Beaumont in *Amboyna* (Dryden), Britannicus in *Nero* (Lee), Pinchwife in *The Country Wife* (Wycherley), Hannibal in *Sophonisba* (Lee), Tribulio in *Love in the Dark* (Fane), Acius in *Lucina's Rape* (Wilmot), the Old Emperor in *Aureng-Zebe* (Dryden), Augustus Caesar in *Gloriana* (Lee), Matthias in *The Destruction of Jerusalem* (2 parts, Crowne), Clytus in *The Rival Queens* (Lee), Edgar in *King Edgar and Alfreda* (Ravenscroft), Ventidius in *All for Love* (Dryden), the title role in *Mithridates* (Lee), Breakbond in *The Man of Newmarket* (Howard), Sir Wilding Frolic in *Trick for Trick* (D'Urfey), and Ismael in *The Loyal Brother* (Southerne).

Mohun was evidently not tall—Lee is supposed to have called him a 'little man of mettle' (Downes)—but his face was handsome and sensitive, with large, liquid, dark eyes. His portrait, probably painted during his military career since its subject is a fairly young man, shows him holding a sword across the front of his body, turned to the left; his head is turned back over his right shoulder to meet the gaze of the observer with a steady, confident command. In the theatre his voice and enunciation were widely admired. By the 1670s he walked with a limp, usually explained as arising from the gout from which he was by then suffering, but perhaps also attributable to his war wounds. His creative partnership with Hart underwent some rupture in late 1667, noted by Pepys. Mohun absented himself from the theatre during the quarrel (which seems to have resolved itself within a week or so), and his wages were withheld.

From 1660 onwards Mohun was a leading participant in theatre business as well as the art of playing. The King's Company played first in a converted tennis court in Vere Street, but in 1661 planned a new building in Bridges Street, in which Mohun bought shares, and to which the company moved in 1663. The property included a number of houses, in the rent of which he had a share. He also held shares in the company itself, and with his fellows Charles Hart and John Lacy effectively managed the troupe for a period after the move to the new theatre. When the building was burnt in 1672 the actors moved for two years to the playhouse in Lincoln's Inn Fields formerly used by the Duke's Company, while a new building, the Drury Lane Theatre, rose on the site of the ruined one. The fire caused a crisis in the company's fortunes, and consequently in Mohun's; he sold his building shares, although he continued to make other investments and to be involved in financial planning. A disruption in the management in 1676 saw Mohun once more, with his colleagues, in charge of running the company, but in the later 1670s he was evidently less active both on stage and in the increasingly difficult financial affairs of the troupe. The union of the two companies in 1682 put Mohun at a financial disadvantage, and he wrote a petition to the king complaining that he had been deprived 'of his share and a quarter in the scenes, clothes, and plays (worth about £4000)', and reduced to the status of a journeyman player; the request was granted, and Mohun was established as a full member of the United Company for the remaining two years of his life.

Mohun's private life away from the playhouse emerges fleetingly and incompletely from surviving records. At what date he married Anne Bird is not known, but they were together for at least twenty-one years and had at least nine children: three daughters and a son were buried at St Giles-in-the-Fields, the Mohuns' parish church, between 1664 and 1679, and Mohun's royal petition of 1682 claims that he was then supporting five children. Mohun lived in the Covent Garden area from the Restoration onwards: in Russell Street in 1675, Bow Street later in the 1670s, and at the time of his death in Brownlow Street (modern Betterton Street). Mohun was buried at St Giles-in-the-Fields on 11 October 1684, evidently with the rites of the Church of England; a letter of 1678, however, reveals him to have been a Catholic, as he perhaps had been throughout his life. It was addressed to Joseph Williamson, secretary of state, requesting exemption from the order banning recusants from within 10 miles of the city in the aftermath of the Popish Plot: 'if I went,' Mohun wryly observes, 'the play-house must of necessity lie still.'

JOHN H. ASTINGTON

Sources Highfill, Burnim & Langhans, *BDA* · J. Milhous and R. D. Hume, eds., *A register of English theatrical documents, 1660–1737*, 1 (1991) · G. E. Bentley, *The Jacobean and Caroline stage*, 7 vols. (1941–68) · J. Downes, *Roscius Anglicanus*, ed. J. Milhous and R. D. Hume, new edn (1987) · D. Thomas, ed., *Restoration and Georgian England, 1660–1788* (1989) · L. Hotson, *The Commonwealth and Restoration stage* (1927) · J. Milhous and R. D. Hume, 'Manuscript casts for revivals of 3 plays by Shirley in the 1660s', *Theatre Notes*, 39 (1985), 32–6 · J. Milhous and R. D. Hume, 'New light on acting companies', *Review of English Studies*, new ser., 42 (1991), 487–509 · *DNB*
Likenesses oils, *c*.1660, Knole, Kent [*see illus.*] · portrait, 1663?; print, 1822 · E. Harding junior, engraving, BM, NPG; repro. in F. G. Waldron, *The biographical mirrour*, 3 vols. (1795–1810)

Mohun, Sir Reginald de (*c*.1206–1258), baron (occasionally erroneously called earl of Somerset), was the son of Reginald de Mohun, lord of Dunster in Somerset, the great-grandson of William de Mohun, earl of Somerset (*d.* *c.*1145). His mother was Alice, fourth daughter and coheir of William *Brewer; she brought a large inheritance to her husband's family, and, before 1228, married as her second husband William Paynel. Reginald was under age at the time of his father's death, which took place in or before 1213, and was a ward of Henry fitz Count (*d.* 1222), son of the earl of Cornwall; the wardship was, apparently, afterwards divided between the crown and William Brewer, his own grandfather.

Mohun had livery of his estates and was knighted on 18 January 1227. He held office under the crown from the mid-1230s and accompanied the king regularly on military expeditions to Wales and the continent. He can occasionally be encountered as a justice in the 1230s and 1240s, though he does not seem to have gone regularly on eyre. From 1 April to 6 May 1242 and (at a fee of 100 marks a year, with the keepership of Sauvey Castle) from 25 October 1252 to 16 February 1253, replacing the unpopular Sir Geoffrey Langley, he was chief justice of the forests south of Trent. In 1253 he received from Henry III rights of warren and of the chase and of a weekly market at Dunster. Among the lands that he inherited from his mother was Torre in Devon, where in 1196 William Brewer had founded a Premonstratensian abbey. Mohun often resided there. The buildings included a court house and, from March 1252, a private chapel for the exclusive use of his family; the abbey bore the Mohun arms, Reginald having confirmed the grants of his grandfather to the convent. His younger brother, William, conveyed to him lands at Torre and Maryansleigh, Devon, at Endicombe, near Dunster, Somerset, and at Clythorn, near Woodstock, Oxfordshire, in order that Reginald might build a Cistercian abbey in a suitable place, and be its founder and patron. On the advice of Alcius of Gisors, abbot of Beaulieu in Hampshire, Mohun founded in 1246, with the grant of Axminster for the souls of himself, his wives, his brother, and William Brewer, the abbey of Newenham at Axminster in Devon, thus breaking with the family's patronage of Bruton, Somerset. Imitating John and Henry III, he placed there a colony of Cistercian monks from Beaulieu, who took possession of their new house with much ceremony in the presence of Reginald and William on 6 January 1247. Mohun generously bound himself to provide annually, for life, 100 marks for building expense at Newenham. In 1247 Mohun's foundation was confirmed by Innocent IV, and a curious later tradition preserved at Newenham records that, when Mohun appeared at the papal court at Lyons, the pope presented him with a rose, or other flower, of gold, and asked him of what degree he was. He replied that he was a plain knight bachelor, on which the pope said that, as such a gift could be made only to kings, dukes, or earls, Mohun should be a count apostolic, and to maintain his title granted him 200 marks a year (the false statement that he styled himself earl of Somerset rests on a forged charter perpetrated in the fourteenth century by the monks of Newenham). He and his brother William joined in laying the foundation-stones of the church of Newenham in 1254; at the ceremony Mohun declared his wish to be buried at Newenham, unless he should die in the Holy Land.

Mohun also made a grant to the convent of Bath for a mass to be said for ever for the souls of his son John, who had recently died, and other members of his house, by a monk of Dunster Priory, a cell of Bath, or by a secular priest, in the chapel of Dunster Castle. He was a benefactor to the Augustinian canons of Bruton and Barlinch, Somerset, the Benedictines of Dunster, and the Cistercians of Cleeve, and gave two charters to the townsmen of Dunster.

Mohun's first wife, Hawise, was dead by 1237; her surname is not known but Maxwell-Lyte cites evidence that she may have been the heir of the Flemyngs of Ottery. With her Mohun had (besides at least three other children, who all married well) a son John, who married Joan, the fifth daughter of William Ferrers, earl of Derby, and died in Gascony in 1254 (his heart was buried at Newenham, his body at Bruton); he left a son, also named John (*d.* 1279), whose son was John *Mohun (1269?–1330). (Joan married as her second husband, in 1256, Sir Robert d'Aiguillon.) Mohun's second wife, whom he married *c.*1242, was Isabel, widow of Gilbert Basset, and daughter of William Ferrers, earl of Derby, and Sybilla, the fourth daughter of William Marshal, earl of Pembroke (*d.* 1219), and so the elder sister of her stepson's wife. By this marriage a part of the inheritance of the earls Marshal fell to the Mohuns; this part included certain lands in Leinster about which Mohun and his wife appear to have been involved in some legal proceedings from 1248 to 1253 with the other Marshal coheirs, especially William de Valence. With Isabel, Mohun had a son named William (aged six or seven in 1258), who inherited part of the Marshal estates. His wardship and marriage were sold to Sir William de la Zouche for 200 marks in 1262.

Mohun died at Torre on 20 January 1258, and was buried on the left side of the high altar at Newenham Abbey. He left 700 marks in his will for Newenham. A long and, no doubt, fanciful, account of his holy death is extant from the mid-fourteenth century, written by a monk of Newenham. He recorded that Mohun, who was wont to hear the whole divine service daily, was confessed by Henry, a Franciscan theologian of Oxford; furthermore, thirty-five years after Mohun's death the writer saw and touched the founder's body, which was then uncorrupt. Mohun was succeeded by his grandson John, a ward of Queen Eleanor, who from 1258 to 1269 received about £100 a year from this custody. His brother William, a knight of the royal household, probably attached to the queen's service, died on 17 September 1265, and was buried in Newenham Abbey. WILLIAM HUNT, *rev.* H. W. RIDGEWAY

Sources *Chancery records* (RC) · *Curia regis rolls preserved in the Public Record Office* (1922–) · C. Roberts, ed., *Excerpta è rotulis finium in Turri Londinensi asservatis, Henrico Tertio rege, AD 1216–1272*, 2 vols., RC, 32 (1835–6) · Dugdale, *Monasticon*, new edn, 5.690–94 · Dugdale, *Monasticon*, new edn, 6/2.926 · H. S. Sweetman and G. F. Handcock, eds., *Calendar of documents relating to Ireland*, 5 vols., PRO (1875–86), vols. 1–2 · H. C. M. Lyte, ed., *Liber feodorum: the book of fees*, 2 (1923), 2.641 · Paris, *Chron.*, 5.340 · *Two cartularies of the Augustinian priory of Bruton and the Cluniac priory of Montacute*, Somerset RS, 8 (1894) ·

H. C. Maxwell-Lyte, *A history of Dunster and the families of Mohun and Luttrell*, 2 vols. (1909), vol. 1 · J. Davidson, *The history of Newenham Abbey* (1843) · M. Howell, 'The resources of Eleanor of Provence as queen consort', *EngHR*, 102 (1987), 372–93, esp. 387

Mohun [Moion], **William de** (*fl.* **1083–***c.***1100**), landowner, was sheriff of Somerset at the time of the Domesday inquest. His name is usually spelt de Moion in contemporary documents and he came from Moyon, near St Lô in western Normandy, which was held by his descendants until the last years of the twelfth century and probably until the French conquest of Normandy in 1204. He succeeded William de Courseulles as sheriff at some time before 1083, for there survives a writ addressed to him by Queen Matilda, who died in that year; and he was replaced by Aiulf, the incumbent sheriff of Dorset, in the early years of William Rufus, probably between 1089 and 1091. (Somerset, as with a number of other counties, saw quite a rapid turnover of sheriffs under the first two Norman kings.)

Nothing is known of William de Mohun's origins or earlier career. The claim by Wace, writing a century after the event, that he was present 'with many companions' at the battle of Hastings should be treated with scepticism. But by the time of Domesday he held in chief lands worth just over £175 a year, comprising fifty-four manors in Somerset, eleven in Dorset, and one each in Devon and Wiltshire. Of these manors, twenty-one (seventeen in Somerset and four in Dorset, with an annual value of almost £91) were retained in demesne and the remainder enfeoffed to subtenants. His Somerset manors were nearly all in the west of the county, in the Quantocks and Exmoor region, and many of them were very small. A number of the more valuable manors along the north Somerset coast and in the neighbourhood of Taunton were retained in demesne, notably Minehead, Cutcombe, West Quantockshead, and East Lydeard, as well as the wealthy manor of North Brewham, near Bruton in the east of the county. His Dorset manors were scattered through the western and northern parts of that county; the four retained by William in his own hands were once again the most valuable of those with which he had been enfeoffed. He appears to have possessed stud farms at Cutcombe and Brewham, where Exon Domesday recorded the presence of thirty-six and twenty-two brood mares respectively. By the time of Domesday, William had built a castle at Dunster, which became the *caput* of his descendants' lordship, passed down in the direct male line until 1375. The *Cartae baronum* of 1166 assessed this lordship, by then held by his grandson, another William de Mohun, at thirty-nine and a half knights' fees under the 'old' (that is pre-1135) assessment.

As sheriff it might be assumed that William de Mohun was 'farming' (or managing) all or most of the royal manors in his county. In fact Exon Domesday records expressly that he was farming twelve royal estates, all of which had been held by Earl Harold and his relatives before 1066, with a total value to the crown of at least £183 (the recorded income of one manor is incomplete), and another £9 from the third penny of the Somerset towns.

At some stage after 1090 William de Mohun gave his manor of Alcombe to the church of St George at Dunster, and tithes from a number of other manors and from his brood mares to the monks of Bath and Bishop John. The charter conveying these donations was witnessed by several members of his family: his wife, Adelisa (or Adeliz), his brother Wimund, and his sons Robert and Geoffrey. However, his other son and eventual successor, William de *Mohun (d. c.1145), was not mentioned in this document; he may therefore have been a younger son, either still unborn or of tender age when the donation was made. The steward Durandus, who witnessed this charter and held three manors not far to the south of Dunster in 1086, was also probably a relative; a 'Durandus le Moiun' was mentioned in a writ of Henry I for Bath Abbey in 1121 (William fitz Durand held five and a half knights' fees in the *Cartae baronum*, though his property was by then more extensive).

The date of William de Mohun's death is unknown. The charter for Bath Abbey, which can only be dated to some time between 1090 and 1122, is the last reference to him, assuming that the William de Mohun mentioned in the 1129/30 pipe roll was his son.   G. A. LOUD

Sources A. Farley, ed., *Domesday Book*, 2 vols. (1783), fols. 72a, 81c–82a, 95c–96c, 110b · *Exon Domesday*, fols. 47a–48b, 355b–364b · W. Hunt, ed., *Two chartularies of the priory of St Peter at Bath*, Somerset RS, 7 (1893), pt 1, p. 38, no. 34 · *Calendar of the manuscripts of the dean and chapter of Wells*, 1, HMC, 12 (1907), 66 · J. H. Round, ed., *Calendar of documents preserved in France, illustrative of the history of Great Britain and Ireland* (1899), p. 178, no. 505 · *Reg. RAN*, 2.302 · *Le 'Roman de Rou' de Wace*, ed. A. J. Holden, 3 vols. (Paris, 1970–73), vol. 2, p. 201, lines 8487–8 · J. A. Green, *English sheriffs to 1154* (1990), 73 · G. A. Loud, 'An introduction to the Somerset Domesday', *The Somerset Domesday*, ed. A. Williams and R. Erskine (1989), 5, 24

Wealth at death £91 p.a. from demesne estates in 1086–7: Farley, ed., *Domesday book*

Mohun [Moyon], **William de**, earl of Somerset (*d. c.***1145**), magnate, was the heir, and almost certainly the son, of the Domesday tenant-in-chief William de *Mohun, who in 1086 held extensive estates, mainly in Somerset, centred on a castle at Dunster. His mother would thus have been Adelisa (or Adeliz), whose parentage is unknown. The family originated from the neighbourhood of Moyon (Manche) where it retained interests until the early thirteenth century.

In September 1131 William de Mohun the younger was in attendance on Henry I at the Council of Northampton and in 1135 witnessed a charter issued by Godfrey, bishop of Bath. There is no evidence that he attended King Stephen's court in the early months of the new reign, and, in 1138 or early 1139, he participated in the general west-country rebellion which followed the formal declaration by Robert, earl of Gloucester, in the late spring of 1138, of support for the Empress Matilda's rival claim to the English throne. William gathered a powerful force within his castle at Dunster, and is said to have 'made raids fiercely and turbulently over all that district of England'. Stephen, on hearing of these disturbances, arrived before the castle, probably in the spring or early summer of 1139; but, finding it impregnable, he built his own castle nearby and left Henry de Tracy, to whom he had recently granted the honour of Barnstaple, to keep William in check.

After Stephen's capture at the battle of Lincoln in February 1141 William de Mohun was in the Empress Matilda's entourage as she advanced on London. On her arrival there at midsummer he witnessed one of her charters as Earl William de Mohun, a title he had not enjoyed a month or two earlier. He stayed with the empress until the siege of Winchester in August when, according to the author of the *Gesta Stephani*, she created him earl of Dorset; but it was as earl of Somerset that she addressed him in a writ issued before the end of 1142, and this was also his style in other charters. By at least the end of 1143 he had deserted her cause, at the same time, apparently, incurring some disgrace. This may be connected with the story, related in the *Gesta Stephani* as a postscript to the account of William's rebellion in 1138–9, of the capture by Henry de Tracy of 104 of William's knights during a cavalry engagement. As a result he humbly and abjectly 'left the country … altogether untroubled by his sedition'.

William founded a house of Augustinian canons at Bruton, in Somerset (in August 1142 according to the priory's lost annals, though Henry I issued a charter in favour of a foundation there between 1127 and 1135), and was a benefactor of the monks whom he, or his father, established at Dunster as a cell of Bath Abbey. He married, in or before 1130, Agnes, daughter of Walter de Gant. Her marriage portion comprised the manor of Whichford, Warwickshire, the church of which William and his wife had granted to Bridlington Priory, Yorkshire, by 1133. He died in obscurity, certainly before 1155 and probably well before 1147, and was succeeded in his estates by his eldest son, William; the earldom lapsed. Other sons were Ralph, who predeceased him, Iwerne, Henry, Peter, and Richard, described together on one occasion as clerks.

ROBERT BEARMAN

Sources R. H. C. Davis, *King Stephen*, 3rd edn (1990) · GEC, *Peerage* · K. R. Potter and R. H. C. Davis, eds., *Gesta Stephani*, OMT (1976) · *Two cartularies of the Augustinian priory of Bruton and the Cluniac priory of Montacute*, Somerset RS, 8 (1894) · L. C. Loyd, *The origins of some Anglo-Norman families*, ed. C. T. Clay and D. C. Douglas, Harleian Society, 103 (1951) · H. C. Maxwell-Lyte, *Dunster and its lords* (1882) · *Reg. RAN*, vols. 2–3 · W. Hunt, ed., *Two chartularies of the priory of St Peter at Bath*, Somerset RS, 7 (1893) · T. Tanner, *Notitia monastica, or, An account of all the abbies, priories, and houses of friers … in England and Wales, and of all the colleges and hospitals founded before AD MDXL* (1744) · Dugdale, *Monasticon*, new edn · J. Hunter, ed., *Magnum rotulum scaccarii, vel, Magnum rotulum pipae, anno tricesimo-primo regni Henrici primi*, RC (1833) · F. M. R. Ramsey, ed., *Bath and Wells, 1061–1205*, English Episcopal Acta, 10 (1995)

Moir, (John) Chassar (1900–1977), obstetrician and gynaecologist, was born on 21 March 1900 at 7 Melville Gardens, Montrose, Angus, in Scotland, the youngest of four children of John Moir (1860–1931), wine merchant and grocer, and Isabella Moir, *née* Pirie (1864–1947). He attended Montrose Academy, taking a particular interest in sciences and in German. He graduated MB, ChB from Edinburgh University in 1922, became FRCS (Edin.) in 1926 and MD with gold medal in 1930, and was elected FRCOG in 1936. He also became MA, DM (Oxon.) in 1938, and was awarded the

(John) Chassar Moir (1900–1977), by Bassano, c.1967

honorary degrees of LLD (Ontario) in 1954, DSc (Edinburgh) in 1970, and DSc (Manchester) in 1972; he was made CBE in 1961.

After graduation and house-surgeon appointments in Edinburgh in 1922, Moir sailed to India as ship's surgeon. On returning to Europe he visited Heidelberg, Vienna, Berlin, and Hungary, becoming proficient in German. For five years he worked as a general practitioner in Redhill, Surrey, where he was also assistant surgeon to the East Surrey Hospital. In 1933 Moir married Grace Hilda Bailey, a nursing sister; they had two sons and two daughters. In 1935 he was appointed reader in obstetrics and gynaecology in the Royal Postgraduate Medical School in Hammersmith (he was the first to hold this readership) and in 1936 he was appointed first assistant to the department of obstetrics and gynaecology at University College Hospital, London, under F. J. Browne. In 1937 he was appointed as the first Nuffield professor of obstetrics and gynaecology in the University of Oxford and a fellow of Oriel College—appointments which he held until his retirement in 1967.

Moir's greatest contribution to medicine was the discovery of the drug ergometrine, an extract of spores containing ergot. Ergot, which contained such a wide variety of substances that it was described as 'a treasure house for drugs', was known from the early nineteenth century for its ability to cause strong contractions of the pregnant uterus. But it was not until the twentieth century that a search began for the active agent or agents which could be extracted and used to prevent post-partum haemorrhage. The physiologist Henry Dale began the search in 1904. Others in Europe entered on a series of often acrimonious claims to have found the active agent, two of which were marketed under the names 'ergotoxine' and 'ergotamine'. They had little practical application, however, until Moir, in 1932, devised a means of recording intra-uterine pressure in the one week post-partum uterus, using an apparatus which he was proud to say cost only 1s. With this apparatus, Moir was able to show that the effects of ergotoxine and ergotamine were much slower than the effects of the crude liquid form of ergot used in the early nineteenth century. For the prevention of post-partum haemorrhage it is essential to have a drug which acts very quickly. Moir believed that the rapidly acting component of ergot had not been discovered because, as he put it, '... the pharmacological dogs had been so absorbed in barking at the cats in the tree in front that they had missed a bigger and altogether more delectable kitten sitting in the tree behind' (Tansey). The rapidly acting component in ergot—the 'delectable kitten'—was isolated and described by Moir and an organic chemist, Harold Ward Dudley FRS, in March 1935. They named it ergometrine, and its rapid introduction into obstetric practice led to a marked fall in deaths from post-partum haemorrhage, saving the lives of countless mothers. The introduction of the sulphonamides in the mid-1930s and the introduction of ergometrine are probably the two most important single advances in the history of obstetrics.

Later, while working at Oxford, Moir also made an outstanding contribution to the gynaecological operation for the repair of vesico-vaginal fistula. Surgical repair of this deeply distressing condition, in which a hole between the bladder and the vagina leads to a continual leakage of urine through the vagina, was often unsuccessful. Moir, who often treated other surgeons' failures, perfected the operation; by slow, meticulous, and extremely skilful surgery, he achieved a cure rate that earned him the admiration and envy of his colleagues. His book, *Vesico-vaginal fistula* (1961), which went into two editions, was the standard work on the subject. Among his other achievements were new methods of pelvimetry, the detection of the placental site by X-rays, and (with Mostyn Embrey) research on prostaglandins. He was also associated with one of the finest textbooks in any branch of medicine in the first half of the twentieth century: J. M. Munro Kerr's *Operative Obstetrics* (1st edn, 1908). Moir joined Munro Kerr as joint author of the fifth edition in 1949, and following Munro Kerr's death Moir was the sole author of the magnificent sixth edition of 1956—a work, incidentally, which reflects the deep historical interest of both authors.

Moir was an unusually handsome man, tall, slim, with aquiline features and high cheek bones suggesting an intellectual, or even perhaps an austere ascetic. In fact he was the kindest, most gentle, and approachable of men, much loved by his staff, students, and especially his patients. At a time when such a thing was rare among senior clinicians, he would go round his gynaecology wards and sit beside his patients to chat to them about their families, their homes, and their worries. Many women returned from the Radcliffe Infirmary in Oxford glowing with praise for the 'great professor' who had showed them such genuine concern and kindness. He died, survived by his wife, on 24 November 1977, at Farnmore, Charlbury, Oxfordshire, and was buried on the 30th in the family grave at Sleepy Hillock, Montrose, Angus. Moir's obituary notice in the *British Medical Journal* described him as 'a great man and a gentle man; a man who did more than anyone living today to save the lives and relieve the miseries of women' (*BMJ*, 1551).

IRVINE LOUDON

Sources private information (2004) · E. M. Tansey, 'Ergot to ergometrine: an obstetric renaissance?', *Women and medicine*, ed. L. Conrad and A. Hardy [forthcoming] · *BMJ* (10 Dec 1977), 1551 · *The Lancet* (10 Dec 1977), 1240 · personal knowledge (2004) · WWW · *CGPLA Eng. & Wales* (1977)
Archives Royal College of Obstetricians and Gynaecologists, London, corresp. and printed material; notes · Wellcome L., corresp. and papers | FILM Royal College of Obstetricians and Gynaecologists, London
Likenesses Bassano, photograph, c.1967, priv. coll. [*see illus.*] · bust, John Radcliffe Infirmary, Oxford, Nuffield Department of Obstetrics and Gynaecology · photographs, priv. coll.
Wealth at death £35,513: probate, 23 Feb 1978, *CGPLA Eng. & Wales*

Moir, David Macbeth [*pseud.* Delta] **(1798–1851)**, physician and writer, was born in Musselburgh, Midlothian, on 5 January 1798, the son of Robert Moir (*d.* 1842) and Elizabeth Macbeth (1767–1842). Having been educated at Musselburgh grammar school, at thirteen he was apprenticed to a local medical practitioner, Dr Stewart, with whom he studied for four years. He also attended classes at the University of Edinburgh, gaining his medical diploma in late 1816 and venturing into private practice in 1817 as a partner of Dr Brown, another Musselburgh doctor.

Moir began writing at an early age, and scored his first publication success with two essays in the Haddington-based *Cheap Magazine* in 1812. After medical qualification in 1816 he undertook further literary work, publishing in the *Scots Magazine* and participating in a local debating society that he founded, called The Musselburgh Forum. His first collection of poems, *The Bombardment of Algiers, and other Poems*, appeared in 1816. Through a connection with Thomas Pringle he began contributing to Constable's *Edinburgh Magazine*, following Pringle's assumption of its editorship in October 1817. His work also began appearing in the *Edinburgh Literary Gazette*, the *Journal of Agriculture*, and *Blackwood's Magazine*. His light satires and poetry in the latter journal, contributed under the pseudonym Delta, were flatteringly attributed to Dr William Maginn, and led to a strong personal friendship between the two. This connection also led to contributions over the next few decades to Maginn's *Fraser's Magazine*, where Moir became part of the Fraserian stable of writers. Similarly his close friendships with John Wilson and the Edinburgh publisher William Blackwood established him within the inner circle of contributors who shaped the contents of the monthly *Blackwood's Magazine* during the first two decades after its founding in 1817. The 'amiable Delta', as he was known, had a natural warmth, loyalty, and friendly personality that proved engaging and

David Macbeth Moir (1798–1851), by Sir John Watson-Gordon, 1850

brought him lasting friendships. As personal physician to Blackwood he was in attendance at his deathbed, in 1834, and was subsequently nominated one of his executors. Moir named two of his sons, John Wilson Moir and William Blackwood Moir (1835–1838), in honour of his close companions.

In 1823 a further important literary friendship sprang up, between Moir and John Galt, who in that year had moved to Eskgrove, near Moir's residence in Musselburgh. Moir played a crucial role in the publication of Galt's novel *The Last of the Lairds* (1826), at a time when Galt was involved in establishing new settlements in Canada. Already an unofficial consultant editor for William Blackwood, advising on and contributing material to *Blackwood's Magazine*, Moir was asked by Blackwood to help to shape the work for publication after Galt's departure for Canada. Moir did so, writing three new concluding chapters for the work, as well as editing and rewriting significant portions of the manuscript. Galt's reaction to this was muted, due in part to the fact that it was a *fait accompli* by the time that he knew of it, and he was later to write an ironic but polite letter of thanks to Moir for his 'various points of minor improvement' (Gordon, 251).

Between his twin roles of medical man and literary critic and editor Moir found time to write and publish widely in various literary periodicals: to *Blackwood's Magazine* alone he contributed over 370 articles, in prose and verse, between 1817 and 1851. 1824 saw the publication of *Legends of Genevieve and other Tales and Poems*, as well as the start in *Blackwood's Magazine* of a series of tales that were to form his best-known work, *The Autobiography of Mansie Waugh*, eventually collected and published in 1828. A humorous account of the sayings and doings of a tradesman in a small Scottish village, it proved extremely popular in the following decades, particularly in England, where readers were fascinated by this portrait of Scots rural life and manners as filtered through carefully Anglicized Scots dialogue. Its caricatures of couthy rural Scotland anticipated the themes and concerns of the kailyard school of Scots literature later in the century. Moir is also credited with being one of the possible originators of the anonymously authored and haunting poem 'The Canadian Boat Song', which first appeared in the pages of *Blackwood's Magazine* in 1829. Other work included studies in medicine and medical history (*Outlines of the Ancient History of Medicine*, 1831, and *Practical Observations on Malignant Cholera*, 1832), biographies (*Biographical Memoirs of John Galt*, 1843), and collections of poetry (*Domestic Verses*, 1843).

In 1829 Moir was offered the editorship of the quarterly *Journal of Agriculture* by William Blackwood but declined it, arguing that it would involve moving from his beloved home town. In that same year, on 8 June, he married Catherine Elizabeth Bell at Carham church, in her native Northumberland. By all accounts theirs was a happy and active union; over the next twenty years they had eleven children, of whom three (including the one named after William Blackwood) died tragically young within eighteen months, in 1838 or 1839. Moir played an active civic role in the Musselburgh community, for which he was awarded the freedom of his native borough in 1831. He played a major part in containing a cholera epidemic that swept the area in 1832, and in 1844 was elected a member of the Church of Scotland kirk session in Inveresk. This led to his election as representative of the Annan burgh in the annual general assembly of the Church of Scotland, a major event in the Scots protestant calendar. He was returned every year until his death, in 1851.

On 22 June 1851 Moir was seriously injured while dismounting from his horse on a visit away from home. He died at Dumfries, of complications resulting from the accident, on 6 July, and was buried on 10 July at Inveresk church, Musselburgh. Those who paid tribute to Moir's character and work included Thomas Carlyle, who described him as having a 'fine melodious character' (*Poetical Works*, cxxi), and his friend George Gilfillan, who wrote of him that 'a better man and a lovelier specimen of the literary character did not exist' (Kunitz, 443). His contribution to Musselburgh life was recognized in 1854, when community leaders unveiled a statue commemorating his life on the banks of the Esk river, which runs through his native town.   DAVID FINKELSTEIN

Sources *Poetical works of D. M. Moir*, ed. T. Aird, 2 vols. (1852) · G. Douglas, *The Blackwood group* (1897) · F. D. Tredrey, *The house of Blackwood* (1954) · Mrs Oliphant, *William Blackwood and his sons* (1897), vols. 1–2 of *Annals of a publishing house* (1897–8) · A. L. Strout, *A*

bibliography of articles in Blackwood's Magazine, 1817–1825 (1959) • I. A. Gordon, 'Plastic surgery on a nineteenth-century novel: John Galt, William Blackwood, Dr D. M. Moir and *The last of the lairds*', *The Library*, 32/3 (Sept 1977), 246–55 • S. J. Kunitz and H. Haycraft, eds., *British authors of the nineteenth century* (1936) • C. Craig, ed., *The history of Scottish literature*, 3: *Nineteenth century*, ed. D. Gifford (1988) • M. M. H. Thrall, *Rebellious Fraser's* (1934) • *DNB* • *IGI*

Archives NL Scot., corresp., literary MSS, and papers | BL, letters to George Thompson, Add. MS 35265 • NL Scot., corresp. with Blackwoods • University of Toronto, Thomas Fisher Rare Book Library, letters to Alexander Balfour

Likenesses D. Maclise, group portrait, lithograph, 1835 (*The Fraserians*), BM; repro. in *Fraser's Magazine* (1835) • J. Watson-Gordon, oils, 1850, Scot. NPG [*see illus.*] • A. F. Ritchie, statue, 1853, Musselburgh • J. Faed, watercolour drawing, Scot. NPG • D. Maclise, lithograph, NPG • D. Maclise, watercolour drawing, Scot. NPG • engraving, repro. in Aird, ed., *Poetical works*, 185 • etching, repro. in Kunitz, ed., *British authors*, 193 • etching, repro. in Thrall, *Rebellious Fraser's*

Moir, Frank Lewis (1852–1904), composer, was born at Market Harborough, Leicestershire, on 22 April 1852. His father was a painter. After working in London and Nottingham, he became an art student at South Kensington. Though he had no musical training, he won a scholarship, in 1876, at the National Training School for Music, where he studied under Ebenezer Prout, John Stainer, and Frederick Bridge; while he was there Boosey & Co. engaged him on a four-year contract to compose ballads. In 1881 he won the Madrigal Society's prize. He possessed a good baritone voice, and gave recitals and taught singing at a studio in Oxford Street.

Moir composed chiefly sentimental drawing-room ballads, many of which were very popular, especially 'Only Once More' (1883) and 'Down the Vale' (1885). He wrote both music and words for many of his works, including a comic opera, *The Royal Watchman* (1877). He attempted more serious pieces, including a harvest cantata, a communion service in D, and some elaborate songs, but they had little success. He also published a work entitled *Natural Voice Production* (1889) and contributed minor organ solos to several contemporary collections.

Moir married Eleanor Farnol, a soprano from Birmingham, on 5 April 1886 and the couple had three children. Moir's career was ruined by the many pirated cheap and illegal copies of his songs which flooded the market before the introduction of stricter copyright laws, and publishers refused his compositions; he fell into financial difficulty, and after a painful illness died at Deal, Kent, on 14 July 1904.   HENRY DAVEY, rev. JAMES J. NOTT

Sources Brown & Stratton, *Brit. mus.* • A. T. C. Pratt, ed., *People of the period: being a collection of the biographies of upwards of six thousand living celebrities*, 2 vols. (1897) • *MT*, 45 (1904), 533 • *Musical Herald* (Aug 1904), 245

Moir, George (1800–1870), literary critic and lawyer, was baptized on 10 April 1800, the second of three children of George Moir, vintner, of the Old Ship inn, Aberdeen, and his wife, Mary Straton. He attended school in Aberdeen and then Marischal College, from 1813 to 1817. Having moved to Edinburgh he worked in a lawyer's office, and on 5 July 1825 was admitted an advocate. But it is clear that by this date he had also developed other interests and

shown considerable drive and ability in acquiring a wide knowledge of Spanish, Italian, and French literature. He had already published anonymously, in 1822, in the *New Monthly Magazine and Literary Journal*, a review of a book of selections from early Spanish poetry; the hitherto tentative attribution is confirmed by the *Edinburgh Review* for January 1824, in which Moir reviews the same book and claims as his own some translations found in the earlier article. These reviews also show a familiarity with Italian and French literature. While working on this article in the Advocates' Library in Edinburgh, Moir made what was to be a lifelong friendship with Sir William Hamilton, who helped him with some related works in German, a language that he said he did not at that time understand (Veitch, 132). He soon made good this deficiency, and in 1827 published *Wallenstein*, containing the verse dramas 'Piccolomini' and 'The death of Wallenstein', the first full translations into English from the German of Schiller; the dedication is to Sir William Hamilton, who revised the proof-sheets. It was well received. In the same year Moir also published *Table-Talk*, comprising 'ana' (Voltairiana, Johnsoniana, etc.) drawn from French, English, Italian, and German literature, and, in the following year, a translation of Schiller's historical works. By 1829 he had become acquainted with Thomas Carlyle. On 12 July 1830 he married Flora (1803/4–1858), daughter of George Tower of Aberdeen; they raised a family of three daughters and one son. Carlyle described Moir at this time as having 'become a conservative, settled everywhere into *dilettante*, not very happy, I think; dry, civil, and seems to feel *unheimlich* in my company' (*DNB*).

A heavy reader of German publications, Moir wrote a forty-seven-page review of G. C. Horst's *Zauber-Bibliothek* for the *Foreign Quarterly Review* (1830) (his later anonymous publication *Magic and Witchcraft*, 1852, is no more than a reprint of this review with a short additional chapter about the ancient world). In his early years he had been whiggish in his politics, but later became a tory. He tried his hand at political satire with *Fragments from the History of John Bull*, published in parts in *Blackwood's Magazine* (1831–5) and then in book form in 1835 (a further part was published in *Blackwood's Magazine* for 1837). He may have written poetry; there survives the privately printed *Sonnet to Clara* (dated from its paper to 1830 or later), which contains a manuscript note of his name (BL, 'Poetical Tracts, 1775–1834, 2', MS 11602.h.14). Altogether he published over forty pieces in *Blackwood's Magazine* between 1831 and 1854, about twenty in the *Edinburgh Review* between 1824 and 1846, and some twenty-six in the *Foreign Quarterly* between 1827 and 1833.

With a name as a critic and with a growing circle of influential friends, in 1835 Moir was appointed regius professor of rhetoric at Edinburgh University. When the seventh edition of *Encyclopaedia Britannica*, eventually published in 1842, was being planned, it was not unexpected that its editor, Macvey Napier, who as editor of the *Edinburgh Review* had known Moir's work since 1829, should select him to write some major articles: 'Treatise on poetry' (which Napier, in the preface to the *Encyclopaedia*, described as 'of no ordinary merit') and 'Modern romance and novel'. They were selected, together with an article by William Spalding, for separate advance publication as *Treatises on Poetry, Modern Romance and Rhetoric* (1839). It was considered that 'in point of easy, fluent, elegant precision, and crystal lucidity of style, whether oral or written, he had no superior and scarcely an equal' (*The Scotsman*). He also had 'a fair practice at the bar' (ibid.), good at opening a case, though not so good at replying, and the law was his main professional interest. In 1840 he resigned his regius professorship and became sheriff of Ross, a post that he held until 1858, when he was appointed sheriff of Stirling. His writing for the *Edinburgh Review* petered out in the mid-1840s. In 1851 he published *The Appellate Jurisdiction of Scotch Appeals*, and there survive manuscript legal opinions dating from the period 1850–58. On 26 March 1864 he took up the post of professor of Scots law in Edinburgh, but resigned it on 14 October 1865 on grounds of serious illness. He was not expected to recover, but in fact regained tolerable health. Carlyle described him as 'in all senses a *neat* man, in none a strong one' (*DNB*). He resigned the sheriffship of Stirling in the autumn of 1868.

Moir lived in Edinburgh's New Town, at 63 Northumberland Street and subsequently at 14 Charlotte Square. He was making arrangements to move to London when he died suddenly, at home, on 19 October 1870. Extracts from his lectures were included in the fourteenth (1870) and later editions of John Erskine's *The Principles of the Law of Scotland*.   BRIAN HILLYARD

Sources Wellesley index · F. J. Grant, ed., *The Faculty of Advocates in Scotland, 1532–1943*, Scottish RS, 145 (1944) · *The Scotsman* (21 Oct 1870) · G. Moir and W. Spalding, *Treatises on poetry, modern romance and rhetoric*, ed. J. V. Price (1995) · A. L. Stout, 'Writers on German literature in Blackwoods Magazine', *The Library*, 5th ser., 14 (1954), 35–44; 16 (1956), 187–201 · J. Veitch, *Memoir of Sir William Hamilton* (1869) · P. J. Anderson and J. F. K. Johnstone, eds., *Fasti academiae Mariscallanae Aberdonensis: selections from the records of the Marischal College and University, MDXCIII–MDCCCLX*, 3 vols., New Spalding Club, 4, 18–19 (1889–98) · T. Crawford, *The Edinburgh Review and romantic poetry (1801–29)* (1955) · *DNB* · *Blackwood* (1831–54) · *EdinR* (1824–46) · *Foreign Quarterly Review* (1827–33) · census returns, 1851 · G. Moir, letter, NL Scot., MS 1765.f.164 · *IGI* · d. cert.
Archives NL Scot., copies of legal opinions, Adv MSS 81.4.15–18 · NL Scot., corresp. | BL, letters to Macvey Napier, Add. MSS 34617–34626, *passim* · NL Scot., corresp. with Blackwoods, verses

Moir, (James) Reid (1879–1944), archaeologist, was born at The Elms, Benslow, Hitchin, Hertfordshire, on 13 June 1879, the second son and youngest of five surviving children of Lewis Moir (1843–1912), a tailor, and his wife, Sarah, *née* Knowles (1841–1910). He was educated at Northgate School, Ipswich, leaving at sixteen to take up an apprenticeship with his father's outfitters' business in the Butter Market, Ipswich. He was never fully committed to his 'chosen' profession.

Moir's 'amateur' pursuits in archaeology dominated his adult life. He did not become interested in archaeology until his mid-twenties, but he quickly made a name for himself locally and by 1910 had attracted international attention. In an audacious letter to *The Times* in October of that year he claimed to have found irrefutable human artefacts beneath the East Anglian crag deposits, thus challenging the orthodox view of the antiquity of human beings in Britain and attempting to push it back into the tertiary period. This opinion plunged Moir into a fractious debate that lasted the rest of his life, but which also brought him the support and friendship of Sir Edwin Ray Lankester.

On 3 March 1909 Moir married Mary Frances Moberly, a widow twelve years his senior; she was the daughter of Robert George Penny, an Anglican clergyman. The match was childless, although Mary had a daughter from her previous marriage. What should have been a comfortable life was jeopardized by Moir's neglect of the family business in order to concentrate on his archaeological researches; in 1912 his father actually gave him notice to quit, but died later that same year, leaving Reid instead central to the business's future. However Moir's continued lack of interest did nothing to improve his or its financial situation, both of which steadily declined. He yearned for full-time employment in palaeolithic archaeology, but none was to be had.

Moir was a force in British palaeolithic archaeology for some thirty-five years. He was a prominent figure in the Prehistoric Society of East Anglia and at Ipswich Museum, acting as president for both institutions (1914–15 and 1932–3 and 1929 respectively). During this long career he published some 233 works, his earlier efforts being summarized in *The Antiquity of Man in East Anglia* (1927). In 1937 his career was crowned by a coveted fellowship of the Royal Society, and in 1939 he delivered the prestigious Huxley memorial lecture at Imperial College, London. The 1930s also saw an upturn in his domestic affairs, when he was awarded a civil-list pension of £100 p.a. with an equal sum coming from Ipswich Museum, both for services to archaeology.

Moir's work comprised two distinct elements, one dealing with evidence for pre-crag or tertiary man, the other with more mainstream palaeolithic archaeology. The first, never well received even in his own time, is now almost universally disregarded, his 'artefacts' discounted as natural and probably the product of marine environments; but in the second he made some genuine and lasting contributions to knowledge. He made several new discoveries—for example the middle palaeolithic sites at Bramford Road and Constantine Road, Ipswich—and undertook new investigations at important known localities, Hoxne, Brundon, High Lodge, and Foxhall Road being among the most famous. Even here, though, the maverick Moir is never far away. A colleague, the geologist Percy Boswell, depicted him as an ambitious, confrontational man who rushed into a series of over-optimistic and premature statements that simply invited attack: the pre-glacial age of the modern human skeleton from Ipswich, which later proved to be an intrusive burial, to cite but one example. Unfortunately, it is with the wilder claims, especially the pre-crag implements, that Moir is today most often, disparagingly, associated.

Moir died of heart failure and coronary thrombosis on 24 February 1944 at his home, the Mill House, Flatford, East Bergholt, Suffolk.   MARK J. WHITE

Sources A. Keith, 'James Reid Moir, 1879–1944', *Obits. FRS*, 4 (1942–4), 733–45 · M. C. Burkitt, 'James Reid Moir, F.R.S.', *Nature*, 153, 368–9 · P. G. H. Boswell, 'James Reid Moir, F.R.S., 1879–1944', *Proceedings of the Prehistoric Society*, 11 (1945), 66–8 · b. cert. · m. cert. · d. cert. · WWW
Archives BM, artefacts and papers · Ipswich Museum, collection · Ipswich Museum, MSS | U. Cam., Museum of Archaeology and Anthropology, letters to L. C. G. Clarke
Wealth at death £641 3s. 6d.: probate, 1944, *CGPLA Eng. & Wales*

Moira. For this title name *see* Rawdon, Elizabeth, *suo jure* Baroness Botreaux, *suo jure* Baroness Hungerford, *suo jure* Baroness Moleyns, *suo jure* Baroness Hastings, and countess of Moira (1731–1808); Hastings, Francis Rawdon, first marquess of Hastings and second earl of Moira (1754–1826).

Moira, Gerald Edward (1867–1959), painter, was born on 26 January 1867 in London, the son of Eduardo Lobo da Moira (1817–1887), a former Portuguese diplomat who became a miniature painter and who was naturalized as a British citizen in 1875, and his half-Spanish wife Eugenia, the daughter of a diplomat. He was privately educated and at the age of eighteen began to attend evening classes to study art; in 1887, the year his father died, he entered the Royal Academy Schools, where he won the Armitage prize for figure composition. He received financial help from Queen Victoria, for whom his father had worked, and as a student he began to earn some money with illustrations for *The Lock to Lock Times*, a pocket guide to the River Thames. He left the RA Schools in 1889 and went to Paris for a period.

Having first exhibited at the Royal Academy in 1891, Moira sprang to prominence as a mural painter with the commission he received from J. Lyons & Co. for decorations at the Trocadero restaurant in Shaftesbury Avenue, London: he painted four large panels (1898) with subjects taken from Tennyson's *Idylls of the King* (1859). The bravura and confidence with which these were composed led to a series of other important murals, many, such as those at the Trocadero, carried out in collaboration with the sculptor L. Lynn Jenkins. He painted ceiling decorations for the library and vestry of the Unitarian church in Liverpool (1898) and for the board-room of Lloyd's Register of Shipping (1901). Most importantly, however, he was recommended by George Frederic Watts to execute three large lunettes and other paintings, as well as two stained-glass windows, for the central criminal court in London (1902–6). Moira painted another lunette during the 1950s following damage to the building during the Second World War; it represents a street scene during the London blitz, with firemen, nurses, and other rescue workers at work. In 1900 he was appointed professor of mural and decorative painting at the Royal College of Art in London, a position he held for twenty-two years. During the First World War he turned to contemporary themes with pictures such as *The War Workers* (1916) and visited France, following which he painted *A War Allegory* (1916) and a triptych (1918) based on observations made at a Canadian stationary hospital at Doullens in Picardy. His approach in these works, fundamentally based on that of the Italian masters of the high Renaissance, expressed a noble idealism rather than horror or destruction; at this period he also painted a purely serene family bathing group on the south coast—*A July Day* (1915, National Gallery of Canada, Ottawa)—in a manner close to impressionism. Moira married Alice Mary, daughter of William Vicary of Newton Abbot, Devon; the couple had four sons.

Principal of the Edinburgh College of Art from 1923 until his retirement in 1932, Moira continued to paint prolifically in oils, tempera, and watercolours, dealing with a wide range of subjects from pure landscape to figure compositions and portraits. His style was vigorous but light, airy, and colourful; he was particularly fond of blue. He was also president of the Royal Institute of Oil Painters, vice-president of the Royal Watercolour Society, a member of the Royal West of England Academy, and a founder member of the National Portrait Society. The Tate collection has his *Washing Day* (1938). A self-portrait of Moira in his early sixties (priv. coll.) depicts him as thin-faced with reddish cheeks, baldheaded but with thick dark hair on his temples and at the back, and having a long nose, elevated eyebrows, and a moustache. Gerald Moira died at his home, 13 Dene Road, Northwood, Middlesex, on 2 August 1959.   ALAN WINDSOR

Sources H. Watkins, *The art of Gerald Moira* (1923) · *The Times* (4 Aug 1959) · *CGPLA Eng. & Wales* (1959) · d. cert.
Archives Edinburgh College of Art, Edinburgh, file · priv. coll. · Royal College of Art, London, file
Likenesses G. Moira, self-portrait, oils, *c.*1930, Stareton House, near Kenilworth, Warwickshire
Wealth at death £33,293 9s. 1d.: probate, 7 Sept 1959, *CGPLA Eng. & Wales*

Moises, Hugh (1722–1806), schoolmaster, was born in Wymeswold, Leicestershire, on 9 April 1722, the second son of Edward Moises (1674/5–1751), vicar of the parish, and his wife, Elizabeth, daughter of Sir James Butler, of Middlesex and Kent. He was educated at home before attending Wrexham grammar school and Chesterfield grammar school, then under the Revd Dr Burroughs. On 12 June 1742 he was admitted sizar at his father's college, Trinity College, Cambridge, where his brother Edward was a fellow. He graduated BA in 1746, with a good reputation as a classical scholar, and was elected a fellow of Peterhouse in 1747; he proceeded MA in 1749. From 1745 to 1749 he worked as an assistant in his old school at Chesterfield. He was ordained deacon on 25 May 1746 and given the curacy of Clifton, in Nottinghamshire.

In March 1749 Moises succeeded the eminent classicist Richard Dawes as headmaster of the grammar school in Newcastle upon Tyne, on the recommendation of the master of Peterhouse, Edmund Keene. He found the school 'almost entirely deserted of scholars' (Brewster, 21) but soon restored pupil numbers; when he left there were 133 pupils in the school. His success in reviving the school's reputation was quickly recognized by the corporation of Newcastle, who in January 1750 raised his salary from £50 to £120. According to his pupil and biographer

John Brewster, Moises conducted his school with 'the dignity of a Busby', yet he 'always tempered necessary severity with affability and kindness' (ibid., 26). Assisted by two under-masters Moises did not confine his pupils to a purely classical curriculum but taught English prose composition, gave regular lectures on the New Testament, and included lessons on astronomy and geography. He was adept at communicating his enthusiasm for the Latin and Greek classics, and 'when the lesson came from Terence, the boys were delighted with the dramatic turn which the master gave to the interpretation' (ibid., 27). He took great pleasure in his pupils' successes. Among his more illustrious pupils were the lawyer brothers John Scott, first earl of Eldon, and William Scott; Baron Stowell; Admiral Cuthbert Collingwood, Baron Collingwood; and the Newcastle antiquary John Brand, who also taught as an usher at the school.

Moises married three times during his years in Newcastle. On 2 February 1754 he married Margaret, sister of Matthew Ridley (1711–1778), landowner and coal magnate, of Heaton Hall. His second wife, whom he married on 6 January 1758, was Isabel, daughter of John Ellison, vicar of Bedlington and lecturer of St Andrew's, Newcastle; their only surviving child was Hugh Moises (d. 1822). Moises married his third wife, Mrs Ann Boag, on 16 August 1764; they had one surviving son, William Bell Moises. On 21 April 1761 the corporation appointed Moises to the morning lectureship of All Saints, Newcastle, and on 14 June 1779 he became master of St Mary's Hospital, which occupied the same site as the school.

In 1787 Moises was presented to the valuable Cumberland living of Greystoke, worth £450 p.a., and soon afterwards resigned from the school. His nephew Edward Moises succeeded as master in June 1787. The boys presented Moises with a diamond ring inscribed with the motto 'Optime merenti'. He lived at Greystoke for several years until, at his patron's request, he gave up the rectory. He died at his home in Northumberland Street, Newcastle, on 5 July 1806 and was buried in St Nicholas's Church. His pupils raised about £400 for a mural memorial by Flaxman that was erected in the church, in St Mary's porch, in 1810; its Latin inscription was composed by William Scott.　THOMPSON COOPER, *rev.* S. J. SKEDD

Sources J. Brewster, *A memoir of the late Revd Hugh Moises MA, head master of the Royal Grammar School, Newcastle upon Tyne* (1823) · Nichols, *Illustrations*, 5.94–129 · *GM*, 1st ser., 76 (1806), 684 · Venn, *Alum. Cant.* · A. R. Laws, *Schola Novocastrensis: a biographical history of the Royal Free Grammar School of Newcastle upon Tyne*, 2 vols. (1932) · B. Mains and A. Tuck, eds., *Royal Grammar School, Newcastle upon Tyne: a history of the school in the community* (1986)

Moivre, Abraham de (1667–1754), mathematician, was born Abraham Moivre on 26 May 1667 at Vitry-le-François, Marne, France, son of the protestant surgeon Daniel Moivre (*fl.* 1665–1685) and his wife, Anne (*fl.* 1665–1685). All knowledge of his early life is derived from the biography by Matthew Maty, parts of which, including the years in France, de Moivre dictated to Maty shortly before he died. Apparently he was educated by the Catholic Pères de la Doctrine Chrétienne (1672–7) before he moved in

1678 to the protestant academy at Sedan, where he studied mainly Greek. After the academy closed in 1681 Moivre continued his studies at a protestant academy at Saumur (1682–4). Interested in the new philosophy of Descartes, which was not taught in Saumur, he went to the Collège d'Harcourt in Paris. There, presumably influenced by Descartes, he turned to mathematics. Hitherto he had studied elementary mathematics and, without mastering it completely, Christiaan Huygens's small tract concerning games of chance, *De ratiociniis in ludo aleae* (1657). In Paris he was taught mathematics by Jacques Ozanam, who made his living as a private teacher of the subject, attracting many students and enjoying a moderate financial success. It seems probable that Moivre later took him as a model when he had to support himself.

After the revocation of the edict of Nantes in 1685, hundreds of thousands of Huguenots who had refused to become Catholic emigrated to protestant countries. Among them was Moivre, who went to England where he and his younger brother Daniel were granted denization in December 1687, and where he began his occupation as a teacher of mathematics. Here both brothers added a 'de' to their names. The most plausible reason for this change is that Abraham for his part wanted the prestige of noble birth in France in dealing with his clients, many of whom were noblemen; Daniel, who became a merchant, presumably felt likewise.

A contemporary anecdote relates that de Moivre cut out the pages of Newton's *Principia* and read them while waiting for his students or walking from one to the other. True or not, the main function of the story was to place de Moivre among the first true and loyal Newtonians. In 1692 he met with Edmond Halley and shortly afterwards with Newton. Halley oversaw the publication of de Moivre's first paper on Newton's doctrine of fluxions in the Royal Society's *Philosophical Transactions* (1695); he was elected to the society in November 1697. His election as fellow of the Kurfuerstlich Brandenburgische Sozietaet der Wissenschaften came only in 1735; five months before his death the Académie Royale des Sciences, Paris, made him a foreign associate member.

Newton's influence on mathematics and natural philosophy in the British universities was such that it seemed profitable to de Moivre to attack the problems posed by the new infinitesimal calculus. In 1697 and 1698 he published the polynomial theorem, a generalization of Newton's binomial theorem, together with applications in the theory of series. Criticized by the Scottish physician George Cheyne in *Fluxionum methodus inversa* (1703), a book on Newton's method of fluents, de Moivre entered into a rather unpleasant fight with Cheyne in the pages of his *Animadversiones in G. Cheynaei Tractatum de fluxionem methodo inversa* (1704). This at least secured him the attention of Leibniz and Johann Bernoulli, with whom he began a correspondence in 1704, hoping to get support for a professorship on the continent. But after 1712, when he became a member of the commission set up by the Royal Society to support Newton's priority in the dispute between Newton and Leibniz and was drawn into the ensuing quarrels between Newtonians and Leibnizians, which lasted until the 1720s, de Moivre saw no reason to continue his correspondence with Bernoulli. He failed to secure a professorship in Great Britain, however, and was obliged to continue as a tutor and consultant in mathematical affairs and as a translator.

Bernoulli's letters had shown de Moivre how difficult it would be to compete with mathematicians of his calibre in the new field of analysis. So he turned to the calculus of games of chance and probability theory, which was of great interest to many of his students and where he had few competitors. Nevertheless, even outside the domain of probability and chance de Moivre could claim mathematical achievements of lasting value. Some of these were published in his *Miscellanea analytica* and its *supplementum* in 1730, such as his expression of cos*n*a as a function of cos*a* equivalent to (cos*a* + isin*a*) = cos*n*a + isin*n*a, which he had found between 1707 and 1722. In stochastics he was involved in two rather fierce disputes about priority with the Frenchman Montmort and with Thomas Simpson, who in two books of 1740 and 1742 exploited the content of de Moivre's *Doctrine of Chances* (1718) and *Annuities upon Lives* (1725).

In the *Philosophical Transactions* for 1711 de Moivre published a long article, 'De mensura sortis', which was followed by the *Doctrine of Chances*. The second, much extended, edition of the *Doctrine* (1738) contained his normal approximation to the binomial distribution that he had found in 1733. This special case of the central limit theorem he understood as a generalization and a sharpening of Bernoulli's *Theorema aureum*, which was later named the law of large numbers by Poisson. De Moivre's central limit theorem is considered as his greatest mathematical achievement and shows that he understood intuitively the importance of what was later called the standard deviation. Crucial to this theorem was a form of the so-called Stirling formula for *n*!, which de Moivre and Stirling had developed in competition which ended in 1730.

De Moivre's representation of the solutions of the then current problems of games of chance tended to be more general than those of Montmort. In addition he developed a series of algebraic and analytic tools for the theory of probability, like a 'new algebra' for the solution of the problem of coincidences which foreshadowed Boolean algebra, the method of generating functions, or the theory of recurrent series for the solution of differential equations. In the *Doctrine* de Moivre offered an introduction which contains the main concepts such as probability, conditional probability, expectation, dependent and independent events, the multiplication rule, and the binomial distribution. In 1738 and 1756 he interpreted his form of the central limit theorem in terms of natural religion as a proof for the existence and constant engagement of God in his creation. With it were connected the function and role of chance in the world.

De Moivre's preoccupation with matters concerning the conduct of a capitalist society, such as interest, loans, mortgages, pensions, reversions or annuities, dated back at least to the 1690s, from which time a short note survives in Berlin containing his answers to a client's questions. In 1693, using the lists of births and deaths in Breslau for each of the years 1687 to 1691, Edmond Halley had published in the *Philosophical Transactions* a life table together with applications to annuities on lives, but the amount of calculation involved in extending this to two or more lives turned out to be immense. De Moivre replaced Halley's life table by a (piecewise) linear function, which allowed him to derive formulas for annuities of single lives and approximations for annuities of joint lives as a function of the corresponding annuities on single lives. He published these formulas, together with the solution of problems of reversionary annuities, annuities on successive lives, tontines, and other contracts that depend on interest and the 'probability of the duration of life', in his book *Annuities upon Lives*. In the second edition of the *Doctrine of Chances* he incorporated part of the *Annuities* together with new material. After three more improved editions of the *Annuities* in 1743, 1750, and 1752, the last version of it was published in the third edition of the *Doctrine* (1756). The *Doctrine*, especially, attracted Lagrange and Laplace to de Moivre's work; it derived from de Moivre's solution of the problem of the duration of play by means of what he called recurrent series, which amounted to the solution of a homogeneous linear differential equation with constant coefficients. In fact, the most effective analytical tool that Laplace developed for the calculus of probabilities, the theory of generating functions, is a consequence of his occupation with recurrent series: thus the most important results of de Moivre's *Doctrine* reappear in Laplace's probability theory represented in a new mathematical form and in a new philosophical context, confirming de Moivre's status as a pioneer in this field.

In his later years, at least, de Moivre was living in the parish of St Anne, Westminster, London. He died in London on 27 November 1754 and was buried on 1 December at St Martin-in-the-Fields, Westminster. He had never married and left his South Sea annuities to be divided among his nieces and nephews.

IVO SCHNEIDER

Sources M. Maty, 'Mémoire sur la vie et sur les écrits de Mr Abraham de Moivre', *Journal Britannique* (Sept–Oct 1755); pubd sep. (1760) · I. Schneider, 'Der Mathematiker Abraham de Moivre, 1667–1754', *Archive for History of Exact Sciences*, 5 (1968–9), 177–317 · K. Wollenschläger, 'Der mathematische Briefwechsel zwischen Johann I Bernoulli und Abraham de Moivre', *Verhandlungen der Naturforschenden Gesellschaft in Basel*, 43 (1933), 151–317 · A. Hald, *A history of probability and statistics and their applications before 1750* (1990), chaps. 19–25 · *GM*, 1st ser., 24 (1754), 530 · parish register (burial), Westminster, St Martin-in-the-Fields, 1 Dec 1754 · will, PRO, PROB 11/811/297 · Huguenot Society of London [pubns of the Huguenot Society of London]

Archives Leibniz-Archiv, Hanover, Germany · RS | University of Basel, Bernoulli corresp.

Likenesses J. Highmore, oils, 1736, RS · Dassier, medal, 1741 · Faber, engraving (after Highmore, 1736)

Wealth at death under £2000; left South Sea annuities of £1600; plus small sundries: will, PRO, PROB 11/811/297

Mole [*née* Jones], **Harriet** [Jeannie] **Fisher** (1841–1912), socialist and women's trade union organizer, was born on 2 May 1841 at Edgeworth Street, Warrington, the daughter of Evan Jones, whitesmith, and his wife, Harriet *née* Fisher. Following 'an exceedingly happy childhood spent in a religious home' (*Labour Annual*, 180), Jeannie, as she was known, married fruit merchant Robert Frederick Willis in 1860 in Blackburn. As a young wife she visited New York, where she became concerned with social issues and worked for black rights. Returning to London with Robert, she worked with a sisterhood active among slum dwellers. However, reading Thomas Carlyle and John Ruskin alerted Jeannie to the causes of the poverty she sought to alleviate, and she converted to socialism.

In London on 2 May 1879 Jeannie married a printer, (William) Keartland Mole, born in Liverpool, where they moved at some point in that year. She found only six other socialists there, so with Robert Frederick Evan (Fred) Willis, the son of her first marriage, she initiated propaganda meetings. These developed into the Workers' Brotherhood, Liverpool's first socialist society, much of whose small membership later helped form the Liverpool Fabian Society (1892). Committedly unsectarian, Jeannie Mole joined the Fabians, the Social Democratic Federation, and the Independent Labour Party. However, it was against the wave of new unionism which swept Merseyside from 1889 to 1891 that she began the work of organizing women's trade unions for which she subsequently became best known. She began this in May 1888, helped by Fred Willis, whose articles in *The Liverpool Review* that month highlighted the plight of Liverpool's sweated women workers. In January 1889 she formed the Liverpool Workwomen's Society, comprising bookfolders, tailoresses, and cigarmakers. Helped by the London-based Women's Provident and Protection League, this relaunched in 1890 as the Liverpool Society for the Promotion of Women's Trade Unions (SPWTU), its membership expanding into unskilled trades.

External organization proved a difficult task, and by October 1894 Jeannie Mole admitted that 'the call should come with the need from the women themselves' (*Liverpool Labour Chronicle*, October 1894). Accordingly, the society became the Liverpool Women's Industrial Council (LWIC) in February 1895, partly inspired by the Women's Industrial Council which was formed in London in November 1894 to collect information about women's working conditions with a view to improving them. As honorary secretary, Jeannie felt the LWIC required an organizing function, and used her position to support a strike and encourage unionization among Liverpool ropeworkers. This proved unpopular with the non-socialist members of the council, and by its AGM of 1897 it was in disarray, with liberal members condemning its 'advanced wing' and socialists seeking a return to the earlier SPWTU (*Liverpool Review*, 13 March 1897). By 1898 Jeannie Mole had largely dissociated from the council, and was encouraging women to join the Liverpool branch of Tom Mann's Workers' Union.

Jeannie Mole felt socialism united her in a common sisterhood with all women. Although she did not participate in local suffrage campaigns, her political work demonstrated a woman-centred approach. She initiated and edited a 'Women's Page' in the *Liverpool Labour Chronicle* whose scope ranged from local disputes involving women to issues of women's health. She also promoted dress reform, and almost exclusively dressed in a Grecian style gown 'becomingly and without corsets' (*The Clarion*, 12 March 1898).

In 1896 Jeannie suffered a serious heart attack through overwork. She recovered sufficiently to attend an international congress that July, but further illness in 1897 effectively curtailed her organizational work. Although she largely withdrew from active life she continued to host activities such as socialist garden parties at her home at Dacre Hill, Rock Ferry, Cheshire, and to provide a home for visiting lecturers from many socialist organizations. Jeannie Mole died suddenly on 15 April 1912 in Paris during a visit intended to improve her health. She was cremated at Père Lachaise cemetery, Paris, her subsequent funeral at Higher Bebington on 22 April being attended by local Fabians and socialists. Predeceased by her son in 1905, she was survived by her husband.

KRISTA COWMAN

Sources *Labour Annual* (1895), 180 · W. Hamling, *A short history of the Liverpool trades council* (1948), 24–6 · K. Cowman, 'Engendering citizenship: women in Merseyside political organisations, 1890–1920', DPhil diss., York, 1994 · S. Maddock, 'The Liverpool trades council and politics, 1878–1918', MA diss., Liverpool, 1948 · *Labour Prophet* (Sept 1893), 85 · *Labour Prophet* (April 1896), 53 · G. Fidler, 'The work of Joseph and Eleanor Edwards, two Liverpool enthusiasts', *International Review of Social History*, 24 (1979), 293–319 · L. Grant, 'Women's work and trade unionism in Liverpool, 1890–1914', *North West Labour History Society Bulletin*, 7 (1950–51), 65–83 · *Liverpool Forward* (4 May 1912) · *Labour Leader* (26 April 1912) · *Liverpool Daily Post and Liverpool Mercury* (23 April 1912) · DLB · b. cert. · CGPLA Eng. & Wales (1912) · m. cert., 1879 · *Liverpool Labour Chronicle* (Oct 1894) · *Liverpool Review* (13 March 1897) · *The Clarion* (12 March 1898)

Archives BLPES, Webb collection, local Fabian societies, Coll. Misc. 375 · Lpool RO, Joseph Edwards MSS · Lpool RO, Trades Council MSS · Nuffield Oxf., Fabian Society MSS

Likenesses photograph, Museum of Liverpool Life

Wealth at death £8694 10s. 1d.: probate, 14 May 1912, CGPLA Eng. & Wales

Mole, John (1744–1827), teacher of mathematics, was born at Old Newton, near Stowmarket, Suffolk, on 10 March 1744, the son of a bailiff whose name is unknown, and his wife, Sarah Martin. His mother taught him to read but he had no formal education and was employed as a worker on local farms.

When he was twenty-seven he displayed extraordinary powers of mental calculation, and was helped in arithmetic by a teacher named Carter in Ipswich. He then taught himself algebra. In 1773 he opened a school at Nacton, near Ipswich. From 1774 to 1779 he contributed to the mathematical section of the *Town and Country Magazine*. His *Elements of algebra … including some new improvements worthy the attention of mathematicians* (1788) was highly commended in the reviews. In April that year Mole paid a visit to London, and was introduced to G. Pretyman Tomline, then bishop of Lincoln, and Horace, Lord Walpole.

In 1793 Mole gave up his school at Nacton, and removed

to Witnesham, on the other side of Ipswich, where he again taught. He occasionally contributed pieces in prose and verse to the *Ipswich Magazine* (1799–1800). His *Treatise on Algebra* (1809) was dedicated to Samuel Vince. In 1811 he returned to Nacton. In 1818 he is found acting as surveyor for a local road diversion. He died in Nacton on 20 September 1827. He was unassuming, independent of mind, a sympathizer with the French revolution and 'far from orthodox' in religion (Nichols, 887–9). He was twice married but nothing is known of his wives, and no children survived him.   THOMPSON COOPER, *rev.* RUTH WALLIS

Sources BL, Add. MS 19167, fol. 162 · BL, Add. MS 19170, fol. 145 · *GM*, 1st ser., 58 (1788), 410–11 · Nichols, *Illustrations*, 6.887–9 · E. G. R. Taylor, *The mathematical practitioners of Hanoverian England, 1714–1840* (1966), 370 · F. W. Steer and others, *Dictionary of land surveyors and local map-makers of Great Britain and Ireland, 1530–1850*, ed. P. Eden, 2nd edn, ed. S. Bendall, 2 vols. (1997)

Mole, John Henry (1814–1886), miniature and landscape painter, was born at Alnwick, Northumberland. He worked as a clerk in a solicitor's office in Newcastle upon Tyne for some years, joining an artists' society in the city before becoming a professional miniature painter in 1835. A regular contributor to exhibitions in Newcastle, he first exhibited in London at the Royal Academy, where he showed four miniatures in 1845 and six in 1846. He turned to landscape painting in watercolour, and this led to his election in 1847 as an associate, and in 1848 as a full member, of the New Society of Painters in Water Colours.

Mole gave up painting miniatures in 1847, and from then on only painted landscapes, and children in landscape settings, mainly in Northumbria, the Lake District, and Scotland, but also in Devon and Surrey. He moved to London, where he exhibited 679 works at the New Watercolour Society (later the Institute of Painters in Water Colours), becoming vice-president in 1884, when it became the Royal Institute of Painters in Water Colours. He occasionally painted in oils and sent an oil painting, *Carrying Peat*, to the Royal Academy in 1879. Three of his watercolours, *Tynemouth*, *Coast of Devon: Gleaners Returning*, and *Hellersdon Wood, Devonshire*, are in the Victoria and Albert Museum, London, and his paintings are also in various galleries in the north of England, including the Laing Art Gallery, Newcastle upon Tyne.

Mole died at his home, 7 Guilford Place, Russell Square, London, on 13 December 1886 and was buried in Brompton cemetery, London.

R. E. GRAVES, *rev.* ANNE PIMLOTT BAKER

Sources M. Hall, *The artists of Northumbria*, 2nd edn (1982), 47–8 · S. Wilcox and C. Newall, *Victorian landscape watercolors* (1992), 91 [exhibition catalogue, New Haven, CT, Cleveland, OH, and Birmingham, 9 Sept 1992 – 12 April 1993] · Wood, *Vic. painters*, 3rd edn, 358 · L. Lambourne and J. Hamilton, eds., *British watercolours in the Victoria and Albert Museum* (1980) · Graves, *RA exhibitors* · J. Johnson, ed., *Works exhibited at the Royal Society of British Artists, 1824–1893, and the New English Art Club, 1888–1917*, 2 vols. (1975) · Boase, *Mod. Eng. biog.* · *CGPLA Eng. & Wales* (1887)

Likenesses McLean & Haes, photograph, carte, NPG · engraving, repro. in *ILN*, 90 (1887), 13

Wealth at death £3483 13*s.* 2*d.*: resworn probate, May 1887, *CGPLA Eng. & Wales*

Molesworth [*née* Carstairs; *other married name* West], **Andalusia Grant**, Lady Molesworth (*c.*1809–1888), society hostess, was the daughter of James Bruce Carstairs (*c.*1770–1845) and his wife, Andalusia. Her family background remains obscure, although she was later to assert a connection with the extinct Bruce of Kinross baronetcy. In June 1824 she passed the entrance examination for the newly founded Royal Academy of Music: as Miss Grant she made her first public appearance at the academy's concert in the Hanover Square Rooms on 5 June 1826. She made her stage début at Covent Garden on 2 June 1827, when her 'remarkably powerful and sweet' soprano voice was favourably received. Further performances as Diana Vernon in *Rob Roy Macgregor*, Lucy Bertram in *Guy Mannering*, and Estelle in *Isidore de Merida* (in which she sang a duet with the celebrated tenor John Braham), and an unsuccessful production of *Edward the Black Prince* with W. C. Macready went to confirm the opinion that, talent as a singer notwithstanding, she was no actress. Singing with Braham in Bath in the winter season of 1830–31, she accepted a proposal of marriage from one of the earliest subscribers to the Royal Academy of Music, Temple West (*c.*1770–1839), a Worcestershire landowner. The wedding took place in London at St George's, Hanover Square, on 2 June 1831.

Andalusia West made her entry into respectable society; she retired from the stage and concert platform, and lived with her ageing husband at his house, Mathon Lodge, Malvern, and in Bath. By his death on 13 April 1839 she inherited all his property outright, and set herself up at 29 Half Moon Street, Mayfair. She made the acquaintance of Sir William *Molesworth (1810–1855), the radical politician, to whom she became engaged on 10 June and married on 9 July 1844. The marriage met with family opposition on account of Sir William's frail health and Andalusia's age—childless in her first marriage, she had few childbearing years before her. Her dubious antecedents and past life, and her social ambitions, caused unfavourable comment in society, and occasioned a permanent breach between her husband and his friend Mrs Harriet Grote.

Molesworth was returned to parliament in the autumn of 1844 after an absence of three years, and his new wife began her career as a hostess in earnest. Sometimes at their Pencarrow estate in Cornwall, but more frequently in their London house (1 Lowndes Square until 1848, thereafter at 87 Eaton Place), Lady Molesworth set out systematically to conquer the prejudices of the social and political élite. During the first years of her marriage her guests included the literary lions W. M. Thackeray, T. B. Macaulay, and Charles Dickens (whose sister Fanny had been a friend at the Royal Academy of Music); by 1850 the political world had given its seal of approval in the presence of Lord Palmerston, Lord Lansdowne, and Lord Granville, and the editor of *The Times*, J. T. Delane, at her dinner table. By the time of Molesworth's death on 22 October 1855 the social world had given its approval also, with some of the grandest of the *grandes dames*, Lady Londonderry and Lady Palmerston, paying their arrears of civility. Of those who did not succumb to her charms her husband's family were the most prominent; indeed, his mother and sister considered that the social whirl in which Lady Molesworth preferred to live, of 'continual excitement for the last year and a half without an hour's repose has destroyed him' (Adburgham, 183).

The breach between the two parts of the Molesworth family was nowhere more clearly visible than in Andalusia Molesworth's will, by which she left everything in her power to leave—and she had inherited from her husband all that was not tied up in trust—to the nephew and heir of the man who became her constant companion after Molesworth's death, George Byng, seventh Viscount Torrington (1811–1885). Within a year of her husband's death the entertainments in Eaton Place had resumed, and they were to be maintained for the following thirty years until her own death, which took place on 16 May 1888 at her London home. She was buried at Kensal Green cemetery.

Making a virtue of her musical background, Lady Molesworth's parties were distinguished for the quality of the musical entertainments she provided, but it was to her dinners, both to intimate groups of six or eight guests and to larger gatherings, that 'Moley' owed her reputation as one of the foremost hostesses in London. Lady Dorothy Nevill recalled that 'although by no means brilliantly intellectual herself, [Lady Molesworth] possessed a mysterious power of drawing out clever people and making them talk' (Reminiscences, 146). Like Frances, Countess Waldegrave, the other great hostess of their generation, who was herself the daughter of that John Braham with whom Miss Grant had sung in the 1820s, Andalusia Molesworth overcame the prejudices of the day against obscure birth, poverty, and the stage to end her life as one of the most successful hostesses. Samuel Wilberforce was heard to remark 'I believe if the King of the Cannibal Islands were to come to England, within twenty-four hours he would be dining with Lady Molesworth' (ibid., 147).

K. D. REYNOLDS

Sources A. Adburgham, *A radical aristocrat … Sir William Molesworth … and his wife Andalusia* (1990) · *Reminiscences of Lady Dorothy Nevill*, ed. R. Nevill (1906) · F. Leveson-Gower, *Bygone years: recollections* (1905)
Archives priv. coll.
Likenesses W. Ross, portrait, 1824, probably Pencarrow House, near Bodmin, Cornwall; repro. in Adburgham, *Radical aristocrat* · A. E. Chalon, portrait, 1844, probably Pencarrow House, near Bodmin, Cornwall; repro. in Adburgham, *Radical aristocrat* · R. Thorburn, portrait, c.1850, probably Pencarrow House, near Bodmin, Cornwall; repro. in Adburgham, *Radical aristocrat* · E. M. Underdown, sketch, 1863, probably Pencarrow House, near Bodmin, Cornwall; repro. in Adburgham, *Radical aristocrat*
Wealth at death £26,140 13s. 7d.: resworn probate, Sept 1889, CGPLA Eng. & Wales (1888)

Molesworth [née St Aubyn], **Catherine** (1760–1836), etcher and painter, was the second daughter of Sir John St Aubyn, fourth baronet, of Clowance in Cornwall, and sister of the MP, amateur mineralogist, and art collector Sir John *St Aubyn. He was a patron and friend of the Cornish artist John Opie, whose pupil Catherine became. Two of her drawings, after Opie's painting of St Michael's Mount and his portrait (1777) of Dolly Pentreath (Dorothy Jeffery),

a Cornish-speaking fishwife, remain at St Michael's Mount. Between 1788 and 1789 she produced a few privately printed etchings including those after the above-mentioned drawings and portraits of Lady St Aubyn after Reynolds and her sister, Mrs Robert White. Two drawings by her of St Michael's Mount were engraved by William Austin (1721–1820). In 1789 she painted her self-portrait wearing a straw hat and a sprig of lilac on her dress. Catherine St Aubyn married, on 26 June 1790, her cousin John Molesworth (d. 1811), rector of St Breocke, Cornwall, second son of Sir John Molesworth, baronet, of Pencarrow. At Pencarrow House near Bodmin there is a painting by Arthur Devis of Catherine and her three sisters showing a distant view of St Michael's Mount (1784). Catherine is shown etching the scene. She died on 21 October 1836. Her eldest son, John (d. 1844), who took the name St Aubyn, succeeded to the St Aubyn estates.

F. M. O'DONOGHUE, rev. ANNETTE PEACH

Sources private information [Lord St Levan] · Redgrave, *Artists* · Dodd, 'Memoirs of English engravers', BL, Add. MS 33394 · Burke, *Gen. GB* · *Parochial history of Cornwall*, 1.272
Likenesses A. Devis, group portrait, 1784 (with her three sisters), Pencarrow House, near Bodmin, Cornwall

Molesworth, John, second Viscount Molesworth (*bap.* 1679, *d.* 1726). *See under* Molesworth, Robert, first Viscount Molesworth (1656–1725).

Molesworth, John Edward Nassau (1790–1877), Church of England clergyman, only son of John Molesworth (d. 1791), of St Clements Strand, London, and his wife, Frances, daughter of Matthew Hill, and great-grandson of Robert, first Viscount Molesworth, was born in London on 4 February 1790, and educated at Dr Alexander Crombie's school in Greenwich. He matriculated from Trinity College, Oxford, on 3 February 1808, graduating BA in 1812, MA in 1817, and BD and DD in 1838.

For sixteen years from 1813 Molesworth was curate of Millbrook, Hampshire. On 28 November 1815 he married Harriet, daughter of W. Mackinnon of Newton Park and sister of W. A. Mackinnon, MP for Lymington. They had six sons and three daughters, of whom the eldest was William Nassau *Molesworth and the youngest son was Sir Guilford Molesworth, engineer. He initially supported his family partly through his writing and also by pressing his claim to the Swords estate of Viscount Molesworth. In 1826, at the instigation of Dr Rennell, dean of Winchester, he wrote a defence of orthodoxy in reply to John Davison's *Inquiry into the Origin and Intent of Primitive Sacrifice* (1826). This work attracted the attention of Dr Howley, then bishop of London, later archbishop of Canterbury. In 1828 Howley presented Molesworth to the living of Wirksworth, Derbyshire, a poorly endowed living which he held only for two months, and then to the rectory of St Martin's and vicarage of St Paul, Canterbury, in 1829. Appointed as one of the 'six preachers' at Canterbury, Molesworth preached on apostolic succession at Howley's primary visitation. Howley also recommended him unsuccessfully for the vicarage of Leeds when W. F. Hook was elected, and in 1839 presented him to the vicarage of Minster in

Thanet, and a few months later (on 3 March 1840) to Rochdale. The last preferment he held for thirty-seven years.

At Canterbury, during the stormy period of the Reform Bill, Molesworth's talents, which were allied with a combative temperament, found abundant occupation. He became recognized as the leader of the church party in the diocese, proclaiming the doctrine of apostolic succession and proposing the revival of convocation. He was no less a zealous parish priest. He was active in trying to break down barriers between parochial and cathedral clergy, and in 1835 established the *Penny Sunday Reader*, a cheap popular periodical which he edited and largely wrote for five years.

At Rochdale Molesworth had an ample field for all his activities. He succeeded an Erastian and absentee vicar, and found the parish church in decline and the local dissenters, led by John Bright, agitating for the abolition of church rates. Molesworth fought on behalf of the rates, with a vigour and determination which, according to Bright (J. Bright, *Speeches on Questions of Public Policy*, ed. J. E. T. Rogers, 2, 1868, 517), was not 'surpassed in any other parish in the kingdom'. Each party published a magazine, and Molesworth issued a stream of pamphlets. Proceedings were taken against those who did not pay, but in the end the rate was never collected. The lack of a rate led to financial difficulties; when the bishop visited in 1845 he found the bell-ringers of Rochdale on strike for lack of pay.

Molesworth was able to augment the value of the living by calling to account the leaseholders of its property, who had neglected to build upon the land according to their covenant; with the increased means at his disposal he promoted church building, giving £1000 to each new church for which the parishioners raised an equal sum. In this way he endowed four churches to add to the original fourteen. He also rebuilt the grammar school founded by Archbishop Parker, and built parish schools. The value of the living, which was £1800 when Molesworth went to Rochdale, was meanwhile rapidly increasing with the spread of factories over the vicarage estate and the erection upon it of the railway station and canal terminus. In 1866, when his income had reached £5000, Molesworth, following Hook's example at Leeds, promoted the Rochdale Vicarage Act, by which the thirteen chapels of ease were converted into parish churches and their endowments raised, some to £200, some to £300, and one to £500. By this act his own income was limited to £4000, while his successor was to receive £1500.

A high-churchman in sympathy with the early Tractarians, Molesworth, like Hook, sometimes differed from the leaders of the Oxford Movement. He was a friend of Hugh James Rose, contributing to the *British Magazine* and the *Encyclopaedia metropolitana*, of which Rose was editor. Molesworth's high-church opinions were not popular in Rochdale. He entered into controversy with Canon Stowell, attacking party societies, such as the Pastoral Aid Society, for interfering with the right of the incumbent to choose his own curate.

A vigorous vicar who fought for what he believed in, Molesworth was not always tactful in what he aired publicly. In 1847 he protested against James Prince Lee's appointment as bishop on the grounds that a charge of drunkenness had been brought against him and remained unrebutted. A libel action subsequently proved the falsity of the accusation. However, another dispute arose when Lee opposed Molesworth's offer to endow and build churches out of his own income, unless the resulting patronage resided with the bishop. Following this, the bishop was determinedly hostile to the vicar during the last twenty years of his episcopate. The points on which Molesworth argued were generally within his legal rights, but were on issues it was publicly unwise to press. In doing so he quarrelled with even natural supporters among the local community. In 1843 in a poll for churchwardens not a single local tory leader supported the vicar.

The closing years of Molesworth's life were spent in comparative peace. Following the death of his first wife in 1850, he was remarried in 1854, his second wife being Harriet Elizabeth (1807–1897), daughter of the Revd Sir Robert Affleck, bt, and widow of John Thomas Bridges (1805–1853) of St Nicholas Court, Thanet and Walmer. She was the mother of Robert Seymour Bridges (1844–1930). Molesworth died at Rochdale vicarage on 21 April 1877, and was buried at St Martin's, Castleton Moor, Lancashire.

H. C. BEECHING, rev. ELLIE CLEWLOW

Sources F. R. Raines, *The vicars of Rochdale*, ed. H. H. Howorth, 2 vols., Chetham Society, new ser., 1–2 (1883), vol. 2 · G. L. Molesworth, *Life of John Edward Nassau Molesworth, DD* (1915) · W. R. Ward, *Religion and society in England, 1790–1850* (1972) · E. J. Speck, *Church Pastoral Aid Society* (1881) · Foster, *Alum. Oxon.*
Likenesses engraving, 1841, repro. in Molesworth, *Life* · two photographs, 1870–75, repro. in Molesworth, *Life* · H. Cook, stipple, BM, NPG
Wealth at death under £60,000: probate, 17 May 1877, *CGPLA Eng. & Wales*

Molesworth [*née* Stewart], **Mary Louisa** (1839–1921), novelist and children's writer, was born on 29 May 1839, the eldest daughter and second child in the family of three sons and three daughters of Charles Augustus Stewart and his wife, Agnes. Her father was the illegitimate son of William Stewart, a Scottish army officer, who was to father three other illegitimate children by different mothers before he married in 1814. He became lieutenant-governor of New South Wales in 1825. Charles Stewart concealed his illegitimacy, of which he was deeply ashamed, from both official authority and his children, who knew only that there was some mystery about his parentage. After three years of school in Inverness he went out to Rotterdam, where his mother was working as a housekeeper to a wealthy Scots businessman, who was to employ the boy in his shipping firm. Here Stewart met and married Agnes Wilson, the sister-in-law of his employer. Mary Louisa, their third child, was born in Rotterdam where the family continued to live until 1840 or early 1841 when they returned to England, first to Preston, Lancashire, and then to Manchester, where Charles Stewart joined the firm of Robert Barbour, a merchant and shipping agent. This background may account for his daughter's distancing herself in her books from the commercial classes and her

Mary Louisa Molesworth (1839–1921), by Walker Hodgson, 1895

somewhat self-conscious identification with the upper classes. From 1841 her childhood was spent near the centre of Manchester—recalled without pleasure as Smokytown in her children's books—though as her father prospered (he was to become senior partner in the Barbour firm) the family was able to move further from the centre of Manchester and finally to the select suburb of Whalley Range. Her early education was at home. In adolescence she attended the private classes of the Revd William Gaskell, the Gaskells being near neighbours of the Stewarts in Manchester, and according to one of her daughters she spent a year studying French in Lausanne.

On 24 July 1861 Mary Louisa Stewart married Captain Richard Molesworth (1836–1900) of the Royal Dragoons, the son of Anthony Oliver Molesworth, a captain in the Royal Artillery. Richard Molesworth's social rank (he was nephew of the seventh Viscount Molesworth) did not compensate in her mother's eyes for the dangers of marrying a man with a violent temper (supposedly caused by a head wound incurred in the Crimean War). There is evidence that the young wife soon realized the truth of this, for there are references in the early adult novels to incompatible marriages and domineering husbands. There was the added disadvantage that he was irresponsible and financially inept. Richard Molesworth retired from the regular army in 1864 with the rank of major, and with financial help from his father-in-law rented Tabley Grange in Cheshire. Though the five years they spent here were to be ultimately clouded by the death of first their eldest daughter in 1869 and then a few months later their infant son, it was probably the happiest period in their

marriage, and they enjoyed social life with the local landowning gentry. During these years Mrs Molesworth was to strike up a close friendship with John Byrne Leicester Warren, poet, numismatist, and botanist, later third Lord de Tabley, whose family lived nearby at Tabley House. He gave her advice about the novel she was trying to write in 1868. The Molesworths had three daughters and two sons who survived into adult life. When the marriage ended in legal separation in 1879, they were living in Caen, France. Mary Louisa Molesworth spent the next four years in France and Germany, but returned to England permanently in 1883.

Lover and Husband was published in 1870, the first of four three-volume novels for adults written under the name Ennis Graham, a deceased friend. Her first children's book, *Tell me a Story*, which included an account of her eldest daughter's death in 1869, was published (still under the name Ennis Graham) in 1875, with drawings by Walter Crane, who was to illustrate many of her books. The use of barely disguised episodes from the lives of children that she knew, and from her own childhood, was to characterize her books. She had limited capacity for invention, and her fairy stories are low on enchantment, but she had unusual talent for entering into a child's feelings. Her second children's book, *Carrots—Just a Little Boy* (1876), for instance, which depicted her own family and included an irascible father, was written with great sympathy from the point of view of a six-year-old. Her own children sometimes suffered from their faults being castigated in their mother's books, for, though tender towards young children and deeply understanding of their need for security, she could be severe towards social failings, such as discontent and ill temper in their elder siblings. She seems to have been a stern mother (she was always a deeply reserved woman) who mellowed when she became a grandmother.

After the success of *Carrots* and of *The Cuckoo Clock* in the following year, which at once established her as a leading writer for children, Mary Louisa Molesworth was to write prolifically, sometimes, as in the 1880s and early 1890s, completing seven books in a year. She wrote more than one hundred books. They were for all ages, from the very young to the schoolroom young lady; some might even be classed as adult fiction, though they were never again to be published as such. The plots are slight and turn on small everyday incidents, but the reader is absorbed in the background, and lives the experiences of her child characters. Algernon C. Swinburne, to whom she sent many of her books as they appeared, was one of her greatest admirers. However, her books, though absorbing to the adult reader, are difficult to revive for the young of another generation because of their preoccupation with social status. Mary Louisa Molesworth died of heart failure in her flat at 155 Sloane Street, London, on 20 July 1921 and was buried on 23 July in Brompton cemetery, London.

GILLIAN AVERY

Sources J. Cooper, *Mrs Molesworth* (2002) · private information (2004) · m. cert. · d. cert. · Burke, *Peerage*
Archives BL, corresp. with Macmillans, Add. MS 54930

Molesworth, Richard, third Viscount Molesworth (1680–1758), army officer, born at Swords, co. Dublin, was the second son of Robert *Molesworth, first Viscount Molesworth (1656–1725), and his wife, Letitia (*d.* 1730), the third daughter of Richard Coote, Lord Coloony. He was destined for the law and was entered at the Middle Temple on 6 August 1700. However, he abandoned his studies and set off with a servant to join the army in the Netherlands, where he presented himself to his father's intimate friend George Hamilton, first earl of Orkney. He was made an ensign on 14 April 1702 in Orkney's regiment, the Royal Scots (1st foot), and was later appointed captain, at which rank he served with the regiment at Blenheim (1704).

Molesworth was one of Marlborough's aides-de-camp, and he saved the duke's life at the battle of Ramillies on 23 May 1706. Different versions of the incident have been given, but the most authentic appears to be that Marlborough, seeing that the allied left, on the open ground to the left of the village of Ramillies, was sore pressed, had ordered reinforcements to proceed thither from the right, and was himself personally leading up some squadrons of horse of the left wing, which he had rallied with great difficulty, when he was unhorsed and ridden over by a body of Dutch cavalry retiring in disorder. His horse galloped away among the Dutch, and Molesworth, seeing his chief in immediate danger of capture from the pursuing squadrons of French, put him on his own horse and persuaded him to ride away. In the ardour of the pursuit Molesworth was overlooked, and the French were presently brought up by the steady fire of Albemarle's Dutch-Swiss, under Colonel Constant. Molesworth recovered Marlborough's horse from a soldier and found his chief in the village of Ramillies, issuing orders. Marlborough attempted to shift back to his own horse, but was stunned by a round-shot which beheaded his principal aide-de-camp, Colonel Bringfield of Lumley's horse, who was holding his stirrup. The affair appears to have been hushed up at the time.

Molesworth remained an aide-de-camp to Marlborough thereafter, and on 5 May 1707 he was appointed captain and lieutenant-colonel in the Coldstream Guards. In August 1708 he was made comptroller of customs at Newcastle (salary £300 p.a.), executed by a deputy. This post was given by the lord treasurer as a small step towards his necessary expenses in the field as an aide-de-camp and kept secret by his family 'that it may not hinder the Duke of Marlborough's good intentions for him in the army. If he have any' (*Various Collections*, 8.238). Molesworth was present at the relief of Brussels in 1708 and Malplaquet in 1709 and was later blown up by a mine at the siege of Mons, but without receiving much injury. In July 1710 he was appointed colonel of a regiment of foot, with which he served in Catalonia under the duke of Argyll. Later the regiment was stationed as the garrison at Port Mahon, Minorca, where it was disbanded at the peace of Utrecht in 1713. Molesworth was placed on half pay. He was made

lieutenant of the ordnance in Ireland on 11 December 1714 and was returned as MP for Swords, co. Dublin, in the same year. During the Jacobite rising of 1715 he raised a regiment of dragoons, with which he served, under General Carpenter, against the rebels in the Scottish borders and at the battle of Preston, where it was reported that he was wounded. The regiment was disbanded in 1718.

Once again on half pay, and in a state of poverty compounded by losses from the South Sea Bubble, Molesworth put his effort into a series of unsuccessful projects to restore his finances. Under the competition set up by act of parliament in 1714 he joined the race to invent a naval chronometer which could plot longitude accurately. His efforts drew the attention of Sir Isaac Newton in March 1722, and after his invention was shown to the Royal Society he was elected a fellow on 15 March. However, by the following year the project was left dormant due to lack of funds. Molesworth's involvement in a new company set up to establish a water supply for London also seems to have come to nothing. At the same time (1723) he was considering a venture into publishing, but his intention to write a biography of the duke of Marlborough was frustrated by the duchess, who refused access to the duke's papers and continued throughout her life to deny any claim by Molesworth upon her for saving the duke's life at Ramillies.

This period of restlessness and financial distress lasted until Molesworth's return to Ireland upon the ill health of his father and the resumption of his military career as colonel of the Royal Inniskilling Fusiliers (17 March 1724). He succeeded to the viscountcy at the death of his elder brother, John *Molesworth, second Viscount Molesworth, ambassador in Tuscany [*see under* Molesworth, Robert], on 17 February 1726 and took his seat on 5 October 1731; on 26 October 1733 he was sworn of the Irish privy council.

On 31 May 1732 Molesworth succeeded General Crofts as colonel of the 9th dragoons (now lancers). On 18 December 1735 he became a major-general, on 19 December 1736 he was sworn one of the lords justices of Ireland, and on 27 June 1737 he succeeded General Wynne as colonel of the 5th dragoons, later the 5th Royal Irish Lancers. He became a lieutenant-general in Ireland in 1739, master-general of the ordnance in Ireland in 1740, a lieutenant-general on the English establishment on 1 July 1742, a general of horse on 24 March 1746, commander-in-chief in Ireland in September 1751, and a field marshal on 29 November 1757. He was also governor of the royal hospital near Kilmainham.

In 1744 Molesworth published *A short course of standing rules for the government and conduct of an army, designed for, or in the field, with some useful observations*, which has been described as a good introduction to the major operations of a unitary army. The inclusion in this work of the full standing orders of his dragoon regiment, dated 1738, is noted by Houlding as an important, if somewhat elementary, source on the training of cavalry.

Molesworth married, first, Jane, the daughter of a Mr Lucas of Dublin. She died on 1 April 1742, having had a son, who died an infant, and three daughters, and was buried at Swords. His second wife was Mary, the daughter of the Revd William Usher, archdeacon of Clonfert, whom he married on 7 February 1744, and with whom he had one son, Richard Nassau, fourth Viscount Molesworth (1748–1793), and six daughters. Molesworth died in London on 12 October 1758 and was buried at Kensington on 16 October. At his death his widow received a pension of £500 per annum, and six of his unmarried daughters pensions of £70 per annum each. The second Lady Molesworth met a tragic fate. She, her brother, who was a captain in the Royal Navy, two of her daughters, and five others were burnt in their beds by a fire at her house in Upper Brook Street, Hanover Square, London, early in the morning of 7 May 1763. A warrant was issued by George III to pay a pension of £390 per annum to the earl of Blessington in trust for the three surviving daughters.

H. M. Chichester, *rev.* Jonathan Spain

Sources GEC, *Peerage*, new edn · J. Lodge, *The peerage of Ireland*, rev. M. Archdall, rev. edn, 5 (1789), 142 · C. Dalton, ed., *English army lists and commission registers, 1661–1714*, 6 vols. (1892–1904) · *Report on manuscripts in various collections*, 8 vols., HMC, 55 (1901–14), vol. 8, pp. 196–568 [Mr M. L. S. Clements] · J. A. Houlding, *Fit for service: the training of the British army, 1715–1795* (1981) · J. Baynes, *The Jacobite rising of 1715* (1970) · *The royal Inniskilling fusiliers: a history of the regiment from December 1688–July 1914* (1934) · T. A. Heathcote, *The British field marshals, 1763–1997: a biographical dictionary* (1999)
Archives NRA, papers | BL, Blenheim MSS
Likenesses J. Brooks, mezzotint (after A. Lee), BM · A. Lee, oils, Pencarrow House, near Bodmin, Cornwall · A. Selvi, copper medal, BM; repro. in C. Dalton, *George the First's army, 1714–27* (1911)

Molesworth, Robert, first Viscount Molesworth (1656–1725), politician and political writer, was born in Fishamble Street, Dublin, on 7 September 1656, the only child of Robert Molesworth (*d*. 1656), merchant, and his wife, Judith (*d*. in or after 1662), daughter of John Bysse. His father, who died four days before Molesworth was born, was English and had served in the royalist army in Ireland until accepting defeat in 1647, becoming a merchant in Dublin, and investing in the parliamentarian war effort. His grandfather John Bysse, recorder of Dublin, was an accomplished time-server, who flourished under the restored monarchy as an Irish judge. Through Bysse, Molesworth acquired a great variety of political connections, both parliamentarian and royalist. He also inherited Bysse's estates, at Brackenstown near Swords, co. Dublin, and Philipstown in King's county, each of which conveyed a controlling electoral interest in a neighbouring parliamentary borough.

Early life and career Molesworth was educated at home, then at Trinity College, Dublin; he graduated BA in 1675. The same year he entered Lincoln's Inn, but he paid little attention to the law and left London by 16 August 1676, the date he married the Hon. Letitia (*d*. 1730), daughter of the prominent Irish privy councillor Richard Coote, Lord Coote, baron of Coloony, whose scapegrace son Richard, later earl of Bellomont, was subsequently to prove a useful political ally. The couple had seventeen children, of whom seven sons and two daughters survived. The eldest

Robert Molesworth, first Viscount Molesworth (1656–1725), by Peter Pelham, 1721 (after Thomas Gibson)

daughter was the poet Mary *Monck (1677?–1715). In 1684, Molesworth later claimed, he began a series of journeys to the continent, 'always taking Holland in my way':

> I had the honour to be well received and esteemed by the Prince of Orange, and to have his great design of coming into England communicated to me as early as to any of the noblemen and gentlemen that waited on him there ... I took many occasions of letting the Prince know that I would serve him to the hazard and loss of life and fortune, and he was pleased to believe and trust me.
>
> Accordingly he sent me into England about six weeks before his intended descent here, to give notice to many of the nobility and gentry to be ready. I came and was believed, and contributed as much to the unanimous rising and appearance of the nation as any gentleman in England. (BL, Add. MS 61639, fol. 3)

Whether or not these boasts could be justified, it is noteworthy that Molesworth was chosen by the new king in 1689 for the important posting of envoy to Denmark. His duties were twofold: to negotiate the hire of Danish troops for William's Irish campaigns, and to counter the machinations of the pro-French party at the Danish court. Although succeeding in both objectives, Molesworth was continually anxious and exasperated: he worried over the course of the war in Ireland and the fate of his own property; suffered periodic shortages of money, and generally poor health; and was appalled at the corruption of the Danish political system and the extent of French influence. He was both temperamentally and politically unsuited to the stifling atmosphere of a petty absolutism, being short-tempered and sharp-tongued, and animated above all by a love of liberty. Inexperience betrayed him into indiscretions, and he was eventually recalled in the summer of 1692.

Back in London, Molesworth did not bother to seek election to the Irish parliament called in the autumn of 1692, but concentrated instead on seeking official employment in England. Bellomont introduced him to various patrons, including the earl of Shrewsbury, but their recommendations proved futile. In truth Molesworth had burnt his boats by writing his *Account of Denmark, as it was in the Year 1692*, a philippic against the Danish monarchy which he himself admitted was composed in a spirit of revenge. First published anonymously in 1693, and sufficiently popular to warrant four more editions within two years, it provoked a rejoinder financed by the Danish government, but even more tiresome to King William than the diplomatic embarrassment were the repercussions in domestic politics, where the *Account* was interpreted and taken up as a warning against authoritarian tendencies in England. Although Molesworth seems not to have intended any slight on William, the enthusiasm with which he pursued a contractarian concept of government, his idealization of the virtue of the Roman republican tyrannicides, and above all his condemnation of 'priestcraft' in all its forms, protestant no less than Catholic, exposed the danger to the English constitution from the contagion of absolutism.

Country whig politician Unable to secure office, Molesworth adopted a different course. He obtained a seat in the new parliament summoned in Ireland in 1695 and set out to make a name for himself there. He was a strong supporter of the party of the lord deputy, Henry, Lord Capell, but exuberance and indiscretion made him a liability. While Molesworth's vehement anti-popery suited the deputy's policies, his devotion to 'country whig' ideals—frequent parliamentary sessions, the constitutional rights of Ireland, even the electoral accountability of the judiciary—led him into what Capell regarded as dangerous territory. He followed a similar path when chosen to the English parliament at the 1695 general election, on the interest of his cousin Sir John Molesworth, second baronet, for a Cornish borough. At Westminster he showed himself a staunch whig, except on issues where the junto ministry departed from 'country' principles, and co-operated closely with the young Lord Ashley, the future third earl of Shaftesbury, leader of a 'club' of country whig back-benchers. Maintaining a seat in both parliaments involved Molesworth in almost constant parliamentary attendance between 1695 and 1698, but brought little reward, except for admission to the Irish privy council on the recommendation of the English-born lord chancellor of Ireland, John Methuen, himself a client of the second earl of Sunderland. Unfortunately further outbreaks of indiscipline during the following parliamentary session at Westminster, 1697–8, including a speech against a standing army and a denunciation of the Danes (in a debate on the Danish subsidy) blotted his copybook with the junto. Then, in the summer of 1698, he not only lost his English parliamentary seat (thanks to his cousin's incompetence) but saw both his patrons, Shrewsbury and Sunderland, edged out of influence.

Molesworth's political career having ground to a halt, he set sail for Dublin. But he was not yet ready to retire to Ireland permanently, observing that the country would prove 'my *pis aller*. I shall perfectly degenerate in that soil' (*CSP dom.*, 1699, 36), and he soon set about acquiring a landed estate, at Edlington in Yorkshire, which would give him a base in England, close to several friends who shared his enthusiasm for building and estate improvement, and for scientific and technological discoveries. Molesworth himself was admitted a fellow of the Royal Society in 1698, and has also been identified as a key member of the so-called 'new junta for architecture', which brought Palladian innovation to both England and Ireland.

The accession of Queen Anne in 1702, and the rise to power of Sidney, Lord Godolphin, and the earl of Marlborough, reawakened Molesworth's interest in politics as an avenue for advancement, as much for his children and dependants as for himself. He flattered Godolphin and was taken under his wing. Soon one of his sons received an army commission. Not that Molesworth could be purchased out of his principles: in the Irish parliament in the winter of 1703–4 he opposed the tory viceroy, Ormond, and was in the vanguard of those 'country' members who pressed for union with England, which would achieve both his prime objectives for Ireland, guaranteeing the liberties of propertied Irishmen and encouraging economic growth. His loyalty to Godolphin never incurred the sacrifice of his virtue, by which he laid great store. Like his friend Shaftesbury, he argued that in supporting this ministry he was contributing to the defence of liberty. In comparison with the corruption of the previous junto ministry, government was now in the hands of the virtuous, and Marlborough's triumphs over the French gave the ministry a heroic dimension. Thus after regaining a seat in the Westminster parliament in 1705 Molesworth continued to vote as a whig on matters of principle, even a country whig on such issues as place bills, but became one of the 'lord treasurer's whigs' who stood by Godolphin as pressure from the junto increased. Again, however, Molesworth had backed the wrong horse. He lost his seat in the 1708 general election, and was obliged to make approaches to the junto lords—unsuccessfully, since he was at best half-hearted, and could not entirely exclude a peevish and self-righteous tone from his letters.

Whig author and peer The downfall of the whigs in 1710 clarified Molesworth's political position. The new tory ministry, headed by Robert Harley, included several old friends, but Molesworth found no favour there, and from despair and isolation came a powerful restatement of his political beliefs as a 'true whig'. In a preface to a translation of François Hotman's *Franco-Gallia*, published in 1711, he defended the right of resistance, attacked standing armies, and reiterated the need for annual parliaments. Moreover, though he no longer enjoyed a seat at Westminster, he took a staunchly whiggish line in the Irish parliament, and in 1713 generated a furious controversy by giving vent to his anti-clericalism in some derogatory public comments against representatives of the lower house of the Irish convocation, which were taken up by convocation itself, by the Irish House of Lords, and in the press. Subsequent tory pressure brought about his removal from the Irish privy council as soon as the parliament was prorogued. But this minor martyrdom (and, no doubt, his previous connections with the Marlborough faction in the English whig party) helped him recover his standing in English politics after the Hanoverian succession, when he regained a seat at Westminster and acquired a position on the Board of Trade. After a brief spell as a court spokesman in the Commons, during which he endured the embarrassment of debating in favour of a standing army and the Septennial Bill, he resigned his place to his eldest son and received in compensation an Irish viscountcy, becoming on 16 July 1716 first Viscount Molesworth of Swords in the peerage of Ireland. By 1718 he was in opposition again, and while his reverence for aristocracy (in terms of political theory and of mere snobbery) induced him to support the Peerage Bill, what was now a heightened sensitivity to Irish constitutional grievances kept him in estrangement from administration: he spoke powerfully in both the Irish and British parliaments against the subordination of the Irish legislature, denouncing the Declaratory Bill of 1720 and procuring a pamphlet against it from his protégé and fellow countryman John Toland.

An active retirement Molesworth lost his Westminster seat in the 1722 general election, and, possibly stung by financial losses in the South Sea Bubble, retired to Brackenstown. He devoted himself to the improvement of his estate and the cultivation of a literary circle, including Toland, which among a variety of advanced intellectual projects helped to bring the ideas of Shaftesbury to an Irish audience, and the principles of 'true' whiggism to a new generation, among whom the best known was perhaps the Presbyterian moral philosopher Francis Hutcheson. Molesworth's influence among Irish dissenters extended in 1722 to Glasgow University, where a number of Irish undergraduates, led by James Arbuckle, proposed him unsuccessfully as their candidate in the rectorial election. His own last effort at authorship, *Considerations for Promoting Agriculture* (1723), blended his long-standing concern for 'improvement' with political objectives in a practical form of Irish patriotism. So far had his understanding of his role as an Irish landowner matured since the 1690s, when he seemed to regard himself as a colonial Englishman and advocated protestant immigration, that he now recognized a community of interest even with native Catholics, who might be brought to civility by economic reconstruction and protestant example. It was as a progenitor of economic patriotism that Swift dedicated to him the fifth of the *Drapier's Letters*.

Molesworth died at Brackenstown on 22 May 1725 and, despite having requested interment at Edlington, was buried at Swords. His estate included much urban property in Dublin, which he had been active in developing. There were small bequests to the established church, including £50 towards building a parish church at Philipstown, which probably reflected his appreciation of the political dividends to be gained from promoting protestantism in Ireland, rather than any weakening in his lifelong antipathy to the clergy.

The eldest of Molesworth's surviving children, **John Molesworth**, second Viscount Molesworth (*bap.* 1679, *d.* 1726), diplomat and government official, was baptized on 4 December 1679. The greatest beneficiary of Lord Treasurer Godolphin's patronage, he was named a commissioner of the stamp office in 1706, and, after being replaced in that post three years later, secured appointment in May 1710 as envoy to Tuscany. He spent two short spells in Florence, in the spring of 1710 and during the following winter, but suffered with his father in the ministerial revolution that brought the tories to power. In December 1715 he succeeded his father as a lord of trade, and held that post until 1720. In September 1718 he married Mary (*d.* 1766), daughter and coheir of Thomas Middleton MP, of Stansted Mountfitchet in Essex, and granddaughter of the first Lord Onslow. They had one daughter, born after Molesworth's death. His loss of office in 1720 was probably in part a retribution for paternal political transgressions, but John's sufferings were moderated by nomination as envoy to the court of Savoy, a position he held until succeeding to the viscountcy in 1725. He returned from Turin to take over the family estates, and his father's seat in the Irish House of Lords, but died within a year, on 17 February 1726, at St James's Street, London, and was buried at Edlington. His title passed to his brother Richard.

D. W. HAYTON

Sources D. W. Hayton, 'Molesworth, Robert', HoP, *Commons, 1690–1715* • E. Cruickshanks, 'Molesworth, Robert', HoP, *Commons, 1715–54* • GEC, *Peerage* • NL Ire., Clements MSS, microfilm, p. 3735 • letters from Copenhagen, 1691–2, BL, Add. MS 36662 • correspondence with Sir William Dutton Colt, BL, Add. MS 34095 • W. Yorks. AS, Leeds, Yorkshire Archaeological Society, Copley papers • will, PRO, PROB 11/612, sig. 239 • R. Molesworth, *An account of Denmark, as it was in the year 1692*, 3rd edn (1704) • R. Molesworth, *The principles of a real whig* (1775) • R. Molesworth, *Some considerations for the promoting of agriculture and employing the poor* (1723) • *An elegy on … Robert, Lord Visct. Molesworth* [1725] • J. Toland, *Collection of several pieces* (1726) • *The life, unpublished letters and philosophical remarks of Anthony, earl of Shaftesbury*, ed. B. Rand (1900); repr. (1995) • *CSP dom.*, 1694–5; 1697–9; 1703–4 • H. Mayo, 'Robert Molesworth's *Account of Denmark*: its roots and its impact', PhD diss., Syddansk Universitet, 2000 • C. Robbins, *The eighteenth-century commonwealthman* (1969) • E. McParland, 'Edward Lovett Pearce and the new junta for architecture', *Lord Burlington: architecture, art and life*, ed. T. Barnard and J. Clark (1995), 151–65 • M. A. Stewart, 'John Smith and the Molesworth circle', *Eighteenth-Century Ireland*, 2 (1987), 89–102 • I. McBride, 'The school of virtue: Francis Hutcheson, Irish Presbyterians and the Scottish Enlightenment', *Political thought in Ireland since the seventeenth century*, ed. D. G. Boyce, R. Eccleshall, and V. Geoghegan (1993), 73–99 • GEC, *Baronetage* • J. Lodge, *The peerage of Ireland*, rev. M. Archdall, rev. edn, 7 vols. (1789) • BL, Add. MS 61639

Archives BL, letters from Copenhagen, Add. MS 36662 • BL, corresp. with Sir W. D. Colt, Add. MS 34095 • Bodl. Oxf., annotated copy of Martin's *Western Islands of Scotland* • TCD, corresp. with William King • W. Yorks. AS, Leeds, Yorkshire Archaeological Society, Copley MSS

Likenesses P. Pelham, mezzotint, 1721 (after T. Gibson), BM, NPG [see illus.]

Wealth at death lands in Ireland, Yorkshire, Dublin; over £5000 to be raised in legacies for younger children: Hayton, 'Molesworth, Robert'

Molesworth, Sir William, eighth baronet (1810–1855), politician, was born on 23 May 1810 at Upper Brook Street, London, the eldest of five children of Sir Arscott Ourry Molesworth, seventh baronet (1790?–1823), landowner, and Mary (1779?–1877), daughter of Patrick Brown of Edinburgh. The Molesworths had resided at Pencarrow, near Bodmin, Cornwall, since the sixteenth century. With estates in Cornwall and Devon, the family's wealth also originally derived from property in Huntingdonshire and Jamaica and from mining and banking interests. In childhood Molesworth suffered from scrofula and a frail constitution, infirmities which elicited no sympathy from a stern father or other boys at the boarding-school in Putney, near London, to where he was dispatched at a tender age. In 1824, after his father's death, his solicitous mother transported the five children to Edinburgh, where William took classes at the university in modern languages. In 1827 he entered St John's College, Cambridge, but soon moved to Trinity College. His stay was short and inglorious. Involvement in a friend's gambling dispute led him to challenge his tutor, Henry Barnard, to a duel. Both parties were bound over to keep the peace and William was sent down from the university in April 1828. The affair was settled at Calais the following year by a harmless exchange of shots. By that time William was seriously pursuing his education in Germany, under the wing of General Sir Joseph Straton, an old family friend. Having a bookish, studious streak, Molesworth applied himself to learning German and reading in mathematics and philosophy, with leisure hours devoted to classes in drawing, painting, and dancing. After a brief return to Britain during 1829, he took up residence in Rome and started Arabic in preparation for an eastern tour. His mother and two sisters joined him in Italy, where particular fascination with the gardens of noblemen's villas stimulated his interest in botany and landscaping, and inspired the creation of an Italianate garden at Pencarrow.

Molesworth returned to Britain early in 1831, when the country was convulsed by the struggle over parliamentary reform. Encouraged by Charles Buller MP, his ebullient Cornish neighbour and an acquaintance from Cambridge, and by exploiting family influence, Molesworth was returned for the new constituency of East Cornwall at the post-reform general election of December 1832. He took his seat in the reformed House of Commons, and declared himself a radical. From a sense of injury and alienation induced by such experiences as his father's 'unkind conduct' and expulsion from Cambridge, he admitted to 'a hatred of all instituted authorities' (Grote, 6, 52). His studies in Scotland and freethinking Germany had also cultivated a sturdy agnosticism in religion, what he once called 'a *cool* and *deliberate* avowal of infidelity' (Molesworth to Harriet Grote, 28 Oct 1834, Pencarrow MSS). From the outset he championed such causes as national education, commutation of tithes, free trade, the secret ballot, triennial parliaments, removal of property qualifications for MPs, and abolition of the House of Lords. In parliament he spoke with uninhibited warmth and displayed an intolerance of those who disagreed with him and their ideas.

Sir William Molesworth, eighth baronet (1810–1855), by Sir John Watson-Gordon, 1854

Although impulsive, he lacked political stamina; his moods oscillated between *élan* and ennui. 'You know I like theory', he explained to his sister, 'but do not care much about practice' (Molesworth to Elizabeth Molesworth, 1835, Pencarrow MSS). Thomas Carlyle found in Molesworth 'the air of a good roystering schoolboy' but shrewdly detected a 'darkness of mind' beneath the surface of such gaiety (*Collected Letters*, Feb 1835, 30 May 1834). Of tall, slender build, with dainty features, expressive blue eyes, and long hair, Molesworth struck Richard Cobden in 1837 as 'a youthful, florid-looking man of foppish and conceited air … and let him *say* what he pleases, there is nothing about him that is democratic in principle' (Morley, 1.137).

As a radical baronet, with youthful enthusiasm and ready wealth, Molesworth soon attracted the attentions of George Grote MP, a City banker who was absorbed in writing a history of Greece, and his formidable wife and political activist Harriet, both Benthamite radicals keen to transform the country's institutions. He was recruited to their circle as a willing disciple, leavening their bourgeois prudence with his patrician recklessness. As Lord Stanley, a Conservative MP, jested, 'The Radicals worship him most humbly and glorify him as their golden calf' (Stanley to Lord Durham, 11 Dec 1836, Lambton MSS). For his part, Molesworth struck up an easy rapport with Mrs Grote, who became his mentor and confidante, while philosophic radicalism gave a dogmatic, doctrinaire edge to his temperamental instability. Through the Grotes he met John Stuart Mill and in 1835 impulsively agreed to finance the launch of the *London Review* and its merger the following year with the *Westminster Review*. During a brief, expensive proprietorship Molesworth wrote articles designed to bestir educated radicals and foster a distinct party. He was also involved in 1836 in establishing *The Constitutional*, a short-lived paper of 'uncompromising liberal principles'. That year, too, he helped to found the Reform Club.

In all these activities Molesworth sought to destroy the nefarious alliance between radicals and the 'loathsome' whigs, 'of hideous sight and pestiferous smell', whose 'influence over our party is of the most demoralising description' (Molesworth to Francis Place, 5 Oct 1836, BL, Add. MS 35150, fol. 167). In the mid-1830s he naïvely expected the whig party to split asunder, producing a realignment in politics between aristocratic and democratic forces. Yet the fortunes of the drifting, disharmonious radicals were already fading both in and out of parliament, as the general election of 1837 and its repercussions starkly demonstrated. Although Molesworth had been re-elected for East Cornwall two years earlier, mounting unpopularity with constituents obliged him in 1837 to migrate to Leeds, where his own return contrasted with the general rout of the radicals, for which he blamed middle-class apathy. His fantasy that 'the people' would coalesce under the leadership of an intellectual élite was, Joseph Parkes remarked, a 'brain-spun' notion of ideologues: 'what Condorcet dreamed political society *would be*, Molesworth and Co. dream it *is*' (Parkes to Edward Ellice, 8 Jan 1837, Lambton MSS). Molesworth's disillusionment with domestic politics drove him back to scholarly pursuits, and in 1838 he began an edition of the works of Thomas Hobbes, which eventually ran to eleven volumes and was for a century the standard edition. He did not seek re-election in 1841.

Nevertheless, Molesworth did not abandon an active and abiding involvement in colonial questions. Like Buller, he was attracted to Edward Gibbon Wakefield's ideas on systematic colonization and from the early 1830s he became associated with a group of colonial reformers. He joined the committee of the South Australian Association (1833) which founded an experimental Wakefieldian colony in 1836. The transportation of convicts to eastern Australia aroused Molesworth's moral outrage and he chaired a parliamentary select committee which investigated the issue in 1837–8. The inquiry assembled a mass of highly coloured, condemnatory evidence to besmirch the penal colonies as 'moral dunghills' and his report contributed to the phasing out of transportation, which finally ceased in 1853.

Maladministration by the Colonial Office also stirred Molesworth's wrath for negating British principles of government and driving colonists to despair and disaffection. Coercive policy towards the Canadas stood condemned, and he reacted to the rebellions in 1837 and suspension of the Lower Canada constitution by championing the French Canadians' struggle for liberty, if necessary by arms—unpatriotic, traitorous sentiments that excited 'very general execration for which I don't care a dam [*sic*]' (Molesworth to his mother, 10 Jan 1838, Pencarrow MSS).

Lord Durham's mission to Canada, of which Buller and Wakefield were members, and the subsequent recommendations for political advance commanded Molesworth's enthusiastic support. Meanwhile, in March 1838, he moved a vote of censure in the Commons on the colonial secretary, Lord Glenelg, castigating Colonial Office rule as 'Government by the misinformed with responsibility to the ignorant' (*Hansard 3*, 41, 6 March 1838, 479). Such motions on misrule overseas became almost annual events in the parliamentary calendar. Molesworth's reiterated prescriptions included slashing imperial expenditure, endowing colonies with free institutions, and differentiating between imperial reserved areas of jurisdiction and colonial control over internal affairs.

Pursuing Wakefieldian schemes of colonization, Molesworth joined the committee of the New Zealand Association (1837) and became a director of the successor New Zealand Company (1839). Early in 1840, as emigrants departed for Wellington, including his brother, Francis Alexander, he rejected Wakefield's proposal that he himself should head a second settlement in New Zealand. Nevertheless, he promoted the auxiliary Plymouth Company (1840–42), for which his solicitor Thomas Woollcombe was the energetic agent. The first migrants to New Plymouth included tenants from Molesworth's estates and the family of a Pencarrow gardener charged with sending back plants and shrubs. One import was an ungainly conifer, genus *Araucaria*, which provoked the barrister Charles Austin to comment: 'That tree would puzzle a monkey' (Adburgham, 61). Thereafter Molesworth was engaged in select committees on New Zealand in 1841 and 1844, parliamentary debates on the colony's affairs, and negotiations with the government surrounding the company's demise. By 1850 his attention had reverted to Australia, as Wakefield embroiled him in the Colonial Reform Society, a ginger group pressing for local self-government.

A decade earlier Molesworth's reclusive habits had been shattered when on 9 July 1844 he married Andalusia Grant [*see* Molesworth, Andalusia Grant (*c*.1809–1888)], daughter of James Bruce Carstairs and widow of Temple West of Mathon, Worcestershire. A professional singer who had studied at the Royal Academy of Music (1824), Andalusia had performed on the London stage until her first marriage in 1831. The Grotes and other acquaintances of Molesworth's expressed disgust at such an inferior match, and old friendships were ruptured. Having ensnared a wealthy baronet, Andalusia was determined to become a celebrated hostess and she drew her husband into a demanding, extravagant social life at Lowndes Square and then at 87 Eaton Place. Her ambitions also goaded him into returning to political life, and in September 1845 he was elected for Southwark, a seat he retained until his death. He supported Lord John Russell's whig ministry, and when Lord Aberdeen formed a government in January 1853, Molesworth hoped to be appointed colonial secretary. He declined the War Office and instead became first commissioner of the board of works with a seat in the cabinet. Cobden and others regarded this as apostasy, the more so when Molesworth defended war in the Crimea and then averred that *The Times* should have censored the graphic reports of horrendous conditions there filed by its correspondent William Howard Russell. As first commissioner, Molesworth opened Kew Gardens to the public on Sundays, initiated ornamental gardens in the London parks, and secured funds for rebuilding Westminster Bridge. In 1854 he received the freedom of the City of Edinburgh for his public services. During Lord Palmerston's administration he moved to the Colonial Office in July 1855, a well-deserved prize, but his tenure was brief. He died in London, probably at 87 Eaton Place, on 22 October 1855 after a bout of gastric fever. His sister, now Mary Ford, and many acquaintances surmised that an unremittingly hectic social life and arduous ministerial labours had placed impossible strains on his delicate health. Parkes was not alone in blaming Andalusia, who had declared, on marrying Molesworth,

> she would raise him into the Cab[inet] and a Peerage. She has been his death. His House, even at Brighton when ill, was a Café—a continual round of company and excitement to a feeble frame, and she kept him in blinkers. (Parkes to Cobden, 1 Dec 1855, Cobden MSS, W. Sussex RO)

Molesworth was buried not, as he had requested, at peaceful Pencarrow, but in the family vault of a mausoleum in Kensal Green cemetery, London. An epitaph referred to his aspiration 'to regenerate the colonial system', and it has been his contribution to antipodean colonization and colonial self-government which contemporaries and later writers have principally acknowledged. They have also recognized a sense of unfulfilment and restlessness, as Harriet Martineau commented, from his 'dying so early, and leaving a general impression of a wild and uncomfortable life' (Martineau to Harriet Grote, 23 Feb 1867, BL, Add. MS 46691). Since Sir William died childless, his cousin the Revd Hugh Henry Molesworth became the ninth baronet, and Andalusia acted the merry widow, often notoriously in the company of George Byng (Viscount Torrington), until her death on 16 May 1888. She bequeathed her personal property to Torrington's heirs, and Mary Ford at last took up residence at Pencarrow, where she died and was buried in 1910.

PETER BURROUGHS

Sources M. G. Fawcett, *The life of the Rt Hon. Sir William Molesworth* (1901) • H. Grote, *The philosophical radicals of 1832: comprising the life of Sir William Molesworth, and some incidents connected with the reform movement from 1832 to 1842* (1866) • A. Adburgham, *A radical aristocrat … Sir William Molesworth … and his wife Andalusia* (1990) • *The Times* (23 Oct 1855), 7 • J. Hamburger, *Intellectuals in Politics: John Stuart Mill and the philosophic radicals* (1965) • W. Thomas, *The philosophic radicals: nine studies in theory and practice, 1817–1841* (1979) • H. E. Egerton, ed., *Selected speeches of Sir William Molesworth on questions relating to colonial policy* (1903) • J. Morley, *The life of Richard Cobden*, 2 vols. (1881) • *The collected letters of Thomas and Jane Welsh Carlyle*, ed. C. R. Sanders and K. J. Fielding, 7–8 (1977–81) • *GM*, 2nd ser., 44 (1855), 645–8 • *DNB* • NRA, priv. coll., Pencarrow MSS • priv. coll., Lambton MSS • BL, Add. MSS 35150, 46691 • W. Sussex RO, Cobden papers

Archives HLRO, corresp. relating to office of works • NRA, priv. coll., Pencarrow MSS • priv. coll., corresp. and papers | BL, corresp. with Lord Aberdeen, Add. MS 43200 • News Int. RO, corresp. with John Thadeus Delane • priv. coll., Lambton MSS • U. Southampton L., letters to Lord Palmerston

Likenesses G. Hayter, group portrait, oils, 1833, NPG • J. Doyle, cartoon, 1838 (*A leading article of the Westminster Review*) • R. Dighton, pencil-and-watercolour sketch, 1840, Pencarrow • W. Behnes, marble bust, 1842, Reform Club, London; version National Gallery of Canada, Ottawa • A. E. Chalon, watercolour, 1844, Pencarrow • wood-engraving, 1851 (after photograph by Kilburn), NPG; repro. in *ILN* (1851) • J. Watson-Gordon, oils, 1854, NPG [*see illus.*] • D. Maclise, lithograph, 1873, NPG • J. Doyle, cartoons, BM • J. Gilbert, group portrait, pencil and wash (*The coalition ministry, 1854*), NPG • E. Landells, wood-engraving (after photograph by B. E. Duppa), NPG; repro. in *ILN* (27 Oct 1855) • D. Maclise, lithograph, BM, NPG; repro. in D. Maclise, *Gallery of illustrious literary characters* (1873) • stipple, NPG; repro. in *Punch* (4 Oct 1845–1846)

Molesworth, William Nassau (1816–1890), historian, eldest son of the Revd John Edward Nassau *Molesworth (1790–1877), vicar of Rochdale, Lancashire, and his first wife, Harriet, *née* Mackinnon (d. 1850), was born on 8 November 1816, at Millbrook, near Southampton, where his father then held a curacy. He was educated at the King's School, Canterbury, and at St John's and Pembroke colleges, Cambridge, where, as a senior optime at the latter, he graduated BA in 1839. In 1842 he proceeded to the degree of MA, and in 1883 the University of Glasgow bestowed on him its LLD degree. He was ordained in 1839, and became curate to his father at Rochdale, but in 1841 the wardens and fellows of the Manchester collegiate church presented him to the incumbency of St Andrew's Church, Travis Street, Ancoats, in Manchester, and in 1844 his father presented him to the church of St Clement, Spotland, near Rochdale, which living he held until his resignation through ill health in 1889. Although a poor preacher, he was a zealous and earnest parish priest; and in 1881 his labours were rewarded by an honorary canonry in Manchester Cathedral, conferred on him by Bishop James Fraser. Ecclesiastically he was a high-churchman; politically a radical. He was the friend of John Bright, who publicly praised one of his histories (G. B. Smith, ed., *The Life and Speeches of … John Bright*, 1881, 2.110), and of Richard Cobden, and was helped—misleadingly, according to J. R. M. Butler (Butler, 429)—by Lord Brougham when writing on the Reform Bill. He was among the first to support the co-operative movement, which he knew through the Rochdale Pioneers. Although described as 'angular in manner', he appears to have been agreeable and estimable in private life. He married, on 3 September 1844, Margaret, daughter of George Murray of Ancoats Hall, Manchester, with whom he had six sons and one daughter. After some years of ill health, he died at Lee Castle, Shawclough, Rochdale, on 19 December 1890, and was buried at Spotland.

Molesworth wrote a number of political and historical works, 'rather annals than history', but copious and accurate. His *The History of the Reform Bill of 1832* (1865) was later incorporated into *The History of England from 1830* (3 vols., 1871–3), which sold well. Molesworth stressed the importance of extra-parliamentary pressure on the passing of the bill, and included many parliamentary speeches. He also wrote an *Essay on the Religious Importance of Secular Instruction* (1857), an *Essay on the French Alliance* (which in

1860 gained the Emerton prize adjudicated by lords Brougham, Clarendon, and Shaftesbury), *Plain Lectures on Astronomy* (1862), and *History of the Church of England from 1660* (1882). He also edited, with his father, the periodical *Common Sense* from 1842 to 1843.

J. A. HAMILTON, rev. H. C. G. MATTHEW

Sources *The Times* (20 Dec 1890) · *Manchester Guardian* (20 Dec 1890) · J. R. M. Butler, *The passing of the great Reform Bill* (1914) · *CGPLA Eng. & Wales* (1891)
Archives Duke U., Perkins L., corresp. | U. Durham L., corresp. with Lord Grey · UCL, letters to Sir Edwin Chadwick
Likenesses wood-engraving (after photograph by E. Debenham), NPG; repro. in *ILN* (3 Jan 1891)
Wealth at death £65,523 14s. 2d.: probate, 26 Jan 1891, *CGPLA Eng. & Wales*

Moleyns. For this title name *see* Hungerford, Robert, third Baron Hungerford and Baron Moleyns (*c.*1423–1464); Rawdon, Elizabeth, *suo jure* Baroness Botreaux, *suo jure* Baroness Hungerford, *suo jure* Baroness Moleyns, *suo jure* Baroness Hastings, and countess of Moira (1731–1808).

Moleyns, Adam (*d.* 1450), administrator and bishop of Chichester, has sometimes been identified as the second son of Sir Richard Molyneux of Sefton, Lancashire, but this association appears decidedly speculative, and in truth his origins remain obscure. In any event, his family background seems to have played little part in his career, which seems rather to have prospered on account of his legal and diplomatic talents, and perhaps also his association with the influential Beaufort family.

Moleyns was presented by the crown to the rectory of Winterbourne Earls, Wiltshire, on 23 November 1423, in advance of his ordination as an acolyte by Bishop John Chaundler of Salisbury on 18 December. Over the next twenty-two years he secured no fewer than fourteen rectories, eleven prebends, two deanships (St Buryan, 1438, and Salisbury, 1441), and two archdeaconries (Salisbury, 1439, and Taunton, 1441), many of which he held only very briefly. Little wonder that Thomas Gascoigne castigated him as an outrageous pluralist. In 1435 the English government proposed Moleyns as a candidate for the archbishopric of Armagh; he finally achieved his bishopric when he was provided to the see of Chichester on 24 September 1445, and was consecrated at Lambeth on 30 November.

Moleyns had received his academic training at Oxford. He was BCL by 1430, LicCL by 1433, and DCL by 1435. It was in 1435, following the death of Bishop Thomas Polton of Worcester in August 1433, that Moleyns represented the government of Henry VI at the papal curia in Rome in supporting the cause of Thomas Bourchier, contrary to the pope's provision of Thomas Brouns. Bourchier was indeed ultimately provided to the see, and Eugenius IV commended Moleyns to the new bishop for his advocacy. In the same year Moleyns had, under royal commission, sought assurance from the pope that the duke of Burgundy would not be released from his oaths to observe the terms of the treaty of Troyes. Moleyns's service in Rome brought him rewards from both king and pope. In April 1435 he was a member of the papal household and clerk of the chamber. He was appointed apostolic protonotary on

5 November 1439, and was already papal sub-collector in England, Ireland, and Scotland by 17 September 1441, when he was named acting collector. He was subsequently commissioned, with others, to investigate the performance of his predecessor, Piero da Monte.

Moleyns was much involved in further diplomatic missions on behalf of Henry VI between England, Rome, and Basel in 1435–7, and in May 1438 he was appointed to offer congratulations to the new emperor, Albrecht II, but appears not to have gone to Germany. He did however lead an English embassy to Frankfurt, under an order of 28 November 1441, and on 12 March 1442 his commission was extended for him to go from Frankfurt to meet Pope Eugenius. Among the issues Moleyns was to raise with the pope were the proposed canonizations of King Alfred and of Osmund, bishop of Salisbury in the late eleventh century, and the king's requests for indulgences for his foundation of Eton College.

There are signs from as early as the 1430s that Moleyns had links with the Beaufort family, and in 1435 he acted as intermediary between Pope Eugenius and Cardinal Henry Beaufort. He was later also to be closely associated with William de la Pole, duke of Suffolk, who came to dominate English politics in the 1440s. Moleyns may have acted as clerk of the royal council from as early as 1436, although he was only formally appointed on 16 May 1438. It was in this capacity that he declared the charges of witchcraft and treason against Eleanor Cobham, duchess of Gloucester, in October 1441. He continued in office until 1443. In the meantime he had been appointed secondary in the privy seal office on 3 June 1441, and became keeper on 11 February 1444. He was a member of the council, rather than simply its clerk, from 27 February 1443, at latest, and was a regular attender for the rest of the decade, as far as his diplomatic commitments allowed.

From 1443 Moleyns's diplomatic talents were extensively employed in pursuit of government policy in France. He acted as intermediary between the council and John Beaufort, duke of Somerset, during preparations for the duke's campaign of 1443, which ultimately ended in ignominious failure. Between 19 February and 27 June 1444 Moleyns accompanied the duke of Suffolk to France in an attempt to secure a lasting peace. A final settlement proved impossible, and only a two-year truce was agreed, together with the marriage of Henry VI and Margaret of Anjou. Moleyns was then among the delegation to meet a French embassy that visited England in July, and was indeed appointed to travel with them when they returned to France, in an attempt to secure the definitive settlement that had continued to prove so elusive.

Moleyns was further commissioned together with John, Lord Dudley, and others, on 20 July 1446 to go to France to resolve difficulties over the surrender of the county of Maine, which the king himself had agreed in December 1445. Political and practical problems over this cession proved to be immense, and Moleyns was among the English representatives who met a powerful French embassy in the summer of 1447. On 31 January 1448 Moleyns and Sir Robert Roos were commissioned to complete the cession of Maine, and a final agreement was signed on 15 March, together with an extension of the truce until 1 April 1450. He was engaged in further diplomatic missions in France later in 1448 and in 1449, as relations continued to deteriorate, culminating in the renewal of the war.

At some point in the negotiations over Anglo-French policy, most likely in the autumn of 1446, Moleyns became involved in a dispute with Richard, duke of York, over the latter's conduct as king's lieutenant in France. York alleged that Moleyns had accused him of financial irregularities, had defamed his reputation, and had blamed him for endangering the security of Normandy. Moleyns denied that he was responsible for such accusations against York, although he did not deny that such rumours were in circulation. In fact, the dispute is indicative of rising tensions over policy in Normandy, and within months York had been replaced as lieutenant-general.

The deteriorating situation in France was a major topic of discussion in the Winchester parliament of 1449, and in the course of debate Moleyns asserted that it would be necessary to establish justice in England before dispatching further troops to France. In the autumn of 1449 he was engaged in diplomatic negotiations with the Scots which culminated in the signing of a four-year truce at Durham on 15 November.

The English military position in Normandy collapsed dramatically following Charles VII's renewal of hostilities in the summer of 1449, and in October Rouen fell. Moleyns's long and intimate association with government policy in France left him exposed to the mounting wave of criticism. He was particularly vilified because of his close identification with the duke of Suffolk, who was to bear the brunt of popular anger. One of several poems that circulated in 1450 following Suffolk's murder comprised an ironic dirge for Suffolk, Moleyns, and Roos.

It was in this hostile atmosphere that Moleyns, on 9 December 1449, obtained a royal licence, pleading failing health and a troubled conscience from neglect of his diocese, to excuse himself from any secular office and to go on pilgrimage. However, it was to be in the course of government business that Moleyns met his death. He was at Portsmouth on 9 January 1450, delivering wages to troops waiting to embark for France, when a dispute erupted and he was attacked and murdered. He was said to have attempted to save himself by accusing Suffolk of being responsible for the loss of Normandy. At the opening of the new session of parliament later that month Suffolk felt obliged to make an open declaration denying the rumours circulating about his conduct as a result of Moleyns's desperate outburst, and indeed, when responding to the articles of impeachment against him, he specifically blamed Moleyns for the surrender of Maine.

Aside from his long career in royal service, Moleyns was one of the most respected of the few English humanist scholars of his day. He was praised for his learning by his friend Poggio Bracciolini, and corresponded with Aeneas Sylvius Piccolomini, later Pope Pius II. Piccolomini asserted that Moleyns's Latin 'was the best written in England since Peter of Blois' (Emden, *Oxf.*, 1291), in the twelfth century. Of Moleyns's own writings only a single letter to Piccolomini survives, but it has been considered sufficient to identify him as the equal of most contemporary Italian humanist scholars. However, the suggestion that Moleyns was the author of *The Libelle of Englyshe Polycye* is now largely rejected.

Moleyns's involvement with his diocese is difficult to assess in the absence of his register but his almost constant employment in secular affairs seems unlikely to have left him able to devote much of his attention to it. He did however secure certain privileges and exemptions for his diocese. Moleyns died intestate. On 15 February 1450 the University of Oxford wrote to the administrators of his estate requesting the fulfilment of the late bishop's promise to donate some of his books to the university, or, failing that, to make some other donation from his property. A contemporary chronicler noted an admiring epitaph for the late bishop, which praised his wise counsel in the affairs of the realm, and his attempts to secure peace.

BILL SMITH

Sources Emden, *Oxf.*, 2.1289–91 · A. C. Reeves, *Lancastrian Englishmen* (1981) · R. Weiss, *Humanism in England during the fifteenth century*, 3rd edn (1967) · M. Harvey, *England, Rome, and the papacy, 1417–1464* (1993) · R. A. Griffiths, *The reign of King Henry VI: the exercise of royal authority, 1422–1461* (1981) · R. A. Griffiths, 'The Winchester session of the 1449 parliament', *Huntington Library Quarterly*, 42 (1978–9), 181–91 · *Chancery records* · A. L. Brown, *The early history of the clerkship of the council* (1969) · J. Ferguson, *English diplomacy, 1422–1461* (1972) · J. A. Giles, ed., *Incerti scriptoris chronicon Angliae de regnis trium regum Lancastrensium* (1848)

Moleyns [Molyns, Molines], **Sir John** (*d.* 1360), administrator and criminal, was the son of Vincent Moleyns and his wife, Isabella; he came from Hampshire, where his father had stood surety for a knight of the shire returned to parliament in 1301. His recorded career began in the royal household, as an adherent of the Despensers. In the autumn of 1325 he accompanied Prince Edward to France, and delivered a letter to the bishop of Winchester there. He married Egidia Mauduit, daughter of Sir John Mauduit and granddaughter of Robert Poges, who claimed a share of the manor of Stoke Poges, Buckinghamshire. Egidia and her husband profited from the murder of Peter Poges, lord of the manor, and his heir in the autumn of 1326, and Moleyns was later indicted of this crime but acquitted, though by a jury partly selected by himself. Stoke Poges became the centre of his estates which extended over thirty-one manors and tenements at the time of their confiscation in December 1340.

After Edward II's fall Moleyns joined William Montagu, future earl of Salisbury. Summoned to a personal interview with Edward III in 1329, he was not only involved in the preparation of the coup against Roger Mortimer, earl of March, but also assisted in Mortimer's arrest in Nottingham Castle on 19 October 1330. As Montagu's retainer and the king's personal friend Moleyns advanced rapidly in the royal household, and exploited his position to become the dominant landholder in Buckinghamshire. He was first referred to as *scutifer* in 1330, and as 'king's yeoman' in August 1331; later in the same year he received the first of a series of royal privileges. In 1335 he was styled *valettus* and had become a knight by March 1336, and steward of the king's chamber by September 1337, while in March 1338 he held the manor of Ilmer in serjeanty as keeper of the king's hawks. He was a member of the royal council in November 1339, and at about this time was made a banneret, receiving additional revenues in March 1340 to support his new status.

Moleyns acted on a number of commissions of oyer and terminer, led inquiries into breaches of the peace, and was entrusted with the inspection of royal castles. In July 1337 he was among those appointed to take alien priories into the king's hands. He travelled abroad on the king's business in August 1337, served briefly in Scotland at the end of that year, and accompanied the king to Flanders in 1338. Not only did he perform military service and provide contingents of archers and horsemen, for which by 1340 he was owed more than £1600, but he also stood surety for loans to the king and organized supplies from England. From November 1338 he was involved in arranging wool exports from England, paying more than £570 into the wardrobe. By July 1340 he was back in London.

After the king's unexpected return from Antwerp on 30 November 1340 Moleyns was among the officials arrested. Refusing to submit to Edward III, who still owed him about £1000, Moleyns escaped from the Tower of London, which led to the confiscation of his estates. A judicial inquest into his conduct began in the following January and implicated him in maintenance and other types of abuse of judicial procedure, partly in collusion with John Inge, a justice of the common bench. Acting on the request of the prior of Canterbury, who was unable to deal with the resistance offered him by a group of his Buckinghamshire tenants, Moleyns was said to have arrested the leaders of the resistance, two of whom did not survive their treatment. Inge and Moleyns later obtained an oyer and terminer commission and procured a false indictment against some of those imprisoned. An entry in the patent rolls (*CPR, 1334–8*, 292) does indeed show that the two acted together on such a commission at the time in question. Among the accusations brought at this time was also an indictment of Moleyns for the murder in 1326 of Peter Poges, his son John, and their cook John Pikerel. He was said to have obtained a fraudulent acquittal of the crime, again in collusion with John Inge. Whereas Moleyns himself was in hiding, his servant Henry Inde was indicted, convicted, and executed for the deed before a commission of gaol delivery justices headed by William de Bohun, earl of Northampton, in 1341. Apart from personal accusations against Moleyns, there were also accusations against his servants of terrorizing neighbouring landholders on his orders. Moleyns, who in the previous decade had obtained seven letters of pardon for felonies and trespasses extending back into the reign of Edward II, escaped arrest and stayed in hiding until August 1345 when his estates were gradually restored to him. He joined Edward III in the 1346 Crécy campaign, and in October 1347 came to a financial arrangement with the king, having received a summons to attend a great council earlier in the same year.

With his inclusion in the commission of the peace for Buckinghamshire in 1350 Moleyns returned to public life, becoming Queen Philippa's steward for her estates south of the Trent in 1352. Until 1354 he again acted as justice of oyer and terminer, but already in 1353 a complaint against him had been made in parliament. In 1356 judicial proceedings were begun against him on the queen's behalf, and in February 1357 indictments of felony were brought against him and his wife. In July 1357 fourteen serious charges were returned into king's bench. This time Sir John was accused of robbery, cattle rustling, and the theft of horses on various occasions, as well as of burglary and the harbouring of felons. No longer immediately attached to the royal household, Moleyns had become involved with criminal gangs operating in and around Buckinghamshire. After a lengthy trial, during which he showed an intimate acquaintance with the criminal law, Moleyns was convicted on seven counts, and escaped execution only by claiming benefit of clergy. From Windsor Castle he was taken to be imprisoned in the castle of Nottingham, and later to Cambridge Castle, where he died on 10 March 1360. His wife received a royal pardon on 30 June, and some of his confiscated estates were returned to her. She died on 21 January 1367. Moleyns and his wife, who were benefactors of Burnham Abbey and other religious houses, had three children: John, who died c.1342; Eleanor, who married John Wodhull (whose wardship Moleyns had obtained in 1336); and William, who married the daughter and heir of Edmund Bacon. The last direct male descendant of Sir John Moleyns, William, was killed during the siege of Orléans in 1429; William's daughter Eleanore married Robert *Hungerford, who became Lord Moleyns and Hungerford. JENS RÖHRKASTEN

Sources *The wardrobe book of William de Norwell*, ed. M. Lyon and others (1983) · G. J. Aungier, ed., *Chroniques de London*, CS, 28 (1844), 83–8 · Chancery records · N. Fryde, 'A medieval robber baron: Sir John Molyns of Stoke Poges', *Medieval legal records edited in memory of C. A. F. Meekings*, ed. R. T. Hunnisett and J. B. Post (1978), 197–221 · GEC, *Peerage*, new edn, 9.36–43 · Tout, *Admin. hist.*, vols. 3–5 · GEC, *Peerage*

Molineaux, Thomas. *See* Molyneaux, Thomas (c.1785–1818).

Molines, Allan. *See* Mullin, Allen (1653/4–1690).

Molines, James. *See* Molins, James (c.1580–1638).

Molines, Sir John de. *See* Moleyns, Sir John (d. 1360).

Molineux, Thomas (1759–1850), stenographer and schoolmaster, was born on 14 May 1759 at Queen Street, Manchester, Lancashire, the son of John and Jannet Molineux. He was educated at a school in Salford kept by Henry Clarke. At the age of fifteen Molineux borrowed, at the cost of 1 guinea, a copy of John Byrom's *Universal English Short-Hand* (1767), and proceeded to teach himself Byrom's shorthand system, thus beginning a long career in what he later described as 'the delightful garden of shorthand writing' (Paterson, 509). By the age of seventeen Molineux became writing master and teacher of accounts and mathematics (subjects of the lower and middle forms) at the free grammar school at Macclesfield, at a salary of £63, exclusive of board and lodging. Molineux married and had at least one child, a daughter, who married John Jackson, vicar of Over, Cheshire.

Molineux published *The Elements of Short-Hand, being an Abridgement of Mr. Byrom's Universal English Short-Hand* (1791) and *An Abridgement of Mr. Byrom's Universal English Shorthand* (1796). This last work, which presented Byrom's shorthand system with a clarity and simplicity lacking in the original, was relatively inexpensive (2s. 6d.), and so disseminated the long-out-of-print work of Byrom to an audience that would not have been able to afford the original at the price of 1 guinea. During this period Molineux also wrote treatises on practical arithmetic and the use of globes, always, as in his works on shorthand, with a view to presenting a subject with clarity and precision.

Molineux, who maintained the first register of students of the free grammar school at Macclesfield, retired from the school in 1802 to set up as writing master and shorthand instructor. Among his pupils was engraver Robert Cabell Roffe. Letters between Molineux and Roffe were published in *The Grand Master* (1860), the title referring to John Byrom.

In response to criticism that Byrom's system was better adapted to literary than to journalistic purposes, and to Thomas Gurney's insinuation that the words of a public speaker could not be recorded verbatim and read immediately with the use of Byrom's system, Molineux recorded and published his transcription *The Trial of W. Davenport [et al.], Journeymen Hatters, of Macclesfield* (1806). The following year he published his transcription of a sermon.

In 1847, in the postscript of a letter to Isaac Pitman, Molineux wrote: 'Written without the use of spectacles, not having as yet begun to use any, although in the 89th year of my age' (Paterson, 509). Molineux died in Macclesfield on 15 November 1850 and was buried at Christ Church, Macclesfield.   PAGE LIFE

Sources A. Paterson, 'Thomas Molineux', *Phonetic Journal*, 59 (1900), 509–10 · J. Corry, *The history of Macclesfield* (1817) · D. Wilmot, *A short history of the grammar school, Macclesfield, 1503 to 1910* (1910) · J. H. Lewis, *An historical account of the rise and progress of shorthand* (privately printed, London, 1825?) · K. Brown and D. C. Haskell, *The shorthand collection in the New York Public Library* (1935); repr. (1971) · *Memoirs of the life and writings of James Montgomery*, ed. J. Holland and J. Everett, 7 vols. (1854–6) · *DNB* · Watt, *Bibl. Brit.* · IGI

Archives NYPL

Likenesses R. C. Roffe, engraving (after Scott)

Molins, Aurelia (*c*.1582–1641). *See under* Molins, James (*c*.1580–1638).

Molins, Edward (1610?–1663), surgeon, was the fourth son of James *Molins (*c*.1580–1638), surgeon, and his wife, Aurelia *Molins, née Florio (*c*.1582–1641) [see under Molins, James], a midwife. He was born in Shoe Lane, London, at a date, possibly late in 1610, between the baptisms at St Andrew's, Holborn, of a brother on 3 March 1609 and a sister on 26 August 1612, perhaps as elder twin of his brother Charles. He said he was about twenty-one for his licence to marry Joanna Tallakerne (*c*.1611–1675) on 6 April 1630 at St Andrew's. She was about eighteen, the orphaned daughter of Devorax Tallakerne, esquire, of Ashdon, Essex. From nine children of the marriage only the first two sons, James *Molins (*bap.* 1631, *d*. 1687) and Edward Molins (*c*.1635–1679), and the two youngest daughters (baptized 1650 and 1654) survived their parents.

Free of the Barber–Surgeons' Company by patrimony in November 1631, Molins was chosen for the livery in the following June and passed the examination as an able surgeon in July 1633. On his father's death in 1638 he succeeded him as surgeon to St Thomas's Hospital at £40 a year and as lithotomist there and at St Bartholomew's Hospital at £15 a year from each. After complaining that the senior warden of his company had maligned him he defied the court of assistants and was fined 40s. in January 1641. The next year, called to join the king's army in York, he arranged for Thomas Hollier, husband of his niece Lucy, to deputize for him at the two hospitals. Molins served with the royalist forces until captured at the siege of Arundel in January 1644, whereupon parliament ordered his dismissal from St Thomas's. He remained in practice in London, though, assisted and consulted several times by Richard Wiseman, and compounded for £18 (twice the value of his house in Shoe Lane) for his part in the civil war.

In spite of his opposition to the government, and reputation for eccentricity, Molins was called for when Cromwell was troubled by a bladder stone in February 1656. He gave him a draught that relieved the pain, but then insisted on turning Cromwell upside down three times, because he had so treated England. Having refused any payment but a drink, Molins toasted King Charles. The report by Francesco Bernardi, the Genoese representative in London, concludes that Cromwell sent Molins £1000 next day as though from the king.

The Restoration allowed Molins to ask for reinstatement, with the king's support, at St Thomas's, which was finally agreed in March 1661, after he had unsuccessfully sued Hollier for the income of the posts since 1644; he was also reinstated at St Bartholomew's. Ironically, it was a surgical misfortune that soon led to the death of 'the famous Ned Mullins', as Pepys called him on 19 October 1663, having heard that a fractured ankle had festered, leading to a bungled amputation of the leg. Molins died about three days later and was buried at St Andrew's, Holborn, on the 27th. By his will dated 14 October his wife, the executor, was to have the property in Helions Bumpstead, Essex, that came from her family, and a life interest in his two houses, one in Shoe Lane and one in Molins Rents, with remainder to their sons James and Edward respectively, while their daughters had £150 each. Joanna Molins lived in Shoe Lane until March 1675 and was buried at St Andrew's on the 16th, four days after adding a codicil to her will dated 7 November 1672, by which £500 was to go between her daughters Frances, wife of Thomas Gooding, and Mary, unhappily married to Edward Littleton, and their children.

G. C. R. MORRIS

Sources G. C. R. Morris, 'Which Molins treated Cromwell for stone – and did not prescribe for Pepys?', *Medical History*, 26 (1982), 429–35 · C. Prayer, ed., 'Oliviero Cromwell dalla battaglia di Worcester alla sua morte', *Atti Società Ligure Storia Patria*, 16 (1882), 366–8 · F. G. Parsons, *The history of St Thomas's Hospital*, 2 (1934), 43, 63, 93, 96 · parish register, Holborn, St Andrew's, GL, MSS 6667/1–3, 6668/1, 6673/4, 5 · Barber-Surgeons' Company, freedoms, court minutes, GL [microfilms] · Pepys, *Diary*, 4.340, 345 · will, PRO, PROB 11/312, sig. 132 [Edward Molins] · will, PRO, PROB 11/347, sig. 27 [Joanna Molins] · PRO, C 10/61/90 [Molins v. Hollier, 1661] · M. A. E. Green, ed., *Calendar of the proceedings of the committee for compounding … 1643–1660*, 1, PRO (1889), 2554 · PRO, C 5/7/89 [Molins v. Turner, 1649] · R. Wiseman, *Several chirurgicall treatises* (1676), 32, 113, 355, 490 · R. Wiseman, *Of lues venerea* (1676), 76, 78
Wealth at death property in Essex; two houses in London; minimum £300 personal: will, PRO, PROB 11/312, sig. 132; PRO, PROB 11/347, sig. 27 [Joanna Molins]

Molins, James (*c.*1580–1638), surgeon, was perhaps the son of John Mullens (*d.* 1603) of London, surgeon, whose oral will on 18 August 1603 left only a seal ring to his son James and everything else to his daughter Marie. Certainly he was the James Mullyns who became free of the Company of Barber-Surgeons on 16 March 1602 after seven years' apprenticeship to William Clowes the elder, surgeon to Elizabeth I. Clowes had probably introduced him to court and so to his future wife, Aurelia [*see below*]. A letter from Queen Anne influenced his precocious appointment as surgeon to St Thomas's Hospital at £30 a year on 11 January 1605. He was the second of her three surgeons at her funeral in 1619, after Peter Chamberlen the elder.

With Peter Chamberlen the younger, Molins was fined by their company in July 1604 for not having presented their dangerously ill patient. Having been chosen for the livery in January and passed the examination in August 1607 he was fined four months later for wearing falling bands with his livery gown and again in 1609 for not attending in livery and hood on the king's day (of accession). He was elected assistant in 1617, examiner in 1624—and warden in the next two years—but not master until 1632 and attended for the last time in February 1636.

Unusually for a surgeon Molins was granted armorial bearings (ermine, a fer du moline azure; crest a watermill wheel or) in 1614 by William Segar, garter. Even more exceptionally he was examined (in Latin) by the College of Physicians in September 1627 and licensed to administer internal remedies in surgical cases. By then his reputation as a lithotomist was established. Operations for stone in the bladder had earned him payments by St Thomas's Hospital in 1621–2 for his extraordinary skill, and negotiations with St Bartholomew's resulted in a joint appointment to the two hospitals at £15 a year from each on 20 January 1623. He undertook the curing by incision of 'the Stone in the yard or Bladder … the rupture or falling downe of the Intestines or gutts into the Codds … the Carnosity or fleshie substance in the Codds … and Wennes', being allowed 2 pounds of tow to dress each patient (Paget, 30). He must have passed on his special skill in the dangerous operation for stone to his son Edward *Molins, as well as

to his last full-term apprentice, Thomas Hollier, each of whom was to follow him in this post. In November 1633 he had persuaded St Thomas's to grant the reversion of his posts there to his son Edward if he died before both Edward and Hollier.

James and Aurelia Molins had eight sons, of whom seven grew up: three went to Oxford, five into his company, though only Edward and William *Molins practised. Their eldest child, Lucy, was the first of only three out of seven daughters who grew up and married. Her daughter Lucy Knowles married Thomas Hollier. James Molins died at his house in Stoke Newington, Middlesex, on 3 December 1638 and was buried in St Andrew's, Holborn, three days later. His will, made five days before death, left the house and garden in Shoe Lane, in which he had lived, and fourteen more there (some in a turning that became called Molins Rents), after life interests in eight to his wife, in tail variously among six surviving sons and his grandson James *Molins (*bap.* 1651, *d.* 1689). There was £5 for the poor of his company and £20 to furnish its new anatomical theatre, £50 for his eldest granddaughter, Lucy Knowles, £5 each for ten other grandchildren and 50*s.* for his sister Marie Pilkington.

Aurelia Molins [*née* Florio] (*c.*1582–1641), midwife, was a daughter of John *Florio (1553–1625), author, and his first wife, and the only child in his will (which said that she exaggerated his debt to her); she was probably born before the Florios' daughter Joan (1585), and had probably married James by 1603. Her boldly flourished signature is the second on the report by ten midwives who examined alleged witches from Lancashire on 2 July 1634 with her husband and five other surgeons, finding nothing to support the allegation. That she was a well-regarded midwife is indicated by the baptizing as Aurelia of eleven girls not of her own family in 1609–39 at St Andrew's, Holborn, where twelve of her own fifteen children were baptized (1605–22) and five were buried. Her father was still living, in the same parish, when Aurelia Florio, wife of James Molins, was granted her own armorial bearings (azure, a heliotrope or issuing from a stalk sprouting out two leaves vert, in chief the sun in splendour or) on 22 August 1614, the day before her husband. Aurelia Molins widow and executor of James, was living in Aldersgate Street with their son William at her death on 12 July 1641; she was buried with her husband next day. Her will, dated the previous 7 February, distributed legacies to her family out of £500 still due to her husband's estate.

G. C. R. MORRIS

Sources Barber-Surgeons' Company, freedoms, court minutes, wardens' accounts, apprentices, GL [microfilms] · F. G. Parsons, *The history of St Thomas's Hospital*, 2 (1934), 18, 30–31 · J. Paget, *Records of Harvey* (1846), 30 · parish register, Holborn, St Andrew's, GL, MSS 6667/1, 2; 6673/1, 2 · annals, RCP Lond., 3.168–9, 193 · will, PRO, PROB 11/102, sig. 63 [John Mullens] · will, PRO, PROB 11/178, sig. 176 [James Molins] · will, 1641, GL, Archdeaconry court of London, MS 9052/10 [Aurelia Molins] · the president of the Funerall of o'late Soveraigne Lady Queene Anne, 1619, PRO, LC 2/5 · PRO, SP 16/271/9 [examination of alleged witches] · BL, Harleian MS 6140, fol. 79 · BL, Add. MS 12225, fol. 82

Wealth at death Fifteen houses in Shoe Lane; £500 owed by John, Alexander, and Hugh Popham on loan outstanding at wife's death.: will, PRO, PROB 11/178, sig. 176; his son Edward's deposition, 1650; will of Aurelia Molins, 1641, GL, MS 9052/10

Molins, James (*bap.* **1631**, *d.* **1687**), surgeon, eldest son of Edward *Molins (1610?–1663) and his wife, Joanna Tallakerne (*c.*1611–1675), and grandson of James Molins (*c.*1580–1638), was born in London and baptized at St Andrew's, Holborn, on 10 March 1631. Brought up as a surgeon under his father's tutelage, he was well enough established to ask to succeed him in October 1663. Petitions to the king shortly before and immediately after Edward's death evoked a letter from Charles II to St Thomas's Hospital on 23 October recommending James as surgeon there for his professional eminence and for his and his father's loyal service to the king and his father. The resulting appointment on 6 November was as surgeon to St Thomas's and as lithotomist, jointly with Thomas Hollier, there and at St Bartholomew's, where they operated on alternate patients and shared the salary of £15 per annum. Surprisingly, he obtained his freedom of the Barber–Surgeons' Company by patrimony only on the following 2 December, and was not chosen for the livery until five years later; he never held office in the company. The first of his seven apprentices, in 1667, was Thomas Hobbs; another, in 1679, was Edward Molins (*d.* 1689), son of the cousin James (1640–1664) who had been apprenticed to William *Molins.

James Molins was probably the 'Moulins' recorded by Pepys as having opened the skull of Prince Rupert on 3 February 1667 to drain an extradural abscess. His operation on the fractured skull of a servant of the Fleet prison in June 1675 was one of those at which his cousin James *Molins (*bap.* 1651, *d.* 1689) assisted. In February 1681 he was sworn surgeon to the household of Charles II, who mandated his degree of MD at Cambridge on 27 September following. He was not the Jacobus Molinaeus incorporated MA there, from Aberdeen, in 1667, who was Jaques du Moulin on his election to the Royal Society later that year. Dismissed from St Thomas's Hospital in December 1683 by order of the commissioners for *Quo warranto*, he continued at St Bartholomew's until his death. He was one of the five surgeons who attended the deathbed of Charles II and was promoted to surgeon-in-ordinary to James II on 1 March 1685.

Molins had lived in Salisbury Court since 1671 and his death on 8 February 1687 was followed by burial in St Bride's, Fleet Street, three days later. Until its destruction in 1940 his memorial there provided the only clue to the identity of his wife, Elizabeth, whose arms (Or, on a bend cotised between six martlets gules three wings argent) suggest that her family name was Warde. In his will, made three days before death, Elizabeth was to have for life the house in Shoe Lane that he had inherited from his grandfather. Its reversion, with any other real estate, was for Henry Molins Davenant, eldest son of their daughter Frances and her husband Charles *Davenant, who was also to have two fifths of the personal estate, like his wife Elizabeth, while the remaining fifth was for the Davenants' daughters.

G. C. R. MORRIS

Sources parish register, Holborn, St Andrew's, GL, MS 6667/2, 10 March 1631 [baptism] · F. G. Parsons, *The history of St Thomas's Hospital*, 2 (1934) · PRO, SP 29/82/28,29 · Pepys, *Diary*, vol. 8 · PRO, LC2/11(1), fol. 5 · G. C. R. Morris, 'On the identity of Jaques du Moulin', *Notes and Records of the Royal Society*, 45 (1991), 1–10 · will, PRO, PROB 11/386, fol. 40 · A. J. Jewers, 'The monumental inscriptions and armorial bearings in the churches within the City of London', 1910–19, GL, MS 2480/2, 357 · St Bride's watch rate, 1670–71, GL, MS 6613/1 · court minutes, St Bartholomew's Hospital, MS Ha 1/5, fol. 356 · Venn, *Alum. Cant.* · PRO, LC 3/56, 8; LC 7/1, fol. 47 · private information (2004)
Wealth at death house in Shoe Lane, parish of St Andrew, Holborn; other real estate: will, PRO, PROB 11/386, fol. 40

Molins, James (*bap.* **1651**, *d.* **1689**), surgeon, second and elder surviving son of William *Molins (1617–1691) and his first wife, Mary Sheppard (1625–1665), was born in Shoe Lane, London, at 10.03 p.m. on 13 May 1651, if he is the 'William Molins junior' in horoscopes by Charles Bernard, and was baptized nine days later at St Andrew's, Holborn. Before he was twenty he had transcribed, as though for publication to help young surgeons, extensive extracts from various books, mainly by Fallopius. To these he added 'Anatomicall practicall observations in St Thomas his hospital', dated from July 1674 to March 1677. This is a record of patients treated while he was an informal assistant at St Thomas's Hospital, London, to his cousin James *Molins (*bap.* 1631, *d.* 1687). The fifty cases described cover a wide range of surgical disorders from fractured skull to fistula in ano, many treated by himself alone, but seven while assisting his cousin, one his father and another an unidentified master (though he was not formally apprenticed to any). Two-thirds of the patients died, most of whom he examined post mortem, describing his findings and relating some of them to published works. The manuscript record was published in 1896 by J. F. Payne.

James Molins obtained his freedom of the Barber–Surgeons' Company on 4 April 1676 by patrimony and he took an apprentice three years later, but gaps in the records make it impossible to trace any further progress in the company. Nor is there evidence of his later development as a surgeon or morbid anatomist. He died unmarried and was buried at St Andrew's, Holborn, from his father's house in Shoe Lane, on 15 July 1689. His will, dated the previous 29 June, shows that he had mortgaged his interest in the rectory of Ratley, Warwickshire, his mother's inheritance, to his cousin Gabriel Dormer (1641–1706), son of his mother's sister Ann and brother of Mary, the wife of James Molins (1640–1664) of Diss, Norfolk, another surgical first cousin of the testator. After an annuity of £5 to his sister Susanna Kinsman, the Ratley property was to go to his brother George (1663–1703), who also became the heir to their father's real estate in 1691.

G. C. R. MORRIS

Sources J. F. Payne, 'Anatomical and practical observations at St Thomas's Hospital, 1674–77', *St Thomas's Hospital Reports*, new ser., 23 (1896), 1–39 · J. Molins, 'Anatomicall practicall observations in St Thomas his hospital', BL, Sloane MS 3293, fols. 242–265 · C. Bernard, 'Astrological schemes', BL, Sloane MS 1684, fol. 92 · parish register, Holborn, St Andrew's, GL, MSS 6667/3; 6673/6 · Barber–

Surgeons' Company, freedoms, apprentices, GL, microfilm · PRO, PROB 11/396, fol. 101 · F. G. Lee, *The history … of the church … of Thame* (1883)
Archives BL, letters, RP2340 · BL, papers, RP2383 [copies] · NMM, corresp. and papers · Norfolk RO, farming and household accounts | BL, letters to Edward Howard, RP1299 [copies] · BL, letters to Royal Literary Fund, loan 96
Wealth at death interest in rectory of Ratley, Warwickshire; other lands: will, PRO, PROB 11/396, fol. 101

Molins, William (1617–1691), surgeon and anatomist, seventh son of James *Molins (c.1580–1638) and his wife, Aurelia *Molins (c.1582–1641) [see under Molins, James], a midwife and daughter of John *Florio (1553–1625), was born in Shoe Lane, Holborn, London, at 2.45 p.m. on 13 February 1617, according to a horoscope by Charles Bernard; he was baptized a fortnight later at St Andrew's, Holborn. The surgeon Edward *Molins (1610?–1663) was his brother. Free of the Barber–Surgeons' Company by patrimony on 20 November 1638, he was chosen for the livery a year later, but was soon in dispute with another surgeon and in 1641 was fined for defiance of the court of assistants. However, he passed the examination in February 1647 and in January 1648 was one of four surgeons allowed to dissect a body privately. He was presumably 'Moulins the great chirurgion' who visited John Evelyn on 8 April 1649 to see his display of blood vessels; five days later Evelyn 'saw a private dissection at Moulin's' (Evelyn, 553–4). Molins's book on muscles had been published in 1648 with the Greek title *Myskotomia*; it was reissued in 1676, and in 1680 with the Latinized title *Myotomia*, each with a *Syllabus musculorum* by Sir Charles Scarburgh; the book was plagiarized by John Browne in *A Compleat Treatise of the Muscles* (1681).

Though Molins's mother died at his house in Aldersgate Street in July 1641, he had by then married Mary, born about March 1625, the posthumous younger daughter of Edward Sheppard of Great Rollright, Oxfordshire, and coheir of his rectory of Ratley, Warwickshire. She was buried on 7 March 1665 at St Andrew's, Holborn, where seven of her nine children were baptized from 1649 to 1663. The second of five sons, James *Molins (bap. 1651, d. 1689), and the youngest, George (1663–1703), the only two who grew up, became surgeons of the third generation living in Shoe Lane. Three daughters survived their father and married, including Mary, his executor, who was the wife of James Molins of Shrewsbury, apothecary, at the time of her will, dated 3 August 1693 and proved 19 May 1694 by her husband (possibly a cousin). William's nephew James (1640–1664), posthumous son of his eldest brother James (1605–1640), rector of Little Dunham, Norfolk, was his penultimate apprentice in 1659 and of Diss, Norfolk, surgeon, at his burial from Shoe Lane; he had married Mary Dormer, niece of William's wife.

William Molins married second, about 1667, another Mary, born about 1640, sixth daughter of Walliston Betham of Rowington, Warwickshire. She survived him and was buried at St Andrew's, Holborn, on 26 December 1695, eight months after her eldest son, Thomas, leaving two other sons and two daughters. Her will, with armorial

seal of Molins impaling Betham, disposed of much personal property, including her own and her husband's pictures, set in gold, to her daughters, Catherine Frankland and Magdalen Taler.

John Aubrey knew William Molins and heard from him that Cromwell walked in May dew in pounced shoes for his gout; he was probably the 'Mr. Molins' who told Aubrey about his grandfather John Florio (*Brief Lives*, 254). John Ward (1629?–1681), in Oxford in 1661, later vicar of Stratford upon Avon, recorded a contemporary surgeon's remark on the two Molins surgeons in Shoe Lane: Edward a skilful lithotomist, William a better surgeon and exquisite anatomist.

William Molins was buried at St Andrew's, Holborn, on 16 August 1691. His will, dated the previous 23 July, left three houses in Shoe Lane and the rectory of Ratley to his eldest surviving son, George, while his personal estate, worth at least £2500, was divided among his wife and nine children. Books and his own portrait went to his son Thomas, who died in April 1695, leaving the portrait to his youngest brother John (1675–1707); but it is not known to have survived.   G. C. R. MORRIS

Sources Barber–Surgeons' Company, freedoms, court minutes, apprentices, GL, microfilm · parish register, Holborn, St Andrew's, GL, MSS 6667/1–4, 6673/3–7 · C. Bernard, 'Astrological schemes', BL, Sloane MS, 1684, fol. 15 · Evelyn, *Diary*, vol. 2 · PRO, C6/126/39 · J. Aubrey, *The natural history of Wiltshire*, ed. J. Britton (1847) · *Brief lives, chiefly of contemporaries, set down by John Aubrey, between the years 1669 and 1696*, ed. A. Clark, 1 (1898) · D. Power, 'John Ward and his diary', *Transactions of the Medical Society of London*, 40 (1917), 1–26 · will, PRO, PROB 11/403, fol. 40 [William Molins, 1691] · will, PRO, PROB 11/420, fol. 105 [Mary Molins, 1684] · will, 1695, archdeaconry court of London, GL, MS 9052/31 [Mary Molins] · will, PRO, PROB 11/425, fol. 77 [Thomas Molins, 1695] · private information (2004)
Likenesses miniature; formerly in possession of his daughter Magdalen Taler · portrait; formerly in possession of his son John
Wealth at death approx. £1000—three houses in Shoe Lane; Rectory of Ratley; approx. £2500—personal estate: will, 1691, PRO, PROB 11/403, fol. 40

Moll, Herman (1654?–1732), geographer and cartographer, was born in the Hanseatic city-state of Bremen and went to London about 1675, possibly as a refugee from the turmoil of the Scanian Wars of 1674 to 1679. Nothing is known of his parents but his German origins seem certain. The antiquary William Stukeley in his *Family Memoirs* cited Moll as being a 'German engraver on copper' (1.134), and in his will Moll left his entire estate, including properties not specifically listed, 'in the Kingdom of Great Britain and Germany or elsewhere' to his daughter Henderina Amelia Moll. In his *Diary*, the scientist Robert Hooke placed Moll in London in 1678–9, working for Moses Pitt as an engraver and frequenting famous Jonathan's Coffee House. Nothing is known of his life before he arrived in London or about where he learned the fine art of engraving, and apart from the mention of his daughter in his last testament, neither is anything known of his family life in London.

As Hooke indicated, Moll first gained notice in London in the late 1670s as a fine engraver working for map publishers such as Moses Pitt, Sir Jonas Moore, the royal hydrographer Greenville Collins, John Adair, [Jeremiah] Seller and [Charles] Price, and others. What can be identified as his two earliest maps—'America' and 'Europe' respectively—and bearing the imprint 'H. Mol schulp.' appeared in Moore's *A New Systeme of the Mathematicks Containing … a New Geography* in 1681. He probably sold his own maps at first from a simple stall set up at various locations throughout London, including Westminster Hall during meetings of parliament to capitalize on the crowds that gathered around them. Moll set up his first shop in 1688 at Vanley's Court in Blackfriars, where he stayed until 1691. Between 1691 and 1710 he was located at the corner of Spring Garden, Charing Cross, after which he moved to Devereux Court, Strand, where he stayed until his death.

Moll worked increasingly independently. He published his first solo volume, the now rare *Atlas Thesaurus* in 1695, and in 1701, by which time he worked completely on his own, he published his first major work, *A System of Geography*, an informative global geography with a full complement of crisp, straightforward maps that sold initially for 18s. a copy. Although relatively traditional and derivative, it helped to establish him as an independent geographer–cartographer. There followed in 1708 *Fifty-Six New and Accurate Maps of Great Britain* and thereafter numerous other lucrative volumes and separate maps of Great Britain and Ireland, and of Europe and its constituent states. In 1711, he founded *Atlas Geographus*, a much imitated monthly magazine which ran until 1717, when it was fully published in five volumes. When the runs of the magazines or volumes were completed, the subscriber had an up-to-date geography of the world, containing maps and other illustrations, which was far more detailed than *A System of Geography*. John Green in his own relatively singular *The Construction of Maps and Globes* in 1717 offered a not wholly favourable critique of *Atlas Geographus*, saying

If something of this Kind had been done before, then there had probably been a Stop put, ere now, to that Swarm of spurious Maps that are abroad. … But that which goes by the Name of *Moll's* Geography, is the most perfect Piece that has been writ yet in any Language, and yet it might be improv'd. (162–4)

In 1709 Moll issued *The Compleat Geographer*, a revised expansion of *A System of Geography*, and the first of two textless global pocket atlases, *Atlas manuale*; the second, *Atlas Minor*, appeared in 1719. They were quite popular, in part because of their comparatively low cost, and consequently went through several editions quickly. These were followed in 1710 by what are probably the greatest rarities among all Moll's maps, a pair of magnificent pocket globes, 7 centimetres in diameter, one terrestrial encased in one celestial. Moll's book *A View of the Coasts, Countries, and Islands within the Limits of the South-Sea-Company*, with accompanying map, published in 1711, provided the historical-geographical background to the formation of the joint-stock South Sea Company by act of parliament in May of the same year. It also contributed to the growing investment frenzy that culminated nine years later in the infamous South Sea Bubble scandal.

Far and away Moll's most consequential work was *The World Described*. Published in nine British and two pirated Irish editions between 1715 and 1754 and usually comprising thirty large two-sheet maps of all parts of the earth, this atlas-folio exhibited Moll's engraving skill at its most distinctive. It contained his most celebrated individual work, 'A New and Exact Map of the Dominions of the KING of GREAT BRITAIN on the Continent of NORTH AMERICA', which incorporated an inset scene of industrious beavers labouring harmoniously on a dam with a great waterfall, probably the Niagara, in the background; consequently the map has become known as the 'Beaver Map'. It is not only one of his cartographic masterpieces, but with its additions, commentaries, and embellishments (for example, post roads) it also offers a ringing endorsement of empire. It also contained some of the best examples of his characteristic and now famous map notations:

The Iroquois consist of four Cantons, Govern'd by so many Kings and are all hearty friends to the English; those Princes came into England in 1710 to offer their services agt the French in Canada, and had it not be for the miscarriage of our Expedition to Quebec in 1711, those People would have been of great service to us, for they joyn'd General Nicholson with 2000 men on his March to attack Montreal.

Moll's cartography also appeared in works other than his own, especially those of members of his intellectual circle. He was associated with the buccaneers William Dampier and Woodes Rogers and provided maps for their voyages round the world and the published accounts of them such as Dampier's *A New Voyage Round the World* (1698) and Rogers's *A Crusing Voyage Round the World* (1712). In turn, they supplied him with current geographic information, particularly from the south Pacific and Indian oceans. Moll provided the maps for Daniel Defoe's *Robinson Crusoe* (1719) and *Tour thro' the Whole Island of Great Britain* (1724) and his maps form the basis for those of the fantastic lands in Jonathan Swift's *Gulliver's Travels* (1726). He dedicated his *Thirty Two New and Accurate Maps of the Geography of the Ancients* (1721) to Stukeley and also engraved classical period maps for him. Moll's maps also illustrated the histories of John Oldmixon, Thomas Salmon, Samuel Simpson, and others.

In the final year of his life Moll issued the first few copies of what was eventually to become a pocket road atlas, *The Roads of Europe* (1732), containing twenty-nine maps on eighteen sheets and covering Britain, Ireland, the English Channel, and the continent; the only known copy is to be found in the King George III topographical collection of the British Library (K. Top.IV.97: 118.c.23). According to his succinct obituary in the *Gentleman's Magazine* and as noted by Stukeley (1.134), after a brief undetermined illness Moll died on 22 September 1732 at his home in Devereux Court, Strand, in the parish of St Clement Danes. Shortly before his death some of his surviving copperplates and map stocks were reportedly purchased by the Bowen family of cartographers and publishers, with whom Moll had done business intermittently.

Moll's reputation rests upon a long and extremely fertile career of almost sixty years that yielded a diverse offering of over two dozen geographies, atlases, and histories and a myriad of individual maps, charts, and globes, spanning the known earth. Through his many works, he had also had an impact beyond geography and cartography on his adopted country and its future by graphically staunchly advocating early British expansion and empire. DENNIS REINHARTZ

Sources D. Reinhartz, *The cartographer and the literati: Herman Moll and his intellectual circle* (1997) · *The family memoirs of the Rev. William Stukeley*, ed. W. C. Lukis, 3 vols., SurtS, 73, 76, 80 (1882–7) · *The diary of Robert Hooke … 1672–1680*, ed. H. W. Robinson and W. Adams (1935) · J. Green, *The construction of maps and globes* (1717) · S. Tyacke, *London map-sellers, 1660–1720* (1978) · *GM*, 1st ser., 2 (1732), 979 · J. N. L. Baker, 'The earliest maps of H. Moll', *Imago Mundi*, 2 (1937), 16 · F. Bracher, 'The maps in *Gulliver's travels*', *Huntington Library Quarterly*, 8 (1944–5), 59–74 · B. Fishman, 'Defoe, Herman Moll, and the geography of South America', *Huntington Library Quarterly*, 36 (1972–3), 227–38 · J. R. Moore, 'The geography of *Gulliver's travels*', *Journal of English and German Philology*, 40 (1941), 214–28 · *DNB* · will, PRO, PROB 11/654/251 · W. Bonacker, *Kartenmacher aller Länder und Zeitens* (1966) · records, Stefan's Church, Bremen, Germany · records, St Clement Danes, London

Archives BL · RGS

Likenesses W. Stukeley, pen-and-ink, 1723, Bodl. Oxf., MS Eng. misc. c. 136, fol. 26

Mollineux, Henry (*d.* 1720). *See under* Mollineux, Mary (1651?–1696).

Mollineux [*née* Southworth], **Mary** (1651?–1696), poet, was born Mary Southworth, probably in 1651 and probably in Lancashire. Her parents' names do not appear on her marriage certificate, but it has been speculated that her mother may have been Alice Southworth of Warrington (Mortimer, 126). Mollineux's cousin Frances Owen (*née* Ridge) was editor and writer of the introduction to her cousin's selection of devotional verses, *Fruits of Retirement* (1702).

Frances Owen observed that Southworth's father 'brought her up to more Learning than is commonly bestowed on our sex' (Mollineux, sig. A4r). She learned about the nature of plants and minerals, in addition to Latin, Greek, 'physick and chyrurgery', and arithmetic. Though seemingly her learning was impeded by 'weak Eyes', her first dated poem puts her at eleven (ibid., sig. A4r–v). She may have been raised a Quaker; Henry Mollineux notes that 'she was Convinced of the Way of Truth in her Youth' (ibid., sig. Br).

In as far as the poetry can be read as biography, Southworth's early work, prior to 1684, extolling the virtues of retirement and retreat, is a pattern of feminine piety. In 1684, however, Southworth was arrested attending a Quaker meeting at James Wright's house in Warrington. Her first experience of imprisonment is rendered in heroic language:

> Tho' the Righteous be in Bonds confin'd,
> They inwardly sweet Satisfaction find.
> (Mollineux, 124)

Southworth met her future husband, Henry Mollineux [*see below*], while in Lancaster Castle. They were married

eleven years—from 10 April 1685 until Mary's death in 1696. John Tomkins describes her as 'a Loving Wife; an Affectionate Mother to her Children' (Tomkins, 50). They had two children, Othniel and Elleazor, both boys. Mollineux compares friendship with the trials of marriage:

> They that are unengag'd in Wedlock, seem
> T'enjoy a Privledge of Liberty
> To act Spontaneously.
> (Mollineux, 162)

The imprisonment of Henry in February 1691, for not appearing before the consistory court over non-payment of tithes, led Mary Mollineux into public conflict with the authorities, whom she engaged in scriptural debate. Answering Bishop Stratford of Chester in August in a way sufficient to convince him that Quakers should be treated with 'kindness' and given their liberty, and arguing with vigour enough to stop the mouth of the bishop's chaplain, she was, nevertheless, accounted a woman with 'so much Learning it makes her mad'. Even despite these victories, Henry was imprisoned, once more, by February 1692 (ibid., sig. B7v–Cr).

Mary Mollineux's poetry was published posthumously since, according to Tryall Ryder, 'she [was] not seeking Praise amongst Men, but to communicate the Exercise of peculiar Gifts amongst her near Friends and Acquaintance' (Mollineux, A7v). Indeed, such is the paradigmatic nature of her meditations on modesty and chastity, her preferment of 'Divine Contemplation' over 'unprofitable Invention', her creative expression is noticeably circumscribed by constrictive notions of pious femininity (ibid., A6r–v).

On her deathbed, Mary Mollineux was 'seized with violent Pain and Sickness'; this continued for a month until she was very weak and rarely achieved consciousness (Mollineux, B2r). She died on 3 January 1696, in Liverpool, 'without any Noise, Sigh, or Groan'; she was forty-four (ibid., B3v).

Henry Mollineux (*d.* 1720) was born at Lydiate, near Ormskirk, Lancashire. His date of birth and parentage are uncertain. He may be either or neither of two Henry Molynex who were baptized in Aughton by Ormskirk: the son of Edward (14 August 1652) or, perhaps less likely, the son of Robert (28 September 1662). He was also a Quaker, and suffered imprisonment in 1684, 1691, and 1692 (Mollineux A8v, B7r, Cr). On his marriage certificate he is listed as a yeoman. He was the author of *Anti-Christ Unveiled* (1695), *An Invitation from the Spirit of Christ* (1696), and *Popery Exposed* (1718), in addition to his testimony to Mary (included in *Fruits of Retirement*, sig. A8 v–B8 v). Henry also contributed to the *Collection of Roger Haydock's Works* (1700). In 1698 he took part in a ministering campaign to Scotland, travelling with Daniel Rigby and Joseph Penington. He died at Lydiate on 16 February 1720. CATIE GILL

Sources J. E. Mortimer, 'An early Quaker poet: Mary (Southworth) Mollineux d. 1696', *Journal of the Friends' Historical Society*, 53 (1972–5), 125–47 · M. Mollineux, *Fruits of retirement* (1702) · J. Besse, *A collection of the sufferings of the people called Quakers*, 1 (1753) · J. J. Green, 'The Quaker family of Owen', *Journal of the Friends' Historical Society*, 1 (1903–4), 28–39, 74–82, 111–20 · J. Tomkins, *Piety promoted … the second part* (1702) · W. F. Miller, 'Stranger Friends visiting Scotland',

Journal of the Friends' Historical Society, 12 (1915), 79–83, 137–45 ·
IGI · DNB

Mollison, James Allan (1905–1959), aviator, was born at 33 Fotheringay Road, Pollokshields, Glasgow, on 19 April 1905, the only child of Hector Alexander Mollison, consultant engineer, and his wife, Thomasina Macnee Addie (*d.* 1965). His childhood was disrupted by his father's alcoholism, which led to his parents' separation and eventual (1915) divorce. He did not see his father again. His mother married again, in 1918; her second husband was Charles Bullmore, a naval officer, and for a while James adopted his stepfather's name. He was educated at the Glasgow and Edinburgh academies, where his record was poor. Family connections enabled him to obtain a short-service commission in the Royal Air Force in 1923 on the nomination of the lord provost of Glasgow, who had been approached by James Mollison's grandfather, a prominent Glasgow engineer. He learned to fly at Duxford, was posted to India in 1925, where he was based on the northwest frontier, but returned to England in September 1926, before completing his tour of duty, for reasons that are unexplained. His subsequent posting to the spartan regime of the Electrical and Wireless School at Flowerdown suggests a penalty for disciplinary shortcomings. He then took the Central Flying School course at Wittering, and went on as an instructor to the Flying Training School at Sealand. On transferring to the reserve in March 1928, after completing five years' service, he went to Australia, where he was first a bathing-beach attendant, next an instructor at the Adelaide branch of the Australian Aero Club, then an airline pilot, from 1929 to 1931 with Kingsford Smith's Australian National Airways.

Lord Wakefield, who helped so many ambitious pilots, gave Mollison the initial impetus in his meteoric career of record-breaking flights by providing him with a Gipsy Moth. Seeking to establish a new record for the solo flight in a light aeroplane from Australia to England, Mollison wrecked his heavily loaded machine on taking off from Darwin (7 June 1931). Wakefield gave him another Moth, a DH60 Gipsy 2, in which Mollison took off from Wyndham on 29 July 1931, and set course for England, making Pevensey Bay on 6 August in just over 8 days 19 hours. As in most of his record-breaking flights, he pushed himself and his aircraft to the limits of endurance.

Mollison's flight from England to the Cape in 1932 again revealed those qualities which were to make him famous. After leaving on 24 March in a De Havilland Puss Moth with Gipsy 3 engine, he took only just over 4 days 17 hours for the flight and arrived over Cape Town aerodrome in the evening in such a state of physical fatigue that double vision caused him to land on an adjacent beach and overturn his machine into the sea.

Small of stature, though with a taste for flashy clothes and with an affected drawl in his speech, Mollison now found the celebrity he craved. A rumoured engagement to Lady Diana Wellesley was followed, amid much publicity, by his marriage on 29 July 1932 to the already famous aviator Amy *Johnson (1903–1941). The press called them 'the Flying Sweethearts' and 'the Air Lovers', and sponsors

James Allan Mollison (1905–1959), by Howard Coster, 1930

were readily found to finance their lavish lifestyle. But the marriage, which enhanced Mollison's own fame, was soon undermined by his heavy drinking and insatiable womanizing.

Intense public interest accompanied Mollison's solo flight east to west across the north Atlantic, not previously attempted and fraught with risk because of prevailing adverse winds. The flight was made in the De Havilland Puss Moth G-ABXY with 120 horsepower Gipsy 3 engine and an extra 160 gallon fuel tank in the cabin. It was named the *Heart's Content* after a town in Newfoundland. He took off on 18 August 1932 from Portmarnock Strand in Ireland; 19 hours 5 minutes afterwards he crossed the Newfoundland coast only 20 miles north of the landfall he had planned. Finally he landed in a field at Pennfield Ridge, New Brunswick, after 31 hours 20 minutes' flying. It was the longest duration flight in a light aircraft, the first crossing of the Atlantic in such a machine, and the fastest east–west crossing. In New York, where he received the freedom of the city, he was fêted as 'England's Lindbergh' (Luff, 178). On his return he published an account of his exploits, *Death Cometh Soon or Late* (1932), with the assistance of a ghost writer, the journalist William Courtenay.

On 6 February 1933 Mollison set out from Lympne to fly the south Atlantic solo from east to west in the *Heart's Content*. He flew by way of Casablanca, Agadir, Villa Cisneros, and Thies in French West Africa, to Port Natal, Brazil, making the 2000 mile ocean crossing in the record time of 17 hours 40 minutes. In recognition of the achievement he was awarded the Britannia trophy. With Amy Johnson on 22–3 July 1933 he flew from Britain to the United States in a De Havilland Dragon. After a flight of 39 hours 42 minutes they ran short of fuel, landed in the dark at Bridgeport, Connecticut, overturned their machine in a swamp, and were slightly injured. Although they failed to reach New York, their intended destination, the city accorded them a ticker-tape reception on 1 August, and the freedom of the city (in Mollison's case, for the second time).

In October 1934 in a De Havilland Comet Mollison and Amy Johnson set a record of 22 hours for the stage from England to India in the England to Melbourne race. But they were unable to complete the race, amid mutual recriminations, and they increasingly led separate lives. An attempted reconciliation in August 1936 failed, and their formal separation was announced. His consorts now included Beryl Markham. In October 1936 in a Bellanca aeroplane Mollison made the first flight from New York to London; the journey took 17 hours, and the north Atlantic crossing 13½ hours. In November and December 1936 he flew from England to the Cape by the eastern route in 3 days 6 hours.

By the late 1930s the scope for spectacular record-breaking flights was diminishing, and with this came a decline in sponsorship and prizes. Desperate for money, Mollison published the sensational *Playboy of the Air* (1937), ghosted by the journalist Victor Ricketts. Its boasts of female conquests confirmed his reputation as a cad, and its dedication to the actress Dorothy Ward heightened Amy Johnson's determination to seek a divorce, which she obtained on 24 August 1938. His second marriage, on 12 November 1938, to Phyllis Louis Verley Hussey (*b.* 1901/2), a wealthy heiress and socialite, offered the prospect of alleviating his money worries; she was the divorced wife of Lieutenant-Commander Thomas Andrew Hussey RN, and a member of the Verley family, which had business interests in the West Indies. Mollison's heavy drinking soon led to their separation.

The Second World War gave Mollison a respite from his personal problems, and provided him with a renewed sense of purpose. He joined the Air Transport Auxiliary, assisting with ferrying aircraft from America across the Atlantic. He undertook many difficult ferrying missions and delivered a vast number of machines for the RAF. In recognition of his wartime service he was appointed MBE in 1946. After the war he was employed as a pilot by Meindert Kamphuis, a Dutch businessman. Mollison began an affair with his wife, and after Kamphuis's death in an air crash he divorced Phyllis and married Maria Clasina Eva Kamphuis (*b.* 1909/10) on 26 September 1949. As a result of his drinking his pilot's licence was revoked in 1953. In 1956 he separated from his third wife, and purchased the Carisbrooke Hotel in Surbiton as a source of livelihood. Suffering from acute alcoholism, he was admitted to The Priory, Roehampton, London, where he died on 30 October 1959. He was cremated at Brookwood cemetery, Surrey. He had no children.

Mollison earned a high reputation both as a pilot and as an especially gifted navigator. His determination not to take things too seriously was indicated by his oft-repeated claim that in an emergency he would rather jettison a navigational instrument than his bottle of brandy. He faced danger with an ironical smile and to the hazardous flights he undertook he always contrived to give his own characteristic faintly humorous flourish. In 1941 a film based on some of the flights by Mollison and Amy Johnson called *They Flew Alone* was made with Robert Newton and Anna Neagle. OLIVER STEWART, rev. M. C. CURTHOYS

Sources C. Collinson and F. McDermott, *Through Atlantic clouds: the history of Atlantic flight* (1934) · *Who's who in British aviation* (1935) · *Royal Aero Club Gazette* (Nov 1963) · *The Times* (2 Nov 1959) · *The Times*

(6 Nov 1959) · private information (1971) · personal knowledge (1971) · D. Luff, *Mollison: the flying Scotsman* (1993) · m. certs. · d. cert.

Archives FILM BFI NFTVA, documentary footage · BFI NFTVA, news footage

Likenesses H. Coster, photograph, 1930, NPG [*see illus.*] · M. Lindsay Williams, portrait, 1932 · photographs, 1932–3, Hult. Arch. · photographs, repro. in Luff, *Mollison*

Wealth at death £8982 15s. 7d.: probate, 7 April 1960, CGPLA Eng. & Wales

Molloy, Charles (1645/6–1690), legal writer and lawyer, was born in King's county, Ireland; nothing is known about his early life. In 1666 he published *Holland's ingratitude, or, A serious expostulation with the Dutch, shewing their ingratitude to this nation*, 'from a faithful and loyal subject to his Majesty, though never in his pay'. This work also contained verses in praise of the duke of Albemarle and Prince Rupert. On 7 August 1667 at the request of the reader, Thomas Powys, Molloy was admitted to Lincoln's Inn, as the son and heir of John Molloy, late of Ireland, deceased. On 28 June 1669 he was admitted to Gray's Inn, with allowance being made for the time he had spent at Lincoln's Inn. There is some evidence that he was called to the bar on 31 July 1669 at the request of the reader of the inn. He may also have been the Charles Molloy who wrote the dedication (to Charles II) in the 1670 *Resusatatio* of Francis Bacon's works.

Molloy's marriage licence of 13 December 1670 gave his address as Lincoln's Inn and his age as twenty-four. He duly married on 17 December 1670, at East Barnet, Elizabeth (*b.* 1651), daughter of William Day. They had at least one son, Charles, born in 1674 and baptized in St Andrew's, Holborn. Molloy wrote an extensive treatise on maritime law, *De jure maritime et navali, or, A treatise of affaires maritime, and of commerce* (1676), which also dealt with naval and military discipline and the prize jurisdiction of the Admiralty. It was a popular work because it catered for the needs of lawyers, and went through many editions. The tenth edition was published in 1778.

There is some evidence that Molloy practised as a barrister. In June 1684 a Mr Molloy was involved in a suit between a Mr Fox and the earl of Clare. Narcissus Luttrell included a Mr Molloy among the counsel for the king in the case against the seven bishops which began on 29 June 1688. This is plausible, as the attorney-general at this juncture was his original patron, Sir Thomas Powys. Molloy was counsel before the House of Lords in a suit in July 1689, and in September was listed as having visited Richard Graham and Philip Burton in the Tower. In June 1690 he was described as counsellor-at-law when being granted access to Charles Turner, then in prison in Newgate.

Molloy died in Crane Lane Court, Fleet Street, London, in 1690, his wife having predeceased him. Administration was granted to his creditors in April 1691. His son edited an edition of his father's work *De jure maritime* (1722).

STUART HANDLEY

Sources W. P. Baildon, ed., *The records of the Honorable Society of Lincoln's Inn: admissions*, 1 (1896), 299 · J. Foster, *The register of admissions to Gray's Inn, 1521–1889, together with the register of marriages in Gray's Inn chapel, 1695–1754* (privately printed, London, 1889), vol. 1, p.

307 • R. J. Fletcher, ed., *The pension book of Gray's Inn*, 2 (1910) • N. Luttrell, *A brief historical relation of state affairs from September 1678 to April 1714*, 1 (1857), 446 • *CSP dom.*, 1690–91, 42 • *The manuscripts of the House of Lords*, 4 vols., HMC, 17 (1887–94), vol. 2, p. 199 • J. L. Chester and J. Foster, eds., *London marriage licences, 1521–1869* (1887), 932 • *IGI* • will, PRO, PROB 6/67, fol. 63*v* • S. C. A. Pincus, *Protestantism and patriotism* (1996), 306–10 • Holdsworth, *Eng. law*, 1.570; 12.627 • C. Molloy, *Holland's ingratitude* (1666), dedication • J. Reddie, *An historical view of the law of maritime commerce* (1841), 431 • *The whole works of Sir James Ware concerning Ireland*, ed. and trans. W. Harris, rev. edn, 2 (1764), 203 • D. R. Coquillette, *The civilian writers of Doctors' Commons, London* (1988), 99, 124, 140–45

Molloy, Charles (*d.* 1767), playwright and journalist, was born probably at Birr, King's county, Ireland. His father was Hugh Molloy, gentleman; nothing is known of his mother. Baker (*Biographia dramatica*, 1.521) says he was educated at Trinity College, Dublin, and afterwards became a fellow there, but he cannot be traced in surviving records.

Molloy moved to London, where three comedies by him were performed with indifferent success at Lincoln's Inn Fields. *The Perplex'd Couple* or *All Jealous, or, Mistake upon Mistake* (February 1715) and *The Coquet, or, The English Chevalier* (April 1718) each ran for three performances: enough to provide one author's benefit. *The Half Pay Officers* achieved seven performances (two author's benefits) in January 1720 and was revived three times: in one memorable case (28 January 1723 at the Haymarket) for the benefit of the actress Peggy Fryar, aged eighty-five, who danced a jig very nimbly at the end of the performance. All three plays were printed: Curll gave 5 guineas for *The Coquet* and a note of hand for another 5 guineas upon the sale of 900 copies (BL, Add. MS 38728, fol. 157).

Molloy was admitted to the Middle Temple on 28 May 1716; it is not known if he practised as a lawyer. Nor is it known when he began writing for the anti-ministerial journals, *Mist's* (1716–28) and its continuation *Fog's Weekly Journal* (1728–31), but his contributions were significant enough to recommend him to James Francis Edward Stuart, the Old Pretender, as a suitable editor for a new opposition journal, funded initially by Jacobites, in which (according to Daniel O'Brien, the Pretender's Paris agent) he would be secretly assisted by Alexander Pope. Molloy himself wrote to the Jacobite King James III on 23 July 1737 to declare his duty and zeal in this project. *Common-Sense, or, The Englishman's Journal*, which ran from February 1737 to November 1743, edited and partly written by Molloy, attracted contributions from the earl of Chesterfield, Lord Lyttelton, and William King the Jacobite, but not from Pope.

Molloy was a political ally of Alderman John Barber (1675–1741) and was remembered in Barber's will along with other tories, including Jonathan Swift, Pope, and Henry Bolingbroke. On 22 July 1742 he married Barber's long-serving, loyal, and resourceful housekeeper and mistress, Sarah Duffkin (*bap.* 1699, *d.* 1758) of Nuneaton, Warwickshire, who had inherited considerably more than £20,000 from her employer and lover. The Molloys, who remained childless, lived in Soho, first in Frith Street, then from 1754 at 18 Soho Square. Sarah died on 3 January 1758 and was buried in the chancel at All Saints, Edmonton, Middlesex, beside her brother Jeremiah Duffkin. On 23 May 1764, aged seventy or over, Molloy was admitted to Gray's Inn. He died at his house in Soho Square and was buried at All Saints, Edmonton, on 20 July 1767.

JAMES SAMBROOK

Sources C. H. Jones, 'The Jacobites, Charles Molloy, and *Common sense*', *Review of English Studies*, new ser., 4 (1953), 144–7 • D. E. Baker, *Biographia dramatica, or, A companion to the playhouse*, rev. I. Reed, new edn, rev. S. Jones, 1 (1812), 521 • E. L. Avery, ed., *The London stage, 1660–1800*, pt 2: *1700–1729* (1960) • A. H. Scouten, ed., *The London stage, 1660–1800*, pt 3: *1729–1747* (1961) • [J. Ralph], *A critical history of the administration of Sir Robert Walpole* (1743), 516 • H. A. C. Sturgess, ed., *Register of admissions to the Honourable Society of the Middle Temple, from the fifteenth century to the year 1944*, 1 (1949), 277 • J. Foster, *The register of admissions to Gray's Inn, 1521–1889, together with the register of marriages in Gray's Inn chapel, 1695–1754* (privately printed, London, 1889), 384 • *The life and character of John Barber, Esq., late lord-mayor of London, deceased* (1741) • E. Curll, *An impartial history of the life, character, amours, travels and transactions of Mr John Barber* (1741) • D. Lysons, *The environs of London*, 2 (1795), 262, 272 • *The parish of St Anne, Soho*, 1 (1966), 69, 152 • W. Robinson, *The history and antiquities of the parish of Edmonton, in the county of Middlesex* (1819), 72, 104–5 • will of Sarah Molloy, PRO, PROB 11/835, sig. 47 • will, PRO, PROB 11/930, sig. 274 • *IGI*

Wealth at death over £16,000—houses in Swallow Street and Soho Square, London; books, pictures, household goods, medals, foreign coins, etc.: will, PRO, PROB 11/930, sig. 274

Molloy, Francis. *See* Ó Maolmhuaidh, Froinsias (*c.*1606–1677?).

Molloy, Gerald (1834–1906), university principal, born at Mount Tallant, Terenure, co. Dublin, on 10 September 1834, was the second son of Thomas Molloy and his wife, Catharine, daughter of Patrick Whelan. After education at Castleknock College he entered St Patrick's College, Maynooth, and there completed his studies for the priesthood. In 1857, when only twenty-three years old, he was appointed professor of theology at Maynooth. His real aptitude, however, was not for theology but for the natural sciences. In 1870 he published a popular work entitled *Geology and Revelation*. In 1874 he resigned his chair at Maynooth (where he received the degree of DD) for the professorship of natural philosophy in the Catholic University, Dublin, founded twenty years earlier by J. H. Newman. Molloy became its rector in 1883 but the title was little more than honorary, the institution having fallen into decay. Molloy had little interest in preparing students for external examinations and enjoyed more success with his public lectures on science which were accompanied by dramatic experiments.

On the establishment of the Royal University of Ireland in 1879 the buildings of the Catholic University housed the new University College of Dublin. Molloy was among the first senators of the Royal University, and was made DSc; in 1882 he resigned the position of senator for a fellowship in the department of physical science at University College, a post which he held until 1887. In 1885 he was appointed to the government commission to inquire into educational endowments in Ireland and to formulate improved schemes for their application. This appointment he held until the commission concluded its work in

1894. In 1890 he was reappointed a senator of the Royal University, and in 1903 became its vice-chancellor. In that capacity he attended the celebrations to mark the quatercentenary of the University of Aberdeen in 1906. During the festivities he died suddenly of heart failure on 1 October 1906. He was buried in Glasnevin cemetery, Dublin.

A man of broad sympathies and genial manners, Molloy was popular with every rank and section of Irish society. His gifts did not lie in the direction of original research, but he had a singular power of lucid exposition. His public lectures in the theatre of the Royal Dublin Society, and elsewhere, attracted large audiences. By his will he left considerable sums for charitable purposes.

T. A. FINLAY, rev. G. MARTIN MURPHY

Sources *A page of Irish history: the story of University College, Dublin, 1883–1909*, ed. Fathers of the Society of Jesus (1930) · W. McDonald, *Reminiscences of a Maynooth professor* (1926), 51–2 · T. J. Morrissey, *Towards a national university* (1983) · P. J. Corish, *Maynooth College, 1795–1995* (1995) · *Freeman's Journal* [Dublin] (2 Oct 1906) · *Irish Times* (2 Oct 1906) · *CGPLA Eng. & Wales* (1906)
Likenesses photograph, repro. in Corish, *Maynooth College*, 470
Wealth at death £1875—effects in England: probate, 23 Nov 1906, *CGPLA Eng. & Wales*

Molloy, James Lynam (1837–1909), composer, born at Cornalaur, King's county, Ireland, on 19 August 1837, was the eldest son of Dr Kedo J. Molloy and his wife, Maria Theresa. His younger brother Bernard Charles Molloy was nationalist MP for King's county (1880–85) and for Birr division (1885–1900). James was educated at St Edmund's College, Old Hall Green, near Ware, and at the Catholic University, Dublin, where he won a junior classical scholarship in 1855, under the rectorship of John Henry Newman, and graduated in arts in 1858. Among his contemporaries were the Roman Catholic archbishop of Dublin (Dr Walsh) and Hugh Hyacinth O'Rorke the MacDermot, the attorney-general for Ireland. He showed much musical ability during his college course, and his singing of the services during Holy Week in 1857 and 1858 attracted attention. As the degree of MA from the Catholic University was not legally recognized by British institutions, Molloy continued his studies at London University, Paris, and Bonn, and was called to the English bar from the Middle Temple on 6 June 1863. He joined the south-eastern circuit and became a member of Brighton sessions, but did not practise. For a time he acted as secretary to Sir John Holker, attorney-general, and settled for several years in London. In 1889 he was made private chamberlain to Pope Leo XIII.

As early as 1865 Molloy issued a number of songs, some of them with words by himself, and he soon grew to be one of the most successful Irish song composers of his time. Later he became more ambitious and composed an operetta, *The Students' Frolic*, to a libretto by Arthur Sketchley. Though the piece was not very successful, the melody of one of the songs, 'Beer, beer, beautiful beer', was subsequently utilized and became extremely popular as 'The Vagabond', with words by Charles Lamb Kenney. In 1873 Molloy brought out an edition of Irish tunes entitled *Songs of Ireland* (enlarged edition, 1882). Between 1865 and 1900

he was responsible for nearly a hundred songs and ballads, many of which were extremely popular. Particularly successful were 'Just a Song of Twilight', 'Rose Marie', 'Songs from Hans Andersen', 'Darby and Joan', 'The Kerry Dance', 'Love's Old Sweet Song', 'Thady O'Flynn', 'The Clang of the Wooden Shoon', and 'By the River'. Molloy also composed the music for one of Sir Francis Burnand's early comic operas, *My Aunt's Secret*. In addition to his music, his prose work *Our Autumn Holiday on French Rivers* (1874) was said to have inspired Robert Louis Stevenson's *An Inland Voyage* (1878).

In 1874 Molloy married Florence Emma (d. 1912), youngest daughter of Henry Baskerville, of Crowsley Park, Henley-on-Thames, deputy lieutenant for Oxfordshire. They had two sons and one daughter, and lived at Woolleys, Hambleden, near Henley-on-Thames, where Molloy died on 4 February 1909.

W. H. G. FLOOD, rev. JAMES J. NOTT

Sources Brown & Stratton, *Brit. mus.* · D. J. O'Donoghue, *The poets of Ireland: a biographical dictionary with bibliographical particulars*, 1 vol. in 3 pts (1892–3) · W. H. G. Flood, *A history of Irish music* (1905) · D. Baptie, *A handbook of musical biography*, 2nd edn (1887) · Allibone, *Dict.* · private information (1912) · Burke, *Gen. GB*
Wealth at death £2083 11s. 7d.: probate, 24 Feb 1909, *CGPLA Eng. & Wales*

Molloy, Joseph Fitzgerald (1858–1908), novelist and historian, born at New Ross, co. Wexford, on 19 March 1858, was the son of Pierce Molloy and his wife, Catherine Byrne. Educated at St Kieran's College, Kilkenny, he was originally intended for the Catholic priesthood, but at the age of twenty decided to try his fortune as a writer and travelled to London, armed with an introduction to the editor Samuel Carter Hall and his wife, Anna Maria Fielding, the author of *Sketches of Irish Character* and a native of co. Wexford. Hall gave Molloy employment on his *Art Journal* as well as the entrée to literary and artistic society. Another of his patrons was Sir Charles Gavan Duffy, former MP for New Ross, who engaged him as his private secretary and later obtained for him a clerkship in the office of the agent-general for New Zealand.

Molloy was a prolific writer and journalist, with a facility for popularization. His first work was a volume of poetry, *Songs of Passion and Pain* (1881), published under the pseudonym of Ernest Wilding. In all he produced some fifteen successful compilations of social, court, and theatrical history, including *Court Life below Stairs, or, London under the First Georges, 1714–1760* (4 vols., 1882), *The Life and Adventures of Peg Woffington* (2 vols., 1884), and *The Russian Court in the Eighteenth Century* (1905); his *Romance of the Irish Stage* (2 vols., 1897) proved especially popular. He published serial novels in leading London and Liverpool papers, as well as in *Temple Bar*, *The Graphic*, and other periodicals; separately published novels included *Merely Players* (2 vols., 1881) and *An Excellent Knave* (1893).

Failing health did not affect Molloy's literary productivity. He died, unmarried, at his home, 40 Norland Square, Notting Hill, London, on 19 March 1908, and was buried in the Roman Catholic section of the Kensal Green cemetery.

G. MARTIN MURPHY

Sources *Freeman's Journal* [Dublin] (20 March 1908) · D. J. O'Donoghue, *The poets of Ireland: a biographical and bibliographical dictionary* (1912) · *DNB* · *CGPLA Eng. & Wales* (1908) · d. cert.
Wealth at death £557 14s. 9d.: administration, 11 May 1908, *CGPLA Eng. & Wales*

Moloney, Sir (Cornelius) Alfred (1848–1913), colonial administrator, the eldest son of Captain Patrick Moloney, was born in 1848, probably in May, possibly in Ireland. He was educated at the Royal Military College, Sandhurst, and entered the 1st West India regiment (in which his father also served). His first posting, in 1867, was to the Quiah district of Sierra Leone, as civil commandant. He then served as aide-de-camp to the governor of the Bahamas, returning to west Africa in 1873. He was promoted captain in 1874 and served in the Second Anglo-Asante War; he was mentioned in dispatches for his services for the abolition of slavery. He continued in the Gold Coast until 1884, serving as secretary to the governor, and later as administrator of Lagos, which was then part of the Gold Coast Colony.

On 28 December 1881 in the Roman Catholic chapel in the Vineyard, Richmond, Surrey, Moloney married Constance Thomson Knight (1860–1891), daughter of William Clifford Knight, Russian consul in the Cape of Good Hope. When on leave from west Africa in the 1880s, and until 1891, he lived in Church Road, Richmond, and while there established contact with leading botanists at the Royal Botanic Gardens, Kew. In 1882 he was made a CMG. From 1884 to 1886 he served as administrator of the Gambia settlement. In 1886 he returned to Lagos, this time as governor of the colony, which was then separated administratively from the Gold Coast; it extended some 300 miles from long. 2° E to 6° E and was linked by fine inland waterways. The colony did not reach far inland but Governor Moloney was much involved with efforts to settle ongoing quarrels between the Yoruba kingdoms. He had a real interest in the local people and their welfare; in 1889 he spoke to a meeting of the British Association about music in west Africa and in 1890 published a major paper about Lagos and the Yoruba people generally in the *Proceedings* of the Royal Geographical Society. In 1887 he published an important book entitled *Sketch of the Forestry of West Africa*, which was much wider in scope than forestry in the modern sense. He was deeply concerned about local agriculture, including crops for export, and in conservation and the need for replanting; in 1887 he established a botanic garden and in 1889 a forestry department in Lagos. He collected many dried plant specimens, and some living ones, which he sent to Kew. Staff at Kew assisted in the preparation of his book, which also lists birds and other animals, in which he also took an interest. He was made a KCMG in January 1890.

Early in January 1891 Moloney left Lagos with the intention of spending three months' leave in Gran Canaria for the benefit of his health. In fact he never returned to west Africa as he was appointed governor of British Honduras. For health and other personal reasons he remained on leave in Richmond until 25 July and then travelled, via New York, to reach Belize on 17 August 1891 with his wife Constance, who died there from yellow fever on 1 September 1891. Moloney was devastated and sought permission to transfer to a more favourable climate, or to retire on pension. In fact he remained as governor of British Honduras until the end of 1896. In co-operation with the Royal Botanic Gardens, Kew, he established in 1892 a botanical station in the grounds of Government House, Belize; its purpose was to promote the use and cultivation of indigenous and imported plants.

On 2 March 1897 Moloney married at Brompton Oratory, London, Frances Isabel Sophia Mary Owen-Lewis (*b.* 1873/4), daughter of Henry Owen-Lewis, and on 1 June 1897 he assumed duty as governor of the Windward Islands, based at St George's, Grenada. In 1898 he welcomed Daniel Morris, who came from Kew Gardens to be commissioner of agriculture in the West Indies. After his service in the Windward Islands Moloney was appointed governor of Trinidad and Tobago, based at Port of Spain. He served there from 4 December 1900 until his retirement in 1904. It was during this period that the water riots took place in Trinidad and, for various reasons, his active interest in agriculture and forestry diminished. He was, however, governor in Trinidad, and no doubt very supportive, when a programme to establish forest reserves was started. He died at Fiesole, near Florence, Italy, on 11 August 1913; his second wife survived him.

R. W. J. KEAY

Sources *WW* (1913) · *GJ*, 42 (1913), 501–2 · E. Thorp, *Ladder of bones* (1956) · S. Johnson, *The history of the Yorubas* (1921) · E. E. Williams, *History of the people of Trinidad and Tobago* (1962) · *The Times* (14 Aug 1913) · *WWW* · *Army List* · *CGPLA Eng. & Wales* (1913) · m. certs.
Archives Bodl. RH, dispatches [copies] · RBG Kew, letters and other MSS sent to Kew by Alfred Moloney and Daniel Morris | Royal Entomological Society of London, corresp. with Herbert Druce
Likenesses photographs, Foreign Office, London
Wealth at death £2787 17s. 7d.: probate, 16 Sept 1913, *CGPLA Eng. & Wales*

Molony, Helena Mary (1883–1967), actress and Irish nationalist, was born at 8 Coles Lane, Dublin, on 15 January 1883, the daughter of Michael Molony, a grocer, and his wife, Catherine McGrath. The family were Catholic, and Helena was educated locally. She first became involved in the Irish nationalist movement at the age of nineteen. After attending a public meeting at the Custom House in Dublin at which Maud Gonne spoke, she joined Inghinidhe na hEireann (daughters of Ireland), founded by Gonne and others in 1900 to mobilize women nationalists who were barred from membership of men's political organizations. In 1908 Molony co-founded and assumed the editorship of *Bean na hEireann* ('Women of Ireland'), a radical journal which advocated militancy, separatism, and feminism. She wrote much of the journal herself, although it attracted support from established writers such as Katherine Tynan and James Stephens, and public figures including Roger Casement, Arthur Griffith, and Constance Markievicz. *Bean* also became a vehicle for Molony's socialist beliefs, and she wrote the labour notes for the journal under the pseudonym A Worker. Molony's support for the labour cause, and her belief in the right of workers to organize, had a significant influence upon the political development of Constance Markievicz, and the two were to work together on a range of political movements.

From 1909 Molony trained under Dudley Digges as an actress in the Abbey Theatre, and she played there regularly until 1913. Her political development continued apace, and in 1911 she was arrested as a result of her protest at the visit of George V to Dublin, in the course of which she had broken a window containing images of the royal party. After her release she was again imprisoned for a seditious speech, but was bailed out by Anna Parnell, sister of Charles Stewart, who wished her to edit her (Parnell's) scathing account of the Land League years.

Between 1909 and 1916 Molony worked closely with James Connolly, the trades union organizer. Molony believed that nationalism and democracy were inextricably linked, a position to which Connolly was eventually to move. In 1913 she was active in the support of those workers taking part in the Dublin lock-out for the right to join trade unions, and she was subsequently asked by Connolly to assist in the organization of women workers, becoming the secretary of the Irish Women Workers' Union (IWWU) in 1915. Her journalistic experience made her an obvious choice as co-worker on Connolly's *Worker's Republic*, although Connolly's request that she be registered as the proprietor made her personally responsible, under the Defence of the Realm Act, for anything published in it. She was one of the founder members of the Irish Citizen Army, the militant workers' group in which women enjoyed equal membership, and fought with them in the 1916 Easter rising. After the surrender of the City Hall garrison, of which she was a part, she was deported to England, one of only six women to be interned. She returned to Dublin in December 1916, and immediately resumed her political work. She joined Cumann na mBan (Society of Women), despite some reservations about its commitment to radical labour and feminist politics, and played a key role in the organization's opposition to the treaty settlement of 1921.

After the civil war of 1922–3 Molony devoted herself full time to the labour cause, having become honorary president of the IWWU in 1917, while still retaining an active role in nationalist politics. In the 1920s and 1930s she opposed attempts to restrict women workers' rights. She fought against the Conditions of Employment Bill of 1935, which sought to limit female industrial workers, as well as the 1937 constitution which implied, through articles 41 and 45, that women should have a restricted public role.

Although Molony continued to actively pursue workers' rights in the inter-war years, serving as president of the Congress of Trade Unions until 1945, she suffered from increasing ill health, and was forced to limit her activities after 1946. She never married, and faced increasing financial hardship in her later years, receiving a pension from the IWWU only after a long struggle. She died at Lungamore, Strand Road, Sutton, Dublin, on 29 January 1967. She was buried in the republican plot, Glasnevin cemetery, Dublin, on 31 January.   OONAGH WALSH

Sources M. Jones, *These obstreperous lassies* (1988) · M. Ward, *Unmanageable revolutionaries: women and Irish nationalism*, pbk edn (1983) · R. M. Fox, *The history of the Irish Citizen Army* (1944) · R. M. Fox, *Rebel Irishwomen* (1935) · *Bean na hEireann* (1908–11) · *Irish Citizen* (1912–20) · *Irish Times* (30 Jan 1967) · R. F. Foster, *Modern Ireland, 1600–1972* (1988) · archival sources, NA Ire. · U. Mac Eoin, *Survivors* (1980) · b. cert. · d. cert.
Archives NL Ire., Mary Hutton MSS · NL Ire., Kent MSS · NL Ire., Sheehy-Skeffington MSS · NL Ire., Máire Nic Shubhlaigh MSS · NRA, priv. coll., Hugh O'Connor collection · NRA, priv. coll., John Manning collection | SOUND BL NSA, documentary recording
Likenesses photograph, repro. in Fox, *Rebel Irishwomen*
Wealth at death impoverished: Jones, *These obstreperous lassies*

Molony, Sir Thomas Francis, first baronet (1865–1949), judge in Ireland, was born in Dublin on 31 January 1865, the youngest son of James Molony, a Dublin hotel proprietor, and his wife, Jane, daughter of Nicholas Sweetman, of Newbawn, co. Wexford. Having received his early education with the Christian Brothers at the O'Connell Schools, North Richmond Street, Dublin, he attended Trinity College, Dublin, where he had a brilliant academic career, obtaining prizes in law and graduating in history and political science as gold medallist and senior moderator in 1886. He was called to the Irish bar in 1887, and he quickly built up a substantial practice. He was a member of the Munster circuit. His court manner was calm, and he was regarded as a painstaking, hardworking, undemonstrative lawyer. In 1899 he took silk, and in 1900 he was called to the English bar by the Middle Temple. He married in 1899 Pauline Mary, daughter of Bernard Rispin, livestock salesmaster, of Eccles Street, Dublin. They had three sons, one of whom was killed in action during the Second World War, and three daughters.

Molony was appointed crown counsel for co. Carlow in 1906 and for the county and city of Dublin in 1907, positions which he held until 1912. In the general election of December 1910 he unsuccessfully contested the West Toxteth division of Liverpool as a Liberal. He became a bencher of King's Inns and successively third and second serjeant-at-law in 1911. He was appointed solicitor-general for Ireland in 1912, and became attorney-general in the following year and, after a short interval, was appointed a judge in the King's Bench Division of the High Court. He was appointed lord justice of appeal in 1915, and in 1918 he became lord chief justice of Ireland. He was the last holder of that office, and fought a determined campaign in 1920 to ensure that the Government of Ireland Act should provide for him to retain that title rather than the proposed one of lord chief justice of southern Ireland.

The final part of Molony's judicial career was set against a background of civil strife, which gave rise to great difficulties in the administration of justice and which required military protection for the judges, in the War of Independence between 1919 and 1921 and then in the civil war between 1922 and 1923. He gave leadership to the judiciary even before he became its titular head in 1922 upon the abolition of the office of lord chancellor of Ireland. He resisted inquiries from the government in 1920 as to whether judges would be prepared to exercise special powers, dispensing summary justice, including the death penalty, in non-jury courts.

Molony is chiefly remembered for a series of judgments which are classic statements on the nature of martial law and its relation to the common law. These judgments were given in respect of applications to the regular courts seeking to prevent the carrying out of executions under sentences of death given by the military courts. In *R. v. Allen* (1921) he stated that:

> it is the sacred duty of this Court to protect the lives and liberties of all of His Majesty's subjects, and to see that no one suffers loss of life or liberty save under the laws of the country; but when subjects of the King rise in armed insurrection and the conflict is still raging, it is no less our duty not to interfere with the officers of the Crown in taking such steps as they deem necessary to quell the insurrection, and to restore peace and order and the authority of the law.

In *R. v. Strickland* (1921) he stressed that the judiciary had the power and the duty to decide whether a state of war existed that justified the application of martial law, and rejected an implication by counsel that the functioning of the assizes in Cork had required the consent of the military, saying that he did not 'sit in Cork by permission of any general. I sat in Cork by virtue of his Majesty's command, which no general could dispute.'

Other issues considered by Molony in judgments arising out of the War of Independence included the question of whether a local authority was obliged to pay compensation under the malicious injuries code for theft resulting from damage to property caused by riotous soldiers, action for false imprisonment arising from the arrest and detention of a possible witness to a murder for the expressed purpose of protecting him from potential malefactors, and the amount and distribution of compensation payable upon the murder of a member of the Royal Irish Constabulary.

Between 1922 and 1924 Molony continued to be chief justice, pending the enactment by the Irish Free State of a new system of court and judicial organization. After the occupation and destruction of the Four Courts in 1922 the courts sat initially at the King's Inns and then at Dublin Castle. The judiciary helped to establish the legal and political authority of the new government, consolidating a tradition of law and order that had been undermined by the years of disorder. When the new Irish Free State judicature was established Molony retired and left Ireland, settling in Wimbledon. He was created a baronet of the United Kingdom in the new year honours list of 1925. A portrait by Sir William Orpen, showing him robed as lord chief justice of Ireland, was presented to him by the solicitors of Ireland in 1925 following his retirement and was exhibited at the Royal Academy in 1925.

Molony had a long association with Trinity College, Dublin, which continued after he took up residence in England. He became a visitor (*ex officio*, as lord chief justice) in 1918 and was appointed vice-chancellor in 1931. In 1925 he became a director of the National Bank. He was chairman of a Home Office committee on the treatment of juvenile offenders, which issued its report in 1927. Between 1920

and 1924 he was president of the Statistical and Social Inquiry Society of Ireland, to which he read papers on a number of legal subjects over the years. He contributed to many social and philanthropic organizations, especially those under the auspices of the Roman Catholic church and/or connected with Ireland. He was a member of the committee for the Irish national war memorial, and subsequently of a committee for Irishmen in Britain to subscribe funds for the Royal Air Force during the Second World War. The honours bestowed on him included appointments as an honorary bencher of the inn of court of Northern Ireland in 1926 and of the Middle Temple in 1933.

Molony died at his home, Shanganagh, 3 The Drive, Wimbledon, on 3 September 1949, and was buried on 7 September. He was survived by his wife, who died on 16 July 1951.   DAIRE HOGAN

Sources W. N. Osborough, 'The title of the last lord chief justice of Ireland', *Irish Jurist*, new ser., 9 (1974), 87–98 · W. N. Osborough, 'Law in Ireland, 1916–26', *Northern Ireland Legal Quarterly*, 23 (1972), 48–81 · *The Times* (5 Sept 1949) · *The Times* (8 Sept 1949) · *Irish Times* (5 Sept 1949) · *Irish Law Times and Solicitors' Journal* (17 Sept 1949) · *The Irish Reports*, 1921 · T. Jones, *Whitehall diary*, ed. K. Middlemas, 3 (1971) · DNB · CGPLA Eng. & Wales (1949) · Burke, *Peerage* · Thom's directories
Likenesses W. Orpen, exh. RA 1925; in possession of H. F. Orpen, 1959 · pastel drawing; in possession of Mrs F. W. Hunt, 1959
Wealth at death £35,398 13s. 10d.: probate, 1949, CGPLA Eng. & Wales

Molteno, Sir John Charles (1814–1886), politician in Cape Colony, the son of John Molteno, deputy controller of the legacy office, Somerset House, and his wife, Caroline Bower, was born on 5 June 1814 in London. The family was of Milanese extraction, but had long been domiciled in England. He was educated at Ewell, Surrey, and after a short period in the office of a City shipbroker he sailed for the Cape in 1831 to take up a post in the public library at Cape Town. In 1837 he started a commercial business of his own, and for ten years worked to open new markets for colonial produce.

A succession of adverse circumstances forced Molteno to abandon his mercantile pursuit in the early 1840s. From 1844 he devoted himself to wool farming on a property which he had acquired in the Beaufort district of the colony. There he prospered (although his first wife, Maria Hewitson, whom he married in 1843, died two years later) and came to know and respect the frontier colonists. He took part as a burgher and commandant in the Cape Frontier War of 1846, and formed a strong opinion of the unsuitability of British troops for such warfare. The incapacity displayed by the British officers was a strong factor in determining his attitude towards the intervention of the British government in colonial military matters.

In 1851 Molteno married Elizabeth Maria, *née* Jarvis, and in the following year settled in the town of Beaufort West, where he founded the mercantile firm of Alport & Co., which he soon combined with a large banking business. This made him one of the wealthiest and most influential

Sir John Charles Molteno (1814–1886), by unknown photographer, 1872

citizens in the Beaufort district. When in 1854 representative institutions were introduced in Cape Colony, Molteno became the first member for Beaufort in the legislative assembly. His skill in debate and his knowledge of the needs of the country soon raised him to the front rank of parliamentarians.

During the governorship of Sir George Grey, Molteno generally supported the executive, but he became a strong opponent of Sir Philip Wodehouse, Grey's successor. The leading cry among Cape politicians was for responsible government, and for many years Molteno took the foremost place in the battle. When, with the approval of the secretary of the colonies, Lord Kimberley, it was conceded in 1872 by Sir Henry Barkly, the new governor, Molteno was designated as the first Cape prime minister.

The first years of Molteno's administration were marked by great prosperity, by a vast increase in railway communications, and by the rehabilitation of colonial finances. The development of the diamond fields played a considerable share in this, but major credit may fairly be attributed to the administrative and financial capacity of Molteno, and to the confidence that he inspired.

While Lord Carnarvon was determined to impose his policy of South African confederation, Molteno insisted that it must come gradually from within and not from without, and that at that time it would impose unduly onerous burdens on the colony. J. A. Froude, the historian, whom Carnarvon sent out as an unofficial representative of the British government in 1875, failed to obtain

Molteno's assistance and started an agitation throughout South Africa which stirred up antagonism between English and Boer settlers. Molteno and his colleagues procured the rejection of a scheme for the holding of a conference on the subject of confederation, and the Cape parliament refused to allow Molteno even to discuss the subject with the British government when he was in England in 1876.

The following year Sir Bartle Frere succeeded Sir Henry Barkly at the Cape. He came out as the special exponent of Carnarvon's views, and it was not long before he came into conflict with Molteno. The latter was a thorough-going advocate of colonial rights, prepared to insist on them to their fullest extent. War with the Gcaleka (Xhosa) beyond the colony's eastern border in 1877–8 brought matters to a crisis. The governor contended that the commander-in-chief at the Cape was the only person who could command the colonial troops; Molteno insisted that, though the governor, as such, had power over the colonial forces, it could only be exercised with and by the advice of his responsible ministers. The ministers were unyielding, and on 6 February 1878 Frere dismissed them.

Molteno had reckoned on the support of a parliamentary majority, which had never failed him hitherto, but in the debate which followed his dismissal the legislative assembly supported his successor, Gordon Sprigg. Deeply chagrined, and feeling helpless before Frere's policy, Molteno retired from public life. After Frere's recall, in 1880 he re-entered the legislative assembly as member for Victoria West, and he served in Thomas Scanlen's administration as colonial secretary (1881–2). In August 1882 he finally retired from politics, and was made KCMG. Molteno's second wife had died, and in 1875 he married his third wife, Sobella Maria, née Blenkins. He had surviving children from his second and third marriages. After a short visit to England, he returned to the Cape and died at Claremont, Cape Town, on 1 September 1886. He was buried at Claremont.

Sir John Molteno was a man of commanding presence and of great physical strength. He was known in the Cape parliament as 'the lion of Beaufort'. In private life he was of simple and unostentatious habits. Though no great orator, Molteno was a skilful debater, and between 1860 and 1872 promoted the cause of responsible government with doggedness. As prime minister he worked to reconcile Boer and British, easterner and westerner, and to promote in every way the self-government of the colony. His opposition to confederation helped ensure its defeat. Though removed as premier after only four years in office, Molteno nevertheless remains one of the most important of the Cape politicians of the late nineteenth century.

J. B. ATLAY, rev. CHRISTOPHER SAUNDERS

Sources P. A. Molteno, *The life and times of Sir John Charles Molteno*, 2 vols. (1900) · *DSAB* · P. Lewsen, 'The first crisis in responsible government in the Cape Colony', *Archives Year Book for South African History*, 5/1 (1942) · C. F. Goodfellow, *Great Britain and South African confederation, 1870–1881* (1966) · C. Saunders, 'The Cape native affairs department and African administration on the eastern frontier under the Molteno ministry', BA diss., University of Cape Town,

1964 · M. W. Spicer, 'The war of Ngcayecibi, 1877–1878', MA diss., Rhodes University, 1978 · P. Lewsen, *John X. Merriman* (1982) · W. E. G. Solomon, *Saul Solomon* (1948) · C. Saunders, 'The annexation of the Transkeian territories', *Archives Year Book for South African History*, 39 (1976) [Pretoria, 1978] · J. Martineau, *The life and correspondence of the Right Hon. Sir Bartle Frere*, 2nd edn, 2 (1895) · *Men of the times: old colonists of the Cape Colony and Orange River Colony* (Johannesburg, 1906) · R. Immelman, 'Sir John Charles Molteno', *Standard encyclopaedia of southern Africa*, ed. D. J. Potgieter, 7 (1972)

Archives BL, corresp. and papers, Add. MS 39299 · Bodl. RH, corresp., letter-books, and papers · National Library of South Africa, Cape Town

Likenesses photograph, 1872, repro. in Molteno, *Life and times*, vol. 1 [*see illus.*] · W. H. Schroder, oils, repro. in R. Kilpin, *The old Cape house* [1918] · L. E. Zoccola, oils, Houses of Parliament, Cape Town, South Africa · photograph, repro. in *Men of the times* · photograph, repro. in *Standard encyclopaedia of southern Africa*, 7 · photograph, Houses of Parliament, Cape Town, South Africa

Molyneaux [Molineaux, Molyneux, Molineux], **Thomas** (*c*.1785–1818), pugilist, was a freed black slave from Virginia and probably a docker before coming to Britain. The least fanciful account of his obscure origins attributes his freedom to his owner's gratitude for the profits of his fighting prowess. Yet he remained virtually unknown in America throughout his life and emerged into black consciousness only in the twentieth century.

Molyneaux is first mentioned as a fighter in 1809, when he appeared in London at the Dolphin tavern, managed by Bill Richmond, another American-born black pugilist, remarkable as both literate and highly regarded. Richmond immediately saw Molyneaux as an exciting prospect, put him first into a pick-up bout after a bull-bait and then a successful fight against a hardy old London pugilist, Tom Blake. He was so impressive there that backing for an early fight against the champion, Tom Cribb, was easily come by. This took place at Cropthorne, near East Grinstead, Sussex, on 18 December 1810. Richmond had by then added a measure of science to Molyneaux's wild, rushing methods, while Cribb, with no apparent challenger in sight in Britain, had put on weight, was out of condition, and made little preparation for the contest. It was closely fought and had enough incidents to fuel later controversy over its fairness. The crowd was certainly with Cribb but the questionable events—the breaking of the ring or delays by his seconds when Cribb was in trouble—were not unusual at the time and none of the several contemporary accounts alleged any unfairness. Nor did Molyneaux's written challenge (almost certainly the work of Richmond) for a return match. Cribb had been treated much worse in his own first London fight. Doubts were only voiced by Pierce Egan some ten years later when he wrote of Molyneaux that 'his *colour* alone prevented him from becoming the hero of that fight' (Egan, 3.493), a view not shared by most later social historians.

For the second fight Cribb went into serious training, following a tough regime supervised by the noted athlete Robert Barclay Allardice ('Captain Barclay'). Molyneaux, by contrast, enjoyed a crowded benefit night at the Fives Court, went on a lucrative but exhausting exhibition tour with Richmond, and took on an unnecessary fight with

Thomas Molyneaux (*c*.1785–1818), by Douglas Guest, *c*.1810

Rimmer, a rough and ready Lancastrian of modest reputation. He went into the rematch jaded and ponderous and on 28 September 1811, at Thistleton Gap, near Leicester, lost without any question to a fit Tom Cribb. From this point Molyneaux's career was all downhill. After a dubious encounter with Jack Carter, another Lancastrian fighter, he was abandoned by Richmond in despair at his lack of discipline. Molyneaux continued to give full rein to his taste for food, drink, flashy clothes, and easy women. His final fight was in Scotland, ironically against William Fuller, who was to be instrumental in promoting pugilism in North America. Molyneaux himself eventually moved to Ireland, where his damaging lifestyle took its final toll. He died on 4 August 1818 in the guardhouse of Galway barracks in the arms of two of his fellow black Americans serving in the 77th regiment.

For all his personal failings Molyneaux was a powerful fighter and a significant figure in the history of boxing. After his contests with Cribb he was the subject of numerous drawings and prints, which were widely circulated. Henry Raeburn complained that engravings after his portrait of Walter Scott were outsold by those of Molyneaux: 'You know the taste of our London beer-suckers: one black bruiser is worth one thousand bright poets, the African sells in thousands, and the Caledonian won't move' (Honour, 30). The prize ring offered one of the few avenues for advancement open to deprived racial minorities, and while he was by no means the first black man to fight there, Molyneaux's performance made the path somewhat easier for the others who followed. His challenge, too, raised the issue of the nature of 'the championship' for which he and Cribb were acknowledged to be fighting, accidentally posing the question of whether it was to be a purely British preserve, making it *de facto* the first ever world championship in any sport.

DENNIS BRAILSFORD

Sources *Pancratia, or, A history of pugilism*, 2nd edn (1815) • H. D. Miles, *Pugilistica: the history of British boxing*, 3 vols. (1906) • P. Egan, *Boxiana, or, Sketches of ancient and modern pugilism*, 5 vols. (1812–29) • F. Henning, *Fights for the championship*, 2 vols. (1902) • *Sporting Magazine* (1810–18) • C. B. Cone, 'The Molineaux-Cribb fight, 1810: wuz Tom Molyneaux robbed?', *Journal of Sport History*, 9/3 (1982), 83–91 • D. Brailsford, 'Morals and maulers: the ethics of early pugilism', *Journal of Sport History*, 12/2 (1985), 126–42 • J. Ford, *Prizefighting: the age of Regency boximania* (1971) • J. C. Reid, *Bucks and bruisers: Pierce Egan and Regency England* (1971) • D. Brailsford, *Bareknuckles: a social history of prize fighting* (1988) • H. Honour, *The image of the black in Western art*, 4, pt 2 (1989) • P. Edwards and J. Walvin, *Black personalities in the era of the slave trade* (1983)
Likenesses H. T. Alken, drawing, 1810 (Cribb v. Molyneaux fight), Brodick Castle, Garden and Country Park, Isle of Arran • D. Guest, portrait, c.1810; Sothebys, 27 June 1973, lot 108 [*see illus.*] • G. Cruikshank, etching, 1812 (of Cribb v. Molyneaux fight) • R. Dighton, etching, 1812 • G. Cruikshank, etching, repro. in Egan, *Boxiana* • T. Rowlandson, drawing, London, Henry Reitlinger Collection • J. Young, mezzotint (after D. Guest) • engraving, repro. in *Sporting Magazine* (Jan 1811) • etching, repro. in Brailsford, *Bareknuckles*, 59 • etching (Cribb v. Molyneaux fight; after T. Rowlandson, Sept 1811), Brodick Castle, Garden and Country Park, Isle of Arran • portrait, repro. in P. Magriel, 'Portraits of the fancy', *Apollo*, 50 (1949) • portraits, repro. in Honour, *Image*

Molyneux, Adam de. *See* Moleyns, Adam (d. 1450).

Molyneux, Caryll, third Viscount Molyneux of Maryborough (1623/4–1700), nobleman, was the second son of Richard *Molyneux, first Viscount Molyneux of Maryborough (*bap.* 1594, *d.* 1636) of Sefton, Lancashire, and Mary (*bap.* 1596, *d.* 1639), daughter and coheir of Sir Thomas Caryll of Bentons in Shipley, Sussex. Throughout his life, unlike his brother Richard *Molyneux, second viscount [*see under* Molyneux, Richard], Caryll was overtly Roman Catholic. It is probable that he attended an English college in Flanders, possibly St Omer, in view of his later transfer of the manor of Euxton to that college.

Caryll Molyneux first came to public prominence in early 1644 when he was a signatory to a petition of royalist officers at Chester. Often mentioned in conjunction with his elder brother, and presumably lieutenant-colonel in the second viscount's horse regiment, Molyneux fought in Rupert's campaign of May to August 1644. He attained especial notoriety at the capture of Liverpool on 11 June 1644, where he, it was later claimed by a former opponent, 'Kild 7 or 8 pore men with his owne hands; good Lord deliver us from the cruelty of bloodthirsty papists Amen' (Heywood, 16). The rest of Molyneux's first war was shadowy but almost certainly tied to his brother's fortunes. In the propositions of Newcastle, 1647, he was included in a list of those whom parliament sought to exclude from pardon. There is no evidence that he fought in either 1648 or 1651.

In or before 1649 Molyneux married Mary Barlow (d. 1662), second daughter of Sir Alexander Barlow of Barlow, Lancashire. They would have three sons and five daughters. Their eldest son, Richard, was aged sixteen in 1665.

Molyneux was granted an income of £1000 from his brother's estate and on 19 September 1654 he became the third viscount on his brother Richard's death. At the Restoration he was reappointed to the local offices held by his brother, that is, the butlership of Lancashire, steward of Blackburn hundred, and constable of Liverpool Castle. In 1662 he was commissioned captain in Lord Gerard's regiment. He was said to be aged forty-one in 1665.

Molyneux achieved some success in rationalizing the family's financial affairs. He sold the family's Sussex lands for £13,000 in 1655. He exacted higher entry fines when granting or renewing leases, and judicious marriages also contributed to financial recovery. The marriage in 1675 of his only surviving son, William, to Bridget, daughter of Lord Henry Arundell, which attracted a dowry of £10,000, is a case in point. Molyneux was involved, unsuccessfully, in attempts to extend his political influence in Liverpool in the 1660s and 1670s and as late as 1699 he suffered a reverse when he failed to prevent the town becoming a separate parish. This signalled a particular setback as until then Liverpool was part of the parish of Walton on the Hill, the patronage of which was in Molyneux's hands.

The accession of James II in 1685 thrust Molyneux, as the leading Roman Catholic in Lancashire, into the centre of events. His appointments as lord lieutenant (13 September 1687), admiral of the high seas, and *custos rotulorum* were controversial as Molyneux was a convicted recusant and had been sequestrated as recently as 1684. As lord lieutenant he pressed upon local office-holders the king's 'three questions' concerning repeal of the penal laws, but in October 1688 he was displaced from the lieutenancy and the earl of Derby was restored to that post as part of James II's attempt to regain tory support. The departure of James led to an investigation of Molyneux's attitude to the new government and accusations of treason. He was placed under house arrest at Croxteth on 15 June 1689 as crippling gout prevented him from facing charges elsewhere. His refusal to take an oath of allegiance to William and Mary led to the loss of all his duchy, palatine, and local offices.

Molyneux was arrested again in July 1694 during the investigation of the Lancashire Jacobite plot of that year. However, after a September hearing in London and a trial at Manchester in October 1694 he was acquitted. Molyneux, who was suffering from defects of memory and hardness of hearing, was a marginal figure in relation to the conspiracy. A staunch defender of his faith and his family's interests Caryll Molyneux was never reconciled to the government of William and Mary. He died on 2 February 1700 at Croxteth and was buried at Sefton on 8 February.

MALCOLM GRATTON

Sources P. R. Newman, *Royalist officers in England and Wales, 1642–1660: a biographical dictionary* (1981) • *VCH Lancashire*, vol. 3 • *DNB* • B. G. Blackwood, *The Lancashire gentry and the great rebellion, 1640–60*, Chetham Society, 3rd ser., 25 (1978) • Gillow, *Lit. biog. hist.* • W. Beamont, ed., *The Jacobite trials at Manchester in 1694*, Chetham Society, 28 (1853) • C. F. Russell, ed., *Parish registers of Sefton*, Lancashire Parish Register Society, 86 (1947) • W. Dugdale, *The visitation of the county palatine of Lancaster, made in the year 1664–5*, ed. F. R. Raines, 3 vols., Chetham Society, 84–5, 88 (1872–3) • J. M. Gratton, 'The parliamentarian and royalist war effort in Lancashire, 1642–1651', PhD diss., University of Manchester, 1998 • E. L. Lonsdale, 'John Lunt and the Lancashire plot, 1694', *Transactions of the Historic Society of Lancashire and Cheshire*, 115 (1963), 91–106 • T. Heywood, ed., *The Moore rental*, Chetham Society, 12 (1847) • G. W. Wall, 'St Helen's Church, Sephton', *Transactions of the Historic Society of Lancashire and Cheshire*, 47 (1895), 37–102 • GEC, *Peerage* • D. H. Hosford, *Nottingham, nobles and the north: aspects of the revolution of 1688* (1976)

Archives JRL, letters to Thomas Legh; letters to Richard Legh
Likenesses G. Morphey, oils, NG Ire.
Wealth at death annual income of £1328 10s.: undated survey of estate, Lancs. RO, DDM 11/37

Molyneux, Sir Edmund (d. 1552), judge, was the eldest son of Sir Thomas Molyneux of Haughton, Nottinghamshire, and his second wife, Catharine, daughter of John Cotton of Hamstall Ridware, Staffordshire, widow of Thomas Powtrell of Hallam, Derbyshire. He is one of the first common lawyers known to have taken a university degree, graduating BA at Oxford on 1 July 1510. He joined Gray's Inn a few years later, presumably after attending an inn of chancery, and was elected an ancient in 1528. He is said to have read in Lent 1532 and again in Lent 1536, the second reading being on the statute 21 Hen. VIII, c. 13, concerning leases by spiritual persons.

After settling at Thorpe, near Newark, Nottinghamshire, Molyneux was from 1526 on the commission of the peace for that county, and from 1536 was recorder of Nottingham. By 1530 he had married Jane, daughter of John Cheney of Chesham Bois in Buckinghamshire, who predeceased him, and they had five sons (including Edmund *Molyneux) and four daughters. On 25 June 1540 Molyneux took the coif. Two years later he was appointed one of the king's serjeants, receiving a knighthood of the Bath at the coronation of Edward VI, and on 22 October 1550 became a judge of the common pleas. He died on 28 August 1552, leaving lands at Thorpe and elsewhere in and around Newark-on-Trent, and other properties further afield. Molyneux is said to have written a treatise on justices of the peace, but only brief extracts survive (BL, Add. MS 25228, fol. 10). J. H. BAKER

Sources Foss, *Judges*, 5.307–9 • Emden, *Oxf.*, 4.387–8 • Baker, *Serjeants*, 168, 526 • W. Stephenson, W. Baker, D. Gray, and W. Walker, eds., *Records of the borough of Nottingham* (1882–1956) • G. W. Marshall, ed., *The visitations of the county of Nottingham in the years 1569 and 1614*, Harleian Society, 4 (1871) • BL, Harley MS 785, fol. 108 • BL, Add. MS 25228, fol. 10 [extracts of lost treatise] • *The reports of Sir John Spelman*, ed. J. H. Baker, 2, SeldS, 94 (1978), pt 2, intro., 126, 303, 390, 396 • inquisition post mortem, PRO, C 142/96/51 • PRO, CP 40/1145, m. 1 [patent as judge] • will, PRO, PROB 11/35, sig. 31 • R. Thoroton, *The antiquities of Nottinghamshire* (1677), 13, 179

Molyneux, Edmund (d. 1605), biographer and politician, was the second of five sons of Sir Edmund *Molyneux (d. 1552) of Thorpe, Nottinghamshire, judge of the common pleas, and his wife, Jane, daughter of John Cheney of Chesham Bois, Buckinghamshire. Probably the Edmund Molyneux admitted of Gray's Inn, London, in 1574, he spent much of his life in the service of the Sidney family, above all as secretary to Sir Henry Sidney. By 1569 he was a clerk to the council in Ireland, frequently carrying messages to England for his master, who was then lord deputy.

In 1577 Sir Henry attempted to have his second son, Robert Sidney, and Molyneux made responsible for framing all orders and bills. Sidney brought Molyneux into parliament through a by-election in 1579 as MP for Bridgnorth. By 1581, as president of the council in Wales, Sidney had obtained the income of the office of clerk of the signet for his servant. Not all Sidney's efforts at patronage were successful, however, for in 1576 he failed to have the privy council appoint Molyneux to supervise the attorneys in Wales, even though he described his secretary as 'honest, dilligent and circumspecte' (Collins, 1.145). It may be that he was the 'one Mollineux' who had 'misused' Cecil while in the latter's employ in 1567, thereby incurring opposition to his future advancement in public office (*Scrinia Ceciliana*, 116).

Molyneux also had dealings with other members of the Sidney family. By 1578 he was 'Mr Ned' to his employer's wife (Collins, 1.272), and in 1582 Robert Sidney described him as 'my very loving frend' (*De L'Isle and Dudley MSS*, 2.99). His relations with Robert's elder brother, Philip Sidney, were uneven. The two men were seemingly on good terms until June 1578, when Molyneux was evidently startled to receive a furious letter from Sidney accusing him of having allowed strangers to read his letters to his father. 'If it be so, yow have plaide the very Knave with me'. Henceforward, Molyneux was told, 'if ever I know yow do so much as reede any Lettre I wryte to my Father, without his Commaundement, or my Consente, I will thruste my Dagger into yow' (Collins, 1.256). Molyneux replied pleading innocence, and eventually the quarrel was made up, so much so that in 1582 Sidney felt able to conclude a letter to Molyneux 'Farewell, even very well, for so I wish you. Your loving Frend, Philip Sidney' (ibid., 1.296).

In 1586 Molyneux provided an account of his late master's life for Holinshed's *Chronicles*. This text, predictably fulsome in its praise, is nevertheless valuable for its personal insights into Sir Henry's travels, daily habits, and sayings. Molyneux also bemoans the failure of his own career, completed 'without anie great wages, fee or other entertainment growing to him in perpetuitie or other waies', claiming that his master attributed 'his hard hap to his owne mishap' (*Holinshed's Chronicles*, 872–3).

Molyneux's whereabouts after 1586 are unknown, but it is likely that he was the 'Mollinax, an inventor of odd devices of ordnance' who offered to demonstrate his 'experiments' in The Hague and concerning whom information was sought from Robert Sidney in 1598 (*De L'Isle and Dudley MSS*, 2.311). Molyneux died, unmarried, in 1605 between 29 September and 23 October. A nuncupative will delivered from his sickbed on the former date was proved on the latter by his brother Thomas, granting his goods to their nephew Edward Molyneux. PETER SHERLOCK

Sources HoP, *Commons, 1558–1603*, 3.60 • *Holinshed's chronicles of England, Scotland and Ireland*, ed. H. Ellis, 4 (1808), 869–80 • *Report on the manuscripts of Lord De L'Isle and Dudley*, 6 vols., HMC, 77 (1925–66), vols. 1–2 • G. W. Marshall, ed., *The visitations of the county of Nottingham in the years 1569 and 1614*, Harleian Society, 4 (1871), 72–4 • G. Molineux, *Memoir of the Molineux family* (1882) • CSP Ire., 1509–73, 422, 443, 462; 1574–85, 99, 142, 203 • R. Flenley, ed., *Calendar of the register of the queen's majesty's council in the dominion and principality of*

Wales and the marches of the same (1916) · *Scrinia Ceciliana: mysteries of state and government … a … supplement of Cabala* (1663) · H. Sydney and others, *Letters and memorials of state*, ed. A. Collins, 2 vols. (1746) · will, PRO, PROB 11/106, sig. 70

Molyneux, Emery (d. 1598), maker of globes and ordnance, came, according to Petruccio Ubaldini, who knew him, 'of obscure and humble family background' (Crinò and Wallis, 14) and was probably the Emery Molynox who was presented as William Cooke's apprentice to the Stationers' Company in October 1557. By the 1580s he had gained a reputation as an able mathematician and maker of mathematical instruments, working in Lambeth, to the south of London. These skills brought him into the company of Richard Hakluyt and the explorers John Davis, Walter Ralegh, and Thomas Cavendish, and the mathematicians Edward Wright and Robert Hues, and led him to accompany Francis Drake, perhaps on the circumnavigation of 1577–80, for Ubaldini reported 'He himself has been in those seas and on those coasts in the service of the same Drake' (ibid., 13). In his *Pathway to Perfect Sayling* (1605) Richard Polter commented that Molyneux had been a skilful maker of compasses and hourglasses.

It seems likely that Davis introduced Molyneux to his own patron, William Sanderson, a rich London merchant. Molyneux and Wright were looking for a sponsor to enable them to build globes promoting England's maritime achievements, and Sanderson provided £1000. Molyneux's globe recorded Drake's track and that of Cavendish, whose own circumnavigation brought him back to England on 9 September 1588. Molyneux gathered information from navigators, and by inspecting rutters and pilots, such as that for Brazil and the West Indies which he gave to Thomas Harriot in 1590. The celestial globe was less original, but was to be used with the terrestrial for oceanic navigation. Wright helped to plot the coastlines and translated some of the legends into Latin; the maps were engraved for printing by Jodocus Hondius. On 10 April 1591 the astrologer and physician Simon Forman visited Molyneux's workshop; he taught Molyneux how to find longitude and claimed to have found an astrological method, which Molyneux challenged him to demonstrate publicly, but to no avail.

The first edition of Hakluyt's *Principal Navigations* (1589) announced the imminent appearance of the globes, describing Molyneux as 'a rare Gentleman in his profession, being therein for divers yeeres, greatly supported by the purse and liberalitie of the worshipfull merchant M. William Sanderson' (Hakluyt, 1.xxx). As made, the globes were just over 2 feet in diameter. They were the first to be constructed so as to be unaffected by humidity at sea, and their flour-paste construction was unusual for the time; Simon Forman remarked that Molyneux's moulding or casting process for the globes was 'the only way to caste [anything] whatsoever in perfecte forme … and yt is the perfectest and trewest waie of all wayes … and this was the wai that Mullenax did use to cast flowere in the verie forme' (Bodl. Oxf., MS Ashmole 1494, fol. 1491). Ubaldini's letters to the duke of Milan detail Molyneux's

progress on their construction: the first pair were presented to Queen Elizabeth at Greenwich in July 1592; another terrestrial globe was presented with entertainments at Sanderson's house in Lambeth. The largest and most prestigious globes, bought by royalty, noblemen, and academic institutions, cost £20 each. One example of this first edition survives at Petworth House, Sussex, and a later one, dated 1603 and bearing the arms which had by then been conferred on Sanderson, is now preserved with its matching celestial globe in Middle Temple Library, London.

Elizabeth immediately realized the propaganda value of these globes, as did other observers: Shakespeare (*The Comedy of Errors*, III.ii) and Thomas Dekker both alluded to them in their plays, Dekker (in *The Gull's Hornbook* of 1609) stating:

> What an excellent workman, therefore, were he that could cast the globe of it into a new mould. And not to make it look like Molyneux his globe, with a round face sleeked and washed over with white of eggs, but to have it in plano as it was at first, with all the ancient circles, lines, parallels and figures. (Dekker, 73)

Sanderson presented a lesser globe to Sir Robert Cecil in 1595, together with Hues's 'Latin booke that teacheth the use of my great globes' (Skelton, 7). No examples either of the smaller globes, priced as low as £2 and intended as practical navigation aids for seafarers and students, or of Molyneux's treatise *The Globes Celestial and Terrestrial Set Forth in plano*, published by Sanderson in 1592, are known.

Molyneux was still associated with Forman in 1595 when the merchant Robert Parkes was to purchase coal, saltpetre, pitch, oils, and waxes for him, perhaps connected to work on his cannon. Molyneux sought the queen's patronage for this 'new invention, of shot and artillery, to be used principally in naval warfare: protection of ports and harbours, a new shot to discharge a thousand musket shot; with wildfire not to be quenched' (*CSP dom.*, 1574–80, 339). This undated document is ascribed to 1570, but is surely later, as Molyneux was issued with a royal warrant in March 1593 and the matter was taken up by the privy council on 4 November 1596, when the lord admiral was urged 'to speak to Molyneux, Bussy and the two Engleberts about their offensive engines' (*CSP dom.*, 1595–7, 303), as part of measures to defend the south coast of England against recusants, a request seemingly ignored. In 1594 Elizabeth granted Molyneux a gift of £200 and an annuity of £50, but these rewards could not prevent him and his wife, Anne, emigrating to Holland in 1597; he surrendered the annuity on his departure. He wished to distribute his globes personally to other European princes, and a base in Amsterdam, fast becoming the centre of globe and map-making, was better for this purpose. Either he or Hondius, who had returned to Amsterdam in 1594, took the printing plates for the globes.

The states general of the United Provinces showed more interest in Molyneux's cannon, granting him a twelve year privilege on a similar invention on 26 January 1598. On 6 June Molyneux lodged a second application, but he died in Amsterdam almost immediately, his wife being granted administration of his estate in England later that month. On 9 April 1599 she was granted a Dutch compassionate pension of 50 florins, suggesting that Molyneux had died in poverty. There appears to have been no surviving family, and the nascent English globe-making industry died with him, though his globes were spoken of in England over forty years later as 'yet in being, great and small ones, celestiall and terrestriall, in both our universities and several libraries, here and beyond the seas' (Sanderson, sig. A3*v*).   SUSAN M. MAXWELL

Sources A. M. Crinò and H. M. Wallis, 'New researches on the Molyneux globes', *Der Globusfreund*, 35–7 (1987), 11–18 • H. M. Wallis, 'Opera mundi: Emery Molyneux, Jodocus Hondius and the first English globes', *Theatrum orbis librorum*, ed. T. C. van Uchelen, K. van der Horst, and G. Schilder (1989), 94–104 • H. M. Wallis, 'The first English globe: a recent discovery', *GJ*, 117 (1951), 275–90 • H. M. Wallis, 'Further light on the Molyneux globes', *GJ*, 121 (1955), 304–11 • R. A. McIntyre, 'William Sanderson: Elizabethan financier of discovery', *William and Mary Quarterly*, 13 (1956), 184–201 • *The voyages and works of John Davis*, ed. A. H. Markham, Hakluyt Society, 59 (1880), introduction, 211 • [R. Hues], *Tractatus de globis et eorum usu … by Robert Hues*, ed. C. R. Markham, Hakluyt Society, 1st ser., 79 (1889), xxvi–xxxiv, xlii • A. M. Hind, *Engraving in England in the sixteenth and seventeenth centuries*, 1 (1952), 154–5, 168–75, 179–81 • L. Kassell, 'Simon Forman's philosophy of medicine, astrology and alchemy in London, *c*.1580–1611', DPhil diss., U. Oxf., 1997, 28–35 • Arber, *Regs. Stationers*, 1.73 • T. Dekker, *The gull's hornbook with other works*, ed. E. D. Pendry (1967) • W. Sanderson, *An answer to a scurrilous pamphlet* (1656) • administration act books, PRO, PROB 6/5, fol. 255*v* • R. Hakluyt, *The principal navigations, voyages, traffiques and discoveries of the English nation*, 2nd edn, 1 (1598) • R. Polter, *Pathway to perfect sayling* (1605) • Bodl. Oxf., MS Ashmole 1494 • *CSP dom.*, 1574–80; 1595–7 • R. A. Skelton and J. Summerson, *A description of maps and architectural drawings in the collection made by William Cecil, first Baron Burghley, now at Hatfield House*, Roxburghe Club (1971)

Molyneux, Richard (d. **1459**), landowner, was the eldest son of Sir Richard Molyneux of Sefton, Lancashire, and his wife, Joan (d. 1440), daughter of Sir Gilbert Haydock. The elder Sir Richard, a major landowner in south-west Lancashire, fought in France under Henry V and was knighted. In 1420 or 1421 he returned to England, and in 1424 engaged in a violent dispute with the Stanleys for control of Liverpool, where the Stanleys had a tower—in 1421 Molyneux had been appointed constable of Liverpool Castle and steward of West Derby and Salford. These offices he retained, and on 10 February 1441 obtained a renewal of the grant of 1421 for the lives of himself and his eldest son, who was by now married to Elizabeth, almost certainly the daughter of Sir Thomas *Stanley. In 1446 the offices were made hereditary, and were subsequently exempted from the Acts of Resumption of 1450 and 1451. But whereas the act of 1450 named Sir Richard Molyneux as beneficiary, that of 1451 excepted 'Richard Molyneux, Esquier, one of the Huishers of oure Chambre' (*RotP*, 5.315), showing that the elder Richard Molyneux had died in the interim.

The younger Richard Molyneux, who received a lease of half of Leyland manor in 1453, remained at court, and was still a gentleman usher of the king's chamber in 1454. A steadfast Lancastrian, he was appointed escheator for Lancashire for life on 12 February 1459, following the death of his father-in-law. Like many of the gentry of Cheshire and Lancashire, he fought for Henry VI at the battle of Bloreheath on 23 September 1459, and was killed there. His heir was his son Thomas, who was knighted by Richard of Gloucester at the siege of Berwick on 5 July 1482, and was one of the pallbearers at Edward IV's funeral the following year.   E. L. O'BRIEN

Sources *VCH Lancashire*, vols. 3–4 • R. Somerville, *History of the duchy of Lancaster, 1265–1603* (1953) • *RotP*, vol. 5 • N. H. Nicolas, ed., *Proceedings and ordinances of the privy council of England*, 7 vols., RC, 26 (1834–7), vol. 6, p. 223 • R. A. Griffiths, *The reign of King Henry VI: the exercise of royal authority, 1422–1461* (1981) • J. Gairdner, ed., *Letters and papers illustrative of the reigns of Richard III and Henry VII*, 2 vols., Rolls Series, 24 (1861–3)

Molyneux, Richard, first Viscount Molyneux of Maryborough (*bap.* **1594**, *d.* **1636**), office-holder and landowner, was baptized at Walton, Lancashire, on 21 February 1594, the eldest surviving son of Sir Richard Molyneux, baronet, of Sefton, Lancashire (1559–1623), and his wife, Frances Gerard, eldest daughter of Sir Gilbert Gerard, master of the rolls. Richard Molyneux attended Brasenose College, Oxford (1609), and Gray's Inn (1613). He was initially betrothed to Fleetwood Barton, daughter of Richard Barton of Barton, but in 1607, when he was about thirteen, the arrangement was dissolved. He married Mary (*bap.* 1596, *d.* 1639), daughter of Sir Thomas Caryll of Bentons in Shipley, Sussex (the marriage settlement was dated 7 December 1614). They had two sons, Richard Molyneux (the second viscount) and Caryll *Molyneux (the third viscount), and three daughters, Frances, Charlotte, and Mary.

Molyneux was knighted in 1613 and was MP for Wigan in 1614; he was knight of the shire in 1625 and 1628 and deputy lieutenant from 1625. He was appointed to the commission of the peace in 1618 and 1629, but was subsequently excluded after his elevation to the Irish peerage as Viscount Molyneux of Maryborough on 22 December 1628. His exclusion followed a deal struck by Charles I to settle a dispute over precedence concerning Irish peers and baronets. Molyneux held office in the administration of the duchy and county palatine of Lancaster. He succeeded his father as receiver-general of the duchy in 1620 and was butler in Lancashire and steward of Blackburn Hundred, Totlington, Rochdale, and Clitheroe from 1621. Molyneux purchased the lordship of Liverpool for £450 and was constable of Liverpool Castle and master forester of West Derby, Toxteth, Croxteth, and Simonswood.

Viscount Molyneux died at Croxteth on 8 May 1636 and was buried at Sefton the next day. Molyneux had incurred debts, as receiver-general, of £7000, beside £9000 to other creditors. The crown held the manors of Sefton and Tarbock as security. His widow married Raphael Tarterean or Tartereau, carver to the queen, and died in 1639 at her house in St Martin's Lane in the parish of St Martin-in-the-Fields.

Molyneux's eldest son, **Richard Molyneux**, second Viscount Molyneux of Maryborough (*c*.1623–1654), royalist army officer, was born about 1623 at Sefton. On his father's death in 1636 Richard was placed under the guardianship of James Stanley, Lord Strange (later seventh earl of Derby). Negotiations regarding Molyneux's marriage to Strange's daughter Henrietta Maria, proved abortive, and he was not to marry until much later in life. A royalist commissioner of array from 11 June 1642, Molyneux became a prominent supporter of the king. Despite the fact that no conclusive evidence exists for the second viscount's Roman Catholicism his regiments contained many Roman Catholic officers. Following the siege of Manchester in late September 1642 he was present at Edgehill on 23 October 1642.

Molyneux, together with Thomas Tyldesley, returned to Lancashire in November and reorganized the royalist war effort. He fought in Derby's campaign of early 1643 which culminated in the disaster at Whalley on 20 April 1643. Thereafter Molyneux left Lancashire for Oxford via the west midlands. He fought at the sieges of Bristol and Gloucester and at the first battle of Newbury (September 1643), but following a reverse at Chipping Campden in mid-October he went north with Lord Byron. Molyneux joined Rupert in Lancashire in May 1644. He helped capture Liverpool on 11 June 1644 and distinguished himself as a brigade commander at Marston Moor on 2 July 1644. Thereafter his service record (Ormskirk, 20 August 1644; Montgomery, 18 September 1644; Naseby, 14 July 1645; and Ludlow, 27 May 1646) reveals tenacity, ill-discipline and misfortune.

In 1646 Molyneux was subjected to a huge fine of £12,280 which was reduced to £9037 in the light of existing debts. Further reduction depended on the permanent maintenance of preaching ministries in certain churches and chapels. The viscount was involved in the 1648 Kingston plot but did not take up arms. He returned north aiming to settle his debts which totalled £10,860 in April 1650. Molyneux was arrested on 17 March 1651 as a precaution and was probably in London during the Wigan Lane and Worcester campaigns. He married Lady Frances Seymour, eldest daughter of William *Seymour, marquess of Hertford, on 28 October 1652. This marriage entailed a settlement of £8000 but Molyneux was unable to enjoy this alleviation of his financial burden for long. He died in the summer of 1654, and was buried at Sefton on 2 July 1654.

MALCOLM GRATTON

Sources J. M. Gratton, 'The military career of Richard, Lord Molyneux, c.1623–1654', *Transactions of the Historic Society of Lancashire and Cheshire*, 134 (1984), 17–37 · T. A. Earle and R. D. Radcliffe, 'The child marriage of Richard, second Viscount Molyneux with some notices of his life, from contemporary documents', *Transactions of the Historic Society of Lancashire and Cheshire*, 43–4 (1891–2), 245–78 · P. R. Newman, *Royalist officers in England and Wales, 1642–1660: a biographical dictionary* (1981) · *VCH Lancashire*, vol. 3 · *DNB* · Lancs. RO, Molyneux deeds, DDM · J. M. Gratton, 'The parliamentarian and royalist war effort in Lancashire, 1642–1651', PhD diss., University of Manchester, 1998 · W. Dugdale, *The visitation of the county palatine of Lancaster, made in the year 1664–5*, ed. F. R. Raines, 2, Chetham Society, 85 (1872) · C. F. Russell, ed., *Parish registers of Sefton*, Lancashire Parish Register Society, 86 (1947) · R. Somerville, *Office-holders in the duchy and county palatine of Lancaster from 1603* (1972) · G. Chandler, *Liverpool under James I* (1960) · GEC, *Peerage* · will, Lancs. RO, DDM 17/122 [of first viscount] · will, Lancs. RO, DDM 17/131, 132 [of second viscount] · T. W. King and F. R. Raines, eds., *Lancashire funeral certificates*, Chetham Society, 75 (1869), 60–61

Archives JRL, letters to Peter Legh

Wealth at death no estate value; debts totalling £16,000: will, Lancs. RO, DDM 17/122, Somerville; *Office-holders* · debts of £10,860 in April 1650; marriage settlement yielded £8000, Richard Molyneux: Lancs. RO, DDM 17/131, 132

Molyneux, Richard, second Viscount Molyneux of Maryborough (c.1623–1654). *See under* Molyneux, Richard, first Viscount Molyneux of Maryborough (*bap.* 1594, *d.* 1636).

Molyneux, Sir Robert Henry More- (1838–1904), naval officer, born on 7 August 1838, was the third and youngest son of James More-Molyneux of Loseley Park, Guildford, and his wife, Caroline Isabella, the eldest daughter of William F. Lowndes-Stone of Brightwell Park, Oxfordshire. After being educated at private schools he entered the navy in 1852. As a cadet and midshipman of the *Sans Pareil* he served in the Black Sea during the campaign of 1854, when he was at the bombardment of Odessa and the attack on Sevastopol on 17 October, and as a midshipman of the *Russell* he took part in the Baltic expedition of 1855. In 1859 he was a mate of the *Vesuvius*, employed on the west coast of Africa in the suppression of the slave trade, and was mentioned in dispatches for services in a colonial gunboat up the Great Scarcies River; in the same year, with two boats, he captured an armed slaver brig off the Congo, and for this was promoted lieutenant (28 June 1859). He served from January 1860 to 1865 on the Mediterranean station, first in the *St Jean d'Acre*, afterwards in the flagship *Edgar*, and on 18 December 1865 was promoted commander.

In June 1866 More-Molyneux was appointed executive officer of the frigate *Doris* on the North America and West Indies station, and while serving in her received the thanks of the Admiralty and of the French government for valuable services rendered to the transport *Gironde*, wrecked off Jamaica; he was also recognized by the Admiralty for services after the great hurricane at St Thomas in 1867. In July 1869 he was appointed to command the *St Vincent*, a training ship for boys, and on 6 February 1872 was promoted captain. More-Molyneux married in 1874 Annie Mary Carew, the daughter of Captain Matthew Charles Forster RN. She died in 1898, leaving a daughter, Gwendolen.

In May 1877 More-Molyneux was appointed to command the *Ruby*, in which he served in the Levant during the Russo-Turkish War (1877–8) and then in Burma. He was captain of the *Invincible*, the flagship of Vice Admiral Sir Frederick Seymour, at the bombardment of Alexandria, and afterwards during the war, and was awarded the Osmanie (third class) and the CB. In May 1884 he was appointed commodore commanding the ships in the Red Sea, and protected Suakin until the arrival of Sir Gerald Graham's expedition in 1885. He was mentioned in dispatches and was advanced to the KCB. He next served as captain-superintendent of Sheerness Dockyard until promoted to his flag on 1 May 1888. He was an aide-de-camp to Queen Victoria from 1885 to 1888.

More-Molyneux's further service was administrative

and advisory. In 1889 he was one of the British representatives at the International Marine Conference at Washington, and from August 1891 to August 1894 he was admiral-superintendent at Devonport. On 28 May 1894 he became vice-admiral, and on 13 July 1899 admiral. From October 1900 until his retirement in August 1903 he was president of the Royal Naval College at Greenwich, and he was promoted GCB in November 1902. He died at Cairo on 29 February 1904. His body was embalmed, sent home, and buried at St Nicholas's Church, Guildford.

L. G. C. LAUGHTON, rev. ROGER MORRISS

Sources *The Times* (5 March 1904) • *The Times* (28 March 1904) • Burke, *Gen. GB* • *WWW, 1897–1915* • R. F. MacKay, *Fisher of Kilverstone* (1973) • A. J. Marder, *The anatomy of British sea power*, American edn (1940) • *CGPLA Eng. & Wales* (1904)
Archives Surrey HC, papers incl. relating to career in Egypt
Likenesses R. T., wood-engraving, NPG; repro. in *ILN* (2 Jan 1886) • four portraits (after photographs), repro. in *ILN* (1886–1904)
Wealth at death £70,885 17s. 2d.: resworn probate, 12 May 1904, *CGPLA Eng. & Wales*

Molyneux, Samuel (1689–1728), astronomer and politician, born at Chester on 18 July 1689, was the third but only surviving child of the experimental philosopher William *Molyneux (1656–1698) and his wife, Lucy (d. 1691), the youngest daughter of Sir William Domville, attorney-general for Ireland. His father zealously undertook his education on Locke's principles, but died in 1698, leaving him to the care of his uncle, Dr Thomas *Molyneux (1661–1733). Having matriculated in his sixteenth year at Trinity College, Dublin, he there formed a friendship with the mathematician George Berkeley (1685–1753), who dedicated to him in 1707 his *Miscellanea mathematica*. Molyneux graduated BA in 1708 and MA in 1710, then spent two years improving his estate in co. Armagh. After leaving Ireland to visit England, he met the duke and duchess of Marlborough at Antwerp during the winter of 1712–13, and was sent by the former on a political mission to the court of Hanover, where he witnessed, in the Herrenhausen Garden, the sudden death of the Electress Sophia on 8 June 1714. He accompanied the royal family to England after the death of Queen Anne, and was made secretary to the prince of Wales, a post which he retained until the prince came to the throne as George II.

Molyneux married in 1717 Lady Elizabeth Capel, the eldest daughter of Algernon, second earl of Essex. She brought with her a fortune of £10,000, and she inherited £18,000 with Kew House, on the death, in 1721, of Lady Capel of Tewkesbury, her great-aunt's widow. They had no children.

Molyneux now turned to the study of astronomy and optics, sciences which had also attracted his father. He made the acquaintance of James Bradley, and together they experimented, from 1723 to 1725, on the construction of reflecting telescopes of Newtonian design. Their first successful speculum, completed in May 1724, was of 26 inches focus. They afterwards turned out one of 8 feet, and Molyneux presented to John V, king of Portugal, a reflector made by himself. He explained his method of speculum manufacture to Edward Scarlett, the king's optician, and George Hearne, a mathematical instrument maker of Fleet Street, London, which helped to bring reflecting telescopes into general use.

Molyneux was a privy councillor in both England and Ireland, he represented the boroughs of Bossiney and St Mawes and the city of Exeter in the English parliaments of 1715, 1726, and 1727 respectively, and was returned in 1727 to the parliament of Ireland as member for the University of Dublin. He was a man of winning manners and obliging temper, uniting Irish wit to social accomplishments. He was elected a fellow of the Royal Society in 1712.

In 1725 Molyneux and Bradley resolved to repeat Robert Hooke's supposed detection of annular parallax for the star Gamma Draconis, for which purpose they ordered a zenith sector of 24 feet radius from the noted instrument maker George Graham. It was set up on 26 November 1725 in Molyneux's observatory at Kew House, but their observations did not confirm those of Hooke. Bradley later obtained a sector with a larger angular range, and made further observations which led to his discovery of the aberration of light, but Molyneux, after his appointment on 29 July 1727 as one of the lords of the Admiralty, was no longer able to assist him.

Molyneux's proposals for the improvement of the navy were actively opposed by his colleagues, and these difficulties perhaps hastened the onset of a disease, supposedly inherited from his mother. He was seized with a fit in the House of Commons, and, after lingering a few days in stupor, died on 13 April 1728. Some time before his death he gave his optical collections and papers to Dr Robert Smith of Cambridge, whom he invited to live in his house and complete his proposed investigations. Smith's book, *A Compleat System of Opticks* (1738), included one chapter by Molyneux on the grinding and polishing of telescope lenses, and another begun by him but finished by John Hadley on the casting and polishing of telescope mirrors. Molyneux's widow married Nathaniel St André in 1730; Kew House was leased to Frederick, prince of Wales, and demolished in 1804.

A. M. CLERKE, rev. ANITA McCONNELL

Sources C. Molyneux, *An account of the family and descendants of Sir Thomas Molyneux*, ed. [T. Phillips] (1820), 32–40 • C. Hutton, *A philosophical and mathematical dictionary*, new edn, 2 vols. (1815) • O. Manning and W. Bray, *The history and antiquities of the county of Surrey*, 1 (1804), 446 • R. H. Scott, 'History of the Kew Observatory', *PRS*, 39 (1885), 37–86 • J. Nichols, *Biographical anecdotes of William Hogarth, and a catalogue of his works chronologically arranged with occasional remarks* (1781), 1.476 • *DSB*, 9.463–4 • J. Locke, *The works of John Locke*, new edn, 9 (1823), 289–472
Archives Southampton Archives Office, letter-books of records accumulated as secretary to prince of Wales, and as one of the lords commissioners of the admiralty • TCD, papers relating to Dublin Philosophical Society | TCD, corresp. with William King

Molyneux, Thomas (1531–1597), administrator, was born at Calais, an only child. His parents, whose identity is unknown, died when he was young, and he was brought up by John Briskin, an alderman of Calais. When that town was taken from the English by the duc de Guise in 1558, Molyneux was taken prisoner. Having ransomed himself by the payment of 500 crowns, he moved to

Bruges, and there, about 1560, married Katherine, daughter of an opulent burgomaster, Lodowick Stabeort. They had two daughters, Katherine and Margaret, and two sons, Samuel and Daniel.

Because of the depredations of the duke of Alva, Molyneux moved to London in 1568, and by about 1576 had settled in Dublin. In 1578, under the patronage of Adam Loftus, archbishop of Dublin, he and his family received a grant in the newly incorporated town of Swords, co. Dublin, with a view to encouraging a settlement there. Most of Molyneux's posts in the Irish administration were connected with the collection and disposition of crown revenues. He was appointed chancellor of the court of exchequer in Ireland in 1590 and in the next year obtained the office of receiver of customs and imposts on wines. The lucrative nature of this levy was demonstrated in Molyneux's account of income of £5230 for the years 1592, 1593, and 1594. He also leased the farm of the customs of the port of Dublin from the widow of the late farmer, Ralph Grimsditch. He showed his support for the project for the foundation of Trinity College, Dublin, in 1592 by contributing £40 towards the building fund.

When the legality of Molyneux's official employment under the queen was impugned on the allegation that he was an alien, an inquiry was instituted in the court of the exchequer at Dublin in 1594. Witnesses examined there before the attorney-general deposed that Molyneux was an Englishman, born in Calais while that town was under the crown of England, and that he was a true and loyal subject, 'of Christian religion, using sermons and other goodly exercises' (*Memoranda Roll*, 2). Molyneux died at Dublin on 24 January 1597 and was buried in the cathedral of Christ Church. Among his descendants were William and Sir Thomas Molyneux, grandsons of Thomas's son Daniel (1568–1632), sometime Ulster king of arms, who married Jane, daughter of Sir William Ussher.

COLM LENNON

Sources C. Molyneux, *An account of the family and descendants of Sir Thomas Molyneux*, ed. [T. Phillips] (1820) · *Extracted from the memoranda roll of the exchequer of Ireland* (c.1850) · 'Calendar of fiants, Henry VIII to Elizabeth', *Report of the Deputy Keeper of the Public Records in Ireland*, 7–22 (1875–90), appxs · CSP Ire., 1592–6 · J. G. Simms, *William Molyneux of Dublin, 1656–1698*, ed. P. H. Kelly (1982) · V. Treadwell, 'The Irish customs administration in the sixteenth century', *Irish Historical Studies*, 20 (1976–7), 384–417 · W. B. Wright, *The Ussher memoirs* (1889) · J. S. Brewer and W. Bullen, eds., *Calendar of the Carew manuscripts*, 3: 1589–1600, PRO (1869) · DNB

Molyneux, Sir Thomas (1661–1733), first baronet, physician and natural philosopher, was born on 14 April 1661 in Dublin, at the New Row near Ormondgate, into the family of five sons (only two of whom outlived their father) and two daughters of Captain Samuel ('Honest Sam') Molyneux (1616–1693), a surveyor and master gunner, who was also a skilled mathematician, and author of *Practical Problem Concerning the Doctrin of Projects*, and his wife, Anne Dowdall (d. 1700), daughter of William Dowdall of Mount Town, co. Meath. Thomas's elder brother William *Molyneux (1656–1698) was one of the founders of the Dublin Philosophical Society, and author of *The Case of Ireland's being Bound by Acts of Parliament in England Stated* (1698).

Daniel Molyneux, his grandfather, was Ulster king of arms from 1597 to 1632.

Little is known of Thomas's early years. From Christ Church School, Dublin, he entered Trinity College, Dublin, in 1676, taking the BA in 1680. To continue his education he sailed to Chester in May 1683, proceeding to London. His movements can be followed in a correspondence with his brother, published by William Wilde in 1841 in the *Dublin University Magazine*. He took lodgings 'at the sign of the Flower-de-luce, over against St. Dunstan's Church in Fleet Street' (*Dublin University Magazine*, 18.315), and visiting Gresham College on a day when the Royal Society was meeting, he was permitted to attend and listen to the discourse: 'I had the opportunity of seeing several noted men as Mr. Evelyn, Mr. Hooke, Mr. Isaac Newton' (ibid., 319). He also met the poet John Dryden, was introduced to Robert Boyle, and called on Elias Ashmole 'at his house beyond Lambeth' (ibid., 324).

Having visited Windsor, Eton College (where he found the rooms were kept 'very nastily stinking, when you come in to them' (*Dublin University Magazine*, 18.321)), Oxford, and Cambridge, Molyneux went in July on to Leiden, where he noticed, among other things, 'that haulting, waddling, and limping men and women and children were extraordinarily frequent and common' (ibid., 470). His teachers included a Dr Margrave, in whose house he settled, and where he had the advantage of the savant's company and advice, and 'the use of his glasses and furnaces whenever I have a mind to do any thing in chymistry myself' (ibid., 475). He published an article on 'the dissolution and swimming of heavy bodies in Menstruums far lighter than themselves' in *Nouvelles de la République des Lettres* in December 1684. He contributed to the *Philosophical Transactions*, compiled a catalogue of the collections of Jan Swammerdam and Paul Herman for the Royal Society, and was elected FRS in 1686, having spent some time in Paris in the previous year.

Back in Dublin in 1687, Molyneux was awarded the MD of Trinity College, Dublin, and elected fellow of the College of Physicians in Ireland. His initial plans to set up in practice being disturbed by the Williamite war, he moved temporarily to Chester, remaining there until the defeat of James II at the Boyne. Without further delay he then established himself as a physician, practising from his father's house. Samuel Molyneux died in 1693, and on 13 May 1694 Thomas Molyneux married Catherine Howard (d. 18 Dec 1747), daughter of Ralph *Howard (1638–1710), professor of physic at Dublin (grandfather of Ralph Howard, Viscount Wicklow (d. 1786)); they had eight daughters and four sons, of whom Samuel died young and William suffered a fatal accident in 1713.

While in Leiden, Molyneux had heard of the progress of the Dublin Philosophical Society from his brother, who wrote:

I have also here promoted the rudiments of a society for which I have drawn up rules ... About half a score or a dozen of us have met about twelve or fifteen times, and we have very regular discourses concerning philosophical, medical and mathematical matters. *(Dublin University Magazine,* 18.472)

William urged Thomas to observe laboratories closely so that on his return 'we shall be the erecters and massers of as good a laboratory as can be desired for all chymical and astronomical operations, together with a convenient place for dissection' (*Dublin University Magazine*, 18.472).

Subsequently Molyneux was active in the Dublin Philosophical Society, his contributions ranging far beyond his medical interests. His papers in the *Philosophical Transactions* are listed by Hoppen, and included 'Concerning a prodigious *os frontis*'; an essay, 'On the late coughs and colds'; and 'Notes on the epidemic of eye-disease' (Hoppen, 221). He published the first scientific account of the Irish elk, the earliest account of the structure of the sea mouse, and 'Notes on the Giant's Causeway'—expressing the opinion that the latter is a natural rather than a man-made phenomenon. He wrote, too, on coal mining in Ireland, on Horace's odes, and on the ancient Greek and Roman lyre; in the sphere of archaeology he granted too much to viking influences. The Dublin Philosophical Society's regular meetings ended about 1697. It was re-founded in 1707 by Molyneux's nephew, Samuel Molyneux (1689–1728), but by August 1708 it was again in decline.

Preferment, meanwhile, had come steadily for Molyneux: he was MP for Ratoath (1695–9), and was one of the seven doctors nominated in 1692 to fellowship of the newly chartered King and Queen's College of Physicians in Ireland, 'being the only Protestant surviving Fellows of the said late College' (Widdess, 34); he was appointed treasurer to the college in 1695 and held the office of president in 1702, 1709, 1713, and 1720. He was regius professor of physic in Dublin University (1711–33), where his portrait by Sir Godfrey Kneller hangs. He was appointed physician-general to the army in Ireland (1718), and state physician (1725).

Having amassed a fortune, Molyneux built a mansion in Peter Street which has been described as being 'a handsome but not very large house, with a central pediment and fine staircase with barley-sugar balusters' (Craig, 55). It was lavishly furnished, and when somebody happened to mention Dr Richard Steevens's wealth, Molyneux boasted that he had spent more than Steevens ever earned.

Molyneux corresponded with Edward Lhuyd, the Welsh naturalist, Hans Sloane, John Locke, whom he had met in Leiden in 1684, and others. Following the death of 'a dear and only brother' in 1698 he received a sympathetic letter from Locke: 'I have lost, in your brother, not only an ingenious and learned acquaintance ... but an intimate and sincere friend, whom I truly loved and by whom I was truly loved' (*Some Familiar Letters*, 290). He was in touch, too, with Irish scholarly notabilities, including Roderic O'Flaherty, but Hoppen points out that it was his nephew, Samuel, who visited the Irish antiquary in Connemara in 1709 (Hoppen, 272).

Widdess refers to a manuscript of fifty pages among Molyneux's unpublished papers, written in 1727 and entitled, 'Some observations on the taxes paid by Ireland to support the government' (Widdess, 70). Molyneux was one of the Royal Dublin Society's early members.

Molyneux was created a baronet in 1730. He died on 19 October 1733, and according to A. M. Fraser was buried in Dublin in St Audoens's churchyard. His wife survived him. Molyneux's full-length statue by L. F. Roubiliac, intended to stand as a family tribute in the grounds of a family estate at Castle Dillon, co. Armagh (bought by his father in 1664), is now in Armagh Cathedral. He was succeeded in the baronetcy by Daniel (1708–1738), his third but oldest surviving son, who died unmarried and was succeeded by Capel (1717–1797).   J. B. LYONS

Sources 'Gallery of illustrious Irishmen, no. XIII: Sir Thomas Molyneux [pts 1–4]', *Dublin University Magazine*, 18 (1841), 305–27, 470–90, 604–19, 744–63 · K. T. Hoppen, *The common scientist in the seventeenth century: a study of the Dublin Philosophical Society, 1683–1708* (1970) · *Some familiar letters between Mr Locke and several of his friends* (1780) · J. D. H. Widdess, *A history of the Royal College of Physicians of Ireland, 1654–1963* (1963) · M. Craig, *Dublin 1660–1860: a social and architectural history* (1969) · J. B. Lyons, *Brief lives of Irish doctors* (1978), 38–40 · A. M. Fraser, 'The Molyneux family', *Dublin Historical Record*, 16/1 (1960–61), 9–15 · GEC, *Baronetage*
Archives RS, letters | BL, case papers and letters to Sir Hans Sloane
Likenesses G. Kneller, portrait, Dublin University, Ireland · L. F. Roubiliac, statue, Armagh Cathedral, Northern Ireland

Molyneux, Sir William (1483–1548), soldier, was the son of Sir Thomas Molyneux (*d.* 1483) and his wife, Anne (*d.* 1521), daughter and coheir of Sir Thomas Dutton. He was himself twice married. His first wife was Jane Rugge, with whom he had three children, Richard, Anne, and Jane. With his second wife, Elizabeth Clifton (*d.* 1547), he had a further three children, William, Thomas, and Anne. He resided in Sefton, Lancashire, where the Molyneux family had once been rivals to the Stanleys for local power. However it was while serving under Sir Edward Stanley, during the Flodden campaign of 1513, that William Molyneux made his own reputation. Although a subordinate commander, he was senior enough to add his signature to that of Thomas Howard, earl of Surrey, and several other captains, in the formal challenge sent to James IV on 7 September, two days before the battle. During the engagement he was credited with the capture of two enemy standards, including that of Alexander Gordon, earl of Huntly. In view of his valour that day he received a personal letter of thanks from the king. Thereafter he played a conspicuous role in military campaigns in the north and, according to Lancastrian tradition, 'he never saw fear but in the backs of his enemies' (Seacombe, 46). In 1536 he led a 400-strong contingent against the rebels of the Pilgrimage of Grace in the army raised by the earl of Derby. He was still active in 1542, when he raised troops for the earl of Norfolk's foray into Scotland. Molyneux died in July 1548, possibly of sweating sickness, at Sefton, and was buried there in St Helen's Church, which the Molyneux family had recently renovated; a monumental brass still exists.   GERVASE PHILLIPS

Sources W. Langton, ed., *The visitation of Lancashire and a part of Cheshire ... AD 1533*, 2, Chetham Society, 110 (1882) · B. Coward, *The*

Stanleys, lords Stanley and earls of Derby, 1385–1672: the origins, wealth and power of a landowning family, Chetham Society, 3rd ser., 30 (1983) · J. Seacombe, Memoirs containing a genealogical and historical account of the ancient and honourable house of Stanley (1767) · E. Baines and W. R. Whatton, The history of the county palatine and duchy of Lancaster, new edn, ed. J. Croston and others, 5 (1893) · LP Henry VIII, vols. 1, 17 · J. L. Thornely, The monumental brasses of Lancashire and Cheshire (1893) · P. Priestly, Monumental brasses at St Helen's Church, Sefton, Merseyside (privately printed, Sefton, 1995) · J. Lofthouse, Lancashire's old families (1972)

Likenesses monumental brass, St Helen's Church, Sefton, Lancashire; repro. in Lofthouse, Lancashire's old families

Molyneux, William (1656–1698), experimental philosopher and constitutional writer, was born in Dublin, near Ormond Gate, on 17 April 1656, the second of five children of Samuel Molyneux (1616–1693), lawyer and landowner, and his wife, Anne, *née* Dowdall. His great-grandfather Thomas *Molyneux (1531–1597) came from the English colony in Calais and settled in Ireland in the 1570s. The family achieved a place in the protestant ascendancy network that controlled the administration and much of the economy, and their prosperity, derived from rents from property in co. Armagh and other counties, freed Molyneux from the need to earn a living.

Early years to foundation of Dublin Philosophical Society
After his early education by private tutor and attendance at a Dublin grammar school (probably attached to St Patrick's Cathedral), on 10 April 1671 Molyneux entered Trinity College, Dublin, as a fellow-commoner. He developed an interest in mathematical and scientific studies, and delighted in the writings of leading figures of the scientific revolution. He was admitted bachelor of arts on 27 February 1674 and, having been sent to London to study law, entered the Middle Temple in June 1675. On his return he married, on 19 September 1678, Lucy (d. 1691), the youngest daughter of Sir William Domville, attorney-general for Ireland. In November she suffered a severe illness that led to the loss of her eyesight. Leading London physicians were unable to help, and Molyneux sought consolation in the study of mathematics and science. In the winter of 1679–80 he translated work by Descartes, which he published as Six Metaphysical Meditations in April 1680. A translation of Galileo's Discorsi remained unpublished. He developed an interest in the study of optics, optical instruments, and astronomical observation. The communication of observations of a lunar eclipse on 1 August 1681 led to a correspondence with John Flamsteed, in which problems of optics, astronomy, ballistics, and tidal observations were discussed.

In 1682 Molyneux undertook to collect material for Moses Pitt's English Atlas. His contributors included the Gaelic Irish antiquary Roderic O'Flaherty. Although the project was aborted in 1685 much valuable material was collected, and Molyneux's correspondence with O'Flaherty led to friendship and an interest in early Irish history. O'Flaherty's learned treatise Ogygia was published in London in 1685 with Molyneux's assistance.

Molyneux has a claim to be considered the founder of modern science in Ireland. In October 1683 he set himself

William Molyneux (1656–1698), attrib. Sir Godfrey Kneller, c.1696

the task of forming a society in Dublin on the design of the Royal Society. As first secretary and treasurer he conducted correspondence and exchanged minutes with the Royal Society and its sister society at Oxford. He took an active part in the proceedings of the society, elucidating discoveries, demonstrating experiments and instruments, discussing books, showing curious objects, undertaking the calculation of solar and lunar eclipses, and recording weather data. The first phase of the society continued until the spring of 1687. By then Molyneux had discoursed on twenty different subjects in optics, astronomy, and natural science. A total of nine of his papers were published in the Royal Society's Philosophical Transactions. Papers of his, or accounts of his books, appeared in the Acta Eruditorum and the Bibliothèque Universelle et Historique. The Dublin Philosophical Society was revived after the Williamite wars but Molyneux no longer held office. As late as 1697, however, he published in the Philosophical Transactions of the Royal Society a scientific paper on the effect of magnetic variation on surveys.

Dioptrics, philosophy, and politics In the summer of 1685 Molyneux visited his brother Sir Thomas *Molyneux, then a graduate medical student at Leiden, and they undertook a three-month tour of the Netherlands and the Rhineland, ending up in Paris. They visited Christiaan Huygens at The Hague, Antoni van Leeuwenhoek at Delft, and Jean-Dominique Cassini at Paris. In September Molyneux spent two or three weeks in London and was invited to Greenwich by Flamsteed. He also took the opportunity to commission an instrument maker, Richard Whitehead, to make a combined dial and telescope. Although the instrument never performed well, Molyneux demonstrated it to the Dublin society, claiming it had improved the art of dialling by application of telescopic sights, and in 1686 he published a small book, *Sciothericum telescopium*, describing it. On 9 December 1685 he was proposed for admission to the Royal Society, and his election as a fellow followed in 1686.

Molyneux secured an official appointment as joint surveyor-general and chief engineer in Ireland (which carried an annual salary of £300) on payment of a sum of £250 to the previous patentee, William Robinson. The new patent was granted on 31 October 1684. In February 1687, when the Catholic Richard Talbot, earl of Tyrconnell, was appointed lord deputy, Robinson left Ireland, leaving Molyneux in sole charge. The major work in hand was the restoration of Dublin Castle, damaged by a fire in April 1684, which Molyneux was left to execute in the eighteen months that remained before his own dismissal by Tyrconnell. In the course of a mass exodus of protestants, Molyneux and his family decided to leave at the end of January 1689. A house was rented in Chester, where they lived for two years until the restoration of the protestant ascendancy following the victory of William III at the Boyne. On returning to Dublin in December 1690 Molyneux was appointed a commissioner of army accounts by the Williamite government. His wife followed in January with their son Samuel *Molyneux, born at Chester on 18 July 1689, but she died on 9 May 1691.

While at Chester Molyneux started assembling material for a book on dioptrics. Previously, between 1683 and 1686, he had discoursed before the Dublin Philosophical Society on the illusion of the different magnitudes of the horizontal and meridional moon, on double vision, and on why four glasses in a telescope show objects erect. His *Dioptrica nova: a Treatise of Dioptricks in Two Parts*, completed in the spring of 1690, appeared early in 1692 (2nd edn, 1709), and was the first treatise on the subject to be published in English. Edmond Halley saw the manuscript through the press and allowed Molyneux to include as an appendix a theorem of his for finding the focus of a spherical lens. At the outset Molyneux paid tribute to John Locke's *Essay Concerning Human Understanding* and acknowledged obligation to Flamsteed. The first part presented 59 propositions on geometrical optics, providing a thorough treatment of the nature of sight and the properties of lenses, telescopes, microscopes, and magic lanterns. The second part consisted of a series of chapters on topics including refraction and light, glasses for defective eyes, and telescopic instruments. In treating refraction, Molyneux highlighted Leibniz's seminal essay of 1682, which marked the beginning of the famous dispute about the principle of least action, or Fermat's principle. He warmly approved of Leibniz's refutation of Descartes's explanation of refraction, and embraced the German's doctrine of final causes. Refraction and the finite velocity of light led Molyneux to conclude that 'Light is a Body'. For certain propositions Molyneux gave the solutions of Flamsteed in addition to his own, but the publication led to a breach between the two, with Flamsteed taking offence probably because the manuscript was not shown to him before publication but entrusted instead to his rival Halley.

Dioptrica nova created no great sensation at first in the learned world. There was no reference to it in the *Philosophical Transactions* of the Royal Society, and the only major journal to notice it was the *Acta Eruditorum* of Leipzig, where Leibniz was a significant influence. Huygens, then the foremost authority on optics, expressed approval and undertook a detailed critique. Leibniz was flattered by Molyneux's use of his paper of 1682, and referred to *Dioptrica nova* as an excellent book on a number of occasions. A gift copy sent to Locke in the summer of 1692 led to a friendship and correspondence that lasted the final six years of Molyneux's life. Most of the correspondence was published after Locke's death as the opening section of *Some Familiar Letters between Mr Locke and Several of his Friends* (1708), and Molyneux's criticisms and suggestions were taken into account in the second and later editions of Locke's *Essay*. In 1695 Molyneux suggested that a Latin translation of the *Essay* be undertaken in Ireland and engaged the Revd Ezekiel Burridge, whose translation was published in 1701. The most notable of Molyneux's contributions to Locke's second edition was the so-called Molyneux problem, included as an addition to the chapter on perception. The question posed was whether a blind man who had learned to distinguish by touch between a cube and a sphere would be able, on gaining his sight, to differentiate the objects without touching them. Molyneux thought not and Locke agreed. The problem had profound philosophical implications and became a key topic in British philosophy.

Other topics that entered the Molyneux–Locke correspondence were morals, ethics, and education. Molyneux's religious views were similar to Locke's—a belief in an all-wise Providence, with a minimum of doctrinal accompaniments and a tolerance of unorthodoxy. Molyneux read Locke's tract *The Reasonableness of Christianity* (1695), and when Locke's religious views were attacked by Bishop Edward Stillingfleet in 1697 he followed the exchanges with interest. In the spring of that year Molyneux conversed with John Toland, finding him to be a candid freethinker and a good scholar. He deplored the indictment of Toland's book *Christianity not Mysterious* by a Dublin grand jury and its condemnation by the Irish parliament.

From the time Molyneux began to correspond with Locke in 1692 he became increasingly involved in political administration and legal work. On 17 September 1692 he was unanimously elected as one of the Dublin University representatives in the Irish House of Commons, which was then exclusively protestant. In November parliament was prorogued, and then dissolved, after a short but stormy session in which protestant reaction prevented the ratification of the treaty of Limerick, seen as being too generous to the vanquished Jacobite Catholics, and in which the Commons challenged constitutional restrictions by asserting its right to prepare draft legislation to raise money. Molyneux supported the government and his conduct was rewarded that month by Lord Lieutenant

Sydney with an appointment as a commissioner for forfeited estates, from which he resigned after a few months, and in July 1693 by the university with a doctorate in laws.

In the summer of 1695 Molyneux was re-elected as one of the university representatives. There was a strong rivalry between the party of the lord chancellor, Sir Charles Porter, which was against toleration for dissenters and supported ratification of the treaty of Limerick, and that of Lord Lieutenant Capel, which had a policy of toleration for dissenters and favoured anti-Catholic legislation. The former party was strong enough to block toleration for dissenters but some penal legislation against Catholics was passed. Molyneux supported Capel's government and presented him with Locke's thoughts on coinage reform. Following the death of Capel in 1696 a new government, appointed early in 1697 under Henri Massue, marquis de Ruvigny and earl of Galway, with John Methuen as lord chancellor, pursued a policy of obtaining ratification of the treaty of Limerick in combination with some anti-Catholic legislation. Molyneux continued to support the government, serving as a member of committees and reporter of bills.

The Case of Ireland Two pressing constitutional issues occupied Molyneux in the last year of his life. Backed by English wool merchants, a bill to prevent the export of Irish woollens to any country other than England passed the English House of Commons on 21 February 1698. About the same time, Bishop William King of Derry was involved in litigation with the London companies that owned large estates in Ulster. King won an appeal to the Irish House of Lords, but early in 1698 the English counterpart ruled that the Irish house had no jurisdiction and reversed the verdict. Molyneux was personally involved in helping the bishop with legal precedents for his appeal. Against this background he wrote his celebrated work *The Case of Ireland's being Bound by Acts of Parliament in England, Stated* early in 1698.

The greater part of this tract was a survey of history, inaccurate or fictitious in places, and a study of precedent supported by considerable legal learning. Molyneux's father-in-law, Sir William Domville, had argued much the same case in a disquisition of 1660. He had provided a wealth of medieval legal precedent, much of which was now incorporated by Molyneux in his tract. He also drew extensively on John Locke's *Two Treatises of Government* (published anonymously in 1690), referring to Locke—much to the latter's displeasure—both as his friend and author of this work. Locke, concerned to preserve anonymity, was displeased at Molyneux's reference to him, but the matter did not, however, ruin the friendship between the two. Having dedicated his tract to William III, and affirmed the loyalty of Irish protestants, Molyneux disclaimed any personal interest in the issues before the houses of the English parliament. He then examined the relationship of the two kingdoms since the Anglo-Norman intervention in Ireland. He maintained that, following the voluntary submission of the Irish kings, nobility, and clergy, Henry II had introduced English common

law to Ireland and granted the freedom of holding parliaments in Ireland as a distinct kingdom, sending a *Modus tenendi parliamenta in Hibernia*. A corresponding medieval document had been published in 1692 by Bishop Anthony Doping, Molyneux's brother-in-law. English laws and liberties had thus, it was claimed, been extended to Ireland under the Plantagenet kings but not by any power of the English parliament. Since that time England and Ireland had enjoyed like forms of government under one and the same monarch, yet both had remained separate and distinct without any subordination of one to the other. Molyneux contended that the records showed that no legislation introducing a new law made in England had been enacted in Ireland down to the year 1641 without passing the Irish parliament. Since then, however, there had been a series of breaches of Ireland's legislative independence, the most troubling being laws introduced since the Restoration, such as the Cattle and Tobacco Acts, the Navigation Act (which obliged ships bringing goods from the plantations to land first in England), and, most recently, the Woollen Act.

Turning to the disputed appellate issues, Molyneux considered a precedent of a writ of error from the king's bench in England that reversed a judgment of its Irish counterpart from which a subordination of Ireland might be inferred. Irish subjects could appeal to the king in England for exposition of the common and statute law of Ireland, but this gave the English parliament no right to legislate for Ireland. The suggestion that Ireland was merely an English colony he rejected out of hand. Ireland, unlike a colony, had a parliament and courts of justice.

That Ireland should be bound by English acts of parliament Molyneux held to be against reason and the common rights of mankind. Consent alone could give laws force, otherwise they offended against rights of liberty and property. The circumstance complained of offended against English common law under which representative government was the right of every subject. Statutes made in England could thus not bind the Irish as they had no representation in the English parliament. Furthermore, the statute laws of both countries were offended against, as was a series of charters of liberties granted to Ireland as a separate and distinct kingdom. That the English parliament should have co-ordinate powers with the king to introduce or repeal legislation in Ireland was repugnant to the constitutional foundation given to the Irish legislature under Poynings' law, passed by a parliament at Drogheda in December 1494, and offended against the royal prerogative itself. In sum he concluded that the Irish constitution, and the rights and liberties granted 500 years earlier to the Irish upon their submission to the crown and inherited by the loyal protestants of English descent, was under attack from the English parliament seeking to extend its power. The happiness of a constitution, he maintained, depended on a proper balance between the king's and the people's rights. Concluding his tract in this tenor, in a passage that reveals the influence of his friend Robert Molesworth, Molyneux likened the pervasive action of the English parliament to that of absolute monarchs in subverting gothic or mixed constitutions considered to have once flourished throughout Europe.

The *Case* was debated in the English House of Commons in May 1698, and a committee was appointed to examine it and to inquire into the circumstances of its composition. On 27 June the house resolved that Molyneux's tract was 'of dangerous consequence to the crown and people of England by denying the authority of the king and parliament of England to bind the kingdom and people of Ireland' (*JHC*, 12, 331). Notwithstanding this condemnation and a complaint to the king, no action was taken by the Irish government to punish Molyneux or his sympathizers. Within a year four replies to the *Case* were published, three of which claimed to vindicate the position of the English parliament. Following the condemnation of Molyneux's *Case*, the leaders of protestant opinion in Ireland for a time decided that their best hope of obtaining redress lay in a union—an option alluded to by Molyneux in his tract—that would give them representation at Westminster and free them from trade restrictions. In the eighteenth century the *Case*, in ten editions, found relevance both in the American struggle for independence and in the movement for constitutional reform in Ireland. Irish patriots of the eighteenth century made repeated, but selective, use of Molyneux's arguments, whereas twentieth-century historians placed him in the vanguard of protestant nationalism.

Reputation and influence Molyneux remains one of the more multifaceted characters of the English-speaking world of his time. Philosophers still discuss the Molyneux problem, historians of science still enjoy his unusually frank correspondence with the scientific centres of his day, and historians of political thought consider him to be a writer that interpreted the principles of the revolution of 1688 in 'Lockean' fashion, and thereby arrived at conclusions more radical than Locke would allow. That his book on the rights of the Irish parliament was burned by the public hangman is an untrue but oft-repeated story whose currency testifies to the work's controversial reputation, as well as to the anachronistic light in which it has often been placed. In the final analysis, perhaps his most interesting—because unexpected—impact was on the American colonies, where, seventy years later, people found his interpretation of British constitutional doctrine much to their liking.

Molyneux spent about five weeks from early August 1698 as Locke's guest at London and Oates. Within a month of his return to Dublin he died, on 11 October, at his home, near Ormond Gate, after a recurrence of a chronic kidney disease. He was buried in St Audoen's Church, Dublin. In what remains of the church today he is commemorated, in an inscription that borrows the philosopher's words, as 'the man whom Locke was proud to call his friend'.   JAMES G. O'HARA

Sources J. G. Simms, *William Molyneux of Dublin, 1656–1698*, ed. P. H. Kelly (1982) • J. I. McGuire, 'Politics, opinion and the Irish constitution, 1688–1707', MA diss., University College Dublin, 1968 • K. T. Hoppen, *The common scientist in the seventeenth century: a study of the*

Dublin Philosophical Society, 1683–1708 (1970) • K. T. Hoppen, 'The papers of the Dublin Philosophical Society, 1683–1708', *Analecta Hibernica*, 30 (1982), 151–248 • P. H. Kelly, 'The printer's copy of the MS of William Molyneux, *The case of Ireland's being bound by acts of parliament in England, stated, 1698*', *Long Room*, 16 (1980), 6–13 • T. W. Moody and others, eds., *A new history of Ireland*, 10 vols. (1976–96), vols. 4, 8 • C. Robbins, *The eighteenth-century commonwealthman* (1959) • J. Locke, *The works of John Locke*, new edn, 10 vols (1823); repr. (1963) • J. P. Kenyon, *Revolution principles: the politics of party, 1689–1720* (1977)

Archives Archbishop Marsh's Library, Dublin • BL, corresp. and papers, Add. MS 4811 • PRO NIre., historical account of Castle Dillon estate • Royal Irish Acad. • RS, papers • Southampton City Archives, corresp. with John Flamsteed, and papers • TCD, papers • Trinity Cam., corresp. and papers | BL, Sloane MSS, letters to E. Borlase and Sir Hans Sloane • NYPL, Carl H. Pforzheimer Collection of Shelley and His Circle, letters to John Locke

Likenesses attrib. G. Kneller, oil on canvas, *c*.1696, NPG [*see illus.*] • R. Home, oils, *c*.1782–1788, TCD • H. Brocas, stipple, 1803 (after R. Home), NG Ire; repro. in Simms, *William Molyneux of Dublin* • E. Scriven, engraving, RS • P. Simms, line engraving, NPG; repro. in Simms, *William Molyneux of Dublin*

Wealth at death probably considerable; rents and land at Castle Dillon, co. Armagh and elsewhere in Ireland; house in Dublin inherited from father

Molyns, John. *See* Mullins, John (*d.* 1591).

Momerie [*formerly* Mummery], **Alfred Williams** (1848–1900), theologian, born in Ratcliffe, London, on 22 March 1848, was the only child of Isaac Vale Mummery (1812–1892), a well-known Congregational minister of Ratcliffe, London, and his wife, a daughter of Thomas George Williams of Hackney. He was descended from a French family of Huguenot refugees, and resumed the original form of his surname—Momerie—in 1879. He was educated at the City of London School and at Edinburgh University, where he won the Horsliehill and Miller scholarship with the medal and the Bruce prize for metaphysics, and graduated MA in 1875 and DSc in 1876. From Edinburgh he proceeded to St John's College, Cambridge, where he was admitted on 17 March 1875 and was senior in the moral science tripos in 1877, graduating BA in 1878 and MA in 1881. He was ordained deacon in 1878, and priest in 1879, as curate of Leigh in Lancashire. On 5 November 1879 he was elected fellow of St John's College, and in 1880, having published *Personality—the Beginning and End of Metaphysics* (1879), he was appointed professor of logic and mental philosophy at King's College, London. In 1883 he was chosen morning preacher at the Foundling Hospital.

Between 1881 and 1890 Momerie published numerous books and collections of sermons on the philosophy of Christianity, which attained considerable vogue. Their style was brilliant, their views latitudinarian. Especially important were *The Origin of Evil* (1881), *Defects of Modern Christianity* (1882), *The Basis of Religion* (1883), and *Inspiration and other Sermons* (1889). As with his predecessor, F. D. Maurice, the broad-church character of his writings (and especially his sermon 'Inspiration') caused trouble with the council of King's College; in 1889 W. E. Gladstone unsuccessfully tried to arrange a compromise (as he had with Maurice a generation earlier); but by 1891 Momerie

Alfred Williams Momerie (1848–1900), by Barraud, pubd 1891

had been dismissed and that year also resigned the Foundling preachership. Edinburgh University, however, gave him an honorary LLD in 1887. With the permission of the bishop of London he subsequently preached on Sundays at the Portman rooms. In 1896 he married Ada Louisa, the widow of Charles E. Herne, who survived him. He died at 14 Chilworth Street, London, on 6 December 1900 and was buried in Kensal Green cemetery.

E. I. CARLYLE, rev. H. C. G. MATTHEW

Sources The Times (8 Dec 1900) · V. Momerie, Dr Momerie: his life and work (1905) · Boase, Mod. Eng. biog. · The Eagle, 22 (1901), 244–6 · Gladstone, Diaries
Archives BL, W. E. Gladstone MSS, Add. MS 44512 · Col. U., H. R. Haweis MSS · University of British Columbia Library, Vancouver, letters to H. R. Haweis
Likenesses Barraud, photograph, NPG; repro. in Men and women of the day, 4 (1891) [see illus.] · Elliott & Fry, photograph, repro. in ILN (15 Dec 1900)

Momigliano, Arnaldo Dante (1908–1987), ancient historian, was born on 5 September 1908 in Caraglio, near Cuneo, Italy, the only son and eldest of three children of Riccardo Salomone Momigliano, grain merchant, and his wife, Ilda Levi. His was a prominent Jewish intellectual family; his father and mother died in a concentration camp in the Second World War. He was educated at home, and from 1925 at Turin University, where he came under the influence of Gaetano De Sanctis in ancient history and Augusto Rostagni in Greek literature.

Immediately after graduating in 1929, Momigliano followed De Sanctis to Rome, where he joined the group of scholars employed on the *Enciclopedia italiana*, for which he wrote over 230 articles, including the long and important 'Roma in età imperiale' (1936). At the same time, from the age of twenty-four he was teaching Greek history at Rome University as assistant and from 1932 as substitute for De Sanctis. He married in 1932 Gemma, daughter of Adolfo Segre, civil servant; they had one daughter, Anna Laura.

Despite his connections with De Sanctis and Benedetto Croce (both openly opposed to fascism) in 1936 Momigliano won the *concorso* for the post of professor of Roman history at Turin University. His inaugural lecture (published posthumously in 1989) was 'The concept of peace in the Graeco-Roman world'. In September 1938 he was dismissed on racial grounds.

Momigliano's second book, on the emperor Claudius (1932), had been favourably noticed by Hugh Last, professor of Roman history at Oxford, who arranged for its translation into English in 1934; he therefore wrote to Last, who applied on his behalf to the Society for the Protection of Science and Learning (founded to assist academic refugees), which responded with an invitation and a small grant for a year to continue his researches in Oxford. He arrived on 30 March 1939, and his wife and daughter followed shortly. In 1940 he was interned briefly as an 'enemy alien' on the Isle of Man. Throughout the war the family lived in rented rooms, supported first by the society, then by research grants from the Rockefeller Foundation arranged through the Oxford University Press. During this period he was preparing a major book under the title 'Liberty and peace in the ancient world' (later abandoned, although substantial fragments survive). He was the youngest (and only Italian) member of that remarkable group of refugee classical scholars who congregated in the library of the Ashmolean Museum, and who subsequently repaid their debt to Britain by transforming classical studies in the Anglo-Saxon world.

After the war Momigliano was reinstated as supernumerary professor at Turin in 1945. In 1947 he was appointed lecturer at Bristol University and in 1949 he was promoted to reader. In 1951 he moved to the chair of ancient history at University College, London, where he remained until 1975. From 1964 he was also professor at the Scuola Normale Superiore of Pisa.

For many years Momigliano played an important part on the editorial boards of the *Journal of Roman Studies*, *Rivista Storica Italiana*, and *History and Theory*. After retirement he was appointed an associate member of All Souls College, Oxford from 1975 to 1982, and from 1983 a visiting (later honorary) fellow at Peterhouse, Cambridge. From 1975 to his death he was Alexander White visiting professor at Chicago, where he spent a semester each year, and he also lectured widely throughout Europe and in Israel. The deaths of most of his family and childhood friends in concentration camps meant that his connections with Germany remained distant.

Momigliano's early work was in the tradition of Italian idealist and critical historical studies, and showed a firm

Arnaldo Dante Momigliano (1908–1987), by unknown photographer

grounding in classical philology. His first book was on the Hellenistic Jewish book of Maccabees (1930); after his biography of Claudius, he wrote a study of Philip of Macedon (1934). These were all highly professional works, distinguished by critical use of sources, sympathy with the subject, and a mastery of the extensive bibliography. By the time of his exile his own bibliography already comprised 208 items (apart from encyclopaedia articles).

The move to England, with the need to master another culture and another language, coincided with a period of deep questioning of the meaning of European history. By the end of the war Momigliano had identified a new subject for research, the history of historiography from antiquity to the present day; his immense learning and sound judgement made him the acknowledged creator and master of a new area of study for a generation. The long delayed publication of the 1962 Sather lectures after his death (*The Classical Foundations of Modern Historiography*, 1990) showed that he had already then established the framework for researches which he pursued in detail over the next twenty-five years; these are included in his *Contributi alla storia degli studi classici e del mondo antico*, which appeared in nine volumes between 1955 and 1992. Many selections from these essays have been published, in English, Italian, French, and German. Some have criticized the fact that he preferred the essay to the book; but his choice relates to his conception of history as a way of life and an attitude of mind, rather than a set of permanent results.

Momigliano's influence was felt in many areas. His work on Edward Gibbon, George Grote, and nineteenth-century continental scholarship is particularly important. He opened up the study of late antiquity in Britain (*The Conflict between Paganism and Christianity in the Fourth Century*, 1963). His work on early Rome inspired a new generation of Italian scholars. In 1972 he helped to establish a joint degree in anthropology and ancient history at University College, London, and comparative themes are evident in his London seminar, culminating in *Alien Wisdom: the Limits of Hellenization* (1975). Since his early contacts with Croce, he had been interested in the idea of liberty and its relation to the concept of the person; this provoked a controversial study, *The Development of Greek Biography* (1971), and towards the end of his life papers on the idea of the person and biography in late antiquity. He retained a lifelong interest in Jewish history, and his latest work centred on the history of ancient religion.

It was in the lecture and the seminar that Momigliano's distinctive combination of immense learning and facility with ideas had most impact. Although his accent remained impenetrably Piedmontese, he wrote English with an unacademic elegance and wit, and Italian 'like an Englishman'. His teaching presented no general theory of history, for he respected too much the autonomy of the past to wish to impose general patterns on it; as he said once: 'I have now lost faith in my own theories, but I have not yet acquired faith in the theories of my colleagues'. To him, theory was created by the historian, not by the facts; it was this emphasis on the role of the observer in the interpretation of history which was one of his most distinctive contributions to the study of history. Another was his insistence that methodology (as opposed to ideology) was the central theme of the history of historiography.

Momigliano's teaching followed the continental tradition of seminars, and his efforts were directed towards the next generation of scholars. In England the main centre of his activity was the Warburg Institute: he contributed many lectures, and from 1967 to 1983 conducted a regular seminar at the institute, which became the centre for young historians throughout Britain. In Italy his annual seminar at Pisa attracted audiences of hundreds, and his Chicago seminar was equally famous. None who presented a paper on these occasions could forget the mixture of awe and fear which he inspired, as he summed up the problem with greater clarity and learning than the speaker could ever hope to achieve.

Widely held to be the most learned man of his age, Momigliano was 'a masters' master' (as George Steiner dubbed him), and one of the dominant figures in European historical studies for a generation, in which he seemed to many to be the embodiment of history itself. Stocky, untidy, and of immense vitality, a non-drinker always on the move, with his pockets full of medicines, carbon copy cash-books (for writing references in), and bunches of keys, his books in a string bag, his scarf attached by a safety pin, he took scant interest in administration, and lived for intellectual discussion. He was immediately approachable, and paid no attention to rank: he lacked all pomposity and most of the social graces, even forgetting his own retirement dinner—an act which he described as 'a triumph of the Id over the Ego'. He would move in a cloud of younger scholars; and an hour with him would often change their lives. He was fascinated by ideas, new and old; in his later years he became more insistent on the need to know, and returned to ancestral traditions of rabbinic learning and exact scholarship, but he never lost his delight in discussion. To those he respected intellectually, especially the young, he was generous to a fault; he would dismiss openly those who did not measure up to his standards. As a result he had many devoted friends and disciples, and not a few enemies. For he was a man of passion, capable of quarrelling magnificently and permanently; yet it must be said that he never did so without good cause, personal or intellectual.

Through his writing and his personality Momigliano made a major contribution to intellectual life in England, Italy, and America. But he remained true to his origins; during a lifetime of exile he retained his Italian citizenship, and as a free thinker was proud of his three inheritances, Celtic Piedmont, Italy of the Risorgimento, and the Jewish tradition of learning.

Momigliano held a number of visiting professorships in America; he became a fellow of the British Academy in 1954, and was president of the Society for the Promotion of Roman Studies in 1965–8; he received many honorary degrees, and an honorary KBE in 1974. Momigliano died on 1 September 1987 in the Central Middlesex Hospital, London, and was buried in the Jewish cemetery at Cuneo. A memorial meeting was held in University College, London, on 4 March 1988.   OSWYN MURRAY, rev.

Sources *Rivista Storica Italiana*, 100 (1988), fasc. 2 · *The Times* (3 Sept 1987) · *The Times* (5 March 1988) · P. Brown, 'Arnaldo Dante Momigliano, 1908–1987', *PBA*, 74 (1988), 405–42 · C. Dionisotti, *Ricordo di Arnaldo Momigliano* (1989) · L. Cracco Ruggini, *Omaggio ad Arnaldo Momigliano* (1989) · *History and Theory* [Beiheft], 30 (1991) · Scuola Normale, Pisa, Momigliano MSS · Bodl. Oxf., Society for the Protection of Science and Learning, MSS Momigliano · Oxford University Press, archives, Momigliano MSS · personal knowledge (1996) · *CGPLA Eng. & Wales* (1989)
Archives Bodl. Oxf., Society for the Protection of Science and Learning MSS · Oxford University Press, archives · Scuola Normale, Pisa
Likenesses photograph, British Academy [*see illus.*]
Wealth at death £303,824 in England and Wales: administration with will, 9 March 1989, *CGPLA Eng. & Wales*

Momma, Jacob (*d.* 1679), copper and brass manufacturer, was born in Stolberg, in the Rhineland of Germany, the son of Leonard and Barbara Momma, members of a group of protestant brass manufacturers. Having previously been settled in Aachen, religious persecution had persuaded them to move to the city outskirts at Stolberg. Several gravestones still commemorate the Mommas and other brassworking families in the town's protestant graveyard.

One branch of the family established brass and copper manufacture under royal patronage in Sweden during the seventeenth century. Jacob Momma, however, moved to England where, with German partners Daniel Demetrius

and Peter Hoet, he leased Esher Mill in Surrey in 1649. The partners adopted traditional European brassmaking methods, using crushed calamine—the zinc carbonate ore, which they obtained from Mendip in Somerset—alloyed with copper, imported from Sweden in the absence of English supplies. Water-powered hammers were employed to flatten brass ingots to produce sheets of the metal and also to form hollowware vessels; and wire was also drawn by water-power.

Momma petitioned unsuccessfully to parliament in 1656 for relief against high duties imposed on imported Swedish copper. A few months later he was brought before the court of the Society of Mineral and Battery Works, the monopoly established in the reign of Elizabeth I, for failing to pay charges for leasing their brass manufacturing rights. Although in defence he pleaded ignorance of this moribund organization, his payments remained outstanding for some years. At some point Momma married and had at least two sons.

Momma was naturalized by 1660 when he purchased the Esher premises outright. A year later he was appointed as constable and served as a juror in 1663, having thus attained the respect of his local community. At this time he and his partners were again petitioning parliament for assistance for the industry, claiming that their manufacturing concerns were almost lost and that their fires were going out. Separately, he pleaded for higher tariffs against imported brass wire. Protection was sought from the price manipulation of exports controlled by powerful Dutch merchants whose practices in England varied from the dumping of cheap foreign brass to the withholding of copper supplies. Momma succeeded in obtaining a degree of support from the Society of Mineral and Battery Works, but neither petition succeeded.

In an attempt to obtain copper at more economic prices, Momma was briefly involved from 1665 in mining copper at Ecton Hill, Staffordshire (later a hugely successful and profitable mine). There he is credited with the introduction of gunpowder to English mining technology and also of a new kind of bellows in smelting his ore at the nearby Ellastone Mill. However, the whole project, managed by his son Jacob, was abandoned at a loss of £300 a few years later when it was found to be unprofitable. The younger Jacob returned to Esher to manage the copper mills, where brass production and manufacture was still surviving in spite of economic pressures. During the 1660s the Esher premises were taxed on twenty hearths, believed to have been related to the brass-making processes. The Momma family appears to have continued this business until the 1670s when two brassworks were demolished. Jacob senior claimed that he had lost £6000 in attempting to make the works pay.

Jacob Momma died in 1679, probably at Esher, and two copper mills at Esher involving both sons, Jacob and William, survived only briefly after their father's death. A failed scheme for producing brass farthings and a business exporting Mendip calamine were also revealed in papers of a dispute in 1686 over family property. In the early 1690s a new company led by William Dockwra, benefiting from political change and technical innovation, succeeded in reviving the Esher brass and copper works of Jacob Momma.   JOAN DAY

Sources J. A. Robey, 'The Ecton copper mines in the seventeenth century', *Bulletin of the Peak District Mines Historical Society*, 4/2 (1969), 145–55 · J. Morton and J. A. Robey, 'Jacob Momma and the Ecton copper mines', *Bulletin of the Peak District Mines Historical Society*, 9/3 (1985), 195–6 · J. Day, 'Copper, zinc, and brass production', *The industrial revolution in metals*, ed. J. Day and R. F. Tylecote (1991), 137–9, 164–5 · J. Morton, 'The rise of the modern copper and brass industry, 1690–1750', PhD diss., U. Birm., 1985 · H. Hamilton, *The English brass and copper industries to 1800* (1926) · *VCH Surrey*, 2.254 · court books of the Society of Mineral and Battery Works, 162–1713, BL, Loan 16 · G. Hammersley, 'Technique or economy: the rise and decline of the early English copper industry, *ca*1550–1660', *Schwerpunkte der Kupferproduktion und des Kupferhandels in Europa, 1500–1650*, ed. H. Kellenbenz (Cologne, 1977), 1–40 · private information (2004) · J. Day and R. F. Tylecote, eds., *The industrial revolution in metals* (1991)

Mompesson, Sir Giles (1583/4–1651×63), projector, was the eldest son of Thomas Mompesson (d. 1587) of Bathampton, Wiltshire, and his second wife, Honor, daughter of Giles Estcourt of Salisbury. He had two younger brothers, Thomas and John, the latter rector of Codford St Mary, Wiltshire. With a first cousin, Jasper Mompesson, two years his senior, Giles matriculated from Hart Hall, Oxford, aged sixteen, on 24 October 1600. Neither seems to have graduated. On 24 October 1601 Giles entered Lincoln's Inn. He does not appear to have been called to the bar. A diarist in 1621 gives a description of Mompesson's appearance: 'a litle black man of a black swart complection with a litle black beard' (Notestein, Relf, and Simpson, 2.160).

The Projector In 1606 or 1607 Mompesson married Katharine (d. 1633), a younger daughter of Sir John St John of Lydiard Tregoze, Wiltshire. The marriage linked Mompesson to a leading county family, and the place he established in Wiltshire society is perhaps indicated by his election (probably unopposed) to the borough of Great Bedwin in 1614. However, the most important connection created by the marriage could not have been foreseen when it took place. About 1612 Katharine's sister Barbara married Edward Villiers, half-brother of George Villiers, subsequently earl, marquess, and duke of Buckingham, who between late 1614 and early 1616 rose rapidly to become the king's powerful favourite. Mompesson rapidly exploited his connection to put forward a variety of profit-making schemes.

In 1616 Mompesson suggested to Villiers the creation of a special commission for the purpose of granting licences to keepers of inns, whereby the pockets of the special commissioners and the king's impoverished exchequer might both benefit. Villiers adopted the suggestion. It was urged that the functions of the new commissioners would clash with those of the justices of the peace, but Sir Francis Bacon, then attorney-general, and three judges were consulted, and the referees were of opinion that the patent for the commission was perfectly legal. Accordingly in October 1616 Mompesson and two others were nominated commissioners for the licensing of inns, and invested with the fullest powers, but the patent was not sealed by Lord Chancellor Egerton until March 1617, and then only under great pressure from the king. The fees which the commissioners were allowed to charge for the grant of licences were practically left to their discretion, although it was stipulated that four-fifths of the sums received were to be paid into the exchequer. To increase his dignity in his new office, Mompesson was knighted by James I at Newmarket on 18 November 1616. Bacon wrote to Buckingham that he was glad that the honour had been conferred on Mompesson: 'he may the better fight with

Sir Giles Mompesson (1583/4–1651×63), by unknown engraver, 1620

the Bulls and the Bears, and the Saracens' Heads, and such fearful creatures' (Spedding, 6.102). Mompesson performed his duties with reckless audacity. He and his agents expanded the scope of their enquiries from the inns specified in the commission, where there were legal anomalies to be resolved, to more modest alehouses where their authority clashed directly with the powers of local JPs. Moreover, Mompesson charged exorbitant fees, exacted heavy fines from respectable innkeepers for trifling neglect of licensing laws, and increased the number of drinking establishments by granting, on payment of heavy sums, new licences to keepers of houses that had been closed on account of disorderly conduct. The entire scheme has been characterized as 'a hit-and-run shakedown operation' (Ruigh, 57).

In the same month as the inns patent, March 1617, Mompesson received a commission to pursue another of his projects, by which he promised to raise £100,000 in four years through the sale of decayed timbers in the royal forests. He was duly authorized to sell the decayed woods from the forests of nine counties with the only condition that he committed no waste or destruction to the coppices and underwoods of the forest. The grant was difficult to police, and inevitably set him against the interests of the tenants and commoners of the forests. In 1621 it was claimed that he had received a £1000 fee from the exchequer at the outset and was due to receive another at the end of the project, and in the meantime had made profits of £10,000 on the sales.

Mompesson thus acquired a very evil reputation, but his close connection with Buckingham and Bacon (who became lord keeper on 7 March 1617 and lord chancellor on 7 January 1618) remained unchanged. At the end of 1619 Bacon frequently consulted him on matters affecting the public revenue, and on 12 December invited him to Kew in order to confer with him the more quietly.

In 1618 Mompesson's functions had been extended still further. Early in the year a commission had been issued for the purpose of imposing heavy penalties on all who engaged in the manufacture of gold and silver thread without a special licence, which the commissioners were empowered to sell at a high price. On 20 October 1618 the punitive powers of the commissioners were enlarged and their number increased by the addition of Mompesson. He at once set energetically to work, and threatened all goldsmiths and silkmen that they should 'rot in prison' unless they proved submissive. His activity satisfied the court. On 19 February 1619 Sir Henry Savile wrote that Mompesson and Sir Albertus Morton were acting as clerks of the council, and on 9 November 1619 James granted the former the office of surveyor of the profits of the New River Company, with an annual income of £200 'from the king's moieties of the profits of the said river' (*CSP dom.*, *1619–23*, 91). On 25 April 1620 he received a licence to convert coal and other fuel, excepting wood, into charcoal. In July he received two commissions for pursuing concealed crown lands. Under one he and his fellow commissioners were authorized to investigate and set the rents, entry fines, and other financial obligations due to the exchequer from their discoveries. The other granted to Mompesson all the concealed lands that he could discover which were worth less than £200. He was later accused, unsurprisingly, of undervaluing his discoveries, claiming that lands worth £2000 were actually only worth £200.

Trial and flight But public feeling was running very high against Mompesson, and his re-election as MP for Great Bedwin in 1620 was quickly followed by retribution, in large part as a consequence of his entanglement with Bacon, and especially with Buckingham. Bacon had fully expected that monopolies would come under fire in the new parliament, counselling pre-emptive action by the privy council to prune back the vigorous growth in grants of letters patent in order to forestall the sharp attack which public opinion increasingly demanded. Bacon particularly singled out the urgency of rescinding Mompesson's patent to license innkeepers. His advice was not only ignored, but Buckingham sought to extend the involvement of his kinsmen in their lucrative farm of government business.

On 19 February 1621 the House of Commons considered William Noy's proposal to inquire into the procedure of all commissions lately created to enforce such monopolypatents as those affecting inns or gold and silver thread. Although that resolution was not adopted, a committee of the whole house opened, on 20 February, an investigation into the patent for licensing inns. Witnesses came forward to give convincing testimony of the infamous tyranny with which Mompesson or his agents had performed the duties of his office. It was found that on one occasion one Ferrett posed as a traveller seeking shelter late at night, throwing himself on the hospitality of a sympathetic alehouse-keeper who gave the stranger his bed and stabled his horse for the night. The agent thereupon prosecuted him for keeping an unlicensed inn. The patent was unanimously condemned. Mompesson at once admitted his fault and, in a petition which was read in the house on 24 February, threw himself on the mercy of the house, but his appeal was heard in silence. In a letter to Buckingham he promised to clear himself of all imputations if the king would direct the Commons to specify the charges in greater detail. On 27 February Sir Edward Coke, when reporting the committee's decision to the house, declared Mompesson to be the original projector of the scheme, to have prosecuted no fewer than 3320 innkeepers for technical breaches of obsolete statutes, and to have licensed, in Hampshire alone, sixteen inns that had been previously closed by the justices as disorderly houses.

Mompesson was summoned to the bar of the house and rigorously examined. He endeavoured to throw the responsibility on the lord chancellor and the judges who had declared the patent to be legal. Finally he was ordered to attend the house every morning, and to render his attendance the more certain he was committed to the care of the serjeant-at-arms. The Commons at the same time invited the Lords to confer with them respecting his punishment. In the meantime investigation proceeded in committees of the Lords into Mompesson's patents for gold and silver thread, and for discovery of 'concealed' crown lands—a source of particular complaint, for so wide was its remit that no man's property seemed safe. He was charged with undervaluing estates; falsely claiming that lands were concealed on which rents were actually being paid to the crown; penalizing people who had drained land; and after claiming to have 'discovered' concealed lands when he had merely copied out the discoveries of Elizabethan predecessors.

New charges against Mompesson accumulated daily, and his fears grew proportionately. On 3 March he managed to elude the vigilance of his gaolers, and before the alarm was raised was on his way to France. Notice was sent to all the ports to stay his flight, a proclamation was issued for his arrest, and he was expelled from his seat in parliament. On 15 March the Commons sent up to the Lords a full account of his offences, and on 27 March the lord chief justice pronounced sentence upon him in the House of Lords, to which the Commons were specially invited for the occasion. Mompesson was to be degraded from the order of knighthood, to be conducted along the Strand with his face to the horse's tail, to pay a fine of £10,000, to be imprisoned for life, and to be for ever held an infamous person. On 30 March a printed proclamation added, not quite logically, perpetual banishment to his punishment.

A rare illustrated tract, entitled *The Description of Giles Mompesson Late Knight Censured by Parliament the 17th of March Aᵒ 1620*, compared him to Sir Richard Empson, the extortionate minister of Henry VII, and credited him with having filled his coffers with his ill-gotten gains. The indictment against Empson had been examined by the Lords when they were proceeding against Mompesson, and a popular anagram on his name was 'No Empsons'. It is probable that Sir Giles Overreach ('a cruel extortioner'), the leading character in Massinger's *New Way to Pay Old Debts*, was intended as a portrait of Mompesson. The play was written soon after his flight.

Investigation of the patent for gold and silver thread raised far-reaching legal and constitutional issues surrounding the right of imprisonment, sparking a debate 'which would culminate in the Petition of Right seven years later' (Russell, 103). Mompesson's case was also crucial in the revival of the parliamentary power of impeachment. Once regarded as a milestone on the high road to civil war, this assertion of ancient parliamentary right was too heavily implicated in the factional politics of the early Stuart court to be regarded as a pristine example of the defence of liberty in the face of regal tyranny. The moves to indict the referees who had maintained the legality of the monopolies were precursors of the attack on Bacon, harried by his long-time rival, Sir Edward Coke, who had led the charge against Mompesson and the others. The episode also revealed a growing inclination to challenge the supremacy of the marquess of Buckingham.

Political circumstances, therefore, helped fix Mompesson's name as 'a byword for corrupt, greedy malpractice' (Hoyle, 327). Mompesson was only one of a number of projectors to whom Elizabethan and early Stuart governments farmed out administrative functions: the granting of such patents and monopolies was in part an effort to remedy defects in existing administrative structures, and even more a quick way of filling the royal coffers. But it was widely perceived as sacrificing the public good for private gain. None of Mompesson's projects was particularly new, and their impact was arguably exaggerated—for instance, the forty or so inn and alehouse licences that Mompesson issued in Kent formed only a small proportion of the county's total. Nevertheless the scale and range of Mompesson's projects made him a particularly dramatic embodiment of this perception, an affront to the Commonwealth on several grounds, crossing the right of local governors to rule (especially through the patent for licensing inns) and challenging the rights of property (through the pursuit of concealed lands) and, indeed, arguably of subsistence. In 1621 his enemies alleged that Mompesson had acquired a commission to license badgers (corn dealers). The charge, whose grounds are obscure and which remained unsubstantiated, concentrated the image of Mompesson as a threat to the Commonwealth, a predator who in licensing men who were themselves regarded ambivalently as potential profiteers in popular and official opinion, was acting against both the authority of the magistrates responsible for policing the market and the needs of the poor. The sentence to ride with his face to the horse's tail drew on popular rituals for other enemies of good order such as husbands beaten or cuckolded by their wives.

Aftermath and later life After her husband's flight to France Lady Mompesson remained in England, and her friends made every effort to secure provision for her out of her husband's estate. On 7 July 1621 the fine of £10,000 due from Mompesson was assigned to his father-in-law Sir John St John, and Edward Hungerford, together with all his goods and chattels, saving the annuity of £200 allowed him by the New River Company. That asset was reserved for Lady Mompesson and her child. In the same year Mompesson petitioned Charles I to recall him so that he might answer the charges alleged against him, and he bitterly complained of the comparison made between him and Dudley or Empson. On 17 February 1623 Lady Mompesson presented a similar petition, on the ground that his presence in England was necessary to settle his estate, most of which was illegally detained by his brother Thomas. Next day this application was granted for a term of three months, on the understanding that Mompesson should not appear at court and should confine himself to his private business. Later in the year (1623) Mompesson was not only in England but was, according to John Chamberlain, putting his patent for alehouses into execution on the ground that it had not been technically abrogated by parliament. On 10 August 1623 a new warrant gave him permission to remain in England three months longer on the old understanding that he should solely devote himself to his private affairs. On 8 February 1624 he was ordered to quit the country within five days. If he did so, he was soon back again. He lived until his death in retirement among his kinsfolk in Wiltshire. On 4 February 1630 he acted with his brother Thomas as overseer of the will of his maternal cousin, Edward Estcourt of New Sarum, and he is mentioned in Thomas's will, which was proved in 1640. He acted as the agent of his sister-in-law Lady Villiers in enclosing and digging pits on land granted to her late husband in the Forest of Dean. On 25 March 1631 commoners of the forest destroyed the enclosure's hedges and ditches, beat up the miners working there, and 'by sound of drum and ensigns in most rebellious manner, carrying a picture or statue apparelled like Mompesson and with great noise and clamour threw it into the coalpits which the said Sir Giles had digged' (Ingram, 91).

In 1639 Mompesson transferred to William Laud's college of St John's, Oxford, through the offices of the archbishop himself, the advowson of Codford St Mary. He seems to have been long on friendly terms with Sir Edward Hyde, afterwards the great earl of Clarendon. He employed Hyde in a lawsuit in 1640, and lent him £104 in September 1643. Although a non-combatant he was a royalist, and in April 1647 went to the king's quarters at Hereford. His property was sequestrated by the parliament, and on 1 May 1647 he was fined £561 9s. The parliamentarian committee for the advance of money assessed him at £800 on 26 December 1645 and at £200 on 2 September 1651.

Mompesson is not heard of again. His will, made on 14 July 1651, was not proved until 3 August 1663. He bequeathed £1 6s. 8d. to Tisbury parish with which to buy canvas for the poor. SIDNEY LEE, rev. SEAN KELSEY

Sources The letters and life of Francis Bacon, ed. J. Spedding, 7 vols. (1861–74), vol. 5, p. 65; vol. 6, pp. 98–9, 102; vol. 7, pp. 68–9, 186 · W. Notestein, F. H. Relf, and H. Simpson, eds., Commons debates, 1621, 7 vols. (1935) · JHL, 3 (1620–28), 72 · JHC, 1 (1547–1628), 532, 536 · CSP dom., 1611–18, 439, 473; 1619–23, 16, 91, 139, 238, 273, 419; 1623–5, 13 · S. R. Gardiner, History of England, 10 vols (1899–1901), vol. 4, pp. 41–2 · E. R. Foster, 'The procedure of the House of Commons against patents and monopolies, 1621–4', Conflict in Stuart England, ed. W. Aiken and B. D. Henning (1960), 57–85 · C. G. C. Tite, Impeachment and parliamentary judicature in early Stuart England (1974) · R. Zaller, The parliament of 1621: a study in constitutional conflict (1971), 23, 56–9, 62–5, 67, 75, 77, 80, 85, 116, 119–20 · C. Russell, Parliaments and English politics, 1621–1629 (1979), 66, 102–3, 105–8 · R. W. Hoyle, ed., The estates of the English crown, 1558–1642 (1992) · will, PRO, PROB 11/312, fols. 46r–47v · W. A. Shaw, Knights of England, 3 vols. (1906) · P. Clark, The English alehouse: a social history, 1200–1830 (1983) · B. Sharp, In contempt of all authority: rural artisans and riot in the west of England, 1586–1660 (1980) · F. H. Relf, ed., Notes of the debates in the House of Lords … AD 1621, 1625, 1628, CS, 3rd ser., 42 (1929) · The works of the most reverend father in God, William Laud, 7, ed. J. Bliss (1860), 582–3 · J. E. Jackson, ed., Wiltshire: the topographical collections of John Aubrey (1862), 175–6 · G. D. Squibb, ed., Wiltshire visitation pedigrees, 1623, Harleian Society, 105–6 (1954) · J. Maclean and W. C. Heane, eds., The visitation of the county of Gloucester taken in the year 1623, Harleian Society, 21 (1885) · W. P. Baildon, ed., The records of the Honorable Society of Lincoln's Inn: admissions, 1 (1896) · R. E. Ruigh, The parliament of 1624: politics and foreign policy (1971) · M. Ingram, 'Ridings, rough music, and the "reform of popular culture" in early modern England', Past and Present, 105 (1984), 79–113 · Foster, Alum. Oxon.

Archives BL, accounts of moneys derived from innkeepers' licences, Add. MS 74241–74242

Likenesses caricature, line engraving, 1620 (The description of Giles Mompesson late knight censured by parliament the 17th of March, A° 1620), BM, NPG [see illus.] · double portrait, funeral monument (with his wife), St Mary's Church, Lydiard Tregoze, Wiltshire

Wealth at death He disposed of miscellaneous real estate and personal effects, none of them valued.

Mompesson, William (1638/9–1709), Church of England clergyman, was born in Yorkshire. He is possibly the William Mompesson who was baptized at Collingham in the West Riding on 8 (or 28) April 1639, the son of John Mompesson; he certainly attended nearby Sherburn in Elmet School. He was admitted sizar at Peterhouse, Cambridge, aged sixteen, on 16 April 1655, and graduated BA in 1658 and proceeded MA in 1662. (His son and grandson were both to be educated at the college.) He became chaplain to Sir George Savile, later Viscount Halifax, was made vicar of Scalby, Yorkshire, in 1662, and in 1664 was presented by his patron to the rectory of Eyam, Derbyshire, a flourishing lead-mining centre. He married first Catherine (d. 1666), daughter of Ralph Carr of Cocken, co. Durham, with whom he had one son, George, born in 1662 or 1663, and subsequently the widow of Charles Newby, with whom he had two daughters. George became rector of Barnburgh, Yorkshire, and had two sons, also clergymen.

An epidemic of bubonic plague broke out in Eyam in September 1665. According to tradition, the infection was brought by its first victim, George Vicars, in a box of cloth from London (which may therefore have contained plague-carrying fleas), but the exact cause remains unknown. Between 7 September 1665 and 11 October 1666, four in ten of the parishioners (and perhaps half of the population of the central township) died; 259 deaths from plague were recorded. Mompesson and his wife Catherine remained at Eyam; they were assisted by Thomas Stanley, the former rector of Eyam, who had been ejected in 1662. The clergymen persuaded the population to confine itself to the parish, receiving food and necessities from neighbouring parishes in exchange for money placed in troughs of running water as a precaution against infection. To avoid close contact, Mompesson read prayers on Sundays in a small valley known as the Delf.

Catherine Mompesson died of the plague on 25 August 1666. Expecting to succumb himself, Mompesson wrote farewell letters to his patron and to his infant child, probably intended as formal records of the events, but the rector survived. The episode is still remembered in Eyam, commemorated in stained glass and in an annual church service, and Mompesson's name is inscribed on Derbyshire's roll of honour. The story of Eyam was first recorded by Dr Richard Mead in his A Short Discourse Concerning Pestilential Contagion of 1720, written amid anxiety over the threat posed by the plague then raging at Marseilles. Mead had spoken to Mompesson's sons about the events at Eyam. The story was brought to popular attention in an account by Anna Seward, written in 1765 and printed in the Gentleman's Magazine in 1801; Seward, who had been born and spent her early years in the parish, drew on letters and local traditions. William and Mary Howitt popularized the tale further in The Desolation of Eyam and other Poems (1827). The fullest account was given by William Wood in The History and Antiquities of Eyam, which went through eight editions between 1842 and 1903.

In the light of more recent knowledge, the parishioners'

isolationist self-sacrifice appears to have been misguided. Bubonic plague is spread by fleas and thus through close contact between people or between people and an animal flea-carrying host. Dispersal would have been the safer option. Mompesson was probably himself under pressure from outside, perhaps from William Cavendish, third earl of Devonshire and lord lieutenant of Derbyshire, to contain the outbreak in exchange for assistance from other parts of the county. A rural outbreak was thus converted into something approaching the intensity of an urban plague. Although memories lingered and one family, the Rileys, had been devastated by many deaths, Eyam's population soon recovered.

In 1669 Mompesson was presented by Savile to the rectory of Eakring, near Ollerton, Nottinghamshire; the parishioners there refused to admit him at first for fear of the plague (so Mompesson was forced to live in a hut in Rufford Park). In 1671 he was made prebendary of Southwell Minster. He is said to have declined the deanery of Lincoln in 1695 in favour of Dr Samuel Fuller. Mompesson died on 7 March 1709 at Eakring, where there is also a memorial window.   DAVID SOUDEN

Sources DNB · W. Wood, *The history and antiquities of Eyam* (1842) · P. Slack, *The impact of plague in Tudor and Stuart England* (1985) · L. Bradley, 'The most famous of all English plagues: a detailed analysis of the plague of Eyam, 1665–6', *The plague reconsidered*, ed. P. Slack (1977), 63–94 [Local Population Studies suppl.] · R. Mead, *A short discourse concerning pestilential contagion* (1720) · W. Howitt and M. Howitt, *The desolation of Eyam* (1827) · W. Seward, *Anecdotes of some distinguished persons: chiefly of the present and two preceding centuries*, 2nd edn, 4 vols. (1795–6); suppl. (1797), vol. 2, pp. 27–44 · J. Clifford, *Eyam plague, 1665–6*, rev. edn (1993) · 'The Derbyshire roll of honour', www.derbycity.com/derby/honour.html · *Calamy rev.*, 459 · 'Instance of Christian heroism, extracted from a juvenile letter of Anna Seard's, written in 1765', *GM*, 1st ser., 71 (1801), 300–04 · Venn, *Alum. Cant.* · IGI

Likenesses stained glass, 20th cent., Eyam church, Derbyshire · oils, Graves Art Gallery, Sheffield

Monahan, James Henry (1803×5–1878), judge, was born at Portumna, co. Galway, Ireland, the eldest son of Michael Monahan, merchant, of Heathlawn, near Portumna, and his wife, Mary, daughter of Stephen Bloomfield of Eyrecourt. He was educated at the endowed school of Banagher in the King's county, and on 1 November 1819 entered Trinity College, Dublin, where in 1823 he graduated in science and was awarded the gold medal. He entered the King's Inns, Dublin, in Easter term 1823, and Gray's Inn, London, on 4 February 1826, and was called to the Irish bar in Easter term 1828. It took him a little while to build up a practice in Dublin and at first he handled mainly chancery cases, but after joining the Connaught circuit he acquired a considerable practice. In 1833 he married Fanny Harrington; they had two sons and four daughters.

In 1840 Monahan was appointed QC, and his career began to take off: he was quickly recognized as one of the leaders in the court of chancery and became a household name as one of the counsel for the defendants in the state trial for conspiracy of Daniel O'Connell and other nationalists in 1844. On the formation of Lord John Russell's government, in 1846, Monahan was appointed solicitor-general for Ireland, and in the following year he was elected a bencher of the King's Inns. At a by-election in February 1847 he was returned as MP for Galway by a majority of four votes, but he lost the seat to the Young Ireland party at the general election in August of the same year. In December 1847 he became attorney-general for Ireland, and in 1848 he was sworn of the Irish privy council.

As attorney-general Monahan conducted in 1848 the prosecutions against the revolutionaries, Smith O'Brien, Meagher and McManus at Clonmel, and Gavan Duffy, Martin, and Mitchel in Dublin. Monahan was accused of excluding Catholics from the jury, but at his speech in Mitchel's trial he repudiated the charge, pointing out that he himself was a Catholic. He emphasized that his instructions were to exclude—not on the basis of religion—only those whom he believed would not give an impartial verdict. In October 1850 Monahan was appointed chief justice of the common pleas in succession to John Doherty. He held the office until January 1876, when he resigned on grounds of ill health. In 1867 he presided at the special commission for the trial of Fenian prisoners at Cork and Limerick.

As a political moderate with a reputation for conscientiousness, Monahan was held in respect by the bar and the general British public alike. In 1860 he received an honorary LLD from Trinity College and was placed on the senate, and in 1861 he was appointed a commissioner of national education. He died on 8 December 1878 at his home, 5 Fitzwilliam Square, Dublin, and was buried on 11 December at Glasnevin cemetery.

J. D. FITZGERALD, *rev.* SINÉAD AGNEW

Sources Boase, *Mod. Eng. biog.* · F. E. Ball, *The judges in Ireland, 1221–1921*, 2 (1926), 290–92, 297, 306, 309, 329, 358 · *Annual Register* (1878) · Burtchaell & Sadleir, *Alum. Dubl.* · J. Foster, *The register of admissions to Gray's Inn, 1521–1889, together with the register of marriages in Gray's Inn chapel, 1695–1754* (privately printed, London, 1889), 431 · J. S. Crone, *A concise dictionary of Irish biography*, rev. edn (1937), 157 · Ward, *Men of the reign*, 636 · *Men of the time* (1875), 733 · Allibone, *Dict.*, suppl. · C. G. Duffy, *Young Ireland: a fragment of Irish history, 1840–1845*, rev. edn, 1 (1896), 17 · *The Times* (13 Jan 1876) · *The Times* (10 Dec 1878) · *Irish Times* (10 Dec 1878)

Likenesses oils, King's Inns, Dublin, Ireland · wood-engraving sketch, NPG; repro. in *ILN* (2 Dec 1843)

Wealth at death under £16,000: administration, 24 Dec 1878, *CGPLA Ire.*

Monamy, Peter (*bap.* 1681, *d.* 1749), marine painter, was born in the Minories, London, and baptized on 12 January 1681 at St Botolph, Aldgate. His father, Pierre or Peter Monamy (*b.* 1652), was a merchant from Guernsey, the family having reached the Channel Islands from France in the early sixteenth century, probably as protestant refugees. In 1676, shortly after arriving in London, Peter Monamy senior was briefly imprisoned for forging customs clearances, from which he obtained considerable profit. He apparently met his wife, Dorothy Gilbert (*b.* 1660), through London engraving contacts used in this activity. Their first son, Peter Gilbert, was born in 1677 but died before 1681: Ann (*b.* 1678), James (*b.* 1680), and Peter followed. His father's other daughter, Charity (*b.* 1679), may have been illegitimate. In September 1696 the Painter–Stainers' Company binding book recorded Monamy being indentured for seven years to William Clarke, a leading house painter and former master of the company, with premises on London Bridge and in Thames Street. He was made a freeman of the company on 1 March 1704 and may at first have assisted other masters.

Monamy first married in 1704/1705. His wife, Margaret, had a daughter of the same name in 1706 but both died. On 9 January 1707 he married Hannah Christopher (b. 1688) at All Hallows, London Wall. Three children—Andrew, Hannah, and another Andrew—born between 1708 and 1712 died in infancy. Another daughter, Mary, was born before 1720 and the last, Anne, was baptized at St Margaret's in 1725.

Vertue says Monamy had 'an Early affection to drawing of ships and vessels of all kinds and the Imitations of other famous masters of paintings … in that manner' and the lack of evidence for decorative work suggests an early focus on marine art; in this 'by constant practice he disti[nguisht] himself and came into reputation … [and] … by many was much esteemd especially sea-faring people, officers and other marchants &c' (Vertue, *Note books*, 3.145). The naming of both his sons Andrew, after his uncle, a successful merchant, may indicate some family support, and he appears to have retained other Channel Islands connections, especially with the Durells of Jersey. The latter, to whom his aunt Marie was connected by marriage, included a number of naval officers and Monamy is said to have had a close link with Captain Philip Durell (1676–1740) and painted his brother Thomas's share in the capture, in 1740, of the Spanish *Princesa*. Although his work and the range of his compositions—calms, storms, shipping, battle and coastal pieces—follows the lead of the van de Veldes, the earliest influence on it is that of Isaac Sailmaker (1633/4–1721) who, after the death of van de Velde the younger in 1707, was the last of the Dutch émigré generation who had introduced marine painting to England in the 1670s. Monamy's talents as a painter are less than van de Velde's but above Sailmaker's rather wooden style, though he emulated both and copied a number of their compositions. He was the first notable English-born painter of marines and, from the 1720s, was recognized as such until Samuel Scott's greater gifts began to challenge him from the mid-1730s.

Monamy lived off Red Lion Street, Minories, until about 1720 when he moved to St Margaret's Lane, Westminster; then he lived in Fish Yard beside Westminster Hall (1723–8). At his death he was living in Old Palace Yard, which possibly had the view of the Thames 'water & sky' which Vertue says drew him to Westminster, although several of his Durell connections lived there and he was probably following his clientele. Vertue also says he travelled round the coasts and ports of England and he probably also visited Ireland and the Channel Islands, and the latter when a boy. In 1726, on becoming a liveryman of the Painter–Stainers he presented them with the large canvas still at Painters Hall, based on van de Velde's portrait of

the *Royal Sovereign* (NMM). He also painted a large view of the fleet in the Downs for the Foundling Hospital, and five large sea pieces in the famous 'supper-box' series at Vauxhall Gardens. These are all lost but the Vauxhall pictures are known from engravings. There are twenty-one paintings, with further drawings, by him in the National Maritime Museum and many others in public and private hands.

About 1730 Monamy's portrait, with him holding a small shipwreck scene, was painted by Thomas Stubley (priv. coll., Jersey). When it was engraved in mezzotint by John Faber junior in 1731, the Latin inscription fairly described him as 'painter of ships and marine prospects, only second to van de Velde'. The print was re-engraved for Walpole's *Anecdotes of Painting* in 1771 (in reverse) and again in 1826. There are two versions of a portrait of him, about 1729, showing a sea piece to a patron, Thomas Walker, with the figures by his friend Hogarth and the seascape by himself: one was Walpole's and is now at Knowsley Hall, near Liverpool, the other is in the Art Institute of Chicago.

Monamy died at his 'dwelling house, next to King Henry VII Chapel in Old Palace Yard', and was buried on 7 February 1749 in St Margaret's, Westminster. He left 'many paintings begun and unfinished', wrote Vertue. 'His works being done for dealers at moderate prices—kept him in but indifferent circumstances to his end' (Vertue, *Note books*, 3.145). On 26 July 1750 his pictures and possessions, including ship models, 'prints and drawings, amongst which are many by William Vandervelde Senior & Junior' were auctioned at his house, prior to its being re-let (Harrison-Wallace, 'Peter Monamy', 113 n. 7). Of his children Anne married Thomas Cornwall in 1745. Their son, the Revd Peter Monamy Cornwall (1747–1828), a scholar of Westminster and Trinity College, Cambridge, later added Durell to his forenames and was for forty years headmaster of the grammar school at Wotton under Edge. Mary married the marine painter Francis Swaine on 29 June 1749 at All Hallows. Their second son, Monamy Swaine, was also a notable marine artist.

PIETER VAN DER MERWE

Sources C. Harrison-Wallace, 'Peter Monamy', *Annual Bulletin* [Société Jersiaise], 23/1 (1981), 97–114 • C. Harrison-Wallace, *Peter Monamy, 1681–1749, marine artist* (1983) [exhibition catalogue, Pallant House, Chichester] • E. H. H. Archibald, *The dictionary of sea painters of Europe and America*, 3rd edn (2000) • A. Russett, 'Peter Monamy's marine paintings for Vauxhall Gardens', *Mariner's Mirror*, 80 (1994), 79–84 • Vertue, *Note books*, 3.14, 145, 157 • P. Van der Merwe, 'Peter Monamy, 1681–1749, and his circle', by F. B. Cockett', *Mariner's Mirror*, 87 (2001), 496 [review]

Likenesses W. Hogarth and P. Monamy, oils, c.1729 (with Thomas Walker), Knowsley Hall, near Liverpool • attrib. W. Hogarth and P. Monamy, oils, c.1729 (with Thomas Walker), Art Institute of Chicago • T. Stubley, oils, c.1730, priv. coll. • J. Faber junior, mezzotint, 1731 (after portrait by T. Stubley), BM, NPG

Monan [St Monan] (*fl.* **6th–7th cent.**), supposed holy man, gave his name to the church of St Monance (or St Monans) in Fife, Scotland. His feast day is 1 March but his dates are unknown; probably he lived in the sixth or seventh century. Of his life virtually nothing is known. *Breviarium*

Aberdonense, published in Edinburgh in 1509–10, states that he was a native of Pannonia 'in Hungary' and a companion of St Adrian who was present when Adrian was martyred by 'vikings' on the Isle of May (where King David I founded a Cluniac, later Benedictine, priory dedicated to St Adrian, between 1142 and 1153). Monan then went to Inverey in Fife (now St Monance) and founded a chapel there, where he was buried. The chapel was rebuilt by David II (*r.* 1329–71) and endowed with lands on 3 April 1370. According to *Breviarium Aberdonense*, this was because David recovered from battle wounds there after praying to St Monan.

Monan's Pannonian origin can be safely discounted, as can the exotic oriental origins claimed for a number of saints venerated in Scotland (for example, St Adrian, St Serf, St Boniface of Rosemarkie, St Regulus); in St Monan's case, they arise because of the unusual spelling of the name of his supposed companion, St Adrian, who is also claimed as a Pannonian. The name Adrian appears in fact to be a corruption of the Pictish name Edarnon or Ethernan.

The Irish martyrologies place a St Moenenn at 1 March; this appears to be the genitive of an -n stem, nominative Moenú. The death of Moenú, bishop of Cluain ferta Brenainn (Clonfert), is recorded in the annals of Ulster, s.a. 572. It is not clear whether St Monance in Fife represents a dedication to St Moenú of Clonfert, or a commemoration of a local saint whose feast day has been assimilated. In the sixteenth century St Monan was confused with St Ninian, because of the hypocoristic form of the latter's name, Mo Ninn. This is, however, unrelated; the first-syllable stress in the name Monan shows that it cannot be a compound of *mo* (literally 'my', but used hypocoristically of many saints) and a name beginning in *nin-* or *nan-*. It is possible, however, that the initial m- does represent hypocoristic *mo*, followed by a name beginning with a vowel.

ALAN MACQUARRIE

Sources *Breviarium Aberdonense* (1509–10), Pars Hiemalis, fols. 59v-60r · *Ann. Ulster* · W. J. Watson, *The history of the Celtic place-names of Scotland* (1926), 294–5 · J. M. Thomson and others, eds., *Registrum magni sigilli regum Scotorum / The register of the great seal of Scotland*, 11 vols. (1882–1914), vol. 1, no. 304, pp. 107–8 · I. B. Cowan and D. E. Easson, *Medieval religious houses: Scotland*, 2nd edn (1976), 120–21 · A. Boyle, 'Notes on Scottish saints', *Innes Review*, 32 (1981), 59–82, esp. 66 · S. Taylor, 'Place names and the early church in eastern Scotland', *Scotland in dark age Britain*, ed. B. E. Crawford (1996), 93–110

Monash, Sir John (1865–1931), army officer and engineer, was born at Richhill Terrace in West Melbourne, Victoria, Australia, on 27 June 1865, eldest of the three children and only son of Louis Monash (1831–1894), a shopkeeper, and his wife, Bertha, *née* Manasse (1841–1885), both Jewish–German immigrants from Krotoschin, Posen, Poland. The young Monash grew up in the Melbourne suburbs of Richmond and Hawthorn in a bilingual German–English household, apart from an interlude from 1875 to 1877 which the family spent at Jerilderie in rural New South Wales where John acquired a lifelong passion for the bush.

Monash was first educated at St Stephen's Church of

Sir John Monash (1865–1931), by Walter Stoneman, 1918

England School, Richmond, Victoria (1872–4), and Jerilderie public school, New South Wales (1875–7). He then attended Scotch College, Melbourne (1877–81), where he was studious and poor at games, but a fair pianist and a good runner. He matriculated at the University of Melbourne in 1882 and eventually took degrees in engineering (1891 and 1893) and arts and law (1895). In his early years at the university his academic work suffered as he spent too much time at the theatre, chasing women, reading on subjects outside the syllabus, and participating in student politics and the university company of the Victorian rifles. He was slim, darkly handsome, charming, very eloquent, and about 5 feet 9 inches tall. In 1886 he found work helping construct the Princes Bridge over the River Yarra and for three years from 1888, despite his youth and still not having his degree, he was appointed to supervise construction of Melbourne's outer circle eastern metropolitan railway. The logistical, leadership, and management skills he thus acquired never left him.

On 8 April 1891, after a heady affair with a married gentile woman, he married 20-year-old Hannah Victoria Moss (1871–1920), and their only child, Bertha, was born in 1893. When depression hit the state of Victoria, Monash took a humdrum post with the Melbourne Harbour Trust but he was retrenched in 1894. Forced into private practice with J. T. Noble Anderson, he eked out a living with occasional minor contracts, but eventually found more rewarding work as an advocate and expert witness in legal–engineering cases. Things looked up from 1898 when Anderson purchased for the firm the Victorian agency for Monier reinforced concrete construction, giving it a virtual monopoly in this latest building technique. It was a stroke of genius, and despite various reverses including the collapse of one of the firm's bridges at Bendigo, Monash had become wealthy enough by 1910 to undertake a long overseas trip to Europe and the United States and even to contemplate early retirement. He moved to a grand house, Iona, in St George's Road, Toorak, Victoria, in 1912.

Monash's consuming private passion was citizen soldiering. In 1886, when the university company disbanded, he joined the garrison artillery, responsible for the harbour defences, was commissioned a year later, and rose to captain in 1895, and major and battery commander in 1897. There he remained for eleven years, before being promoted lieutenant-colonel in 1908 in charge of the Victorian section of the newly formed Australian intelligence corps (militia). Monash initiated a vigorous programme of military mapping, attended schools in military science at the University of Sydney, and wrote a prize-winning essay on the Wilderness campaign of 1864. In 1913 he was made colonel and commander of the 13th infantry brigade. As early as 1894, as a young lieutenant (and professional engineer) addressing the United Services Institution of Victoria, he had adumbrated a key element of his military philosophy: physical force and individual courage had been replaced by 'the perfect unity' of 'forces … acting together as a machine'. Good leadership would ensure the machine's optimal operation. A training pamphlet Monash wrote along these lines in 1913, *100 Hints for Company Officers*, eventually became a classic, and the efficiency it helped engender during manoeuvres in early 1914 won the praise of visiting Inspector-General Sir Ian Hamilton.

When war broke out, Monash was appointed after a month as deputy chief censor to command the 4th infantry brigade, Australian Imperial Force (AIF). To his pro-German cousin in the United States he wrote: 'I am Australian born … my whole interests and sympathies are British … in this horrible war … every man … must do his best for his country' (Serle, *John Monash*, 202). Monash's brigade was in the reserve during the Gallipoli landings of 25 April 1915 and took its place in the line over the ensuing week. On the night of 2–3 May, against Monash's better judgement, they were thrown unprepared into a disastrous assault on the key position of Baby 700. The correspondent Charles Bean described this experience as leaving Monash 'unstrung, as well it might' (Serle, *John Monash*, 220), though Monash and the brigade recovered sufficiently to help repel the major Turkish attack on 19 May. In July Monash was promoted to brigadier-general.

Monash's bleakest time of the war came on the nights of 6–7 and 7–8 August 1915. With the New Zealanders and Indians, 4th brigade made a hopelessly optimistic attempt to take the critical Sari Bair Ridge. The New Zealand guides steered Monash's men up the wrong gully, and Monash, whose eye for ground was uncanny, found himself unable to do anything about the error, as he had been ordered to place himself too far back in the column to discover it. Daylight found them in impossible terrain and very exposed, though they held the position. An ill-judged push the next night was foredoomed and the 4th brigade were forced to leave their wounded in the chaos of the retreat. Overwrought, and frustrated at the poor planning of his superiors, Monash momentarily lost his grip—'I thought I could command men' (Rhodes James, 272), he told a Gurkha major. But Bean reported percipiently that men were saying that, given the chance, Monash the gifted planner 'would command a division better than a brigade and a corps better than a division' (Serle, *John Monash*, 251).

His opportunity came in July 1916, when Monash was made major-general and commander of the 3rd division, then assembling on Salisbury Plain. Dubbed 'deep thinkers' for their lateness in enlisting, or 'Lark Hill lancers' by Australians already at the front, these generally older men responded well to Monash's solid training regimen and they impressed George V at a review the publicity conscious Monash arranged at Bulford Field. Monash was lucky to miss the battle of the Somme and to benefit from the doctrinal lessons derived from it, such as 'the limited objective', more complex and continuing artillery and machine gun support, detailed and realistic rehearsals, proper comforts and medical evacuation, and, above all, sound planning and its percolation through to all ranks.

Monash's first battle as divisional commander was Sir Herbert Plumer's great victory at Messines in June 1917, during which the untried 3rd division was entrusted with the important southern flank. On 4 October he won a notable victory at Broodseinde by using leap-frogging tactics to maintain pressure on the enemy, but two weeks later his division suffered the mud and carnage of Passchendaele. In March 1918 the division moved very quickly to plug a 10-mile hole in the line before Amiens, helping to blunt the German spring offensive. During these battles Monash developed his habit of remaining at his headquarters, 'seeing through other men's eyes', and sustaining directive control (Pedersen, 158).

1st Anzac corps had been formed in November 1917. On 1 June 1918 Field Marshal Haig, who had been watching Monash for some time, promoted him lieutenant-general in command of the corps, thus satisfying Australian desire to have their corps under Australian command, just as the Canadians had been under a Canadian since June 1917. Monash more than rewarded Haig's trust. On 4 July—a date whose significance was not lost on Monash, who arranged to have some American troops under his command for the battle—Monash fought a model setpiece, 'limited objective' action at Hamel. Nothing was left to chance in an all-arms, co-ordinated effort which anticipated the warfare of twenty years later. Everyone knew his role. The German defenders were blinded by smoke. Tank crews fraternized with the infantry well beforehand, and their tanks were used in unprecedentedly close support of the infantry, not only with firepower, but also by transporting a great deal of ammunition and by crushing the wire. Aircraft masked the sound of the approaching tanks, strafed the German line, and dropped ammunition to forward positions. The artillery and machine-gun fireplans were superlative and each battalion carried thirty Lewis guns. It was all over in 93 minutes, at a cost of 1400 casualties on each side; 1600 German prisoners were taken and 177 German machine guns captured.

As Monash later wrote in his *The Australian Victories in France, 1918* (1920): 'A perfected modern battle plan is like nothing so much as a score for an orchestral composition, where the various arms and units are the instruments and the tasks they perform are their respective musical phrases' (Pedersen, 232). And again: 'the true role of the Infantry … was to advance under the maximum possible protection of the maximum possible array of mechanical resources' (ibid., 166–7). This was the war-winning formula of the British expeditionary force (BEF) by 1918 and Monash, a modern 'scientific' general, and his Australian corps were among its leading exponents. They played a central role in the break-out battle of Amiens on 8 August—Ludendorff's 'black day of the German army'—and went on to the more fluid battles of Mont-St Quentin and Péronne on 1–2 September. Finally, with 200,000 men under his control, Monash helped breach the Hindenburg line near Bellicourt a month later. A rest period followed, and the armistice came before the Australians were again required in the line. Under Monash in 1918 Anzac corps constituted less than a tenth of the BEF but they captured over a fifth of the enemies' ground, prisoners, and guns.

Monash had been made CB in the new year honours of 1916 and KCB in January 1918. His finest moment came when the king conferred his knighthood on the steps of the Anzac corps headquarters at the Château de Bertangles on 12 August 1918—600 men formed a guard of honour and hundreds of trophies of war, from howitzers to searchlights, were dragged into the courtyard for the occasion.

Monash, who supervised the repatriation of the AIF, returned himself in November 1919 to a hero's welcome. This was marred, however, by his wife's death on 27 February 1920. Four months later, having disposed of his engineering company, he became general manager of the state electricity commission of Victoria; and he spent the next decade rescuing the Yallourn brown coal project and establishing Victoria's electricity grid. Much to the relief of the politicians, who feared his huge popularity, Monash eschewed politics, but he was always ready to speak on behalf of returned soldiers. He died at his home, Iona, St George's Road, Toorak, of coronary vascular disease on 8 October 1931. Some 250,000 people attended his state funeral and he was buried in Brighton cemetery, Melbourne, on 11 October. The military commentator Sir Basil Liddell Hart perhaps exaggerated a little when he wrote in an obituary that Monash 'probably had the greatest capacity for command in modern war among all who held command' (Serle, *John Monash*, 377) in the BEF, but that he deemed Monash a contender is praise enough. Another tribute came in 1958 with the establishment of the university in Victoria that carries his name. CARL BRIDGE

Sources G. Serle, *John Monash: a biography* (1982) · P. A. Pedersen, *Monash as military commander* (Melbourne, 1985) · G. Serle, 'Monash, Sir John', *AusDB*, vol. 10 · P. A. Pedersen, 'General Sir John Monash: corps commander on the western front', *The commanders*, ed. D. M. Horner (Sydney, 1984) · P. Dennis and others, 'Monash, General John', *The Oxford companion to Australian military history* (1995), 404–6 · J. Terraine, *The smoke and the fire* (1981) · E. M. Andrews, *The Anzac illusion: Anglo-Australian relations during World War I* (1993) · J. Grey, *A military history of Australia*, rev. edn (1999) · C. E. W. Bean and others, *The official history of Australia in the war of 1914–1918*, 12 vols. (1921–43) · R. Rhodes James, *Gallipoli* (1965) · B. Liddell Hart, *Through the fog of war* (1938)

Archives Australian War Memorial, Canberra, papers · NL Aus., papers | Australian War Memorial, Canberra, C. E. W. Bean papers · Australian War Memorial, Canberra, Field Marshal Lord Birdwood papers · King's Lond., B. H. Liddell Hart papers · NL Aus., Sir Keith Murdoch papers | FILM Australian War Memorial, Canberra · BFI NFTVA, documentary footage · IWM FVA, 'King's visit to France, August 1918', Topical Film Company, 1918, IWM 289 · IWM FVA, actuality footage · IWM FVA, documentary footage | SOUND Australian War Memorial, Canberra · IWM SA, oral history interview

Likenesses W. Stoneman, photograph, 1918, NPG [*see illus.*] · I. M. Cohen, oils, *c*.1919, National Gallery of Victoria, Melbourne · J. Longstaff, oils, *c*.1919, Australian War Memorial, Canberra · J. Quinn, oils, *c*.1919, Australian War Memorial, Canberra · J. S. Sargent, group portrait, oils, 1922 (*General officers of World War I*), NPG · P. Mountford, bronze bust, 1928, Australian War Memorial, Canberra · P. White, oils, *c*.1928, State Electricity Commission, Melbourne, Monash House · W. L. Bowles, bust, *c*.1934, Australian War Memorial, Canberra · W. L. Bowles, equestrian statue, The Domain, Melbourne

Wealth at death approx. £27,000: Serle, *John Monash*, 533

Monboddo. For this title name *see* Burnett, James, Lord Monboddo (*bap.* 1714, *d.* 1799).

Monck, Charles Stanley, fourth Viscount Monck of Ballytrammon (1819–1894), governor-general of Canada, was born at Templemore, co. Tipperary, Ireland, on 10 October 1819, the eldest son of Charles Joseph Kelly Monck, third Viscount Monck of Ballytrammon (1791–1849), a barrister, and Bridget (*d.* 1843), the youngest daughter of John Willington of Killoskehane, co. Tipperary. Educated at Trinity College, Dublin, he graduated BA in 1841, and was called to the Irish bar at King's Inns in June of the same year. On 22 July 1844 he married his cousin Elizabeth Louisa Mary (*d.* 1892), the fourth daughter of Henry Stanley Monck, first earl of Rathdowne. They had two sons, of whom the elder, Henry Power, succeeded to the peerage, and two daughters, including Frances, whose *Canadian Leaves* is an interesting account of the country in 1864–5. On 20 April 1849 Monck succeeded as fourth viscount in the Irish peerage.

In 1848 Monck unsuccessfully contested the county of Wicklow as a Liberal, but he was elected member for Portsmouth in July 1852. He became a lord of the Treasury in Lord Palmerston's government (7 March 1855) and held the office until the government fell in 1858. Defeated in the general election of 1859, he decided to leave active politics.

On 30 August 1861 Monck was appointed by Palmerston captain-general and governor-in-chief of Canada and governor-in-chief of British North America. Scarcely had he entered on his duties on 28 November than news broke of the *Trent* affair, which threatened to embroil England

Charles Stanley Monck, fourth Viscount Monck of Ballytrammon (1819–1894), by John Watkins, 1868

and the United States in a war. Monck's considerable diplomatic skill dispelled the cloud. Three years later more serious trouble arose, when certain confederates, having found refuge in Canada during the American civil war, plotted to turn their asylum into a basis for petty attacks on the United States. By patrolling the 2000 mile long frontier and setting small armed craft on the Great Lakes, Monck kept the peace between the nations and received the approbation of the imperial authorities, although not of the United States. Controversy flared up again in 1865, when the reciprocity treaty of 1854 was denounced by America. The American government also suffered, if it did not encourage, the armed attacks of the Fenian Brotherhood against British North America. Once more the militia was called out and the frontier patrolled. At the Niagara peninsula some nine hundred Fenians attacked Canadian territory and were repulsed with considerable loss by the militia on 2 June 1866. Difficulties with the United States continued for most of Monck's term of office, but his shrewdness and practical common sense helped him guide the colonies peacefully through the crises.

Monck was also a strong proponent of the confederation of all British North American colonies, and, in 1864, urged on the Canadian cabinet the forming of the 'Great Coalition', devised to carry the project. He also took an active interest in the conferences on the subject held at Charlottetown and Quebec (1864), and in the conduct of the Quebec resolutions, which embodied the federal constitution, through the Canadian houses of parliament (1865). Likewise he brought his influence to bear in favour

of the union on the lieutenant-governors of Nova Scotia and New Brunswick. In the autumn of 1866 he went to England to assist at the Westminster conference and advise the imperial authorities. On 4 June following, his appointment was renewed under 30 Vict. c. 3, and his title declared to be governor-general of the dominion of Canada. He took the oath of office and constituted the privy council of Canada on 1 July 1867. Having thus inaugurated the federation successfully, he resigned office on 13 November 1868.

On 12 July 1866 Monck was created a peer of the United Kingdom as Baron Monck of Ballytrammon, co. Wexford. To reward his achievements in Canada, he was created a knight grand cross of St Michael and St George on 23 June 1869, and was called to the privy council on 7 August the same year. In 1870 Trinity College, Dublin, awarded him the degree of LLD. After his return to Ireland Monck was appointed a member of the church temporalities and national education commissions (1871); he continued to administer the former until 1881. The following year he was chosen to effect the Irish Land Acts, and sat on the commission until 1884. From 1874 to 1892 he was lord lieutenant and *custos rotulorum* in and for the county of Dublin. He died at his home at Charleville, Enniskerry, co. Wicklow, on 29 November 1894.

T. B. Browning, *rev.* Jacques Monet

Sources W. L. Morton, *The critical years: the union of British North America, 1857–1873* (1964) · R. H. Hubbard, *Rideau Hall* (1967) · E. Batt, *Monck: governor general, 1861–1868* (1976) · F. Monck, *My Canadian leaves: an account of a visit to Canada in 1864–5* (1891) · Burke, *Peerage* (1890) · R. G. Trotter, 'Lord Monck and the Great Coalition of 1864', *Canadian Historical Review*, 3 (1922), 181–6 · C. P. Stacey, 'Lord Monck and the Canadian nation', *Dalhousie Review*, 14 (1934–5), 179–91 · *CGPLA Eng. & Wales* (1895)
Archives NA Canada, corresp. and papers · NL Ire., corresp. and papers · NRA, priv. coll., corresp. and papers · University of British Columbia Library, Vancouver, diary [copy] | BL, corresp. with duke of Buckingham, Add. MSS 41860, 43742 · BL, corresp. with W. E. Gladstone, Add. MSS 44375–44388 · Bodl. Oxf., corresp. with Lord Kimberly · New Brunswick Museum, Saint John, corresp. with Sir William Fenwick Williams · PRO, corresp. with Lord Carnarvon, 30/6 · U. Nott., corresp. with duke of Newcastle
Likenesses J. Watkins, photograph, 1868, NA Canada [*see illus.*] · oils, Rideau Hall, Ottawa, Canada · photographs, NA Canada · wood-engraving, NPG; repro. in *ILN* (3 Feb 1867) · wood-engraving, NPG; repro. in *ILN* (6 March 1869)
Wealth at death £40,391 0s. 9d.: probate, 19 Jan 1895, *CGPLA Eng. & Wales*

Monck, Christopher, second duke of Albemarle (1653–1688), army officer and colonial governor, was born in London on 14 August 1653, the only surviving son of George *Monck (1608–1670), first duke of Albemarle and the general whose army and political influence helped make possible the restoration of Charles II in 1660, and his seamstress wife, Anne Radford, *née* Clarges (1619–1670). Monck struggled all his life to equal his father's distinction in both military and political affairs. At first, however, birth and title brought him a succession of offices and honours: knight of the Garter in 1670, when he also inherited the ducal title, colonel of a foot regiment (1673), privy councillor (1675), lord lieutenant of Devon and (jointly) of both Essex (1675) and Wiltshire (1681), and colonel of the Queen's regiment in 1678. On 30 December 1669 he married Lady Elizabeth Cavendish (1654–1734), eldest daughter of Henry Cavendish, second duke of Newcastle, and his wife, Frances Pierrepoint. In the 1670s he was a member of the duke of Monmouth's violent gang of young rakes, and in 1671 both men had to take out pardons for the killing of a beadle during a brawl in a brothel. Albemarle tried unsuccessfully to see active service in the wars of 1673 and 1678. In the Popish Plot and exclusion crises he remained completely loyal to the king, and was rewarded with honours taken from the disgraced duke of Monmouth: colonel of Horse Guards in 1679 and chancellor of Cambridge University in 1682. By then, however, his extravagant lifestyle forced him to sell his London residence, Albemarle House, and his wife was showing the first signs of the intermittent insanity which was to last for the rest of her life.

Then in 1685 came Albemarle's great opportunity to prove himself the equal as a soldier of his renowned father. The duke of Monmouth landed at Lyme Regis in Dorset to begin his rebellion against the newly crowned James II, and as commander of the Devon militia Albemarle found himself responsible for the government's initial response, which might have snuffed out the rising before it had really begun. In this he signally failed. Troops of his militia were successively chased out of Bridport, Axminster, and Bridgwater, and Lyme Regis and Taunton were both occupied by him long after the rebels had left. For most of the rebellion his troops were several days' march distant from the rebels, and Colonel John Churchill (later duke of Marlborough) complained to the king about this lack of offensive spirit. Finally, Albemarle missed the climax at Sedgemoor because he had rushed back to Exeter upon a wild rumour that the French were about to land and attack the town. Ordered to obey the earl of Feversham (commander of the king's regular troops in the west) in all things, angry at the promotion of the energetic Colonel John Churchill, and upbraided by the king for his slack performance, Albemarle resigned his army commission and his lord lieutenancies, and after sulking in the countryside for a year in worsening health he unexpectedly begged and received the governorship of Jamaica, which had become vacant in 1686.

This move was connected with Albemarle's leading role in a successful expedition to recover the treasure of a sunken Spanish galleon. From this venture he may have netted anything up to £40,000, but though his fortune was thus restored he did not live long to enjoy it. On arriving in Jamaica in December 1687 he was soon embroiled in fierce local disputes relating to the suppression of piracy and to the power of the court-backed Royal Africa Company over the settlers. These stresses, together with continued heavy drinking and an enervating tropical climate, plus the bleeding prescribed by his physician, Dr Hans Sloane, steadily weakened him, and he died on 6 October 1688 in his thirty-sixth year. His body was brought back to England for burial in Westminster Abbey on 4 July 1689. Albemarle had no children, and conflicting wills dating from

1675 and 1687 led to prolonged legal disputes, with his father's friend the earl of Bath ultimately benefiting. His widow married Ralph Montagu, first duke of Montagu, in 1692, but they too had no children.   ROBIN CLIFTON

Sources E. F. Ward, *Christopher Monck, duke of Albemarle* (1915) • R. Clifton, *The last popular rebellion* (1984) • DNB • CSP dom., 1670–88 • will, PRO, DEL 10/30
Archives Palace House Archives, Beaulieu, corresp. • PRO, legal, estate, and personal corresp. and papers, C 107/25–29, 61–62; C 116/2–8, 163–171, 174, 183–188 | PRO, corresp. relating to testamentary dispute, PROB 36/5
Likenesses L. Crosse, miniature, 1680, priv. coll. • T. Murray, oils, c.1682, probably Old Schools, Cambridge • I. Beckett, mezzotint (after T. Murray), BM, NPG • G. Bower, silver medal, BM
Wealth at death under £100,000: Ward, *Christopher Monck*

Monck [Monk], **George, first duke of Albemarle** (1608–1670), army officer and naval officer, the fourth child and second son of a Devon gentleman, Sir Thomas Monck, was born at the latter's manor house of Great Potheridge, north Devon, on 6 December 1608. He was baptized at the nearby parish church of Landcross five days later. His mother was Elizabeth, daughter of one of the richest Exeter merchants, Sir George Smyth of Maydworthy. This classic alliance between old lineage and new money reaped an extra dividend when Sir Thomas found himself too encumbered by debt to be capable of supporting young George, and the boy was sent to the Smyths for a time to be brought up. Of his education it is only known that one biographer, Skinner, stated that he attended an unnamed local school.

The younger son, 1608–1641 Given his situation it is hardly surprising that Monck turned to one of the most obvious ways of earning a living then open to a younger son of impoverished gentry: the profession of arms. It was a profession, moreover, which clearly suited his own temperament. In 1625, when just sixteen, he volunteered to join the English expedition against Cadiz. He is known to have accompanied his cousin Sir Richard Grenville, who commanded a foot company, but it is not clear whether he served in that company or indeed what part he played in the campaign. He was also involved in the next English military expedition, for the relief of La Rochelle in 1627. This time Monck had a further reason to join the army, to escape a prosecution for homicide. In September 1626 he and his elder brother had met in a tavern in Exeter an under-sheriff who had arrested their father for debt. They cudgelled the man and George, chasing him into the street, stabbed him as he was lying fallen on the ground, thrusting so hard 'that his sworde turned almost double' (Stoyle, 'Early incident', 13). The under-sheriff later died of his wounds. The incident, toned down to a richly deserved thrashing administered by the outraged George, became part of the story of how he became a soldier told by his earliest biographers.

On the expedition to relieve La Rochelle, Monck was once again associated with Grenville, this time being formally commissioned as an ensign in the foot regiment of Sir John Burroughs, where Sir Richard served as a captain. The youth distinguished himself by bravely carrying the

George Monck, first duke of Albemarle (1608–1670), by Sir Peter Lely and studio

the form of two vivid stories designed to emphasize his physical courage and his savage and impulsive temper.

After the second expedition to France, Monck vanishes completely from the records for three years, to reappear in 1631. Once again he was serving as an ensign, but this time in the foot regiment of the earl of Oxford, employed in the Dutch forces operating against the Spanish in the Netherlands. He presumably shared in the prominent part played by that unit at the siege of Maastricht in 1632, where Oxford was killed. By 1634 his reputation had grown to the point at which the new colonel, George Goring, gave him command of its largest company, with the rank of captain-lieutenant. No trace of him is then found for another three years, until the celebrated siege of Breda in 1637. Monck became one of the heroes of that event, leading the storming of the breach in a hornwork which precipitated the surrender of the town. Having won this distinction he proceeded to throw away any immediate advantage in a fit of rage. His regiment had been assigned to winter quarters at Dordrecht (Dort), where some of its men were accused of misconduct towards the townspeople. He insisted that they be tried by court martial, but the states general determined that the city magistrates would hear the case. Monck subsequently resigned his commission in disgust and returned to England, presumably early in 1638.

It was fortunate for Monck that within a year Charles I had gone to war against the Scottish covenanters and so furnished him with an excellent opportunity for employment at home. He received with it promotion to the rank of lieutenant-colonel in the foot regiment of the earl of Newport; but like most of Charles's army he saw no action before his men were disbanded after the treaty at Berwick in June 1639. With the resumption of war in 1640 his command and his unit were restored together, and this time he was invited to participate at times in the army's council of war. He was at Newburn on 28 August when the Scots routed the English advance guard, and was the only officer in it to win credit; he saved the ordnance by deploying his regiment to cover its retreat. This, however, did nothing to save the war, and, although Monck was later said to have urged its continuation, the king sued for peace. George was left with another bitter memory of incompetent English generalship.

Monck was also left unemployed again, and passed another year in obscurity until the Irish rising of October 1641 opened a new theatre of war. The newly appointed lord lieutenant of Ireland was the earl of Leicester, who happened to be a kinsman of Monck, a relationship augmented by a personal friendship which George had developed with the earl's son Lord Lisle. This piece of luck, compounded by Monck's conduct at Newburn, won him the position of colonel of the foot regiment which the earl himself raised as part of the expeditionary force sent against the rebels. In this fashion Monck attained the rank of a regimental commander at the age of thirty-three, a respectable though not sensational achievement for a man of his social origins. It was more remarkable that he had gained such a varied experience of warfare, including

colours in an unsuccessful attack on a French fort. Grenville later credited him also with having carried a message from the king in England to the commander of the expedition, the duke of Buckingham, which involved a daring passage through the French royal army besieging La Rochelle. As a firsthand witness, Sir Richard's account must be respected, but it is hard to understand how such an obscure youth could have been chosen for such an important mission. The death of Burroughs during the campaign opened the way to promotion for them both. When a second expedition to La Rochelle was launched in 1628 Grenville had been made colonel of the regiment and Monck commanded a company, but the English force was never landed and they had no opportunity to see action.

These three campaigns represented an important initial experience of warfare for George Monck. All were complete failures, which in later years he remembered with anger and bitterness. They remained object lessons for him in incompetent leadership, even while they provided a crucial practical training. It is also significant that when others later recalled his connection with them it was in participation in some notably dangerous actions, without sustaining a wound. He had proved himself a brave and steady officer, and also a lucky one.

The earl's commander, 1642–1644 Monck's regiment landed at Dublin on 21 February 1642, and with 1200 men it was one of the largest to operate in the British Isles during the decade. It was immediately added to the royal army based in the city under the earl of Ormond, who chose George to command the 2500 foot soldiers in that force. They marched together in April to relieve the settlements holding out against the rebels in western Leinster. Monck distinguished himself by a feint which enabled Ormond's army to cross the River Nore on the 12th, and he showed notable courage in the action which forced the passage of the Barrow three days later. After the return to Dublin, Monck was employed until the end of the year on a series of raids into rebel occupied territory to the west, on which he relieved loyal castles and reduced and destroyed those held by enemies, and burnt houses and hanged prisoners with the ruthlessness common in this war. He defeated a rebel force in another skirmish at Tymachoe in December. In June 1642 his patron Leicester tried to appoint him to govern Dublin itself, but King Charles preferred another man.

This experience could have done nothing to endear his monarch further to Monck, and his loyalty was strained further by the outbreak of the English civil war in late 1642. In this conflict Leicester was more or less neutral, Lisle a parliamentarian, and Ormond a royalist. It is not surprising that Monck was among the officers who urged successfully that the royal army in Ireland should take no oaths of allegiance to either side. Ormond made him commander of the foot once again in the expeditionary force which set out to relieve Wexford on 1 March 1643. On the 3rd he was detached to reduce the rebel garrison at Timolin and used a field gun to do so, being his first recorded employment of artillery. On the 18th he took part in the repulse of a rebel army at Old Ross. After the successful return of the expedition he returned to leading raids, failing to save some besieged castles in co. Kildare in June, ravaging co. Wicklow in August, and facing enemy forces in co. Meath in September. The relative lack of achievement during these sallies reflected the manner in which the rebels, less well trained and equipped, were now preferring guerrilla warfare to pitched battles.

Monck's first stint of Irish service ended abruptly on 15 September 1643, when Ormond concluded an armistice with the rebels, which freed the royal army in Ireland for deployment against Charles's English opponents. The earl now demanded that its officers swear unequivocal allegiance to the king, and Monck refused. As a result he was dismissed from his command and sent a prisoner to Bristol with a letter from Ormond extolling his virtues and expressing the hope that he would give proof of his loyalty. Charles duly sent for him and gave him a personal interview at Oxford in which Monck won the king's trust sufficiently to be commissioned to raise and command a new foot regiment which would be added to those now sent over from Ireland.

Monck rejoined the latter on 24 January 1644 at the siege of Nantwich in Cheshire, just as a parliamentarian relief force was approaching. The royalists were outnumbered, divided by a river, and caught between the oncoming army and the garrison, but their commander, Lord Byron, still committed them to battle on the 25th. Monck had not yet recruited any men of his own, and so rejoined his former regiment as a volunteer. He led it into a charge with a pike in his hand, but was surrounded and captured as the parliamentarians overwhelmed the royalist units. Having so recently and reluctantly decided to engage himself in the king's cause, he now found himself a prisoner of parliament. His known experience and ability, moreover, made him seem a particularly dangerous one. For six months he was held at Hull, and was then sent to London where, on 8 July, the House of Commons committed him to the Tower, to remain there during its pleasure. His physical luck had held—once again he had come through a fierce action without a scratch—but in every other respect he had been profoundly unfortunate. For the fifth time he had followed an English royal commander to humiliating defeat, and now it had cost him his liberty.

The parliament's commander, 1645–1649 It was later reported that the king himself contributed to Monck's upkeep in the Tower of London, but it is certain that he depended there upon the generosity of his elder brother, Thomas, who had now inherited their father's estate. It could not have helped his mood that having taken up a military career to stop being a burden upon his indebted family, he was now thrown back upon its resources. Many a prisoner and exile has whiled away time with authorship, and Monck was no exception; he wrote a military manual which was published after his death as *Observations upon Military and Political Affairs*. It is very much the work of a foot commander with a special expertise in siege warfare, and is distinguished by sound sense rather than originality. He placed great stress on logistics and morale, on quartering soldiers in purpose-built accommodation, and on the importance of outworks to fortresses and of mining to siegecraft. His comments upon the context in which wars were fought were generally platitudes, although it speaks for his breadth of vision that he attempted to provide them at all. With understandable bitterness he asserted that civil wars could be prevented only if governments kept up strong garrisons and full treasuries, prevented differences of opinion in religion, and operated successfully against foreign enemies.

Monck's prospects began to brighten with parliament's final victories over the king in 1646, when old friends made efforts on his behalf. Both Charles's lord lieutenant of Ireland, Ormond, and Lisle, who had now been appointed as his parliamentarian rival, recommended that Monck be sent back to fight the rebels there. Faced with this prospect, and with the English royalist cause clearly lost, Monck certainly proved willing to swear never to fight against parliament again, and probably took the solemn league and covenant, which endorsed its aims in fighting the king. On 12 November the House of Lords resolved that he be released for Irish service. Later tradition had it that on leaving the Tower he secretly promised a fellow royalist prisoner, Bishop Wren, that he would still do his best to serve King Charles, but this remains unconfirmed. What is certain is that promotion came with freedom, for Lisle expressed his confidence in his old companion by making him adjutant-general in the force with which he sailed for Cork in February 1647.

The immediate consequence of the expedition was a political disaster, for the local protestant commanders in Munster refused to accept Lisle's authority, and he returned, frustrated, to England in May 1647. Monck repaid his kindness by supporting him throughout this episode and retiring with him. Parliament was clearly impressed by Monck's conduct, for during the summer it resolved to appoint him to command all the forces loyal to it in eastern Ulster, with the rank of major-general. He landed at Dublin on 5 September 1647 with the promise of £7000 to fund his campaign, but it may be presumed that at least some of the money never arrived; at any rate, his first independent command was marked by nothing except minor raids.

In September 1648 Monck gave the first proof of his abilities, when parliament ordered him to arrest all the officers in Ulster who had supported the king in the second civil war which had been waged in England during the summer. Monck had remained faithful to his engagement to parliament, sitting out the conflict in Ireland, and the crushing victory obtained by his new masters must have confirmed him in his loyalty. He accordingly acted with remarkable speed and decision against those who had sent soldiers to support the royalists, who in the case of Ulster were confined to the leaders of the Scottish army stationed there. Until this point these had been allies in the common cause against the rebels, and they seem to have suspected no danger from him when he suddenly led an attack upon their bases at Belfast and Carrickfergus. Both places were easily overwhelmed, the Scots commander, Robert Munro, being seized in his bed at Carrickfergus and sent as a prisoner to England. The gratitude of parliament was immediate and generous; on 4 October 1648, Monck was voted a personal gift of £500 and was appointed to govern both the captured strong points. These rewards doubtless helped him to accept the execution of Charles I and proclamation of a Commonwealth early in 1649. On 21 March he informed the officers under his command in Ulster that they should sign a declaration of loyalty to the new regime and be prepared to fight anybody who opposed it.

This was, however, easier said than done. Many of his own officers refused to sign the required declaration, while Ormond was building a powerful coalition of Catholic rebels, Scots, and former royalists and parliamentarians to secure Ireland for the exiled Charles II. Monck's soldiers were starved of money and supplies as the Commonwealth concentrated on aims more immediately important to its own survival. In April 1649 he retired to Dundalk, whence he could strike into Ulster or Leinster as required, and from there he watched his achievements

slipping away. Belfast and Carrickfergus were lost to a rising of local Scots allied to Ormond, and with them all eastern Ulster. Monck's last stronghold at Dundalk was itself threatened by the approach of an Irish army under Owen Roe O'Neill; lacking the strength to fight it, Monck employed diplomacy instead. His only advantage lay in the fact that O'Neill was the one Catholic commander who had refused to join Ormond's coalition, finding the security which it offered to his religion to be inadequate. Monck held out to him the somewhat fantastic hope that the Commonwealth would offer him better terms, and the Irishman was desperate enough to listen. After six weeks of talks an armistice was agreed between the two on 8 May 1649, to last three months in order to allow negotiations between O'Neill and the English parliament to proceed. In this interim Monck also promised to sell gunpowder to the Irish. He kept this deal secret from most of his own soldiers, and not until 25 May did he nerve himself to inform the government in England of his action, and to forward the Irish general's proposals. He was perfectly aware that they had no reasonable prospect of acceptance, pleaded direst military necessity in concluding the agreement, and sent this message in the first instance to Oliver Cromwell. The latter had been selected by the new regime in England to lead the reconquest of Ireland, and Monck now pleaded with him to represent his actions to the government with the kindest possible gloss.

It was all in vain. In June 1649 some of O'Neill's men arrived to collect the gunpowder, and this exposed Monck's dealings with the Catholics to his own men. The latter were thus already demoralized when one of Ormond's protestant generals arrived to besiege Dundalk in July. Monck surrendered after just two days on terms which allowed him and his officers to withdraw to England. Only a few, of minor rank, elected to accompany him, the rest defecting to the victors. In this humiliating manner the town was handed over, and his command extinguished, on 17 July.

Monck had now, moreover, to face an inquiry into his conduct. Having landed at Chester on 26 July 1649, he made at once for Milford Haven in another attempt to enlist the support of Cromwell. The two men met on 4 August, and although the event is of historic significance in view of what followed, its only immediate result was that Cromwell formally referred Monck to the council of state. Monck arrived in London forty-eight hours later, and reported to the council on the next day. On 10 August it referred him in turn to the judgment of the house of parliament, which was now the sovereign authority of the Commonwealth. After a long debate, in which Monck spoke in his own defence at the bar of the house, the MPs condemned his dealings with O'Neill. They also resolved, however, that his conduct had been sufficiently excused by his circumstances as to leave him deserving of no worse punishment than a reprimand. The vindictive anger which his failure in Ulster had left in Monck is revealed in a letter which he sent in December to parliament's new commander in the east of the province; he urged the latter to ensure that some of his former officers lost their estates, and that Scottish ministers were never allowed again to preach in the region.

The Commonwealth's commander, 1650–1653 After his reprimand Monck was unemployed once more. Fortunately for him his elder brother had died in 1647 and he had thus now inherited the family lands. They remained encumbered by debts and annuities, but they afforded him a home and an income. He passed the winter quietly in Devon, and then a new campaigning season afforded new opportunities, as the Commonwealth declared war on Scotland. Cromwell was to lead the invasion force, and now the attempts which Monck had made to ingratiate himself with this key soldier paid off handsomely. He was commissioned as a colonel of foot, and joined Cromwell as he advanced northward at the end of June 1650. The invasion meant that he was fighting directly against Charles II, who had been accepted as king in Scotland, but he showed no sign of scruples in doing so, and the animosity which he now bore towards Scotsmen probably sweetened the service. For the first time in his life, also, he was answering directly to an exceptionally fine general.

Cromwell's opinion of his new protégé is vividly illustrated by his determination to find Monck a unit to command. The first regiment to which he was appointed refused to accept him, as a former royalist. Cromwell's prompt reaction was to form another for him from scratch by deducting five companies each from two existing regiments; the new one was formally added to the establishment on 30 July 1650. Monck was also put in effective charge of the artillery train, and distinguished himself on 24 August by leading the capture of a Scottish outpost, Red Hall. He was added to the council of war which planned the battle of Dunbar on 3 September, and during that action played a key part by leading the infantry brigade which attacked the Scottish centre. After the victory he was put to work as a siege expert, attacking the key fortresses of south-eastern Scotland which were now left in the rear of Cromwell's advance. Between November 1650 and March 1651 he reduced the castles of Dirleton, Edinburgh, Tantallon, and Blackness, and was made the military governor of Edinburgh.

For all these services Monck was promoted to the rank of lieutenant-general of the ordnance on 6 May 1651 at the opening of the new summer offensive. When Cromwell's army crossed into Fife, Monck was detached from it to reduce two more strongholds in that region, taking Inchgarvie Castle on 24 July and Burntisland on the 29th. Charles II now made his great gamble of dashing for England with his field army, and Cromwell followed him on 4 August, leaving Monck to continue the conquest of Scotland with 5000 to 6000 men who were reinforced to 12,000 before the end of the year. He bullied Stirling into surrender on 6 August and used mortars to bring in its castle on the 14th. On the 26th he summoned Dundee. Hearing that the provisional government which Charles had left behind him to run Scotland was meeting within striking distance, at Alyth, he sent a party of horse to surprise its members. All were captured on the 28th, thereby repeating the tactic which he had used against Munro in 1648, and leaving Scottish resistance leaderless and fragmented. By 1 September 1651 the defences of Dundee had been breached by bombardment, and Monck had them stormed. He then made an example of the town, allowing no quarter until the market place was reached and giving his men freedom to plunder for twenty-four hours. Up to 800 Scots were killed and sixty shiploads of booty sent to England.

These actions demoralized the Scots, and Monck's forces were able to occupy the rest of the lowlands and seal off the highlands before the end of the year. He began the work of reconciling the conquered population by granting protection to individual notables and setting up courts martial to discipline his soldiers. He himself, however, had fallen seriously ill on 5 September 1651, either because his frenetic activity in August had broken his health, or because of sheer bad luck. In February 1652 he had to resign his command and retire to Bath in order to recover, which he had begun to do by the summer. The council of state made use of him during his convalescence by sending him to inspect the fortifications of Yarmouth. The parliament had also rewarded him with confiscated Scottish land worth £500 a year.

This sudden concern for sea defences was due to the outbreak of war with the Dutch, and, on 26 November 1652, Monck was brought directly into that war by being appointed a general-at-sea. This gamble—of employing his proven talent as an artillery commander in the naval theatre—made him one of the three joint commanders of the English fleet. His colleagues were the experienced sailor Robert Blake, and another artillery expert from the Scottish war, Richard Deane. On 8 February 1653 they joined their ships at the mouth of the Thames, having been instructed to attack a convoy of Dutch merchantmen being escorted home by Van Tromp. Ten days later the latter were located off Portland. Monck, commanding the rear squadron, was separated from the others and took time to reach the battle. Once there he hurled his ships against the Dutch rear, sustaining damage to his own which killed many of his crew, including his captain. Getting the worst of the fight, Van Tromp ran for home and reached it after two more days of pursuit; Monck could fairly be claimed to have turned defeat into victory by his intervention.

After the fleet had been repaired, Monck and Deane set sail again from the Downs on 2 May 1653 and spent a month hunting the North Sea for an enemy. On 2 June Van Tromp's fleet was sighted off Suffolk. Monck and Deane were commanding the central squadron together on the same flagship, which came under heavy fire. Deane was killed at the side of George, who threw his cloak coolly over the body and carried on directing the battle alone, regaining the wind and counter-attacking. On the following day he attacked again, altering his tactics from long- to close-range fire, and chased the enemy back to their ports. For a month, rejoined by Blake, he blockaded the Dutch coast, and then returned to refit. Blake was now taken ill, and on 27 July 1653 Monck resumed the blockade in sole command. Two days later he launched an attack on Van Tromp's fleet off the Texel. High winds delayed a full engagement until the 31st, when the Dutch were routed again and Van Tromp killed. The damage sustained by the English was still considerable, and Monck's fleet had to be refitted. At the end of August he sailed to the Dutch coast again, but found neither an enemy nor prizes, and so took his fleet home to be laid up for the winter.

The battles of 1653 marked a notable episode in British naval history, whereby the fleet gradually abandoned the traditional loose order of combat to sail to the attack in a formal line. This tactic is clearly a copy of methods long used in land warfare. All the three generals-at-sea had been trained on land, but of them Monck was the one in most consistent command, and was in sole charge at the Texel, when the new formation was fully deployed from the start of the engagement. He may therefore plausibly be given the chief credit for it. The innovative pragmatism of his seamanship can be seen in the change of tactics between 2 and 3 June, and he was also noted for the care with which he consulted his flag-officers and took their advice. He may be considered one of the ablest, and most significant, of seventeenth-century English naval leaders, and this is the more impressive in view of his lack of prior experience.

It is also significant that in the course of 1653 Monck had managed to come through three bloody battles unscathed; his passage of the political upheavals of the year was even smoother. In April 1653 Cromwell expelled the regicide parliament, and two days later Monck and Deane issued a formal statement on behalf of their fleet that their concern was with fighting the Dutch, and that therefore they accepted the event without further comment. Monck's attitude towards the nominated assembly of late 1653 was presumably sweetened by the facts that he was named to sit in it as a member for Devon, that it voted him a gold chain worth £300 for his victory off the Texel, and that on 1 October 1653 he received the formal thanks of the assembly for all his services. He now took his seat, but is not recorded as being active in debate. The only glimpse of him at this period is an encounter with a group of unpaid sailors demonstrating in Whitehall: he struck the leader with his sword and persuaded them to desist. Monck seems to have been completely passive during the coup of December, in which the nominated assembly was replaced by the Cromwellian protectorate; but then Cromwell had salvaged his career, and if the assembly had voted him the gold chain, Oliver had hung it round his neck.

This momentous year also saw a further crucially important development in Monck's own life: on 23 January 1653, at St George's, Southwark, he married a Londoner, Anne Radford (1619–1670). She had been born on 25 March 1619, the daughter of a farrier at the Savoy, John Clarges, and his wife, Anne Leaver. On 28 February 1633 she had wed another farrier, Thomas Radford, from whom she separated in 1649. Radford seems then to have disappeared, so that there was no absolute proof of her widowhood when she married Monck. A whiff of scandal thus hung around their union, and even in view of his status as a landed gentleman, let alone as a republican general, he was marrying beneath his class. John Aubrey stated that she had been Monck's seamstress when he was imprisoned in the Tower, and that they had become lovers then. As this had been the only period in which George had lived in London hitherto, there is much plausibility in the story. Theirs was clearly a lasting love match, which was formalized when there seemed reasonable presumption that Radford had gone permanently missing.

The new hammer of the Scots, 1654–1659 On 2 December 1653, Monck's commission as general-at-sea was renewed for the coming year, but the establishment of the protectorate altered his prospects. Cromwell and his advisers wanted peace with the Dutch, while a serious uprising had broken out among Scottish royalists; and on 17 January 1654 Monck was recalled from the fleet to discuss the latter. On 8 April, Cromwell commissioned him as commander-in-chief of all the forces in Scotland, with powers to collect taxes, fine and imprison at will, and issue proclamations. This made him effective dictator of the country, and represented an authority greater than that given to any previous republican general operating there. He was also given about 3000 more soldiers and £50,000 with which to quell the rising.

Monck was thus equipped with considerable legal and physical resources for his new job, and made the most of them. The Scottish rebels were waging a guerrilla war like the Irish before them, and Monck showed that he had learned to the full the lessons furnished by his encounter with similar tactics in Ireland. First he sealed off the highlands, which were the centre and stronghold of the revolt. Then he deployed his army to invade the mountains in separate columns, with sufficient supplies to keep them moving fast through the passes, unhampered by any need to return to bases to revictual. Each soldier had a week's bread in his knapsack, while packhorses carried more bread and cheese with them. In this fashion his divisions marched almost 1000 miles between June and September, burning the crops of the rebels, killing their cattle, and chasing them relentlessly. By autumn, exhausted and starving, they were surrendering in large numbers. A few held out through the winter, but by May 1655 the last had submitted or fled abroad. Monck now stepped over the line between ruthlessness and brutality, by advising the protector and council to execute the leaders, but the latter preferred to pardon them as a gesture of conciliation, and this clemency proved justified.

In September 1655 Monck's dictatorship was ended by the establishment of a council to govern Scotland, on which he sat with some of his officers, English civilians, and Scots, under the presidency of an Anglo-Irishman, Lord Broghill. He retained direct control of the occupying army, and put most of his energy during the next year into fortifying strategic strongpoints while the other councillors settled the civil and religious affairs of the country. He also weeded out officers who expressed doubts concerning the actions of the government. From the autumn of

1656 the most prominent of the council were drawn away to serve in the second protectorate parliament. In 1657 Monck himself was created one of the lords qualified to sit in its 'other house', but never took up the honour. Instead he remained at his post in Scotland, and the departure of other councillors made him once again the dominant figure in the country. He lobbied for a reduction in its level of taxation proportionate to that given to England in this period, and restructured the occupying army on a smaller scale to take account of the fall in funding.

During the second half of the 1650s Monck displayed three overriding concerns in his role as military supremo north of the border. One was to ensure that control of the appointment of officers in his army remained in his own hands as much as possible, turning it into something like a private patronage system. The second was with security. In part this was manifested in the obvious respect of monitoring information concerning possible royalist plots, but it also had an aspect which was much more peculiar to George himself: when Quaker missionaries entered Scotland they were arrested and deported to England on his personal orders. Thus the man who had written in the Tower that states should not tolerate different varieties of religious belief manifested his hostility to those who opposed the concept of a national church. In doing this he was displaying a significantly narrower sense of what was acceptable in British religion than many of Cromwell's other supporters, especially among military men.

The third aspect of Monck's activities was that he continued to manifest a strong personal loyalty to, and affection for, the protector himself. When Cromwell died in September 1658 he immediately transferred that loyalty to Oliver's son and successor, Richard, having him proclaimed protector throughout Scotland, obtaining an address of recognition for him from the army there, and working to ensure that supporters of the regime were elected to represent Scotland in the parliament called for January 1659. He also sent Richard himself a private letter of advice, which reveals him beyond question to have belonged to that faction or tendency in the leadership of the protectorate which favoured more conservative or reactionary policies. He advocated strengthening the Church of England by favouring moderate presbyterian ministers and calling an assembly of divines to achieve greater unity within the church and find a means of attracting separatist groups back into it. He hinted that the prevailing tolerance of such groups should be curtailed. In political affairs he advised the young protector to favour the more conservative of the advisers bequeathed by his father, such as Broghill, and to reorganize the army in England in such a way as to get rid of 'some insolent spirits' among the officers. In the context of the letter these were fairly clearly the radicals (Thurloe, *State papers*, 7.37).

His expressed views make it easy to imagine Monck's private dismay at the events of April and May 1659, when the English army deposed Richard and recalled the regicide parliament which had been expelled in 1653, with a powerful if vague mandate to lead the nation into more radical courses. His public reaction, however, was to safeguard his own position, and it may well have been rooted in older loyalties. This parliament was, after all, the body which had first promoted him to the rank of general, and in whose name he had first fought the Scots and the Dutch. As he reminded it in the fulsome profession of support which he now made, he had been trained in the service of a republic, that of the Netherlands, and so was at ease with a regime less monarchical than that of the protectorate. Richard's submission to the coup absolved him of his former commitments, and some of his own junior officers were enthusiastic allies of those in England. He therefore made the best of things.

Tension between Monck and the new regime was still considerable, as the restored parliament set about replacing those officers in his army whom it suspected of being politically unreliable with its own trusted supporters. This represented a considerable blow to Monck's own patronage network, and his control over the units occupying Scotland, and he protested strenuously. The only concession made was that his own foot regiment, and a horse regiment now raised in his name to partner it, were left almost unchanged. Even this gesture was probably made, and Monck's command itself continued, only because of the knowledge of a royalist rising brewing in Britain, which made it desirable to keep Scotland in George's capable and experienced hands. In the summer of 1659 Charles II indeed made his first attempt to win over Monck himself, using as intermediaries George's cousin Sir John Grenville and his own younger brother Nicholas *Monck, who had been royalists since the civil war. Nicholas carried a personal appeal from the king to George in August, as Charles's supporters rose in England. Monck seems to have temporized, hinting to his brother that he might co-operate, while arresting Scottish royalists and keeping an eye on events further south. By the end of the month the English rebels had been crushed, and George showed no further interest in the overture from Charles. The episode was a first indication of his capacity for duplicity.

Monck's growing distaste for the regime, and probable sympathy for the rebels, is indicated by the fact that on 3 September 1659 he offered his resignation to the speaker of parliament. The latter, having seen only the efficiency with which he had secured Scotland in parliament's interests, and concerned with growing tension between the parliament and the army in England, refused. This moment was to be the turning point of Monck's career.

Parliament's champion, 1659–1660 It has already been noted that Monck had expressed hostility towards officers in the army of England. That hostility could only have been increased when the protectorate fell and the English army was purged of men who had prominently supported Richard, their places generally being taken by others of more radical reputation. Thus, when that army began to attempt to prescribe policies to parliament, in September 1659, Monck expressed his support for the MPs, and may have emboldened them to deal severely with the military commanders in England. The response of the latter was to expel the parliament once more, on 13 October 1659. When the news reached Monck, four days later, he decided immediately and without advice to condemn this action and mobilize his own army to oppose it. His first action was to form a flying column of trusted supporters who toured the bases into which the forces in Scotland were dispersed, taking each by surprise, arresting unreliable officers, and replacing them with picked men of his own. In this fashion he remodelled his army into a force loyal to him and his objectives. The process took a month, but by 20 October was already far enough advanced for him to send a declaration of defiance to the council of officers in England.

It seems likely that the reasons for this precipitate action will never be firmly established, but weight must be given to Monck's own assertion that he believed himself to be acting against a 'fanatical party' of religious radicals who wished to dismantle the Church of England (Firth, *Clarke Papers*, 4.151). The English army had become commonly identified with such views, which were anathema to Monck, and the parliament had apparently rejected them. The expulsion of the MPs thus seemed to many to remove the last defences of the church, and it is likely that Monck indeed acted impulsively to save it. When dealing with the English army, however, he had a vested interest in delay. He needed to complete the purging of his own forces. Scotland was still relatively overtaxed in comparison with England, and he had just been sent a lump sum by the council of state. His soldiers were thus better paid and supplied than their prospective enemies, and had time on their side. As the military leaders in England were shocked by his reaction to their coup, and hoped to win him over, he found it easy to arrange a truce with them during which talks with his representatives could proceed in London. When those talks seemed to end in agreement on 15 November he bought further time by requesting additional negotiations to amend certain details.

By the end of the month Monck had perfected the remodelling of his army into a force loyal to himself and to the church, and on 8 December 1659 he advanced to the border at Coldstream. There he waited while the military regime in England disintegrated in the face of lack of revenue to pay their soldiers and a series of risings against their authority. The most significant of these, from Monck's point of view, was that led by Lord Fairfax in Yorkshire in the closing days of December, which took in the rear the army assembled around Newcastle ready to invade Scotland. The military leaders in London had already resigned their power to the parliament once more on 26 December, and when Fairfax took York the hostile forces which blocked Monck's route into England started to mutiny and disintegrate. He had a perfect legal right to advance, because on 24 November members of the former council of state, meeting in secret, had sent him a commission as commander-in-chief of all military units in Britain. He executed this on 2 January 1660, by leading 5000 foot and 2000 horse across the Tweed, and following

the regiments which had opposed him as they retreated and dispersed. This process he supervised, replacing many of the officers, until nine days later he reached York and halted, the job done, to await orders. His role in the defeat of the English generals had been decisive, for not only had he first set the example of resistance to them, with a credible force, but he had pinned down their best officers and most loyal forces near the border, facing him, while their rule collapsed further south.

The new orders reached Monck in the form of an invitation to bring his army onward to London, to guard the MPs while they secured their rule over the country. With this parliament voted a set of rewards consisting of land worth £1000 a year, the custody of St James's Park, and the honour of *custos rotulorum* of his native Devon. His chaplain was made provost of Eton and his brother-in-law and friend, Thomas Clarges, won the post of commissary-general. These favours may have strengthened his loyalty to the restored Commonwealth as he began his march south on 16 January with a total of 5800 men. *En route* he was left in no doubt of the unpopularity of the parliament which he was called to protect, as he received seven successive petitions from counties or cities, calling for a free (freshly elected) parliament or for the readmission of the MPs removed from the Long Parliament in 1648, in the purge which had made the regicide possible. In response he issued a declaration which rejected both courses, on the ground that the existing parliament would fill its own vacant seats, and thus he appeared to confirm his loyalty to it.

Monck was still maintaining this stance when his army reached Westminster on 2 February 1660. On the 6th he attended parliament with every sign of respect, urging it to fill itself up swiftly and to protect the nation from both royalists and religious radicals. Three days later the council of state ordered him to cow London, where the common council had repudiated the regime's authority, by destroying its defences and arresting eleven leading citizens. His response was to obey, but with the suggestion that the City gates be spared as a conciliatory gesture. He received a curt instruction to destroy them as well. This response clearly irritated him, for on 10 February he carried out the order but then called his officers to discuss the political situation. His purge had ensured that none of them were men who had personally been involved in the revolution of 1649 or had any emotional ties with the parliament that it had produced. The officers were joined by Monck's wife and Clarges, who all urged him to resist the parliament and win general popularity. The next day the chief of the officers joined him in writing to parliament expressing their dislike of the policy of repression and instructing it to issue writs for recruiter elections within a week and to provide for a new general election as soon as it was filled up. Monck then moved his army into London as a gesture of solidarity, receiving a hero's welcome from the corporation. The MPs, with suicidal folly, deprived him of his post of commander-in-chief and reduced him to being one of a commission appointed to manage the armed forces. This removed his last reason for loyalty to them.

In a sense Monck's policy had been consistent since he wrote his advice to Richard Cromwell: to stabilize the country by winning over moderate opinion. What had changed was that he had hoped that first the young protector and then the regicide parliament might be the instruments to effect this, and he had lost faith in both, successively. For ten days more he considered his options, dealing amicably with the MPs, who pressed ahead with the writs for elections, and trying to persuade them to reach agreement with those purged in 1648. Increasingly, his wife, chaplain, and Clarges united with the City's presbyterian clergy and the more moderate members of the existing parliament to convince him that a new general election could be obtained much more swiftly if he readmitted the purged MPs on condition that they called one immediately. This he did on 21 February 1660, adding the demands that they recognize him as commander-in-chief and preserve the Commonwealth, with a presbyterian church which tolerated separatist groups; the second and fourth requirements being clearly calculated to reassure radicals and discourage them from desperate action. Now constituting a majority, the readmitted MPs followed his wishes to the letter, and added further honours for him, of appointment to the new council of state, of the stewardship of Hampton Court Palace, and of a grant of £20,000. The City of London gave him the command of its militia.

Restoration, 1660 Between late February and late May 1660 Monck consistently followed three policies. The first was to wait upon the consequences of the election and to accept whatever settlement of the nation the new parliament made. The existing one dissolved according to its promise on 16 March. In the new one Monck himself was returned for both Devon and Cambridge University, and chose to represent the former again. It met on 25 April, and immediately recognized a House of Lords composed of civil war parliamentarians. The following day the Commons agreed also to endorse the right to sit of peers who had come of age since the war, and who were mostly royalist, and on 1 May both houses voted the restoration of the Stuart monarchy. At each stage Monck ensured that the Commons' will was carried out: for example, he warned the young peers not to attend the Lords until the other house had pronounced upon them.

Monck's second policy was to ensure that the soldiers in Britain were as willing as himself to acquiesce in events. Since his arrival at London he had made sure that units commanded by officers with strongly republican views were widely scattered through the provinces and were watched by others loyal to himself. When he readmitted the purged MPs he circulated a declaration assuring soldiers that the act was intended to secure the Commonwealth more swiftly and ensure them their pay. Three prominent commanders expressed disquiet, whereupon Monck persuaded two to join him in London and dismissed them there, while a strike force formed from his own guards arrested the third. A mobile brigade of other loyal troops toured the provinces replacing suspected officers. At the same time Monck ostentatiously ordered military units not to interfere with the meetings of peaceful religious separatists, and made speeches to gatherings of officers assuring them that the Commonwealth would continue. On 9 April 1660 he felt confident enough to impose an engagement upon every officer, to avoid meetings and to accept whatever the new parliament decided. Any who refused it were discharged without their arrears of pay. Monck's own army from Scotland was kept massed around the capital ready for action, while he sent detachments to patrol the provinces; one of these put down the only republican rising, led by John Lambert, in mid-April. By the time of the restoration of the monarchy, both soldiers and civilians were quiet.

Monck's third policy was a private one: to ensure that, as the Stuart restoration became ever more likely, he would reap the maximum personal benefit from it. This entailed making the right responses to approaches from the exiled king at each stage of the process, which he did. A channel of secret communication was easily opened through his network of west country kin. Charles II wrote another appeal for support to Monck in early March, and entrusted it once more to Grenville. The latter contacted a Devon cousin also related to Monck, William Morice, who was one of the MPs readmitted to parliament and had become firm friends with the general. Morice arranged a private meeting once parliament was dissolved, at which Grenville delivered the royal letter with promises of high office and Monck replied that he had always been secretly working in the royalist cause. A few days later he specified his own requests of the king, which were designed to ensure that the latter returned with the minimum of difficulty, especially from the soldiers: to promise indemnity for past deeds, full payment of wages owed to the army, confirmation of possession of former crown and church land, and toleration of peaceful separatist religious groups. He then settled back to await a response, and the result of the parliamentary election, thus keeping his options open if the king proved tactless and the new parliament republican.

Neither eventuality occurred. Charles and his advisers accepted Monck's terms, but on condition that they be endorsed by a parliament, to which he could hardly object. The new parliament itself found them acceptable, and so the Restoration duly occurred. On 25 May 1660, when Charles landed at Dover, Monck was the first person to embrace him, and the next day the king fastened the insignia of the Garter upon him with his own hands. He was also made master of the horse in the restored royal court. On 7 July he was created Baron Monck of Potheridge, Beauchamp, and Teyes, earl of Torrington, and duke of Albemarle. Two of these titles were references to his Devon roots, but the rest paid homage to aristocratic forebears of the Monck line. The dukedom itself was a royal one, made possible by the fact that George descended from Arthur, an illegitimate son of Edward IV. These honours were supported by grants of land worth £7000 a year and an annual pension of £700. The land included a former royal palace, Theobalds, to which Monck later added a handsome country seat at New Hall, Essex, while he was allotted the part of Whitehall known as The Cockpit for his town residence. On 3 August his control of any British army was confirmed with a life patent for the office of captain-general, and an alternative career was made possible by that of lord lieutenant of Ireland, although for the time being deputies and commissioners were appointed to govern that kingdom. He was made one of the trusted inner ring of the new privy council. Of his relatives and clients, Morice became one of the two secretaries of state, Grenville was created earl of Bath, Clarges was knighted, and Nicholas Monck was made bishop of Hereford. As the army was disbanded under his supervision during the rest of 1660, a troop of his cavalry regiment was incorporated into the Royal Horse Guards, while his infantry regiment was preserved entire and still survives as the Coldstream Guards of the crown.

The king's general, 1660–1665 If Monck was the person who made the Restoration possible, by breaking the power of the Commonwealth's army, and the one who reaped its largest harvest of honours, then his impact on the political affairs of the restored monarchy was much more muted. In part this was simply because he had never been greatly interested in politics, but it is also likely that he was shrewd enough to realize that he could obtain a permanent hold on the king's trust and favour by playing the part of the obedient servant. It is true in addition, however, that the temper of the Convention Parliament of 1660, and even more that of the Cavalier Parliament which followed from 1661, was less inclined to moderation and conciliation than he, as one who had fought successively in the royalist, parliamentarian, and Cromwellian causes would have wished.

Monck himself proposed that only five persons be excepted from indemnity, but had to accept the much longer list decided by parliament, and he duly served as a judge in the trials of the regicides condemned to death in late 1660. His one success was to save the life of one notable Commonwealthsman who had appealed for his aid, Sir Arthur Hesilrige. The king himself overruled his wish that royalist peers created since 1642 be kept out of the Lords. Monck proposed that purchasers of former crown and church land should be compensated with long leases of it on easy terms. In the end he had to settle for the restriction of this favour to soldiers who had marched from Scotland with him and who owned former crown estates. He took part in the Worcester House conference which patched up a temporary compromise settlement of the Church of England between episcopalians and presbyterians. In 1662 he supported the bid of Charles to dispense leading presbyterians from the Act of Uniformity which was forcing them out of that church; but the Cavalier Parliament thwarted it. In Scotland he had unwillingly to accept the restoration of episcopacy and the removal of English garrisons. His one decisive intervention there was an illustration of his skill in political trimming: on discovering that Charles was absolutely set on

destroying the marquess of Argyll he helpfully produced letters which proved Argyll's collaboration with the protectorate. These ensured the execution of the marquess, with whom Monck had no personal quarrel and who had actually been of help to him in his own days as a Cromwellian satrap. It was precisely that help, of course, which had enabled Monck to send him to his death when times changed.

In other fields the general was even less effectual. Monck never took up his great office of lord lieutenant of Ireland, nor made any attempt to intervene personally in the affairs of that country, and he resigned it in 1661. His impact on foreign policy was minimal, being apparently restricted to adding his voice to the already considerable support for the king's marriage to the Portuguese princess Catherine of Braganza. He was not noted as having been especially influential in the king's decision to accept this bride, which was swayed principally by the extraordinary richness of the dowry offered by Portugal. He unavailingly opposed the sale of Cromwell's main foreign conquest, Dunkirk, to the French. After the first year of the restored monarchy, although he continued to sit on the privy council and to be reckoned one of the realm's most important men, he tends to recede into the background of the government.

In part this may have been due to Monck's state of health. In August 1661 he contracted the second serious illness of his life, a fever, and was ever after prone to shortness of breath and swellings of his body. His partial eclipse may also, however, have been due to his general distaste for several aspects of the Restoration settlements of England and Scotland, mentioned above. If his instincts probably warned him that the king's favour could best be retained by carrying himself modestly, the ineffectuality of so much of the counsel which he had given may well have deterred him from offering more. There was probably an even deeper reason for his lack of impact during the first half of the 1660s; that for most of the previous forty years he had operated in states which were either at war or upon a war footing. For a professional soldier this was an ideal situation, and explains the fairly steady progress of his career, which now reached its apex. He found himself in a nation at peace, in which the land forces were reduced to a few thousand royal guards. His only notable action between 1661 and 1664 was in May 1663, when he drank an entire dinner party under the table and then walked away. The title of captain-general must have seemed an empty one to him during this period, and it is not surprising that he gives the impression of a ship becalmed.

It was in ships that Monck came to place his faith as a means of rescuing himself. During 1664 the government of Charles II became increasingly resolved upon a new war with the Dutch as a means of promoting English trading and colonial interests and increasing its prestige at home and abroad. Monck was one of the major shareholders in the Royal African Company, the chief instrument by which rivalry between the two nations was fomented, as it was chartered in that year specifically to break into the Dutch markets in west Africa. As the Dutch reacted, he was prominent among those who argued for strong retaliatory measures to the king and to parliament. When the Second Anglo-Dutch War was formally declared on 4 March 1665, it was certain to be a naval conflict, and Monck may have had high hopes of a return to active service in it.

Initially these were thwarted, as the commands at sea were given to the king's own brother, James, with the foremost royalist soldier of the civil war, Prince Rupert, and Cromwell's favourite naval expert, Edward Montagu, now the earl of Sandwich. Monck was relegated to managing James's administrative business as lord high admiral while the latter was with the fleet, a task which he performed as industriously and reliably as any which he undertook. When he was given a command in July 1665 it was in unique and particularly nightmarish circumstances. The last great plague epidemic to strike London had erupted in that summer, and as the king and court fled the city Monck was left behind to supervise its affairs and watch in particular for any sign of republican plots, designed to seize it in collusion with the Dutch while it was paralysed, and largely emptied, by the disease.

Despite the horrific nature of the assignment, it is difficult to resist the feeling that it was very well suited to that grim tenacity which was a feature of Monck's nature. From his headquarters at The Cockpit, in the otherwise deserted palace of Whitehall, he deployed a strong force of soldiers whom he quartered in tents in Hyde Park to keep them clear of the infected city. The tactic did not save a third of them from dying of the plague, while many of the officers deserted their men and their posts and fled the region. Monck, predictably, was not one of them, and kept the survivors to a relentless round of searches and interrogations. He was rewarded in August by the discovery of a small group of plotters who were planning a rising, and most were duly captured and consigned to prison and then the gallows. Monck's traditional animosity against religious nonconformists, carefully controlled during the first year of the Restoration when it was politically expedient to do so, was now given full rein in the wake of new laws prohibiting meetings outside the national church. Repeatedly his soldiers relieved their work of hunting for conspirators by arresting dissenters, especially Quakers, and committing them to gaols where many died of plague.

As the epidemic, and Monck's work in the capital, began to wind down during the autumn, his prospects of active service steadily improved. In the course of the summer's naval campaign the king had decided to recall his brother for the sake of the latter's own safety, and to divide the command between Prince Rupert and Sandwich. Rupert refused to share the supreme authority in this fashion, and so Sandwich was left in sole charge of the fleet between July and September 1665. He returned at the end of the season with some rich prizes, but also the makings of a considerable scandal, as it became public knowledge that he had taken some of the prize goods for himself and distributed others among his flag officers. Gossip was soon rife that the value of these had been considerably greater than that which the earl had officially declared.

In this situation it became crucially important that Sandwich had enemies at court, and one of the most active in fomenting opinion against him over the prize goods affair was Monck himself. Despite (or perhaps because of) their common service to Cromwell, the two men had long shared a hearty mutual dislike, and this was now almost certainly compounded by George's realization that if his rival was dismissed, then he stood a good chance of inheriting his command. This is precisely what occurred, as in November he was summoned to meet the king at Oxford and informed that during the next year he would be given charge of the fleet.

The king's admiral, 1666–1667 Monck was not the sole commander for the 1666 naval campaign, for Rupert had also been intriguing with determination to secure Sandwich's position, and the king compromised by offering him joint authority with Monck. The prince accepted this situation, which he had professed to be intolerable with Sandwich as a partner; it may be that he had now given up hope of an undivided command, or it may be that he liked and respected Monck more than the other man. If the latter suggestion is correct, then it would explain why the two of them worked together without any apparent tension throughout the course of their partnership. The person most openly distressed by the pattern of events was Monck's wife, Anne, who expressed a quite natural horror and resentment at the prospect of seeing her husband depart once more to a particularly dangerous form of military employment.

In March 1666 the joint appointment of the two admirals was confirmed, and in late April they joined the fleet at the mouth of the Thames estuary. After three weeks of hard work they had it ready for war. Intelligence had brought reports that a French fleet was on its way up the channel to reinforce a Dutch one ready to set sail, and so on 13 May Monck and Rupert agreed to divide their own force. It is possible that each was still happier to operate independently of the other; what is certain is that on the 29th the prince took twenty ships to look for the French, and to destroy them if found, while Monck remained with sixty to guard the English coast. The separation was made at the worst possible moment, for a Dutch fleet of eighty-three vessels immediately bore down upon Monck's reduced force.

Monck's reaction was to call a council of officers at which it was resolved to attack the enemy at once, rather than retire or wait for Rupert to return. The formal justification for this decision was that the enemy was too close to make either of the latter courses a safe one. This may well have been true, although it is noteworthy that one of the charges which Monck had levelled against Sandwich in his campaign of criticism had been that of cowardice. It is possible that at all costs he wished to avoid attracting the same accusation, and even that the lassitude of the past few years, and the decay of his body, made the prospect of death in action hold even fewer fears than before. At any rate, he launched his fleet against the Dutch in the middle of the North Sea, as soon as the wind permitted it. As the two forces closed, on 1 June, the English were handicapped not merely by inferior numbers but by the fact that, having the weather gauge in a high sea, they had to keep their lower gun decks closed as they turned broadside for action. They manoeuvred in formation, as they had not done in 1665; another sign that this innovation may be chiefly credited to Monck. This, and a slight advantage in ship size and in discipline, saved them from destruction in the three days of desperate fighting which ensued. On the third day Monck's fleet had suffered so much the worst of it that he gave the signal to run for home, only to meet Rupert's returning squadron. On 4 June the two attacked the Dutch again, until their ships began to run out of ammunition towards evening, by which time the enemy vessels had been battered enough to enable them to retire unpursued.

Technically, therefore, the battle had been indecisive, but the English fleet had lost twice as many ships, and more than twice as many men, and was completely unfit for further action. Monck's own amazing physical luck had held by the narrowest of margins, when a cannon-ball grazed his leg before tearing off that of a secretary standing behind him. A public sense of defeat was reinforced when the Dutch returned to blockade the Thames after only three weeks. Any criticism, however, was suspended as the duke and the prince played their part in a huge administrative effort to repair their ships. By mid-July the latter were ready to be sent forth from the Thames once again, now equal in number to their opponents. Monck and Rupert led them out on the 19th, and reached the Dutch off Suffolk on the 25th, St James's day. Once again the English kept better formation than their enemy, and broke the latter fairly quickly. The Dutch were chased back to port, and this time had lost twice as many ships and men and suffered much more damage. After this they avoided battle, and the two English commanders cruised off the coast of the Netherlands for long periods up to the opening of September, when a gale blew their fleet down to Portsmouth.

It was from there, on 6 September 1666, that Monck received an urgent summons from the king to lend his talents to the effort of fighting the great fire of London. It is a measure of how highly Charles valued his expertise in any crisis that he automatically called him to this one; and also an insight into George's character that he wept on being denied the opportunity to lead out his ships on another campaign. Rupert was left to patrol the channel alone, while Monck reached the capital too late to do more than organize his soldiers into squads to make safe the ruins which were still smouldering. This work continued until the sailing season was over, and during the winter Monck was obliged to deploy his regiments in the still more depressing duty of dispersing sailors who were rioting in and around London because of the non-payment of their wages. The shortage of money was, in fact, so severe that the government decided to lay the fleet up during the fighting season of 1667 and negotiate an end to the war.

Monck was mollified with an appointment to lead the commission set up to manage the Treasury on 25 May. He had never shown any interest in high finance, and his membership of the board was accordingly no more than honorific. Instead he was called almost at once to a task more to his taste, although its outcome was not: to superintend the defence of the River Medway in early June, as a Dutch fleet fought its way upstream to attack the uncrewed English warships laid up there. The fiscal crisis had left the fortifications of the river either inadequate or unbuilt, and the Dutch attacked fast and efficiently enough to create serious confusion as Monck's orders clashed with those issued by lesser military and naval officials on the spot. The raid therefore destroyed three important ships, while the flagship itself was taken as a prize. Monck remained on the Medway afterwards, securing it against a further assault, but none came and his efforts proved to be both needless and too late.

Monck's main business now was to make sure that he did not become one of the scapegoats of the inquiry launched by the Cavalier Parliament as soon as the war was ended, and designed to expose the causes of the various mistakes and miscarriages of the conflict. He prepared a formal statement in his own defence which laid full blame for those in which he had been involved, such as the division of the fleet in 1666 and the Medway disaster of 1667, on bad intelligence and faulty support systems. His reputation was still so high that he was formally absolved from all blame, and thanked for his services, by the Commons before his statement had even been heard by them. Instead, public opinion settled on the lord chancellor, Clarendon, as its preferred victim. Charles decided to sacrifice Clarendon, and employed Monck as his messenger to ask for the chancellor's resignation, as a person of high social and official rank who had no personal quarrel with the doomed man. As Clarendon refused, was dismissed, and duly became the object of an ever increasing royal anger, Monck turned against him as ruthlessly and dutifully as he had in the case of Argyll. When the impeachment of the fallen minister reached the House of Lords in November, Monck became one of a small number of royal servants to vote for it, despite its patent injustice, because it accorded with the wishes of the monarch.

The old soldier, 1668–1670 During the winter of 1667–8 Monck's physical debility worsened. He continued to swell, and his shortness of breath increased to the point at which he was unable to sleep lying down, and had to do so propped up in a chair. He more or less retired from public life to his country estate of New Hall, where the expansive grounds, with their deer park, gardens, spacious walks, and avenue of lime trees, provided appropriate recreation for an invalid. The beauty of the property was noted in detail by the most distinguished visitor to be entertained there during the period of Monck's retirement, the grand duke of Tuscany, who stayed there in the summer of 1669. Endearingly to modern minds, he noted that the duchess, Anne, still betrayed her lower-class origins in her speech and manners. The Italian potentate, of course, regarded this as a matter for regret, as he did also the fact that the couple were obviously fabulously wealthy but still parsimonious in their treatment of guests; if true, this would not be an uncommon pattern in people who had worked their way to riches after growing up in straitened circumstances.

Monck's decline continued, until by the next winter he was a dying man. He expired at The Cockpit on the morning of 3 January 1670, propped up in his chair as was now his habit and surrounded by army officers as if on campaign; the military tone of his life endured until the end. The cause of death was stated as dropsy. His wife collapsed with his passing, and died herself on 29 January. Charles II undertook to give the dead hero a state funeral, but this ran into the perennial difficulties of royal finance. As a result, while Anne was buried at Westminster Abbey on 28 February, George had to wait almost four months. For the first three weeks of that time his coffin was placed on view at Somerset House, surmounted by an effigy in armour with a golden baton in its hand. Hundreds of people paid their respects to it. His body at last followed that of his wife into a vault of the Henry VII chapel of the abbey on 29 April, and the official funeral was held on the next day. Those attending included Ormond, Sandwich, and the whole regiment of Coldstream Guards. Anne had borne two sons, of whom the younger, George, had died in infancy. The survivor, Christopher *Monck, now succeeded to Monck's titles and property, and was chief mourner at the funeral.

Reputation and assessment George Monck's posthumous reputation was well served by his friends and clients because his brother-in-law, his former chaplain, and two of his physicians all left adulatory biographies or memoirs. All supported his own story, which the Restoration made more or less compulsory to his admirers, that he had a long-term project to rescue the Stuart monarchy and that this bore fruit in 1660. This interpretation of events may fairly be doubted, although it can never be conclusively disproved. Monck's version has also been more or less accepted with an admiring view of his personality by his later biographers François Guizot (1837), Sir Julian Corbett (1889), Griffith Davies (1936), and Maurice Ashley (1977). The only hostile tradition was that of presbyterians, who felt betrayed by him at the Restoration, and this died out with J. D. Reid in the late eighteenth century. It is true that two of the most frequently consulted sources for Restoration history, the memoirs of Clarendon and the diary of Pepys, were written by people who had cause to dislike him, but they have generally been discounted by scholars who have dealt with him at length, and have been swayed more by his friends. On the whole, his twentieth-century reputation has been a good one, of a fine soldier and skilful politician, while remaining somewhat enigmatic.

Some aspects of Monck's character and career, at least, are clear. One is his remarkable physical and moral courage, and steadiness under pressure, which was manifested repeatedly both in military and in political action. Also manifest is his devotion and attention to duty, and determination to carry out to the most perfect degree each task which he was set by a commander or sovereign power. To these can be added a skill in sizing up a terrain, and then manoeuvring to take best advantage of it, which was displayed both in literal terms in his military and naval campaigns, and in figurative terms in political affairs. In those latter affairs, likewise, he can be said to have maintained certain fixed principles throughout life: a partiality for ordered, stable, and disciplined government, which had to include a secure and well-regulated national church and to enjoy the support of most of the people over whom it ruled. He had an equivalent instinctual dislike of disorder and of variety and novelty in opinion. Within these limitations he was in practice quite prepared to serve a range of different regimes, from the Dutch republic and the British Commonwealth to the protectorate and the Stuart monarchy.

Most of these traits can be related to Monck's vocation as a soldier, which was the keynote of his life. He seems to have enjoyed battle for its own sake, and sought active service for the pleasure of living through it as well as for the promotion and reward which it offered. To a great extent political activity was forced upon him, and his chief aim when engaging in it was to serve the master or masters to whom he had acquired a habit of loyalty, or in default of these to restore a stable regime as efficiently as possible and then to resume his career as a military commander. As well as a habit of good service to leaders whom he recognized—and especially to those whom he respected—he always manifested a care for the men under his own authority. Whether as a commander of soldiers or of sailors, he worked hard to ensure that they were paid, clothed, and fed, and he seems to have inspired an equivalent devotion in them. The manner in which clients and friends eulogized him after his death testifies to his ability to inspire affection and loyalty in them as well. One of the most attractive aspects of his nature, to a modern commentator, is his love for his wife and the deeply, mutually, happy marriage which resulted and which stood up to all his changes of fortune, even though in the terms of his own time it was a social misalliance.

When these qualities are noted, there remains a darker side to the man. Much of this can perhaps be related to an apparent experience of poverty and humiliation as a child, when Monck's indigent father was forced to lodge him with his mother's family. Such a background would explain his prickliness, with its outbreaks of violent temper, his driving ambition, and the manner in which he accumulated wealth—he died owning estates in twelve different English and Irish counties, worth a total of £60,000—while being careful of his expenditure. The parsimony in entertainment noted by the duke of Tuscany was the subject of similarly indignant comment by Pepys. In political affairs he could be absolutely ruthless, as is demonstrated by the cold-blooded way in which he turned upon Argyll and Clarendon to please his royal master. His most conspicuous act of generosity was his intercession on behalf of Hesilrige, but even this was accompanied by a rather grim jest: he informed the fallen Commonwealthsman that he would help him if he were paid 2*d*. for the service. As a military commander he regarded terrorism as a device to be employed whenever circumstances suggested that it might be profitable. His hanging of prisoners in Ireland was typical of behaviour in that especially unpleasant conflict, and his sack of Dundee was in harmony with the conventions of warfare at the time. His systematic devastation of land in both Scotland and Ireland was arguably a necessary response to guerrilla tactics which could hardly be quelled by any other means. None the less not every general who operated in either country proceeded with such severity, and in two respects—his sinking of captured vessels in the First Anglo-Dutch War and his attempt to secure the execution of the leaders of the Scottish royalist rebels—he was noted as outrunning the general appetite for brutality. There was a vicious streak in George Monck.

Monck's contribution to the history of warfare was muted but still significant. As a subordinate commander of infantry and artillery he was superb, but the same is true of several others who operated in the same wars, let alone the same century. His Scottish campaign of 1654–5 was a model of counter-insurgency measures conducted in mountain country and establishes him as a first-rate strategist and tactician. There is no sign, however, that it was used as an example by any later general. His claim to a place in the development of his profession must therefore rest upon his naval campaigns and here, as argued above, he can probably be credited with the decisive adoption by the English navy of battle plans based on co-ordinated formations. This said, his true place in history derives from his impact on politics. There is no doubt that the Stuart Restoration would not have occurred when it did, and with as little bloodshed, had not Monck been in command of the army of Scotland at a crucial juncture of affairs.

Monck's portraits bear out the impression of stolidity given by his actions, showing a thickset man of middle height with dark hair and heavy jowls. They also convey that sense of reserve which emanates from the literary sources, of a brooding, taciturn person who kept his thoughts very much to himself. Both in political and in military affairs he was the master of the surprise attack and unexpected reaction. If historians have found him enigmatic, this is largely because he worked very hard to be so. RONALD HUTTON

Sources T. Gumble, *The life of General Monck, duke of Albemarle* (1671) · J. Price, *The mystery and method of his majesty's happy restauration* (1680) · R. Baker, *A chronicle of the kings of England*, rev. edn (1670) · *The Clarke papers*, ed. C. H. Firth, 4 vols., CS, new ser., 49, 54, 61–2 (1891–1901) · J. R. Powell and E. K. Timings, eds., *The Rupert and Monck letter book, 1666*, Navy RS, 112 (1969) · G. Monck, *Observations upon military and political affairs* (1671) · J. Toland, *The art of restoring, or, The piety and probity of General Monk in bringing about the last restoration evidenc'd by his own authentic letters* (1714) · Thurloe, *State papers*, vols. 3–4, 7 · S. R. Gardiner and C. T. Atkinson, eds., *Letters and papers relating to the First Dutch War, 1652–1654*, 6 vols., Navy RS, 13, 17, 30, 37, 41, 66 (1898–1930) · C. H. Firth, ed., *Scotland and the protectorate: letters and papers relating to the military government of Scotland from January 1654 to June 1659*, Scottish History Society, 31 (1899) · *Two original journals of Sir R. Granville* (1724) · T. Skinner, *The life of General Monk, late duke of Albemarle* (1723) · M. Ashley, *General Monck* (1977) · M. Stoyle, 'The honour of General Monck', *History Today*, 43/8 (1993), 43–8 · M. Stoyle, 'An early incident in the life of General George Monck', *Devon and Cornwall Notes and Queries*, 37 (1992–6), 7–14 · F. Sandford, *The order and ceremonies used for, and at the solemn interment of … George duke of Albemarle* (1670) · E. Peacock, *The Monckton papers*, Philobiblon Society Miscellanies, 15 [n.d.] [preface dated 1884] · GEC, *Peerage* · *Fifth report*, HMC, 4 (1876), appx, 154 · *Brief lives, chiefly of contemporaries, set down by John Aubrey, between the years 1669 and 1696*, ed. A. Clark, 2 vols. (1898)

Archives BL, letters, Add. MS 19399 · BL, letters and papers, Sloane MSS 970, 1052, 1519, 1956, 3299 · Bodl. Oxf., account of sea battles against the Dutch · Hunt. L., financial and business MSS · NMM, letter-book · NRA, priv. coll., letters · PRO, legal and estate corresp. and MSS, C 107/25–9, 61–2; C 116/2–8, 163–71, 174, 183–8 · Worcester College, Oxford, corresp. and papers; papers of and concerning; letters | BL, letters to Oliver Cromwell, George Downing, and John Thurloe, Add. MSS 4156–4158 · BL, corresp. with duke of York and others, Add. MS 32094, Egerton MS 2618 · Derbys. RO, letters to Sir Ralph Knight · NL Scot., letters to Sir Thomas Morgan

Likenesses S. Cooper, watercolour miniature, *c*.1660, Buccleuch estates, Selkirk; unfinished version, Royal Collection · P. Lely, oils, *c*.1660, NPG · P. Lely, oils, *c*.1660, Chatsworth House, Derbyshire · T. Simon, electrotype of medal, 1660, BM · D. Loggan, print, 1661, BM, NPG · P. Lely, oils, *c*.1665–1666, NMM; version NPG · J. M. Wright, oils, 1668, Longleat House, Wiltshire · W. T. Fry, stipple, pubd 1816 (after P. Lely), BM, NPG · R. Gaywood, etching (when General Monck; after F. Barlow), BM, NPG · R. Gaywood, etching, BM, NPG · P. Lely and studio, oils, Scot. NPG [*see illus.*] · oils, Guildhall, Exeter

Wealth at death £60,000: Ashley, *General Monck*, 253–4

Monck [*née* Molesworth], **Mary** (1677?–1715), poet and translator, was the second daughter in the family of seventeen children of Robert *Molesworth, first Viscount Molesworth (1656–1725), of Brackenstown, co. Dublin, and Laetitia (*d*. 1729), daughter of Richard, Lord Coote of Coloony. She married George Monck, member for Philipstown in the Irish parliament from 1703 to 1713. Family correspondence suggests she had children, but their number or ages are not known.

Monck's literary manuscripts consisting of original poetry and translations of Tasso, Della Casa, Guarini, Quevedo, Marino, and Petrarch were printed after her death by her father in a volume entitled *Marinda: Poems and Translations upon Several Occasions* (1716). In his dedication to Caroline, princess of Wales, her father declared that Mary Monck had taught herself Latin, Italian, and Spanish, and that the poems printed were the result of a 'remote Country Retirement' and a good library. The sixty-three poems also record her participation in a coterie, social literary environment, and contain eleven poems addressed to her as Marinda. Her own verses include epigrams, madrigals, 'Mocoli', a landscape poem dated 1711 addressed to her brother Colonel Richard Molesworth serving in Catalonia, and occasional verse. The verses addressed to her praise her abilities as a translator and as a discerning reader of others' work, and give interesting insights into the reciprocal nature of authorship.

Monck died in Bath in 1715, after a lengthy illness. Her

unpublished deathbed poem to her husband, who apparently suffered from mental disorders, was first printed along with several other selections from *Marinda* by Coleman and Thornton in *Poems by Eminent Ladies* (1755).

MARGARET J. M. EZELL

Sources G. Ballard, *Memoirs of several ladies of Great Britain* (1752), 418–22 · R. Shiels, *The lives of the poets of Great Britain and Ireland*, ed. T. Cibber, 3 (1753), 201 · *Report on manuscripts in various collections*, 8 vols., HMC, 55 (1901–14), vol. 8, pp. 243–68, 318–19 · GEC, *Peerage*, new edn · J. Giles, *Historical account of the English poets* (1720), 2.106–8 · R. Lonsdale, ed., *Eighteenth-century women poets: an Oxford anthology* (1989) · G. Coleman and B. Thornton, eds., *Poems by eminent ladies*, 2 vols. (1755)

Monck, Nicholas (*c.*1610–1661), bishop of Hereford, was the fifth-born and third surviving son of Sir Thomas Monck of Great Potheridge, Devon, and Elizabeth, daughter of Sir George Smyth; he was thus the younger brother of George *Monck, first duke of Albemarle (1608–1670). He entered Wadham College, Oxford, on 25 May 1628, and lived at Buller's Inn. He graduated BA on 3 March 1631 and proceeded MA on 23 October 1633. Having been ordained he was on 23 July 1640 instituted to the rectory of Langtree, 5 miles from his home in Devon, a living in the crown's gift. On 7 October 1642 he had licence to marry Susanna (*d.* 1666), daughter of Thomas Payne, rector of Plymtree, and widow of Christopher Trosse (*d.* 1635). Monck served as curate to his father-in-law, and after his death in October 1646 succeeded to his benefice. In 1649 he was recorded as preaching minister of both Langtree and Plymtree, and so a suggestion that he was ejected cannot be sustained.

On 7 December 1653 Monck was instituted to the much richer rectory of Kilkhampton, Cornwall, through the presentation of his cousin Sir John Granville, later first earl of Bath, who was active in the royalist cause. Granville's patronage was given with the intention that Monck might at some future date make contact with his brother George, whom Granville believed could be induced to change sides. Nicholas's potential usefulness was reported to Edward Hyde in Brussels; meanwhile he resigned Plymtree and lived at Kilkhampton. From there he was called to London in July 1659. Granville had received a letter from the king, with another to be sent to General Monck in Scotland. It was agreed that Nicholas Monck should be the messenger, under pretext of discussing the marriage of his daughter Mary, who was staying at her uncle's headquarters at Dalkeith. He left London on 4 August and arrived at Dalkeith on the eighth. His brother was not able to see him immediately, and Nicholas indiscreetly revealed his mission to the first person he met, the general's chaplain John Price. Fortunately Price was sympathetic, though 'strangely suprized' (Price, 10). Others in the general staff were suspicious of Nicholas's cover. At least he had been cautious enough not to carry the king's actual letter, and when he did meet his brother he conveyed the contents verbally. George Monck was said to be 'wary and reserved' and 'not ... to listen over-much' (Gumble, 104), and took a fortnight before agreeing to accept the king's overtures. Before decisive action could

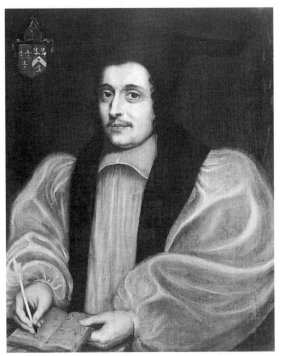

Nicholas Monck (*c.*1610–1661), by unknown artist, 1661

be taken news came on 22 August of the defeat of Booth's rising. It was not the time for George Monck to accept or acknowledge his brother's mission. When Nicholas returned to London (by 12 October) he had no answer for Granville; the only message he brought was the general's promise to support the Rump. It would nevertheless be maintained by George's first biographers, Price and Thomas Gumble, that his conversion to the king's cause dated from Nicholas's visit. Some recent historians have been sceptical of these claims, published after the Restoration when it was necessary to trace Monck's rediscovered royalism back to its earliest source, but the original accounts seem mutually corroborative.

The honours which Nicholas Monck received from Charles II reflected his new status as a duke's brother, but can also be interpreted as rewards for his own role in the Restoration. On 7 July 1660 the king appointed him provost of Eton, not allowing the fellows even the pretence of an election. On 1 August Monck was created DD at Oxford by virtue of the king's letters alluding to his 'particular and eminent sufferings for our self and the church during the late distractions' (Wood, *Ath. Oxon.: Fasti*, 2.236). John Walker was understandably dubious about including him among the suffering clergy on the strength of this citation, but governments necessarily disguise rewards to their secret servants. On 1 January 1660 Monck was elected bishop of Hereford; he was consecrated in Westminster Abbey on 6 January 1661. He never visited his diocese, but died at his house in Old Palace Yard, Westminster, on 17 December. After lying in state in the Jerusalem chamber of the abbey, he was on 20 December buried with 'a decent solemnity' in St Edmund's Chapel, a silver mitre being carried before his hearse, which was followed by his brother and his fellow bishops (Evelyn, 3.307).

Monck's widow lived until 1666. Their only son, Nicholas, had died aged thirteen in 1652, but Monck was survived by his daughters Elizabeth and Mary. Elizabeth's son Christopher *Rawlinson (1677–1733) raised a vast monument over his grandfather's grave in 1723.

C. S. KNIGHTON

Sources Wood, *Ath. Oxon.*: *Fasti* (1815), 454, 469 · Wood, *Ath. Oxon.*: *Fasti* (1820), 236 · Wood, *Ath. Oxon.*, new edn, 4.815–17 · Clarendon, *Hist. rebellion*, 6.154–6 · T. Gumble, *The life of General Monck, duke of Albemarle* (1671), 2–3, 104 · J. Price, *The mystery and method of his majesty's happy restauration* (1680), 4–5, 8–10, 18–19, 34, 36, 38, 41–2 · J. Walker, *An attempt towards recovering an account of the numbers and sufferings of the clergy of the Church of England*, pt 2 (1714), 306 · *Walker rev.*, 119 · F. B. Troup, 'Nicholas Monk, the king's messenger, and the honest clergyman', *Report and Transactions of the Devonshire Association*, 31 (1899), 305–25 · H. C. Maxwell Lyte, *A history of Eton College, 1440–1898*, 3rd edn (1899), 259–62 · Evelyn, *Diary*, 3.266, 307 · J. L. Chester, ed., *The marriage, baptismal, and burial registers of the collegiate church or abbey of St Peter, Westminster*, Harleian Society, 10 (1876), 155, n. 3 · G. Davies, *The restoration of Charles II, 1658–1660* (1955), 140n. · M. Ashley, *General Monck* (1977), 160–65, 167, 168 · R. Hutton, *The Restoration: a political and religious history of England and Wales, 1658–1667* (1985), 69 · R. Scrope and T. Monkhouse, eds., *State papers collected by Edward, earl of Clarendon*, 3 vols. (1767–86), vol. 3, p. 618 · will, 16 Dec 1661, PRO, PROB 11/307, fols. 304v–305 [proved 13 March 1662] · memorial, St Edmund's chapel, Westminster Abbey

Archives Hereford Diocesan Registry, episcopal register, unclassified MS, fols. 177–184v

Likenesses oils, 1661, bishop's palace, Hereford [*see illus.*] · R. Dunkarton, mezzotint, pubd 1811 (after D. Loggan), NPG

Wealth at death over £4000—£2000 to elder and £1000 to younger daughter; £1000 to wife: will, PRO, PROB 11/307, fols. 304v–305, proved 13 March 1662

Monck, (Walter) Nugent Bligh (1877–1958), actor and theatre director, was born at Welshampton, Shropshire, on 4 February 1877, son of the Revd George Gustavus Monck, vicar of Welshampton and later a curate and incumbent in parishes in Liverpool, and his wife, Hester Isabella, *née* Nugent. He was educated at the Royal Institution, Liverpool, and the Royal Academy of Music, London (which he entered in 1892). His first intention had been to follow a musical career, either as a singer or as a violinist, but in 1895 he changed his mind and transferred to the academy's actor training course. He graduated from the academy in 1898 and was immediately accepted into a theatre touring company, with which he stayed until 1901, when he played in London for the first time: the role was that of Pastor Jensen in Björnstjerne Björnson's *Beyond Human Power (I)* at the Royalty Theatre. Shortly after this he met William Poel, the founder of the Elizabethan Stage Society and the first English promulgator of revolutionary modern theories of Shakespearian staging. At the age of twenty-five he became Poel's stage manager and fervent disciple.

In January 1909 Monck was invited by Rex Rynd, the precentor of Norwich Cathedral (who had been Monck's fellow student at the Royal Academy of Music), to direct a programme of historical tableaux at St Andrew's Hall, Norwich. The production was so successful that Monck was offered a handsome house in Norwich and invited to come back the following year to direct what became the first of many masques presented by him at Blickling Hall. He returned, briefly, to London for the 1909–10 theatre season when, among other things, he stage-managed for Poel a production of *Two Gentlemen of Verona* presented at His Majesty's Theatre on the invitation of Herbert Beerbohm Tree. It was his last piece of work for Poel because the following year Norwich claimed him for her own: though in the future he was to work, temporarily, in many other cities—London, New York, and Dublin among them—his theatrical centre of gravity and his permanent personal home for the rest of his life was to be Norwich.

During the latter part of 1910 and the beginning of 1911 Monck produced several plays with various groups of amateur players in Norwich. One of these plays was W. B. Yeats's *The Countess Cathleen* (1892). Yeats was persuaded to make the journey to Norwich to see the play and was so pleased with the production that he returned six months later to see Monck's adaptation of *The Book of Job*, presented by him in the Blackfriars' Hall. On the strength of this Yeats invited Monck to Dublin to take over as the director of the Abbey Theatre's 'second company' for a year while their first-line company toured in the United States. The following year Monck himself took an Abbey company to play in New York.

Nugent Monck's interest was never primarily in acting as such—and certainly not in acting as a vehicle for self-display. His fanatically concentrated attention was always focused on the play; and the degree of *popular* approval enjoyed by one play or another interested him not at all. In 1911 (the same year as a similar venture was launched by Barry Jackson and John Drinkwater in Birmingham) Monck formed the Guild of Norwich Players for 'the presentation of Mysteries, Moralities and Plays of Merit'. In the earlier days of the guild its performances were presented in the large drawing-room of Monck's house and, a little later, in various public buildings around the city, but in 1921 Monck was able to raise enough local money to convert a disused Roman Catholic chapel, originally built in 1794, into a minute replica (or near-replica) of an Elizabethan stage. The influence of Poel is, of course, paramount and obvious in this, and the resultant playhouse was the first attempt in Britain to provide, on a permanent basis, modern productions of Jacobean and Elizabethan plays with the physical stage relationships for which they were originally intended and designed. The little theatre, when finished, seated 220 but was enlarged in 1953 to seat 324. Monck insisted on an austere aesthetic: actors' names never appeared on house programmes or posters and the cast never took a curtain call at the end of the performance (or at any other time). The audience should be applauding the *play*, Monck argued. He acquired the reputation, among his amateur company, of being something of a martinet, but this seems to have endeared him to them rather than otherwise. Among them he was, apparently, always known as Moncklet (he was a man of only slight stature physically).

Monck named his new theatre the Maddermarket, after

the madder plant (*rubia tinctorum*) which grows wild locally and which was, in medieval times, the source of the madder dye used for the distinctive red woollen cloth that was exported from Norwich to Holland. The company of amateur actors, still retaining its name as the Norwich Players, moved into the new theatre in July 1921, opening with a production of *As You Like It*. From that time they presented a new production every month, even during wartime; between December 1939 and May 1945 they presented fifty-six plays. The Elizabethan-style theatre greatly enhanced the theatrical qualities of the many Elizabethan and Jacobean plays that were performed, making for an intimacy with the audience and speed of performance. Yet it did not inhibit the presentation of pieces from many other eras and from several cultures and countries.

Monck had served with the Royal Army Medical Corps during the First World War and had spent three years (1915–18) in Egypt, where he produced five Shakespeare plays with the troops, but was back in Norwich by mid-1919 and producing *Much Ado about Nothing* with the Norwich Players at the Music House. Between 1920 and 1927 he directed all Shakespeare's plays with his company in Norwich, as well as plays by many other dramatists: by 1950 the total number of his productions had risen to a little over two hundred. And, as the importance of his work, especially on Shakespeare, became recognized both nationally and internationally (he was appointed OBE in 1947), he was increasingly invited to direct at other theatres—Toller's *The Machine Wreckers* for the Stage Society in London in 1923; the Cardinal Wolsey pageant for the city of Ipswich in 1930; *Timon of Athens* at the Westminster Theatre, London, in 1935; *Cymbeline* at the Shakespeare Memorial Theatre, Stratford upon Avon, in 1946; *Pericles* at Stratford in 1947; *King Lear* at King's Theatre, Hammersmith, in 1953; and so on.

Monck was not so original a thinker as William Poel, nor so bold a director as Granville Barker; and he did not have Barker's gift for trenchant and imaginative written criticism of Shakespearian texts. At the daily level of practical Shakespeare production, however, he probably did as much as, or even more than, these other pioneers to make audiences and Shakespeare-lovers outside London aware of the necessity for a new, more imaginative, more vigorous approach to the producing and performing of Shakespeare's plays. Though much of his work was done with amateur actors, Monck must be numbered among that small group of innovators who, in the first quarter of the twentieth century, rescued Shakespeare from the antiquated influence of the Victorian actor–managers and restored him to the living theatre.

Monck retired as director of the Maddermarket in 1952, having made arrangements for the establishing of the Maddermarket Theatre Trust to take over the property and the future management of the playhouse in Norwich. He himself received the very modest pension of £500. Even after his retirement he continued to direct occasional productions in Norwich: in 1955, at the Maddermarket, *The Big Field* (which was the text of the Mancroft

pageant that he had directed in Norwich in 1910 in aid of the restoration of St Peter Mancroft Church); in 1957 Ben Jonson's *The Masque of Cupid* in the gardens of Blickling Hall; in 1958 he was planning a series of annual festivals to feature theatre works and music from the Restoration, the eighteenth century, the Victorian age—one period each year for the next three years. The plans were never realized: on 21 October 1958, in the middle of a conversation with friends in Norwich about the festival plans, he died very suddenly, at 6 Ninhams Court, Bethel Street. He had been appointed CBE a few months before he died. He never married.   ERIC SALMON

Sources *The Times* (23 Oct 1958) · I. Herbert, ed., *Who's who in the theatre*, 17th edn, 2 vols. (1981) · M. Banham, ed., *The Cambridge guide to world theatre* (1988) · P. Hartnoll, ed., *The Oxford companion to the theatre*, 2nd edn (1957) · *The Maddermarket Theatre* (1971) · R. Speaight, *William Poel and the Elizabethan revival* (1954) · F. J. Hildy, 'Nugent Monck', PhD diss., U. Mich., 1980 · N. Marshall, *The producer and the play* (1957) · private information (2004) · d. cert. · *CGPLA Eng. & Wales* (1959)

Archives Norfolk RO, papers | BL, corresp. with League of Dramatists, Add. MS 63416 · priv. coll., production prompt copies

Likenesses photographs, repro. in *The Maddermarket Theatre*

Wealth at death £1081 12s. 11d.: probate, 29 Jan 1959, *CGPLA Eng. & Wales*

Monckton, (John) Lionel Alexander (1861–1924), composer and songwriter, was born in London on 18 December 1861, the eldest son of Sir John Braddick Monckton (1832–1902), town clerk to the City of London, and his wife, Maria Louisa Long (d. 1920). Lady Monckton was an enthusiastic amateur actress. The young Monckton was educated at Charterhouse School and at Oriel College, Oxford (1880–85), where he took part in college theatricals and composed music for the dramatic society's productions. Called to the bar at Lincoln's Inn in 1885, he subsequently practised as a lawyer but worked simultaneously as a theatre critic and a songwriter. His first stage piece, an operetta called *Mummies and Marriage*, was produced by amateurs in 1888.

Monckton broke through in the professional theatre when George Edwardes put his song 'What will you have to Drink?' into the burlesque *Cinder-Ellen up-too-Late* (1891), and he afterwards had individual songs heard in several other London shows before Edwardes gave him the job of supplying additional numbers to Ivan Caryll's score for the Gaiety Theatre's *The Shop Girl* (1894) [see Caryll, Ivan]. Monckton's 'Beautiful Bountiful Bertie' and 'Brown of Colorado' proved to be among the show's favourite numbers. The association with Edwardes, the Gaiety, and Caryll thus established continued for some fifteen years: the tuneful Monckton by and large supplied the melodies for featured songs while the musically educated Caryll took care of the more plotful pieces and the ensemble work. During the period in which the pair provided the Gaiety's music, Edwardes's theatre was the most popular musical house in London, and the shows produced there—*The Circus Girl* (1896), *A Runaway Girl* (1898), *The Messenger Boy* (1900), *The Toreador* (1901), *The Orchid* (1903), *The Spring Chicken* (1905), *The Girls of Gottenberg* (1907), *Our Miss*

Gibbs (1909)—went round the world, popularizing Monckton's songs such as 'Soldiers in the Park', 'Maisie', 'Keep off the Grass', and 'Moonstruck' not only throughout the English-speaking world, but even around Europe, as the product of the Gaiety Theatre established itself as the favourite musical-theatre entertainment of the *fin-de-siècle* years.

Alongside his contribution to the Gaiety's lightweight musical comedies, Monckton wrote additional numbers for Edwardes's other major theatre, Daly's, where a more substantial kind of romantic musical play was produced, and where the house's chief composer was Sidney Jones. Monckton began his Daly's career by supplying several numbers for Jones's *The Geisha* (1896, 'Jack's the Boy', 'The Toy Monkey'), and, while that show went on to become the most internationally successful English-language musical play of the nineteenth century, he followed up with numbers for *A Greek Slave* and another major worldwide hit, *San Toy*.

In 1902, when Jones moved on, Edwardes gave Monckton his first opportunity to compose a full score for the London stage. *A Country Girl* (1902, for which the additional numbers were by the rising Paul Rubens) gave the producer and composer another enormous success. Its successor *The Cingalee* (1904), however, brought all sorts of problems with it, and Edwardes switched to importing continental shows for Daly's. As a result Monckton ended up composing his next show score for Robert Courtneidge. The outcome was *The Arcadians* (with Howard Talbot), the classic musical play of the Edwardian era. Like *The Geisha*, and like *A Country Girl*, *The Arcadians* (1909) became a worldwide success, and its favourite songs—'The Pipes of Pan', 'The Girl with the Brogue', and 'All Down Piccadilly'—held their own with the melodies of the now fashionable Viennese operetta as the song hits of the period.

When Edwardes purchased the lease of the Adelphi Theatre, Monckton and his wife, the Gaiety star *ingénue* Gertie *Millar, whom he had married on 20 December 1902, were deployed there, and Monckton supplied the music for the house's biggest success, *The Quaker Girl* (1910, 'The Quaker Girl', 'Come to the Ball', 'Tony from America'). He nevertheless wrote music for only three more book shows for the London stage after *The Quaker Girl*. After providing Courtneidge with the score for a *Geisha* clone called *The Mousmé* (1911) and the Adelphi and Miss Millar with the pretty but unexceptional *The Dancing Mistress* (1912) he had one last major hit when he combined once more with Talbot to provide the songs for *The Boy* (1917), a musical version of Sir Arthur Wing Pinero's *The Magistrate*, which was one of the greatest hits of the wartime years.

The death of George Edwardes and the changing fashions in popular music sparked by the introduction of syncopated American dance music to British shores in the years before the war had, however, discouraged the composer and, although he for a while tried his hand at writing for the newly popular genre which called itself revue (*Bric à Brac*, *We're All in it*, *Airs and Graces*), he soon renounced and went into retirement. He died at his home, 49 Golden Square, London, on 15 February 1924. His widow remarried later that year, becoming the countess of Dudley.

One of the most successful writers of popular melodies of the Victorian era (his arrangements and orchestrations were inevitably left to everybody's favourite arranger, Carl Kiefert), Monckton contributed materially to the success of a quarter of a century of musical shows.

KURT GÄNZL

Sources A. Staveacre, *The songwriters* (1980) · K. Gänzl, *The encyclopedia of the musical theatre*, 2 vols. (1994) · K. Gänzl, *The British musical theatre*, 2 vols. (1986) · will of Lionel Monckton · *CGPLA Eng. & Wales* (1924) · J. Parker, ed., *Who's who in the theatre*, 6th edn (1930) · Foster, *Alum. Oxon.* · m. cert. · *WWW* · d. cert.
Wealth at death £79,517 12s. 1d.: probate, 16 April 1924, *CGPLA Eng. & Wales*

Monckton, Mary. *See* Boyle, Mary, countess of Cork and Orrery (1746–1840).

Monckton, Sir Philip (*bap.* 1622, *d.* 1679), royalist army officer, was baptized at Howden in the East Riding of Yorkshire on 19 January 1622, the eldest son of Sir Francis Monckton (*d.* in or after 1655), gentleman landowner, of Cavil and Hodroyd in the East Riding, and his wife, Margaret, daughter of Thomas Savile of Northgate Head, Wakefield, and his wife, Sarah. Monckton matriculated at University College, Oxford, on 8 June 1638 but did not proceed to any degree. He became a committed royalist in 1642, serving as a commissioner of array and a captain in Sir Thomas Metham's foot regiment. He later recalled his service at the siege of Hull in July 1642: 'I had the fortune to command the first party, that gave fier in that warr' (*Monckton Papers*, 14). He was a major of horse at Adwalton Moor on 30 June 1643, later boasting 'if I did not win the day I saved it' (ibid., 15). Monckton participated in defeating the Scots at Corbridge on 19 February 1644, and was knighted in the same year for gallantry at Newcastle upon Tyne. Sent to Shrewsbury in April 1644 to urge Rupert to relieve York, he fought at Marston Moor, finally leaving the field with Sir Marmaduke Langdale. He served in Langdale's 'Northern horse' at the relief of Pontefract and at Naseby, before commanding them at Rowton Heath, where he was wounded. He finally compounded for his estates on 6 May 1646.

During the second civil war Monckton joined the royalist council of war at Pontefract on 17 June 1648. On 30 June he left Pontefract with 600 men, with whom he captured the bishop's palace at Lincoln. On 5 July his forces were routed at Willoughby Field, where he was captured by Colonel Rossiter before being imprisoned in Belvoir Castle. Rossiter wrote to Lord Fairfax recommending mercy and Monckton later believed he owed his life to Fairfax's intervention. He was permitted to pass overseas and compound for his estate for £220 14s. 6d. On 13 January 1649 he began an unsettled exile, travelling to Louvain, Brussels, Rotterdam, Paris, Blois, and Orléans and finally returning to London by December 1651.

Having endeavoured to draw Fairfax into royalist conspiracy in 1654, Monckton was implicated in the 1655 uprising, and revealed much under questioning, including his opposition to royalist schemes for Cromwell's

Sir Philip Monckton (*bap.* 1622, *d.* 1679), by unknown artist

murder. In January 1657 he planned an uprising with Lord Belasyse, but he was arrested, brought before Cromwell on 7 June, and imprisoned in Lambeth House for over ten months. Subsequently gaoled in Hull, he alleged only Cromwell's death prevented his deportation to Jamaica. Released in 1658, he married Anne (*d.* in or after 1675), daughter of Robert Eyre of Highlow, esquire, high sheriff of Derbyshire. Claiming to have enlisted men to support Booth's rising in August 1659, he later co-ordinated a citizen uprising in York Minster which facilitated Lord Fairfax's takeover of York on 1 January 1660. Grossly exaggerating, he claimed his actions saved Fairfax's life and ensured the Restoration's success.

In 1660 Monckton was commissioned captain in Hull's garrison and comptroller of customs at Dunkirk, with a salary of £150 per annum. Claiming to be suffering from former republicans' lawsuits, he was the archetypal 'embittered and disillusioned cavalier' (Newman, 260), and clearly 'suffered from a persecution complex' (Underdown, 336). When Albemarle suggested him for preferment, Clarendon answered that Monckton was mad and unfit for employment, a diagnosis supported by Monckton's claim in 1673 that he 'was more instrumentall in his Ma[jes]ties restauration than any man now alive' (*Monckton Papers*, 100). Another hostile contemporary described him as 'beggarly but outrageously insolent' (HoP, *Commons, 1660–90*, 3.76). He went to court in 1667 to gloat at

Clarendon's downfall, even reminding the king that he had saved him from assassination in 1662. On 26 March 1668 he was rewarded with a captaincy in the 1st foot guards.

An East Riding JP from 1660 to 1679, Monckton was appointed high sheriff of Yorkshire in 1669, in which capacity he was accused of lenience to dissenters. He was elected MP for Scarborough in November 1670, and his daughter Margaret received the seignory of Howdenshire in 1673 in recognition of his service. In 1674 his guards company was moved to Portsmouth, so he sold his captaincy, receiving a pension of £300 per annum compensation. After 1674 his hostility to Catholics grew, particularly Lord Belasyse whom he insinuated had informed on him to Cromwell and from whom he demanded financial reparations. Heavily in debt, he was gaoled for seven weeks on 5 July 1676 for writing a libel that defamed government ministers. In 1678 Shaftesbury listed him 'worthy' and he spoke out against papists and the French, but never committed himself to Exclusion, privately assuring the duke of York of his fidelity. Monckton was buried at St Nicholas's Church, North Newbald, in the East Riding of Yorkshire on 21 February 1679.

ANDREW J. HOPPER

Sources *The Monckton papers*, ed. E. Peacock (1885) · HoP, *Commons, 1660–90*, vol. 3 · P. R. Newman, *Royalist officers in England and Wales, 1642–1660: a biographical dictionary* (1981) · D. Underdown, *Royalist conspiracy in England, 1649–1660* (1960) · *Dugdale's visitation of Yorkshire, with additions*, ed. J. W. Clay, 2 (1907) · Foster, *Alum. Oxon.*, 1500–1714, vol. 3 · G. Fox, *The three sieges of Pontefract Castle from the manuscript compiled and illustrated by George Fox* (1987) · 'A journal of the first and second sieges of Pontefract Castle, 1644–5, by Nathan Drake', ed. W. H. D. Longstaffe, *Miscellanea*, SurtS, 37 (1861) · *CSP dom.*, 1655–77 · *VCH Yorkshire East Riding*, vol. 4 · G. E. Weddall, ed., *The registers of the parish of Howden*, 1 (1904) · J. W. Clay, ed., *Yorkshire royalist composition papers*, 2, Yorkshire Archaeological Society, 18 (1895) · will, Borth. Inst., vol. 58, fol. 698 · *DNB* · J. W. Clay, ed., *Abstracts of Yorkshire wills in the time of the Commonwealth*, Yorkshire Archaeological Society, 9 (1890) · A. H. Woolrych, 'Yorkshire and the Restoration', *Yorkshire Archaeological Journal*, 39 (1956–8), 483–507 · J. Foster, *The peerage, baronetage, and knightage of the British empire for 1882*, 2 vols. [1882]

Archives U. Nott. L., memoirs, corresp. and other papers, Ga | BL, Add. MSS 22230, 22253, 40133 · BL, Harley MS 7020 · BL, account of the rebellion, Lansdowne MS 988 · Notts. Arch., DDSR 221/94

Likenesses portrait, repro. in E. Hailstone, ed., *Portraits of Yorkshire worthies* (1869) · portrait, priv. coll. [*see illus.*]

Wealth at death lands at Wakefield to be sold to pay debts and legacies: will, Borth. Inst., vol. 58, fol. 698 · excise pension of £300 p.a. granted 1674: HoP, *Commons, 1660–90* · inherited manors of Cavil and Birland worth £147 3s. p.a. from father: Clay, ed., *Yorkshire royalist composition papers*, 2 (Yorkshire Archaeological Society, Records Ser., 18) (1895), pp. 67–70

Monckton, Robert (1726–1782), army officer and colonial administrator, was born on 24 June 1726, the second son of John Monckton, later first Viscount Galway (1694/5–1751), of Cavil and Hodroyd in Yorkshire, and his wife, Lady Elizabeth Manners (*c.*1709–1730). He entered Westminster School in 1737. In 1741, at the age of fifteen, he was commissioned as an ensign in the 3rd foot guards. Monckton saw extensive service during the War of the Austrian Succession, experiencing victory at Dettingen in 1743 and

Robert Monckton (1726–1782), by Thomas Hudson, c.1759–60

defeat at Fontenoy two years later; he remained in Flanders when the duke of Cumberland returned to Britain to counter the threat of the Jacobite rising of 1745. He enjoyed rapid promotion: to captain in the 34th foot in 1744, to major in 1747, and to lieutenant-colonel of the 47th foot in 1751; that November, following the death of his father in July, he was elected MP for the family borough of Pontefract, a seat he retained until 1754. In 1752 he joined his regiment in Nova Scotia; and it was in North America, where he was destined to remain for more than a decade, that he made his reputation as a soldier.

Monckton arrived in Nova Scotia at a time of growing tension between Britain's settlements and their French-Acadian neighbours. In August 1753, following a stint as commander of Fort Lawrence in the Bay of Fundy, he was nominated a member of the provincial council at Halifax. Soon afterwards he volunteered to lead 200 men against rioting German settlers at Lunenberg, and pacified the outbreak through a combination of humanity and firmness. On 21 August 1754 he was appointed lieutenant-governor of Annapolis Royal, in the place of Charles Lawrence, who became lieutenant-governor of Nova Scotia. He wintered in Boston, where he helped to plan a surprise attack against the French possessions in Nova Scotia. Unlike Britain's other North American operations of 1755, Monckton's expedition proved a signal success; his force of 2000 Massachusetts volunteers and 280 British regular troops landed at Fort Lawrence on 2 June, besieged Fort Beauséjour, and secured its surrender within two weeks. Another French outpost, Fort Gaspereau, capitulated soon

afterwards. Lawrence attributed the outcome of the operations to Monckton's 'military skill, and good conduct' (*GM*, 1st ser., 25, 1755, 332).

Encouraged by these successes, Lawrence now demanded that the Acadians swear an unconditional oath of allegiance to Britain; when they refused, Monckton executed Lawrence's commands to round up and deport them to Britain's mainland colonies in an episode of 'ethnic cleansing' that remains controversial. In December, upon Lawrence's appointment as governor, Monckton replaced him as lieutenant-governor. Both men were at Halifax through much of 1756–7 as skirmishing continued with the French and their Native American allies. On 20 December 1757 Monckton was appointed colonel-commandant of the 2nd battalion of the 60th or Royal American regiment. While Lawrence joined Major-General Jeffrey Amherst's victorious expedition against Louisbourg in the summer of 1758, Monckton remained at Halifax. In September Amherst ordered Monckton on an expedition to destroy French settlements along the St John's River. Early in 1759 Monckton received orders from Amherst to assume command in the south in place of the ailing Brigadier-General John Forbes; however, Pitt had already appointed Monckton second in command of the expedition bound for Quebec under the command of Major-General James Wolfe.

By 27 June Wolfe's command had been transported up the River St Lawrence by a powerful fleet under Vice-Admiral Charles Saunders and landed unopposed on the Île d'Orléans, some 3 miles below Quebec. As Wolfe's senior subordinate, Monckton took an active part in the coming campaign. On 30 June his brigade of four battalions occupied Point Levis on the south shore of the St Lawrence. This position, immediately opposite Quebec, was of immense strategic importance; artillery batteries were soon constructed, and on 12 July commenced a destructive fire upon the city. Elements of Monckton's command participated in Wolfe's attempt of 31 July to lure the French defenders into a confrontation by landing troops on the Beauport shore, between Quebec and the Montmorenci River; the first wave of grenadiers attacked without waiting for their supports and were repulsed with heavy losses. Monckton's troops subsequently landed in good order, and covered the withdrawal of the survivors. As the siege dragged on through the summer with little prospect of success, rifts developed between the sickly Wolfe and his brigadiers. Of the trio, only Monckton appears to have enjoyed the general's complete confidence. Indeed, while his contacts with both George Townshend and James Murray grew increasingly frosty, Wolfe remained keen to maintain a cordial relationship with his second in command; in mid-August he wrote two letters apologizing for any offence he might have caused and emphasizing the value he placed upon Monckton's continuing friendship. The sentiment was apparently reciprocated; of the three brigadiers, Monckton alone figures in Benjamin West's celebrated painting *The Death of Wolfe*.

At the end of August Wolfe invited the brigadiers to comment upon his latest proposals to bring the enemy to action; he remained convinced that this goal could best be achieved by another assault upon the Beauport lines. By contrast, the brigadiers were adamant that the solution lay above the city itself: they argued that a landing there would rupture Quebec's supply line, so obliging Montcalm to emerge and fight. Although it was at odds with his own plans, Wolfe quickly accepted the brigadiers' reasoning; on 13 September he implemented a modified version of their scheme, with a landing closer to the city than had been suggested. During the ensuing battle on the Plains of Abraham, Monckton commanded the right of the line and was badly wounded while at the head of his old regiment, Lascelles's 47th foot. Having been obliged to leave the field, he was taken on board the frigate *Lowestoft* at 10.30 a.m.—shortly before the corpse of his late commander.

In Monckton's absence the command devolved upon Townshend. On 18 September Quebec capitulated on terms negotiated by Townshend and Saunders; to his chagrin, Monckton was not consulted. On 24 October Monckton became colonel of the 17th foot. Two days later, after organizing the Quebec garrison for the approaching winter, he sailed to New York for 'the re-establishment of his health' (Knox, 2.243). Early in 1760 he was sent to Philadelphia to command the troops in the southern department. In February 1761 he received promotion to major-general, and the following month he became governor and commander-in-chief of New York province.

Late that year Monckton was chosen to lead 13,000 troops against Martinique, an objective which had resisted British assault in 1759. Rear-Admiral George Rodney's warships covered the first landings on 16 January 1762, and within two days the entire army had disembarked at Cas des Naviers, some 4 miles west of the chief town of Fort Royal. The French were entrenched upon the dominating heights of Morne Tartenson. On 24 January British troops stormed this position, pushing the defenders back to an even stronger one at Morne Garnier. Three days later the French attacked Monckton's batteries; this sortie was repulsed and Morne Garnier swiftly captured. Deserted by the island's militia, the regulars besieged in the citadel of Fort Royal surrendered on 4 February. In his dispatch to the earl of Egremont, Monckton showed characteristic generosity in paying tribute to 'the true Valour and persevering ardor of His Majesty's Troops', who had conquered an enemy 'possessed of every advantage, that art or nature could give them' (letter from Fort Royal, Martinique, 9 Feb 1762, PRO/CO/166/2 fol. 29). Grenada, St Lucia, and St Vincent fell soon afterwards. Monckton and Rodney received the thanks of the House of Commons, and by 12 June the general had returned to New York.

On 28 June 1763 Monckton sailed for England. In the following year he was brought before a court martial after Colin Campbell, the major-commandant of the 100th foot, accused him of misconduct on Martinique; he was honourably acquitted, the court finding the allegations to be 'groundless, malicious and scandalous in the highest degree' (*Proceedings of a General Court Martial*, 87). On 14 June 1765, when Sir Henry Moore succeeded him in the

governorship of New York, Monckton was appointed governor of Berwick upon Tweed and Holy Island. Promotion to lieutenant-general followed on 30 April 1770. In 1769, after unsuccessful speculation in East India Company stock, Monckton sought to recoup his losses by volunteering to command the company's troops; the bid failed, as did an effort in 1773 to gain appointment as commander-in-chief in India. Sympathetic to the American colonists, Monckton declined an alternative offer to take command in North America. Between March and September 1774 he was once again member of parliament for Pontefract. In 1778 he became governor of Portsmouth, and he represented the town in parliament from August until his death in London on 21 May 1782. He was buried on 26 May at Kensington parish church. Although he was unmarried, Monckton was survived by three sons and a daughter.

STEPHEN BRUMWELL

Sources *The Northcliffe collection* (1926) · C. P. Stacey, *Quebec, 1759: the siege and the battle* (1959) · *Correspondence of William Pitt, when secretary of state, with colonial governors and military and naval commissioners in America*, ed. G. S. Kimball, 2 vols. (1906); repr. (1969) · J. Knox, *An historical journal of the campaigns in North America, for the years 1757, 1758, 1759, and 1760*, ed. A. G. Doughty, 3 vols. (1914–16) · *GM*, 1st ser., 25 (1755), 332 · *GM*, 1st ser., 52 (1782), 263, 357, 576 · Monckton to the earl of Egremont, Fort Royal, Martinique, 9 Feb 1762, PRO, CO/166/2, fols. 28–9 · W. Wood, ed., *The logs of the conquest of Canada* (1909) · *Proceedings of a general court martial 1764 … for the trial of a charge preferred by Colin Campbell esq. against … Major General Monckton* (1764) · GEC, *Peerage* · J. Brooke, 'Monckton, Hon. Robert', HoP, *Commons, 1754–90* · *DCB*, vol. 4
Archives L. Cong., corresp. and papers · NA Canada, personal and family corresp. and papers · PRO, Colonial Office MSS · PRO, War Office MSS · U. Nott. L., corresp. | BL, corresp. with Henry Bouquet, Add. MS 21638 · BL, corresp. with first earl of Liverpool, Add. MSS 38211, 38217, 38306–38309 · Northants. RO, Monckton of Fineshade records · PRO, corresp. with Sir Jeffrey Amherst, WO 34 · U. Nott., Galway MSS
Likenesses T. Hudson, oils, *c.*1759–1760, priv. coll. [*see illus.*] · B. West, oils, *c.*1764, priv. coll.; on loan to NAM · B. West, group portrait, oils, 1770 (*Death of general Wolfe*), National Gallery of Canada, Ottawa · J. McCardell, mezzotint (after T. Hudson), BM, NPG; repro. in Doughty, ed., *Historical Journal*, vol. 1, facing p. 162 · J. Tassie, paste medallion, Scot. NPG · J. Watson, mezzotint (after B. West), BM · oils, NA Canada

Monckton, Walter Turner, first Viscount Monckton of Brenchley (1891–1965), lawyer and politician, was born on 17 January 1891 at Plaxtol in Kent, the eldest child of Frank William Monckton (1861–1924), a paper manufacturer, and his wife, Dora Constance (d. 1915), a daughter of William Golding. From 1899 he attended a preparatory school, The Knoll, at Woburn Sands, where he became head boy in 1903. From 1904 to 1910 he was at Harrow School, where his charm, debating skills, good looks, and cricketing prowess made him popular. Though clever, he was not highbrow or pretentious, and throughout his life had few cultural interests. But already the capacity for winning trust and affection that sustained him through his public work had become fully apparent; he was 'the perfect schoolboy, becoming by gentle transition the don's delight' (Birkenhead, 13). In 1910, despite winning

Walter Turner Monckton, first Viscount Monckton of Brenchley (1891–1965), by Sir Cecil Beaton, 1944

an exhibition to Hertford College, Oxford, he chose to enter Balliol College as a commoner; there his contemporaries included Julian Grenfell, Cyril Asquith, Aldous Huxley, and (at Magdalen College) Edward, prince of Wales, who became a lifelong friend. He obtained a third in classical moderations (1912) and a second in history (1914), and was elected president of the Oxford Union in 1913. Though ostensibly an orthodox Conservative in this period, Monckton was regarded by some contemporaries as leaning towards radical views.

Marriage, the law, and adviser to the nizam of Hyderabad Just after leaving Oxford, Monckton married, aged twenty-three, on 18 July 1914 at Igtham church in Kent. His wife, Mary Adelaide Somes (Polly; 1892–1964), a childhood friend, was the daughter of Sir Thomas Colyer-Fergusson, third baronet. They had two children, Gilbert, born in 1915, and Valerie, born in 1918. Shortly after the wedding, when war broke out, he volunteered for service in the army, navy, and Royal Flying Corps, but in vain because of defective vision in one eye. Finally the medical officer of the Queen's Own West Kent regiment advised him to read the tests with his good eye and memorize them, so that he could recall them when using his bad eye. Sporting a monocle in the trenches, Monckton won the affection of his men and used his forensic talents to good effect as defending officer in courts martial. After taking part in the third battle of Ypres in June 1917 he suffered from nervous exhaustion, to which he was prone throughout life; he

was demobbed in February 1919 and awarded the Military Cross in June.

During the period when he was frustrated in his attempts to join the army, Monckton had taken the preliminary law examinations in the autumn of 1914, and he was called to the bar at the Inner Temple in 1919. As a lawyer he habitually worked through the night, mastering his briefs with ease. In court his gift for lucid exposition and his ability to disarm witnesses by sheer courtesy brought him great success. The absence of histrionics and the distaste for confrontation which characterized Monckton as a lawyer represented a drawback later in his political career; after the war his partisanship faded, leaving him ill-suited to a system increasingly polarized between two major parties.

In 1927 Monckton was appointed legal adviser to the Simon commission, then investigating constitutional reform in India; he took silk in 1930 and served as attorney-general to the prince of Wales from 1932 to 1936. It was this royal connection that prompted the nizam of Hyderabad to employ him as his constitutional adviser in 1933 at a time when the round-table conference was attempting to draft a scheme for a federal government for India. Subsequently Monckton visited India in 1935 and 1936 when the passage of the Government of India Act had placed the princes under pressure to accede to an all-India federal government. His objects were to assist the nizam to retain most of his existing powers, to persuade him to join the federation, and to encourage him to give a lead to the other princes. In this he largely failed, despite his negotiating skills, because as a Muslim ruler in a Hindu state the nizam feared the trend to democracy and nationalism, and preferred to make a bid for independence following a British departure from India.

Confidant of Edward VIII Monckton's success in his career obscured an increasingly unhappy private life. Totally absorbed by his legal work, he showed little interest in his family, even to the extent of avoiding holidays with his children. His chief leisure activity was hunting with the West Kent regiment, but Polly took no interest in this or in his hunting friends; they had married without really getting to know one another. Consequently, they lived separate lives and had effectively become estranged by the early 1930s, though they did not divorce until 1947.

Following the accession of the prince of Wales as King Edward VIII, Monckton had been appointed attorney-general to the duchy of Cornwall, a position he retained until 1951 except during the years 1947–8. Lonely and lacking confidence in his private secretary, the new king quickly came to rely on Monckton's friendship and support, often smuggling him into Buckingham Palace in order to prevent his official staff from seeing him. Monckton's romantic nature and the collapse of his own marriage led him to sympathize strongly with the king. 'From the moment when the King spoke to me about Mrs Simpson', he wrote, 'I recognised that here was a subject upon which a frontal assault could never be successfully delivered' (Birkenhead, 126). As a result, even though he had initially assumed that marriage to her was out of the question, Monckton never attempted to dissuade the king from his intentions. When the crisis deepened in December 1936 he became so heavily involved that he decided to give up his legal work in order to be constantly with the king at Fort Belvedere. He also acted as go-between for the king and the prime minister, Stanley Baldwin, sometimes using his daughter, Valerie, to convey messages from Downing Street to Fort Belvedere. Monckton urged Baldwin to resolve the issue by passing not one bill but two—one giving effect to the abdication and the other making Mrs Simpson's decree nisi absolute forthwith—in order to avoid the danger that the king might sacrifice his crown but not become free to marry. This, however, was rejected by the cabinet. More successfully, Monckton negotiated with the duke of York for a financial settlement and for the retention of a royal title after the abdication. He was responsible for the first draft of the abdication message which the king broadcast on 11 December from Windsor Castle. When it was over, the former king put his arm round Monckton's shoulder saying, 'Walter, it is a far better thing I go to!' (Monckton's account of the abdication, quoted in Birkenhead, 152). When the Windsors entered their exile abroad Monckton remained in regular contact with them. Although Mrs Simpson had been denied a royal title, he always bowed to her: 'it does no harm and it makes the little man so happy' (Roberts, 245). It was a sign of his tact that he managed to remain on friendly terms with both sides in the crisis, so much so that he became KCVO in the January 1937 honours list and was dubbed the first knight of King George VI's reign.

Wartime offices On the outbreak of war in 1939 Monckton became director-general of the press and censorship bureau in the Ministry of Information. A shrewd choice, he succeeded in charming the newspapers and was appointed director-general for the entire ministry in December 1940. In July of that year the coalition government sent him to Lisbon to persuade the duke of Windsor to accept an appointment as governor of the Bahamas. In November 1941 he became head of propaganda and information services in Cairo and a member of the Middle East war council. Following the departure of Oliver Lyttelton he acted as a minister of state in February–March 1942. After he had filled so many roles it was not surprising that Monckton was invited by Churchill to become solicitor-general in the short caretaker government he formed after the breakup of the coalition in May 1945. However, though Monckton had been offered seats in parliament in the late 1930s and 1940s, he was not by temperament a politician, and, moreover, had largely lost his original conservative views. But Churchill swept aside his reservation, saying that it made no difference. As a result Monckton served as solicitor-general without taking a seat. His long years in the law had detached him from his youthful loyalties, and his friendship with Sir Stafford Cripps, another successful barrister who had abandoned his tory background for the Labour Party, doubtless compounded the change of heart. Moreover, like many Conservatives, Monckton had been influenced by the experience of two world wars, which he felt had been fought to secure social justice for ordinary people. By 1945 he favoured the nationalization of the coal mines, but declined Cripps's suggestion of standing for the Labour Party. In effect, Monckton had become part of the liberal-minded élite, incorporating men of all three parties, who adopted a consensus view of post-war politics.

Indian independence; second marriage After the general election of July 1945 Monckton plunged into his legal practice once again and appeared frequently before parliamentary committees and public inquiries. He also made further trips to India in January, April, and November 1946 to assist the Hyderabad delegation in its negotiations with the cabinet mission sent out by the new Labour government to devise a scheme for handing over power. This proved as frustrating as ever. Monckton described his relation to the nizam as that of 'nurse to a difficult child of suicidal tendencies, my main task to prevent or postpone suicide' (Birkenhead, 221). Following the arrival of Lord Mountbatten as viceroy in January 1947 Monckton attempted unsuccessfully to persuade the nizam to accept that independence for his state was impossible. Though the nizam continued to negotiate with the new Indian government, his refusal to compromise eventually resulted in the entry of Indian troops into Hyderabad territory in September 1948.

It was during his time in India that Monckton met the Hon. Bridget Helen (Biddy; 1896–1982), eldest daughter of Walter Patrick Hore-Ruthven, ninth Lord Ruthven; she was the wife of George Josslyn L'Estrange Howard, eleventh earl of Carlisle. During the Second World War she served with the ATS, and from 1944 to 1946 she was director of the Women's Auxiliary Corps of India. In 1947 she was appointed CBE (military) for her war work. Soon after the dissolution of their existing marriages, they married on 13 August 1947.

Minister of labour Meanwhile the pressure to enter politics mounted. In 1949 Monckton's application to become a candidate in South Oxfordshire was humiliatingly rejected by the local Conservatives despite the personal recommendation of Churchill. But he accepted the offer of a safe Conservative seat at Bristol West when a by-election vacancy occurred in February 1951, thus becoming an MP at sixty. When Churchill returned to power in October that year he was expected to appoint Monckton to a legal post. But to his surprise the prime minister greeted him with the words: 'Oh my dear … I have the worst job in the Cabinet for you!' (Birkenhead, 274). The Ministry of Labour, which had grown in importance under Ernest Bevin during the war, was of especial significance for the new Conservative government. The party had returned to office with fewer votes than Labour, and Churchill thought it essential to avoid conflict between the government and the trade unions—a strategy which left the new minister little room for manoeuvre. According to Churchill, Monckton was well qualified for the post because he lacked a political past, to which he replied: 'I take it you do not expect me to have a political future' (*DNB*).

In the short term this pessimistic view proved very wide of the mark, for Monckton won golden opinions from politicians, unions, and businessmen as minister for labour from 1951 to 1955. However, in the long run he became a victim of the reaction against consensus politics in the Conservative ranks. This was reflected in the bitter attack on him in *Eminent Churchillians* (1994) by Andrew Roberts, who accused him of 'appeasement' towards the unions, of fuelling inflation by accepting excessive wage increases, and of effectively promoting the rise of the left within the trade unions.

Yet at the time Monckton's appointment seemed shrewd and successful. His own instinct was to uphold the wartime practice of involving the unions in the process of government and employing his undoubted skills as a lawyer and negotiator to conciliate them. As a result his work at the Ministry of Labour involved very little legislation, and he neglected party policies designed to curtail the closed shop and impose strike ballots. His energies were largely absorbed by the settlement of industrial disputes. Monckton's methods involved negotiating with the employers in one room and with the union leaders in another so that he and the chief industrial commissioner could move freely between them. He liked to keep things as informal as possible and to reduce the area of disagreement to the narrowest limit. Only then would he appoint an inquiry. Monckton had to cope with some major disputes, including those in engineering in 1952 and 1954 and those among electricity and railway workers in 1953. Typically the workers demanded 15 per cent pay rises and the inquiries offered 5 per cent or more. Under the circumstances the settlements were not excessive, since the unions had been kept on a tight rein under Attlee's government. The end of the Korean War and the removal of food subsidies pushed up inflation; moreover, full employment inevitably strengthened the workers' bargaining powers.

Thus, despite criticism from the tory right and the Labour left, Monckton was generally felt to have done a fine job. His civil servants admired his conscientiousness and mastery of detail. He enjoyed the confidence and friendship of Vincent Tewson, the TUC president, and other union leaders. 'He left the Ministry of Labour a better place than he found it', wrote Tom O'Brien of the TUC (*The Times*, 19 Jan 1965). The political significance of Monckton's work was encapsulated by Arthur Deakin of the Transport and General Workers' Union in 1953: 'I believe Sir Walter Monckton has given us a square deal and we have been able to do things that were difficult under our own people' (Seldon, 202). At the 1955 election the Conservatives retained a good deal of working-class support, which made possible their return with a higher vote and a larger majority.

Retirement from politics and peerage However, the pressure of work left Monckton sleepless, weary, and often close to breakdown. After settling the railway dispute he entered hospital in January 1954 suffering from eczema,

gout, and nervous exhaustion. It was a relief to leave the Ministry of Labour in December 1955 for ten months at defence. There, despite his reservations about military intervention in Suez in 1956, he remained outwardly loyal to the government, and became paymaster-general in October 1956. But following the retirement of Sir Anthony Eden, Monckton decided to leave politics in January 1957 and was made first Viscount Monckton of Brenchley. He then became director and chairman of the Midland Bank (1957–64) and chairman of the Iraq Petroleum Company. At the Midland Bank he was responsible for introducing personal cheque book accounts and the personal loans scheme, which became fashionable banking policy. Apart from acting as president of the MCC in 1956–7 and as the first chancellor of Sussex University in 1963, Monckton's most important role in this period was as chairman of the advisory committee on the constitution of the federation of Rhodesia and Nyasaland in 1959–60. The African majorities in Northern Rhodesia and Nyasaland had begun to demand the right to withdraw from the federation, which was dominated by the white minority under Sir Roy Welensky. The report reflected Monckton's characteristically ambivalent views in arguing that it would be a mistake to break the federation and also that it could not be maintained in its present form.

By June 1964, when he retired from the Midland Bank, Monckton's health had deteriorated sharply; he had had a kidney removed in 1963 and was suffering from arteriosclerosis. As a result he left London to spend his time in the country at Folkington in Sussex, surrounded by his children and grandchildren. He died there on 9 January 1965. Monckton was buried four days later among his forebears at All Saints' Church, Brenchley, Kent, where one of his ancestors, the Revd John Monckton, had been vicar in 1651; a memorial service was held on 14 January at Southwark Cathedral.

Monckton's widow claimed succession to her father's peerage in 1956, and her claim was recognized in 1967. Active since the 1950s in promoting family planning, as Baroness Ruthven of Freeland she took a leading part in the all-party group of peers who persuaded the government to introduce a universal and free family planning service in 1973. She died on 17 April 1982.

MARTIN PUGH

Sources Lord Birkenhead, *Walter Monckton* (1969) · A. Roberts, *Eminent Churchillians* (1994) · *The Times* (11 Jan 1965) · *The Times* (19 Jan 1965) · DNB · A. Seldon, *Churchill's Indian summer: the conservative government, 1951–55* (1981) · P. Ziegler, *King Edward VIII* (1990) · F. Donaldson, *Edward VIII* (1974) · H. Montgomery Hyde, *Walter Monckton* (1991) · H. Pelling, *Churchill's peacetime ministry, 1951–55* (1997) · Burke, *Peerage* (1959) · *The Times* (20 April 1982) [obit. of Lady Ruthven of Freeland] · *The Times* (26 April 1982) [obit. of Lady Ruthven of Freeland]

Archives Bodl. Oxf., corresp. and papers · PRO, DEFE 13/25–70 · Royal Arch. | Bodl. Oxf., Woolton MSS · HLRO, corresp. with Lord Beaverbrook · JRL, corresp. with Sir Claude Auchinleck · NL Wales, corresp. with Thomas Jones · U. Birm. L., corresp. with Lord Avon | FILM BFI NFTVA, documentary footage · BFI NFTVA, news footage · IWM FVA, actuality footage · IWM FVA, news footage | SOUND IWM SA, oral history interview

Moncreiff, Sir Henry. *See* Wellwood, Sir Henry Moncreiff, eighth baronet (1750–1827).

Moncreiff, Henry James, **second Baron Moncreiff of Tulliebole** (1840–1909), judge, was born on 24 April 1840 in Edinburgh, the eldest son of James Wellwood *Moncreiff, first Baron Moncreiff of Tulliebole (1811–1895), and his wife, Isabella (1813–1881), daughter of Robert Bell, advocate. He was educated at Edinburgh Academy and Harrow School before going on to Trinity College, Cambridge in 1857. From the latter he graduated BA and LLB in 1861, taking a first in the law tripos. From there he went on to attend law classes at Edinburgh University and was admitted to the Faculty of Advocates in July 1863. He was also active as a member of the Speculative Society at this time and acquired a reputation as a better than average sportsman, becoming well known at Musselburgh links.

Moncreiff had been born into a family with a long-standing political and legal tradition, and it was apparently a matter of little surprise and comment when, in a rapid promotion, he was made an advocate-depute by his father in 1865. This office he held until the resignation of the Russell ministry in the following year, and then again from 1868 until 1874 and from 1880 to 1881, when he became sheriff of Renfrew and Bute. He built up a good practice at the bar and wrote *Review in Criminal Cases*, which appeared in 1877 and became something of a standard text.

On 3 April 1866 Moncreiff married Susan Wilhelmine (1843–1869), third daughter of Sir William Dick Cunningham of Prestonfield, Midlothian. After her death (on 29 October 1869) he married, on 26 March 1873, Millicent Julia (1845–1881), eldest daughter of Colonel Frederick Daniel Fryer of Moulton Paddocks, Newmarket, Suffolk. There were no children of either marriage.

Moncreiff, like his father, sympathized with the Liberal Unionists on the issue of Irish home rule and there was therefore nothing to stand in the way of his appointment to the bench in 1888, the same year in which his father retired, with the courtesy title of Lord Wellwood. This title he kept until his father's death on 27 April 1895, at which time he succeeded to the peerage as the second Baron Moncreiff as well as to the two family baronetcies.

As a lord ordinary in the outer house of the Court of Session Moncreiff was popular, with a reputation for being painstaking and, owing to his indifferent health, for occasional irritability. His elevation to the second division of the inner house in 1896 saw him enter an environment in which he did not prosper. In an atmosphere of struggle and strife, marked especially by the impatience of Lord George Young, Moncreiff's judgments may have been open to the charge of undue caution, but were nevertheless regarded as careful and thorough. He took a special interest in the principles of the law of testing. In January

1905, after frequent absences due to ill health in the previous two years, he gave up the fight and retired at the comparatively early age of sixty-four. In 1901 Moncreiff had been appointed lord lieutenant of Kinross-shire, in which Tulliebole lies. He was a contributor to the periodical press and was otherwise active as an author and poet. His sporting interests were reflected in 'The golfer at home' which appeared in the *Cornhill Magazine* in 1867 and in contributions on the same subject to the volume on golf in the Badminton Library. He also specialized in humorous short stories. Collections of his work were printed for private circulation in 1898 and in 1907.

Dividing his time mainly between Edinburgh, London, and North Berwick, Moncreiff continued to suffer from ill health after his retirement. On a visit to Bournemouth for health-related reasons he caught pneumonia, and died there on 3 March 1909. He was buried in the Grange cemetery, Edinburgh, on 8 March. His brother, Robert Chichester Moncreiff, a Church of England clergyman, succeeded to the family titles.   GORDON F. MILLAR

Sources *The Scotsman* (4 March 1909) · *Scottish Law Review*, 25 (1909), 99–100 · *Scottish Law Review*, 21 (1905), 43, 167–9 · S. P. Walker, *The Faculty of Advocates, 1800–1986* (1987), 129 · F. J. Grant, ed., *The Faculty of Advocates in Scotland, 1532–1943*, Scottish RS, 145 (1944), 153 · *The Scotsman* (9 March 1909) [funeral report] · F. Moncreiff and W. Moncreiffe, *The Moncreiffs and the Moncreiffes*, 1 (1929) · Burke, *Peerage* (1970) · [W. M. Watson], ed., *The history of the Speculative Society, 1764–1904* (1905), 151 · DNB
Likenesses F. Watt, oils (shortly before death)
Wealth at death £70,428 1s. 10d.: confirmation, 14 April 1909, CCI

Moncreiff, Sir Henry Wellwood, **tenth baronet** (1809–1883), Free Church of Scotland minister, was born at Edinburgh, on 21 May 1809, eldest son of Sir James Wellwood *Moncreiff, ninth baronet, later Lord Moncreiff (1776–1851), and his wife, Ann Robertson (d. 1843). Moncreiff attended Edinburgh high school and Edinburgh University before travelling to Martley rectory in Worcestershire in 1826, where he received tuition from an evangelical clergyman, Henry James Hastings. He matriculated at New College, Oxford, in April 1827 (graduating BA in 1831), where he befriended W. E. Gladstone. He returned to the University of Edinburgh to study divinity under Thomas Chalmers. Licensed by the presbytery of Edinburgh, he was ordained minister of Baldernock, Stirlingshire, in March 1836, transferring to East Kilbride, Lanarkshire, in November 1837. He married, on 8 March 1838, Alexina Mary (d. 1874), daughter of George Bell. He married again on 19 August 1875, his second wife being Lucretia (d. 1885), daughter of Andrew Murray, sheriff of Aberdeen. There were no children of either marriage.

Moncreiff joined the Free Church after the Disruption of 1843, and remained in East Kilbride until, in 1852, he was called to Free St Cuthbert's, Edinburgh, his grandfather's congregation, if not his church. He succeeded to his father's baronetcy in 1851, at which time he assumed the name Wellwood. In 1855 he became joint principal clerk of the Free Church general assembly. Honoured with the award of DD from Edinburgh University in 1860, he became secretary to the Bible Board in 1862, and in 1869 he served as moderator of his church. He took a leading role in the negotiations which led to union with the Reformed Presbyterian church in 1876. Although his church's procedural manual was drawn up by a committee, the work was largely his.

Moncreiff became more influential as time thinned the ranks of the Disruption ministers and he played a leading role in the prosecution of the Robertson Smith case. Principal Rainy's biographer recognized him as:

> less the leader than the counsellor, but in the latter capacity he was invaluable. He had much knowledge, a trained judgement, and was the soul of integrity and purity of motive in all he did. He was a fine type of the old Scottish gentleman—with a rubicund countenance, a portly presence, a stentorian voice, and an honest heart. (Simpson, 49–50)

He died, probably at his home, 6 Merchiston Crescent, Edinburgh, after a short illness, on 4 November 1883 and was buried in the Dean cemetery on 8 November.

LIONEL ALEXANDER RITCHIE

Sources J. A. Wylie, *Disruption worthies: a memorial of 1843*, ed. J. B. Gillies, new edn (1881), 419–28 · *Fasti Scot.* · *The Scotsman* (5 Nov 1883) · *The Scotsman* (9 Nov 1883) · *Biograph and Review*, 4 (1880), 107–8 · *The Bailie* (5 June 1878) · Burke, *Peerage* · *DNB* · P. C. Simpson, *The life of Principal Rainy*, 2 (1909), 49–50
Archives BL, corresp. with W. E. Gladstone, Add. MSS 44357–44617, *passim* · NRA Scotland, priv. coll., letters to Lord Moncreiff
Likenesses caricature, repro. in *The Bailie* · lithograph, repro. in Gillies, ed., *Disruption worthies*, 419
Wealth at death £3288 16s. 4d.: confirmation, 5 Dec 1883, CCI

Moncreiff, Sir James Wellwood, ninth baronet, Lord Moncreiff (1776–1851), judge, was born on 13 September 1776, the second son of the Revd Sir Henry Moncreiff *Wellwood, eighth baronet (1750–1827), of Tulliebole, Kinross-shire, and Susan (*d.* 1826), daughter of James Roberston Barclay of Keavil, Fife. This family of lairds had long been prominent in the Church of Scotland, to which it had given five ministers in previous generations. James Moncreiff attended school in Edinburgh and went on to Glasgow University (1788–93); he then held an exhibition at Balliol College, Oxford, from which he graduated BCL in 1800. He was called to the Scottish bar on 26 January 1799.

The Moncreiffs belonged to the popular party in the kirk, which opposed lay patronage, and to the small whig faction in Scottish politics; James shared his family's views. In 1795, when a youth of nineteen, he attracted attention by carrying a lighted tallow candle to allow the face of Henry Erskine, dean of the Faculty of Advocates, to be seen at a meeting of protest against the war with France; Erskine was afterwards deposed from the deanship. Moncreiff returned from Oxford as strong a Presbyterian and whig as when he went there. As a lay elder he spoke for the popular party in the general assembly of the Church of Scotland. Since that party formed only a minority, he was defeated when in 1806 he stood for the office of procurator. On 19 June 1808, Moncreiff married Ann (*d.* 1843), daughter of Captain George Robertson RN, and granddaughter of Principal William Robertson. They had five sons and three daughters. The eldest son was the Revd Sir Henry Wellwood *Moncreiff, tenth baronet; the second son was James Wellwood *Moncreiff, first Baron Moncreiff of Tulliebole.

By now Moncreiff had acquired a good practice at the bar. The ministry of All the Talents gave the Scots whigs their first preferment in twenty years, and on 7 February 1807 Moncreiff was appointed sheriff of Clackmannan and Kinross. He also mixed in the liberal literary circle associated with the *Edinburgh Review*, becoming a friend of Francis Jeffrey and Henry Cockburn, whose *Memorials* recorded:

> while grounded in the knowledge necessary for the profession of a liberal lawyer, [Moncreiff] was not a well-read man. Without his father's dignified manner, his outward appearance was rather insignificant … Always simple, direct, and practical, he had little need of imagination … He added to these negative qualities great powers of reasoning, unconquerable energy, and the habitual and conscientious practice of all the respectable and all the amiable virtues … Everything was a matter of duty with him, and he gave his whole soul to it. Jeffrey called him the whole duty of man! (*Memorials*, 250)

Moncreiff took a leading part in the agitation for reform in Scotland. On 19 December 1820 he presided at the Pantheon meeting, which passed resolutions in favour of a petition to the crown for the dismissal of the tory ministry of Lord Liverpool. On 22 November 1826 he was elected dean of the Faculty of Advocates; Jeffrey, though his senior, gracefully ceded his claim in favour of his friend. On 9 August 1827, on the death of his father (his unmarried elder brother had also died) Moncreiff succeeded to the baronetcy. In 1828, following a custom of the bar that no criminal however poor should be undefended nor without the services even of its professional head if necessary, Moncreiff defended the 'resurrectionist' William Burke. In March 1829 he spoke at a great meeting in Edinburgh in favour of Catholic emancipation. On 24 June of the same year he was made a judge of the court of session by Sir Robert Peel.

After the Reform Act of 1832, Moncreiff turned to reform of the church, for which other whigs had little taste. He continued to sit in the general assembly. It was he who in 1834 carried the motion, marking the new ascendancy of the popular party, for a congregational veto on ministers appointed by lay patronage. This unleashed the conflict between church and state in Scotland which was to lead to the Disruption in 1843. In the Auchterarden case in 1838, Moncreiff gave judgment in the minority in favour of the kirk. At the Disruption in 1843 he joined the Free Church of Scotland. He died a widower on 30 March 1851.

A. J. G. MACKAY, rev. MICHAEL FRY

Sources *Memorials of his time, by Henry Cockburn*, another edn, ed. H. A. Cockburn (1910) · G. Brunton and D. Haig, *An historical account of the senators of the college of justice, from its institution in MDXXXII* (1836) · Burke, *Peerage* (1970) · C. Robertson, ed., *Report of the Auchterarder case*, 2 vols. (1838) · Foster, *Alum. Oxon.*
Archives NRA, priv. coll., papers | NL Scot., letters to Andrew Rutherford · U. Edin., New Coll. L., letters to Thomas Chalmers
Likenesses S. Joseph, plaster bust, 1823, Scot. NPG; [on loan from trustees of William Moncreiff] · W. Brodie, marble bust, 1863, Parliament Hall, Edinburgh, Faculty of Advocates · J. W. Gordon, oils,

Parliament Hall, Edinburgh, Faculty of Advocates · C. Holl, stipple (after H. Raeburn), NPG

Wealth at death £448 4*s.* 6*d.*: 1851

Moncreiff, James Wellwood, first Baron Moncreiff of Tulliebole (1811–1895), lawyer and politician, was born at Edinburgh on 29 November 1811, the second of the eight children of Sir James Wellwood *Moncreiff, ninth baronet (1776–1851), lawyer, and Ann (*d.* 1843), daughter of George Robertson, a naval officer. He was educated at Edinburgh high school and Edinburgh University, where he was a member and president of the Speculative Society. He won the principal honours at both institutions, including the medal in Professor John Wilson's moral philosophy class in 1828. He married, on 12 September 1834, Isabella (1813–1881), only daughter of Robert Bell, procurator of the Church of Scotland, and sheriff of Berwickshire and East Lothian; they had five sons and two daughters.

Moncreiff was called to the Scottish bar in 1833 and within a few years had gathered a large practice, but from natural bent and family background he showed even more interest in politics than in the law. Moncreiff's father had presided at the Pantheon meeting in 1820, the first great whig public meeting in Scotland, and James was very much in this tradition—a free-trader, a supporter of the property-based franchise, and in favour of moderate reform in the interests of efficiency. Moncreiff was also in the thick of the struggle over the claims of the non-intrusionists to independence from lay patronage in the Church of Scotland and their defiance of the civil courts in the matter. He was engaged as counsel in the leading conflicts of that time, notably in the Marnoch and Auchterarder cases. With his father and his elder brother, Sir Henry Wellwood *Moncreiff, he came out with the seceders in 1843 and therefore helped to found the Free Church of Scotland. During this period he became one of the first contributors to the *North British Review*, which was started in the free-church interest in 1844.

In February 1850 Moncreiff was appointed solicitor-general for Scotland in Lord John Russell's administration, and in April 1851 he succeeded Andrew Rutherford as lord advocate. This made it necessary for him to find a seat in the House of Commons, which he did by taking over Leith burghs from Rutherford. This constituency, claimed by some inhabitants to be too firmly in the hands of lord advocates, he represented until 1859.

In February 1852 Moncreiff left office when the Russell ministry resigned, but he was made lord advocate again in Lord Aberdeen's coalition government in December 1852. This began the most fruitful and yet frustrating period of Moncreiff's parliamentary life. He introduced and carried an act to abolish almost all religious tests in Scottish universities in 1853 and was instrumental in preparing the way for the act reforming these institutions more generally passed by Lord Advocate Inglis in 1858. Also passed were acts to amend the bankruptcy laws (1856), and to streamline the registration of burgh voters (1856). All these measures stood in the whig reforming tradition, to which Moncreiff belonged.

In February 1854 Moncreiff introduced an education bill for Scotland which was intended to establish a national and less sectarian system of elementary education. This had been made a pressing question by the split in the Scottish church in 1843, which had greatly intensified sectarian rivalries in educational provision, and by the rapid growth of the population in urban areas, which had overwhelmed the traditional system of parish schools in Scottish towns. Moncreiff's bill was defeated, in common with his other proposals in the two following years, mainly by Conservative hostility and that of the established church, both Scottish and English; the suspicions within English nonconformism and the Scottish voluntary church also played a part.

When the coalition ministry fell in February 1855, and Lord Palmerston succeeded Aberdeen, Moncreiff was kept on as lord advocate, and in the following month he reintroduced a modified version of his Education Bill, which was passed by the Commons but thrown out by the Lords. Moncreiff had no more success with two separate bills, one for burgh and the other for parish schools, in 1856. Indeed, only in 1861 was he able to carry the modest reform of opening the parish schools up to teachers from other presbyterian denominations by abolishing the Church of Scotland's religious test. He then served between 1864 and 1867 as a member of the Argyll commission, set up to investigate Scottish education. Ironically, and despite yet another effort to reform Scottish education along the lines suggested by the commission in 1868, it was his successor as lord advocate, George Young, who finally succeeded in 1872 in passing a measure to create a national education system.

A powerful speaker, with a sonorous, bell-like voice, Moncreiff was also put up to speak for the governments he served on non-Scottish questions. He defended the Palmerston government, for example, on James Whiteside's motion accusing it of want of energy in preventing the fall of Kars during the Crimean War in 1856.

Except for the year of the Derby–Disraeli administration (February 1858–June 1859), Moncreiff was lord advocate until July 1866. His only other year of political office was from December 1868 to October 1869. The limits of his reforming creed were shown by his defence of this office against those, such as Sir James Fergusson and W. E. Baxter, who wanted to take the administration of non-legal Scottish business away from the lord advocate and give it to a 'Scottish secretary'. His legislative activity, apart from the field of education, continued in the 1860s to be concentrated on non-controversial administrative reforms, such as the County Voters Registration Act (1861), which cleaned up county electoral rolls considerably, and the General Police and Improvement Act (1862), which increased the powers available to Scottish local authorities.

During this later period of his parliamentary career Moncreiff was forced to change constituencies on two occasions, as Scottish whiggery came under pressure from more radical forms of Scottish urban Liberalism. Divisions in the Leith Liberal Party led him to move to Edinburgh in place of the retiring Charles Cowan in 1859.

Moncreiff's position in Edinburgh was then undermined partly by his continuing adherence to a limited, property-based franchise but mainly by others' opposition to his attempt to reform the Edinburgh annuity tax in an act of 1860. Anger at Moncreiff's failure totally to remove general public financial support for the city's Church of Scotland ministers was exploited by Duncan McLaren and Edinburgh's independent Liberals, and it led to the defeat of Moncreiff's fellow whig, Adam Black, in 1865, and to Moncreiff's retreat to the newly created, safer seat of Glasgow and Aberdeen Universities, in 1868.

From 1858 to 1869 Moncreiff was dean of the Faculty of Advocates, the leading position at the Scottish bar, and alongside his political career he continued work as an advocate. For example, he had defended the accused in the Chartist sedition trials of 1848 shortly before entering government. In 1856 he defended the whig *Scotsman* in a famous libel action raised by Duncan McLaren, his fellow Liberal and later political adversary in Edinburgh. As lord advocate he was engaged as public prosecutor in prominent cases, notably the trial of Madeleine Smith for murder in 1857. In 1861 he defended the Free Church in the Cardross case against interference from the civil courts.

In 1869 Moncreiff accepted the position of lord justice-clerk and president of the second division of the Court of Session. Although in his early years as a judge he had to work hard to compensate for a certain unfamiliarity with case law, important for appeals work in the Inner House, Moncreiff's long experience in the administration of the criminal law as lord advocate helped to make him a highly respected criminal judge. For the next nineteen years Lord Moncreiff presided, alongside his appeals work, over such criminal trials in the justiciary court as those of the directors of the City of Glasgow Bank, in 1878, and of the crofters, in 1886.

Moncreiff published anonymously in 1871 a novel entitled *A Visit to my Discontented Cousin*. At the time of his death his memoirs, in which he had invested some time, were unfinished. He was a frequent contributor to the *Edinburgh Review* and wrote articles for the *North British Review*. In 1858 Edinburgh University awarded him an honorary degree of LLD and from 1868 to 1871 he was its rector. He received another honorary LLD degree from Glasgow University in 1879. In 1869 he was sworn of the privy council. On 17 May 1871 he was created a baronet in his own right; on 1 January 1874 he was made a baron of the United Kingdom; and in 1883 he succeeded his brother as eleventh baronet, of Tulliebole.

Lady Moncreiff died on 19 December 1881. In September 1888 Moncreiff resigned the position of lord justice-clerk and in the same year his eldest son, Henry James *Moncreiff, later second Baron Moncreiff, became a lord of session, taking the title Lord Wellwood. Moncreiff himself died on 27 April 1895 at 15 Great Stuart Street, Edinburgh, and was buried on 1 May at Dean cemetery, Edinburgh. His pall-bearers included the serving lord advocate, his son-in-law J. B. Balfour, who had married Marianne Elizabeth Moncreiff in 1877. Moncreiff's undoubted importance in nineteenth-century Scotland sprang mainly from his

many years as holder of the office of lord advocate, with which he was said to be fascinated. He is credited with guiding more than a hundred measures onto the statute book and, before becoming a judge himself, appointing nearly a dozen others to the bench and twice as many sheriffs. However, his most significant contribution lay in his repeated attempts, which in his case remained unfulfilled, to reform Scottish elementary education.

GORDON F. MILLAR

Sources *The Scotsman* (29 April 1895) · *Glasgow Herald* (29 April 1895) · *The Times* (29 April 1895) · *Scottish Law Review*, 11 (1895), 153–72 · G. W. T. Omond, *The lord advocates of Scotland, second series, 1834–1880* (1914), 147–202, 226–59 · J. Moncrieff, *An educational retrospect* (1886) · W. H. Bain, 'The life and achievements of James, first baron Moncrieff, 1811 to 1895', MLitt diss., 1977 · *The Scotsman* (2 May 1895) · *Dod's Parliamentary Companion* (1867), 257 · G. Seton, *The house of Moncrieff* (1890), 156–9 · F. Moncreiff and W. Moncreiffe, *The Moncreiffs and the Moncreiffes*, 1 (1929), 170–72 · Burke, *Peerage* (1970) · *Hansard 3* (1856), 141.1684–8 · *DNB*

Archives NRA, priv. coll., corresp. and papers · Tulliebole Castle, Kinross-shire | BL, corresp. with Lord Aberdeen, Add. MS 43201 · BL, corresp. with W. E. Gladstone, Add. MSS 44356–44787 · NA Scot., lord advocate's MSS · NL Scot., letters to Andrew Rutherford · PRO, corresp. with Lord John Russell, PRO 30/22

Likenesses T. Atkinson, mezzotint, pubd 1872 (after D. Macnee), NPG · G. Reid, oils, exh. 1887, Parliament House, Edinburgh · J. Archer, pastel drawing, Dundee City Art Gallery · Caldesi, Blanford & Co., carte-de-visite, NPG · H. Délié, photograph, repro. in *Scottish Law Review*, 153 · W. Holl, stipple (after G. Richmond), BM, NPG · wood-engraving, NPG; repro. in *ILN* (17 April 1869)

Wealth at death £21,003 7s. 2d.: confirmation, 31 May 1895, CCI

Moncreiffe, Sir (Rupert) Iain Kay, of that ilk, eleventh baronet (1919–1985), herald and genealogist, was born on 9 April 1919, in the parish of Hampton Court, Middlesex, the only child of Lieutenant-Commander (Thomas) Gerald Auckland Moncreiffe RN (1886–1922) and his first wife, Hinda, daughter of Frank Meredyth, styled Comte François de Miremont. His father, who had settled in Kenya as a coffee planter before the First World War, died in 1922; his mother left her son's upbringing to nurses and later to uncles, aunts, and elderly relatives in London and Scotland. She remarried in 1923, her new husband being Captain Geoffrey Lionel Smith of Kenya. Moncreiffe was educated at Stowe School, briefly at Heidelberg University, and from 1938 at Christ Church, Oxford, where he read French and history. He served in the Scots Guards throughout the Second World War, saw much active service, attained the rank of captain, and was injured in Italy. After the war he became an attaché in the British embassy in Moscow, but soon returned to study Scots law at Edinburgh University (LLB, 1950), being admitted to the Faculty of Advocates in 1950. His legal practice was small but his distinction in peerage and related matters enabled him to take silk in 1980.

From an early age Moncreiffe had displayed a strongly genealogical and heraldic cast of mind, which derived in part from the great antiquity of his own family and partly from wide historical interests that took his researches far beyond Scots ancestry and gave him an enviably synchronous view of historical development. These instincts

Sir (Rupert) Iain Kay Moncreiffe of that ilk, eleventh baronet (1919–1985), by Dudley Reed, 1983

were emphasized by his marriage, in 1946, to Diana Denyse (called Dinan or Puffin) Hay (1926–1978), in her own right countess of Erroll and hereditary lord high constable of Scotland, and later by his inheritance in 1957 from a cousin of the baronetcy of Moncreiffe of that ilk ('of that ilk' means 'of that same place'). His wife was the daughter of Josslyn Victor *Hay, twenty-second earl of Erroll (1901–1941), notoriously killed near Nairobi, Kenya. They had two sons and a daughter.

Moncreiffe joined the court of lord Lyon king of arms as Falkland pursuivant in 1952, and became Kintyre pursuivant (in ordinary) from 1953, Unicorn pursuivant from 1955, and Albany herald from 1961. Although the chief office of the Lyon court eluded him, to his disappointment, he was widely recognized as an expert authority. He was appointed CVO in 1980.

Such resounding titles appealed to the popular press, which increasingly came to regard him as an (eminently quotable) super-snob, and he teasingly played up to this designation in an unguarded way that did little justice to his wide view (based on his deep understanding of Scottish clan history) of the importance of individual ancestry and of the universal bonds of tradition and continuity, themes which were well displayed in his writings.

In collaboration with the heraldic artist Don Pottinger, Moncreiffe published *Simple Heraldry* (1953), a considerable success that was followed by *Simple Custom* (1954) and *Blood Royal* (1956). Each was 'cheerfully illustrated', but their lightness of manner disguised a great deal of sound learning that was also shown in later writings, including the excellent *The Highland Clans* (1967) and many discursive book reviews. Most of his best work, however, remains unpublished, including his Edinburgh University PhD

thesis (1958), 'Origins and background of the law of succession of arms and dignities in Scotland'. He gave many expert opinions in peerage cases, and was frequently consulted, formally and informally.

Moncreiffe was a well-known figure in London clubland, and in Edinburgh founded his own club, Puffin's (named after his first wife), as a resort for Scottish country gentlemen. Quite short, with hair latterly almost white and a bristling moustache curved like a tilde, the quietly spoken baronet and chieftain had nothing overbearing in his appearance or manner. His neat little handwriting was described by a friend as 'like the footprints of a wren'. In conversation, as well as in his published work, he relied on a marvellously retentive memory that was unimpaired even by a considerable intake of alcohol. Conviviality that could prostrate others left him in full command of detail and only increased his extraordinary range of allusiveness.

Moncreiffe's first marriage was dissolved in 1964, and in 1966 he married Hermione Patricia, daughter of Lieutenant-Colonel Walter Douglas Faulkner, Irish Guards, and his wife, Patricia Katherine, later countess of Dundee. He had long lived at Easter Moncreiffe, near Perth, on lands held by his family from time immemorial, but it was at his London flat, 117 Ashley Gardens, Westminster, that he died on 27 February 1985. His elder son, Merlin Sereld Victor Gilbert, twenty-fourth earl of Erroll (b. 1948), succeeded to the baronetcy; to the younger, Peregrine, devolved the style of 'Moncreiffe of that ilk', which his father had done so much to enhance in the memory of a wide public. Moncreiffe's wife also survived him.

ALAN BELL, *rev.*

Sources J. Jolliffe, ed., *Sir Iain Moncreiffe of that ilk: an informal portrait* (1986) · H. Montgomery-Massingberd, ed., *Lord of the dance: a Moncreiffe miscellany* (1986) · personal knowledge (1990) · Burke, *Peerage* · CCI (1985)
Likenesses D. Hill, portrait, 1970, repro. in Montgomery-Massingberd, ed., *Lord of the dance*, facing p. 49; priv. coll. · D. Reed, photograph, 1983, NPG [*see illus.*]
Wealth at death £278,938.02: confirmation, 12 June 1985, CCI

Moncrieff, Sir Alan Aird (1901–1971), paediatrician, was born at East Cliff Manse, St Johns Wood Road, Bournemouth, on 9 October 1901, the second in the family of three sons of William Moncrieff, a Congregational minister of Bournemouth but formerly of Perth, and his wife, Isabella, daughter of John Masterson, who was in the army. He was educated at Caterham School and trained at the Middlesex Hospital, qualifying at the age of twenty-one and graduating MB BS (London) in 1923 with honours and a gold medal. He became MD and MRCP in 1925 and FRCP in 1934. In 1928 he married Honor Mary Constance (d. 1954), daughter of Cecil Wedmore, an author; they had a daughter and two sons.

Moncrieff held house officer and registrar appointments at the Middlesex Hospital and the Hospital for Sick Children, with a year in Paris (1923) working for the Red Cross. He later spent a year in clinics in Germany (1930), studying respiratory failure in the newborn. He was appointed paediatrician to Queen Charlotte's Maternity

Sir Alan Aird Moncrieff (1901–1971), by Elliott & Fry, 1948

Hospital (1933), and physician to the Hospital for Sick Children, the Middlesex Hospital, and the British Postgraduate Hospital, Hammersmith (1934), where he developed the renowned premature baby unit in 1947. These appointments were combined with a private practice based at 121 Harley Street. Moncrieff joined the Emergency Medical Service during the Second World War and never returned to his Harley Street practice.

In addition, Moncrieff worked in school medical and infant welfare clinics and as consultant for newborn babies to the Infectious Diseases Hospital, Willesden. None of these appointments brought a regular salary and he supplemented his income by medical journalism; for a time he was joint editor of *The Practitioner* and for many years was medical correspondent to *The Times*. He wrote numerous articles in journals relating to children's health, and was editor and part author of a number of textbooks, including *Nursing and Diseases of Sick Children* (1930). *Child Health and the State* (1953) was based on his three Newsholme lectures (1953).

Moncrieff was appointed to the first Nuffield chair in child health in the University of London in 1946 and held this post at the Hospital for Sick Children, Great Ormond Street. This brought a further surge in activity in addition to his clinical and teaching duties. He served on numerous Home Office and Ministry of Health committees, including the central training council in childcare under the Home Office and the Ingleby committee for children and young persons. He was on the clinical research board of the Medical Research Council and served as chairman of the Central Midwives' Board in 1967. He was also on the executive board of UNICEF and on the WHO maternal and child health panel. He was president of the British Paediatric Association (BPA) in 1962. As director of the Institute of Child Health from 1946 he was responsible for its rapid development and for the innovative departments of growth and development, and tropical medicine. He was also a keen JP, chairing a juvenile court until well after his retirement.

Moncrieff was a simple man, proud of being a son of the manse, with a retentive memory and a quick mind, capable of discarding irrelevant details without hesitation. His interest in the social aspect of child health did much to shape the nature of British paediatrics. He loved children and was a keen observer who possessed the ability to make correct deductions. He was appointed CBE in 1952 and knighted in 1964. He was made an honorary FRCOG in 1958, and chevalier of the Légion d'honneur in 1968. In 1952 he was Charles West lecturer at the Royal College of Physicians, and received the James Spence medal of the BPA in 1961. He retired in 1964 with the title professor emeritus of the University of London.

In 1955 Moncrieff married his recently deceased wife's cousin Mary Katherine (d. 1996), daughter of Ralph Wedmore, a businessman. She nursed him through his final illness until his death on 24 July 1971 at his home at Waterford Lodge, Waterford, Hertfordshire.

A. P. NORMAN, rev.

Sources *The Times* (26 July 1971) · Munk, *Roll* · personal knowledge (1993) · private information (1993 and 2004) · b. cert. · d. cert. · *BMJ* (31 July 1971) · *WWW*
Likenesses Elliott & Fry, photograph, 1948, NPG [see illus.] · J. Mendoza, oils, 1953, Royal College of Paediatricians · photograph, repro. in *BMJ*
Wealth at death £53,892: probate, 12 Oct 1971, *CGPLA Eng. & Wales*

Moncrieff, Alexander, of Culfargie (1695–1761), minister of the Secession church, born at Culfargie, Abernethy, Perthshire, was the eldest son of the laird of Culfargie and Margaret Mitchell, of the Bahbardie family from Fife. As his father died when Alexander was a boy he became heir to the estate. His grandfather Alexander Moncrieff of Scoonie, Fife, was the companion of the martyr James Guthrie, whose history and character deeply influenced Moncrieff. After studying at the grammar school in Perth he went to the University of St Andrews, where he graduated MA in 1714 and then entered the Divinity Hall. In 1716 he went to Leiden, where he pursued his theological studies, returning in August of the following year. He was licensed as a preacher by the presbytery of Perth in 1718, and in September 1720 he was ordained in his native parish of Abernethy. On 8 March 1722 he married Mary Clerk, daughter of Sir John Clerk of Penicuik. The Marrow controversy, in which Thomas Boston of Ettrick was a leading figure, began shortly after Moncrieff's ordination, and, although he took little part in the controversy itself, his theological sympathies lay firmly with Boston and the Marrow men. Moncrieff joined the Erskine brothers, Ralph and Ebenezer, in denouncing attempts to subvert the right of congregations to choose their own pastors. He was one of the four ministers whom the Church of Scotland's general assembly suspended in November 1733. Having formally separated themselves from the authority of the general assembly the four men formed, on 6 December 1733, at Gairney Bridge, Kinross-shire, the Secession Church of Scotland. With his fellow founder members Ebenezer Erskine, William Wilson, and James Fisher, Moncrieff jointly authored the Secession's 'judicial testimony' against the Church of Scotland in December 1736.

The new denomination met with widespread sympathy and success, and was soon not only licensing young men as preachers for different parts of the country, but even organizing a theological hall for the training of its future ministers. In February 1742 Moncrieff was unanimously chosen professor of divinity, a position which he filled with great ability and zeal. When the controversy over the burgess oath split the Secession church in 1747 into the Burghers and Anti-Burghers, Moncrieff played a leading role on the Anti-Burgher side, and served the new General Associate (Anti-Burgher) Synod as its theology professor until his death. He justified the breach with the Burghers in his influential *The Warrantableness of the Associate Synod's Sentence* (1747). Moncrieff was by this date married to his second wife, Jane Lyon (d. c.1791), daughter of William Lyon of Ogle; they had fifteen children, eight of whom died in infancy. In 1749 his son William (d. 1786) was ordained as his pastoral colleague and successor in the charge of the congregation at Abernethy. Moncrieff published in 1756 *England's Alarm*, which provided a warning of the wickedness to be found not only in England but also Scotland and Ireland. He died on 7 October 1761 at Culfargie, and was buried there.

Moncrieff, who was generally referred to as Culfargie, from his estate, left behind him an enduring reputation as a spiritually minded man of prayer, but he also had a name for resolution and daring and was jocularly called 'the lion of the Secession church' by his colleagues. He was survived by his two eldest sons, Matthew (d. 1767) and William, as well as his second wife. His *Practical Works* in two volumes were published posthumously in 1779 in Edinburgh.   T. B. JOHNSTONE, rev. N. R. NEEDHAM

Sources D. Young, *Memorials of the Rev. Alexander Moncrieff* (1849) · J. M'Kerrow, *History of the Secession church*, rev. edn (1848) · D. C. Lachman, 'Moncrieff, Alexander', *DSCHT* · *Fasti Scot.* · R. Small, *History of the congregations of the United Presbyterian church from 1733 to 1900*, 2 vols. (1904)
Likenesses line drawing, repro. in Young, *Memorials*, frontispiece

Moncrieff, Sir Alexander (1829–1906), army officer and engineer, born at 27 George Square, Edinburgh, on 17 April 1829, was the eldest son of Captain Matthew Moncrieff of Culfargie, of the Madras army, and Isabella (d. 1880), daughter of Archibald Campbell. His father was a descendant of Alexander Moncrieff: he retained the 'superiority' and designation of Culfargie (in Perthshire), but the estate had been sold to Lord Wemyss, and he lived at Barnhill near Perth.

Moncrieff was educated at Edinburgh and Aberdeen universities, and spent some time in a civil engineer's office, but did not settle down to a profession. He was commissioned lieutenant in the Forfarshire artillery (militia) on 16 April 1855, and obtained leave to go to the Crimea during the siege of Sevastopol. He was promoted captain on 16 September 1857, was transferred to the City of Edinburgh artillery on 9 November 1863, became major on 26 March 1872, and was made colonel of the 3rd brigade, Scottish division, Royal Artillery, on 20 February 1878.

As he watched the bombardment of 6 June 1855, and the silencing of the Russian guns in the Mamelon by shots through the embrasures, Moncrieff's mind turned to the problem of raising and lowering guns, so that they might fire over the parapet and then descend under cover for loading. He conceived the idea of mounting guns on curved elevators, which would allow them to recoil backwards and downwards, the energy of recoil being used to raise a counterweight which would bring the gun up again to the firing position. This method had the further advantage that it lessened the strain on the platform by interposing a moving fulcrum between it and the gun. He carried out experiments at his own expense for several years, and a 7 ton gun mounted on his system was tried at Shoeburyness and favourably reported on in 1868.

From 1867 to 1875 Moncrieff was attached to the Royal Arsenal, to work out the details of his disappearing carriage, adapt it to heavier and lighter guns, and devise means of laying and sighting guns so mounted. He received £10,000 for his invention and for any improvements on it. In 1869 he submitted designs for a hydropneumatic carriage, in which air was compressed by the recoil of the gun and formed a spring to raise it again. This was intended for naval use in the first instance, but it was adapted to siege and fortress guns, and eventually superseded the counterweight system. It met with opposition at first, as too complicated, and Moncrieff complained bitterly of the obstacles placed in his way. He had controversy also with officers of the Royal Engineers, who held that he claimed too much for his system, and was not entitled to dictate how and where it should be used. There was widespread agreement, however, as to the merit of his inventions, and in the 1880s and 1890s—despite their cost, complexity, and the relatively low rate of fire—his disappearing mountings were used in the coastal defences of Britain and the colonies. He published in 1873 a pamphlet on the Moncrieff system, which he explained or defended in lectures at the Royal Institution (7 May 1869) and the United Service Institution, in the *Proceedings of the Royal Artillery Institution* for 1868, and the Royal Engineers' professional papers of 1870. He was a member of the Institution of Civil Engineers, was elected FRS in 1871, and was made CB in 1880 and KCB in 1890. He was also a supporter of the Oxford Military College (1876–96) at Cowley, and a member of its building committee.

On 20 April 1875 Moncrieff married Harriet Mary (d. 17 Feb 1907), only daughter of James Rimington Wilson of Broomhead Hall, Yorkshire. They had five sons and two daughters. The eldest son, Malcolm Matthew (6th dragoon guards), and a younger son, Alaric Rimington (6th Inniskilling dragoons), served in the Second South African War. A man of many interests, genial and sociable, Moncrieff went to South Africa and Canada for sport, and exhibited at the Scottish Academy as an amateur artist. He was captain of the Wimbledon golf club in 1894. In later life he was a director of two banks, acquired wealth, and bought the estate of Bandirran in Perthshire. He claimed to be head of his family as the heir male of William Moncrieff, who died in 1570; but this claim affected the title to the baronetcy created in 1626, and was opposed by Lord Moncreiff of Tulliebole, the holder of the baronetcy. The case came to court in June 1905, and the evidence produced led to the withdrawal of his petition. He died at Bandirran on 3 August 1906, and was buried at Abernethy, Perthshire.

E. M. LLOYD, *rev.* M. G. M. JONES

Sources *The Times* (6 Aug 1906) · G. Seton, *The house of Moncrieff* (1890) · Burke, *Gen. GB* · private information (1912) · *WWW* · Kelly, *Handbk* · J. Tecklenborough [H. Naidley], *Seven years' cadet-life: containing the records of the Oxford Military College* (1885)
Likenesses J. H. Lorimer, pencil drawing, 1891, Scot. NPG
Wealth at death £95,146 15s. 9d.: confirmation, 26 Nov 1906, *CCI*

Moncrieff, Charles Kenneth Michael Scott (1889–1930), translator, was born on 25 September 1889 at Weedingshall, Polmont, near Falkirk, Stirlingshire, the third son of William George Scott Moncrieff (1846–1927), advocate and sheriff substitute for Stirlingshire, and his wife, Jessie Margaret (1858–1936), daughter of Robert Scott Moncrieff, merchant of Calcutta. The Moncrieffs (variously spelt) are an ancient Scottish family; Scott Moncrieff, a keen genealogist, traced their history in the introduction to his translation (1925) of *The Adventures of Zeloïde and Amanzarifdine* by an eighteenth-century French cousin, Paradis de Moncrif. He never used the form Scott-Moncrieff, by which he is often known.

Scott Moncrieff's boyhood was spent in Scotland in a number of different places. His father was transferred successively to Inverness and Lanark, and he himself, who was proud of his Scottishness, wrote ruefully in 1929 that he had no place of his own: 'it is a grim thing to be homeless' (Scott Moncrieff, 189).

Being considerably younger than his brothers, Scott Moncrieff had a somewhat solitary childhood, developing a taste for books and starting early to write poetry. He went to school in Inverness and Nairn, and in 1903 won a scholarship to Winchester College, from where in 1908 he went to Edinburgh University; he took a first degree in law, was awarded a bursary in Old English in 1913, and graduated with first-class honours in English language and literature in 1914. Among his teachers was Professor George Saintsbury, who was to become a valued friend.

A keen officer cadet, Scott Moncrieff was commissioned second lieutenant in 1913; in August 1914 he joined the King's Own Scottish Borderers. He served in Flanders for more than two years, though with long periods of sick leave, and won the admiration and affection of his fellow soldiers through his concern for them and his bravery. In 1915 he was promoted captain. In April 1917 he was

Charles Kenneth Michael Scott Moncrieff (1889–1930), by unknown photographer, c.1916

severely wounded in the leg while leading his battalion into an attack; the wound left him permanently lame. In May 1917 he was awarded the Military Cross for gallantry. After convalescing he served in the War Office until the end of the war.

The experience of war left its mark on Scott Moncrieff, not only physically, but through the loss of many friends. His translation (1919) of the Old French *Chanson de Roland* contains dedicatory poems to three of these, including Wilfred Owen, to whom he became deeply attached in 1918. The *Song of Roland* was followed by a translation of another epic, *Beowulf*, in 1921. In the immediate post-war period he moved in London literary circles, reviewing regularly in G. K. Chesterton's *New Witness*, and publishing occasional stories and poems. He worked for a time as private secretary for Lord Northcliffe and as a journalist on *The Times*, but from 1923 lived entirely on his earnings as a translator.

In 1919 Scott Moncrieff had discovered Marcel Proust's *A la recherche du temps perdu* (rendered in his translation as *Remembrance of Things Past*). Over the next ten years he published *Swann's Way* (2 vols., 1922), *Within a Budding Grove* (2 vols., 1924), *The Guermantes Way* (2 vols., 1925), *Cities of the Plain* (2 vols., 1927–9), *The Captive* (1929), and *The Sweet Cheat Gone* (1930). (The final volume of Proust's sequence, *Time Regained*, was done by his friend Sydney Schiff after his death.) Although Scott Moncrieff joked irreverently about

Proust, he set great value on him and after Proust's death edited *Marcel Proust: an English Tribute* (1923).

Scott Moncrieff translated much else besides: four major works of fiction by Stendhal (*The Charterhouse of Parma*, 2 vols., 1925; *Scarlet and Black*, 2 vols., 1926; *The Abbess of Castro and other Tales*, 1926; *Armance*, 1928); three volumes of Pirandello; the Latin letters of Abelard and Héloïse; the memoirs of Lauzun; a frivolous tale by Paradis de Moncrif; a novel by Jean-Richard Bloch. He translated quickly, for modest financial rewards, and some of his authors (for example, Bloch and Abelard) he found less congenial than Proust. The bookseller Orioli described his way of working in these terms:

> He carried in his left hand the French volume he was translating, read a few lines of it, interrupted his reading in order to talk to me, and then took a notebook out of his pocket and wrote in English the few lines he had just read, leaning against a pine tree.   (Orioli, 228)

From 1923 until his death Scott Moncrieff lived principally in Italy, first in Tuscany, mainly in Pisa, and from 1928 in Rome. His friend the German scholar E. R. Curtius wrote that 'he was a Roman body and soul', loving 'the everyday life of the city'. He returned to Britain from time to time, and cultivated a wide circle of friends. He loved conversation; according to Curtius, 'a dominating, brilliantly humorous mood was his usual attitude' (Scott Moncrieff, 179). His reviewing was combative and caustic, notably in a prolonged polemic with the Sitwell circle begun in *New Witness* in 1919 and culminating in the pamphlet *The Strange and Striking Adventures of Four Authors in Search of a Character*, published under the name of P. G. Lear and L. O. in 1926. Some found him malicious, but the *Times* obituarist insisted on the goodness and kindness beneath the surface. He remained close to his mother and supported the families of his brothers, giving as his recreation in *Who's Who* 'nepotism'.

Scott Moncrieff was a handsome, well-built man, with a fine head and a remarkable voice. Having converted to Roman Catholicism during the war, he practised assiduously and fervently. At the same time he had a marked taste for the scandalous, writing an enthusiastic preface for a reissue (1923) of the *Satyricon* of Petronius, with whom he compares Proust for his frank description of unorthodox morals (Scott Moncrieff shared Proust's homosexual orientation).

Vyvyan Holland, in his obituary, wrote that Scott Moncrieff did much to raise the profession of translator to an honourable position in the world of literature. He is, with Constance Garnett, the most celebrated of twentieth-century translators into English. He attempted in *Beowulf* and in the assonant verse of the *Song of Roland* to respect both form and meaning, bringing readers into contact with something foreign and archaic. These versions were much praised in his day, but it was in the translation of modern writing that he made his lasting contribution to English literature. His Stendhal, vigorous and witty though it is, was partly superseded by other versions, but his Proust, later revised to take account of new French editions, was the classic text which exerted an incalculable

influence on readers and on literature in English in the twentieth century. There are errors and omissions in the translation, but it is generally scrupulous, rendering Proust's rhythms and images with remarkable flair. His English has acquired a not inappropriate period flavour; although some feel that his version prettifies Proust, he creates in language an attractive and witty narrator worthy of the original.

In November 1929 Scott Moncrieff was admitted to hospital in Rome, suffering from terminal cancer. He suffered great pain and died there on 28 February 1930. His funeral service was held in the baptistery of the church of St John Lateran, and he was buried in the Verano cemetery on 2 March. His estate after death (almost entirely books and currency) was estimated at £418.   PETER FRANCE

Sources C. K. Scott Moncrieff, *Memories and letters*, ed. J. M. Scott Moncrieff and L. W. Lunn (1931) · C. R. Gale, 'Charles Scott Moncrieff: a biography', PhD diss., U. Cal., Berkeley, 1969 · 'The translator as artist', *The Times* (3 March 1930) · V. Holland, *London Mercury*, 21 (1929–30), 529–36 · V. Payen-Payne, 'The translator of Marcel Proust: C. K. Scott-Moncrieff and his work', *The Bookman*, 79 (1930–31), 176–7 · G. Orioli, *Adventures of a bookseller* (1938) · M. M. Stuart, 'Ink in their veins', *Scottish Genealogist*, 29 (1982), 120–22 · private information (2004) · CGPLA Eng. & Wales (1930)
Archives NL Scot., notebooks and translations · U. Reading L., Chatto and Windus archive, letters about publication | Faber and Faber, archives, letters to T. S. Eliot · NYPL, Berg collection, letters to Sir Edward Marsh
Likenesses photograph, c.1913, repro. in Payen-Payne, 'The translator of Marcel Proust', 176 · photograph, c.1916, repro. in Scott Moncrieff, *Memories and letters*, frontispiece [*see illus.*] · E. S. Mercer, 1919, Scot. NPG
Wealth at death £418: administration, 20 May 1930, CGPLA Eng. & Wales

Moncrieff, James (1744–1793), army officer and military engineer, was the son of James Moncrieff of Sauchop, Fife. He attended the Royal Military Academy, Woolwich, between 11 March 1759 and 28 January 1762, when he was appointed practitioner engineer and ensign. During the earl of Albemarle's expedition to capture Havana he served as an ensign in the 100th foot, into which he was commissioned on 10 July 1762. On the disbandment of the regiment, on 18 November 1763, he transferred to the Royal Engineers, and was promoted sub-engineer and lieutenant on 4 December 1770. Much of his early military career was spent in the West Indies and North America, and he was promoted captain in the Royal Engineers on 10 January 1776, shortly after the commencement of the American War of Independence.

In 1777 Moncrieff constructed a bridge across the Raritan river near New York which was of sufficient interest for a model to be made and deposited at Woolwich. The same year he participated in General William Howe's Philadelphia campaign and the American defeat at Brandywine (11 September 1777). He is reputed to have assisted the advance of the 4th foot by leading them across one of the many fords on the battlefield, and later the same month he was commended for his part in the capture of the American frigate *Delaware*. In 1778 he was briefly captured by the Americans at Flatbush (a village on

Long Island, near New York). It was in the southern campaign, however, that he achieved prominence, initially with Major-General Augustine Prevost's forces in Georgia and South Carolina in 1779. He was a member of Prevost's rearguard stationed on James Island after the failed attempt to take Charles Town (11–12 May 1779). When this force was attacked by the Americans at Stono Ferry (20 June 1779) it succeeded in beating them off and inflicted heavy losses. Moncrieff took an active part in the pursuit and captured an ammunition wagon.

Prevost's forces retired on Savannah, Georgia, and it was during the defence against the allied force of the American General Benjamin Lincoln and the French Admiral comte d'Estaing that Moncrieff distinguished himself as the chief engineer responsible for the fortifications and artillery. Such was his activity that the French declared his batteries sprang up like mushrooms in the night. Moncrieff's services in successfully resisting the siege were rewarded by his promotion to brevet major on 27 December 1779, the date the dispatches recounting the operation were presented to the king.

Moncrieff remained with the troops at Savannah until they were joined by an expedition commanded by Lieutenant-General Henry Clinton in February 1780. The expedition had been sent to capture Charles Town and commenced siege operations on 1 April under Moncrieff's direction. By the end of April the British proximity to the defenders' positions made surrender inevitable; this followed on 12 May. The American losses were significant, and included no fewer than seven generals and a considerable amount of ordnance stores, though the exact number of prisoners is disputed.

Moncrieff remained at Charles Town as chief engineer and was promoted lieutenant-colonel in the army on 27 September 1780. Aside from his official role, he was elected president in 1781 of the St Andrew's Society, a social and philanthropic enterprise founded in Charles Town in 1729. He recognized the crown's obligations to the many hundreds of black workers employed in the engineering and ordnance departments, among others, but his proposal of raising a brigade of black soldiers was never realized. The Americans were to accuse him of personal profit when the British evacuated Charles Town in December 1782 and took with them 800 black slaves: he had reputedly boasted that he would carry at least 200 of them to his own estates in East Florida.

Moncrieff spent the years after the American War of Independence engaged primarily in engineering duties in southern England, where he received the appointment of deputy quartermaster-general on 14 July 1790. During this period he was promoted colonel in the army (18 November 1790). When France declared war on Great Britain on 1 February 1793 he was selected by the king as one of the key staff officers chosen to advise the young duke of York, who commanded the expeditionary force sent to Belgium. Moncrieff was appointed quartermaster-general to the duke on 25 February 1793, and in addition acted as *de facto* chief engineer, a position he owed to his technical abilities and experience in America. He arrived with the army

at the end of March, and according to one subordinate had 'Very much got the ear of the Duke of York' (Leslie, 26).

The allied armies spent much of 1793 attacking the series of barrier fortresses ranged along the northern French border. Moncrieff's abilities came into their own during the siege of Valenciennes (13 June–28 July 1793) at which York commanded the primarily Anglo-Austrian attacking force. Regular siege operations culminated in a successful assault on the Mons hornwork fortifications delivered on 25 July, and with the allies now firmly established in the outworks of the town the French position became untenable: they surrendered on 28 July. Moncrieff was promoted regimental lieutenant-colonel near the beginning of the siege (18 June 1793).

York's force now engaged in the siege of Dunkirk. However, the operation started and continued badly, since the siege train did not arrive from England until long after the date promised, thus allowing the French to counter-attack, and the naval support arrived too late to prevent enemy gunboats from enfilading the allied siege works. The allied besieging force was subjected to increasing French pressure, and, despite one sortie by the garrison being repulsed on 5 September, a second attack on the following day caused heavy casualties to the 14th foot (fifty-two of all ranks) and mortally wounded Moncrieff. As the duke of York described in a letter to the king, 'I have however greatly to lament poor Colonel Moncrief who was shot through the head with a grapeshot towards the end of the action' (*Later Correspondence of George III*, 2.88). Moncrieff was buried with full military honours at Ostend on 10 September, the funeral being attended by the duke of York, General George Ainslie, the town's governor, and the officers there.

Few contemporary descriptions of Moncrieff exist, though the general opinion held of him was summarized by Herbert Taylor, a junior member of York's staff, as 'An able and very gallant man (indeed, he exposed his person uselessly) … He spoke only English, or rather Scotch' (*Taylor Papers*, 27). Moncrieff had died unmarried, and he left his estate at Airdrie and property in the West Indies to his five sisters.

R. N. W. THOMAS

Sources *GM*, 1st ser., 63 (1793), 869, 884, 955, 976 · Fortescue, *Brit. army* · *Army List* (1759–93) · in-papers, commander-in-chief, British army on the continent, 1793, PRO, WO 1/166, 167 · *The later correspondence of George III*, ed. A. Aspinall, 5 vols. (1962–70), vol. 2 · M. Duffy, ' "A particular service": the British government and the Dunkirk expedition of 1793', *EngHR*, 91 (1976), 529–44 · J. H. Leslie, 'Campaigning in 1793: Flanders', *Journal of the Society for Army Historical Research*, 8 (1928), 2–32 · G. S. McCowen, *The British occupation of Charleston, 1780–82* (1972) · J. S. Pancake, *This destructive war: the British campaign in the Carolinas, 1780–1782* (1985) · *The Taylor papers, being a record of certain reminiscences, letters and journals in the life of Lieut.-Gen. Sir Herbert Taylor*, ed. E. Taylor (1913) · James Moncrieff letterbook, U. Mich., Clements L. · *Report on American manuscripts in the Royal Institution of Great Britain*, 4 vols., HMC, 59 (1904–9), vols. 1–3 · E. W. H. Fyers, 'General Sir William Howe's operation in Pennsylvania, 1777', *Journal of the Society for Army Historical Research*, 9 (1929), 28–9 · W. Porter, *History of the corps of royal engineers*, 1 (1889) · M. M. Boatner, *Cassell's biographical dictionary of the American War of Independence, 1763–1783* (1973)

Archives U. Mich., Clements L., letter-book | PRO, commander-in-chief in-papers

Wealth at death left estates in West Indies and at Airdrie, Scotland, to five sisters: *GM*, 869

Moncrieff, William Gibbs Thomas [*formerly* William Thomas Thomas] (**1794–1857**), playwright and theatre manager, was born William Thomas Thomas in London on 24 August 1794, the son of a tradesman of Newcastle Street, Strand. About 1804 he was put to work in a solicitor's office, and later became a clerk with the firm of Moses Hooper, Great Marlborough Street. He is said to have written the spectacle drama *Moscow, or, The Cossack's Daughter* (Regency Theatre, 1810), but in the period up to about 1815 he began to earn a livelihood as a law stationer, to write songs, including the popular 'Pretty star of the night all others outstanding', and to contribute theatre criticism to *The Satirist* and *The Scourge*. His dramatic career proper began when he was introduced to Robert William Elliston, the lessee of the Olympic, for whom, under his adopted name William Thomas Moncrieff (he also used the name William Gibbs Thomas Moncrieff), he wrote in his first season the lively musical farces *The Diamond Arrow* (1816) and *All at Coventry* (1817). In the second season he produced the slightly risqué burlesque *Giovanni in London* (1817), which, when its hero's role was turned into a breeches part, gave Madame Vestris one of her greatest successes. Moncrieff asserted later that the piece 'was written before I arrived at years of discretion' and ought never to have been licensed by the Lord Chamberlain ('Select committee on dramatic literature', 178). For the ensuing season Moncrieff wrote the opening night address and the musical comedy *Rochester, or, King Charles the Second's Merry Days* (16 November 1818), which ran for more than eighty nights.

After becoming manager at Astley's, Moncrieff staged the equestrian drama *The Dandy Family*, which ran for nearly a hundred nights. He also wrote for the Adelphi and Coburg theatres, including, at the latter, *The Lear of Private Life* (1820), a drama ostensibly founded on Mrs Opie's *Father and Daughter*, but in reality a domestication of Shakespeare, and, also in 1820, *The Shipwreck of the Medusa*, which exploited intense popular interest in Géricault's painting, then being exhibited in London.

Moncrieff's propensity for adapting novels for the stage, sometimes before their conclusions had appeared in print, later to arouse Dickens's wrath, was first shown by his dramatization of Pierce Egan's picaresque novel *Life in London* as *Tom and Jerry* (Adelphi, 1821), which achieved a success second only to that of *The Beggar's Opera* and generated almost as much controversy; even the Lord Chamberlain came to see it after 'a great outcry' as to its immoral tendency ('Select committee', 178). Moncrieff returned to write for Elliston, newly installed as the lessee of Drury Lane, in 1819–20 'as a sort of hack author' on a weekly salary of £10 to supply any piece the theatre required (ibid., 175). Under this regime, which lasted about three years, until he quarrelled with Elliston over unfulfilled promises, he wrote *The Spectre Bridegroom* and *Monsieur Tonson* (both 1821). His most famous drama was *The Cataract of the Ganges* (1823), written at Elliston's request for an afterpiece combining water and horses, which concluded with the hero ascending a waterfall on horseback, carrying the rescued heroine, while fire rages all round. This huge spectacle was denounced by several commentators as foreshadowing the death of drama: the *Morning Chronicle* (28 October) dismissed it as 'tinsel and trumpery'. The same trend continued with Moncrieff's *Zoroaster* (1824), which, with its enormous Egyptian diorama advertised as 482 feet long, had to be scaled down for the scene shifters and carpenters to manage.

In 1827 Moncrieff undertook the management of Vauxhall Gardens, and in 1828, in partnership with John Barnett, he opened a music shop in Regent Street. With Nicholas Bochsa he edited *The Minstrel's Offering* (1831?), a collection of songs. He wrote a number of pieces for the Surrey Theatre from 1828, including *Shakespeare's Festival, or, A New Comedy of Errors* (1830), partly a reworking of Garrick's *Jubilee*, and dramatized Bulwer-Lytton's Newgate novel *Eugene Aram* (1832). He also wrote for the New City Theatre, Milton Street, of which he was lessee between 1833 and 1835, and for the Coburg (renamed the Victoria), where he was acting and stage manager, between 1835 and 1837. His sight began to fail, but he accepted an engagement with W. J. Hammond at the Strand Theatre, where he produced his first Dickens adaptation, *Sam Weller* (1837), as the final part of *Pickwick Papers* was being published. He also dramatized W. H. Ainsworth's *Jack Sheppard* (Victoria, 1839). Moncrieff is generally thought to have been the original of the 'literary gentleman' who dramatized any novel to order in *Nicholas Nickleby* (which Moncrieff dramatized in May 1839, six months before Dickens finished the novel). In a 'manifesto' to the public (5 June 1839) Moncrieff vigorously defended his practice by observing that he was only one of a crowd of playwrights who did the same thing and that novels in any case were always considered fair game.

Moncrieff had money problems—he was arrested for debt twice in 1829, appearing before the insolvent debtors' court in 1830—and also struggled with progressive blindness, which by 1842 became total. His inability to afford to employ an amanuensis severely curtailed his literary and dramatic activity after 1840, when he applied to the Literary Fund for assistance and received a grant of £25. A second grant of £10 came in 1842. By then he was a widower, with no living children, and he expressed his despair now that 'the cold gloom of poverty is added to the darkness that half shuts out life' (Royal Literary Fund archive, letter, 5 April). However, he completed a twelve-part series on his old employer Elliston ('Ellistoniana', *New Monthly Magazine*, 1843).

In 1844, on the presentation of the queen, Moncrieff became a brother of the Charterhouse, in Aldersgate Street, and received partial board and a pension of 10s. a week. This austere institution, regulated by Carthusian asceticism, was totally unsuited to Moncrieff, who could not venture out of his room without a guide. A final burst of activity in 1851—when his dramatic reminiscences were sold to the *Sunday Times* and a subscription edition of his selected dramatic works (three volumes, containing twenty-four plays, all previously published) was issued by

Lacy—fuelled his frustration at his living conditions. His application to the Literary Fund described the Charterhouse as not 'in unison with the liberal spirit of the age' and having not 'progressed with the march of civilisation' (Royal Literary Fund archive, letter, 4 February). These criticisms were communicated to Buckingham Palace and some attempt appears to have been made to investigate them. Lonely and ill, Moncrieff received £30 between April and July 1851 and spent six weeks at Herne Bay, Kent, vainly trying to recover his health and even alleviate his blindness, which some oculists of the day represented as the consequence of a general physical prostration. He died at the Charterhouse on 3 December 1857, aged sixty-three. The *Sunday Times* commented that, though suffering much in latter years, 'he was the same cheerful and chatty companion when a friend called in to see him, as he ever had been' (6 Dec 1857).

Moncrieff wrote several non-dramatic works, among them guidebooks to Leamington (1822) and Stratford (1824), an elegy in imitation of Gray called 'Prison Thoughts' (1821), a volume of poems (1829) privately printed when he owned a press (at Saville House, Lambeth), and a comic poem 'The Triumph of Reform' (1832). By his own estimate in 1840, he wrote upwards of 200 dramatic pieces, only a minority of which, between sixty and seventy, were printed. Some were included in *Richardson's New Minor Drama* (4 vols., 1828–31), which he edited and for which he supplied biographical and critical prefaces in an attempt to raise the profile of minor theatre drama. He had an unerring instinct for what his audiences wanted. But Moncrieff's own description of himself as a hack, and the fact that he wrote to order and too much, belies his overall achievement, which challenged the unwritten boundaries on what was permissible as minor theatre drama, to the extent that, as the *Theatrical Inquisitor* (December 1818) noted, Moncrieff's early contributions to the Olympic were 'far superior' to much of what was produced at the regular theatres. At his best, as in *Rochester*—claimed as 'the first regular drama produced at a minor theatre without an accompanying tinkle of the piano' ('Remarks', *Richardson's New Minor Drama*, 1)—it has been suggested by a modern commentator that he shows 'the tone and energy of a Farquhar' (Donohue, 132). In his spirited version of *Tom and Jerry*, deservedly successful over 300 nights, Moncrieff shows unusual linguistic verve in the handling of gambling and auctioneering slang.

JOHN RUSSELL STEPHENS

Sources *Sunday Times* (6 Dec 1857) · Royal Literary Fund archive, file no. 1008, vol. 31 · 'Select committee on dramatic literature', *Parl. papers* (1831–2), vol. 7, no. 679 · *Reynolds's Miscellany*, 9 (1853), 28–9 · C. Murray, *Robert William Elliston, manager* (1975) · J. Donohue, *Theatre in the age of Kean* (1975) · *The Times* (5 April 1830) · letters, *The Times* (20 Jan 1837) · letters, *The Times* (22 Jan 1837) · E. B. Watson, *Sheridan to Robertson* (1926) · T. E. Pemberton, *Dickens and the stage* (1888) · J. R. Stephens, *The profession of the playwright: British theatre, 1800–1900* (1992) · A. Nicoll, *Early nineteenth century drama, 1800–1850*, 2nd edn (1955), vol. 4 of *A history of English drama, 1660–1900* (1952–9), 358–61, 600 [incl. bibliography]
Archives BL, Add. MSS 42866–43017 · University of Rochester, New York, Rush Rhees Library, corresp. and financial papers | BL, letters to C. Mackay, Add. MS 29905, fols. 102–53 · BL, letters to Royal Literary Fund, loan 96 · BL, letters to J. Winston and R. W. Elliston, Add. MS 33964, fols. 295–351
Likenesses engraving, 1819, Harvard TC · stipple, 1819, BM · J. K. Meadows, lithograph, BM · J. K. Meadows, vignette, Harvard TC · B. Reading, vignette, Harvard TC · portrait (after engraving), repro. in Donohue, *Theatre*, 119 · portrait, repro. in *Reynolds's miscellany*

Mond family (*per.* 1867–1973), chemical manufacturers and industrialists, came to prominence with the life and career of Ludwig Mond, chemical technologist, manufacturer, and collector of works of art. He was the first of a notable dynasty of science-based businessmen, some of whom are better known under the name of Melchett (the family's title). The Monds played a leading role in the growth of large-scale industrial enterprise, but they also made themselves felt in other fields such as politics and the philosophy of management. They were patrons of the arts and respecters of scholarship. Judaism played a varying role in the family, insignificant for some, dominant for others.

Founder of the family Ludwig Mond (1839–1909) was born on 7 March 1839 at Kassel, Germany, son of a Jewish merchant, Moritz B. Mond, and his wife, Henriette (*née* Levinsohn). He was educated at first in Kassel, at the *Realschule* and the polytechnic school. This was followed by university studies at Marburg, under Hermann Kolbe, and at Heidelberg, under Robert Wilhelm Bunsen. He then pursued a lifetime of industrial work, first in factories in Germany and the Netherlands, moving to England to John Hutchinson & Co. in Widnes in 1862 and, from 1864 to 1867, extending his experience in Utrecht. In 1866 he married his cousin Frida Löwenthal (1847–1923). They had two sons, Robert Ludwig and Alfred Moritz.

In 1867 Mond began his involvement in chemical business affairs by forming a partnership with John Hutchinson to promote a process for recovering sulphur from the waste products of the clumsy and uneconomic Leblanc process for making soda (a substance of central importance in many manufactures) from salt. From now on England was his home and he became a naturalized British subject in 1880. His success began, however, with another process. In 1872 he met Ernest Solvay, a Belgian chemist who was perfecting a better process of making soda (the ammonia-soda process, originated by H. G. Dyer and J. Hemming in 1838). Mond purchased rights to operate Solvay's process. He entered into partnership with John Tomlinson *Brunner, a friend from his Hutchinson days, to set up a Solvay process factory at Widnes. It took time to bring the process to commercial profitability, but by its success it turned the firm, within twenty years, into the largest producer of soda in the world.

Mond recognized the economic importance in all industry of energy sources and put his mind and inventive capacity to processes such as that for making producer gas, in which inconvenient solid fuel is converted into convenient gaseous fuel. He was also able to convert the nitrogen of the solid fuel into ammonia. Following the original efforts of William Grove he also made attempts to produce electrical energy direct from gaseous reactions, but was no more successful than many others before and after him.

Ludwig Mond's other most important, commercially fruitful, discovery originated in the study of failed experiments on the recovery of the chlorine lost in the calcium chloride waste of the ammonia-soda process. Nickel components and nickel compounds had been used in the apparatus. With two assistants, C. Langer and F. Quincke, Mond traced the faults to the conversion by carbon monoxide of the nickel to a hitherto unknown substance, nickel carbonyl. This was remarkable in being the first identified gaseous compound of a metallic element. Since the nickel carbonyl could easily be decomposed to yield pure nickel, Mond saw in this a completely novel metallurgical extraction process and proceeded to commercialize it with great success. He exploited Canadian nickel ores, which were given a preliminary enrichment in Canada and then shipped to a new works at Clydach, near Swansea, for the final purification by the carbonyl route. Several personal accounts of his work, presented in the first place as lectures, were later published. The work on nickel opened up new fields of investigation which were explored by his son Robert.

Allied with Brunner's business and political acumen, Mond's discoveries and his genius for developing their practical applications led to the establishment of the British chemical industry on a scale capable of challenging that of any other country. All the same, in spite of his identification with great industrial enterprises, he always maintained that scientific education should be centred on pure science, not on its profitable application, the industry growing out of the science, not the other way round. He made a personal statement of his convictions in this respect in an address to students at the opening of the Schorlemmer Laboratory at Manchester University on 3 May 1895. His own research was carried out in privacy. He bought a farm at Combe Bank, Sevenoaks, intending it for the use of his sons, and there built a useful laboratory.

Mond was very active in the organization and support of scientific societies, taking a lead (with Sir Henry Roscoe) to expand the small Lancashire Chemical Society into the nationwide Society of Chemical Industry, established in 1881. He supported this body financially until it could stand on its own feet, and acted as its foreign secretary until elected to its presidency in 1888. The society honoured him with its Messel medal, recognizing his leadership in the development of large-scale British chemical industry.

Mond was a man of impressive presence, not tall, but full-bearded and clearly of Jewish extraction, as is seen in a painting and several sculptures. He was elected to fellowship of the Royal Society in 1891, and to membership of the German Chemical Society, of the Società Reale of Naples in 1908, and of the Prussian Akademie der Wissenschaften in 1909. He received honorary doctorates from the universities of Padua (1892), Heidelberg (1896), Manchester (1904), and Oxford (1907). He was awarded the grand cordon of the Crown of Italy in 1909. Throughout his industrial career he was much concerned with the welfare of his employees, a care which extended into their retirement years. He was generous in his lifetime to scientific organizations, giving the Royal Society £16,000 in support of its *Catalogue of Scientific Papers* and funding a prize at the Italian Accademia dei Lincei in memory of Stanislas Cannizzaro. His most notable benefaction was that to the Royal Institution of Great Britain, providing a house next door to its main premises to be used for research purposes under the name of the Davy-Faraday Laboratory.

In his will Ludwig Mond left £20,000 to the town of Kassel, with an additional £5000 for a Jewish charitable foundation. This was only one of many charitable gifts, to Jewish as well as other beneficiaries, many of them anonymous. One bequest was to the Munich Akademie der bildenen Kunst, a reflection of a personal enthusiasm. From 1892 onwards he was able to indulge his taste for works of art, and built up a fine collection, mainly early Italian. In this he was advised by Dr J. P. Richter who published a two-volume account of it in 1910. Subject to a life interest for his wife, the greater portion of his collection was left to the National Gallery.

After the birth of his sons Mond's main British residence was at Winnington, Cheshire, until 1884 when he moved to London. In addition he spent most of his winters in Rome, at the Palazzo Zuccari which he had bought and restored. He suffered from heart disease, from which he died on 11 December 1909 at his house, The Poplars, 20 Avenue Road, Regent's Park, London. In his later years he had given much thought to the Jewish religion, in which he had been brought up but whose observances he had neglected. He was buried with Jewish rites at the St Pancras cemetery, Finchley. His sons later erected a mausoleum there for all the family remains.

The second generation The elder of Ludwig Mond's two sons, **Sir Robert Ludwig Mond** (1867–1938), chemist and archaeologist, was born at Farnworth, near Widnes, Lancashire, on 9 September 1867. He was educated at Cheltenham College, at Peterhouse, Cambridge, at Zürich Polytechnic, at Edinburgh University, and at Glasgow University, where he worked under Sir William Thomson. He became a good chemist and eventually had a number of papers to his credit on subjects which related to his father's discoveries, such as metal carbonyls, and the electrolytic production of zinc. He was the originator of a number of patents. However, he was not by temperament a solitary investigator and was less interested in novel discovery than in application and the encouragement of colleagues. For a time after his father's death he made trials of scientific farming methods at Combe Bank, Sevenoaks (which his father had bought with Robert's needs in mind), pioneering the production of high-quality milk from a selected herd of dairy cows. It was at Combe Bank, in the laboratory installed by his father, that he did most of his scientific investigation. He continued the connection with the Davy-Faraday Laboratory at the Royal Institution, was its honorary secretary for life (an appointment which had been a condition of his father's gift), and contributed substantially to its reconstruction and re-equipment in 1931. His industrial connections included a directorship of Brunner Mond & Co. and chairmanship of the Mond Nickel Company. His work with the nickel mines at Sudbury, Ontario, led him to make a close relationship with the Royal Ontario Museum in Toronto, of which he became a trustee. He made it gifts of money and, later, of important objects from his archaeological investigations in Egypt.

Robert Mond was twice married, first, in 1898, to Helen Edith, third daughter of Julius Levis. They had two daughters. She died in 1905 following the birth of the second daughter, and in her memory Robert Mond founded the Infant's Hospital, Vincent Square. His second marriage, in 1922, was to Marie Louise, daughter of Guillaume Jean Le Manach, of Belle-Île-en-Terre, Brittany, and widow of Simon Guggenheim.

Robert Mond was greatly attached to life in France, having homes in Paris and at Dinard. He contributed largely towards the conversion of the town house of the ducs d'Estissac in the rue Dominique in Paris into the Maison de la Chimie, for meetings of French chemical societies and work on the documentation of chemical literature. He founded a Société des Amis de la Maison de la Chimie. He was a benefactor of the British Institute in Paris and an active supporter of the France-Grande Bretagne Association. He also contributed to the National Council for Chemistry and supported the cause of a 'chemistry house' for Great Britain. In 1937 he helped to found a society for the history of alchemy (at present the Society for the History of Alchemy and Chemistry) and its journal, *Ambix*. He was one of the original subscribers to the Hill Observatory Corporation for the establishment of an observatory at Sidmouth, Devon, later named the Norman Lockyer Observatory. He was personally responsible for some buildings and novel photographic astronomical equipment. He also made large benefactions to the universities of Liverpool, Manchester, and Toronto.

Convalescence in Egypt after a serious illness led Robert Mond to develop a lifelong and creative interest in Egyptian archaeology, to which he made considerable contributions not only as benefactor but also as a worker in the field. He collaborated first with Percy Edward Newberry, and then with Howard Carter and Arthur E. P. B. Weigall. Following his assistance in a first publication on the Theban tombs by Alan Gardiner and Weigall, he played a large part in the restoration and protection of the Theban necropolis. Resuming work after the interruption of the First World War, he initiated the preservation of the tomb of Rameses, in association with the University of Liverpool Institute of Archaeology. His work in this and other excavations brought him into close and sometimes active collaboration with some of the most distinguished archaeologists of his time, as for example a joint publication on *The Bucheum* (1934) with Oliver Myers. He was a discriminating collector, exhibiting his collection magnificently in his own home in London and then bequeathing much of it to the British Museum. His support extended to the development of archaeological work by British scholars in Palestine when this became a British mandated territory under the League of Nations. He stimulated and gave financial help to the foundation of a British School of Archaeology in Jerusalem.

Another interest was that in model soldiers. Robert Mond gave the United Services Institution a gift of 900 figures representing all the regiments in Napoleon's army, a collection it had taken him thirty-five years to build up. With his brother Alfred he set up the mausoleum at the St Pancras cemetery, Finchley, which their father had envisaged, for the burial of members of the family. Eventually it was to receive both Jew and Christian.

Mond was knighted in 1932. Among the many honours he received, from academic bodies and governments, were the honorary degrees of LLD from the universities of Liverpool and Toronto, an honorary DSc from the University of London, the presidency of the Faraday Society, and the Messel medal of the Society of Chemical Industry, which his father had helped to found. He was elected fellow of the Royal Society of Edinburgh and fellow of the Royal Society. He also received French honours, first officer and later commander of the Légion d'honneur, and then member of the Académie des Inscriptions et des Lettres, thus becoming a member of the Institut de France. He was elected president of the Société de Chimie Industrielle. He died in Paris on 22 October 1938, was cremated at the cemetery of Père Lachaise, and his ashes buried at Belle-Île-en-Terre.

Ludwig Mond's younger son, **Alfred Moritz Mond**, first Baron Melchett (1868–1930), industrialist, financier, and politician, was born at Farnworth on 23 October 1868. He was educated at Cheltenham College, and at St John's College, Cambridge. He began his adult life with the shock of failing his natural sciences tripos, but went on to Edinburgh University to study law with some success. He was called to the bar by the Inner Temple in 1894. Although his ambitions were mainly political he first made use of his considerable scientific ability. He put politics on one side for a while and in 1895 joined his father's business, Brunner Mond & Co., becoming a director in 1895 and, soon after, managing director. He combined this with being managing director of the Mond Nickel Company. In 1894 he married Violet Florence Mabel, daughter of James Henry Goetze, coffee merchant of Mincing Lane, London. They had one son, Henry Ludwig, who succeeded his father, and three daughters.

Alfred Mond's future success came from possessing a harmonious mixture of talents, which enabled him to look at the overall structure of industry in relation to its political relevance; he expressed his views in a book, *Industry and Politics* (1927). He advocated and put into practice processes of rationalization and amalgamation, exemplified in his gradual dominance of the Welsh anthracite coal industry through Amalgamated Anthracite Collieries. He added to his directorships those of the International Nickel Company of Canada, the Westminster Bank, and the Industrial Finance Investment Corporation. He gradually took on a leading role in the creation by amalgamation and development of what must be considered his most long-lasting achievement—one of the world's largest industrial corporations, ICI (Imperial Chemical Industries). An important factor in this success was his ability to encourage organization and research in the manufacturing process. He always advocated close co-operation between employer and employed. He believed that industry worked better in large units than in small and the aim of industry should be the achievement of greater units, and the effective joint use of resources. Nevertheless, he realized that there are limits to the size of enterprise that can be controlled effectively. From this stemmed his opposition to the ideas of socialism and of nationalization. He was anxious that there should be good relations between management and workforce and to this end insisted on good arrangements for the comfort and welfare of both blue-collar and white-collar workers wherever he was able to have an influence. He tried to encourage this attitude in others from both sides of industry.

Alfred Mond did his best to avert the coal strike of 1926 by bringing coalowners together in a joint selling organization and, following the general strike of 1926, he initiated meetings between leaders of the Trades Union Congress and of employers' organizations. He held meetings with Ben Turner, who was then chairman of the general council of the Trades Union Congress, and they established a method of conciliation, but there was not at the time sufficient cohesion between the various employers' organizations for this to lead anywhere.

Mond was not an immediately engaging character in appearance and manner, having remnants of the family German accent and a forbidding personal bearing. However his honesty and sincerity carried him through any social barriers and he was always eventually listened to with respectful attention. This was particularly true of his political career. He sat as a Liberal, first for Chester in 1906, then for Swansea from 1910, when he was created a baronet, to 1923 and then from 1924 to 1928. He was sworn of the privy council in 1913. He was not outstanding as a party man but was effective in office, as first commissioner of works (1916–21) in Lloyd George's coalition ministry, and then as minister of health from 1921 to 1922. In 1926, convinced he should adhere to the Conservative policy of protection, he joined the Conservative and Unionist Party.

Sir Alfred Mond's parliamentary life took a new turn in 1928 when he achieved a long-standing ambition to enter the House of Lords, as Baron Melchett of Landford in the county of Southampton. The spelling Melchett was a deliberate modification of the name of his home. He expounded a principle of imperial economic unity, was chairman of the Empire Economic Union, and in 1930 published a book, *Imperial Economic Unity*, on the subject. His argument was, that in addition to tariff preferences, common action could produce large imperial combines through which production and marketing could be systematically allocated.

Sir Alfred Mond was generous to good causes and in 1924 provided for the housing at the National Gallery of his father's bequest of forty-two pictures. In 1929 he bought ground in Chelsea for the Chelsea Health Society, of which his wife was president. A deeply rooted enthusiasm which developed after the First World War came out of Mond's Jewish heritage. In 1921 he visited Palestine in company with Dr Chaim Weizmann. He became an enthusiastic Zionist, contributed a large sum to the Jewish Colonization Corporation for Palestine in 1928, and wrote for Zionist publications. He was an active member of the Jewish agency set up to administer the British mandate but resigned in 1930 in protest against a change in the British government's attitude to the national home in Palestine which followed the riots in Jerusalem. He was elected fellow of the Royal Society in 1928, and received honorary degrees from Oxford, Paris, and other universities. He died at his London home, 35 Lowndes Square, on 27 December 1930.

The third generation **Henry Ludwig Mond**, second Baron Melchett (1898–1949), industrialist and financier, only son of Alfred Mond, was born in London on 10 May 1898. He was educated at Winchester College and served from 1915 in the First World War, in the South Wales Borderers, entering before he was strictly old enough; he was wounded in 1916. He had ambitions to become a writer and poet but he had neither the talent nor the connections to make a success of this as a career, although his skill was later shown in political writing. His wife was (Amy) Gwen Wilson, whose origin is obscure but who described herself as daughter of John Wilson of Klerksdorp, Transvaal. She came from South Africa to study art, and was for a time involved with Augustus John. She later went to live with the writer Gilbert Cannan. Cannan was married to Mary (the former wife of J. M. Barrie), who cited Gwen as co-respondent in an action for judicial separation. Henry Mond crashed his motorcycle outside the Cannan flat in St John's Wood, was cared for by Gwen, and set up a *maison-à-trois* with her and Cannan. Alfred regretted the arrangement and Henry's attempt to make a living in literature but went on supporting him. Eventually Cannan gave up Gwen to Henry and they were married on 30 January 1920. Henry then began to play an effective part in the family enterprises. He and Gwen had two sons and one daughter. The elder son, Derek, was killed in a flying accident on active service with the Royal Naval Volunteer Reserve in 1945.

Henry Mond entered some of his father's businesses, becoming a director of ICI (of which he was deputy chairman in 1940–47), of the Mond Nickel Company, and of Barclays Bank. He was elected member of parliament as a Liberal for the Isle of Ely from 1923 to 1924, in which year he left the Liberal Party. He returned to parliament as a Conservative for the East Toxteth division of Liverpool in 1929 but vacated this seat on the death of his father and his succession to the peerage. (His wife was asked to fill the vacancy but was unable to accept.) Henry Mond was faced with the task of restoring the family finances since Alfred had made investments which were very vulnerable to the damage inflicted on them by the worldwide recession of the early 1930s. Henry patiently put his inheritance on a sound footing through a talent for finance which he exercised in all his many appointments.

On leaving the Commons, Mond shifted the balance of his interests away from politics and concentrated mainly on economics and industry. He believed that formal consultation, in a kind of third chamber, between some industrialists and financiers, some scientists and economists, and some ministers, could solve economic problems. He published two books on these issues: *Why the Crisis?* (1931) and *Modern Money* (1932).

Henry Mond had been brought up as a not very active member of the Church of England but in 1933 reflection on his family history and the news of the treatment of the Jews in Germany persuaded him to accept formal conversion to the Jewish religion of his forebears. He became a champion of Zionism, but held that Jew and Arab could be persuaded to live harmoniously together, making his views public in a book, *Thy Neighbour* (1937). He hoped for a time when the Jews could be established in their own land as an independent state. He advocated the evacuation of all Jews from Germany and some from other countries for transfer to Palestine, believing that this would lead to among other things the reconciliation of Germany to the rest of Europe. During the Second World War he continued to press the British government to facilitate the transfer of Jews to Palestine, there to form an independent state as part of the British Commonwealth. He later made visits to Palestine, was chairman of the British Agency for Palestine, and took a great interest in the Maccabean Jewish youth organization.

In addition to other books on economic subjects Henry Mond wrote one entitled *Hunting and Polo*, which reflects his enthusiasm for riding: he was master of the Oakley Hounds. When his father died he closed Melchet Court and went to live at Colworth, Bedfordshire, which in 1941 he turned into a rest home for American nurses. He brought his industrial career to a close by resigning from ICI in 1947, when the condition of his health became clearly life-threatening. He died at Miami Beach, Florida, USA, on 22 January 1949, and was succeeded by his surviving son, Julian Edward Alfred.

The fourth generation **Julian Edward Alfred Mond**, third Baron Melchett (1925–1973), industrialist, the son of Henry Ludwig Mond, was born in London on 9 January 1925. He was educated at Eton College and, although ready to go to Oxford, chose instead to go straight into the Fleet Air Arm in 1942, first in the lower deck and then commissioned, becoming senior pilot in his squadron. After training in Canada and South Africa he served in the Atlantic and on the Russian convoys. During his time in the Fleet Air Arm he took a correspondence course in farming which prepared him for what he was long to consider his most important activity. He founded a farming company (British Field Products Ltd) which specialized in grass-drying and animal feed-stuffs. On 26 April 1947 he married Sonia Elizabeth, daughter of Lieutenant-Colonel R. H. Graham, Royal Army Medical Corps. They had one son and two daughters. He and his wife lived between a mews house in London and a farm, Courtyard, Ringstead, Hunstanton, in Norfolk.

In 1947 Julian Mond joined the merchant bankers M. Samuel & Co. and by 1960 had become a significant influence in the financial world. He was an adviser to the export credits guarantee department and the British Transport Docks Board, and was on the council of administration of the Malta Dockyard. He became a director of the Guardian Assurance Company and of the Anglo-American Shipping Co. Ltd. In 1965 M. Samuel & Co. merged with Philip Hill, Higginson, and Erlanger Ltd, and Melchett (he had inherited the title in 1949) became director in charge of the banking and overseas departments. It was not an entirely easy life because tensions developed from time to time between the two components of the merged company. In his early forties he had thus acquired over a dozen directorships and was on the council of the Confederation of British Industry and the National Economic Development Council.

British Field Products expanded in size and variety and Melchett persuaded Guardian Assurance to become a major shareholder. In 1964 the company acquired Weasenham Farm, with more than 14,000 acres of Norfolk farmland. During the same period he was a member of the British Transport Docks Board, which gave him a valuable insight into the operation of a nationalized industry. This extra work was to a great extent a relaxation. He made certain of being able to get home to the Norfolk countryside by flying there in his own single-engined plane after office hours. He rode and sailed and in the summer took family holidays in Majorca where he had built a villa.

In April 1966 his career took a new turn. The prime minister, Harold Wilson, asked Melchett to be chairman of the committee to plan the nationalization of the British steel industry. He took this on in spite of misgivings about government intervention in the conduct of the affairs of any new industrial organization. From 1967 until his death he was chairman of what was eventually called the British Steel Corporation. The task was enormous: the bringing together of fourteen major iron and steel companies and other smaller ones employing more than a quarter of a million workers with a variety of traditions, methods, and loyalties. Among many innovations which helped harmonious progress was his introduction of worker-directorships—members of trade unions being appointed to boards.

Melchett's leadership survived the change of government in June 1970. The new prime minister, Edward Heath, and his cabinet accepted Melchett's plans for a massive modernization and its funding. By 1973 he had clearly established himself as an international influence in this leading industry, and was even being proposed for election as the next president of the International Iron and Steel Institute. He was much respected for his hard work and for his open manner. It was clear that the load needed to be eased and he was supported by the appointment as chief executive and deputy chairman of Dr H. M. Finniston. However, some of his colleagues on the board of British Steel differed from him and looked to an eventual return to separation of functions and to private ownership. Melchett had accepted appointment as non-executive director of Orion Bank in 1972, and his future seemed to be undecided. In 1973 he went on holiday to the villa in Majorca, where he died of a heart attack in June 1973. He was buried in the family mausoleum at Finchley. A memorial service was held in Westminster Abbey. He was succeeded by his son, Peter Robert Mond.

The family's influence Four generations of the Mond family, German in origin, but British by choice and further descent, played a powerful role in the development of the chemical and metallurgical industries of the United Kingdom and of other countries. Ludwig Mond saw the possibilities of exploiting the advances in alkali manufacture made possible by contemporary discovery. His appreciation of the markets led him to make his home in England. One son advanced Ludwig Mond's scientific discoveries and applied them to industry, but devoted much of his energy in later life to historical scholarship. His other son, who entered parliament, became a minister, and was raised to the peerage, led in the creation of a great international industry (Imperial Chemical Industries). A grandson showed a family gift for high finance and politics, a gift exhibited so fully by a great-grandson that he was invited to head the establishment of the first great nationalized industry (the British Steel Corporation). Thus over four generations, science, as the backbone of industry, played its part in the forefront of Mond family life, first in the expansion of manufacture and then as the basis for enterprise in the worlds of finance and politics, a clear example of one of the main trends in twentieth-century history. On his deathbed Ludwig said he hoped Henry would make himself necessary. Alfred adapted these words for the motto in the Melchett coat of arms: 'Make yourself necessary'. The four generations of Monds described here did just that. FRANK GREENAWAY

Sources J. M. Cohen, *The life of Ludwig Mond* (1956) · H. Bolitho, *Alfred Mond, first Lord Melchett* (1933) · J. Goodman, *The Mond legacy: a family saga* (1982) · T. E. Thorpe, *Nature*, 82 (1909–10), 221–3 [Ludwig Mond] · *The Times* (13 Dec 1909) [Ludwig Mond] · *The Times* (29 Oct 1930) [Alfred Moritz Mond] · *The Times* (18 March 1938) [Sir Robert Ludwig Mond] · F. G. Donnan, *JCS* (1931), 3374–9 [Alfred Moritz Mond] · J. F. Thorpe, *JCS* (1939), 215–19 [Sir Robert Ludwig Mond] · archives, Royal Institution of Great Britain, London · J. F. Thorpe, 'Sir Robert Mond', *Obits. FRS*, 2 (1936–8), 627–32 · W. J. Reader, *Imperial Chemical Industries: a history*, 1: *The forerunners, 1870–1926* (1970) · D. W. F. Hardie, *A history of chemical industry in Widnes* (1950) · D. W. F. Hardie, *The chemical industry on Merseyside* (1961) · H. E. Armstrong, 'The Monds and the chemical industry', *Nature*, 127 (1931), 238–40 · d. cert. [Ludwig Mond] · *CGPLA Eng. & Wales* (1938) [Sir Robert Ludwig Mond] · b. cert. [Sir Robert Ludwig Mond] · m. cert. [Sir Robert Ludwig Mond and Helen Edith Levis] · m. cert. [Sir Robert Ludwig Mond and Marie Louise Guggenheim] · d. cert. [Sir Robert Ludwig Mond] · m. cert. [Alfred Moritz Mond] · d. cert. [Alfred Moritz Mond] · m. cert. [Henry Ludwig Mond] · d. cert. [Henry Ludwig Mond] · *CGPLA Eng. & Wales* (1949) [Henry Ludwig Mond] · b. cert. [Julian Edward Alfred Mond] · m. cert. [Julian Edward Alfred Mond] · *CGPLA Eng. & Wales* (1973) [Julian Edward Alfred Mond]
Archives Ches. & Chester ALSS, corresp. and papers; personal papers [Ludwig Mond] · Egypt Exploration Society, London, corresp. of him and his wife with Egypt Exploration Society [Robert Mond] · Imperial Chemical Industries Archive · NRA, family papers · NRA, corresp. and papers [Alfred Mond] · Royal Institution of Great Britain, London, archives · U. Oxf., Griffith Institute, archaeological papers, incl. notes on Theban tombs, notebook and notes, photographs [Robert Mond] | BL OIOC, letters to Lord Reading, MSS Eur. E. 238, F 118 [Alfred Mond] · Bodl. Oxf., corresp. with J. L. Myres [Robert Mond] · Bodl. Oxf., corresp. with Viscount Addison [Alfred Mond] · HLRO, corresp. with Lord Beaverbrook [Henry Mond] · HLRO, corresp. with Lord Beaverbrook [Alfred Mond] · HLRO, corresp. with David Lloyd George [Alfred Mond] · Nuffield Oxf., corresp. with Lord Cherwell [Henry Mond] · U. Birm. L., corresp. with Austen Chamberlain [Alfred Mond] · U. Oxf., Griffith Institute, letters to Sir A. H. Gardiner [Robert Mond]
Likenesses E. Lanteri, bronze statuette, 1912 (Robert Ludwig Mond), NPG · W. Stoneman, photograph, 1917 (Alfred Moritz Mond), NPG · F. O. Salisbury, oils, *c*.1920 (Robert Ludwig Mond), Westminster Hospital, London · Quiz [P. Evans], pen-and-ink caricature, 1926 (Alfred Moritz Mond), NPG · E. Kapp, drawing, 1929 (Alfred Moritz Mond), Barber Institute of Fine Arts, Birmingham · W. Rothenstein, drawing, 1929 (Alfred Moritz Mond), NPG · A. Wysard, double portrait, watercolour drawing, 1929 (Henry Ludwig Mond with his wife, Gwen), NPG · W. Stoneman, photograph, 1938 (Robert Ludwig Mond), NPG · R. von Marientreu, oils, *c*.1955 (Alfred Moritz Mond, 1929; after J. Lavery), Imperial Chemical Industries Ltd, London · B. Partridge, pen-and-ink and watercolour caricature (Alfred Moritz Mond), NPG; repro. in *Punch Almanack* (1 Nov 1926) · group portrait, half-tone reproductions of photographic originals (with Löwenthal family), repro. in Cohen, *Life of Ludwig*, 48
Wealth at death £1,000,000—Ludwig Mond: probate, 1910, CGPLA Eng. & Wales · £381,958 17s. 9d.—Sir Robert Ludwig Mond: resworn probate, 1938, CGPLA Eng. & Wales · £96,968 0s. 2d.—Henry Ludwig Mond: probate, 1949, CGPLA Eng. & Wales · £310,500—Julian Edward Alfred Mond: probate, 27 Sept 1973, CGPLA Eng. & Wales

Mond, Alfred Moritz, first Baron Melchett (1868–1930). *See under* Mond family (*per.* 1867–1973).

Mond, Henry Ludwig, second Baron Melchett (1898–1949). *See under* Mond family (*per.* 1867–1973).

Mond, Julian Edward Alfred, third Baron Melchett (1925–1973). *See under* Mond family (*per.* 1867–1973).

Mond, Ludwig (1839–1909). *See under* Mond family (*per.* 1867–1973).

Mond, Sir Robert Ludwig (1867–1938). *See under* Mond family (*per.* 1867–1973).

Mone, Hawise (*fl.* 1428–1430). *See under* Lollard women (*act.* c.1390–c.1520).

Mo-nennius. *See* Mo Nennus (*fl.* 5th–early 6th cent.).

Money, John (1739/40–1817), military theorist and balloonist, of whose parents nothing is known, began his military career in the Norfolk militia in 1760. He served in Germany as a volunteer with the 15th light dragoons in 1761 and was at the battle of Vellinghausen. On 11 March 1762 he joined the 6th dragoons as a cornet, eventually transferring in 1770 to the 9th foot as a captain. He served in Canada in 1777 as General John Burgoyne's quartermaster-general, being captured at Saratoga. Promoted major in 1781, Money went on half pay in 1784 but continued to receive regular promotions, becoming brevet lieutenant-colonel on 18 November 1790, colonel on 21 August 1795, major-general on 18 June 1798, lieutenant-general on 30 October 1805, and general on 4 June 1814.

In 1785, just two years after Montgolfier's first aerial voyage, Money made two ascents by hot air balloon. The second, on 22 July, began at Norwich but ended in the sea, from which he was rescued several hours later. In 1790 he offered his services to the ill-fated uprising in the Austrian Netherlands and was eventually given a commission as a major-general: he commanded some 5000 men at Tirlemont and fought one sharp engagement. In July 1792 the offer of his sword was accepted by the French. According to his published account, he was in the Tuileries ready to defend King Louis XVI when that palace was stormed by the Parisian mob on 10 August 1792. He then served for the remainder of that year under generals Valence and Dumouriez against the Prussians and Austrians.

During these campaigns Money was struck by the efficacy of French light troops operating in the enclosed frontier country and later called for the creation of British forces capable of countering them. His open letter to the secretary at war was subsequently elaborated upon and published as *On a Partial Reorganization of the British Army* (1799). It formed an important contribution to the contemporary debate about the reform of the British army in general and the need for specialist light infantry forces in particular.

Money retired to his residence, Crown Point, Trowse Newton, Norfolk, where he farmed 300–400 acres, and later acted as colonel of the East Norfolk yeomanry. He died at his home on 26 March 1817 aged seventy-seven; his sister Elizabeth and the children of his brother Philip (d. 1795) inherited his estate.

LEONARD DARWIN, *rev.* DAVID GATES

Sources D. Gates, *The British light infantry arm, c.1790–1815* (1987) • J. Philippart, ed., *The royal military calendar*, 3 vols. (1815–16) • J. Money, *The history of the campaign of 1792* (1794) • R. H. Mason, *The history of Norfolk* (1884) • will, PRO, PROB 11/1594 (376) • *GM*, 1st ser., 87/1 (1817), 376 • M. Mason, *Aeronautica* (1838)

Money, Sir Leo George Chiozza (1870–1944), politician and author, was born in Genoa on 13 June 1870, the son of Giuseppi Antonio Chiozza (d. 1882), a naval engineer, and his wife, Fawnia (d. 1886), the daughter of Edward Allwright. His original name was Leone Giorgio Chiozza, which he changed in 1903. He was educated privately, and at some time moved to England. On 31 March 1892 he married Gwendolen Maria (b. 1873/4), the daughter of George Elliott Stevenson, a clerk, of Hackney.

In London, Chiozza Money established himself as a journalist writing on economic, social, and political issues, with a particular penchant for statistical analysis. From 1898 to 1902 he was managing editor of Henry Sell's *Commercial Intelligence*, a weekly journal dedicated to reviewing the trade of the world for the benefit of British trade, finding new markets by intelligence and information. In 1902 his first book, *British Trade and the Zollverein Issue*, appeared under its imprint, arguing against imperial preference on

the grounds that the empire offered neither a sufficient market for British goods, nor adequate supplies of food and raw materials. His traditional defence of free trade continued in *Elements of the Fiscal Problem* (1903), which developed a simple Cobdenite argument of exploiting a country's natural advantages. Free trade, he argued, would prevent the growth of unsuitable industries and the development of monopolies. His statistical expertise meant that he advised on the revision of the Board of Trade returns in 1903.

In 1906 he was elected Liberal MP for North Paddington, losing the seat in the election of January 1910; in December 1910 he was returned as Liberal member for East Northamptonshire and he held the seat until 1918. His free-trade credentials were well established, but he soon started to move in a more radical direction, towards eventual membership of the Labour Party. He made his greatest impact with his analysis of the distribution of income and wealth in *Riches and Poverty* in 1905, which was reissued in a cheap, popular edition, with striking graphics. He emphasized the 'error of distribution', using Inland Revenue data to show that a large amount of the aggregate income of the United Kingdom—£585 million—went to a mere 1,250,000 rich people, with a further £245 million for 3,750,000 'comfortable' people, so that £880 million was left for the remaining 38 million poor people. In Chiozza Money's view, the error of distribution led to serious social, political, and economic problems—a demand for wasteful luxuries by the rich, a misuse of capital, a misappropriation of power. Rather than a demand for 'worthy' commodities, consumption was directed to unworthy things, and labour was degraded. He moved away from a simple Cobdenite vision of free trade as allocating capital and labour in the most efficient way, for he now argued that 'the error in the distribution of income connotes an error in the distribution of our population amongst useful and useless, noble and ignoble, industries'. Further, industries could fall into the hands of monopolists, so that free trade alone was not enough to prevent exploitation.

Chiozza Money did not reject free trade, but he argued that the distribution of income and wealth should be corrected by the use of redistributive taxation, especially a graduated income tax. In 1906 he gave evidence to the select committee on income tax, presenting data on the distribution of income in 1904 to suggest that the rich could afford to pay much higher taxes. He disputed the statistics produced by the Inland Revenue which claimed to show that incomes over £5000 accounted for a mere £121 million, with a relatively modest yield from a graduated tax; he argued that they amounted to £250 million. He was also in favour of improvements in the organization of industries and the imposition of minimum wages in the 'sweated' trades. In 1907–8 he served as a member of the select committee on home work. Where he differed from other 'new Liberals' was in his early advocacy of nationalization. He stressed the existence of waste in distribution, and the efficiency to be achieved by converting all common services into monopolies owned by the public. Hence the milk trade should be municipalized to produce cheap, clean supplies; and coalmines should be brought into public hands to offer better terms of employment, and to ensure cheap distribution of coal by local authorities. He was already arguing in 1905 that public ownership offered the only way of securing 'for each worker in the hive the full reward of his labour'.

During the First World War, Chiozza Money was a member of the restriction of enemy supplies committee in 1914–15; parliamentary private secretary to David Lloyd George at the Ministry of Munitions in 1915; and a member of the retrenchment committee in 1915, and of the war trade advisory committee from 1915. He was parliamentary secretary to the Ministry of Pensions in 1917, where he drafted the new pensions scheme, and to the Ministry of Shipping from December 1916 to January 1919, chairing the tonnage priority committee and National Maritime Board, and serving as a member of the shipping control committee. He was knighted in 1915.

By the end of the war, Chiozza Money's support for nationalization and redistributive taxation took him away from the Liberal Party; in 1918 he stood (unsuccessfully) as Labour candidate for South Tottenham. In 1919 he was appointed to the royal commission on the coal industry, serving alongside R. H. Tawney and Sidney Webb as an advocate of nationalization. In 1920 he again stood (unsuccessfully) as Labour candidate for Stockport. Any prospect that he would become a leading figure within the party was destroyed by sexual scandal. He was involved in a notorious incident in April 1928, when he and Miss Irene Savidge were arrested for indecent behaviour in Hyde Park. He claimed to be giving her career advice, and they were both acquitted. She was later taken from work by detectives and interrogated at Scotland Yard, which led to a debate in the Commons and a tribunal of inquiry chaired by Sir John Eldon Bankes, the minority report of which condemned the police for excessive zeal. He was less fortunate when, in September 1933, he was again arrested for indecent behaviour, with a lady in a railway carriage. On this occasion, he was found guilty.

Chiozza Money's political career was finished, and he made a living as an editor of the fourteenth edition of the *Encyclopaedia Britannica*. He continued to publish, but he was a marginal figure using his statistics for idiosyncratic ends. In *The Peril of the White* (1925), he showed the small number of people of British stock in the world's population, and the dominance of all white people by a huge number of other peoples. He argued that white civilization could survive only by uniting: the real danger was not a yellow or black peril, but the internal divisions of white people in the First World War. He argued for racial understanding within the white races and also with non-white peoples. He stressed that the leadership of the white peoples could only be sustained by respect for others, and by ensuring that past errors of slavery or economic exploitation were not repeated. He developed his argument in *Can War be Averted?* (1931), where he argued for universal compulsory arbitration, equal economic opportunity for all peoples, a cancellation of war debts, general disarmament, a world court of justice, freedom of the seas, a better use of sparsely populated areas, and freedom of commerce. None of these plans could work, he remarked, unless children had knowledge and admiration of all the peoples of the world, a realization that their love of their own kind was part of a love of humankind.

In 1935 Chiozza Money attempted to resolve the problems of the world depression through a new concept of 'product money', based on certificates granted to producers so that they and their workers became consumers to purchase the output of other concerns. Production would automatically lead to consumption, and supply would be equated with demand, so that the mass of producers were no longer poverty-stricken. Although the book was announced as a sequel to *Riches and Poverty*, it was now far from the mainstream of political debate. Chiozza Money's Edwardian new liberalism, and his own political career, came to a sad end. He died at his home, the Old Quarry, Bramley, Surrey, on 25 September 1944.

MARTIN DAUNTON

Sources A. J. P. Taylor, *English history, 1914–45* (1965) · WWBMP · WWW · m. cert. · d. cert. · Kelly, *Handbk* (1917) · Walford, *County families* (1919) · Burke, *Peerage* (1924) · H. Montgomery Hyde, *Norman Birkett* (1964), 229–45
Archives Bodl. Oxf., memoranda relating to an imperial policy for British supplies · CUL, corresp. and papers, incl. autobiography · CUL, political corresp. and papers · Labour History Archive and Study Centre, Manchester, papers | BLPES, letters to Edwin Cannan · BLPES, corresp. with The Fabian Society · HLRO, letters to David Lloyd George · JRL, letters to *The Manchester Guardian* · U. Edin. L., corresp. with Charles Sarolea, Sar. coll. 28
Likenesses L. C. Money, photograph, repro. in *Product Money* (1933)
Wealth at death £14,843 11s. 1d.: probate, 20 Dec 1944, CGPLA Eng. & Wales

Moneyers (*act. c.*1180–*c.*1500) served in a profession that included a wide range of different types of people employed, chiefly in London, in the production of currency.

The mint and its staff At its most comprehensive the mint could employ both illiterate labourers at the bottom of the scale, and figures of the stature of Peter de *Rivallis (*d.* 1262), Gregory of *Ruxley (*d.* 1291), and John *Sandale (*d.* 1319) at the top. These distinguished men all served as wardens of the mint and exchange, but theirs was essentially a civil service, supervisory post, which could be exercised by deputy, and which monitored the work of mint staff and accounted for the king's seigniorage (the fee received by the crown for every pound of coin struck). Thus **William Hardel** (*d. c.*1248), deputy to Peter de Rivallis, who ran the mints and exchanges of London and Canterbury from 1234 until his death, was an important royal clerk who also served as controller of the wardrobe. But it was the master of the mint who directed day-to-day production, and whose developing combination of financial experience and practical metallurgical knowledge made him the chief mint worker during the thirteenth and fourteenth centuries.

The recoinage of 1180 and its aftermath Although William I had retained most of the Anglo-Saxon moneyers who had served his predecessors, the Plantagenets often looked abroad for their senior mint staff. The central part played by **Philippe Aimer** (*fl.* 1180–1181) in the recoinage of 1180 conformed to this practice, but also marks a significant stage in the evolution of the office of master. Aimer was brought from Tours by Richard of Ilchester, bishop of Winchester (*d.* 1188), and between August 1180 and May 1181 he was paid 16*d.* a day—double the rate paid to other senior moneyers. His son Aimer was paid 4*d.* a day. Although Philippe Aimer's employment was terminated rather suddenly, on 2 May 1181, his reputation throughout the Angevin empire, his overall direction of the recoinage—Ralph de Diceto suggests that he bore some general responsibility for the moneyers' shortcomings, and that he was sent home to France unpunished only thanks to the indulgence of the king—and his exalted salary all mark him out from ordinary moneyers.

After the recoinage of 1180 for many years the production of coin was left increasingly in the hands of moneyers, with no master formally appointed over them. Their number at London, the largest mint, fluctuated according to the pressure of work, from a dozen or more at a time of recoinage, to less than half that number at other times. Some scores of labourers were in turn employed by the senior moneyers for most of the less technical manual work. And keepers of the dies and assayers were appointed as a check on the moneyers. In fact moneyers, assayers, and die-keepers came from very similar kinds of social background, and sometimes men moved from one grade to another when vacancies arose. Thus **Henry of Frowick** (*d.* 1286?), a leading citizen of London, was made assayer at the London mint in 1247, and promoted moneyer in 1248. Henry owned property in various parts of the city, and rose to the rank of alderman and sheriff. He married Isabel, daughter of Thomas of Durham, another alderman and sheriff, with whom he had six sons and three daughters.

Thirteenth-century developments There were strong family and professional links binding all these mint workers together. Ralph of Frowick had been moneyer at London from 1218 until after 1222, and **Roger Frowick** (*fl.* 1292–1327), goldsmith and moneyer, was active from 1292. Exchanger at the London mint from 1297 to 1327, Roger was involved in city politics as alderman of Langbourn ward from 1312 to 1324, served as assessor of the fifteenth in 1313, and is known to have mixed socially, as well as professionally, with John Sandale. John Hardel, appointed keeper of dies in 1247, was no doubt related to William Hardel, warden of the mint and exchange at that time.

Not surprisingly, many moneyers were goldsmiths. **Adam of Bentley** (*fl.* 1230–1246), sheriff of London in 1246, is a case in point. Appointed moneyer in 1230, he and his wife, Maud, had an interest in a house in Friday Street, which appears in the wills of several Bentley goldsmiths

into the fourteenth century. **Richard Bachelor** (*fl.* 1235), another goldsmith, paid 100*s.* to have the die of Richard of Necton in 1235, but it is not clear whether he received it. Bachelor owned property in the parish of St Andrew, Holborn, later released by his widow, Isabella, and son, Thomas.

Nicholas of St Albans (*d.* in or before 1253), who acquired a controlling interest in the mints of London and Canterbury from about 1237 until his death, was another goldsmith. Nicholas's father, John, described by Matthew Paris as *aurifaber incomparabilis*, made the exterior of the shrine at St Albans before taking employment under the king of Denmark. Nicholas succeeded him, and ran the Danish mint for many years before returning to England to take up a similar position for Henry III. He seems to have bought out several other moneyers, and been almost solely responsible for the London and Canterbury mints in the early 1240s when activity continued at a very high level. A will in the name of Nicholas of St Albans, goldsmith, was enrolled on 25 July 1258, and mentioned a wife, Joan, and sons, Richard and Michael, though the moneyer–goldsmith is known to have died by 1253.

William of Gloucester and his circle William of Gloucester (*d.* 1269), a Londoner who became a king's serjeant, seems also to have achieved a remarkable concentration of power within the mint and exchange. The great seal in use from 1259 until 1272 was his work, and he carried out a number of royal commissions at Westminster Abbey, including a golden shrine for St Edward. He married Joan, daughter of Michael de St Helen, and with her had a daughter, Joan, and two sons—John, who became a draper, and Henry, who was a goldsmith. William owned a goldsmithery in the parish of St Vedast. In May 1255 he received the London die formerly held by Nicholas of St Albans, and in 1256 was apparently a leading figure in the consortium of moneyers that took on all the London dies. Then in 1257 he also acquired the Canterbury die of the moneyer Robert, launched the gold penny of Henry III (the first English gold coin since before the conquest), and became warden of the exchanges of London and Canterbury, simultaneously with his moneyer role.

Other members of the London consortium included John Hardel and Henry of Frowick, already mentioned, and Walter of Brussels, who held property in Pentecostlane, in St Nicholas Shambles, and was still living there in 1281. **David of Enfield** (*d. c.*1260), a citizen and goldsmith, was also one of the consortium. He had a son and two daughters, and is most often recorded in the property transactions of his children, which reveal his ownership of half a shop in Cheap, in the parish of St Peter, and a tenement in St Sepulchre, probably consisting of three houses and a shop. He also owned a stone house in Wodestrete in the parish of St Michael, Wood Street. **Richard Bonaventure** (*fl.* 1250–1260) was a citizen and goldsmith, married to Hawise, with whom he had two known sons and a daughter. He witnessed a deed giving land in Aldersgate for a dowry on the occasion of a marriage involving a goldbeater, and the other witnesses included William of Gloucester, Henry of Frowick, and David of Enfield. In

1253 Bonaventure was holding property fronting on Cheapside in the parish of St Vedast, which was a centre for goldsmiths and the location for the London mint before its establishment in the Tower. He also bought a shop further east in Cheapside, and rented accommodation in Gutter Lane, known also as Guthrens Lane, a centre for the purest assays of silver in England. Indeed the property records of the consortium indicate that they all occupied property within a quarter mile of Old Change, which lay east of St Paul's running north into West Cheap.

Reform and reorganization in the later thirteenth century

This group of moneyers seems to have operated successfully until June 1260, when a judicial inquiry was set up under Hugh Bigod (d. 1266), justiciar of England, and John Mansel (d. 1265), Henry III's principal adviser. They were to hear moneyers' pleas and to amend errors in the mint. Apparently there were many errors and defects in the exchange of London, with contention among the moneyers and possible damage to the king. The upshot was that William of Gloucester was replaced as warden in January 1262, and thereafter the wardens' accounts begin to concern themselves with the profits of the foundry for the first time. It then becomes apparent that there was a significant margin of about 3d. in the pound between the sums charged to the merchant for mintage and the actual costs of the operation. This margin—the profits of the foundry—was after 1262 claimed by the crown, but before this date had fallen to the moneyers, and made them very rich.

William surrendered the wardenship, but he continued to hold office as royal goldsmith, and as keeper of the works of the shrine of St Edward, a mark of royal favour which even survived his involvement, with much of the city, on the side of the barons and Simon de Montfort. After the battle of Evesham in 1265 he was imprisoned at Windsor, but was soon restored to royal favour, and to his work at Westminster. His privileged position was confirmed in 1267. In 1268 he and Henry of Frowick were executors of a colleague's will, and in the same year he was sent to France on urgent royal business. He died in 1269.

Perhaps as a result of the excesses of Gloucester's moneyer consortium, there followed a general tightening up. Under Edward I the old distinction between the exchange and mint was reactivated with the warden of the exchange collecting the royal seigniorage, supervising the purchase of bullion and issue of new coin, and checking up on the master moneyer, who took charge of all aspects of minting according to a detailed written indenture. The earliest surviving indenture for a master of the mint, dated 1279, is that of **William de Turnemire** (fl. 1279–1284). William and his brother Peter (who fled abroad in 1286) were from Marseilles, and formed part of a team of continental mint-masters brought in to supervise Edward I's recoinage of 1279. The senior master was initially Hubert Alion d'Asti, who was paid £200 per annum for his services, twice the sum William and Peter received. However, Hubert soon left England, and by 1283 he was working in the Namur mint for the count of Flanders. On Hubert's departure William took charge in England. As well as the master's indenture, details of work at the mint survive from a *Treatise on the New Money* written about this time. This treatise was formerly attributed to William but is now known to have been written in 1286 or 1287, after he had resigned on 28 January 1284 to take charge of the Anglo-Gascon mint at Bordeaux. The treatise describes the division of responsibilities between the master and the warden, and the types of quality control in use at the mint. It also contains authoritative information on assaying, and on the calculation of the correct alloy and appropriate mint charges.

Italian moneyers in England The employment of foreign experts who ran the mints at particularly busy times but soon moved on, either to avoid prosecution or to take up minting opportunities elsewhere, was common. Occasionally, however, men stayed in England for life. One such was **Lapinus Roger** (fl. 1292–1331), a Florentine, who succeeded to his uncle's post as assayer and exchanger at Canterbury in 1292, and subsequently also worked at London when his brother Philip was dismissed for faulty record keeping. In due course he was to hold the senior post of master of the mint at both London and Canterbury. In addition to, or perhaps as a consequence of, his professional services he also acquired some 300 acres of marsh in Kent. It is not clear if this land was a deliberate investment of the profits of commerce, or security for an unpaid debt, but in either case it illustrates both his great prosperity and his attachment to Kent. He married a Kentish woman and was admitted a freeman of Canterbury, where he worked for Edward I, Edward II, and Edward III. Roger's conduct seems to have been exemplary, and although he quarrelled with the influential treasurer, Walter *Langton (d. 1321), over wages, no charges of misconduct were ever suggested. Though occasionally deprived of office as a consequence of political changes during this period, he was consistently reinstated, and in addition was frequently called on to resolve crises at the London mint. In 1331 he was put in charge of an exchange at Dover. His son Robert also subsequently became a moneyer at Canterbury, the third generation of this family employed at the mint there.

Another long-serving foreigner was **Walter Barde** (fl. 1360–1390), son of Filippo de Barde. Walter held the mastership at London from the 1360s to the 1390s. He also ran the exchange of the city of London, despite oft repeated injunctions against such dual appointments, and managed the Calais mint by deputy. Since he was also one of the most frequent sellers of bullion to the exchange, he was simultaneously one of the chief customers of the mint, and the controller of both bullion purchase and coin production. Like Lapinus Roger, Walter held office at a time of considerable political unrest, and despite serious parliamentary interest in the workings of the mint, his expertise seems to have made him indispensable. It has been suggested that Walter may have owed his survival to the importance of the society of the Bardi to crown finances, but it has also been argued that he tried to dissociate himself from the family to build a truly English career. The society, for its part, was anxious not to incur any liability for Walter's mint dealings.

English master moneyers of the fifteenth century English master moneyers sometimes competed with the Italians for the mints in the fourteenth century, but they became dominant in the fifteenth. The best example is **Bartholomew Goldbeter** [Seman] (d. 1430/31), the name Goldbeter deriving from his trade. From his earliest indenture of 1422, until his death in 1430 or 1431, Goldbeter dominated the mints of London and Calais. He also ran a mint at York in 1423–4, but never took up his option to coin in Bristol. He may have found the work involved in the provincial mints unattractive compared with the very large sums he was coining at London and Calais. He certainly seems to have driven a hard bargain, both with the crown about the terms on which he ran the mints and exchanges, and with individual merchants who brought bullion to the mints. A Commons inquiry of 1423 into Goldbeter's handling of the mints reveals the unusually favourable terms on which he worked, but he managed to hold on to office until his death. He was buried in the London church of St John Zachary. Goldbeter was one of a number of London goldsmiths, such as Louis John (1413), William Rus (1431), and John Paddesley (1434), who were appointed to run the mint at this time. But from the middle of the century a new trend developed, as rather more exalted crown servants were entrusted with the mint. The most famous was Sir William (later first Baron) *Hastings (d. 1483), an especial confidant of Edward IV.

In summary a typical medieval moneyer was often a goldsmith with knowledge of precious metals; he was frequently a property owner of some standing; he might be English or continental, but in either case he had to be able to enjoy the confidence of the international bankers and merchants as well as that of the crown and the local community. It was a technically demanding profession, which offered great rewards to the successful.

N. J. MAYHEW

Sources C. E. Challis, ed., *A new history of the royal mint* (1992) · M. Male, 'Mint officials under Edward I and II', *Edwardian monetary affairs, 1279–1344*, ed. N. J. Mayhew (1976), 32–44 · J. D. Brand, *The English coinage, 1180–1247: money, mints and exchanges* (1994) · J. Craig, *The mint: a history of the London mint from AD 287 to 1948* (1953) · T. F. Reddaway, 'The king's mint and exchange in London, 1343–1543', *EngHR*, 82 (1967), 1–23 · R. R. Sharpe, ed., *Calendar of wills proved and enrolled in the court of husting, London, AD 1258 – AD 1688*, 2 vols. (1889–90) · G. Galster, 'Notes on the Danish mint-masters in the middle ages before 1377', *Centennial publication of the American Numismatic Society*, ed. H. Ingholt (1958) · D. F. Allen, *A catalogue of English coins in the British Museum: the cross and crosslets ('Tealby') type of Henry II* (1951) · J. Cherry, *Medieval craftsmen: goldsmiths* (1992) · *CPR, 1232–1485* · *'De moneta' of Nicholas of Oresme and English mint documents*, ed. C. Johnson (1956)
Archives BM, department of coins and medals · PRO, exchequer accounts

Mongredien, Augustus (1807–1888), corn merchant and political economist, was born in London, the son of John Adrien Mongredien, a French officer who had fled to England after Bonaparte's *coup d'état* in 1798 and was later described as an 'agriculturalist'. Educated at the Roman Catholic school at Penn, Buckinghamshire, Mongredien 'entered commercial life at an early age' (*DNB*), was in 1831 a member of the National Political Union, and by 1839, president of the London Chess Club (a position he held for over thirty years). He married on 1 May 1840 at the Independent Chapel of Thomas Raffles, Jeanette Ann, the daughter of William Lockerby, a Liverpool merchant. By 1840 he was established in Liverpool as a cornbroker, and he later acted as agent for the enterprising Greek firms who had opened up the south Russian grain trade after the repeal of the corn laws in 1846. In the late 1840s Mongredien himself owned several of the first screw steamers to the Levant, but about 1850 he moved back to London, operating as a cornbroker on his own account, as a member of H. and J. Johnston (1859–64) and later of Ellerby, Mongredien & Co.

In 1862 Mongredien purchased Heatherside, a 300 acre estate at Bagshot Heath, Surrey, where his botanical interests flourished with the creation of a leading nursery, noted for its Wellingtonias. This was floated as a limited company in 1873 (with the naturalists Viscount Walden, A. R. Wallace, and Robert Fortune among its directors) but failed in 1877, at great cost to Mongredien. He also owned an experimental farm at Bratton Clovelly, Devon, in the 1870s. By this time, however, tariffs rivalled trees in his interests. In 1871 he had already shown a strongly radical approach to foreign policy, and after joining the Cobden Club in 1872 he became one of its most prolific authors. In a series of much reprinted books and pamphlets, 'calculated to do good among general readers', he lucidly provided the standard popular history and defence of free trade in the later nineteenth century, with translations into both French and Japanese. In 1883 he published a notable scheme for the 'privatisation' of the government's Suez Canal shares, which attracted his friend Lord Granville but roused Gladstone's suspicions. A firm believer in the future alliance of the Anglo-Saxon race, Mongredien was also a convinced advocate of a United States of Europe, having a colloquial knowledge of seven languages. In July 1886, at the instance of the outgoing Liberal government he was granted a civil-list pension for 'the merits and utility of his literary work'.

Mongredien was an energetic and versatile man, one of the foremost amateur chess players of his day (an opponent of the great American player Morphy and a founder of the British Chess Association in 1862), a considerable linguist, a good musician, a great conversationalist, and 'somewhat of a *bon vivant*'. Mongredien died on 30 March 1888 at his home, 31 Park Road, Forest Hill, London, survived by his wife, son (Augustus, a commercial clerk), and two 'intellectual' daughters.

A. C. HOWE

Sources *The Times* (4 April 1888) · *The Athenaeum* (7 April 1888), 437 · Boase, *Mod. Eng. biog.* · S. E. Fairlie, 'The Anglo-Russian grain trade, 1815–61', PhD diss., U. Lond., 1959 · E. J. Willson, *Nurseryman to the world* (privately printed, 1989) · P. W. Sergeant, *A century of British chess* (1934) · A. R. Wallace, *My life: a record of events and opinions*, 2 vols. (1905) · *The political correspondence of Mr Gladstone and Lord Granville, 1876–1886*, ed. A. Ramm, 2 (1962) · m. cert. · *DNB*
Archives PRO, Heatherside Nurseries Co. Ltd, BT 31/1918/7873

Likenesses portrait, repro. in *Illustrated News of the World*, 8 (1861), 164
Wealth at death £3240 13s. 5d.: probate, 14 April 1888, *CGPLA Eng. & Wales*

Moninne [St Moninne, Darerca] (d. **517**), nun, was an Irish saint who has been identified with St Modwenna of Burton [see below]. According to the life of the saint contained in the fourteenth-century Codex Salmanticensis, which appears to preserve the earliest account, Moninne, or Darerca, was the daughter of Mochta, a nobleman of the Conailli Muirthemne, an Irish population group settled in the area of modern co. Louth. She took the veil at the hands of St Patrick, founded the monastery of Killevy in south Armagh, and, according to the annals of Ulster, died in 517.

Moninne's original religious community consisted of eight virgins and a widow, with the widow's child, Luger, later a bishop. This group received instruction, first from a local priest, later from St Ibar, and lived under his tutelage successively in the western islands, at Begerin (Wexford), and at the unidentified 'Ard Conais'. Attracted by the reputation of St Brigit, Moninne and her companions also spent time at her monastery at Kildare. The community eventually returned from Leinster to the north of Ireland, settling first at Faughart, then at Killevy. Here the number of nuns grew to over 150 and here Moninne died on 5 July 517. The miracles attributed to her include the production of food and drink, protection against robbers, prophecy, and converse with angels. According to the life in the Codex Salmanticensis, her hoe, spade, rough garments, and comb were preserved in her monastery of Killevy and were brought out as war talismans when invaders threatened the region. The nunnery survived until the Reformation and the annals of Ulster mention the death of a 'coarb [successor] of Moninne' in 1077.

Another account of Moninne's life, written by Conchubranus (about whom nothing is known except that he wrote prior to 1100), transforms this simple story. Conchubranus introduces more Irish saints, including, in defiance of all chronology, Columba. He transforms Brigit from Moninne's model into one of her early followers, here presumably using statements about the relative status of the two saints to make claims about the relative status of their two churches, Killevy and Kildare. Most significantly, Conchubranus attributes to Moninne a much wider geographical range of activity. In addition to three trips to Rome, the saint is now endowed with a southern Scottish career and also brought to Mercia, the west midlands, where she is tied in with the neighbourhood of Burton upon Trent. Most modern commentators assume, with plausibility, that three separate saints have been conflated in this new career spanning the three kingdoms.

Conchubranus also elaborates upon Moninne's genealogy, giving the name of her mother as Coman, daughter of King Dallbronach, and depicting her father as an important ruler in Ulster and identifying him as a member of the lineage of 'Hilech' (perhaps Ailech, the seat of the kings of Cenél nEogain, although Dallbronach does not appear in their genealogies). The saint's Scottish activities in this developed version include the founding of numerous churches, including some at such significant 'high status' sites of central Scotland as Dumbarton, Stirling, and Edinburgh. The site of her death is transferred to another of her foundations, 'Lonfortin' (perhaps Luncarty in Perthshire). No Scottish religious house of the later middle ages can be traced back to any of her supposed foundations.

It is not clear when and how the identification was made between the founder of Killevy, who died in 517, and **St Modwenna of Burton** (*fl.* before 12th cent.), whose bones were enshrined in the abbey of Burton upon Trent. Conchubranus's version, in the sole surviving manuscript (a copy made at or for Burton in the early twelfth century), reports that, after the saint had cured Alfred, son of an English king, she came to England and was rewarded by the grant of land in the Forest of Arden. Her bones, according to this account, lay on the island of Andresey, in the Trent by Burton. Local tradition, as represented by the version of the saint's life and miracles written by Geoffrey, abbot of Burton (1114–50), asserted that the saint was translated into the abbey church of Burton in the eleventh century and that her shrine there became the centre of miraculous healing and of miraculous punishments of those who intruded upon Burton's rights and property. Later medieval evidence of the cult at Burton includes a thirteenth-century Anglo-Norman version of Modwenna's life by Geoffrey, a chapel on the island of Andresey, and, within the abbey, an altar and an image, which were removed at the Reformation.

ROBERT BARTLETT

Sources W. W. Heist, ed., 'Vita sanctae Darercae seu Moninnae abbatissae', *Vitae sanctorum Hiberniae ex codice olim Salmanticensi nunc Bruxellensi*, Subsidia Hagiographica, 28 (Brussels, 1965), 83–95 · 'The *Life of St Monenna* by Conchubranus', *Seanchas Ardmhacha* [Ulster Society for Medieval Latin Studies], 9 (1978–9), 250–73; 10 (1980–82), 117–41, 426–54 · M. Esposito, 'The sources of Conchubranus' Life of St Monenna', *EngHR*, 35 (1920), 71–8 · A. T. Baker and A. Bell, eds., *St Modwenna*, Anglo-Norman Text Society, 7 (1947) · *Ann. Ulster*, vol. 1

Monk. *See also* Monck.

Monk, James Henry (1784–1856), bishop of Gloucester and Bristol and classical scholar, was born on 12 December 1784 at Buntingford, Hertfordshire, the only son of Charles Monk, an officer of the 40th regiment, and his wife, daughter of Joshua Waddington, vicar of Harworth, Nottinghamshire. He went to school first at Norwich and then, from 1799 to 1800, at Charterhouse. He entered Trinity College, Cambridge, in October 1800, and was elected a scholar in 1801. He graduated BA as seventh wrangler in 1804 and was also second chancellor's medallist. He became MA in 1807, BD in 1818, and DD in 1822. In 1805 he was elected fellow of Trinity and became an assistant tutor in 1807. In January 1809 at the age of twenty-five he was elected regius professor of Greek in succession to Richard Porson.

Although he did not match his predecessor in scholarly distinction, Monk was an influential college tutor and published several pamphlets advocating the establishment of a classical tripos, with public examinations and

James Henry Monk (1784–1856), by William Gush, 1842

honours open only to those who had obtained a place in the mathematical tripos. His chief work, like Porson's, was on the text of Euripides. His editions of *Hippolytus* (1811) and *Alcestis* (1816) were regularly reprinted. The Latin notes are learned and appreciative of the work of earlier critics, especially Porson. They also show something of the austerity of the Porsonian school in their concentration on the textual tradition and points of linguistic and metrical usage. He was one of the editors of Porson's *Adversaria* (1812) and of the short-lived but influential Cambridge journal *Museum Criticum*. His most important contribution to the history of classical scholarship was his *Life of Richard Bentley*, which appeared in 1830 and remains the fullest assessment of the greatest of English classical scholars.

Monk was ordained deacon in 1809 and priest in 1810. In 1812 he was Whitehall preacher, and attracted the attention of the prime minister, Lord Liverpool, who appointed him to the deanery of Peterborough in 1822. He hoped to retain his professorship, but was unable to do so since he had become a doctor of divinity on his decanal appointment, and the statutes of the university laid down that the professor of Greek should not be a doctor.

In right of his deanery, Monk nominated himself to the rectory of Fiskerton, Lincolnshire, in 1822, and afterwards held the rectory of Peakirk-cum-Glinton, Northamptonshire, from 1829. In 1823 he married Jane Smart, only daughter of the Revd Hugh Hughes, rector of Hardwick, Northamptonshire. They had three daughters and a son, Charles James (1824–1900), who became MP for Gloucester.

As dean, Monk collected £6000 for the restoration of Peterborough Cathedral, himself contributing substantially. In 1830 he was given a canonry at Westminster and in the same year consecrated bishop of Gloucester. In 1836 the see was amalgamated with Bristol by the recommendation of the ecclesiastical commission, of which Monk was an original member.

Monk was an old-fashioned conservative, equally suspicious of nonconformity and Tractarianism, and distrusted the social and political changes of his times. Although he spoke very rarely in the House of Lords (one of his few set speeches was a reply to the earl of Shrewsbury during the last debate on the Reform Bill in 1832), his diocesan charges to his clergy show that he was well aware of wider issues in church and state. While generally hostile to reform, he accepted nomination by the bishop of London, his Trinity contemporary the classical scholar C. J. Blomfield, onto the ecclesiastical commission, where his toryism was ridiculed by Sydney Smith in his *Third Letter to Archdeacon Singleton* (1839).

Although forced to admit that some redistribution of resources was necessary when confronted with the realities of religious life in the towns, Monk never conceded that the problems of the day were to a great extent the result of clerical negligence. He was, however, one of the instigators of the Pluralities Act of 1838, which sought to curb some of the most notorious abuses in the church.

Within his own diocese Monk was troubled by the increasing influence of evangelicals, particularly in Bristol, Cheltenham, and Clifton, but supported the demand of the Bristol Church Union for the revival of convocation. He gave considerable sums of money to charities, contributing part of his income towards the restoration of churches, the augmentation of clergy stipends, and the building of parsonages and church schools.

For some years before his death Monk suffered from partial blindness, although he produced editions of Euripides' *Iphigeneia in Aulis* (1840) and *Iphigeneia in Tauris* (1845). He died at the palace, Stapleton, near Bristol, on 6 June 1856, and was buried in the north aisle of Westminster Abbey on the 14th.   RICHARD SMAIL

Sources GM, 3rd ser., 1 (1856), 115–17 · R. L. Arrowsmith, ed., *Charterhouse register, 1769–1872* (1974) · C. O. Brink, *English classical scholarship: historical reflections on Bentley, Porson, and Housman* (1986) · R. A. Soloway, *Prelates and people: ecclesiastical social thought in England, 1783–1852* (1969) · M. L. Clarke, *Greek studies in England, 1700–1830* (1945) · P. Virgin, *The church in an age of negligence: ecclesiastical structure and problems of church reform, 1700–1840* (1989) · Boase, *Mod. Eng. biog.*

Archives Glos. RO, corresp. and papers · priv. coll. · Trinity Cam., corresp. and papers | BL, corresp. with Samuel Butler, Add. MSS 34583–34590 · BL, corresp. with Sir Robert Peel, Add. MSS 40512–40575, *passim* · Bodl. Oxf., corresp. with Sir Thomas Phillipps · Bodl. Oxf., corresp. with Frederick Pollock · LPL, letters to Christopher Wordsworth · Trinity Cam., corresp. with William Whewell

Likenesses W. Gush, portrait, 1842, bishops palace, Gloucester [*see illus.*] · F. Bacon, mezzotint, pubd 1843 (after W. Gush), BM · G. Parker, stipple (after J. Moore), BM, NPG; repro. in W. Jerdan, *National portrait gallery of illustrious and eminent personages* (1832) · portrait, repro. in W. Jerdan, *National portrait gallery of illustrious and eminent personages* (1833), no. 21 · portrait, repro. in W. C. Taylor, *National Portrait Gallery* (1846), 3.76–9

Monk, Richard (*fl.* 1434–1439), astronomer and writer on the calendar, was a London chaplain who in 1434 compiled calendrical tables at Oxford. Whether their date has anything to do with the movement for calendar reform that was then in full spate at the Council of Basel it is impossible to say, but it coincides exactly with the church's establishment of a commission to look into that long-running question.

Nothing is known of Monk's personal circumstances, either of birth or of death. His calendrical tables, which apparently survive in only a single manuscript (Bodl. Oxf., MS Laud misc. 594), are all that remain of him, and they are accompanied by almost no explanation. They are intelligently thought out, however, and unusually radical for the time. They use the Egyptian year of 365 days, which some astronomers have preferred for its logicality, although since it makes for a more rapid drift of the seasons through the resulting calendar than the very calendars that the church wished to replace, it cannot have found favour with many churchmen. Monk's system, like those of Nikolaus von Kues (*d.* 1464), Paul van Middelburg (*d.* 1534), Joseph Justus Scaliger (*d.* 1609), and Petavius (*d.* 1652), was heavily bound up with certain numerological ideas. He gave the 'true year of the world' which he believed ran in seven cycles of 924 years each, this being subdivided into cycles of thirty-three years. His months have thirty or thirty-one days, according to a simple rule. At worst, with the final scheme he proposed, the seasons would have oscillated within the calendar with an amplitude of eight days. There are faint echoes here of a calendar reform proposed in 1079 at Esfahan by the polymath ʿUmar Khayyam (al-Khayyami), which also used a thirty-three-year cycle. Monk's scheme would have caused Easter to shuttle back and forth in new ways, and there would have been problems with the placing of saints' days. Yet another measure of Monk's freedom from traditional thinking is that he chose as a standard meridian not Oxford, nor London, nor Rome, nor Jerusalem, but 'the place of the world between east and west'. He had in mind an Indian and Persian tradition whereby the town of Arin was taken as the centre of the world.

Much of this must have irritated Monk's academic acquaintances. All that is known of his life comes from records in the close rolls of a lawsuit that hints at the controversial nature of some unknown aspect of his astronomy. On 4 December 1439 he gave recognizance to Thomas Gosse, mercer, for £20 to be levied from his lands, chattels, and church goods, to abide by an award by John Stopyndoun (clerk keeper of the chancery rolls) 'concerning all debts, trespasses, debates, etc., between the parties to this date, and certain opinions of certain articles of the science of astronomy' (*CClR, 1435–1441*, 349). Gosse—perhaps an angry parishioner—was similarly bound. A terser judgement was that of John Dee, who, in a manuscript he owned (now Bodl. Oxf., MS Ashmole 369), simply wrote 'falsum' over the top of a statement he found there, that according to R. M. (fairly certainly Monk) the world was created 4909 years before the birth of Christ.

J. D. NORTH

Sources J. D. North, 'The western calendar —"Intolerabilis, horribilis et derisibilis": four centuries of discontent', *Gregorian reform of the calendar: proceedings of the Vatican conference to commemorate its 400th anniversary* [Vatican 1982], ed. G. V. Coyne, M. A. Hoskin, and O. Pederson (1983), 75–113, esp. 89–94 • Emden, *Oxf.*, 2.1294 • *CClR, 1435–41*, 349
Archives Bodl. Oxf., MS Laud misc. 594

Monk, William Henry (1823–1889), organist and hymnist, the son of William and Anna Coleman Monk, was born at Brompton, London, on 16 March 1823. He studied music under Thomas Adams, J. A. Hamilton, and G. A. Griesbach, and became church organist and choirmaster at, successively, St Peter's, Eaton Square (1841–3), St George's, Albemarle Street (1843–5), and St Paul's, Portman Square (1845–7). He succeeded Robert Druitt as editor of the *Parish Choir* (1846–51), the journal of the Tractarian Society for Promoting Church Music, and contributed articles advocating the revival of plainsong as part of the Anglican service. He was appointed choirmaster at King's College, London, in 1847, and in 1849 took up the post of organist there. In 1851 he became professor of music at the School for the Indigent Blind. From 1850 to 1854 Monk gave lectures on music at the London Institution, and he also lectured at similar establishments elsewhere. In 1852 he became organist at the church of St Matthias, Stoke Newington, where he established a daily choral service with a voluntary choir. Monk set high standards, demanding good discipline and giving his choirs challenging music. He wished also to foster congregational music, using the organ for support rather than for display.

In 1857 Monk was appointed music editor of *Hymns Ancient and Modern*. The first edition was published in 1861, and was an immediate success, achieving wide circulation in this and many subsequent editions. Monk was assisted in his editorial work by Sir Frederick Ouseley and later by Charles Steggall. For the first edition he wrote fifteen original hymn tunes, including 'Eventide' for Henry Francis Lyte's text 'Abide with me'. Although this tune, the one for which Monk is best remembered, has been derided for its supposed sentimentality, its expressive warmth and directness of appeal typify the best of high Victorian hymnody. Monk himself criticized sentimentality in church music, believing that music in currently popular styles was unfit for church use. Most of his hymn tunes are relatively austere, and his shorter anthems, services, and chants follow similar principles. Their textures are simple and chordal, characterized for the most part by the deliberately conservative harmony that Tractarians considered proper for church use. Monk also arranged music from other sources for the 1861 edition of *Hymns Ancient and Modern*: the best known of these tunes is 'Dix', named after the author of the Epiphany hymn text 'As with gladness men of old', for which it was arranged from a German chorale.

In 1874 Monk was appointed professor of vocal music at King's College, London. He was also professor at the National Training School for Music (1876), and at Bedford College, London (1878). He acted as music editor to numerous further collections of church music, including Bishop

William Henry Monk (1823–1889), by W. & A. H. Fry, 1870

Christopher Wordsworth's *The Holy Year* (1865), the Church of Scotland's *Book of Psalms in Metre and the Scottish Hymnal* (1872 and later editions) and *Book of Anthems for Use in Public Worship* (1875 and later editions), the 1886 edition of Dr Henry Allon's *The Congregational Psalmist Hymnal*, and *The Book of Common Prayer, Edited with Plain Song and Appropriate Music* (1891). He also edited works by Handel and Palestrina.

In 1882 Monk received the honorary degree of MusD from Durham University. He died at his home, Glebe Field, Clissold Road, Stoke Newington, London, on 1 March 1889, and was buried in Highgate cemetery, where a memorial cross, erected by public subscription, marked his grave. He was survived by his wife, Hope Isidora Monk.

JUDITH BLEZZARD

Sources DNB · *New Grove* · B. Rainbow, *The choral revival in the Anglican church, 1839–1872* (1970) · N. Temperley, *The music of the English parish church*, 1 (1979) · I. Bradley, *Abide with me: the world of Victorian hymns* (1997) · N. Temperley, ed., *Music in Britain: the romantic age, 1800–1914* (1981); repr. (1988), vol. 5 of *The Blackwell history of music in Britain*, ed. I. Spink · L. Baillie and R. Balchin, eds., *The catalogue of printed music in the British Library to 1980*, 62 vols. (1981–7), vol. 40 · W. J. Gatens, *Victorian cathedral music in theory and practice* (1986) · M. Frost, ed., *Historical companion to 'Hymns ancient and modern'* (1962) · J. Blezzard, *Borrowings in English church music* (1990) · A. Hutchings, *Church music in the nineteenth century* (1967)

Likenesses W. & A. H. Fry, photograph, 1870, NPG [*see illus.*] · photograph, repro. in Frost, ed., *Historical companion* · portrait, repro. in *Musical Herald* (April 1889)

Wealth at death £1614 7s. 3d.: administration with will, 3 April 1889, CGPLA Eng. & Wales

Monk Bretton. For this title name *see* Dodson, John George, first Baron Monk Bretton (1825–1897).

Monkhouse, William Cosmo (1840–1901), poet and art critic, born in London on 18 March 1840, was the son of Cyril John Monkhouse, a solicitor, and his wife, Amelia Maria Delafosse, who was of a Huguenot family which came to England after the revocation of the edict of Nantes. He entered St Paul's School, London, on 3 October 1848 and left in 1856 to take up a nomination to a supplementary clerkship in the Board of Trade, then under the presidency of Lord Stanley of Alderley.

Monkhouse's literary career began early. He wrote much verse while at school, and he was an early contributor to *Temple Bar*, *The Argosy*, the *Englishwoman's Review*, and other magazines. In 1865 he married Laura, daughter of John Keymer of Dartford, Kent, but they appear to have divorced soon afterwards. It was also in 1865 that Moxon published his first volume of poetry, *A Dream of Idleness, and other Poems*. The volume was of promise, and poems such as 'The Chief Ringer's Burial' and 'The Night Express' found their place in anthologies. But it had no great success, pecuniary or otherwise, and the moment was perhaps unfavourable to Monkhouse, who was a disciple of Wordsworth and Tennyson. After an attempt at the three-volume novel with *A Question of Honour* (1868), he for some years practically abandoned poetry for literary and art criticism. He became a frequent contributor to *The Academy*, the *Magazine of Art* (then under the editorship of W. E. Henley), and eventually the *Saturday Review*. In 1869 he published *Masterpieces of English Art*; in 1872 he edited and prefaced a photographic edition of William Hogarth's works; in 1877 he produced a *Handbook of Précis Writing*; in 1879 an excellent short life of Turner for Cundall's Great Artists; and in 1887 a guidebook on the Italian Pre-Raphaelites in the National Gallery. He published a significant volume, *Earlier English Water Colour Painters*, in 1890 (2nd edn 1897). His analysis of the life and works of Edwin Landseer was reprinted in 1990.

Meanwhile Monkhouse continued to rise through the ranks in the Board of Trade; at his death in 1901 he was assistant secretary to the finance department. In 1870–71 he was sent to South America in connection with seamen's hospitals; and in 1894–6 he was a member of the committee on the mercantile marine fund. In 1873 he married his second wife, Leonora Eliza, the daughter of Commander Blount RN; they had two sons and six daughters.

Corn and Poppies, some portions of which had appeared in the *Magazine of Art*, marked Monkhouse's return to poetry in 1890. This volume contained many of his best pieces, perhaps the most famous of which is 'Dead March'. A limited edition was issued of the ballad 'The Christ upon the Hill', with etchings by William Strang in 1895; after his death the ballad was included in the publication of a slender volume entitled *Pasiteles the Elder and other Poems*. His other works included *A Memoir of Leigh Hunt* (1893) in the Great Writers series, *In the National Gallery* (1895), *British Contemporary Artists* (1899; chiefly from contributions to *Scribner's Magazine*), and *A History of Chinese Porcelain* (1901). He was also a diligent contributor of lives of artists to the *Dictionary of National Biography*, including the biographies of Turner and Sir Joshua Reynolds. As a critic, he had the happy faculty of conveying a well-considered and weighty opinion without suggesting superiority or patronage; as a poet, though he lacked the leisure to realize his full ambition, he left much of value. Monkhouse died at Skegness on 2 July 1901; he was survived by his second wife.

AUSTIN DOBSON, *rev.* SAYONI BASU

Sources *The Times* (4 July 1901) · Allibone, *Dict.* · E. Gosse, 'Cosmo Monkhouse as an art critic', *Art Journal*, new ser., 22 (1902) · J. Sutherland, *The Longman companion to Victorian fiction* (1988), 443 · *CGPLA Eng. & Wales* (1901)
Archives Royal Holloway College, Egham, Surrey, corresp. | LUL, letters to Austin Dobson and notes
Likenesses W. Strang, etching, 1892, NPG · J. M. Hamilton, oils, 1898, NPG · H. Furniss, pen-and-ink sketch, NPG
Wealth at death £747 13*s*.: probate, 9 Aug 1901, *CGPLA Eng. & Wales*

Monkswell. For this title name *see* Collier, Robert Porrett, first Baron Monkswell (1817–1886); Collier, Mary Josephine, Lady Monkswell (1849–1930).

Monmouth. For this title name *see* Carey, Robert, first earl of Monmouth (1560–1639); Carey, Henry, second earl of Monmouth (1596–1661); Scott, James, duke of Monmouth and first duke of Buccleuch (1649–1685); Middleton, Charles, styled second earl of Middleton and Jacobite first earl of Monmouth (1649/50–1719); Scott, Anna, duchess of Monmouth and *suo jure* duchess of Buccleuch (1651–1732); Mordaunt, Charles, third earl of Peterborough and first earl of Monmouth (1658?–1735); Robinson, Anastasia, countess of Peterborough and Monmouth (*d.* 1755).

Monmouth, Geoffrey of [Galfridus Arturus] (*d.* **1154/5**), bishop of St Asaph and historian, is of obscure origins, and very little of substance is known about his life. Later historians, notably the author of the Welsh *Brut*, have assigned him many roles, some of which must be regarded as impossible (for example, monk of Monmouth and bishop of Llandaff) or at least highly unlikely (chaplain of Gloucester or chaplain of Monmouth). There is no reliable evidence for his date of birth, but it seems likely that he was born within ten years of 1100, and had reached adulthood no later than 1129, when his existence is first recorded as a witness to a charter.

Life and learning Geoffrey's cultural background has occasioned some discussion, partly because it impinges on the relationship of his work to Celtic sources. Earlier generations of scholars thought of him as Welsh, or at least Welsh-speaking. He has been credited with Welsh paternity: contemporaries called him not Geoffrey of Monmouth but Geoffrey Arthur (Galfridus Arturus, or Galfridus Artur), which, if the Arturus is a patronymic, would suggest that Geoffrey's father bore a Welsh name. However, as Arturus does not appear in the form expected for a patronymic (the genitive case), this argument looks decidedly weak, and the name is usually regarded as a nickname reflecting Geoffrey's scholarly interests. Geoffrey himself laid claim to Celtic connections, using the toponymic Monemutensis—of Monmouth—and advertising two of his three works as translations. His grasp of the Welsh language has been shown to have been slight, however, and he is best located among the French-speaking élites settled on the Welsh border since 1066, to whose ranks belonged the distinguished authors Walter Map and Gerald of Wales. Monmouth had been held by Breton lords since William I granted it to Wihenoc before 1086, so it is possible that Geoffrey's ancestors were Breton rather than Norman, having originally settled on the border as part of the entourage of Wihenoc or his successor, William fitz Baderon.

Most, if not all, of Geoffrey's adult life must have been spent outside Wales, although the details remain very sketchy. Between 1129 and the time of his election to the see of St Asaph he can be traced periodically to the Oxford area, where he attested a number of charters in favour of local foundations. By 1139 he is sometimes styled *magister*, which indicates a level of learning unlikely to have been attained in England at this date. Geoffrey had probably been educated at Paris or one of the other continental schools, perhaps before his first attested connection with Oxford in 1129 when he appears, unstyled, in the witness list of the foundation charter of Osney Priory, an institution set up in that year. His occupation in Oxford remains unclear. Some have envisaged him as one of the small number of schools-educated teachers active in the city in the 1130s. Most agree in counting him among the canons of the church of St George in Oxford Castle. He witnessed charters in the company of another canon, Walter, archdeacon of Oxford, and appears among the witnesses to an alleged charter of Robert d'Oilly in favour of the canons of St George's. Although this latter document has been shown to be a forgery, Geoffrey's association with St George's should not be dismissed. Osney and Thame, two of the three institutions whose documents Geoffrey witnessed, enjoyed the patronage of the d'Oilly family, founders and patrons of St George's, who continued to influence appointments there until the second half of the twelfth century: Robert d'Oilly (*d.* 1142), sheriff of Oxfordshire, nephew and heir of the founder of the castle chapel of St George, founded Osney Priory in 1129, whose foundation charter Geoffrey witnessed, and his wife was a significant patron of Thame. In addition, Geoffrey dedicated his last work to a former canon of St George's, Robert de Chesney.

Friends and patrons A handful of men can be identified as Geoffrey's friends and associates. Archdeacon Walter (*d.* 1151) of Oxford, who features as witness or issuing authority in all of the documents attested by Geoffrey in his lifetime, must be regarded as an influential friend. Geoffrey named Walter in the second chapter of his *Historia regum*

Britanniae, describing him as a man learned in the rhetorical art and in exotic histories, who had supplied him with a key text, the ancient book in the British language that Geoffrey claimed to have translated into Latin. Ralph of Monmouth, who held a canonry at Lincoln, attests alongside Geoffrey in every charter in which he appears except the first, from 1129, and can therefore be counted another associate. The nature of Ralph's associations with Monmouth, like Geoffrey's, remains hazy, but it is at least possible that their association antedates their time at Oxford. Indeed, a patronage network may have extended from Monmouth into the west midlands of England. Geoffrey chose to dedicate his most important work, the *Historia*, to marcher magnates. The main dedicatee was Robert, earl of Gloucester (*d.* 1147), bastard son of Henry I, whose lands included Glamorgan and Gwynllŵg in southeast Wales, just west of Monmouth. In one version of the *Historia*, the dedication is shared with Robert's rival and neighbour, Waleran, count of Meulan (*d.* 1166), a man who would have offered Geoffrey the prospect of further powerful local patronage. Waleran's acquisition of the city of Worcester in 1135 and subsequently, in 1138, the earldom of the same name, has been interpreted as an attempt by the king to check Robert's power in his home territory. Geoffrey's career, like that of Ralph, was also influenced by the diocese of Lincoln within whose boundaries Oxford lay. Geoffrey dedicated the *Prophetie Merlini* ('The prophecies of Merlin'), which form the core of his *Historia*, to Alexander, bishop of Lincoln (*d.* 1148). Geoffrey's last work, his *Vita Merlini* ('Life of Merlin'), was offered to Alexander's successor, Robert de Chesney (*d.* 1166), whose charter in favour of Thame (refounded in 1139 by Alexander) Geoffrey witnessed as bishop-elect in 1152. Geoffrey's courting of Robert's favour has been interpreted as a desperate move to find new support after the death of Robert of Gloucester in 1147.

Political sympathies as well as geography may find reflection in the network of patronage that underlay Geoffrey's career. When war broke out between Matilda and Stephen in 1139 Geoffrey almost certainly found himself within the Angevin sphere of influence. From 1139 Robert of Gloucester led Matilda's cause in England. The lords of Monmouth were Robert's most powerful allies, and by 1140 Oxford offered a stronghold for Angevin sympathizers after another Breton lord, Brian fitz Count of Wallingford, had declared for Matilda. Robert d'Oilly was slow to come over to the Angevins but he did so in 1141, losing his life in 1142. Geoffrey had probably completed his *Historia* before Robert of Gloucester renounced his allegiance to Stephen in 1138. In fact, the allegiances of Geoffrey's chosen dedicatees provide the best indications for the dating of the *Historia*. While most copies bear a dedication to Robert alone, one manuscript is dedicated to Robert and King Stephen, and nine to Robert and Waleran. These dedications almost certainly predate Robert's rift with Stephen's party which dates from 1137, and suggest that the *Historia* was available in some form before 1138 (although not necessarily preserved in the texts prefaced by surviving examples of these dedications).

The best documented part of Geoffrey's life is its end. He gained election to the see of St Asaph, north Wales, on 24 February 1151 (his episcopal profession survives), having been ordained priest a week before. His appointment coincided with a period of extreme instability for the Anglo-Normans in Powys, the kingdom in which his diocese was situated. In 1149 Madog ap Maredudd, prince of Powys, took Oswestry, and in 1152 his son killed Stephen Fitzbaldwin, lord of Montgomery. Such inroads into regions of Anglo-Norman control in eastern Powys may have prevented Geoffrey from taking up residence in his see. Whatever the circumstances, Geoffrey did not live long after his elevation. He is usually held to have died between 25 December 1154 and 24 December 1155 when his presumed successor, Richard, took office (although doubts have been cast upon the date of Richard's episcopate).

The *Prophetie Merlini* Geoffrey's posthumous fame depends entirely on his literary output. He is celebrated as the author of one of the most popular and influential historical works of the middle ages, the *Historia regum Britanniae* ('The history of the kings of Britain'). Allegedly a translation from an ancient 'British' book, the *Historia* brought such figures as Arthur, Merlin, and kings Leir and Coel to an international Latin-reading public, and reached more widely still after translation into Anglo-Norman, French, English, Welsh, and Norse. The only one of his works in which Geoffrey declared his authorship, the *Historia* was in fact one of three works circulating in the middle ages that were connected with his name, the others being the hugely popular *Prophetie Merlini* ('Prophecies of Merlin'), written, like the *Historia*, in Latin prose, and the less well-known *Vita Merlini*, composed in Latin verse. None of his writings can be dated precisely, but the *Historia* had been completed by 1139, and the others are presumed to have been written in the 1130s and 1140s. He has also been associated, purely speculatively, with the collection of spurious charters and saints' lives known as the Book of Llandaff, the *Liber Landauensis*, which was compiled in the 1130s.

The *Prophetie Merlini* has been called Geoffrey's earliest work. This series of increasingly obscure animal prophecies may date in its earliest form from the mid-1130s (an interpolated passage contains information about Henry I's death in 1135). Although Geoffrey claimed to have translated the *Prophetie* (from an unspecified, presumably Celtic, language), it contains transparent references to Anglo-Norman history and politics up to Geoffrey's own lifetime—for example the wreck of the *White Ship* in 1120 when Henry I's son and heir was killed—and little, if any, of his material can be regarded as inherited from Celtic sources. The *Prophetie* circulated widely as a self-standing text and bears its own dedication, to Alexander, bishop of Lincoln. However, it is far from clear whether it was written before the *Historia*, or was extracted from it later. Orderic Vitalis, writing *c*.1136–7, cites the prophecies as a *Libellus Merlini*, but as his text is close to that in the *Historia*, which was being completed at just that time, his testimony does not guarantee the prior and independent existence of the *Prophetie*.

The *Historia regum Britanniae* Whenever it was completed, the *Prophetie* is best understood as part of Geoffrey's *Historia*, in which it occupies a key position. The *Historia* provides a vivid, uninterrupted account of the early history of Britain from the foundation of the island's population and monarchical tradition by Brutus, a Trojan émigré, via a series of royal dynasties, some of whose members enjoyed later fame, to the last glorious British kings, notably Uther Pendragon and Arthur, before the population of the island succumbed to Saxon aggression. Geoffrey concluded his work in approximately the seventh century AD, where Bede's *Historia ecclesiastica* begins as a continuous history (Geoffrey chose not to encumber his narrative with dates). Merlin's prophecies occur before the last, greatest, days of the British monarchy, but after the island has begun to be threatened by the Saxons, some time in the fifth century. Vortigern, who has usurped the throne of Britain, has built a tower to save himself from the Saxon fighters whose entry into his kingdom he had permitted. When the tower repeatedly collapses, he seeks advice from his court magicians and, when they advise him to find a fatherless boy, he locates in Wales one Merlin Ambrosius. Merlin tells him that the subsidence of the tower has been caused by a pool in which two dragons are sleeping. When Vortigern's men drain the pool the two dragons, one red, one white, begin to fight, and Merlin explains that the red dragon represents the British and the white the Saxons. He goes on to utter a long series of prophecies, beginning with the known—predicting the final part of Geoffrey's *Historia*, Anglo-Saxon history to the Norman conquest, Anglo-Norman history until the time in which Geoffrey was writing—and then moving into the unknown with a series of vague and apocalyptic prophecies.

The *Vita Merlini* The last work attributed to Geoffrey, the *Vita Merlini* ('Life of Merlin'), is the least securely associated with his name. A long Latin poem, the *Vita* describes Merlin's old age as a crazed and grief-stricken outcast in the Scottish woods. Some commentators have doubted Geoffrey's authorship. The *Vita* concerns a Merlin character, Merlin of the Woods (Merlinus Sylvestris) or the Scottish Merlin (Merlinus Caledonius), recognized as early as the 1150s as a figure distinct from the young Merlin of Geoffrey's earlier work (Merlinus Ambrosius). The external evidence for authorship is certainly late—a colophon appended to the only complete manuscript of the work, the late thirteenth-century BL, Cotton MS Vespasian E.iv. The opening lines of the poem name one Robert, bishop of Lincoln, as dedicatee, but Geoffrey's acquaintance from Oxford, Robert de Chesney, is not the only candidate: Robert Grosseteste (*d.* 1253) has also been suggested. However, for most critics these doubts have been outweighed by recognizably Galfridian elements in the construction and the details of the poem. Geoffrey would have written the *Vita* after Robert's elevation to Lincoln, and perhaps before his

own elevation to St Asaph *c*.1151. The *Vita Merlini* apparently circulated poorly, but Geoffrey's earlier works—the *Prophetie* and the *Historia*—had already propelled Merlin, together with Arthur, into the mainstream of medieval historical literature.

The creation of legend: King Leir Merlin and Arthur do at least have a recognized autonomy of identity outside Geoffrey's works. This can hardly be said of **Leir** [Lear] (*supp. fl. c.*820 BC), king of Britain, who must be regarded as arguably the most successful of Geoffrey's creations. Commentators have scoured Indo-European myth, Celtic literature, even the sixth-century history of Gregory of Tours (book 2, chapter 28, contains a story similar at some points), in the hope of finding a source for Geoffrey's Leir, but with no satisfactory outcome. Indeed, Tatlock described the Leir story 'along with the vogue of Arthur' as 'Geoffrey's greatest contribution to the world'. Leir appears early in Geoffrey's *Historia*, in chapter 31, as the tenth ruler of Britain after Brutus. Finding himself old and without a male heir, he decides to provide for the succession by finding suitable husbands for his three daughters and dividing the kingdom between them. In order to establish the most deserving of his daughters, he asks each of the three who loves him most. Goneril and Regan protest that he is dearer to them than anyone; Cordeilla, the youngest, refuses to exaggerate her love and so incurs Leir's wrath and loses her share of the kingdom. Goneril and Regan marry the dukes of Albany and Cornwall and hold half the kingdom between them. However, instead of waiting to inherit the remainder at Leir's death, they usurp his power and reduce him to seeking hospitality at their courts. Both daughters resent the expense of his entourage and finally Leir seeks refuge with Cordeilla, now married (without dowry) to Aganippus, king of the Franks. Aganippus raises an army, ousts Leir's other sons-in-law, and restores Leir to his kingdom. On Leir's death Cordeilla inherits the throne of a united Britain.

Later medieval writers who took up the story seem to have relied on Geoffrey's version, which they embellished or abbreviated. Leir is mentioned in numerous Latin, French, English, and Welsh chronicles, from the earliest vernacular versions of Geoffrey's *Historia* by Wace (French, *c*.1155) and Layamon (English, *c*.1200), through Latin works like Matthew Paris's *Chronica majora*, into the printed chronicles of the sixteenth century—Robert Fabyan (1516), Richard Grafton (1568), Ralph Holinshed (1577)—and beyond—John Taylor (1622). In contrast to Arthur, Leir remained a sparsely documented figure until Elizabeth's time, when Edmund Spenser included the story in his *Faerie queene*. An anonymous play, the *True Chronicle History of King Leir and his Three Daughters*, registered in 1605, has been attributed to about the same time, the years around 1590. William Shakespeare's *King Lear*, first performed at court in 1606, drew on Holinshed, Spenser, and the anonymous *King Leir*, but raised the story to a new plane. It is curious to reflect that its tragic hero, like many of the early kings in Geoffrey's *Historia*, may have started life as little more than an eponym: Geoffrey made Leir founder of Kaerleir (Leicester).

Contemporary and later responses Both the *Prophetie* and the *Historia* enjoyed enormous popularity, reaching libraries all over western Europe. The reception of the *Historia* in particular has aroused curiosity, partly because of Geoffrey's apparently impossible claims to be translating from an ancient source, and partly because of the strikingly unhistorical nature of his subject matter. On both counts medieval readers faced fewer difficulties than their modern counterparts. The translation claim is best regarded as a literary topos. No British book has ever been found despite the efforts of scholars but other medieval 'historical' works, notably the very popular history of Troy ascribed to Dares the Phrygian (a translation from 'Trojan' into Latin), carried similar declarations of authenticity. Geoffrey's readers, too, would have been less surprised than modern readers by the historical panorama which his *Historia* offers: in embryo it existed in a work already in circulation, the Latin *Historia Brittonum* ('History of the Britons') composed by an anonymous ninth-century Welsh cleric who, by Geoffrey's time, had become known as Nennius; it was in its scale, detail, and grandeur that Geoffrey's vision had no precedent.

The first datable reaction to the *Historia* comes from Henry of Huntingdon, Geoffrey's fellow historian and a fellow client of Alexander of Lincoln, who in 1139 travelled to Rome in the company of Archbishop Theobald of Canterbury (d. 1161). Stopping on the way at the Norman monastery of Bec, he was shown the work by Robert de Torigni, another historian and later abbot of Mont-St Michel. Henry expressed his astonishment at finding an account of a period for which he had found no sources when researching his own *Historia Anglorum* and he provided a very full, only slightly edited, summary of the contents in a letter addressed to Warinus Brito (Guérin the Breton) which serves as a supplement and preface to his work. Two late twelfth-century writers, Gerald of Wales and William of Newburgh, launched diatribes against the *Historia*, primarily, it would seem, because of Geoffrey's treatment of Arthur, increasingly the focus for Celtic resistance against Norman encroachment, whose glorious life and mysterious death Geoffrey had endorsed. However, Geoffrey's work had already entered the historical canon on the continent and in England, and, as their exploitation of the story of Lear shows, historians, poets, and dramatists continued to plunder it until the sixteenth century. The fact that thereafter the Arthurian cycle was mediated primarily through the mid-fifteenth-century *Morte d'Arthur* of Sir Thomas Malory should not detract from the position of Geoffrey of Monmouth as its great originator.   J. C. Crick

Sources H. E. Salter, 'Geoffrey of Monmouth and Oxford', *EngHR*, 34 (1919), 382–5 · L. Thorpe, 'The last years of Geoffrey of Monmouth', *Mélanges de langue et littérature françaises du moyen âge offerts à Pierre Jonin* (1979), 663–72 · M. D. Legge, 'Master Geoffrey Arthur', *An Arthurian tapestry: essays in memory of Lewis Thorpe*, ed. K. Varty (1981), 22–7 · J. E. Lloyd, 'Geoffrey of Monmouth', *EngHR*, 57 (1942), 460–68 · *The Historia regum Britannie of Geoffrey of Monmouth*, ed. N. Wright, 1: *Bern, Bürgerbibliothek, MS 568* (1985) · 'Geoffrey of Monmouth's Vita Merlini', ed. J. S. P. Tatlock, *Speculum*, 18 (1943), 265–87 · J. C. Crick, *The Historia regum Britannie of Geoffrey of Monmouth*, 4: *Dissemination and reception in the later middle ages* (1991) · T. D. Crawford, 'On the linguistic competence of Geoffrey of Monmouth', *Medium Ævum*, 51 (1982), 152–62 · D. M. Smith, 'The episcopate of Richard, bishop of St Asaph: a problem of twelfth-century chronology', *Journal of the Historical Society of the Church in Wales*, 24 (1974), 9–12 · D. Crouch, 'Robert, earl of Gloucester, and the daughter of Zelophehad', *Journal of Medieval History*, 11 (1985), 227–43 · E. M. R. Ditmas, 'Geoffrey of Monmouth and the Breton families in Cornwall', *Welsh History Review / Cylchgrawn Hanes Cymru*, 6 (1972–3), 451–61 · O. J. Padel, 'Geoffrey of Monmouth and Cornwall', *Cambridge Medieval Celtic Studies*, 8 (1984), 1–28 · W. Perrett, *The story of King Lear from Geoffrey of Monmouth to Shakespeare* (1904) · *The tragedy of King Lear*, ed. W. J. Craig, 4th edn (1905) · W. R. Elton, *King Lear and the gods* (1966) · W. W. Greg, 'The date of *King Lear* and Shakespeare's use of earlier versions of the story', *The Library*, 4th ser., 20 (1939–40), 377–400 · J. S. P. Tatlock, *The legendary history of Britain: Geoffrey of Monmouth's Historia regum Britanniae and its early vernacular versions* (1950)
Archives BL, Cotton MS Vespasian E.iv

Monmouth, John of (*c.*1182–1248), baron, son of Gilbert of Monmouth and his wife Bertha, was the great-great-grandson of William fitz Baderon, who is recorded in Domesday Book as the possessor of many lands and lordships in Gloucestershire, Herefordshire, and the Monmouth area. Rose or Roysya of Monemue, daughter of Gilbert fitz Richard de Clare, and wife successively of Baderon of Monmouth (d. 1170×76) and Hugh de Lacy (d. 1186), was his grandmother. In 1201–2 Monmouth was a minor in the wardship of William (III) de Briouze, and the latter in 1206 was placed in possession of Grosmont, Whitecastle, and Skenfrith castles, probably belonging to the Monmouth family.

Monmouth came of age before 1205, when he held fifteen knights' fees, and in 1208 his two infant sons, John and Philip, were demanded by King John as hostages for his good behaviour, probably as a precaution against Monmouth's joining William de Briouze in his rebellion; he paid a large fine for restoration to royal favour, and his children were liberated. In 1213 another son, William, appears to have been held as a hostage by John, but Monmouth remained to the end an active and faithful partisan of the king. In 1214 he was ordered to attend John at Cirencester, and received a completely equipped horse for his prompt obedience. On 10 February 1215 he was appointed one of the custodians of William de Lacy, half-brother of Monmouth's cousin Walter, Lord Lacy, and was commissioned to negotiate with the barons of Herefordshire, and in April to raise a loan in Gloucestershire. On 21 August he was made governor of St Briavels Castle, Gloucestershire, and later in that year and in 1216 he was granted custody of the castles of Elmley in Worcestershire, Bramber in Sussex, which had belonged to William de Briouze, Grosmont, Whitecastle, and Skenfrith, as well as the Forest of Dean, and lands in Bedfordshire and Cambridgeshire forfeited by Hugh Malebisse, besides those of his sister-in-law, Albreda de Boterel, who had sided with the barons, and of the wife of Walter of Stoke. During 1216 Monmouth owned a ship in John's service; he was present at the king's deathbed and was one of the executors of his will.

After the accession of Henry III, Monmouth received further promotion. In 1218 he escorted the magnates of north and south Wales to do homage to the king, and served as a justice itinerant on the west midlands circuit in 1220–21. On 8 August 1224 he was present at Bedford, when the castle of Falkes de Bréauté was besieged. The next year he was witness to the reissue of Magna Carta. In 1226 he founded the Cistercian abbey of Grace Dieu in his lordship of Monmouth (*Ann. mon.* 2.302), and in May stood security for his cousin Walter de Lacy; on 2 September he was appointed to attend the meeting of Llywelyn, prince of Gwynedd, William (II) Marshal, and other barons at Shrewsbury, and to report on the result. In 1228 Monmouth was made sheriff of Wiltshire and briefly in 1229 of Shropshire and Staffordshire; also in 1228, apparently by right of his wife, Cecilia, daughter and heir of Walter de Walerand, he was keeper of New, Clarendon, Panchet, and Buckholt forests, offices held by his father-in-law. In 1229 he mediated between the town and abbey of Dunstable, and witnessed a grant from Henry to Dafydd, son of Llywelyn, and other charters. On the death of William Marshal, in 1231, the castles and honours of Striguil and Hereford were committed to his custody, and in December he negotiated the truce that was patched up with Llywelyn.

On the revolt of Richard Marshal in 1233 Monmouth bore the brunt of his attack. In command of the king's Poitevin mercenaries in south Wales, on 26 December he collected a large force, intending to make a secret attack on Marshal. The earl, however, learning his design, set an ambush for Monmouth in a wood near Grosmont, and completely routed his forces; Monmouth himself escaped only by a hasty flight. Marshal proceeded to destroy Monmouth's lands and buildings, including, at the instigation of his Welsh allies, the abbey of Grace Dieu. On 28 March 1234 Henry informed him that he had concluded a truce with Marshal and Llywelyn, and in July Monmouth was ordered to besiege the castles in the hands of Peter des Rivaux, should he refuse to give them up. At the marriage of Eleanor and Henry III on 14 January 1236 Monmouth claimed the right as a lord marcher to carry the canopy. In the same year he witnessed the confirmation of Magna Carta, and rebuilt the abbey of Grace Dieu. At Easter 1238 he was summoned to parliament at Oxford to advise Henry on the probable outbreak of war with Llywelyn, and in 1240 he was appointed one of the arbiters to decide on the disputed points between Dafydd II and the king. He played a key role in Henry III's policies in south Wales in the 1240s. On 30 October 1241 he was appointed chief bailiff of the new counties of Carmarthen and Cardigan and was subsequently referred to as the king's justiciar or lieutenant in south Wales. He was in charge of the key castle of Builth and was later appointed constable of Dinefwr Castle. With the earl of Gloucester he resisted Dafydd's invasion in 1244; he received a grant of 300 marks on 3 June for that purpose, and inflicted a severe defeat on the

Welsh; in January the next year he was directed to summon the Welsh barons to answer for the depredations they had committed. He died in 1248. In addition to the Cistercian abbey of Grace Dieu he also founded two hospitals at Monmouth, the one dedicated to the Holy Trinity, the other to St John.

Monmouth and his wife, Cecilia, apparently had five sons, John, Philip, Walter, Henry, and William. Of these John alone survived, and had livery of his father's lands in September 1248. This John had two daughters, but no male issue, and died in 1257, leaving the castle and honour to Prince Edward. Another **John Monmouth** (*fl.* 1320) was a supporter of the marcher lords during the conflict with Edward II in 1321–2 and was imprisoned successively at York, Berkhamsted, and Berkeley castles; a third was vice-chancellor of the University of Oxford and in 1294 was appointed bishop of Llandaff. He died on 8 April 1323 after a long and notable episcopate.

A. F. POLLARD, *rev.* R. R. DAVIES

Sources Dugdale, *Monasticon*, new edn · *Chancery records* [PRO and RC] · Paris, *Chron.* · *Ann. mon.* · J. G. Edwards, *Calendar of ancient correspondence concerning Wales* (1935) · R. W. Banks, ed., 'Cartularium prioratus s. Johannis evang. de Brecon', *Archaeologia Cambrensis*, 4th ser., 13 (1882), 275–308 · R. W. Banks, ed., 'Cartularium prioratus s. Johannis evang. de Brecon', *Archaeologia Cambrensis*, 4th ser., 14 (1883), 18–49, 137–68, 221–36, 274–311 · Emden, *Oxf.* [John Monmouth] · G. Williams, *The Welsh church from conquest to Reformation*, rev. edn (1976)

Monmouth, John (*d.* 1323), bishop of Llandaff, was a man of marcher stock—one chronicler refers to him as John Ludlow, and he was also known as John Eaglescliffe. Though not Welsh-speaking, as a bishop he learned Welsh and showed strong Welsh sympathies in his diocese. The pupil and protégé of Robert Winchelsey at Oxford, he had graduated MA by 1276, and by 1290 had become regent master in theology. He was elected chancellor of the university on 6 June of the latter year, an office he held until December 1291. Clearly a theologian of some distinction, he is recorded as taking part in disputations, while his library included works by Anselm and Thomas Aquinas, which he bequeathed to Merton College. Ordained subdeacon in 1277 and priest in 1285, he was rector of Wolferlow, Herefordshire, from 1276 to 1284 or 1285, and of Upton-on-Severn, Gloucestershire, from 1284 to 1294. From 1289 he was dean of the collegiate church of Westbury-on-Trym, where Godfrey Giffard, bishop of Worcester, was seeking to establish a second base for episcopal administration in his diocese. He continued to hold this office after his consecration. He was also a canon of Lincoln (1290–94), holding the prebend of Milton Ecclesia.

After the death of Bishop William de Briouze on 19 March 1287 Llandaff was vacant until February 1297. Briouze's death was followed by a disputed and ineffective election in 1287, and by an unsuccessful attempt in October 1290 to appoint a bishop by papal provision. When, in the summer of 1294, Archbishop Winchelsey went to Rome, Celestine V initiated a third attempt to fill the see and delegated to him the nomination of a bishop. Winchelsey nominated John Monmouth. After Celestine V's resignation in December 1294, Boniface VIII rescinded all his predecessor's acts, and the validity of Monmouth's appointment was impaired.

This ecclesiastical controversy was matched by a clash of secular interests in the diocese. Edward I challenged the claim of Gilbert de Clare, as lord of Glamorgan, to the temporalities of the see during a vacancy, and limited that right in 1290 to the lifetime of Earl Gilbert and his wife. After Monmouth was nominated in 1294, Clare still chose to defy a royal instruction to hand over the temporalities, which were not surrendered until August 1295. Even then, the archbishop was slow to act. In July 1296 Winchelsey asked Boniface VIII for a clear directive: was Celestine V's provision valid? Reassured, he consecrated Monmouth at Canterbury on 10 February 1297.

On the national scene Monmouth was Winchelsey's friend and close ally. Together they incurred royal displeasure by opposing Edward I's taxation of the clergy in 1297, when Monmouth's refusal to submit to the king's demands resulted in his having to pay a higher fine for the restitution of his temporalities than almost any other bishop. He remained Winchelsey's supporter and confidant thereafter, acting as the archbishop's vicar-general in spirituals in the months immediately before Winchelsey's death, and officiating and preaching at the primate's funeral on 22 and 23 May 1313. In his will Winchelsey left Monmouth a ring and 100 marks. In secular politics, Monmouth was one of the *lords ordainer appointed on 16 March 1310, in response to baronial demands for the banishment of Piers Gaveston and the reform of the king's finances and administration. However, the summary execution of Gaveston on 19 June 1312, at the behest of the earls of Lancaster, Hereford, and Warwick, divided the ordainers, and Monmouth dissociated himself from Edward II's hardline opponents, led by Lancaster, to take up a broadly royalist position.

The bishops had often in the past acted as peacemakers in times of political strife, and it was probably inevitable that Monmouth should have become engaged in efforts to bring about a settlement between Edward II and Lancaster; perhaps the fact that he had earlier been active in resisting the demands of the crown helped to make him acceptable as a mediator to the king's opponents. Early in 1316 he was a member of a commission appointed to reform the realm and royal household. In the following year, probably in August, he was one of the envoys whom Edward sent to try to reach an agreement with Lancaster. And in April 1318 he attended the assembly at Leicester whose programme of reform helped pave the way for the treaty of Leake, which temporarily settled the differences between the king and his adversaries. In the years that followed, Monmouth, who may have felt in need of protection against the younger Despenser's ambitions in Glamorgan, moved closer to the king, securing a loan for Edward from the hospitallers in 1320, censuring the king's critics and praying for the king's victory in 1321, and obtaining small grants from Edward II.

The scanty records of his episcopate show that Monmouth continued to develop the organization of his cathedral at Llandaff and was active in visitation in the diocese. From 1297, perhaps because of his link with the college at Westbury-on-Trym, he acted as assistant in the diocese of Worcester, where Bishop Godfrey Giffard was handicapped by illness. From April 1301 until Giffard's death in January 1302 he assumed the whole range of the latter's episcopal duties. His standing in Wales was made clear when Llywelyn Bren, a cultured Welsh magnate in Glamorgan, rebelled against the king in 1316. He placed his books and personal effects in Llandaff Cathedral for safe keeping. In government circles it was suggested that Bishop John allowed outlaws and malefactors to seek sanctuary in the cathedral. But it was also reported, in less critical terms, that Monmouth had lived long in Wales, spoke Welsh, and was known and loved by the people of his diocese. He died on 8 April 1323. DAVID WALKER

Sources Emden, *Oxf.*, 2.1295 · J. W. W. Bund, ed., *Register of Bishop Godfrey Giffard, September 23rd, 1268, to August 15th, 1301*, 2 vols., Worcestershire Historical Society, 15 (1898–1902) · G. Williams, ed., *Glamorgan county history*, 3: *The middle ages*, ed. T. B. Pugh (1971) · G. Williams, *The Welsh church from conquest to Reformation* (1962) · J. R. H. Moorman, *Church life in England in the thirteenth century* (1945) · W. Greenway, 'The election of John of Monmouth, bishop of Llandaff, 1287–97', *Morgannwg*, 5 (1962), 3–22 · *Ann. mon.*, 4.324 · J. H. Denton, *Robert Winchelsey and the crown, 1294–1313: a study in the defence of ecclesiastical liberty*, Cambridge Studies in Medieval Life and Thought, 3rd ser., 14 (1980) · J. R. S. Phillips, *Aymer de Valence, earl of Pembroke, 1307–1324: baronial politics in the reign of Edward II* (1972) · J. R. Maddicott, *Thomas of Lancaster, 1307–1322: a study in the reign of Edward II* (1970)

Monmouth, John (*fl.* 1320). *See under* Monmouth, John of (*c*.1182–1248).

Monnington, Sir (Walter) Thomas (1902–1976), painter, was born in Westminster, London, on 2 October 1902, the younger son of Walter Monnington, barrister, and his wife, Catherine Brown. He grew up in Sussex, where he attended Brunswick School, Haywards Heath, but developed heart trouble at the age of twelve. Invalided for a year, he set himself to draw and paint. Later he spent eighteen months at a farm school near Ross-on-Wye, a period congenial to his fundamentally practical turn of mind. In January 1918 he entered the Slade School of Fine Art. At the Slade, Henry Tonks decisively influenced Monnington's development, particularly through insisting that artists should be as objective as possible—like Ingres, 'who always drew as nearly as possible what he saw in front of him'. Encouraged by Tonks, Monnington specialized in decorative painting, and in 1922 won the scholarship in decorative painting offered by the British School at Rome.

Monnington spent most of the years 1922–5 in Italy. Artists of the quattrocento deeply influenced him, particularly Piero della Francesca, to whose mathematical principles and muted colours he instinctively responded. A reproduction of a single authoritative figure from one of the Arezzo frescoes hung in Monnington's house all his life.

In Rome, on 23 April 1924, Monnington married the

painter **Winifred Margaret Knights** (1899–1947), eldest daughter of Walter Henry Knights, sugar merchant, of Streatham, London, and his wife, Mabel Gertrude Knights. Born on 5 June 1899, she was educated at James Allen's Girls' School, Dulwich, and preceded Monnington both at the Slade School of Fine Art (1915–17; 1918–20) and at the British School at Rome (1920–23). In 1920 she became the first woman to win the prix de Rome, with a then unfinished painting, *The Deluge* (reproduced in the *Daily Graphic*, 8 February 1921, over the caption 'Girl artist remodels the flood'), eventually purchased for the Tate Gallery in 1989. Knights's fastidious draughtsmanship and reverence for natural forms (both evident in one of her finest works, *Santissima trinita*, c.1924–1930: priv. coll., Italy) influenced Monnington's own early work.

Monnington's chief work in Italy was the large tempera painting purchased in 1925 by the Contemporary Art Society, presented to the Tate Gallery in 1939, and known (since Monnington declined, in correspondence with Tate curators, to explain it more precisely than as 'an attempt to express in pictorial form my attitude to life—almost my faith') simply as *Allegory*. This work made his early reputation.

From 1925 to 1937 the Monningtons lived in London, first in Putney and then in a studio flat in Tonks's house in The Vale, Chelsea. Monnington taught part-time at the Royal College of Art and later in the Royal Academy Schools. He was involved between 1926 and 1937 with other artists—including Sir David Cameron, Sir George Clausen, A. K. Lawrence, Sir William Rothenstein, and Colin Gill—in two major decorative schemes, for St Stephen's Hall, Westminster, and for the new Bank of England designed by Sir Herbert Baker. Monnington's contributions are distinguished by their austere linear style. Meanwhile he completed (1931) a *Supper at Emmaus* for a reredos in Bolton parish church.

In the early 1930s Monnington received several commissions for portrait drawings of eminent contemporaries, including Sir James Barrie and Sir Joseph Thomson (both NPG) and Stanley Baldwin, later Earl Baldwin of Bewdle (Trinity College, Cambridge). As a portraitist Monnington was objective, accurate, and, since he was incapable of an ingratiating line, often devastatingly candid. A portrait in oil, *Admiral of the Fleet Lord Jellicoe*, commissioned for presentation to HMS *Excellent* and exhibited at the Royal Academy in 1934, was rejected after objections from Lady Jellicoe (Monnington eventually sold it in 1960 to the National Maritime Museum).

In 1931 Monnington was elected an associate of the Royal Academy. After Tonks's death in 1937, the Monningtons moved to Leyswood Cottage, Groombridge, Sussex, Monnington's home for the rest of his life; but his work now faltered, and he envied other professions. Despite his lack of training, physics and higher mathematics deeply interested him. He liked to gaze on pylons, radio transmitters, and television masts; he loved cars and fast, accurate driving, and he took flying lessons. His election as Royal Academician in 1938 seemed to Monnington himself an unreal event; as his diploma work he deposited *Piediluco*, an Umbrian landscape painted fifteen years earlier.

In May 1939 Monnington joined the Ministry of Defence's camouflage team, and for the next four years was chiefly responsible for designing camouflage for aircraft production airfields. He threw himself into this with energy, indeed with relief. From 1943 he flew as an official war artist with a Yorkshire training squadron and later with light Mitchell bombers over Germany. He spent winter 1944–5 in the Netherlands with the 2nd Tactical Air Force, drawing pioneer mobile radar equipment.

After the war Monnington found it impossible to return to his former representational work. He taught at Camberwell School of Arts and Crafts until 1949, then at the Slade until 1967. Winifred Knights died on 7 February 1947. Her work, by her own choice rarely exhibited during her lifetime, remained comparatively unknown for nearly half a century, when it was the subject of an exhibition presented by the Fine Art Society in association with the British School at Rome (Rome and London, 1995).

On 6 December 1947 Monnington married Evelyn Janet, daughter of Bernard Hunt, mining engineer and silver prospector. Monnington had one son by each marriage. His second marriage proved very happy; but for a while he produced little work. Contemporaries, observing his sparse Royal Academy exhibits between 1946 and 1953, believed he had 'dried up'; in fact he was essaying new directions.

Monnington's early work and the very different geometric paintings of his last twenty-five years are linked by his consistent interest in Piero della Francesca's mathematical principles. The metamorphosis was slow, and accompanied by periods of waning self-confidence. A commission in 1953 to paint the ceiling of the conference hall in Bristol's new council house provided just the stimulus he needed. A suggestion by the Bristol city fathers that he should do 'something connected with the Merchant Adventurers' fell on deaf ears. Monnington's design instead symbolizes twentieth-century progress in nuclear physics, electronics, aeronautics, and biochemistry. The Bristol ceiling (over 4000 sq. ft) is one of the largest painted ceilings in Britain, and one of the few painted in true fresco technique; it was completed in 1956. In 1959 he began fourteen *Stations of the Cross* for Brede parish church.

In the 1960s most of Monnington's works were geometric designs. He had become a fellow of University College, London, in 1957; in 1964 he completed two murals, painted in polyvinyl acetate, for the University of London Students' Union. *Square Design* (1966) was purchased for the Tate Gallery under the terms of the Chantrey bequest. All Monnington's geometric paintings were based on drawings as exact and fastidious as his earlier representational studies.

Monnington was elected president of the Royal Academy on 6 December 1966; he was knighted the following year, and in 1968 presided over the academy's bicentenary celebrations. He proved a popular president, and was annually re-elected. He was chiefly responsible for opening the treasures of the academy's private rooms to the public; but exhibitions such as 'Big Paintings for Public Places', 1969, and 'British Sculptors '72' demonstrated equal concern for living artists. He continued his lively interest in the Royal Academy Schools, and contributed to the *Dictionary of National Biography* the notice of Sir Walter Russell, under whom he himself had first taught there. He was a warm-hearted man, and a shrewd and perceptive teacher, who well understood what Tonks called 'the difficulties of doing'. It was characteristic of Monnington that on Christmas eve he should telephone the academy night watchman to make sure he was not lonely.

The presidency, added to his long commitments to the British School at Rome (1926–72) and the National Art Collections Fund (1941–76), left Monnington little time for painting, though he himself remarked in 1972 that its complexities were 'in some ways less difficult than trying to paint'. Monnington died in office in London on 7 January 1976.   JUDY EGERTON

Sources *The Times* (8 Jan 1976) · J. Egerton, *Drawings and paintings by Sir Thomas Monnington PRA* (1977) [exhibition catalogue, Royal Academy, London] · papers, IWM · private information (1986, 2004) · A. Powers and others, *Sir Thomas Monnington, 1902–1976* (1997) [exhibition catalogue, British School at Rome] · *CGPLA Eng. & Wales* (1976)
Wealth at death £44,611: probate, 5 April 1976, *CGPLA Eng. & Wales*

Monnoyer, Antoine (*bap.* 1672, *d.* 1747). *See under* Monnoyer, Jean-Baptiste (*bap.* 1636, *d.* 1699).

Monnoyer, Jean-Baptiste (*bap.* 1636, *d.* 1699), painter, was baptized in Lille, France, on 12 January 1636, the son of Charles Monnoyer and Marie Pancoucq. An elder brother, also called Jean-Baptiste, baptized on 19 July 1634, died in infancy; the painter has often been given his brother's baptismal date. According to Vertue he was 'brought up at Antwerp. His business there was history-Painting; but afterwards he returned to Lisle, & applied himself to painting Flowers' (Vertue, *Note books*, 2.135). His French biographer, d'Argenville, makes no mention of this Antwerp phase in his career, saying instead that he moved early to Paris. It is sometimes claimed that he was painting at the Hôtel Lambert in Paris about 1650; but this seems hard to believe, since he would have been just fourteen years old. In 1658 he was making important connections; he worked with Charles Le Brun on the decoration of the Château de Vaux-le-Vicomte, and he painted at the Château de St Cloud for Philippe d'Orléans, brother of Louis XIV. Thereafter his career can be followed in a long series of payments in the *Comptes des bâtiments du roi*. Monnoyer's speciality was floral interior decoration; flower pieces, placed above doors and mantlepieces, on ceilings and between pilasters, became fashionable in France in the second half of the seventeenth century, and Monnoyer was the leading exponent of the décor. He worked for the king at numerous royal palaces including the Louvre, the Tuileries, and Versailles, and also contributed floral borders to tapestries at the Gobelins from 1666 onwards. In 1665 he was received as a member of the Académie Royale

de Peinture et Sculpture. His *morceau de réception* was a still life (now in the Musée Fabre, Montpellier) containing flowers, fruit, a painter's palette, a globe half-covered by a carpet, two urns, a ewer, a clock, and a sphinx. Some allegory of fame was perhaps intended. Monnoyer exhibited four flower pieces in the first salon of 1673; in 1679 he was honoured by being elected *conseiller* of the academy. He was married twice; his first wife, sister of the history painter Pierre Monnier, died before 1667, leaving two children, Jean-Baptiste and Marie. The former was first a history painter and then a Dominican friar, while the latter married Monnoyer's best pupil, Jean-Baptiste Blin de Fontenay. In 1667 the artist married Marie Pétré. In seeming commemoration of this event, he painted a portrait (now priv. coll.) of himself at the easel, in the act of portraying his wife holding a basket of flowers: there is presumably a reference to the story of the ancient painter Pausias, who fell in love with the garland weaver Glycera (Pliny, *Natural History*, 35.xl.125). The couple had five daughters and three sons.

In 1690 Monnoyer went to London to work for Ralph, first duke of Montagu. Initially he intended to spend just three months in London, but, apart from brief trips back to France, he remained in England for the rest of his life. According to Vertue, the artist left France in irritation after learning that his works had been retouched by his son-in-law, Blin de Fontenay; but it may also be, as Faré suggests, that he disliked the art-political climate in Paris after the death of Charles Le Brun in 1690. In London as in Paris he was not short of work. He helped decorate Burlington House, Kensington Palace, and Hampton Court, although all of these paintings have since been dispersed. 'The most curious of all,' Vertue wrote, 'is the Looking-Glass at Kensington House, which he painted for the Late Queen Mary, of Glorious Memory, her Majesty sitting by him almost all the while' (Vertue, *Note books*, 2.135). Monnoyer died in London on 16 February 1699, and was buried two days later in St James's, Piccadilly (as John Baptist).

Monnoyer's son **Antoine Monnoyer** (*bap.* 1672, *d.* 1747) was baptized on 8 April 1672 in Paris. He worked with his father in London in the 1690s, where he lived on and off until 1734. He became a member of the Académie Royale in 1704. He travelled over much of western Europe during the course of his career, being recorded in Amsterdam (where he was married on 7 November 1699), Rome, Copenhagen, and possibly Stockholm; Vertue claimed that he also travelled to Lisbon, Vienna, and Poland, and thought he had 'a roving unsettled or unsatisfyd mind' (Vertue, *Note books*, 3.38). Art historians tend to attribute to him poor imitations of his father's work. He died at St Germain-en-Laye in 1747.   PAUL TAYLOR

Sources M. Faré, *Le grand siècle de la nature morte en France* (1974) · S. H. Pavière, *Jean Baptiste Monnoyer, 1634–1699* (1966) · Vertue, *Note books*, vols. 2–3 · parish register, St James Piccadilly, City Westm. AC, 18 Feb 1699 [burial] · J. Guiffrey, *Comptes des bâtiments du roi sous le règne de Louis XIV*, 5 vols. (1881–1901) · A. J. Dezallier d'Argenville, *Abrégé de la vie des plus fameux peintres*, 4 (1762) · Thieme & Becker, *Allgemeines Lexikon* · *DNB* · C. Salvi, 'Trois peintres de fleurs à Meudon: Jean-Baptiste Monnoyer, Antoine Monnoyer et Jean-

Baptiste Blin de Fontenay', *Bulletin de la Société de l'Histoire de l'Art Français* (1998), 19–42
Likenesses J. B. Monnoyer, self-portrait, oils, 1667 (with his wife), priv. coll.; repro. in Faré, *Le grand siècle* · G. Kneller, chalk drawing, *c*.1697–1699, Courtauld Inst. · G. White, mezzotint, 1715 (after G. Kneller), BM, NPG

Monocled Mutineer, the. *See* Toplis, (Francis) Percy (1896–1920).

Monoux, George (*b.* in or before **1465**, *d.* **1544**), merchant and local politician, was born by 1465, probably in London, the youngest of the five sons of Richard Monoux, of the Salters' Company. He was descended from John Monoux, of Stanford, Worcestershire, and the family was probably of Welsh marcher origin. He is first recorded (1485–6) in Bristol, where he exported cloth to Bordeaux, Lisbon, and Spanish ports in return for wine, oil, salt, and sugar. He rose to be mayor (1501) and there married his first wife, Joan, with whom he had three children (who predeceased him).

At the end of his mayoralty Monoux returned to London and became a freeman of the City (1503) as a member of the Drapers' Company. By 1508 he had remarried, his new wife being Anne, *née* Wood, the widow of Robert Wattes, sheriff of London and a fellow draper. From 1510 he lived in Crooked Lane, New Fish Street, not far from Drapers' Hall. He was master of the company in 1508–9 and was re-elected five times between 1516 and 1539. In 1507 he became alderman of Bassishaw ward, which office he held until 1541, and in 1524 became the City's senior alderman. He was sheriff (1509), auditor (1512), and mayor of London (1514), and in 1514 he received a grant of arms. He was appointed one of the commissioners to sell the goods of Scots in London (1513), and he was also a commissioner for collecting five subsidies (1512–24). He petitioned Henry VII over cloth-making irregularities in 1508 and was on deputations seeking remission of new customs rates in 1508–9. In 1512 he lobbied parliament over a new corporation bill, so he had some parliamentary experience when in 1523 he was elected one of the four MPs for the City. He was re-elected mayor the same year, but he declined the mayoralty on grounds of ill health and was fined £1000; the fine was remitted in 1524.

Monoux's wealth was considerable, and he invested his profits in land. His ledger traces (from 1508) the increase of his estate in London, which included ex-monastic property and well-known taverns, such as the Pope's Head. He acquired manors in ten counties, especially Bedfordshire, Essex, Norfolk, and Yorkshire. In the subsidy valuation of 1523 he was assessed at £1000, and his contribution to the loan of 1535–6 (£3000) was the highest in London. Monoux was a hard-headed and somewhat devious businessman. In 1508 he fell foul of the law banning payments to foreigners in gold coin, but escaped financial penalty. Sir Richard Gresham's plans (1537–8) for a bourse in Lombard Street to rival that in Antwerp were stalled partly because Monoux haggled over the sale of property he owned. It took Henry VIII's intervention, which Gresham said should be 'sharply made, for he ys of no gentyll nature' (*LP Henry VIII*), to browbeat Monoux into acquiescence, though the scheme was temporarily abandoned.

As a country seat Monoux bought in 1507 the moated mansion Moones in Walthamstow, and he became a local benefactor. He built a causeway and two bridges over the Lea marshes to avoid floods on the journey into London, he provided a feast room (1527) for the proper celebration of parish weddings and holy days, and for St Mary's Church he reconstructed the tower and north aisle and built the Monoux chantry chapel. He died at Moones on 9 February 1544. His altar tomb is gone, but the mural memorial brass of him and his second wife, originally above the tomb, is now (with later inscription) in the north aisle of St Mary's. His heir, George Monoux, was the great-grandson of his eldest brother, Humfrey. In 1527 Monoux had bought land in Walthamstow churchyard on which to build a school and almshouses, and his will left City property worth £50 a year as an endowment to pay the salaries of a schoolmaster and parish clerk, who were to pray for the souls of Monoux and his wives and to teach up to thirty children. The school is today the Sir (a local posthumous courtesy title) George Monoux Sixth Form College, now on another site in Chapel End, Walthamstow.   BASIL MORGAN

Sources G. F. Bosworth, *George Monoux: the man and his work*, Walthamstow Antiquarian Society, 17 (1927) · L. Naylor and G. Jagger, 'Monoux, Sir Humphrey, 2nd bt (1640–85)', HoP, *Commons, 1640–60* [draft] · *LP Henry VIII*, vol. 13 · G. F. Bosworth and C. D. Saunders, eds., *Original documents relating to the Monoux family*, Walthamstow Antiquarian Society, 19 (1928) · C. C. Pond, *George Monoux's school, Walthamstow, 1527–1977*, Walthamstow Antiquarian Society, new ser., 20 (1977) · *CPR, 1494–1509* · A. H. Johnson, *The history of the Worshipful Company of the Drapers of London*, 5 vols. (1914–22) · will, PRO, PROB 11/30, sig. 5
Likenesses print, *c*.1800 (after monumental brass), repro. in Bosworth, *George Monoux* · monumental brass (with his second wife), St Mary's Church, Walthamstow, Essex

Monro. *See also* Munro.

Monro, Alexander (*d.* **1698**), episcopalian clergyman, was probably born in Ross-shire, the fourth son of Hugh Munro of Fyresh, Ross-shire (*d. c.*1668), and his wife, Isobel Munro. He perhaps matriculated at St Andrews in 1666 and graduated MA in 1669. He is known to have visited France, giving rise to persistent rumours of his conversion to Roman Catholicism while abroad. In 1673 he was appointed to the second charge of Dunfermline, and on 6 May 1673 married Anna Logan, who died on 16 May 1674. On 26 March 1676 he entered the charge of Kinglassie, and on 11 April 1676 married Marion Collace, who bore him eight children.

In 1678 Munro's rising reputation led to his appointment as successor to James Nairn in Wemyss parish. In 1682 he became professor of divinity in St Mary's College, St Andrews, and in 1683 doctor of divinity. On 9 December 1685 Edinburgh town council elected him principal of the University of Edinburgh and nominated him to the second or collegiate charge of the high church. Installed on 30 December, his success in fostering academic standards during a turbulent period was overshadowed by his successors' achievements, and belittled by charges of weak discipline and partiality. On 24 October 1688 he was nominated bishop of Argyll, but he was probably not elected, and certainly not consecrated, before the revolution.

After the privy council enjoined prayers for William and Mary as sovereigns Monro demitted his charge on 24 April 1689 and began to hold popular private services in Edinburgh using the Book of Common Prayer. On 3 December the council interrogated him and released him without charge. On 25 September 1690 he was deprived of his principalship by a commission of visitation of the universities for refusing to take the requisite civil tests and to subscribe the Confession of Faith, although various charges of instances of sympathy for Roman Catholicism were also heard. Monro soon quit Edinburgh for London, only returning, in 1691, to accompany the widow of his friend Sir George Mackenzie of Rosehaugh to his funeral.

Becoming a leading apologist for the nonjuring episcopalians Monro exchanged stinging but not always sophisticated attacks with his presbyterian antagonists, starting with the fourth part of *An Account of the Present Persecution of the Church in Scotland* (1690), and *Presbyterian Inquisition* (1691) about the university visitations. His *Sermons* (1693) evinced his piety and faith in passive obedience and the divine right of episcopacy. Suspicious of Jacobite intrigue, in February 1693 the authorities searched his house and papers, and on 1 March 1696 gaoled him for about five months after a forced denunciation by Simon Wyld, his nonjuring associate. Monro's letters to John Mackenzie, clerk of session, who sustained his indigent friend, reveal his classical learning, wit, and dismay at his ever active enemies in London and Scotland. He preferred to remain in London, struggling to raise his surviving children, Elizabeth and James *Monro (1680–1752), the distinguished specialist in mental health. After suffering declining health Monro died in London between 11 July and 22 September 1698. TRISTRAM CLARKE

Sources *Fasti Scot.*, new edn, vol. 1 · 'Letters to John Mackenzie of Delvine from the Rev. Alexander Monro, 1690 to 1698', ed. W. K. Dickson, *Miscellany ... V*, Scottish History Society, 3rd ser., 21 (1933), 197–290 · *Historical notices of Scotish affairs, selected from the manuscripts of Sir John Lauder of Fountainhall*, ed. D. Laing, 2 vols., Bannatyne Club, 87 (1848) · *Reg. PCS*, 3rd ser., vol. 14 · D. Reid, ed., *The party-coloured mind* (1982) · T. Smith, correspondence, 1698, Bodl. Oxf., MSS Smith 48, 59 · A. Mackenzie, *History of the Munros of Fowlis* (1898) · A. Grant, *The story of the University of Edinburgh during its first three hundred years*, 2 vols. (1884)

Archives NL Scot., Mackenzie of Delvine MSS

Monro, Alexander, primus (1697–1767), surgeon and anatomist, was born in London on 8 September 1697, the only surviving son of John Monro (*bap.* 1670, *d.* 1740), an army surgeon, and his wife and first cousin, Jean Forbes (*d. c.*1710), daughter of Captain James Forbes, second son of Duncan Forbes, laird of Culloden, and Agnes Monro. John Monro was the youngest son of Sir Alexander Monro of Bearcrofts (1629–1704), an advocate and a member of the Scottish parliament who had fought in the battle of Worcester (1651) on the royalist side.

John Monro resigned from the army and moved his family to Edinburgh in 1700, where he was admitted a burgess in 1702 and to the Incorporation of Surgeons in 1703; he

Alexander Monro primus (1697–1767), by Allan Ramsay, 1749

served as deacon 1712–14. He harboured great ambitions for his son Alexander, who received a thorough education in Greek, Latin, French, natural philosophy, and mathematics before becoming an apprentice to his father about 1713. Alexander Monro attended the University of Edinburgh between 1710 and 1713 but did not obtain a degree. In 1715 he assisted his father in treating the wounded after the battle of Sheriffmuir. Early in 1717 he travelled to London where he remained for about a year, attending the natural philosophy lectures of Francis Hawksbee the younger and William Whiston, and the anatomy course of William Cheselden. Monro and Cheselden became good friends, and Monro also made the acquaintance of the Scottish anatomist James Douglas. Monro sent his father some examples of his dissecting skills, which the elder Monro presented to the College of Physicians and the Incorporation of Surgeons. From London, Alexander Monro went on to Paris in the spring of 1718, where he attended various courses at the Jardin du Roi and the Hotel-Dieu; he studied anatomy with Bourquet at the latter institution, but did not take an anatomy course with either Jacques-Benigne Winslow or Joseph-Guichard Duverney, the two most prominent anatomists of the time.

On 16 November 1718 Monro enrolled as a medical student at the University of Leiden, where he remained for another year, studying chemistry and clinical medicine with Herman Boerhaave. He continued to dissect with his fellow students but the ailing J. J. Rau did not offer his anatomy course. However, on Boerhaave's recommendation Monro visited the anatomist Frederik Ruysch in Amsterdam, from whom he learned the art of making anatomical preparations. He did not take a degree from Leiden.

Monro returned to Edinburgh in September 1719 and soon after passed the examinations for admission to the Incorporation of Surgeons. He was admitted as a burgess on 18 November 1719 by right of his father (erroneously named Alexander in the records). On 21 January 1720 the joint professors of anatomy, Adam Drummond and John McGill, resigned their professorship in favour of Monro. The professorship had been established in 1705 by the town council, who paid the surgeons' dissector to offer an annual public dissection; by Monro's time this had dwindled to once every two or three years. Monro's position, unlike that of his predecessors, was clearly defined as a university chair. Many historians have viewed this appointment, therefore, as the beginning of the Edinburgh medical school. While Monro's talents were evident, his rapid rise owed much to the efforts of his father and the patronage of George Drummond, a dominant figure on the town council.

Monro began his first course of anatomy in the autumn of 1720 with fifty-seven students. He offered a yearly course from that date until 1758, when he retired (except for his clinical course) in favour of his son, Alexander *Monro secundus. From 1720 until 1725 Monro primus taught his course in the anatomy theatre in Surgeons' Hall. However, suspicions of grave robbing by Monro and his students caused public rioting outside Surgeons' Hall, and in 1725 Monro petitioned the town council to provide for him a more secure site within the university walls. Monro was given a room on the ground floor of the so-called 1617 building. By 1751 attendance had reached almost 200 students and he had to offer the course in two shifts, one later taught by his son Alexander secundus.

Monro's lecture course, which ran from October to April, began each year with the history of anatomy and went on to human anatomy. He employed only one or two cadavers for this part of the course, an indication of the continuing shortage of bodies for dissection. This was followed by comparative anatomy, physiology, and surgical operations. Monro's lecture style was widely described as compelling: he had learned much about style and technique from the popular natural philosophy lecturers in London and Paris, and he made full and ingenious use of animals, waxes, and anatomical preparations. A sturdy man of middle stature he was a gifted technician of great manual skill. Many volumes of student notes of his lectures survive, often carefully copied out and sold to the next generation of students. While generally inclining toward mechanical explanations, Monro subscribed to no particular school of thought, and carefully outlined competing theories to his students, offering often pungent opinions on their fallacies. He did not hesitate to admit his own lack of conclusive knowledge on controversial points. He lectured in English rather than Latin.

Meanwhile, in 1722 Monro petitioned the town council to make his professorship a life appointment, which was granted. On 27 June 1723, at Cheselden's nomination,

Monro was elected a fellow of the Royal Society of London, but he never travelled to London to be admitted. On 3 January 1725 Monro married Isabella MacDonald (1694–1774), third daughter of Sir Donald MacDonald of Sleat in the island of Skye, baronet. MacDonald had been a prominent Jacobite. They had three sons and five daughters; only one of the daughters, Margaret (1727?–1802) survived to adulthood. In 1739 Monro wrote for her *An Essay on Female Conduct Contained in Letters from a Father to his Daughter* which remained in manuscript until 1996. Their eldest son, John (1725–1789), became an advocate, and the two other sons, Donald *Monro (1728–1802) and Alexander secundus (1733–1817), entered medicine. Donald became physician to St George's Hospital, London, and Alexander secundus's son, Alexander *Monro tertius (1773–1859), also joined the medical profession.

Monro's move to a university site led to his formal inauguration as a university professor on 3 November 1725 with an inaugural lecture *De origine et utilitate anatomiae*. The Edinburgh medical school began to take form. In February 1725 four physicians—John Rutherford, Andrew St Clair (or Sinclair), Andrew Plummer, and John Innes—had begun teaching chemistry and other medical subjects out of a house they had bought near the university physic garden. A year later they petitioned the town council to appoint them professors in the university. With their appointments the medical school formally began. The professors were without salary, since they were expected to make their income from student fees. Monro himself had assumed the £15 salary of his predecessors in anatomy, but this seems to have ceased in 1725, and at £3 3s per student he made £500 per annum in fees by the 1740s, although he kept lengthy lists of students whose payments were in arrears and sometimes never paid.

In 1729 Monro rented a house in Robertson's Close, off Cowgate, with six beds for the sick poor to provide clinical training for medical students. This was the origin of the Edinburgh Infirmary, one of a number of voluntary hospitals in eighteenth-century Britain. It was chartered by George II as the Royal Infirmary in 1736, and a large new building, designed by William Adam, opened for patients in 1741.

In 1726 Monro published his first and only major book, *The Anatomy of the Humane Bones*, an unillustrated text intended as a commentary on his demonstrations. While it contained no new discoveries it displayed Monro's fine observational and expository skills. In the second edition (1732) he added treatises on the nerves, heart, and lacteals. This continued to be a popular text for a century in English and other languages; the French translation of 1759 by Jean-Joseph Sue was illustrated. In 1744 an unauthorized edition of Monro's lectures of comparative anatomy was published in London. He also published a few pamphlets, including *An Account of the Inoculation of Smallpox in Scotland* (1765). However, the majority of his published work, some of it anonymous, was contained in the six volumes of *Medical Essays and Observations* (1732–44) which he edited as secretary of the Society for the Improvement of Medical Knowledge, which he had helped found in 1731.

This society was a predecessor of the Royal Society of Edinburgh. His son Alexander secundus published his father's collected works in 1781, with a biographical introduction by his brother Donald.

Monro was an active citizen of Enlightenment Edinburgh and friend and associate of many of its brightest lights, including Hume and Maclaurin. While a strong supporter of the Hanoverians, he assisted the wounded on both sides at the battle of Prestonpans (1745) and helped obtain a pardon for the Jacobite Dr Cameron. He was critical to the success of the Edinburgh medical school, and trained generations of physicians and surgeons from many countries. A 1749 portrait of him by Allan Ramsay, in the Scottish National Portrait Gallery, Edinburgh, conveys his considerable personal magnetism. An engraving of this portrait by Basire is a frontispiece to the 1781 *Works*.

In 1756 Monro was awarded the degree of MD (*honoris causa*) by the University of Edinburgh. In 1762 he began to show signs of the rectal cancer which caused his death five years later. He none the less continued to be active in civic and university life, and never retired to the estate he had purchased at Auchenbowie, Stirlingshire. Monro died at his house in Covenant Close, Edinburgh, on 10 July 1767, and was buried in Greyfriars churchyard.

Monro's will, written on 12 March 1750, was proved on 28 October 1767. The executor was the professor's eldest son, John, advocate of Auchenbowie. He inherited the bulk of the estate, with 12,000 marks left to Monro's widow, Isabella MacDonald, to distribute to her children as she saw fit. Debts owed to Monro, totalling over £1500 sterling, were noted. While it is impossible to assess the exact extent of Monro's wealth, he was evidently quite successful, and apart from the estate at Auchenbowie he had also purchased a house at Carolside, Berwickshire, for his father. He was known as a benefactor to many charitable causes.

ANITA GUERRINI

Sources R. E. Wright-St Clair, *Doctors Monro: a medical saga* (1964) · H. D. Erlam, 'Alexander Monro, *primus*', *University of Edinburgh Journal*, 17 (1953–5), 77–105 · A. Bower, *The history of the University of Edinburgh*, 2 (1817) · D. W. Taylor, *The Monro collection in the medical library of the University of Otago: a descriptive catalogue with annotations and introduction* (Dunedin, 1979) · *The works of Alexander Monro*, ed. A. Monro (1781) · *DNB*
Archives RCS Eng., lecture notes · Royal College of Physicians of Edinburgh, lecture notes · U. Edin. L., lecture notes; treatises · University of British Columbia Library, Woodward Biomedical Library, notebook · University of Otago, Dunedin, medical library, papers · Wellcome L., lecture notes
Likenesses A. Ramsay, oils, 1749, Scot. NPG [*see illus.*] · J. Basire, line engraving, 1775 (after Ramsay), Wellcome L. · J. Basire, engraving, 1781 (after Ramsay), BM, NPG; repro. in Monro secundus, ed., *Works* · T. Cook, line engraving, 1786 (after Ramsay), Wellcome L. · J. C. Lavater, pencil, c.1792, Wellcome L. · P. Thomson, line engraving, 1793 (after Ramsay), Wellcome L. · A. Bell, line engraving (after Ramsay), Wellcome L.
Wealth at death 12,000 marks left to wife: will, NA Scot., CC 8/8/120/2.1766

Monro, Alexander, secundus (1733–1817), anatomist, was the third son of Alexander *Monro primus (1697–1767),

Alexander Monro secundus (1733–1817), by James Heath, pubd 1800 (after Sir Henry Raeburn)

professor of medicine and anatomy at Edinburgh University, and Isabella, second daughter of Sir Donald MacDonald bt, of the Isle of Skye. He was born in Edinburgh on 20 May 1733. He and his elder brother Donald *Monro (1728–1802) attended James Mundell's school. Professorships at Edinburgh were formally filled by the town council, but throughout the eighteenth century they were commonly regarded as the property of their holders, who treated them like other pieces of valuable property, to be protected, augmented, and passed on to their sons. From an early age young Alexander was designated as his father's successor as professor of medicine, and Monro primus took seriously the task of educating his son to fill his position with distinction. Monro secundus's name first appears on his father's anatomy class list in 1744. The following year he matriculated in the faculty of arts at Edinburgh University, where he heard lectures in Latin, Greek, philosophy, mathematics, physics, and history. In 1750 he began attending medical lectures. In 1753, still a student, he took over the teaching of his father's summer anatomy class, and at Monro primus's petition he was named joint professor of medicine and anatomy on 10 June 1754. He graduated MD in 1755 with a thesis 'De testibus et semine in variis animalibus'. He then went on an anatomical grand tour, studying anatomy in London with William Hunter and in Berlin with Johann Friedrich Meckel. He matriculated on 17 September 1757 at Leiden University and became friends with the noted anatomist Albinus. His tour was interrupted in the same year when he had to return to Edinburgh to assist his father in the anatomy course; his father's recurring illness brought Monro secundus home to take up the duties of the professorship in

January 1758. He became a fellow of the Royal College of Physicians of Edinburgh in 1759.

In the fifty years he taught at Edinburgh University Monro secundus became the most influential anatomy professor in the English speaking world, lecturing daily from 1 to 3 p.m. during the six-month winter session. He spent every morning preparing for his class anatomical specimens from his own extensive collection, and his lectures were praised for their clarity and strength of argument. Not even his extensive medical practice interfered with the zealous discharge of his professorial obligations. He was equally assiduous in defending what he regarded as his professorial prerogatives. Monro's course was an ongoing argument for the value of the philosophical anatomist, who used his detailed understanding of anatomy to develop new surgical procedures, and he paid comparatively little attention to standard surgical operations. When the Royal College of Surgeons of Edinburgh attempted to institute a professorship of surgery, however, Monro acted vigorously to protect his chair, protesting vehemently to the town council against such a step. He succeeded in 1777 in having the title of his own professorship formally changed to the chair of medicine, anatomy, and surgery, preventing the establishment of a course of surgery in Edinburgh for thirty years.

A philosophical anatomist had to be a distinguished anatomical researcher, and Monro secundus began his detailed anatomical studies in his MD thesis, when most MD theses were based only on printed sources. His philosophical ambitions led him to controversy. His first publication beyond his thesis was *De venis lymphaticis valvulosis* (Berlin, 1757), in which he argued that the lymphatic system was absorbent, and separate from the circulatory system. His former teacher William Hunter objected that he had been teaching the same theory for many years, and accused Monro of stealing the idea from him; Monro countered by insisting that Hunter must have stolen the idea from his, Monro's, thesis. Careful examination of the controversy has shown that though Monro had published first, Hunter had in fact been teaching the idea for some years; both, however, had been preceded by other medical writers, most notably Friedrich Hoffman and Francis Glisson. Monro continued to defend what he considered his intellectual property against encroachment as vigorously as he defended his professorship: priority claims led him to publish *A state of facts concerning the first proposal of performing the paracentesis of the thorax … and the discovery of the lymphatic valvular absorbent system of vessels, in oviparous animals. In answer to Mr Hewson* (1770) and *Observations on the muscles, and particularly on the effects of their oblique fibres: with an appendix, in which the pretension of Dr. Gilbert Blane, that he first demonstrated the same effect to be produced by oblique muscles … is proved to be unfounded* (1794), both directed against former students.

The anatomical research which secured Monro's posthumous medical reputation was his description of the communication between the lateral ventricles of the brain, now known as the foramen of Monro. He first noted it in a paper read before the Philosophical Society of Edinburgh in 1764, as it appeared unusually enlarged in the post-mortem dissection of a case of hydrocephalus. He described it in detail in *Observations on the Structure and Functions of the Nervous System* (1783, German edn, Leipzig, 1787). His other major anatomical works are *The structure and physiology of fishes explained, and compared with those of man and other animals* (1785), *A Description of all the Bursae murcosae of the Human Body* (1788, German edn, Leipzig, 1799), *Experiments on the nervous system, with opium and metalline substances, made chiefly with the view of determining the nature and effects of animal electricity* (1793), and *Three Treatises. On the Brain, the Eye, and the Ear* (1797).

Monro was an active member of Edinburgh intellectual and civic life: he was a member of the Harveian Society (a medical supper club), secretary to the Philosophical Society of Edinburgh, a manager of the Royal Infirmary, and district commissioner for the city of Edinburgh. He enjoyed the theatre and was proud to have been consulted by the actress Mrs Siddons. He bought the estate of Craiglockhart, on the Water of Leith, to cultivate a model farm, but always spent the night in his town house in case he was called to a patient. Monro married Katherine, daughter of David Inglis, treasurer of the Bank of Scotland, on 25 September 1762, and they had two daughters and three sons. The eldest son, Alexander *Monro tertius (1773–1859), succeeded his father as professor of medicine, anatomy, and surgery. Monro secundus had an attack of apoplexy in 1813, and he died on 2 October 1817. He was survived by his wife.

LISA ROSNER

Sources C. P. Finlayson, 'Monro, Alexander (secundus)', *DSB* · R. E. Wright-St Clair, *Doctors Monro: a medical saga* (1964) · N. Eales, 'The history of the lymphatic system, with special reference to the Hunter–Monro controversy', *Journal of the History of Medicine and Allied Sciences*, 29 (1974), 280–94 · D. W. Taylor, 'The manuscript lecture-notes of Alexander Monro, *secundus* (1733–1817)', *Medical History*, 22 (1978), 174–86 · A. Monro tertius, memoir, *Essays and heads of lectures in anatomy, physiology, pathology and surgery* (1840) · D. W. Taylor, *The Monro collection in the medical library of the University of Otago: a descriptive catalogue with annotations and introduction* (Dunedin, 1979) · *DNB*

Archives Exeter Cathedral, medical MSS · McGill University, Montreal, Osler Library of the History of Medicine, lecture notes · RCS Eng., lecture notes and treatises · Royal College of Physicians of Edinburgh, lecture notes and corresp. · U. Edin. L., lecture notes · University of Kansas Medical Center, Kansas City, Clendening History of Medicine Library and Museum, lecture notes · University of Otago, Dunedin, medical library, papers · Wellcome L., lecture notes

Likenesses J. Kay, etching, 1790, Wellcome L.; repro. in J. Kay, *A series of original portraits and caricature etchings* (1837–8) · J. Heath, coloured stipple, pubd 1800 (after H. Raeburn), BM, NPG, Wellcome L. [*see illus.*] · E. Calvert, oils, U. Edin. · J. Kay, etching, BM, NPG, Wellcome L. · H. Raeburn, portrait, Auchenbowie House · J. T. Seton, portrait, Auchenbowie House · plaster bust, Scot. NPG

Monro, Alexander, tertius (1773–1859), anatomist, son of Alexander *Monro secundus (1733–1817) and his wife, Katherine, daughter of David Inglis, treasurer of the Bank of Scotland, and grandson of Alexander *Monro primus (1697–1767), was born at Edinburgh on 5 November 1773. He attended the high school there, and graduated MD from Edinburgh University in 1797 with a thesis 'De

Alexander Monro tertius (1773–1859), by David Octavius Hill and Robert Adamson, 1843–8

dysphagia'. Though professors at Edinburgh were formally appointed by the town council, in practice professorships were treated as the property of their holders, who often arranged to have them passed on to their sons with only perfunctory outside review. In this way Monro tertius was appointed to assist his father in 1798. To prepare for the appointment he studied anatomy in London and Paris, returning to Edinburgh in 1800, when he was appointed conjoint professor (with his father) of medicine, surgery, and anatomy. From 1808 he delivered the whole course, and on his father's death in 1817 he was duly appointed sole professor. He held this position until 1846. Monro married, on 20 September 1800, Maria Agnes (d. 1833), the daughter of Dr Carmichael Smyth; they had twelve children, one of whom was Sir David *Monro (1813–1877). His second wife, whom he married on 15 July 1836, was Jessie, the daughter of David Hunter.

The anatomy course was the cornerstone of medical studies, and Monro carried on his family's tradition of providing a thorough grounding for students. There is no truth to the often repeated story that he lectured from his grandfather's notes. However, he was criticized for devoting so little attention to surgery while successfully opposing the establishment of a separate course in it, and in an era of excellent anatomists he did little to advance the subject. Faced with competition from private lecturers and more exacting standards in anatomical teaching he

began offering a course in practical dissection in 1815. He published *Observations on Crural Hernia* (1803), *Morbid Anatomy of the Human Gullet, Stomach, and Intestines* (1811), *Outlines of the Anatomy of the Human Body* (1813), *Engravings of the Thoracic and Abdominal Viscera* (1814), *Observations on the Different Kinds of Small-Pox* (1818), *Morbid Anatomy of the Brain*, volume 1, *Hydrocephalus* (1827), *Anatomy of the Pelvis of the Male* (1827), *The Anatomy of the Brain* (1831), *Essays and Heads of Lectures of A. Munro secundus, with Memoir* (1840), and *Anatomy of the Urinary Bladder and Perinaeum in the Male* (1842).

Monro tertius died at his home in Craiglockhart, near Edinburgh, on 10 March 1859; he was survived by his second wife. His reputation has suffered by comparison with his father and grandfather. His chief fault was to occupy a prestigious and lucrative chair of medicine while fulfilling its obligations with mere competence rather than brilliance. The fault was compounded by the genteel nepotism by which he had obtained the position and was exacerbated by continuing comparisons with his more eminent contemporaries. LISA ROSNER

Sources R. E. Wright-St Clair, *Doctors Monro: a medical saga* (1964) · *Edinburgh Medical Journal*, 4 (1858–9), 961–2 · *The life of Sir Robert Christison*, 1 (1885), 68 · C. J. Lawrence, 'The Edinburgh medical school and the end of the "old thing", 1790–1830', *History of Universities*, 7 (1988), 265–8 · DNB
Archives Exeter Cathedral, medical MSS · RCS Eng., lecture notes · Royal College of Physicians of Edinburgh, corresp. and lecture notes · U. Edin. L., lecture notes
Likenesses group portraits, silhouettes, c.1830, Wellcome L. · D. O. Hill and R. Adamson, calotype, 1843–8, NPG [*see illus.*] · B. W. Crombie, coloured etching, 1848, NPG; repro. in *Modern Athenians* (1882) · A. Edouart, cut paper silhouette, Scot. NPG · A. Geddes, portrait, Auchenbowie House · J. W. Gordon, oils, U. Edin., Faculty of Medicine · D. O. Hill, carbon photograph, NPG; related daguerreotype, BM · K. Macleay, oils, Royal College of Surgeons, Edinburgh · K. Macleay, watercolour, Auchenbowie House · F. Schenck, lithograph (after W. Stewart), Wellcome L. · J. S. C. Syme, portrait, Auchenbowie House
Wealth at death £2806 17s. 0d.: confirmation, 30 June 1859, NA Scot., SC 70/1/101/201–9

Monro, Sir Charles Carmichael, baronet (1860–1929), army officer, was born at sea on the *Maid of Judah* on 15 June 1860, the youngest son of Henry Monro (d. 1869), a businessman, and his wife, Catherine, daughter of Alexander Power, who was a direct descendant of the poet Edmund Spenser. Destined for the army, Charles attended Sherborne School (1871–8) before he was admitted to the Royal Military College, Sandhurst, on 1 September 1878.

There was little in Monro's attitude and performance at Sandhurst to mark him as a future general. He was described in a report as somewhat below average, frequently unpunctual, and a bad rider. But he managed to pass out of Sandhurst, 120th on the list, and as a second lieutenant he was posted to the 2nd foot, later the 1st battalion the Queen's Royal (West Surrey) regiment, on 13 August 1879. Slowly he pulled himself together and two years after joining his battalion was appointed adjutant, a post he held until July 1886. He studied at the Staff College, Camberley, in 1889–90, where he distinguished himself only as captain of the cricket eleven. After passing out

Sir Charles Carmichael Monro, baronet (1860–1929), by Walter Stoneman, 1921

of the Staff College he rejoined his battalion and accompanied it to Malta, serving first as aide-de-camp to the governor and then as brigade major.

From Malta, Monro moved with his battalion to India in 1897 and continued his duties as company commander. In quick succession he served with the Malakand field force, and in the Mohmand and Tirah field expeditions. Having been promoted major in February 1898, he received his first staff appointment when he went to Gibraltar as brigade major. He had barely settled in when he was appointed deputy assistant adjutant general (DAAG) at Guernsey; and a few months later he was on the move again, taking up a similar appointment at Aldershot. Shortly after the outbreak of the Second South African War, Monro was appointed DAAG of the 6th division, which began to mobilize as soon as news of Lord Methuen's reverse at Magersfontein (December 1899) became known.

Monro set sail for South Africa with his divisional commander, General Thomas Kelly-Kenny, and arrived on 10 January 1900, in time to participate in Lord Roberts's march to Pretoria. Monro was on the scene when the British besieged and forced the surrender of a Boer convoy at Paardeberg. He was also present at the battles of Poplar Grove and Driefontein and, following the capture of Pretoria on 5 June, went with his division to Cape Colony; he remained there until the end of the year. For his services he was promoted brevet lieutenant-colonel.

Monro returned to England and became the chief instructor at the School of Musketry at Hythe in February 1901. He assumed command of the school eighteen months later. It was here that Monro first developed a reputation as an energetic and clear-thinking infantry officer. His experience in South Africa had convinced him that the teaching of musketry fire in the army was outdated. During his six years at Hythe he was the main force behind the evolution of a new system of infantry fire tactics which would be the salvation of the British army in the opening battles of the First World War.

Having been promoted substantive colonel in November 1903, Monro left Hythe in March 1907 to take command of the 13th infantry brigade at Dublin with the rank of brigadier-general. He showed the same hands-on approach to training as at Hythe and his brigade became renowned, particularly for its skill in fire tactics. The high standard of Monro's work brought him a promotion to major-general in 1911 and to the command of the 2nd London division, Territorial Force, in the spring of 1912. Monro's friendship with Mary Caroline Towneley-O'Hagan, daughter of the first Lord O'Hagan, whom he had met in Gibraltar, blossomed into a closer union and the two married on 1 October 1912.

War in Europe On the outbreak of the First World War Monro was put in charge of the 2nd division which, along with the other three regular British divisions, proceeded to France during the second week in August 1914. The 2nd division formed part of Haig's 1st corps, which was actively involved in all the early battles—Mons, the Marne, and the Aisne. In October the British expeditionary force (BEF) was transferred to Flanders to take up a position on the left of the French army. Monro played a key role in the first battle of Ypres, holding his own against a much larger enemy force. During desperate fighting on 31 October Monro and the commander of the 1st division, Major-General S. H. Lomax, and their staffs, were in conference when their building was demolished by four heavy shells. Lomax was fatally wounded and seven staff officers of the two divisions were killed. Monro was badly shaken but otherwise unhurt. After seeing the way Monro had dealt with the trials and stress of the early weeks, Haig could not have been more pleased by his steadiness and judgement. Monro was never hurried or flustered, and he invariably made the right decisions.

At the close of 1914 the expanded British contingent was divided into two armies with Haig as the obvious choice to command one of them. As a result, Monro was given command of the 1st corps with the temporary rank of lieutenant-general. His corps did not play a prominent role in the battles of Aubers Ridge and Festubert in the spring of 1915. In July he was placed in charge of the newly formed Third Army and promoted temporary general. His tenure of office in the Third Army was brief, however, and he took no part in the ill-fated battle of Loos in September. The following month he learned that he had been appointed commander-in-chief of the Mediterranean expeditionary force in succession to General Sir Ian Hamilton. As the new commander Monro was instructed to report on whether it would be better to evacuate the Gallipoli peninsula, or try again to carry it.

Evacuation of Gallipoli Monro, like practically all the other senior British officers, had no use for side-shows, having become convinced that the war could only be won by defeating the main German army in France. That attitude invited Churchill's often cited comment, 'he came, he saw, he capitulated' (Churchill, 2.516). While Monro was not the block-headed westerner that Churchill made him out to be, it would be idle to pretend that he approached his task with an unbiased mind.

Monro insisted on being briefed before leaving, spending several days at the War Office reading the available data and meeting Lord Kitchener, the secretary for war, on four occasions. Monro reached Gallipoli on 27 October 1915 and devoted the next three days to inspecting the battle zones on the Peninsula and conferring with the staff of his dismissed predecessor. Kitchener did not give Monro much time, telegraphing on 29 October that he wanted an early answer to the main question, namely 'leaving or staying?'. Monro wired his report on 31 October, advising evacuation and estimating that in the process casualties could run as high as a third of the force. Monro half expected to be sacked, for he knew there was a powerful element in the cabinet that desperately wanted to keep the campaign alive. That he was willing to risk dismissal for giving an opinion as he saw it—and with no certainty that he would ever receive a comparable command— speaks volumes for his integrity and courage.

Kitchener, who had put so much effort in the operation, decided to go out and see for himself whether Monro was right in recommending withdrawal. On arrival Kitchener visited the Gallipoli fronts, spoke to the local commanders and, after some soul-searching, came to the same conclusion as Monro. The British cabinet accepted his recommendation. Under Monro's general supervision a withdrawal plan was worked out and carried out with such skill that not a single man was lost. The retirement of so large a force without alerting the enemy, credit for which Monro generously gave to subordinates, was the only efficiently conducted phase of the operation.

Commander-in-chief, India Monro returned to France in January 1916, and took charge of the First Army, a post he held for eight months. During that period the First Army's front was relatively quiet, except for a minor action involving the 4th corps under General Sir Henry Wilson. In the autumn of 1916 Monro was appointed commander-in-chief of the army in India, where he faced a colossal task. The Indian army was not prepared for a major war outside India in 1914. It was not only short of modern equipment, but also had no plans for a large-scale expansion of its establishment which stood at 155,000. Nevertheless Indian units were sent to fight in France, east Africa, Egypt, Gallipoli, and Mesopotamia. Initially there had been universal support in India for the British cause so that there was an ample flow of recruits for the regular army. But by 1916 the scale of casualties caused by modern weapons, together with a weakening of British prestige following setbacks on the western front, Gallipoli, and Mesopotamia, made finding new replacements difficult. It was left to Monro to raise new native formations, and find non-commissioned officers to train them and officers to lead them. The problem was magnified by necessary corresponding increases in the supply of munitions, accommodation, medical services, equipment, and mechanical transport.

Prior to Monro's arrival the pattern of raising units had followed pre-war tradition. Recruiting officers were appointed for different classes and enlistments were confined to 'martial areas' and carried on independently of civil administration. Monro altered the old system, drawing in more recruits from non-martial areas, appointing officers to recruit by areas rather than by classes, and seeking the help of civil government. Monro felt that one of the most effective ways to stimulate recruiting would be to end the age-old custom by which men paid for their own rations. With the co-operation of the viceroy a measure was quickly passed, sanctioning free rations for the Indian army. In 1917 the Indian Defence Force Act was passed, making all British European subjects between the ages of 18 and 41 liable for military service. Lastly a central recruiting board, consisting of civil and army personnel, was set up to consider military requirements and how they could best be met, as well as co-ordinate recruiting so as to ensure that the men enlisted were not needed in essential war industries. The various steps taken by Monro resulted in a substantial expansion of the army, which was to rise to 573,000 by the armistice. Of the new units raised, most served and played important roles in the victorious campaigns in Mesopotamia and Palestine.

The end of the war did not ease Monro's problems or anxiety. Amid the mounting agitation of Indian nationalists, Monro conducted two major campaigns, one against the Afghans and the other against the Wazirs. The Third Anglo-Afghan War, sparked by the aggressive action of the new amir of Afghanistan, Amanullah Khan, in May 1919, lasted less than a month. The war against the Wazirs, who were conducting frequent raids against defenceless villages along the border, was initiated at Monro's insistence. An Indian force invaded Waziristan in November 1919, but because of the inexperience of the troops, the tenacity of the defenders, and the nature of the terrain, the campaign proved more arduous than anyone had expected. The fighting dragged on until May 1920 when the tribesmen accepted terms imposed by the British government. In both instances Monro had skilfully managed the campaigns, although at the end of the Third Anglo-Afghan War there was some criticism, mostly unjustified, that the wounded had been left on the battlefield for an extended period and that inadequate arrangements had been taken to cope with an outbreak of cholera.

Retirement In August 1920 Monro, worn down by the stress and sheer volume of work, resigned his post and returned to London to live on half pay. During the next few years his time was occupied in leisure pursuits, such as unveiling war memorials and speaking at gatherings of military organizations. In the autumn of 1923 he succeeded General Sir Horace Smith-Dorrien as governor of Gibraltar. Here he showed his usual tact, good sense, and personal interest in dealing with various matters associated with his office. He was held in such high esteem that the chamber of commerce took the unusual step of petitioning the secretary of state for the colonies for an extension of his stay beyond the regular five-year term. To immense disappointment, the request was not granted and Monro returned to his home in London in August 1928. Troubled by internal disease, Monro underwent an operation on 30 November 1929, but the cancer had metastasized and, a week later, on 7 December, he died in his home, 54 Eaton Square, London. Following his funeral service at Westminster Abbey, he was buried in Brompton cemetery on 11 December.

Although Monro did not attract as much notice as some of his contemporaries, he was a fine soldier, typical of many relatively unknown career officers who served Britain faithfully and effectively during its imperial age. While he could not be described as brilliant or especially imaginative, he had a thorough knowledge of warfare, much common sense, and a retentive memory; he was bold and courageous without being reckless. By all accounts he was shy, shunned publicity, and was modest and kind, and quick to give credit to others for his successful ventures. During his career he received numerous honours and appointments: CB in 1906; KCB in 1915; GCMG in 1916; and GCSI and GCB in 1919. In addition he was aide-de-camp to the king (1918–22); appointed colonel to the Queen's regiment in 1920; created baronet and appointed Bath king of arms in 1921; and finally selected as a trustee of the Imperial War Museum in 1928. Monro and his wife had no children and the baronetcy became extinct on his death.   GEORGE H. CASSAR

Sources G. de S. Barrow, *The life of General Sir Charles Carmichael Monro* (1931) · *The Times* (9 Dec 1929) · *DNB* · C. F. Aspinall-Oglander, ed., *Military operations: Gallipoli*, 2, History of the Great War (1932) · R. R. James, *Gallipoli* (1965) · J. E. Edmonds, ed., *Military operations, France and Belgium, 1914*, 2, History of the Great War (1925) · M. Hickey, *Gallipoli* (1995) · C. C. Trench, *The Indian army and the king's enemies, 1900–1947* (1988) · J. Terraine, *Douglas Haig: the educated soldier* (1963) · *The private papers of Douglas Haig, 1914–1919*, ed. R. Blake (1952) · C. Miller, *Khyber* (1977) · V. Schofield, *Every rock, every hill* (1984) · W. S. Churchill, *The world crisis*, another edn, 6 vols. (1951–9), vol. 2 · *CGPLA Eng. & Wales* (1930)
Archives BL OIOC, corresp. and MSS, MSS Eur D 783 · NAM, notebooks | IWM, corresp. with Sir Henry Wilson |FILM IWM FVA, actuality footage; documentary footage
Likenesses W. Stoneman, two photographs, 1917–21, NPG [*see illus.*]
Wealth at death £46,878 9s. 6d.: resworn probate, 5 April 1930, *CGPLA Eng. & Wales*

Monro, Charles Henry (1835–1908), jurist and benefactor, was born in London on 17 March 1835, the second of three sons of Cecil Monro, chief registrar of the court of chancery, and his wife, Elizabeth, the daughter of Colonel Henry Howe Knight-Erskine of Pittodrie. He was a descendant of Alexander Monro, principal of Edinburgh University in 1685. He entered Harrow School in 1847, proceeded as Sayer scholar to Gonville and Caius College, Cambridge, in 1853, graduated BA in 1857 with a first class in classics, and in the same year was elected to a fellowship, of which he resigned the payments in 1897. He entered Lincoln's Inn on 14 April 1858 and was called to the bar on 17 November 1863, but did not practise. Instead he continued his study of law, though his work was hampered by ill health, requiring much residence abroad. From 1872 to 1896 he was law lecturer at his college. In 1900 he represented Cambridge University at the 500th anniversary of the second foundation of the University of Cracow.

Between 1891 and 1902 Monro published annotated translations of portions of Justinian the First's *Digest of Roman Law*. Meanwhile he had begun the heavy task of translating the whole *Digest*. One volume of this work appeared in 1904 and another, posthumously, in 1909. They covered altogether about one-fourth of the book.

Monro died, unmarried, at the Grand Hotel, Eastbourne, Sussex on 23 February 1908, and was buried in Eastbourne. An accomplished linguist with a special interest in Celtic, by his will he left a large endowment to Gonville and Caius College, which has been used to fund, at different times, a Monro fellowship, a Monro lecturership in Celtic, a Monro endowment to the Squire Law Library in Cambridge, and a Monro extension to the college library.

W. W. BUCKLAND, *rev.* ERIC METCALFE

Sources J. Foster, *Men-at-the-bar: a biographical hand-list of the members of the various inns of court*, 2nd edn (1885), 322 · J. Venn and others, eds., *Biographical history of Gonville and Caius College*, 2: 1713–1897 (1898), 310 · W. W. B., *The Caian*, 17 (1907–8), 161–71 · Burke, *Gen. GB* · F. C. Cass, *Monken Hadley* (1880), 181 · personal knowledge (1912) · C. N. L. Brooke, *A history of Gonville and Caius College* (1985)
Archives LMA, corresp. with family
Wealth at death £39,223 13s. 3d.: resworn probate, 16 April 1908, *CGPLA Eng. & Wales*

Monro, Sir David (1813–1877), doctor and politician in New Zealand, was born in Edinburgh on 27 March 1813, the seventh of the twelve children of Alexander *Monro tertius (1773–1859) and his first wife, Maria, the daughter of Dr Carmichael Smyth. He attended Edinburgh Academy and the University of Edinburgh, from where he graduated MD in 1835, then studied on the continent before practising in Edinburgh. He settled in Nelson, New Zealand, in 1842. On 7 May 1845 he married Dinah, the daughter of J. Secker of Widford, Gloucestershire, with whom he had seven children.

Monro soon entered politics, and in 1853 was elected to the first general assembly. He was speaker of the house of representatives from 1861 for ten sessions, and was knighted in 1866. At the general election in the latter year he was elected member for Cheviot. On his retirement as speaker in 1870 he was incensed at the failure of the premier, William Fox, to propose any vote of thanks for his services; he stood in opposition in 1871, but was unseated by an electoral petition. The move by the house of representatives to appoint Monro to the legislative council as a mark of favour for his long service was blocked by Fox. Monro was then elected to the house for Waikouaiti, and opposed Fox's government. He resigned in 1873, and died on 15 February 1877 near Nelson.

J. A. HAMILTON, rev. JANE TUCKER

Sources R. E. Wright-St Clair, 'Monro, David', *DNZB*, vol. 1 · R. M. Allen, *Nelson: a history of early settlement* (1965) · P. Mennell, *The dictionary of Australasian biography* (1892) · *The Times* (2 May 1877) **Archives** Auckland Public Library, letters to Sir George Grey · NL Scot., corresp. with Blackwoods **Wealth at death** £53,337 12s. 4d.: testamentary records, 1877, Archives New Zealand

Monro, David Binning (1836–1905), classical scholar, was born at Edinburgh on 16 November 1836, the eldest child of the four sons and two daughters of Alexander Binning Monro, writer to the signet (1805–1891), of Auchenbowie, Stirlingshire, and Softlow, Roxburghshire, and his wife and cousin, Harriet, daughter of Alexander *Monro MD of Craiglockhart. On his marriage his father assumed his wife's surname, which his own ancestors had borne, and on his death in 1891 his Scottish estates passed to his eldest son. Monro was educated privately as a boy. He entered Glasgow University in 1851, and there distinguished himself in logic and mathematics, but the influence of Edmund Lushington, professor of Greek, determined the direction of his studies for life. He matriculated at Oxford as scholar of Brasenose College on 16 June 1854, and in November of the same year was elected to a scholarship at Balliol College, where he afterwards held a Snell exhibition. He was placed in the first class in moderations, both in classics and mathematics, in 1856, in the first class in the final classical school, and the second class in the final mathematical schools in 1858. He won the Ireland scholarship (1858) and the prize for a Latin essay (1859), and was elected fellow of Oriel in the same year. He entered at Lincoln's Inn as a student, but was not called to the bar, returning to Oxford in 1862 as lecturer of Oriel College. He became tutor in 1863, and was elected vice-provost in 1874, on the retirement of Dr Edward Hawkins from Oxford. On Hawkins's death in 1882 Monro was chosen provost of Oriel.

As tutor at Oriel, Monro raised the standard of the teaching, and won the regard of his pupils by his devotion to their best interests. He lectured, as the manner then was, on a great variety of subjects, comparative philology, early Greek history and philosophy, Homer, Thucydides, Herodotus, early Roman history, Roman constitutional history, and Roman public law, and though his delivery was weak and he lacked fluency, his lectures were valued. Here, as with his pupils in his rooms, his strength lay not merely in the abundance and accuracy of his knowledge, but even more in his method of interpreting an author and of marshalling his facts. As provost he ruled his college in a wise and liberal spirit; a sound judgement and a rare grasp of principle were linked to fine courtesy and warmth of heart. In the life and work of the university he played a leading part. He was more than once public

David Binning Monro (1836–1905), by Sir William Quiller Orchardson, 1897

examiner; he served on the delegacy of the press, was a curator of the museum, and a member of the hebdomadal council, and he filled the office of vice-chancellor (1901–4).

Meanwhile Monro devoted his literary interests and energies to the elucidation of the Homeric poems, and to questions arising out of them. In October 1868 he wrote in the *Quarterly Review* an article entitled 'The Homeric question', which he recast for the *Encyclopaedia Britannica* (1880 edn). He collated the Venetian MSS of scholia to the *Iliad* for Dindorf's edition (1875–7); published a school edition of the *Iliad* book i (1878), a *Grammar of the Homeric Language* (1882), and a school edition of the *Iliad* (i–xii, 1884; xiii–xxiv, 1889). A complete text of *Homeri opera et reliquiae* appeared in 1896, and in 1902 there followed, in collaboration with T. W. Allen, a text of the *Iliad* with an apparatus criticus. The later years of his life were given to an edition of the last twelve books of the *Odyssey* (1901), with notes and introductions embodying the results of his work. He contributed papers on Homeric questions to *The Academy*, the *Journal of Philology*, the *Journal of Hellenic Studies*, and other periodicals. If the quantity of his published work is small, this is due to his powers of compression, to his self-criticism, and his reluctance to put out anything for which he could not vouch. His school edition of the *Iliad* book i embodied the results of years of work, and gives concisely the writer's views on disputed points of interpretation and the principles underlying them. The *Homeric Grammar* was the standard work on that subject for seventy years, and remains fundamental to the study of Homeric syntax.

Monro held that the solution of all Homeric questions must be found in philology. He was thoroughly familiar with the work of archaeologists and the contribution made by them to classical knowledge, but he did not hold it to be of equal value or certainty. Unwearying industry, a sound judgement, and a true sense of literary form combined to make him an influential interpreter of his author; his dislike of anything premature or superfluous, his wide range of knowledge of comparative philology, and his clearness of statement gained for his writings considerable authority among his contemporaries. Monro spoke French, German, and Italian with accuracy of idiom and accent, having a very sensitive ear, while his *Modes of Greek Music* (1894), a lengthy and influential treatment of a generally neglected subject, attests his fondness for music and his knowledge of it.

Monro was a founder member of the Oxford Philological Society in 1870, and was for many years its president; he took part in founding the Hellenic Society and the Classical Association, and was vice-president of both. He was a member of the council of the British School at Athens, officier de l'instruction publique in France, and an original fellow of the British Academy. He was created honorary DCL of Oxford in 1904, LLD of Glasgow in 1883, and DLitt of Dublin in 1892. He died suddenly of heart disease at Heiden, Switzerland, on 22 August 1905, and was buried in Holywell cemetery, Oxford. He was unmarried.

L. R. PHELPS, rev. RICHARD SMAIL

Sources J. C. Wilson, *David Binning Monro* (1907) · *The Times* (23 Aug 1905) · *CGPLA Eng. & Wales* (1905)
Archives Oriel College, Oxford, corresp. relating to college and university affairs
Likenesses W. Q. Orchardson, oils, 1897, Oriel College, Oxford [*see illus.*]
Wealth at death £13,344 13s. 4d.: confirmation, 3 Nov 1905, *CCI*

Monro, Donald (*d.* in or after **1575**), Church of Scotland minister and author, was a younger son of Alexander Monro (or Munro) of Kiltearn, on the north side of the Cromarty Firth, and of Janet Maclean. The Monros had a tradition of service in the church (an uncle and namesake was provost of Tain in 1534–46), and Donald also had early associations with the Western Isles through his mother's family. He is usually assumed to be the Donald Monro who in 1526 was appointed vicar of Snizort in the Trotternish district of Skye, which was then held along with the island of Raasay as a joint charge. Competing claims to ownership of lands in Skye by the MacLeods and MacDonalds, and continuing attempts to restore the lordship of the Isles, ensured constant civil disturbance in the area. Although misnamed Archibald in the privy seal register, Donald was presumably the Monro chaplain presented in the name of the child Queen Mary to the archdeaconry of the Isles on 2 March 1548, when it should be vacated by Roderick MacLean (who was raised to the bishopric in 1550). There is documentary evidence that Monro was 'archdean', that is, archdeacon, in 1553, and he was still being styled archdeacon ten years later.

In August 1560 Monro's cousin and clan chief Robert Munro of Foulis was one of the lairds who attended the Reformation Parliament, and he is himself commonly regarded as the first professing protestant of the family. Four of the bishops and many clergy accepted the new order of church government; Monro was admitted to the charge of Kiltearn parish, later extended to include Limlair and neighbouring Alness. Superintendents answerable to the kirk's general assembly were appointed instead of bishops, but men considered suitable for that office were few, especially in the highlands, and commissions for one year only were granted to some ministers, without releasing them from parish duties. Monro was the only highlander chosen, with the further duty of helping the bishop of Caithness to preach and to 'plant kirks' in the far north, although it was to be complained that he 'was not prompt in the Scottish tongue' (Thomson, 1.176). He was regularly reappointed for Ross until 1575, when another man took his place. Thereafter Monro's name disappears, not only from the higher councils of the church but also from the parish ministry, and it is supposed that he died about this time. He is said to have been buried at Kiltearn.

Monro's *Description of the Western Isles* is the first account of that region known to have resulted from personal observation, and it provided the basis for the discussion of the Hebrides by George Buchanan in his *Rerum Scoticarum historia* of 1582. No holograph manuscript of the original *Description* seems to have survived, but several copies are preserved in the National Library of Scotland; an incomplete version was published at Edinburgh in 1774 and reprinted five times, before being supplanted by an edition (first published in 1961 and reprinted in 1999 as an addendum to Martin Martin's *Description*) based on a more complete copy and a careful comparison with Buchanan's text. Monro is said to have travelled through most of the islands which he describes in 1549, but it is not explained what purpose his account was intended to serve. Whatever this may have been, Monro's text would have reminded him of particulars which could have been useful for any senior churchman unfamiliar with the diocese of the Isles, and thanks to him far more is known of the general appearance of these islands in Queen Mary's reign than of any other part of Scotland. Monro also wrote *Genealogies of the Chieff Clans of the Isles* (1774); in the earliest dated copy of his writings, made in 1642, he is styled 'high dean of the isles', apparently an informal allusion to an office which had in fact disappeared at the Reformation.

R. W. MUNRO and JEAN MUNRO

Sources R. W. Munro, ed., *Monro's Western Isles of Scotland* (1961) · R. W. Munro, ed., *The Munro tree* (1978) · G. Buchanan, *Rerum Scoticarum historia* (1582) · P. Hume Brown, ed., *Scotland before 1700* (1893) · T. Thomson, ed., *Acts and proceedings of the general assemblies of the Kirk of Scotland*, 3 pts, Bannatyne Club, 81 (1839–45), pt 1
Archives NL Scot., MSS, Adv MS 31.2.6, 33.2.3, 33.3.20 [copies]

Monro, Donald (**1728–1802**), military physician, born in Edinburgh on 15 January 1728, was the second surviving son of Alexander *Monro primus (1697–1767), and Isabella, second daughter of Sir Donald MacDonald of Sleat. He was the elder brother of Alexander *Monro secundus (1733–1817). He was educated at James Mundell's private school in the West Bow, Edinburgh. In 1746 he entered his father's anatomy class at Edinburgh University, and he graduated MD on 8 June 1753. His dissertation on the subject of dropsy was published in 1756 as *An Essay on Dropsy and its Different Species*. He was one of the first to relate dropsy to disease of the heart valves.

After graduation Monro settled in London and established a practice in Jermyn Street. In April 1756 he became a licentiate of the Royal College of Physicians, and on 3 November 1758 he was elected physician to St George's Hospital. As part of his duties he gave lectures on materia medica, which formed the basis of his textbook *A Treatise on Medical and Pharmaceutical Chemistry and the Materia medica* (1788).

In December 1760 Monro was appointed physician to the British Military Hospital in Germany during the Seven Years' War (1756–1763). In *An Account of the Diseases which were most Frequent in the British Hospitals in Germany* (1764), Monro described the administrative and medical problems facing army physicians during the campaign. He suggested that staff surgeons should be stationed at brigade headquarters in order to perform early surgery. He also raised the issue of rank, which led to direct hospital control for medical officers.

At the end of the war Monro returned to St George's. In 1766 he became a fellow of the Royal Society, and in November 1783 he was made a fellow of the Royal Society of Edinburgh. On 30 September 1771 he was elected a fellow of the Royal College of Physicians by special grace (fellowship was usually restricted to Oxford and Cambridge graduates). He held a number of offices in the college, and delivered the Croonian lectures in 1774 and the Harveian lectures in the following year.

At St James's Church, Piccadilly, on 29 August 1772 Monro married Dorothea Maria Heineken, a German lady-in-waiting to Queen Charlotte. Isabella Margaret, their only child, went on to marry Colonel Hugh Scott.

In June 1778, at the time of the American War of Independence, Monro was recalled to army service, though he did not serve overseas. Two years later he published *Observations on the Means of Preserving the Health of Soldiers*, a second and enlarged version of his earlier work on army health. John Millar's *Observations on the Management of the Diseases of the Army and Navy During the American War, 1783* (1784) was partly a response to Monro's work.

Ill health forced Monro to resign his hospital post in 1786 and he then moved to a house in Argyle Street. In June 1793 he once again reverted to the full-pay ranks of the army, though the details of the appointment are unknown. At the time of his death, at his home on 9 June 1802, he was senior physician to the forces. Of his publications, those dealing with the health of the army are his most celebrated, and they are rendered more valuable in the absence of official accounts of army health in the period.

CLAIRE E. J. HERRICK

Sources R. E. Wright-St Clair, *Doctors Monro: a medical saga* (1964), 62–8 · A. Peterkin and W. Johnston, *Commissioned officers in the medical services of the British army, 1660–1960*, 1 (1968), 33 · N. Cantlie, *A history of the army medical department*, 1 (1974), 106–9, 121, 126–31, 232 · R. E. Wright-St Clair, 'Donald Monro (1727–1802)', *Medical History*, 15 (1971), 95–6 · Munk, *Roll* · S. Devlin-Thorp, ed., *The Royal Society of Edinburgh: one hundred medical fellows elected, 1783–1844* (1982), vol. 3 of *Scotland's cultural heritage* (1981–4) · J. D. Comrie, *History of Scottish medicine*, 2nd edn, 2 (1932), 432 · Chambers, *Scots.* (1835) · W. S. Craig, *History of the Royal College of Physicians of Edinburgh* (1976), 392, 958 · P. J. Wallis and R. V. Wallis, *Eighteenth century medics*, 2nd edn (1988) · *GM*, 1st ser., 72 (1802), 687 · *The Monro collection in the medical library of the University of Otago* (1979)

Archives BL · RS · University of Otago, Dunedin, collection

Monro, Edward (1815–1866), Church of England clergyman and theologian, eldest son of Edward Thomas Monro MD (1790–1856), physician at Bethlem Hospital, grandson of Thomas *Monro (1759–1833) and brother of Henry *Monro (1817–1891), was born in London. He was educated at Harrow School, and from 1833 at Oriel College, Oxford, where his early evangelical sympathies were replaced by a lifelong devotion to the teachings of the Tractarians. He graduated in 1836, and was ordained in 1837. In 1838 he married Emma, daughter of Dr Hay of Madras. They had no children. From 1842 to 1860 he was perpetual curate of Harrow Weald, Middlesex, and from 1860 until his death vicar of St John's, Leeds. He quickly attained a wide reputation as a preacher, and was select preacher at Oxford in 1862.

Monro was one of the first Tractarians to recognize the particular pastoral needs of those living in the new industrial areas of Victorian England. This led him to visit many such areas, recording his observations and ideas about ministering to colliers, carpet weavers, and navvies in *The Church and the Million* (five parts, 1857–9). In Harrow Weald he established an agricultural college for boys, outlining his theories in *Agricultural Colleges* (1850). In this venture he received support from lords Selborne and Nelson, and C. J. Blomfield, bishop of London. The boys were boarded and educated free of charge, but the great expense of the college led the enthusiastic founder into debts from which he was extricated with difficulty by friends and admirers. The institution was without endowment, and the large and elegant buildings disappeared after Monro left Harrow Weald. Monro was a spontaneous storyteller and most of the stories and allegories for which he became famous were delivered impromptu to village boys.

In response to an article in *The Guardian* of 25 April 1849, lamenting the absence of practical guides for parish priests, Monro wrote *Parochial Work* (1850), a pioneering volume of Tractarian pastoral theology. This was followed by *Sermons Principally on the Responsibilities of the Ministerial Office* (1850); *The Parish* (1853), a long narrative poem; and *Parochial Papers for the Clergyman, the Schoolmaster, and the Family* (1856). In all these works Monro argued that the clergy should seek to acquire a deep and sympathetic understanding of their parishioners, a quality he called 'elasticity', through such means as frequent visiting, personal intercourse, and the building of schools, all of which should lead to the development of the sacramental life and the reconciliation of the poor to God. At Leeds, Monro put into effect on a larger scale the ideal of parochial work described in his books: the numbers of candidates for confirmation and communicants in his parish increased greatly. But overwork damaged his health, and he died at Leeds on 13 December 1866, after two years of illness. He was buried at Harrow Weald.

GEORGE HERRING

Sources B. Heeney, 'Tractarian pastor: Edward Monro of Harrow Weald', *Canadian Journal of Theology*, 13 (1967), 241–53 · B. Heeney, 'Tractarian pastor: Edward Monro of Harrow Weald', *Canadian Journal of Theology*, 14 (1968), 13–27 · B. Heeney, *A different kind of gentleman: parish clergy as professional men in early and mid-Victorian England* (1976) · A. Russell, *The clerical profession* (1980) · Foster, *Alum. Oxon.* · CGPLA Eng. & Wales (1867)
Archives BL, corresp. with W. E. Gladstone, Add. MSS 44364–44392
Likenesses photograph, Leeds City Libraries; repro. in Heeney, *A different kind of gentleman*, following p. 34
Wealth at death under £3000: probate, 14 Feb 1867, CGPLA Eng. & Wales

Monro, Sir George, of Culrain and Newmore (d. 1694), army officer, was the third son of Colonel John Monro (d. 1633) of Obsdale and his wife, Catherine, daughter of John Gordon of Embo. The tradition that he served in the Swedish forces from the late 1620s appears false, as in a letter of 31 October 1635 his uncle Colonel Robert Monro writes that 'My nephewe, Mr George, haid a greatt mynd to have quatt his biuck [quit his books] and to have followit wares.' Thus George was already a university graduate, and his uncle now sent him to Leiden 'to pass his course in the lawes' (W. Fraser, *Sutherland Book*, 3 vols., 1892, 2.160). However, he soon escaped from study to the German wars, enlisting as an ensign in a Scottish regiment in the Swedish army in 1637 and reaching the rank of lieutenant-colonel by 1639. He left the Swedish service in August 1640 and in 1642 he was appointed a lieutenant-colonel in the Scottish army sent to Ireland (commanded by his uncle Robert) to resist the Irish Catholics. He was given command of the army's garrison in Coleraine, which he retained for six years. Local assessment of him as 'a surly Mercenarie' (Fitzpatrick, 263) accords well with later opinions. In 1644 he took a leading role in negotiating on behalf of the army with the covenanters' government in Edinburgh. A proposal in November 1645 that he should bring 2100 men from Ireland to Scotland and take command of the forces employed against the royalist marquess of Montrose, with the rank of major-general, was soon abandoned. Further negotiations designed to secure the army's future in an increasingly complex political situation included, in October and November 1646, unsuccessful approaches to Monro by the marquess of Ormond (the king's lord lieutenant of Ireland) for the occupation of Dublin by the Scots, and attempts to secure aid from the English parliament.

When, in 1648, the Scottish engagers raised an army to invade England on Charles I's behalf, Monro was commissioned (24 June) as major-general of forces to be brought to Scotland from the army in Ireland. By the time he reached Scotland, with about 2000 men, the duke of Hamilton's army had already entered England, and Monro followed it south. But he was then ordered not to join the main army, as he had disputed the right of the lieutenant-general, the earl of Callander, to give him orders. 'For all practical purposes Monro might as well have remained in Ireland' (S. R. Gardiner, *Civil War*, 4 vols., 1893–4, 4.181). After Hamilton's defeat at Preston, Monro sought briefly to uphold the collapsing engager regime in Scotland. In negotiations on 18 September he sought to be allowed to return his men to Ireland, but on 26 September was forced to agree to disband. Monro fled to the Netherlands, but he was back in Ireland by January 1649, when he was knighted by Ormond at Kilkenny. Commissioned to command royalist forces in Ulster, he helped the earl of Clanricarde to subdue Sligo before moving north and seizing Coleraine and (4 July) Carrickfergus. Soon most of Ulster was in royalist, rather than parliamentary, hands, but after Cromwell's sack of Drogheda (11 September) and a defeat suffered by Monro on 16 September royalist resistance crumbled. Monro retained Enniskillen until April 1650 but then returned to Scotland. He was one of a group of frustrated nobles and officers who protested, in the 'northern band' of 24 October, against their exclusion from the army opposing Cromwellian invasion. Subsequently he negotiated about declaring his repentance for having joined the engagement, but the completion of the Cromwellian conquest rendered the matter irrelevant.

Monro again fled abroad, but early in 1654 he landed in the north of Scotland with John Middleton, Charles II having appointed them respectively lieutenant-general and general of his forces in Scotland. Many of the royalists, led by the earl of Glencairn (who had formerly been in command), were deeply resentful of Monro's promotion, and in April the latter's arrogance led to a duel with Glencairn. He was wounded, and Glencairn had to be restrained from killing him, but Monro still 'carried so high' (Young and Tucker, 80–85) in his usual haughty manner that Glencairn withdrew with his men from the rising. In August it was reported that the main reason that royalists in the highlands would not unite was dislike of Monro's position, 'he being a person generalli hated of all men' (Firth, 170). The rising collapsed in confusion and bitter recriminations, with Middleton denouncing Monro and others in December for having 'baselie deserted us' (Thurloe, *State papers*, 2.42).

During the Restoration period Monro sat in parliament for Ross-shire (1661–3, 1685–6) and Sutherland (1685–6), but he was excluded from the Act of Indemnity of 1662, being fined £360 sterling. This was doubtless a punishment for his 1653 'desertion' of Middleton, who had become the king's commissioner to parliament, but it may also reflect suspicion of Monro's Presbyterian sympathies, which were encouraged by his second wife. Monro had married, first, Anne, the daughter of his uncle Robert Monro, in 1638 or 1639. She died on 3 March 1647 leaving two sons; she had been predeceased by five other children of the marriage. In 1649 or 1650 Monro married Christian Hamilton, daughter of Sir Frederick Hamilton of Manner Hamilton (Manorhamilton), co. Leitrim; they were to have at least one son and seven daughters. She was staunchly Presbyterian, and it was rumoured that in the 1660s she and her husband sometimes helped dissidents escape persecution. During the Second Anglo-Dutch War there were fears of trouble among Scots Presbyterians, and in August 1665 Monro, among others, was briefly imprisoned. However, by 1674 the regime was sure enough of his allegiance for him to be appointed major-general of the forces in Scotland (August) and admitted as a member of the privy council there (September). He was active in the suppression of dissidents, but in December 1677 his commission was cancelled, possibly because his enthusiasm for the increasingly harsh persecution was suspect.

However, on 24 October 1688 he was hauled out of retirement, being again appointed major-general, with a pension of £200 sterling. As all regular troops had been sent to England to help James VII oppose the invasion of Prince William of Orange, Monro's forces consisted of an untrained militia, which could do nothing to prevent the collapse of the regime. The earl of Balcarres claimed that Monro was not much better in the military trade 'than these new-raised men, having lost by age, and being long out of service, anything he had learned [in Germany], except the rudeness and austerity of that service' (Lindsay, *Memoirs*, 12). It may have been a hostile editor rather than the earl himself who subsequently altered the text to produce the even harsher verdict that all that Monro had retained from Germany was 'affected Nastiness, Brutality and Fanaticism' (Lindsay, *An Account of the Affairs of Scotland*, 30). Such judgements by Jacobites reflect the fact that Monro was quick to abandon that cause once it was clear that all was lost. The 1688–9 revolution might offend his royalism, but it gratified his underlying Presbyterianism. In December 1689 he was appointed a member of King William's Scottish privy council, with a £300 pension, and he was one of three generals charged with organizing the forces in Scotland. He sat in parliament for Ross-shire in 1689–90, and took an active part in the restoration of Presbyterian church government.

Monro died in his castle of Newmore in Ross-shire on 26 February 1694 and was buried at Rosskeen, Ross-shire. He was survived by his wife. In his many years of military employment he showed himself to be a forceful, determined soldier, but arrogant and quarrelsome, 'a proud and self-willed man' (Adair, 133). No contemporary commented favourably on his personality, but an account of the greeting he and his 'Presbiterian Lady' gave to Lord Lovat at Newmore in 1669 suggests a more attractive side to his character: 'I am a souldier, my entertainment will be course [coarse] but very cordiall, and you are sure of the hidden dish: a free welcom' (Fraser, 481).

DAVID STEVENSON

Sources DNB · *Reg. PCS*, 1st ser. · *Reg. PCS*, 2nd ser. · *Reg. PCS*, 3rd ser. · D. Stevenson, *Scottish covenanters and Irish confederates* (1981) · C. Dalton, ed., *The Scots army, 1661–1688* (1909) · A. Mackenzie, *History of the Munros of Fowlis* (1898) · E. M. Furgol, *A regimental history of the covenanting armies, 1639–1651* (1990) · J. Fraser, *Chronicles of the Frasers: the Wardlaw manuscript*, ed. W. Mackay, Scottish History Society, 1st ser., 47 (1905) · H. Munro, *Foulis Castle and the Monroes of Lower Iveagh* (1929), 76–7 · C. H. Firth, ed., *Scotland and the protectorate: letters and papers relating to the military government of Scotland from January 1654 to June 1659*, Scottish History Society, 31 (1899) · R. W. Munro, *The Munro tree: a genealogy and chronology of the Munros of Foulis* (1978) · Thurloe, *State papers* · T. Fitzpatrick, *The bloody bridge*

(1903) · *Report on manuscripts in various collections*, 8 vols., HMC, 55 (1901–14), 5.146–7 · P. Young and N. Tucker, eds., *Military memoirs of the civil war* (1967) · P. Adair, *A true narrative of the rise and progress of the Presbyterian church in Ireland (1623–1670)*, ed. W. D. Killen (1866) · [C. Lindsay, earl of Balcarres], *An account of the affairs of Scotland* (1714) · NA Scot., PA 11/6, fol. 40v · C. Lindsay [earl of Balcarres], *Memoirs touching the revolution in Scotland*, ed. A. W. C. Lindsay [earl of Crawford and Balcarres], Bannatyne Club (1841) · W. A. Shaw, *The knights of England*, 2 (1906), 221 · *Decennial indexes to the services of heirs in Scotland*, 1 (1863), 23 · S. Murdoch and A. Grosjean, 'Scotland, Scandinavia and Northern Europe, 1580–1707', www.abdn.ac.uk/ssne/

Monro, Harold Edward (1879–1932), poet and bookseller, was born on 14 March 1879 at 137 chaussée de Charleroi, St Gilles, Brussels, the youngest of the three surviving children of Edward William Monro (1848–1889), civil engineer, and his wife and first cousin, Arabel Sophia (1849–1926), daughter of Peter John Margary, civil engineer, and his wife, Emma. Monro belonged to the Monros of Fyrish, a London-based branch of the clan Munro. He inherited a small income from a family-owned lunatic asylum, originally bought by his direct ancestor Dr John *Monro. He was first educated in Belgium, becoming bilingual; after his father's death from tuberculosis he attended prep schools in England before following his father, two uncles, and brother to Radley College in 1892. His brother died of tuberculosis in 1893.

Monro went up to Gonville and Caius College, Cambridge, in 1898. He became intimate with Maurice Browne, later well known as a theatre director, and they decided to become the poets of the new, post-Victorian age. After graduating with a third in French and German in 1901 Monro became a student at Lincoln's Inn, London, but soon left to write poetry in a remote Irish cottage. Browne arranged a walking tour in Germany for himself, his sister, and Monro, hoping a romance would ensue. On 2 December 1903 Monro duly married Dorothy Elizabeth Browne (1885–1960), daughter of the Revd Frederick H. Browne and Frances Anna, *née* Neligan; their only child, Nigel, was born a year later. In 1906 they moved from Ireland to Haslemere, Surrey.

The early deaths of his father and brother left Monro painfully aware of mortality; finding no comfort in religion, despite intensive questioning, he longed for a terrestrial state where human frailties could be overcome. He and Maurice Browne were inspired by H. G. Wells's *A Modern Utopia* (1905) to start an order of 'Samurai', Wells's voluntary ruling class. Browne also set up the Samurai Press (1907–9), a utopian venture which published work by himself, Monro, Wilfrid Gibson, John Drinkwater, and others. The nascent order collapsed, as did Monro's marriage, early in 1908.

Monro then set out on the walk from Paris to Milan described in his *Chronicle of a Pilgrimage* (1909), the prelude to three years abroad, mostly spent in Florence and the freethinking community at Monte Verità, Ascona. Psychoanalysed in Zürich in 1908, he seems to have accepted that he was homosexual and that his marriage was beyond rescue. The separation became permanent, ending in divorce in 1916.

Harold Edward Monro (1879–1932), by unknown photographer, 1926 [at the Poetry Bookshop, 38 Great Russell Street, London]

only group ever to meet there regularly was T. S. Eliot's *Criterion* Club in the twenties; Monro and Eliot became close friends.

The Poetry Bookshop remained in business until 1935, known throughout the English-speaking world. Readings were given regularly in winter, often by famous poets. Gibson was the first lodger, followed by two leading modernists, T. E. Hulme and Jacob Epstein. The shop published numerous rhyme sheets and nearly fifty books and pamphlets, including all five volumes of *Georgian Poetry* (1912–22), and first books by Richard Aldington, Robert Graves, and Charlotte Mew. Monro lost control of the *Poetry Review* at the end of 1912, the Poetry Society having taken fright at his support for innovation, so in March 1913 he started his own quarterly, *Poetry and Drama* (1913–14).

Impending conscription drove Monro to volunteer in June 1916. Commissioned into the Royal Garrison Artillery, he was posted to anti-aircraft stations in Manchester, London, and Coventry, hating his servitude. A desk job in the Ministry of Information in September 1918 came too late to save his health and ideals. The shop was kept going by Alida Klemantaski (1892–1969), the daughter of Sigismund Klemantaski, a Polish–Jewish trader, and his English wife, Lizzie, *née* Phillips. Alida had met Monro in 1913 and had fallen in love with him, sharing some of his ideals.

Against all his instincts, but out of a sense of obligation, Monro married Alida on 27 March 1920. She had by then discovered he was drinking heavily, a weakness exacerbated by the war, and she soon realized that he had male lovers. She never lived with him, but he took a house for her in Bloomsbury and they spent weekends together in the country; he always had a cottage somewhere, rural escapes being important to him.

Monro revived the shop after the war and relaunched his periodical as the (*Monthly*) *Chapbook* (1919–25). Bookshop parties became famous; despite his chronic melancholy, the reverse side of his idealism, he was a generous host and kindly listener, delighting in serious conversation. Some people thought him handsome, others said he looked like an intelligent horse; he was tall, lean, and upright, with sleek dark hair, thick moustache, long face, and sad eyes. His tactless survey, *Some Contemporary Poets* (1920), shows little critical insight; his greatest service to his fellow poets was as an enabler.

Monro published his own work from the shop in four small collections: *Children of Love* (1915), *Strange Meetings* (1917), *Real Property* (1922), and *The Earth for Sale* (1928). The first contains some of his most popular poems, including 'Overheard on a Saltmarsh' and 'Milk for the Cat', and the quartet 'Youth in Arms', which influenced Wilfred Owen (who stayed at the shop in 1916). The 1916–17 poems, notably 'Strange Meetings', 'Trees', and 'Week-end', explore the relationship between humans and the earth. The 1928 book is as pessimistic as *Before Dawn* had been optimistic, lamenting individual isolation and environmental destruction.

When the Devonshire Street lease ran out in 1926 the

Few British people can have experienced so much of the alternative lifestyles that were being tried out on the continent. Monro's *Before Dawn: Poems and Impressions* (July 1911) declares boundless faith in the future, advocating sexual and social freedom, Wellsian socialism, and the Nietzschean ideal of the superman living at one with the earth. Armed with this manifesto Monro arrived in London in the autumn of 1911, determined to make a practical contribution to Utopia by finding the poets of the future. He launched the monthly *Poetry Review* for the Poetry Society in January 1912 and published work by many of the younger poets and critics, including Ezra Pound's manifesto, 'Prolegomena', and F. S. Flint's monumental study of recent French poetry, two contributions which gave rise to Pound's brief imagist movement. Monro was strictly neutral, to Pound's annoyance; the *Poetry Review* also published Rupert Brooke's 'Grantchester' and other work by the poets soon to be known as the Georgians.

The success of the *Review* led Monro to establish a 'Poetry House', containing a shop, a room for readings, an editorial office, and accommodation for himself and poets in need of cheap lodgings. He took a Queen Anne house at 35 Devonshire Street in a seedy area of Bloomsbury; in December 1912 the Poetry Bookshop received its first customers and published its first book, *Georgian Poetry 1911–1912*. This anthology, edited by Edward Marsh with advice from Monro, Brooke, Gibson, and Drinkwater, proved immensely successful. Yet Monro's efforts to unite poets contributed to a schism, by bringing out the differences between imagists and Georgians. He deplored such divisions, always striving to disprove the myth, still current, that the bookshop was a Georgian headquarters. The

Poetry Bookshop moved to 38 Great Russell Street, opposite the British Museum. Financial troubles soon forced a further move to the rear of the building. By now Monro was a disappointed man, appalled at the state of Europe and feeling forgotten by the poets he had helped. He had used up most of his money in subsidizing the shop. His drinking bouts worsened. Early in 1932 an operation revealed advanced tuberculosis, and Monro died at the Cliff Combe Nursing Home in Broadstairs, Kent, on 16 March 1932, and was cremated at Golders Green crematorium, Middlesex, on 21 March. Perhaps no one did more for the advancement of twentieth-century British poetry.

DOMINIC HIBBERD

Sources BL, Monro and Poetry Bookshop MSS, Add. MSS 57734–57768 · U. Cal., Los Angeles, Harold Monro MSS · H. Monro, letters, U. Mich., Van Volkenburg-Browne MSS (Monro) · Ransom HRC · State University of New York, Buffalo · NYPL, Humanities and Social Sciences Library, Berg collection · letters to Robert Bridges, Bodl. Oxf. · correspondence with S. Cockerell, BL, Add. MS 52737 · J. Grant, *Harold Monro and the Poetry Bookshop* (1967) · R. Tomalin, preface, in H. Monro, *Collected poems*, ed. A. Monro (1970) · J. H. Woolmer, *The Poetry Bookshop, 1912–1935: a bibliography* (1988) · D. Hibberd, *Harold Monro: poet of the New Age* (2001) · *DNB* · General Register Office for England

Archives Ransom HRC, letters · U. Cal., Los Angeles · U. Mich. | BL, corresp. with Sydney Cockerell, Add. MS 52737 · BL, corresp. and papers, incl. material relating to Poetry Bookshop, Add. MSS 57734–57768 · Bodl. Oxf., letters to Robert Bridges · NYPL, Berg collection

Likenesses J. Kramer, ink and chalk drawing, 1923, NPG · photograph, 1926, NPG [*see illus.*] · E. M. Kauffer, drawing, repro. in H. Monro, ed., *The Chapbook* (Oct 1924) · photograph (after drawing by P. W. Lewis, 1923), NPG · photographs, BL, Monro and Poetry Bookshop MSS, Add. MSS 57734–57768

Wealth at death £12,771 4s. 7d.: probate, 28 April 1932, *CGPLA Eng. & Wales*

Monro, Henry (1758–1798), Irish nationalist and linen draper, was born in May or June 1758 in Lisburn, co. Antrim, Ireland, the second of three children. His father (1733–1793) was a Presbyterian, and his mother, Margaret Gorman (d. 1832), the daughter of a country gentleman of co. Down and later a grocer in Lisburn, a member of the Church of Ireland. Monro and his two sisters were brought up in the Anglican tradition of their mother. He was educated in Lisburn and served his apprenticeship in the linen industry, becoming a prosperous linen draper based in Market Square, Lisburn. He joined the Lisburn Volunteers shortly after their foundation in 1778, and served as a drill sergeant and later an adjutant. In 1795 he married Margaret (d. 1840), fourth daughter of Robert Johnston, a linen bleacher from Seymour Hill, near Belfast. Madden's assertion that they had two children who died in infancy is contradicted by his sister-in-law, who states that Monro's daughter married a clergyman called Hanson (Madden, 227, 246). Monro was not a man of literary tastes and preferred an active life of hunting and shooting. It is recorded that he was of medium build, with a fair complexion, intelligent features, and large blue eyes.

Monro was master of freemasons' lodge 193, a forum for radical ideas in Lisburn which he joined on 11 October 1795. A supporter of Catholic emancipation and parliamentary reform, he joined the United Irishmen in 1795. When the rising spread to Ulster in June 1798, his name was forwarded as one of three possible candidates to fill the vacant command in co. Antrim, a post eventually assumed by Henry Joy McCracken. Monro, however, was acclaimed leader of the co. Down insurgents after they had ambushed government troops at Saintfield. He took charge on 10 June, and soon after encamped at Creevy Rocks, near Saintfield, where he began to organize and drill his force. He sent an advance rebel party to occupy Ballynahinch, and the main body arrived in the afternoon of the 12th to take up position on the high ground in the Montalto demesne of Lord Moira. The advancing government army under Major-General George Nugent met stiff resistance at Windmill Hill in Ballynahinch. The rebels later retreated, allowing Nugent to position his men on the hill, facing the insurgent army. Monro is said to have resisted suggestions of a night attack on the government forces, some of whom (the Monaghan militia) were engaged in drunken looting in Ballynahinch. Substantial numbers of insurgents deserted in protest.

At daylight on 13 June Monro's basic artillery bombarded the government positions and initial forays of pike-wielding insurgents into Ballynahinch proved successful. However, the rebels' inferior artillery and their inexperience, contrasted with the superior discipline of the government army, which captured rebel supplies, combined to make defeat inevitable. A bugle call created confusion in the United Irish ranks, whereupon the government forces turned and put the rebels to flight. Monro and one William Kean sought refuge at a farm owned by William Holmes, who betrayed them to the authorities. Monro was arrested by local yeomen and taken to Lisburn, where he was imprisoned in the Huguenot church and refused visitors, with the exception of his father-in-law. Monro's rector, the Revd Snowden Cupples, who was a strong supporter of Orangeism, conveyed meals to his parishioner, despite their differing political allegiances.

Monro was court-martialled in his home town on 16 June 1798. Three witnesses confirmed his leadership at the battle of Ballynahinch. In his defence Monro claimed that he had been forced into that role by a United Irish emissary, James Townsend, and he offered to assist the authorities in subduing the disturbances in co. Down. Monro was hanged on 16 June 1798 in the Market Square, Lisburn, within sight of his front door with both his mother and one of his sisters looking on. According to an eyewitness, he settled his business accounts before ascending the gallows. His last words were 'tell my country I deserved better of her' (Paterson, 197). His head was cut off, impaled on a pike, and displayed for several weeks. His papers were destroyed by the military. The precise location of Henry Monro's grave is unknown, but it is believed to be unmarked in Lisburn Cathedral churchyard.

KENNETH L. DAWSON

Sources R. R. Madden, *Antrim and Down in '98* (1888) · K. L. Dawson, 'Henry Monro, commander of the United Irish army of Down', *Down Survey* (1998), 12–26 · W. T. Latimer, *Ulster biographies relating*

chiefly to the rebellion of 1798 (1897) • M. Hill, B. Turner, and K. L. Dawson, *1798 rebellion in county Down* (1998) • C. H. Teeling, *History of the Irish rebellion of 1798: a personal narrative* (1876) • C. Dickson, *Revolt in the north: Antrim and Down in 1798* (1960) • T. G. F. Paterson, 'Lisburn and neighbourhood in 1798', *Ulster Journal of Archaeology*, 3rd ser., 1 (1938), 193–8 • A. T. Q. Stewart, *The summer soldiers* (1995) • R. M. Young, *Ulster in '98: episodes and anecdotes* (1893) • H. Monroe, *Foulis Castle and the Monroes of Lower Iveagh* (1929) • H. M. McCall, *Our staple manufacturers* (1855) • *DNB* • NA Ire., Rebellion MSS, 620 series • PRO NIre., Downshire MSS

Monro, Henry (1791–1814), portrait and subject painter, was born in London on 3 August 1791, the second of the five sons and a daughter of Dr Thomas *Monro (1759–1833) and his wife, Hannah or Elizabeth Woodcock, of Bath. After two years at Harrow School he entered the navy, but quitted it from distaste after a few days on board the frigate *Amelia*. His inclinations then wavered between the army and art, but he finally chose the latter. On 13 January 1807 Farington noted that 'Dr. Monro's 2d. son, a youth 15 years of age, now attends the Royal Academy regularly' (Farington, *Diary*, 8.2945). Here and at the colour school of the British Institution he studied with great diligence and distinction.

In 1811 Monro exhibited *A Laughing Boy*, *Boys at Marbles*, and three portraits, including one of his father, and in the following year *Boy Grinding Colours*, *Lace-Maker*, and four portraits, including one of Thomas Hearne and another of himself. In 1813 he sent a *Head*, some studies from nature in pen and ink, and *Othello, Desdemona, and Iago* to the Royal Academy, and *The Disgrace of Wolsey* to the British Institution; for the latter he was posthumously awarded a premium of 100 guineas. In 1811 he had visited Scotland, and sustained serious injuries by a fall from his horse, and in January 1814 he was seized with a cold, which affected his lungs, and cut short his promising career at the age of twenty-three. A pastel portrait by him of his father in the robes of the Royal College of Physicians remains in the college collection. A drawing by Monro of his father (NPG), probably used in preparing this portrait, was singled out by the watercolourist Thomas Girtin in a letter dated 26 May 1842 to one of Thomas Monro's executors:

> There is no signature but it was a matter of a moment to pick it out from a mass of drawings by Dr Thomas Monro, John and Alexander Monro, and a very few Henry Monros, for this young man's merit was quite outstanding and his work very easily recognisable amongst all the other family stuff. (Walker, 1.340–41)

Similar drawings are in the Mellon collection, Pantzer collection, Indianapolis, and the British Museum, London. Walker notes that 'another drawing by Henry Monro— "Dr Thomas Monro, Miss Sally Monro, Miss Charlotte Monro and the Artist on Horseback", inscribed: "HM fecit Oct 24, 1820, Bushey", was at Christie's 18 December 1973 (155)' (ibid.). He died on 5 March 1814, and was buried at Bushey, Hertfordshire, where a monument was erected to his memory.

W. C. MONKHOUSE, rev. JOHN-PAUL STONARD

Sources E. J. G. Jefferiss, *Dr Thomas Monro (1759–1833) and the Monro Academy* (1976) [exhibition, V&A] • J. Turner, ed., *The dictionary of art*, 34 vols. (1996) • artist's file, archive material, Courtauld Inst., Witt Library • *IGI* • Farington, *Diary*, 8.2945 • *GM*, 1st ser., 84/1 (1814),

414 • R. Walker, *National Portrait Gallery: Regency portraits*, 1 (1985), 340–341
Likenesses H. Monro, self-portrait, etching, 1813, BM • H. Monro, self-portrait (aged seventeen), Collection of the Dean of York • H. Monro, self-portraits; copies, Witt Library, Courtauld Inst. • negatives, Paul Mellon Foundation

Monro, Henry (1817–1891), physician specializing in the treatment of the insane, born in London on 10 January 1817, was the second son of the physician Edward Thomas Monro (1790–1856) and Sarah Cox Monro, and grandson of Thomas *Monro. Two of his three brothers became clerics: the eldest, Edward *Monro (1815–1866), became curate of Harrow Weald, Middlesex (1842–60), and vicar of St John's, Leeds (1860–66), and the youngest, Percy (d. 1883), became vicar of Colden Common, Hampshire (1851–83). Monro was educated at Harrow School and then, like his father and grandfather before him, at Oriel College, Oxford, matriculating on 27 November 1834 and graduating BA in 1839. After studying medicine at St Bartholomew's Hospital from 1840 he graduated BM in 1844, but did not gain his DM (Oxon.) until 1863. He became a fellow of the Royal College of Physicians in 1848, and officiated at various times as councillor and was censor in 1861. Monro married Jane Eliza, the fourth daughter of Sir William Russell, bt, of Charlton Park, Gloucestershire, on 5 April 1842. They had five sons; only the youngest, Henry Theodore, followed family tradition and entered the medical profession, although not into the mental science branch. Monro's first published work was *On Stammering and its Treatment* (1850), an early neurological study published anonymously, possibly because it was a condition from which he himself suffered mildly throughout his life.

Unlike his predecessors, who were physicians to Bethlem Hospital over four successive generations, Henry was, in 1854, appointed joint physician to St Luke's Hospital, the institution which had long been Bethlem's rival and historically something of a thorn in the family's side. Monro was to serve as physician for twenty-eight years. In order to ensure a more constant supervision of patients Monro and his colleague were required to visit patients at St Luke's on alternate days of the week, instead of once a week as had previously been the requirement. After retiring from active service as physician he was elected consulting physician to St Luke's in 1882. Some mark of recognition for his contribution to the speciality is signalled by the fact that he was the first in the Monro family to be elected president of the Medico-Psychological Association in 1864.

Besides his public duties at St Luke's, Monro also enjoyed an extensive private practice and was proprietor of a private madhouse, Brooke House, Clapton, which he had inherited as the family business. In 1841 severe aspersions were cast by Richard Paternoster on Monro's management of this asylum, which he left under the charge of the Misses Pettingal, he 'going only occasionally to Clapton to give general orders and arrange accounts' (Paternoster, 9). Brooke House, licensed for fifty patients, was described as the inverse of the up-to-date, model madhouse: 'old-fashioned and dilapidated', in a 'low and damp' situation, totally devoid of views and with a small high-walled airing court, condemned as a 'green swamp', and with nothing in the way of pleasure gardens for patients to walk in comfortably. Its cells and layout bore much in common with old Bedlam, being mostly 'wretchedly furnished with old-fashioned latticed windows, letting the wind in', defying 'all attempts to keep warm', their 'thick iron bars' underlining the carceral nature of the building (ibid., 30).

Despite such criticisms Monro was an active campaigner for improving the condition of the insane, something he saw as attainable in particular via the expansion of asylum accommodation specifically for the middle classes. His physicianship at St Luke's encouraged the hospital's movement towards the same goal. Indeed Monro was among a number of contemporary reformers who advocated establishing self-supporting asylums for the lower middle classes unable to afford the charges in existing private proprietary asylums. However, this proposal, contained in his *Articles on Reform in Private Asylums* (1852), was never fully implemented. Neither was his appeal for civil responsibility for a patient's detention in a private asylum to be passed from the proprietor to the lunacy commissioner. Other proposals, such as that 'the Commissioners and other public inspectors' should be 'as responsible as possible for the conduct of private lunatic asylums' (p. 2), and suggesting measures for the reform of the education and character of attendants (including increasing their salaries; pp. 74–87), echoed the thoughts of reformers like John Conolly, and were received more sympathetically by the profession in general. The quality of asylum attendants was one of the subjects inquired into by a parliamentary committee on lunacy in the 1850s. But these and other of Monro's proposals were only partially implemented through subsequent lunacy legislation and changes in asylum administration. Monro also lent advocacy to the recommendations of the Alleged Lunatics' Friend Society, including increasing the number of lunacy commissioners and the regularity of their inspections, and enlarging the official reports on private asylums. In this set of proposals Monro added his voice to a volley of early criticisms of the limited work being carried out by the lunacy commission since its establishment in 1845. However, such recommendations were strongly resisted in *The Lancet* and elsewhere by medical professionals concerned about central interference and loss of status for asylum practitioners.

The year previous to the appearance of his *Articles*, Monro had published his major work on insanity, entitled *Remarks on Insanity: its Nature and Treatment* (1851). Published originally in two parts, it was one of a number of contemporary works which were tending to define insanity as essentially a matter of 'deficient' or 'loss of nervous tone' and 'consequent loss of vitality' (or, alternatively, 'nervous and vital depression') and of 'the wear and tear of … ordinary life' (pp. v, 1, 112). Monro argued against the previously dominant and still resilient doctrine that located the pathological seat of insanity in inflammation of the brain. He also dissented from the antiphlogistic therapeutics this theory had justified and which previous generations of his own family had remained wedded to for so long. Contrariwise, for Henry, strongly influenced as he was by the physiological researches of William Benjamin Carpenter (1813–1885), the main foundation of therapy in order to 'subdue excess, and raise depressed tone' consisted in 'air, exercise and diet' (Monro, *Remarks*, vi, 128–44). And he deployed statistics from Bethlem (presumably provided by his father) in support of his arguments. Monro regarded insanity also as a congenital disorder, 'primarily of bodily origin', with attendant exciting causes which were not sufficient 'alone' to account for it (ibid., iv, 20–21). He was disposed to be critical of phrenological theory, and, like J. E. D. Esquirol (1772–1840), he regarded women as much more subject to insanity than men. However, Monro's postulations in this work were, on the whole, relatively unoriginal, as he himself admitted.

In a series of lectures on the nomenclature, classification, and forms of insanity, published in the *Asylum Journal* (1855–6) and later in pamphlet form, Monro publicized his own nosology of insanity. Intent on affording his students a simple, easily assimilable classificatory system, he divided insanity into emotional, notional, intelligential, and motor forms of derangement. In so doing he was careful to chart a middle course between more radical views, such as those of John Abercrombie (1780–1844), which saw insanity as 'a spiritual matter, independent of organic change', and those which vice versa regarded mind as 'nothing more than a function of brain' (Monro, 'Classification', 2–3). There is little evidence, however, that his nomenclature (which was strongly influenced by the work of Daniel Noble (1810–1885) on insanity), had much impact on the thinking of other contemporary specialists.

Monro's philanthropic concerns saw him in 1846 found the House of Charity in Rose Street, Soho, as a home for the destitute; he was also a promoter of the Walton Convalescent Home, founded by his younger brother, Theodore Monro.

Continuing the artistic pursuits of his forebears, Monro took a passionate interest in art and artists, and was a regular attender at Christies picture auctions. He was himself a relatively accomplished artist, and painted a number of self-portraits, some of which survive in the private collection of the Jefferiss family. Henry donated one of these self-portraits, plus others of four previous generations of the Monros, including one he had painted himself of his father, to the College of Physicians. He also took a considerable interest in Scottish history. Monro lived at 13 Cavendish Square, London, but later moved to 14 Upper Wimpole Street, London, and he also had a house at Orchard Leigh, Bonchurch, Isle of Wight. Monro was struck down by the influenza epidemic that was raging in the 1890s, and after a brief illness (worsened by his contracting pleurisy) he died at his Wimpole Street house on 18

May 1891. A memorial service held on the Sunday following at St Peter's, Vere Street, testified to the deep religious sentiment Monro had displayed during his lifetime. He was survived by his wife.   JONATHAN ANDREWS

Sources H. Monro, 'On improving the condition of the insane', *London Medical Gazette*, [3rd] ser., 13 (1851), 751–8, 963–9 · H. Monro, 'On improving the condition of the insane', *The Lancet* (3–17 Jan 1852), 3–4, 33–5, 68–70 [see also *Psychological Journal* (Oct 1851)] · H. Monro, *Remarks on insanity: its nature and treatment* (1851) · review of Monro, *Remarks*, *The Lancet* (23 Nov 1850), 577 · review of Monro, *Remarks*, *The Lancet* (8 Feb 1851), 157–8 · review of Monro, *Remarks*, *London Medical Gazette*, [3rd] ser., 12 (1851), 203 · review of Monro, *Remarks*, *The Lancet* (3 July 1852), 17–18 · H. Monro, *Articles on reform in private asylums* (1852) · H. Monro, 'On the nomenclature of the various forms of insanity', *Asylum Journal of Mental Science*, 2 (1855–6), 286–305 · H. Monro, 'On the classification and forms of insanity', *Asylum Journal of Mental Science*, 3 (1856–7), 193–218 · *BMJ* (6 June 1891), 1282 · *The Lancet* (23 May 1891), 1170 · *Journal of Mental Science*, 37 (1891), 496–7 · W. L. Parry-Jones, *The trade in lunacy: a study of private madhouses in England in the eighteenth and nineteenth centuries* (1972), 23, 100 · R. Paternoster, *The madhouse system* (1841), 9, 30 · Foster, *Alum. Oxon.* · St Luke's Hospital, Woodside, London, archives · *DNB* · *IGI* · Burke, *Peerage* (1857) · *CGPLA Eng. & Wales* (1891)

Archives priv. coll. | St Luke's Hospital, Woodside, London

Likenesses H. Monro, self-portrait, oils, *c*.1848, RCP Lond. · H. Monro, self-portrait, oils, *c*.1870, RCP Lond. · H. Monro, self-portraits, oils, priv. coll.

Wealth at death £20,752 18s. 4d.: probate, 7 July 1891, *CGPLA Eng. & Wales*

Monro, **Sir Horace Cecil** (1861–1949), civil servant, was born on 14 May 1861 at Highmore, Henley-on-Thames, the eldest son of the vicar, Horace George Monro (*d*. 1920), and his wife, Margaret Isabella, daughter of Archibald Hamilton Duthie, rector of Deal. He was educated at Repton School and at Clare College, Cambridge, where he was a scholar. He was placed in the second class in the classical tripos in 1883. He entered the civil service by open competition in 1884 and was appointed to the Local Government Board. He was soon chosen private secretary to the permanent secretary, Sir Hugh Owen, and was afterwards private secretary to successive presidents of the board. In 1897 he became an assistant secretary to the board, and in 1910 permanent secretary.

Monro was a notable administrator, courageous, practical, and patient, ready to listen to suggestions and criticisms, and always concerned to avoid friction and unnecessary expenditure. He was, perhaps, old-fashioned in his distrust of propaganda and in his view that publicity was not the business of a civil servant. His courtesy, unselfishness, and disinterestedness earned him the devotion of those who worked with him and he enjoyed at all times the full confidence of his political chiefs.

A wholehearted believer in local government, Monro was opposed to undue centralization and took pains to establish good relations with local authorities and their associations. This policy did much to ensure smooth administration and bore fruit in the contribution made by local authorities to the solution of many problems arising out of the First World War. Monro's own activities during the war were many and varied, for in the change from peace to wartime conditions his immense knowledge of local government proved invaluable. He did considerable work in the preparation of the Military Service Bill, and he was made a commander of the order of Leopold in recognition of his services on behalf of Belgian refugees. He personally took in hand the arrangements made for dealing with them when war broke out and was later, with Lord Gladstone, primarily responsible for the organization concerned with their welfare. As the war drew to a close he was involved in the planning and arrangements for the general election, which was to be held under the terms of the 1918 Representation of the People Act.

In 1919 the Local Government Board was abolished and Monro retired, somewhat before the usual age. The board's functions were transferred to the newly constituted Ministry of Health, to which Sir Robert Morant was appointed permanent secretary:

> Monro was a civil servant of the old school, competent and industrious, without perhaps great driving power, and certainly without the initiative of his vigorous successor. Of a modest disposition, he used to say genially that such success as he had had in the service had been largely a matter of luck. (*The Times*, 26 April 1949)

In his day the work of the board had embraced many subjects which were now transferred to other ministries. He had, for instance, played an important part in devising the machinery of the first Old Age Pensions Act, 1908, and in the earliest arrangements for the regulation of motor traffic. After his retirement he continued to do much valuable work as chairman of government committees, on many and various subjects, such as the use of preservatives in food, and land drainage, in particular the commission on Ouse drainage. Under his skilful direction these committees did a great deal of pioneer work, much of which forms the basis of existing law and practice.

Monro had many interests outside his official work. He was a member of the 'Corner' at the National Club about which Austin Dobson wrote 'A Whitehall Eclogue'. Sir Owen Seaman, who had been a scholar of Monro's year at Cambridge, was his lifelong friend and Monro for many years attended the weekly dinners of *Punch* to which from time to time he contributed light verse. He had an attractive sense of humour. A man of middle height with the carriage of a tireless walker, Monro was of fair complexion with a pronounced aquiline nose; quite late in his long life there were still a few who continued to refer to him affectionately as Beaker Monro of Clare. For the great part of his days he was a keen botanist and ornithologist—'he was on the friendliest terms with the Whitehall pigeons' (*The Times*, 26 April 1949)—and when failing eyesight and hearing made identification of birds difficult, he continued almost to the end an ardent collector of plants in England and the Pyrenees. He never married, and passed much of his time in the company of his sisters in France.

Monro was called to the bar by the Middle Temple in 1900, appointed CB in 1902 and promoted KCB in 1911. He died on 23 April 1949, at Meadow House, Crowborough, Sussex.   E. R. FORBER, *rev.* MARK POTTLE

Sources *The Times* (4 Nov 1918) · *The Times* (26 April 1949) · personal knowledge (1959) · private information (1959) · Venn, *Alum. Cant.* · *CGPLA Eng. & Wales* (1949)
Archives BL, corresp. with Lord Gladstone, Add. MSS 46078–46083
Likenesses W. Stoneman, photograph, 1917, NPG
Wealth at death £27,367 19s. 9d.: probate, 17 Oct 1949, *CGPLA Eng. & Wales*

Monro, James (1680–1752), physician and specialist in insanity, was born in Scotland on 2 September 1680, the son of Alexander *Monro DD (d. 1698), the Jacobite principal of Edinburgh University, and his wife, Anna Logan (d. 1674). His family moved to London in 1691, after Alexander was removed from the see of Argyll by William III's government. James matriculated as a commoner at Balliol College, Oxford, but was admitted as a commoner and Snell exhibitioner on 13 July 1699, graduating BA on 15 June 1703, MA on 3 June 1708, and BM on 25 May 1709. He did not take his DM degree until 9 July 1722, subsequently pursuing private practice in Greenwich. He was admitted candidate of the Royal College of Physicians on 23 December 1728, becoming a fellow the following year, 22 December 1729, but did not achieve higher office in the college.

James was the first of four generations of Monros who were to hold the post of physician to Bridewell and Bethlem hospitals between 1728 and 1853. Monro was appointed to Bethlem (or Bedlam, England's oldest public hospital for the insane), on 9 October 1728, having failed in his candidature for physician to St Bartholomew's Hospital three years earlier. Monro prevailed over seven other applicants, most of them first-class opposition for this post. Yet Monro was far from unknown, having contributed during the 1720s to one of the first experiments in smallpox inoculation in England.

Monro was to preside as physician at Bethlem for the next twenty-four years. Bethlem's records show that James was a regular presence at hospital meetings, attending roughly three times a week, and presiding over almost every admission. He served on committees responsible for a number of medical initiatives at Bethlem, including the establishment of an infirmary, and a review of the costs and quality of medicines which saw the appointment of a resident apothecary and the erection of an apothecary's shop. His physicianship also coincided with the establishment of incurables' wards for men and women at the hospital.

Monro's attendance at Bethlem met with stinging criticism from some quarters. In 1742 he was sued unsuccessfully before the king's bench by Thomas Leigh, a former Bethlem patient, and was defended at the hospital's expense. The Methodists, led by John Wesley and George Whitefield, expressed particular antipathy for the Bethlem regime during Monro's physicianship. They complained, for example, that they were banned by the Bethlem committee on which Monro normally sat from visiting any patient, 'for fear', commented Wesley sardonically, 'of driving them mad' (*Works of … John Wesley*, 26). Wesley's mother called Monro 'that wretched fellow' (Hunter and Macalpine, *Three Hundred Years*, 423). Wesley himself portrayed the standard medical treatments of bleeding, blistering, and confinement to a dark room, prescribed on Monro's orders, as harsh, useless, and debilitating.

Monro was to publish nothing on madness. His only publication was the Harveian oration he gave before the Royal College of Physicians in 1737, which provides very limited insight into his ideas about medical practice. His silence about the subject of insanity, his lack of commitment to broadening knowledge and debate about madness, as well as his uncritical espousal of traditional evacuative medicaments, were to meet with posthumous censure in the 1758 *Treatise on Madness* of William Battie, physician to St Luke's. Although James's eldest son, John *Monro, jumped to an immediate defence of his father's record, historical assessments have found considerable substance in Battie's charges against the deceased doctor.

By virtue of his Bethlem position Monro was to gain public recognition as an expert on insanity. He was summoned as a witness in a number of controversial legal proceedings on lunacy and idiocy. In the 1740s Monro wrote to the lord chancellor, and testified vainly as to Henry Roberts' sanity, alongside Drs Frank Nicholls and Richard Mead, and the Bethlem governor and apothecary, John Markham. Monro was also approached to vouch before the chancellor for the sanity of Lady Frances Erskine Mar, alongside Mead and Dr John Arbuthnot, in the 1720s.

Rather than any major contribution to medical knowledge of insanity it was probably Bethlem's increasing exposure to the prying eyes of visitors and the preoccupation of Augustan literary satirists and newspaper hacks with madness and folly as metaphors which ensured that Monro became something of a household name. Pope's *Dunciad* immortalized rather ambivalently Monro's role at Bethlem:

Where Folly holds her throne,
And laughs to think Monro would take her down

Physicianships at contemporary hospitals like Bethlem being somewhat honorary, visiting posts, James and all the Monros were to devote most of their time to their more profitable private practice. The reputation of the mad-doctor appears to have been fragile here too. Monro's attendance on Alexander Cruden, the compiler of the long definitive biblical *Concordance*, while the latter was confined in Wright's Bethnal Green madhouse, was to provoke a torrent of published abuse from the disaffected patient. Substantial evidence in Cruden's writings of severe mental disturbance casts some doubt on their reliability as a source, and Cruden also lost the case he brought before the king's bench against Monro and others. However, a deal of mud still sticks to Monro. Monro evidently prescribed medicine for Cruden before he had even seen him and made no inquiry into the ill treatment to which his patient alleged he was being subjected. Nevertheless, the severe mechanical restraint imposed on Cruden was removed on each of Monro's four visits, Cruden once even being 'by Dr Monro's advice, allowed … to walk in the garden'.

Despite such published criticisms Monro seems to have experienced little trouble attracting wealthy clients.

While customers complained about his fees, Cruden accusing him of being grasping and the lawyer Joseph Girdler protesting to Lord Fermanagh about the devouring of his father's estates by the mad-doctor's demands, Monro succeeded in carving out a prosperous private practice to bequeath to his eldest son. Lord Galloway and John Newport, son of the third earl of Bradford, were among James's other wealthy private clients. According to Horace Walpole, James was held in great regard by his father, Sir Robert, for whom he had prescribed and whose patronage must have helped to bolster James's practice.

James had five children with his wife, Elizabeth: two sons, John *Monro (1715–1791) and Thomas, and three daughters, Marion, Ann, and Elizabeth. Ann married the physician George Randolph. James had donated a customary £100 to the charity of Bridewell and Bethlem on being elected a governor in 1747. While he was in ailing health during 1751 his son John was appointed joint physician, virtually securing the Monro succession to the sole physicianship. Monro died on 4 November 1752 at Sunninghill, Berkshire, where he was buried. His assets were bequeathed in two equal shares, one to his wife, and the other divided equally between his two sons and unmarried daughter. He had already provided for his married daughters and their family members, but apologized in his terse will for the guinea he bequeathed to each of them, 'because I do not Expect to dye in Circumstances able to do more'.   JONATHAN ANDREWS

Sources J. Andrews, *The history of Bethlem* (1997) · Munk, *Roll* · Bethlem Royal Hospital Archives and Museum, Monk's Orchard Road, Eden Park, Beckenham, Kent, Bethlem court minutes and sub-committee minutes · A. Cruden, *The London-citizen exceedingly injured* (1739); repr. in A. Ingram, ed., *Voices of madness: four pamphlets, 1683–1796* (1997) · W. Wale, ed., *Whitefield's journals* (1905) · PRO, PROB 11/798, q.n. 302, fols. 250–51 · Walpole, *Corr.*, vol. 5 · J. Munro, *Remarks on Dr Battie's Treatise on madness, by William Battie, M.D., and Remarks on Dr. Battie's Treatise on madness, by John Monro*, ed. R. Hunter and I. Macalpine (1962) [introduction by R. Hunter and I. Macalpine] · Lady Percival, letter to Claude Amyand, 6 Aug 1725; C. Amyand, letter to James Jurin, 16 Aug 1725; J. Monro, letter to James Jurin, 14 April 1726, RS, classified letters: inoculation · R. Hunter and I. Macalpine, *Three hundred years of psychiatry, 1535–1860* (1963) · *The works of the Rev John Wesley*, another edn, ed. J. Benson, 17 vols. (1809–18), vols. 2–3 · *The case of Henry Roberts, esq: a gentleman, who, by unparalleled cruelty was deprived of his estate, under the pretence of idiocy* (1747) · P. de St Pierre, trans., *The sufferings and death of Henry Roberts Esquire* (1748) · J. Andrews, 'Bedlam revisited: a history of Bethlem Hospital, c.1634–c.1770', PhD thesis, U. Lond., 1991 · J. Andrews, 'A respectable mad doctor? Dr Richard Hale, FRS (1670–1728)', *Notes and Records of the Royal Society*, 44 (1990), 169–203 · admission book, Balliol Oxf. · A. Cruden, *Mr Cruden greatly injured: an account of a trial between Mr. Alexander Cruden … and Dr Munro … July 17, 1739, on an action of trespass, assault and imprisonment … to which is added a surprising account of several other persons who have been most unjustly confined in private madhouses* (privately printed, London, 1739) · Foster, *Alum. Oxon.* · D. Leigh, *The historical development of British psychiatry* (1961), 48–9 · Cambridge, Hunter Collection, letter from James Monro entitled 'Success of vaccination against smallpox' · *DNB* · R. Porter, *Mind-forg'd manacles: a history of madness in England from the Restoration to the Regency* (1987) · M. M. Verney, ed., *Verney letters of the eighteenth century*, 2 vols. (1930), vol. 2

Archives Bethlem Royal Hospital, Beckenham, Kent, archives and museum

Likenesses J. M. Williams, oils, 1747, RCP Lond.

Monro, John (*bap.* **1670**, *d.* **1740**), surgeon, was baptized in Edinburgh on 19 October 1670, the third son of Sir Alexander Monro (1629–1704), commissary of Stirling, of Bearcrofts, near what later became Grangemouth, Stirlingshire, and his wife, Lillias Eastoun. He was initially apprenticed on 8 April 1687, the start of the Monro family's involvement with medicine, as a servant to William Borthwick, a leading Edinburgh surgeon. Borthwick at that time could not, under existing regulations, take on any new full apprentices. However, Monro became fully apprenticed to him as surgeon in January 1689, largely as a result of his father's influence over the Incorporation of Chirurgians (later the College of Surgeons). He duly completed his apprenticeship in April 1692. On 11 October 1692 he matriculated at the University of Leiden. This experience was to inspire him with an aim to found a faculty of medicine at Edinburgh University, since no university in Britain had a medical school like those on continental Europe.

Monro returned to Scotland in 1694 and the next year became surgeon to Lieutenant-General Sir Henry Belasyse's 22nd (Cheshire) regiment of foot, where he stayed until 1700. However, he was on active service abroad with the regiment only during the summers, spending winters in London, where he probably practised surgery in the hospitals. He then returned to Edinburgh, where he established an apothecary's shop. He became a burgess of the city on 19 August 1702, a precondition of membership of the Incorporation of Chirurgians of Edinburgh, which would enable him to practise surgery within the burgh. He was elected a member on 11 March 1703. Monro was elected as boxmaster (treasurer) to the incorporation from 1708 to 1710 and as deacon (president) from 1712 to 1714. As deacon he had a seat on the town council of Edinburgh, which controlled many aspects of civic life. He was also deacon convener of the trades in Edinburgh and represented the town on the convention of royal burghs of Scotland. Queen Anne died shortly before his term of office as deacon ended in 1714, and he took part in proclaiming George, elector of Hanover, as king, showing his support. Monro was surgeon to the poor in Edinburgh from 1713 to 1720.

Monro married twice; first, in 1694, Jean Forbes (*d.* c.1710), with whom he had a son, Alexander *Monro primus (1697–1767); and second, in 1721, Margaret Main, *née* Crichton. Monro still retained the idea of establishing a medical school in Edinburgh and arranged Alexander's education with the plan that he should play an important role in any such school. Monro told the physicians and surgeons of Edinburgh of 'a plan which he had long formed in his own mind, of having the different branches of Physic and Surgery regularly taught at Edinburgh, which was highly approved by them' (Craig, 361). Early in 1720 Monro used his power in the Incorporation of Chirurgians of Edinburgh 'to force the two demonstrators of anatomy to resign in favour of his son, who was appointed by the town Council as professor of anatomy on 29 Jan. 1720'

(Morrell, 50). He also encouraged Charles Alston, one of Alexander's fellow students, to amass a collection of plants and to advertise public lectures in Edinburgh which became known as materia medica. Hence the faculty of medicine of Edinburgh University was born.

Monro died at Carolside, near Earlston, Berwickshire, in 1740. ALISON M. STEVENSON

Sources Records of the chirurgians of Edinburgh, Royal College of Surgeons, Edinburgh, 8 April 1687, 9 Jan 1689, 11 March 1703 · R. E. Wright-St Clair, *Doctors Monro: a medical saga* (1964) · J. A. Inglis, *The Monros of Auchinbowie and cognate families* (1911) · R. W. Innes Smith, *English-speaking students of medicine at the University of Leyden* (1932) · W. S. Craig, *History of the Royal College of Physicians of Edinburgh* (1976) · J. Morrell, 'The Edinburgh town council and its university, 1717–1766', *The early years of the Edinburgh medical school*, ed. R. Anderson and A. Simpson (1976), 46–57 · parish register (baptism), Greyfriars church, Edinburgh, 1670
Likenesses W. Aikman, oils, *c*.1712–1713, Royal College of Surgeons, Edinburgh, Sir Jules Thorn Museum · T. Rowlandson, etching, 1784, Wellcome L.

Monro, John (1715–1791), physician and specialist in insanity, was born on 16 November 1715 at Greenwich, Kent, the eldest son of James *Monro (1680–1752), later physician to the Bethlem Hospital, and his wife, Elizabeth. His family were of Scottish extraction, descended from a branch of the house of Foulis. His paternal grandparents were Alexander *Monro (*d*. 1698), Jacobite principal and high-church minister at Edinburgh University, and Anna Logan.

Monro's early education was at Merchant Taylors' School, London. He graduated BA from St John's College, Oxford, on 13 May 1737 and MA on 11 July 1740. The following April, allegedly through the patronage of Sir Robert Walpole, Monro gained election as a Radcliffe travelling fellow, a ten-year appointment requiring the incumbent to pursue the study of medicine on the continent. Monro's medical education commenced at Edinburgh, whence he gravitated to Leiden, the most famous of the continental medical schools, where he attended the lectures of Boerhaave. After taking his BM in Oxford on 10 December 1743 he returned to Europe, living for a period in Paris and spending subsequent years travelling through France, the Netherlands, Italy, and Germany. His DM was conferred on him in absentia by diploma on 27 June 1747. While Monro was in Rome in 1745–6 Horace Mann claimed he was one of a number of 'Jacobites abroad' in the habit of frequenting the pretender's court; his grandfather's Jacobitism evidently continued to taint Monro's early career (Walpole, 191, 196, 400). According to Munk he did not return to England from France until 1751, but the records of Bethlem Hospital make it clear that he spent substantial parts of 1748–52 attending committee meetings at both Bethlem and Bridewell. On returning permanently to live in England, John was made a candidate of the Royal College of Physicians on 25 June 1752, becoming a fellow exactly a year later. In 1757 he presented the Harveian oration. Monro also enjoyed high office for some time at the college, serving as censor in 1754, 1759, 1763, 1768, 1772,

1778, and 1785. Monro had four sons with his wife, Elizabeth: John, Charles, James, and Thomas *Monro (1759–1833), and a daughter, Charlotte.

Monro's career at Bethlem and Bridewell began formally on 21 June 1751, when he was elected as a joint physician to assist his ailing father. He was already familiar with affairs at the united hospitals, having been officiating as a governor since 1748. After the death of his father John succeeded him as sole physician, being appointed on 5 November 1752. Monro appears to have done what was asked of him at Bethlem and Bridewell. He vetted nearly every admission to Bethlem on official Saturday morning 'views' of patients, and visited the hospital three times a week as he was required to do by its rules. Monro probably had an important role in a number of the initiatives at Bethlem which took place in the second half of the century, including substantial overhauls in 1765 and 1769 of the regulations governing the hospital, its officers and servants, and the building of an infirmary for women patients.

Monro's physicianship embraced the period when Bethlem lost a significant part of its virtual monopoly over the institutional treatment of insanity to the rival institution of St Luke's established in 1751. Monro shared in the hostility of the Bethlem governors to its competitor. The first physician appointed to St Luke's was one of Bethlem's very own governors, William Battie, whose *Treatise on Madness* (1758) was replete with veiled criticisms of Bethlem's practice and of Monro's father. Against his inclination Monro was stung into a quick response, but his *Remarks on Dr Battie's Treatise* (1758) has been appropriately characterized by historians as reactionary and rather narrow minded. Repudiating Battie's main motive in publishing a detailed examination of madness Monro argued that such discussions would only confuse a public insufficiently educated to grasp their meaning. For Monro madness was intelligible only via empirical experience, a perspective which rested awkwardly alongside Bethlem's continuing refusal to admit medical students. His judgement that 'madness is a distemper of such a nature, that very little of real use can be said concerning it' has been oft quoted as the encapsulation of hidebound medical negativism towards insanity, although other assessments, including his accompanying statement that 'care … depends on management as much as medicine', were rather more in tune with the subsequent development of the speciality (Monro, 21–3, 35, 38). Battie's and St Luke's ban on unregulated public visiting of the insane met with stonewalling from Monro and Bethlem until the practice was finally curtailed in 1770. Monro had earlier stated in his reply to Battie's *Treatise* that he did not think it advisable for patients to receive visitors—a view he seems to have restricted to his private practice.

Despite enduring tensions between Battie and Monro, employment in the same business required that relations did not become too unsettled. Both doctors presented similar testimony when summoned before the House of Commons madhouses inquiry of 1763. Monro's summons is indicative of his standing as England's premier mad-doctor. However, while he endorsed Battie's earlier testimony as to the need to tighten up regulations governing private madhouses, especially with respect to licensing, committal, and visitation, it was another eleven years before an act of parliament was passed to this effect. Battie gave evidence to the same inquiry in Monro's favour during the controversial case of Mr Wood, who had accused Monro of having illegally detained him in Hoxton madhouse, Battie helping to reveal the plaintiff's insanity. Monro's casebook also records his summons alongside Battie before the court of king's bench in the case of Mrs Hannah Mackenzie, in which false confinement was alleged.

As physician to Bethlem, Monro was required to pronounce on the mental state of a number of famous cases, including Earl Ferrers, who was accused of murdering his factor. Summoned by Ferrers to testify to his insanity before the Lords in 1760, the discomfort Monro displayed in his testimony was more a result of the ill-judged nature of Ferrers's examination, than of forensic inexperience. Monro also gave expert testimony as to the insanity of Richard Hyde, who was accused of riotous assembly and destruction of property in 1780 and acquitted as insane. In addition Monro certified as insane the attempted regicide, Margaret Nicholson. Nicholson's attempt to stab George III in 1786 saw her committed to Bethlem for life, Monro declaring her the worst case he had ever seen.

Three years later Monro received his one and only consultation from the royal court, during the first bout of George III's supposed madness, in 1788–9; Monro never attended the king in person. He assured Sir Lucas Pepys that most cases 'did recover', while in response to Sir Richard Warren's enquiry as to the 'symptoms of incurability', he dictated his opinion from his sickbed in politically expedient terms, careful not to take sides (Macalpine and Hunter, *George III*, 56).

Having, like his father, been appointed to Bethlem in a visiting, quasi-honorary capacity, Monro's hospital duties left him ample time to prosecute a lucrative private practice. Monro's famous private patients included Horace Walpole's nephew, Lord Orford. His private practice is partially documented in an extant casebook which details one year's attendance during 1766 on more than a hundred cases of mental disorder. This source reveals that while Monro attended the aristocracy, prominent city aldermen, politicians, and tradesmen, and their female relations, the majority of his customers were from the middling and lower ranks of society. Monro was particularly well acquainted with John or Jonathan Miles (being mentioned in his will), and with his son (later Sir Jonathan), who ran the enormous Hoxton madhouse where Monro recommended many patients and was in regular attendance. Fully appreciating the rich pickings to be had in the private mad trade, Monro acquired an interest in Brooke House, Hackney, in the 1760s, and after the 1774 act became the licensee. Relinquishing the licence to Mary Hawkins in 1784, Monro retained financial control over the madhouse until his death, while his son Thomas became the licensee on Mary Hawkins's death in 1790.

Hawkins's legacies of around £11,000 in value, including a bequest of £1000 to Monro and his family, are evidence of the prosperity of the business and of the Monros' continuing involvement with it. Beside Brooke House, Monro had also taken over a Clerkenwell madhouse, formerly owned by Battie, which Thomas Monro continued to run for a few years after his father's death. Monro's will left explicit instructions for the preservation of what he saw as his 'business' in his sons' partnership.

Apart from the mad business, Monro was also renowned for his interest in the fine arts, which he had probably acquired while travelling in Europe. He was particularly interested in engraving and its history, and had gathered a substantial collection of books and engravings, which he appears to have bequeathed mostly to his son Thomas, who became an even more zealous patron of the arts. John Monro had helped the engraver Joseph Strutt in the preparation of his *Biographical Dictionary of Engravers*. He was also scurrilously depicted in the combined guise of both art connoisseur and mad-doctor in a Rowlandson caricature which portrayed him examining Charles James Fox (in the guise of a lunatic) with an eye-glass. Monro's casebook shows that artists and members of their households also appeared among his patients. Monro attended Mrs Walker, a servant in the household of the watercolourist and etcher Joseph Goupy, and also visited Elizabeth Moreati, wife of an Italian craftsman brought over by Richard Dalton, art collector, librarian, and antiquary to George III. Monro was also an admirer of classical and more modern literary works, from Horace to Shakespeare, and his research into the latter was of assistance to George Steevens in his edition of Shakespeare's works.

Monro was struck down by a paralytic stroke in 1783, and although he recovered sufficiently to continue to practise he became increasingly infirm and gradually delegated his Bethlem duties to his youngest son, Thomas, who was officially appointed as his assistant in 1787. Thus, as his father had before him, Monro secured the succession to the Bethlem physicianship for his son. Thomas had to wait four years to take on the position. Having retired from city life earlier in the year, John Monro died at Hadley, near Barnet, on 27 December 1791.

JONATHAN ANDREWS

Sources J. Munro, *Remarks on Dr Battie's Treatise on madness*, in *A treatise on madness, by William Battie, M.D., and Remarks on Dr. Battie's Treatise on madness, by John Monro*, ed. R. Hunter and I. Macalpine (1962) · W. Battie, *Treatise on madness*, in *A treatise on madness, by William Battie, M.D., and Remarks on Dr. Battie's Treatise on madness, by John Monro*, ed. R. Hunter and I. Macalpine (1962) · J. Andrews and A. Scull, eds., *Customers of the mad trade: the 1766 case book of Dr John Monro, physician to Bethlem Hospital* (1999) · J. Andrews, *The history of Bethlem* (1997) · Bethlem Royal Hospital Archives and Museum, Monk's Orchard Road, Eden Park, Beckenham, Kent, Bethlem court minutes and sub-committee minutes · A. Cruden, *The adventures of Alexander the Corrector* (1954) · 'A report from the committee appointed (upon the 27th day of January, 1763) to enquire into the state of the private madhouses in this kingdom', *JHC*, 29 (1761–4), 486–9 · letters relating to the illnesses of George III in 1789 and 1811, RCP Lond., MS 3011/46–48 · I. Macalpine and R. Hunter, *George III and the mad-business* (1969) · *Parish of Hackney*, 1, Survey of London, 28 (1960), 63–6 · Walpole, *Corr.*, vol. 5 · PRO, PROB 11/1213, q.n.

32, fols. 256–8 · J. Andrews, 'Bedlam revisited: a history of Bethlem Hospital, c.1634–c.1770', PhD thesis, U. Lond., 1991 · R. M. Christy, *Joseph Strutt, author, artist, engraver, and antiquary, 1749–1802: a biography* (1912) · 'Report from the committee appointed to examine the physicians who have attended his majesty during his illness touching the state of his majesty's health', *JHC*, 44 (1788–9), 6–11, 47–87 · *The whole proceedings on the king's commission of the peace* (1780) [Old Bailey sessions papers] · *State trials*, vol. 22 · R. Hunter and I. Macalpine, *Three hundred years of psychiatry, 1535–1860* (1963) · *GM*, 1st ser., 61 (1791), 1237 · D. Leigh, *The historical development of British psychiatry* (1961) · Nichols, *Lit. anecdotes*, vol. 8 · R. Porter, *Mind-forg'd manacles: a history of madness in England from the Restoration to the Regency* (1987) · N. Walker, *Crime and insanity in England*, 1 (1968) · *The plays of William Shakespeare*, ed. S. Johnson and G. Steevens, 10 vols. (1773)

Archives Bethlem Royal Hospital, Beckenham, Kent, archives and museum · priv. coll., casebook | CUL, Hunter collection **Likenesses** N. Dance, oils, 1769, RCP Lond. · T. Rowlandson, etching, 1784, Wellcome L. · oils, Bethlem Royal Hospital, Beckenham, Kent

Monro, Matt [*real name* Terence Richard Parsons] (**1930–1985**), popular singer, was born on 1 December 1930 in Shoreditch, London, the youngest in the family of four sons and one daughter of Frederick Parsons, druggist packer, and his wife, Alice Mary Ann Reed. He began singing when he joined the army in 1947 at the age of seventeen. He became a tank instructor and divided his time between tanks and talent contests while serving in Hong Kong. It was there that he decided to become a professional singer. After demobilization in 1953 he worked as a long-distance lorry driver, electrician, coalman, bricklayer, stonemason, railway fireman, layer of kerbstones, milkman, baker, offal boy in a tobacco factory, plasterer's mate, builder's mate, and general factotum in a custard factory. Using the name Al Jordan, he took a semi-professional job with Harry Leader and his orchestra. It meant months of travelling from town to town, and for a time he abandoned the work to become a London bus driver instead. However, the desire to become a fully professional singer persisted and he recorded a demonstration disc of 'Polka dots and moonbeams' with a small rhythm section. One of its members was so impressed that it was forwarded to the pianist Winifred Atwell, who arranged a number of important meetings. At this point he decided on a change of name. Terence Parsons became Matt Monro—Matt from Matt White, the first journalist to write about him, and Monro from the first name of Winifred Atwell's father.

For the newly named Matt Monro there followed a series on Radio Luxemburg in 1956, a regular singing spot with Cyril Stapleton's show band, and a recording contract with Decca. However, his career took off almost by accident. The record producer George Martin, of EMI/Parlophone, was at this time making a name for himself in the comedy record field, and was looking for someone to sound like Frank Sinatra for an LP for Peter Sellers, *Songs for Swingin' Sellers*. He chose Matt Monro with his rich, clean-cut baritone voice. Everyone connected with the recording was impressed, especially Martin, who asked if he would like to record under his new professional name (on the LP he had used the name Fred Flange).

Matt Monro (1930–1985), by Larry Ellis, 1966 [on stage at the royal variety show]

Monro's first single, 'These things happen', was followed by 'Love walked in'. His third recording, 'Portrait of my love', which he thought one of the least commercial songs he had ever heard, entered the list of British best-selling records in December 1960 and reached number three. This was followed by further chart successes, including 'My kind of girl', which climbed to number five in 1961, 'Softly as I leave you' (1962), 'From Russia with love' (1963), 'Walk away' (1964), and 'Yesterday' (1965). He was to achieve his final singles chart hit in Britain with 'And you smiled' (1973). Oddly, 'Born free' and 'We're gonna change the world', two of his most requested records on radio programmes, never achieved success in the British best-seller lists, although the former won an Academy award for the best song in a motion picture in 1965. Among his best-known albums were *Walk Away*, *I have Dreamed*, *My Kind of Girl*, *The Late Late Show*, and *Softly*. Monro came second in the Eurovision song contest in 1964 and was voted best male singer in England in 1965.

Monro spent a considerable amount of time in the United States of America, where he turned increasingly to cabaret. His first visit was in 1960 on a special exchange agreement: he sang at the Pentagon in Washington, while Ella Fitzgerald appeared in Great Britain. In 1966 Monro signed with Capitol Records and he resided in the United States during 1967. He was a constant traveller, and appeared in cabaret and concerts in Australia, New Zealand, Japan, Hong Kong, the Philippines, Malaysia, Canada, South Africa, Scandinavia, and most European countries. He travelled approximately 150,000 miles a year.

Monro's hobbies were golf, the cinema, and watching television: he once said that 'the worst fate that can befall me is to be stranded in a town without a television set'. His favourite film was *The Magnificent Seven*. He was a man of great natural charm and was highly respected by his colleagues, including Frank Sinatra, Tony Bennett, and Bing Crosby, who all regarded him as 'a singer's singer'. According to his friend George Martin, best known as the producer of the Beatles, he 'had the rare gift of getting to the heart of a lyric and delivering it in such a way that it became a personal message to his audience'. Occasionally dogged by comparisons to Sinatra in his lifetime, Monro's reputation has benefited from a posthumous reappraisal.

On 15 January 1955 Monro married Iris Patricia Jordan, a textile machinist, the daughter of Frederick Jordan, factory wallpaper dyer. A son, Mitchell, was born the same year. The marriage was dissolved in 1959 and on 15 April that year Monro married Renate Annette Daisy Giles (known as Mickie), the daughter of Adolph (Dolly) Schuller, a dentist. They had a daughter, Michele, in 1959 and a son, Matthew, in 1964. Monro died of liver failure in the Cromwell Hospital, Kensington, London, on 7 February 1985.   DAVID JACOBS, *rev.*

Sources personal knowledge (1990) · private information (1990) · *The Times* (8 Feb 1985) · m. certs. · d. cert. · P. Gambaccini, T. Rice, and J. Rice, *British hit singles*, 10th edn (1995)
Archives FILM BFI NFTVA, performance footage | SOUND BL NSA, performance recordings
Likenesses L. Ellis, photograph, 1966, Hult. Arch. [*see illus.*] · photograph, repro. in *The Times* · photographs, Hult. Arch.
Wealth at death £425,529: probate, 17 July 1985, *CGPLA Eng. & Wales*

Monro, Robert, of Foulis [*called* the Black Baron] (d. **1633**), army officer in the Swedish service, was born in Scotland, the son of Hector Monro and his wife, Anne Fraser, who was the daughter of Hugh, fifth Lord Fraser of Lovat. Monro of Foulis, who was the cousin of the famous Colonel Robert *Monro of Obsdale, became laird of Foulis as a minor upon the death of his father in 1603. Complaints were soon made in Monro's name to the privy council of Scotland: in 1607 a George Ross of Balnagown was charged with not abiding by a contract signed by Monro's father concerning fishing rights. This was only the first of many dealings between Monro and the privy council in Edinburgh, and indeed Monro's behaviour so disturbed two Stuart kings that they both ordered the council to summon Monro to answer charges. During the attempts of James VI and I to control his independent subjects in the highlands and islands Monro's name was always among the 'northern lairds' noted by the council to be under pain of caution from 1609 to 1610 if they harboured any known thieves on their lands. Monro was likewise charged with the liability of apprehending two highland outlaws for murder in 1614.

Between these two events Monro married his first wife, Margaret Sutherland, the daughter of William Sutherland of Duffus: their marriage contract was dated 24 November 1610. However, Margaret died in childbirth in 1616. Shortly after this Monro travelled south and married Mary Haynes in England. Within a year he had used up her fortune of £600 and the couple soon headed for Scotland. *En route*, however, Monro persuaded Haynes to stay behind in Newcastle and promptly abandoned her there to her fate. Despite her desperate attempts to find him she met with silence in Edinburgh and returned to England to give birth to their child, a daughter. Monro soon met and married Marjorie McIntosh, but his irresponsible financial habits led him to resign the lands and barony of Foulis in 1618 and Simon Fraser, sixth Lord Fraser of Lovat, received a crown charter for the lands. This obviously did not sit well with Monro who was again brought up in the privy council meetings. Fraser lodged a complaint with the council against Monro in 1619 for taking armed accomplices and entering his castle by force and taking possession of it. The council's decision was to denounce Monro as a rebel if he did not henceforth leave the property, and as no further reference was made to the matter, it would seem he complied with the demands. Little is known of Monro between 1619 and 1624, although he apparently became a guild burgess of Aberdeen in 1619, and in 1623 his brother was appointed one of the JPs for Inverness and Cromarty. Monro was again involved in duties to apprehend an outlaw the following year, just as his major troubles with the council were to begin.

James VI and I commanded that Monro be called before the council to be tried for charges of bigamy against Mary Haynes in May 1624. A month later the council recorded the king's letter and noted that Monro would receive a summons. However, nothing seems to have resulted from this as Haynes herself petitioned the council for financial relief in November 1625, at which point the whole story of Monro's behaviour emerged. Haynes believed that Monro was living with Marjorie McIntosh on the income of his estate—£900 sterling per annum—and she sought a share of this money. Again no action appears to have been taken, and half a year later the council informed George, Lord Gordon, that he was to apprehend Monro who had been put to the horn at the king's command. Shortly after this Monro was registered as engaged to apprehend another outlaw. In an attempt to escape his predicament Monro tried to join the Scottish recruits being levied for Danish service in June. However, the council wrote to Colonel Sir Donald Mackay and warned him not to take Monro into his company, which was about to be transported abroad.

Monro must have realized his impossible situation and surrendered to the council. He obtained a month-long respite from his horning in order to meet Haynes in Edinburgh and resolve the issue. Monro again was charged to apprehend a number of men accused of stealing cattle, butter, and cheese from Hector Monro of Balgonie. He must have made his escape from Edinburgh because on 29

July 1626 Lord Gordon was once again ordered to apprehend Monro. Haynes resorted to royal intercession a second time. On 3 March 1627 Charles I informed the Scottish privy council that although Haynes had obtained the right to life-rent and escheat from Monro, as an English national she had no recourse to Scottish law and therefore all obstacles for her compensation were to be removed. No further news of this affair appears in the council records, suggesting that Monro must finally have become financially liable for Haynes. He soon escaped to the continent by levying a company in 1628, although he had to cede his commission to John Beaton that year.

Monro began his military career as a private gentleman in the French guards and was once punished for missing his exercise by being made to stand on duty from 11 a.m. to 8 p.m. on a hot summer's day in full battle uniform. Monro then entered the service of the Swedish crown as the colonel of a Dutch regiment, and is noted as commanding two regiments, one of horse and the other of infantry. Monro's regiment was engaged in the vanguard at the battle of Breitenfeld near Leipsig in 1631, along with Sir James Ramsay's forces. His troops also served at Nuremburg and became part of the largely Scottish Green brigade. Monro died from wounds sustained in battle at Ulm in April 1633 and is said to be buried in the Franciscan church at Ulm. On his death the barony of Foulis passed to his brother Hector.   A. N. L. GROSJEAN

Sources military muster rolls, Krigsarkivet, Stockholm, MR 1629/14, 16, 18, 20, 1630/22–28 · G. Lind, *Danish officers, 1614–1662*, no. 1573 [computer database, Danish data archives 1573] · *Reg. PCS*, 1st ser., vols. 7–8, 10–12 · *Reg. PCS*, 2nd ser., vol. 1 · R. Monro, *Monro his expedition with the worthy Scots regiment (called Mac-Keyes regiment) levied in August 1626* (1637); new edn, with introduction by W. S. Brockington (1999) · T. Riis, *Should auld acquaintance be forgot … Scottish–Danish relations, c.1450–1707*, 2 (1988) · J. Grant, *The Scottish soldiers of fortune, their adventures and achievements in the armies of Europe* (1890) · J. Mackay, 'Mackay's regiment', *Transactions of the Gaelic Society of Inverness*, 8 (1878–9), 128–89, esp. 128–9 · T. Fischer, *The Scots in Germany* (1902), 284

Wealth at death estate valued at £900 p.a. in 1625: *Reg. PCS*, 1st ser., vol. 13; 2nd ser., vol. 1

Monro, Robert (*d.* 1675?), army officer, was the second son of George Monro of Obsdale and Catherine Monro, daughter of Andrew Monro of Milntown. His father is said to have died in 1589, but as Robert matriculated at St Andrews University in 1610, and in 1615 was travelling in France to complete his education, it seems likely that he was born in the later 1590s (Monro, 2.75; Mackie). He served in the French army in 1625–6 before enlisting in 1626 under Sir Donald Mackay (later Lord Reay) to fight for the Danes in Germany, being wounded at Stralsund in 1628. By 1629 he had reached the rank of lieutenant-colonel, and when Denmark withdrew from the Thirty Years' War that year he and 1400 other Scots transferred to the Swedish service. Appointed colonel in 1632, he returned to Scotland the following year to raise recruits, and in 1634 he obtained the support of Charles I and the Scottish privy council for the founding of a hospital for old and wounded soldiers, of which he himself would be master for life. Nothing came of the plan, but Monro's

strong sense of the services and sufferings of Scots soldiers abroad led him to commemorate them through an account of the campaigns in which he had taken part: *Monro his Expedition with the Worthy Scots Regiment (called Mac-Keyes Regiment) Levied in August 1626 … Collected and Gathered together at Spare-Houres by Col. Robert Monro …* (1637; reissued in 1644 entitled *The Scotch Military Discipline, as Learned from the Valiant Swede*). Monro has been dismissed as 'a rude soldier' (S. R. Gardiner, *History of the Great Civil War*, 4 vols., 1893–4, 1.115), but his book reveals a man with a great respect for book-learning. However, his erudition all too often leads to ambiguity and ponderous platitudes.

By May 1637, when Monro received permission to levy a further 800 men to serve the Swedes, his earlier services had been recognized by appointment as a gentleman of Charles I's privy chamber. But though Monro had commented on the Danish king being 'of absolute authority in his Kingdome, as all Christian Kings ought to be' (Monro, 1.86), when the covenanters rebelled against Charles I he showed no hesitation in serving the enemies of absolutism. His regiment was the first unit raised by the covenanters, and he helped in the capture of Edinburgh Castle in March 1639. Later in the same year he was on the borders, and from May to September 1640 he was based in Aberdeen, taking punitive action against royalists in the north-east of Scotland. He was then sent to command forces in the south-eastern borders, and when the rest of the army was disbanded in August 1641 his regiment was one of four that were retained.

When it was decided to send a Scottish army to Ireland after the Irish rising of October 1641, Monro was appointed its major-general, under the earl of Leven as general. Landing at Carrickfergus on 3 April 1642 with the first regiments of the army (including his own), Monro joined with 'British' forces (raised by Ulster protestants) and soon cleared much of co. Down of rebels, in a campaign of skirmishes marked by much indiscriminate killing to revenge alleged Irish atrocities. A garrison was established in Newry, and Monro then moved north, driving the Irish out of Antrim, arresting the earl of Antrim, and garrisoning Coleraine. However, Monro's activities were from the first hampered by problems that were to persist throughout his six years in Ulster. His army was supposed to be paid and supplied by the English parliament, but the latter seldom fulfilled its obligations. Moreover, he faced a conflict of loyalties: was his prime duty to Scotland, to his English paymasters, or to the 'British' protestants of Ulster? Already by June 1642 Monro was being blamed for inactivity, and his commitment to attempts to take the strategic Irish stronghold of Charlemont was questioned.

Leven landed in Ireland on 4 August to take up command of the army, which had then reached its full strength of over 10,000 men, but in November he returned to Scotland, leaving Monro to lead a discontented army, many of whose officers were near to mutiny over lack of pay. The year 1643 saw Monro undertaking a number of further expeditions from his base at Carrickfergus, but he again failed to capture Charlemont. Civil war in England was a new restraint on his activities, for both sides considered employing him and his army on the British mainland. The covenanters and parliament contemplated transferring the army to England to fight against the king, while the recapture of the earl of Antrim (who had escaped the previous October) in May 1643 led to the revelation that he had intended to bribe Monro to join his men to an Irish army which would fight for the king in England. In September 1643 the marquess of Ormond, the lord lieutenant of Ireland, signed a cessation or truce with the Irish. The news led Monro to withdraw from a proposed attack on Charlemont, fearing that many of the British commanders in Ulster would obey the truce and refuse to support him.

The plans of covenanters and parliament to employ Monro in England were soon abandoned, for fear of a threat to both Scotland and England from Ireland if his army withdrew. In negotiations on the issue Monro appears to have been forced into a subsidiary role by his army's council of officers, whose priority was redress of their grievances. At first they rejected the idea of leaving Ulster unless they were paid, but when it was decided the army should indeed stay, they switched to threatening to leave unless paid. On 13 February 1644, in spite of Monro's opposition, a meeting of officers decided that the army should return to Scotland immediately, but amid a confusion of orders and counter-orders only three of the ten regiments left Ulster.

Monro's determination to stay in Ireland was probably in part personal. He had married, first, Jean Maver, daughter of Walter Maver of Maverston (Morayshire), some time before 1622, but she died early in 1642 (leaving one son and one daughter), and late in 1644 Monro married Jean Alexander (d. 1670), daughter of William *Alexander, first earl of Stirling, and widow of the second Viscount Montgomery of the Ards. Leaving Ireland would have meant abandoning the Montgomery family estates in co. Down. But the position of his weakened army was precarious. Several garrisons had to be abandoned, and the attitude of many of the British to the Scots was doubtful, for reluctance to fight the Irish was widespread now that the king had agreed the cessation. The covenanters' invasion of England in January 1644 and the Scots army's imposition of the solemn league and covenant in Ulster further intensified tensions between the Scots army and royalist-inclined British. On 9 March 1644 the English parliament appointed the commander of the army (nominally Leven, in effect Monro) to be its commander-in-chief in Ireland, and in May Monro's officers forced him to assert his authority by seizing Belfast, expelling the British garrison. Most of the British then agreed to continue the war against the Irish, and with their help Monro advanced south into co. Meath in June and July, attempting to bring a new Irish army being formed by the earl of Castlehaven to battle before it was fully prepared. Monro had over 10,000 men under his command, more than on any other campaign, but though he threw the Irish into disarray, he failed to force a decisive encounter. When Castlehaven eventually advanced, in August, Monro compelled him to withdraw to Charlemont, and in spite of great scarcity he maintained his army in the field until mid-October, when Castlehaven finally withdrew.

The 1644 campaign partly restored the flagging reputation of Monro's army, but his ability to confront the Irish was soon further diminished by withdrawals of men to Scotland, to resist the successful royalist rising of the marquess of Montrose. One regiment left about the end of 1644, 1400 more men three months later. In August 1645 Monro was ordered to bring his whole army back to Scotland and become commander of all forces there, but the intervention of the English parliament prevented any more men from being sent to Scotland. With victory now in sight in the English civil war, parliament foresaw future conflict with its Scots allies, and wished to limit the resources Scotland had available for intervention in England. It therefore insisted that Monro remain in Ireland, while simultaneously limiting his influence by revoking the 1644 agreement that he act as parliament's commander-in-chief there.

In 1646 the remnants of Monro's army became increasingly isolated. Pleas to send more men back to Scotland continued to be refused through opposition from the English parliament. Monro advanced yet again towards Charlemont in May, and perhaps the political pressures on him to prove his army's value led him to behave with less than his usual caution, attacking an Irish army under Owen Roe O'Neill at Benburb on 5 June. The result of this, the only pitched battle Monro fought in his six years in Ulster, was decisive defeat, with the loss of perhaps a third of his 6000 or so British and Scottish troops. He sought to blame others for his disastrous attack: 'all our army, both Horse and Foot did earnestly covet fighting, which was impossible for me to gainstand, without being reproached of Cowardice', he explained, and 'for ought I can understand, the Lord of Hosts had a controversie with us to rub shame on our faces … till once we shall be humbled' (J. Rushworth, *Historical Collections*, 1701, vol. 4, pt 1, 399). After Benburb, Monro's army stubbornly hung on to north-east Ulster, motivated largely by determination to get its arrears paid before leaving. In 1648 he supported the engagement, whereby Scotland agreed to help the now imprisoned Charles I against the English parliament. His officers and men were divided, but in the end the army sent about 2000 men to Scotland to support the engagement under Monro's nephew George Monro. As a result, George Monck seized Carrickfergus for the English parliament on 13 September, aided by dissident officers in Monro's own army. Monro himself was ignominiously captured in 'bed with his ladye' (*Two Biographies of William Bedell*, ed. E. S. Shuckburgh, 1902, 174), and the remnants of his army disintegrated. He was imprisoned in the Tower of London, and, when his release was ordered on 31 August 1653, his plight was such that he was given £10 sterling to cover the costs of his return to Scotland. However, the confiscated property of his wife, the dowager Lady Montgomery, and his stepson William Montgomery, third Viscount Montgomery, was restored, and Monro evidently spent the rest of his life in their household at

Comber in co. Down. In later years he was described as 'honest, kind Major-general Munro' (*Montgomery Manuscripts*, 213). His wife died in 1670, and Monro's own death probably followed in 1675.

Monro has often been blamed for his failure to achieve more in Ireland, but considering his problems of supply and the conflicting political pressures that he faced, the fact that he maintained his hold on eastern Ulster in 1642–8 was notable. He was repeatedly frustrated in his attempts to engage the Irish in pitched battle—with the disastrous exception of Benburb—by the Irish tactics of dispersing their forces when he took the offensive, regathering them once he had withdrawn. His best memorial is his *Expedition*, and the value of this work as a source was recognized by Sir Walter Scott, for he was much influenced by Monro's book in creating the character of Dugald Dalgetty, the battered old mercenary in *A Legend of the Wars of Montrose* (1819).

DAVID STEVENSON

Sources W. S. Brockington, 'Robert Monro: professional soldier, military historian and Scotsman', *Scotland and the Thirty Years' War, 1618–1648*, ed. S. Murdoch (2001), 216–39 · D. Stevenson, *Scottish covenanters and Irish confederates* (1981) · R. Monro, *Monro his expedition with the worthy Scots regiment (called Mac-Keyes regiment) levied in August 1626* (1637) · R. Monro, *Monro his expedition with the worthy Scots regiment (called Mac-Keyes regiment) levied in August 1626* (1637); new edn, with introduction by W. S. Brockington (1999) · A. Mackenzie, *History of the Munros of Fowlis* (1898) · *Reg. PCS*, 1st ser. · *Reg. PCS*, 2nd ser. · *Reg. PCS*, 3rd ser. · *The Montgomery manuscripts, 1603–1706*, ed. G. Hill (1869) · E. M. Furgol, *A regimental history of the covenanting armies, 1639–1651* (1990) · R. W. Munro, *The Munro tree: a genealogy and chronology of the Munros of Foulis* (1978) · J. D. Mackie, 'Dugald Dalgetty and Scottish soldiers of fortune', *SHR*, 12 (1914–15), 221–37, esp. 224n · J. Spalding, *Memorialls of the trubles in Scotland and in England, AD 1624 – AD 1645*, ed. J. Stuart, 2, Spalding Club, [23] (1851), 122 · S. Murdoch and A. Grosjean, 'Scotland, Scandinavia and Northern Europe, 1580–1707', www.abdn.ac.uk/ssne/
Archives NL Scot., letters to Sir Robert Gordon

Monro, Robert, of Foulis. *See* Munro, Sir Robert, of Foulis, sixth baronet (1684–1746).

Monro, Thomas (1759–1833), physician and patron of art, the youngest son of Dr John *Monro (1715–1791), physician, and his wife, Elizabeth, was born in London. He was the grandson of Dr James *Monro. Educated at Harrow School, under the classicist and divine Dr Samuel Parr, and then at Oriel College, Oxford, he graduated BA on 4 December 1780; MA on 15 July 1783; MB on 24 January 1785; and MD on 24 May 1787. He became a candidate of the Royal College of Physicians on 29 March 1790 and FRCP on 18 April 1791. He was censor in 1792, 1799, and 1812, and Harveian orator in 1799, and he was named an elect in 1811. Monro married (Hannah) Elizabeth, the daughter of the Revd P. Woodcock of Bath, and they had five sons and one daughter. His eldest son, Edward Thomas, was the father of Edward Monro (1815–1866) and Henry Monro (1817–1891); his second son was the artist Henry *Monro (1791–1814). Monro's other children were named Robert, John, Alexander, and Mary. Monro was appointed as physician to the Bridewell and Bethlem (Bedlam) hospitals on 2 February 1792, having served as assistant physician to his father since 19 July 1787. Apart from

this public office, Monro's main source of income came from private practice, he having inherited the management of the private madhouse Brooke House, Hackney, from his father.

Monro's post at the Bethlem, the nation's most prominent madhouse, made him a recognized expert on insanity. With his father, in 1786, he attended Margaret Nicholson, who had attempted regicide. Twenty-five years later, Monro was asked to attend Nicholson's former target, George III, during his second bout of madness in 1811–12, in a joint consultation of independent 'specialists', alongside John Willis and Samuel Foart Simmons. However, the queen's opposition to interference in the king's case ensured that Monro's involvement remained merely that of a passive observer. Some had raised questions as to the delicacy of the king's being attended by the physician of Bedlam, and the king (being blind) was unaware of Monro's presence at consultations as Monro (along with Simmons) remained unannounced. Monro was to charge £500 for his 'frequent' attendance, and for the advice he tendered—much of which he confided to friends during social gatherings, opining almost from the outset that the king's recovery was improbable. Monro was also called on by counsel to give evidence as to the state of mind of John Bellingham, prior to the latter's trial for the assassination of the prime minister, Spencer Percival, in 1812, but he failed to return any answer.

Monro was most notorious, however, for his unconvincing testimony in 1815–16 before the House of Commons committee on madhouses, concerning scandalous abuses at Bethlem. His responses to questioning emphasized the rather supine nature of Bethlem's medical regime, though clearly deeply rooted in long traditions of part-time hospital attendance and antiphlogistic medicine. Monro confessed that patients received little medical treatment beyond spring evacuations, that his therapeutic approach had been entirely derived from that of his father, and that he knew no better. To criticisms of excessive use of mechanical restraint at the hospital, he replied that chains were quite appropriate in an understaffed, public madhouse which was mainly for paupers, though he admitted that 'there is no such thing … in my [private] house' and that 'if a gentleman was put into irons, he would not like it' ('Select committee … better regulation of madhouses', 95). The main charges levelled against him were that he was 'wanting in humanity' towards his patients; that he had 'pursued a course of medical treatment' that was 'indiscriminate … cruel … useless … and injurious'; and that he had been negligent in his attendance and performance of duties at Bethlem; Monro defended these charges in a subsequently published series of *Observations* (originally addressed to the governors in April 1816), but his defence mostly rested on trying to pass responsibility to the hospital's apothecary, John Haslam, and to the governors (Monro, *Observations*, 2–3). The hospital's own records suggest that Monro had been a rather more energetic physician than his critics allowed (Andrews, 73–4), but in 1818 further weight was added to the Commons committee's findings following a publication by an ex-patient, Urbane Metcalf.

As a result of the scandal Monro felt obliged, in June 1816, alongside Haslam, to resign his post, and soon after he left medical practice altogether. Monro had been strongly urged by Edward Wakefield, the major force behind the Commons inquiry, to resign, but had initially resisted, realizing how 'prejudicial' it 'would be … to His reputation as a Physician and probably to Him in other respects' (*Farington Diary*, ed. Greig, 8.59). He was, nevertheless, succeeded by his son Edward, the fourth and last in a 'nepotistic' dynasty of Monros at the hospital (Porter, 123). Apart from his *Observations*, Thomas Monro published nothing on the treatment of insanity.

Monro's activities in the art world were somewhat more to his credit. Inheriting his father's passion and much of his large art collection, Thomas became one of the best-known connoisseurs of his day, as well as a patron and teacher, and an amateur artist. He had himself been a pupil of John Laporte. Encouraging a host of young artists who were later to become household names, Monro has been distinguished as a major founder of the British school of watercolourists. Assisting and training artists in the techniques of landscape watercolour, Monro turned his town house into an evening studio, paying a few shillings and providing supper for artists in return for retaining their work. About 1793 he moved from Bedford Square, where his father had lived until his death in 1791, to the house at 8 Adelphi Terrace. He additionally owned country houses, first at Fetcham, Surrey, and, from about 1805, at Bushey, Hertfordshire, where he also invited artists. Monro was one of the first to recognize the talents of J. M. W. Turner. Among others who benefited from his patronage were Thomas Girtin, John Varley, Joshua Cristall, Peter DeWint, William Henry Hunt, and John Linnell. Monro's roles as patron and mad-doctor blended when he attended John Robert Cozens after Cozens became deranged. Monro arranged the burials of, and erected monuments to, the artist Thomas Hearne, and, in Bushey churchyard, Henry Edridge.

Monro died aged seventy-four at Bushey, on 14 May 1833, and was buried in Bushey churchyard close to other members of his family who had died and whose memory was celebrated in a stained-glass window in the church. His large collection of watercolours, many by Turner, was sold at Christies in June 1833.   JONATHAN ANDREWS

Sources Court of Governors minutes and sub-committee minutes, Bridewell and Bethlehem Hospital, Bethlem Royal Hospital Archives, Beckenham, Kent · T. Monro, *Observations of Dr Monro (physician to Bethlem Hospital) upon the evidence taken before the committee of the hon. House of Commons for regulating mad-houses* (1816) · will, PRO, PROB 11/1819/465, fols. 120–23 · E. T. Monro, diary, priv. coll. · *The Farington diary*, ed. J. Greig, 8 vols. (1922–8) · 'Select committee appointed to consider provisions for better regulation of madhouses', *Parl. papers* (1814–15), 4.801, no. 296 · 'Report from the committee appointed to examine the physicians who have attended his majesty during his illness', *Parl. papers* (1812), 2.5, no. 7 · letters relating to the illnesses of George III in 1789 and 1811–12, RCP Lond., MS 3011, 1–62, esp. 49–56 · J. Andrews, '"Hardly a hospital, but a charity for pauper lunatics": therapeutics at Bethlem during the seventeenth and eighteenth centuries', *Medicine and charity before the welfare state*, ed. J. Barry and C. Jones (1991), 63–81 · Munk, *Roll* · R. Porter, *Mind-forg'd manacles: a history of madness in England from the Restoration to the Regency* (1987) · I. Macalpine and R. Hunter, *George III and the mad-business* (1969); repr. (1991) · U. Metcalf, *The interior of Bethlem Hospital* (1818) · *GM*, 1st ser., 103/1 (1833), 477 · D. Leigh, *The historical development of British psychiatry*, 1 (1961) · A. P. Oppé, *Alexander and John Robert Cozens* (1952)
Archives Bethlem Royal Hospital, Beckenham, Kent, Archives and Museum · priv. coll., diary · RCP Lond.
Likenesses H. Monro senior, pastel drawing, *c*.1810, RCP Lond. · H. Monro, pencil drawing, 1813, BM · J. Henderson, pen-and-ink drawing, BM · H. Monro, pencil and wash drawing, NPG

Monro, Thomas (1764–1815), Church of England clergyman and writer, was born on 9 October 1764, the son of the Revd Thomas Monro of Wargrave, Berkshire. He was a nephew of Alexander Monro primus (1697–1767), and first cousin of Dr Alexander Monro secundus (1733–1817). He was educated in the free schools of Colchester and Norwich under Dr Samuel Parr, and on 11 July 1782 he matriculated at St Mary Hall, Oxford. In 1783 he was elected to a demyship at Magdalen College, which he resigned on his marriage to Sarah Jane Hopewood on 7 June 1797. He graduated BA in 1787 and MA in 1791. He was curate of Selborne, Hampshire, from 1798 until 1800, when he was presented by Lord Maynard to the rectory of Little Easton, Essex. Monro always had a literary bent, and while at Oxford had founded and edited a periodical entitled *Olla Podrida*, which ran to forty-eight weekly numbers. He was assisted in the conducting of this journal by Bishop Horne, then the president of Magdalen College, and it appeared in volume form in 1787 and 1788, with a reprint in volume twenty-eight of Lynam's edition of the *British Essayists* (1827). He also published *Essays on Various Subjects* (1790), and, with William Beloe, a translation entitled *Alciphron's Epistles* (1791). His other works included *Modern Britons, and Spring in London* (1792), and *Philoctetes in Lemnos* (1795), the latter a play published under the name Oxoniensis. Thomas Monro died on 25 September 1815 at the rectory of Little Easton, Essex.

THOMPSON COOPER, rev. M. CLARE LOUGHLIN-CHOW

Sources [J. Watkins and F. Shoberl], *A biographical dictionary of the living authors of Great Britain and Ireland* (1816) · Foster, *Alum. Oxon.* · J. R. Bloxam, *A register of the presidents, fellows … of Saint Mary Magdalen College*, 8 vols. (1853–85), vol. 7, pp. 77, 81 · *GM*, 1st ser., 85/2 (1815), 378 · *N&Q*, 7th ser., 2 (1886), 407, 449–50 · *IGI*

Monroe, Elizabeth (1905–1986), journalist and scholar of the Middle East, was born at the Nurses' Home, Great Malvern, Worcestershire, on 16 January 1905, daughter of Horace Granville Monroe (1872–1933) and his wife, Francis Alice (d. 1932), daughter of the ecclesiastical historian George Thomas Stokes. Elizabeth Monroe's father was rector of Great Witley, Worcestershire, and later, in London, vicar of Wimbledon, and canon of Southwark Cathedral; she remained a loyal member of the Church of England all her life. She was educated at Putney high school and the Society of Oxford Home Students (which became St Anne's College, of which she was to be made an honorary fellow), where she read modern languages, graduating in 1926. She worked for two years (1931–3) in the secretariat of the League of Nations in Geneva and then, in 1933, joined the information department of the Royal Institute of International Affairs, Chatham House. She was there when the Abyssinian crisis blew up in 1935, and an urgent need was felt to tell the public something about a country which Mussolini was determined to grab; the league was rather less determined in trying to stop him from doing so. The result was *A History of Abyssinia* (1935) by A. H. M. Jones and Monroe, she contributing the later chapters. Though produced in a hurry, her share was carefully researched and in a lively style that was to characterize all her writings.

The next year the Rockefeller Foundation gave Monroe a fellowship which enabled her to travel in the Middle East and north Africa, the outcome being her first full book, *The Mediterranean in Politics*, published in 1938 on the eve of a war which was to make that sea and its shores a five-year battleground. In 1938 Monroe married Humphrey Neame (1887–1968), consulting ophthalmic surgeon at University College Hospital. He had two sons from a previous marriage, but they had no children of their own.

On the outbreak of war in 1939 Monroe joined the Ministry of Information, becoming director of its Middle East division. In 1944 she began a long career in journalism, first as diplomatic correspondent of *The Observer* and the next year joining the staff of *The Economist*, where she was to remain until 1958. After 1950 she shared with Albert Hourani in setting up the Middle East Centre at St Antony's College, Oxford. This was a new department of a new college and a new area of the world which had not hitherto been academically institutionalized. Her status was that of a research fellow, but when in 1963 the college decided to admit women she was one of the first two to be so recognized.

Both as a journalist and as an academic—indeed, also as a philanthropist, being much involved in Musa Alami's Arab Development Society, which took boys out of the refugee camps and trained them in agriculture and other useful skills, and in Bir Zeit University at Ramallah—Monroe made regular visits to the Middle East and got to know most of the principal politicians, diplomats, and businessmen there. She now planned to turn this knowledge into a book. Her first idea was to write a study of how the peoples of the area were adjusting old traditions to the challenges of a complex new world, but she decided she lacked the personal experience of Arab societies to justify such an undertaking. Instead she settled on a study of the rise and fall of British power in an area where briefly it had no serious rivals. This resulted in *Britain's Moment in the Middle East, 1917–1956* (1963), that is from the capture of Baghdad and Jerusalem to the Suez catastrophe. In it she wrote

> Forty years is only a moment in the life of a region with a recorded history of four millennia. Britain's time of dominance will seem short in the eyes of later centuries. But to those who took part in it, the moment seemed long enough for the performance of services useful both to Britain and to certain Middle Eastern peoples.

A second edition with a new chapter on post-Suez appropriately entitled 'Nightfall' appeared in 1981. In 1969 Monroe won a Leverhulme research fellowship to write a biography of that dramatic character H. St John Philby, explorer, convert to Islam, friend of Ibn Saʿud, Indian civil servant turned scourge of empire. She sometimes said that she regretted having spent so much time on someone 'subjective to a fault', but *Philby of Arabia*, published in 1973, was another extremely readable book.

At St Antony's, as well as taking infinite pains with the students of all nationalities, mostly engaged in postgraduate work, for whom she was responsible, Monroe took particular joy in arranging for the collection of unpublished papers from many of those who had been principal actors in the events she had described in her books. This grew into a unique archive of photographs as well as documents. She retained an active interest in this collection after her retirement in 1972.

Monroe's house at West Hendred, Berkshire, became a centre known and cherished by many in the 1950s and 1960s. She described her recreation in *Who's Who* as 'entertaining', but that was an inadequate description of all that went on there. She loved company, particularly of the young; she loved finding people jobs and listening to their troubles; she loved gardening, cooking, and embroidery, pictures and music. Small in stature, eager in manner and speech, she retained a modesty which made her truly delighted when recognition came her way—as well as the honorary fellowship at St Anne's College, the Lawrence of Arabia medal from the Royal Society for Asian Affairs in 1980, and the CMG in 1973. She died on 10 March 1986 at the Sutton Veny House Nursing Home, Sutton Veny, near Warminster, Wiltshire.   E. C. HODGKIN

Sources personal knowledge (2004) · *WWW* · b. cert. · *CGPLA Eng. & Wales* (1986)

Archives St Ant. Oxf., Middle East Centre, corresp. and papers | King's Lond., Liddell Hart C., corresp. with Sir B. H. Liddell Hart

Wealth at death £182,131: probate, 1986, *CGPLA Eng. & Wales*

Monsarrat, Nicholas John Turney (1910–1979), writer, was born at 11 Rodney Street, Liverpool, on 22 March 1910, the second son and fourth child of the distinguished surgeon Keith Waldegrave Monsarrat (1872/3–1968), who was of French descent, and his wife, Ada Marguerite, daughter of Sir John Turney, a wealthy leather merchant who was mayor of Nottingham in 1889. His mother preferred the spelling Montserrat, which she recorded on Nicholas's birth certificate and which caused much confusion throughout his life. It was at the family country home in Anglesey that over the years he developed his mastery of sailing and his love of the sea. His elder brother was killed in a cliff fall here in 1908; another brother, born in 1914, died in the Second World War. Monsarrat's early childhood and youth were spent in well-to-do circumstances in Liverpool. He was educated at St Christopher's School for Boys, at The Leas in Cheshire, and at Winchester College, where he was relentlessly bullied. He called his time at school his 'season in hell'. At Trinity College, Cambridge, where he obtained a third class in law in 1931, he began to

Nicholas John Turney Monsarrat (1910–1979), by unknown photographer, 1978

compose short stories. He was articled to a firm of Nottingham solicitors, but was determined to live by his pen.

Monsarrat moved to London with a typewriter and £40 and occasionally slept on the Thames embankment. He had left-wing views: he sold the *Daily Worker* on the streets of London and took part in pacifist marches. He published a number of articles for *Yachting World* and *London Week*, and three novels of little consequence (*Think of To-Morrow*, 1934; *At First Sight*, 1935; *The Whipping Boy*, 1937). He also experimented with the theatre: his play *The Visitor* (1936) starred Greer Garson but closed after a few shows. In 1938 he wrote *This is the Schoolroom*, which related a young man's political development through capitalism and communism. It had the misfortune to appear days before the declaration of war, but it received considerable critical acclaim and (although the sales figures may later have appeared small) sold out its comparatively large edition. He married Eileen Violet Martin Rowland (*b.* 1914/15) on 7 September 1939. They had one son.

With war begun, Monsarrat's conscience directed him to the St John Ambulance Brigade. But the disasters of 1940 changed his mind and when he saw an advertisement advising 'gentlemen with yachting experience' to apply for commissions in the Royal Naval Volunteer Reserve, he put his name forward and was accepted. Within a few weeks he was at sea as a temporary probationary sub-lieutenant on a corvette in the Atlantic. He

remained in the western approaches for the rest of the war, commanding corvettes and, at the end, captaining a frigate as lieutenant-commander; he was mentioned in dispatches. In 1953 he received the Coronation Medal. During his service he wrote three small books about his ships which were brought together in one volume, *Three Corvettes* (1945). In contrast *Leave Cancelled* (1945), a novella about a British officer's wartime honeymoon, provoked both censure and praise for its sexual content.

On his release in 1946 Monsarrat went into government service and was appointed director to open the UK information office in Johannesburg, where he remained until 1953. Towards the end of this time he was required to answer questions about Mau Mau atrocities in Kenya. He refused to be pressed by the world's journalists into giving an account of what he had witnessed.

Monsarrat wrote two more books before his life changed radically: *Depends What You Mean by Love* (1947) and *My Brother Denys* (1948). In 1951 *The Cruel Sea*, the novel on which he had spent three years, appeared. It was an overwhelming success throughout the world and won the Heinemann award for literature in 1952. But popular acclaim always exceeded critical praise: Monsarrat was a fine observer of physical surroundings but critics noted that he seemed uninterested in psychological drama. By 1981 his English publishers alone had sold over 1,330,000 copies of *The Cruel Sea* in hardback—there having been no cheap edition. Sales figures were similar around the world, and it was filmed in 1953, starring Jack Hawkins in the role of the captain of the ill-fated corvette. Monsarrat was immediately a wealthy man, enjoying an affluence greater than that in which he had been brought up as a child, and he unashamedly set out to enjoy every moment of it. *The Story of Esther Costello* (1953) followed and received mixed reviews for its treatment of a deaf, dumb, and blind Irish girl exploited by an American woman. In 1952 he was divorced and in the same year married the South African journalist Philippa Crosby. They had two sons.

In 1953 Monsarrat was transferred to Ottawa as British information officer, where he remained until 1956, when he resigned to devote the rest of his life to writing. He bought an island in the middle of St Lawrence Seaway, Canada, on which he lived for a while. Before he retired from public service he occupied various offices: a councillor of Kensington borough council in London, 1946; chairman of the National War Memorial Health Foundation (South Africa), 1951–3; a governor of the Stratford Festival of Canada, 1956; and a director of the board of the Ottawa Philharmonic Orchestra, 1956. In 1956 he fictionalized his experiences in South Africa in *The Tribe that Lost its Head*, an attempt to deal with racial conflicts which does not now stand up to political scrutiny. *The Ship that Died of Shame* (1959) confirmed him as a skilled practitioner of adventure fiction. His most impressive work of this period, however, was his two volumes of autobiography, *Life is a Four-Letter Word* (1966–70), and *The Master Mariner* (1978), an innovative and epic but unfinished series of novels based on a favourite subject which told of a sailor condemned to sail the seas for ever.

Monsarrat was a handsome man of medium height, dark with blue eyes. He was quiet—even the barbs of his uproariously sardonic sense of humour reached their target in a low tone—but wilful. Publicly, when he had brushes with the media, he could be abrasive but he emerges from his autobiographies as a romantic who realizes he is out of place in the present.

In 1961 Liverpool mounted in the City Library a one-man exhibition of Monsarrat's work: the first time it had so honoured one of its sons; happily his father, at nearly ninety the doyen of the city's surgeons, was able to be present. Monsarrat was also a fellow of the Royal Society of Literature. Monsarrat's second marriage was dissolved in 1961 and on 22 December of that year he married Ann Griffiths (b. 1937/8), journalist, the daughter of a chartered accountant.

Monsarrat went to Gozo in Malta in the late 1960s to research for *The Kapillan of Malta*. He found the island so agreeable that he decided to linger for a while, writing and gardening. But eventually his health declined and his wife brought him back to die of cancer in King Edward VII Hospital for Officers, Beaumont House, Beaumont Street, London, on 8 August 1979. After cremation at Golders Green his ashes were scattered at sea by the Royal Navy. He left the second volume of *The Master Mariner* unfinished.

DESMOND FLOWER, *rev.* CLARE L. TAYLOR

Sources B. Oldsey, ed., *British novelists, 1930–1959*, 2 pts, DLitB, 15 (1983) · N. Monsarrat, *Life is a four-letter word*, 1 (1966) · N. Monsarrat, *Monsarrat at sea* (1975) · m. certs. · d. cert. · *The Guardian* (11 Aug 1979) · *Daily Telegraph* (9 Aug 1979)

Archives Lpool RO, corresp. and literary papers

Likenesses E. I. Halliday, portrait, 1929, repro. in N. Monsarrat, *Life is a four-letter word* · photographs, 1953–78, Hult. Arch. [*see illus.*]

Wealth at death £57,708: administration with will, 1 Feb 1980, CGPLA Eng. & Wales

Monsell, Bolton Meredith Eyres, first Viscount Monsell (1881–1969), politician, was born at home at Hamble Cottage, Hamble, Hampshire, on 22 February 1881. His Anglo-Irish ascendancy family was a branch of the Monsells of Tervoe, who had settled in co. Limerick in 1644 and were represented in the senior line by the extinct barons Emly. His father, Bolton James Alfred Monsell (1840–1919), was an army officer and then chief constable of the Metropolitan Police from 1886 to 1910, and his mother, Mary Beverley Ogle (d. 1929), was the second daughter of General Sir Edmund Ogle, sixth baronet; Monsell was the younger of their two sons in a family of six children. Although his father had an army background, Monsell was destined for the senior service. After preparatory schooling at Stubbington House, Fareham, he entered HMS *Britannia* as a cadet in 1894. He went to sea as a midshipman in 1896 and specialized as a torpedo lieutenant in 1903, but his marriage to an heiress brought his naval career to a close. On 3 December 1904 he wed Caroline Mary Sybil (1881–1959), the only child of Henry William Eyres of Dumbleton Hall, near Evesham in Worcestershire. The names were joined together as Eyres Monsell, and the match enabled him to retire from the navy in 1906 and embark instead upon a political career.

Monsell was elected Conservative MP for Evesham in January 1910, and in the following year became a whip at the suggestion of Bonar Law. During the war he returned to active duty in the navy, and was awarded the order of the Nile for service in Egypt in 1915 before being promoted to commander in 1917. Monsell became deputy chief whip, as treasurer of the household, on 5 February 1919. On 1 April 1921 he moved to the Admiralty, where he was civil lord up to the fall of the coalition and then parliamentary and financial secretary. He was on good terms with Stanley Baldwin, who sat for the adjacent Bewdley division, and with other Conservative anti-coalitionists. It was therefore not surprising that Bobby (as he was known to his friends) should be chosen as chief whip when that post became vacant shortly after Baldwin's succession to the Conservative leadership. Monsell was sworn of the privy council on 7 July 1923 and took over as chief whip on 25 July.

Monsell served as chief whip for more than eight years, and was considered one of the most successful holders of this office. He possessed enormous charm and impeccable manners, was amusing and intelligent, and liked to be liked. Noted as being the best-dressed man in the House of Commons, he was tall, elegant, and strikingly handsome. He was cultivated and sociable, and enjoyed the parties of the 'smart set' and the company of women, but he was also very particular and easily bored, when a sardonic note might surface. He enjoyed yachting and holidays at friends' houses on the Mediterranean. He also loved life in the country, where shooting was his favourite pursuit; he took great trouble in shaping the Dumbleton woods into one of the best and most difficult shoots in the country.

Monsell enjoyed his work as chief whip, and was closely consulted by Baldwin on appointments and parliamentary strategy. Under his command the whips' office ran with smooth efficiency; in the 1924–9 parliament the huge Conservative majority was organized in a rota system which gave MPs some leisure while ensuring a government majority. Although Monsell was normally a patient man, tempers can fray in the summer heat and in July 1928 his exasperation with Sir Basil Peto, a notably awkward 'die-hard', led to the unusual step of withdrawing the whip for several months. This explosion was untypical: dissidents were normally handled with 'a nice admixture of polite persuasion and hints of party discipline', applying 'the spur and bridle, when needed, with a deft touch' (*The Times*, 24 March 1969). He encouraged the development of both the 1922 committee and the party's official back-bench committee system which began in 1924. He faced a more difficult period while the Conservatives were fractious and dispirited in opposition between 1929 and 1931. Dissatisfaction with Baldwin's leadership and policy, whipped up by the press lords, led to two party meetings being held in 1930, the first of which Monsell chaired. The critics were outmanoeuvred, but unrest continued into the spring of 1931. Monsell, who had been knighted on 28 June 1929, acted as chief whip during the first emergency National Government and then joined the cabinet as first lord of the Admiralty on 5 November 1931.

The longest-serving first lord of the 1930s, Monsell began by restoring confidence after the shock of the Invergordon mutiny (September 1931) and the uncertainty of Sir Frederick Field's period as first sea lord (1930–33). In 1932 Monsell decided to replace him with the outstanding service figure of the 1930s, Admiral Sir Ernle Chatfield, with whom he established a good working relationship based on mutual respect for their complementary roles. Under the economic pressures of the early 1930s, Monsell 'had to struggle on behalf of the Navy against his old friends in the Cabinet, a severe trial to his nature'. By the end of his tenure, a programme of replacement and expansion had begun. In Chatfield's view 'no one could have done more, few could have achieved so much' (Chatfield, 2.98).

The Anglo-German naval agreement of 1935 was the most controversial event of Monsell's career. Although he signed it on Britain's behalf, it originated as a German offer and was shaped by many hands. The agreement was attacked by Churchill at the time and in his memoirs, and for many years after the Second World War it was regarded as a defining example of the folly of appeasement. The terms negotiated allowed Germany to build up to same strength in submarines, but her overall naval tonnage was limited to only 35 per cent of Britain's. Recent research has suggested that the Admiralty was mainly concerned with countering the danger that Germany would build large surface warships, and in this respect the agreement was successful. The German navy never posed a serious surface threat in the Second World War, while no treaty could have prevented the rapid building of submarines in wartime.

Monsell's intention to retire had been known since the middle of 1935, but he was persuaded to remain owing to the approaching international naval disarmament conference; as this met in London, he had the further burden of acting as its chairman. He retired from the House of Commons at the 1935 general election, and was raised to the peerage as Viscount Monsell on 30 November 1935. He eventually stood down as first lord on 5 June 1936, by which time the negotiations for the London naval treaty had been concluded. The conference failed to secure any significant disarmament, but even a partial continuation of the Washington treaty system had some advantages and was better than an unbridled naval arms race.

From 1941 to 1945 Monsell served as regional controller of civil defence for south-east England. He had one son and three daughters, but was something of a remote figure to his children. By the late 1940s his first marriage was effectively over, and he did not defend his wife's suit for divorce on grounds of adultery. A decree *nisi* was granted on 25 May 1950, and exactly two months later Monsell remarried. His second wife, Essex Leila Hilary (1907–1996), was a granddaughter of the first earl of Ypres and daughter of Lieutenant-Colonel Edward Gerald Fleming French; her marriage to Captain Vivyan Drury of Castle Kevin, co. Wicklow, was dissolved in 1935. Monsell died on 21 March

1969, and was cremated at a ceremony held on 28 March, after which the ashes were scattered at sea from a warship. He was succeeded by his only son, Henry Bolton Graham Eyres Monsell (*b.* 1905), who died unmarried in 1993 and the title became extinct. STUART BALL

Sources private information (2004) [Hon. Mrs Joan Leigh Fermor] · *Parliament and politics in the age of Baldwin and MacDonald: the Headlam diaries, 1923–1935*, ed. S. Ball (1992) · T. Jones, *Whitehall diary*, ed. K. Middlemas, 2 (1969) · *The Times* (24 March 1969) · N. Chamberlain, diary, U. Birm. L., Neville Chamberlain MSS · A. E. M. Chatfield, *The navy and defence: the autobiography of Admiral of the Fleet Lord Chatfield*, 2: *It might happen again* (1947) · S. W. Roskill, *The period of reluctant rearmament, 1930–1939* (1976), vol. 2 of *Naval policy between the wars* · J. Maiolo, *The Royal Navy and Nazi Germany, 1933–1939* (1998) · S. Ball, *Baldwin and the conservative party* (1988) · K. Martin, ed.: *a second volume of autobiography, 1931–1945* (1968) · b. cert. · GEC, *Peerage* · Burke, *Peerage* (1967)

Archives NRA, papers | NMM, Chatfield MSS · PRO, corresp. with Sir Roger Keyes, ADM 230 · U. Cam., Baldwin MSS

Likenesses Fayer, photograph, NPG

Wealth at death £106,074: probate, 25 July 1969, *CGPLA Eng. & Wales*

Monsell [*née* O'Brien], **Harriet** (1811–1883), founder of the Community of St John Baptist, Clewer, was seventh of the nine children of Sir Edward O'Brien, fourth baronet, of Dromoland in co. Clare, and his wife, Charlotte, *née* Smith, whose father was an attorney. She had three sisters and five brothers, one of whom was William Smith *O'Brien MP (1803–1864). Like her sisters, she was educated at home by governesses. Following the death of her father in 1837, she married on 21 September 1839 Charles Monsell, third son of the Revd Thomas Bewley Monsell, archdeacon of Derry and rector of Dunboe, and subsequently accompanied her husband to Oxford, where he studied for ordination. Here they were influenced by the Tractarian movement, Dr Pusey becoming a friend. Six years after his ordination Charles Monsell developed consumption, and he and Harriet left Ireland for Italy, where he was to recuperate. While there a friendship with William and Catherine Gladstone flourished, which continued throughout Harriet's life. Charles died in Naples on 20 January 1851, aged thirty-four; Harriet was forty.

A devout woman, Harriet Monsell dedicated her life to God's service at Charles's deathbed, and on returning to England she became companion to her invalid sister Katherine (*d.* 1865), whose husband the Revd Charles Amyand Harris was a curate in the parish of Clewer. With the support of the rector of Clewer, Thomas Thellusson Carter, Mariquita Tennant had founded in 1849, in the nearby garrison town of Windsor, the Clewer House of Mercy for women seeking moral refuge, but early in 1851 ill health had forced her retirement. Here Harriet Monsell saw her vocation. With Carter she refounded the House of Mercy as a sisterhood dedicated to rescue work. She was clothed as a Sister of Mercy on Ascension day, 29 May 1851—the only member of the sisterhood. Two others soon joined and on 30 November 1852 she was installed as mother superior. The Community of St John Baptist grew rapidly, numbering 200 sisters by the time of her death in 1883. The work came to include orphanages, hospitals, schools,

Harriet Monsell (1811–1883), by Sir Frederic William Burton

and parish missions in many places, including America and India.

With Carter as warden, Harriet Monsell as mother superior, and Samuel Wilberforce, bishop of Oxford, as visitor, the community developed along soundly Anglican lines. Harriet Monsell's personality drew women to Clewer, many of whom were from titled backgrounds (as indeed was she, having been granted the courtesy title 'the Honourable' in 1862). Henry Woodyer's vast Gothic revival buildings which arose between 1855 and 1881 were a testimony to the growing importance of sisterhoods in the church. During her twenty-five years as superior Harriet Monsell grew in stature: her counsel was available to all at Clewer, both sisters and women in the penitentiary, and her opinion was sought and respected by churchmen at all levels, including Gladstone (who referred many 'rescue' cases to Clewer), Lord Addington (whose daughter joined the community), and Dr J. M. Neale. She was also widely consulted by those founding other communities. She was cousin by marriage to Archbishop Tait, whose friendship she cherished and whom she admonished more than once for his treatment of high-church clergy. In 1864 Queen Victoria made a private visit to the House of Mercy and was impressed with all she saw, confiding to her journal (6 July 1864) that 'Mrs Monsell the Mother Superior is an excellent person'. At a time when sisterhoods were still controversial, Harriet Monsell did much to allay suspicion and win respect.

Age brought increasing ill health, and in 1875 Harriet Monsell resigned as superior and retired to Folkestone, where the sisters had work and where her interest in the community continued. She died peacefully on 25 March (Easter Sunday) 1883 and was buried at Folkestone on 30 March. St Saviour's, Folkestone, a mission church in which she had shown great interest, was eventually completed as her living memorial. VALERIE BONHAM

Sources V. Bonham, *A place in life: the Clewer House of Mercy, 1849–83* (1992) · T. T. Carter, *Harriet Monsell: a memoir* (1884) · Gladstone, *Diaries*

Archives Community of St John Baptist, Clewer, Berkshire | Clwyd RO, Gladstone–Glynne MSS, G-G 814 · LPL, letters to A. C. Tait

Likenesses F. W. Burton, portrait, priv. coll. [*see illus.*] · photographs, Community of St John Baptist, Clewer, Berkshire

Monsell, John Samuel Bewley (1811–1875), hymn writer, was born at St Columb's, Londonderry, on 2 March 1811, the son of Thomas Bewley Monsell, archdeacon of Derry and precentor of Christ Church Cathedral, and brother-in-law of Harriet Monsell. He entered Trinity College, Dublin, graduating BA in 1832, and LLB and LLD in 1856. He was ordained deacon in 1834 and priest in 1835, and was successively chaplain to Bishop Richard Mant (1776–1845); chancellor of the diocese of Connor; rector of Ramoan, co. Antrim; vicar of Egham, Surrey (1853–70); and rector of St Nicholas, Guildford (1870–75). He died on 9 April 1875, at Guildford, after being struck by a stone falling from the roof of his church, then in the course of reconstruction. He left at least one son.

Monsell was a prolific writer, producing eleven volumes of verse, which included 300 hymns, 70 of which came into common use. A fine preacher of happy disposition, he urged that hymns should be fervent and joyous, and that congregations should abandon their sense of distance and reserve in singing. From this reasoning emerged those hymns for which he is best known: 'O worship the Lord in the beauty of holiness' and 'Fight the good fight with all thy might'. He also believed in spontaneity in writing and relevance to parish concerns; as he stated in his preface to *Parish Musings* (1850), his work consisted of 'the unpremeditated aspirations and utterances of the heart of one engaged in the active service of parish labour'. Monsell was also a writer who felt a compulsion to edit; therefore various versions of his hymns exist. His most important collections of hymns are *Hymns and Miscellaneous Poems* (1837), *Spiritual Songs* (1857), *Hymns of Love and Praise for the Church's Year* (1863), and *The Parish Hymnal* (1873). D. J. O'DONOGHUE, *rev.* LEON LITVACK

Sources F. P. Green, 'J. S. B. Monsell (1811–1875)', *Hymn Society Bulletin*, 133 (June 1975), 120–22 · J. Julian, ed., *A dictionary of hymnology*, rev. edn (1907); repr. in 2 vols. (1915) · M. Frost, ed., *Historical companion to 'Hymns ancient and modern'* (1962) · J. Miller, *Singers and songs of the church* (1869) · J. I. Jones and others, *The Baptist hymn book companion*, ed. H. Martin (1962) · J. Moffatt and M. Patrick, eds., *Handbook to the church hymnary, with supplement*, 2nd edn (1935) · K. L. Parry, ed., *Companion to 'Congregational praise'* (1953)

Archives BL, corresp. with W. E. Gladstone, Add. MSS 44363–44436 · Keble College, Oxford, letters to H. P. Liddon · U. Reading L., letters to George Bell & Sons

Wealth at death under £5000: probate, 7 July 1875, *CGPLA Eng. & Wales*

Monsell, William, first Baron Emly (1812–1894), politician, born on 21 September 1812, was the only son of William Monsell (*d.* 1822) of Tervoe, co. Limerick, who married in 1810 Olivia, second daughter of Sir John Allen Johnson Walsh of Ballykilcavan, Queen's county. Monsell was educated at Winchester College from 1826 to 1830, and among his schoolfellows were Roundell Palmer (afterwards earl of Selborne) and W. G. Ward. On 10 March 1831 he matriculated from Oriel College, Oxford, but he left the university without taking a degree. On 11 August 1836 he married Anna Maria Charlotte Wyndham Quin (1814–1855), daughter of Windham Henry Wyndham Quin, the second earl of Dunraven and his wife, Caroline. She died childless at St Leonards, Sussex, on 7 January 1855.

At the general election in August 1847 Monsell was returned to parliament for the county of Limerick, and represented it, as a moderate Liberal, without a break until 1874. A member of the Tractarian lay organization, the Engagement, he joined the Roman Catholic church in 1850 over the Gorham judgment, and subsequently spoke as the leading representative of its hierarchy. In 1855 he married, in Paris, Berthe, the youngest daughter of the comte de Montigny Boulainvilliers and his wife, Victoire. He became a close friend of J. H. Newman and was associated with Montalembert's liberal Catholic movement, contributing articles to the *Home and Foreign Review*.

As a resident and conciliatory landlord Monsell was popular with his tenantry, and in the House of Commons he promoted the cause of agricultural reform. His prominence in parliament is shown by his selection to propose the re-election of Speaker Denison in 1866. Monsell filled many offices but never reached the cabinet. He was clerk of the ordnance from 1852 until the office was abolished in February 1857, and from that date to September 1857 was president of the Board of Health. On 13 August 1855 he was sworn a privy councillor. For a few months (March to July 1866) he was vice-president of the Board of Trade and paymaster-general. He served as under-secretary for the colonies from December 1868 to the close of 1870, and as postmaster-general from January 1871 to November 1873. His name is identified with the abortive scheme for the establishment of an Irish national university which Gladstone had brought forward in 1873, and on 12 January 1874 Gladstone raised him to the peerage as Baron Emly.

With the rise of the Land League, Emly lost his popularity. He opposed the movement for home rule (though he did not vote in the Lords division in 1893) and he was accordingly removed from the chairmanship of the board of poor-law guardians. He had been high sheriff of Limerick in 1835, and he was made lord lieutenant of the county in 1871. He was also vice-chancellor of the Royal University of Ireland.

Emly died at Tervoe on 20 April 1894, and was buried in the family vault at Kilkeedy. His second wife died on 4 November 1890, leaving one son, Thomas, who succeeded to the peerage, and one daughter.

W. P. COURTNEY, *rev.* H. C. G. MATTHEW

Sources *The Times* (21 April 1894) · W. Ward, *William George Ward and the Catholic revival* (1893); repr. (1969) · *The Tablet* (28 April 1894) ·

William Monsell, first Baron Emly (1812–1894), by John & Charles Watkins

GEC, *Peerage* · J. Garnett and C. Matthew, eds., *Revival and religion since 1700: essays for John Walsh* (1993) · Gladstone, *Diaries* · R. Palmer, first earl of Selborne, *Memorials*, ed. S. M. Palmer, 2 pts in 4 vols. (1896–8)

Archives NA Ire., corresp. · NL Ire., corresp. | Birmingham Oratory, corresp. with J. H. Newman · BL, corresp. with Lord Aberdeen, Add. MSS 43249–43253 · BL, corresp. with W. E. Gladstone, Add. MS 44152 · Bodl. Oxf., letters to Lord Kimberley · Limerick University Library, letters to Lord Dunraven · PRO NIre., Dunraven MSS · PRO NIre., Emly MSS · PRO NIre., corresp. with Lord O'Hagan · U. Nott. L., letters to duke of Newcastle

Likenesses Ape [C. Pellegrini], chromolithograph caricature, NPG; repro. in *VF* (11 Feb 1871) · Faustin, chromolithograph caricature, NPG · J. & C. Watkins, photograph, NPG [*see illus.*] · R. Taylor, wood-engraving (after photograph by London Stereoscopic Co.), NPG; repro. in *ILN* (11 Feb 1871)

Wealth at death £6244 7s. 3d.: probate, 10 July 1894, CGPLA Eng. & Wales

Monsey, Messenger (*bap.* 1694, *d.* 1788), physician, was baptized in the parish of Hackford with Whitwell, Norfolk, on 30 October 1694, the eldest son of Robert Monsey, sometime rector of Bawdeswell, Norfolk, but ejected as a nonjuror, and his wife, Mary, daughter of the Revd Roger Clopton. (The family name Monsey or Mounsey may have Norman origins.) Monsey was educated at home, and later at Pembroke College, Cambridge, where he graduated BA in 1714. He studied medicine at Norwich under Sir Benjamin Wrench, and was admitted as an extra-licentiate of the College of Physicians on 30 September 1723. He then

Messenger Monsey (*bap.* 1694, *d.* 1788), by Mary Black and Thomas Black?, 1764

settled in practice at Bury St Edmunds, never earning more than £300 p.a. While at Bury, Monsey had the good fortune to marry a wealthy widow (*d.* before 1788), and to be called in to attend the earl of Godolphin, who had been taken ill on a journey. Monsey recommended himself so well by his skill or by his wit (despite the latter's being considered gross and inelegant) that Godolphin induced him to go to London and ultimately obtained for him the appointment of physician to Chelsea Hospital. Monsey held this post until his death.

Through Godolphin's influence Monsey was introduced to Sir Robert Walpole, Lord Chesterfield, and other members of the whig party, whose principles he supported. Always eccentric and coarse-mannered, he treated his noble patrons with ostentatious familiarity. Walpole once asked how it was that no one but Monsey ever contradicted him or beat him at billiards; 'They get places,' said Monsey (*Life and Eccentricities*, 29). Monsey also acquired literary connections. For many years he and the earl of Bath were rivals for the affections of the literary hostess Mrs Elizabeth Montagu, with whom Monsey was reported to be in love. Monsey's friendship with David Garrick was broken off after a quarrel, and he was never in favour with Dr Johnson, who disapproved of his loose conversation. His rhymed letters to Mrs Montagu, in the style of Swift, show him to have been a lively correspondent.

In religion Monsey was a freethinker. Late in life his increasing eccentricity made him the subject of innumerable anecdotes. Noted for his 'disgusting language', 'unseemly deportment', and 'vitiated taste' (*Life and Eccentricities*, 106), it is reported that in his old age he was wont

to receive with savage delight those who hoped to succeed him as physician at Chelsea Hospital. When they came to inspect the place, Monsey was inclined to prophesy to each that he would die before him, and in most cases his predictions proved correct. He quarrelled with his colleagues, and eventually lived the life of a morose hermit in Chelsea College. He had given directions that his body was to be dissected after death and the remnants thrown away. On 12 May 1787, when seriously ill, and thinking that he was about to die, he wrote to William Cruikshank, the anatomist, begging him to dissect his body after death, as he was afraid that his own surgeon, Mr Forster, would not arrive from Norwich in time to carry out the task. Monsey died at Chelsea College on 26 December 1788. The post-mortem examination was, it is said, performed by Mr Forster before the students of Guy's Hospital.

Despite having lost money in investments during his lifetime, Monsey was still able to leave his only daughter £16,000. In 1868 a memorial to him was erected in the church at Hackford, Norfolk, but he is now mostly remembered as the possessor of a wit which was not a 'keen, shining, well-tempered weapon', but more like a sabre 'which at the same time that it cuts down by the sharpness of its edge, demolishes by the weight of the blow' (*Life and Eccentricities*, 106). J. F. PAYNE, *rev.* MICHAEL BEVAN

Sources *A sketch of the life and character of the late Dr Monsey* (1789) · *Life and eccentricities of the late Dr Monsey FRS* (1804) · Munk, *Roll* · J. C. Jeaffreson, *A book about doctors* (1860) · J. Doran, *A lady of the last century* (1873) · Venn, *Alum. Cant.*
Archives Norfolk RO, papers | BL, letters to duke and duchess of Newcastle, Add. MSS 32716–33083 · Hunt. L., letters to Elizabeth Montagu · Norfolk RO, letters to W. W. Bulwer
Likenesses M. Black and T. Black?, oils, 1764, RCP Lond. [see illus.] · W. Bromley, line engraving, 1789 (in old age; after T. Forster), BM, Wellcome L.; repro. in *European Magazine* (1789) · J. Gillray, coloured etching, 1789, Wellcome L. · stipple, 1804 (after T. Forster), Wellcome L. · Rivers, line engraving (after T. Forster), Wellcome L. · J. Wolcot, crayon drawing, Sir John Soane Museum, London
Wealth at death approx. £16,000: *Life and eccentricities*

Monson [*née* Vane; *other married name* Hope-Vere], **Lady Anne** (*c.*1727–1776), botanist and collector of plants and insects, was the eldest daughter of Henry Vane, first earl of Darlington (*c.*1705–1758), and his wife, Lady Grace Fitzroy (1697–1763); she was thus a great-granddaughter of Charles II. In 1746 she married Charles Hope-Vere of Craigiehall (1710–1791). They had two sons before the marriage was dissolved by act of parliament in 1757. That same year she married Colonel George *Monson (1730–1776) of Lincolnshire, third son of John Monson, first Baron Monson. Since her new husband's career lay with the Indian military, she thereafter spent most of her time in Calcutta, where she became prominent in Anglo-Indian society and 'a very superior whist player' (*DNB*, 'Monson, George'). Her interest in natural history, however, predated her arrival in India: by 1760 she was already well known to James Lee, the nurseryman of Hammersmith, as a remarkable lady botanist.

J. E. Smith claims that it was Lady Anne who assisted Lee

in translating Linnaeus's *Philosophia botanica*, the first work to explain Linnaean classification to English readers (Smith, 12). Although Lee published the book under his own name in 1760, he handsomely acknowledged an anonymous patron in the preface. At Lee's nursery a few years later Lady Anne was introduced to the Danish entomologist John Christian Fabricius, one of Linnaeus's pupils. Later, she gave her collection of Bengal insects to Lee's daughter Ann, who may have been named after her, and Lee mentioned her in letters to Linnaeus. In 1774, on the way out to Calcutta, she visited the Cape of Good Hope where she met another of Linnaeus's pupils, C. P. Thunberg, a seasoned collector of South African plants. Thunberg described her appreciatively as 'a lady about sixty years of age, who, amongst other languages, had also some knowledge of Latin, and had, at her own expense, brought with her a draughtsman, in order to assist her in collecting and delineating scarce specimens of natural history' (Thunberg, 2.132). Thunberg accompanied her on several expeditions around Cape Town and considered her collection very fine. She presented him with a ring in remembrance.

One of the South African plants collected by Lady Anne was named *Monsonia* by Linnaeus. He wrote to her in sprightly Latin:

> This is not the first time that I have been fired with love for one of the fair sex, and your husband may well forgive me so long as I do no injury to his honour. Who can look at so fair a flower without falling in love with it, though in all innocence? … should I be so happy as to find my love for you reciprocated, then I ask but one favour of you: that I may be permitted to join with you in the procreation of just one little daughter to bear witness of our love—a little *Monsonia*, through which your fame would live for ever in the Kingdom of Flora.　(Blunt, 224)

Specimens of *Monsonia*, an attractive flowering shrub, were sent to Kew Gardens in 1774 by Masson and introduced as a hothouse plant by Lee's nursery in 1788. Another genus to bear her name, previously chosen by Koenig, was thus superseded. She further sent Indian plants to Linnaeus. In 1775 her husband's vendetta against Warren Hastings made life intensely difficult. She died in Calcutta on 18 February 1776.　　　　　　　　JANET BROWNE

Sources J. Britten, *Journal of Botany, British and Foreign*, 55 (1917), 145–51 • E. J. Willson, *James Lee and the Vineyard Nursery, Hammersmith* (1961) • C. P. Thunberg, *Travels* (1796) • J. E. Smith, *English flora* (1824) • J. Lee, *Philosophia botanica* (1760) • M. Gunn and L. E. Codd, *Botanical exploration of southern Africa* (1981) • A. Rees and others, *The cyclopaedia, or, Universal dictionary of arts, sciences, and literature*, 45 vols. (1819–20), vol. 23 • W. Blunt and W. T. Stearn, *The compleat naturalist: a life of Linnaeus* (1971) • Burke, *Peerage* • GEC, *Peerage*

Monson, Sir Edmund John, first baronet (1834–1909), diplomatist, was born at Chart Lodge, Seal, near Sevenoaks in Kent on 6 October 1834, the third son of William John Monson, sixth Baron Monson (1796–1862), and his wife, Eliza (1803–1863), the youngest daughter of Edmund Larken. After attending a private school in the Isle of Wight he went to Eton College and then Balliol College, Oxford, where he graduated with a first class in law and

modern history in 1855; in 1858 he was elected fellow of All Souls College.

Monson entered the diplomatic service early in 1856, and was appointed unpaid attaché in Paris, where he served for nearly two years. Described by Lord Cowley, ambassador in Paris, as one of the best and most intelligent attachés he ever had, his reputation for hard work led to his being chosen in December 1858 as private secretary to Lord Lyons, who had just been appointed British minister in Washington. He served there for five years and in 1863 was transferred to Hanover and then to Brussels as third secretary of legation. Discouraged by the slowness of promotion, he left the diplomatic service in 1865 to try to enter parliament as member for Reigate in Surrey but was unsuccessful.

In 1869 Monson was appointed consul in the Azores and two years later he was promoted to be consul-general at Budapest and second secretary to the British embassy in Vienna. In the following years he served in various posts. During the eastern crisis he was sent as special envoy to Dalmatia and Montenegro (1876–7), and then he was transferred to South America, where he acted as minister-resident and consul-general in Uruguay (1879–84), and later as minister in Argentina and Paraguay (1884). During his stay in Uruguay, aged forty-seven, he married, on 6 July 1881, Eleanor Catherine Mary Munro (*d.* 1919), the daughter of a former British consul-general in Montevideo, Major James St John Munro; they had three sons.

On his return to Europe, Monson became envoy successively to Copenhagen (1884–8), Athens (1888–92), and Brussels (1892–3) before being promoted ambassador to Vienna, where he stayed three years (1893–6). Soon after this promotion he was sworn of the privy council (1893). In October 1896 he succeeded the marquess of Dufferin as ambassador in Paris, although Lord Salisbury feared Monson's readiness to take offence, and the queen had some qualms as to how Monson's wife would be received by the French, as she had proved herself quite inadequate in the role of ambassadress when in Vienna.

Monson took over the embassy at a very difficult period in Anglo-French relations. France's colonial expansion had brought it into conflict with Britain in several parts of the world, and the rivalry between the two countries had been embittered by the Egyptian question, as no French government could reconcile itself to the fact that Britain would not leave the Nile. Complaining that French interests in Egypt were being unfairly treated, the French demanded the end of British occupation there. Conflict arose also in Asia (over Siam) and in Africa (over the upper Nile and the middle Niger).

A compromise was reached between the two countries on the Niger boundary in June 1898, but almost immediately a new crisis developed at the village of Fashoda on the White Nile, where the French had dispatched, from the Congo, a mission led by Captain Marchand. Soon afterwards Kitchener's army, which had embarked on the reconquest of the Sudan in 1896, appeared and demanded its withdrawal. The press in both countries became violent in their denunciations and in September 1898 a war between Britain and France was thought to be near. From mid-October until early November the crisis was at its height as the French foreign minister, Théophile Delcassé, argued with Salisbury that if Britain insisted on humiliating France the latter might be driven to conflict. However, the British government firmly refused to enter into territorial discussions as long as the French remained in Fashoda.

From Paris, Monson insisted that the situation was highly volatile. France was being torn apart by the Dreyfus affair and the Brisson government's tenure of power was very shaky. Monson believed that a demand for French compliance with British demands would lead to a rupture between the two countries. Unlike Salisbury, he also took seriously Delcassé's hints that France could rely on Russian support in the crisis. On the day the Brisson government resigned (26 October) Monson sent to London reports of French military and naval preparations and on the following day the fleet was placed on a war footing.

Tension remained high in the following days. In London, Salisbury stood firm, insisting that the presence of a French flag at Fashoda made compromise impossible. On 2 November the new French cabinet bowed to British pressure and withdrew the Marchand mission. Anglo-French tension did not relax, however, as both sides continued to fear attack. Monson may not have been the best man to change this climate. In December 1898 he delivered a speech at the British chamber of commerce in Paris. Going beyond his brief, he told the French that if they wanted peace they must 'abstain from the continuance of a policy of pin-pricks' (Gladwyn, 152). Monson's speech was seen in Paris as an indication that Britain might be tempted to attack France. Some French ministers pressed for his recall, and the incident was finally closed only by a statement from the embassy that the ambassador's speech had not been presented with sufficient clearness. Monson seemed to have been startled by the storm he had raised and, although he gave assurances that he had had no intention of giving offence to France, he shortly afterwards went to the Riviera to allow the storm to blow itself out. This incident did little to enhance Monson's reputation with Salisbury.

Although Anglo-French conflicts in west Africa and in the Sudan were resolved in 1898–9, the settlements of these colonial disputes had not dissipated the resentments and fears felt on both sides of the channel. Monson's reports from Paris were despondent as the French press heaped abuse on Britain during the Second South African War. He warned the government that war with France was possible and told Salisbury in September 1900 that Britain should make 'herself so strong, both on land and sea as to afford no temptation to France to attack her' (PRO FO 27/497). Relations between the British embassy and the Quai d'Orsay were also made difficult by the fact that Monson could not get on with Delcassé, the French foreign minister, who stayed in office until 1905.

The early years of the twentieth century brought a reorientation of French foreign policy. Discussions between Britain and France, begun as early as 1902, ended with the *entente cordiale* of April 1904. Edward VII's state visit to Paris in April 1903 and the warmth of his welcome did much to reconcile the two countries. This visit left Monson bitter, however, as he felt aggrieved that the king never thanked him for his efforts in making the visit a success.

In February 1905 Monson retired and was rewarded for his services with a baronetcy. He had already received other decorations, including the KCMG (1886), the GCB (1896), and the GCVO (1903). He was replaced in Paris by Lord Bertie of Thame. Monson died at his home, 4P Bickenhall Mansions, London, on 28 October 1909, having been ill for some time. He was buried on 3 November in the family mausoleum in South Carlton church, near Lincoln.   BERNARD SASSO

Sources B. Willson, *The Paris embassy: a narrative of Franco-British diplomatic relations, 1814–1920* (1927) · C. Gladwyn, *The Paris embassy* (1976) · K. Eubank, *Paul Cambon: master diplomatist* (1960) · P. J. Rolo, *Entente cordiale: the origins and negotiations of the Anglo-French agreements of 8 April 1904* (1969) · J. A. S. Grenville, *Lord Salisbury and foreign policy: the close of the nineteenth century* (1964) · G. W. Monger, *The end of isolation: British foreign policy, 1900–1907* [1963] · Z. S. Steiner, *The foreign office and foreign policy, 1898–1914* (1969) · S. R. Williamson, *The politics of grand strategy: Britain and France prepare for war, 1904–1914* (1969) · K. M. Wilson, *Empire and continent: studies in British foreign policy from the 1880s to the First World War* (1987) · K. M. Wilson, ed., *British foreign secretaries and foreign policy from the Crimean War to the First World War* (1987) · D. Bates, *The Fashoda incident of 1898* (1984) · *CGPLA Eng. & Wales* (1909)
Archives Bodl. Oxf., corresp., diaries, and papers · Duke U. · Lincs. Arch. · NRA, priv. coll. · Ohio University, Athens, diary and letter-books | All Souls Oxf., letters to Sir William Anson · Bodl. Oxf., corresp. with Lord Kimberley · Duke U., Perkins L., letters to William Monson · U. Birm. L., corresp. with Joseph Chamberlain
Likenesses carte-de-visite photo, All Souls Oxf.
Wealth at death £1884 7s. 4d.: probate, 13 Dec 1909, *CGPLA Eng. & Wales*

Monson, George (1730–1776), army officer and administrator in India, was born in Arlington Street, London, on 18 April 1730, the third and youngest son of John *Monson, first Baron Monson of Burton (1693?–1748), and his wife, Lady Margaret (d. 1752), youngest daughter of Lewis Watson, first earl of Rockingham. The Monson family had country seats at Burton Hall in Lincolnshire and at Broxbournebury in Hertfordshire. George Monson was sent to Westminster School in 1738. He went on the grand tour during the years 1747–9 before commencing a military career. He was commissioned ensign in the 1st foot guards in November 1750, obtaining a lieutenant's commission with the rank of captain in 1754. In the course of the 1750s Monson strengthened his court and political links despite at one time being too poor to find £1200, the purchase price of a majority. He headed the poll in a corrupt election at Lincoln in 1754, and in 1756 was appointed a groom of the bedchamber to the prince of Wales (subsequently George III), relinquishing the office in 1763. Even allowing for an absence of six years' military service in the East, Monson's participation in the business of the house was negligible, and he did not stand for re-election in 1768.

Monson married Lady Anne Hope-Vere [see Monson, Lady Anne (c.1727–1776)], the eldest daughter of Henry

Vane, first earl of Darlington (*c*.1705–1758). In 1746 she had eloped with Charles Hope-Vere, a Scottish member of parliament and a son of the earl of Hopetoun, whom she had married. They were divorced in 1757, and in the same year she married Monson. There were two sons from her first marriage but no children from the second. Through her mother, *née* Lady Grace Fitzroy, Lady Anne was a great-granddaughter of Charles II. In India she became a prominent and popular figure in Calcutta society, where her death on 18 February 1776 was widely lamented.

In 1757 Monson transferred from the guards into Lieutenant-Colonel William Draper's regiment (first the 64th, from 1759 the 79th), and was appointed major. He sailed for India with his regiment on 5 March 1758, arriving in Madras in February 1759. He was second in command at the siege of Pondicherry in 1760. He briefly replaced Colonel Eyre Coote in the command but it reverted to Coote when Monson was obliged to relinquish it on being wounded. Pondicherry surrendered on 15 January 1761. Monson later distinguished himself at the capture of Manila by Draper's force in 1762. He became lieutenant-colonel in September 1760, and on 20 January 1761 was given command of the 96th foot. He received the rank of brigadier-general (India only) on 7 July 1763. He returned to England in December 1764. On 30 November 1769 he became full colonel and aide-de-camp to the king.

After the peace of Paris in 1763 Monson's military career was becalmed. In 1768 he solicited Lord Barrington, the secretary at war, for appointment as quartermaster-general in America, and between 1769 and the spring of 1773 wrote to him five times seeking employment in the East. 'The immense Fortunes acquired in the East do not allure me', he explained, 'any small Employment at Home or in America would give me infinitely more satisfaction and I only solicit Service in the East, as being the first Scene that presents itself' (Monson to Barrington, 27 May 1773, BL, Add. MS 73556). Monson's nomination as third member of the Bengal supreme council, which was established by the East India Regulating Act of 1773, did not quench his military aspirations. On 11 November 1773 he solicited Barrington's recommendation for the colonelcy of the 6th foot 'on the Death of General Gore who is not expected to live many Days', adding that his motive 'in accepting the Indian Appointment was not Avarice or an Idea of accumulating Wealth'; indeed, he offered to 'relinquish the Indian Appointment so much envied by others, for the military Line to which I wish to adhere' (Monson to Barrington, 11 Nov 1773, BL, Add. MS 73556). Monson believed himself personally slighted, even humiliated, in the matter of military rank. He was going to a country where in 1760 'I stood in the first Rank of Estimation', while now the commanding officers in Bengal and Madras had served under him at Pondicherry (Monson to Barrington, 26 Nov 1773, BL, Add. MS 73556). On 1 December 1773 Monson wrote to request an interview with Barrington 'to explain the Ground, on which I did place my illusive military Pretensions' (Monson to Barrington, 1 Dec 1773, BL, Add. MS 73556); and on 10 March 1774, on the eve of his

departure for Calcutta, he yet again solicited Barrington for a vacant regiment, fearing that 'I shall be esteemed by all Persons degraded, as I return without the same Degree of Honor and Confidence from His Majesty as when I was last there' (Monson to Barrington, 10 March 1774, BL, Add. MS 73556).

Monson agreed to serve on the Bengal council on condition that he would succeed Lieutenant-General John Clavering as commander-in-chief, should he die or quit. He appears to have underrated the appointment in terms of both prestige and income (to most men of modest means and abilities a salary of £10,000 a year would have been welcome), and to have overrated his military capacities. He left England disgruntled, suspecting that Lord Barrington had neglected his interests. Two years after Monson's death Philip Francis wrote that no man could have gone out to serve on the council 'with less Inclination to it' (Weitzman, 295). Furthermore, Francis Sykes thought that Monson harboured 'great prejudice against the [East India] Company' (ibid., 207). However, his appointment pleased the king who considered him 'desirous of Service, and though not a shewy Man, has excellent Sense' (*Correspondence of George III*, 2.496). It is evident that Monson went to Calcutta neither for what he could do for Bengal, nor for what Bengal could do for him, but *faute de mieux*, because he could not obtain more congenial employment.

Monson arrived at Calcutta, with his wife, on 19 October 1774. A gallant if unremarkable middle-ranking soldier, he was hardly equal to so complex a task as the government of Bengal. Neither Clavering nor he could match the acumen and dynamism of their colleague Philip Francis who, with his own decided ideas on Indian government, incited 'the Majority', as the three became known collectively, to challenge Hastings's policies in council. But Monson possessed a certain dogged single-mindedness of his own. Hastings came to consider him the most formidable of his adversaries. He wrote on 25 March 1775:

> Colonel Monson, with a more guarded temper and a more regular conduct, now appears to be the most determined of the three. The rudeness of General Clavering and the petulancy of Francis are more provoking, but it is from the former only that I apprehend any effectual injury. (Gleig, 1.517)

Monson's opposition to Hastings was registered both in letters sent home and in transactions in Calcutta. He wrote to the marquess of Rockingham of the deplorable state of affairs in Bengal and of Hastings's high-handedness. Hastings was dismayed by the lengths to which Monson seemed prepared to go to pursue accusations of corruption against him, in particular the use of Nandakumar, a Brahman, an old enemy of Hastings, as a prime source of such accusations. However, Monson, along with the others of the Majority, did not attempt to halt Nandakumar's execution for forgery. Monson signed the Majority's protest on the Rohilla war and, during the first half of 1775, censured the judges' conduct of proceedings in the supreme court. He also endorsed Francis's revisionist revenue plan of January 1776.

On 21 August 1776 Francis wrote: 'Col. Monson has been dangerously ill, and not able to attend Council these six weeks ... and he has now formally communicated to us his Resolution to resign' (Weitzman, 284). The following month Monson was 'obliged to go to Sea to save his Life' (ibid., 292). He died at Hooghly on 25 September 1776, and was buried in South Park Street cemetery, Calcutta. Military advancement came too late. In 1775 Monson was appointed colonel of the 50th foot and, before his death became known in England, on 11 February 1777 he was promoted to lieutenant-general in the East Indies.

T. H. BOWYER

Sources S. Weitzman, *Warren Hastings and Philip Francis* (1929) · *Memoirs of the life of the Right Hon. Warren Hastings, first governor-general of Bengal*, ed. G. R. Gleig, 3 vols. (1841) · HoP, *Commons, 1754–90*, 3.151–2 · BL, Barrington MSS, Add. MSS 73546–73769A: Add. MS 73556 · Fortescue, *Brit. army*, 2nd edn, 2.481–2, 553–4 · J. Parkes and H. Merivale, *Memoirs of Sir Philip Francis*, 2 vols. (1867) · F. Hill, *Georgian Lincoln* (1966), 87–92 · Charles, second marquis of Rockingham, correspondence, Sheff. Arch., Wentworth Woodhouse muniments · H. E. Busteed, *Echoes from old Calcutta*, 4th edn (1908) · *The correspondence of King George the Third from 1760 to December 1783*, ed. J. Fortescue, 2 (1927), 496 · *Bengal Past and Present*, 30 (1925), 215 · GEC, *Peerage* · *GM*, 1st ser., 22 (1752), 93 · *GM*, 1st ser., 16 (1746), 164 · *The historical register*, 11 (1726), 23 · *Old Westminsters*, 2.653–4 · DNB
Archives BL OIOC, corresp., minutes as member of supreme council, Bengal · NAM, orderly book | BL, Barrington MSS · Sheff. Arch., letters to Charles, second marquess of Rockingham
Likenesses silhouette, repro. in Busteed, *Echoes from old Calcutta*, facing p.163
Wealth at death estate at Ely

Monson, Sir John, second baronet (1599–1683), politician and financier of fen drainage, was born in St Sepulchre, London, the eldest son of Sir Thomas *Monson, first baronet (1563/4–1641), of South Carlton in Lincolnshire, and his wife, Margaret (1569–1630), daughter of Sir Edmund *Anderson, lord chief justice of the common pleas. His father was at court under James I, and John, who was not entered at either Oxford or Cambridge, may have studied law in London. He represented the city of Lincoln in the first parliament of Charles I in 1625 and the county of Lincolnshire in the parliament of 1626, and was made knight of the Bath by Charles at his coronation on 2 February 1626. In 1625 he married Ursula (d. 1692), daughter of Sir Robert Oxenbridge of Hurstbourne in Hampshire. Through his wife he gained in 1645 the manor of Broxbourne in Hertfordshire, which was the seat of the family for many years.

Monson appears to have been imprisoned briefly in 1631, possibly in connection with allegations concerning his mishandling of the Lincolnshire grain supply in those lean times. In 1635, in view of the necessity of reclaiming and draining the low-lying lands by the banks of the River Ancholme in Lincolnshire, the commissioners for the fens endeavoured to negotiate with 'some foreign undertakers' for the carrying out of the works, but failed to come to terms. Thereupon Monson offered himself as undertaker, 'out of a noble desire to serve his country', and his services were accepted (Dugdale, 151). The drainage was completed to the satisfaction of the commissioners on 19 February 1639, and 5827 acres of the

reclaimed land were allotted to Monson on 4 March, in accordance with a previous arrangement. Complaints and dissatisfaction, however, had arisen in the meantime among the neighbouring landlords. In 1639 the ditches and sluice gates came under attack, the riotous resumption of common rights in the Ancholme Fen being winked at subsequently by parliamentarians with little patience for court-backed projectors such as Monson.

Earlier, Monson had found that his strongest support lay in making common cause with Archbishop Laud, and in consequence he had been drawn yet closer to the court's 'new counsels'. In 1633 he became embroiled in Laud's attack on John Williams, bishop of Lincoln. Having cast doubt on the moral character of Williams's key supporter, his registrar, John Pregion, Monson found his own good name impugned. As a result he was himself awarded 1000 marks out of the massive fine imposed on Williams, the king himself ordering that his recompense be proportionable to the damage done to his reputation by the bishop and his supporters.

In 1641 Monson succeeded to his father's baronetcy. His legal acumen had been noticed by the king, and he offered Charles much useful advice during his disagreements with parliament in the lead-up to the civil war. On the departure of Charles from London, Monson retired to Oxford, where on 1 or 2 November 1642 he was created DCL. In 1643, when the proximity of the armies threatened the safety of Oxford, he sent his wife to London while he remained behind to take part in the negotiations. In May 1646 Fairfax demanded the surrender of the town, and Monson and Philip Warwick were sent to confer with him. Monson was one of the fourteen commissioners for Oxford who met the parliamentary commissioners on 18 May, and for a month was actively occupied in framing the articles for the surrender of the town. His conduct throughout gained for him the respect of both parties. Subsequently he applied for and was granted permission to compound for his estates on the terms granted by the Oxford articles, according to which the fine should not exceed two years of the revenue. In his *Short Essay of Afflictions* (1647) he was able therefore to look forward confidently to passing on at least 'a competent measure' of his fortune to his son, to whom the essay was addressed. (At this time he also wrote a religious tract entitled *An Antidote Against the Errour in the Opinion of Many*.) But he failed to pay the composition in full and the estate was ordered to be sequestered on 8 March 1648. Sir Thomas Fairfax and Cromwell both deemed his usage needlessly severe, but it was not until July 1651 that parliament removed the sequestration. Monson was again in difficulties at the end of 1655, when he refused to pay the decimation tax, levied to meet insurrection, and was imprisoned in his own house, but the protector's council ordered that he be discharged from further proceedings on 22 September 1656. Only ill health appears to have prevented his playing a fuller role in Sir George Booth's rising in 1659.

During the civil wars Monson's drainage works were injured and neglected. On his petition to parliament in

December 1654 the business was referred to the committee for the fens, without result, but he petitioned the convention in November 1660, and the Cavalier Parliament on 14 May 1661, whereafter, despite the opposition of two of the fen towns—Winterton and Bishop Norton—a bill confirming Monson's former privileges was passed by both houses in March 1662 and received royal assent in May. Having claimed losses totalling £30,000, and having been promised a peerage (possibly now denied him because of his younger brother William's complicity in the regicide), parliamentary confirmation of his Ancholme interest was the very least he might have hoped for.

As guardian and trustee for John Sheffield, third earl of Mulgrave (and later first duke of Buckingham and Normanby), Monson undertook in December 1663 to farm the earl's alum mines at Mulgrave in Yorkshire, allowing the king almost half the profits. His involvement in the earl's affairs earned him little but trouble at the hands of the litigious dowager countess.

Care should be taken after 1661 to distinguish between the second baronet and his son, Sir John Monson, kt. Certainly it was Sir John junior who sat throughout the Cavalier Parliament, during all which time his father appears to have been indisposed through ill health. Monson was, nevertheless, predeceased by his son. In 1680, Monson ventured some thoughts in print in a *Discourse Concerning Supreme Power and Common Right*, an early repudiation of exclusion. He died in 1683, and was buried on 29 December at South Carlton. He built and endowed a free school in South Carlton and a hospital in Burton, and left money to the towns in Lincolnshire of which he was lord.

BERTHA PORTER, rev. SEAN KELSEY

Sources GEC, *Baronetage*, 1.39 · J. Foster, *The register of admissions to Gray's Inn, 1521–1889, together with the register of marriages in Gray's Inn chapel, 1695–1754* (privately printed, London, 1889), 173 · W. A. Shaw, *The knights of England*, 2 vols. (1906), 1.162 · *Members of parliament: return to two orders of the honorable the House of Commons*, House of Commons, 1 (1878), 464, 470 · *CSP dom.*, 1625–6, 565; 1627–8, 578; 1629–31, 481; 1631–3, 24, 63, 65; 1637, 309, 311, 415; 1637–8, 61; 1639, 232; 1655–6, 50; 1661–2, 213; 1663–4, 365–6; 1665–6, 372; 1667–8, 77, 196, 408 · J. Rushworth, *Historical collections*, new edn, 2 (1721), 416ff. · Foster, *Alum. Oxon.*, 1500–1714, 3.1021 · Wood, *Ath. Oxon.*: *Fasti* (1820), 40–41 · M. A. E. Green, ed., *Calendar of the proceedings of the committee for compounding … 1643–1660*, 5 vols., PRO (1889–92), 1431–3 · M. A. E. Green, ed., *Calendar of the proceedings of the committee for advance of money, 1642–1656*, 3 vols., PRO (1888), 745 · *JHL*, 4 (1628–42), 254 · *JHL*, 10 (1647–8), 222–3, 225 · *JHL*, 11 (1660–66), 395, 397–9, 406, 473 · *JHC*, 6 (1648–51), 610–11 · *JHC*, 7 (1651–9), 402 · *JHC*, 8 (1660–67), 186, 248, 252, 257, 296, 374 · Worcester College, Oxford, Clarke MS 66, fols. 22–23v · *Calendar of the Clarendon state papers preserved in the Bodleian Library*, ed. O. Ogle and others, 5 vols. (1869–1970), vol. 4, p. 236; vol. 5, pp. 112, 359 · C. Holmes, *Seventeenth-century Lincolnshire*, History of Lincolnshire, 7 (1980), 127–8, 150, 151, 156, 202, 226–8, 238 · M. W. Helms and J. S. Crossette, 'Monson, John', HoP, *Commons, 1660–90*, 3.79–80 · will, PRO, PROB 11/375, fols. 46v–49r · W. Dugdale, *The history of imbanking and drayning of divers fenns and marshes* (1662)

Archives Lincs. Arch., MSS

Wealth at death property in Lincolnshire; two houses at Burton and Broxbourne, jewels, plate, coaches, and other personal estate; legacies worth over £6000 to be paid largely from mortgages worth £4000: will, PRO, PROB 11/375, fols. 46v–49r

Monson, John, first Baron Monson (1693?–1748), politician, was the son of George Monson (*c*.1658–1726) of Broxbourne, Hertfordshire, and his wife, Anne, the daughter of Charles Wren of the Isle of Ely. He was educated at Christ Church, Oxford, where he matriculated on 26 January 1708. On 4 April 1722 he was returned to parliament for the city of Lincoln, and was re-elected on 30 August 1727. On 8 April 1725 he married Margaret (1696?–1752), the daughter of Lewis Watson, first earl of Rockingham. He was created a knight of the Bath (17 June 1725), when that order was reconstituted by George I, and he succeeded to the family baronetcy on 7 March 1727, following the death of his uncle Sir William, a former guardian of the duke of Newcastle. On 28 May 1728 he was created a peer, with the title of Baron Monson of Burton, Lincolnshire.

In June 1733 Monson was named captain of the band of gentlemen pensioners, and on 31 July 1737, through Newcastle's influence, he was sworn of the privy council. In the previous month he had been appointed commissioner of trade and plantations. His office was confirmed when the board was reconstituted in 1745, and he continued to hold it until his death. Many historians have viewed his presidency as the lowest ebb of the board's influence. Monson also continued his family's involvement in Newcastle's private affairs; in 1738 he and his brother Charles were among the trustees appointed by Hoare's Bank to manage the duke's assets.

Monson died on 18 July 1748 in Piccadilly, London, and was buried in South Carlton, Lincolnshire. The duke of Newcastle, in a letter to the duke of Bedford dated 12 August 1748, wrote of 'the loss of so valuable a man and so amiable a friend', and Bedford in reply uses similar expressions of regret (*Correspondence*, 1.440–41). He was survived by his widow, Margaret, who died on 24 February 1752, and their three sons: John, second Baron Monson [*see below*]; Lewis Thomas, who assumed the name of Watson, and was created Baron Sondes in 1760; and George *Monson.

John Monson, second Baron Monson (1727–1774), politician, born on 23 July 1727, was awarded an LLD from Cambridge University in 1749. On 23 June 1752 he married Theodosia (1725–1821), the daughter of John Maddison of Stainton Vale and Stanford, Lincolnshire. He continued his family's close association with Newcastle, and by 1765 had become part of the 'hard core of peers and their clients' at the centre of the Rockingham party (Langford, 270–71). On 5 November 1765 he was appointed warden and chief justice in eyre of the forests south of the Trent. On the fall of the first Rockingham ministry he was offered an earldom on the condition that he would relinquish the position. He rejected the proposal, but ultimately resigned with Portland and other whigs on 27 November. According to Walpole, he later voted with the court on Bedford's motion that the privy council should acknowledge the Massachusetts assembly's pardoning of the late insurrection. In 1768 he signed a protest against the bill to limit the dividends of the East India Company.

Monson died at his house in Albemarle Street, London,

on 23 July 1774 and was buried at South Carlton, Lincolnshire. His widow, with whom he had five sons and two daughters, died on 20 February 1821.

G. Le G. Norgate, *rev.* Matthew Kilburn

Sources GEC, *Peerage*, new edn, vol. 2 · H. Walpole, *Memoirs of King George II*, ed. J. Brooke, 3 vols. (1985) · *GM*, 1st ser., 3 (1733), 328 · *GM*, 1st ser., 35 (1765), 539 · *GM*, 1st ser., 44 (1774) · R. Browning, *The duke of Newcastle* (1975) · J. A. Henretta, *Salutary neglect: colonial administration under the duke of Newcastle* (1972) · P. Langford, *The first Rockingham administration, 1765–1766* (1973) · Foster, *Alum. Oxon.* · Venn, *Alum. Cant.* · *Correspondence of John, fourth duke of Bedford*, ed. J. Russell, 1 (1842), 440–41

Archives BL, corresp. of second Baron Monson, Add. MSS 18988

Wealth at death wealthy; family estates of Carlton and Barton, Lincolnshire, and Broxbourne, Hertfordshire

Monson, John, second Baron Monson (1727–1774). *See under* Monson, John, first Baron Monson (1693?–1748).

Monson, Sir (William Bonnar) Leslie (1912–1993), colonial official, was born on 28 May 1912 at 2 Comely Bank Street, Edinburgh, the only son of John William Monson (1881/2–1929), tax inspector, and his wife, Selina Leslie, *née* Stewart (*d.* 1958). His parents came originally from Ulster, but had settled in Edinburgh after their marriage. Monson's father died prematurely in 1929 before his son had completed his education. Fortunately, however, Monson was blessed with academic ability, and scholarships helped his progress through Edinburgh Academy and Hertford College, Oxford. He was dux at Edinburgh in 1930 with prizes in history, English, and classics (though under physical activity he could only record 'corporal in the OTC'). At Oxford he gained a second class in classical moderations, followed by a first in modern history in 1934. The following year he passed into the administrative grade of the home civil service and was posted to the Dominions Office as an assistant principal. In 1938 he became private secretary to the permanent undersecretary, Sir Edward Harding. In 1939 he transferred to the much larger Colonial Office as a principal, securing promotion to assistant secretary in charge of the production and marketing department in 1944.

A chance to make a real mark came in 1947 with Monson's appointment as chief secretary to the west African council, based in Accra. This council comprised the secretary of state for the colonies and the governors of the British west African colonies, and their task was to co-ordinate British policy in west Africa. While based in Accra he married, on 2 October 1948, Helen Isobel, daughter of Roland Francis Browne, of Ceylon; she was at that time working for the British Council in west Africa (for which she was in 1949 made MBE). His quiet tact had previously been demonstrated by his promptly vacating a British Council house he had been lent which she claimed to be rightfully hers. His sensitivity to racial issues was demonstrated at this time when, producing *The Pirates of Penzance*, he arranged for the very modern major-general to have six white and six black daughters. District officers far up country were surprised but gratified to find that Monson, despite his wide-ranging task, knew of and

Sir (William Bonnar) Leslie Monson (1912–1993), by Walter Bird, 1964

encouraged their efforts to improve their districts. He was appointed CMG in 1950.

On returning to the Colonial Office in 1951 Monson was promoted to assistant under-secretary, initially supervising the work of the production, marketing, and research departments, and leading colonial delegations to international conferences on sugar, rubber, and tin. In 1959 he returned to geographical responsibilities. His supervision of the east and central African departments was later extended to cover Aden and southern Africa, and Monson attended the relevant independence conferences at Lancaster House. At the conference leading to Zambian independence Kenneth Kaunda came to have great respect for Monson, and may have asked that he should be Britain's first high commissioner in Lusaka. At any rate he was so appointed, serving there from 1964 to 1966. He was appointed CB in 1964 and advanced to KCMG in 1965. As later high commissioners were to find, good relations between Britain and Zambia were hard to maintain because of the bedevilling factor of the declaration of unilateral independence by Southern Rhodesia. There was also the particular problem of the unpredictability of Wilson's government. For example, President Kaunda would hear on the BBC that Wilson's government was to hold talks with the Rhodesian rebels many hours before Monson had been officially briefed about such a change of policy. Kaunda would then refuse to see Monson. At other times Kaunda would press Monson for news of Wilson's intentions which he was unable to supply. It was not long before security grilles had to be installed at the high commission.

On his return to London, Monson was advanced to deputy under-secretary in 1967, supervising the Commonwealth Office departments for sub-Saharan Africa. With the merger of the Commonwealth and Foreign offices in 1968 his responsibilities extended to all sub-Saharan departments from both offices. During this period the problem of oil sanctions against Rhodesia was prominent, and Monson and others were subsequently featured in the Bingham report on that subject, though without harm to Monson's career. His status as one of the most experienced and able members of the former Colonial Office was recognized in his next and last posting, in 1969, to supervise the remaining dependent territories (as the remnants of the colonial empire had been titled). There he was able to maintain continuity with the welfare outlook of his old department until his retirement in 1972.

After retirement Monson was asked to serve on a commission on the future of the Gilbert and Ellice islands (now Kiribatu and Tuvalu), requiring some journeys by canoe. In 1975 he was made a knight of St John and director of the overseas relations branch of St John Ambulance, liaising with more than forty overseas branches and introducing regional conferences. He gave up this post in 1981. Former colleagues and friends continued to visit the Monsons at their home in Blackheath thereafter.

In later life Monson acquired an avuncular aura: tall, moustached, pipe smoking, unthreatening in manner, and tactful but decisive. He was a man of considerable ability and humane in outlook, who played a significant but unobtrusive part in the largely peaceful transition of British colonies to independence. He died at his home, Golf House, Goffers Road, Blackheath, London, on 3 July 1993. He was survived by his wife. They had no children.

LEONARD ALLINSON

Sources Edinburgh Academy records · *The Times* (26 July 1993) · *Daily Telegraph* (12 July 1993) · personal knowledge (2004) · private information (2004) [W. Peters, Sir D. Scott, S. R. J. Bottomley, Revd C. Morris] · *WWW* [forthcoming] · Burke, *Peerage* · R. C. Good, *VDI: the international politics of the Rhodesian rebellion* (1973) · b. cert. · *CGPLA Eng. & Wales* (1993) · d. cert. [J. W. Monson]
Likenesses W. Bird, photograph, 1964, NPG [*see illus.*] · photograph, repro. in *The Times*
Wealth at death £182,845: probate, 22 Oct 1993, *CGPLA Eng. & Wales*

Monson, Robert (*c*.1525–1583), judge, was the third son of William Monson (*d. c.*1558) of South Carlton, Lincolnshire, and Elizabeth, daughter of Sir Robert Tyrwhit of Kettleby in the same county, of which he was a native. He is said to have attended Cambridge University before he was admitted to Lincoln's Inn in 1546. After a slightly unruly student career he was called to the bar in 1552, and in 1556 was fined for failing to keep most of the exercises while he was reader of Thavies Inn. His first reading in Lincoln's Inn, in 1565, was on the 1549 statute concerning tithes and was sufficiently well regarded to circulate in manuscript. He acted as treasurer in 1567–8 but managed to avoid giving a second reading in 1572 by pleading a broken leg. He was elected a member of parliament for Dunheved in 1553 and served continuously through Mary's reign for three Cornish constituencies, and then in the following reign as member for Lincoln and Totnes. The Cornish elections may have resulted from a strong Lincoln's Inn connection with that county; but Monson's home was at South Carlton near Lincoln, where he was counsel to the city by 1559 and recorder from 1570. He was also a justice of the peace for the county of Lincoln.

On 12 September 1559 Monson married Elizabeth, daughter and heir of John Dyon of Tathwell, attorney and filazer of the common pleas. In the Elizabethan parliaments Monson was active on law reform committees and

showed a particular interest in religion and the succession. He spoke boldly on the succession question, and in 1566 offended the queen by pressing for an answer to a petition of both houses praying for her to marry and to nominate her successor in the event of her dying without issue. Nevertheless, this did not prevent his advancement. In 1571 he became an ecclesiastical commissioner in the dioceses of Lincoln and Peterborough, and then in October 1572 he received the distinction of being appointed a justice of the common pleas without having practised as serjeant. He was indeed the first puisne judge to be appointed from outside the order of the coif, and the necessary qualification was achieved by a private graduation ceremony the week before his judicial patent was sealed. In 1577 he became, in addition, chief justice of the county palatine of Lancaster.

However, Monson again attracted the queen's displeasure in 1576, and in 1579 his career was brought to an end by his protest against the punishment of John Stubbe. Stubbe, a puritan barrister of Lincoln's Inn, had suffered the loss of his right hand on the scaffold in Westminster market place for writing a pamphlet opposing the marriage between the queen and the duc d'Alençon, under a statute prohibiting false, seditious, or slanderous news. Since the prosecution was in the queen's bench, Monson's opposition must have been extrajudicial, and it doubtless arose from his implication in a Lincoln's Inn circle with strong views on the succession. James Dalton, a bencher of the inn, was sent to the Tower, and Monson to the Fleet prison. Monson was later allowed to return to Lincolnshire, and was finally released from house arrest on 2 March 1580. Nevertheless he did not return to the bench. He was paid as a judge until Lady day 1580, when he presumably resigned, though he was not replaced until February 1581. After three years in retirement he died without issue on 23 September 1583 and was buried in Lincoln Cathedral, where until the civil war there was a brass effigy of him in judicial robes. J. H. BAKER

Sources HoP, *Commons, 1509–58*, 2.613; 3.66–7 · Foss, *Judges*, 5.527–8 · W. P. Baildon, ed., *The records of the Honorable Society of Lincoln's Inn: the black books*, 1 (1897) · Baker, *Serjeants*, 172, 304, 527 · Sainty, *Judges*, 73 · *APC*, 1578–80, 404 · BL, Harleian MS 5265, fols. 27–56v · CUL, MS Dd. 11. 87, fols. 136–150v · *CPR*, 1558–60, 151 · PRO, C142/204/116 · R. E. G. Cole, ed., *Lincolnshire church notes*, Lincoln RS, 1 (1911) · F. Peck, ed., *Desiderata curiosa*, new edn, 2 vols. in 1 (1779), 305 · BL, Loan MS 38, fol. 92 [drawing of monument]
Likenesses brass effigy, repro. in Dugdale's book of monuments, BL, Loan MS 38, fol. 92

Monson, Theodosia, Lady Monson (1803–1891), dilettante and promoter of women's rights, was born on 23 July 1803 at Warkworth, Northumberland, fifth and youngest child of Major Latham Blacker (1765–1846) of Drogheda, Ireland, and subsequently of Newent, Gloucestershire, and his wife, Catherine (1769–1823), daughter of Colonel George Maddison of Lincolnshire. Bred in country residences, Theodosia became a spirited horsewoman and a talented landscape painter. In her mid-twenties she was courted by a younger maternal kinsman, Frederick John, fifth Baron Monson of Burton (1809–1841), a Christ Church undergraduate who amused her, indulged her with jewellery, and married her at St James's, Westminster, on 21 June 1832. They made an extraordinary pair: she self-reliant, he the darling of a protective mother; she an atheist, he a devout Christian; she a vehement whig, he among the last tory stalwarts to vote against reform. In 1834 the duchesse de Dino contrasted this 'little figure of a man or rather a child, shy and taciturn because embarrassed by his small stature and physical weakness', with that 'tall blonde Englishwoman, stiff and bony, with long features, broad hands, a large flat chest, a spinsterly appearance, angular movements' (Dino, 1.39–40). The contradiction became hard to bear and led to a separation of ways; on Lady Monson's side there may also have been infidelities. Frederick Monson went on collecting pictures for his gallery at Gatton Park, Surrey, wandered about Europe making sketches, published travel books and sermons on renunciation and suffering, and became provincial grand master of freemasons. He is said to have lived in a world of his own, prey to delusions caused perhaps by an organic disease, the last manifestation of which was ascites; he died in his mother's arms at Brighton on 7 October 1841, leaving everything he could to her and nothing to Theodosia beyond the ample settlement they must earlier have agreed.

Lady Monson herself led a peripatetic existence, living for months on end with ladies who found in her a suitable companion to tour Scotland or to take as a guide to the continent. Among her closest friends were Fanny Kemble, Anna Jameson, and Jean Mitchell of Carolside, Berwickshire. An assiduous patron of the theatre, she sought out actresses and singers, including Pasta, Rachel, Ristori, and Viardot, as well as both Fanny and Adelaide Kemble. For a time she championed Eliza Lynn Linton, who would later recall her as that 'most unhappy woman whose head and neck were so strangely the human representation of the Ionic column. ... Sex with her determined everything. To be a man was to be a monster; to be a woman was to be probably a saint and certainly a victim' (Linton, 2.179, 182).

In the autumn of 1855 Theodosia Monson undertook a trip to the Crimea with Mrs Mitchell, whose sons were fighting there. She then wintered in Paris, where she associated with the Brownings and Monckton Milnes and was introduced to Dickens (who is wrongly thought to have based Betsey Trotwood in *David Copperfield* on her). Through Pauline Viardot she met George Sand, and acted as a go-between for her English devotees; she also affected to dress like her, and smoked. She was invited to each stage of the production of *Comme il vous plaira*, Sand's adaptation of *As You Like It*, and translated her famous *Letter to M. Regnier* (1856) in which English and French drama were compared; Theodosia's preface regretted that Shakespeare, 'every man's countryman, the whole world's teacher', was insufficiently venerated in his native land.

Perhaps by a shared admiration for George Sand, Lady Monson now became intimate with Matilda *Hays, joint editor with Bessie Rayner Parkes of the *English Woman's Journal* (1858–64). She set enthusiastically to work in its tiny reading-room at 14A Princes Street, Cavendish Square. Some of her grandiose ideas, for instance to build homes for single women, came to nothing, but her shrewdness and honesty of purpose overcame what others saw as her wilder side; towards the end of 1859 she generously procured and furnished very comfortable premises at 19 Langham Place for the use of the journal (and its reading-room) and the Society for Promoting the Employment of Women, guaranteeing them a fair trial with indemnity from debts. Bessie Parkes described the new establishment as 'a regular Ladies' Institute', 'a very Queen of Clubs' (Parkes to B. Bodichon, 19 Oct 1859 and 8 Jan 1860, Parkes MSS). Visitors were able not only to consult newspapers and periodicals they could not afford to buy but also to enjoy luncheon, coffee, tea, and a place of recreation during breaks from their work. Theodosia was appointed a director in March 1860, and in general her contribution seems to have been administrative rather than authorial, though she probably made at least one perspicacious contribution to the 'deceased wife's sister' debate and wrote angrily about laws that assigned a woman's property to her husband. Most significantly, the so-called Langham Place group of early feminists was facilitated by her. Despite clashes of temperament with her colleagues, she refitted the house at the end of 1863. Little is known about her life thereafter. Perhaps the excitableness of which everyone spoke turned her head; by some, already in the 1860s, she was considered slightly unhinged. She died of chronic gastritis and cardiac failure on 3 July 1891 at Essington's Hotel, Malvern Wells, where for many years she had been residing in season, and was buried four days afterwards at Oxenhall, near Newent.

PATRICK WADDINGTON

Sources Duchesse de Dino [D. de Talleyrand-Périgord], *Chronique de 1831 à 1862*, ed. A. Radiziwill, 4 vols. (1909–10) • E. L. Linton, *The autobiography of Christopher Kirkland*, 3 vols. (1885) • F. A. Kemble, *Record of a girlhood*, rev. edn, 3 vols. (1879) • F. A. Kemble, *Records of later life*, 3 vols. (1882) • F. A. Kemble, *Further records, 1848–1883: a series of letters*, 2 vols. (1890) • G. Sand, *Agendas*, ed. A. Chevereau, 1 (1990) • *Correspondance: George Sand*, ed. G. Lubin, 27 vols. (Paris, 1964–95) • L. Héritte-Viardot, *Memories and adventures* (1913) • *Anna Jameson: letters and friendships*, ed. B. S. Erskine (1915) • J. Rendall, '"A moral engine"? Feminism, liberalism and the *English Woman's Journal*', *Equal or different: women's politics, 1800–1914*, ed. J. Rendall (1987), 112–38 • GEC, *Peerage* • *The George Eliot letters*, ed. G. S. Haight, 9 vols. (1954–78) • *Elizabeth Barrett Browning: letters to her sister, 1846–1859*, ed. L. Huxley (1929) • *The letters of Charles Dickens*, ed. M. House, G. Storey, and others, 8 (1995) • *Letters of Anna Jameson to Ottilie von Goethe*, ed. G. H. Needler (1939) • T. W. Reid, *The life, letters, and friendships of Richard Monckton Milnes, first Lord Houghton*, 2 vols. (1890) • IGI • d. cert. • Girton Cam., Parkes MSS

Archives Lincs. Arch. • priv. coll., family MSS • Warks. CRO | CUL, letters to W. S. Greg • Girton Cam., Bessie Rayner Parkes MSS • Trinity Cam., Houghton MSS

Likenesses Hadley & Son, print (after drawing, c.1832), priv. coll.

Wealth at death £66,192 6s. 7d.: probate, 8 Sept 1891, *CGPLA Eng. & Wales*

Monson, Sir Thomas, first baronet (1563/4–1641), courtier, was the eldest surviving son of Sir John Monson (c.1546–1593) of South Carlton, Lincolnshire, and his wife, Jane (d. 1624), daughter of Robert Dighton of Little Sturton. Thomas was educated at Magdalen College, Oxford, matriculating at the age of fifteen in December 1579, and at Gray's Inn, where he was admitted student in 1583. In July 1590 he married Margaret Anderson (1569–1630), daughter of Sir Edmund *Anderson, lord chief justice of common pleas. During their forty-year marriage the couple had nine children, four sons and five daughters.

Sir John Monson, a fairly prominent Lincolnshire gentleman, served as high sheriff in 1577 and was knighted in 1586, but his son's fortunes far outstripped Sir John's achievements. The story of Thomas Monson's meteoric rise and calamitous fall begins on the local stage. He succeeded to his father's estates late in 1593, about the same time that he began to enjoy important local office. He was a JP in his native county from about 1592, and sheriff in 1597–8. He was chosen MP for Lincolnshire in 1597 and was probably knighted in the same year. In February 1599 he was appointed surveyor of royal lands in Lincolnshire and the city of Lincoln, and in 1599–1600 he was colonel of 300 horse levied in the county.

By the death of Elizabeth I, Sir Thomas Monson was clearly a figure of significant local standing. In the new reign he, along with his brother William *Monson, acquired office and renown at the very centre of power. Under the patronage of Henry Howard, earl of Northampton, Monson spent the first decade of Jacobean rule accumulating court office. He became chancellor to Queen Anne and master falconer to the king. In 1611 he was appointed keeper of the armoury at Greenwich and master of the armoury at the Tower of London. In 1612 he was appointed keeper of the naval munitions. He also sat in the first two Jacobean parliaments. He was selected MP for Castle Rising in 1604, and in 1614, having contested and lost the election for Lincolnshire, he took a seat as MP for Cricklade. His court offices and connections also led to honours. He was created MA by the University of Oxford in 1605, and in June 1611 became one of the first of the new order of baronets.

Monson's heady days of court success—of office, access, influence, and wealth—came to an abrupt and nearly catastrophic end in the autumn of 1615. On 10 September 1615 Sir Gervase Elwes, lieutenant of the Tower, submitted to the king a document revealing all he knew concerning Sir Thomas Overbury's death in the Tower two years before. Elwes confessed that Overbury had been poisoned through the machinations of his keeper, Richard Weston. Elwes stated that Weston had been appointed Overbury's keeper on the recommendation of Sir Thomas Monson, though Elwes insisted that Monson was unaware of Weston's intentions: 'in this business in my conscience', Elwes wrote, Monson was 'as clear as my own soul' (PRO, SP 14/81/86). Elwes's confession triggered a massive investigation into Overbury's death that resulted in the most sensational court scandal of the age. Weston implicated the royal favourite, Robert Carr, earl of Somerset; his wife, Frances Howard; and a handful of accomplices. Elwes's evidence connecting Monson to Weston meant that Sir Thomas was soon ensnared in the investigation.

The truth of the plot against Overbury is difficult to disentangle from the surviving evidence. According to the investigators, led by Sir Edward Coke, Monson had been a crucial intermediary in the poison plot, working at the behest of Overbury's political and personal enemies the earl of Northampton (now dead) and the earl and countess of Somerset. Monson vigorously denied the charge. He admitted that he had recommended Weston to Elwes at the request of Frances Howard, then countess of Essex, and with the knowledge and consent of her great-uncle Northampton. He admitted, too, that on their instructions he had made sure Elwes and Weston strictly controlled the flow of letters and information into and out of Overbury's cell. But he denied all knowledge of a plot to poison Overbury. Nevertheless, he was committed into custody at the house of a London alderman.

It seems likely that Monson understood the political need to have Overbury in the Tower and under close supervision during the summer of 1613. Frances Howard had sued for an annulment of her marriage to Robert Devereux, third earl of Essex, and intended to marry Carr, then Viscount Rochester. Overbury, Carr's friend, opposed the marriage and the closer alliance with the Howard family it would entail. Northampton, leader of the Howard faction, obviously felt quite differently. His correspondence with Carr during Overbury's imprisonment reveals that the two men plotted to coerce Overbury into accepting closer ties with the Howards, and that they used the privileged access afforded by Weston and Elwes to keep close watch on the prisoner's mood. Monson was clearly an intermediary in this political manoeuvring, helping in the appointment of Elwes as lieutenant, recommending Weston, and advising Elwes on controlling access to Overbury. At the same time someone—perhaps Northampton but almost certainly Frances Howard—wanted Overbury dead and used Weston and a variety of other intermediaries to arrange the poisoning. It is more than likely that Monson knew nothing of the poison plot, though in his willingness to serve Northampton's political ends he may unwittingly have contributed to its ultimate success.

Indicted as accessory to Overbury's murder, Monson was arraigned at the Guildhall on 30 November 1615, but the proceedings were postponed because of disorder in the crowded courtroom. On 4 December Monson returned to the Guildhall only to have proceedings once again aborted—this time after he had entered a not-guilty plea—when Coke declared that important new discoveries necessitated a delay. Coke's hints from the bench that these discoveries 'make our deliverance as great as any that happened to the children of Israel' (State trials, 2.949) helped fuel wild rumours that the Overbury investigators had unearthed a massive popish plot. Coke made it quite clear that he thought Monson part of that conspiracy, declaring that the prisoner was a liar and a papist and comparing him to the notorious Henry Garnet. Taken from the Guildhall, Monson was remanded to the Tower, a move that, along with Coke's comments, encouraged rumours that he was to be tried for a more serious crime than just Overbury's murder.

Monson remained in the Tower until October 1616,

nearly five months after the earl and countess of Somerset had been convicted, and long after the fears of a popish plot had subsided. In December Sir Francis Bacon recommended that Monson be pardoned, the evidence against him being 'doubtful' and 'conjectural' (Spedding, 6.120). And in February 1617 Thomas Monson came to the bar for the last time, declaring that his pardon had been granted for 'the insufficiency of the proofs and evidences against me' and asserting before God that he was 'guiltless in the blood of that man, for which I stand here indicted, guiltless of the fact, guiltless of the procurement thereof, guiltless of the privity, or consent thereto, directly or indirectly' (common place book of Sir John Holles, b.32, 62–6).

Guiltless of murder he most likely was, but financially and politically Thomas Monson never recovered from the Overbury affair. Stripped of his offices, his friends displaced at court, he tried to begin again. In 1618 he acquired the stewardship of the duchy of Lancaster, but in the same year his chances of political recovery were damaged by the Howard faction's misguided attempt to promote his nephew, William *Monson, as a rival to the current royal favourite, George Villiers. In 1620 Sir Thomas was allowed to kiss the king's hands, encouraging gossip that he was to be reappointed as falconer, but nothing came of it. Financial worries began to consume him. During his years of affluence he had given nearly £14,000 in loans and sureties to the master of the ordnance, Sir Roger Dallison, with Dallison's Lincolnshire estates as security. By 1621 Monson's loans were still unpaid, but he could not take Dallison's lands because the crown had seized them to cover Dallison's large debts to the ordnance office. At the same time Dallison had defaulted on a loan from the crown for which Monson had stood surety, and the crown had put an extent on Monson's manor at Long Owersby. These financial troubles were compounded by a claim from the duchy of Lancaster that Monson had misappropriated £2000 of duchy money. Lacking options, Monson cut an unfavourable deal with Lord Treasurer Middlesex. In a complicated and crooked scheme, which was used against him during his impeachment in 1624, Middlesex persuaded the ordnance office to let him buy Dallison's lands in return for paying off Dallison's debts to the crown. Middlesex then bought off Monson's claim with a four-part financial deal that gave Monson £1000 in cash, cleared his £2000 arrears with the duchy of Lancaster, lifted the extent on Long Owersby, and granted him the right to sell six baronetcies. This last part of the arrangement fell through and was exchanged in February 1625 for the right (estimated at £200 a year) to enfranchise the copyholders of the manor of Wakefield in Yorkshire. The death of James I, however, left the exchange unimplemented, and for the rest of his life Monson struggled in vain to secure compensation from the crown. In 1628, for instance, he petitioned for the right to sell a barony—which he intended for himself—but the king turned him down.

The last phase of Monson's career was played out on the local stage. In 1626 he acquired minor office as clerk for the king's letters before the president and council of the north. During the personal rule, his son and heir, Sir John *Monson, played an increasingly prominent role in Lincolnshire politics, and Sir Thomas seems to have sided with his son and the Laudian faction in the local disputes surrounding John Williams, bishop of Lincoln. In 1633, in another bid for compensation, Monson advertised to the king his ongoing usefulness in Lincolnshire, but with the exception of an appointment as a commissioner for the trained bands in 1637, Thomas Monson's days of public service were over. His wife, Margaret, had died in the summer of 1630, and by the mid-1630s Thomas himself had become increasingly frail. He died in May 1641 and was buried on 25 May at South Carlton.

ALASTAIR BELLANY

Sources Burke, *Peerage* (1975), 1857 · R. C. Gabriel, 'Monson, Sir Thomas', HoP, *Commons, 1558–1603* · Foster, *Alum. Oxon.* · *CSP dom.*, 1603–10, 184, 386; 1611–18, 15, 40, 153, 606; 1619–23, 163; 1623–5, 369, 389–90, 485; 1625–6, 290, 565; 1631–3, 494; 1633–4, 376–7; 1637, 176 · M. Prestwich, *Cranfield: politics and profits under the early Stuarts* (1966) · L. Stone, *The crisis of the aristocracy, 1558–1641* (1965), 108–9 · materials relating to the Overbury investigation, PRO, SP 14/81/86; 14/82/20, 29, 30, 32, 37 · Earl of Northampton, letters to R. Carr, summer 1613, CUL, MS Dd.3.63 · BL, Add. MS 32092, fol. 226r · *Report on the manuscripts of the marquis of Downshire*, 6 vols. in 7, HMC, 75 (1924–95), vol. 5, pp. 383–4 · *Letters from George Lord Carew*, ed. J. Maclean (1860), 17–20, 44, 47–8 · *The letters and life of Francis Bacon*, ed. J. Spedding, 7 vols. (1861–74), vol. 6, pp. 120–21 · J. Holles, commonplace book, Yale U., Beinecke L., Osborn MS b.32, 62–6 · *State trials*, 2.949–52 · J. W. F. Hill, *Tudor and Stuart Lincoln* (1956), 122 · A. R. Maddison, ed., *Lincolnshire pedigrees*, 2, Harleian Society, 51 (1903), 682 · *The letters of John Chamberlain*, ed. N. E. McClure, 2 (1939), 144, 313 · R. Lockyer, *Buckingham: the life and political career of George Villiers, first duke of Buckingham, 1592–1628* (1981), 35 · L. L. Peck, *Northampton: patronage and policy at the court of James I* (1982), 52, 173
Archives Lincs. Arch., papers

Monson, Sir William (1568?–1643),

naval officer, was the third but second surviving son of Sir John Monson (d. 1593) of South Carlton, Lincolnshire, and Jane, daughter of Robert Dighton of Little Sturton, Lincolnshire. He was probably raised as a Catholic, as both he and his brothers, Sir Thomas and Sir John, were all described as such in their adult lives. He matriculated at Balliol College, Oxford, on 2 May 1581, aged about twelve-and-a-half (and not fourteen, as the university admission registers record).

Privateering In September 1585, aged almost seventeen (as he later recalled), he ran away to sea in a privateer, being 'led thereunto by the wildness of my youth' (BL, Add. MS 9298, fol. 33v). His vessel and its consort sailed for the Spanish coast, where they encountered a well-armed Biscayner of 300 tons, recently returned from Newfoundland, which refused to yield. She was boarded at 8 p.m. but, the sea growing rough, the English vessels were forced to ungrapple, leaving the boarding party, which included Monson, to contest possession of the ship throughout the night. The Spaniards mounted a stiff resistance, twice attempting to blow up the decks on which Monson and his fellows stood, but were forced to capitulate the following morning.

Monson again served in a privateer in 1586. His reputation grew, and in 1587 he commanded three small ships financed by Sir George Carew. Before sailing Monson consulted the famed astrologer Simon Forman, who predicted that he would take a dazzling prize. Sure enough at Easter, Monson came upon a Catalonian vessel at anchor, trading in the north African port of Salé. However, he was persuaded not to seize her by English merchants resident in the port, who feared retaliation by the local authorities. A subsequent cruise along the Barbary coast proved fruitless and Monson made for the Canaries. His provisions soon ran low and he was forced to head for home. After narrowly escaping shipwreck off southern Ireland he reached England on 26 May 1588, in time to serve as a volunteer aboard the queen's pinnace *Charles*, part of the fleet that opposed the Armada.

Though the 1587 voyage had proved unprofitable Monson continued to consult Forman, who assured him that had he taken the Catalonian vessel at Salé the earlier prophecy would have been fulfilled. In 1589 Monson served as vice-admiral in the earl of Cumberland's expedition to the Canaries and the Azores. Eight prizes were taken at Flores, three of which Monson described as being 'of reasonable good value' (*Naval Tracts*, 5.177), but the expedition failed to prevent ships of the West Indian *flota* from reaching the safety of Terceira. On the return voyage Monson (and his men) went without drink for several days and when he reached southern Ireland his health collapsed. To make matters worse one of the valuable prizes was cast away.

Monson remained unwell throughout 1590 but had recovered by the following spring, when he again went to sea, this time as Cumberland's flag captain. Soon after the earl's squadron reached the Spanish coast Monson was put in charge of a Dutch ship laden with Portuguese spices, which had fallen into Cumberland's hands. However, she was recaptured and Monson was imprisoned in one of the galleys based at Lisbon. There he hatched a plan of escape, which was thwarted when his galley unexpectedly put to sea. He subsequently attempted to smuggle out intelligence to England concerning the homeward route to be taken by the Spanish Indies fleet but his scheme was betrayed by his English interpreter and he was transferred to Lisbon Castle. His capacity for mischief-making remained undiminished, however, as he proceeded to aid the escape of Manuel Fernandez, a servant of the Portuguese pretender, Don Antonio, whose cell adjoined his own. During the ensuing investigation by the Spanish authorities he initially denied helping Fernandez on the grounds that he could not speak Spanish. He subsequently adopted a more robust line of defence, maintaining that as a prisoner of war he was duty-bound not to neglect any opportunity to do his queen service. After his interrogation orders were given for him to be more closely guarded. At the end of November Monson witnessed the triumphant entry into Lisbon harbour of the Spanish galleon *St Andrew*, which had recently taken Grenville's *Revenge*, and swore that he would one day be present at the taking of the *St Andrew* herself.

The circumstances behind Monson's release in July 1592 are obscure. In 1593 he resumed his association with Cumberland. The two men captured a fleet of twelve hulks laden with powder bound for Spain, and Monson was left to examine half of them while Cumberland took the rest out to sea. Towards night the earl released them but they returned to attack Monson who, having no adequate force with him, narrowly escaped capture by jumping into his boat on one side as they boarded on the other. He sustained an injury to his leg which troubled him for the rest of his life. Monson returned to England later that year, soon after which his father died. As a younger son he inherited only a small amount of property.

Monson remained ashore throughout 1594, possibly suffering from another bout of illness for, when in August Sir John Hawkins contemplated sharing the treasurership of the navy with another, he discounted Monson on health grounds. On 9 July 1594 Monson was awarded an MA by the University of Oxford. Later, on 8 August, he was granted (honorary) admission to Gray's Inn. Early in the following year he married Dorothy, daughter of Richard Wallop of Bugbrooke, in Northamptonshire, and widow of Richard Smith of Shelford, Cambridgeshire. They had three sons (including William *Monson) and two daughters. Before his marriage Monson had agreed to undertake a further privateering voyage with Cumberland, a decision which he soon came to regret. Shortly after putting to sea Cumberland returned to England, as he was no longer convinced that the expedition required his personal attendance, leaving James Langton in command. Monson was so furious at being overlooked that he sailed alone to the Spanish coast. Buffeted by storms, his ship was driven back to Plymouth; there he met Sir Francis Drake, whom he joined in a fruitless search for some Spanish ships which had recently sacked Penzance.

Royal service Monson's anger with Cumberland proved long-lasting and precipitated his entry into royal service. In April 1596 he was appointed flag captain to the earl of Essex. In the subsequent expedition to Cadiz, during which time he was knighted (27 June), Monson helped to take the Spanish galleon *St Andrew*, fulfilling his earlier pledge to be present at her capture. During the voyage to the Azores the following year he again served under Essex. That same year he wrote a paper advocating the establishment of a settlement on the west African coast rather than in South America. In February 1598 Monson challenged Cumberland to a duel after hearing that the earl blamed him for the failure to capture the treasure ships at Terceira nine years earlier but Cumberland ignored him. During the invasion scare of 1599 Monson commanded a queen's ship in the Downs under Lord Thomas Howard but saw no action. Howard's wife, Lady Catherine, was by birth a Knyvett and it was doubtless through her influence that Monson was elected to parliament for the Knyvett-controlled borough of Malmesbury in 1601. He took no recorded part in this, his only parliament.

On 26 March 1602 Monson sailed for Spain as vice-admiral to Sir Richard Leveson, who had departed with his own squadron a week earlier. Their orders were to forestall an invasion of England or Ireland by preventing the

Spanish navy from putting to sea and to intercept the plate fleet. Before Monson could link up with his superior Leveson had encountered the treasure ships and their escorts but, being heavily outnumbered, he was forced to retreat. Despite this disappointment Leveson, now joined by Monson, espied in Lisbon harbour the carrack *St Valentine*, bearing cargo worth almost £130,000. Leveson entered the harbour first but his ships missed their station and were carried out of the road. Next came Monson, who engaged eleven enemy galleys drawn up under the guns of the nearby castle. His ordnance did fearful execution on these closely-packed vessels 'for when I hit one of them my shot passed through most part of the rest' (*Naval Tracts*, 4.114); the Spanish inflicted minimal damage, killing only five of Monson's crew. Nine of the galleys fled; the two that remained (one of which had earlier held Monson prisoner) were captured and burnt. There was still the carrack to be dealt with. Under a flag of truce Monson went aboard and treated with her Portuguese officers, who agreed to surrender their ship in return for their own freedom. Following this action a delighted Leveson wrote to the queen, desiring her to 'take notice of Sir William Monson', who had shown himself 'a very gallant, worthy gentleman' (*Salisbury MSS*, 12.184).

On returning to England, Monson reported in person to the queen, and in mid-July, in recognition of his outstanding service, he was given his own command. He was instructed to return to the Spanish coast, where he was to link up with a Dutch squadron under Opdam to prevent the enemy from concentrating his naval forces for invasion. Though impatient to put to sea Monson remained wind-bound throughout August, and by the time he sailed the threat of invasion had receded, the last remaining rebel stronghold in Ireland having surrendered. On reaching the Spanish coast he found no sign of Opdam, who had consumed most of his provisions in awaiting Monson's arrival and was on his way home. Matters were made worse by a storm on 22 September, which scattered his ships. When Monson arrived off the rock of Lisbon four days later he was accompanied by just two of his eight escorts. He remained undaunted, and that night, when he espied the lights of an enemy fleet, he gave pursuit. Bearing up to the flagship, however, he was horrified to discover her immense size and the number of her escorts. He avoided detection in the darkness by employing a Spaniard then aboard to hail the enemy but one of his consorts was less fortunate and was badly mauled. The following day Monson extricated himself with some difficulty and went to lie off Cape St Vincent. On 21 October he attempted to cut out a galleon that had taken refuge under the guns of Sagres Castle but in the ensuing artillery duel he lost ten men. Forced to give over the fight when an enemy squadron appeared to the westward he returned to Plymouth on 24 November. Over the winter he advised Sir Robert Cecil, in writing, on how to continue prosecuting the war. In the event his lines were not needed; in March 1603, just as he and Leveson were making ready to intercept the plate fleet, the queen died, and in the following year England made peace with Spain.

On 1 July 1604 Monson was appointed admiral of the narrow seas, doubtless on the recommendation of the new lord chamberlain, Thomas Howard, now earl of Suffolk. It was to Howard's wife that Monson owed his former parliamentary seat, and in June 1604 he was described by a Spanish diplomat as 'a creature of the countess of Suffolk' (Loomie, 54). As commander of the channel squadron one of Monson's main duties was to preserve the peace in English waters. Given the continuing conflict between Spain and the Dutch this was never going to be easy. Even so Monson's willingness to remain even-handed must be doubted, not least because he was a closet Catholic and hated the Dutch. Moreover, in the summer of 1604 Spain, aware of his sympathies, granted him a secret annuity of 4000 crowns (later increased to 5500) in the hope that this would encourage his partiality towards them. Monson always denied showing favour towards Spain in the performance of his duties but in May 1606, after protesting at the behaviour of several Dutch captains who had chased a Dunkirker into Sandwich harbour, he was officially reprimanded for failing to remove the Englishmen who formed part of the Dunkirker's crew.

Fall from office Monson helped to prevent the escape to France of Arabella Stuart in June 1611. In May 1614 he was sent to Scotland to suppress pirates but, on discovering their numbers had been exaggerated, he sailed to Ireland, where he found richer pickings. Monson's fortunes changed abruptly towards the end of 1615, at which time the power of his court patrons, the earl and countess of Suffolk, was diminished as a result of the Overbury murder scandal. Early in December he was arrested after the king learned of his Spanish pension; after being questioned at Hatton House, the London home of the lord chief justice, Sir Edward Coke, he was sent to the Tower on the night of 12 January 1616. The following day he was stripped of office. Coke interrogated him again on 24 January and desired to know, *inter alia*, whether he was in treasonable communication with the government of the Spanish Netherlands. In mid-April he was subjected to a final examination by Lord Chancellor Ellesmere and Attorney-General Bacon, when he made no attempt to conceal his hatred of the Dutch. Indeed he promised to provide a paper detailing the outrages committed by the Dutch during his period of office. No charges were brought against him and he was released in mid-July.

Despite his fall from office Monson harboured hopes of reinstatement. Instead he was left to languish at Kinnersley, his Surrey estate near Reigate; in 1617 the only official duty he performed was to counsel the government against mounting an attack on the pirate base at Algiers. By the beginning of 1618 Monson was so frustrated at his continued exclusion from office that he evidently consented to a scheme devised by the Suffolk faction to topple the new royal favourite, George Villiers, marquess of Buckingham. It involved his own second son, William, a youth of eighteen, whose handsome features it was thought would divert the gaze of the king from Villiers. In the event the flaunting of young Monson merely served to irritate James, who ordered the young man to be banished from his presence. Any hopes that Monson may have entertained thereafter of recovering favour were finally dashed in July 1619 with the fall of the Howards.

Fisheries and naval affairs In March 1623 Monson was consulted by the government over his enthusiastic support for plans to wrest control of the North Sea's fisheries from the Dutch. Monson's interest in this matter was of long standing for he had frequently lobbied the late Henry Howard, earl of Northampton, on the subject and had supported the publication in 1614 of Tobias Gentleman's pamphlet *England's Way to Win Wealth*, which had argued for the strengthening of England's fishing industry. Henceforth much of Monson's time was taken up in writing. The first of his six books was completed in 1624 (though later revised); comprising an account of the Elizabethan war at sea, which has achieved notoriety for its many inaccuracies, it circulated in manuscript form only. It clearly had a practical purpose, for England in 1624 was again on the verge of war with Spain. A further book (book 3), dealt with 'the state of his Majesty's navy and the abuse that is crept in by inexperienced carelessness' and was drafted shortly after the abolition of the navy commission in February 1628. Among its contents is 'A proposition to the parliament', wherein Monson anticipated the ship-money levies of the 1630s by advocating that parliament authorize the raising of £20,000 each year for the benefit of the navy.

Monson's advice was sought prior to the foundation of a royal fishery society in 1632. Despite his enthusiasm for the project he did not agree to invest in the new company until 1636 and had to be pursued to pay his £100 subscription in 1637. In 1635 Monson, now in his late sixties, was permitted to serve as vice-admiral of the first ship-money fleet under the earl of Lindsey. At the end of his cruise, which was largely uneventful, he submitted a paper of criticisms to the admiralty on the management of naval affairs. Its contents were taken seriously. Monson's opposition to the large number of watermen employed as mariners in the first ship-money fleet may help to explain why proportionally fewer were employed in 1636, and it was undoubtedly at Monson's suggestion that the admiralty permitted an under-treasurer to accompany the fleets of 1636 and 1637, an officer whose purpose was to pay for the needs of sailors put ashore for reasons of sickness or injury. In addition to his formal submission to the admiralty Monson wrote a separate, rather more candid paper based upon his observations of the first ship-money fleet. It formed an addition to his earlier book on naval administration and contained sly digs at admiralty commissioner Sir John Coke, of whose success he was obviously jealous. Some of the criticisms contained within this second paper were quite unjust. For instance Monson's view that the navy board had interfered in the victualling of the ships ignored the fact that for most of 1635 there had been no surveyor of marine victuals and that the board had therefore been acting under admiralty orders.

Monson was not employed in subsequent ship-money fleets, probably because of failing health, but he was appointed, on 9 May 1637, to the newly revived council of war. His final years were spent largely in writing. In 1638 he wrote a paper, 'How to make war upon Scotland if they follow their rebellious courses', while soon after the battle of the Downs (October 1639) he composed a short treatise in defence of ship money. A book containing various projects on how to make war on France, Spain, or the Dutch was being written as late as 1641. Monson never saw any of his work through the press, however. He died intestate in the Westminster parish of St Martin-in-the-Fields, where he was buried on 13 February 1643. Letters of administration were granted to his eldest surviving son, William, Viscount Castlemaine.

In 1682 part of Monson's book on the Elizabethan war with Spain appeared alongside Heywood Townsend's *Debates in Parliament*; all six of Monson's books were eventually published in 1704 by Messrs A. and S. Churchill. Since Monson evidently never achieved a final text, the publishers collated two variant copies of the manuscript, both of which are apparently now lost. The Churchill edition was itself collated with other known copies of the manuscript by Michael Oppenheim at the beginning of the twentieth century, and the end result was published in five volumes by the Navy Records Society between 1902 and 1914. At least one of Monson's tracts, hitherto unidentified as his and written at some time during the early 1630s, escaped inclusion in book 5 and is now in the Public Record Office (SP 9/202/24). Presented to Charles I, it advocated a pre-emptive naval strike on the Dutch in conjunction with Spain. Besides his naval writings Monson is said by Oppenheim to have penned 'Certain considerations that are not worthy of the name of history that happened to England since the year 1588 and a little before', several copies of which apparently are in the British Library. Sadly Oppenheim failed to specify their catalogue numbers. Monson also wrote a detailed account of his interrogation by the Lisbon authorities regarding his part in the escape of Manuel Fernandez 'at the request of my friends' (*Naval Tracts*, 5.159) but this is not known to have survived.

ANDREW THRUSH

Sources *The naval tracts of Sir William Monson*, ed. M. Oppenheim, 5 vols., Navy RS, 22–3, 43, 45, 47 (1902–14) · BL, Add. MS 9298, fol. 33v · E. G. R. Taylor, 'Sir William Monson consults the stars', *Mariner's Mirror*, 19 (1933), 22–6 · D. M. Loades, *The Tudor navy* (1992) · J. S. Corbett, *The successors of Drake* (1900) · A. J. Loomie, *Toleration and diplomacy: the religious issues in Anglo-Spanish relations, 1603–05* (1963), 54–5 · PRO, SP 9/202/24 · S. Usherwood and E. Usherwood, *The counter-Armada, 1596: the journall of the Mary Rose* (1983) · *Calendar of the manuscripts of the most hon. the marquis of Salisbury*, 12, HMC, 9 (1910); 16 (1933); 18 (1940) · *Report on the manuscripts of the marquis of Downshire*, 6 vols. in 7, HMC, 75 (1924–95), vol. 5 · *The manuscripts of the Earl Cowper*, 3 vols., HMC, 23 (1888–9), vol. 1, p. 15 · *The works of Francis Bacon*, ed. J. Spedding, R. L. Ellis, and D. D. Heath, 14 vols. (1857–74), vol. 5 · *The letters of John Chamberlain*, ed. N. E. McClure, 2 (1939), 127, 144 · Foster, *Alum. Oxon., 1500–1714*, 3.1021 · PRO, E351/2254, 2276, 2278 · *CSP dom., 1619–37* · HoP, *Commons, 1558–1603* · M. Fitch, ed., *Index to administrations in the prerogative court of Canterbury*, 6: *1631–1648*, British RS, 100 (1986), 287 · R. B. Wernham, *The return of the armadas: the last years of the Elizabethan war against Spain, 1595–1603* (1994) · R. T. Spence, *The privateering earl* (1995)

Archives Southwark Roman Catholic Diocesan Archives, London, naval diaries

Monson, William, first Viscount Monson of Castlemaine (*d.* 1673?), politician, was the second son of Admiral Sir William *Monson (1568?–1643) and Dorothy Smith (*fl.* 1595), daughter of Richard Wallop of Bugbrooke, Northamptonshire. He was promoted unsuccessfully as a court favourite in 1618 by the earl of Suffolk, but was knighted on 12 February 1623, and was created Viscount Monson of Castlemaine, co. Kerry, on 23 August 1628. He acquired substantial property in Reigate, Surrey, through his marriage on 25 October 1625 to Lady Margaret (*d.* 1639), daughter of James *Stewart, earl of Moray, and widow of Charles Howard, first earl of Nottingham. He entered Gray's Inn on 13 August 1633.

MP for Reigate in 1626, Monson was reported to the privy council in August 1626 as a muster defaulter in Surrey, and in 1638 and 1639 he was named as a defaulter on the county's 1636 ship money assessments. He was elected member of the Long Parliament for Reigate on 21 October 1640, and sided with parliament on the outbreak of civil war. Although named as a member of Surrey's county committee in several ordinances in 1643 and 1644, he did not begin to attend committee meetings with any regularity until January 1645. In May 1646 he married Frances, daughter of Sir Thomas Alston of Polstead, Suffolk. Their son, Alston, was born the following year.

On 21 May 1647 Monson was appointed to the committee of indemnity, and became active in its proceedings. He was among the MPs who fled parliament, faced with the London mob, to the New Model Army in July 1647, and in July 1648, at the time of the earl of Holland's rising in Surrey, he garrisoned Reigate Castle to prevent it from falling into the hands of the insurgents. He was later reprimanded by the parliamentarian executive committee at Derby House for taking it upon himself to sequester local inhabitants who were suspected of involvement in the rising. He continued to attend the House of Commons after Pride's Purge, and in January 1649 he was nominated one of the king's judges. He attended the high court on 20, 22, and 23 January 1649, but withdrew from the proceedings on 26 January and did not sign the king's death warrant. On 1 February he was placed by parliament on the committee appointed to receive and take note of the dissent of any member from the vote taken on 5 December 1648, that the king's latest terms were a sufficient basis for further negotiation with him.

Monson's financial difficulties became increasingly evident at this time. On 19 July 1649 he sought to persuade the house that £4500 was owing to him as arrears of the pension due to his first wife, but he lost his motion by two votes. Following the dissolution of the Rump in April 1653, and consequently his loss of parliamentary privilege, a judgment for debt was obtained against him by Richard Nunnelly of Westminster. In May 1654 Monson petitioned the protector for an order to help free him from restrictions imposed by his 1646 marriage settlement, claiming that he was unable to dispose of any part of his estate to pay his debts or to provide for his children.

The protector's council chose not to act on his petition. When the Rump was restored in May 1659 it was rumoured that Monson, along with Henry Marten, had to be sent for from the Fleet prison in order to form a quorum.

Monson's third wife, whom he married before the Restoration, was Elizabeth (*d.* 1695), second daughter of Sir George Reresby of Thrybergh, Yorkshire, and widow of Sir Francis Foljambe, bt, of Aldwark, Yorkshire, and of Edward, younger son of Sir John Horner of Mells, Somerset. Her nephew Sir John Reresby later claimed that she left Monson when his political influence began to wane, 'having sufficiently enriched herselfe by severall jewels and a greate part of his personall estate' (*Memoirs of Sir John Reresby*, 25). It was she who was accused in lampoons of having, with the help of her maidservants, tied her husband naked to a bedpost and whipped him.

At the Restoration, Monson was excepted out of the Bill of Pardon and reserved for future parliamentary resolution as to his punishment. On surrendering himself on 21 June 1660 he was recommitted to the Fleet. By the July 1661 act of pains and penalties he was brought before the House of Commons and was degraded of all his honours and titles and deprived of his property. He was also sentenced to be imprisoned for life and to be drawn from the Tower through the city of London to Tyburn, and back again, with a halter about his neck. In petitioning the House of Lords on 25 July 1661 to remit this 'most ignominious' part of the sentence, Monson claimed that he had attended the king's trial in order, if possible, to prevent 'that horrid murder' (*Seventh Report*, HMC, appx, 1, 150). The ignominious part of the sentence was, however, duly carried out on the anniversary of the king's execution. His estate at Reigate was granted to James, duke of York.

Monson appears to have died in the Fleet prison in 1673. His widow was restored to her rank as a peeress in April 1673 at the intercession of Sir John Reresby. She married Sir Adam Felton, bt, before 1676, and died in December 1695. Stewart Monson (*b.* 1628), Monson's son from his first marriage, did not outlive his father; Alston, his second son, died in 1675.

GORDON GOODWIN, *rev.* JOHN GURNEY

Sources GEC, *Peerage* · S. T. Bindoff, 'Monson, Sir William', HoP, *Commons, 1558–1603* · R. K. G. Temple, 'Monson (or Mounson, Munson), Sir William', Greaves & Zaller, *BDBR*, 244–5 · J. Gurney, 'The county of Surrey and the English revolution', DPhil diss., U. Sussex, 1991 · *Memoirs of Sir John Reresby*, ed. A. Browning, 2nd edn, ed. M. K. Geiter and W. A. Speck (1991) · Pepys, *Diary*, vol. 3 · *The journal of William Schellinks' travels in England, 1661–1663*, ed. M. Exwood and H. L. Lehmann, CS, 5th ser., 1 (1993) · JHC · JHL · C. H. Firth and R. S. Rait, eds., *Acts and ordinances of the interregnum, 1642–1660*, 3 vols. (1911) · *The letters of John Chamberlain*, ed. N. E. McClure, 2 vols. (1939) · *Fourth report*, HMC, 3 (1874) · *Seventh report*, HMC, 6 (1879) · CSP dom., 1654 · J. Foster, *The register of admissions to Gray's Inn, 1521–1889, together with the register of marriages in Gray's Inn chapel, 1695–1754* (privately printed, London, 1889) · VCH Surrey · *N&Q*, 3rd ser., 6 (1864), 252

Wealth at death deprived of property at the Restoration

Monson, William (1760–1807), army officer, fourth son of John *Monson, second Baron Monson (1727–1774) [*see*

under Monson, John, first Baron Monson], and his wife, Theodosia (1725–1821), daughter of John Maddison of Harpswell, Lincolnshire, was born on 15 December 1760. He was educated at Eton College (1769–74) and Harrow School (1774–5). In 1777 he was commissioned ensign in the 12th foot, and became lieutenant in 1778 and captain in 1780. By 1785 he had transferred to the 52nd foot in India. Monson married at Calcutta, on 10 January 1786, Anne, youngest daughter of John Debonnaire, merchant, of Lisbon and Calcutta. She died on 26 February 1841.

During the war carried on by the English against Tipu, sultan of Mysore, Monson commanded a light company of the 52nd regiment, which successfully attacked the southern entrenchment of Seringapatam on 22 February 1792. Monson continued in India, and had by September 1795 reached the rank of major. In 1797 he exchanged into HM 76th regiment, which had recently arrived in India, and obtained the rank of lieutenant-colonel. On the outbreak of the Second Anglo-Maratha War in 1803 Monson was appointed by Lord Lake to command the 1st infantry brigade of the army for the invasion of the Maratha dependencies in northern India, and he led the storming party which took Aligarh on 4 September 1803, receiving a severe wound, which incapacitated him from field duty for six months. In April 1804 Monson, in high favour with Lord Lake, was sent, with a mainly sepoy force, to keep watch on the large army of Jaswant Rao Holkar Ali, who was threatening the raja of Jaipur, an ally of the British. Monson reached Jaipur on 21 April. After an over-bold advance, his force of some 4000 men was defeated, only a few hundred surviving.

Monson's retreat was a blow to British prestige and he himself was considerably to blame. On the other hand, Lake has been rightly censured for sending Monson out with so small a force, and for not coming to his assistance when the retreat began. In spite of his defeat Monson was again employed by Lake in the final operations against Holkar in northern India. At the victory of Dig (14 November 1805) he was second in command to General Fraser, and on the latter being wounded Monson obtained the chief command. On 21 February 1806 Monson was chosen by Lake to head the last of the four unsuccessful assaults on Bharatpur. He subsequently returned to England, and in December 1806 entered parliament as member for Lincoln. He died at Bath on 26 December 1807. His only son, William John (1796–1862), became sixth Baron Monson in 1841, and the sixth baron's son and successor, William John Monson (1812–1898), was created Viscount Oxenbridge in 1886, and was master of the horse in Gladstone's fourth ministry.   G. P. MORIARTY, *rev.* JAMES FALKNER

Sources *Army List* · *GM*, 1st ser., 77 (1807), 1235 · J. Philippart, *East India military calendar*, 3 vols. (1823–6) · G. Malleson, 'Lord Lake', *Calcutta Review*, 43 (1866), 1–56 · HoP, *Commons*
Likenesses D. Gardner, pastel drawing, 1780 · photograph (after D. Gardner), NAM, Army Museums Ogilby Trust collection

Mont, Christopher (1496/7–1572), diplomat, was born in Koblenz near Cologne in Germany; the identity of his parents is unknown. Almost nothing is known of his background and early life. By his own testimony he entered English service in 1527 aged thirty. He attained a doctorate in civil law in the mid-1540s, and in addition to his fluency in Latin he probably had a reasonable grasp of English. The first records concerning him deal with his denization as an English citizen on 4 October 1531 and a payment made to him by Sir Thomas Cromwell, king's secretary, in 1533 for the translation of some German texts into Latin. It was also in 1533 that the first evidence of Mont's work as an English diplomatic agent comes to light.

As Henry VIII's struggle against the papacy and Charles V grew more implacable and England's position in Europe increasingly isolated, the need for new allies to lend support in the face of growing Habsburg hostility became more pressing. Additionally, Henry's rejection of Roman Catholicism left the king and Cromwell in need of a new religious settlement. It was in these circumstances that the king, very probably at Cromwell's suggestion, began to explore the idea of an alliance with the protestant princes of the Schmalkaldic League. In this context Mont's use as a diplomatic agent was threefold. As a native German he understood the language, politics, and geography of a land largely unknown to Henry's councillors and diplomats. As a protestant scholar he could introduce the king's overtures to German rulers and theologians with enthusiasm and competence. And finally, as a social and political nonentity he could broach negotiations for a military and religious alliance with men whom most of Europe's leaders, very possibly including Henry, regarded as heretics, without attracting undue attention.

The nature of Mont's service, not only to Henry but also to his children, is perhaps best summarized in the instructions he received for his first mission in July 1533. In company with Stephen Vaughan he travelled to Augsburg from where he dispatched reports on the imminent dissolution of the Swabian League and the ongoing plans to drive the Habsburgs out of Württemberg. After the diet's conclusion Mont performed the second part of his mission, which was to offer himself to Ludwig Wittelsbach, duke of Bavaria, as Henry's resident diplomatic agent. Should his offer be accepted he was:

> to explore, ensearch and know the state of the whole country of Germany and of their minds, intents and inclinations towards the king's highness and this realm. And also … ye can explore and ensearch to know the minds and intents of the princes of the Germanys, how they be inclined aswell towards the emperor as the king of the Romans. (PRO, SP 1/80, fol. 55r)

In the event Ludwig declined the offer and Mont returned to England, yet for much of the next forty years his work in Germany echoed these first instructions.

Mont's efforts to shape an alliance between Henry and the protestant princes began in earnest with his second embassy in January 1534. Having failed to meet his colleague, Nicholas Heath, he travelled to Munich alone, where he was given audiences with among others Johann Friedrich, elector of Saxony, and Philip, landgrave of Hesse, the leaders of the Schmalkaldic League. His remit was to justify to the princes Henry's actions concerning the divorce including an encomium on the suitability of

Anne Boleyn as queen. Furthermore, he was to defend the king's opposition to Clement VII and to seek the advice of the princes on how best to proceed. Somewhat distracted with their occupation of Württemberg, the princes failed to match Henry's enthusiasm for his new queen and offered little advice on his continuing struggles with Rome. Nevertheless, the embassy served as a signal to the league that Henry valued their opinion and took seriously the idea of closer co-operation. Consequently, Mont was rewarded with an annuity of £20 on 26 June.

Over the next five years Mont performed three more embassies. The first to Paris, between August and December 1535, with Simon Haynes, was intended to find the protestant theologian Philip Melanchthon in order to persuade him to leave the French court and to go to England. Henry and Cromwell no doubt hoped that with one of Germany's foremost theologians personally advising them their credibility in the eyes of their would-be allies would increase considerably. In the event little came of the mission. Between February and May 1538 Mont performed one of his rare solo missions to Philip of Hesse and Johann Friedrich of Saxony, primarily to advise them against attending the forthcoming general council. Finally, in January 1539 he visited Johann Friedrich, duke of Saxony, in order to seek his support for Henry's marriage to his sister-in-law, Anne of Cleves. He and his colleague, Thomas Paynell, were also instructed to gather information about Anne's personal attributes and the degree to which William, duke of Cleves, was committed to Rome.

On two further occasions, between August and October 1539 and March and August 1540, Mont was appointed Henry's special diplomatic agent in Germany, but his work was largely limited to dispatching reports from imperial diets and delivering messages. Although still employed as the king's agent, from 1540 he was largely inactive in the diplomatic sphere and served Henry mainly as an expert correspondent on German affairs. In truth even at the high point of Anglo-German relations Mont's status was not significant. Usually he accompanied more senior diplomatic colleagues on low-profile missions. His main role was as a guide, interpreter, and intelligence gatherer. Yet within this context he served the king well. Respected by prominent protestant theologians including Melanchthon, Martin Bucer, and Heinrich Bullinger, and known to the leading princes of the Schmalkaldic League, he served as an invaluable point of first contact for English envoys who might otherwise have floundered in the bewildering network of German politics and religion. He resided mainly in Strasbourg from 1544 and continued to receive his annuity.

After Henry's death Mont provided the regency government of Edward VI with news on German affairs and performed an embassy to Bern and Zürich in October 1549 to consult with the Swiss about the possibility of convening a protestant council. He married Rosina Quinter in January 1549. They had at least one son. He was involved in the odd negotiations instigated by the English to bring about a universal peace, especially between the emperor and the French, in May 1553. Dismissed after Mary's accession in July, he was called back to service in December 1558 by Elizabeth I. In addition to the newsletters which he continued to dispatch, Mont also offered support to English envoys sent to Germany such as Sir Henry Knollys in August 1562, and certain important private individuals, like Thomas Cecil, the somewhat dissipated eldest son of the queen's chief adviser, Sir William Cecil, principal secretary. He died between 8 July and 15 September 1572, probably in Strasbourg. News of his death reached the English government in November.

LUKE MACMAHON

Sources LP Henry VIII · CSP for., 1547–53 · CSP for., 1558–74 · E. Doernberg, Henry VIII and Luther: an account of their personal relations (1961) · E. Hildebrandt, 'Christopher Mont, Anglo-German diplomat', Sixteenth Century Journal, 15 (1984), 281–92 · R. McEntegart, 'England and the league of Schmalkalden, 1531–1547', PhD diss., U. Lond., 1992 · L. MacMahon, 'The ambassadors of Henry VIII: English diplomatic personnel, c. 1500–1550', PhD diss., University of Kent, 1999 · DNB
Archives BL, Royal MSS, letters

Montacute, John de. See Montagu, John, third earl of Salisbury (c.1350–1400).

Montacute, Nicholas (supp. fl. 1466), supposed chronicler, owes his existence to a misapprehension on the part of John Bale, who found in the library of Eton College a copy of the versified list of popes, De incorruptis pontificum Romanorum nominibus, by Nicholas de Maniacutia, or Maniacutius, a canon of St John Lateran during the papacy of Alexander III (r. 1159–81). Originally extending down to the reign of Eugenius III, the list was continued by a number of later hands. Perhaps the fact that copies were found in English collections (for example BL, Cotton MSS Vespasian A.xvi, fols. 15–17; Domitian A.xiii, fols. 98v–100) was a consideration prompting Bale to Anglicize Maniacutius as Montacute. Bale attributes to Montacute three other historical works, presumably all occurring in the same volume: De nominibus episcoporum Britannie majoris, incipit 'Augustinus Arelate consecratus est'; De regibus Anglorum, incipit 'Alphredus filius Edelwolphi junior'; Scalam temporum a Christo nato, incipit 'Christus natus est xlij anno regni Octaviani'. The fact that he saw these works at Eton was doubtless the reason for Bale's placing Montacute in the reign of Henry VI. However, John Pits, speculating that Montacute was a teacher at Eton, gives him a more precise floruit in 1466, while Thomas Tanner adds a collection of epigrams to his literary output. The identity of these other writings, which probably had a more concrete existence than their nominal originator, remains unknown.

HENRY SUMMERSON

Sources R. Sharpe, A handlist of the Latin writers of Great Britain and Ireland before 1540 (1997), 329–30 · Bale, Index, 307 · Bale, Cat., 1.597–8 · J. Pits, Relationum historicarum de rebus Anglicis, ed. [W. Bishop] (Paris, 1619), 656–7 · Tanner, Bibl. Brit.-Hib., 531 · N. Maniacutius, 'Ex Arnaldi cronica Londoniensi', [Ex rerum Anglicarum scriptoribus saec. XIII], ed. F. Liebermann and R. Pauli, MGH Scriptores [folio], 28 (Hanover, 1888), 529–30 [list of popes] · BL, Cotton MSS, Vespasian A.xvi, fols. 15–17; Domitian A.xiii, fols. 98v–100 [copies of the above]

Archives BL, Cotton MSS Vespasian A.xvi, fols. 15–17, Domitian A.xiii, fols. 98v–100

Montacute, Simon de. *See* Montagu, Simon de, first Lord Montagu (1259?–1316).

Montacute, William de. *See* Montagu, William, second Lord Montagu (*c*.1285–1319).

Montagu. For this title name *see* individual entries under Montagu; *see also* Neville, John, Marquess Montagu (*c*.1431–1471); Pole, Henry, Baron Montagu (1492–1539); Browne, Anthony, first Viscount Montagu (1528–1592); Browne, Magdalen, Viscountess Montagu (1538–1608).

Montagu, Ashley (1905–1999), anthropologist, was born Israel Ehrenberg on 28 June 1905 at 45 New Road, Mile End, London, the son of Charles Ehrenberg, tailor, and his wife, Mary, *née* Plotnik. Both parents were Jewish, his father from Russian Poland and his mother from Russia. He was educated at the Central Foundation School, London, and began while still young to collect the works of John Stuart Mill, Thomas Henry Huxley, and Friedrich Nietzsche from the used book stalls that lined Whitechapel Road. At fifteen he was given an old skull unearthed by a workman on the banks of the Thames. He took the skull in a paper bag to Sir Arthur Keith, conservator of the Royal College of Surgeons and England's leading evolutionary anatomist of the period. The famous scientist spoke to the young East End boy as if to a learned professor, thus beginning a friendship that lasted until Keith's death.

In 1922 Ehrenberg went up to University College, London, where he studied anthropology and psychology with Grafton Elliot Smith, Charles Spearman, and Karl Pearson, founders of the British eugenics movement. Sensing that class bias might impede his career, and in honour of a much admired Montague, he changed his name, originally to M. F. Ashley-Montague (subsequently dropping the initials, hyphen, and terminal e). By his early twenties he was attending the famous seminars led by the social anthropologist Bronislaw Malinowski at the London School of Economics. In 1926 he became a research worker at the British Museum (natural history), and in 1929 (on Keith's recommendation) he was appointed a scientific assistant at the Wellcome Historical Medical Museum. Nevertheless, sensitive to the struggle of the British working classes after the crushing of the 1926 general strike, he emigrated in 1931 to America, believing that it would be more congenial to social justice, as well as to the career of a young anthropologist. On the ocean crossing he met a young American woman, (Helen) Marjorie Peakes; they married six weeks later. They had three children: Audrey, Barbara, and Geoffrey.

In America, Montagu was appointed assistant professor of anatomy and director of the division of child growth and development at New York University, posts which he held from 1931 to 1938. He also continued his association with seminal figures in early twentieth-century anthropology, studying at Columbia University with Franz Boas and Ruth Benedict, where he enrolled in the graduate programme in 1934. He completed his doctorate in 1937 on the very Malinowskian issue of paternity knowledge among Australian Aborigines. After serving as associate professor of anatomy at Hahnemann Medical College and Hospital, Philadelphia, from 1938 to 1949, he was in the latter year appointed professor of anthropology at Rutgers University, where he developed the anthropology programme over the next six years. Because he was an outspoken anti-racist and opponent of McCarthyism during a retrograde period in American political life, some powerful academic and non-academic people considered his views dangerously un-American. He could also be a difficult colleague, and never suffered fools gladly. He left Rutgers under pressure from its president, Lewis W. Jones, in 1955, and never again held a regular teaching position, often remarking that true scholarship and the academic life were incommensurate pursuits.

Montagu wrote prodigiously for a popular audience (including a regular column for the *Ladies Home Journal*), educating the American public about the negative impact of social deprivation and stress on the development of children, the importance of a nurturing environment, the desirability of breast feeding, and the immense creative capacities of the young. In 1953 he published the early feminist classic *The Natural Superiority of Women*, which argued for complete equality of the sexes at a time when this was a controversial topic. (A fifth edition was published posthumously in 1999.) He was an accomplished author, writing the first modern account of the life of Joseph Merrick—*The Elephant Man* (1971)—who, like Montagu, had grown up in London's East End.

Montagu's most significant contribution was to demystify the concept of race. As early as 1926 he was publishing articles on the mistake of viewing races as typological, bounded categories. In 1942 he published what was arguably his most influential book, *Man's Most Dangerous Myth: the Fallacy of Race*, which called into question the entire basis of race as a biological category. The book went through six editions by 1997. In 1950 he was asked to become rapporteur (lead writer) of the first *UNESCO Statement on Race* (1951). He also published *Race, Science and Humanity* (1963), *The Idea of Race* (1965), and *What we Know about Race* (1985), and edited *Race and IQ* (1975, expanded edn 1996).

Montagu had a lighter side, and wrote a number of humorous books and articles, including a history of swearing (*The Anatomy of Swearing*, 1967). He appeared frequently on television, with a regular guest spot on Johnny Carson's *Tonight Show*. As a result he was sometimes erroneously thought of as a mere popularizer. While his writing was witty and accessible, rigorous scientific research and scholarship always informed his books.

An evolutionary anthropologist and public intellectual, Montagu brought to his many writings, whether about the first dissection of a great ape or the role of co-operative behaviour in human evolution, a wit shaped by a largely autodidactic education. He worked in three major domains of interest over seven decades of a prolific career: the integration of evolutionary biology and behaviour in the study of human development; the deconstruction of the category 'race' as biologically meaningful; and the social and ethical implications of anthropology's role in public education. As his friend the anthropologist C. Loring Brace said, 'Montagu has done more than anyone except Margaret Mead to bring the findings of anthropology to the attention of the public' (Harnad, 536). He died in Princeton, New Jersey, on 26 November 1999, and was survived by his wife Marjorie and their three children. SUSAN SPERLING

Sources A. P. Lyons, 'The neotenic career of M. F. Ashley Montagu', *Race and other misadventures: essays in honor of Ashley Montagu in his ninetieth year*, ed. L. Lieberman and L. T. Reynolds (1996), 3–22 · S. Harnad, 'Ashley Montagu', *International encyclopaedia of the social sciences*, 18 (1980), 535–7 [biographical supplement] · J. Marks, 'Ashley Montagu, 1905–1999', *Evolutionary Anthropology*, 9/6 (2000), 225–6 · S. Sperling, 'Ashley Montagu', *American Anthropologist*, 102/3 (Sept 2000), 583–8 · *The Guardian* (1 Dec 1999) · WWW · personal knowledge (2004) · private information (2004) [Mrs Helen Montagu] · b. cert.
Archives priv. coll.
Likenesses photograph, *c*.1949, Hult. Arch. · photograph, *c*.1957, Hult. Arch. · photograph, repro. in *The Guardian* · photograph, repro. in Sperling, 'Ashley Montagu', 583

Montagu, Lady Barbara (*c*.1722–1765). *See under* Scott, Sarah (1720–1795).

Montagu, Basil (1770–1851), author and legal reformer, was born on 24 April 1770, the acknowledged son of John *Montagu, fourth earl of Sandwich (1718–1792), and his mistress, Martha *Ray (*d*. 1779). The latter, the daughter of a stay maker, was a talented singer, who was murdered in 1779 by James Hackman. Montagu was brought up in his father's house at Hinchingbrooke, Huntingdonshire. He was educated at Charterhouse School and at Christ's College, Cambridge, where he matriculated in 1786 and graduated BA (sixth wrangler) in 1790 and MA in 1793. Montagu was admitted a member of Gray's Inn, London, on 30 January 1789 but continued to live in Cambridge. On 4 September 1790 he married Caroline Matilda Want (*d*. 1793) of Brampton, Huntingdonshire. This improvident marriage antagonized his father, who seems at that point to have stopped subsidizing him. It may have contributed to his impecuniosity during the 1790s, which culminated in this future authority on bankruptcy being threatened in 1798 with imprisonment for debt. In 1795, having been deprived in chancery of the inheritance from his father, he went to London to read law; he was called to the bar on 19 May 1798.

Montagu first travelled on the Norfolk circuit. He was not an eminent pleader but acquired an extensive practice in chancery and bankruptcy. His second marriage, in 1806, was to Laura Rush (*d*. 1806), eldest daughter of Sir William Beaumaris Rush of Roydon, Suffolk, and Wimbledon, Surrey. Like his first wife she died in childbirth. In 1808 Montagu married his housekeeper and children's governess, Anna Dorothea Benson Skepper, widow of Thomas Skepper, a lawyer in York, and daughter of Edward

Basil Montagu (1770–1851), by unknown artist

Benson, a York wine merchant. Montagu thereby became the stepfather of Anne Benson Skepper, who married the poet Bryan Waller Procter and became a gifted literary socialite and whose own daughter, Adelaide Ann *Procter, was also to become a poet. Edward Irving gave Montagu's third wife the sobriquet 'noble lady', and she is remembered in the correspondence of both Burns and Carlyle. Montagu had one son, Basil, with his first wife (mentioned in Wordsworth's 'To my Sister' and 'Anecdotes for Fathers', where he is called Edward), three sons with his second (one of whom, Algernon Sidney Montagu, became a judge in Australia), and two sons and a daughter with his third.

Montagu's writings on bankruptcy date from his four-volume *Digest of Bankruptcy Laws*, compiled between 1805 and 1807. On the strength of this work, which ran into several editions, Lord Erskine appointed him a commissioner in bankruptcy in 1806. For the next twenty-five years Montagu dedicated himself to the reform of bankruptcy administration. During this period he published numerous books and pamphlets on the subject. In 1825, when a major bankruptcy reform was being debated in parliament, Montagu attacked the delay and expense involved in the existing bankruptcy procedure in his timely *Inquires Respecting the Courts of Commissioners of Bankrupts, and Lord Chancellor's Court*. In July of the same year he suggested reforms of the system before the chancery commission. Although Montagu's *Inquires* contained few original suggestions, it did provide a handy collection of previous proposals for reform.

Montagu, a close friend of the law reformer Samuel Romilly, actively participated in other efforts to reform the law. In 1809, along with the Quaker philanthropist

William Allen and others, he formed the Society for the Diffusion of Knowledge upon the Punishment of Death and the Improvement of Prison Discipline (re-established in 1829 as the Society for the Diffusion of Information on the Subject of Capital Punishments). As part of this effort he wrote *The Opinion of Different Authors upon the Punishment of Death* (1813). Montagu also served in 1816 with Allen, James Mill, David Ricardo, and John Herbert Koe on the committee for investigating the causes for the alarming increase of juvenile delinquency in the metropolis. Later in the same year the committee published its report, in the fourth volume of Allen's periodical, *The Philanthropist*.

In 1835 Montagu was made a king's counsel, and soon afterwards he became accountant-general in bankruptcy. During his tenure, which lasted until 1846, he successfully convinced the Bank of England to pay interest on bankruptcy deposits which, until then, had never been paid. In 1837, with the assistance of Scrope Ayrton, he published *The Law and Practice in Bankruptcy as Altered by the New Statutes, Orders, and Decisions*. In co-operation with others, Montagu also published several series of bankruptcy case reports between 1830 and 1845.

Montagu is remembered for his close associations with some of the leading literary figures of his day. He came to know Samuel Taylor Coleridge in his undergraduate years; and after settling in London in 1795 he formed friendships with a number of intellectuals, including Charles Lamb, Henry Crabb Robinson, Robert Southey, Samuel Parr, and William Wordsworth. It was during this period that Montagu became one of the earliest pupils of William Godwin, and he was so impressed with Godwin's *Political Justice* that he temporarily gave up his legal studies. He toured the midland counties with Godwin in the autumn of 1797. Although Montagu later distanced himself from Godwin's teachings, he continued to be a regular visitor to Godwin's home and was present at the death of his wife, Mary Wollstonecraft.

Wordsworth, however, had the more lasting influence on Montagu. He lived with Montagu in Lincoln's Inn from February to August 1795, and Montagu's early papers on geometry probably stimulated Wordsworth's interest in mathematics. In an unpublished autobiography located at Grasmere, Montagu refers to his meeting Wordsworth as 'the most fortunate event of my life'. As evidence of their friendship, upon the death of Montagu's first wife in 1793 Wordsworth and his wife undertook the care of Montagu's young son during his infancy. Two years later Wordsworth lent Montagu £300, later increased to £400, secured by an annuity, the principal of which was not repaid until 1814. Montagu's acquaintance with Wordsworth and Coleridge is perhaps best remembered for the role he played in the estrangement of the two poets in 1810. According to Coleridge's contemporaneous recording of the incident in his notebooks and letters, Montagu claimed that Wordsworth had authorized him to tell Coleridge that Wordsworth had no hope in him and that he was a 'nuisance'. Although what Montagu actually said to Coleridge remains uncertain, the discussion precipitated the two-

year estrangement of Wordsworth and Coleridge. Wordsworth summed up Montagu in 1808 as a very kind, generous, and humane man who was, however, inept in the practical business of life.

Montagu also made the acquaintance of other luminaries such as Thomas Carlyle, William Hazlitt, Leigh Hunt, Edward Irving, and Percy Bysshe Shelley. He served as one of Shelley's counsel in the chancery proceedings over the custody of Shelley's children. These acquaintances frequently visited the Montagu home in 25 Bedford Square, London, for, as Robinson relates in his diary, Montagu was fond of playing the patron.

Montagu's own attempt at literary achievement is exemplified best by his 16 volume *Works of Francis Bacon*, which he edited between 1825 and 1837, assisted by Francis Wrangham and William Page Wood. While at Cambridge he had noticed how little attention the works of Bacon had received, and he set out to publish a complete edition. In 1821 he contributed to the *Retrospective Review* two articles on Bacon's 'Novum organum'. Montagu's edition of Bacon's works was severely criticized by Thomas Macaulay in the *Edinburgh Review* in July 1837. Montagu responded in 1841 with the publication of a series of letters to Macaulay.

Montagu published numerous other works on a wide variety of subjects. In the field of law, in addition to works on bankruptcy he wrote on set-off (1801), partnerships (1815), liens (1816), and pleading and equity (1824). He undertook, but never published, a translation of Étienne Dumont's *Traités de législation civile et pénale*. In addition he wrote more than twenty-five books and pamphlets on other diverse subjects ranging from the effects of fermented liquors, in 1814, to the funerals of Quakers, in 1840. Montagu died at Boulogne on 27 November 1851.

V. MARKHAM LESTER

Sources *GM*, 1st ser., 60 (1790), 858 · *GM*, 1st ser., 76 (1806), 590 · *GM*, 2nd ser., 37 (1852), 410 · D. Wu, 'Basil Montagu's manuscripts', *Bodleian Library Record*, 14 (1991–4), 246–51 · *The Athenaeum* (6 Dec 1851), 1282 · M. C. Crum, 'Literary work and literary friends of Basil Montagu QC', BLitt diss., U. Oxf., 1950 · K. Coburn, ed., *The notebooks of Samuel Taylor Coleridge*, 3 (1973) · M. Moorman, *William Wordsworth, a biography*, 2: *The later years, 1803–1850* (1965) · V. M. Lester, *Victorian insolvency: bankruptcy, imprisonment for debt, and company winding-up in nineteenth-century England* (1995) · N. Roe, *Wordsworth and Coleridge: the radical years* (1988) · W. Knight, *The life of William Wordsworth*, 3 vols. (1889) · *Collected letters of Samuel Taylor Coleridge*, ed. E. L. Griggs, 3 (1959) · W. C. Metcalfe, ed., *The visitations of Essex*, 2, Harleian Society, 14 (1879) · C. Kegan Paul, *William Godwin: his friends and contemporaries*, 2 vols. (1876) · *Memoirs of the life of the Right Honourable Sir James Mackintosh*, ed. R. J. Mackintosh, 2nd edn, 2 vols. (1836) · J. Wells, ed., *Four letters to Anna and Basil Montagu* (1995)

Archives BL, considerations on the removal of Jewish disabilities, Add. MS 20041 · CUL, papers relating to edition of works of Francis Bacon | NMM, letters to fourth earl of Sandwich relating to his education · University of Bristol, Pinney MSS · Wordsworth Trust, Dove Cottage, Grasmere

Likenesses Opie, portrait; formerly in possession of Bryan Walter Proctor, 1894; lent to the third Loan exhibition, No. 183 · portrait, priv. coll. [*see illus.*]

Montagu, Charles, earl of Halifax (1661–1715), politician, was born on 16 April 1661 at Horton, Northamptonshire, and baptized at St Margaret's, Westminster, on 12 May, the

Charles Montagu, earl of Halifax (1661–1715), by Sir Godfrey Kneller, c.1703–10

sixth, but fourth surviving, son of George Montagu (*bap.* 1622, *d.* 1681), politician, a younger son of Henry Montagu, first earl of Manchester, and his wife, Elizabeth (1623x31– 1684), daughter of Sir Anthony Irby of Whaplode, Lincolnshire.

Early years Montagu entered Westminster School in 1675, distinguishing himself with the quality of his 'extempore epigrams' (Montagu, 4). He was admitted to Trinity College, Cambridge, on 8 November 1679, proceeding MA in 1682 and being elected a fellow in 1683, following Charles II's order to the college to confer the next fellowship upon Montagu notwithstanding any statute or custom to the contrary. His verses commemorating the death of Charles II were published in *Moestissimae ac laetissimae academiae Cantabrigiensis affectus* (1685). These drew him to the attention of Charles Sackville, sixth earl of Dorset, a notable patron of literature, who invited him to London and introduced him to the wits of the town, where he acquired what the duchess of Marlborough later called 'a great knack at making pretty ballads' (*Private Correspondence*, 2.144). In 1687 he joined with Matthew Prior to write a parody of John Dryden's *Hind and the panther*, entitled *The hind and the panther travers'd to the story of the country mouse and the city mouse*, in which a mouse was substituted for the hind, and which earned him the nickname Mouse Montagu.

Montagu was living in Channel Row, Westminster, when he married shortly before 18 February 1688 Anne (*b.* after 1630, *d.* 1698), daughter of Sir Christopher Yelverton, first baronet, of Easton Maudit, Northamptonshire, and

the widow of Robert *Montagu, third earl of Manchester (*d.* 1683) [*see under* Montagu, Edward, second earl of Manchester]. This match considerably augmented the rather meagre estate of £50 per annum which was all Montagu had inherited from his father as a younger son. Montagu supported the revolution of 1688, joining the forces at Northampton commanded by his stepson, Charles *Montagu, fourth earl of Manchester, in the company of his brothers George and Christopher.

The House of Commons Montagu was able to take advantage of the new political opportunities which opened up following William's invasion. He obtained Dorset's recommendation to Aubrey de Vere, twentieth earl of Oxford, in order to smooth his election to the Convention for Maldon in Essex, aided by some support from Manchester, who had an interest in the nearby Leighs Priory estate. In February 1689 he was able to purchase a clerkship of the privy council for £1500, reputedly owing to the influence of George Savile, marquess of Halifax. He retained this office until his appointment to the Treasury. Montagu was clearly perceived as a rising star by the whigs, not least because of his 'natural quickness, eloquence and good address' (Knights, 851). However, these talents were insufficient as yet to bring him further preferment as in June 1691 he failed to obtain the secretaryship of the Treasury, which was vacant following the sudden death of William Jephson.

In the House of Commons, Montagu generally supported the court, particularly on financial matters. He seems to have been given a leading role by the Commons in the conferences with the Lords over the bill regulating trials for treason. Following his report from a conference on 29 December 1691, on 31 December he opposed the Lords amendments to the Treason Trials Bill on the grounds that the upper house was attempting to set up an aristocracy instead of a monarchy. Possibly owing to his own experience at Cambridge, Montagu tried unsuccessfully on 22 February 1692 to amend the bill confirming the charters of Cambridge University to allow some fellows not to take orders. His appointment on 21 March 1692 to the Treasury board was indicative both of his own ability and of William III's shift towards the whigs. The first lord of the Treasury, Sydney Godolphin, Baron Godolphin, was clearly impressed by his ability and henceforth Montagu was a major government spokesman in the House of Commons. This involved much attention to financial detail and generally pushing forward the government's supply needs. Montagu also continued to defend his fellow whigs from attack, most notably defending Admiral Edward Russell on 20 December 1692 by proposing a motion that he had 'behaved himself with fidelity, courage and conduct during the whole summer's expedition' (*Parliamentary Diary of Narcissus Luttrell*, 331) and on 23 January 1693 opposing the motion that Bishop Gilbert Burnet's *Pastoral Letter* be burned by the common hangman. His ministerial position also involved such unpopular tasks as defending the king's use of the royal veto of the place bill in January 1694.

Montagu was at the heart of the Treasury when the legislation founding the Bank of England was devised in the 1693–4 session. Although the plans were based on the ideas of William Paterson and Michael Godfrey, Montagu played an important role in the negotiations and his performance was recognized in May when he was appointed to succeed the ailing Richard Hampden as chancellor of the exchequer, and was sworn a privy councillor; both appointments were dated 10 May 1694. He was thus in post in time to oversee the subscriptions to the bank which took place in June, and in which he invested £2000 of his own money. Political considerations were never far from Montagu's calculations and in the 1694–5 session he was in the vanguard of attacks on tories Henry Guy, speaker Sir John Trevor, and Thomas Osborne, first duke of Leeds, for taking bribes from the East India Company. At this point Montagu overreached himself in his bid for political dominance by trying to remove Robert Spencer, second earl of Sunderland, from power, the failure of which attempt led to an insincere reconciliation between the two men.

Montagu had resided in Jermyn Street since 1689, and at the 1695 election he decided to contest the more prestigious parliamentary constituency of Westminster, obtaining the support of Princess Anne, William Russell, first duke of Bedford, and John Holles, duke of Newcastle. By switching seats he was able to set up his brother Irby Montagu at Maldon, using tactics which one opponent called 'fighting some and bribing and corrupting others' (*Autobiography*, 390). Such was Montagu's prestige that he was elected on 30 November 1695 to the Royal Society (although he had been approved for membership in May 1688), and served as president for the next three years. The 1695–6 parliamentary session saw Montagu grapple with the recoinage question and face opposition to the court over the establishment of a Board of Trade. In the case of the former, Montagu won the parliamentary debate about the desirability of a recoinage and managed the resultant bill through the house. On the Board of Trade he supported Thomas Wharton's wrecking amendment to the bill establishing the board which required the office-holders to take the abjuration oath. The amendment failed, although the parliamentary board was eventually lost in the furore surrounding the assassination plot. However, in the summer he saw off the attempts to create a land bank to rival the Bank of England and when the land bank failed to raise sufficient subscriptions he was on hand with an alternative scheme to ease the shortage of funds by issuing exchequer bills. He was also able to raise funds in the City of London to pay the troops in Flanders and stave off a military disaster. In November 1696 he supported the attainder of Sir John Fenwick, defending in debate Russell, Charles Talbot, duke of Shrewsbury, and John Churchill, earl of Marlborough, from Fenwick's accusations, 'shewing how improbable this fiction was to any of you' (*Letters Illustrative*, 1.49), and ensuring that the main issue in the debate remained the security of the government.

On 1 May 1697 Montagu became first lord of the Treasury, holding off the claims of Sir Stephen Fox to precedence in the new board, and in November he was sworn a member of the cabinet council. In 1697 he also became high steward of Cambridge University. By the beginning of the 1697–8 parliamentary session Montagu was the only member of the junto group of leading whigs remaining in the Commons and in December James Vernon predicted an attack in the Commons on him, 'he being the person they have the greatest mind to lower, as one that stands in their way' (*Letters Illustrative*, 1.461). The session began with a defeat for Montagu over the standing army, MPs voting to reduce it to the number employed in 1680 despite his arguments. In January 1698 Montagu was attacked for falsely endorsing exchequer bills, but rather than retreating he retaliated by 'carrying the war into the enemy's country' (ibid., 1.475), and he was able to turn this attack upon himself into a successful parliamentary prosecution of his accuser, Charles Duncombe, who ended up being sent to the Tower and then facing a bill of pains and penalties. A further attack in February 1698, this time on his grant of £12,000 in Ireland, resulted in a resolution of the Commons that Montagu had deserved the king's favour because of his services to the government. The session ended with Montagu piloting through the Commons an innovative piece of financial legislation raising £2 million, and a bill settling the East India trade. Following the end of the session, on 16 July 1698 Montagu was named one of the lords justices charged with governing the kingdom in William's absence abroad.

Montagu faced a stern challenge in the election for Westminster in July 1698. He was assisted by the court interest and obtained from the king the great bell known as Tom of Westminster, the sale of which was used to aid the poor of the parish of St Margaret, Westminster. However, the election coincided with his wife's final illness and his victory at the polls coincided with her death. She was buried on 28 July, whereupon Montagu retreated to the house of Richard Jones, earl of Ranelagh, at Chelsea to recover. He also lost the use of her jointure of £1500 per annum, which fell to her son, the earl of Manchester. The prospects of further parliamentary pressure on his position, and perhaps the need for a steady income to replace the lost jointure, may explain why on 5 September 1698 he used his powers of patronage as the head of the Treasury to appoint his brother Christopher to the lucrative office of auditor of the receipt in the exchequer. This was widely seen as being for his own financial benefit and as providing a line of retreat from his more onerous Treasury post as peace brought a different set of political problems for Montagu. It also brought him into conflict with the duke of Leeds, who had been granted the reversion of the office for his son in Charles II's reign. The 1698–9 session saw Montagu fail to prevent the Disbanding Bill and consequently lose some of the king's confidence. At the end of the session Montagu relinquished the chancellorship, but he remained first lord and he was named in June 1699 as a lord justice. With a potentially troubled session ahead, on

15 November 1699, on the eve of parliament's reassembly, he retired from the Treasury altogether. Two days later he received a life patent for the auditorship of the receipt, which carried with it a house close to St Stephen's Chapel in New Palace Yard. Almost immediately Leeds began legal proceedings to try to force Montagu to relinquish his new office.

The House of Lords In December 1699 Joseph Addison had written to Montagu of his continental fame, in which 'your name comes in upon the most difficult subjects, if we speak of the men of wit or the men of business, of poets or patrons, politicians or parliament men' (*Letters*, 12–13). However, in politics at least Montagu was no longer pre-eminent in the Commons and on 13 December 1700 he was created Baron Halifax, with a special remainder to his nephew George Montagu and his male heirs. His choice of title, in recognition of another of his early patrons, drew a somewhat barbed response from the tory Francis Gwyn, who wrote, 'I cannot help begrudging him the title of our poor friend Halifax' (*Portland MSS*, 3.637), the second marquess having died earlier that year. Halifax took his seat in the Lords on 11 February 1701. On 14 April 1701 he was impeached by the House of Commons in an indictment containing six articles, most of which referred to the procurement of grants, but which included as the most serious charge his role in the first partition treaty, which James Vernon had communicated to him in August 1698. The case collapsed and the impeachment was discharged in June 1701.

The accession of Queen Anne saw Halifax dismissed from the privy council in March 1702, and for the next eight years his claims to high financial office were blocked by the incumbent lord treasurer, Lord Godolphin. In July 1702 Godolphin ruled that the dispute between Halifax and the duke of Leeds should be decided through the normal course of the law, and in December 1702 Halifax nearly fought a duel with Peregrine Osborne, marquess of Carmarthen, the eldest son of the duke of Leeds, occasioned in part by the ongoing dispute over the auditorship and in part by the duke's public remark that Montagu's family 'was raised by rebellion, but his own suffered by it' (*London Diaries of William Nicolson*, 142). Halifax remained a whig partisan and in January 1703 the tory majority in the House of Commons passed a motion accusing him of circumventing the traditional accounting procedures in the exchequer. Halifax defended his actions on the ground that more efficient methods were required given the vast sums of money which had to be audited in wartime. Although the House of Lords vindicated Halifax in February 1703 by voting him 'a person diligent and faithful in his office' (ibid., 198), he had to face prosecution by the attorney-general in a case which eventually petered out in June of the following year with a *nolle prosequi* after Halifax had not answered the information and stood on his parliamentary privilege. Twice in 1703 he opposed bills aimed at penalizing the practice of occasional conformity. Although an important member of the whig junto his

chances of a return to the Treasury remained bleak, particularly as the whigs gradually grew closer to the Marlborough–Godolphin ministry. Fortunately his frustrations were allayed to some extent by his other interests. He chaired most meetings of the House of Lords committee on the public records, which complemented his own antiquarian interests. In November 1704 Bishop William Nicolson noted Halifax as 'beginning a vast design in collecting the public records' (ibid., 231), which no doubt appealed to a man already known for his private library, 'a gallery nobly furnished with curious books placed under statues as in Cotton's. His lordship has transcripts of all the rolls of parliament, journals of the Lords and Commons etc.' (ibid., 277).

Halifax played a key role with his junto colleagues in protecting Godolphin following his advice in August 1704 that the Act of Security passed by the Scottish parliament should be granted the royal assent, which was then attacked in parliament because it threatened the Hanoverian succession north of the border. In particular he was one of those seen negotiating with Godolphin during the debate of 29 November 1704 in the House of Lords in which the whigs stepped in to divert the debate away from censuring the lord treasurer. On 6 December Halifax was on hand 'with great gaiety of oratory and elocution' (*London Diaries of William Nicolson*, 245) to support the deal recently done between Godolphin and the junto over Scotland. On 11 December he proposed the Aliens Act, which was designed to force the Scots to come to terms. During the queen's visit to Cambridge University in April 1705 Halifax was awarded the degree of LLD.

When the new parliament assembled Halifax sprang a trap on the tories by noting on 30 November 1705 that there had been much misrepresentation of 'persons of honour and quality as disaffected to the present establishment of the Church of England' (*London Diaries of William Nicolson*, 315). A subsequent debate on 6 December on the 'Church in danger' saw Halifax dismiss tory attacks on the ground that 'there's always a cry for the Church when a certain faction is disregarded' (ibid., 321). On 9 December Halifax's old quarrel with the Osbornes reared its head again and a duel with Carmarthen in Hyde Park was prevented only after the intervention of a captain of the guards. The queen's husband, Prince George, then intervened to prevent further trouble. Halifax took an important role in February 1706 in persuading sufficient country whigs to drop their advocacy of certain aspects of the Regency Bill, such as the place clause, to ensure their defeat. In April 1706 he was named as one of the English commissioners to negotiate the union with Scotland. In May 1706 he was chosen as the representative of the queen to compliment the Electress Sophia of Hanover with copies of the acts of parliament passed in her favour and to institute the electoral prince (the future George II) with the Order of the Garter. On both the outward and return trips he stopped at The Hague to engage in negotiations with the Dutch about a barrier treaty providing protection from France and the English succession. His aim, as he recounted to Lord Somers, was that 'their barrier should be as good as we can get for them; and if they insist upon too much, it will be the greater tie on them, not to make peace till it is procured for them' (Hill, 103). Halifax was to be disappointed that Charles, second Viscount Townshend, was to be chosen as a peace plenipotentiary in March 1707. Frustrated political ambition may explain his intention in April 1707 of forming an assembly of 'beaux esprits' (Spens, 309). Certainly his literary fame was growing for in his will of August 1707 his old school friend George Stepney left Halifax the choice of 100 'tomes if there be any which may deserve to have a place in his library' (ibid., 317).

In July 1707 Halifax recommended one Robert Barton to the duke of Marlborough for a captain's commission. He was the nephew of Halifax's friend Sir Isaac Newton and the brother of Catherine Barton, who was Halifax's house-keeper following the death of his wife, and reputed by some to be his mistress. Thinly disguised accusations appeared in print under the pen of Delariviere Manley, whose character, Bartica, in her *Memoirs* (1710) was taken to represent Catherine Barton. To Sarah, duchess of Marl-borough, Montagu 'was a frightful figure, and yet pre-tended to be a lover, and followed several beauties, who laughed at him for it' (*Private Correspondence*, 2.147).

Halifax was still willing to embarrass the ministry for party ends, thus on 5 February 1708 he supported the abo-lition of the Scottish privy council. On the 9th he was elected to the Lords committee to investigate William Gregg, the former under-secretary in Robert Harley's office, who had been convicted of spying. A more con-structive piece of legislation sponsored by Halifax in Feb-ruary 1708 was the bill encouraging privateers in the West Indies, which he drafted after consulting naval and Lon-don mercantile opinion. Halifax was not averse to flatter-ing Marlborough, noting after the battle of Oudenarde in July 1708 that 'we shall never get Spain, unless your grace conquerors it by way of Flanders' (*Marlborough–Godolphin Correspondence*, 2.1039–40). As the other members of the whig junto acquired office, Halifax became more trouble-some to Marlborough and Godolphin. In November 1708 Marlborough opined 'if he had no fault but his unreason-able vanity, that alone would be capable of making him guilty of any fault' (ibid., 2.1150). Thus Halifax was not appointed as a peace plenipotentiary in 1709 and had to make do with appointment on 3 June to the rangership of Bushey Park, Hertfordshire. His frustrations were no doubt amplified by the entrenched position of Lord Treas-urer Godolphin and Halifax's evident belief 'that nobody can execute that office so well as himself' (ibid., 3.1207).

Halifax had maintained good relations with Robert Har-ley, so he was an early target when Harley began to intrigue against the Godolphin ministry in the wake of the prosecution of Dr Henry Sacheverell, a measure which Halifax had supported in March 1710. During the intrigues which preceded Godolphin's fall, Harley engin-eered Halifax's appointment in July as a peace plenipot-entiary at The Hague, a role which Halifax had previously coveted. However, when Harley came to power in August, the ministry's peace negotiations were conducted in

secret and Halifax never took up his post. Indeed, Halifax received no office from Harley and spent the last four years of Anne's reign in opposition. There is little doubt that he was effective in this oppositional role: in June 1711 John Elphinstone, fourth Lord Balmerino, reported that there was 'not a man in our house that speaks more hand-somely nor that understands trade, taxes and all things concerning the public revenue better' (*London Diaries of William Nicolson*, 65). On 15 February 1712 Halifax moved an address against the peace and on 28 May 1712 he led the whig attack on the ministry for issuing orders restraining James Butler, second duke of Ormond, from offensive action in Flanders. Despite maintaining contact with Har-ley (earl of Oxford from 1711), Halifax joined in the whig opposition to the peace of 1713 and its attendant commer-cial treaty with France. He opposed the address on 9 April 1713 because it gave thanks for the peace when the terms had yet to be announced. He was also not prepared to back the Scots in supporting the motion of James Ogilvy, fourth earl of Findlater, on 2 June 1713 for leave to bring in a bill to dissolve the Union. In the next session Halifax voted against the Schism Bill in June 1714.

Final year Upon Queen Anne's death it was revealed that Halifax was one of the regents appointed by George I to govern the kingdom until his arrival in England, and he duly served as a lord justice until 18 September. On 23 Sep-tember 1714 he was appointed to the privy council. On 30 September he surrendered his office of auditor of the exchequer, which was then granted to his nephew, George, although it was believed that Halifax 'reserves the profits during his life' (*Wentworth Papers*, 425). This surren-der was in preparation for Halifax's return to the Treasury as he was named first lord on 13 October, much to his chag-rin as he had coveted the more prestigious position of lord treasurer. Further honours followed: he was nominated to the Order of the Garter on 16 October, and on 19 October he was created earl of Halifax, but without a special remainder in his nephew's favour. On 24 December he was appointed lord lieutenant of Surrey.

Halifax was taken ill on 15 May 1715 while visiting the house of Mynheer Duvenvoord, one of the Dutch ambas-sadors. He died of an inflammation of the lungs on 19 May and was buried on 26 May in Westminster Abbey. His will, written on 10 April 1706, contained a codicil dated 12 June 1706 leaving £3000 and his jewels to Catherine Barton. In a further codicil of 1 February 1713 this was augmented to £5000 plus his interest in the rangership of Bushey Park and his manor of Apscourt in Surrey. All this 'as a token of the sincere love, affection and esteem, I have long had for her person, and as a small recompense for the pleasure and happiness I have had in her conversation' (*N&Q*, 430), which led to renewed speculation that she had been his mistress. She subsequently married John Conduitt, later an MP and master of the Royal Mint. The other main bene-ficiary of the will was his nephew, George, who also suc-ceeded as second Baron Halifax, and for whom the Halifax earldom was shortly to be revived.

Significance Montagu was a major politician in the twenty-five years following the revolution of 1688. Few contemporaries were without an opinion of him. To his friends and admirers he was the founder of the national debt and Bank of England, and rescuer of a debased currency, and a veritable political genius. To his enemies he was greedy and insincere, 'a party-coloured, shallow, maggot-headed statesman' (Knights, 850). Initially Montagu used his natural abilities to interest a series of patrons and took the opportunities of office to demonstrate his talents. By all accounts he was a prickly man, owing perhaps to his lack of inches and the disadvantages of being the younger son of the younger son of a peer. Nevertheless, his ability made him a key member of the group of young whigs—with John Somers, Thomas Wharton, and Edward Russell—known collectively as the junto, which formed the backbone of the government between 1694 and 1700 and which continued to be influential politically until 1714. Indeed, such was Halifax's power as an orator that William Legge, first earl of Dartmouth, thought him partly responsible for the change in the nature of debates in the Lords after 1700, when he 'brought up a familiar style' (*Bishop Burnet's History*, 5.234) from the Commons. A favourable marriage and Treasury and exchequer office transformed his material fortune and by the reign of Queen Anne he had become a patron of letters, numbering William Congreve, Richard Steele, and Joseph Addison among his protégés. He received thirteen sets of Thomas Rymer's *Foedera* in recognition of his financial support for that project, and was a member of the Kit-Cat Club. Not surprisingly, it was Addison who provided one of the most fulsome assessments of Halifax's character and career when he wrote to a friend in November 1708:

> you have in it greatness of birth and natural parts, a consummate knowledge of Belles Lettres in all their branches and a celebrated patronage of them in others. His lordship's management of the Treasury in King William's reign when all the money of the kingdom was recoined has made him looked upon universally as one of our greatest ministers as his many excellent speeches in the House of Commons and since in the House of Lords have gained him the reputation of one of our greatest orators. (*Letters*, 122)

STUART HANDLEY

Sources GEC, *Peerage*, new edn, 6.245–6 · Venn, *Alum. Cant.* · G. Hampson, 'Montagu, Charles', HoP, *Commons, 1660–90* · M. J. Knights, 'Montagu, Charles', HoP, *Commons, 1690–1715* · D. B. Horn, ed., *British diplomatic representatives, 1689–1789*, Camden Society, 3rd ser., 46 (1932) · *The parish of St James, Westminster*, 1/2, Survey of London, 30 (1960) · C. Montagu, *The poetical works of the Rt. Hon. Charles, late earl of Halifax with his lordship's life*, 2nd edn (1716) · *The London diaries of William Nicolson, bishop of Carlisle, 1702–1718*, ed. C. Jones and G. Holmes (1985) · *The Marlborough–Godolphin correspondence*, ed. H. L. Snyder, 3 vols. (1975) · H. Horwitz, *Parliament, policy and politics in the reign of William III* (1977) · G. S. Holmes, *British politics in the age of Anne* (1967) · M. Hunter, *The Royal Society and its fellows, 1660–1700: the morphology of an early scientific institution* (1982) · *Private correspondence of Sarah, duchess of Marlborough*, 2 (1838) · *The parliamentary diary of Narcissus Luttrell, 1691–1693*, ed. H. Horwitz (1972) · *The autobiography of Sir John Bramston*, ed. P. Braybrooke, Camden Society, 32 (1845) · *Letters illustrative of the reign of William III from 1696 to 1708 addressed to the duke of Shrewsbury by James Vernon*, ed. G. P. R. James, 3 vols. (1841) · *The letters of Joseph Addison*, ed. W. Graham (1941) · *The manuscripts of his grace the duke of Portland*, 10 vols., HMC, 29 (1891–1931), vols. 2–9 · B. W. Hill, *Robert Harley: speaker, secretary of state, and premier minister* (1988) · S. Spens, *George Stepney, 1663–1707: diplomat and poet* (1997) · J. J. Cartwright, ed., *The Wentworth papers, 1705–1739* (1883) · *Bishop Burnet's History* · N&Q, 8 (1853), 429–53 · J. Sainty, *Treasury officials, 1660–1870* (1972) · J. Sainty, *Officials of the exchequer*, List and Index Society, special ser., 18 (1983) · W. L. Sachse, *Lord Somers: a political portrait* (1975) · N. Luttrell, *A brief historical relation of state affairs from September 1678 to April 1714*, 6 vols. (1857)

Likenesses G. Kneller, oils, c.1690–1695, NPG · G. Kneller, oils, 1699, Trinity Cam. · G. Kneller, oils, c.1703–1710, NPG [see illus.] · G. Kneller, oils, c.1703–1710, Knole, Kent · attrib. M. Dahl, c.1710, Bank of England, London · J. Faber junior, mezzotint, 1732 (after G. Kneller), BM, NPG · J. Smith, mezzotint (after G. Kneller), BM, NPG

Montagu, Charles, first duke of Manchester (c.1662–1722), diplomat, was the third and eldest surviving son of Robert *Montagu, third earl of Manchester (bap. 1634, d. 1683) [see under Montagu, Edward, second earl of Manchester], and his wife, Anne (d. 1698), the daughter of Sir Christopher Yelverton of Easton Maudit, Northamptonshire. He was educated at St Paul's School, London, and Trinity College, Cambridge, where he matriculated in June 1678 and received an MA in 1680. He was styled Viscount Mandeville until he succeeded as earl of Manchester on the death of his father on 14 March 1683. He was appointed lord carver to the queen at the coronation of James II (23 April 1685) and on 12 May of the following year took his seat in the House of Lords. Soon afterwards he embarked on a tour of the continent, during which he had an audience with the prince of Orange. After returning to England he raised a cavalry troop in Nottinghamshire and joined the prince on his landing. At the coronation of William and Mary (11 April 1689) he carried St Edward's staff, and the same year he was made captain of the yeomen of the guard and lord lieutenant of Huntingdonshire. He accompanied the king to Ireland in June 1690, and fought at the Battle of the Boyne.

On 26 February 1691 Manchester married Dodington (1672–1721), the second daughter and coheir of Robert Greville, fourth Baron Brooke. The couple had four daughters and two sons. In the winter of 1697 he was sent to Venice on an extraordinary mission to obtain the release of detained English seamen. Although the doge and signory welcomed and entertained the earl lavishly, they proved unwilling to negotiate substantively, and the prisoners had not been released when, in the spring of 1698, he was recalled.

On his return to England, Manchester was appointed a privy councillor (9 June 1698), and in the following year he succeeded Lord Jersey as ambassador-extraordinary at the court of France. He arrived in Paris on 5 August 1699, and had his first audience with Louis XIV on 15 November. His principal function was to watch and, as far as possible, counteract the efforts of the exiled Stuart court of St Germains. On the death of James II and the recognition of his son as James III (James Francis Edward Stuart) by Louis, Manchester was promptly recalled (September 1701). From 4 January to 15 May 1702 he held the seal of secretary

Charles Montagu, first duke of Manchester (c.1662–1722), by Sir Godfrey Kneller, c.1710–12

of state for the northern department. In 1707 he was again ambassador-extraordinary at Venice, sent to negotiate the republic's attachment to the grand alliance. Travelling by way of Vienna, where he had an audience with the emperor (27 April), he arrived in Venice on 30 June. His attempts to reach terms with the Venetians proved as fruitless as his negotiations in 1697–8, and in September 1708 he was recalled. On the accession of George I he was readmitted to the privy council and appointed lord of the bedchamber. He again performed the role of lord carver, this time for George I, at the coronation on 20 October 1714. On 30 April 1719 he was created duke of Manchester. His wife died on 6 February 1721, and he on 20 January 1722, at his home in Arlington Street, London. He was buried at Warwick on 3 March. The title passed in turn to his two sons, William (1700–1739) and Robert (d. 1762).

J. M. RIGG, rev. MATTHEW KILBURN

Sources GEC, *Peerage*, new edn · *The Marlborough–Godolphin correspondence*, ed. H. L. Snyder, 3 vols. (1975) · P. Grimblot, ed., *Letters of William III and Louis XIV and their ministers*, 2 vols. (1848) · C. Cole, *Historical and political memoirs* (1735)
Archives BL, diplomatic and general corresp. · Cambs. AS, family papers · PRO NIre., papers as ambassador to Paris | CKS, corresp. with Alexander Stanhope · Longleat House, Wiltshire, corresp. with Matthew Prior · U. Nott. L., letters to William Blathwayt
Likenesses G. Kneller, oils, c.1710–1712 (*Kit-Cat Club*), NPG [*see illus.*] · stipple and line engraving, pubd 1864, NPG · J. Faber, engraving (after G. Kneller, c.1710)
Wealth at death Kimbolton Castle and estates, Huntingdonshire: GEC

Montagu, Lord Charles Greville (1741–1784), colonial governor and politician, was born in England on 29 May 1741, the second son of Robert Montagu, third duke of Manchester (c.1710–1762), and his wife, Harriet (d. 1755), daughter of Edmund Dunch of Little Wittenham, Berkshire, and Elizabeth Godfrey. Through his mother's side Montagu was the great-nephew of John Churchill, first duke of Marlborough. Like most second sons of high-ranking aristocrats, he had the advantages of family connections and money, but did not have the convenience of a life that was mapped out as carefully as that of his elder brother, George *Montagu, fourth duke of Manchester.

Montagu entered Christ Church, Oxford, in 1759 and married Elizabeth, daughter of James Balmer of Huntingdon, on 20 September 1765. They had one son and two daughters. He succeeded his elder brother as a member of parliament for Huntingdonshire in June 1762, and voted both with government and with the opposition before settling in as a supporter of the Rockingham administration. Rockingham rewarded Montagu in 1765 with an appointment as governor of South Carolina. After vacating his seat at the end of the session in December, Montagu set his affairs in order and set sail for Charles Town, arriving on 12 June.

Montagu's South Carolina was a land in turmoil. The combination of the proclamation of 1763, which severely restricted the colonies' westward expansion, and the Stamp Act of 1765, by which the British government sought directly to tax internal colonial American commerce, had created substantial tensions between the South Carolinians and the British. As an associate of the Rockingham administration, which had repealed the Stamp Act, Montagu was received in South Carolina with great favour and expectation, but the initial rejoicing soon wore off as new problems with Britain arose and the colonies marched down the road to revolution. Moreover, the Carolinas had numerous internal problems, the worst of which was between the eastern counties, which were wealthier and disproportionately represented in the colony's assembly, and the poorer frontier counties, which erupted in the regulators' rebellion. As governor, Montagu sought to ease tensions by pardoning seventy-five of the failed rebellion's leaders, but this only agitated further the colonists of the more settled areas of the colony, who were becoming increasingly critical of British rule.

Although he remained the governor in title, Montagu effectively had given up by the summer of 1769, and on 29 July he set sail for England, where he worked as hard for a new position as the South Carolina assembly did for his recall. He returned briefly, arriving on 15 September 1771, but found a colonial assembly more hostile to British rule than ever. Part of the assembly's tax bill, put forward the day after his arrival, included the £10,500 that the assembly had already advanced to John Wilkes's fund, for the support of that English radical's flagrant attacks on the king and his government. At stake was control of the colony's purse. Montagu was under strict instructions from the king and Wills Hill, first earl of Hillsborough, secretary of state for the American colonies, not to allow the assembly to dispose of public money without the consent of the governor and council. The assembly resented such interference as unacceptable infringements on its authority. In the face of such intransigence, Montagu had no choice but to dissolve the assembly time and again. Either unable or unwilling to suffer the situation any further, he left the colony without leave, and officially resigned his post in the first months of 1773.

Montagu made a bid in the general election of 1774 for a Southampton seat, but without the North administration's support was soundly defeated. With the assistance of his brother, he was placed in charge of raising a corps from among the American prisoners of war for the king's service against the colonies of Spain, which had entered the war in 1779. In New York he toured the prison ships and recruited upwards of 500 men to form the duke of Cumberland's provincial regiment. When it was disbanded in 1783 Montagu and a number of his men, along with thousands of other loyalists, resettled in Nova Scotia. He died in Halifax, Nova Scotia, on 4 February 1784 and was buried there in St Paul's churchyard.

TROY O. BICKHAM

Sources R. M. Weir, *Colonial South Carolina: a history* (1983) · J. B. O. Landrum, *Colonial and revolutionary history of upper South Carolina* (1959) · E. McCrady, *The history of South Carolina under the royal government, 1719–1766* (1899) · M. E. Sirmans, *Colonial South Carolina: a political history, 1663–1763* (Chapel Hill, NC, 1966) · W. R. Smith, *South Carolina as a royal province, 1719–1776* (1970) · GEC, *Peerage* · L. B. Namier, 'Montagu, Lord Charles Greville', HoP, *Commons, 1754–90* · Foster, *Alum. Oxon.* · www.montaguemillennium.com/research/h_1783_charles.htm, 11 Jan 2002 · Burke, *Peerage* (1999)
Archives PRO, Colonial Office papers, ser. 5
Wealth at death unknown, but substantial

Montagu, David Charles Samuel, fourth Baron Swaythling (1928–1998), merchant banker, was born on 6 August 1928 at 8 Grosvenor Crescent, Westminster, London, the eldest son and heir of Stuart Albert Samuel Montagu, third Baron Swaythling (1898–1990), and his first wife, Mary Violet Levy (d. 1983). His father was briefly a partner in the family firm Samuel Montagu & Co., but his principal interests were his herd of English Guernsey cattle and road safety: a Liberal peer, his foremost legislative achievement was to make rear lights on bicycles compulsory.

David Montagu was educated at Eton College and Trinity College, Cambridge, where he studied English literature, having tried law and economics but found them too dull. Upon graduation in 1949 he reported for work at the family firm founded by his great-grandfather in 1853. He was interviewed by Louis Franck, the abrasive Belgian who ran the City merchant bank: 'He saw this young pip-squeak who he thought had been born with a silver spoon in his mouth', Montagu recalled; 'his first words to me were: "you have no future in banking"' (*Financial Times*, 20 May 1998). Goaded by Franck's disdain, Montagu applied himself to mastering the business of merchant banking, and in 1954 he was admitted to the partnership. It was while a trainee in Paris in 1951 that he met and married, on 14 December, Christiane Françoise (Ninette) Dreyfus, with whom he had two daughters and a son.

While Franck focused on the firm's traditional foreign exchange and bullion trading, Montagu developed its corporate finance, capital markets, and investment management activities. Among his achievements were the invention of the split-level investment trust and a pioneering presence in the Euromarkets. When Franck retired in 1970, Montagu became chairman and chief executive at the early age of forty-one. Between his arrival at Samuel Montagu & Co. in 1949 and his departure in 1973, the staff grew from sixty to 4000.

The firm's dynamic expansion and its new activities necessitated greater capital, so in 1967 Montagu persuaded Midland Bank to take a minority shareholding, at the time a radical departure for a merchant bank. Six years later Midland purchased full ownership and Samuel Montagu & Co. became its merchant banking subsidiary. In view of the family tie, Montagu was offered the non-executive chairmanship for life, a banking equivalent to allowing the ancestral family to live on as tenants in a wing of a house acquired by the National Trust. Montagu was outraged and resigned: 'I wanted nothing to do with it', he fulminated; 'a greater insult has never been offered' (personal knowledge). He was immediately recruited as chairman and chief executive of Orion, a joint-venture 'consortium bank' established in 1970 by six of the major banks, including the National Westminster, Chase Manhattan, and the Royal Bank of Canada, to operate in the burgeoning Eurobond and syndicated loan markets. Montagu took the helm at a particularly turbulent moment in the international financial markets, but under his leadership Orion prospered and became a powerful and profitable player in petro-dollar recycling and the Eurobond market. Orion's success inspired its shareholders to develop their own Euromarket activities, resulting in mounting conflicts of interest, a common fate of the consortium banks. But the shareholders refused to accept Montagu's advice that one of them should buy out the others, leading to an acrimonious parting in 1979. His strategic judgement was vindicated when the Royal Bank of Canada became sole owner eighteen months later.

After Orion, Montagu worked briefly and unhappily for the American brokerage firm Merrill Lynch and then for J. Rothschild Holdings, where he had charge of Ailsa Investment Trust. In 1988 he became chairman of the tobacco giant Rothmans International, a position he retained until a few months before his death in 1998. He succeeded as fourth Baron Swaythling in 1990.

Swaythling was much sought after as a director of banks, investment trusts, and companies, including London Weekend Television (LWT), Bovis, and the *Daily Telegraph*. His friend the broadcaster John Freeman, whom Montagu helped to establish LWT, once described him as 'someone I trust entirely, a man with whom I would go tiger shooting' (*Daily Telegraph*, 2 July 1998). He was often consulted by government and was a member of the Bank of England's board of banking supervision and its inquiry into the collapse of Barings.

Swaythling was a man of fastidious, civilized tastes who described himself as 'a lobster-eating Jew' (*Daily Telegraph*,

2 July 1998). He was an art collector, a theatre lover, a connoisseur of fine wine and cigars, a keen bridge player, and an excellent shot. He was an active supporter of a variety of causes, among them the National Theatre, and was president of the Association for Jewish Youth. But his passion was racing. He kept a string of racehorses near his Newmarket home, a house called The Kremlin. The high point of his racing career was in 1979, when his horse Zongalero finished second in the Grand National. He was proud to be a founder member of the British Horseracing Board. He had a sharp wit, which was a delight for companions but did not endear him to its targets, first and foremost commercial bankers. On one occasion when asked to justify his first-class airline ticket by an Orion shareholder he replied, 'I'm afraid a private jet wasn't available' (personal knowledge). His tongue made him a few enemies, but they were greatly outnumbered by friends, and he inspired remarkable admiration and affection among colleagues. He possessed a genuine *joie de vivre* and instilled a sense of fun and excitement in every undertaking in which he was involved. Lord Swaythling died at his home, 14 Craven Hill Mews, Westminster, London, on 1 July 1998, and was succeeded by his son, Charles Edgar Samuel Montagu.   RICHARD ROBERTS

Sources personal knowledge (2004) · *Financial Times* (3 July 1998) · *The Times* (6 July 1998) · *Daily Telegraph* (2 July 1998) · *The Independent* (13 July 1998) · National Westminster Bank, records of Orion · C. Harris, 'Banking with a lucky lord', *Financial Times* (20 May 1998) · R. Roberts, *Take your partners: Orion, the consortium banks and the transformation of the Euromarkets* (2001) · Burke, *Peerage* (1999) · b. cert. · d. cert.

Archives SOUND BL NSA

Likenesses photograph, repro. in *Daily Telegraph* · photograph, repro. in *The Times* · photograph, repro. in *The Independent*

Montagu, Sir Edward (1480s–1557), judge, the second son of Thomas Montagu (*d.* 1517), of Hemington, Northamptonshire, and Agnes, daughter of William Dudley of Clopton, near Oundle, was born in the royal manor house of Brigstock. His father, an attorney representing Northamptonshire clients in the common pleas from the 1470s until at least 1505, had prospered sufficiently to acquire the manors of Hemington and Hanging Houghton. Edward is said to have spent some time at Cambridge before 1506, when he was admitted to the Middle Temple, an inn with a strong Northamptonshire presence perhaps attributable to the benchership of Richard Empson. Little is known of his early career, save that he is mentioned as an attorney in the court of requests from 1519 and was a justice of the peace for his native county from 1523. A tradition that he was speaker of the Commons in 1523 has not been corroborated by any contemporary source, though it is possible that he was a member of parliament that year.

In 1524 Montagu became a bencher of the Middle Temple and delivered his first reading in the autumn. He was the second most junior serjeant at the call of November 1531, and as the junior serjeant-elect from his inn gave a second reading in that capacity. One of his principal arguments at the bar as a serjeant was made on behalf of Lord Dacre in the great case of 1535 which led to the Statute of Uses. In the same year he was counsel for Sir John Melton in another case of high importance, concerning the earl of Northumberland and the Lucy inheritance, a case that incidentally helped to establish the validity of contingent remainders. On the eve of the dissolution of the monasteries Montagu was steward for several houses, including the abbey of Peterborough, which had retained his father. He profited largely by the dissolution, receiving among other properties the numerous estates held in Northamptonshire by the abbey of Bury St Edmunds. On the outbreak of the Pilgrimage of Grace in 1536 Montagu acted as commissioner to the royal forces in Northamptonshire, and the following year Audley recommended him to the king as an honest and learned man fit to become king's serjeant, an office that he was granted on 16 October 1537 with a knighthood two days afterwards. He was assigned as an assize commissioner to the Oxford circuit, transferring to the Norfolk in 1540.

On 22 January 1539 Montagu received his writ of appointment as chief justice of the king's bench, and presided over the court at a time when its fortunes revived markedly and its commercial jurisdiction began to flourish. The speech that he made to the call of serjeants in 1540, on the text *Diligite justiciam qui judicatis terram*, is an eloquent argument that law without justice is inadequate. Just as good conscience without knowledge of the law did not equip a lawyer for practice, so much learning without good conscience could easily lead him astray. Montagu drew from the Bible and the classics to demonstrate that 'great encreace had chaunced to empires and realmes for embracinge of justice', and utter destruction to those that had disregarded it, such as Sodom and Gomorrah or more recent examples: 'Who so listethe to marke contreis adjacent unto us, where is more povertie and miserye then where misrule is? An example of the wilde Yrishe and such other which livethe more like beastes then men, and all for lacke of good rule and justice' (BL, Harley MS 361, fol. 80). On 6 November 1545 Montagu was transferred to the less onerous but more lucrative post of chief justice of the common pleas. He is credited with having tried to bring some of the king's bench innovations with him, and the court certainly enjoyed a similar boom during his presidency. Although he did not stay long enough to convert the common pleas from its conservative mood, it seems in his time to have accepted some innovations, such as the wider use of special verdicts and the awakening of the dormant action of ejectment, both of which bore fruit in later periods.

Montagu was a member of the council of regency appointed by Henry VIII's will to carry on the government during the minority of Edward VI. In the council he acted with the party adverse to Somerset, whose patent as protector he refused to attest, and in October 1549 he concurred in his deposition. On 12 June 1553, in the council at Greenwich, he was apprised of the duke of Northumberland's scheme for altering the succession in favour of Lady Jane Grey and asked to draft the necessary clauses for insertion in the king's will. He objected that they would be void, as contravening the act of parliament settling the succession, and obtained leave to consult his colleagues.

The judges met at Ely House, and after a day in conference resolved that the project was treasonable. This resolution Montagu communicated to the council on 14 June, but was answered that the sanction of parliament would be obtained and peremptorily ordered to draft the clauses. He still hesitated, but his scruples were removed by a commission under the great seal and the promise of a general pardon. He not only drafted the clauses, but appended his signature to the will as one of its guarantors. On the accession of Mary he was committed to the Tower, on 26 July, but was discharged on 6 September with a fine of £1000 and the forfeiture of some of his estates. Although he apologized for his conduct and declared in favour of Mary, she declined to reappoint him as chief justice and he retired to the manor of Boughton, Northamptonshire, which he had bought in 1528. A supporter of the queen branded him *avarus judex* ('a covetous judge'), but conceded that he possessed a powerful reputation among commoners and nobility alike (MacCulloch, 200).

Montagu married three times: first Cicely (or Elizabeth), daughter of William Lane of Orlingbury, Northamptonshire; second, following Cicely's death, Agnes, daughter of George Kirkham (d. 1527) of Warmington in the same county, a chancery clerk and member of parliament for Stamford in 1515; and third, after the death of Agnes, Eleanor (or Helen), daughter of John *Roper (d. 1524), chief clerk of the king's bench and attorney-general to Henry VIII, who was the widow of John Moreton. With his third wife he had five sons and six daughters. The eldest, Sir Edward Montagu (d. 1602), was father of Edward *Montagu, first Baron Montagu (d. 1644), of James *Montagu (d. 1618), bishop of Winchester, of Henry *Montagu, first earl of Manchester (d. 1642), chief justice of the king's bench, and of Sidney Montagu (d. 1644), bencher of the Middle Temple and master of requests.

Montagu died at Boughton on 10 February 1557 and was buried on 5 March with much pomp (including a 'hearse of wax') in the neighbouring church of St Mary, Weekley, where there is an altar tomb with his full-length effigy in robes and collar of SS and the motto 'Pour unge pleasoir mille dolours' ('For every pleasure, a thousand sorrows'). There exists also a portrait in private dress by a follower of Eworth, formerly attributed to Holbein. His widow married Sir John Digby as her third husband and died in May 1563. J. H. BAKER

Sources PRO, CP 40/1133, m. ix · Baker, *Serjeants*, 168, 294–304, 527 · C. H. Hopwood, ed., *Middle Temple records*, 1: *1501–1603* (1904) · J. H. Baker and S. F. C. Milsom, eds., *Sources of English legal history: private law to 1750* (1986), 82–3, 108–10, 244, 450 · introduction, *The reports of Sir John Spelman*, ed. J. H. Baker, 2, SeldS, 94 (1978) · *The diary of Henry Machyn, citizen and merchant-taylor of London, from AD 1550 to AD 1563*, ed. J. G. Nichols, CS, 42 (1848), 35, 128 · *Report on the manuscripts of Lord Montagu of Beaulieu*, HMC, 53 (1900), 4–5 · L. Abbott, 'Public office and private profit: the legal establishment in the reign of Mary Tudor', *The mid-Tudor polity, c.1540–1560*, ed. J. Loach and R. Tittler (1980), 137–58, esp. 137–40 · W. K. Jordan, *Edward VI*, 2: *The threshold of power* (1970), 516–20, 527 · J. Caley and J. Hunter, eds., *Valor ecclesiasticus temp. Henrici VIII*, 6 vols., RC (1810–34), vol. 4, pp. 274, 282, 283, 288, 295; vol. 5, p.13 · D. MacCulloch, 'The *Vita Mariae Angliae Reginae* of Robert Wingfield of Brantham', *Camden miscellany, XXVIII*, CS, 4th ser., 29 (1984), 181–301, esp. 200 · PRO, REQ 1/4, fol. 156 · N. H. Nicolas, ed., *Testamenta vetusta: being illustrations from wills*, 2 (1826), 743 · will, PRO, PROB 11/39, fols. 40v–43 · *LP Henry VIII*, 12/2, no. 805 · Sainty, *Judges*, 9, 48 · C. Wise, *The Montagus of Boughton* (1888) · HoP, *Commons, 1558–1603*, 3.68–71

Likenesses oils, 1539, Middle Temple, London · effigy on monument, c.1557, Weekley church, Northamptonshire · J. Van der Eyden, oils, 17th cent., Boughton House, Northamptonshire; [Buccleuch estates], Selkirk, Scotland] · oils, 17th cent., Boughton House, Northamptonshire · oils, 17th cent., Peterborough City Museum · oils, Boughton House, Northamptonshire

Montagu, Edward, first Baron Montagu of Boughton (1562/3–1644), politician and local administrator, was the second son of Sir Edward Montagu (c.1532–1602) of Boughton Castle, in the parish of Weekley, Northamptonshire, and his wife, Elizabeth (c.1542–1618), daughter of Sir James Harington of Exton, Rutland. He matriculated at Christ Church, Oxford about 1574, supplicated for the degree of BA on 14 March 1579, and was a student of the Middle Temple in 1580. On 21 September 1585 he married Elizabeth (c.1568–1611), daughter and heir of Sir John Jeffrey of Chiddingly, Sussex, chief baron of the exchequer; this was the first of three marriages. She died on 6 December 1611 and within three months, on 24 February 1612, Montagu married Frances, daughter of Thomas Cotton of Conington, Huntingdonshire. She was buried at Weekley on 16 May 1620. On 16 February 1625 Montagu married Anne (1572/3–1648), daughter of John Crouch of Corneybury, in Layston, Hertfordshire, and widow in turn of Robert Wyncoll, Richard Chamberlain, and Sir Ralph Hare. He represented Bere Alston in the parliament of 1584, Tavistock in 1597, Brackley in 1601, and then Northamptonshire in the parliaments of 1604, 1614, and 1621. He was made a knight of the Bath on 24 July 1603 and was raised to the peerage as Baron Montagu of Boughton on 29 June 1621.

Northamptonshire magnate Montagu was an influential figure in Northamptonshire from the time he succeeded his father in 1602 until his death. His family had been settled in the county since the fifteenth century, but its principal estates had been acquired by Edward's grandfather Sir Edward *Montagu, who became lord chief justice in 1539 and purchased a cluster of manors centred on the family's principal seat at Boughton. Edward's father consolidated the family's local position, establishing himself as one of the wealthiest landowners in the shire and earning a considerable reputation for wisdom and piety for his service as JP and deputy lieutenant under Elizabeth. In spite of his regular attendance in parliament, Edward's own priorities remained essentially local and dynastic—to maintain the unity and prosperity of his family and establish them as the leaders of the gentry in the eastern half of the shire. He himself acted as JP (from 1595), deputy lieutenant (from 1602), sheriff (1595–6), and deputy keeper of Rockingham Forest (from 1593), and again became renowned for his conscientious service. When the midland revolt broke out in May 1607 he took a leading role in its suppression, commanding the contingent of trained bands which dispersed the rebels at the battle of Newton Field and then presiding over the hanging of the ringleaders at Kettering. He was also much involved in

Edward Montagu, first Baron Montagu of Boughton (1562/3–1644), by unknown artist, 1630s

schemes for poor relief and in 1630 provided his brother Henry *Montagu, first earl of Manchester and lord privy seal, with information on local procedures which helped in the formulation of the Book of Orders.

For much of James's reign Montagu's position as leading magnate in the eastern half of the shire was unchallenged. He and his friend Robert Spencer, Lord Spencer, from Althorp in the western half, presided over the shire's affairs, dominating the county bench, settling local quarrels, and determining who should represent the shire in parliament. This changed, however, when Sir Francis Fane (later earl of Westmorland) arrived in the shire in 1617 having married the heiress of Sir Anthony Mildmay of Apethorpe. He set about challenging Montagu's primacy in a series of disputes which arose out of the enforcement of James I's declaration of sports and jurisdiction in Rockingham Forest. Montagu tried, unsuccessfully, to have him punished in Star Chamber. These quarrels had repercussions for the county elections when, in 1624 and again in 1626, Spencer and the western gentry took offence at Fane's contentiousness and abandoned the long-standing arrangement whereby one candidate was returned from each half of the county. Montagu was caught in the middle, apparently powerless to uphold the claims of the eastern half, and he felt snubbed and humiliated. Westmorland's death in 1628, however, allowed tensions to subside and after this Montagu re-established his dominance of the east.

Puritan patron Much of Montagu's status in Northamptonshire rested on his reputation as a patron of godly ministers. He used his patronage in the area around Kettering to promote a string of puritan preachers to local livings,

including Joseph Bentham, Nicholas Estwick, William Spencer, and the renowned Robert Bolton. He was also the patron of the puritan lecture at Kettering, making great show of regular attendance at the sermons and trying, unsuccessfully, to defend it against the bishop of Peterborough's efforts at suppression. Montagu can best be described as a moderate puritan. The ministers he sponsored all conformed to the ceremonies of the Church of England and, like Montagu, tended to direct most of their energies into combating various forms of sinfulness—notably sabbath-breaking, swearing, simony and usury (which were particular preoccupations of Montagu), and, above all, popery. James I got the measure of Montagu when he told him he 'smelt a little of puritanism' (HoP, *Commons, 1558–1603*, 3.70). In 1605, however, Sir Edward got caught up in a more radical puritan initiative when he, with Sir Richard Knightley and his son, presented James I with a petition, signed by forty-five gentlemen, requesting the reinstatement of ministers who had recently been deprived of their livings. The king regarded the petition as tantamount to rebellion and immediately had Montagu removed from the commission of the peace. He was only restored after making a personal submission, arranged by his brother James *Montagu who was dean of the Chapel Royal.

Religion was also the principal theme of Montagu's interventions in parliament. As an MP he spoke sparingly but regularly, and he was a diligent attender of Commons' committees. He looked after the interests of his constituents, at the opening of the 1604 parliament reporting 'the cry of the country' against abuses such as 'depopulation' and 'conversion of tillage'. But it was religious matters which concerned him most. He sponsored a bill against pluralities and was a mainstay of committees to deal with issues such as sabbath observance and drunkenness; however, he perhaps made his greatest mark in January 1606 when he initiated the bill for a public thanksgiving every 5 November for the king's deliverance from the Gunpowder Plot. This summed up the basis of his political beliefs—loyalty to the monarch combined with an absolute abhorrence of popery.

The crown's servant Montagu never displayed any ambition for high office; however, his personal affection and gratitude towards James I, his dependence on the support of his brothers Henry and James, and his need for backing from the duke of Buckingham in his local quarrels ensured that he forged strong links with the royal court. On several occasions during James's parliaments he proposed the grant of royal subsidies. He also backed the king's project for union with Scotland in 1606 and in 1614 attempted to defuse the row over undertaking. His support for the crown became particularly apparent during the forced loan of 1626–7 when he joined with Henry in launching the collection in Northamptonshire. As a result he was castigated by his neighbours, who contrasted his apparent subservience to the wishes of Buckingham with the resistance of local 'patriots', like Richard Knightley and Lord Spencer. This episode destroyed Montagu's earlier reputation as a spokesman for 'the country'; but, undeterred, he continued to serve the crown loyally, taking a leading role in the levying of knighthood fines in 1630–31 and supporting the collection of ship money, after initially complaining about the unfairness of the assessment imposed on the eastern division. In early 1639 he was even prepared to travel to York to serve the king in person against the covenanters, until he was talked out of it on account of his age. As civil war approached in 1642 Montagu found himself torn between conflicting loyalties. He attended the Short Parliament and joined the opposition peers' protest against its dissolution. He also strongly supported the measures taken by the Long Parliament to dismantle Laudianism. However, when he was summoned to execute the king's commission of array in June 1642 he responded positively. He thought long and hard about it and desperately hoped for accommodation between king and parliament. But, eventually, he decided that his personal duty to serve his king outweighed all other obligations.

Montagu's support for the king led to his arrest in August 1642 and imprisonment in the Tower of London. He was eventually allowed to move to more comfortable quarters in the Savoy, but he remained in London, where he died on 15 June 1644, aged eighty-one. He was buried at Weekley eleven days later. He was succeeded by his eldest son, Edward.

Edward Montagu, second Baron Montagu of Boughton (1616–1684), nobleman, was born on 11 July 1616 and baptized on 25 July at Weekley, the son of Sir Edward Montagu (later first Baron Montagu of Boughton) and his second wife, Frances Cotton. He was educated at Oundle School and at Sidney Sussex College, Cambridge, where he matriculated in 1631 and was created MA the following year. He married in 1633 Anne, the daughter of the Jacobean secretary of state Sir Ralph Winwood of Ditton, Buckinghamshire.

Montagu sat as MP for Huntingdon from the start of the Long Parliament until his elevation to the House of Lords on his father's death in 1644. He was not a very active MP and he appears to have had misgivings about subscribing to the solemn league and covenant, but he was a staunch supporter of parliament. As a commissioner from the House of Lords, he took charge of the king's person after he was surrendered by the Scots in January 1647 and attended on him until his escape later in the year. He took no part in Charles's trial and strongly disapproved of his execution; this resulted in his virtual exclusion from politics during the 1650s. He welcomed the restoration of Charles II, but did not return to public life. He died on 10 January 1684 and was buried at Weekley. His eldest son, Edward, predeceased him and he was succeeded by his second son Ralph *Montagu, later first duke of Montagu.

Edward Montagu (1635/6–1665), naval officer, was the eldest son of Edward, second Baron Montagu of Boughton and his wife, Anne Winwood. He was educated at Westminster School, and matriculated in June 1651 at Christ Church, Oxford, aged fifteen, and the following year at Sidney Sussex College, Cambridge. In 1656 he attended the University of Padua. He was created MA at Oxford in 1661. In 1659 Montagu joined the navy in the service of his cousin, Admiral Edward *Montagu, and he was instrumental in bringing the admiral over to the royalist cause. He sat as MP for Sandwich in the Cavalier Parliament, but devoted most of his energies to the pursuit of influence at court. In 1662 he was sent to Lisbon with the fleet commanded by his cousin, now earl of Sandwich, to bring the king's bride, Catherine of Braganza, to England. On her arrival he was made master of the queen's horse; however, his clumsy efforts to gain control of her household and his amorous advances towards her, which were reported to Charles, led to his dismissal from court in 1664. He rejoined Sandwich's fleet during the Second Anglo-Dutch War and was killed in the attack on Bergen on 2 August 1665. He was buried at Weekley on 13 October 1665.   RICHARD CUST

Sources E. Cope, *The life of a public man: Edward first Baron Montagu of Boughton, 1562–1644* (1981) · HoP, *Commons, 1558–1603,* 3.69–70 · 'Montague, Sir Edward (1562–1644)', HoP, *Commons* [draft] · Barclay, 'Edward Montagu (1616–1684)', HoP, *Commons* [draft] · B. D. Henning, 'Montagu, Edward', HoP, *Commons* · Keeler, *Long Parliament,* 275 · *Report on the manuscripts of his grace the duke of Buccleuch and Queensberry … preserved at Montagu House,* 3 vols. in 4, HMC, 45 (1899–1926), vols. 1, 3 · *Report on the manuscripts of Lord Montagu of Beaulieu,* HMC, 53 (1900) · J. Wake, ed., *The Montagu musters book, 1602–1623,* Northamptonshire RS, 7 (1935) · papers of the dukes of Buccleuch and Queensberry, Northants. RO, vol. 186 [incl. a life of Lord Montagu by Joseph Bentham] · A. J. Fielding, 'Conformists, puritans and the church courts: the diocese of Peterborough, 1603–1642', PhD diss., U. Birm., 1989 · P. G. Lake, '"A charitable christian hatred": the godly and their enemies in the 1630s', *The culture of English puritanism, 1560–1700,* ed. C. Durston and J. Eales (1996), 145–83 · R. P. Cust, *The forced loan and English politics, 1626–1628* (1987) · W. C. Metcalfe, ed., *The visitations of Northamptonshire, 1564 and 1618–19* · Foster, *Alum. Oxon.* · GEC, *Baronetage*
Archives Northants. RO, dukes of Buccleuch and Queensberry MSS, corresp. and papers · Northants. RO, corresp. · Beaulieu, Beaulieu archives, corresp. and papers | Bodl. Oxf., Carte MS 74
Likenesses portrait, *c.*1620, Boughton House, Northamptonshire; repro. in Wake, ed., *Montagu musters book,* frontispiece · portrait, 1630–39, Boughton House, Northamptonshire [*see illus.*]

Montagu, Edward, second earl of Manchester (1602–1671), politician and parliamentarian army officer, was the eldest son of Henry *Montagu, first earl of Manchester (*c.*1564–1642), judge and government official, and his first wife, Catherine (*d.* 1612), second daughter of Sir William Spencer of Yarnton, Oxfordshire. On 27 January 1618 he was admitted as a fellow-commoner at Sidney Sussex College, Cambridge, and he later graduated MA. He accompanied Prince Charles to Spain in 1623 in the latter's quest for the infanta's hand in marriage. His reward was to be created a knight of the Bath at Charles's coronation in February 1626. He represented his county of Huntingdonshire in the parliaments of 1623–4, 1625, and 1625–6. With the duke of Buckingham's help he was elevated to the House of Lords in his father's barony as Lord Kimbolton on 22 May 1626. In the same year he was granted the courtesy title of Viscount Mandeville when his father was created earl of Manchester.

Opposition peer Mandeville's first marriage, on 6 February 1623, was to Susanna (*d.* 1625), daughter of John Hill of

Edward Montagu, second earl of Manchester (1602–1671), by Sir Peter Lely, c.1661–5

Honiley, Warwickshire, and cousin of the duke of Buckingham. The union, which took place in the king's bedchamber, was politically important since it secured the powerful Buckingham interest for the Montagu family. The couple had no children, however, and Susanna died in January 1625. On 1 July the next year, at Stoke Newington, Mandeville married Anne (d. 1642), daughter of Robert *Rich, second earl of Warwick. They had three children: his heir, Robert [see below]; Frances, who married Henry, son of Robert Sanderson, bishop of Lincoln; and Anne, who married Robert Rich, second earl of Holland and fifth earl of Warwick. This second marriage brought Mandeville into the orbit of puritan peers dominated by the Rich family. Perhaps to express his disapproval of Mandeville's new associates, his father allowed him only a slender income. However, his sociability and desire for popularity, perhaps reflecting his parvenu status among the aristocracy, led Mandeville to adopt an extravagant style of life, with the inevitable consequence of heavy debts.

Like Warwick, Mandeville soon found himself out of favour at court because of his association with the fraternity of disaffected peers who included the earl of Bedford, Viscount Saye and Sele, and Lord Brooke. He would have joined the latter two in refusing to fight the Scots in the first bishops' war had his father not threatened to disinherit him. On 24 April 1640, during the Short Parliament, he was one of the minority of twenty-five who voted against the king on the question of the precedency of supply, and he was part of the pro-Scottish group that worked behind the scenes for the parliament's failure. Despite his later denial, he was almost certainly one of the

seven noble signatories to the letter that Lord Savile forwarded to the Scots promising them support if they invaded England that summer.

After the king's defeat at Newburn in the second bishops' war Mandeville also signed the petition of the twelve peers (28 August 1640) urging him to summon parliament again, and with Lord Howard of Escrick presented the petition to Charles on 5 September. That same month he attended the king's grand council of peers, where he expressed surprise that the king had entered a war without knowing how he would pay for it, and opined that it would be 'more for the honour and safety of the king to come to an accommodation' with the Scots (Hardwicke, 266). Overlooking the oppositional role Mandeville was playing, the king appointed him a commissioner to negotiate with the Scots at Ripon. While he spoke little during the negotiations, he played a key role in reporting to the king and preparing draft texts of the treaty that brought an end to the hostilities between the two kingdoms. He also supported the Scots' demand to have the negotiations transferred to London, in effect so that the treaty could be taken out of Charles's hands and dealt with by parliament.

During the early months of the Long Parliament, Mandeville was an active member of the radical party, working closely with Saye and Sele, Brooke, Pym, Hampden, St John, and others. Secretary Edward Nicholas reported to the king that 'there are divers meetings att Chelsey att the Lo. Mandevilles house and elsewhere by Pym and others to consult what is best to be donne at their next meeting in P'liamt' (Evelyn, 4.76). Mandeville was one of the four peers to whom Colonel George Goring leaked the details of the first army plot in May 1641 to capture the Tower of London and release the earl of Strafford from captivity. The House of Lords then dispatched him to Portsmouth with a warrant to examine Goring and send him to London to appear before parliament. He was also one of sixteen peers chosen to transact business during the parliamentary adjournment from 9 September to 20 October 1641. On 24 December he protested against the adjournment of the debate over the removal of Sir Thomas Lunsford from the command of the Tower.

In view of Mandeville's activities over the previous two years it was not a complete surprise that his name was among the six members whom the king impeached for high treason on 3 January 1642. When the articles of impeachment were read out Mandeville at once offered 'with a great deal of chearfulness' to obey the commands of the house, and demanded that, 'as he had a public charge, so he might have a public clearing' (JHL, 4, 1628–42, 501). Since the king subsequently waived the charges, no 'public clearing' turned out to be necessary, but two months later a bill was passed by both houses absolving Mandeville from the accusation. Meanwhile, on 13 January Mandeville and John Pym had addressed speeches to their supporters in the City, promising that the Lords and Commons 'will never desert you, but will stand by you, with their lives and fortunes, for the preservation of the city' (Harleian Miscellany, 5.219).

Mandeville's second wife, Anne, died in February 1642 and was buried at Kimbolton Castle, Huntingtonshire, the family seat. On 20 December that year at St Mary Aldermanbury, London, he married his second wife's cousin, Essex (d. 1658), widow of Sir Robert Bevill of Chesterton, Huntingdonshire, and daughter of Thomas Cheke, of Pirgo, Essex, and Essex, daughter of Robert Rich, first earl of Warwick. He thereby continued and reinforced his close connection with the radical Rich family. He and Essex had six sons and two daughters over the next fifteen years.

Parliamentarian commander Mandeville was one of the few peers who stayed with parliament in August 1642 when the king raised his standard and declared war at Nottingham. The earl of Warwick, fearful that his mild character would not stand up to the rigours of war, wrote to Mandeville the following month, exhorting him to:

> stand well upon your guard both military and politic, for you will never get the like opportunity if you slip this which God hath put into your hands. And loose not the business with civilities and compliment … do the work thoroughly and look to yourselves. (*Eighth Report*, HMC, 2.59)

There is no evidence that Mandeville (who inherited the earldom upon his father's death in November 1642) needed the advice. He at once took command of a foot regiment in the earl of Essex's army, and saw action at Edgehill where his men unfortunately left the field with unseemly haste. The regiment was then disbanded, and the new earl returned to London. There he was appointed to the committee for the advance of money, and concentrated on financing the parliamentary war effort. Befitting his status as one of the leading radical parliamentary peers, he was invested with other important offices and responsibilities. Appointed lord lieutenant of Huntingdonshire and Northamptonshire, and one of the ten peers who sat as lay members of the Westminster assembly of divines, he was also involved in the negotiations for a cessation of arms under the abortive Oxford treaty of early 1643.

When rumours surfaced of a plot to seize London for the king in May of that year, Manchester's and Saye and Sele's interrogation of one of the suspects blew open the conspiracy, which was then crushed. Manchester presided at the court martial of the ringleaders in June and July. By his skilful and moderate conduct of the trials he helped to weaken the parliamentary peace party at a critical moment.

In August 1643 parliament dismissed the ineffectual Lord Grey of Wark as major-general of the eastern associated counties and named Manchester in his place. The appointment brought him into intimate contact with Oliver Cromwell. The two men already knew each other, being from the same county, and educated at the same Cambridge college. In 1640 Mandeville had been called before a Commons committee to defend his enclosures in the eastern counties against loud complaints from the tenants. Cromwell was there as the tribune of the tenants, and whenever Mandeville testified he:

> did answer and reply upon him with so much indecency and rudeness, and in language so contrary and offensive, that every man would have thought, that as their natures and their manners were as opposite as it is possible, so their interest could never have been the same. (Hyde, 1.74)

Harrowing though this experience must have been, Manchester did not let the memory of it eclipse his appreciation of Cromwell's military talent. The commander of the Ironsides became Manchester's lieutenant-general of horse, and the two men worked together effectively until the summer of 1644.

With a mandate to conscript up to 20,000 men for military service, Manchester soon demonstrated administrative and organizational gifts of a high order. In September 1643 he took back King's Lynn from the royalists who had seized it in August. In October he joined Cromwell and Sir Thomas Fairfax in Lincolnshire, and routed the royalists at Winceby, killing 300 and taking 800 prisoner. In his letter to the House of Lords he lavished generous praise on his two fellow commanders. A few days later the city of Lincoln surrendered to him. In the House of Commons, Cromwell repaid Manchester's compliment by moving that Lord Willoughby of Parham, who had had military responsibility for Lincolnshire, should be under Manchester's authority. Willoughby fiercely resented the implied judgement of his performance, and challenged Manchester as he was on his way to the House of Lords. A committee of the upper house dominated by Manchester's friends reprimanded the upstart lord and upheld Manchester's authority in Lincolnshire. This and other enhancements of his power were embodied in an ordinance of 20 January 1644. The legislation, for which Manchester and his friends had lobbied intensively over the preceding three months, increased the assessments on the eastern association by 50 per cent and established a centralized financial organization at Cambridge. It also released Manchester from the authority of the earl of Essex. At the same time he was empowered to purge the clergy of the seven counties of the association, and regulate Cambridge University. Over the succeeding months he worked efficiently to accomplish the tasks set for him. After taking up residence at Cambridge, he personally selected the group of commissioners, socially heterogeneous but united in their puritanism, who were to work for him. He also deployed his considerable diplomatic skills to win the co-operation of the local gentry in building up a centrally controlled Treasury system which greatly increased the funds at his disposal. Manchester and Cromwell saw eye to eye in choosing and promoting able, politically committed, and 'godly' officers who 'love[d] Christ in sincerity', without respect for their origin or social status (*Camden Miscellany, VIII*, 3). The worth of these efforts would be seen at the epochal battle of Marston Moor.

Before that climactic moment Manchester also found time to purge the University of Cambridge, remove scandalous ministers in the associated counties, and issue a commission to William Dowsing to take down and 'deface … crosses, crucifixes, and other superstitious images and pictures … within the associated counties' (*N&Q*, 324).

Dowsing accomplished his assignment with a thoroughness that Manchester would have commended.

In February 1644 Manchester was elected to the new English-Scottish committee of both kingdoms that was charged with directing the war against the king. In April he was with his army watching the movements of Prince Rupert. In May, responding to Rupert's march towards York, he led an 8000-strong force to the aid of the northern parliamentarian army under Ferdinando Lord Fairfax and the Scottish army under Alexander Lord Leven, who were besieging the city. On the same day that the three allied armies came together (3 June), the committee of both kingdoms sent Sir Henry Vane to York, ostensibly to urge the generals to send forces into Lancashire to stop Rupert's advance, but also, it was reported, to win their support for a plan to depose the king. The three generals were unanimous in their rejection of Vane's proposals; Cromwell was more receptive, and his quarrel with Manchester and the Scots may have dated from this time.

At Marston Moor, Manchester exercised a general control as a field officer, while Cromwell and Lawrence Crawford commanded the eastern association horse and foot respectively. To the other chief commanders Manchester confessed 'that because himselfe was no experienced Souldier, therefore he would rather be guided, then guide' (Ashe, 2). Manchester did not attempt to detract from Cromwell's brilliant performance at Marston Moor, and more to his credit, while the other two senior generals (Leven and Fairfax) fled, he remained on the field until the battle ended, at which time he rode about thanking his men and exhorting them to give the honour to God alone.

Manchester then joined in the siege of York, which fell on 16 July 1644. From there he marched to Doncaster, and with Major-General Crawford overran Sheffield, Welbeck, and Bolsover castles. From that point he perplexed his colleagues by refusing to seize military opportunities, ignoring or disobeying orders from London, and generally subsiding into inaction. He passed by Pontefract Castle without summoning it; excoriated John Lilburne for taking Tickhill Castle contrary to orders; disregarded the committee of both kingdoms' directive to pursue Prince Rupert through Lancashire; and turned a deaf ear to his officers' entreaty to blockade the royalist stronghold at Newark.

What accounted for the sudden lethargy and distaste for warfare that overtook Manchester shortly after Marston Moor? In part it stemmed from his eirenic temper, reflected in the motto he had chosen for his battle standard: 'Truth and peace' (BL, Sloane MS 5247, fol. 75v). More than that he was revolted by the terrible carnage and misery that he had witnessed at Marston Moor and throughout Yorkshire. His army was much weakened by battle casualties, desertion of the conscripted infantry, and disease. By the late summer of 1644 too, the coffers of the eastern association were bare, and this financial crisis meant that its soldiers went unpaid, unclothed, and unfed. The splendid fighting force that he had put together the previous spring had declined into a gaunt shadow of its former self.

Even the radical Henry Ireton shared Manchester's reluctance to move his troops westward, because their condition was so 'miserable' (BL, Add. MS 63788B, fol. 11). The earl's nightmarish experiences on the battlefield brought him to the conclusion not merely that 'this war would not be ended by the sword'; but that 'it would be better for the Kingdom if it were ended by an accommodation' (*CSP dom.*, 1644–5, 152). As he insisted 'with vehemence' to Oliver Cromwell after his failure to stop the king's relief of Donnington Castle, 'if we fight [the king] 100 times and beat him 99 he will be King still, but if he beat us but once, or the last time, we shall be hanged, we shall lose our estates, and our posterities be undone' (ibid., 159). Over the previous year he had also witnessed the shattering of his ideal of a godly, unified army in which Independents should, in the words of his publicist John Dillingham, 'close with the honest Calvinest and Scot and go on unanimously against the common enemy' (*Parliament Scout*, 20–27 June 1644, 427). By the late summer of 1644 he had to contemplate the reality of an army divided into two factions, each loathing and seeking the destruction of the other. His bitter realization that 'it was easy to begin a war, but no man knew when it would end, and that this was not the way to advance religion' prompted his decisive realignment with the peace party (*CSP dom.*, 1644–5, 152). Hence Manchester's flouting of sixteen directives from the committee of both kingdoms and three orders from the House of Commons between August and October. Though constantly urged to advance westward to assist the earl of Essex, he did nothing until it was too late, did not reach Reading until the end of September, and did not unite with Sir William Waller and Essex until 21 October.

At the second battle of Newbury on 28 October 1644 Manchester's performance was abysmal. He put off the attack that had been assigned to him until too late in the day, which caused him to fail in his attempt on Shaw House. Under cover of darkness the royalist army withdrew westward, within 'little more than musket shot' of the earl's position (*CSP dom.*, 1644–5, 150). At the council of war held the following day he opposed Waller's and Cromwell's advice to pursue the enemy, preferring to summon Donnington Castle. His attempt to storm the castle was repulsed, and so he fell back, allowing the king to relieve it a few days later. On 17 November he left Newbury, ostensibly to assist the siege of Basing House. But he never got there. His starving men were deserting him, and so with the remnant of his army he turned back to Reading. This caused the abandonment of the siege of Basing House.

Self-denial and interregnum career Cromwell and Waller were by this time so fed up that they launched a wholesale political attack on Manchester in the House of Commons, demanding his removal as commander-in-chief of the eastern association. On 25 November 1644 the house spent a good part of the day hearing Cromwell's allegations. They were referred to the committee of the army, which was instructed to report back speedily. Manchester now unexpectedly showed the steel that was in his soul, hitting back hard against Cromwell in the upper house and in a letter a few days later. He accused his lieutenant-general of being an intolerant man, a sower of division, who had said 'that he hoped to live to see never a Nobleman in England', and 'could as soone draw his sword against [the Scots] as against any in the king's army' (*Camden Miscellany, VIII*, 2). To the accusations of military inaction, he replied that Cromwell too had been unwilling to bring his cavalry into action at Donnington Castle.

Dissatisfaction in the war party at the dismal record of both aristocratic generals was the impetus for the resolution for a self-denying ordinance under which the members of both houses would resign their military and civil offices. For several months Manchester and Essex strenuously resisted the passage of the ordinance and the creation of the New Model Army. Eventually they were forced to admit defeat, resigning their commissions on 2 April 1645, the day before the ordinance became law. Manchester may have derived some comfort from the petition of forty of his officers in January for his exemption from self-denial on the ground that his removal would 'breed a great confussion amongst them by reason of the differences between the Presbiterians and Independants' (BL, Add. MS 31116, fol. 185v).

Loss of Manchester's commission did not mean retirement from public affairs. He remained active in the committee of both kingdoms, and frequently acted as speaker of the House of Lords. At the end of 1645 the Commons recommended in its peace proposals to the king that he should be made a marquess. He was one of those to whom Charles said he was willing to entrust the militia in accordance with the Uxbridge propositions, and was a commissioner for framing the articles of peace known as the Newcastle propositions, which were presented to Charles in July 1646. He was given joint custody, with William Lenthall, of the great seal from 30 October 1646 to 15 March 1648. Early in 1647 he and other presbyterian peers were occupied in designing a peace settlement more likely to appeal to the king. When a counter-revolutionary, crypto-royalist crowd attacked the houses of parliament on 26 July 1647, Manchester executed a political volte-face. He could see that there was no Scottish army on the way to save the presbyterians, and that the New Model was invincible despite its lack of pay. He therefore swallowed his pride and joined Warwick and the other mainly Independent members in fleeing to the army at Hounslow Heath west of the capital. On 4 August he signed the engagement pledging 'to live and die with Sir Thomas Fairfax and the Army in the vindication of the Honour and Freedom of Parliament' (Rushworth, 7.754). On the 6th, escorted by Sir Thomas Fairfax, he and the other peers rode in their coaches at the end of a long procession of MPs and New Model regiments, back to the Palace of Westminster where he resumed his duties as speaker of the upper house.

When the ordinance for the king's trial came before the House of Lords at the beginning of January 1649 Manchester spoke strongly against it, saying that to call the king a traitor contradicted the fundamental principles of the law. With the establishment of the republic he was stripped of various offices and retired from public life.

Although he had been made chancellor of the University of Cambridge on 15 March 1649, he was dismissed from the post two years later for refusing to take the engagement of loyalty to the Commonwealth. In 1657 Cromwell extended an olive branch in the form of a summons to his upper house, but Manchester turned his back on the offer. On 28 September 1658 he lost his third wife, Essex, to pleurisy at Twickenham, Middlesex; she too was buried at Kimbolton. Preserving once again his connection with the Riches, in July 1659 he married his fourth wife, Eleanor (*d.* 1667), widow of his erstwhile political colleague and mentor Robert Rich, second earl of Warwick, and previously of Sir Henry Lee and Edward Ratcliffe, and daughter of Sir Edward Wortley.

Restoration and last years When in 1659 the protectoral regime began to unravel and the restoration of monarchy seemed imminent Manchester sprang into political action once again. As speaker of the Lords he welcomed the king back to his throne on 3 May 1660, and was soon again showered with honours. Already in the previous month he had been appointed a commissioner of the great seal; in May he was restored to his lord lieutenancy of Northamptonshire and Huntingdonshire, and to the chancellorship of Cambridge. Immediately after the king's arrival at the end of May he was made lord chamberlain of the household, privy councillor, and also chamberlain of south Wales. Later in the same year he was engaged in a grave responsibility: judging the captured regicides. His one recorded intervention during all the trials, when he urged his fellow judges who were relentlessly hounding the accused, 'I beseech you, my Lords, let us go some other way to work', seems to reveal an inclination towards leniency (*An Exact and most Impartial Accompt*, 53b).

Both Manchester and Charles II must have enjoyed the rich irony of the former rebel against monarchy taking an active part, as lord chamberlain, in the preparations for the royal coronation. On the day itself, 23 April 1661, Manchester bore the sword of state, and was made a knight of the Garter. The office of lord chamberlain also permitted him to indulge his penchant for old-fashioned moral values. In July 1661 he issued an order for the suppression of the 'manie and very great disorders and abuses' committed by 'companies of stage players, tumblers, vaulters, dauncers on the ropes, and … such as goe about with motions and shewes' (BL, Add. MS 19256, fol. 69). He became joint commissioner for the office of earl-marshal on 16 May 1662, and was incorporated MA at the University of Oxford on 8 September 1665. In 1667, during the Second Anglo-Dutch War, he was commissioned a general and given a regiment to command. He was also a fellow of the Royal Society from 1667 until his death. His fourth wife, Eleanor, died on 20 January 1667. The following August he married his last wife, Margaret (*d.* 1676), widow of James Hay, earl of Carlisle and daughter of Francis Russell, fourth earl of Bedford. Manchester died suddenly of 'cholic' at Whitehall on 7 May 1671, and was buried at Kimbolton church on 13 May. His will revealed that for all his political adroitness he had not accumulated great riches.

Besides household belongings which he left to his wife and daughter Lucy there was the ancestral estate at Kimbolton, pastures worth 500 marks a year at Keyston in the same county, and a sum of £4000 'due to mee from his Majestie in trust' (will, fol. 205). Unlike other men of similar standing at that time he left nothing to his friends, nothing to the poor, nothing to the clergy, and only a year's wages to his servants.

Reputation Yet despite the apparent meanness of his will, almost everyone who knew him was agreed on Manchester's affable, generous, gentle temper. A man of 'natural civility, good manners, and good nature, which flowed towards all men, he was universally acceptable and beloved', according to the royalist earl of Clarendon (Clarendon, *Hist. rebellion*, 1.243). Everyone recognized the genuineness of his piety, though some found it vitiated by a weak personality and the lack of a systematic education. The Scottish presbyterian clergyman Robert Baillie called him 'a sweet, meek man', and his English presbyterian chaplain, Simeon Ashe, enthused, 'I know no man … lesse self-seeking, and more desirous to issue the warres in comfortable peace' (Baillie, 2.229; Ashe, 11). Sir Philip Warwick took a more jaundiced view: 'a gentleman of good parts, … and of a debonair nature, but very facile or changeable; and had the misfortune to fall into ill company' (Warwick, 246). The dyspeptic royalist Anthony Wood dismissed him as a time server who always looked out for his own interests, 'a thorough-pac'd dissembler … and never a loser for his high actings against the royal family' (Wood, *Ath. Oxon.: Fasti*, 2.284). A fairer estimate comes from Richard Baxter, who though disappointed by Manchester's defence of episcopacy after the Restoration could still qualify him as 'a good man' (*Reliquiae Baxterianae*, 278). This goodness was manifested particularly during the supreme crisis of his life in 1644. Under withering attack by his political enemies, he responded that 'my endeavours shalbe, as farr as it may stand with the vindication of my owne integritie, to returne good for evill' (*Camden Miscellany, VIII*, 3).

His detractors were right in one respect: Manchester was graced with the ability always to land on his feet. In his youth a friend of the heir to the throne and an ally of the duke of Buckingham, by the 1630s he had fallen under the spell of the earl of Warwick, a tough-minded radical. Under Warwick's influence he joined the cabal of aristocratic enemies of monarchy, and when civil war was unleashed he took up arms without hesitation. As commander-in-chief of the eastern association he exploited his administrative skills and his engaging personality to create a superbly effective military instrument between 1643 and 1644. The army that he assembled showed its mettle in the bloodiest, most decisive battle of the civil war, Marston Moor. Then, in spite of this shining victory, he suddenly lost all appetite for warfare. His unexpected about-face was partly the product of his horror at the slaughter of the battlefield, and partly the fruit of his compassion for the exhausted, unpaid, hungry, disease-ridden soldiers of his army. But it also came from his realization that the radical officers and politicians with whom he was in daily contact would stop at nothing to achieve their revolutionary objectives. Under their influence the army which he had striven to fashion into a beacon of godliness had degenerated into a cauldron of bitter sectarian strife. By the late summer of 1644 Manchester had come to see with blinding clarity that the sword was a poor weapon with which to advance the cause of true religion. From that moment on he worked for peace, and distanced himself from his former political allies. Much later, having sat out the interregnum as a matter of principle, he was well placed to welcome the exiled king back to his throne in 1660. A firm royalist at the beginning and the end of his life, and a political firebrand in the middle, this modest, pious nobleman emerged as a consummate practitioner of the art of political survival.

Manchester's eldest son and heir, **Robert Montagu**, third earl of Manchester (*bap.* 1634, *d.* 1683), politician, was born in the parish of St Margaret, Westminster, and baptized there on 25 April 1634, a child from the second earl's second marriage to Lady Anne Rich (*d.* 1642); he was styled Viscount Mandeville from the time of his father's succession to the earldom. Little is known of his early years or education. He travelled abroad between 1649 and 1654, and shortly after his return married, on 27 June 1655, Anne (*d.* 1698), daughter of Sir Christopher Yelverton, bt, of Easton Maudit, Northamptonshire. The couple had five sons, two of whom, Edward and Henry, predeceased their father, and four daughters.

Mandeville had no political experience prior to his election in April 1660 to the Convention Parliament for Huntingdonshire. In May he was a member of the deputation sent by the Commons to The Hague to invite the return of Charles II. A train bearer at the king's coronation in the following year, he was re-elected to the Cavalier Parliament but was largely inactive. In 1663 he was sent to France on the occasion of Louis XIV's illness and in 1665 was created MA of Oxford University. While the Dutch lay off the coast of the eastern counties of England in 1666 and 1667 Mandeville commanded a troop of horse. Yet having been appointed gentleman of the bedchamber to the king in 1666, he was characterized as 'a bedchamber pimp', content to live off the financial benefits of the court (Helms and Edwards, 3.89).

However, after succeeding his father Manchester became an opposition peer. Shaftesbury noted him 'worthy' in 1679, and following his support for the second Exclusion Bill in the following year he was removed from all his offices. After rumours in 1681 that he was consorting with prominent exclusionists in Northamptonshire he fled the country. He died at Montpellier on 14 March 1683 and was buried at Kimbolton. His wife survived him and later married Charles Montagu, the future first earl of Halifax. Manchester was succeeded by his third but first surviving son Charles *Montagu, first duke of Manchester.   IAN J. GENTLES

Sources C. Holmes, *The eastern association in the English civil war* (1974) · I. Gentles, *The New Model Army in England, Ireland, and Scotland, 1645–1653* (1992) · *Eighth report*, 2, HMC, 7 (1910) [Manchester MSS] · BL, Add. MS 15567 [second earl of Manchester's memoirs] ·

J. Bruce and D. Masson, eds., *The quarrel between the earl of Manchester and Oliver Cromwell*, CS, new ser., 12 (1875) • S. Ashe, *A true relation of the most cheife occurrences, at, and since the late battell at Newbery … to vindicate the earle of Manchester from many undeserved aspersions* (1644) [Thomason tract E22] • 'A letter from the earl of Manchester to the House of Lords, giving an opinion on the conduct of Oliver Cromwell', ed. S. R. Gardiner, *Camden miscellany, VIII*, CS, new ser., 31 (1883), 1–3 • J. Bruce, ed., *Notes of the treaty carried on at Ripon between Charles I and the Covenanters of Scotland, AD 1640*, CS, 100 (1869) • *A continuation of true intelligence from the army, under the command of the Right Honourable the earle of Manchester, from July 27 to August 16th* (1644) [Thomason tract E6 (17)] • *CSP dom.*, 1640, 1644–5 • *JHL*, 3–12 (1620–75) • GEC, *Peerage*, new edn • A. Collins, *The peerage of England*, ed. B. Longmate, 5th edn, 8 vols. (1779), vol. 2 • will, PRO, PROB 11/336, fols. 204v–205 • *DNB* • J. Nalson, *An impartial collection*, 2 (1683) • P. Hardwicke, *Miscellaneous state papers*, 2 (1778) • William Cole's collections, vol. 28, BL, Add. MS 5829 • Baker's history of St John's College, BL, Add. MS 5850 • Master of the revels MSS, BL, Add. MS 19256 • papers for the committee for the eastern association, BL, Add. MS 22169 • 'A rolle of his majesties royal proceeding through London, the 22 of April 1661', BL, Add. MS 29774 • Lawrence Whitacre's parliamentary diary, 1642–7, BL, Add. MS 31116 • civil war papers, 1640–47, BL, Add. MS 34253 • civil war MSS, BL, Add. MS 63788B • Nicholas papers, BL, Egerton MS 2546 • Barrington papers, BL, Egerton MSS 2643, 2647 • minutes of the great council of peers, 1640, BL, Harley MS 456 • BL, Harley MS 2224, fols. 12–16 [on the quarrel between Lord Willoughby and the earl of Manchester] • original letters of state, etc., 1633–1724, BL, Harley MS 7001 • T. Baker, miscellaneous collections, BL, Harley MS 7038 • original letters, 1574–1667, BL, Sloane MS 1519 • '"Cornetes", or flags and arms in colors … in the time of the commonwealth', BL, Sloane MS 5247 • Bodl. Oxf., MSS Tanner 16, 49, 57, 62, 63, 64 • CUL, Baker MSS, vols. 27, 30, 36 • J. Rushworth, *Historical collections*, new edn, 7 (1721) • Clarendon, *Hist. rebellion* • Thurloe, *State papers*, vol. 1 • M. A. E. Green, ed., *Calendar of the proceedings of the committee for compounding … 1643–1660*, 1, PRO (1889) • *The whole works of the Rev. John Lightfoot*, ed. J. R. Pitman, 13 vols. (1822–5), vol. 13 • *The letters and journals of Robert Baillie*, ed. D. Laing, 2 (1841) • Cobbett, *Parl. hist.*, vol. 3 • T. Gumble, *The life of General Monck, duke of Albemarle* (1671) • *An exact and most impartial accompt of the … trial … of nine and twenty regicides* (1660) [Thomason tract E1047 (3)] • Wood, *Ath. Oxon.*, new edn, vol. 4 • *Reliquiae Baxterianae, or, Mr Richard Baxter's narrative of the most memorable passages of his life and times*, ed. M. Sylvester, 1 vol. in 3 pts (1696) • P. Warwick, *Memoires of the reigns of King Charles I* (1701) • *The life of Edward, earl of Clarendon … written by himself*, 2 vols. (1857) • Evelyn, *Diary*, vol. 4 • *Harleian miscellany*, 5 (1810) • *N&Q*, 3rd ser., 12 (1867) • D. Scott, '"Hannibal at our gates": loyalists and fifth-columnists during the bishops' wars—the case of Yorkshire', *BIHR*, 70 (1997), 269–93 • J. Morrill, 'William Dowsing, the bureaucratic puritan', *Public men and private conscience in seventeenth-century England*, ed. J. S. Morrill, P. S. Slack, and D. Woolf (1993) • M. W. Helms and E. R. Edwards, 'Montagu, Robert', HoP, *Commons, 1660–90*, 3.89

Archives BL, memoirs, Add. MS 15567 • BL, corresp. and papers, Add. MS 34253 • Cambs. AS, Huntingdon, letters and papers • CUL, corresp. relating to University of Cambridge | Bodl. Oxf., Tanner MSS • CUL, Baker MSS • Derbys. RO, Matlock, corresp. with Derbyshire committee regarding lead trading and exchange of prisoners

Likenesses silver medal, *c.*1643, NPG • P. Lely, oils, *c.*1661–1665, NPG [*see illus.*] • studio of P. Lely, oils, *c.*1661–1665, NPG; version, Woburn Abbey, Bedfordshire • Hollar, portrait, pubd 1694 • Benoist, engraving, repro. in T. Smollett, *A complete History of England*, 2nd edn (1758–60), vol. 7, p. 209 • Dean, engraving (after painting by unknown artist), repro. in E. Lodge, *Portraits of illustrious personages of Great Britain*, vol. 3 • W. Hollar, portrait, NPG • Houbraken, engraving, repro. in T. Birch, *The heads of illustrious persons of Great Britain* (1751), 31 • Van Dyck, portrait; in possession of the duke of Manchester in 1894 • M. Vandergucht, engraving, repro. in

E. Hyde, earl of Clarendon, *The history of the rebellion and civil wars in England*, 1/1 (1721), 54 • engraving, repro. in J. Ricraft, *A survey of Englands champions and truths faithfull patriots* (1647), 17 • engravings, repro. in J. Vicars, *England's worthies under whom all the civill and bloody warres since anno 1642 to anno 1647 are related* (1647), 16

Wealth at death £4000 due to him from the king; his ancestral estate at Kimbolton; pasture worth 500 marks p.a.: will, PRO, PROB 11/336, fols. 204v–205

Montagu, Edward, second Baron Montagu of Boughton (1616–1684). *See under* Montagu, Edward, first Baron Montagu of Boughton (1562/3–1644).

Montagu [Mountagu], **Edward, first earl of Sandwich** (1625–1672), army and naval officer and diplomat, was born at Barnwell, Northamptonshire, on 27 July 1625, the second but eldest surviving son of Sir Sydney Montagu (*c.*1571–1644) of Hinchingbrooke, Huntingdonshire, MP for Huntingdonshire, master of requests, and groom of the bedchamber to James I, and his wife, Paulina, formerly Pepys (*d.* 1638). Edward spelt his surname Mountagu, though the family name later settled in the form Montagu.

Early life, civil war, and protectorate Edward Montagu was educated at the grammar school in Huntingdon; he was entered on the books of the Middle Temple in 1635, aged ten, but never studied there. He married Jemimah Crew (1625–1674) at St Margaret's, Westminster, on 7 November 1642. Although his ageing father supported the king in the recently declared civil war, his new in-laws were parliamentarians, and his cousin the earl of Manchester commanded the army of the eastern association. In June 1643 he became a deputy lieutenant of the association, and on 20 August he was commissioned to raise his own regiment of foot, a colonel at eighteen. He first fought at the attack on Hillesden House in March 1644, and early in May took part in Manchester's recapture of Lincoln. His regiment then marched to join the siege of York, fighting in the battle of Marston Moor on 2 July and at the second battle of Newbury on 27 October. Despite his family connections, Montagu was one of the colonels who supported Cromwell's denunciation of Manchester for indecisiveness, giving evidence to the effect that Manchester had opposed the war from the beginning.

Montagu spent much of the winter of 1644–5 at Henley, where he became governor on 10 January 1645. His regiment fought at Naseby on 14 June, and in the following month Montagu effectively became acting major-general in the west in Skippon's absence, participating in the successful siege of Bristol. In the assault on 10 September, Montagu led the attack through the breach at Lawford's Gate and on to the castle gates. He was one of the two colonels who bore the news of Bristol's surrender to parliament on 12 September, receiving the thanks of the house. On 13 October he returned to parliament on a more permanent basis, having been elected MP for Huntingdonshire. Thereafter, the self-denying ordinance of 1645 precluded further military command, but Montagu played only a limited role in parliament, withdrawing from it entirely at Pride's Purge.

Montagu spent the early part of the Commonwealth in

General at sea The fleet sailed on 15 March 1656, shortly after the first surviving piece of correspondence between Montagu and his relatively new servant, his distant kinsman Samuel Pepys. Blake and Montagu flew their flag in the new first-rate *Naseby*. After reconnoitring Tangier, Tetuan, and Gibraltar, and exacting compensation for English merchants in Lisbon from the Portuguese crown (partly by threatening the returning Brazil fleet), Montagu returned home in October. He carried with him much of the Spanish treasure captured by Richard Stayner in the previous month, and on 4 November unjustly received parliament's thanks for an action in which he had taken no part.

Montagu became one of the leading members of the 'new Cromwellian' faction which advocated the offer of the crown to Cromwell in 'The humble petition and advice' of April 1657. On 17 July he rejoined the *Naseby* to command the fleet designed to support the attacks on Dunkirk and Mardyke, promised to England under Cromwell's treaty with Mazarin. From 19 to 22 September his ships supported Marshal Turenne's successful attack on Mardyke. He returned to England in October and joined Cromwell's privy council, becoming additionally (in January 1658) a baron and member of the controversial 'other house' created by 'The humble petition and advice'. He returned to his command at sea on 1 June, supporting Turenne's attack on Dunkirk; after the town's surrender on 24 June he was presented to Louis XIV and entertained Mazarin aboard the *Naseby*.

Montagu strongly supported the protectorship of Richard Cromwell following Oliver's death on 3 September, and presented an address of loyalty to the new regime from the navy. He was made a colonel of horse on 16 September, and in October briefly took a squadron to sea to suppress the Dunkirk privateers. His strong personal commitment to Richard made him enemies, notably major-generals Fleetwood and Desborough, who at the privy council in December accused Montagu of plotting to kidnap and perhaps kill them. Montagu denied the charge, which was based on anonymous information, and Desborough walked out of the meeting in disgust.

In March 1659 Montagu returned to the *Naseby* to take command of a fleet intended for the Baltic. The ongoing conflict between Sweden and Denmark threatened England's substantial trading interests in that area, especially as the Dutch, who sympathized with Denmark, had sent a large fleet to 'mediate'. The prospects of the Dutch gaining greater control of Baltic trade, and of England's ally Sweden's being defeated, were unacceptable to Richard Cromwell's council, and Montagu was sent with forty ships to provide England's input into the mediation effort. He arrived at Elsinore on 6 April to find the forces of Charles X of Sweden besieging Copenhagen, and his first efforts were directed towards persuading the Dutch not to intervene on Denmark's side, and persuading the Swedes to negotiate at all. Montagu's efforts were temporarily stymied by the fall of Richard Cromwell at the end of April, and the fleet withdrew to await the outcome of events in England.

Edward Montagu, first earl of Sandwich (1625–1672), by Sir Peter Lely, *c*.1670

retirement at Hinchingbrooke, although he continued to act as a county commissioner. He returned to public life in July 1653 as a member of the nominated, or Barebone's Parliament, becoming a member of the council of state on 14 July. His increasingly close association with his Huntingdonshire neighbour Oliver Cromwell became apparent after the establishment of the protectorate. Montagu became one of the fifteen members of Cromwell's council, and was appointed a treasury commissioner on 3 August 1654 with a salary of £1000 p.a. He was employed in a number of high-profile diplomatic roles, such as the reception of the Dutch ambassadors at Whitehall on 20 March 1654. He was a leading government spokesman in the debates over military and naval expenditure in December, and in October 1655 was appointed to the admiralty committee. With Cromwell intent with war on Spain, Montagu was appointed joint general at sea on 2 January 1656. He shared the position with Robert Blake, whose illness—and the need to have someone personally loyal to Cromwell in authority in the fleet—prompted Montagu's elevation.

Montagu made it plain that he regretted Richard's fall, but promised to follow the orders of the newly restored Rump Parliament. The royalists immediately seized the opportunity to approach Montagu, using direct letters from Charles and the agencies of two intermediaries, the general at sea's eponymous cousin Edward Montagu and the former naval captain Thomas Whetstone (a nephew of Oliver Cromwell). Royalist doubts about Montagu's loyalty to the Rump were shared by that body itself, which removed him from the admiralty commission on 31 May, sent the known republican John Lawson to command a fleet off Flanders as a counterweight to Montagu's, and dispatched three commissioners, led by the leading republican Algernon Sidney, ostensibly to assist Montagu with the negotiations but in reality at least partly to monitor his activities. The new commissioners and their government were less inclined towards Sweden, and agreed to form a joint Anglo-Dutch fleet to enforce their proposed treaty. Montagu opposed this, arguing that the rapidly diminishing level of provisions in the fleet made its immediate return to England essential. Sidney suspected that Montagu was in touch with the royalists—he had seen Whetstone ashore in Copenhagen—and that the real reason for taking the fleet home would be to assist that cause. The fleet sailed on 24 August, arriving in Hollesley Bay on 6 September. The fact that Montagu had persistently rejected the option of obtaining provisions ashore, and that a nationwide royalist uprising took place during August (albeit abortively, except in the case of Sir George Booth's revolt in Cheshire), led to immediate suspicions that he had covertly planned to use the fleet for the royalists, perhaps by blockading the Thames. Montagu argued his case before the Rump and no hard evidence could be found against him. Nevertheless, he ceased to command at sea and retired to Hinchingbrooke.

The Restoration Montagu's agents in London, notably Samuel Pepys and John Creed, kept him informed of the bewildering pace of political change over the winter of 1659–60. On 5 December he was named one of the fleet's representatives at projected talks on a new constitution, but he decided to remain at home. In February 1660 the arrival in London of George Monck's Scottish army, and the subsequent recall of the 'secluded members' to parliament, signalled Montagu's recall to public life. He was appointed to the council of state on 23 February and made general at sea jointly with Monck on 2 March, although the latter's enforced presence in London meant that Montagu was effectively in sole command. He was reappointed to the admiralty commission on 3 March. His first task was to oversee a purge of known republican officers from the fleet; his first list of casualties and their replacements (many of them his own clients) was approved by the council on the 7th. Montagu was certainly amenable to a restoration of the monarchy by this point, although in a pragmatic rather than an idealistic way: on 6 March 1660 Pepys noted his belief that the king would return, but would not last long 'unless he carry himself very soberly and well' (Pepys, 1.79). Montagu was in regular correspondence with Charles II by this time. On 23 March he joined the fleet, and continued to work on the purge of the officer corps, engineering the dismissals of several potential dissidents and sending off others in command of distant convoys. He was elected to the Convention for both Weymouth and Dover, choosing to sit for the latter, where he was also made a freeman. On 14 May the fleet under his command dropped anchor off Scheveningen, having decided not to wait for parliament's commissioners—an action that made him a number of lifelong enemies, or so Clarendon alleged. On the 23rd the royal party went aboard, landing at Dover on the 25th.

The inevitable honours quickly followed. Within forty-eight hours of the king's landing Montagu was an earl (subsequently choosing Sandwich for his title on 12 July) and a knight of the Garter. To maintain an earl's dignity, he was granted an estate of £4000 p.a. He was reappointed to the treasury commission, where he had previously served between 1654 and 1659. In June he was sworn of the privy council and made master of the wardrobe and warden of Trinity House (serving as master in 1661–2). He commanded the squadrons which brought Princess Mary from the Netherlands in October 1660, that which conveyed the queen mother, Henrietta Maria, and Princess Henrietta to France in January 1661, and that which brought the queen mother back in July 1662. On the first voyage to France he fell out with the duke of Buckingham, challenging him to a duel when the duke refused to pay his losses to Sandwich at cards; only the direct intervention of the queen mother and her entourage settled the quarrel. Sandwich was one of the Garter knights who bore the canopy over the king's head at the coronation (23 April 1661). Additionally, he was elected to the Royal Society on 13 February 1661 and appointed master of the king's swans on 10 May, having become 'lieutenant, or admiral and general of the narrow seas' (*Journal*, xxix)—effectively vice-admiral of England—on 18 March. The perennial disputes with the north African Barbary regencies over freedom of the seas, and the imminent marriage of Charles II to Catherine of Braganza, led to Sandwich's being sent with a fleet to the Mediterranean, with the additional title of ambassador-extraordinary to Portugal. He sailed in June 1661 and after recovering from a fever anchored before Algiers on 29 July and engaged in a desultory exchange of fire with the town. From September he was at Lisbon to begin the arrangements for the royal wedding, sailing on 3 October to take possession of Tangier, part of Catherine's dowry. His fleet oversaw the Portuguese evacuation and the arrival of the English garrison before sailing once more for Lisbon on 18 February. After a spectacular ceremonial entrance into the city, he spent two months conducting the protracted negotiations over the payment of Catherine's dowry. The fleet sailed on 15 April, arriving at Spithead on 14 May, and Sandwich attended the subsequent marriage ceremony at Portsmouth. He was a strong advocate of the sale of Dunkirk to France (October 1662), believing from his Mediterranean experiences in the 1650s that the possession of Tangier offered England far better opportunities, but he bore the brunt of some of the public outcry against the sale.

Sandwich spent much of the period 1661–4 rebuilding Hinchingbrooke, consolidating his estates, and supervising the work of the wardrobe from the London house pertaining to the master. He took little part in politics, although he sat on a number of Lords' committees and was identified (as, indeed, he was throughout the period 1660–67) as a close political ally of the lord chancellor, Clarendon. An illness forced his retirement to Chelsea for much of 1663, where rumours of a liaison with his landlady's daughter led Pepys to send him an ill-judged letter of reproof, one of the factors that probably contributed to the gradual cooling of the relationship between the cousins in the period covered by Pepys's diary.

The Second Anglo-Dutch War In July 1664 Sandwich hoisted his flag in the *London*, taking command of a small squadron intended to monitor Dutch movements. He cruised in the channel in the following months, and when the fleet was enlarged in November he became admiral of the Blue squadron under the overall command of the duke of York. In February 1665 he moved to the *Revenge* for a brief and abortive cruise to intercept Banckert's Dutch squadron in the North Sea. At the end of March he hoisted his flag aboard the *Royal Prince*, his flagship for the main campaign of 1665. Aboard her, he commanded the rear squadron in the battle of Lowestoft (3 June), playing a prominent part in the victory, especially when his squadron successfully broke through the Dutch centre. Despite this, Sandwich received little credit in the printed accounts of the battle, and blamed York and Prince Rupert for denigrating him. As it transpired, York's departure from the fleet after the victory and Rupert's refusal to contemplate a joint command handed Sandwich the position of sole admiral for the remainder of the campaign. His main objectives, as laid down in his instructions, were to be the interception of the returning Dutch East Indies ships and De Ruyter's fleet which had been cruising off Africa, even if they took refuge in neutral harbours in Norway. The belief that the king of Denmark–Norway, Frederick III, had been persuaded by the English envoy, Sir Gilbert Talbot, to acquiesce in such an attack in return for part of the proceeds led to the over-hasty departure of a badly prepared fleet on 5 July. Sandwich cruised on the Dogger Bank until all his reinforcements had arrived, then moved slowly northeast towards Norway. While he did so, De Ruyter evaded him by slipping along the Danish coast to the Ems. However, Sandwich was informed on 23 July that the Dutch merchant fleet from the Mediterranean was certainly in Bergen, and on the 30th he received intelligence that ten East Indiamen had just come into the same port. Trusting in Talbot's diplomacy, on 30 July Sandwich detached a squadron under Sir Thomas Teddeman to attack the shipping in Bergen. When the attack was made, on 2 August, the Danish governor refused to co-operate with Teddeman, and the Dutch and Danes jointly manned the shore batteries. The hail of fire forced Teddeman's withdrawal with over 400 casualties. Although public opinion criticized Sandwich, he retained the support of the court, and the real responsibility for the failure seems to have lain in

a breakdown of communications and series of misunderstandings between Talbot and Frederick III, and then between Talbot, his political masters, and Sandwich.

Sandwich's fleet, containing Teddeman's battered contingent, returned to Southwold Bay on 21 August. He sailed again seven days later, intending to intercept De Ruyter as he escorted home the merchantmen at Bergen. Although the English failed in their main objective, they had a major success on 3 September when a number of Dutch vessels, separated from De Ruyter by storms, were taken off the Texel. The prizes included two East Indiamen, the *Phoenix* and *Slothany*, and two other large merchant ships. Sandwich fought a further brief and successful engagement with the Dutch on 9 September before returning to the buoy of the Nore on 13 September. The hugely lucrative cargoes of the prizes guaranteed Sandwich's triumphant reception, but this quickly turned sour. Legally, the prize goods should have been turned over to the officials of the prize commission, but, on the voyage to the Nore, Sandwich was persuaded (notably by Sir William Penn) to order an immediate distribution of part of the cargoes to the flag officers of the fleet. His action quickly triggered jealousy among the captains who had not benefited, and some of the flag officers, in particular Sir George Ayscue, repudiated their shares. Sandwich sought retrospective authorization for his actions from the king and duke of York, but this had not arrived before the flagmen started to ship their goods ashore. His rivals, the duke of Albemarle prominent among them, used Sandwich's indiscretion to undermine his position, and his decision on 1 October to lay up the fleet for the winter only encouraged the (entirely unjustified) popular perception of him as a cowardly and avaricious admiral. This impression was heightened by Sandwich's departure from the fleet to attend the court at Oxford, despite the fact that the Dutch spent much of October on the English coast, and by the seizure of some of his prize goods by the customs at King's Lynn, whence they were to be taken upriver to Hinchingbrooke. It had already been decided, thanks largely to Albemarle's urging, that Sandwich would hold no further command at sea in the forthcoming campaigns.

Ambassador to Spain In late October or early November 1665 it was decided that Sandwich should go to Spain as ambassador-extraordinary. The appointment removed him from the political storm over the prize goods affair, but also presented him with a major challenge. The new ambassador would be expected to mediate in the ongoing war between Spain and England's ally Portugal, and to conclude a commercial treaty which had been stalled throughout 1665. Moreover, England desperately needed Spanish support, or at least sympathy, to prevent her complete diplomatic isolation (relations between her and both France and Denmark–Norway were deteriorating rapidly, leading to outbreaks of war early in 1666). The situation was complicated by the fact that the Spanish government was itself in a state of flux, with the recent death of King Philip IV having brought to the throne the sickly four-year-old Charles II under the regency of his mother, Maria Anna. Sandwich received his official appointment as ambassador on 20 February, said his farewells to his family and to Pepys on the 25th, and sailed on 2 March. On arrival off Corunna on 12 March Sandwich was informed that he and his retinue would have to be quarantined owing to fears of the plague spreading from England, and he was put up in quarters in Burgos. He finally set off for Madrid on 27 April, entered the city on 18 May, and was presented privately to the queen regent on 27 May and publicly on 20 June.

Sandwich's negotiations were bedevilled by the factional divisions among the Spanish ministers, by their insistence on ratifying the highly favourable commercial treaty that the previous ambassador, Sir Richard Fanshawe, had been prepared to concede, and by their categorical refusal to allow Alfonso of Portugal recognition as a reigning monarch. Moreover, the French diplomats in Madrid attempted to undermine Sandwich's efforts at every turn, as war between Spain and Portugal served Louis XIV's purpose. Sandwich eventually persuaded the Spanish to decouple the commercial treaty from the Portuguese question, and that treaty was signed in May 1667. By its most important clause, English goods imported into Spain could be re-exported without paying a second set of customs duties, and this proved an immensely valuable boost to the English carrying trade to and from the Mediterranean. Meanwhile, Sandwich's hand on the outstanding issues was strengthened by the Franco-Portuguese alliance of March 1667, and by the French invasion of Brabant in May. Sandwich attempted to exact substantial concessions from the Spanish before he would agree to a full alliance; above all, he sought access for English shipping to the lucrative trade of the Spanish Americas. The Spanish could not contemplate such sweeping concessions, but the ending of the Second Anglo-Dutch War (and the concomitant Anglo-French war) by the treaty of Breda in July 1667 panicked the Spanish, as it seemed to free the French to turn all their attentions to Spain. Within two days of the news of Breda reaching Madrid, the Spanish government had agreed to recognize Portugal as a kingdom. Moreover, a coup in Lisbon in November effectively sidelined Alfonso and installed, as regent, his brother Pedro, who rejected the pro-French line of the previous government. Sandwich himself set out for Madrid on 26 December to hasten matters, arriving in Lisbon on 12 January 1668. Despite the inevitable last-minute arguments over individual clauses, he was able to engineer the signing of the treaty on 3 February. The Portuguese war of independence, which had lasted since 1640, was over.

Sandwich returned to Madrid on 22 March 1668, and made his formal farewell to the king and queen regent on 23 April. He left Madrid on 10 July, bound for Cadiz and a tour of inspection of Tangier. He arrived in the English colony on 14 August and undertook a rigorous examination of the defences, population, and facilities of the town, as well as presenting it with a new charter. He sailed from Tangier aboard the *Greenwich* on 29 August, and, after a short stay in Cornwall, returned to Spithead on 28 September. He was received by the king at Audley End on 11 October, returning finally to Hinchingbrooke two days later. In his absence, both the Bergen and prize-goods affairs had been raised in parliament, and in April 1668 Sandwich had been threatened with impeachment. In the summer of 1668 the 'Brooke House committee', which was investigating the alleged miscarriages of the Dutch war, demanded his responses to the allegations against him over the prize goods. His answer, sent to the committee on 10 September, failed to satisfy it, and in February 1669 he was pressed for further information, but his stalling tactics prevailed: the committee was dissolved before it obtained a fuller response from him. Sandwich spent much of 1669 and the early months of 1670 at Hinchingbrooke and in attendance at the House of Lords, and at the privy council's committee for trade and the plantations which he had joined on 13 January 1669. In May 1670 he escorted Princess Henrietta to Dover, unaware of the secret treaty which her visit entailed, and on 30 July became president of the newly created council for foreign plantations, a smaller, more efficient replacement for the previous committee.

The Third Anglo-Dutch War Sandwich reportedly disliked the war which Charles II and Louis XIV began against the Dutch in 1672. He told John Evelyn that he 'was utterly against this war from the beginning', and seems to have regarded his own prospects with fatalism: when he parted from Evelyn, 'shaking me by the hand he bid me good-bye, and said he thought he should see me no more … "No", says he, "they will not have me live … I must do something, I know not what, to save my reputation"' (Evelyn, 3.616). However, unknown to Evelyn or the earl's subsequent biographers, Sandwich, along with the French ministers Seignelay and Colbert de Croissy, had signed the naval treaty of January 1672, which set out the arrangements for the conduct of the naval campaign. On 21 April 1672 the earl hoisted his flag aboard the *Royal James*, a new 100-gun first-rate built in the previous year. He was to be admiral of the blue in a combined Anglo-French fleet. The two English squadrons sailed from the Nore on 2 May, joining with the French at Spithead on 5 May. After attempts to bring the Dutch to an engagement were frustrated by the weather, the allied fleet entered Southwold Bay, or Solebay, on 21 May. Believing the Dutch had retired to their own coast, the fleet began to revictual. However, in the early morning of 28 May the Dutch fleet was sighted. The fact that Sandwich's Blue squadron was the most northerly of the anchored allied squadrons meant that when the combined fleet got under way it formed the van, rather than the rear, and would therefore bear the brunt of De Ruyter's attack. Van Ghent's squadron of Amsterdam ships engaged Sandwich just before seven, and the *Royal James* gradually became detached from her support: her chief second, Captain Francis Digby's *Henry*, was taken, and the vice- and rear-admirals' divisions were both too far away to help. About nine, Sandwich's ship was engaged by Captain Jan van Brakel's *Groot Hollandia*, which got into such a position that she could rake the *Royal James* from the bows. An hour later van Ghent and the *Dolfijn* attempted to attack Sandwich's stern, but in the light winds she was unable to manoeuvre, and in the subsequent pounding from the *Royal James*'s guns van Ghent was killed. At the suggestion of his wounded flag captain, Richard Haddock, Sandwich managed to get clear of the *Groot Hollandia*, only to come under renewed attack from the *Olifant* and from a Dutch fireship, which succeeded in grappling onto the *Royal James*. With her crew already decimated, the flagship was unable to repel the attack. Sandwich rejected all suggestions that he should abandon the ship, and, by midday, the last of those who survived had left him. By the end of the afternoon, the ship had burnt to the water-line.

Sandwich's body, recognizable from the Garter ribbon that he had worn during the battle, was recovered from the sea on 10 June. The absence of any evidence of burning suggested that he had probably attempted to swim away from the wreck at the last moment, but that his middle-aged weight ensured he was soon overcome by the sea. The body lay at Landguard Fort until 22 June when it was taken by sea to Deptford. The funeral took place on 3 July. An impressive flotilla escorted the coffin up the Thames to Westminster Abbey, where the earl was laid to rest in Henry VII's chapel. In his will, Sandwich made bequests of £3000 to each of his three daughters, and of £2000 to each of his six sons, who included John *Montagu; the estate at Brampton passed to his wife; but the bulk of his inheritance passed naturally to his eldest son, Lord Hinchingbrooke, who became the second earl of Sandwich. It was a sign of how estranged the first earl and his old servant, Samuel Pepys, had become by the time the will was drawn up, in August 1669, that the diarist—an obvious candidate to be an executor—is named nowhere in it.

Conclusion If Sandwich was often the subject of popular and political attack in life, his reputation was fortunate in death. The publication of Pepys's diary presented a picture of his 'my lord' almost as a true Renaissance man: the generous patron, the cheerful if sometimes moody companion, the hopeless manager of money, the competent artist and musician. He had an ear for languages, mastering Spanish by the end of his embassy, and his fascination with topography, mathematics, astronomy, and navigation emerges clearly from his manuscript journals, which are still held by his family. These formed the main sources for two sympathetic twentieth-century biographies, by F. R. Harris (1912) and Richard Ollard (1994).

Sandwich's religious beliefs changed over time. His youthful sympathy for the independents and more radical sects in the 1640s gave way by 1660 to the scepticism and indifference noted by Pepys, and he became a pragmatic supporter of the established church. Politically, he never regained the level of influence he had possessed under the Cromwells from about 1657 to 1659, especially in Richard Cromwell's protectorate. His firm belief in strong rule, ideally of a single person, enabled him to make the transition from lingering adherence to Richard (whom he was still addressing as 'your highness' months after his fall) to a qualified support for the return of Charles II. Although he could handle certain political situations masterfully—

for instance, his treatment of Algernon Sydney in the Baltic, or his concealment from an incredulous Pepys of his early dealings with the royalists—he never truly came to terms with the new situation after the Restoration. He was at best a reluctant courtier, and his steady adherence to Clarendon made him many enemies. He did not suffer fools gladly, as his obviously hostile attitude to his political masters in 1659 suggests, and this did not stand him in good stead at a post-Restoration court where dissembling was commonplace. Ultimately, his naïvety in the prize-goods affair destroyed much of his public reputation, and his undoubted successes as ambassador in Spain only partially regained his standing in the country and at court.

Sandwich's career as an admiral was his most enduring achievement. Although modern writers give him less credit than some of their predecessors for the development of the line of battle as the main tactic of the Second Anglo-Dutch War, it is clear that the fighting instructions he issued to his squadron on 1 February 1665, modifying and clarifying the duke of York's of the previous November, were an important step in the process of working through the implications of what was still a very new way of fighting a naval action. Sandwich's belief that less well-armed ships and hired merchantmen should not be placed in the line of battle at all foreshadowed the emphasis on power and weight of broadside that dominated tactical thinking in the French wars from 1689 to 1815. His consistent belief in the necessity for Britain to have a forward Mediterranean strategy, focused on a permanent fleet base, originated during his cruise with Blake in 1656, was refined by his later experiences at Tangier, and again foreshadowed the strategic thinking that led ultimately to the capture of Gibraltar. Sandwich was not the only high-ranking officer to hold such views, but his clarity of thinking on a range of naval matters was a comparative rarity in the seventeenth century.

Ultimately, the epitaph by his friend John Evelyn still provides one of the best summaries of the character of Edward Montagu, first earl of Sandwich:

> My Lord Sandwich was prudent as well as valiant, and always governed his affairs with success, and little loss, he was for deliberation and reason … deplorable was the loss of one of the best accomplished persons, not only of this nation but of any other: he was learned in the Mathematics, in Music, in Sea affairs, in political … was of a sweet obliging temper; sober, chaste, infinitely ingenious and a true noble man, an ornament to the court, and his prince.   (Evelyn, 3.616–19)

J. D. DAVIES

Sources F. R. Harris, *The life of Edward Montagu … first earl of Sandwich*, 2 vols. (1912) • R. Ollard, *Cromwell's earl: a life of Edward Mountagu, 1st earl of Sandwich* (1994) • Bodl. Oxf., MSS Carte 73–75, 223 • *The journal of Edward Mountagu, first earl of Sandwich, admiral and general at sea, 1659–1665*, ed. R. C. Anderson, Navy RS, 64 (1929) • Pepys, *Diary* • NMM, Sandwich papers [uncatalogued] • B. Capp, *Cromwell's navy: the fleet and the English revolution, 1648–1660* (1989) • Bodl. Oxf., MS Rawl. A. 468 • Evelyn, *Diary* • *The life of Edward, earl of Clarendon … written by himself*, new edn, 3 vols. (1827) • Bodl. Oxf., MSS Clarendon 64–72 • Longleat House, Wiltshire, Coventry MS 95 • PRO, Admiralty papers [esp. ADM 2/1731 and 2/1745] • NMM, LBK/47 • J. D. Davies, *Gentlemen and tarpaulins: the officers and men of the Restoration navy* (1991) • A. W. Tedder, *The navy of the Restoration* (1916) • C. H. Hartmann, *Clifford of the Cabal* [1937] • R. C. Anderson, ed., *Journals and narratives of the Third Dutch War*, Navy RS, 86 (1946) · GEC, *Peerage* · HoP, *Commons, 1660–90*, 3.82–3 · Cambs. AS, Huntingdon, Hinchingbrooke MS 7/34

Archives Bodl. Oxf., corresp. and papers, Carte MSS 73–75 · Bodl. Oxf., notebook on navigation and places visited · Mapperton House, Dorset, MS journals · NMM, papers · NRA, priv. coll., corresp., journal, and papers | BL, Sloane MSS, corresp. · RS, letters to Lord Brouncker **Likenesses** P. Lely, oils, *c.*1649, repro. in Ollard, *Cromwell's earl*, following p. 142 · P. Lely, oils, *c.*1655–1659, NPG; repro. in Ollard, *Cromwell's earl*, jacket · P. Lely, oils, *c.*1658–1659, NMM · P. Lely, oils, *c.*1667–1668, NMM · Feliciano, oils, 1668, Gov. Art Coll. · P. Lely, oils, *c.*1670, repro. in Ollard, *Cromwell's earl* · P. Lely, oils, *c.*1670, Yale U. CBA, Paul Mellon collection [*see illus.*] · T. Flatman, miniature · school of P. Lely, three paintings · miniature · oils, Hampton Court Palace · oils, Sandwich town hall **Wealth at death** £3000 to each daughter; £2000 to each son; Hinchingbrooke to successor, second earl; estates at Lyveden and Oundle to second son; Brampton to widow; also jewels, incl. presents from the king of Sweden and queen of Spain; over £4000 worth of jewels, plate, and other goods lost in the *Royal James*: Harris, *Life of Edward Montagu*, vol. 2, p. 288

Montagu, Edward (1635/6–1665). *See under* Montagu, Edward, first Baron Montagu of Boughton (1562/3–1644).

Montagu, Edward (1755–1799), army officer, was born on 20 February 1755, the fourth son of Admiral John *Montagu (1718/19–1795), kinsman of the duke of Manchester, and his wife, Sophia, daughter of James Wroughton of Wilcot, Wiltshire. Having been educated at the Royal Military Academy, Woolwich, he went to Bengal as an infantry cadet in 1770. Since no commission was available on his arrival he was placed in the 'select picket', a unit composed of the cadets at Calcutta. On 12 April 1772, as a cadet, he was moved from the infantry to the Bengal artillery, where he was made fireworker on 16 May 1772, lieutenant on 28 September 1777, and captain-lieutenant on 20 March 1780. During the Maratha campaign of 1773 he was attached to Brigadier-General Goddard's army and was successfully employed against forts on the Rohilkhand border; he was severely wounded in the face by an arrow. In 1782, during the Second Anglo-Mysore War, he commanded the artillery with the detachment led by Colonel T. D. Pearce that was sent to join Sir Eyre Coote in the Carnatic against Haidar Ali and the French. Montagu apparently distinguished himself and commanded the British artillery at the unsuccessful siege of Cuddalore, a strong Carnatic fortress held by the French.

Following the end of the war in the Carnatic, Montagu returned to Bengal and was promoted captain on 13 October 1784 (major on 14 September 1790). In the Third Anglo-Mysore War (1790–92), against Tipu Sultan, he took a prominent part in Lord Cornwallis's invasion of Mysore in 1791 and successfully commanded the artillery at the sieges of Nandidroog (stormed 19 October) and Savanadrug (stormed 21 December). On 17 May 1792 at Masulipatam he married Barbara (d. 1848), daughter of John Fleetwood; together they produced a family. Montagu was promoted lieutenant-colonel on 5 November 1796 and brevet colonel on 1 January 1798.

At the beginning of the Fourth Anglo-Mysore War, in 1799, Montagu commanded the Bengal artillery in the expedition against Tipu Sultan that culminated in the siege of his capital, Seringapatam. On 2 May, during the siege, Montagu was struck by cannon shot; one arm was amputated but he died from his wounds on 8 May 1799. A memorial was placed in Lacock church, Wiltshire. John *Montagu (1797–1853), army officer and colonial official, was his youngest son.　　G. P. MORIARTY, rev. D. L. PRIOR

Sources J. Philippart, *East India military calendar*, 3 vols. (1823–6) · V. C. P. Hodson, *List of officers of the Bengal army, 1758–1834*, 4 vols. (1927–47)

Montagu, Edward Wortley (1713–1776), traveller and criminal, was born in London on 16 May 1713, the elder child and only son of Edward Wortley Montagu (1678–1761), MP, diplomat, and entrepreneur, and Lady Mary Wortley *Montagu (*bap.* 1689, *d.* 1762), writer and traveller. In 1716 Montagu's mother took him on a hair-raising journey across Europe to Constantinople, where his father had been posted. There in March 1718 Montagu achieved early fame when he was inoculated against smallpox according to the practice of Turkish folk-medicine.

Early years and army career Montagu attended Westminster School, but he ran away several times. According to the highly coloured saga of his adventures which he told years later to the Revd John Forster (his tutor) his parents sent him to the West Indies for three years but he was in England in 1730 when he inexplicably married 'a woman of very low degree, considerably older than himself' (M. W. Montagu, *Letters and Works*, 1861, 1:iii), said to be a washerwoman and named Sally. He very soon left his wife; the marriage was hushed up; his parents sent him abroad again and his increasingly wealthy father took advice about disinheriting him.

Montagu was sent to Europe with a Scottish tutor, John Anderson. Between bouts of indulgence with drink and women he had phases of marathon praying and expressed a desire to enter a monastery. He later spoke romantically of earning his keep around Europe as a postilion, ploughman, and in other humble jobs, but in fact made something approximating the grand tour, visiting Italian cultural centres, and leaving debts behind him everywhere. In autumn 1734, having come of age, Montagu gave Anderson the slip and returned to England to claim a legacy from his paternal grandfather and some entailed estates. He set lawyers to work on his behalf and left the country again.

Back in the Netherlands with Anderson, Montagu was forbidden to approach his father until he could 'act with more prudence than a downright Idiot' (that is, live within his income; *Complete Letters of Lady Mary Wortley Montagu*, 2.189). He sought a settlement with his parents while they enquired in vain for some haven where a debtor might live unmolested. Montagu's allowance was well below what a young man of his class could expect, even from a less exceptionally wealthy father, but the latter, though mean, was apparently paying annuities to two women discarded by his son (besides the wife). His father knew him to be in debt and believed him to be in league with foot-pads or highwaymen: one named Warren was among his creditors; and Montagu's name came up in 1750 during the trial of another, James McLean or Maclaine. Montagu enrolled at Leiden University in September 1741 to study oriental languages under the eminent Dr Schultens. He was already a skilled linguist and a book collector. But within three months he left Leiden (having run up the usual debts) for London, where he stayed for three months more to cultivate patrons, especially Edward Montagu (MP, coal magnate, and first cousin of Edward Wortley Montagu senior) and John, second Baron Carteret (1690–1763), secretary of state, neither of whom had a male heir. Montagu visited the French court disguised as a French officer in order to write a report for Edward Montagu.

With the War of the Austrian Succession impending Montagu wanted an army commission. In 1742, after another visit to London and a spell in debtors' prison, he was commissioned a cornet in Sir John Cope's dragoon regiment, the seventh hussars; he later became a captain-lieutenant, then captain, in the 1st foot. He left London for the Low Countries after the battle of Dettingen, and fought a successful campaign. He distinguished himself at the battle of Fontenoy on 12 May 1745, being mentioned in dispatches. That autumn he became aide-de-camp to the British commander-in-chief. After the siege of Brussels (1746) he was taken prisoner by the French and was confined at Liège until freed by exchange.

Diplomatic career and criminal ventures Montagu now felt himself passed over for younger men and decided to leave the army for a diplomatic career. He visited London to solicit fellow-members of the 'Divan' (a club of young Englishmen who affected admiration for the Turks, which Montagu had joined in 1744). He resigned from the army in 1748 to become secretary (with another cousin, Richard Montagu), to John Montagu, earl of Sandwich. Sandwich was appointed minister-plenipotentiary at the peace negotiations at Aix-la-Chapelle where Montagu's command of languages proved valuable. Sandwich arranged for his uncontested election to parliament for Hunting-donshire in 1747.

Once peace was established Montagu aimed at the post of secretary to the British embassy in Paris, but did not get it. As a member of parliament, however, he could, without fearing arrest for debt, pass between London and Paris, where he was suspected of gathering intelligence contrary to British interests. He lived fashionably, frequented the Divan Club, and was elected to the Royal Society.

On 21 July 1751 Montagu bigamously married a fellow-adventurer, Elizabeth Ashe, close friend of Elizabeth Chudleigh the future bigamist. He left her within three months, and was horrified when required by a court to contribute to the maintenance of their son, Edward Wortley Montagu the third, one of his several illegitimate children. His children also included another son, George, as well as Mary, and another unnamed daughter. Another boy, Massoud (later Fortunatus), was spoken of as his own son, but may have been adopted.

Montagu turned large profits as a gamester in London and Paris. In London he tallied, or kept the bank, at faro parties in the house of Madame de Mirepoix, the French ambassadress. In Paris in 1751 he was partnered in an extortion business by his new wife, by Thomas, second Baron Southwell, and by a fellow member of parliament, Theobald Taaffe. Their activities became known when one of their victims resisted. A young Jewish merchant, Abraham Payba or James Roberts, was lured to the gaming table by Montagu's rank and connections. In Payba's account (published in English in 1752) they got him drunk, kept him gambling after he tried to stop, and caused him to chalk up large losses. He refused to pay, alleging harassment and inaccurate reckoning. They threatened to slash his face. Payba fled Paris, enabling them to ransack his lodgings, doing expensive damage as well as purloining every item of value they could find. Montagu and Taaffe were arrested and brought to trial. Payba won the first case; the two MPs appealed and in August 1752 were cleared, while Payba was successfully charged with defamation and false accusation.

Montagu was on bail from Paris when Horace Walpole graphically described him: 'he plays, dresses, diamonds himself'—even to separate sets of diamond shoe-buckles for each costume—'and has more snuff-boxes than would suffice a Chinese idol with an hundred noses' (Walpole, *Corr.*, 9 Jan 1752, 9.129). Montagu's father had evidently softened towards him, as he increased his allowance and in 1754 saw him elected for Bossiney, a Cornish borough in his possession. The son borrowed money on his expectations, and his debts grew to well beyond £50,000. He was perhaps bidding for the favour of his father (who had scholarly leanings) in *Reflections on the Rise and Fall of the Antient Republicks* (1759) which sets forth his classical learning, his flourished and ornamented prose style, and a whiff of opposition politics. (Lord Bute, who had married his sister, was now both head of the government and his rival for the inheritance.) He contrasted the civic virtue of ancient republics with contemporary luxury and degeneracy. Reviewers were respectful and the book went through four editions by 1778, despite persistent rumours that John Forster was its real author.

When Edward Wortley Montagu senior died in January 1761 he left his son an increased annual allowance, but the residue of his estate (estimated at £1,350,000) went to Montagu's sister, Lady Bute. This was a severe blow. Montagu said that he would be reduced to 'pauperly banishment abroad' (HoP, *Commons, 1754–90*, 3.662). In fact the Butes were willing to pay for peace. They made over to Montagu large sums in cash, and an estate of £8000 p.a. Lord Bute secured his re-election for Bossiney. Having unsuccessfully challenged the will, Montagu shook (in his phrase) 'the dust of an ungrateful country' from his feet (Curling, 161).

Final years abroad The rest of his life, spent abroad, is what made Montagu famous. He took with him his daughter Mary. In February 1761 he re-enrolled at Leiden University, where he made lavish purchases of scientific instruments, as *linguarum orientalum cultor*. The following year he was in Venice, but after this it is as difficult to pin down his movements as it was during his earlier European period. He mixed with scholarly individuals (like Winckelmann, who was at first much impressed by him) and published small antiquarian pieces. At Alexandria he persuaded Caroline Dormer Feroe, wife of the Danish consul, a Roman Catholic, that her husband had died, and married her. He took her on a tour of Armenia, Sinai, and Jerusalem and was received into the Roman Catholic church; when she learned that her husband was alive he told her that her marriage to a protestant was in any case invalid. His secretary, Nathaniel Davison, wrote up their travels for the Royal Society. In 1765 he was again in Venice and then back in Alexandria; he lived some time at Rosetta, and drew or collected views of Egypt (now in Stanford University Library); he travelled through Greece and made plans of ancient battlefields. In 1767 he visited Zante and Salonica, and stayed in Constantinople with the child Massoud and Massoud's mother, Ayesha. Dressing *en Turque* with a beard and turban, he professed himself a Muslim. He finally settled at Padua.

In November 1775 Montagu made his will in preparation for a visit to Mecca. He left his Arabic and Turkish library to Massoud (now Fortunatus), and provided for him to be educated in England.

In February 1776 Montagu heard a false report of his wife Sally's death. Mindful of the money that would accrue to his legal male heir under the terms of his father's will, he advertised in the *Public Advertiser* (16 April) and elsewhere that he had 'no objection to marry any widow or single lady, provided the party be of genteel birth, polished manners and five, six, seven or eight months gone in her pregnancy'. By then, however, he was ill. An ortolan or beccafica eaten in early March had pierced his throat with a tiny, broken bone. An abscess developed, and despite the care of Fortunatus he died in Padua on 29 April 1776. Montagu's advertising for a wife had revived his former notoriety, and many magazine articles followed his death. Fortunatus Montagu reached London that June. He died in 1787, leaving the oriental library to John English Dolben, a friend of Edward Wortley Montagu III, who sold his books and manuscripts years later through Leigh and Sotheby, including an important manuscript of the *Arabian Nights* cycle now in the Bodleian Library.

Achievements and assessment Besides his skill in languages, Montagu was a noted graphologist. Letters from him survive in various collections, including the British Library. Some have been printed in the collections of others such as Maximilien, comte de Lamberg, *Le memorial d'un mondain*, new edn, 1776, 19–21, and J. Nichols, *Literary Anecdotes of the Eighteenth Century*, 1812, 4.640n. Several fictional accounts of his life appeared: the first, compiled from his own papers, was *Memoirs of the late Edw. W—ly M—tague, esq., with remarks on the manners and customs of the oriental world*, 2 vols. (1779). Others are H. Coates, *The British Don Juan … the Hon. Edward W. Montagu* (1823) and E. V. H. Kenealy's novel *Edward Wortley Montagu, an Autobiography*, 3 vols. (1869). Montagu liked to tell gullible visitors that his

real father was the Turkish sultan (though he had been almost four when his mother reached Turkey). His spectacular 'going native' was the culmination of a career of conspicuous social nonconformity. His considerable talent and undoubted oriental scholarship left few tangible traces, but he claims a place in any gallery of notable eccentrics. ISOBEL GRUNDY

Sources J. Curling, *Edward Wortley Montagu, 1713–1776, The man in the iron wig* (1954) • *GM*, 1st ser., 47 (1777), 376–7; 48 (1778), 220–1; 50 (1780), 122, 124, 174; 67 (1797), 1020 • I. Grundy, *Lady Mary Wortley Montagu* (1999) • [Maximilien, comte de Lamberg], *Le memorial d'un mondain* (Corsica, 1774); (London, 1776) • C.- P. d'Albert, duc de Luynes, *Mémoires … sur la cour de Louis XV, 1735–1758* (1860) • G. S. Maxwell, 'Highwayman's heath, the story in fact and fiction of Hounslow Heath in Middlesex', *Middlesex Chronicle* (1935) • E. W. Montagu, *Reflections on the rise and fall of the antient republicks. Adapted to the present state of Great Britain* (1759) • E. W. Montagu, *Observations upon a supposed antique bust at Turin* (1763) • E. W. Montagu and T. Taaffe, *A memorial, or humble petition presented to the judge in the high court of the Tournelle, in Paris … against Abraham Payba alias Abraham Roberts and Louis Pierre, jeweller, appealing from sentence given in favour of those two on 14 June 1752* (1752) [trans. from the Fr. orig.] • *The complete letters of Lady Mary Wortley Montagu*, ed. R. Halsband, 3 vols. (1965–7) • Stanford University, Montagu MSS • Sheff. Arch., Wharncliffe muniments • *Monthly Review*, 7 (1752), 232 • J. Moore, *A view of society and manners in Italy: with anecdotes relating to some eminent characters* (1781) • F. Moussa-Mahmoud, 'A manuscript translation of the *Arabian Nights* in the Beckford papers', *Journal of Arabic literature*, 7 (1973), 12–13 • HoP, *Commons, 1754–90* • Nichols, *Lit. anecdotes* • A. Payba, *The memorial presented to the high court of La Tourelle at Paris, in favour of Abraham Payba, Jew, a native of London; against E—d W—y M—u, Esq; and T—d T—e, Esq.* (1752) [trans. from the Fr. orig.] • *Remarks on the sentence given in favour of E— W— M—, and T— T—, Esqs; by the L—t C—l at Paris* (1752) • *Scots Magazine*, 30 (1768), 41; 38 (1776), 279; 39 (1777), 399–400, 625–6 • [W. Ouseley], *The oriental collections* (1797–8) • HoP, *Commons, 1715–54*, 2.556–7 • J. Waldie, *Sketches descriptive of Italy in the years 1816 and 1817: with a brief account of travels in various parts of France and Switzerland* (1820), iii • Walpole, *Corr.* • *Weekly Magazine, or, Edinburgh Amusement*, 32 (1776), 341 • 'Anecdotes of the late Edward Wortley Montague, Esq.', *Westminster Magazine* (May 1776)

Archives PRO, accounts and inventories of effects at Padua and Venice, and legal papers • RS, corresp. | E. Sussex RO, letters to John Bridger • Harrowby Manuscript Trust, Sandon Hall, Staffordshire • Hunt. L., letters to Elizabeth Montagu • Sheffield Central Library, Wharncliffe MSS • Stanford University, California, Montagu MSS • Swiss Cottage Public Library, London, Beattie MSS, B 826. 51 W. B. 86

Likenesses M. W. Peters, oils, NPG • J. Pillement, caricature, etching, NPG • G. Romney, oils, Warwick Castle, Warwickshire • Vanmour, double portrait (as a child, with his mother), NPG

Montagu, Edwin Samuel (1879–1924), politician, was born on 6 February 1879 at 12 Kensington Palace Gardens, London. He was the second son of Samuel *Montagu, the first Baron Swaythling (1832–1911), a millionaire banker and later Liberal MP, and his wife, Ellen (1848–1919), daughter of Louis Cohen, a member of the prominent Jewish banking family of Liverpool. Henrietta *Franklin (1866–1964) and Lilian Helen *Montagu (1873–1963) were his elder sisters.

Education and early years From 1887 to 1891 Montagu attended Doreck College, a preparatory school in Kensington Gardens Square. In 1891 he was sent to a boarding-school, Clifton College, where he did not settle, suffering from frequent bouts of homesickness, especially missing his mother, to whom he was very close. Severe headaches resulted in his being sent on a recuperative sea voyage round the world from December 1891 to April 1892, accompanied by a young tutor, J. D. Israel. His personal unhappiness was reflected in increasingly poor grades and he was removed from Clifton on 7 April 1893, being enrolled soon after in the City of London School.

Though an intelligent student with an interest in the sciences, Montagu was not strongly academic and his full potential was not reflected in school reports. He cared little for sport, but took a keen interest in ornithology, shooting, and walking, which became lifelong passions. In December 1895 he entered University College, London, specializing in biology, and in June 1896 was placed in the first division, being awarded an exhibition and gold medal in the bachelor of science examination. Although he failed in his attempt to pass the inter-science degree exam in July 1897, he succeeded a year later. After briefly attending University College Hospital as a medical student, he entered Trinity College, Cambridge, in October 1898.

Montagu's years at Cambridge were eventful. In strictly academic terms he was an undistinguished student, obtaining a second in part 1 (1900) and a third in part 2 (1902) of the natural sciences tripos. Instead, he made his mark in the extracurricular field as a witty and eloquent debater, editor, and amateur dramatist. He was elected librarian (and later acting president) of the Amateur Dramatic Club in 1900, president of the Magpie and Stump (the celebrated Trinity College debating society); and secretary (1902) then president (1903) of the prestigious Liberal club. Finally, after two unsuccessful attempts, he was elected president of the Cambridge Union in 1902.

Liberal politics Montagu increasingly focused his energies in two areas—the law and politics. In 1903 he started work with Messrs Coward Hawksley and Chance, solicitors, at 30 Mincing Lane, London, and later in 1904 in the chambers of Mr Pollock QC. In November 1905 he passed the constitutional law section of the bar examination. However, he disliked studying law and realized that the legal profession did not appeal to him as a short cut into politics. Instead, he paid greater attention to the political arena itself. In autumn 1903 he went to Canada with Auberon Herbert in order to test the 'imperial value' of Joseph Chamberlain's imperial preference proposals. Montagu and Herbert were free-trade imperialists and their book, *Canada and the Empire: an Examination of Trade Preferences* (1904), argued vigorously that Canada did not wish to receive imperial preference.

While at Cambridge, Montagu had come to the attention of Liberal leaders, especially H. H. Asquith, as an intelligent and eloquent debater at the Liberal club. He also began speaking for the Liberal Party at meetings throughout the country, earning a reputation as an up-and-coming Liberal of radical opinions. He was rewarded for his exertions when he was adopted as the Liberal candidate for the West Cambridgeshire (Chesterton) constituency, and was elected to parliament as part of the Liberal landslide of

1906. He held the seat until 1918, representing the combined county of Cambridgeshire from 1918 until November 1922.

Montagu rose to prominence under Asquith's wing, beginning a close political and personal partnership that lasted until the end of Asquith's premiership, serving as his parliamentary private secretary when the latter was chancellor of the exchequer from February 1906, and retaining his post when Asquith became prime minister in 1908. Among Montagu's chief concerns during these years was land reform, in which his constituency's strongly rural character gave him a special interest. He took an interest, also, in fiscal issues, and his calls for the reform of the tax system (and especially income tax), while not always successful, highlighted his radicalism.

India Office, Treasury, and war cabinet Montagu's official connection with India began in early 1910 when he was appointed under-secretary of state at the India Office, serving under lords Morley and Crewe until February 1914. His maiden Indian budget speech in July 1910 was a *tour de force* and marked him out for a considerable political future. Apart from financial issues, Montagu concerned himself with political matters, particularly the growing unrest in India. While acknowledging that demands for increasing political participation emanated from a small section of the educated intelligentsia, he nevertheless asserted the importance of responding to the challenging nationalist climate constructively in order to avoid major conflagration, for 'the amount of yeast necessary to leaven a loaf is very small'. In 1912 he left for his first tour of the Indian subcontinent, being keen to establish a personal understanding of the land, its people, and its problems. Accompanied by his brother Lionel, Montagu's visit enabled him to make valuable contacts with several influential Indians (including politicians and princes) that endured for the rest of his career and cemented a growing passion for the Indian empire.

In February 1914 Montagu became financial secretary to the Treasury, and held several posts between 1914 and 1917. He joined the cabinet (and was sworn of the privy council) in February 1915 as chancellor of the duchy of Lancaster. However, in May he was replaced by Winston Churchill and returned to his former post at the Treasury with the formation of the first coalition ministry. During his second tenure at the Treasury he played a leading role in popularizing the first war loans and in establishing voluntary war savings associations and the issue of war savings certificates (February 1916). In July 1916 he was appointed minister of munitions with a seat on the war committee of the cabinet. An agreement he made with J. P. Morgan & Co. saved the allies millions of pounds in their American purchases.

Forced to resign with the fall of Asquith's coalition in December 1916, Montagu continued to harbour hopes of re-entering the government. The opportunity first arose in January 1917 when the new prime minister, Lloyd George, offered him a cabinet post as minister without portfolio in charge of reconstruction. Montagu accepted, much to the annoyance of the Asquithian Liberals, becoming vice-chairman of a second reconstruction committee with Lloyd George as its titular head.

Secretary of state for India, 1917–1922 These were eventful years in the history of the subcontinent, with a growing nationalist movement and an increasing realization among the British ruling élite that more co-operation and political reform were urgently required. Such concerns were made more acute by India's immense contribution to the war effort. Montagu was impatient to play an active part in this process and hoped to succeed Lord Hardinge as viceroy in 1915. 'Indian problems attract me with an intensity—which I can find for no other problems. I have no other ambition save to go to India' (Kaul, 'Press and empire', 112). Although unsuccessful in his bid to become viceroy, his interest in the governance of India found unexpected fulfilment when, following the resignation in July 1917 of the Conservative secretary of state, Austen Chamberlain, Montagu was appointed in his place. Montagu was the last Liberal and only Jew to become secretary of state, and his period of office constituted a turning point in the history of the raj.

Montagu inherited a difficult situation, and one of his first acts was to make a clear statement of the government's position on future constitutional advance for India, a position which had broad cross-party support and had been drafted by the former viceroy, Lord Curzon. His historic pronouncement in the Commons in August 1917 declared that:

> The policy of His Majesty's Government, with which the Government of India are in complete accord, is that of the increasing association of Indians in every branch of the administration, and the gradual development of self-governing institutions with a view to the progressive realisation of responsible government in India as an integral part of the British Empire. ('Report on Indian constitutional reforms', *Parl. papers*, 1918, 8.60, Cd 9109; also S. Char, ed., *Readings in the Constitutional History of India*, 1983, 457)

Montagu was personally committed to this process, and his enthusiasm was evidenced by his decision in winter 1917–18 to undertake an extensive tour of India in order to ascertain public opinion at first hand and formulate with the viceroy, Lord Chelmsford, a concrete scheme for constitutional reform. Apart from a brief visit by Crewe accompanying the king for the Delhi durbar in 1912, no secretary of state had officially visited the subcontinent over whose destinies they presided, and Montagu's tour proved a landmark. He kept a daily record of the visit, published posthumously as *An Indian Diary* (1930). The *Diary* reveals his frank opinions on a range of issues, including the nature of the political problems confronting India; the need for major reforms and an overhaul of the machinery of empire; the hundreds of Indian political delegations he received; his frustration at what he considered unnecessary bureaucracy and the inherent conservatism of the Indian Civil Service; his fluctuating and often less than charitable views of Chelmsford; as well as the pleasures of dining, shooting, and birdwatching with his many friends in princely India.

The Montagu–Chelmsford reforms The resultant Montagu–Chelmsford report of July 1918 formed the basis of the Government of India Act, which formally entered the statute book in December 1919. One of the major innovations was the introduction of diarchy, or dual government (the concept being first mooted by Lionel Curtis and the Round Table organization), under which there was to be a devolution of power and responsibility in the executive and legislative spheres to Indian administrators elected on a restricted franchise at the provincial level. Subjects 'transferred' to Indian ministers included education, agriculture, and local self-government, although several 'reserved' subjects such as irrigation, police, the press, finance, and justice were retained under British control. Reserve powers were also vested in the governors and the viceroy, and the central government retained overriding powers. A bicameral system was set up at the centre with the legislative assembly having elected majorities but no control over ministers. The electorates were enlarged to 5.5 million in the provinces and 1.5 million in the imperial legislature.

Apart from the moderates, most Indian nationalist leaders criticized the report and subsequent act for promising much but delivering little actual power into Indian hands, given the impractical division of duties through diarchy, the fact that politically less important departments were transferred to Indians with limited funds, the extension of the system of separate electorates, and the extensive veto powers retained by the British. Provincial diarchy was, in fact, subsequently revoked in the 1935 act. Nevertheless, the Montagu–Chelmsford reforms did represent an important step in the advance of self-government and a stage on the road to the complete devolution of constitutional power.

The constitutional process was jeopardized, however, by the political repercussions of the government of India's clumsy handling of disturbances during 1919, and in particular by the massacre at Jallianwalla Bagh in Amritsar. The officiating General Dyer was eventually dismissed from the army and the Hunter committee report (1920) was critical of official actions. Montagu was appalled by the massacre and by the justifications offered by Dyer and his supporters, and in the Commons spoke out against the evils of racial arrogance and government by 'terrorism'. However, his emotional outburst was resented by a significant section of the Conservative-dominated Commons, and die-hard back-benchers called for his resignation. He withstood the opposition, but his political position was severely shaken.

The non-cooperation movement (1920–22) was a further testing period for the secretary of state as the raj witnessed unprecedented India-wide opposition. Montagu, as head of the government of India, was increasingly blamed in parliament for the troubles, while Lord Reading, the new viceroy, adopted a cautious policy, preferring to avoid or postpone confrontation. To Montagu's critics this implied weakness and a lack of decisive leadership, and his position in the Commons grew increasingly precarious. Ironically, Montagu enjoyed a more harmonious relationship with Reading. They were friends and liberal Jews who shared a common approach to imperial policy and governance, had worked together during the war, and were temperamentally better suited—Reading's charm, diplomacy, and political pragmatism proving a useful counterfoil to Montagu's impetuousness and idealism.

Montagu was eventually compelled to resign from the India Office on 9 March 1922, following his decision to publish the views of the Indian government on the revision of the treaty of Sèvres without previously consulting his cabinet colleagues—thus flouting the principle of collective responsibility. These views were critical of Lloyd George's anti-Turkish stance in the conflict between Greece and Turkey, an attitude which aroused strong feeling among the Muslim population of India. Montagu felt he had been harshly treated by Lloyd George at the instigation in particular of Curzon, the foreign secretary. Montagu and Lloyd George were not close, and when the prime minister's position as the Liberal head of a Conservative-dominated coalition became more precarious Montagu, who was increasingly seen as a political liability, represented a convenient scapegoat. His earlier betrayal of Asquith meant that he was now politically isolated, and in the general election of November 1922 he lost his seat.

Personal life, family, and religion Montagu was a tall, slim man with a reflective and studious manner. His appearance was striking rather than handsome, with large eyes, black moustache, dark hair, and a receding hairline on a large head, a dark and faintly pock-marked complexion, with a monocle producing a slightly owlish effect. His first love was the natural world. He was a keen ornithologist and was active in the pursuit of country sports, especially shooting. He devoted considerable time and expenditure to renovating his country residence, Breccles Hall near Attleborough in Norfolk, which he purchased in 1916. Along with Lord Grey of Fallodon he established a bird sanctuary at nearby Hickling Broad.

Despite an apparently abundant and successful life, Montagu frequently appeared a solitary and insecure figure. His incisive eloquence and often abrupt manner won him few political friends and helped to alienate potential allies. He was rarely relaxed, was painfully self-deprecating, and suffered a range of health, marital, familial, and religious problems. After a protracted, and not always smooth, courtship Montagu married on 26 July 1915 the Hon. Beatrice Venetia (1887–1948), youngest daughter of Edward Lyulph Stanley, fourth Baron Sheffield and Baron Stanley of Alderley [see Stanley, (Beatrice) Venetia]. Their relationship lacked passion, and Montagu bravely tolerated his wife's many indiscretions—her affair with Lord Beaverbrook being only the most prominent—and her profligate and expensive lifestyle. The triangular relationship between Asquith, Montagu, and Venetia created a major stir in society circles and widened the rift between mentor and protégé. Montagu's close personal friendship with the Asquith family, including Asquith's wife, Margot, meant that his marriage to Venetia and subsequent decision to join Lloyd George's government were highly damaging personally as well as politically.

Montagu had always had a tempestuous relationship with his father, finding his insistence on the strict observance of the Orthodox Jewish faith intellectually and temperamentally hard to countenance. His relationship with his father remained a source of strain, both emotional and financial, into adulthood, as Samuel Montagu used his monetary control over his son to enforce his Orthodox opinions. Samuel Montagu had financed his son's university and legal studies, and paid £500 p.a. as support for his political career. The result was conflict and resentment and a continual financial straightjacket for Montagu. Even after his father's death, when he had an annual income of £10,000 p.a., Venetia was compelled to convert to Judaism upon marriage in order to save his inheritance. For Montagu, religion was a purely personal affair; he had no formal religious beliefs, was anti-Zionist, and constantly emphasized his foremost identity as a Briton.

Antisemitism It has been contended that, although Montagu was not a practising Jew, religious persecution afflicted him throughout his life and helped to destroy his career. His case exemplifies a fundamental paradox in English society: namely, that while England permitted Jews to climb to the pinnacle of economic and political success, it condoned antisemitism (Levine, 4–5). However, concrete links between religious persecution and the ultimate fate of Montagu as a politician are tenuous and can be exaggerated, as no doubt they often were in Montagu's own mind. Personal and political differences were often confused, and developments in his career owed more to a combination of factors within and outside his control than to overt religious bigotry.

This is not to deny that antisemitism was a constant undermining factor in his political life. Conservative critics often portrayed him as unreliable, disreputable, and corrupt on grounds of his religion. In 1913, while under-secretary at the India Office, Montagu had to endure antisemitic taunts in parliament and in the press in connection with the contracts of his cousin, Sir Stuart Samuel, and his father's firm, Samuel Montagu & Co., to supply silver to the Indian government. Montagu had played no part in these proceedings, but though cleared of all charges of corruption he was tainted by the connection. Subsequently, during the Dyer debates in parliament, Montagu riled the Conservative back-benchers. Although his words were insensitive, there is no doubt that antisemitism was a component of the strong reaction they evoked. However, it is important to consider the fate of Montagu in the light of other factors, including the momentous changes that he helped to effect in India, his advanced and idealist views on Britain's imperial mission, his penetrating criticism of Indian government officials, his popularity among Indian politicians, his alienation of key political affiliations in the domestic context, and no doubt his overall political tactlessness. As he himself noted to Chelmsford:

> You see you and I are so much more vulnerable than any other Secretary of State and Viceroy because we have set our signatures to plans and proposals which are controversial … when beaten in the attacks on our scheme, they find it easier to attack us. (Kaul, 'Press and empire', 121)

Twilight years, 1922–1924 India had been Montagu's lifelong passion and after his dismissal he was, in significant respects, a broken man. He continued to work halfheartedly on a number of business ventures and always planned to revisit India, though he never did. In February 1923 he became vice-chairman of the board of De Beers, and later that year joined the board of the Underground Electric Railways and the board of the Metropolitan and District Railway Company. He was a deeply unhappy man in the last years of his life, and continued to suffer from stress and a variety of medical symptoms. Though these were not always serious, he remained preoccupied with premonitions of an early death. On his return from a trip to Brazil (December 1923 to January 1924), undertaken in his capacity as chairman of a British financial mission sent to advise the government on financial and banking reforms, he complained of sickness.

Montagu's condition worsened, though doctors were unable to agree on a diagnosis. He was admitted to a nursing home at 7 Queen Anne Street, London, in autumn 1924, and died there on 15 November 1924. The cause of death was given as a combination of arteriosclerosis and septicaemia coma. He was buried, in accordance with his wishes, in the grounds of his beloved Breccles, on 20 November, in a private ceremony without a religious service—though a rabbi, Vivian G. Simmons, officiated at the gravesite. A public memorial service, at the behest of his family, was held on 21 November in the West London Synagogue, which Venetia did not attend. He left his property equally divided between Venetia and a daughter, Judith, born in February 1923, though there is some weight in the speculation that her father was, in fact, Eric Ednam, the third earl of Dudley. CHANDRIKA KAUL

Sources S. D. Waley, *Edwin Montagu* (1964) · *The Times* (17 Nov 1924) · *DNB* · BL OIOC, Montagu MSS · Trinity Cam., Montagu MSS · N. Levine, *Politics, religion and love: the story of H. H. Asquith, Venetia Stanley and Edwin Montagu, based on the life and letters of Edwin Samuel Montagu* (1991) · *H. H. Asquith: letters to Venetia Stanley*, ed. M. Brock and E. Brock (1982) · E. S. Montagu, *An Indian diary*, ed. V. Montagu (1930) · C. Kaul, 'Press and empire: the London press, government news management and India, circa 1900–1922', DPhil diss., U. Oxf., 1999 · C. Kaul, 'A new angle of vision: the London press, governmental information management and the Indian empire, 1900–1922', *Contemporary Record*, 8 (1994) · C. Kaul, *Reporting the raj: the British press and India, c.1880–1922* (2003) · R. J. Moore, *Liberalism and Indian politics* (1966) · K. O. Morgan, *Consensus and disunity: the Lloyd George coalition government, 1918–1922* (1979) · G. R. Searle, *Corruption in British politics, 1895–1930* (1987) · *Hansard* · *CGPLA Eng. & Wales* (1925)

Archives BL OIOC, papers as secretary of state for India, MS Eur. D 523 · NA Scot., journal of tour of Egypt and India · Trinity Cam., corresp. and papers | BL OIOC, corresp. with Lord Chelmsford, MS Eur. E 264 · BL OIOC, letters to Sir L. Kershaw, MS Eur. D 1056 · BL OIOC, letters to second earl of Lytton, MS Eur. F 160 · BL OIOC, Reading collection · BL OIOC, corresp. with Lord Willingdon, MS Eur. F 93 · Bodl. Oxf., corresp. with Herbert Asquith · Bodl. Oxf., corresp. with Margot Asquith [copies] · Bodl. Oxf., corresp. with Lord Selborne · CUL, corresp. with Lord Hardinge · Herts. ALS, family letters, mainly to Lady Desborough · HLRO, corresp., incl. wife's corresp., with Lord Beaverbrook · HLRO, corresp. with David Lloyd George · HLRO, corresp. with A. Bonar Law · HLRO, letters to H. Samuel · King's AC Cam., letters to Oscar Browning · U. Birm. L., corresp. with Austen Chamberlain and relating to his resignation · U. Newcastle, Robinson L., corresp. with W. Runciman

Likenesses K. Kennet, statue, Calcutta, India · W. Orpen, group portrait, oils (*The signing of peace in the Hall of Mirrors, Versailles, 1919*), IWM · E. Riccardi, statue, Jamnagar, Gujarat, India

Wealth at death £44,969 1s. 8d.: administration with will, 2 Jan 1925, CGPLA Eng. & Wales

Montagu [*née* Robinson], **Elizabeth** (1718–1800), author and literary hostess, was born at York on 2 October 1718, the first daughter and fifth child of Matthew Robinson (1694–1778) of Edgeley and West Layton, Yorkshire, and his wife, Elizabeth (*c.*1697–1746), daughter of Robert Drake, recorder of Cambridge, and his wife, Sarah Morris. A second daughter, Sarah (1720–1795) [*see* Scott, Sarah], three infants who did not survive, and three more living sons completed the Robinson family. The families of both parents were wealthy and well connected. Elizabeth's eldest brother, Matthew (1713–1800) [*see* Morris, Matthew Robinson-], succeeded his father's cousin, Richard Robinson, archbishop of Armagh, as second Baron Rokeby in the Irish peerage in 1794. Mrs Robinson's brother Morris Drake *Morris inherited the large Kent holdings of their maternal grandfather, Thomas Morris, about 1717.

Early life and education The Robinson family at the time of Elizabeth's birth lived for part of the year in York and the rest at Coveney, Cambridgeshire, a part of her mother's inheritance. In 1710 her grandmother Sarah Drake had married as her second husband Dr Conyers *Middleton, a noted Cambridge classical scholar. The Middletons maintained a large house in Cambridge where the Robinson family often visited; the three youngest sons were born there. The Robinsons were not particularly involved or attentive parents: Elizabeth Robinson was obviously much involved with her pregnancies and childbearing; Matthew Robinson was an intelligent and well-educated man, although as he appears in his children's letters he was also very selfish. He preferred London and urban pleasures to those of the country; though comfortably off, he could not afford to live permanently in town. He expected entertainment from his family; young children were of little interest to him.

Between the ages of six and thirteen Elizabeth made long stays with Dr and Mrs Middleton in Cambridge. It was there presumably that she received her introduction to classical and English literature and history. Both she and her sister learned Latin, French, and Italian. Elizabeth and Sarah were very close as girls, so much so that they were sometimes referred to as the peas, although Elizabeth's was always the dominant personality. Elizabeth was also close to her older brothers, especially Morris (1715/16–1777) and Robert (1717–1756), the nearest to her in age. There was a gap of six years between Sarah and the three

Elizabeth Montagu (1718–1800), by Allan Ramsay, 1762

youngest sons; the girls were not much involved with them. Elizabeth and her brother Matthew corresponded in French while he was at Cambridge. Both in the Middleton household and with her parents she gained an appreciation for lively intellectual conversation and encouragement to participate in it.

Elizabeth's acquaintance with Lady Margaret Harley, the only surviving child of Edward Harley, second earl of Oxford, dated from the Cambridge years. Lady Margaret, lively and well-educated, was three years older than Elizabeth. The two girls began a friendship that brought Elizabeth into contact with a more exciting and glamorous world. She visited the Oxford household at Wimpole Hall where her vivacity won the nickname Fidget from the countess. When they were apart the girls corresponded regularly. After Lady Margaret married William Bentinck, second duke of Portland, in 1734, Elizabeth visited them in London and at the duchess's favourite country seat, Bulstrode. Through the duchess she met Mary Pendarves, later Mrs Delany, her sister Ann Dewes and friend Ann Donnellan, the poet Edward Young, and Gilbert West and his wife. The combination of aristocratic ambience and intellectual conversation by men and women participating equally was a model Elizabeth would recreate in her assemblies. Relations between Elizabeth and the duchess cooled in the late 1740s for reasons not now clear; their correspondence ceased in 1753. After 1760 they resumed their friendship; they corresponded and visited occasionally but never again on the intimate basis they had once enjoyed.

The family fortunes improved in the 1730s when Mrs Robinson inherited the Morris estate from her brother.

Mount Morris at Monks Horton, Kent, became their chief residence. Elizabeth was not pleased with being isolated in the country; the amusements of Canterbury and Tunbridge Wells were pale in comparison to those being enjoyed by the duchess of Portland in London. By the late 1730s the family usually made a spring visit to London where she could visit the Portlands and her other friends, go to court, and attend the theatre and other entertainments. They also made at least one visit to Bath. These experiences helped clarify Elizabeth's notions of what she wanted and expected to achieve.

Marriage Like most females of her class Elizabeth Robinson expected to marry, although she did not have a particularly high opinion of men or the institution of marriage. Writing to the duchess of Portland in 1738 she admitted that she 'never saw one man that I loved', and she could not imagine being able to find all the qualities one wanted in a single husband. What did she want?

> He should have a great deal of sense and prudence to direct and instruct me, much wit to divert me, beauty to please me, good humour to indulge me in the right, and reprove me gently when I am in the wrong: money enough to afford me more than I can want, and as much as I can wish; and constancy to like me as long as other people do.   (Johnson, 40–41)

She wished to live in London and move in the great world, to be known and acknowledged for her accomplishments and social position. The twenty-year-old who began to form such ambitions had never known passion and could not imagine throwing away her life for love. For the remaining fifty years of her life, these views did not change. Marriages were made for prudent and rational reasons, for financial independence and social position; her own certainly illustrated this view.

On 5 August 1742 Elizabeth Robinson married Edward Montagu (1692–1775). They had probably met in London during the previous year. Montagu was a fifty-year-old bachelor, a grandson of Edward Montagu, first earl of Sandwich, the owner of coalmines and estates in Northumberland, Yorkshire, and Berkshire, with scholarly interests, particularly in mathematics. He was a member of parliament for Huntingdon, a family seat, from 1734 to 1768. Their son, John, called Punch, was born on 11 May 1743 in London. Elizabeth had a long recovery from childbirth but was much pleased with her apparently sturdy child. Her letters about him are among the most intimate and personal that she wrote. The family spent time at their Berkshire estate, Sandleford Priory, near Newbury, as well as at Allerton, Yorkshire, where the young boy died unexpectedly in September 1744. Elizabeth was devastated. During the next few years she also experienced the deaths of her mother, who had suffered from cancer for several years, and of her brother Thomas. She made long stays at Sandleford and visits to Bath and Tunbridge Wells. She and her husband were frequently apart; they remained friendly but there were no more children.

After 1750 the Montagus established a routine that lasted until his death. They lived in their London house in Hill Street, Mayfair, with visits to Sandleford in the spring and summer. He went nearly every year to Yorkshire and Northumberland, where he had a house near his colliery at Denton, outside Newcastle; she accompanied him on some of these visits. From time to time she took the waters at Bath or Tunbridge Wells, places which Edward Montagu did not enjoy. In London her reputation as a hostess grew during these years as she brought together such acquaintances as Gilbert West, George, first Baron Lyttelton, Elizabeth Vesey, and Frances Boscawen.

The bluestockings Elizabeth Montagu's parties began as literary breakfasts but by 1760 had become large evening assemblies or conversation parties at which card playing and heavy drinking were barred. Guests were encouraged to exchange witty conversation on literary and philosophical subjects. The success of these parties attracted many famous names; Samuel Johnson, Sir Joshua Reynolds, who painted her portrait, Edmund Burke, David Garrick, and Horace Walpole could be seen at Mrs Montagu's house, the closest parallel in England to contemporary French salons. Literary visitors to London were brought to Hill Street; Elizabeth Carter became close friends with Montagu after their introduction in 1758. In 1760 William Pulteney, earl of Bath, became another of Montagu's inner circle. By the 1770s an introduction to Hill Street could be the route to securing patronage from its wealthy, assertive, and respected hostess. James Beattie, Hannah More, Frances Burney, Anna Laetitia Barbauld, Sarah Fielding, Hester Chapone, and Anna Williams were recipients of Montagu's bounty. Hester Thrale was also introduced to Hill Street, but she and her hostess were more often rivals than friends.

Elizabeth Montagu has been called the 'queen of the blue stockings', although Elizabeth Vesey is probably as deserving of the title. Together the two women created the assemblies; Vesey seems to have been the personality who made them successful. But as Montagu had a large house and the money to pay the expenses, and was never loath to take the credit, she was at the time and later perceived as the leading figure among that group of friends often called the bluestockings. In fact she was probably less dominating in that group than in any other. With such women as Vesey, Carter, and Boscawen and such men as Lyttelton, Bath, and West, she generally functioned as an equal; these were people who sometimes allowed her to lead but were not dependent on her. The origins of the term bluestocking are obscure; by the 1760s Montagu, Vesey, and others referred to their group of friends as the bluestocking philosophers. Vesey seems to have started the usage; bluestocking was probably meant to describe the informality of the assemblies and the emphasis placed on wit and conversation rather than on dress and etiquette. The wearing of blue stockings at the gatherings may first have been associated with the botanist Benjamin Stillingfleet. The original bluestocking circle included members of both sexes, although the women were at its centre.

In 1763 Montagu visited Paris for several weeks; she impressed the Paris literati and deeply appreciated their admiration. In the same year—accompanied by her husband, Elizabeth Carter, and Lord and Lady Bath—she toured the Rhineland and the Low Countries. They enjoyed new experiences and new sights but remained convinced that England and English ways were best. Montagu made an extended visit to Scotland in 1766, visiting Henry Home, Lord Kames, at Blair Drummond, touring the highlands, and meeting all the Edinburgh celebrities. Dr John Gregory, professor of medicine at Edinburgh University, whose late wife was a Montagu connection, was her host and guide for the northern trip.

There is little evidence of devotion to or appreciation of music or art in Montagu's correspondence. The theatre was her preferred public entertainment, but above all literature of all varieties found in her a great consumer and promoter. Like most of her contemporaries she delighted in the novels of Samuel Richardson, John and Sarah Fielding, and Frances Burney. She enjoyed the works of Laurence Sterne and was pleased to find him a distant connection of her family. Older literature found in her a champion; she was an early subscriber to Thomas Percy's *Reliques of Ancient Poetry* and wrote enthusiastically about Spenser's works. Both ancient and modern history were favourite subjects for her reading. She also read widely in Latin, French, and Italian.

It was apparently Lyttelton who encouraged Montagu herself to write for publication. He added three selections by her to his *Dialogues of the Dead* (1760), a series of critiques of modern society. In dialogue 26 Montagu portrayed Hercules and Cadmus discussing the meaning and value of virtue. In dialogue 27 Mrs Modish is so occupied with countless worldly diversions that she cannot go with Mercury to the Elysian Fields; in 28 a modern bookseller tells Plutarch how much money he has lost on a new edition of the Roman author's *Lives* because modern readers of both sexes want only to be entertained. These were common mid-eighteenth-century criticisms of society and its standards. Less conventional was her other publication, *An Essay on the Writings and Genius of Shakespear* (1769), written at the urging of Elizabeth Carter. This work was the result of several years of study of both drama and criticism. Full of nationalistic pride, the *Essay* defended Shakespeare against the attacks of foreign critics such as Voltaire, comparing him with classical Greek and more modern French dramatists, none of whom had all of his virtues. Another particular target was Samuel Johnson, whose *Preface to Shakespeare* had appeared in 1765. Montagu argued that 'he should have said more or have said nothing' (Clarke, 141); in concentrating on the historical context in which the plays were written and their subsequent treatment by editors and critics, he had failed to engage with the texts of Shakespeare's plays and to use them to argue for Shakespeare's superiority as a dramatist. The *Essay* sought to remedy what Montagu argued was Johnson's neglect of Shakespeare's 'dramatic genius' (ibid.). It was praised by a number of reviewers and translated into French and Italian, but on a personal level permanently injured her friendship with Johnson. Like the *Dialogues*, the *Essay* was first published anonymously.

Some reports attributed it to Joseph Warton and other men, but within a few months of publication Montagu was recognized as the author, and her name appeared on the title-page by the fourth edition in 1777.

Although it was apparently never a primary subject of discussion at her assemblies, Elizabeth Montagu was always interested in politics. Edward Montagu was listed by John Stuart, third earl of Bute, in December 1761 as a tory, but his attendance in parliament was irregular. She took an active part in the management of her husband's interest in Newcastle upon Tyne. During the campaign of 1760 she visited Northumberland ladies and entertained the wives of the members of Newcastle corporation at tea, as well as attending local society occasions. After her husband's death she continued to keep close watch on political developments in Newcastle, and deployed her influence in favour of her chosen candidate in parliamentary elections. She exchanged correspondence and visits with Hester, wife of William Pitt the elder, and her politics before the 1770s were probably close to his, although by 1777 she seems to have become a supporter of Lord North's administration and backed Sir John Trevelyan, a government supporter, in Newcastle. She was always loyal to the crown and opposed threats to the *status quo*, from Jacobites to supporters of John Wilkes and the American revolutionaries.

Widowhood and family By the late 1760s Edward Montagu was in very poor health. His wife conscientiously cared for him, though she sometimes fretted at the loss of her independence. She took more and more responsibility for the management of the collieries and estates. The continuing support of such friends as Carter and Boscawen and the resumption of relations with the duchess of Portland and Mary Delany helped her deal with the deaths of Lord Bath in 1764 and Lord Lyttelton in 1773, as well as the restrictions imposed by her husband's condition. Edward Montagu died in London on 12 May 1775. He left his entire estate to his wife except for £3000 left to Matthew Robinson (1762–1831), the second son of Elizabeth's brother Morris. Matthew was adopted by his aunt and took the surname Montagu in 1776. Elizabeth Montagu's inheritance from her husband was reported to be worth £7000 a year.

Montagu was now in the most advantageous position possible for a woman in the eighteenth century. She was a wealthy widow; no person could legally exercise any control over her and there were no financial limitations which could stand in her way. She continued to manage her business affairs with considerable success. She visited the Northumberland and Yorkshire properties from time to time, paid close attention to the economic circumstances of the coal industry, and stayed in constant correspondence with her managers. She was a generous employer, so long as her orders were followed, and like other ladies of great estates she took measures to alleviate the poverty of her employees and tenants, through customary measures such as annual feasts and providing basic education. By the time of her death in 1800 her coal was the most popular on the market, and her estate was said to be worth £10,000 a year. She also used her wealth to aid her friends when in need. After her husband's death she established annuities for Elizabeth Carter and Anna Williams. Among her charities was an annual May day entertainment for climbing boys.

Throughout her life Montagu remained close to most of her family. Her father moved to London after his wife's death in 1746, setting up an establishment with his housekeeper as his mistress. His children were all horrified but had no success in changing his conduct. Robinson was reluctant to spend any more money than he had to on his children. When Sarah's marriage to George Lewis Scott broke down, not only would he not give her an adequate settlement, but he also refused to allow Elizabeth and Morris to advance her any money. Elizabeth with the support of her husband had succeeded in getting her younger brothers properly educated. William *Robinson (*bap.* 1727, *d.* 1803), later a clergyman, and John (1729–1807) were sent to Westminster School and afterwards to Cambridge. Charles (1731–1807) was sent to sea with his older brother Robert, a captain with the East India Company. Several of the Robinson brothers were trained as lawyers, including the legal writer Thomas *Robinson (*d.* 1747). Morris was a solicitor in chancery in Ireland. Charles left the sea after a few years and read law at the inns of court. He became recorder of Canterbury and represented that borough in parliament from 1780 to 1790. John fell victim to mental illness while still at Cambridge; he was in custodial care for the remainder of his life. Robert died at sea.

Montagu maintained friendships with many distinguished men and women over a number of years, but she can never have been an easy person to live with. She expected to rule her household and seldom seemed to make any accommodation for those who were dependent on her. Like many women of her class, she often had a female companion to fetch and carry, to accompany her out, to do her bidding. Such a person was not a servant but was certainly a dependent. Her sister Sarah sometimes acted in this position between their mother's death and her own marriage in 1752. There seems good reason to think that Sarah made this unsatisfactory marriage, which lasted not quite a year, in part to escape from Elizabeth. In 1772 seventeen-year-old Dorothea Gregory, daughter of Dr John Gregory of Edinburgh, was taken by Montagu to live as her ward. Gregory travelled with her benefactor in Britain and to France, was introduced to society, and treated almost as a daughter. Montagu's dream was that Dorothea would ultimately marry Matthew Robinson, who was eight years younger. However, Gregory fell in love with and became engaged to Archibald Alison (1757–1839), an altogether worthy though penniless young man. Montagu, who never believed in marrying for love, stormed and threatened to no avail. After her marriage in 1782 Dorothea was cast off; the two women were only partially reconciled several years later. Montagu was particularly annoyed when several of her friends supported the couple and helped Alison find employment. Elizabeth Montagu always wanted to be in charge and to have her opinions prevail. She befriended the shoemaker poet James Woodhouse and became his patron for twenty years. But disagreements with him over religious and political matters led her to dismiss him from his post as steward at Sandleford in 1788. He at least had the satisfaction of delineating his unflattering version of her character in his autobiographical poem, *The Life and Lucubrations of Crispinus Scriblerus*.

During her early years Montagu's immediate family members do not seem to have had any strong religious beliefs, though they were nominally members of the Church of England. There are no references to churchgoing, to religion, or theological reading and discussion in her earlier letters, although she would no doubt have said she was a Christian. Edward Montagu would not have admitted to that, a fact which came to worry his wife. In the years following the death of her son Elizabeth began to take a greater interest in religion; her friendship with Gilbert West was important in her developing this aspect of her studies. West had been a nonbeliever but by the time he and Montagu became acquainted he had become a practising Anglican. They corresponded about religion and exchanged books on religious topics. Montagu was not ostentatious in her religious observances and there are seldom any references to them in her letters. But she was one of the friends who worried about Elizabeth Vesey's having no faith, and surely it was her own faith that was one of the links in her most significant friendships with Carter, Lyttelton, and Bath.

Sandleford and Montagu House After her husband's death Montagu engaged in a programme of building, enlarging the house and improving the grounds at Sandleford as well as building a great new mansion in London. She had remodelled and redecorated the Hill Street house several times. In the early 1750s with the help of Gilbert West she fitted out her great dressing-room in the fashionable chinoiserie style. A decade later she hired Robert Adam, who brought classicism into fashion, to design a new ceiling, carpet, and furnishings for the chamber which was, despite its name, a large room where the assemblies were held. In the early 1770s the walls of this room were decorated with flowers and cupids; it was often referred to as her Cupidon Room. Elizabeth and Edward Montagu had also employed Adam to build an addition to Sandleford in 1765. Clearly she always wanted to be in style, to have the most currently fashionable architect and decoration.

Shortly after her husband's death Montagu signed a ninety-nine-year lease on a plot on the north-west corner of Portman Square. In 1777 she contracted with James 'Athenian' Stuart to build her new house. Stuart was not a very satisfactory employee in terms of finishing on schedule. She had hoped to occupy her new mansion in the spring of 1779; it was not until late 1781 that she was able to move in. Montagu House was large and impressively decorated. Angelica Kauffman and Biago Rebecca painted panels for the interior, some of which represented scenes from Shakespeare's plays, an allusion to the owner's book. The building process seemed to go on and on. Montagu wrote in 1790:

> things of these kinds are tedious in their process, my House is full of Carvers, Guilders, Carpenters etc, which is certainly no very agreable circumstance … As I pay the workmen as fast as they proceed, one should think they wd be more expeditious.   (Blunt, 2.242)

The ballroom was completed by Joseph Bonomi from Stuart's original designs in 1791. It featured scagliola columns in antique vert and a decorated ceiling probably by Giovanni Battista Cipriani. A special room also completed in 1791 contained Montagu's feather work. This was a large tapestry designed by James Wyatt and the Wright family, the royal embroiderers; it was made entirely of feathers of all kinds by Montagu and a number of other women who had worked for years on this project. The feathers were collected from friends and correspondents; they were stored and worked in a large room at Sandleford. The feather tapestry seems to have been Montagu's only effort at handicrafts; it was visited and praised by Horace Walpole. Queen Charlotte accompanied by five of her daughters made a visit to Montagu House to see it. The house passed into the possession of Matthew Montagu after his aunt's death. In 1874 the lease reverted to the ground landlord, and the structure became known as Portman House. It was badly damaged by bombing in 1942, and the remnants of the walls were pulled down after 1945.

Sandleford was the favourite country house of both Edward and Elizabeth Montagu. It was not too far from London and was about halfway along the road to Bath. She regarded the enlargement by Adam, however, as only sufficient to house a few friends; a house party of any size would require more space, especially for dining. She had suggested making the house more Gothic in the 1760s in keeping with its origins as a priory and the few remaining medieval elements, but Adam had convinced her and her husband that it would cost too much. Her dream persisted; in 1780 she requested James Wyatt to make a proposal for a rebuilt house in the Gothic style. They agreed on the plan, but the reshaping of the house was not finally completed for some years. Montagu found that Wyatt was as dilatory as Stuart, but she ultimately enjoyed the former chapel converted to a salon with a Gothic window, a new eating chamber, and her own apartment. More satisfactory was the remaking of the grounds. In 1781 Montagu hired Lancelot 'Capability' Brown to make plans for her landscape; Sandleford was the great gardener's last major commission before his death in 1782. Montagu and all her friends agreed that his work enhanced the house and produced in visitors the proper thoughts of the beautiful and sublime.

Death and lasting reputation In her last years Montagu found comfort and company in her nephew Matthew and his family, although they did not share her house except for visits to Sandleford. In 1785 Matthew Robinson Montagu married Elizabeth Charleton, a suitable and amiable heiress; they had ten children. He sat as a member of parliament for various boroughs from 1786; in 1829 he succeeded his brother Morris as fourth Baron Rokeby. Elizabeth Montagu died at Montagu House on 25 August 1800. Her entire estate was left to Matthew.

Like others among her contemporaries Montagu was a

great letter writer, in terms of both quantity and quality. She wrote regularly to family members and friends; the letters are lively, full of gossip, comments on her reading, news of others, and of what she was doing. Her letters, like those of Horace Walpole and Mary Delany, are among the most important surviving collections from the eighteenth century. Unlike Delany, she seldom wrote of domestic details, handiwork, art, or music. Montagu's ambition, her awareness of her own success, and her domineering personality are seldom disguised in her letters. Readers often do not like her. To her closest friends she did not hesitate to describe her jaundiced view of marriage and of most men, and about what women can do if given the opportunity. A letter to Elizabeth Carter in 1782 summed up many of these opinions. Commenting on the second marriage of a friend, she wrote:

> I always thought her the perfection of the female character, formed to become the domestick situation and disposed to obedience. She could not stir till she received the word of command. ... She would have preferred her husband's discourse to the angels. I am afraid you and I dear friend should have entered into some metaphysical disquisitions with the angel. We are not so perfectly the rib of man as woman ought to be. We can think for ourselves, and also act for ourselves. When a wife I was obedient because it was my duty, and being married to a man of sense and integrity, obedience was not painful or irksome, in early youth a director perhaps is necessary if the sphere of action is extensive; but it seems to me that a new master and new lessons after ones opinions and habits were formed must be a little awkward, and with all due respect to the superior sex, I do not see how they can be necessary to a woman unless she were to defend her lands and tenements by sword or gun. (Blunt, 2.119–20)

Fortunately a very large part of Montagu's correspondence has survived; the bulk of it is at the Huntington Library in San Marino, California, and there are smaller collections elsewhere. Some of the letters, or edited parts of them, have been published in various biographies of her, in accounts of the bluestocking circle, and works on eighteenth-century women. Two volumes of the correspondence were published in 1809 and two more in 1813 by her nephew. They were not particularly well received then; Montagu belonged to an earlier age. They were still being denigrated through the nineteenth century; Sidney Lee in the *Dictionary of National Biography*, for example, characterized them as having 'too much prolixity to be altogether readable'. More recent scholars, however—especially those interested in women and their lives—have found Montagu's letters, written over nearly seventy years, a major source for any study of the eighteenth century.   BARBARA BRANDON SCHNORRENBERG

Sources B. Rizzo, *Companions without vows: relationships among eighteenth-century British women* (1994) • S. Harcstark Myers, *The bluestocking circle: women, friendship, and the life of the mind in eighteenth-century England* (1990) • *Elizabeth Montagu, the queen of the bluestockings: her correspondence from 1720 to 1761*, ed. E. J. Climenson, 2 vols. (1906) • *Mrs Montagu, 'Queen of the Blues': her letters and friendships from 1762 to 1800*, ed. R. Blunt, 2 vols. (1923) • R. B. Johnson, ed., *Bluestocking letters* (1926) • *DNB* • B. Rizzo, ed., *The history of Sir George Ellison* (1996) • L. B. Namier, 'Montagu, Edward', HoP, *Commons, 1754–90* • R. S. Lea, 'Montagu, Edward', HoP, *Commons, 1715–54* •

E. H. Chalus, 'Women in English political life, 1754–1790', DPhil diss., U. Oxf., 1997 • N. Clarke, *Dr Johnson's women* (2000)
Archives BL, family corresp., Add. MS 40663, RP2393 • Hunt. L., corresp. and papers • Princeton University, New Jersey, corresp. • Yale U., Farmington, Lewis Walpole Library, letters from her | BL, corresp. with Lord Lyttleton, RP2377 [copies] • BL, letters to Messenger Monsey, RP1277 [copies] • BL, Portland Loan • BL, corresp. with Frances Reynolds, RP196 [copies] • Bodl. Oxf., letters to Elizabeth Carter [copies] • Hants. RO, letters to Lady Wallingford • JRL, letters to Hester Lynch Thrale • Longleat House, Warminster, letters to duchess of Portland • NA Scot., letters to Lord and Lady Kames • PRO, letters to Lord and Lady Chatham, PRO 30/8/50 • U. Aberdeen L., corresp. with James Beattie • U. Nott. L., letters to duchess of Portland • V&A NAL, corresp. with David Garrick
Likenesses A. Ramsay, portrait, 1762, priv. coll. [*see illus.*] • Wedgwood medallion, 1775, Wedgwood Museum, Stoke-on-Trent • J. R. Smith, mezzotint, pubd 1776 (after J. Reynolds), BM, NPG • line engraving, pubd 1776 (after T. Holloway), BM, NPG • R. Samuel, group portrait, oils, exh. 1779 (*The nine living muses of Great Britain*), NPG • W. Lowry, line engraving, pubd 1787 (after unknown artist), NPG • W. Ridley, stipple, 1800 (after Rivers), BM, NPG; repro. in *Lady's Monthly Museum* (1800) • T. Cheesman, stipple, pubd 1809 (after J. Reynolds), BM, NPG • R. Cooper, stipple, 1809 (after C. F. Zincke), BM; repro. in Wraxall, *Memoirs* • C. Townley, stipple (after F. Reynolds), BM, NPG
Wealth at death £10,000 p. a.: *DNB*

Montagu, Ewen Edward Samuel (1901–1985), judge and intelligence officer, was born on 29 March 1901 in Kensington, the second of the three sons (there was also a younger daughter) of Louis Samuel Montagu (1869–1927), banker, who succeeded his father, Samuel *Montagu (1832–1911), founder of the family firm, as second Baron Swaythling in 1911. His father's younger brother was Edwin Samuel Montagu (1879–1924), the politician; his own younger brother Ivor Goldsmid Samuel *Montagu (1904–1984) became a leading communist intellectual. His mother was Gladys Helen Rachel (d. 1965), daughter of Colonel Albert Edward Williamson Goldsmid. The children were brought up at Stoneham House, later swallowed by the suburbs of Southampton, in lavish circumstances. He was at Westminster School during the First World War, and spent a year at Harvard before going up to Trinity College, Cambridge, in 1920. There he gained second classes (division two) in both part one of the economic tripos (1922) and part two of the law tripos (1923).

Just before he went down in 1923 Montagu married Iris Rachel, daughter of Solomon Joseph Solomon, the portrait painter; her first cousin had married Victor Gollancz. They had a son and a daughter; all three survived him. In 1924 he was called to the bar from the Middle Temple, and after fifteen years' hard work on the western circuit took silk in 1939.

Montagu spent many holidays yachting, and his interest in small boats led him to a commission in the Royal Naval Volunteer Reserve that September. As a naval intelligence officer at Hull he attracted the attention of Rear-Admiral J. H. Godfrey, who summoned him in 1941 to join the naval intelligence division at the Admiralty. There Montagu ran a highly secret sub-branch, NID 17(M), which handled counter-espionage. He accompanied Godfrey to the W board, the informal committee that ran the most secret intelligence war, and sat as the naval member of the XX

Committee which supervised the playing-back of captured Abwehr agents. Extreme caution and extreme daring had to be combined for this work to be effective; Montagu displayed both.

The best known of several coups Montagu organized was operation Mincemeat. This involved the floating ashore on 30 April 1943 in south-west Spain of what appeared to be the body of a Royal Marine officer, carrying documents which indicated an imminent allied attack on Sardinia rather than Sicily. Through the deciphering service, Montagu was able to trace enemy reactions; this ploy reached at least as high as Admiral Canaris, head of the Abwehr, and the chiefs of staff telegraphed to the absent prime minister 'Mincemeat swallowed whole'. No one can quantify the results of such work, but it undoubtedly saved thousands of lives.

At the end of the war Montagu returned to law, becoming judge advocate of the fleet in 1945, a post he held until 1973. He had been appointed recorder of Devizes in 1944 and held this post until 1951. He was then recorder of Southampton for nine years more, and became deputy lieutenant in that county in 1953. He served also for fourteen years as assistant chairman, deputy chairman, and chairman of quarter sessions for Middlesex, and became a bencher of the Middle Temple in 1948 and treasurer in 1968.

This work was interrupted in 1952. A novel by A. Duff Cooper (later Viscount Norwich) was based on operation Mincemeat, of which Cooper had had official knowledge. Word leaked out that the story might be true; important secrets were held to be at risk. The government was worried that too much would come out, about both the existence and the methods of the deception service. The Admiralty appealed to Montagu. In forty-eight hours, from a Friday evening to a Sunday evening, he dictated an account that was at once accurate, exciting, and circumspect: it revealed nothing the government wanted kept secret. As *The Man who Never was* (1953) it sold over 2 million copies and inspired a film of the same name (1955). At more leisure, after the principal secret he protected had been released, Montagu wrote *Beyond Top Secret U* (1977), a war autobiography in which he explained what he had left out of his best-seller—how much of his work had depended on the deciphering done at Bletchley Park.

Montagu was a devout Jew, long active in charitable works, and president of the United Synagogue from 1954 to 1962. He was appointed OBE in 1944, for his work on operation Mincemeat, and advanced to CBE in 1950; he also received the order of the crown of Yugoslavia in 1943. He was a tall, spare, handsome man, who kept his good looks and gentle manners into old age. He died at his flat at 24 Montrose Court, Exhibition Road, Westminster, on 19 July 1985. M. R. D. FOOT, *rev.*

Sources *The Times* (20 July 1985) · *The Times* (30 July 1985) · E. Montagu, *The man who never was* (1953) · E. Montagu, *Beyond top secret U* (1977) · private information (1990) · Burke, *Peerage* · *CGPLA Eng. & Wales* (1985)

Wealth at death £207,363: probate, 19 Nov 1985, *CGPLA Eng. & Wales*

Montagu, Frederick (1733–1800), politician, was born in July 1733, the only surviving son of Charles Montagu (d. 1759), a politician and landowner, of Papplewick, Nottinghamshire, and his wife, Ann (c.1700–1780), the daughter of Sir Theodore Colladon (1650–1712), a physician at the Tower of London and then the Chelsea Hospital. As a widow living with her devoted son in Hanover Square, his mother was esteemed in London society and was a close friend of Mary Delany and Mary, dowager Countess Gower. Montagu, who had one sister, was educated at Eton College (1742–8), at Trinity College, Cambridge, and at Lincoln's Inn (both from 1751). He proceeded MA and was called to the bar in 1757. His prizewinning Latin oration in praise of Francis Bacon was published at Cambridge in 1755. There he befriended the poets Thomas Gray and William Mason, and he retained literary interests, as appears from Horace Walpole's correspondence with George Montagu, Frederick's cousin. He became a bencher at Lincoln's Inn in 1782, was elected FSA in 1782, and was awarded a DCL at Oxford in 1793.

Montagu succeeded his father, late auditor in turn to the prince and princess of Wales, as MP for Northampton on 6 June 1759, on the interest of their kinsman the second earl of Halifax. Politically well connected, he supported successively the ministries of Newcastle, Bute (also a kinsman), Grenville, and Rockingham, like his parliamentary patron, who tried in November 1763 to get Grenville to 'grace our cause' (*Additional Grenville Papers*, 67–8) by appointing Montagu to the Board of Trade. This overture failed, and to Halifax's annoyance he refused the vacant post of groom porter in October 1764, as he was ambitious for a more businesslike office. His attachment to the duke of Newcastle, whom he defended in debate against the barbs of Pitt the elder, prevented him from supporting Pitt as premier. In 1768, no longer sponsored by Halifax for his troublesome constituency, he transferred to Higham Ferrers, a safe one-member borough, with Rockingham as patron, and retained it unopposed for twenty-two years. He took Rockingham's line in debate, and became prominent in opposition counsels. While he was a kinsman of the new premier, Lord North, he did not think it honourable to be lured into office, being sure that Rockingham would disapprove. On 25 February 1772 he gave notice of, and a week later introduced, a bill to abolish once and for all the public commemoration of Charles I's martyrdom, which was defeated by 125 votes to 97. He spoke in favour of relief measures for protestant dissenters (3 April 1772; 10 March 1779) and supported the removal of subscription to the Thirty-Nine Articles as a basis for university entry (23 February 1773).

Montagu consistently opposed the administration's American policy: he voted against taxation by means of tea duties on 19 April 1774, supported the amendment to the address on 30 November, and seconded the motion of his friend Lord John Cavendish for further intelligence from North America on 5 December. In February 1775 he defended the Nottingham hosiers' petition against war with the American colonies, and, although he was reported to be conciliated by Lord North's show of penitence over the conflict in February 1778, his continued opposition to it, particularly when he chaired a Commons committee on the conduct of the war in May 1779, flustered North. The premier made him his intermediary with the Rockingham squadron in June 1780, hoping to secure a coalition. When this manoeuvre failed, North offered Montagu the speakership in October: he was by then regarded as something of an expert on parliamentary procedure, which prompted several of his speeches, notably one of 16 December 1778. Rockingham had no objection to the offer, but Montagu, disliking the imputation of turning coat, declined for health reasons—which George III condoned, being sure of Montagu's personal regard for him despite political commitments. Montagu objected to interference with the provisions of the Grenville Act of 1770 for controverted elections to the house (23 January 1781), but later found reason to alter his views on this (7 April 1785). In Rockingham's brief administration he served as a lord of the Treasury (April–July 1782), and on Rockingham's death he defended his leader's probity, which was questioned on 9 July 1782 on account of the grant of a pension to Isaac Barré.

After opposing the Shelburne ministry, Montagu returned to the Treasury board with a privy councillorship, awarded on 14 April 1783, under the duke of Portland, with whom he resigned in December later that year. He was to have been a commissioner under Fox's abortive India Bill of the same year. He acted with the Portland whigs in opposition to Pitt the younger's administration, defending his former department's financial record on 23 July 1784. In the debate on the Westminster election scrutiny he showed himself to be a purist for the separation of constitutional powers, and on 9 February 1785 criticized the presence, and intervention, of judges in parliament. He supported the efforts of Edmund Burke to impeach Warren Hastings for his conduct in India, and was one of the Commons committee on the subject: it was on his motion of 14 May 1787 that Burke, his friend for twenty-four years, moved the impeachment at the bar of the Lords. Although he left the committee for health reasons, he became one of the managers of the impeachment early in 1788, when he was apparently portrayed as a diminutive chimney sweep in Gillray's cartoon *State Jugglers*. On 1 May 1789 he defended Burke's charges against Hastings, publicizing Burke's letter to him on the subject. He seconded the opposition's choice of Sir Gilbert Elliot as candidate for the twice vacant speaker's chair on 5 January and 8 June 1789, and on 15 March 1790 readily proposed to the house an enhanced speaker's salary of £5000. On 14 May 1790 he supported compensation for displaced American loyalists, particularly the Penn family. He retired from parliament that year, commended for his integrity, and soon afterwards approved Burke's *Reflections on the French Revolution*.

Montagu, who was never robust and had suffered from gout from the age of twenty-five, died on 30 July 1800 at Papplewick, the Nottinghamshire residence he had inherited and rebuilt in 1787; he was buried there the following month. In his mansion he had displayed a bust of Rockingham, inscribed with a poetic tribute and surrounded by Montagu family portraits; Rockingham's mausoleum at Wentworth Woodhouse, Yorkshire, reciprocally featured a bust of Montagu among those of his eight principal adherents. As he was unmarried, Montagu left his 3300 acre estate, and name, to Richard Fountayne Wilson, the grandson of his sister, Ann, and her husband, John Fountayne, dean of York. Montagu's heir succeeded to his own paternal estate of Melton, Yorkshire, in 1802, and Papplewick was let to tenants.   ROLAND THORNE

Sources J. Brooke, 'Montagu, Frederick', HoP, *Commons, 1754–90* · *The autobiography and correspondence of Mary Granville, Mrs Delany*, ed. Lady Llanover, 1st ser., 2 (1861); 2nd ser., 2–3 (1862) · Walpole, *Corr.* · *The correspondence of Edmund Burke*, ed. T. W. Copeland and others, 10 vols. (1958–78), vols. 1–6 · *The historical and the posthumous memoirs of Sir Nathaniel William Wraxall, 1772–1784*, ed. H. B. Wheatley, 5 vols. (1884), vol. 2, p. 348; vol. 4, p. 446 · GM, 1st ser., 70 (1800), 801 · J. Stockdale, ed., *The debates and proceedings of the House of Commons: during the sixteenth parliament of Great Britain*, 19 vols. (1785–90) · J. Almon, ed., *The parliamentary register, or, History of the proceedings and debates of the House of Commons*, 17 vols. (1775–80) · J. Debrett, *The history, debates and proceedings of both houses of parliament … from 1743 to … 1774*, 7 vols. (1792) · Cobbett, *Parl. hist.*, 17.315, 319, 433, 753, 1272; 18.43; 20.240; vol. 21, 23 Jan 1781; vol. 23, 9 July 1782; 25.397, 1184; 26.45, 882, 1149; 27.621, 906, 1374; 28.150, 506, 514, 814 · J. Debrett, ed., *The parliamentary register, or, History of the proceedings and debates of the House of Commons*, 112 vols. (1775–1813) · L. Jacks, *The great houses of Nottinghamshire and the county families* (1881), 97 · *Eighth report*, 2, HMC, 7 (1910), 128, 136 · *Additional Grenville papers, 1763–1765*, ed. J. R. G. Tomlinson (1962), 67–8 · *Thoroton's history of Nottinghamshire*, ed. J. Throsby, 2nd edn, 3 vols. (1790–96), vol. 2, p. 288 · K. G. T. Meaby, ed., *Nottinghamshire: extracts from the county records of the eighteenth century* (1947), 55 · *The last journals of Horace Walpole*, ed. Dr Doran, rev. A. F. Steuart, 2 vols. (1910), vol. 1, pp. 39, 332, 412; vol. 2, pp. 116, 424, 426, 456, 513 · GM, 1st ser., 3 (1733), 379

Archives BL, letters to Lord Camelford, Add. MS 69293 · BL, corresp. with duke of Newcastle, Add. MSS 32922–33070 · Sheff. Arch., corresp. with Lord Rockingham · U. Nott. L., letters to third duke of Portland

Likenesses J. Gillray, caricature, 1788 · bust; formerly at Wentworth Woodhouse, West Yorkshire

Wealth at death under £10,000: will, PRO, PROB 11/1347, sig. 675

Montagu, George, fourth duke of Manchester (1737–1788), politician, was born on 6 April 1737, the eldest son of Robert Montagu, third duke of Manchester (*c*.1710–1762), courtier, and Harriet (*d*. 1755), daughter and coheir of Edmund Dunch MP, and Elizabeth Godfrey, of Little Wittenham, Berkshire. A ready and effective speaker, he became a politician of some consequence but was handicapped by an income which, he confessed, was not commensurate with his rank, and by a small electoral interest which gave him precarious command over only one seat in Huntingdonshire, where the family resided at Kimbolton Castle. His inheritance was, for most of his life, saddled with a substantial jointure for his aunt, Isabella, the dowager second duchess, and he spent much time trying to obtain places for his younger brother, Lord Charles Montagu, who sat as MP for Huntingdonshire from 1762 to

1765. During one of his many scrapes, Sarah Byng Osborn wrote in March 1767:

> Duke of Manchester must seek another country, the house in this square [Berkeley] is to be sold, the castle in the country to be let, but who is there can take it? He has not paid a tradesman since his father died.

Two months later she reported that 'Duke Manchester's house is sold to Child the banker for 10,000 guineas' (*Political and Social Letters*, 167, 170).

Montagu began as an ensign in the county militia in 1757. At the general election of March 1761 he was returned to parliament for Huntingdonshire and at the coronation of George III in September 1761 supported the king's train. His stay in the Commons was brief. He does not appear to have spoken, but was appointed to a number of committees. On succeeding to the dukedom on 10 May 1762, he inherited the sinecure of collector of the subsidies of tonnage and poundage outwards in the Port of London, worth £1500 p.a., and was appointed lord lieutenant of Huntingdonshire. He married on 23 October 1762 Elizabeth (1740/41–1832), eldest daughter of Sir James Dashwood, second baronet, of Kirtlington Park, Oxfordshire, and Elizabeth Spencer. In November 1762 he succeeded Rockingham as a lord of the bedchamber and it looked as if his line of advance was at court. He was presumably being groomed when Rockingham reported to the king in November 1765 that he had seconded the address 'very well' (*Correspondence of George III*, 1.203, letter no. 163). But in January 1770, when Camden and Grafton left the government, he resigned his post and went into immediate opposition. He voted in the minority with Rockingham on 9 January 1770 on the address of thanks, and again with the minority on the Wilkes issue on 2 February, joining in the printed protest. He protested again in May 1770 on Chatham's motion to remedy the grievances of the Middlesex petitioners. In December 1770 he was reported speaking with 'an uncommon degree of eloquence' in an attack upon supine ministers, and the following day accused them of 'incapacity and pusillanimity' (Cobbett, *Parl. hist.*, 16.1317, 1322). The following March, he paid a well-publicized visit with Rockingham, Portland, and Burke to Lord Mayor Crosby in the Tower of London to demonstrate support for the Middlesex grievances over the Wilkes affair.

Growing trouble with the American colonists in the 1770s brought Manchester into greater prominence and he moved into the heart of Rockinghamite counsels. On 20 April 1774 he wrote to Rockingham suggesting that it might not be wise to oppose the bill suspending the charter of Massachusetts Bay since the public was so inflamed against the colonists. Rockingham bridled, insisting that the bill was 'very strong and arbitrary', but Manchester did not sign the protest on 11 May (*Memoirs*, 2.245). In January 1775 he begged Rockingham not to allow Chatham's eccentricities to make a breach in the opposition: 'while the man treads this earth, his name, his successes, his eloquence, the cry of the many, must exalt him into a consequence perhaps far above his station' (ibid., 2.266). He

spoke in support of Chatham on 1 February and his warning of great perils to the nation was said to have 'drawn the attention of every side of the House' (Cobbett, *Parl. hist.*, 18.215). He was now one of the mainstays of opposition in the Lords, particularly since Rockingham was so reluctant a debater. Manchester gave strong opposition to the bill to restrain American trade, and in May 1775 was involved in a protracted procedural wrangle when attempting to present a memorial from the assembly of New York. His speech of 1 November 1775 against the employment of Hanoverian troops was printed as a pamphlet. But, as hostilities in America developed, he was reduced to the role of chorus, prophesying doom. On 5 March 1776 he warned that America would not be conquered, and a fortnight later that France and Spain would intervene. His advice within the opposition was usually sensible—in March 1777 he was one of the first to point out that the opposition's secession from parliament had produced no effect whatever on the public. In May 1779 he assured ministers that Ireland might well follow the example of the Americans. He took an active part in the Yorkshire Association campaign for economical reform in 1779–80: Sandwich, his rival for influence in Huntingdonshire, reported a speech at Huntingdon in April 1780 in which Manchester had dissociated himself from the more radical Westminster committee. Towards the Gordon rioters, who erupted in June 1780, Manchester showed some sympathy, telling Rockingham that he had always thought that concessions to the Catholics in 1778 would lead to mischief: 'the tenets of the Papists do make it indispensably necessary to put stronger restrictions upon them than upon men of any other faith' (*Memoirs*, 2.417). In the Lords, on 19 June, while not defending violence, he thought it absurd that the rioters were being charged with treason. In the abortive negotiations conducted in July 1780 by Frederick Montagu (a distant cousin) for a coalition between North and the opposition, he was marked for a place, the king replying that 'the duke of Manchester in a lucrative office I could not object to' (*Correspondence of George III*, 5.97).

Permanent opposition did nothing for Manchester's finances and in January 1781 he was downhearted, demanding from Rockingham 'a change of system on our side' and 'a little unanimity in our mode of attacks' (*Memoirs*, 2.432). His zeal in the Lords seems to have dwindled, but, when Rockingham came to power in April 1782, Manchester was appointed lord chamberlain in succession to Lord Hertford and was sworn of the privy council. His finances still did not permit handsome gestures and, in July 1782 when most of the Rockinghamites resigned after the death of their leader, he stayed in office. When the Fox–North coalition took power in the spring of 1783 his post was needed again for Lord Hertford, but Manchester was appointed ambassador-extraordinary to France to supervise the conclusion of the peace treaty. The detailed negotiations were conducted by plenipotentiaries and the treaty was too far advanced for Manchester to be able to win many concessions. In September 1783 Portland offered him the post of governor-general of Bengal in succession to Warren Hastings under the new arrangements which the coalition was planning. Manchester declined, pleading ill health, his growing family, and reluctance to leave his wife. But he was quick to perceive that the reorganization of India might be dangerous for the ministry, warning Portland on 30 September 1783 that

> His Majesty, perhaps, might be induced to acquiesce without being thoroughly convinced of the fitness of the measure, and should he coldly support it at the outset, means at the same time might be found to thwart it before it could be brought to maturity. (*Eighth Report*, HMC, appx 2, 134a)

He returned to England to take part in the critical vote in the Lords on the India Bill, but ran into a debating ambush: rising in anger to deplore the violent protest of the City of London, he was told by Richmond that it was based upon the Rockinghamites' own protest of 1773. He voted with the minority and was dismissed when the coalition was turned out at the end of 1783.

Manchester continued to work with Portland and the opposition to Pitt after 1784 but his interventions in debate were less frequent. He did however offer strong criticism on 5 March 1787 of the commercial treaty with France, warning of the implacable hostility of the French. He was reported to have caught cold at the trial of Warren Hastings which worsened at a cricket match at Brighton, and he died at Brighton on 2 September 1788 at the age of fifty-one, and was buried at Kimbolton on 14 September. Although he was comparatively young, his political career in a hopeless opposition was no longer promising. Wraxall was unduly dismissive in writing of Manchester on his appointment as ambassador that 'though a man of very dissipated habits and unaccustomed to diplomatic business, he did not want talents', and on his death he wrote that although the opposition had lost a steady adherent, 'his person and manner were most dignified, but neither his abilities nor his fortune corresponded with his figure' (*Historical and Posthumous Memoirs*, 3.59, 5.172). He was survived by his wife, who died aged ninety-one on 26 June 1832, and by their three daughters and two surviving sons, the eldest of whom, William *Montagu, succeeded as fifth duke. JOHN CANNON

Sources GEC, *Peerage* · Cobbett, *Parl. hist.* · G. Thomas, earl of Albemarle [G. T. Keppel], *Memoirs of the marquis of Rockingham and his contemporaries*, 2 vols. (1852) · *Eighth report*, 1, HMC, 7 (1907–9), pt ii · *The manuscripts of the earl of Dartmouth*, 3 vols., HMC, 20 (1887–96) · *The historical and the posthumous memoirs of Sir Nathaniel William Wraxall, 1772–1784*, ed. H. B. Wheatley, 5 vols. (1884) · 'Montagu, George', HoP, *Commons* · JHC, 29 (1761–4) · Walpole, *Corr.* · *The correspondence of King George the Third from 1760 to December 1783*, ed. J. Fortescue, 6 vols. (1927–8) · *The correspondence of Edmund Burke*, ed. T. W. Copeland and others, 10 vols. (1958–78) · *Political and social letters of a lady of the eighteenth century, 1721–1771*, ed. E. F. D. Osborn [1890] · F. O'Gorman, *The rise of party in England: the Rockingham whigs, 1760–1782* (1975)

Archives Bodl. Oxf., reports on French warships · Cambs. AS, corresp. and papers · Portsmouth Museums and Records Service, notebook · U. Mich., Clements L., corresp. and papers | BL, corresp. with Charles James Fox, Add. MS 47563 · BL, corresp. with duke of Newcastle, Add. MSS 32918–33072 · NMM, corresp. with Lord Sandwich · NRA, priv. coll., letters to Lord Shelburne · Sheff.

Arch., letters to marquess of Rockingham · U. Nott. L., letters to duke of Portland

Likenesses J. Jones, mezzotint, pubd 1790 (after G. Stuart), BM, NPG · W. Leney, stipple, pubd 1796 (after W. Peters), BM · J. S. Copley, chalk drawing (head), Metropolitan Museum of Art, New York · attrib. A. R. Mengs, oils, Kimbolton Castle, Cambridgeshire · M. Peters, portrait · G. Stuart, portrait

Wealth at death comparative poverty; £4000 p.a., heavily encumbered: letter of 1739, Osborn, *Political and social letters*

Montagu, Sir George (1750–1829), naval officer, was born on 12 December 1750, the second son of Admiral John *Montagu (1718/19–1795) and Sophia (*d.* 1802), daughter of James Wroughton of Wilcot, Wiltshire. He was the brother of Captain James *Montagu and Edward *Montagu. In 1763 he entered the Royal Naval Academy at Portsmouth, and was thence appointed to the *Preston* with Captain Alan Gardner, going out to the Jamaica station with the flag of Rear-Admiral William Parry. He continued in the *Preston* for three years, was afterwards in the *Levant* with Captain Gardner, and returned to England in 1770. He passed his examination on 2 October 1770, and on 14 January 1771 was promoted to be lieutenant of the *Marlborough*. In February he was moved into the *Captain*, going out to North America as the flagship of his father. The elder Montagu on 9 April 1773 made him commander in the *Kingfisher* sloop, and on 15 April 1774 he was posted to the *Fowey*. In her he continued on the North American station during the early years of the War of Independence, actively co-operating with the army in the embarkation at Boston in March, and in the reduction of New York in October 1776. Shortly afterwards he returned to England in bad health. From 1777 to 1779 he commanded the *Romney*, as flag-captain to his father at Newfoundland. On his return he was appointed to the frigate *Pearl* (32 guns), in which, cruising near the Azores, he captured the Spanish frigate *Santa Monica*, of equal force, on 14 September 1779. In December the *Pearl* sailed with the fleet under Sir George Rodney, and assisted in the capture of the Caracas convoy; but, having sprung her foremast, was ordered home with the prizes. She was afterwards sent out to North America, and on 30 September 1780, while on a cruise off the Bermudas, captured the *Espérance*, a frigate-built privateer of 32 guns. In Marriot Arbuthnot's action off Cape Henry, on 16 March 1781, the *Pearl* performed as repeating frigate. She was not with the fleet at the Chesapeake on 5 September, but joined it, still off Cape Henry, on the 14th, and Rear-Admiral Thomas Graves left her to keep watch on the movements of the French until the 25th, when she sailed for New York. On 19 October she sailed again with the fleet, and on the 23rd, according to her log, was stationed ahead as a look-out. She returned to England in 1782.

In the armament of 1790 Montagu was appointed to the *Hector* (74 guns), and, continuing to command her, went out to the Leeward Islands in 1793 with Rear-Admiral Gardner, and thence to Jamaica, to convoy the homeward-bound trade. He was afterwards with the squadron in the Downs, under the orders of Rear-Admiral John Macbride, until 12 April 1794, when he was promoted to the rank of rear-admiral. Hoisting his flag in the *Hector*, he joined the Grand Fleet under Richard, Earl Howe.

On 4 May Montagu was detached, with a squadron of six sail of the line, to convoy a large fleet of merchant ships as far as Cape Finisterre. His further orders were to cruise to the west until 20 May, in the hope of meeting the French provision convoy daily expected from America. The convoy, however, did not arrive at that time, and Montagu, after making several important captures, returned to Plymouth on 30 May. He had extended his cruise for several days beyond the prescribed limit, but had not been able to communicate with Howe. On 2 June he received orders from the Admiralty to put to sea again with every available ship, and to cruise off Brest in order to intercept the French provision fleet. On the 3rd the *Audacious* came in with news of the partial action of 28 May; but Montagu, having no other orders, put to sea on 4 June with nine sail of the line. On the evening of the 8th he chased a French squadron of eight ships into Brest, and at daybreak on the 9th he found a French fleet of nineteen ships of the line a few miles to the west of him. Though several of these were under jurymasts, or in tow of others, they all appeared capable of defending themselves, and fourteen of them seemed to be ordinarily effective. Of Howe's success on 1 June Montagu had no information. All he could hope was that by stretching to the south, with a northerly wind, he might tempt the French so far to leeward of their port that Howe, if following them up, might be able to secure them. However, the French commander, Villaret, was not inclined to run such a risk, and, after a slight demonstration of chasing him, resumed his course and steered for Brest. Montagu, after looking unsuccessfully for Howe to the north-west, bore away for the channel, and on the 12th anchored in Cawsand Bay.

In relating these events in the first volume of his *Naval History of Great Britain*, published in 1823, Captain Edward Brenton attacked Montagu's conduct in not bringing on a general action, and maintained that Lord Chatham and the Board of Admiralty had been displeased at his conduct, ordering him to strike his flag. In the same year Montagu responded with *A refutation of the incorrect statements and unjust insinuations contained in Captain Brenton's 'Naval history of Great Britain'*. Montagu was perhaps too old, too angry, and too little practised in literary fence to punish Brenton as he deserved; but he had no difficulty in showing that Brenton's facts were untrue.

Indeed, Lord Howe and the Admiralty fully approved of Montagu's conduct. When, in bad health, rendered worse by the shock of his brother James's death on 1 June 1794, he applied for permission to resign his command, they both expressed their regret and a hope that his absence might be short. On 1 June 1795 he was promoted to be vice-admiral, and in March 1799 he was offered the command at the Nore, which he declined, as beneath his rank. In April 1800 Lord St Vincent offered him the post of second in command in the channel; but other officers were appointed by the Admiralty, and there was no vacancy. On 1 January 1801 he was made admiral; but when shortly afterwards he applied for a command, St Vincent, now

first lord of the Admiralty, replied that he had learned there was 'an insuperable bar' to his 'being employed in any way' (BL, Add. MS 31158). He refused to elucidate but it would appear that the obstacle was some misunderstanding of his conduct in 1794, as it gave way on a perusal of the official letters which Montagu had received at the time, and in 1803 he was appointed commander-in-chief at Portsmouth. He held this post for five and a half years and in August 1810 was presented with 'a superb piece of plate' as 'a tribute of respect and esteem' by the captains who had fitted out at Portsmouth during his command. On 2 January 1815 he was nominated a GCB, but he had no service after the peace.

In 1783 Montagu had married his first cousin, Charlotte, daughter and coheir of George Wroughton of Wilcot, Wiltshire; the couple had one daughter, Georgiana (d. 1836), who married Vice-Admiral Sir John Gore, and four sons: George Wroughton (d. 1871), army officer, who assumed the name of Wroughton in 1826; John William (d. 1882) and James (d. 1868), both retired admirals; and Edward (d. 1820), a Church of England clergyman. Montagu died on 24 December 1829.

J. K. LAUGHTON, *rev.* RUDDOCK MACKAY

Sources J. Marshall, *Royal naval biography*, 1/1 (1823), 39–43 • W. L. Clowes, *The Royal Navy: a history from the earliest times to the present*, 7 vols. (1897–1903) • B. Tunstall, *Naval warfare in the age of sail: the evolution of fighting tactics, 1650–1815*, ed. N. Tracy (1990) • D. Syrett and R. L. DiNardo, *The commissioned sea officers of the Royal Navy, 1660–1815*, rev. edn, Occasional Publications of the Navy RS, 1 (1994) • M. Duffy, 'The man who missed the grain convoy: Sir George Montagu and the escape of Vanstabel's convoy from America in 1794', *Les marines française et britannique face aux États-Unis, de la guerre d'Indépendance à la guerre de Sécession (1776–1865)* [Brest 1998] (Vincennes, 1999)
Archives BL, John Jervis MSS, Add. MS 31158 • NMM, letters to Lord Keith • PRO, Admiralty records
Likenesses portrait, *c*.1782–1783, NMM

Montagu, George (1753–1815), naturalist, was born on 8 June 1753 at Lackham House, Lackham, Wiltshire, the ninth of the thirteen children and third surviving son of James Montagu and his wife, Elizabeth Eleanor, daughter of William Hedges of Alderton Hall. He was descended from Henry Montagu, first earl of Manchester (*c*.1564–1642). He went to school at Urchfont, Wiltshire, but his lively temperament was thought to be unsuited for a professional career and his health too delicate for service at sea with the East India Company. In June 1770, when seventeen, he enlisted in the 15th foot East Yorkshire regiment, was promoted lieutenant in 1773 and captain in December 1775 when the regiment was ordered to America during the War of Independence. On returning to England in November 1777, he resigned his commission, to the consternation of his parents. One reason for his resignation was a wish to be re-united with his wife: in 1773, he had eloped to Scotland and married Ann(e) Courtenay, niece of the earl of Bute; their first son was born while he was with the army in America.

Montagu spent the next twenty years as a country gentleman living in various parts of Wiltshire, and served as an officer of the Wiltshire militia from 1781. He became lieutenant-colonel in 1791. Stationed throughout Britain, he used the opportunity for making useful observations of the local natural history. During this period he progressed from a liking for field sports to serious research; his *Sportsman's Directory* (1792) was succeeded by a paper to the Linnean Society (1796) and various ornithological publications which reveal the gradual switch from the gun to observation as a means of obtaining information. Over this period he became estranged from his brother, separated from his wife and six children, and met (*c*.1794) Elizabeth Wolff, the wife of John Dorville. These events offended the influential social circles to which he belonged, causing gossip which culminated in the loss of his chance to inherit the family estates and finally resulted in litigation over the property. In addition, this relationship, formed as the militia moved around the south coast, provoked the incidents that led to his court martial in 1799, at Plymouth, and his dismissal from his position in the Wiltshire militia. The decision was not a reflection on his military abilities for, later, on the threat of invasion, he was given command of the south Devon corps. He remained attached to Mrs Dorville for the rest of his life and they settled at Kingsbridge, Devon, whose climate and marine location he regarded as ideal for the study of natural history.

Montagu is recognized as the 'father of British ornithology' through his papers and the *Ornithological Dictionary* (1802) and supplement (1813) in which he established scrupulous standards for observation and description. Edward Forbes acknowledged his role as one of the founders of British zoology, considering him one of the most practical naturalists of his time. Later recognition as an early pioneer of the study of British crabs and crustaceans, and his work on British sponges and British Foraminifera, serve to emphasize his wide interests. His work on British mollusca, *Testacea Britannica* (1803), was the first to deal with these fauna by personal research conducted in a comprehensive scientific manner; it drew attention to the beauty of the opisthobranchs; and described the more minute molluscan taxa that his thoroughness had discovered. He was also one of the few naturalists with a knowledge of both land and freshwater mollusca and his species descriptions were only predated by the work of Draparnaud. As a fellow of the Linnean Society (1795) he had an outlet for his scientific papers (eleven in all), and sought information, specimens, and advice through correspondence with other fellows. Unfortunately, several of his correspondents did not follow his own standards on provenance and thus many molluscs described in his supplement (1808) are spurious exotic shells.

Montagu's name is still associated with a variety of British species, including Montagu's harrier, Montagu's blenny, Montagu's ray, Montagu's sucker, and Montagu's sea snail. The detailed examination of numerous specimens of other taxa, for example the Thornback ray, and observations made when rearing young birds to become adults, such as the Cirl bunting and the Ringtail/Hen harrier, enabled him to resolve nomenclatorial problems caused by sexual dimorphism. A persistent researcher, he

not only discovered the callianassid shrimp in its beach tunnels, but also its specific parasite. He was one of the first British naturalists to exploit the use of the microscope to describe smaller species. Later papers published posthumously confirm the continuation of a youthful interest in small vertebrates; and he also developed an interest in the physiology and parasitism of game birds (on which six papers of his were published in the *Transactions* of the Wernerian Society). Undoubtedly, his natural history contributions were made with the assistance and talent of the resourceful Eliza Dorville, who was also the mother of four of his ten children. Montagu died at his home, Knowle House, Kingsbridge, Devon, on 20 June 1815, from lockjaw caused by accidentally stepping on to a rusty nail a few days before. He was buried at Kingsbridge church on 24 June.

Montagu devoted his life to natural history and diligently endeavoured to establish the extent of the British fauna with the resources available to him. His contemporaries acknowledged his sincere qualities and meticulous research; and subsequent researchers in zoology have recognized the value of his work. His collection of birds was purchased by the British Museum in 1816 for £1200. His lifestyle led to some social prejudice against him, which may have been the cause of his rejection for membership of the Royal Society, after a ballot in 1808.

R. J. CLEEVELY

Sources R. J. Cleevely, 'Some background to the life and publications of Colonel George Montagu (1753–1815)', *Journal of the Society of the Bibliography of Natural History*, 8 (1976–8), 445–80 · B. F. Cummings, 'A biographical sketch of Colonel George Montagu (1755–1815)', *Zoologisches Annalen Würzburg*, 5 (1913), 307–325 · B. F. Cummings, 'Colonel Montagu, naturalist', *Proceedings of the Linnean Society of London*, 127th session (1914–15), 43–8 · E. W. Swanton, 'Colonel George Montagu', *Journal of Conchology*, 12/7 (1908), 161–6 · W. Cunnington, 'Memoir of George Montagu', *Wiltshire Archaeological and Natural History Magazine*, 3 (1857), 87–94 · L. M. Crawford, 'Autobiographical sketches connected with Laycock Abbey', *Metropolitan Magazine*, 12 (April 1835), 400–02; 14 (Nov 1835), 306–18; 22, 317; 23 (Oct 1838), 189–94 · B. Mearns and R. Mearns, 'George Montagu (1753–1815)', *Biographies for bird watchers: the lives of those commemorated in western palearctic bird names* (1988), 263–447 · *DNB* · *Kingsbridge Gazette* (7 July 1899) · E. A. S. Elliott, 'Recollections of Colonel Montagu', *The Field* (24 July 1897) · 'A century's work on ornithology in the Kingsbridge district', *Rept. Trans. Devon. Ass. Advmt Sci.*, 29 (1897), 167–74 [Montagu p. 167] · 'Account of Montagu's coffin in Kingsbridge church', *Rept. Trans. Devon. Ass. Advmt Sci.*, 31 (1899), 326–30

Archives BL, ornithological catalogue and notes, Add. MS 33495 · Linn. Soc., ornithological and conchological papers · NHM, family papers and notebook containing natural history notes | Dorset RO, Thomas Rackett corresp. · NHM, Richard Pulteney corresp. · NHM, letters to members of Sowerby family

Likenesses miniature (in uniform), Linn. Soc., Montagu MSS; repro. in Mearns and Mearns, 'George Montagu'

Wealth at death wife had to dispose of various assets to meet costs, debts, and legacies of husband: BM, Montagu MSS

Montagu, George Brudenell, duke of Montagu (1712–1790), courtier, was born on 26 July 1712 at Cardigan House in Lincoln's Inn Fields, London, and baptized George Brudenell on 1 August at St Giles-in-the-Fields, the eldest son of George Brudenell, third earl of Cardigan (*d*. 1732), courtier, and his wife, Lady Elizabeth (*c*.1689–1745), the eldest daughter of Thomas Bruce, second earl of Ailesbury. At the age of thirteen, on 1 July 1726, he was admitted to Queen's College, Oxford, where he was made an MA on 31 January 1730. On 7 July 1730 he married Lady Mary (1710/11–1775), the daughter and coheir of John *Montagu, second duke of Montagu (1690–1749), and his wife, Mary Churchill (1689–1751). They had one son, John (1735–1770), who was created Baron Montagu of Boughton in 1762, and three daughters, Elizabeth, Mary, and Henrietta. Elizabeth was the only child to marry: her husband was Henry *Scott, third duke of Buccleuch (1746–1812). Following his father's death on 5 July 1732 Brudenell succeeded as fourth earl, and on the death of his father-in-law in July 1749 he assumed the name and coat of arms of Montagu, although the dukedom became extinct. However, on 5 November 1766 he was created marquess of Monthermer and duke of Montagu of the second creation; a barony of Montagu of Boughton, with remainder to a grandson, was bestowed on him in 1786.

Montagu took little part in politics but enjoyed a long career at court. He began as a page at George II's coronation in 1727. From 1742 to 1752 he served as chief justice in eyre, north of the Trent, and was then appointed governor and captain of Windsor Castle. He was made a knight of the Garter in 1762 and was the first person to be invested in absentia, being abroad at the time. In 1776 he was appointed governor to the prince of Wales and the duke of York, and on 5 June that year he was sworn of the privy council. Montagu resigned as governor in 1780, whereupon he became master of the horse. He was elected fellow of the Royal Society on 7 December 1749, and served as president of the Royal Society of Arts, president of St Luke's Hospital, and vice-president of St George's Hospital.

Montagu died at his home in Privy Gardens, London, on 23 May 1790. As there were no surviving male heirs, the earldom of Cardigan and the entailed estates devolved on his brother James Brudenell and the barony of Montagu of Boughton passed to his grandson Henry James Montagu Scott, but his other titles became extinct. The personal estate and family jewels, which together were valued at £150,000, were inherited by his daughter Elizabeth, the duchess of Buccleuch.

H. M. CHICHESTER, rev. M. J. MERCER

Sources GM, 1st ser., 60 (1790), 482 · GEC, Peerage · B. Burke, A genealogical history of the dormant, abeyant, forfeited and extinct peerages of the British empire, new edn (1883), 375 · Foster, Alum. Oxon.
Archives BL, lawsuits | BL, letters to General Haldimand · BL, letters to first Lord Hardwicke · BL, letters to second Lord Hardwicke · BL, letters to R. Keith · BL, letters to Sir R. M. Keith · BL, letters to duchess of Newcastle · BL, corresp. with duke of Newcastle, Add. MSS 32718–32883 · BL, letters to Lord Strafford
Likenesses H. van der Myn, oils, 1732, Deene Park, Northamptonshire · T. Gainsborough, oils, c.1768, Buccleuch estates, Selkirk · W. Beechey, oils, 1789–90, Hatfield House, Hertfordshire · T. Gainsborough, pastel drawing, BM · T. Hudson, oils, Buccleuch estates, Selkirk · J. Miers, silhouette on plaster, Royal Collection · attrib. E. Seeman, oils, Buccleuch estates, Selkirk · oils, Beaulieu Abbey, Hampshire
Wealth at death £100,000 personal estate; £50,000 family jewels: DNB

Montagu, Henry, first earl of Manchester (c.1564–1642), judge and government official, was born at Boughton, Northamptonshire, the third surviving son of Sir Edward Montagu (c.1532–1602) of Boughton and his wife, Elizabeth (c.1542–1618), daughter of Sir James Harington of Exton, Rutland. His grandfather was Sir Edward *Montagu (1480s–1557), chief justice of king's bench. Henry was intended for the law, and after matriculating at Christ's College, Cambridge, in March 1583 entered the Middle Temple on 6 November 1585. Three years later he lent his father support during his shrievalty, and may have been his under-sheriff. He was called to the bar on 9 June 1592, and was elected autumn reader at the Middle Temple in 1606. Like his eldest brother, Edward, he sat in the parliaments of 1593, 1598, and 1601, each time returned for Higham Ferrers; another brother, Sidney, also sat in two of them, creating difficulties over identification in reports of proceedings. It was, however, almost certainly Henry Montagu who in the 1601 Commons dismissed Serjeant Hele's rash contention that the subsidy was something that the queen could demand of right, by confidently asserting that it was by way of a free gift.

A rising lawyer, 1603–1620 Montagu was elected recorder of London in May 1603, and was knighted by James at Whitehall on 23 July. His relations with the new king were usually sound, although James received 'less satisfaction than wee expected' from the firmly Calvinist Montagu's response to an urgent request to tighten regulation in London against recusants in February 1605 (Correspondence of Dr Matthew Hutton, 171–5). He sat for the City of London in both early Jacobean parliaments, in 1614 encountering difficulties over a potential clash of interest since he was now a king's serjeant while, at James's wish, retaining his recordership. The City's disquiet was aggravated by a rumour, in the end effectively denied by the crown, that another of its candidates, Sir Thomas Lowe, was to be chosen speaker. In the 1614 Commons, Montagu showed himself anxious to prevent undue influence by unscrupulous minorities by speaking strongly for the bill to make all elections free and so reduce the risk of patrons packing the Commons with their clients; characteristically, he thought it 'a fit subject for a necessary law' (Hirst, 67, 229). Having invested for the first time in 1606, as a director of the new Virginia Company venture, he adopted a similarly open view in his attitude to joint-stock companies, consistently supporting those who welcomed a wide range of clients. With Sir Francis Bacon, then the solicitor-general, he took part in a detailed inquiry under the direction of Salisbury and Northampton in 1612 into the customs in general, and those of the French and Rhenish wines in particular. Here too he supported open trade. His links with Bacon strengthened when, after resigning the recordership of London, he became chief justice of king's bench in succession to Sir Edward Coke in November 1616, paying, it was thought, at least £10,000 for an office he had wanted for some time. Both of them were committed to the development of the New River project for providing London with fresh water, an enterprise for what might be termed the public good into which James, like

Henry Montagu, first earl of Manchester (c.1564–1642), after John Riley

Montagu, had put money. Montagu held the first meeting of the reconstituted company in his chambers in Serjeants' Inn in 1619.

While a serjeant, Montagu had regularly served as a justice of assize, since 1612 riding the midland, home, and western circuits, leaving impressive signs of his busyness in the Devon order books. But it was while chief justice of king's bench, riding the Norfolk circuit and presiding over the Middlesex sessions, that he did most to affirm, and try to improve, the administrative standards advocated by Popham, Ellesmere, and others from the 1590s onwards. He was, above all, anxious to sharpen the mechanisms for delivering systematic enforcement of existing statutes, especially those addressing pauper apprenticeship, control of alehouses, and punishment of rogues and vagabonds. He did not seek new laws, but steady use of the many already available. In his Star Chamber charge in June 1618 Bacon noted that over 2000 apprentices had recently been bound out in Norfolk, and other evidence shows that 500 had been apprenticed there during 1618–19 alone. Michael Dalton, author of *The Countrey Justice* (1618), a handbook 'for such JPs as have not been much conversant in the studie of the Lawes of this Realme', dedicated it to Montagu in acknowledgement of his interest and encouragement on the Norfolk circuit. Montagu was among the judges who had begun to advocate the use of public service informers in the counties to identify breaches of economic statutes; and in 1619 he, rather than the attorney-general, was entrusted by James with superintending the drawing of a proclamation intended to reintroduce into alehouse licensing a degree of central control and profit to the exchequer, last tried unsuccessfully in 1608. Two patentees were appointed for five years to manage the scheme, one of them Montagu's servant Robert Dixon; but it proved even less acceptable in the localities than the previous venture, and its end was apparent when Montagu, like Dixon and his partner, was attacked in the 1621 parliament.

By then Montagu had shared in an initiative which was to bear fruit, in different circumstances, a decade later. As a new year's gift for 1620, Bacon had presented James with the outline for an ambitious series of interrelated committees, intended to remedy the ills of the commonweal. Montagu had taken the opportunity of suggesting one, particularly likely to appeal to James, for quickening the JPs, drawn from his experience as a circuit judge. Based on the privy council, it addressed what he was already calling 'services for the public good', laying some emphasis on relief of the poor and suppression of vagabonds, and proposing rules for, and regular accounting by, JPs (Quintrell, 568). It proved to be the only part of the programme which had its commission, but not its directions to JPs, drawn and sealed before the scheme was set aside on Bacon's fall in 1621.

Minister of the crown, 1620–1642 In December 1620 Montagu gave up the chief justiceship and became lord treasurer, potentially closer to the inner workings of royal government than any of his family since the premature death in July 1618 of his brother James, bishop of Winchester, dean of the chapels royal since 1603 and a close confidant of the king. It was to prove an unsettling experience. Even though he became a privy councillor on 3 December and soon afterwards was created Baron Montagu of Kimbolton and Viscount Mandeville, he had paid no less than £20,000 for an office which had little to offer its buyer, so hedged about was it by reversions, leases, and prior grants of lands to the prince of Wales, with much of the revenues anticipated. Cranfield judged it worth half as much; and the transaction formed part of the tenth article of Buckingham's impeachment in 1626. In later life, as he began to take stock of his public service with an eye to posterity, Montagu in 1634 wrote a lengthy, and rather self-serving, account of his term as lord treasurer; but, as his term lasted no more than ten months, the most that can be said is that he furthered reforms already underway, and provided more clear money for immediate spending wherever he could.

At Buckingham's urging, James replaced him with Cranfield on 28 September 1621, and Montagu found himself instead the first lord president of the council since Northumberland in 1553, 'a place long out of use and of no great necessitie' as Chamberlain put it (*Letters of John Chamberlain*, 2.399). Although concerned at his financial loss, he maintained a cordial relationship with Buckingham and was duly rewarded. On the eve of his departure for Madrid in February 1623 the duke, busy mending political fences, abruptly invited himself to dinner at Montagu's London house in Aldersgate Street. Subsequently he provided his host with a security for the recovery of £10,000 on the marriage of his impoverished niece Susannah Hill to Montagu's heir, Edward; and on 7 February 1626, as parliament convened, Montagu was created earl of Manchester, with Edward joining him in the Lords as Baron Kimbolton with the courtesy title of Viscount Mandeville. In 1621 the elder

Montagu stoically threw himself into his new office, by the king's special warrant signing privy council orders on 28 September before the formalities of his appointment had been completed. Although his powers, as defined by the council's standing orders in 1628, were circumscribed and sometimes shared with the secretaries of state, he soon developed an effective role at its head in unstable times. He did what he could to contain the mettlesome but unproven lord keeper, John Williams, appointed less than three months before he became lord president to an office Montagu might have relished, and shouldered some of Secretary Calvert's domestic responsibilities now that he was preoccupied with foreign business. When James retreated to Newmarket after the prince and Buckingham had set out for Spain, Montagu, rather than Calvert, provided him with weekly accounts of council proceedings of a quality which quickly won his approval, and while he remained president he continued to supply them whenever necessary, as he did for Charles in the summer of 1627. Much of the administrative business of the council in these years had a bearing on commerce and settlement; and, as an investor in five joint-stock ventures by 1620, Montagu was able to add his mercantile experience to his concern for responsible government in his dealings with the wayward Virginia Company of London. James followed the discussions closely; but, after numerous attempts at reform proved fruitless, Montagu presided over the commission which wound the company up in July 1624. His appointment in October 1624 to the lord lieutenancy of Huntingdonshire, where he had settled at Kimbolton Castle in 1619, proved more durable; either jointly or alone, he held the office until his death in 1642, strengthening his ties with Huntingdonshire in 1627 when he and Sidney Montagu bought Hinchingbrooke from the Cromwells.

On a constitutional plane Montagu did what he could in the later 1620s to preserve the polity from prerogative excess, striving to maintain the traditional concept of ruling with parliament, deflecting Charles's attempts at early dissolution in the spring of 1626 and later raising the possibility of further parliaments despite the king's obvious antipathy to the idea. He regarded the forced loan of 1626–7 as an exceptional measure in response to an immediate emergency, and sought to curb its more disturbing aspects. He and Coventry combined in March 1627 to prevent Gloucestershire loan refusers from being pressed for military service overseas, and in June that year he took advantage of Charles's absence to release leading loaners, temporarily and under supervision, from their close confinement in the Gatehouse at Westminster into healthier country air nearby, thus confirming his reputation as the prisoners' friend. With other moderates in the council, he drew freely on the advice of Sir Robert Cotton and made use of the precedents in his library in the search for compromise and common ground. His role in the two sessions of the parliament of 1628–9 was similarly constructive: both in his speeches and his contributions to conferences between the houses he showed the concern he shared with members anxious to preserve the integrity of the

prerogative without damaging the liberties of the subject, as over the petition of right and the case of the five knights. He and Coventry did not help their chances of major political influence in the personal rule by their determination to keep alive hopes of future parliaments after 1629.

Shortly after the end of the first session, Manchester was on 15 July 1628 appointed to what he seemed to sense would be his last office, that of lord privy seal. He was relieved to be free from the accumulating burdens of an ill-defined post. As he told his brother Edward, 'I have put myself at some ease by putting off the Presidency; nor do I repent the change; nor will I be too forward to ease others' (*Buccleuch MSS*, 1.267). Having served 'so many offices in severall professions'—in his will he claimed to have 'borne and executed all the great offices and places of this kingdome one after another'—he took time to take stock, and decided to record, in neo-stoical vein, his thoughts on death and immortality. The work first appeared anonymously in 1631 as *Contemplatio mortis et immortalitatis*; its authorship was revealed in the third edition of 1633, and its title amended to announce *Manchester al mondo*. It was reissued several more times before the civil war. Late in 1630 Manchester had also revisited his past in a more practical way. Prompted by an unsolicited enquiry from Edward Cecil, Viscount Wimbledon, the council had in November 1630 appointed a working party, with Manchester at its head, to consider what more might be done for the poor in difficult times. He thus had a belated opportunity to dust off his 1620 proposal for quickening the JPs. By 5 January 1631 he had produced a revised version of his stillborn commission of 1620, directed to all active members of Charles's council and basing its orders and directions to JPs, which he now hurriedly added, on working practices already familiar in many counties. Six hundred copies of the Book of Orders were printed and distributed throughout England and Wales, providing for the first time for regular and continual reporting by JPs to the council as a matter of routine, year after year, in a manner James I would have welcomed. In essence the Caroline Book of Orders remained Jacobean, raising concerns and expressing values which deserved a timely reiteration, even if Charles's own priorities soon threatened to divert his council's attention elsewhere. Its impact in the localities was to prove less emphatic than Manchester might have wished; arguably, he had more obvious success in presiding, as lord privy seal, over the court of requests. The court provided comparatively quick and cheap justice for those of modest means, and by the 1630s was proving increasingly popular with its users. It had acquired a strong Montagu association: Manchester's brother Sidney was one of the masters of requests from 1616 to 1640, and the most prominent counsellor in the court during the later 1630s was Robert Barnard, steward to the young Viscount Mandeville and, in time, an executor of Manchester's will. As recorder of Huntingdon in 1630, Barnard had been one of the parties roughly challenged by Oliver Cromwell in a factional dispute arising from the borough's new charter, and to Cromwell's discomfort he was among those vindicated by Manchester on reference from the privy council.

Manchester married three times. His first wife was Catherine, daughter of Sir William Spencer of Yarnton, Oxfordshire. Married on 1 June 1601, she died on 7 December 1612 and was buried in St Botolph's, Aldersgate. They had four sons, the heir, Edward *Montagu, Walter *Montagu, James and Henry, and two daughters, Elizabeth, Lady Mansell and Lucy, Lady Coleraine. He married secondly, about September 1613, Anne, daughter of William Wincot of Langham, Suffolk, widow of Sir Leonard Haliday, lord mayor of London in 1605–6. She died childless around November 1618 and was also buried at St Botolph's. His third marriage, on 26 April 1620 at Totteridge, Hertfordshire, was to Margaret (d. 1653), one of the daughters of John Crouch of Corneybury in Layston, Hertfordshire, widow of Allen Elvine, a London bookseller, and of John Hare, clerk of the court of wards. She survived him, dying in December 1653. They had two sons, George and Sidney, and at least one daughter, Susannah, Lady Chandos. Manchester's brother Edward, Lord Montagu, subsequently married Anne, one of Margaret's sisters; and both brothers came to enjoy the expertise and friendship of Ralph Freeman, the widowed husband of Joan, a third Crouch sister. Freeman was a wealthy clothworker and alderman of London, active in overseas ventures, who obligingly handled many of the brothers' routine business affairs before dying during his mayoralty in 1633–4. Margaret Crouch took pains to bind Henry's immediate family together, made much of Manchester House in Cannon Row (once Hertford House), London, and kept in touch with the wider kinship beyond. In the 1620s Henry came to occupy a more central role in the family than had once seemed likely.

At heart Manchester was always an administrator, more concerned with dispensing justice, enforcing statute law, and quickening the machinery of government than with the play of court politics. In his unspectacular way, he became a pillar of the privy council. Remarkably, between December 1620 and December 1641 he attended four in every five of its routine meetings as well as others concerned with policy, served on the bench in Star Chamber, and attended its standing committees for trade and plantations and, briefly, for Ireland (1623–5). He was continuously in demand as a referee for all manner of domestic problems and disputes brought to the council's notice, providing his capacious memory with regular exercise. No other early Stuart councillor was so much involved over so lengthy a period in the everyday business of England. But he was less familiar with foreign affairs, and lacked the political stature of those Hispanophile ministers, such as Weston and Cottington, who acquired a close understanding of the relationship between royal finances and foreign policy. Like other councillors of firmly protestant inclinations he welcomed the final collapse in 1634 of any prospect of a Spanish subsidy for Charles's growing English fleet, and helped Coventry and John Coke in managing the preliminaries to levying ship money each year during the remainder of the personal rule; but how far he

understood the king's purposes is unclear, and at least initially he may, like Coke, have believed the primary concern was to protect English commerce. Perhaps, like Noy in his last days, he glimpsed the possibility that active support for the new fleet might draw peers and gentry closer to the king and encourage a community of interest in, as well as out of, parliament. Always a moderate, he had little time for factious activity. Unlike Coventry and Laud he did not encourage the use of the forest courts to harass Lord Treasurer Portland in 1634, and had earlier viewed the revival of the forest laws as being entirely in the interests of law and order, whereas his country brother Edward sensed a money-making exercise. His son Wat's conversion to Rome, relayed from Paris on 21 November 1635, hit him hard, particularly when he realized that before Wat's letter reached him several copies were not only in circulation but, to his embarrassment, were already in use as Catholic propaganda. Even so, he was determined to receive the news in silence, hurt as he was that Wat had failed to consult him before making his decision; after seven months, however, he felt impelled to respond

> lest those of your now profession should think, as some of them say, that a new lapsarian was more able by a few day's discipline to oppose our religion than an old father and a long professor was able to defend it.

He set out in detail the fundamentals of his protestant faith, grounded in Christ and renouncing 'all men alike as inventors of our religion', among them Luther, to whom Wat had particularly objected, and maintaining 'only the apostolical doctrine of the ancient primitive and catholic Church' (Eighth Report, HMC, 2.51–2). He would not abandon Wat, but wanted him to return to the Church of England of his own accord. Before the end of 1636, however, he had become so depressed that the countess of Leicester reported him 'drunke everie Meall' (Collins, 2.454). One of his rare absences from the council table was on 22 October 1637 when, in the king's presence, Laud bluntly attacked Catholic influence at court, evident in the recent wave of conversions among courtiers around the queen and exemplified by the pernicious influence of, among others, Wat Montagu (Works of ... William Laud, 3.229). Predictably, Laud once more upset Henrietta Maria; but it is quite possible that he had taken the trouble to warn Wat's father of what he was about to say.

Last years Despite his advancing years, Manchester headed delegations of councillors to the City in search of gifts or loans to underpin Charles's expeditions to the north in 1639 and 1640, and personally lent him £4000 and pledged more. He drew on Tudor precedent and recent example, and in the autumn of 1640 made much of the covenanters' rough treatment of Thomas Morton, the gentle and aged bishop of Durham, a few weeks earlier. But the City was in no mood to be generous. His eldest son, Edward, Viscount Mandeville, meanwhile showed himself to be no more inclined than Wat to heed his advice, preferring instead to associate with Pym and his allies: Edward was one of the twelve peers hustling for a parliament in September 1640, became a treasonable accomplice of the five members, and in due course commanded a parliamentary army. The final pages of Henry's compendious will, completed on 22 March 1642, necessarily lacked the certainty of its opening remarks, their provisions contingent on the resolution of difficulties which, he thought, Edward and Wat had wilfully created; neither was named as an executor. As he said there of Edward, 'I cannot but blame him that would not be advised by me to desist from medling in matters that might be ill construed by the king and be a danger to them that medled therein' (will, PROB 11/192, sig. 47). He was still attending the House of Lords in June 1642; but, although he took an optimistic view of the king's answer to the nineteen propositions, he was tired of business and increasingly bewildered by the dismaying shifts of contemporary politics. He died on 7 November 1642 and was buried at Kimbolton, in the chancel of the church where he had already set up a small monument 'of what I was in my being' (ibid.).

Manchester had spent heavily in establishing his station in life, without entirely realizing the promise of earlier years, and died a man of respectable, rather than abundant, means. After disposing of his landed estate in Huntingdonshire and London among his older children, he was able to provide almost £5000 a year for his widow and younger sons, with gifts of £2000 to each of his two granddaughters. Yet he fretted that it was not more. As his will shows, he never forgot what he regarded as his underprivileged beginnings as a younger brother, and seemed determined that his children should not do so either. As late as 1616 his nose had reportedly been set 'somewhat awrie' by the news that his eldest brother, Edward, had at last got a male heir; and, in Clarendon's opinion, he came to care too much about advancing his fortune 'by all ways which offered themselves' (*Letters of John Chamberlain*, 2.16; Clarendon, *Hist. rebellion*, 1.68). Nevertheless, with 'a faire portion of God's blessing' on his labours, and 'never gain[ing] anything by corruption, cavillation or oppression', Henry Montagu had prospered sufficiently by 1642 to show those of his posterity who cared to heed his words what might be achieved by conscientious service to king and country (will, PROB 11/192, sig. 47).   BRIAN QUINTRELL

Sources will, PRO, PROB 11/192, sig. 47 · [H. Montagu], *Contemplatio mortis et immortalitatis* (1631) · *Report on the manuscripts of his grace the duke of Buccleuch and Queensberry … preserved at Montagu House*, 3 vols. in 4, HMC, 45 (1899–1926), vols. 1, 3 · *Report on the manuscripts of Lord Montagu of Beaulieu*, HMC, 53 (1900) · *Eighth report*, 2, HMC, 7 (1910) · *The manuscripts of Rye and Hereford corporations*, HMC, 31 (1892) [Wodehouse MSS] · *The manuscripts of the Earl Cowper*, 3 vols., HMC, 23 (1888–9), vols. 1–2 · *Report on the manuscripts of Lord De L'Isle and Dudley*, 6, HMC, 77 (1966) · *CSP dom.*, 1591–1642 · *The letters and life of Francis Bacon*, ed. J. Spedding, 7 vols. (1861–74) · *Cabala, sive, Scrinia sacra: mysteries of state and government in letters of illustrious persons* (1654) · M. Dalton, *The countrey justice* (1618) · *The letters of John Chamberlain*, ed. N. E. McClure, 2 vols. (1939) · *The works of the most reverend father in God, William Laud*, ed. J. Bliss and W. Scott, 7 vols. (1847–60) · Clarendon, *Hist. rebellion* · R. Scrope and T. Monkhouse, eds., *State papers collected by Edward, earl of Clarendon*, 3 vols. (1767–86) · A. Collins, ed., *Sydney state papers*, 2 vols. (1746) · W. Notestein, F. H. Relf, and H. Simpson, eds., *Commons debates, 1621*, 7 vols. (1935) · J. F. Larkin and P. L. Hughes, eds., *Stuart royal proclamations*, 2 vols. (1973–80), vol. 1 · *The correspondence of Dr Matthew Hutton, archbishop of York*, ed. [J. Raine], SurtS, 17 (1843) ·

P. Slack, *From Reformation to improvement* (1999) · D. Hirst, *The representative of the people?* (1975) · R. P. Cust, *The forced loan and English politics, 1626–1628* (1987) · L. J. Reeve, *The road to personal rule* (1989) · B. W. Quintrell, 'The making of Charles I's Book of Orders', *EngHR*, 95 (1980) · G. E. Aylmer, *The king's servants: the civil service of Charles I, 1625–1642* (1961) · F. C. Dietz, *English public finance, 1558–1641* (1932) · R. Lockyer, *Buckingham: the life and political career of George Villiers, first duke of Buckingham, 1592–1628* (1981) · E. Cope, *The life of a public man* (1981) · T. K. Rabb, *Enterprise and empire … 1575–1630* (1967) · T. K. Rabb, *Jacobean gentleman: Sir Edwin Sandys* (1998) · A. Brown, ed., *The genesis of the United States*, 2 vols. (1890) · W. R. Prest, *The rise of the barristers: a social history of the English bar, 1590–1640* (1986) · M. Prestwich, *Cranfield* (1966) · J. Morrill, ed., *Oliver Cromwell and the English revolution* (1990) · Venn, *Alum. Cant.* · GEC, *Peerage*

Archives Beaulieu, Hampshire, letters · BL, letter-book and accounts, Add. MS 4147 · BL, office and estate MSS, Egerton MS 3881 · Northants. RO, family corresp. · PRO, letters, SP 14 and SP 16

Likenesses F. Delaram, line engraving, BM, NPG · W. Faithorne, line engraving, BM, NPG · F. H. Van Hove, line engraving, BM, NPG; repro. in H. Montagu, *Manchester al Mondo: contemplatio mortis et immortalitatis*, 6th edn (1656) · engraving (after unknown artist, then at Kimbolton), repro. in Duke of Manchester [W. D. Montagu], *Court and society from Elizabeth to Anne* (1864), frontispiece · engraving, repro. in *Manchester al Mondo: contemplatio mortis et immortalitatis*, 4th edn (1639), preface [NewSTC 18028.5] · oils (after J. Riley), Middle Temple, London [*see illus.*] · portrait (while lord privy seal) · portrait, repro. in Brown, *Genesis of the United States*, vol. 2, facing p. 650

Wealth at death nearly £5000 p.a. for widow and younger children; plus Kimbolton Castle and Manchester House: will, PRO, PROB 11/192, sig. 47

Montagu, Henry Robinson-, sixth Baron Rokeby (1798–1883),

army officer and landowner, was born at Great Cumberland Place, London, on 2 February 1798, the fifth son of Matthew Montagu, formerly Robinson, fourth Baron Rokeby (1762–1831), and his wife, Elizabeth Charlton (*d.* 1817). He was also the great-nephew of Matthew Robinson-*Morris, second Baron Rokeby (1713–1800), and the brother of Edward Montagu, fifth Baron Rokeby (1787–1847). He was commissioned ensign in the Scots Fusilier Guards on 21 April 1814, and served at Quatre Bras and Waterloo. He was promoted lieutenant and captain (by purchase) in June 1823, captain and lieutenant-colonel (by purchase) in September 1832, and colonel in November 1846. On 18 December 1826 he married Magdalen (*d.* 1868), the eldest daughter of Lieutenant-Colonel Thomas Huxley and the widow of Frederick Croft. They had one son, Edward (1835–1852), and four daughters.

Robinson-Montagu succeeded to the peerage on 7 April 1847. He was promoted lieutenant-colonel commanding the regiment in 1854, and major-general on 20 June 1854. In 1855 he was sent to the Crimea, where he arrived in February, to command the guards brigade, replacing the duke of Cambridge who had gone home. He called the guards officers together to read them letters from the queen, and the sight of so few and such haggard faces caused him to burst into tears. One night his patent water-closet was stolen, allegedly by Zouaves, perhaps to make soup in. From November 1855, with the local rank of lieutenant-general, he commanded the 1st division. He was made KCB in May 1856 (GCB May 1875) and a commander of the Légion d'honneur, and was awarded the Turkish order of the Mejidiye (third class). From July 1856 he was general commanding the brigade of guards. He was promoted lieutenant-general in 1861 and general in March 1869, and retired in October 1877. He was colonel of the 77th foot from 1861 to 1875, and of the Scots Guards from May 1875 until his death. He was the last to have the letter W, denoting service at Waterloo, before his name in the *Army List*. He owned 4863 acres in the North Riding of Yorkshire, Hertfordshire, Cambridgeshire, and Kent, worth £9180 a year in 1883, and more before the agricultural depression. Rokeby died on 25 May 1883 at 7 Stratford Place, Marylebone, London, and was buried on 31 May at Clewer cemetery, Berkshire. At his death his peerage became extinct.

ROGER T. STEARN

Sources GEC, *Peerage* · *The Times* (26 May 1883) · *The Times* (21 June 1883) · *ILN* (2 June 1883) · Burke, *Peerage* (1879) · *Dod's Peerage* (1878) · *Hart's Army List* (1854) · Boase, *Mod. Eng. biog.* · C. Hibbert, *The destruction of Lord Raglan* (1963) · R. Muir, *Britain and the defeat of Napoleon, 1807–1815* (1996) · A. D. Lambert, *The Crimean War: British grand strategy, 1853–56* (1990)
Likenesses G. Zobel, mezzotint, pubd 1858 (after F. Grant), BM, NPG · lithograph, BM, NPG
Wealth at death £41,681 1s. 1d.: probate, 4 Oct 1883, *CGPLA Eng. & Wales*

Montagu, Ivor Goldsmid Samuel (1904–1984), film producer and writer, was born on 23 April 1904 in Kensington, London, the third of four children, and the youngest of three sons of Louis Samuel Montagu, second Baron Swaythling (1869–1927), banker, and his wife, Gladys Helen Rachel (d. 1965), daughter of Colonel Albert Edward Williamson Goldsmid. He was educated at Westminster School, the Royal College of Science, London, and King's College, Cambridge, where he gained a pass degree in 1924. From an early age he cultivated the widely different interests that he pursued for over sixty years—zoology, sport, most of all table tennis, film, and socialism. At Cambridge he was a film critic for *Granta*. By the time he was twenty-two he had already published his first book (*Table Tennis Today*, 1924), founded the English Table Tennis Association, made two zoological expeditions to the Soviet Union, and co-founded the Film Society in 1925 with Sidney Bernstein, Adrian Brunel, Iris Barry, Hugh Miller, Walter Mycroft, and Frank Dobson. The society marked the crucial first recognition of film as an art form in Britain, and numbered among its sponsors Augustus John, J. M. Keynes, G. B. Shaw, and H. G. Wells. It provided a means of bypassing film censorship and Montagu remained its chairman until 1939.

Montagu wrote some of the earliest London newspaper film reviews for *The Observer* and wrote notes for the Film Society's programmes, 1925–9. In 1926 he was invited to re-edit *The Lodger*, directed by Alfred Hitchcock. Two years later, with his partner Adrian Brunel, he directed his first films, *Bluebottles* (1928), *Daydreams* (1929), and *The Tonic* (1930), comedy shorts adapted from stories by H. G. Wells, which starred for the first time together Charles Laughton and Elsa Lanchester. Although he continued to live at this pace for the next thirty years, Montagu never quite fulfilled the promise of this tumultuous beginning to his career.

Montagu's first visits to the USSR confirmed his early enthusiasm for Soviet-style socialism, and he moved from the Fabian Society and the British Socialist Party into the British Communist Party, on whose behalf he spoke and wrote vividly. This move and his marriage in January 1927 to a secretary, Eileen Hellstern (affectionately known as 'Hell'), the daughter of a south London bootmaker (Francis Anton Hellstern), completed the abandonment of the patrician life, Liberal politics, and Jewish orthodoxy of his family background. Until they died within a month of each other in 1984, Ivor and Hell were inseparable partners, together with Hell's daughter Rowna. There were no children of the marriage.

On a visit to Switzerland in 1929 Montagu was captivated by the Russian film director Sergey Eisenstein. He travelled to Hollywood and prepared the way for a contract for Eisenstein to work on a film at the Paramount studios. Eisenstein arrived with his assistant Aleksandrov and the cameraman Tisse, and moved into a house with the Montagus, where Ivor Montagu acted as manager, script writer, mentor, and disciple, as recorded in his book *With Eisenstein in Hollywood* (1968). After six confused months Paramount terminated the contract. Montagu disagreed with Eisenstein's plans to film in Mexico, and the two men parted company, friends but no longer partners, with their great projects 'Sutter's Gold' and 'An American Tragedy' unmade.

On his return to Britain, Montagu began the move from film to a mixture of film and political activity that led later to his main concentration on politics and writing. He was a founder member of the film trade union the Association of Cine Technicians in 1933. He also campaigned against the system of film censorship which operated in Britain, criticizing its political role. In the early 1930s he helped establish a progressive film institute, which played an important role in distributing Soviet films in Britain.

In addition Montagu worked as an associate producer for Michael Balcon on five of Hitchcock's British feature films of the 1930s, including *The Man Who Knew Too Much* (1934) and *The 39 Steps* (1935). He also produced the left-wing documentary films *Free Thälmann* (1935), *In Defence of Madrid* (1938), *Spanish ABC* (1938), and *Behind the Spanish Lines* (1938), after a visit to the Spanish republican front. *Peace and Plenty* was a brilliantly satirical attack on the Chamberlain government made in 1939 for the Communist Party.

During the Second World War, Montagu was on the editorial staff of the *Daily Worker*, an adviser to the Soviet Film Agency, and producer of a film for the central office of information, *Man, One Family* (1946) on the theme of racial harmony. A short post-war reunion with Balcon at Ealing Studios, where he co-wrote *Scott of the Antarctic* (1948), was almost the end of his association with commercial cinema. After the Wrocław peace conference in 1949 he was caught up in the peace movement, as a writer and speaker, travelling extensively in communist Europe, China, and Mongolia (for which he had a special affection). Montagu remained steadfast to the Communist Party to the end. He was awarded the Lenin peace prize in 1959, many other socialist decorations, and was a tireless, colourful dignitary at conferences and film festivals in eastern Europe.

In the late 1960s Montagu gave up active office in many of the organizations he had supported, even established, such as the International Table Tennis Association, the Association of Cine and Television Technicians, and the World Council of Peace, but he stayed in the wings as a respected elder statesman. From his home in Watford and his retreat in Orkney he translated plays, novels, and works by 'new wave' Soviet film-makers such as Andrey Tarkovsky. He helped launch Eisenstein's *Ivan the Terrible* (part 2) when it appeared belatedly in 1957–8 (after Khrushchov's 'secret speech'). In addition Montagu wrote political pamphlets and produced his own major books, *Film World* (1964), *With Eisenstein in Hollywood* (1968), and *The Youngest Son* (1970). Unfortunately these autobiographical sketches about his family and intellectual adventures up to the late 1920s were never complemented by a second volume of autobiography, which he worked on up to his death.

Montagu listed his recreations in *Who's Who* as 'washing up, pottering about, sleeping through television', modest occupations for a man who had started life with so many social and intellectual advantages. He did 'potter about' in a wide range of activities but always with a passionate energy and often with striking effect. A tall, strongly built man, Montagu dressed carelessly but distinctively, often in a shaggy pullover, buried beneath the long black leather overcoat he had picked up in Mongolia. He played tennis with more energy and craft than skill at Cambridge, the Queen's Club, and in Hollywood with Eisenstein and Charles Chaplin. His causes included cricket (he was a member of the MCC and Hampshire County Cricket Club) as well as communism, and Southampton United Football Club as well as the Zoological Society of London. With his friends in all social classes he communicated vividly in many languages and endlessly over the telephone from Watford, Orkney, Moscow, or Beijing (Peking). He died in Watford on 5 November 1984, shortly after his wife.   D. J. WENDEN, *rev.* SARAH STREET

James Montagu (1568–1618), by unknown artist

Sources I. Montagu, *The youngest son* (1970) · I. Montagu, 'The Film Society', *Sight and Sound*, 44 (1974–5), 220–24 · I. Montagu, *Film world* (1964) · I. Montagu, *With Eisenstein in Hollywood* (1968) · *WW* · Burke, *Peerage* (1980) · D. Macpherson and P. Willemen, *Traditions of independence: British cinema in the thirties* (1980) · *CGPLA Eng. & Wales* (1985)

Archives BFI, corresp. and papers relating to his career in the cinema · Labour History Archive and Study Centre, Manchester, corresp. and papers, mainly relating to his political activities | BFI, Film Society collection | FILM BFI NFTVA, 'Before hindsight — Ivor Montagu interview', 1977 · BFI NFTVA, 'Ivor Montagu interview', 1980 · BFI NFTVA, performance footage

Wealth at death £137,138: probate, 12 April 1985, *CGPLA Eng. & Wales*

Montagu, James (1568–1618), bishop of Winchester, was born at Boughton, Northamptonshire, the fifth son of Sir Edward Montagu (*c.*1532–1602) and his wife, Elizabeth, daughter of Sir James Harington of Exton and his wife, Lucy Sidney. Edward *Montagu, first Baron Montagu (1562/3–1644), and Henry *Montagu (*c.*1564–1642) were his elder brothers. His family connections with the Sidney circle strongly influenced Montagu's career at university, court, and in the church. He matriculated a fellow-commoner at Christ's College, Cambridge, in June 1585. Montagu's great-aunt, Frances Radcliffe (*née* Sidney), countess of Sussex (1531–1589), provided in her will for the foundation of Sidney Sussex College, Cambridge. Her principal executors, Montagu's grandfather Harington and Henry Grey, earl of Kent, chose Montagu as the first master after securing the cautious approval of the vice-chancellor and other heads for such a young master. He laid the foundation-stone in May 1595, and meticulously oversaw the building works until their completion in 1602. He served as master from 1596 to 1608, during which time the college earned a reputation for puritanism. He was created DD 'by special grace' in 1598, and never held a parochial living.

Upon the accession of James I and VI, Montagu was swiftly preferred first to a royal chaplaincy (between April and July 1603, formally sworn 23 December), and then to the deanery of the Chapel Royal. The chapel deanery had lapsed under Elizabeth, but was revived by Archbishop John Whitgift and Bishop Richard Bancroft in 1603 as a safeguard against Scottish presbyterian influence in James's English court. Though without any prior court service, Montagu probably appealed as a mediator between ecclesiological extremes: he had strong Calvinist credentials and was sympathetic to those of godly conscience, but yet committed to episcopacy and the royal prerogative over church discipline. As such, Montagu was the epitome of mainstream Jacobean conformist Calvinism. His intimacy and favour with the new king was immediate and lifelong. He attended the king constantly, and no cleric had more direct personal contact with James than Montagu; Francis Bacon judged him one of the three most influential servants in the king's household. This intimacy might be seen as part of James's revival of the Essex circle's fortunes, which included the appointment of Montagu's uncle John Harington, first Baron Harington, as guardian of Princess Elizabeth, and the prominence at court of Montagu's first cousins, Lucy Russell, countess of Bedford, and her brother John Harington.

Montagu was an effective dean of the Chapel Royal. He was sworn dean on Christmas day 1603 in the vestry at Hampton Court, the marginal gloss in the minute book providing the only record of his familiar name: 'Bertie Mountague sworne Deane of the Chapell' (Ashbee and Harley, 1.82). In his first year as dean he issued orders for the election and attendance of the gentlemen and children of the chapel, and for the appointment of music for services, and persuaded a royal commission to augment all chapel wages by a third, the first increase since Henry VIII's reign. As dean he presided or assisted at the baptism of the princesses Mary and Sophia (1605, 1606), and Queen Anne's churchings thereafter, as well as at the confirmations of the surviving royal children, Henry (1607), Elizabeth (1610), and Charles (1613), and preached at the marriage of Elizabeth to the elector palatine (1613). The chapel 'cheque books' show Montagu's continued routine involvement with the business of the chapel to within a year of his death.

However, Montagu also used his court position to further puritan interests in the church. Two near-disasters taught him that the king did not share his sympathies: in 1604 the puritan John Burgess was sent to the Tower for preaching before the king against ceremonies in a sermon arranged by Montagu as an audition for a chaplaincy to Prince Henry; in 1605 Montagu was openly accused of sympathizing with ministers deprived for ceremonial nonconformity. Yet he had already given signs that his personal preferences were otherwise. He had ordered that the surplice be worn in his college chapel for the first time in 1604, and spoken in favour of ceremonies at the Hampton Court conference.

In July 1603 Montagu had been instituted dean of Lichfield, with the prebendal stall of Brerewood, which he resigned upon presentation to the deanery of Worcester on 20 December 1604. In September 1606 James promised Montagu the next vacant bishopric, and doubled his chapel dean's annual stipend to £400. Bath and Wells fell vacant in February 1608, and Montagu accepted the king's offer of it, but begged not to be forced to surrender the chapel deanery. He offered instead to forfeit his stipend, the Worcester deanery, and his college mastership to ensure 'that I may not too suddenly be drawn from the breasts of so dear and precious a master' (Salisbury MSS, 20.86). This proposal was accepted. Montagu was consecrated at Lambeth by Bancroft on 17 April, 1608; the sermon (soon printed) was preached by the reconciled puritan, George Downame, Montagu's contemporary at Christ's. In spite of his court obligations Montagu was an assiduous bishop, immersing himself in diocesan administration during annual residence in his see from July to September. His only surviving visitation articles (1609) are notable for strict attention to excommunication, Sunday observance, and keeping 'holy' the anniversaries of the Gowry and Gunpowder plots. Montagu spent large private sums on roofing the nave of Bath Abbey, and restoring the chapel of the bishop's palace at Wells. On 3 July 1616 he was translated to Winchester. Remaining dean of the Chapel Royal, he continued the pattern of residence and service that he had established in his former see.

Later in the same year appeared Montagu's lavish folio edition of King James's *Workes*, a project he claimed, in the dedication to Prince Charles, was his brainchild; a Latin edition appeared posthumously in 1619. The long panegyrical preface is his only surviving original work. His influence at court remained strong. He accompanied James to Scotland in the summer of 1617, and was appointed to the privy council in October. He furthered the appointment of his brother Henry as lord chief justice (1616), and brother Sidney as master of requests (1618). At Christmastide 1617–18 he held a lavish entertainment to mark his restoration of Winchester House in Southwark. Active at court until March, by April he lay dangerously ill of dropsy. Samuel Daniel's fine verse epistle to him, first printed 1623, dates from this time.

Montagu died at Greenwich on the morning of 20 July 1618, attended by his brother, Sir Charles, who on the same day reported the death personally to the marquess of Buckingham and the king. In his will dated 1 April, Montagu remembered the king's favour as 'the greatest comforte of my life', and left him a gold cup of £100 value; to Buckingham, 'the most faithful friend that ever I had', he left a diamond ring. Montagu estimated in his will that he had already bestowed over £5000 on his episcopal properties; further bequests included rents and 'all my bookes' to Sidney Sussex College, and legacies to his brothers and servants. He also set aside £300 for 'a Monument in the bodye of the churche of Bathe' that would 'stirre up some more Benefactors to that place' (PRO, PROB 11/132, sig. 71, fols. 37–8). His executor, Sir Charles Montagu, commissioned the tomb, with canopied recumbent effigy of the bishop by William Cure and Nicholas Johnson, that stands in the nave of Bath Abbey. Montagu's bowels were buried in the chancel at Greenwich; after lying at Winchester House, his body was taken to Bath for burial in the abbey church on 20 August 1618. His death marked a turning-point in the influence of anti-Spanish Calvinism at court.   P. E. MCCULLOUGH

Sources K. Fincham, *Prelate as pastor: the episcopate of James I* (1990) • P. E. McCullough, *Sermons at court: politics and religion in Elizabethan and Jacobean preaching* (1998) [incl. CD-ROM] • A. Ashbee and J. Harley, eds., *The cheque books of the Chapel Royal*, 2 vols. (2000) • D. Beales and H. B. Nesbit, eds., *Sidney-Sussex College, Cambridge: historical essays* (1996) • E. P. Shirley, ed., 'Will, inventories, and funeral expenses of James Montagu', *Archaeologia*, 44 (1873), 398–421 • Calendar of the manuscripts of the most hon. the marquis of Salisbury, 24 vols., HMC, 9 (1883–1976) • Report on the manuscripts of his grace the duke of Buccleuch and Queensberry … preserved at Montagu House, 3 vols. in 4, HMC, 45 (1899–1926), vol. 1, pp. 202, 237, 239, 240–41,

252–3 · *Report on the manuscripts of the marquis of Downshire*, 6 vols. in 7, HMC, 75 (1924–95), vol. 6, pp.17–18, 300, 375 · *Calendar of the manuscripts of the dean and chapter of Wells*, 2, HMC, 12 (1914), 355–8, 362, 372 · K. Fincham, ed., *Visitation articles and injunctions of the early Stuart church*, 2 vols. (1994–8) · G. M. Edwards, *Sidney Sussex College* (1899) · S. Daniel, *Works* (1623), vol. 1, pp. 294–6 · will, PRO, PROB 11/132, sig. 71 · *The letters of John Chamberlain*, ed. N. E. McClure, 2 vols. (1939) · *The diary of John Manningham of the Middle Temple, 1602–1603*, ed. R. P. Sorlien (Hanover, NH, 1976) · BL, Stowe MS 76, fol. 244 B

Archives Bodl. Oxf., papers · Sidney Sussex College, Cambridge, his library | Northants. RO, letters to Edward Montagu · Sidney Sussex College, Cambridge, building accounts and corresp. relating to construction of Sidney Sussex College, box 1

Likenesses oils, *c*.1616; Christies, 28 June 1946, no. 89 · S. de Passe, line engraving, 1617, BM, NPG · W. Cure & N. Johnson, marble recumbent effigy on monument, Bath Abbey · Passe, line engraving, BM, NPG; repro. in Holland, *Herōologia* (1620) · line engraving (after Passe), BM, NPG; repro. in Boissard, *Bibliotheca Chalcographica* (1650) · oils, Sidney Sussex College, Cambridge [*see illus.*] · oils, second version, bishop's palace, Wells

Wealth at death £3225 9s. 6d.: will, PRO, PROB 11/132, sig. 71

Montagu, Sir James (1666–1723), politician and judge, was born on 2 February 1666, the seventh (but fifth surviving) son of the Hon. George Montagu (*bap.* 1622, *d.* 1681) of Horton, Northamptonshire, and his wife, Elizabeth, daughter of Sir Anthony Irby of Whaplode, Lincolnshire. Montagu's father was half-brother to the second earl of Manchester, the parliamentarian general. After being admitted to Trinity College, Cambridge, and the Middle Temple in 1683, Montagu chose the law as his profession, being called to the bar in 1689. In 1698 he proceeded MA at Cambridge.

His first official post, in 1694, was as secretary to his elder brother Charles *Montagu, earl of Halifax (1661–1715), then chancellor of the exchequer. On 6 October 1694 he married Tufton (*bap.* 1663, *d.* 1712), daughter of Sir William Wray, first baronet, of Ashby, Lincolnshire. The following year he was elected to parliament for Tregony. Not surprisingly he followed the lead of his brother, becoming a loyal supporter of the whig junto. Clearly an able lawyer, he was counsel of Cambridge University by 1698, and chief justice of Ely the same year. After losing the 1698 election he soon returned to the Commons at a by-election for Bere Alston, but was unable to find a seat in 1701. However, Montagu proved just as useful to the whigs outside the Commons, his legal talents being put to good use in the defence of the party cause. In November 1701 he acted for the Kentish petitioner David Polhill in the court of king's bench, and in 1704 he successfully defended John Tutchin for a libel published in *The Observator*. More famously, he was committed to the custody of the serjeant-at-arms of the Commons on 26 February 1705 for committing a breach of privilege in acting for the Aylesbury men in the *Ashby* v. *White* case.

With the revival of whig fortunes in 1705 Montagu re-emerged into favour, receiving a knighthood on 16 April when the queen visited Cambridge University. The following month he re-entered the Commons for Carlisle, and on 5 November became a QC. On 25 April 1707 Montagu was appointed solicitor-general, and promoted to attorney-general on 21 October 1708. As such he opened

the case against Dr Sacheverell on 27 February 1710. When the tories returned to power later in 1710 he was compensated for the loss of his office with a royal pension of £1000 p.a. He retained his seat in parliament, continued to support the whigs, and contributed to Kit-Cat Club activities. After his wife died in 1712 he married, on 6 October 1713, Lady Elizabeth Montagu (1665–1730/1735), the daughter of Robert, third earl of Manchester. They had a son, Charles Montagu, later MP for St Albans.

On the Hanoverian succession Montagu was made a baron of the exchequer (20 November 1714), being used in April and May 1718 as a stopgap commissioner of the privy seal following the resignation of Lord Chancellor Cowper. On 8 May 1722 he was advanced to the position of chief baron of the exchequer, which he held until his death on 30 October 1723 at Lincoln's Inn Fields, London.

STUART HANDLEY

Sources HoP, *Commons* · Foss, *Judges*, 8.43 · Sainty, *Judges*, 97, 128 · Sainty, *King's counsel*, 64, 90 · A. Boyer, *The political state of Great Britain*, 1 (1711) · IGI · Venn, *Alum. Cant.*

Likenesses G. Vertue, oils, 1722 (after G. Kneller), BM, NPG

Montagu, James (1752–1794), naval officer, was born on 12 August 1752, the third son of Admiral John *Montagu (1718/19–1795) and Sophia, daughter of James Wroughton of Wilcot, Wiltshire, and the brother of Admiral George *Montagu and Edward *Montagu (1755–1799), army officer. Following eight years at sea (or, at least, on the muster books), rated as able seaman and midshipman in the *Dragon*, *Launceston*, *Bellona*, and *Alarm*, he passed his lieutenant's examination on the *Captain* at Boston on 17 August 1771; next day his father appointed him lieutenant of the *Mercury* (24 guns). On 11 September 1773 he was given command of the sloop *Tamar*. In her, and afterwards in the *Kingfisher*, he continued on the North American station, and on 14 November 1775 he returned to the *Mercury* as her captain.

In December 1776 Montagu was sent to England with the dispatches announcing the capture of Rhode Island by Sir Peter Parker and General Clinton. He then returned to North America; but on 24 December 1777, coming down the Hudson River, the *Mercury* struck on a hulk which the enemy had sunk in the fairway, and was wrecked. Montagu was acquitted of all blame by a court martial at New York, and in July 1778 he was appointed to the frigate *Medea* (28 guns), which he commanded for the next two years. On 20 October 1778, cruising off Finisterre in company with the *Jupiter* (50 guns), he encountered the French *Triton* (64 guns), which escaped in darkness after a fierce two-hour engagement.

In October 1780 Montagu moved to the *Juno*, and in February 1782 he sailed with Sir Richard Bickerton for the East Indies. The *Juno* arrived at Bombay in August 1782, and on 20 June 1783 was present at the action off Cuddalore, the last between Sir Edward Hughes and the *bailli* de Suffren. Montagu returned to England at the beginning of 1785, and being unable to obtain further employment afloat he went, in October 1786, to France on a year's leave.

In October 1787 Montagu was back in England, but had

no employment until the outbreak of the French Revolutionary War, when at his own request—apparently on account of the ship's name—he was appointed to the *Montagu* (74 guns), one of the Grand Fleet under Lord Howe during the campaigns of 1793 and 1794. Montagu was killed in her, off Ushant, at the battle of 1 June, in 1794.

J. K. LAUGHTON, *rev.* RANDOLPH COCK

Sources commission and warrant books, PRO, ADM 6/20, 21, 22 · lieutenant's passing cert., PRO, ADM 6/87 · W. L. Clowes, *The Royal Navy: a history from the earliest times to the present*, 7 vols. (1897–1903) · W. James, *The naval history of Great Britain, from the declaration of war by France, in February 1793, to the accession of George IV in January 1820*, 5 vols. (1822–4)
Likenesses Bartolozzi, Landseer, Ryder & Stow, line engraving, pubd 1803 (*Commemoration of the victory of June 1st 1794*; after R. Smirke) · H. R. Cook, stipple, pubd 1805 (after statue on monument by Maynard), BM · J. Bacon, ink drawing (design for monument), BM · J. Flaxman, statue on monument, Westminster Abbey

Montagu [Montacute], **John**, **third earl of Salisbury** (*c*.1350–1400), magnate and courtier, was the son and heir of John, first Lord Montagu (*d*. 1390), and nephew of William *Montagu, second earl of Salisbury (*d*. 1397). His mother, Margaret (*d*. 1395), was the daughter and heir of Thomas, Lord Monthermer. Between 2 November 1381 and 4 May 1383 the younger John Montagu married Maud (*d*. 1424) [*see* Montagu, Maud, countess of Salisbury], daughter of Adam *Fraunceys, former mayor of London, from whom she inherited Middlesex properties; Maud was the widow of the London alderman Andrew Aubrey, and of the recently deceased king's knight Alan Buxhull, from whose inheritances she held dower in, respectively, Hertfordshire and Essex, and Dorset and Sussex. In 1369, when war broke out again with France, Montagu was probably on the small expedition that Edward III's son Edmund of Langley, earl of Cambridge, and the earl of Pembroke took to Aquitaine to reinforce the prince of Wales. Montagu distinguished himself in the siege and capture of Bourdeilles in Périgord, and was knighted there by Langley. In 1370 Montagu was on the expedition led by Langley and Pembroke that attempted to relieve Belleperche in the Bourbonnais, and there first displayed his banner. His father was steward of the royal household from 1381 to 1387, and this must have eased Montagu's subsequent passage from a military to a courtly career. In or before 1383 he was appointed a king's knight.

Under the year 1387 the St Albans chronicler Thomas Walsingham accuses Montagu of being the leading knightly patron of Lollards, citing such evidence of heterodox activity at his house in Shenley, Hertfordshire, as the presence there of Wyclif's Oxford disciple Nicholas Hereford, and Montagu's removal from the chapel of sacred images placed there by Aubrey, Buxhull, and other previous owners, and then his casual disposal of them. Walsingham is the sole contemporary accuser of Montagu; but he is persistent in his allegations, and has the advantage of local knowledge. In 1391 Montagu was indeed behaving in a notably orthodox manner, by obtaining a licence to go on crusade to Prussia, but, as others among the so-called *Lollard knights also went on crusade

at about this time, it may be that their expeditions should be regarded as moved less by spiritual conformity than by a shared militant asceticism, by a readiness to fight for the love of God which could be justified by reference to Wyclif's teaching. In 1394 Montagu went on Richard's first Irish expedition, but returned before the main force, since Walsingham says that he was one of the four knights who presented a bill in favour of Lollard views to the parliament that met in January 1395, and that the king, after his return, berated them soundly. Although the death of his father, on 25 January 1390, led to Montagu's succeeding to the former's peerage title, until after Montagu inherited his uncle's earldom in 1397 Richard showed him no favours, and may, indeed, have had well-founded doubts about his usefulness. His early military promise appears to have faded. In 1397 he gave up an important inherited role in the defence of the realm by selling the castle and lordship of Wark-on-Tweed on the Scottish border to Ralph Neville. Richard may have suspected his links with Thomas of Woodstock, duke of Gloucester: in the parliament of 1399 Thomas, Lord Morley, alleged that he had been the duke's chief counsellor, and had betrayed his trust; Montagu denied having revealed his counsel. Gloucester and Montagu had some interests in common. Not only was the former interested in Lollard doctrine, but in his youth he had formed a company to celebrate the coming of May, which suggests that he would have appreciated Montagu's courtly accomplishments. Christine de Pisan, who met Montagu in Paris in 1398, praised him as a lover of poetry, and as a fine poet himself. She sent her son, thirteen-year-old Jean de Castel, to be educated in Montagu's household, with his son Thomas. The French squire Jean Creton joined Montagu's retinue in 1399 because of his courtly reputation. Clearly, rumours of Montagu's Lollardy had not reached Paris.

William Montagu died on 25 February 1397, and his nephew inherited the earldom of Salisbury, a large inheritance whose nucleus was in the west country. John Montagu now emerged as a leading royal partisan, probably in the hope of recovering parts of the impressive inheritance that his uncle had either lost or sold. At Nottingham on 5 August 1397 he agreed, with seven other lords, to appeal the duke of Gloucester and the earls of Arundel and Warwick of treason in parliament. On 24 September he petitioned in parliament to be allowed to sue the earl of March for the lordship of Denbigh, which Edward III had forced his uncle to relinquish in 1354. Richard granted him permission to sue for a writ. According to Henry Bolingbroke, in his accusations against Thomas (I) Mowbray in 1398, Salisbury was one of the royal favourites whom Mowbray in December accused of plotting the destruction of Bolingbroke and his father, John of Gaunt, duke of Lancaster. Indeed, Salisbury did have a family motive for hostility towards the Lancastrians: in 1365 his uncle had been obliged to give up to Gaunt the former Lancastrian lordships of Trowbridge and Aldbourne, Wiltshire. In January 1398 Salisbury was one of the commissioners appointed to terminate parliamentary business, and in September was made marshal of the realm for three years. In December he was commissioned to go to Paris to receive dower for Richard's queen, Isabella. The king also wished him to scotch the rumoured negotiations for a match between the exiled Bolingbroke and the duke of Berri's daughter, Marie. This Salisbury succeeded in doing, but at the cost of infuriating Bolingbroke, whom he refused to meet—and whose lordships of Trowbridge and Aldbourne were put in his keeping on 22 March 1399. In that month he was appointed to negotiate with the Scots, and in May he accompanied the king on his second Irish expedition.

After news reached Richard at Dublin of Bolingbroke's landing in England, he dispatched Salisbury with a small retinue on about 17 June to rally support in north Wales and the principality of Chester—the earl was appointed steward of the latter by July. In the face of Bolingbroke's successful advance through the marches, Salisbury signally failed to keep his levies together, and retreated from Chester to Conwy Castle, where he was soon joined by Richard and a few companions, who had travelled via south Wales. Salisbury vainly advised the king to take ship to Bordeaux—sensible advice, since it was a centre of anti-Lancastrian feeling. He loyally accompanied the king to meet Bolingbroke at Flint, where the latter refused to speak to him, and made him a prisoner. Summoned to Henry IV's first parliament, he was accused with other lords for their part in the prosecutions of 1397. Salisbury was sent to the Tower of London on 20 October, and tried before parliament with the others on the 29th. He pleaded that he had acted through fear, but he was not sentenced, because Lord Morley challenged him to combat for complicity in Gloucester's death.

Released from the Tower on surety, in December 1399, Salisbury plotted with Richard's kinsmen—John Holland, earl of Huntingdon, the latter's nephew Thomas Holland, earl of Kent, and Edward, earl of Rutland—to seize Henry IV and restore Richard. The plot misfired—Salisbury and Kent retreated westwards from Windsor, probably hoping to make their way to the Ricardian stronghold of Cheshire, but on 6 January were seized by the townsfolk of Cirencester, and lodged in the abbey there. Fear that they might be rescued caused the townspeople to take them out and execute them, probably on 8 January. Walsingham, persisting in his view of Salisbury as an incorrigible heretic, says that he refused the last rites. This contrasts with the care the earl had taken, presumably in anticipation of hazardous travels, to secure papal indults, dated 23 January 1399, to choose his own confessor, have a portable altar, and have mass celebrated before daybreak. The canons of Cirencester allowed him burial within their church, but in 1420 his widow was licensed to transfer the remains to his family's place of burial, Bisham Abbey, Berkshire. Although Salisbury was attainted in the parliament of March 1401, his elder son, Thomas *Montagu, was subsequently able to succeed both to the earldom and to his father's entailed estates. ANTHONY GOODMAN

Sources Chancery records · GEC, Peerage, new edn, 11.391–3 · CEPR letters, vol. 5 · [J. Creton], 'Translation of a French metrical history of the deposition of King Richard the Second … with a copy of the original', ed. and trans. J. Webb, Archaeologia, 20 (1824), 1–423 · Chroniques de J. Froissart, ed. S. Luce and others, 7 (Paris, 1878) · Johannis de Trokelowe et Henrici de Blaneforde … chronica et annales, ed. H. T. Riley, pt 3 of Chronica monasterii S. Albani, Rolls Series, 28 (1866) · Thomae Walsingham, quondam monachi S. Albani, historia Anglicana, ed. H. T. Riley, 2 vols., pt 1 of Chronica monasterii S. Albani, Rolls Series, 28 (1863–4), vol. 2 · RotP, vol. 3 · K. B. McFarlane, Lancastrian kings and Lollard knights (1972) · R. Delachenal, Histoire de Charles V, 4 (Paris, 1928) · G. A. Holmes, The estates of the higher nobility in fourteenth-century England (1957) · J. C. Laidlaw, 'Christine de Pizan, the earl of Salisbury and Henry IV', French Studies, 36 (1982), 129–43 · The chronicle of Adam Usk, 1377–1421, ed. and trans. C. Given-Wilson, OMT (1997) · C. Tyerman, England and the crusades, 1095–1588 (1988)

Montagu [Mountagu], **John** (1654/5–1728), college head and dean of Durham, was the son of Edward *Montagu (or Mountagu), first earl of Sandwich (1625–1672), and his wife, Jemimah (1625–1674), eldest daughter of John *Crew, first Baron Crew of Steane. He and his father spelt their name Mountagu, though the family later settled on the form Montagu. John Montagu was the fourth son in a family of six sons and four daughters, and had a twin, Oliver. The twins went to school initially at Huntingdon grammar school, from where the twelve-year-olds were summoned one afternoon in October 1667 to be examined by family friend Samuel Pepys. He found them 'but little, and very like one another; and well-looked children'. Pepys was deeply impressed by how advanced they were in their Latin and Greek, 'and so grave and manly as I never saw, I confess, nor could have believed—so that they will be fit to go to Cambridge in two years at most' (Pepys, 8.472). In fact it was five years later, after further education at Westminster School, that John was admitted fellow-commoner at Trinity College, Cambridge, on 12 April 1672. He proceeded MA jure natalium in 1673 and was elected fellow of the college on 2 October 1674. He was ordained priest on 21 December 1679. There followed two preferments in the gift of his uncle Nathaniel Crew, third Baron Crew of Steane and bishop of Durham: in 1680 he was made master of Sherburn Hospital, and in 1683 a prebendary of Durham Cathedral. On 12 May of the latter year he was made master of his college, and DD on 27 September 1686, both by royal mandate. He served as vice-chancellor of the university in 1687–8, a tenure that called on him to contribute to the university's publication of commemorative Latin poems on two rather different royal occasions: the birth of James Francis Edward, the first son of James II, and the accession of William and Mary. These were to remain his only publications. He was appointed clerk of the royal closet in 1695, due to the efforts of Archbishop Tenison. He ended his otherwise uneventful career at Cambridge late in 1699, resigning his mastership to become dean of Durham.

Assessments of Montagu's mastership at Trinity vary from 'amiable' and 'open-handed' (White, 114, 124) to having 'enjoyed an ill repute' (Manuel, 102–3), depending on the degree to which Montagu was used to set in relief his successor, Richard Bentley. It is certainly true that college records indicate a somewhat distant relation to its affairs, especially after 1695. But Montagu's compliance to royal mandates for fellowships during James's reign, apparently his principal failing, was scarcely imprudent, and indeed was the invariable practice at Cambridge during those years in particular, and almost without contrary precedent generally. In the university's passage through the revolution of 1688, there were distinct advantages for Cambridge in having an 'amiable' vice-chancellor and master of its wealthiest college.

Although Montagu does not appear to have been particularly active in the building of the college's Wren Library, he donated several French and Latin historical works, subscribed £228, and seems graciously to have parted with a further £170 due to him upon leaving the college, but claimed by Bentley for furnishing the master's lodge. In 1720 he further aided Bentley in lending him manuscripts from the chapter library at Durham for his projected edition of the New Testament. Montagu is recognized by his college in the display of his coat of arms on the vaulted ceiling of the main staircase leading to the library, along with those of the other masters during whose mastership the library came into being, Isaac Barrow and John North. His portrait, hung in the dining room of the master's lodge, Trinity College, Cambridge, shows him as being of medium stature, clean shaven with brown curly hair, and dressed in black gown with broad bands.

The Spalding Gentlemen's Society welcomed Montagu as a member on 22 August 1723. He died, unmarried, at his house in Bedford Row, Holborn, London, on 23 February 1728 and was buried at Barnwell, Northamptonshire, his family's burying-place. Montagu's career of academic and ecclesiastical preferment, marked as it was by a conspicuous absence of visible signs of either incident or industry, nevertheless is of interest in that it involved the courts of three very different monarchs and the patronage of two very different bishops (the notoriously negligent Crew and the conscientious Tenison). If nothing else, his career illustrates how lines of patronage could cross over historians' subsequent ecclesiastical and political boundaries.

IAN G. STEWART

Sources *DNB* · conclusions book, 1646–1811, Trinity Cam. · admissions and admonitions, 1560–1759, Trinity Cam. · Venn, *Alum. Cant.* · J. Gascoigne, *Cambridge in the age of the Enlightenment* (1989) · J. Twigg, *The University of Cambridge and the English Revolution, 1625–1688* (1990) · R. J. White, *Dr Bentley: a study in academic scarlet* (1965) · F. E. Manuel, *A portrait of Isaac Newton* (1968) · H. M. Wood, ed., *Registers of Sherburn Hospital* (1914) · *VCH Berkshire* · C. H. Cooper and J. W. Cooper, *Annals of Cambridge*, 5 vols. (1842–1908) · Pepys, *Diary* · GEC, *Peerage*

Likenesses oils, Trinity Cam.

Montagu, John, second duke of Montagu (1690–1749), courtier, was born on 29 March 1690 at Boughton, Northamptonshire, and baptized on 11 April at Weekley. He was the third and youngest but only surviving son and heir of Ralph *Montagu, first duke of Montagu (*bap.* 1638, *d.* 1709), diplomatist, and his first wife, Elizabeth, countess of Northumberland (1649?–1690), the daughter of Thomas Wriothesley, fourth earl of Southampton, and the widow of Joceline Percy, eleventh earl of Northumberland. Upon the death of his brother Windwood in May

1702 he was styled Lord Monthermer. In 1709 he succeeded his father as second duke of Montagu.

There is little known about Montagu's education in the formative years, but it is known that Pierre Sylvestre, later physician to William III, became his tutor in 1702, and accompanied him on a tour through France and Italy. He married, on 20 March 1705, Mary (1689–1751), the fourth and youngest daughter and coheir of John *Churchill, first duke of Marlborough, and Sarah *Churchill, duchess of Marlborough. The couple had two sons, both of whom died at a young age, and three daughters, one of whom died in infancy. Montagu volunteered in the spring of 1706 for Flanders with Marlborough, but soon returned home, for he had little taste for war's carnage. In 1709 he assumed the office of the master of the great wardrobe, an office once his father's, which honour he held until his death. He officiated as lord high constable at the coronation of George I on 20 October 1714, and served as colonel of the 1st troop of Horse Guards (1st Life Guards) from 1715 to 1721 and as master forester and warden of Rockingham and lord lieutenant of Northamptonshire and Warwickshire from 1715 until his death.

A fair scholar, Montagu liked to be considered erudite, and was well pleased at being made a fellow of the Royal Society and admitted doctor of physic at Cambridge in 1717. That same year, at his own request, he was made a fellow of the Royal College of Physicians, and he often attended the Harverian lectures and banquets. On 31 March 1718 he was nominated a knight of the Garter, and was installed on 30 April. In 1721–2 he functioned as grand master of the grand lodge of England freemasons. On 22 June 1722 he obtained a grant of the islands of St Lucia and St Vincent, in the West Indies, and was appointed governor and captain-general and attempted to settle these islands. However, his endeavours were thwarted both by the failure of the British fleet to support the undertaking and by the opposition of the French on the grounds that the islands were by treaty to be neutral. It is said that Montagu lost a rather large sum of money, over £40,000, in this vain attempt to colonize.

New honours awaited the duke, whose whig credentials made him a suitable recipient of government patronage. On 27 May 1725 he was created a knight of the Bath, being grand master of that order, and on 11 October 1727 he was appointed bearer of the sceptre with cross at the coronation of George II. He was governor of the Isle of Wight (1733–4), captain of the gentlemen pensioners (1734–40), a member of the privy council (1735), master-general of the ordnance (1740–41, 1742–9), and one of the lords justices (regents) of the realm (1745, 1748). In 1735 he was appointed major-general in the army, in 1739 lieutenant-general, and in 1740 colonel of the 3rd cavalry regiment (later 2nd dragoon guards, or Queen's Bays). In 1745 he was promoted to the rank of general, and in the same year he raised a cavalry regiment of horse called the Montagu carabiniers and a regiment of 'ordnance foot', both of which were disbanded after the battle of Culloden.

The duke seems by all accounts to have been a kindhearted and benevolent man. Evidence of this may be seen in his funding of the education at Cambridge of the Jamaican slave Francis Williams and patronage of the young Ignatius Sancho. He was at the same time of a whimsical, fun-loving bent and was said to have been puckish and eccentric from birth. Still, he was essentially a man of noble nature to whom any form of suffering was abhorrent, and was thus highly esteemed for his great charity and his pleasant company was sought after. However, his mother-in-law, Sarah, duchess of Marlborough, was rather hard on him and did not appreciate his sense of humour. She considered that he was immature and reserved his enthusiasm for infantile enterprises. In part she was correct. He seems to have believed that the quest for happiness was the main purpose of life and that the struggle for wealth, honours, fame, and power simply destroyed a more generous nature. With this as his guiding principle he became a lover of the practical joke and a creator of hoaxes (for example, the hoax of a man squeezing himself into a quart bottle at the Haymarket Theatre, January 1749), and thus was considered rather frivolous. He was a man of many parts: philanthropist, a patron of the opera and drama, the protector of freemasonry, and the proponent of a gentler way of life, all hidden under a devil-may-care attitude and style of life.

The duke's country home, Boughton House, which later passed to the Buccleuch family, was originally laid out by his father in the style of Versailles. He later had a direct and extensive hand in the expansion of the gardens and as a result is often referred to as the Planter. His town residence, Montagu House, became the site of the British Museum and opened to the public in 1759. Montagu died, aged fifty-nine, of a violent fever (pneumonia) at another London house, in Privy Gardens, Whitehall, on 6 July 1749 and was buried on 20 July at Warkton, Northamptonshire. He was survived by his wife, who died on 14 May 1751, and his two daughters. Isabella (*d.* 1786) married, first, William, duke of Manchester, and secondly Edward Hussey, earl of Beaulieu. Mary (*d.* 1775) married George Brudenell, earl of Cardigan, who after the death of his father-in-law was created marquess of Monthermer and duke of Montagu. Under her father's will Mary was made heir to all his estates.   EDWARD CHARLES METZGER

Sources GEC, *Peerage* · B. Burke, *A genealogical history of the dormant, abeyant, forfeited, and extinct peerages of the British empire*, new edn (1883); repr. (1978) · Boughton House, Northamptonshire, Buccleuch MSS · BL, Add. MSS 61450 and 61451 · G. S. Thomson, *The Russells in Bloomsbury, 1669–1771* (1940) · *The letters of St Evremond*, ed. J. Hayward (1930) · B. Falk, *The way of the Montagues* (1947) · M. Petherick, *Restoration rogues* (1951) · L. Baillie and P. Sieveking, eds., *British biographical archive* (1984) [microfiche] · J. Redington, ed., *Calendar of Treasury papers*, 6 vols., PRO (1868–89) · J. Redington and R. A. Roberts, eds., *Calendar of home office papers of the reign of George III*, 1: *1760–1765*, PRO (1878) · J. Cornforth, 'The making of the Boughton landscape', *Country Life*, 149 (1971), 536–9 · DNB

Archives Northants. RO, corresp.; corresp. mainly with his steward | BL, Marlborough collection, Add. MSS 61450–61451 · Boughton House, Northamptonshire, Buccleuch MSS · CUL, letters to Sir Robert Walpole · U. Nott. L., letters to Henry Pelham and letters as master-general of the ordnance

Likenesses G. Kneller, oils, 1699, Boughton House, Northamptonshire · G. Kneller, oils, 1709 (*Kit-Cat Club*), NPG · attrib. J. Verelst, group portrait, oils, 1712, NPG · G. Kneller, oils, 1715, Petworth House, Sussex · M. Dahl, oils, 1716, Beaulieu Abbey, Hants · attrib. C. Jervas, oils, 1720–29, Boughton House, Northamptonshire; version, Beaulieu Abbey, Hants · oils, 1740–49 (with Garter George), Boughton House, Northamptonshire · oils, 1740–49, Beaulieu Abbey, Hants · Shalk, oils, 1747, Buccleuch estates, Selkirk, Scotland · L. F. Roubiliac, medallion on monument, 1752, St Edmund's Church, Warkton, Northamptonshire; terracotta models, V&A, Westminster Abbey · J. A. Dassier, medal, BM · M. Laroon, group portrait, pen-and-ink (*Concert at Montagu House, 1736*), BM · J. Macardell, mezzotint (after T. Hudson), BM, NPG; version, Beaulieu Abbey, Hants · attrib. J. Verelst, oils (in his teens), probably Boughton House, Northamptonshire · oils (as a young man), Boughton House, Northamptonshire

Wealth at death wealthy; total income of £17,000: Falk, *Way of the Montagues*, 264, 286

Montagu, John, fourth earl of Sandwich (1718–1792), politician and musical patron, was born in London on 13 November 1718, the eldest son of Edward Richard Montagu, Viscount Hinchingbrooke (1692–1722), and his wife, Elizabeth Popham (*d.* 1761). His grandfather had been insane for some time before he died in 1729, leaving his ten-year-old grandson very little but the earldom. His widowed mother had already remarried and effectively abandoned her sons; John had boarded at Eton College since he was seven. There he displayed the ambition and ability which marked him all his life, leaving in 1735 with a classical education unusually complete for an eighteenth-century public schoolboy, and especially for a nobleman. After two years at Trinity College, Cambridge, he left for the continent, but not for a conventional grand tour. The following year he and a small group of friends sailed in a chartered ship for a tour of the Turkish empire, including numerous sites of Greek antiquity, several months in Constantinople (where Sandwich studied the language and customs of the country), and a visit to Egypt. He returned with a learned manuscript full of new information, and a collection of antiquities including what proved to be the oldest dated Greek inscription then known. This unusual and dangerous voyage made his reputation as a traveller, scholar, and orientalist. Soon after returning to England he married on 3 March 1741 the Hon. Dorothy Fane (1716/17–1797), sister of the British minister to Tuscany, whom he had met at Florence in 1737. She was the younger daughter of a minor Irish peer; neither brought much money to the marriage, which was evidently one of love rather than convenience, and they were admired as a model young couple, living modestly on a modest income. Their eldest surviving son John *Montagu was born in 1744.

Admiralty and diplomacy Meanwhile Sandwich had become part of the duke of Bedford's opposition whig group, and with his patron he joined the ministry in December 1744 as a member of the Admiralty board. Already keenly interested in the navy, Sandwich threw himself into his work with his usual ferocious energy. Since the duke preferred Woburn to his desk, most of the daily running of the Admiralty and navy fell on Sandwich as his deputy, and their colleague George Anson. This team was responsible for a series of important naval

John Montagu, fourth earl of Sandwich (1718–1792), by
Thomas Gainsborough, 1783

reforms, embracing tactics, training, discipline, strategy,
ship design and the management of the dockyards,
among other subjects. Anson took the lead in the strictly
professional subjects, but Sandwich was fully involved in
the development of the western squadron, the most
important strategic development of the century and the
key to British naval success. This was the more noteworthy since they were both working part-time, for in
summer Anson was usually at sea, and in the autumn of
1745 Sandwich briefly went on campaign as an officer of
the regiment Bedford raised for service against the Young
Pretender. Then in August 1746 Sandwich was sent to the
continent as British representative at the peace talks
opening at Breda, which two years later led to the peace of
Aix-la-Chapelle. He had no experience of diplomacy, and
his task was delicate as he was receiving contradictory
instructions from a divided ministry, only a minority of
which was seriously seeking peace. The restoration of the
Dutch stadholderate in April 1747, of which Sandwich was
a close observer if not promoter, seemed to boost the
chances of victory, but by the end of that year the war had
turned sharply against Britain and her allies. The ministry
now panicked, accusing Sandwich (with some justice) of
over-optimistic reports, and begging him to conclude a
peace at once on any terms. He kept his head, played a

weak hand with skill, and in the end secured a much better peace than anyone expected. Diplomats were
impressed: 'He has great coolness and great fire in him,
both subservient to great sense … he did not believe it was
possible for a young man, so new in affairs, to have acted
so thoroughly both like a man of business and parts. He
must be a great man' (G. S. H. Fox Strangways, ed., *Letters of
Henry Fox, Lord Holland*, 1915, 29).

Meanwhile, in February 1748, Sandwich had succeeded
Bedford as first lord of the Admiralty. He continued to
work closely with Anson, who acted for him in his absence
at Aix-la-Chapelle. In 1749, when they were both back at
the Admiralty, their reforming efforts reached a climax.
The death in March of the surveyor of the navy, Sir Jacob
Acworth, the dominant figure on the Navy Board,
removed a major obstacle to change, and in June the
Admiralty embarked on the simple but revolutionary procedure of a personal tour of the dockyards. There they
found ample evidence of mismanagement, and took the
opportunity to push Sandwich's favourite measure of
task-work (meaning piece-work). The visitation was followed by a stream of orders which the Navy Board
received with very little enthusiasm. Nor were Sandwich's
cabinet colleagues overjoyed by the energy with which he
argued for the navy estimates, and in June 1751 he was dismissed in a successful manoeuvre to force the resignation
of his patron, Bedford, as secretary of state. Anson succeeded him at the Admiralty, where he remained for most
of the next eleven years, advancing many of the reforms
for which they had worked together, but leaving the dockyards well alone.

Unemployment, diplomacy and music Sandwich remained
out of major office for twelve years. Unemployment did
not bring out the best in him, and his marriage was
already in difficulties, though his wife's developing insanity was not yet obvious. He does not appear to have been
much of a gambler, though it was the vice of the age, and
he continued to live frugally, but he began to acquire the
reputation of libertine which has never left him. Neither
religion nor fidelity were fashionable in his age and class,
and his discreet amours attracted no particular notice at
the time. Otherwise his boisterous energy was spent on
his favourite sport of cricket (of which he was an important early patron), on yachting, punting, and fishing. Amateur theatre was another enthusiasm, and with the help of
his friend David Garrick he mounted substantial productions at his house at Hinchingbrooke, outside Huntingdon.

Sandwich returned to major office in April 1763 as first
lord of the Admiralty again. He at once threw himself into
his old projects, notably of dockyard reform, but he had
hardly begun when in September he was removed to be
the junior secretary of state, responsible for relations
with the states of northern Europe. He conducted diplomatic business with skill, and contributed much to the
firmness with which the Grenville administration
deterred French aggression in the West Indies. A good deal

of his time was occupied, however, by a piece of domestic business inherited from his predecessor: the prosecution of John Wilkes, a young MP whose newspaper had accused George III of lying, to the king's fury. Wilkes was highly popular out of doors, the prosecution had been bungled, and the government position appeared weak, but with great political skill Sandwich exploited Wilkes's blasphemous private writings to discredit and ruin him. The episode restored Sandwich's reputation as a major politician of ruthless ability, but for the Wilkite opposition it made him into 'Jemmy Twitcher', the character in *The Beggar's Opera* who betrayed his friend. In fact it is very uncertain whether he and Wilkes, though certainly acquainted, had ever been close. They had both been involved in Sir Francis Dashwood's disreputable country club, the 'monks of Medmenham', but Wilkes had been expelled before Sandwich became a member.

Sandwich lost office again with the fall of Grenville in July 1765. He continued to hope for employment, but a clever and ruthless colleague was not wanted in the weak and unstable Chatham and Grafton ministries. In these years, however, his private life regained some of its equilibrium. Long parted from his wife, who was now completely insane, Sandwich took as his mistress about 1761 the seventeen-year-old Martha *Ray (d. 1779), with whom he lived contentedly for eighteen years in as near a regular married life as propriety permitted. They had five children, with whom Sandwich's relations were notably warmer than with his legitimate family. These years also saw a new flowering of another of Sandwich's interests, music. By 1767 the annual Christmas music meetings at Hinchingbrooke assembled sixty or seventy amateur performers with a stiffening of professionals, for an ambitious programme centred on the oratorios of Handel. In these performances Sandwich played the drums, and Martha Ray sang the soprano solos. From these meetings grew the Concert of Ancient Music, founded in 1776 by Sandwich and Sir Watkin Williams Wynn to preserve the music of the remote past, and above all the music of Handel, who had died in 1759 and (in an age when composers had not abandoned their public and all music was modern music) was already half forgotten. The Ancient Concerts were an outstanding success both socially and musically. They were managed by Sandwich's private secretary, Joah Bates, the young scholar and musician who was the outstanding Handelian of his generation.

The Admiralty and the American War of Independence Meanwhile the formation of Lord North's ministry in 1770 and the Falkland Islands crisis which immediately followed had given Sandwich a further chance in public life. Another poor nobleman who had risen on his abilities, but one who sat in the Commons during his father's lifetime, North could appreciate Sandwich's abilities without feeling threatened by his ambition. Briefly Sandwich replaced Lord Weymouth as secretary of state, but after three weeks, in January 1771, he was back at the Admiralty for the third time. At once he took up what he rightly

regarded as the great work of his life, the reform of the dockyards. The tardy mobilization of the previous year had recently underlined the long-term problems of which he was already well aware. The seagoing fleet had grown 65% in twenty years, but the capacity of the yards remained much the same as it had been in Queen Anne's time, and its distribution, mainly on the Thames and Medway, quite inadequate for the new strategic situation in which the main fleet operated in the western approaches. To meet this Lord Egmont, Sandwich's Admiralty colleague in the Grenville ministry, had planned to expand Portsmouth and Plymouth. This programme Sandwich inherited and vigorously pushed forward. He immediately revived the visitations of the dockyards which he had pioneered in 1749, and which none of his successors had imitated. There was, however, a significant difference of practice. Then the Admiralty had attacked a reactionary and obstructive Navy Board, with limited success. Now, with a new and more flexible generation at the Navy Board, Sandwich took a mixed party of both boards and enlisted the Navy Board's co-operation in his schemes.

At the heart of these were the linked problems of timber and shipbuilding. Sandwich understood what few of his contemporaries appreciated, that the size of the navy had long outpaced the capacity of the dockyards, and that far more ships were being built than could be maintained. The result was that much of the paper strength of the fleet could not be translated into reality on mobilization, and that expensive wartime new building took the place of economical peacetime repairs. These emergency wartime orders had to be given to private yards for want of dockyard capacity, and built of green timber for want of time to season, thus producing defective ships with short lives which made the problem worse. A large number of those built in this way during the Seven Years' War were decaying fast in the early 1770s. Sandwich's ambition was to increase the shipbuilding capacity and timber stocks of the dockyards to a level which would allow them to build every ship for the navy, slowly and carefully of seasoned timber, following a regular cycle of replacement which would provide the maximum strength for the minimum expense. Otherwise he could see no possibility of maintaining the needful naval power on any navy estimates parliament was likely to grant. His difficulty was that much time and money would be needed to reach this happy state. Even in the face of continuous pressure for economy from North, within three years of taking office he had achieved his target of timber stocks sufficient to allow everything to season properly before it was used. He had less success with increasing the number of building slips, and none with increasing the number of shipwrights to work on them. Moreover he bought time for these reforms by building some more ships in private yards, and allowing the nominal size of the fleet to fall slightly. In order to achieve his reforms Sandwich had to make better use of the existing dockyard workforce. He therefore revived his old scheme of task-work, which was introduced in the spring of 1775, in return for a substantial increase in pay. Unfortunately it was met with strikes at Portsmouth and Plymouth, though accepted in the Thames yards.

Sandwich's closest colleague in reforming the dockyards was the controller, and head of the Navy Board, Captain Hugh Palliser. Though inherited from Sandwich's predecessor, Palliser was typical of Sandwich's appointments: an able man of plain manner and obscure background. In April 1775 Sandwich took him into the Admiralty, replacing him with Captain Maurice Suckling. Suckling soon fell ill, and when he died in July 1778 Sandwich chose Captain Charles Middleton to replace him. An obscure Scot with an undistinguished service career, Middleton was a surprising choice, but none ever better vindicated Sandwich's judgement, for Middleton became the outstanding naval administrator of the century—though he was always a difficult colleague, cantankerous, egocentric, and disloyal, and only Sandwich was able to manage him successfully.

Meanwhile Sandwich's reforms had been overtaken by the American crisis. Initially the navy was called on only for a major logistical effort to support the troops sent to North America, but Sandwich was alert to the risk of French intervention, and urged on his colleagues the vital importance of early mobilization. Instead they chose appeasement, ignored French preparations, and when war broke out in the spring of 1778 the Royal Navy, for the first and last time in the eighteenth century, was substantially behind in the mobilization race. Worse still, the expanded and reformed Spanish navy was fully mobilized and threatened to join the French, giving them overwhelming superiority. The cabinet now agreed that the war in America was a lesser priority than survival at home, but it proved unable to keep to its decision. George III did not want and North could not impose cabinet unity, while Lord George Germain, the American secretary, constantly undermined Sandwich and diverted resources to America. Sandwich, for his part, in spite of his unequalled experience, does not seem to have argued clearly enough the essential importance of building up the western squadron to achieve command of European waters before allowing strength to be dispersed around the world.

Thus in April 1778 Vice-Admiral Byron was detached from the main fleet to pursue the French Toulon squadron across the Atlantic—a wild-goose chase which achieved nothing, but weakened Keppel's main fleet before it met the French off Ushant on 27 July, and threw away the only chance of establishing an initial superiority over the French before Spain entered the war. Instead the evenly matched fleets fought an indecisive action. What was worse, Keppel, though the inevitable choice in terms of seniority and experience, was a leading member of the opposition, and Palliser his third in command was still Sandwich's colleague at the Admiralty. Mischief-making by Keppel's political friends, which he was too weak to resist, and Palliser's touchy honour, combined to produce an inflammatory quarrel between them, leading to the resignation of both, and courts martial which the opposition exploited to divide the main fleet between 'Montagus' and 'Capulets'. This led to a violent attack on Sandwich in parliament, and a proposal to pacify the navy by transferring Sandwich to secretary of state and replacing him with Vice-Admiral Lord Howe, which foundered on the unacceptably high price demanded by Howe for his services. In the midst of these troubles Sandwich's private happiness was shattered on 7 April 1779 when Martha Ray was murdered by a deranged admirer. In August the Admiralty underwent its most severe crisis yet, when the Channel Fleet, now under Sir Charles Hardy, faced a Franco-Spanish fleet twice its size. The prospect of imminent invasion reduced several senior officers to panic, but Hardy kept his head and manoeuvred with skill, and the enemy was presently obliged to withdraw.

In this case and throughout the war, the squadrons in home waters were outnumbered because so much of the navy's strength was overseas, and if Sandwich argued the case for concentrating on the western squadron he certainly did not persuade his colleagues. Instead repeated detachments were made to answer different demands in America or the West Indies, sometimes with local success, but with no possibility of effective strategic co-ordination. Communications were so slow that, with no command of home waters to control the situation overseas, both French and British squadrons in the Americas were blundering about more or less at random. Germain (followed by modern historians) frequently accused Sandwich of being too 'defensive', by which he meant not sending enough ships to support his plans in America. His real mistake was not being defensive enough, not concentrating in the western approaches to achieve victory where it really mattered, as Anson had done in the two previous wars. So far from appreciating the fact, Sandwich and his naval advisers were seriously proposing in 1782 to send the bulk of the main fleet to the West Indies, leaving only a small squadron to cover against invasion.

Before they could do so, the North ministry had fallen as a result of the disaster of Yorktown, itself an indirect result of the navy's failure to win the battle of the Chesapeake, which in turn was just such an 'accidental' battle as the ministry's strategy had made likely. By the time Sandwich left office, in March 1782, the navy had recovered its full strength and equalled or surpassed the Franco-Spanish forces. With a better strategy it might have done more, but even so Sandwich could claim some credit for the preservation of Canada, the West and East Indies, Gibraltar, and above all Britain itself, all of which had been gravely threatened. He left his successors a fleet larger and in better condition than ever before, newly fitted with copper bottoms.

Last years Sandwich never again held high office, though as late as the 1788 regency crisis he had hopes of returning to the Admiralty. His public life, however, was not over, for in 1784 he was the leading promoter of the great Handel commemoration, in which the largest collection of musicians and singers ever seen in England collected under Bates's direction to sing the music of Handel before the largest and most distinguished audience, led by the royal family. These concerts completed the work of the Ancient Concerts in fixing Handel, and above all *The Messiah*, in the centre of national life, and arguably the English Handelian tradition is Sandwich's most enduring monument.

Sandwich died on 30 April 1792 at his home in Hertford Street, London, and was buried at Barnwell, Northamptonshire, on 8 May. His obituaries were respectful. It was nineteenth-century whig historians, the heirs of his political opponents, who effectually blackened his name, and only the publication of some of his papers in the 1930s began the process of rehabilitation. Sandwich's career as a politician was only partly successful, and for much of it he was a controversial figure. He suffered in part from his ill-concealed ability and ambition, uncomfortable to the second-rate; and illegitimate in a peer, whose political position was supposed to rest on independent wealth. A poor earl who needed his salary was always open to the suspicion of corrupt dependence. The unequalled skill with which Sandwich sustained his parliamentary interest in Huntingdon and Huntingdonshire without the money normally considered essential reinforced the impression of a clever but dangerous man. At the Admiralty his austere impartiality in promoting only on merit and refusing the requests of the influential earned him many enemies. A knowledge of the navy and its officers eventually extending back nearly forty years made him a much more effective manager than many of the admirals wanted. As a strategist and wartime minister he was less effective. He cannot be blamed for the disastrous failure to mobilize early in 1776–7, but he shared responsibility for a muddled and misconceived strategy. He tried hard but did not succeed in insulating the navy from the destructive political passions of the 1770s. Though he was never able to complete the thorough overhaul of the dockyards and naval shipbuilding policy which he aimed for, his greatest achievement was undoubtedly the flourishing condition of the fleet he left his successors.   N. A. M. RODGER

Sources N. A. M. Rodger, *The insatiable earl: a life of John Montagu, fourth earl of Sandwich* (1993) · *The private papers of John, earl of Sandwich*, ed. G. R. Barnes and J. H. Owen, 4 vols., Navy RS, 69, 71, 75, 78 (1932–8) · D. A. Baugh, 'Why did Britain lose command of the sea during the war for America?', *The British navy and the use of naval power in the eighteenth century*, ed. J. Black and P. Woodfine (1988), 149–69 · D. A. Baugh, 'The politics of British naval failure, 1775–1777', *American Neptune*, 52 (1992), 221–46 · J. H. Broomfield, 'Lord Sandwich at the admiralty board: politics and the British navy, 1771–1778', *Mariner's Mirror*, 47 (1961), 195–207 · J. A. Davies, 'An enquiry into faction among British naval officers during the war of the American revolution', MA diss., U. Lpool, 1964 · D. A. Baugh, *British naval administration in the age of Walpole* (1965) · *The fourth earl of Sandwich: diplomatic correspondence, 1763–1765*, ed. F. Spencer (1961) · J. M. Haas, 'The pursuit of success in 18th century England: Sandwich, 1740–71', *BIHR*, 43 (1970), 56–77 · R. J. B. Knight, 'The royal dockyards in England at the time of the war of American independence', PhD diss., U. Lond., 1972 · R. J. B. Knight, 'Sandwich, Middleton and dockyard appointments', *Mariner's Mirror*, 57 (1971), 175–92 · J. M. Haas, 'The rise of the Bedfords, 1741–1757: a study in the politics of the reign of George II', PhD diss., University of Illinois, 1960 · P. D. G. Thomas, *John Wilkes, a friend to liberty* (1996) · A. T. Patterson, *The other armada: the Franco-Spanish attempt to invade Britain in 1779* (1960) · N. A. M. Rodger, 'Instigators or spectators? The British government and the restoration of the stadholderate in 1747', *Tijdschrift voor Geschiedenis*, 106 (1993), 497–514 · J. Cooke, ed., *A voyage performed by the late earl of Sandwich round the Mediterranean in the years 1738 and 1739 …* (1799) · D. Syrett, *The Royal Navy in American waters, 1775–1783* (1989) · D. Syrett, *The Royal Navy in European waters during the American revolutionary war* (1998) · N. Tracy, *Navies, deterrence and American independence: Britain and seapower in the 1760s and 1770s* (1988) · W. Weber, *The rise of the musical classics in eighteenth-century England* (1992)

Archives Cambs. AS, Huntingdon, corresp. · Mapperton, near Beaminster · NMM, appointment books and corresp. · NMM, corresp. and papers · NRA, priv. coll., corresp. and papers | BL, letters to Lord Anson, Add. MS 15957 · BL, corresp. with George Grenville, Add. MS 57810 · BL, corresp. with earls of Hardwicke, etc., Add. MSS 35431–35681 · BL, corresp. with Lord Holland, Add. MS 51386 · BL, corresp. with Lord Liverpool, Add. MSS 38198–38217, 38306–38309, 38570 · BL, corresp. with duke of Newcastle, etc., Add. MSS 23823–23830, 32704–32987 · Captain Cook Memorial Museum, Whitby, corresp. with Lord Mulgrave and others · NMM, corresp. with Thomas Lewis · NMM, corresp. with Sir Charles Middleton · NRA, corresp. with Sir Joseph Banks · PRO, letters to Admiral Rodney, PRO 30/20 · PRO, corresp. with Lord Stafford, PRO 30/29 · U. Nott. L., corresp. with duke of Newcastle, etc. · V&A NAL, letters to David Garrick · Warks. CRO, corresp. with Lord Denbigh · Woburn Abbey, Bedfordshire, fourth duke of Bedford's MSS

Likenesses J. Highmore, oils, 1740, NPG · G. Knapton, oils, 1745, Society of Dilettanti, Brooks's Club, London · T. Gainsborough, portrait, *c*.1770, Captain Cook Museum, Whitby · V. Green, mezzotint, pubd 1774 (after J. Zoffany), BM, NPG · R. Stewart, mezzotint, pubd 1779 (after his earlier work), BM, NPG · J. Sayers, etching, pubd 1782 (after his earlier work), NPG · T. Gainsborough, oils, 1783, NMM [*see illus.*] · J. S. Copley, oils (*The collapse of the earl of Chatham in the House of Lords, 7 July 1778*), Tate collection; on loan to NPG · J. E. Liotard, oils, Gov. Art Coll. · G. Townshend, pencil, ink, watercolour caricature, NPG · oils (after Zoffany), NPG · Wedgwood medallion, BM

Wealth at death £624 5*s*. 1*d*.: PRO, C 38/824

Montagu [Mountagu], **John** (1718/19–1795), naval officer and politician, was the fourth son of James Montagu (*d.* 1747) of Lackham, Wiltshire, a cousin of the fourth earl of Sandwich; his mother was Elizabeth, daughter of Sir John Eyles of Southbroom, Bishop's Canning, Wiltshire. He entered the Royal Naval Academy at Portsmouth on 14 August 1733, and subsequently served for six years as volunteer, able seaman, and midshipman in the *Sunderland*, *Sheerness*, *Oxford*, and *Princess Caroline*, under captains Man, Martins, and Griffin. Montagu (or Mountagu as he was known until the late 1740s) passed his lieutenant's examination on 5 June 1740, and was appointed fourth lieutenant of the *Buckingham* on 22 December 1740, and third lieutenant on 2 February 1741. Vice-Admiral Richard Lestock was on the *Buckingham* during the action off Toulon on 11 February 1744, and Mountagu gave evidence against him at the subsequent court martial. To Lestock's accusation that his evidence was dictated by Captain Towry, Mountagu replied 'I never ask any man's opinion, but go by my own' (*Minutes of the Proceedings of a Court-Martial Assembled on the 23rd of September, 1745*, 1746).

Shortly afterwards Mountagu moved to the *Namur*, flagship of Admiral Thomas Mathews. On 2 March 1745 he was given command of the *Hinchinbroke*, and on 15 January 1746 he became captain of the *Rose* (20 guns). He moved to the *Ambuscade* (40 guns) on 11 August, and was present at the battle of Finisterre on 3 May 1747, though in the rear and not engaged. On 29 December 1747 he moved to the *Tilbury* (58 guns), and over the next two years he commanded the *Greenwich*, *Bristol*, *Kent*, and *Mermaid*, before returning to the *Kent* and commanding her from 10 January 1750 to January 1753.

On 2 December 1748 Mountagu married Sophia Wroughton (*d.* 1802) of Wilcot, Wiltshire; they had one daughter and four sons, two of whom—George *Montagu (1750–1829) and James *Montagu (1752–1794)—became naval captains, and one, Edward *Montagu (1755–1799), a lieutenant-colonel in the Royal Artillery. About the time of his marriage he changed the spelling of his name from Mountagu to Montagu. From 10 November 1748 to 1754 he was the MP for Huntingdon, standing as the deputy for Lord Sandwich's brother-in-law, Kelland Courtenay.

Upon the outbreak of the Seven Years' War, Montagu was again at sea, commanding the *Elizabeth* (64 guns) from 4 February 1755, and moving to the *Monarch* (74 guns) at Portsmouth on 27 January 1757. He therefore superintended the execution of Admiral John Byng, who was shot on the *Monarch*'s quarterdeck on 14 March 1757. Two months later the *Monarch* left for the Mediterranean, and in the action off Cartagena on 28 February 1758, in company coincidentally with the *Montagu* (64 guns), she drove ashore the *Oriflamme* (50 guns).

Montagu took the *Raisonable* to the West Indies on 16 February 1759 and brought home the *Panther* (60 guns). On 19 November he took over the *Terrible* (74 guns); from her he moved on 14 April 1760 to the *Newark* (80 guns) and shortly afterwards to the *Princess Amelia* (80 guns), in which he cruised off Brest in a squadron under Captain Matthew Buckle, during Keppel's expedition against Belle-Île in 1761. On 22 June 1762 he moved to the *Magnanime*, before taking possession of the brand new *Dragon* (74 guns) on 6 May 1763, which was a guardship at Chatham until 1766.

Montagu was appointed to the *Bellona* (74 guns) on 26 July 1769, and on 18 October 1770 he became a rear-admiral of the blue. On 16 January 1771 he was appointed commander-in-chief in the Downs and hoisted his flag in the *Romney* at Spithead, but from 3 March 1771 he was commander-in-chief on the North American station. In January 1773 at Newport, Rhode Island, Montagu sat on a commission of inquiry into the seizure and burning of the *Gaspee* by a mob in June 1772. On 7 December 1775 he became vice-admiral of the blue, and for three years from 28 February 1776, as commander-in-chief at Newfoundland, he maintained a system of active cruising against privateers. On the outbreak of war with France he detached a squadron to take the islands of St Pierre and Miquelon.

Having returned to Portsmouth in time to sit on Keppel's court martial, Montagu became admiral of the blue on 18 April 1782 and admiral of the white on 24 September 1787; and he was port admiral at Portsmouth between 1783 and 1786. He died at his home in Fareham, Hampshire, on 7 September 1795, with the 'universal reputation of a man possessing the strictest integrity, and a most benevolent heart, unhappily alloyed by some intemperance' (Charnock, 5.480).   RANDOLPH COCK

Sources DNB · commission and warrant books; lieutenant's passing certificate, PRO, ADM 6/15, 17, 18, 19, 20, 21; ADM 107/3, p. 385 · W. L. Clowes, *The Royal Navy: a history from the earliest times to the present*, 7 vols. (1897–1903) · D. Syrett and R. L. DiNardo, *The commissioned sea officers of the Royal Navy, 1660–1815*, rev. edn, Occasional Publications of the Navy RS, 1 (1994) · W. E. May, 'The Gaspee affair', *Mariner's Mirror*, 63 (1977), 129–35 · J. Charnock, ed., *Biographia navalis*, 5 (1797), 480 · *Annual Register* (1776) · *Annual Register* (1783) · J. K. Laughton, ed., *The naval miscellany*, 1, Navy RS, 20 (1902), 116 · N. A. M. Rodger, *The insatiable earl: a life of John Montagu, fourth earl of Sandwich* (1993)
Archives NMM, letters to Lord Sandwich · PRO, commission and warrant books, ADM 6/15, 17–21; ADM 107/3

Montagu, John, fifth earl of Sandwich (1744–1814), politician and landowner, was born on 26 January 1744, the second but first surviving son of John *Montagu, fourth earl of Sandwich (1718–1792), politician, and his wife, Dorothy (1716/17–1797), daughter of Charles Fane, first Viscount Fane, and his wife, Mary Stanhope. Styled Viscount Hinchingbrooke from birth, at the age of four he was sent to board with his father's old master at Eton College, where he was a scholar from 1753 to 1758. In 1759 he entered the army and in 1761, through his father's influence, he was sent to Germany as aide-de-camp to General Earl Waldegrave and promoted lieutenant and captain in the Scots guards. He retired from the army in 1767.

Hinchingbrooke was a man of no real ability, but through the connections of his powerful father he became MP for Brackley in 1765. On 1 March 1766 he married Lady Elizabeth (Betty) Montagu (*d.* 1768), daughter of George Montagu, second earl of Halifax, and Anne Dunk; they had two children before her early death. In the year of her death, 1768, his father moved him to the Huntingdonshire constituency, which was dominated by the Montagu interest, and though his first election was hard fought there were no further contests until he succeeded his father to the earldom on 30 April 1792. On 25 April 1772 he married Lady Mary Powlett (1753–1779), daughter of Harry Powlett, sixth duke of Bolton, and his first wife, Mary Munn; they had four children, only two of whom survived infancy.

Hinchingbrooke's public life was undistinguished. He seldom spoke in parliament, and in the Commons divisions he at first merely followed his father's line. He held the court appointment of vice-chamberlain of the household from 1771 to 1781 and was made master of the buckhounds by the Fox–North coalition in May 1783. In November 1783 he announced his intention of withdrawing his support from the coalition on the grounds that 'he could not prevail upon himself to give additional strength to a combination of men whose purpose was to establish their own power in order to keep the King in perpetual subjection' (Martelli, 282–3). His father soon made him see that he could not oppose a ministry that had appointed him to a lucrative court post but Hinchingbrooke certainly felt easier in his mind when Pitt became prime minister and continued him in his place. Thereafter he remained a

Pittite and continued as master of the buckhounds until 1806. From 1807 until his death he enjoyed the post of joint postmaster-general.

Like his father Hinchingbrooke spent much of his life heavily in debt, and the family's financial problems were the cause of friction between father and son. After the old earl's death an astute agent and a long-anticipated windfall revived the family fortunes, and the fifth earl remained in possession of the Huntingdonshire estates and the family seat of Hinchingbrooke House, continuing to manage and control local parliamentary elections. He died in Upper Wimpole Street, London, on 6 June 1814, passing his earldom and estates to his only surviving son, George John Montagu (1773–1818).   W. R. MEYER

Sources GEC, *Peerage* · L. B. Namier, 'Montagu, John, Visct. Hinchingbroke', HoP, *Commons, 1754–90* · R. G. Thorne, 'Montagu, John', HoP, *Commons, 1790–1820* · P. Rowley, 'Owsley Rowley and the Sandwich family, 1778–1792', *Records of Huntingdonshire*, 2/7 (1987), 29–32 · P. Rowley, 'Owsley Rowley and the Sandwich family, 1778–1792', *Records of Huntingdonshire*, 2/8 (1988), 22–32 · P. Rowley, 'Owsley Rowley and the Sandwich family, 1778–1792', *Records of Huntingdonshire*, 2/9 (1990), 35–9 · *VCH Huntingdonshire*, 2.42–7, 64–5 · N. A. M. Rodger, *The insatiable earl: a life of John Montagu, fourth earl of Sandwich* (1993), 70–71, 73, 76, 89, 122, 304–5, 317 · Burke, *Peerage* (1970), 2379 · R. A. Austen-Leigh, ed., *The Eton College register, 1753–1790* (1921), 271–2 · will, PRO, PROB 11/1558, sig. 377 · *GM*, 1st ser., 84/1 (1814), 699 · G. Martelli, *Jemmy Twitcher: a life of John Montagu, 4th earl of Sandwich, 1718–1792* (1962)
Archives NRA, priv. coll., corresp. and papers · priv. coll., Sandwich papers | BL, corresp. with C. Whitefoord, Add. MSS 36593–36595 · Cambs. AS, Huntingdon, corresp. and papers relating to elections · Cambs. AS, Huntingdon, Hinchingbrooke papers · priv. coll., Rowley MSS
Likenesses portrait, Hinchingbrooke House, Cambridgeshire

Montagu, John (1797–1853), army officer and colonial official, born on 21 August 1797, was the youngest son of Lieutenant-Colonel Edward *Montagu (1755–1799) and his wife, Barbara, *née* Fleetwood. He was educated at Cheam in Surrey and at Parson's Green, London. On 10 February 1814 he was appointed, without purchase, to an ensigncy in the 52nd foot. He was present at Waterloo, and on 9 November 1815 was promoted to a lieutenancy by purchase; he also bought his company in the 64th foot in November 1822, but exchanged into the 40th foot on 7 August 1823. In April 1823 he married Jessy, daughter of Major-General Edward Vaughan Worseley, and the same year went to Van Diemen's Land (later Tasmania) with the lieutenant-governor, George Arthur, his wife's uncle, whose private secretary he became. This post he retained until 1827, while holding his captaincy on half pay.

In 1826 Van Diemen's Land, which had been part of New South Wales, was constituted as a separate colony, and Montagu became clerk of the executive and legislative councils. In 1829 his military duties recalled him to England, but in 1830 Sir George Murray, secretary of state for the colonies, offered to reappoint him if he left the army. He accordingly sold out and returned to Van Diemen's Land. In 1832 he took charge for a year of the colonial treasury, and in 1835 he was appointed colonial secretary,

having previously carried out the duties of the post owing to the indisposition of his predecessor.

From February 1839 to March 1841 Montagu was absent on a visit to England, and on his return he was involved in differences with the governor, Sir John Franklin. Franklin had been appointed in 1837, and found the government of Van Diemen's Land in the hands of an 'Arthurite clique'. As early as 1838 Montagu had clashed with Franklin over the assignment of convicts. After his visit to England, which Montagu used to enhance his status with the Colonial Office, their differences intensified: among the issues in dispute were the dismissal of a number of officials, the siting of Christ's College, and the addition of a tower to St George's Church at Battery Point. Montagu ceased to co-operate with the governor, openly accused Franklin of being influenced by his wife, and called into question the reliability of his statements. On 17 January 1842 Montagu was suspended from office, and he returned to England the following month. Colonial sympathy was largely on his side, and Lord Stanley, after investigation, came to the conclusion that Franklin was not justified in his action and that Montagu's dismissal was unmerited. Montagu subsequently circulated all the documents in the case, which proved damaging to Franklin's reputation.

In 1843 Montagu accepted the colonial secretaryship at the Cape of Good Hope, where he arrived on 23 April. He introduced a scheme for improving the financial condition of the colony, which met with considerable, and sustained, success. He also realized the importance of encouraging immigration, and by a system of bounties nearly 1700 settlers were brought into the colony in three years. During the government of Sir Peregrine Maitland, Montagu distinguished himself by his able conduct of the financial arrangements necessitated by the Cape frontier wars. He promoted the construction of good roads across the mountain passes into the interior, chiefly by convict labour. The road carried over Cradock's kloof was named Montagu Pass, a part of the great trunk line between the western and eastern districts. The scene of another great engineering feat, Bain's kloof, in the mountain range which separated Worcester and the districts beyond from the Cape division, was designated Montagu Rocks.

On the outbreak of the Cape Frontier War in December 1850, the governor, Sir Harry Smith, was besieged in Fort Cox. Montagu reorganized the methods of recruitment to the army, which was a significant factor in the outcome of the war. Ill health caused him to depart from Cape Colony on extended leave in 1852, and he died in London on 4 November 1853. He was buried in Brompton cemetery on 8 November. Montagu's finances were in considerable disorder, and he left his family relatively impoverished; in 1854 his wife received a civil-list pension of £300.

E. I. CARLYLE, *rev.* LYNN MILNE

Sources W. A. Newman, *Biographical memoir of John Montagu* (1855) · J. J. Breitenbach, 'Montagu, John', *DSAB* · J. Reynolds, 'Montagu, John', *AusDB*, vol. 2 · J. Fenton, *A history of Tasmania, from its discovery in 1642 to the present time* (1884) · J. Franklin, *Narrative of some passages in the history of Van Diemen's Land during the last three years of Sir John Franklin's administration* (privately printed, 1845)

Archives State Library of New South Wales, Sydney, Dixson Wing, letters and memoranda | Rhodes University, Grahamstown, South Africa, Cory Library for Historical Research, letters to R. Southey
Likenesses A. Elliott, print, repro. in G. E. Cory, *The rise of South Africa*, 2 (1926) • engraving, South African Public Library, Cape Town • lithograph, South African Public Library, Cape Town
Wealth at death £600: *AusDB*

Montagu, John Walter Edward Douglas-Scott-, second Baron Montagu of Beaulieu (1866–1929), promoter of motoring, was born on 10 June 1866 at 3 Tilney Street, London, the eldest son of Lord Henry John Montagu-Douglas-Scott (1832–1905), landowner, and his wife, the Hon. Cecily Susan, younger daughter of John Stuart-*Wortley, second Baron Wharncliffe [*see under* Wortley, James Archibald Stuart-, first Baron Wharncliffe]. His father was the second son of the fifth duke of Buccleuch and was raised to the peerage in 1885 as Lord Henry John Douglas-Scott-Montagu, first Baron Montagu of Beaulieu. On Lord Henry's marriage in 1866 he was given the family estate of Beaulieu, Hampshire, which provided the background to Montagu's childhood and stimulated his interest in rural life.

In childhood Montagu developed asthma, which caused him to be educated by private tutors until deemed strong enough at fourteen to go to Eton. As well as rowing, he enjoyed shooting and captained the school's shooting eight for three successive years. He joined the Eton College Volunteers, becoming a colour sergeant, and proceeded to a commission in the 4th battalion, Hampshire volunteers, after leaving school. His interest in transport developed while at Eton, in the form of cycling. At New College, Oxford, from 1886 Montagu led an active sporting and social life, stroking the college boat to the head of the river in 1887 and joining in Oxford amateur dramatics. However he had no commitment to the subject of his studies, history, and left in 1889 without a degree. By this time he had already shown his dedicated enthusiasm for another form of transport by training as a competent engine driver and fitter. On 4 June 1889 he married Lady Cecil Victor Constance Kerr (*d.* 1919); they had two daughters.

In 1890 Montagu was adopted as the tory candidate for the New Forest constituency and he was returned in the 1892 general election. In the same year he visited southern Africa, where his father had business interests. On his return he championed Cecil Rhodes and became a director of six companies operating in Africa; his interest in and business connections with Rhodesia remained strong for many years. These interests prompted a visit of several months to South Africa in 1896, when he combined some journalism with military action.

In the months following Montagu's return in July 1896 the Locomotives on Highways Bill moved towards its passage into law in November 1896. During this period he developed the passion for motor cars which was to dominate his life. He acquired his first, a Daimler, in 1898 and in January of the following year joined the Automobile Club of Great Britain and Ireland (later the RAC), becoming a member of its committee six months later. In 1899 Montagu established the right of MPs to drive their cars into Palace Yard and took the prince of Wales for a drive, which seems to have confirmed the latter in his intention to acquire a car. Montagu also took part in the Paris–Ostend race in 1899, finishing third despite mechanical problems. In 1900 he participated in the Automobile Club's Thousand Miles Trial, with its object of proving the general safety and reliability of the motor car under a variety of conditions.

The motor car was by now Montagu's primary interest and he took steps to establish a new publication, having first sought advice (including a temporary placement on the staff of the *Daily Mail*) from Alfred Harmsworth, who had underwritten the Thousand Miles Trial. At the end of May 1902 Montagu launched *Car Illustrated* as a 'quality' weekly. Subtitled 'A Journal of Travel by Land, Sea and Air', it necessarily drew on a wide range of contributors, including Charles Rolls, known to Montagu as a fellow competitor in the Paris–Ostend race and participant in the Thousand Miles Trial. The *Car Illustrated* offered readers the benefit of insurance and travel and technical information, and motoring-related guides and books, written or edited by Montagu. It remained in Montagu's ownership for fourteen years, but only made a profit in five of those years; a sister monthly, the *Car Magazine*, had to be abandoned, but *Car Illustrated* proved to be influential. For all his enthusiasm, Montagu was realistic and moderate in his advocacy of motoring interests. Thus, in return for the abolition of the speed limit (of 12 m.p.h.), his Motor Vehicles Registration Bill of 1902, supported by the legislative committee of the Automobile Club, provided for the registration of motor vehicles and the display of registration plates to enable motoring offenders to be identified. Montagu's original bill failed to get a second reading, but in July 1903 the cabinet introduced its own Motor Car Bill, which included a speed limit, determined, as a compromise, at 20 m.p.h. Montagu's unwillingness to oppose the government's introduction of a speed limit aroused strong criticism from some of his motoring colleagues. The decision led to a major shake-up within the Automobile Club, Montagu leading a successful reform movement.

Montagu's journalistic ambition led him in 1904 into an abortive attempt, in collaboration with Harmsworth, to purchase the *Standard* from the Johnstone family. After protracted and complex negotiations Montagu's efforts were beaten by a high bid from Arthur Pearson, but Montagu eventually negotiated with Harmsworth an annual retainer as a parliamentary journalist, contributing a nightly article to the *Daily Mail* while parliament was in session. Meanwhile another form of transport took up Montagu's enthusiasm and energy in 1904–5, the motor boat or 'sea racer', a version of which he had proposed for naval reconnaissance in November 1902. In partnership with Lionel de Rothschild, he had two successful seasons' racing in 1905 and 1906, but he had succeeded to the title and the Beaulieu estates on his father's death on 4 November 1905. New responsibilities and journalistic commitments left him little time to continue with competitive power boating.

The motor car made an additional claim on Montagu through his involvement with Rolls-Royce and Brooklands, the racing circuit at Weybridge developed by H. F. Locke-King in 1907. *Car Illustrated* gave publicity both to the Rolls-Royce Silver Ghost and to the circuit and Montagu opened the new Rolls-Royce factory at Derby in 1908. With Charles Rolls he attended the International Road Congress in Paris in 1908, then visited Wilbur Wright's flying demonstration at Camp d'Auvours. The short demonstration he saw reinforced his belief in the supremacy of air power. He was a founder member of the Aerial (later Air) League, a pressure group for the commercial as well as military use of aviation.

Shortly after the outbreak of war Montagu was gazetted to command the 7th Hampshire reserve battalion, which was sent out to India early in 1915; however, on arrival he was appointed to the army general staff as inspector of motor vehicles. In that capacity Montagu produced a critical report on the Indian armoured car force and advocated a chain of air bases. He also strongly urged the mechanization of army transport, with the prerequisite of an improved road network. In the summer of 1915 Montagu returned to England to plead India's case for military vehicles, and also for aeroplanes for the north-west frontier.

Sailing back to India at the end of 1915 Montagu narrowly escaped death when the SS *Persia* was torpedoed. His long-time secretary and mistress, Eleanor Velasco Thornton, who was travelling with him as far as Port Said, died in the disaster. This loss was deeply felt by Montagu, the more so in that its severity could not be openly acknowledged. Eleanor Thornton was reputed to have inspired the famous Rolls-Royce figurehead (carried on the bonnet of every car), and she and Montagu had a daughter. Although fostered, the girl was later befriended by Montagu as her 'uncle'.

During a subsequent visit to England, Montagu organized military transport for India, including 'Indian standard lorries'. He also entered the fierce air power debate, reviving his pre-war charges of national unreadiness for war in the air, arguing for the establishment of an air ministry, and proposing to the Air Board that aero-engine components should be made by motor manufacturers. Montagu gave evidence to the Bailhache committee of 1916 on the efficiency of the Royal Flying Corps but some of his allegations against the Royal Aircraft Factory failed to impress. He returned to India at the end of 1916 but the Admiralty's proposed purchase of Ditton Park, one of his family estates, brought him home once again in March 1917. The Gotha bombing offensive of 1917 then involved Montagu in a contentious public debate on aerial warfare and the need for enhanced air defences. He also served on the civil aerial transport committee of the Air Board.

After a speaking tour in Canada, advocating an imperial air service, Montagu returned to India, not finally leaving until April 1919. During his time there he had successfully implemented the motorization of military transport. His wife died in September 1919 and on 10 August the following year he married Alice Pearl Barrington-Crake; they had three daughters and a son.

Although he had failed to secure the future of the road board in 1919, Montagu re-established himself as a leading spokesman for road transport, partly through a series of articles in *The Times* in the summer of 1921. From 1923 to 1925 he was chairman of a syndicate which sought to build a private enterprise motorway, albeit with some public financial support, from London to Liverpool via Birmingham and Manchester. The project became enmeshed in political discussion about its delaying effects on local authority road-building schemes and its implications for other projects to reduce unemployment, as well as the principle of private enterprise road provision. The final objection came from a surprising quarter: in December 1924 the president of the Commercial Motor Users' Association wrote to *The Times* expressing his total opposition to the project and supporting through traffic on improved railways. Two further transport projects then engaged Montagu. In 1925 in collaboration with Sir Samuel Instone he proposed a Thames express service of large diesel launches, but this foundered over proposed funding of new piers by the London county council. Then, at the request of the Anglo-Persian Oil Company, Montagu visited Persia and Iraq with his wife in 1927 to advise the company on transport problems.

By the end of the following year Montagu was increasingly troubled by ill health and he died on 30 March 1929 at 29 Wimpole Street, Marylebone, London, from pneumonia and a post-operative chest infection. He was succeeded as third baron by Edward John Barrington Douglas-Scott-Montagu (b. 1926), who created the National Motor Museum at Beaulieu in his memory. Montagu, who was survived by his wife, was buried in Beaulieu Abbey church.   RICHARD A. STOREY

Sources P. Tritton, *John Montagu of Beaulieu, 1866–1929: motoring pioneer and prophet* (1985) · W. Plowden, *The motor car and politics in Britain, 1896–1970* (1973) · *CGPLA Eng. & Wales* (1929) · C. A. M. Press, *Hampshire and Isle of Wight leaders* (1903) · Lord Montagu and D. Burgess-Wise, *Daimler century* (1995) · d. cert. · b. cert.
Archives King's Lond., Liddell Hart C., military and political papers, First World War · Palace House, Beaulieu, Hampshire, family MSS | BL, corresp. with Lord Northcliffe, Add. MS 62165 · CUL, corresp. with Lord Hardinge
Likenesses E. U. Eddis, chalk drawing, 1870, Palace House, Beaulieu, Hants · L. Ward, drawing, 1900, Palace House, Beaulieu, Hants · W. Stoneman, photograph, 1917, NPG · J. Collier, oils, c.1921–1922, Palace House, Beaulieu, Hants; repro. in Tritton, *John Montagu*, 227 · Spy [L. Ward], caricature, lithograph, NPG; repro. in *VF* (8 Oct 1896) · Lady Welby, bronze bust, Palace House, Beaulieu, Hants
Wealth at death £86,000: resworn probate, 2 Nov 1929, *CGPLA Eng. & Wales*

Montagu, Katharine, countess of Salisbury (d. 1349). *See under* Montagu, William, first earl of Salisbury (1301–1344).

Montagu, Lilian Helen [Lily] (1873–1963), feminist and social worker, was born at 96 Lancaster Gate, London, on 22 December 1873, the sixth of the ten children of Samuel *Montagu, first Baron Swaythling (1832–1911), and his wife, Ellen Cohen (1848–1919). Her father, Liberal MP for Whitechapel (1885–1900), was a staunchly Orthodox Jew, uncompromising in his beliefs and in his religious practices, which he expected all members of his household to follow without question. The oppressive atmosphere that this engendered reacted upon his children in different ways. Louis, his eldest son, inherited his title but not his religious beliefs, while Edwin *Montagu, as a member of Lloyd George's wartime cabinet, did his best to sabotage the Zionist movement. Lily, as she was known, was without doubt the most spiritual and religious of all Samuel's offspring: her reaction took the form of a rebellion against what she perceived to be her father's callous disregard of and contempt for those Jews who were not as religious as him. 'My father', she recalled in a speech in 1950, 'saw all around him the lax Jews, and considered them as dead leaves … I began to worry about the dead leaves' (Alderman, 202). Her sister Henrietta *Franklin was of a like mind.

Lilian Montagu was privately educated. At the age of fifteen she appears to have suffered a mental crisis, from which she emerged convinced that her destiny was to minister to her fellow Jews. Within Jewish Orthodoxy it is not possible for a Jewess to become a rabbi (that is the religious leader of a congregation). Montagu turned instead to social work in the Jewish East End of London; in 1893 she established the West Central Jewish Girls' Club as a place where young Jewish girls from the East End could meet in a friendly and supportive girls-only atmosphere. Meanwhile, at the fashionable New West End Synagogue she began conducting a children's service based upon an English liturgy. Now in her mid-twenties, this excessively plain, nominally Orthodox Jewess was drawn to the personality and the pronouncements of the handsome Claude Goldsmid Montefiore, the gentleman scholar who was in the process of inventing a new form of Judaism, denationalized and devoid of ritual; on 1 February 1896 Montefiore proclaimed the tenets of Liberal Judaism from the pulpit of the West London Reform Synagogue. In the January 1899 issue of the *Jewish Quarterly Review* (of which Montefiore was co-editor), Montagu published an essay condemning the 'materialism and spiritual lethargy' into which Anglo-Jewry had lapsed, and calling for a new form of Judaism in which 'all that was valuable and lovely in the ancient faith' would be preserved, but in 'forms acceptable to emancipated minds' (Alderman, 204).

It is clear that Montagu had formed an emotional attachment to Montefiore (then a widower); it is equally clear that this affection was not reciprocated. Montagu spent the better part of the next three years persuading Claude to agree to become president of the Jewish Religious Union (JRU), established on her initiative in February 1902 as a vehicle for energizing debate about the future of Jewish Orthodoxy in Britain. Montagu's amorous advances were rebuffed (Montefiore married his first wife's former

Lilian Helen Montagu (1873–1963), by unknown artist

tutor at Girton College, Cambridge). But Montefiore agreed to accept the headship of the JRU, with Lily as one of its vice-presidents.

To begin with, the JRU had leading members of the nominally Orthodox United Synagogue on its governing body—for example Rabbi Simeon Singer—thus signalling that its existence was not meant to be schismatic. It began holding Saturday afternoon services at the premises of the West London Synagogue, but rejected a set of conditions demanded by the West London, including the recitation of a number of Hebrew prayers, a prohibition on the employment of hymns not composed by Jews, and the strict separation of sexes. Underlying the insistence of the JRU on the equality of the sexes at prayer, Lily Montagu and Claude Montefiore nurtured a passionate belief in the part that the JRU could play in the emancipation of the Jewish woman. Chief Rabbi Hermann Adler issued a condemnation of the JRU, and was joined in this condemnation by Samuel Montagu, who became estranged from Lily and from her sister Marian, who had joined in her venture. In his will Montagu stipulated that each daughter was to lose three-quarters of her share of his estate should she persist in the promotion of 'a movement known as "Liberal Judaism" the objects of which I strongly disapprove' (Alderman, 207). It is a tribute to the sincerity of Lily and Marian that neither of them capitulated to this threat.

In 1909 the JRU became the Jewish Religious Union for the Advancement of Liberal Judaism. Members of Orthodox congregations who had identified with it were induced to resign after Hermann Adler had condemned its form of religious services as contrary to Jewish law. The JRU acquired a former chapel in Hill Street, Marylebone, as its place of worship, and the Liberal Jewish Synagogue, as it was called, came into being in 1911, when it acquired its first minister, Israel Mattuck. Some parts of the service were in Hebrew, but for the most part English was used. A few verses were chanted from the Torah scroll: no one was 'called' to the reading of the law, as in Orthodox synagogues. There was an organ and a mixed-sex choir. Men and women sat together—of course. Two years later the West Central Club was reorganized as a section of the JRU. In due course affiliate congregations of the JRU were established in other parts of London and in the provinces. Meanwhile, Lily began preaching at the Hill Street place of worship; in 1925 the congregation moved to larger premises in St John's Wood Road, and in 1944 she was formally ordained there as a lay minister.

Side by side with her work for Liberal Judaism, both in England and worldwide, Lily Montagu pursued a career as a social worker. She was one of the first women to be made a justice of the peace, becoming in time chair of the Westminster magistrates. In 1937 she was appointed OBE. In spite of her many acts of open and proud rebellion against Jewish Orthodoxy, Montagu remained in some respects a remarkably Orthodox Jewess. She adhered throughout her life to the Orthodox dietary laws and recited (at the New West End Synagogue) the memorial prayer for her parents. She died on 22 January 1963 at St Mary's Hospital, Paddington, London, and was buried, in strict accordance with Orthodox Jewish practice, beside her parents at the Edmonton cemetery of the Federation of Synagogues, Middlesex. She never married.

GEOFFREY ALDERMAN

Sources C. Berman, *The cousinhood* (1971) · E. Umansky, *Lily Montagu and the advancement of Liberal Judaism* (1983) · L. G. Kuzmack, *Woman's cause: the Jewish woman's movement in England and the United States, 1881–1933* (1990) · E. Conrad, *Lily H. Montagu* (1953) · G. Alderman, *Modern British Jewry* (1992) · b. cert. · American Jewish Archives, Cincinnati, Ohio, USA, Lily Montagu MSS · *The Times* (24 Jan 1963) · WWW · CGPLA Eng. & Wales (1963)
Archives American Jewish Archives, Cincinnati, Ohio, MSS [microfilm] · LMA, corresp. and papers, incl. sermons and MS lectures
Likenesses oils, Liberal Jewish Synagogue, London [see illus.]
Wealth at death £24,151 8s. od.: probate, 11 March 1963, CGPLA Eng. & Wales

Montagu, Lady Mary Wortley [née Lady Mary Pierrepont] (*bap.* 1689, *d.* 1762), writer, was baptized at St Paul's, Covent Garden, London, on 26 May 1689. She was the eldest child of Evelyn *Pierrepont, later first duke of Kingston (*bap.* 1667, *d.* 1726), and his first wife, Lady Mary Feilding (1668/9–1692). Her mother had three more children before dying late in 1692. The children were brought up by their Pierrepont grandmother until Mary was nine. (She was now Lady Mary, her father having succeeded his surviving brother as earl of Kingston in 1690.)

On her grandmother's death, Lady Mary passed to the care of her father. In the library of his mansion, Thoresby Hall in the Dukeries of Nottinghamshire, she set herself

Lady Mary Wortley Montagu (*bap.* 1689, *d.* 1762), by Sir Godfrey Kneller, 1719–20

to 'stealing' her education, studying Latin when, she said, 'everyone thought I was reading nothing but romances' (Spence, *Letters*, 357; Spence, *Observations*, no. 743). At about fourteen she filled two albums with writings: poems, a brief epistolary novel, and a prose-and-verse romance modelled on Aphra Behn's *Voyage to the Isle of Love* (1684). She had a circle of literate female friends of her own age, and apparently corresponded with two bishops, Thomas Tenison and Gilbert Burnet, who supplemented the instruction of a governess whom she despised.

Marriage and embassy to Constantinople In 1710 Lady Mary's friend Anne Wortley died, and Anne's brother Edward Wortley Montagu (1678–1761), who had already been dictating his sister's letters to Lady Mary, became her correspondent in his own person. He formally offered himself to her father as a suitor for her, but was rejected because of his conscientious objection to entailing his estate on his hypothetical future eldest son. To family estates at Wortley near Sheffield he and his father were fast adding great holdings of mines in both the Barnsley and the Durham coalfields. To him, over more than two years, Lady Mary addressed a remarkable series of courtship letters, constructing herself as a serious-minded and submissive potential wife to a demanding, even querulous, potential husband.

What provoked their eventual marriage was her father's pressure on Lady Mary to marry another candidate, Clotworthy Skeffington, heir to an Irish peerage. The father (by now marquess of Dorchester) was inflexible. Lady Mary had fallen in love with another, unidentified man, who seems to have been out of the question for marriage. She and Edward Wortley Montagu eloped and were married at Salisbury, apparently on 23 August 1712. (The date comes from an anniversary letter, written by her and annotated by him: he altered the date he first wrote.) For the rest of her life she felt beholden to the husband who had taken her without a portion.

The first two and a half years of Lady Mary's marriage were spent mostly in the country, latterly at Middlethorpe

Hall near York. She bore her son (Edward Wortley *Montagu the younger) on 16 May 1713, on one of her visits to London. Writings from these years include a poem of wifely submission beginning 'While thirst of power' (*Essays and Poems*, 179), a critique of Addison's *Cato*, an epilogue to the same play, and the only contribution to *The Spectator* to be written by a woman.

The accession of George I revolutionized the Wortley Montagus' fortunes. Lady Mary arrived in London at new year 1715 and plunged into both intellectual and court society. For a year she courted both George I and the prince of Wales, as well as striking up friendships with literati like Alexander Pope, John Gay, and the visiting Abbé Antonio Conti. Struck down by smallpox in December 1715, she surprised her circle by surviving. Disgrace at court followed, for during her illness someone circulated the satirical 'court eclogues' she had been writing. One of these was read as an attack on Princess Caroline (a reading which disregards the fact that the 'attack' is voiced by a character who is heavily satirized). Three of the six poems were illicitly printed by Edmund Curll, upon which Pope, professedly defending Lady Mary, conspired to dose Curll with an emetic, and wrote up and published a grisly account of the outcome.

Lady Mary left London in August 1716 to accompany her husband on his embassy to Constantinople, seat of the Ottoman empire. Owing to the transformation of European politics by the battle of Peterwardein shortly after they set out, and a requirement that Wortley Montagu pick up further instructions at both Hanover and Vienna, they travelled overland, criss-crossing Europe on the way. They reached Turkey in spring 1717, after a fearsome journey through wolf-infested forests and across the battlefield of Peterwardein (where bodies of men, horses, and camels still lay deep-frozen in the snow). Lady Mary sent home long letters describing her travels, and she kept copies for future reworking as a travel book. She laid a foundation of expertise in Turkish culture in three weeks billeted in Belgrade with an efendi, or Islamic scholar, with whom she had wide-ranging conversations on oriental languages, literature, religions, and social customs. She was delighted with the civility of women at a public bath building in Sofia, socially poised and graciously welcoming although stark naked.

Lady Mary's time in Turkey (divided between Adrianople, Constantinople, and Belgrade Village, a country retreat near the latter) turned out to be brief. Her husband, hoping to win great national and personal benefit by brokering a peace between the Ottoman and Austrian empires, found himself recalled, purely, it seems, because of a change of ministry at home. Very reluctantly, the Wortley Montagu family (with a new addition, a baby born on 19 January 1718: the future Mary Stuart, countess of Bute) sailed for home on 5 July 1718. Lady Mary was consoled for leaving Constantinople by the scholarly pleasures of a Mediterranean voyage. She and her husband disembarked at Genoa, crossed the Alps, and made a last stop in Paris, where she observed the peak period of John Law's Mississippi scheme.

1720s: Pope and smallpox Back at home Lady Mary seems not to have taken up her court career with the same seriousness as before. Her husband acquired houses in Covent Garden and at the newly fashionable Twickenham. He sat in parliament and spent much of his time pursuing business in Yorkshire, whither Lady Mary did not accompany him. Instead she read, wrote, gardened, embroidered, and oversaw the education of her daughter. She edited her travel letters, but decided not to publish them. She wrote a series of outspoken poems on the topic of society's unjust treatment of women. Her friendship with Pope turned to bitter animosity, for reasons which are no better understood today than they have ever been. She formed new friendships: with Molly Skerrett, who became the mistress and eventually the second wife of Sir Robert Walpole, with Lady Stafford, a Frenchwoman settled in England, and with John, Lord Hervey, Walpole's right-hand man in the House of Lords. She included among her friends both Mary Astell and Sarah, duchess of Marlborough. She wrote funny, excoriating letters about the vagaries of fashionable people to amuse her next sister, Frances Erskine, countess of Mar, who was living in penury in Paris with her husband, leader of the first Jacobite rising.

Lady Mary's most important activity during the 1720s, for the world if not for herself, was the introduction to Western medicine of inoculation against smallpox. She had lost her only brother to this dread disease as well as nearly dying of it herself. In Turkey she had discovered that inoculation (with live smallpox virus) was a common procedure in folk medicine, administered to all comers by an old woman who made it her business. Lady Mary and Charles Maitland, the Aberdeen-educated surgeon at the embassy, looked carefully into the local practice, and then with Maitland's help and support she had her nearly five-year-old son inoculated.

Lady Mary was not the first Western European to have a child inoculated while resident in Turkey. But she was the first to bring the practice home. In spring 1721, with an epidemic raging in England, she persuaded a reluctant Maitland to inoculate her small daughter. Maitland, with his career to protect, stipulated the attendance of medical witnesses. One of these, James Keith, had lost several children to smallpox already, and had a little son whom he immediately had inoculated. The practice of inoculating children spread rapidly among those who knew Lady Mary and who had already been bereaved by the disease. Lady Mary made herself available for proselytizing: she visited sickbeds and supported anxious parents, using her own daughter's immunity as a teaching aid. She interested Caroline, princess of Wales, in the procedure; Caroline arranged the famous experiment on prisoners in Newgate gaol. Hard-hitting and frequently slanderous media warfare broke out, abusing and defending the procedure in newspapers and pamphlets, and even from the pulpit. Lady Mary contributed a single, pseudonymous essay to this vituperative controversy. The whole affair made her well enough known for the common people to be 'taught to hoot at her as an unnatural mother' who had gambled with her children's lives (*Essays and Poems*, 35–6). She carried on at least one correspondence (now lost) with a country apothecary on the topic of inoculation.

The year 1728 marked a nadir in Lady Mary's life. Lady Mar (by now her only surviving sibling) succumbed to some form of madness under the strain of her husband's debts and his career as a political turncoat. Lord Mar's brother, Lord Grange (who is known for subsequently immuring his wife on the uninhabited island of St Kilda), wanted to get custody of her to ensure that her pension from the crown would remain with the Erskine family, as the only, inadequate substitute for Mar's confiscated estates. Lady Mary fought Grange in court and had the better of the fight. When he mustered a posse of friends to escort Lady Mar from London to Scotland, Lady Mary secured a warrant and pursued them on horseback, intercepting them at Barnet to bring her sister back.

Pope attacked Lady Mary in his *Dunciad* that same year: not his first printed attack, but the one which, appearing in a major poetic statement, set the scene for a decade in which almost no important publication of his failed to toss out some damaging allegation against her. Typically, his allegations are false in the main, but fantastically encrusted around some tiny grain of truth. She attempted in vain to silence him by enlisting the aid of shared friends, and wrote a number of ripostes which she did not publish (some of them in collaboration with her cousin the young Henry Fielding, whose patron she was). Among the flood of printed attacks on Pope it is possible that some by her still lie unidentified; but only one is known as almost certainly hers: *Verses Address'd to the Imitator of Horace*, attributed (on good grounds though without incontrovertible evidence) to her and Lord Hervey as joint authors. This was very probably put into a publisher's hands by Pope himself, who may well have judged that its appearance in print would mitigate the damage that its manuscript circulation was doing him.

1730s: family troubles and love Information about Lady Mary's life is far sparser for the 1730s than for the 1720s. The younger generation gave trouble. Her son, who had already run away from Westminster School several times, was entrusted to the care of a tutor who had orders to keep him abroad. When he turned twenty-one he came home without permission, and had (in his father's absence) several public, acrimonious rows with his mother. Her niece Lady Frances Pierrepont (daughter of her late brother) eloped from her care, through her daughter's connivance, with a man whom Lady Mary regarded as a gold-digger. Next her daughter reached marriageable age, and Lady Mary found her husband had ambitious plans to secure a wealthy son-in-law. It fell to Lady Mary to give a polite brush-off to one suitor (Lord Egmont's heir), and preserve some surface of civility towards the successful candidate, Lord Bute, who was her daughter's choice but not her husband's. Wortley Montagu followed family tradition and withheld the dowry his daughter had been led to expect. During the courtship, it seems, Lady Mary wrote a play, 'Simplicity', an adaptation of *Le jeu d'amour et du hasard* by Marivaux, which depicts a heroine permitted, even

encouraged, by her father to test her suitor under his benevolent supervision.

In 1736, the year of her daughter's wedding, Lady Mary fell in love. The object of her affection was Francesco *Algarotti, Count Algarotti (1712–1764), a brilliant young middle-class Venetian who later became a respected critic of literature and the arts. He came to England fresh from impressing Voltaire and Mme du Châtelet, and was immediately elected to membership in the Royal Society and the Society of Antiquaries. Lady Mary wrote him love letters which are eloquent, hyperbolic, and frequently in French (the language both of love and of Enlightenment learning). She also wrote him poems. Her friend Lord Hervey was almost as badly smitten with him as she was, and Hervey's letters as well as hers pursued Algarotti when he left England.

Algarotti was slow to return, writing of his intention to come but not carrying it out. It appeared that Lady Mary's life went on as before, or that its most important new direction was her writing and (anonymously) publishing a pro-Robert Walpole periodical entitled the *Nonsense of Common-Sense*, which ran for nine issues in 1737–8. In its witty and resourceful essays, she challenges lords Chesterfield and Lyttelton (the moving spirits behind the antigovernment journal *Common Sense*) and addresses some topics seldom met with in women's writing, such as industrial wages, interest rates, and censorship.

But at this time her life was bitter to Lady Mary. Her daughter was married and living in Scotland; her son was apparently written off; she had handed over custody of her sister to the sister's now adult daughter. Pope's attacks continued. Molly Skerrett (now Lady Walpole) died in June 1738, Lady Stafford in May 1739. While Lady Stafford lay ill, Algarotti appeared on another brief visit to England. Lady Mary, who had already proposed joining him in Italy, now began seriously planning to do so.

Lady Mary managed her departure with elaborate deceit: nobody but Hervey knew of either her motivation or her intentions. The story told to her husband and others was that she was travelling for her health, and would probably winter somewhere in the south of France. Recurrent rumours that her husband had banished her (according to the painter Joseph Farington, for losing money in financial speculation) are unsubstantiated. Lady Mary wrote to a new correspondent, Henrietta Louisa Fermor, countess of Pomfret, of her eagerness to join her abroad. She packed up her possessions, to be stored for the moment and later, perhaps, to follow her, and had a catalogue made of her library (an informative document which, however, lumps together as 'pamphlets' 137 titles which probably included her annotated copies of Pope's individually published poems).

Once she was abroad, Lady Mary's health and spirits improved. She travelled directly to Venice (while hinting to her husband at several episodes of indecision). There she rented a house, explored the city, picked up a number of old friendships (particularly with the savants Antonio Conti and Pietro Grimani, procurator of St Mark, whom she had met at Vienna), and made some enduring new ones (notably with Chiara Bragadin Michiel). She was warmly welcomed into Venetian society, and began holding a weekly salon. Venice pleased her both socially, as a place of freedom, and politically, as an aristocratic republic. All the while, however, she was waiting for Algarotti (who had travelled to Russia) either to join her or to name some other rendezvous.

Next year Lady Mary was on the move. She went from Venice to Florence, where she stayed two months with the Pomfrets. While there she met Horace Walpole (whom she erroneously believed to be full of friendliness and respect). From there she went on to Rome (for sightseeing), to Naples (where she failed to secure admittance to the recently opened ruins of Herculaneum), and back to Rome. On her second spell there her salon was much frequented by British grand tourists. Joseph Spence (tutor to Lord Lincoln, and future professor of poetry at Oxford) interviewed her for his collection of literary anecdotes and transcribed a number of her poems, which were published in 1747–8. She then travelled to Leghorn to receive her baggage, and thence to Turin, where Algarotti was currently an envoy from the court of Berlin, trying to enlist the kingdom of Savoy and Sardinia as an ally of Frederick the Great in the War of the Austrian Succession. (It was Frederick's summons, on his father's death, which had put paid to any intention Algarotti might have entertained of a life with Lady Mary.) During three months of spring 1741, these two odd lovers came to the end of their probably unconsummated affair.

Lady Mary spent that summer at Genoa, where she intervened on behalf of the republic in an international incident which involved a British breach of Genoese law. In the end a British court concurred with her in taking the Genoese side.

1742–1756: Avignon and Brescia For two years Lady Mary's erratic movements had been dictated by her expectations of Algarotti. They were now dictated by the progress of European war. Italy expected invasion, so she crossed the Alps again, tried Geneva (which she disliked), and wintered at Chambéry. In 1742 she settled at Avignon, where she stayed for four ill-documented years. She did not particularly like the place, but because it was under the dominion of the pope it was safe from attack. By the time of the second Jacobite rising she was finding its population of exiled Scots and Irish dissidents an intolerable irritation, but she did not know how to get away.

In Avignon, Lady Mary mapped out the solitary life she led for the next decade or more. Her gift for languages enabled her to mingle in continental society more than most visiting English, but she preferred to be often alone. The town council made her a grant of a tower in the citadel (now destroyed) and here she lodged some of her books and constructed a belvedere. She made forays away from Avignon: to Orange in 1742 to meet her errant son and write an assessment of him for her husband; and to Nîmes in 1743, for a social function where she petitioned the governor of Languedoc (the duc de Richelieu) for clemency for persecuted Huguenots.

In 1746 Lady Mary made concerted attempts to get away from Avignon. She travelled around Languedoc seeking a place to settle; she discussed possible plans for travel. Finally she arranged with a native of the Venetian province of Brescia, Count Ugolino Palazzi, to escort her as far as Brescia, whence she planned to go on to Venice. She had to pay Palazzi's debts before they could leave; but still she judged the bargain worth while, since a few days later their path led right through the retreating Spanish and advancing Austrian armies. But after arriving at Brescia, at the house of Palazzi's mother, she fell gravely ill; and she got no further on her journey for ten whole years.

Brescia was a singularly lawless province, with a high murder rate. Ugolino Palazzi and his brothers were among the most notorious of its upper-class bandits, who lived largely by extortion backed with threats of violence. Lady Mary was not to know this. She rented a house from the Palazzis, in the Po valley town of Gottolengo. Because the house was dilapidated she improved and furnished it; since it lacked a garden she bought, through Palazzi's agency, a 'dairy-house' with gardens and vineyards, several miles off. When all her jewels were stolen during her first autumn in Gottolengo, she suspected Palazzi, yet she did nothing.

During these isolated years Lady Mary sent to her daughter her most personal, philosophical letters, expatiating on topics like the education of girls and the works of the modern novelists. She described her walks, her fishing, her gardening, her farming, and the social habits of her neighbours. She described also the beauties of Lovere on Lago d'Iseo, a holiday resort where she bought another palazzo and lived for months at a time. Many of her undated writings probably belong to these years, though she told Lady Bute that when she wrote the history of her own times she destroyed each section as she completed it. Her letters to her daughter and her husband make no mention of the harassment and anxiety which she later described in a document drawn up with the intention of suing Palazzi. Indeed, midway in her northern Italian sojourn, when a traveller who had attempted to visit her complained of violence from Palazzi, and the Venetian governor of the province enquired into her position, she maintained that she was perfectly at her ease and under no compulsion or restraint.

That was in 1750. From early 1754 she was trying to get away, but something always intervened. Either she fell ill (she had a dreadful bout with gum disease, but was saved by having her mouth cauterized), or her trusted woman-servant fell ill, or floods were up or bridges broken, or the roads were said to be infested with bandits. In spring 1756 she finally realized she was a prisoner. She made her escape with the aid of her secretary, Dr Bartolomeo Moro, and of one of Palazzi's aunts. She did not get off scot-free: all the title-deeds to property she had bought were stolen, and she was informed that in any case most of the sales had been legally invalid.

Final years But Lady Mary reached her goal, and she shook off Palazzi. She bought a house in Venice and one in Padua, and spent a last few years among society as well as books. Many old friendships were restored (including that with Algarotti, with whom she exchanged letters of wit and philosophic speculation). She made new ones too, many of which are known only from the summaries of letters sent, which she kept at this time as she had done in Turkey. One correspondence which survives is that with Sir James Steuart, the political economist, and his wife, Lady Frances, who were exiled Jacobites. Lady Mary's brilliant, exuberant letters to Sir James suggest something of what must have been the quality of her lost letters to Pope, William Congreve, Hervey, Conti, Montesquieu, and other literary and Enlightenment figures.

Lady Mary's late years in Venice were marred only by a bitter feud with John Murray, the British resident, and Joseph Smith, the art collector, who was British consul there. The grounds for this quarrel seem to have been political, having to do with support for or opposition towards William Pitt; but the mode of it was to torment Lady Mary with insinuations that her learning was not respectable. This made her position harder when in 1761 news reached her of her husband's death, followed by the news that her son had contested the will, not in his own name but in hers.

The activities of Edward Wortley Montagu junior are much canvassed in surviving letters between his parents (who remained on the best of epistolary terms)—although a large batch of letters about him were later destroyed. Lady Mary encountered in many European cities the traces of his passage, in confidence tricks perpetrated and debts unpaid. She had come to believe that her husband ought to disinherit their son and leave his by now immense fortune to their daughter, Lady Bute, the mother of a large family. She had feared he might waver in his purpose to do this; now that he had done it, his will was challenged. This was the reason for her last journey, undertaken late in the season in 1761, when Europe was again at war, and she was suffering from advanced breast cancer.

En route from Venice to London, Lady Mary deposited the manuscript of her *Embassy Letters* with a protestant clergyman at Rotterdam, Benjamin Sowden, whom she apparently trusted to direct it into the hands of a publisher. (In fact he gave it up to Lord Bute, but not before it had been illicitly copied by two men, one of them the son of the publisher Thomas Becket.)

After arriving in London early in 1762, Lady Mary was a social sensation, like a revenant from another age. But she was not happy: if she had been well enough, she would have set off again for Venice. She evidently made yet more new friendships, since she left to Joshua Reynolds a ring engraved with both their names. She died at Great George Street, Mayfair, Westminster, on 21 August 1762, and was buried the next day in the vault of Grosvenor Chapel in South Audley Street.

Lady Mary was painted many times: by Charles Jervas as a shepherdess in 1710; by Sir Godfrey Kneller in 1715 (a painting which exists in almost innumerable versions or copies) and again in 1722 (a portrait done for Pope, in which she wears authentic Turkish dress brought back from her travels); by Jean-Baptiste Vanmour while she was in Turkey; by Jonathan Richardson once in unobtrusive

travelling dress and once in dazzling gold with attendant black boy; and by Carlo Francesco Rusca among emblems including a skull. Another portrait ascribed to Kneller seems to show her in the identical costume to that she wears in Pope's picture, against a background encampment of Serbian tents. Costume and tents are strong circumstantial evidence that this is Lady Mary; but since another version of this picture (at Dulwich Art Gallery) bears the arms of her friend Dorothy (Walpole), Countess Townshend, the National Gallery (which owns a third version) does not accept it as Lady Mary.

Other pictures which claim to be of Lady Mary are too numerous to mention here. Turkish costume, which became widely popular, seems to have been regarded as sufficient grounds for attributions, of which some are feasible but many are not. The authenticated pictures have been often engraved. One particularly interesting engraving shows her portrait in an oval frame, along with matching portraits of the duke and duchess of Portland (son-in-law and daughter of her friend Henrietta Harley, countess of Oxford); the picture of Lady Mary is embellished with attributes to mark her talents and achievements: a trumpet and oak leaves for fame, a globe for travel, a caduceus for medicine, and a mahlstick for painting (or possibly for needlework design).

A number of Lady Mary's poems were printed in her lifetime, either without or with her permission or connivance: in newspapers, in miscellanies, and independently. Though she later told her daughter she had never published anything, this is demonstrably false, even if the only proven case of her active involvement is the *Nonsense of Common-Sense*. After Curll, Anthony Hammond included her in his *New Miscellany of Original Poems, Translations and Imitations, by the most Eminent Hands* (1720). It remains unknown whether she engineered the publication of *Verses Address'd to the Imitator of Horace*, *The Reasons that Induced Dr Swift to Write a Poem call'd the 'Lady's Dressing Room'*, and the *Answer to the Foregoing Elegy*, the last of which is only probably hers. While she was abroad the *London Magazine* printed a number of her poems, one by one. Horace Walpole was responsible for her *Six Town Eclogues, with some other Poems* (1747), and in part responsible for Dodsley's inclusion of her the next year in his influential *Collection of Poems*.

Lady Mary's diary for the years since her marriage was long preserved by her daughter but was finally destroyed, as an act of filial piety. Meanwhile her *Letters Written during her Travels* appeared in three volumes from Becket and De Hondt (transcribed from the manuscript then held by Sowden) in the year after her death. An apparently pirated edition of her *Letters* (1764; said to be 'Printed for A. Homer in the Strand, and P. Milton in St. Paul's Church-yard') added some inauthentic material, which in 1767 was joined as a fourth volume to the Becket and De Hondt edition. Her *Poetical Works* (1768) collected pieces which had already appeared in print. In 1803 appeared her *Works*, edited by James Dallaway, published by Richard Phillips: a skimpy and deplorably edited selection from manuscripts in her family. Their appearance was a concession to Phillips, to prevent him from publishing other manuscripts not held by the family, which were then destroyed. During the nineteenth century two more editions repaired some but not all of Dallaway's inaccuracy. During the twentieth century Lady Mary's letters were edited separately from her essays, poems, and play, and from her longer fictions.

Montagu (like her literary predecessors Aphra Behn and Margaret Cavendish, duchess of Newcastle) had both the capacity and the serious ambition of a major writer. With these went inconsistent social responses, both conformist and resistant, to the path in life marked out by her rank and gender. She defied convention most memorably by her pioneering of inoculation, a course of action unparalleled in the annals of medical advance. Her letters and her poetry, which were admired by her contemporaries and successors, have more recently been overshadowed by her political periodical the *Nonsense of Common-Sense* (authorship unknown until the mid-twentieth century) and by her longer fiction (particularly the novella entitled in English *Princess Docile*; authorship unknown until near the end of the twentieth century). Scholarship has yet to catch up with the task of evaluating Montagu as author. But at the same time, the fascination of her life story—including its least visible parts: her quarrel with Pope, her relationship with the north Italian bandit Ugolino Palazzi—continues to upstage her writing in the public mind.

ISOBEL GRUNDY

Sources I. Grundy, *Lady Mary Wortley Montagu* (1999) · *The complete letters of Lady Mary Wortley Montagu*, ed. R. Halsband, 3 vols. (1965–7) · Farington, *Diary* · J. Spence, *Observations, anecdotes, and characters, of books and men*, ed. J. M. Osborn, new edn, 2 vols. (1966) · J. Spence, *Letters from the grand tour*, ed. S. Klima (Montreal, 1975) · *Lady Mary Wortley Montagu: essays, poems and 'Simplicity: a comedy'*, ed. R. Halsband and I. Grundy (1977); rev. edn (1993) · M. Wortley Montagu, *Romance writings*, ed. I. Grundy (1997) · M. Wortley Montagu, *Selected letters*, ed. I. Grundy (1996) · J. McLaverty, '"Of which being publick the Publick judge": Pope and the publication of *Verses address'd to the imitator of Horace*', *Studies in bibliography* (1998)
Archives Harrowby Manuscript Trust, Sandon Hall, Staffordshire, corresp., notes, literary MSS and MSS · Holborn Library, Camden, London, Local Studies and Archives Centre, letters written on travels in Europe, Asia, and Africa · Hunt. L. · JRL, papers · NL Scot., notes · priv. coll., letters | Biblioteca Civica, Udine, Italy, Manin MSS · Bodl. Oxf., letters to Francesco Algarotti · Col. U., Halsband MSS · Lincs. Arch., letters to P. Massingberd · Lincs. Arch., Monson MSS · Lincs. Arch., Mundy MSS · NA Scot., Mar and Kellie MSS · Sheff. Arch., Wharncliffe MSS
Likenesses C. Jervas, portrait, 1710 · portrait, *c.*1712–1715 (after G. Kneller), Stratfield Saye, Hants. · G. Kneller, portrait, 1715 · J.-B. Vanmour, group portrait, oils, *c.*1717, NPG · G. Kneller, portrait, 1719–20, priv. coll. [*see illus.*] · G. Kneller, portrait, 1722 · C. F. Rusca, oils, *c.*1739, Gov. Art Coll. · G. Vertue, print, 1739, repro. in Wortley Montagu, *Romance writings* · C. Watson, stipple, 1803 (after G. Kneller), BM; repro. in *The works of the Right Honourable Lady Mary Wortley Montagu*, ed. J. Dallaway, 5 vols. (1803) · C. Watson, stipple, 1817 (after J. Richardson), NPG · J. Richardson, portrait, Sheffield Central Library · J. Richardson, portrait · C. Watson, stipple, BM, NPG; repro. in *Works*, ed. Dallaway · print, repro. in Wortley Montagu, *Complete letters*, 1.400

Montagu [*née* Fraunceys], **Maud, countess of Salisbury** (d. **1424**), magnate and wealthy widow, was the daughter of Adam *Fraunceys (*c.*1310–1375), a wealthy mercer and

mayor of London, and his wife, Agnes (d. after 1392). She first appears in the records named alongside her brother, Adam junior, in a series of remainder clauses in charters to her father concerning the manor of Edmonton, issued between October 1369 and July 1371. About 1373 she became the second wife of an eminent London citizen, John Aubrey (d. 1381), a grocer, and son of the former mayor, Andrew Aubrey. In June 1374 she and her husband acquired lands in Essex, strikingly close to the manors of Ruckholts and Chobhams which her father had purchased some twenty years earlier. They also acquired estates in Hertfordshire, among which was the manor of Shenley, near St Albans, which was probably their principal residence outside London and with which Maud was to have a close association for the rest of her life. Aubrey died shortly before 18 March 1381, granting all his moveables to his widow. They appear not to have had any surviving children, and Maud inherited all the lands that they held together. Already blossoming into that most attractive of medieval women, a wealthy widow, Maud was not left to mourn for long, and within a few months was married to Sir Alan *Buxhull (1323?–1381), himself a widower, who held lands in Sussex and Dorset. Tragically Buxhull died on 2 November the same year, while Maud was already pregnant, leaving his lands to be divided among the two surviving daughters from his first marriage. Maud received a third of the manor of Bryanston, Dorset, as dower on 19 October 1383. By then Maud had married for the third time, with expectations of a longer union than her previous two marriages. It is likely that both Aubrey and Buxhull were substantially older than their bride. Both had been married before and Buxhull died leaving a married daughter aged about thirty.

Maud's new husband, John *Montagu (d. 1400), son of John, Lord Montagu, the younger brother of the earl of Salisbury, was still a young man of thirty-two or thirty-three when he married her, some time before 4 May 1383. His cousin, William, only son and heir of the earl, had died in a tilting accident on 6 August 1382, whereupon John's father became heir to the earldom, and it is conceivable that John's future prospects were already known before their marriage. He eventually became third earl of Salisbury in 1397 on the death of his uncle, his own father having died in 1390. Of Maud's life with Montagu little is known, although it is evident that her wealth was a significant attraction. In 1389, for example, Montagu was bound to his father in the sum of £666 13s. 4d., pledging his wife's property as security for the loan. Maud's particular problems concerning her estate, however, came following her husband's part in the conspiracy against Henry IV in January 1400. Salisbury was arrested and summarily executed by the townsfolk of Cirencester; all his goods and lands were confiscated, including those held by Maud in her own right. Maud immediately petitioned against such action and an interim arrangement was made on 28 February 1400 whereby the manor of Stokenham in Devon, together with some other lands previously held by her husband to a total value not exceeding £100, was granted to Maud for the maintenance of herself and her children. By 6 July she had had her own lands restored to her and on 27 November was granted the manor of Yalhampton, Devon, up to the value of £80. On 7 June 1404 the reversion of her own lands in Ham, Essex, and Shenley, Hertfordshire, was granted to the king's son, John. Her own son, Thomas *Montagu, entered into his inheritance on 14 June 1409 after he came of age, and almost two years later his mother was granted a joint life interest with certain other parties in manors held by him in Wiltshire, Hampshire, and the Isle of Wight, so that he could raise money to support her and his sisters, since she had no dower following Salisbury's death. Maud was never entirely destitute, however. She was assessed at £26 14s. 6d. in the subsidy return for London of 1411, and her will demonstrates that she was able to dispose of goods amounting to a tidy sum. Her last service for her third husband was to move his remains from the abbey of Cirencester to his own foundation at Bisham Montagu in Berkshire some time after 12 November 1420. Maud died on 30 July 1424 at Shenley and was buried there.

STEPHEN O'CONNOR

Sources S. J. O'Connor, ed., *A calendar of the cartularies of John Pyel and Adam Fraunceys*, CS, 5th ser., 2 (1993) · *Chancery records* · PRO · GEC, *Peerage*, new edn · J. C. L. Stahlschmidt, ed., 'Lay subsidy temp. Henry IV: original documents', *Archaeological Journal*, 44 (1887), 56–82

Montagu, Ralph, first duke of Montagu (*bap.* 1638, *d.* 1709), politician and diplomat, was born at his grandmother's (Lady Winwood's) house in London and baptized on 24 December 1638 at St Bartholomew-the-Less, London, the second son of Edward *Montagu, second Baron Montagu of Boughton (1616–1684) [*see under* Montagu, Edward, first Baron Montagu of Boughton], nobleman, and his wife, Anne (*d.* 1642), daughter of Sir Ralph Winwood. Little is known about his early life other than that he received an education along classical lines at Westminster School, beginning in 1649, under the careful guidance of Dr Richard Busby. There is no record of his having attended either Oxford or Cambridge, but it is possible that he undertook the customary tour of the continent.

Early years at court, 1661–1672 In 1661 the young Montagu became joint keeper of Hartleton Lodge in Richmond Park along with his future brother-in-law, Daniel Harvey. The next year found Montagu at court in the service of Anne, duchess of York, as a gentleman of the horse, and, upon the death of his elder brother Edward, in December 1665 he succeeded to the post of master of the horse to Queen Catherine, a position he held until 1678. He soon gained a reputation for gallantry at court and was rumoured to be the lover of the beautiful Jane *Myddelton (*bap.* 1646, *d.* 1692x1703). Anthony Hamilton described him as a person not at all good-looking but to be feared on account of his wit and his many other talents. In later years he was described as 'of a middle stature, inclining to fat, of a coarse dark complexion' (*Memoirs of the Secret Services*, 44). According to Hamilton, Montagu's rise in court society owed much to the favour of the ladies. He was soon noticed by Charles II who appointed him as an envoy on a five-month mission from October 1662 to February 1663 to

Ralph Montagu, first duke of Montagu (*bap.* 1638, *d.* 1709), attrib. John Riley

seek closer co-operation with France, giving Montagu his first taste of foreign diplomacy.

From 1665 to 1668 Montagu remained at court in his post of master of the horse, awaiting an opportunity which he could turn to his advantage. Finally, on 1 January 1669 Montagu was appointed ambassador-extraordinary to France:

> for which Embassy he prepared a very splendid Train, with which he sail'd ... where he was received with great Magnificence, and a vast Equipage was preparing for him to make his Publik Entry, which he did on the 25th of *April*, in most splendid manner, that the like had never been seen in *France* before. (*The Court in Mourning*, 2)

Originally kept deliberately ignorant of Charles's true intent in foreign policy, he did eventually learn of the intended secret alliance with France against the Dutch, but although he determined to have a part in the intrigue he was not in fact admitted to any of the secret negotiations that led to the alliance with Louis XIV known as the treaty of Dover. Present in June 1670 at the death of Charles's sister, Henriette Anne, duchess of Orléans, he carefully enquired into the rumour that she was poisoned but he found no evidence that it was true.

Montagu made a visit to England from summer 1671 to January 1672. While there he purchased, on 12 August 1671, the post of master of the great wardrobe from his cousin the earl of Sandwich for the sum of £14,000, holding this office until 1685 and again from 1689 until his death. He was admitted to the privy council on 2 January 1672 and relieved of his diplomatic post in May 1672.

Marriage, diplomacy, and fall, 1673–1678 On 24 August 1673 Montagu married the very wealthy Elizabeth (*d.* 1690), sixth and youngest daughter of Thomas Wriothesley, fourth earl of Southampton, and his second wife, Elizabeth, daughter of Francis Leigh, first earl of Chichester, and widow of Joceline Percy, eleventh earl of Northumberland, who reportedly had intended herself for the widowed duke of York. She supposedly fled England in order to avoid the advances of the king and married Montagu in France. In fact the marriage took place at Titchfield, Hampshire, in the face of opposition on the part of the lady's family. The marriage was soon reported to be rather stormy and there was talk of a separation, but they did go on to have three sons and a daughter.

In December 1673 Montagu was sent to the Tower for several days for challenging the duke of Buckingham to a swordfight after Buckingham had roughly attempted to push past him to speak to the king in the queen's drawing room at Whitehall. On 1 September 1676 Montagu was again appointed ambassador-extraordinary to the court of Louis XIV and became actively involved in the negotiations concerning the price of England's neutrality in the war between France and the Netherlands. Ever ambitious, Montagu soon desired something higher than an embassy and in autumn of 1677 began to press his claims for the post of secretary of state. In spring 1678 he agreed with Sir Henry Coventry to pay £10,000 for his place. Thomas Osborne, earl of Danby, the lord treasurer, had, however, another candidate in mind, and consistently blocked Montagu's negotiations. Having made a brief visit to England in November and December 1677 Montagu had returned to Paris and there engaged in further intrigues to obtain increasingly large subsidies for Charles from the French. However, Montagu's diplomatic career soon came to an end after a bitter quarrel with Barbara *Palmer, duchess of Cleveland (*bap.* 1640, *d.* 1709), the king's former mistress, then living in Paris, who may have had a brief affair with Montagu. The quarrel arose over Cleveland's affair with another man which Montagu betrayed to the king, and Montagu's subsequent alleged affair with Cleveland's and the king's daughter, Anne, countess of Sussex. In June 1678 the duchess denounced him to Charles II, claiming that Montagu had revealed to her that he intended to use the secretaryship of state as a means to become lord treasurer, thus allowing him to:

> easily supply Charles with money for his pocket and his women and lead him by the nose. For he has neither conscience nor honour, and has several times told me, that in his hart he despised you and yr Brother; and that for his part he wished with all his hart the Parliament wd send you both to travell, for you were a dull governable fool, and the Duke a willful Fool. (BL, Harley MS 7006, fols. 171–3)

She also accused him of 'corrupting' a French astrologer, Abbé Pregnani, in whom Charles had great confidence in order to influence the king according to his desires. Intending to defend himself personally before the king Montagu left his post on 1 July without the leave of the monarch and returned to England. Charles, however, refused to discuss the affair, removed Montagu from the privy council, replaced him as ambassador to France with the earl of Sunderland, and dismissed him from the mastership of the horse.

Parliament and whig politics, 1678–1687 Montagu, hoping to shield himself from further penalty and to avenge himself on Danby, whom he blamed for his misfortunes, planned Danby's destruction. He entered into negotiations with Barrillon, the French ambassador, on 24 October 1678, promising the fall of Danby within six months if given a pension of 40,000 livres a year. The proposal accepted, Montagu stood and won a seat as a whig candidate for Northampton in the first Exclusion Parliament, and prepared to accuse Danby in the House of Commons. On 19 December 1678, at a meeting of the privy council, Danby, trying to destroy Montagu first, accused Montagu of having private conferences with the papal nuncio while in Paris and ordered the seizure of Montagu's papers. The House of Commons, however, stood by Montagu, who informed it that the seizure of his papers was designed to silence him and that he had important information regarding a leading minister. Montagu had hidden the crucial letters by Danby about the French negotiations and, on being demanded by an excited Commons to produce his papers he selected two letters which showed Danby to have requested 6 million livres as the price of England's peace with France and the prorogation of Parliament. Parliament behaved as Montagu hoped and by a vote of 179 to 116 demanded the impeachment of the lord treasurer and refused to read the letters that proved Montagu to be equally guilty of secret dealings with France. With the dissolution of parliament on 30 December 1678 Montagu's political career seemed to be temporarily checked. Afraid of being sent to the Tower for his part in the Danby affair he hid for three weeks in London and subsequently attempted to flee to France in disguise, but was arrested at Dover and forced to give surety not to leave the kingdom. Perhaps the attempted flight was also attributable to his championing the cause of the duke of Monmouth: he apparently hoped to gain Louis XIV's support for the scheme to replace the Catholic duke of York with the protestant duke of Monmouth in the succession.

Elected for Huntingdon in March 1679 and again for Northampton in October 1679 and 1681, Montagu continued to intrigue in support of excluding the duke of York from the throne. He had no qualms in becoming involved in Ambassador Barrillon's dealings with the English. In this he was aided by his sister Elizabeth, wife of Sir Daniel Harvey, who willingly entered into political intrigue and showed herself as adept as her brother, but even with her help Montagu's schemes were not always successful. His involvement in the Danby affair, his advocacy of the exclusion bills, and his support of the duke of Monmouth's pretensions only caused him great difficulties, and an attempted alliance with the earl of Shaftesbury as a political ally was doomed from the start. Shaftesbury detested Montagu, considering him a rogue and a possible rival. Despite the tensions between them Montagu did not abandon Shaftesbury when the latter was sent to the Tower. Montagu visited him there and offered to stand bail for him. Not at all involved in the Rye House plot of 1683 to assassinate the king Montagu was nevertheless suspected of disaffection and thought it prudent to go to France in August 1683. There he had great difficulty in obtaining the promised 6 million livres for which he had sold his services to the French crown: in Paris he unsuccessfully sought an audience with Louis XIV and petitioned for full payment for his past services. While in Paris Montagu succeeded his father, on 10 January 1684, as third Baron Montagu of Boughton.

Upon the accession of James II in 1685 Montagu lost the post of master of the great wardrobe to Lord Preston. Undaunted, and still hoping for a position at court, he openly declared his intention of attending the coronation:

> so I hope his majesty will be pleased to think the king is not to remember anything that has passed in relation to the Duke of York, for whatever my opinions were when I delivered them, … they are altered now I am become his subject, knowing myself obliged, by the laws of God and man, to hazard life and fortune in the defence of his sacred person, crown and dignity. (*Correspondence of Henry Hyde*, 1.114)

Surprisingly he was allowed to return to England and was courteously received by James; it was even rumoured that he was once again to serve the court, as secretary of state or as ambassador to France, but the hoped for post did not materialize.

Revolution, return to office, second marriage, 1688–1702 After the flight of the king in 1688 Montagu took an active part in the debates in the House of Lords during the Convention Parliament and was one of the first to espouse the revolution, voting for bestowing the crown on William and Mary and supporting the Bill of Rights. On 14 February 1689 Montagu was appointed to the privy council and on 9 April 1689 was created Viscount Monthermer and earl of Montagu. This was not reward enough for him and on 18 May 1694 he wrote to William asking for elevation to the title of duke, claiming that his family history (one of the oldest in England) and his tenacious support of William, especially in winning over three wavering peers who voted against the regency, entitled him to a dukedom. The request was denied. However, a lawsuit against Lord Preston restored Montagu to the lucrative mastership of the great wardrobe.

On 19 September 1690 Montagu's wife died at Boughton and was buried on 26 September at Warkton, Northamptonshire. Two years later, on 8 September 1692, Montagu married Elizabeth (1654–1734), eldest daughter and coheir of Henry *Cavendish, second duke of Newcastle upon Tyne, and his wife, Frances, daughter of the Hon. William Pierpont, and widow of Christopher Monck, second duke of Albemarle. Very rich and apparently insane, according to some reports she had stated that she would marry no one but a monarch and accepted Montagu only after he had courted her in the guise of the emperor of China. After the marriage she was kept in such strict seclusion that it was rumoured that she had died and that Montagu concealed her death in order to continue to enjoy her income of £7000 a year. They had no children. The marriage engendered many lawsuits over the Albemarle estates. Perhaps the most lengthy, lasting from 1693 to 1699, and widely known was that between Montagu and the duke of Bath, which cost both litigants some £20,000. The suit was clouded by the accusation of perjury on the part of four of Montagu's witnesses, suborned, so it was claimed, by one of his chaplains. From 1693 to 1695 Montagu enjoyed the post of captain of the band of gentlemen pensioners; in 1695 he was created commissioner of Greenwich Hospital and that same year he entertained William III at Boughton House, Northamptonshire, in a most splendid fashion. He was made lord lieutenant of Northamptonshire in 1697, which post he held until 1702.

Patron of the arts Montagu's political activity declined in his later years. Although he continued to attend the House of Lords after 1690 on an almost daily basis he was not involved in any significant legislation and spoke rarely in debates. His main concern during these years was the refurbishing and extension of his houses to create architectural masterpieces adorned with the best in art and surrounded with gardens of great beauty. Montagu was known for two great buildings, one at Boughton, Northamptonshire, the Montagu family seat which he extensively remodelled, imitating the style of Versailles, and the other, Montagu House at Bloomsbury, said to be without comparison and the finest building in London. The Bloomsbury house burnt down on 19 January 1686 due to the negligence of a servant. After an unsuccessful lawsuit with his tenant at the time, the earl of Devonshire, Montagu rebuilt the mansion with very little alteration. It was purchased in 1753 by the government to establish the British Museum but was demolished between 1840 and 1849 and was replaced by the present museum building.

At his residences Montagu hosted social gatherings which were renowned for elegance and delightful entertainment. He was a most amiable host, with a ready wit which made him an excellent conversationalist. The French philosopher the seigneur de Saint-Evremond received a pension of £100 a year from Montagu and on one occasion wrote that one of his greatest joys was to visit Boughton and to be 'with my Lord *Montagu*, to enjoy his conversation twice a day, before and after the best cheer in the world' (*Letters of Saint Evremond*, 356). Montagu also invited the great names of the English theatre; the playwright William Congreve dedicated his play *The Way of the World* to Montagu, claiming that if he found a better turn of phrase or expression than formerly, he had to ascribe this to participating in the conversations of Montagu and his friends:

> If I am not mistaken, Poetry is almost the only Art, which has not yet laid Claim to your Lordship's Patronage. Architecture, and Painting, to the great Honour of our Country, have flourish'd under your influence and protection. In the mean time, Poetry the eldest Sister of all Arts, and Parent of most, seems to have resign'd her Birthright, by having neglected to pay her duty to your Lordship. (*Complete Works*, 9–11)

Last years, 1703–1709 On 20 March 1705 Montagu's son John *Montagu married Lady Mary, youngest daughter of John Churchill, duke of Marlborough. It has been suggested that the marriage, first proposed by Montagu in 1703, was a political alliance, agreed to by Marlborough as security against a possible combination of whigs and tories against himself. Given Montagu's declining political influence, however, it seems more likely that the motive was financial. For Montagu it meant the achievement of a long desired goal; through Marlborough's influence he was elevated on 12 April 1705 to the dignity of marquess of Monthermer and duke of Montagu. He was not, however, to enjoy his triumph for long. He died of pleurisy at Montagu House, Bloomsbury, on 9 March 1709 and was buried on 16 March at Warkton, Northamptonshire. Montagu was survived by his wife, who died on 28 August 1734, his third son, John, and a daughter, Anne, who married Alexander Popham of Littlecote, Wiltshire. His first son, Ralph, born on 8 August 1679, had died before his father became an earl, while Winwood Montagu, styled Lord Monthermer, Montagu's second son, apparently died in Flanders about 1 May 1702 and was buried at Warkton.

Montagu was an opportunist in public as well as in private life. Early on he determined to pursue a career that led to wealth and titles and was willing to use any means necessary to obtain his ends. Service at court appeared to be the way to rise in the world and Montagu used the court to enrich and advance himself, but at the expense of the public good. One historian has commented that 'In a corrupt age … [he] … had acquired a singular reputation of profitable dishonor' (Gregg, 195). A rogue even by the standards of the day, it would seem that Montagu did not concern himself with any future evaluations of his political activities. He was, however, concerned to demonstrate his credentials as a patron of the arts and he spent the wealth he accumulated with style, earning the praise of those men of letters whom he encouraged and leaving a lasting legacy in the architectural grandeur of Boughton House.   EDWARD CHARLES METZGER

Sources GEC, *Peerage*, new edn · *Fifth report*, HMC, 4 (1876) · *Sixth report*, HMC, 5 (1877–8) · *Seventh report*, HMC, 6 (1879) · *Eighth report*, 3 vols. in 5, HMC, 7 (1881–1910) · A. Hamilton, *Memoirs of the comte de Gramont*, trans. P. Quennell (1930) · *Bishop Burnet's History* · N. Mignet, *Negotiations relatives à la succession d'Espagne*, 4 vols. (1864) · *CSP dom.*, 1665–6; 1673–5 · A. Boyer, *The history of the reign of Queen Anne digested into annals*, 10 vols. (1710) · E. M. Thompson, ed., *Correspondence of the family of Hatton*, 2 vols., CS, new ser., 22–3 (1878) · J. Dalrymple, *Memoirs of Great Britain and Ireland*, new edn, 3 vols. (1790) · *The right honorable earl of Arlington's letters to Sir W. Temple, bar, from July 1665*, ed. T. Bebington (1701) · W. D. Cooper, ed., *Savile correspondence: letters to and from H. Savile*, CS, 71 (1858) · *DNB* · C. H. Firth and S. C. Loomis, *Notes on the diplomatic relations of England and France, 1603–1688* (1908) · letters to Lord Danby, Charles II, Hon. C. Bertie from Ralph Montagu, BL, Add MS 39757 · *Calendar of the manuscripts of the marquess of Ormonde*, new ser., 8 vols., HMC, 36 (1902–20), vol. 4 · A. Grey, ed., *Debates of the House of Commons, from the year 1667 to the year 1694*, new edn, 10 vols. (1769) · E. R. Edwards, 'Montagu, Ralph', HoP, Commons, 1660–90 · *The correspondence of Henry Hyde, earl of Clarendon, and of his brother Laurence Hyde, earl of Rochester*, ed. S. W. Singer, 2 vols. (1828) · G. Agar-Ellis, ed., *The Ellis correspondence: letters written during the years 1686, 1687, 1688, and* addressed to John Ellis, 2 vols. (1829) · N. Luttrell, *A brief historical relation of state affairs from September 1678 to April 1714*, 6 vols. (1857) · B. Falk, *The way of the Montagues* (1947) · M. Petherick, *Restoration rogues* (1951) · *Memoirs of Sarah, duchess of Marlborough*, ed. A. T. Thompson, 2 vols. (1839) · J. Granger, *A biographical history of England, from Egbert the Great to the revolution*, 4th edn, 4 vols. (1804) · *Letters illustrative of the reign of William III from 1696 to 1708 addressed to the duke of Shrewsbury by James Vernon*, ed. G. P. R. James, 3 vols. (1841) · *Diary of the times of Charles the Second by the Honourable Henry Sidney (afterwards earl of Romney)*, ed. R. W. Blencowe, 2 vols. (1843) · *Memoirs of Sir John Reresby*, ed. A. Browning (1936) · A. Browning, *Thomas Osborne, earl of Danby and duke of Leeds, 1632–1712*, 3 vols. (1944–51) · Evelyn, *Diary* · *The court in mourning: being the life and worthy actions of Ralph, duke of Montague, master of the great wardrobe to Queen Anne* (1709) · W. D. Christie, ed., *Letters addressed from London to Sir Joseph Williamson*, 2 vols., CS, new ser., 8–9 (1874) · C. H. Hartmann, *Charles II and Madame* (1934) · E. C. Metzger, *Ralph, first duke of Montagu* (1987) · *Memoirs of the secret services of John Macky*, ed. A. R. (1733) · E. Gregg, *Queen Anne* (1980) · BL, Harley MS 7006, fols. 171–6 · G. F. Barker, *Memoir of Richard Busby D. D. (1605–1695) with some account of the Westminster School in the seventeenth century* (1895) · *Letters of Saint Evremond, Charles Marguetel de Saint Denis, seigneur de Saint Evremond*, ed. J. Hayward (1930) · *The complete works of William Congreve*, ed. M. Summers (1964)

Archives Northants. RO, corresp. and papers · V&A NAL, estimates for furniture, etc., at Hampton Court, signed by Montagu as a master of the great wardrobe · Yale U., Beinecke L., diary | BL, corresp. with Lord Danby, Add. MS 28054; Egerton MS 3326 · BL, letters to Lord Danby and Charles II, Add. MS 39757 · Bodl. Oxf., letters to Lord Danby, Charles II, C. Bertie · Longleat House, Wiltshire, Coventry papers; Portland papers; Thynne papers

Likenesses attrib. J. Closterman, oils, Boughton House, Northamptonshire · B. Gennari, oils, Boughton House, Northamptonshire · G. Kneller, oils, priv. coll. · attrib. J. Riley, oils, Boughton House, Northamptonshire [*see illus.*] · oils, Beaulieu Abbey, Hampshire

Montagu, Richard. *See* Mountague, Richard (*bap.* 1575, *d.* 1641).

Montagu, Robert, third earl of Manchester (*bap.* 1634, *d.* 1683). *See under* Montagu, Edward, second earl of Manchester (1602–1671).

Montagu, Lord Robert (1825–1902), politician and religious controversialist, born at Melchbourne, Bedfordshire, on 24 January 1825, was the second son of George Montagu, sixth duke of Manchester (1799–1855), and his first wife, Millicent (1798–1848), daughter and heir of Brigadier-General Bernard Sparrow of Brampton Park, Huntingdonshire. Educated privately, he graduated MA from Trinity College, Cambridge, in 1849.

In April 1859 Montagu was returned as a Conservative MP for Huntingdonshire and held the seat until February 1874. He quickly made his mark as a speaker, championing church rates and retrenchment. In 1852 he published *Naval Architecture: a Treatise on Ship-Building* and advocated the establishment of a naval school of architecture and engineering on the model of the Royal Military Academy. In foreign affairs Montagu was no less active. His *Few Words on Garibaldi* (1861) attacked its subject as an adventurer. He opposed Roebuck's resolution (30 June 1863) for recognition of the Confederacy, and he spoke strongly in favour of non-intervention between Denmark and the German powers (5 July 1864). In later years he gave much attention to the Eastern question. On political reform,

Montagu showed characteristic individuality. He advocated plural voting, with additional franchises to property and the professions to balance the increase in the numbers enfranchised. On social questions his attitude was more liberal. As early as 1860 he supported a measure for a council of conciliation in labour disputes; and in 1875, in a debate on the Employers and Workmen Bill, he declared trade unions to be 'not only a natural right but a preservative of order'. On his motion (April 1864) a select committee on which he sat inquired into the disposal of sewage in large towns; and subsequent legislation on the subject owed much to his labours. On 19 March 1867 Montagu was made, on the reconstruction of Lord Derby's third ministry, vice-president of the committee of council on education, and was appointed first charity commissioner, being sworn of the privy council. He held office until Disraeli's resignation in December 1868. As education minister Montagu sought vigorously to enforce the conscience clause in all schools that received grants from public funds, and advocated the extension of technical education. But he was an awkward colleague. Lord Stanley observed: 'though industrious and quick, his total want of tact makes it impossible that he should be entrusted with the conduct of an important measure' (Vincent, 327). He carried a bill assimilating the vaccination procedure of England to that of Scotland and Ireland, and took effective measures to deal with a serious cattle plague which had spread from the continent to England.

While in opposition Montagu voted against Irish disestablishment in 1869. But in 1870 he became a Roman Catholic and in 1873 he was formally expelled from the Conservative Party (Thornley, 200). He became a Conservative home-ruler, sitting for County Westmeath from 1874 to 1880, later claiming that the tories had promised him a cabinet seat if he endorsed home rule (Thornley, 201). He quickly proved an unreliable member of Isaac Butt's party and by 1877 had left it, but without a reconciliation with the tories, whose Eastern and Indian policy he condemned. *Foreign Policy* (1877) was a substantial and quite well-documented attack on the tory government's policy.

On his retirement from parliament in 1880 Montagu devoted himself to religious controversy. In 1864 he had defended church establishments and upheld Anglicanism in *The Four Experiments in Church and State and the Conflicts of Churches*; but his conversion to Roman Catholicism in 1870 prompted several pamphlets from a different point of view. However, in 1882 he rejoined the Church of England on ethical and political rather than on theological grounds (see his *Reasons for Leaving the Church of Rome*, 1886). Thereupon he pursued a vigorous campaign against Romanist doctrine and practice, professing in a series of pamphlets—notably *Scylla or Charybdis, which? Gladstone or Salisbury?* (1887)—to expose a conspiracy, in which the leaders of both political parties were involved, to bring England under the dominion of the papacy. *The Sower and the Virgin* (1887) was an exhaustive confutation of the doctrines of the immaculate conception and papal infallibility. *The Lambeth Judgment, or, The Marks of Sacerdotalism* (1891) minutely analysed Bishop King's case.

Montagu married first, on 12 February 1850, Mary (d. 1857), only child and heiress of John Cromie, of Cromore, co. Antrim, with whom he had two sons and two daughters; second, on 18 October 1862, Elizabeth Catherine (d. 1897), daughter of William Wade, with whom he had three sons and two daughters. Not surprisingly, Montagu's violent switches of political and religious allegiance baffled his colleagues in public life and are still hard to explain. He died at his home, 91 Queen's Gate, London, on 6 May 1902, and was buried at Kensal Green cemetery.

G. Le G. Norgate, *rev.* H. C. G. Matthew

Sources *The Times* (7 May 1902) · *The Times* (12 May 1902) · Venn, *Alum. Cant.* · D. Thornley, *Isaac Butt and home rule* (1964) · *Disraeli, Derby and the conservative party: journals and memoirs of Edward Henry, Lord Stanley, 1849–1869*, ed. J. R. Vincent (1978) · DNB
Archives BL, letters to W. E. Gladstone, Add. MSS 44398–44464 · Bodl. Oxf., letters to Benjamin Disraeli
Likenesses Ape [C. Pellegrini], chromolithograph caricature, repro. in *VF* (1 Oct 1870), pl. 64
Wealth at death £38,171 11s. 1d.: probate, 12 June 1902, CGPLA Eng. & Wales

Montagu, Samuel, first Baron Swaythling (1832–1911), merchant banker and philanthropist, was born Montagu Samuel in Liverpool on 21 December 1832, the second son and youngest child of Louis Samuel (1794–1859), watchmaker and silversmith of Liverpool, and his wife, Henrietta, daughter of Israel Israel of Bury Street, St Mary Axe, London. The Samuel family had emigrated from Mecklenburg-Strelitz in northern Germany in the mid-eighteenth century. Both of Montagu's parents were Orthodox Jews and he was to remain a strict adherent of Orthodox Judaism.

Montagu's parents altered his given name of Montagu Samuel to Samuel Montagu as soon as he completed his education at the Mechanics' Institution (later the Liverpool Institute). His name change was confirmed by royal licence in 1894. After Louis Samuel retired from business in 1847, the family moved to London, where Montagu joined the money-changing business of his brother-in-law Adam Spielmann. In 1850 or 1851 he was appointed London manager of V. Monteaux & Co., a private bank in Paris, but in 1852 he persuaded his father to provide £5000 to start his own firm. This investment was on condition that Montagu—not yet twenty-one—should run the business in partnership with his elder brother, Edwin Samuel, who was a bullion merchant and banker in Liverpool. On this basis the firm of Montagu and Samuel was founded at 142 Leadenhall Street, London, in February 1853. The brothers took on Monteaux's lease at 21 Cornhill in 1862 and in 1865 moved to 60 (later renumbered 114) Old Broad Street, which remained the firm's address until 1987.

The new firm specialized in bullion and exchange services, bill collection, and bankers' drafts. Montagu's experience and expertise in bullion and foreign exchange were the key factors in the business, and within two decades the firm had 'assumed an undisputed lead in the silver market' (*Jewish Chronicle*, 20 Jan 1911). His skilful use of fine margins in foreign exchange gave him the reputation of founding his fortune on 'the quarter-pfennig and the half-centime' (Franklin, 4).

Samuel Montagu, first Baron Swaythling (1832–1911), by Sir
Benjamin Stone, 1898

Edwin Samuel played little part in the development of
the firm, remaining in Liverpool until he wound up his
own bank in 1872. Montagu's main support came from
Ellis Abraham Franklin, who had been the firm's first
employee. Franklin married Montagu's sister Adelaide in
1856 and became a partner in 1862. The business was then
renamed Samuel, Montagu & Co. (the comma was
dropped from the title when Edwin died in 1877). In 1868
the three partners, who were each to have four sons,
founded and financed the independent firm of A. Keyser &
Co. at their old office in Cornhill; it was later agreed that
two sons of each partner in Samuel, Montagu & Co. would
be admitted to the new concern.

By the 1870s Montagu had diversified into the market
for foreign loans and bills. He cultivated this new interest
by frequent visits to western Europe, where he acted as
'the bank's courier' (Montagu, 61). In 1896 these international contacts led to the appointment of Samuel Montagu as the issuing house for the Belgian government's £1
million 3 per cent loan. By that time the financial success
of the firm was assured. Montagu himself admitted in
1896 that 'we have a capital of at least £1,000,000. Some
people give us credit for having more than this' (Green,
299). 'For practical purposes', reported one London
banker in the same year, 'they are as good as Rothschilds'
(HSBC Group Archives, M153/44).

Throughout his career Montagu maintained direct and
narrow control over the firm. Procurations, for example,
were not granted to members of staff; consequently for
the first fifty years of the firm's existence it was necessary
for Montagu or Franklin to sign every letter and every
cheque issued by the bank. Montagu was also famously
impatient with staff or customers who would not accept
instructions and advice. Outside the partnership he was
an active shareholder in many British and overseas companies. As an investor in the Chartered Mercantile Bank of
India, for example, he was a powerful influence in the successful reconstruction of the company as the Mercantile
Bank in 1893.

Montagu was elected Liberal MP for the Whitechapel
division of Tower Hamlets in 1885. Although he was 'far
from being a brilliant speaker' (Montagu, 67), he was a
popular figure in his East End constituency and in the
Commons. In 1888 he was a member of the select committee of the House of Commons on alien immigration, an
issue on which he opposed over-restriction and spoke for
the interests of persecuted Jews. A devoted follower of
Gladstone, he was active as a 'home-ruler' (he contributed
to the Parnell expenses fund) and as an advocate of free
trade. He was chief author of the Weights and Measures
Act 1897 which legalized the use of metric weights and
measures, and he ensured that the Finance Act of 1894
exempted from death duties bequests to public libraries,
museums, and art galleries. An ardent supporter of bimet-
allism, he was a member of the gold and silver commission (1887–90) and president of the Decimal Association;
he advised both Liberal and Unionist governments on
financial issues and gave evidence to the national monetary commission in the USA.

In his activities outside business and politics, Montagu
was equally tenacious and purposeful. He was closely
identified with the work of the Anglo-Jewish community.
He was a life member of the council of the United Synagogue, a prominent member of the Board of Deputies of
British Jews (from 1862), and a member of the board of
guardians and the religious education board. In 1870 he
founded and became president of the Jewish working
men's club in Aldgate. He was until 1909 president of the
Shechita board (for supervising the slaughtering of animals according to Jewish practice) and he was chairman of
the building committee of the New West End Synagogue
in Bayswater (his own place of worship). One of his greatest services to the Jewish community was the formation in
1887 of the federation of the smaller East End synagogues,
where he insisted that English became the official language. He was a seat holder at no fewer than forty synagogues.

Montagu worked energetically in the interests of the
east London poor, both Jewish and non-Jewish. He was
treasurer of the Jews' Temporary Shelter, founder of the
East London Apprenticeship Fund in 1887, trustee of the
People's Palace at Mile End, member of the house committee at the London Hospital, and a director of the Four Per
Cent Industrial Dwellings Company. In 1903 he gave
£10,000 to London county council for its housing scheme
for the poor of Tottenham.

Montagu frequently travelled overseas in the interests
of his co-religionists. In 1875 he visited the Holy Land and
later founded with Lord Rothschild the first secular and

industrial school in Jerusalem. In 1884 he visited the United States to assist the formation of Jewish agricultural colonies in the far west, and two years later he visited all the chief towns of Russia in order to investigate the condition of the Jews there—an enterprise which on his arrival in Moscow led to his expulsion from Russia at forty-eight hours' notice. Thereafter he was prominent in the affairs of the Mansion House Fund (later the Russo-Jewish Committee), and he served as president from 1896 to 1909.

Samuel Montagu, who was made a baronet on 23 June 1894, retired from the House of Commons in 1900 and was succeeded there by his nephew and partner Stuart Montagu Samuel. On Campbell-Bannerman's recommendation, in 1907 he was raised to the peerage as Baron Swaythling, taking his title from Swaythling near Southampton, where he had a country house, at South Stonham.

In 1862 Montagu married Ellen (1848–1919), the youngest daughter of Louis Cohen, a merchant and stockbroker. They had ten children, including Henrietta *Franklin (1866–1964), educationalist and suffragist Edwin *Montagu (1879–1924), later secretary of state for India, and Lilian *Montagu (1873–1963), vice-president of the Jewish Religious Union. Over several decades Montagu amassed a large and celebrated collection of antique silver and a fine collection of English paintings (including works by Reynolds, Turner, and Morland). He was elected a fellow of the Society of Arts in 1897 and he was a conscientious contributor to Palgrave's *Dictionary of Political Economy*, the *Encyclopaedia Britannica*, and the *Jewish Chronicle*. He retired from active business life in 1909 and died on 12 January 1911 at his London home, 12 Kensington Palace Gardens, leaving an estate with a gross probate value of £1,150,000. He was buried at the Federation Jewish cemetery at Edmonton, Middlesex, and was survived by his wife, four sons, and six daughters. Most of his fortune was left in trust for his children on the condition that they should neither leave nor marry outside the Jewish faith.

EDWIN GREEN

Sources DNB · E. Green, 'Montagu, Samuel', *DBB* · *The Samuel family of Liverpool and London* (1958) · L. H. Montagu, *Montagu, Baron Swaythling: a character sketch* (1913) · *Jewish Chronicle* (13 Jan 1911) · *Jewish Chronicle* (20 Jan 1911) · *The Times* (13 Jan 1911) · S. E. Franklin, 'Samuel Montagu & Co: a brief account of the development of the firm', memoir, 1967, HSBC Group Archives, London, Samuel Montagu archives · K. Grunwald, *Studies in the history of the German Jews in global banking* (1980) · Samuel Montagu Archives, HSBC Group Archives, London, Samuel Montagu archives · d. cert. · HSBC Group Archives, London, Midland Bank archives
Archives HSBC Group Archives, London · LMA · U. Southampton L., papers | Bodl. Oxf., letters to Sir William Harcourt and Lewis Harcourt · HLRO, letters to Herbert Samuel · HSBC Group Archives, London, Midland Bank archives · NL Scot., corresp. with Lord Rosebery
Likenesses B. Stone, photograph, 1898, NPG [*see illus.*] · photograph, c.1900, HSBC Group Archives, London, Midland Bank archives · Lib [L. Prosperi], caricature, chromolithograph, NPG; repro. in *VF* (6 Nov 1886) · W. Q. Orchardson, oils, repro. in *Jewish Chronicle* (20 Jan 1911) · photograph, repro. in *Bankers' Magazine*, 48 (1888) · photograph, repro. in *Bankers' Magazine*, 88 (1909) · photograph, repro. in *Jewish World* (July 1907)

Wealth at death £1,150,000: probate, 2 March 1911, *CGPLA Eng. & Wales*

Montagu [Montacute], **Simon de**, first Lord Montagu (1259?–1316), soldier and baron, was descended from Drogo de Montagu, a Norman who came to England with William the Conqueror. Simon was the son of William de Montagu, a Somerset landowner, and his wife, Berthe. He was under age at his father's death, in 1270, but fought in Edward I's wars in Wales in 1277 and 1282, and in 1283 was summoned to parliament at Shrewsbury. In 1290 he surrendered his lands in Dorset, Devon, Buckinghamshire, and Oxfordshire to the king, and was then regranted them with remainders to his sons William and Simon. He was summoned to fight in Gascony in 1294, where he served as marshal at Blaye. In 1296 he succeeded in breaking the French siege of Bourg-sur-Mer, taking a ship loaded with victuals through the line of French galleys. He returned to Gascony with John Hastings on royal service in 1302. It was in Scotland, however, that Montagu served the crown most. In 1298 he attended the parliament at York at which the Scottish war was discussed, and may have been present on the Falkirk campaign later that year. He certainly took part in the Caerlaverock expedition of 1300; the poet who described the army placed him at the rear of the 3rd division. Montagu's particular contribution to the wars lay in naval warfare in the Irish Sea and around the Western Isles. In 1300 he provided two substantial ships for the Scottish war, a galley and a barge, manned by 100 men between them. In 1307 he was captain and governor of the English fleet, and admiral in 1310. He continued to be summoned to campaign against the Scots until his death.

Montagu did not receive many rewards for his services. In 1299 he was given charge of Corfe Castle, jointly with Richard de Bosco, a post he held until 1301. It was later claimed that the hall had suffered damage amounting to 100 marks during his tenure; he was granted permission to pay off his debts to the crown at the rate of £10 a year in 1302. In 1309 he was given custody of Beaumaris Castle in Anglesey. His baronial status is testified to by his witnessing the barons' letter to the pope in 1301. Montagu's first marriage, about 1270, was to Hawise, daughter of Amaury de St Amand. Shortly after her death in 1287 he married Isabel, whose parentage is unknown. It seems probable that in 1304 he married Aufrica de Connoght, who claimed to be heir to the Isle of Man, for in that year she handed over her rights in the isle to him. Man had come under Scottish control in 1265, but was annexed to England by Edward I in 1290. In 1311 Montagu was imprisoned for a time in Windsor; perhaps this was because he had attempted to seize the Isle of Man, an action for which he was pardoned in 1313. He died on 27 September 1316, and was buried in Bruton Priory, Somerset. His being summoned to parliament in 1299 and afterwards has led to his being conventionally styled first Lord Montagu. He left a son William *Montagu (c.1285–1319), who became second Lord Montagu.

MICHAEL PRESTWICH

Sources *Chancery records* · GEC, *Peerage*, new edn, 9.78–80 · T. Stapleton, 'A brief summary of the wardrobe accounts of the tenth, eleventh and fourteenth years of King Edward the Second', *Archaeologia*, 26 (1836), 318–45, esp. 339 • [W. Rishanger], *The chronicle of William de Rishanger, of the barons' wars*, ed. J. O. Halliwell, CS, 15 (1840) • J. Topham, *Liber quotidianus contrarotulatoris garderobae: anno regni regis Edwardi primi vicesimo octavo* (1787) • S. Duffy, 'The "continuation" of Nicholas Trevet: a new source for the Bruce invasion', *Proceedings of the Royal Irish Academy*, 91C (1991), 303–15

Montagu [Montacute], **Simon** (1304?–1345), bishop of Ely, was the second son of William *Montagu, second Lord Montagu (c.1285–1319), and his wife, Elizabeth de Montfort (d. 1354). He was probably born in 1304, to judge from a request to the pope in November 1318 for a dispensation for Montagu, as one who had not completed his fifteenth year. The same petition describes him as a student at Oxford, where he had proceeded MA by 1329. By that time he was also a king's clerk. His rise in the church, then and later, was unquestionably smoothed by family connections—his father was loyal to Edward II, while his elder brother, William *Montagu (1301–1344), was the leading agent in the *coup d'état* of October 1330 whereby Edward III overthrew Roger Mortimer and Queen Isabella. As early as 15 October 1317 a royal grant had secured for Simon the prebend of Bugthorpe in York Minster. Attempts to secure the archdeaconry of Wells for him between 1329 and 1332 came to nothing, but during 1330 he received prebends in Salisbury and Exeter, and by 1332 he was a papal chaplain. Before March 1332 he was provided to the prebend of Stow Longa in Lincoln Cathedral, in response to a petition in which Edward III described Montagu as his familiar clerk, and on 15 July following he was provided to the archdeaconry of Canterbury. Following the translation of John Stratford to Canterbury in November 1333, Edward even tried to secure for Montagu the great see of Winchester, but was thwarted by Pope John XXII, who translated Adam Orleton thither from Worcester; by way of compensation, Montagu was on 11 December provided to the latter see. The temporalities were restored on 15 March 1334, and the bishop of Lincoln consecrated him at Thame, Oxfordshire, on 8 May.

Montagu did not enter his diocese until 25 September 1334, but once there he seldom left it—he is recorded as attending parliament in May 1336 and March 1337. In 1335–6 he conducted a thorough primary visitation, preaching an unusually large number of sermons in the course of it. He was usually on good terms with his cathedral priory, restoring the Worcestershire manor of Crowle Syward to the monks, and assisting the work then in progress on Worcester Cathedral. In return the chapter admitted him to confraternity and made provision for a perpetual obit. He was supported by a distinguished body of diocesan officers, several of whom accompanied him when, on 14 March 1337 (just two days before his elder brother was created earl of Salisbury), he was provided to the wealthy see of Ely. The temporalities were restored on 11 June. As bishop of Ely, Montagu was occasionally involved in public affairs. He attended parliaments in 1339, 1340, and 1343, and in the crisis of 1340–41 he stood by Archbishop Stratford to the extent of acting as his

cross-bearer; but this was probably more to show his support for ecclesiastical rights than a gesture of political partisanship. Otherwise he seems to have devoted himself principally to diocesan business. He gave important statutes to Peterhouse, Cambridge, deriving some material from those of Merton College, Oxford, but showing due regard for the Cambridge house's relative poverty. As at Worcester, he earned the high regard of his cathedral monks, for whom he was 'our most kindly father and pastor Lord Symon' (Wharton, 1.651). He gave large sums towards the building of the cathedral's lady chapel, and, although he did not live to see its completion, when he died, on 20 June 1345, he was buried before its altar. No tomb or memorial now survives.

HENRY SUMMERSON

Sources Emden, *Oxf.*, 2.1295–6 • R. M. Haines, ed., *Calendar of the register of Simon de Montacute, bishop of Worcester, 1334–1337*, Worcestershire Historical Society, new ser., 15 (1996) • R. M. Haines, *The administration of the diocese of Worcester in the first half of the fourteenth century* (1965) • R. M. Haines, *Archbishop John Stratford: political revolutionary and champion of the liberties of the English church*, Pontifical Institute of Medieval Studies: Texts and Studies, 76 (1986) • [H. Wharton], ed., *Anglia sacra*, 1 (1691) • *Fasti Angl., 1300–1541*, [Monastic cathedrals] • *VCH Cambridgeshire and the Isle of Ely*, vols. 3–4 • H. Rashdall, *The universities of Europe in the middle ages*, ed. F. M. Powicke and A. B. Emden, new edn, 3 (1936), 296–9 • GEC, *Peerage*, new edn, 9.80–2

Montagu, Thomas [Thomas de Montacute], **fourth earl of Salisbury** (1388–1428), soldier, was the elder son of John *Montagu, third earl of Salisbury (d. 1400), and his wife, Maud *Montagu (d. 1424), daughter of Adam Franceys, mayor of London, and widow of John Aubrey, and of Sir Alan Buxhull (d. 1381). Earl John died in the aftermath of the abortive plot to murder Henry IV, planned for 4 January 1400. Despite his father's subsequent attainder for treason in 1401, Thomas Montagu was granted an annuity out of the comital lands for his maintenance, and was already styling himself earl. On 14 June 1409 he proved his age, performed fealty, and was restored to all that his father had held in fee tail. In October next he was summoned to parliament as the earl of Salisbury, and in 1414 he petitioned for full restoration, to which the king all but acquiesced in 1421 after the Commons had added their support.

The reason for this return to royal favour was Salisbury's service in France in which he was engaged almost continuously under Henry V and Henry VI, thus playing little role in domestic high politics. In 1412 he served on the expedition sent under Thomas, duke of Clarence. Created a knight of the Garter in April 1414, he was involved in negotiations with the French and discussions in the royal council about Gascony before serving on the Agincourt campaign. In 1416 he was assigned with Humphrey, duke of Gloucester, to greet Emperor Sigismund at Dover, and also served on the naval expedition under John, duke of Bedford. In the following year he crossed with the king for the conquest of Normandy, where he took part in Henry's sieges of Caen and Falaise before accompanying Clarence on an expedition along the Risle. At the siege of Rouen he was stationed at the Mont-St Catherine. He was later

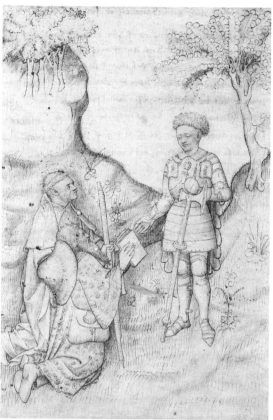

Thomas Montagu, fourth earl of Salisbury (1388–1428), tinted drawing [standing right, with John Lydgate and a palmer]

responsible for the capture of Fécamp, Montivilliers, Gournay, Eu, and Honfleur (of which he was captain, 1419–20). His military prominence is confirmed by his appointment on 26 April 1419 as the king's lieutenant-general in Normandy and in the marches south of the Seine. On 13 November 1420 his charge was redefined as the whole duchy in addition to Maine. The level of royal trust is also revealed by his involvement in diplomatic activities in the autumn of 1418 and spring of 1419. Having accompanied Henry V on his entry to Paris on 1 December 1420, he was appointed on 25 December to the governorship of Alençon, Essay, Exmes, Bonsmoulins, and Verneuil, places he continued to control until Michaelmas 1423. He also benefited from royal largesse under Henry and his son: he was created count of Perche on 26 April 1419, and enjoyed a series of major land grants in France between 1418 and 1427.

Salisbury accompanied Clarence on his campaign into Maine and Anjou in the spring of 1421. According to Jean de Waurin (d. 1473/4), the duke advanced against the French and Scots at Baugé without waiting for the rear guard under Salisbury. All the earl could do was to drive off the victorious French in order to retrieve Clarence's body, and to conduct his own brief raid into Anjou. He continued in service in France after the death of Henry V, assisting in the recovery of Meulan and Orsay, and holding

the captaincy of Falaise from 25 December 1422 to his death. In June 1423 Bedford appointed him governor of Champagne, Brie, Auxerrois, Nivernois, and the Mâconnais, and in this capacity he laid siege to Montaguillon, near Provins. When the French army of relief advanced against Cravant, Salisbury was sent with reinforcements to assist the Burgundians, and together they defeated the French on 30 July 1423, with the earl in command of the left flank. He continued to campaign successfully in Champagne over the next year. In preparation for the *journée* of Verneuil, John, duke of Bedford, ordered Salisbury to take up an initial position four leagues from the enemy. Waurin, who was an eyewitness, claimed that without the earl's personal example of valour, which spurred on those who fought under his banner, the battle might have gone quite differently. In September and October 1424 he attempted with William de la Pole, earl of Suffolk (d. 1450), and reinforcements from England to recover Nogent le Rotrou, Senonches, Rambouillet, and Rochefort. He afterwards took over the captaincies of Nogent and Montigny. By the summer of 1425 the situation in Champagne was secure enough to allow him to take up command of the advance into Maine and Anjou. He conducted a highly successful campaign whereby all of the key places, including Le Mans, were captured. At Bedford's departure for England in September 1425 conduct of the war was entrusted to Richard Beauchamp, earl of Warwick, and the earls of Suffolk and Salisbury, with the latter being given charge of much of Normandy as well as Anjou, Maine, the Vendômois, the Chartrain, and Beauce. Warwick was assigned to the 'marches et pays de France', thus replacing Salisbury in the theatre of the Vermandois, Champagne, Brie, and the Gâtinais. In February 1426, however, Salisbury resigned his command to go on pilgrimage to Jerusalem in accordance with a vow made during the course of a battle. By July he had changed his mind; he obtained a dispensation from the pope which released him from his vow, and returned to the field, resuming his activities in Champagne while Warwick maintained the advance into Maine. From October 1426 Salisbury also held the captaincy of Meulan. When Bedford returned to France in April 1427, Warwick was appointed lieutenant of Normandy, Anjou, Maine, and the marches of Brittany while Salisbury returned to England, perhaps in search of reinforcements. His return had been anticipated by his appointment as a privy councillor in November 1426 and he attended the council regularly from July 1427 to 1 June 1428, as well as the parliament of 1427–8, where he took the opportunity to present a joint petition with Gloucester concerning wages still owing from the Agincourt campaign. His stay was dominated by the planning and raising of a major expeditionary force with which he sailed in July 1428.

Bedford had hoped to use Salisbury's reinforcements along with troops raised within Normandy and France for a final thrust into his own duchy of Anjou, but the campaign which ensued was directed instead towards Orléans, perhaps with its ultimate goal an assault on Bourges. Why the change in plan occurred and whether

Salisbury was instrumental in it have been the subject of much debate. The attack on Orléans was most certainly against the interests and the will of the duke of Burgundy, Philip the Good, who, according to Fenin, had made amorous advances towards the countess of Salisbury during the wedding celebrations of the seigneur de Toulongeon in Paris in November 1424, offending the earl and leading him to support Gloucester's anti-Burgundian activities in the Low Countries. Further clashes with Philip had arisen over the administration of Champagne. Salisbury was also in dispute with Bedford over rights in the duchy of Alençon, but it is perhaps going too far to see the earl deliberately acting against Bedford in the war policy of 1428. The earl met Bedford at Paris before conducting a swift and successful campaign southwards, skilfully establishing a forward base at Janville and isolating Orléans by capturing the Loire towns of Jargeau, Beaugency, and Meung. By 12 October he had drawn his army up to besiege Orléans and within eleven days had forced the French to abandon the fortification of Les Tourelles which controlled the bridge. While observing the city from Les Tourelles on 27 October he was seriously wounded in the face by a cannon shot from the city. Salisbury's death at Meung on 3 November 1428 deprived the English of their most talented and experienced commander. His body was taken back to England; after a mass at St Paul's on 29 November he was buried at Bisham Abbey in accordance with his will.

Salisbury married twice. His first wife, whom he married on or before 23 May 1399, was Eleanor, daughter of Thomas *Holland, earl of Kent (d. 1400), and Alice, daughter of Richard (III) Fitzalan, earl of Arundel. Neither Eleanor's date of death nor the date of Salisbury's marriage to his second wife, Alice *Chaucer (c.1404–1475), daughter of Thomas *Chaucer (d. 1434) and Maud Burghersh (d. 1437), is known. Eleanor was definitely dead by 10 June 1424; thus it must have been his second wife, Alice, who aroused the passions of the duke of Burgundy in November 1424. It has been suggested that Salisbury may already have been married, or at least contracted, to Alice by May 1421 when her father was speaker of the parliament in which the Commons petitioned with some success for the full restoration of the earl's lands. Alice had been married as a child to Sir John Philip who died at Harfleur in 1415 and was sole heir to her father's fortune. After Salisbury's death she married, in November 1430, William de la Pole, earl of Suffolk (d. 1450). With his first wife, Salisbury had one daughter, Alice (c.1406–1462), who married in or before February 1421 Richard Neville (d. 1460), younger son of Ralph Neville, earl of Westmorland, and Joan Beaufort. Neville seems to have been styled earl of Salisbury from the time of his father-in-law's death; the privy council confirmed his right to the earldom in May 1429. There was also an illegitimate son, Sir John Montagu (Bastard Salisbury), who served in France; he was captain of Gournay and Gerberoy (1430–31), of Argentan (1431–4), lieutenant at St Lô (1434–5), and captain of Fresnay (1446–8).

ANNE CURRY

Sources GEC, *Peerage* · *RotP* · N. H. Nicolas, ed., *Proceedings and ordinances of the privy council of England*, 7 vols., RC, 26 (1834–7) · PRO · BL · Bibliothèque Nationale, Collection Clairambault, manuscrits français · Archives Nationales, série K, série JJ, série Xia · *Chancery records* · Rymer, *Foedera* · *Recueil des croniques … par Jehan de Waurin*, ed. W. Hardy and E. L. C. P. Hardy, 5 vols., Rolls Series, 39 (1864–91), vols. 2–4 · *Mémoires de Pierre de Fenin*, ed. Mlle Dupont (Paris, 1837) · J. Stevenson, ed., *Letters and papers illustrative of the wars of the English in France during the reign of Henry VI, king of England*, 2 vols. in 3 pts, Rolls Series, 22 (1861–4) · E. F. Jacob, ed., *The register of Henry Chichele, archbishop of Canterbury, 1414–1443*, 2, CYS, 42 (1937) · C. T. Allmand and C. A. J. Armstrong, eds., *English suits before the Parlement of Paris, 1420–1436*, CS, 4th ser., 26 (1982) · M. Warner, 'The Montagu earls of Salisbury, 1300–1428', PhD diss., U. Lond., 1991 · M. W. Warner, 'Chivalry in action: Thomas Montague and the war in France, 1417–1428', *Nottingham Medieval Studies*, 42 (1998), 146–73 · *Chronique de Jean Le Fèvre, seigneur de Saint-Remy*, ed. F. Morand, 2 vols. (Paris, 1876–81) · HoP, *Commons, 1386–1421* · Archives Municipales de Troyes, série BB · Archives Départementales de la Marne, série E · S. Guilbert, ed., *Registre de délibérations du Conseil de ville de Reims (1422–36)* (Reims, [1993]) · A. Desplanque, 'Projet d'assassinat de Philippe le Bon par les Anglais, 1424–25', *Mémoires publiés par l'Académie royale des sciences, des lettres et beaux arts de Belgique*, 33 (1865–7) · inquisition post mortem, PRO, C 139/41 · inquisition post mortem, PRO, E 149/142/1 · inquisition post mortem, PRO, E 152/522, 568
Archives GL, letter-book K | BL, Harley MSS · BL, Cotton MSS · BL, Lansdowne MSS · PRO, ancient correspondence, SCI
Likenesses tinted drawing, BL, MS Harley 4826, fol. 1* [paste-in] [see illus.]
Wealth at death over £311—from lands in England: PRO, C 139/41; E 149/142/1; E 152/522, 568; will

Montagu, (Beatrice) Venetia. *See* Stanley, (Beatrice) Venetia (1887–1948).

Montagu, (Alexander) Victor Edward Paulet, tenth earl of Sandwich (1906–1995), politician, was born on 22 May 1906, the elder son and oldest of four children of George Charles Montagu, ninth earl of Sandwich (1874–1962), Unionist MP for south Huntingdonshire from 1900 to 1906, and his first wife, Alberta (d. 1951), daughter of William Sturges, of New York. Victor became Viscount Hinchingbrooke on his father's succession as earl of Sandwich in 1916, and thereafter was known as 'Hinch'. Although his 1962 succession to the peerage was to dramatically destroy his career as the maverick Conservative MP for South Dorset, he was fascinated by his family's history. Sydney Montagu had become groom of the bedchamber to his fellow Scot James I, and, even more lucratively, master of the court of bequest to Charles I, fleeing to the continent on the latter's downfall. His son Edward threw in his lot with parliament, but went over to King Charles in 1660, and was rewarded by being made the first earl of Sandwich. Hinch enjoyed reading the description by another relative, Samuel Pepys, of the duels of Edward Montagu, cousin of the first earl. Hinch was, however, most attracted to another ancestor, the fourth earl of Sandwich, who became first lord of the admiralty during the war against the American colonies, and the patron of Captain Cook. Cook named as the 'Sandwich Islands' both the Hawaiian Islands and a small volcanic group southeast of South Georgia.

Hinchingbrooke was educated at Eton College and Trinity College, Cambridge, where, unlike most Etonians, he opted for the natural science tripos. During vacations, at his father's insistence, he worked on the factory floor of an engineering works, which made him, for a Conservative MP, unusually sympathetic to factory workers in later life. In 1932–4 his father's influence enabled him to work as an assistant private secretary to Stanley Baldwin, lord president of the council. He then worked for the Junior Imperial League, which later joined the Young Conservatives. He married, on 27 July 1934, (Maud) Rosemary, only daughter of Major Ralph Harding Peto. There were two sons and four daughters of the marriage, which was dissolved in 1958.

During the Second World War, Hinchingbrooke served with the Northamptonshire regiment in France, and then on the general staff of the home forces. In 1941 he was elected, unopposed, MP for South Dorset. His first book, *Full Speed Ahead*, elegantly laying out his views of post-war tory ethics and philosophy, appeared in the same year. In 1943 he became chairman of the Tory Reform Committee, which included Peter Thorneycroft and Thelma Cazalet-Keir, and sought to find a 'new conservatism'. In 1944 they helped defeat the coalition government on the issue of equal pay for women teachers.

The conviction which made Hinchingbrooke the post-war stormy petrel and most unbending of 'Suez rebels' of Sir Anthony Eden's and Harold Macmillan's premierships was his attempt to retain the Commonwealth as the central focus of Britain's loyalty against the encroaching challenges of Europe, the Anglo-American alliance, and nationalist insurrectionaries in Africa and Asia. He came into national prominence in 1954 as the most outspoken of the small band of the 'Suez group' right wing Conservative MPs seeking to resist Britain's withdrawal of its garrison from the Suez Canal bases. In 1956 he urged 'gunboat diplomacy', aligning himself with the ailing Sir Anthony Eden, who had secretly planned with France and Israel to invade Egypt to reverse President Nasser's seizure of the Anglo-French Suez Canal company. Eden kept his friend, the pro-British President Eisenhower, in the dark. After Washington retaliated for this 'betrayal' by selling sterling, and Eden's doctors forced his unexpected retirement, Harold Macmillan accepted the need to withdraw British troops. This brought the Suez rebels to a peak, with Hinch and seven others resigning the Conservative whip in May 1957 on the ground of the government's 'capitulation to Nasser'. His constituency backed him overwhelmingly, singing 'For he's a jolly good fellow' following the defeat of a motion of no confidence in him, backed by his own executive committee. After sitting for a year as independent Conservatives, under the chairmanship of Hinch, the rebels had the whip restored.

Hinchingbrooke's next major rebellion was over Harold Macmillan's attempt from 1961 to join the Common Market. He and his colleagues immediately declared their opposition, with Hinch becoming president of the Anti-Common Market League in 1962. On 15 June the same year his ancestors' axe fell on his political neck: his father died and he succeeded to his unwanted earldom. Under the law as it stood he had to yield his seat. In 1963, however, Tony Benn succeeded in reversing the law, enabling Hinch to disclaim his peerage in 1964. His loss of constituency was a terrible wrench. He had been an outstanding local MP, genuinely loved by his constituents, one of whom (a Labour supporter) said 'He may be an eccentric, but he is *our* eccentric!' (*The Independent*, 2 March 1995). He had resisted fiercely the attempt by Enoch Powell in 1956, as parliamentary secretary for housing, to 'dump' former urban-dwellers in overspill towns in his beloved countryside. On 7 June 1962 he married Lady Anne Holland-Martin (*d.* 1981), youngest daughter of Victor Christian William Cavendish, ninth duke of Devonshire, divorced wife of Lieutenant-Colonel Henry Philip Hunloke, and widow of Christopher John Holland-Martin, Conservative MP for Ludlow from 1951 to 1960. The marriage was ended by divorce in 1965.

Hinchingbrooke made the unforgivable error of his career in 1962. Instead of backing Angus Maude, the official Conservative candidate, as his successor (who happened to be an anti-marketeer), he backed the Anti-Common Market League candidate, Sir Piers Debenham, a former local Conservative county councillor. The split tory vote secured the election of Labour's Guy Barnett. Hinch was never forgiven by local tories. He disclaimed his titles for life in July 1964, and immediately set about attempting to return to the Commons, but without success. He fought marginal Accrington in distant Lancashire in 1964 but failed. When the perfect opening came in North Dorset in 1970, the local tories turned him down as 'too old' at sixty-four. Having rejected the Lords and been rejected by local tories, he knew his active political life was over, though his comments remained sharp. When Enoch Powell refused to contest his Wolverhampton seat again in February 1974, urging a vote for Labour as a way of opposing the EEC, Hinch was scathing. He deplored Powell's silence on the EEC in 1962 and 1967: 'Much trouble might have been saved, if Mr Powell's thinking on either of these two occasions had been as needle-sharp as it is today' (*Parliamentary Profiles* files).

Hinch died on 25 February 1995, and was survived by the six children of his first marriage. His disclaimed peerages were resumed by his elder son, John Edward Hollister Montagu (*b.* 1943), a charity worker for Christian Aid and the Save the Children Fund, who became the eleventh earl of Sandwich. A memorial service was held at St James's, Piccadilly, on 25 April 1995.   ANDREW ROTH

Sources L. D. Epstein, *British politics in the Suez crisis* (1964) · A. Roth, *Enoch Powell: Tory tribune* (1970) · *The Independent* (2 March 1995) · *The Times* (27 Feb 1995) · *WWW*, 1991–5 · *Debrett's Peerage* · Burke, *Peerage* · Open University, *Parliamentary Profiles* files
Archives NRA, priv. coll., papers
Likenesses photograph, repro. in *The Times* · photograph, repro. in *The Independent*
Wealth at death £2,276,201: probate, 27 Sept 1995, *CGPLA Eng. & Wales*

Montagu, Walter (1604/5–1677), courtier and abbot of St Martin, was born in the parish of St Botolph Aldgate, London, the second of four sons of Henry *Montagu, first earl of Manchester (*c.*1564–1642), and his first wife, Catherine (*d*. 1612), second daughter of Sir William Spencer of Yarnton, Oxfordshire; Edward *Montagu, second earl of Manchester (1602–1671), was his elder brother.

On 27 January 1618 Montagu entered Sidney Sussex College, Cambridge, as a fellow-commoner. Upon leaving Cambridge he travelled to the continent (France and Italy) in order to improve himself both in languages and in the graces considered necessary to the formation of a nobleman. Returning to England he found employment in the service of the duke of Buckingham and was sent to France in 1624 in relation to the planned marriage of the future Charles I and the French princess Henrietta Maria. At this time Montagu met Marie Aimée de Rohan, duchesse de Chevreuse, but although he appears to have been involved in her later intrigues against Richelieu 'it was not until the summer of 1647 that their relations were to take on an intimate character' (Falk, 29). In March 1625 he returned with the news that, with regard to the marriage negotiations, 'all is forward, and the lady should be delivered in thirty days' (Montagu, 2.2). The 21-year-old agent was rewarded for his efforts with the sum of £200 and began a devoted service to Henrietta Maria which ended only at her death. Later in 1625 he was dispatched to France with regard to the arbitrary seizure of some English vessels and returned with France's promise both of the restitution of the seized ships and of peace between the French government and the Huguenots. For his efforts he again received £200 and in March of 1627 another sum (£400) was granted him in recognition of his 'secret' service to the crown.

By now England's relations with France were deteriorating. Following his creation as MA of Cambridge in 1627 Montagu was sent to Lorraine and Italy, this time to seek allies for England against France, against whom war had already broken out. He enjoyed little success in this endeavour and was forced to report to Charles I that if he became involved in a continental war England would have no allies. While passing through Lorraine, considered neutral territory, Montagu was arrested by Richelieu's agents and along with his papers was carried off to Paris and lodged in the Bastille, though accorded a large degree of freedom. He returned to England in April 1628 and was warmly received by Charles I. As a consolation for his troubles he and his brother Edward received the office of chief ranger of the forest of Waybridge, Huntingdon, with a fee of £20 per annum. In addition he was also granted a quarter-share of an office registering chancery writs. In August 1628 he was present at the assassination of the duke of Buckingham at Portsmouth. Later that same year he was again sent to France on the pretext of negotiating an exchange of prisoners and afterwards returned to England carrying Richelieu's conditions for coming to terms with England—which Charles rejected. Montagu travelled back to France, this time staying until 1633. About this time he emerged as a dramatist, penning the comedy or pastoral *The Shepherd's Paradise* which was privately presented before Charles and the court by the queen and her ladies of honour. This long prose pastoral, considered both stilted and tedious, drew the ire of Sir John Suckling

and others in sharp ridicule. Montagu seemed destined never to become a dramatist or poet of real worth.

Having returned once more to France, Montagu resided in Paris, attached to the English embassy. Out of curiosity he travelled to Loudun to witness the exorcisms of some Ursuline nuns, an experience which resulted in a spiritual conversion. He embraced the Catholic faith and in 1635 announced his departure to Rome and his intention to join the fathers of the Oratory. His conversion caused a stir at court and the letter containing this announcement to his father, and giving his reasons for embracing the Roman Catholic faith, was passed from hand to hand. In 1636 he was sent to Rome where he campaigned for a papal agency to England. In turn the papal agent, George Con, negotiated Montagu's return to England in 1637. He had been secretly ordained abroad and was appointed chamberlain to the queen at Somerset House, her residence, and began to urge her to actively participate in the propagation of the Catholic religion. By 1638 he appears to have aspired towards the rank of cardinal, though in 1639 he again spoke of entering the Roman Oratory. With Con's death in 1640, the queen lent her support, but the plan won the favour neither of the king nor of Rome. In April 1639 Montagu and Sir Kenelm Digby, as the queen's agents, collected a contribution from Catholics to defray the cost of the royal army in the struggle with the Scots, a contribution which raised £20,000. Montagu was to expend much energy on behalf of the royal cause but action against him was swift. On 16 March 1640 parliament petitioned the king to remove all recusants from court and by the beginning of 1641 the Long Parliament had ordered Montagu, Digby, and John Winter (the queen's secretary) to give an account of their part of the collection of the money. In the same month Montagu was banished and went again to France.

In October 1643 Montagu re-entered England by subterfuge, clumsily disguised as a member of the French ambassador's entourage. He reached Rochester but was captured and taken to London, where he was ordered by the House of Commons to be detained as a close prisoner in the Tower, evidently due to the fact that he was carrying sealed letters with the arms of France directed to the king and queen of England. He suffered a long imprisonment before being released in 1647. On 9 February 1644 the Commons ordered all his goods seized and sold and the proceeds sent to the army of Lord Fairfax. While in prison Montagu occupied his time in penning the first book of *Miscellanea spiritualia, or, Devout Essaies* and engaging in religious disputations with John Bastwick, and was permitted from time to time to go to Tunbridge Wells to drink the waters.

On 31 August 1649 the Commons declared that Montagu, Digby, and Winter were 'doomed to perpetual banishment with confiscation of estate and with menace of the penalty of death if either should dare to return to England without the authority of Parliament' (Montagu, 2.12). After returning to France once more Montagu took time during these difficulties to engage in literary endeavours, composing verses which were to be prefixed to Edward

Benlowes' *Theophila, or, Love's Sacrifice*, (1652) and *The Accomplished Woman* (1656), translated from the French. Shortly thereafter, due to the influence of Anne of Austria, regent of France, he was created abbot of the Benedictine monastery of Nanteuil in the diocese of Metz. He subsequently became abbot of St Martin, near Pontoise, in the diocese of Rhoan. He was made a member of the regent's cabinet council and was perhaps the chief instrument in bringing Cardinal Mazarin into her favour. Henrietta Maria's chamberlain now became Anne of Austria's almoner; the former secret service man was now consulted by the French on matters of state and he was, at least temporarily, acceptable to Mazarin, who had often regarded him with cold indifference and suspicion. Ever the fertile schemer, Montagu once suggested to Charles II that the surest way of gaining Mazarin's adherence to the cause of his restoration and, in Montagu's mind, of the re-establishment of the old religion was for him to marry Mazarin's niece, Hortense Mancini. However, Mazarin would not hear of it since Charles's 'affairs were not in order' (MacPherson, 12).

High in Henrietta Maria's regard, in 1654 Montagu was entrusted with the care of her son Henry, duke of Gloucester. At the queen's constant urging he tried with the utmost intensity to present the teachings of the Catholic religion with a view to Henry's conversion. Entertaining Henry at Pontoise, Montagu sought to keep him sequestered from anyone who might confirm him in his opposition to conversion. Charles, Henry's older brother, became troubled as to his younger brother's 'orthodoxy' and endeavoured with success to thwart Montagu's efforts. Charles regarded Montagu as the 'queen's evil genius', for she had made him her 'spiritual director'. Montagu hoped that with her influence he would attain the office in the church that he most desired—that of cardinal—which he saw as a means better to serve his church. For him the one great reality that transcended everything else was the Catholic church and its propagation, making reconciliation between the church and England his one goal. He made known that he was always ready to mediate between Charles and Louis XIV should his services be desired, and he was at times consulted.

For his remaining years Montagu lived quietly in France with the one known exception of a journey to England in 1660, when he enjoyed a friendly visit to his brother Edward. Not long after the death of Henrietta Maria in 1669 he was asked to resign the office of abbot of St Martin, and upon his so doing the abbacy was given to Cardinal Bouillon. However, Montagu was allowed to keep his furniture and continued to enjoy the revenues of the abbey. His income as commendatory abbot (£5000), together with gifts, had allowed him to give monetary aid to his fellow countrymen, Catholic and protestant, whom the civil war in England had forced to flee. His life at Pontoise appeared to be tranquil and happy. He was employed by Louis XIV in the translation of documents relating to the secret treaty of Dover of 1670, from English to French and from French to English. Close upon the signing of the treaty (August 1670) he was to mourn the death of the

duchess of Orléans, Henriette Anne, sister of Charles II, with whom he had closely collaborated in the writing of the treaty and who was his close confidant and supporter. He refused to believe rumours of her being poisoned and was present at the autopsy which refuted any suggestion of foul play. In 1672 he published *Exposition of the Doctrine of the Catholic Church*, his translation from Bossuet. Five years later, on 5 February 1677, he died in Paris at the Hospital of the Incurables in his seventy-third year. He was probably buried at Pontoise.

Montagu was deeply committed to the cause of his church; her welfare came before all else, leading to the general suppression of his personal desires. This did not mean that he lacked ambition—he would dearly have loved to have been made a cardinal—but advancement was not the sole or even the main driving force of his efforts; rather, the compelling motivation of his actions was his religious conviction and not the immediate opportunity of reward.

THOMPSON COOPER, rev. EDWARD CHARLES METZGER

Sources Wood, *Ath. Oxon.*, 2nd edn • W. D. Montagu, duke of Manchester, ed., *Court and society from Elizabeth to Anne*, 2 vols. (1864) • E. Hyde, earl of Clarendon, *The history of the rebellion and civil wars in England*, 7 vols. (1849) • B. Falk, *The way of the Montagues* (1947) • J. Macpherson, ed., *Original papers: containing the secret history of Great Britain*, 2 vols. (1775) • *Collins peerage of England: genealogical, biographical and historical*, ed. E. Brydges, 9 vols. (1812) • *CSP dom.*, 1628–9 • W. A. Shaw, ed., *Calendar of treasury books*, [33 vols. in 64], PRO (1904–69) • *Dodd's Church history of England*, ed. M. A. Tierney, 5 vols. (1839–43) • F. C. Montague, *The history of England: from the accession of James I to the Restoration (1603–1660)* (1909) • J. Granger, *A biographical history of England from Egbert the Great to the revolution*, 5th edn, 6 vols. (1824) • S. R. Gardiner, *History of England from the accession of James I to the outbreak of the civil war*, 10 vols. (1883–4) • J. Dalrymple, *Memoirs of Great Britain and Ireland*, new edn, 3 vols. (1790) • H. Chapman, *Great Villiers: a study of George Villiers, second duke of Buckingham, 1628–87* (1949) • J. Cartwright, *Madame: a life Henrietta, daughter of Charles I and duchess of Orleans* (1901) • M. M. Motier, *The secret history of Henrietta, princess of England*, trans. J. M. Shelmerdine (1919) • C. Oman, *Henrietta Maria* (1936) • C. H. Firth and S. C. Loomis, *Notes on diplomatic relations of England and France, 1603–1688* (1906) • M. R. Smuts, *Court culture and the origins of a royalist tradition in early Stuart England* (1987) • C. M. Hibbard, *Charles I and the Popish Plot* (1983)

Likenesses W. Marshall, line engraving, NPG; repro. in W. Montagu, *Miscellanea spiritualia, or, Devout essaies* (1648)

Montagu, William, second Lord Montagu (*c.*1285–1319), soldier and courtier, was the son of Simon de *Montagu, first Lord Montagu (1259?–1316), and either Hawise, daughter of Amaury de St Amand, or his second wife, Isabella. William Montagu was descended from a prominent west-country family which traced its origins back to the conquest. The patrimony was concentrated in Somerset with the manors of Jerlington and Thurlbear as principle residences. During the thirteenth century the family had extended its holdings beyond the south-west, most notably acquiring the manor of Aston Clinton, Buckinghamshire, in 1252. William's father, Simon, had an impressive record of military service under Edward I, and was personally summoned to parliament between 1299 and 1316. Between 1301 and 1304 William Montagu too made his mark in the Scottish wars. In 1302, described as king's yeoman, he was entrusted with the supervision of shipping for the war. In 1306, like many of his illustrious contemporaries, he was knighted along with Edward, prince of Wales. In 1314 he was keeper of Berwick. This military experience served him well, for it is as 'commander of the royal cavalry' (*prefectus militie regis*) in 1316, a description accorded to him by the *Vita Edwardi secundi*, that he first emerged as an important servant of the king (*Vita Edwardi secundi*, 68). In that year he played a leading part in suppressing the revolt of Llywelyn Bren (*d.* 1318) in Glamorgan and in settling the disputes between the townspeople of Bristol and Bartholomew Badlesmere (*d.* 1322), the constable of the castle there. In November 1316 he was appointed steward of the royal household. The material rewards of his stewardship included a pension of 200 marks, the absolution of his father's debts, forfeited lands in Cumberland, a quay on the Thames, and the marriage of Joan, one of the heirs of Theobald de Verdon, which he bestowed upon his younger son. He also acted as a channel of patronage for others and a number of grants were made on his information. By influencing the king and making himself a lynchpin in the relationships which bound Edward II to his courtier supporters Montagu developed the importance of the stewardship, which after his death became an important focus of contention among the rival magnates and the particular object of the earl of Lancaster's ambitions.

Montagu was relieved of the stewardship on 16 November 1318 and replaced by Badlesmere. This was almost certainly a concession to Thomas of Lancaster who had accused Montagu of combining with Roger Damory to plot against his life, a factor which delayed his reconciliation with the king. Lancaster's deep suspicion of Montagu is one of the clearest signs that the courtiers around Edward II were his ardent supporters, rather than a 'middle party' as was once thought. On 20 November Montagu was appointed seneschal of Gascony and Aquitaine and governor of the Île d'Oléron. Although prestigious, this appointment was an effective demotion since it withdrew him from the centre of affairs, so reducing his influence over the king. He died in Aquitaine at the end of October 1319 and was buried there. The permanent loss of his forceful presence and military experience disadvantaged the king in the troubled years which followed. Montagu had four sons with his wife, Elizabeth, daughter of Peter de Montfort. The eldest, John, predeceased his father before August 1317. Of the others, William *Montagu (1301–1344) succeeded as third Baron Montagu, Simon *Montagu (*d.* 1345) was successively bishop of Worcester and Ely, and Edward made his career in the wars of Edward III. Elizabeth later married Sir Thomas Furnival whose son Thomas Furnival the younger had married John Montagu's widow, Joan de Verdon.

ANTHONY GROSS

Sources R. Douch, 'William Montague, earl of Salisbury, 1301–1344', MA diss., U. Lond., 1958 · GEC, *Peerage* · J. R. Maddicott, *Thomas of Lancaster, 1307–1322: a study in the reign of Edward II* (1970) · Chancery records · CDS, vol. 3 · VCH Somerset, 6.246 · VCH Buckinghamshire, 2.312–16 · N. Denholm-Young, ed. and trans., *Vita Edwardi secundi* (1957), 68 · H. R. Luard, ed., *Flores historiarum*, 3 vols., Rolls Series, 95 (1890) · CIPM, 6, no. 238
Wealth at death sixteen manors in seven counties: CIPM, 6, no. 238

Montagu, William [William de Montacute], **first earl of Salisbury** (1301–1344), soldier and magnate, was the second, but first surviving, son of William *Montagu, second Lord Montagu, and Elizabeth, daughter of Sir Piers de Montfort of Beaudesert, Warwickshire, and Maud, daughter and heir of Matthew de la Mare. Born at Cassington, Oxfordshire, he was under age at his father's death in 1319 and his lands were taken into the custody of the crown; he was made a ward of the king and was created a yeoman of the royal household in the same year. He was allowed seisin of part of his inheritance in May 1321, though still under age, and was granted full possession on 21 February 1323, proof of age having been taken some time after 29 June 1322.

As a member of the royal household Montagu served abroad with Edward II in 1320 and 1325, and he received a knighthood in 1326. Summoned to provide military service on the first Scottish campaign of Edward III's reign in 1327, he was elevated to the rank of knight-banneret of the household by June 1328 and was granted the manor of Wark on the River Tweed in January 1329, in part payment for his agreement to serve the king in peace and war for life with a personal retinue of twenty men-at-arms. In October 1329 he was made keeper of the king's stannary and the water of Dartmouth.

Montagu clearly established a close friendship with the young Edward III. He accompanied the king on a journey to Amiens in May–June 1329 and was sent to France in June of the same year to negotiate a marriage alliance with Philip VI. More particularly, in September 1329 he was sent to discuss certain secret business with Pope John XXII at Avignon, as a result of which Edward III wrote to the pope indicating that only those written instruments containing the words *pater sancte*, written in his own hand, should be considered to express the king's personal wishes, and specifying that only Montagu and Richard Bury, the royal secretary, were apprised of this business. The implication was that the king's mother, Queen Isabella, and her lover, Roger Mortimer, earl of March, who controlled the government, were preventing the king from taking charge of his own regime.

When Edward and his friends were interrogated by Mortimer before a great council at Nottingham in October 1330, Montagu is reported to have advised the king, 'It was better that they should eat the dog than that the dog should eat them' (Gray, 157). Montagu clearly took a leading part in the subsequent coup of 19 October, when the king and his closest associates entered Nottingham Castle by way of an underground passage, seized the earl of March, and removed him to London for trial and execution. The same parliament that condemned Mortimer in January 1331 also gave formal recognition to the role played by Montagu, along with Edward de Bohun, Robert

Ufford, and John Neville, in the palace revolution, and the grateful king distinguished Montagu by making him an exceptionally generous grant of land to the value of £1000, including the valuable lordship of Denbigh lately confiscated from the earl of March.

Throughout the 1330s Montagu was probably Edward III's closest political ally and personal friend. He accompanied the king on a secret expedition to France in April 1331, when both men travelled incognito, disguised as merchants. In September of the same year Montagu organized a magnificent tournament at Cheapside in which he, the king, and their team appeared dressed as Tartars. Edward's reliance on and confidence in Montagu is demonstrated by the use of the latter's seal to validate royal letters; Montagu also claimed to act as the spokesman for the royal council in communicating its decisions to the chancery, and occasionally intervened directly to authorize minor administrative matters such as the appointment of judicial commissions.

It was, however, as a soldier that Montagu was doubtless most valued by his friend the king. From 1333 to 1338 he served regularly in the Scottish wars. He distinguished himself at the siege of Berwick in 1333 and was rewarded with royal recognition of his right, inherited from his grandfather, to possession of the Isle of Man. It was in his capacity as lord of Man that he was appointed to the commission sent to Edinburgh in February 1334 to demand the homage of Edward Balliol. He served on the Roxburgh campaign of 1334–5 and provided the largest single contingent—180 men-at-arms and 136 mounted archers—for the summer campaign of 1335. It was during this campaign that he was granted the right to bear the king's crest of an eagle (a privilege that Montagu later surrendered to his godson, Prince Lionel), and was awarded a series of manors to support this new dignity. Following the cession of the lowlands to Edward III, Montagu was granted the forest of Selkirk and Ettrick with the town and county of Peebles, including all royal rights save pleas of the crown. In November 1337 he was appointed joint commander of another northern campaign. However, his siege of Dunbar proved a failure, the castle being vigorously defended by Black Agnes, wife of the Scottish earl of March, and he quickly negotiated a truce, not least because the king now required his services in the impending war against France.

On 16 March 1337, in parliament, Montagu was made earl of Salisbury and promised additional lands to the value of 1000 marks per annum. This was one of six new comital creations deliberately designed by Edward III to restock the aristocracy in preparation for a major military engagement against the French. Despite his commitments in the north Montagu became quickly and actively involved in this new project. He had already served as keeper of the Channel Islands between 1333 and 1337 and was admiral of the western fleet between January and August 1337; in April 1337 he was dispatched to Valenciennes with the bishop of Lincoln and the earl of Huntingdon to treat with the French and to negotiate alliances with Flanders and with the princes of the Holy Roman

empire. In July 1338 he accompanied Edward and his household to the continent, once again providing the largest retinue in the accompanying army, representing at its maximum a force of some 123 men-at-arms and 50 mounted archers. In September he succeeded the king's uncle, Thomas of Brotherton, as marshal of England, and in the same month took part in the attack on the Cambrésis. In 1339 he undertook engagements near Liège and Laon and was one of the English commanders at the battle of Buirenfosse.

At the end of the year, when the king prepared to return to England to negotiate with parliament, Montagu was left in the Low Countries to act as surety for the king's debts to the duke of Brabant and to take care of the queen and her young children, who remained at Ghent. For these responsibilities he was paid at the remarkable rate of 5 marks per day over the period between 17 November 1339 and 11 April 1340. During the king's absence, however, Earl William was taken prisoner by the French at Lille in April 1340 and imprisoned in Paris. He was apparently released under the terms of the truce of Esplechin of September 1340, though only on parole: in May 1342 Edward III allowed him to negotiate a final settlement with Philip VI by swearing, if necessary, never to fight in France again, and in the following month Earl William was pardoned his formal obligations to the French king in return for the release from English custody of the earl of Moray and Herman, lord of Léon in Brittany.

Montagu apparently returned directly to England following his release from captivity in 1340, being summoned to attend a council on 6 November 1340, and was not therefore part of the small group of royal friends and advisers who accompanied Edward III when the latter arrived home unexpectedly on 30 November 1340 and dismissed many of the leading members of the domestic administration. Earl William seems to have kept out of the conflict that erupted between the king and John Stratford, archbishop of Canterbury, before and during the parliament of April–May 1341, though he was appointed to the lords' committee established in this assembly to examine the king's charges against Stratford. He quickly resumed his military career, and fought in Brittany with Robert, count of Artois, in 1342–3, being one of the sponsors of the truce of Malestroit. Tradition has it that it was shortly after this episode that the earl finally confirmed his lordship of Man by conquest and was crowned king there, though there is no evidence that he used the latter title outside the island. Later in 1343 he was sent on an embassy to Castile with the earl of Derby and took part in Alfonso XI's siege of Algeciras. He is reputed to have fallen ill during this period (*Œuvres de Froissart*, 4.460), but he was apparently present at the tournament held by Edward III at Windsor early in 1344, when the king founded his round table of 300 knights. The well-informed chronicler Adam Murimuth attributed Montagu's death, which occurred on 30 January 1344, to the wounds that the earl had received while fighting in this tournament (*Adae Murimuth*, 232).

Montagu married, in or before 1327, Katharine [**Kathar-ine Montagu**, countess of Salisbury (*d.* 1349)], the youngest daughter of William, first Lord Grandison, and Sybil, daughter and coheir of Sir John Tregoz. The marriage brought Montagu into contact with Katharine's brother, John Grandison, bishop of Exeter, who corresponded with him on both personal and political matters. Montagu and Katharine had six children: William *Montagu, second earl of Salisbury (1328–1397); John Montagu (1330–1390), who married his father's ward, Margaret, heir of Thomas de Monthermer; Elizabeth Montagu (*d.* 1359), who married successively Giles Badlesmere, Hugh Despenser, and Guy de Bryan; Philippa Montagu (*d.* 1381), who married Roger (VI) Mortimer, second earl of March; Sibyl Montagu, who married Edmund Fitzalan, the disinherited eldest son of the earl of Arundel; and Agnes Montagu, who was contracted to marry John, eldest son of Roger, Lord Grey of Ruthin. The prestigious marriages of his children are a mark of Montagu's political ascendancy. His brothers Simon, bishop of Worcester and Ely, and Edward, Lord Montagu, also rose to prominence through his good offices.

After Montagu's death Katharine made a vow of chastity; she died on 23 April 1349. She has sometimes been identified with the elusive figure of Alice, countess of Salisbury, whom certain continental chroniclers alleged to have been raped by Edward III during William Montagu's captivity in France, and who appears in English historical writings from the time of Polydore Vergil as the lady whose garter became the emblem of Edward's celebrated order of chivalry (*Œuvres de Froissart*, 4.458–62). However, neither of these stories is attested in contemporary English sources and the rape allegations seem almost certainly to have originated in French attempts to defame the character of Edward III.

Both William Montagu and his wife were buried at the Augustinian priory at Bisham (Berkshire) which he had founded in 1337. Montagu's close friendship with Edward III is tangibly demonstrated in a surviving memorial inscription recording that the king himself laid the foundation stone of the priory. In spite of this relationship Montagu's fortunes were not unclouded: he never obtained possession of all the lands promised him by the king and had to invest heavily in the military enterprises undertaken on Edward's behalf. At his death Montagu was owed a total of £11,720 by the crown, of which some £6374 was formally written off by his executors in 1346.

W. M. ORMROD

Sources GEC, *Peerage* · R. Douche, 'The career, lands and family of William Montague, earl of Salisbury, 1301–44', MA diss., U. Lond., 1950 · R. Nicholson, *Edward III and the Scots: the formative years of a military career, 1327–1335* (1965) · *The wardrobe book of William de Norwell*, ed. M. Lyon and others (1983) · *Chancery records* · C. G. Crump, 'The arrest of Roger Mortimer and Queen Isabel', *EngHR*, 26 (1911), 331–2 · *Scalacronica, by Sir Thomas Gray of Heton, knight: a chronical of England and Scotland from AD MLXVI to AD MCCCLXII*, ed. J. Stevenson, Maitland Club, 40 (1836) · *Œuvres de Froissart: chroniques*, ed. K. de Lettenhove, 25 vols. (Brussels, 1867–77) · *Adae Murimuth continuatio chronicarum. Robertus de Avesbury de gestis mirabilibus regis Edwardi tertii*, ed. E. M. Thompson, Rolls Series, 93 (1889), 232 · W. M. Ormrod, *The reign of Edward III* (1990) · A. Gransden, 'The alleged rape by Edward III of the countess of Salisbury', *EngHR*, 87 (1972), 333–44 · F. C. Hingeston-Randolph, ed., *The register of John de Grandisson, bishop of Exeter*, 3 vols. (1894–9)
Wealth at death substantial; owed £11,720 by the crown

Montagu, William [William de Montacute], **second earl of Salisbury** (1328–1397), lord of Man and the Isle of Wight, was born on 28 June 1328 at Donyatt, Somerset, the elder son of William *Montagu, first earl of Salisbury (1301–1344) who had two sons and four daughters with his wife, Katharine *Montagu (*d.* 1349) [*see under* Montagu, William, first earl of Salisbury], third daughter of William, Lord Grandison. The theory that he was actually the son of Edward III and a brother of William Montagu is based on inaccurate French sources, which are explicitly contradicted by better English ones (Gransden, 333–44).

Montagu was raised by his parents together with other young aristocrats, including Edward, prince of Wales, and *Joan of Kent (*c.*1328–1385), the eventual heir of her father, Edmund, earl of Kent. Montagu contracted a marriage with Joan before 10 February 1341. In 1347 Thomas Holland, Montagu's steward, sought the nullification of the Montagu marriage on the grounds of a prior informal but valid marriage between Joan and himself *c.*1339. Montagu resisted this suit but was commanded to permit Joan to testify, which she apparently did in Holland's favour. The annulment was granted on 17 November 1349, and Montagu promptly married Elizabeth (1343–1415), daughter of John, Lord Mohun of Dunster, with whom he had one son, also William. Following Holland's death in 1360 Joan married Edward, prince of Wales (*d.* 1376), and was the mother of Richard II.

William Montagu had become earl of Salisbury on the death of his father from tournament injuries on 30 January 1344. He was then a minor, but received livery of his inheritance in July 1349. He had been knighted on Edward III's landing at La Hogue in July 1346 to commence the Crécy campaign; authorities differ on whether Montagu was knighted by Edward III or his son Edward, prince of Wales, himself newly knighted. A few years later Montagu was a founder member of the Order of the Garter. The suggestion that Joan of Kent (then still Montagu's ostensible wife) was the lady whose garter inspired the order's emblem is probably mistaken (Gransden, 333–44).

Montagu served in the defeat of the Castilian fleet off Winchelsea in 1350, but his most notable service was in 1356, when he and the earl of Suffolk were the two commanders of the rearguard in Prince Edward's march through southern France which culminated in the battle of Poitiers, and Montagu is mentioned alone as its commander during the battle. The first major French attack at Poitiers, led by the marshals Clermont and d'Audenham, was heavily defeated by Montagu, who is credited by Baker with choosing the strong defensive position along the gap of a hedge which proved valuable to the English. Clermont was killed and other French leaders were captured.

Montagu served in further fighting, including King

Edward's expedition of 1359, and took part in the negotiations for the peace of Brétigny in 1360. During the quiet interlude that followed Montagu served as justice of the peace in Hampshire and Somerset in 1361, and in Dorset in 1362 and 1364. In 1367 he served on a commission of array in Somerset and a special commission to perambulate the border between Somerset and Devon. The next year he was again justice of the peace in Dorset.

During this period Montagu became deeply involved in a suit against the Mortimer earls of March over claims to Denbigh, which had been granted to the elder William Montagu for his part in overthrowing Roger Mortimer in 1330. Montagu did homage for it in 1353, but by 1355 the Mortimer heir (Roger) had recovered it by royal favour, and it remained in Mortimer hands despite repeated petitions by Montagu. When he petitioned in 1372, the answer was postponed due to the minority of another Mortimer heir (Edmund (III), earl of March). When Edmund Mortimer had come of age, Montagu petitioned again in 1378 but was put off with other technicalities until 1380 when Mortimer departed for Ireland. His death soon afterwards led to another minority and a delay in negotiations until 1396. At that time the earl was prepared to give the Mortimers a quitclaim, but this remained undelivered at his death, and the matter was left for his nephew and heir to settle.

King Edward's policy of political reconciliation apparently took precedence over gratitude to the Montagus, at least after the death of the first earl, who had been his close companion. William Montagu could obtain neither Denbigh nor the compensation for it which had originally been promised, even in the 1370s when he was one of the leading defenders of the increasingly desperate English position in France. When the war resumed, Montagu served in the futile raid led by John, duke of Lancaster, in 1369, and then in 1373 himself commanded the English fleet which destroyed seven Spanish ships in the harbour of St Malo and then relieved Brest, whose defenders had promised to yield if not relieved within forty days. The earl's fleet arrived in time and challenged the French (led by Bertrand du Guesclin) to battle; after elaborate negotiations no battle was fought, but Montagu's expedition was able to revictual Brest and prevent its capture. The earl also served in fruitless peace negotiations with the French between 1375 and 1377.

Montagu was appointed to commissions of array and of peace in Dorset in early 1377, and took part in a great council on 17 April. The same year Montagu served with the earl of Arundel in a raid near La Rochelle which was beaten off by local French forces. As captain of Calais in 1379 he captured and burned the French fortified monastery of Beaulieu. On his return to England Earl William was appointed to commissions of array and of peace in Dorset again in 1380, and to commissions of the peace in Wiltshire in 1381. He is said to have been with Richard II in London during the peasants' revolt of June 1381 and to have advised the king to show mercy to the rebels after their defeat. Despite this moderation Montagu served on

commissions to suppress the revolt in Dorset and Wiltshire later in 1381. In 1382 he was also given custody of Carisbrooke Castle and the Isle of Wight, and served on commissions against the rebels (which were evolving into commissions of the peace) in that island, Somerset, Dorset, and Wiltshire.

That year proved disastrous for Montagu. He accidentally killed his only son in a tournament on 6 August 1382, and in the same year became involved in a very bitter dispute with his own brother, John Montagu the elder, in a case in the court of chivalry concerning a statute merchant whose conditions were violated by John. William won the first round of this case, but John appealed in November 1384, and continued to evade a final judgment for some time. The court of chivalry at this time was led by the constable, the earl of Buckingham, soon to be duke of Gloucester, while the commissions included the earl of Oxford (later duke of Ireland) and other leading courtiers who were apparently in no hurry to condemn John Montagu, steward of the king's household.

In 1385 the earl also found himself prosecuted by his wife's kinsman Otto de Grandson the younger, but Buckingham intervened in his favour. Meanwhile the case against his brother, John, still dragged on. More positively, the earl's grant of Carisbrooke Castle and Wight was now converted from a single year to life. This year the duke of Lancaster suspected certain courtiers of plotting to kill him; eventually Joan of Kent persuaded him to forgive the supposed plotters, who are said to have included the earls of Oxford and Salisbury, though Earl William's brother is perhaps a more likely candidate.

The year 1386 saw more commissions appointed to handle John Montagu's appeal of the case with his brother, but finally, in November 1387, Gloucester was authorized to pass judgment on John and collect the expenses from him despite his appeal, which he did in January 1388, although the case was not finally settled until after John's death in 1390: John's son surrendered the disputed statute merchant in 1391. This case seems to have completely alienated William from his brother and his nephew. These men (John Montagu the elder and younger) were the earl's heirs following the death of his son, William, in 1382, but the earl seems never to have accepted them as such.

Although the appellants had apparently favoured the earl of Salisbury, loyalty to the crown was his family's tradition, and when Richard II resumed power on a more moderate basis Montagu co-operated with him. Despite his own troubles with an appeal, Montagu served on the commission in 1389 to hear an appeal from the chivalry court in the case of *Scrope* v. *Grosvenor*, as well as others including an admiralty case. This last may have led to his appointment in 1390 to a commission on shipping disputes with Prussia. That year he served again on commissions of the peace in Wiltshire, Dorset, and Somerset, renewed in Wiltshire in 1391, in Somerset in 1392, and in Dorset, Somerset, and Wiltshire in 1394. He also served on a special commission on crimes in Southampton in 1395, and on a peace commission there in 1396. The same year he served on peace commissions in Dorset and Wiltshire; his last such appointment was in Southampton in 1397.

These years also saw Montagu sell off substantial parts of his property, most notably the Isle of Man to William Scrope in 1393. It is likely these sales were intended to keep the property out of the hands of his heir, John Montagu the younger, but one of the sales was to John's brother Richard, so the old earl's bitterness did not include the entire junior branch of the family. The earl made a will leaving half his goods to his wife and the rest to servants and the church, with nothing of his disposable property to John Montagu the younger, although the latter did inevitably inherit the title and landed estates not mentioned in the will. These family disputes are the most likely explanation for Earl William's failure to play a role in Ricardian politics commensurate with his earlier glory; by his death on 3 June 1397, however, he was the last survivor of Edward III's great captains. He was buried in Montacute Priory, Bisham, Somerset, but nothing remains of his tomb.   JOHN L. LELAND

Sources *Chancery records* · PRO, SC 1, SC 8, DL 28, E 101, E 401, E 403, C 81 · LPL, Arundel Register I, fols. 159–60 [will] · M. Warner, 'The Montagu earls of Salisbury, 1300–1428', PhD diss., U. Lond., 1991 · *Chronicon Galfridi le Baker de Swynebroke*, ed. E. M. Thompson (1889) · J. Froissart, *Chronicles of England, France, Spain, and the adjoining countries*, trans. T. Johnes, 2 vols. (1874) · *Thomae Walsingham, quondam monachi S. Albani, historia Anglicana*, ed. H. T. Riley, 2 vols., pt 1 of *Chronica monasterii S. Albani*, Rolls Series, 28 (1863–4) · V. H. Galbraith, ed., *The Anonimalle chronicle, 1333 to 1381* (1927) · Chandos herald, *Life of the Black Prince by the herald of Sir John Chandos*, ed. M. K. Pope and E. C. Lodge (1910) · M. Packe, *Edward III* (1983) · R. Delachenal, *Histoire de Charles V*, 5 vols. (Paris, 1909–31) · A. Gransden, 'The alleged rape by Edward III of the countess of Salisbury', *EngHR*, 87 (1972), 333–44 · M. Galway, 'Joan of Kent and the order of the Garter', *University of Birmingham Historical Journal*, 1/1 (1947), 13–50 · A. Burne, *The Crécy war* (1955) · R. Barber, ed. and trans., *The life and campaigns of the Black Prince: from contemporary letters, diaries and chronicles* (1979) · E. F. Jacob, ed., *The register of Henry Chichele, archbishop of Canterbury, 1414–1443*, 2, CYS, 42 (1937), 14–18 · *CIPM*, vols. 15–23 · GEC, *Peerage*

Wealth at death approx. £1000 p.a. from estates: will, LPL, Arundel Register I, fols. 159–60; *CIPM, Richard II*, 15–23, nos. 313–24

Montagu, William (1618/19–1706), judge and politician, was the second son of Edward *Montagu, first Baron Montagu of Boughton, Northamptonshire (1562/3–1644), and his second wife, Frances (c.1586–1620), daughter of Thomas Cotton of Conington, Huntingdonshire, and half-sister of Sir Robert Bruce *Cotton. He was educated at Oundle School, and was admitted to Sidney Sussex, Cambridge, on 13 April 1632, aged thirteen. He then entered the Middle Temple on 22 October 1635, being called to the bar on 9 July 1641. Montagu was elected to the Short Parliament for Huntingdon, on the interest of his uncle the first earl of Manchester, but stood down in favour of his brother, Edward, at the election later in 1640. Montagu remained in London during the first civil war, and presumably concentrated on building up his legal practice.

Following the death of his father in 1644, Montagu inherited an estate at Little Oakley, Northamptonshire. His first marriage, on 18 June 1646, to Elizabeth (d. 1647), daughter of Ralph Freeman of Aspenden, Hertfordshire,

William Montagu (1618/19–1706), by unknown artist, 1680

was short-lived; his second, on 7 December 1651, was to Mary (d. 1700), daughter of Sir John Aubrey, first baronet, of Llantriddyd, Glamorgan. The first marriage produced a son, Christopher, the second a son, William (d. 1690), and a daughter, Elizabeth. Montagu did not serve in local office until 1657, when he was named as a commissioner of assessment for Northamptonshire.

As a cousin of the chancellor of Cambridge University, the second earl of Manchester, Montagu was returned for the university at a by-election to the Convention on 22 June 1660. He appears to have supported modified episcopacy. In the general election of 1661 he was returned for Stamford. On 10 June 1662 he was appointed attorney-general to Queen Catherine of Braganza, whose affairs he dutifully protected in parliament. Montagu was generally a supporter of the court, and on 13 June 1670 he was appointed a king's counsel. A defender of the earl of Danby in 1675, he was appointed chief baron of the exchequer on 12 April 1676, and consequently resigned his seat in parliament. Soon afterwards he was made a serjeant-at-law, with Danby acting as one of his patrons.

As a judge, Montagu took part in some of the trials consequent on the Popish Plot, particularly those of William Ireland and Thomas Pickering on 17 December 1678. Subsequently he attested that he 'had never any great faith' (*DNB*) in Titus Oates. He also sat as assessor to the House of Lords when William Howard, Viscount Stafford, was impeached in November 1680, and was a member of the court which tried Lord William Russell on 13 July 1683. On the western circuit in March 1684 Montagu sentenced to death Alicia Welland, almost the last person executed for witchcraft in England. He was reappointed following the death of Charles II, despite offending James II by giving his opinion that collection of the excise needed parliamentary sanction. Montagu accompanied Jeffreys on the 'bloody assizes', but he was removed on 20 April 1686 because of his equivocal stance on the dispensing power.

Montagu apparently returned to the bar and was nominated on 22 January 1689 as an assessor to the House of Lords; he was reported to be active in lobbying several peers, possibly for his old place on the bench. When an opportunity arose to replace his recently deceased son-in-law, Sir William Drake, Montagu won the by-election at Amersham on 8 October 1690. However, he did not stand again in 1695. His wife died on 10 March 1700, and Montagu himself died on 26 or 27 August 1706 and was buried at Weekley, Northamptonshire.   STUART HANDLEY

Sources HoP, Commons, 1690–1715 [draft] · HoP, Commons, 1660–90, 3.90–92 · Sainty, Judges · Baker, Serjeants · Sainty, King's counsel · J. Bridges, The history and antiquities of Northamptonshire, ed. P. Whalley, 2 (1791), 348 · R. Clutterbuck, ed., The history and antiquities of the county of Hertford, 3 (1827), 348 · will, PRO, PROB 11/490, sig. 197 · G. W. Keeton, Lord Chancellor Jeffreys and the Stuart cause (1965), 237, 263, 272, 290, 312, 315, 356 · Foss, Judges, 7.258–60 · DNB · GEC, Peerage · W. E. Riley, The parish of St Giles-in-the-Fields, ed. L. Gomme, 1, Survey of London, 3 (1912), 36–7 · H. I. Longden, The visitation of the county of Northampton in the year 1681, Harleian Society, 87 (1935), 138
Archives PRO, corresp. and papers, C 108/62–3
Likenesses oils, 1680, Gov. Art Coll. [see illus.]

Montagu, William (1720?–1757), naval officer, was the son of Edward Richard Montagu, Viscount Hinchingbrooke (1692–1722), politician and army officer, and Elizabeth (d. 1761), daughter of Alexander Popham of Littlecote, Wiltshire, and younger brother of John *Montagu, fourth earl of Sandwich. His mother seems to have effectively abandoned him when he was very young, and sent him to sea at the age of eleven. On 20 September 1740 he was promoted lieutenant of the *Defiance*, one of the ships going out to the West Indies with Sir Chaloner Ogle, and in her he was present at the unsuccessful attack on Cartagena in March–April 1741. He was afterwards moved into the *Launceston*, one of the squadron with Commodore Peter Warren at the Leeward Islands, and by Warren he was promoted, on 23 May 1744, to the command of the sloop *Mercury*. As a result of an incident in which a sentry of the *Mercury* shot a person in a boat, Admiral Charles Knowles suspended Montagu from command, refused him a court martial, and ordered him back to England. Montagu in the *Eltham* was carried to New England, where, after he had been seven months under arrest, he was released and promoted by Warren to the post-ship *Mermaid* on 23 May 1745. He played a full part in Warren's squadron during the siege of Louisbourg, and when the place fell in June he carried Warren's dispatches to England, and received the customary reward of £500. On arriving in England in August he vainly petitioned the first lord of the Admiralty to try Knowles, who had just returned to England, for his tyrannical conduct, but succeeded in a civil suit (25 June 1752).

In the meantime Montagu was appointed to the *Prince Edward* on 20 August 1745, and in July 1746 to the *Bristol* (50 guns), one of the ships in the squadron under Vice-

Admiral George Anson in the following spring. In the action of 3 May 1747 Montagu's conduct was described by an anonymous correspondent of the *Gentleman's Magazine* as extremely brilliant. But neither in his official letter to the Admiralty, nor in his private letter to the duke of Bedford, does Anson say anything about it or about Montagu, nor was his brother Lord Sandwich at the Admiralty aware that he had distinguished himself.

Already Montagu's agitation and intriguing for an independent cruise (with the prospect of rich prizes) had embarrassed and infuriated his brother. After the battle the easier strategic situation persuaded Warren to let the troublemaker go. On 12 December Montagu fell in with Rear-Admiral Edward Boscawen in the *Namur* off Madeira, and anchored there with him. Boscawen, who had charge of a large convoy of East Indiamen, wrote to Anson on 21 December that he had been obliged to confine Montagu, at the desire of the governor, for threatening the life of one of the captains of the Indiamen.

In March 1748 Montagu finally found his prize, a rich Spanish register ship, and at once applied for leave on grounds of ill health. On 13 November 1749 he married Charlotte Naylor, daughter of a gentleman of Offord Darcy, near Huntingdon. His cruelty to her distressed Sandwich, who tried unsuccessfully to arrange a separation in 1754. Although Montagu subsequently commanded guardships in port, he had no further sea service. Montagu was brought into parliament by his brother on a by-election for Huntingdonshire in May 1745, but by 1747 his violent and erratic behaviour had considerably embarrassed Sandwich, and he was dropped. In 1752 he was elected for Bossiney under the auspices of his cousin Edward Wortley, and served until the dissolution of 1754. Sandwich then contemplated proposing Montagu for Huntingdonshire again, but his public insults against his brother, and his conduct in leading a drunken mob to attack the mayor of Huntingdon, swiftly killed the idea.

With a brother effectively running the Admiralty from 1745, 'Mad Montagu' had every advantage a sea officer could desire, and threw them all away. It is unlikely that he would have lasted as long as he did in the navy, had not several commanders-in-chief treated him more gently than he deserved on Sandwich's account. His brutal, aggressive, and drunken behaviour towards his family, his brother officers, and his wife eventually alienated everyone he had to deal with, and his early death on 10 February 1757 aroused few regrets.

J. K. LAUGHTON, rev. N. A. M. RODGER

Sources N. A. M. Rodger, The insatiable earl: a life of John Montagu, fourth earl of Sandwich (1993) · R. S. Lea, 'Montagu, William', HoP, Commons · J. Gwyn, ed., The Royal Navy and North America (1973) · Elizabeth Montagu, the queen of the blue-stockings: her correspondence from 1720 to 1761, ed. E. J. Climenson, 2 vols. (1906)
Archives NMM, Sandwich MSS | BL, Anson MSS, Add. MS 15957 · BL, Newcastle MSS, Add. MS 32808 · Woburn, fourth duke of Bedford MSS

Montagu, William, fifth duke of Manchester (1771–1843), colonial governor, the second son of George *Montagu, fourth duke of Manchester (1737–1788), and his wife,

William Montagu, fifth duke of Manchester (1771–1843), by Sir William Beechey, 1790

Elizabeth Dashwood (d. 1832), was born on 21 October 1771 at St Marylebone, Middlesex. His elder brother having died at the age of eight in 1772, he succeeded to the dukedom on his father's death in 1788. Described as 'the most beautiful statue-like person that ever was seen in flesh and blood' (Strachey, 90), when he was a child his portrait was painted by Sir Joshua Reynolds, who depicted him as Cupid and his mother as Diana.

After being educated at Harrow School, Montagu was gazetted ensign in the 35th foot (27 October 1787) and then lieutenant in the 76th foot (25 December 1787). He also held a commission in the 50th foot from January 1788 to May 1790, and exchanged into the 73rd regiment on 29 February 1792. He attained the rank of colonel in the army on 14 March 1794, having been gazetted colonel of the Huntingdonshire militia on 8 March of the preceding year. His youth and early manhood seem to have been passed in travel and field sports. He specially excelled as a rower, and is said to have pulled a wherry from London to Gravesend without a rest.

On 7 October 1793 Manchester married Lady Susan Gordon (1774–1828), the third daughter of Alexander *Gordon, fourth duke of Gordon, and his wife, Jane Maxwell. They had two sons and six daughters before the marriage broke down; the duchess of Manchester was reported to have run off with one of her footmen some years before their final separation in 1813. In 1808 Manchester was made governor of Jamaica, where he arrived, without his wife, in March. The nineteen years of his government of the colony were times of great distress and anxiety. Two months after his arrival, on 30 May 1808, a mutiny of the 2nd West India regiment, a black corps, led to a quarrel between Carmichael, the commander-in-chief, and the colonial assembly. Manchester applied to the home authorities, and prorogued the assembly when it ordered Carmichael into custody. Five months later the general, under orders from the crown, apologized to the assembly, and Manchester's discretion was generally commended.

In 1811 Manchester paid a visit to England, but returned to Jamaica in 1813. During the following year attempts were made to reform the law courts and Post Office by fixing the amount of all fees, and a law was passed allowing 'free people of colour' to give evidence, but precluding them from holding offices. In 1815 Manchester sought to alleviate the distress caused by the destruction of Port Royal by fire on 13 July, and by the hurricanes and floods which destroyed the sugar and coffee plantations of the island on 18 and 19 October. He showed great administrative ability during the panic which prevailed in the colony following an insurrection of slaves in Barbados, and by his personal influence pacified the Jamaica slaves. The colony gratefully voted him an addition to his personal establishment. In 1816 he risked his popularity with the planters by vigorously supporting a bill for the registry of slaves, in accordance with the recommendation of the imperial government.

In 1820 Manchester was thrown from his carriage and fractured his skull. The assembly voted 500 guineas to the surgeons who attended him. After recuperating in Europe, Manchester returned in 1822, and the last years of his administration were marked by the introduction of measures preparatory to the emancipation of the slaves, which the planters solidly resisted. The Jamaica government was called upon by the Colonial Office to abolish Sunday markets, to forbid the carrying of whips, and to exempt women from flogging. All these reforms were carried out with great difficulty. In 1824 there was a slave insurrection in the west of the island, and a plot was apparently discovered for the massacre of the white inhabitants in the north and east. In 1825 the assembly rejected a bill allowing slaves to give evidence, but in the following year Manchester succeeded in securing a temporary measure to be in operation for five years. In this form, however, the law was vetoed by the home government, but before the imperial decision was known a conviction for murder was obtained by the evidence of slaves given under the temporary law. In the midst of the consequent confusion Manchester finally left Port Royal on 2 July 1827.

Soon after his return to England, on 27 September 1827, Manchester was appointed postmaster-general in the duke of Wellington's ministry. He voted with his leader on Catholic emancipation, but against the Reform Bill in the House of Lords on 7 October 1831, and again when the second reading was carried on 13 April 1832. He also voted for Lord Lyndhurst's motion to postpone the disfranchisement clauses. In autumn 1841 he resigned the lord lieutenancy of Huntingdonshire, which he had held since 1793, owing to failing health, which had never recovered from the accident of 1820. He died from fever at Rome on 18 March 1843.   G. LE G. NORGATE, *rev.* LYNN MILNE

Sources GEC, *Peerage* · G. W. Bridges, *The annals of Jamaica*, 2 vols. (1827–8) · T. Southey, *Chronological history of the West Indies*, 3 vols. (1827) · *Memoirs of a highland lady: the autobiography of Elizabeth Grant of Rothiemurchus*, ed. J. M. Strachey (1898) · A. C. Burns, *History of the British West Indies*, 2nd edn (1965)
Archives Cambs. AS, corresp. and papers | LPL, corresp. with William Howley · PRO NIre., corresp. with Lord Castlereagh · Royal Mail Heritage, London, letters to Francis Freeling
Likenesses W. Beechey, portrait, 1790; Sothebys, 9 July 1997, lot 60 [*see illus.*] · G. Hayter, pencil drawing, BM · J. Reynolds, double portrait, oils (with his mother), priv. coll.; in possession of the duke of Manchester, 1894 · Saunders, oils, priv. coll.; in possession of the duke of Manchester, 1894 · Watson, engraving (after Reynolds), priv. coll.; in possession of the duke of Manchester, 1894
Wealth at death under £60,000: will, 1843

Montague. *See also* Montagu, Mountagu.

Montague, Charles Edward (1867–1928), journalist and novelist, was born at Ealing, Middlesex, on 1 January 1867, the third of the four sons of Francis Montague (d. 1892/3) and his wife, Rosa McCabe (d. 1906), daughter of a merchant in Drogheda, Ireland. His father renounced his priesthood in the Roman Catholic church and settled in England. Montague was educated at the City of London School (1879–85) and at Balliol College, Oxford, where he obtained a first class in classical moderations in 1887 and a second in *literae humaniores* in 1889. He was recruited to the staff of the *Manchester Guardian* in 1890 by its editor, Charles Prestwich Scott; six years later Montague became chief leader writer. He opposed the Second South African War, and his commitment to the great Liberal causes was demonstrated during the Edwardian era in his leaders on protectionism, female suffrage, home rule, and the constitutional crisis. His novel *A Hind Let Loose* (1910), which was first written as a farce during the Second South African War, angrily condemned 'rotten journalism' and was inscribed 'To C.P.S., through whom an English paper is clear of these stains'.

Although Montague was often acting editor after 1906, when C. P. Scott was an MP, their differences of outlook became more apparent. In August 1914 Montague's leaders quickly noted that Germany was responsible for the war and that 'Prussian Junkerdom' must be defeated (*Manchester Guardian*, 24 Aug 1914). Conversely, C. P. Scott worked for peace and feared the 'impossibility of harmony of feeling' with Montague on this vital issue (C. P. Scott to L. T. Hobhouse, 12 Dec 1914, Guardian archives 132/186). In the autumn months of 1914 Montague, aged forty-seven, astonished his colleagues by his urgent attempts to enlist. In 1898 he had married Madeline, daughter of C. P. Scott, at Platt Unitarian Chapel, Rusholme, and they had five sons and two daughters. In December 1914 he dyed his white hair—a widely cited action in the literature of the First World War—and succeeded in joining a unit for 'elderly' sportsmen. This battalion, the 24th service battalion, Royal Fusiliers, appeared as the king's own Middlesex fusiliers in his later writings. He joined as an alpinist, as mountaineering was his favourite recreation, made clear in *The Morning's War* (1913).

In 1915 Montague revelled in the comradeship of soldier-sportsmen, who sacrificed comfortable standards of living and believed, with crusading innocence, in the cause of defending small nations. His personal experience of enlistment, training, embarkation, and a brief period of front-line service, up to February 1916, provided raw material for his post-war writing. After slow recovery from a bombing incident and a wretched period at base depot, Montague was posted to a reserve battalion at Leith.

In June 1916 he was commissioned into the intelligence department at general headquarters, where he accompanied war correspondents to the front line and censored their daily reports. Captain Montague courteously and quietly fulfilled the role of a conducting officer and he also guided guests such as H. G. Wells and Bernard Shaw on their journeys on the western front.

Montague was demobilized in January 1919, appointed OBE (military), and returned to the *Manchester Guardian*, but not to the role of chief leader writer, for L. T. Hobhouse, J. L. Hammond, and Ted Scott were more influential adjuncts of C. P. Scott's seemingly endless editorship. Instead, in short leaders, Montague became the voice of the demoralized provincial middle class. The years before 1914 became 'a lost Golden age' (*Manchester Guardian*, 30 Dec 1920) when compared with the 'discordant, blatant and vulgar' post-war years, characterized by revolution, industrial unrest, decadence, and the loss of self-control ('Armistice day meditation', *Manchester Guardian*, 11 Nov 1920).

Disenchantment was an episodic and impressionistic commentary on the course and impact of the war, comprising articles published in the *Manchester Guardian* between April 1920 and November 1921. As an early liberal perspective on the war in France it has no equal, but its title has erroneously been used to identify a school of anti-war writers. Montague opposed the *conduct* of the British war effort and the lack of generosity and decency in the post-war years. The delicate allusiveness, romanticized treatment of voluntary recruiting, and pungent wit did not mask the moral indignation in *Disenchantment*. As a highly contemporary manual for living it had a didactic purpose, and character stereotypes were used to explore the themes of idealism and cynicism.

Montague revisited these themes in a collection of short stories, *Fiery Particles* (1923), in which the moral shallowness of the political élite featured strongly. *The Right Place* (1924) continued the condition of England theme, but conveyed with much enjoyment the propinquity of landscape. In those years Montague expressed the interests and distinctiveness of Manchester in a newspaper which had begun to emphasize political news from London. The closure of Miss Horniman's Gaiety Theatre in 1920 effectively ended his work as a theatre critic, which earlier in his career was published in *The Manchester Stage, 1880–1900* (1900) and *Dramatic Values* (1911). In December 1925 he departed from the *Manchester Guardian* with much dignity and regret.

Rough Justice was published in 1926. It presented in fiction the message of *Disenchantment*, but was much more popular; in 1926 20,000 copies were sold. Montague made much use of his war diary in this depiction of England at war. Molly and Auberon were hero types, but social 'betters' had generally failed the test of war and the only redeeming feature of English society was the 'ineradicable decency of the plain man' (Montague MSS I.8). As an old Liberal Montague expended much literary effort in charting institutional failure, a dysfunctional social structure, and a cultural shift which affronted his adherence to individualism and anti-modernism. He was a diffident writer, whose elliptical phrasing and awkward rendition of vernacular idiom provided feats of linguistic contortion.

After *Rough Justice*, which is full of his own experiences, Montague could not think of another plot for a novel and feared that he would be remembered primarily as an essayist. After the publication of *Right off the Map* (1927), an allegorical study of the causes and consequences of war, Chatto and Windus suggested that a further opportunity for reflections on Englishness would lie in a series of semi-historical essays. However, his final, posthumously published works were *Action and other Stories* (1928) and *A Writer's Notes on his Trade* (1930).

In retirement Montague lived at Burford, Oxfordshire, and in 1926 he received the honorary degree of LittD from the University of Manchester. He remained a director of Manchester Guardian Ltd. He died of pneumonia at The Firs, Fallowfield, Manchester, on 28 May 1928, and was cremated on 30 May at the Manchester crematorium. His wife survived him.

KEITH GRIEVES

Sources C. E. Montague, *Disenchantment* (1922) · JRL, Montague MSS I.8; II.22–5; IV.3 · O. Elton, *C. E. Montague: a memoir* (1929) · K. Grieves, 'C. E. Montague, Manchester, and the remembrance of war, 1918–25', *Bulletin of the John Rylands University Library*, 77 (1995), 85–104 · K. Grieves, 'C. E. Montague and the making of *Disenchantment*, 1914–21', *War in History*, 4 (1997) · K. Grieves, 'War correspondents and conducting officers on the western front from 1915', *Facing Armageddon: the First World War experienced*, ed. H. Cecil and P. Liddle (1996), 719–35 · L. Tillier, 'A study of C. E. Montague', Diplôme d'Études Supérieures diss., Université de Lille, JRL, Montague MSS IV.3 · *TLS* (11 March 1926), 180 [review] · *TLS* (25 Oct 1928), 778 · *TLS* (26 Sept 1929), 733 · JRL, Alexander MSS, box V [letters of C. E. Montague to S. Alexander] · H. M. Tomlinson, *Out of soundings* (1931) · *The Times* (29 May 1928) · Man. CL, C. E. Montague cuttings collection · J. B. Atkins, *Incidents and reflections* (1947) · N. Cardus, *Autobiography* (1947) · *Manchester Guardian* (21 Dec 1925) · 'Fiery particle: a radio portrait of C. E. Montague', *Manchester Guardian* (23 June 1955) · D. Ayerst, *Guardian: biography of a newspaper* (1971) · D. Scott, *Men of letters* (1916) · *DNB* · C. E. Montague, army service record, PRO, WO 339/63410
Archives JRL, corresp., literary MSS, and papers | BL, letters to Francis Dodd, Add. MS 45910 · Bodl. Oxf., J. L. Hammond MSS · IWM, British artists at the front, 1916–18, letters by Montague · JRL, Samuel Alexander MSS · JRL, letters to Allan Monkhouse · JRL, letters to C. P. Scott · NL Scot., John Buchan MSS · U. Reading, Chatto and Windus archive
Likenesses F. Dodd, drawing, 1905, repro. in Elton, *C. E. Montague*, facing p. 56 · P. Evans, drawing, 1928, repro. in *London Mercury*, 18 (1928), 347 · B. Cracowski, drawing, JRL, Guardian archive, 223/49/13 · F. W. Schmidt, photograph, repro. in Elton, *C. E. Montague*, frontispiece · chalk drawing, *The Guardian* offices, London
Wealth at death £22,244 9s. 1d.: probate, 18 Aug 1928, CGPLA Eng. & Wales

Montague, Francis Charles (1858–1935), historian, was born in London on 31 August 1858, the eldest son of Francis Montague, of St Margaret's, Twickenham, and his wife, Rosa McCabe, daughter of a Drogheda merchant; Charles Edward *Montague was his brother. He was a precocious child, reputedly able to read Greek at the age of eight. From University College School and University College, London, he went to Balliol College, Oxford, as an exhibitioner in 1875. After gaining a first class in classical moderations (1877) and in *literae humaniores* (1879), he graduated BA and became a prize-fellow of Oriel College in 1881, having also been elected fellow of University College, London, in 1880. He then took up law as a profession and was called to the bar by Lincoln's Inn in 1883, but returned to Oxford in 1891. There he lectured on law and was later lecturer in modern history at Oriel (1893–1927), simultaneously acting as professor emeritus of history at University College, London; he travelled regularly between Oxford and London to deliver his lectures. He also played an important part in the training of candidates for the Indian Civil Service (1892–1920), and was curator of the Indian Institute from 1900 to 1913.

For about twenty years Montague maintained a steady output of historical publications, all of them judicious, accurate, and well written. Besides reviews, an elementary textbook on English constitutional history, and contributions to the Cambridge Modern History, he published an essay entitled *The Limits of Individual Liberty* (1885) and a *Life of Sir Robert Peel* (1888). He also edited Bentham's *Fragment on Government* (1891) and Macaulay's *Essays* (1903) and wrote volume 7 (the history of England in the Stuart period, 1603–60) for Longman's *Political History of England* (1907). In 1930 he was elected an honorary fellow of Oriel and was considered one of the most gifted members of the common room society.

Montague was a widely read and cultured man, with much of the eighteenth century in his mind and outlook: he was a tolerant rationalist and a blameless epicurean. A self-absorbed scholar, he seems to have been unsuited not only to his first profession of law but also to that of teaching and lecturing, only enjoying the company of his best pupils. Perhaps it is not surprising that in later life he became something of a recluse. He died, unmarried, at his home, 177 Woodstock Road, Oxford, on 8 April 1935, and was buried at Wolvercote cemetery on 11 April.

NILANJANA BANERJI

Sources *The Times* (9 April 1935) · J. Foster, *Men-at-the-bar: a biographical hand-list of the members of the various inns of court*, 2nd edn (1885) · Foster, *Alum. Oxon.* · personal knowledge (1949) [*DNB*] · *CGPLA Eng. & Wales* (1935)
Archives UCL, notes on French history
Wealth at death £15,579 5s. 4d.: probate, 22 June 1935, *CGPLA Eng. & Wales*

Montague [*formerly* Mann], **Henry James** (1843–1878), actor, was born on 20 January 1843 in Forebridge, Staffordshire, the son of Henry Mann, an accountant, and his wife, Ann, *née* Bentley. At an early age he held an appointment in the Sun Fire Office, but after some experience as an amateur actor he appeared at Astley's Theatre under Dion

Boucicault on 26 January 1863 as the Junior Counsel for the Defence in *The Trial of Effie Deans*, extracted by Boucicault from *The Heart of Midlothian*. At the St James's, in 1864, he played in *The Adventures of a Love Letter*, an adaptation by Charles Mathews of Sardou's *Pattes de mouche*, and was Valentine in F. C. Burnand's burlesque *Faust and Marguerite*, and Christopher Larkins in J. Maddison Morton's *Woodcock's Little Game*. Various engagements followed at the Adelphi and the Olympic, among which were the roles of Captain Trevor in Tom Taylor's *White Boy*, Frank Aldersley in Wilkie Collins's *Frozen Deep* (1866), and Mars in Burnand's burlesque *Olympic Games* (1867).

Montague's first appearance at the Prince of Wales's, converted from the old Queen's under the management of the Bancrofts, took place as Dick Heartley, an original part, in Boucicault's *How she Loves him* (December 1867). This was followed by Frank Prince in T. W. Robertson's *Play* (February 1868). At the Princess's, in August 1868, he was the original Sir George Medhurst in *After Dark*, an adaptation by Boucicault of *Les oiseaux de proie* of D'Ennery and Grangé. Back at the Prince of Wales's, in December 1868, he took the part of Biddles in Edmund Yates's *Tame Cats*, and in January 1869 he made his first distinct mark as Lord Beaufoy in Robertson's *School*. In partnership with David James and Thomas Thorne, Montague opened the Vaudeville Theatre on 16 April 1870, when he spoke an address by Shirley Brooks and played George Anderson in Andrew Halliday's comedy *For Love or Money*. In James Albery's *Two Roses* (June 1870) he made a hit as Jack Wyatt to the Digby Grant of Henry Irving. In August 1871 he seceded from the management, and became sole lessee of the Globe. He opened there on 7 October 1871 with H. J. Byron's comedy *Partners for Life*, in which he played Tom Gilroy, a young barrister. Here he remained until 1874, playing numerous original parts, from Claude Redruth in Albery's *Forgiven* and Walker in Byron's *Spur of the Moment* (1872) to Alfred Trimble in *Committed for Trial*, W. S. Gilbert's adaptation of *Le réveillon* (January 1874). This was the last original character he played in England. He had also played Charles Courtly in Boucicault's *London Assurance*, Cyril in Byron's *Cyril's Success*, Careless in *The School for Scandal*, John Hawksley in Taylor's *Still Waters Run Deep*, and Claude Melnotte in Bulwer-Lytton's *The Lady of Lyons*, besides giving dramatic readings at Hanover Square Rooms.

In 1874 Montague started for the United States, and first appeared there at Wallack's Theatre, New York, on 6 October 1874, as Tom Gilroy in *Partners for Life*. His career in America lasted for less than four years, during which he confined himself mostly to plays of his own period, appearing as Julian Beauclerc in *Diplomacy*, by B. C. Stephenson and Clement Scott, and Tom Denter in Taylor's *The Overland Route*, and occasionally trying out the roles of Gratiano in *The Merchant of Venice*, Harry Dornton in Thomas Holcroft's *The Road to Ruin*, and Captain Dudley Smooth in Bulwer-Lytton's *Money*. He revisited London just once, in July 1876, and assumed for a benefit his original part of Jack Wyatt in *Two Roses* at the Vaudeville; he then returned to America. He died in San Francisco of a haemorrhage of the lungs on 11 August 1878, while on tour with a company playing *Diplomacy*. Funeral services were held in San Francisco and in New York, and a monument was erected to his memory by Lester Wallack in Greenwood cemetery, Brooklyn, where Montague was buried.

A bright, versatile man, with a pleasant face, good figure, and sociable manners, Montague was a favourite on and off the stage. He founded convivial clubs in both London and New York. He had some earnestness and force, but was seen to most advantage in juvenile parts; he was not very successful in serious roles.

JOSEPH KNIGHT, rev. NILANJANA BANERJI

Sources *The Era* (18 Aug 1878) · *DAB*, vol. 13 · *The life and reminiscences of E. L. Blanchard, with notes from the diary of Wm. Blanchard*, ed. C. W. Scott and C. Howard, 2 vols. (1891) · P. Hartnoll, ed., *The Oxford companion to the theatre* (1951); 2nd edn (1957); 3rd edn (1967) · P. Hartnoll, ed., *The concise Oxford companion to the theatre* (1972) · *Who was who in America: historical volume, 1607–1896* (1966) · Hall, *Dramatic ports.* · *Era Almanack and Annual* (1879) · b. cert. · personal knowledge (1894)

Likenesses Elliott & Fry, carte-de-visite, NPG · portrait, repro. in *The Hornet* (23 Aug 1871) · portrait, repro. in *San Francisco Newsletter*, pl. 69 · portrait, repro. in W. R. Denhoff, *Something in the city* (1876) · prints, Harvard TC · woodburytype carte-de-visite, NPG

Wealth at death under £1000: administration with will, 15 May 1879, *CGPLA Eng. & Wales*

Montaigne, George. *See* Mountain, George (1569–1628).

Montalba, Henrietta Skerrett (1856–1893), sculptor, was born in London, the youngest of the four daughters of the Swedish painter Anthony Rubens Montalba and his British wife, Emmeline. All four sisters and their brother practised art, with Clara Montalba (1842–1929) in particular becoming a very successful painter. From 1868 Henrietta studied at the South Kensington School of Design (where she won a medal in 1872 for modelling the figure from life) and then at the Accademia delle Belle Arti in Venice, where her family lived in 1873 and also resided from the late 1880s. She continued her studies at South Kensington, distinguishing herself by winning further medals in 1874, 1875, and 1876 for life modelling, and studied there under Jules Dalou from 1877 to 1880. She made the acquaintance of her fellow student Princess Louise, visiting her later in Canada for three months in 1879 while the princess's husband, the marquess of Lorne, was governor-general. Princess Louise sculpted and painted a portrait of Montalba; the latter (National Academy of Canada) was exhibited at the Grosvenor Gallery, London, in 1882.

Montalba won prizes for fans with her sister Hilda Montalba (d. 1919) at the 1871 International Exhibition in London, but her first work of sculpture, with which she made her exhibition début at the Royal Academy in 1875, was a portrait of her father. She exhibited subsequently at the Grosvenor Gallery (1880–89) and its successor, the New Gallery (1890–93); other notable exhibition appearances included those at the Glasgow International Exhibition at Kelvingrove Park (1888) and the World's Columbian Exhibition at Chicago (1893).

Chiefly a portrait sculptor in terracotta (for example, *Robert Browning*, 1883), Montalba's principal work (which

Henrietta Skerrett Montalba (1856–1893), by Ellen Montalba

was also her last), *Venetian Boy Catching a Crab* (Victoria and Albert Museum, London), was a full-length bronze recumbent figure exhibited in 1893 at the Royal Academy and in Chicago. Busts in marble, including those of the masseur Doctor Mezger (1886) and George F. White (1893), and in bronze (*The Marquess of Lorne*, 1880), also attracted attention and critical praise. Excursions into the literary field included the companion busts *Tito* and *Romola* (both 1880) and an illustration of Edgar Allan Poe's poem 'The Raven' in the form of a likeness of that bird sitting on a bust of Pallas (1888).

Montalba lived with her family all her life and, like her sisters, remained unmarried. Her prolonged residence in Venice from the late 1880s, when the family left Britain permanently, did not prevent her from maintaining her presence at London exhibitions. She was a frequent traveller to other parts of Italy and to Sweden. Her pleasing and attractive personality made her very popular, and she was praised by her contemporaries for her good looks, charm, and graciousness. In 1892 her health began to fail and she died, after a long illness, in Venice on 14 September 1893. She was buried at San Michele, Zattere, Venice.

PAMELA GERRISH NUNN

Sources *DNB* · M. Hepworth-Dixon, 'Henrietta Montalba: a reminiscence', *Art Journal*, new ser., 14 (1894), 215–17 · S. Beattie, *The New Sculpture* (1983) · *Letters of Frances Hodgkins*, ed. L. Gill (1993)

Likenesses Princess Louise, oils, 1882, National Academy, Ottawa, Canada · E. Montalba, oils, priv. coll.; repro. in Hepworth-Dixon, 'Henrietta Montalba', 215 [*see illus.*] · H. Montalba, oils, priv. coll.

Monte, Piero da [Pietro del Monte] (1400×04–1457), scholar and papal diplomat, was born in Venice, where his father, Nicolò da Monte, was a citizen of substance. He pursued humanistic studies under Guarino da Verona and then law in Padua, under the famous jurists Prosdocimo de Conti and Giovan Francesco di Capodalista. His writings as a young man (speeches and letters survive) show all the conventional interests of early fifteenth-century humanists; he retained throughout his career a concern with such studies, for instance collecting books and arranging for copying. He corresponded later with Poggio Bracciolini, Ambrogio Traversari, Pietro Barbo, and Pier Candido Decembrio, among others. On 15 July 1433 he graduated as doctor of both civil and canon law.

Da Monte then attended the Council of Basel as ambassador for Venice, where his defence of Pope Eugenius IV, *De summi pontificis, generalis concilii et imperialis majestatis origine et potestate*, a work much influenced by Cardinal Francesco Zabarella, won him considerable support from the Venetians round the pope. In it, as in all his polemics, he strongly supported a high doctrine of papal power, stressing in particular the papacy as a monarchy. He was thus made (21 April 1435) a protonotary apostolic and given the collectorship (of papal revenues) in England, which he exercised in person between 1435 and 1440. Da Monte's major task was not to collect money but to keep the English from siding with the Council of Basel, as it became increasingly hostile to the pope. Speeches by him on the subject remain. His main letter collection gives an incomparable picture of his work and of the ecclesiastical politics of the country, though he probably exaggerated his own importance to his employers. He commented several times on the country's wealth, and presented an admiring picture of the young Henry VI, describing him as pious, patient, continent, and hostile to obscenity, in all more like a monk than a secular prince; his second-hand account of the death in 1437 of James I, king of Scots, was much less flattering, the dead ruler being stigmatized as a cruel tyrant. He was inclined to report what the Roman curia wanted to hear, and this may have coloured his description of a council meeting in May 1438 at which a delegation from the Council of Basel was rebuked by Archbishop Chichele, Humphrey of Gloucester, and others, and also his picture of England as so devoted to the papacy that, as Chichele put it, a choir of angels would be unable to separate the realm from the Roman obedience.

But da Monte was clear-sighted and truthful when he spelt out for Eugenius IV the king's overriding control of ecclesiastical appointments, and recommended that the pope accept the government's appointments. And he passed on English criticism of the curia's provision of unworthy nominees to benefices, and its misuse of dispensations to permit the holding of livings in plurality. He noted the hatred of the English for Italians in 1439, and later reported on such matters as the divisions among the monks of Westminster as they elected a new abbot, and a quarrel over precedence between the archbishops of Canterbury and York. Later he was accused of having pocketed some of the collected money, but this was almost certainly an invention of his enemies, of whom he had several, in Rome and England. He dedicated to Humphrey, duke of Gloucester, *De virtutum et vitiorum inter se differentia* (Bodl. Oxf., MS Auct. F.5.26 is a copy), and introduced the duke to Italian scholars, including Tito Livio dei Frulovisi and Antonio Beccaria, whom Humphrey employed. Beccaria was da Monte's sub-collector and dedicated to him a translation of Plutarch's life of Pelopidas.

On his return to Rome da Monte was made nuncio with some legatine powers for France (1442–4) and bishop of Brescia in 1442. His task in France was to use his experience to work for Anglo-French peace and to obtain the abrogation, in return for a concordat, of the Pragmatic Sanction of Bourges (1438)—legislation embodying 'the Gallican liberties', acceptance of certain reforms of Basel, and, in particular, a denial to the pope of a major part of his claims to appoint to benefices in France. Da Monte considered himself on good terms with Charles VII and discussed literature with him; he is also recorded presiding at the betrothal (on 24 May 1444, at Tours) of Margaret of Anjou to Henry VI. But, though an assembly of churchmen at Bourges in the summer of 1444 seemed favourable to the pope's revision of the concordat, the French government raised its demands and the plan failed. Da Monte returned to continue his career in Italy. He dedicated to Pope Nicholas V (*r.* 1447–55) his next important polemic, *Contra impugnantes sedis apostolicae auctoritatem.* Between May 1451 and April 1453, while keeping Brescia, he was governor of Perugia, returning afterwards to Rome, where Calixtus III (*r.* 1455–8) made him a referendary. Between 1451 and 1453 he produced his most famous work, *Repertorium utriusque iuris*, also known as *Brixiense*, which exists in many manuscripts and printed editions before 1500. A legal dictionary or encyclopaedia, it contains interesting references to England and English practice. Da Monte was hoping to be promoted cardinal, but may have missed this because of rivalries in the curia. He died in Rome on 12 January 1457 and was buried there in the church of Santa Maria Maggiore.

MARGARET HARVEY

Sources J. Haller, ed., *Piero da Monte: ein Gelehrter und päpstlicher Beamter des 15. Jahrhunderts* (Rome, 1941) • D. Quaglioni, *Pietro del Monte a Roma: la tradizione del 'Repertorium utriusque iuris' c.1453* (Rome, 1984) • A. Sottili, *Studenti tedeschi e umanesimo italiano nell'Università di Padova durante il Quattrocento, 1: Pietro del Monte nella società accademica padovana (1430–1433)* (1971) • G. Tournoy, 'Un nuovo testo del periodo padovano di Pietro da Monte', *Quaderni per la Storia dell'Università di Padova*, 8 (1975), 67–72 • A. Zanelli, 'Pietro da Monte', *Archivio Storico Lombardo*, 4th ser., 7 (1907), 317–78 [pt 1] • A. Zanelli, 'Pietro da Monte', *Archivio Storico Lombardo*, 4th ser., 8 (1907), 46–115 [pt 2] • J. W. O'Malley, *Praise and blame in Renaissance Rome: rhetoric, doctrine and reform in the sacred orators of the papal court, c.1450–1521* (1971)
Archives Biblioteca Apostolica Vaticana, Vatican City, MSS Vat. Lat. 373, 2347, 2694, 4872 • Biblioteca Nazionale Marciana, Venice, MS Lat. xiv 179 • Bodl. Oxf., MS Auct. F.5.26

Monteage, Stephen (*bap.* 1623, *d.* 1687), writer on accounting, was baptized on 1 February 1623 at St Giles Cripplegate, London. He was the son of Stephen Monteage of Buckingham, a goldsmith. As a young man he was apprenticed to the merchant James Houblon, but after the Restoration he became a steward in the service of the second duke of Buckingham. He was agent to Christopher, Viscount Hatton; and he was succeeded in this role after his death by his son Dean. Monteage married Jane Deane at some point before 1654; they had one daughter and two sons, the last of whom was born in 1657. After Jane's death, of which no date is recorded, Monteage married a second wife, called Martha, with whom he had at least one daughter.

During the period 1659–61 Monteage wrote a manuscript discourse on accounting techniques; intended first for private circulation, this was published in 1675 as *Debitor and Creditor Made Easie*. Most of the writings on accounting then available were written for wealthy merchants, who kept a variety of journals, cash books, petty-charge lists, and invoice registers. Ordinary people were not familiar with such procedures, and if they kept accounts at all they probably used a charge–discharge system. Monteage's treatise addressed middle-class merchants. They were advised to keep detailed accounts in a simplified system, based only upon two records, a 'waste' book, or record of first entry, and a general ledger, where these entries were reconciled in a double-entry system. In 1664 this treatise caught the eye of the scrivener bankers Robert Clayton and his partner John Morris, who brought Monteage into their mortgage banking operations and estate management. Monteage devised a system of accountability whereby a network could be reconciled which extended from a remote shepherd in the country to the scriveners' counting-house in the Old Jewry. After many years of close involvement in all aspects of the scriveners' elaborate hierarchy of financial operations, Monteage published the fruits of his experience in 1683 as *Instructions for Rent-Gatherers' Accompts … Made Easie*, which he dedicated to Clayton. In approving the system which Monteage described in simple language, Clayton and the high finance that he represented helped to promote the same practices of accounting to groups other than merchants.

Monteage died in London on 21 October 1687 and was buried at All Hallows, London Wall. He was the founder of a family of accountants. His son Dean Monteage was accountant-general to the commissioners of the excise. Dean Monteage's son, also Stephen Monteage, was the first accountant of the Bank of England, and later he became an accountant to the York Buildings Company, the South Sea Company, and the customs.

FRANK MELTON

Sources F. T. Melton, *Sir Robert Clayton and the origins of English deposit banking, 1658–1685* (1986) • Bank of England, Clayton MSS • E. B. Jupp and R. Hovenden, eds., *The registers of christenings, marriages, and burials of the parish of Allhallows, London Wall … 1559 to 1675* (1878) • parish register, London, St Giles Cripplegate, 1623, GL
Archives GL, diaries and accounts | Bank of England, London, Clayton MSS

Likenesses E. Le Davis, line engraving, BM, NPG; repro. in S. Monteage, *Debitor and creditor made easie* (1675) [prefixed]

Monteagle. For this title name *see* Stanley, Edward, first Baron Monteagle (*c*.1460–1523); Parker, William, thirteenth Baron Morley and fifth or first Baron Monteagle (1574/5–1622); Rice, Thomas Spring, first Baron Monteagle of Brandon (1790–1866).

Monteath, George Cunningham (1788–1828), physician and oculist, was born on 4 December 1788 at Neilston, Renfrewshire, the son of John Monteath, minister of that parish. He attended medical classes at the University of Glasgow, and graduated MA in 1805 and MD in 1808. He was a clerk at the Glasgow Royal Infirmary during his student days, and then studied under Sir Astley Cooper in London, where he was licensed as a practitioner by the Royal College of Surgeons. From 1809 to 1813 Monteath was surgeon to the Northumberland regiment of militia. He married Anne Colquhoun Cunningham of Craigends, and set up house at 15 George Square, Glasgow.

Monteath commenced in practice with his uncle, James Monteath, in Glassford Street, and rapidly became the city's leading oculist. As the first specialist in eye diseases to practise in Glasgow, difficult cases from elsewhere in the west of Scotland were brought to him for treatment. His translation of Weller's textbook on ophthalmology, *Manual of Diseases of the Human Eye* (2 vols., 1821), became a standard work and was notable for its coloured illustrations of eye diseases.

When William Mackenzie proposed forming a specialist eye hospital in Glasgow, Monteath gave it his wholehearted support. The Glasgow Eye Infirmary was founded in 1824, but Monteath's association with it was brief; he died of fever on 25 January 1828, and was buried in the graveyard at Houston. Monteath's widow later met Lord John Campbell and became fond of his children; when he was widowed, they married, and in due course she became duchess of Argyll.

GEORGE STRONACH, *rev.* ANITA MCCONNELL

Sources A. M. W. Thomas, *The history of the Glasgow Eye Infirmary, 1824–1962* (1963) · W. I. Addison, ed., *The matriculation albums of the University of Glasgow from 1728 to 1858* (1913), 196 · Chambers, *Scots.* (1835)
Likenesses portrait, repro. in Thomas, *History of the Glasgow Eye Infirmary*, facing p. 33

Monteath, Sir James (1847–1929), administrator in India, was born at Guileburn, Lockerbie, on 7 September 1847, the fourth son of Thomas Monteath, of the Bank of Scotland, who came from an old Perthshire family, and his wife, Hannah Johnstone. Monteath attended the Royal Belfast Academical Institution, and afterwards Queen's College, Belfast, where he graduated MA. In 1868 he passed the open competition for the Indian Civil Service and in November 1870 arrived in Bombay to begin a career in the Bombay presidency.

Monteath was initially posted to Dharwar as an assistant collector and thence, in October 1871, to Kanara, where for several months in 1873 he was engaged on the Kanara land assessment case. Subsequently he wrote chapters on the

land revenue administration and history of Kanara for the *Bombay Gazetteer* (1883). On 9 December 1872, while still based at Kanara, he married Amelia (*d*. 1927), daughter of Thomas Hunter of Belfast, a member of a Scottish family long settled in Ireland, with whom he had five sons and three daughters.

In April 1874 Monteath began a short stint as undersecretary to the government in the revenue, financial, and general departments, the first of many postings in the secretariat. He returned to Kanara in February 1875, but was called back to the secretariat in 1878, after which he undertook only one extensive period of district work as the collector of Bijapur from 1892 to 1895. He was private secretary to Lord Reay, governor of Bombay, from 1885 until 1890, and in July 1896 was appointed chief secretary to the government of Bombay.

As chief secretary it fell to Monteath to deal with the Bombay famine of 1896–7, an onerous duty for which he was created a CSI. In spite of the official recognition, however, implicit criticism of his famine administration appeared in the reports of the two famine commissions of 1899 and 1901, each of which castigated the Bombay government for over-enthusiastic collection of land revenue during the crisis.

In August 1900 Lord Northcote, governor of Bombay, appointed Monteath revenue member of his council with special responsibility for famine. Monteath was thus in charge again throughout the famine years of 1899–1902, during which time his health began to falter from overwork. As both Northcote and Lord Curzon noted with some dismay, Monteath lacked the instincts of a politician and often blundered, not least when he sent a curtly worded letter to *The Times of India* in July 1900 stating that he would take no notice of anonymous complaints about the famine administration. In May 1901 he introduced a land bill into the Bombay legislative council which, in the aftermath of famine indebtedness, was designed to limit the transfer of land from cultivating castes to moneylending castes by prohibiting the alienation of land by tenants whose revenue payments were in arrears. Possibly because he had little faith in the bill himself, Monteath promoted it with such ineptitude that its attempt to free peasants from the grip of moneylenders was perceived instead as an attack by the state on the occupancy rights of indebted tenants. Opposition came from many quarters, but Monteath persisted with the bill, provoking a walkout on 23 August 1901 by five Indian members of the council when he accused them of opposing it on the grounds of economic self-interest.

Monteath retired in August 1905. He had served as acting governor of Bombay from 6 September to 13 December 1903 and in January of that year had been promoted to KCSI, an honour which Northcote had requested for him on account of his loyalty in implementing a revenue policy he personally disliked and the intense public criticism to which his work had been subject. A Conservative, he was delighted to receive a farewell letter from Curzon praising his devotion to duty.

After retirement Monteath lived at Buckerell Lodge,

Honiton, Devon, where he died on 19 April 1929; he was buried on 23 April. His wife, Amelia, had died in 1927. Of their five sons, two followed their father into the Bombay civil service, a third joined the Indian forest service, and a fourth entered the India Office and became private secretary to the secretary of state.

A. C. McWATTERS, rev. KATHERINE PRIOR

Sources The Indian civil service list (1880) · J. R. McLane, *Indian nationalism and the early congress* (1977) · letters from Lord Northcote, governor of Bombay, to Lord Curzon, viceroy of India, BL OIOC, Curzon MSS · *The Times* (22 April 1929), 1, 16 · R. I. Cashman, *The myth of the Lokamanya* (1975) · ecclesiastical records, BL OIOC
Archives BL OIOC, Curzon MSS
Wealth at death £6455 9s. 10d.: resworn probate, 30 May 1929, CGPLA Eng. & Wales

Montefiore, Claude Joseph Goldsmid- (1858–1938), scholar and founder of Liberal Judaism, was born in London on 6 June 1858, the youngest of four children born to Nathaniel Mayer Montefiore (1819–1883), medical practitioner, and his wife, Emma, *née* Goldsmid (1819–1902). On his father's side Montefiore was a nephew of Sir Moses Montefiore; on his mother's he was the grandson of Isaac Lyon *Goldsmid. His roots were thus firmly planted within some of the wealthiest Anglo-Jewish families. A delicate, thoughtful child, his early ambition was to enter the rabbinate. Educated privately and then at Balliol College, Oxford, where he graduated BA with a first in classics (1881), he came under the influence of liberal ideas, particularly the religious liberalism of the then master of Balliol, Benjamin Jowett. In 1881–2 he studied Jewish subjects in Berlin, at the Anstalt für Wissenschaft des Judentums, where he met, and from which he brought to England as his tutor in rabbinic literature, the Romanian-Jewish academic Solomon Schechter, later reader in rabbinic and Talmudic literature at Cambridge. Schechter was a thoroughly Orthodox Jew, but one who was not afraid of approaching Jewish texts in a critical manner.

Montefiore's own religious leanings had already veered away from the nominal orthodoxy of his father and were at this time heavily influenced by the Reform Judaism of his mother. Montefiore, like her, questioned and found wanting the eternal truths of Orthodox Judaism. In 1886 he married, at the West London Synagogue of British [Reform] Jews, Thérèse (d. 1889), daughter of Lazar Schorstein of Reuter's agency, London. Three years later Thérèse died in childbirth. Montefiore abandoned plans to become a rabbi, and instead used the leisure his private wealth secured to deepen and broaden his religious studies, which were now taking him well beyond the modest radicalism of the West London Synagogue. In 1891, at Jowett's invitation, he delivered the Hibbert lectures at Oxford, entitled 'The origins of religion as illustrated by the ancient Hebrews'. In these he set out the prospectus for a new form of Judaism, the doctrine of which he developed to maturity over the next decade.

The essence of Montefiore's theology was to be found within an entirely de-nationalized and de-ritualized Judaism. He rejected the central tenet of Orthodox Judaism, that the Hebrew Bible was the revealed word of God, and

he rejected the claim that the Talmud represented the definitive interpretation of that word. What was left was simply an amalgam of moral and ethical values, based on a vague monotheism: the good Jew was the good citizen, charged with the task of bearing witness to 'righteousness in action and truthfulness of the heart' (*Jewish Quarterly Review*, 1/2, 152). Such were the intellectual origins of Liberal Judaism, the founding tenets of which Montefiore proclaimed from the pulpit of the West London Synagogue on 1 February 1896. The condemnation of him, and his philosophy, from the world of Orthodox Judaism was almost without qualification. However, he found a number of kindred spirits, especially in Lily Montagu, a daughter of the ultra-Orthodox Jewish banker and MP, Sir Samuel Montagu. Lily's rebellion against the oppressive Orthodox observance which she had to endure in her father's house could not have been more complete or more public. Lily warmed to Montefiore; in truth she wished to marry him, but was rebuffed. She formed the idea of founding an organization to promote his religious views, and hers. On 16 February 1902 the Jewish Religious Union (from 1909 the Jewish Religious Union for the Advancement of Liberal Judaism) was born. Montefiore was its president and philosopher-in-chief from its foundation until his death.

Scarcely less important to Montefiore than his Liberal Judaism was his anti-Zionism. In common with most members of the emancipated Anglo-Jewish gentry, Montefiore harboured and articulated a strong aversion to Jewish nationalism, which he regarded as quite incompatible with his status as a Briton of the Jewish persuasion. In his capacity as president of the Anglo-Jewish Association from 1896 to 1921 he was one of the two signatories of a letter published in *The Times* of 24 May 1917, which argued that Jews were not 'a homeless people' and had 'no separate national aspirations'. The appearance of the letter created a sensation within Anglo-Jewry: Montefiore's co-signatory, David Lindo Alexander, was compelled to resign as president of the Board of Deputies of British Jews. But at the Anglo-Jewish Association, a self-appointed body whose membership reflected the views of like-minded British Jews, Montefiore was assured of support. Later that year, following the promulgation of the Balfour declaration, he became a founder member of the League of British Jews, dedicated to resisting the allegation that Jewish people constituted a separate political entity. In his anti-Zionist faith Montefiore was unshakeable, even when Nazism cast its shadow across Europe. Under his influence the Liberal Jewish Synagogue in London became a bastion of anti-Zionist propaganda. Montefiore blamed Zionism, in part, for Hitler's rise to power.

Montefiore was a prolific writer, especially on biblical subjects and in popularizing the Jewish origins of Christianity. From 1888 to 1908 he served as joint editor of the *Jewish Quarterly Review*. In 1909 he published *The Synoptic Gospels*, the following year *Some Elements of the Religious Teaching of Jesus*, and in 1914 *Judaism and St Paul*. His *Bible for Home Reading*, a work of some 1400 pages, first published in 1897, went into three editions. In 1921 he received an honorary DD from Manchester University, and in 1930 he was awarded the British Academy medal for biblical studies. Montefiore was also deeply interested in educational matters and in social welfare. For a few months in 1888 he served as a co-opted member of the London school board. He was instrumental in the establishment of the Froebel Institute at Roehampton and in 1913 he became president of Hartley College, precursor of Southampton University.

Montefiore assumed the additional surname of Goldsmid by letters patent in 1883. In 1902 he married his first wife's tutor, Florence Fyfe Brereton (d. December 1938), daughter of Richard James Ward; she had been a vice-principal of Girton College, Cambridge, and underwent a formal conversion to Judaism. He died at his London home, 42 Portman Square, on 9 July 1938 and was survived by Leonard (1889–1961), the son of his first marriage.

GEOFFREY ALDERMAN

Sources C. Bermant, *The cousinhood: the Anglo-Jewish gentry* (1971) · W. R. Matthews, *Claude Montefiore: the man and his thought* (1956) · L. Cohen, *Some recollections of Claude Goldsmid Montefiore, 1858–1938* (1940) · E. M. Umansky, *Lily Montagu and the advancement of Liberal Judaism* (1983) · E. Kessler, ed., *An English Jew: the life and writings of Claude Montefiore* (1989) · *CGPLA Eng. & Wales* (1938)
Archives LMA, corresp. and papers, incl. sermons and MS lectures · U. Southampton L., papers | Bodl. Oxf., letters to H. A. L. Fisher · JRL, letters to Samuel Alexander · Liberal Jewish Synagogue, London, archives · U. Southampton L., corresp. with J. H. Hertz
Likenesses G. F. Watts, oils, 1903, Watts Gallery, Compton, Surrey · O. Birley, oils, 1925, Liberal Jewish Synagogue, London · B. Elkan, bronze bust, 1934, U. Southampton · W. Rothenstein, sanguine drawing, NPG · photograph, repro. in Bermant, *The cousinhood* · photograph, NPG

Montefiore [*née* Fuller], **Dora Frances Barrow** (1851–1933), suffragist, was born on 20 December 1851 and baptized (as Dora Frances) on 18 January 1852 at St Nicholas's Church, Tooting Graveney, the eighth of thirteen children of Francis *Fuller (1807–1887), surveyor and railway entrepreneur, and his wife, Mary Ann, *née* Drew. Educated at home at Kenley Manor, Surrey, and then at a private school in Brighton, Dora Fuller became her father's amanuensis. In 1874 she went to keep house for her eldest brother in Australia, where she met George Barrow Montefiore, a merchant. After their marriage on 1 February 1881, they lived prosperously in Sydney, where their daughter was born in 1883 and their son in 1887. On being widowed on 17 July 1889, Dora Montefiore discovered that she had no rights of guardianship over her own children unless her husband had willed them to her. She therefore became an advocate of women's rights. The first meeting of the Womanhood Suffrage League of New South Wales was held at her home on 29 March 1891. Dora Montefiore became its corresponding secretary but by 1892 had returned to Europe with her children, first to Paris and finally to England.

Dora Montefiore's suffragism continued through a range of organizations: the National Society for Women's Suffrage, the League of Practical Suffragists, and later the Women's Social and Political Union (WSPU). Never just a member on paper she was on the executive of the first, wrote a pamphlet, *Women Uitlanders* (1899), for the second,

and was for a time an active WSPU organizer in London. She was also part of a network of correspondents centred on Elizabeth Wolstenholme Elmy. In 1906 Dora Montefiore's Hammersmith home was besieged by bailiffs for six weeks because of her refusal of taxation without representation. Later that year she was sent to Holloway prison after being arrested at a WSPU lobby of parliament. This experience, coupled with severe doubts concerning the WSPU, prompted her resignation even though it cost her cherished friends. In 1907 Montefiore joined the Adult Suffrage Society and was elected its honorary secretary in 1909.

The vote was never an isolated issue for Dora Montefiore. From the 1890s she sought an organization which reflected her evolving politics. Although for a time a member of the Women's Liberal Association, working for the election of women to local government, Montefiore was soon moving towards socialism and the Marxist Social Democratic Federation (SDF). In 1903 she was elected for the first time to the party's executive. Within the SDF she developed a woman-focused socialism and helped set up the party's women's organization in 1904. An energetic although often dissident worker for the SDF until the end of 1912, Montefiore resigned from what had become the British Socialist Party as an anti-militarist, only to return in 1916. She spoke at the Leeds 'Soviet' in 1917 and was a founder member of the Communist Party of Great Britain in 1920, serving on its first executive. Having become politically active in her late forties, Montefiore sustained her passion and principle into her seventies, only becoming less active when her sight deteriorated.

Internationalism was also important to Dora Montefiore's politics. Attendance at international suffrage and socialist congresses led to strong links with other activist women, as did her travels throughout the United States, Australia, and South Africa from 1910 to 1912. While in Australia in 1911 she edited the *International Socialist Review of Australasia*.

Dora Montefiore's writing knitted together all her political activities. Although she published poetry and translated Maksim Gorky, she was pre-eminently a journalist and pamphleteer. She wrote a women's column in *New Age* (1902–6) and in *Justice* (1909–10). Her pamphlets were on women and socialism while *Our Fight to Save the Kiddies* (1913) described her activities in the Dublin lock-out, which had resulted in her arrest on kidnapping charges. She published an autobiography, *From a Victorian to a Modern*, in 1927. Although there were those who found her difficult, it was hard to deny Dora Montefiore's energy and commitment. There were unsubstantiated rumours of drug abuse and gossip about an 'inappropriate' relationship with a married working-class man, George Belt.

Dora Montefiore died on 21 December 1933 at her home, Melbourne, Edwin Road, Clive Vale, Hastings, and was cremated at Golders Green, Middlesex. She was survived by her daughter, her son having died from the effects of mustard gas in 1921.

KAREN HUNT

Sources D. B. Montefiore, *From a Victorian to a modern* (1927) · K. Hunt, *Equivocal feminists: the Social Democratic Federation and the* *woman question, 1884–1911* (1996) · correspondence of Mrs Wolstenholme Elmy, BL, Add. MSS 449–455 · BLPES, Francis Johnson MSS, Independent Labour Party Archive · autograph collection, Women's Library, London · *The Times* (1 Jan 1934) · *Daily Herald* (28 Dec 1933) · *Daily Worker* (27 Dec 1933) · D. B. Montefiore, *Our fight to save the kiddies* (1913) · E. S. Pankhurst, *The suffragette movement: an intimate account of persons and ideals* (1931); repr. (1977) · D. Mitchell, *Queen Christabel: a biography of Christabel Pankhurst* (1977) · C. Collette, 'Socialism and scandal: the sexual politics of the early labour movement', *History Workshop Journal*, 23 (1987), 102–11 · L. Stanley, 'Feminism and friendship in England from 1825 to 1938: the case of Olive Schreiner', *Studies in Sexual Politics*, 8 (1985), 10–46 · d. cert. · *CGPLA Eng. & Wales* (1934) · *AusDB*

Archives BL, corresp. of Mrs Wolstenholme Elmy, Add. MSS 449–455 · BLPES, Francis Johnson MSS · Women's Library, London, autograph collection

Likenesses photograph, 1923, repro. in Montefiore, *From a Victorian to a modern*, frontispiece · photograph, repro. in D. B. Montefiore, *Some words to Socialist women* (1907), cover · photograph, repro. in Countess of Aberdeen, ed., *International congress of women of 1899* (1900) · photograph, repro. in *Social Democrat* (Aug 1911), 372

Wealth at death £1284 16s. 5d.: probate, 23 April 1934, *CGPLA Eng. & Wales*

Montefiore, Sir Moses Haim (1784–1885), financier and Jewish community leader, the eldest son of Joseph Elias Montefiore, a London businessman, and Rachel, the daughter of Abraham Lumbroso de Mattos Mocatta, was born in Leghorn, Italy (during a visit there by his parents), on 24 October 1784. On his father's side Montefiore's ancestors were Italian merchants, his paternal grandfather having emigrated from Leghorn to London in the early 1750s. His mother was descended from a family of Marranos who had settled in London to escape the Inquisition. It seems that Montefiore was educated privately. For a time he worked as a clerk with a firm of tea merchants in the City of London, and in 1803 he became a member of the London stock exchange. His early years in this profession were not particularly hopeful: in 1806 he was the victim of a fraud which cost him £30,000, and it was not until February 1815 that he was able to pay off all his creditors.

His marriage on 10 June 1812 to Judith (1784–1862), a daughter of Levi Barent Cohen and the sister-in-law of Nathan Mayer Rothschild, proved a watershed, both personally and financially. The marriage probably brought him a large dowry, but, more importantly, it led to his becoming Rothschild's stockbroker. Montefiore remained a member of the London stock exchange until 1845, but his business interests had by then widened considerably. He underwrote Rothschild's loan flotations, and in the 1820s undertook a series of highly profitable overseas speculations. He was a founder of Alliance Assurance (1824), was instrumental in establishing the Provincial Bank of Ireland (1825), and became a major shareholder in the Imperial Continental Gas Association. Directorships of other companies followed. By the time of Rothschild's death in 1836 Montefiore had himself amassed a very large fortune, so large that he was able gradually to retire from business and devote himself to the service of his fellow Jews both in England and in the wider world.

Montefiore was a *ba'al teshuvah*—a Jew who was once lax

Sir Moses Haim Montefiore (1784–1885), by Elliott & Fry

in terms of religious observance but who rediscovered and returned to his Orthodox roots. As such, he became obsessed with the minutiae of Orthodox Jewish observance, and grew intolerant of those who remained less observant. As late as 1823 he and his wife had no compunction about eating non-kosher food, but his first visit to the Holy Land in 1827 appears to have played a part in reinforcing his sense of Jewish identity and commitment. His Sephardic origins, and Ashkenazic marriage, made him uniquely well placed to assume the effective lay leadership of Anglo-Jewry. In the period 1835 to 1874 he held the presidency of the London Committee (later Board) of Deputies of British Jews for all but fifteen years, during eleven of which others simply deputized for him during his foreign travels. These foreign excursions established his reputation worldwide as the champion of oppressed Jewries, and made his name a household word throughout the British empire. At home, he became no less renowned as the champion of unbending religious orthodoxy, using his authority to stunt, insofar as he could, the early growth of Reform Judaism.

In 1845 the Orthodox Ashkenazi communities of Britain, which comprised the overwhelming majority of British Jews, elected for themselves a new chief rabbi, Nathan Marcus Adler. Montefiore shared Adler's view that in Britain orthodoxy was too weak to permit the establishment of self-governing Jewries, as were commonplace on the European mainland; what was needed, indeed, was a highly centralized religious authority (the chief rabbinate) working in full co-operation with a highly centralized lay authority (the London Committee of Deputies). However, on 15 April 1840, at the Bedford Hotel, Southampton Row, a meeting of twenty-four members of the leading Jewish families in London resolved to establish a place of worship which was to be neither Ashkenazi nor Sephardi, but 'British'; this synagogue, the West London Synagogue of British Jews, opened its doors on 27 February 1842. Although these dissidents could boast no coherent theology of their own, they inclined towards the reform movement that had sprung up in Germany at the beginning of the century, a direction confirmed by the appointment of David Wolf Marks, an anti-Talmudist, as their first minister. But the establishment of the West London Synagogue also had a political dimension, and must be viewed, from one perspective, as an episode in the history of the struggle for Jewish political equality in Britain—or, rather, in the struggle within British Jewry over whether political emancipation should be pursued, and, if so, at what pace. By declaring themselves to be 'British' the West London seceders proclaimed publicly that they were prepared to depart from orthodoxy, and so jettison their religious particularisms, in order to make themselves more acceptable as 'British' citizens.

Like Adler, Montefiore did not oppose emancipation, but he could never bring himself to give it a place of high priority. He felt that the rights to vote at local and parliamentary elections, and to be elected to municipal authorities and to the House of Commons itself, were important at an abstract level, but believed that, since Jews enjoyed complete economic equality and a large measure of social integration, political emancipation would be of little practical benefit. Montefiore's diaries reveal a preoccupation with the fear that involvement in political life would lead, inevitably, to clashes between the requirements of Orthodox observance and the demands of public office. He was not prepared to permit the London Committee of Deputies to be catapulted into a public agitation, as was demanded by the reformers and by the Orthodox radicals, led by David Salomons and Rothschild's son Lionel. This reticence had led, in 1838, to a break between the London committee and the emancipationists, and, in 1845, to Montefiore and Isaac Goldsmid leading rival deputations to Robert Peel, the prime minister, on the emancipation question.

Montefiore had already (1836) informed the government that the London committee was 'the only official channel of communication for the secular and political interests' of British Jewry. The passage, that year, of the Registration Act gave him a powerful new weapon to use against both the reformers and any dissident Jews who might choose to challenge the authority of the chief rabbinate. That measure recognized the president of the London committee as the sole authority competent to certify to the registrar-general the names of marriage secretaries of synagogues 'of Persons professing the Jewish Religion'. Montefiore established the principle that such certification would not be given without authorization from

either the spiritual head of the Spanish and Portuguese Jews or the chief rabbi of the Ashkenazim. In 1842 these ecclesiastical authorities issued a *herem*, or ban, against the reformers, who, Montefiore agreed, could not be considered authentic Jews. He thus supported Chief Rabbi Solomon Hirschell and his successor, Nathan Adler, in refusing to grant recognition for marriage purposes to the reformers, and in 1853, when a small number of provincial congregations elected reformers as deputies, he used his casting vote to keep them out. This ban was not lifted until 1874, the year of Montefiore's ultimate retirement from the presidency, and it was not until 1886, the year following his death, that the first reform deputies took their seats.

Montefiore, in short, allowed his personal prejudices to interfere with his duty to uphold the representative status of the London committee. But his attitude towards this representative status was in any case ambivalent. When Montefiore was first elected president, the committee (dating from 1760) comprised twenty-two deputies, all representing the large, and wealthy, London congregations. In 1836 the committee acquired its first formal constitution, permitting the affiliation of other London congregations and of provincial communities. By nature an autocrat, Montefiore found it difficult to come to terms with this enlargement and very limited democratization. He seems to have looked upon the conduct of the committee's business as almost a private, family affair, and could never adjust properly—or positively—to its necessary reform to meet changing circumstances. When the enlarged committee met for the first time, on 12 August 1838, his friend and secretary Louis Loewe noted from Montefiore's diary that the president appeared 'to have apprehended some difficulty in managing' the new body. He had little liking for the details of administration, and delayed too long the appointment of a professional secretary (the solicitor Sampson Samuel, appointed 1838). The collection of basic communal statistics, relating to synagogue membership, births, deaths, and marriages, was not commenced until 1849. Although the board resorted to *ad hoc* standing committees from time to time, it was not until 1854 that a standing general purposes committee was created.

Montefiore saw to it that, in the struggle for political emancipation, the committee did not play the central role that might have been expected of the body that claimed to be the representative organ of British Jewry. Others made the running, while Montefiore busied himself with journeys to foreign parts in order to take up what he regarded as the far more pressing claims of oppressed Jewries abroad. These epic voyages—to the Middle East over the Damascus Blood Libel (1840), to Rome over the Mortara affair (the abduction of a Jewish child by Catholic conversionists, 1859), to Russia (1846 and 1872), to Constantinople and Morocco (1863–4), and seven times to the Holy Land (1827, 1838, 1849, 1855, 1857, 1866, and 1875)—were productive of little concrete good (the release of Damascus Jews accused of ritual murder being the one exception worthy of mention), though they probably had an uplifting effect upon the morale of those co-religionists on whose behalf they were undertaken.

With hindsight, it may appear difficult to understand the very genuine popularity—bordering on adulation—which Montefiore enjoyed during his lifetime. His hundredth birthday was an occasion of national rejoicing; *The Times* devoted a leader to it. Montefiore was a living symbol of Victorian liberal values: the Orthodox Jew who, without sacrificing his religious scruples, played a full part in public life, and who acted almost as a roving ambassador for his country. Physically he was a most imposing figure, standing 6 feet 3 inches tall. A captain in the Surrey local militia (1809–14), he served as sheriff of the City of London (1837–8), and was at that time knighted by Queen Victoria; he was elected a fellow of the Royal Society in 1836 and was created a baronet in 1846.

Montefiore died on 28 July 1885 at his country estate, East Cliff Lodge, Ramsgate, and was buried there, on 31 July, in the mausoleum he had constructed to house the remains of his wife. There were no children of the marriage, but strong family tradition identifies Montefiore as the father of C. F. Moberly *Bell, manager of *The Times*.

GEOFFREY ALDERMAN

Sources S. Lipman and V. D. Lipman, eds., *The century of Moses Montefiore* (1985) • M. Samet, *Mosheh Montifyori: metsi'ut ve-agadah* [Moses Montefiore: reality and myth] (Jerusalem, 1989) • *Diaries of Sir Moses and Lady Montefiore*, ed. L. Loewe, 2 vols. (1890) • R. Sebag-Montefiore, *A family patchwork* (1987) • G. Alderman, *Modern British Jewry* (1992) • V. D. Lipman, ed., *Sir Moses Montefiore: a symposium* [Oxford 1980] (1982) • G. Collard, *Moses, the Victorian Jew* (1990)
Archives CUL, letters • U. Southampton L., transcripts of corresp. • UCL, corresp., letter-books, diaries, and account books | Jewish Museum, London, letters to Lewis Emanuel • UCL, letters to Moses Gaster • Wellcome L., corresp. with the Hodgkin family
Likenesses R. Dighton, caricature, coloured etching, 1818, NPG, V&A • E. Kruger, two lithographs, 1840–46, BM • S. A. Hart, oils, 1848, Spanish and Portuguese Synagogue, London • S. A. Hart, oils?, 1869, Ramsgate Public Library, Kent • H. Weigel, oils?, 1881, NPG • R. Blind, lithograph, NPG • Elliott & Fry, cabinet photograph, NPG [*see illus.*] • Lunois, lithograph (aged ninety-nine), BM • W. Wilson, pen-and-ink drawing, repro. in *The Graphic* (27 Oct 1883) • lithograph, BM
Wealth at death £374,421 2s. 5d.: probate, May 1886, CGPLA Eng. & Wales (1885)

Monteith, Charles Montgomery (1921–1995), publisher, was born on 9 February 1921 in Lisburn, co. Antrim, the elder son of James Monteith, draper, and his wife, Marian, *née* Montgomery. He was educated at the Royal Belfast Academic Institution and at Magdalen College, Oxford (demy, 1939; senior demy, 1948). His university education was interrupted by war service. Before it he studied English and, afterwards, law; in both he obtained first-class honours. In 1948 he graduated MA and won a prize fellowship at All Souls College, Oxford; the following year he graduated BCL and was called to the bar at Gray's Inn.

Monteith had five years in the army, from 1940 to 1945; he was commissioned into the Royal Iniskilling Fusiliers and, as a major, served with his regiment in India and Burma. It was in Burma that a mortar explosion severely wounded him in the legs. He suffered the effects of this for the rest of his life; he limped, though not very noticeably, and could never walk fast or long.

At the age of twenty-four Monteith returned to Oxford, with a greater feeling of urgency about the need to choose and pursue a career. He chose the bar, but soon realized that it was not going to satisfy him. Although quick with thoughts and words, he lacked the instinct of attack. Meanwhile he had found a spiritual home in All Souls, where he was a fellow from 1948 to 1988 and sub-warden from 1967 to 1969. He relished the society there and was fully able to hold his own in the lightly erudite, often amusing, conversation in which it excelled.

It was through All Souls that he became a publisher. An older fellow, Geoffrey Faber, whose two sons had opted for careers other than in the family publishing firm, was looking for somebody who could eventually take over from him and his immediate successors. Invited to join Faber and Faber in 1953, Monteith became a director in 1954. Twenty years later he was vice-chairman, before becoming head of the firm from 1977 to 1980. As chairman, however, he was not wholly successful. He was not a born businessman, nor felt himself to be so, and he preferred to leave finance to others; where he was not deeply interested, he tended to lack drive. He could also be exigent in his demands on other people and was not always good with staff. On the other hand, when fully engaged, he was both conscientious and committed; he had great loyalty to the firm and affection for its founder.

What made Monteith an outstanding publisher was his exceptional editorial flair. At least as familiar with modern, as with classical, English writing, he was always open to new literary fashions and ideas. He took great trouble with his chief authors (William Golding, Philip Larkin, Seamus Heaney, Samuel Beckett, John Osborne, Ted Hughes, Thom Gunn, Tom Paulin, Jan Morris, and P. D. James, among others) and had personal friendships with them. He was particularly close to Golding, Larkin, and Heaney, who all recognized their debt to him. He attracted science fiction and Northern Irish writers to the firm and could always find the right academic contact when an expert opinion was needed. The best-known of his editorial successes was his realization that Golding's book, which became *Lord of the Flies* (a grubby and rejected manuscript when it reached the firm), was a potential masterpiece. The original work, called *Strangers from within*, had begun with a description of an atomic explosion; this was expunged and the title was changed.

Apart from his work at Faber and Faber, Monteith was a director of the Poetry Book Society from 1966 to 1981, a member of the literature panel of the Arts Council from 1974 to 1978, and a member of the Library Advisory Council for England from 1979 to 1981. He remained a senior editorial consultant of the firm, and an emeritus fellow of All Souls, after his retirement. He received honorary DLitt degrees from the New University of Ulster in 1980 and from the University of Kent in 1982.

Monteith preferred to publish other people's books than to produce his own. But he was an active correspondent; he also wrote a few essays in volumes honouring authors on his list, a delightful account of 'Eliot in the office', and the entry on Geoffrey Faber in the *Dictionary of National Biography*. In religion he came to feel more affinity with the Church of England than with the Presbyterianism in which he had been brought up; intellectually, however, he remained an agnostic. In politics, although he had voted Labour as a young man, he moved to the right as he grew older. He admired Thatcher's handling of the Falklands War and liked to predict that, with advancing years, the queen would be universally venerated, like her great-grandmother. In all his attitudes there was a blend of cultivated liberalism and northern Irish patriotism. His tastes were discerning, catholic, and by no means rigidly highbrow. He liked good food and drink, good architecture, and good pictures; he was also fascinated by films and motor racing; he enjoyed travel and learned to cook and garden. He had virtually no musical sense, but his excellent visual judgement was always shown by his surroundings.

Although he did not inherit money, Monteith was left a charming villa in St John's Wood by an aunt (on his mother's side) who had lived there in what he supposed was 'a high-minded lesbian relationship' with the daughter of a successful late Victorian painter. This came to him in middle age and gave him much pleasure. When gardening became too difficult he sold it and moved to a comfortable flat, Flat G, 38 Randolph Avenue, where he remained until his death.

He suffered much illness in later life. He bore this uncomplainingly and made light of it to his many friends. In middle life he went through an unhappy period when he was persecuted by a failed author with a grudge against Faber and Faber. This caused him much distress and shook his self-confidence; but in due course he recovered his aplomb and the experience seemed to deepen his sympathy and understanding. His heart gave the worst of his physical problems. He had a bypass operation and it was of a heart attack that he died, alone in his flat, on 9 May 1995; his body, discovered by his cleaning lady, was cremated and the ashes were taken to Castlederg to be buried with his parents.

Monteith was tall and heavy, with a presence that could not be ignored. His talk was full of humour and anecdote; his Irish jokes (delivered in the most authentic accents) were particularly effective; he would imitate chancellor Harold Macmillan, using the old English pronunciation of Latin at Oxford University, with unfailing gusto. At bottom he was always both kind and shy. But, as a young man, he displayed a kind of surface brilliance which could be slightly intimidating; one sometimes got the impression that he would rather be talking to more interesting people. Later on, he became humbler and mellower. He had always enjoyed life, in spite of some inner melancholy; looking back he must have felt that he had largely realized the promise of his youth. After his death, indeed, his reputation grew. He came to seem one of the last representatives of an earlier age of publishing, when literary judgement could sometimes prevail against commercial expectations. RICHARD FABER

Sources *The Times* (12 May 1995) · *The Independent* (13 May 1995) · *Daily Telegraph* (13 May 1995) · *The Guardian* (11 May 1995) · P. Howard, *The Times* (22 Sept 1995) · personal knowledge (2004) · private information (2004) [Seamus Heaney; Gerard Irvine]
Archives Bodl. Oxf., corresp. with R. B. Montgomery | SOUND BL NSA, performance recordings
Likenesses photograph, repro. in *The Independent* · photograph, repro. in *The Times*
Wealth at death £387,796: probate, 11 July 1995, CGPLA Eng. & Wales

Monteith, Henry (1765–1848). *See under* Monteith, Robert (1811–1884).

Monteith, Robert (1811–1884), politician and philanthropist, was born in Glasgow on 23 December 1811, one of fourteen children, but the only surviving son, of the marriage between **Henry Monteith** (1765–1848) and Christina Cameron (1768–1818). Henry Monteith was a merchant landowner, twice lord provost of Glasgow (1814–16 and 1818–20), and an MP; he owned huge textile mills at Barrowfield, Glasgow, and at Blantyre, and made his fortune with the Turkey-red dye process. His home, Carstairs House (built in 1818), was one of the first neo-Gothic buildings in Scotland. In 1820 he defeated Robert Owen for the Lanark burghs parliamentary seat. Briefly MP for Saltash in 1826, he was returned again for Lanark burghs in 1830, holding the seat until 1832.

Robert Monteith, after studying at Glasgow University, proceeded, with his cousin Francis G. Garden, to Trinity College, Cambridge, matriculating in 1829. A member of the Apostles, he became a close friend of Richard Monckton Milnes (later Lord Houghton), Alfred Tennyson, John Sterling, Henry Hallam, Richard Chenevix Trench, A. J. C. Hare, William Palgrave, and many others. He was acquainted with W. E. Gladstone, W. M. Thackeray, Coventry Patmore, and François Rio, the French art critic, and shared in many literary and artistic endeavours, such as the 1839 Eglinton tournament, the restoration of Glasgow Cathedral, and the Burns and Scott memorials in Edinburgh. His hospitality was always lavish. He was prevented from going to support the Spanish liberal cause in 1830, but he travelled the continent and visited Rome in the 1830s: he passed many winters there in Catholic aristocratic circles in the 1850s. After unsuccessful attempts to win a seat in Glasgow in the tory interest twice in 1837, he refused to stand later on at least two occasions. He unsuccessfully contested Bewdley in 1841. In 1844, at Morden parish church, Monteith married Wilhelmina Catherine Anne (*d.* 1884), the third daughter of Joseph Charles Mellish, a former consul-general at Hamburg and translator of Schiller's *Mary Queen of Scots* (1801). They had two sons and three daughters.

Various influences encouraged the development of Monteith's social Romanticism: Kenelm Digby; his association with French liberal Catholicism; Bishop Gillis's mutual improvement and benefit society; the Holy Guild of St Joseph, Edinburgh; Catholic notions of international law; and the patient suffering of the Irish workers in his textile mills. In the debates over the established churches of Scotland and England, he fell under Romantic rather than rational German influences. He consulted John Henry Newman at Littlemore, who received him into the Roman Catholic church in 1846. His wife followed shortly afterwards. His godfather was Ignatius Spencer, an earlier convert and Passionist priest. Monteith came deeply under the influence of David Urquhart, the renowned Russophobe, whose Glasgow visit in 1838 made Monteith a close supporter. Urquhart and Monteith believed that Russia had infiltrated the British government, fomented unrest among workers, and destroyed their sense of community: they argued that a just international order would bring domestic peace. Monteith championed the poor. He attended the great Birmingham Chartist gathering of 1840, and worked with Chartists such as Robert Lowery and William Cardo to prevent an Anglo-French war in 1841. If poverty horrified him, pauperism, or state-induced dependence, he believed to be worse. He and Urquhart pressed their views on Catholic clergy and Oxford scholars: they hoped to establish a chair of international law at Oxford. From the 1850s Monteith supported Urquhart's working men's foreign affairs committees and newspaper, the *Free Press*, to which Karl Marx was a contributor. With Thomas Chisholm Anstey MP, and Urquhart, he campaigned against Russian expansion, British imperialism, and the despoiling of the highlands. He promoted savings banks for workers. With Urquhart he supported the introduction of Turkish baths into Britain for social harmony and health: he addressed the National Association for the Promotion of Social Science on the subject in 1874. He also patented several early forms of refrigeration for foodstuffs. A peace advocate, if not a pacifist, to his death, he bitterly opposed the military conscription common in continental states in the nineteenth century. His campaign for the reassertion of the law of nations at the Vatican Council of 1870–71 was a logical development of his view that conscription encouraged war as a regular arm of policy. Using a variety of influences—the *Diplomatic Review*, Bishop Mermillod of Geneva, the French sociologist Frédéric Le Play, a visit to Turkey to win over the Armenian bishops, and, not least, lavish Roman hospitality—he won the attention of the pope, and the issue reached the council. In a similar vein, Monteith led a delegation of working men to the French national assembly in 1873 to promote social peace and international harmony. He also showed great interest in the Italian Don Bosco and his work with poor boys.

Prominent in the Scottish Catholic revival, Monteith was a member of the Catholic Poor Schools Committee and the Catholic Defence Association, which worked against the Ecclesiastical Titles Act of 1850. He had earlier established the Association of St Margaret (1848) to bind together the aristocratic, convert, and Irish elements in Scottish Catholicism in order to support Catholic legal defences, education, vocations, and the poorer parishes of Scotland. He saw congregational singing as part of his schemes for social unity and composed hymns to promote this aim. He brought some 10 tons of religious statues to Scotland, and encouraged and financially supported the return of religious orders: Franciscan and Good Shepherd

nuns, Jesuits, Passionists, and, unsuccessfully, Christian Brothers. His financial backing was important in many endeavours: he was largely responsible for St Mary's, Lanark, and the Smyllum orphanage and hospital. His influence was significant in a poverty-stricken church: Rome found it useful in the bitter public clash between Scottish and Irish Catholics in the 1860s.

The ill health of his wife and his own decline meant that Monteith was less active in his last years, wintering in France. He died at his home, Carstairs House, Lanarkshire, on 31 March 1884, having played an important, if idiosyncratic, role in the revival of Roman Catholicism in Scotland. His wife died within days of him.

BERNARD ASPINWALL

Sources *The Times* (10 April 1884) · *The Tablet* (12 April 1884) · B. Aspinwall, 'Robert Monteith, 1812–84', *Clergy Review*, 63 (1978), 265–72 · B. Aspinwall, 'The Scottish dimension: Robert Monteith and the origins of modern Catholic social thought', *Downside Review*, 97 (1979), 46–68 · B. Aspinwall, 'Before Manning: some aspects of British social concern before 1865', *New Blackfriars*, 61 (1980), 113–27 · B. Aspinwall, 'David Urquhart, Robert Montieth and the Catholic church: a search for justice and peace', *Innes Review*, 31 (1980), 57–70 · M. C. Bishop, *Memoir of Mrs Urquhart* (1897) · B. Harrison and P. Hollis, *Robert Lowery, radical and chartist* (1980) · J. F. White, *The Cambridge movement: the ecclesiologists and the Gothic revival* (1962) · J. H. Gleason, *The genesis of Russophobia in Great Britain* (1950) · R. Shannon, 'David Urquhart and the Foreign Affairs Committee', *Pressure from without in early Victorian England*, ed. P. Hollis (1974) · J. Butt and J. T. Ward, 'The promotion of the Caledonian railway', *Transport History*, 3 (2 July 1970), 164–92 · J. Butt and J. T. Ward, 'The promotion of the Caledonian railway', *Transport History*, 3 (3 Nov 1970), 225–57 · G. Robinson, *David Urquhart* (1920) · b. cert. · m. cert.

Archives Scottish Catholic Archives, Edinburgh | Balliol Oxf., Urquhart MSS · Birmingham Oratory, Newman MSS · BL, Gladstone MSS · English College, Rome, Talbot MSS · Lincs. Arch., Tennyson MSS · Sacra Congregazione di Propaganda Fide, Rome · Trinity Cam., Houghton MSS · Dublin, Vincennan Provincial House MSS · Cambridge, Massachusetts, Artemas Ward MSS

Likenesses portrait; formerly in possession of sisters of St Joseph of Peace at Carstairs House

Wealth at death £31,604 12s. 7d.: confirmation, 5 Dec 1884, *CCI* · £2000 in his wife's estate: NA Scot.

Monteith, William (1790–1864), army officer in the East India Company, diplomatist, and historian, son of William Monteith and his wife, Janet Goodwin, was born in the Abbey parish, Paisley, Renfrewshire, on 22 June 1790. On 18 March 1809 he was appointed a lieutenant in the Madras engineers, and became captain on 2 May 1817, lieutenant-colonel on 4 November 1824, and colonel on 13 May 1839 (brevet on 18 June 1831). He accompanied Sir John Malcolm's embassy to Persia, and when at Tabriz in February 1810 was sent to reconnoitre the Russian frontier posts on the Arras, near Megri, at the request of Abbas Mirza, the prince royal of Persia. When Malcolm's embassy quitted Persia, Monteith was one of the officers who stayed behind. He went with Abbas Mirza to Erivan, and accompanied the unsuccessful Persian military expedition into Georgia. During four succeeding campaigns against the Russians in 1810–13 Monteith commanded a frontier force of cavalry with six guns as well as the garrison of Erivan. He took part in many skirmishes, and was wounded. The war against Russia was supported by the British minister Sir Harford Jones Brydges, but Napoleon's 1812 campaign brought about a reversal of British policy. When Henry Ellis and David Richard Morier concluded the treaty of Tehran between Great Britain and Persia (25 November 1814), which remained in force until the Anglo-Persian War of 1857, Monteith acted as secretary to Morier. He was still in Persia in 1819, and acted as aide-de-camp to Sir William Grant Keir, commanding the Bombay force sent against the Wahabi pirates of the Persian Gulf, which destroyed their stronghold of Ras al-Khaimah. He was with the Persians during the war with Turkey, which was ended by a cholera epidemic in 1821. He was then employed to determine the boundary between Persia and Turkey.

In 1826 the Russian attack came, and during the unsuccessful operations of the Persians Monteith was at the Persian headquarters. Peace was signed between Russia and Persia on 21 February 1828, and Monteith was appointed commissioner for the payment of the indemnity of £400,000 exacted from Persia, part of which was conveyed by him personally into the Russian camp. He was thus brought into contact with the Russian commander, Prince Paskevich, which led to his presence at the Russian headquarters at Tiflis during the war between the Russians and Turks in 1828. He was ordered to remain in Persia until the settlement of the Russo-Persian boundary. He left Persia in October 1829, and on his way home was with the French army at the capture of Algiers in July 1830. Monteith married on 23 March 1831. He returned to India in July 1832, and was appointed chief engineer at Madras, but in January 1834 was superseded by the arrival of Colonel Gurnard, who was ten years his senior. Monteith then became superintending engineer at the presidency, but on Gurnard's death (2 September 1836) he again became chief engineer, and, *ex officio*, a member of the military board, a position he held to 18 July 1842. He became a major-general on 23 November 1841, retired in 1847, and attained the honorary rank of lieutenant-general in 1854. Monteith was FRS and FRGS London, a member of various foreign learned societies, and a knight of the Persian order of the Lion and Sun. His publications included *Kars and Erzeroum, with the Campaign of Prince Paskiewitch* (1856) and articles in the journal of the Royal Geographical Society. Monteith died at his residence, 11 Upper Wimpole Street, London, on 18 April 1864.

H. M. CHICHESTER, rev. JAMES FALKNER

Sources *Indian Army List* · *East-India Register* · *GM*, 3rd ser., 16 (1864), 378 · H. M. Vibart, *The military history of the Madras engineers and pioneers*, 2 vols. (1881–3)
Archives BL OIOC, notebook and papers related to travels in Middle East, MSS Eur. B 24–25 · PRO, account of French expedition to Algiers, PRO 30/12
Wealth at death under £6000: probate, 12 May 1864, *CGPLA Eng. & Wales*

Montez, Lola [*real name* Elizabeth Rosanna Gilbert] (1821–1861), adventuress, was born on 17 February 1821 at Grange, co. Sligo, Ireland, the only child of Edward Gilbert (*c*.1797–1823), an ensign of the 25th foot regiment, and his wife, Eliza Oliver (*c*.1805–1875), the illegitimate daughter

Lola Montez (1821–1861), by Albert Sands Southworth and Josiah Johnson Hawes, *c*.1850

of Charles Silver Oliver MP and Mary Green. Before the girl was two years old her father exchanged into the 44th foot regiment, which had already departed for service in India; he died there on 22 September 1823, almost immediately upon his arrival with his wife and daughter at Dinajpur, near Patna. The widow soon married Lieutenant Patrick Craigie of the 19th native infantry, and in late 1826 the child was sent to live with Craigie's relatives in Montrose, Scotland. In the autumn of 1832 she was placed in a boarding-school at 20 Camden Place in Bath, and remained there until the spring of 1837, when her mother arrived to take her back to India. By this time Elizabeth had grown into a very beautiful young woman, with jet black hair, a striking figure, and large, dark blue eyes. According to Montez, her mother told her she was to be married to an old man in India, but the sixteen-year-old eloped to Ireland with a thirty-year-old officer of the 21st native infantry her mother had met on the ship from India, Lieutenant Thomas James (1807–1871). They were married at Rathbeggan, outside Dublin, on 23 July 1837. James returned with his bride to India in 1838, but the marriage failed, and Mrs James sailed alone from Calcutta on 3 October 1840 to return to England, where it had been arranged she would live with a brother of her stepfather. During the voyage, however, she began an adulterous affair with Lieutenant George Lennox (1821–1844) of the 4th Madras cavalry, a nephew of the duke of Richmond. When this news reached India, Lieutenant James sued his wife for divorce, and on 15 December 1842 the court of arches entered a decree of divorce specifically forbidding each of the parties to remarry during the lifetime of the other.

By this time the affair with Lennox was over, and Eliza Gilbert James, now publicly branded as an adulteress, had resolved to go on the stage. She claimed she studied acting briefly at Fanny Kelly's school in Soho but was advised that dancing might better suit her talents. The new divorcée travelled to Cadiz, Spain, where she learned the rudiments of Spanish dancing and of the Spanish language, and returned to England in the spring of 1843 having transformed herself into Lola Montez, a noble Spanish dancer. Montez gained the patronage of the third earl of Malmesbury, who convinced Benjamin Lumley, the impresario of Her Majesty's Theatre, to allow her to make her début at a gala performance on 3 June 1843. Her dance, which combined Spanish elements with miming the pursuit and destruction of a spider, was a great success and immediately encored; but after the performance Lumley was informed that his new 'Spanish' star was a fraud, and he refused to allow her to appear again. Montez mounted a vehement but futile campaign in her own defence, publicly swearing she was a native Spaniard and had never been Mrs James.

After sailing for Germany, Lola Montez obtained an engagement at the Royal Theatre in Dresden, where critical reaction was sharply divided, as it would be throughout her career, between enraptured praise of her beauty and magnetic stage presence and scornful condemnation of her technique as a dancer. An engagement in Berlin followed, and she was invited to dance before Friedrich Wilhelm IV and his guest, Tsar Nicholas I, at a private gala held in the Neues Palais at Potsdam. Her stay in Berlin ended with an episode that began the legend of Lola Montez as a fiery and unconventional woman, when, at a troop review before the king and Tsar, she lashed out with her riding whip at a mounted gendarme who prevented her from riding unbidden into the royal enclosure. Her legend grew at her next stop, Warsaw, where during her engagement she began feuding with the impresario, who was also the chief of police. At a performance on 14 November 1843 she denounced the impresario from the stage, and the subsequent uproar threatened to become a patriotic demonstration against the Russian occupation. After barricading herself in her hotel room and assaulting one of the guards placed outside her door, Montez was deported to the Prussian border.

The incidents in Berlin and Warsaw had made her notorious, and Montez had no trouble arranging engagements in Stettin, Danzig, Königsberg, and Riga. She apparently travelled to St Petersburg, but the Tsar was well aware of her activities in Warsaw, and no engagement was forthcoming in the Russian capital. By Montez's own account, she now hit upon the idea of attaching herself to Franz Liszt (1811–1886), then at the peak of his fame as a virtuoso, and raced by post coach along the frozen Baltic coast to intercept him at a concert near Berlin. She convinced the famous Hungarian to allow her to travel with him to Dresden. There she met the composer Richard

Wagner on 29 February 1844, during a special performance of his *Rienzi* arranged at Liszt's request. Wagner was repelled by her, but following the performance Montez introduced Liszt to the fourteen-year-old Hans von Bülow, whom she had met in Berlin and who later, like Wagner, would become Liszt's son-in-law. Montez's liaison with Liszt ended, apparently amicably, after only about a week, and she left Dresden for Paris with letters of recommendation to Liszt's influential friends. She arranged a début at the Opéra, then ballet's most prestigious stage, before she had been in Paris a month. At her first appearance, on 27 March 1844, Montez began her dance by tossing a garter into the audience, but this unorthodox gesture could not save her from failure before the critical French audience. An equally ill-received performance two days later definitively ended her career at the Opéra, and she temporarily abandoned the stage to enjoy the life of a beautiful demimondaine in Paris.

Montez became the mistress of Alexandre Henri Dujarier (1815–1845), the wealthy co-owner of the influential newspaper *La Presse*, and he probably played a role in the resumption of her dancing career, at the Théâtre de la Porte-Saint-Martin on 7 March 1845. Although the critical reception was not as hostile as before, Dujarier's death in a duel a few days later once again suspended Montez's dancing career. She was seen prominently at the festival Liszt arranged in August 1845 to dedicate Beethoven's statue at Bonn and shortly thereafter was expelled from fashionable Baden-Baden, reportedly for outraging decency by demonstrating publicly that she carried a dagger in her garter. After making a dramatic appearance at Dujarier's murder trial in March 1846, she travelled to the spas of Belgium and Germany. On 5 October 1846 she arrived in Munich, where she applied for an engagement at the Royal Theatre.

Thus began the central episode of Montez's life, her liaison with the sixty-year-old Ludwig I of Bavaria (1786–1868). The king, who had a deep interest both in beautiful women and in things Spanish, was quickly enthralled by her, and after she had danced twice he established her in her own small villa at Barerstrasse 7, promising to make her a countess. Once Montez recognized her influence over the king, she was unrestrained in attempting to advance her supporters and secure the dismissal of her foes. 'The Spanish woman' was soon hated and feared in Munich. Although the king refused to allow her to interfere in matters of political importance, his promise to make her a Bavarian countess led him to ignore the recommendation of his cabinet against granting her citizenship, and the cabinet resigned on 11 February 1847, bringing an end to nearly ten years of conservative Catholic government. The ministers' private remonstrance to King Ludwig was published throughout Europe, increasing Montez's international notoriety; and the appointment of a more liberal government seemed to give her a political importance that was belied by her apolitical self-interest. King Ludwig created her countess of Landsfeld on 25 August 1847, when his initial platonic interest had become frankly erotic, although Montez usually rewarded his desires with frustration. As countess she became even more arrogant, establishing a corps of university students to act as her bodyguard and undermining the new cabinet until it too was replaced. The final crisis began on 9 February 1848, when Montez attempted to defy a mob attacking her student corps and was saved from assassination only by the arrival of troops. Two days later she fled Munich as an enraged mob stormed her villa. She ultimately found refuge in Switzerland, where she corresponded with King Ludwig, encouraging him to abdicate and join her. Depressed by her absence and the concessions forced from him by the revolutionary events of 1848, King Ludwig did abdicate on 19 March 1848. But after he learned how Montez had betrayed and manipulated him, the king broke off contact with her.

Montez moved from Switzerland to London, where, on 19 July 1849, at St George's, Hanover Square, she married 21-year-old Cornet George Trafford Heald (1828–1856) of the 2nd Life Guards, the wealthy heir of a London barrister. Heald's aunt and former guardian, having learned that Lieutenant James was still alive in India, prosecuted her for bigamy. Montez and Heald fled England, and led a stormy existence in France, Italy, and Spain, until Heald finally abandoned her in Paris in August 1850. She returned to dancing with a tour of France and Belgium in the autumn of 1851, and, seeking new worlds to conquer, she crossed the Atlantic to dance in New York city on 29 December 1851. Five months later New York saw her first appearance as an actress, when she played herself in a new work entitled *Lola Montez in Bavaria*, written to perpetuate the myth that she had attempted to bring liberal reforms to Bavaria. Her successful American tours eventually brought her to California in the midst of the gold rush, and in San Francisco, on 2 July 1853, she married Patrick Purdy Hull (1821–1858), a newspaper editor, from whom she separated after a few weeks.

Montez retired to Grass Valley, a small mining town in the California mountains, for nearly two years before leaving in June 1855 to tour Australia. Her acting and the famous 'Spider Dance' won her large audiences in Sydney, Melbourne, and Adelaide, as well as the gold-mining towns of Victoria; horsewhipping encounters with a newspaper editor and the wife of her manager added to the legend of her fiery temper and eccentricity. Following a brief second tour of California, she returned to New York city and continued to perform widely in the United States and Canada. In the summer of 1857 she abandoned the stage to become a very successful lecturer on topics such as 'Gallantry', 'Fashion', and 'Heroines and strong-minded women of history', in which she scorned the feminist movement in favour of individual self-assertion. During this period Montez, who had always been generous in private charity, became increasingly religious and was attracted particularly to the spiritualist movement. Her first lectures were published in June 1858 as *Lectures of Lola Montez Including her Autobiography*, which was quickly followed by her popular health and beauty advice under the title *The Arts of Beauty* (1858). In November 1858 she arrived in Ireland to begin an extensive lecture tour of the British Isles, which concluded the following spring in London. There she used her substantial earnings to purchase the lease of a large house at 26 Park Lane West with the intention of operating it as a fashionable boarding house. Her mismanagement and ill health soon brought her to bankruptcy, but she returned to New York city in October 1859 and recouped her fortune with another successful lecture tour.

Montez suffered a crippling stroke on 30 June 1860, but had nearly recovered when she contracted pneumonia and died at 194 West 17th Street, New York, on 17 January 1861, leaving word for King Ludwig that she had died a good Christian and had never forgotten his friendship. She was buried two days later under the name Mrs Eliza Gilbert in Brooklyn's Greenwood cemetery.

BRUCE SEYMOUR

Sources B. Seymour, *Lola Montez: a life* (1996) · R. Rauh and B. Seymour, eds., *Ludwig I und Lola Montez: der Briefwechsel* (1995) · L. Montez, *Memoiren von Lola Montez, Gräfin von Landsfeld*, trans. L. Fort (1851) · *Lectures of Lola Montez: including her autobiography* (1858) · H. Gollwitzer, *Ludwig I von Bayern: Königtum in Vormärz: eine politische Biographie* (1986) · E. Corti, *Ludwig I von Bayern* (1937) · H. von Bülow, *Briefe und Schriften*, 6 (1904) · C. Wagner, *Die Tagebücher*, 1 (1976) · B. Lumley, *Reminiscences of the opera* (1864)
Archives Bayerische Staatsbibliothek, Munich, König Ludwig I Archiv · Harvard TC, Lola Montez collection · U. Cal., Berkeley, Bancroft Library, Lola Montez collection | BL OIOC, journals of Sir Jasper Nicolls, Eur. MS F175 · LMA, file of the consistory court in the case of *James v. James*, Acc. 73.77
Likenesses W. von Kaulbach, oils, 1847, Stadtmuseum, Munich, Germany · A. Leeb, plaster bust, 1847, Neue Pinakotek, Munich, Germany; marble copy, Neue Pinakotek, Munich, Germany · J. Stieler, oils, 1847, Bayerische Verwaltung der staatlichen Schlösser, Gärten und Seen, Munich, Germany, Schloss Nymphenburg · A. S. Southworth and J. J. Hawes, daguerreotype, *c.*1850, Metropolitan Museum of Art, New York [*see illus.*] · M. Root, daguerreotype, 1852, Harvard TC · M. Root, double portrait, daguerreotype, 1852 (with Chief Light in the Clouds), priv. coll. · A. S. Southworth and J. J. Hawes, daguerreotype, 1852, Boston Museum of Fine Arts, Boston, Massachusetts · J. Skipper, pencil and wash sketches, 1855, Mortlock Library of South Australiana, Adelaide, Australia · Meade Bros., daguerreotype, *c.*1856–1857, Harvard TC · Meade Bros., daguerreotype, *c.*1858, Smithsonian Institution, Washington, DC, National Portrait Gallery · salt print photograph, *c.*1858, Museum of the City of New York · Meade Bros., two photographs, *c.*1858–1860, Harvard TC · London Stereoscopic Co., photograph, 1859, Harvard TC · A. Adam-Salomon, photograph, *c.*1860, Bibliothèque Nationale, Paris, France · theatrical prints, Cambridge, Massachusetts
Wealth at death $1247: letter to editor of *New York Sun* (25 April 1897)

Montfichet, Richard de (*b.* after 1190, *d.* 1267), baron and forest administrator, was the eldest son of Richard de Montfichet (*d.* 1203), an important servant of Richard I, and his wife, Millicent. He was a descendant of William de Montfichet (*d.* before 1156), whose barony of Stansted Montfichet comprised nearly fifty knights' fees, and from whom he inherited a claim to the custody of the royal forests in Essex, forfeited by his grandfather Gilbert de Montfichet (*d.* 1186/7), probably for his part in the rebellion of Henry, the Young King, in 1173. The younger Richard de Montfichet was about ten years old at the death of his father and was sold in wardship to Roger de Lacy, constable of Chester, in return for a proffer of £1000 which seems never to have been paid. In 1210 his wardship was resold to his mother for a fine of 1100 marks paid in full within a year. Montfichet had come of age by 1214, when he served on King John's expedition to Poitou, but shortly afterwards he joined the rebel barons, perhaps in the hope of recovering the rights forfeited by his family under Henry II, perhaps also because of his close kinship to the baronial leaders Robert Fitzwalter and Richard, earl of Clare. His grandfather Gilbert had married Avelina de Lucy, Robert Fitzwalter's aunt, while William de Montfichet, the first baron, had been married to Margaret, daughter of Gilbert de Clare, first earl of Hertford (d. 1152).

On 21 June 1215, at the field of Runnymede, Montfichet was restored to custody of the forests of Essex once held by his ancestors. At the same time he was one of the twenty-five barons appointed to enforce the observance of Magna Carta, promising the service of thirty knights. His lands were confiscated, and Montfichet himself was taken prisoner at the battle of Lincoln in May 1217. In the following October he returned to loyalty and recovered his lands, including his hereditary custody of the Essex forests, which he retained for the remainder of his life. In 1225 he witnessed the reissue of Magna Carta, and in 1230 he sailed on the king's expedition to Brittany. Despite a brief eclipse under the regime headed by Peter des Roches, he was admitted to sit as a baron of the exchequer in 1234, and in 1237 witnessed a further confirmation of Magna Carta. He was appointed chief justice of the forests for nineteen southern counties in 1236, and from 1242 to 1246 served as sheriff of Essex and Hertfordshire. One of the baronial representatives appointed to consider the king's demand for a subsidy in 1244, he probably had a share in drafting the remarkable scheme of reform of that year, recorded by the chronicler Matthew Paris. At some time before October 1252 his custody of the Essex forests was challenged in the king's court by the chief forester, Robert Passelewe, but Richard was restored to office in hereditary fee. Throughout the political storms of the 1260s he remained active as forester, apparently without compromising himself with either the royalist or the Montfortian party. He died late in 1267, the last survivor of the baronial twenty-five of 1215.

Although Montfichet had been married at least twice, to Alice (*fl.* 1217), and later to a woman named Jousa or Joyce who outlived him, he left no issue, so that his estates were partitioned among the children and grandchildren of his three sisters. Shortly before his death, with royal assent, he conveyed his hereditary custody of the Essex forests to Thomas de Clare, son of the earl of Gloucester and Hertford, a distant kinsman. Richard de Montfichet's coat of arms, or, three chevrons gules, a label of five points azure, derived from the Clare arms, is recorded by Matthew Paris and on Richard's seal.　　　NICHOLAS VINCENT

Sources Chancery records · Pipe rolls · Paris, *Chron.* · I. J. Sanders, *English baronies: a study of their origin and descent, 1086–1327* (1960) · W. Farrer, *Feudal Cambridgeshire* (1920) · L. C. Loyd, *The origins of some*

Anglo-Norman families, ed. C. T. Clay and D. C. Douglas, Harleian Society, 103 (1951) · J. C. Holt, *Magna Carta*, 2nd edn (1992) · L. Landon, *The itinerary of King Richard I*, PRSoc., new ser., 13 (1935) · D. J. C. King, *Castellarium Anglicanum: an index and bibliography of the castles in England, Wales, and the islands*, 2 vols. (1983) · *Sir Christopher Hatton's Book of seals*, ed. L. C. Loyd and D. M. Stenton, Northamptonshire RS, 15 (1950) · W. R. Fisher, *The forest of Essex* (1887)

Montfort. For this title name *see* Silva, Francisco Dias da, marquess of Montfort in the nobility of the Holy Roman empire (1634–1688) [*see under* Silva, Duarte da (1596–1677)].

Montfort, Amaury de, styled eleventh earl of Leicester (1242/3–c.1300), ecclesiastic, was the third son of Simon de *Montfort, earl of Leicester (c.1208–1265), and his wife, *Eleanor (1215?–1275), daughter of King *John. Like his brother Henry de *Montfort he was for a time brought up in the household of Robert Grosseteste, bishop of Lincoln, and from an early date he was marked out for a clerical career. In April 1259 he was already a chaplain and property-holder in Évreux, where he subsequently acquired a canonry, and in July 1260 his father's friend Eudes Rigaud, archbishop of Rouen, conferred a prebend on him in his cathedral. Like Simon de Montfort's other sons, he did especially well out of his father's period of power between 1263 and 1265, acquiring a prebend at St Paul's, London, probably in 1263, the wealthy Cornish rectory of St Wendron, probably in 1264, the treasurership of York (one of the richest benefices in England) in February 1265, and at some stage a prebend at Lincoln. Throughout this period he remained in minor orders, below the subdiaconate, for it was only in December 1267 that he was given a licence by Eudes Rigaud to be ordained to major orders by any bishop anywhere. It may not have been his father's influence alone that commended him to so many bishops, but also his scholarly qualities. Described by a contemporary chronicler as 'a clerk of eminent learning' (*Flores historiarum*, 3.67), he had for a teacher one Master Nicholas, whom Roger Bacon placed among the best mathematicians of the day, and was himself the author of an alchemical tract.

After his father's death at Evesham Montfort was immediately deprived of the treasurership of York by Henry III and took refuge in France, together with his mother and his younger brother Richard. In 1268 he went to Italy, and for the next three years studied at the University of Padua; he was also made a papal chaplain. In April 1271 he was charged with complicity in the murder of Henry of Almain at Viterbo, but the bishop and chapter of Padua, the university, and the city's friars cleared him by joining in a written declaration that he had never been out of Padua since October, and that at the time of the murder he was at death's door with fever. On 19 April 1272 he was at Rome, whence he returned to the abbot of Monte Cassino three books on medicine which he had borrowed, probably for his studies at Padua. By this time he had taken the title of earl of Leicester, presumably after the death of his elder brother Simon de *Montfort the younger.

Late in 1275 or 1276, when escorting his sister *Eleanor

(c.1258–1282) to Wales for her marriage to Llywelyn ap Gruffudd, Montfort was captured and imprisoned by Edward I, first at Corfe Castle, then at Sherborne, then at Taunton. He was released only in April 1282. During his time in prison he compiled three theological treatises which still survive in his own holograph copy and with his signature. They reveal much about his own hopes and fears and include an unusually personal set of confessions. After his release, on condition of abjuring the realm, he wrote to the king from Arras on 22 May, thanking him for his grace, promising fidelity, and asking for liberty to 'recover his rights' by processes of law in England. When this demand was refused or ignored, in December 1284 he began a suit in the court of Rome against Edmund of Lancaster, the king's brother, for restitution of his inheritance. In June 1286 he was in Paris, dealing with business arising from the will of his mother, whose executor he was. He made his own will in 1289 at Montargis, the house of Dominican nuns, south of Paris, where his mother had died. In it he granted his hereditary rights in England to the pope and cardinals, making them responsible for the will's execution and for the restoration of the Montforts' rights in England. After the death of his brother Guy de *Montfort in 1291/2 he is said to have renounced his orders and become a knight. It is reported that he afterwards travelled to Italy and acted as tutor to Guy's two daughters. Since the pope, Boniface VIII, obtained a certified notarial copy of Amaury de Montfort's will in 1302 it is likely that he died shortly before this date.   J. R. MADDICOTT

Sources *Chancery records* · Bibliothèque Nationale, Paris, MS Lat. 9213, no. 19 [for Amaury as chaplain of Évreux] · Bodl. Oxf., MS Auct. D.4.13 [holograph copy of subject's theological works] · will, Vatican Archives, AA. Arm. I–XVIII, 123 · C. Bémont, *Simon de Montfort, earl of Leicester, 1208–1265*, trans. E. F. Jacob, new edn (1930) · *Rogeri de Wendover liber qui dicitur flores historiarum*, ed. H. G. Hewlett, 3 vols., Rolls Series, [84] (1886–9) · L. E. Boyle, 'E cathena et carcere: the imprisonment of Amaury de Montfort, 1276', *Medieval learning and literature: essays presented to R. W. Hunt*, ed. J. J. G. Alexander and M. T. Gibson (1976), 379–97 · J. R. Maddicott, *Simon de Montfort* (1994)
Archives Bodl. Oxf., MS Auct. D.4.13
Wealth at death see will, Archivio Vaticano, Vatican City, AA. Arm. I–XVIII, 123

Montfort, Eleanor de. *See* Eleanor (c.1258–1282).

Montfort, Guy de (c.1244–1291/2), soldier and administrator, was the fourth son of Simon de *Montfort, earl of Leicester (c.1208–1265), and his wife, *Eleanor (1215?–1275), daughter of King *John. He first appears as one of the commanders, with his brother Henry de *Montfort, of a division of his father's army at the battle of Lewes on 14 May 1264, and after the battle he was given custody of the Devon and Cornwall lands of Richard of Cornwall, the king's brother. At the battle of Evesham on 4 August 1265 he was wounded and taken prisoner. Confined first in Windsor, and afterwards in Dover Castle, he escaped to France in April or May 1266.

Two or three years later Montfort went to Italy and took service with Charles of Anjou, with whose Italian ambitions, as the French conqueror of the kingdom of Naples, the whole of his future career was to be involved. Two factors probably led him in this direction: his father's earlier friendship with Charles (the St Albans chronicle says that they were sworn brothers), and the example of his cousin Philip de Montfort, who was already Charles's vicar in Sicily. Guy de Montfort was with Charles at the battle of Tagliacozzo in August 1268, where Conradin, grandson of the emperor Frederick II, was defeated and Charles's conquest of Sicily secured. He supported Charles's subsequent consolidation of his control in Sicily and was rewarded with important fiefs in the mainland kingdom of Naples and, in March 1270, with appointment as Charles's vicar-general in Tuscany. In August 1270 he married Margherita Aldobrandesca, daughter and heir of Count Ildebrandino of Pitigliano, the most powerful man in southern Tuscany. They had two daughters, Thomasina and Anastasia, through whom alone the line of the English Montforts was to be preserved.

Then followed the crime which made Guy de Montfort notorious. On 13 March 1271 he and his brother Simon de *Montfort the younger, who had joined him in Italy, murdered their cousin Henry of Almain, son of Richard, earl of Cornwall, in the church of San Silvestro at Viterbo, in vengeance for Almain's desertion of their father during the barons' wars. The crime was all the more shocking because Henry of Almain had been sent as a peacemaker to restore the two Montfort brothers to the favour of their other cousin, Edward, Henry III's eldest son; its heinousness led Dante to place Guy de Montfort among the murderers in his *Inferno*, in the seventh circle of Hell.

After the murder Montfort became a fugitive. Deprived of his lands and offices by Charles of Anjou, he was given shelter near Siena by his father-in-law. In April 1273 he was excommunicated by Gregory IX. Submitting to the pope in July, he was placed in a papal prison in the castle at Lecco, on Lake Como, though in Charles's custody. From this prison it was rumoured that he escaped, and certainly he had returned to Charles's service by 1281, after abortive negotiations between Charles of Salerno, Charles's heir, and Edward I for his rehabilitation. His reascent was eased by the accession of a French pope, Martin IV, in 1281, and by 1283 he was in charge of the papal forces in the Romagna. In 1284, on the death of his father-in-law, he returned to Tuscany to secure his wife's inheritance, but he was soon back in the service of the Angevins. Charles of Anjou died in 1285, his position undermined by the Sicilian Vespers of 1282, the popular rising which freed the island from French control and brought it under that of Peter, king of Aragon. Angevin attempts to regain Sicily continued, however, and it was during one such attempt that Guy de Montfort was captured at sea in 1287 by the great Aragonese admiral Roger Loria. He was sent to a Sicilian prison, and although his cousin Philip's son, John de Montfort, tried to have him ransomed, nothing came of this, possibly because Edward I intervened to prevent it. He died a prisoner in 1291 or 1292, reputedly (so a Sicilian chronicle asserts) by his own hand. Ambitious, violent, the acquisitive accumulator of wide lands, but also a talented soldier and administrator, and one capable of winning the friendship of great men, Montfort had to some extent followed in his father's footsteps, though on a different stage and to a different sort of failure.

J. R. MADDICOTT

Sources Chancery records · Ann. mon. · C. Bémont, Simon de Montfort, earl of Leicester, 1208–1265, trans. E. F. Jacob, new edn (1930) · F. M. Powicke, 'Guy de Montfort, 1265–1271', TRHS, 4th ser., 18 (1935), 1–23 · F. M. Powicke, King Henry III and the Lord Edward: the community of the realm in the thirteenth century, 2 vols. (1947) · S. Runciman, The Sicilian Vespers (1958) · J. R. Maddicott, Simon de Montfort (1994)

Montfort, Sir Henry de (1238–1265), soldier, the eldest son of Simon de *Montfort, earl of Leicester (c.1208–1265), and his wife, *Eleanor (1215?–1275), daughter of King *John, was born in Kenilworth Castle on about 26 November 1238. He was the boyhood companion of his cousin Edward, his near contemporary and Henry III's eldest son and heir, and was partly brought up in the household of Robert Grosseteste, bishop of Lincoln. In June 1252 he accompanied his father to Gascony, and again travelled to France, probably to meet his father, in August or September 1256. When the king's Lusignan half-brothers were expelled from England in June 1258, Henry de Montfort secretly followed them to Boulogne and stirred up his father's friends to besiege them there. On 1 January 1259 he was in France with his father and with his own hand wrote his father's will. The county of Bigorre in southwest France, which his father acquired at this time, may have been intended as an appanage for him. On 13 October 1260 he and his brother Simon de *Montfort the younger were knighted by their cousin Edward, afterwards going to France to tourney in his company.

During the disorders of June 1263 both Henry de Montfort and his brother Simon took part in the devastation of the Kentish lands of Boniface of Savoy, archbishop of Canterbury. In January 1264 he was one of the deputies sent to represent the barons before Louis IX at Amiens. When Louis's judgment was rejected in England he commanded a body of troops dispatched to attack his father's enemies among the marcher barons on the Welsh border. On 28 February he stormed and sacked Worcester, and soon afterwards took Gloucester, but on Edward's approach he misguidedly made a truce with him and retired to Kenilworth. In thus allowing Edward to escape he incurred his father's bitter anger. At the battle of Lewes on 14 May 1264 he and his brothers Simon and Guy de *Montfort were among the leaders of their father's first division.

After the victory, on 28 May, Henry de Montfort was made constable of Dover Castle, governor of the Cinque Ports, and chamberlain of Sandwich; and until 23 July he was also escheator south of Trent. His command of the channel ports allowed him to enforce the prohibition laid by the new government on the export of wool to his own profit, and his seizures of wool earned him the nickname of 'the Wool Merchant'. In January 1265 he was at Chester, part of Edward's appanage appropriated by his father probably for Henry's use. He fought and fell at Evesham

on 4 August 1265, by his father's side, and was buried with him in the neighbouring abbey. Like his brother Simon, he had been exceptionally close to his father, sharing in many of his activities and, in 1264 and 1265, profiting from his command of the kingdom's resources. He possessed all his father's violent and acquisitive tendencies without any of his compensating qualities, and the growing baronial hostility to both brothers was one factor in his father's fall.

J. R. MADDICOTT

Sources Chancery records · Paris, Chron., vols. 3–5 · Ann. mon. · C. Bémont, Simon de Montfort, comte de Leicester (Paris, 1884) · C. Bémont, Simon de Montfort, earl of Leicester, 1208–1265, trans. E. F. Jacob, new edn (1930) · J. R. Maddicott, Simon de Montfort (1994) · R. C. Stacey, Politics, policy and finance under Henry III, 1216–1245 (1987), 124, n.168 · D. C. Cox, The battle of Evesham: a new account (1988), 18

Montfort, John de, fourth earl of Richmond and duke of Brittany (d. 1399), magnate, was the only son of John, count of Montfort, and Joan of Flanders, daughter of Louis, count of Nevers.

Background and childhood Probably born in November or December 1339, John de Montfort is first mentioned in a document of November 1341 which claimed that John (III), duke of Brittany, his childless uncle, had made provision for him to receive 20,000 livres from his patrimony. But when the duke died on 30 April 1341, his half-brother (John's father) and Charles de Blois (husband of John (III)'s niece, Jeanne de Penthièvre) disputed his succession. Civil war broke out and was soon subsumed in the larger conflict already raging between England and France, because Edward III supported the elder Montfort while Philippe VI backed Blois, his nephew. War and political intrigue dominated Montfort's life thereafter. If his English connections should naturally be emphasized here, the main significance of his career lies in his promotion of policies that eventually enabled Brittany to achieve a large measure of autonomy within the late medieval French polity.

Montfort's earliest days were inauspicious; in November 1341 his father was captured and his mother forced to assume leadership of the Montfortist cause. Although Edward III sent troops and secured some strongholds, following his own largely fruitless campaign in the duchy in late 1342, he withdrew leaving a lieutenant and minimal forces to defend Anglo-Breton interests. Montfort, his mother, and sister Joan, who later married Ralph, Lord Basset of Drayton (d. 1390), accompanied Edward back to England. Here, although she did not die until 1374, Montfort's mother lapsed into chronic illness and Queen Philippa took John de Montfort into her care. A revival of family fortunes when the elder John broke parole, fled to England, and paid homage to the king at Easter 1345, proved ephemeral since he died unexpectedly while leading another small force to the duchy in September 1345, leaving his son in *Edward III's guardianship.

The duchy attained The capture of Charles de Blois by Sir Thomas Dagworth at the battle of La Roche Derrien on 20 June 1347 marked a new stage in the Breton civil war. While his release was being negotiated, there was renewed discussion of the succession issue. For a period it seemed that Edward III might sacrifice his ward's interests for diplomatic advantage. In March 1353 a treaty was drafted with Blois that would have deprived Montfort of most of his rights. But it was not implemented, and by the time Blois was released in 1356 (for a huge ransom) Edward was resolved on firmly maintaining his ward's claims in Brittany. Here Montfort's first major military experience came when he joined Henry, duke of Lancaster, to besiege Rennes from October 1356 to July 1357; he later took part in the Rheims campaign of 1359–60.

By the treaty of Brétigny (1360) it was agreed that separate discussions should be held over the Breton succession. But talks attended by Montfort and Blois at St Omer in March 1361 (about the time when Montfort married Edward III's fourth daughter, Mary), and again in April 1362, achieved no lasting solution. In June 1362 Edward finally recognized Montfort's majority and allowed him to return to Brittany where he was advised in government by a small but influential group led by William, Lord Latimer (d. 1381). After further exchanges with Blois in July 1363, Edward, the Black Prince, called the two rivals together at Poitiers in November and again in February 1364. Proposals to partition the duchy failed, probably because of the intransigence of Jeanne de Penthièvre, and decisive military confrontation followed. Leading an Anglo-Gascon force, commanded by Sir John Chandos, to the relief of Auray (Morbihan), Montfort forced Blois to give battle on 29 September 1364. The defeat and death of Blois there broke Penthièvre resistance. Charles V of France acknowledged John de Montfort as duke. In the treaty of Guérande (12 April 1365) terms were reached with Jeanne de Penthièvre, while in December 1366 Montfort performed homage at Paris.

Rebellion and exile During Montfort's early years as duke ties with England remained strong. Although his first wife, Mary, had died after a few months (1361), in 1366 he married Joan Holland, the stepdaughter of *Edward, the Black Prince. He continued to rely largely on English councillors, while English troops manned Breton garrisons. His financial debts and other obligations ensured that he pursued policies largely acceptable to Edward III. But renewal of the Anglo-French war in 1369 posed an awkward dilemma. Charles V demanded acknowledgement of his sovereignty and became increasingly angry at Montfort's prevarications, while his Breton subjects, many in royal employment, likewise grew restive. When in reciprocation for a continuing alliance with Edward III Montfort received various grants, including the return of the earldom of Richmond (1372), discontent turned to revolt.

By April 1373 Montfort's position was untenable and he fled to England as Brittany was overrun by a powerful French force. His part in a *chevauchée* with John of Gaunt, marching from Calais to Bordeaux later that summer, increased French animus and eventually led to his trial for treason in the Paris *parlement* in December 1378 when Charles V decreed confiscation of his duchy. In the interim Montfort and his English allies had tried to recover it by force (1375, 1377, 1378) and diplomacy; in 1376 and again in 1377 he visited Flanders to seek support. But most of his six-year exile was spent on his English estates or at court, where he was present for state occasions like the funeral of Edward III, the coronation of Richard II, parliament and Garter ceremonies, being the first foreign prince to be promoted knight of the Garter in 1374.

The duchy regained: diplomacy and politics In 1378 Montfort released Brest, one of his few remaining castles in Brittany, to the English for the duration of the war with France, and received Castle Rising in recompense. His return to Brittany in August 1379 resulted, however, not from military success but from a change of heart by his Breton subjects, fearful that Charles V's efforts to incorporate Brittany more closely into the royal demesne would jeopardize the province's traditional privileges and limit their own freedom of action. A league of nobles and townsmen thus invited Montfort to reassume rule; the Breton constable of France, Bertrand du Guesclin, sympathetic to his compatriots' aspirations, failed to oppose his landing. Subsequently, through the mediation of the count of Flanders and Louis, duke of Anjou, after the death of Charles V in September 1380 peace was reached with France in the second treaty of Guérande in April 1381.

Montfort now distanced himself from England, giving full rein to his considerable diplomatic skills in which brinkmanship and duplicity are very evident. He agreed to oppose his former allies Richard II and Charles II of Navarre in September 1381, and fought alongside Charles VI against Bishop Despenser's army in Flanders in 1383, earning remission from financial penalties imposed in 1381. The English occupation of Brest and difficulties in drawing revenues from his English estates (now normally in the hands of crown nominees) were constant sources of acrimonious debate for almost two decades. Duchess Joan only returned to Brittany in 1382 after some vigorous exchanges. Her death in November 1384 removed an important link with the English court. Prudence dictated that Montfort should ally with other powerful French princes like the dukes of Berri and Burgundy and the king of Navarre and that his policies should not unduly antagonize his sovereign, but his own interests were always uppermost. Despite moments of crisis—his impetuous capture of Olivier de Clisson, constable of France, in 1387, and suspected implication in an attempted assassination of the constable in 1392—most disputes with his domestic enemies (often owing their origins to the civil war) were generally resolved to Montfort's advantage.

Montfort's hold on Brittany after 1381 was further reinforced by institutional developments and increasing wealth; many new taxes were devised, minting rights exploited, and trade encouraged. By skilful use of visual symbolism, especially associated with an ambitious building programme, literary propaganda, expansion of court culture (he had a passion for music and gardening), and well-directed patronage (for example, by appointment to his chivalric order, the Ermine), he encouraged loyalty to his dynasty, the future of which was finally secured by marriage to *Joan of Navarre in September 1386 and the birth of a long-desired heir in 1389. Although the latter was contracted under protest to marry a French royal princess in 1392, Montfort continued to press for the return of his English lands. An improvement in the Anglo-French diplomatic situation facilitated an alliance with John of Gaunt, duke of Lancaster, in 1395, which complemented a proposed marriage of a daughter to a son of the earl of Derby; Montfort attended the wedding of Richard II and Isabella of France in 1396. Brest was returned to him in 1397 and in 1398 he paid a last nostalgic visit to England, when he took formal possession once again of Richmond, attended the Garter ceremony at Windsor, and then accompanied Richard II to Bristol and the midlands before returning home.

Death and English legacy Montfort died, active almost to the last, on 1 November 1399 at Nantes, where in 1409 an alabaster tomb, exported from England (but unfortunately destroyed during the French Revolution), was erected in the cathedral by his widow, since 1402 queen of England. The couple, who held each other in high mutual affection, had eight children. Seven survived to adulthood: John (V), duke of Brittany (d. 1442); Arthur de Richemont, duke of Brittany, constable of France (d. 1458); Gilles (d. 1412); Richard, count of Étampes (d. 1439); Marie, countess of Alençon; Blanche, countess of Armagnac; and Marguerite, vicomtesse de Rohan. Among mementoes of John de Montfort's presence in England are 'King John's cup', owned by the mayor and corporation of King's Lynn (in fact a probable gift of the duke, holder of nearby Castle Rising) and Montfort's arms in a window erected by Sir William Etchingham in the rebuilt parish church of Etchingham, a reminder that Montfort also held the rape of Hastings, which with his other lands returned on his death to the crown. His descendants continued throughout the fifteenth century to style themselves earls of Richmond, but the territorial and personal links that had existed between the honour and the rulers of Brittany since the conquest were extinguished in 1399.

MICHAEL JONES

Sources GEC, *Peerage* · M. Jones, ed., *Recueil des actes de Jean IV, duc de Bretagne*, 3 vols. (Paris, 1980–2001) · M. Jones, ed., *Recueil des actes de Charles de Blois et de Jeanne de Penthièvre, duc et duchesse de Bretagne, 1341–1364* (Rennes, 1996) · M. Jones, *Ducal Brittany, 1364–1399* (1970) · M. Jones, 'The Breton civil war', *Froissart: historian*, ed. J. J. N. Palmer (1981), 64–81, 169–72 · M. Jones, *The creation of Brittany: a late medieval state* (1988) · J. Kerhervé, *L'État Breton aux 14e et 15e siècles: les ducs, l'argent et les hommes*, 2 vols. (Paris, 1987) · P. H. Morice, *Mémoires pour servir de preuves à l'histoire ecclésiastique et civile de Bretagne*, 1 (Paris, 1742), 80

Montfort, Peter de (c.1205–1265), magnate, was the son of Thurstin de Montfort (d. 1216) and his wife, a daughter of William (I) de *Cantilupe, a steward of King John. A leading supporter of Simon de Montfort, earl of Leicester (but no relation), Montfort was technically not a baron, for he held little directly from the king. He was, however, a substantial magnate. His chief seat was at Beaudesert, a low hill above Henley in Arden in Warwickshire, where extensive earthworks of the family castle still remain. Another important base was at Preston in Rutland.

In 1166 Montfort's great-grandfather, another Thurstin

de Montfort, had held ten fees from the earl of Warwick, which made him the second greatest of his tenants. The connection with the earls of Warwick, however, played no discernible part in Peter's career, partly because the earldom was held from 1242 until 1263, in right of his wife, by a Poitevin favourite of the king, John de Plessis, who established few local roots. Much more important for Montfort was the family of his grandfather William (I) de Cantilupe (d. 1239), whose principal residence was at Aston Cantlow, only 4 miles from Beaudesert. His father died in 1216 and Montfort spent many years as Cantilupe's ward, developing what was to be a lifelong friendship with his son Walter de Cantilupe, bishop of Worcester from 1238 to 1266. The fleurs-de-lis of the Cantilupe coat of arms were incorporated into Montfort's seal.

It was probably ties of neighbourhood that drew both Montfort and Walter de Cantilupe into the circle of Simon de Montfort, for Beaudesert and Aston Cantlow are respectively 9 and 12 miles distant from Kenilworth, after 1244 Earl Simon's great base in England. In 1248 Montfort was in Earl Simon's retinue when the latter went out to Gascony as seneschal and thereafter there are numerous instances of the close connection between the two men. Peter de Montfort attested many of the earl's charters and was probably often in his company; in 1259 he was named as an executor of Simon de Montfort's will. His faithful service was rewarded with a grant of the manor of Ilmington in Warwickshire. Part of that service was doubtless to help Earl Simon build up his following of midlands knights, for Montfort was well connected locally—in 1260–62 six knights of Warwickshire and Leicestershire acted as his pledges (PRO, JUST 1/953, mm. 1d, 7; 954, m. 23d).

From 1254 onwards, while Montfort remained close to Earl Simon, his career developed independently. He was employed by Henry III on diplomatic missions, was given an important command in the Welsh marches, and by 1257 was on the royal council. He was also closely connected with Edward, the king's son, whom he had accompanied to Spain for his marriage to Eleanor of Castile in 1254. Fear of being ousted from Edward's entourage by the king's Poitevin half-brothers perhaps gave him a personal interest in the political upheaval of 1258, which began with the half-brothers' expulsion from England. In that upheaval Peter de Montfort played a leading part. He was one of the seven magnates whose confederation in April 1258 began the revolution; he was one of the baronial twelve who were to draw up the plans of reform; and he was one of the council of fifteen set up by the provisions of Oxford to govern England in the king's name. In all these capacities Earl Simon was a colleague. However, unlike the earl (who withdrew to France), Peter de Montfort accepted the king's recovery of power in 1261, and in the following year served the king and Edward as custodian of Abergavenny, which he tried in vain to protect from the attacks of Llywelyn ap Gruffudd. None the less, when Earl Simon returned to England in April 1263 and raised once more the standard of the provisions of Oxford, Peter de Montfort joined him. This time he was to remain with him to the end. When the civil war commenced in March 1264, he was in command of the Montfortians in Northampton and was captured when the town fell to the king on 5 April. Released after Earl Simon's great victory at Lewes (14 May), Peter de Montfort was one of the council of nine imposed on the king (June 1264) and thenceforth played a major part in the direction of central government. In September he was one of those appointed to negotiate with the king of France and the papal legate in the abortive hope of finding some political settlement. His rewards during this period of power included a grant from the king of the manor of Garthorpe in Leicestershire. Montfort accompanied Earl Simon throughout his final campaign and died with him at the battle of Evesham on 4 August 1265. His eldest son, from his marriage with Alice, daughter of Henry *Audley, was wounded in the battle but survived to recover eventually the bulk of his father's properties. The direct male line of the family died out in 1367.

The support Peter de Montfort gave Earl Simon was of the first importance. While a close personal friend and follower, he also enjoyed his own power base in the midlands and an independent career in the service of the king and his son Edward. He possessed considerable abilities as a soldier, diplomat, and councillor. It is highly significant that Earl Simon retained the loyalty of such a man to the last. D. A. CARPENTER, rev.

Sources Chancery records · Ann. mon. · R. F. Treharne and I. J. Sanders, eds., Documents of the baronial movement of reform and rebellion, 1258–1267 (1973) · private information (1993) · H. W. Ridgeway, 'The Lord Edward and the Provisions of Oxford (1258): a study in faction', Thirteenth century England: proceedings of the Newcastle upon Tyne conference [Newcastle upon Tyne 1985], ed. P. R. Coss and S. D. Lloyd, 1 (1986), 89–99

Montfort, Simon de, eighth earl of Leicester (c.1208–1265), magnate and political reformer, was the third son of Simon de Montfort (c.1170–1218), lord of Montfort l'Amaury in the Île-de-France, and of Alice (d. 1221), daughter of Bouchard de Montmorency.

Family and youth Despite the general obscurity of his early years Montfort was almost certainly brought up in southern France, where his father waged war against the Albigensian heretics from 1209 until his death. He first appears assenting to a charter made by his mother in 1218. After his father had died, he seems to have returned with her to the family's northern estates, though he may have returned to the south for his first grounding in arms during the renewed Albigensian war of 1226–9.

Two factors in Montfort's early life played an important part in determining his future. First, Simon senior had inherited a claim to the earldom of Leicester through his mother, Amicia, sister and coheir of Robert de Breteuil, earl of Leicester, who had died childless in 1204. Three years later the Leicester lands were divided between Simon and Amicia's sister Margaret, wife of Saer de Quincy, earl of Winchester. But Anglo-French hostilities meant that the new earl of Leicester never took possession of his inheritance. The claim subsisted none the less, to be transmitted after Simon's death to his eldest son,

Simon de Montfort, eighth earl of Leicester (c.1208–1265), seal, 1258

Amaury. By 1230 Amaury had transferred some or all of his rights in the earldom to his younger brother Simon junior, and it was this transferred claim that brought Simon onto the stage of English politics. Second, Simon senior had been a man of intense and aggressive piety: the disciple of the reforming Parisian evangelist Foulques de Neuilly, a participant in the fourth crusade, and the close friend of St Dominic, as well as the leader of militant orthodoxy against the heretics of the south. His wife, Alice, was a zealot of a similar sort. The religious fervour of his upbringing, the product of both circumstance and parental influence, marked out the course of Simon junior's future career just as surely as his family claim to the earldom of Leicester.

Relations with Henry III, 1230–1248, and marriage Simon de Montfort first went to England in 1230 to pursue his claim to his inheritance. In this he was remarkably successful. The value placed by Henry III on his service and connections, particularly in northern France, and the willingness of Ranulf (III), earl of Chester, to hand over the Leicester lands, which had been in his custody since 1215, both help to explain the king's acceptance of his homage in August 1231. Montfort now held his family's portion of the Leicester estate, though not yet the earldom that should have gone with it. From this point until 1239 he rose at Henry's court, first gradually and then with increasing momentum. His close association with Ranulf of Chester until Ranulf's death in 1232 aligned him with the earl's opposition to Hubert de Burgh, Henry's unpopular justiciar. This allegiance also led him towards the party of Peter des Roches, bishop of Winchester, which ruled the court and country after Hubert de Burgh's disgrace in 1232; but he was not so close to des Roches as to be imperilled when the bishop himself fell from power in 1234. The dissolution of these factional rivalries cleared the way for Simon's own entrée to the heart of the court. He attended meetings of the great council from 1234, forwarded Henry's diplomacy in Wales and Scotland, and acted as steward—an office traditionally attached to the earldom of Leicester—at the king's marriage to Eleanor of Provence in 1236. In that year Henry was already speaking of him as earl, though there had as yet been no formal conferment of the title. His closeness to Henry, and to a regime whose combination of financial improvidence and fiscal oppressiveness was proving increasingly unpopular, made him enemies, whose hostility increased after the culminating move in his upward progress: his marriage in January 1238 to *Eleanor, the 23-year-old sister of the king, and widow of William (II) Marshal, earl of Pembroke (d. 1231).

Montfort's marriage to Eleanor, rushed through by Henry without any attempt to consult the magnates on what was a matter of national business, outraged those conventions of baronial consent to royal policy that had been hardening since Magna Carta. It was equally offensive to the church, since Eleanor had taken a vow of chastity in the early days of her widowhood. The marriage provoked a short-lived baronial revolt, led by Richard, earl of Cornwall, the king's brother; yet events were to prove that Montfort was less vulnerable to the opposition of his fellow magnates than to the withdrawal of royal favour. At the root of his first great quarrel with Henry lay the question of money. Possessing only half of the original earldom of Leicester, worth about £500 p.a., Montfort was not especially wealthy. His buying-out of his brother's claims to the earldom, not fully achieved until Amaury ceded his rights in England in April 1239, had been expensive, and his impending crusade, after he had taken the cross probably in 1237, added to his financial difficulties. The result was a heavy burden of debt. In 1239 Montfort found himself owing 2000 marks to Thomas of Savoy, the queen's uncle, and in order to extricate himself from this imbroglio he presumed on his relationship with Henry by pledging the king's name for the debt's repayment. When this became known, in August 1239, Henry reacted with explosive anger, stirring the pot by accusing Montfort, almost certainly unjustly, of having seduced Eleanor before their marriage. Montfort and his pregnant wife were forced to flee abroad.

Despite its unfortunate sequel Montfort's marriage to Eleanor contributed powerfully to his establishment in England and in English political life. First, it added greatly to his wealth. Eleanor's position as the widow of William Marshal had left her with a dower income of some £930 p.a. in cash and land. This was far more than Montfort's income from his Leicester inheritance, and the disposition of the dower lands through southern England, with concentrations in Wiltshire and Berkshire, extended his influence beyond the Leicestershire and Warwickshire core of his ancestral holdings. Second, the marriage provided him with a family. Henry de *Montfort, the couple's first son, was born in November 1238, his name marking the bonds of affection between Montfort, Eleanor, and the king; and three other sons, Simon de *Montfort, Amaury de *Montfort, and Guy de *Montfort, followed c.1245. Their only daughter, *Eleanor de Montfort, was born

c.1258. New lands and a growing family provided one means by which Montfort put down roots and became assimilated, however imperfectly, into the English governing class.

Yet they also added to the tensions already evident in Montfort's relations with Henry, and again the problems were financial. In Eleanor's widowhood her brother Henry had taken over responsibility from the Marshal heirs for the payment of an annual fee of £400 in respect of Eleanor's dower lands in Ireland and Wales: a sum which the couple claimed, from 1244 onwards, was entirely inadequate compensation for the widow's customary third. Henry had similarly failed to settle any marriage portion on Eleanor at the time of her marriage to Montfort, thus making no provision for the endowment of their family. These deficiencies left Montfort precariously placed, for on Eleanor's death her dower would revert to the Marshal heirs, leaving Montfort with inadequate means to maintain his position or that of his sons. In 1244–5 Henry made arrangements which went some way towards meeting these grievances. But they were never fully met, and in the years up to 1258 the question of Eleanor's dower and marriage portion, more than any political or constitutional matter, proved a constant source of disharmony between Montfort, his wife, and his brother-in-law.

On crusade, 1240–1241 Montfort was away on crusade from the summer of 1240 until the autumn of 1241, when he returned to France. His contingent had been preceded by a larger French force, led by his elder brother Amaury, and by an English army under Richard of Cornwall; but the achievement of these forces in the Holy Land was small. In another way, however, the crusade bore witness to Montfort's prestige, for during its course the barons of the kingdom of Jerusalem asked the emperor Frederick II to appoint Montfort as their governor: a request which probably testified to his military skills as well as his wider reputation. He came back to another war, that waged in 1242 and 1243 by Henry III against Louis IX for the recovery of Poitou. Montfort was summoned to Henry's aid in June 1242 and the rift between the two men patched up, thanks to Henry's proffers of cash and to his need for Montfort's generalship which underlay them. But despite their military partnership, Henry was humiliated by a narrow escape from the French at Saintes, and no territory was regained. Both men returned to England in 1243, when the king's capricious generosity brought Montfort and his wife lavishly back into favour. Some attempt was made to settle their grievances over Eleanor's dower and marriage portion; Montfort was given custody of the great midlands castle of Kenilworth; and in 1244–5 he became an assiduous attender at court. As far as can be seen, he was strongly royalist in his sympathies at this time, taking no part in the parliamentary opposition to Henry's financial methods and use of patronage which characterized these years. As so often, his position owed much to his value as a negotiator with the French, and in 1247 he was sent to

Louis IX to see if Louis could be induced to surrender Normandy before his departure on crusade. By this time, however, he was once again moving away from the centre of affairs, coming to court less frequently, and receiving Henry's gifts less regularly, though without any dramatic rupture with his brother-in-law.

Religion Montfort's rise in England, his early quest for patrons, and his later pressure on Henry to meet his financial claims, all suggest the talent for aggressive self-advancement which was to emerge as one of the leitmotifs of his career. But he was also a devoutly religious man, whose Christian principles were often at odds with his voracious pursuit of his own interests. Here he was deeply influenced by three of the leading churchmen of the day: Robert Grosseteste, bishop of Lincoln (1235–53), whom he probably first met in 1231, when Grosseteste was archdeacon of Montfort's newly acquired borough of Leicester; Walter de Cantilupe, bishop of Worcester (1236–66), a neighbour in the west midlands and, like Grosseteste, a notably energetic pastor; and Adam Marsh (*d.* 1259), the leading Oxford Franciscan scholar of his generation. All three of these men stood for a new sort of fervent reforming Christianity. Its aim was the salvation of the laity through their attendance to the teachings of an educated clergy and their disciplined observance of the religious practices, such as regular confession and reception of the eucharist, laid down in the Lateran Council of 1215.

Many of the features of Montfort's religious life were shaped by his friends' teaching. Personally very close to each of them, and cherishing Grosseteste 'with heartfelt affection', according to William Rishanger, he particularly shared their respect for conscience and for the process of confession by which conscience was regulated. This was shown most clearly in the doubts which emerged in his mind during the 1240s about the propriety of his marriage to one who had previously taken a vow of chastity. In his private life he seems to have been similarly attentive to Christian moral teaching, practising austerities which may have owed as much to the general example of the Franciscans and of his friend Louis IX as to that of his three spiritual advisers. According to sources written after his death, and which therefore need to be treated judiciously but not necessarily sceptically, he used to spend much of the night in prayer, was frugal in food, drink, and clothing, wore a hair shirt, and after his oath to the provisions of Oxford in 1258 even abstained from relations with his wife. The hair shirt is widely vouched for. A more humane trait, but one that also owed much to his clerical friends, was his interest in education and learning. He was almost certainly literate, and even able to read Latin, so that Marsh could send him to the book of Job for consolation at a particularly difficult time in his life. That two of his sons, Henry and Amaury, were brought up with other noble children in Grosseteste's household, testified to his respect both for his mentor and for his mentor's ideal of a devout and learned laity.

His friends saw Montfort as an exemplar of the type of layman whom they hoped to create: pious, given to prayer, attendant to conscience, and, in Montfort's case, holding a position in worldly affairs which made him a potential force for good. That he was also a crusader was an additional commendation, for all three of his guides had an intense concern for the enterprise of the crusade. But in many ways Montfort must have disappointed their expectations. In politics his own claims and interests often took priority over all else. In his private life he proved to be a harsh and exacting lord, extorting 500 marks from a Leicester burgess in 1239, for example, in a way which earned him a devastating rebuke from Grosseteste. Although he had a more than conventional respect for the religious orders, attested by the confraternity agreement that he made with St Albans in 1257, his few recorded gifts to monastic houses do not suggest that he was a particularly open-handed benefactor; nor did he show the exceptional generosity to the poor that characterized the religious lives of Henry III and Louis IX. In public as in private the contrast between the ideals which he strove for and intermittently attained, and the more consistent quest for his own advantage, was one of the most salient features of his career.

In Gascony, France, and England, 1248–1258 In 1247 Montfort once more took the cross, intending to join the other English crusaders journeying to relieve the Holy Land after the fall of Jerusalem in 1244. His departure was forestalled, however, by Henry's recalling him from semi-retirement in May 1248 to serve as his lieutenant in Gascony for seven years. At this time the English position in Gascony was under threat both from neighbouring powers—the kings of France, Castile, Aragon, and Navarre—and from the province's own disorderly magnates who threatened to ally with them. Although Montfort was able to make peace with these powers, and thus to secure the duchy for the king, the five and a half interrupted years which he spent in Gascony did much to undermine his relations with Henry and to explain his later alignment with the reform movement of 1258.

There were two essential reasons for Montfort's growing differences with Henry. First, he took full advantage of the independent power given to him by his lieutenancy: he ruled Gascony like a commissar, imposing order by military methods—imprisoning enemies, besieging castles, destroying vineyards—which rode roughshod over local rights and aristocratic privileges. Second, the cost of these activities greatly outran the total income of the duchy which Henry had set aside for its restoration to order. As a result Montfort had both to draw on his own private resources and repeatedly to turn to Henry for financial assistance. Henry's reaction was understandable if also perfidious. He was dismayed at the grievances which his lieutenant's methods had provoked and which seemed merely to have exacerbated the internal unrest which Montfort had been sent to quell. By November 1249 Henry was receiving complaints from the embittered Gascons, contrary to the terms of Montfort's commission, and even pardoning and releasing robber barons like Gaston de Béarn whom Montfort had imprisoned. Later, in January 1252, he went further, sending envoys to Gascony to inquire into Montfort's conduct and to summon Gascon representatives to London to state their case.

Their work was the preliminary to Montfort's trial, which took place at Westminster in May and June 1252. Charged essentially with brutal high-handedness in his government of Gascony, he responded both by justifying his conduct and by accusing Henry of contravening the terms of his commission and of leaving him out of pocket. Support for Simon de Montfort from the English magnates prevented Henry from getting his way, and his lieutenant remained unconvicted, though from Montfort's viewpoint the trial itself was a humiliation and an inexpungeable breach of faith. On its conclusion he returned to Gascony, probably to take revenge on his accusers, only to be bought out in November 1252 by a generous financial settlement which terminated his seven-year commission. Assessing Montfort's character correctly, Henry had seen how best to quieten his grievances. But Montfort's subsequent withdrawal from Gascony left the province without effective government, and in the summer of 1253 a new expedition, headed by the king himself, had to be organized hastily to put down a further rebellion led by Gaston de Béarn. In the campaign which followed Henry evidently judged Montfort's military support to be indispensable, and he was once again summoned to the colours. This time he was able to strike a very hard bargain with Henry. In return for his assistance, Henry had to promise him, *inter alia*, an annual fee of £400, to be replaced by land of the equivalent value at a later date. This was a testimony to Montfort's military weight and to the value which Henry set on it, and the king's judgement was vindicated by the successful outcome of the campaign. When Montfort left Gascony for France in January 1254, the province had been pacified and Henry ruled once again in precarious security.

Montfort's time in Gascony soured his whole relationship with Henry III. As he saw it, the king had subverted his position, given comfort to his own and to Henry's enemies, and unjustly dismissed him. Even Henry's enforced generosity, the price of Montfort's appeasement and co-operation, had a sharp edge to it, for Henry's commitment to exchange his money fee for land could not possibly be met. From the time of the king's return to England in December 1254 his financial position deteriorated. Not only did the Gascony expedition leave him heavily in debt, but in March 1254 he had accepted Pope Innocent IV's offer of the throne of Sicily for his second son, Edmund, undertaking in exchange to pay the debts already incurred by the papacy in its Sicilian wars against the Hohenstaufen. Henry's insolvency had a direct effect on his dealings with his brother-in-law. Both the annual fee of £400 due for Eleanor's dower and the money due for the termination of Montfort's Gascon appointment fell into arrears; land could not be found to exchange for the second fee of £400; and the claim of both Montfort and

Eleanor for the full value of the dower remained outstanding. To make matters worse, Montfort's developing interest in the Pyrenean county of Bigorre had, by a complicated process, put Henry still more deeply in his debt. Henry was desperately anxious to pay what he owed—a sign of the nervous apprehension with which he regarded Montfort—but he had no means of doing so.

Although Henry's financial obligations did most to determine his relationship with Montfort, that relationship was also governed by the course of national politics. Here three factors were especially important: the rise of the king's Lusignan half-brothers; the deepening crisis over Sicily; and the attempts to secure a lasting peace with France. Montfort's opinions on the first two of these issues had much in common with those of his fellow magnates, leading them all towards a united demand for political reform in 1258. By the early 1250s the four Lusignans, William de Valence, Aymer, Guy, and Geoffrey, had become the dominant faction at court, taking the lion's share of Henry's limited patronage and using their connections without scruple to enlarge and defend wide estates in the countryside. It was a special grievance of Montfort that their leader, William, had been granted a fee with the promise of land in exchange. He was, therefore, placed similarly to Montfort; but, unlike Montfort, he had been able for the most part to secure the required land. The Lusignans, too, supported Henry's Sicilian ambitions. These were opposed by almost all the magnates, and not least by Montfort, the settlement of whose outstanding claims was jeopardized by Henry's huge obligations to the papacy. On neither of these matters could Henry afford to ignore Montfort's antagonism. It was not only that his grievances, energies, and abilities constituted a powerful destabilizing force in politics. The king also needed to draw on his diplomatic expertise and knowledge of the French court in the negotiations for a permanent peace with France. These began in 1257 and were seen by Henry as a necessary condition for his intended conquest of Sicily. With Montfort closely involved in the peace process, Henry could not afford his hostility.

Montfort was not yet, however, so alienated from Henry as this definition of their differences might suggest. In 1256 and 1257 he received a number of minor royal grants (some compensation perhaps for Henry's failure to meet his major obligations), and in 1257 he was frequently at court. Although not one of Henry's inner circle, he remained more royalist than outsider, with an interest in some of Henry's aims: for example, he may have hoped that a French peace would promote the reclamation of his own family lands in France. There is no sign that he contributed to the local and parliamentary opposition to the harsh fiscal regime which resulted from Henry's penury and which bore down on county society through the sheriff's exactions and the judicial eyre. His grievances were private and financial, not constitutional and fiscal. They were nevertheless unappeased and drove him towards a common position with his fellow magnates. Others besides him—men such as John Fitzgeoffrey and Richard de Clare, earl of Gloucester—had their private quarrels with the Lusignans, with whose leader, William, Montfort himself came into violent conflict in May 1257. It was these discontents, in combination with a deeper exasperation at the folly of Henry's policies, that led in April 1258 to a demand for general reform.

Reforming principles, parliaments, and private grievances from 1258

The reform movement of 1258–9 began within the court and was directed against both the Lusignans and Henry's conduct of affairs. But it soon became much more comprehensive, not only in the support that it attracted but also in the remedies that it offered. It drew in the minor baronage, knights, and local freeholders who had been among the chief sufferers from royal misgovernment and Lusignan power, and in the provisions of Oxford, of June 1258, it attempted to place Henry's kingship under organized control through the institution of a baronial council of fifteen. The whole authority of the crown was virtually placed in commission, its operations to be supervised and its local workings investigated.

Montfort was from the start at the centre of these great events. He was among the seven confederate lords who, at the Westminster parliament of April 1258, launched the movement by demanding the expulsion of the Lusignans and the establishment of a committee of twenty-four to reform the realm. At the Oxford parliament, which followed in June, he personally renewed the call for the Lusignans' expulsion, successfully accomplished soon afterwards, and saw some of his chief supporters, including Walter de Cantilupe, placed on the various reforming committees. He took the new oath to the provisions of Oxford, though with a reluctance which suggested some apprehension about the consequences of so solemn and religious an obligation. Finally, in the months which followed the Oxford parliament, he became thoroughly caught up in the practicalities of reform and of the business of governing which was reform's corollary, acting with the council, negotiating with the Scots, and working for Henry's release from his Sicilian obligations. Flanked by John Fitzgeoffrey and the earl of Gloucester, he had a central place in what was still a collective leadership.

It was already evident that the reform movement had become something like a religious enterprise. The majority of the bishops had participated in the oath taking at Oxford, and already promises had been made in the provisions to deal with complaints against baronial as well as royal officials. The initial action of a party had insensibly become a broader campaign, imbued with the ideal of justice for all. Montfort's religious convictions, now brought to bear on politics, led him to share in that ideal and almost certainly to contribute to it. But at the same time he followed his own more private course. The preliminary committee of twenty-four had been commissioned to discuss not only reform but also the king's debts to Montfort and his obligation to turn Montfort's fee into land. The continuing French negotiations gave Montfort a lever to advance these grievances, for Louis IX had demanded Eleanor de Montfort's renunciation of her family claims, as King John's daughter, to the former royal possessions in France, and Eleanor had as yet failed to comply. Meanwhile, in October and November the new council began to clear the backlog of Henry's debts to Montfort. So from the earliest days of the reform movement public ideals and private interests became deeply entwined in Montfort's activities.

France and the treaty of Paris, 1258–1259

The difficulty of deciding whether he gave priority to the one or the other is shown by Montfort's activities in France between November 1258 and February 1259. He had gone there to forward the French peace, but when negotiations foundered he remained behind to promote his own business. In Paris in November he secured a grant of Bigorre in fee from its current lord, probably with the intention of conferring the county on his eldest son, Henry. Six weeks later, still in Paris, he made his will, calling exigently on his executors to clear his debts and to make restitution to the peasant tenants whom he had wronged, in words that suggest a pressing sense of religious anxiety. He had already taken steps to pay one particular debt, that to the nuns of St Antoine's, Paris. His long stay abroad, where his concerns appear to have been wholly personal, left the baronial council 'mutilated', according to Matthew Paris, and certainly seems to have held up the progress of reform: testimony to the value placed on his advice and experience.

When Montfort returned for the parliament of February 1259, however, his idealist's enthusiasm seemed undiminished. Shortly after parliament had disbanded, two sets of reforming proposals were published which made extensive concessions to under-tenants and others with grievances against their lords. When Gloucester, never more than a lukewarm reformer, backed away from these self-denying restraints, Montfort rounded on him with a sharp reminder of their common oath to the provisions. Yet Montfort himself was now to back away from the whole reforming process. From March to December 1259 he was almost continuously in France. The French treaty still hung fire, but from the time of the February parliament it had come to depend explicitly on Eleanor's renouncing her claims to the old Angevin lands. This she now refused to do until the Montforts' grievances over Henry's debts, the promised land grant, and, above all, her own dower claims, had been satisfied.

The conciliation of the Montforts thus became imperative, as they had certainly intended, before any final settlement with France could be made. With great difficulty this was partly accomplished. In May the king's debts were fully paid and land was found to replace Montfort's fee. The dower was a less tractable problem. Arguing from its inadequacy, the Montforts now put in a huge claim for arrears, together with a full settlement in land or a future payment of 2000 marks a year: demands that Henry could not remotely meet. Meanwhile the work of reform continued, though without Montfort's assistance, to culminate in the further concessions to local society published as the provisions of Westminster at the conclusion of the October parliament. Montfort returned to England for that parliament, but only to enlist the help of Edward, Henry's eldest son, in supporting his claim; he did not stay for the publication of the provisions. But, despite Eleanor's continuing refusal to renounce, Henry was now preparing to meet Louis and to make peace. When the final treaty was published, at a Paris meeting between the two kings in December 1259, it contained a compromise proposal by which Louis was to withhold some of the money due to Henry under the treaty's terms until Henry's disputes with the Montforts had been settled. This was enough to induce Eleanor at last to renounce her claims.

The treaty of Paris was a defeat for Montfort. Not only had he made no real progress over the dower question, but the Anglo-French peace meant that Henry no longer needed him as an ambassador. When he returned to England in December 1259 his grievances as well as his principles brought about the revival of a reforming zeal that had been in complete abeyance for some nine months. Taking his stand on the provisions of Oxford, and in defiance of Henry's prohibition, issued from France, he insisted that the Candlemas parliament of February 1260 should meet as the provisions required, despite the king's absence. Successfully countered by the more moderate councillors, who were not prepared to challenge the king, he now struck up a close alliance with Edward, directed chiefly against Henry and the more royalist councillors, especially Gloucester. When Henry came home in April, Montfort's blatant defiance of his directions in the preceding months, together with his earlier obstruction of the French treaty, formed the central charges made against him at a second trial. This took place at Westminster in May and from it Montfort emerged unscathed, thanks partly to the support which he received from Louis IX and partly to the trial's curtailment by a rising in Wales. But he was now politically isolated, dependent for support largely on Edward alone, and bitterly opposed to Gloucester and the court. Only at the October parliament was he restored to a central place in politics: an upturn in his fortunes which owed much to his unexpected reconciliation with Gloucester and probably to a weakening of the reforming programme, now moving in favour of lords rather than tenants, that was the price of Gloucester's friendship. Reform was not abandoned, for the council governed and the great officials were changed during the parliament, in accordance with the provisions. But it had certainly been diluted by its champion's restoration.

The crisis of 1261–1262 In December 1260 Montfort returned to France, partly to pursue Eleanor's claim to her share in the French inheritance of her mother, Isabella of Angoulême. His departure was one among several factors which allowed Henry to move steadily towards the recovery of his power. The baronial council virtually ceased to act; royal patronage was used to suborn some of its leading members; the king appealed to Pope Alexander IV for absolution from his oath to the provisions; and, finally, he launched a long indictment against what he saw as the council's misgovernment of his kingdom. Running in parallel with this programme, and closely connected with it, was Henry's attempt to secure Louis IX's arbitration on his differences with Montfort; for the king clearly believed, perhaps correctly, that satisfying Montfort's personal

grievances might temper the reforming enthusiasm that was the greatest threat to Henry's position.

But such a settlement with Montfort proved unnecessary for Henry's re-establishment. This was accomplished in June 1261, when he received his papal absolution, immediately dismissed the council's men from the great offices of state, and followed this up by dispatching the unpopular general eyre to the counties and ousting the baronial sheriffs. To match what he had already achieved at the centre he thus sought the local power that was all he now needed for unhindered rule. What he had not reckoned on, however, was the reaction to these measures from the gentry of the counties who had been among the chief beneficiaries of reform. The eyres and the sheriffs were rejected in the localities, in a display of defiant opposition to royal government which Montfort moved quickly to exploit. He had returned to England in 1261 and had so far been a passive witness to Henry's recovery. Now he took charge, negotiating for help from the Welsh, Louis IX, and even the papal curia, and summoning knights from the counties to meet at St Albans in September. Montfort's marshalling of the opposition showed his energy, his organizational skills, and his sharp political eye. But in attempting to construct what looked increasingly like a military coalition he had overreached himself. Few of his supporters wanted a civil war, and in the treaty of Kingston, made in November 1261, Henry was able to buy them off with empty promises of reform. Even Montfort's closest friends, such as Walter de Cantilupe, conceded defeat, and Montfort himself crossed to France, in bitterness of spirit against those who had abandoned their oaths.

The events of 1261 had shown that, in the pursuit of reforming ideals which interlocked closely with personal grievances, Montfort could expect more backing from the gentry than from the magnates. But he had little immediate chance to apply the lesson. Despite the unappeased resentments of the counties, Henry was now apparently in full control and able to move on to the offensive against his brother-in-law. Montfort, enjoying Louis's hospitality in France from January 1262, was willing to accept the arbitration of Louis's queen, Marguerite, in his quarrel with Henry; but Henry's own aims were more aggressive. In July 1262 he too crossed to France, intending to present to Louis a full case against Montfort's conduct which would dislodge Montfort from what had repeatedly been proved to be a safe refuge at the French court. The indictment that Henry had drafted reached back to Montfort's earliest days in England and lingered longest over his supposed misgovernment in Gascony. Montfort, in reply, emphasized his services to the crown, the financial losses that they had brought him, and the unanswered claim for Eleanor's dower. Both arbitrations, personal and political, came to nothing, and in October 1262 Montfort suddenly appeared in England to present to parliament a papal bull apparently confirming the provisions. That he did so only when negotiations on his own claims had broken down was an uncomfortable reminder of how the barometer of his public principles moved in response to the pressures of his private interests.

It was not the revival of the reforming programme that brought Montfort back to England, however, but a series of fortuitous events. Henry's return from France in December 1262 coincided with a Welsh rising which threatened him with loss of territory and reputation. His swift reissuing of the provisions of Westminster, in January 1263, showed both his weakness and his need to rebuild support among the shire gentry. On hand were equally disgruntled but more powerful men who were better placed to exploit his difficulties. In 1261–2 some of Edward's leading retainers, mainly marcher barons, had been dismissed by Queen Eleanor in an attempt to reassert royal control over her son's household and finances. Cut off from lordship and patronage, these men now wanted revenge on the queen and the court and restoration to favour. When Edward himself returned from abroad in February 1263 to deal with the Welsh, accompanied by a large foreign retinue, their grievances intensified. It was their leaders, probably Roger Leyburn and Roger Clifford, who now, in April, summoned Simon de Montfort back to England.

The captain of a cause Montfort returned as the public champion of the provisions and of the local interests they protected. That he was also the chosen leader of the ex-Edwardians, men who had little or no interest in reform, was not an immediate disadvantage, for all could unite on the prosecution of Edward's aliens and Henry's courtiers, their common enemies and (it could plausibly be said) the enemies of the provisions. After the dissidents had met at Oxford in May 1263 and demanded the provisions' enforcement from Henry, predictably refused, nationwide attacks began to be launched against the royalists, the queen's friends, and their lands. While they were under way Montfort showed his generalship by moving from the midlands to take control first of Kent, vital for links with France, and then of London, which he entered in mid-July. His progress seemed all the more assured because of his gathering support. He had now secured the backing of some of the leading bishops and Londoners, and had initiated a novel campaign for the expulsion of all aliens: a move designed to exploit the widespread opposition to aliens throughout the country. Here he displayed the political skills of the populist. But at the same time the spread of disorder had damaged his cause, for many besides royalists had suffered from what had become almost formless devastation. That he had personally benefited, through the bestowal of the lands of the exiled royalist John Mansel on his second son, Simon, threw some doubt on his own motives.

Superficially, however, it seemed that Montfort's cause had triumphed. Henry once more confirmed the provisions; some of the great officials were changed; and conciliar rule resumed. Montfort sought to confer a degree of legitimacy on the baronial government which he now headed by emphasizing his inherited position as steward of England. But in reality he was precariously placed. Those dispossessed during the summer's disorders were clamouring for restitution, while their Montfortian dispossessors saw no reason to disgorge—a conflict of interests and political morality which surfaced in the September parliament. It was partly in the interests of the dispossessed, as well as in the expectation of a favourable verdict, that Henry now appealed again to Louis's arbitration; yet although Louis pronounced in favour of restitution, his friendship with Montfort seems to have led him to endorse the provisions. This was the last success of Montfort's ministry. In July Edward's alien knights had been summarily dismissed, facilitating the return of his former followers to their old allegiance and depriving Montfort of further support from those who had brought him to power. Edward himself was now an active enemy and from mid-October held Windsor Castle for the king. Between Henry and Montfort a state of armed truce prevailed. Its outcome depended on a further arbitration by Louis, to whom both sides appealed in November to settle their differences. Henry meanwhile attempted unsuccessfully to seize Dover Castle and almost captured Montfort at Southwark in December. Both the political and the military advantages now seemed to lie with the king.

Yet Montfort's position was by no means hopeless. He retained the allegiance of most of the bishops, a large section of knightly society, particularly in eastern England, and of his own powerful retinue; nor did he have any reason to think that Louis IX, his supporter in September, would desert him. Here he was wrong. Louis's religious susceptibilities had been wounded by the attacks on churchmen during the disorders and his family affections outraged by the insults offered to his sister-in-law, Henry's queen, by the London mob. Skilfully presented to him, the baronial case turned on Henry's repeated confirmations of Magna Carta and on the status of the provisions as an outgrowth of the charter. Unfortunately for Montfort it was a case he could not argue in person, since he was detained in England by a broken leg, and at Amiens in January 1264 Louis rejected it utterly, quashing the provisions without reservation. He had lost the backing of the French court, on which he had previously been able to depend, and could now rely on force alone for the salvation of the provisions.

Defeat of Henry at Lewes, 1264, and its aftermath Force was immediately deployed, though only ambivalently in the provisions' defence. On hearing of Louis's decision, Montfort dispatched an army under his two sons Henry and Simon to attack Edward's marcher allies, who had seized Montfort's own marcher manors in December. This was the start of a civil war. Henry returned home in February 1264, summoned troops to Oxford, and then marched against the important baronial stronghold of Northampton, the control point for the midlands. On 5 April he won a great victory there, capturing some of the leading Montfortians, including the younger Simon. Simon senior had been at Kenilworth in the early part of the year, but had moved to London in March, in an attempt to draw Henry's army southwards. Henry's victory showed the failure of this tactic, and Montfort now sought to consolidate his position in the south-east, where he remained strong. In mid-April he laid siege to the royal castle at Rochester, but was forced to retreat to London on Henry's approach. It was now Henry's turn to seek control of the channel coast, a move which Montfort had to forestall if he was to hold on to power. On 6 May he left London with a small army and on 14 May he decisively defeated Henry at Lewes, below the Sussex downs. Most of the royalists who escaped fled to France, but Henry, Edward, and Richard of Cornwall were all captured.

Lewes seemed to have delivered the country into Montfort's hands. The author of the 'Song of Lewes' probably reflected the views of many when he saw the victory as a divine vindication of all that Montfort stood for. The provisions had been confirmed in the aftermath of the battle, and with the leading members of the royal family effectively his prisoners and the offices of state at his command, he had the means to control the kingdom. Yet his position was far less secure than the scale of his victory might suggest. By the post-battle agreement known as the mise of Lewes, he had committed himself both to an arbitration on the provisions and to a second arbitration, to be initiated by Louis IX and to lead to a final settlement with Henry. In appealing once more to France, with the uncertainties that entailed, he sought to legitimize rule which essentially rested on *force majeure*. Still more immediate were the military dangers which faced him. Some castles remained in enemy hands, Edward's friends, the marchers, remained at large, and Louis, far from co-operating in the planned arbitration, supported the invasion force which Queen Eleanor was gathering in France. In this emergency Montfort turned to parliament and to the local forces which had always sustained him. The famous assembly of June 1264 established a narrow council of nine, headed by a triumvirate (Montfort himself, the bishop of Chichester, and Gilbert de Clare, the new earl of Gloucester), to rule the country; while the knights who had been summoned to parliament were seemingly allowed to nominate the sheriffs for their counties. As baronial enthusiasm for reform declined, so Montfort nurtured its local supporters.

Danger of invasion, 1264–1265   From July to November 1264 England stood in real danger of invasion. That the danger eventually subsided owed much to Montfort's leadership in holding together a coalition of baronial, episcopal, and knightly allies, whose opinions differed on what ought to be done, and to the inability of Queen Eleanor indefinitely to fund a mercenary army. Montfort's assets lay both in the possession of the royal family and in the nationalist fervour which he emotively exploited against the threat from abroad. Against these resources were deployed not only an army poised for attack but also the papal legate, Guy Foulquois, friend of Louis IX, who, from France, threatened Montfort's party with the excommunication and interdict which would have destroyed their already weakened claims to be standing for religion and righteousness. During these months cross-channel negotiations with the legate, conducted mainly by the English bishops, were almost continuous; but since Louis and the

legate wanted nothing less than the abrogation of the provisions and the restoration of the king to full power, compromise was hardly possible. Montfort drew strength from an increasingly close partnership with the bishops, whose unease at defying the pope was overridden by their concern for justice and for the country's defence. By December, when the legate had retired and the opposing army disbanded, this broad alliance had been vindicated, and, with it, Montfort's commanding qualities.

Yet, as on the morrow of Lewes, Montfort was less well placed than he appeared to be. The marchers were still unchecked, although he had fought two campaigns against them in July and November and had apparently brought them to terms at Worcester in December. Once the country had been saved, moreover, his own leadership, accepted unquestioningly during the emergency, began to generate its own discontents. They sprang largely from the accumulation of land and power which had, since Lewes, steadily passed to him and his family. His leading position had given full play to his characteristic avarice, seen most notably in the takeover of Richard of Cornwall's lands for his sons. The earlier claims for Eleanor's dower, though not forgotten, were superseded by the scale of what he now acquired. Yet he could still claim, with justice, to be defending the reforms of 1258–9. The provisions of Westminster had been defended all through the negotiations with the legate and were confirmed in December 1264; the new council of June 1264 shared in the country's government; and the knights (and burgesses) were summoned to the parliament of January–March 1265 and their grievances redressed. At the same time, however, his own powers were greatly enlarged. A scheme for the release of Edward from captivity, confirmed in parliament, was used to transfer a large part of Edward's appanage to Montfort's permanent control, and the one major obstacle to these dubious proceedings, Robert de Ferrers, earl of Derby, was seized and imprisoned. Criticism came to focus on Montfort's sons Henry and Simon, the lawless and indulged beneficiaries of their father's rule. Their conduct was instrumental in losing Montfort the support of the earl of Gloucester, his one remaining marcher ally.

Death at Evesham, 1265   Gloucester's desertion in March marked a crucial step towards Montfort's downfall. Leaving young Simon to protect the south-east, he advanced westwards in April, taking with him Henry, Edward, and a substantial army. He had to settle with Gloucester and the marchers or risk the establishment of a permanently disaffected western frontier. But this he was unable to do. After inconclusive negotiations at Gloucester in early May, he moved to Hereford. There his own incaution allowed Edward to escape. Immediately Edward assumed the headship of his old following and became the military leader of a marcher alliance. Montfort summoned help from the younger Simon, but he moved westwards too slowly to help his father. In June Gloucester fell to the royalists, leaving Montfort trapped west of the Severn. After an abortive attempt to cross to Bristol his forces began to move towards Kenilworth, hoping to link up with those of the young Simon. But at Evesham on 4 August 1265 they found themselves cut off by the River Avon and by Edward's advancing troops. In the ensuing battle Montfort, his eldest son, Henry, and his leading retainers were killed. In the aftermath his widow, Eleanor, fled to France, where she was eventually joined by her remaining sons. This was the end of the Montfort family as an effective force in English politics.

Cult and reputation In the period after his death Simon de Montfort's politics and the manner of his dying rapidly gave him the reputation of a saint and martyr. It was fostered by the Franciscans who had always been among his supporters. The cult was most active at Evesham, at the abbey where he was first buried and on the battlefield, and within months of the battle miracles were reported from both locations. In the dictum of Kenilworth, published in October 1266, the king and the new legate, Cardinal Ottobuono, forbade all reference to Montfort as a saint and all talk of his 'vain and fatuous miracles'. But although the cult peaked in 1265–6, it continued probably until at least the late 1270s and, in a much attenuated form, until the Reformation. It was notable for the numbers who resorted to the Montfortian sites (some two hundred miracle stories are recorded in a collection compiled at Evesham), for the social range of the visitors (village constables, a tailor, a carpenter, knights, abbots, priors, an earl, and a countess, to name but a few), and for their often distant origins (in East Anglia, Kent, and Lancashire, as well as the west midlands). Even as late as 1323, and in Yorkshire, Edward II could be entertained by women 'singing of Simon de Montfort'.

Montfort's popular reputation cannot quite be endorsed by the judgement of history. He was a man of commanding abilities, high political intelligence, verbal dexterity, and exceptional skills as a general. His range of experience—as crusader, soldier, military governor, the counsellor of kings, and the friend of scholars and saints—was unrivalled among his contemporaries. In geographical terms it stretched from Oxford to Paris, from southern France to the Holy Land, from the Welsh hills to the Palace of Westminster. His cosmopolitan outlook and interests, together with his origins and continuing friendships in France, made him always something of an outsider in English politics. His religious fervour cannot be doubted, nor can his oath-driven dedication to the reforming principles of 1258–9, which was partly an outgrowth of his religion. Yet he was at the same time hard and acquisitive, powered by the need to build a position for himself and his family which would eradicate his own early insecurity as a younger son and as a magnate excessively dependent on his wife's lands and income. Those who stood closest to him, especially Grosseteste and Marsh, pointed out the contradictions in his character, but his conversion to their ways was never more than partial. Nor was his work as a reformer entirely disinterested, for it was fuelled by personal grievances against Henry III which the reformed constitution offered the best means of satisfying. Even so, his friends were not entirely wrong to see him as standing for a code of political morality, promising justice to all, which Henry had denied. This tension in his mentality and career between the idealist and the adventurer, present from start to finish, is one which has given his political odyssey its enduring fascination. From at least the seventeenth century, with its echoes of his own time, Montfort has figured prominently in the British historical consciousness. Seen first as a would-be dictator, then as the visionary initiator of parliamentary government, he came to occupy a key position in the nineteenth-century school of constitutional history. Scholars of the twentieth century have exploited unpublished archives to fill out the picture of this complex personality. He remains one of the best-known figures of the British middle ages. In 1992 the new De Montfort University at Leicester was named after him.

J. R. MADDICOTT

Sources accounts various, PRO, E.101 · memoranda rolls, PRO, E.368 · *Chancery records* · R. F. Treharne and I. J. Sanders, eds., *Documents of the baronial movement of reform and rebellion, 1258–1267* (1973) · C. Bémont, *Simon de Montfort, comte de Leicester* (Paris, 1884) · *Paris, Chron.* · [W. Rishanger], *The chronicle of William de Rishanger, of the barons' wars*, ed. J. O. Halliwell, CS, 15 (1840) · *Ann. mon.* · A. O. Anderson and M. O. Anderson, eds., *The chronicle of Melrose* (1936) · J. R. Maddicott, *Simon de Montfort* (1994) · D. A. Carpenter, 'Simon de Montfort: the first leader of a political movement in English history', *History*, new ser., 76 (1991) · R. F. Treharne, *The baronial plan of reform, 1258–1263*, [new edn] (1971) · C. Bémont, *Simon de Montfort, earl of Leicester, 1208–1265*, trans. E. F. Jacob, new edn (1930) [does not incl. sources printed in 1st edn]
Likenesses seal, 1258, BL, Add. ch. 11296 [*see illus.*]

Montfort, Sir Simon de, the younger (1240–1271), soldier, was the second son of Simon de *Montfort, earl of Leicester (c.1208–1265), and his wife, *Eleanor (1215?–1275), daughter of King *John. He was born near Brindisi about April 1240, while his mother awaited her husband's return from the crusade. With his brother Henry de *Montfort he accompanied his father to France in November 1258 and was knighted by Edward, the king's eldest son, in October 1260. During the disorders of 1263 both he and Henry de Montfort took part in the devastation of the Kentish property of Boniface of Savoy, archbishop of Canterbury. When peace had been restored, in August, he received from his father, who now controlled the government, the extensive lands of the exiled royalist John Mansel. In February 1264, after Louis IX's mise of Amiens had been rejected, he and Henry led a force to the marches to attack their father's enemies there; on his return he was sent to Northampton, where he was among the Montfortians captured by the king after the battle of 5 April. Released after his father's victory at Lewes on 14 May, he was given command of some important castles, including Gloucester, Nottingham, and Porchester, and during the winter and spring of 1264–5 he was charged by his father with the siege of Peter of Savoy's castle at Pevensey in Sussex, still in royalist hands.

During the period of his father's supremacy Montfort was thus one of the props of the new regime. He also shared in the malpractices which contributed to its fall. He sought unsuccessfully to abduct Isabella de Forz, the richest woman on the marriage market, and was more successful in ousting the royalist magnate William (VI) de Briouze, by a combination of force and the perversion of judicial procedures, from his Sussex lordship of Bramber. When Montfort's father withdrew to the west in April 1265, in pursuit of the marchers, he was left in charge of south-east England, and was summoned thence to his father's rescue in May. From Dover he moved to London to gather troops and then proceeded westwards, sacking Winchester, and travelling via Oxford and Northampton to Kenilworth which he reached on 31 July. There his forces were surprised and routed by Edward, and he was lucky to escape. On 3 August he set out to join his father with his remaining troops, but was too late to relieve him at Evesham. After the battle he saw his father's head go by on a spear and withdrew, heartbroken, to Kenilworth.

At Kenilworth, Montfort freed Richard of Cornwall, the king's brother and formerly the prisoner of the elder Montfort. After fruitless negotiations with Henry he left Kenilworth in November to join some of the remaining Montfortians in the Isle of Axholme, in Lincolnshire. In December Edward, at the head of an army, forced him to come to terms and to undertake to surrender Kenilworth and to abjure the realm in return for an annual pension. But the rebels at Kenilworth refused to give in, and Montfort was taken to London. On 10 February 1266, fearing treachery, he escaped, first to Winchelsea and then to France. In the autumn he was rumoured to be mustering forces for an invasion of England. In September 1267 Louis IX was negotiating with Henry III for Montfort's return, but Henry was willing to readmit him only on unacceptable conditions, and nothing came of this initiative. By December 1270 he had joined his brother Guy de *Montfort in the service of Charles of Anjou, the French conqueror of southern Italy. There he became notorious, sharing with his brother in the vengeful murder of their cousin Henry of Almain, in the church of San Silvestro at Viterbo on 13 March 1271. He died later that year in a castle near Siena, 'like Cain, cursed by God, a wanderer and a fugitive' (Maddicott, 371).   J. R. MADDICOTT

Sources Chancery records · Ann. mon. · H. R. Luard, ed., Flores historiarum, 3 vols., Rolls Series, 95 (1890), vol. 3, p. 22 · F. M. Powicke, King Henry III and the Lord Edward: the community of the realm in the thirteenth century, 2 vols. (1947) · J. R. Maddicott, Simon de Montfort (1994) · Paris, Chron., 7.44n.

Montgomerie, Alexander (early 1550s–1598), poet and

courtier, was born at Hazlehead Castle, Ayrshire, the son of John Montgomerie (d. 1558), laird of Hazlehead or Hessilheid, and Margaret Fraser, daughter of John Fraser of Knok. His father belonged to a cadet branch of the influential Eglinton family, whose roots lay in south-west Scotland, and through his maternal grandmother Alexander was descended from John Stewart of Derneley, and so was distantly related to James VI. As his parents married in 1548, and as most authorities name him as the second of three sons in a family of five, this makes a birth date in the early 1550s seem likely.

Little is known about Montgomerie's early life. There is no evidence that he went to university or that he married. As befitted a younger son in a noble family, he underwent military training, gaining expertise that would equip him in later life for involvement in a series of plots aimed at strengthening the Catholic cause. His purchase of a Southampton barque, the James Bonaventor, on 20 December 1580 may be the first of these ventures. Certainly the transaction coincided with efforts to restore Mary, queen of Scots, and was conducted by a man already suspected of 'being of Don John's faction for the old Queen's sake' (Stevenson, 273 n. 3).

Montgomerie had also made a precocious reputation as a poet prior to James VI's period of personal rule. It is, therefore, not surprising that the young king on assuming power made him master poet, or laureate, of his newly formed Castalian poetic band at the Edinburgh court. In 1585 James set out his programme for a Scottish poetic renaissance. Based on the practice of the French Pléiade, the movement was defined primarily in musical terms, with a heavy emphasis placed on lyricism and the ability to range over a wide variety of stanzaic forms. When illustrating this range in his published work The Essayes of a Prentise in the Divine Arte of Poesie (1585), James uses Montgomerie's lyrics as his major source. Indeed, the very title of the book specifically defines their poetic relationship within the game of courtly culture played out in the nation's capital at this time. Apprentice and master even exchanged poetic nicknames. James was called William Mow, and Montgomerie might be either Rob Stene or 'beloved Sanders'.

Concern over the unreliability of Fortune emerges as a thematic leitmotif in Montgomerie's writing. Given the major misfortunes that befell him, such an obsession is unsurprising. In the later 1580s, as a trained soldier, he was granted a royal licence to travel throughout Europe, and so joined his elder brother among the troops marshalled against Spain by the master of Gray. Later, he would be a captain in Leicester's Scottish regiment— again ostensibly on the protestant side. But fears that his Catholic connections made him unreliable were expressed at this time and borne out by future events.

In June 1586 the Montgomerie 'nere in place and credytt and place to the kynge of Skottland' (Jack, 9), whose ship, full of contraband, was captured off the Brielle, is certainly the poet. When the case was brought before Robert Cecil, the English diplomat described him as a 'taking man'. James, in a letter of March 1588, records that the poet had visited Spain during his absence and had been imprisoned despite acting under the royal 'saufgaird'. That letter, by writ of the privy seal, is a major attempt by the king to prevent further misfortune befalling 'his gude servitour' (Reg. PCS, 1st ser., 4.367).

Prior to his period abroad, Montgomerie had drawn an annual income of 300 merks from the revenues of Glasgow Cathedral. Even then the grant had caused protestant outrage because it involved ratifying James Beaton, a proclaimed Catholic, as archbishop of Glasgow. Montgomerie, however, returned at a time when anti-Catholic feeling was much more intense, and the protestant claimant William Erskine had laid claim to all revenues associated with the archbishopric. As these included the poet's pension, Montgomerie was forced to bring a counter-case himself. A long litigation process followed, with the court finally upholding Erskine's cause in 1593.

The poet charted the case's progress in a series of sonnets in which the 'master' turns against the 'apprentice', ironically using the very form whose wider thematic range had been advocated by James as a sign of the distinctive 'Scottishness' of his courtly renaissance. In these 'Pensioun Sonnets', Montgomerie refers pointedly to the 'povertie, imprisonment and pane' he had suffered abroad, and prophesies a future abroad, 'If I must begge, it sall be far fra hame'. Finally, he accuses his erstwhile friend of treachery:

> Is this the frute, Sir, of your first affectione
> My pensioun perish under your protectione?

His case having failed, Montgomerie fulfilled his threat of going into exile. A series of Latin poems by Thomas Duff reveals that he sought spiritual retreat at the abbey of Würzburg. But he soon returned to his native Ayrshire, where his support for Catholic causes continued. He plotted to provide support for the earl of Tyrone by capturing the strategically important island of Ailsa Craig in the Firth of Clyde. On his involvement being revealed, he was summoned to answer charges of treason. He failed to appear in Edinburgh and was officially outlawed on 14 July 1597.

The events following Montgomerie's death were just as melodramatic as his life. His health had been deteriorating and on 22 August 1598 the presbytery of Edinburgh requested the bailies of the Canongate 'to ansuer for the bureing of umquhill Alexander Montgomerie poet, a papist in their kirk, contrare the actis of the general assemblie' (Durkan, 92). Duff's Latin poems explain that the Catholic nobility and the common people had urged the king to grant Montgomerie the burial in consecrated ground usually denied to an outlaw. That this request was granted, and a royal cortège provided, suggests that the king did feel guilt at the fate of his once 'beloved' Sanders. In a poetic epitaph James even pleads that Montgomerie's poetic skills may be appreciated by posterity:

> Though to his buriall was refused the bell,
> The bell of fame shall aye his praises knell.
> (*Poems of James VI*, 2.108)

It seems that this prophecy is at last being fulfilled. Until Helena Shire's *Song, Dance and Poetry at the Court of Scotland under King James VI* (1969), most critics damned Montgomerie with faint praise as the last and least of the Middle Scots makars. By setting him firmly within the specific performance culture of James's renaissance, Shire allowed him to be judged on his own terms. Later critics have built upon this base, emphasizing his stylistic and thematic range in particular. This virtuosity is most obvious in his shorter lyrics, where praise of the Trinity and stern moral diatribes mingle with romance, political satire, and bawdry. But variety of another kind is offered in his major long work, *The Cherrie and the Slae*. That poem's

central theme is whether human beings will find happiness in high aspiration or easy contentment. Montgomerie does not provide a simple answer. Instead he uses the techniques of personification allegory to show how the same issue, regarded from personal, political, moral, and divine viewpoints, may provide differentiated although ultimately complementary answers. If the test for a professional court poet be to demonstrate verbal skill across a wide gamut of styles and forms, then James's 'maister poete' deserves the recognition his apprentice-monarch wished for him.   R. D. S. JACK

Sources D. J. Parkinson, introduction, in *The poems of Alexander Montgomerie*, ed. D. J. Parkinson, 2 vols., STS, 4th ser., 28–9 (2000) · G. Stevenson, appx, in *Poems of Alexander Montgomerie*, ed. G. Stevenson, STS, 59 (1910) · R. D. S. Jack, *Alexander Montgomerie* (1985) · H. M. Shire, *Song, dance and poetry at the court of Scotland under King James VI*, ed. K. Elliott (1969) · J. Durkan, 'The date of Alexander Montgomerie's death', *Innes Review*, 34 (1983), 91–2 · R. J. Lyall, 'Alexander Montgomerie and the Netherlands, 1586–89', *Glasgow Review*, 1 (1993), 52–66 · M. Dilworth, 'New light on Alexander Montgomerie', *The Bibliotheck*, 4 (1963–6), 230–35 · *DNB* · T. Pont, *Cunninghame topographized*, ed. J. Dobie, Maitland Club (1876) · *The poems of James VI of Scotland*, ed. J. Craigie, 2 vols., STS, 3rd ser., 22, 26 (1955–8) · T. Duff, *Cerasum et sylvestre prunum* (1631) · NA Scot., Edinburgh presbytery records, CH 2/121/2 · *Scots peerage*

Archives Magd. Cam., Maitland Quarto MS · NL Scot., Bannatyne MS · U. Edin., Ker MS · U. Edin., Laing MS · U. Edin., Thomas Wode's partbook

Montgomerie, Alexander. *See* Montgomery, Alexander, sixth earl of Eglinton (1588–1661).

Montgomerie, Alexander, **ninth earl of Eglinton** (*c.*1660–1729), politician, was the eldest son of Alexander, eighth earl of Eglinton (*d.* 1701), landowner, by his first wife, Lady Elizabeth Crichton (*d.* 1673), eldest daughter of William, second earl of Dumfries. From the time of the death of his grandfather Hugh *Montgomery, seventh earl of Eglinton, in 1669, he was boarded with Matthew Fleming, the minister of Culross, Perthshire, who supervised his education at Culross School until 1673. He was then sent to the University of St Andrews, where he remained until August 1676.

A few months after leaving the university Montgomerie married Lady Margaret, eldest daughter of Lord Cochrane, son of the first earl of Dundonald. The marriage produced three sons, all of whom died young, and six daughters, including Catherine, who married James, fifth earl of Galloway; Euphemia, who married George Lockhart of Carnwath; Grace, who married Robert, sixth earl of Carnwath; and Jean, who married Sir Alexander Maxwell of Monreith. Following his marriage Montgomerie's father made over to him the encumbered Eglinton estates.

Only after achieving solvency did Montgomerie enter public life, and office remained a financial necessity. After the revolution of 1688 he was appointed a lord of the Treasury and was sworn of the privy council by William III. In 1700 he obtained a letter from the king to sit and vote in the Scottish parliament in place of the lord high treasurer, and in the following year he succeeded to the earldom on his father's death. On Queen Anne's accession in 1702 he was again chosen a privy councillor, and in 1711 he was named one of the commissioners of the chamberlain. By now his second wife, Lady Anne Gordon (*bap.* 1675, *d.* 1708), daughter of George, first earl of Aberdeen, had died; she was buried on 16 December 1708. Details of the marriage are unknown, though it did produce one daughter, Mary, who married Sir David Cuningham of Milncraig, Ayrshire. In June 1709 he married his third wife, Susanna (1689/90–1780), daughter of Sir Archibald Kennedy of Culzean and Elizabeth, daughter of David Leslie, first Lord Newark [*see* Montgomerie, Susanna, countess of Eglinton]. They had three sons and seven daughters.

In 1710, and again in 1713, Eglinton was elected one of the Scottish representative peers. His income at that time was estimated at £4000, a figure which, however modest, exceeded that of all other elected Scottish peers save the duke of Hamilton. According to George Lockhart, Eglinton supported his son-in-law's bill to resume the bishops' revenues to the episcopal clergy in Scotland and reassured Anne that the Presbyterians would not actively oppose the measure. This is corroborated by Wodrow, who asserts that Eglinton, either in the House of Lords or in the privy council, proposed 'that as we are one in civil we should be one in church matters' (Wodrow, 1.318). Wodrow also states that his speech on patronage and toleration was 'so very good' that it was supposed 'it was done by somebody for him' (ibid., 320). In June 1712 Eglinton proposed a bill for prolonging the time for taking the oath of abjuration until 1 November.

Lockhart affirms that Eglinton at last professed himself a Jacobite, and promised him three thousand guineas 'to help the Pretender in his restoration' (*Lockhart Papers*, 2.9). Wodrow relates that shortly before the rising in 1715 Eglinton 'was at a meeting of the Jacobites where the rebellion, as to the manner of carrying out, was concerted, and heard all their proposals' (Wodrow, 2.359). Nevertheless, during the crisis he raised and disciplined the Ayrshire fencibles, with whom on 22 August 1715 he joined the earls of Kilmarnock and Glasgow and Lord Semple at Irvine in support of the government. Prudence may have tempered his alleged Jacobitism in view of the leadership of the rising (the earl of Mar was first and foremost a politician not a soldier) and the overwhelming support in Ayrshire for the protestant succession.

The purchase of land to settle on his many children caused the earl to leave debts of £18,000 upon his sudden death at Eglinton on 18 February 1729. Between 900 and 1000 beggars are stated to have attended his funeral on 20 March, £50 being divided among them. Eglinton was survived by his wife, who died on 18 March 1780, and, among their children, Alexander *Montgomerie, tenth earl of Eglinton, and Archibald *Montgomerie, the eleventh earl.   RONALD M. SUNTER

Sources G. Lockhart, *The Lockhart papers: containing memoirs and commentaries upon the affairs of Scotland from 1702 to 1715*, 2 vols. (1817) · GEC, *Peerage* · *Letters of George Lockhart of Carnwath, 1698–1732*, ed. D. Szechi, Scottish History Society, 5th ser., 2 (1989) · R. Wodrow, *Analecta, or, Materials for a history of remarkable providences, mostly relating to Scotch ministers and Christians*, ed. [M. Leishman], 4 vols., Maitland Club, 60 (1842–3) · G. S. Holmes,

British politics in the age of Anne (1967) · D. Hayton, 'Traces of party politics in early eighteenth-century Scottish elections', *The Scots and parliament*, ed. C. Jones (1996) · W. Fraser, *Memorials of the Montgomeries, earls of Eglinton*, 2 vols. (1859) · J. Paterson, *History of the county of Ayr: with a genealogical account of the families of Ayrshire*, 2 vols. (1847–52) · W. Robertson, *Ayrshire, its history and historic families*, 2 vols. (1908) · J. T. Ward, 'Ayrshire landed estates in the nineteenth century', *Ayrshire Archaeological and Natural History Collections*, 8 (1969), 93–145 · P. W. J. Riley, *The English ministers and Scotland, 1707–1727* (1964) · *DNB*

Archives Hunt. L., letters to earl of Loudoun · NA Scot., letters to duke of Montrose

Wealth at death in debt: Ward, 'Ayrshire landed estates'

Montgomerie, Alexander, tenth earl of Eglinton (1723–1769), politician and agricultural improver, was born on 10 February 1723, the son of Alexander *Montgomerie, ninth earl of Eglinton (*c.*1660–1729), politician and landowner, and his third wife, Susanna (1689/90–1780) [*see* Montgomerie, Susanna, countess of Eglinton], daughter of Sir Archibald Kennedy of Culzean, Ayrshire. Alexander succeeded his father as tenth earl on 18 February 1729. After attending Irvine grammar school, he and his younger brother Archibald *Montgomerie (later the eleventh earl) left in May 1737 to continue their education at Haddington. In October 1738 Alexander left for England to continue his studies at Winchester College, which he finally left in October 1740. By August 1742 he was in Paris, where his social activities and increasing interest in antique artefacts aroused concerns over his expenditure.

Eglinton was the scion of one of the most powerful landed families in west central Scotland. Some indication of their political and social clout in the counties of Ayr and Renfrew can be sensed from the fact that, as compensation for the loss of his private heritable jurisdictions in 1748, Eglinton received £7800, though he had in fact earlier claimed £12,000 from the crown. Indeed, the tenth earl very much reflected the modernizing, 'improving' ethos that underpinned the Heritable Jurisdictions Act. Problems of credit and banking, for instance, attracted his attention. Having published on the subject as early as 1754, he heavily influenced the 1765 parliamentary act that ensured Scottish banks dealing and lending through paper credit could no longer defer specie payments for six months. Above all Eglinton exemplified the tendency for Scotland's often politically reactionary aristocracy not only to countenance but, indeed, actually to implement and promote revolutionary agrarian change. He was responsible for substantial tenurial developments and enclosures on his own lands by the early 1750s, and created Ayrshire's first local agricultural society; his epitaph was to be 'the reviver of agriculture in Ayrshire' (Strawhorn, *History of Irvine*, 71). Clearly, however, not everybody saw his actions as progressive and patriotic. Indeed, it appears that in the aftermath of his untimely death local folklore quickly interpreted the event as evidence of divine judgement.

Like many improvers Eglinton was determined to exercise fully the socio-economic powers that fell to him as feudal superior. In 1751, heartened, no doubt, by the general assembly's increasing willingness to discipline presbyteries that refused to accept ministers presented by feudal patrons, he made full use of his legal rights to nominate the new parish minister of Irvine—creating much local hostility in the process. Unsurprisingly he also sought to involve himself in wider political affairs. However, certain key circumstances undermined what could have been a prestigious and successful career in Scottish politics. His character, for example, was personable and genial in many respects, but he lacked the application and attention to detail required for the fractious and often Byzantine nature of Scottish county politics. Indeed, one contemporary described him as a 'worthless and silly … wretch' (Shaw, 7–8). More seriously, however, Eglinton's political pretensions ran contrary to the other electoral interest that dominated the county of Ayr—namely, John Campbell, fourth earl of Loudoun, a close political associate of the third duke of Argyll. The result was frustration in the election of 1754, when the administration of the duke of Newcastle, anxious to secure Argyll's client MPs, strongly supported Loudoun's candidate. As was so often the case in other Scottish localities, the balance of power was so evenly distributed that it took the emergence of a new political interest at London to alter the *status quo*. Thus, while Eglinton was forced on the defensive in October 1759 as Argyll sought to resurrect the old Scottish administrative post of lord lieutenant and bestow it upon Loudoun, the rising influence of John Stuart, third earl of Bute, already signalled a temporary shift in favour of Eglinton. Having sought Bute's influence as early as 1757, the tenth earl was appointed, first, as a gentleman of the king's bed chamber in 1760 and, second, as a Scottish representative peer in February 1761. These successes were crowned when, on 28 April 1761, in alliance with other local notables such as the earl of Glencairn, Eglinton's brother Archibald won the parliamentary seat for Ayrshire.

The performance of the Eglinton interest through its association with Bute reveals something of the important process whereby Scottish politics, while very much retaining its own distinctive players and local agendas, was also increasingly integrated into a more obvious British framework. None the less, the earl failed to consolidate his position. His lack of attention to individual voters enabled the Loudoun interest to challenge successfully in the election of 1768. On 21 March Eglinton's brother was defeated by forty-five votes to twenty-seven. Precisely how far this bad electoral blood between the Montgomeries and Loudoun Campbells formed a subtext to the strained relationship between the tenth earl and Mungo Campbell, excise officer at Saltcoats, and the man responsible for the earl's shooting is impossible to say. What is known is that when, on 24 October 1769, Eglinton saw Campbell on Ardrossan beach with a musket, he had already warned him against carrying weapons on his land. The earl rode up with some servants and challenged Mungo to hand over his piece, chiding him in the process for suspected poaching. Campbell refused absolutely, and backed away from the earl, who continued to demand the weapon while also calling for his own musket to be

brought to him. As the stand-off continued Campbell stumbled over a rock and discharged his weapon as he fell. The ball struck the earl in the stomach, inflicting what he himself immediately recognized as a fatal wound. Having been taken back by carriage to Eglinton Castle the earl died of his wounds in the early hours of 25 October. Campbell himself was found guilty of murder at the high court of justiciary in Edinburgh on 27 February 1770, but escaped execution by hanging himself in his cell on the night of 1 March. Although he was engaged to Jane Maxwell, daughter of Sir John Maxwell of Pollock, Eglinton died without an heir and the estate passed to his younger brother Archibald.   ANDREW MACKILLOP

Sources BL, Newcastle MSS, Add. MS 33049, fol. 306 • W. Fraser, *Memorials of the Montgomeries, earls of Eglinton*, 2 vols. (1859), vol. 1 • A. Murdoch, 'The people above': politics and administration in mid-eighteenth-century Scotland (1980) • E. Haden-Guest, 'Montgomerie, Archibald', HoP, *Commons, 1754–90*, 3.157–8 • J. S. Shaw, *The management of Scottish society, 1707–1764: power, nobles, lawyers, Edinburgh agents and English influences* (1983) • J. Strawhorn, *Ayrshire: the story of a county* (1975) • J. Strawhorn, *The history of Irvine Royal Burgh and New Town* (1982) • J. Sinclair, *Statistical account of Scotland, 1791–1799*, [new edn], ed. J. Withrington and I. R. Grant, 20 vols. (1977–83), vol. 6 • *Scots Magazine*, 31–2 (1769–70)

Archives NL Scot., legal and financial papers | BL, Newcastle MSS, Add. MS 33049, fol. 306 • NL Scot., letters to James Stuart of Torrance

Montgomerie, Archibald, eleventh earl of Eglinton

Montgomerie, Archibald, **eleventh earl of Eglinton** (1726–1796), army officer and politician, was born on 18 May 1726, the third son of Alexander *Montgomerie, ninth earl of Eglinton (*c*.1660–1729), and his third wife, Susanna (1689/90–1780) [see Montgomerie, Susanna, countess of Eglinton], daughter of Sir Archibald Kennedy, bt, of Culzean, Ayrshire. Having been educated at Scottish grammar schools, Eton College, Winchester College, and Geneva, Montgomerie joined the army in 1743, and rose to major in the 36th foot by 1751. In 1757 he raised a new regiment of highlanders, the 77th foot, 1460 strong, having been commissioned lieutenant-colonel-commandant on 4 January. He commanded the regiment in the capture of Fort Duquesne in 1758, and in 1760 it formed the main part of an expeditionary force he commanded against the insurgent Cherokees. Despite fighting a running battle at Echoe and burning several Cherokee towns, the expedition was inconclusive; next year, under its second in command, Lieutenant-Colonel James Grant, a new expedition won a decisive victory. The regiment was disbanded in 1764, and Montgomerie went onto half pay.

Montgomerie was by then MP for Ayrshire, having been elected in 1761 against the Loudoun interest. He was a silent member who was counted as a supporter of the Bute, Grenville, and Rockingham ministries. In 1764 he was made governor of Dumbarton Castle. Having neglected his constituents he was defeated in the general election of 1768, but succeeded to the title in the following year on the murder of his brother Alexander *Montgomerie, tenth earl. He was elected as a Scottish representative peer in 1774, a result generally taken to show the end of ministerial control of this election process. As a peer he was not inclined to support the government: at the risk to

Archibald Montgomerie, eleventh earl of Eglinton (1726–1796), by Sir Joshua Reynolds, c.1783–4

his military career he supported the Fox–North coalition government only briefly, and in 1789 supported the prince of Wales in the regency dispute. In 1780 he successfully promoted his cousin Hugh *Montgomerie (later twelfth earl of Eglinton) as MP for Ayrshire.

Montgomerie became colonel of the 51st foot in 1767, and gradually ascended by seniority to general in 1793, though he remained inactive. He exchanged his governorship of Dumbarton for that of Edinburgh Castle in 1782, and replaced the colonelcy of the 51st with that of the 2nd dragoon guards in 1795.

Eglinton was a Scot of the type who, according to James Boswell, despised Englishmen in the same way that Dr Johnson criticized the Scots. Hard-drinking, hot-tempered, without intellectual interests, Eglinton was a man of limited ability in all his roles. He married twice: on 30 March 1772, Lady Jane Lindsay (1756–1778), daughter of George, twenty-first earl of Crawford, and second, on 9 August 1783, Frances, daughter of Sir William Twysden, bt, of Royden Hall, Kent; they had two daughters, and were divorced in 1788. Eglinton died on 30 October 1796, and was succeeded as earl by his cousin Hugh.

JOHN D. GRAINGER

Sources DNB · E. Haden-Guest, 'Montgomerie, Archibald', HoP, Commons, 1754–90, 3.157–8 · GEC, Peerage · D. Stewart, Sketches of the character, manners, and present state of the highlanders of Scotland: with details of the military service of the highland regiments, 2 (1822), 14–17 · J. R. Alden, John Stuart and the southern colonial frontier (1944) · E. L. Lee, Indian wars of North Carolina (1988) · M. W. McCahill, 'The Scottish peerage and the House of Lords in the late eighteenth century', SHR, 51 (1972), 172–96 · J. Ferguson, The sixteen peers of Scotland: an account of the elections of the representative peers of Scotland, 1707–1959 (1960) · will, PRO, PROB 11/1289, sig. 258

Archives NA Scot., Eglinton MSS | Yale U., Beinecke L., corresp. with James Boswell

Likenesses J. Reynolds, oils, c.1783–1784, Royal Collection [see illus.] · S. W. Reynolds, mezzotint, pubd 1797 (after C. F. von Breda), BM · J. Scott, mezzotint (after J. Reynolds), BM · W. S. Watson, group portrait, oils (The inauguration of Robert Burns as poet laureate of the Lodge Canongate, Kilwinning, 1787), Scot. NPG

Wealth at death annuity yielding £165; property in Ayrshire, Perthshire, Edinburgh, Middlesex: will, PRO, PROB 11/1289, sig. 258

Montgomerie, Archibald William, thirteenth earl of Eglinton and first earl of Winton (1812–1861), politician and racing patron, was born on 29 September 1812 at Palermo, Sicily, the second surviving son of Major-General Archibald Montgomerie, Lord Montgomerie (1773–1814), and his cousin, Lady Mary Montgomerie (1787–1848). As heirs of, respectively, Hugh *Montgomerie, twelfth earl of Eglinton, and Archibald *Montgomerie, eleventh earl, the Montgomeries' combined rights to the family estates and title ensured that considerable wealth would pass undivided to their heir. Lord Montgomerie died of consumption at Alicante, Spain, in January 1814, and in January 1815, against the wishes of the twelfth earl, his widow married Charles Montolieu Lamb (1785–1860), who became second baronet in 1824 and knight marshal of the royal household the following year. In retaliation the twelfth earl took away guardianship of her two sons and brought them up at Eglinton Castle, his Gothic-revival seat in Ayrshire. There the elder boy, Hugh (b. 1811), died of croup on 13 July 1817, and Archibald became Lord Montgomerie and heir, succeeding as thirteenth earl at his grandfather's death on 14 December 1819.

By his grandfather's will Eglinton's upbringing and management were controlled by five trustees, against whom he and his mother frequently rebelled. He was educated ineffectually by tutors at Eglinton Castle, wretchedly at a private school in Mitcham (1821–5), and riotously at Eton College (1825–8). In 1826, at fourteen, enabled under Scottish law to take partial control of his own affairs, he firmly did so, and in 1828 left Eton to live and travel with his mother and stepfather, spending the next five years mainly in claret drinking, debauchery, and steeplechasing. When he reached his majority, on 29 September 1833, he settled at Eglinton Castle to devote himself to sport. In token of future earnestness, however, he took his seat in the Lords as Baron Ardrossan on 1 May 1834, and became colonel of the Ayrshire militia (1836–52) and lord lieutenant of Ayrshire in 1842. At this time, although he reputedly drank nothing but champagne, he was robust and fit, with a lively eye and fine dark mutton chop whiskers.

Eglinton's wealth and interest in horses coincided happily with a large-scale expansion of horse racing as a popular recreation. He bought well, employed good trainers and jockeys (who had to ride in patriotic tartan), and won many classic races, including the Derby and St Leger. His best horse, The Flying Dutchman, beat Lord Zetland's Voltigeur in a historic match at York in May 1851. Elected to the Jockey Club in 1838, he helped to establish organized steeplechasing in England, and campaigned with

Archibald William Montgomerie, thirteenth earl of Eglinton and first earl of Winton (1812–1861), by George Sanders (after C. Smith)

Lord George Bentinck against betting fraud. Both he and Bentinck, however, heavily backed their own horses, and in 1843 two victims of their reforms, the Russell brothers, brought an action against Eglinton, Bentinck, Charles Greville, and other Jockey Club members under the obscure *Qui tam* statute (9 Anne c.14), which technically limited wagers to minute amounts. Closing ranks, the sporting establishment rushed a bill through parliament in February 1844 which removed all limits.

The Eglinton Tournament of 1839, the outstanding example of early Victorian medievalism in action, secured his fame. Beginning as a private gesture, it so catered to public appetite for pageantry and heroism that it grew into a national event. In June 1838 the whig government had for reasons of economy omitted some traditional ceremonies from Queen Victoria's coronation. In Conservative reproof, Eglinton, enthusiastically urged on by friends and family, announced in August a medieval tournament and banquet at Eglinton Castle. He originally planned only an amusement for his race meeting in the spring of 1839, but the unexpected public response forced postponement for adequate organization and for rehearsal of unskilled knights. The number of these gradually fell from an initial 150 to thirteen, but on 28 August 100,000 spectators gathered, their presence at this medieval spectacle made possible by the prime symbols of Victorian mechanical progress, railways and passenger steamers. Unfortunately, the prevailing weather pattern of western Scotland held: torrential rain fell, and knights, ladies, and spectators fled the field. Eglinton's fortitude

(or obstinacy) redeemed what might have been total fiasco—he hospitably detained his guests until the weather improved, and on 30 August successfully held his tournament, banquet, and ball. The costs were enormous, Eglinton's own expenditure probably approaching £40,000. But, although the tournament was ridiculed by some critics, its enactment of chivalric metaphor is now seen to have inspired Victorian imagination in art and literature, as well as public and private standards of behaviour.

Eglinton himself owed his subsequent political career to the fame of his Tournament. Before that, however, he married, on 17 February 1841, Theresa (d. 1853), widow of Richard Cockerell RN, and one of eight illegitimate children of Thomas, second and last Viscount Newcomen, and Harriet Holland. Lady Eglinton's pathological jealousy made it an unhappy marriage—in his own words, 'the great, the most important, error of my life'—but it produced four children: Archibald William, fourteenth earl (1841–1892), Egidia (later Lady Rendlesham; 1843–1880), Seton Montolieu (1846–1883), and George Arnulph, fifteenth earl (1848–1919). In these years Eglinton became more active in parliament. He was a protectionist, and in 1846 spoke against corn law repeal, joined in attempts at a whig–protectionist coalition, and was assistant whip in the Lords. His reform of the election of Scottish representative peers (1847) was in part nationalistic but was also intended to increase protectionist numbers, as were his frequent banquets and house parties. In 1848 he prevented the pope being able to appoint a priest as his British envoy, and he opposed the abolition of Jewish disabilities. In February 1851 he was part of Lord Derby's unsuccessful attempt to form a protectionist government and in Derby's first administration was lord lieutenant of Ireland (February–December 1852), where his fairness and liberality (reputedly spending £50,000) made him extremely popular. He was elected lord rector of Marischal College, Aberdeen (1851–3), and of the University of Glasgow (1852–4), and for his work in Ireland was made DCL of Oxford University and a knight of the Thistle in June 1853. In December 1853 Lady Eglinton died.

During Derby's second administration Eglinton was again lord lieutenant of Ireland (February 1858 – June 1859). In November 1858 he married Lady Adela Caroline Harriet Capel (1828–1860), only daughter of Arthur, sixth earl of Essex, and his first wife, Caroline; by this very happy marriage he had two daughters, Sybila Amelia Adela (1859–1932) and Hilda Rose (later Baroness Anslow; 1860–1928). In Ireland he continued to work for protectionist interests, although he rejected on principle Disraeli's suggestion to appoint Roman Catholics to patronage positions. He resigned with the tory government in June 1859, and was created earl of Winton, a dormant title to which he had been made heir male general in 1840.

On 31 December 1860 Eglinton's wife died of rheumatic fever, and in July 1861 he spoke for the last time in the Lords. For some months he had complained of intermittent disturbances of vision, and on 1 October, at Mount Melville House, St Andrews, he had a stroke, from which he never regained consciousness. He died at Mount Melville on 4 October 1861 and was buried on 11 October in the family vault at Kilwinning, Ayrshire.

At his death Eglinton was the most popular nobleman in Scotland, while Disraeli described him as 'the most honest man, & the most straightforward, I ever dealt with'. Edward Stanley (future fifteenth earl of Derby), testily examining a list of hereditary peers, found that only eighty-one out of 380 actually did any significant work: one of them was Eglinton. Amiably, probably uncomprehendingly, but consistently, he applied chivalric values to Victorian life.   MARY S. MILLAR

Sources I. Anstruther, *The knight and the umbrella* (1963) · M. Girouard, *The return to Camelot: chivalry and the English gentleman* (1981) · GEC, *Peerage* · *Benjamin Disraeli letters*, ed. J. A. W. Gunn and others (1982–), vols. 3, 5–6 · J. H. Harris [third earl of Malmesbury], *Memoirs of an ex-minister: an autobiography*, 2 vols. (1884), vol. 2 · A., Lord Lamington, *In the days of the dandies*, [new edn] (1906) · R. Longrigg, *The history of horse racing* (1972) · *The Times* (5 Oct 1861) · *The Scotsman* (5 Oct 1861) · *The Scotsman* (11 Oct 1861) · *The Scotsman* (14 Oct 1861) · R. Stewart, *The foundation of the conservative party, 1830–1867* (1978) · *Disraeli, Derby and the conservative party: journals and memoirs of Edward Henry, Lord Stanley, 1849–1869*, ed. J. R. Vincent (1978) · *Morning Post*
Archives NA Scot., corresp. and papers | Ayrshire Archives, Ayr, corresp. with Archibald Hamilton · BL, corresp. with Sir Robert Peel, Add. MSS 40513, 40527 · Bodl. Oxf., corresp. with Benjamin Disraeli · Durham RO, corresp. with Lord Londonderry · Lpool RO, letters to fourteenth earl of Derby · NL Scot., corresp. with Blackwoods; corresp. with Sir Thomas Cochrane; letters to William Mure · NRA, letters to sixth earl of Mayo · NRA, priv. coll., corresp. with John Morgan · NRA, priv. coll., corresp. with S. H. Walpole · U. Glas., Hamilton MSS · W. Sussex RO, letters to fifth duke of Richmond
Likenesses Blackburn, portrait, 1833, Rozelle Mansion, Ayrshire · Ferneley, portrait, 1836, Courtauld Inst. · E. H. Corbould, portrait, c.1839, repro. in Girouard, *Return to Camelot*, 99 · E. Burton, mezzotint, pubd 1850 (after J. G. Gilbert), BM · C. Silvy, carte-de-visite, 1861, NPG · M. Noble, statue, 1865, Ayr · P. MacDowell, statue, 1866, St Stephen's Green, Dublin, Ireland · Cotterill & Sebron, silver figure (on testimonial), priv. coll.; on loan to Irvine District Council · Laporte, oils, Upton House, Warwickshire · H. Raeburn, oils (as a boy), Upton House, Warwickshire · G. Sanders, mezzotint (after C. Smith), NG Ire., NPG [*see illus.*] · S. C. Smith, oils, Dublin Castle, Ireland · J. & C. Watkins, photograph, repro. in *ILN* (19 Oct 1861), 394 · two portraits, repro. in W. Fraser, *Memorials of the Montgomeries* (1859), 1.396–7
Wealth at death £105,933 4*s.* 9*d.*: confirmation, 6 May 1862, NA Scot., SC 6/44/29/615–50 · £3937 0*s.* 3*d.*—effects in England: Scottish probate sealed in London, 6 June 1862, CGPLA Eng. & Wales

Montgomerie, Hugh. See Montgomery, Hugh, first earl of Eglinton (1460?–1545); Montgomery, Hugh, third earl of Eglinton (1531?–1585); Montgomery, Hugh, seventh earl of Eglinton (1613–1669).

Montgomerie, Hugh, twelfth earl of Eglinton (1739–1819), politician and army officer, was born on 5 November 1739 in Tarbolton, Ayrshire, and baptized there on 29 November. He was the son of Alexander Montgomerie (*d.* 1783) of Coilsfield, Ayrshire—the 'Castle of Montgomerie' celebrated by Burns—descended from Colonel James Montgomerie, fourth son of Alexander Montgomerie, sixth earl of Eglinton; his mother was Lillias (*d.* 1783),

daughter of Sir Robert Montgomery of Skelmorlie, eleventh baronet. After studying at Edinburgh University he entered the army in 1756; he served in the American War of Independence in the 78th highlanders and afterwards as captain in the 1st Royals.

On 3 June 1772 Montgomerie married his cousin Eleonora (*c.*1743–1817), daughter of Robert Hamilton of Bourtreehill, Ayrshire. They had three sons and three daughters: Archibald, Lord Montgomerie, a major-general from 1809 employed in military and diplomatic posts in Sicily, died at Alicante in Spain on 4 January 1814; Roger, a lieutenant in the Royal Navy, died in Port Royal, Jamaica, in January 1799; Alexander; Jane (*d.* 1860), married to Edward Archibald Hamilton of Blackhouse; Lillias (*d.* 1845), married first to Robert Dundas Macqueen of Braxfield and then to Richard Alexander Oswald of Auchincruive; and Mary, who died young.

In 1780 Montgomerie was elected to parliament as member for Ayrshire. In 1783 he succeeded his mother in the estate of Skelmorlie, and his father in that of Coilsfield. He was re-elected in 1784 and is recorded as supporting Pitt in 1784–5, but he opposed the latter's Regency Bill in 1788. If the testimony of Burns is trusted, Montgomerie's oratorical power was less conspicuous than his courage:

> I ken if that your sword were wanted,
> Ye'd lend your hand;
> But when there's ought to say anent it,
> Ye're at a stand.
> ('The Author's Earnest Cry and Prayer')

He resigned his seat in parliament in 1789 on being appointed inspector of military roads in Scotland.

When war with France broke out in 1778 Montgomerie was appointed major in the Argyll, or western, fencibles, raised jointly by the Argyll and Eglinton families, with Lord Frederick Campbell as colonel. On the outbreak of the French Revolutionary War in 1792, Montgomerie was appointed lieutenant-colonel of the fencibles, but almost immediately he resigned his commission on his appointment as colonel of the revived West Lowland fencible regiment, one of the seven regiments that provided for the internal security of Scotland, which then lacked a militia. Soon afterwards, while retaining his fencible colonelcy, he raised a regiment of the line called the Glasgow regiment, which was disbanded, the soldiers being drafted into other corps, in 1795. This was done over the strong objections of Montgomerie, who complained to Henry Dundas that he had been obliged to 'incur very heavy expence' (Melville Castle MSS, NA Scot., GD 51/1/871) for his recruits. It may have been as a gesture of compensation that Montgomerie was appointed lieutenant-governor of Edinburgh Castle at this time.

In 1796 Montgomerie was again returned as member of parliament for Ayr. On 30 October he succeeded to the earldom of Eglinton on the death of Archibald *Montgomerie, eleventh earl. Part of the estates devolved on the eleventh earl's daughter Lady Mary Montgomerie; but as on 28 March 1803 she married Archibald, Lord Montgomerie, eldest son of the twelfth earl, the whole estates were again joined with the earldom. In 1798 Eglinton was elected a representative peer of Scotland on a vacancy caused by the death of the earl of Erroll, and was re-elected in 1802. On 15 February 1806 he was created a peer of the United Kingdom, as Baron Ardrossan of Ardrossan, Ayrshire. He was also made a knight of the Thistle in 1812 and one of the state councillors to the prince regent. The earl was lord lieutenant of Ayrshire from 1796 until his death.

Soon after his accession to the earldom, Eglinton began to rebuild the castle of Eglinton as one of the finest examples of modern castellated architecture. Completed in 1802, it became the principal residence of the family. It was abandoned in 1925, and little remained after the ruin was destroyed by special forces in training during the Second World War. Besides continuing the agricultural improvements begun by his predecessors, Eglinton commenced work on a great scale for a harbour and new town at Ardrossan, to be connected to Glasgow by the Glasgow, Paisley, and Johnstone Canal. The deepening of the Clyde and the advent of steam navigation proved the downfall of his elaborate scheme, and after more than £100,000 had been spent the work was suspended upon his death. The canal was constructed only from Glasgow to Johnstone, but the harbour of Ardrossan with its new town was ultimately completed by the thirteenth earl at a cost of £200,000; it became a popular resort and transportation centre.

Eglinton died on 14 December 1819 at Eglinton Castle. He left a debt of £269,000, and had been obliged to sell portions of his estates. He spent most of his life in Ayrshire, devoting his efforts to the improvement of the community and its welfare. In the army he was a strict disciplinarian, but though he had a conservative temperament his public spirit and enterprise deserve the highest praise. He had cultivated tastes, being a musician and composer of considerable ability; a *Selection of Songs and Marches* by him was published in Glasgow by John Turnbull about 1838.

RONALD M. SUNTER

Sources *Edinburgh Magazine and Literary Miscellany*, 85 (1820), 91–2 · GEC, *Peerage* · W. Fraser, *Memorials of the Montgomeries, earls of Eglinton*, 2 vols. (1859) · J. Paterson, *History of the county of Ayr: with a genealogical account of the families of Ayrshire*, 2 vols. (1847–52) · W. Robertson, *History of Ayrshire* (1908) · A. Valentine, *The British establishment, 1760–1784: an eighteenth-century biographical dictionary*, 2 vols. (1970) · J. Paterson, *Kay's Edinburgh portraits: a series of anecdotal biographies chiefly of Scotchmen*, ed. J. Maidment, 2 vols. (1885) · D. Johnson, 'Eglinton, 12th earl of [Montgomerie, Hugh]', *New Grove* · D. Baptie, ed., *Musical Scotland, past and present: being a dictionary of Scottish musicians from about 1400 till the present time* (1894) · J. T. Ward, 'Ayrshire landed estates in the nineteenth century', *Ayrshire Archaeological and Natural History Collections*, 8 (1969), 93–145 · NA Scot., Melville Castle MSS, GD 51/1/871 · J. Strawhorn and K. Andrew, *Discovering Ayrshire* (1988) · *DNB* · *Scots peerage*
Archives Mitchell L., Glas., Glasgow City Archives, corresp. with Hugh Crawford · NA Scot., letters to Hugh Hamilton of Pinmore · NA Scot., letters to Melvilles · NL Scot., letters to Lord Melville
Likenesses J. S. Copley, oils, *c*.1780, Scot. NPG; version, County Art Museum, Los Angeles · J. Kay, etching, BM
Wealth at death £269,000 in debt

Montgomerie, John (*bap.* **1680**, *d.* **1731**), politician and colonial governor, was born in Dumfriesshire and baptized on 11 September 1680, the son of the Hon. Francis Montgomerie, politician, of Griffen, and his second wife, Elizabeth Primrose, daughter of Sir Robert Sinclair, first baronet, of Longformacus, Berwick. He was educated at Glasgow in 1694. On 28 September 1704 he married Lady Mary Carmichael, daughter of John, first earl of Hyndford; they had one daughter. He was possibly the John Montgomery who joined Colonel Brudnall's regiment of foot in March 1702 and was taken prisoner at the battle of Almanza (1707). In 1710 he was elected MP for Ayrshire, which he represented for the next seventeen years, and in the same year became master of the mint in Scotland. Four years later he was appointed groom of the bedchamber to George, prince of Wales. His relationship with the prince earned him promotion to the rank of lieutenant-colonel in 1723. When George became king in 1727 he offered his aide a choice of offices in Britain or in the colonies. Montgomerie now gave up his Ayrshire seat in favour of the governorship of New York and New Jersey.

Montgomerie, who replaced William Burnet, arrived in New York on 15 April 1728 and quickly allied with Burnet's opposition, the mercantile, or 'country', faction. Montgomerie was a weak governor and a poor defender of the royal prerogative, as charged by the opposition, the landowners, or 'court', faction, who had supported Montgomerie's predecessors, Robert Hunter and William Burnet.

Montgomerie called for assembly elections and the popular appeal of the merchant faction was evident when landowners lost seats. The new assembly, led by the merchant Stephen DeLancey as speaker, assured government revenue for five years, including the governor's salary, but at the same time reduced the salary of the opposition leader, the chief justice, Lewis Morris senior, from £300 to £250 a year. By setting the salary of a crown official the assembly was intruding on the privileges of the governor and the royal prerogative he represented. Morris was outraged at both the reduction of salary and at Montgomerie's acceptance of the assembly's actions, which set a dangerous precedent for future assemblies.

Morris was further disturbed when Montgomerie sought to placate local interests by refusing to take the oath as chancellor or to erect a chancery court, as was customary, until ordered to do so by the home government. Morris and his allies rightly interpreted Montgomerie's failure to exercise his authority as a weakening of the royal prerogative. The outspoken criticism of Montgomerie by Morris and his son caused the governor to suspend the younger Morris from his council seat. To strengthen mercantile control of the council further, Montgomerie appointed Stephen DeLancey's son James to that body, and also named the young DeLancey as puisne judge on the supreme court.

Montgomerie's governorship of New Jersey was as lacklustre as his tenure in New York. The Board of Trade had instructed Montgomerie to persuade the New Jersey assembly to repeal an act that permitted it to use surplus money for government expenses, including the governor's salary. The unpopular alternative to using this source of money was to raise taxes in New Jersey. Montgomerie ignored the issue. He did not, however, ignore the assembly's attempt to petition the home government for a separate governor. Alarmed by their proposal because it might affect him personally, he refused to permit the assembly to send a petition to the crown until 1730. At the same time he approved an act to continue the use of surplus money for government expenses. In exchange the assembly guaranteed support of government for five years.

Montgomerie's anxiety to bolster his own fortune made him indifferent to the decline of royal authority in the colonies. He was not helped by an administration in Britain that was concerned primarily with fostering trade and often thwarted its own best imperial interests. Proof of this lack of concern came during Montgomerie's term, when the crown disallowed the act passed during Burnet's administration outlawing the Albany–Montreal trade. The royal rejection was achieved at the urging of New York's merchants who were reluctant to lose the immediate profits of that trade, which was enriching the French enemy. The merchants cared little for the imperial consequences.

Montgomerie, who died of a stroke on 1 July 1731 in New York city, represented one of the worst of the colonial appointments that were made during the tenure of Sir Robert Walpole as first lord of the Treasury. All too often placemen were appointed as royal governors not on the basis of ability but because the king or one of his ministers owed that person a favour. Such officials, in America to line their pockets, often made extravagant concessions to local interests that weakened the royal prerogative. The result among colonists was declining respect for the king's governor, which fostered defiance and resistance to royal authority. MARY LOU LUSTIG

Sources colonial office, PRO, CO/S · colonial MSS, New York State Library, Albany, New York · E. B. O'Callaghan and B. Fernow, eds. and trans., *Documents relative to the colonial history of the state of New York*, 15 vols. (1853–87) · E. B. O'Callaghan, ed., *The documentary history of the state of New York*, 4 vols. (1849–51) · C. Z. Lincoln, ed., *Messages from the governors, 1683–1776* (1909) · *The colonial laws of New York from the year 1664 to the revolution*, 5 vols. (1894) · *CSP col.*, vols. 22–38 · W. A. Whitehead and others, eds., *Documents relating to the colonial, revolutionary and post-revolutionary history of the state of New Jersey*, 1–10 (1880–86) · *Minutes of the common council of the city of New York, 1675–1776* (1905) · *The papers of Lewis Morris*, ed. E. R. Sheridan, 2 vols. (1991–3) · W. Smith, *The history of the province of New-York* (1757); repr. M. Kammen, ed., 2 (New York, 1972) · P. A. Stellhorn and M. J. Birkner, eds., *The governors of New Jersey, 1664–1974* (1982) · J. M. Simpson, 'Montgomerie, John', HoP, *Commons, 1715–54*

Montgomerie, Robert (*d.* 1609×11), archbishop of Glasgow, is of unknown origins. Nineteenth-century claims that he belonged to the family of Montgomerie of Hazlehead, Ayrshire, and that he was the brother of the poet Alexander Montgomerie (*d.* 1598), cannot be sustained. Nor can anything certain be said of his education and early career; it seems unlikely that he was the Robert

Montgomerie recorded at St Salvator's College, St Andrews, in 1534, or the man of the same name who was archdeacon of Argyll from 1554 to 1601. The earliest reliable record of him dates from 20 December 1560, when at the first general assembly of the kirk he was listed as one thought able to minister. Soon afterwards he was appointed to the parish of Cupar, where he remained until 1564. By 1567 he was minister of Dunblane, and he translated in 1572 to Stirling. He was a member of a commission which met in John Knox's house in 1572 to arrange for certain articles to be presented to the regent and council; in 1580 he was appointed to warn the bishops of Argyll and the Isles to appear before the general assembly; and in 1581 he was a commissioner for the establishment of presbyteries in Stirling and Linlithgow.

Following the death of James Boyd, archbishop of Glasgow, on 21 June 1581, James VI named Montgomerie as his successor, on the advice of the duke of Lennox. The result was a *cause célèbre* in relations between crown and kirk. Montgomerie had made a deal with Lennox, whereby in return for £1000 Scots per annum he would lease to the duke all the lands of the diocese. Licence to elect was not issued until 1 August, and did not mention a name; when Montgomerie's name was put forward the chapter refused to elect him, whereupon the king provided him, on 3 October. He does not appear to have been consecrated. The general assembly which met that autumn was one of a series bent on the abolition of bishops, and though James forbade it to proceed against Montgomerie on that score, it was still able to attend to charges against him arising from his ministry at Stirling, where his association with Lennox had also caused disquiet. The accusations included drunkenness, lending money at high rates of interest, and the promulgation of eccentric doctrines, as when he broached 'the question tuiching the circumcision of weomen; and, in the end, concluded that they were circumcised in the foreskinne of their forehead' (Mullan, *Scottish Puritanism*, 163–4). In Glasgow itself there were student riots against Montgomerie's appointment (the archbishop was *ex officio* chancellor of the university), and the university principal, Thomas Smeaton, preached on the text 'He that enters not by the door but by the window is a thief and a robber' (Kirk, 133). In March 1582 the presbytery of Stirling suspended Montgomerie from his ministry, a sentence confirmed by the general assembly shortly afterwards, but royal intervention prevented his excommunication for the time being.

On 12 April 1582 the privy council reasserted the crown's right to present to Glasgow after the chapter had failed to present. However, Montgomerie appeared before the general assembly on 24 April and submitted himself, promising to desist from attempting anything further concerning the bishopric. But he soon changed his mind, under pressure from Lennox and the earl of Arran, and proceeded to Glasgow, where his arrival caused serious disturbances. The moderator of the presbytery was ejected from his chair, the university beadle was imprisoned, and Montgomerie entered the cathedral accompanied by soldiers from the royal guard, who pulled

David Wemyss, the city minister, out of the pulpit on the 'day of the communion in the presence of the haill congregation' in order to make way for him (Durkan and Kirk, 336). Once more the students rioted. On 23 May, Montgomerie was denounced in Edinburgh by John Durie as 'an apostate and mayn sworne traytor to God and his churche' (*CSP Scot.*, *1581–3*, 121) and on 10 June he was finally excommunicated by the presbytery of Edinburgh, a sentence upheld by the general assembly at the end of the month. In the meantime he was received in the house of the earl of Gowrie (who was subsequently disciplined by the kirk) and preached at court, delivering sermons described as 'invectives against the ministers' (ibid., 135). Nevertheless, he was obliged to leave Edinburgh. The townspeople lined the streets, armed with sticks, stones, and rotten eggs, but he escaped with the assistance of the provost. An account of his enforced departure greatly amused King James.

Montgomerie still had the support of the duke of Lennox, before whom he preached at Dalkeith, and as long as Lennox retained control of government Montgomerie had hopes of securing his see. On 2 July the king declared null the sentence of excommunication against him, and on 20 July he was confirmed in the emoluments of his diocese. But the Ruthven raid on 22 August, which replaced Lennox with a hard-line protestant regime, made Montgomerie's position untenable. In a proclamation of 12 September the king effectively withdrew from opposition to the assembly, and on 13 November, Montgomerie himself presented a petition to the Edinburgh presbytery, confessing his offences and asking to be restored back into the kirk. He was referred to the general assembly. Following the end of the Ruthven government early in 1584 Montgomerie had hopes of restoration, and on 22 May his excommunication was nullified in parliament. But the prospect of his return was once again resisted in Glasgow, leading to the temporary closure of the university and the imprisonment of some of the masters, and was effectively ended by the fall of the earl of Arran in November 1585. On 7 December King James promised that Montgomerie should be produced for trial before the next general assembly he should appoint, and by 21 December he had been formally deprived, to be replaced by William Erskine.

Montgomerie was reconciled to the kirk only in June 1587, following a request by James to the general assembly for his readmission. The assembly assented on conditions, and in 1588 agreed to Montgomerie's own request that he be admitted pastor over a flock, provided that he should be found to be qualified in life and doctrine; in the same year he was admitted to the parish of Symington, Ayrshire, and in 1589 he was translated to Stewarton. He demitted his charge in 1607 in favour of his son-in-law William Castlelaw, husband of his daughter Katherine. Montgomerie had married Beatrice Jamieson, with whom he also had two sons and a second daughter. On 20 June 1582, following his appointment to Glasgow, his son Robert obtained a grant under the privy seal of a life pension of £200 from the thirds of benefices at Stirling and elsewhere, but this was revoked on 1 November 1583. The elder Robert Montgomerie died between 25 March 1609 and April 1611. The anti-episcopalian historian William Scot, looking back from the 1630s, recalled him as 'a stolid asse and arrogant' (Mullan, *Episcopacy*, 142).

Duncan Shaw

Sources *Fasti Scot.*, new edn, 3.124–5, 7.321 · C. H. Haws, *Scottish parish clergy at the Reformation, 1540–1574*, Scottish RS, new ser., 3 (1972), 56, 69, 80, 155, 224 · D. E. R. Watt, ed., *Fasti ecclesiae Scoticanae medii aevi ad annum 1638*, [2nd edn], Scottish RS, new ser., 1 (1969), 151 · D. Calderwood, *The history of the Kirk of Scotland*, ed. T. Thomson and D. Laing, 8 vols., Wodrow Society, 7 (1842–9), vol. 2, p. 46; vols. 3–4 · J. Spottiswood, *The history of the Church of Scotland*, ed. M. Napier and M. Russell, 2, Bannatyne Club, 93 (1850) · *The autobiography and diary of Mr James Melvill*, ed. R. Pitcairn, Wodrow Society (1842), 468, 639, 569f. · T. Thomson, ed., *Acts and proceedings of the general assemblies of the Kirk of Scotland*, 3 pts, Bannatyne Club, 81 (1839–45) · *Reg. PCS*, 1st ser., vols. 3–4 · *Register of the secret seal of Scotland, 1581–4* · *CSP Scot., 1581–5* · D. Mullan, *Episcopacy in Scotland* (1986) · D. Mullan, *Scottish puritanism* (2000) · J. Kirk, *The Second Book of Discipline* (1980) · A. R. Macdonald, *The Jacobean kirk, 1567–1625* (1998) · J. Durkan and J. Kirk, *The University of Glasgow, 1451–1577* (1977) · *Poems of Alexander Montgomerie*, ed. G. Stevenson, STS, 59 (1910)

Montgomerie, Robert. *See* Montgomery, Robert (d. 1684).

Montgomerie, Robert Archibald James (1855–1908), naval officer, born at Rothesay, Isle of Bute, on 11 September 1855, was the son of James Montgomerie MD, of Edinburgh, and his wife, Mary Campbell of Lochnell. He entered the navy on board the *Britannia* in August 1869 and became sub-lieutenant in September 1875; while serving on the *Immortalité* in the detached squadron, on 6 April 1877 he jumped overboard to save life. It was a dark night, the sea was rough, the ship was before the wind, and the latitude was infested with sharks. Montgomerie therefore, in addition to the Albert medal and the silver medal of the Royal Humane Society, was awarded the Stanhope gold medal for the act of greatest gallantry during the year, and shortly afterwards was appointed to the royal yacht. From her he was promoted lieutenant on 13 September 1878. He was serving in the *Carysfort*, under Captain H. F. Stephenson, during the Egyptian campaign of 1882, and, landed with the naval brigade, was present at the battle of Tell al-Kebir on 13 September.

In January 1885 the naval brigade under Lord Charles Beresford was organized to help attempt the relief of Gordon at Khartoum, and Montgomerie, then a lieutenant of the *Inflexible*, joined it at Gubat and served in the gunboat *Safieh* in some of the operations above Metemmah. From March to July 1885 he was naval transport officer at Dongola, and was specially mentioned in Lord Wolseley's dispatches; from August 1885 to June 1886 he served on the staff of General Sir Frederick Stephenson, and was placed in command of all the armed steamers on the Nile and appointed to superintend the river transport. He was then assigned to the royal yacht, an appointment almost invariably awarded for services which otherwise would go unrequited. From the yacht he was promoted commander on 24 August 1887, and served on the East India station in the

Boadicea, the flagship of Sir E. R. Fremantle. In October 1890 he took part in the Witu expedition, commanding the field battery, which was actively engaged. He was again mentioned in dispatches, and in May 1892 was made a CB.

In September 1891 Montgomerie was appointed to command the training ship *Lion*, and on 1 January 1894 was promoted captain. After commanding the cruiser *Bonaventure* on the China station and the battleship *Prince George* in the channel, he was appointed to the *Charybdis* in November 1901 for the North American station, and was commodore in Newfoundland waters during the fishery season. He served as commodore under Sir Archibald Douglas during the Venezuelan operations of December 1902, and blockaded the coast and bombarded Puerto Cabello. In April 1904 he was appointed a naval aide-de-camp to Edward VII, and in May became inspecting captain of boys' training ships. In 1904 he was created CMG, and on 5 July 1905 he was promoted rear-admiral. He hoisted his flag on 1 January 1907 in command of the destroyers and submarines in commission with nucleus crews, an appointment he held for a year. In August 1907 he was created CVO.

Montgomerie married in 1886 Alethe Marian, the eldest daughter of Spencer Charrington, of Hunsdon House, Hertfordshire; they had one son. Montgomerie was a distinguished athlete, and at one time was heavy-weight boxing champion of the navy. A keen sportsman, he hunted big game in many parts of the world. He died at his home, 22 Embankment Gardens, Chelsea, in London, on 1 September 1908, survived by his wife, and was buried at Hunsdon, Hertfordshire.

L. G. C. LAUGHTON, rev. ROGER MORRISS

Sources *The Times* (3 Sept 1908) · *WWW, 1897–1915* · E. R. Fremantle, *The navy as I have known it, 1849–1899* (1904) · *CGPLA Eng. & Wales* (1909)

Likenesses J. K. Robertson, portrait, 1908; in possession of his widow, 1912

Montgomerie [*née* Kennedy]**, Susanna, countess of Eglinton** (1689/90–1780), literary patron and society hostess, was the daughter of Sir Archibald Kennedy (*c*.1656–1710) of Culzean in Ayrshire and his wife, Elizabeth, daughter of David *Leslie, first Lord Newark, and his wife, Anna. According to family tradition Susanna expected from childhood that she would one day be countess of Eglinton. While she was playing in the gardens at Culzean, a hawk landed on her shoulder. The name of its owner was engraved on its bells: Alexander, ninth earl of Eglinton. Her family took this as a sure sign that she would one day become the earl's wife, unlikely though that seemed. He was certainly an old friend of the Kennedy family, for his estates, like theirs, were in Ayrshire, but he was nearly forty, had been married before Susanna was even born, and was the father of eight children. As time passed, her prospects of becoming Lady Eglinton receded still further, for about 1703, after the death of his first wife, Margaret Cochrane, he married Anne Gordon, eldest daughter of the first earl of Aberdeen.

When Susanna was about sixteen, her father took her to Edinburgh to introduce her to society. She was an immediate sensation. A striking 6 foot beauty, she soon attracted a satisfying number of suitors. One of the most enthusiastic was Sir John Clerk of Penicuik, a handsome and romantic man. Knowing that she was musical, he sent her the gift of a flute. When she tried to play it no sound came, and she discovered inside a scroll of paper with a poem of his own composition, beginning:

> Go, happy pipe and ever mindful be
> To court bewitching Sylvia for me.
> (Graham, 167)

She liked him and was delighted by his proposal, but of course the marriages of aristocratic ladies were not decided by personal attraction. Sir John may have been wealthy, but Susanna's father knew that his handsome daughter could find someone of higher social status than a mere baronet. He consulted his old friend the earl of Eglinton, whose advice was brief but to the point: 'Bide a wee, Sir Archie', he said, with a twinkle in his eye, 'My wife's very sickly' (ibid., 168). To Susanna's chagrin, her father rejected Sir John's proposal, and, sure enough, the countess of Eglinton died soon afterwards, in December 1708. In the following June, Susanna married Alexander *Montgomerie, ninth earl of Eglinton (*c*.1660–1729).

Lord Eglinton's three sons had all died before reaching adult life: he was left with six daughters but was very anxious to have male heirs. Usually a kind and indulgent husband, he was angry and disappointed when his first child with Susanna, born on 4 July 1710, proved to be another daughter, whom they named Elizabeth. She was followed by still more girls, Susanna, Margaret, and Frances. Losing all patience, the earl declared that he would divorce his wife if she could not give him a son. Susanna replied calmly, 'By all means, but first of all, give me back all that I brought you'. He would give her back every penny of her dowry, he blustered. She smiled. 'Na, na, My Lord' she retorted. 'That winna do. Return me my youth, my beauty and my virginity and then dismiss me whenever you please' (Graham, 169). That silenced him, and the following year James, Lord Montgomerie (1718–1724), their first son was born; eventually, they had three sons and four more daughters. Their time was divided between Eglinton Castle in Ayrshire and their town house, on the west side of the Old Stamp Office Close in Edinburgh. Susanna was famous for the magnificence of her entertaining, and she became the patron to a circle of literary friends. The poet Allan Ramsay dedicated *The Gentle Shepherd* to her, praising her 'superior wit and sound judgement' (Fraser, 108), while William Hamilton of Bangour described her as:

> Pure in thy thought, and spotless in thy deed
> In virtues rich, in goodness unconfin'd.
> (ibid., 111)

The earl died suddenly at Eglinton on 18 February 1729, aged about sixty-nine, and Susanna became the guardian of her six-year-old son Alexander *Montgomerie, tenth earl of Eglinton, who inherited his father's titles. She had him carefully educated, locally and then at Winchester College, before sending him to study in Paris. At the same time she busied herself finding husbands for her daughters. Charlotte, her youngest, had died in childhood, but the others were growing up with their mother's graceful good looks. They always attracted attention when they went to dance at the Edinburgh assembly, and people spoke admiringly of 'the Eglinton air' which combined dignity with beauty. The girls also had Susanna's quick wit. 'What would you give to be as pretty as I?' she asked her eldest daughter teasingly one day. 'Not half so much as you would give to be as young as I!' Lady Elizabeth retorted.

Susanna found husbands for six of her seven surviving daughters, but by 1769 Helen, Susanna, Frances, Christian, and Grace had all died, and that year brought an even greater family tragedy. Her son Alexander, a lord of the bedchamber and one of Scotland's representative peers, was deeply interested in agriculture and an enthusiastic improver of his estates. On 24 October 1769 he was shot by a poacher whom he had disturbed on his land near Ardrossan. He was carried back to Eglinton and Susanna was summoned urgently from Auchans House, where she now lived, but he died a few hours later. He had devoted himself to his public duties and never married, and was succeeded by his younger brother, Archibald *Montgomerie, eleventh earl of Eglinton. Mungo Campbell, the former exciseman who fired the fatal shot, was convicted of murder and committed suicide while awaiting execution.

Susanna never really recovered from her son's death, but even in her eighties she retained her handsome appearance and her independent spirit. Lonely with so many of her family gone, she made pets of the rats that lived in the walls at Auchans House, summoning them for scraps after a meal by rapping on the panelling, then sending them away again with another signal. When friends shuddered at her strange pets, she would say defiantly that the rats were better than many of her human guests, for at least they knew when the time had come to leave. One visitor whose departure she did regret was Samuel Johnson. He came to see her with James Boswell in 1773, and they took to one another right away. She told him playfully that, as she had married a year before he was born, she could have been his mother. 'My dear son, farewell!' she cried, embracing him when he went. He later told his friend Mrs Thrale 'I was sorry to leave her'.

Susanna died at Auchans House on 18 March 1780, at the age of ninety. Johnson commented that the countess of Eglinton 'for many years gave the laws of elegance to Scotland' (Graham, 177). She also typified those wealthy women of character who, while lacking an academic education, were figures of influence in the intellectual circles of eighteenth-century Edinburgh, by virtue of their intelligence, their humour, and indeed their eccentricity.

ROSALIND K. MARSHALL

Sources W. Fraser, *Memorials of the Montgomeries, earls of Eglinton*, 2 vols. (1859) · R. Chambers, *Traditions of Edinburgh*, new edn (1847) · H. Graham, *A group of Scottish women* (1908) · *Scots peerage*
Archives NA Scot., Eglinton muniments
Likenesses W. Aikman, portrait, oils, Scot. NPG · G. Hamilton, oils · G. Hamilton, oils, Scot. NPG · G. Hamilton, oils · attrib. M. Verelst, oils (in widow's garments), priv. coll. · oils, priv. coll. · oils (after W. Aikman), priv. coll.

Montgomerie, Thomas George (1830–1878), army officer and geographer, fourth son of Colonel W. E. Montgomerie of the Ayrshire yeomanry and of Annick Lodge, Ayrshire, was born on 23 April 1830. He was educated at Addiscombe College for the East India Company's army, and passed out first of his term, winning the Pollock medal as the most distinguished cadet. He was gazetted a second lieutenant in the Bengal Engineers on 9 June 1849. After training at Chatham, he went to India in 1851 and, having served for a year at Roorkee with the headquarters of the Corps of Bengal Sappers and Miners, was posted to the great trigonometrical survey. Among his earlier duties on the survey he assisted in the measurement of the bases of verification on the plain of Chach (near Attock on the Indus) in 1853, and at Karachi in 1854–5. He was promoted first lieutenant on 1 August 1854.

On the conclusion of the Karachi measurement Montgomerie was given the charge of the trigo-topographical survey of the whole dominions of the maharajas of Janin and Kashmir, including the Tibetan regions of Ladakh and Balti, an area of about 70,000 square miles of rugged and little known country. Many of the stations of observation exceeded 15,000 feet in height, while some were at close to 20,000. Besides the triangulation of the particular country in hand, peaks were fixed rising out of distant and inaccessible regions, such as those to the west of the Indus, towards Upper Swaton, in the ranges beyond Gilgit, which were either unknown or known only in inaccurate generalities. Further difficulties arose from the constant need to train fresh hands and from the work's being carried on in the territory of a quasi-independent prince. The tact and ability which Montgomerie exercised in maintaining amicable relations with the court, and in preserving discipline among his own large staff (which continued work throughout the mutiny), earned just praise from the government. A permanent result of his survey work was the naming K1, K2, and so on, of peaks in the Karakoram.

Montgomerie was promoted captain on 27 August 1858. A degree sheet of the survey was sent to England in August 1859 by Lord Canning, who wrote to Sir Roderick Murchison from Calcutta to praise both the map and its author. The survey was completed, without a single casualty or serious failure, in 1863–4, and Montgomerie, whose health had broken down, went to Europe on medical certificate. In 1864 he married Jane Farrington; they had three children. In May 1865 he received the founder's medal of the Royal Geographical Society.

Montgomerie returned to India early in 1867, and in May was appointed to take charge of the Himalayan survey in Kumaon and Garhwal. Long before the completion of the Kashmir survey he had considered how to achieve accurate reconnaissance beyond the Indian frontier. It was not possible to extend the survey itself, or any work of European officers, without the risk of political complications, but there was no reason why Indian surveyors should not pass into Tibet and neighbouring regions to conduct secret surveys and reconnaissance missions. His scheme

Thomas George Montgomerie (1830–1878), by unknown photographer

Lhasa. He was disguised as a Buddhist holy man: his prayer beads numbered only 100, instead of the normal 108, and were in fact used to record paces; inside his prayer wheel notes and calculations took the place of the prayer scroll; inside his pilgrim's staff was a thermometer; and hidden about his person and in his baggage were other surveying instruments. He reached Lhasa one year after setting out and spent three months there, keeping himself by teaching accounts, while he established the position and altitude of the capital, and gathered general intelligence about the city. He even attended an audience with the Dalai Lama, secretly surveying his palace. After witnessing the public beheading of a Chinese who had entered Lhasa without permission, and having been forced to reveal his true identity to two Muslim traders, Nain Singh thought it prudent to leave in April 1866 with the same caravan with which he had arrived. Continuing to survey on his route home, he reached India eighteen months after having set out. He had surveyed some 1200 miles and his findings forced a complete revision of the map of Tibet since they proved D'Anville's plan to be unreliable.

In 1867 Nain and Mani Singh and a third pandit, Kalian, set off on a trip to the Tibetan goldfields. They passed safely into Tibet, but were forced to leave Mani with a suspicious headman as a surety against their return. Kalian went west up the Indus River until bandits forced him to turn back when he was quite near its source. Nain Singh went east, spending four days in the productive goldfields of Thok Jalung, surveying as he went. The two men returned to the camp where Mani was being held and they all returned safely to India. Their 800 mile survey allowed Montgomerie to extend the map of Kashmir into Tibet.

Montgomerie and his superior, Colonel James Walker, reported the findings of the pandits in the *Journal* and *Proceedings* of the Royal Geographical Society between 1868 and 1877, a somewhat surprising decision given the need for secrecy, but the missions continued. In 1877 Nain Singh was awarded the Royal Geographical Society's patron's medal and, in his absence, was warmly commended for his contribution to the geography of trans-Himalaya, and particularly for having determined the position of Lhasa in 1865–6. He continued to undertake journeys himself and to recommend others for training as pandits. In the course of his work his health, particularly his eyesight, had suffered and he retired in 1878. He was awarded a small government pension and a grant of land. He died in January 1882.

Kishen Singh [*known as* A. K.] (1849/50–1921) was the youngest of Montgomerie's pandits, who continued to survey after Montgomerie had left the country. After making two successful missions he was dispatched to the north-east corner of Tibet, close to the Chinese and Mongolian borders, in 1878. He spent a year in Lhasa during which time he prepared the most accurate map to that date of the capital before setting off for Mongolia. Robbed of most of his trading goods by bandits, he pressed on, reaching Tunhuang (Dunhuang) in the Gobi Desert. He aroused the suspicions of the Chinese and was imprisoned for seven months before being allowed to

won the approval of the government and in the summer of 1863 the first pandit (as these surveyors came to be called), Abdul Hameed (Mohamed-i-Hameed), a clerk trained as a surveyor, was sent to survey the route to Yarkand. He spent six months at Yarkand, gathering intelligence, but perished in the Karakoram passes on his way home. His notes were recovered and fixed accurately the position and altitude of Yarkand and other towns, as well as giving useful intelligence on Russian activity. This was so valuable that Montgomerie persisted with the scheme, which is now seen as his greatest, and certainly his most spectacular, achievement. He recruited many Indians, long known only by names such as 'the Havildar' and 'the Mullah'. They suffered appalling hardships for little reward, covering thousands of miles recording distances, altitudes, and bearings of previously unmapped regions, with extraordinary devotion to duty and a high degree of accuracy and competence.

The most famous of Montgomerie's emissaries was **Nain Singh** (1829/30–1882), known as the Pandit, or Pandit Number One, or the Chief Pandit. He was the headmaster of a village school at Milam in the Himalayas, and, like his elder cousin **Mani Singh** (*b.* in or before 1829, *d.* after 1868) known as Pandit Number Two, or the Second Pandit, was an experienced mountain traveller, having accompanied a German expedition some years previously. They were taken to Dehra Dun about 1863 and for two years were trained in the basic surveying techniques which India chain men normally learned, but were also taught how to survey secretly using instruments specially contrived at Dehra Dun and, particularly, how to keep a pace of constant length, because on this depended the whole system of distance measurement. In January 1865 they set out for Lhasa. After two abortive attempts to enter Tibet together, the cousins agreed to separate. Mani made one further attempt to enter the country, but then turned back. He attributed his failure to poor health and bad luck, Montgomerie to lack of determination. Nain pressed on to return to Tibet. He surveyed the wild south-eastern corner of Tibet, before heading for northern India, reaching Darjeeling some four and a half years after leaving. He had surveyed about 2800 miles and greatly added to what was known of this area: but he returned to find his son dead and his home broken up and, like many of the pandits, his health ruined. The Royal Geographical Society presented him with a gold watch for his achievements. He was granted a small government pension and lived on this until he died in 1921.

Montgomerie himself was acting superintendent of the great survey in the absence of Colonel Walker in 1870–3. He was promoted major in 1872, but was compelled by ill health to return to England in 1873. He was elected fellow of the Royal Society in 1872, and of several foreign geographical societies. Promoted lieutenant-colonel in 1874, he retired as colonel in 1876. From 1873 he lived at Bath, where he died at his home, 66 Pulteney Street, on 31 January 1878. His papers in the publications of the Royal Geographical Society remain an important record of discovery in trans-Himalaya and the activities of his pandits continue to capture the imagination, being the inspiration for Rudyard Kipling's *Kim*, in which book he was the model for Colonel Creighton, the spymaster and co-ordinator, and for later travel books.

R. H. Vetch, *rev.* Elizabeth Baigent

Sources Sir R. Alcock, *Journal of the Royal Geographical Society*, 48 (1878), cxlv–cxlviii · P. Hopkirk, *Trespassers on the roof of the world* (1982) · R. H. Phillimore, ed., *Historical records of the survey of India*, 4 vols. (1945–58) · R. Alcock, 'Address to the Royal Geographical Society', *Proceedings* [Royal Geographical Society], 21 (1876–7), 454–9 · G. F. Heaney, 'The story of the survey of India', *Geographical Magazine*, 30 (1957–8), 182–91 · P. Hopkirk, *The quest for Kim* (1996)
Likenesses photograph, RGS [*see illus.*]
Wealth at death under £14,000: resworn probate, May 1879, *CGPLA Eng. & Wales* (1878)

Montgomery. For this title name *see* individual entries under Montgomery; *see also* Herbert, Philip, first earl of Montgomery and fourth earl of Pembroke (1584–1650); Clifford, Anne, countess of Pembroke, Dorset, and Montgomery (1590–1676); Herbert, Thomas, eighth earl of Pembroke and fifth earl of Montgomery (1656/7–1733); Herbert, Henry, ninth earl of Pembroke and sixth earl of Montgomery (c.1689–1750); Herbert, Henry, tenth earl of Pembroke and seventh earl of Montgomery (1734–1794); Herbert, Elizabeth, countess of Pembroke and Montgomery (1737–1831); Herbert, George Augustus, eleventh earl of Pembroke and eighth earl of Montgomery (1759–1827); Herbert, George Robert Charles, thirteenth earl of Pembroke and tenth earl of Montgomery (1850–1895).

Montgomery family (*per.* c.1350–c.1485), nobility, was important in the history of Renfrewshire and Ayrshire (in particular the region of Cunningham in north Ayrshire) in the south-west of Scotland. Persons bearing the name Montgomery first appear in Scotland in the twelfth century, in the retinue and lands of the Stewarts in Renfrewshire and Ayrshire, and their rise to prominence in the late fourteenth and fifteenth centuries probably owed much to the Stewart accession to the crown in 1371. They

also had links with the Douglases. **John Montgomery of Eaglesham** (d. 1400/01) is the first member of the family who achieved more than local eminence and from whom its descent can be followed with some certainty. Froissart's account of the battle of Otterburn in 1388 narrates how Montgomery captured Sir Henry Percy (Hotspur) in the course of hand-to-hand fighting. Montgomery is also said to have built the castle of Polnoon at the *caput* of his principal estate of Eaglesham in Renfrewshire, near Glasgow, as or with the proceeds of Percy's ransom. Although these stories gain no support from record evidence, Montgomery did have 'ix hunder punde of Inglish gold' to lend James Lindsay in 1389 (Fraser, *Eglinton*, 2, no. 22). He married Elizabeth, the only daughter and heir of Sir Hugh *Eglinton of Eglinton, prominent servant of both David II and Robert II. Through Elizabeth, Montgomery acquired the neighbouring west Cunningham estates of Eglinton and Ardrossan, together with the offices of bailie of Cunningham and chamberlain of the burgh of Irvine, which Sir Hugh had been granted by Robert Stewart before he became king.

John received a pension for the year to May 1400, but was dead by 4 July 1401, when his son **Sir John Montgomery of Ardrossan** (d. 1427×9) was in possession of his lands. He styled himself lord of Ardrossan and also held the estate of Giffen in Kyle Stewart in Ayrshire. He was bailie not only of Cunningham but also of the barony of Kilbride (once held by the future Robert III) in the sheriffdom of Lanark. His first wife, Agnes, was a daughter of John, lord of the Isles, while his second wife, Margaret, was a Maxwell of Carlaverock, in Dumfries-shire. Sir John was taken captive by the English at the battle of Homildon in 1402, and spent a good deal of the next six years as a prisoner or hostage in England. Subsequently he seems to have managed Cunningham on behalf of the Stewart dukes of Albany, governors of Scotland during the captivity of James I in England between 1406 and 1424. He also engaged in overseas trading activity and apparently owned a ship called *La Wynyne*. In 1424 James I returned to Scotland. He probably resented the services that Montgomery, formerly a retainer of his father and elder brother, the duke of Rothesay, had rendered to the Albany Stewarts. Consequently Sir John was arrested at parliament in March 1425 along with Murdoch Stewart, duke of Albany, and the latter's family. He was quickly released, and subsequently demonstrated his loyalty to the king by serving on the assize that convicted Murdoch and others at Stirling in May 1425, and by being one of the joint leaders of an expedition which at Loch Lomond in June crushed a rebellion led by James Stewart, a surviving son of Duke Murdoch, but the king probably remained suspicious. One of the other leaders of this expedition was Sir John's neighbour in Cunningham, Sir Robert Cunningham of Kilmaurs, who had also served on the Stirling assize. It is likely that the king arranged the indenture that on 6 June 1425 Sir John entered into with Sir Robert for the latter's marriage with Sir John's daughter Anna. This provided for a life grant of the office of bailie of Cunningham to Sir Robert, with reversion to Sir John and his heirs on Sir Robert's death. This document also seems to anticipate what in fact happened a couple of months later (which may also have been a sign of royal displeasure), the sending of Sir John into England in exchange for a hostage returning to Scotland. He seems not to have returned to Scotland, and to have died in England, possibly at Pontefract Castle.

Sir John was succeeded by his eldest son, **Alexander Montgomery**, first Lord Montgomery (d. 1470). Alexander's wife, Margaret, was a daughter of Sir Thomas Boyd of Kilmarnock, head of another important Cunningham family. As part of the king's assertion of control over the territories under the sway of the lordship of the Isles, Alexander was in February 1430 appointed joint keeper of Kintyre and Knapdale in Argyll with his brother-in-law, Sir Robert *Cunningham of Kilmaurs [see under Cunningham family (per. c.1340–1631)]; in this role the pair had custody of castles Sween and Skipness. Sir Robert seems to have been dead by February 1431, and in 1447 Alexander Montgomery rendered an account at the king's exchequer for the last twelve years as bailie of Cunningham, having presumably regained possession of the office under the indenture of 1425. From 1436 on Alexander was a frequent envoy to England, and during the minority of James II, c.1445, he became a lord of parliament as Alexander, Lord Montgomery, probably by 1438 and certainly by 1445. Between 1442 and 1444 he was keeper of Brodick Castle on Arran, and he seems to have held other lands on the island, as well as receiving various further grants of land from the crown.

On 31 January 1449, just before the end of the king's minority, when governance was still in the hands of the Livingstons and the earl of Douglas, Lord Montgomery's son Alexander, master of Montgomery, received a royal grant of the office of bailie of Cunningham, thereby sparking a feud with the Cunninghams of Kilmaurs, which was to continue murderously for over 150 years until settled by royal arbitration in 1609. The initial phase of the feud was ended in the winter of 1454–5, after the death in 1452 of the master of Montgomery (who thus predeceased his father). The king, who was now of age to act for himself, ratified the families' agreement that Alexander Cunningham of Kilmaurs should exercise the office until the lawful age of Alexander Montgomery, the master's son, at which point the matter would be put to 'a declaration of rycht' before the king and his council, who would declare who should 'bruik office fra thinefurth for ever maire' (NA Scot., GD 148/1/12). Alexander was the son of the master's marriage with Catherine, daughter of Gilbert *Kennedy of Dunure and Cassillis [see under Kennedy family] in Carrick, south Ayrshire. In June 1466 the younger Alexander was retoured heir to his father in the bailiary of Cunningham. Significantly, this process did not take place in Ayrshire but before sheriffs *in hac parte* at Linlithgow, suggesting that trouble with the Cunninghams of Kilmaurs was anticipated. Nothing is known of any process of right concerning the office at this time or, indeed, about whether Alexander was ever able to make good his claim to be bailie of Cunningham. He seems to

have been dead before 1470, the year of the death of his grandfather, Lord Montgomery. When Alexander's son Hugh *Montgomery, later first earl of Eglinton, was infeft in the principal family estates of Eglinton, Ardrossan, and Eaglesham in 1484, it was as heir to Lord Montgomery rather than to his father, suggesting that the latter had predeceased the former.

The Montgomerys provide a good example of a long-established landowning family in the south-west of Scotland achieving political significance following the ascent of the Stewarts to the throne, which left something of a power vacuum locally, but also drew the family closer to the central government of the day. The feud with the Cunninghams of Kilmaurs is the main illustration of the local power struggle, but there was an interaction with national politics inasmuch as royal favour (as well as the premature deaths of successive heirs) clearly played a significant part in determining which family held the upper hand in that struggle from time to time.

HECTOR L. MACQUEEN

Sources W. Fraser, *Memorials of the Montgomeries, earls of Eglinton*, 2 vols. (1859), vol. 2 · J. M. Thomson and others, eds., *Registrum magni sigilli regum Scotorum / The register of the great seal of Scotland*, 11 vols. (1882–1914), vols. 1–2 · G. Burnett and others, eds., *The exchequer rolls of Scotland*, 3–9 (1880–86) · Froissart, 'Chronicles', ed. and trans. G. Brereton (1968), 345 · *CDS*, vols. 2–5 · *APS*, 1124–1567 · S. I. Boardman, 'Politics and the feud in late medieval Scotland', PhD diss., U. St Andr., 1989, 171–8 · W. H. Bliss, ed., *Calendar of entries in the papal registers relating to Great Britain and Ireland: petitions to the pope* (1896) · W. Fraser, ed., *The Douglas book*, 4 vols. (1885) · Eglinton muniments, NA Scot., GD 148/1/12

Archives NA Scot., Eglinton muniments, GD 3; GD 148/1/12

Montgomery, Alexander, first Lord Montgomery (d. 1470). See under Montgomery family (per. c.1350–c.1485).

Montgomery [Montgomerie; *formerly* Seton], **Alexander**, sixth earl of Eglinton (1588–1661), army officer, was born at Seton Palace, Seton, Haddingtonshire, the third (but second surviving) son of Robert Seton, first earl of Wintoun, and his wife, Lady Margaret Montgomery, eldest daughter of Hugh Montgomery, third earl of Eglinton. The third earl's grandson, Hugh Montgomery, fifth earl of Eglinton (1584–1612), was Alexander's first cousin.

Early years Alexander first appears in the records as Sir Alexander Seton of Foulstruther. On 2 July 1606 he and his elder brother George *Seton (later third earl of Winton), master of Wintoun, were summoned to appear before the privy council to answer for an attack on James Cunningham, seventh earl of Glencairn, at Perth. The matter was eventually settled on 23 December when the master and Glencairn received an order to subscribe an assurance.

The fifth earl of Eglinton, childless and estranged from his wife, made a resignation and settlement of the earldom and entail on his cousins, the younger sons of Lady Margaret—Alexander, Thomas, and John—to them successively and to their heirs male, with the Seton heir taking the name Montgomery. The settlement was confirmed by a charter under the great seal on 28 November 1611. The newly made heir rapidly acquired a wife: on 22 June 1612

Alexander married Anna Livingstone (d. 1632), eldest daughter of Alexander *Livingstone, first earl of Linlithgow. The couple had five sons and three daughters: Hugh *Montgomery, the future seventh earl of Eglinton, and Robert *Montgomery were the eldest and the youngest sons.

Within five months of his marriage Alexander had succeeded his cousin as earl of Eglinton: Hugh died on 4 September 1612 and Alexander was infeft in the earldom on 30 October. King James, however, challenged the transference of the title as having occurred without his authority. On 28 April 1613 the privy council decided Seton should be cited to appear on 18 May, to 'hear and see him discharged of all assuming unto himself the style, title, and name of earl' (Reg. PCS, 32). This he refused to do, but ultimately on 15 March 1615 he appeared before the council, apologized for having used the title without the king's permission, and resigned it to the king. Consequently James, by the previous arrangement, conferred the earldom of Eglinton on Seton, under the designation Alexander Montgomerie, earl of Eglinton, Lord Montgomerie and Kilwinning. Tradition states that the king finally agreed owing to the plea of his favourite, Robert Carr, earl of Somerset, after Eglinton had told him that, though ignorant of the intricacies of the law, he knew the use of the sword, and had intimated that he would challenge the favourite to a duel unless the opposition to his assumption of the title was withdrawn. From the incident Eglinton, who was a very skilful swordsman, received the nickname 'Graysteel'. Meanwhile in 1614 the new earl had entered into a feud with the archbishop of Glasgow over the patronage and teinds of eight parishes, which lasted until 1621. In assuming control of the earldom, Alexander had to buy the lordship of Kilwinning from Lord Balfour of Burleigh for 8000 merks. In 1617 James visited Eglinton during his Scottish tour. In alliance with the earl of Rothes, Eglinton opposed the introduction of the five articles of Perth in 1617–21, and at the parliament of 1621 he was one of the commissioners who voted against them. Despite his dissent from royal policy, Eglinton was one of the Scots nobles who on 7 May 1625 attended the funeral of King James in Westminster Abbey. He formed one of the procession of the state entry of King Charles into Edinburgh on 15 June 1633; at the coronation on 18 June he carried the spurs; and at the rising of the parliament on 24 June he carried the sword.

A staunch Presbyterian As his opposition to the five articles indicates, despite an upbringing and an early adulthood as a Roman Catholic, Eglinton became one of the first staunch presbyterian nobles, chiefly through the influence of David Dickson (or Dick), minister of Irvine from 1618 to 1640, whom he affirmed was 'the instrument to reclaim him from popery', the traditional faith of the Setons (DNB). At Eglinton Castle the earl kept a serious and elaborate estate. After Dickson was deprived of his ministry at Irvine for publicly protesting against the articles, the earl obtained for him liberty 'to come to Eglinton and to visit then and now his family at Irvine, but not to preach there' (Calderwood, 7.541). On Dickson's arrival Eglinton

arranged that he should preach in the hall of the castle, and afterwards in the close, when the crowd who gathered to hear him became too large for the hall. After two months he was ordered to proceed to prison. Eglinton, however, eventually gained consent for the minister's return to Irvine. Countess Anna shared her husband's presbyterian commitment, and was a patroness of godly ministers. 'I sie clearlie the Lord hes appointed yow to be a wessel of honore. This is the crosse of Christ that is upon your ladyship and it will sanctifie the domestick', Robert Bruce of Kinnaird assured her, while from Temple Patrick, co. Antrim, the presbyterian minister Josias Welsh addressed her as 'elect ladye' (Eglinton MSS, 46).

Eglinton's commitment to presbyterianism remained strong owing to his conversations with Robert Baillie, minister of Kilwinning (1631–42). After the riot at St Giles's Church, Edinburgh, against the introduction of the new prayer book in July 1637, Eglinton joined other nobles in a petition condemning the offending book and took an active part in the plans for the preparation of the national covenant, acting as a witness to the oaths of those subscribing to it in March 1638. He also enlisted William Keith, sixth Earl Marischal, the husband of his niece, Lady Elizabeth Seton, to the cause. As an elder commissioner from the presbytery of Glasgow he attended the general assembly of 1638. There he served on the committee appointed for receiving complaints against the bishops.

Meeting invasion from Ireland and Irish insurgency, 1639–1642 In May 1639 the Tables appointed him and John Kennedy, sixth earl of Cassillis, to defend Galloway and Ayrshire against Lord Wentworth's Irish army. Summoned to join Lord General Alexander Leslie's army at Duns Law, Berwickshire, Eglinton 'came away with the whole country at his back', bringing 1000 foot soldiers, and mounted men including 100 gentry and 200 tenants (Letters and Journals of Robert Baillie, 1.201). In April 1640 the convention of estates deputed him and Archibald Campbell, eighth earl of Argyll, to protect the western parts of Scotland from the landing of Irish forces, with Eglinton taking responsibility for the lands south of the Clyde. On 29 August Argyll ordered him to gather boats and ships at Ayr as part of the defensive measures. After the treaty of London between the king and covenanters, Eglinton was nominated to the Scottish privy council on 17 September 1641, and parliament confirmed his selection on 13 November. He was also one of the committee appointed to inquire into 'the incident', the plot against Argyll, Hamilton, and Lanark. In the aftermath of the Ulster rising by the Irish Roman Catholics in October 1641 the earl sent officers from his former regiment to the province to train the foot regiment of Lord Montgomery of the Ards. On 11 March 1642 the privy council commissioned Eglinton as a colonel of foot from the southern lowlands in the army paid for by the English to suppress the Irish rising. The earl accepted the charge four days later. The regiment of 1116 officers and men in ten companies reached Ulster in May. The earl only accompanied the regiment between 4 August and November. On 28 February 1643 he contributed £6000 to the voluntary loan for the supply of the army. In March

1644 he lost the colonelcy to his lieutenant-colonel, James Montgomery. Meanwhile on 5 July 1642 the privy council named him to the Ayrshire commission for the apprehension of Roman Catholics. On 3 March 1643 it appointed Eglinton one of the conservators of peace, a joint Anglo-Scottish body for the maintenance of the treaty of London.

At arms in England and Scotland, 1643–1650 In autumn 1643 the convention of estates appointed Eglinton colonel of horse for the shires of Ayr, Renfrew, and Lanark in the army being raised to assist the English parliamentarians against the king. The regiment entered England on 19 January 1644 in the earl of Leven's army. By some time in February the earl and his officers had levied all the regiment's eight troops. Eglinton was present at the siege of York in April–June; he entered the city during one assault with 4000 Scots, and helped to repulse bloodily a sally by the defenders. At the battle of Marston Moor on 2 July his regiment served as the reserve of Fairfax's cavalry on the right wing. Following the destruction of the parliamentarian horsemen, Eglinton and his officers kept the regiment in place, anchoring the right of the allied line. Shortly afterwards he returned to Scotland, and attended the parliament that met on 28 July. Some time in 1645 the colonelcy of Eglinton's cavalry regiment passed to his son, Lieutenant-Colonel Robert Montgomery. After the covenanter debacle at Kilsyth on 15 August 1645 he raised levies to oppose the royalists, but they fled on the approach of Alasdair MacColla. Later that year he was one of the committee of estates appointed to consider the petition of General William Baillie for a trial over his conduct at the battle of Kilsyth. On 30 January 1646 he was named one of the committee of estates.

In 1648 Eglinton strongly disapproved of the engagement to march an army into England for the relief of the king. In March he fought a duel over the matter with William Cunningham, eighth earl of Glencairn. In late May at Irvine he joined with other kirk party leaders to discuss a rising against the engagers, but abandoned the idea. When word of the engagers' defeats in the north-west of England reached Ayrshire in late August, his son Robert raised a force of Ayrshire who started the Whiggamore raid by attacking a troop of the earl of Lanark's horse. Eglinton joined with John Campbell, first earl of Loudoun, in raising 6000 men from Kyle, Cunningham, Renfrewshire, and Lanarkshire. The earl took Edinburgh Castle on 5 September, then marched north to Falkirk on 12 September. Following the engager surrender the earl led his men home on 29 September. In January 1649 he attended the kirk-party-dominated parliament as one of only sixteen nobles. On news of the execution of Charles I he supported the proposal for the recall of Charles II as a 'covenanted king'. On 22 July 1650, following the king's arrival in Scotland, the estates appointed Eglinton colonel of his majesty's life guard of horse. Previously, on 28 June, he had been named to the purging committee (to free the army of royalists and openly sinful soldiers). Despite his staunch commitment to the kirk party, the earl does not seem to have paid much attention to the quality of his new recruits. Thus, while the regiment quickly reached full strength, its reputation for indiscipline became renowned. On 29 July the king came from Stirling to the army's camp at Leith on the earl's urging. At Dunfermline on 13 August Eglinton attended the first council held by the king since his arrival in Scotland. After the defeat at Dunbar on 3 September, the earl returned to Ayrshire and levied reinforcements for the army, but he refused to serve under the radical Colonel Gilbert Ker and disbanded most of his men; nevertheless 146 of his cavalry recruits had joined his son (now Major-General) Robert Montgomery's horse by December. In early October, when the king tried to join the royalists in the north of Scotland, Eglinton joined with other nobles in Perth and sent him a polite letter asking him to return. Eglinton joined Argyll and other members of the moderate kirk party in opposing the extreme covenanters of the south-west. He proposed that the western remonstrance be condemned as treasonable and scandalous, and be burnt by the public hangman. In his appointment with Argyll and Loudoun to persuade the remonstrant lairds to agree to a union of forces he met with no success.

Imprisonment in England and final years In spring 1651 Eglinton raised troops for the king but while in Dumbarton with his son Colonel James Montgomery of Coilsfield, Ayrshire, English soldiers captured them in their beds. For betraying them one Archibald Hamilton was hanged at Stirling in April 1651. Eglinton and his son were taken first to Edinburgh Castle, then to Hull, and finally to Berwick. While a prisoner Eglinton was widowed a second time. Some ten years after the death of his first wife on 11 November 1632 he had married Margaret Scott, eldest daughter of Walter *Scott, first Lord Scott of Buccleuch, and widow of James Ross, lord of Buccleuch (the marriage took place between November 1642 and March 1644). The flavour of her rigorous piety is caught by a letter to her husband commending his action in sacking a female servant whose misbehaviour was suspected but not proved in which she expressed the wish that 'God Almighti send a gud tryell of all the wichtis, and send them a hotte fire to burne them with' (*Eglinton MSS*, 57). She died at Hull on 3 October 1651. On 15 October 1652 he received the liberty of the town of Berwick. Subsequently his liberty was increased, for on 18 July 1654 the governor of Berwick was ordered to secure him and his eldest son, Hugh, Viscount Montgomerie, until they produced Robert Montgomery and handed him over to the English, or until they gave security that he would leave the Commonwealth. Although his heir the viscount was excluded from the act of grace and pardon, the earl was included, and his estates returned to him after two years' sequestration. On the viscount's marriage in 1631 Eglinton had settled the estates on him, reserving for himself only a life-rent, but in 1635 the heir promised not to interfere with the estates during his father's lifetime. Not being forfeited Eglinton settled them in 1655 on the viscount's eldest son, Alexander.

In August 1659 General George Monck had Eglinton imprisoned to prevent him from rebelling in favour of the king. However, he was freed by December 1659, when the

Scottish shire commissioners at Berwick selected him as one of five direct negotiators with Monck. He lived to see the restoration of the king, but fortunately not of episcopacy. He died at Eglinton Castle on 7 January 1661 and was buried at the parish kirk in Kilwinning on 14 February.

EDWARD M. FURGOL

Sources *Scots peerage*, vol. 3 · GEC, *Peerage*, new edn · *The letters and journals of Robert Baillie*, ed. D. Laing, 3 vols., Bannatyne Club, 73 (1841–2) · D. Calderwood, *The history of the Kirk of Scotland*, ed. T. Thomson and D. Laing, 8 vols., Wodrow Society, 7 (1842–9) · J. Balfour, *Works*, 4 vols. (1823–5) · *Reg. PCS*, 1st ser. · *Reg. PCS*, 2nd ser. · J. Nicoll, *A diary of public transactions and other occurrences, chiefly in Scotland, from January 1650 to June 1667*, ed. D. Laing, Bannatyne Club, 52 (1836) · *CSP dom.*, 1651–60 · J. Spalding, *Memorialls of the trubles in Scotland and in England, AD 1624 – AD 1645*, ed. J. Stuart, 2 vols., Spalding Club, [21, 23] (1850–51) · J. Gordon, *History of Scots affairs from 1637–1641*, ed. J. Robertson and G. Grub, 3 vols., Spalding Club, 1, 3, 5 (1841) · *The memoirs of Henry Guthry, late bishop*, ed. G. Crawford, 2nd edn (1748) · P. Gordon, *A short abridgement of Britane's distemper*, ed. J. Dunn, Spalding Club, 10 (1844) · D. Stevenson, *Scottish covenanters and Irish confederates* (1981) · *Reports on the manuscripts of the earl of Eglinton*, HMC, 10 (1885), 1–58 · W. Stewart, *A full relation of the late victory obtained … against his Majesties forces … on Marstam-Moor … on the second of July, 1644* (1644) · J. Paterson, *History of the county of Ayr: with a genealogical account of the families of Ayrshire*, 2 vols. (1847–52) · W. M. Metcalfe, *A history of the county of Renfrew from the earliest times*, New Club, 13 (1905) · G. Burnet, *Memoirs of the lives and actions of James and William, dukes of Hamilton and Castle Herald* (1852) · B. Whitelocke, *Memorials of English affairs*, new edn, 4 vols. (1853) · *A list of the severall regiments and chief officers of the Scottish army quartered neer Newcastle* (1644) · *Supplementary parliamentary papers, 1650*, NA Scot., PA Fif · M. Russell, *Life of Oliver Cromwell*, 2 vols. (1829) · C. S. Terry, ed., *The army of the covenant*, 2 vols., Scottish History Society, 2nd ser., 16–17 (1917)
Archives Eglinton Castle, Irvine, Ayrshire | NA Scot., parliamentary papers
Likenesses engraving, repro. in W. Fraser, *Memorials of the Montgomeries: earls of Eglinton*, 2 vols. (1859)

Montgomery, Arnulf de (*c.*1066–1118x22), magnate, was the sixth and youngest son of Roger de *Montgomery, vicomte of the Hiémois in Normandy and earl of Shrewsbury, and Mabel, daughter and heir of Guillaume Talvas of Alençon. His career illustrates the opportunities which were available to younger sons of the Norman aristocracy as the Norman settlement of England was consolidated. In the 1090s during the first Norman penetration of west Wales he was established at Pembroke. Here he built a castle whose chapel of St Nicholas he gave to his family foundation of St Martin-de-Sées in southern Normandy, to which he had also granted a tithe of his property around Argentan in Normandy. He was closely associated with his elder brother Hugh de *Montgomery, earl of Shrewsbury, but on his death in 1098 William II granted Hugh's lands and title to their eldest brother, Robert de *Bellême, with whom the king had worked closely in Normandy. None the less Arnulf received the title of *comes* (earl or count) and lands in Holderness in the late 1090s, and had achieved a considerable position by 1101, when he acted as a surety for the new king, Henry I, in the treaty of Dover, but his career in royal service was cut short when he joined his brother Robert's rebellion against the king in 1102. Arnulf approached the Irish king, Muirchertach Ó Briain, from whom he sought help for the rebels and

whose daughter Lafracoth he married in the same year. When the rebellion failed Arnulf joined his brother in his conflict with the duke of Normandy, Robert Curthose, but then seized the family stronghold of Alménêches and handed it over to the duke.

Arnulf then began a peripatetic career of some twenty years. In 1103 his Irish father-in-law asked for his help against the Norseman Magnus Bareleg, and Arnulf led the first Norman campaigns in Ireland which defeated the Norse raids. He was reconciled with King Henry by Archbishop Anselm, to whom Arnulf was particularly attached, and in the 1110s he attested several acts of Foulques, count of Anjou. In 1114 he was in the south of France where he witnessed an act involving his greatniece, Philippa, duchess of Aquitaine, and it is quite possible that his constant travelling may have been the result of diplomatic initiatives, for he was described as a man of great probity and the highest reputation. His influence at the court of Count Foulques is indicated by the fact that in 1118 the townsfolk of Alençon, the former centre of his family's power in Normandy, asked him to approach the count for help in their rebellion against Stephen, count of Mortain, King Henry's nephew. He died before 1122, leaving no verifiable descendants.

KATHLEEN THOMPSON

Sources Ordericus Vitalis, *Eccl. hist.*, vol. 6 · Évêché de Sées, Livre blanc de Saint-Martin de Sées · V. Chandler, 'The last of the Montgomerys: Roger the Poitevin and Arnulf', *Historical Research*, 62 (1989), 1–14 · E. Curtis, 'Muchertach O'Brien, high king of Ireland, and his Norman son-in-law, Arnulf of Montgomery, c.1100', *Journal of the Royal Society of Antiquaries of Ireland*, 6th ser., 11 (1921), 116–24 · Eadmer, *The life of St Anselm, archbishop of Canterbury*, ed. and trans. R. W. Southern, 2nd edn, OMT (1972), 146–7 · 'Epistolae Anselmi', ed. F. S. Schmitt, *S. Anselmi Cantuariensis archiepiscopi opera omnia*, 3–5 (1938–61), *ep.* 426 · L. Delisle, ed., *Rouleaux des morts du IXe au XVe siècle* (1866), 281–2, 325 · K. Thompson, 'Note de recherche: Arnoul de Montgommery', *Annales de Normandie*, 45 (1995), 49–53

Montgomery, Bernard Law [*known as* Monty], **first Viscount Montgomery of Alamein** (1887–1976), army officer, was born on 17 November 1887 in St Mark's vicarage, Kennington Oval, London, third son and fourth of the nine children of the Revd Henry Hutchinson *Montgomery (1847–1932) and his wife, Maud Farrar (1865–1949).

Early life, 1887–1918 The Montgomerys, staunch protestants, came from Moville, near Londonderry, where the Revd Henry Montgomery, in the same year as Bernard's birth, inherited New Park, the extensive property of his father, Sir Robert Montgomery, former deputy commissioner of the Punjab during the Indian mutiny, and later its lieutenant-governor. Bernard's mother, Maud, was a Farrar: third daughter of the celebrated English educator and cleric, Dean F. W. Farrar (author of *Eric, or, Little by Little*), and his wife, Lucy, from whom Maud inherited looks and fecundity. (The Farrars had ten children, Maud nine.)

Maud Farrar had become engaged to Henry Montgomery, her father's former curate, at fourteen and had married him at age sixteen in 1881. Sexually ignorant and often lonely (her husband looked after a parish of 14,000 souls), she bore five children in the following eight years. In 1889, as an infant turning two, Bernard Montgomery travelled with his parents and four siblings to Tasmania, of which territory his father had been promoted Anglican bishop. Save for one spell in England in 1897, Bernard spent the next twelve years in Tasmania, living at Bishopscourt, the bishop's residence in Hobart, overlooking the Derwent estuary. The house had a private chapel and a private schoolroom in the garden, where the children were taught by tutors shipped from England. They were not beaten by the tutors, however, but by their mother.

Maud had always been proud; in Hobart, in the absence of her husband who was often away for six months of the year doing missionary work, she became a martinet of fearsome obstinacy and wilfulness. Being mother to nine of her own children as well as quasi-mother to the children of numerous relatives parked with the Montgomerys, she became crime-and-punishment obsessed. 'The Rule was all. Sin had to be closely watched … Little by little the rules grew up until every corner of the day was organized and disciplined' (Moorehead, 26). The effect on Bernard was profound. 'Certainly I can say that my own childhood was unhappy' he wrote in his memoirs (p. 17), after her death. His claim that he had begun to know 'fear early in life, much too early' (ibid.) was contested by his youngest brother, Brian (*Field Marshal in the Family*, 111), but it helps explain the tortured psyche of the 'colonial' Australian boy (the colony of Tasmania became a constituent state of Australia in 1901) who became the 'black sheep' of the family. Having 'taken his beating' from his mother in her bedroom, he would 'come down again, still in control of himself but with a trembling lip'—a clash of wills that left him 'lonely and unhappy' (Moorehead, 28)—solaced only by his kind but domestically ineffectual father, who was allowed 10s. a week by Maud out of his episcopal earnings. Certainly Bernard's early relationship with his mother, and his repeated confrontations with her, would be replicated throughout a lifetime of scrapes and clashes with authority that characterized his controversial career.

In 1901 Bishop Montgomery was rewarded for his evangelical and missionary zeal by being made secretary of the Society for the Propagation of the Gospel, and the family moved back to London. His boys Donald and Bernard were sent to St Paul's School in Hammersmith—in 1944 to become Montgomery's headquarters during the preparations for the D-day landings in the Second World War.

Freed from Maud's tyrannous upbringing, the fourteen-year-old Bernard chose the school's army class in direct opposition to the wishes of his parents, who had hoped he

Bernard Law Montgomery [Monty], **first Viscount Montgomery of Alamein (1887–1976)**, by Frank O. Salisbury, 1945

might settle down and become a priest. Instead he threw himself into competitive sports and ignored his studies. His brother Donald went to Cambridge as a scholar, while Bernard, standing 5 feet 7 inches with piercing blue-grey eyes and a somewhat foxy nose, passed into the Royal Military College, Sandhurst, without distinction but without difficulty also, in autumn 1906 (72nd out of 170). As a cadet Montgomery showed outstanding powers of leadership and was quickly promoted with a view to his becoming colour-sergeant of his company, but he deliberately set fire to the backside of a fellow cadet in an armed fight with pokers. He was reduced to the ranks; only the timely intercession of his mother—terrified of another scandal in the family (her brothers had been arraigned for acts of homosexuality)—saved him from being expelled. He was made to stay a third term, and though attempting to reform, did not pass out high enough (thirty-sixth) to get into the coveted Indian army, where an officer could live on his pay. Instead Montgomery joined a county regiment (Royal Warwickshire) with a battalion in India, claiming foreign service supplement.

For four years (1908–13) Montgomery learned to know and despise the arcane traditions of regimental messes and the Indian army. 'An expression heard frequently was that so-and-so was a "good mixer"', he later recalled. 'A good mixer of drinks, I came to believe. … Overall, by the time I left India in 1913, I was glad that fate had decided against my passing high enough out of Sandhurst to be elected for the Indian army' (Montgomery, *Memoirs*, 29). Montgomery's scorn for all products of the Indian army was typical of the prejudices that came to rule his life as much as they did his mother's. In the event it was the First World War that changed Montgomery from a bumptious, querulous infantry subaltern, constantly at odds with authority, into a decorated company commander, outstanding staff officer—and trainer of men.

The 1st battalion Royal Warwickshire regiment (RWR) was thrown into the tail end of the retreat from Mons on 26 August 1914, at Le Cateau, where half the men were killed or captured, and the battalion commander cashiered for offering to surrender to the Germans. It was an inauspicious start to modern warfare. Montgomery himself evaded capture by hiding by day with a party of survivors, and retreating by night between the British and German lines. Thrown back into action at Meteren during Joffre's allied counter-offensive on the Marne on 13 October 1914, Montgomery was shot by a sniper through the right lung, and a grave was dug for him. He survived, however, was awarded the DSO for gallant leadership, and in February 1915 became a brigade-major in Lancashire (112th, redesignated 104th 'Bantams'), helping to prepare Kitchener's New Army of volunteers for war. His gifts of courage, energy, confidence, and analytical clarity then earned him steady promotion as an operations staff officer during the bloody battles of the Somme, Arras, and Ypres. 'The Germans have lost enormously and they can't afford to', he wrote in March 1916 to his mother—whose respect, if not her love, he hoped to win—before the tragic battle of the Somme (Hamilton, *Monty*, 1.103). He still did

not question, at this stage in his professional career, the gruesome casualties that ensued, or the British high command. Even in the following spring he shared the confidence of the British commander-in-chief, General Sir Douglas Haig, that the battle of Arras would be successful. 'The Hindenburg line is very strong, too strong to attack frontally. So we broke through at the North end of it and are rolling it up sideways', he wrote as the number two operations staff officer (GSO2) at 33rd division (ibid., 1.120). In the event there was no breakthrough, Haig squandering a further 120,000 men as casualties, without positive result.

After promotion to GSO2 of 9th corps in July 1917, however, Montgomery came under a New Army commander, General Sir Herbert Plumer. Montgomery was placed in charge of the 9th corps battle-training programme. By his issuing a sixty-page training manual, arranging preliminary rehearsal of all troops behind the lines, and integrating artillery and engineer support, the infantry were able to achieve their tactical objectives (Polygon Wood, Menin Road, and Broodseinde) with a minimum of casualties. After Sir Douglas Haig's vast and futile casualties on the Somme and at Arras, Plumer's offensive operations were salutary in their tactical achievements—though Haig thereupon insisted, against the advice of his corps commanders, on a do-or-die battle for the Passchendaele Ridge, which resulted in further gruesome losses.

Watching the doomed Canadians undertake this battle Montgomery finally saw where the generals had gone wrong. As he wrote of his brother Donald's corps, on 8 November 1917, the Canadian soldiers were 'magnificent' at 'straightforward fighting', but 'they forget that the whole art of war is to gain your objective with as little loss as possible' (Hamilton, *Monty*, 1.129). This was the art that Montgomery would perfect, and which made him the outstanding British field commander of the twentieth century.

After serving throughout spring 1918 on the western front in the battles of the Lys and Chemin-des-Dames, confronting the Ludendorff offensive, Montgomery was again promoted, becoming on 16 July chief-of-staff of a division, the 47th (London), as a temporary lieutenant-colonel, aged thirty.

The allies having resumed the offensive on the western front, Montgomery was able to translate the crucial lessons of modern continental war into a series of outstanding training pamphlets and instruction manuals. Having been dismissed contemptuously by his English teachers at school, he began to realize that he possessed a remarkable ability to see through the fog of war: to pick out the essentials of twentieth-century combat, and to articulate those essentials in a way that amateur soldiers—volunteers and conscripts—could immediately understand. By a process of simplification, repetition, and sharpness of intellect he managed to dramatize complex aspects of modern battle—the co-operation of all arms, from engineers to artillerymen, cooks to machine-gunners—and render them transparent. He became, in effect, a brilliant teacher of combat, in the midst of combat. Critics were later incensed at his bravado, boastfulness, and egomania, but for a democratic country waging a second world war with inferior equipment and disastrous separation of arms, it was an education of immense significance.

The inter-war years With the withdrawal of the German armies and the armistice agreed on 11 November 1918, Montgomery was posted to the British army of the Rhine in Cologne on 24 March 1919, and from September to November of that year commanded the 17th battalion of the Royal Fusiliers. He was desperate, however, to go to the army's Staff College in Camberley, and distraught when not chosen for the one-year course of 1920. During a tennis game with Field Marshal Sir William Robertson, the commander-in-chief of the British army of occupation (a post Montgomery was to hold twenty-five years later), the 31-year-old temporary lieutenant-colonel made sufficient impression that he was added to the list. He could not contain himself once there, and became 'a bloody menace', as his brother Brian recorded (B. Montgomery, 17), leading a group of younger officers demanding radical changes in military thinking. It became a punishment to have to sit beside him at breakfast. As Montgomery himself later admitted, 'I was critical and intolerant; I had yet to learn that uninformed criticism is valueless' (B. L. Montgomery, 38).

The inter-war years informed Montgomery. On graduation from the Staff College in December 1920 he was posted to Cork, Ireland, as a brigade-major of the 17th infantry brigade during the troubles—an experience of martial law and guerrilla warfare that caused Montgomery to rethink many of his attitudes. He was himself protestant and half-Irish; the family seat was still at Moville, just outside the six counties; his own first cousin Lieutenant-Colonel Hugh Montgomery was assassinated by the IRA in Dublin—yet Montgomery came away from the Irish struggle for independence (in which he was the chief staff officer responsible for the operations of nine battalions) with the conviction that Sinn Féin was right. He had run the brigade with such exemplary efficiency that his divisional commander, Major-General Sir Peter Strickland, noted in his diary that 'We had a perfect organization and had "them" beat' when the Truce was declared on 11 July 1921. 'A short time more' Strickland claimed (Hamilton, *Monty*, 1.158–9), would have sufficed to complete the smashing of the IRA, but Montgomery did not agree. As he wrote shortly afterwards to one of his intelligence officers, A. E. Percival (who was to surrender Singapore to the Japanese in the Second World War), 'My own view is that to win a war of that sort you must be ruthless; Oliver Cromwell, or the Germans, would have settled it in a very short time'—but as a twentieth century democracy, Britain could not behave in such a militaristic way. 'I consider that Lloyd George was right. ... The only way therefore was to give them some form of self-government and let them squash the rebellion themselves' (ibid., 1.160).

Given his later reputation for ruthlessness and high-toryism (pro-apartheid, anti-European Common Market), this may seem inconsistent, but it provides a measure of

Montgomery's quirky realism and willingness to adopt unpopular stances when convinced of a moral cause. In a class-divided, imperialist post-war Britain he remained a superlative staff officer and soldier (he even issued a book of his own orders as brigade-major to help officers arriving in Ireland), yet also a Christian with a deep social conscience and interest in the welfare of ordinary people. His later popularity with his men as an army and army group commander contrasted markedly with the distant generals of the First World War—a popularity that was often ascribed to a gift for public relations (Ralph Ingersoll, *Top Secret*, 1946; Correlli Barnett, *The Desert Generals*, 1960; and J. Ellis, *Brute Force*, 1990); in truth it derived from something much deeper, namely a primary loyalty to his own men, a questioning moral conscience, and ruthless realism. After the carnage of the First World War, he reasoned, men could no longer be expected to fight for a cause that was not explained to them, and which could not be seen to be just. This was the challenge to modern high command—and another twenty years elapsed before Montgomery deployed the weapon of PR to meet it.

In the meantime he concentrated on gaining experience, and teaching 'masterclasses' for younger officers hoping to enter the Staff College. The Geddes 'axe' required a drastic reduction in British military spending; Montgomery was posted in 1923 as GSO2 to a territorial division (49th) in Yorkshire, where he first met Lieutenant Francis de Guingand—later to become his most famous chief of staff. Scorning the conventional importance attached to drill in Britain's part-time army, he concentrated on the winter training of individual leaders, using sand-tables to rehearse tactical approaches to combat, which could then be tried out in summer camps and manoeuvres. He saw Britain's army as a single body of men, though divided into regular and territorial categories. Fascinated by the challenge of teaching 'spare time' soldiers, he told Basil Liddell Hart in 1924: 'Personally, I take my hat off to those in category 2 every time' (Hamilton, *Monty*, 1.173)—for it would be the territorials, he knew, who would have to win a future war on the continent.

Montgomery's reputation spread, and after a brief spell back with his battalion as a company commander, Major (brevet Lieutenant-Colonel) B. L. Montgomery was made in January 1926 an instructor at the Staff College, Camberley, where he taught alongside Alan Brooke, later his corps commander and chief of the Imperial General Staff (CIGS), and Bernard Paget, who would later precede him at Twenty-First Army group.

Montgomery had calculated that by 1934 he ought to get one of the two battalion commands in his regiment, and had recognized that his chances would be immeasurably improved if he married. In the spring of 1925 he had already begun a campaign to win the affections of a beautiful girl whom he met in Dinard, on a golfing holiday with his battalion colonel. Loath to waste time, the innocent 37-year-old Major Montgomery proposed to the innocent 17-year-old music student, Betty Anderson, at the end of his first dance with her, giving rise to a reckless series of proposals which Betty turned down, to the disappointment of her parents who saw Montgomery as a man with a future. Betty recalled:

> He never discussed books or anything at all. It just seemed his whole mind was geared on how he was going to win this [next] war and, I mean, I never thought there'd be a war, I wasn't thinking of wars—I mean one didn't.   (Hamilton, *Man Behind the Legend*, 42)

Undaunted, Montgomery pursued Betty the following winter to Lenk in Switzerland. Dressing as Napoleon for the fancy dress ball he again proposed to her. Rejected, the emperor finally accepted defeat, saying 'I shall wash you out of my life. You're the first thing I've not conquered' (ibid.).

Better luck met Montgomery's next romantic campaign. Resuming his didactic imperative he began to teach the children in the winter sports party to ski, and befriended the widowed mother of two of them, a second Betty, whose Olympic-athlete husband, Waldo Carver, had been killed at Gallipoli. This Betty, *née* Hobart, was his own age, not beautiful, but intelligent and artistic and loved by all who knew her. She had studied at the Slade under Henry Tonks, and had a wide circle of bohemian friends in Chelsea. Winter friendship deepened, and after another trip to Lenk the following Christmas, Montgomery proposed to her and was accepted. The confirmed bachelor, virginal and devoted heart-and-soul to soldiering, had finally found love.

Betty's brother Patrick Hobart was a colonel in the army, a pioneer of mechanization and modern armoured warfare. Betty was thus well-versed in matters military and was not put off by Montgomery's dedication to his art, while determined to introduce her shy husband to other arts, as well as artists such as her best friends Gwen and Alan Herbert. The change did nothing but good for Montgomery, who found Alan Herbert's novel, *The Secret War*, to be 'the best story of front-line war I have read' (Hamilton, *Monty*, 1.199).

Marital happiness allowed Montgomery to make peace with his mother, and with the more vindictive as well as reckless parts of his nature. His love for Betty was so whole-hearted that even sceptical observers, alarmed at the way he took charge even of the family's laundry, found themselves touched—as when, after Betty gave birth to a son and heir in August 1928, Montgomery would move a china rabbit to one or other side of the shelf above the bed to remind his wife with which breast to begin her next feed. They did everything together, and when Montgomery was given command of the 1st battalion RWR in January 1931—three years before he had reckoned—it seemed as if fate were compensating for his lonely and unhappy childhood in a remarkable way.

Betty travelled with her husband for the following six years, while the battalion was stationed in Palestine (1931), Egypt (Alexandria, 1931–3) and India (Poona, 1933–4), followed by another spell for Montgomery as a teacher, this time as chief instructor of the Staff College). Often resented by his superiors for his arrogance and dictatorial ways (such as setting up a battalion brothel, regularly inspected by his own battalion medical officer, for the 'horizontal refreshment' of his soldiers who were not permitted to take their wives abroad), Montgomery's genius for training and his marriage to Betty ensured him a charmed life until one day in 1937 when, promoted to command of 9th infantry brigade in England and taking part in (and taking over) the all-important summer manoeuvres on Salisbury Plain, he insisted on Betty's going on a holiday with their nine-year-old son David, while their Portsmouth garrison house was redecorated. On the beach at Burnham-on-Sea, Betty was bitten by an insect. The wound became infected and before she could be moved to the military hospital at Portsmouth her leg had to be amputated, and she died in his arms on 19 October 1937 of post-operative septicaemia.

Montgomery, heartbroken, shut himself away, refusing to allow any member of the family to attend her funeral, or share his grief. He had always taken his punishment as a child—and could not bear the idea of being seen to break down and weep uncontrollably, as he now did. 'It was the only time during our long friendship that I ever saw him less than in control of himself', recalled his brigade-major, F. Simpson—the only witness, together with a staff captain, of the funeral (Hamilton, *Monty*, 1.276).

The following night, however, having insisted on driving back to Portsmouth alone, Montgomery pulled himself together, and ordered his brigade-major to have 'all the papers on my desk at 9 a.m. and we'll get down to work' (Hamilton, *Monty*, 1.279). Montgomery devoted the remainder of his life to a demonstration of the art of high command in the field. He had spent years perfecting the art of training: of inspiring, instructing, and guiding younger officers towards the goal of professional warfare: warfare in which officers must become masters of modern weaponry, co-operation between all arms, the organization of large forces, and tactical manoeuvre. Night fighting became his speciality, as well as close air support. In the spring of 1938 he organized an amphibious combined operations landing exercise, supported by bomber aircraft and naval cruisers and destroyers, that would bear a remarkable likeness to the D-day landings six years later—an initiative witnessed by the new commander-in-chief, southern command, General Wavell. Although Wavell said nothing (typically), he was impressed—and when calls came for Montgomery to be sacked over the unauthorized leasing of government property to a fairground operator at Easter—the proceeds going into the garrison welfare fund—Wavell was able to fend them off and obtain promotion for his protégé, as commander of 8th division in Palestine for a year, from 1938 to 1939, to be followed by command of the famed 3rd (Iron) division at home.

Montgomery's command in northern Palestine, exercised in tandem with Major-General Richard O'Connor who commanded 9th division in the south, began in December 1938 and was ruthlessly effective. After visiting the whole of his divisional area he decided that the Arab revolt against the British mandate was different from his earlier experience in Ireland. This was not a 'national movement' and most Palestinian Arabs, he claimed, would be content to remain under British rule 'so long as Jewish immigration is limited to a fixed total (say of 500,000)' (Hamilton, *Monty*, 1.292). The Arab 'gangs' were therefore hunted down and largely destroyed, ensuring relative peace in Palestine as world war loomed. No one foresaw the immigration pressures that would result from the Holocaust, however—and it would be Montgomery's distressing job, nine years later, as head of the British army, to order the evacuation of British troops from a Palestine exploding into civil war, as Arabs fought against a Jewish population that had grown beyond all hope of peaceful co-existence.

In the meantime, having quashed Arab unrest, Montgomery became restless to get back to England and start retraining the 3rd division, which had become, he felt, lethargic and unfit for modern combat under its 'useless' commander, General Denis (Podge) Bernard. It was at this moment, however, that Montgomery was struck down by an illness so crippling (fever, pleurisy, and physical collapse), that it was assumed by all that he would never serve again in the field. Whether it was tuberculosis, as suspected, was unclear, for he could not—or perhaps would not—bring up enough sputum to be tested. Instead he was airlifted to Egypt and sent home on the SS *Ranchi* in July 1939, accompanied by his sister Winsome who watched as he recovered, it seemed, by sheer willpower, insisting he be carried onto the deck by his male nurses and taking longer walks each day. By the time the ship docked at Tilbury, Montgomery was able to walk unassisted. At the medical board at the Military Hospital, Millbank, on 14 July he was pronounced completely free of infection—'causal organism unknown' (Hamilton, *Monty*, 1.311).

Determined to take over his new division, Montgomery attempted a quasi-coup—as he would in the desert prior to Alamein—by travelling to Portsmouth in August 1939, setting up headquarters in a hotel, and running the 3rd division in the absence of its commander, General Bernard, who was fishing in Ireland, regardless of the rising tension in Danzig and Poland. As all appointments were then frozen by part-mobilization, Montgomery was ordered to join a pool of unemployed major-generals. General Bernard, it was understood, would take 3rd division to France as part of the British expeditionary force (BEF) as soon as war was declared.

Dunkirk Montgomery's protests bore fruit, and after a certain amount of string-pulling at the request of the 2nd corps commander, General Alan Brooke, General Bernard was sent abroad to Bermuda as governor, and Montgomery took official command of 3rd division. Though farcical, it was a historic turnabout, for 3rd division's extraordinary performance in the retreat to Dunkirk, nine months later, helped save the BEF: a masterly performance planned, rehearsed, and conducted by Montgomery, that would eventually go down in the military annals of the Second World War—for instead of training the 3rd division to conduct offensive operations, Montgomery

predicted an allied catastrophe, as in 1914, and was determined, this time, that his division would not be found wanting. Once war was declared and the BEF had taken up its positions along the Franco-Belgian border, on the left flank of the French army, Montgomery concocted a unique series of exercises in retreat—instead of offence—which were carried out through the winter of 1939–40. These full-scale rehearsals, involving fighting by day and withdrawing by night, were conducted backwards into France during the 'phoney war', using rivers and waterways as defensive lines, exercising the intimate co-operation of artillery and motorized infantry, and employing leap-frogging techniques, all in the face of vociferous local French protests.

The British commander-in-chief, Lord Gort, who had never commanded a unit higher than a brigade in the field, chose to remain almost throughout this period at his BEF headquarters, as distant from his troops as French or Haig, his predecessors in the First World War. How the BEF would fight if the Germans invaded Belgium remained a mystery to him as to his subordinates, and he contented himself with boots-and-polish inspections, interesting himself in Montgomery's command of 3rd division only when a scandal brewed over the issuing of a highly explicit divisional warning about venereal disease.

Montgomery's training techniques were thus wholly ignored by the BEF commander, yet inspired the men of 3rd division—who, once the Germans invaded Belgium and the Netherlands on 10 May 1940, performed their advance to the Dyle and subsequent withdrawal to Dunkirk with a professionalism that astounded even Brooke, the corps commander.

By contrast Gort's failure as a higher commander was tragically exposed—his BEF headquarters totally unrehearsed in movement or communications exercises. As a result Gort was relieved of his command, while Brooke was made commander-in-chief southern command, then commander-in-chief, home forces. Montgomery had managed to bring his entire division home with only nominal casualties and succeeded Brooke as 2nd corps commander for a few days on the beach at Dunkirk. When he marched into the War Office in Whitehall on his return, saying that the BEF had never been properly commanded, indeed had not been commanded at all, his criticisms aroused the deepest enmity in the corridors of military power. Despite his superlative performance in Belgium and France he was only created CB and relegated to divisional command. Although he was soon promoted to command 5th corps, he fell out with General Auchinleck, the outgoing commander and now commander-in-chief southern command, concerning Auchinleck's static beach-defence strategy. A lasting feud began between the two generals, culminating in Montgomery's promotion, two years later, to command of Eighth Army in Egypt, following the defeats of the two army commanders appointed by Auchinleck, as commander-in-chief Middle East, in the struggle against Rommel.

Alamein and the desert war Auchinleck, having had to take command of Eighth Army himself after the British rout at

Gazala, was fully cognizant of the need for a new field commander, if the allies were to hold on to Egypt and the Suez Canal. Having managed to stabilize the position at Alamein, only 60 miles west of Alexandria, Auchinleck planned to appoint his chief staff officer in Cairo, General Corbett, as his third appointee to command Eighth Army. However, Churchill, after flying out to Egypt early in August 1942 and making a personal tour of the Alamein front with the new CIGS, General Brooke, was neither impressed by Auchinleck's field headquarters, nor by Auchinleck's selection of field commander. Brooke recommended Montgomery, but Churchill—who discouraged egos as large as his own—disliked Montgomery. By contrast he had heard good things from Anthony Eden, the minister of war, about General Richard Gott, a young corps commander already serving in Eighth Army, but a soldier exhausted by the 1400-mile retreat before Rommel's axis army. Tired by Churchill's working hours and methods, Brooke gave way, and after a personal interview Gott was appointed by Churchill to command Eighth Army, while General Auchinleck was sacked and replaced as commander-in-chief Middle East, by General Harold Alexander. (Auchinleck was offered the Persia–Iraq command, which he refused.)

In one of the strange fortunes of war Gott was killed flying back to Cairo for a bath on 7 August 1942 and Brooke, relieved, was finally able to persuade a reluctant Churchill to summon Montgomery later that night.

Montgomery's peremptory assumption of command of Eighth Army was deeply resented by Auchinleck and his departing entourage, but became, for the men of Eighth Army, one of the miracles of the desert war. Seizing command two days earlier than authorized by Auchinleck (13 August 1942), ordering up immediate reinforcements from Cairo against Auchinleck's wishes, instructing the vital heights of Alam Halfa to be defended in strength, joining army and air headquarters together in a single operating unit, and instructing all contingency plans for retreat to be destroyed, Montgomery's edict that Eighth Army would stand and die where it stood told everything. 'No Withdrawal and No Surrender' became the army's buzzword, as the new, white-kneed, evangelical commander toured the units of his army, acquiring multiple cap badges for his Australian bush hat as he did, and spreading a new gospel of victory.

By the time Churchill had returned to the desert on 19 August 1942, the 'complete change in atmosphere' was so marked that Churchill could hardly credit the transformation. Brooke was equally surprised. 'I knew my Monty pretty well by then', he wrote later, 'but I must confess I was dumbfounded by the situation facing him, the rapidity with which he had grasped the essentials, the clarity of his plans, and above all, his unbounded self-confidence— a self-confidence with which he inspired all those that he came into contact with' (Bryant, *The Turn of the Tide*, 478).

Montgomery's lack of subsequent magnanimity towards General Auchinleck later served to obscure his historic transformation of a beaten body of men into the legendary Eighth Army that fought its way from Alamein to Tunisia between August 1942 and May 1943. Had Betty lived, Montgomery's egoism might perhaps have been less bombastic, his comments on others less scandalously quotable. Yet at the time his messianic vitality and vanity were, as his later chief of intelligence, E. T. Williams, put it, 'Eighth Army's dynamo' (Hamilton, *Monty*, 2.173). Above all, Montgomery understood soldiers' hearts and minds, thousands of miles from home, in a 'citizen army'. Such men looked to their commander for leadership— leadership that was not a matter of suavity, but of man-management and clear command. The men of Eighth Army wanted to know what they were required to do in order to defeat Rommel, as the enemy was known; Montgomery gave them an immediate answer.

For two years, in relative obscurity outside the confines of his general's posts in England (5th corps, 12th corps, south-east army) Montgomery had laid down the principles of successful combat by a democratic nation in modern war against a professional enemy—and had relentlessly rehearsed his units and formations in a series of exercises from sand-tables to manoeuvres. These exercises had culminated in Exercise Tiger in May 1942, involving 100,000 troops in the Kent–Sussex area, co-ordinating infantry, armour, artillery and air forces. In flying out to the desert Montgomery felt he had rehearsed to his satisfaction the problems of tactical co-operation between all arms, and of mobile command and communications in modern battle conditions on a significant scale. His faith in himself thus rested upon a professionalism in the organization and command of large bodies of men unequalled by any British commander in home forces. All he needed was army command in the field of battle, against a skilled adversary, to prove himself.

Churchill's satisfaction with the new spirit pervading Eighth Army proved well placed. ULTRA decryptions of German high-grade signals had confirmed Montgomery's instantaneous orders to defend in depth the Alam Halfa Ridge, which Rommel hoped to encircle. In the battle of Alam Halfa, which began on 31 August 1942, Rommel's attempt to smash through the British front line with 234 tanks and encircle the Eighth Army was dealt a fatal blow by secret minefields, concealed hull-down Grant tanks (known as 'Egypt's last hope') at Alam Halfa, and close air support by RAF bombers and fighter bombers. The German Afrika Korps commander was wounded, the commander of 21 Panzer division killed, and it was all Rommel could do to extract his Panzerarmee Afrika from potential annihilation. The threat to Egypt—and by extension, a German pincer movement to seize the Persian oilfields from north and south—had been lifted. Eighth Army rejoiced in its well-earned defensive victory.

It was now Eighth Army's turn to mount an offensive: the battle of Alamein, which in many people's view marked the turning of the tide. Here Montgomery's skills in organization and training were to be tried in one of the decisive battles of the Second World War. Not only did the Martuba airfields need to be recaptured in order to provide air protection for the crucial convoy resupplying Malta in November, but the planned allied invasion of

French north-west Africa, operation Torch, was predicated upon British victory in the Egyptian desert—making it possible to evict axis forces in north Africa between the two.

The British had never won a major offensive battle against the Germans in the Second World War; nor had the Russians. Blunting Rommel's attempt to seize Cairo and the Suez Canal, then breaking through the German–Italian defences at Alamein, therefore, had a psychological and morale-raising significance that exceeded even its strategic importance. Working on the lines of Exercise Tiger, Montgomery insisted the Eighth Army undergo a massive retraining programme, both to assimilate the new Sherman tanks pouring into Suez from America, and to retrain the men in night fighting. Ignoring Churchill's impatience—based upon ULTRA evidence of massive German minefields that would become more difficult to penetrate with each day's delay—Montgomery laid down his plan of battle, revised it when rumours of timidity among the British tank commanders reached his ears—and visited every single unit that would be participating in the offensive. By 23 October, when the largest British artillery barrage of the Second World War commenced, Montgomery was confident he would win—but by a ruthless battle of tactical surprise and then gradual mutual attrition, rather than by manoeuvre. He forecast the number not only of days of battle—twelve—but even of British casualties: 13,500, almost to the man. His long experience in the First World War was paying off.

Montgomery's conduct of the battle—his imperturbability at his forward command headquarters (Tac headquarters) and his daily display of confidence—inspired his subordinates, but not Whitehall. By early November, when news that Montgomery was withdrawing tanks from the battle leaked back to London, Eden began to scare the prime minister, and fears grew that the battle would end in stalemate—an alarming prospect in relation to the Torch invasion of Morocco and Algeria, set for 8 November and relying on Vichy French compliance as the Anglo-American forces landed.

Montgomery's faith in his men was rewarded, however. The tanks had been pulled out in order to deliver a powerful *coup de grâce*, once the Australian, New Zealand, and highland infantry had crumbled the German forces opposing them in the break-in sector in the north. By 2 November, Rommel was signalling to Berlin that he wished to retreat. Hitler, recognizing the immense significance which defeat would have on other German forces in Africa, Europe, and Russia, intervened and ordered a 'victory or death' stand. It did no good—and was largely ignored as German motorized units fled, leaving more than 30,000 axis infantry (mostly Italian, but including the commander of the Afrika Korps, General von Thoma) to surrender as Eighth Army's forces broke beyond the battlefield and threatened to cut off Rommel's retreat. 'I wish I were just a newspaper vendor in Berlin' Rommel told his aide-de-camp (Irving, 221).

Montgomery, by contrast, became Sir Bernard Montgomery (KCB), as well as a full general. Churchill ordered

the ringing of church bells across England as news of his victory spread throughout the world. Montgomery's caution, during the subsequent advance across open desert, disappointed many younger staff and armoured officers in north Africa and England, and the codebreakers at Bletchley Park became incensed at the apparent caution of the Eighth Army at a time when Rommel was down to eleven tanks. The Germans were, however, withdrawing onto their own lines of communication and stores—while the British line of communication became daily longer until it stretched over 1000 miles. 'I thought he was very cautious considering his immensely superior strength', von Thoma remarked in retrospect, adding, though, that the 'decisive factor is the organization of one's resources—to maintain the momentum' (Liddell Hart, 173). This momentum Montgomery maintained throughout the north African campaign, refusing to take unwarranted risks and conducting a methodical advance that, if it did not impress the pundits, gave the western world the sense that the tide of war had really turned: that Britain had at last learned how to deploy its resources, and would win not occasional battles, but, inexorably, the necessary campaigns that would end in Hitler's defeat. Thus Montgomery kept the initiative, applying superior strength as and when it suited him, bouncing Rommel out of each successive axis position.

The difficult situation facing the allies under Eisenhower in north-west Africa meanwhile presented a vivid contrast. When, fresh from his triumphant check to the American forces at Kasserine, where the 'green' Americans suffered 10,000 casualties, Rommel attacked an overstretched Eighth Army at Medenine on 6 March 1943 Montgomery was completely unfazed. Forewarned by air reconnaissance and ULTRA of the general German intention, Montgomery raced up more tanks and artillery to face the largest concentration of German armour ever assembled in north Africa (three Panzer divisions) and fought one of the best one-day defensive battles of the Second World War—having disposed his forces in such a way that he could face attack from any direction. 'The Marshal has made a balls of it', he calmly observed of Rommel during the morning of 6 March. 'I shall write letters' (N. Hamilton, *Master of the Battlefield: Monty's War Years, 1942–1944*, 1984, 169).

At Mareth (20–27 March 1943), however, Montgomery encountered fiercer frontal opposition than he had anticipated, and was forced to switch his major effort into an outflanking inland pincer under Lieutenant-General Horrocks, backed by low-flying RAF fighter-bomber support, pioneered by the young Air-Vice-Marshal Harry Broadhurst: a spectacular demonstration of British *blitzkrieg*, and a harbinger of what allied ground forces could achieve when working in real tandem with co-operative airmen.

This campaign, demonstrating the battle-winning ingredients of morale, intimate co-operation of all arms including the air weapon, first-class logistical back-up and clear-cut orders, would be Montgomery's legacy to modern field command, ending in a brilliant infantry attack at the Wadi Akarit, and—once the advance came to a halt before the difficult Enfidaville position—a switch of Eighth Army armoured divisions to Eisenhower's field deputy, General Alexander, for his First Army assault on Tunis, which fell on 12 May 1943.

Montgomery's achievement, then, was to refashion a dispirited and defeated Eighth Army, and make it the most victorious allied army of the war in north Africa, legendary in its morale to the point that there was virtually no sickness or absenteeism; everyone wanted to fight. This was no mean accomplishment, after years of British failure, extending from Norway, Dunkirk, Crete, Burma, and Singapore to Tripoli and Tobruk. Nevertheless Montgomery's strengths would also prove to be his weaknesses, once Eighth Army had to co-operate with American forces in the invasions of Sicily and the Italian mainland. Ironically Montgomery sided with the American view about the soft Italian 'underbelly'—that it would be better to make the axis powers defend a vast Mediterranean coastline from possible allied attack than commit the allies to arduous campaigns in easily defended mountainous countries. Better, he reasoned, to invade France in a cross-channel operation—the so-called Second Front—that would compress and ultimately crush German forces between Soviet and Western offensives. Neither Alan Brooke, the CIGS, nor Churchill agreed, however, and Montgomery was required to conduct a series of amphibious assaults and land campaigns in the Mediterranean that did little to win the war, and often threatened—as at Salerno and later Anzio—to lose it.

Montgomery's exasperation at the strategic bungles of 1943 was compounded by his frustration with the lack of clear planning and professionalism at Eisenhower's and Alexander's headquarters. Montgomery felt he had proved a master of the art of modern war by absolute concentration upon essentials, and focusing of all arms on specific tactical tasks. He was thus an enemy of the opportunism and muddle that had for so long characterized allied operations and failures—and the mixture of Churchill's wild projects and dispersion of allied effort in the Mediterranean proved an ominous rehearsal for the great strategic and tactical controversies that would arise in France in the late summer of 1944.

Although Montgomery managed to recast plans for the invasion of Sicily, which was conquered in five weeks (10 July–17 August), inter-allied tensions grew as Americans—Eisenhower, Patton, Bradley, and Clark—took umbrage at Montgomery's know-all attitudes and boastfulness. Eager to make their own marks on military history, they resented him, while accepting his remarkable skills as a general. The Italian mainland campaign, from 3 September 1943, was thus a shambles, under Eisenhower's overall direction and General Alexander's Fifteenth Army group command in the field. There was little or no co-ordination of British and American efforts, and when Montgomery, having laboriously slogged from Reggio in the southern tip of Italy to the River Sangro, above the latitude of Rome, was recalled to England on 23 December 1943 to lead the D-day landings, he was delighted to leave what he considered, not without justice, 'a dog's breakfast'.

D-day and the Battle of Normandy There followed Montgomery's greatest contribution to the Second World War, and arguably the greatest military achievement of the twentieth century. Not for nine centuries had any attempt at an opposed landing across the English Channel proved successful, despite attempts by a fleet of Spanish warships in the sixteenth century, and recurrent French and German threats during the Napoleonic wars and in the first and second world wars. On taking over the D-day landings as land forces commander-in-chief, Montgomery became, for the first time, an army group commander (Twenty-First Army group), responsible for 2 million British, American, Canadian, Polish, Free French, and other allied troops who would land on the French coast, bring the German armies in the West to battle, and, it was hoped, defeat them.

This Montgomery achieved, over the ensuing eight weeks. Ruthlessly reviewing and recasting the Normandy invasion plan within the first days of his arrival in Britain, Montgomery insisted on a vastly increased assault landing astride the Carentan estuary, supported by parachute divisions, and he laid down a proposed ninety-day battle, once the troops were ashore, with the British and Canadian armies forming a left shoulder, pivoting on Caen, while the two American armies (First and Third) wheeled through the bocage on the British right, seizing the ports of Cherbourg and St Malo, and forming a southern flank along the Loire. As in all his previous commands he insisted upon strenuous training and rehearsal by all forces participating in the assault—not only the troops, but also the commanders. Thus, at two great presentations of plans at his St Paul's School headquarters on 7 April and 15 May 1944, Montgomery set out his strategy and the anticipated response of the enemy—commanded by his old desert adversary, Field Marshal Rommel.

In this way Montgomery's clarity, energy, confidence, professionalism, and lifetime's experience in the training of others transformed an operation of war in which the planners, working since 1942, had little confidence, into an invasion project that could not, in the hearts and minds of those participating in the landings, fail. Keeping the peace between warring airmen, naval commanders, and the anxious British and American chiefs of staff, Eisenhower spread a mantle of bonhomie as supreme commander that was invaluable in such a multi-national undertaking, but he left the entire planning and direction of the land forces to Montgomery. Both Eisenhower and his chief of staff, Lieutenant-General Bedell Smith, privately acknowledged to the American military correspondent, Drew Middleton, after the war, that D-day would have failed without Montgomery's personal command. 'No one else could have got us across the Channel and into Normandy … Whatever they say about him, he got us there' (Hamilton, *Monty*, 3.946–7).

Despite stormy weather and fierce opposition on the American Omaha beach, the D-day landings on 6 June 1944 proved more successful than could have been hoped, with more than 156,000 soldiers ashore by nightfall. Montgomery embarked for the beaches at 9.30 p.m., but his destroyer got lost in the night and went aground the next day: prelude to two-and-a-half months of bitter fighting in Normandy, and continual sniping from England, as air commanders, having been promised French airfields from which to operate, were compelled to fly their forces from Britain. Fear of stalemate—exactly as during the long battle at Alamein—tested everyone's patience; at one point in July 1944 it was thought Churchill was flying to Montgomery's Tac headquarters to sack him, at the request of Eisenhower—who, like the air commanders, remained quartered in England throughout the battle, watching from the sidelines.

To his credit Montgomery never showed the least signs of wavering or dissatisfaction with the slow unfolding of his ninety-day strategy. By the last week in July he was certain of victory, and once Hitler ordered a counter-offensive at Mortain—which was easily defeated by US First Army—the parallel with Alamein became obvious. The break-out of Patton's US Third Army to the Loire, as envisaged in Montgomery's planning before D-day, became the *coup de grâce*. By the end of August the Germans had lost, by British calculations, over 450,000 casualties, by American in excess of 500,000. The survivors were fleeing back towards Germany, and the only question left was: by which route should the allies end the war?

Montgomery's command in Normandy had ensured German defeat; equally, it had exposed almost insurmountable personality problems in the allied command hierarchy. Montgomery had always treated Eisenhower as a likeable but innocent schoolboy; Bradley, Hodges, and Patton had served with remarkable success under his British command, and he felt proud of them. Now that the United States was providing the bulk of reinforcements and *matériel*, however, Anglo-American rivalry threatened to vitiate the rewards of the great allied victory in Normandy—and did. For this Montgomery drew much of the blame. Though he happily flew to see his British, American, Canadian, and other subordinates in his little Miles Messenger to discuss the operational situation and to give orders, he refused to go back to Eisenhower's rear headquarters, arguing that it was the duty of a supreme commander to visit his front-line commanders. The truth was, he hated to discuss issues in any sort of committee or group of which he was not the boss, or where the boss was vague or incompetent. Unfortunately he saw Eisenhower as the latter ('His ignorance as to how to run a war is absolute and complete; he has all the popular cries, but nothing else' he commented at the height of the battle of Normandy; Hamilton, *Monty*, 2.791). Montgomery behaved, in other words, like the ruthless tactical field commander he was, ignoring and ignorant of the wider world. As Brooke noted of Montgomery, 'He is probably the finest tactical general we have had since Wellington. But', Brooke added with a shake of his head, 'on some of his strategy, and especially on his relations with the Americans, he is almost a disaster' (Hamilton, *Monty*, 2.799).

Arnhem, the Ardennes, and Lüneburg It was precisely such disaster that now overshadowed the allies at the very moment of their triumph in late August and early September 1944, as allied troops liberated Paris and reached the docksides of Antwerp. Montgomery was made a field marshal in the field; it seemed as if the war in the West would, in the wake of his great victory in Normandy, be won by Christmas. Instead Eisenhower took over from Montgomery as land force commander, split the allied advance into separated thrusts, and the allied advance towards Germany petered out in a series of reverses from Metz to Arnhem that left little hope of the western allies beating Soviet troops to Berlin.

Arnhem, the so-called 'bridge too far', was Montgomery's only defeat in the Second World War—a nightmare attempt between 17 and 25 September 1944 to outflank the Ruhr by aerial *coup de main*, before the German front could stabilize. Planned in haste and poorly supported, despite heart-breaking courage on the part of the airborne troops, it symbolized the end of allied initiative. Montgomery was ordered to take the approaches to Antwerp and forget the Rhine, and the war in the West settled down into a broad-front strategy which the western allies could not ultimately lose, given their greater industrial potential and the resolve of the Soviets in the East. Yet on 16 December 1944 they very nearly did, as Hitler launched a secret force of twenty-eight divisions straight through the Americans' weakest sector in the Ardennes, threatening to seize Antwerp and cut off the British and Canadian armies as they had once cut off the British at Dunkirk.

Pride would dictate that no American could ever accord Montgomery the laurels due to him in cauterizing the German onslaught, yet the battle of the Ardennes (or Bulge) was in many respects the greatest example of his army group generalship in defence in the war and a brilliant counterpoint to his offensive battle in Normandy. Eisenhower, the nominal land forces commander, panicked and was virtually imprisoned at his headquarters at Versailles in fear of German assassination parties working behind the allied lines; Bradley, the American Twelfth Army group commander, was similarly incarcerated at his headquarters in Luxembourg. It was thus left to Montgomery, on 20 December 1944, to take official command of all four allied armies from Givet to the channel, leaving Bradley with only Patton's US Third Army to direct. By dint of personal visits to all divisional, corps, and army field commanders, and by using his unique stable of 'gallopers' or liaison officers operating in jeeps and Auster aircraft every day as personal emissaries to all fighting headquarters under his command, Montgomery ended the American rout, created a strategic reserve, and brought the German offensive involving two Panzer armies to a halt before it reached the Meuse.

For this one great defensive battle alone, Montgomery would and perhaps should have gone down in history, but it was not to be. Once he had restored allied order out of chaos, American *amour propre* demanded retaliation in the form of an immediate counter-offensive victory. Loath to sacrifice more men than necessary in the strategically irrelevant forests of the Ardennes, Montgomery refused to do more than force the Germans back by air, tank, and artillery bombardment, saving his infantry for the more crucial battles necessary in order to reach and cross the Rhine. For this, for an interview on Christmas day 1944 in which he made Bradley eat humble pie, for insisting that Eisenhower hand back to him the role of land forces commander, as well as for an unwise press conference on 6 January 1945 in which he congratulated himself on saving the Americans in the battle of the Bulge, Montgomery became the *bête noire* of patriotic Americans at Eisenhower's, Bradley's, and Patton's headquarters, and elsewhere. Far from according Montgomery overall allied field command, a chastened Eisenhower rewarded him by threatening the allied chiefs of staff with resignation, and restoring one of Montgomery's two American armies (US First) to Bradley's command immediately after the battle. Moreover when, having crossed the Rhine on 24 March 1945, Montgomery seemed poised to race to Berlin with the armoured troops of General Simpson's US Ninth Army, Eisenhower transferred that army too to Bradley's command—and halted it on the Elbe, allowing the Russians to capture the whole of Berlin.

Montgomery, reduced to commanding the British and Canadian armies, made do with the task of sealing off the Danish peninsula at Wismar, east of Lübeck, on 2 May 1945, before the Soviets got there. Two days later, however, he received the unconditional surrender, on Lüneburg Heath, of all German armed forces in Holland, northwest Germany, and Denmark. This was not Berlin, but beneath the canvas of the special tent that had been erected, reminiscent of Eighth Army headquarters in the desert, it had an appropriately campaign-style quality wholly different from the general German surrender to Eisenhower at Rheims three days afterwards. Montgomery had summoned the BBC, which recorded the historic moment. 'His lips were firm, and as he finished signing', one war reporter described, 'he sighed faintly, sat back and removed his tortoiseshell rims, relaxed. "That concludes the surrender" he said. The tent flaps were let down and we walked away over the brown heather' (Hamilton, *Monty*, 3.513). The war, for Montgomery and the British, was over.

Post-war Fighting from Egypt to the Baltic, Montgomery had made mistakes, exhibited great dislike of opportunism and dispersal of effort, and had upset his allied colleagues and superiors on many occasions. Above all, he had attempted to call the military tune at a time when the British contribution to the allied armies amounted to only 13 divisions compared with 72 American; as Bradley's staff complained in the aftermath of their catastrophe in the Ardennes, he had become in American eyes simply too big for his boots. 'You may be great to serve under, difficult to serve alongside, but you sure are hell to serve over!', Lieutenant-General Bedell Smith, Eisenhower's chief of staff, once remarked to Montgomery in exasperation (Hamilton, *Monty*, 2.xxv). Yet he had made an incalculable contribution to winning the war. By dedication and supreme professionalism he had developed what he saw as the art of war to its highest point: minimizing the loss of human life in achieving allied objectives. He was justly revered by his men—ordinary soldiers as much as officers—because he cared about them in deed as well as word. No sooner had he won the battle of Medenine than he was writing to Brooke to urge the repatriation of long-serving soldiers. 'When a man hasn't seen his wife and family for 6 years, he has some grounds for a grievance' (Hamilton, *Monty*, 2.178). Even before Alamein, in home forces, he had declared the most important people in the army to be 'the Nursing Sisters and the Padres—the Sisters because they tell the men they matter to us—and the Padres because they tell the men they matter to God. And it is the men who matter' (Smyth, 232). Identifiable everywhere by his black beret with two badges and universally known as Monty, his raising of public morale, especially in whistle-stop speeches given at crucial munitions factories in Britain before D-day, made him as popular as the tiring prime minister—indeed by autumn 1944, according to Alan Brooke, a visibly ailing Churchill became almost paranoid about Montgomery 'filling the Mall' with worshipping crowds if he went to Buckingham Palace to receive his field marshal's baton (Bryant, *Triumph in the West*, 301).

In the context of post-war Europe and Britain's retreat from empire, however, Montgomery's battle-winning qualities were of little use, while his lack of diplomacy became a grave failing. As CIGS from 1946 to 1948, raised to the peerage as a viscount in the new year's honours of 1946, Lord Montgomery proved a dictatorial but ineffective successor to Brooke—not least because he could not bring himself to sit in the same room as his fellow chief of staff, Air Marshal Lord Tedder, the head of the RAF, who had intrigued against him throughout the Normandy campaign and as Eisenhower's deputy thereafter. In 1948 Montgomery even attempted to stop Attlee, the prime minister, from appointing General Sir William Slim as his successor as CIGS, lest Slim outshine him—which Slim promptly did.

Dispatched to France as supreme commander or chairman of the western union's commanders-in-chief committee, successor organization to the wartime Supreme Headquarters, Allied Expeditionary Force (SHAEF), and charged with presenting a credible European defence organization in the event of war with the Soviet Union, Montgomery found himself entirely unable to handle his French subordinate, Marshal de Lattre de Tassigny, and equally unable to pledge Britain to a continental defence commitment. Although he became an awe-inspiring inspector-general of European military forces, and mounted memorable exercises and manoeuvres, he found politicking in a post-war world simply beyond his capabilities, indeed began to yearn for Eisenhower's help in creating an American-led NATO force in Europe. Eisenhower obliged in 1951, and Montgomery—despite all their wartime disagreements—became his grateful number two, as deputy supreme commander, allied powers in Europe. This he remained until his retirement in 1958, after fifty years' service in the British army.

There followed publication of Montgomery's controversial and best-selling *Memoirs*, in which he attempted, like Churchill, to win the war all over again. Although riveting in its self-portrayal and its clarity of presentation, it was thought self-serving and lacking in magnanimity, quite apart from the *lèse-majesté* in a post-war period, of criticizing a serving president of the United States (by poor leadership in the field of battle, Monty claimed, Eisenhower had unnecessarily prolonged the Second World War by a year). In America, Montgomery was never really forgiven, and his reputation plummeted, as it did in England among historians tired of hearing his boastful banalities in the House of Lords on homosexuality, or of reading his articles applauding apartheid in South Africa and the glories of Chinese socialism under Mao Zedong. He died at his home, Isington Mill, Alton, Hampshire, on 24 March 1976. So low had his stock fallen that Sir Michael Howard, the regius professor of history at Oxford, writing in *The Times*, could see it as 'doubtful whether he will be regarded by posterity as one of the great captains of history, or even as one of the truly outstanding figures of the Second World War' (*The Times*, 25 March 1976).

'The rats will get at me', Montgomery had always predicted—and in historiographical terms they did. Gradually, however, retrospective outrage at his vanity diminished. As more documents emerged from the archives, it became clearer how much the western democracies owed to Montgomery's leadership and professionalism in the Second World War, however arrogant the man. Fame had turned his head, reigniting his childhood insecurities; he had not even attended his mother's funeral in 1949, claiming he was 'too busy'. Without his beloved Betty he had become, in the sophisticated world of politics and diplomacy, even of normal human relations, a failure; but in the grim business of total war in the twentieth century he had proved himself, in the eyes of many, the greatest British field commander since the Iron Duke, and had left a legacy of professionalism (training, rehearsal, clarity of orders, first-class planning and the co-operation of all arms) that still marks and inspires his country's army. As General Sir David Fraser wrote in his history of the Second World War, in 1983, Montgomery had 'dominated the collective consciousness of the British Army'. His achievement, Fraser felt, 'was to keep iron control of operations: to inspire with confidence all those who served under his command; and to make sure that his soldiers were never puzzled, frustrated or unsure of victory' (Fraser, 395–6). For a leader of millions in a modern democracy, charged to pit his troops against the combined forces of the Third Reich, it was a fitting epitaph.

Montgomery's state funeral took place in St George's Chapel, Windsor, and he was buried under a simple granite gravestone in Binstead churchyard, near Alton, Hampshire, close to the converted mill at Isington where he lived in retirement for the last eighteen years of his life.

NIGEL HAMILTON

Sources N. Hamilton, *Monty*, [3 vols.] (1981–6) · B. L. Montgomery, *The memoirs of field-marshal the Viscount Montgomery of Alamein* (1958) · B. Montgomery, *A field marshal in the family* (1973) · A. Moorehead, *Montgomery: a biography* (1973) · *DNB* · N. Hamilton, *Monty: the man behind the legend* (1987) · A. Bryant, *The turn of the tide, 1939–1943: a study based on the diaries and autobiographical notes of Field Marshal the Viscount Alanbrooke* (1957) · D. Irving, *The trail of the fox* (1977) · B. Liddell Hart, *The other side of the hill* (1962) · J. Smyth, *In this sign we conquer* (1968) · A. Bryant, *Triumph in the West, 1943–1946* (1959) · M. Howard, *The Times* (25 March 1976) · D. Fraser, *And we shall shock them* (1983) · *CGPLA Eng. & Wales* (1976)

Archives IWM, papers · St Paul's School, London, papers | Bodl. Oxf., corresp. with Clement Attlee · Bodl. Oxf., corresp. with Lord Monckton · Durham RO, corresp. with Virginia Surtees · HLRO, corresp. with Lord Beaverbrook · IWM, letters to Sir Arthur Bryant · IWM, letters to Lord Harding · IWM, letters to Sir Frank Simpson · IWM, letters to T. Warren · IWM, corresp. with Sir Edgar Williams · King's Lond., Liddell Hart C., corresp. with Viscount Alanbrooke · King's Lond., Liddell Hart C., corresp. with Sir B. H. Liddell Hart · King's Lond., Liddell Hart C., corresp. with Major John North · U. Birm. L., corresp. with Lord Avon |FILM BFI NFTVA, 'Command in battle' (seven parts), 1958–9 · BFI NFTVA, *The Levin interview*, 5 Sept 1966 · BFI NFTVA, documentary footage · BFI NFTVA, news footage · BFI NFTVA, propaganda film footage (Ministry of Information) · IWM FVA, 'Desert victory', March 1943, CVN 307 · IWM FVA, *Reputations*, BBC2, 18 Sept 1994, 384.2 · IWM FVA, actuality footage · IWM FVA, news footage |SOUND BL NSA, 'The human factor in my life', 13 Oct 1970, P511WBD1 · BL NSA, current affairs recordings · BL NSA, documentary recordings · BL NSA, news recordings · IWM SA, 'British field marshal discusses his memoirs with Brigadier E. T. Williams and Charles Collingwood', 16 Nov 1958, 3752 · IWM SA, 'British field marshal discusses command in battle with Richard Dimbleby and Charles Collingwood', 16 Nov 1958, 3753 · IWM SA, 'Command in battle' (parts 1, 2, 3, 4, and 6), BBC, 1958–9 · IWM SA, 'Leadership', Cyprus Broadcasting, 6 Aug 1961, 12008 · IWM SA, 'Field Marshal reminisces about his career and discusses music', 20 Dec 1969, 11971 · IWM SA, 'About my life', BBC, 6 March 1970, 11984 · IWM SA, 'British field marshal's philosophical reflections on his life ...', BBC, 1 Oct 1970, 3761 · IWM SA, 'Speech made before the final assault ... in the western desert, 1943', Deutsches Rundfunkarchiv, 1983, 7238 · IWM SA, oral history interview

Likenesses W. Stoneman, photograph, 1939, NPG · S. Morse-Browne, pencil drawing, 1943, IWM · A. Gross, pen and wash drawing, 1944, IWM · A. John, oils, 1944, Hunterian Museum and Art Gallery, Glasgow · F. O. Salisbury, oils, 1945, NPG [*see illus.*] · J. Stafford-Baker, watercolour drawing, 1945, IWM · J. Worsley, oils, 1946, IWM · Y. Karsh, three photographs, 1946–54, NPG · W. Stoneman, photograph, 1947, NPG · O. Birley, oils, 1948, IWM · D. D. Eisenhower, oils, 1952, Gov. Art Coll. · D. Fildes, oils, 1956, St Paul's School, London · M. Gerson, photograph, 1967, NPG · G. Argent, photographs, 1969, NPG · T. Cuneo, oils, *c*.1972, Staff College, Camberley · O. Nemon, bronze statuette, *c*.1976, IWM · O. Nemon, bronze statue, 1980, Whitehall · photographs, IWM · photographs, Hult. Arch.

Wealth at death £159,983: probate, 27 Aug 1976, *CGPLA Eng. & Wales*

Montgomery, (Robert) Bruce [*pseud.* Edmund Crispin] **(1921–1978)**, composer and detective novelist, was born on 2 October 1921 at Blackwood, Bois Lane, Chesham Bois, Buckinghamshire, the fourth child and only son of Robert Ernest Montgomery (1878–1962), sometime secretary to the high commissioner for India, and his wife, Marion Blackwood, *née* Jarvie (1888–1971). Although Montgomery was accomplished as a composer of concert and film music, his reputation rests higher under his pseudonym Edmund Crispin as the author of nine stylish detective novels and many short stories.

Montgomery was educated at Merchant Taylors' School,

(Robert) **Bruce Montgomery** [Edmund Crispin] (**1921–1978**), by Lida Moser, 1953

Northwood, Middlesex, from 1934 to 1940, and St John's College, Oxford, where he read modern languages and, in the absence at war of the elected undergraduate, acted as organ scholar. He graduated BA in 1943. After a chance encounter with *The Crooked Hinge* by John Dickson Carr, Montgomery was moved to write his first detective novel, *The Case of the Gilded Fly* (1944), which he completed in fourteen days during the Easter vacation of 1943. It was immediately accepted for publication by Gollancz. The novel featured as detective Gervase Fen, professor of English language and literature in the University of Oxford, and was full of the high spirits and erudition which mark all his work (typical is a parrot which, on hearing certain lines by Mallarmé, can be induced to recite Heine). A further seven novels appeared almost annually until *The Long Divorce* in 1951. Montgomery inclined temperamentally to the so-called Golden Age authors, and his work was welcomed as much for its humour, social satire, and idiosyncratic characters as for its detection. Julian Symons called him 'the last and most charming of the Farceurs' (Symons, 142). The early novels make use of milieux with which Montgomery was familiar: Oxford, a repertory company, the church and its music, opera, and schoolmastering all feature. His seventh novel (*Frequent Hearses*, 1950) has a film studio as its setting at a time when Montgomery was beginning to make his mark as a composer of film scores.

Montgomery's career as a composer rose in tandem with his literary success. Within a few months of his first novel being accepted, Oxford University Press published an anthem ('My joy, my life, my crown!') and two piano pieces. A steady stream of works followed. His major work, *An Oxford Requiem*, was commissioned by the Oxford Bach Choir to celebrate the Festival of Britain and was first performed with the London Symphony Orchestra in May 1951. *The Times* said: 'It is Montgomery's most considerable achievement to date; it confirms the suspicion that he is a composer with something of real significance to say' (*The Times*, 25 May 1951).

Montgomery tended towards choral music (only three of his twenty-four published titles are purely instrumental), and was particularly fond of setting poetry of the late sixteenth and early seventeenth centuries. He was most successful with smaller forms. His highly chromatic and romantic language is often characterized by sudden short harmonic 'swerves'. His songs, which include eight to texts by Shakespeare, may be considered his best work.

After a brief period of schoolmastering, Montgomery moved to Devon in 1945 to compose and write full-time. Early in the 1950s his rapid production of novels and concert music ceased as he turned to the more lucrative field of film music. Directors soon appreciated his ability to point the action for comedy, and he became type-cast (much to his chagrin). He composed scores for many of the leading comedies of the 1950s, including four in the series started by *Doctor in the House* (1954) and the first six *Carry on* films. In 1961 Montgomery was responsible for both screenplay and score of *Raising the Wind*, a comedy about music students, but the following year he reached the disastrous culmination of a growing trend in his work when he failed to honour the demanding deadline for completion of the music for *Carry on Cruising*. The film world closed its doors to him.

In his remaining years Montgomery wrote and composed little. His musical and literary styles were nostalgic, and he felt little enthusiasm for contemporary trends. Increasingly poor health, fuelled by alcoholism and osteoporosis, led to frequent stays in clinics and to financial insecurity. The sociable man of the 1950s, with whom Philip Larkin, a friend from Oxford days, recalled 'spending most of our time together swaying about with laughter on bar-stools' (Larkin, 18–19), turned into a frail, apparently morose, semi-recluse. His reaction to the rising careers of Larkin and Kingsley Amis, another Oxford friend, was to 'feel like an ageing hare overtaken by squads of implacable tortoises' (letter to Larkin, 19 June 1956, Larkin MSS). Even so, Montgomery was an influential reviewer of crime fiction for the *Sunday Times* for many years, and the anthologies of science fiction he edited established critical standards for the genre. The major achievement of his last years was the completion of his ninth and final novel, *The Glimpses of the Moon* (1976). Its riotously bucolic and irreverent tone, supported by a cast of rustic half-wits, made it a natural successor to the early novels: 'It is in the line that goes back not only through Innes but through N. F. Simpson, through Beachcomber, through Wodehouse, through a major strain of Dickens, through Sterne, to Urquhart's punch-drunk rendering of Rabelais' (Keating).

On 19 February 1976 Montgomery married Barbara Ann Clements (*d.* 1986), the daughter of Charles Camille Dornat Youings, mineral water manufacturer. She had previously been his secretary. He died from heart failure in a Plymouth hospital on 15 September 1978 and was buried in Dartington, Devon.   DAVID WHITTLE

Sources Bodl. Oxf., MSS Montgomery · *The Times* (25 May 1951) · H. R. F. Keating, *The Times* (12 May 1977) · *The Armchair Detective* (spring 1979), 183 · U. Hull, Brynmor Jones L., Larkin papers · J. Symons, *Bloody murder* (1985) · P. Larkin, *Jill* (1975) · personal knowledge (2004) · private information (2004) · WWW
Archives Bodl. Oxf., corresp. and literary papers · University of Bristol, corresp. and literary papers | U. Hull, Brynmor Jones L., letters to Larkin
Likenesses L. Moser, photograph, 1953, NPG [*see illus.*] · photographs, priv. coll.

Montgomery, Florence Sophia (1843–1923), novelist and children's writer, was born at 2 Halkin Terrace, Chelsea, London, on 17 January 1843, the second child of the five daughters and two sons of Admiral Sir Alexander Leslie Montgomery, third baronet (1807–1888), who succeeded his brother in the baronetcy in 1878, and his wife, Caroline Rose Campbell (*bap.* 1818, *d.* 1909), daughter of James Campbell of Hampton Court, Middlesex, and his wife, Eliza. There were also a brother and a sister who died in infancy. Her father, who was a first cousin of Jemima Montgomery, Baroness von Tautphoeus (1807–1893), the novelist, was an MP and a serving naval officer; he was placed on the reserve list in 1871 as a vice-admiral. As one of the older children in a long family (her youngest brother was born in 1859), Montgomery began her career telling tales to the little ones. A story of hers printed for sale at a charitable bazaar, about a little golden-haired girl whose mother dies of scarlet fever, was published on the advice of the novelist G. J. Whyte-Melville, as *A Very Simple Story* (1867). It was illustrated by her first cousin, Sibyl Montgomery, marchioness of Queensbury (*d.* 1935), mother of Lord Alfred Douglas (1870–1945). Its morbidity is typical of Montgomery's later work, as is the fact that the central characters are children although the implied reader is an adult.

Montgomery's breakthrough was with her third work, *Misunderstood* (1869), whose preface states (p. v): 'The following is not a child's story. It is intended for those who are interested in children.' It is the story of Humphrey Duncombe, whose widowed father thinks him naughty and thoughtless, but whose high spirits conceal deep thoughts and yearning for the love of the father and the dead mother. There is just time for the father to appreciate how wrong he has been before the boy's heart-rending death. This book remained in print throughout her life, and her later fiction appeared as 'by the author of *Misunderstood*'. A notorious tear-jerker, it invites the reader to identify with the neglected child who makes the grown-ups feel guilty. Such stories, Montgomery made clear in the preface to *Thrown together* (2 vols., 1872), were not suitable for children to read as she was obliged 'to side, as it were, with the children against the parents'. Nothing so dangerous happens in *The Children with the Indian Rubber Ball: a Little Story for Children* (1872), a rather sternly moralistic tale about a little girl on holiday by the seaside, which was addressed to children, and later collected with others in *The Town-Crier* (1874). *Moral Tales for Children* (1886) is preceded by a note that: 'The Author is anxious to distinguish between her Stories *about* Children and her Stories *for*

Children.' By the same token *Wild Mike and his Victim* (1875), one of the 'waif' stories popular in the seventies, is prefaced with the statement: 'The Following Story is not a continuation of the "Town Crier Series", nor is it intended for children.' *Seaforth* (1878) was one of several full-length novels for adults with romance plots; its heroine begins as the lonely unwanted child of a noble house. *The Fisherman's Daughter* (1889) is the story of a spoilt girl who becomes a fashionable dressmaker, and *Colonel Norton* (1895) is about the transformation of a frivolous orphan into a virtuous wife.

Montgomery's fiction is markedly pious in tone, and its usual setting is fashionable society. Though the comforts of the rich are often contrasted with the privations of the very poor, one of Montgomery's favourite types is the society lady who is also a ministering angel and a paragon of both virtue and charm, like the heroine's mother in *A Very Simple Story* or the duchess of Grinstead in *A Fisherman's Daughter*. An important theme is the neglect of some of the children of the rich, and the feelings of those, such as the hero of *Misunderstood* or the heroine of *Seaforth*, who are disliked by one or both parents. Towards the end of her career an undercurrent of animosity against the modern young woman emerges, for example Lady Jane Marton in *Tony: a Sketch* (1898), a hard, selfish, bicycling creature, who rediscovers her femininity by saving the life of a schoolboy she meets on a train.

Montgomery's correspondence with Macmillans, her publishers during the latter part of her life, indicates the considerable currency of her books well into the twentieth century, and that almost all of them had been translated into German and French, and some also into Italian, Dutch, and Russian. In an undated letter she says, 'I have no answer from the applicant for the "film rights" of "Misunderstood"' (BL, Add. MS 54955, fol. 110). I have not, however, traced any film version of any of her works earlier than Jerry Schatzberg's *Misunderstood* (MGM/United Artists, 1984).

Montgomery's nephew, Sir Hughe Montgomery Knatchbull-Hugessen (1886–1971), implies in his memoirs that his aunts led unusually sheltered and circumscribed lives. Some of Montgomery's energy was devoted to charitable work among the London poor. Aged thirteen, in 1856, she moved with her family to 56 Cadogan Place, Belgravia, London. This house (in which her father and mother both died) was her home, and that of her two unmarried sisters, for sixty-seven years until she herself died there, of breast cancer, on 8 October 1923. She was buried on 12 October at Brompton cemetery, London.

CHARLOTTE MITCHELL

Sources *The Times* (1 Feb 1909), 1 · *The Times* (17 March 1909), 13 · *The Times* (15 June 1888), 5 · *The Times* (11 Oct 1923), 1 · *The Times* (13 Oct 1923), 15 · *Boyle's Court Guide* · GM, 2nd ser., 19 (1843), 197 · Burke, *Peerage* (1921) · BL, Add. MS 54955 · H. M. Knatchbull-Hugessen, *Diplomat in peace and war* (1949) · E. Baskin and M. Hicken, eds., *Enser's filmed books and plays, 1928–1991* (1993) · WW · IGI · b. cert.
Archives BL, letters to Bentley, Add. MSS 46625, 59631 · BL, corresp. with Macmillans, Add. MS 54955

Wealth at death £23,180 16s. 6d.: probate, 14 Jan 1924, *CGPLA Eng. & Wales*

Montgomery, George (1569/70–1621), Church of Ireland bishop of Meath and Clogher, was the second son of Adam Montgomery, laird of Braidstane, Ayrshire, while his mother was a daughter (whose name is unrecorded) of John Montgomery, laird of Hazlehead. He was born in 1569 or 1570, if one may judge from an inscription on his tomb, which stated that he died at fifty-one years of age in early 1621. His brother Hugh became the laird of Braidstane and first Viscount Montgomery of the Great Ardes, in Ulster. On the eve of the accession of James VI of Scotland to the English throne George Montgomery was the rector of Chedzoy, Somerset. He had married his first wife, Susan Steynings (d. 1614), a member of a local gentry family, in 1597. They were to be survived by a daughter called Jane.

James I had not been in London long when he appointed Montgomery as one of his chaplains. It has been suggested that this promotion was a reward for his communicating news from the English royal court to his brother Adam in the Scottish royal court in Elizabeth's final days. The king also promoted him to the deanery of Norwich, in which he was installed on 7 June 1603 and which he held until his resignation therefrom on 20 September 1614. Montgomery 'resided much at court' in the first years of James's reign in England (*Montgomery Manuscripts*, 20). According to later testimony from his daughter, the Church of Ireland archbishop of Armagh and some other of his colleagues in Ireland employed Montgomery as their agent at court. It seems to have been at their suggestion that James I appointed him bishop of the Ulster dioceses of Derry, Raphoe, and Clogher on 15 February 1605.

Montgomery was sent to Ireland to survey the condition of the Catholic church in his three dioceses and to make recommendations to the king as to how it might be transformed into a protestant establishment. His work was thorough and systematic. It formed the basis for the creation of the new Church of Ireland in western and central Ulster. Montgomery was zealous in his efforts to recover the church's ancient patrimony from the local Irish nobility and English servitors alike. He had already succeeded in forcing Sir Cahir O'Doherty to recognize his title to certain church lands in Inishowen, co. Donegal, before O'Doherty rebelled in April 1608 and sacked the colonial settlement at Derry. Montgomery's house was looted and his library was destroyed by the rebels. His wife was detained as a hostage for three months by the Irish before being released. O'Doherty's failed rebellion, following the flight of the earls of Tyrone and Tyrconnell to mainland Europe, prompted James I to embark on the plantation of Ulster.

Montgomery was given a commission to assist in the survey and demarcation of the plantation estates. This put him in a strong position to represent the church's interests in the plantation project. Crucially, he managed to secure the *erenagh* lands, episcopal lands held by paraclerical tenants, for the Church of Ireland bishops despite attempts to classify them as 'monastic' lands forfeited to the crown. By the summer of 1610 the plans for the Ulster plantation were almost finalized. However, Montgomery's insistence on recovering the island of Derry for the church brought him into conflict with the crown, which intended to make Derry the chief British stronghold in Ulster. James I obliged the bishop to resign from Derry and Raphoe, after making a composition with the crown whereby he ceded the church's title to the island of Derry in return for a royal charter confirming his title to the remainder of the church's patrimony in Derry diocese. As a reward for his instrumental role in the establishment of the Church of Ireland in Ulster the king made him bishop of Meath, a diocese in the most Anglicized and prosperous part of Ireland. He was allowed to retain Clogher, an extensive but poor diocese, *in commendam*.

Montgomery built a new episcopal residence at Ardbraccan, co. Meath, the chief manor of his predecessors in Meath diocese. He re-roofed the local parish church, but it does not appear that he was an overly zealous pastor. He was often absent. The royal visitation of Meath diocese in 1622 implies that the churches there were in far worse order shortly after his death than they had been seven years earlier. He had failed, too, to increase the church's resident, let alone its preaching, ministry.

Montgomery arranged for his daughter to marry Nicholas St Lawrence, Lord Howth and one of the leading noblemen of the pale in Ireland, in 1615. He settled £3000 sterling on her as a marriage portion—a 'great burden', as he was to acknowledge to a brother-in-law. He married Elizabeth (d. 1639), daughter of Edward Brabazon, baron of Ardee, some time after the death of his first wife. Elizabeth, in turn, remarried after the bishop's death.

According to the late seventeenth-century Montgomery manuscripts Montgomery commended James Ussher to James I, and the king was persuaded by his 'black Ireland bishop' that Ussher should succeed him in co. Meath (*Montgomery Manuscripts*, 107). Bishop George Montgomery died in Westminster on 15 January 1621. In accordance with his will his body was sent to Ireland to be interred beside his first wife in the vault he had constructed within the parish church at Ardbraccan, co. Meath.

HENRY A. JEFFERIES

Sources *The Montgomery manuscripts*, ed. J. Macknight (1830) · W. C. Trevelyan and C. E. Trevelyan, eds., *Trevelyan papers*, pt 3, CS, 105 (1872) · *CSP Ire.*, 1603–25 · T. F. Colby, ed., *Ordnance survey of the county of Londonderry: parish of Templemore* (1837) · A. F. O'D. Alexander, ed., 'The O'Kane papers', *Analecta Hibernica*, 12 (1943), 67–127 · 'Bishop Montgomery's survey of the parishes of Derry diocese', ed. H. A. Jefferies, *Seanchas Ardmhacha*, 17 (1996–7), 44–76 · visitation report, 1615, TCD, MS 566 · visitation report, 1622, TCD, MS 550 · T. W. Moody and J. G. Simms, eds., *The bishopric of Derry and the Irish Society of London, 1602–1705*, 2 vols., IMC (1968–83), vol. 1 · J. C. Erck, ed., *A repertory of the inrolments on the patent rolls of chancery in Ireland, commencing with the reign of James I*, 1/1 (1846) · H. A. Jefferies, 'George Montgomery, first protestant bishop of Derry, Raphoe and Clogher (1605–1610)', *History of the diocese of Derry*, ed. H. A. Jefferies and K. Devlin (1999) · A. Ford, *The protestant Reformation in Ireland, 1590–1641*, 2nd edn (1997)

Archives TCD, accounts of dioceses of Clogher, Derry, and Raphoe

Likenesses portrait, *c.*1606–1620, Clogher Cathedral, Clogher, Northern Ireland

Montgomery, Henry (1788–1865), a founder of the Remonstrant Synod of Ulster, was born on 16 January 1788 at Boltnaconnel House, Killead, co. Antrim, the fifth son and youngest child of Archibald Montgomery, lieutenant in the volunteers, and his wife, Sarah, daughter of William Campbell of Killealy, Killead. He was educated at the Crumlin Academy by the Revd Nathaniel Alexander and entered Glasgow University in November 1804, graduating MA in 1807. In the following year (1808) he returned to Glasgow for a year's study of divinity. He was licensed by the Templepatrick presbytery on 5 February 1809. In May he was a candidate for the pulpit at Donegore, but, refusing to subscribe to the Westminster confession of faith, was unsuccessful. His chief opponent of later years within the synod of Ulster, Henry Cooke (1788–1868), was the successful candidate. On 9 July he received a call from the congregation of Dunmurry, near Belfast, and was ordained there by the Bangor presbytery on 14 September as successor to Andrew George Malcolm. In this charge he remained until his death.

From the beginning of his settlement at Dunmurry, Montgomery engaged in tuition. Shortly after his marriage on 6 April 1812 to Elizabeth (1794–1872), fourth daughter of Hugh Swan and his wife, Lilian (*née* Dickey) of Summerhill near Antrim, Montgomery took up residence at The Glebe, Dunmurry, and, from 1815 boarded pupils in his house. On 3 October 1817 he was elected headmaster, in succession to James Knowles, of the English school in the Belfast Academical Institution, his congregation agreeing that he should reside there. He had just declined an invitation, made through Archibald Hamilton Rowan, to preach on trial at Killyleagh, co. Down, the charge to which Henry Cooke was subsequently elected. He held the mastership until June 1839 and exercised great influence, teaching the children of all Presbyterian ministers without fee.

Montgomery was strongly influenced by his family's support of the United Irishmen (two brothers, William and John having been at the battle of Antrim, and the family home having been destroyed by the yeomanry), and this undoubtedly led him to defend the former United Irishman Dr William Steele Dickson during his first major debate in the General Synod of Ulster in 1813. In 1816 Montgomery was a candidate for the clerkship of synod, but withdrew in favour of William Porter (1774–1843) of Newtownlimavady, co. Londonderry. At the unusually early age of thirty he was elected moderator of the general synod on 30 June 1818.

A strong supporter of the whig interest in politics, Montgomery also maintained a staunchly liberal position in theology. Synodial acts of 1698 and 1705 required candidates for the ministry to subscribe to the Westminster confession of faith, but by the end of the eighteenth century these were largely ignored. Ten of the fourteen presbyteries treated subscription as optional, and the differences between them and the presbytery of Antrim, founded in 1725 on the principle of non-subscription,

Henry Montgomery (1788–1865), by John Prescott Knight, exh. RA 1846

were widely disregarded. Montgomery advocated the continuation of this position. He described the synod at the time of his ordination as

> an assembly of Christian freemen … where amid the variety of creeds there was unity of spirit … I gloried in the name Presbyterian and rejoiced in my church … where the Bible was the only standard of faith and the conscience of man was free. (*Irish Unitarian Magazine*, 1847, 353)

Henry Cooke found this liberalism intolerable, and determined to enforce unqualified subscription.

In 1815 classes at the Belfast Academical Institution had been recognized by the synod as appropriate for the training of its students. Montgomery, a staunch supporter of the institution, was clearly allied to those liberals or non-subscribers who exercised strong influence there. In 1821 William Bruce was appointed to the chair of Greek and Hebrew. He was a well-known liberal and self-confessed Arian, joint minister of the First Presbyterian Church, Belfast, and a member of the non-subscribing presbytery of Antrim. Cooke was incensed, believing that the value of these classes would be undermined and future generations of ministers rendered theologically and politically suspect. Thus began his crusade against liberalism in all its forms. Henry Montgomery became his chief opponent.

The non-subscribing principle had many supporters. Cooke determined to isolate and discredit the Arians among them by emphasizing belief in the doctrine of the Trinity. Montgomery responded in a notable speech on Christian liberty, delivered before the synod at Strabane in 1827, in which he advocated religious tolerance without compulsory subscription to any creed. Leading news-papers in Ireland and London published the speech, and 30,000 copies were circulated. Montgomery was presented with a service of plate, costing over £600, by inhabitants of Belfast and the adjoining counties, representing various denominations including Roman Catholics. The address which accompanied it referred to his 'manly, honest and talented efforts' in the cause of theological toleration.

Cooke, having isolated the Arians, realized however that he could not expel the many other non-subscribers from the General Synod of Ulster, and so adopted a policy which would ensure that non-subscribers would never be ordained in the future. Montgomery protested against what he called the 'heart searching committee' set up to investigate students by the synod of 1828. Despite his outstanding eloquence, and a speech which lasted three hours, Montgomery could not overturn this decision. On 16 October 1828 he and his friends adopted a 'Remonstrance' at a meeting of Presbyterians, held in the meeting-house of the Second Congregation in Belfast, and attended by Cooke. The last of Montgomery's outstanding speeches in the general synod was delivered at Lurgan on 3 July 1829. The Remonstrance was presented at a special meeting of synod, held at Cookstown on 18 August, and terms of separation were agreed at a conference on 8 September. The first meeting of the Remonstrant Synod of Ulster was held on 25 May 1830. It consisted of three presbyteries, containing seventeen congregations, and retained the 1824 code of discipline. Its ministers were secured in the possession of the *regium donum*.

When the Remonstrants were derided as 'a body of avowed Arians, driven from the Synod of Ulster' Montgomery challenged the remark as untrue: 'So far from being a body of avowed Arians', he said:

> we have constantly disavowed any such bond of union: and we were not expelled from the Synod of Ulster. Many ministers holding our religious views are still members of that body, and had we been so inclined we could have remained in it until this hour. (Crozier, *Life*, 592–3)

This debate continued outside the synod. In 1841 Montgomery successfully opposed Cooke's endeavour to exclude Arian professors from the Belfast Academical Institution. He also led the campaign to remove legal disabilities from non-Trinitarian dissenters, and again defeated Cooke's endeavours. The Dissenters Chapels Act of 1844 resolved the issue: Sir Robert Peel asserted that the passing of the act was largely due to Montgomery's efforts.

Montgomery's politics, like his theology, invited Cooke's opposition. 'Our opponents', he said:

> raised against us the cry of heresy and when this unjust accusation failed, they truly and more injuriously branded us as Catholic Emancipators. Certain fanatics had the ingenuity to identify Orthodoxy with Orangeism, and thus to array against us the most powerful engines of hostility; religious bigotry and political intolerance. (Crozier, *Life*)

As a staunch supporter of Catholic emancipation, Montgomery travelled to England, where he was influential in achieving this reform. It was a cause to which he was 'zealously attached' on the grounds of 'political right, religious liberty and love of country' (ibid., 534). On his return to Ireland he was hailed by the Roman Catholic community and accepted an invitation to speak from the altar in St Patrick's Roman Catholic Church in Belfast. He was also guest of honour at a public dinner and was toasted by Dr William Crolly, Roman Catholic bishop of Down and Connor and later archbishop of Armagh, who spoke of him as:

> a man of distinguished talents who has long been regarded as the champion of civil and religious liberty … a gentleman who has done more service to our cause in his late visit to our sister country than the whole deputation of the Catholic body could have effected. (*Northern Whig*, 29 Jan 1829, Supplement)

At Montgomery's insistence the Remonstrant Synod of Ulster petitioned parliament in 1845 in favour of an increased grant to the college at Maynooth.

These actions encouraged Daniel O'Connell to believe that Montgomery and the Remonstrants would support his movement for the repeal of the union. He was mistaken. Montgomery replied: 'I am no wild innovator. I wish not to see the constitution overthrown' (*Northern Whig*, 6 Dec 1830). It was his constant theme that the friends of reform were the enemies of revolution. Montgomery's stand alienated many Irish liberals from O'Connell's cause. But Montgomery's liberal views embraced many causes. Three articles in the *Northern Whig* written by him in 1829–30 foreshadowed the later tenant right movement. His sympathies also extended to Jewish disabilities, the Irish famine, the marriage laws, the poor laws, and many social concerns connected with the city of Belfast.

In 1835 the Association of Irish Non-Subscribing Presbyterians was founded. This consisted of the Remonstrant Synod of Ulster, the presbytery of Antrim, and the synod of Munster. Dr Montgomery (he had received the degree of LLD from Glasgow University in 1832) was appointed the association's professor of ecclesiastical history and pastoral theology on 10 July 1838. The office was without salary until 1847, when the government endowed the chair with £150 per annum from the *regium donum*.

In appearance Montgomery was a giant of 6 feet 4 inches in height, and built in proportion; he was given the nickname long Harry by his students. He had fair hair and grey penetrating eyes. His dress was always immaculate. A portrait shows a carefully arranged cravat with a diamond breast-pin, watch-ribbon and seal, silk knee-breeches, an ebony walking-stick, and tassled hessian boots reaching almost to the knees. As an orator he was unsurpassed. Cooke said of him 'he is one of the most eloquent men of any age. He has more command of the English language than any man I know of' (*Non-Subscribing Presbyterian*, May 1958, 69). His major speeches were always delivered extemporaneously, though transcriptions in the press seem often to have been edited by him. An original editor of the *Bible Christian* with Fletcher Blakely, he also contributed 'Outlines of the history of Irish Presbyterianism' to the *Irish Unitarian Magazine* in 1846–7. His theological opinion was firmly stated in 'The creed of an Arian' published in 1830. Shortly before his death he wrote of this: 'It is the belief that has been the support and guide of my own heart through the passage of life, as it is that which imparts to me now, unutterable peace and strength in the presence of death' (*Northern Whig*, 11 May 1870).

In later years Montgomery opposed radical theological tendencies among his own students. To curb these 'wild irresponsible spirits' he inserted certain theological questions into the Remonstrant Synod's new code of discipline of 1857 which led to bitter controversy and the secession of several congregations from the synod. It also divided the presbytery of Antrim. Maligned by former friends, he was also scorned by Cooke for 'manufacturing a little creed of his own' (*Belfast News-Letter*, 4 Sept 1858). He defended his position by claiming that genuine Christian liberty was not 'licence to believe or disbelieve the great truths of the Gospel'. The controversy continued until his death and caused him great sadness. Of his family of four sons and six daughters, five predeceased him, and a trying illness caused by renal calculus precipitated his death on 18 December 1865 at The Glebe, Dunmurry. He was buried on 20 December in the graveyard attached to his meeting-house at Dunmurry; the funeral was attended by his old adversary, Henry Cooke. Following his death, in recognition of his services as an advocate of civil and religious liberty, the government settled a pension of £100 per annum on his widow.   WILLIAM MCMILLAN

Sources J. A. Crozier, *The life of the Rev. H. Montgomery LLD* (1875) · J. A. Crozier, *Henry Montgomery LLD* (1888) · *DNB* · R. Allen, 'Henry Montgomery', *Essays in British and Irish history in honour of James Eadie Todd*, ed. H. A. Cronne, T. W. Moody, and D. B. Quinn (1949) · F. Holmes, *Henry Cooke* (1981) · W. McMillan, *A profile in courage* (1965) · W. McMillan, 'The subscription controversy in Irish Presbyerianism', MA diss., University of Manchester, 1958 · private information (2004) · C. Porter, *Irish Presbyterian biographical sketches* (1883) · minutes of General Synod of Ulster and Remonstrant Synod · *Christian Unitarian* (Jan 1866) · minute book, Dunmurry Presbyterian Congregation · *Belfast News-Letter* (1788–1865) · *Northern Whig* (1788–1865) · *Irish Unitarian Magazine* (1847)
Archives Non-Subscribing Presbyterian Church of Ireland, synod records | BL, corresp. with Sir Robert Peel, Add. MSS 40531–40600
Likenesses engraving, 1845, repro. in Crozier, *Life* · J. P. Knight, oils, exh. RA 1846, priv. coll. [*see illus.*] · J. P. Knight, oils, priv. coll. · pastels, session room, Dunmurry
Wealth at death under £3000: probate, 8 Jan 1866, *CGPLA Ire.*

Montgomery, Henry (1847–1943), minister of the Presbyterian Church in Ireland and evangelist, was born in Bangor, co. Down, Ireland, on 12 October 1847. After education in the town, he worked with his brother in Belfast during the 1870s. His decision to train for the Presbyterian ministry was influenced by the visit in September 1874 of the American evangelists Dwight L. Moody and Ira D. Sankey. While studying at Queen's College, Belfast, Montgomery became interested in the work of the Belfast Town (from 1895 City) Mission. This had begun in 1827 as an interdenominational mission aimed at the large number of workers flooding into Belfast to seek employment in the expanding textile industry. The mission appointed agents to visit the poor in their homes, distribute tracts, and invite them to attend church and Sunday school. It also established 'stations' visited by local clergy two evenings a week for Bible reading and tract distribution. As a student, Montgomery worked at the mission's hall in McClure Street. The Belfast Town Mission, which after 1843 was a Presbyterian organization, undoubtedly provided Montgomery with a model for his later mission work on the Shankill Road. He continued his connection with the Town Mission for the rest of his life, serving as its honorary secretary from 1897 until his death forty-six years later.

Montgomery was ordained in August 1882 and took charge of the Albert Street congregation as its fourth successive minister. This congregation had been formed in the early 1850s as a result of the work of the Town Mission. Running between the Falls Road and Durham Street, Albert Street bordered the area known as The Pound, where Catholics from Divis Street and the Falls had regularly clashed with the protestants of Sandy Row and the Shankill since the 1830s. Montgomery's church was thus located on one of nineteenth-century Belfast's bitterest sectarian fault lines. The 1886 anti-home rule riots, the worst of the century, soon acquainted Montgomery with the violence that was endemic to the Albert Street area.

The Albert Street Church had been erected in 1854 by the congregation's first minister, John Browne Wilson. After taking charge of the congregation, Montgomery immediately set about building a larger church, which was opened in 1884, and establishing a mission hall in Percy Street, which was opened in 1889. The population of the area had grown rapidly since the 1850s, spurred by the development of heavy industry in Belfast. Many in Montgomery's congregation worked in the linen mills, foundries, engineering works, and distilleries that were scattered around the western edge of the town centre, and many had recently migrated to Belfast from the Ulster countryside. Montgomery sought to preserve and revive the faith among this dislocated working class. He criticized the rich for ignoring the spiritual and material needs of such people, warning in 1895: 'if we do not reach the masses, the masses will reach us, and in a way some may not like' (Murray, 30).

To further his mission work, Montgomery established the Shankill Road Mission in a tent in spring 1896. With money raised by his congregation, he was able to build the Albert Hall on the site in 1898, with a capacity for 2000 people. Holiday homes for Belfast women and children were subsequently opened by Montgomery on the co. Down coast. At first he carried on his evangelical work in conjunction with his congregational duties. But in September 1902, wishing to devote all his time to the mission, he resigned the charge of Albert Street. The Belfast presbytery approved this step and placed the mission under the care of the presbytery's church extension committee. But, within five years, his efforts had been so successful that he decided he wanted to raise the mission to the status of an organized congregation. A committee of the general assembly gave permission for this step in 1907, on condition that Montgomery be installed as the first minister and that future ministers be directly selected by the Belfast presbytery. The new congregation was officially organized on 10 July 1907, designated the Shankill Road Mission, and Montgomery was installed on 24 September 1907.

By 1912 the congregation had increased to 500 families. In that same year Montgomery was elected to the moderatorship of the general assembly and received the degree of doctor of divinity from the Presbyterian Theological Faculty.

Montgomery retired from the ministry in April 1924, but continued to superintend the evangelical work of the Shankill Mission until January 1936. His wife, who had borne him thirteen children, several of whom became overseas missionaries, died in 1937 at the age of eighty-one. Montgomery died on 17 February 1943 at his son's home, 56 Osborne Park, Belfast, and, after a funeral service at the Albert Hall, was buried in the city cemetery on 19 February 1943.   ELIZABETH MALCOLM

Sources R. M. Sibbett, *For Christ and crown: the story of a mission* (1926) · S. W. Murray, *The City Mission story* (1977) · *A history of congregations in the Presbyterian Church in Ireland, 1610–1982*, Presbyterian Church in Ireland (1982) · J. E. Davey, *The story of a hundred years, 1840–1940* (1940) · D. Hempton and M. Hill, *Evangelical protestantism in Ulster society, 1740–1890* (1992) · A. Jordan, *Who cared? Charity in Victorian and Edwardian Belfast* [1993] · A. Boyd, *Holy war in Belfast* (1969) · J. Bardon, *Belfast: an illustrated history* (1982) · *Belfast News-Letter* (18–19 Feb 1943) · E. Corkey, *David Corkey* [1926] · *CGPLA Ire.* (1943)
Likenesses photograph, repro. in Davey, *Story of a hundred years*, facing p. 69
Wealth at death £5045 4s. 7d.: probate, 20 May 1943, *CGPLA NIre.*

Montgomery, Sir Henry Conyngham, second baronet

(1803–1878), administrator in India, was born in Donegal, Ireland, on 10 March 1803, the eldest son of Sir Henry Conyngham Montgomery, first baronet (d. 1830), and his wife, Sarah Mercer (d. 1854), daughter of Leslie Grove of Grove Hall, Donegal. His father was a cavalry officer in India, and was created a baronet in 1808. Montgomery was educated at Eton College and at the East India College, Haileybury, to which institution he was nominated as a student on 1 August 1821. He was permitted to leave Haileybury early in 1822 for the purpose of serving as assistant private secretary on the staff of Lord Wellesley, who was at that time lord lieutenant of Ireland. Early in 1824 he returned to Haileybury, passing through the college at the end of that year.

In 1825 Montgomery proceeded to India, reaching Madras on 3 November. It was customary then for young civil servants to remain for two years at the presidency town, studying Indian languages. Montgomery was therefore not appointed to the public service until 16 January 1827, when he was gazetted assistant to the principal collector and magistrate of Nellore. On 3 March 1827 he married Leonora (d. 1889), daughter of General Richard Pigot, and on 31 January 1830 he succeeded his father as second baronet. He subsequently served in various grades of the revenue department in several different districts, completing his revenue service in the provinces as collector of Tanjore. In all these districts he had made his mark as an able administrator, and in 1843 he was sent on a special commission to Rajamundry district to inquire into the causes of its impoverished condition. It was on his recommendation, based upon his experience in Tanjore, that Captain Arthur Cotton was deputed to Rajamundry to investigate the question of utilizing the waters of the Godavari River for a large-scale deltaic irrigation project. This project, together with parallel works on the adjacent Kistna River, were to transform the region into a rice-bowl for southern India.

Montgomery's report and recommendations on the condition of the Rajamundry district elicited high commendation from the government of Madras, and two years later he was selected by the marquess of Tweeddale to fill a vacancy in the government secretariat. He served as secretary to government in the revenue and public works departments until 1850, when he was promoted to the chief secretaryship. In 1855 he was appointed by the court of directors a member of the Madras legislative council, which post he held until 1857, when, his health failing, he returned to England, and in the course of that year resigned his appointment and retired from the East India Company service. In the following year, on the establishment of the Council of India in London, Montgomery was appointed to be one of the first members of the new council, and this position he retained until 1876, when he finally retired from official life. On the occasion of his retirement he was sworn of the privy council, an honour which was very rarely conferred upon Indian civil servants.

Montgomery's official career was eminently successful. He was regarded as one of the ablest district officers in the Madras presidency. He certainly had the advantage of possessing influential friends. Lord Wellesley had formed a high opinion of him when he worked in Dublin in the lord lieutenant's private office, and did not fail to exert his influence on his behalf. Sir John Malcolm was also a kind friend to him. But he fully justified their recommendations. By his report upon the Rajamundry district, and by the recommendations which he made for improving its condition, he helped to confer a major benefit on southern India. In the higher posts which he subsequently filled in Madras, as secretary and chief secretary to government and member of council, he maintained his previous reputation. During his long service in the Council of India, extending over eighteen years, he was highly esteemed both by successive secretaries of state and by his colleagues in the council. He maintained a studied independence of view and was not afraid to dissent from the decisions of the secretary of state and the majority of the council. He retained to the last a keen interest in the presidency in which the whole of his Indian service had been passed and advocated its claims strongly. He helped to obtain sanction for the Madras harbour project, in spite of its costs and lack of returns on government investments. On political questions concerning the south of India he was an authority. When the nawab of the Carnatic died in 1858, Montgomery supported Lord Harris in advocating the extinction of the titular nawabship. But he was not opposed in principle to the maintenance of Indian dynasties. In 1863 he wrote a cogent minute dissenting from the refusal of the secretary of state in council to restore to the raja of Mysore the administration of that state. The policy which on this occasion Montgomery opposed had been supported by two successive governors-general, the marquess of Dalhousie and Earl Canning, but was subsequently reversed.

Montgomery died suddenly at his home, 5 Manchester Square, London, on 24 June 1878. He left no children, and was succeeded as third baronet by his brother Admiral Sir Alexander Leslie Montgomery (1807–1888).

A. J. ARBUTHNOT, rev. DAVID WASHBROOK

Sources F. Hemingway, *Godaveri District Gazetteer* (1909) · Burke, *Peerage* (1939) · personal knowledge (1901) · private information (1901) · *CGPLA Eng. & Wales* (1878)
Archives CUL, Mayo MSS
Wealth at death under £14,000: probate, 17 July 1878, *CGPLA Eng. & Wales*

Henry Hutchinson Montgomery (1847–1932), by George Charles Beresford, 1902

Montgomery, Henry Hutchinson (1847–1932), bishop of Tasmania and missionary society administrator, was born on 3 October 1847 at Cawnpore, Uttar Pradesh, India, the second of five children of Sir Robert *Montgomery (1809–1887), lieutenant-governor of the Punjab, and his second wife, Ellen Jane (1824–1920), daughter of William Lambert JP, an administrator in India. After an evangelical preparatory education he entered Harrow School in 1861 where he imbibed public-school athleticism as 'a real education for life' (M. Montgomery, 9). He matriculated at Trinity College, Cambridge in the autumn of 1866, graduated BA in 1869, and subsequently prepared for ordination in London under the conservative churchman Charles Vaughan, master of the Temple. Ordained deacon 1871 and priest in 1872, he was successively curate at Hurstpierpoint, Sussex (1871–4), Christ Church, Southwark, London (1874–6), and St Margaret's, Westminster (1876–9), and priest at St Mark's, Kennington (1879–89), where he was known for his comprehensive organization of the parish. At St Margaret's he associated closely with the popular author and broad church evangelical Canon (later Dean) Frederick William Farrar and became the intimate and secretary to the dean of Westminster, A. P. Stanley, sympathizing with his commitment to the ideal of a comprehensive national church. On 28 July 1881 he married Maud (1864–1949), Farrar's third daughter, who came to command the domestic affairs of the family; they had three daughters and six sons, the most notable being Bernard Law *Montgomery, the future field marshal and first Viscount Montgomery of Alamein.

Henry Montgomery was consecrated bishop of Tasmania on 1 May 1889 and took up residence in Hobart, throwing his considerable energy and visionary enthusiasm into diocesan reorganization and especially missionary work. While Montgomery nearly doubled the number of churches in his diocese, many of his other initiatives were frustrated by lay apathy, economic recession, and

party opposition from radical evangelicals who suspected him of ritualism. He nevertheless became an important advocate of invigorating colonial Anglicanism and extending its pan-imperial connections, particularly emphasizing global missionary co-operation in the Australian board of missions and synod. Because of his activism, in July 1901 he was appointed by a committee of six English bishops, led by his friend and Harrow schoolmate Randall Davidson of Winchester, to the secretaryship of the Society for the Propagation of the Gospel (SPG). Despite misgivings over abandoning his colonial bishopric, Montgomery became convinced of the importance of creating 'a sort of Foreign Office' for world Anglicanism at the SPG (circular letter, autumn 1901, Temple MSS, vol. 49, fols. 115–16).

Montgomery's impact at the SPG as a reformer was substantial. A traditional high-church society, the SPG did not cater to the party enthusiasms of either evangelicals or Anglo-Catholics. In order to dispel well-known lethargy at the SPG, Montgomery allied himself with progressive younger clergy and female supporters. Despite opposition from an 'old guard', he drew activists into a reorganized central administration, launched new publications, built a new society headquarters proximate to Church House in Westminster, emulated and co-operated with Anglican evangelicals, and established a new emphasis at the SPG on service to the British empire. Broad in his religious views, warm in his spirituality, and generous in his humour, Montgomery sought to recreate the Church of England as an 'Imperial Church' (Montgomery to SPG standing committee, 17 Aug 1901, Davidson MSS, vol. 151, fols. 322–3) in order to increase enthusiasm for foreign missions, remedy Anglican party factionalism, and reverse the decline of Anglican observance and ordination. As the archbishop of Canterbury's (Davidson) adviser on foreign missions, he proposed and led arrangements for the Pan-Anglican Congress of 1908. In 1902 Montgomery was made prebendary of St Paul's, in 1906 prelate of the Order of St Michael and St George, and a knight commander of the order in 1928. Under his guidance SPG incomes increased sharply, and the society gained a new reputation for innovation. Yet his more ambitious goal of creating imperial unity in the church was thwarted by the local preoccupations of Anglican clergy, differences within the communion over imperial methods and attitudes to race, and the re-emergence of tension between Anglican evangelicals and high-churchmen, especially following the 1913 Kikuyu Controversy in east Africa. In this final evangelical/high-church controversy of the pre-war period, in which the Anglo-Catholic bishop of Zanzibar accused the evangelical bishops of Mombasa and Uganda of heretically ecumenical associations with nonconformists, Montgomery retreated from an earlier ecumenism out of fear for the authority and distinctiveness of the Anglican communion.

Montgomery served the SPG with patriotic verve through the war years, and finally resigned the secretaryship in 1918, retiring in 1921 to the family property at New Park, Moville, co. Donegal. He spent his final decade in occasional church and SPG work, and writing. He died at New Park on 25 November 1932, and was buried in the Moville church cemetery on 30 November. His wife survived him.

Montgomery was the author of twenty-five books on theological or missionary subjects, most notably *The Light of Melanesia* (1896), *Foreign Missions* (1902), *Life's Journey* (1916), and *Life and Letters of George Alfred Lefroy* (1920).

STEVEN S. MAUGHAN

Sources M. M. [M. Montgomery], *Bishop Montgomery: a memoir* (1933) · B. Montgomery, *A field-marshal in the family: a personal biography of Montgomery of Alamein* (1973) · S. Maughan, 'Regions beyond and the national church: domestic support for the foreign missions of the Church of England in the high imperial age, 1870–1914', PhD diss., Harvard U., 1995 · B. Montgomery, *Monty's grandfather: Sir Robert Montgomery … a life's service for the raj* (1984) · G. Stephens, *H. H. Montgomery: the mutton bird bishop* (1985) · *The Times* (28 Nov 1932) · LPL, Frederick Temple MSS, vol. 49 · LPL, Randall Davidson MSS, vol. 151
Archives Bodl. RH, United Society for the Propagation of the Gospel archives, home series, especially classes H3 and H37 · Bodl. RH, United Society for the Propagation of the Gospel archives, miscellaneous (X) series copy letter-books, Montgomery X 366 and X 382 · diocesan registry, Hobart, Tasmania, diocesan letter-books | LPL, reports on Church of England in Australia and Tasmania, and corresp. with Randall Thomas Davidson, archbishop of Canterbury · LPL, corresp. with F. Temple
Likenesses photograph, 1895, NPG · G. C. Beresford, negative, 1902, NPG [*see illus.*] · photographs, 1907, Bodl. Oxf. · S. P. Hall, oils, 1915, Bodl. RH, United Society for the Propagation of the Gospel archives · photograph, *c.*1916, NPG · F. Salisbury, oils, 1932, priv. coll.
Wealth at death £2777 15*s*. 4*d*.: probate, 3 Oct 1933, *CGPLA Éire*

Montgomery, Hugh de, second earl of Shrewsbury

(*d.* 1098), magnate, was the third, but second surviving, son of Roger de *Montgomery (*d.* 1094), the first earl, and his first wife, Mabel de Bellême (*d.* 1077). A Welsh source (*Brenhinedd y Saesson*) calls Hugh 'Goch' ('the Red'). As the second son he was destined to inherit his father's acquisitions in England, and is accordingly found in Britain as early as 1074, when he laid waste Ceredigion during a raid

presumably launched from, or at any rate through, the region of Arwystli in central Wales. But Hugh was back in Normandy at least once in the Conqueror's reign, for in December 1077 it was he, and not one of his brothers, who pursued, vigorously but in vain, the men who had murdered his mother at Bures-sur-Dives. At Caen in the summer of 1080 Hugh attested a charter for Troarn. In England there is nothing to link him with his father's lordship in Sussex; but in 1086 he held of the king the large and lucrative manor of Worfield, then in Staffordshire but near two centres of his father's Shropshire power at Morville and Quatford. The annual value of Worfield was given as £18, a sum interestingly almost equal to the £18 5*s*. assigned to the support in prison of his brother Robert de *Bellême in the pipe roll of 1130, and thus apparently the level of maintenance required for the son of a substantial magnate. In 1088 Hugh may have been one of the sons of Earl Roger who supported Duke Robert Curthose against William Rufus. In 1092 Hugh was again in Normandy, involved as a peacemaker in a local feud.

Hugh de Montgomery succeeded his father as earl in July 1094. The way had been opened for the resumption of activity in south Wales by the death of Rhys ap Tewdwr in the previous year; but in 1094 Hugh had to fight the resurgent mid-Welsh, who the next year took Montgomery and slaughtered the garrison. Earl Hugh next comes to notice as a confederate of Robert de Mowbray in the latter's revolt against William Rufus of 1095; Orderic Vitalis, who alone mentions this, gives no details, except to say that Rufus spoke 'privately' with Hugh, and took him back into favour for £3000 (Ordericus Vitalis, *Eccl. hist.*, 4.284). Hugh was lucky. In Shropshire he continued to support his father's foundation of Shrewsbury Abbey: standing before his father's tomb, he issued a charter of liberties to the abbey; he further gave the abbey the tithe of the earl's hunting in the county, except for the woods of St Mildburg. A decline of comital interest in the south-east of the county may be inferred from Earl Hugh's gift of Quatford church to the abbey of La Sauve Majeure near Bordeaux.

In 1098 Hugh de Montgomery, with Hugh d'Avranches, earl of Chester ('the Brave' and 'the Stout', according to the *Heimskringla*), led a large expedition against the Welsh of Gwynedd (now more powerful than their neighbours to the south whom Hugh de Montgomery had raided more than twenty years before). Accounts of the events of the summer are muddled, but the two earls had no difficulty in putting the Welsh to flight and occupying Anglesey. However, Magnus Bareleg, king of Norway (son of Harald Hardrada), after forays in Hebridean waters, appeared with a large fleet. In Orderic's account it was the threat from Magnus which provoked the invasion by the two earls, but it seems clear from the sources as a whole that Hugh de Montgomery, after waiting—sensibly enough—at Deganwy for his fellow earl, pushed westwards towards Anglesey and met his death at the end of July off Aberlleiniog, near Beaumaris. He was struck in the right eye by an arrow or javelin, or some other missile, perhaps aimed by Magnus himself, and fell lifeless from his horse into the sea. His body was recovered with difficulty and taken back to Shrewsbury; in mid-August, seventeen days after his death, he was buried in the abbey. This death, followed by Hugh of Chester's retreat and death, set back the Norman penetration of Gwynedd beyond Conwy for over a century.

Hugh de Montgomery never married and was succeeded in his English lands and title by his eldest brother, Robert de Bellême. According to Orderic Vitalis, he was the only 'mild and lovable' (*mansuetus et amabilis*; Ordericus Vitalis, *Eccl. hist.*, 5.24) son of his mother, Mabel; Welsh writers leave no doubt of his cruelty towards their people, but this was natural enough. Hugh's knowledge of the politics, geography, and warfare of Wales was good; it is ironic that he was killed in an encounter with a chance Scandinavian intruder, whose concern was with neither Welsh lands nor Norman but with former Norwegian possessions, or even—according to Orderic—with an invasion of Ireland.

J. F. A. MASON

Sources Ordericus Vitalis, *Eccl. hist.* · T. Jones, ed. and trans., *Brut y tywysogyon, or, The chronicle of the princes: Red Book of Hergest* (1955) · T. Jones, ed. and trans., *Brut y tywysogyon, or, The chronicle of the princes: Peniarth MS 20* (1952) · T. Jones, ed. and trans., *Brenhinedd y Saesson, or, The kings of the Saxons* (1971) [another version of *Brut y tywysogyon*] · Snorri Sturluson, *Heimskringla, or, Chronicle of the kings of Norway*, ed. and trans. S. Laing (1844); 2nd edn (1889), vol. 3, pp. 129–33 · D. S. Evans, ed. and trans., *A mediaeval prince of Wales: the life of Gruffudd ap Cynan* (1990) [Eng. trans. of *Historia Gruffud vab Kenan*, with orig. Welsh text] · F. Barlow, *William Rufus* (1983) · GEC, *Peerage*, new edn

Montgomery [Montgomerie], **Hugh, first earl of Eglinton** (1460?–1545), magnate, was the eldest son of Alexander Montgomery, master of Montgomery (*c*.1445–1468) and his wife, Katherine Kennedy (*d*. in or after 1486), daughter of Gilbert, first Lord Kennedy. He succeeded his great-grandfather Alexander *Montgomery, first Lord Montgomery [*see under* Montgomery family], as a minor about 1470 and was infeft in the family estates on 5 June 1484, when he was said to be not yet twenty-four. Hugh married Helen Campbell (*b. c*.1460), third daughter of Colin, first earl of Argyll and James IV's first chancellor, at Dollar parish church on 21 April 1478. They had five sons and seven daughters: John, master of Eglinton and grandfather of Hugh, second earl of Eglinton; William, laird of Greenfield; Sir Neil, laird of Langshaw, Hugh, who was killed at the battle of Pinkie in 1547; Robert, first rector of Kirkmichael and bishop of Argyll; Margaret, first wife of William, second Lord Semple; Matilda, who married Colin Campbell of Ardkinglas; Isobel, married to John Mure of Caldwell; Helen, wife of John Blair of that ilk; Janet, who married George Campbell of Cessnock; Agnes, married to John Ker of Kersland; and Katherine, wife of George Montgomerie of Skelmorlie. Montgomery also had an illegitimate daughter, Janet.

In 1484 Montgomery murdered the fifteen-year-old James, second Lord Boyd. The violent streak in his personality also found an outlet in his family's contest with the Cunninghams for pre-eminence in north Ayrshire, by now some forty years old. On 11 June 1488 he fought with the rebels at the battle of Sauchieburn, where Alexander Cunningham, recently made earl of Glencairn by James

III, was killed, possibly by Montgomery himself. The latter was rewarded by the new king, James IV, with a remission for razing the Cunningham castle at Turnlaw in Lanarkshire, and in the following year received a commission, also directed against the Cunninghams, to repress crime in Ayrshire. In addition he had grants of crown lands in Arran and Bute, joined the lords of council, and was appointed constable of Rothesay Castle, bailie of Cunningham, and chamberlain of Irvine. When the Cunninghams resisted his authority as bailie Montgomery retaliated by personally killing Alexander's son Robert, second Lord Kilmaurs. Following Argyll's death in 1493 and the succession of the earl of Angus as chancellor, Montgomery's influence in Ayrshire diminished to the extent that following the king's act of revocation of 1498 he was willing to contract his eldest son to marry Elizabeth, the daughter of Sir Archibald Edmonstone, a royal favourite, and pay a composition of £1666 13*s*. 4*d*., in order to be confirmed in the supposedly hereditary office of bailie of Cunningham. He was appointed to a royal commission to set lands in the lordship of the Isles in April 1500, and was created earl of Eglinton between 3 and 20 January 1506. Following the king's death at Flodden, he attended the Stirling parliament, preceding James V's coronation, where he was elected to council. He acted as an ambassador to London in February 1515.

The Montgomerys and Cunninghams continued to pursue their vendetta throughout James V's minority with frequent violence, the duke of Albany as governor seeking unsuccessfully to pacify the feud by arranging a marriage between the master of Glencairn's heir and a Montgomery, in decreet arbitrals of 22 May 1517 and 13 March 1524. The master of Eglinton was killed on 30 April 1520 in the battle fought on the High Street of Edinburgh called Cleanse the Causeway. In the summer of 1526 Eglinton and his son Neil were outlawed for the murder of Edward Cunningham of Auchenharvie, though later acquitted. On 2 February 1527 the earl was appointed justice-general of the northern parts of Scotland and in June 1528 joined James V at Stirling, after the latter's escape from the Douglases. On 28 May the lords of council had ordered Eglinton to pay Glencairn £1000 for breaking the 1524 decreet, but he failed to pay, prompting the master of Glencairn to burn Eglinton Castle in November, destroying the family charters in the process, though the king made good this loss with a new charter of the lands on 23 January 1529. On 18 August 1533 the earl of Bothwell, as great-admiral of Scotland, appointed Eglinton admiral-depute within the bounds of Cunningham. During the king's absence in France in 1536–7 to bring home his bride, Princess Madeleine, he acted as a member of the council of regency and in August 1540 he sat on the assize which condemned Sir James Hamilton of Finnart. He died between 23 September and 3 October 1545 and was buried at Kilwinning Abbey, Ayrshire.

JOHN SIMMONS

Sources Eglinton muniments, NA Scot., GD3 · W. Fraser, *Memorials of the Montgomeries, earls of Eglinton*, 2 vols. (1859) · R. K. Hannay, ed., *Acts of the lords of council in public affairs, 1501–1554* (1932) · APS, 1424–1567 · M. Livingstone, D. Hay Fleming, and others, eds.,

Registrum secreti sigilli regum Scotorum / *The register of the privy seal of Scotland*, 1 (1908) · GEC, *Peerage*, new edn, 5.17–18; 9.134–5 · *Scots peerage*, vol. 3 · N. Macdougall, *James IV* (1989) · J. M. Thomson and others, eds., *Registrum magni sigilli regum Scotorum* / *The register of the great seal of Scotland*, 11 vols. (1882–1914), vols. 2–3 · *RotS*, vol. 2 · J. Cameron, *James V: the personal rule, 1528–1542*, ed. N. Macdougall (1998) · G. Burnett and others, eds., *The exchequer rolls of Scotland*, 9–18 (1886–98)

Wealth at death left 2500 marks in gold: Fraser, *Memorials* 2.132

Montgomery [Montgomerie]**, Hugh, third earl of Eglinton** (1531?–1585), nobleman, was the eldest son of Hugh Montgomery, second earl of Eglinton (*c*.1510–1546), and his wife, Marion Seton (*c*.1515–1558×61), daughter of George, third Lord Seton. He was probably born in 1531 and was not yet sixteen when he succeeded to the earldom following his father's death on 3 September 1546. In 1552 he enrolled with his brother William as a student in St Mary's College at the University of St Andrews. In February 1554 he married Jean Hamilton (*c*.1535–1596), daughter of James, duke of Châtelherault (previously third earl of Arran), in accordance with a marriage contract dated 13 February. Eglinton, though strongly Catholic, initially followed his father-in-law's political lead and was among the nobles who gathered in Edinburgh in October 1559 to depose Mary of Guise as regent and elect a protestant council. However, Eglinton's marital problems soon soured his relations with Châtelherault and by February 1560 he was reported to be 'wholly addicted unto the Queen in this cause' (*CSP Scot.*, *1547–63*, 321). Though he attended the parliament at Stirling in June the English ambassador remarked that Eglinton 'loves his wife so well he will do nothing for her father's sake' (ibid., 471). After the death of Queen Mary's husband, François II, in December, Eglinton attended a convention of the queen's supporters at Dunbar on the 10th and signed a bond promising aid. By now Châtelherault was pressing Eglinton to divorce his daughter. Jean Hamilton complained of her husband's alleged impotence, while he sought to be divorced on the grounds of his own adultery, claiming that since she had left him he had got a wench with child.

In February 1561 Eglinton crossed to France with the abbot of Dunfermline; he returned with Queen Mary in August. The ship on which he travelled out was intercepted by the English, but released once it became clear that the queen was not on board. In September 1561 Eglinton further infuriated his father-in-law by hearing mass within the duke's Clydesdale bounds; at the end of the month he issued a revocation of deeds issued during his minority. In the following April he raised an action for divorce on the ground of consanguinity and the marriage was duly dissolved by papal decree on 30 May 1562. Jean Hamilton responded by obtaining a divorce from the kirk on 25 June, citing her husband's adultery. Eglinton promptly married Margaret Drummond (*c*.1535–1590), daughter of Sir John Drummond of Innerpeffrey and widow of Sir Hugh Campbell of Loudoun. They had four children: Hugh, later fourth earl of Eglinton; Robert, laird of Giffen; Margaret, wife of Robert Seton, first earl of Winton, celebrated by the poet Alexander Montgomerie as

the 'flour of feminine most fair' (Montgomery, 161); and Agnes, who married Robert, first Lord Sempill.

Throughout the summer of 1562 Eglinton continued to hear daily mass in defiance of the government's proscription, and in June 1563 he received a commission of justiciary through the influence of Mary's secretary, William Maitland of Lethington. Although he is unlikely to have favoured the restitution of the earl of Lennox, with whom he disputed land at the parliament of December 1564, he approved the marriage of the queen to Lennox's son Lord Darnley in July 1565, and was one of the peers who waited on Darnley at the marriage banquet. When Châtelherault and the earl of Moray rebelled in August he joined other lords from the west of Scotland in signing a bond pledging their support to the queen, and rode in the vanguard of the crown forces during the chaseabout raid. He attended the Roman Catholic celebration of Candlemas in Holyrood Chapel in 1566, and also the baptism of Mary's son James in the Chapel Royal at Stirling Castle on 17 December.

Eglinton was not implicated in Darnley's murder in February 1567, and though he dined at the supper given by the earl of Bothwell in Ainslie's tavern on 19 April 1567 he slipped away without signing the bond in favour of the earl's marriage to the queen. After Bothwell abducted Mary he joined the nobles who gathered in Stirling resolved to rescue her and to safeguard the young prince's life. He took the field against Mary and Bothwell at Carberry, but, when the queen was imprisoned by the confederate lords, withdrew his support and stayed away from the parliament held by Moray in December. By March 1568 he had joined Moray's council, but following Mary's escape from Lochleven Castle he signed the Hamilton bond and fought for her on 13 May at Langside. His son, the master of Eglinton, was taken prisoner, but he himself avoided capture by hiding in a house under straw until nightfall. Resisting demands to surrender his castles of Eglinton and Ardrossan, he assembled with other Marian supporters at Largs in July.

Throughout Moray's regency and after his assassination in January 1570 Eglinton stayed loyal to Mary, and when Lennox was elected the new regent in July he was reported to remain 'constantly at the Queen's obedience and cause all courts and other things to be set forward in her name' (*CSP Scot.*, *1569–71*, 219). However, when the regent descended in force on Ayrshire in April 1571 Eglinton was forced to submit and was sent to ward in Doune Castle in May. Released in July, Eglinton was present in Stirling for the parliament called by Lennox when the burgh was raided by the queen's supporters in the early hours of 4 September. The earl was taken prisoner in his lodgings, but later rescued by townsmen during the fighting in which Lennox was killed. Days later he joined his peers in electing the earl of Mar as the new regent and in the coming months assisted in the siege of the queen's forces in Edinburgh. After Mar's death in October 1572, Eglinton was thought to favour Argyll for the regency. However, though absent from the convention which elected Morton in November he appears to have approved of the choice, for he shortly after joined the new regent's council. At the parliament of February 1573 he protested against the new religious legislation, advocating a policy of toleration for Roman Catholics, but none the less attended protestant service with Morton.

Eglinton successfully dominated his locality through control of the Cunninghame bailiary court at Irvine and the office of bailie of the regality of Kilwinning Abbey, which he had acquired in 1559 from the then commendator, Gavin Hamilton, a kinsman of his first wife. The position at Kilwinning altered when Alexander Cunningham of Montgreenan, son of his territorial rival the fifth earl of Glencairn, succeeded as commendator in 1571 and sought to obstruct Eglinton. In May 1578 the earl garrisoned the steeple of the abbey church and both parties were called before the privy council to explain their actions. Ultimately, a working relationship was established and outwardly there remained little sign of the tensions between the kindreds which resurfaced with the murder of Eglinton's heir a year after his death.

After Morton was deprived of the regency in March 1578 Eglinton attended the Stirling convention which affirmed the new settlement, but he reappeared in the council of Morton's revived government. When the government prosecuted the Hamiltons for the murders of Moray and Lennox in May 1579, Eglinton was appointed to the commission empowered to proceed against them and took part in the siege of Hamilton Castle. When Morton was in turn charged in 1581 for his part in Darnley's death Eglinton sat on the assize which condemned him. Eglinton was excluded from the parliament later that year which confirmed the advancement of Esmé and James Stewart to the dukedom of Lennox and earldom of Arran respectively. He co-operated with the Ruthven raid against Lennox and Arran in August 1582, but following its collapse in June 1583 was again chosen to sit in council. Eglinton was a political conservative who throughout his career had balanced a consistent defence of the Roman Catholic faith with a pragmatic acceptance of the existing state of affairs. He died on 3 June 1585 and was buried with his ancestors in Kilwinning Abbey. JOHN SIMMONS

Sources CSP Scot., 1547–86 · NA Scot., Eglinton muniments, GD 3 · Reg. PCS, 1st ser. · W. Fraser, Memorials of the Montgomeries, earls of Eglinton, 2 vols. (1859) · G. Donaldson, All the queen's men (1983) · APS, 1424–1592 · Scots peerage, 3.439–42 · GEC, Peerage, 5.19 · J. M. Thomson and others, eds., Registrum magni sigilli regum Scotorum / The register of the great seal of Scotland, 11 vols. (1882–1914), vols. 3–5 · A. Montgomery, The poems of Alexander Montgomery (1821)
Wealth at death see will, 1563, NA Scot., GD 3/7/5

Montgomery [Montgomerie], **Hugh, seventh earl of Eglinton** (1613–1669), army officer, was the eldest son of Alexander *Montgomery (formerly Seton), sixth earl of Eglinton (1588–1661), and his first wife, Lady Anna Livingstone (d. 1632), daughter of Alexander *Livingstone, first earl of Linlithgow. He was born on 30 March 1613 at Eglinton Castle, Ayrshire, and baptized on 18 April. Until he succeeded to the earldom he was known as Viscount Montgomery. Robert Baillie, whom he afterwards had appointed to the parish of Kilwinning, Ayrshire, was his

tutor for some years. On 29 February 1628 Montgomery was enrolled as a student at the University of Glasgow. In 1631 he married (under a marriage contract dated 7–13 April) Lady Anne Hamilton, eldest daughter of James *Hamilton, second marquess of Hamilton, and Lady Anne Cunningham, daughter of James Cunningham, seventh earl of Glencairn. Anne Hamilton died at Struthers, Fife, on 16 October 1632, and was buried on 15 November at Kilwinning. In 1633 Montgomery went to Paris, where he spent over a year studying, especially the art of fortification while serving in the French army during 1634. In 1635 (the contract was dated 17–24 December) he married, second Lady Mary Leslie, daughter of John *Leslie, sixth earl of Rothes, and his wife, Anne Erskine, daughter of John Erskine, earl of Mar.

Like his father, Montgomery took a prominent part in opposing the ecclesiastical policy of Charles I in the assembly of 1638, strongly supporting the proposals against the bishops. When the covenanters in 1639 determined to resist the march of Charles northwards, Montgomery was chosen colonel of the men of the Cunningham district of Ayrshire, Paisley, and Glasgow. In 1640 he raised 300 infantry in Renfrewshire, and joined the army which under Alexander Leslie marched into England in August. He commanded a brigade of 1800 men at the battle of Newburn. On 15 September 1640 he was sent to garrison the castle of Tynemouth. He remained with his brigade in England during most of the army's occupation. By 3 August 1641 he was back in Scotland, where he was one of four earls' heirs who tried to sit in the estates, but he was expelled. Some time afterwards he was suspected by the covenanters of lukewarmness, and it was greatly feared that he would join Montrose.

However, in the spring of 1644 Montgomery received command of a regiment of horse, which he raised by May in Ayrshire. He entered England with his cavalry as part of Callendar's army on 25 June. With Major-General Sir James Ramsay he led an unsuccessful attack on Gateshead in late July. On 11 October he joined the rendezvous at Glasgow against Montrose. Along with other Scottish lords in Leven's army, Montgomery after the battle of Naseby made vain attempts on 21 July to open communications with Charles. His regiment, if not the viscount himself, served in the Philiphaugh campaign against Montrose.

In 1646 Montgomery served in the northern campaign under Middleton, and on 27 April entered Aberdeen with four troops of horse and two companies of dragoons. In addition to his 240 horsemen he had under his command two regiments of foot (700 men) and he was entrusted with the duty of holding the city. But on 14 May the marquess of Huntly entered the town with 1500 foot and 500 horse; he defeated Montgomery and took over 300 of his men prisoner. Nevertheless a council of war declared on 8 June that Montgomery had conducted himself in the affair 'with as much prudence and gallantry as could have been expected' (Stuart, 2.64). Suspicions about his loyalty to the covenanters continued to dog him in 1646 owing to his correspondence with the king's intermediary Sir William Fleming. Montgomery did not, as is sometimes stated, join the engager army under his brother-in-law, the duke of Hamilton, for the rescue of the king. However, on 26 May 1648 he was one of only two members who refused to sign the Ayrshire committee of war's anti-engagement petition. Furthermore on 4 May the estates nominated him colonel of horse for Ayrshire and Renfrewshire. A week later he received command of his younger brother Robert *Montgomery's Scottish New Model Army horse troop. On 10 June the committee appointed him colonel of horse for Ayrshire but he does not seem to have levied the regiment. By the Act of Classes he was disqualified for all public service as having been accessory to the engagement; but while admitting that he had consented to nominate officers, he declared that he declined to go into England on finding that the 'malignants' had been invited to join in the scheme. He also denied that he had given any support to William Hamilton, second earl of Lanark, or Colonel George Monro on their retreat to England. Consequently on 16 October 1650 he petitioned the estates to be restored to office, producing a recommendation from the commission of the kirk in his favour, and he was finally, on 17 December, declared by parliament to be capable of public employment.

On 1 January 1651 Montgomery secured a place on the committee of estates. Later that year he defended himself in his house of Cumbrae against Cromwell, Baillie taking shelter with him. Montgomery was taken prisoner. He was subsequently released, but on 18 July 1654 the governor of Berwick was ordered to secure him and his father until they procured his brother Robert, who had escaped from the Tower of London after his capture at the battle of Worcester, or gave security that he should leave the kingdom. Although Robert was recaptured, Lord Montgomery was still in prison on 1 September 1656. Hugh Montgomery had been excepted from Cromwell's Act of Grace in 1654. The yearly value of his estate was then stated to be £271 3s. 11d., and the charges on it £5236 18s. 0d. In addition to the fine on his own estates he was also fined £1400 in the summer of 1657 for his interest in the estate of his father, but he petitioned to be relieved and the petition was granted on 1 June 1658. In 1659 Montgomery took the engagement not to take up arms against the Commonwealth.

Montgomery succeeded his father as earl of Eglinton on 7 January 1661. On 13 July he became a member of the Scottish privy council, and on 1 January 1662 he obtained from the king the citadel of Ayr. He consistently attended parliament from 1661 to 1667. In 1663 he served as one of the estates' lords of articles and became a JP for Ayrshire and Renfrewshire. He died towards the close of February 1669.

Eglinton and his first wife, Lady Anne Hamilton, had one daughter. He and his second wife, Lady Mary Leslie, had two sons and five daughters. Alexander, the eighth earl (d. 1701) was a staunch supporter of the covenanters and afterwards a privy councillor of William III. Alexander and his first wife, Lady Elizabeth Crichton, daughter of

William, second earl of Dumfries, were the parents of Alexander *Montgomerie, the ninth earl. Eglinton's younger son, Francis, was a commissioner of the Treasury under William III and one of the commissioners for the union with England. Of the daughters, Mary was married to George Seton, fourth earl of Wintoun; Margaret to James Campbell, second earl of Loudoun; Eleonora to Sir David Dunbar of Baldoon, Wigtownshire; Christian to John Elphinstone, fourth Baron Balmerino; and Anne to Sir Andrew Ramsay of Abbotshall.

T. F. HENDERSON, rev. EDWARD M. FURGOL

Sources The letters and journals of Robert Baillie, ed. D. Laing, 3 vols., Bannatyne Club, 73 (1841–2) • APS • J. Balfour, Works, 4 vols. (1823–5) • A. F. Mitchell and J. Christie, eds., The records of the commissions of the general assemblies of the Church of Scotland, 3 vols., Scottish History Society, 11, 25, 58 (1892–1909) • CSP dom., 1654 • Eleventh report, HMC (1887) • H. W. Meikle, ed., Correspondence of the Scots commissioners in London, 1644–1646, Roxburghe Club, 160 (1917) • J. Stuart, ed., Extracts from the council register of the burgh of Aberdeen, 1625–1747, 2 vols., Scottish Burgh RS, 8–9 (1871–2) • F. D. Dow, Cromwellian Scotland, 1651–1660 (1979) • J. Spalding, Memorialls of the trubles in Scotland and in England, AD 1624 – AD 1645, ed. J. Stuart, 2 vols., Spalding Club, [21, 23] (1850–51) • Thurloe, State papers, vol. 1 • E. Kimber, The peerage of Scotland: a complete view of the several orders of nobility, of that ancient kingdom (1767) • GEC, Peerage • Scots peerage • NA Scot., PA. 11.11, fol. 54r–v

Likenesses engraving, priv. coll.; repro. in W. Fraser, Memorials of the Montgomeries, earls of Eglinton (1859)

Montgomery, Hugh, first earl of Mount-Alexander (b. in or before 1626, d. 1663), nobleman, was the eldest son of Hugh Montgomery, second Viscount Montgomery (1598/9–1642), and his wife, Jean (d. 1670), first daughter of William *Alexander, first earl of Stirling, and his wife, Lady Janet Erskine. His grandfather, also Hugh, the first viscount, was originally from Braidstone in Ayrshire and migrated to Ireland and accumulated extensive properties, mostly in co. Down, where his family played a leading role in the development of Scottish settlement in east Ulster. In his late teens Hugh travelled in France and Italy, and, returning through London, was visited by William Harvey, dispatched to see him by Charles I on reports of Montgomery's unusual medical condition. Harvey reported how a fall in childhood had left him with a 'large open space in his chest, into which I could readily introduce three of my fingers and a thumb' and touch the 'apex of the heart'. The wound was covered with an 'old and extensive ulcer, beyond the reach of art, but brought by a miracle to a kind of cure'. Montgomery, who wore a metal plate on his chest, led a 'pleasant life in perfect safety' (Hill, 152).

Montgomery was elected to the Irish parliament of 1640 for Newtownards, co. Down, but requested resignation on the grounds of ill health. With the outbreak of the rising of 1641 his father was commissioned by Charles I to raise a regiment to oppose the insurgents, drawing largely upon his own tenants. The second viscount died on 15 November 1642 and Montgomery inherited not only the title and lands, but also command of his father's regiment. As such he served in successive campaigns in Ulster, wherein local protestant forces co-operated with the army sent from

Scotland under Major-General Robert Monro, who married Montgomery's widowed mother. In 1643 he petitioned the general assembly of the Church of Scotland to supply a chaplain for his regiment and a minister for his family living at Newtownards. In June 1646 Monro's combined forces were defeated at the battle of Benburb, and Montgomery, serving as commander of the cavalry, was captured and held a prisoner in Cloughoughter Castle, co. Cavan, until 1648. His release followed representations on his behalf by the presbyterian clergy in Ulster. Monro's army was effectively destroyed, while local protestant forces frayed under the impact of political developments in England, Scotland, and Ireland. In 1648 Montgomery supported the engagers among the Scottish government, and by the end of the year his arrest had been ordered by the forces of the English parliament. In December that year he married Mary (1631–1655), eldest daughter of Charles, second Viscount Moore, with whom he had one daughter, Jean, and two sons, Hugh and Henry.

By 1649, with the death of Charles I, Montgomery headed a coalition of those protestant forces in Ulster ready to declare for Charles II, but faced the opposition of troops loyal to the nascent English republic. He received a commission (dated 14 May 1649) from the exiled king as commander-in-chief in Ulster but, despite early successes, his forces were racked by division. His ambiguous attitude to the aims of the presbyterian clergy in the province was interpreted by them as treachery, and the withdrawal of their support seriously undermined the strength of his forces. In October 1649 he was defeated by a detachment of Cromwell's army sent into Ulster under Colonel Venables, and fled south to join Ormond, the king's lord lieutenant. He surrendered to Cromwell at Clonmel, was sent a prisoner to Kilkenny about March 1651, and then banished to Holland.

In 1652 Montgomery secured permission to return to England, and later to Ireland. He was, however, one of the few Ulster Scots individually excepted from pardon under Westminster's 1652 legislation, and in 1653 his name headed a list of Scottish landowners whom the Commonwealth regime planned to transplant from Ulster to Tipperary. The scheme did not take effect, however. Nevertheless, with recurrent anxieties about disaffection, he again came under suspicion. He was reported to be a prisoner in Kilkenny again in December 1655; in April 1656 he was freed but confined to Dublin city and county, having given a pledge not to act against the present government. In February 1657 he was allowed to compound for his estates at a cost of £3000. His arrest was ordered again on 5 August 1659. Certainly he appears to have been involved in conspiracy against the regime later in that year, despite being confined to Dublin.

Montgomery's fortunes revived somewhat with the restoration of Charles II. In September 1660 he was appointed master of the ordnance for Ireland, in November was appointed governor of counties Londonderry, Tyrone, Fermanagh, and Cavan, and a month later named to the Irish privy council. Following the death of his wife, he married on 20 October 1660 Catherine (d. 1675), widow of Sir William Parsons, bt, and daughter of Arthur Jones, second Viscount Ranelagh. He took his seat in the Irish House of Lords on its assembly in May 1661 and within days had moved for a declaration that all subjects conform themselves to episcopal church government and the Book of Common Prayer. On 28 July 1661 he was created earl of Mount-Alexander, the title taken from the family's home, Mount-Alexander House, built by his father and named after his mother. But the damage inflicted on the family fortunes owing to losses incurred in the 1650s was severe, and debts were incurred leading to sales of land and the effective demise of the family as major landowners. The government planned to award lands as recompense, but arrangements had not been finalized at his death.

Mount-Alexander died 'suddenly' at Dromore, co. Down, on 15 September 1663, 'little past the thirty-eighth year of his life' (Hill, 254), and was buried at Newtownards on 29 October. He was succeeded by his son Hugh. Mount-Alexander was described as 'among the properest of middle-sized men, well shaped, of a ruddy sanguine complexion, his hair had been reddish and curled ... his eye grey and quick, and his countenance smiling and complacent' (Hill, 254–5). Given the state of his health, he was perhaps destined for an early death, a fate made more likely by his misfortunes in the 1640s and 1650s. His political and military ventures showed few successes, his ability to inspire trust and support not being matched with corresponding abilities to balance the multitude of factions necessary to success when at the apogee of his influence in 1649. If a consistent royalist, such an allegiance was hardly an uncomplicated one for someone who at all times needed to balance the conflicting demands of political and religious alignments in Ireland, in Scotland, and in England.   R. M. ARMSTRONG

Sources G. Hill, ed., *The Montgomery manuscripts* (1869) · GEC, *Peerage* · B. McGrath, 'A biographical dictionary of the membership of the Irish House of Commons 1640–1641', PhD diss., University of Dublin, 1997 · A. Clarke, *Prelude to Restoration in Ireland* (1999) · R. Gillespie, 'Landed society and the interregnum in Ireland and Scotland', *Economy and society in Scotland and Ireland, 1500–1939*, ed. R. Mitchison and P. Roebuck (1988) · D. Stevenson, *Scottish covenanters and Irish confederates* (1981) · P. Adair, *A true narrative of the rise and progress of the Presbyterian church in Ireland (1623–1670)*, ed. W. D. Killen (1866) · J. S. Reid and W. D. Killen, *History of the Presbyterian church in Ireland*, new edn, 3 vols. (1867) · R. Dunlop, ed., *Ireland under the Commonwealth*, 2 vols. (1913) · St J. D. Seymour, *The puritans in Ireland, 1647–1661* (1921)

Archives Hunt. L., corresp.

Montgomery, Hugh Maude de Fellenberg (1870–1954), army officer and politician, was born on 5 December 1870, eldest son of Hugh de Fellenberg Montgomery (1844–1924), politician, of Blessingbourne, Fivemiletown, co. Tyrone, and his wife, Mary Sophia Juliana (d. 1928), youngest daughter of the Revd. Hon. John Charles Maude. A brother of Field Marshal Sir Archibald Armar Montgomery-*Massingberd (chief of the Imperial General Staff 1933–6) and Major-General Sir Charles Hubert Montgomery (British minister at The Hague 1933–8) he was also a cousin of General Sir Stanley Maude and second cousin of the actor Cyril Maude. Educated at Eton College and at the Royal Military Academy, Woolwich, Montgomery was commissioned in the Royal Regiment of Artillery in 1891. In 1894 he married Mary, (d. 1950), daughter of Edmund Langton. They had three sons and three daughters.

Montgomery served in the Second South African War (1899–1900) where he was awarded the queen's medal with three clasps and was mentioned in dispatches. Promoted captain in 1900 and major in 1908, he was assistant embarkation commandant at Southampton at the outbreak of war in 1914. Three weeks later he went to France to serve as a general staff officer of the 7th division. He held this appointment until 11 November 1915, by which time the 7th division had almost ceased to exist. Montgomery was assistant adjutant and quartermaster-general of the 8th division from November 1914 to March 1915, general staff officer at headquarters in France from March to August 1915, brigadier-general on the staff of the Eleventh Army from August to October 1915, assistant quartermaster-general, 5th army corps, from October 1915 to June 1916, and deputy assistant adjutant and quartermaster-general, 5th army corps, until the end of the war. He was mentioned in dispatches eight times, and was awarded the Russian order of St Anne (third class), made a member of the légion d'honneur, and awarded the Croix de Guerre. In 1918 he was made a CB and in 1919 a CMG. At the end of the war he served on the staffs of the Rhine army and southern command. After the death of his father he retired to the family estate of Blessingbourne in February 1925.

When Montgomery succeeded to the Blessingbourne estate he followed family tradition by taking an active part in local public affairs. He represented the Fivemiletown division on the Clogher board of guardians, the Clogher rural council, and the regional education committee. Like his father he was a prominent Anglican churchman, not only in his own parish but in diocesan circles. He was a patron of the Boy Scouts and assisted in the formation of the Fivemiletown company, whom he provided with a hall on his own land, and took an interest in the progress of the movement in the Clogher valley area where he held the office of commissioner for a lengthy period. He was instrumental in acquiring a grant for equipment for the King George playing field in Fivemiletown and provided the land for the playground. Montgomery was also involved in the local British Legion and was president of the local branch in the twenty-five years from its inauguration until his death. On 7 July 1927 he was appointed deputy lieutenant for co. Tyrone, and on 30 December 1927 high sheriff of co. Tyrone. He was a director of Clogher Valley Railway Company and strongly opposed government plans to buy out shareholders and close the railway. Unusually for a member of his class, Montgomery felt an 'element of remorse for the sins committed by our class—sins by which many of us are still benefiting—against the ancestors of our Roman Catholic neighbours'.

In June 1930 Montgomery was unsuccessful in an attempt to have a Catholic nationalist reappointed as deputy vice-chairman of Clogher board of guardians. This led to a dispute with members of the local Unionist Association, and he was subsequently excluded from membership of the regional education committee. Though he was a personal friend of the future prime minister of Northern Ireland, Sir Basil Brooke, the two were on opposing wings of the Ulster Unionist Party. In 1933 Montgomery began a correspondence with another Liberal Unionist, Lord Charlemont, Northern Ireland minister of education, in which they discussed protestant–Catholic relations in Northern Ireland, relations between Northern Ireland and the free state and between Britain and Ireland, and the ways in which these relationships could be improved. This correspondence was given a greater sense of urgency by the outbreak of sectarian riots in Belfast in July 1935, and in the wake of these riots Montgomery first suggested the idea of establishing an organization which might help improve relations between nationalists and Unionists. As a result of his correspondence with Charlemont and other like-minded individuals Montgomery launched the far-sighted Irish Association for Cultural, Economic and Social Relations in December 1938. In 1938 an *ad hoc* group inspired by Montgomery prepared a leaflet setting out the aims of the proposed association. Briefly they were these: to further better relations between Catholics and protestants in Northern Ireland, the people of Northern Ireland and the Irish Free State, and the people of Great Britain and Ireland. Strikingly, these principles continued to underpin attempts at reconciliation until the end of the century, and may be said to lie at the heart of the Belfast agreement of 1998. Lord Charlemont became president of the association, with Montgomery as treasurer. The primary aim of the association was:

> To organise and give effective expression to the body of opinion known to exist among Irish people in favour of conciliation, and to foster, through the initiative of its individual members, more neighbourly relations between Irishmen who differ from each other in politics and religion.

Since its inauguration the Irish Association has continued to promote understanding and mutual respect between people of diverse political opinions throughout Ireland.

In the last years of his life Hugh Montgomery was confined to a wheelchair. He died at his home, Blessingbourne, co. Tyrone, on 22 January 1954, and was buried in the parish church of Fivemiletown three days later.

GORDON GILLESPIE

Sources family and estate papers, PRO NIre., Montgomery MSS, D 627 [Montgomery family, Blessingbourne] · PRO NIre., Irish Association MSS, D 2661 · P. Bew, K. Darwin, and G. Gillespie, eds., *Passion and prejudice: nationalist/unionist conflict in Ulster in the 1930s, and the origins of the Irish Association* (1993) · *Belfast Telegraph* (23 Jan 1954) · *Belfast News-Letter* (23 Jan 1954) · *Tyrone Constitution* (29 Jan 1954) · *Tyrone Constitution* (5 Feb 1954) · *Tyrone Courier* (28 Jan 1954) · *Tyrone Courier* (4 Feb 1954) · *CGPLA NIre.* (1954) · *Belfast Gazette* (1927–8) · Burke, *Peerage* (1967) · d. cert.
Archives Bodl. Oxf., corresp. · PRO NIre., family and political papers · PRO NIre., MSS of Irish Association for Cultural, Economic and Social Relations, D.2661 | PRO NIre., corresp. with Lord Belmore · UCL, letters to Sir Edwin Chadwick

Wealth at death £901 3*s.* 1*d.*: probate, 29 Nov 1954, *CGPLA NIre.*

Montgomery, Sir James, of Skelmorlie, fourth baronet (*c.*1654–1694), politician and Jacobite conspirator, tenth laird of a cadet branch of the lords Montgomery (later earls of Eglinton), was the eldest of ten children of Sir Robert Montgomery, third baronet (*d.* 1684), landowner, and his wife, Anna (*d.* 1687), daughter of Sir James Scott of Rossie, Fife. Sir Robert and Anna married in 1653, and in 1654 Sir Robert succeeded to the baronetcy, inheriting the family seat at Skelmorlie in northernmost Ayrshire, and lands in Ayrshire, neighbouring islands, and Renfrewshire.

Youth and persecution On the covenanting side during the civil war period, after the Restoration the family were excluded by their presbyterianism and debts from public life. James Montgomery was sent to university, matriculating in 1669 at Edinburgh, but he did not graduate, probably to avoid the oaths required; and he supposedly also studied abroad. On 27 September 1678 he married at Ceres, Fife, Lady Margaret (1654–1726), second daughter of James Johnstone, first earl of Annandale. They had two sons, one of whom was the author Sir Robert *Montgomery.

The earl of Shaftesbury listed Sir Robert in 1679 among the whigs' potential Scottish allies, and James by 1682 was reputed disaffected. He succeeded his father on 7 February 1684. In April that year his mother appealed to him to make suitable provision for her and his siblings, but he replied that, for the sake of peace, he had already done more than was legally required. When on 7 May 1685 they were both prosecuted for conventicles that Sir Robert had kept, each argued for laying the fine on the other.

From 1678 Montgomery attempted to reduce the family's debts by coalmining, and in 1684 he invested deeply in the new Scottish colony in Carolina, appointed his friend William Dunlop to manage his estate there, and bought a ship to trade to America. That summer he attempted to emigrate there to escape religious repression. However, on 10 October 1684 he was one of many western gentry arrested at Glasgow and was imprisoned at Edinburgh awaiting trial for illegal presbyterian worship, and for harbouring 'rebels', that is, covenanters. He submitted to the government's demands, and was acquitted on 24 December. J. H. Halliday suggests that this humiliation provoked his disastrous obstinacy in later crises. Obliged to bear arms against the ninth earl of Argyll's rising in 1685, he was one of the friends who attended Argyll on the scaffold on 30 June.

Although Montgomery appeared to co-operate with James VII and II he secretly organized a subscription in 1688 to send his cousin Archibald, later tenth earl of Argyll, to join William of Orange. Montgomery was far less deeply involved in the plotting for the revolution than he afterwards pretended, although from October 1688 he did organize the cutting of communications between James and his privy council at Edinburgh.

Parliament and 'the club' Montgomery was elected to the convention of 1689 as a member for Ayrshire. He spoke there 'with great force and eloquence, although a country gentleman, not used to great affairs' (Balcarres, 59), vying with Sir John Dalrymple in obtaining the vote that James had forfeited the throne. Montgomery inserted an article denouncing episcopacy into the claim of right but he retreated from supporting the attempts of Sir Patrick Hume and Duncan Forbes to limit royal prerogative in appointments to office. One of the delegation to London that offered William the crown, Montgomery hoped to become secretary of state for his services in the convention, but William, considering him too hostile to episcopacy, selected the undistinguished George, Lord Melville. He merely made Montgomery a privy councillor and lord justice clerk, a legal post that he quickly lost for his opposition that summer.

Montgomery also shared his parliamentary colleagues' alarm that William's proposed reforms fell far short of the convention's demands. In particular, the 'articles', the committee through which the Stuarts had dominated parliament, was merely to be reformed, not abolished. Montgomery became the main leader of 'the club', the first post-Restoration 'country' opposition that relied on success in parliament itself rather than strengthening some court faction. During the session of 1689 the club seized the initiative from the lord commissioner, William, duke of Hamilton, and the ill-organized government supporters. Overall (though never simultaneously) about 70 of the 125 attending parliament supported it, mainly shire and burgh members. Among the nobles, Argyll usually co-operated; but Montgomery's closest followers were his brother-in-law William *Johnstone, second earl of Annandale, and William, Lord Ross. In particular, the club steered debate away from the church, which William was ready to settle, for fear the primarily presbyterian members might then disregard the civil grievances.

After Hamilton ended the session on 2 August, the club prepared an address to William, which Hume, Forbes, Montgomery, Annandale and Ross carried up in September, asking him to pass the five main acts voted, but he refused. Through the machinations of the Jacobite Henry Nevile Payne, Montgomery became convinced that William's favourite the earl of Portland was plotting his downfall and death, and consequently sabotaged further negotiations with William, alienating Hume and Forbes. In November, he claimed, William offered to compromise and follow the future advice of the club but this exceptional (for him) concession was rejected by Montgomery, Annandale, and Ross. Montgomery also at some time, when alone with the king, insulted him personally in a way William never forgave.

The renewed offer, if genuine, was partly a response to Montgomery's nuisance value in England. His warnings helped persuade the Commons whigs not to settle the revenue permanently. He collaborated with the Jacobite Robert Ferguson on a pamphlet that justified the address and insinuated distrust of William. Yet meanwhile he pretended to Anglican tories that the Scottish presbyterians were too weak to force William to establish their church against his will and offered to abandon a presbyterian settlement in the next session in return for the support of the Episcopalians in redressing civil grievances.

The Montgomery plot Having approached the Jacobites, Montgomery in December 1689 organized a plot into which lords Annandale and Ross blindly followed him. In the next session of parliament they planned to force a break with William and, under Jacobite and Cameronian military protection (assisted by arms and money from France), to restore James. A council of five was to rule Scotland, including Montgomery as secretary and earl of Ayr. James, when informed of it, agreed to the plot, including the demand that he never again employ his unpopular Scottish minister, the earl of Melfort. When parliament opened on 15 April 1690, however, Montgomery and his allies found they could not get the upper hand. The government, led by Lord Melville, now lord commissioner, proved stronger, and made more concessions, than expected, and the plot quickly began to unravel. Montgomery wildly proposed restoring the near-theocratic 1649 presbyterian church; in parliament he and Dalrymple scolded each other 'like watermen' (Balcarres, 59), but finally, in desperation he sent to France to request an invasion of Scotland. Since the plot had failed, however, James held himself absolved from particular promises.

Montgomery's plot was exposed after the capture of Payne in May and the confession of Lord Ross in June. Montgomery was dismissed from the privy council, and throughout July negotiated with Lord Melville, offering to confess but not be a witness. Melville was willing to save him, writing 'he is a man of very good parts, and may be very serviceable' (Leven and Melville, 482). Montgomery went south on 3 August 1690 but failed to appear before Queen Mary until 6 September, and then mumbled a nonsensical story; from fear or honour, he would not denounce his English whig associates. He was allowed to slip away, but his pardon was destroyed and he retreated into the London Jacobite underworld. He dared not return to Scotland, where judicial torture was legal, and forfeited his parliamentary seat on 28 April 1693. His wife and family also went to London, where she bought goods on commission for Scottish noble families to supplement their meagre income.

Jacobite conspirator In June 1691 Montgomery formed a second conspiracy at London, drawn from various Scottish politicians, particularly Argyll and the marquess of Atholl. Their intrigues assisted in sabotaging the government's agreement that summer with the highland clans for a pacification, thus helping to bring about the massacre of Glencoe. Montgomery, though high in James's favour that summer, was secretly betraying some English fellow conspirators to Queen Mary, in a last unsuccessful attempt to regain his natural place on William's side. Ferguson discovered this and warned St Germain; Montgomery lost James's favour and his plot fell apart, severing his links with Argyll. That winter he organized yet another short-lived plot, the details of which are obscure.

A Jacobite mainly from lack of alternatives, Montgomery now ironically became a major Jacobite propagandist, though his first unaided pamphlet, a defence for an English audience of the uncompromising general assembly of 1692, apparently remained unpublished. After the French invasion attempt in May was crushed at La Hogue, he revived the movement's morale in August with the lengthy *Great Britain's Just Complaint*, which presented James as trustworthy, his worst policies as based on deliberately bad advice from ministers who betrayed him, and William as tyrannical at home (with apparently the first British denunciation of Glencoe) but duped by his European allies. James, who was sent a presentation copy, gave him no thanks, while Lord Melfort remained implacable towards him. The French court, in contrast, now trusted him almost blindly.

Montgomery therefore in autumn 1692 became active among the compounders, the Jacobite faction which worked for restoration through negotiations with the widest possible spectrum of politicians and concessions by James, rather than through a French invasion. Though hunted by king's messengers and creditors, Montgomery wrote a few short pamphlets to influence English MPs during the parliamentary session of 1692–3 before illness drove him to the country. In October he sent the French a long draft conciliatory letter to parliament for James to sign, declaring that it would gain him widespread support. James refused. He helped frame the compounders' demands, though James vetoed his main addition, that nonjuring bishops should raise the prince of Wales as a protestant, and in February 1693, he held discussions in the Netherlands with the peace party led by the Halewijn brothers, also former Williamites. On his own initiative, Montgomery negotiated with Denmark and with Sweden, whose Charles XI asked for a formal Jacobite envoy. In April 1693 Charles, earl of Middleton, crossed to France and became senior secretary and chief minister to James, who issued the declaration the compounders had prepared. But Middleton refused Montgomery's own request to cross to St Germain, claiming that the French opposed it.

The compounders' initiative faltered as William, under the pressure of wartime defeats, turned from the tories to the whigs. Montgomery was increasingly the spokesman for seventeen tory Jacobite peers and Anglican bishops who, fearing whig dominance, wrote urging Louis to invade. He resumed attacks on Lord Melfort, who had now reverted to violently anti-compounding attitudes. When, therefore, Montgomery, about to carry over the invasion plan along with Major-General Sir Theophilus Oglethorpe, was captured in London on 9 January 1694, apparently by chance, Melfort was generally blamed.

Knowing his peril, Montgomery vainly offered to confess all he knew provided he was not made a witness. Oglethorpe rescued him by bribing the sentries guarding him, and, after sheltering at the Swedish embassy, they secretly crossed to France. Their proposal for an immediate invasion of Kent was ignored; but their accusations against

Melfort contributed heavily to his final dismissal in June 1694.

Montgomery again hoped to become a Jacobite secretary of state, but the post went to John Caryll. Disillusioned, Montgomery applied in August to William for permission to return home and live quietly but was refused. That autumn he obtained a French pension but three days later, on 6 October 1694 NS, he died of tuberculosis, possibly in Paris but more probably in the country nearby. He was succeeded by his eldest son, Sir Robert *Montgomery. His younger son Lieutenant-Colonel William Montgomery went into Queen Anne's army and was killed at the battle of Almenara in Spain on 27 July 1710 NS.

Montgomery was probably the individual most responsible, after William himself, for the shape of the revolution settlement in Scotland. He excelled as a parliamentary leader, but at the same time his distortions, lies, and deceptions were exceptional even among late Stuart Scottish politicians, and his public career was consequently short-lived, 'So fatally did ambition and discontent hurry a man to ruin who seemed capable of greater things' (*Bishop Burnet's History*, 4.113). Turning reluctantly to Jacobitism, Montgomery had a significant impact on the movement in the early 1690s. He greatly encouraged the compounding faction, and while almost all Jacobites looked for foreign help from Catholic France, Montgomery negotiated with the protestant Netherlands, Sweden, and Denmark on the basis of national interest, foreshadowing Jacobite policy after 1715. Ironically, his own final Jacobite proposal was for a French invasion; and it was not surprising it failed. Few Jacobites had done more to damage French confidence in the movement, by denigrating Melfort as a traitor and James and his court, for not realizing this, as more foolish than they were. The general prejudice outlived Montgomery, Melfort, and James.

PAUL HOPKINS

Sources P. A. Hopkins, 'Aspects of Jacobite conspiracy in England in the reign of William III', PhD diss., U. Cam., 1981 · J. A. Halliday, 'The career and political significance of Sir James Montgomerie of Skelmorlie, 1654–1694', BLitt. diss., U. Glas., 1962 · J. A. Halliday, 'The Club and the revolution in Scotland', *SHR*, 45 (1966), 143–59 · P. A. Hopkins, 'Sir James Montgomerie of Skelmorlie', *The Stuart court in exile and the Jacobites*, ed. E. Cruikshanks and E. Corp (1995), 39–60 · W. H. L. Melville, ed., *Leven and Melville papers: letters and state papers chiefly addressed to George, earl of Melville … 1689–1691*, Bannatyne Club, 77 (1843) · NA Scot., Leven and Melville papers, GD26 · W. Fraser, ed., *The Melvilles, earls of Melville, and the Leslies, earls of Leven*, 3 vols. (1890) · W. Fraser, ed., *Memorials of the Montgomeries earls of Eglinton*, 2 vols. (1859) · NA Scot., Eglinton papers, GD3 · H. B. Duff, ed., *Culloden papers … from the year 1625 to 1748* (1815) · C. Lindsay [earl of Balcarres], *Memoirs touching the revolution in Scotland*, ed. A. W. C. Lindsay [earl of Crawford and Balcarres], Bannatyne Club (1841) · F. Ravaisson, ed., *Archives de la Bastille*, 19 vols. (1866–1904), vol. 9 · Bibliothèque Nationale, Paris, Renaudot papers, Nouvelles acquisitions françaises MSS 7487–7492 · [J. Montgomery], *Great Britain's just complaint* (1692) · *Bishop Burnet's History* · U. Nott. L., Portland MSS, PwA · Nairne MSS, Bodl. Oxf., MSS Carte 181, 209, 256 · J. Macpherson, ed., *Original papers containing the secret history of Great Britain*, 2 vols. (1775) · Melfort letterbooks, BL, Lansdowne MS 1163A–C; Add. MS 37661 · Halifax's 'Holland House' notebook, BL, Add. MS 51511 · *CSP dom.*, 1689–95 · P. A. Hopkins, *Glencoe and the end of the highland war* (1986); rev. edn (1998) · *APS* · *Reg. PCS*, 3rd ser. · R. Morrice, 'Ent'ring book', DWL, Morrice MS Q–R [vols. 2–3] · J. Montgomery, 'A representation and vindication of the presbyterians', NL Scot., Wodrow MS Oto 30 · G. Crawford, genealogical notes, NL Scot., Adv. MS 34.3.8 · *Memoirs of Thomas, earl of Ailesbury*, ed. W. E. Buckley, 2 vols., Roxburghe Club, 122 (1890) · *The life of James the Second, king of England*, ed. J. S. Clarke, 2 vols. (1816) · *Memoirs of the secret services of John Macky*, ed. A. R. (1733) · R. Taylor, 'An account of wt passed', NL Wales, Celynog 24 Additional MS 550 B · C. Dalton, ed., *English army lists and commission registers, 1661–1714*, 6 vols. (1892–1904) · matriculation rolls, U. Edin. L., special collections division, university archives, 1.61 · *Scots peerage* · m. reg. Scot. · Margaret Montgomery to Lady Murray, 8 May 1694, 8 Dec 1694, Blair Castle, Atholl MSS, box 29 I (7), 71, 93

Archives Bibliothèque Nationale, Paris, Renaudot papers · NA Scot., Eglinton papers · NA Scot., Leven and Melville papers · NL Scot., Wodrow MSS

Likenesses mezzotint, 1690–1694?, Bibliothèque Nationale, Paris; copy, Scot. NPG · oils, Scot. NPG; formerly in possession of Hon. H. Dalrymple, 1925

Wealth at death estate valued at little or nothing: *Leven and Melville papers*, ed. Melville, 480 · estates in Ayrshire, Renfrewshire, the Cumbraes, and Arran outweighed by debts: Fraser, ed., *Memorials*, vol. 1, p. 167

Montgomery, James (1771–1854), hymn writer and poet, was born on 4 November 1771 in Irvine, Ayrshire, the second of the four children of John Montgomery (1734–1791), and his wife, Mary, *née* Blackley (d. 1790). His family, originally from Scotland, had been settled for several generations in Ulster, and his father had come under the influence of the Moravians (a protestant sect founded in the early eighteenth century), who had established a community, Grace Hill, near his birthplace, in Ballykennedy, co. Antrim. John Montgomery became a Moravian minister and took charge of the Moravian congregation at Irvine just before the birth of James. The family returned to Grace Hill in 1775 and there James Montgomery received his earliest education before being sent in 1777 to school at the Moravian establishment at Fulneck, Leeds. James did not see his parents after 1783, when they went to Barbados as missionaries; they were to die there when James was about twenty.

Although indolent in regular studies, the young James Montgomery was a compulsive and prolific writer. By the age of fifteen he had composed three volumes of sacred poems, a very long mock heroic poem and an 'Ode on the General Judgement'. Deciding that he would make neither minister nor teacher, the community placed him in 1787 as an apprentice with a baker in nearby Mirfield. Here he continued his writing and spent much time also in playing his oboe and composing music. Notwithstanding the tolerance of his master, after eighteen months in the occupation James impulsively ran away with three and sixpence in his pocket and a bundle of verses. He found himself in Wentworth, near Rotherham, where he was offered employment in a general store in nearby Wath. Walking in Wentworth Park, the precocious lad, in a chance encounter with Earl Fitzwilliam, presented one of his poems and received a guinea in return.

Anxious to secure a publisher for his writings Montgomery went to London, where he worked in a bookseller's. But, having no success, within six months he was back in Wath. In April 1792 he responded to an advertisement in

James Montgomery (1771–1854), by Charles Turner, pubd 1819 (after John Raphael Smith)

the *Sheffield Register* and was appointed clerk and book-keeper in the office of that newspaper. This change marked out the path for Montgomery's future. He quickly established himself as a regular contributor to the paper and became well known in the town. However, the days of the *Register* were numbered. Joseph Gales, the radical reformist proprietor and editor of the paper, fled to America to escape prosecution for alleged sedition and the paper ceased publication. Gales's misfortune was Montgomery's opportunity. In July 1794 the paper was relaunched with a new title, the *Sheffield Iris*, a less radical editorial line, and with Montgomery as editor. Capital was provided by Benjamin Naylor, a Unitarian minister and wealthy sleeping partner in a silversmithing firm. Within a year Naylor withdrew from the paper on his marriage and ownership passed to Montgomery.

Although much less of a radical than Gales, Montgomery was soon in trouble with the authorities. In January 1795 he was prosecuted for publishing a supposedly seditious poem celebrating the fall of the Bastille. He was sentenced to three months' imprisonment at York. A second prosecution, for malicious libel, followed in January 1796, as a result of Montgomery's report of the use of the militia to fire on a riotous crowd in Sheffield, with consequent loss of life. Convicted, he served six months at York. It later became clear that the prosecutions had been instigated by government sources to bring pressure to bear on radical political societies in Sheffield. The convictions in no way blackened the young Montgomery's reputation and character and he was strongly supported, both in

prison and subsequently, by influential friends. Even Colonel Athorpe, whom Montgomery had libelled as commander of the militia, later showed his respect. In prison he wrote *Prison Amusements*, published in 1797, mostly light-hearted pieces, but conveying some indication of the trauma of his prison experience. *The Whisperer*, a volume of essays written under the pseudonym Gabriel Silvertongue which Montgomery subsequently sought to suppress, followed in 1798.

The *Iris*, worthy newspaper though it was, lacked the reforming zeal and vitality of the *Register*, although Montgomery established a successful business as publisher and printer enabling him to live in gentlemanly comfort in the palatial setting of The Mount and to look after Gales's three sisters. But other newspapers entered the field and in 1825 Montgomery sold the business, remaining until his death active in Sheffield affairs and devoting himself to his writings, his voluminous correspondence, and his many friendships. He was the mainspring of missionary support in Sheffield, the founder of the Sheffield Literary and Philosophical Society, the chairman of the board of management of the infirmary for twenty-five years, and a director of the Sheffield Gas Company; he supported movements for the abolition of the slave trade and the betterment of conditions for sweeps' climbing boys, and tirelessly promoted education through Sunday schools, a working men's library, and new schools. No public platform was complete without him, no major issue in the city was resolved without his participation. A deeply religious man, he was truly ecumenical, moving freely between Methodist and Baptist chapels and Anglican churches. After a short period of wavering doubt, in his twenties, his faith remained firm. He never lost touch with his Moravian roots and was readmitted as a member of the Moravian church in 1814.

But Montgomery's heart was in his writings—his poems, his hymns, and reviews. *The Ocean* was published in 1805, making little impact, but the publication in 1806 of *The Wanderer of Switzerland and other Poems* placed Montgomery on the national scene. Savaged by Jeffrey in the *Edinburgh Review*, it was nevertheless popular and quickly reprinted and, by 1850, had run to thirteen editions in Britain. Southey and Scott were among those who spoke highly of the poem and Byron wrote that *The Wanderer* 'was worth more than a thousand Lyrical Ballads' (Byron, *Complete Poetical Works*, ed., J. J. McGann, 1980, 1.407). *The Wanderer* is a political poem and although set in the context of Napoleon's subjugation of Switzerland, it spoke directly to a Britain concerned for its own liberty and freedom threatened by Napoleonic conquest. Following the success of *The Wanderer*, Montgomery was commissioned to write a poem in support of abolishing the slave trade. His poem 'The West Indies' appeared with others on the same subject in 1809 and achieved great popularity when published separately. *The World before the Flood* (1812) is Montgomery's attempt at a religious epic, interwoven, not very successfully, with a romantic theme. It was well received and sold well. *Greenland* (1819), an uncompleted poem in five cantos, seeks to celebrate the achievements of Moravian missionaries in Greenland. While having some interesting descriptive passages, the poem, in heroic couplets, is of limited appeal. Montgomery's last important longer poem, *The Pelican Island* (1827), develops, in blank verse, a grand evolutionary theme. It contains some of his best descriptive passages but lacks a compelling narrative and is not brought to a successful conclusion.

Apart from these longer poems, Montgomery was prolific in shorter pieces, some of which were popular in his day, but none has entered modern anthologies. Among these are some finely crafted poems of feeling, such as 'The Grave' (1806) and 'The Peak Mountains' (1812). He was much in demand as a reviewer. A regular contributor to the *Eclectic Review*, he delivered a series of lectures on poetry at the Royal Institution which were published in 1833. He wrote substantial articles on Dante, Ariosto, and Tasso for Lardner's *Cabinet Cyclopaedia*. As a critic he is fair and balanced and always offers a sound appreciation of his subject, seeking not to destroy or wound, but to commend.

Montgomery's reputation today rests on his hymns, which are well represented in modern hymnals. He stands worthily alongside Wesley and Watts. A prolific writer of hymns for all occasions, many produced to order, he played a significant role in establishing the use of hymns in worship. His *The Christian Psalmist* (1825), a collection of hymns of many writers, contains an introduction which is a fine essay on hymn composition. He not only contributed original compositions to Thomas Cotterill's collection, but his support and encouragement helped to ensure official sanction of this, the first authorized hymnal of the Church of England. Firmly established in the hymnals of many denominations are: 'Angels from the realms of glory', 'Songs of praise the angels sang', 'Stand up and bless the Lord', 'Hail to the Lord's anointed', and others. In his hymns Montgomery displays a mastery of rhythm and an extensive knowledge of scripture and Christian doctrine. Above all, his better hymns display discipline and inspiration, qualities that much of his poetry conspicuously lacks.

During his lifetime Montgomery was revered in Sheffield and respected by many nationally. He was granted a government pension of £150 in 1835 on the recommendation of Sir Robert Peel. Many thought he might be nominated poet laureate on the death of Southey (a great personal friend) and he declined to be nominated as professor of rhetoric at Edinburgh University and as Conservative candidate for Sheffield. His death at The Mount on 30 April 1854 put Sheffield into mourning. His funeral on 11 May was a grand public occasion, the hour-long procession including every individual and organization of note in the town, its industry and commerce stilled in memory of its adopted son. A tasteful monument, with a full-sized bronze of Montgomery, designed by John Bell, was erected over his grave in the Sheffield general cemetery. It now stands in a prominent position adjacent to Sheffield Cathedral, the large east window of which is dedicated to his memory.

Overrated in his lifetime as a poet, Montgomery nevertheless deserves better than the near oblivion into which his poems have sunk. He wrote too much, as did many of his contemporaries, but here and there he displays a fine lyrical quality, though insufficiently sustained. He was, ultimately, constrained by his circumstances—the rigidity of his Moravian upbringing, the sturdy insularity of a provincial city and his comfortable existence as a moderately successful small businessman. Only his recurrent melancholy and hypochondria indicate the tensions that ran beneath the surface. A man with a great capacity for friendship—he never married—he showered friends and acquaintances with letters of enormous length, but must have been good company and a stimulating conversationalist. He was, perhaps, too sociable, too fond of local position, to be a really good poet. But his best hymns are of fine and lasting quality. 'He has bequeathed to the Church of Christ wealth which could only have come from a true genius and a sanctified heart' (Julian, 1.765).

G. TOLLEY

Sources *Memoirs of the life and writings of James Montgomery*, ed. J. Holland and J. Everett, 7 vols. (1854–6) • H. F. Beutner, 'By fraternal feelings fired', PhD diss., Northwestern University, Evanston, Illinois, 1967 • J. W. King, *James Montgomery: a memoir, political and poetical* (1858) • H. C. Knight, *Life of James Montgomery* (1857) • S. Ellis, *Life, times and character of James Montgomery* (1864) • J. Marratt, *James Montgomery: Christian poet and philanthropist* (1879) • W. Odom, *Two Sheffield poets: James Montgomery and Ebenezer Elliott* (1929) • E. D. Mackerness, 'Mary Ann Rawson and the *Memorials of James Montgomery*', *Transactions of the Hunter Archaeological Society*, 8 (1960–63), 218–28 • J. Wigley, 'James Montgomery and the *Sheffield Iris*, 1792–1825', *Transactions of the Hunter Archaeological Society*, 10/3 (1975), 173–81 • A. S. Holbrook, 'The life and work of James Montgomery', *London Quarterly and Holborn Review* (April 1954), 134–7 • J. A. Kay, 'The poetry and hymns of James Montgomery', *London Quarterly and Holborn Review* (April 1954), 138–45 • J. Julian, ed., *A dictionary of hymnology*, rev. edn (1907) • J. R. Watson, *The English hymn: a critical and historical study* (1997), 304–20

Archives Sheff. Arch., corresp., account book, and literary MSS • University of Sheffield, literary MSS, corresp., and papers | JRL, MS of Leonard Dober, and related papers • RS Friends, Lond., letters to Henry Wornall • Sheff. Arch., corresp. and memoir relating to death of George Bennett • Sheff. Arch., letters to Samuel Roberts

Likenesses H. Meyer, stipple, pubd 1819 (after T. Westoby), BM, NPG • C. Turner, mezzotint, pubd 1819 (after J. R. Smith), BM, NPG [*see illus.*] • T. Barber, oils, 1824, Graves Art Gallery, Sheffield • E. Smith, marble bust, 1843, Cutlers' Hall, Sheffield • W. Ellis, bronze medallion, 1852, Sheffield City Art Gallery • W. Ellis, marble bust, 1855, Royal Hallamshire Hospital, Sheffield • J. Bell, bronze, 1861, outside Sheffield Cathedral • H. Adlard, stipple (aged fifty-five; after J. Jackson), BM, NPG; repro. in Holland and Everett, *Memoirs*, vol. 4 • Ridley and Blood, stipple (after F. Chantrey), BM; repro. in *Monthly Mirror* (1807) • F. A. Roberts, stipple (after T. H. Illidge), NPG • Roffe, stipple and line engraving (after Pickering), NPG; repro. in J. Montgomery, *Poetical works*

Montgomery, James (1794–1880), cotton manufacturer and author, was born on 2 December 1794 at the cotton mill village of Blantyre on the Clyde in Lanarkshire, son of William Montgomery, employed in Taylor's cotton mill, and his wife, Helen, *née* Reid. Little is known of Montgomery's early life. Raised in the first generation of Scottish children to be inducted into the machine-dominated discipline of the cotton factory, he not only learned to read and write, but also acquired a thorough knowledge of cotton spinning, weaving, and finishing. By the mid-1830s he was working as a cotton mill manager for MacLeroy, Hamilton & Co. of Calton, Glasgow, where the Scottish cotton industry flourished before fading in the railway age.

Montgomery came to public notice in 1832 with the publication of his *The Carding and Spinning Master's Assistant, or, The Theory and Practice of Cotton Spinning*. This was an invaluable practical handbook—the first of its kind. Compiled from notes made for Montgomery's own use as a mill manager, it presented rules, illustrated with worked examples, for calculating speeds, drafts, and settings for cylinders, rollers, and spindles, and ways of adjusting them to suit various cotton qualities, or to produce yarns differing in fineness, a knowledge jealously guarded by the first generation of mill overseers and managers. A second edition appeared in 1833 and a third in 1836, which was enlarged and retitled *The Theory and Practice of Cotton Spinning, or, The Carding and Spinning Master's Assistant*, all from the same publisher, John Nixon of Glasgow. In addition Montgomery prepared a small pocket manual of rules, calculations, and worked examples for use by mill overseers. Entitled *The Cotton Spinner's Manual, or, A Compendium of the Principles of Cotton Spinning* and issued by his publisher in 1835, and again in 1850, it was similar to George Galbraith's *The Cotton Spinner's Companion*, published in Glasgow in 1834.

Through his publications, Montgomery's reputation spread abroad. When, in 1835, Daniel Treadwell, inventor, entrepreneur, and Rumford Professor at Harvard University, visited Britain, he was commissioned *inter alia* to secure economic and technical information. Finding Glasgow manufacturers far more open than those in Manchester, Treadwell gleaned what he could from Montgomery and relayed his information to one of his sponsors, Samuel Batchelder (1784–1879), a prominent New England cotton manufacturer. This led Batchelder to invite Montgomery to become superintendent of the York Manufacturing Company at Saco in Maine, USA. In 1836, or soon after, Montgomery emigrated with his family, which, by the time of the US census of 1840, comprised two males beside himself and six females.

Whereas in Glasgow Montgomery had managed a factory with 11,000 spindles and 200 power-looms, all steam-driven, in Maine he had charge of three (later four) factories of 3000–6000 spindles each, and a total of several hundred water-powered looms. While at Saco, Montgomery wrote his most important book, *A Practical Detail of the Cotton Manufacture of the United States of America, and the State of the Cotton Manufacture of that Country Contrasted and Compared with that of Great Britain*, which was published in Glasgow in 1840. It responded to British worries about American competition in overseas textile markets, and the debate over relative cotton manufacturing costs in Britain and the USA. The volume gave precise estimates, unmatched elsewhere and derived from first-hand experience in both countries. Montgomery concluded that overall American running costs were 3 per cent less than British ones. When he came to revise the volume he

brought the differential of American advantage down to 1 per cent. Both figures were much lower than British commentators had earlier alleged. One unexpected result of the publication of his *Practical Detail* was a vigorous, and at times slanderous, debate in the Boston newspapers about the relative costs of steam power and water power in manufacturing cotton. Montgomery was accused of underestimating the cost of water power as compared with steam power. His opponent Justitia, who gave his pseudonym to the debate, has been identified as Charles Tillinghast James (1805–1862), a mill engineer from Rhode Island.

Montgomery left Maine in 1843, and worked in New York state until 1850. He then joined the sporadic migration of workers from New England to the south and became superintendent and treasurer of the Graniteville Manufacturing Company's factory in South Carolina. Sponsored by William Gregg (1800–1867), the well-known promoter of southern manufacturing, the mill started in 1849, when it ran 10,000 spindles and 300 power-looms, driven by water turbines. Montgomery stayed there until 1863. In 1867 he was superintendent of the Batesville Manufacturing Company in the South Carolina piedmont. Montgomery retained strong Presbyterian convictions, but was recalled as tolerant of others. His wife, whose identity is unknown, died in 1876. Montgomery died at Pliny, Greenville county, South Carolina, on 27 December 1880.   DAVID J. JEREMY

Sources D. J. Jeremy, *Technology and power in the early American cotton industry: James Montgomery, the second edition of his 'Cotton manufacture' (1840) and the Justitia controversy about relative power costs*, American Philosophical Society (1990)

Montgomery, Sir James William, first baronet (1721–1803), judge and politician, was born at Magbie Hill, Peeblesshire, in October 1721, the second son of William Montgomery, advocate, and his wife, Barbara, daughter of Robert Rutherford of Bowland, Edinburghshire. After attending Linton parish school he studied law in Edinburgh and was called to the Scottish bar on 19 February 1743. He was appointed the first sheriff of Peeblesshire in 1748, under the new system of local government, and in 1761 his influential friend Robert Dundas, lord president, secured for him the appointment as solicitor-general, jointly with Francis Garden. In 1764 he became sole solicitor-general and in 1766 lord advocate. He held the parliamentary seat for the Dumfries burghs in 1766–8 and that for Peeblesshire in 1768–74.

On 13 January 1763 Montgomery married Margaret (*d.* 1806), daughter and heir of Robert Scott of Killearn, Stirlingshire; they had four sons and two daughters. The eldest son, William, a lieutenant-colonel in the 43rd foot, predeceased him, the second son, James, became lord advocate and succeeded him in the baronetcy, the third, Archibald, went to the East Indies, and the fourth, Robert, practised at the English bar. At his marriage Montgomery bought from the heir of Lord Ilay a half-reclaimed estate, The Whim, in the parish of Newlands, which became his favourite residence, complementing Queensberry House, Canongate, in Edinburgh. In 1767 he paid £40,000 for the estates of Stanhope and Stobo, also in Peeblesshire, and from this time he was able to indulge in his favourite pursuit, the science of agriculture. He travelled widely through England to study improvements in farming, introducing early species of oats and peas, and the use of the light horse plough. His improvement of the road between Peebles and Edinburgh earned him the title of 'the father of the county'.

Montgomery was one of the most active members of the board of trustees for the encouragement of arts, manufactures, and commerce in Scotland, he was elected a fellow of the Society of Antiquaries of Scotland, and he was one of the original fellows of the Royal Society of Edinburgh, established in 1783. As landlord, lawyer, and member of parliament, he was well qualified to deal with the matter of entails, which discouraged long-term improvements of the land and imposed restrictions on the families owning such estates. He accordingly introduced a bill in 1770, which passed into law (10 Geo. III c. 51), embodying many of the needed reforms. In June 1775 he was created lord chief baron of the Scottish exchequer; he resigned his judgeship in April 1801, and in July was made a baronet.

Henry Cockburn remarked of Montgomery that:

> though a remarkably kind landlord, he thought it his duty to proceed sometimes with apparent severity against poachers, smugglers ... but as it generally ended in his paying the fine himself, in order to save the family, his benevolence was supposed to do more harm than his justice did good. (Memorials ... by Henry Cockburn, 161)

Kay described him as 'tall and slender, not undignified, and more ... of a winning grace than of overawing command' and wrote that in old age he was 'of clear complexion, serene and cheerful' (Kay, 190–92). He died on 2 April 1803.   J. A. HAMILTON, rev. ANITA MCCONNELL

Sources W. Chambers, A history of Peeblesshire (1864) · G. W. T. Omond, The lord advocates of Scotland from the close of the fifteenth century to the passing of the Reform Bill, 2 (1883), 223–4 · Memorials of his time, by Henry Cockburn, 2 (1872), 161–3 · J. Foster, Members of parliament, Scotland ... 1357–1882, 2nd edn (privately printed, London, 1882), 257 · Anderson, Scot. nat. · J. Kay, A series of original portraits and caricature etchings ... with biographical sketches and illustrative anecdotes, ed. [H. Paton and others], new edn [3rd edn], new edn [3rd edn], 1 (1877), 190–92 · G. W. T. Omond, ed., The Arniston memoirs: three centuries of a Scottish house, 1571–1838 (1887) · E. Haden-Guest, 'Montgomery, James', HoP, Commons, 1754–90 · F. J. Grant, ed., The Faculty of Advocates in Scotland, 1532–1943, Scottish RS, 145 (1944)
Archives NA Canada, corresp. and papers [copies] · NL Scot., legal corresp. | NA Scot., corresp. with John Spottiswood
Likenesses J. Kay, caricature, etching, 1788, NPG · H. Raeburn, oils, 1801, Kinross House, Tayside · J. Brown, pencil drawing, Scot. NPG · G. Willison, oils, Kinross House, Tayside

Montgomery, John, of Eaglesham (d. 1400/01). See under Montgomery family (per. c.1350–c.1485).

Montgomery, Sir John, of Ardrossan (d. 1427×9). See under Montgomery family (per. c.1350–c.1485).

Montgomery [married name Macdonald], **Lucy Maud** (1874–1942), novelist and diarist, was born on 30 November 1874 in Clifton, Prince Edward Island, Canada, the only child of Hugh John Montgomery (1841–1900), shopkeeper and land agent, and Clara Woolner, née Macneill

(1853–1876). After her mother's early death from tuberculosis, the child Maud was placed in the care of her maternal grandparents, while her father moved west, eventually remarrying, settling, and raising a second family in Alberta. Life in her grandparents' farmhouse at Cavendish, Prince Edward Island, was quiet, but Montgomery was part of an extended family with a tradition of storytelling. She learned and practised the craft during visits to her Montgomery grandparents and her aunt Annie Macneill Campbell's lively family. Montgomery was especially close to her youngest Campbell cousin, Frederica; Frede's death in 1919 ended Montgomery's closest relationship.

Montgomery was educated in the local one-room school; when nine she began to write poetry and to keep a diary. Her first published poems and stories appeared in 1890–91, a year she spent in Alberta with her father's second family. After a teacher-training course in Charlottetown in 1892–3, she taught in a rural school, continuing to write and publish her stories. She studied for one year at Dalhousie University in 1895–6, but returned to teaching until needed upon her grandfather's death in 1898 to look after her grandmother. The young schoolteacher had rejected two possible partners, a Presbyterian minister who had been suitable and a farmer to whom she had been passionately attracted. Neither offered her the possibilities she longed for, but life with her grandmother was even narrower. The romantic fiction she was writing and selling to Canadian and American magazines was her major occupation: among her output were stories she liked enough to rework into later fiction. Increasingly confident in her talent and professionalism, and supported by her closeness to Frede and by the interest of another Presbyterian minister, Ewen Macdonald (1870–1943), she wrote her first novel, Anne of Green Gables. Published in 1908, the book was a critical and commercial success, and was followed by a sequel as well as a continuing stream of stories and poems. On her grandmother's death in 1911 Montgomery married Macdonald, to whom she had been engaged for five years, and joined him in Leaskdale, Ontario, where he was minister.

For more than thirty years Montgomery was both a successful and admired writer and a minister's wife. She wrote at the dining-room table in the mornings, and spent her afternoons and evenings in such activities as choir practice, congregational entertaining, and Red Cross war work. The couple had two sons, Chester in 1912 and Stuart in 1915. A stillbirth in 1914, the near-death of Frede in 1915, and the impact of the First World War distressed her, but she continued to write, bringing out more Anne books and a volume of poetry. The Alpine Path (1917), an autobiographical essay, asserted her place as a highly disciplined and professional writer. Annual visits to her beloved Prince Edward Island maintained an essential link. Unhappily, a series of lawsuits with her first publisher over royalties and an unauthorized collection of stories began in 1918, and the dispute was not finished until 1928. More devastating were Frede's death and the first of her husband's series of mental breakdowns, the full extent of which she managed to conceal from his parishioners.

Throughout the period between the wars Montgomery's life was a public success and a private struggle, the duality echoed in her two main writing projects, the fiction and the journal. The one was deft, amusing, and positive, though with a strong subversive streak and a sure knowledge of both the originality and the commonality of women's lives. The other was also crafted and edited, constructing and controlling the shadow side of her life, critical, despairing, painful. It was a side that shocked those who knew the public or literary woman when the first journal selections were published in 1985. She published her last novel in 1939, and worked on another collection of stories in 1940, but the now-fragmentary journals recorded her loss of hope for herself, her family, and for a world once again sunk in international war. Her physical and mental decline ended with her death in Toronto on 24 April 1942. She was buried in Cavendish, Prince Edward Island, on 29 April.

Montgomery's fictions, both novelistic and autobiographical, have increasingly drawn serious critical attention, while continuing to be popular. Widely read, not only in Canada, her books have been turned into film and television, as well as into a tourist industry. Translated into a dozen languages, her novels are particularly popular in Poland and Japan. Their strong appeal derives in part from their celebration of the natural beauty of Prince Edward Island, but more especially from their celebration of women's lives, and the quiet challenge to the authority of the structures within which those lives are lived.

SUSAN DRAIN

Richard Montgomery (1738–1775), by Charles Willson Peale

Sources M. Rubio and E. Waterston, *Writing a life: L. M. Montgomery* (1995) · M. Rubio and E. Waterston, eds., *The selected journals of L. M. Montgomery, 1889–1935*, 4 vols. (1985–98) · G. Åhmansson, *A life and its mirrors: a feminist reading of the life of L. M. Montgomery* (1991) · M. Gillen, *The wheel of things: a biography of L. M. Montgomery* (1975) · L. M. Montgomery, *The alpine path: the story of my career*, [new edn] [1974] · M. Rubio, ed., *Harvesting thistles: the textual garden of L. M. Montgomery* (1994) · E. R. Epperly, *The fragrance of sweet-grass: L. M. Montgomery's heroines and the pursuit of romance* (1992) · F. W. P. Bolger, *The years before 'Anne'* (1974) · F. W. P. Bolger and E. R. Epperly, eds., *My dear Mr. M: letters to G. B. Macmillan* (1980) · K. McCabe, *The Lucy Maud Montgomery album*, ed. A. Heilbron (1999) **Archives** Confederation Center of the Arts, Charlottetown, Prince Edward Island, MSS · NA Canada, corresp. · University of Guelph, Ontario, journals **Likenesses** photographs, repro. in McCabe, *Lucy Maud Montgomery album*

Montgomery, Philip de (d. 1097/8). *See under* Montgomery, Roger de, first earl of Shrewsbury (d. 1094).

Montgomery, Richard (1738–1775), revolutionary army officer, was born on 2 December 1738 at Swords, co. Dublin, the third of four children of Sir Thomas Montgomery, baronet, former army officer and MP for Lifford, and his wife, Mary Franklin (or Franklyn). He attended St Andrews School and enrolled in Trinity College, Dublin, in 1754. On 21 September 1756, following the advice of his father and his eldest brother, Alexander, he left college and became an ensign in the 17th regiment. He served with his regiment under General Jeffrey Amherst at the siege of Louisbourg in 1758 and was promoted lieutenant on 10 July. A year later he was part of Amherst's expedition against forts Ticonderoga and Crown Point. Appointed adjutant on 15 May 1760, he was in the forces of Colonel William Haviland, sent from Crown Point to join the armies under Amherst and Brigadier-General James Murray converging on Montreal. After the fall of Montreal he was present with his regiment when Major-General Robert Monckton captured Martinique in early 1762. Promoted captain on 6 May 1762, he served the following summer under General George Keppel, earl of Albemarle, at the siege and capture of Havana. After peace was declared in 1763, he went with the 17th from Cuba to New York, and in 1765 returned home.

Over the next few years Montgomery made the acquaintance of Colonel Isaac Barré, Edmund Burke, Charles James Fox, and other men of liberal views who were friends of the Americans. Despite these connections he became convinced that he had no prospects of professional advancement in England: having sought promotion to major in 1771 he lost the opportunity to a protégé of the prime minister, Lord North. So he sold his captain's commission on 6 April 1772 and a year later bought a farm of 67 acres at Kings Bridge, now a part of the city of New York. Developing a passion for agriculture, he settled into a life of ease as a gentleman farmer and became reacquainted with Janet Livingston (1735–1824), whom he had met eight years earlier. On 24 July 1773 they were married, and Montgomery began building a handsome house,

Grasmere, the completion of which was delayed by growing tensions between Britain and the colonies in the early 1770s. Meantime, they lived at her more modest residence near Rhinebeck, New York. They had no children.

Upon his arrival in New York, Montgomery had joined his neighbours in resisting British policies, and they had come to trust him as a man of steady whiggish views. On 16 May 1775 they chose him to represent them in the New York provincial congress, called in protest at repressive ministerial measures against Massachusetts. Because of his military experience, on 22 June he was commissioned by congress as a brigadier-general in the continental army, ranking second among the eight chosen. Reluctantly he consented to part from his young wife, consoled by the reflection that the will of an oppressed people, compelled to choose between liberty and slavery, must be respected. Four days later General George Washington appointed him second in command in New York under Major-General Philip Schuyler, and on 29 June congress ordered Schuyler and Montgomery to invade Canada. After organizing their army at Fort Ticonderoga in August, they took Isle aux Noix and besieged St Johns and Chambly in early September. Schuyler fell sick, and on 16 September Montgomery assumed command of the army. The troops (chiefly New England men) were not of high quality, 'every man a general, and not one of them a soldier', Montgomery wrote. Supplies were low and desertion rife. Nevertheless, Montgomery took Chambly and St Johns, and captured Montreal on 11 November. He moved down the St Lawrence River to Quebec, and on 2 December effected a junction with Benedict Arnold, who had led an army through Maine.

For three weeks Montgomery and Arnold besieged Quebec, but failed to force its surrender. Smallpox was in their camp, and the men's enlistments were to end on the last day of the year. Hence they decided to try an assault. Early in the morning of 31 December 1775 Montgomery, in a blinding snowstorm, led an attack on the lower town, while Arnold attacked the upper town. Calling on the 'men of New York' to follow, Montgomery dashed on, but was instantly killed by a discharge of grapeshot. The Americans, thrown into confusion, withdrew, leaving Montgomery's frozen corpse in the snow. He died without knowing that congress had promoted him major-general on 9 December. Arnold drew off to the Plains of Abraham, where he kept up a fitful blockade until spring 1776, when the Americans withdrew from Canada. Montgomery's body was recovered by the British on 1 January 1776 and was buried with full military honours inside St Louis Gate, Quebec. On 25 January congress ordered that a memorial in marble be erected to Montgomery in the graveyard of St Paul's Episcopal Church, New York. In 1818 the Canadian government permitted the removal of his remains, which were laid next to his monument at St Paul's Church. An inscription on the rocks at Cape Diamond shows where he fell.   H. M. Chichester, *rev.* Paul David Nelson

Sources H. T. Shelton, *General Richard Montgomery and the American Revolution: from redcoat to rebel* (1994) · J. Armstrong, *Life of Richard Montgomery* (1836), vol. 1 of *Library of American Biography*, ed.

J. Sparks · G. W. Cullum, *Biographical sketch of Major-General Richard Montgomery of the continental army* (1876) · P. K. Fitzhugh, *The story of General Richard Montgomery* (1906) · C. W. Allen, *Memoir of General Montgomery* (1912) · A. L. Todd, *Richard Montgomery: rebel of 1775* (1967) · *Major-General Richard Montgomery: a contribution toward a biography from the Clements Library* (1970) · P. Force, ed., *American archives: a collection of authentick records, state papers, debates, and letters and other notices of publick affairs*, 4th and 5th ser., 9 vols. (1837–53) · J. H. Smith, *Our struggle for the fourteenth colony: Canada and the American Revolution*, 2 vols. (1907) · P. D. Nelson, 'Montgomery, Richard', *ANB*
Archives New York Historical Society, papers · PRO NIre., papers [copies] · U. Mich., Clements L., papers | L. Cong., George Washington papers · NYPL, Philip Schuyler
Likenesses C. W. Peale, oils, New York Historical Society · C. W. Peale, portrait, Independence National Historical Park, Philadelphia [*see illus.*]
Wealth at death owned land near New York City; married rich lady: Shelton, *General Richard Montgomery*, 37, 39, 176

Montgomery [Montgomerie], **Robert** (*d.* 1684), army officer, born at Eglinton, Ayrshire, was the fifth son of Alexander *Montgomery or Montgomerie, sixth earl of Eglinton (1588–1661), and his first wife, Lady Anna Livingstone (*d.* 1632), daughter of Alexander, first earl of Linlithgow. He was educated at the University of Glasgow, where he was enrolled a student on 1 March 1637. Subsequently he served as a mercenary on the continent. In the autumn of 1643 his father selected him to serve as lieutenant-colonel of his horse regiment, levied from Ayrshire, Lanarkshire, and Renfrewshire for the army of the solemn league and covenant, intended to join with the English parliamentarians. He fought under his father at the battle of Marston Moor (2 July 1644), was severely wounded in the arm, but kept the regiment in order despite the destruction of the other cavalry units on the right wing. In 1645 he served in the Hereford and Philiphaugh campaigns and replaced his father as colonel. In 1646 he held, under Major-General John Middleton, the command of a regiment of horse and dragoons in the north of Scotland, with which on 3 January 1646 he entered the city of Aberdeen. He served in the campaign which involved the relief of Inverness, besieged by Montrose, and which subdued Montrose's allies the Mackenzies. In February 1647 he was given command of a horse troop in Scotland's New Model Army and served in David Leslie's north-eastern and Argyll campaigns.

Montgomery opposed the December 1647 engagement and the resulting expedition under the duke of Hamilton in 1648 in the king's interest, losing his troop to his brother Hugh, Lord Montgomerie, on 11 May 1648. When the defeat of Hamilton at Winwick, near Preston, on 19 August became known, he gathered a body of western covenanters opposed to the engager regime, with which he routed a number of horse under the earl of Lanark, quartered in Ayrshire. He became a major-general in the kirk party aligned whiggamore forces. His action led the committee of estates to call out the fencible men, but their action was anticipated by the march to Edinburgh of the western whiggamores under his father, the earl of Eglinton, on 5 September. After the arrival of Cromwell in Edinburgh in support of the kirk party, Montgomery, in

1648, set out for London, carrying a letter from Cromwell recommending him, since there were none 'more active against the late invaders of England' (*Writings and Speeches*, 1.667), and seeking an order to deliver to him 2000 of the Scottish prisoners taken at Preston (ibid.). His purpose was to sell them to the king of Spain for service in the Low Countries, but negotiations with both Spain and France proved abortive.

In February 1649 the estates, now dominated by the kirk party, commissioned him major-general of horse, and colonel of horse for Ayrshire and Renfrewshire. By the following summer the regime had formalized its support for Charles II and raised forces to defend Scotland against attack by the English republic. Montgomery took a prominent part in the ensuing contest against Cromwell. On 31 July 1650 he attacked Cromwell's forces in the early morning near Musselburgh, beat in his guards, and 'put a regiment of horse in some disorder', but failed in his attempt to surprise them and was forced to retreat towards Edinburgh. Cromwell asserted that, so far as he had heard, his own loss was only a cornet and four men, but Sir James Balfour represented the Cromwellian loss as very severe (*Writings and Speeches*, 2.300–01). Montgomery fought at the battle of Dunbar on 3 September, and after the battle he retired with the other troops under David Leslie beyond the Forth. When Charles, in October 1650, suddenly left Perth intending to abandon the kirk party and join royalists in the north, in an incident known as the Start, Montgomery was in the neighbourhood of Forfar, in command of two regiments of horse. Being informed of his flight, Montgomery marched towards Atholl, where two of his officers discovered Charles in a poor cottage belonging to the laird of Clova. On the appearance of Montgomery with his troops, Charles consented to accompany him back to Huntly Castle, in the Carse of Gowrie.

On 14 October, Montgomery was ordered by the committee of estates to join Lieutenant-General Leslie, who was to employ him in any way he thought most advantageous to the country and hurtful to the enemy, and on 25 October he was ordered to take a cavalry force under his command and move to the west. By now it was apparent that the forces of the western association were increasingly inclined to support the remonstrant party, suspicious of the intentions of the king and the governing regime. Apparently to counter such divisions on 28 November it was agreed that there should be a union of the forces in the west under Montgomery's command, and on 2 December it was ordered by parliament that the three radical western regiments of Kirkcudbright, Galloway, and Dumfries be joined to his. Montgomery was at this time in Stirling, whence he was proceeding with four or five regiments of horse to carry out the commission entrusted to him, when, according to Cromwell, 'he was put to a stand' by the news of the defeat of Colonel Gilbert Ker, in command of the western forces, at Hamilton on 1 December. Nevertheless, he shortly afterwards forced his way by Kilsyth, killing seven of the enemy and taking four prisoners.

With the rank of major-general Montgomery was appointed to the command of the 3rd cavalry brigade in the army, which in the autumn of 1651 marched under David Leslie and Charles II into England. At the battle of Worcester on 3 September his brigade was posted opposite Powick bridge on the right flank of the southern force. Although furiously attacked by Fleetwood, he maintained his post with great determination until his ammunition was expended and Major-General Colin Pitscottie's retreat on the left uncovered his flank, when he retreated towards the city. He was taken prisoner either at or after the battle and sent to the Tower, from which in July 1654 he made his escape. On it becoming known that he had returned to Scotland, orders were given to arrest the earl of Eglinton, his father, and Lord Montgomerie, his brother, and detain them until they either delivered him up or gave security that he should leave the country. Shortly afterwards Montgomery was arrested in Renfrewshire, and confined in the castle of Edinburgh, but on 29 February 1657 made his escape in coalman's clothes. In October 1657 he went to Leghorn to offer his services to the king of Sweden and subsequently obtained the offer of employment in Denmark, but refused service because he was offered only a foot regiment, not one of horse. In October 1658 he was at Tours in France. After the Restoration he was made by Charles II a lord of the bedchamber, but his strong Presbyterian sympathies subsequently lost him the king's favour. In August 1665 an order was on this account made for his imprisonment and it was not until 22 January 1668 that he obtained his liberty. By his marriage, in 1662, to Elizabeth Livingstone (d. in or after 1688), daughter of James, Viscount Kilsyth, he had a daughter and two sons. He died in December 1684.

T. F. HENDERSON, *rev.* EDWARD M. FURGOL

Sources *The historical works of Sir James Balfour*, ed. J. Haig, 4 vols. (1824–5) · *The letters and journals of Robert Baillie*, ed. D. Laing, 3 vols. (1841–2) · *A list of the severall regiments and chief officers of the Scottish army quartered neer Newcastle* (1644) · J. Turner, *Memoirs of his own life and times, 1632–1670*, ed. T. Thomson, Bannatyne Club, 28 (1829) · APS, 1124–1707 · J. Stuart, ed., *Extracts from the council register of the burgh of Aberdeen, 1625–1747*, 2 vols., Scottish Burgh RS, 8–9 (1871–2) · J. Nicoll, *A diary of public transactions and other occurrences, chiefly in Scotland, from January 1650 to June 1667*, ed. D. Laing, Bannatyne Club, 52 (1836) · Thurloe, *State papers* · W. Stewart, *A full relation of the late victory obtained … against his Majesties forces … on Marstam-Moor … on the second of July, 1644* (1644) · J. Paterson, *History of the county of Ayr: with a genealogical account of the families of Ayrshire*, 2 vols. (1847–52) · CSP dom., 1649–85 · R. Wodrow, *The history of the sufferings of the Church of Scotland from the Restoration to the revolution*, ed. R. Burns, 4 vols. (1828–30) · W. Fraser, *Memorials of the Montgomeries, earls of Eglinton*, 2 vols. (1859) · Scots peerage · GEC, *Peerage* · *The writings and speeches of Oliver Cromwell*, ed. W. C. Abbott and C. D. Crane, 2 (1939)

Montgomery, Sir Robert, of Skelmorlie, fifth baronet (1680–1731), property speculator and author in America, was born at Skelmorlie Castle, Ayrshire, the son of Sir James *Montgomery of Skelmorlie, fourth baronet (c.1654–1694), and Lady Margaret (1654–1726), second daughter of James Johnstone, second earl of Annandale.

Robert married Frances (*d.* 1759), eldest daughter of Colonel Francis Stirling. He entered the English army and saw service in the War of the Spanish Succession (1702–13). Like his father he was interested in practical schemes of colonization, and after the peace turned his attention to America.

On 19 June 1717 Montgomery received from the Carolina lords proprietors a grant of land between the rivers Allatamaha and Savannah. In the same year he published a full prospectus, *A Discourse Concerning the Designed Establishment of a New Colony to the South of Carolina*, in which he set out his plans for the territory, which he intended to call the margravate of Azilia. He proposed a form of feudal colony devoted to the cultivation of tea, coffee, almonds, and other exotic goods currently imported from Mediterranean states. On 20 February 1718 the lords proprietors recommended that Montgomery be appointed to the council as life governor of the southern part of Carolina. Before the council he stated that he had raised £30,000 to finance his scheme and needed no additional money from the royal government, and on 24 July the scheme was approved.

In 1720 Montgomery published a second treatise for the proposed colony, *A Description of the Golden Island* (1720). However, by this date the project was clearly at an end and the crown took control of the land. On 15 September 1720 an application was made to the council to restrain action 'upon some advertisement now published by Sir Robert Montgomery' that suggested that he was sending persons 'to the Golden Islands, one of which islands lies in the mouth of the River Allatamaha, which has been proposed to be secured'.

Montgomery died in Ireland in August 1731, and in the following year the first moves were made by the Georgia trustees (among them James Oglethorpe) to establish, under the name of Georgia, the territory that had formerly belonged to Montgomery. He was survived by his wife, who died at Skelmorlie on 9 June 1759. One of their three daughters, Lillias (*d.* 1783), married Alexander Montgomerie and was the mother of Hugh, twelfth earl of Eglinton. On Sir Robert's death his title devolved on his uncle, Sir Hugh Montgomery, MP for Glasgow, and became extinct on his death on 14 January 1735.

C. A. HARRIS, *rev.* PHILIP CARTER

Sources *Scots peerage* · K. Coleman, 'The founding of Georgia', *Forty years of diversity: essays on colonial Georgia*, ed. H. H. Jackson and P. Spalding (1984), 4–20 · T. Reese, ed., *The most delightful country of the universe: promotional literature of the colony of Georgia, 1717–1734* (1972)

Montgomery [*formerly* Gomery], **Robert** (1807–1855), poet and Church of England clergyman, was born at Bath, the illegitimate son of Robert Gomery (*d.* 1853), who was at that time resident clown at the Bath theatre, but who also performed at the Haymarket (1814) and in the English Opera at the Lyceum (1816), and of an unnamed woman who may have been a schoolteacher and who appears to have taken no part in Montgomery's upbringing. He was educated at Dr Arnot's school in Bath and began early to

Robert Montgomery (1807–1855), by Charles Baugniet, 1845

produce evidence of literary ambition. At sixteen he founded a weekly paper called *The Inspector*, which ran for a few issues, and in 1825 he published his first collection of verse, *Poetical Trifles*, which boasted Joanna Baillie and Thomas Haynes Bailey among its subscribers. It was also during his adolescence that his name was extended by the prefix Mont, and although the reasons for this change remain obscure, there can be little doubt that the poet derived some benefit, especially in the early part of his career, from inevitable confusion with the already established, and unrelated, James Montgomery (another of the subscribers to his first book).

Robert Montgomery's next publication, a topical satire entitled *The Age Reviewed*, appeared anonymously in 1827, but his popular reputation was established in the following year with *The Omnipresence of the Deity* and *A Universal Prayer; Death; a Vision of Heaven; and a Vision of Hell*. *The Omnipresence*, in particular, was extravagantly praised by a number of influential writers including Crabbe, Southey, and John Wilson, and within a year the poem had gone through eight editions. This immediate success may owe something to the vogue for religious epic established by Pollok's *The Course of Time*, published in the previous year, and both poems appealed to a (largely evangelical) taste for grandiose restatements of traditional Christian wisdom, generally with an apocalyptic bent, in a decade troubled by the prospect of imminent social and political catastrophe. The years of Montgomery's triumph were also those in which Edward Irving preached the coming millennium to packed congregations at Hatton Garden (several of Irving's works, extensively annotated, were included in Montgomery's library) and in which the gigantic canvases of John Martin (whom Montgomery enthusiastically described as a 'second Milton' (R. Montgomery, *Satan, or, Intellect without God*, 1830, 344–5)) were being hailed as masterpieces of the sublime. Montgomery's most committed admirer, Edward Clarkson, indeed, wrote of a 'great crisis … now at hand' and conjectured that the poet might well be the 'harbinger' of the 'Star in the East' (Clarkson, 146–7).

Montgomery's next major productions were another satirical poem, *The Puffiad*, and *Satan, or, Intellect without God*, both published in 1830. The latter poem consists of three books of blank verse in which the Prince of Darkness surveys the precarious moral and spiritual condition of England, and it was hailed by the *Evangelical Magazine* for February 1830 as conclusive proof that Montgomery had become a writer of enduring value. Adverse criticism, however, appeared in *Fraser's* and in April Macaulay (who had been described by Montgomery as 'pert' (R. Montgomery, *The Age Reviewed*, 1828, 111)) launched a devastating attack in the *Edinburgh Review*. Macaulay, believing that the poet was a beneficiary both of ill-educated popular taste and of assiduous puffing, subjected passages from *The Omnipresence of the Deity* to a close textual analysis which remorselessly exposed its essentially vacuous basis. The poet considered a libel action, but instead contented himself with incorporating a lengthy rejoinder among the notes to *Oxford* (1831), in which he labelled Macaulay the 'hired assassin of a bigoted review' (R. Montgomery, *Selections from the Poetical Works*, 1836, 323) and with a few further sentences in the preface to *The Messiah*.

In 1830, with the encouragement of William Lisle Bowles and Sharon Turner, Montgomery matriculated at Lincoln College, Oxford, from which he graduated with fourth-class honours in Greats in 1833 (proceeding MA in 1838). His stay at the university, almost inevitably, resulted in a long poem, *Oxford*, and this prompted an anonymous *Poetical Epistle Addressed to Robert Montgomery* (1831) in which the poet was described as a byword 'for all that is vacant, vague, and inane' (*GM*, 311). After publishing two further epics (*The Messiah* appeared in 1832 and *Woman, the Angel of Life* in 1833), in May 1835 Montgomery was ordained at St Asaph and took a curacy at Whittington in Shropshire, which he left late in 1837 or early in 1838 to become minister to the episcopal congregation which then assembled at Buchanan Street, Glasgow, but which shortly afterwards moved to the newly erected church of St Jude. Here he swiftly established himself as a dramatic and popular preacher and he took visiting engagements at Leeds and at such fashionable resorts as Cheltenham and Bath in order to assist in fundraising for his new church. It was also during his years in Glasgow that Montgomery began to supplement his poetical labours (his last long poem, *Luther*, appeared in 1842) with a copious series of theological works, including collections of sermons (1843, 1845) and *The Church of the Invisible* (1847), a 'Manual for Christian Mourners' which went into four editions.

Montgomery left St Jude's in December 1842 and in October of the following year became minister at Percy Chapel, Charlotte Street, Bedford Square (where the pew rents were a source of disappointment). On 7 October 1843 he married Rachel Catherine Andrews McKenzie, youngest daughter of Alexander Douglas McKenzie of Bursledon, Hampshire; they had one child. Although Montgomery continued to produce verse, his principal efforts in his final decade were directed towards his theological writing and the consolidation of his position as a successful preacher for such charitable causes as the St Anne's Society schools in Brixton. His manner in the pulpit was described by John Dix as 'very affected' and his sermons as 'a tissue of laborious conceits, wrapped up in very hard words' and containing 'nothing like argument' (Hopkins, 362), while the comic actor Wybert Reeve recalls him likening dead humanity to a 'decayed Stilton cheese' which would be restored to its former consistency by the angel trumpets on the Last Day (Reeve, 86–7). Montgomery died at 21 Preston Street, Brighton, after a short illness, on 3 December 1855.

Aside from his personal vanity (and Macaulay was not alone in noticing the poet's assiduous efforts to enhance a fancied resemblance to Byron), Montgomery seems to have been a hard-working and well-liked clergyman, generous of time and energy in support of good works. Moreover, his unenviable position as the general butt of reviewers did little to damage the widespread appeal of his verse. Despite Macaulay's onslaught, the British Library catalogue lists twenty-eight editions of *The Omnipresence*, eight of *Satan*; multi-volume collections appeared in 1840 and 1841, and as late as 1856 E. Farr produced a volume of selected passages 'for School and Family Use'. As Macaulay himself acknowledged, Montgomery's works were bought and admired by a large and relatively new class of readers whose tastes and expectations were very different from those of the cultural élite. For such an audience, the value of Montgomery's verse lay in its grandiloquent presentation of conventional religious truth, and the slipshod thought and mixed metaphor which appalled a classically educated critic like Macaulay may well have gone unremarked beneath the stately procession of dignified abstract nouns. Montgomery's unquestioning confidence, both in his own inspiration and in the evangelical convictions he expressed, offered welcome reassurance to a generation whose intellectual leaders were becoming increasingly sceptical about the traditional bases of spiritual, political, and moral belief. It was thus, in a sense, his very banality which ensured Montgomery's position as one of the two or three best-selling poets of the second quarter of the nineteenth century.

ROBERT DINGLEY

Sources *GM*, 2nd ser., 45 (1856), 310–14 · *Annual Register* (1855) · *DNB* · K. Hopkins, 'Reflections on Satan Montgomery', *Texas Studies in Literature and Language*, 4 (1962–3), 351–66 · W. Bates, *The Maclise portrait gallery of illustrious literary characters*, new edn (1898) · Foster, *Alum. Oxon.* · *Catalogue of the theological and miscellaneous library of the late Robert Montgomery, AM* (1856) · W. Reeve, *From life* (1892) · E. Clarkson, *Robert Montgomery and his reviewers* (1830) · BL cat. · d. cert.

Archives BL · NL Scot., letters · University of Leicester · Wordsworth Trust, Dove Cottage, Grasmere

Likenesses J. Romney, line engraving, 1828 (after C. Grant), NPG · Thomson, stipple, pubd 1828 (after Derby), NPG · Thomson, stipple, pubd 1828 (after Hobday), NPG · D. Maclise, caricature, c.1830, repro. in Bates, *Maclise portrait gallery* · R. Montgomery, self-portrait miniature, oils, c.1830, Holburne of Menstrie Museum, Bath · C. Baugniet, lithograph, 1845, AM Oxf., BM, NPG [*see illus.*] · Finden, engraving (after portrait by D. Macnee), repro. in R. Montgomery, *The omnipresence of the deity and other poems*, 21st edn (1841) · prints, NPG · wood-engraving, NPG; repro. in *ILN* (24 March 1855)

Montgomery, Sir Robert (1809–1887), administrator in India, born on 2 December 1809 at New Park, Moville, co. Donegal, was the son of Samuel Law Montgomery, rector of Lower Moville. He was educated at Foyle College, Londonderry, Wraxall Hall School, north Wiltshire, and Addiscombe College, Croydon, Surrey. He was appointed to the Bengal civil service in 1827 under the patronage of Joseph D. Alexander—although he was trained as a military cadet, he never joined the army. He filled various junior posts in the North-Western Provinces, including one at Azamgarh under James Thomason, whose sister, Frances Mary, he married on 17 December 1834. They had three surviving children before her death from smallpox in Allahabad on 23 March 1842. He was appointed magistrate and collector at Allahabad in 1838, and published a report on the settlement of the Allahabad district in 1839. He was on leave from 1843 to 1846, during which time he married, in 1845, Ellen Jane, daughter of William Lambert of Woodmansterne, Surrey. On his return to India, he was appointed collector of Cawnpore through the patronage of James Thomason, by now lieutenant-governor of the North-Western Provinces.

On the recommendation of Henry Miers Elliot, Dalhousie's foreign secretary, Montgomery became one of the new divisional commissioners of the Punjab in 1849, and in 1851 he replaced Charles Grenville Mansel on the board of administration of Punjab, at the instance of his old friend and schoolfellow, Henry Lawrence. He took a large part in organizing the newly annexed province, eventually (in 1853) becoming judicial commissioner, his duties being not merely legal, but including the superintendence of education, roads, police, and municipalities.

On the outbreak of the mutiny in May 1857, Montgomery acted swiftly to disarm the sepoys in Lahore, whom, he had learned, intended to rise as soon as they heard of the rising in Delhi. Montgomery's actions were of great significance because Lahore was strategically vital for defending British rule in the Punjab, from which region lower India was first reconquered. Following the relief of Lucknow and the re-establishment of order there, Lord Canning appointed him to succeed Sir James Outram as chief commissioner of Oudh in April 1858, and there he enforced Canning's confiscation proclamation. Thanks to his great administrative skill with respect to the aggrieved talukdars, and his realization that these landowners had a genuine grievance stemming from Dalhousie's 1856 annexation and administration, he effected a new settlement by February 1859, with the support of Sir Hope Grant and his force. In 1859 he was appointed lieutenant-governor of the Punjab, and held that post until 1865, when he resigned and returned to England on pension. He had been made a civil KCB on 19 May 1859. On 20 February 1866 he was made a GCSI, and in 1868 was appointed a member of the Council of India. This office he held until his death on 28 December 1887 at his home, 7 Cornwall Gardens, London, from bronchitis; he was buried in his family vault in Londonderry Cathedral on 3 January 1888. He was survived by his wife. In addition to the three children of his first marriage, Montgomery and his second wife had four sons and three daughters. The second son, Henry Hutchinson *Montgomery, became a bishop, whose son, Bernard Law Montgomery, became first Viscount Montgomery of Alamein.

J. A. HAMILTON, *rev.* PETER PENNER

Sources B. Montgomery, *Monty's grandfather: Sir Robert Montgomery ... a life's service for the raj* (1984) · P. Penner, *The patronage bureaucracy in north India* (1986) · P. Penner, *Robert Needham Cust: a personal biography* (1987) · R. Temple, *James Thomason* (1893) · R. B. Smith, *Life of Lord Lawrence*, 2 vols. (1883) · J. W. Kaye, *The administration of the East India Company* (1853) · C. Hibbert, *The great mutiny, India, 1857* (1978); repr. (1980) · *The Times* (29 Dec 1887) · *The Times* (30 Dec 1887) · *The Times* (31 Dec 1887) · J. W. Kaye, *A history of the Sepoy War in India, 1857–1858*, 3 vols. (1864–76) · *CGPLA Eng. & Wales* (1888)

Archives BL OIOC, semi-official, and personal corresp. and papers, MS Eur. D1019 | BL, corresp. with H. Bruce, Add. MS 43993 · BL OIOC, letters to Sir Richard Temple, MSS Eur. F83, 86 · BL OIOC, letters to Lord Elgin, MSS Eur. F83 · Bodl. Oxf., corresp. with Lord Kimberley · W. Yorks. AS, Leeds, letters to Lord Canning

Likenesses A. B. Joy, marble bust, exh. RA 1893, BL OIOC · A. B. Joy, medallion, St Paul's Cathedral, London · A. Rendall, oils (after F. Grant, 1865), BL OIOC

Wealth at death £24,431 12s. 1d.: probate, 30 Jan 1888, *CGPLA Eng. & Wales*

Montgomery, Roger de, **first earl of Shrewsbury** (*d.* 1094), soldier and magnate, came from St Germain de Montgommeri and St Foy de Montgommeri (modern French usage prefers Montgommery) near Troarn in Calvados, in an area between Caen and Rouen where place names suggest intensive Scandinavian settlement: in a charter to Troarn Abbey of as late as c.1080 Roger proudly described himself as a Norseman of Norsemen—'ex Northmannis Northmannus' (Round, no. 465).

A loyal servant in ducal Normandy Roger de Montgomery's father was also Roger, whose tenure of lands round the lower reaches of the River Dives can be traced to Duke Robert (I)'s time (1027–35), and his mother (still alive in 1068) may have been called Emma. The elder Roger's descent is among the most problematical of all the connections of the Duchess Gunnor, second wife of Duke Richard (I) (*d.* 996), who were so prominent in the landed aristocracy of eleventh- and twelfth-century Normandy and England. However, the problem is soluble in his case by acceptance of the outline genealogy given at the end of a letter written a century later by Ivo, bishop of Chartres, to prevent a marriage within the prohibited degrees of a descendant of Earl Roger's daughter Mabel. According to this, one of Gunnor's sisters (Wevie, not Senfrie) herself had a daughter, Joscelina, who married c.990–1000 Hugh de Montgommeri (of whom otherwise nothing is known) and was mother by him of Earl Roger's father. Whatever the exact relationship to the dukes, who hoped to find Gunnor's kin more loyal supporters than members of the ducal house itself, the elder Roger was a leading member (1033) of Duke Robert's administration as vicomte of the Hièmois. Under Robert's son William, the younger Roger (according to Orderic Vitalis) eventually held the same position and was a frequent witness of ducal *acta* (usually after his kinsman *William fitz Osbern but once immediately before him). The two made their mark as youths (*tirones*) by loyalty to the equally youthful duke at the siege of Domfront (of uncertain date but perhaps 1051–2).

Probably about 1050, the younger Roger had married Mabel de Bellême (*d.* 1077), daughter of Guillaume Talvas and ultimately heiress of Bellême, on the south-eastern frontier of the duchy. His reputation in the duchy was made by his success in enforcing his wife's rights as heiress, thus showing that constant activity on a borderland which his overlord was to require of him elsewhere after 1066. Mabel, however, was hostile to the monastery of St Evroult, in the Pays d'Ouche, as a result of the Talvas feud with the family of Giroie, benefactors of St Evroult; and this hostility gained for her the strong dislike of the historian Orderic Vitalis, a monk of St Evroult, who, though a prime source for her husband, Roger, never concealed his distaste for Roger's violent and aggressive wife, as Orderic (rightly) thought her. In Roger himself, however, Orderic found much to praise: his benefactions to St Evroult, his expulsion from Troarn of the secular canons established there by his father and his foundation of an abbey in their place, his foundation of the nunnery at Alménêches, and his foundation, with Mabel, of a priory at Sées in the sphere of influence of Mabel's family.

Lordships in Anglo-Norman England In the years before 1066 Roger de Montgomery extended his influence in the Hièmois and the Alençonnais; his career culminated, in the duchy at least, in his appointment as adviser (with Roger de Beaumont, (*d.* in or after 1090)) to Duchess Matilda in the government of Normandy during Duke William's invasion of England (1066–7). Hence neither Roger himself nor his teenage elder sons were present at Hastings. When King William returned to England in November 1067 after his visit to Normandy, Roger returned with him, and grants to him of lands in England quickly followed. Orderic says twice that this happened in two stages: Roger received first Arundel and Chichester, and afterwards Shropshire. With responsibilities on both the south coast and the Welsh border, Roger was thus put in the same position as that already held by his kinsman and associate William fitz Osbern (in the Isle of Wight and Herefordshire), and by no one else. By Arundel and Chichester are meant the rapes in west Sussex of those two titles, but not the earldom of Arundel, which Roger de Montgomery never held; the grant must be dated to 1067–8 and Roger may temporarily have held somewhat more land than the two rapes covered in Domesday Book. The grant to Roger of most of Shropshire probably followed in 1070–71, after the revolt and defeat of Earl Eadwine of Mercia. Fairly soon afterwards Roger was made earl of

Shrewsbury, thus becoming one of two vicomtes from Normandy who in England received the higher title of earl, the other being Hugh d'Avranches who became earl of Chester. The date of Roger's creation was long thought to be 1071, but L. C. Loyd deduced from charters that it took place between 1 and 24 December 1074. More recently, however, C. P. Lewis has argued for 1068 as the date of Roger's creation as earl, perhaps even of the grant of Shropshire lands. There is no warrant for describing Roger's comital status as 'palatine'.

Roger de Montgomery's eminence is reflected in the fact that among his vassals were a dozen men who were themselves tenants-in-chief of varying levels of endowment. His sixty or so tenants in Sussex included very few tenants-in-chief and, with one important exception, do not seem to have followed him to Shropshire, where, however, his vassals included no fewer than eleven tenants-in-chief. Three of these, in the south of the county, had probably secured a footing in Herefordshire before Roger's advent; further north there were three others from much further afield, among them one kinsman of Roger (William de *Warenne) who was himself nearly as well endowed as Roger himself. Perhaps even Roger was running out of followers of his own to whom he could enfeoff his estates.

Curiously, men connected with Roger de Montgomery in Normandy are found not so much in Sussex (where his Domesday tenants are seldom given toponymic or patronymic descriptions), as in Shropshire. It was three of these who were enfeoffed by the earl with fairly compact holdings on the border with the Welsh of Powys: north of the Severn, Warin and then Reinaud de Bailleul-en-Gouffern, successive husbands of the earl's niece Amieria and also successive sheriffs of Shropshire, held manors in Ruesset hundred between the Severn and Cheshire, notably Oswestry with its new castle, Luvre (*L'oeuvre*), built by Reinaud; Corbet, possibly from the Pays de Caux, was installed in the broken country south of the river round Caus and Longden; and Picot de Sai, from near Argentan, in the valleys of the Clun and Onny rivers. (A similar eye for country had been shown in west Sussex: of Roger's leading tenants there, Robert fitz Tetbald, sheriff of the rape of Arundel, held over thirty manors north of the Downs, including Pulborough, which commanded an important ford over the marshy Arun; and William de Ansleville, perhaps from Valognes in the Cotentin, held about half of that number south of the Downs, some of them straddling the line of Stane Street, which led from Chichester to London.) Of 230 hides held by the earl in the Shropshire border hundreds, 196 were held by these three vassals, whose descendants or representatives were dominant in western Shropshire for some centuries.

Wealth and power on the Shropshire march In the valley of the Severn, Roger de Montgomery had three main centres of power and administration. The selection of Shrewsbury itself, in the middle of the county, as the site of a castle had been made before the arrival of the earl. Further up the Severn, Roger, possibly before 1073, began the construction of the Hen Domen ('the old mound') near the ford at Rhydwhiman, 2 miles from Montgomery. This timber castle was to have a life of over a century and shows how durable and complex such a wooden fortress might be, with its first-floor hall, large granary, and about seventy other buildings. In the south-east of the county, Roger had in 1086 a new house (*nova domus*) at Quatford, built on the first eminence commanding a ford over the Severn in Shropshire on the approach from the south. The earl's interest in his final years in this corner of his earldom is also evidenced by the story of his foundation nearby of Quatford church, allegedly (though the tale follows a well-known pattern) at the spot where he met his second wife on her coming to Shropshire.

From his forward base at Montgomery, supported by the vassals who held border tenancies behind him, Earl Roger was well placed to harry the Welsh. The versions of the Welsh *Brut* state two facts about Roger: that he ill-treated the Welsh, and that he began a castle at 'Dingeraint' (Cardigan). The castle may have resulted from one of the expeditions of 'Franci' dispatched by Roger in 1073 or 1074, or more probably from his last thrust in 1093. The earl aimed to control the Welsh of Powys by a steady penetration along the upper valleys of the Dee and Severn. In the north, the commotes of Cynllaith and Edeyrnion bordering the Dee were by 1086 subject to Roger's sheriff, and nephew by marriage, Reinaud, the castellan of Oswestry. The tenure of the nearby commote of Ial by the earl of Chester as Earl Roger's vassal is among the evidence that the Normans could co-operate with each other in these efforts. Roger himself held Arwystli in the very centre of Wales, through which ran the main lines of approach to the Welsh coast at Aberystwyth and Cardigan; and his forces once went even further afield, when his sheriff Warin led a raid into Llŷn.

Earl Roger's extensive lands were administered with the help of a number of officials. There appear to have been three distinct sets of these, one in Normandy, one in Sussex, and one in Shropshire. He had a sheriff in Sussex; and in Shropshire another sheriff, probably a steward, a landless constable, two huntsmen, and a butler, each of the last three holding (as though in conformity with the rules of some unknown establishment) tenancies assessed at 10 hides. The earl was served by various clerks (including those in the castle chapels of Arundel and Shrewsbury) and by others, including Odelerius, who was the father of the historian Orderic Vitalis, and, probably, Richard de Belmeis, who was to be in effect the successor in Shropshire of Roger's two eldest sons.

Roger de Montgomery was forward-looking in the economic exploitation of his lands: for instance he founded *bourgs* in Normandy and new towns in Shropshire, brought French burgesses to Shrewsbury, and exploited his demesnes profitably. In consequence he and his sons had at their disposal considerable amounts of cash, and could employ large numbers of knights, import horses, and pay the fines demanded by kings.

In England, Earl Roger's major ecclesiastical benefactions were limited to Shropshire; in Sussex he granted manors to Norman houses, notably to his own foundation of Alménêches. In Shropshire, probably with the aid of monks from La Charité sur Loire, he refounded (*c*.1079–82) the existing well-endowed minster of secular clerks at Much Wenlock as a Cluniac priory. In 1083 he publicly and ceremoniously announced his intention to found a Benedictine abbey at Shrewsbury itself, on the site of the wooden church of St Peter and St Paul, just east of the English bridge; this church was then held by Odelerius. Work was begun on a new stone church and two monks from Sées were brought in to begin the new foundation, which was endowed with the churches of Roger's Shropshire demesne manors and two-thirds of the tithes of his demesnes in the county. Lastly, Roger founded a collegiate church at Quatford as a companion foundation to his new house and borough there; the church was dedicated at an impressive ceremony in 1086. At Montgomery, with its more exposed site, the earl did not set up a new religious house.

The richest tenant-in-chief of William I and William II His lands in west Sussex and Shropshire, with a number in ten other scattered counties (especially in Staffordshire), made Roger de Montgomery one of the eleven best-endowed tenants-in-chief of William I in 1086. By C. W. Hollister's calculations of the figures given in Domesday Book, the total annual value of Earl Roger's honour at that date (£2078) was exceeded only by that of the honour of Odo of Bayeux, the Conqueror's half-brother, and the value of the estates still held in demesne by Roger in that year (£1031) was greater, often considerably greater, than that still held in demesne by Odo himself or by any other of William's greatest non-ecclesiastical tenants-in-chief. As Odo had been in disgrace since 1082, Roger thus disposed of more landed wealth than anyone in England after the Conqueror, and was therefore a key figure in any alignment of political forces.

Earl Roger spent the last fifteen years of the Conqueror's reign on his estates in England, at the king's court in England and Normandy, and on the affairs of Wales. The death of William I posed for Roger the same conflict of loyalties as it did for many of the Anglo-Norman baronage: in his case, Orderic Vitalis says that William I and his son William Rufus had an affection for both the earl and Mabel, but also that Roger was among those who pleaded with the Conqueror on behalf of the king's eldest son, Robert Curthose. In 1088 the earl was openly in rebellion against Rufus, as were some of his sons; Roger joined at the persuasion of Rufus's uncles, Odo of Bayeux and *Robert de Mortain, who was the earl's son-in-law (and contemporary). Orderic implies that the conspiracy was hatched in Normandy and that Roger then crossed to England. He soon went over to Rufus, probably because his eldest son, Robert de *Bellême, who had been assigned a chief place in the plot, had been arrested by Duke Robert; with Rufus's permission Roger rushed to Normandy to fortify his own castles against the duke. Roger's efforts on his son's behalf were successful and he resumed support of the king. Rufus wisely imposed no penalty on Roger, who was taken back into favour; so too, at about that time, was his third son, Roger the Poitevin [*see below*]. In 1093 the earl dispatched another raid into west Wales; and at the very end of that year he was again at court. The final scenes took place at Shrewsbury Abbey, which Roger had founded. Here, as death approached, he took the monastic habit and here he died, on 27 July 1094, probably in his mid-sixties; he was buried 'between the altars', in a fine tomb which no longer survives.

Orderic Vitalis once, when first noting Earl Roger's rise in England, pauses to record his merits: 'sapiens et moderatus et amator aequitatis fuit, et comitatem sapientium atque modestorum dilexit' ('a wise and prudent man and lover of justice, who loved the company of learned and sober men'; Ordericus Vitalis, *Eccl. hist.*, 2.262–3). This was admittedly a prelude to recording the earl's reliance on Orderic's own father, but he goes on to note Roger's wise choices of men for positions of authority and command. Orderic allows a conclusion that Roger was (despite problems) uxorious and that he cared for the interests of his children. R. W. Eyton caught up Orderic's first words on Roger, whom he called 'wise and politic' (Eyton, 2.191). H. F. M. Prescott, the only novelist to use Roger in a novel (*Son of Dust*, 1938), stresses the earl's loyalty; in this regard wisdom deserted him only once, in 1088, but his position, connections, and past services were such that prudence dictated that no penalty could be imposed. Alone of all the Conqueror's vassals, Roger de Montgomery gave his name to a British county, appropriately in Wales.

Wives and younger sons Earl Roger's first wife, Mabel de Bellême, has been depicted unforgettably for posterity by Orderic Vitalis, though that historian never saw her. He describes her as 'a forceful and worldly woman, cunning, garrulous, and extremely cruel', 'a perfidious woman', and 'a cruel woman, who had shed the blood of many and had forcibly disinherited many lords' (Ordericus Vitalis, *Eccl. hist.*, 2.48–9; 3.134–7); and he recounts several stories to her discredit related to him by colleagues at St Evroult. Whatever allowances can be made for Mabel there must have been something particularly aggressive and brutal about her for four of her vassals to ride at night into her castle at Bures [-sur-Dives] and cut off her head as she lay in bed after a bath (Chibnall, 107–8). Her murderer Hugh Bunel was among those whom she had disinherited and was never caught. The date of the murder must be December 1077, not 1082 as long accepted from a marginal note in the *editio princeps* of Orderic. There is evidence that Mabel, like a very few other baronial wives, was a tenant-in-chief in England, but no evidence that she ever visited that land or the Montgomery estates there.

Roger quickly remarried, probably by 1080; his second wife was the high-born Adelais du Puiset from the Île-de-France, who survived him. Orderic naturally made the most of the differences between Mabel and Adelais; he could have added that Adelais (admittedly in a much later account) did come to England, indeed to Shropshire, where she was the cause not of disinheritance but of the foundation of a church, and where probably she witnessed a land-grant of 1085 by the bishop of Hereford.

Orderic gives Roger and Mabel five sons and four daughters, and lists the sons first, as Robert de Bellême, Hugh de

*Montgomery, Roger the Poitevin, Philip [*see below*], and Arnulf de *Montgomery. Robert, Hugh, and Roger attested a charter in that order; but Orderic's list omits the eldest son, also Roger, who attested a Le Mans charter as *Rogerio parvulo* and presumably lived a few years; on his death a younger brother was given his baptismal name.

Roger the Poitevin (*b. c.*1065, *d.* before 1140), the third surviving son of Earl Roger and Mabel, was probably born in the mid-1060s. In Domesday Book he appears as Roger the Poitevin (*Pictavensis*), by reason of his marriage, made on his father's advice, to Almodis, sister of Boso (III), count of La Marche (*d.* 1091); but the Domesday entries for his large honour present problems. In five counties (Hampshire, Nottinghamshire, Lincolnshire, Essex, and Suffolk) he is entered as a normal tenant-in-chief; but in four others (the land between the Ribble and the Mersey, Derbyshire, Yorkshire, and Norfolk) his tenure is entered as a thing of the past: thus at the end of his Derbyshire fee is a note that Roger used to hold the lands, but they are now in the hand of the king. This and other entries suggest that Roger's lands were all ordered to be taken into the king's hand late in 1086, but that in some cases the order was not known locally in time to be recorded in Domesday, or recorded in full. In view of his age, Roger cannot have held this honour for long; why he should so soon have lost it, at a time when as far as is known he and his father were loyal to the Conqueror, is not stated. The land between the Ribble and the Mersey was later enlarged to become modern Lancashire. By 1086 Roger had installed a body of tenants and built a castle at Penwortham, at a crossing of the Ribble which might be used by an invading king of Scots; at Lancaster he later founded a priory with the aid of monks from his parents' foundation at Sées.

Roger the Poitevin may have joined the revolt of 1088 against William Rufus, but if so soon made his peace; Rufus restored all or most of the honour which Roger held before Domesday and soon added to it the honour of Eye (mainly in East Anglia), previously held by Robert Malet. Rufus entrusted him with two demanding tasks: a military command in 1088 against William of St Calais, bishop of Durham, with whom Roger also negotiated on the king's behalf before the bishop came to trial, and in 1094 the defence of Argentan. Roger's quick surrender of the town to Philippe I of France, despite the size of his own forces, has been thought 'pathetic', but is explained if the French king was then his direct overlord. Roger continued loyal to Rufus, but in 1102 joined, ineffectively, his eldest brother's unsuccessful rebellion against Henry I. In consequence he was expelled from England, which he visited again only in 1109. The rest of his life was spent in the politics of La Marche; his sons bore names (Aldebert, Boso) which do not appear in the Montgomery family tree. Roger died before 1140.

Earl Roger's fourth surviving son, **Philip de Montgomery** (*d.* 1097/8), was presumably named after King Philippe of France. He is variously styled *clericus* and *grammaticus* ('the grammarian') by Orderic Vitalis, but for some years at least was destined for a secular career: he joined his two eldest brothers in confirming a paternal grant, and in another charter is described as the holder of an island in Normandy. He may have supported Robert Curthose in 1088, being indeed imprisoned, according to John of Worcester, and followed him on the first crusade, dying at Antioch, presumably in 1097 or 1098. He was the only son of Earl Roger to die while actually serving Curthose. It is not known whether he ever married, but his daughter Matilda succeeded her aunt Emma as abbess of Alménêches in 1113.

Orderic's list of four daughters of Roger and Mabel follows that of their brothers, in an order which is probably that of their birth: Emma (d. 1113), a nun at and later (perhaps as early as c.1074, when she was probably in her early twenties) abbess of her father's foundation at Alménêches; Matilda (d. 1082x4), who married before 1066 the Conqueror's half-brother Robert de Mortain; Mabel, who married Hugues de Châteauneuf-en-Thymerais; and Sybil, who married Robert fitz Hamon from south Wales.

With his second wife Earl Roger had one son, Ebrard, who was described by Orderic Vitalis, writing in 1127, as well educated and as among the royal chaplains in the households of William II and Henry I. If Ebrard served Rufus he was probably born soon after his parents' marriage; but his tentative identification with the Everard, or Eborard (d. 1147), who became bishop of Norwich in 1121 seems most unlikely.   J. F. A. MASON

Sources Ordericus Vitalis, *Eccl. hist.* · A. Farley, ed., *Domesday Book*, 2 vols. (1783) · D. R. Bates, *Normandy before 1066* (1982) · R. R. Davies, *Conquest, coexistence, and change: Wales, 1063–1415*, History of Wales, 2 (1987), chap. 2 · D. C. Douglas, *William the Conqueror* (1964) · F. Barlow, *William Rufus* (1983) · J. F. A. Mason, 'Roger de Montgomery and his sons (1067–1102)', *TRHS*, 5th ser., 13 (1963), 1–28 · J. F. A. Mason, 'The officers and clerks of the Norman earls of Shropshire', *Transactions of the Shropshire Archaeological Society*, 56 (1957–60), 244–57 · K. Thompson, 'The Norman aristocracy before 1066: the example of the Montgomerys', *Historical Research*, 60 (1987), 251–63 · GEC, *Peerage*, new edn, 11.682–7; and appx k · C. W. Hollister, 'The greater Domesday tenants-in-chief', *Domesday studies: papers read at the novocentenary conference of the Royal Historical Society and the Institute of British Geographers* [Winchester 1986], ed. J. C. Holt (1987), 219–47 · P. A. Barker and R. Higham, *A timber castle on the east Wales border* (1988) · P. A. Barker and R. Higham, *Timber castles* (1992), chap. 9 · J. H. Round, ed., *Calendar of documents preserved in France, illustrative of the history of Great Britain and Ireland* (1899) · M. Fauroux, ed., *Recueil des actes des ducs de Normandie de 911 à 1066* (Caen, 1961) · T. Jones, ed. and trans., *Brenhinedd y Saesson, or, The kings of the Saxons* (1971) [another version of *Brut y tywysogyon*] · A. Jones, ed. and trans., *History of Gruffydd ap Cynan* (1910) · R. Charles and M. d'Elbenne, eds., *Cartulaire de l'abbaye de St Vincent du Mans*, 2 vols. (1886–1913) · Ivo Carnotensis, *Patrologia Latina*, 162 (1854) · Symeon of Durham, *Opera*, vol. 1 · R. W. Eyton, *Antiquities of Shropshire*, 12 vols. (1854–60) · V. H. Galbraith, 'An episcopal land-grant of 1085', *EngHR*, 44 (1929), 353–72 · V. H. Galbraith, *The making of Domesday Book* (1961) · J. F. A. Mason, *William I and the Sussex rapes* (1966) · V. Chandler, 'The last of the Montgomerys: Roger the Poitevin and Arnulf', *Historical Research*, 62 (1989), 1–14 · C. P. Lewis, 'The king and Eye: a study in Anglo-Norman politics', *EngHR*, 104 (1989), 569–89 · C. P. Lewis, 'The early earls of Norman England', *Anglo-Norman Studies*, 13 (1990), 207–23 · M. Chibnall, 'Women in Orderic Vitalis', *Haskins Society Journal*, 2 (1990), 105–21

Montgomery, Walter [real name Richard Tomlinson] (1827–1871), actor, is said to have been a descendant of an old Norfolk family. The tenth son of William Tomlinson and Charlotte Montgomery, he was born on 25 August 1827, at Gawennis, Long Island, in New York state, but soon settled in England. While occupied in business in Cheapside with a shawl manufacturer named Warwick he took part in amateur entertainments, and appeared at the Soho Theatre, later known as the Royalty, in *Othello*. Having been engaged by J. H. Chute, the manager of the Bath stage, he played at that house under the name of Montgomery, and later went on to Bristol, Birmingham, Manchester, Norwich, and Yarmouth. In Nottingham, where he became a favourite, he also entered into management, and opened a new theatre. Montgomery's first appearance in London took place at the Princess's, on 20 June 1863, as Othello to Ellen Terry's Desdemona; on 24 June he played Romeo to the Juliet of Stella Colas. Under his own management at the same theatre he appeared as Shylock (22 August 1863), but incurred heavy losses. In the following March he gave, at the St James's Hall, readings from Shakespeare, Hood, Tennyson, Macaulay, and the *Ingoldsby Legends*. He continued with Shakespearian roles during the next few years, playing Posthumus Leonatus in *Cymbeline* and Cassius in *Julius Caesar* at Drury Lane (1865) and Hamlet at the Haymarket, the management of which he undertook, not very successfully, from July to November 1865. He also played Claude Melnotte in Bulwer-Lytton's *The Lady of Lyons*, King John, Shylock, and Iago, to the Othello of Ira Aldridge and was the original Lorenzo in *Fra Angelo*, a tragedy in blank verse by William Clark Russell. In November 1866 Helen Faucit began a twelve-night engagement at Drury Lane, and Montgomery was Orlando to her Rosalind and Sir Thomas Clifford in Sheridan Knowles's *The Hunchback* to her Julia. He made soon afterwards some reputation in America and Australia, being well received as Louis XI and Sir Giles Overreach. In July 1871 he began with *Hamlet* a short and unprosperous season at the Gaiety, in the course of which he played, besides other characters, Sir Giles Overreach, Louis XI, and Meg Merrilies.

On 30 August 1871 Montgomery married Laleah Burpee Bigelow, an American actress who had appeared twice at the Gaiety as Pauline in *The Lady of Lyons* and was scheduled to do so again to her husband's Claude Melnotte at Rochdale on 4 September before the two of them sailed for America on the 7th. But on 1 September, at his home, 2 Stafford Street, Bond Street, Montgomery shot himself, while, according to the verdict given at an inquest, of unsound mind. He was buried in Brompton cemetery on 5 September. His acting was pleasing if not very subtle, his appearance good, and his voice powerful.

JOSEPH KNIGHT, rev. NILANJANA BANERJI

Sources *The Era* (10 Sept 1871) · *The Times* (4 Sept 1871) · *The life and reminiscences of E. L. Blanchard, with notes from the diary of Wm. Blanchard*, ed. C. W. Scott and C. Howard, 2 vols. (1891) · *Era Almanack and Annual* (1878) · CGPLA Eng. & Wales (1872)

Wealth at death under £300: probate, 18 June 1872, CGPLA Eng. & Wales

Montgomery, William (1633–1707), historian, first son of Sir James Montgomery (d. 1652) of Rosemount, co. Down, and Katherine, daughter of Sir William Stewart, was born on 27 October 1633 at Aughantain, co. Tyrone. Raised by his maternal grandparents in Tyrone he was hurriedly sent to Scotland via Derry in October 1641 following the outbreak of a massive rebellion in Ireland. He returned to Derry after spending a year studying Latin at Glasgow high school, and in 1644 went to the family seat at Rosemount for the first time. There he mostly remained until the successes of parliament's forces in Ulster in late summer 1649 prompted his flight to Scotland. He studied at Glasgow University, but was again forced to flee in 1650, this time to the Dutch republic, where he studied philosophy at Leiden University. Despite the political and military upheavals that formed the backdrop to his youth William's family never neglected his education. A good student, he was fluent in Latin, Greek, French, and Dutch.

After hearing of his father's death fighting pirates Montgomery travelled to London to petition for restoration to his family lands, remaining in the capital from June 1652 to May 1653. He also pleaded on behalf of his cousin, Hugh Montgomery, third viscount of Ards. After failing to recover his lands he returned to Ireland where he purchased land debentures worth £500. He spent the rest of the 1650s in Down, Dublin, and London trying to have these debentures satisfied in the form of his father's lands at Florida manor in Castlereagh barony, co. Down. However, Colonel Barrow, a Cromwellian soldier, was in possession of these lands and refused to yield them. From 1656 William was also engaged in litigation with Sir Bryan O'Neill for possession of Ballyhoran, co. Down. During this period Montgomery lacked a steady source of income and ran up heavy debts.

As the Cromwellian regime collapsed throughout the three kingdoms in late 1659 Montgomery was heavily engaged in various royalist conspiracies. Following the royalist coup in Dublin he hurried to Down and forcibly seized Rosemount and the castle at Quintin Bay on 12 February 1660. This left him in full possession of his father's holdings for the first time. In 1660 he married his cousin Elizabeth, daughter of Hugh, second Viscount Montgomery of the Ards. They had one son, James. Montgomery became JP for co. Down and sat as MP for Newtown from 1661 to 1667. During the early 1660s he acted as an agent for Ards, who became earl of Mountalexander and who appointed Montgomery his deputy in the office of *custos rotulorum pacis* for co. Down in 1660. A zealous Anglican he was also active in the early 1660s in investigating presbyterian plots against the government. Upon Mountalexander's death in 1663 Montgomery became *custos rotulorum pacis* of Down, and, in February 1664 he travelled to England to press the new Mountalexander's claim to property in co. Kildare. Through Montgomery's efforts a clause was included in the 1665 Act of Explanation granting the land in question to Mountalexander. Another clause granted Montgomery forfeited lands to satisfy his debentures. He spent over a year in London, during which time he was replaced as *custos rotulorum* of Down.

By 1668 Montgomery was a trustee for the 1649 officers and in the same year he received small grants of land in Down and Fermanagh in compensation for his losses during the civil war and interregnum. Thereafter he was high sheriff of co. Down (1670) and deputy *custos rotulorum* of Down again (1683–8). He effectively retired from public life in 1688 due to ill health. The upheavals of 1689 prompted him to flee to Scotland, but he returned later in the year. Throughout his life Montgomery was a prolific writer and has left many works of poetry and of a religious nature. In 1683 he wrote a topographical description of the Ards peninsula for William Molyneux's planned atlas of Ireland. He also wrote a treatise on the post of *custos rotulorum*.

However, Montgomery is best remembered for his account of the history of the Montgomery family in Ireland, which he began in 1697. The 'Memoirs of the Montgomerys of Ireland' was based around the lives of the leading members of the Montgomerys of Ards, starting with Hugh, first Viscount Montgomery, and includes an account of the author's own life. The memoirs are an invaluable source for modern historians and provide a wealth of detail on the experiences of a British colonial family in seventeenth-century Ireland. He used very little documentary material, relying mainly on his own personal experiences and on family lore. As a result they make for rewarding and at times far more revealing reading than more impersonal sources. Aside from two academic dissertations published in Leiden in 1652, none of Montgomery's works was published during his lifetime. His only intended audience appears to have been family, friends, and perhaps posterity. Montgomery died on 7 January 1707 and was buried at Greyabbey.

TERRY CLAVIN

Sources G. Hill, ed., *The Montgomery manuscripts* (1869) · R. Gillespie, 'The making of the Montgomery manuscripts', *Familia*, 2 (1986), 23–9 · D. B. Quinn, 'William Montgomery and the description of Ards, 1683', *Irish Booklore*, 2 (1972), 29–43

Monthermer, Ralph de, first Lord Monthermer (*d.* 1325), soldier and courtier, and for several years earl of Gloucester and Hertford, is said to have been born in the bishopric of Durham, but his parentage is unknown. Before 1296 he was a squire in the service of Gilbert de Clare, earl of Gloucester (1243–1295), whose widow, *Joan of Acre, daughter of Edward I, fell in love with him, and, after inducing her father to knight him, married him privately early in 1297. When in April Joan was forced to reveal the marriage, the king had Monthermer imprisoned at Bristol. The *Song of Caerlaverock* says that Monthermer 'acquired, after great doubts and fears, the love of the countess of Gloucester, for whom he a long time endured great sufferings.' Eventually Edward's wrath was appeased and Monthermer released.

Monthermer did homage at Eltham on 2 August 1297, when he is styled *miles* ('knight'). On 8 September he was summoned to appear with horse and arms at Rochester. After this time he is styled earl of Gloucester and Hertford, in right of his wife. Under this title he was present with his wife at the parliament held at York on 14 January 1298, and took part in the subsequent invasion of Scotland under

Earl Warenne, when Berwick and Roxburgh were relieved. When the earls of Norfolk and Hereford demanded the reconfirmation of the charters, Gloucester was one of those nominated to swear on the king's behalf. He was with Edward in Scotland in June, and was presumably present at Falkirk on 22 July. He fought at the siege of Caerlaverock in June 1300, and again served in Scotland in 1301, 1303, 1304, and 1306. In the last year, on 12 October, he received the earldom of Atholl in Scotland, together with the lands of Annandale. During the winter he was one of the three wardens in Scotland, and was besieged by Robert Bruce in the castle at Ayr.

On 23 April 1307 Joan of Acre died; after this time Monthermer was no longer styled earl of Gloucester, and in March 1308 his stepson was summoned under that title. In June 1307, just before the death of Edward I, Monthermer also surrendered his Scottish earldom of Atholl in return for 10,000 marks with which to buy land to the value of 1000 marks for the support of himself and his children. On 24 June of the same year he was given the custody of the Clare lands in Wales during Gilbert de Clare's minority. On 4 March 1309 he was again summoned to parliament as Baron Monthermer, and on 16 September 1309 and 24 December 1310 received grants of land at Warblington and Westenden and other manors in Devon, Wiltshire, and Hampshire for himself and his sons. In 1311 and 1312 Monthermer served as warden and lieutenant for the king in Scotland, and received 300 marks in reward for his services. He was taken prisoner at Bannockburn, and owed his release without ransom to his former acquaintance with Robert Bruce. On 19 February 1315 he was appointed warden of the royal forests south of the Trent, an office which he held until 18 May 1320. On 30 December 1315 he had royal permission to appoint a deputy while on a pilgrimage to Santiago de Compostela, and earlier in 1315 he had held an inquest on the claim of John, earl of Richmond, to the towns of Great Yarmouth and Gorleston, but after this there is no mention of Monthermer in public affairs. Probably in 1318 Monthermer married as his second wife Isabella Despenser (d. 1334), the widow of John Hastings (1262–1313). He had pardon for this marriage on 12 August 1319. He was summoned to parliament as a baron until 30 October 1324, and was summoned to attend a great council in the spring of 1325, but died on 5 April before it met.

Monthermer had two sons with Joan of Acre, Thomas and Edward, and a daughter, Mary, who married Duncan, earl of Fife. Thomas de Monthermer was never summoned to parliament. During the early troubles of the reign of Edward III he supported Henry of Lancaster, for which he received pardon on 30 July 1330. He served in Scotland in 1333, 1335, and 1337, and was killed in the naval battle off Sluys on 24 June 1340. Edward de Monthermer served in Scotland in 1334, and, although the second son, was summoned to parliament in 1337; he accompanied Edward III to Antwerp in 1338, and fought at Vironfosse in 1339. He died in December 1339 and was buried near his mother in the church of the Augustinian friars at Clare. With his wife Isabella Ralph de Monthermer left a daughter, Margaret, who married Sir John Montagu, the second son of William, earl of Salisbury. Montagu was summoned to parliament in 1357, apparently in the right of his wife. This barony was afterwards merged in the earldom of Salisbury, and was finally forfeited at the death of Richard Neville, earl of Warwick, in 1471. The titles of viscount and marquess of Monthermer were borne in the first half of the eighteenth century by the dukes of Montagu, who claimed descent from Thomas de Monthermer.

C. L. KINGSFORD, rev. JENNIFER C. WARD

Sources GEC, *Peerage* · M. Altschul, *A baronial family in medieval England: the Clares, 1217–1314* (1965) · *The chronicle of Walter of Guisborough*, ed. H. Rothwell, CS, 3rd ser., 89 (1957) · A. Gransden, ed. and trans., *The chronicle of Bury St Edmunds, 1212–1301* [1964] · [Walter of Exeter?], *The siege of Carlaverock … with a translation, a history of the castle and memoirs of the personages commemorated by the poet*, ed. and trans. N. H. Nicolas (1828) · *Willelmi Rishanger … chronica et annales*, ed. H. T. Riley, pt 2 of *Chronica monasterii S. Albani*, Rolls Series, 28 (1865) · *Johannis de Trokelowe et Henrici de Blaneforde … chronica et annales*, ed. H. T. Riley, pt 3 of *Chronica monasterii S. Albani*, Rolls Series, 28 (1866) · *Adae Murimuth continuatio chronicarum. Robertus de Avesbury de gestis mirabilibus regis Edwardi tertii*, ed. E. M. Thompson, Rolls Series, 93 (1889) · Rymer, *Foedera* · F. Palgrave, ed., *The parliamentary writs and writs of military summons*, 2 vols. in 4 (1827–34) · CClR · *Calendar of the fine rolls*, 22 vols., PRO (1911–62) · CPR · CDS · PRO, E 357/1 m.16

Monti, Raffaelle (1818–1881), sculptor and writer on art, was born at Iseo in Ticino, Switzerland, the son of the sculptor Gaetano Monti (1776–1847) of Ravenna, who worked on Milan Cathedral and on monuments initiated under Napoleon. Raffaelle studied under his father and with the sculptor Pompeo Marchesi at the Accademia di Belle Arti di Brera in Milan. His period of study stood on the brink of the emergence of a new realism in Milanese sculpture, but Monti was averse to this trend. His first successes were with subjects taken from the classical repertory. After exhibiting his group *Ajax Defending the Body of Patroclus* in 1838, he was invited to Vienna. During his four-year stay there, he collaborated with the Munich sculptor Ludwig Schaller on a monumental pediment (in zinc) for the National Museum in Budapest. Monti was once again in Milan between 1842 and 1846, after which he made his first visit to London, where in 1847 he executed a marble statue of *A Veiled Vestal* (Compton Place, Eastbourne, Sussex) for the duke of Devonshire. (Monti's name would henceforth be associated with veiled female figures.) After completing the statue he returned to Italy, where he joined the popular party and, as one of the chief officers of the national guard, was sent on a confidential mission to King Carlo Alberto of Savoy. When the Italian insurgents were defeated by the Austrian army at Custozza in 1848, Monti fled back to London, where he was to remain for the rest of his life.

Between 1859 and 1861 Monti contributed a series of 'Letters from London' to the newly established French art journal *Gazette des Beaux-Arts*. In these he diagnosed some of the tendencies of the British art world. The artist had to conform to 'a calm and systematic taste, taking into account both Puseyism and Quakerism' ('Correspondance particulière', *Gazette des Beaux-Arts*, 1, 1860, 105). Nudity and classical mythology, he sensed, were still experienced as an alien import. Monti effectively mingled sensuality and contrition in *Eve after the Fall* (marble, formerly Grittleton House, Wiltshire), shown at the Great Exhibition of 1851 at the Crystal Palace, and he fell in with the Victorian taste for idealized genre in the group *Sister Anglers* (1851). He also entered the market for tomb sculpture, where his most ambitious creation was the conspicuously highchurch monument to Lady de Mauley (marble, 1848) at Hatherop, Gloucestershire.

During his years in Britain, Monti also identified with what he saw as the practical genius of the nation, in allying himself with architects and manufacturers of ornamental sculpture. His own practice assumed industrial proportions when he became involved with the Crystal Palace Company, which transferred Joseph Paxton's exhibition building to Sydenham, Kent, in 1853. Monti provided allegorical statuary for the palace and its grounds, and was responsible for the installation and colouring of the reconstructions of the Parthenon sculptures in its Grecian court. In 1857 he embellished the great hall of the Rothschilds' country house, Mentmore, Buckinghamshire, in collaboration with Paxton. His largest architectural work is the relief over the proscenium arch of the Royal Opera House, Covent Garden, London (plaster, 1858). Here a colossal profile portrait of Queen Victoria is flanked by scenes showing Orpheus and Ossian as embodiments of music and poetry. The firms with which Monti collaborated in the production of decorative items were Copeland for ceramics (principally statuary porcelain statuettes and busts) and C. F. Hancock for silverware. For the latter he extended his subject repertory to include ancient history and exotic animals.

Monti was especially prominent in the public eye in the early 1860s. In 1861 his equestrian bronze statue of the marquess of Londonderry in hussar's uniform was inaugurated in Durham. This unusually florid public statue was cast by electrotype after four years of experiment. In 1862 he exhibited at the London International Exhibition his poetic allegory of the Italian Risorgimento, *The Sleep of Sorrow and a Dream of Joy*. This extravagantly fanciful marble group, now in the Victoria and Albert Museum, London, marked the climax of his exploration of the veiled effect. It unsurprisingly impressed the starchy art critic Francis Turner Palgrave as a startling example of 'how far sculpture must fall, when it has once admitted any taint of the sensational' ('Sensational art', *Essays on Art*, 1860, 201). Raffaele Monti died in London on 16 October 1881.

P. WARD-JACKSON

Sources *Art Journal*, new ser., 1 (1881), 352 • R. Gunnis, *Dictionary of British sculptors, 1660–1851*, new edn (1968) • A. Radcliffe, 'Monti's allegory of the Risorgimento', *Victoria and Albert Museum Bulletin*, 1/3 (July 1965) • 'Inauguration of the Londonderry monument in this city', *Durham County Advertiser* (6 Dec 1861), 2 • [R. Monti], 'Letters from London', *Gazette des Beaux-Arts*, 1–11 (1859–61) [series of articles] • Graves, *RA exhibitors*
Likenesses C. Silvy, carte-de-visite, NPG • wood-engraving, repro. in *ILN* (25 Oct 1851), 536

Montibus [Monte], **William de** (*d.* 1213), theologian, was born in Wigford, a suburb of Lincoln. There is evidence of

a de Montibus family in Wigford in cartularies of the thirteenth century. The surname under which he was once known—'of Leicester'—seems to have been first applied to William, erroneously, by John Bale, who confused William with one of his students, Richard Wetheringsett of Leicester, who quotes William copiously in his very popular *summa*, *Qui bene presunt* (Goering, 153). As a youth William was raised in the household of Gilbert of Sempringham (*d.* 1189). He travelled to Paris, perhaps in the 1160s, where he studied theology under Peter Comestor and other masters, and then opened his own school of theology on Mont-Ste Geneviève, just outside the walls of Paris. Gerald of Wales and Alexander Neckam both knew him there. William was one of a number of famous theologians at Paris during the last part of the twelfth century whose teachings were characterized by their interest in practical, pastoral theology and in the training of clergy for exercising the care of souls. In the 1180s William was invited back to England by Bishop Hugh of Lincoln (*d.* 1200). He spent the last thirty years of his life at the head of the cathedral school in Lincoln, which was, during William's time, among the most famous in England. He served as chancellor of the cathedral from at least 1194 until his death in 1213.

Gerald of Wales asserts that he was first called William de Monte because of his school on Mont-Ste Geneviève, and that he came to be called William de Montibus when he began teaching on the second 'mount', in the cathedral close at Lincoln. William de Montibus was perhaps the most famous theologian of his day in England. He composed four encyclopaedic *summae* to aid students in his school. One is an introduction to theology entitled *Numerale* (Goering, 230–35), wherein William discusses basic theological topics arranged according to the numbers from one to twelve (One God, Two testaments … Twelve articles of faith). Three of his *summae* make use of the new experiments in alphabetical organization. His *Distinctiones theologice* (ibid., 265–7) collects theological and scriptural terms and distinguishes their usages. His *Proverbia* (ibid., 338) organizes more than 5000 Latin proverbs and quotations under 281 alphabetically ordered subject headings. One of his latest and most ambitious works is the *Versarius* (ibid., 397–8), in which nearly 4400 lines of verse, many of them composed and commented upon by the author himself, are presented under some 900 alphabetically ordered headings. One of William's poems, known by its first words, *Peniteas cito peccator*, circulated independently as a guide to hearing and making confessions; it became one of the most popular didactic poems in Europe in the following centuries, and was printed, along with William's gloss, at least fifty-one times between 1485 and 1520. His other writings include several treatises on penance, a guide to theological tropes and scriptural interpretation, a commentary on the Psalms, theological questions on the seven sacraments, and a verse summation of the sacraments, several collections of sermons, and a number of pastoral letters addressed to the nuns of the Gilbertine order.

William de Montibus died in Scotland in April 1213,

while England was under papal interdict, and his body was transferred to Lincoln Cathedral for reburial in 1214 after the interdict was lifted. Matthew of Rievaulx composed four sets of memorial verses in William's honour, comparing him favourably with Augustine and Gregory the Great. Alexander Neckam praised William in his *Laus sapientie divine* as a 'steadfast mountain and a pillar of the faith, who gave himself wholly to the study of theology' (*Alexandri Neckam*, 460).   JOSEPH GOERING

Sources J. Goering, *William de Montibus (c.1140–1213): the schools and the literature of pastoral care*, Pontifical Institute of Medieval Studies: Texts and Studies, 108 (1992) · *Alexandri Neckam de naturis rerum libri duo*, ed. T. Wright, Rolls Series, 34 (1863)

Montmorency [Mount Maurice], **Hervey de** (*fl. c.*1135–*c.*1189), adventurer, became involved in Ireland through his association with his nephew, Richard fitz Gilbert de *Clare (*c.*1130–1176), earl of Pembroke and lord of Striguil (Strongbow). Their relationship stemmed from the marriage of Adeliz, daughter of Hugh, count of Clermont, widow of Gilbert de Clare (*d.* 1117) to Hervey's father, surnamed de Montmorency, whose first name may have been Bouchard, and who probably was related to the French house of Montmorency (among whom the name Hervé occurs). Gerald of Wales states that Hervey previously had fought in France, and that when he went to Ireland he 'was a fugitive from fortune, unarmed and destitute' (*Expugnatio*, 30–33). He certainly appears to have inherited nothing from his own father, while his mother's first marriage had produced four sons and three daughters as heirs to the Clare estate to which Hervey had no entitlement. Before his intervention in Ireland, Hervey de Montmorency is found witnessing charters linked to his half-brothers and -sisters: about 1136–8 he witnessed his mother's charter in favour of Thorney Abbey, suggesting that he may have come of age by that date, and that he may therefore have been born about 1120; he witnessed a charter of his half-brother, Gilbert de Clare, earl of Pembroke (*d.* 1148), granting Parndon in Essex to Southwark Priory. He witnessed a charter of his nephew Strongbow, when earl of Pembroke, to Tintern Abbey which probably predates 1154; about 1164–5 he witnessed a charter of Henry II at Oxford in favour of Stratford Langthorne Abbey, Essex, his half-sister, Margaret, being married to the abbey's founder, William de Montfichet. In a charter of Richard I granted on 7 December 1189 he is mentioned as a benefactor of Beeleigh Abbey, Essex, previously located at Parndon during which time Montmorency made a grant that was confirmed by Strongbow.

In May 1169 Montmorency accompanied Robert fitz Stephen to Ireland and took part in the capture of Wexford. Diarmait Mac Murchada, king of Leinster, then assigned him two coastal cantreds between Wexford and Waterford, which were probably equivalent to the grant of Uí Bairrche subsequently allocated to him by Strongbow. He took part in raids into Osraige and Uí Failge alongside Diarmait and clearly was more important in the early years of the invasion than Gerald of Wales admits, though Gerald later numbers him among the four great pillars of the conquest of Ireland along with Robert fitz Stephen,

Raymond fitz William Fitzgerald (Raymond le Gros), and John de Courcy. Gerald gives a very negative portrayal of Montmorency, describing him as spying on Robert fitz Stephen in the interest of Strongbow: his hostility stemmed from partiality for his cousin, and the rivalry he perceived between Montmorency and Raymond le Gros for leadership of Strongbow's troops. Immediately after Raymond le Gros had landed in Ireland about May 1170 Montmorency joined forces with him and participated in the defeat of the men of Waterford at Dún Domnaill where more than 500 were killed and at which 70 prisoners were taken. Gerald reconstructs a tendentious debate between Raymond and Montmorency about how the prisoners should be treated. Raymond supposedly argued for their release, whereas Montmorency held that they should be condemned to die; his arguments won out and the prisoners had their limbs broken and were thrown from cliffs into the sea. It is likely that Gerald was protecting, at Montmorency's expense, the reputation of Raymond for the incident appears to have been notorious; it is recounted also in the so-called *Song of Dermot and the Earl* which, however, does not attribute any decisive role to Montmorency. When Raymond's mission to Henry II on Strongbow's behalf failed in 1171, Montmorency was dispatched to the king probably in July 1171 when Robert de Torigni records messengers from Strongbow at the court of Argentan. On his return to Ireland, Montmorency met Strongbow at Waterford and advised him to go to the king in person. Both men travelled to meet Henry at Newnham, Gloucestershire, where Montmorency mediated on Strongbow's behalf. In 1173, when Strongbow was summoned by the king to fight in Normandy, Montmorency commanded his troops in his absence; on Strongbow's return to Ireland, Gerald depicts the troops unanimously requesting the removal of command from Montmorency and its transfer to Raymond, threatening that otherwise they would abandon Strongbow's service. With Raymond as leader the troops began to build up resources, but Raymond returned to Wales, and when Montmorency was once more in charge of the garrison, he led an expedition towards Cashel, on which according to Gerald four knights and over 400 Ostmen were killed in an engagement with Domnall Ua Briain, king of Thomond, at Thurles (Irish annals variously put numbers slain at between 700 and 1700). Thereafter Strongbow recalled Raymond to Ireland and, according to Gerald, Montmorency, recognizing that Raymond's reputation was growing and that he could not harm him on the battlefield, sought other means to do so: Gerald suggests that Montmorency's marriage to Nest, daughter of Maurice *Fitzgerald (*d.* 1176), had the sole purpose of forging closer bonds with the Geraldines in order to do them greater mischief. Following the taking of Limerick by Raymond le Gros in 1175 Gerald accused Montmorency of spreading false rumours about Raymond, sending messages to Henry II asserting that Raymond was usurping royal authority and planning to seize all of Ireland for himself, and that he had put the army under oath to produce all booty shared in common, setting aside a portion for their leader. Henry thereupon dispatched royal envoys to recall Raymond.

In his charter to Dunbrody Abbey, Montmorency styled himself 'marescallus domini regis de Hibernia et seneschallus de tota terra Ricardi comitis' ('Marshall of the lord king of Ireland and seneschal of all the land of Earl Richard'; Gilbert, *Chartularies*, 2.151), while in a charter in favour of Osbert son of Robert, the form 'marescallus domini regis totius Hiberniae' ('Marshall of the lord king of all Ireland'; Halstead, 446) occurs. When this office was conferred on him, and how long he may have held it, is unknown. It might have related to the period in 1173 when Strongbow was absent in Normandy, or the period between Strongbow's death in April 1176 and the appointment of William fitz Aldelin as custodian of Leinster at the Council of Oxford in May 1177, at which Montmorency was present, as evidenced by his attestation, without title, of Henry's charter granting the kingdom of Cork to Robert fitz Stephen and Miles de Cogan. In the arrangements made for the administration of Leinster by the crown during the minority of Strongbow's heirs, Montmorency's lands between Wexford and Waterford were assigned to the service of Wexford.

Gerald attributes Montmorency's failure to produce legitimate children to his lack of generosity to the church; however, Gerald does not give due notice to his monastic benefactions. Montmorency became a monk of Christ Church, Canterbury (in 1179 according to the annals of St Mary's Abbey, Dublin, about 1182–5 according to Gerald), to which community he donated the churches of his lands between Waterford and Wexford, as well as the lands of Kilmore, Kilturk, Bannow, and the Saltee Islands. His attempt some time before 1176 to persuade Reginald, prior of the Benedictine community of Walden, Essex, to found a monastery at Bannow failed and the lands subsequently passed to Christ Church, Canterbury; when in 1245 Christ Church transferred the lands to Tintern Abbey, Wexford, it was stipulated that Tintern should maintain a chaplain in St Brendan's Chapel, Bannow, to celebrate masses for Montmorency's soul. A Cistercian foundation at Dunbrody, intended as a daughter house of Buildwas, but in November 1182 taken over by St Mary's Abbey, Dublin, was to be more successful. The anniversary of his death (year unknown, but a reference to him in a charter of Richard I of 1189 may imply that he was dead by that date) was celebrated at Christ Church, on 12 March; he is described as *conversus et benefactor* in an early thirteenth-century martyrology (BL, Cotton MS Nero C.ix, 2, fols. 5, 6; cf. BL, Cotton MS Galba E.iii, 2, fol. 32). An erroneous descent from the Montmorency family, which hinged on a false interpretation of Gerald of Wales, was claimed by the family of Morres and viscounts Mountmorres and certified on 29 June 1815 by Sir William Betham, Ulster herald, which resulted in much confusion and the proliferation of variants of his name, including de Monte Marisco, Mountmaurice, Mo(u)nt Maurice, Mountmorris, Mount Morriss.   M. T. FLANAGAN

Sources Giraldus Cambrensis, *Expugnatio Hibernica / The conquest of Ireland*, ed. and trans. A. B. Scott and F. X. Martin (1978), 30–35, 58–65, 88–9, 135–9, 142–3, 158–61, 180–81, 188–9 · G. H. Orpen, ed. and trans., *The song of Dermot and the earl* (1892), lines 457, 606, 749, 930, 1140, 1496, 3071 · J. T. Gilbert, ed., *Chartularies of St Mary's Abbey, Dublin: with the register of its house at Dunbrody and annals of Ireland*, 2 vols., Rolls Series, 80 (1884), vol. 1, p. 79; vol. 2, pp. 98, 141, 143, 151–2, 304 · R. Halstead [H. Mordaunt, second earl of Peterborough], *Succinct genealogies of the noble and ancient houses* (1685) · W. Stubbs, ed., *Gesta regis Henrici secundi Benedicti abbatis: the chronicle of the reigns of Henry II and Richard I, AD 1169–1192*, 2 vols., Rolls Series, 49 (1867), 1. 163–4 · *Chronica magistri Rogeri de Hovedene*, ed. W. Stubbs, 2, Rolls Series, 51 (1869), 134 · *The historical works of Gervase of Canterbury*, ed. W. Stubbs, 1: *The chronicle of the reigns of Stephen, Henry II, and Richard I*, Rolls Series, 73 (1879), 234 · J. B. Sheppard, ed., *Literae Cantuarienses: the letter books of the monastery of Christ Church, Canterbury*, 3, Rolls Series, 85 (1889), 361–2 · J. H. Round, *Feudal England: historical studies on the eleventh and twelfth centuries* (1895), 392–7 · H. G. Richardson, 'Some Norman monastic foundations in Ireland', *Medieval studies presented to Aubrey Gwynn*, ed. J. A. Watt, J. B. Morrall, and F. X. Martin (1961), 29–43 · R. Howlett, ed., *Chronicles of the reigns of Stephen, Henry II, and Richard I*, 4, Rolls Series, 82 (1889), 252 · F. M. Stenton, ed., *Facsimiles of early charters from Northamptonshire collections*, Northamptonshire RS, 4 (1930), 52–4 [no. 18] · G. F. Warner and H. J. Ellis, eds., *Facsimiles of royal and other charters in the British Museum* (1903), no. 17 · *Sir Christopher Hatton's Book of seals*, ed. L. C. Loyd and D. M. Stenton, Northamptonshire RS, 15 (1950), no. 413 · G. Lyttelton, *The history of the life of King Henry the Second*, 2nd edn, 6 (1773), 406–8 [citing J. Ware, *De Hibernia et antiquitatibus ejus disquisitiones* (1654), 237–9] · GEC, *Peerage* · *Calendar of the charter rolls*, 6 vols., PRO (1903–27), vol. 3, p. 97; vol. 5, p. 186 · J. T. Gilbert, ed., *Register of the abbey of St Thomas, Dublin*, Rolls Series, 94 (1889), 370 · *VCH Essex*, 8.216 · W. Stokes, ed., 'The annals of Tigernach [8 pts]', *Revue Celtique*, 16 (1895), 374–419; 17 (1896), 6–33, 119–263, 337–420; 18 (1897), 9–59, 150–97, 267–303, 374–91; pubd sep. (1993) · S. Mac Airt, ed. and trans., *The annals of Inisfallen* (1951), s. a. 1174.3

Montmorency, James Edward Geoffrey de (1866–1934), jurist, was born at Greenwich on 6 December 1866, the third son of James Lodge de Montmorency, a member of the hospital staff there, and his wife, Susan Kiddel. Educated at Blackheath proprietary school, he was admitted to Peterhouse, Cambridge, in 1886, and graduated BA in 1889 and LLB in 1890; in 1909 he was awarded the Seatonian prize for an English poem on a sacred subject. In 1892 he was called to the bar by the Middle Temple and went into chambers on the Chancery side. He married in 1899 Caroline Maud Saumarez, third daughter of Major-General James de Havilland; they had one son and two daughters.

Having a strong inclination towards the more academic aspects of the law, at an early stage in his career de Montmorency was inspired with enthusiasm for comparative legal studies by the influence of John Macdonell, Quain professor of comparative law in the University of London. In 1902 he was Quain prizeman in comparative law at University College, London, and in 1911 and 1912 King Edward VII legal research scholar of the Middle Temple. In 1920 he succeeded Macdonell as Quain professor and he held the chair until his retirement in 1932. From 1930 to 1932 he was also dean of the faculty of laws in the University of London.

De Montmorency's activities covered a wide area and, in addition to those already mentioned, he was for many years literary editor of the *Contemporary Review*. He acted as assistant secretary of the royal commission on divorce and matrimonial causes from 1910 to 1912, and from 1918 to 1920 as joint secretary and member of the attorney-general's committee of inquiry into breaches of the laws of war. He was a prolific writer, but much of his published work is of a somewhat miscellaneous and transient character. He was one of the principal contributors to the series of monographs published by the Society of Comparative Legislation under the title of Great Jurists of the World, and he wrote the section 'Sea-policy and the *Alabama* claims' in the *Cambridge History of British Foreign Policy*, volume 3 (1923). Selections of the articles which he contributed to *The Times* and the *Contemporary Review* were published under the titles of *The Never-Ending Road* (1916), *The White Riders* (1918), and *The Admiral's Chair* (1921).

De Montmorency met with considerable success as a teacher of the law. He was of a warm-hearted and generous disposition, which endeared him to students, and he was untiring in his efforts to assist them. A keen churchman, he was invaluable as a governor and manager of church schools. He died at his home, 31 Lee Terrace, Blackheath, on 9 March 1934; he was survived by his wife.

H. C. GUTTERIDGE, rev.

Sources *The Times* (10 March 1934) · *The Times* (13 March 1934) · WWW · private information (1949) · CGPLA Eng. & Wales (1934) · personal knowledge (1949)
Wealth at death £3940 10s. 10d.: probate, 24 April 1934, CGPLA Eng. & Wales

Montmorency, Raymond Harvey de, third Viscount Frankfort de Montmorency (1835–1902), army officer, born at Theydon Bower, Epping, Essex, on 21 September 1835, was the only son of Lodge Raymond, second viscount (1806–1889), and his wife, Georgina Frederica (d. 1885), daughter of Peter Fitzgibbon Henchy QC, of Dublin. Educated at Eton College and at the Royal Military College, Sandhurst, he was commissioned as ensign in the 33rd (Duke of Wellington's) regiment on 18 August 1854, promoted lieutenant on 12 January 1855, and served with his regiment during that year in the Crimea. He was in the trenches at the siege of Sevastopol and took part in the storming of the Redan on 8 September. For his gallantry at the assault he was recommended for the Victoria Cross, but he did not receive it. De Montmorency then accompanied his regiment to India. During the mutiny in 1857–8 he commanded a detachment against the mutineers in central India.

Promoted captain on 29 March 1861, de Montmorency exchanged into the 32nd (Cornwall) regiment, and from 6 December 1861 to 31 December 1864 was aide-de-camp to his uncle by marriage, Major-General Edward Basil Brooke, who commanded the troops in the Windward and Leeward islands. From 4 June 1865 de Montmorency was aide-de-camp to Lieutenant-General Sir John Michel, commanding the troops in British North America, and in 1866 took part in the repulse of the Fenians. He married on 25 April 1866, at Montreal, Rachel Mary Lumley Godolphin, eldest daughter of Sir John *Michel. They had two sons and three daughters.

While travelling in Abyssinia in 1867 de Montmorency volunteered under Sir Robert Napier in the campaign against King Theodore. He accompanied the expedition to the gates of Magdala, when all volunteers were recalled. He commanded the frontier force during the 1886–7 Sudan operations, and in 1887, while commanding the troops at Alexandria with the local rank of major-general, he directed the operations of the British field column of the frontier force during the Nile operations. He was mentioned in dispatches. He was promoted major-general on the establishment on 30 November 1889, and succeeded to the peerage on the death of his father on 25 December.

From 1890 to 1895 Lord Frankfort commanded a district in Bengal, and from 1895 to 1897 the Dublin district; he retired on 21 September 1897. A keen soldier, strict disciplinarian, and master of drill, and a kind and generous man, he died suddenly of apoplexy at his home, 30 Bury Street, St James's, London, on 7 May 1902, and was buried on the 12th in the village churchyard of Dewlish, Dorset. His wife survived him. Their eldest son, Raymond Harvey de Montmorency (1867–1900), captain 21st lancers, won the Victoria Cross in the charge near Omdurman in 1898. He was killed in action in February 1900 at Molteno, Cape Colony, while commanding the corps of scouts he had organized and which bore his name.

R. H. VETCH, rev. JAMES FALKNER

Sources *The Times* (8 May 1902) · Burke, *Peerage* · Army List · Hart's Army List · private information (1912)
Wealth at death £9671 16s. 9d.: resworn probate, April 1903, CGPLA Eng. & Wales (1902)

Montresor [*formerly* Le Trésor], **James Gabriel** (1702–1776), military engineer, was, according to a paper in the family archive, born on 19 November 1702, the only son of Major James Gabriel Le Trésor (c.1667–1724) and Anne (d. 1738), daughter of Gabriel d'Hauteville. The baptism of one Jacques Gabriel Le Trésor at Le Quarré Chapel, Little Dean Street, London, on 23 November 1704, may be identified with him. Of Huguenot origin, his father came to Britain and entered the English service prior to 1691 and was married in London in 1699. The surname Montresor seems to have been adopted at an early date by the family in Britain.

Montresor was serving as a matross in the artillery at Minorca in 1724 and remained there until 1726. He was present as a bombardier at Gibraltar for the siege of 1727. At Gibraltar he gained experience as an overseer attending the various works and was rewarded on 2 October 1731 with a commission as practitioner engineer. On 5 April 1732 Montresor was commissioned an ensign in the 14th foot. In August 1732 he took several months' leave in England before returning to Gibraltar. Montresor served at Gibraltar for the next ten years during which time he was promoted lieutenant in his regiment in 1737, sub-engineer in 1739 and engineer-extraordinary in 1742. During his time at Gibraltar, Montresor surveyed the town and fortifications and drew large-scale, detailed plans. He also married there, on 10 June 1735, Mary (d. 1761), daughter of Robert Haswell, master attendant of the royal dockyard at Gibraltar. They had several children, including John *Montresor, who followed in his father's footsteps with distinction.

On 5 October 1743 Montresor was promoted to engineer-in-ordinary and transferred to Minorca. Late in 1746 he returned to Gibraltar as chief engineer in succession to William Skinner and was active in carrying out improvements to the fortifications. In 1752 he made a special report on the defences and on 17 December of that year was promoted to sub-director. Montresor's health had begun to fail and in November 1753 he was relieved at Gibraltar and given leave of six months to travel in France. Making good use of this time he made observations on the places he passed through in his travels between Gibraltar and Paris and submitted a report to the Board of Ordnance.

Returning to England by summer 1754, Montresor was appointed, on 7 October, chief engineer on the expedition to North America under Major-General Edward Braddock. The expedition reached Waterford in Ireland on 10 December with Montresor once again in poor health. Unable to proceed, Montresor made his way to Bristol to take the waters where, following disputes with the board, he eventually sailed about 7 August 1755 with his wife and some of his family, arriving at Hampton, Virginia, on 11 October, where he heard of the fate of Braddock and his forces at Fort Duquesne.

Montresor proceeded to Albany where he remained some months preparing plans and projects for the ensuing campaign. He designed a typical field redoubt for use against the Indians, which was ordered to be generally adopted. Montresor was much consulted by General William Shirley and attended his councils of war at Albany. John Campbell, fourth earl of Loudoun, who assumed the command in North America in mid-1756, formed a poor opinion of the engineers at his disposal, including Montresor, by whom he claimed to be ill-served, accusing him of shifting 'so often from one thing to another' (Loudoun to Cumberland, 22 Nov–26 Dec 1756, in Pargellis, *Military Affairs*, 265) and not completing the barracks so urgently required. He further declared that Montresor's experience was all 'in drawing and directing in his room' (ibid., 266) and 'I dare not trust a Siege to [him]' (ibid., 277).

In the early part of 1757 Montresor was based at New York. Montresor was one of those engineers to write to the board expressing the inconveniences 'his poor, abandoned branch' (Pargellis, *Lord Loudon in N. America*, 318) suffered as a result of having no army rank. On 14 May 1757 this disadvantage was done away with, the equivalent for Montresor as sub-director being major. In May 1757 he was ordered to put all forts and frontier posts in a proper state of defence against the possibility of a French attack. He visited Fort Edward on 24 June where he remained a month setting men to work on fascines and otherwise improving the defences. With General Daniel Webb, who was in command, he went on to Fort William Henry on 25 July where a French attack was even more anticipated. Montresor set to work on defensive measures decided upon at a council of war, but they proved insufficient to prevent the fort's fall following Montresor's and Webb's departure on 29 July, and the subsequent siege.

Montresor supervised the strengthening of the defences of Fort Edward before proceeding to similar works at Saratoga and Stillwater. In October he returned to Albany and early in 1758 went to New York. He was promoted director of engineers and lieutenant-colonel on 4 January 1758. Montresor subsequently had to deal with the problems that ensued when the new commander-in-chief, James Abercromby, altered the disposition of the engineers, thereby exceeding his command as the duties of engineers were the responsibility of the Board of Ordnance. Montresor also experienced predicaments with individual engineer officers who made difficulties as to where and under which officers they were prepared to serve, or kept Montresor, who was responsible for the overall accounting for expenditure of ordnance funds and materials, insufficiently apprised of their disbursements. He was authorized by the board to put under arrest any officer who refused his orders and try them accordingly.

In April 1759 Montresor was present at the Indian conference held at Philadelphia and in June he accompanied General Jeffrey Amherst and his army as chief engineer on the campaign to the Lake Country, where the two planned, and Montresor supervised until December, the construction of Fort George on the lake of the same name. Montresor was incapacitated for a large part of October as a result of an accident. While at Fort George he was in command of the troops and outposts on the lines of communication between Albany and Lake George.

Montresor's health was still unsatisfactory and he had obtained the board's consent to return home when the campaign was over. He was at New York for the first months of 1760 before sailing for home, arriving at Falmouth with his family at the end of June. The board lost little time in finding other employment for him, appointing him on 1 October chief engineer on the expedition against Belle Île, but while awaiting embarkation in November he was suddenly struck with a palsy and was unable to proceed. The board ordered him 'to be struck off the list of the staff' (PRO, WO 47/56, fol. 388) and he was given no employment for two years. His wife died on 5 March 1761 and was buried at St James's, Westminster.

In 1763 the board employed Montresor at Purfleet designing and erecting the new powder magazines to replace those at Greenwich, ordered demolished by act of parliament. On 25 August 1766, at St Marylebone, Middlesex, he married Henrietta Eleanor, forty-one years his junior, the daughter of Henry *Fielding. She was buried on 11 December 1766 at St James's, Westminster. On 10 November 1767, at Teynham, Kent, Montresor married Frances (1731/2–1810), daughter of Henry Nickoll, of Barham, Kent, and widow of William Kemp of New Gardens, Teynham. They had no children. In 1768 Montresor was made chief engineer at Chatham. In 1772 he was promoted colonel in the army. He died at his home, New Gardens, Teynham, Kent, on 6 January 1776. He was buried at Teynham. Montresor's widow and his daughter Augusta were both granted pensions by the Board of Ordnance.

PAUL LATCHAM

Sources J. W. S. Connolly, 'Notitia historica of the corps of royal engineers', *c.*1860, Royal Engineers Corps Library, Chatham · F. M.

Montresor, 'Memoirs of the Montresors', 1941, Society of Geneal-ogists, London [vol. 1] · 'Journals of Col. James Montresor, 1757-1759', *Collections of the New York Historical Society* (1881) · E. B. O'Cal-laghan, ed., *The documentary history of the state of New York*, 4 vols. (1849-51) · S. M. Pargellis, *Lord Loudoun in North America* (1933) · S. Pargellis, ed., *Military affairs in North America, 1748-1765: selected documents from the Cumberland papers in Windsor Castle* (1936) · W. Porter, *History of the corps of royal engineers*, 2 vols. (1889) · memorial tablet, Teynham parish church, Kent
Archives BL, observations in France, Add. MS 32849, fols. 78-82 [also in PRO, SP 78/249] · Royal Engineers, Brompton Barracks, Chatham, Kent, family archive [microfilm] | Hunt. L., letters to James Abercromby · PRO, Amherst papers, WO34/75, 76, 77, 78, 80, 81, 82 · PRO, board of ordnance minutes, WO47 · PRO, SP 78/249
Likenesses oils, repro. in *Collections of the New York Historical Society*

Montresor, John (1736-1799), military engineer, was born on 6 April 1736 at Gibraltar, the eldest of the three sons of James Gabriel *Montresor (1702-1776), a colonel of engin-eers, and his first wife, Mary (*d.* 1761), the daughter of Rob-ert Haswell, master attendant of the royal dockyard at Gibraltar. Apart from four years (1746-50) at Westminster School, London, his early life was spent in Gibraltar, where he learned the basics of military engineering from his father. In 1754 Colonel Montresor returned to England and, having been appointed engineer-in-chief to General Edward Braddock's expedition to America, arranged for his son to accompany him. As was the case with engineers at this time, Montresor obtained a commission in a line regiment (48th), although he never served as a regimental officer; only in 1758, when the engineers were established as a permanent branch of the army with royal commis-sions, was he gazetted ensign and practitioner engineer. Until that time he served first as an additional engineer with Braddock's disastrous expedition against Fort Duquesne, when he was wounded, then on building works in northern New York and with Lord Loudoun in Halifax, Nova Scotia. He was with General Jeffrey Amherst at the capture of Louisbourg in 1758, with General James Wolfe at Quebec the following year, and with General James Murray on the final Quebec campaign. In 1761 and 1762 he made difficult overland trips from Quebec to the old colonies, mapping hitherto unexplored territory in the process. His maps and diaries formed the guide for Benedict Arnold's 1775 expedition against Quebec.

With the start of Pontiac's rising in 1763 Montresor was ordered to the besieged outpost of Detroit with dispatches and supplies. His small party was shipwrecked at the east-ern end of Lake Erie and had to fight off attacks from Native Americans before eventually getting through. A year later he was back at Niagara, where he constructed fortifications along the portage route past the falls and built the first Fort Erie. On 1 March 1764, in New York, he married Frances Tucker (1744-1826), the only child of Thomas Tucker of Bermuda. They had ten children, six of whom survived infancy.

In 1766 Montresor returned to Britain on leave and on petition was promoted captain-lieutenant and engineer-extraordinary. His request for the brevet rank of major was turned down, but he did receive an appointment as chief barrackmaster of the ordnance for North America.

John Montresor (1736-1799), by John Singleton Copley, *c.*1771

Having made his married home in New York, where he purchased an island in the East River (Montresor's Island, renamed Ward Island), he engaged in such tasks as the rebuilding of Castle William at Boston, the construction of Mud Fort in the river below Philadelphia, and surveying the New York–New Jersey boundary.

Montresor was engineer-in-chief in America and with the army in Boston when the American War of Independ-ence broke out. He was present at Lexington and Bunker Hill and, in 1776, the battle of Long Island. In 1777 he was with General Sir William Howe's expedition against Phila-delphia and organized the siege of the fort—renamed Fort Mifflin—that he had built there less than ten years earlier. He organized both the defences of Philadelphia and their subsequent destruction when the city was abandoned in 1778. Health problems and an inability to get along with General Sir Henry Clinton led to his return to Britain later the same year and the resignation of his commission as captain and engineer-in-ordinary.

For his retirement Montresor purchased a house in Port-land Place, London, and the estate of Belmont near Faver-sham, Kent. In the 1780s he travelled in Europe and put two of his sons through military school there.

Although he was a man of strong character with consid-erable skills as an engineer, a surveyor, a draughtsman, and an artist, there was a dark side to Montresor's life. As chief engineer in America he drew funds for his depart-ment's expenses, and he had to submit accounts to the Audit Office after relinquishing his commission. When he did so in 1783 it was common knowledge that corruption was rife in the army service departments in America, with huge fortunes being made. The auditors subjected Mon-tresor's accounts to intense scrutiny and in the end rejected £50,000 of claimed expenses. Montresor fought the auditors for fifteen years, calling their investigations 'a court of inquisition' (Scull, 127), but ultimately his estates were confiscated, and he died in Maidstone prison on 26 June 1799.

Although it is claimed that Montresor's children cleared his name and recouped £40,000 from the government, the evidence suggests that the auditors were correct in substance if not in detail. Judge Thomas Jones, a New York loyalist, believed that Montresor had profited to the tune of £100,000 and Lord Charles Cornwallis, when asked to intercede with the government in Montresor's favour, wrote to Pitt that, while Montresor was an amiable person, 'in his official situation he … followed the inviting examples of the times' (PRO, 30/8/327, 205–6). It is the case, moreover, that in 1779, when Montresor gave evidence to a parliamentary committee while still requiring approval of his accounts by General Howe, he could remember nothing critical of Howe's performance in America, notwithstanding the many sharp criticisms of him in his journals. The observer must also wonder how he could afford the lifestyle he adopted in retirement. When his troubles with the Audit Office began, Montresor made a long list in his journal of 'Extra services by me' (Scull, 117–28). It reveals intense bitterness over his lack of recognition and preferment after long years of hard and meritorious service, and can be read as a rationalization of his surrender to temptation.   R. ARTHUR BOWLER

Sources G. D. Scull, ed., *The Montresor journals* (1882) · 'Lt John Montresor's journal of an expedition in 1760 across Maine from Quebec', *New England Historical and Genealogical Register*, 36 (1882), 29–36 · F. M. Montrésor, 'Captain John Montrésor in Canada', *Canadian Historical Review*, 5 (1924), 336–40 · J. C. Webster, 'Life of John Montrésor', *Proceedings and Transactions of the Royal Society of Canada*, 3rd ser., 22 (1928), 1–31 [incl. 'Journal of John Montresor's expedition to Detroit in 1763'] · *DNB* · *DAB* · *DCB*, vol. 4 · R. A. Bowler, *Logistics and the failure of the British army in America, 1775–1783* (1975), 175–8 · Burke, *Gen. GB* (1863) · F. H. Severance, 'The achievements of Captain John Montresor on the Niagara and the first construction of Fort Erie', *Buffalo Historical Society Publications*, 5 (1902), 1–19 · T. Jones, *History of New York during the revolutionary war*, ed. E. F. de Lancey, 1 (1879) · I. D. Gruber, *The Howe brothers and the American Revolution* (Chapel Hill, NC, 1972) · H. M. Lydenberg, ed., *Archibald Robertson: lieutenant-general, Royal Engineers* (1930); repr. as *Archibald Robertson: his diaries and sketches in America, 1762–80* (New York, 1971) · PRO, audit office 12 · PRO, 30/8/327, 205–6

Archives BM, maps and plans · CKS, journal · L. Cong., Peter Force map collection, maps · NA Canada, map | BL, Haldimand MSS, Add. MSS 21661–21892 · PRO, AO 12 · PRO, corresp. with commander-in-chief, North America, WO 34 · PRO, Ordinance Office, WO 44 · PRO, WO 1 · U. Mich., Clements L., Gage MSS

Likenesses J. S. Copley, oils, *c*.1771, Detroit Institute of Arts, Michigan [*see illus.*]

Wealth at death real property confiscated to make up for his accounting shortages during Revolutionary war; but must have transferred assets to family for there are records in Audit Office files of payments in cash to government for years after death

Montrose. For this title name *see* Lindsay, David, fifth earl of Crawford and duke of Montrose (1440–1495) [*see under* Lindsay family, earls of Crawford (*per. c.*1380–1495)]; Graham, William, first earl of Montrose (1462/3–1513) [*see under* Graham family (*per. c.*1250–1513)]; Graham, John, third earl of Montrose (1548–1608); Graham, John, fourth earl of Montrose (1573–1626); Graham, James, first marquess of Montrose (1612–1650); Graham, James, second marquess of Montrose (1633–1669); Graham, James, first duke of Montrose (1682–1742); Graham, James, third duke of Montrose (1755–1836); Graham, James, fourth duke of Montrose (1799–1874); Graham, Caroline Agnes, duchess of Montrose (1818–1894); Graham, James, sixth duke of Montrose (1878–1954); Graham, (James) Angus, seventh duke of Montrose (1907–1992).

Monty. *See* Montgomery, Bernard Law, first Viscount Montgomery of Alamein (1887–1976).

Monypenny, William, first Lord Monypenny (*d.* in or before **1488**), diplomat, was the son of Sir William Monypenny and Margaret or Marjorie Arbuthnott, only daughter of Philip Arbuthnott of that ilk. Born shortly after 1410 he probably went to France in 1436 as part of the entourage of Margaret Stewart, daughter of James I, who married the dauphin Louis in that year, and by 1439 he was in the French king's service. In July 1447 Monypenny was described as *escuier d'escuieres* of Charles VII of France; he took a prominent part in the expulsion of the English from Normandy and was knighted on 16 October 1449 for his role in the siege of Rouen; rewarded by Charles VII in 1450 following the recovery of Normandy, he received the lordship of Concressault in Berry between 1451 and 1458.

Monypenny's French rewards were, if anything, exceeded by those from the Scottish crown. On 1 May 1450 he was given the lands of the Halls of Airth in Stirlingshire, specifically for ambassadorial services to James II's sisters and father; further grants of land in Stirlingshire, Aberdeenshire, and Kirkcudbrightshire were made in the 1450s. He was probably created a lord of parliament towards the end of James II's reign, about 1458; he is first described as Lord Monypenny in a grant of 17 July 1464.

Monypenny's career as a diplomat spanned more than three decades. After his entry into French service he acted as an ambassador for the Scottish crown in the negotiations leading to the marriage of James II's sister Isabella to François, count of Montfort (later duke of Brittany), in 1441–2. In 1447 he sank a great deal of money into the abortive and tasteless French scheme to marry the recently widowed dauphin to Eleanor Stewart, younger sister of his widow, Margaret who had died as recently as 1445. Monypenny was Charles VII's ambassador in Scotland in 1456 and at Bourges in the summer of 1460 he presented James II's demands for a marriage alliance and for the Orkneys and Shetlands in full sovereignty to the astonished Danes. Such cosmopolitan activities involved a high degree of risk; in November 1451 he was captured by the English at Whitby, and ransomed only for an enormous sum put up jointly by Bishop William Turnbull of Glasgow and Charles VII of France.

Monypenny's later ambassadorial tasks, in association with his son Alexander (the child of his marriage to Catherine Stewart (*d.* 1486)), were almost wholly in the service of Louis XI, who gave him an annual pension of 1200 livres tournois and in October 1473 made him seneschal of Saintonge, the French county to which successive kings of

Scots had laid claim—in vain—since 1428. Alexander had succeeded his father as second Lord Monypenny by 4 July 1488.

NORMAN MACDOUGALL

Sources F. Michel, *Les écossais en France, les français en Écosse*, 2 vols. (1862) · J. M. Thomson and others, eds., *Registrum magni sigilli regum Scotorum / The register of the great seal of Scotland*, 11 vols. (1882–1914), vol. 2 · G. Burnett and others, eds., *The exchequer rolls of Scotland*, 6 (1883) · *Scots peerage*, vol. 6 · [T. Thomson], ed., *The acts of the lords of council in civil causes, 1478–1495*, 1, RC, 41 (1839) · A. I. Dunlop, *The life and times of James Kennedy, bishop of St Andrews*, St Andrews University Publications, 46 (1950) · N. Macdougall, *James III: a political study* (1982) · C. McGladdery, *James II* (1990) · [T. Thomson], ed., *The acts of the lords of council in civil causes, 1478–1495*, 1, RC, 41 (1839), 197
Archives Scot. RO, exchequer rolls · Scot. RO, register of the great seal

Monypenny, William Flavelle (1866–1912), journalist and biographer, came of an Ulster protestant family of Scottish extraction, which until 1898 spelt the surname Monypeny. The second son of William Monypeny, a small landowner, of Ballyworkan, co. Armagh, and of Mary Anne Flavelle, his wife, he was born probably at Dungannon, co. Tyrone, or possibly in co. Armagh, on 7 August 1866. Educated at the Royal School, Dungannon, and at Trinity College, Dublin, where he graduated with high distinction in mathematics, he proceeded to Balliol College, Oxford; but temporary ill health compelled him, after a short residence (1889–90), to leave Oxford for London, and he became a regular contributor to *The Spectator*. In 1893 he joined the editorial staff of *The Times*, where his outstanding abilities were quickly recognized.

Early in 1899 Monypenny was offered unexpectedly the editorship of the Johannesburg *Star*, the foremost organ of the Uitlanders, who were suffering under the oppressive rule of President Kruger. The offer was accompanied by an assurance of unhampered editorial freedom. It was specially attractive to a man 'inspired by a lofty imperial patriotism and a keen interest in practical politics' (*The Times*, 9f). He accepted it, and made the journal a power in the political struggle that ensued. This was not achieved without personal risk. Threats were made against his life, and on one occasion he was assaulted in his office. When, later, he learned that a warrant for high treason had been taken out against him, he reluctantly withdrew to the sanctuary of British territory. On the outbreak of the Second South African War he obtained a commission in the Imperial light horse, fought in Natal, and, to the detriment of his health, endured the siege of Ladysmith. Later, under Lord Milner's high commissionership, he became director of civil supplies and a member of the committee for regulating the return of refugees after the annexation of the Transvaal. When the *Star* was again published he resumed the editorship, and marshalled the paper behind Milner's imperial vision for South Africa in the aftermath of the war. However, he resigned from the *Star* in 1903 from a scrupulous sense of honour, finding himself unable to countenance the importation of indentured Chinese labour. He made his way from Lake Victoria by an exhausting tramp past Wadelai and Dufile and down the White Nile to Khartoum, and thence to England, where he rejoined the staff of *The Times*. He contributed the opening chapter, 'The imperial ideal', to the collection of essays published in 1905 as *The Empire and the Century*. It is a statement of Monypenny's belief that by maintaining its empire, Britain could play a moderating role in world affairs, which would ensure its continued pre-eminence. In 1908 he was appointed an original director of the Times Publishing Company.

Monypenny's great opportunity came when he was chosen by *The Times* to write the authoritative biography of Disraeli, from the 'vast mass of papers' (*The Times*) that had been bequeathed to Lord Rowton. The choice was greeted with surprise by some, who thought that Monypenny lacked the necessary experience of people and affairs. He had, though, taken a lifelong interest in the greater issues of politics, imperial and domestic, and he brought to bear a judgement of conspicuous sagacity, fortified by close observation, penetrating shrewdness, and a natural gift for separating the essential from the accidental. These qualities gave weight to a lucid style, charged with thought.

The first volume of Monypenny's *Life of Benjamin Disraeli* appeared, to critical acclaim, in October 1910, and the second, delayed by failing health, in November 1912. Ten days later, on 23 November, Monypenny died suddenly of heart failure in a nursing home in the New Forest, Lingford, Ringwood, Hampshire. The biography was continued, and completed in four more volumes, by George Earle Buckle, the editor under whom Monypenny had served on *The Times*. Buckle also wrote the inscription for the memorial tablet in the parish church of Farnham Royal, Buckinghamshire, where Monypenny was buried on 27 November 1912. Monypenny never married.

J. B. CAPPER, rev. MARK POTTLE

Sources *The Times* (25 Nov 1912) · personal knowledge (1927) · private information (1927) · W. F. Monypenny, 'The imperial ideal', *The empire and the century*, ed. C. S. Goodman, reissued 1998 (1905), 5–28 · *CGPLA Eng. & Wales* (1913) · d. cert.
Archives Bodl. Oxf., corresp. and papers · News Int. RO, papers | PRO NIre., letters to Lady Londonderry
Wealth at death £175 5s.: administration, 15 Jan 1913, *CGPLA Eng. & Wales*

Moodie, Donald (1794–1861), colonial official, was born in Melsetter, Hoy Island, Orkney, on 25 June 1794, the third child of Major James Moodie, laird of Melsetter (1757–1820), and his wife, Elizabeth Dunbar. He entered the Royal Navy in 1808 at the age of fourteen as a first-class volunteer in the flagship at Leith, and served in the North Sea, off America, and in Spanish waters. After becoming a midshipman in 1811, he mainly served in the Mediterranean. He participated in the attack on Leghorn in 1814. After being made a lieutenant in December 1816 he was retired on half pay. His father had fallen into debt, and his older brother Benjamin (1789–1856) organized an emigration scheme and went out to the Cape in 1817. Although his scheme ran into difficulties, Benjamin had by 1819 settled in the district of Stellenbosch, east of Cape Town, and was beginning to prosper, and Donald's younger brother John [see below] went out to the Cape in that year. Donald had remained in Melsetter to look after his blind father, but in 1820, following the death of his father, he sailed for India. At the Cape he was persuaded by his brothers to go no further.

After a large party of British settlers arrived in the eastern Cape, the Moodie brothers went east and were themselves given land on the frontier. Their first venture, east of the Fish River in the 'ceded territory', was not a success, but they were then granted farms in the Bushman's River area in the district of Uitenhage. Moodie came to public attention when in December 1823 he wrote to the commissioners of eastern inquiry deploring the policies being pursued against the Xhosa. With his farming hopes dashed by flood damage, and having on 25 March 1824 married Eliza Sophia Pigot (1804–1881), the daughter of a British settler of 1820, he abandoned farming to become acting magistrate at Port Frances on the Kowie River in 1825. That post fell away when it was decided not to develop a harbour there, and in 1828 Moodie became clerk of the peace for Albany and then acting resident magistrate of the rapidly growing Grahamstown. The government, however, decided to appoint a more experienced person as magistrate, and in 1830 he succeeded his father-in-law as protector of slaves for the eastern division of the Cape Colony and moved to Graaff-Reinet. The preceding year he had conducted a series of interviews with the Khoi-Khoi which have led to his being called 'South Africa's pioneer oral historian'.

With the emancipation of the slaves in 1834, Moodie's post as protector ceased, but the governor, Sir Benjamin D'Urban, on the grounds that he had not completed his final report, continued to employ him and asked him to translate and transcribe early official Dutch sources in order to compile an 'authentic history' of interaction between the colonists and the indigenous people. This was intended to constitute a reply to the charges which John Philip of the London Missionary Society had made against the colonists in his *Researches in South Africa* (1828). After some years of work in Cape Town, in records never before sorted or used, Moodie produced a seminal work, which he entitled *The record, or, A series of official papers relative to the condition and treatment of the native tribes of South Africa*. It was published in Cape Town in a number of parts between 1838 and 1841. (It was not to appear as one book until reprinted in 1960.) *The Record* was controversial, for Moodie chose material to support settler interpretations of the past against those of the missionaries and the British government. He won a libel action which he brought against John Fairbairn, the editor of the *South African Commercial Advertiser*, who challenged his work. In a number of lesser booklets relating to his project Moodie expressed his opinions vigorously. He was thus at the centre of what has been called the 'great debate' beginning South African historiography, and *The Record* was to form a basis for much later historical writing about the early Cape.

When support from the government for his historical researches ceased, Moodie became in 1840 acting president of the government bank in Cape Town. Having restored it to solvency, he was sent as acting commissioner to the district of George to sort out problems there. In August 1845 he was appointed secretary to the government of the new colony of Natal where he remained for the rest of his life.

In the late 1840s Moodie was virtually ruler of the new colony. His administrative duties as secretary included establishing an office of colonial treasurer and of registrar of deeds. He worked closely with Governor Martin West until 1849, in which year he did much to assist the arrival of a large group of British settlers. But the new Natal colonists criticized his work as a member of the Natal land commission and accused him of being too keen to advance the claims of Africans to land in Natal. He then clashed with Governor Benjamin Pine, and his career as a colonial civil servant ended unhappily, when he was forced out of office in 1851. He then hoped to return to his historical work. He did begin publishing a series of *South African Annals*, one of which concerned the origin of the Bushmen, but he failed to persuade the Cape parliament or governor to support financially the continued publication of the records of the Cape. In 1856 he was elected to the first legislative council of Natal, and he became the first speaker of the house in 1857. He died at Pietermaritzburg, Natal, on 27 August 1861.

Moodie and his wife, who was ten years younger than he, had fourteen children. Among the seven sons and five daughters who survived to adulthood was Duncan Campbell Francis Moodie (1838–1891), historian and poet, whose best-known work was *The history of the battles and adventures of the British, the Boers and the Zulus in southern Africa* (1879, new edn, 1888).

John Wedderburn Dunbar Moodie (1797–1869), army officer and farmer, the younger brother of Donald Moodie and the fourth son, was born on 7 October 1797 at Melsetter. He was appointed second lieutenant, 21st regiment, Royal North British Fusiliers, on 24 February 1813, and promoted lieutenant in 1814. He was severely wounded in the left wrist in the disastrous night attack on Bergen-op-Zoom (8 March 1814) when attempting to rescue comrades from a canal. In March 1816 he was placed on half pay. He followed his elder brother Benjamin (1789–1856) to the Cape, arriving there in September 1819, and described his experiences in South Africa in *Ten Years in South Africa, Including a Particular Description of the Wild Sports* (2 vols., 1835), an important work of Africana. Elephant Moodie, as he was known, stayed on at Hoy in the Bushman's river valley after his brothers abandoned farming there, but himself came to see no long-term future in farming, and so in August 1829 sailed for England. There he published *The Campaigns in Holland in 1814* (1831) and on 4 April 1831 married Susanna Strickland (1803–1885), whom he met at the home of Thomas Pringle, a friend from the Cape. She was the daughter of Thomas Strickland and his wife, Elizabeth, *née* Homer, and the youngest sister of Agnes Strickland. She published *Enthusiasm, and other Poems* in 1831, the year before they emigrated to Upper Canada. In October 1832 they bought a farm in Hamilton township in the forest country inland from Belleville, but they lost money by unwise investment in a steamboat company, and in 1834 moved to uncleared land in Douro township, north of Peterborough. Moodie served as captain of the militia on the Niagara frontier, then paymaster of military detachments along the shores of Lake Ontario. After he had helped suppress the rebellion of 1837 he was in November 1839 made sheriff of Victoria district (later Hastings county), Ontario. Local residents resented his appointment. Unsuccessful at pioneer farming through bad luck and misjudgement, Moodie abandoned it and in January 1840 moved to the small town of Belleville itself, where in the 1840s he and his wife edited *The Victoria Magazine*, to which he contributed verse, stories, and essays. He was involved in a long vexatious litigation over the appointment of a deputy sheriff and in 1861 suffered an attack of paralysis of his left side, from which he never wholly recovered. He retired in 1863 and published his memoirs, *Scenes and Adventures as a Soldier and Settler, during Half a Century* (1866), a 'plaintive tome' (Dunae, 24) very different from the more positive memoirs of some of his contemporaries. In his later years he regretted having emigrated to Canada. He died, disappointed, at Belleville on 22 October 1869. His wife, with whom he had seven children, in 1852 published the classic *Roughing it in the Bush*, about the difficulties of pioneering life in Canada; it was followed by lesser non-fiction works and novels. After Moodie's death she remained in Canada and died in Toronto on 8 April 1885.   CHRISTOPHER SAUNDERS

Sources D. Moodie, ed. and trans., *The record, or, A series of official papers relative to the condition and treatment of the native tribes of South Africa* (1838–41); repr. with introduction by A. H. Smith (1960) · B. J. T. Leverton, 'Moodie, Donald', *DSAB* · J. W. D. Moodie, *Ten years in South Africa*, 2 vols. (1835) · *DNB* · V. C. Malherbe, 'Donald Moodie: South Africa's pioneer oral historian', *History in Africa*, 25 (1998) · R. Ross, 'Donald Moodie and the origins of South African historiography', *Beyond the pale: essays on the history of colonial South Africa* (1993) · E. H. Burrows, *Overberg Outspan* (1952) · *The journals of Sophia Pigot, 1819–1821*, ed. M. Rainier (1974) · O. H. Spohr, 'Notes from letters and pamphlets about Donald Moodie, W. H. Bleek and *The Record*', *Africana Notes and News* (March 1965) · A. Bank, 'The great debate and the origins of South African historiography', *Journal of African History*, 38 (1997), 261–81 · L. Young, 'The native policy of Benjamin Pine in Natal', *Archives Yearbook for South African History* (1951), vol. 2 · *Colonial services of Donald Moodie* (1862) · V. M. Fitzroy, *Dark bright land* (1955) · E. H. Burrows, *Overberg origins* (1988) · *DCB*, vol. 9 · P. A. Dunae, *Gentlemen emigrants: from the British public schools to the Canadian frontier* (1981) · Boase, *Mod. Eng. biog.* · *DSAB*
Archives Cape Archives, Cape Town, Moodie MSS, VC 864–889 · PRO, Colonial Office MSS
Likenesses photograph, repro. in Moodie, *The record*, frontispiece

Moodie, John Wedderburn Dunbar (1797–1869). *See under* Moodie, Donald (1794–1861).

Moodie [*née* Strickland], **Susanna** (1803–1885), autobiographer and short-story writer, was born at Bungay, Suffolk, on 6 December 1803, the daughter of Thomas Strickland (1758–1818), an importer and former dock manager, and his second wife, Elizabeth, *née* Homer (1772–1864). Susanna was the youngest of six daughters, including Agnes *Strickland and Catharine Parr *Traill; she also had

two younger brothers. In 1808 the family moved to Reydon Hall, near Bungay, where the younger daughters were educated by their elder sisters and by their own apparently unrestricted reading. The Stricklands' pleasant life as country gentry was cut short in 1818 with the death of Thomas Strickland, following some serious financial losses. While the family managed to retain Reydon Hall there was little money, a fact that may have spurred Agnes Strickland, the second daughter, into establishing what was to be a very successful career as a novelist and a writer of popular history. (She was sufficiently well known for Anthony Trollope to parody her as Lady Carbury, a fashionable, self-promoting author of romanticized biographies, in *The Way we Live now*.) By the late 1820s Susanna Strickland was following her elder sister's lead, attempting to support herself as a gentlewoman on the precarious income from her writing. She initially had reasonable success in this career, publishing work in annuals and in periodicals such as *The Athenaeum*. She was willing to experiment in almost any literary genre; her output in the 1820s and early 1830s includes, in addition to her poems, sketches, and stories for magazines, several children's stories; a novel (*Spartacus*, 1822), which she claimed to have written when she was thirteen; and a volume of poetry inspired by her conversion to congregationalism (*Enthusiasm, and other Poems*, 1831). She also helped the former slave Mary Prince to write her autobiography (1831), which was to become an important document in the abolition debate.

On 4 April 1831 Susanna Strickland married John Wedderburn Dunbar Moodie (1797–1869), an Orkneyman and former soldier who, after attempting to settle in South Africa (he eventually published an account of his time there), had returned to Britain in 1830. Neither had an income sufficient to support a family in England and so they decided to emigrate to Canada, where John Moodie was entitled to a grant of uncleared land and where Susanna Moodie's younger brother Samuel Strickland had already settled. It was a painful and difficult decision; Susanna Moodie recalled years afterwards that in the months before they left she 'seldom awoke without finding [her] pillow wet with tears' (Moodie, *Roughing It*, 61). They were, however, somewhat encouraged by the accounts of Canada provided by William Cattermole, a pamphleteer who promoted emigration and who is probably the figure whom Susanna Moodie had in mind when she later bitterly attacked 'interested parties' who 'prominently set forth all the *good* to be derived from a settlement in the Backwoods of Canada; while they carefully concealed the toil and hardship' and who were therefore answerable for 'a mass of misery' (ibid., xvii–xviii).

The Moodies initially settled on some cleared land near Cobourg, Ontario, but difficulties with their farm and with uncongenial neighbours led them to decide to move into the bush and clear a tract of land near Susanna Moodie's brother and her sister Catharine Parr Traill, who had also decided to emigrate with her husband, setting out shortly before the Moodies. For six years, from early in

1834 until late in 1839, Susanna Moodie lived in the backwoods outside what was then the tiny settlement of Peterborough, raising her children and, with her husband, attempting to clear and farm their land. They soon realized that they were entirely unsuited for life as pioneers, and after seeking work for some time John Moodie eventually found a government place in the town of Belleville. There Susanna Moodie was able to concentrate more fully on her writing than she had at any time since arriving in Canada, although she had continued to publish the occasional story and poem during her first years in the country. In 1847 she became editor of the *Victoria Magazine*, a short-lived periodical (thirteen issues) for which she and her husband wrote most of the material; she was also contributing stories and journalistic work to magazines such as the *Literary Garland*. In 1852 she published the work that established her reputation, *Roughing it in the Bush*. An unflattering and unsentimental account of her first years in Canada, she concluded it with the grim observation that if her book 'should prove the means of deterring one family … from shipwrecking all their hopes, by going to reside in the backwoods of Canada, I shall … feel that I have not toiled and suffered in the wilderness in vain' (Moodie, *Roughing It*, 515). The book was generally well reviewed in England—*Blackwood's Magazine* for example exhorted its female readers to take a lesson from 'one, gently nurtured as yourselves … unrepiningly enduring hardships you never dreamed of' (vol. 51, p. 355)—but Moodie was unsurprised to find the book poorly reviewed in the Canadian press and herself thoroughly 'unpopular with the natives' (Moodie, *Letters*, 127). She was, however, both surprised and disappointed by the reaction of her sister Agnes Strickland, to whom she had dedicated the book but who strongly disapproved of Moodie's decision to be so frank about her poverty. Strickland's disapproval notwithstanding, the book was popular enough to have gone into a third edition, 'with additions', by 1854. Moodie followed this book with a sequel, *Life in the Clearings* (1853), as well as with a number of short stories, including some based on her own life, and four novels: *Mark Hurdlestone* (1853), *Flora Lyndsay* (1854), *Matrimonial Speculations* (1854), and *The Moncktons* (1856). None of these works achieved either the success or the notoriety of *Roughing it in the Bush*.

John Moodie died suddenly in October 1869, leaving Susanna a widow with two daughters, three surviving sons (two other sons had died, one in infancy and one in an accident as a child), and numerous grandchildren. It was a literary family. Moodie's second daughter, Agnes, by then a widow herself, also did some writing; likewise Catharine Parr Traill, to whom Moodie remained close all her life, had considerable success writing about her Canadian experiences. Susanna Moodie died on 8 April 1885 at 52 Adelaide Street, Toronto, and was buried in Belleville, Ontario. By that time her family was well established in the Canadian literary scene and she herself was recognized as one of the important early figures in Canadian literature, even though she always considered herself

British and in 1861 had declined, rather stiffly, an invitation to have her name included in a 'list of Canadian worthies' (Moodie, *Letters*, 191). None the less *Roughing it in the Bush* remains a central work in the literary history of Canada, and five separate critical editions were published between 1962 and 1997. Moodie's grim account of a middle-class woman's attempt to settle in the Ontario wilderness has continued to catch the imagination of Canadian writers including Margaret Atwood and Carol Shields.

PAM PERKINS

Sources *Susanna Moodie: letters of a lifetime*, ed. C. Ballstadt, E. Hopkins, and M. Peterman (Toronto, 1985) · S. Moodie, *Roughing it in the bush* (1988) · 'Forest life in Canada west', *Blackwood*, 71 (1852), 355–65 · W. H. New, ed., *The Victoria Magazine, 1847–48* (Vancouver, 1968) · *Voyage: short narratives of Susanna Moodie*, ed. J. Thurston (Ottawa, 1991) · R. L. McDougal, ed., *Life in the clearings* (Toronto, 1959) · C. Gray, *Sisters in the wilderness: the lives of Susanna Moodie and Catharine Parr Traill* (Toronto, 1999)
Archives NA Canada · Public Archives of Ontario, Toronto, letters · Queen's University, Kingston, Ontario, Douglas Library, letters · Suffolk RO, Ipswich, commonplace book · U. Cal., Los Angeles, letters | BL, Bentley papers · National Library of Canada, Ottawa, Patrick Hamilton Ewing collection, letters · Suffolk RO, Ipswich, John Glyde papers · Toronto Public Library, Boys and Girls House, letters · University of Illinois, Bentley papers
Likenesses T. Cheesman, miniature, 1820–29, priv. coll.; repro. in Ballstadt, Hopkins, and Peterman, eds., *Susanna Moodie* · miniature, c.1820–1829, NA Canada · G. Stanton, photograph, c.1850, NA Canada · photographs, NA Canada

Moodie, William [*pseud.* Adam Whyte] (1759–1812), Church of Scotland minister and university teacher, was born on 2 July 1759 in Gartly, Aberdeenshire, the eldest of the seven children of Roger Moodie (*d.* 1775), parish minister of Gartly and later of Monimail in Fife, and his wife, Margaret Scott (*d.* 1806). He was educated at Monimail parish school and enrolled at St Andrews University in 1773. After a further period of study at Edinburgh University, Moodie was licensed to preach in 1781. He was ordained and inducted as the minister of Kirkcaldy, Fife, on 9 June 1784, having been presented to the charge through the influence of James Oswald of Dunnikier, in whose family he had been employed as tutor. On 10 November 1786 he married Johanna Lindsay (*d.* 1796). They had two sons (neither of whom survived childhood) and two daughters.

Moodie was translated on 25 October 1787 to the prominent charge of St Andrew's Church in the New Town of Edinburgh. There, 'in his spare time' ('A short account', xix), he studied oriental languages. On 11 September 1793 he was appointed to the chair of Hebrew and oriental languages in the University of Edinburgh in conjunction with his parish duties. He was said to have been skilled in Hebrew and Chaldaic, producing a revised edition of Wilson's *Hebrew Grammar*, and also 'intimately acquainted' (ibid., xx) with several other languages, most notably Persian.

Moodie wrote two pamphlets on political and ecclesiastical subjects during the 1790s: *Political Preaching* (1792), published under the pseudonym Adam Whyte, which condemned the use of sermons to advocate political reform or radicalism, and *A Cobler's Remarks on a Journal of a Tour through the Northern Counties of Scotland* (1798), which attacked itinerant evangelical lay preachers such as James Haldane for not holding clerical licences, for excluding reason from the interpretation of scripture, and for anti-nomianism in denying that man can do anything to render himself acceptable to God. Moodie also published four single sermons between 1794 and 1799, and a collection of his *Sermons*, which he had begun editing before his death, was published posthumously in 1813. He was awarded the degree of DD by the University of Edinburgh on 6 February 1798, and he was chosen as moderator of the general assembly of the Church of Scotland in 1799.

Moodie's preaching was held in high regard, as was his enthusiastic teaching of eastern languages. He was said to have been a gentle pastor, and in general a kind, cheerful, and unassuming man. He was not endowed with a robust constitution, and he frequently suffered from stomach complaints. In 1801 the Revd David Ritchie, professor of logic at Edinburgh University and an old friend, was appointed to assist him at St Andrew's Church. Moodie suffered particularly violent illnesses during the summer of 1803 and most of 1810, both of which rendered him temporarily incapable of preaching. His final illness began in May 1812, and he died in Edinburgh on 11 June.

EMMA VINCENT MACLEOD

Sources 'A short account of the life and character of Dr William Moodie', W. Moodie, *Sermons* (1813) · *Fasti Scot.*, new edn, 1.88, 5.166 · A. Bower, *The history of the University of Edinburgh*, 3 (1830) · *Caledonian Mercury* (18 June 1812)

Moody [*née* Dunch], **Deborah**, **Lady Moody** (*c*.1585–1658/9), colonist in America, was born in the mid-1580s, the eldest of five children of Walter Dunch (*c*.1552–1594), barrister and landowner and MP for Dunwich in 1584 and 1588, and Deborah, daughter of James Pilkington, bishop of Durham. Deborah Dunch remarried after her husband's death. In 1606, her daughter Deborah married Henry Moody (*d*. 1629), later first baronet, who, like her family, held lands in Wiltshire, where he served as sheriff in 1618–19. He represented Malmesbury in the parliaments of 1625, 1626, and 1628–9. They appear to have had at least two children, Henry and Catherine.

By 1635 Lady Moody was resident in London and was included in the 21 April Star Chamber order requiring more than 200 named members of the nobility and gentry to live on their country properties rather than in the city. About 1639 she emigrated to Massachusetts where she was granted property near Lynn in 1640, expanded by the purchase of Swampscott a year later. In April 1640 she had joined the congregation at Salem. Late in 1642, however, her rejection of infant baptism was reported and, rejecting congregational admonishment, she and her associates left Massachusetts the following year, moving to Dutch New Netherland.

Governor Willem Kieft, hoping to populate Long Island and thereby establish safety from the American Indians around Manhattan, offered patents for settlements. Lady Moody accepted the offer and founded Gravesend, just north of Coney Island. Attacks by Mohicans in retaliation for the loss of land drove the settlers out of Gravesend soon afterwards but the ending of warfare in 1645 saw

them return. Again taking advantage of Kieft's desire to secure increased settlement in the area she secured a new town charter, including the town's right to choose its officers (subject to the governor's approval) and 'free libertie of conscience according to the costome and manner of Holland' (Biemer, 20), though not the right to public worship.

Lady Moody's continued position of influence in Gravesend was apparent in her dealings with Kieft's successor, Pieter Stuyvesant. In 1654, following the outbreak of war between the English and the Dutch, he sought to bar as traitors two of Gravesend's elected magistrates. In 1655 when the two attempted to claim Gravesend for the English she mediated an agreement between Stuyvesant and the town to secure magistrates acceptable to both, 'binding that which is broken' in a divided community. In 1655 she voted in the election as a householder, being the first European woman known legally to have voted in North America.

In the later 1650s Lady Moody appears to have shielded Quakers in Gravesend, sometimes being described as a convert. Her commitment to religious freedom was notable at a time when the New Netherland authorities were becoming increasingly concerned about dissent from the Dutch Reformed church. She died about five years before New Amsterdam was taken by the English, between November 1658 and May 1659, at which time her son sold some of the property of his late mother. It is believed that this 'dangerous woeman' as she was described by John Endecott, governor of Massachusetts (Biemer, 20) or 'first Lady Liberty' as later admirers dubbed her, was buried in old Gravesend cemetery. The settlement later became a part of Brooklyn, New York.

CAROL BERKIN

Sources V. H. Cooper, *A dangerous woman: New York's first Lady Liberty (1586–1659?)* (1995) · E. G. Burrows and M. Wallace, *Gotham: a history of New York city to 1898* (1999) · J. W. Gerard, *Lady Deborah: a discourse delivered before the New York Historical Society* (1880) · A. Sheehan, 'Moody, Lady Deborah', *ANB* · L. B. Biemer, *Women and property in colonial New York: the transition from Dutch to English law, 1643–1727* (1983), 11–31 · J. C. Henderson, 'Dunch, Walter', HoP, *Commons, 1558–1603*, 2.65–6

Archives Brooklyn Historical Society · New York Historical Society

Moody, Dwight Lyman (1837–1899), evangelist, was born in Northfield, Massachusetts, on 5 February 1837, the sixth of nine children of Edwin Moody (1800–1841), a bricklayer, who died early, and his forceful wife, Betsey, *née* Holton (1825–1895). He was educated at the local grammar school and at Northfield Academy for Boys. Becoming a shoe salesman, he was converted in 1855, joined a Congregational church in the following year, and moved to the rising city of Chicago, where he prospered. There he soon launched an undenominational Sunday school that developed into the unattached Illinois Street Church. In 1860 he abandoned his business to become a full-time employee of the Chicago Young Men's Christian Association, acting chiefly as a zealous city missionary but also visiting troops during the civil war. On 28 August 1862 he married the nineteen-year-old Emma Charlotte Revell (*d*. 1903), a calm and self-controlled Baptist who was to

Dwight Lyman Moody (1837–1899), by Edward Clifford, 1884

accompany him on his main trips to Britain. They had one daughter and two sons.

Between 1866 and 1870, while president of the Chicago YMCA, Moody became an experienced convention speaker. In 1867 he crossed the Atlantic, basing himself for four months at the London YMCA. He established contact with the circle of evangelicals associated with the annual Mildmay conference and particularly R. C. Morgan, the Brethren publisher and editor of *The Christian*. In 1871 his home, church, and YMCA were destroyed in the great Chicago fire, but a decisive spiritual experience nerved him for fresh ventures. During a brief visit to London in 1872, when he spoke at Mildmay, he discussed with Morgan a plan for an evangelistic tour of Britain. On 17 June 1873 Moody arrived at Liverpool, unannounced, to mount the enterprise. After missions in York, Sunderland, and Newcastle, he opened a campaign in Edinburgh on 23 November that lasted until late January. Boosted by publicity in *The Christian*, Moody took Edinburgh by storm. Crowds flocked nightly to the Corn Exchange, which held nearly 6000, attracted in part by the singing of his partner, Ira D. Sankey [*see below*]. From 8 February Moody enjoyed even greater celebrity in Glasgow, where until April he

regularly spoke four times a day. Missions followed in other Scottish towns, in Belfast, Dublin, and Manchester during the autumn, and in Sheffield, Birmingham, and Liverpool in the new year. The climax took place in London between 9 March and 21 July 1875, when he addressed altogether over 2½ million people at four venues: the Agricultural Hall, Islington; the Royal Opera House, Haymarket; Camberwell Green; and Bow Common. In June an attempted evangelistic visit to Eton College was transferred to an adjacent garden after protests in the House of Lords. Criticized by the secular press for vulgarity, by hyper-Calvinists for distorting the gospel, and by Anglo-Catholics for both, he nevertheless enjoyed enormous popularity and (contrary to some accounts) did make an appreciable impact on non-churchgoers and the working classes.

Moody sustained similar campaigns in America for the rest of his life. He founded a girls' school (1879), a boys' school (1881), an annual Bible conference (1880) on the Mildmay model (all three at Northfield), and a Bible institute for lay workers in Chicago (1889). During 1881–3 he was again in the United Kingdom, holding missions in Newcastle, Edinburgh, Glasgow, and elsewhere, perhaps the most notable being a visit to the University of Cambridge in November 1882. Between November 1883 and June 1884 he preached in temporary iron tabernacles on eleven successive sites in London, receiving less acclaim than in 1875 but quietly meeting many metropolitan notables. On a final visit to Britain in 1891–2 Moody gave addresses briefly in London and more extensively in Scotland. He collapsed in 1899 while conducting a campaign in Kansas City, and died of heart failure on 22 December 1899 in Northfield, where he was buried on 26 December.

Ira David Sankey (1840–1908), Moody's singing colleague, was born on 28 August 1840 at Edinburgh, Pennsylvania. He was educated at the high school in Newcastle, Pennsylvania, and entered his father's bank there in 1857. In 1863 he married Fanny, *née* Edwards. A lifelong Methodist, he encountered Moody at a YMCA conference in 1870 and, though without vocal training, joined his missions to 'sing the gospel'. After congregational singing, led whenever possible by a mass choir, Sankey accompanied his own baritone solos on a harmonium. Rousing or plaintive melodies possessing memorable choruses reminiscent of the music hall were interspersed with anecdotal sermonettes. His immensely popular *Sacred Songs and Solos* (1873 and many subsequent editions) came to include a few of his own compositions, especially 'There were Ninety and Nine'. Sankey visited Britain without Moody in 1898–9 and 1901, eventually dying at Brooklyn, New York, on 14 August 1908.

Moody and Sankey successfully adapted the American revivalist tradition to a respectable urban world, dropping the inherited 'anxious seat' for potential converts in favour of less threatening enquiry rooms and organizing increasingly careful preparations such as domestic visitation. Moody insisted on interdenominational co-operation, helping to draw together the Free Church and United Presbyterians in Scotland. His preaching was deliberately compatible with both Calvinism and Arminianism, but he did adopt the increasingly widespread belief in a premillennial second advent. Although he normally consorted with businessmen, he encouraged measures of civic responsibility such as temperance efforts, free breakfasts for the poor, and refuges for destitute children. In Britain his message seemed radical because of its democratic populism. Strong, square-shouldered, and sporting a long brown beard, Moody used simple language, homely illustrations, and a dash of Yankee humour to bring Bible stories alive. His published sermons circulated widely. Moody and Sankey probably represent the chief cultural influence of the United States on Britain during the nineteenth century.   D. W. BEBBINGTON

Harold Arundel Moody (1882–1947), by Ronald Moody, 1946

Sources J. F. Findlay, *Dwight L. Moody: American evangelist, 1837–1899* (1969) · J. Coffey, 'Democracy and popular religion: Moody and Sankey's mission to Britain, 1873–5', *Citizenship and community: liberals, radicals and collective identities in the British Isles, 1865–1931*, ed. E. F. Biagini (1996), 93–119 · J. Kent, *Holding the fort: studies in Victorian revivalism* (1978) · J. C. Pollock, *Moody without Sankey: a new biographical portrait* (1963) · P. B. Morgan, 'A study of the work of American revivalists in Britain from 1870–1914 and of the effect upon organized Christianity of their work there', BLitt diss., U. Oxf., 1961 · I. D. Sankey, *My life and sacred songs* (1906) · S. S. Sizer, *Gospel hymns and social religion* (1978) · W. G. McLoughlin, *Modern revivalism: Charles Grandison Finney to Billy Graham* (1959) · W. H. Daniels, *D. L. Moody and his work* (1875) · W. R. Moody, *The life of Dwight L. Moody* · *The London discourses of Mr D. L. Moody: as delivered in the Agricultural Hall and Her Majesty's Opera House* (1875) · J. H. Hall, *Biography of gospel song and hymn writers* (1914), 201

Archives L. Cong. · Moody Bible Institute, Chicago · Northfield School for Girls, Massachusetts

Likenesses G. P. A. Healy, portrait, 1867, repro. in Pollock, *Moody without Sankey*, frontispiece · W. & D. Downey, photograph, 1873? (Ira Sankey), repro. in Daniels, *D. L. Moody and his work*, facing p. 229 · photograph, 1875, repro. in Daniels, *D. L. Moody and his work*, frontispiece · E. Clifford, watercolour, 1884, Smithsonian Institution, National Portrait Gallery [see illus.] · photographs, repro. in Findlay, *Dwight L. Moody*, 246–7 · photographs (Ira Sankey), repro. in Sankey, *My life and sacred songs*

Moody, Harold Arundel (1882–1947), physician and founder of the League of Coloured Peoples, was born on 8 October 1882 at 8 Rum Lane, in Kingston, Jamaica, the eldest of six children of Charles Ernest Moody (1861–1920) and his wife, *née* Christina Emmeline Ellis (d. 1951), who kept a drug store. Moody, a diligent student at Wolmer's Free School, went on to study medicine at King's College, London, in 1904.

Moody qualified MB, BS in 1912 and gained an MD in 1919. Although well qualified, he was refused a post at King's College Hospital because of his colour; eventually he was employed as medical superintendent of the Marylebone Medical Mission in London. On 10 May 1913 Moody married Olive Mabel Tranter (1889–1965), a white nurse, who worked closely with him in a long and happy marriage which produced two girls and four boys. That same year he opened a practice in Peckham, London, eventually moving to 164 Queen's Road, where he lived and worked for the rest of his life. Moody revisited Jamaica on only three occasions, in 1912, 1919, and finally in 1946–7.

As a teenager Harold Moody became a Christian and his faith was the mainspring of his life and activities. Until the late 1920s Moody concentrated on his family, medical work, and various Christian activities mainly within the Congregational Union and as chairman of the Colonial Missionary Society. Racial prejudice was widespread and overt, and Moody sought to counter this by using his professional influence and preaching opportunities, although with few results. In 1931 he founded the League of Coloured Peoples (LCP), a multiracial organization, to press for black civil rights. Moody regarded the LCP as a Christian body pursuing a Christian purpose, and he pressed these claims in his preaching and as president of the Christian Endeavour Union (1936) and chairman of the London Missionary Society (1943). In its early years the league engaged mainly in a range of social and welfare roles, while Moody sought the support of influential people, who were invited to address its meetings and conferences.

The Italian invasion of Ethiopia in 1935 politicized the league and gave it a sharper pan-African edge. The league lobbied on a variety of national and international issues: the treatment of black British seamen as aliens, land and labour questions in British colonial Africa, the labour and political unrest in the Caribbean in the late 1930s, and the 'colour bar' in Britain and the colonies. In these protests the LCP was often allied to other black groups, including those led by radicals, although relations were never easy: there was tension between Moody and African students in the mid-1930s over who should control a London hostel for west African students, for example.

The wartime influx of black workers and soldiers into Britain led to increased racial animosity and helped give the LCP greater purpose and influence. Moody became a frequent visitor to government departments. Some officials regarded him as pompous and interfering but invariably he was listened to with respect. In 1943 he joined advisory bodies on the training of nurses in the colonies and on the welfare of colonial people in Britain. At the 1944 London conference of the LCP a 'charter for coloured peoples' demanded 'full self-government' for colonial peoples 'at the earliest possible opportunity' and that racial discrimination in Britain be made illegal. The charter foreshadowed some of the demands made at the Pan-African Congress in Manchester in 1945, which Moody helped to prepare but did not attend.

Moody wrote several pamphlets on race relations, while a league committee report of 1944 advocated radical changes in school curricula in an attempt to counter racial prejudice. In the winter of 1946–7 Moody made an extended speaking and preaching tour of the West Indies in order to raise money for a colonial culture centre in London. It was a tiring and disappointing journey. Moody returned ill to his London home and died there of acute influenza on 24 March 1947; he was cremated at the South London crematorium.

Moody was a tall, bespectacled, and imposing figure with a dominating personality. A bronze bust, executed by his brother Ronald Clive *Moody in 1953, is in the National Portrait Gallery, London. The league continued until the early 1950s, faltered, and then closed; it had been Moody's personal creation, largely sustained and directed by his enthusiasm, energy, and income.

DAVID KILLINGRAY

Sources private information (2004) · priv. coll., Moody MSS · D. A. Vaughan, *Negro victory: the life story of Dr Harold Moody* (1950) · *The Keys* [Journal of the League of Coloured Peoples] (1933–9) · League of Coloured Peoples, *Letter* [continued as *Newsletter*] (1939–47) · b. cert. · m. cert. · d. cert. · *Wolmer's bi-centenary souvenir* (1924), 40 · King's College registers, King's Lond. · D. Killingray, *Race, faith and politics: Harold Moody and the League of Coloured Peoples* (1999) **Archives** Bodl. RH, Anti-Slavery Society MSS · NRA, priv. coll., notes, newspaper cuttings, photographs · PRO, CO, DO, WO, HO | Bodl. RH, Arthur Creech Jones MSS · Bodl. RH, Lord Lugard MSS · Bodl. RH, Margery Perham MSS **Likenesses** R. Moody, bronze bust, 1946, NPG [see illus.] · R. Moody, bronze bust, London Missionary Society **Wealth at death** £5304 17s. 4d.: probate, 8 June 1947, CGPLA Eng. & Wales

Moody [*formerly* Cochran]**, John** (1726/7–1812), actor and singer, was born in Cork, the eldest son of a hairdresser named Cochran. He later hid his Irish origins in order to be accepted as an Englishman and claimed that he had been born in Stanhope Street, Clare Market, London. He followed his father's trade in Tuckey's Lane, Cork, for several years before travelling to Jamaica—to avoid, it is said, conscription during the 1745 uprising. In Kingston he joined a theatre company and performed Hamlet, Romeo, and Lear. He returned to England with some 'property of consequence', which he subsequently augmented. Kelly claimed that Moody had told him 'that he worked his passage home as a sailor before the mast' (Kelly, 199). In 1758 he became a principal actor on the Norwich circuit, specializing in heroes and lovers. He was playing Claudio in *Measure for Measure* when Joseph Peterson, playing the Duke, died while performing the speech 'Reason thus with life'. (Coincidentally in 1766 Mrs Jefferson died in

John Moody (1726/7–1812), by Johan Zoffany, c.1763–4 [as Father Foigard in *The Beaux' Stratagem* by George Farquhar]

Moody's arms during a rehearsal in Plymouth.) Tate Wilkinson remembers acting Lord Townly to Moody's Manly in John Vanbrugh's and Colley Cibber's *The Provok'd Husband* at Portsmouth on 20 June 1759, soon after Moody had returned from Jamaica. Wilkinson adds that Garrick saw him play Lockit in John Gay's *The Beggar's Opera* during the same engagement and hired him at 30s. per week, although Moody stipulated that he should first appear as Henry VIII. Wilkinson's ordering of these events, however, is somewhat confused. Moody made his first appearance in London on 12 January 1759, given 5 guineas by Garrick to act Thyreus in Edward Capell's version of *Antony and Cleopatra* when Holland became ill. He was again billed as making his début on 22 May 1759, when he acted Henry VIII at Drury Lane. The prompter there noted that 'one Moody, a Stroler' (Highfill, Burnim & Langhans, *BDA*) was formally engaged by the theatre on 12 September 1759; with the exception of one season at the Haymarket, a few performances at Covent Garden, and touring engagements Moody remained at Drury Lane until the end of his career. In his first season he was the original Kingston in James Townley's *High Life below Stairs*, he created his first great Irish character, Sir Callaghan O'Brallaghan in Macklin's *Love à-la-Mode*, and he played the first clown in Garrick's pantomime *Harlequin's Invasion*.

In 1760–61 Moody played Teague in *The Committee* by Robert Howard, one of his most successful parts and the subject of several paintings, engravings, and a Delftware wall tile. During this season he also created Captain O'Cutter in George Colman's *The Jealous Wife* and played Vulture in *Woman's a Riddle*, Father Foigard in *The Beaux' Stratagem*, and Obadiah Prim in Susanna Centlivre's *A Bold Stroke for a Wife*. On 24 April 1761 he sang his specialty number, 'Teddy Wolloughan's whimsical oratorical description of a man o' war and sea fight, with Hibernian notes on the whole', with which he continued to entertain audiences for many years.

Moody's fourth season at Drury Lane, which followed a summer of acting in Birmingham, began well with Peachum in *The Beggar's Opera* on 21 September 1762. However, on 25 January 1763, when he was scheduled to act the Host in *The Two Gentlemen of Verona*, a great deal of undesirable publicity was thrust upon him. During the 'half-price riot' led by the Irishman Fitzpatrick against Garrick, Moody seized and extinguished a torch intended to burn down the theatre. An apology was demanded the next night from Fitzpatrick's followers. Moody used his specialist dialect, the low-bred Irishman, to say that 'he was very sorry he had displeased them by saving their lives in putting out the fire' (Davies, 2.6). His sense of irony only further infuriated the mob, who insisted that he beg their forgiveness on his knees. According to Thomas Davies, Moody exclaimed, 'I will not, by God' (ibid.) and stormed off the stage to be embraced by Garrick, who declared that while he had a guinea he would pay Moody his salary. Unfortunately, in order to appease the audience the following night, Garrick promised that Moody would not appear on the Drury Lane stage while suffering their displeasure. Eventually Moody compelled Fitzpatrick to withdraw the prohibition and to promise the support of his friends on the actor's reappearance, which did not take place until 15 February 1763. A full account of these events can be found in the *Thespian Dictionary* (1805).

Under Garrick, Moody was considered a serviceable actor and was popular in the earlier part of his career. Churchill devotes ten lines to him in *The Rosciad*, which Moody 'always considered as his passport to the Temple of Fame'. According to Doran he was 'the first who brought the stage Irishman into repute, and rendered the character one of distinct line whereby a performer might acquire a reputation' (Doran, 337). Moody excelled in such comic roles, especially those written for him, like Major O'Flaherty in Richard Cumberland's *The West Indian* (first performed 19 January 1771), Sir Patrick O'Neale in Garrick's *The Irish Widow* (23 October 1772), Connolly in Hugh Kelly's *The School for Wives* (11 December 1773), and McCormuck in Cumberland's *The Note of Hand, or, A Trip to Newmarket* (9 February 1774). William Hawkins said he was 'capital' in many low comedy roles, insisting that one could not find a better Commodore Flip, Adam, or Vamp: 'There is considerable ease and propriety in his manner of acting' and that he had 'become no less a favourite with the boxes, than he is with the galleries' (Highfill, Burnim & Langhans, *BDA*).

After Garrick's retirement in 1776 Moody remained at Drury Lane under Sheridan and Kemble, adding many new roles to his repertory. Like many other employees of the theatre he had trouble claiming his wages from Sheridan. According to Anthony Pasquin he was fired for attempting to 'enforce the payment' of £500 due to him (Pasquin, 41–2). Moody's last appearance at Drury Lane was as Sir Patrick O'Neale on 13 June 1796, the same night that Dodd, playing Kecksey, also retired from the stage. As late as November 1800 Moody was still suing for back pay in the court of the king's bench; Lord Kenyon found on his behalf, praising him as 'a frugal and prudent man' (Highfill, Burnim & Langhans, *BDA*).

By the time of Moody's retirement, however, he was known as a lethargic, limited, and lazy actor. The anonymous author of *The Modern Stage Exemplified* wrote in 1788:

Moody devoid of spirit, humour, grace!
No strong expression of his face we find;
No passion marks the features of his mind.
Dull, sluggish, cold insensible and tame,
He gives no pleasure, and deserves no fame.

The *Monthly Mirror*, in a 1797 retrospective of Moody's career, described him as 'tall and bulky': 'We believe no one had a desire to see Moody twice; he was perfectly uniform in his representations, and one part was a sample of all'.

Moody retired in comfort to Barnes Common, where despite his rheumatism he grew and sold vegetables and retained his interest in theatre. He belonged to the actors' society, the 'School of Garrick', and in 1805 he became the chairman of the Drury Lane Actors' Fund, which he had helped to form in 1774. On 26 June 1804 he returned to the stage for the benefit of Bayswater Hospital, announced as 'his first appearance these ten years, and positively his last on any stage'. The following year, on 12 May, his wife, Anne, died at the age of eighty-eight, and on 22 May 1806 he married Kitty Ann Worlock (1763–1846), a dancer whose stage name was Elizabeth Armstrong, at St Dionis Backchurch. Moody died at the age of eighty-five, on 26 December 1812, either at Shepherd's Bush (according to the *Gentleman's Magazine*) or in Leicester Square (according to the *European Magazine*). Though he had requested burial in the parish of St Clement Danes, London, where he claimed to have been born, the cemetery was full and he was interred instead in Barnes churchyard.

ROBERTA MOCK

Sources *The thespian dictionary, or, Dramatic biography of the present age*, 2nd edn (1805) · T. Wilkinson, *Memoirs of his own life*, 4 vols. (1790) · Genest, *Eng. stage* · W. C. Russell, *Representative actors* [1888] · C. Churchill, *The Rosciad* (1772) · J. Boaden, *Memoirs of the life of John Philip Kemble*, 2 vols. (1825) · [J. Haslewood], *The secret history of the green rooms: containing authentic and entertaining memoirs of the actors and actresses in the three theatres royal*, 2 vols. (1790) · T. Davies, *Memoirs of the life of David Garrick*, 2 vols. (1808) · J. Doran, 'Their majesties' servants', or, Annals of the English stage, 2nd edn, 2 vols. (1865) · *Theatrical biography, or, Memoirs of the principal performers of the three Theatre Royals*, 2 vols. (1772) · G. W. Stone and C. B. Hogan, eds., *The London stage, 1660–1800*, pts 4–5 (1962–8) · A. Pasquin [J. Williams], *The pin basket to the children of Thespis* (1796) · M. Kelly, *Reminiscences*, 2nd edn, 2 vols. (1826); repr., R. Fiske, ed. (1975) · Highfill, Burnim & Langhans, *BDA* · tombstone, Barnes parish church · *N&Q*, 5th ser., 3 (8 May 1875)
Archives Garr. Club, letters, notes, receipt, marriage certificate

Likenesses J. Zoffany, portrait, *c.*1763–1764; Sothebys, 13 April 1994, lot 68 [*see illus.*] · B. Vandergucht, oils, exh. RA 1775, Garr. Club · T. Hardy, engraving, 1792 · T. Hardy, mezzotint, pubd 1792 (after his earlier works), BM, NPG · P. Audinet, engraving, repro. in J. Bell, *Bell's British theatre* (1792) · W. Bromley, engraving (after S. Drummond), repro. in *European Magazine* (1790) · S. De Wilde, oils (as Commodore Flip in *The fair Quaker*), Garr. Club · Dighton, watercolour drawing, Harvard TC · S. Drummond, oils (as Jonson in *The devil to pay*), Garr. Club · J. Roberts, drawing (as Teague), BM · B. Vandergucht, double portrait, oils (with John Hayman Packer in *The register office*), Leicester Museum and Art Gallery · gouache drawing, Garr. Club · portrait, Garr. Club · prints, BM, NPG

Wealth at death unspecified amounts in public funds; freehold estate at Barnes; will, Highfill, Burnim & Langhans, *BDA*

Moody, Richard Clement (1813–1887), army officer and colonial governor, second son of Colonel Thomas Moody RE (*d.* 1849), who served extensively in the West Indies, and his wife, formerly Miss Clement, was born in St Ann's garrison, Barbados, on 13 February 1813. Colonel Hampden Blaimire Moody RE (*d.* 1869), and Revd James Leith Moody (*d.* 1896), an army chaplain, were his brothers. Educated at private schools and by a tutor at home, Moody entered the Royal Military Academy, Woolwich, on 24 April 1827, and in accordance with contemporary practice was appointed, on 23 December 1829, to the Royal Engineers for specialized training before being commissioned second-lieutenant on 5 November 1830. On 30 May 1832 he joined the Ordnance Survey in Ireland, but early the following year became ill, and on recovery was stationed at Woolwich. In October 1833 he sailed for the West Indies, where he advanced to first-lieutenant (25 June 1835) on St Vincent. Moody went to England in September 1837, following a debilitating attack of yellow fever; while on sick-leave he toured the United States with Sir Charles Felix Smith. For a short time afterwards he served at Devonport, then in June 1838 was appointed assistant instructor in fortification at the Royal Military Academy, Woolwich, where he remained for three years.

Meanwhile, after a lengthy period of international dispute and recent violence ashore involving Argentinian settlers, in 1833 the United Kingdom asserted authority over the Falkland Islands, which had been named after a seventeenth-century first lord of the Admiralty and where the union flag had been hoisted in 1765. Moody left England on 1 October 1841 for the Falklands as lieutenant-governor, advancing in 1843 to be its first British governor and commander-in-chief. Given extensive powers to secure and maintain order, he governed firmly and sensibly, and took some steps to develop the area's resources. A detachment of sappers and miners, assisted by civilian labourers, erected government offices, a school and barracks, dwellings and storehouses. Jetties and sea walls further enhanced poor facilities to encourage trade, and a new road system facilitated expansion of farming and fishing. However, the settlers, though they liked him, considered that he did insufficient for development: no survey was made and no system of land tenure devised. Among his achievements, in 1845 Moody introduced tussock grass into Great Britain, for which he received the gold medal of the Royal Agricultural Society. Moody Creek, near Port Stanley, was named after him. Moody progressed to second-captain on 6 March 1844 and first-captain on 19 August 1847. In February 1849, his tour of duty in the Falklands having ended the previous autumn, he returned to England, where he was employed by the Colonial Office until November. Subsequently, after resuming his military career for a year in Chatham, he was appointed commanding engineer at Newcastle upon Tyne. While he was in the northern district a reservoir dam burst at Holmfirth, Yorkshire, on 5 February 1852, causing much loss of life and damage to property. Moody produced an official report on the incident, and in the cause of safety also inspected other dams and reservoirs in the district. Meanwhile, at Newcastle upon Tyne on 6 July 1852, he married Mary Susanna, daughter of Joseph Hawks JP, deputy lieutenant, and banker: they had eleven surviving children.

Moody went to Malta in 1854. Without ever having been major he was promoted lieutenant-colonel on 13 January 1856, but took sick-leave in Germany four months later after an attack of fever. Following his recovery Moody served in Scotland as commanding engineer. An accomplished draughtsman, he personally drew up plans for the restoration of Edinburgh Castle which so pleased the secretary of state for war, Lord Panmure, that he was ordered to Windsor to show them to the queen and Prince Albert. Moody became brevet colonel on 28 April 1858, and that autumn was appointed lieutenant-governor and chief commissioner of lands and works (with a £1200 salary) in British Columbia, a new colony; he was sworn in at Victoria on 4 January 1859. Moody founded the capital, New Westminster, having drawn up plans for it when the area was a dense pine forest. He designed other settlements and roads throughout the colony, during a difficult period of development, but opinion of him varied: he was widely considered to have been inefficient and extravagant. During his term of office the Canadian and Pacific Railway terminated at the head of Burrards inlet at Port Moody, named in his honour. Moody became regimental colonel on 5 December 1863, returned to England that month, and took a post as commanding engineer of Chatham district in March 1864. Promoted major-general on 25 January 1866, he retired to Lyme Regis, Dorset, where he acted as commissioner for the extension of the municipal boundaries in 1868. He hoped to return to British Columbia but, while visiting Bournemouth, died of apoplexy at the Royal Bath Hotel on 31 March 1887. He was survived by his wife.   JOHN SWEETMAN

Sources *Army List* · H. D. Buchanan-Dunlop, *Records of the Royal Military Academy, 1741–1892*, 2nd edn (1892) · archives, Royal Military Academy, Sandhurst · T. W. J. Conolly, *Role of officers of the corps of royal engineers, 1660–1898* (1898) · *DNB* · M. A. Ormsby, 'Moody, Richard Clement', *DCB*, vol. 11 · Boase, *Mod. Eng. biog.* · CGPLA Eng. & Wales (1887)

Archives British Columbia Archives and Records Service, Victoria, corresp.

Wealth at death £24,289 10s. 4d.: probate, 13 May 1887, *CGPLA Eng. & Wales*

Moody, Ronald Clive (1900–1984), sculptor, was born on 12 August 1900 at 122 King Street, Kingston, Jamaica, one

Ronald Clive Moody (1900–1984), by Val Wilmer, 1963 [with Father from his *Concrete Family*]

of six children of Charles Ernest Moody (1861–1920), dispensing chemist, and his wife, Christina Emmeline, *née* Ellis (d. 1951). Harold Arundel *Moody was his eldest brother. After education at Calabar College, Jamaica, he arrived in London in 1923 to study dentistry at King's College. He qualified in 1930 and later established his practice in Cavendish Place, London, but worked as a dentist only infrequently thereafter. By chance he encountered the collection of Egyptian sculptures at the British Museum, and was struck by 'the tremendous inner force, the irresistible movement in stillness' they displayed (Walmsley, 2); he later claimed that Egyptian sculpture encouraged him to be an artist. He taught himself by experimenting with dentistry plaster. He also found time to read Indian and Chinese philosophy. While at King's College he had joined John G. Bennett's Institute for the Comparative Study of History, Philosophy, and the Sciences, which studied the teachings of G. I. Gurdjieff. He wanted his art to reflect his interest in philosophy.

Moody's first important sculpture, *Wohin* (1935; priv. coll.), was made from wood, as were *Johanaan* (1936; Tate), *Midonz* (1937; priv. coll.), and *Tacet* (1938). All these works engaged with the human essence which is essential to Eastern philosophy. He exhibited at the Adams Gallery, London, in 1935, and at the Walker Art Gallery, Liverpool, in 1936. Through a mutual friend he met the film director Alberto Cavalcanti, who arranged exhibitions of his work at the Galerie Billiet-Vorms in Paris in 1937 and at the Kunstzaal van Lier in Amsterdam the following spring. Moody's work received much praise, especially from G. Charensol, editor of *Les Nouvelles Littéraires*. In 1938, Moody moved to Paris and on 22 July he married Helene Coppel-Cowan (1902–1978), an English painter. In 1939 he

shipped twelve works to the Harmon Foundation in New York, which displayed them at the Boyer Gallery, the Baltimore Museum of Art, and the Museum of Fine Arts in Boston. In 1940 the German invasion of France forced Moody to flee. He travelled through Spain, before eventually returning to Britain in 1941.

After settling back in Britain, in 1943 Moody was interviewed by Una Marson for the BBC radio programme *Closeup*. In the same year this was followed by three lectures, 'A sculptor', 'The artist's environment', and 'The artist's education', then in 1949–50 by a series of lectures for the overseas service, beginning with 'What is called primitive art' and ending with 'Modern art'. He started to experiment with concrete in the early 1950s but soon contracted tuberculosis, which forced him to give up sculpture for several years. In 1951 he collaborated with Gulla Kell, a German philosopher, to produce a collection of short stories entitled *Amadu's Bundle*, based on the traditional tales of the Fulani tribe; the stories were eventually published in 1972 by Heinemann. Meanwhile, when he recovered from his illness he resumed his artistic career. In 1964 he was commissioned to make a metal sculpture by Professor A. L. Cochrane from the epidemiological research unit in Cardiff, to be presented to the University of the West Indies and installed on its Mona campus. He produced *Savacou*, a stylized mythological bird based on a parrot from the Solomon Islands and a bird from a Chinese drawing. The bird represented the Carib idea of a god who came down to earth to look after the storms and the sea, and later returned to heaven and became a star.

In 1967 Moody became actively involved with the Caribbean Artists Movement, taking part in its many activities, including the controversial exhibition held at the House of Commons in 1968. He was awarded the 1977 Musgrave gold medal; this was Jamaica's most prestigious cultural award. His sculptures were included in the 'Commonwealth Artists of Fame '52–'77' exhibition held at the Commonwealth Institute in 1977, and he served as chairman of the UK visual arts subcommittee for the Festival of Art and Culture 77 in Lagos. In 1980 he received the Jamaican Institute centenary medal for contributions to the arts. Three years later his work was included in an exhibition at the Commonwealth Institute entitled 'Remembrance'.

Moody died of bronchopneumonia and pulmonary embolism on 6 February 1984 at the Westminster Hospital, Westminster, and was cremated on 12 February at Golders Green. His wife had died in 1978. To honour his life achievements his niece, Cynthia Moody, established the Ronald Moody sculpture award to fund an outstanding sculpture student from Jamaica or the Caribbean Commonwealth who had completed a diploma at the Edna Manley College of the Visual and Performing Arts (formerly the Jamaica School of Art). His work was included in 'The Other Story', an exhibition at the Hayward Gallery in 1989, and in 'Representing Britain, 1500–2000: 100 Works from the Tate Gallery' in 2000. A monographic display of his early sculptures in wood was exhibited at Tate Britain and Tate Liverpool in 2003–4. PAULINE DE SOUZA

Sources C. Moody, *Ronald Moody: sculpture catalogue*, 2 vols. [n.d.] · C. Moody, 'Ronald Moody: a man true to his vision', *Third Text*, 8/9 (autumn/winter 1989), 5–24 · C. Moody, 'Midonz', *Transition*, 77 (1999), 10–18 · A. Walmsley, *The Caribbean Artists Movement, 1966–72* (1992) · *The other story: Afro-Asian artists in post-war Britain* (1989) [exhibition catalogue, Hayward Gallery, 1989] · d. cert. · private information (2004) [Cynthia Moody]

Archives priv. coll., corresp., writings, diaries, exhibition files, sketchbooks, *c*.1930–1984 · Tate collection, corresp., writings, diaries, exhibition files, sketchbooks, *c*.1930–1984

Likenesses V. Wilmer, photograph, 1963, priv. coll. [*see illus.*] · photograph, 1968, University of East London, London, African and Asian Visual Artists Archive · photographs, priv. coll.

Wealth at death £45,961: administration, 1984, *CGPLA Eng. & Wales*

Moody, Theodore William (1907–1984), historian, was born in Belfast on 26 November 1907, the second child and only son of William John Moody and his wife, Ann Isabella Dippie, members of the Plymouth Brethren sect. A scholar and teacher of eminence, 'he was driven by an inner force elevated by a dedication which was not just scholarship but which embraced it' (Martin, 5).

Moody is principally renowned as a major influence on the development of research-based Irish history and its dissemination. He was educated at the Royal Belfast Academical Institution from 1920 to 1926, when he entered the Queen's University of Belfast; he received a BA there in 1930 after an outstanding undergraduate career. That same year he went to the Institute of Historical Research and King's College, University of London, to begin research under the direction of Eliza Jeffries Davis. R. H. Tawney was a formative influence on him in London. He was awarded a PhD and elected a fellow of the Royal Historical Society in 1934. While in London he met Margaret Robertson, whom he married in 1935. They had four sons and a daughter. In 1932 he returned to Queen's to take up an appointment as assistant in history to James Eadie Todd, his former tutor, before becoming a lecturer in Irish history in 1935.

Moody was among a handful of university academics who sought to transform Irish historical scholarship, and their efforts 'took on a distinctly institutional—even bureaucratic form' (Brady, 3–4). In February 1936 he was the chief impetus behind the founding of the Ulster Society for Irish Historical Studies. Together with Robin Dudley Edwards, a contemporary at the Institute of Historical Research, he created the Irish Committee of Historical Sciences in March 1938 so that Ireland could be represented on the Comité International des Sciences Historiques. Perhaps the most significant consequence of their collaboration was the founding of *Irish Historical Studies*; the first issue appeared in March 1938 with Moody and Edwards as co-editors. Moody remained joint editor until 1977. Consciously modelled on prestigious academic journals in Germany, France, the United States, and Great Britain, the journal was intended to provide an outlet for Irish scholarship dedicated to the 'scientific' study of history. It contained scholarly articles, contributions on research methods, edited documents, critical bibliographies, historical

Theodore William Moody (1907–1984), by unknown photographer, 1968

revisions, notices of library collections, reviews of books, and listing of theses, along with inventories of books and articles in other Irish journals.

Moody's revised PhD thesis was published in 1939 under the title *The Londonderry Plantation, 1609–41: the City of London and the Plantation in Ulster*. On 5 June 1939 he was appointed to a fellowship in Trinity College, Dublin, and succeeded to the Erasmus Smith chair of history a few months later. In 1940 he was elected a member of the Royal Irish Academy. He held numerous offices within Trinity College (tutor, 1939–52; senior tutor, 1952–8; senior lecturer, 1958–64; and the first dean of the arts faculty, 1967–9), and dedicated himself to bringing it into the 'mainstream of national life' (Martin, 6). On the death of Edmund Curtis in 1943 Moody took on the chief responsibility for managing the school of history, and he remained chairman of its committee until 1977. In 1944 with Dudley Edwards and David B. Quinn he edited Studies in Irish History, a series of monographs on Irish history which concluded in 1957; he also edited the second series between 1960 and 1975. As a protestant (he began attending the meetings of the Society of Friends in 1960, his wife in 1963), Moody might have chosen to restrict his role to Trinity College, then something of a pariah within the new Irish state, a situation intensified by the Roman Catholic hierarchy's ban on Catholics attending it, but he laboured long and devotedly for the ultimately successful mission of reconciling the college, the Catholic church, and the state. Moody served on the Irish Manuscripts Commission

(1943–84), the Irish Broadcasting Council (1953–60), the Irish Broadcasting Authority (1960–72), the advisory committee on cultural relations (1949–63), and the government-appointed commission on higher education (1960–67); this last proved a frustrating experience. From 1972 he was a member of the academic council of the Irish School of Ecumenics. He was particularly interested in radio and television as a medium for education. This grew out of his interest in the curriculum followed in Ireland's schools and in public dissemination of specialist scholarship. In 1969 he wrote 'if history at its best is not made available to the educated public as a whole, it fails in one of its essential social functions' (Brady, 39). Moody suggested to the Irish Broadcasting Council the motif for what became the annual Thomas Davis lectures, first aired in 1953, which present the best in Irish scholarship for a non-specialist audience. With his former pupil at the Queen's University of Belfast J. C. Beckett he edited two series of broadcasts on Ulster, the first made in later 1954 (*Ulster since 1800: a Political and Economic Survey*) and the second in 1957 (*Ulster since 1800, Second Series: a Social Survey*).

In collaboration with Beckett, Moody wrote *Queen's, Belfast, 1845–1949: the History of a University* (2 vols., 1959), which serves as a model for this type of study. That year he was awarded an honorary DLitt. by the Queen's University. Undoubtedly the largest project of Moody's career—the multi-volume *A New History of Ireland*, in a format similar to the *New Cambridge Modern History*—began with his presidential address to the Irish Historical Society in 1962. He chaired the board of editors from 1968 until his death. The first volume appeared in 1977. From 1964 to 1966 he was a Leverhulme research fellow, and spent 1965 at the Institute of Advanced Studies at Princeton. In 1966, with Professor F. X. Martin, he initiated a series of twenty-one lectures published as *The Course of Irish History* (1967), a striking attempt to bring scholarship to the people.

Much of Moody's historical writing is found in articles. However, his short book *The Ulster question, 1603–1973* was published in 1974. In 1977 Moody retired; he was elected a corresponding fellow of the British Academy that year and in 1978 awarded a DLitt. by the National University of Ireland. In a much cited lecture (published in 1978) which retrospectively attempted to define his career-long objectives he proclaimed 'the mental war of liberation from servitude to the myth is an endless and it may be an agonising process. It is, I believe, one in which Irish historians are called on to take an active part' (Brady, 24).

Moody was a fastidious scholar, and the combined weight of college, public, and historical burdens led as the years progressed to a legendary dilatoriness. His commitment to fostering 'inclusiveness' in Irish life fostered a parochialism which blinded him to influential scholarly innovations in Great Britain, Europe, and the United States. His most substantial authored work, *Davitt and Irish Revolution, 1848–1882*, did not appear until 1981. His scholarly reputation will probably remain linked to this study. Although Moody's earlier interest was in the seventeenth and eighteenth centuries, he was entrusted by Michael

Davitt's son with his father's voluminous papers. Constructing a biography of Davitt was to be his chief personal scholarly preoccupation. This huge tome, a model of meticulous research, was as much a history of the times as of the man. Overall, the volume reveals Moody's great strengths and limitations. On the negative side it is often excessively detailed, nor could it be termed 'value-free' history, given that it reflects the author's own preference for liberal-nationalist sentiment. Possibly Moody's enduring works published posthumously will prove to be the collaborative editions: *Florence Arnold-Foster's Irish Journal* (1988) and the multi-volume *The Writings of Theobald Wolfe Tone, 1763–98* (from 1998). Moody's historical project began to come under scrutiny during the 1980s, a process that culminated in Brendan Bradshaw's critique 'Nationalism and historical scholarship in modern Ireland', published in *Irish Historical Studies* (1989). Bradshaw took issue with Moody's austere methods and consciously directive agenda, and suggested that he was intellectually and politically naïve; the net effect in Bradshaw's estimation was to desensitize Irish historical writing. Although this verdict itself has been contested, there is no doubt that Moody's work has subsequently been viewed in a different light.

As a teacher and supervisor of research, Moody commanded affection. A childhood stammer sometimes affected his delivery in lectures but he was known as a fine and committed tutor. A number of the ablest Irish historians learned their craft under his guidance as a research supervisor. Moody retired in 1977 with his health deteriorating. He died in Dublin on 11 February 1984 and was buried in the Quaker burial-ground, Temple Hill, Blackrock. His wife survived him.   ALAN O'DAY

Sources F. X. Martin, 'Theodore William Moody', *Hermathena*, 136 (1984), 5 · C. Brady, ed., *Interpreting Irish history: the debate on historical revisionism, 1938–1994* (1994) · F. S. L. Lyons and R. A. J. Hawkins, eds., *Ireland under the union: varieties of tension* (1980) · *Irish Times* (13 Feb 1984) · *Irish Independent* (13 Feb 1984) · *Belfast Telegraph* (13 Feb 1984) · H. F. Mulvey, 'Theodore William Moody (1907–84): an appreciation', *Irish Historical Studies*, 24 (1984–5), 121–30
Archives CUL, corresp. with Sir Herbert Butterfield · TCD, F. S. L. Lyons MSS |SOUND BBC Northern Ireland
Likenesses photograph, 1968, Royal Irish Acad. [*see illus.*] · photograph, repro. in Brady, ed., *Interpreting Irish history* · photograph, repro. in Lyons and Hawkins, eds., *Ireland under the union*
Wealth at death £113,091: probate, 9 Aug 1984, *CGPLA Éire*

Moon, Sir Francis Graham, first baronet (1796–1871), printseller and publisher, was born at Holborn Bar, London, on 28 October 1796, the youngest son of Ann Withry and Christopher Moon, a gold and silver smith. In 1810 his father died leaving the family 'ill-provided for', so the fourteen-year-old was placed with a bookseller and stationer named Tugwell with premises in Threadneedle Street. He was apparently a diligent and well-liked employee and, working his way through the ranks, on his master's retirement he was able to take over the business in 1817. Under his guidance it continued to prosper. On 28 October 1818 he married Ann Chancellor (d. 1870).

In 1825 Moon's fortunes improved when he purchased the bankrupt stock of Messrs Hurst, Robinson & Co., which also contained high-quality material that had come from the celebrated eighteenth-century publishers Boydell & Co. This decision was made on the advice of Henry Graves and Thomas Boys, who both had connections with the floundering company; together these three men founded the separate company of Moon, Graves, and Boys, which operated from 6 Pall Mall, London, though Moon also continued his business in Threadneedle Street.

Specializing in engraved reproductions of some of the most celebrated paintings of the period, the business of Moon, Graves, and Boys soon became renowned for its high-quality engravings of works after Reynolds, Landseer, and Turner. While it was willing to invest huge sums in the production of such plates its profit was ensured by a policy of purchasing the copyright of the paintings; this was also the case with its publication of a line engraving of *The Chelsea Pensioners* (1828) by David Wilkie.

In 1836 Moon left this partnership, preferring to concentrate his attention on his original business, and his commercial success was based upon his winning the attention of Queen Victoria, who allowed him rights to publish engravings of most of the royal portraits and commissions of the period. 'Moon was ever ready to exploit the advantages that this strong "establishment" aura gave him' (Fox, 404) and he readily described himself as 'Publisher in Ordinary to her Majesty'. With its dedication to the queen, his publication of David Roberts's twenty-part series of tinted lithographs, *The Holy Land* (3 vols., 1842–5), was undoubtedly the most costly and lavish, and potentially risky, publishing enterprise that Moon had ever undertaken. Investing £50,000 in the project, he exhibited the drawings across England and by 1841 had raised an enormous subscription list for the lithographs, which were executed by Louis Haghe, one of London's leading lithographers. Like many of the artists Moon dealt with, Roberts was pleased with the results, but critics found fault with a variety of aspects of the work, Lady Eastlake alleging that Moon was no more than a vulgar, uneducated 'buffoon' (Fox, 401) who put his own interests above those of art.

At the beginning of 1853 Moon retired from business to his new, fashionably situated home at 69 Oxford Terrace, Edgware Road, London. He remained active in public life, having long been involved in local office, as a sheriff of London and Middlesex in 1843 and as an alderman of Portsoken ward in 1844. A self-made man from a modest background, Moon had achieved the position of a wealthy gentleman and to this he added the status of civic dignitary when he ran successfully for lord mayor in 1854: 'The high point of his year in office was his reception at the Guildhall … of the Emperor and Empress of the French' (Fox, 411), for which he was honoured with a baronetcy; this was complemented in 1859, when as a guest of the French he was appointed to the Légion d'honneur by Napoleon III.

One year after the death of his wife, Sir Francis Graham Moon died on 13 October 1871 at his home in Brighton, Western House, and was buried on 20 October 1871 at Fetchingham in Surrey. The following year, in April 1872,

Christies, Manson, and Wood held two crowded sales of Moon's proof engravings and collections of diverse objects of virtu; together these sales realized £10,421 10s.

LUCY PELTZ

Sources J. R. Abbey, *Scenery of Great Britain and Ireland in aquatint and lithography, 1770–1860* (1952); repr. (1972) · *Annual Register* (1871) · P. A. H. Brown, *London publishers and printers, c.1800–1870* (1982) · A. Dyson, *Pictures to print: the nineteenth-century engraving trade* (1984) · D. Bank and A. Esposito, eds., *British biographical archive*, 2nd series (1991) [microfiche] · Foster, *Alum. Oxon.* · C. Fox, 'Mr Moon the printseller of Threadneedle Street', *Collectanea Londiniensia: studies in London archaeology and history presented to Ralph Merrifield*, ed. J. Bird and others (1978), 401–14 · *ILN* (21 Oct 1871) · *ILN* (28 Oct 1871) · E. Lodge, *Peerage, baronetage, knightage and companionage of the British empire*, 81st edn, 3 vols. (1912) · A. Davies, *Dictionary of British portraiture*, 1 (1979) · *Engraved Brit. ports.* · D. Robertson, *Sir Charles Eastlake and the Victorian art world* (1978) · C. R. Leslie, *Autobiographical recollections*, ed. T. Taylor, 2 vols. (1860) [repr. as *Autobiographical recollections by Charles Robert Leslie* (1978), with new introduction by R. Hamlyn] · *The Times* (15 April 1872) · M. Twyman, *Lithography, 1800–1850* (1970) · Walford, *County families* (1888) · *DNB*

Likenesses Smyth, wood-engraving (after portrait by Fr. Skill), repro. in *ILN* (11 Nov 1854), 460 · line engraving (after photograph by Messrs Maul & Co.), repro. in *ILN* (28 Oct 1871), 401 · line engraving, NPG

Wealth at death under £160,000: probate, 22 Jan 1872, *CGPLA Eng. & Wales*

Moon, Keith John

Moon, Keith John (1946–1978), musician, was born in Central Middlesex County Hospital, Willesden, on 23 August 1946, the eldest child and only son of Alfred Charles Moon (*d.* 1974), a motor mechanic, and his wife, Kathleen Winifred, *née* Hopley. Moon had two sisters, Linda and Lesley. He grew up in Wembley, north London. At the age of twelve he joined the local sea cadet band, playing the bugle, but quickly moved on to the drums. While still a schoolboy he joined a local band, the Beachcombers. Leaving school at fifteen he began working as an electrician, but in 1964 auditioned to join another, more successful, local band, then known as the Detours, comprising Roger Daltrey, Pete Townshend, and John Entwhistle. The Detours soon changed their name to the High Numbers and in July 1964 released their first single, 'I'm the face'. Shortly afterwards the band's name was changed again, conclusively, to the Who.

The Who became especially popular among the mods who were then at the cutting edge of youth culture, and they were renowned for the loudness and aggression of their stage performances, which frequently ended with guitars smashed into speakers. Moon typified the band's energy with his unconventional, frenetic style of drumming, which many admired but few tried to imitate—he used a huge kit, which often included two bass drums, as well as a forest of cymbals. In January 1965 the band released their first single as the Who, 'I can't explain'; it was followed by 'Anyway, anyhow, anywhere' in May 1965 and the anthemic 'My generation' that November. Hits in 1966, 'The kids are alright' and 'Substitute', confirmed the Who's status as a major force in contemporary music. Between 1966 and 1978 Moon recorded nine studio albums with the Who, including *My Generation*, *Who's Next*, and *The Who by Numbers*. The first of many visits to the USA came early in 1967, supporting Herman's Hermits. The

Keith John Moon (1946–1978), by unknown photographer

Who achieved worldwide acclaim with the release in 1968 of the double album *Tommy*, Townshend's tale of the tribulations of a deaf, dumb, and blind orphan, presented as the first ever rock opera. A film of *Tommy* was made in 1974, directed by Ken Russell, in which Moon took the part of the pervert Uncle Ernie. Moon also received offers of parts in other films, and accepted small roles in *That'll Be the Day* (1973) and its sequel, *Stardust* (1975). In 1976 he appeared in *Sextet* with Mae West and Ringo Starr. His last appearance on celluloid was in the Who's own biographical film *The Kids are Alright*. In 1973 the Who released *Quadrophenia*, another rock opera that was an expression of Townshend's unique perspective on the Who's generation (it was made into a film in 1979).

In 1964 Moon had met Maryse Elizabeth Patricia (Patsy) Kerrigan (*b*. 1948), a model, always known as Kim, whom he married on 7 March 1966. In order not to enrage Moon's fans, the marriage was kept secret for nearly two years. The couple had a daughter, Mandy, born in 1967. In July 1971 they settled at Tara House, Chertsey, Surrey. The house was never really a family home, however, but a repository for Moon's ever-changing collection of cars, and of hangers-on. His turbulent behaviour finally induced Kim to leave him in autumn 1973, taking Mandy with her; Kim was granted a decree nisi in April 1975, on the grounds of Moon's unreasonable behaviour. Though he rarely admitted it, Moon was deeply affected by the departure of his wife. In 1975 he began a relationship with the Swedish model Annette Walter-Lax, to whom he became engaged more than once, though they never married.

Moon moved to California in the middle of 1974 to begin work on his solo album *Two Sides of the Moon*, assisted by, among others, Harry Nilsson and Ringo Starr, and featuring songs by Pete Townshend and Lennon and McCartney. Although three singles were released from it in the USA, it was not a success. Moon lacked the versatility for a solo career; rather, his reputation for madcap antics such as the destruction of hotel rooms, usually fuelled by alcohol, helped the Who to project the exuberant, anarchic image that made the group famous. But with time, as his drinking became more intense, Moon displayed ever greater irresponsibility, ever less regard for the people around him. Occasionally events stopped him in his tracks—the departure of his wife and the death, in January 1970, of his chauffeur in a still unexplained and bizarre accident—but to such examinations of his character he always ultimately responded with another binge of drinking and exhibitionism. He usually had a bodyguard to protect him against physical harm. He spent recklessly, buying a string of expensive cars, many of which were soon forgotten, sold on, or wrecked. He often shared his exploits with other boisterous personalities from the entertainment world—Vivian Stanshall, Ringo Starr, Oliver Reed, and Graham Chapman (whose autobiography includes a notably sympathetic portrait of Moon)—but had few close friends in any real sense, at least outside the Who.

Throughout late 1975 and most of 1976 the Who toured intensively, partly because its members' legal wrangles with their management meant that much of their income was frozen. At a concert in Boston, Moon collapsed on stage after he had overdosed on sedatives. In August 1976, during a short tour of the USA, he was placed under psychiatric observation. Moon lived in California for most of 1977, but moved back to England towards the end of that year and joined the Who to record a new album, *Who are You*. But his drumming, until then reliable even when he was inebriated, became erratic. He was placed on medication to help wean him from alcohol. On 7 September 1978 he took thirty-two tablets of heminevrin, a sedative used to treat acute mania and alcoholic withdrawal, at his London flat—9 Curzon Place, Mayfair. He was pronounced dead on arrival at the Middlesex Hospital; an open verdict was recorded. He was cremated at Golders Green, London, on 13 September.   MARIOS COSTAMBEYS

Sources I. Waterman, *Keith Moon: the life and death of a rock legend* (1979) • D. Butler, C. Trengove, and P. Lawrence, *Moon the Loon: the amazing rock and roll life of Keith Moon* (1981) • R. Barnes, *The Who: maximum R'n'B* (1982) • G. Chapman, *A liar's autobiography*, 2nd edn (1991) • T. Fletcher, *Dear boy: the life of Keith Moon* (1998) • *The Times* (9 Sept 1978) • *CGPLA Eng. & Wales* (1979) • b. cert. • m. cert. • d. cert.
Archives FILM BFI NFTVA, 'The real Keith Moon', Channel 4, 26 Aug 2000 • BFI NFTVA, documentary footage • BFI NFTVA, performance footage | SOUND BL NSA, documentary recordings • BL NSA, performance footage
Likenesses photographs, Hult. Arch. [*see illus.*]
Wealth at death £357,599: administration, 12 June 1979, *CGPLA Eng. & Wales*

Moon, Lorna. *See* Low, (Helen) Nora Wilson (1886–1930).

Moon, Sir (Edward) Penderel (1905–1987), administrator in India and writer, was born on 13 November 1905 in

Green Street, Mayfair, London, the only son and second of five children of Robert Oswald Moon, consultant cardiologist, and his wife, Ethel Rose Grant Waddington. Dr Moon wrote about philosophy and Greek medicine as well as diseases of the heart; he stood several times as a Liberal candidate for parliament.

Penderel Moon followed his father to Winchester College and to New College, Oxford, was placed in the first class in *literae humaniores* (1927), and in the same year was elected to a fellowship at All Souls College, Oxford, which he held until 1935. In 1929 he was appointed to the Indian Civil Service, arriving in India on 29 November. He was posted to the Punjab and attached for instruction to Gurdaspur district under Evan Jenkins, later private secretary to the viceroy and governor of the Punjab, who formed very early a high opinion of his administrative ability. By the time he had charge of the difficult district of Multan, it was known that Moon decided quickly and acted firmly but was not notably tolerant of the opinions of others, even his elders. None the less, he was appointed in 1938 private secretary to the governor of the Punjab, Sir Henry Craik; he was young for this key position and was also unusual in winning races on the governor's horses.

After his spell as private secretary, Moon was posted in 1941 as deputy commissioner to Amritsar, the focal point of the Sikh religion and of special importance in war in view of the Sikh contribution to the Indian army. Like many young British officers in the Indian Civil Service, Moon considered that the government of the second marquess of Linlithgow was dragging its feet about Indian advance towards self-government. In November 1942 he addressed to the Punjab government a letter arguing that those imprisoned for preaching civil disobedience should receive better treatment; this was in order, but when he received an unsympathetic reply, explaining the critical war situation, Moon's reaction was not. He sent a copy of the government's letter, with his own acid comments, to a brother of Rajkumari Amrit Kaur, secretary to M. K. Gandhi. He was at the time in gaol. This letter was intercepted and Moon was in serious trouble. Eventually the new governor, Sir Bertrand Glancy, persuaded him not to insist on dismissal, but to resign; he refused the suggestion of a proportionate pension.

Moon returned to England in April 1943, on six months' leave pending retirement, but in 1946 Viscount Wavell, now viceroy, on the advice of his private secretary, Sir Evan Jenkins, invited him to return, on contract, as secretary to the boards of development and planning. In April 1947 he became revenue minister of the state of Bahawalpur and stayed on after India's independence, serving as chief commissioner of Himachal Pradesh, as chief commissioner of Manipur state, and as adviser to the planning commission. The tone of an address to the Indian Administrative Staff College suggests that he was sometimes as critical of the new rulers of India as of the old.

During the Second World War Moon had published *Strangers in India* (1944), in which he argued that the ills of India could not be solved by a foreign government; it was followed by *Warren Hastings* (1947), brilliantly written in a simple, lucid style and notable for its sympathy with Hastings.

Moon's last appointment in India ended in 1961. He was knighted in 1962 for services to good relations between Britain and India, to which indeed he had notably contributed. After his return to England he held brief appointments with the World Bank and as adviser to the government of Thailand but soon put the main thrust of his life into scholarly work on India. In 1961 he published *Divide and quit*, which he later believed the most likely to survive of any of his books. It contains a lucid account of the events leading up to the partition of India and Pakistan, and an unflinching assessment of responsibility together with a day-by-day account of his own actions and observations as revenue minister and district magistrate in the border state of Bahawalpur during the months immediately following the division of the Punjab and the slaughter that followed. There can be no doubt that his power of swift decision, and his application of common sense amounting to brilliance, saved many lives; his account constitutes first-hand historical evidence of a high order. His *Gandhi and Modern India* is an admirable counterpoise to his *Warren Hastings*.

From 1965 to 1972 Moon was a fellow of All Souls, being the college's estates bursar from 1966 to 1969, and from 1972 to 1982 he was at the India Office Library and Records, preparing for publication, with Nicholas Mansergh, the India Office documents on *The Transfer of Power 1942–7* (12 volumes). He found time also to edit *Wavell: the Viceroy's Journal* (1973), a labour of love carried out with his usual clarity and distinction. When he died his last and most substantial book, *The British Conquest and Dominion of India* (1989), was still in proof. It was written, as always, with clarity, detachment, and mastery of complex material. In 1966 he married Pauline Marion, daughter of the Revd William Everard Cecil Barns; the marriage was not a success and was soon dissolved; there were no children.

Moon's life was not all spent toiling at a desk. Before retiring from All Souls he bought a mixed farm near Aylesbury, which he later enlarged. He employed a manager, but took pleasure not only in the business of the farm but in the physical work of haymaking and harvest; he was a generous employer. He was a good horseman and enjoyed both hunting and racing. He sang in Oxford in the Bach Choir and had a particular admiration for the music of Handel.

Penderel Moon resembled in many ways an aristocrat of the Enlightenment. In appearance he was trim and slight; in personal habit, ascetic. In scholarship, as in farming, he combined the confident mastery of the professional with the detachment of the amateur of independent means. He was decisive in his opinions and often autocratic, a champion of the peasant but no egalitarian. In youth, he liked to surprise and even to shock, but he never took up a position merely for effect. He died on 2 June 1987 at home at Manor Farm, Wotton Underwood, Buckinghamshire.

PHILIP MASON, *rev.*

Sources E. P. Moon, *Divide and quit: on the partition of India and Pakistan in 1947* (1961) · *The Times* (4 June 1987) · private information (1996) · personal knowledge (1996) · *CGPLA Eng. & Wales* (1987)
Archives BL OIOC, corresp. and papers, Eur. MS F 230
Wealth at death £1,570,611: probate, 5 Aug 1987, *CGPLA Eng. & Wales*

Moon, Philip Burton (1907–1994), nuclear physicist, was born at 116 Leahurst Road, Lewisham, London, on 17 May 1907, the only son of Frederick Dolman Moon, ship's mate and later master mariner, and his wife, Clara Charlotte, daughter of George Burton, a farmer at Southill, Bedfordshire. After his secondary education at Leyton county high school Moon was awarded a scholarship to Sidney Sussex College, Cambridge, where he took the natural sciences tripos with physics in part two and graduated in 1928. Supported by a Department of Scientific and Industrial Research grant and a college scholarship he joined the Cavendish Laboratory under Sir Ernest Rutherford. His doctoral research, supervised by Mark Oliphant, concerned the interaction of positive ions with metal surfaces at various temperatures and low ion energies.

In 1931 Moon took up a post as assistant lecturer at Imperial College, London, under G. P. Thomson. At the Cavendish James Chadwick had recently identified the neutron as an atomic particle and in Rome Enrico Fermi's team was studying its behaviour. Fermi's work led Moon and his colleague J. R. Tillman to place a neutron source at the centre of a cube of paraffin wax cooled to 90° K (the temperature of liquid oxygen), the purpose being to slow down the neutrons by their elastic scattering with the hydrogen atoms of the paraffin wax. They found that the emerging neutrons were dominantly thermal, with a temperature of 90° K rather than room temperature. This was the first demonstration of 'neutron thermalization'. Moon and Tillman then placed a slab of material on the upper face of the cube, to absorb neutrons emitted from the cube, and another slab of material on top of that to act as a neutron detector. The absorption values varied widely and they were greatest when the two slabs were of the same material. Moon and Tillman termed this behaviour 'selective absorption'. Their findings, published in the journal *Nature* in 1935 (135.904 and 136.66–7) and in the *Proceedings of the Royal Society* in 1936 (series A, 153.476–92) and widely confirmed by others, were a shock to the theoreticians, who had predicted resonance effects in nuclear physics to be broad and widely spaced, on the basis of the two-body theory then current. The Moon–Tillman results came to the attention of Niels Bohr, who in 1936 proposed his 'compound nucleus' model, which implied that nuclear resonances would be numerous, narrow, closely spaced, and characteristic of the materials used—as Moon's and Tillman's experiments had shown.

Moon's marriage on 18 September 1937 to Winifred Florence Barber (1912–1971), a bank clerk, brought them two children, Anthony Edward and Sarah Elinor. Moon took up a lectureship in Oliphant's department of physics at Birmingham University the following year, but when G. P. Thomson obtained a ton of uranium oxide in 1939 Moon

returned to Imperial College to work with it. By the autumn, however, Moon and Thomson had shown that a self-sustaining chain reaction could not be obtained using unenriched uranium and a water moderator, so Moon returned to Birmingham to assist Oliphant in his Admiralty funded project to develop high power microwave transmitters for radar.

As an experienced neutron physicist Moon became a member of the MAUD committee in June 1940, and later of the 'Tube Alloys' directorate (dealing with both civil and military uses of atomic science). At the end of 1941 he was seconded to the British central scientific office in Washington DC, on behalf of the Admiralty, until his return to Birmingham in June 1942. By agreement with Oliphant, Moon was left in charge of the microwave and nuclear work at Birmingham until it became clear that the small UK-based projects were making too little difference to matter. He then left Birmingham, and arrived at Los Alamos in March 1944. At Los Alamos he worked on site preparation and on the instrumentation needed to make a full record of the first atomic explosion. He was present at the Trinity test on 16 July 1945 when an implosion-type weapon was detonated in the desert at Alamogordo. In 1946 he was a foundation member of the Atomic Scientists' Association, being its first secretary and later its vice-president, until its dissolution about 1958. He was elected a fellow of the Royal Society in 1947 for his slow neutron studies, and served on the society's council in 1953–5.

After returning to Birmingham in 1946 Moon was appointed to a second chair of physics where Oliphant had two major constructions under way. The Nuffield-funded 60-inch cyclotron (a particle accelerator) was completed in 1950, when Moon's students began to use it for nuclear physics experiments. In 1946 Oliphant had obtained further funding for a new type of accelerator, the proton synchrotron, but he moved to Canberra in 1950, taking with him many key synchrotron personnel. Moon succeeded Oliphant as Poynting professor. After much discussion Moon concluded that he would have to complete the synchrotron himself, and he did so, handing over a functioning apparatus in 1953, a remarkable achievement. Data-taking began at the end of 1953 and the apparatus ran regularly until its beam was finally turned off in August 1967.

After the war Moon's special interest was the development and possible uses of high-speed rotors. These consisted of a pair of blades or paddles, their faces in a vertical plane, spinning about a vertical axis. With their aid Moon was able to explore the kinetics of chemical reactions, and later to detect resonant scattering of gamma radiation by using a source mounted on the tip of a high-speed rotor. Moon's early rotors were manufactured from a special steel alloy and could attain tip velocities of up to 80,000 centimetres per second, beyond which they became unstable and disintegrated. By changing to carbon fibre reinforced plastics and magnetic suspension, Moon was able to increase the rotor speed to attain tip velocities up to 220,000 centimetres per second, a velocity registered in the *Guinness Book of Records* (1975) as a world record.

Moon took a prominent role in the introduction of new courses, and the overseeing of new building works. He headed the physics department until 1970, and was dean of the faculty of science and engineering in 1969–72. He loved university life and found fulfilment as a researcher and teacher; his lively encouragement of his students ensured that his department was a friendly place and gained him their admiration and respect. A keen cricketer, he played regularly for his department at Edgbaston, and he enjoyed the challenge of solving the *Times* crossword.

Following the death of his first wife Moon married, on 9 April 1974, Lorna Margaret Aldridge, a Bristol schoolteacher. He retired the same year, and in 1975 went on a lecture tour of Australia. The family moved to Church Stretton, Shropshire, in 1984, then in 1993 to Droitwich, Worcestershire. Both his wives were musicians, and Moon himself played the piano. Not a religious man, he nevertheless had a deep interest in Christianity and a familiarity with the Bible. However, physics remained his abiding passion and his favourite topic of conversation. He was awarded the Royal Society's Hughes medal in 1991. Moon died at the Royal Infirmary, Ronkswood, Worcester, on 9 October 1994.   R. H. Dalitz

Sources W. E. Burton and G. R. Isaak, *Memoirs FRS*, 42 (1996), 249–64 · *WWW* · *The Independent* (19 Oct 1994) · *The Times* (24 Oct 1994) · papers of P. B. Moon, 1997, University of Bath Library, National Cataloguing Unit for the Archives of Contemporary Scientists; biographical abstract, NCUACS 69/7/97 · b. cert. · m. certs. [Winifred Florence Barber; Lorna Margaret Aldridge] · d. certs. [Winifred Florence Moon; Philip Burton Moon] · *CGPLA Eng. & Wales* (1994)
Archives U. Birm. L., corresp. and papers · University of Bath Library, National Cataloguing Unit for the Archives of Contemporary Scientists, papers
Likenesses photograph, 1964, repro. in *Memoirs FRS*, 248 · photograph, repro. in *The Independent* · photograph, repro. in *Times*
Wealth at death under £125,000: probate, 19 Dec 1994, *CGPLA Eng. & Wales*

Moon, Sir Richard, **first baronet** (1814–1899), railway company chairman, was born on 23 September 1814, the elder son of Richard Moon (1783–1842), of Liverpool, merchant, and his wife, Elizabeth, who was the daughter of William Frodsham. The family of Moon was settled at Newsham, in Woodplumpton, Lancashire, before the end of the sixteenth century.

Richard was educated at St Andrews University, but left without taking a degree. He intended when a young man to take holy orders, but his father opposed this, and so he entered his father's firm. He married Eleanor (1820–1891) daughter of the major shipowner, John Brocklebank, of Hazelholm, Cumberland on 27 August 1840. They had six children, of whom two died in infancy. Little is known of Moon's early adult life, but he appears to have withdrawn from the family firm by 1851. However, his family had invested early in railway shares, and in 1847 Richard Moon was elected a director of the London and North Western Railway Company (LNWR). He became chairman in June

1861, holding that position until he retired in February 1891.

The London and North Western Railway Company came into being on 16 July 1846 by the amalgamation of the Grand Junction, the London and Birmingham, and the Manchester and Birmingham railway companies. The chairman of the new company was George Carr Glyn. The marquess of Chandos became chairman in 1853. He was forced to resign in 1861, and was briefly succeeded by Admiral Moorsom, who died in May of that year, and Moon was elected chairman. Since joining the board in 1847 he had established a reputation as an outstandingly able administrator with little time for the senior executives of the company. He brought about the resignation in 1858 of Captain Mark Huish, the first general manager of the new company.

Moon was essentially conservative in his outlook, but could be innovative when he thought it in the best interests of the company. He certainly ran it very tightly, constantly looking for means of cutting costs, but he could also spend lavishly if this appeared to him to be justified—for example, on the expansion of the works at Crewe. Annual receipts of the company rose from £4.3 million in 1841 to £11.8 million in 1891, and the dividend from 4.25 per cent to 7 per cent, while the network grew from 1030 miles to 1830 miles. The company was employing 55,000 men in 1885, and was, at that stage, the largest joint-stock company in the world. Under Moon's guidance it became famous for the punctuality of its trains, the courtesy of its staff, and the creation of two new towns, Crewe and Wolverton; and in all of this he took a close personal interest.

Both the Grand Junction and the Manchester and Birmingham Railway Co. had reached Crewe before the amalgamation. The town began as a wayside station in the parish of Church Coppenhall, in Cheshire, in 1837. It was the Grand Junction that opened railway works there in 1843. The company set about building a new town, and this was continued after the amalgamation. It was administered at first from Euston, but the Crewe local board was formed in 1860, and the town was incorporated in 1877. The company provided everything: housing, water, gas, churches, and schools. It presented the municipal park to the town in 1887, the year of Queen Victoria's golden jubilee, when Moon was created baronet and became the first freeman of the town. Bessemer steel works were opened in 1864 and four years later the Siemens–Martin openhearth furnaces were added. After 1864 carriage building was concentrated in Wolverton and locomotive building at Crewe, where locomotives were manufactured from raw materials, everything being made on site.

The London and Birmingham Railway Company had acquired 8 acres of land at Wolverton, a small village and parish in Buckinghamshire, in 1837. It began to build houses in 1839. Further land was bought in 1840, and by 1847 a new station had been built, and new streets laid out. As at Crewe, the company provided everything: housing, gas, a building society, a savings bank, market house, shops, and church, and opened a park in 1885. The company itself withdrew from building houses in 1860, preferring to lay out the plots and control the type and standard of those built.

Richard Moon retired from the board of the LNWR on 22 February 1891, his wife having died on 31 January. He died at his home, Copsewood Grange, Stoke, Warwickshire, on 17 November 1899. His eldest son, Edward, had died in 1893, and so he was succeeded in the baronetcy by his grandson, Cecil Ernest Moon, born in 1867.

Sir Richard Moon was described by his obituarist in *The Times* as 'the hardest of hard workers and the sternest of stern disciplinarians'. He was said to combine 'an assured confidence in the correctness of his own judgement with an autocratic spirit which hardly recognized the possibility of that judgement being criticized by others'. At the same time he was of 'a singularly retiring disposition' (*The Times*, 18 Nov 1899). He was Conservative in his politics, and remained a devout Anglican throughout his life.

MICHAEL REED

Sources M. C. Reed, 'Moon, Sir Richard', *DBB* · Burke, *Peerage* (1980) · Boase, *Mod. Eng. biog.* · *WWW*, 1897–1915 · *The Times* (18 Nov 1899), 11, 14 · O. S. Nock, *The London and North Western Railway* (1960) · D. K. Drummond, *Crewe: railway town, company and people, 1840–1914* (1995) · M. Reed, *The Buckinghamshire landscape* (1979) · Burke, *Gen. GB* (1964) · T. R. Gourvish, *Mark Huish and the London–North Western Railway* (1972) · *CGPLA Eng. & Wales* (1900) · d. cert.

Archives PRO, corresp., RAIL 1008/101

Likenesses portrait, National Railway Museum

Wealth at death £395,844 0s. 4d.: resworn probate, Aug 1900, *CGPLA Eng. & Wales*

Moon, William (1818–1894), inventor of typography for blind people, was descended from an old Sussex family seated at Rotherfield. He was born at Horsmonden, Kent, on 18 December 1818, the son of James Moon of Horsmonden and his wife, Mary Funnell Moon. During his childhood his parents moved to Brighton, but William remained for some time at Horsmonden. At the age of four he lost his sight in one eye through scarlet fever, and the other eye was seriously affected. He was educated in London, and when about eighteen years old he settled at Brighton with his widowed mother. He was studying with the intention of taking holy orders, but his sight in the remaining eye gradually failed, in spite of several operations. In 1840 he became totally blind.

Moon had previously made himself familiar with various systems of embossed type, and now started a day school in Egremont Place, Brighton, where he taught blind children, and a number of deaf mute children. In the system devised by James Hatley Frere, and in the other systems used at that time for teaching blind people, contractions were very extensively used; Moon, after some years' teaching, judged this to be too complicated for the vast majority of blind persons, especially the aged, and accordingly constructed a system of his own in 1845, using a simplified system of roman lettering. By the help of friends interested in the blind, type was procured, and Moon began a monthly magazine. His first publication, *The Last Days of Polycarp*, appeared on 1 June 1847; *The Last Hours of Cranmer* and devotional works followed. Next he

began to prepare the entire Bible, discontinuing the monthly issues for a time. As his supply of type was insufficient for such an extensive undertaking, he tried stereotyping, and after much experimenting succeeded in inventing a process by which he could produce a satisfactory plate at less than a sixth of the ordinary price. He put his process into use in September 1848, and the stereotyper then engaged was employed on the work until after Moon's death. The publications were always sold under cost price, the deficiency being made up by charitable contributions. In 1852, when the greater part of the Bible was still unprinted, Moon published a formal report with a defence of his system against objectors, who had sneered at the cost and bulk of his publications; he argued that the Frere and other systems depending upon contractions complicated the notation to such an extent that the books were useless to the majority of blind people. He soon extended his system to foreign languages, beginning with Irish and Chinese; the principal languages of Europe were next used, and before his death either the Lord's prayer or another portion of scripture had been embossed in 476 languages and dialects, for all of which the original nine characters were sufficient. As well as the scriptures, Moon printed many devotional works, some scientific treatises, and selections from Shakespeare, Milton, Burns, Scott, Longfellow, and other standard authors.

After meeting a girl born blind who believed that horses stood upright and walked with two legs, Moon devised his embossed book, *Pictures for the Blind*, which taught blind people by touch to understand the forms of common objects. He also issued embossed diagrams for Euclid, music, and maps, both geographical and astronomical. He was made a fellow of the Royal Geographical Society in 1852, a fellow of the Society of Arts in 1859, and in 1871 the University of Philadelphia created him LLD. He supported home-teaching societies for blind people, which by his efforts were founded in many places, and lending libraries of Moon's books were common in the late nineteenth century. Moon travelled widely to promote his system; in 1882 he visited the United States and in 1885 Sweden. He received great help, especially in the matter of lending libraries, from Sir Charles Lowther, with whom he became friendly in 1855. On 4 September 1856 Sir Charles laid the foundation stone of a new building at 104 Queen's Road, Brighton, where the embossed books were produced. In addition to his other publications Moon wrote *A Memoir of Harriet Pollard, Blind Vocalist* (1860), *Blindness* (1868), and *Light for the Blind* (1873).

Moon was twice married, first, in 1843 to Mary Ann Caudle (d. 1864), daughter of a Brighton surgeon, and second, in 1866, to Anna Maria Elsdale, a granddaughter of William Leeves, the composer of 'Auld Robin Gray'. His first marriage produced two children. His son, Robert, was of great assistance to him in arranging his types to set foreign languages, and became a physician in Philadelphia. His daughter, Adelaide Eliza Clara, took over his publishing business. Moon had a slight stroke in the autumn of 1892, which reduced his level of activity. He died suddenly at 104 Queen's Road, Brighton, on 10 October 1894, and was buried on 15 October in the cemetery outside Brighton. Books have continued to be produced using Moon's system and in the late twentieth century there was a revival of interest in it.

HENRY DAVEY, rev. H. C. G. MATTHEW

Sources *Brighton Herald* (13 Oct 1894) · *Brighton Herald* (20 Oct 1894) · *Record* (3 June 1894) · *ILN* (20 Oct 1894) · J. Rutherfurd, *William Moon and his work for the blind* (1898) · M. Fison, *Darkness and light, or, Brief memorials … [of] the origin of Moon's system of reading for the blind* (1859) · E. Stroud, *Blind faith as portrayed in the life of William Moon* (1992) · C. T. Burt, *The Moon Society: a century of achievement, 1848–1948* (1949) · *CGPLA Eng. & Wales* (1895)

Likenesses portrait, repro. in Rutherfurd, *William Moon and his work for the blind* · portrait, repro. in *ILN*

Wealth at death £912 7s. 7d.: probate, 11 Feb 1895, *CGPLA Eng. & Wales*

Moone, Peter (*fl.* 1548–1556), poet, is of unknown origins. He headed a theatrical troupe that regularly performed polemical protestant mystery and morality plays in the tradition of John Bale's *King John* and others. Uncorroborated evidence suggests that this company was based in Ipswich, a centre for protestant ideas and publishing during the reign of Edward VI, and Moone himself probably lived there. John Oswen printed Moone's only surviving work, *A Short Treatise of Certain Things Abused in the Popish Church, Long used, but now Abolished* at Ipswich in 1548 (simultaneously published at London by William Copland), at a time when Oswen joined Anthony Scoloker in a fledgeling provincial printing trade in the production of protestant books both by English 'gospellers' and by continental reformers such as Calvin and Melanchthon. An artisan poet like John Ramsey, Moone was also known as a 'hot gospeller' because of his evangelical zeal.

The mission of Oswen's press and the Ipswich book trade was to disseminate protestant ideas in vernacular publications by employing popular literary techniques and conventions. Written in thirty-seven stanzas of eight lines rhyming ababbcbc, Moone's *Short Treatise* satirizes ecclesiastical practices and 'ceremonies' of the Church of Rome, for example papal overlordship, the priesthood, the mass, and belief in non-scriptural traditions. It also draws on current events, making reference to the government of Edward Seymour, duke of Somerset, protector of the realm during the minority of Edward VI. The *Short Treatise* is characteristic of the Ipswich printing trade by amalgamating proletarian anti-clericalism with emergent Reformation theology.

Moone is found six years later in the records of the privy council on 2 September 1554. Along with John Ramsey, Christopher Goodwyn, and William West, he was charged with having been 'the first and chefest styrrers in a commotion intended in Yppiswiche' (*APC, 1554–6*, 70). They were committed to the Tower, and remained there until 24 December that year.

Moone next appears in Foxe's *Acts and Monuments*, among the protestants examined by Bishop Hopton during his 1556 visitation of Ipswich. Foxe's fairly lengthy narrative describes how first Moone and then his wife were questioned about their non-attendance in church, but providentially escaped punishment when the bishop

left before he had time to examine them a third time. According to Foxe, Moone was a tailor. Neither Foxe nor the privy council records makes any reference to Moone's *Treatise*.

JOHN N. KING

Sources A. G. Dickens, *The English Reformation*, 2nd edn (1989); pbk edn (1991) · A. G. Dickens, 'Peter Moone: the Ipswich gospeller and poet', *N&Q*, 199 (1954), 513–14 · J. N. King, *English Reformation literature: the Tudor origins of the protestant tradition* (1982) · *STC, 1475–1640* · *DNB* · *APC, 1554–6* · *The acts and monuments of John Foxe*, new edn, ed. G. Townsend, 8 (1849), 223

Moor, Edward (1771–1848), writer on Hindu mythology, was appointed a cadet on the Bombay establishment of the East India Company in May 1782, and sailed for India in the September following, being then under twelve years of age. Adverse winds caused the fleet in which he sailed to put into Madras in April 1783, and Moor was temporarily transferred to the Madras establishment. Back on the Bombay establishment, he was promoted lieutenant in September 1788, and three months later adjutant and quartermaster of the 9th battalion native infantry. Though then only seventeen, his 'very great proficiency' in the native tongue was noticed in the certificate of the examining committee.

On the outbreak of war in 1790 Moor resigned his adjutancy, and proceeded in command of a grenadier company of the 9th battalion to join the brigade under Captain John Little, then serving with the Maratha army at the siege of Dharwar. He was of the storming party on the assault of that stronghold on 7 February 1791, and on 13 June he was shot in the shoulder while heading the leading company in an assault of the hill fort Doridroog, near Bangalore. He rejoined his corps within four months, and on 29 December 1791 led the two flank companies of the 9th battalion at the battle of Gadjmoor, where he was especially complimented for his gallantry in renewing the British attack on the right. In this engagement Moor received two wounds, and was eventually compelled to return home on sick leave. During his consequent leisure in China and Europe he wrote, and dedicated to Little and his fellows in arms, *A narrative of the operations of Captain Little's detachment and of the Mahratta army commanded by Purseram Bhow during the late confederacy in India against the nawab Tippoo Sultan Bahadur* (1794). This lively account, extending over more than 500 quarto pages, went beyond military and tactical matters into details of the geography, history, and ethnography of the Maratha territory the men traversed.

Moor married, on 10 July 1794, Elizabeth (*d.* 13 Dec 1835), daughter of James Lynn of Woodbridge, surgeon. They had a son, Edward Jacques Moor, who became rector of Great Bealings, and a daughter, Charlotte, who married William Page Wood, afterwards Baron Hatterley and lord chancellor. He re-embarked for Bombay in April 1796, with the brevet rank of captain, and in July 1799 he was appointed garrison storekeeper (commissary-general) at Bombay, a post which he held with credit until his departure from India in February 1805. In 1800, at the request of Governor Duncan, he compiled a *Digest of the Military Orders and Regulations of the Bombay Army*; this was printed at the expense of the government, which, on 14 September 1800, awarded him 10,000 rupees for the original work, and 2000 more for the additions subsequently made to it. Since the state of his health precluded his return to India, Moor retired from the company's service in 1806, receiving a special pension for his distinguished service in addition to his half-pay.

In 1810 Moor published in London his most significant scholarly contribution, the *Hindu Pantheon*, a work later largely superseded but of considerable value in its time, being for more than fifty years the only authoritative book on the subject in English. A collection of pictures and engravings of Hindu deities formed the nucleus of the book. Around these the author accumulated a mass of information, partly gathered by himself, but largely derived from Charles Wilkins and other correspondents, and supplemented from the works of Sir William Jones and other orientalists. The book, though unduly prolix and overweighted with Western classical parallels and irrelevancies, was nevertheless of sufficient value to carry it through several editions. Its nearly 2000 mythological figures, with additional remarks on sectarian variants, symbols, and religious practices, were widely consulted. A beautiful series of illustrative plates (engraved by J. Dadley after drawings by M. Houghton), edited by the Revd A. P. Moore, was published in London in 1861, and another edition with fresh plates appeared at Madras in 1864. Moor's other works on Indian subjects were *Hindu Infanticide: an Account of the Measures Adopted for Suppressing the Practice* (1811), and the diverting miscellany *Oriental Fragments* (1834), comprising descriptions of gems and inscriptions and general reflections on Indian mythology, religion, etymology, and folklore. During his retirement at Great Bealings, in Suffolk, Moor also wrote *The Gentle Sponge* (1829), a proposal for reducing the interest on the national debt, and a collection entitled *Suffolk Words and Phrases* (1823), containing many elaborate articles (for example, 'cantle' and 'sibrit') of some interest but little etymological value, as well as several pamphlets. He also contributed Indian articles to Rees's *Cyclopaedia*.

Moor was a member of various learned societies in India, England, and France. He was elected a member of the Asiatic Society of Bengal in 1796, of the Royal Society in 1806, and of the Society of Antiquaries in 1818. Of the Royal Asiatic Society he was one of the original founding members, and he regularly attended its meetings.

Moor died at the house of his son-in-law in Great George Street, Westminster, on 26 February 1848. A set of memorial verses was written in the year of his death by his acquaintance, the Quaker poet Bernard Barton.

THOMAS SECCOMBE, *rev.* J. B. KATZ

Sources J. Philippart, *East India military calendar*, 3 vols. (1823–6), vol. 1, pp. 339–48, vol. 3, p. 470 • *GM*, 2nd ser., 29 (1848), 549–50 • *Journal of the Royal Asiatic Society of Great Britain and Ireland*, 9 (1848), iv–v • J. G. Duff, *History of the Mahrattas*, 2 (1873), 2.492 • B. Barton, *A brief memorial of Major Edward Moor, FRS* (1848) • K. Teltscher, *India inscribed: European and British writing on India, 1600–1800* (1995), 14off. • P. Mitter, *Much maligned monsters: history of European reactions to Indian art* (1977), 178ff. • Allibone, *Dict.*

Archives BL, letters to Major and Mrs David Price, Add. MS 63091
Likenesses Mrs D. Turner, etching, 1810, BM, NPG
Wealth at death £5000: administration, PRO, PROB 6/224

Moor, Sir Frederick Robert (1853–1927), politician in South Africa, was born at Pietermaritzburg, Natal, on 12 May 1853, the eldest son of Frederick William Moor (*b.* 1830), a farmer and settler under the Byrne immigration scheme of 1850, and his wife, Sarah Annabella, the daughter of Robert Ralfe. He was educated at Hermannsburg School, near Greytown, Natal. As a young man of nineteen, he was attracted to the recently discovered diamond fields at Kimberley. There he met, and in 1878 married, Charlotte Mary St Clair Moodie (*d.* 1930), daughter of William James Dunbar Moodie and granddaughter of Donald Moodie, first colonial secretary of Natal. They had three sons and four daughters. Moor remained on the diamond fields for seven years. As the amalgamation and consolidation of claims gathered momentum, he realized that it would be increasingly difficult for the individual digger to prosper. Like many others, he sold out his claims, and in 1879 returned to Natal, where he farmed near Estcourt.

Moor's election on two occasions to the mining board in Kimberley fostered an interest in public life. In 1886 he was elected as member of the Natal legislative council for Weenen county. He attached himself to the party which advocated responsible government for the colony and, from 1893, when this was conceded, he served two terms as minister of native affairs (1893–7 and 1899–1903), interrupted by two years in opposition.

Moor resisted any modification of the long-standing policy of upholding customary law and the authority of local chiefs. He considered this essential—under the supervision of white officials—for the effective control of Natal's black majority. He consequently discouraged the granting of exemptions from customary law, disapproved of the Cape Colony's non-racial franchise, opposed the acquisition of land by black people on freehold tenure, and wanted to extend governmental control over the mission reserves.

Subsequently, as leader of the opposition, Moor criticized the ministry of C. J. Smythe (1905–6) for increasing the taxation of the black population, and particularly the ill-advised poll tax which sparked the uprising of February 1906. On succeeding Smythe as prime minister in November of that year, Moor's handling of the delicate situation created by the 1906 disturbance was unimpressive. The trial of the heir to the Zulu throne, Dinuzulu ka Cetshwayo, provoked criticism in Britain and elsewhere. This tarnished Natal's image at the time of the 'closer union' negotiations.

Moor consistently urged the necessity for some measure of unification in South Africa. He had been impressed by the enthusiasm he encountered as delegate for Natal to the inaugural ceremonies of the Australian commonwealth in 1901. He represented the colony at customs conferences in Cape Town (1898), Bloemfontein (1903), Pietermaritzburg (1906), and also in Pretoria (1908), where he wholeheartedly supported the proposal that a national convention should be held to formulate a draft South African constitution. Natal's white minority electorate favoured federation in preference to union but Moor and his colleagues were outvoted in the national convention which met at Durban in October 1908. He eventually approved the large discretionary powers granted to the union government, believing that public opinion would safeguard the interests of the provinces. His insistence that isolation would be suicidal in view of the colony's dependence upon the transit trade into the interior was persuasive, and in the referendum of June 1909 Natal accepted union.

In General Botha's ministry of 1910, Moor assumed the portfolio of commerce and industries, but he was defeated at the first election after union. His previous experience as minister of native affairs in Natal secured him a seat in the senate which he retained for ten years (1910–20) before retiring to his farm, Greystone, near Estcourt, where he died on 18 March 1927. A funeral service was held the next day at St Matthew's Anglican church in Estcourt.

Moor was not a popular parliamentarian, even though he was a fluent speaker with a commanding physical presence, and a keen sportsman. His deep commitment to the interests of Natal was acknowledged by his opponents and his political services were rewarded with a privy councillorship on the occasion of the Imperial Conference of 1907, which he attended as premier of a self-governing colony. He was knighted on 1 January 1911.

W. R. GUEST

Sources *Debates of the Legislative Assembly* [Natal] (1893–1910) · *Debates of the Legislative Council* [Natal] (1886–93) · S. Marks, *Reluctant rebellion: the 1906–1908 disturbances in Natal* (1970) · L. M. Thompson, *The unification of South Africa, 1902–1910* (1960) · U. S. Dhupelia, 'Frederick Robert Moor and native affairs in the colony of Natal, 1893–1903', MA diss., University of Durban-Westville, 1980 · *Natal Witness* (19 March 1927) · A. Duminy and B. Guest, eds., *Natal and Zululand from earliest times to 1910* (1989) · Pietermaritzburg Archive Repository, Pietermaritzburg, deceased estate, 1840–1968, Moor F. R. IZI80/1927 · Pietermaritzburg Archive Repository, Pietermaritzburg, deceased estate, 1840–1968, Moor C. M. St C. 16177/1930
Archives University of Natal, Durban, Campbell collections, Charlotte Moor MSS · University of Natal, Durban, Campbell collections, Shirley Moor MSS
Likenesses photograph, 1906, repro. in *The Natal who's who* (1906) · photograph, 1907, repro. in *ILN* (20 April 1907) · group portraits, photographs, Kwa-Zulu Natal Museum Services · photograph, repro. in F. H. Gale, ed., *Who's Who in the Union Parliament* (1911) · photograph, repro. in *Souvenir of the union of South Africa* (1910)
Wealth at death £58,549 9s. 7d.—after death duties: deceased estate, 1840–1968, Pietermaritzburg Archive Repository, Pietermaritzburg, Moor F. R. IZI80/1927

Moor, James (*bap.* 1712, *d.* 1779), classical scholar, was baptized James Moore in Glasgow on 22 June 1712, the son of James Moore, or Muir, a Glasgow mathematics teacher, and Margaret Park. Despite the loss of an eye from measles, Moor read voraciously as a boy, especially at the shop of the bookseller Andrew Stalker. He matriculated from the University of Glasgow in November 1725, distinguishing himself in natural philosophy and mathematics, which he studied with 'the justly celebrated Doctor Robert Simson, ... my most excellent master in Geometry' (J. Moor, commonplace book, Edinburgh University Library, La.III.567). After Francis Hutcheson assumed the duties of the chair of moral philosophy in 1730 Moor became his student and disciple; he graduated MA in 1732. He subsequently taught at a school in Glasgow, travelled to Europe as tutor to the earls of Selkirk and Erroll, and served as tutor to the fourth earl of Kilmarnock.

In June 1742 Moor published anonymously an extensively annotated English translation of the *Meditations* of Marcus Aurelius; a joint translation with Hutcheson, it was printed in Glasgow by Robert *Foulis, who would marry Moor's sister, Elizabeth (*d.* 1750), in September 1742, and subsequently would marry Moor's first cousin, Euphan Boutcher (*d.* 1774). From 11 November 1742 to 1747 Moor was the librarian of Glasgow University. After having failed to become professor of moral philosophy at Edinburgh University in 1745, he was again recommended by Hutcheson for the vacant Glasgow University chair of Greek the following summer. To secure the post Moor and his patron Hutcheson had to win the support of the powerful third duke of Argyll, and to persuade the elderly occupant of the Greek chair, Hutcheson's old ally Alexander Dunlop, to retire; Dunlop retained his academic salary and his college house, together with an additional £600 from Moor, advanced on his behalf by the fourth earl of Selkirk. Moor also had to undergo a competency test on 9 July 1746 when he was asked to provide a critical explication of a chapter by Longinus. After Dunlop's death on 27 April 1747 Moor finally received the full benefits of his professorship, which he held for another twenty-seven years.

Moor was a principal member of a club which met in the village of Anderston under the direction of his mathematics professor, now colleague, Robert Simson. In 1752 he was among the twelve founding members of the Glasgow Literary Society, a university club at which scholarly discourses were read and discussed; there he subsequently presented discourses on a range of classical and modern literary topics. In 1759 he published three of his discourses as *Essays; Read to a Literary Society; at their Weekly Meetings within the College, at Glasgow*, in which he argued various Hutchesonian themes about the importance of classically defined notions of aesthetics for the cultivation of virtue and culture. Four years later he published another paper he had previously delivered at the Glasgow Literary Society, *On the End of Tragedy, According to Aristotle*, and in 1766 he issued two more discourses, on Virgil and on Greek prepositions, that derived from the same source. All these works were published by the Foulis brothers, Robert and Andrew, who were themselves members of the Glasgow Literary Society. The brothers were also the publishers of Moor's popular Greek grammar, *Elementa linguae Graecae* (1766), which first appeared in 1753 under a different title and passed through many editions during its long life as a standard school text in Britain and America, including English translations in the nineteenth century.

Moor also collaborated with the Foulis brothers on editions of the classics for which they became famous, such as the magnificent 4-volume folio edition of Homer that appeared in 1756 (*Iliad*) and 1758 (*Odyssey*), meticulously edited by Moor and his colleague, George Muirhead. This was part of a scheme by Moor and the other Glasgow professors to promote 'at their own expence, & intirely under their own direction, a Compleat sett of the best Greek & Latin Classicks' which would be 'correct, Splendid, Elegant & Sizeable' (letter from William Rouet to [John Nourse?], 19 July 1756, Edinburgh University Library, La.II.511). Among the other Foulis editions that Moor edited were the heroic *Spartan Lessons, or, The Praise of Valour; in the Verses of Tyrtaeus* (1759), later satirized in William Thom's *Donaldsoniad*, and the 9-volume Greek and Latin edition of Herodotus that appeared in 1761. He also assisted Robert Simson with the editing of his editions of Apollonius of Perga (1749) and Euclid's *Elements* (1756), and he planned an edition of Archimedes that was never completed. A grander unfinished work, projected to be the crowning glory of the Foulis classics, was Moor's multivolume edition of Plato. Proposals and specimens were issued in 1750–51, and Moor penned a summary of materials used in the project in 1759, but the edition never appeared.

A man of diminutive size, with a patch over one eye, Moor is easily picked out in the foreground of David Allan's well-known painting of the inside of the Foulis brothers' fine arts academy about 1760. One contemporary made reference to his 'gaiety and levity' (D. Stewart, 1.10), which is evident in his poetry. He was one of several professors who made James Boswell and General Paoli feel welcome when they visited Glasgow on 6 September 1771. But his personality also had a darker, more aggressive side. In 1760 he was fined £20 and temporarily suspended by the faculty for a tavern quarrel with another cantankerous professor, John Anderson, that almost escalated into a duel. In 1763 his belligerent behaviour in another episode provoked a severe rebuke from his colleagues. As he grew older this irascible, violent tendency developed into a serious personality disorder, which his arch-enemy, Anderson, blamed on his being 'often Drunk and sometimes mad in the latter period of his life' (Butt, 12), though one modern commentator has suggested that it may have been caused by 'a neurasthenic condition' (Hilson, i).

In his more rational periods Moor took an active part in university affairs, serving as dean of faculty from 1756 to 1758 and as vice-rector in 1759 and again in 1761. On the latter occasion he was appointed by the rector, his former pupil, the earl of Erroll, to whom he had dedicated his *Essays*. At this time he supported the rector in a power struggle in the university, but later he switched to the side of the principal, William Leechman. In April 1763 he received the degree of LLD from his university, and three years later he was appointed university clerk. By then his health had begun to decline noticeably and from October 1766 his Greek classes were regularly taught by assistants. He suffered a financial crisis, and when Robert Foulis, hard-pressed for cash himself, called in a debt that Moor could not repay, Foulis was obliged to claim possession of Moor's beloved library, which consisted of almost three thousand items, with especially fine holdings in mathematics and Greek literature. It was later purchased from the Foulis estate and in February 1779 auctioned by James Spotiswood as the *Bibliotheca Mooriana*. In 1767 Moor's household goods were repossessed by a creditor, and two years later he was forced to sell his collection of medals to the university for £32. Meanwhile, Moor's problems at the university were growing more serious. On 25 January 1766 he was obliged to make a formal apology before his colleagues for directing such harsh abuse at the professor of divinity, Robert Trail, that the latter had begun legal proceedings against him. In March 1773 he was censured by his colleagues for beating an innocent student with a heavy candlestick four months earlier, and on 25 March 1774 he avoided being tried by the faculty for another, undisclosed, violation only by offering to resign his chair. The resignation was delayed more than a month by the unwillingness of the faculty to accept his stipulation that he be permitted to dictate the terms governing his arrangement with his successor, his former teaching assistant, John Young. But the faculty was willing to allow Moor to retain his college house and salary, and on 5 May 1774 he finally resigned on those terms. That he eventually lost control of his faculties is clear from a review of the third volume of Lord Monboddo's *On the Origin and Progress of Language* by John Gillies (who had also served as one of Moor's Greek teaching assistants), where Monboddo is accused of lifting certain ideas from Moor's lectures at a time 'when this learned and ingenious man was languishing under infirmity and misfortune, unconscious of the insult, and unable to punish it' (*Edinburgh Magazine and Review*, 5, June 1776, 258). Moor died of unknown causes on 17 September 1779. Although nothing is known of his wife, a son was reported to be the head of the grammar school at Irvine in 1784.

RICHARD B. SHER

Sources W. I. Addison, *A roll of graduates of the University of Glasgow from 31st December 1727 to 31st December 1897* (1898) · Anderson, *Scot. nat.* · J. Butt, *John Anderson's legacy: the University of Strathclyde and its antecedents, 1796–1996* (1996) · [A. Carlyle], review of the Foulis edition of *The Iliad*, *Scots Magazine*, 19 (1757), 570 · Chambers, *Scots.* (1835) · J. Coutts, *A history of the University of Glasgow* (1909) · *The correspondence of Adam Smith*, ed. E. C. Mossner and I. S. Ross, 2nd edn (1987), vol. 6 of *The Glasgow edition of the works and correspondence of Adam Smith* · W. J. Duncan, *Notices and documents illustrative of the literary history of Glasgow* (1831), ch. 4 · *Edinburgh Evening Courant* (3 Feb 1779) · *Edinburgh Evening Courant* (21 June 1784) · *The Edinburgh Magazine and Review* (1773–6) · [J. B. Neilson], ed., *Fortuna domus: a series of lectures delivered in the University of Glasgow in commemoration of the fifth centenary of its foundation* (1952) · P. Gaskell, *A bibliography of the Foulis Press*, 2nd edn (1986) · J. C. Hilson, introduction, in J. Moor, *An essay on historical composition* (1978) · A. Hook and R. B. Sher, eds., *The Glasgow Enlightenment* (1995) · J. D. Mackie, *The University of Glasgow, 1451–1951: a short history* (1954) · J. Maclehose, *The Glasgow University Press, 1638–1931* (1931) · D. Murray, *Robert and Andrew Foulis and the Glasgow press* (1913) · D. Murray, *Memories of the old college of Glasgow: some chapters in the history of the university* (1927) · *N&Q*, 2nd ser., 3 (1857), 21–2, 121–2, 506; 4 (1857), 104, 276, 333–4, 354, 362, 417 · I. S. Ross, *Lord Kames and the Scotland of his day* (1972) · I. S. Ross, *The life of Adam Smith* (1995) · [J. Robertson], *Lives of Scottish poets*, 3/1 (1822) · www.origins.net, 26 March 2000 · W. R.

Scott, *Francis Hutcheson: his life, teaching and position in the history of philosophy* (1900); repr. (1966) • R. B. Sher, 'Commerce, religion and the Enlightenment in eighteenth-century Glasgow', *Glasgow*, ed. T. M. Devine and G. Jackson, 1: *Beginnings to 1830* (1995), 312–59 • R. B. Sher, 'Professors of virtue: a social history of the chair of moral philosophy at Edinburgh', *Studies in the philosophy of the Scottish Enlightenment*, ed. M. A. Stewart (1990), 87–126 • D. Stewart, 'Account of the life and writings of Thomas Reid', in *The works of Thomas Reid*, ed. W. Hamilton, 8th edn, 1 (1895); repr. as *Philosophical works: Thomas Reid* (1967), 10 [introduction by H. M. Bracken] • M. A. Stewart, 'The origins of the Scottish Greek chairs', *Owls to Athens*, ed. E. M. Craik (1990), 391–400 • W. Thom, *Donaldsoniad* (1763) • *A vindication of Mr Hutcheson from the calumnious aspersions of a late pamphlet* (1738)

Archives NL Scot., notes on the *Iliad* • NL Scot., notes on Greek authors and geometry • NL Scot., revised proofs of *E tou Omerou Ilias* • U. Edin. L., commonplace book • U. Glas., summary of papers and books used in the preparation of the Foulis edition of Plato (never published) | U. Glas., Archives and Business Records Centre • U. Glas., minutes of the Literary Society in Glasgow College, 1764–79 [typescript]

Likenesses D. Allan, group portrait, repro. in Murray, *Robert and Andrew Foulis and the Glasgow press*, facing p. 68

Moor [*alias* Cross], **John** [*name in religion* Joannes de Sancta Cruce] (**1629?–1689**), Franciscan friar, was born in Norfolk. He may have been the son of a John Moore, and been baptized on 13 December 1629 at Wymondham, Norfolk. He entered the order of Friars Minor (Franciscans) in 1646 or 1647, taking the name in religion Joannes de Sancta Cruce, which supplied his alias of John Cross. He was made STD (doctor of divinity) by his order on 12 October 1672. He published a number of devotional works of which *Contemplations of the Life and Glory of Holy Mary* (1685) went through several editions, and copies of his *Dialecta admentum Joannis Scoti* (1673) were ordered to be given to every professed father. He was also asked to write a life of the Franciscan martyr John Wall, who was put to death at Worcester in 1679. He was twice elected provincial of the English province (1674–7 and 1686–9). In 1687 he established a Franciscan community of ten members at Lincoln's Inn Fields. But the landing of the prince of Orange on 4 November 1688 provoked rioters to attack this residence for a day and a night; they were eventually dispersed by a body of soldiers sent by the king. The rioters contemplated a renewal of the attack, but the king sent an order, through Bishop Leyburn, to the provincial, directing him and the rest of the fathers to retire from the place 'for prevention of future dangers and inconveniences'. This they did on 16 November 1688, having first removed their goods and obtained a guard of soldiers from his majesty for the security of the house and chapel. Their loss is said to have been upwards of £3000. Moor died at St Bonaventure's, Douai, on 13 December 1689 and was buried before the high altar in the old church, St Bonaventure's, Douai.   THOMPSON COOPER, *rev.* J. T. RHODES

Sources R. Trappes-Lomax, ed., *The English Franciscan nuns, 1619–1821, and the Friars Minor of the same province, 1618–1761*, Catholic RS, 24 (1922), 277–8 • Father Thaddeus [F. Hermans], *The Franciscans in England, 1600–1850* (1898) • 'Acta capitulorum, 1625–1746', Franciscan Friary, London, Franciscan Archive, English province • T. H. Clancy, *English Catholic books, 1641–1700: a bibliography* [1974]; rev. edn (1996) • IGI

Moor, Michael (1640–1726), university teacher, administrator and principal, was born in Bridge Street, Dublin, the son of Patrick Moore, a Roman Catholic merchant, and his wife, Mary Dowdall of Mountown. His initial education took place in Dublin and subsequently at the College of the Oratorians in Nantes, France. From about 1656 he studied philosophy and theology at the University of Paris. He graduated BA and was admitted a member of the German nation on 11 November 1662, having proceeded MA.

Renowned for his skill in Greek, Moor was quickly appointed to the Collège des Grassins, Paris, where he taught philosophy and rhetoric for ten years. He was subsequently appointed to the even more prestigious position of professor of Latin and Greek, and master of students in the Collège de Navarre. During his tenure he was elected to the office of rector of the University of Paris in 1677—an offer he declined at this time. University records demonstrate that he left for Ireland in 1685, rather than in 1684 as was previously thought.

Once in Ireland, Moor was ordained in 1685 by Luke Wadding, the bishop of Ferns, and was advanced to the prebend of Tymothan in St Patrick's Cathedral, Dublin. Patrick Russell, the archbishop of Dublin, made him his titular vicar-general. Although he published no work of his own at this time, he undertook to translate into Latin *Lettre de Monseigneur le Cardinal le Camus*. This was published in London in 1687 under the title *A pastoral letter; written in French by the Lord Cardinal le Camus, bishop and prince of Grenoble, to the curates of his diocese*. His appointment as chaplain to Richard Talbot, earl of Tyrconnell, led to further advancement when Moor came to the attention of James II. Initially this attention proved beneficial, as the king followed Moor's suggestion that the Jesuits should not be given charge of Trinity College, Dublin. Indeed, Moor himself was made provost of the college in 1689—on the recommendation of Tyrconnell and with the unanimous approval of all the Roman Catholic bishops. During his brief sojourn there Moor and another Roman Catholic priest, Teigue MacCarthy (one of James II's chaplains), played a vital role in preserving the library from the depredations of the king's army, and he more generally gained renown for his attempt to mitigate the suffering of protestant prisoners in Dublin. Moor's provostship came to an abrupt end when Jesuits managed to gain the ear of the king and persuaded him that one of Moor's sermons was critical of him. As a result, he was forced to leave Ireland.

By 1691 records of the University of Paris place Moor in that city, and in the following year there appeared at a Paris press his first work, *De existentia Dei, et humanae mentis immortalitate, secundum Cartesii et Aristotelis doctrinam, disputatio, in duobus libris divisa*, an attack on Cartesian philosophy which James Ware declares was later translated into English by a Mr Blackmore. However, the arrival in Paris of the defeated James II again necessitated a move, this time to Rome, where Moor was appointed censor of books, and then on to Montefiascone, in Italy, where he was elevated to the rectorship of Cardinal Barbarigo's seminary. In his position there he came to the attention of two popes—Innocent XII and Clement XI—who supported him unreservedly. During this relatively tranquil period he published his textbook *Hortatio ad studium linguae Graecae et Hebraicae recitata coram eminent M. Ant. Barbarigo Cardinale, archiepiscopo Montisfalsci* (1700).

On the death of James II in 1701, Moor was called back to France and was appointed rector of the University of Paris on the recommendation of Cardinal de Noailles. Indeed, so highly was he esteemed that he was appointed for the entire year of 1702—rather than for the customary trimester. Other honours quickly followed. On May 16 1702 he was asked to deliver the panegyric oration in honour of Louis XIV in the Collège de Navarre, and he later helped to remodel the university for the king. While rector of the university he was appointed rector of the Collège de Navarre and royal professor of philosophy, Greek, and Hebrew.

During this period Moor continued his critique of Cartesianism and in 1716 published his *Vera sciendi methodus*—a treatise in a dialogue format which sets him firmly in the circle of Cambridge Platonists. Along with John Farrelly, rector of the Irish College in Paris, Moor also played an important role in encouraging the education of Irish youths in Paris by purchasing accommodation for them close to the Irish College. No doubt with this aim in mind he bequeathed his library to the Irish College—a library which had, unfortunately, been much depleted by a duplicitous servant. Moor died on 22 August 1726 in his rooms in the Collège de Navarre, aged eighty-seven, and, according to his own request, was buried in the vault of the chapel of the Irish College. ELIZABETHANNE BORAN

Sources P. Boyle, 'Dr Michael Moore: sometime provost of Trinity College and rector of the University of Paris (AD 1640–1726)', *Archivium Hibernicum*, 5 (1916), 7–16 • *The whole works of Sir James Ware concerning Ireland*, ed. and trans. W. Harris, 3/1 (1746), 288 • L. Moréri, *Le grand dictionnaire historique*, 18th edn, 8 vols. (1740), vol. 6, p. 467 • H. L. Murphy, *A history of Trinity College, Dublin from its foundation to 1702* (1951), 174–6 • C. Maxwell, *A history of Trinity College Dublin, 1591–1892* (1946), 84–5 • J. W. Stubbs, *The history of the University of Dublin, from its foundation to the end of the eighteenth century* (1889), 134 • *DNB* • L. W. B. Brockliss, *French higher education in the seventeenth and eighteenth centuries: a cultural history* (1987), 347–8, 351, 459, 464 • C. Jourdain, *Histoire de l'Université de Paris au XVIIe et au XVIIIe siècle*, 2 pts (Paris, 1862–6), 285 • W. B. S. Taylor, *History of the University of Dublin* (1845), 54–5, 245–6

Moor, Sir Ralph Denham Rayment

Moor, Sir Ralph Denham Rayment (1860–1909), colonial official, was born on 31 July 1860 at The Lodge, Furneux Pelham, Buntingford, Hertfordshire, son of William Henry Moor (*c*.1830–*c*.1863), surgeon, and his wife, Sarah Pears. Educated privately after his father's death, he worked in the tea trade before entering the Royal Irish Constabulary as a cadet on 26 October 1882, becoming in due course a district inspector. After involvement in a divorce case, he resigned on 9 February 1891, and undertook to raise a constabulary force of Hausa and Gold Coasters to serve in the Oil Rivers protectorate.

Having impressed the consul-general, Sir Claude Macdonald, by his military efficiency, Moor was in 1892 transferred to political duties as vice-consul. He soon showed

himself prepared to act forcefully to assert British authority, and on 1 February 1896 succeeded Macdonald as commissioner and consul-general of what was now called the Niger Coast protectorate. Moor recorded his intention of extending British influence to the interior by peaceful expeditions and collaboration with African rulers, but first saw it necessary to enforce their acknowledgement of British supremacy. Already in 1894, as Macdonald's deputy, Moor had enforced the deposition and exile of the Itsekiri chief Nana Olomu; he now resolved to take strong measures against the Edo kingdom of Benin, and encouraged his deputy, James R. Phillips, in his ill-fated mission of January 1897. Returning from leave, Moor joined the expeditionary force of Admiral H. H. Rawson which within a month avenged the deaths of Phillips's party, looted the art works of Benin city, and established British control. In May Moor was appointed KCMG.

The British government now decided to establish unified and effective colonial administration over a wider region. In January 1900 Moor became high commissioner (under the Colonial Office) for the protectorate of Southern Nigeria. This comprised a union of the Niger Coast protectorate with the former territories of the Royal Niger Company, but not, as Moor had hoped, with the Lagos protectorate. Moor tried to create a structure for peaceful development by extending Macdonald's practice of designating warrant chiefs to form native councils and native courts. These expedients, devised with little knowledge of how these small-scale societies governed themselves, were to cause problems to his successors, but immediately they provided sufficient stability to permit rapid growth in exports. Moor remained very ready to use armed force, notably in the Aro expedition of 1901, but his commitment to economic development is acknowledged by Nigerian historians. He hoped to substitute currency transactions for barter and to encourage reluctant British traders to move inland by improving transport, but could not persuade the British government to invest in railways. The forestry department which he founded served the cause of conservation by supervising and controlling the tapping of wild rubber and the felling of hardwoods.

On 1 October 1903 Moor retired on grounds of ill health. He had hoped for more than the minor committee appointments offered by the Colonial Office, but he became a director of Alfred Lewis Jones's African Steam Ship Company, and worked for the British Cotton Growing Association. In 1898 he had married Mrs Adrienne Burns, *née* Shapland (*b. c.*1871), an attractive divorcee, but does not seem to have found happiness. On 14 September 1909 he was found dead at his home, The Homestead, Church Road, Barnes, having committed suicide by poison. His wife survived him. JOHN D. HARGREAVES

Sources A. E. Afigbo, 'Sir Ralph Moor and the economic development of Southern Nigeria, 1896–1903', *Journal of the Historical Society of Nigeria*, 5/3 (1970), 371–97 • A. E. Afigbo, *The warrant chiefs: indirect rule in southeastern Nigeria, 1891–1929* (1972) • R. Home, *City of blood revisited: a new look at the Benin expedition of 1897* (1982) • T. N. Tamuno, *The evolution of the Nigerian state: the southern phase, 1898–1914* (1972) • J. C. Anene, *Southern Nigeria in transition, 1885–1906: theory and practice in a colonial protectorate, 1885–1906* (1966) • O. Ikime,

Merchant prince of the Niger delta: the rise and fall of Nana Olomu, last governor of the Benin river (1968) • *DNB* • *CGPLA Eng. & Wales* (1909) • *The Times* (17 Sept 1909)

Likenesses photograph, repro. in Tamuno, *Evolution*, 144 • photograph, repro. in Home, *City of blood*, 1

Wealth at death £2671 1s. 1d.: administration, 25 Oct 1909, *CGPLA Eng. & Wales*

Moor, Robert (1567/8–1640), Church of England clergyman and author, was born at Holyrood, Southampton; nothing is known of his parents. He was elected a scholar of Winchester College in 1579 and matriculated from New College, Oxford, in July 1588, aged twenty. He was elected a perpetual fellow of the college the following year and 'at length was numbered among the best of preachers in that house' (Wood, *Ath. Oxon.*, 2.654). He graduated BA on 16 April 1591 and proceeded MA on 15 January 1595, the year in which his long Latin poem, *Diarium historicopoeticum*, was published. As its title suggests, this was an account of events in classical, medieval, and contemporary history, structured according to the passage of the year, in which Moor paid particular attention to the past of Winchester and New College.

In 1597 Moor became rector of Milbrooke, Hampshire, and resigned his fellowship. From 1601 he was rector of West Meon and of Chilcombe. He added to these livings the vicarage of Hambledon in 1603 and that of East Meon in 1612. Appointed a canon of Chichester in 1612, on 4 June 1613 he was installed prebendary of Winchester. He proceeded BD and DD on 5 July 1614. By 1618 he had married, but his wife's name is unknown; their son Robert was baptized at East Meon on 11 August.

Following the election of Richard Neile as bishop of Winchester in December 1627 Moor found himself engaged in frequent controversy. Neile reprimanded him for the anti-papal tone of his preaching at court, remarking that 'You have pleased King James with some pretty passages against Papists but you must not preach soe now' (Notestein and Relf, 50–52). Moor's opposition to bowing at the name of Jesus led to an attempt to force him to surrender the texts of his sermons at a cathedral chapter held on 26 November 1629. He eventually resigned his canonry in January 1632. He died on 20 February 1640 and was buried in the chancel of the church at West Meon.

SCOTT MANDELBROTE

Sources *The diary of John Young STP, dean of Winchester, 1616 to the Commonwealth*, ed. F. R. Goodman (1928) • Foster, *Alum. Oxon., 1500–1714*, 3.1025 • Wood, *Ath. Oxon.*, new edn, 2.654 • A. Milton, *Catholic and Reformed: the Roman and protestant churches in English protestant thought, 1600–1640* (1995) • W. Notestein and F. H. Relf, eds., *Commons debates for 1629* (1921), 50–53, 203 • *IGI* [parish register of East Meon, Hampshire]

Moor, Thomas (*b.* 1648/9, *d.* in or after 1713), religious controversialist and barber, was born to unknown parents, and brought up by his grandfather, who wanted him to be a lawyer, and sent him to Abingdon School, Berkshire. Moor wanted to be a barber, and he was apprenticed to his uncle by marriage, a barber in Bristol. Terrified by the doctrine of predestination to damnation, from the age of thirteen Moor questioned people on doctrine, receiving no satisfactory answers. He travelled through France and Italy, and served as a surgeon's mate in the Third Anglo-Dutch War. At the end of the war in 1674 he took ship from London to Barbados and Jamaica. Upon arrival in Jamaica, Moor opened a barbershop in Port Royal. Moor claimed that while returning from Legui to Port Royal at an unspecified date he saw a vision of a fiery globe and sword, ten days later receiving a revelation answering his religious questions. He returned to England around 1680.

Moor's religious questioning continued, sometimes combined with his professional duties—he tested his arguments on a visit to Cambridge by questioning the scholars as he cut their hair. Moor was dissatisfied with both the Anglican and dissenting theology of his day, which he believed overemphasized moralism at the expense of theological truth. He announced his heresies in an anonymous letter to the *Athenian Mercury*, John Dunton's periodical based on answering readers' questions. Moor's letter and *The Mercury*'s hostile reply were printed in the 21 June 1691 edition. Moor's heresy, later put forward in *Clavis aurea* (1695) and the first and second *Additions* in 1696 and 1697 was a denial of free will, and a belief in universal salvation. He suggested but did not insist that he was Elijah returned to announce the second coming, in *A disputation: whether Elijah, in Malachi 4. be any other prophet than what hath already been in the world?* (1695), which reprinted material from the *Athenian Mercury*. Moor loathed the orthodox doctrine of hell.

> I have lately met with some who will have all the Scripture to be taken in a Literal Sense; but then they make God both the Cause of our Sins, and the Eternal Punishment in a real Fire for unavoidable Sins, and let them say worse of the Devil if they can. (T. Moor, *Second Addition*, 28)

He attempted to confront leading Anglican and dissenting divines with his arguments, including Bishop Edward Stillingfleet in 1695 and Nathanael Vincent soon after. Moor did not attract many followers, although one publication was devoted to confuting him, *An impartial examination and refutation of the erroneous tenents of Thomas Moor, in his dangerous writings, intituled 'Clavis aurea', &c* by T. Curtis (1698). Moor's last and very rare work, *The wonderful and delightful doctrine of predestination not only proved from the scriptures, but also from a union of the scriptures* was self-published in 1713, when he described himself as aged sixty-four. It combined a restatement of his theological position with an autobiography that constitutes the chief source for his life.

According to the 1696 addition to *Clavis aurea*, Moor was then living 'at the sign of the Harrow' in St Thomas's parish, Southwark; he was still residing in the parish in 1713. Children were mentioned in the 1697 additions, but their names, and details of his wife, if any, are unknown, as is the date of his death.

WILLIAM E. BURNS

Sources T. Moor, *A second addition to the Clavis aurea, wherein the mysteries of the scripture are clearly broken open in this present year 1697, according to Dr. Beverley's calculation in his scriptural line of time* (1697) • T. Moor, *The wonderful and delightful doctrine of predestination not only proved from the scriptures, but also from a union of the scriptures* (1713) • T. C. [T. Curtis], *An impartial examination and refutation of the erroneous tenents of Thomas Moor, in his dangerous writings, intituled Clavis aurea, &c.* (1698) • *ESTC* • T. Moor, *An addition to the Clavis aurea* (1696) • W. E.

Burns, 'London's Barber-Elijah: Thomas Moor and universal salvation in the 1690s', *Harvard Theological Review*, 95 (2002), 277–90

Moorcroft, William (*bap.* **1767**, *d.* **1825**), veterinary surgeon and traveller, was the illegitimate son of Ann Moorcroft (*bap.* 1747), and an unknown father. Baptized on 25 June 1767 he lived with his mother in the house of her parents, Richard and Dorothy Moorcroft, who farmed land near Ormskirk, Lancashire. In September 1784 he was apprenticed to the Liverpool surgeon John Lyon. In 1788, having seen the effects of a cattle disease in his home parish, he turned to veterinary studies, enrolling at the veterinary school in Lyons in 1790. He was the first English person to complete a period of formal veterinary training.

Moorcroft returned home and in March 1792 he set up practice as a horse veterinarian in London at 224 Oxford Street. For six weeks in 1794 he was professor at the London Veterinary College but he resigned for unknown reasons, devoting himself thereafter to his thriving practice. He acquired a reputation as a humane vet who worked from scientific principles. He was the first to experiment with neurotomy as a cure for lameness, but unlike others he recognized the risks involved. In 1796 and 1800 he took out patents for improved horseshoes which he claimed could be mass-produced and which would protect the horse from brutal farriers, but schemes to produce the shoes ended in his losing as much as £16,000. His professional reputation grew but he wrote only two minor veterinary works, *The Horse Medicine Chest* (1795) and *Methods of Shoeing Horses* (1800).

His activities were enough to bring Moorcroft to the notice of the East India Company, for whom he began to buy breeding-horses. In 1807 he agreed to go to India to take charge of the company's stud operations at the remarkably large salary of 30,000 sicca rupees or £3000 a year. Leaving behind Mary (*née* Pateshall, *d.* 1819), of whom little is known but who was almost certainly his wife, he sailed for India in 1808; he reached the stud at Pusa, Bengal, in December that year. The stud was in a dismal state: though absorbing large amounts of money, it had never produced horses of the right quality in the right numbers. Moorcroft began management improvements immediately but it was clear that fundamental progress could not be made until bigger, bonier horses could be secured to improve quality. In 1811 Moorcroft set off to the north-west; he travelled 1500 miles, buying stock and collecting information. The trip convinced him that the answer to the stud's problems lay in the horses coming through the markets beyond the north-west frontier.

In April 1812 Moorcroft set off again, this time with Captain Hyder Young Hearsey, an experienced traveller. Moorcroft was disguised as Mayapoori, a physician and holy man. With them was Pandit Harkh Dev, from whose regular pace measurements and with his own calculations Hearsey was later to produce a fine map. Having crossed the Himalayas by July 1812 the group arrived in Tibet. Moorcroft noted everything of interest in his copious journals and reports, from which emerged themes which were to dominate the rest of his life. He was a keen observer, and always had an eye to practical improvement in

the interests of both the local people and British commerce. He saw signs of Russian expansion in trans-Himalaya and thought that these should be immediately countered by what came to be known as a 'forward' policy of pushing the sphere of British influence ever north-westwards. He gathered information and sent intelligence south, and he established contacts on his travels to further British political as well as commercial ends. Moorcroft returned from this trip with no horses and little else to convince his employers of the value of his trip. The Kashmir goats which he brought back died later in Scotland, and although his botanical collections were helpful they were not of central concern.

After returning to Pusa, Moorcroft formed an alliance with Purree Khanum, whose affection, along with the birth of their daughter Anne in January 1816 and of their son Richard in October 1818, consoled him during a difficult time at the stud; this was in a worse state than before and official patience was wearing thin, though the need for horses was more pressing than ever with war looming and with little stock to be bought on the open market. In May 1819 Moorcroft received permission to go to Bukhara, where he hoped to barter goods for horses, thus improving the stud and opening up the area to British goods. (He arranged for his wife, with whom he was still in contact, to take care of his daughter at her Paris home; however, Mary died on 27 November 1819 and both his children went to guardians in London.) Taking 8 tons of luggage and fifty permanent staff Moorcroft set off for Bukhara in 1819. In September 1820 he became the first European for a century to reach Leh. Again noting signs of Russian activity, he negotiated a trade treaty with the Ladakhis and wrote to the company urging that Ladakh be taken as a British protectorate. Later, both his treaty and his political suggestions were firmly repudiated. His copious dispatches were full of observations, projects, and schemes, a mixture of the far-sighted and the half-baked. They rarely included information about horses, the ostensible reason for his travels, and taxed the patience of his employers considerably.

In November 1822 Moorcroft reached Kashmir, and he set off the following year via the Hindu Kush for Afghanistan, which he reached in December 1823. Receiving there a letter from Calcutta recalling him unless he were near Kabul, he deemed himself to be near and carried on; he reached Kabul in June 1824, still leading his huge, unwieldy convoy, still dispatching reports, and still writing in his journal. Delayed by the authorities he finally reached Bukhara in February 1825, the first Briton to do so for some four hundred years and the first ever to reach it from the south. He found his goods unsaleable there and few horses to buy because of the prevailing war. His journey was a commercial failure, but improving the stud had long ceased to be its main purpose. Having established a network of spies to report on the activities of the Russians he set off home in July 1825. He reached only as far as Balkh, Afghanistan, where he died of a fever, on 27 August 1825, his health broken by the extraordinary demands of his expedition. He was buried outside the walls of the city, the Muslim and Jewish authorities having refused to grant him burial in their cemeteries. His caravan broke up in disarray and the survivors straggled home.

The task of editing for publication Moorcroft's all too abundant papers fell to Horace Wilson. Moorcroft was observant but his prose style was cumbersome. When Wilson's edition of his works finally appeared in 1841 he proved to have compounded Moorcroft's failings, producing a work which was lifeless and which missed out some of the most important of his observations. Even worse, by that time Alexander Burnes had reached Bukhara and his was the book which captured the public imagination. None the less, those interested in the region recognized Moorcroft's contribution. Considered by Sven Hedin as being one of the greatest of all high-Asian explorers, Moorcroft was soon acknowledged as a prescient geopolitical observer and is now seen by many as the earliest player of the 'great game'.   ELIZABETH BAIGENT

Sources E. Alder, *Beyond Bokhara: the life of William Moorcroft* (1985) · E. Alder, 'Standing alone: William Moorcroft plays the Great Game 1808–25', *International History Review*, 2 (1980), 172 · P. Hopkirk, *The great game: on secret service in high Asia* (1990) · H. Hearsey, 'Mr Moorcroft's journey to Balkh and Bokhara [pt 1]', *Asiatic Journal*, new ser., 18/1 (1835), 106–19, 171–82, 278–87 · H. Hearsey, 'Mr Moorcroft's journey to Balkh and Bokhara [pt 2]', *Asiatic Journal*, new ser., 19/1 (1836), 35, 95 · S. Hedin, *Trans-himalaya*, 3 vols. (1910–13) · S. Hedin, *Southern Tibet*, 9 vols. (1917–23) · P. J. Wallis and R. V. Wallis, *Eighteenth century medics*, 2nd edn (1988)
Archives BL OIOC, corresp., journals, and papers, MSS Eur. A 20–21, B 50–51, C 39–45, 68–9, E 113, F 35–41, G 27–31 · LUL, notes on agriculture in Kashmir | NL Scot., letters to Lord Minto
Likenesses H. Y. Hearsey, watercolour drawing, 1812, BL OIOC; repro. in Alder, *Beyond Bokhara*, pl. 18 · drawing, c.1820, repro. in Alder, *Beyond Bokhara*, pl. 1
Wealth at death over Rs240,000: Alder, *Beyond Bokhara*, 362

Moore. *See also* Moor, More.

Moore, Adolphus Warburton (1841–1887), civil servant and mountaineer, was born on 12 July 1841, the son of Major John Arthur Moore, a director of the East India Company. Educated at Harrow School, in August 1858 he became a junior clerk in the India Office, on the heels of the abolition of the East India Company. By 1867 he was senior clerk in the financial department, and in 1874 he joined the political department, where in the following year he became assistant secretary. In 1885 he became private secretary to the secretary of state, Lord Randolph Churchill, who placed great confidence in his advice; Moore followed him to the Treasury in 1886. His health broke down under the pressure of work, and he was sent abroad to recuperate, but died of typhoid fever on 2 February 1887 at the Hotel Victoria, Monte Carlo, before he could take up his new appointment as political secretary at the India Office. Sir Arthur Godley of that office provided his political obituary in a letter to Lord Dufferin, the viceroy of India:

> He was a most remarkable man, extremely able and clear headed, with 'an infinite capacity for taking trouble', great experience and knowledge of his subject, and a very strong will. He was invaluable to Lord R. Churchill ... in fact he was, during those six months, quite as much Secretary of State as his master (Foster, 188)

Moore's relaxation was mountaineering, in which area his lasting significance lies. He first visited the Alps in 1860, the golden age when there were many new peaks to climb and passes to cross. Equipment was primitive, maps inadequate, and expeditions often involved nights in herdsmen's huts or rocky bivouacs. Moore's usual partner was Horace Walker; sometimes they joined Horace's sister Lucy. They always climbed with guides, chiefly the Oberlanders Christian Almer, and Melchior and Jakob Anderegg. The guides supplied skill and experience—cut steps, led on rocks, navigated glaciers; the amateurs provided the strategy and the ambition to discover new routes. Moore was short-sighted and by his own admission no great cragsman, but he had great stamina and a ferocious appetite for exploration. Among his party's first ascents were the Gross Viescherhorn (1862), the Écrins (with Whymper in 1864), and in 1865 Piz Roseg, Obergabelhorn, and Mont Blanc by the Brenva glacier, his most celebrated climb. Moore relished it as providing 'the highest, as it is certainly the grandest, pass across the chain of Mont Blanc' (Moore, 360), and his energies were increasingly directed to finding and crossing new passes, among them the Jungfraujoch, the Sesiajoch, the Moming Pass, and many between the Great St Bernard and the Simplon. According to Horace Walker (p. 258), Moore's 'knowledge of the Western and Central Alps was for long unsurpassed, and his ingenuity in planning new and interesting routes inexhaustible. He had an extraordinary gift too for topography.' His detailed and lively accounts in the privately printed *The Alps in 1864*, and his many articles in the *Alpine Journal*, with his own maps, helped to establish the topography of the high Alps of Dauphiné, Valais, and Oberland.

Moore was a pioneer of winter climbing: from Grindelwald in December 1866 he crossed the Finsteraarjoch, and from La Grave in December 1867 the Brèche de la Meije. In 1868, as a member of an expedition to climb and explore the Caucasus, he made first ascents of Kazbek and Alborz; he revisited the range in 1874. Moore was elected to the Alpine Club in 1861; as secretary in 1872–4 he did much to regenerate the club. Highly regarded by fellow mountaineers, he was twice offered the presidency, but on account of official duties had to refuse.   JANET ADAM SMITH

Sources H. Walker, 'In memoriam: A. W. Moore', *Alpine Journal*, 13 (1886–8), 258–61 · A. L. Mumm, *The Alpine Club register*, 1 (1923) · A. W. Moore, *The Alps in 1864: a private journal* (1867) · CGPLA Eng. & Wales (1887) · Boase, *Mod. Eng. biog.* · *The Times* (3 Feb 1887), 6 · R. F. Foster, *Lord Randolph Churchill: a political life* (1981)
Archives Alpine Club, London
Likenesses group portrait, photograph, Alpine Club, London; *see illus. in* Walker, Lucy (1836–1916) · photograph, repro. in *Alpine Journal*, 29 (1915), facing p. 106
Wealth at death £1750 18s. 7d.: probate, 18 Feb 1887, CGPLA Eng. & Wales

Moore, Albert Joseph (1841–1893), painter, born at York on 4 September 1841, was the youngest of the fourteen children of William *Moore (1790–1851), a portrait painter, and his second wife, Sarah Collingham (d. 1863).

Four of his brothers also became artists, the most successful of whom was the marine painter Henry *Moore (1831–1895), and much of his early artistic training came from his father and brothers. He was educated in York at Archbishop Holgate's and St Peter's schools, and at the York School of Design (c.1853–c.1855). After his widowed mother moved to London with her younger sons in 1855 he attended Kensington grammar school until 1858. In 1857, at the age of fifteen, he exhibited two watercolour studies of dead birds at the Royal Academy, and in the following year he entered the Royal Academy Schools, where he remained only briefly. He also joined a sketching club with several fellow students including Frederick Walker, William Blake Richmond, Marcus Stone, Henry Holiday, and Simeon Solomon. In the summers of 1857 and 1858 he visited the Lake District, and in 1859 he travelled in northern France with the architect William Eden Nesfield, who in subsequent years would be an important source of patronage. His only other recorded significant period abroad was spent in Rome for several months in the winter of 1862–3.

Among the earliest works by Moore now known is a watercolour *Study of an Ash Trunk* (1857; exh. RA, 1858; Ashmolean Museum, Oxford), which shows foliage drawn in microscopic Pre-Raphaelite detail. Starting in 1861 he exhibited Old Testament subjects at the Royal Academy, most of them modest in scale, but culminating in *Elijah's Sacrifice* (exh. 1865; Art Gallery and Museum, Bury) and *The Shulamite Relating the Glories of King Solomon to her Maidens* (exh. 1866; Walker Art Gallery, Liverpool). During this period, however, his main activity was decorative painting, much of it in conjunction with Nesfield. Between 1860 and 1867 Moore painted at Croxteth Hall, near Liverpool; Claremont, near Manchester; Shipley Hall, Derbyshire; Combe Abbey, Warwickshire; and Cloverley Hall, Shropshire. His largest single undertaking, the chancel of St Alban's, Rochdale, occupied him for most of 1864–5. Little of this work survives, but related drawings are preserved, mainly in the Victoria and Albert Museum in London. In ruinous condition is a huge painting in tempera (80 × 347 inches), *A Greek Play* (Victoria and Albert Museum, along with preparatory drawings), which was installed in 1867 over the proscenium of the Queen's Theatre in Long Acre, London. His last major decorative project was a frieze of peacocks painted in 1872–3 for the drawing-room of Frederick Lehmann in Berkeley Square. In the 1860s Moore also made unrealized designs for an altarpiece for the Dutch church in Austin Friars, for mosaics in the central hall of the houses of parliament, and for the exterior frieze of the Albert Hall.

While Moore's decorative commissions ceased, they laid the foundation for the distinctive equation of decoration and art which would characterize his easel paintings for some twenty years. These paintings show figures, predominantly women, in classical dress, without narrative or other recognizable subject and without concern for personality, natural detail, or archaeological accuracy, in two-dimensional and seemingly simple compositions, painted with sumptuous and inventive texture, pattern, and colour. Although always figurative, the pictures usually bear names of flowers or the like, taken from incidental accessory details, as titles; they are full of deliberate and conspicuous anachronisms, which confounded conventional Victorian expectations about content and meaning by restricting content to an essentially abstract exploration of the formal richness inherent in the medium.

Moore's first painting in this vein, which showed four figures of the Seasons (exh. RA, 1864), was catalogued as a fresco, and its description by Sidney Colvin as a scheme for mosaic suggests its origins in architectural decoration. Beginning with *Azaleas* (exh. RA, 1868; Hugh Lane Municipal Gallery of Modern Art, Dublin) and concluding with *Blossoms* (exh. Grosvenor Gallery, London, 1881; Tate collection) he depicted single standing women in pictures so repetitive in subject and format—while differing in refinements of colour, pose, and details of drapery and setting—that they effectively constitute a set of variations upon a theme. In 1875 he painted three small pictures of sleeping girls, *Beads* (exh. RA, 1876; National Gallery of Scotland, Edinburgh), *Apples*, and *A Sofa* (both priv. coll.), with identical compositions but in each instance different colours. These works preceded two larger and more complex compositions of sleeping or reclining figures, *Dreamers* (exh. RA, 1882; City of Birmingham Museum and Art Gallery) and *Reading Aloud* (exh. RA, 1884; Glasgow Art Gallery and Museum). In the painstaking preparation of a major picture Moore normally made numerous oil studies to test different colour schemes. These, which he completed, exhibited, and sold as smaller independent works, constitute a large part of his œuvre; there are no fewer than seven such variant treatments of the individual figures in *Dreamers*.

Praise of *Azaleas* in a review of the Royal Academy show of 1868 by Algernon Swinburne, and an article by Sidney Colvin in the first issue of the periodical *Portfolio* in 1870 established Moore as the paradigmatic artist of the emerging aesthetic movement. Swinburne linked his 'faultless and secure expression of an exclusive worship of things formally beautiful' (Rossetti and Swinburne, 32) with the verse of Théophile Gautier, the chief progenitor of the underlying ideas of aestheticism, and Moore's title for another painting of this time, *A Quartet: a Painter's Tribute to the Art of Music, A.D. 1868* (exh. RA, 1869; priv. coll.), suggests his allegiance to those ideas. This tribute anticipates Walter Pater's axiom 'All art constantly aspires towards the condition of music', and, not coincidentally, the musical titles of J. M. Whistler, a close friend from 1865 onward. Moore absorbed from Whistler awareness of Japanese art, and Whistler clearly emulated Moore in his never-completed *Six Projects* of 1867–8 (Freer Gallery of Art, Washington, DC). In 1878 Moore testified on Whistler's behalf in his suit against Ruskin, and Whistler dedicated the ensuing *Whistler v. Ruskin: Art and Art Critics* (1878) to Moore, later proclaiming him 'The greatest artist that, in the century, England might have cared for and called her own' (Baldry, 25).

Moore exhibited at the Royal Academy throughout his

career but was never made a member; he also showed regularly at the Grosvenor Gallery from its inception in 1877. In 1884 and 1885 and subsequent years he painted and exhibited works in watercolour and in pastel, and he did become an associate of the Society of Painters in Water Colours. He continued to paint in much the same manner until the end of his life, but allegory, narrative, and mood reappear in *Midsummer* (exh. RA, 1887; Russell-Cotes Art Gallery and Museum, Bournemouth) and *A Summer Night* (exh. RA, 1890; Walker Art Gallery, Liverpool). His last painting, *The Loves of the Winds and the Seasons* (Museum and Art Gallery, Blackburn), is a charming allegory for which he wrote accompanying explanatory verse. Stylistically his late work shows no decline, but content of a sort which he had previously eschewed costs it the single-minded focus on formal qualities which had been the most noteworthy feature of his art from the mid-1860s to the mid-1880s.

During his last years Moore suffered from cancer, for which he had operations in 1890 and 1892. He died on 25 September 1893 at his home, 2 Spenser Street, Westminster, London and was buried in Highgate cemetery. He had never married and had gained a reputation as a solitary eccentric, living from 1877 until 1891 in an odd and shabby house in Holland Lane, Kensington. Moore possessed a 'splendid Christ-like head', with broad brows and visionary brown eyes, set upon an awkward little body (Robertson, 57). Dante Gabriel Rossetti dismissed him as 'a dull dog' (D. G. Rossetti, *Letters of Dante Gabriel Rossetti*, ed. O. Doughty and J. R. Wahl, 4 vols., 1965–7, 2.497), but he is described with respect and affection in the memoirs of his one-time pupil Graham Robertson. Another devoted pupil, Alfred Lys Baldry, wrote the basic monograph on the artist.   ALLEN STALEY

Sources A. L. Baldry, *Albert Moore: his life and works* (1894) · W. M. Rossetti and A. Swinburne, *Notes on the Royal Academy exhibition, 1868* (1868) · S. Colvin, English painters of the present day, 2: Albert Moore, *The Portfolio*, 1 (1870), 4–6 · W. G. Robertson, *Life was worth living* (1931) · [R. Green], *Albert Moore and his contemporaries* (1972) [exhibition catalogue, Laing Art Gallery, Newcastle upon Tyne, 23 Sept – 22 Oct 1972] · R. Green, 'Albert Moore: recent discoveries', *The Moore family pictures: paintings, watercolours and drawings by Albert and Henry Moore, their brothers William, John Collingham and Edwin and their father William Moore snr* [1980], 21–37 [exhibition catalogue, York City Art Gallery, 2–31 Aug 1980, Julian Hartnolls Gallery, 22 Sept – 10 Oct 1980] · R. Asleson, *Albert Moore* (2000) · DNB

Likenesses S. P. Hall, two pencil sketches, NPG · F. Hollyer, photograph, National Museum of Photography, Film and Television, Bradford, Royal Photographic Society collection; repro. in J. Maas, *The Victorian art world in photographs* (1984), 130 · F. Hollyer, photograph, repro. in Baldry, *Albert Moore*, facing p. 1 · R. Taylor, woodcut (after photograph), NPG; repro. in *Magazine of Art* (1885)

Wealth at death £1184 13s. 6d.: probate, 24 Nov 1893, CGPLA Eng. & Wales

Moore [*née* Peg], **Ann** (*b.* 1761), the fasting woman of Tutbury, was born on 31 October 1761 at Rosliston, Derbyshire, the daughter of a labourer and sawyer, William Peg. She went into domestic service, and in 1788 married a fellow farm servant, James Moore, the illegitimate son of a woman named Laikin. It was apparently a shotgun wedding and Moore—who may have believed that the child

was not his—was probably unwilling to marry her; whatever the circumstances, the couple appear to have soon separated. Ann Moore went back into service, eventually becoming housekeeper to a widowed farmer at Aston, near Tutbury. She bore her employer at least two children, a girl and a boy. About 1800, apparently after conversion by a local sect of Calvinists, she left the farmer to live in Tutbury, working as a cotton beater.

Here Ann Moore's long fasts began to attract attention, both from her neighbours and from the national medical community. From November 1806 she was said to have lost all interest in food. By March 1807 she was suffering from hysterical fits and stomach cramps, and in April she took to her bed; in May 1807 she attempted to swallow a biscuit, but was in great pain and vomited. The last solid food which she took was said to have been some blackcurrants in June 1807; her diet then subsequently seemed to consist of gradually diminishing doses of tea without milk or sugar. In September 1808 two local surgeons, Robert Taylor and John Allen, organized a watch of sixteen days to test the claims she was now making of total abstinence. She appeared to take no food or water in this time, and both men subsequently published letters in the *London Medical and Physical Journal* supporting her claims. Varied explanations were given for her loss of appetite, both by her and her audience. She seems to have claimed initially that nausea, caused by washing the sheets of a man who had died of scrofulous ulcers, had destroyed her appetite; later she declared that extreme want had driven her to semi-starvation, or that her illness had come on gradually. One account claimed that her fasts represented miraculous intervention: in this version Ann Moore, unable to feed both herself and her children, asked God to take away her appetite and he obligingly complied. Meanwhile, medical opinion suggested that her anorexia was caused by a disease of the oesophagus or a stomach complaint.

Debate also raged over Moore's apparent ability to survive without food. 'Air appears to be the means by which life is still maintained' (*An Account of the Extraordinary Abstinence of Ann Moor, of Tutbury*, 25) claimed one commentator, adopting a well-worn medical theory, while others cited similar cases from literature and recent history (it is possible that Moore's fasts were inspired by local traditions concerning the late seventeenth-century anorexic Martha Taylor of Bakewell). The accounts by medical observers outline her physical condition, mentioning her frequent perspiration, limited excretion of urine, flatulence, and extreme emaciation; visitors also commented on her cheerful and pious frame of mind. She was said to have received as much as £400 from her visitors, although her finances were apparently depleted by her daughter's extravagance and her own expenses.

On 31 March 1813 Legh Richmond, the well-known evangelical rector of Turvey, instituted a second watch. A committee was established under Sir Oswald Mosley and a group of watchers—consisting entirely, at Moore's request, of clergymen and doctors—was appointed. Moore herself seems to have been reluctant to submit to a second watch, and in particular objected to the introduction of a weighing machine. The watch began on 21 April; by 30 April Ann Moore was so feverish and emaciated that her death was expected. At her daughter's request the watch was discontinued. Moore initially persisted in her claims, but the evidence of excreta on her bedclothes and sheets was held to invalidate them. On 4 May she confessed to perpetuating a fraud before a local magistrate, signing her confession with a cross. Further investigation by Richmond suggested that her daughter, who had visited her daily during the first watch, had somehow smuggled in some food; it was also revealed that during the period of her earlier fasts tea, sugar, and milk were left within her reach and were apparently consumed by her. Nevertheless, it was clear that she was able to survive for some time on small amounts of liquids alone.

Moore's subsequent fate is unclear. According to Mosley she left Tutbury with her daughter, amid hooting from a crowd, and the pair settled in Macclesfield; they were afterwards sent to the Knutsford house of correction for robbing their landlord, but nothing further is known of either. Her fasts are reminiscent of the ascetic practices of the medieval woman religious; comparisons with modern sufferers from anorexia nervosa are also tempting. Some modern commentators have classified her as one of the 'miraculous maidens' who starved themselves as a means to gain money or attention, embodying the tensions of early modern European society undergoing the beginnings of secularization. But this comparison, helpful as it is, obscures aspects of Moore's case which are rooted in the peculiar climate of early nineteenth-century England, at war with France, troubled with social and political unrest among the working classes, and swept by evangelical religiosity. While her contemporaries offered medical and religious interpretations of Moore's behaviour, a modern historian may prefer to view both her fasting and her fraud as a form of social protest, an early hunger strike, witnessing to intense frustration at the situation in which her class, gender, and unfortunate personal history left her. A labouring woman with a disreputable past, Ann Moore could catch the public attention only as a religious celebrity—a minor Joanna Southcott—or as a criminal: ironically, she eventually appeared in both roles.

ROSEMARY MITCHELL

Sources L. Richmond, *A statement of facts, relative to the supposed abstinence of Ann Moore* (1813) · [L. J.], *An account of the extraordinary abstinence of Ann Moor, of Tutbury*, 2nd edn (1809) · *A full exposure of Ann Moore, the pretended fasting woman of Tutbury*, 3rd edn (1813) · E. Anderson, *The life of Ann Moore of Tutbury …: her wonderful existence without food* (c.1810) · O. Mosley, *History of the castle, priory, and town of Tutbury* (1832), 320–24 · *DNB* · W. Vandereycken and R. van Deth, *From fasting saints to anorexic girls: the history of self-starvation* (1990), 54, 68, 107–8
Likenesses wax, exh. early 19th cent. · A. Cardon, stipple, pubd 1812 (aged fifty-eight), BM · stipple and line engraving, pubd 1813, NPG · J. Ward, etching, BM · engraving, repro. in G. H. Wilson, *Wonderful characters* (1842)

Moore, Arthur (d. 1730), financier and politician, was probably born in Monaghan town, co. Monaghan, Ireland. If his critics are to be believed, he was a son of the gaoler there (*Political Merriment, or, Truths Told to some Tune*, 1714, 14), and may have been born in the public house at the prison gate. No more is known of his family than that he had a brother (later Colonel Thomas Moore) and two sisters, Jane and Mary. Nothing is known of his early life: he may have begun his professional life as a groom, or 'a footman without any education' who rose 'to be a great dealer in trade' (*Bishop Burnet's History*, 6.1232).

In 1695 Moore was elected MP for the borough of Great Grimsby, Lincolnshire. He lost his seat in the disputed election of 1700–01, but soon regained it and continued to represent the borough for the next twenty years. He was chosen in 1702 to be one of the managers of the newly amalgamated East India companies, and two years later when Henry St John (later Viscount Bolingbroke) was made secretary at war, Moore was appointed comptroller of the army accounts. On 30 September 1710 he was made one of the commissioners of trade and plantations, and in 1711 he became a director of the South Sea Company which the tories set up as a counter to the whig-dominated Bank of England. It seems clear that Moore was thought to be possessed of considerable ability. Arthur Onslow, later speaker of the House of Commons, observed:

> [he] had very extraordinary talents, with great experience and knowledge of the world, very able in parliament, and capable of the highest parts of business, with a manner … equal to almost any rank … He was generous and magnificent; wrote and spoke accurately and politely; but his figure was awkward and disadvantageous. If he had raised himself by a course of virtue, he would have justly been deemed one of the greatest among those who have wrought their own fortunes. But *vendidit hic auro patriam* … (*N&Q* 1st ser. 11.197)

The suggestion that 'he sold his country for gold' arose from Moore's role in drafting the proposed commercial treaties which followed the peace of Utrecht. Whether or not Moore was associated with Matthew Prior in the secret negotiations with France which led to the peace, it seems certain that the articles of the projected commercial treaties with France and Spain were mainly drawn up by Moore, particularly the eighth and ninth clauses of the treaty of commerce, under which France and Britain would accord each other most favoured nation status. Since similar provisions were considered between France and the Netherlands, Moore's initiative can be seen as leading towards European free trade. These clauses effectively removed tariffs previously introduced by statute and therefore required parliamentary approval. Moore was the most frequent speaker in their support throughout the furious debate which they provoked. St John wrote to the duke of Shrewsbury on 25 January 1712:

> Never poor proposition was so bandied about as this of using each other reciprocally, *ut amicissima gens*, has been … surely we from the first should have stuck to that plain article, which is contained in the papers drawn by Mr. Moore, and on which the last draught which I sent your Grace is grounded. (*Letters … Bolingbroke*, 3.336–7)

While he has therefore been seen as possessing

'advanced views', it seems likely that Moore was a spokesman for tory policy, rather than an early advocate of the economic principles of free trade. The articles were eventually cancelled, in part due to Moore's unconvincing defence of the proposal in parliament during June 1713. His stance, not surprisingly, made him a target for subsequent attack by the whigs.

There is no proof that Moore had a personal stake in the projected French treaty, but the case may be otherwise where the Spanish treaty of commerce is concerned. The attack on him was initiated by a committee of the South Sea Company appointed on 10 June 1714 to investigate charges against Moore, particularly that he had pressed Captain Robert Johnson, of the *Bedford*, to take on board 20 or 30 tons of Dutch linen to be sent to the West Indies on his personal account. Though clandestine private trading was not unusual at the time, Moore insisted on his complete innocence. Fearing the verdict might go against him, however, he took the precaution of transferring all the South Sea stock in his possession on 11 June, a proceeding which was generally looked upon as a plain indication that he was not altogether innocent. On 7 July 1714 he was dismissed from the employment of the company on the grounds of breach of trust.

Early in 1714 Moore narrowly escaped parliamentary censure for his management of clothing contracts in 1706 while he was comptroller of army accounts. On 8 July the treaty of commerce with Spain came under scrutiny, when it was alleged that Moore was an interested party in the Asiento contract, the purpose of which was to give the South Sea Company a monopoly of shipping slaves to Spanish colonies in the New World. When Treasury officials were examined in the House of Lords it emerged that they were only nominal assignees for the quarter part of the Asiento contract reserved for the queen, which was actually to go to some unknown persons, strongly suspected to be Bolingbroke, Abigail Masham, and Arthur Moore. Queen Anne was deeply embarrassed, and moved quickly to prorogue parliament, in the process forestalling action on the allegation that 'Mr. Arthur More ... had a Promise from the King of Spain, to be one of his Commissioners; but that M. Orry had writt, that his Commission (worth 2,000 louis d'or a year) was not to be sign'd till the three Articles on which all hinged, were Sign'd' (Hamilton, 62).

Moore lost his seat in the election that followed, and retired from parliament to improve the property he had bought at Fetcham, near Leatherhead in Surrey. The expense of this, which included a house designed by Tallmen and ornamented by Louis Laguerre, and a park and waterworks said to rival Fontainebleau, together with the litigation in which he was involved, ate up his fortune and in his will, dated 6 November 1729, Moore feared that his personal estate would not suffice to defray his bequests—these included an annuity of £400 a year to his widow, and a sum of £2500 to each of his two younger sons, as well as provisions for his property in Surrey, Gloucester, and Middlesex.

On 17 March 1691 Moore had married at St Bride's, London, Susanna (*d.* 1694), eldest daughter of the physician and traveller, Edward Browne, and granddaughter of the physician Sir Thomas *Browne; they had two children, Jane (*b.* 1693) and Susanna (*b.* 1694), both of whom died in early infancy. His wife, who had been baptized at St Bride's on 4 September 1673, herself died on 23 February 1694; she was buried at St Bride's on 2 March, but the body may have been removed to Northfleet in Kent, where a monument was erected to her memory. At Westminster Abbey on 4 November 1696 Moore married for a second time, his wife being Theophila (*c.*1676–1739) of Epsom, daughter and heir of William Smythe of the Inner Temple, paymaster of the band of pensioners, and Lady Elizabeth, eldest daughter of George, earl of Berkeley. By this marriage there were six children, of whom the best known was the third son, James Moore [*see* Smythe, James Moore], a minor dramatist and wit, referred to in Alexander Pope's 'Epistle to Dr Arbuthnot' as 'Arthur's giddy Son', who assumed his maternal grandfather's surname of Smythe in 1720. Arthur Moore died in London on 4 May 1730, broken in all respects except in his ability and spirit, and was buried at Fetcham on 10 May.

EDWARD H. THOMPSON

Sources DNB · *N&Q*, 11 (1855), 157–9, 177–8, 197–8, 295 · A. Boyer, *The history of Queen Anne* (1735) · *Bishop Burnet's History of his own time*, new edn, ed. T. Burnet, 6 vols. (1725–34) · *Letters and correspondence, public and private, of ... Henry St John, Lord Viscount Bolingbroke, during the time he was secretary of state to Queen Anne*, ed. G. Parke (1798) · *The diary of Sir David Hamilton, 1709–1714*, ed. P. Roberts (1975) · *N&Q*, 2nd ser., 5–6 (1858), 8–9; 13–14 · *N&Q*, 4th ser., 9 (1872), 307 · P. Rapin de Thoyras, *The history of England*, ed. and trans. N. Tindal, 2nd edn, 5 vols. (1732–47) · S. Bidde, *Bolingbroke and Harley* (1975) · J. A. Downie, *Robert Harley and the press* (1979) · G. S. Holmes, *British politics in the age of Anne*, rev. edn (1987) · E. Gregg, *Queen Anne* (1980) · I. Kramnick, *Bolingbroke and his circle* (1968) · G. de F. Lord and others, eds., *Poems on affairs of state: Augustan satirical verse, 1660–1714*, 7 vols. (1963–75), vol. 7
Archives Bodl. Oxf., letters and papers | GL, papers relating to subsidies assessed upon City of London · North East Lincolnshire Archives, Grimsby, letters mainly relating to Grimsby elections
Wealth at death probably bankrupt; estates in Surrey (Fetcham and Randalls), and the farm of Polesden at Great Bookham; estates in Gloucester and Middlesex, and a house at Grimsby, Lincolnshire; probably had stock in the United East India Company, and at one time held shares in South Sea Company: will, *N & Q*, 1st ser., 197–8, 1730

Moore, Arthur William (1853–1909), historian and Manx scholar, born on 6 February 1853 at Cronkbourne, Douglas, Isle of Man, was the eldest of the ten children (five sons and five daughters) of William Fine Moore (1814–1895) JP, proprietor of the Tromode Sailcloth Mills and, from 1857 to 1875, a member of the House of Keys (self-elected until the reforms of 1866), and his wife and cousin, Hannah Christian (1827–1914). The Moores, of Ballakilley, Marown, a leading family of ancient and complicated lineage, were rooted in the island, and Moore claimed descent from the Christians of Milntown and the Manx patriotic hero William Christian, Illiam Dhône (1608–1663), through both his mother and his father. After Rugby School, which he entered in February 1867, he went on to Trinity College, Cambridge, where he matriculated in

1872 and was bracketed first in the historical tripos in 1875; he graduated BA in 1877 and MA in 1880. He also distinguished himself at athletics and won his blue for rugby football. He married, on 24 February 1887, Louisa Elizabeth Wynn (1864–1937), the daughter of Dr Joshua Hughes-Games, then archdeacon of Man and later vicar of Hull.

Following extensive travel in Europe, Asia, and the West Indies in the early 1870s Moore devoted his adult activities to the concerns of his native island. In business he followed his father in the profitable management of the Tromode Sailcloth Mills, until the competition of steamships inevitably led to their decline and eventual closure. He developed the family farms, and his interest in advancing Manx agricultural practices, particularly his attempt to introduce high quality cheesemaking, was marked by his membership and, in 1883, his presidency of the Isle of Man Agricultural Society. He was also a director of the Isle of Man Steam Packet Company and the Isle of Man Banking Company, the two most important commercial institutions in the island's resort development of the nineteenth century.

Moore began his life in public service on his appointment as a justice of the peace at the age of twenty-four, and in 1881, at the age of twenty-eight, he was made captain of the parish of Onchan and elected a member of the House of Keys for the sheading of Middle, which he represented for the rest of his life. He served as a member of the Manx council of education, the Manx Harbour Board, and the Manx diocesan church commissioners and was appointed deputy receiver-general in 1905. An authority on the procedures and precedents of the House of Keys, in 1898 he was elected its speaker, a post he held until his death. A staunch defender of the Keys' rights and privileges against their erosion by the governor and legislative council, he guided the house's first moves in the battle for constitutional reform towards Manx home rule with ability, tenacity, and tact. He led the first Keys' deputation on that issue to the Home Office in February 1907, when his health was already in decline.

Moore's achievements in business and political life were notable but they were overshadowed by the range and quality of his services to Manx cultural and intellectual life in a relatively short career. His rigorously professional, record-based *History of the Isle of Man* (1900) continues at the end of the twentieth century to underpin most historical investigations, and his many works on the language, music, and social culture, published on the island and in Britain, are the foundations of modern Manx studies, the essential scholarly basis for the definition of the particular Norse and Celtic-influenced national identity of the Manx. They include *The Surnames and Place-Names of the Isle of Man* (1890), *Folk-Lore of the Isle of Man* (1891), *Manx Carols* (1891), *The Diocese of Sodor and Man* (1893), *Manx Ballads and Music* (1896), *Manx Worthies* (1901), *Bishop Hildesley's Letters* (1904), *Douglas 100 Years Ago* (1904), and *Extracts from the Records of the Isle of Man* (1905). He edited the elegant illustrated periodical the *Manx Notebook* (1885–

7) and contributed many articles to that and other learned magazines.

Moore learned Manx in adult life at a time when it was unfashionable and undervalued by the educated classes, and his keen interest in the language linked him with the popular, native-speaking side of the movement for Manx studies as well as the scholarly antiquarians of the Manx Society for the Publication of Historical Documents, the Fine Arts and Industrial Guild, the Isle of Man Natural History and Antiquarian Society, and the trustees of the projected Manx National Museum, all of which he actively supported. In 1899 he founded the Manx Language Society, which drew all the elements of Manx culture together. Influenced by the example of the Welsh eisteddfod, it was not confined to the pursuit of language studies, but defined in his first presidential address to the society (November 1899) as dedicated 'to the preservation of everything that is distinctively Manx, and above all to the cultivation of a national spirit'.

In 1902 Moore was created commander in the Royal Victorian Order by Edward VII on a visit to the island and in 1905 he was enthroned as bard at Caernarfon, gratifying acknowledgements of the two sides of his life's work, in politics, and as a leader of the Manx cultural revival. He was still speaker and still working on his latest project, 'The vocabulary of the Anglo-Manx dialect', in spite of prolonged ill health, when he died at his home, Woodbourne House, Douglas, on 12 November 1909 at the age of fifty-six. He was buried at Kirk Braddan on 15 November. He left one son and two daughters.   A. M. HARRISON

Sources *Manx Quarterly*, 7 (1909) · *Celtic Review*, 6 (1909–10), 283–7; repr. in *Peel City Guardian* (26 Feb 1910) · S. M. [S. Morrison], 'The origin of the Manx Language Society', *Manx Quarterly*, 14 (1914), 132–3 · T. W. Cain, 'Constitutional reform in the twentieth century', *Isle of Man Natural History & Antiquarian Society*, 10/3 (1993–5), 201–24 · N. G. Crowe, 'The Moores of Ballakilley, Marown', *Isle of Man Natural History & Antiquarian Society*, 10/10 (1993–5), 17–40 · *I.O.M. Weekly Times* (13 Nov 1909) · *I.O.M. Examiner* (20 Nov 1909) · W. Cubbon, *Bibliography of the literature of the Isle of Man*, 2 vols. (1933–9)
Archives Manx National Heritage Library, Douglas, Isle of Man, corresp. and collections · Manx National Heritage Library, Douglas, Isle of Man, Manx Museum MSS | CAC Cam., corresp. with Lord Randolph Churchill
Likenesses F. M. Taubman, bust, 1911, House of Keys chamber, Douglas, Isle of Man · R. E. Morrison, oils, House of Keys chamber, Douglas, Isle of Man · photographs, Manx Museum, Library and Art Gallery, Douglas, Isle of Man
Wealth at death £6105 7s. 2d.: administration with will, 12 Feb 1910, CGPLA Eng. & Wales

Moore, Aubrey Lackington (1848–1890), theologian and philosopher, was born at 13 North Terrace, Camberwell, Surrey, on 30 March 1848, the second son of Daniel Moore (1809–1899), vicar of Holy Trinity, Paddington, and prebendary of St Paul's, and his wife, Fanny Henrietta Lackington. He was educated at St Paul's School (1860–67), which he left with an exhibition, and matriculated as a commoner of Exeter College, Oxford, in 1867. After obtaining first-class honours in classical moderations and *literae humaniores* he graduated BA in 1871 and MA in 1874. He was a fellow of St John's College, Oxford, from 1872 to 1876, became a lecturer and tutor in 1874, and was assistant tutor at Magdalen College in 1875. On 3 August 1876 he married Catherine Maria, daughter of Frank Hurt, a merchant; they had three daughters.

Moore was rector of Frenchay, near Bristol, from 1876 to 1881, when he was appointed a tutor of Keble College, Oxford. He was examining chaplain to bishops Mackarness and Stubbs of Oxford, select preacher at Oxford (1885–6), Whitehall preacher (1887–8), and an honorary canon of Christ Church (1887). A few weeks before his death he accepted an official fellowship as dean of divinity at Magdalen, and when nominated simultaneously to examine in the final honour schools of both theology and *literae humaniores* he accepted the latter post. He died from influenza, after a very brief illness, on 17 January 1890 at 2 Keble Road, Oxford, and was buried in Holywell cemetery, Oxford, on 21 January. His wife survived him.

At Oxford, Moore lectured mainly on philosophy and the history of the Reformation; in 1890 his *Lectures on the History of the Reformation* were published posthumously. But his real contribution to the intellectual life of the university lay in his exploration of the impact of modern philosophical and scientific thought on traditional theology. A liberal high-churchman, he contributed the second essay, 'The Christian doctrine of God', to *Lux mundi* (1889), demonstrating in it his conviction that new philosophical and scientific ideas could enrich and confirm theological doctrine. An unusual knowledge of science was apparent in his essays on the relationship between Darwinism and natural theology, *Science and Faith* (1889) and *Essays Scientific and Philosophical* (1890). These won him, despite his early death at the age of forty-two, a prominent place among Anglican apologists of the day; leading British biologists, including W. H. Flower, E. R. Lankester, E. B. Poulton, and G. J. Romanes, praised his work. Several volumes of his sermons were published after his death, and a fund of nearly £1000 was subscribed to his memory by friends, from which an Aubrey Moore studentship in theology, open to graduates of Oxford, was founded in 1890. More recently, his theological and philosophical treatment of teleology has been considered in a study of the post-Darwinian controversies.

RICHARD ENGLAND

Sources E. S. Talbot, W. Lock, and G. J. Romanes, 'Memoirs of the author', in A. L. Moore, *Essays scientific and philosophical* (1890) · *Oxford Times* (25 Jan 1890) · J. R. Moore, *The post-Darwinian controversies* (1979) · W. D. Macray, *A register of the members of St Mary Magdalen College, Oxford*, 8 vols. (1894–1915), vol. 7 · R. B. Gardiner, ed., *The admission registers of St Paul's School, from 1748 to 1876* (1884) · B. M. G. Reardon, *From Coleridge to Gore: a century of religious thought in Britain* (1971), 436–7 · b. cert. · m. cert. · *CGPLA Eng. & Wales* (1890)
Archives BL, Gladstone MSS · Bodl. Oxf., Liddon MSS
Likenesses C. W. Furse, oils, 1892, Keble College, Oxford · engraving, repro. in *London Figaro* (25 Jan 1890), 4
Wealth at death £4879 7s. 7d.: resworn administration with will, Sept 1892, *CGPLA Eng. & Wales* (1890)

Moore, Brian (1921–1999), writer, was born on 25 August 1921 at 11 Clifton Street, Belfast, the fourth of nine children (six girls and three boys) born to James Bernard Moore (1867–1942), and Eileen *née* McFadden (*c.*1890–1957). Theoretically at least, Ireland was still within a united kingdom, but this formality was rapidly being superseded by partition. In family lore, Brian's birth was brought on by a fusillade of shots by British soldiers outside the house, causing his shocked mother to go into labour. He was known as 'the Bomb' as a result. His mother, a former theatre nurse, was from Gweedore, co. Donegal. His father, born in Ballymena, co. Antrim, was a successful surgeon at the Mater Infirmorum Hospital, and a university examiner. He was an Irish nationalist and Anglophobe, who insisted on buying bread and other commodities from Catholic rather than protestant businesses, though he was sufficiently well respected to become a member of the senate of Queen's University. Like Simon Dedalus in James Joyce's *Portrait of the Artist as a Young Man*, he wore a monocle. 'It had a black ribbon that went down over his ear', Moore later recalled (Chevrefils, 247). The family had a resident children's nurse (and a car), in a household where the children were encouraged to read.

The expectation of academic success was strong. Brian (pronounced Breean) Moore was initially educated at Newington elementary school, Belfast, where the headmaster asked him at the age of 'seven or eight' (*Contemporary Literary Criticism*, 260) to write 'seven or eight essays' (ibid., 261), which became class models for some years afterwards. In the 1930s at St Malachy's College, a Jesuit establishment, Moore showed further writing ability by composing essays for schoolfriends for 6d. each, but in the main he found his education a brutish experience, 'beating and teaching by rote' (Dahlie, 5). At odds with his father, he became opposed to both the Catholicism and the protestantism on offer in Northern Ireland. Moore's failure to matriculate for Queen's University, because of inadequate mathematics, was a severe family disappointment. Some London University correspondence courses came to nothing, as Moore pursued interests in politics and theatre. Although he sold left-wing newspapers, he refused to join the Trotskyite party publishing them. 'My childhood … made me suspicious of faiths, allegiances, certainties', he wrote much later (Mulholland).

Early in the Second World War Moore served in the Belfast air raid precautions unit, and later in the National Fire Service in the city. After the death of his father he joined the Ministry of War Transport as a civilian and was sent as a junior port clerk to Algiers. Soon afterwards he was in Naples on promotion, then in Marseilles (after the allied invasion of southern France), where he saw collaborators shot in the streets. Adept at problem solving and dealing with fluctuating circumstances, he was engaged by moral courage rather than heroics in the many situations that he dealt with or heard of. His Francophilia grew as his Anglophilia diminished. At the war's end he joined the United Nations Relief and Rehabilitation Administration (UNRRA) and was due to go to China, when he was explicitly rejected for being Irish. Instead he developed his experience and international perspectives by going to Poland for UNRRA early in 1946.

In Gdynia and Zapot, Auschwitz and Warsaw, Moore saw

the devastated country at close range, working as (by his own admission) an inefficient statistical officer. He had an intense love affair with a hard-drinking older woman, Margaret Swanson, a Canadian economist. But he was reminded too of the great Russian writers while working for a Russian, Colonel Poulnikov, coping with chaos and associating with planners, relief workers, black marketeers, foreign correspondents, and many others. Moore realized that Polish communists could be as antisemitic as other Poles, and that his socialist views made him a joke to them. The multiple disjunctions provided a good grounding in shifting relativities and ambiguous loyalties. An American photographer friend, John Vachon, wrote of him in March 1946: 'Brian Moore is a fine fellow—a literary Irishman, and a student of Joyce—also acquainted with Thomas Wolfe and Dos Passos. It was a good night, and we sang lots of Irish songs' (Vachon, 45). Two articles by Moore on Polish tension in the face of incipient Stalinism were smuggled out in the British diplomatic bag and published in Dublin. After this he worked as a freelance journalist in Scandinavia and France.

By late 1947 Moore was back in Belfast and London with a quasi-Beckettian sense that life in parochial Ireland was not bearable and would not change. The following year he followed his lover to Canada, but in vain. He found work as a dam construction camp clerk at Thessalon, Ontario. Later he became a proof-reader (at C\$27 a week), and then a notably efficient reporter and feature writer, for the *Montreal Gazette*. Some of Moore's early fiction appeared in the *Weekend Magazine* (Montreal). He became friendly with one of its staff writers, Jacqueline Sirois, *née* Scully (1921–1976), of Irish–French descent, and on 25 February 1951 they were married. He was uxorious, and for some years the couple were very close. By 1953 he had become a Canadian citizen, and in November 1953 they had a son, Michael, Moore's only child.

Under the pseudonyms Bernard Mara and Michael Bryan, Brian Moore wrote several hard-boiled thrillers, including *French for Murder* (1954). Mordecai Richler became a long-standing friend, one of a growing number. Moore's first serious work of fiction, written in a cabin in the Laurentides mountains of Quebec, was *Judith Hearne* (1955)—also known as *The Lonely Passion of Judith Hearne*—a study in psychological isolation. Its (eventual) first publication in London by André Deutsch met with great and continuing acclaim and helped both his reputation and his income, except in the Irish Republic, where the novel was formally banned.

As a natural exile, Moore was by 1959 living in the United States, at Amagansett, Long Island, where he wrote *The Luck of Ginger Coffey* (1960) on a Guggenheim fellowship. The problematic meaning of metropolitan success was anatomized in *An Answer from Limbo* (1962), written in Greenwich Village. After extended stays in London, Italy, and Canada, Moore was back in New York City in 1963. Among the Moores' newer friends were Franklin Russell, a Canadian nature-writer five years younger than Moore, and his wife Jean, formerly Denney (*b. c.*1930), an actress with the stage name Jean Lewis. A plan to share a property in rural New Jersey foundered in June 1964 when the *partie carrée* reconstituted itself adulterously and then matrimonially. The split divided the Moores' friends and caused him to be estranged from a number of them, and from his son and his unhappy wife. She resisted divorce but eventually consented, and later married Russell.

A timely invitation to work with Alfred Hitchcock brought Moore and his future second wife to Hollywood in early 1965. (The result was the cold war thriller *Torn Curtain*, one of a number of screenplays by Moore, which were to include his own *Black Robe*, directed by Bruce Beresford, and an adaptation of Simone de Beauvoir's *Le sang des autres* for Claude Chabrol.) His next novel, *The Emperor of Ice Cream* (1965), confronted the pressures of his arid upbringing and was hopefully dedicated 'to Jean'. By 1966 the couple had a remote house on the Pacific Coast Highway at Malibu, California. Moore said of these years that he was much happier than in his late thirties, a period when he was suffering from ulcers and in which he wrote his dark, Dostoevskyan sketch 'Preliminary pages for a work of revenge'. He and Jean were married in October 1967 at New York City Hall. Moore continued to be based mainly in the United States, but was happy to be known as a Canadian writer.

With some exceptions Moore was only rarely an autobiographical novelist. He became noted for not writing the same novel twice. Periods, locations, themes, and treatments were unpredictable, though not his skill in driving the narrative. Like Graham Greene and Anthony Burgess, he could harness popular genres (such as the political thriller) for his own ends, though he pointed out that subverting readers' expectations was not a recipe for bestsellers, rather the reverse. 'I live as I choose, and I wrote about various items and places', he said (*Irish Times*, 12 Jan 1999). Some of his work, such as *Fergus* (1970) and *Cold Heaven* (1983), treated elements of the supernatural or 'the Godgame'. Moore had an abiding interest in the forces that act on people's self-awareness, a perspective that made humble characters no less important than grander ones. 'A good writer must feel sympathetic with the least of his characters', he said (Dahlie, 10). A connoisseur of human foibles and also a natural gossip, he often focused on the point in a person's life at which what has sustained them is removed, and reassessment is necessary. There is often a quasi-religious dimension to such a crisis: 'I am not a believer, but I am fascinated by belief. Not just belief in God, but belief in something. A hope that one's life will have some meaning, some fulfilment' (Sullivan, 3). Bearing this out, Moore's 1968 novel *I am Mary Dunne* (working title 'A woman of no identity') is a monologue about masks. Moore writes as the female narrator, Mary Dunne, who is on the edge of a breakdown, juggling and reliving her multiple identities. Harassment and confusion are her lot, and she reacts against the objectification of women. In this way, the novel was a deft anticipation of the feminist concern of the 1970s, known generally as 'the male gaze'. His writings won him many awards and honours, including a doctorate from Queen's, his father's old university.

Nineteen novels, a number of other books, eight screenplays, and other writings make up his literary output. Among the teaching posts he held were regents' professor at the Los Angeles campus of the University of California, writer-in-residence at the University of Toronto, and visiting fellow at the University of Stirling. He was also a fellow of the Royal Society of Literature.

As a former journalist, Moore recognized the advantages of discreet publicity. He gave interviews and tended to co-operate, albeit on his own terms, with projects affecting him. 'I am not a colourful character', he said in 1967. 'I dislike personal publicity and I have contempt for those writers who become "personalities"' (Dahlie, 8–9). Graham Greene stated that Moore was his favourite living novelist, a label that Moore came to regard as 'a bit of an albatross' (*Irish Times*, 13 Jan 1999). His style of careful simplicity was harder to achieve than it seemed: a number of projects were abandoned. Moore acquired the barbed compliment of being a writer's writer. Among those writers who praised his work were Julian Barnes, Derek Mahon, Joyce Carol Oates, Kingsley Amis, Laurie Lee, and Joan Didion. Others occasionally alleged unevenness.

Moore's businesslike approach to his work showed itself in the careful records that he kept, and in his fondness for good suits. He was disciplined, but also convivial. Socially he was talkative and charming, though he could delight in being provocative, having a 'wicked tongue' like his irreverent mother (Sampson, 17, 71). His editor and friend Diana Athill described him in the mid-1950s as 'instantly likeable: a small, fat, round-headed, sharp-nosed man resembling a robin, [with a] flat Ulster accent' (Athill, 139). The fatness was due to the milk he took for his ulcers and his enthusiasm for his wife's cooking. In later life he became much slimmer, and sounded more North American. Despite his sociability he also guarded his privacy, especially in his markedly happy second marriage.

In his later years Moore and his wife built a house near Lunenburg, Nova Scotia, where he liked to spend his summers by a tree-lined bay. He died at his main home in Malibu late on Sunday 10 January 1999 of pulmonary fibrosis, a lung clot caused by emphysema. His last (unfinished) project was a novel about Arthur Rimbaud. Of himself Moore said, 'I am the sort of person who passionately wishes to have one reader a hundred years from now rather than hundreds of readers now' (Sale, 78).

BERNARD McGINLEY

Sources D. Sampson, *Brian Moore: the chameleon novelist* (1998) · H. Dahlie, *Brian Moore* (1969) · D. Athill, *Stet: an editor's life* (2001) · A. Vachon, ed., *Poland 1946: the photographs and letters of John Vachon* (1995) · M. Chevrefils, J. F. Tener, and A. Steele, eds., *The Brian Moore papers, first accession and second accession: an inventory of the archive at the University of Calgary Libraries* (Calgary, 1987) · B. Moore, 'Bloody Ulster: an Irishman's lament', *Atlantic Monthly* (Sept 1970) · J. Chapman and others, eds., *Contemporary Literary Criticism*, 90 (1996) · N. Mulholland, 'Brian Moore, 1921–1999: cool prose craftsman', *Socialism Today*, 36 (March 1999) · R. Fulford, 'Brian Moore', *Globe and Mail* [Toronto] (12 Jan 1999) · R. Sullivan, *A matter of faith: the fiction of Brian Moore* (1996) · *Irish Times* (12 Jan 1999); (13 Jan 1999) · *New York Times* (12 Jan 1999) · R. B. Sale, 'An interview in London with Brian Moore', *Studies in the Novel*, 1/1 (spring 1969), 67–80 · P. Craig, *Brian Moore: a biography* (2002)

Archives Ransom HRC, papers · University of Calgary Library, Alberta, archive | FILM 'A view from across the water', *Writers and Places* series, BBC documentary, (4 March 1980) · Canadian quasi-documentary: *The lonely passion of Brian Moore* (1986)—made by Alan Handel · *South Bank Show* (London): apparently treated Moore in late 1981 | SOUND BL NSA [12 recordings]
Likenesses J. Vachon, photograph, 1946, repro. in Vachon, ed., *Poland* · photographs, repro. in Chevrefils, ed., *Brian Moore papers*

Moore, Charles, second Viscount Moore of Drogheda (1603–1643), soldier, was the third and eldest surviving son of Garret *Moore, Baron Moore of Mellifont and first Viscount Moore of Drogheda (1565/6–1627), and his wife, Mary (d. 1654), daughter of Sir Henry Colley of Carbery Castle, co. Kildare. He was knighted by the lord deputy of Ireland, Viscount Falkland, in 1623. At some time before 21 June 1626 he married Alice Loftus (d. 1649), younger daughter of Adam *Loftus, first Viscount Loftus of Ely, lord chancellor of Ireland. Moore and his wife had nine children. Moore succeeded his father as second viscount in 1627, and in January 1628 was made a member of the Irish privy council, supposedly one of a smattering of Old English noblemen admitted to sit in this somewhat bloated assembly of the New English protestant ascendancy in Ireland. However, it is clear that he became an active member of the council when his father-in-law's faction came to prominence after the arrival of Lord Deputy Thomas Wentworth in 1633.

Moore was present at the opening of parliament on 14 July 1634, and was a member of the lords' committee of grievances. During an outbreak of smallpox at Dublin in 1636 both he and his wife were reported to have been 'in a dreadful state' (*CSP Ire.*, 1625–32, 126). In 1638 Moore's niece, Lettice, daughter and heir of his deceased elder brother, Sir Edward, petitioned the king to complain that Moore had detained from her certain lands to which she was entitled. The case was referred to Wentworth, who upheld Lettice Moore's claims in 1640, and gave opinion that the viscount should pay her £1062 10s. in satisfaction.

At the outbreak of the uprising of October 1641 Moore threw himself immediately and energetically into the defence of Drogheda, which he secured until the arrival of Sir Henry Tichborne on 4 November with 1000 foot and 100 horse. Tichborne's arrival relieved Moore of further responsibility, but did not cause him to relax his exertions to place the town in a defensive posture; and fearing that the force at the governor's disposal would be insufficient to resist attack, he took advantage of the reassembling of parliament on 16 November to make a fresh appeal to the government. His offer to raise 600 men at his own expense on condition that the four independent companies in Drogheda were embodied in one regiment and placed under his command for the defence of the county, though approved by the earl of Ormond, was not accepted by the lords justices. But by an ordinance of the two houses he was appointed a commissioner 'to confer with the rebels in Ulster and other parts, touching the causes of their taking arms' (*DNB*).

The Irish, influenced no doubt by the well-known friendship that existed between the earl of Tyrone and

Moore's father and grandfather, made several ineffectual efforts to win him over to their side. On 21 November Mellifont was attacked, and, after a short but brave defence, captured and looted. Towards the end of the month Drogheda was invested on all sides. The siege lasted several months. Putting himself at great personal danger, Moore led a sally on 5 March which shifted the rebels from their possession of the north side of the town, and a few days later, they withdrew altogether in the face of Ormond's advance. Although the earl was ordered by the lords justices not to pursue the rebels, Moore and Tichborne resolved to do so, recapturing Dundalk in the process. Tichborne remained there, while Moore returned to Drogheda, where he assumed responsibility for the town's defence once again.

During the summer Moore was active in the suppression of the rebellion in co. Meath, for which services he received the king's personal thanks in a letter written on 11 May at York. He attacked a troop concentration on 25 April in the neighbourhood of Navan, and in August he captured the castle of Siddan. That summer, evidently to the dislike of the lords justices, Moore was appointed governor of co. Louth and the barony of Slane by the king's letters patent, dated 30 June and 20 August. He was subsequently entrusted, on 11 January 1643, with a commission to meet with the leaders of the confederate Catholics, and to receive their remonstrance, the first step in a train of events which issued in the agreement of a cessation of arms the following September. However, Moore did not live to see this development, neither is it entirely clear that he would have welcomed it.

In the month when the cessation was finally agreed Moore had advanced against Owen Roe O'Neill, leader of the revolt in Ulster. In an engagement at Portlester, on the Blackwater, in co. Meath, on either 7 August or 11 September 1643 he was knocked off his horse and killed by a cannon ball, fired, it was said, by O'Neill himself. His corpse was taken to Mellifont, and subsequently interred in St Peter's Church, Drogheda. Shortly afterwards his wife, appalled that the king's representatives in Ireland were negotiating a truce with the Catholic rebels, was involved in a plot to betray that town into the hands of the Scots commander in Ulster, Robert Monro. She and several accomplices were imprisoned in Dublin Castle, and it is clear from her deposition that she feared the consequences of a cessation because her husband had been so stout in his opposition to the rebels. Lord and Lady Moore's eldest son, Henry, succeeded to the viscountcy, as well as his father's military and civil offices, and was created earl of Drogheda in 1661.   SEAN KELSEY

Sources DNB · CSP Ire., 1625–47

Moore, Charles, first marquess of Drogheda (1730–1822), army officer and politician, born on 29 June 1730, was the eldest son of Edward Moore, fifth earl of Drogheda (1701–1758), and his first wife, Sarah (bap. 1711, d. 1736), fourth daughter of Brabazon Ponsonby, first earl of Bessborough. Styled Viscount Moore from 1752 to 1758, he entered the army in 1744, carried the colours at the battle of Culloden

(16 April 1746), and in January 1755 was promoted brevet lieutenant-colonel. He was MP for St Canice (Irishtown) in the Irish parliament in 1756–8, and was grand master of freemasons in Ireland from 1758 to 1760. Following his father's death (28 October 1758) by drowning on a voyage from England to Dublin, he succeeded as sixth earl of Drogheda, taking his seat in the Irish House of Lords on 16 October 1759. On 12 January 1759 he was made governor of co. Meath, and on 7 December he was appointed lieutenant-colonel commandant of the 19th, afterwards the 18th light dragoons, of which he was colonel from 3 August 1762 until its disbandment in September 1821. On 29 August 1760 he became a member of the Irish privy council. He was very active during 1762–4 in repressing the activities of the Whiteboys, a southern Irish agrarian insurgent movement of labourers, cottiers, and small farmers against enclosures, tithes, and other grievances. He succeeded William Gerard Hamilton (known as Single-Speech Hamilton) as secretary to the lord lieutenant on the appointment of Hugh Percy, second earl of Northumberland, as viceroy in 1763, and in April 1766, during the absence of Francis Seymour-Conway, first marquess of Hertford, he was appointed a lord justice. He married on 15 February 1766 Anne Seymour-Conway (b. 1744), daughter of the marquess of Hertford, and with her, had ten children; she died on 4 November 1784.

His ambition was to become an Irish marquess. In general Moore was a consistent supporter of government, but in 1769, during the viceroyalty of George, fourth Viscount Townshend, disappointed in his expectation of a marquessate, he placed his parliamentary influence on to the side of the opposition. He was, nevertheless, that year made governor and custos rotulorum of Queen's county. He was promoted major-general on 30 August 1770, lieutenant-general on 29 August 1777, general on 12 October 1793, and field marshal on 19 July 1821, but apparently never saw active service. He was master-general of the ordnance (Ireland), and concurrently colonel-in-chief of the Royal Irish regiment of artillery, from 1770 to 1797: Ireland then had a separate military establishment. Henry Ingram, seventh Viscount Irwin, owned the majority of the burgages in the burgage borough of Horsham, Sussex, and controlled both seats. He placed them at the disposal of the government, and Drogheda was an MP for Horsham from October 1776 to July 1780, after which he did not again stand. From 1776 to 1779 he was apparently mostly abroad and no votes of his were reported, but in March 1780 he voted with the administration on economical reform and on abolition of the Board of Trade. By 1790 he also controlled the Irish parliamentary borough of Ballynakill. He was created a knight of the Order of St Patrick on 17 March 1783, one of the fifteen original knights, and on 5 July 1791 he was created marquess of Drogheda. He was joint postmaster-general (Ireland) from 1797 to 1806, and, in reward for his support in parliament for the union, on 17 January 1801 he was created Baron Moore of Moore Place in Kent in the United Kingdom peerage. This was reluctantly conceded to him by the duke of Portland,

and only to facilitate Marquess Cornwallis's arrangements for the representative peers. 'He is,' wrote Cornwallis to Major Ross on 3 July 1800, 'perfectly insignificant in respect to weight and interest in the country, and I only recommended him as being the oldest marquis in order to assist me in providing room for friends in the representative peerage' (*Correspondence of … Cornwallis*, 3.269). Moore was muster-master-general (Ireland) from May to November 1807. He was a heavy gambler, and in 1763 was reported to have broken the bank at Spa. In November 1784 Horace Walpole wrote that he was 'ruining his health through drink and play' (Drummond, 160). In his later years, heavily in debt, he was 'subjected to great pecuniary embarrassments' (GEC, *Peerage*, 4.466). He died in Sackville Street, Dublin on 22 December 1822, and was buried with great pomp on 3 January 1823 in St Peter's Church, Drogheda, where he had been the oldest freeman of the city.

Drogheda's children were Edward, seventh earl and second marquess, who was born on 23 August 1770, was insane for his last forty-five years, and died unmarried on 6 February 1837; Henry Seymour (*d.* 1825), who married on 28 September 1824 Mary Letitia, second daughter of Sir Henry Brooke *Parnell, afterwards first Baron Congleton; Isabella (*d.* 1787); Elizabeth Emily, who married George Frederick Nugent, seventh earl of Westmeath; Mary (*d.* 1842), who married Alexander Stewart of Ards, brother of Robert, first marquess of Londonderry; Gertrude; Alice (*d.* 1789); Anne (*d.* 1788); and Frances, who married in 1800 John Ormsby Vandeleur and died on 28 November 1828.

ROBERT DUNLOP, rev. ROGER T. STEARN

Sources *Correspondence of Charles, first Marquis Cornwallis*, ed. C. Ross, 3 vols. (1859) · J. A. Froude, *The English in Ireland in the eighteenth century*, 3 vols. (1872–4) · W. E. H. Lecky, *A history of England in the eighteenth century*, new edn, 7 vols. (1892) · *The manuscripts and correspondence of James, first earl of Charlemont*, 1, HMC, 28 (1891) · M. M. Drummond, 'Moore, Charles', HoP, *Commons, 1754–90* · GM, 1st ser., 93/1 (1823), 83 · GEC, *Peerage* · Burke, *Peerage* (1967) · J. Philippart, ed., *The royal military calendar*, 3rd edn, 1 (1820), 280 · J. J. Crooks, *History of the royal Irish regiment of artillery* (1914) · R. B. McDowell, *Ireland in the age of imperialism and revolution, 1760–1801* (1979) · T. W. Moody and others, eds., *A new history of Ireland*, 4: *Eighteenth-century Ireland, 1691–1800* (1986) · R. F. Foster, *Modern Ireland, 1600–1972* (1989) · T. Bartlett and K. Jeffery, *A military history of Ireland* (1996)
Likenesses J. Reynolds, oils, 1761, NG Ire. · J. K. Sherwin, group portrait, line engraving, pubd 1803 (*The installation banquet of the knights of St Patrick in the Great Hall, Dublin, 1783*), NG Ire. · R. B. Parkes, mezzotint, pubd 1865 (after J. Reynolds), NG Ire. · R. B. Parkes, mezzotint (after J. Reynolds), BM, NPG

Moore, Charles (1815–1881), geologist, was born at Ilminster, Somerset, on 8 June 1815, the second son in the family of three sons and three daughters of John Moore (1768–1844), bookseller and printer, and his wife, Anna (*née* Eames). He was educated at the commercial school in Ilminster, and at the free grammar school for one year from 1827. He then worked with both his father and his uncle (a bookseller and printer in Castle Cary). About 1837 he joined a Mr Meyler, a bookseller in Abbey Churchyard, Bath, but following the death of his father in 1844 he returned to Ilminster to help his eldest sister run the family business. In 1853 Moore moved back to Bath and on 14 January 1854 he married Eliza Maria Deare (1813/14–1894), only daughter of James Deare of Widcombe, Bath. The marriage enabled him to retire from business, live in Bath, and devote himself to geology. He became active in the Unitarian community, and was elected a councillor for Lyncombe and Widcombe in 1868 and an alderman in 1874.

As a schoolboy Moore had found fossil fish and ammonites in the rocks around Ilminster and from this grew a fascination with geology and with fossil collecting. In the succeeding two decades he discovered and excavated a series of large Jurassic reptiles (ichthyosaurs, plesiosaurs, and crocodiles). When he settled in Bath he made the acquaintance of many local geologists and explored intensively the strata within a 25 mile radius, collecting thousands of fossils and recording in detail the geological succession. Despite his total lack of formal training, his knowledge of geology was said to equal or exceed that of professionals. He had a highly original mind and this he combined with unbounded enthusiasm and the eye of a born collector. His careful examination of strata enabled him to recognize the existence of the Rhaetian stage in Britain for the first time, a discovery grudgingly acknowledged by the professionals.

Moore collected sands from Dundry Hill near Bristol, long thought to be barren of fossils. However, by washing and sieving the sands he recovered microfossil brachiopods; it was a highly innovative technique with enormous potential. His greatest contribution was the study of 'mineral veins' in the Carboniferous limestones of the Mendip hills; he washed and sieved these clay-infilled fissures to yield a rich harvest of early Mesozoic fossils. Among thousands of small fish teeth he recovered two dozen teeth of *Microlestes*, one of the earliest known mammals. The Moore principle of searching fissure infillings, physically processing them, and searching residues has become a standard method worldwide for fossil recovery. Moore published more than sixty scientific papers.

An accident in a Mendip cave in 1873 caused severe damage to one lung and afterwards Moore's activities became increasingly limited. He died at his home, 6 Cambridge Place, Widcombe, on 7 December 1881 and was buried in the Lyncombe Unitarian burial-ground a week later. His vast collections were purchased from his widow by public subscription for the Bath Royal Literary and Scientific Institution, where Moore had himself set out the display cases.

ROBERT J. G. SAVAGE

Sources H. H. Winwood, 'Charles Moore F.G.S. and his work, with a list of the fossil types and described specimens in the Bath Museum by Edward Wilson, F.G.S.', *Proceedings of the Bath Natural History and Antiquarian Field Club*, 7 (1892), 232–92 · C. J. T. Copp, M. A. Taylor, and J. C. Thackray, 'Charles Moore (1815–1881): Somerset geologist', *Proceedings of the Somersetshire Archaeological and Natural History Society*, 140 (1996) · F. S. Wallis, 'Charles Moore F.G.S., "the Somerset Geologist"', *Somerset Countryman*, 8/3 (1938) · R. J. Cleevely, *World palaeontological collections* (1983) · R. J. G. Savage, 'Vertebrate fissure faunas with special reference to Bristol Channel mesozoic', *Journal of the Geological Society*, 150 (1993), 1025–34 ·

R. Etheridge, *Quarterly Journal of the Geological Society*, 38 (1882), 51–2 · H. Woodward, *Geological Magazine*, new ser., 2nd decade, 9 (1882), 94–6 · C. J. T. Copp, 'The Charles Moore geological collection', *Newsletter of the Geological Curators' Group*, 1 (1975), 109–16 · H. S. Torrens, 'Note on the date of birth of Charles Moore', *Newsletter of the Geological Curators' Group*, 1 (1978), 483 · m. cert. · d. cert.
Archives GS Lond., scientific corresp. and papers | NHM, corresp. with Sir Richard Owen and William Clift
Likenesses photograph, *c*.1860, repro. in Wallis, 'Charles Moore F.G.S.'
Wealth at death £1591 6s. 11d.: probate, 24 Feb 1882, *CGPLA Eng. & Wales*

Moore [Moir, Muir], **David** (1808–1879), horticulturist and botanist, was born on 23 April 1808 at Dundee, Forfarshire, Scotland, the eldest son of Charles Moir (*b*. 1782), gardener, and Helen Rattray (1784–1832); David's baptismal record has their surname spelled Moir, but by 1830 the family had adopted the spelling Moore, and David also, about 1828, signed his name Muir.

Moore was taught locally; in particular, he learned botany from Douglas Gardiner, conservator of Dundee Rational Institution's museum. To receive horticultural training he was apprenticed to Mr Howe, head gardener of the Camperdown estate near Dundee, and after two years proceeded elsewhere, including James Cunningham's nursery at Comely Bank, Edinburgh. In November 1828 he was appointed foreman in Trinity College Botanic Gardens, Ballsbridge, Dublin, where he was assistant to James Townsend Mackay (1775–1862). Moore was an unsuccessful candidate during 1834 for the post of head gardener in the Botanic Gardens, Glasnevin, Dublin, but in June that year he joined the Irish Ordnance Survey as botanist. Based in Belfast, he explored the flora of north-eastern Ireland, making several discoveries including the narrow small-reed *Calamagrostis stricta*, and the club-sedge *Carex buxbaumii*, both now extinct in the wild. His observations were reported in Thomas Colby's *Memoir of the City … Londonderry, Parish of Templemore* (1835; 2nd edn with illustrations by George Victor du Noyer, 1837).

In October 1838, following Ninian Niven's resignation, Moore was elected curator of the Botanic Gardens, Glasnevin. His position was upgraded to director by the Royal Dublin Society in May 1865, but the Department of Science and Art which financed the gardens withheld sanction until November 1869.

Moore, alerted by reports in a horticultural periodical, observed symptoms of late blight on potatoes growing at the Glasnevin Gardens, on 20 August 1845; this was the first verified record in Ireland of the disease that led to the destruction of the potato crops during 1845, 1846, and 1847, and thereby caused the great famine. Moore observed that this disease also killed other members of the potato family (Solanaceae) growing in the gardens' glasshouses during the winter and spring of 1846, and changed his views about the nature of the blight, to agree with the Revd Miles J. Berkeley that a minute fungus, named *Phythophthora infestans*, was the cause. Very few other scientists at the time agreed with Berkeley and Moore; the predominant opinion attributed the blight to 'atmospheric conditions' or to the 'degeneration' of the

potato from its intensive cultivation in Europe. At Glasnevin, Moore experimented with treatments to prevent the spread of blight, and although he was not successful, his understanding of the fungal nature of the disease made his approach more promising than most contemporary attempts.

Moore supervised two significant horticultural advances at Glasnevin. Orchids were raised from seed to flowering stage between 1845 and 1849. In the early 1870s hybrid pitcher plants, namely *Sarracenia* x *moorei* (named after Moore) and *Sarracenia* x *popei* (named after the gardens' propagator, William Pope), were produced by artificial pollination. As a botanist interested in Ireland's native flora, Moore's most significant contributions were the publications of his latter years, especially on mosses. His collaboration with Alexander Goodman More on *Cybele Hibernica* (1866) and related papers produced the earliest examples of maps showing the distribution of plant species in relation to climatic factors.

Moore received little recognition in his native or adopted countries. His doctorate was awarded (1863) by the University of Zürich. Among plants named after him are a Natal lily, *Crinum moorei*, and a hybrid horsetail, *Equisetum* x *moorei*.

Moore was married three times; on 7 April 1836 to Hannah Bridgford who died of typhus at Glasnevin in December 1840 (they had two daughters); in 1843 to Isabella Morgan who died on 7 November 1847 (they had two children); and on 7 December 1854 to Margaret Baker, who survived her husband and with whom he had five children. Their second child, Frederick William Moore (*b*. 1857), succeeded his father as curator (later upgraded to keeper) of the Botanic Gardens, Dublin. Thus father and son ran the Glasnevin Gardens for eighty-four years (1838 to 1922). Moore died at the Glasnevin Gardens, still in post, on 9 June 1879 following a bladder operation. He was buried at Mount Jerome cemetery, Harold's Cross, Dublin.

E. CHARLES NELSON

Sources E. C. Nelson and E. M. McCracken, *The brightest jewel: a history of the National Botanic Gardens, Glasnevin, Dublin* (1987) · E. C. Nelson, 'David Moore's date of birth — a correction', *Glasra*, 7 (1983), 24 · E. C. Nelson, 'David Moore, Miles J. Berkeley and scientific studies of potato blight in Ireland, 1845–1847', *Archives of Natural History*, 11 (1982–4), 249–61 · E. C. Nelson, *The cause of the calamity: potato blight in Ireland, 1845–1847, and the role of the National Botanic Gardens, Glasnevin* (1995) · E. C. Nelson, 'Irish arts and crafts: the cultivation of orchids in the National Botanic Gardens, Glasnevin, Dublin, 1795–1922', *14th World Orchid Conference* [Glasgow 1993], ed. A. Pridgeon (1994), 342–52
Archives National Botanic Gardens, Glasnevin, Dublin, notes and catalogues | RBG Kew, Hooker MSS
Likenesses photograph, *c*.1865, repro. in Nelson and McCracken, *Brightest jewel*, p. 129 · engraving, repro. in Nelson and McCracken, *Brightest jewel*, p. 139

Moore, (Lilian) Decima (1871–1964), actress, was born on 11 December 1871 at 21 Regency Square, Brighton, one of the family of nine daughters (three of whom died in childhood) and one son of Edward Henry Moore, chemist, and his wife, Emily Strachan. Her sisters Eva (1870–1955) and Jessie (*d*. 1910) were also successful actresses. She was educated at Miss Pringle's school in Brighton, and sang in the church choir; she won a scholarship to Blackheath Conservatory. At seventeen she approached Richard D'Oyly Carte at the Savoy Theatre for a voice trial, and was offered the part of Casilda in the original production of *The Gondoliers*, the last great success of the partnership of W. S. Gilbert and Sir Arthur Sullivan, which opened on 7 December 1889 and ran for eighteen months with 554 performances. She took part in the command performance before Queen Victoria at Windsor Castle on 6 March 1891, the first theatrical entertainment to take place at court since the death of Prince Albert thirty years earlier. After her success as Casilda she appeared in another operetta, *Captain Billy*, at the Savoy Theatre. This opened in June 1891 and when it closed in January 1892 she moved on to take over the title role in the comic opera *Miss Decima* by F. C. Durand at the Criterion Theatre, and acted in *A Pantomime Rehearsal* by Cecil Clay at the Royal Court before heading the cast of *The Wedding Eve*, and starring in the title role in a revival of *Dorothy* by B. C. Stephenson. Returning to the Savoy Theatre in May 1893, she played the schoolgirl Bab in *Jane Annie*, a new comic opera, with a libretto by J. M. Barrie and Arthur Conan Doyle and music by Ernest Ford, which was poorly received and closed after six weeks.

Moore came under the influence of the theatre manager George Edwardes when she created the ingénue role of Rose Brierly in *A Gaiety Girl* by Owen Hall, with music by Sidney Jones, one of the first of the new musical comedies; it opened at the Prince of Wales Theatre on 14 October 1893 and ran for eleven months. She remained in the cast of *A Gaiety Girl* when Edwardes sent the company to New York in September 1894 for a two-month season on Broadway, with Granville Bantock as musical director, before touring the United States, covering eight more American cities in four months. When the company moved on to Australia she starred as Bessie Brent in *The Shop Girl* by H. W. Dam (music by Ivan Caryll and Lionel Monckton) and the Prima Donna of the Ambiguity Theatre in *In Town* by Adrian Ross and J. T. Tanner, when these were added to the repertory.

After returning to England, Moore left Edwardes and pursued a singing career in the theatre for the next ten years, starring in *The White Silk Dress* by A. McLean (1896) at the Prince of Wales Theatre; *Lost, Strayed or Stolen* (1897); Sir Arthur Sullivan's operetta *The Rose of Persia* (1899) at the Savoy Theatre; and the musical comedy *Florodora* (1900–01) by Owen Hall at the Lyric Theatre. She played the Swineherd in the Christmas musical *The Swineherd and the Princess* (1901) at the Royalty Theatre, toured in the 1902 production of *The Gay Cadets*, and took the role of Alice Coverdale in *My Lady Molly* by G. H. Jessop (music by Sidney Jones) (1903), which ran for 341 performances. About 1892 she married Cecil Ainslie Walker-Leigh, but they separated in 1902 and divorced two years later; they had a son.

On 15 August 1905 Moore married Sir (Frederick) Gordon *Guggisberg (1869–1930), son of Frederick Guggisberg, merchant, of Galt, Ontario, Canada. She was his second wife. Guggisberg, an officer in the Royal Engineers, was appointed director of surveys in the Gold Coast in 1905, returning to England in 1908. She accompanied him

to the Gold Coast, and together they published an account of their survey journeys, *We Two in West Africa* (1909). When in England she made occasional appearances in the theatre, but no longer in musicals; she appeared in Ben Jonson's *The Vision of Delight* in 1908, his masque *The Hue and Cry after Cupid* in 1911, and for the last time on the London stage in a matinée performance of *Vantage out* in 1914.

At the outbreak of the First World War Guggisberg rejoined the army, and Decima Moore set up the Women's Emergency Corps, a clearing-house for women's voluntary war work, with its headquarters at the Little Theatre. Thousands of women enrolled, ready to be called on to meet any emergency. She attached herself to the French army in January 1915, and ran the Leave Club in Paris for British soldiers. After the armistice, she was one of the first women to enter Cologne, where she organized a club for the army of occupation, before travelling across the battlefields, from Ypres to Verdun. She was appointed CBE and awarded the overseas medal and the *Médaillon de reconnaissance*.

In 1919 Guggisberg was appointed governor of the Gold Coast and Moore spent the next decade with him there. They then lived briefly in British Guiana, where he was governor from 1928 until his resignation in 1929, when they returned to England. Guggisberg died in 1930, and his widow lived on until her death, aged ninety-three, on 18 February 1964 at 92 Redcliffe Gardens, London.

ANNE PIMLOTT BAKER

Sources K. Gänzl, *The encyclopedia of the musical theatre*, 2 vols. (1994) · E. Moore, *Exits and entrances* (1923) · C. Rollins and R. J. Witts, *The D'Oyly Carte Opera Company in Gilbert and Sullivan operas: a record of productions, 1875–1961* (1962) · J. P. Wearing, *The London stage, 1890–1959* (1976–93) · G. Bantock and F. G. Aflalo, *Round the world with 'A gaiety girl'* (1896) · F. Gaye, ed., *Who's who in the theatre*, 14th edn (1967) · b. cert. · m. cert. [Sir F. G. Guggisberg] · d. cert. · *CGPLA Eng. & Wales* (1964)

Likenesses W. & D. Downey, photographs, repro. in Cellier and Bridgeman, *Gilbert, Sullivan and D'Oyly Carte* (1927), facing p. 278 · M. Talma, photograph, repro. in Bantock and Aflalo, *Round the world*, facing p. 84 · double portrait, photograph (with her husband), repro. in *We two in west Africa* (1909), frontispiece · photograph (as Casilda), repro. in *100 years of D'Oyly Carte and Gilbert and Sullivan* (1975)

Wealth at death £50,041: probate, 8 April 1964, *CGPLA Eng. & Wales*

Moore, Doris Elizabeth Langley (1902–1989), writer on fashion and museum founder, was born on 23 July 1902 in Liverpool, the second daughter in the family of three daughters and one son of Joseph Langley Levy, writer and newspaper editor, and his wife, Mabel Ada Rushden, theatrical designer. The family moved to South Africa when she was eight, and she was educated at convent schools there. In *Pleasure: a Discursive Guide Book* (1953) she described her comfortable and indulged childhood. Although she had no formal education, she read widely, under the guidance of her father.

Moore moved to London in the early 1920s, and her first book, *Anacreon: 29 Odes* (1926), was a verse translation from the Greek. This was followed by *The Technique of the Love Affair* (1928) by 'a Gentlewoman', a manual of advice to a woman on how to catch a husband. *Pandora's Letter Box, being a Discourse on Fashionable Life* (1929) was written for her two-year-old daughter. She wrote six romantic novels between 1932 and 1959, and several books on household management, including *The Bride's Book* (1932, revised in 1936 as *Our Loving Duty*). Her biography of Edith Nesbit (1933; revised, 1967) drew on extensive conversations with members of the novelist's family and family letters, transcripts of which were invaluable for later biographers.

Moore was passionately interested in clothes, and dressed in the height of fashion each season. She loved hats, and early in life decided that, when depressed, one should go out and buy a hat. Her own clothes formed the basis of a collection of costumes, to which she added historical costumes, discovered in salerooms, country house auctions, and attics. She admitted to a certain amount of bargaining, plotting, and machination in obtaining such items. Her most exciting acquisition was the Albanian costume bought by Lord Byron on his grand tour of 1809, which he wore for the portrait painted by Thomas Phillips in 1814. She was one of the first to study the history of fashion seriously, and all her life she wrote and lectured on it, organized exhibitions, and produced television programmes. In 1949 she brought out *The Woman in Fashion*, a history of fashion in which some of the most famous beauties of the day, most of them personal friends, were photographed wearing costumes from her collection. In 1955 followed *The Child in Fashion*.

Moore campaigned for many years for a museum of costume to be founded in London, persuading Christian Dior to bring his collection over from Paris in order to raise money for the project. The museum was opened in 1955, housed temporarily in Eridge Castle, near Tunbridge Wells, Kent, and then in the Brighton Pavilion. It moved permanently to the rebuilt assembly rooms in Bath in 1963.

Moore was anxious to keep the museum up to date, and created a modern room for clothes from 1907 to the current year. Each year new specimens were added, chosen as representative of current fashion, and a different fashion expert was asked to choose one outfit as 'dress of the year'. The dress for 1963 was designed by Mary Quant, and the 1967 'dress' was a trouser suit. Moore retired as adviser to the museum in 1974, and left her collection to the city of Bath.

Moore's interest in costume extended to the stage and to films, but the décor for her ballet *The Quest*, first performed at Sadler's Wells in 1943, was done by John Piper. The scenario was adapted by her from Edmund Spenser's *The Faerie Queene*, showing the victory of St George over the forces of evil. William Walton wrote the score especially for the ballet, Frederick Ashton was the choreographer, and the soloists were Margot Fonteyn, Robert Helpmann, Beryl Grey, and Moira Shearer in her first role. Moore also worked as a costume designer for the theatre and films, and designed Katharine Hepburn's dresses for *The African Queen* (1951).

Doris Langley Moore first came across Byron when she was fifteen, when her father gave her a copy of *Don Juan*. She remained devoted to him all her life. 'I was perhaps the only woman to whom nothing but pleasure has come from loving that poet.' In 1924, the centenary of Byron's death, she was invited to join the commemoration committee, and in 1931 she accompanied the Greek prime minister on a visit to Byron's tomb. She was present when his tomb in Hucknall church was opened in 1938 to see if he really was buried there. She became a founding vice-president of the Byron Society in 1971. She was the first person, apart from Byron's family, to be allowed access to the large collection of uncatalogued Wentworth and Lovelace papers in the possession of Lady Wentworth, Byron's great-granddaughter. Her last novel, *My Caravaggio Style* (1959), about the forgery of the lost Byron memoirs, was written while she was immersed in these papers.

The first of her three scholarly works on Byron, *The Late Lord Byron*, appeared in 1961. *Lord Byron, Accounts Rendered* (1974) won the British Academy's Rose Mary Crawshay prize in 1975. Based on Byron's accounts, found among the papers of his Italian secretary, this book examines Byron's finances as a means of gaining insight into his domestic life. *Ada, Countess of Lovelace* (1977) is a biography of Byron's daughter. The publication of these works had enormous influence on the subsequent course of Byron studies. Doris Langley Moore was appointed OBE in 1971.

Moore was an attractive woman, with a high forehead and a handsome profile. She moved in fashionable London circles, but she was a difficult person, and some of her friendships ended in bitterness. In 1926 she married Robert Sugden Moore, wool merchant, the son of Fred Denby Moore, also a wool merchant. They had one daughter, Pandora. They were divorced in 1942. She died in the Middlesex Hospital, London, on 24 February 1989.

ANNE PIMLOTT BAKER, rev.

Sources *The Independent* (28 Feb 1989) · *The Guardian* (2 March 1989) · D. L. Moore, *The Museum of Costume: guide to the exhibition and commentary on the trends of fashion* (1967) · D. Moore, *Pleasure: a discursive guide book* (1953) · *CGPLA Eng. & Wales* (1989)
Likenesses F. Fonteyn, photograph, c.1948, Hult. Arch. · photograph (in later life), repro. in *The Guardian*
Wealth at death £69,856: probate, 11 April 1989, *CGPLA Eng. & Wales*

Moore [née Feilding], **Lady Dorothy Mary Evelyn** (1889–1935), ambulance driver, was born at Newnham Paddox, Warwickshire, on 6 October 1889, the second daughter of Rudolph Robert Basil Aloysius Augustine Feilding, ninth earl of Denbigh (1859–1939), a colonel in the Territorial Army, and his wife, Cecilia Mary Clifford (1860–1919). She was educated at home and at Assumption Convent, in Paris. She had six sisters, of whom Clare, Bettie, and Victoria also served in the First World War, and three brothers, Major Rudolph, Viscount Feilding, Coldstream Guards, who survived the war; Lieutenant-Commander the Hon. Hugh Feilding, Royal Navy, killed in action on 31 May 1916 at the battle of Jutland; and Captain the Hon. Henry Feilding, Coldstream Guards, who died on 9 October 1917 from wounds received in action in Flanders.

Lady Dorothy, who was a tall brunette, had a deep sense of patriotism and was determined to 'do something' in the war (Foster and Cluley, 1). At the earliest opportunity, in August 1914, she joined the Munro British Red Cross Motor Ambulance Corps (founded by Dr Hector Munro) and, after a short training course at Rugby Hospital, went to the front as an ambulance driver the following month. She served with the corps in Flanders until June 1917. This corps, comprising a convoy of motor ambulances, was officially attached to the allied armies; its work consisted of bringing wounded men from the firing lines to the casualty clearing hospitals.

Lady Dorothy's devotion to duty and her bravery were recognized at an early stage in the war. Admiral Ronarc'h, who commanded the French brigade of *fusiliers marins* in Flanders, published a special order of the day on 31 December 1914, thanking her for her work in removing wounded men in the neighbourhood of Ghent and Dix-mude, 'showing, almost every day, the finest example of devotion and of disregard for danger' (Leslie, 7). A letter from the admiral accompanied this order, saying that all the men under his command would ever bear in remem-brance '*la gracieuse ambulancière*' who had so often risked her life in their relief.

Throughout her stay in Flanders Lady Dorothy wrote let-ters home, and some 250 of these survive. Most were addressed to her mother, with the exception of a few to her father. They were often written in a hurried scrawl but had an intimate and conversational style. Many aspects of her daily life were included in her writing. She gave eye-witness accounts of air raids and shelling, and descrip-tions of the perilous work of collecting casualties and driving them to hospital, often under fire. She told stories about her pet terrier, Charles, made rude remarks about the military censors, and commented on the beauty of the wild poppies and cornflowers that she saw growing near the battlefields. Her letters display her resilience and cheerfulness.

After the fall of Antwerp, Ghent had to be evacuated, and Lady Dorothy wrote angrily from Dunkirk, where all was chaos: 'I have had to run the whole dam [*sic*] show' (Foster and Cluley, 2). She describes Dr Munro as 'losing his silly head and running round in circles'. Her chance encounter with an acquaintance, who was a relative of Baron de Broqueville, the Belgian war minister, changed the fortunes of the Munro ambulance corps and saved it from being sent back to England. The baron arranged for the setting up at Furnes of a field hospital that was to be fed by the Munro corps. Lady Dorothy was delighted at the outcome: 'Ripping and I'm so glad we have a job' (ibid.).

In one of her letters she admits how greatly affected she was by the scenes she witnessed: 'It just despairs one and makes one rage when you see this endless stream of shat-tered humanity, and see the ghastly work a shell can make of their poor bodies'. Although she was a devout Roman Catholic her faith in an afterlife was destroyed by these experiences: 'I think that there is an endless blank that begins after death and that all things finish there. I try to believe that there is a future, but I can't any more' (Foster and Cluley, 6).

In September 1916 Lady Dorothy became the first Eng-lishwoman to be awarded the Military Medal for bravery in the field. The award was notified in the *London Gazette* of 1 September 1916; she was decorated with the medal by George V at Windsor Castle on 6 September. She also received the bronze star in 1914, the French Croix de Guerre (bronze star), and was made a knight of the Belgian order of Leopold II.

Early in 1917 Lady Dorothy complained about the mud, the cold, and the gas attacks. 'It's a dirty business gas and rather frightening—comes in great foggy waves and makes you cough your head off' (Foster and Cluley, 7). She left the front in June 1917 and, on 5 July, married Captain Charles Moore MC (1880–1965), of the Irish Guards, from Mooresfort, co. Tipperary, at the church of the Sacred Heart, Newnham Paddox. In one of her last letters to her mother she expressed her thoughts about the previous three years: 'Here right at the heart and pulse of things one finds realities and greatness' (ibid.).

After the war Lady Dorothy and her husband, who had succeeded his father as second count of Rome, went to live at Mooresfort, where they ran the estate. They had four daughters and one son. Lady Dorothy died at Mooresfort on 24 October 1935.   ROY TERRY

Sources R. Foster and C. Cluley, *Warwickshire women: a guide to sources in the Warwickshire County Record Office* (2000) · Warks. CRO, Feilding papers · J. H. Leslie, ed., *An historical roll (with portraits) of those women of the British empire to whom the military medal has been awarded during the great war, 1914–18*, pt 1 (Jan 1919) · b. cert. · m. cert. · *Debrett's Peerage*
Archives Warks. CRO, Feilding collection
Likenesses photographs, Warks. CRO, Feilding family photo-graph albums

Moore, Dugald (1805–1841), poet, was born in Stockwell Street, Glasgow, on 12 August 1805, the son of a private sol-dier. After receiving some rudimentary education from his mother, who had been left almost destitute by the death of her husband, he was apprenticed to a tobacco manufacturer. He later entered the copper-printing branch of Messrs James Lumsden & Sons, booksellers, of Glasgow. He had been writing verse for some time, and Lumsden helped him to secure subscribers for his first vol-ume, *The African, a Tale, and other Poems* (1829). Over the next ten years Moore was remarkably prolific. He published four more volumes of verse, including *The Bridal Night and other Poems* (1831), and *The bard of the north, a series of poetical tales, illustrative of highland scenery and character* (1833). He also published dramatic works, including *The Hour of Retri-bution and other Poems* (1835). He was felt by contemporaries to have had a genuine gift for lyrical expression; John Wil-son (Christopher North) considered his *Bard of the north* especially powerful.

On the strength of profits accruing from his publica-tions, in 1832 Moore started a successful business in Glas-gow as a bookseller. He died unmarried, after a short ill-ness, in Glasgow on 2 January 1841, leaving a competence to his mother, with whom he had lived all his life. His burial-place in the Glasgow necropolis was marked by a stately monument.   T. W. BAYNE, *rev.* JAMES HOW

Sources Anderson, *Scot. nat.* · R. Inglis, *The dramatic writers of Scot-land* (1868) · Allibone, *Dict.* · C. Rogers, *The modern Scottish minstrel, or, The songs of Scotland of the past half-century*, 6 vols. (1855–7) · Ward,

Men of the reign • Irving, *Scots.* • J. G. Wilson, ed., *The poets and poetry of Scotland*, 2 vols. in 4 (1876–7)

Moore, Sir Edward (*c.*1530–1602), administrator, was the second son of John Moore of Benenden in Kent, and Margaret, daughter and heir of John Brent, and widow of John Dering of Surrenden in Pluckley. He was a kinsman of Sir Henry Sidney who also described him as 'the earl of Warwick's man' (H. Sydney, P. Sydney, and others, 1. 282), but the exact relationship is unclear. Moore arrived in Ireland about the beginning of Queen Elizabeth's reign, probably in Sidney's entourage, with his three brothers: Owen, the eldest, who became clerk of the check, and died in 1585; George, who was killed at Glenmalure in August 1580; and Thomas, the youngest, afterwards Sir Thomas of Croghan in the Offaly, who was ancestor of the earls of Charleville, and died in December 1598. By May 1564 Edward Moore was being referred to as 'of Mellifont', from which it would appear that he had already obtained a lease of the dissolved abbey of Mellifont, co. Louth. Besides being one of the richest of the monasteries of the northern pale, Mellifont was a post of considerable strategic importance for the policing of the Gaelic districts of southern Ulster. Even before he became a government official Moore frequently furnished information to the government on the movements of the Irish in the north, and on more than one occasion he assisted the marshal of the army, Sir Nicholas Bagenal, in his campaigns against those perceived to be obstructive to English expansion into the region. He supported the unsuccessful colonization scheme of Walter Devereux, first earl of Essex, in the north of the province in 1573–5. Warmly commended by the lord deputy, Sir William Fitzwilliam, his services were recognized by leases of lands and properties in the neighbourhood of Mellifont, including those of the former hospital of Ardee, co. Louth.

Firmly established as a leading landowner in Louth, of which county he became sheriff in 1571, Moore had already extended his influence by a prudent alliance with the Brabazon family. He married Elizabeth (*d.* 1581), daughter and coheir of Nicholas Clifford of Chart in Kent, who had been widowed three times, her previous husbands being Christopher Blunt, Humphrey Warren, and Sir William Brabazon, sometime vice-treasurer of Ireland. They had at least four children, including Garret *Moore (*d.* 1627), his heir. A marriage between another son, Henry, and Mary, daughter of Francis Agard, one of the most prominent government servitors of Elizabethan Ireland, reflected the Moores' growing ascendancy among the newly settled English. In May 1574 he was appointed governor of King's county in place of Henry Colley, and immediately entered on his charge, campaigning vigorously against the O'Connors. He was absent in England during the greater part of 1575, but on 24 May 1576 he obtained a grant during pleasure of the office of constable of Philipstown, King's county. Among the many commissions that he held during his tenure for a quarter of a century were those for concealed lands in 1576, for ecclesiastical causes in May 1577, and for the peace in Ulster,

Leinster, and Connaught. He was rewarded with a knighthood in 1579, and in the same year he obtained additional leases of lands in the counties of Louth, Meath, Kildare, and Queen's county. He also acquired the goods of Nicholas Nugent, sometime chief justice of the common pleas, who had been executed for treason in 1582. By 1580 his friendship with Hugh O'Neill, baron of Dungannon, was being officially acknowledged by government approval of their co-operation in the preservation of the pale from the depredations of Turlough Luineach O'Neill and others. O'Neill's bond with Moore was consolidated by the latter's role as stepfather to Henry and William Warren, to whom the Ulster lord was very close. Even after the death of his first wife, their mother, and his subsequent marriage in 1589 to Dorothy Wentworth (*née* Southwell), Moore retained his ties with his Warren stepsons.

Moore's serviceability in the administrative reforms planned for southern Ulster led him to play a more important role in civic and diplomatic affairs in the region from the mid-1580s. Apart from the period from 1587 to 1589, during which he sojourned in England, probably in connection with an inheritance from his cousin Nicholas, he was engaged in negotiations with political leaders, including Hugh O'Neill, now earl of Tyrone. Lord Deputy Perrot, who employed him to collect payment in kind of the composition levy in Ulster, commended him highly to Sir Francis Walsingham, and in recognition of his service he was created a privy councillor on 28 September 1589.

When Perrot's regime was being investigated in 1590 at the behest of his successor, Sir William Fitzwilliam, Moore sat on a commission that exculpated the former governor of charges of conspiracy. In the subsequent proceedings against Perrot on charges of treason Moore, described by Fitzwilliam as 'grown to be a man of party in his quarters' (*CSP Ire.*, *1588–92*, 322), narrowly escaped a trial in the court of castle chamber for his firm support of the discredited governor.

Moore's 'strong link of amitie' (Morgan, 97) with the increasingly suspect earl of Tyrone did not assist his cause at this juncture; but when he returned to Ireland in September 1594 after the Perrot investigations, he was regarded as a valuable agent in government efforts to prevent O'Neill from taking up arms against the state. Although he was unsuccessful in this respect, he was recognized as having displayed great prudence in his management of the negotiations. He was given responsibility again for treating with O'Neill in 1596 and his meeting with the earl was instrumental in the concluding of a truce that lasted until 1597. Thereafter, contrary to reports of his partiality for the earl's party, Moore was a staunch antagonist of the rebels. His estate at Mellifont was devastated in the intensification of the fighting in the later stages of the war, and he wrote to Robert Cecil in 1601 claiming to have been 'utterly undone' by the depredations of the 'archtraitor' which had cost him £3000 (*CSP Ire.*, *1601–3*, 149). Despite his advanced years, he was still active militarily, retaining his constableship of Philipstown and acting as commissioner of the peace in Leinster in the absences of the earl of Essex in 1599 and Lord

Mountjoy in 1601. On 1 October 1601 his son, Sir Garret, was referred to as his 'successor' in the constableship (ibid., 289). He died early in 1602, and was probably buried in St Peter's Church, Drogheda.   COLM LENNON

Sources *CSP Ire., 1509–1602* · 'Calendar of fiants, Henry VIII to Elizabeth', *Report of the Deputy Keeper of the Public Records in Ireland*, 7–22 (1875–90), appxs · H. Morgan, *Tyrone's rebellion: the outbreak of the Nine Years' War in Tudor Ireland*, Royal Historical Society Studies in History, 67 (1993) · *DNB* · C. Brady, *The chief governors: the rise and fall of reform government in Tudor Ireland, 1536–1588* (1994) · J. S. Brewer and W. Bullen, eds., *Calendar of the Carew manuscripts*, 2: 1575–1588, PRO (1868) · H. Sydney and others, *Letters and memorials of state*, ed. A. Collins, 2 vols. (1746) · J. Lodge, *The peerage of Ireland*, rev. M. Archdall, rev. edn, 7 vols. (1789) · GEC, *Peerage*, 4.462

Moore, Edward (1712–1757), playwright and writer, was born at Abingdon, Berkshire, on 22 March 1712, the third of seven children of Thomas Moore (*d.* 1721), dissenting pastor at Abingdon, and Mary, daughter of Thomas Alder of Drayton in the same county. His grandfather was the Revd John Moore, pastor of the dissenting congregation at Bridgwater, Somerset, where he founded an academy for the 'tuition of youth designed for the ministry' (Caskey, 3). Following his father's death, Moore was raised by his paternal uncle, John, who conducted the Bridgwater seminary. After a strict, classical education, Moore's decision to become apprenticed to a wholesale linen draper in London was no doubt influenced in part by his knowledge of the flax industry, the most important in his native Abingdon. Moore spent some years as a linen factor in Ireland and returned to London to set up business with an Irish partner. The business failed and Moore turned to literature.

Moore's first published work was the libretto to William Boyce's best-known composition, *Solomon: a serenata* (1743), a musical setting of the Song of Solomon. This quasi-dramatic secular and pastoral work, which was premièred in public performances (after private performances under the auspices of the Apollo Academy) at Ruckholt House, Essex, in August and September 1743, and in London at the New Wells in November, relies on Samuel Croxall's *The Fair Circassian* (1720) and the Authorized Version to dramatize the airs and recitatives of the shepherd and shepherdess about the charms and anxieties of love, 'thou soft invader of the soul' (Boyce, xlviii).

Initially published anonymously in May 1744, Moore's *Fables for the Female Sex* had its third edition by 1746 and at least sixteen other editions in the eighteenth century, four of which were American; it was translated into French in 1764 and German in 1772. Influenced by but inferior to John Gay, the sixteen verse fables, three of which were contributed by Henry Brooke, the author of *Gustavus Vasa*, whom Moore had met in Ireland, were 'intended', according to Moore's 'Preface', 'for the reading of those whose only business is amusement'. Moralizing cautions warn women against coquetry, since

> Pity may mourn, but not restore,
> And woman falls, to rise no more
> (120)

and unkemptness:

> from hence proceed aversion, strife,
> And all that sours the wedded life
> (26)

as well as vanity, which

> from six to sixty, sick or sound,
> rule[s] the female world around.
> (152)

Conduct is proscriptively gendered, with 'weaker woman', being assigned 'that soft'ning gentleness of mind' and man, 'with useful arts … inform'd', given

> knowledge, taste, and sense,
> And courage for the fair's defence.
> (48)

Moore's first play, *The Foundling: a Comedy* (1748), was acted at the Theatre Royal, Drury Lane, for eleven nights in February 1748, with David Garrick as Belmont, the rake hero, Charles Macklin as Faddle, the foppish knave, and Mrs Cibber as Fidelia, the virtuous orphan reunited with her true father. The play was performed throughout the eighteenth century and was produced in America for over twelve years, beginning in 1788. It was translated three times: twice into French and once into German. Adapting the situation of Richard Steele's *The Conscious Lovers* and the improbable twists of Terentian and Plautine comedies, *The Foundling* suffers from the implausibility of Belmont, who initially rescues Fidelia from rape and then plots to have her removed from the protection of his father's house so that he can debauch her himself. Calling himself 'a fellow of Principle, some time or other', he adds: 'these Appetites are the Devil—and at present I am under their Direction' (III.v). Although Fidelia's influence makes Belmont 'a Convert to Honour' (v.v), the 'Epilogue' underscores the bitter comic lesson that

> savage Man, the wildest Beast of Prey,
> Assumes the Face of kindness to betray.

Moore's panegyrics and society verse in defence of friends and potential patrons, such as *The Trial of Selim the Persian* (1748) for Lord George Lyttleton, were clearly attempts to secure patronage.

Lacking money and facing a wealthy country squire as his rival, Moore married Jane, daughter of Charles Hamilton of St James's, table decker to the princess, on 17 May 1750, in Grosvenor Chapel in South Audley Street, London. For over half a year their courtship had been the subject of a series of witty poems, full of puns on his name, in the *London Magazine*, some by Moore and others attributed to Miss Hamilton and her friend Miss Duck, daughter of the poet Stephen Duck. The *General Evening Post* (17–19 May 1750) described the bride as 'a Lady of great Beauty and fine Accomplishments' (Caskey, 72). Their only child, Edward, who was educated and pensioned by Lord Chesterfield, entered the naval service and died at sea in 1773.

Although it had a run of nine nights at Drury Lane in a production by Garrick, Moore's second comedy, *Gil Blas* (1751), adapted from Tobias Smollett's translation of Le Sage's romance, from whose popularity Moore wished to profit, was a dismal failure. The *London Magazine* (February

1751) published the opinion of the council at George's Coffee House about this 'unmeaning drama' and 'confounded stuff' in which

> the dialogue is all alike;
> Nor scarce a sentiment to strike
> (Caskey, 74–5)

With an initial run of ten nights at the Drury Lane with Garrick in the lead role, Moore's domestic tragedy *The Gamester* (1753), adapted from Aaron Hill's *The Fatal Extravagance* (1721) and extending the experiment of stage prose of George Lillo's *George Barnwell* (1731), remained popular to the middle of the nineteenth century, enjoying more performances in America than England. Striving to save her weak but good husband, who is pathetically addicted to gambling, Mrs Beverley is the archetypal long-suffering but undervalued wife. As Beverley's moral paralysis increases and the prospect of direct divine intervention disappears, his suicide becomes inevitable. Mrs Beverley's surprise inheritance and the exposure of the 'thousand frauds' and 'false dice' (v.xi) of the villainous Stukley temper the tragedy, as does the closing eulogy of Beverley, whose 'life was lovely, save but one error and the last fatal deed'. With translations and adaptations in French, German, and Italian, *The Gamester* remains in the opinion of his biographer, J. H. Caskey, 'Moore's best work' (Caskey, 134).

Through the influence of Lord Lyttleton, Moore became the editor of a weekly periodical, *The World* (1753–6), under the *nom de plume* of Adam Fitz-Adam. Although Moore, who wrote sixty-one numbers, was permitted to take the entire profits of the venture in his memorandum with the bookseller Robert Dodsley, other contributors to the 210 numbers included men of fashion, among them, lords Lyttleton, Bath, and Chesterfield, Soame Jenyns, Horace Walpole, and Edward Lovibond. Announcing his design 'to ridicule, with novelty and good-humour, the fashions, follies, vices, and absurdities of that part of the human species which calls itself the World' (vol. 1, no. 1) and promising to be 'very sparing of mottos' (ibid.), Fitz-Adam chattily covered a wide range of topics: the search for happiness, revival of Italian opera, need of calendrical reform, erection of a hospital for decayed actors and actresses, adroit use of face paint, and fashions for curling the hair for a month without combing. He also included and commented on real and fabricated letters to the editor from both unidentified and allegorized correspondents, such as Rebecca Blameless, Toby Frettabit, Mary Muzzy, and Sir Tunbelly Guzzle.

A minor, mainly derivative writer, Moore died in poverty at his home in South Lambeth on 1 March 1757 and was buried without a memorial in the South Lambeth parish graveyard. He was survived by his wife.

PATRICIA DEMERS

Sources W. Boyce, *Solomon: a serenata*, ed. I. Bartlett (1996) · J. H. Caskey, *The life and works of Edward Moore* (1927) · *The dramatic works of Mr Edward Moore* (1765) · E. Moore, *The gamester*, facs. edn (1948) · E. Moore, *The World, by Adam Fitz-Adam*, 3rd edn, 4 vols. (1756) · *DNB*
Likenesses J. Neagle, line engraving (after T. Worlidge), BM, NPG; repro. in *The dramatic works of … Edward Moore* (1788)

Moore, Edward (1835–1916), college head and literary scholar, was born at Cardiff, where his father practised as a physician, on 28 February 1835. He was the elder son of Dr John Moore and his second wife, Charlotte Puckle. He was educated at Bromsgrove School, and at Pembroke College, Oxford (1853–7). In 1858, after obtaining four first classes (classics and mathematics) in moderations and the final schools, he was elected to an open fellowship at Queen's College. He was president of the Oxford Union Society in 1860.

Moore was ordained in 1861, and three years later was appointed by Queen's College to the principalship of St Edmund Hall, which he held for nearly fifty years. Brought up in an evangelical home, he remained a low-churchman and maintained this aspect of the hall's tradition. Under his headship the reputation of the hall as a home of 'true religion and sound learning' was greatly increased, the numbers were more than doubled, and it was represented in almost every honours list. He lectured on Aristotle's *Ethics* and *Poetics*, producing student handbooks on both, although his early scholarly interest was more towards mathematics.

The university commission of 1877 prepared a new scheme for St Edmund Hall, to take effect on the retirement or death of the existing head. Moore made it his object to defeat this scheme, which would have brought the hall under the control of Queen's College and ended its separate existence. In 1903, on Moore being nominated to a canonry at Canterbury, J. R. Magrath, the provost of Queen's, carried through the university's hebdomadal council a statute which would have resulted in the absorption of the hall by the college. Moore successfully opposed the statute in congregation, and, retaining the headship with the sanction of the prime minister, A. J. Balfour, set himself to preserve the independence of the hall. After a prolonged struggle, and with the decisive assistance of Lord Curzon, the university chancellor, a statute was passed in 1913 preserving St Edmund Hall as an independent institution. He at last felt free to resign, and settled permanently at Canterbury, where he was an active member of the chapter, taking a special interest in the library.

To the world at large Moore was best known as a Dante scholar. His interest was awakened by a visit to Italy in 1863 and developed by his friendship with H. F. Tozer. In 1876 he founded the Oxford Dante Society, thereby giving a powerful impulse to the study of Dante in Oxford and beyond. In 1886 he was appointed Barlow lecturer on Dante at University College, London, an appointment which he held in all for seventeen years; in 1895 a Dante lectureship was specially created for him at the Taylor Institution at Oxford. Two of his earliest works on Dante, *The Time References in the 'Divina Commedia'* (1887) and *Dante and his Early Biographers* (1890), were the outcome of the Barlow lectureship. In 1889 appeared his monumental *Contributions to the Textual Criticism of the 'Divina Commedia'*. This work, which at once placed Moore among the leading Dante scholars of his time, was the first serious attempt to deal scientifically and methodically with the complicated problems presented by the text of the *Commedia*. In response to a proposal from the Clarendon Press for a single-volume edition of the works of Dante, Moore, in collaboration with Paget Toynbee, brought out in 1894 the *Oxford Dante*, of which a fourth edition, revised by Toynbee, appeared in 1924. It was accepted as the standard of reference throughout the world until the publication in 1921 of the critical edition sponsored by the Società Dantesca Italiana of Florence. The *Oxford Dante* was followed in 1896–1903 by three series of *Studies in Dante*. A fourth series was on the eve of publication at the time of Moore's death, and carried through the press by Toynbee. A new impression of the four volumes was published in 1968–9. Especially noteworthy among the essays contained in these four volumes were: 'Scripture and classical authors in Dante', accompanied by elaborate tables, in the first volume; the closely reasoned article on the *Quaestio de aqua et terra*, which finally established the authenticity of the treatise, and the masterly vindication of the letter to Can Grande, in the second and third; and the lengthy series of studies on the textual criticism of the *Convivio*, which constitute the *pièces justificatives* of the emended text as printed in the *Oxford Dante*, in the posthumously published fourth volume.

Moore's close acquaintance with the whole range of Dante's writings, his attainments in the many fields covered by his subject, his acute yet cautious critical judgement, his sound scholarship, and indefatigable industry gained him a European reputation, which was recognized by his election, among other distinctions, as a corresponding member of the Accademia della Crusca in 1906 and as a fellow of the British Academy in the same year.

Moore was twice married: first, in 1868, to Katharine Edith (d. 1873), daughter of John Stogdon, solicitor, of Exeter; second, in 1878, to Annie (d. 1906), daughter of Admiral John Francis Campbell Mackenzie. He had one son and two daughters from each marriage. Moore died of a stroke at Chagford, Devon, on 2 September 1916, and was buried at Canterbury Cathedral.

P. J. TOYNBEE, *rev.* M. C. CURTHOYS

Sources E. Armstrong, 'Edward Moore, 1835–1916', *PBA*, [7] (1915–16), 575–84 · P. Toynbee, 'Preface', in E. Moore, *Studies in Dante, fourth series* (1917), v–vi · C. Hardie, 'Preface', in E. Moore, *Studies in Dante, first series*, new impression (1969), v–vii · *The Times* (5 Sept 1916) · personal knowledge (1927) · J. N. D. Kelly, *St Edmund Hall: almost seven hundred years* (1989) · C. Firth, *Modern languages at Oxford, 1724–1929* (1929) · J. Foster, *Oxford men and their colleges* (1893) · C. S. Singleton, 'Preface', in P. Toynbee, *A dictionary of proper names and notable matters in the works of Dante*, rev. edn (1968)

Archives Bodl. Oxf., letters relating to Dante · Bodl. Oxf., papers · U. Oxf., Taylor Institution | BL, letters to W. E. Gladstone, Add. MSS 44499–44526

Likenesses oils, St Edmund Hall, Oxford · photograph, repro. in E. Moore, *Studies in Dante, first series*, new impression (1969), frontispiece

Wealth at death £17,938 8s. 2d.: resworn probate, 30 Sept 1916, *CGPLA Eng. & Wales*

Moore, Edwin (1813–1893). *See under* Moore, William (1790–1851).

Moore, Eleanora [Nelly] (1844/5–1869), actress, of unknown parentage, was always known on the stage as Nelly Moore. She appeared in Manchester and made her London début at the St James's Theatre on 29 October 1859 as the original Winifred in Leicester Buckingham's *Cupid's Ladder*, a part in which she displayed much promise. A year later she was the first Margaret Lovell in Tom Taylor's *Up at the Hills* at the same theatre. She was seen at the Haymarket for the first time on 29 March 1864 as Venus in F. C. Burnand's *Venus and Adonis*, and on 30 April, also at the Haymarket, she was the original Ada Ingot in T. W. Robertson's *David Garrick*. It was here that she obtained her chief success, her performances being lauded in verse by H. S. Leigh in his 'Châteaux d'Espagne' in *Carols of Cockayne*. She was again Venus, this time in J. R. Planché's *Orpheus in the Haymarket*, on 26 December 1865. In the following year, on 2 April, she played the original Lucy Lorrington in Westland Marston's *The Favourite of Fortune*, and continued with a variety of roles until March 1867. In June 1867 she was at the Princess's as Mabel in a revival of *True to the Core* by A. Slous. In 1868 she made her first appearance at the Queen's as Nancy in *Oliver Twist* to Henry Irving's Bill Sikes and the Artful Dodger of J. L. Toole. On 29 June of the same year she played the original Marian Beck in *Time and the Hour* by J. Palgrave Simpson and Felix Dale (Herman Merivale) and on 24 July 1868 was Ruth Kirby in H. J. Byron's *A Lancashire Lass*. This was her last performance. She died of typhoid fever on 22 January 1869 at 31 Soho Square, London, and was buried on 1 February at Brompton cemetery. Her sister and others of her family were also connected with the stage. She was fair, with bright yellow hair, well proportioned, and a pleasant and sympathetic actress of great promise.   JOSEPH KNIGHT, *rev.* J. GILLILAND

Sources Boase, *Mod. Eng. biog.* · H. S. Leigh, *Carols of Cockayne* (1869) · *The life and reminiscences of E. L. Blanchard, with notes from the diary of Wm. Blanchard*, ed. C. W. Scott and C. Howard, 2 vols. (1891) · *The Era* (31 Jan 1869) · personal knowledge (1894)

Moore, Eleanor Allen (1885–1955). *See under* Glasgow Girls (*act.* 1880–1920).

Moore, Eva [*married name* Eva Moore Esmond Jack] (1868–1955), actress and suffragist, was born on 9 February 1868 at 67 Preston Street, Brighton, the eighth of ten children of Edward Henry Moore, a chemist, and his wife, Emily Strachan. She was educated in Miss Pringle's school in Brighton and went to Liverpool to study gymnastics and dancing under Madame Michau. She returned to Brighton to teach dancing, and one of her pupils was the young Winston Churchill. Eva was given her first professional role by Tom Thorne at the Vaudeville Theatre in London in a play called *Partners*, a comedy drama by Robert Buchanan. Her sisters Jessie and Decima were to join her on the stage. In 1890 Arthur Pinero gave her a part as the countess of Drumdurris in his play *The Cabinet Minister* at the Court Theatre. Emboldened by money they had won in a bet at the races, on 19 November 1891 Eva married the Irish actor and playwright Henry Vernon *Esmond (1869–1922), son of Richard George Jack, a physician and surgeon. Her husband's real name was Harry Esmond Jack.

They had three children: a baby, Lynette, who did not survive, and Jack and Jill, who both made careers in the theatre.

Eva Moore was an active suffragist and a founder and vice-president of the Actresses' Franchise League, a non-party grouping of actresses working for votes for women, formed in 1908. She did not go to prison but had the deepest respect for women who did. A familiar figure marching in the suffrage processions in London with contingents of other well-known actresses including Cissy Loftus, May Whitty, and Lena Ashwell, she was called as a witness when Emmeline Pankhurst was on trial. However, she resigned from the Actresses' Franchise League when members took exception to her acting in a sketch written by her husband called *Her Vote*, in which the heroine was shown to prefer kisses to votes.

When the First World War broke out the Women's Emergency Corps was formed, with the actress–manager Gertrude Kingston lending the Little Theatre as its premises. Eva Moore played at the Vaudeville Theatre in the evening and worked as a volunteer at the Little Theatre during the day. Members of the Actresses' Franchise League also founded the British Women's Hospital in 1914. In the following year she met the 'Women of Pervyse', Mairi Chisholm and Elsie Knocker. An appeal Eva Moore made at a Birmingham theatre raised 1500 balaclava helmets; another appeal raised thousands of sandbags. In 1918, when the Germans were making their last big offensive, she paid a visit to Belgian trenches to see the dressing station at Pervyse. She was one of a delegation who presented to the queen a cheque for £50,000 raised for the British hospital. Five of the Moore sisters worked for the British war effort at home and abroad and all received decorations for their services. Moore was honoured with the ordre de la Reine Elisabeth. After the war she toured the battlefields of France and Belgium and also visited Germany.

Although many touring companies were disbanded at the beginning of the First World War, Eva Moore and her husband carried on performing. In 1914 she went to New York to play the title role in his play *Eliza Comes to Stay*, which was poorly received, and in the following year they visited Ireland. In 1918 Eva Moore played Mrs Culver in Arnold Bennett's play *The Title*, at the Royalty Theatre under the direction of J. E. Vedrenne, then stayed on at that theatre to take the part of Mrs Etheridge in W. Somerset Maugham's *Caesar's Wife* and the title role in *Mumsie*. In 1920 she joined the Trans-Canada Company, which took British plays and actors across Canada in a tour of forty-eight towns and cities.

Eva Moore was one of the best-known actresses of her day. Between 1887 and 1923, when her book of reminiscences *Exits and Entrances* was published, she acted in approximately ninety plays, thirteen of which were written by her husband. The two appeared together in fourteen plays. Eva Moore had parts in a number of films, including *Flames of Passion*, *Of Human Bondage*, and *La vie parisienne*. She visited Berlin to act in *Chu Chin Chow* and went to Hollywood in 1942 before returning to Britain in 1945. Her friends included W. S. Gilbert, Sir Herbert Tree, Sir Henry Irving, Anthony Hope, Clemence Dane, Marie Loftus, and Marie Lloyd. She retired from the theatre in 1945. In the latter part of her life Apple Porch, Henley Road, Bisham, Maidenhead, Berkshire, was her home; she died there of myocardial degeneration on 27 April 1955.

MAROULA JOANNOU

Sources E. Moore, *Exits and entrances* (1923) · *WWW* · J. Holledge, *Innocent flowers: women in the Edwardian theatre* (1981) · b. cert. · m. cert. · d. cert.
Archives BL, corresp. with Society of Authors, Add. MS 63238
Likenesses Biograph Studio, photograph (*Kahlie*), repro. in Moore, *Exits and entrances* · Dover Street Studio, photograph (*Eliza*), repro. in Moore, *Exits and entrances* · A. Ellis, photograph (*Pepita*), repro. in Moore, *Exits and entrances* · Foulsham & Banfield, photograph (*Mumsie*), repro. in Moore, *Exits and entrances* · Gabell & Co., photograph (*Wedding bells*), repro. in Moore, *Exits and entrances* · C. Harris, photograph, repro. in Moore, *Exits and entrances* · F. Vandamon, photograph (*Miss Van Gorder*), repro. in Moore, *Exits and entrances*

Moore, Frances (1788/9–1881), historian and novelist, was born at Carlingford, co. Louth, the daughter of Peter *Moore (1753–1828), a former Indian civil servant who became MP for Coventry in 1803, and his wife, Sarah (*d.* before 1798), daughter of Lieutenant-Colonel Richmond Webb of Bandon, co. Cork. She was one of a family of five sons (only one of whom survived his father) and two daughters. Her father was the director of several shaky companies, which crashed in 1824–5, and after the loss of his seat in 1826 he was forced to flee to France to escape arrest. At his death, in 1828 at Abbeville, he is said to have left his two daughters 'respectably provided for' (*GM*, 568); in 1881 her income was derived from annuities and land.

Frances Moore's short literary career began with the publication of several novels, under the pseudonym 'Madame Panache'. Her second novel, *Manners* (1817), commented on the work of other novelists and examined social distinctions in an English village and in Ireland. *A Year and a Day* (1818) is a well-written and restrained silver-fork novel, which deals with the love of a fashionable man for the fascinating, unconventional, but ultimately virtuous wife of an elderly aristocrat. It was possibly inspired by the less reputable career of Lady Caroline Lamb.

Moore's most important publication, however, is her *Historical Life of Joanna of Sicily* (1824). This substantial biography begins with a long introductory digression on the history and literature of Provence and Italy in the thirteenth and fourteenth centuries. Controversially, Moore portrayed Joanna as entirely innocent of the murder of her first husband, Andrew of Hungary, viewing her as the victim of treacherous men. The critic of the *Quarterly Review* of December 1824 firmly opposed her interpretation of Andrew's assassination, and criticized her inclusion of superfluous material. The *Eclectic Review* was more sympathetic, describing the work as an 'elaborate and elegant historical miscellany' (p. 412) and professing an open mind with respect to Andrew's murder. Despite its shortcomings, all subsequent English-language biographies of Joanna are substantially based on Moore's *Life*. Moore's only subsequent publication seems to have been a translation of two volumes of Carlo Botta's *History of Italy*, published in 1828, with a useful preface considering Botta's career and its influence on his account of Italy under Napoleon.

Frances Moore's later life is very obscure. She seems to have lived for some years in Carlingford, co. Louth. Then she moved to 16 Park Street in Taunton, where she may have resided with a nephew. In 1881 she was living at 6 Queen's Terrace, Exeter, with her three nieces. She died at Queen Square, Mount Radford, in Exeter on 6 June of that year at the age of ninety-two. ROSEMARY MITCHELL

Sources Blain, Clements & Grundy, *Feminist comp.*, 755–6 · *The Times* (13 June 1881) · *Trewman's Flying Post* (15 June 1881) · HoP, *Commons* · *GM*, 1st ser., 98/1 (1828), 567–8 [obit. of Peter Moore] · review, *QR*, 31 (1824–5), 65–76 · *Eclectic Review*, new ser., 23 (1825), 385–412 · Boase, *Mod. Eng. biog.* · census returns, 1881
Wealth at death £48: probate, 29 Sept 1881, *CGPLA Eng. & Wales*

Moore, Sir Francis (1559–1621), lawyer and politician, was the sole and posthumous son of Edward Moore (*d.* 1558/9), a yeoman of East Ilsley near Wantage, and Elizabeth Hall of Tilehurst, Berkshire. After attending Reading grammar school he may have been a commoner at St John's College, Oxford, in 1574. Awarded the degree of MA as under-steward to the university in 1612, Moore took no undergraduate degree, but rather entered New Inn some time before his admission to the Middle Temple in August 1580. At an unknown date he married Anne Twitty.

Called to the bar in 1587, Moore made his parliamentary début two years later via the Yorkshire constituency of Boroughbridge, possibly benefiting from connections with the influential Englefield family. While he had some notable north-country clients, and in 1597 was proposed for the post of attorney at York, Moore's personal and professional activities centred on London and Berkshire, especially after Thomas Egerton became lord keeper in 1596. As Egerton's known favourite, Moore long enjoyed pre-eminence among counsel practising at the chancery bar. On Egerton's request, joined by Chief Justice Popham, he was associated to the bench of the Middle Temple in 1603, while the introductory speech to his reading of 1607 fulsomely acknowledged 'that great Lorde, my patron and protector' (Jones, 245). He was created serjeant in 1614. It was only Egerton's declining influence at court towards the end of his life that prevented Moore's gaining a Welsh judgeship, according to a hostile James Whitelocke, who also noted that Moore's knighthood was conferred in March 1617, the month of Egerton's death. By then Moore had spent some £10,000 on land purchases in Berkshire alone, and built himself a new house at South Fawley. He was among the most financially successful common lawyers of his time.

As member for Reading in the parliaments of 1597, 1601, 1604, and 1614, Moore defended the economic interests of his constituents, notably by attacking monopolies, a cause pursued throughout his parliamentary career. His committee memberships and speeches ranged from private bills and detailed law reform proposals to broad issues of religious and social policy. Despite his support of stricter anti-recusant legislation in 1601, Moore's personal religion was conservative; oversight of his will with its markedly non-Calvinist preamble was entrusted to the Catholic Sir Francis Englefield, he married a daughter into another popish family, and his widow, Anne, was herself later accused of recusancy.

Moore is credited with inventing the lease and release, a widely adopted conveyancing technique, but less credence attaches to his supposed drafting of the Statute of Charitable Uses (1601), on which he read in 1607. Several abridgements and extracts of this reading have been published. Moore's extensive collected reports of cases were also highly regarded, circulating widely in manuscript both before and after their compiler's death on 21 September 1621, and their first printing in 1663. He was buried at Great Fawley, Berkshire. WILFRID PREST

Sources HoP, *Commons, 1558–1603* · *DNB* · W. R. Prest, *The rise of the barristers: a social history of the English bar, 1590–1640*, 2nd edn (1991) · C. G. Durston, 'Berkshire and its county gentry, 1625–1649', PhD diss., U. Reading, 1977 · 'Digest of the legal title to his estates in the Co. Berks. compiled by Sir Francis Moore', Berks. RO, D/EW E17 · C. T. Martin, ed., *Minutes of parliament of the Middle Temple*, 4 vols. (1904–5) · G. Jones, *History of the law of charity, 1532–1827* (1969) · Baker, *Serjeants* · T. Clendinnen, 'The common lawyers in parliament and society: a social and political study of the common lawyers in the first Jacobean parliament', PhD diss., University of North Carolina at Chapel Hill, 1975 · *Liber famelicus of Sir James Whitelocke, a judge of the court of king's bench in the reigns of James I and Charles I*, ed. J. Bruce, CS, old ser., 70 (1858) · M. Jansson, ed., *Proceedings in parliament, 1614 (House of Commons)* (1988) · *VCH Berkshire* · Hunt. L., MS E1.2475 · PRO, PROB 11/138, sig. 98
Archives Folger · Harvard U., law school | Berks. RO, 'Digest of the legal title to his estates in the Co. Berks. compiled by Sir Francis Moore' · BL, Harley MSS, Add. MSS 25191–25192 · BL, Lansdowne MSS, Add. MS 1059 · CUL, 'Sir Francis Moore's ten rules of advice for Lord Keeper Williams'
Likenesses W. Faithorne, line engraving, BM, NPG; repro. in F. Moore, *Reports* (1663)
Wealth at death among the most financially successful common lawyers of his time; land in Berkshire; bequeathed two daughters portions of £1500 each: 'Digest of the legal title to his estates', Berks. RO, D/EW E17; Hunt. L., MS E1.2475; will, PRO, PROB 11/138, sig. 98

Moore, Francis (1657–1714?), astrologer and medical practitioner, was born on 29 January 1657 in Bridgnorth, Shropshire. He may have been a student of the astrologer John Partridge (1644–1715). His first practice in 1698 was at the sign of 'Dr. Lilly's Head'—undoubtedly named after the late famous astrologer—in Crown Court, near Cupid's Bridge, Lambeth. By 1702 he was based 'near the old Barge House in Christ-Church Parish, Southwark', advertising himself as a 'Licensed Physician and Student in Astrology … [who] gives Judgment by Urine or the Astrological way, which is surest, without seeing the Patient' (Advertisement in Coley): that is, diagnosis from a horoscope for the moment the physician receives a sample of the patient's urine.

Little is known about Moore's life. His astro-medical practice did not differ from that of his peers, such as William Salmon, or those of the preceding generation, like Richard Saunders, and Joseph Blagrave. His politics too, like theirs, were populist and, within the bounds of loyalty to the king, radical whig.

But Moore is notable for one thing, and that is his annual almanac, entitled *Vox stellarum*, better known as *Old Moore's Almanack* in the mid-nineteenth century. *Vox stellarum* was preceded by an almanac for 1699 with the less felicitous title of *Kalendarium Ecclesiasticum*. The first issue, for 1700, was dedicated to Sir Edward Acton (*c*.1650–1716), MP for Bridgnorth. It consisted of a simple daily ephemeris (listing the moon's sign and sun's sign and degree in the zodiac); lunar quarters and times of rising and setting, and the major aspects to the planets, to which were added weather predictions; some social and political commentary; often, a section of judicial astrology and of simplified astronomy (concerning eclipses, for example); lists of fairs, tides, and so on; a chronology of important dates and historical events; and an enigmatic hieroglyphic that portended coming events.

In its concerns and its approach to them, *Vox stellarum* faithfully reflected its semi-literate, labouring readers. Without patronizing or trying to reform them in any way—which perhaps partly explains its acceptability—Moore's almanac also played a significantly educational role, bringing to many readers issues of contemporary natural philosophy, astronomy, and medicine, in readily accessible form.

Moore produced *Vox stellarum* until his death, but there is conflicting evidence about when that occurred. The records of Christ Church, Southwark, show that a Dr Francis Moore was buried on 20 July 1714; but according to the conscientious Henry Andrews, writing in 1788, Moore died 'about the year 1724' (*Vox stellarum*, 1788).

Although the chronology is unclear, a succession of editors took over Moore's creation, without, however, making any significant changes to the basic formula: John Wing, Tycho Wing, William Harvey, and notably, from about 1783 until his death in 1820, Henry Andrews. Having begun life as simply one of the pack, by 1738 *Vox stellarum* was outselling all rivals at 25,000 copies a year. By 1768 it was selling twice the number of all the other titles combined, and at the century's end the print-run stood at 353,000 a year. It peaked in 1839 at 560,000. A few years earlier, John Clare had described the typical reading-matter in a rural cottage as the Bible, a few chapbooks, *The Whole Duty of Man*, and Moore's almanac. Nor was its readership confined to the rural population, as the reformer Charles Knight indignantly recalled: 'There was scarcely a house in Southern England in which this two shillings worth of imposture was not to be found' (Knight, 151).

Along with John Gadbury, and John Partridge, Moore was one of the last eminent (which is to say, nationally known) astrologers before the subject's long decline of the eighteenth and early nineteenth centuries. He recognized and strove to meet the needs of a readership which still exists, and his literary creation is accordingly still in circulation, with new predictions added annually.

PATRICK CURRY

Sources E. Howe, 'The Stationers' Company almanacks: a late eighteenth-century printing and publishing operation', *Buch und Buchhandel in Europa im achtzehnten Jahrhundert / The book and the book trade in eighteenth-century Europe* [Wolfenbüttel 1977], ed. G. Barber and B. Fabian (1981), 195–209 · *DNB* · B. S. Capp, *Astrology and the popular press: English almanacs, 1500–1800* (1979), 320 · P. Curry, *Prophecy and power: astrology in early modern England* (1989) · H. Coley, *Merlinus Anglicus junior* (1708) · C. Knight, *Passages of a working life during half a century*, 3 vols. (1864–5), vol. 1, p. 151 · H. Andrews, ed., *Vox Stellarum* (1788)

Likenesses M. Nickson, pen drawing, 1810 (after J. Drapentier), Wellcome L. · J. Drapentier, print, BM

Moore, Francis (*bap.* **1708**, *d.* in or after **1756**), geographer, was baptized in Worcester on 11 July 1708, the son of William Moore and his wife, Elizabeth. In July 1730, then employed as a writer in London, he entered the service of the Royal African Company, a chartered company with a royal monopoly of trade with west Africa, and was appointed a writer at James Fort, the company's local headquarters, near the mouth of the Gambia River. He remained in the company's service until 1735, was promoted to be a factor and eventually a chief factor, and served in most of the company's trading establishments (or factories) established along the banks of the river. During these years he kept a regular journal, recording an account of his official duties and the daily events of his life. These included anecdotes of his colleagues' vagaries in these isolated outstations, where many found solace only in heavy drinking. He, however, kept his mind alert by filling out his journal with detailed descriptions of the manners and customs of the African peoples he dealt with, and of the local flora and fauna, illustrating them with his own drawings, and including a rudimentary vocabulary of the Mandinka language.

Moore was also interested in the still unsolved mystery of the course of the Niger and its possible geographical relation to the Gambia. Though he did not himself venture beyond its already known reaches, which he estimated as 500 miles, double its real extent (an estimate repeated in the *Dictionary of National Biography*), on his return to England he collected together the various published sources on this theme, mostly dating from the sixteenth and seventeenth centuries, adding the unpublished account of a voyage up the river by Bartholomew Stibbs in 1723. These he incorporated as an appendix to his own journal which he published in 1738 under the title *Travels into the Inland Parts of Africa*. In it he gave his readers the most comprehensive account of west African geography yet to appear in English which, with the similar compilation published by J. B. Labat in Paris in 1728, remained the most authoritative source until the publication of Mungo Park's *Travels* in 1799.

In 1735 Moore was appointed storekeeper for the settlement of Frederica on the coast of Georgia, founded by colonists brought out by General James Oglethorpe. Here too he kept a journal, describing the flora and fauna and the neighbouring 'Nations of Indians', but on a much smaller scale than his Gambia journal and covering only eight months, up to June 1736 when he went home. He returned to Georgia in 1738, remained there until 1743, and in 1744 published his journal under the title *A Voyage to Georgia*. A further volume, containing the journal of his second visit, and including an account of the Spanish invasion of 1743, was projected but never published. He went back to live in Worcester. On 27 January 1756 at Feckenham, Worcestershire, he married Elizabeth Chillingworth. It is not known when or where he died.   CHRISTOPHER FYFE

Sources F. Moore, *Travels into the inland parts of Africa* (1738) · F. Moore, *A voyage to Georgia* (1744) · IGI

Moore, Garret [Gerald], **first Viscount Moore of Drogheda** (1565/6–1627), politician and soldier, was the second but first surviving son of Sir Edward *Moore (c.1530–1602) and his first wife, Elizabeth (d. 1581), widow successively of Humphrey Warren, Christopher Blunt, and Sir William Brabazon, and daughter and coheir of Nicholas Clifford of Chart in Kent. The Moores were originally from Benenden in Kent but early in Elizabeth's reign Garret's father moved to Ireland, where he rose to prominence as a government official and leading landowner. Sir Edward was a long-standing friend of Hugh O'Neill, earl of Tyrone, and his eldest surviving son also became closely associated with the Ulster lord. Garret probably received some form of legal education in his youth for he was admitted to King's Inns in Dublin in 1610. He was first noted in 1591 when he entertained—at his home at Mellifont in co. Louth—Tyrone's son, Hugh Roe O'Neill, who had recently escaped from Dublin Castle. By this date he had probably already married Mary (d. 1654), daughter of Sir Henry Colley of co. Kildare. The couple had seven sons and five daughters.

Alongside his father Moore assisted the crown authorities in Dublin in 1594 and again in 1596 in treating with Tyrone, helping to secure a rapprochement with the earl on the later occasion. Sir Edward had supplied the government with useful intelligence on O'Neill for a number of years and it is likely that his son did likewise. Having in 1595 been appointed register and scribe of the supreme commissioners for ecclesiastical causes and clerk of recognizances, in 1598 Moore served on the martial law commissions for Louth and co. Meath. Joining his father in opposing Tyrone's resumption of arms against the government he was said to have distinguished himself against the earl's forces in 1599. As a result he was knighted by the earl of Essex, lord lieutenant of Ireland, on 6 September that year. Succeeding his father in 1602 he replaced him in several of his public offices, including the constableship of Philipstown. In the same year he was involved in negotiations between Tyrone and the government, and escorted the earl to Mellifont in March 1603 where his final surrender took place.

Despite his appointment to the Irish privy council in 1604 Moore's renewed friendship with Tyrone prompted suspicions of his loyalty. The earl's final visit to Mellifont was in September 1607, when he collected his infant son John, who had been fostered with Sir Garret, prior to fleeing Ireland for exile on the continent later that month with the rest of his family, the earl of Tyrconnell, Cúchonnacht Óg Mag Uidhir (Maguire), and their followers. This visit provided a plausible pretext for Moore's enemies to reflect on his loyalty. In 1608 Lord Howth charged him with treason on grounds of his intimacy with Tyrone and his schemes. Howth's persistency with the accusations eventually forced Lord Deputy Chichester to place Moore under bonds to the extent of £9000. Upon investigation in the following year the charges were found to be groundless and the king ordered Chichester to restore Sir Garret to his favour.

From this point on, and despite renewed accusations from Howth, Moore's loyalty to the government was no longer questioned. He was a servitor in the plantation in the O'Hanlon lands of Orier in co. Armagh and was elected MP for Dungannon in 1613. After serving as president of Munster in 1615, in the following year he was created Baron Moore of Mellifont, and Viscount Moore of Drogheda in 1622. He died, aged sixty-one, at Drogheda on 9 November 1627, and was buried there at St Peter's Church on 13 December. His wife survived him and later married Charles, Viscount Wilmot. During the late 1640s she was a staunch supporter of parliament and at her death on 3 June 1654 she was buried in Drogheda with her first husband. Moore's two eldest sons, Sir Edward and Sir Thomas, had both predeceased him, leaving his third son, Charles *Moore, to succeed to his titles.   HAROLD O'SULLIVAN

Sources A. Moore [countess of Drogheda], *History of the Moore family* (1902), chaps. 1–4 · J. Lodge, *The peerage of Ireland*, rev. M. Archdall, rev. edn, 7 vols. (1789) · DNB · Father Columcille OCSO, *The story of Mellifont* (1958), 195–202, and appx 3, possessions · H. Morgan, *Tyrone's rebellion: the outbreak of the Nine Years' War in Tudor Ireland*, Royal Historical Society Studies in History, 67 (1993), pts 2–3 · H. O'Sullivan, 'Rothe's castle, Dundalk and Hugh O'Neill', *Journal of the County Louth Archaeological Society*, 15 (1963), 281 · J. L. J. Hughes, ed., *Patentee officers in Ireland, 1173–1826, including high sheriffs, 1661–1684 and 1761–1816*, IMC (1960), 92–3 · *Calendar of the Irish patent rolls of James I* (before 1830); facs. edn as *Irish patent rolls of James I* (1966), 67–9, 230–32 · G. Hill, *The plantation in Ulster* (1877), 570–71, 310n. · *Inquisitionum officia rotulorum cancellariae Hibernice* (1826–9) · H. O'Sullivan, 'Women in county Louth in the seventeenth century', *Journal of the County Louth Archaeological Society*, 23 (1995), 356–8 · GEC, *Peerage*
Archives NL Ire., Drogheda papers

Moore, (Charles) Garrett Ponsonby, eleventh earl of Drogheda (1910–1989), newspaper proprietor and opera manager, was born at 40 Wilton Crescent, London, on 23 April 1910, the elder child and only son of Henry Charles Ponsonby Moore, tenth earl of Drogheda, diplomatist, and his wife, Kathleen, daughter of Charles Maitland Pelham Burn, of Grange Park, Edinburgh. He was educated at Eton College and at Trinity College, Cambridge, which he left early, without a degree. After two years' bookkeeping at the Mining Trust, the first turning-point of his career came in 1932 when, at Brooks's Club in London, he met Brendan Bracken, and went to work for him at the *Financial News*, selling advertising space. He worked hard at mastering the detail of the newspaper business, made a considerable impression on Bracken, and developed a long, close relationship with him. In 1935 he married Joan Eleanor, daughter of William Henry Carr, who left her mother when she was born. She was an excellent pianist, whose immaculate musical taste stood him often in good stead. They had one child, a son.

In the Second World War he served briefly in France, as a

captain with the 53rd battalion of the heavy anti-aircraft regiment, Royal Artillery, and was then appointed to the staff of the war cabinet secretariat (1941) and later the Ministry of Production (1942–5). By the end of the war he was back at the *Financial News*, as managing director.

In 1945, at Bracken's instruction, he went out and bought the *Financial Times*. The two newspapers merged under the one title. For twenty-five years, as managing director of the *Financial Times* (1945–70), Drogheda (who succeeded his father in 1957) devoted himself to its commercial expansion and editorial improvement, taking particular pleasure in stimulating its coverage of the arts, the other great passion and interest of his life. He allowed the editor, Sir L. Gordon Newton, to edit, but pursued him daily with a string of memoranda, demanding answers to pertinent questions. If none was received Drogheda persisted.

Drogheda used the same tactic at the Royal Opera House, Covent Garden, where, after serving as secretary to the board from 1951, he was its chairman from 1958 to 1974. He bombarded the general administrators, Sir David Webster and later Sir John Tooley, with similar missives, which were known as Droghedagrams. At Covent Garden Drogheda attempted to insist that the board was entitled to approve executive artistic decisions, such as the choice of designer for a particular opera. Webster resisted and Georg Solti, engaged by Drogheda as musical director from 1961, never tolerated such interference. Solti's appointment, the decision to give opera in the original language rather than in English, and the high standards that resulted were the principal achievements of Drogheda's chairmanship, which also saw the birth and growth of the Friends of Covent Garden. The Droghedagrams were addressed also to those critics on the *Financial Times*'s pages and elsewhere whose views did not, in the author's opinion, do the opera house justice. These would arrive by messenger on a motor cycle early in the morning the review appeared. It was not unknown for them to be brought round, should the victim live close enough to his house in Lord North Street, by Drogheda himself, in slippers, pyjamas, and dressing-gown.

Drogheda's handsome looks and languid appearance concealed an iron determination to secure his ends. Charming, but obdurate; a dandy, but determined; debonair, but persistent, he would stop at nothing on the newspaper's or the opera house's commercial behalf, pursuing advertisers or possible benefactors without compunction. He struck up friendships with employees of every rank, and treated very many with great personal kindness. He had an acute mind, which expressed itself fluently and clearly on paper, but was guided, he himself thought, always by instinct.

Drogheda was chairman of Financial Times Ltd (1971–5) and of the Newspaper Publishers' Association (1968–70). He chaired the London celebrations committee for the queen's silver jubilee in 1977. From 1941 he served as a director of *The Economist*, to which he was much attached. He was a commander of the Légion d'honneur (1960) and of the order of merit of Italy (1968) and was grand officer of the order of Leopold II of Belgium (1974). He was appointed OBE in 1946, KBE in 1964, and knight of the Garter in 1972.

Drogheda died on 24 December 1989 (eight days after his wife), at Englefield Green, Surrey. He was succeeded in the earldom by his son, Henry Dermot Ponsonby Moore (b. 1937).   JEREMY ISAACS, rev.

Sources *The Times* (28 Dec 1989) · *Daily Telegraph* (27 Dec 1989) · D. Kynaston, *The Financial Times: a centenary history* (1988) · F. Donaldson, *The Royal Opera House in the twentieth century* (1988) · Lord Drogheda [C. G. P. Moore], *Double harness: memoirs* (1978) · *CGPLA Eng. & Wales* (1990) · private information (1996) · personal knowledge (1996)

Archives CAC Cam., corresp. with Sir E. L. Spears · King's AC Cam., letters and postcards from him and his wife to G. H. W. Rylands

Wealth at death £819,145: probate, 18 July 1990, *CGPLA Eng. & Wales*

Moore, George (1803–1880), physician, born on 11 March 1803 at Plymouth, was possibly the son of William Moore, a druggist. After attending John Abernethy's lectures and surgical practice at St Bartholomew's Hospital in London, Moore studied anatomy in Paris in company with Erasmus Wilson and attended G. Dupuytren's practice. In 1829 he became MRCS in London, in 1830 LSA, in 1841 MD at St Andrews, in 1843 LRCP, and in 1859 MRCP. He settled first at Camberwell, Surrey, where he practised successfully for eight years. In March 1835 he obtained the Fothergillian gold medal for his essay, 'Puerperal fever', which was favourably reviewed in the *British and Foreign Medical Review*. He was a fellow of the Hunterian Society, the Medico-Chirurgical Society, and the Medical Society of London.

In 1838 Moore's health failed and he moved to Hastings, where he remained for ten years. During part of this time he was physician to the Hastings Dispensary, with his friend James Mackness as a colleague. In 1845 Moore published the most popular of his books, *The Power of the Soul over the Body*, which reached a sixth edition in 1868. In 1848 his health obliged him to go into partial retirement at Tunbridge Wells, but he returned to Hastings in 1857. Moore spent the rest of his life there, engaged in literary work, and, until within a few years of his death, in medical practice.

Moore was married three times (his first wife died very shortly after their marriage), and with his second wife, who died in 1850, he had several children, who survived him. His son Daniel was the father of the philosopher G. E. *Moore (1873–1958) and the poet Thomas Sturge *Moore (1870–1944). Moore was a man of high moral and religious character, and of considerable learning. In 1840 he published *Infant Baptism Reconsidered*; he was a Baptist by conviction, but in his latter years he attended congregational or Church of England services.

Moore's principal work was *The lost tribes and the Saxons of the east and of the west, with new views of Buddhism, and translations of rock-records in India* (1861), in which he endeavoured to demonstrate the connection of the Buddhists with the Israelites, and of both with the *Sacae* (or *Sakai*), and of the *Sacae* with the Saxons. Some of his other works were: *The*

Use of the Body in Relation to the Mind (1846); *Man and his Motives* (1848); *Health, Disease, and Remedy* (1850); *Ancient Pillar Stones of Scotland* (1865); *The First Man and his Place in Creation* (1866); and *The Training of Young Children on Christian and Natural Principles* (1872). He also published, in 1826, *The Minstrel's Tale, and other Poems*, and in later life he composed hymns and short religious poems, some of which appeared in the *Hastings and St Leonards News*. Moore died at his home, 2 Baldslow Road, Hastings, on 30 October 1880.

W. A. GREENHILL, *rev.* KAYE BAGSHAW

Sources *London and Provincial Medical Directory* (1853–80) · P. J. Wallis and R. V. Wallis, *Eighteenth century medics*, 2nd edn (1988) · *CGPLA Eng. & Wales* (1880) · personal knowledge (1894) · private information (1894) · *Hastings and St Leonards News* (5 Nov 1880) · *Hastings and St Leonards News* (12 Nov 1880)
Archives Herts. ALS, letters to Lord Lytton
Wealth at death under £7000: probate, 7 Dec 1880, *CGPLA Eng. & Wales*

Moore, George (1806–1876), philanthropist and businessman, was born on 9 April 1806 at Mealsgate, a farm of about 60 acres in Cumberland, the third of the five children of John Moore, statesman, and his wife, Peggy Lowes. His life, as memorialized by Samuel Smiles and many other collectors of nineteenth-century success stories, followed a classic pattern. In his youth he played truant from the village school, took his father's horse to go hunting with the legendary John Peel, and during his apprenticeship as a draper began gambling in the public house where he was lodging. He won a wrestling bout on the day after his arrival in London, in April 1825, to seek his fortune. It was less easy to succeed in business. But he applied himself and eventually found a position through a Cumberland connection in the firm of Flint, Ray & Co. Wanting to transfer from the retail to the wholesale trade, he moved through Ray's recommendation in 1826 to Fisher, Stroud, and Robinson of Watling Street, then said to be the first lace-house in the City. He went to evening school and helped his brother William, who had also come up to London to work for Flint, Ray. He became a commercial traveller; after eighteen months he was transferred to the Liverpool and Manchester circuit, and was so successful that he became known as the 'Napoleon of Watling Street'. After about a year he was given Ireland to cover as well. He entered into partnership with Groucock and Copestake, a young rival firm, and worked sixteen hours a day. Tales spread of his success in winning customers and of the dangers he overcame in doing so (once being almost thrown out of a boat at Dublin). At the end of three years he was put on an equal footing with the other partners. The business flourished, for some time doubling itself annually, and Groucock and he travelled to Belgium and France to buy lace and broaden their range of connections. On 12 August 1840, having been rejected once, he married Eliza Flint Ray, the daughter of his first employer.

In 1841 Moore largely gave up travelling but city life did not suit him and he was recommended to take a long rest. In 1844 he went to America, establishing a daily regime on the ship of reading six chapters of the Bible immediately after breakfast. Apart from trips to lace importers and to public philanthropic institutions there he made a visit to the grave of Benjamin Franklin, whose maxims formed a key part of Victorian self-help literature. On his return he took up hunting again, joining Lord Lonsdale's hunt in Tring for two days a week in winter, a passion that he combined with raising subscriptions for good causes in the area through which the hunt passed. When he gave up travelling he started to go regularly to church and worked to improve the spiritual condition of his firm, which was expanding and opening branches in all the larger towns of the country. In 1856 he appointed in London a chaplain who had worked for the firm; the chaplain involved some of the young employees in ragged and Sunday schools, and helped to start a young men's mutual improvement society and Sunday morning Bible class. Moore organized libraries and lectures by eminent clergy and ministers, and set up similar projects for employees elsewhere.

Moore plunged into philanthropy with the same zeal that he gave to business. He was always very committed to education: he was actively involved in the establishment of the commercial travellers' schools in Pinner, while continuing throughout his life to encourage the development of schools in Cumberland and to help boys from there to find a commercial position. The warehousemen's and clerks' schools started on the premises of his firm. He visited prisons and started a short-lived reformatory for young men. He also worked with Robert Hanbury MP in setting up a refuge for fallen women, and helped to establish the British Home for Incurables, of which he was treasurer until the year of his death. He was a governor of Christ's Hospital; a member of the Committee of Almoners; treasurer of the Field Lane ragged schools; supported the London City Mission, the Reformatory and Refuge Union, the County Towns Mission, and the Porters' Benevolent Society; he was an active member of the Royal Free Hospital; supported the Industrial Dwellings Company, founded to build cheap housing for the working classes; and was one of the chief promoters of the Cabmen's Mission. He was the leading figure in the Cumberland Benevolent Institution and gave liberally to local charities. He funded the building of Christ Church, Somers Town (consecrated in 1868), and helped to fund ancillary institutions; he also supported the Wesleyans and the Baptists, and counted many prominent nonconformist ministers among his friends. He supported broadly-based evangelical initiatives. His diary recorded incessant attendance at religious or reforming meetings—of worn-out needlewomen, city missioners, the YMCA—and he often went down to St George-in-the-East or Wapping to work with the poor. He held Bible readings and committee meetings at his houses in London and in Cumberland, where he also invited young men and philanthropic workers to visit regularly. To commemorate the new year in 1876 he gave £40,000 of his private money in gifts to employees of the firm.

A moderate Liberal in politics, Moore strongly supported free trade. In 1845 he and five others bought a small freehold in Middlesex and for more than twenty years all voted for free-trade candidates. He canvassed for Liberal friends (including Lord John Russell in his campaigns in the City of London in 1852 and 1857). He refused to take on political office himself, however, on the ground that he had too many other commitments. He paid a fine of £500 rather than be sheriff of Middlesex in 1844 and six times refused to stand for parliament, though invitations came from the City of London, Middlesex, Nottingham, Mid-Surrey, and East Cumberland. He did accept other public offices: he was JP for Wigton and for Middlesex; was chosen to be prime warden of the Fishmongers' Company; acted as commissioner to Paris for the distribution of the Mansion House Relief Fund during the Franco-Prussian War (for which he was awarded the cross of the Légion d'honneur); and agreed to be high sheriff of Cumberland in 1873. He served on various public committees of investigation into City or mercantile business and chaired the select committee on postal telegraphs, which reported in 1875.

Moore permitted himself some personal extravagance, though not without a great deal of soul-searching. In 1854 he moved from Oxford Terrace, in London, to a mansion that he had built in Kensington Palace Gardens, then becoming 'a colony of new money' (Crook, 170). He claimed that he had done it to please his wife but that it was 'wicked and aggrandizing—mere ostentation and vain show' (Smiles, 173). His wide-ranging hospitality—extending to porters and cabmen—was in part a justification of such luxury. His sentimental attachment to Cumberland was crowned by his purchase—in 1858 for £40,000—of the Whitehall estate, near Wigton. Supposed to be the Whiteladies of Walter Scott's novel *Redgauntlet*, it had been admired from afar by Moore as a young man; now he became the proud owner, and in 1862 commissioned Anthony Salvin to extend the house in Tudor-bethan style. Moore's first wife died on 4 December 1858; on 28 November 1861 he married Agnes, second daughter of Richard Breeks of Warcop, Westmorland. There were no children by either marriage. On his second wedding tour he bought works of art in Rome. Other enthusiasms were short-horn cattle and flowers; he tried to encourage cottage gardeners to grow old-fashioned flowers—sweet william, southernwood, mint, and lavender.

Moore died on 21 November 1876, after being knocked down by a horse on the previous day, when he was on his way to speak to a meeting of the Nurses' Institution at Carlisle. He died at the Grey Goat, Carlisle, the inn where he had slept on his way to London in 1825, and was buried in the mortuary chapel in All Hallows Church, near Whitehall, Cumberland, on 25 November. George Moore was a Smilesian hero on a grand scale. Inexhaustibly energetic and intolerant of idleness, he was involved in a remarkable range of activities, even by the standards of his day. He retained the foibles of the self-made man: extraordinarily generous, he could throw his counting-house into a ferment because no voucher could be found for an omnibus fare. Yet he evidently won genuine respect and affection from those with whom he worked. At Wigton church a memorial window represented him as the good Samaritan. Also at Wigton his wife commissioned a fountain in his memory. Round the plinth were bronze reliefs by Thomas Woolner, showing various acts of charity: clothing the naked, teaching the ignorant, consoling the afflicted, and feeding the hungry. The gilding is kept burnished by Agnes Moore's endowment, and until recently the granite was washed weekly by the town's fire-engine.

JANE GARNETT

Sources S. Smiles, *George Moore, merchant and philanthropist*, 2nd edn (1878) · A. H. Japp, *Successful business-men: short accounts of the rise of famous firms, with sketches of the founders* (1892) · J. Burnley, *Sir Titus Salt and George Moore* (1885) · J. Burnley, *Summits of success: how they have been reached, with sketches of the careers of some notable climbers* (1901) · H. A. Page, *Leaders of men: a book of biographies specially written for youth* (1880) · P. S. O'Brien, *Two sermons preached at Christ Church, Somers Town on Sunday November 26th, 1876, on the occasion of the death of George Moore* [1876] · J. M. Crook, *The rise of the nouveaux riches: style and status in Victorian and Edwardian architecture* (1999) · J. M. Robinson, *The architecture of northern England* (1986) · Boase, *Mod. Eng. biog.*

Likenesses P. Anderson, stipple (after photograph by V. Blanchard), NPG · G. F. Watts, portrait, repro. in Smiles, *George Moore*, frontispiece · memorial window, Wigton church, Cumbria · wood-engraving (after photograph by Maull & Co.), NPG; repro. in *ILN* (2 Dec 1876)

Moore, George Augustus (1852–1933), writer, was born on 24 February 1852 at Moore Hall, overlooking Lough Carra, co. Mayo, in the west of Ireland, the eldest son of George Henry *Moore (1810–1870) and Mary Blake Moore (1830–1895). The Moores, originally English protestants, migrated to Ireland in the seventeenth century, then through marriage turned Roman Catholic, a faith which from childhood grew more distasteful to Moore until in middle life he publicly renounced it.

There probably never was a more unlikely candidate for literary fame than the younger George, who received little formal education aside from seven unhappy and unsatisfactory years at St Mary's College, a Roman Catholic school in Oscott, near Birmingham. The reedy lake in front of Moore Hall was the scene of many youthful excursions, and throughout his life it was never far from his mind, its beauty inspiring some of his finest descriptive writing. His father had a notable racing stable and here the impressionable youth spent many happy days, both before and after his miserable days at school, as a fascinated spectator of its bustling activities, which years later supplied the authentic background for *Esther Waters* (1894).

Informal education in Paris In 1868 the Moores were living in London, where George became enamoured of painting and enrolled in art classes. His family saw no future for him as an artist and so a military career was ordained, a fate from which he was spared by the unexpected death of his father in 1870. As eldest son he inherited the bulk of the Irish estates and their revenues and, when he came of age in 1873, left for Paris to continue his art studies. In the studios, behind the would-be bohemian, there always lurked the Irish landlord, but in spite of this, as he frequently proclaimed, his true education was obtained at the Nouvelle Athènes, a café frequented by artists and

George Augustus Moore (1852–1933), by Sir William Orpen

writers, where he met and became friends with many who supplied him with his artistic criteria and whose works he promoted on his return to London.

These years in Paris were probably the most important in Moore's life, influencing much of his subsequent career. He soon realized that his artistic talent was at best mediocre and in desperation he turned to the literary scene. Art, however, remained a vital interest and throughout his life artists, rather than writers, were his closest associates, to whom he was known as GM. Moore was a man of words rather than action, so the story of his life is not so much what he did as what he wrote. Charles Morgan, his designated biographer (though never his actual one), suggested in his *Epitaph on George Moore* that 'Twice George Moore recreated the English novel' (Morgan, 2)—and be that as it may, Moore laboriously did re-create himself as an egocentric man of letters, which led to Oscar Wilde's frequently quoted witticism, 'George Moore has conducted his whole education in public' (F. Harris, *Oscar Wilde*, 1959, 278).

In a constant search for perfection Moore continuously passed on to new forms of self-expression rather than repeating a successful formula as did so many of his contemporaries, leading step by step from the 'naturalism' of the early novels to the tapestry-like quality of his final works. Few authors of modern times revised to the extent that Moore did, as he habitually recast material seeking a more perfect form, which frequently resulted in some later editions being completely rewritten, producing a bibliographic jungle. Perhaps this is the reason that the works of this once-brilliant Anglo-Irish star of the English literary firmament, whose writings have been translated

into a dozen foreign languages, are now almost forgotten by the general public. On the other hand, perhaps this multiplicity of texts explains the extensive scholarly interest, which has resulted in hundreds of books and articles in English and other languages, suggesting that English literature in the twentieth century would have been quite different had he not lived.

Frequently Moore was the storm centre of literary controversies, making him the target of spiteful comments, and his unusual physical features, particularly his flaxen hair and sloping shoulders (which led Yeats to describe him as 'carved from a turnip, looking out of astonished eyes'; W. B. Yeats, *Dramatis Personae*, 1935, 24), are perhaps better known today than his books. He was a subject for several generations of artists, from Manet in Paris to his late-life contemporaries in London and Dublin, as well as a favourite model for caricaturists, particularly Max Beerbohm, who found him one of his preferred subjects. His first attempts at writing were negligible and included unproduced dramas and two volumes of verse, *Flowers of Passion* (1878) and *Pagan Poems* (1881), the latter including poems revised from the earlier volume, the onset of his lifelong habit of pursuing perfection.

First novels Due to landlord–tenant hostilities in Ireland, income from Moore's estates was greatly reduced, forcing him to return to London in 1879, where he turned to journalism and fiction to make a living. While still living in Paris, a vital factor in his decision to turn to literature had been his meeting with Émile Zola, whose 'disciple' he soon became, with the avowed intention of introducing the French writer's 'naturalism' to England. In Moore's first realistic novel, the three-volume *A Modern Lover* (1883)—subsequently rewritten as *Lewis Seymour and some Women* (1917)—he translated into an English setting the French art scene he had known so well. The book met with scant commercial success, partly due to the reluctance of the circulating libraries adequately to stock it. To circumvent such censorship, he persuaded Zola's English publisher, Henry Vizetelly, to issue his next book, *A Mummer's Wife* (1885), in an inexpensive one-volume format. It was the first truly 'naturalistic' novel with an English background, dealing as it did with alcoholism and the tawdry side of the theatrical world. Reviews were mixed, but it was generally agreed that a new and distinctive, if somewhat abrasive, voice had arrived on the London literary scene.

In these two early works Moore was the first English novelist to break away from the content, structure, techniques, and style of the Victorians. Other works followed, including *A Drama in Muslin* (1886) (rewritten as *Muslin*, 1915), a story of the Dublin marriage market and of Irish life in one of the rural 'big houses' during the land war in the late 1870s and early 1880s; *A Mere Accident* (1887), an examination of bachelorhood; and *Parnell and his Island* (1887), a collection of critical and pugnacious denunciations of his native land. Following these was the pseudo-autobiographical novel, *Confessions of a Young Man* (1888), in which the transplanted Anglo-Irishman set out to shock his readers. What it did in fact was to create a legend and establish Moore's reputation as a recognized authority on impressionism and symbolism, based on his first-hand knowledge of the contemporary French art and literary scene. Next came *Spring Days* (1888), a story of pale love in suburban villas; and *Mike Fletcher* (1889), his 'Don Juan' novel, which received hostile reviews and which its author quickly tried to forget and suppress.

During the same period Moore emerged as a crusading journalist, in the forefront of the fight to break the power of the 'select' circulating libraries, those self-appointed literary censors who imposed strait-laced moral standards on English literature by arbitrarily banning some customary three-volume novels from their discreet shelves. Moore's spirited attacks, 'A New Censorship of Literature' in *Pall Mall Gazette* (10 December 1884), and his influential pamphlet, *Literature at Nurse, or, Circulating Morals* (1885), were among the earliest blows against the powerful libraries and helped prepare the way for the more liberated spirit of the period and the final break with literary Victorianism.

The works of the 1890s The 1890s were an extremely productive period for Moore and the decade was the high point of his career as a journalist, as he continued his crusade to introduce the new French art and literature to the English public in articles published in various periodicals, some of which were collected in *Impressions and Opinions* (1891) and *Modern Painting* (1893), two works which increased his reputation as a significant critic.

Moore's novel *Vain Fortune* (1891), serialized as being by Lady Rhone, is the story of a writer who can neither write nor give up writing. It met with critical disdain and failed to satisfy its author even after three revisions, though it made a deep impression on James Joyce, who described it in his youthful 'The day of the rabblement' as a 'fine, original work'; it was later the inspiration for 'The Dead', the final story in Joyce's *Dubliners* (1914), according to Richard Ellmann, Joyce's biographer.

Moore's interest in the theatre led to controversial articles attacking the conventional melodramas being offered to the British public, contrasting them with the innovative drama being developed in Europe. He became one of the founders of the Independent Theatre, established in London to introduce the 'new' European drama of Ibsen, Strindberg, and others to the British play-going public. His own three-act play, *The Strike at Arlingford*, was presented for two performances and published in 1893. A one-act play, *Journeys End in Lovers Meeting*, by Moore and John Oliver Hobbes (Mrs Pearl Craigie), was used for a number of years by Ellen Terry as a curtain-raiser. Next, after partial serialization, *Esther Waters* (1894) was published, a story which broke new ground in its presentation of its subject matter by making a servant the sympathetic title-character. This book, with its non-judgemental depiction of 'the fallen woman', is considered by many to be Moore's greatest achievement, as well as a turning point in the English novel. It was his most successful book and has not been out of print since its first publication. At the 1994 Cheltenham festival it was awarded a spoof centennial '1894 Booker prize'.

Moore continued to restructure his material, publishing *Celibates* (1895), a collection of three stories, one a revision of *A Mere Accident*. For the next few years he was chiefly concerned with revising *Esther Waters* and in writing and rewriting the story of an opera singer, *Evelyn Innes* (1898), which, with its sequel, *Sister Teresa* (1901), marked a change in his artistic aims.

Due to the practical experience he had gained from his association with the Independent Theatre, Moore was enlisted in 1899 by William Butler Yeats to assist in the launching of the Irish Literary Theatre, for which he served as a stage director and playwright, turning Edward Martyn's *The Tale of a Town* into his *The Bending of the Bough* (1900) and collaborating with Yeats on *Diarmuid and Grania*. In 1901, disgusted with British atrocities in the Second South African War (confided to him by his brother, Maurice, then serving in South Africa), plus his interest in the emerging Irish literary renaissance, he moved to Dublin. Once there he aspired to create a literature for his native land, writing a series of stories to be translated into Irish, six of which were published as *An T-Úr-Gort* (1902). English versions of these and other stories were included in *The Untilled Field* (1903), a book considered by some to be the progenitor of the modern Irish short story. This was followed by *The Lake* (1905), a study of an Irish priest gaining consciousness of himself and abandoning his calling, and *Memoirs of my Dead Life* (1906), a semi-autobiographical book of reveries which marked a new direction in Moore's writing, leading to the polished 'oral narrative' style of his later years.

Hail and Farewell and last writings Discovering that he was not the 'messiah' of a new Irish literature he had hoped to be, Moore returned to London in 1911, settling in Ebury Street and living as a 'man of letters'. The publication of *Ave* (1911), *Salve* (1912), and *Vale* (1914), the three sections of his autobiographical *Hail and Farewell* (which includes his account of the Irish Literary Theatre), infuriated Yeats, Lady Gregory, and other of his former associates in the project, all of whom failed to be amused at the satire and frequently malicious humour of his account or to observe that he made as much fun of himself as of the others. Ironically Yeats paid him the compliment of imitating the style of the trilogy in his own account of the venture.

In 1914 Moore travelled to the Holy Land to see at first hand the setting for his next book, *The Brook Kerith* (1916), the story of an unrisen Christ and his dramatic meeting with Paul twenty years after the crucifixion. On its publication an attempt was made to have the book banned as blasphemous, and this, coupled with an unsuccessful libel suit when the rewritten *A Modern Lover* of 1883 was republished in 1917 as *Lewis Seymour and some Women*, caused Moore to issue his books in expensive limited editions under the sign of the fictitious Society of Irish Folklore. The first was *A Story-Teller's Holiday* (1918), part autobiography but primarily a retelling of Irish folk-tales and the creation of others.

Moore's previous critical periodical writings served as the basis for sections in *Avowals* (1919) and *Conversations in Ebury Street* (1924). He again turned to the past as he retold the love story of *Héloïse and Abélard* (1921) and, in his final fiction, *Aphrodite in Aulis* (1930), an imaginative tale of ancient Greece. *In Single Strictness* (1922; partially reprinted as *Celibate Lives*, 1927) was a collection of stories, both new and revised. The celibacy theme was not autobiographical, for although Moore never married, he detailed numerous amours in many of his writings. These were once thought to be fictitious, but a number are verified in his letters.

In spite of Moore's long interest in the theatre, he never achieved his ambition to write a truly successful play, and all were collaborations, not always revealed. Shortly after his return to London a dramatization of *Esther Waters* (1911) and *Elizabeth Cooper* (1913), a comedy, were produced by the Stage Society for limited runs. The latter was revised as *The Coming of Gabrielle* and presented for three matinee performances in 1923. Two other plays were produced. *The Making of an Immortal*, an imaginative account of the authorship of Shakespeare's plays, had two performances in 1927. The second, *The Passing of the Essenes* (a revision of *The Apostle*; 1911 and 1923), his final attempt to dramatize *The Brook Kerith*, had a limited run in 1930.

At the time of his death Moore was writing *A Communication to my Friends* (1933), which was posthumously published. It was composed of recollections of his early life, which he described as being 'the story of how literature hailed me'. He died on 21 January 1933 at his home at 121 Ebury Street, Belgravia, London; his body was cremated following services at Golders Green attended by members of his family, a few of his closest friends (mostly artists), and the prime minister, Ramsay MacDonald, with whom he was to have dined shortly before his death. On 27 May his ashes were buried on Castle Island in Lough Carra, co. Mayo, where he had played as a boy. Over his crypt was erected a wooden marker inscribed 'He deserted his family and friends for his art'; however, 'deserted' was softened to 'forsook' when carved on a permanent stone monument.

Perfection was Moore's constant goal and his place in literature should eventually be secure, if for no other reason than his pioneer efforts in freeing English prose from Victorian inhibitions and the example he set of absolute devotion to his art.   EDWIN GILCHER

Sources E. Gilcher, *A bibliography of George Moore* (1970) · E. Gilcher, *A supplement to 'A bibliography of George Moore'* (1988) · J. Hone, *The life of George Moore* (1936) · J. Hone, *The Moores of Moore Hall* (1938) · C. Morgan, *Epitaph on George Moore* (1936) · R. Langenfeld, *George Moore: an annotated secondary bibliography of writings about him* (1987) · private information (2004) [H. E. Gerber] · *George Moore in transition: letters to T. Fisher Unwin and Lena Milman, 1894–1910*, ed. H. E. Gerber (1968) · *George Moore on Parnassus: letters (1900–1933) to secretaries, publishers, printers, agents, literati, friends and aquaintances*, ed. H. E. Gerber (1988) · H. E. Gerber, 'George Moore', *Anglo-Irish literature: a review of research*, ed. R. J. Finneran (1976), 138–66 · R. S. Becker, 'The letters of George Moore, 1863–1901', PhD diss., U. Reading, 1980 · 'George Moore: collected letters', ed. R. S. Becker, vol. 1 · private information (2004) [A. Frazier] · private information (2004) [K. Gow, P. Deane] · private information (2004) [F. Fayant] · A. Frazier, *George Moore, 1852–1933* (2000)

Archives Arizona State University · Bibliothèque Nationale, Paris · BL · Boston College, Massachusetts · Boston PL, letters · Boston University · Col. U., letters, mainly to agents, and literary MSS · CUL · Emory University, Atlanta, Georgia · Folger · Harvard U. · Hunt. L., letters and literary MSS · Indiana Library · Institut de France · Johns Hopkins University, Baltimore · Letterkunding Museum · LUL, letters · New York University · NL Ire., letters, mainly to his mother · NRA, corresp. and literary papers · Ohio University · Pennsylvania State University · Princeton University, New Jersey · Ransom HRC, corresp. and papers · TCD, revised proofs for *The brook Kerith* · U. Cal., Los Angeles · U. Glas. · U. Leeds · University of Florida · University of Kansas, Lawrence · Washington University, St Louis, Missouri, corresp. · Yale U. | BL, letters to William Archer, Add. MS 45293 · BL, corresp. with Society of Authors, Add. MS 56757 · Duke U., Perkins L., letters to Sir Edmund Gosse · Harvard U., Houghton L., corresp. with Thomas Smith and Horace Liveright; literary MSS and papers · NL Ire., letters to R. L. Best · NL Ire., letters to Mark Fisher · NL Ire., letters to Edmund Gosse [copies] · NL Ire., letters to Marquise Clara Lanza · NL Ire., letters to duchess of Marlborough · NL Ire., letters to Max Meyerfield · NL Ire., letters to Maurice Moore · NL Ire., letters to Baroness Ripp · NL Ire., letters to Mr Wigram · NYPL, corresp. with John Balderston · NYPL, Berg collection · TCD, corresp. with Thomas Bodkin · U. Glas. L., letters to D. S. MacColl · U. Leeds, Brotherton L., letters to Sir Edmund Gosse · U. Leeds, Brotherton L., letters to Philip Gosse · University of Rochester, New York, Rush Rhees Library, corresp. with Leon Lion · University of Washington, Seattle, Joseph Hone MSS

Likenesses E. Manet, oils, *c*.1879, Metropolitan Museum of Art, New York · J. E. Blanche, oils, 1887, Musée Rouen, France · W. R. Sickert, oils, 1890–91, Tate collection · W. Rothenstein, chalk drawing, 1896, NG Ire. · AE [G. Russell], pastel drawing, 1900, Ransom HRC · H. Tonks, pencil drawing, 1901, NPG · J. B. Yeats, pencil, 1904, NYPL, Berg collection · J. B. Yeats, oils, 1905, NG Ire. · A. L. Coburn, photogravure, 1908, NPG; repro. in A. L. Coburn, *Men of mark* (1913) · W. Orpen, group portrait, oils, 1909 (*Homage to Manet*), Man. City Gall. · W. Orpen, group portrait, oils, 1911–12, Nicols Bar, Café Royal, London; copy, Musée d'Art Moderne, Paris · F. L. Harris, oils, 1920, FM Cam. · H. Tonks, pastels, *c*.1920, NPG · H. Tonks, group portrait, oils, 1928–9 (*Saturday night in the Vale*), Tate collection · F. Dodd, pencil drawing, 1932, NPG · E. Kapp, drawing, 1933, Barber Institute of Fine Arts, Birmingham · M. Beerbohm, caricature, Museum of Modern Art, Dublin · M. Beerbohm, caricature, Savile Club, London · M. Beerbohm, caricature, Harvard TC · M. Beerbohm, caricature, U. Cal., Los Angeles · M. Beerbohm, caricature, U. Texas · M. Beerbohm, crayon and pencil, London Library · M. Beerbohm, ink and wash, AM Oxf. · M. Beerbohm, pen and wash caricature, Hugh Lane Municipal Gallery of Modern Art, Dublin · M. Beerbohm, pencil, Ransom HRC · S. C. Harrison, oils, Ransom HRC · E. Manet, pastel drawing, Metropolitan Museum of Art, New York · W. Orpen, pencil, NPG [*see illus.*] · Sic [Sickert], chromolithograph caricature, NPG; repro. in *VF* (21 Jan 1897) · R. P. Staples, pencil, Ulster Museum · P. W. Steer, oil on panel, Ransom HRC · plaster death masks, NG Ire., NPG

Wealth at death £68,816 2*s*. 8*d*.: resworn probate, 2 March 1933, *CGPLA Eng. & Wales*

Moore, George Belton (1805–1875), landscape painter and drawing-master, a pupil of A. C. Pugin, exhibited pictures of foreign scenery at the Royal Academy, British Institution, and Society of British Artists, Suffolk Street, from 1830 until his death. He was drawing-master at the Royal Military Academy, Woolwich, and at University College, London. In 1850 he published *Perspective, its Principles and Practice*, and in 1851 *The Principles of Colour Applied to Decorative Art*. Moore died at his home, 221 Burrage Road, Plumstead, London, on 4 November 1875. He left a widow, Ann, and a daughter and a son.

L. H. CUST, *rev.* EMILY M. WEEKS

Sources Wood, *Vic. painters*, 3rd edn · Graves, *Artists*, 1st edn · *CGPLA Eng. & Wales* (1875)

Wealth at death under £3000: probate, 23 Nov 1875, *CGPLA Eng. & Wales*

Moore, George Edward (1873–1958), philosopher, was born on 4 November 1873 at Hastings Lodge, Upper Norwood, Surrey, the third son and fifth child of the eight children of Daniel Moore (1840–1904), physician, and his second wife, Henrietta Sturge (1839–1903). His paternal grandfather was George *Moore (1803–1880); Joseph Sturge was a great-uncle. His eldest brother was Thomas Sturge *Moore, the poet. G. E. Moore much disliked his forenames and during his academic career he was called just Moore, though his wife called him Bill.

From the age of eight Moore attended Dulwich College as a day boy (1882–92); there he was educated almost exclusively in the Latin and Greek classics. His parents were Baptists, and at home his upbringing was religious. At about the age of twelve he went through a spell of evangelical enthusiasm which lasted two years. He emerged from this a convinced agnostic and later wrote: 'For my part I never did get much comfort from religion, and never felt very sorry at disbelieving: indeed I find it hard to understand how it can make much difference to most people' (letter to Desmond MacCarthy's mother, 1900, Moore MSS).

Philosophical influences In 1892 Moore won a scholarship to study classics at Trinity College, Cambridge, and obtained a first class in part one of the classical tripos in 1894. He then decided to combine further study of classics with the study of philosophy and in 1896 he obtained a second class in part two of the classical tripos and a first class in part two of the moral sciences tripos (which was by then primarily concerned with philosophy).

Moore's new interest in philosophy had been stimulated by his new friends and acquaintances at Trinity, particularly Bertrand Russell and J. M. E. McTaggart. Russell later wrote concerning his time as a student at Trinity:

> In my third year I met G. E. Moore, who was then a freshman, and for some years he fulfilled my ideal of genius. He was in those days beautiful and slim, with a look almost of inspiration, and with an intellect as deeply passionate as Spinoza's. (Russell, 68)

In his autobiography Moore himself tells the story of his meeting with McTaggart, who was then a prize fellow of Trinity:

> Russell had invited me to tea in his rooms to meet McTaggart; and McTaggart, in the course of conversation had been led to express his well-known view that Time is unreal. This must have seemed to me then (as it still does) a perfectly monstrous proposition, and I did my best to argue against it. (Moore, 'Autobiography', 13–14)

Russell and McTaggart were already members of the Cambridge Conversazione Society, commonly known as the Apostles, and in 1894 Moore was elected a member. The meetings of the Apostles, which comprised short philosophical papers followed by uninhibited discussion, provided Moore with the ideal context for the development of his philosophical interests. Moore was at this time studying philosophy with, among others, Henry

George Edward Moore (1873–1958), by unknown photographer, 1899

Sidgwick; but although Moore's early writings are much indebted to Sidgwick, Moore found him remote and rather dull, and never enjoyed a close intellectual relationship with him. Instead it was McTaggart whose influence was at first dominant, so much so that, despite his account of their first meeting, Moore's first published paper (published in 1897) is a defence of the unreality of time.

Following his success in part two of the moral sciences tripos in 1896 Moore decided to try to follow in the footsteps of McTaggart and Russell by winning a prize fellowship at Trinity College on the basis of a dissertation. Moore's first attempt in 1897 was not successful; but in the following year he was elected to a prize fellowship which lasted until 1904. Moore preserved his two dissertations, and through them one can trace the course of his influential break with the idealist philosophy he had learned from McTaggart. Moore's main thesis in his second dissertation is the need to distinguish sharply, as idealists do not, between thought and its objects, and this distinction is the subject of his first important paper, 'The nature of judgment' (1899; *Selected Writings*, 1–19), which is in fact largely excerpted from this dissertation. Moore here also propounds a programme of conceptual analysis—maintaining that 'A thing becomes intelligible first when it is analysed into its constituent concepts' (p. 8) and in retrospect the paper can be seen to be the starting point of the Cambridge school of analytical philosophy.

Moore's time as a prize fellow at Trinity College (1898–1904) was the most productive period of his life. He published a series of papers critical of the dominant idealist metaphysics of the period, of which the best known is 'The refutation of idealism' (1903; *Selected Writings*, 23–44). Russell acknowledged the impact of these writings when he wrote in the preface to *The Principles of Mathematics* (1903) that 'on fundamental questions of philosophy, my position, in all its chief features, is derived from Mr. G. E. Moore' (p. xviii). The central themes of this new philosophy are, first, that thoughts of all kinds, even simple sensations, require objects distinct from the thoughts themselves. Second, Moore vehemently denounces the idealist conception of an 'organic whole' (G. E. Moore, *Principia ethica*, 1903, 82), the conception of a whole whose parts are intrinsically dependent upon each other, and especially the claim that the world itself is such a whole. But, third, Moore carries over from his own brief idealist phase his rejection of the naturalistic thesis that everything exists in space or time. Instead, according to Moore, there are plenty of things which are not in space or time, such as numbers, meanings, and values.

Principia ethica Moore's development of this new philosophy culminates in his most famous book, his ethical treatise *Principia ethica* (1903; rev. edn, 1993). He maintains here that almost all previous philosophers have been guilty of a fallacy, the 'naturalistic fallacy' (p. 62) of treating ethical values as if they were natural properties and thereby seeking to reduce ethics to psychology, sociology, or some other science (or indeed to metaphysics). Instead, according to Moore, there are truths concerning the things that are good which are irreducibly different from all other kinds of truth. Ethical theory has its own distinctive domain, the study of goodness, which is 'simple' and 'unanalysable' (p. 72); but when its results are combined with knowledge of the potential consequences of the courses of action open to us, it should be possible to reach conclusions concerning those actions whose consequences are best, and these are the actions which we ought to perform.

The validity of Moore's arguments in *Principia ethica* remains much disputed. But it is beyond dispute that Moore inaugurated a new approach to ethical theory, in which an analytical concern with the structure of ethical concepts is sharply separated from debates about the substance of morality. This analytic concern within ethical theory was enormously influential during the twentieth century, though it was also much criticized. It is important to recognize, however, that Moore did also advance a substantive scheme of moral values in *Principia ethica*, for he ends the book with an emphatic affirmation of the values of friendship and art:

> by far the most valuable things which we know or can imagine, are certain states of consciousness which may be roughly described as the pleasures of human intercourse and the enjoyment of beautiful objects … it is only for the sake of these things—in order that as much of them as possible may at some time exist—that anyone can be justified in performing any public or private duty. (pp. 237–8)

It is easy to see here the influence of the discussions in which Moore had participated through his membership of the Apostles. Indeed throughout his time as a prize fellow Moore took a leading role in running this group, and in this context he developed friendships with several younger students which were to become central to all their lives thereafter—with Desmond MacCarthy, Leonard Woolf, Lytton Strachey, and J. Maynard Keynes. This is, of course, the group of Cambridge friends who formed the original nucleus of the Bloomsbury Group, after moving in 1904 into Bloomsbury where the Stephen sisters Vanessa and Virginia were setting up house. Moore was never himself a member of this group; but if he took from them a profound, and perhaps exaggerated, sense of the value of friendship and art, they took from him the thought that lives dedicated to these values were indeed lives well spent. As Keynes later put it, *Principia ethica* provided them with their 'religion' (Keynes, 436).

In 1904, when Moore's young friends were moving to London, he too moved away from Cambridge, having failed to secure an extension to his fellowship at Trinity. He went first to live in Edinburgh with his friend A. R. Ainsworth, where he continued writing philosophy while living off some private income inherited from his mother. This situation was, naturally, a challenge to his self-confidence, and the characteristic assertiveness of his early writings was now replaced by a rather tedious determination to make himself *absolutely* clear. Leonard Woolf's description of Moore writing his second book, *Ethics* (1912), during a holiday in 1911 captures well his state of mind at this time:

> in another part of the garden sat Moore, a panama hat on his head, his forehead wet with perspiration, sighing from time to time over his literary constipation as he wrote *Ethics* … Moore said that his mental constipation came from the fact that as soon as he had written down a sentence, he saw that it was just false or that it required a sentence to qualify the qualification. (Holroyd, 234)

Lectureship, marriage, and Cambridge chair By 1911 Moore's relative isolation had in fact come to an end. In 1908 he moved to London, and in the winter of 1910–11 gave an important series of public lectures in London under the title *Some Main Problems of Philosophy* (he wrote out the lectures in full, and they were published in 1953). Finally in 1911 he was appointed to a university lectureship in moral sciences at Cambridge, though at this time the salary for a lectureship was only £50 p.a., and even when it was supplemented by further fees he still needed to draw on his private income until 1925, when he was appointed professor of mental philosophy and logic at Cambridge and elected to a fellowship at Trinity College. Moore then stayed on in Cambridge throughout his academic career, and indeed for almost all the rest of his life. In 1916 he married Dorothy Mildred Ely (1892–1977), who had been a student of moral sciences at Newnham College. They had two sons, Nicholas (1918–1986) and Timothy (1922–2003), and lived at 86 Chesterton Road, Cambridge, where for years they welcomed visitors who had come to study with Moore. Nicholas Moore was a poet; his works include *The Glass Tower* (1944), with illustrations by Lucian Freud. Later he became a gardener and wrote a guide to garden irises.

Timothy Moore became a teacher and composer of music; for many years he was head of music at Dartington School.

Despite Moore's crabbed writing style there are many testimonies to his personal impact in philosophical discussions and lectures. Here, first, is Lytton Strachey, describing Moore's contribution to a discussion of a paper given by Karin Costelloe at a meeting of the Aristotelian Society in London in 1913:

> the excitement came with Moore ... and the intellectual display [was] terrific. But display isn't the right word. Of course it was the very opposite of brilliant—appallingly sensible, and so easy to understand that you wondered why on earth no one else had thought of it. The simplicity of genius! But the way it came out—like some half-stifled geyser, throbbing and convulsed, and then bursting into a towering gush—the poor fellow purple in the face, and beating his podgy hands on the table in desperation. The old spinsters in the background tittered and gasped at the *imprévu* spectacle. (Holroyd, 279)

Second, here is I. A. Richards, who studied moral sciences at Cambridge during the years 1912–15 and 1918–19, describing Moore as a lecturer:

> [Moore] was not like any other lecturer I have heard or heard of. He made sure that what was going on mattered enormously—without your necessarily having even a dim idea as to what it could be that was going on. We were, in truth, undergoing an extraordinarily powerful influence, not one that I would suppose Moore could for a moment conceive. He was not at all interested in that. He was interested in the problem in hand: more interested in it than, I think, I have ever seen anyone interested in anything ... He could take a single sentence from James Ward's *Encyclopaedia Britannica* article on psychology and stay with it for three weeks ... underlining the key words perhaps seventy times, gown flying, chalk dust rising in clouds, his intonations coruscating with apostrophes, and come out by the same door as in he went, looking up to heaven and shaking his head in despair. (Richards, 109)

Another of those who attended Moore's lectures on Ward in 1912 was Ludwig Wittgenstein, who reputedly told Moore that he should not waste his lectures on criticisms of Ward but should use them to develop his own ideas. Moore later wrote that he quickly came to feel that Wittgenstein was 'much cleverer at philosophy ... but also much more profound' (Moore, 'Autobiography', 33). During this early period Moore did not in fact have much contact with Wittgenstein, although he visited Wittgenstein in Norway in 1913 and took an important dictation from him; but after Wittgenstein returned to Cambridge in 1929 the two of them met regularly, and some of Wittgenstein's later writings show the importance he attached to Moore's views. This is indicative of the fact that from 1910 onwards Moore had in fact begun to develop new positions of his own in which he in effect acknowledged that the emphatic realism of his earlier 'refutation' of idealism had been too simple. One central concern of these later writings is with the structure of perception and belief: Moore seeks to show how we can accommodate the existence of illusory appearances and false beliefs within a non-illusory world which does not include objective falsehoods. Another central concern is with the issues raised

by sceptical arguments: Moore maintains that scepticism is an absurd doctrine, but recognizes that he has to demonstrate that there are mistakes in sceptical arguments.

The analysis of common sense The best way to characterize this mature philosophy is as 'the analysis of common sense'. Moore was one of the first philosophers to grasp the significance of the new logic developed by Russell, and he became an effective practitioner of that branch of applied logic that has come to be known as 'philosophical analysis'. Although it was never his view that such analysis by itself yields the resolution of philosophical problems, his writings bear witness to its effectiveness in setting the stage for further argument. At the same time he identified himself as a defender of what he called 'the Common Sense view of the world' by composing his famous paper 'A defence of common sense' (1925; *Selected Writings*, 106–33) for a collection of 'personal statements' on philosophy. This marked a change in his philosophical position—*Principia ethica* is certainly not a defence of common-sense ethical thought. The climax of this development comes in his most famous, and almost his last, paper, 'Proof of an external world' (1939; *Selected Writings*, 147–70). This is the text of a lecture in which Moore returns to the task of refuting idealism and finally accomplishes his 'proof' by means of a startling theatrical gesture in which he simply holds up his hands before his audience and challenges them to deny their reality.

Moore held his professorship at Cambridge from 1925 until 1939. This was the golden period of Cambridge philosophy, when distinguished students from home and abroad came to study with him and with Wittgenstein, and then travelled afar to spread their new way of doing philosophy. Moore's influence among British philosophers of the period was unrivalled. One vehicle of this was his editorship of the philosophical journal *Mind*, of which he was editor from 1921 until 1944. But, as ever, it was in discussion that he really captured his audience, especially those of a younger generation, such as Gilbert Ryle:

> For some of us there still lives the Moore whose voice is never quite resuscitated by his printed words ... He gave us courage not by making concessions, but by making no concessions to our youth or to our shyness. He would explode at our mistakes and muddles with just that genial ferocity with which he would explode at the mistakes and muddles of philosophical high-ups, and with just the genial ferocity with which he would explode at mistakes and muddles of his own. He would listen with minute attention to what we said, and then, without a trace of discourtesy or courtesy, treat our remarks simply on their merits ... sometimes, without a trace of politeness or patronage, crediting them with whatever positive utility he thought they possessed. (Ryle, 270–71)

In 1939 Moore retired, and then spent the war years 1940–44 in the United States; again there are many testimonies from his time there to his impact as a teacher. Thereafter he lived quietly in Cambridge. In 1951 he was appointed to the Order of Merit. He died at the Evelyn Nursing Home, Cambridge, on 24 October 1958 and was buried in St Giles's cemetery. His son Nicholas wrote this epitaph for him:

Here lies the great philosopher
Who did not like the world to err,
Who did not err himself, but died
Forever not quite satisfied
That he was not a silly, though
His wise friends never thought him so.

THOMAS BALDWIN

Sources G. E. Moore, *Selected writings*, ed. T. Baldwin (1993) · G. E. Moore, 'Autobiography', *The philosophy of G. E. Moore*, ed. P. A. Schilpp (1942), 3–39 [incl. bibliography of Moore's writings] · CUL, Moore MSS · J. M. Keynes, 'My early beliefs', *The collected writings of John Maynard Keynes*, ed. D. Moggridge and E. Johnson, 10 (1972) · P. Levy, *Moore* (1979) · M. Holroyd, *Lytton Strachey: a new biography* (1994) · B. Russell, *'Portraits from memory' and other essays* (1956) · I. A. Richards, *Complementarities: uncollected essays*, ed. J. P. Russo, [another edn] (1977) · G. Ryle, *Collected papers: Gilbert Ryle*, 1 (1971) · private information (2004) [Sir H. Bondi]
Archives CUL, corresp. and papers | King's AC Cam., letters to John Maynard Keynes · King's AC Cam., letters to W. G. H. Sprott · LUL, corresp. with Thomas Sturge Moore · McMaster University, Hamilton, Ontario, corresp. with Bertrand Russell · Trinity Cam., paper on Aristotle's *Ethics* by F. M. Cornford, annotated by subject; letters to Norman Malcolm · U. Sussex, corresp. with Leonard Woolf | SOUND BL NSA, performance recording
Likenesses photograph, 1899, Trinity Cam. [*see illus.*] · W. Stoneman, two photographs, 1921–45, NPG · P. Horton, chalk drawing, 1947, Trinity Cam. · P. Horton, pen and chalk drawing, 1947, NPG · P. Horton, pencil drawing, 1947, NPG · H. A. Freeth, etching, 1952, NPG · H. A. Freeth, pen and wash drawing, 1952, FM Cam. · photographs, CUL, Moore MSS · photograph, U. Cam., faculty of philosophy
Wealth at death £5243 7s. 6d.: probate, 2 April 1959, *CGPLA Eng. & Wales*

Moore, George Henry (1810–1870), politician, son of George Moore and his wife, Louisa Browne, granddaughter of the first earl of Altamont, was born at Moore Hall, co. Mayo, on 1 March 1810. The family was Catholic and landed, with mercantile antecedents. Having been a pupil at Oscott College, Birmingham, from *c*.1817, he entered Christ's College, Cambridge, in 1828 but did not graduate. Legal studies begun in London in 1830 were also left uncompleted. From 1834 to 1837 he travelled in Russia, the Caucasus, and the Middle East. Subsequently he became immersed in hunting and horse-racing, along with his brother Augustus, who was killed in a fall at Aintree racecourse in April 1845. Winning the Chester Cup and £17,000 on 6 May 1846 was the high point of Moore's racing career. In 1851 he married Mary, daughter of Maurice Blake of Ballinafad, co. Mayo.

In 1847 Moore was elected Liberal MP for his native county. His brilliant oratorical gifts soon brought him to the fore, and in 1851 he initiated a policy of obstructive opposition to the Ecclesiastical Titles Bill which was taken up by a group of Catholic MPs known as the Irish brigade; they became the nucleus of the Independent Opposition Party. When in 1853 other leading members broke ranks and accepted office, Moore's prominence in the party was enhanced. Although he lost his seat on petition in 1857, he was one of a small circle of notables involved in subsequent years in endeavouring to lay plans for a nationalist movement. At the general election of 1868 he regained a co. Mayo seat and subsequently was the first MP to begin the undermining of Gladstone's stature in the eyes of

Irish Catholics, who had initially seen in the new prime minister the embodiment of concession to their demands. Publicly Moore supported the campaign for an amnesty for Fenian prisoners and secretly he discussed co-operation with the Fenian leadership. He was about to launch a new nationalist initiative when he died suddenly on 19 April 1870 at home at Moore Hall. He was survived by his wife.

By political necessity an advocate of tenant-right legislation, Moore was nevertheless unbending as a landlord and was in bitter dispute with some of his tenants at the time of his death. Mischievously his son George *Moore, the celebrated novelist, suggested that Moore's tenants had driven him to suicide, an interpretation not consistent with the evidence adduced by his other son, and biographer, Maurice Moore. Moore was buried four days after his death in the family mausoleum at Moore Hall, despite calls for a public funeral in Dublin. He was widely esteemed but had forfeited much goodwill by reason of cantankerousness and a sharp tongue.

R. V. COMERFORD

Sources M. Moore, *An Irish gentleman: George Henry Moore, his travels, his racing, his politics* (1913) · J. Whyte, *The Irish independent party, 1850–59* (1958) · R. V. Comerford, *The Fenians in context: Irish politics and society, 1848–82* (1985) · *Freeman's Journal* [Dublin] (22 April 1870) · *Freeman's Journal* [Dublin] (23 April 1870) · *Freeman's Journal* [Dublin] (25 April 1870) · *The Nation* (23 April 1870) · *CGPLA Eng. & Wales* (1870)
Archives NL Ire., corresp., draft speeches, travel journals | Bodl. Oxf., letters to Benjamin Disraeli · NL Ire., Butt MSS · NL Ire., William Smith O'Brien MSS · NL Ire., A. M. Sullivan MSS
Likenesses engraving, repro. in *The Nation* (8 Aug 1868)
Wealth at death under £200—in England: Irish probate sealed in England: probate, 23 June 1870, *CGPLA Eng. & Wales* · under £4000: probate, 23 June 1870, *CGPLA Ire.*

Moore, Gerald Frederick (1899–1987), pianist and accompanist, was born on 30 July 1899 in Watford, Hertfordshire, the eldest in the family of three sons and a daughter, who died in childhood, of David Frank Moore, who owned a men's outfitting establishment, and his Welshborn wife, Chestina Jones. He was educated at Watford grammar school. Musical, with perfect pitch, he learned the piano locally with Wallis Bandey. When, owing to a financial crisis, the family decided to emigrate to Toronto, Canada, the thirteen-year-old Gerald had to start again with his piano studies. His mother arranged an audition with Michael Hambourg, founder of a school of music in Toronto. This resulted in a scholarship and much expert coaching. Hambourg's cellist son, Boris, later took Moore as his accompanist on a tour of forty engagements in western Canada. When Moore finally was shipped back to London in 1919, it was another Hambourg son—the pianist Mark Hambourg—who offered to take over his training.

But Moore was not cut out for a career as a soloist and on the advice of Landon Ronald, then principal of the Guildhall School of Music, he concentrated on accompanying. He went on tour with baritone Peter Dawson and was engaged on an exclusive basis by the tenor John Coates. Coates taught him to work and awakened his realization

Gerald Frederick Moore (1899–1987), by Elliott & Fry, 1958

of the importance of the piano part in the basic structure of the song: Moore said he owed everything to him.

In 1921 Moore made his first record (for HMV), with Renée Chemet, the French violinist. The studio had a large horn contraption into which the violinist played. In spite of the piece being a gentle lullaby Moore had to play fortissimo throughout in order to be heard at all on the record.

A vital step forward for Moore was the arrival on the recording scene of the microphone. At last his playing would be faithfully reproduced on records. At first he was greatly shocked by hearing himself. But by listening carefully he was able to improve, technically and musically, and raise his playing to a new standard, which took him to the top. Apart from many instrumentalists, his famous vocal partners included Elena Gerhardt, Elisabeth Schumann, Maggie Teyte, John McCormack, Hans Hotter, Kathleen Ferrier, Elisabeth Schwarzkopf, Victoria de los Angeles, Dietrich Fischer-Dieskau, and Janet Baker.

When Myra Hess started her series of lunchtime concerts in the National Gallery, during the Second World War, she asked Moore to give a talk at the piano on his experiences as an accompanist. He revealed a sense of verbal timing of which any professional comic would be proud. His unique blend of wit and wisdom not only pleased the cognoscenti but also won over ordinary people who had no idea that classical music could be fun. This kind of treatment has its dangers, but not with Moore, who always put the music first and used the jokes to sugar the pill. The talk became immensely popular. His first book, *The Unashamed Accompanist* (1943; 3rd edn, 1984) grew out of these talks.

Moore played throughout the world as an accompanist and included many tours of the United States as a lecture-recitalist. His favourite festivals included Edinburgh, Salzburg, and King's Lynn (where he played piano duets with Ruth, Lady Fermoy).

Moore retired from the concert platform in 1967, at the comparatively early age of sixty-seven, when he was at the top of his form. A farewell concert, which was recorded, was given in his honour at the Royal Festival Hall on 20 February 1967. After Moore gave up public playing his great affection for Schubert became an obsession: he embarked on the huge task of recording over 500 Schubert songs. Three sets of these—*Die schöne Müllerin*, *Winterreise*, and *Schwanengesang*, all with Fischer-Dieskau—were issued on compact disc and form a lasting tribute to his work. His playing was remarkable for flawless technique and a rare ability to make the piano 'sing'.

Moore was a talented writer. His best-known book was the autobiography *Am I Too Loud?* (1962). He became CBE (1954), honorary RAM (1962), FRCM (1980), honorary DLitt, Sussex (1968), and honorary MusD, Cambridge (1973).

Moore was a stocky, thickset figure not readily associable with the ravishingly delicate effects he could obtain from the piano. His zest for living, his enormous vitality, and his sense of humour were strong preservatives in a very hard-working life. Away from music Moore enjoyed in early life tennis and golf and, later, bridge, gardening, and watching cricket. He had an ideal partner in his wife, Enid Kathleen (d. 1994), daughter of Montague Richard, ironmonger, of Beckenham, whom he called 'the most perfect of all accompanists'. They had no children. Moore had had a previous marriage, in Canada in 1929, which lasted only three or four years and which ended in divorce. Moore died in his sleep at his home, Pond House, Elm Road, Penn, Buckinghamshire, on 13 March 1987.

JOSEPH COOPER, rev.

Sources G. Moore, *Am I too loud?* (1962) · G. Moore, *Furthermoore* (1983) · G. Moore, *Collected memoirs* (1986) · *The Times* (17 March 1987) · *The Independent* (17 March 1987) · *The Times* (21 Feb 1967) · personal knowledge (1996) · *CGPLA Eng. & Wales* (1987)
Archives Bodl. Oxf., letters to Jack Lambert
Likenesses Elliott & Fry, photograph, 1958, NPG [*see illus.*]
Wealth at death £140,301: probate, 14 May 1987, *CGPLA Eng. & Wales*

Moore, Sir Graham (1764–1843), naval officer, the third surviving son of Dr John *Moore (1729–1802) and his wife, Jean Simson (1735–1820), and the younger brother of both Lieutenant-General Sir John *Moore and James Carrick *Moore, was born in Glasgow. He entered the navy in 1777, and served in the West Indies, on the North American station, and in the channel. On 8 March 1782 he was promoted lieutenant of the *Crown*, one of the fleet with Lord Howe at the relief of Gibraltar and in the rencounter with the allied fleet off Cape Spartel in October 1782. After the peace he went to France to study the language, but was recalled by an appointment to the *Perseus*, in which, with the *Dido* and the *Adamant*, the flagship of Sir Richard

Hughes at Halifax, he served continuously until promoted commander of the sloop *Bonetta* (22 November 1790); in her he returned to England in 1793. On 2 April 1794 he was promoted captain and posted to the frigate *Syren*, employed during the year in the North Sea, and afterwards on the coast of France, as one of the squadron under the orders of Sir Richard John Strachan. In September 1795 he was moved into the *Melampus* (42 guns), and, remaining on the same station, cruised with distinguished success against the French privateers and coasting trade. In the summer of 1798 he was attached to the squadron on the coast of Ireland under Sir John Borlase Warren; he assisted in the defeat of the French squadron on 12 October, and on the 14th captured *La Résolue* (40 guns), with 500 men, including soldiers, on board. In February 1800 he went out to the West Indies, but after eighteen months his health broke down under the trial of a summer in the Gulf of Mexico, and in August 1801 he was invalided out.

On the renewal of the war in 1803 Moore was appointed to the frigate *Indefatigable* (46 guns), attached to the fleet off Brest under Admiral Cornwallis. In September 1804, because of the threatening attitude of Spain and intelligence that a large quantity of treasure expected at Cadiz was intended for the service of France, Moore, in command of a small frigate squadron, four in all, was sent to watch off Cadiz and intercept the treasure ships. On 4 October they were sighted, four frigates under the command of Rear-Admiral Bustamente. The two squadrons approached each other in line of battle. On a shot being fired across his bows the Spanish admiral brought to, and Moore sent an officer on board to say that he had orders to detain the ships and take them to England, that he wished to do so without bloodshed, but the admiral's decision must be made at once. The Spanish admiral refused to yield to a nominally equal force. A sharp action took place, three of the Spanish frigates were captured, and the fourth was blown up, with the loss of nearly all on board. The treasure taken amounted to upwards of 3.5 million silver dollars, and was condemned as the prize of the captors, although war was not declared until 24 January 1805, more than three months afterwards. Moore used his share to purchase Brook Farm, at Cobham in Surrey.

In August 1807 Moore was appointed to the *Marlborough* (74 guns) on the coast of Portugal. In November he was ordered to hoist a broad pennant and escort the royal family of Portugal to Brazil. With a squadron of four British and five Portuguese ships of the line, besides frigates, smaller vessels, and a large number of merchant ships, he sailed from the Tagus on 27 November and arrived at Rio de Janeiro on 7 March 1808. Before leaving again for Europe he was invested by the prince regent with the order of the Tower and Sword.

In the autumn of 1809 the *Marlborough* formed part of the force under Sir Richard Strachan in the Walcheren expedition, and when the island had to be evacuated Moore was assigned the task of destroying the basin, arsenal, and sea defences of Flushing. In August 1811 he was offered the command of the yacht *Royal Sovereign*, but he declined it, preferring active service, and in January 1812 he was appointed to the *Chatham* (74 guns). That year he married Dora (1789–1875), the daughter of Thomas Eden, deputy auditor of Greenwich Hospital, the brother of William Eden, first Baron Auckland. They had one son. On 12 August 1812 Moore was promoted rear-admiral, after which for a short time he commanded in the Baltic, with his flag in the *Fame*. In 1814 he was captain of the fleet to Lord Keith in the channel. On 2 January 1815 he was nominated KCB, and on the escape of Napoleon from Elba was ordered to the Mediterranean as second in command. The appointment was cancelled on the abrupt termination of the war, and on 24 May 1816 Moore was appointed one of the lords of the Admiralty. He remained in this post for four years, rising to be the senior lord in 1818.

On 12 April 1819 Moore was promoted vice-admiral, and in March 1820 he went out as commander-in-chief in the Mediterranean to replace Sir Thomas Fremantle, who had died suddenly, with his flag in the *Rochefort*. Shortly after his arrival on the station he took the king of Naples to Leghorn (Livorno) on his way to attend the congress at Laibach. On his return to Naples the king wished to confer on Moore the grand cross of the order of St Ferdinand and Merit for the important services rendered to the king and the royal family by the British squadron during the revolution. Moore, however, declined it as contrary to British regulations. He was nominated GCMG on 28 September 1820. He returned to England in 1823, was made a GCB on 11 March 1836, and became admiral on 10 January 1837. From 1839 to 1842 he was commander-in-chief at Plymouth. During the latter part of the time his health deteriorated and he lost his hearing entirely. He died at Brook Farm, Cobham, on 25 November 1843, and was buried there in the churchyard, where there is a plain monument to his memory. His son, John Graham, born on 16 January 1822 at Malta, was promoted to the rank of commander in the navy three days before his father's death. He served with distinction in the Crimean War and died a captain in 1866.

Moore was a brave and resourceful sea officer. Although he commanded fleets and served extensively, he missed all the great fleet actions. His early career benefited, like that of his more famous brother, from the patronage of the eighth duke of Hamilton, whom his father had accompanied on the grand tour in the 1770s. Moore was always close to his brother, and his politics were also whig, which explains his relationship with Lord Keith and his final appointment in 1839. However, he was not so much a political figure as to exclude himself from the Admiralty in 1816. His service there was unremarkable, chiefly from his failure to take a seat in the House of Commons.

J. K. LAUGHTON, rev. ANDREW LAMBERT

Sources C. Oman, *Sir John Moore* (1953) · *The Creevey papers*, ed. H. Maxwell, 3rd edn (1905); rev. edn, ed. J. Gore (1963) · H. R. V. Fox, third Lord Holland, *Further memoirs of the whig party, 1807–1821*, ed. Lord Stavordale (1905)

Archives CUL, diaries; letter-book; Brook Farm accounts, naval journal | BL, corresp. with Sir William A'Court, Add. MS 41536

Likenesses T. Lawrence, oils, 1793, NPG

Moore, Sir Henry, first baronet (1713–1769), colonial governor, was born in Vere, Jamaica, on 7 February 1713, the eldest son of Samuel Moore, a planter in Jamaica, and Elizabeth, daughter of Samuel Lowe of Goadby, Leicestershire. Samuel Moore's father, John, had settled in Barbados during Charles II's reign, and later migrated to Jamaica. Henry Moore was educated at Eton College—presumably he was the Moore attending between 1725 and 1728—and at Leiden University in the Netherlands, where he matriculated in 1731. On 13 December 1751 he married Catharine Maria Long (1727–1812), eldest daughter of Samuel Long of Longville (a member of the council of Jamaica), and sister of Edward *Long, the island's renowned historian. Henry and Catharine had a daughter, named Susanah Jane, who was married to Alexander Dickson at the time of her father's death, and a son, Sir John Henry *Moore (b. 1756), who died unmarried on 16 January 1780.

Henry Moore's political career began when he joined the Jamaica militia. After serving several terms in the assembly, he became a member of the council (1752), island secretary (1753), and lieutenant-governor (c.1755) under a dormant commission. When the governor, Admiral Sir Charles Knowles, was recalled in June 1756, Moore became acting governor. A sensible, tactful, yet firm administrator, Moore judiciously managed the assembly, especially when its conduct threatened to provoke civil discord. In 1759, when war with France led Moore to impose martial law, the council countered by attempting to obstruct his administration. Moore resolutely suspended the trouble-makers. Later in 1759 the appointed governor, Sir George Haldane, superseded him. When Haldane died several weeks later, Moore resumed office.

On Easter Monday 1760 a bloody slave revolt erupted, and soon became a guerrilla war that lasted for more than a year. Moore handled the situation capably and courageously. He promptly declared martial law and personally commanded two British regiments. His decisiveness, speed, and tactical skills were critical elements in crushing the revolt. Twice he nearly lost his life in ambushes. On another occasion, when he was discovered reconnoitring alone, his marksmanship saved his life. In February 1762 his administration ended, and he sailed for England, where he was made a baronet on 28 January 1764.

In July 1765 Moore was appointed governor of New York. He arrived there in November amid the Stamp Act disturbances. He handled the crisis much more adroitly than his predecessor, Lieutenant-Governor Cadwallader Colden. Moore took steps, such as dismantling Fort George, which appeased the public. However, he refused to reopen the port so long as the Stamp Act was not being enforced, and hoped thereby to make the people pay for their disobedience. Although he allegedly had a streak of indolence, he was a shrewd politician who adeptly governed the province during a tense period in imperial relations. When parliament passed the Restraining Act (1767), which threatened to suspend the New York assembly until it obeyed the Quartering Act (1765), Moore secretly and successfully worked with both provincial parties to evade the act and thereby save the assembly. Moore also aided New Yorkers in their fruitful effort to have parliament amend the Currency Act (1764) so that the province could issue paper money. He also engaged in a struggle with General Thomas Gage, the commander-in-chief of the British army in America, over which official (the civil or the military) should take precedence at official functions. Moore likewise attempted to settle New York's boundary disputes with other colonies, and did so successfully with Quebec. He strove to maintain good relations with New York's Native American population, and twice visited the Five Nations in this quest.

Following a sixteen-day illness, Moore died at Fort George, New York city (where he lived), on 11 September 1769, and was buried at Trinity Church, New York city, on 12 September. His widow later married Richard Vincent, and died in England on 8 June 1812. The *New-York Gazette* concluded that Moore had governed 'with such a Degree of *Wisdom* and *Temper*, as to gain the Approbation of his Sovereign and the Esteem of the People committed to his care' (*New-York Gazette*). JOSEPH S. TIEDEMANN

Sources GEC, *Baronetage*, 5.130 · *New-York Gazette, or, The Weekly Post-Boy* (18 Sept 1769) · W. J. Gardner, *A history of Jamaica* (1873); repr. (1971) · M. Jensen, *The founding of a nation: a history of the American Revolution, 1763–1776* (1968) · J. S. Tiedemann, *Reluctant revolutionaries: New York city and the road to independence, 1763–1776* (1997) · E. B. O'Callaghan, ed., *The documentary history of the state of New York*, 4 vols. (1849–51) · E. B. O'Callaghan and B. Fernow, eds. and trans., *Documents relative to the colonial history of the state of New York*, 15 vols. (1853–87), vols. 7–8 · *The Colden letter books*, 2 vols. (1877–8) · *The letters and papers of Cadwallader Colden*, 6–7 (1922–3) · W. S. Pelletreau, ed., *Abstract of wills on file in the Surrogate's office: city of New York*, 7 (1899), 279–80 · G. W. Bridges, *The annals of Jamaica*, 2 (1828); facs. edn (1968) · T. Jones, *History of New York during the revolutionary war*, ed. E. F. De Lancey, 2 vols. (1879)
Archives BL, corresp. and papers, Add. MSS 12440, 22679 | BL, letters to Lord Holdernesse, Egerton MS 3490
Wealth at death Pelletreau, ed., *Abstract of wills*, 279–80 · estate large enough to provide wife with yearly income of £600

Moore, Henry (1732–1802), Presbyterian minister and hymn writer, son of Henry Moore (d. 1762), minister of Treville Street Presbyterian congregation, Plymouth, was born at Plymouth on 30 March 1732; his mother was the daughter of William Bellew of Stockleigh Court, Devon. He received his rudimentary education from his father, after which he attended the grammar school in Plymouth run by the Revd Bedford, afterwards vicar of St Charles the Martyr, Plymouth. In 1749 he entered Doddridge's academy at Northampton, and after Doddridge's death he moved, on 9 November 1752, to Daventry Academy, under Caleb Ashworth; there he remained until 1755, when he became minister of a small Presbyterian congregation at Dulverton, Somerset, after which he moved in 1757 to the Presbyterian congregation at Modbury, Devon. He was at this time an Arian. It was not until 6 July 1768 that he was ordained at Plymouth. His congregation at Modbury went over to Methodism, and towards the end of 1787 he moved to the Presbyterian congregation at Liskeard, Cornwall. He seems to have retired from active duty before 1792, when Thomas Morgan, one of the founders of the Western Unitarian Society, is described as minister at Liskeard.

As a writer Moore possessed true poetical talent but he was scarcely known to the general public. He first gave evidence of his talent in an elegiac poem written in 1752 in affectionate memory of his revered tutor, Philip Doddridge. The poem was spoken of as 'a tribute of elegant fancy and warm affection' (Hatfield). He also wrote several hymns of great beauty, such as 'Supreme and Universal Light' and 'My God thy boundless love I praise', both of which still appear in most Unitarian hymn books. His critical abilities were also of a high order, as is apparent in his numerous contributions to the two volumes of *Commentaries and Essays* published by the Society for Promoting the Knowledge of the Scriptures. He was persuaded in the last year of his life to prepare a manuscript volume of his poems for publication but the paralysis he suffered shortly before his death prevented him from completing the task. He died, unmarried, at Liskeard on 2 November 1802 and was buried there. The Revd Dr John Aikin, a friend and admirer, undertook to oversee the publication of his work, which was issued in 1803 with the title *Poems, Lyrical and Miscellaneous*.

ALEXANDER GORDON, *rev.* M. J. MERCER

Sources J. Murch, *A history of the Presbyterian and General Baptist churches in the west of England* (1835) · E. F. Hatfield, *The poets of the church: a series of biographical sketches of hymn writers* (1884) · R. Spears, *Record of Unitarian worthies* (1877) · G. E. Evans, *Vestiges of protestant dissent* (1897) · J. Julian, ed., *A dictionary of hymnology*, rev. edn (1907)
Archives DWL, letters to Philip Doddridge

Moore, Henry (1751–1844), Methodist minister and biographer, only surviving son of Richard Moore (1716/17–1763), farmer and grazier, was born near Dublin on 21 December 1751. He was educated at Oxmantown Green under a clergyman named Williamson and proved himself to be a good classical scholar. He was prevented from going to university by his father's death and instead was apprenticed to a wood-engraver. He practised this skill during visits to London in 1771 and 1773–6, where he was attracted by the gaiety of its social life, and especially by the theatre. When still very young he had heard John Wesley preach in Dublin, but was not impressed by his oratory. However, he frequented the Methodist services from time to time, and back in Dublin in February 1777 was converted through reading the epistle to the Romans, hearing Samuel Bradburn preach, and attending a watch-night service. He became a local preacher and opened a school providing instruction in the classics. But when this showed signs of prospering, he gave it up, fearing the temptation of worldliness. In 1779 he married Ann (Nancy) Young (*bap.* 1756, *d.* 1813) of Coleraine, a great favourite with John Wesley; the marriage produced no children.

In the spring of 1779, while employed in Liverpool, Moore was called by Wesley into the itinerant ministry and appointed to Coleraine, co. Londonderry. Here he met and became a friend of Alexander Knox, whose parents were Methodists. After serving in several other Irish circuits, in 1784 he was transferred to London and acted for two years as Wesley's assistant, travelling companion, and amanuensis. His knowledge of French, which Wesley 'had very much forgotten', made him especially useful in his correspondence with France. In 1785 he turned down the possibility of going to the United States out of a sense of duty to his mother, and instead returned to the Dublin circuit in 1786–8. While there he began, on the advice of a physician, to study medicine, but soon abandoned it as incompatible with his circuit responsibilities. Between 1788 and 1790 he was again closely associated with Wesley who, he recorded, 'never treated me as his assistant in the work; his spirit and conduct had a kindness with an appearance of friendship, notwithstanding the disparity of years'. He could hold his own with the older man when the need arose, and Wesley said to him, 'No man in England has contradicted me so much as you have done, and yet, Henry, I love you still.' He had resisted the suggestion of Charles Wesley that he should take Anglican orders, but on 27 February 1789 John Wesley, with the assistance of two other Anglican priests, James Creighton and Peard Dickinson, ordained him and two other preachers, the first to be ordained for work in England.

At the time of Wesley's last illness Moore was stationed in Bristol, but came up to London the day before he died (2 March 1791) and was with him at the end. By his last will (dated 5 October 1789) Wesley had made Moore one of his literary executors, together with Dr Thomas Coke and John Whitehead, with power to burn or publish his manuscripts 'as they see good'. This very soon brought Moore much anxiety and trouble. It was agreed by the executors that a biography should be brought out as soon as possible, since John Hampson, a former itinerant, had already announced the publication of his *Memoirs of Wesley*. Whitehead, Wesley's physician and a local preacher in the London circuit, was deputed to write the life and was entrusted with all Wesley's papers, but refused to comply with the instruction of the conference that the executors should examine and cull the papers. An acrimonious dispute ensued, which led to the hasty compilation of an 'official' biography, published in 1792. Coke and Moore were named as the joint authors on the title page, though in fact the work was almost entirely Moore's and is said to have been prepared in little more than four weeks, and without access to the sources in Whitehead's hands. It met with some success, despite its limitations and defects. Moore ultimately obtained access to the bulk of Wesley's papers, though some had by then (1797) been destroyed by John Pawson as 'worthless lumber', and used them when many years later he rewrote and substantially enlarged his own biography. This was published in two volumes in 1824–5, this time under his name alone, and drew quite heavily (often without acknowledgement) on both Whitehead's and Hampson's work.

Moore was one of the preachers who held a clandestine meeting in Lichfield in April 1794 to consider the future government of Methodism. Though he supported the proposal to provide Methodism with a hierarchy of 'bishops', he successfully opposed any move being made without conference approval, which in the event was not forthcoming. Later that year he found himself at the centre of another dispute, in which two fundamental issues coalesced: the question of the administration of the sacrament by the Methodist preachers and the division of authority between the conference and local chapel trustees. During the conference which met in Bristol that year he had assisted at a celebration of the Lord's Supper, and was informed by the trustees of the New Room at Bristol that in consequence of this he would not be allowed into the New Room pulpit. When he was physically debarred from it, he left for the new Portland Chapel, accompanied by a majority of the congregation. A split ensued, which led to the building of King Street Chapel and the closure of the New Room as a Methodist place of worship.

Moore's difficulties during these years after Wesley's death were compounded by the fact that Wesley had named him in his will as one of twelve preachers (including four Anglican clergymen) permitted to preach at his new City Road Chapel in London and to be responsible for appointing the preachers at the chapel in Bath, apparently without reference to the conference or the local trustees. In 1812 one of the City Road trustees, Harvey Walklate Mortimer, disputed his right to read prayers at the chapel and once again a lengthy dispute arose, resolved only by Mortimer's death in 1819. Even then it was not until May 1826 that Moore and Joseph Entwisle became the first Methodist preachers not in Anglican orders to administer the sacrament there.

Moore was committed to the authority of conference, and was deeply unhappy about the concessions made in the 'miscellaneous regulations' of 1797, which he saw as an abandonment to the laity of conference's authority and its responsibility for spiritual discipline. He remained loyal to the conference even when he disagreed with its decisions, as he did over the establishment of a theological institution for the training of ministers in 1834 and over the setting up of a centenary fund in 1839. He himself was twice elected president of the conference, in 1804 and 1823.

Moore had no personal ambition and refused engagements that might interfere with his circuit duties as an itinerant, including the editorship of the *Arminian Magazine* in 1789. But, in addition to his biographies of Wesley, he also wrote a life of Mary Fletcher (1817). He did not retire from the active ministry until 1833, when he was eighty-two. By then he had outlived all his contemporaries and was revered as a representative of the devout simplicity characteristic of Methodism in its earliest years. Nevertheless, when the conference determined in 1836 to adopt the practice of ordination by laying on of hands, Moore, as the only surviving preacher ordained by Wesley himself, was passed over and the possibility of a 'Methodist apostolic succession' was missed.

After the death of his first wife in 1813, Moore married Mary Ann Hind (*d.* 1834) in August 1814; as before, this marriage did not produce any children. His last years were spent in a house in Brunswick Place, City Road, London,

where, after suffering for two years from paralysis, he died on 27 April 1844. He was buried in the City Road Chapel graveyard.

ALEXANDER GORDON, *rev.* JOHN A. VICKERS

Sources M. A. Smith, *The life of the Rev Mr Henry Moore* (1844) · letters, JRL, Methodist Archives and Research Centre · G. Smith, *History of Wesleyan Methodism*, 2 vols. (1857–8) · *Minutes of the Methodist conferences, from the first, held in London by the late Rev. John Wesley …*, 20 vols. (1812–79) [1844 conference] · G. J. Stephenson, *City Road Chapel* (1872) · G. J. Stephenson, *Methodist worthies*, 6 vols. (1884–6) · H. D. Rack, *Reasonable enthusiast: John Wesley and the rise of Methodism* (1989)

Archives JRL, Methodist Archives and Research Centre, corresp.; letters, plus some items relating to his wives; letters to him, sermon notes and register · Wesley College, Bristol, corresp., shorthand diary · Wesley's Chapel, London, letters

Likenesses W. T. Fry, stipple, NPG · W. Ridley, stipple (aged forty-four), BM, NPG; repro. in *Methodist Magazine* (1797) · line engraving (aged thirty-two), BM, NPG; repro. in *Arminian Magazine* (1785) · portrait, repro. in *Arminian Magazine* (1797) · portrait, repro. in *Methodist Magazine* (1824)

Moore, Henry (1831–1895), marine painter, was born at 14 Castlegate, York, on 7 March 1831, the second son of the portrait painter William *Moore (1790–1851) and his second wife, Sarah Collingham (*d.* 1860), and the ninth son and tenth child in the family of fourteen children. Four of his brothers were artists, including John Collingham *Moore (1829–1880) [*see under* Moore, William] and Albert Joseph *Moore (1841–1893). Henry Moore was taught painting by his father and in 1851 entered York School of Design. His early work was clear and vigorous, and as well as landscapes that show a Pre-Raphaelite influence, he painted flowers in watercolours and animals in oils. In spring 1853 he joined his brother John Collingham in lodgings near Oxford Street, London, and that summer he made his début at the Royal Academy with the landscape *Glen Clunie, Braemar*. He was admitted to the Royal Academy Schools in December 1853 but baulked at the training and stayed only a few months. In 1854 he exhibited *Study in Gowbarrow Park* at the Royal Academy and thereafter hardly ever failed to send one or more works each year. In 1855 he also exhibited many works with the Society of British Artists in Suffolk Street, of which he became a member in 1867. He took an active interest in the society's affairs until 1875, when he resigned and ceased to exhibit. In addition he exhibited at the Portland Gallery (1855–60), the British Institution (1855–65), the Dudley Gallery (1865–82), and, in later years, the Grosvenor Gallery and the New Gallery. He was well represented in provincial galleries throughout his career. Moore sent fifty-five works to the Old Watercolour Society, of which he became an associate in 1876 and a full member in 1880. In total he exhibited 550 works—testimony to his great industry.

In the summers of 1855 and 1856 Moore painted mountain scenes at Servoz, near Chamonix. In 1857 he made the first of a series of prolonged visits to the fishing village of Clovelly in north Devon. This marked a new epoch in his career, as at Clovelly he became inspired with the open sea, something that he 'never saw truly given in a painting' (Maclean, 33). Gradually he turned to marine painting, having by 1860 established himself as a successful landscape painter. In that year he married, on 19 July, Mary (1834/5–1890), the daughter of Robert and Elizabeth Bollans, of York; they had two daughters, one of whom also became a painter. From 1860 until 1873 Moore painted landscapes as well as coastal scenes and sea pieces, but in the last twenty years of his life his major works were almost all seascapes.

Moore's high reputation as a marine painter was built on careful observation of the sea in all weathers. He made painstaking pencil studies, initially from land but from 1873 on board ship as well, mostly in the English Channel. Always in his work the sea itself was more important than anything upon it. He used short decisive brush strokes to create form and colour, rarely resorting to the palette knife. As he progressed his technique became more fluid, and his colours developed from cold greys to rich, deep blues and greens. With *Mid-Channel* (exh. RA, 1881) he began a series of works remarkable for their precise 'observation of atmosphere and wave form' (Maclean, 51). For these he made careful pencil studies of the movement of waves and ships. His marine paintings did not fit into any established genre, and galleries found his intense colours difficult to hang. But Moore would not be deflected, and his determination to pursue his scientific interest in wave form in his art perhaps caused his election to an associateship at the Royal Academy to be delayed.

Moore was elected an associate of the Royal Academy in 1885 after the purchase, under the terms of the Chantrey bequest, of *Catspaws off the Land* (exh. RA, 1885; Tate collection). As much a landscape as a seascape, it depicts two fishing sloops against a headland. With this Moore exhibited *The Newhaven Packet* (Birmingham City Art Gallery), 'a pure blue sea-piece, and perhaps Moore's master-work in this direction', subsequently purchased by the corporation of Birmingham (Maclean, 81). Moore was finally elected Royal Academician in 1893. He exhibited 107 works at the academy, including *A White Calm* (1858), *The Launch of the Lifeboat* (1876; Walker Art Gallery, Liverpool), *A Breezy Day in the Channel* (1888), and *Summer at Sea* (1893).

In the 1880s and 1890s Moore was recognized as a fine colourist and one of the most able marine painters of his day. In 1887 the Fine Art Society staged an exhibition, entitled 'Afloat and Ashore', of ninety of his pictures and watercolour drawings. His work was exhibited throughout Europe and he was one of the few English painters of his day to seek and obtain French honours: at the Universal Exhibition in Paris in 1889 *Clearness after Rain* (exh. RA, 1887) won the grand prix (medaille d'honneur), and he was made chevalier of the Légion d'honneur. Moore continued to paint until the last, in spite of breaking both arms in a fall from a London omnibus in September 1891. He lived for many years at Hampstead, and died of apoplexy on 22 June 1895 at the High Cliff Hotel, Margate. He was buried in Highgate cemetery. Shortly before his death an exhibition was held at York of the works of his father, William Moore, and his five artist sons.

Henry Moore was of medium height with a strong frame, 'full-bearded, with high intellectual forehead, crowned by thick, dark hair … keen eyes, and aquiline nose' (Maclean, 124). His search for accuracy in sea painting led him to a strong realism which many admired. Others, though, criticized his painting for a lack of imagination, dismissed as crude and violent his use of brilliant blues and greens, and held him to be an imitator of J. C. Hook, whom he met at Clovelly in May 1858. 'It would be very doubtful', ventured the *Art Journal* at the time of his death, 'if Henry Moore's great reputation will be permanent'. Hook undoubtedly influenced Moore, but in spite of their similar use of colour the latter's mature seascapes demonstrate an original approach to sea painting. Moore was 'among the first English artists to treat the sea as a subject sufficient in itself, rather than simply the background of a battle, shipwreck, or even landscape' (Maclean, 2). Examples of his work are in the British Museum and the Victoria and Albert Museum, London, and Portsmouth City Art Gallery.

CAMPBELL DODGSON, *rev.* MARK POTTLE

Sources F. Maclean, *Henry Moore, R.A.* (1905) · *Art Journal*, new ser., 15 (1895), 280–82 · *The Athenaeum* (29 June 1895) · *The Times* (24 June 1895) · Mallalieu, *Watercolour artists* · Wood, *Vic. painters*, 2nd edn · Bryan, *Painters* (1903–5) · A. Wilson, *A dictionary of British marine painters* (1967) · H. M. Cundall, *A history of British water colour painting* (1908) · S. W. Fisher, *A dictionary of watercolour painters, 1750–1900* (1972) · *Daily Graphic* (24 June 1895) · private information (1901) · Graves, *RA exhibitors* · m. cert. · d. cert. · CGPLA *Eng. & Wales* (1895)
Likenesses G. Pilotell, drypoint, BM · R. W. Robinson, photograph, NPG; repro. in *Members and associates of the Royal Academy of Arts* (1891) · wood-engraving, NPG; repro. in *ILN* (4 July 1885)
Wealth at death £19,960 8s. 11d.: probate, 8 Aug 1895, CGPLA *Eng. & Wales*

Moore, Sir Henry Monck-Mason (1887–1964), colonial governor, was born in Wimbledon on 16 March 1887, the youngest of the seven children of the Revd Edward W. Moore and his wife, Laetitia M. Monck-Mason. As a youth Moore, who was affectionately known to his friends as Monkey, attended Rokeby preparatory school, King's College School in Wimbledon, and then received Rustat and Skinner scholarships to Jesus College, Cambridge, where he was awarded the BA degree in 1909 in classics. After failing the Indian Civil Service examination, Moore obtained an eastern cadetship in the Ceylon civil service. In November 1910 he arrived in Ceylon and was attached to the secretariat and then to the Colombo *kachcheri*. During his years in Ceylon he served in a variety of positions in Colombo, Negombo, and Avisawela. In 1914 he received a promotion to fourth assistant colonial secretary.

During the First World War Moore, who had initially enlisted in the Royal Horse Artillery as a gunner and driver, held a temporary commission in Royal Garrison Artillery. He served in the Salonika campaign and the British expeditionary force. In August 1919 he returned to Ceylon and became assistant colonial secretary. The following year he worked as the private secretary to the governor. In December 1921 he married Daphne Ione Viola, the only daughter of W. J. Benson, who was in the consular service; the couple had two daughters. Moore became colonial secretary in Bermuda in 1922. Two years later he became principal assistant secretary in the Lagos secretariat, Nigeria, and in 1927 was promoted to deputy chief secretary. During his tenure in Lagos he served as secretary to two committees for Northern and Southern Nigeria.

In 1929 Moore went to Kenya to assume the post of colonial secretary. At that time the colony was in the throes of a political crisis because its Indian population was struggling for equality and demanding to be placed on a common roll with the European settlers instead of on an Indian communal roll. As colonial secretary Moore served as the leader of the official majority in the legislative council and repeatedly conducted negotiations with representatives from the Indian and European settler communities. Additionally, in 1930, he served as the colony's acting governor.

In 1934 Moore became governor and commander-in-chief of Sierra Leone. Among other achievements, he facilitated the protectorate's social and economic development, ended forced labour, built roads, improved medical and sanitary facilities, and introduced African administration. He served a tour in 1937–40 as assistant and then deputy under-secretary of state at the Colonial Office. Initially he was in charge of the West Indian and Far Eastern departments and the economic section. Additionally, he was the Colonial Office's representative on committees investigating civil aviation and oil distribution.

In January 1940 Moore succeeded Air Chief Marshal Sir Robert Brooke-Popham as governor of Kenya. During his tenure he allowed the European settlers to make considerable political and economic gains. In 1942 he became chairman of the east African supply and defence council, which co-ordinated the defences of Kenya, Tanganyika, and Uganda. More importantly, his common-sense wartime leadership enabled Kenya to enlarge its military establishment, participate in the allied victories in Ethiopia and British and Italian Somaliland, and deploy King's African rifles units to north Africa, Madagascar, and southeast Asia. His wife served as chair of the joint Red Cross and St John committee and as president of Kenya's Women's Emergency Organisation.

After leaving Kenya, Moore served as governor of Ceylon from 1944 to 1948. In this position he facilitated the decolonization process and the emergence of an independent Ceylon 'in an atmosphere of general peace and good will' (The Times, 28 March 1964). He co-operated closely with D. S. Senanayake, the Ceylonese leader; and he in particular facilitated the implementation of the Soulbury constitution, which provided for a two-chamber parliament and for full internal self-government. He also served as Ceylon's first governor-general in 1948–9 under the new order.

Although not as well remembered as some colonial governors, Moore nevertheless made significant contributions in several of the countries in which he served. In Sierra Leone, for example, he helped to lay the foundation of a more extensive administrative system, which previously had been centred primarily in the capital, Freetown, and had extended no further than a small group of minor chiefs. During his wartime service in Kenya, Moore proscribed the Kikuyu Central Association, a nationalist group led by Jomo Kenyatta, and jailed many of its leaders. This was a politically unpopular step, especially with much of the Kikuyu community which was seeking to expand the political role of Africans, but one that Moore deemed necessary because of the ongoing military campaign in neighbouring Ethiopia. However, his most enduring legacy was his success in engineering a peaceful transition to independence in Ceylon.

In recognition of his numerous contributions Moore received many awards, the most significant of which included appointments as CMG in 1930, KCMG in 1935, and GCMG in 1943. He also received an honorary LLD degree from the University of Ceylon. In 1949 Moore, who had been suffering from arthritis, retired to Cape Town, South Africa. He died on 26 March 1964 at the Volkshospital, Hof Street Gardens, Cape Town, South Africa. Lady Moore survived him. His Times obituarist described Moore as 'a first-class administrator, with a tidy mind and a fund of common sense' (28 March 1964).

THOMAS PAUL OFCANSKY

Sources The Times (28 March 1964) • H. A. J. Hulugalle, British governors of Ceylon (1963) • A. H. M. Kirk-Greene, A biographical dictionary of the British colonial governor (1980) • A. Clayton and D. C. Savage, Government and labour in Kenya, 1895–1963 (1974, [1975]) • WWW • CGPLA Eng. & Wales (1965)

Archives Bodl. RH, papers • PRO, corresp. relating to Kenya, CO 967/55–56, 62, 158–62

Likenesses W. Stoneman, photographs, 1934, NPG • photograph, repro. in Hulugalle, British governors

Wealth at death £21,637 effects in England: administration with will, 8 Feb 1965, CGPLA Eng. & Wales

Moore, Henry Spencer (1898–1986), sculptor, was born on 30 July 1898 at 30 Roundhill Road, Castleford, Yorkshire, the fourth son and seventh of the eight children of Raymond Spencer Moore (1849–1922), miner, and his wife, Mary (1858–1944), daughter of Neville Baker, miner, of Burntwood, Staffordshire.

Early life Raymond Moore was born in the county of Lincolnshire. A self-improving man, with an interest in music and literature, he had taught himself enough mathematics and engineering to qualify as a pit deputy, and later as an under-manager at the Wheldale colliery in Castleford. Moore's father, proud, conscientious, and fiercely ambitious for his children, was determined that they should not 'have the suffering, the drawbacks and the restricted life he'd had, and he saw that we didn't' (Berthoud, 22). Moore's relationship with his strict, authoritarian father—who showed no outward signs of warmth and affection towards his children—was one of respect rather than of mutual love.

Mary Moore was a handsome woman of remarkable character, humorous, affectionate, and with tremendous physical stamina. Moore later commented: 'She was to me the absolute stability, the rock, the whole thing in life that one knew was there for one's protection' (Henry Moore: Writings, 33). Of the many anecdotes about his childhood, one of the best-known was Moore's account of one of his earliest and most significant sculptural experiences. His

Henry Spencer Moore (1898–1986), by Ida Kar, 1954 [detail]

mother suffered from severe rheumatism of the back and he would often massage her back with liniment. He never forgot the contrast between the soft, yielding, fleshy parts of the back and the hard framework of bone beneath. Moore always explained his preference in his sculpture for matronly women by his relationship with his mother.

Moore's childhood was happy, full of physical exercise, games, and excursions to the surrounding countryside. The most impressive element of landscape which he experienced as a boy was Adel Rock (as he later called it), an enormous outcrop of rock, part of Alwoodley Crags, some 5 miles north of Leeds.

> For me, it was the first big, bleak lump of stone set in the landscape and surrounded by marvellous gnarled prehistoric trees. It had no feature of recognition, no element of copying of naturalism, just a bleak, powerful form, very impressive. (*Henry Moore: Writings*, 36)

Moore's schooling began at the age of three when he attended the infants' section of Temple Street elementary school; he transferred to the main section of the school when he was eight. He and his siblings were baptized and brought up in the Church of England, though his parents were not regular churchgoers. At fifteen or sixteen Moore was confirmed and experienced a strong religious phase,

which was short-lived. Earlier, at about ten or eleven years old, while attending Sunday school, at the nearby Congregational chapel, an episode occurred which in later life Moore recounted in countless interviews and conversations, when he was asked when exactly he had decided to become a sculptor. The Sunday school superintendent would end the class with a moral story, and one such self-improving tale concerned Michelangelo; however, it was not the moral of the story which stuck in Moore's mind, but the description of Michelangelo as 'the greatest sculptor who ever lived' (Berthoud, 26). Moore returned home, read the entry on Michelangelo in the encyclopaedia his father had given him, and from that day forward, he always maintained, when asked what he wanted to be, he replied 'a sculptor'.

In 1910 Moore was accepted at Castleford secondary school, having been awarded, at his second attempt, a county minor scholarship. There he encountered two mentors, the headmaster, T. R. Dawes, and Alice Gostick, the art teacher. One of Dawes's interests was English church architecture, and it was probably with him, rather than on a visit with his family, that Moore came to appreciate the grotesque Gothic corbels and the two effigies in St Oswald's Church, Methley. Dawes also saw to it that every pupil participated in the school plays, which always included something from Shakespeare. This whetted Moore's appetite for theatre, and a few years later, probably in 1916, Moore wrote *Narayana and Bhataryan*, a play influenced by the orientalism of James Elroy Flecker. The most influential figure in Moore's formative years as a student was undoubtedly Alice Gostick. Gostick was in touch with the work of the European avant-garde and, when invited to her house for Sunday tea, Moore could browse through her art books and current copies of such magazines as *Colour* and *Studio*. Some years later he joined her evening pottery classes. He explored his artistic potential under her guidance and their affectionate friendship lasted until her death in 1960.

When Moore completed his five years as a student at Castleford in July 1915 and said that he wanted to become a sculptor, his father disapproved and advised, Henry recalled: 'First become qualified as a teacher like your brother and sisters have done and then change to art if you wish. Be sure that you have some living in your hand' (*Henry Moore: Writings*, 31). Moore became a student teacher at his old elementary school in Castleford; he later described his first teaching experience as the most miserable period of his life. In 1916 he was asked to carve the Castleford secondary school roll of honour, using Alice Gostick's wood-carving tools.

War service and the Leeds School of Art In February 1917 Moore left home and joined the Civil Service Rifles as a volunteer. It was probably in mid-August 1917 that Private H. S. Moore was sent to France for training in trench warfare near Arras. On 30 November Moore and some 400 men of the Civil Service Rifles were gassed at Bourlon Wood in the battle of Cambrai and then subjected to a major German assault. The losses were appalling and

Moore was fortunate to survive. He was sent back to England as a stretcher case and spent the next six weeks or so recuperating at the Lansdowne Road Hospital in Cardiff. After further convalescence he volunteered for a course in physical training at Aldershot where as a lance corporal he qualified as a bayonet instructor. As a teacher Moore was entitled to early demobilization, and returned to Castleford in February 1919. Both in his letters from the battlefield and particularly in his descriptions of his experiences many years later, Moore almost always conveyed the impression that the conflict was little more than a glorified, romantic adventure. But in a letter to a friend, written in 1919 or 1920, he did describe the horrors of war. If God were 'Almighty', he wrote, 'the things I saw & experienced, the great bloodshed & the pain, the insufferable agony & depravity, the tears & the inhuman devilishness of the war, would, could never have been' (letter, Sothebys, London, 15 Dec 1988, English Literature and History, lot 242, catalogue, p. 182). Late in life, he summed up his attitude very differently: 'I was not horrified by the war, I wanted to win a medal and be a hero' (Henry Moore: Writings, 40).

In March 1919 Moore briefly resumed teaching at Temple Street elementary school, but with the help of Alice Gostick he successfully applied for an ex-serviceman's grant, and was accepted at the Leeds School of Art for the autumn term. Within his first year there, Moore managed to complete the two-year drawing course. The curriculum included architectural drawing and drawing from memory, from life, and from the antique.

On his first day at college Moore met fellow student Raymond Coxon, who became a lifelong friend. At the end of the first year of the drawing course, Moore and Coxon won a third of the prizes for the nine categories of drawing. Edna Ginesi, known as 'Gin', was another student whom Henry met during his first year. He later fell in love with her, but Gin was in love with Coxon, whom she married in 1926. In the autumn of 1920 Barbara Hepworth arrived at the Leeds School of Art. Moore was rather 'sweet on her' and they had 'a bit of an affair' (private information), which was probably nothing more than a mild flirtation. Their friendship flourished for the next two decades, from 1921 to 1924 when they were students together at the Royal College of Art in London, and in the 1930s when they were living in close proximity in Hampstead.

During his second year at Leeds, Moore asked Hayward Ryder, the principal, if he could study sculpture. Reginald Cotterill was hired to set up a department with Moore as its only full-time student. As carving was not taught, Moore concentrated on modelling in clay. The two small painted plasters now in the Leeds City Art Gallery are his earliest surviving sculptures. At the end of that year Moore won a royal exhibition scholarship worth £90 a year, which enabled him to achieve his goal, entrance to the Royal College of Art in London.

Two encounters during his two years of study in Leeds had far more impact than the academic courses at college on forging and shaping Moore's imagination. At the home of Sir Michael Sadler, vice-chancellor of Leeds University,

Moore saw for the first time original examples of modern art, and was particularly excited by the work of Gauguin and Van Gogh. Here he also saw his first examples of African sculpture. The second event was Moore's discovery in 1921 of Roger Fry's Vision and Design (1920), arguably the most influential book in shaping his ideas about sculpture during his formative years, particularly the chapters entitled 'Negro sculpture' and 'Ancient American art'. Fry praised African sculptors for conceiving fully three-dimensional forms, and for their handling of material. What Moore later called 'full three-dimensional realisation', and the doctrine of truth to material were the two most important tenets of his art during the 1920s and 1930s. Moore later acknowledged his debt to Fry, and said that he 'opened the way to other books and to the realisation of the British Museum. That was really the beginning' (Henry Moore: Writings, 44).

London Moore arrived in London in September 1921 to begin the three-year course in sculpture at the Royal College of Art. William Rothenstein, who had been appointed principal the previous year, had lived in Paris and brought a fresh international outlook to what had become primarily a teachers' training college. He gave Moore the same kind of encouragement and support that Alice Gostick had offered during the previous decade.

From the outset Moore recognized the importance of an academic training based on drawing and modelling from life. The sculptor Leon Underwood, the drawing instructor at the Royal College of Art, was passionate about life drawing. Moore was so impressed with Underwood's teaching that he later attended his life drawing class at his studio in Hammersmith. As a student, Moore was leading a double life: drawing and modelling from the nude model at college, with the weekends and holidays free to develop what appealed to him in sculpture, constantly nourished by the books he had bought and by those he borrowed from the library of the Victoria and Albert Museum, and above all by his frequent visits to the British Museum. 'One room after another in the British Museum took my enthusiasm' (Henry Moore: Writings, 45), Moore commented in 1947. It was a period when he thought that the classical/Renaissance ideal was the enemy and that he should look to non-Western traditions and 'primitive' art for inspiration. At the British Museum Moore was drawn to Egyptian, Assyrian, and Sumerian sculpture, as well as prehistoric European and archaic Greek sculpture. But above all he was excited by the ethnographical gallery, with its profusion of African, Oceanic, North-West Coast, Inuit, and pre-Columbian carvings. Pre-Columbian stone sculpture was by far the most important influence on Moore's early carvings, from the 1924 marble Snake (priv. coll.) to the 1930 Hornton stone Reclining Woman (National Gallery of Canada, Ottawa). The notebook drawings of the early to mid-1920s record the sculptures and artefacts in the British Museum, and those illustrated in some of the earliest books on primitive art, which Moore particularly admired.

In 1921, during their first term at the Royal College of Art, Moore and Raymond Coxon visited Jacob Epstein, the leading avant-garde sculptor in Britain. They must have seen his superb collection of African, Oceanic, and north-west coast art, as well as works from other non-Western cultures and traditions—pre-Columbian, Peruvian, Egyptian, and Chinese sculpture. Moore would also have seen examples of Epstein's stone carvings of 1912–13 and experienced for the first time the blatant borrowings from primitive art of the sort which were to inform his own wood and stone sculptures of the 1920s. That Moore does not appear to have mentioned this visit—he recalled that he met Epstein about 1928—is in keeping with 'an almost compulsive need to ablate the memory of those artists [his contemporaries] who had significant short-range influence upon him' (Fuller, 26).

Both the sculpture and writings of the French-born sculptor Henri Gaudier-Brzeska made a considerable impact on several of Moore's carvings from the early 1920s and on his ideas about sculpture. Ezra Pound's *Gaudier-Brzeska: a Memoir* (1916), which Moore probably read in 1921 or 1922, left, like Fry's *Vision and Design*, an indelible impression. His marble *Dog* (1922; Henry Moore Foundation) is distinctly reminiscent of Gaudier-Brzeska's Vorticist sculptures of 1913–14, and his comment that the sculpture that moved him most gives out 'something of the energy and power of great mountains' (*Henry Moore: Writings*, 188) seems unmistakably to echo the French sculptor's most famous dictum: 'Sculptural energy is the mountain'.

At Whitsun 1922, Moore and Raymond Coxon decided to go to Paris to see some original Cézannes. Rothenstein suggested they visit the collection of Auguste Pellerin, who owned more than one hundred works by the French artist. Moore was bowled over by the monumental *Large Bathers* of 1906 (Philadelphia Museum of Art). Years later he described the tremendous impact of 'the triangular bathing composition with the nudes in perspective, lying on the ground as if they'd been sliced out of mountain rock' (*Henry Moore: Writings*, 50).

Moore was awarded his diploma from the Royal College of Art at the end of the summer term of 1924 and received a six-month travelling scholarship to be spent in Italy studying the old masters. He planned to set off in the autumn; however, the resignation of Derwent Wood, professor of sculpture, and his assistant led to Rothenstein appointing Moore as assistant in the sculpture department for a period of seven years. The salary of £240 a year for teaching two days a week gave him the freedom to pursue his career, and financial security. At the outset Moore enjoyed his teaching: 'I remember I used to be very surprised quite often at the things I discovered while teaching, the actual sentences I used' (Berthoud, 87), but after a few years he found the repetition of his beliefs a deadening thing. Moore was now living at 3 Grove Studios, Hammersmith, which he shared with Raymond Coxon.

When Ernest Cole was hired to replace Wood as professor of sculpture, Moore set off for Italy in early February 1925. He spent about a week in Paris *en route* for Italy. He visited the Louvre, where he particularly admired the work of Mantegna, but he was most excited by the Indian sculptures he saw at the Musée Guimet. He visited Genoa, Pisa, and Rome before settling in Florence some time before 12 March, when he wrote to Rothenstein giving an account of his travels and his reactions to the work of the Italian masters. Among the painters, Giotto and Masaccio made the biggest impact, particularly *The Tribute Money* in the Brancacci chapel, Florence. Moore still maintained that 'what I know of Indian, Egyptian and Mexican sculpture completely overshadows Renaissance sculpture—except for the early Italian portrait busts, the very late work of Michelangelo and the work of Donatello' (*Henry Moore: Writings*, 52). Moore returned to London in June, having spent only three and a half months of the six-month scholarship abroad. Both emotionally and in terms of his artistic development, the Italian journey had been stressful and disorientating, so much so that years later he admitted that it was the closest he had come to a nervous breakdown. Henry had fallen in love with Edna Ginesi and in March was rejected when he had confessed his love to his best friend's fiancée. Of his struggle to come to terms with the art of the Italian Renaissance, he commented:

> For about six months after my return I was never more miserable in my life. Six months' exposure to the masterworks of European art which I saw on my trip stirred up a violent conflict with my previous ideals … I found myself helpless and unable to work. Then gradually I began to find my way out of my quandary in the direction of my earlier interests. I came back to ancient Mexican art in the British Museum. (*Henry Moore: Writings*, 54)

Before leaving for Italy, Moore had begun work on the Hornton stone *Mother and Child* (1924–5; Manchester City Galleries), a massive, brooding representation of one of the two themes which would obsess him for the rest of his life. It was his most impressive carving to date, although he was not as yet fully in control of the material. As in much of his early work, the forms are all buried inside each other and the head is given no neck 'simply because I was frightened to weaken the stone' (Hedgecoe, *Henry Spencer Moore*, 45). As with almost all Moore's sculptures executed between 1921 and the early 1950s, the 1924–5 *Mother and Child* was based on a preparatory drawing.

Dorothy Warren was the first of a line of influential art dealers to promote and market Moore's sculpture and drawings. Although he had already exhibited in two mixed exhibitions in London, at St George's Gallery in 1926 and at the Beaux-Arts Gallery the following year, his first major exhibition was a one-man show in January 1928 at the Warren Gallery, Maddox Street, London, with a brochure listing forty-two sculptures and fifty-one drawings. Moore described Warren, whom he had met through his first patron Charles Rothenstein (William Rothenstein's brother), as a 'remarkable person with tremendous energy and real verve, real flair' (*Henry Moore: Writings*, 55). She sold £90 worth of Moore's work, including 'thirty drawings at £1 each, several to Epstein, several to Augustus John, and Henry Lamb—it was mostly other artists, and established ones, who bought, and that was a great encouragement to me' (ibid.). Looking back, Moore often focused on the hostile notices, such as the one in the *Morning Post* (28 January 1928), which suggested that the exhibition 'must raise furious thoughts in the minds of those responsible for the teaching at the Royal College of Art'. And yet the reviewer of the *Daily Herald* (28 January 1928) found the sculpture 'simply staggering'; the exhibition was a 'very "advanced" show and one that will shock the orthodox, it contains much sculpture of almost overwhelming power'. The public controversy that his work continued to incite for many years had begun in earnest. But one thing was certain: Henry Moore had established himself as a forceful presence, whose reputation gradually eclipsed the older generation of British sculptors, namely Jacob Epstein, Frank Dobson, and Eric Gill.

The year 1928 not only saw Moore's successful one-man exhibition, but also brought his first public commission. The architect Charles Holden, on Epstein's recommendation, chose Moore as one of six sculptors to carve eight reliefs symbolizing the four winds for the new headquarters of London Underground at St James's Park station, Westminster. Epstein had already been asked to produce two carvings representing *Night* and *Day* to be placed above the entrance. The relief sculptures were to be attached to the building some eighty feet above street level. At first Moore was reluctant to accept the commission because relief sculpture was the antithesis of the full, three-dimensional spatial richness he was striving to achieve, and also because it 'symbolised for me the humiliating subservience of the sculptor to the architect, for in ninety-nine cases out of a hundred, the architect only thought of sculpture as a surface decoration, and ordered a relief as a matter of course' (*Henry Moore: Writings*, 252). But Holden was persuasive, and Moore filled almost an entire sketchbook with studies for the 1928 Portland stone *West Wind* relief. He realized that a sculpture personifying the west wind could not be static, 'and then I hit on the idea of a figure suggesting a floating movement' (ibid., 253). Some nine and a half feet in length, the *West Wind* was by far the largest carving he had so far attempted, and probably his only sculpture representing the human figure in motion.

Moore regarded the 1929 Hornton stone *Reclining Figure* (Leeds City Art Gallery) as one of the earliest 'of some ten or twenty works which I know have been keyworks and which I know have solved some directions that I wanted to be satisfied with' (*Henry Moore: Writings*, 254). This carving embodies the quite sudden and dramatic influence of the Toltec-Maya Chacmool reclining figure in the Museo Nacional de Antropología, Mexico City, which Moore described as 'undoubtedly the one sculpture which most influenced my early work' (Wilkinson, *Drawings*, 1977, 77). Moore explained what he admired about the pre-Columbian stone carving: 'Its stillness and alertness, a sense of readiness—and the whole presence of it, and the legs coming down like columns' (*Henry Moore: Writings*, 98). Unlike the 1924–5 *Mother and Child*, the forms are no longer buried in the block-like mass of the stone. The neck is clearly defined and a naturalistic space has been confidently carved out between the head and the upraised left arm. No longer afraid to weaken the stone, Moore was now in complete control of his material. If the analogy between the female figure and landscape is hinted at in the Leeds carving, in its pendant, the Hornton stone *Reclining Woman* of 1930 (National Gallery of Canada, Ottawa), the similarity is so striking that at one time the sculpture was called simply *Mountains*. On the one hand, the Leeds and Ottawa reclining figures marked the culmination of a decade largely informed by pre-Columbian sources; on the other hand, they proclaimed in no uncertain terms the reclining figure as one of Moore's principal themes.

At a college dance in the autumn of 1928 Moore met Irina Anatolia Radetzki (1907–1989), a student in the painting school of the Royal College of Art. She was born in Kiev, the daughter of Anatol Radetzki (disappeared 1917), a member of a wealthy, upper-class mercantile family. She and her mother settled in England in 1921 or 1922. Henry and Irina were married in London on 29 July 1929, and moved to 11a Parkhill Road, Hampstead, which they had found through Barbara Hepworth and her first husband, the sculptor John Skeaping, who were living close by at 7 The Mall Studios. During their long and happy marriage Irina was, Moore said, 'a tremendous inspiration, my most valuable constructive critic' (*Henry Moore: Writings*, 57). 'Nitchka', as she was known to her friends, was unimpressed by the fame, flattery, and the many honours which were later bestowed on her husband. In her rather shy, quiet but firm way, 'she keeps my feet on the ground' (ibid.). They had one daughter, Mary, born on 7 March 1946. Irina died in 1989.

The 1930s The 1930s represent the most innovative and original years of Moore's career. They also saw a proliferation of exhibitions at home, and Moore's work was included for the first time in exhibitions abroad. In 1930 Moore, with Jacob Epstein and John Skeaping, was invited to represent British sculpture at the XVIII Venice Biennale. In the following year Moore exhibited three works at an international sculpture exhibition at the Kunsthaus, Zürich. It was also in 1931 that Dr Max Sauerlandt, director of the Museum für Kunst und Gewerbe, Hamburg, made the first purchase by a museum of a Moore sculpture. By the end of the decade, examples of his carving had been acquired by the Albright-Knox Art Gallery, Buffalo, the Museum of Modern Art, New York, and the Tate Gallery, London.

In April 1931 Moore held his second one-man exhibition in London, this time at the Leicester Galleries in Leicester Square, the best-known of the London galleries specializing in modern art. In his brief foreword to the modest catalogue, Epstein wrote: 'Before these works I ponder in silence … For the future of sculpture in England, Henry Moore is vitally important' (Berthoud, 110–11). As with his first one-man show in 1928, the notices ranged from 'A Genius of the First Order' (*Jewish Chronicle*, 1 May 1931) to an attack by his old enemy at the *Morning Post*: 'The cult of ugliness triumphs at the hands of Mr Moore' (11 April 1931). By far the most serious and influential review was Herbert Read's article in *The Listener* (22 April 1931), which was reprinted almost verbatim later that year in *The Meaning of Art*. In this book Read, who became one of Moore's closest friends, was responsible for helping to spread the sculptor's fame throughout the English-speaking world.

Moore's ten-year association with the Royal College of Art had ended earlier in the year when Rothenstein accepted his resignation. With the continuing attacks on his work in the *Morning Post*, in an effort to remove him from the staff, Moore may well have felt that his teaching at the college put the principal in an awkward position. Before he resigned Moore may already have been approached to start a sculpture department at the Chelsea School of Art, where he began teaching in the autumn of 1931.

One of the most marked features of Moore's warm and gregarious personality was his capacity to form and nourish lasting friendships. Many of his closest friendships, as well as the most influential in terms of his career and reputation, were formed during the 1920s and 1930s. Raymond Coxon, E. C. ('Peter') Gregory, the joint managing director of the Bradford printing firm Lund Humphries, and Herbert Read were probably his closest friends. During the thirties, living in Hampstead among what Herbert Read described as 'a nest of gentle artists' (H. Read, *Art in Britain, 1930–1940*, 1965, 7), Moore's friends included, among artists, Naum Gabo, Barbara Hepworth, Ivon Hitchens, Bernard Meadows, Paul Nash, Ben Nicholson, Roland Penrose, John Piper, John Skeaping, and Graham Sutherland; among architects, Wells Coates, Walter Gropius, and Serge Chermayeff; among poets and writers, T. S. Eliot, Geoffrey Grigson, Stephen Spender, and Adrian Stokes; and among art historians, Alfred Barr, Kenneth Clark, and Philip Hendy.

In English art the 1930s was the decade of group manifestos and group exhibitions. In 1931 Moore joined the Seven and Five Society, possibly as a result of the summer holiday which he and Irina had spent in 1931 at Happisburgh on the Norfolk coast with Ivon Hitchens and Ben Nicholson, who were already members. He exhibited with the group in the following year, and again in 1935 at the society's last show.

In 1931 Moore produced a Hornton stone sculpture called simply *Composition* (priv. coll.), in which the human form has been subjected to disturbing and violent distortions utterly unlike anything found in his previous work. This radical change in direction was almost certainly provoked by Picasso's sculpture of 1928 entitled *Metamorphosis*, and by his drawings of the late 1920s. During the rest of the decade Moore's sculpture and drawings continued to reflect the influence of Picasso and the surrealist sculpture of Arp and Giacometti. Their work liberated Moore's imagination in the direction of a more elusive, more evocative, organic abstraction.

The Moores bought Jasmine Cottage at Barfreston, near Canterbury, Kent, in 1931. This changed dramatically the routine of their lives; the couple spent weekends and holidays there, Moore completing a good half of his year's work in the country. He particularly enjoyed being able to work on his carvings out of doors in the small garden. This

pattern of dividing his time between his Hampstead studio, his teaching at the Chelsea School of Art, and a cottage in Kent continued until 1940. In August 1935 the Moores sold Jasmine Cottage and bought Burcroft, a modern bungalow near Kingston, not far from Canterbury. 'The cottage had five acres of wild meadow. Here for the first time I worked with a three or four mile view of the countryside to which I could relate my sculptures' (*Henry Moore: Writings*, 59). Living and working at Burcroft clinched Moore's interest in trying to make sculpture and nature enhance each other.

It was at Burcroft, probably in the summer of 1935, that Moore employed his first assistant, Jack Hepworth, a first cousin of Barbara Hepworth. The following year he took on the young sculptor Bernard Meadows, who lived with the Moores at Burcroft during the summer holidays and was given full board and lodging but no pay. He worked for Moore from 1936 to 1940, from 1946 to 1948, and intermittently during the 1950s. Meadows did much of the initial roughing out of the stone or wood sculptures, and was allowed to carve down to about a quarter inch of the final surface. During the 1950s Moore hired two young English sculptors who went on to achieve brilliant careers—Anthony Caro in 1951 and Phillip King in 1959.

Herbert Read's *Henry Moore, Sculptor: an Appreciation*, the first monograph on the artist, was published in 1934. The author was unreserved in his praise of Moore's achievement at this relatively early stage in his career, eulogizing that 'in the fulness of his powers, he offers us the perfected product of his genius' (p. 16).

The birth of Unit One was announced by Paul Nash in a letter to *The Times* in June 1933, although the group's first exhibition, at the Mayor Gallery, Cork Street, London, was not held until April 1934. The show coincided with the publication of *Unit One: the Modern Movement in English Architecture, Painting and Sculpture*, edited by Herbert Read, to which each of the eleven members contributed a statement. Moore and Hepworth were the two sculptors in the group. In Moore's statement, his most expansive airing to date of his views on the art of sculpture, he discussed five qualities in sculpture which had become of fundamental importance to him: truth to material, full three-dimensional realization, observation of natural objects, vision and expression, and vitality and power of expression. Throughout his life, in his extensive writings, and in his countless conversations and interviews, Moore never seemed to tire of surveying the history of sculpture, of describing the work of his favourite painters, sculptors and draughtsmen, or of helping others to understand his own sculptures and drawings. He was an engaging conversationalist, with a great ability to communicate in a direct and vivid way.

In the summer of 1934 the Moores and the Coxons set off on a motoring holiday to the continent. They drove to Bordeaux, crossed the border, and headed for the Altamira caves in northern Spain. It was not just the prehistoric paintings that interested Moore. Caves had held a fascination for him since childhood when he explored the sand holes in the sides of hills in Castleford. In 1937 he associated the holes in his sculpture with 'the mysterious fascination of caves in hillsides and cliffs' (*Henry Moore: Writings*, 196). They moved on to Toledo to see the El Grecos and then to the Museo del Prado in Madrid. On the way home they visited the cave paintings at Les Eyzies and Font de Gaume in the Dordogne.

Moore's sculptures and drawings of the mid-1930s continued to reflect the influence of the Parisian avant-garde, as well as the uncompromising abstraction of Nicholson's white reliefs and Hepworth's first abstract carvings. By 1933–4 Moore had created several sculptures in which the holes carved through the stone were abstract spaces, rather than naturalist voids between, for example, the arm and the head or torso. The Cumberland alabaster of 1934, *Four Piece Composition: Reclining Figure* (Tate collection), anticipated the monumental two- and three-piece reclining figures of 1959–64. In the 1934 pynkado wood *Two Forms* (Museum of Modern Art, New York), in which the semi-abstract pelvic form looms over the smaller rounded form, the mother and child theme is represented on a symbolic level. At this stage Moore believed that in making his sculptures more abstract he could 'present the human psychological content of my work with the greatest directness and intensity' (*Henry Moore: Writings*, 198). On a completely different note, the serene life drawings of Irina of 1933–5 marked the culmination of some fifteen years of continuous study of the human figure.

1936 was an important year for group exhibitions at home and abroad. In London Moore's work was included in 'Abstract and Concrete' at Alex. Reid and Lefevre and in the International Surrealist Exhibition at New Burlington Galleries, and in New York in Alfred Barr's pioneering exhibitions 'Cubism and Abstract Art' and 'Fantastic Art, Dada, Surrealism'.

Unlike his article for *Unit One*, Moore made only a minimal contribution to the 1937 *Circle: International Survey of Constructivist Art*, edited by J. L. Martin, Ben Nicholson, and Naum Gabo. He never fully embraced the ideals of abstraction and constructivism, any more than he did those of surrealism. From each he borrowed and absorbed what he needed. 'The sculptor speaks', published in *The Listener* (18 August 1937), was the most important statement of Moore's career on the art of sculpture. In it he described sculpture as the most difficult of the arts to appreciate, and recommended that a sculptor should think of and use form in its full spatial completeness. In a surprising remark, he stated, 'Since the Gothic, European sculpture had become overgrown with moss, weeds—all sorts of surface excrescences which completely concealed shape' (*Henry Moore: Writings*, 194), effectively dismissing the sculpture of Donatello, Michelangelo, Bernini, and Rodin. With echoes of surrealist doctrine, he acknowledged that 'There are universal shapes to which everybody is subconsciously conditioned and to which they can respond if their conscious control does not shut them off' (ibid., 195). He discussed the importance of the human figure and of natural forms as his primary sources of inspiration. The succinct statements about holes in sculpture—'The first

hole made through a piece of stone is a revelation' (ibid., 195)—are among the most frequently quoted passages from the article. Moore concluded with an explanation of the importance of drawing as a means of generating ideas for sculpture, a condemnation of what he saw as the unnecessary quarrel between the abstractionists and the surrealists, and an affirmation of his commitment, however abstract his work may appear, to retaining links with human and occasionally animal forms: 'I think the humanist organic element will always be for me of fundamental importance in sculpture, giving sculpture its vitality' (ibid., 197).

The mid- to late 1930s saw Moore, like many British artists and writers, deeply affected by the rise of Nazism in Germany and of fascism in Italy, and by the outbreak of the Spanish Civil War in July 1936. This, the politically most active period of his life, began with his association with the Artists International Association (AIA), a Marxist-orientated group of artists. Moore exhibited in the AIA's first exhibition, 'The Social Scene', held in London in 1934, and the following year in their second London show, 'Artists against Fascism and War'.

In an interview a few years before his death, Moore recalled: 'I was approached by the Communists in the 1930s when a lot of people did join them. But I didn't go that far' (Berthoud, 144). There is no doubt, however, of his allegiance at the time to communist ideals. After the outbreak of the Spanish Civil War in 1936 Moore was one of ten signatories of the English Surrealist Group's *Declaration on Spain*, accusing the government of duplicity and anti-democratic intrigue, and calling for arms for the people of Spain. The horrors of the Spanish Civil War were brought home to Moore in 1937 when he and Irina visited Picasso in his studio in Paris to see the as yet unfinished *Guernica*, the greatest anti-war painting of the twentieth century, which was inspired by Picasso's outrage at the German bombing of the Basque town. In a long letter published in the *Yorkshire Post* on 3 March 1938, Moore urged attendance at a mass demonstration in Leeds on 3 April under the banner 'Collective security—the people's answer to dictators'. It was the most public and impassioned political statement of his career.

Moore described the stringed figures of 1937–40 as his most abstract sculptures and yet maintained that the forms were based on living creatures. These highly inventive works were inspired by the mathematical models developed by J. F. Lagrange in Paris, 'that have geometric figures at the ends with coloured threads from one to the other to show what the form between would be' (*Henry Moore: Writings*, 256). In his own stringed figures, Moore liked the contrast between the transparent strings and the solid form. The ingenious wood *Bird Basket* of 1939 (Henry Moore Foundation, Much Hadham, Hertfordshire) was so called 'because it has the handle of a basket over the top and strings that show the little inner piece as a bird inside a cage' (ibid., 257).

In the 1938 Hornton stone *Recumbent Figure* (Tate collection), with its large, opened-out space beneath the breasts, Moore has achieved in the more fragile medium of stone what he had managed in wood in the 1935–6 *Reclining Figure* (Albright-Knox Art Gallery, Buffalo). The 1938 carving was commissioned by the Russian architect Serge Chermayeff for the terrace of his house at Halland in Sussex, which had an open view of the South Downs. This was the first sculpture which Moore created for a specific rural setting, 'and it was then that I became aware of the necessity of giving outdoor sculpture a far-seeing gaze' (*Henry Moore: Writings*, 259). When Chermayeff moved to America in 1939, he returned the carving and the deposit to Moore. On the advice of Kenneth Clark, director of the National Gallery, the Contemporary Art Society purchased *Recumbent Figure* for £300 and presented it to the Tate Gallery in 1939. Clark, whom Moore had probably met in early 1938, was to become one of his most influential patrons and a close friend.

Moore produced a maquette based on a drawing both for the Tate *Recumbent Figure* and for the 1939 elm wood *Reclining Figure* (Detroit Institute of Arts). Previously, large carvings had evolved directly from the drawings. Moore described the Detroit sculpture as 'my most "opened out" wood carving—you can look from one end to the other through a series of tunnels' (*Henry Moore: Writings*, 259–60). These two works are representative of Moore's greatest achievements in stone and wood.

Between 1938 and 1940 Moore and Bernard Meadows cast some twenty-four small-size lead sculptures at Burcroft in Kent. This not only marked a radical break from his commitment to direct carving, but also meant that by modelling in wax he could create much thinner, more open forms than were possible in stone or wood. *Three Points* (1939–40; cast iron, Henry Moore Foundation, Much Hadham, Hertfordshire), where the three sharp forms practically touch, reminded Moore of the fingers of God and Adam in Michelangelo's fresco in the Sistine Chapel. *The Helmet* (1939–40; lead cast, National Galleries of Scotland) was the first of Moore's internal–external form sculptures. The motif had first appeared in a drawing of 1935 in which Moore copied a Malanggan figure from New Ireland, a style of wood carving which he greatly admired for the delicate, intricately carved forms within forms. *The Helmet*, however, would appear to derive from two hollowed-out, prehistoric Greek implements which Moore had sketched in a 1937 notebook.

The 1940s When war was declared in September 1939 Moore was living and working at Burcroft in Kent. In October the Moores gave up 11a Parkhill Road, London, and rented the less expensive 7 The Mall Studios from Barbara Hepworth and Ben Nicholson, who had moved to Cornwall with their three children. By 1940 Moore's teaching had all but ended. Late one evening in September 1940, Moore and Irina were forced to remain on the platform at Belsize Park underground station for about an hour until a bombing raid subsided. They found themselves in the company of Londoners, men, women, and children who were spending the night sheltering from the blitz. Moore was fascinated by what he saw: 'I saw hundreds of Henry Moore Reclining Figures stretched along the platforms' (*Henry Moore on Sculpture*, 212, 216), and 'even the train tunnels seemed to be like the holes in my sculpture' (Hedgecoe, *Henry Spencer Moore*, 134). Within a few days he produced the first of his shelter drawings.

In October 1940 the Moores spent a weekend with the Labour MP Leonard Matters and his wife at their house in South-End, next to the hamlet of Perry Green, near Much Hadham, Hertfordshire. On their return to London they found that 7 The Mall Studios had been badly damaged by a bomb and was uninhabitable. They returned to their friends in South-End and were soon able to rent half of a seventeenth-century house, Hoglands, in Perry Green. A few months later, having just sold for £300 the 1939 elm-wood *Reclining Figure* to Gordon Onslow-Ford, Moore bought Hoglands for £900 and he lived there for the rest of his life.

At home Moore began filling the first of two shelter sketchbooks with scenes drawn from memory of what he had seen on his frequent visits to various London underground stations. As he recounted some years later: 'the only thing at all like those shelters that I could think of was the hold of a slave-ship on its way from Africa to America, full of hundreds and hundreds of people who were having things done to them that they were quite powerless to resist' (*Henry Moore on Sculpture*, 218). The War Artists' Advisory Committee, which had commissioned the shelter drawings, purchased seventeen large versions based on the sketchbook studies. When the shelter drawings were exhibited in 1941, 1942, and 1944 in three exhibitions under the title 'War Pictures' at the National Gallery, they reached and touched the general public in a way that his earlier sculpture and drawing never could.

Leeds and Castleford were the focal points of two important events in 1941. The first was the exhibition of thirty-nine sculptures and fifty-six drawings organized by Philip Hendy and shown with the works of Graham Sutherland and John Piper at Temple Newsam House, part of the Leeds City Art Gallery. The second was Moore's visit to Castleford, following Herbert Read's suggestion that he might consider doing a series of drawings of coalminers, 'Britain's underground army'. Early in December Moore began sketching miners at the coalface in the depths of the Wheldale colliery where his father had worked. Moore had never willingly drawn the male figure before, but now he was confronted with the challenge of doing so, and of representing the figures in action. In his wartime drawings he adopted a more naturalistic approach to the human figure, which he later saw as 'perhaps a temporary resolution of that conflict which caused me those miserable first six months after I had left Masaccio behind in Florence and had once again come within the attraction of the archaic and primitive sculptures of the British Museum' (*Henry Moore: Writings*, 266).

Moore produced no sculptures between September 1940 and June 1942 when he was working on his wartime drawings. In 1941 he did find time to write an important article, 'Primitive art', published in *The Listener* on 24 April.

He was a trustee of the Tate Gallery from 1941 to 1948, and again from 1949 to 1956. Over the years Moore gave generously of his time, serving on various public bodies: he was a trustee of the National Gallery for three consecutive terms from 1956 to 1971; he also served on the boards of the Arts Council of Great Britain, the Royal Fine Arts Commission, and the National Theatre.

In 1943 the Revd Walter Hussey commissioned Moore to create a sculpture of the Madonna and child for the fiftieth anniversary of St Matthew's Church, Northampton. From twelve terracotta maquettes, Moore chose one which served as the model for the massive 5 foot high stone carving, his first religious sculpture. The *Madonna and Child* was unveiled in February 1944 to a mixture of praise and condemnation of the sort that had greeted his first one-man exhibition in 1928. The naturalism of the figures and the use of drapery reflected the influence of the shelter drawings. Moore succeeded in giving the *Madonna and Child* what he described as 'an austerity and a nobility, and some touch of grandeur (even hieratic aloofness) which is missing in the everyday "Mother and Child" idea' (*Henry Moore: Writings*, 267).

By the mid-1940s Moore's achievements were recognized at home and abroad. In 1945 he was created honorary doctor of literature by the University of Leeds, the first of some two dozen honorary degrees bestowed on him during the next forty years. In December 1946 Moore was in New York for the opening of his retrospective at the Museum of Modern Art. The show attracted 158,000 visitors in three months, before travelling to the Art Institute of Chicago and the San Francisco Museum of Art. There was extensive coverage, mainly favourable, in the New York press, as well as in *Newsweek*, *Time*, *Life*, and *Vogue*. The fine arts department of the British Council arranged for a much reduced version of the exhibition to tour to Australia. Moore's international reputation was firmly established.

In 1944 Moore began a series of maquettes of family groups which culminated in the large bronze *Family Group* (1948–9) commissioned for Barclay School, Stevenage, Hertfordshire, by the county's education officer. The subject was first suggested when the educationist Henry Morris approached Moore about a sculpture for one of his village colleges at Impington, Cambridgeshire, but failed to raise the necessary funds. Two other outdoor sculptures date from the mid- to late 1940s: the Hornton stone *Memorial Figure* (1945–6), beautifully sited at Dartington Hall, Devon, and the Darley Dale stone *Three Standing Figures* (1947–8), in Battersea Park, London.

Moore won the international prize for sculpture at the XXIV Venice Biennale of 1948, firmly establishing his reputation in Europe. The exhibition was under the auspices of the British Council, who over the years helped to organize and supported on a cost-sharing basis many Henry Moore exhibitions. As the sculptor commented: 'the British Council did more for me as an artist than any dealer' (Berthoud, 214). In 1949 the largest exhibition to date was shown at the Wakefield City Art Gallery and at the Manchester City Art Gallery, before the British Council organized a tour to Brussels, Paris, Amsterdam, Hamburg, Dusseldorf, and Bern. The inexorable flood of Moore exhibitions had begun. In the early days Moore often travelled to several venues to supervise the installation and attend the opening ceremony. His infectious charm and his willingness to discuss his work at these events did much to promote his sculpture and to enhance the growing reputation abroad of contemporary British art.

The 1950s On 5 December 1950, Moore wrote to decline the offer of a knighthood; he was concerned that it might change his conception of himself and of his work. Two greater honours were later bestowed: the Companion of Honour in 1955 and the Order of Merit in 1963.

The bronze *Reclining Figure: Festival* (1951; cast held at the Scottish National Gallery of Modern Art, Edinburgh) was commissioned by the Arts Council of Great Britain for the festival of Britain; it was installed opposite the main entrance of the South Bank site. The sculpture marked a turning point in Moore's exploration of solids and voids: 'This figure was perhaps my first conscious effort to make space and form absolutely inseparable' (*Henry Moore: Writings*, 276). The Arts Council also arranged Moore's first London retrospective, which opened at the Tate Gallery on 1 May, two days before the festival itself. The works were selected and the catalogue was written by the art critic David Sylvester, who had worked as Moore's part-time secretary in 1944. To coincide with the Tate exhibition, John Read wrote and produced for the BBC a film on Moore's work. In 1951 Moore began a series of internal–external form sculptures which culminated in the large elmwood *Upright Internal/External Form* (1953–4; Albright-Knox Art Gallery, Buffalo). The reclining figure and mother and child were the two most important themes in Moore's work; a third was the internal–external form motif, many examples of which were inspired by Malanggan carvings. He discussed the theme in symbolic terms of 'an outer protection to an inner form, and it may have something to do with the mother and child idea' (*Henry Moore: Writings*, 214).

Moore and Irina visited Greece in late February 1951 on the occasion of his British Council exhibition at the Zappeion Gallery, Athens. He later remarked that if asked for his ten greatest visual experiences, three or four would come from Greece, including the Parthenon, Delphi, and Mycenae. Towards the end of 1953 Moore visited Brazil, again as a guest of the British Council; he won the international sculpture prize at the second São Paulo Bienal. From there he travelled to Mexico City, saw the pyramids at Teotihuacan and Cuernavaca, and met the painter Diego Rivera.

Between 1952 and 1956 Moore created three of his greatest bronzes, which are as different from each other as they are from his earlier work. The *King and Queen* (1952–3)—of which a cast is dramatically sited at Glenkiln, Dumfriesshire—is probably Moore's best-known sculpture. The idea for these two regal seated figures was triggered by the stories of kings and queens and princesses which Moore was reading at the time to his six-year-old daughter. In contrast to the quiet dignity of this work, the mutilated *Warrior with Shield* (1953-4; cast held at Art Gallery of Ontario, Toronto), Moore's first sculpture of a separate male figure, with bony, masculine, tense forms, is wounded yet still defiant. The idea 'evolved from a pebble I found on the seashore in the summer of 1952, and which reminded me of the stump of a leg, amputated at the hip' (*Henry Moore: Writings*, 283). By the mid-1950s Moore was no longer using drawing as a means of generating ideas for sculpture. During the last thirty or so years of his working life natural forms—bones, shells, and flint stones— were the principal sources of inspiration from which sculptural ideas evolved. *Upright Motive No. 1: Glenkiln Cross* (1955-6; cast at Glenkiln, Dumfriesshire) is the largest and the most figurative of five upright motives, each of which was enlarged from one of thirteen maquettes made in 1955 for what turned out to be an abortive commission for Olivetti's new office building in Milan. Moore began by balancing organic forms 'one above the other—with results rather like the Northwest American totem poles … and then one in particular (later to be named the *Glenkiln Cross*) took on the shape of a crucifix—a kind of worn- down body and a cross merged into one' (*Henry Moore on Sculpture*, 253). The *Glenkiln Cross* is rich in associations: seen from afar an eroded Celtic cross; on closer inspection a single primeval eye above truncated arms balancing on the smooth torso with the sensuous conjunction of waist and hip; and viewed between upright motives nos. 2 and 7, a crucifixion scene.

The *UNESCO Reclining Figure* (1957-8) was one of Moore's last public commissions created for a specific site, the new UNESCO headquarters in Paris. The massive carving, his largest sculpture to date, was made from four blocks of Roman travertine weighing some 39 tons and took four- teen months to complete. The unveiling in Paris in November 1958 may be said to mark the end of Moore's public role as sculptor. As a spokesman on the inter- national stage, his speech 'The sculptor in modern soci- ety', delivered in Venice in 1952 at the International Con- ference of Artists, was his first and last major public address. Moore's role as an adjudicator, which had included membership of the organizing committee for the Unknown Political Prisoner sculpture competition in 1952, came to an end in 1958 when, as president of the jury, he reported on the progress in selecting a sculpture to be erected on the site of Auschwitz–Birkenau concen- tration camp, which he visited in 1958.

The year 1958 was a watershed. From this date forward Moore's work became more personal. As Alan Bowness pointed out, 'Moore has seemed more inclined to please himself, exploiting all the possibilities of working on a grand scale that were now open to him as a successful sculptor, indifferent to fashion and caring little about what other people might think' (*Henry Moore: Writings*, 27). This late period began abruptly in 1959, when he created the first in the series of rugged two- and three-piece reclin- ing figures, which were a continuation, but on a much larger scale, of the multi-part compositions of the

mid-1930s. The analogies between the female figure and landscape had never been so strongly stated.

> I realised what an advantage a separated two-piece composition could have in relating figures to landscape … Knees and breast are mountains … Once these two parts become separated, you don't expect it to be a naturalistic figure; therefore, you can more justifiably make it like a landscape or a rock. (*Henry Moore: Writings*, 288)

Several figurative carvings of the 1930s and 1940s echoed elements of landscape; the metaphor was now reversed. The imagery of cliffs, rocks, caves, and dramatic head- lands dominated, but with enough legible, figurative ref- erences to enable each of the sections to be read as form- ing part of a single, fragmented human form. In *Two Pieces Reclining Figure No. 1* (1959; cast held at Chelsea College of Art and Design, London), the first in the series, the dynamic thrust of the leg section reminded Moore of Adel Rock, which he had visited as a boy, and also of Seurat's painting *Le Bec de Hoc, Grandcamp* (1885; Tate collection), which he had often seen on visits to Kenneth Clark.

The 1960s In 1961 Moore was asked if he would create a sculpture for the pool in front of the new Lincoln Center for the Performing Arts in New York. It was a commission, but he was free to produce what he liked. The two-piece Lincoln Center *Reclining Figure* (1963-5) was so large that, in order to make and protect the plaster from which the bronze would be cast, Moore built a large outdoor studio in his garden. The sculpture was cast in West Berlin by Hermann Noack.

Moore's 1961 *Standing Figure: Knife Edge* was based dir- ectly on a small bone, to which he added a clay head and a stump-like arm. In 1967 one of the bronze casts of this sculpture was unveiled in St Stephen's Green, Dublin, in memory of the Irish poet W. B. Yeats.

Paradoxically, it was during the personal and private late period—private in the sense that the abundant maquettes developed in the seclusion of his studio were created for their own sake—that many of Moore's best- known public sculptures evolved. In December 1963 Pro- fessor William McNeil and two other committee mem- bers from the University of Chicago visited Moore in the hope of commissioning a sculpture to commemorate Enrico Fermi's achievement in producing the first con- trolled nuclear chain reaction. Moore showed them a small maquette which he had made recently, with a smooth, dome-shaped head that related to the earlier hel- met series. It was agreed that if enlarged, the sculpture might be a suitable memorial. Moore said that he would make it anyway, and if the committee liked it, well and good. Based on the 1964 *Maquette for Atom Piece*, a plaster working model was made, and from this the 12 foot-high bronze *Nuclear energy* (1964-6; University of Chicago) with its sinister suggestions of a human skull and a mushroom cloud.

Three Way Piece No. 2: (the) Archer (1964-5) began life as a maquette and working model. The Finnish architect Viljo Revell, on a visit to Hoglands on 23 November 1964, told Moore that an enlarged version would be ideal for the civic square in front of the new city hall he had designed for Toronto. Revell returned home and died in Finland the following day. Moore went ahead and enlarged the sculpture. Toronto city council refused to buy *The Archer* but the necessary funds (£40,000) were raised from private sources, and the large bronze was unveiled on 27 October 1966. In March 1967, during a reception for Moore at the new city hall, the idea for a Moore gallery as part of a planned expansion programme of the Art Gallery of Ontario was born. During the late 1960s and early 1970s, Moore was closely involved with the design and plans for the Henry Moore Sculpture Centre, which opened on 26 October 1974. The sculptor donated 100 original plasters and bronzes, 57 drawings, and an almost complete collection of his graphic work. Today, some 900 sculptures, drawings, and prints comprise the largest public collection of Moore's work.

On 26 February 1967 it was announced in the *Sunday Telegraph* that Moore had offered between twenty and thirty sculptures to the nation, which would probably go to the Tate Gallery. Late in April, the government agreed to give £200,000 towards a proposed extension, provided that the trustees could match the grant. On 26 May *The Times* published a letter signed by forty-one artists protesting against the allocation of funds and exhibition space for the work of an individual artist. Moore was deeply hurt by the letter, among whose signatories were his former assistants Anthony Caro and Phillip King. The special gallery to display his work was never built. In 1978, on the occasion of his eightieth birthday, Moore donated thirty-six bronzes and original plaster casts to the Tate Gallery.

One of the most obvious characteristics of Moore's late style is the highly charged erotic and overt sexual nature of some of the work. This is particularly true of the sculpture of the 1960s, such as the intertwining, embracing forms of *Locking Piece* (1963–4; cast held in Tate collection); the thrusting, phallic form in *Two Piece No. 7: Pipe* (1966; cast held in Tate collection); and the sense of coupling, past or imminent, in the sensual *Large Two Forms* (1966 and 1969; cast held at Art Gallery of Ontario, Toronto). Another characteristic of his late work is the sheer size of some of the bronzes. *Large Two Forms* was one of the first works constructed using large, lightweight blocks of polystyrene, rather than by building an armature and adding heavy wet plaster.

During the 1960s the two most important Moore exhibitions were held in London: 'Henry Moore: Sculpture, 1950–1960' opened in November 1960 at the Whitechapel Art Gallery, and in 1968 Moore's second retrospective at the Tate Gallery was held on the occasion of his seventieth birthday. David Sylvester once again selected the works and wrote the Tate catalogue. Of the many books, catalogues, and articles on Moore that had appeared in startlingly increasing numbers since 1945, none was more influential than *Henry Moore on Sculpture: a Collection of the Sculptor's Writings and Spoken Words* (1966), edited by Philip James.

In 1969, a year after he had been given an African elephant skull by Juliette Huxley, Moore began a series of etchings of the skull, the largest and most impressive item among the hundreds of natural forms which filled many boxes and were strewn about among the plaster maquettes on every available surface in the Hoglands maquette studio. Once he had made several etchings of the entire skull, Moore found so much fascinating imagery in the structural details—a Doric column, underground dungeons, a desert landscape—that he produced thirty-eight etchings for the *Elephant Skull* album, which marked the beginning of a sustained interest in printmaking, an activity which had occupied him intermittently since he produced his first graphic work in 1931. During the next fifteen years, the sale of individual prints, print albums and portfolios generated a substantial income. Between 1931 and 1984, Moore produced 719 prints, mainly in editions. His activities as a printmaker coincided almost exactly with a renewed interest in drawing, which had declined in the early 1950s when he was no longer using drawings as a way of generating ideas for sculpture. In 1970 he made some sixty-five pen exercises, and during the next sixteen years he produced an astonishing number of drawings, particularly during the early 1980s when he was too ill to work on his sculpture. The range and variety of subject matter is equally astonishing: sheep in the field near one of the studios; a log pile at Hoglands; trees and hedges; shipwrecks; ethereal landscapes; drawings of his grandson Gus; reclining figures; mother and child studies; and Dorothy Hodgkin's hands. He was able to draw freely, enjoying it for its own sake.

The 1970s In 1972 a retrospective exhibition of Moore's work was held in the magnificent setting of the Forte di Belvedere, Florence. Moore commented that 'No better site for showing sculpture in the open-air, in relationship to architecture, & to a town, could be found anywhere in the world' (*Henry Moore: Writings*, 75). The exhibition attracted 345,000 visitors. Other notable, if less spectacular, exhibitions included 'Henry Moore: Sculptures et Dessins' at the Orangerie des Tuileries, Paris (1977), and 'The Drawings of Henry Moore', shown at the Art Gallery of Ontario, Toronto, in 1977 and in 1978 at four venues in Japan and then at the Tate Gallery, London, as part of the celebrations marking Moore's eightieth birthday. It was also during the 1970s that the demand for Moore's sculpture among private collectors, museum directors, and architects reached its zenith. In May 1978 he was in Washington, DC, to help with the installation of the monumental bronze *Mirror Knife Edge* (1977), at the entrance to I. M. Pei's new East Building of the National Gallery of Art. In December of that year Moore was in Dallas for the unveiling of the gigantic bronze *Three Forms Vertebrae* (1978), in front of Pei's new city hall, and in 1979 he was in Bonn to supervise the placement of *Large Two Forms* (1966 and 1969) in front of the new chancellery building. Examples of Moore's carvings and bronzes are sited in many public locations around the world. Some 285 museums, municipalities, and institutions own examples of his work.

In 1977, with the help of his daughter, Mary, Moore established the Henry Moore Foundation funded by the enormous profits from the sale of his work. The foundation was set up 'to advance the education of the public by the promotion of their appreciation of the fine arts and in particular the works of Henry Moore'. It now operates from Dane Tree House, Perry Green, and the Henry Moore Institute, Leeds. The foundation is responsible for conserving and expanding their vast holdings of Moore's work, which comprise some 650 carvings and bronzes, 3500 drawings, and 6000 prints, and for making the collection available for exhibitions, scholarly study, and publication. The institute supports students and artists, and organizes conferences, seminars, and exhibitions. Moore's charitable foundation is one of his enduring legacies. In March 1980 Moore's daughter left England to settle in South Africa with her husband and son. Even though their relationship had at times been difficult, it was the most upsetting event in Moore's adult life.

Final years The largest Moore exhibition ever assembled, again organized with the assistance of the British Council, was shown at three locations in Madrid in 1981. In November 1982 Moore attended the opening by Queen Elizabeth II of the Henry Moore Centre for the Study of Sculpture, an extension of Leeds City Art Gallery which had been funded by the Henry Moore Foundation. In 1983 Moore's second New York retrospective, 'Henry Moore: 60 Years of his Art', was held at the Metropolitan Museum of Art. It was also in the 1980s that two prestigious honours were bestowed upon Moore: in 1980 he was presented with the West German grand cross of the order of merit and in October 1984 he was invested commander of the Légion d'honneur.

On 8 August 1983 Moore was taken to hospital in Cambridge, where he underwent a prostate operation; he was discharged on 17 August but returned to hospital soon afterwards. Following his daughter's return from South Africa, Moore returned to Hoglands, where he gradually recovered and was able to do some drawing. Henry Moore died at Hoglands on 31 August 1986. His funeral was held on 4 September at St Thomas's Church, Perry Green, and a service of thanksgiving took place at Westminster Abbey on 18 November 1986.

Working methods, character, reputation, and assessment In his early career, Moore had an almost fanatical belief in truth to materials, carving his sculptures. However, by the mid-1940s his working methods had radically changed. Although he did not give up carving, he created more and more sculptures in clay, but more usually in plaster, many of which were destined to be cast in bronze. The small plaster maquettes were made by Moore in the privacy of his studio. He would select a maquette which he wanted to be enlarged and his assistants would, under his supervision, make the large version or versions by constructing an armature of wood, scrim, wire, or wire netting, onto which the wet plaster was applied. From the mid-1940s to the mid-1960s Moore would take over once the assistants had built up the plaster to within an inch or so of the final measurements, but during the last twenty or so years of his life he worked less and less on the working model and large-scale plasters. As the scale of Moore's work increased dramatically in the mid-1960s, the assistants worked with large blocks of polystyrene to create the working models and very large sculptures.

Practical, down-to-earth, open and friendly, Moore had a boyish charm, beguiling conversation, and sense of fun that enchanted his many friends and the thousands of visitors whom he welcomed over the years to Hoglands. Bernard Meadows described working with him during the late 1930s: 'Henry was like a boy, jokey, singing bawdy army songs he had learnt in the First World War. There was a *simplicity* about him, not a naiveté' (Berthoud, 136). Short and stocky of build, he never lost his light Yorkshire accent. A genuine modesty masked a supremely confident and ambitious artist, addicted to his work, and deeply concerned about his place among the greatest sculptors in the history of Western art. He rarely acknowledged the considerable influence on his own work of such contemporaries as Picasso, Arp, and Giacometti. Moore was extraordinarily generous in many ways, yet rarely gave a sculpture or drawing to a friend, or to those who had worked for him for many years. He was financially less than generous towards his assistants, without whose help the very profitable large sculptures could never have been made. Despite his becoming a very wealthy man, in the many years that Henry and Irina lived at Hoglands, their lifestyle changed very little. What mattered most to Moore was that he could readily afford to hire more assistants when needed, in later years to employ highly skilled stone carvers at the Henraux marble works at Querceta, and to meet the considerable cost of having the hundreds of original plasters cast in bronze editions. In the tributes and obituaries following Moore's death, there was almost as much praise for the man as for his work. The *Daily Telegraph* (1 September 1986) declared in a leading article: 'Since the death of Sir Winston Churchill, Henry Moore had been the most internationally-acclaimed of Englishmen, honoured by every civilized country in the world', and in *The Guardian* (1 September 1986) Norbert Lynton commented that 'Time will show which was his greater achievement, his life or his art'.

From 1928, the year of his first one-man show and his first public commission, until 1939, when his first sculpture to enter a national collection was accepted as a gift by the Tate Gallery, Moore's reputation as one of the most important avant-garde artists in England grew steadily and inexorably. Although the British public may have been baffled and affronted by the holes and distortions of the human figure, and the hermetic, semi-abstract carvings of the mid-1930s, Moore had the support of such influential artists, art historians, and collectors as Jacob Epstein, Augustus John, Herbert Read, R. H. Wilenski, Alfred Barr, Kenneth Clark, Philip Hendy, Michael Sadler, Roland Penrose, and Robert Sainsbury. The carvings from these years represent Moore's most significant contribution to the modernist movement in England, and their importance and originality have rarely been questioned. It was the shelter drawings of 1940–41, exhibited during the war at the National Gallery, which almost overnight transformed Moore's reputation with the public from that of an avant-garde outsider to an artist whose work Londoners could readily identify with and admire.

The first serious challenge to Moore's brand of modernism was voiced in 1947 by the influential American formalist critic Clement Greenberg. He labelled Moore 'a sincere academic modern', deplored his attachment to the past, and described his work as 'not too far from classical statuary' (Kosinski, 23). Greenberg championed the new American sculpture of David Smith and his colleagues, who had rejected the traditional materials of sculpture in favour of welding and commercial steel, often brightly coloured with industrial paints. By the early 1960s, influenced by David Smith and supported by Greenberg, Moore's former assistant Anthony Caro and his students at St Martin's School of Art were constructing sculptures made of painted steel or synthetic materials. Moore's work was deemed conservative and irrelevant. However, Caro recognized and paid tribute to Moore's importance for his generation, and in so doing summed up one of the older sculptor's most important legacies: 'His success has created a climate for all of us younger sculptors and has given us confidence in ourselves which without his efforts we would not have felt' (ibid., 27). While the steel constructions of Smith and Caro had an enormous stylistic influence on the evolution of sculpture during the second half of the twentieth century, Moore's work involved closure, marking the end of a tradition and leading nowhere, so thoroughly had he explored, in stone, wood, and bronze, the human figure and biomorphic forms inspired by natural objects: bones, shells, pebbles, and flint stones.

From the late 1940s until the end of Moore's career, the increasing adulation of the public, collectors, architects, and the boards of multinational corporations ran parallel to the growing hostility of a number of critics and of the younger generation of sculptors. When in the early 1950s he had all but abandoned the sacred doctrine of truth to material so that he could have his work cast in bronze editions, his detractors compared his working method, whereby assistants were given a maquette to be enlarged in plaster, to the use of mechanical pointing machines by skilled stone carvers, a practice which Moore had deplored as a young student. Some of the monumental late bronzes were criticized for their grandiose inflation of scale and for the large editions in which they were cast. There was also the question of over-exposure. In the 1960s and 1970s, almost as if by right, a large Moore bronze was frequently the inevitable choice for new public spaces or office towers of multinational companies. To his friends and admirers, Moore could do no wrong, while the anti-Moore camp found nothing to praise or admire. And yet nobody can doubt the enormous influence of the man and his work. No sculptor since Rodin enjoyed such world-wide fame and no artist of his era has done as much as Henry Moore to explain and promote the art of sculpture.

Moore was an instinctual not an intellectual artist, whose work has a high seriousness, a gravitas, with an almost total absence of wit or humour. Throughout his life he was striving to achieve a vitality and power of expression in his work. As he wrote in 1934, 'I want to make sculpture as big in feeling & grandeur as the Sumerian, as vital as Negro as direct & stone like as Mexican as alive as Early Greek & Etruscan as spiritual as Gothic' (*Henry Moore: Writings*, 200). The diversity of Moore's imagery stems from the plethora of sources which he assimilated into his art. In focusing on the human figure, Moore extended the frontiers of the Western humanist tradition. In exploring the reclining figure theme, he created profoundly moving, poetic images of the human body as a metaphor for landscape. In the mother and child motif and family groups, he celebrated nurturing and the bonds of family life. Moore's sculpture embodies the dignity and resilience of the human spirit, and the will to survive.

Moore never belonged to a school. Nor was he in the 1930s a true surrealist or a true abstractionist: although he took from both camps what he needed, he always retained his independence. He was as much a successor to the sculpture of classical Greece and the work of Michelangelo and Rodin as he was to the disparate styles of 'primitive' art. Throughout the more than sixty years of his prolific creative life, whether working in stone, wood, clay, or plaster, Moore's single-minded obsession was the exploration of three-dimensional form and space. In the final analysis, it is for the richness and inventiveness of his personal form language, and its power to move and to evoke rich associations with the human body, with landscape and the forms in nature, that the sculptor would wish to be remembered. ALAN WILKINSON

Sources *Henry Moore: writings and conversations*, ed. A. Wilkinson (2002) · R. Berthoud, *The life of Henry Moore* (1987) · A. G. Wilkinson, *The drawings of Henry Moore* (1977) · *Henry Moore on sculpture*, ed. P. James (1966) · A. G. Wilkinson, *Henry Moore remembered* (1987) · S. Spender, *Henry Moore OM* (1987) [memorial address] · A. Davis, ed., *Henry Moore bibliography*, 1–5 (1992–4) · H. Moore, *Henry Spencer Moore*, ed. J. Hedgecoe (1968) · H. Moore and J. Hedgecoe, *Henry Moore: my ideas, inspiration and life as an artist* (1986) · H. Read, *Henry Moore, sculptor: an appreciation* (1934) · H. Read, *Henry Moore: a study of his life and work* (1965) · H. Read, 'Henry Moore', *The Listener* (22 April 1931), 688–9 · G. Grigson, *Henry Moore* (1943) · J. J. Sweeney, *Henry Moore* (1946) · A. D. B. Sylvester, 'The evolution of Henry Moore's sculpture', *Burlington Magazine* (June 1948), 158–65 · A. D. B. Sylvester, *Sculpture and drawings by Henry Moore* (1951) · J. Russell, *Henry Moore* (1968) · D. Hall, *Henry Moore: the life and work of a great sculptor* (1966) · E. Neumann, *The archetypal world of Henry Moore* (1959) · H. Seldis, *Henry Moore in America* (1973) · K. Clark, *Henry Moore drawings* (1974) · B. Robertson, *Henry Moore: sculpture, 1950–1960* (1960) · *Henry Moore: sculpture and environment* (1976) [photographs and text by D. Finn, foreword by K. Clark, commentaries by H. Moore] · H. Moore, *Henry Moore at the British Museum* (1981) · *Henry Moore: sculptures in landscape* (1978) [photographs and foreword by G. Shakerley, text by S. Spender, introduction by H. Moore] · D. Sylvester, *Henry Moore* (1968) · A. G. Wilkinson, *The drawings of Henry Moore* (1984) · 'Henry Moore: an interview by Donald Hall', *Horizon* (Nov 1960), 102–15 · W. Forma, *Five British sculptors: work and talk* (1964) · J. Freeman, *Face to face with John Freeman: interviews from the BBC TV series* (1989) · D. Carroll, *The Donald Carroll interviews* (1973) · C. Lake, 'Henry Moore's world', *Atlantic Monthly* (Jan 1962), 39–45 · W. Grohmann, *The art of Henry Moore* (1960) · E. Roditi, *Dialogues on art* (1960) · J. Russell and V. Russell, 'Conversations with Henry Moore', *Sunday Times* (17–24 Dec 1961) · G. Levine, *With Henry Moore: the artist at work* (1978) · G. Levine,

Henry Moore: wood sculpture (1983) • P. Fuller, *Henry Moore: an interpretation* (1993) • W. Packer, *Henry Moore: an illustrated biography* (1985) • A. G. Wilkinson, 'Henry Moore', *'Primitivism' in twentieth-century art: affinity of the tribal and the modern*, ed. W. Rubin (1984), vol. 2, pp. 595–612 • R. Melville, *Henry Moore: sculpture and drawings, 1921–1969* (1970) • *Celebrating Moore: works from the collection of the Henry Moore Foundation* (1998) [sel. by D. Mitchinson] • D. Kosinski, ed., *Henry Moore: sculpting the twentieth century* (2001) • A. Garrould and V. Power, *Henry Moore: tapestries* (1988) • J. Hedgecoe, *A monumental vision: the sculpture of Henry Moore* (1998) • A. Garrould, *Henry Moore drawings* (1988) • *Henry Moore: mother and child etchings* (1988) [introduction by G. Gelburd] • D. Mitchinson, ed., *Henry Moore sculpture* (1981) • *Henry Moore's sheep sketchbook* (1980) [comments by H. Moore and K. Clark] • J. Read, *Henry Moore: portrait of an artist* (1979) • W. Strachan, *Henry Moore: animals* (1983) • *Auden poems: Moore lithographs* (1974) • P. Gilmour, *Henry Moore: graphics in the making* (1975) • *Mostra di Henry Moore* (1972) • D. Sylvester, *Henry Moore at the Serpentine* (1978) • J. Russell, *The Henry Moore gift* (1978) • *Henry Moore: drawings, 1969–79* (1979) • *Tapestry: Henry Moore and West Dean* (1980) • *Henry Moore: early carvings, 1920–1940* [texts by A. Garrould, T. Friedman, and D. Mitchinson] • G. Gelburd, ed., *Mother and child: the art of Henry Moore* (1987) • S. Compton, ed., *Henry Moore* (1988) • N. Lynton, *Henry Moore: the human dimension* (1991) • W. S. Lieberman, *Henry Moore: sixty years of his art* (1983) • *Henry Moore at the National Gallery* (1998) • *Henry Moore: war and utility* (2001) • *Moore in the Bagatelle Gardens, Paris* (1993) [exhibition catalogue]

Archives Henry Moore Foundation Archive and Library, Hertfordshire • Henry Moore Institute, Leeds, corresp. and papers | priv. coll., corresp. with Sir Robert Sainsbury and Lady Sainsbury, and relating to exhibitions of his works • Tate collection, corresp. with Lord Clark • Tate collection, letters to Gustav Kahnweiler and Elizabeth Kahnweiler • Tate collection, corresp. with Sir Michael Sadler • Tate collection, corresp. relating to Unit One • University of East Anglia Library, Norwich, corresp. with J. C. Pritchard • V&A, corresp. with Bernhard Baer, publisher, collographs, and papers • V&A, questionnaire completed for Kineton Parkes • W. Sussex RO, letters to Walter Hussey and related papers | FILM Henry Moore Foundation | SOUND Henry Moore Foundation

Likenesses R. J. Coxon, oils, 1924, Man. City Gall. • H. Coster, photographs, 1930–39, NPG • H. Coster, twelve negatives, 1944, NPG • Y. Karsh, photographs, 1949–73, NPG • I. Kar, bromide prints, 1950–c.1960, NPG [*see illus.*] • D. Low, pencil, in or before 1952, NPG • M. Gerson, photograph, 1960, NPG • W. Bird, photograph, 1963, NPG • J. Lewinski, bromide print on card mount, 1964, NPG • J. S. Lewinski, photograph, 1964, NPG • M. Marini, bronze cast of head, 1969, NPG • G. Argent, photograph, 1970, NPG • D. Hockney, pen-and-ink drawing, 1972, Café Royal, London • J. Fraser, wax figure, 1973, Madame Tussauds Ltd, London • F. Kormis, plaster model for medallion and bronze cast, 1978, FM Cam. • A. Newman, photograph, 1978, NPG • H. Moore, self-portrait, drawing, 1982, NPG • C. Beaton, photograph, NPG • J. Hedgecoe, bromide print, NPG • D. Low, caricatures, pencil sketches, NPG

Wealth at death £1,284,570: probate, 23 March 1987, *CGPLA Eng. & Wales* • most of wealth tied up in Henry Moore Foundation

Moore, James, junior (1675×80–1724), army officer and politician in America, was born in South Carolina, the son of James Moore (c.1650–1706), governor of South Carolina, and his wife, Margaret Berringer. He began his political career as a soldier instead of a politician. He served in the South Carolina Commons house of assembly (1706–8) but rose to prominence in 1713 as a militia commander during the Tuscarora War. He led an army of white Carolinians and their Creek, Cherokee, and Catawba American Indian allies, into North Carolina where his force defeated the Tuscarora people in the battle of Nooherooka. The battle broke the strength of the Tuscarora and the war subsided.

Defeated, the Tuscarora migrated north and joined the Iroquois confederation.

Moore's outspoken opposition to the lords proprietors barred him from elected and appointed offices for a decade. But he took a leading role as a soldier and a diplomat with the American Indians during the Yemassee War in South Carolina. In April 1715 the Yemassee, allied with the Catawbas, Creeks, and other south-eastern American Indians, tried to kill or drive out all whites from the colony. Moore served as lieutenant-general of the colonial forces and was successful in defeating the colony's enemies.

In the aftermath of the Yemassee War anti-proprietary feeling grew strong. The proprietors had given the province little assistance during the fighting and, after the warfare had subsided, sought to strengthen their control over the province. They voided popular local legislation and appointed Robert Johnson, son of the former governor Nathaniel Johnson, to reassert proprietary authority as the new governor. During the autumn of 1719 the threat of Spanish attack on the province increased internal tensions. The Commons house election of November 1719 triggered active, organized resistance to the proprietary government. Moore and other prominent colonial leaders formed an 'association', an extra-legal organization that sought to oust the proprietary government and place the Carolina colony under direct British royal authority. Moore was a leader of the association and of the convention of the people that succeeded it.

Association members first invited Johnson to keep the governorship in the king's name but he refused. When the convention met in December it named Moore interim governor of South Carolina in the name of George II, although he had no official royal backing. He accepted the post and kept it until May 1721. As acting governor Moore convened general assemblies, made executive appointments, and issued ordinances. He and the revolutionary government sent numerous petitions and reports to the British Board of Trade reporting conditions in South Carolina and justifying the revolution. Most of these petitions concluded with a plea for the crown to take over the government. The crown and privy council assumed royal authority over the former proprietary colony in August 1720 and appointed a royal governor.

In the spring of 1721 Carolinians learned that Sir Francis Nicholson would soon leave Britain to take up his post as the colony's first royal governor. This news stirred former governor Johnson and some of his supporters, including Nicholas Trott and William Rhett, to undertake a brief resistance to Moore's royal government. Until that time Johnson and his allies had boycotted the interim government and obstructed its proceedings on occasion. But at this juncture they gathered in public a small armed force to intimidate Moore and his government. Johnson's force marched to the government offices but was met by a company of militia loyal to the revolution. Johnson and his supporters dispersed. Sir Francis arrived in the colony in May 1721 and took up his appointment. Moore relinquished the governorship and returned to a leadership position in the Commons house of assembly. He was elected speaker of the house and held that post until his death.

Moore married Elizabeth Beresford, whose brother, Richard Beresford, was one of his political allies, and the couple had six children. Moore died at his plantation in the Goose Creek region of South Carolina on 3 March 1724. An inventory of his estate recorded the total value of his chattels personalty as £7684 2s. 9d. Included in this total were the values of forty-four African and American Indian slaves.

ALEXANDER MOORE

Sources L. H. Roper, 'Moore, James jr.', ANB · W. B. Edgar and N. L. Bailey, eds., *Biographical directory of the South Carolina house of representatives*, 2 (1977) · M. Webber, 'The first Governor Moore and his children', *South Carolina Historical and Genealogical Magazine*, 37 (1936), 1–23 · V. W. Crane, *The southern frontier, 1670–1732* (1929) · R. M. Weir, *Colonial South Carolina: a history* (1983) · J. A. Moore, 'Royalizing South Carolina: the revolution of 1719 and the evolution of early South Carolina government', PhD diss., University of South Carolina, 1991 · F. Yonge, *A narrative of the proceedings of the people of South Carolina, in the year 1719: and of the true causes that induced them to renounce their obedience to the lords proprietors, as their governours, and to put themselves under the immediate government of the crown* (1726)
Archives L. Cong., James Moore jun., letter-book · South Carolina Archives and History Center, Columbia, sessional papers, S16525
Wealth at death £7684 2s. 9d.: inventory, Charleston county wills, inventories and miscellaneous records, South Carolina Archives and History Center, Columbia, 60 (1724–5), 55–8

Moore [later Carrick-Moore], **James** (1762–1860), surgeon and biographer, was born on 21 December 1762 in Glasgow, the son of John *Moore (1729–1802), physician and writer, and Jean (1735–1820), daughter of John Simson, professor of divinity at Glasgow University. Moore followed his father into medicine and studied in Edinburgh, and in London as a pupil and later house surgeon at St George's Hospital. He served as an army medical officer in 1781 during the American War of Independence, and returned to Britain in early 1782. By 1784 Moore had become a member of the Surgeons' Company of London, and had set up in practice in the city. He later also held the post of surgeon to the 2nd regiment of Life Guards. Moore married a daughter of John Henderson, a distinguished actor, and had at least three children.

Moore published on a variety of topics in both medicine and surgery, including a speculative work on the processes of wound healing, a critical survey of William Cullen's categorization of drugs, and an analysis of quack medicine. In *A Method of Preventing or Diminishing Pain in Several Operations of Surgery* (1784) he described experiments to induce anaesthesia by compressing the nerves in the arm and leg, a technique which was successfully used by John Hunter. Moore's most significant contribution to medicine came through his involvement in the new practice of vaccination. Around the turn of the century Moore took part in debates over the safety and immunity conferred by the procedure. As a result he met Edward Jenner, the discoverer of vaccination, and joined Jenner's circle of friends and allies. In 1806 Moore defended the new practice in two pamphlets, *A Reply to the Antivaccinists* and

Remarks on Mr. Birch's Serious Reasons for Uniformly Objecting to the Practice of Vaccination. The following year he published a satirical pamphlet, *Pethox parvus: dedicated, without permission, to the remnant of the blind priests of that idolatry* (1807), under the pseudonym Iconoclastus. In these works Moore argued that introducing a vaccine, produced from cowpox, into the human body did not induce bovine diseases, and that the procedure conferred permanent immunity to smallpox. After the initial dispute had died down, Moore helped to consolidate support for vaccination by publishing *A History of Smallpox* (1812), reminding the public of the dangers of the disease, and *A History of Vaccination* (1817), a comprehensive account of the history of the practice. Through Jenner's patronage Moore was appointed assistant director to the new National Vaccine Establishment in 1808, and on Jenner's rapid resignation he became director of the institution. During his tenure Moore ensured that the establishment fulfilled its remit to provide free vaccination and a guaranteed supply of vaccine lymph, and to investigate cases where vaccination had apparently failed to prevent smallpox. After 1821 Moore gradually gave up his medical practice. In that year he inherited, through his wife, the property of Robert Carrick, a wealthy Glasgow banker, including land in southwest Scotland. He then adopted the name Carrick-Moore.

Moore probably achieved his greatest fame as the biographer of his elder brother, Lieutenant-General Sir John *Moore, who died at the battle of Corunna in 1809. Shortly after his death Moore published *A Narrative of the Campaign of the British Army in Spain* (1809), incorporating letters and extracts from his brother's journals, which defended John Moore's role in the action. In 1833 he also produced a lively two-volume *Life of Lieutenant-General Sir John Moore*. Carrick-Moore died on 1 June 1860 at 9 Clarges Street, London.

DEBORAH BRUNTON

Sources DNB · *Scottish Nation*, 7 [n.d.] · Chambers, *Scots.*, rev. T. Thomson (1875) · Irving, *Scots.* · *New Biographical Dictionary* (1825) · *The Times* (5 June 1860) [death notice] · CGPLA Eng. & Wales (1860)
Archives BL, corresp. with second earl of Liverpool, Add. MSS 38243, 38321, 38571, *passim*
Wealth at death under £40,000—in UK: probate, 1860, CGPLA Eng. & Wales

Moore [née Gobeil], **Jane Elizabeth** [Jeanne Elizabet] (b. **1738**), writer and businesswoman, was born in London on 30 September 1738, the elder of two daughters of Abraam Gobeil (1711–c.1765), leather manufacturer, and his wife, Jeanne Marie (c.1719–1741), eldest daughter of Monsieur G—r of St Onge, France. Both her parents were French, living in England at the time of her birth. She was baptized at St Martin Orgar French Huguenot church, Martin Lane, on 15 October 1738. Gobeil's mother, tricked into an unhappy marriage, died young and about two years later her father remarried. Her stepmother, according to Gobeil, 'had forsaken the path of virtue … and every scheme was agitated to destroy the reputation of the house' (*Genuine Memoirs*, 38–9; 43–4). After a series of adulterous affairs, the stepmother left when Gobeil was ten years old.

Brought up speaking only French, Gobeil claimed to have begun her schooling at the age of twenty months. She rapidly learned English and at five could read the Bible in both languages. She was removed from school in 1743 and spent a year at home with her stepmother where unsuccessful attempts were made to teach her needlework and 'most indelicate novels' were read aloud to the servants in her presence. Gobeil was later to accuse her stepmother of underfeeding her during this period. After a spell at a school for young ladies in Bromley, she moved first to her godfather's house where she was tutored by a French refugee, then to a seminary for young women and finally to a school in Wandsworth. She completed her formal education in 1753, but later taught herself accounting in order to keep her father's books.

Returning home on the completion of her schooling, Gobeil found that her father resented her because she was a girl. She nevertheless began to work in his business, turning down several proposals of marriage in order to remain with him. In 1760 she first met Mr Moore (c.1717–1781), her future husband, when he visited her father's warehouse. He became interested in her and, according to Gobeil, 'pretended to have knowledge of books' and 'flattered her' (Genuine Memoirs, 291). Although her father opposed the match, they were married on 10 October 1761.

Upon marrying, Moore became stepmother to her husband's son from a previous marriage. Two children were born to the couple but both died in infancy.

Moore participated in her husband's leather manufacture business and travelled extensively around Britain studying trade and manufacture. By 1772, however, both the business and the marriage were in serious difficulty.

Mr Moore died in 1781 leaving considerable debts. In 1784 Jane Moore was imprisoned as a bankrupt and remained in prison for eight months. After her release, she turned to writing as a way to support herself. Her Genuine Memoirs, 3 vols. (1786?) alternate sensationalized details of Moore's life with details of her travels and observations; the third volume consists of essays on subjects such as agriculture, fisheries, education, trade, and the law. The Monthly Review (December 1786) described the book as 'a silly tale of trifling adventures, related in a most vulgar style' and complained that the 'journey through Great Britain is neither sentimental nor instructive' (Monthly Review).

Moore had written poetry for years and published a number of poems (some anonymously) in the Sentimental and Masonic Magazine (1792–5). Visiting Dublin in 1795 on business, she met the poet and satirist Henrietta Battier and the poet Thomas Moore, the latter describing her as 'of the largest and most vulgar Wapping mould … making havoc with the v's and w's' as she read her poems to the assembled company (Memoirs, ed. Russell, 41–2). Her Miscellaneous Poems, on Various Subjects was published by subscription in 1796; a second edition followed in 1797. Generally considered to be better than her prose, it included poems to the royal family, biblical paraphrases, a set of songs and poems from an opera, 'The Female Hermit'

(lost), and an entertaining poetic correspondence with an anonymous freemason on the refusal of the Society of Freemasons to admit women as equal members.

ELIZABETH HAGGLUND and PEARL FOGELL

Sources J. E. Moore, *Genuine memoirs of Jane Elizabeth Moore, late of Bermondsey, in Surry. Written by herself: containing the singular adventures of herself and her family, her sentimental journey through Great Britain; specifying the various manufactures carried on at each town. A comprehensive treatise on the trade, manufacture, laws and police of this kingdom, and the necessity of a county hospital, to which is prefixed a poetic index*, 3 vols. (1786?) · 'Review of Moore's *Genuine memoirs*', *Monthly Review*, 75 (1786), 473–4 · *Memoirs, journal and correspondence of Thomas Moore*, ed. J. Russell, 8 vols. (1853–6) · *The Sentimental and Masonic Magazine* (1792–5) · Ordnance Survey of England, book reference to the plan of the parish of St Mary Magdalen, Bermondsey (Hundred of Brixton) in the county of Surrey. Containing 627:445 acres (1875) · J. R. de J. Jackson, *Romantic poetry by women: a bibliography, 1770–1835* (1993) · T. de Vere White, *Tom Moore, the Irish poet* (1977) · A. Carpenter, ed., *Verse in English from eighteenth-century Ireland* (1998) · Blain, Clements & Grundy, *Feminist comp.* · IGI

Moore, John (d. 1619), Church of England clergyman and author, is said to have been a member of the Moore family of Moorehays, near Cullompton, Devon. According to Wood he entered University College, Oxford, as a commoner in or before 1572; he was probably the member of that college who graduated BA on 16 December 1573 and MA on 2 July 1576. He may also have been the John More MA who was ordained priest by the bishop of Exeter on 24 August 1582 and who was curate of Thurlangton, or Langton Tur, Leicestershire, in 1585. But it is certain that in 1586, on presentation of Frances, widow of Sir George Turpin, Moore became rector of Knaptoft, Leicestershire, listed in 1603 as a parish of 300 communicants, a living valued at £34 12s. 6d. per annum.

In 1604 Moore was an objector against the new constitutions and canons promulgated by James I. On 3 October 1604, and again on 22 November, he appeared before the bishop of Lincoln and asked for time to deliberate; on 30 January 1605, having been admonished four times, Moore was reported to be 'more and more confirmed in his opinions and therefore hath not yet conformed himself, neither can he conform himself' (C. W. Foster, cxxx). On 10 April he appeared again. Action was postponed until 19 June, but he was then granted time to confer with Ambrose Sacheverell, vicar of Ratcliffe, Buckinghamshire. Further respites were granted on 31 July and 18 September 1605. On 23 October he and others, 'in hope of their conformity, were dismissed until they shall be cited again' (ibid., 368). Moore was cited again in 1607 for refusing to wear the surplice, but he held on to his benefice until his death in 1619.

In 1617 Moore published a theological treatise, *A Mappe of Man's Mortalitie*, but his interests were not narrowly clerical. In 1612 he had issued *A Target for Tillage*, directed against enclosure, a movement which seems to have had more serious effects in Leicestershire than elsewhere, and not least in the area of Knaptoft. Moore dedicated his book to Sir William Turpin, his 'patron and very good friend', dating it from Sheasby, Leicestershire, April 1611. It is ironic indeed that Turpin was reported to have later become a leading local encloser. Moore explains in his preface that he does not intend to defend spendthrifts or 'idle drones' but rather to take up 'the pitiful case of the painful ploughmen, tradesmen, and poor labourers' who are unable to provide for their families, and who, on that account, 'sometimes break out into fearful clamours, against the tyrannous dealing of unjust enclosers'; the work embodies his 'second thoughts to my former meditations', perhaps occasioned by the midland revolt of 1607, though no earlier edition is known. He seeks to present a patriotic rationale for reform against those who seek mere repression: 'let not the courtier, I say, condemn the carter, by whose toil and tillage of the earth both king and state consisteth' (Moore, 51). This outlook and commitment was continued by his son, also John *Moore (1594/5?–1657), who became rector of Knaptoft in 1638.

STEPHEN WRIGHT

Sources Foster, *Alum. Oxon.* · C. W. Foster, ed., *The state of the church in the reigns of Elizabeth and James I*, Lincoln RS, 23 (1926) · J. Moore, *A target for tillage* (1612) · M. Beresford, 'Glebe terriers and open field Leicestershire', *Transactions of the Leicestershire Archaeological Society*, 24 (1948), 77–126 · Wood, *Ath. Oxon.*, new edn, 2.163–4

Moore, John (1594/5?–1657), Church of England clergyman and author, was the son of John *Moore (d. 1619), rector of Knaptoft, Leicestershire. A clergyman's son of that name and county matriculated at Exeter College, Oxford, on 9 May 1617 aged twenty-two. Moore became rector of Knaptoft on the death of his father in 1619 and just after his marriage to Eleanor Kirk of Northamptonshire. They had two sons, John and Thomas, baptized at Knaptoft on 30 January 1619 and 3 June 1621 respectively; Thomas was the father of John *Moore (1646–1714), bishop successively of Norwich and of Ely.

In 1634, during the metropolitical visitation of Archbishop Laud, it was discovered that Knaptoft was 'all enclosed by Sir W. Turpin deceased and the glebe withall and the parsonage house'. At Sheasby, a chapelry of the parish, 'the parson Mr More hireth a house and dwelleth and hath a lease of a ground to stop his mouth, quaere of the glebe' (*Architectural Societies*, 513). Perhaps Moore's involvement in the arrangement was forced upon him. However that may be, it seems that this illegal alienation of church property led to official action against both the rector and the patron, Ralph Turpin, and that lengthy civil proceedings were also initiated in respect of the rectory and glebe. On 5 May 1638, following the lapse of Turpin's right of patronage, and on presentation of Charles I, William Farrowe was instituted as rector of Knaptoft by Archbishop Laud, acting during the vacancy caused by the suspension of Bishop John Williams of Lincoln. On 23 January 1640 Moore appeared before the court of high commission, which suspended the taxation of costs 'till it appear what the promoter will further do at common law', though the following day Moore was granted a 'certificate of having passed his purgation before his ordinary' (PRO, SP 16/434/57).

Moore returned, under unknown circumstances, to the rectory of Knaptoft. It was one John Moore, minister of Knaptoft, who preached two sermons 'in the lecture at Lutterworth', but this cannot have been the John Moore, incumbent of Clavering, Essex, between 1643 and 1662 who was appointed rector of Lutterworth in 1647 and who on 17 September that year complained of having been forcibly prevented from taking its possession. Neither is John Moore of Knaptoft the same man as the author of *A Lost Ordinance Restored* (1654). But John Moore of Knaptoft did publish pamphlets, on the very issue which had worried his father and led him into trouble with the church authorities. In September 1653 he issued a violent attack on enclosure, *The Crying Sin of England*, based on two of his lectures at Lutterworth. Inveighing largely against the oppression of the poor, Moore drew especially on the experience of Leicestershire. He urged Barebone's Parliament to the view that enclosure 'doth unpeople towns and uncorn fields' and was 'arraigned, convicted and condemned by the word of God'; indeed, it corroded humanity itself, for 'the poor is hated even of his own neighbour … but the rich hath many friends'. The elect—God's poor—were sharply to be distinguished from the 'devil's poor', but even these must be cared for 'as our own flesh'; begging was condemned, but the enclosers were condemned more passionately, as the 'makers of beggars': 'I wish I could cry so loud in their ears that I could awake their consciences to repentance' (J. Moore, *The Crying Sin of England*, 1653, 3–4, 7).

Before the year's end Moore's book was criticized, chiefly on the grounds of efficiency, in *Considerations Concerning Common Fields* by Joseph Lee, the rector of Cottesbach, Leicestershire, who himself had been involved in enclosing lands in his village. Further exchanges took place which culminated in the autumn of 1656 in Moore's *A Scripture Word Against Enclosure* (1656) and his opponent's *A Vindication of a Regulated Enclosure*. John Moore died shortly after the controversy, and was buried at Knaptoft on 2 August 1657.

STEPHEN WRIGHT

Sources J. Nichols, *The history and antiquities of the county of Leicester*, 4/1 (1807) · F. Blomefield and C. Parkin, *An essay towards a topographical history of the county of Norfolk*, [2nd edn], 11 vols. (1805–10), vol. 3 · J. H. Green, 'Notes on Mowsley and Knaptoft', BL · Foster, *Alum. Oxon.* · VCH Leicestershire, 5.253–5 · Calamy rev. · *Associated Architectural Societies' Reports and Papers*, 29 (1908), 479–534 · C. Moore, 'Bishop Moore', *Transactions of the Leicestershire Architectural and Archaeological Society*, 6 (1888), 134–49 · J. Ainsworth and others, eds., *Index to administrations in the prerogative court of Canterbury*, 2, ed. C. H. Ridge, Index Library, British RS, 74–5 (1952)

Likenesses J. Drapentier, line engraving (after unknown artist), NPG

Wealth at death £268: administration, 1657, Ridge, ed., *Index to administrations*

Moore, John (c.1599–1650), parliamentarian army officer and regicide, was the eldest son of Edward Moore (c.1577–1632), merchant of Bank Hall, Walton, Lancashire, and his wife, Katherine (d. 1641), daughter of John and Margaret Hockenhull of Prenton on the Wirral, Cheshire. The Moores were a well-established family in Liverpool, wielding both commercial and political influence; they also possessed extensive landholdings in south-west Lancashire. In 1630 John Moore was bailiff of Liverpool. In 1633 he became mayor, was appointed a justice of the peace for Lancashire, and married Mary, daughter of the future royalist Alexander Rigby of Burgh and Layton, Lancashire. Moore led the opposition in Liverpool to the first levy of ship money in 1634. He was admitted to Lincoln's Inn in 1638.

Elected to the Long Parliament in 1640 as MP for Liverpool, Moore had lucrative commercial interests which were reflected in service on parliamentary committees concerning trade, monopolies, and navigation. His extensive but indecipherable parliamentary diaries date from this period. Moore indicated strong support for parliament in 1642 and on 24 March he was named deputy lieutenant for Lancashire.

Moore's contribution to parliament's war effort was divided between Lancashire and London. He was in Lancashire in April 1642 to help organize resistance to Lord Strange (the future earl of Derby), but from August 1642 to December 1645 Moore spent just over half his time in Lancashire, the rest in the capital. Moore missed the early fighting in Lancashire because he was made colonel and captain of the guard of horse and foot in Westminster, a position he held from 6 August 1642 to 25 July 1643. Effectively in charge of security in the City, Moore was instrumental in searching and seizing deserters and potential subversives. Moore returned north in August 1643 as colonel of a foot regiment, captain of a horse troop, and governor of Liverpool. His importance was confirmed by his appointment as vice-admiral for Lancashire and Westmorland in November 1643.

Despite a stubborn defence Moore was unable to prevent the fall of Liverpool to Prince Rupert on 11 June 1644; he himself escaped by boat to the north Lancashire coast. Attempts were made within Lancashire to remove Moore from the governorship of Liverpool. These reflected tensions among the county's parliamentarians. Moore gained the support of Sir John Meldrum, chief commander in Lancashire from the summer of 1644. Nevertheless, despite Liverpool's recapture on 1 November 1644, an inquiry held on 5 March 1645 into the port's surrender revealed that Moore's conduct was still in question. Under the terms of the self-denying ordinance Moore relinquished all his military posts by 24 July 1645 and was replaced as Liverpool governor by Major John Ashurst, younger brother of the prominent Lancashire MP William Ashurst, on 16 May 1645.

Back in parliament in the summer of 1645 Moore threw himself into committee work. Between June and October Moore sat on several committees which investigated the disposing of prisoners after the battle of Naseby, affairs in Ireland and Munster, the organization of presbyterianism in Ireland, the reduction of Chester, abuses in the sequestration system, the relief of Leicester, and the continuation of the business of the admiralty and Cinque Ports. He returned to Lancashire in October 1645 and helped secure parliament's triumph there.

Following the king's defeat in May 1646 Moore recruited a new regiment and arrived in Ireland the following autumn. His wife's family had substantial interests in Ireland as earls of Meath. By the start of 1647 Moore was styled governor of both co. Louth and Dundalk and a commissioner for Ireland. The colonel returned to England in January 1648 with his military reputation enhanced.

As a political radical and a consistent 'war party' man Moore was both a supporter and beneficiary of Pride's Purge (6 December 1648) for afterwards he sat on some highly important committees such as those of the army, for advance of money and for settling courts of justice. He seems to have resumed his former security role in Westminster and was named a commissioner to the high court of justice to try Charles I. He attended most of the court's sittings and signed the death warrant [*see also* Regicides]. Thereafter he was added to committees for delinquents, excise, and sequestration.

Early in 1649 Lancashire Independents suggested the reappointment of Moore as governor of Liverpool in order to counteract strong presbyterian influence. However, Moore left for Ireland in June 1649 and another Lancashire radical, Colonel Thomas Birch, took the post in September. A trip to England saw Moore become a member of the committee of the army. Back in Ireland Moore was both a parliamentary commissioner and colonel. He became governor of Dublin and fought at the parliamentarian victory at Rathmines on 2 August 1649. After a brief interlude at Liverpool in December 1649 Moore returned to Ireland and in May 1650 besieged Tecroghan Castle, co. Meath. The castle surrendered on 16 June, about which time Moore had died either of pleurisy or of fever. He left three sons and a daughter.

Moore died with debts of £10,000. In the summer of 1649 he was still owed 53% of his pay reckoned from August 1642 onwards. Parliament had lost a determined, energetic, and wholly committed supporter.

MALCOLM GRATTON

Sources J. M. Gratton, 'The parliamentarian and royalist war effort in Lancashire, 1642–1651', PhD diss., University of Manchester, 1998 · Lpool RO, Moore deeds and papers, 920 MOO · G. Chandler and E. Wilson, *Liverpool under Charles I* (1965) · *The manuscripts of the earl of Westmorland*, HMC, 13 (1885); repr. (1906) [Capt. Stewart] · J. Brownbill, *A calendar of … deeds and papers of the Moore family*, Lancashire and Cheshire RS, 67 (1913) · R. Stewart-Brown, 'Moore of Bankhall', *Transactions of the Historic Society of Lancashire and Cheshire*, 63 (1911) · *The letter books of Sir William Brereton*, ed. R. N. Dore, 1, Lancashire and Cheshire RS, 123 (1984) · *The letter books of Sir William Brereton*, ed. R. N. Dore, 2, Lancashire and Cheshire RS, 128 (1990) · Greaves & Zaller, *BDBR*, vol. 2 · Keeler, *Long Parliament* · T. Heywood, ed., *The Moore rental*, Chetham Society, 12 (1847)

Archives Birkenhead Central Library, corresp. and papers · BL, parliamentary journals, Harley MSS 541, 476–479 · Lpool RO, deeds and papers, 920 MOO · U. Lpool, family corresp. and papers

Wealth at death debts of £10,000: Heywood, ed., 'The Moore rental'

Moore, Sir John (*bap.* 1620, *d.* 1702), merchant and local politician, the second son of Charles Moore (*d.* 1654) and his wife, Cicely Yates, was baptized at Norton, near Twycross, Leicestershire, on 11 June 1620. His father, who had

Sir John Moore (*bap.* 1620, *d.* 1702), by James Macardell (after John Closterman)

six children, was descended from the Moores of Lancashire, but came from Stretton, Derbyshire, and also owned land in Applebee Parva, Leicestershire.

Moore migrated to London, where he established himself in Mincing Lane and by 1649 was a member of the Grocers' Company. Around 1652 he married Mary Maddox (*d.* 1690). He was involved in both the domestic and foreign trades and in lending. Scattered correspondence to him from his country and foreign agents, with bills, invoices, and balance statements, has survived from the period 1666–87, but not the bulk of his outgoing correspondence or his principal ledgers. His primary business was the lead trade and his connections stretched to Derbyshire, Yorkshire, and Cornwall. He exported to Amsterdam and Rotterdam through Kingston upon Hull and petitioned against certain provisions in a new charter for Hull. His associates included Robert Richbell of Southampton, James Johnson of Great Yarmouth, Thomas Bludworth, a Levant merchant, and the banker Thomas Vyner. He owned shares in ships and had assets in the Mediterranean trade when, on 22 February 1677, he was warned that war with France was imminent. That same year he commanded a premium of £500 from an apprentice.

By 1689 Moore was the second largest holder of East India Company stock (£25,509), often purchased in small amounts, and he engaged in the private trade in diamonds and coral and supplied lead and ships to the company. Between 1669 and 1701 he served on all the committees of the company in rotation, and on 3 October 1693 put up a bond of £10,000 to guarantee an undertaking by the company that £100,000 in goods would be exported. He was also a shareholder of the New River Company and an assistant of the Royal African Company (1687–9; 1700–02). Although he lent £5000 to the new regime on 11 February 1689, this was undoubtedly political insurance, and his later loans, such as £1000 in 1692/3, were modest.

Moore, as a nonconformist, was initially unwilling to take the sacramental test. On 25 September 1666 he was elected alderman for Farringdon Without, but on 30 April 1667 was discharged with a fine of £520. He was, however, a common councilman (1667–71), and he served on numerous committees of the City. In 1671 Sir John Lawrence, the leader of the dissenters in the City, and Sir William Turner nominated him for Walbrook ward. Moore conformed and served as alderman (26 September 1671 – 9 August 1687; 3 October 1688–1702). In 1693, as senior alderman, he became father of the City. Having been elected for London to the parliament of 1685, he sat on five committees and supported a bill to levy an imposition on coals to rescue the Orphans' Court from bankruptcy.

Moore was master of the Grocers' Company in 1671–2, and in 1672, when Sir Jonathan Dawes died in office while sheriff, Moore was elected in his place; he was knighted by Charles II on 13 May 1672. In 1675 he accepted the post of gentleman of the privy chamber, which he held until 1685. Having been a captain of the militia of London since October 1660, he was commissioned as colonel of the Yellow regiment on 30 May 1681, which rank he held until 1687. He was a commissioner for assessment (1666–80), served as deputy lieutenant of London (1681–7; October 1688–1689; 1690–1702), and was acting president of Christ's Hospital (1684–6) and then president (1686–1702).

Moore's City career was bedevilled by the vicious factional struggles in London which followed the crisis over the succession to Charles II. In 1681 he was next in seniority for the mayoralty, but, since he was regarded as friendly to the court, the whigs attempted to prevent his election. The king and Secretary Jenkins intervened on his behalf by leaning on the tradesmen who catered to the court, and Burnet claimed that the preachers delivered dissenting votes for Moore, who topped the poll by 300 votes in a rowdy election. Ballads celebrated the victory, as did King Charles by attending the inauguration festivities, and the Grocers' Company mounted a lavish pageant designed by Thomas Jordan.

The court now expected Moore to secure the election of a tory sheriff in 1682. By ancient custom the lord mayor could nominate one of the sheriffs, but this right was contested and had been exercised irregularly and usually to raise revenue from fines. Moore drank to Dudley North at the bridgemasters' feast on 18 May 1682 and Ralph Box was put up as the second candidate. The whigs, determined to retain jury selection in their hands, put up two of their own candidates, Thomas Papillon and Dubois, for election by the whole livery. Although Moore declared North and Box duly elected at the common hall which he summoned on 19 June 1682, the whig sheriffs then in office insisted on taking a poll. Moore responded by successive adjournments, and the tumult was such on 24 June 1682 that he had his hat knocked off in the crowd. When the whig sheriffs declared Papillon and Dubois elected by a majority on 5 July, Moore conferred with the privy council. Secretary Jenkins instructed him to dissolve both common hall and the court of aldermen if necessary. Moore ordered another poll, and after more adjournments the court party eventually gained the day. North was declared sheriff on 14 July and Box on 15 July. Moore rejected petitions from the whigs, and after Box was allowed to fine off on 5 September Rich was declared sheriff in his place on 19 September. When Moore could not silence the clamour he closed the Guildhall, and Rich and North were sworn in on 28 September. On 16 January 1683 common council passed a vote of thanks for Moore's handling of the crisis, but the struggle continued, and on 28 April 1683 Moore was arrested on the suit of Papillon and Dubois.

A huge and partisan pamphlet literature discussed the constitutional niceties of Moore's actions. According to Roger North, Moore was a grave man of very few words, cautious but loyal. Moore himself told Secretary Jenkins that some accused him of lacking courage and others of being drunk with passion and revenge. He skilfully used his power of adjournment to outmanoeuvre the opposition. There is little doubt that he followed directions from the court, though it is possible that he chose North hoping that he would fine off. He was on the committee of common council which drew up a loyal address after the Rye House plot, and in recognition of his services King Charles, on 25 August 1683, authorized his family to augment their arms with the royal lion.

Burnet later wrote that Moore abandoned his nonconformity when he grew rich and politically ambitious. But Moore continued to dress plainly and to sympathize with the dissenters. He was always a moderate. He voted against surrender of the City's charter and he consistently opposed Catholicism. As steward of the Artillery Company in October 1673 he had sought to avoid entertaining James, and after being closeted in 1687 he was temporarily removed from his aldermancy for opposing the declaration of indulgence.

James II granted Moore a general pardon on 22 October 1688, but after the revolution Moore had to defend his actions before a committee of the Commons. In March 1689 he was voted a betrayer of the City's liberties, and the tories put him up for the mayoralty in protest. Pilkington and Bethel failed to have him punished, but Pilkington was elected mayor by a majority of two to one.

Moore's wife died on 16 May 1690, and a sumptuous marble monument was raised over her remains in St Dunstan-in-the-East. In his old age, when he suffered much from gout, many of his business affairs were handled by his nephew John, a cheesemonger, who lived at Mincing Lane. The French war hit him hard, and he had a cash-flow problem when he endowed his charities. On 24 December 1695 he told his nephew Thomas that he had lost heavily in the Guinea trade and £15,000 in the East Indies. He gave £500 to Bridewell and Bethlem hospitals, and in 1695 built for £10,000 the writing and mathematical school at Christ's Hospital. In 1697 he founded a free grammar school at Applebee, initially for local boys but extended, under the statutes of 1706, to all England. Both buildings were designed by Christopher Wren. The correspondence between Moore and his nephews Thomas and George contained detailed instructions and advice on how the construction of Applebee should proceed and included accounts for labour and materials and negotiations with prospective schoolmasters. Moore took a personal interest in every detail, from the choice of site to the weathercock, mouldings, and boarding facilities. He insisted that there be no vainglory and that costs be firmly contained. He set aside the revenue from land at Upton to pay the salaries of three masters, who were allocated gardens but not allowed to keep hens, cows, or swine.

In 1682 Moore defrayed nearly the entire cost (£500) of rebuilding Grocers' Hall, and in acknowledgement his portrait was painted and hung in the hall. Other portraits and statues with memorial inscriptions were set up at Christ's Hospital and Applebee.

Moore died in London on 2 June 1702 and was buried in the church of St Dunstan-in-the-East. His fortune at the time of his death was probably between £80,000 and £100,000, and included the manor of Shalford. Since he had no surviving children, his estate passed to two nephews, both named John, one the son of his brother Charles and the other of his brother George, who was also appointed Moore's executor and residuary legatee.

RICHARD GRASSBY

Sources R. North, *Examen, or, An enquiry into the credit and veracity of a pretended complete history* (1740) · E. Cruickshanks, 'Moore, Sir John (1620–1702)', HoP, *Commons* · J. B. Heath, *The Grocers' Company of London*, 3rd edn (1869) · J. R. Woodhead, *The rulers of London, 1660–1689* (1965) · A. B. Beaven, ed., *The aldermen of the City of London, temp. Henry III–[1912]*, 2 vols. (1908–13) · N. Luttrell, *A brief historical relation of state affairs from September 1678 to April 1714*, 6 vols. (1857) · *Memoirs of Thomas Papillon, of London, merchant*, ed. A. F. W. Papillon (1887) · *Le Neve's Pedigrees of the knights*, ed. G. W. Marshall, Harleian Society, 8 (1873) · R. R. Sharpe, *London and the kingdom*, 3 vols. (1894–5) · W. B. Bannerman and W. B. Bannerman, jun., eds., *The registers of St Stephen's, Walbrook, and of St Benet Sherehog, London*, 1, Harleian Society, register section, 49 (1919) · *The manuscripts of the House of Lords*, 4 vols., HMC, 17 (1887–94) · S. Lee, ed., *A collection of the names of the merchants living in and about the City of London* (1677) · CSP dom. · E. B. Sainsbury, ed., *A calendar of the court minutes … of the East India Company*, [11]: 1677–1679 (1938) · *Memoirs of Sir John Reresby*, ed. A. Browning, 2nd edn, ed. M. K. Geiter and W. A. Speck (1991) · W. A. Shaw, ed., *Calendar of treasury books*, [33 vols. in 64], PRO (1904–69) · *Bishop Burnet's History* · P. Morant, *The history and antiquities of the county of Essex*, 2 vols. (1768) · G. S. De Krey, *A fractured society: the politics of London in the first age of party, 1688–1715* (1985) · J. Nichols, *The history and antiquities of the county of Leicester*, 4 vols. (1795–1815) · K. G. Davies, *The Royal Africa Company* (1957) · [E. Hatton], *A new view of London*, 2 vols. (1708) · will, PRO, PROB 11/465, sig. 101

Archives BL, Add. MSS 22185, 28930 · GL, family and business papers · GL, personal estate and business papers · Leics. RO, personal and family corresp. and papers, mainly relating to Appleby School · U. Lpool, letters · U. Lpool L., family corresp. and papers | BL, Add. MS 19819

Likenesses J. Linton?, oils, 1694–5, Christ's Hospital, Horsham, Sussex · G. Gibbons, statue, 1695, Christ's Hospital, Horsham, Sussex · W. Wilson, statue, 1701, Appleby grammar school, Leicestershire · Clamp, engraving (after Harding) · Harding, portrait ·

J. Macardell, mezzotint (after J. Closterman), BM, NPG [*see illus.*] • portrait, Grocers' Hall

Wealth at death approx. £80,000–£100,000: will, PRO, PROB 11/465, sig. 101

Moore, John (*b.* in or before **1621**), Church of England clergyman, is an obscure figure. Nothing is known of his parentage or education, and indeed all that is known of him is derived from his only known work, *The Banner of Corah, Dathan, and Abiram, Display'd, and their Sin Discover'd* (1696). This contains a head and shoulders likeness of the author at the age of seventy-five, which records that he was born in the city of Worcester. The book consists of sermons published during his years as curate of Brislington, Gloucestershire, a suburb of Bristol, and may perhaps have been published posthumously. Moore was a conservative in politics and religion. He warned against factions and schisms, the dangers of which led to 'unspeakable miseries' during the 'reign of that pious prince, King Charles I', and says that 'our Common Prayer book is the surest visible bulwark to keep out Popery' (Moore, 118, 120). Nothing else is known of him.   STEPHEN WRIGHT

Sources J. Moore, *The banner of Corah, Dathan, and Abiram, display'd, and their sin discover'd* (1696)

Likenesses engraving, repro. in Moore, *The banner of Corah*

Moore, John (*fl.* **1669**), Church of England clergyman and author, is of unknown parentage and origins. He may perhaps have come from Cornwall or Devon, since he dedicated his one book, *Moses Revived … wherein the Unlawfulness of Eating Blood is Clearly Proved* (1669), to 'the worshipfull, my ever honoured brother, Hugh Jones, esq, one of his majesty's justices of the peace for the County of Cornwall' and to his 'beloved brother Mr John Jones, a citizen and merchant of the once famous city of London'. There follows a verse to 'my ever honoured, prudent and virtuous sister, Mrs Dorothy Jones'. Hugh Jones has been identified as Hugh Jones alias Valence of Sennen, near Land's End, who married Alice Gould of Lewtrenchard, near Exeter, and died at Sennen in 1715.

Of Moore's own life hardly anything is known. He might perhaps be the John Moore, son of John Moore of Helston, Cornwall, who matriculated from Exeter College, Oxford, on 24 May 1664, aged sixteen—but he gives the impression of being older than that, if only because he seems to have married Jones's sister by 1669. His book is signed as curate of West Cowes in the Isle of Wight, published so that 'I might leave testimony behind me, (If God either by death or any other dispensation of providence should call me from you) that in the work of my ministry my chief aim was God's glory' (Moore, sig. F4). The chief purpose of the book is to urge abstention from the eating of blood. To it is appended 'An hundred and seventy six sacred observations, upon the several verses of … the 119th psalm', dedicated 'to the People of west Cowes, in the Isle of Wight, being the exercise of my Publicke Ministry, in their new chappel'. This building, erected in 1657, was consecrated by the bishop of Winchester, George Morley, in 1662. A previous curate of West Cowes, Simon Pole, was indicted for nonconformity at the winter assizes of 1663 for Somerset and imprisoned. Perhaps Moore arrived soon afterwards as his successor. Nothing else is known of his activities, nor anything of his death.   STEPHEN WRIGHT

Sources J. Moore, *Moses revived … wherein the unlawfulness of eating blood is clearly proved* (1669) • Boase & Courtney, *Bibl. Corn.*, vol. 3 • J. L. Vivian, ed., *The visitations of Cornwall, comprising the herald's visitations of 1530, 1573, and 1620* (1887) • J. L. Vivian, ed., *The visitations of the county of Devon, comprising the herald's visitations of 1531, 1564, and 1620* (privately printed, Exeter, [1895]) • R. Worsley, *The history of the Isle of Wight* (1781) • *VCH Hampshire and the Isle of Wight*, vol. 5 • *Calamy rev.* • Foster, *Alum. Oxon.*

Moore, John (*bap.* **1643**, *d.* **1717**), Presbyterian minister and nonconformist tutor, the son of John Moore of Musbury, Devon, was baptized there on 5 August 1643. He was educated at the grammar school at Colyton, Devon. From there he went to Brasenose College, Oxford, where he was admitted plebeian on 9 June and matriculated on 13 July 1660, but did not apparently graduate. He was ordained in the Church of England and in 1662 became vicar of Long Burton, Dorset, and curate at Holnest chapelry in that parish. Moore remained in these livings until 1667, when he resigned: under the influence of Thomas Crane, the former incumbent of Rampisham, Dorset, and other local ejected ministers he had become a nonconformist. While at Long Burton, Moore married; his eldest daughter, Margaret, was baptized there on 2 August 1667.

On leaving Long Burton, Moore retired to his small estate at Ottery St Mary, Devon, where on 18 April 1672 he was licensed as a Presbyterian minister under the declaration of indulgence. After its withdrawal he continued to preach to the people of the neighbourhood, often at great risk to himself. While at Ottery his wife gave birth to several more children but it would appear that only his two sons, John Moore [*see below*] and Thomas Moore (1675?–1720) survived him, and a daughter, Anastace. In 1676 Moore became assistant to John Gardner, pastor to the presbyterian meeting at Bridgwater, and in 1679 he succeeded him. Moore laboured there as minister for thirty-six years, years which saw the town's welcome to the forces of the duke of Monmouth in 1685 and the building of a meeting-house for Moore's congregation three years later. Bridgwater's dissenting population, according to Edmund Calamy, came to include 'the whole magistracy of the town till the latter end of Queen Anne's reign' (Palmer, 2.132), an increase in numbers and social respectability which he ascribed to Moore's ministry though it probably reflects as much the existing strength of presbyterianism in the town. Together with John Weekes and Alexander Sinclair of Bristol, Moore was instrumental in establishing a union of Somerset dissenting ministers which was later extended to Devon, a move parallel with and if anything a little in advance of the Happy Union in London. Moore diligently attended the union assemblies in Somerset and sometimes, even in old age, travelled to those held in Exeter.

In 1688 Moore opened an academy in Bridgwater for the training of nonconformist ministers. It was open to both Independents and Presbyterians and between 1703 and

1720 four students received grants from the Presbyterian Fund. Under Moore the academy enjoyed a reputation as one of the best in the country, and its students included such distinguished figures as the nonconformist controversialist Samuel Chandler and Joseph Jeffries, editor of *The Library*. Students underwent a four-year course of instruction in divinity, Latin, Greek, Hebrew, and natural philosophy and went on to complete their studies at the Scottish universities. From 1698 Moore was assisted at the academy by his son John. Even after the passing of the Toleration Act in 1689 dissenting academies and their tutors were not entirely free from persecution. On one occasion during the reign of William III, Moore was arrested and fined £30 for keeping an academy, while in 1714 upon the passing of the Schism Act the academy was, like several others, suspended for a short time. During the latter years of his life Moore was in almost constant pain from a gallstone. He died at Bridgwater on 23 August 1717. His funeral sermon was preached by Edmund Batson of Taunton.

His son **John Moore** (1673–1747), Presbyterian minister and nonconformist tutor, who had graduated MA from Edinburgh University in 1693, succeeded Moore both as pastor of the congregation and head of the academy. The younger Moore did not achieve the same measure of success as his father. He adopted Arian views which led to a fall in the number of students and to the secession of some of the orthodox members of the congregation. Nevertheless he was a competent and respected tutor and minister, and the nineteenth-century historian of nonconformity in the west country, Jerom Murch, claimed that Moore's students 'enjoyed great advantages from his attainments in science and his methods of conveying knowledge' (Murch, 178). Moore published one work, *Propositions of Natural and Revealed Religion* (1736). He died at Bridgwater in 1747 and was succeeded in his dual roles of pastor and tutor by Matthew Towgood, son of Michaijah.

M. J. MERCER

Sources *Calamy rev.*, 353 • A. Gordon, ed., *Freedom after ejection: a review (1690–1692) of presbyterian and congregational nonconformity in England and Wales* (1917), 313–14 • J. Murch, *A history of the Presbyterian and General Baptist churches in the west of England* (1835), 177–9 • Surman, index of nonconformist ministers, DWL • H. McLachlan, 'Bridgwater Academy, 1688–1756?', *Transactions of the Unitarian Historical Society*, 3 (1945), 93–6 • *The nonconformist's memorial … originally written by … Edmund Calamy*, ed. S. Palmer, [3rd edn], 2 (1802), 130–32 • Foster, *Alum. Oxon.* • J. Hutchins, *The history and antiquities of the county of Dorset* (1861–74), vol. 4, pp. 139–40 • [C. B. Heberden], ed., *Brasenose College register, 1509–1909*, 2 vols., OHS, 55 (1909), 206 • will, PRO, PROB 11/560, sig. 175

Archives BL, letter to R. Ellis, Add. MS 28884, fol. 179

Wealth at death see will, PRO, PROB 11/560, sig. 175

Moore, John (1646–1714), bishop of Ely, was born at Sutton-juxta-Broughton, Leicestershire, the eldest son of Thomas Moore (1621–1686) and his wife, Elizabeth, daughter of Edward Wright of Sutton-juxta-Broughton. His father, an ironmonger at Market Harborough, was the son of John *Moore (1594/5?–1657). Moore was educated at the free school in Market Harborough and at Clare College, Cambridge, where he was admitted as 'sizer and pupil to Mr. Mowsse' (*DNB*) on 28 June 1662. He graduated BA in

John Moore (1646–1714), by Sir Godfrey Kneller, 1705

1665–6 and proceeded MA in 1669 and DD in 1681. On 17 September 1667 Moore was elected fellow of Clare. In 1670 he became chaplain to Heneage Finch, subsequently lord chancellor and first earl of Nottingham. He was ordained priest by Benjamin Laney, bishop of Ely, on 24 September 1671. This and his subsequent elevation to the episcopate were, according to Robert Martin of Stamford, displeasing to Moore's father, who was of a 'Rigid perswasion', opposed to the episcopal settlement following the restoration of Charles II, and who 'tho' he gave his Son the university Education, yet he never intended him for the Episcopate order', and obliged Moore to repay the cost of his education (Robert Martin to John Strype, 5 March [1695], CUL, Add. MS 2, no. 148). In 1673 he was incorporated MA at Oxford. In 1676 Moore was presented to the rectory of Blaby, Leicestershire (a royal advowson), which he held until 1687. Through Finch's interest he was nominated a canon of Ely in September 1677, but Bishop Peter Gunning claimed the preferment, and Moore was not installed until 28 June 1679. On 22 May that year he had married Rose (d. 1689), fifth daughter of Nevill Thomas Butler of Barnwell Priory, Cambridgeshire, and Mary, daughter of Sir Gilbert Dethick. She died on 18 August 1689, and was buried in the chancel of St Giles-in-the-Fields, London. They had three sons and three daughters, the eldest of whom, Rose (d. 1707), married Thomas *Tanner (1674–1735).

Moore's services as a popular preacher were often employed in the London pulpits, and when the new church of St Anne's, Soho, was consecrated in 1686 he officiated as its minister. He was drawn permanently to London by his appointment as rector of St Augustine by St

Paul on 31 December 1687, and on 26 October 1689 migrated to the rectory of St Andrew's, Holborn, which he held with his canonry at Ely until 1691. As chaplain to William III and Mary II from 1689, he often preached before them. Among the sermons which he preached before William and Mary, one, on 14 July 1689, was interpreted as charging protestant dissenters with schism and elicited a reply, *The Charity and Loyalty of some of our Clergy, in a Short View of Dr. M's Sermon*, published that year.

When the see of Norwich became vacant by the deprivation of the nonjuror William Lloyd (1636/7–1710), Moore was appointed to the bishopric. He was consecrated at St Mary-le-Bow, London, on 5 July 1691. About this time he married as his second wife Dorothy, daughter of William Barnes of Darlington, and widow firstly of Michael Blackett of Morton Palms, co. Durham, and second of Sir Richard Browne. They had three sons. He continued to preach before the king and queen: a sermon on religious melancholy preached before the queen on 6 March 1692 was published, and reached a seventh edition in 1708. Many of his sermons were warnings against Catholicism, and a collection, translated into Dutch by W. van Schie, was published in Delft in 1700. In 1704 he edited *A Form of Prayer used by ... King William III when he Received the Holy Sacrament*, which was an instant success, and Dutch and French editions quickly followed. Although 'he wrote nothing himself beyond the call of duty' (McKitterick, 88), he was alleged to have written the preface to *An Introduction to a Breviary of the History of England* by Sir Walter Ralegh, published in 1693, and prepared it for the press. During his period as bishop of Norwich he acquired most of the books and manuscripts for his extensive library: 'he was relieved of much of the necessity of dealing in person with payments to booksellers, and on many occasions the task, with sundry other mundane ones, fell to his chaplains' (ibid., 58). Among the latter were Samuel Clarke and Thomas Tanner, who both made extensive use of Moore's library and did much to organize and catalogue it. John Bagford was the chief assistant in its formation, and in return Moore obtained for him a place in the Charterhouse. Another chaplain was William Whiston, who later observed that Moore 'was ever ambitious of being, and of being esteemed a Patron of Learning, and learned men' (*Historical Memoirs of the Life of Dr Samuel Clarke*, 1730, 7). Moore's books and manuscripts were consulted by prominent scholars in England, such as Richard Bentley, Gilbert Burnet, John Strype, George Hickes, and Thomas Hearne, and he answered queries from overseas scholars. He was alleged by some antiquaries, such as William Cole and Richard Gough, to have built up his collection by taking books from the clergy of his diocese, but this was a frequent allegation made against book-collecting bishops of the period. An early account of the library appeared in Edward Bernard's *Catalogi librorum manuscriptorum Angliae et Hiberniae in unum collecti* (1697); a copy at Cambridge University includes annotations giving details of the collection's development until 1714.

Moore was a low-churchman, and many of his chaplains went on to express anti-trinitarian views outside conventional Church of England theology. None the less, on 31 July 1707 Queen Anne translated Moore to the diocese of Ely. This promotion to a wealthier diocese was at odds with Anne's preference for high-church clergy, but was part of a wider struggle over preferment with the lord treasurer, Sidney Godolphin, first earl of Godolphin, whose nominees Anne was by this stage ignoring. In 1708 Moore made his first visitation of Cambridge as bishop of Ely; the address presented to him by his college refers to his munificent gifts to Clare Library, and to the help which he had given in the rebuilding of the college. Immediately after his confirmation he began to rebuild and repair the episcopal house in Ely Place, Holborn. He brought his collection of books and manuscripts together there, and arranged them, as Ralph Thoresby observed in 1712, in 'eight chambers (as I remember) that almost surround the quadrangle' (*Diary*, 2.116); he was never happier than when he could show a visitor to London the treasures of his library. When it was proposed in 1709 that his friend Richard Bentley should be appointed bishop of Chichester, Moore's support was enlisted on Bentley's behalf. In May and June 1714, as visitor of Trinity College, Cambridge, he presided at the trial of Bentley, then master of Trinity, for encroaching on the privileges of the college fellows. During the long sittings at Ely House, London, which the trial demanded, he caught cold, and died (presumably at Ely House) on 31 July 1714, before he could pass judgment on Bentley. A draft sentence of deprivation was found among his papers. He was buried in Ely Cathedral on 5 August in the north choir aisle, near the vault of his immediate predecessor as bishop of Ely, Simon Patrick. A monument, with a Latin epitaph ascribed to Samuel Knight, was erected near by, but was moved to the south choir aisle c.1850. Twelve of his printed sermons were collected after his death by Samuel Clarke, and published in one volume as *Sermons on Several Subjects* in 1715. A second issue in two volumes appeared under the same editorship in 1724, the first volume being a reprint of the previous set, and the second consisting of sixteen discourses, none of which had been printed before. About 1740 a pamphlet was published commending Moore's views on justification by faith alone to the followers of George Whitefield.

At Moore's death his library was 'universally and most justly reputed the best furnish'd of any (within the Queen's Dominions) that this Age has seen in the Hands of any private Clergyman' (W. Nicholson, *The English Historical Library*, 2nd edn, 1714, xii). He had accumulated nearly 29,000 books and 1790 manuscripts. The library was offered to Robert Harley, earl of Oxford, in 1714 for £8000. Following Oxford's refusal it was eventually sold for £6450 to King George I, who gave it to the University of Cambridge in 1715, on the instigation of his secretary of state, Charles, second Viscount Townshend. The donation, which immediately became known as the Royal Library, brought the university library into international prominence, such was the richness of Moore's collection in manuscripts and early printed works.

PETER MEADOWS

Sources DNB · D. McKitterick, *Cambridge University Library, a history: the eighteenth and nineteenth centuries* (1986), 47–152 · C. Moore, *"The father of black-letter collectors": memoir of the Rt. Rev. John Moore …* (1885) [reprinted from *The Bibliographer*] · J. Ingamells, *The English episcopal portrait, 1559–1835: a catalogue* (privately printed, London, 1981) · E. F. Carpenter, *Thomas Tenison, archbishop of Canterbury* (1948), 179–83 · J. R. Wardale, ed., *Clare College: letters and documents* (1903), 143–7 · D. R. Hirschberg, 'Episcopal incomes and expenses', *Princes and paupers in the English church, 1500–1800*, ed. R. O'Day and F. Heal (1981), 211–30 · A. F. Johnson, 'John Bagford, antiquary, 1650–1716', in A. F. Johnson, *Selected essays on books and printing*, ed. P. H. Muir (Amsterdam, 1970), 378–80 · J. Ringrose, 'The Royal Library: John Moore and his books', *Cambridge University Library: the great collections*, ed. P. Fox (1998), 78–89 · Venn, *Alum. Cant.* · *The diary of Ralph Thoresby, 1677–1724*, ed. J. Hunter, 2 vols. (1830), 1.334–5, 342; 2.116, 220 · E. Gregg, *Queen Anne* (1980)

Archives Bodl. Oxf., corresp. · Cambs. AS, Cambridge, letterbook · CUL, Ely diocesan records, personal account books, EDR D5/19–20 · CUL, diaries, Adv. e.38.7–16

Likenesses portrait, *c.*1700–1705, LPL · G. Kneller, oils, 1705, Clare College, Cambridge [*see illus.*] · J. Kersseboom?, portrait, *c.*1705–1710, Clare College, Cambridge · W. Faithorne, mezzotint (after G. Kneller), BM, NPG · T. Hodgetts, engraving (after R. White), repro. in J. Ames, *Typographical antiquities*, ed. T. Dibdin (1810–19), vol. 2 · R. White, engraving (after his portrait) · I. Whood, portrait (after G. Kneller), CUL · portrait (after G. Kneller), bishop's house, Ely

Moore, John (1673–1747). *See under* Moore, John (*bap.* 1643, *d.* 1717).

Moore, Sir John, baronet (1718–1779), naval officer, was born on 24 March 1718. He was the grandson of Henry, third earl of Drogheda, and the third son of Henry Moore, rector of Malpas in Cheshire, and Catherine, daughter of Sir Thomas Knatchbull, baronet, and widow of Sir George Rooke. Moore received his early education at Whitchurch grammar school in Shropshire, and in 1729, when aged eleven, he was entered on the books of the *Lion*, going to the West Indies with the flag of his kinsman Rear-Admiral Charles Stewart. Before the ship sailed Moore was transferred to the *Rupert*, and afterwards to the *Diamond*, commanded in 1731 by George Anson.

After twelve months in the *Diamond* Moore was for a short time in the *Princess Amelia*, with Captain Edward Reddish, and then for three and a half years in the *Squirrel*, with Anson, on the coast of Carolina. He was afterwards for some months in the *Edinburgh*, carrying Vice-Admiral Stewart's flag in the channel, and then in the *Torrington*, with Captain William Parry. He passed his examination on 6 April 1738, and was promoted lieutenant of the *Lancaster*, one of the fleet off Cadiz or in the Mediterranean, with Rear-Admiral Nicholas Haddock. When Vice-Admiral Thomas Mathews succeeded to the command he moved Moore into the *Namur*, his flagship, but presently he sent him to England in the *Lennox*, to be promoted by his kinsman, the earl of Winchilsea, first lord of the Admiralty. On 24 December 1743 Moore was accordingly posted to the frigate *Diamond*, one of the squadron which sailed for the East Indies in May 1744, with Commodore Curtis Barnett. On leaving Madagascar the *Diamond*, with the *Medway*, under the command of Captain Edward Peyton,

Sir John Moore, baronet (1718–1779), by Ridley, pubd 1804

was detached to the Strait of Malacca, where they captured a rich French ship from Manila, and a large privateer, which had been fitted out from Pondicherry, and was now brought into the British service as the *Medway's Prize*. In March 1745 Moore was moved into the *Deptford*, Barnett's flagship, in which, after Barnett's death, he was sent to England.

In 1747 Moore was appointed to the *Devonshire*, the ship in which Rear-Admiral Edward Hawke hoisted his flag for his autumn cruise in the Bay of Biscay, and in the action with L'Etanduère on 14 October, after which he was sent home with the dispatches. 'I have sent this express', Hawke wrote, 'by Captain Moore of the *Devonshire* … It would be doing great injustice to merit not to say that he signalized himself greatly in the action' (*Hawke Papers*, 55). During the peace Moore commanded the yacht *William and Mary*, and in April 1756 he was again appointed to the *Devonshire*. About this time he married Penelope, daughter of General Matthews; the couple had one son, who died young, and four daughters. In January 1757 Moore was a member of the court martial of Admiral John Byng, and he was afterwards one of those who petitioned to be released from the oath of secrecy. It is said that he was 'on intimate terms with Byng's family' (Keppel, 1.248). He was shortly afterwards moved to the *Cambridge*, and appointed commodore and commander-in-chief on the Leeward Islands station.

In January 1759, with a force of eleven ships of the line, besides frigates and small craft, Moore convoyed the expeditionary army under General Hopson from Barbados to Martinique, reduced Fort Negro, and covered the landing of the troops in Fort Royal Bay. Hopson, however, worn with age and infirmities, seems to have been unequal to the exigencies of his position; and on intelligence from a deserter that the ground in front of the town was mined, he promptly abandoned the undertaking (*GM*, 1st ser., 29, 1759, 286–7). He proposed to attack St Pierre, but on Moore's advice it was resolved rather to attempt the reduction of Guadeloupe. On 22 January the fleet was off Basseterre. During the early morning of 23 January the ships took up their assigned positions, and at seven o'clock opened fire on the sea defences. Moore hoisted his broad pennant in the frigate *Woolwich*, the better to see what was going on, and to consult Hopson, who was also in the *Woolwich*.

For several hours the fire was extremely heavy on both sides, but before night the batteries were silenced, and the town, with its warehouses of rum and sugar, was in flames. The next day the troops were landed, and occupied the ruins. The French maintained their ground in the hill country, where they were secretly supplied with provisions by the Dutch. On 11 March, on intelligence that a strong French fleet had arrived at Martinique, Moore took up his post in Prince Rupert's Bay in Dominica, the better to flank any attempt that might be made to relieve Guadeloupe, and also for the health of his men, who were falling sick. On 1 May Guadeloupe capitulated, and with it the small islands adjacent, the Saints and Deseada. In 1760 Moore returned to England.

On 21 October 1762 Moore was promoted rear-admiral, and for the rest of the war he was commander-in-chief in the downs. He was afterwards commander-in-chief at Portsmouth for three years. He was created a baronet on 4 March 1766, and was made vice-admiral on 18 October 1770, a KB in 1772, and admiral on 29 January 1778. His health had for some time been failing; gout had troubled him since the 1760s and by 1777 the attacks had become violent. His last public duty was, in December 1778, to sign the protest against holding a court martial on Admiral Augustus Keppel, his signature coming second, immediately below Hawke's. He died on 2 February 1779.

J. K. LAUGHTON, *rev.* RUDDOCK MACKAY

Sources passing certificates, PRO, ADM 107/3, pp. 324, 360 · W. L. Clowes, *The Royal Navy: a history from the earliest times to the present*, 7 vols. (1897–1903); repr. (1996–7), vol. 3 · R. F. Mackay, *Admiral Hawke* (1965) · *The Hawke papers: a selection, 1743–1771*, ed. R. F. Mackay, Navy RS, 129 (1990) · N. A. M. Rodger, *The wooden world: an anatomy of the Georgian navy* (1986) · T. R. Keppel, *The life of Augustus, Viscount Keppel*, 2 vols. (1842) · NMM, SAN F 35, fol. 24

Archives NMM, Sandwich MSS · PRO, Admiralty records

Likenesses Ridley, engraving, pubd 1804, NPG [*see illus.*] · T. Gainsborough, oils

Moore, John (1729–1802), physician and writer, second child and eldest son of Charles Moore (1680?–1736), an early moderate Presbyterian minister, and his wife, Marion, daughter of John Anderson the younger of Dowhill, a member of a prominent merchant family in Glasgow, was born at Stirling on 7 December 1729 and baptized on the same day.

Education and medical practice On her husband's death in 1736 his mother took her family back to Glasgow, where,

John Moore (1729–1802), by Sir Thomas Lawrence, 1790–91

after education at the grammar school, Moore matriculated at the university in 1742. In 1744 he was apprenticed to William Stirling and John Gordon, surgeons in a large practice and formerly masters to Moore's distant cousin Tobias Smollett. Besides attending the medical lectures of William Cullen and others, Moore devoted himself to literature and philosophy, attending the lectures of Francis Hutcheson.

In 1747 Moore was released from his apprenticeship to serve as surgeon's mate in the north British fusiliers. His initial service was at Maastricht, where hospitals were filled with the wounded from the battle of Laffeldt. David Middleton, the director-general of military hospitals, recommended him to George Keppel, third earl of Albemarle, colonel of the Coldstream Guards. Moore became assistant to the surgeon of that regiment, Peter Triquet, attending its sick at Flushing, and went into winter quarters at Breda in 1748 under General Braddock, with whom he returned to England when peace was made in the spring.

In London Moore attended the anatomy lectures of William Hunter and then went to Paris with William Fordyce to study surgery under Sauver-François Morand (1679–1773) at the Hôpital de Charité; he also studied diseases of women and children under Jean Astruc (1684–1766) at the Academy of Medicine. The earl of Albemarle, then British ambassador, appointed Moore surgeon to his household. In the summer of 1749, when Smollett came to Paris, Moore and his cousin visited St Cloud and Versailles together. In the summer of 1750 Gordon, his former master, invited him to become his partner in Glasgow. Moore consented reluctantly because he had been hoping for a commission as surgeon to another regiment. On his way back he attended another course of Hunter's lectures in London and a course in midwifery taught by William Smellie.

Moore practised in Glasgow first with Gordon and then with Thomas Hamilton, who eventually became professor of anatomy. On 17 June 1754 he married Jean Simson (d. 1820), eldest daughter of John *Simson (1667–1740), late professor of divinity at Glasgow, who had twice been prosecuted for heretical teaching. The couple had eleven children, six of whom reached adulthood. Their sons achieved singular success: General Sir John *Moore (1761–1809), of Corunna fame, was one of the most highly regarded military leaders of his age; James Carrick *Moore (1762–1860) founded the National Vaccine Institute; Admiral Sir Graham *Moore (1764–1843) had a distinguished career in the Royal Navy and earned considerable prize money; Francis Moore rose to become deputy secretary of war; and Charles Moore, bred to the English bar, became auditor of the public accounts. The eldest child, Jane, never married.

After his marriage Moore worked hard at his profession, but as he declared in an unpublished autobiographical fragment, 'I had uneasiness & disgust in that of rolling thro' the Streets from Morning [to evening] from [one] disease to another' (Moore, 'Sketches') and was always seeking some means of escaping from medicine. As a city surgeon he had an extensive practice, attracting clients from all ranks of society. Following John Gordon's example he was very active in the concerns of public health and with Gordon popularized the practice of smallpox variation in the area. Moore was one of the founders of the Hodge-Podge Club, and on two occasions tried unsuccessfully to secure a professorship at his university. His closest friends at this time were William Mure, baron of the Scottish exchequer; John Millar, professor of civil jurisprudence; and Frances Dunlop, who later became a well-known correspondent of Robert Burns. He also corresponded frequently with Smollett in London.

In 1769, at the recommendation of Cullen, Moore attended James George, seventh duke of Hamilton, who died of phthisis in his fifteenth year. Moore wrote his epitaph, and his mother, Elizabeth Gunning, duchess of Argyll, placed her remaining son, Douglas, the eighth duke, under Moore's care. In 1772 Moore was appointed tutor to the duke for a residence of study on the continent, concluding with the traditional grand tour. (As part of his credentials he was awarded a doctorate by Glasgow University and was thereafter known as Dr Moore.) Accompanying them was Moore's eldest son, Jack (Sir John). After two years of private tutoring in Geneva they toured the major German courts, Vienna, and the Italian cities. Moore did not reach the British Isles until early in 1777, by which time a £300 annuity, added to the value of his holdings of city property in Glasgow, allowed him to leave off practice entirely. By late 1777 he had moved his entire family (save his sons Jack and Graham, who were already in military service) to London, first taking a house in Clarges Street. He formally retired from medical practice, though he occasionally ministered to families of close friends.

From this time on he devoted his life to the careers of his children, to his investments, to the deliberations of parliament, to the theatre, and, mostly, to writing.

Travel writings In 1779 Moore published *A View of Society and Manners in France, Switzerland, and Germany*, in two volumes; this proved immensely popular, going through twenty-one editions in his lifetime. In 1781 he published a sequel, *A View of Society and Manners in Italy*, in two volumes, which was equally popular. These works are arranged in a series of letters, and relate in an informal style the observations of Moore's travels with the duke of Hamilton. Some of his most frequently excerpted passages were his accounts of visits to the ageing Voltaire at Ferney. Equally notable were his conversations at Potsdam with Frederick the Great, a ruler virtually inaccessible to British visitors. The letters from Vienna featured accounts of the empress and her son, Joseph II, as well as a description of the fabulous estate of Esterhaza. Moore's description of Venice includes a lengthy digression on the rise and fall of that powerful city-state. There is an amusing account of the visit the duke and he paid to the pope. At Florence they often saw Prince Charles Edward Stuart and his still attractive spouse.

These volumes earned Moore a considerable reputation. His principal friends at this time were Edmund Burke, the MP John 'Fish' Craufurd, the duke and duchess of Devonshire (who obtained a clerkship in the Foreign Office for his son Francis), Sir Joshua Reynolds, and the duke of Hamilton, who was like another son in the household. On 30 May 1784 he met Samuel Johnson; he recorded their conversation in his preface to an edition of Smollett's works (see below).

Moore and his family next moved to Clifford Street, and in 1786 he published *Medical Sketches*, a series of essays that attempted to be candid about contemporary medical practice. It was not popular. By this time Frances Dunlop had introduced herself to Robert Burns, and she initiated a correspondence between the poet and Moore which climaxed in Burns's entrusting to the London physician a revealing account of his life and education; however, the relationship never developed beyond their correspondence. In addition Moore joined the circle of friends that gathered around Mrs Piozzi after her second marriage, and he was also called to the sickbed of the writer Helen Williams, with whom he became close friends. He was intimate with the poet Samuel Rogers and with the fiery Liberal in the House of Lords, the earl of Lauderdale, and at weekends he and his sons could frequently be found at the estate of the Locks of Norbury Park in Surrey.

Zeluco In 1789 Moore published his most famous work, a novel entitled *Zeluco: Various Views of Human Nature, Taken from Life and Manners, Foreign and Domestic*, in two volumes. The broad title suggests that even in fiction Moore was as interested in comparing the customs and manners of various peoples as he was in his travel literature. The first chapter begins by stating:

> Religion teaches, that Vice leads to endless misery in a future state; and Experience proves, that in spite of the gayest and most prosperous appearances, inward misery accompanies

her; for, even in this life, her ways are ways of wretchedness, and all her paths are woe. (J. Moore, *Zeluco*, 1789)

The protagonist is a Sicilian nobleman raised by his mother without restraint and discipline who, by the time he reaches adulthood, is virtually a monster, subject to bouts of rage and constant jealousy. He dies of a wound received in a duel. For an obviously didactic work, this is finely done, and narrated with pronounced irony. This too was popular; thirteen editions appeared in Moore's lifetime. However, his successful delineation of a villain cost him some reputation in the eyes of his public, so he planned his next novel to feature a protagonist of unquestioned virtue. (In the preface to *Childe Harold* Byron said he hoped to make his hero 'perhaps a poetical Zeluco'.)

Edward and Mordaunt Moore's second novel was delayed by the outbreak of the revolution in France, which consumed his attention for the next six years. Moore became greatly preoccupied with the prospects for a constitutional monarchy in the nation he had come to love, whose language he spoke fluently. Although he never joined any society that encouraged constitutional reform in Great Britain, or corresponded with the assemblies in France, he followed developments in parliament in the early 1790s closely, especially the debates over slavery and the proposed repeal of the Test and Corporation Acts. Moore kept company with the Foxite whigs; he was entertained by the MP William Smith, and his name appears in the guest books of Holland House. In 1791 he met Thomas Paine. Moore's political sentiments at this time embraced some form of republic for France or a constitution on the British model. Letter 59 of his *Manners in Italy* expresses his approval of revolution: after stating the natural rights of the poor, who are willing to labour for food and raiment, he writes:

> If their governors, whether from weakness or neglect, do not supply them with these, they certainly have the right to help themselves.—Every law of equity and common sense will justify them, in revolting against such governors, and satisfying their own wants from the superfluities of lazy luxury. (J. Moore, *Manners in Italy*, 1781, no. 59)

Following the earl of Lauderdale's notorious duel with Benedict Arnold in 1792, Moore and his youngest son, Charles, travelled with Lauderdale to France in the late summer in time to witness the attack on the Tuileries, the September massacres, the rise of the Jacobins, and the humiliation of the French monarchy. They returned on 5 December, before the trial of Louis XVI. In 1793 Moore published the first volume of an account of this experience, *A journal during a residence in France from the beginning of August to the middle of December 1792* (the second volume was delayed until 1794, when he had obtained material on the king's trial). The narrative is a simple and obviously exact account of what he saw, and was often quoted by Carlyle in his *French Revolution*. In 1795 Moore published *A View of the Causes and Progress of the French Revolution* (2 vols.), which assesses the financial conditions that led to events in 1789.

Moore's second novel, *Edward: Various Views of Human Nature, Taken from Life and Manners, Chiefly in England*, finally appeared in two volumes in 1796 and was intended to appease those who suspected that he could not draw the manners of a virtuous man. As a satire of contemporary English manners it is far less interesting than *Zeluco*, and did not sell well, though it featured some episodes in France. However, in 1797 Moore was approached by London booksellers to compose a biography of Smollett for a projected edition of his works. The result was an influential profile of the character of the novelist, though it is otherwise deficient in detail about Smollett's life: hardly anyone else remained alive who had known him, and Moore had last seen his cousin some thirty years before. To this work Moore added 'A view of the commencement and progress of romance'.

The last years of Moore's life were consumed mainly by events associated with the war with France and by his involvement with three of his children. In 1795 Francis shocked his parents by marrying Frances Twysden, the divorced countess of Eglinton, who had once been the mistress of the duke of Hamilton. Moore was suffering from difficulties with his eyes, and his heart began to weaken. Disagreements arose between him and his children about the benefits of his parental authority. He quarrelled unreasonably with his wife over money. His relationship with his daughter was often more critical than loving, and near the end of his life she converted to Roman Catholicism. In every other way the family remained close. In 1799 Moore, his wife, and his daughter moved one last time—to Marshgate House, Richmond, Surrey—though he kept a room in town where he could write and make his customary London rounds.

Moore's last novel, *Mordaunt: sketches of life, character, and manners in various countries, including the memoirs of a French lady of quality* (1800), in three volumes, is another satire on contemporary manners of the fashionable in London, set against the horror of events in France. It is the only work of Moore's that has been recently reprinted (1967). Moore died at his house in Richmond on 21 February 1802 of congestive heart failure; all his children were at his side. At the time of his death he had two comedies for the stage in manuscript; they were destroyed by his children. He was buried at Paradise cemetery, St Mary Magdalene's, Richmond. His wife died in London on 25 March 1820.

Moore was very much a product of the Scottish Enlightenment—in university study, in friendships, and in training. Educated at a time when Latin was going out of favour in schools, he remained an avid reader of the classics and was otherwise well read for his time in English, Scottish, and French literature. As a parent he guided his children according to the recipe for happiness he learned from Hutcheson's lectures; as a writer he reflected in many works the principles of cultural analysis he found in Montesquieu. At a time when the government repressed popular sentiments about reform, his views remained liberal, though his long-standing sympathy for France was betrayed by the rise of Napoleon and the empire.

Portraits of the mature John Moore depict a slightly florid face, the most prominent features of which were heavy, bristly eyebrows, a somewhat prominent nose, and a slightly protruding lower lip. He was broad-shouldered and bulky. He wore his own hair powdered, curled on the side, and pulled back in a queue, the fashion of the time. His conversation was frequently facetious, and even after moving to London he continued to speak with a Scottish accent.   H. L. FULTON

Sources parish register (birth), Stirling, 7 Dec 1729 [490/2, 458, New Register House, Edinburgh] · R. Anderson, *The works of John Moore, M.D., with memoirs of his life and writings*, 7 vols. (1820) · parish register (marriage), Glasgow, 17 June 1754 [644 1/25] · Duke of Argyll, ed., *Intimate society letters of the eighteenth century*, 2 vols. [1910] · P. W. Clayden, *The early life of Samuel Rogers* (1887) · G. Heath, *Records of the Carrick Moore family* (1912) · C. Oman, *Sir John Moore* (1953) · *Thraliana: the diary of Mrs. Hester Lynch Thrale (later Mrs. Piozzi)*, 1776–1809, ed. K. C. Balderston, 2nd edn, 2 vols. (1951) · [W. Mure], ed., *Selections from the family papers preserved at Caldwell*, 3 vols., Maitland Club, 71 (1854) · V. C. Caetani, *The Locks of Norbury* (1940) · J. Strang, *Glasgow and its clubs*, rev. edn (1857) · *The journals and letters of Fanny Burney (Madame D'Arblay)*, ed. J. Hemlow and others, 12 vols. (1972–84), vols. 1–7 · J. Moore, 'Sketches of my own birth', priv. coll.

Archives BL, family corresp., Add. MSS 57320–57321 · CUL, journal · Inveraray Castle, Argyll · NL Scot., letters | Carmarthenshire RO, letters to John Vaughan · Chatsworth House, Derbyshire, letters to Lady Devonshire · NL Wales, letters to William Mure · NRA Scotland, priv. coll., letters to the duchess of Argyll

Likenesses P. de Neuchatel, group portrait, oils, 1774 (with the duke of Hamilton and Sir John Moore) · G. Hamilton, group portrait, oils, 1775, Lennoxlove, Lothian region · Cochrane, engraving, 1775–6, Scot. NPG · W. Bromley, line engraving, 1790 (after S. Drummond), BM, Wellcome L.; repro. in *European Magazine* (1790) · T. Lawrence, oils, 1790–91, Scot. NPG [*see illus.*] · W. Lock, pastel ?, after 1791 · A. Vestier, oils, 1792? (dated 1774–95), Musée Carnavelet, Paris, France · G. Dance, pencil-and-ink drawing, 1794, NPG · etching, 1804, Wellcome L. · W. Daniell, soft-ground engraving, 1808, Wellcome L. · J. Edgar, group portrait, wash drawing, *c*.1854, Scot. NPG · J. Cochran, stipple (after W. Cochrane), BM, Wellcome L. · Hopwood, engraving, repro. in J. Moore, *Mooriana* (1803) · W. H. Lizars, line engraving (after G. Hamilton), BM, Wellcome L.; repro. in Anderson, *Works of John Moore* · Wedgwood medallion, Wedgwood Museum, Barlaston, Staffordshire

Wealth at death approx. £30,000—in government securities, interest-bearing loans, and a tontine: will, PRO; ledgers, Royal Bank of Scotland, London

Moore, John (*bap.* 1730, *d.* 1805), archbishop of Canterbury, son of George (*d.* 1775) and Jane Moore, formerly Cook (*d.* 1772), was baptized in St Michael's Church, Gloucester, on 13 January 1730. Like his predecessor Cardinal Wolsey, Moore was the son of a butcher and grazier; his father had a shop in Gloucester and held pasture lands at Sandhurst, close by. Moore was educated at the free grammar school of St Mary de Crypt, Gloucester, and he matriculated at Pembroke College, Oxford, with a Townsend closed scholarship on 25 March 1745. He graduated BA in October 1748 and proceeded MA in June 1751.

After his ordination Moore was engaged to work in the household of the third duke of Marlborough as tutor to the duke's younger sons, lords Charles and Robert Spencer. On the duke's death in 1758 he settled £400 per annum on Moore, who also tactfully declined to court the widowed duchess; she was smitten by the family chaplain's handsome features. This early patronage connection with the Blenheim family was the making of Moore's career in the Church of England. Moore travelled with

John Moore (*bap.* 1730, *d.* 1805), by Sir Thomas Lawrence, 1794

Lord Robert as his tutor in central Europe and Italy during 1766–7, by which date he had already accumulated two important capitular posts: he received the fifth prebendal stall at Durham on 21 September 1761 and a canonry of the first prebend from the king at Christ Church, Oxford, in April 1763. He took the degrees of BD and DD on 1 July 1763 and was appointed rector of Ryton, co. Durham, in 1769.

Moore had a brief first marriage to the sister of Sir James Wright, first baronet, of Ray House, Woodford, Essex, British minister to the republic of Venice from 1766 to 1773. After her death he married for a second time on 23 January 1770. His bride was Catherine, daughter of Sir Robert Eden, third baronet, of West Auckland, co. Durham, and the match brought him into the circle of a highly competent political family. In September 1771 Moore became dean of Canterbury following the direct request to the king of the fourth duke of Marlborough, but he resigned after less than four years to become bishop of Bangor in February 1775. He resided in his see during the summer, conducted visitations at regular intervals, and found that his young family much enjoyed their stays in north Wales. Eight years later he was advanced to the primacy itself, a surprise choice of a relatively junior bishop. Although bishops Hurd and Lowth had both declined the honour they agreed that the king should send for Moore, who was duly translated to the archbishopric of Canterbury on 26 April 1783 and installed and enthroned by proxy on 10 May.

Moore's primacy of twenty-two years was steady and cautious, with the defence of the establishment as its main hallmark. The key role of his brother-in-law, William Eden, first Lord Auckland, in the circle of William

Pitt the younger ensured the archbishop was party to state deliberations at the highest level. Moore was opposed to hazarding the repeal of the Test and Corporation Acts and he convened a gathering of sixteen of the twenty-six bishops in London on 10 February 1787 to test and concert opinion against parliamentary moves for repeal. The archbishop spoke out on 9 June 1789 in the House of Lords against Earl Stanhope's Toleration Bill for its dangerous vagueness that would 'serve to cover every species of irreligion' (Ditchfield, 'Dissent and toleration', 63). Though Moore cautiously accepted the Roman Catholic Relief Act of 1791, the outbreak of the French Revolution intensified his conviction that the times were inappropriate to reducing the privileges of the religious establishment, and he was reluctant to take further Pitt's interest in tithe commutation. In late 1800 the archbishop deployed his influence in strengthening the king's dislike of conceding Catholic emancipation. Similarly, although he was initially sympathetic to the campaign for the abolition of the slave trade, he withdrew his support in 1792 in a move that was a severe blow to Wilberforce. Though cautious of the evangelicals and the new Church Missionary Society, Moore was in principle sympathetic to the expansion of Anglican missionary activity and he promoted the Sunday school movement. It was during his primacy that the Episcopalian church in the United States was settled. Though it was inexpedient for Moore to consecrate Samuel Seabury from Connecticut as an American bishop in 1784, he privately made clear he had no objection to the nonjuring Scottish bishops—whose orders he considered valid—undertaking that office. In due course, on 4 February 1787 Moore presided at Lambeth Palace over the consecration of William White and Samuel Provoost—elected by the Philadelphia convention of United States episcopalians—as bishops of New York and Philadelphia respectively. In May 1786 Moore and Bishop Lowth had petitioned the crown for a bishop for Canada. The choice eventually fell on Charles Inglis of Nova Scotia, whom the archbishop consecrated on 12 August 1787. Moore took this step only after extensive soundings of interested parties; equally characteristically, once this was done he gave the infant Canadian church his full support. He allowed other bishops, such as Samuel Horsley, to take the lead in denouncing the politics of republican, regicide France in the 1790s, and was reluctant to allow individual clerics to take up arms during the invasion scare of 1798.

Throughout his primacy Moore's administrative competence, astute patronage, and impeccable orthodoxy made him many friends and few enemies. It was typical that he and Wilberforce remained on affectionate terms despite their differences over the slave trade. His relationship with the royal family was cordial; he married the prince of Wales to Princess Caroline of Brunswick on 8 April 1795. Moore was, as Bishop Porteus observed on 23 January 1805, 'a very aimiable and worthy man' (Nichols, *Lit. anecdotes*, 7. 880), and he was president of both the Society for Propagation of the Gospel and the Corporation of the Sons of the Clergy. A man of considerable presence, though not pompous, Moore was conscious that his office

gave him an extended pastoral responsibility for the whole kingdom. Accordingly, near the end of the harsh winter of 1799–1800, he proposed a national agreement to be signed voluntarily to relieve want among the poor and destitute. Moore himself enjoyed a net annual income of £11,000 which allowed him to live in some style. He and his second wife had a number of children, and were both distraught when two daughters died of consumption in the last seven years of Moore's life. The two of his four sons who entered the church undoubtedly benefited from their father's scope for patronage. At Lambeth he undertook a minor remodelling of the grounds to open up the views and built a more convenient carriage-approach road. The archbishop died at Lambeth Palace on 18 January 1805 after some months of senility, and he was buried in Lambeth church on 25 January after a ceremonial funeral. Moore was an administrator rather than a scholar, and only three of his sermons were published separately in his lifetime.

NIGEL ASTON

Sources GM, 1st ser., 33 (1763), 258 · GM, 1st ser., 40 (1770), 46 · GM, 1st ser., 45 (1775), 40 · GM, 1st ser., 53 (1783), 605 · GM, 1st ser., 75 (1805), 94 · C. Lepper, *The Crypt School, Gloucester, 1530–1989* (1989), 24–6 · Foster, *Alum. Oxon.* · chronology, *Annual Register* (1805), 80–82 · *Fasti Angl.* (Hardy) · *Fasti Angl., 1541–1857*, [Canterbury], 11, 14 · *Fasti Angl., 1541–1857*, [Bristol], 8.89 · A. W. Rowden, *The primates of the four Georges* (1916) · Nichols, *Lit. anecdotes* · Nichols, *Illustrations*, 8.380 · *The historical and the posthumous memoirs of Sir Nathaniel William Wraxall, 1772–1784*, ed. H. B. Wheatley, 5 vols. (1884), vol. 3, pp. 33–5 · *The journal and correspondence of William, Lord Auckland*, ed. [G. Hogge], 4 vols. (1861–2) · P. Thicknesse, *Memoirs and anecdotes of Philip Thicknesse* (1790), 332–7 · baptism register, St Michael's Church, Gloucester, Glos. RO [baptism] · G. M. Ditchfield, 'Dissent and toleration: Lord Stanhope's bill of 1789', *Journal of Ecclesiastical History*, 29 (1978), 51–73 · G. M. Ditchfield, 'The parliamentary struggle over the repeal of the Test and Corporation Acts, 1787–90', *EngHR*, 89 (1974), 551–77 · W. Sachs, *The transformation of Anglicanism: from state church to global communion* (1993) · B. E. Steiner, *Samuel Seabury, 1729–1796: a study in the high church tradition* (1971), 196–212, 308–10 · P. M. Doll, 'American high churchmanship and the establishment of the first colonial episcopate in the Church of England: Nova Scotia, 1787', *Journal of Ecclesiastical History*, 43 (1992), 35–59 · W. White, *Memoirs of the Protestant Episcopal church in the United States of America* (1820) · J. Fingard, *The Anglican design in loyalist Nova Scotia, 1783–1816* (1972) · B. Cuthbertson, *The first bishop: a biography of Charles Inglis* (1987) · A. E. Nimmo, 'Bishop John Skinner and the resurgence of Scottish episcopacy', PhD diss., U. Aberdeen, 1996 · J. Ehrman, *The younger Pitt*, 2: *The reluctant transition* (1983), 85 · J. Ehrman, *The younger Pitt*, 3: *The consuming struggle* (1996), 505 and n. · *Public characters*, 10 vols. (1799–1809), vol. 1, p. 276 · F. C. Mather, *High church prophet: Bishop Samuel Horsley (1733–1806) and the Caroline tradition in the later Georgian church* (1992) · D. Gardiner, *The story of Lambeth Palace: a historic survey* (1930), 208–9 · J. Ingamells, ed., *A dictionary of British and Irish travellers in Italy, 1701–1800* (1997)

Archives BL, corresp. as a trustee of the British Museum, MSS 63090, fol. 138; 70839, fols. 5–14 · Bodl. Oxf., MSS 37825, fols. 88–91; 49423, fols. 241–2; 40957, fols. 185–7 · LPL, corresp. and papers · LPL, corresp. relating to the Society for the Propagation of the Gospel | BL, letters to Lord Auckland, MSS 34412–34413, 34415, 34417–34419, 34421–34429, 34441, 34443, 34446, 34452–34454, 34456–34461 · BL, Blenheim MSS, MSS 61668; 61670, fols. 36–199b · Bodl. Oxf., letters to first earl of Guilford · CUL, Pitt MSS, 6958, (1033), boxes 3–9 · PRO, Chatham MSS, corresp. with Pitt the younger, 30/8/161, 195, 199

Likenesses G. Romney, oils, 1776–83, deanery, Canterbury · G. Romney, oils, 1788–92, LPL · T. Lawrence, oils, 1794, Southampton City Art Gallery [*see illus.*] · attrib. W. Hamilton, oils, 1796 ·

R. Dighton, coloured etching, pubd 1803, NPG · H. Ashby, portrait, exh. RA 1804 · H. Edridge, portrait, exh. RA 1804 · S. P. Hall, portrait (after G. Romney, 1788–92), Pembroke College, Oxford · attrib. G. Hamilton, oils, LPL · T. Stewart, portrait (after G. Romney, 1788–92), Christ Church Oxf. · H. Thomas I, portrait (after G. Romney, 1788–92), Old Vicarage, Bangor, Wales

Moore, John (1742–1821), biblical scholar, was born in London on 19 December 1742, the son of John Moore, rector of St Bartholomew-the-Great and incumbent of St Sepulchre, London, and his wife, Susanna (*bap.* 1703), daughter of Peter and Anne Surel of Westminster. He was educated at Merchant Taylors' School, where he became head scholar in 1756. He matriculated from St John's College, Oxford, on 28 June 1759, and graduated BA on 15 April 1763; he subsequently proceeded LLB. During his time at Oxford he assisted Benjamin Kennicott in collating the Hebrew manuscripts of the Old Testament.

After he was ordained, Moore gained many ecclesiastical preferments. On 11 November 1766 he became sixth minor prebendary in St Paul's Cathedral, London, and in 1783 he was made twelfth minor prebendary and appointed sacrist. He also became priest of the Chapel Royal; lecturer of St Sepulchre; rector of St Michael Bassishaw, London (19 October 1781) and rector of Langdon Hills, Essex (1798). He also served as an examiner of Merchant Taylors' School, and as president of Sion College, London, from 1800. He married Sarah Lilley, and their daughter, Mary Anne, was the wife of Harry Bristow *Wilson (1774–1853), under-master of Merchant Taylors', and the mother of Henry Bristow *Wilson (1803–1888), the historian of the school.

Moore was the author of several religious works and dedicated *An attempt to recover the original reading of 1 Sam. xiii. 1, to which is added an enquiry into the duration of Solomon's reign* (1797) to the dean and chapter of St Paul's; it was translated into French in 1800. He also wrote on the Septuagint and on Isaiah. Moore argued for the rights of the clergy, and his *Case Respecting the Maintenance of the London Clergy* (1802) was revised and reprinted in 1812 and 1818. He unsuccessfully attempted to publish by subscription one of Brian Walton's lesser-known works on the ecclesiastical history of London.

Moore died at the parsonage house, Langdon Hills, Essex, on 16 June 1821. An obituary in the *Gentleman's Magazine* praised his efforts on behalf of his fellow Church of England ministers.

THOMPSON COOPER, *rev.* EMMA MAJOR

Sources Foster, *Alum. Oxon.* · *GM*, 1st ser., 91/1 (1821), 478 · J. Moore, *An attempt to recover the original reading of 1 Sam. xiii. 1, to which is added an enquiry into the duration of Solomon's reign* (1797) · *IGI* · *ESTC* · private information (1897) · Nichols, *Lit. anecdotes*, 1.344 · J. P. Malcolm, *Londinium redivivum, or, An antient history and modern description of London*, 4 vols. (1802–7), vol. 1, pp. 38–9; vol. 3, pp. 29, 148; vol. 4, p. 495 · C. J. Robinson, ed., *A register of the scholars admitted into Merchant Taylors' School, from AD 1562 to 1874*, 2 (1883), 105 · H. B. Wilson, *The history of Merchant-Taylors' School*, 2 vols. (1814), 453–54, 525, 1142–1143, 1211, 1220

Moore, Sir John (1761–1809), army officer, was born in the Trongate, Glasgow, on 13 November 1761, the eldest surviving son of the eight sons and three daughters of the

Sir John Moore (1761–1809), by Sir Thomas Lawrence, *c.*1800–04

physician and writer John *Moore MD (1729–1802) and his wife, Jean (1735–1820), daughter of the Revd Professor John *Simson of Glasgow University. James *Moore and Sir Graham *Moore were his brothers. Tradition links the Moore family with the younger branch of the Mures of Ruellan, which had fourteenth-century royal connections.

Youth, education, and early military service After attending Glasgow high school, in February 1772 John Moore (known as Jack in the family) travelled to London with his father. Two months later he went with him when the elder John Moore accompanied the fifteen-year-old duke of Hamilton as his tutor and doctor on the grand tour, visiting France, Switzerland, Germany, and Italy. His father wrote that 'he dances, rides and fences with unusual address' (*DNB*), and he also became proficient in German. The younger Moore danced with princesses at Potsdam, was presented at the Austrian court, and suffered painful burns from cinders when venturing too close to the crater of Vesuvius. He had decided on a military career but, officially, a British commission could not be obtained before he reached the age of sixteen. Briefly, entry into Prussian or Austrian service was, therefore, contemplated. His father, perhaps deliberately, mistook his date of birth, for Moore was only fourteen when gazetted ensign in the 51st foot, on 2 March 1776, through the duke of Argyll's influence. Having at once obtained leave of absence, he did not return to London until September. He had hoped to spend three or four weeks (in the event, seven) with his mother, whom he had not seen for 'almost five years' (Wylly, 110), before joining the regiment, which he did at Minorca in January 1777. From Georgetown he assured his mother the following month: 'I have got into one of the best regiments in the service; as to officers I never knew such a number of fine, gentlemanly lads' (ibid., 111). When the duke of Hamilton raised the 82nd foot Moore was appointed captain-lieutenant and captain (10 January 1778), serving with it in Nova Scotia as regimental paymaster. The day after landing at Penobscot Bay, on 29 July 1779, when in charge of an outlying picket and unsupported, he held firm and was almost captured during an American foray, 'a great deal startled … [and] develishly [sic] frightened' (Oman, 48). In 1783, at the close of the American War of Independence, the 82nd was disbanded and, having acquired command of a company in 1780, Captain Moore went on half pay.

Politics and active service, 1784–1796 Through the duke of Hamilton's interest, in 1784 Moore entered parliament for the Linlithgow burghs. He generally supported Pitt's administration and apparently made no speech in the house. He did not seek re-election in 1790. Meanwhile, he had resumed his military career. On 23 November 1785 he returned nominally to the active list in the 100th foot, the same day purchasing a majority in the 102nd, which was soon disbanded, leaving him an unattached major on full pay. On 16 January 1788 he secured a majority in the 60th Royal American foot, which practised a less rigid form of drill and movement than was normal in line regiments. He was stationed at its depot in Chatham, and the regimental historian Lieutenant-Colonel Lewis Butler later recorded the legend that he used this experience to develop his system of light infantry training. Moore exchanged, on 1 October 1788, into his first regiment, the 51st foot, which he joined in Ireland. He found it in a poor state, apparently disapproved of the methods of the commanding officer, and, though second in command, spent all but fifty-four days in twenty-six months away from the regiment on 'Lord Lieutenant's leave'.

After assuming command himself as lieutenant-colonel (30 November 1790), Moore worked hard to improve discipline and morale. He dealt severely with drunkenness and noted that when a lieutenant 'went rioting about the town and was absent from his guard all night' (Wylly, 134), Moore obliged him to sell his commission. Refusing to confine his men to barracks on the eve of embarkation, he was rewarded when the regiment paraded 'perfectly sober' (ibid., 136), finally disembarking at Gibraltar on 25 March 1792. The 51st remained there until ordered to reinforce Major-General Sir David Dundas at Toulon in December 1793, but when they arrived they found the British force already withdrawn.

Almost immediately Moore was ordered to Corsica with Sir Gilbert Elliot, British commissioner in the Mediterranean, where anti-French forces under the Corsican patriot Pasquale Paoli had appealed for help. Elliot and Moore landed on 14 January 1794 and were misled by Paoli into believing that the French garrisons totalled 2600 men and not the actual 7000. They agreed to a British invasion, for which Moore stayed to prepare. On arrival of the main body on 7 February, he assumed command of a brigade for an assault on San Fiorenzo in the north, only to discover

that the French positions had been unexpectedly strengthened. After the adjacent Martello tower had been bombarded into submission, Moore successfully charged the dominant Convention redoubt at a cost of forty casualties. The French were thus forced to abandon the crucial Fornoli heights and retreat 9 miles east to Bastia. On reconnoitring Bastia, Moore found a garrison of an estimated 1400 men, supported by two French frigates, and cautioned against a rash attack by saying: 'I do not think our force equal to the attempt' (*Life and Letters*, 38). Bastia subsequently surrendered, following naval action, without Moore being involved. Elliot has described Moore during these weeks:

> His bed consists of some loose straw covered with meadow hay, and there he has slept in his clothes ever since our arrival at San Fiorenzo, generally making a tour of a mile or two himself in the course of the night. He is in love with his profession. (ibid.)

When Lieutenant-General Sir Charles Stuart arrived to command the British troops, he determined to attack the last French stronghold at Calvi in the west; and on 9 June Moore was appointed to lead the reserve corps of grenadiers. Reinforced by a small naval detachment under Captain Horatio Nelson, Stuart launched his assault on 28 June, Moore concentrating on the critical Mozello Fort, which proved a long and daunting task. In his diary (13 July 1794) he recorded bitter exchanges the previous day and night: 'We were fortunate enough to have but three or four men touched. Captain Nelson was wounded by stones in the face. It is feared he will lose one of his eyes' (*Life and Letters*, 44). Previously, Nelson had written somewhat equivocally to Admiral Lord Hood, who commanded the naval covering force, hoping that Stuart 'will not be led wrong, but Colonel Moore is his great friend' (*DNB*). Moore himself was wounded by a shell splinter in the head in the final attack on the Mozello on 19 July, and Calvi surrendered on 10 August. Noting this success in a letter to his mother, he mused: 'You have heard how the thickness of my skull saved my life. The last plaster fell off to-day; and as soon as the hair, which has been shaved, grows, there will not remain any trace of the hurt' (*Life and Letters*, 46). In his dispatch Stuart wrote: 'I am much indebted to Lieut.-Colonel Moore for his assistance upon every occasion; it is only a tribute to his worth to mention that he has distinguished himself upon this Expedition for his Bravery, Conduct and Military Talent' (Wylly, 156).

Moore became brevet colonel on 21 August 1795 and local brigadier-general on 9 September; after Stuart had left Corsica, on 7 February of that year, he had been appointed adjutant-general. However, he soon clashed with Sir Gilbert Elliot, the viceroy, who accused him of meddling in politics by maintaining contact with Paoli, of whom Elliot disapproved. Following a painful interview 'during which my feelings were so strong and my indignation such as to bring tears to my eyes' (*Life and Letters*, 49), he was ordered from the island. He reached London on 25 November 1795, to discover ministers 'embarrassed' by Gilbert's action, and 'a few days afterwards [he] was appointed brigadier-general in the West Indies' (ibid., 52).

In February 1796 Moore sailed from Portsmouth to join Lieutenant-General Sir Ralph Abercromby's expedition to recover the islands; he arrived at Barbados on 13 April, though not before his mother had unsubtly hinted that he should marry an old friend, Peggy Coates. He led a brigade under Abercromby during the capture of St Lucia in May, distinguishing himself on the heights of Chabot and Chasseau. Despite his reservations—'of all things I dislike a garrison … to attend to the army is more to my taste' (ibid., 59)—with a force of 4500 and a daily allowance of 30s. 6d., at Abercromby's request he remained as governor when the expeditionary force moved on. Several armed bands of black men, supporting the French, were still at large, the rainy season prevented swift movement, many white troops fell ill, and there was no hospital. Moore felt strongly that Abercromby had been guilty of 'running away' without properly securing the island. As he noted: 'ten days would have secured a conquest which it took an army of 11,000 men a month to make'. St Lucia was now 'in the most precarious state' (ibid., 61). Not only were the insurgents a danger, but he feared invasion from Guadeloupe and deplored the fact that 'the regiments are ill-commanded … [and have] very few officers upon whom I can depend' (ibid., 63). Nevertheless, he tirelessly visited outposts, sleeping in the open and sharing the same sparse rations as his men in a determined attempt to regain control of the region. In the midst of these efforts he recounted that he 'cried like a child' (ibid., 62) to learn that his mother had been distressed by graphic reports of casualties during the fight for St Lucia. In November 1796 Moore suffered an attack of yellow fever; and Abercromby offered to recommend him for the less arduous governorship of Grenada or the military post of quartermaster-general in the West Indies. He declined both offers, making clear his preference for a field command, and reluctantly agreed to continue at St Lucia. However, on 16 May 1797 he admitted that an abscess on his right hip and a return of the fever had weakened him, and by the end of the month he had sailed for home, reaching Falmouth on 9 July. Five days later he joined his family in Clifford Street, London, whither they had moved from Scotland almost twenty years previously.

Ireland, The Helder, and Egypt, 1797–1801 For four months, to his chagrin, Moore held no military appointment. In November 1797 the new commander-in-chief in Ireland, Sir Ralph Abercromby, offered him a post as brigadier-general on his staff. Moore recognized that 'there was no alternative but Ireland, or idleness at home, of which I was already tired' (Life and Letters, 76). He arrived in Dublin on 4 December and assumed command of the forts at Cork, Kinsale, and Midleton before taking over a force of 3000 (mostly militia) at Bandon. He was unimpressed with the 'profligate and idle' officers, whom he believed to the 'serving for the emolument … [not] from a sense of duty nor of military distinction' (ibid.). Insurrection had begun and a French invasion was feared. While marching to relieve Wexford, Moore routed a strong force under Father Philip Roche at Foulkes's Mill on 20 June 1798, and the following day he took Wexford without resistance.

Lieutenant-General Gerard Lake praised his initiative: 'General Moore, with his usual enterprize and activity, pushed on to this town, and entered it so opportunely as to prevent it from being laid in ashes, and the massacre of the remaining prisoners' (London Gazette, 26 June 1798). A tedious expedition to clear the Wicklow hills followed. On 18 June Moore advanced to major-general and on 6 September became colonel of the 9th West India regiment. Fretting about the climate of 'perpetual damps' and 'being far from well … no appetite, yellow, etc. … [though] I am averse to try Trim's recipe, burned whiskey, or radical heat' (Life and Letters, 86), he ached to be free from 'the continued broils of this distracted people, when active service is going on elsewhere' (Oman, 19).

Moore remained in Ireland until June 1799, when he was ordered to England to command a brigade in the vanguard of the expeditionary force to free the Netherlands from French control. He left the Downs on 13 August and landed fourteen days later on the Helder peninsula. He then moved south parallel to the sea and on 10 September led his brigade against a strong force among the dunes, having a finger of his right hand broken by a shot deflected from his spyglass. After the duke of York arrived with reinforcements, Moore became embroiled in a costly encounter near Egmont-op-Zee on 2 October, during which he sustained a serious thigh injury and a second wound caused by a shot which entered behind his ear and came out of his cheek under his left eye. He was taken, semi-conscious, back to his quarters, where he mistakenly drank a solution of sugar of lead, intended for dressing his wounds; only quick action by his aide-de-camp, Major Paul Anderson, with an emetic saved his life. Thoughtfully, when able to write, he assured his parents, now living in Richmond, that his condition was neither painful nor dangerous. When he had recovered sufficiently he was invalided back to England, but convalesced so swiftly that he resumed command of his brigade at Chelmsford on 24 December. Meanwhile, on 25 November, he had been appointed colonel-commandant of the 2nd battalion of the 52nd foot.

In May 1800 Moore commanded part of General Sir Ralph Abercromby's expedition to the Mediterranean, landing at Minorca on 22 June and immediately being sent to support the Austrian garrison at Genoa. Finding that Genoa had fallen, he was ordered back to Minorca, where he laboured to improve discipline and practise troops in rapid movement, without unnecessary baggage. He left Minorca once more, on 1 September, and sailed via Gibraltar to join a force off Cadiz. On 6 October, with his men in boats ready to land, the attack on the Spanish port was cancelled, the British thereby cutting a 'ridiculous figure' (Life and Letters, 107), as he observed to his father. He then joined, at Marmarıs Bay in southern Turkey, Abercromby's expeditionary force destined for Egypt, which had been invaded by Napoleon. On 3 January 1801 he learned that 'Major-General Moore is to proceed to the Turkish Army near Jaffa, where he will endeavour to make himself the master of the real state and condition of the Ottoman Army' (Oman, 237). He returned on 20 January with the news that 'the plague' was virulent and the opinion that the Turks were 'a wild, ungovernable mob, incapable of being directed to any useful purpose' (*Life and Letters*, 113). None the less, Abercromby determined to oust the French from Egypt, and Moore, in command of the reserves, was prominent during the opposed landing on 8 March, after which the enemy retired to fortified heights near Alexandria, from which they counter-attacked on 21 March. In the ensuing battle Abercromby fell mortally wounded, and Moore had a horse shot under him and was wounded in the left leg, which caused prolonged fever and incapacitated him for five weeks, during which amputation was considered. He recovered in time to take part in the capture of Cairo on 29 June, and with his column to escort French prisoners to the coast. He took part in the successful siege of Alexandria, which ended on 2 September. After resisting pressure to become the garrison commander, he reached England on 10 November and received the thanks of parliament and the Turkish order of the Crescent. On 8 May 1801 he had been appointed colonel of the 52nd foot.

Shorncliffe, the Mediterranean, and Sweden, 1802–1807 While Moore was commanding a brigade at Brighton, his father died on 21 February 1802. Hostilities with France were resumed in May 1803, and on 9 July Moore took command of a brigade centred on Shorncliffe, near Folkestone in Kent, where he established his celebrated training camp for light infantry. Whether he did profit from his brief service in the 60th foot is moot. But in Minorca in 1800 Abercromby had certainly drawn attention to the need for a light infantry corps to challenge the French *voltigeurs*, and Moore had observed with special interest the deployment of the 90th into skirmishers, supports, and reserves, and had exercised his own troops with light equipment. Although responsible for the coast of Kent from Deal to Dungeness, he was primarily concerned with the threat of invasion, which did not recede until 1805. He found time, however, to bring his elderly mother and his sister Jane to Sandgate, near his house at Hythe, for the summer of 1803. In December 1804 he sailed to Spain to advise on the feasibility of landing at Ferrol, which on closer examination he discouraged. He had been appointed KB on 14 November 1804, choosing as supporters of his arms 'a light infantry soldier, as being colonel of the 1st light infantry regiment, and a 92nd highlander, in gratitude and acknowledgment of two soldiers of that regiment who saved my life in Holland, 2 Oct 1799' (*DNB*). His officers presented him with a diamond star of the Bath, worth 350 guineas. Moore advanced to lieutenant-general on 2 November 1805, and the following month, based at Canterbury, he took charge of the southern district. His close personal friendship with William Pitt, then living at Walmer, gave rise to rumours of a romantic connection with Pitt's eccentric niece, Lady Hester Stanhope.

In March 1806 Moore felt that 'there is a chance of my going with the command to India. I wish it; for I am tired of the trifling details of a home command. But there are difficulties in the way' (Oman, 362). In fact, objections were raised about sending him to India as commander-in-

chief, because of the state of affairs in Europe. Instead, on 14 June 1806, he sailed for Sicily as second-in-command to Lieutenant-General Henry Fox. There he recognized that 'possession of Sicily is a most important object, whether as a military post, or as a valuable colony' (*Life and Letters*, 163), but he advised against an invasion of Calabria, in support of the kingdom of Naples. Privately, in a letter to Major Paul Anderson, he admitted a deep attraction to Fox's seventeen-year-old daughter Caroline Amelia, but he concluded that 'my high position here, my reputation as a soldier of service and my intimacy with her father, may influence her to an irretrievable error for her own future contentment', if he proposed marriage, and that 'my present feelings must therefore be suppressed' (ibid., 170). He succeeded Fox in July 1807. Two months later, though not before he had sharply condemned William Drummond, British minister in Palermo, for his perceived inept dealings with the Neapolitan royal family, he relinquished command and went to Gibraltar with 7000 men, prepared to help Portugal resist French invasion. When this proved impossible, he sailed on to England, and was dispatched to Sweden with a force of 10,000 to assist Gustavus IV Adolphus, whose country was being threatened by France, Russia, and Denmark. Moore arrived off Göteborg on 17 May 1808 but found himself forbidden to land the troops. After exchanging letters with the secretary for war and the Horse Guards in London, in June he went to Stockholm, where he found the king obsessed with co-operative schemes to seize Zealand and fight the Russians in Finland. Moore demurred, suggesting that he return to his men and consult his government. The king forbade him to leave Stockholm, but Moore escaped in disguise to Göteborg and quickly sailed for England. He confided to his mother that the whole experience had been 'most painful' (ibid., 186).

The Peninsula, 1808–1809 On reaching London, Moore discovered that he was to go to Portugal in a post junior to lieutenant-generals Sir Hew Dalrymple and Harry Burrard. Fruitlessly, he protested to the secretary for war, Lord Castlereagh, that he had held independent commands in Sicily and Sweden, and he complained 'of the unhandsome treatment that I have received from you' (*Life and Letters*, 192). His forthright manner hardly invited ministerial approbation and, indeed, shortly afterwards Lieutenant-General Sir Arthur Wellesley gently reproved him for 'some unpleasant'—and by implication unwise— 'discussions with the King's ministers' (*Dispatches*, 4.156). Towards the end of July 1808 Moore sailed from Portsmouth as Burrard's second in command. Burrard found that Wellesley was already in action ashore, so he left Moore with the transports and made directly for Oporto. Moore did not land until the battles of Roliça and Vimeiro were over and French evacuation had been agreed by the convention of Cintra. Dalrymple and Wellesley went back to England, leaving Moore and Burrard at Lisbon. On 6 October Moore learned that Burrard would remain in Portugal while he was to command an army of 35,000 men in northern Spain, 15,000 of which would be reinforcements from England under Lieutenant-General Sir David Baird via Corunna. Faced with the decision of either sending his own force by sea to Corunna or marching overland to a convenient rendezvous with Baird, he chose the overland route. Poor roads determined that the main body from Lisbon should advance north-east in three columns, with the intention of converging at Valladolid with Baird and another column under Brigadier-General John Hope, then in Spain near Elvas. Moore himself left Lisbon, on 27 October, having been promised an additional 60,000–70,000 Spanish troops in support. He advanced through Almeida across the Spanish frontier to an enthusiastic reception at Ciudad Rodrigo and reached Salamanca on 13 November.

Moore quickly realized that little, if any, Spanish military assistance would materialize and he was, too, running seriously short of money. He therefore decided to retire into Portugal, ordering Hope to join him and Baird to fall back on Corunna, explaining to Castlereagh: 'I conceive the British troops were sent in aid of the Spanish armies; but not singly to resist France, if the Spaniards made no efforts' (*Life and Letters*, 221). However, on 2 December General Thomas Morla wrote to Moore stating that the Spanish were determined to protect their capital and that the junta wanted his army to help defend Madrid, a plea independently supported by the British plenipotentiary, J. H. Frere. Moore soon discovered, however, that Madrid had fallen. Nevertheless, he countermanded orders for the retreat and decided instead to attack Marshal Soult. Moore's various columns at length came together at Sahagún on 23 December, but shortly before he planned to close on Soult he discovered that an overwhelming French force was gathering against him. It appeared that his route back to Portugal was also blocked. He had no option but to head north for Vigo or Corunna, more than 200 miles away, over mountainous terrain in the depths of a bitter winter. His journal entry for 24 December correctly foresaw 'a country without fuel [where] it is impossible to bivouac; the villages are small, which obliges us to march thus by corps in succession. Our retreat, therefore, becomes much more difficult' (ibid., 237). His depleted and exhausted force, ravaged by sickness and constantly harassed by the enemy, finally reached Corunna on 11 January 1809, in Moore's words 'so completely disorganized. Its conduct during the late march has been infamous beyond belief' (Oman, 587). *En route*, he had needed strict discipline to keep his army together and had narrowly avoided a fatal pincer movement between Soult and Napoleon. Now the transports were not ready and he had insufficient men to occupy a range of hills overlooking the port. His last letter to Castlereagh, sent back with Brigadier-General Charles Stewart on 13 January, assured him 'that I shall accept no terms that are in the least dishonourable to the Army, or to the Country' (*Life and Letters*, 260). The next day he reflected that 'I have often been thought an unlucky man by my friends, in consequence of my being generally wounded in action' (Oman, v). As embarkation was under way on 16 January 1809, three French columns began to descend the surrounding heights. While encouraging a vigorous counter-attack, Moore fell from his horse, fatally wounded. An eyewitness, his military secretary, Major John Colborne, recorded: 'General Moore was struck in his left breast and shoulder by a cannon shot, which broke his ribs, his arm, lacerated his shoulder and the whole of his left side and lungs' (Oman, 605). He was carried to his quarters in the town and laid on a mattress, where he heard that the French had been repulsed. During the evening, as he lay dying, he said: 'I hope the people of England will be satisfied. I hope my country will do me justice' (*Life and Letters*, 268). When an aide-de-camp came into the room, he said: 'Stanhope, remember me to your sister' (ibid.), fuelling speculation that the relationship between Moore and Lady Hester had indeed been close. He died shortly before 8 p.m.

Moore wished to be buried where he died, not conveyed to England. Therefore, a grave was dug, within the landward bastion of the citadel, at midnight by soldiers of the 9th foot. At 8 a.m. on 17 January, to a background of gunfire, the chaplain to the brigade of guards, the Revd J. H. Symons, conducted the burial service, and Moore's body, wrapped in a military cloak and blanket, was laid to rest.

Memorials, character, and judgement On 1 February 1809 a general order from the Horse Guards read:

> During the seasons of repose, [Moore's] time was devoted to the care and instruction of the officers and soldiers. In war he courted service in every quarter of the globe … his virtues live in the recollection of his associates, and his fame remains the strongest incentive to great and glorious actions. (*Life and Letters*, 271)

Colborne wrote simply about 'my friend. He was a noble fellow' (Oman, 603), the duke of York (commander-in-chief of the army) appeared 'much affected', and the king mourned 'a national loss' (ibid., 607). Attempts were made by opponents to undermine Moore's military reputation by pointing to his failure in Spain, but, in 1824, Soult confounded them by paying generous tribute to his skill in the Peninsula.

Parliament ordered a public monument to be erected in St Paul's Cathedral; and a statue, paid for by public subscription, was placed in George Square, Glasgow. Shortly after Moore's death Corunna was occupied by Spanish troops under the marqués de La Romana. A wooden column was painted to resemble stone and placed over the grave on a pediment of guns and shells, the impressive unveiling ceremony being attended by military and civil authorities. Romana wrote an inscription on the column in black chalk. Subsequently, the British converted this memorial into a more permanent structure of marble, with a Latin inscription. In 1834 the site was further modified, with a railing installed around a plain granite urn, which marked the grave.

Tall, erect, and graceful, with hazel eyes and brown hair, Moore never married. His copious correspondence with his family, and especially his mother, showed an affection beyond mere duty. Dedicated to his profession, he could be tactless to civilian ministers; and, despite a brief period as an MP, he displayed no political ambitions. He showed particular irritation and sensitivity when he believed himself slighted. But he was exceptionally popular with his officers and inspired fierce loyalty among those who knew him well. In the Peninsular period, and long after, to have been 'one of Sir John Moore's men' conferred special prestige. From his death onwards through the nineteenth century he was famous and much admired. The Revd Charles Wolfe's 'Funeral of Sir John Moore' (first published in 1817)—with its poignant opening,

Not a drum was heard, not a funeral note,
As his corse to the rampart we hurried

— was long one of the most popular poems in the English language and remains one of its best elegies. Moore's greatest military legacy was the system of light infantry training that he established at Shorncliffe.

JOHN SWEETMAN

Sources *Army List* · *The life and letters of Sir John Moore*, ed. B. S. Brownrigg (1923) · *The diary of Sir John Moore*, ed. J. F. Maurice, 2 vols. (1904) · C. Oman, *Sir John Moore* (1953) · R. Parkinson, *Moore of Corunna* (1976) · J. F. C. Fuller, *Sir John Moore's system of training* (1924) · *The dispatches of ... the duke of Wellington ... from 1799 to 1818*, ed. J. Gurwood, 4: *Peninsula, 1790–1813* (1835) · H. C. Wylly, *History of the king's own Yorkshire light infantry*, 1 (1926) · L. Cooper, *The king's own Yorkshire light infantry* (1970) · L. Butler, *The annals of the king's royal rifle corps*, 1 (1913) · HoP, *Commons* · DNB
Archives BL, corresp. and diaries, Add. MSS 57320–57332, 57539–57554 · CUL, letter-book and essay · NAM, order book · Suffolk RO, Bury St Edmunds, extracts from journal relating to battle of Canyser Duyn and Egyptian campaign | BL, letters to Lord Auckland, Add. MSS 34412–34461, *passim* · BL, corresp. with Sir James Willoughby Gordon, Add. MS 49482, *passim* · BL, letters to Sir Hudson Lowe, Add. MSS 20107, 20162–20166, 20189 · National War Museum of Scotland, Edinburgh, letters to Sir David Baird · NL Scot., corresp. with Kenneth Mackenzie · NL Scot., letters to Mure family · NRA Scotland, priv. coll., letters to Lord Hopetoun · priv. coll., letters to Lord Cathcart · PRO NIre., corresp. with Lord Castlereagh · U. Aberdeen L., corresp. with A. M. Fraser · U. Nott. L., letters to Lord William Bentinck
Likenesses T. Lawrence, c.1800–1804, NPG [*see illus.*] · J. Northcote, oils, c.1801 (*Sir John Moore at the battle of Alexandria*), Scot. NPG · T. Lawrence, c.1804, NAM; repro. in Brownrigg, ed., *Life and letters of Sir John Moore*, frontispiece · A. Cardon, stipple, pubd 1809 (after A. J. Oliver), BM · C. Turner, mezzotint, pubd 1809 (after T. Lawrence), BM, NPG · C. Turner, mezzotint, pubd 1811 (after J. J. Halls), BM · J. Bacon jun., monument, St Paul's Cathedral, London · G. Hamilton, group portrait, oils, Toronto Art Gallery, Canada · J. Northcote, oils (fragment of the *Death of Abercromby*), Scot. NPG · J. Tischbein jun., soft-ground etching (as a boy), BM · statue, George Square, Glasgow

Moore, John Bramley- (1800–1886), dock administrator, was probably born at Pontefract, Yorkshire (some authorities say Leeds), the youngest son of Thomas Moore, but little else is known about his origins. He went to Brazil at an early age, possibly when he was only fourteen years old, and lived in Rio de Janeiro where he successfully learned the business of a merchant. In 1830 he married Seraphina Hibernia, daughter of William Pennell, the British consul-general for Brazil; they had two sons.

Moore returned to England in 1835, and established himself in Liverpool as a Brazilian merchant. He assumed the additional name of Bramley, and in 1841 he was elected an alderman by the borough council, not resigning until 1865. The council was the trustee body for Liverpool docks and rapidly appointed him to the dock

committee, to which most of the trustees' powers were delegated. In 1843 he was elected chairman, a meteoric rise which prompted some unfavourable comments. Immediately before his chairmanship, the 'reform party' had been following a policy of retrenchment in the docks, restraining the pace of new construction and resolving to close the dockyard (engineer's depot) in favour of putting work out to contract. Under Bramley-Moore, this policy was rapidly and dramatically reversed: expenditure almost quadrupled between 1841 and 1845. If Bramley-Moore, was fortunate in having the services of Jesse Hartley (1780–1860), the most accomplished and prolific dock engineer of his generation, Hartley benefited from working for a chairman whose ambitions for the port of Liverpool exceeded even his own.

Under Bramley-Moore, Liverpool dock committee was the largest and fastest-growing port authority in the country and he recognized that even greater expansion was possible and desirable, provided that new investment continued. To some contemporaries, the escalating corporate debt indicated not vision but recklessness. In 1843 he made a most unusual agreement with the earl of Derby which secured 2 miles of foreshore for dock extension. After the benefits became apparent, the fact that he had negotiated largely on his own initiative and in secret was eventually forgiven.

The Liverpool Dock Act of 1844 enabled the construction of the first five of the new docks to be built there. All were opened together on 4 August 1848: one was unprecedentedly named 'Bramley-Moore', which caused some hostile comments. That year he was elected mayor, albeit at the second attempt, and resigned from the dock committee. Such, however, were his achievements in just six years that he remained an honoured guest at functions of the Mersey Docks and Harbour Board (successor to the dock trustees) until 1885.

Bramley-Moore was a forceful character, sometimes antagonizing people by being arbitrary and dogmatic. His greatest admirers could not claim that he was an intellectual, but before several parliamentary select committees on local dock bills, he proved an effective witness, making his case clearly and conceding little to hostile cross-examination by counsel for the rival undertaking at Birkenhead. He had several subsidiary business interests: he was chairman of the Brazilian chamber of commerce, the Bank of Egypt, the General Credit Company, the Rio Improvements Company, as well as the Montevideo Gas Company. Bramley-Moore, in addition, served as deputy chairman of the North Staffordshire Railway and was a director of the London North Western Railway.

A committed tory, Bramley-Moore was heavily defeated as parliamentary candidate for Hull in 1852, and more heavily in Liverpool in 1853. He was MP for Maldon from 1854 to 1859, then represented Lincoln from 1862 to 1865. In 1863, his speech in parliament on Anglo-Brazilian relations so pleased the emperor of Brazil as to gain him the order of the Rose.

Nathaniel Hawthorne described Bramley-Moore as 'a

moderately bulky and rather round-shouldered man, with a kindly face enough' (Hawthorne, 56) but considered him an ungentlemanly parvenu. The story that he declined a knighthood in 1846 (*DNB*) certainly seems out of character. He retired from business about 1865, becoming only an occasional visitor to Liverpool. He died at 116 Marine Parade, Brighton on 19 November 1886, aged eighty-six, and was buried at St Michael's-in-the-Hamlet, Liverpool. He was predeceased by his wife, but was survived by his two sons, John Arthur Bramley-Moore, who continued his father's business, and the Revd William Bramley-Moore.　C. W. SUTTON, *rev.* ADRIAN JARVIS

Sources B. G. Orchard, *Liverpool's legion of honour* (1893) · *Liverpool Daily Post* (23 Nov 1886) · N. Ritchie-Noakes and M. Clarke, 'The dock engineers and the development of the port of Liverpool', *Liverpool shipping, trade and industry*, ed. V. Burton (1989), 91–108 · H. Shimmin, *Pen-and-ink sketches of Liverpool town councillors* (1866) · N. Hawthorne, *The English notebooks*, ed. R. Stewart (1941), 55–7 · *CGPLA Eng. & Wales* (1886)
Archives U. Lpool L., corresp. and papers | Merseyside Maritime Museum, Liverpool, Mersey Docks and Harbour Board collection
Likenesses E. Benson, oils, 1846, Walker Art Gallery, Liverpool · bust
Wealth at death £167,815 15*s.* 0*d.*: resworn probate, April 1887, *CGPLA Eng. & Wales* (1886)

Moore, John Collingham (1829–1880). *See under* Moore, William (1790–1851).

Moore, John Francis (*d.* 1809), sculptor, was a native of Hanover and arrived in England about 1760. Definitely from 1765, but probably earlier, he worked in Berners Street, London. He was a member of the Free Society of Artists, where he exhibited every year from 1766 to 1776 showing a variety of sculpture, including models in clay and works in marble, designs for monuments, bas-reliefs, among them some for chimney-pieces, animals, portrait busts, and statues—notably, in 1769, a statue of Apollo. In 1763 he made several chimney-pieces for Audley End, Essex, including one for the library with Doric columns, after a design by Robert Adam, for which in January 1764 he was paid £111 14*s.* 3*d.* (priv. coll., Ireland). In 1765 Moore was making chimney-pieces for Alderman William Beckford's house, Fonthill Splendens, in Wiltshire. The one for the music room is carved with two whole figures of piping fauns; another, for the saloon, was seen in Moore's studio in 1765 by a French visitor, P. T. Grosley, who described it thus: 'remarkable on account of its high finishing … All the most remarkable deaths in the Iliad were presented … intermixed with figures in basso-relievo representing the deaths of less consequence' (Grosley, 69; priv. coll.).

In 1766 Moore presented to the Society of Arts a marble bas-relief entitled *Britannia, reviver of Antique and Prompter to Modern Arts* (Progress House, Coventry). The next year he exhibited a full-length marble statue of his patron William Beckford, showing the latter when lord mayor of London, delivering a speech. The statue (at Ironmonger's Hall, London, since 1833) is well animated and among his best works. He also exhibited a number of portrait busts,

most of which are lost today. That of William Ponsonby, second earl of Bessborough, which is probably the 'bust of a Nobleman' exhibited at the Free Society in 1775 and at the Royal Academy in 1776, is now at Spencer House, London. For the Revd Thomas Wilson, the eccentric rector of St Stephen Walbrook, London, Moore made a statue of the bluestocking Mrs (Catharine) Macaulay in the character of *History*. It was unveiled in that church on 8 September 1777, but without the permission of the churchwardens, who very soon had it removed; its present whereabouts is unknown.

When Alderman Beckford died in 1770, the City of London held a public competition for a monument to be set up in Guildhall, for which they set aside £1000. There were seventeen competitors, including Agostino Carlini and Nathaniel Smith, but it seems that, through influence, Moore had already been chosen as sculptor. His monument, which had been estimated to cost £1300, shows Beckford at full length delivering the impromptu speech in May 1770 which confused and angered George III; below are figures representing Trade and Navigation. It is not an attractive work, and J. T. Smith called it 'a glaring specimen of marble spoiled' (Smith, 2.204). The monument was engraved by Grignion in 1771 and erected in 1772.

Moore made a number of church funeral monuments, ranging from simple tablets to elaborate architectural constructions. Among the great ones are those to Field Marshal Lord Ligonier (1773) at Westminster Abbey, London; Washington Shirley, second Earl Ferrers (1775) at Ettington, Warwickshire; and Admiral Lord Hawke (*d.* 1781) at North Stoneham, Hampshire. Generally, the figures on the monuments lack animation and the draperies are unconvincing, but the formal sculpture is well executed and Moore made good use of coloured marbles. Nineteen drawings by Moore for monuments were acquired in 1866 by the Victoria and Albert Museum, London. With their good draughtsmanship and clear bright colouring, they would doubtless have attracted patrons.

Three of Moore's sons are known by their exhibits at the Free Society of Artists between 1767 and 1775. James, probably the eldest, was a sculptor; Charles was a painter. The youngest, John, born in March 1758, was a painter and entered the Royal Academy Schools in December 1777, aged nineteen. Francis Moore, who won a silver palette at the Society of Arts in 1769 for a figure drawing, may have been another son. James Moore became assistant to his father, and together they signed the monument to Jonas Hanway (*d.* 1786) at Westminster Abbey. Evidently James died shortly afterwards, and Moore senior took as partner an unidentified J. Smith, whose signature is on some late monuments. Then of York Buildings, New Road, London, Moore died on 21 January 1809 at Wells Street, Oxford Street. In his will, dated 21 November 1805, he settled three houses, nos. 9, 28, and 29 Welbeck Street, London, and left an annuity of £520 to his wife, Barbara, and bequests to the wife of James and grandson Charles Moore, and to three married daughters.

JOHN KENWORTHY-BROWNE

Sources R. Gunnis, *Dictionary of British sculptors, 1660–1851* (1953); new edn (1968) · *Catalogues* of the summer exhibitions, Free Society of Artists, London, and Royal Academy, London (1766–77) · *GM*, 1st ser., 79 (1809), 94 · Redgrave, *Artists* · J. D. Williams, *Audley End: the restoration of 1762–1797* (1966) · P. T. Grosley, *A tour to London* (1772), vol. 2, pp. 68–9 · J. Harris, 'Fonthill, Wiltshire—I', *Country Life*, 140 (1966), 1373 · J. Hardy, 'Fonthill Splendens: an iconographical chimneypiece rediscovered', *Apollo*, 130 (July 1989), 40–42 · M. Trusted, 'Agostino Carlini, part II', *Burlington Magazine*, 135 (1993), 190–91 · R. Dossie, *Memorials of agriculture*, 2 (1782), 440 · F. G. White, *History of Walbrook Ward* (1904), 386–7 · restoration of the house, bills, etc., 1763–4, Essex RO, Southend, Audley End archives, D/D By, A248 · J. T. Smith, *Nollekens and his times*, 2 vols. (1828) · *European Magazine* (1809), 83 · will, PRO, PROB 11/1491, sig. 47

Archives Essex RO, Southend, Audley End archives, restoration of the house, bills, etc.

Moore, Sir John Henry, second baronet (1756–1780), poet, was born in Jamaica, the only son of Sir Henry *Moore, first baronet (1713–1769), colonial governor, and Catharine Maria (1727–1812), eldest daughter of Samuel Long of Longville, Jamaica, and sister of Edward *Long, author of the *History of Jamaica*. John succeeded to the baronetcy in 1769 while still at Eton College, before proceeding to Cambridge, where he graduated from Emmanuel College BA in 1773 and MA in 1776.

In 1777 Moore issued, anonymously, through John Almon, a volume of poems entitled *The New Paradise of Dainty Devices* (named after Richard Edwards's popular Elizabethan miscellany), which provoked a justifiable sneer from the *Critical Review* (43.232–3). It contains, however, some fair occasional verses. The best of these, including an early parody of Thomas Gray's famous *Elegy Written in a Country Churchyard* entitled 'Elegy Written in a College Library', together with a few new pieces, and an excruciating palinode deprecating the vigour of the reviewers John Langhorne and William Kenrick, and beseeching them to 'untwist their bowels of commiseration', were issued again in 1778 as *Poetical Trifles*. Some lines 'To Melancholy' evidently inspired Samuel Rogers's 'Go, you may call it madness, folly'. Moore frequently resided at Bath, where he wrote verses for Lady Miller's coterie and took part in the other harmless fooleries of the group. He died unmarried at Taplow on 16 January 1780, when the baronetcy became extinct. A third edition of his *Trifles* appeared posthumously in 1783, edited by his friend Edward Jerningham. His poems appear between those of Francis Hoyland and Henry Headley in volume 73 of *The British Poets* (1822), and in similar company in volume 35 of Thomas Park's *British Poets* (1808).

THOMAS SECCOMBE, *rev.* DAVID KALOUSTIAN

Sources R. A. Davenport, 'The life of Sir John Henry Moore', *The British poets*, 73 (1822), 37–9 · S. Halkett and J. Laing, *Dictionary of anonymous and pseudonymous English literature*, ed. J. Kennedy and others, new edn, 4 (1928) · *The poetical works of Sir John Henry Moore*, ed. T. Park (1808) · Nichols, *Lit. anecdotes*, 8.433–4 · *Critical Review*, 43, 232–3 · J. Burke and J. B. Burke, *A genealogical and heraldic history of the extinct and dormant baronetcies of England, Ireland and Scotland*, 2nd edn (1841); repr. (1844) · [E. Brydges], *Censura literaria*, 7 (1808)

Likenesses P. Condé, stipple (after R. Cosway), BM, NPG

Moore, Sir Jonas (1617–1679), mathematician and patron of astronomy, was born on 8 February 1617 at White Lee

Sir Jonas Moore (1617–1679), by Thomas Cross, pubd 1650 (after Henry Stone)

(now Higher Whitelee Farm) near the village of Higham in Pendle Forest, Lancashire, the second (or second surviving) son of Hugh Moore (d. 1649) and his wife, Mary Aspinall (d. 1623). Both the Moore and Aspinall families included some minor gentry, but Hugh Moore seems to have had the status of a prosperous yeoman. Three years after Mary Moore died Hugh married Frances (née Whitaker), the widow of William Starkie, second son of Edmund Starkie of Huntroyd.

It is probable that Moore went to a local grammar school. He appears not to have attended a university, but furthered his education by reading mathematical books, assisted and encouraged by friends, especially members of the Presbyterian (and later parliamentarian) Shuttleworth family of nearby Gawthorpe Hall. He later said that the inventor William Gascoigne, of Middleton, near Leeds, had given him 'good information in mathematicall knowledge' (*Brief Lives*, 2.80), and that he had used the library of the antiquarian Christopher Towneley of Carr Hall, but there is no evidence that he was in contact with them, or with other members of the Towneley family, before the 1640s.

On 24 November 1637 Moore was appointed clerk to Thomas Burwell, who, as spiritual chancellor and vicar-general, presided over the ecclesiastical courts of the diocese of Durham. The post proved short-lived, as the courts ceased to function when the region was invaded by the Scots in August 1640, and formally ceased to exist in October 1642. A signature on the Durham Protestation of February 1642 shows that Moore was then still in the city, but he probably left before the end of that year. His whereabouts during the civil war period are unknown, though it appears that he initially sent his family back to Lancashire. On 8 April 1638 at St Giles, Durham, Moore married Helenora (probably Eleanor, baptized on 2 October 1604), the daughter of Ralph Wren of Durham, a relation of the wealthy and locally influential Wrens of Binchester. The Moores' elder daughter, Mary, was baptized at St Mary-le-Bow, Durham, on 24 March 1639, and the younger, Helen or Ellen, at Padiham, Lancashire, on 1 January 1641. A son, Jonas, was the youngest of the three children; the date and place of his birth and baptism are unknown, as are the date and place of Eleanor's death and burial, though there is evidence that she predeceased her husband.

During the time of the Scots invasion Moore furthered his mathematical studies by visiting William Milburne at Brancepeth. He then found the subject a useful resource when he needed a livelihood, and established himself as a teacher with the aid of the figurehead of English mathematics, William Oughtred, settling in London by the late 1640s. In the 1647 *Key of the Mathematics*, the first English edition of Oughtred's famous *Clavis*, an authorial preface pays glowing tribute to Moore and Thomas Wharton for the 'exceeding great paines and expense', they had bestowed in correcting and proof-reading the volume. In the same year, when the royal children were in the custody of parliament, Moore briefly held the post of tutor in 'Arithmetick, uses of the Globes, and Geography' to James, duke of York; the several dedications to his 1650 *Arithmetick* show that he had other well-connected pupils. Its preface was dated from the house of Elias Allen, a leading instrument maker and close friend of Oughtred.

Moore later attributed his rise in the world to his work as surveyor to the fifth earl of Bedford's fen drainage company. He was first mentioned in the company's minutes, and perhaps briefly employed, in June 1649; on 26 August 1650 his appointment as surveyor from 2 September following was confirmed. He went on to serve for four years at £200 per annum and for at least one more at £100. He was probably peripatetic at first, but in February 1652 brought his family to live in the fens, at March, Cambridgeshire; in 1653 they moved to Southery, on the fenland edge of Norfolk. The surveyor's duties were 'to sett out the works and see that they bee done' (Bedford Level Corporation records, R 59.31.9.3, fol. 31*r*), to measure land for compensation and completed work so that it could be paid for, to help resolve legal disputes, and to convince the commissioners appointed to judge the project's success.

Moore was thus much more closely involved in day-to-day management of the work than was the nominal director, Sir Cornelius Vermuyden; recent research has indicated that he and not Vermuyden was responsible for commissioning the massive sluice at Denver in 1655. He

also eventually produced the general map that the company had requested from the start. A single-sheet version (*c*.1654) appeared in a variant form in William Dugdale's *History of Embanking and Drayning* (1662), and provided the basis for a two-sheet map (1685). In late 1657 or early 1658 Moore published a huge sixteen-sheet *Mapp of the Great Levell* of the fens, displaying the coats of arms of Cromwellian drainage investors (the sole known copy is in the Public Record Office: MPC 88). This map's large scale and claims to mathematical accuracy earn it a unique place in English cartographical history. A new edition lacking arms was issued by Moses Pitt (1684) and later reprinted (*c*.1706).

Moore marked his return to London by publishing *Resolutio Triplex* (1658), an answer to a French geometrical challenge, followed by a pamphlet, *Short Introduction into the Art of Species* [algebra] (1660), and a revised edition of his *Arithmetick* (1660). As this last appeared after the Restoration, Moore used it to claim royalist credentials (not altogether convincingly); the duke of York was the principal dedicatee. The author's address was advertised as in Stanhope Street, on the fashionable western side of London; he went on to occupy a succession of nearby houses in Blackamore Street, Drury Lane, and Kings Head Court. For the next few years he derived his income from teaching and from a variety of short-term projects, such as surveying the manor of Woburn (1661) and mapping the Thames for the Navy Board (1662). In 1663 he joined an expedition to the new English possession of Tangier to help plan a fortified harbour wall, known as 'the Mole'; on his *Mapp of the Citty of Tanger* [1664] he is termed surveyor to the duke of York.

On 19 June 1665, during the Second Dutch War (1665–7), Moore was appointed temporary assistant surveyor of the royal ordnance. He succeeded to the permanent post of surveyor general on 28 July 1669 and held it until his death ten years later. The surveyor was one of the principal officers of the Board of Ordnance, with particular responsibility for incoming stores and fortifications, duties which were burdensome only in wartime; Moore undertook them himself rather than appointing a deputy. From 1665 he lived near the Tower of London and from 1669 in an official house in its grounds. The Third Dutch War (1672–4) placed heavy demands upon the office; meeting them helped earn Moore his knighthood, conferred on 28 January 1673, and the reversion of the surveyorship for his son.

During the war Moore published *Modern Fortification* (1673). *A General Treatise of Artillery* (1673), translated from the Italian, is sometimes attributed to him but was in fact produced by his son. Then he reverted to more general mathematical concerns: his notes were edited by his Ordnance second clerk, Nicholas Stephenson, to form a pocket-book, *Mathematical Compendium* (1674). Stephenson was also deputed by Moore to compile the *Royal Almanack* (annually, 1674–8), a strictly non-astrological almanac containing astronomical tables by John Flamsteed, tide-tables, and other practical information.

Moore first met Flamsteed in 1670, through their

mutual acquaintance John Collins. They corresponded occasionally after Flamsteed's return to Derby, and from March 1674 more frequently, with Moore offering 'to assist yow with eyther Bookes or Instrumentes' (Royal Greenwich Observatory archives, RGO 1/37, fol. 73*r*) and financially; most of these letters survive among Flamsteed's papers. By the autumn of 1674 Moore was planning to provide Flamsteed with a permanent income, perhaps by 'moveing his Majesty for a yearly Annuity' (ibid., fol. 78*r*). In the meantime he considered establishing an observatory at Chelsea College, which belonged to the Royal Society; this proved impractical, but the society's interest in the project led to Moore's election as a fellow on 3 December 1674. In February 1675 a committee appointed by the king to assess a proposed astronomical means of finding longitude at sea co-opted Flamsteed as an adviser; its members accepted his claims about the inadequacy of all existing data, and, in Flamsteed's words, 'readily joined with Sir Jonas Moore to move the King that an Observatory might be built ... and myself to be employed in it ... which his Majesty was graciously pleased to grant' (Baily, 125–6). The warrant was signed on 4 March 1675, and the building of an observatory at Greenwich was authorized in the following June.

The leading role Moore played in the foundation, constructing, and equipping of the observatory was acknowledged in an inscription placed near its door, and in a plate accompanying views of the park, buildings, and instruments, commissioned by Moore from the draughtsman Robert Thacker and engraver Francis Place (*c.*1676). The observatory's key instruments—a large sextant, a 7 foot mural quadrant designed by Robert Hooke, and two sophisticated clocks by Thomas Tompion—were paid for by Moore personally, at a cost of several hundred pounds. In return he exercised considerable influence over the institution's work, and continued to intervene in its affairs until his death; his attempts to make Flamsteed publish results caused much friction between them.

During the same period Moore was also involved with the management of the Royal Mathematical School at Christ's Hospital, having been made a governor of the hospital in December 1676. He began to compile a textbook for the school's use, writing parts himself and incorporating contributions by Flamsteed, Halley (another of his protégés), and the school's master, Peter Perkins. Moore's sons-in-law, William Hanway and John Pottenger, saw the work completed and posthumously published, in lavish style, as *A New Systeme of the Mathematicks* (2 vols., 1681).

Moore's death was described by an Ordnance colleague's wife as follows:

> Joaney Moore had but three fitts of a fever, and the fourth carried him away; he died ... coming from that rotten place Portsmouth, whither he was very unwilling to goe, but nothing would satisfy the imperious Governor but he must come. (Lady Newton, 80)

He died at Godalming, Surrey, during the night of 26–7 August 1679; on 2 September his body was buried in the Tower chapel of St Peter ad Vincula, where a monument was later set up by his elder daughter. Since he had made no will, a legal battle between his son and daughters followed; two extensive probate inventories of his goods and funeral expenses survive (PRO PROB 4/18757 and 5/4229). Jonas Moore junior succeeded to the surveyorship but died in 1682; his father's outstanding mathematical library was sold at auction in 1684. An anonymous verse eulogy *To the Memory of my most Honoured Friend Sir Jonas Moore* was published soon after the elder Moore's death. Another tribute came from his friend John Aubrey, whose brief life terms him 'a good mathematician and a good fellow'. Aubrey noted details not recorded elsewhere, and described his appearance later in life as 'tall and very fat, [with] thin skin, faire, clear grey eie'.

FRANCES WILLMOTH

Sources F. H. Willmoth, *Sir Jonas Moore: practical mathematics and Restoration science* (1993) [incl. bibliography] · F. Baily, *An account of the Revd John Flamsteed, the first astronomer-royal* (1835); repr. (1966) · *The correspondence of John Flamsteed, the first astronomer royal*, ed. E. G. Forbes and others, 1 (1995) · *The preface to John Flamsteed's Historia coelestis Britannica, or, British catalogue of the heavens*, ed. A. Chapman, trans. A. D. Johnson (1982) · *The diary of Robert Hooke ... 1672–1680*, ed. H. W. Robinson and W. Adams (1935) · *Brief lives, chiefly of contemporaries, set down by John Aubrey, between the years 1669 and 1696*, ed. A. Clark, 2 (1898), 79–81 · Lady Newton, *Lyme letters* (1925), 80 · Cambs. AS, Cambridge, Bedford Level Corporation records, R 59.31 · CUL, Royal Greenwich Observatory papers, RGO 1/36; 1/37
Archives Cambs. AS, Bedford Level corporation records · CUL, Royal Greenwich Observatory archives, Flamsteed MSS
Likenesses T. Cross, line engraving (after H. Stone), BM, NPG, V&A; repro. in J. Moore, *Moore's arithmetick* (1650), frontispiece [see illus.] · line engraving, BM; repro. in J. Moore, *Moor's arithmetick* (1660), frontispiece
Wealth at death over £4750—incl. revenue from sale of library: inventories, PRO, PROB 4/18757; PRO, PROB 5/4229

Moore, Jonas (*d.* 1741), military engineer, was possibly related to the mathematician Sir Jonas Moore FRS (1617–1679) and his son, Sir Jonas Moore (*d.* 1682), both of whom served as surveyor-general of the ordnance, though the name is common in this period.

Moore became a probationer engineer in October 1709. On 1 January 1711 he was appointed sub-engineer at Gibraltar and attached to David Colyear, first earl of Portmore, the governor, for special service. He then served in Minorca before returning to Gibraltar in August 1720. On 18 November he was appointed chief engineer and commander-in-chief of the artillery at Gibraltar; on 1 October 1722 he became sub-director of engineers. He was chief engineer at Gibraltar during the siege which lasted from 11 February to 23 June 1727. Moore minimized British losses by building resilient cover from brushwood obtained on a visit to Morocco. On 19 March 1728 he was given the local rank of director of engineers.

Moore remained at Gibraltar until 1740, many of his plans for the fortifications still surviving. The regard in which Moore was held was shown by the issue of a dormant commission from John, second duke of Montagu, master-general of the ordnance, dated 24 July 1740, placing him at the head of the Royal Artillery should the two senior officers of the corps die. In October he was appointed chief engineer of the expedition to South America under Admiral Sir Chaloner Ogle and General Lord

Cathcart. Moore took part in the attack on Cartagena, which began on 9 March 1741, and made a breach in Fort St Louis which defended the harbour mouth, but he was hit by a shell fragment on 22 March and died on the following day. He was unmarried and administration (of Lambeth, Surrey) was granted to his next of kin, an unmarried sister, Anna Marie Moore.   STUART HANDLEY

Sources T. W. J. Connolly, *Roll of officers of the corps of royal engineers from 1660 to 1898*, ed. R. F. Edwards (1898), 2–3 · W. Porter, *History of the corps of royal engineers*, 1 (1889), 70–71, 151 · R. Harding, *Amphibious warfare in the eighteenth century: the British expedition to the West Indies, 1740–1742*, Royal Historical Society Studies in History, 62 (1991), 63, 102–5 · administration, PRO, PROB 6/118, fol. 148r · R. Beatson, *Naval and military memoirs of Great Britain*, 2nd edn, 1 (1804), 94 · *DNB*

Moore, Joseph (1766–1851), benefactor and impresario, was born at Shelsley Beauchamp or Shelsley Walsh, Worcestershire. Details of his parentage and exact date of birth are not known, but he was educated in Worcester. In 1781 he was sent to Birmingham to learn die-sinking, and afterwards entered into a partnership in the button trade. On acquiring an independent position he devoted his leisure to works of charity. In conjunction with Thomas Hawkes and others he founded a dispensary in the building of Christ Church for the sick poor. He came to know Matthew Boulton of the Soho works, who introduced him to James Watt. At Boulton's instigation Moore formed a society for the performance of private concerts, the first of which took place in February 1799 at the Royal Hotel in Birmingham. These became known as the Royal Hotel Concerts and, being well patronized, became an index of high-class musical taste in the city. However, with the increasing repertory of more challenging music and the growing number of professional musicians (who replaced the decreasing number of amateurs), the cost of these concerts increased. To meet the growing financial burden, recommendations were made by Moore to the proprietors of the hotel to enlarge the room, but, after objections, these were abandoned. The concerts lingered on until 1844, when they ceased. The popularity of the Royal Hotel Concerts encouraged the Birmingham Festival (which was sponsored by the general hospital) to boost its profits and audiences. In 1799 the festival committee engaged Moore to select the music and direct the festivals. That year profit to the general hospital grew from £897 (taken at the 1796 festival) to £1470. By 1823 the profit had risen to £5806. In recognition of his services to the hospital Moore was presented, on 6 April 1812, with a service of plate, and his portrait by Wyatt was also purchased for the hospital.

Under Moore's direction the Birmingham Triennial Festival became increasingly ambitious. To enhance the standard of local singers engaged for the festivals he founded the Birmingham Oratorio Choral Society in 1808. Handel oratorios remained the staple diet of the programme, but other works, such as Beethoven's *Christus am Ölberge* and Mozart's *Requiem*, were given in 1817 and 1820 respectively. Moore was also able to secure the services of conductors such as William Crotch (1808), Samuel Wesley (1811), Thomas Greatorex (1820), William Knyvett (1834–

43), Mendelssohn (1837, 1840, and 1846), Moscheles (1846), and Michael Costa (1849).

The success of the initial festivals under Moore's management encouraged other centres, such as York, and Malvern's Three Choirs festival to expand their own operations. Indeed, during the 1820s York enjoyed the position of holding the largest festival of its kind in the country, while further expansion in Birmingham was prevented by the lack of a sufficiently capacious building, sacred oratorios being performed at St Philip's Church and secular music at the King's Street Theatre. In 1832 Moore began actively to agitate for the erection of a new town hall and, through public subscription, for the construction of an organ. Both were used for the first time at the 1834 festival, which was cast on a grand scale with a chorus of 184, a semi-chorus of 34, 19 soloists, and an orchestra of 147.

In order to gather information for the building of the town hall and the organ, Moore visited Holland and Germany. While in Berlin, where he had gone to hear the city's Sing-Academie, he befriended Mendelssohn and induced him to conduct his oratorio *St Paul* at the 1837 festival. Mendelssohn visited Birmingham again in 1840 to conduct the first English performance of *Lobgesang*, but Moore's greatest *coup* was the commission of *Elijah*, which received its first performance under the composer's direction on 26 August 1846. The net profits arising from the festivals while under Moore's management (1802–49) amounted to £51,756.

Moore died at his house, Crescent, 10 Cambridge Street, Lady Wood, Birmingham, on 19 April 1851, and was buried in the Church of England cemetery there. A monument was erected to his memory by subscription.

GORDON GOODWIN, *rev.* JEREMY DIBBLE

Sources G. Hogarth, 'The late Joseph Moore: his public-spirited labours for the advantage of Birmingham', *Birmingham festival of 1855*; repr. in *Aris's Birmingham Gazette* (1855), 7–9 · N. Temperley, 'Birmingham', *New Grove* · C. Mackeson, 'Birmingham Festival', *Grove, Dict. mus.* · d. cert.
Archives Birm. CA, corresp. relating to Birmingham Triennial Music Festival
Likenesses Wyatt, portrait, *c*.1812; purchased for the Birmingham General Hospital

Moore, Joseph (1817–1892), medallist and die-sinker, was born at Eastbourne, Sussex, on 17 February 1817, the son of Edwin Moore, a builder of hothouses, who temporarily left his business during the Peninsular War (1807–14) and in a fit of enthusiasm joined the 10th hussars, with which he saw active service. A few weeks after Joseph Moore's birth his parents moved to Birmingham, where he continued to live all his life. On 27 August 1839 he married Mary Ann Hodgkins at Aston.

Moore showed an early aptitude for drawing, and was apprenticed to Thomas Halliday, die-sinker, of Newhall Street, Birmingham. He also attended the drawing classes of Samuel Lines of Temple Row, Birmingham. For many years Moore was engaged in the production of dies for commercial uses, mainly for buttons. In 1844 he entered into partnership with John Allen, a fellow apprentice. The partners traded as Allen and Moore in Great Hampton Row, Birmingham, and manufactured articles of papier mâché, and also metal vases, cups, and boxes. These metal wares, produced on machines invented by Allen, incorporated coloured patterns in low relief which were chiefly designed by Moore. A selection of their products were shown at the Great Exhibition of 1851, and they were awarded a prize medal for their metal buttons. Partly owing to changing fashions the business folded, and Moore, having lost all he had, began trading again by himself in 1856 as a die-sinker, first in Summer Lane and afterwards, and until his death, in Pitsford Street, Birmingham.

Moore's first medal, produced in 1846, was a large piece, nearly 4 inches in diameter, bearing the *Salvator mundi* of Leonardo da Vinci as the obverse, and the *Christus consolator* of Ary Scheffer as the reverse. Only a few copies of this medal, which was highly praised by Scheffer, were produced. From this time Moore had a large number of commissions for die-sinking and designing, and executed numerous prize and commemorative medals. Many of these, made for English and colonial trading firms, do not bear Moore's name. He employed his son, Joseph Edwin Moore, and other assistants in his business, but the best of his works were cut by his own hand. A selection of his medals was presented by Moore to the Corporation Art Gallery of Birmingham.

Moore had the reputation of being an honourable and kind-hearted man, fond of music and art, and intensely devoted to his work. He was a founder member and the first president of the Midland Art Club. In March 1892 he fell ill, and died on 7 September 1892 in his house at 13 Pitsford Street, Birmingham, which adjoined his workshops. He was buried at Key Hill cemetery, Birmingham. The Joseph Edwin Moore, die-sinker, named on his probate record as executor, was probably his son.

W. W. WROTH, *rev.* CHRISTOPHER MARSDEN

Sources Birmingham Weekly Post (10 Sept 1892) · The Times (9 Sept 1892) · private information (1894) · L. Forrer, ed., Biographical dictionary of medallists, 1 (1902), 17–19; 4 (1909), 136–41; 8 (1930), 74 · L. Brown, A catalogue of British historical medals, 1760–1960, 2 (1987) · Boase, Mod. Eng. biog., 2.951 · Exhibition of the works of industry of all nations 1851: reports by the juries on the subjects of the thirty classes into which the exhibition was divided (1852), 503 · CGPLA Eng. & Wales (1892)
Likenesses W. T. Roden, oils, Birmingham Museums and Art Gallery · photograph, repro. in Forrer, Biographical dictionary of medallists, 4.137
Wealth at death £10,810 15s. 11d.: probate, 3 Nov 1892, CGPLA Eng. & Wales

Moore, Mary Charlotte [*married name* Mary Charlotte Wyndham, Lady Wyndham] (**1861–1931**), actress and theatre manager, was born in Islington, London, on 3 July 1861, the fifth child and third and youngest daughter of Charles Moore of Dublin and his wife, Haidée Sophie Acland. When Mary was born her father was a prosperous parliamentary agent, but financial ruin hit the family in 1873. Mary, aged twelve, had to collect rents from slum

Mary Charlotte Moore (1861–1931), by Barraud, pubd 1889

houses in Hoxton, an experience which taught her the value of money (and, incidentally, gave her a reputation in later life for stinginess). Her education was interrupted by lack of money though she did attend Warwick Hall, Maida Vale, when a German couple needed someone to accompany their daughter to the school. She learned a little German, which would be useful during her career.

Although untrained, Mary Moore could sing and at fifteen she joined the chorus of *The Bohemian Girl* and *Little Doctor Faust* (by H. J. Byron) at the Gaiety Theatre. On 12 June 1878, aged sixteen, she married the dramatist James *Albery (1838–1889); they lived for a time in his bachelor chambers in Southampton Street off the Strand. Three sons were born and they moved to Fairlawn, Stone, Greenhithe, Kent. They subsequently returned to London, taking 11 Bentinck Terrace facing Regent's Park. This was not a wise move, being close to the temptations of the West End which Albery was unable to resist. For the second time in her life Mary experienced a collapse in family fortunes; by the mid-1880s James Albery, owing to ill health and alcoholism, could no longer write, so Mary had to support him and the children. She had known Charles (later Sir Charles) *Wyndham (1837–1919) when he commissioned Albery to adapt *Dominos roses* and other French plays, so she nervously approached him for work. He was so shocked by her changed appearance that he doubted whether he could engage her. When he did it was as an understudy on tour. Mary quickly realized that he did not intend to do more than this (out of kindness) and pay her £4 a week. She told him she must be allowed to appear if her career was to progress. Wyndham gave her two small parts in farces at the Criterion Theatre and when he saw what she could do he gave her the leading part of Lady Amaranth in John O'Keeffe's *Wild Oats*, in which he played Jack Rover. When he followed this with a revival in November 1886 of T. W. Robertson's *David Garrick*, with Mary as Ada Ingot, their stage partnership was established. With this encouragement her good looks returned and she retained her slim figure for many years. They played *David Garrick* at Sandringham and were invited to take it to Berlin, where they played in German. Wyndham was fluent in the language but Mary had to study. One German critic commented: 'Miss Moore does not speak our language as well as her talented companion, but with what a consoling charm!' (Moore, 60). They also played—in German—before the tsar in St Petersburg. *David Garrick* would be their most enduring production.

The Alberys separated four years before James's death from cirrhosis of the liver in 1889. When an obituarist accused Mary of neglecting him, she was tempted to sue, but received a written apology.

Recognizing that Mary Moore had a superior head for business, Wyndham sealed their business partnership in 1896 and together they planned to enlarge their empire by building two theatres on land occupied by old houses between Charing Cross Road and St Martin's Lane. The marquess of Salisbury, then prime minister, was the ground landlord, and stated that no theatres should be built there unless they were for Charles Wyndham, whose acting he admired; Wyndham's Theatre opened in 1899 and the New Theatre in 1903.

Mary Moore was a woman of good sense who excelled at playing the opposite—the sillier the woman the better, and such parts were written for her by Henry Arthur Jones in *The Case of Rebellious Susan* (1894), *The Liars* (1897), and *Mrs Dane's Defence* (1900), and by Hubert Henry Davies in *Mrs Gorringe's Necklace* (1903) and *The Mollusc* (1907), in which she gave a remarkable performance, seldom moving from the sofa on which she reclined. As Irene Vanbrugh, who appeared with her in *The Liars*, said of her: she 'still held without effort after a number of years the title of the perfect *ingénue*' (I. Vanbrugh, *To Tell my Story*, 1949, 38).

The acting partnership continued until 1913; Wyndham also preserved a youthful spirit and figure until failing memory compelled his retirement at the age of seventy-six. Mary acted little without him. On 1 March 1916, after the death of Wyndham's wife, she married her business partner in order to be able to take care of him. After Wyndham's death in 1919 she made one successful appearance in a new play and then devoted herself to managing her theatres (she founded Wyndham Theatres Ltd in 1924) with the assistance of her stepson, Howard Wyndham, and her son, Bronson *Albery. When no one attempted to write a biography of Wyndham she wrote her own memoirs, *Charles Wyndham and Mary Moore* (1925), which her family insisted should be privately printed as they feared the prejudice against a mistress. In her last years she suffered a disfiguring illness and died in London on 6 April 1931.   WENDY TREWIN

Sources W. Trewin, *All on stage: Charles Wyndham and the Alberys* (1980) · Lady Wyndham [M. Moore], *Charles Wyndham and Mary Moore* (privately printed, Edinburgh, 1925) · *DNB* · J. Parker, ed., *Who's who in the theatre*, 6th edn (1930) · *CGPLA Eng. & Wales* (1931)
Likenesses S. P. Hall, pencil drawings, 1887, NPG · Barraud, photographs, c.1889, NPG [*see illus.*] · A. Ellis, cabinet photograph, c.1895, NPG · A. Ellis, photograph, 1895, NPG · M. Beerbohm, caricature, V&A · H. van Dusen & Hassall, lithograph, NPG · Ellis & Walery, photograph, NPG
Wealth at death £161,686 8s. 8d.: resworn probate, 5 May 1931, *CGPLA Eng. & Wales*

Moore, Mary Elizabeth Constance (1860–1933), headmistress and writer on Natal, was born on 7 February 1860 in Middleham, Yorkshire, one of three children of William George Moore, a solicitor's clerk, and his wife, Mary Ann Smith Holdich. Little is known of her family and early life but she attended Newnham College, Cambridge, and taught at St Mary's School, Paddington, London. On 19 September 1890 she sailed for Natal, to teach at St Anne's Diocesan College in Pietermaritzburg. She was made headmistress in 1898 and in 1904 she played a major part in relocating the school to its permanent site at Hilton, Natal. She left St Anne's in 1905 to found her own girls' school in Pietermaritzburg, which she named Wykeham. After a notable career as its headmistress she retired in 1919, and in 1926 she settled in Greytown, Natal, where she was joined by her only sister, Florence Maud Gurden Moore.

Moore's manuscript letters and diaries from Natal to her mother and sister in Lincoln, England—of which those from September 1890 to December 1892 and from July 1897 to June 1902 survive—constitute a valuable holding of the Killie Campbell Library in Durban. They are rich in detail and opinion on social and cultural matters, Zulu custom, racial dynamics, education, the church, the military, travel, nature, fauna, flora, people, prejudices, and gossip in Natal life. An intrepid walker and astute observer, Moore described and often illustrated her forays with friends into the remote areas of the colony. A mark of this adventurous spirit was her month-long tour of the Second South African War battlefields in northern Natal in July 1900.

Of particular interest are her observations throughout the Second South African War (1899–1902) as a British civilian woman running a school in wartime. Added to this is her almost obsessive interest in the detail of warfare itself and her lengthy descriptions of battles. She commented on strategy and tactics, made judgements on generals and soldiers, and often expressed the wish to participate actively in the war, lamenting that women were not yet allowed to fight. She nevertheless accepted the female role, working tirelessly for the troops, hosting nurses and refugees at St Anne's, and visiting the wounded at Fort Napier, the nearby imperial regimental headquarters. Her sense of gendered conflict emerges in her letter of 29 October 1899, when after a day of sewing at St Anne's she remarked, 'I stuck to the machine as I should like to stick to a Gatling or a Maxim, mowing them all down before me' (Vietzen, 9).

Moore was a conventional Victorian woman, fiercely pro-British, certainly imperialist, unequivocally high-church Anglican, and of establishment leanings, who found her friends within the old Natal family network that controlled the government, the law, the military, and the private schools. Yet in various ways this petite, fair-haired, blue-eyed, lively, humorous, sociable, and intelligent woman seriously challenged the passive, non-combatant Victorian female stereotype. She died, unmarried, on 2 March 1933 at her home, Resthaven, Durban Street, Greytown, and was buried the following day in Greytown cemetery. A memorial plaque in St George's Anglican Church commemorates her pioneering work in Pietermaritzburg.   SYLVIA VIETZEN

Sources M. Moore, correspondence, Killie Campbell Library, Durban, KCM 93/2 · Wykeham Collegiate Archives, Pietermaritzburg, South Africa, Wykeham School papers · *Natal Witness* (11 March 1933) · private information (2004) · d. cert., Natal Archives Repository, Pietermaritzburg · will, Natal Archives Repository, Pietermaritzburg · C. Midgley, ed., *Gender and imperialism* (1998) · N. Chaudhuri and M. Strobel, eds., *Western women and imperialism: complicity and resistance* (1992) · M. Cooke, *Women and the war story* (1996) · S. Vietzen, 'Mary Moore writes of war', *Natalia*, 29 (1999), 6–15 · b. cert.
Archives University of Natal, Durban, Killie Campbell Africana Library, corresp., KCM 93/2 | St Anne's College, Hilton, Kwa Zulu-Natal, South Africa, photographs · Wykeham Collegiate Archives, Pietermaritzburg, South Africa, Wykeham School papers
Likenesses attrib. J. Pope-Ellis, oils, 1960–69 (after photograph), Wykeham Collegiate Archives, Pietermaritzburg
Wealth at death £12,384

Moore, Sir Norman, first baronet (1847–1922), physician and Irish scholar, was born at Higher Broughton, Manchester, on 8 January 1847, the only child of Robert Ross Rowan *Moore (1811–1864), barrister and political economist, of Kilmainham, Dublin, and his wife, Rebecca (1819–1905), daughter of Benjamin Clarke Fisher, a Quaker of Lifford, co. Tipperary. Robert Moore, a campaigner with Cobden and Bright against slavery and the corn laws, left his wife before his son's birth. Moore was brought up by his mother, supported by her circle of Manchester Liberal nonconformist friends. She ran a Froebel kindergarten until her retirement in 1877.

Moore left Chorlton high school at fourteen to work in a cotton mill, then attended Owens College, 1862–5, to study for London matriculation. From both choice and necessity he explored much of northern England and Ireland on foot. A Manchester friend recalled him 'leaving my house at midnight, a hawk on my wrist, to walk the 50 miles to Lancaster' (*Manchester Guardian*, 16 Dec 1922). At fourteen Moore undertook his first long walking tour in Ireland, a country for whose people, history, and language he had an intense attachment, perhaps to replace the father he admired but never met. He spoke Irish fluently, having learned the rudiments in childhood from an Irish shoemaker in Manchester, and achieved an international reputation as an Irish scholar and historian. In 1863 Moore visited Walton Hall, Wakefield, to see the natural history collection of the explorer Charles Waterton, author of

Wanderings in South America (1825). A friendship ensued which influenced the boy profoundly. Waterton regarded him as a second son, and Moore was with him when he died in 1865.

From 1865 to 1868 Moore read natural science at St Catharine's College, Cambridge, where he formed lifelong friendships with Charles Darwin's son Francis, and the Revd Whitwell Elwin, rector of Booton, Norfolk, among others. A former editor of the *Quarterly Review*, Elwin gave Moore valuable introductions to the literary world, including the publishers John Murray, father and son, Leslie Stephen, and W. J. Craig, the Shakespearian scholar. Moore's natural history interest was encouraged by the zoologist Professor Alfred Newton, the anti-Darwinian Professor Richard Owen, and by Charles Darwin. Having gained an eight-year residential scholarship at St Catharine's, Moore was invited by George Murray Humphry, the anatomy professor, to help establish the Cambridge school of science. However, the master, the Revd C. K. Robinson (notorious for having voted himself into office), unjustly rusticated Moore after a minor scuffle in hall. Elwin initiated a vigorous pamphlet war and Moore was allowed to sit the tripos, but lost his scholarship. In 1869 he enrolled at St Bartholomew's Hospital, London, to study comparative anatomy. A year later he wrote to Elwin's son 'The sages have decided I am to give up science and stick to medicine'. In 1909 St Catharine's made him an honorary fellow.

Moore obtained his MD in 1876. His thesis, *The Causes and Treatment of Rickets*, noted the value of cod-liver oil, foreshadowing the discovery of vitamins. At St Bartholomew's he was warden of the college from 1873 to 1891, lecturer in anatomy, pathology, and medicine, and physician to the hospital in 1902. He was elected fellow of the Royal College of Physicians in 1877. He visited Ireland annually, increasing his already extensive knowledge of its language and history. He corresponded with Owen on bone cancer in deer, with Francis Darwin on electrical impulses in plants, with Standish Hayes O'Grady on ancient Irish texts, and learned palaeography from Henry Bradshaw, Cambridge University librarian. He published a life of Waterton in a new edition of his *Essays in Natural History* (1871); *The Loss of the Crown of Loegaire Lurc*, a translation from the Book of Leinster (1881); and in 1882 a translation from the German of Windisch's *Concise Irish Grammar*. In 1876 Leslie Stephen asked Moore to contribute to a new project, a dictionary of national biography, for which Moore wrote 459 lives. Field Marshal Sir Evelyn Wood VC, another lifelong friend (and patient), fostered his interest in military history. Moore's son recorded that 'next to native Irish speakers & well-read old ladies, he most enjoyed meeting & listening to military men of mark'.

One of Rebecca Moore's friends was Barbara Leigh Smith Bodichon, cousin of Florence Nightingale, a founder of Girton College, and campaigner for women's rights. She introduced Moore to artists and writers: H. B. Brabazon, William de Morgan, the Rossettis, Helen and William Allingham, George Eliot, and Mme Belloc and her children, Hilaire and Marie. In 1876 Moore proposed to

Barbara Bodichon's seventeen-year-old niece Amy Leigh Smith (1859–1901), who accepted. Her parents objected, forbidding all communication. When they eventually relented Norman and Amy were married by Elwin at Westfield, Sussex, on 30 March 1880. They lived in the Warden's House, Little Britain, West Smithfield, until 1891, then at 94 Gloucester Place, west London. They had two sons, Alan Hilary (1882–1959) and Gillachrist (1894–1914), who was killed in the first battle of Ypres, and a daughter, Ethne Philippa (1885–1968). Moore was a skilled pathologist, diagnostician, and teacher. His casebooks show that he complemented physical examination with conversation about the patient's work and daily life. He advised students to remember that medicine concerned the 'whole man'. Moore was instrumental in establishing medical education in the restructured University of London, first through the royal commission, later on the board of advanced medical studies. In 1900 Amy, who was dying of tuberculosis, converted to Roman Catholicism. Moore, though a nonconformist by upbringing and an Anglican by inclination, followed her. He was devout but disliked discussing theology. 'If they teach what is ridiculous you don't believe it' (private information). Amy died on 25 August 1901, and in 1903 Moore married her first cousin, Milicent Ludlow (1868–1947).

Moore, a short, fair haired, bearded man, never smoked and rarely drank. He was considered a fascinating conversationalist, though some found the flow of talk overwhelming. His enemies were few, but powerful. In 1915 he was unexpectedly defeated for the presidency of the Royal College of Physicians. A grudging and inaccurate *Times* obituary said his work 'lacked that deeper scholarship' which would 'render it lasting'. M. R. James, provost of Eton College, refuted this, adding 'I have never met any man whose erudition was so varied, lay so ready to hand, or was so delightfully enlivened by human and humorous touches' (*The Times*, 8 Dec 1922).

Moore inspired lifelong and devoted friendship among a wide circle in all walks of life. He had two happy marriages; he was amused and amusing. 'His laughter was accompanied by a moistening of the eyes', wrote E. V. Lucas, 'which his friends found very well worth striving after' (private information). He impressed and delighted children by reciting all the rhyming page headings in Thackeray's *The Rose and the Ring*. A friend's small daughter recalled the joy of his visits: 'He made the very dullest subject amusing, because to him nothing was dull, and he had the power of taking away the dullness from the person he was talking to' (private information). Moore's circle of 'well-read ladies' included the gardening expert Edith Willmott, and the scholarly Ethel Portal, a close friend who helped with his research.

On retirement in 1911 Moore was appointed consulting physician to St Bartholomew's, emeritus lecturer in medicine, and hospital governor. He published numerous papers, served on medical and educational committees, was secretary of the Literary Society, and librarian of the Royal Society of Medicine (1899–1918). At the Royal College of Physicians he became Harveian librarian, served

on its conjoint board, and for twenty-one years represented the college on the General Medical Council, where he supported the interests of patients rather than the profession. He was the 1901 Harveian orator, and was elected senior censor in 1908. His many official lectures included the Linacre (*The Physician in English History*, 1913), Lumleian, Bradshaw, FitzPatrick (*The History of the Study of Medicine in the British Isles*, 1908), and Hunterian, and in 1914 the Cambridge Rede lecture, all of which were published. In 1918 Moore—'the then pre-eminent British physician' (Linnett, 15)—became president of the Royal College of Physicians and a trustee of the British Museum. His monumental *History of St Bartholomew's Hospital*, in two volumes, was published the same year. He read, and copied by hand, nearly 1000 medieval charters, and would walk the ancient City streets at night to reconstruct its links with twelfth-century London.

Moore was created a baronet in 1919 and in 1920 received an honorary LLD from Cambridge. His powers began to decline, his writing showing early signs of Parkinsonism. The war had aged him: he never wholly recovered from the loss of his younger son, Gillachrist. On 30 November 1922 he died at his wife's house, Hancox, Whatlington, near Battle. He was buried on 5 December in the churchyard of St John the Baptist, Sedlescombe, Sussex. His son Alan succeeded him as second baronet.

ANN MOORE

Sources Moore family MSS: letters, journals, casebooks, notebooks, reminiscences, NRA, priv. coll. • M. J. Linnett, 'Life and works of Sir Norman Moore', *St Bartholomew's Hospital Journal*, 51 (1947–8), 92–5, 106–10, 128–31, 150–54 [Wix prize essay, 1947] • 'Moore, Robert Ross Rowan', *DNB* • 'Waterton, Charles', *DNB* • 'Elwin, Whitwell', *DNB* • P. Hirsch, *Barbara Leigh Smith Bodichon: feminist, artist and rebel* (1998) • N. G. Annan, 'The intellectual aristocracy', *Studies in social history: a tribute to G. M. Trevelyan*, ed. J. H. Plumb (1955), 241–87 • N. Moore, *The history of St Bartholomew's Hospital*, 2 vols. (1918) • Munk, *Roll* • N. Moore, 'Essays and addresses', RCP Lond., Ref. 2825 • E. V. Lucas, *Postbag diversions* (1934) • C. Woodham-Smith, *Florence Nightingale, 1820–1910*, new edn (1951) • P. Gosse, *The squire of Walton Hall* (1940) • G. Raverat, *Period piece* (1952) • *The Times* (1 Dec 1922) • private information (2004) • d. cert.

Archives CUL, Irish MSS, Add. 6472–6568, 6624, 7089 • NRA, priv. coll., corresp. and papers • Wellcome L., lecture notes

Likenesses A. E. Verlag, photogravure, c.1900–1910, RCP Lond. • R. G. Eves, oils, 1913, St Catharine's College, Cambridge; copy, RCP Lond. • W. Russell, oils, 1922, RCP Lond. • photograph, RCP Lond. • photographs, Hancox, Whatlington, Battle, Sussex

Wealth at death £18,786 2s. 10d.: probate, 18 Jan 1923, CGPLA Eng. & Wales

Moore, Peter (1753–1828), politician, was born on 12 February 1753 at Sedbergh, Yorkshire, the second son of the Revd Edward Moore (d. 1755), vicar of Over, Cheshire, and his wife, Mary. He was two years old when his father died and so was educated at Sedbergh School under the aegis of Edward Moore, his elder brother by eighteen years, who secured him a position as indexer of the *House of Commons Journals* through a connection with the first Lord Holland. As a result of Holland's patronage Moore went to India in 1769 as a writer, and subsequently as collector, factor, and commissioner of police in the East India Company's service. When in India he married at Patna on 8 or 10 January

1774 Sarah Webb (*b. c.*1750, *d.* before 1797), daughter and coheir of Lieutenant-Colonel Richmond Webb of Bandon, co. Cork, and Sarah Griffiths. They had five sons, four of whom predeceased their father, and two daughters, including Frances *Moore. His wife, whose sister Amelia was grandmother of the novelist William Makepeace Thackeray, also died some time before 1797.

Moore arrived back in England in July 1785 with a substantial fortune and settled at Hadley, Middlesex, as lord of the manor. He joined the more radical section of the parliamentary opposition, and from his Indian experience was able to supply useful information to Burke and Sheridan for their attack on Warren Hastings. He also helped to maintain the whig party's interests in the Westminster constituency. His house at Hadley was a rendezvous for their leading members. Sheridan often stayed with him, and in 1784 Fox took refuge from the bailiffs in his house.

In 1796 Moore stood as a parliamentary candidate at Tewkesbury, where the franchise was disputed between the householders, and the freemen and freeholders. Though elected with a majority of the former, the House of Commons determined in favour of the latter and he was unseated. A further attempt at Tewkesbury in 1797 was also unsuccessful. In 1802 he contested Coventry without success, but he won a by-election there in March 1803. His election was said to have cost £25,000 in all. He also won support from the Coventry weavers by backing a project to import Bengal silks and muslins at a cheap rate for their benefit.

Moore immediately demonstrated his whig allegiance by voting with Fox on 24 May 1803 against the renewal of hostilities against France and he took a prominent part in the Westminster election of 1804, when he was Fox's proposer. He also voted against Pitt's second ministry in 1804–5. He spoke frequently in the house on a variety of subjects. He supported, and proposed, Burdett in the Middlesex election of 1804 when he was Burdett's 'busiest advocate' and in the subsequent dispute he took a leading role at the freeholders' meeting to contest the sheriff's return of Mainwaring (Hone, 142). He also continued, as member for Coventry, to concern himself with the interests of the clothworkers and printers against the employers. He presented petitions on behalf of the calico printers in May 1805 and July 1806 and from the clothiers of York and Lancaster on 4 March 1806. When Fox and Grenville formed the 'ministry of all the talents' in 1806 a family tradition maintains that it was intended to appoint him to an office in India with a peerage, but the fall of the ministry in April 1807 put an end to his prospects.

Moore remained a staunch and indefatigable member of the whig party after Fox's death, attached as before to the radical wing of the party. He supported Melville's impeachment in 1805 but in 1806, together with other Foxites, he turned against Burdett in Middlesex when the latter accused both government and opposition parties of writing against the people. He supported the abolition of the slave trade in March 1807 and spoke frequently on Indian and Irish questions, favouring Catholic emancipation, the reform of Irish tithes, and the grant to Maynooth College. Despite personal differences he remained an advocate of campaigns by Cochrane and by Burdett for radical reform, against sinecures, and for enquiry into allegations of corruption in high places. In 1809 and 1810 he voted for parliamentary reform, presenting a petition from his constituents in its favour on 13 June 1810. He championed the freedom of the press and supported the case for the discharge from prison of the radical journalist John Gale Jones.

Moore was a close friend of Sheridan and was active in the affairs of Drury Lane Theatre. He sat on the management committee and was a member of the board of trustees. He chaired a parliamentary inquiry into the London theatres in 1811, helping to defeat a proposal to build a rival theatre to Drury Lane after the latter had been burnt down. He was instrumental in 1810 in raising the funds to rebuild Drury Lane and he became a director of the new theatre in 1815. He supported other improvements in London, including the Highgate Tunnel and the Imperial Gas Light Company, and was a patron of the bill to provide a canal between Woolwich and Erith, but he failed in 1812 to carry a bill to provide a sea water baths near the capital. A busy promoter and skilful manager of private bills in this area, he was much in demand by projectors of many companies.

After 1812 Moore continued to participate in debates on such radical and reformist issues as Catholic relief, retrenchment of government expenditure, the repeal of the property tax, and the resumption of cash payments by the bank. Parliamentary reform, the restoration of habeas corpus, and the protection of civil liberties remained dear to his heart, as did the relief of the poorer classes from economic distress and high taxation. In 1819 he was presented with a gold cup by 2000 of his electors in recognition of his services. In 1820 he again joined Burdett in supporting Queen Caroline, and moved resolutions in her favour at the Middlesex freeholders' meeting of 8 August. He also played a part in the campaign against the combination laws and introduced a bill for their abolition in 1823, but his measure attracted too much controversy and Joseph Hume, on Huskisson's advice, substituted in 1824 a motion for a committee on artisans and the export of machinery, which achieved the objective by indirect means. His political career was blighted, however, by his fascination for speculative ventures, which led to bankruptcy. When he lost his seat in parliament in 1826 he had to flee to Dieppe to escape arrest for debt. He surrendered most of his assets to his creditors and never returned to England.

Moore was a friend of many leading members of whig political society, a promoter of worthy causes, and defender of popular liberties. He was attached to traditional manners, and was said to have been the last wearer of a pigtail in society. He could be an abrasive character: 'Moore is not a man to be put aside'. Place wrote in 1824: 'I know Mr. Moore well, know how pig-headed he is, that he will be sure to go in the opposite way to which he is pulled'

(Wallas, 209). Perhaps his pre-eminent claim to remembrance may rest in his friendship with Sheridan. He had chaired Sheridan's election committee at Westminster in November 1806. He took charge of Sheridan's chaotic financial affairs in 1810 and was endlessly supportive of his activities and in his troubles. Thomas Hammersley wrote to Sheridan in 1809 that he and Moore were 'the best friends you ever had' (*Letters of Richard Brinsley Sheridan*, 3.53). This friendship continued until the end of Sheridan's life and, when he died, in poverty and some degree of squalor, Moore organized his funeral in Westminster Abbey; the funeral procession started from Moore's house in Great George Street and was so immense that the last of the mourners had not left the house when the head of the cortège entered the abbey. It was Moore who placed the memorial stone over Sheridan's grave as 'the tribute of an attached friend'. He is also known as Thackeray's guardian.

Moore died at Abbeville on 5 May 1828.   E. A. SMITH

Sources R. G. Thorne, 'Moore, Peter', HoP, *Commons, 1790–1820* · *Hansard 1* (1805–10), vols. 3, 5–6, 9, 16–17 · W. S. Sichel, *Sheridan, from new and original material*, 2 vols. (1909) · *The letters of Richard Brinsley Sheridan*, ed. C. Price, 3 vols. (1966) · J. A. Hone, *For the cause of truth: radicalism in London, 1796–1821* (1982) · G. Wallas, *The life of Francis Place, 1771–1854*, 4th edn (1925) · W. F. Rae, *Sheridan: a biography*, 2 vols. (1896) · *GM*, 1st ser., 98/1 (1828), 567–8 · M. W. Patterson, *Sir Francis Burdett and his times (1770–1844)*, 2 vols. (1931) · *DNB* · 'Webb, John Richmond', *DNB* · *Morning Chronicle* (Oct 1815) · *A full report of the Middlesex county meeting … to take into consideration the propriety of presenting an address to the queen* (1820) · IGI
Archives BL, corresp. with Lord and Lady Holland, Add. MS 51811
Likenesses T. Gainsborough, oils, probably Frampton Hall, Lincolnshire · two portraits, priv. coll.

Moore, Philip (*fl.* 1564–1573), medical practitioner, practised at Halesworth, Suffolk. He wrote *The hope of health, wherein is contained a goodlie regiment of life: as medicine, good diet, and the goodly vertues of sondrie herbes* (1565). The dedication, dated 1 May 1564, is to Owen Hopton, then JP for Suffolk and later lieutenant of the Tower of London. Prefixed to the book are a Latin epistle and some verses in mixed Latin and English by William Bullein, who calls Moore his 'well-beloved friend'. The book aimed to disseminate the knowledge of medicinal herbs among the poor, and to encourage their cultivation. It also included a 'Table for xxx yeres to come'. Moore also published *An Almanack and Prognostication for xxxiiii. Yeares* (1573).

GORDON GOODWIN, *rev.* SARAH BAKEWELL

Sources P. Moore, *The hope of health* (1565) · O. Hopton, 'Moore, Philip', HoP, *Commons*

Moore, Philip (1705–1783), headmaster and Manx scholar, was born at Pulrose and baptized on 10 September 1705 at Kirk Braddan on the Isle of Man, the sixth son of Robert Moore, of Pulrose, and Catherine Kelly. He was educated at Douglas grammar school under the Revd Peter Lancaster until 1716 and then under the Revd Anthony Hall until 1726 when he moved to the Academic School in Castletown. After being prepared for the Church of England ministry by Thomas Wilson, bishop of Sodor and Man, he was ordained deacon in 1729. He remained a friend of Wilson's until the latter's death in 1755, and preached at his funeral. During his time as curate of Marown from 1731 to 1735, however, he was reprimanded by Wilson for masquerading one night in the ruins of St Trinian's in order to scare the local people and demonstrate how foolish was their fear of the *buggane* or bogey.

Moore was not ordained priest until 1739, apparently because he refused to believe that the unbaptized were damned. From 1735 onwards he obtained many preferments and became a noted pluralist. He was simultaneously chaplain of Douglas, private chaplain to the duke of Atholl, and rector of Ballaugh and Bride in succession. He was also headmaster of Douglas grammar school for over forty years and, shortly before he died, boasted that with four exceptions all the Manx clergy had been his pupils. Moore was on very good terms with Mark Hildesley, Wilson's successor, although the bishop was compelled to rebuke him for neglecting his pastoral duties. Moore is chiefly remembered for having been general editor of the Manx Bible, which was published at Whitehaven between 1771 and 1775. He also published a Manx translation of the Book of Common Prayer (1777). He died in January 1783 and was buried in the churchyard at Kirk Braddan on 22 January 1783. A tablet to his memory was set up in the church. His wife, whose name is unknown, had predeceased him in 1767 or early 1768.

N. J. A. WILLIAMS

Sources A. W. Moore, *Manx worthies* (1901) · D. Craine, *Manannan's isle: a collection of Manx historical essays* (1955) · IGI · R. L. Thomson, *The study of Manx Gaelic* (1969) · W. Butler, *Memoirs of Mark Hildesley, D.D.* (1799), 186ff. · *DNB*
Likenesses photograph (of portrait), Manx Museum, Douglas; repro. in *Journal of the Manx Museum*, 2/35 (June 1933), facing p. 120 · portrait; at Bishop's Court, Isle of Man, until 1940s

Moore, Raymond Ethelbert (1920–1987), photographer, was born on 26 August 1920 at 43 Liscard Road, Wallasey, Cheshire, the son of Alfred Ethelbert Moore, an architect's assistant, and his wife, Winifred Ethel Agnes Mayne; he had one brother. Nothing is known of Moore's early education but in 1937, intending to become a painter, he enrolled at the Wallasey School of Art. In 1940 he joined the RAF, spending the war years in the Middle East. After winning a scholarship to study painting, he enrolled in 1947 at the Royal College of Art (RCA) in London, graduating in 1950 as an ARCA. While at the RCA Moore began to experiment more with photography, a medium familiar to him since his teenage years: examples of this early work are found in the Moore archive. Among his influences at this time were Henri Cartier-Bresson, Edward Weston, Walker Evans, Hugo Van Wadenoyen, and the two publications *Subjektive Fotografie* (1950) and *Subjektive Fotografie 2* (1956). The work in these books by international photographers emphasizes modernist trends and displays a strong graphic awareness. It tends to consider the photographic potential within the mundanities of man-made and natural phenomena, rather than the conventionally beautiful.

From 1950 to 1975 Moore taught lithography and painting at the Watford School of Art, while continuing his interest in photography. In 1956 the principal of the school asked him to start a photography course for graphic design students. He based the course on Ansel Adams's books, later published as *The Camera* (1980), *The Negative* (1981), and *The Print* (1983), and simultaneously gave up painting, destroying all but one of his works, *Skomer 1949*. With the painter Ray Howard-Jones, he spent nine summers on Skomer, off the Pembrokeshire coast. There, among the craggy rock formations and tactile stretches of sand, he began to develop his photographic 'voice'. His first exhibition of seventy prints was held in 1959 in the architectural department of the Regent Street Polytechnic, but more significant was an exhibition in 1962 which he shared with painter Malcolm Hughes and sculptor Peter Startup at the Artists' International Association Gallery in Soho. At this event he met the renowned photo-historian Helmut Gernsheim, who bought some prints and became a supportive lifelong friend.

In 1967 Moore was invited to participate in Modfot 1 by a breakaway group from the Croydon Camera Club; other exhibitors included Don McCullin and Roger Mayne. The exhibition was opened by the Arts Council chairman, Lord Goodman, and was a valiant attempt to balance the preponderance of pictorialism then prevalent by showing radical, modern photography. In 1968 the Welsh Arts Council asked Moore to mount a retrospective exhibition of his work at its principal gallery in Museum Place, Cardiff. It was the first time a British arts council exhibited work by a living British photographer, and it marked the first time Moore's work would be seen in such an auspicious gallery. The exhibition subsequently toured Wales.

In 1970 Moore visited America where he met Minor White, Harry Callahan, and Aaron Siskind, three of the most influential American photographers of the time. Although the nature of their work differed greatly within the genre of the black and white fine print, they all had in common with Moore a need to express an inner, personal truth through their photography. In America Moore found stimulus and support: six exhibitions of his work were mounted there during the 1970s. Appreciation in America bolstered his reputation at home and in 1973 the Photographers' Gallery in London mounted a one-man show. In 1975 eight prints were included in 'The Land', selected by Bill Brandt for the Victoria and Albert Museum. Also in 1975 Moore became senior lecturer on the diploma in creative photography course at Trent Polytechnic and moved to Clipstone. However, his career here was brief: in 1977 he was awarded a bursary by the Arts Council to pursue personal work, which he did after resigning from Trent Polytechnic and moving to Carlisle in 1978.

In 1979 Moore took part in 'Three Perspectives on Photography', a controversial exhibition at the Hayward Gallery which included politically slanted work. He was invited back to the Hayward in 1981 to mount a major retrospective, becoming the second living British photographer, after Bill Brandt, to be given this honour. A book, *Murmurs*

at every Turn, was published to coincide with the exhibition. A further book of Moore's photographs, *Every so Often*, was published in 1983 by BBC North East to coincide with a film portrait of that title.

Raymond Moore found his mature photographic voice working in the abandoned areas between town and country and deserted seaside towns out of season, where man's presence was only apparent in the traces left—the marks of car tyres, litter, or a game of hopscotch abandoned in the sand. He said 'For me—the no-man's land between the real and fantasy—the mystery in the common place—the uncommonness of the commonplace' (Moore, 12). Moore's work observed those forgotten, overlooked fragments of life, making the viewer aware of the extraordinary residing within the ordinary. It was founded on a strong sense of design and impeccable technique, and he cast magic on the most immemorable scene. Latterly working exclusively with a 35 mm camera in black and white, he meticulously crafted prints which annotated the tones of the grey scale with the precision of the notes in a musical score. He has been described as the first 'independent' photographer to have made his mark in British photography during a career founded upon personal, artistic work, rather than that dependent on commissions.

Raymond Moore was of medium build, with piercing eyes set in a somewhat hawk-like face. He was an essentially private person whose strength of character enabled him to develop his photographic voice in a cultural environment which was not sympathetic to 'art' photography. He was twice married: first to Pauline in the late 1960s at Hemel Hempstead and then, on 11 November 1978, to Mary Margaret Cooper (b. 1954/5) at Mansfield register office. Moore moved to Chapelknowe, Canonbie, Dumfriesshire, in the early 1980s, where he died on 6 October 1987. He was buried at Chapelknowe, and was survived by his second wife. Posthumously Moore was represented in two major exhibitions in London mounted to commemorate photography's 150th anniversary in 1989, 'The Art of Photography' at the Royal Academy and 'Through the Looking Glass' at the Barbican Centre. His work is held in several American collections, as well as major British institutions including the Victoria and Albert Museum and Welsh Arts Council.   JANET HALL

Sources Sothebys sales rooms, London, Moore archive · R. Moore, *Murmurs at every turn* (1981) · M. M. Evans, ed., *Contemporary photographers* (1995) · private information (2004) · personal knowledge (2004) · *Creative Camera* (Jan 1988), 30 · H. Gernsheim and A. Gernsheim, *A concise history of photography* (1965) · I. Jeffrey, *Photography: a concise history* (1981) · D. McClelland, 'The light and the vision: the work of Raymond Moore', *British Journal of Photography* (29 Aug 1969), 822–5 · *The Independent* (9 Oct 1987) · b. cert. · m. cert. [Mary M. Cooper]
Archives priv. coll.
Likenesses photograph, repro. in Moore, *Murmurs*, back fly-leaf

Moore, Richard (1619–1683), nonconformist minister, son of William and Janne Moore, was born in Alvechurch, Worcestershire, where he was baptized at St Laurence Church on 8 August 1619. His mother died shortly after Richard's birth and was buried on 18 August 1619. Member of a prominent local family, Moore matriculated at Magdalen Hall, Oxford, on 30 June 1637, and graduated BA on 12 November 1640. Although Moore served as preacher and lecturer in Worcester, there is as yet no evidence of his ordination in the Church of England. In 1649–50 Moore, 'preacher of God's word', leased a house belonging to the cathedral in Worcester on the west side of the College Green next to the Lead House (Cave and Wilson, 171).

Moore married Susanna Seaborne (d. 1701) on 16 August 1649 in Alvechurch. Baptisms for an unnamed son (1653) and three daughters, Mary (1654), Sary (1657), and Susannah (1660), were recorded in the parish register of St Laurence, Alvechurch.

Moore was chosen in 1650 to replace the previously sequestered William Hollington as rector of St Laurence, Alvechurch. While rector of Alvechurch, Moore became a member of Richard Baxter's Worcestershire Association. Although not one of the original members Moore joined the association before 1656, and was a signatory to the second edition of Baxter's *The Agreement of Divers Ministers*. As an association member Moore may have attempted to develop a parish-wide system of catechizing, pastoral oversight, and church discipline, and would have had opportunity to meet regularly with like-minded area ministers.

After the Restoration the sequestered former incumbent William Hollington successfully petitioned to have Moore removed from the rectory, and himself restored. Following his removal Moore was given a licence to preach in a room adjoining his house. When George Morley, bishop of Worcester, discovered in 1662 that Moore's house and adjoining room were actually the curate's chamber over the sanctuary of the Bromsgrove chapelry of Wythall, his licence was revoked. Moore continued his preaching ministry from an upper window of his house at the foot of Weatheroak Hill, Moor Green Hall. In an effort to circumvent the laws against nonconformist preaching he had a hole cut in the upper wall of the house to enable him to preach without leaving his residence. Moore would climb a flight of stairs inside the building and address the congregation that had assembled below on a covered cartway connecting the house to the barn. The hole has been bricked over, but is still visible from the inside. The barn and covered cartway are still standing.

Following the Act of Indulgence Moore was licensed as a presbyterian on 22 April 1672 and restored to Wythall Chapel, where he ministered for two years. He published a small volume entitled *A Pearl in an Oyster-Shel, or, Pretious Treasure Put in Perishing Vessels* (1675), the first part of which contains a sermon preached in Wythall Chapel in 1673. The second part, entitled 'Abel redivivus, or, The dead speaker', is a memorial sermon for his friend Thomas Hall (1610–1665), the presbyterian minister of King's Norton, Worcestershire.

After the indulgence was revoked Moore continued to preach privately at his home at Moor Green Hall. Moore died in September 1683 and was buried at King's Norton parish church on 27 September 1683. His wife survived him. The 'Richard Moore Clarck' who was buried in Alvechurch on 31 January 1706 is probably the unnamed son of Richard and Susanna who was baptized on 17 August 1653.

J. WILLIAM BLACK

Sources W. English, 'A history of St Laurence Church Alvechurch', 1990, Bearhill House, Alvechurch · W. English, *Alvechurch: 1200 years of history* (1997) · T. Nash, *Collections for the history of Worcestershire*, 1 (1781) · parish register, Alvechurch, 8 Aug 1619, 17 Aug 1653, 19 Dec 1654, 13 Jan 1658, 12 June 1660 [baptism], 16 Aug 1649 [marriage], 14 Feb 1701 [burial] · G. F. Nuttall, 'The Worcestershire Association: its membership', *Journal of Ecclesiastical History*, 1 (1950), 197–206 · parish register, King's Norton, 27 Sept 1683 [burial] · *Calamy rev.* · private information (2004) [W. English] · T. Cave and R. A. Wilson, eds., *The parliamentary survey of the lands and possessions of the dean and chapter of Worcester … 1649* (1924) · *CSP dom.*, 1662, 613 · *Walker rev.* · J. Noake, *The rambler in Worcestershire, or, Stray notes on churches and congregations* (1851) · J. Noake, *Guide to Worcestershire* (1868) · *DNB*

Moore, Richard (1810–1878), radical, was born in London on 16 October 1810. He was a woodcarver of no mean skill, and eventually employed a considerable staff. He became in 1831 a member of the council of Sir Francis Burdett's National Political Union, and assisted Robert Owen in his projects for working-class education at the Institute of the Industrious Classes, Gray's Inn Lane. In 1834 he was the principal member of a deputation to Lord Melbourne on the question of the social condition of the people. He was a member of the committee for which William Lovett drew up the People's Charter in 1837. In 1839 he was a member of the national convention which met to promote the passing of the Charter, was secretary of the testimonial committee which greeted Lovett and Collins on their release from gaol in 1840, and joined Lovett in the Working Men's Association in 1842. He took an active part in its meetings in the National Hall (later the Royal Music Hall), Holborn, and was also active in the Chartist cause, though he never approved of physical force, or professed to believe that the Charter could remedy all the grievances of the working classes. When the People's Charter Union was formed on 10 April 1848, he was appointed its treasurer, and conducted its affairs with moderation and discretion.

In 1849 Moore took up the reform with which he was most practically connected, the abolition of newspaper stamps, and urged Cobden to adopt it in order to keep the working classes and the middle classes in touch on the subject of financial reforms. The Charter union appointed a committee on the question, which met at his house, and of which he became permanent chairman. This committee was afterwards absorbed into the Association for Promoting the Repeal of Taxes on Knowledge, of which Moore was one of the most active members. Between 7 March 1849, when the first committee was formed, and June 1861, when the paper duty was repealed, Moore attended 390 meetings on the subject. During the same period he took part in almost every advanced radical movement, and was the constant colleague of Lovett, Henry Hetherington, and James Watson. He was also a member of the Society of the Friends of Italy, the Jamaica Committee, and the Financial Reform Union, and was an executive member of the Travelling Tax Abolition Committee. He worked hard to promote electoral purity in Finsbury, where he had lived from 1832, and assisted in managing the Regent's Park Sunday band. Moore had married, on 9 December 1836, Mary Sharp of Malton, Yorkshire (a niece of James Watson, the publisher and Chartist), who with four children survived him, after his death in Finsbury on 7 December 1878. He was buried five days later in Highgate cemetery.

J. A. HAMILTON, *rev.* MATTHEW LEE

Sources C. D. Collet, *Life of Richard Moore* (1879) · W. J. Linton, *Century Magazine*, 21 (1882), 428 · Boase, *Mod. Eng. biog.* · Ward, *Men of the reign* · private information (1894) [Mrs M. E. Heath, daughter of Richard Moore] · H. L. Malchow, *Agitators and promoters in the age of Gladstone and Disraeli: a biographical dictionary* (1983)

Archives BL, corresp., Add. MS 46345

Likenesses portrait, repro. in *Century Magazine*

Moore, Robert Frederick Chelsea [Bobby] **(1941–1993)**, footballer, was born in Upney Hospital, Barking, Essex, on 12 April 1941, the only son of Robert Edward Moore, a railway signalman, and his wife, Doris Joyce, *née* Buckle. He was brought up in a typical street of working-class housing at 43 Waverley Gardens, Barking. After Barking primary school he passed the eleven-plus examination to the Tom Hood Grammar School in Leyton. Although not an outstanding schoolboy footballer—indeed at one time it seemed he might be a more successful cricketer—he had already been noticed by West Ham United and was taken to Upton Park for training. There he met and was influenced by Malcolm Allison, Malcolm Musgrove, Noel Cantwell, and his manager at West Ham in the 1960s, Ron Greenwood—all of whom taught the importance of ball control, accurate distribution, and intelligent movement. As a young man he was also impressed by Ray Barlow, the cultured left half of West Bromwich Albion, by the penetrating passing of Johnny Haynes, and by the spectacular athleticism of Duncan Edwards, whom he once played

truant from school to watch at Tottenham. He signed a professional contract with West Ham at the age of seventeen and played his first match for the first team against Manchester United in 1958. It took two years to earn a regular first-team place, after which he became the first footballer to experience the iconic status of the other stars of 1960s popular culture. On 30 June 1962 he married Christina Elizabeth Dean (*b.* 1942/3); they had a son and a daughter.

Moore had already played eighteen times for the England youth team and eight more for the under-twenty-threes when at twenty-one he was chosen for the squad which went to the world cup in Chile in 1962. He returned an established international, having played in all four matches against Argentina, Bulgaria, Hungary, and Brazil. When Alf Ramsay became England manager in 1963, Moore became both captain and the second central defender in the new manager's new system. Their partnership was the key to one of the most successful periods for any England team. The world cup was won at Wembley in 1966, England finished third in the European championship in Italy in 1968, and in the 1970 world cup in Mexico England reached the quarter-finals, in which they played some of the most impressive football before losing 3–2 to West Germany after being two goals up. Moore had been voted player of the tournament in 1966 and appointed OBE in 1967, but was probably at his peak in 1970, when he gave a particularly assured performance against Brazil in Guadalajara which led Pele to say that he was the most accomplished defender against whom he had played. His international reputation was symbolized by a famous photograph of his exchange of shirts with the world's leading player after the match. Between 1962 and 1973 Moore played 108 times for England, 90 as captain. Of those 90 games 57 were won, 20 drawn, and only 13 lost.

Yet success at club level proved elusive. The West Ham of the 1960s, often containing three members of England's

Robert Frederick Chelsea [Bobby] **Moore (1941–1993)**, by Bippa Pool, 1966 [centre, holding the trophy after England won the world cup]

world cup-winning team, could play exciting and effective football. They won the FA cup in 1964 and Moore was elected footballer of the year; they took the European cup winners' trophy in 1965, but they never finished higher than eighth in the first division. Local wags characterized the team as 'erratic as dock work'. Moore was disappointed not to win a league championship and annoyed that West Ham refused to release him when real contenders such as Brian Clough's Derby County and Tottenham made serious offers. Though an admirer of Greenwood's footballing philosophy, he was not always impressed by his signings or, as he got older, by his man management. Greenwood in turn sometimes suggested that Moore concentrated harder for England than he did for West Ham, and it seems clear that Moore relished the stiffer challenges of the international game.

Moore eventually completed 1000 senior games, including 544 for West Ham and 124 for Fulham, whom he joined in March 1974. Ironically he found himself captaining Fulham against West Ham in the 1975 cup final, when West Ham won. He also played briefly for Herning Football Club in Denmark and San Antonio Thunder and the Seattle Sounders in the United States. After his retirement he was expected to have a successful career in football management, but it never happened. Brief spells at Oxford City (1978–81) and Southend United (1983–6) ended in disappointment. It is worth noting that the only member of the England world cup-winning team to succeed as a manager was Jack Charlton, perhaps providing support for the well-worn footballing cliché that good players do not necessarily make good managers.

That Moore was a great footballer is beyond argument. His balance, timing, and anticipation, his ability both to win the ball with certainty and to deliver it to a team-mate tellingly far outweighed the lack of pace which severe critics pointed to as a fatal flaw. Moreover his skill reflected an unruffled temperament as well as intelligence. In the world cup of 1970 he played the game of his life against Brazil, when only a few days before he had been under house arrest in Bogotá, his training watched by local policemen after he had been unjustly accused of stealing a gold bracelet from a shop. On the field he rarely appeared flustered or hurried, his play a byword for style, poise, and sportsmanship. If, in the late 1960s or 1970s, a recreational footballer won a tackle at the back and then strode forward, chest out, looked up and attempted a 40 yard diagonal pass inside the opposing full back, there would have been no doubt whom he was trying to imitate.

Life after football could never quite provide the same excitement or measurable achievement, though Bobby Moore's celebrity meant that he was in continual demand. A man who always enjoyed a drink, he part-owned pubs and clubs in east London, notably Mooros. He did coaching stints in Hong Kong and North Carolina and for three years from 1986 was sports editor of the *Sunday Sport*, perhaps the raunchiest of all the tabloids. In 1990 he joined Capital Radio as a football match analyst. He was also involved in a sports marketing and promotions company

called Challenge, which went into liquidation in the early 1990s. Perhaps he needed longer to understand the ways of the business world. In 1986 Moore was divorced from his wife, Christina; on 4 December 1991 he married his partner Stephanie Parlane-Moore (b. 1948/9). In April 1991 he had an operation for suspected cancer of the colon. Only he and his closest family were aware that the disease was terminal. He continued his radio work until shortly before his death on 24 February 1993, at his home, 12 Seaton Close, Putney Heath, London.

This sad event produced a public reaction that was only partly related to the fact that Moore was still only fifty-one. The powerful televisual image of the England team captain lifting the world cup at Wembley on 30 July 1966 was engraved on the minds of many people who would not have thought of themselves as followers of football. The moment when he wiped his grimy, sweaty hands on his shorts so that he would not soil the white gloves worn by the queen as she presented the Jules Rimet trophy to him particularly forced itself into the collective memory. It also symbolized this polite, cool, and composed young man, who seemed to represent the best side of a sport not always noted for its sensitivity. Compared to many professionals, Moore was the epitome of fair play, a man of exemplary character both on and off the field. He was a good-looking but modest star and one with a powerful sense of team identity. He was anxious not to let anyone down and did not like those who did. He was a hero as the English like them, a captain who led by example to the last, epitomized by the courage and dignity he showed in the face of death.

Bobby Moore's many fans built a shrine of flowers, candles, cards, and scarves in West Ham's claret and blue colours at the gates of Upton Park, the first of many tributes paid to him. A memorial service was held in Westminster Abbey on 28 June; West Ham opened the Bobby Moore stand at Upton Park at a memorial match on 7 March 1994, and a bridge at Wembley Stadium was also named after him. His widow, Stephanie Moore, set up the Bobby Moore Fund for Cancer Research UK, to support research into the disease which carried off 'football's greatest gentleman' at such an early age.

TONY MASON

Sources J. Powell, *Bobby Moore: the life and times of a sporting hero* (1993) · *The Independent* (25–6 Feb 1993); (29 June 1993) · *The Times* (25–6 Feb 1993); (26 March 1993); (29 June 1993) · b. cert. · m. certs. · d. cert.
Likenesses photographs, c.1962–1981, Hult. Arch. · B. Pool, photograph, 1966, Hult. Arch. [*see illus.*] · photograph, repro. in *NPG book of British sporting heroes* · photograph, repro. in *The Times* (25 Feb 1993) · photograph, repro. in *The Independent* (25 Feb 1993)
Wealth at death £134,528: probate, 13 May 1993, CGPLA Eng. & Wales

Moore, Robert Ross Rowan (1811–1864), political economist, born in Dublin on 23 December 1811, was the eldest son of William Moore, from whom he inherited a taste for literature. His father was the head of a branch of the family of Rowallan which had settled on a small estate in

Ulster in 1610. His mother, Anne Rowan, who was her husband's first cousin, was daughter of Robert Ross Rowan of Mullaghmore, co. Down, a lieutenant in the 104th foot.

Moore was sent in 1828 to the Luxemburg School, near Dublin, one of those established by Gregor von Feinagle. He was a successful student, and in 1831 entered Trinity College, Dublin, where he graduated BA in 1835. He spoke regularly at the Dublin University Debating Society, and was one of the chief opponents of his friend Thomas Osborne Davis, maintaining that Ireland's prosperity would be better secured by general toleration, free trade, and closer relations with Great Britain than by political independence. Despite the differences between the two men, their friendship was uninterrupted until the death of Davis. After teaching private pupils at Carlow, Moore read law, and was called to the bar as a member of Gray's Inn on 28 April 1837. Political economy, however, was the subject to which he devoted most of his time, and he also took an interest in a wide range of movements for social improvement. On 15 August 1839 he gave a lecture in Dublin 'On the advantages of mechanics' institutions', which was later published. He became a member of an Irish antislavery society, and in 1841 visited Limerick, where he successfully opposed a scheme for exporting apprentices to the West Indies.

Moore's economic studies led him to take an interest in the movement for the repeal of the corn laws. George Thompson introduced him to John Bright, with whom, along with Richard Cobden, he soon became closely allied. He joined the Anti-Corn Law League, and Bright is supposed later to have stated on several occasions that a large share of the success of the agitation was due to Moore's lucid exposition of economic principles, and his convincing public illustration of the benefits that would flow from free trade. Bright and George Thompson visited Ireland in December 1841, and Moore's first important public speech on free trade was at a meeting held at the Mansion House, Dublin, on 23 December, when he moved a resolution in favour of the total and immediate repeal of the corn laws. From this date until the repeal in May 1846 he devoted his whole time and energy to the cause, speaking repeatedly as the representative of the league at meetings held in the major towns and cities of England and Scotland. With both Bright and Cobden he spoke several times at Salisbury, and often had dinner there with the father of Henry Fawcett. At Cupar in Fife, in January 1844 the freedom of the town was conferred upon Cobden and Moore.

A month later Moore spoke at the great series of meetings in Covent Garden Theatre in London, and was invited to be a parliamentary candidate for Hastings. In March 1844 he contested that borough at a by-election, but was defeated, receiving 174 votes. He was presented with a silver inkstand by his supporters, and an enthusiastic elector, Benjamin Smith, MP for Norwich, had a list of the 174 free-trade voters printed in letters of gold and distributed as a record of the contest. The working men of Exeter in 1845 presented Moore with a piece of plate, with an inscription commemorating their admiration for his speeches in favour of free trade. Medallions of his head in relief were also sold at the Anti-Corn Law League bazaar held in Covent Garden Theatre in May 1845.

On 1 January 1845 Moore married Rebecca (1819–1905), daughter of B. C. Fisher, but left her before the birth of their son, Sir Norman *Moore (1847–1922), and moved to a house near Manchester, as the most convenient centre for his work in relation to the league. There he assisted J. L. Ricardo in the preparation of a book published in 1847, entitled *The Anatomy of the Navigation Laws*.

When the corn laws were repealed in 1846, Moore found it difficult to resume his professional career, though his prospects of success in Ireland were apparently very good. He remained in England, visiting Ireland occasionally, but withdrew completely from public life. The constant exertion of public speaking and of travelling in the league agitation had broken down an already weak constitution and cost him a large amount of money.

In the latter years of his life Moore wrote a volume of fables in rhyme for children, but they were not published. He went to Bath, and died there on 6 August 1864, of angina faucium. He was buried with his father in Mount Jerome cemetery, Harold's Cross, Dublin.

NORMAN MOORE, *rev.* MATTHEW LEE

Sources Boase, *Mod. Eng. biog.* · A. Prentice, *History of the Anti-Corn-Law League*, 2 vols. (1853) · J. Morley, *The life of Richard Cobden*, 2 vols. (1881) · H. Ashworth, *Recollections of Richard Cobden … and the Anti-Corn-Law League* (1876) · H. Jephson, *The platform: its rise and progress* (1892) · G. J. Holyoake, *Sixty years of an agitator's life*, 3rd edn, 2 vols. (1893) · *Anti-Bread-Tax Circular* (1841–3) · *The League* (1843–6)
Likenesses C. A. Duval, portrait · relief medallion; sold by Anti-Corn Law League in 1840s

Moore, Roger. *See* O'More, Rory (*b. c.*1592, *d.* in or after 1666).

Moore, Samuel (*fl.* 1680–1720), draughtsman and engraver, appears to have been employed at the customs house in London. He designed and engraved two of the plates for Francis Sandford's magnificent *History of the Coronation of James II … and of … Queen Mary* (1685) and the plates in the *Coronation Procession of William and Mary*. George Vertue's notes imply that he thought Moore to have been the inventor of the medley, a *trompe-l'œil* montage of imitations of various drawn, written, and printed materials. He presented one of these, deceptively copying various prints, to Robert Harley while the latter was speaker of the House of Commons between 1701 and 1704. Medleys subsequently became quite fashionable. Moore also engraved some costume plates. Beyond this intriguing report very little is known of the artist's life and work. L. H. CUST, *rev.* TIMOTHY CLAYTON

Sources Vertue, *Note books*, 6.246 · G. Vertue, 'Common-place books, notes on art and artists, artistic tours, etc.', BL, Add. MS 23078, fol. 42

Moore, Samuel James (1810–1876), revivalist preacher, was the son of David Moore, Presbyterian minister of

Markethill, co. Armagh, and was educated at Belfast Academic Institution. He was ordained minister of Ballycopeland Secession Church on 9 May 1838, and on 28 October 1845 was installed in Donaghmore, co. Down. His sermons, which were described as eloquent, were said to have had a direct effect on his congregation, who held him in particularly high esteem. Indeed, when on 20 August 1850 he accepted a call to Third Ballymena Presbyterian, the Donaghmore congregation opposed his move at presbytery level, their protests culminating in '11 reasons of protest' presented to the synod meeting at Dublin on 2 May 1851. Moore, however, believed that 'the finger of God' directed him to Ballymena (*History of Congregations*), and was determined to follow the wishes of the Almighty.

The move was indeed timely. Moore continued to make an impact, regularly preaching on street corners and holding open-air services for the poor throughout the local area. In the spring of 1859, when revivalist fervour spread from Connor, where Moore's brother, John Hamilton, had played a leading role, his own groundwork ensured an enthusiastic response. A flourishing town, described in this period as 'a principal seat of the linen trade', Ballymena was at the very heart of the revivalist movement, and Moore's zeal and enterprise made him a central figure in this period of hectic religious activity. Like his brother, he presided over many emotionally powerful meetings, at least one of which resulted in the 'striking down' of affected worshippers. Such physical manifestations were the subject of heated controversy both within and outside the church. Moore himself contributed to the growing body of revivalist literature with a strongly supportive pamphlet, *The history and prominent characteristics of the present revival in Ballymena and its neighbourhood* (1859). It has been noted as one example of the revival's success that increasing numbers in Moore's congregation necessitated the building of the Third Presbyterian Church in Wellington Street, Ballymena. Completed at a cost of £5000, West Church opened on 1 January 1863.

As a member of the general assembly's committee on psalmody, Moore also gave a series of discourses on this issue, and in 1856 published a pamphlet entitled *Zion's Service of Song: its Importance, Improvement and Posture* in which he approved of the standing posture. It is, however, as a tireless worker for revival that Moore is best remembered: a memorial window in West Church commemorates the extraordinary events of 1859 in which he played a key role. He died at the manse, Ballymena, on 8 April 1876 and was buried in the parish graveyard on 14 April. Although the dramatic claims of mass conversions made by contemporaries have been significantly qualified by recent historians of the revival, its importance as a landmark in Ulster religious history remains undisputed.

MYRTLE HILL

Sources *A history of congregations in the Presbyterian Church in Ireland, 1610–1982*, Presbyterian Church in Ireland (1982) · A. R. Scott, 'The Ulster revival of 1859', PhD diss., TCD, 1962 · W. Gibson, *The year of grace: a history of the Ulster revival of 1859* (1869) · I. R. K. Paisley, *The 'fifty-nine revival* (1968) · M. Hill, 'Assessing the awakening: the 1859 revival in Ulster', *Church and people in Britain and Scandinavia* [York 1995], ed. I. Brohed (1996) · *The Witness* (14 April 1876)
Likenesses photograph, repro. in Paisley, *The 'fifty-nine revival*, 65

Moore, Stuart Archibald (1842–1907), antiquary and barrister, was born in September 1842, the fourth son of Barlow Brass Moore of The Lawn, South Lambeth, Surrey, and his wife, Harriet Adcock. Educated at the Philological School, Marylebone Road, Marylebone, London, he became secretary to Sir Thomas Duffus Hardy, deputy keeper of the public records, and afterwards practised as a record agent. Elected FSA on 2 May 1869, he contributed in 1886 a paper—'The death and burial of King Edward II'—to *Archaeologia*. Moore's services were retained in legal disputes relating in particular to foreshore, fishery, and cognate matters. On 24 January 1880, when well established in this career, he became a student of the Inner Temple, and was called to the bar on 25 June 1884.

Moore came to the bar at a time when the crown, through the office of woods, forests, and land revenues, and after 1866 the Board of Trade, had consistently asserted over the past fifty years a claim to presumptive ownership of the foreshore of most of the United Kingdom, excluding the duchies of Cornwall and Lancaster, putting lords of coastal manors in England and Wales, and owners of coastal baronies in Scotland, to strict proof of their alleged titles. The crown's assertion was supported in particular by Robert Gream Hall's essay *Rights of the Crown and the Privileges of the Subject in the Sea Shore of the Realm* (1830), re-edited by Loveland in 1875. Moore accepted an invitation from its publishers to produce a third edition. He observed that on starting this task he became aware of the unfairness and bias of Hall's arguments and obtained the publisher's permission to preface the new edition with a 'brief treatise' of his own. The result, in 1888, was a single volume comprising a treatise of over 600 pages, *A History of the Foreshore and the Law Relating Thereto*, which included the text of Sir Matthew Hale's 'Touchinge the customes' and 'De jure maris' printed from the Hargrave manuscripts, together with Loveland's edition of Hall's essay with additional footnotes by Moore, mostly critical of Hall's text. The thesis of Moore's treatise, described by a reviewer as a 'crusade' (*Solicitors' Journal*, 313), was that before the conquest most of the English foreshore had been granted to subjects and thereafter formed part of the waste of coastal manors; furthermore, the crown's assertion of presumptive ownership had been advanced for political reasons as late as Elizabethan times by 'title hunters', in particular Thomas Digges, and had been endorsed by compliant Stuart judges. Moore considered that not until 1849 did the crown's presumptive title acquire authority in Scotland, through statements by Anglocentric judges in the House of Lords. Moore, who described his treatise as a 'counterblast' against Digges, Hall, and government officials, and as 'a brief for the subject against the Crown' (*A History of the Foreshore and the Law Relating Thereto*, xlv), sought to support his case by a wealth of citation from medieval rolls, charters, and manorial records. Moore's historical theory was not original, for in 1849 Henry Merewether had argued at length before the court of chancery that the crown's claim was unsupported by authority. This address was reproduced in Loveland's edition, but not by Moore.

Moore's treatise was published while he was engaged as counsel to the lord of the manors of Great and Little Wakering in Essex, against whom the crown claimed ownership of the Maplin Sands. However, Moore's theory was not put to the test as the lord was able to win the case on the ground that he could prove a good title from the crown. Moore's satisfaction at his client's victory must have been tempered by the unanimous statement of the House of Lords that 'it is beyond dispute that the Crown is prima facie entitled to every part of the foreshore between high and low-water mark' (*Attorney-General* v. *Emerson*, 1891). Moore continued a lucrative practice in foreshore disputes, defending the subject against the crown, to the extent that he was described in one obituary as 'a thorn in the side of Government officers' (*The Times*, 6 July 1907).

Moore loved yachting, and was one of the finest amateur seamen of his time; he commanded his own 80 ton fishing ketch, in which he carried the vice-commodore's flag of the Royal Cruising Club all round Great Britain and the greater part of Ireland, with little regard for weather. He was a frequent correspondent of *The Times*, chiefly on yachting and other seafaring matters. He married Isabel Kate, daughter of John Knight Higgins of Northamptonshire, and had two sons; the elder, Hubert Stuart Moore (1869–1951), followed him both into chambers and into scholarship as a writer and editor on matters of water, land drainage, and fishery law.

Besides his treatise, Moore also published *The Thames Estuary: its Tides, Channels, &c., a Practical Guide for Yachts* (1894) and (with Hubert Stuart Moore) *The History and Law of Fisheries* (1903). He edited *The Letters and Papers of J. Shillingford, 1447–50*, for the Camden Society (1871), and *Cartularium monasterii sancti Johannis Baptiste in Colecestria*, for the Roxburghe Club (1897), as well as *The Domesday Book for Northamptonshire, Extended and Translated* (1863). The library of the Inner Temple has a collection of his professional papers, including extensive notes and transcripts for his foreshore research.

About two years before his death Moore was seized with paralysis of his lower limbs and retired to his vessel, where he continued to be a genial host. Shortly before his death he wrote two letters to *The Times*, on secret commissions (8 January 1907) and on the channel tunnel (8 February 1907). He died on 29 June 1907, on board his yacht *Gwalia* at Southwick, near Hove, and was buried at Southwick on 2 July.   GEOFFREY MARSTON

Sources *The Times* (6 July 1907) · *Law Times* (13 July 1907) · *Sussex Daily News* (3 July 1907) · *Proceedings of the Society of Antiquaries of London*, 2nd ser., 22 (1907–8), 289 · *Law Times* (1 Dec 1888) · review, *Solicitors' Journal*, 33 (1888–9), 313–14 · J. Foster, *Men-at-the-bar: a biographical hand-list of the members of the various inns of court*, 2nd edn (1885), 324 · *DNB*

Archives Inner Temple, London, collections relating to manorial, fisheries, and foreshore rights | Exeter Cathedral, MS calendar of archives of dean and chapter of Exeter
Wealth at death £9489 16s. 7d.: probate, 31 July 1907, *CGPLA Eng. & Wales*

Moore, Temple Lushington (1856–1920), architect, the eldest son of Captain George Frederick Moore (1818–1884) and his wife, Charlotte (1826–1922), youngest daughter of John Lushington Reilly, of Scarvagh House, co. Down, was born on 7 June 1856 at Tullamore, King's county, Ireland, where his parents were then living. His early education was at Glasgow high school, where his father, now a major, had become staff officer of pensioners for the army. In 1872 the boy, whose health was delicate, was sent as a pupil to the Revd Richard Wilton of Londesborough, Yorkshire. Three years later he was articled to the architect George Gilbert Scott junior, son of Sir George Gilbert Scott. Although nominally beginning in independent practice in 1878, Moore's career remained closely bound up with Scott for several years. Scott's mental health deteriorated and he became incapable of effective work for long stretches. Moore, therefore, faithfully completed many of his master's commissions, including the major church of St Agnes, Kennington, London, and all the income from such work went to support Scott's wife, Ellen, and her family. Moore's own career began slowly, partly because of these difficulties, and partly because it took time for his style and talents to mature.

In 1884, after a long engagement, Moore married Emma Storrs Wilton (1856–1938), elder daughter of his former tutor. Family and clerical contacts in Yorkshire remained important to Moore and explain many commissions, especially during his early career. By about 1890 his reputation was growing rapidly and over the next twenty-five years he built some forty churches which established him as England's leading ecclesiastical architect from the mid-Edwardian years. As an Anglo-Catholic himself, much of his work was for high-church clients who required beautiful settings and fine furnishings for worship. He was a very private man who lived for his family and architecture and never sought the limelight by aggressive self-promotion or involvement in architectural institutions or politics. He chose to remain based in London but much preferred working at home than doing so from his office. Gradually it became apparent that Moore's artistic destiny was not to preserve an attenuating tradition but to bring to maturity a development which otherwise would have remained incomplete. The following are the more important new churches he designed: All Saints', Peterborough (1886–1901); St Peter's, Barnsley (1891–1911); Sledmere church, Yorkshire (1893–8); St John's, Hendon, Middlesex (1895–6); Carlton in Cleveland church, Yorkshire (1896–1900); St Mark's, Mansfield (1896–7); St Cuthbert's (1897–1901) and St Columba's, Middlesbrough (1900–02); All Saints', Tooting Graveney, London (1904–6); St Wilfrid's, Lidget Green, Bradford (1904–5); St Wilfrid's, Harrogate (1904–14); St Luke's, Eltham (1906–7); St Margaret's, Leeds (1907–9); St Anne's, Royton, Lancashire (1908–9); Uplands church,

Temple Lushington Moore (1856–1920), by unknown photographer

Stroud, Gloucestershire (1908–10); Canwell church, Staffordshire (1910–12); St James's, Clacton-on-Sea, Essex (1912–13); and All Saints', Basingstoke (1915–17). Moore designed the Anglican cathedral at Nairobi (1917–18), the chapel at the Bishop's Hostel, Lincoln (1906–7), and the nave of Hexham Abbey (1907–8) and Pusey House, Oxford (1913–18). He also carried out numerous church restoration and furnishing schemes.

Although primarily a church architect, Moore undertook over seventy commissions for other building types (especially during the early part of his career). Major works include South Hill Park, near Bracknell, Berkshire (1891–8), the 'Eleanor Cross' at Sledmere, Yorkshire (1896–9), and the Hostel of the Resurrection, Leeds (1907–28). He also gained great credit from his contemporaries for his restoration of Treasurer's House (1897–1901) and of St William's College (1902–11) at York. Among his miscellaneous works are some schools, parsonages, and parish halls, the court house at Helmsley, and a hospital at Woodhouse Spa.

Moore's work, like that of the younger Scott, is important in the history of English architecture not only for its beauty but also for its development of the Gothic revival. Assuming an essential incompatibility between medieval architecture and modern life, A. W. N. Pugin, the pioneer of the Gothic revival, had striven to lead people back to medievalism; his successor, like Sir Gilbert Scott, had striven to bring medieval architecture up to date. The school identified with the name of the younger Scott and pioneered by G. F. Bodley held that both of these processes were unnecessary, that the Gothic style was still the most natural medium for the church architect to employ, and that its resumption meant not the adoption but the abandonment of a restrictive convention. Moore, even more than Bodley and Scott, seems to have thought and built in Gothic without any effort at stylism. His designs are indistinguishable in kind from those of the middle ages, and as independent of exact precedent as they. The limits of his style were the limits of his predilections: his buildings, although purely Gothic, appear to have been designed with no constraint save that of his vigilant good taste. Everything depends, not on elaborate detail and ornament, but on subtle planning, fine vistas, and what a contemporary critic called 'good proportion and sweetness of line' (Building News, 82, 1902, 657). The church of St Wilfrid, Harrogate, and that of St Peter, Barnsley, show Moore's style at its grandest; the village churches of Carlton in Cleveland and Canwell reveal it at its most intimate and delicate.

Moore died at his home, 46 Well Walk, Hampstead, on 30 June 1920 and was buried at St John's, Hampstead. He had intended that his only son, Richard, who had been articled to him about 1913, should take over the practice. However, Richard died in 1918 when the SS Leinster was torpedoed, and the following year Moore took on his son-in-law Leslie Thomas Moore (1883–1957). The partnership was known as Temple Moore and Moore, and Leslie continued in practice, often carefully adding to and furnishing the older man's works, until the mid-1950s. Among Temple Moore's pupils was, from 1899, Giles Scott, the son of his master.

H. S. GOODHART-RENDEL, *rev.*
GEOFFREY K. BRANDWOOD

Sources G. K. Brandwood, *Temple Moore: an architect of the late Gothic revival* (1997) · H. S. Goodhart-Rendel, 'The work of Temple Moore', *RIBA Journal*, 35 (1927–8), 470–92 · H. S. Goodhart-Rendel, 'The churches of Temple Moore, with a note on the use of styles', *ArchR*, 59 (1926), 11–17, 55–63 · *CGPLA Eng. & Wales* (1920) · private information (2004)
Archives Borth. Inst., drawings relating to churches at Old Malton and Lidget Green · priv. coll., photographs, sketchbooks, account books
Likenesses photographs, priv. coll. [*see illus.*]
Wealth at death £5635 8s. 9d.: probate, 7 Dec 1920, *CGPLA Eng. & Wales*

Moore, Sir Thomas (1663–1735), playwright, was born at Richmond, Surrey, on 9 October 1663, the son of Anne Agar, daughter of Thomas Agar and John Milton's sister Anne, and David Moore (b. 1619). Moore was knighted by George I in 1716, 'on what occasion is not recorded; but as some writers have observed, it was scarcely on account of his poetry' (Baker, 1.326). He wrote *Mangora, King of the Timbusians, or, The Faithful Couple* (1718), a tragedy in blank verse, which was played at Lincoln's Inn Fields Theatre on 14 December 1717. The scene is laid in Paraguay, the action full of 'love, battle, murder, and worse, between the Spaniards and South American Indians' (Doran, 1.351), and has been described as 'remarkable only for its absurdities' (Baker, 1.326). Moore, it is said, stimulated the actors during rehearsals by inviting them to supper. Genest asserts that there is 'no particular fault to be found with the plot of the play' (Genest, *Eng. stage*, 2.628), which, nevertheless, provoked the ferocious *Reflections on Mangora* (1718). A reply, probably by Moore, was entitled *The Muzze Muzzled, in Answer to 'Reflections on Mangora'* (1719). Moore died at Leatherhead, Surrey, on 16 April 1735.

THOMAS SECCOMBE, rev. FREYA JOHNSTON

Sources D. E. Baker, *Biographia dramatica, or, A companion to the playhouse*, rev. I. Reed, new edn, 2 vols. (1782) · Genest, *Eng. stage*, vol. 2 · J. Doran, *'Their majesties' servants', or, Annals of the English stage*, 2nd edn, 2 vols. (1865) · *N&Q*, 2 (1850) · J. F. Arnott and J. W. Robinson, *English theatrical literature, 1559–1900* (1970) · private information (2004) [G. Campbell]

Moore, Thomas (1700?–1788), hosier and carpet-maker, was born in Dulverton, Somerset. Nothing is known of his family except the existence of a sister, Grace, who married John Norman of Winsford, Somerset, and predeceased her brother leaving two sons, James and William. William became Moore's apprentice. Thomas Moore married and had one surviving child, Jane (c.1736–1815). His wife may have died before Moore moved to London, for her burial was not recorded on his tomb.

Rate books of St Luke's, Old Street, Middlesex, establish Thomas Moore's residence in Chiswell Street, Moorfields, just north of the City, from 1739. At the sign of the Bishop Blaze, according to his trade-cards, he made stockings, caps, purses, and frame-knit pieces for breeches and waistcoats. Appointed framework-knitter to Frederick, prince of Wales, in September 1750, Moore was described in Thomas Mortimer's *Universal Director* of 1763, as 'Stocking-manufacturer, carpet-maker and Framework-knitter to his Majesty', a post clarified on Moore's French trade-card as 'Marchand fabricant de Bas et Bonnetrie de sa Majesté Brittanique'. Moore's reputation, however, rests on his manufacture of hand-knotted pile carpets and furnishings like those of the Savonnerie at Chaillot, near Paris. He and Peter Parisot, both of whom supported and employed Savonnerie workmen defecting to London in 1750, each claimed in their advertisements to be the first to establish this manufacture in England. Whoever was right, Parisot's enterprises failed, while Moore's flourished for over forty years. Moorfields carpets sold widely: to Horace Walpole for Strawberry Hill, to George, prince of Wales, for Carlton House; even reaching America.

Like the Axminster carpet maker Thomas Whitty, Moore received publicity from the competition of 1756–7 promoted by the Society for the Encouragement of Arts, Manufactures, and Commerce to produce 'the best Carpet in one Breadth, after the manner of Turkey Carpets'. The judges found 'Mr Moore's was the finest in Pattern and Colour and Mr Whitty's came nearest in Staple'; being 'equally good in proportion to their Price', £40 and £15 respectively (minute book of the society for 1757, 31). Patterns for Moore's hand-knotted carpets—and for the

cheaper cut and uncut looped-pile strip-carpeting Moore made from the 1760s—were mainly in the fashionable neo-classical style. Robert Adam designed several Moorfields carpets, including one at Syon House, signed 'by Thomas Moore 1769', and three documented carpets of 1775–8 still surviving at Osterley Park. Moore employed his own painter, Thomas Wyth, to enlarge designs to carpet-size, bequeathing him 1 guinea a month for life.

Moore died on 21 January 1788, aged eighty-seven, and was buried in the dissenters' burying-ground, Bunhill Fields, on 30 January. He left a considerable fortune, thoughtfully distributed. £20,000 and several properties including Moore Place, his new house and shop, designed by George Dance, were shared out among his daughter, her husband, Joseph Foskett, worsted-weaver, and their seven children. The business was left in trust for Moore's grandchildren, William and Thomas Moore Foskett. Among many smaller bequests, Moore left £200 for each of his two principal workmen, encouraging them to set up in business; and £100 to succour residents in the Framework-Knitters Company almshouses that he had helped to administer since 1756. Friends given mourning included the dissenting minister Dr Abraham Rees. Moore's will shows generous support of protestant dissenters, particularly in Dulverton (where he still had a correspondent), contributing towards the meeting-house, Sunday school, and the minister's salary.

An engaging picture of Thomas Moore is provided by his obituary in the *Gentleman's Magazine*: 'In his stature, Mr M. was rather below the common size, but of a manly aspect. Easily accessible, without … pride … His address was pleasing, if not completely polished' 'Mr Moore … was by Nature formed for industry'.

WENDY HEFFORD

Sources W. Hefford, 'Thomas Moore of Moorfields', *Burlington Magazine*, 119 (1977), 840–49 · *GM*, 1st ser., 58 (1788), 86, 177 · will, PRO, PROB 11/1161 · trade cards, BM, department of prints and drawings, Banks collection · rate books, parish of St Luke, Old Street, Grubb Street Liberty, Finsbury public library · *Public Advertiser* (24 May 1755) · *Public Advertiser* (7 Jan 1756) · S. Sherrill, *Carpets and rugs of Europe and America* (1996) · T. Mortimer, *The universal director* (1763) · commercial directories (Kent, Lowndes), 1752–97 · D. Stroud, *George Dance, architect, 1741–1825* (1971) · register, Bunhill Fields, London

Archives CLRO, Dance portfolio, surveyor's miscellaneous plans, 96–192 [detailed plans of Moore's house; drawings of shop-front]

Wealth at death £10,000 in 3% bond annuities; plus funds to finance other annuities of £178 p.a.; £10,400 in bequests; two freehold tenements, five leasehold properties; new house and shop built at est. cost of £3500; warehouse and three other houses: will, PRO, PROB 11/1161; Dance portfolio, CLRO

Moore, Thomas (d. 1792), music teacher, lived in the Pool Fold in Manchester and was teaching music there in 1750, when he published *The Psalm Singer's Compleat Tutor and Divine Companion*. In 1755 the town council of Glasgow appointed him precentor of 'the new church in Bell's yeard' (Blackfriars) and teacher of psalmody and church music in the town's hospital (Renwick, 438). In 1756 he was elected a burgess, and subsequently he taught free music classes by order of the magistrates (in addition to his usual duties) in Hutcheson's Hospital. In 1758 Moore was effectively granted a monopoly of church music in Glasgow: the various other precentors in the town were admonished to attend his music classes and, as far as possible, nobody was to teach church music there unless 'sufficiently qualified upon Mr Moores plan [of instruction]' (Renwick, 523).

Moore continued to publish collections of psalmody in Glasgow, and he played a significant part in the revival of the practice of choral singing in Scotland. His collections included *The Psalm Singer's Pocket Companion* (Glasgow, 1756) and *The Psalm Singer's Delightful Pocket Companion* (Glasgow, [1762]) as well as *The Vocal Concert* (Glasgow [n.d., c.1761]). The Glasgow collections presented, probably for the first time in Scottish publications, a large number of psalm tunes which subsequently became popular in Scotland. Moore himself composed a handful of the tunes in these books, notably one called 'Knutsford'; he may have had connections with the town of that name, since his 1756 publication was to be sold by various booksellers including 'Randle Moore in Knutsford'. Moore also owned a bookseller's shop in Glasgow, first in Princes Street and later in Stockwell Street. He resigned his offices of precentor and psalmody teacher in 1787. From an advertisement in the *Glasgow Courier* of 17 November 1792 it appears that he died in Glasgow earlier that year.

J. C. HADDEN, *rev.* GORDON J. MUNRO

Sources R. Renwick, ed., *Extracts from the records of the burgh of Glasgow*, 6 (1911) · *Glasgow Courier* (17 Nov 1792) · W. H. Hill, *History of the hospital and school in Glasgow founded by George and Thomas Hutcheson of Lambhill* (1881), 206 · H. Parr, *Church of England psalmody* (1880) · J. D. Brown, *Biographical dictionary of musicians: with a bibliography of English writings on music* (1886), 432 · J. Love, *Scottish church music* (1891), 215 · M. Patrick, *Four centuries of Scottish psalmody* (1949), 162 · N. Temperley, *The hymn tune index*, 1 (1997), 292 · [J. Pagan], ed., *Glasgow, past and present: illustrated in dean of guild court reports and in the reminiscences and communications of Senex, Aliquis, J.B., &c*, 3 vols. (1851–6); rev. D. R. [D. Robertson], 3 vols. (1884)

Moore, Thomas (1779–1852), poet, was born on 28 May 1779 at 12 Aungier Street, Dublin, the only son and eldest child of John Moore (1741–1825), a grocer and wine merchant, and Anastasia Codd (1749–1832).

Education and first writings Moore's first school was conducted by a Mr Malone, his second by the Samuel Whyte who years earlier had taught R. B. Sheridan, the playwright. Whyte was much involved with Dublin's theatrical life, and encouraged Moore's talents as an elocutionist. It was at this time also that Moore had his first poems published, in the *Anthologia Hibernica*, a short-lived monthly magazine. Moore and his family were Catholics, and subject therefore to the penalties imposed on Ireland's majority community by her protestant rulers. The French Revolution had reinforced resistance to this regime, and one of Whyte's assistants, Donovan, not only gave Moore a good grounding in Latin but encouraged his Irish patriotism, with his 'ardent passion for poor Ireland's liberties, and a deep and cordial hatred to those who were then lording it and trampling her down' (Russell, 1.21). These sentiments were further encouraged after he entered Trinity College, Dublin, in 1795, when he became a close friend of Robert

Thomas Moore (1779–1852), by Sir Thomas Lawrence, 1829

Emmet, afterwards executed for treason. Emmet discouraged Moore from involving himself in the conspiracies that led to the rising of 1798, but the young poet acquired some reputation as a political speaker, and presided over a meeting protesting against the removal of an enlightened viceroy—Lord Fitzwilliam—and his replacement by the sternly protestant Lord Camden.

At Trinity, Moore became a sound classical scholar, and undertook the translations from Anacreon which he published in 1800. He had offered them to Dr Kearney, the provost of Trinity, in the hope that they might earn him an academic award, but the provost felt they were too amatory and convivial for this purpose. But amatory and convivial poetry admirably suited the taste of the fashionable London to which Moore was introduced in the spring of 1799, when he was enrolled in the Middle Temple with a view to a legal career.

Travels and early publications, 1799–1806 Moore had been introduced to Joseph Atkinson, secretary to the Irish ordnance board and in his spare time a playwright, who in turn introduced him to Francis Rawdon Hastings, earl of Moira, a friend of the prince of Wales. Moira's patronage was of immediate service to Moore, for he persuaded the prince to allow the poet to dedicate his translations of Anacreon to him. Moira also invited Moore to spend long periods at Donington Park, his palatial country house in Derbyshire, where he spent his days reading in the library, walking, shooting rooks, and on one occasion going down a coalmine. In London there was a round of parties, and his songs were in great request. His performances were brilliant, his face 'sparkling with intelligence and pleasure, whilst Beauty crowded enamoured around him and hung with infectious enthusiasm upon his every tone' (Jerdan, 91). Moore's social success reinforced the sale of his poetry. His songs began to be published and were well received. His *Poetical Works of the Late Thomas Little* appeared in 1801 and was a commercial success, although its mildly erotic flavour eventually caused him some embarrassment. But he rested his chief hopes of advancement on the patronage of Lord Moira, and when Moira's interest served to offer him the post of Irish poet laureate he was half tempted to accept, although the appointment was hardly compatible with his Irish patriotism. Temptation was resisted when Moore's father made strong objections.

There was no such objection to Moore's appointment, in 1803, as registrar of the naval prize court in Bermuda, employment moderately lucrative in time of war, though hardly secure. Moore sailed first to Norfolk, Virginia, and then on to Bermuda, where he stayed only until the end of April 1804. While there he made a notable contribution to the colony's social life, but saw little future in the business of the prize court. So he appointed a deputy, and spent some five months travelling in North America. He found the United States barbarous and disorderly, although he formed a more favourable impression of Philadelphia, where his reception was 'extremely flattering' (*Letters*, 1.69). In Washington he was presented to President Jefferson, who received him in complete silence. Moore arrived home in November.

Moore set to work on his *Epistles, Odes, and other Poems* (1806). It was reviewed in the *Edinburgh Review* by Francis Jeffrey, who denounced both the poet ('the most licentious of modern versifiers') and his book ('a public nuisance') (Jeffrey, 456). He elaborated these charges with such zest that Moore's Irish blood was roused, and, learning that Jeffrey was in London, Moore challenged him to a duel. This was about to take place in woodland near Chalk Farm when the contest was interrupted by police officers, who took both men into custody. Newspapers turned the whole affair into ridicule by alleging that the ammunition to be used consisted of paper pellets, and although the allegation was evidently untrue, it remained to mortify Moore for some years. When Byron repeated the story in *English Bards and Scotch Reviewers* (1809), Moore proceeded to challenge him as well, but fortunately Byron was touring the eastern Mediterranean, and was unaware of Moore's anger. Both challenges, as it happens, led to warm and lasting friendships, remarkable evidence of the charm and good nature of the Irish poet.

Irish Melodies and whig satire After the embarrassment of the duel, Moore withdrew to Dublin, where he spent the winter of 1806–7. His letters at the time were depressed, describing the city as 'desperately vulgar and dreary' (*Letters*, 2.111), but it was at this time that he was approached by two music publishers, William and James Power, to take part in a venture which proved astonishingly successful: the series of *Irish Melodies* (1808–34). He was to write words for characteristic Irish airs arranged by Sir John Stevenson, and Moore's splendid performances were more than enough to recommend the songs to fashionable society. But while this project was very congenial, Moore also saw some prospect in gaining a reputation as a satirist. He told Lady Donegal in April 1808 that he was hoping to 'catch the eye of some of our patriotic politicians', and at least one poem published at this time in the *Morning Chronicle* is very much in his briskly animated manner. It attacked the bombardment of Copenhagen by a British fleet in 1807, a politically controversial event. But his first formal appearance as a satirist was in a pair of poems in heroic couplets, *Corruption: an Epistle* and *Intolerance* (1808), both pleas for better treatment of Ireland. In an appendix he relates the story of the emperor Theodosius and his repressive measures against the people of Antioch. Reasoned appeals for clemency had no effect on him, but their mournful songs were irresistible. Evidently Moore hoped the *Irish Melodies* might have a similar softening effect on the harsh, scornful, or indifferent English.

At this time Moore also saw some prospect of success in the theatre. Joseph Atkinson had persuaded him to visit Ireland in the autumn of both 1808 and 1809 to take part in the lively theatrical season then held in Kilkenny. His performances in roles such as David in Sheridan's *The Rivals* were vivacious, and he used his enhanced familiarity with the theatre to good effect in his own musical comedy, *M.P., or, The Blue-Stocking*. It was performed in London's Lyceum Theatre in September 1811, and was well received.

On 25 March 1811 Moore married Elizabeth Dyke (1796–1865)—Bessy, as he always called her. In the Kilkenny season of 1809 she was one of the visiting actresses, and that is presumably where they met. Little is known of how their relationship developed, though in the summer of 1823 Moore revisited Kilkenny and recalled the days of his courtship: 'I used to walk with Bessy on the banks of the river' (Russell, 4.103). The wedding itself, at St Martin's Church, was so private that not even Moore's parents were told of it until months later. The couple lived for a time in Bury Street, but in May 1812 moved to Kegworth in Leicestershire, not far from Donington Park. This gave Moore continued access to Lord Moira's library, and might have suggested continued hopes of advantage from Moira's patronage if the political situation had not blighted his prospects in that quarter. The prince of Wales had been confidently expected to install a whig ministry when he became prince regent early in 1812, giving people like Moira the disposal of many places and pensions. The prince did no such thing, retaining the tory ministers in office for reasons outlined in a letter to his brother the duke of York. Moore composed (anonymously) a scathing parody of this letter which was widely circulated among whig politicians and greatly admired. It confirmed his standing as a leading literary partisan of the whig opposition, a status reinforced by the close friendship that developed with Lord Byron, whom he had met for the first time in November 1811. For many years Moore contributed his lively and accomplished verses to the *Morning Chronicle* and for a while *The Times*. It was a useful source of income, *The Times* paying him £400 in 1826 and 1827, and

£200 thereafter. Then there was the £500 a year he received from James Power in consideration of the continued publication of new numbers of *Irish Melodies*. As he remarked to John Dalby on 10 March 1812, he had 'every certainty of making an ample livelihood by literature' (*Letters*, 1.181).

Lalla Rookh and the period of exile But the amplitude of Moore's livelihood was never quite sufficient to cover the expenses of the fashionable society in which he moved, or of his continuing generosity to his parents in Ireland. This was in spite of his regular sources of income being handsomely supplemented by some outstandingly successful publications. The first of these, which appeared in March 1813, was *Intercepted Letters, or, The Twopenny Post-Bag*, a set of verse epistles purportedly written by associates of the prince regent. A rapid succession of new editions, coupled with the reputation Moore already enjoyed from *Irish Melodies*, established his position as a leading poet, and when word went round that he was writing an elaborate oriental romance, the two principal London publishers, John Murray and Longman, competed recklessly for the privilege of obtaining it. In December 1814 *Lalla Rookh*, as it was called, was assigned to Longman for £3000.

By this time Moore had left Kegworth, Lord Moira having departed for India, and was settled in Mayfield Cottage, pleasantly situated near Ashbourne. He was occupied in rewriting *Lalla Rookh* for many months, still referring to it as unfinished as late as December 1815. It did not appear until May 1817, although a final delay was caused by the difficult conditions of publishing in the immediate aftermath of the French wars. This monument of romantic orientalism, its four tales illustrating different aspects of a sensuously exotic enthusiasm, was immensely successful, going into many editions, and judged by Thomas Longman after twenty years to be the 'cream of the copyrights' (*Letters*, 2.821, 23 Nov 1837).

Moore had moved to Hornsey near London to oversee the printing of his poem, and stayed there until September, when the death of his first child, Barbara (then six years old), made the place intolerable to both parents. In November they settled into the home that was to be theirs for the rest of their lives, Sloperton Cottage, near Calne in Wiltshire. It was close to Bowood, the seat of Lord Lansdowne, Moore's most considerate and loyal patron in his later years. Politically Lansdowne was congenial, being a supporter of Catholic emancipation and sympathetic to Irish aspirations. He also brought to Bowood some of the fashionable society in which the poet found most fulfilment. Better still, there was a fine library. Moore now returned to his satirical mode in *The Fudge Family in Paris* (1818), a set of verse epistles attributed to writers ranging from a servile creature of the tories to a passionate champion of Ireland, with some light relief from Miss Biddy Fudge, a young lady of fashion. This too enjoyed considerable success, but Moore now found himself in serious financial difficulties. His deputy in Bermuda absconded, leaving Moore responsible for a debt of £6000. As he could not possibly pay this sum, he went abroad to avoid arrest,

and spent three years in France and Italy. It was an unproductive time for him, apart from the pedestrian continuation of the Fudge family travels later published as *Rhymes on the Road* (1823), and the verse letters (first published as *Alciphron* in 1839) which were the basis of his prose romance *The Epicurean* (1827). When in Italy he visited Byron, who presented him with the manuscript of his memoirs, a gift that had troublesome consequences for Moore, but that eventually led to the writing of his biography of the poet.

Later career Moore's friends were active in extricating him from his difficulties, and in 1821 Lansdowne was able to arrange a settlement which allowed him to return to England. Here he continued to exploit his talent for exotic sensuousness in *The Loves of the Angels* (1823), and to confirm his reputation as a political satirist in *Fables for the Holy Alliance* (1823) and *Odes upon Cash, Corn, Catholics, and other Matters* (1828). But he embarked on a new career as a biographer in his *Memoirs of the Life of the Right Honourable Richard Brinsley Sheridan* (1825), an elaborate work which made a genuine attempt to be fair to its sometimes disreputable subject. On the whole it was well received, and made it all the more possible for Moore to extract a handsome fee for the biography of Byron: 4000 guineas from John Murray. Byron had given his manuscript memoirs to Moore in the expectation that his friend might profit from them should he survive him. Moore later sold the manuscript to Murray on the understanding that he would write a biography after Byron's death, but then questions were raised about the propriety of this arrangement, and the money from the sale was converted into a loan, with the manuscript as security. After Byron's death in April 1824 the ownership proved a matter of great perplexity, and the consequent acrimonious legal disputes ended only when agreement was reached to burn the memoirs, much to the relief of Byron's family. Moore none the less remained the best qualified person to write a definitive biography and to edit Byron's poetry. He went diligently in search of materials, and received an abundance of letters and anecdotes from those who had known the poet. The title, *Letters and Journals of Lord Byron* (1830), distracts attention from the skill with which Moore constructed his portrait. 'Biography', he told Samuel Rogers, 'is like dot engraving, made up of little minute points, which must all be attended to, or the effect is lost' (*Letters*, 2.608, 21 April 1828). Moore did attend to them, and his biography remains indispensable for students of Byron. His edition of the poetry followed in 1832–3.

During the 1820s the condition of Ireland had increasingly forced itself on the attention of British politicians, and although Moore had no liking for pugnacious nationalists like Daniel O'Connell, he was keenly aware of the centuries of oppression that had generated such a nationalism. A visit with Lord Lansdowne to Ireland inspired him to write his *Memoirs of Captain Rock* (1824), a fierce indictment of the misgovernment of Ireland. The book established him as a leading Irish patriot, a reputation reinforced by his respectful treatment of a leader of the 1798 rising in *The Life and Death of Lord Edward Fitzgerald* (1831).

Moore insisted that his *Travels of an Irish Gentleman in Search of Religion* (1833), though offered as a defence of the ancient national faith, was 'in its bearings on the popular cause of Ireland deeply political' (*Letters*, 2.786, 26 Sept 1834). In 1832 he was invited to stand for parliament in the Limerick constituency. He refused, but spent the last years of his active life in writing a *History of Ireland* (1835–46), illustrating the impressive cultural achievements of Irish people before the blight of an alien rule afflicted them, and narrating in detail the acts of often appalling injustice committed by those alien rulers.

Moore's wife gave him unstinting support and understanding through frequently harassing financial difficulties and domestic distress. They outlived all their children: like Barbara, Anastasia died young, just before her sixteenth birthday; the two sons, Tom and John Russell, died abroad, in Algiers and India respectively. In his last years Moore was overcome by senile dementia: 'I am sinking here into a mere vegetable', he told Samuel Rogers in one of his last letters (*Letters*, 2.889, 23 June 1847). Fortunately he had been granted a literary pension in 1835 and a civil-list pension in 1850. He died at Sloperton Cottage on 25 February 1852 and was buried on 3 March in Bromham churchyard. Bessy lived on until September 1865.

Moore's contemporaries saw him as a major poet. In Ireland he was pre-eminent, and on his visits there could rely on an ecstatic welcome at any public occasion. Through much of the nineteenth century *Lalla Rookh* was admired and reprinted, and the popularity of some of the songs from *Irish Melodies* and its companion series *National Airs* (1818–27) persisted well into the twentieth century. In the twenty-first century, however, he is remembered mainly as an associate of Byron, although there is some specialist interest in his political poetry and in his orientalism as a vehicle for his Irish sympathies. His *History of Ireland* remains important for anyone who wants to understand the intractable difficulties of Irish politicians in their dealings with the British inheritance.

GEOFFREY CARNALL

Sources *Memoirs, journal and correspondence of Thomas Moore*, ed. J. Russell, 8 vols. (1853–6) · *The letters of Thomas Moore*, ed. W. S. Dowden, 2 vols. (1964) · H. M. Jones, *The harp that once —* (1937) · *Letters and journals of Lord Byron, with notices of his life*, ed. T. Moore, 2 vols. (1830) · *Works of Lord Byron*, ed. T. Moore, 17 vols. (1834) · T. Moore, *Poetical works*, ed. A. D. Godley (1915) · S. Smiles, *A publisher and his friends*, 2 vols. (1891) · S. Gwynn, *Thomas Moore* (1904) · W. Jerdan, *The autobiography of William Jerdan: with his literary, political, and social reminiscences and correspondence during the last fifty years*, 4 vols. (1852–3), vol. 4 · F. Jeffrey, review of *Epistles, odes, and other poems*, *EdinR*, 8 (1806) · T. de V. White, *Tom Moore the Irish poet* (1977) · G. Carnall, 'Robert Southey and Thomas Moore on the battle of Copenhagen', *Bulletin of the New York Public Library*, 73 (1969)
Archives Boston PL, corresp., commonplace book, and literary MSS · FM Cam., notes in *Anthologia hibernica* · Hunt. L., letters, literary MSS · Knox College, Galesburg, Illinois, papers · NL Ire., commonplace book and journal [copy] · NL Ire., literary MSS and letters · NL Scot., journal of a visit to Scotland · Rice University, Houston, Texas, Woodson Research Center, corresp. · St John's Seminary, Camarillo, papers · TCD, papers · U. Reading L., corresp., diaries, and papers, Longman Archive II 26B · University of Florida Libraries, papers · University of Virginia, Charlottesville, papers · Yale U., Beinecke L., letters | Birm. CA, letters to Joseph Strutt · BL, letters to A. Bain, RP 1495 [copies] · BL, letters to Sir John Easthope, with related papers, M/508 [copies] · BL, corresp. with Lord Holland, Add. MS 51641 · BL, letters to Houlton family, Add. MS 27425 A–C · BL, letters to Leigh Hunt, Add. MS 37210 · BL, letters to Macvey Napier, Add. MSS 34615–34616, 34618 · BL, letters to Royal Literary Fund, loan 96 · Bodl. Oxf., letters to E. R. Moran, with related papers · CKS, letters to Lord Stanhope · Fox Talbot Museum of Photography, Lacock, Wiltshire, letters to William Henry Fox Talbot and Lady Elizabeth Fox Strangeways · Leics. RO, letters to John Dalby · Morgan L., letters to John Wilson Croker · NL Scot., letters to J. G. Lockhart · PRO, corresp. with Lord John Russell, PRO 30/22 · TCD, letters to Sir Philip Crampton · Wilts. & Swindon RO, letters to Horatio Nelson Goddard
Likenesses oils, *c.*1800, NPG · stipple, 1800–40, NG Ire. · E. Hayes, pencil drawing, 1815, NG Ire. · J. Jackson, oils, 1818, NG Ire. · H. H. Meyer, stipple, pubd 1818 (after miniature), NG Ire. · M. A. Shee, oils, 1818, NPG; version, NG Ire. · T. Kirk, bust, 1821, Royal Irish Acad. · G. S. Newton, chalk drawing, 1821, Athenaeum Club, London · J. Thomson, stipple, pubd 1824 (after J. Jackson), NG Ire. · stipple, 1825 (after J. Comerford, 1808), NG Ire. · T. Lawrence, oils, 1829, John Murray collection, London [*see illus.*] · D. Maclise, lithograph, pubd 1830 (after drawing by D. Maclise), NG Ire. · B. Holl, stipple, pubd 1833, NG Ire. · D. Maclise, oils, 1837, NG Ire. · G. Mulvany, oils, 1837, NG Ire. · W. Essex, oils, 1838, NG Ire. · J. Kirkwood, etching, pubd 1842 (after D. Maclise), NG Ire. · C. Moore, marble bust, 1842, NPG; version, NG Ire. · G. Richmond, chalk drawing, 1843, NG Ire. · J. Hogan, plaster statuette, 1852, NG Ire. · W. Denning, watercolour drawing, NG Ire. · D. Maclise, pencil and watercolour drawing, V&A · C. Moore, statue, College Street, Dublin · G. S. Newton, oils, Bowood, Wiltshire · oils, NG Ire. · watercolour drawing, NG Ire.

Moore, Thomas (1821–1887), gardener and writer on horticulture, was born on 21 May 1821 at Stoke, near Guildford, Surrey. He worked for several years at Dickinson's nursery in Guildford before being employed at Fraser's Lea Bridge nurseries in Leyton, Essex, in 1839. He moved to Park Hill, Streatham, as an under-gardener, in 1842, and two years later he became clerk to Robert Marnock, who was laying out the Botanic Society gardens in Regent's Park. In 1845 he also became sub-editor of *The United Gardeners' and Lord Stewards' Journal*, which was edited by Marnock. While at Regent's Park, Moore attracted the attention of John Lindley, and in 1848, through Lindley's influence, Moore was appointed curator of the Society of Apothecaries' botanic garden in Chelsea (the Chelsea Physic Garden). He remained at Chelsea for the rest of his life, a period during which the reputation of the Chelsea garden declined, partly as a result of the decision of the Society of Apothecaries to scale it down in order to reduce the financial burden on the society.

Moore spent much of his time on horticultural journalism. He was editor of the *Gardeners' Magazine of Botany* in 1850–51, the *Garden Companion and Florists' Guide* in 1852, the *Floral Magazine* in 1860–61, the *Gardeners' Chronicle* from 1866 to 1882 (with Lindley), the *Florist and Pomologist* from 1868 to 1874, and the *Orchid Album* from 1881 to 1887.

Moore's speciality was ferns, and he published extensively in this field, but he was also an expert on garden plants and florists' flowers, and in the 1870s he named more than 100 varieties of holly. He was elected a fellow of the Linnean Society in 1851. He was exhibition secretary of the International Horticultural Exhibition in London in

1866, and for many years was secretary to the floral committee and floral director of the Royal Horticultural Society. He was appointed one of the directors of the Chiswick garden in 1866. He was also a member of the Pelargonium, Carnation, Auricula, and Dahlia societies. He was in much demand as a judge at horticultural shows, and only a short time before his death was engaged in classifying the narcissi for the Daffodil Congress.

Moore's chief publications included his *Handbook of British Ferns* (1848, 3rd edn 1857), *Ferns of Great Britain and Ireland*, edited by J. Lindley, and nature-printed by H. Bradbury (1855), *Index filicum*, in twenty parts, ending at the letter G (1857–63), *Illustrations of Orchidaceous Plants* (1857), and *The Treasury of Botany*, with John Lindley (1866; 2nd edn, 1874). Moore also wrote the article 'Horticulture' in the ninth edition of the *Encyclopaedia Britannica*, with Dr Maxwell Masters, which was later expanded into *The Epitome of Gardening* (1881).

Moore died at his home at the Chelsea Physic Garden on 1 January 1887, and was buried in the Brompton cemetery. He left a widow, Elizabeth. They had at least one child, a son. Moore's collection of ferns was bought by the Kew herbarium.   ANNE PIMLOTT BAKER

Sources M. Hadfield, *A history of British gardening*, 3rd edn (1979) · M. Hadfield, R. Harling, and L. Highton, *British gardeners: a biographical dictionary* (1980) · Desmond, *Botanists* · *Journal of Horticulture, Cottage Gardener and Home Farmer*, 14 (1887), 3 · *The Garden*, 31 (1887), 36–7 · *Gardeners' Chronicle*, 3rd ser., 1 (1887), 48 · *Proceedings of the Linnean Society of London* (1886–7), 41–2 · d. cert.
Archives Chelsea Physic Garden, London, herbarium and letters · NHM, herbarium · RBG Kew, ferns and letters
Likenesses portrait, repro. in *Gardeners' Chronicle*, 1 (1882), 709 · portrait, repro. in *Gardeners' Chronicle* · portrait, repro. in Hadfield, Harling, and Highton, *British gardeners*, 209
Wealth at death £3234 12s. 9d.: probate, 31 Jan 1887, CGPLA Eng. & Wales

Moore, Thomas Edward Laws (*c.*1820–1872), naval officer and polar explorer, was born in Brompton, Chatham, Kent. Nothing is known of his family or youth. He entered the Royal Navy as volunteer of the first class on 19 October 1833, but his early years in the service cannot be traced. From 1839 to 1843 he took part in James Clark Ross's Antarctic expedition as mate and magnetic observer on the *Terror*, and was promoted lieutenant on 4 October 1843 on his return. In 1845 he was sent to the Cape of Good Hope with Lieutenant Henry Clerk RA; they were to make a magnetic survey between the Greenwich meridian and 140° E, towards the Antarctic continent, to fill in a gap left by Ross in 1839–43. In the hired barque *Pagoda* Moore sailed to within 100 miles of the continent, making detailed observations, despite the very poor conditions and the fact that he was working without supporting vessels. He reported his findings very briefly in the *Nautical Magazine* (1846) and they were described more fully in Clerk's account, communicated by Edward Sabine, in the *Philosophical Transactions of the Royal Society* (1846). In 1846 Moore was sent to Hudson Bay in the *Prince Albert* to make similar observations. He was elected fellow of the Royal Society on 1 June 1854 for his 'skill, zeal, success in making magnetic observations at sea' (certificates of candidates

for election to the Royal Society, 1801–81, no. 42). His sponsors were John Barrow junior, Francis Beaufort, F. W. Beechey, and James Clark Ross.

On 11 January 1848 Moore was promoted commander and in the same year set out in the *Plover* to the Bering Strait to seek Franklin and help his search for the northwest passage. On this voyage he earned the disapproval of John Rae for having 'an Esquimaux girl in his cabin for purposes which were too evident' and 'selling spirits to the natives' (Jones, 'Governor Moore', 38). He returned in 1852, having discovered nothing as Franklin's ships had been lost some years earlier, but he did some useful surveying. He was promoted to captain on 15 January 1852.

In 1855, with no prospect of further commands at sea, Moore was appointed governor of the Falkland Islands. Despite the company of his wife, Eliza (whom he had married at some point before 1854), and his first daughter, and his secretary, Captain John Sibbald RN (who had been in the *Terror* with him), he found the place desolate, his duties monotonous, the people 'worse than savages', and 'drunkenness the prevailing habit' (Jones, 'Governor Moore', 39). Even the clergyman and his wife were often drunk, and Moore had to suspend the surveyor for insubordination. After a year he could write 'the officers have taken a turn and are behaving better' (ibid., 39) and when he left the islands in 1862 the colony was in a better condition: drunkenness was less rife, thanks in part to Moore's reading room and temperance hall, and a new surveyor and clergyman proved more co-operative.

Moore was promoted to rear-admiral in the retired list in 1867. In 1871 he had a stroke and he died on 10 April 1872 at his home at 5 Victoria Place, Stonehouse, Plymouth, from congestion of the lungs. He was buried in St George's Church, Stonehouse. He was survived by his wife, three daughters, and a son.

Moore's promotion was slow, partly for lack of influence and partly because he was retiring by nature. Although relatively little known today, his magnetic observations were a useful contribution to polar exploration.   A. G. E. JONES

Sources A. G. E. Jones, 'Lieutenant T. E. L. Moore, RN, and the voyage of the *Pagoda*, 1845', *Mariner's Mirror*, 56 (1970), 33–40 · A. G. E. Jones, 'Governor Moore, 1855–1862', *Falklands Islands Journal* (1977), 37–40 · A. G. E. Jones, 'Lieutenant T. E. L. Moore, RN, and the voyage of the *Pagoda*, 1845', *Falkland Islands Journal* (1976), 43–8 · *Navy List* (1839–72) · O'Byrne, *Naval biog. dict.* · reports and correspondence, *Parl. papers* (1849–51) [arctic expeditions] · H. R. Mill, *The siege of the south pole* (1905) · d. cert.
Archives PRO, Admiralty series, logbooks
Likenesses S. Pearce, oils, 1860, NPG
Wealth at death under £5000: probate, 2 Oct 1872, CGPLA Eng. & Wales

Moore, Thomas Laurence de la. *See* More, Sir Thomas Laurence de la (*fl.* 1327–1358).

Moore, Thomas Sturge (1870–1944), writer and designer, was born at 3 Wellington Square, St Mary in the Castle, Hastings, on 4 March 1870, the eldest of the four sons (one of whom was the philosopher G. E. *Moore) and four daughters of Daniel Moore (1840–1904), a physician, and his second wife, Henrietta, *née* Sturge (1839–1903). The family moved to Norwood in 1871, and he attended Dulwich College from 1879 to 1884, but, dogged by ill health, fell behind academically. In 1885 he enrolled in the Croydon Art School, where he lost his Baptist faith and where he met the artist Charles Shannon. After two years he transferred to Lambeth Art School; there Shannon's lover, Charles Ricketts, was a teacher. When Shannon and Ricketts moved into The Vale, Chelsea, in 1888, Moore rented workrooms there and they introduced him to artistic London at their 'Friday Evenings'. He contributed to their periodical *The Dial*, and helped to edit and translate a number of books for the Vale Press, which Ricketts started in 1894. In 1895 Moore's parents moved to Torquay, but he remained in London, living mainly off an annuity from an uncle. In 1893 he had privately published *Two Poems*, and in 1899 issued *The Vinedresser and Other Poems*, which impressed Laurence Binyon. Binyon introduced him to W. B. Yeats in 1899, and the two became lifelong friends.

In 1885 Moore began regular visits to his French relatives and fell in love with his cousin Marie Appia, daughter of George Appia, a Lutheran minister. In 1895, however, she became engaged to his brother Harry, but he was training to be an Anglican clergyman and, assailed by religious scruples about her nonconformity, soon broke off the engagement. Moore declared himself in June 1897, but was rebuffed; he persisted and the two finally married in 1903. Their son Daniel was born in 1905, and their daughter Henriette (Riette) in 1907.

Moore's developing interest in drama led to his association with a number of societies, notably the Literary Theatre Club, which he helped found in 1901 with Florence Farr and Ricketts, and resuscitated as a limited company in 1905. In April 1906 it staged his one-act *Aphrodite against Artemis*, based on the Phaedra–Hippolytus story. Although the play was savagely attacked by the reviewers, productions of Wilde's *Salomé* and *A Florentine Tragedy* (in Moore's adaptation) followed in June 1906. He joined the Stage Society in 1908, shortly after appearing in its production of *The Persians*, and in 1912 was appointed to its council.

Moore designed and illustrated books throughout his life (notably his own works and those of Yeats), and in May 1904 he was elected a member of the Society of Twelve, a group of wood-engravers and lithographers. He published books on Altdorfer (1900), Dürer (1905), and Correggio (1906), and in 1910 formulated his aesthetic ideas in *Art and Life*. His story 'A Platonic Marriage' was attacked by the Vigilance Society on its appearance in the *English Review* in January 1911, but later that year he was elected to the Royal Society of Literature. In the following year he joined Harold Monro's Poetry Bookshop, and contributed 'A Sicilian Idyll' to the first volume of *Georgian Poetry*. At this time he helped translate works by Rabindranath Tagore, then becoming popular in England.

In 1919 Moore moved his family from 40 Well Walk, Hampstead, London, where they had lived since 1912, to Steep in Hampshire, where his children attended the progressive Bedales School. In the following year he was awarded a civil-list pension of £75 per annum and published *The Powers of the Air*, which propounds his aesthetic in mythological terms, and a play, *Medea*. He gave classes in aesthetics at Bedales, and in 1929 these formed the basis of *Amour for Aphrodite*, in which he argued that beauty is an intrinsic value. The family had returned to Well Walk in 1927, where he began to keep open house on Friday evenings. His numerous volumes of poems were gathered into *The Poems of T. Sturge Moore*, issued in four volumes from 1931 to 1933, and a *Selected Poems* appeared in 1934. His *Judith* had been staged in January 1916, but there were no more performances of his plays until *Psyche in Hades* in 1927 and *Niobe* and *Medea* in 1930. He underwent a Steinach rejuvenating operation in 1936, and at the outbreak of the Second World War moved to Dorking. He suffered from chronic ill health from 1942, and died in Windsor of kidney infection on 18 July 1944, following an operation.

JOHN KELLY

Sources F. L. Gwynn, *Sturge Moore and the life of art* (1952) · W. B. *Yeats and T. Sturge Moore: their correspondence, 1901–1937*, ed. U. Bridge (1953) · S. Legge, *Affectionate cousins: T. Sturge Moore and Marie Appia* (1980)
Archives Indiana University, Bloomington, Lilly Library, MSS · LUL, corresp., diaries, literary MSS, papers · NRA, corresp. and literary papers | BL, corresp. with Sir Sydney Cockerell, Add. MS 52737 · BL, letters to Michael Field, Add. MS 45856 · BL, corresp. with Macmillans, Add. MS 55000 · BL, corresp. with Charles Ricketts and Charles Shannon, Add. MS 58086 · BL, corresp. with Shri Purohita Svami, Add. MS 45732 · BL, corresp. with Society of Authors, Add. MS 63306 · CUL, letters to G. E. Moore · LUL, letters to Wyndham Lewis · LUL, literary papers relating to Moore's family life collected by Sylvia Legge · LUL, letters and postcards to Llewellyn Jones, MS poems by Moore edited by Jones · LUL, letters to Llewellyn Jones · Royal Society of Literature, London, letters to the Royal Society of Literature · Trinity Cam., letters to R. C. Trevelyan · U. Reading L., corresp., mainly with John Gawsworth, and other papers
Likenesses C. H. Shannon, portrait, 1896 (*Thomas Sturge Moore in a cloak*) · C. H. Shannon, chalk drawing, 1925, NPG · W. Stoneman, photograph, 1932, NPG · G. C. Beresford, photograph, NPG · H. Murchison, photograph, NPG · C. H. Shannon, two lithographs, Carlisle City Art Gallery

Moore, William (*bap.* 1590, *d.* 1659), librarian and collector of manuscripts, was baptized on 29 November 1590 at Gissing, Norfolk, the son of William Moore; his mother's name is unknown. He was educated at Moulton School under Mr Machet and was admitted to the scholars' table of Gonville and Caius College, Cambridge, on 22 June 1606. He graduated BA in 1610 and proceeded MA in 1613; a man of this name incorporated a Cambridge MA degree at Oxford on 13 July 1619. Moore was university rhetoric lecturer in 1614, and also for some time Greek and Hebrew lecturer. He became a junior fellow of Caius at Michaelmas 1615 and a senior fellow from Michaelmas 1621. In accordance with the prescriptive statutes of the refounding master, John Caius, Moore compiled annals of the college starting from the year 1603 and continuing until 1648. He was also an important collector of dispersed monastic manuscripts, and he gave these, nearly 150 in number, together with historical papers of the sixteenth and seventeenth centuries, to his college library; the gift was presumably made during his lifetime, since it is not mentioned in his will.

Moore resigned his fellowship in 1647, perhaps upon marriage, though the date of his marriage and the maiden name of his wife, Sibella, are unknown. He continued to live in Cambridge, taking private pupils, and was elected university librarian in 1653. The university library, temporarily enriched with the contents of Lambeth Library, thrived under his librarianship and received numerous donations, notably the collection of books and papers relating to the Waldensian church and formed by Samuel Morland (1625–1695).

Moore died in the spring of 1659 of an ulcer in the bladder. At his funeral on 24 April Thomas Smith, his successor as university librarian, delivered a sermon eulogistic of Moore's piety and diligence. According to Smith, Moore had 'delivered to me a *catalogue* of all the manuscripts in that library (except the Oriental)'; this is no longer extant. Of his librarianship, Smith said 'we never before had such a custos, and I believe hereafter never shall' (Smith). Moore was buried in Great St Mary's Church; he had wished to be buried in Caius College, but the master, William Dell, would not allow him to be buried 'by the Liturgy' of the Church of England. By his will, dated 15 April, Moore left his property in Norfolk to his wife, Sibella, and made her his executor. There were evidently no children.

R. JULIAN ROBERTS

Sources J. Venn and others, eds., *Biographical history of Gonville and Caius College*, 1: 1349–1713 (1897), 192–3 · J. C. T. Oates, *Cambridge University Library: a history from the beginnings to the Copyright Act of Queen Anne* (1986) · T. Smith, *The life and death of Mr William Moore … a sermon* (1660) · J. Caius, *The annals of Gonville and Caius College*, ed. J. Venn (1904) · M. R. James, *A descriptive catalogue of the manuscripts in the library of Gonville and Caius College*, 1 (1907), viii, 106–241 · M. R. James, *A descriptive catalogue of the manuscripts in the library of Gonville and Caius College*, 2 (1908), xix · will, PRO, PROB 11/290
Wealth at death see will, 21 May 1659, PRO, PROB 11/290

Moore, William (*fl. c.*1806–1823), mathematician and rocket theorist, is a person of whom little is now known. His publications showed his mathematical competence, but he was not an Oxford or Cambridge graduate and was probably self-taught and thus near the end of a long line of similar men typified by Benjamin Robins (1707–1751) or Charles Hutton (1737–1823). He is shown among the preliminary appointments in the records of the Royal Military Academy, Woolwich, for 1741–1892, as becoming the sixth mathematical assistant in 1806 and as remaining on the mathematical staff until he was either retired or discharged when staff cuts were made in 1822 or 1823. The examining board that appointed him consisted of Charles Hutton and two others. According to a transcript dated October 1806, Moore and Peter Barlow (1776–1862), also then appointed, were thought 'capable of becoming very useful Masters'.

There is no published recognition by Charles Hutton of Moore, despite their teaching and researching in the same academy, supposedly side by side for several years. In Hutton's article 'Rockets' in volume 2 of his *Philosophical and Mathematical Dictionary* (1815) there is no mention of Moore or of his publications. Woolwich was then the centre of British rocket research and development, and Moore probably personally knew Sir William Congreve, inventor and rocket pioneer, and was presumably influenced by his work on rockets.

In 1811 Moore published *A Treatise on the Doctrine of Fluxations*. His *Treatise on the Motion of Rockets [and] an Essay on Naval Gunnery* (1813) is acknowledged as the first publication on rocket mechanics which correctly proceeds from Newton's principles, calculating on the basis of equations following from Newton's third law of motion, that 'action and reaction are equal and opposite'. The second topic in the title, the penetration of wood by round shot, was then already well researched. The aim was to predict gunpowder charges which would cause solid iron round shot, projected at speeds of about 1500–2000 feet per second, to penetrate the 'wooden walls' of ships in action at sea.

In September 1807 Copenhagen was successfully bombarded by British Congreve rockets. In 1810 the academy of Copenhagen proposed a prize essay on the related topics of rocket trajectories when projected in an oblique direction, the effects of perturbations on them, and certain matters pertaining to Congreve rocket combustion. Moore did not submit a competition essay but wrote four short incomplete papers, published in the *Journal of Natural Philosophy* (1810–12). The questions set in the competition were so wide-ranging as to deter all but two entrants. This led Moore to write his *Treatise*, essentially an extension and refinement of his papers, but also including naval gunnery theory. He did not himself experiment, and admitted that his results were theoretical and needed to be tested by experiment.

Moore's date and place of death are now unknown. German bombing in the Second World War destroyed invaluable documents with data on men, presumably including Moore, who had worked at Woolwich.   W. JOHNSON

Sources DSB · F. G. Guggisberg, *'The shop': the story of the Royal Military Academy* (1902) · W. Johnson, 'Comments and commentary on William Moore's *A treatise on the motion of rockets and an essay on naval gunnery*', *International Journal of Impact Engineering*, 16/3 (1995), 449–521 · F. H. Winter and M. R. Sharpe, 'William Moore: a pioneer in the theory of rocket dynamics', *Space Flight* (1976), 179–82 · F. H. Winter, *The first golden age of rocketry: Congreve and Hale rockets of the nineteenth century* (1990) · S. Clyens and W. Johnson, 'Fra Leipzig til London', *International Journal of Impact Engineering*, 16/1 (1995), 171–84

Moore, William (1790–1851), portrait painter, was born at Birmingham on 30 March 1790. He studied under Richard Mills in that city, but after some employment decorating japanned objects, he turned his hand from about 1810 to portrait painting, and achieved some success and repute in London. In 1829 he settled at York, where he obtained considerable patronage in the city and its neighbourhood. Moore worked in oil, watercolours, and pastel.

Moore was twice married: first, on 12 March 1812, to Martha Jackson of Birmingham; second, in 1828, at Gainsborough, to Sarah (*d.* 1863), daughter of Joseph Collingham of Newark. By them he was the father of fourteen children, including thirteen sons; five of the latter, besides Albert Joseph *Moore and the well-known painter Henry *Moore

RA, followed his example to become professional artists. In 1845 Moore fell ill from lead and vermilion poisoning, contracted from pastel pigment, which resulted in his death at York on 9 October 1851.

Edwin Moore (1813–1893), painter, eldest son of William Moore and his first wife, Martha, was born on 29 January 1813 at Birmingham. He studied watercolour painting under David Cox the elder, and also under Samuel Prout. Edwin Moore married Jane Oates on 23 June 1837, at St Michael-le-Belfry, York. He was employed for many years as a teacher of painting in watercolours at Bootham School, York, and at other Society of Friends schools there; he received a pension from the society after fifty-seven years' work for them. Moore was an occasional exhibitor at the Royal Academy, and died at York on 27 July 1893. He was survived by his wife, Jane.

John Collingham Moore (1829–1880), painter, the eldest son of William Moore and his second wife, Sarah, was born at Gainsborough, Lincolnshire, on 12 March 1829. He practised early as a painter, studying under his father at the York School of Art and later, in 1851, in the Royal Academy Schools. He was a constant exhibitor in London at various galleries and at the Royal Academy from 1853 to the year of his death. Moore was best known for his work in watercolour, and especially in his later years for his portraits of children and landscape views in or near Rome, which he visited in 1858, and Florence. John Moore married in 1865 Emily Simonds of Reading, and died at his home, Northbrook Hause, Grove Road, St John's Wood, London, on 12 July 1880. He was survived by his wife. Examples of his work are in the Victoria and Albert Museum, London, and the Fitzwilliam Museum, Cambridge.   L. H. CUST, *rev.* JOHN-PAUL STONARD

Sources *The Moore family pictures: paintings, watercolours and drawings by Albert and Henry Moore, their brothers William, John Collingham and Edwin and their father William Moore snr* [1980] [exhibition catalogue, York City Art Gallery, 2–31 Aug 1980, Julian Hartnolls Gallery, 22 Sept – 10 Oct 1980] · J. Turner, ed., *The dictionary of art*, 34 vols. (1996) · B. Stewart and M. Cutten, *The dictionary of portrait painters in Britain up to 1920* (1997) · *CGPLA Eng. & Wales* (1880) · *CGPLA Eng. & Wales* (1893) · *IGI* · D. Child, *Painters in the northern counties of England and Wales* (1994)
Likenesses J. C. Moore? or W. Etty?, oil on unstretched canvas, priv. coll.
Wealth at death under £800—John Collingham Moore: probate, 20 Oct 1880, *CGPLA Eng. & Wales* · £839 1s., Edwin Moore: probate, 30 Aug 1893, *CGPLA Eng. & Wales*

Moorehead, Alan McCrae (1910–1983), author and journalist, was born on 22 July 1910 in Melbourne, Australia, the youngest of three children and second son of Richard McCrae Moorehead, journalist, and his wife, Louise Edgerton. Educated at Scotch College, Melbourne, and Melbourne University, where he gained a BA degree in law, he displayed an early interest in newspapers as a student contributor to the *Melbourne Herald*. He later claimed that his awareness of journalism as a profitable career was awakened by the discovery that the *Herald* would pay linage rates even for the interminable lists of final results that he supplied to them. After six years as a reporter for the *Herald*, ambition and his intense curiosity about the

Alan McCrae Moorehead (1910–1983), by Francis Goodman, 1950 [in Florence]

wider world persuaded him in 1936 to sail for England, where he gained a job with the *Daily Express*. In the next ten years, although Moorehead's relations with the Beaverbrook press proved as stormy as those of many other writers, he became one of its star reporters. He made his reputation as a war correspondent in the western desert and later in north-west Europe. He was mentioned in dispatches in 1939 and 1945. His series of books on the desert campaign were collected in a single volume, *African Trilogy*, in 1944. In 1946 he produced an early biography of Montgomery.

As Moorehead confessed with engaging honesty in his fragment of autobiography, *A Late Education* (1970), he arrived in England before the war as a gauche and lightly educated provincial. He developed his cultural interests avidly, not least through his friendship with his talented fellow correspondent Alex Clifford, with whom he enjoyed one of the closest relationships of his life. His charm and intelligence gained him many friends, not least among women. He married on 29 October 1939, in Rome, Lucy Martha (*d.* 1979), a journalist, daughter of Vincent Milner, a medical practitioner, of Torquay, and Isabella Mary Milner. They had two sons and a daughter.

Jealousy of his success and dislike of his unembarrassed ambition made Moorehead a controversial figure among Fleet Street colleagues. But even his enemies could not dispute his brilliant gifts as a descriptive writer and military analyst, which also won him respect among senior soldiers. Most journalism is immediately forgettable, but Moorehead's wartime dispatches still seemed models of vividness and insight half a century later.

In 1946, weary of daily journalism, Moorehead defied the imprecations of Lord Beaverbrook and resigned from the *Daily Express*. His enthusiasm for Europe was undiminished, but he had little patience with English weather. He departed for Italy with his young children and wife, Lucy, a former women's editor of the *Daily Express*. In the next four years, at the house they had rented outside Florence, he wrote two forgettable novels which taught him his own limitations as a writer of fiction. He was on the verge of returning to England, nursing failure, when he received a cable from the *New Yorker* announcing its acceptance of a long extract from a non-fiction book he had written about the occupants of his Florence house in the fifteenth century, *The Villa Diana* (1951). The generous American cheque that followed was insufficient to save him from returning to England and accepting an improbable job for some months as a Ministry of Defence press officer. But it restored his confidence in his own abilities. In 1952 he achieved his first substantial commercial success with *The Traitors: the Double Life of Fuchs, Pontecorvo, and Nunn May*. The pattern of his career was then set, founded upon intensely disciplined work on a succession of historical books. In 1957 he built a house at Porte Ercole where the family spent several months every year thereafter. Yet he remained a restless, almost compulsive traveller, with little interest in developing permanent roots.

Moorehead's reputation as a major historical writer was made by *Gallipoli* in 1956. *The Russian Revolution* and *No Room in the Ark* followed in 1958 and 1959. In 1960 he published what is generally regarded as his finest work, *The White Nile*, a study of the nineteenth-century search for the sources of the greatest river in Africa, based upon archival research and extensive personal travel in the heart of the continent. Written with Moorehead's customary precision and literary grace, the book sold 50,000 hardback copies in its first British edition. *The Blue Nile* followed in 1962. In 1963 he produced *Cooper's Creek*, a study of R. O'H. Burke's and W. J. Wills's journey across Australia in 1860, which reflected his reawakening interest in his own country. In 1966 came *The Fatal Impact*, a study of the coming of westerners to the south Pacific. But in that year, while still in his mid-fifties, Moorehead suffered a stroke. This deprived him of the power to write or speak coherently. He retained sufficient comprehension to read widely by the simultaneous use of text and aural tape. He mitigated the terrible frustration of his condition by painting, and still found some pleasure in travel. But his tragedy was compounded by the death in a car accident in 1979 of his wife, whose role as typist, editor, critic, and business adviser had been essential to his career.

Moorehead was an outstanding example of the writer as professional. Some colleagues in his early years rebuked his indifference to ideology. He was single-mindedly dedicated to the job in hand, whatever this might be. Though he lost his Australian accent at an early age, there remained about him an underlying raw, outsider's quality. He used his gifts—above all as a writer of descriptive prose—to earn a living rather than to pursue any personal passion. In his youth, he seemed somewhat careless of personal relationships, although he valued those with other successful men and women: Ernest Hemingway, the Australian painters Sidney Nolan and G. Russell Drysdale, the television tycoon Sidney Bernstein. He mellowed towards his fellow men as he grew older, above all after his stroke. He was one of the most admired non-fiction writers of his generation, who also achieved great popularity in America. He was appointed OBE in 1946 and CBE in 1968. He became an officer of the Order of Australia in 1978. He was awarded the *Sunday Times* gold medal and Duff Cooper memorial award for *Gallipoli*, and received the Royal Society of Literature award in 1964. Moorehead died in London on 29 September 1983.

MAX HASTINGS, *rev.*

Sources A. Moorehead, *A late education: episodes in a life* (1970) • private information (1990) • *WWW* • *The Times* (30 Sept 1983) **Likenesses** F. Goodman, photograph, 1950, NPG [*see illus.*]

Moorehead, John (*d.* 1804), violinist and composer, was born in Ireland, where he received some musical instruction. He went to England while young, and played the violin in the orchestras of various provincial theatres. He was one of the violinists at the Worcester festival of 1794, and the following year Thomas Dibdin took him to London as principal viola player at the Sadler's Wells Theatre. Moorehead composed music for many of the entertainments there, including *Alonzo and Imogene*, *Birds of a Feather* (1796), *Old Fools*, and *Blankenberg*. In 1798 he moved to Covent Garden, playing in the band and writing music for such pieces as *The Naval Pillar* (1799), *The Dominion of Farce* (1800, with Thomas Attwood), *The Cabinet* (1802, with Reeve, Davy, Corri, and Braham), and *Family Quarrels* (1802, with Braham and Reeve). During 1802 Moorehead became insane and was confined in Northampton House, Clerkenwell, and then in Tothill Fields prison. After his release he joined the navy as a sailor, and was in 1803 heard of as bandmaster on board HMS *Monarch*. About March 1804, during a walk in the neighbourhood of Deal, Kent, he hanged himself with a handkerchief on the bar of a gate. His brother, Alexander, leader of the Sadler's Wells orchestra, died in 1803 in a Liverpool lunatic asylum.

L. M. MIDDLETON, *rev.* K. D. REYNOLDS

Sources *New Grove* • Grove, *Dict. mus.* (1927) • T. Dibdin, *The reminiscences of Thomas Dibdin*, 2 vols. (1827) • *St James's Chronicle* (5 April 1804)

Moores, Cecil (1902–1989), businessman, was born on 10 August 1902 in Manchester, the fifth child and third son in the family of four sons and four daughters of John William Moores (1871–1919), builder, and his wife, Louisa Fethney (1873–1959). He completed state elementary and secondary education, and in the early 1920s worked in a variety of jobs, which included training as an analytical chemist.

In 1924 Cecil joined his brother John *Moores in helping to run the Littlewoods Pools business, which the elder brother had already started. By 1932 it was so thriving and successful that John Moores decided to concentrate his attention on diversification and left the core pools business in the safe control of his brother. Cecil Moores's name became synonymous with what was Britain's, indeed probably the world's, largest football pools business. He was also a director of the Littlewoods organization, lending his considerable experience and talents to the progress of the other major businesses in the group, such as chain stores and mail order.

Moores was a loyal Briton, buying the famous Bapton herd of dairy shorthorn cattle in the early 1950s to prevent its being exported to America. Under his direction the herd won many prizes in national competitions and when he eventually came to sell it he imposed a rigid condition that it should stay in Aberdeenshire, to which he had moved it after its acquisition.

Moores's devotion to the work ethic was profound, but he also believed in enjoying life. His philosophy managed to combine both approaches: 'it is fun to work hard and to build a business'. His care of his employees embraced both these precepts also: he wanted to give them chances for 'fun' as well as for 'improvement'. His concern for them and their working conditions provided the company's employees with numerous social benefits long before the welfare state became a reality. This concern was extended to his customers—for example, in 1957 he initiated a 'winners' advisory service' to help winners of very large sums to adjust to and cope with a sudden and unexpected fortune. He believed in practical involvement in management and his personal presence was manifest daily throughout the pools company. He arrived before most of the staff and usually did not depart until long after they had gone home.

Moores's drive and organizing ability came to fruition with the outbreak of the Second World War in 1939. Virtually overnight the pools company was turned into an efficient war production machine, manufacturing and supplying everything from parachutes to Wellington bombers. The speed and efficiency with which a largely female clerical labour force was retrained and applied to these new activities were due in very large measure to the abilities of Cecil Moores. After the war he speedily guided Littlewoods Pools back to its pre-eminent position. He oversaw all the major developments in the pools industry, including, for example, the mechanization of the business, the provision of a nationwide coupon collector service (from 1957), and the use of Australian fixtures during the summer (from 1949). A shrewd man, he was once described as 'beady-eyed and on the ball' (private information).

Moores was also keenly interested in many sports. As a young man he was an amateur soccer player for Hyde United and later played for the amateur Liverpool side the Azoics. Throughout his life he was a supporter of both Liverpool and Everton football clubs. He was also a horse-racing enthusiast and pursued numerous other sporting activities, including golf, snooker, shooting, and salmon and trout fishing—at all of which he characteristically became proficient. In 1975 he was the driving force behind the formation of the Football Ground Improvement Trust (later the Football Trust), which provided about £40 million a year to help football at all levels.

Cecil Moores was of medium height and stocky build, with straight brown hair and blue eyes. Totally without 'side', he could get on with people from all walks of life. On 11 June 1930 he married Doris May (d. 1988), daughter of Thomas Steel, electrician. They had a daughter and two sons, the elder of whom, Nigel, died as a result of a motor accident in 1977. Moores was a devoted family man. He was also a generous host who enjoyed entertaining his friends and relatives in the house that he loved, which he had bought in Freshfield, Lancashire, before the Second World War. He could also entertain in other circumstances, and it was said of him that he was 'the best after-dinner speaker I've ever heard' (private information).

Although Moores retired in 1979 as chairman of Littlewoods Pools, in old age he continued, as president of the business, to attend his office daily, maintaining regular contact with the family business. He died on 29 July 1989 while on a fishing holiday at Loch Trool in Kirkcudbrightshire, Scotland, one year after the death of his wife.

MALCOLM A. DAVIDSON, rev.

Sources *The Times* (31 July 1989) · personal knowledge (1996) · private information (1996) · m. cert. · *CGPLA Eng. & Wales* (1989)
Likenesses statue (with brother Sir John), Church Street, Liverpool
Wealth at death £1,946,440: probate, 30 Oct 1989, *CGPLA Eng. & Wales*

Moores, Sir John (1896–1993), businessman and philanthropist, was born on 25 January 1896 at the Church Inn, Eccles, Lancashire, the first son and second among the eight children of John William Moores (1871–1919) and his wife, Louisa, *née* Fethney (1873–1959), a millworker. On the birth certificate his father's occupation is registered as 'licensed victualler', but John William had been trained as a bricklayer, and before long he was back in the building trade again. He was a hard worker, but his health was poor and he had started to drink too much. The family had difficulty making ends meet. Young John Moores's ambition was born: he wanted to look after his mother and to make the family fortune.

Early years Louisa, a highly intelligent woman, had recognized her son's potential early. He left his higher elementary school at thirteen to become a Post Office messenger boy, but the front room at home, otherwise sacrosanct, was opened up for him every evening so that he could work there in peace: he was doing a correspondence course for the civil service. He also went to night school to learn telegraphy, which finally led to a job as trainee telegraphist with the Commercial Cable Company. In 1916 he volunteered for the navy and was posted to a shore station in Aberdeen as a telegraphist. He was demobilized in 1919. His father had died earlier that same year, and John was now head of the family.

Moores returned to the Commercial Cable Company again, first in Liverpool, then to a posting in Ireland. The Waterville cable station was an isolated base in co. Kerry, where the cable came out of the Atlantic. There was a nine-hole golf course nearby, but no library or sports shop for miles, and very soon Moores had embarked on his first business venture. In his spare time he formed the Waterville Supply Company, to import bulk-purchased books; before long it also became Dunlop's 'sole agent in Waterville for the supply of golf requisites'. John had discovered that there was a good profit to be made on golf balls, and

Sir John Moores (1896–1993), by David J. Poole, 1992

he wanted some to practise with himself; sport of all kinds always interested him. Eighteen months later he was moved back to Liverpool.

Littlewoods Pools Now Moores had another plan. He had heard of a football pool being run by a man in Birmingham, and he persuaded two friends to join him in starting a football pool of their own. They risked the sack if found out, as the Commercial Cable Company's rules did not permit outside employment: they used the name Littlewood (the birth name of one of the trio) to disguise their identities from their employer.

A few months earlier Moores had married: major steps in his career often coincided with important happenings in his private life. Ruby Knowles (1894–1965), a waitress, was the daughter of the family where he was in digs. Her father, William Albert Knowles, was a clerk in a shipping firm, but the family came of fairly prosperous farming stock and had once owned a sizeable acreage near Chester. Ruby's qualities were warmth and kindliness and, even more importantly, strength of character. It would be needed in the risky times that lay ahead. The couple were married on 19 September 1923.

Littlewoods Pools—a system of betting on the outcome of football matches—was to be run on the French *pari-mutuel* system, in which 10 per cent of the total stake is subtracted for management costs. The three young men had to lay out their own money to rent an office, engage a typist, and pay for the coupons to be printed. Of those first 4000 coupons distributed in 1924, only thirty-five were returned. They had 10,000 coupons printed for a big match in Hull. Only one came back. By Christmas each of them had put £200 of his own money into the kitty, and

the two friends had had enough. John had not, and Ruby backed him, saying: 'I'd sooner be the wife of a man who has gone broke than a man who is haunted by regret' (*The Independent*). He took on overtime for the Commercial Cable Company, working on Sundays; he also paid back each former partner his £200, stopped renting the office, dismissed the typist, and called on the family. From now on coupons were marked by his brothers and sisters, who came over to his house every weekend, while Ruby cooked meals for them. She was still doing this the following season, as well as looking after a small baby; their first child, a daughter, had been born at the beginning of June. And the enterprise was still losing money. John decided to drop the *pari-mutuel* system. Instead he deducted expenses, plus a commission, before paying out, and the business began to take off. He rented an office again, took on staff, and devised a security system to prevent cheating. In 1928—the year in which his second child, a son, was born—he acquired his own printing firm to produce the pools coupons. By the 1990s it had diversified and become one of the largest printers in the north of England.

The world slump from 1929 to 1934 caused mass unemployment everywhere, but Littlewoods continued to engage more staff and acquire more buildings. And as their incomes increased the family began to enjoy life: they took up golf, shooting, and fishing, and started to travel abroad. The seeds of Moores's two lifelong interests, languages and painting, were sown now, although he did not have time to indulge them fully for many years. What he did do was to make sure that his workforce, in many ways his extended family, was also benefiting. Canteens were installed, with good food at subsidized prices; there was a medical welfare department, a contributory pension scheme, a social club for activities such as ballroom dancing and snooker matches, and a staff sports ground.

Moores was now a millionaire, at thirty-six. But he had to prove to himself that his success had not just been a matter of luck: he would start a new and entirely different business, from scratch. And on 23 January 1932, three months before the birth of his second son, Littlewoods Mail Order Stores was incorporated.

The mail-order business The idea may have come from the little mail-order firm Moores had started years earlier in Ireland, and he knew that the enormous mailing list which pools had built up would be very helpful; but it was also inspired by the hardship and poverty prevalent everywhere in the bleak depression years at the beginning of the 1930s. And he could remember only too well the difficulties with which his mother had to cope when feeding, clothing, and bringing up a large family on a small income. There had for some time been institutions in existence, such as the Co-operative Society, and the tallyman of the north, which enabled the poorer members of society to buy things they needed. Moores's originality lay in applying a mix of these schemes to a large-scale business enterprise.

As usual all the family were involved. They researched

and planned catalogues and helped to choose the merchandise, and Moores visited the United States to get information from big American mail-order firms such as Sears Roebuck. At the end of the first year the turnover was £100,000. A year later, in 1934, it had risen to £400,000; and by early 1936 mail order was grossing £4 million a year. Moores had made his second million.

It was not enough to satisfy him. Moores wanted to do more for Liverpool, the city to which he had given his abiding loyalty. For seven years, from 1933 to 1940, he served as a Conservative city councillor. He also stood twice for parliament, on each occasion fighting a safe Labour seat, and so failing to get in. But he still had another major business success ahead, the Littlewoods chain stores.

Moores's timing was impeccable: the economy had begun to pick up in the second half of the 1930s, and the firm already had buying experience and supplier contacts. On 4 July 1937 his fourth and last child, a daughter, was born. And on 6 July the first store was opened in Blackpool. Three years later, in 1939, there were twenty-five stores in operation, and further sites had been acquired. Then war was declared.

The war years and austerity Moores had seen it coming. After the Munich conference in September he had already started to consider air-raid precautions, and had organized an ambulance division at his own expense. Less than forty-eight hours after the outbreak of war the new pools building, complete with all office equipment, was handed over to the government censorship department, and a great many of the Littlewoods vehicles were donated for use as ambulances. But Moores wanted the whole organization converted to war work.

The first contract was for parachutes. A Littlewoods warehouse was transformed into a factory; groups of pools girls were instructed by experts in the techniques of cutting, sewing, rigging, and assembly. The first parachute was produced on 11 December 1939, only a month after work had started on the building conversion. One month after that the first 20,000 parachutes were delivered to the Air Ministry.

It seems extraordinary that a paperwork-based firm such as Littlewoods could switch to mass production, often of a very technical nature, in the way that it did. But the records show that its sixteen factory conversions, employing 14,000 workers, produced among other things 12 million shells, 5 million parachutes, 50,000 dinghies, 20,000 barrage balloons, and more than 40,000 pontoons and storm boats. It could be put down to Moores's leadership, to the research he had done into time study on his visits to the United States, to his organizing ability. But his own explanation was simpler: 'The ordinary man or woman can do anything if they want to badly enough' (private information). He always regarded himself as an ordinary man.

When victory was finally won it brought little respite on the work front. Moores's businesses had to adapt to a new and changing world. The pools building which had been handed over in 1939 was not returned for nearly ten years.

There was an acute paper shortage, so pools coupons could not be produced. The mail-order business had difficulty finding enough manufacturers, let alone enough paper for catalogues. The stores took the longest to recover. Building restrictions were not relaxed until October 1945, and not lifted completely for a further nine years. All the sites which had been acquired before the war lay undeveloped, and some were even compulsorily purchased by the government, having been first valued as 'derelict' land.

In spite of the difficulties, by buying up old properties and shops Moores had managed to get six new stores going by the end of 1947. But the non-stop work involved took its toll. He was fifty, and was driving himself hard. There was panic throughout the organization when, at the beginning of that year, he became seriously ill with meningitis.

Moores had recovered in time for his eldest daughter's wedding in April, but the specialists were far from satisfied with his condition and prescribed a good rest and some sunshine. Moores and his wife went to Bermuda. During the holiday he came across an enormous disused hotel on the island's best ocean beach, and before long he had decided to buy it himself and build it up into a profitable concern. (As a follow-on, Littlewoods also became involved in the hotel business for a time, acquiring two in Harrogate and a loch and fishing lodge in Scotland. The family had to pay to take holidays there, but groups of long-serving employees who needed a break were sent free of charge.) Moores's initial action had not been entirely due to business acumen; he had an ulterior motive. Should anything happen to him, the Bermuda hotel could be sold and the proceeds used to pay off his death duties on Littlewoods. His concern was to keep the business intact for his descendants, and his recent illness had made him only too aware of his own mortality. A great many of his shares were put in trust for his offspring at this point.

The 1950s saw a resurgence in all three core businesses. New catalogue titles were created in mail order; more stores were opened (there were now more than sixty in the chain). Moores had produced a formula which could withstand almost any economic conditions: the cash flow from the pools was continuous; in good times the stores thrived; if there was a recession, then mail order got the benefit. Two of the divisions were always able to support the third when necessary.

Philanthropic work Moores's charitable works increased at an equal rate. In 1956 he became chairman of the Liverpool Motorists' Outing for Handicapped Children. In 1957 the John Moores Liverpool Art Exhibition was founded, a biennial competition with a top prize of £20,000. Moores had taken up painting himself, and wanted to do what he could to assist young and aspiring artists. Those the competition helped to launch included David Hockney, Peter Blake, and R. B. Kitaj.

After his mother's death from cancer in 1959, the pace of Moores's activities grew even more hectic. In 1960 he became chairman of Everton Football Club, attending nearly every match: he even left for one in the middle of his younger daughter's wedding reception. In 1963 he funded a school of business management studies at Liverpool University. He became involved in the funding and building of boys' clubs and youth clubs. And his charities went on growing.

What few people knew, even within the family, was that Ruby, like John's mother, had suffered from cancer herself. She had had a mastectomy two years before Louisa's death, going into hospital under an assumed name, and timing it carefully so that two weeks later she could attend a family party without anyone realizing. She never liked a fuss. Now the cancer was recurring. Moores resigned his chairmanship of Everton to be with her as much as possible, but she died in 1965, seven weeks before her seventy-first birthday. At first Moores seemed almost stunned; they had been married for nearly forty-two years. Then he forced himself back to work again.

A few weeks later Moores had a bad fall. His hip gave him considerable pain for the next year or two, which restricted his fishing and shooting activities. But nothing could make him restrict his workload. In 1966 he had an IBM computer installed. In 1967 Littlewoods took over Sherman's Pools. New stores were being built and bought every year: there were eighty-four by the end of the 1960s, and three years later the number had grown to more than 100. Then Moores decided on a hip replacement operation. Artificial hip joints were still a recent development, but the operation was a great success. He was not allowed to ski again, or to water ski (a sport which he had taken up at the age of sixty-nine), but otherwise he was back to normal.

Later years In 1970 Moores was made a freeman of the city of Liverpool, the honour, probably, which gave him the greatest pleasure of all. A year later he was appointed CBE. In 1980 he received a knighthood and chose as the motto for his coat of arms 'Opportunity made, not found'.

On doctor's orders Moores was beginning to take more holidays. He was enjoying his great hobby, painting. But, even after resigning the chairmanship and handing over to his younger son in 1977, he still went in to his office every day and continued his flying visits to stores all over the country. Three years later he was back at the helm: handing over was something he always found difficult to do. When he did finally resign the chairmanship, he was elected president for life, remaining involved until 1986. In that year he had two operations, one after another, first on his Achilles tendon, and then for an enlarged prostate. He was never quite the same again.

Sir John Moores died on 25 September 1993 at his modest four-bedroomed home, Fairways, Shireburn Road, Formby, Liverpool, at the age of ninety-seven, and was cremated on 1 October at Southport crematorium, Scarisbrick; his ashes were interred in Dove Glade on 11 May 1994. He was reputedly one of the wealthiest men in Britain, and left an estate valued at over £10 million. Moores was the archetype of the self-made man, in the paternalist, Victorian manner: his business acumen was matched by a concern for his workforce, and, while his family was at the centre of his world, he had a practical interest in the welfare of other young people. Liverpool Polytechnic was renamed Liverpool John Moores University in 1992, a testimony to his success, his philanthropy, and his devotion to the city of Liverpool.   BARBARA CLEGG

Sources B. Clegg, *The man who made Littlewoods* (1993) · Littlewoods company records, Littlewoods Organisation, 100 Old Hall Street, Liverpool, Group Corporate Communications · private information (2004) [family, executives, and retired staff] · b. cert. · m. cert. · d. cert. · *The Times* (27 Sept 1993) · *The Independent* (28 Sept 1993) · B. West, 'Moores, Sir John', *DBB*
Likenesses D. J. Poole, oils, 1992, priv. coll. [*see illus.*] · photograph, repro. in *The Times* · photograph, repro. in *The Independent*
Wealth at death £10,208,599: probate, 3 Dec 1993, *CGPLA Eng. & Wales*

Moorhead, Ethel Agnes Mary (1869–1955), suffragette and painter, was born on 28 August 1869 at Fisher Street, Maidstone, Kent, one of six children of George Alexander Moorhead (*d.* 1911/12), an army surgeon of Irish extraction, and his wife, Margaret Humphries (1833–1902), an Irishwoman of French Huguenot extraction. She spent a peripatetic childhood in India, Mauritius, and South Africa, before the family returned to Scotland towards the end of the nineteenth century. Ethel Moorhead's elder sister, Alice, encouraged by their father, qualified as a doctor in 1893 and practised in Dundee. She married a doctor in Leith in 1908 and died a year later. According to Ethel Moorhead's memoir, 'Incendiaries', while her siblings spread their wings in different parts of the globe, Ethel was the stay-at-home daughter who looked after their parents (her mother died in 1902). One of her brothers, Arthur, died in Batheaston, Somerset, in 1916 and left the residue of his estate to her, thus providing her with an income. Another brother, Rupert (*d.* 1939), worked as a doctor, also in Batheaston.

Although her main role was perceived as one of caring for her parents, Ethel was permitted to study painting in Paris during the 1890s, financially supported by her sister Alice. Although it was never considered that she would become a professional artist, she apparently studied painting under Whistler and drawing under Mucha. The first paintings she exhibited at Dundee Graphic Arts Society (in 1901) were said to be 'the gems of the collection', 'notable for their dark tones and strength of colour' (Henderson). She had a studio in Dundee and exhibited widely, acclaimed as 'a most refined and distinguished artist' (*Celtic Annual*, 16). During that period she kept house for her father, who encouraged her painting and to whom she was very close.

Ethel became involved in the women's suffrage movement in 1910, joining the militant, Pankhurst-led Women's Social and Political Union. In December she threw an egg at Winston Churchill at a political meeting in Dundee. In January 1911 she became Dundee's first tax resister (on the principle adopted by many in the suffrage movement that if they were not admitted to full citizenship women should not be held liable for taxes). The bailiffs came to the house to remove all the household goods but were persuaded to take a silver candelabrum. Her friends bought it back, and her father 'was delighted when she marched in with it' (Moorhead, 251). After her father's death 'the loneliness was terrible' (ibid.) and she moved to Edinburgh and threw herself into the women's suffrage campaign. In March 1912 she was arrested in London for damaging two windows but was discharged for lack of evidence. In September she smashed the glass at the Wallace monument; when she was arrested she gave her name as Edith Johnston and served a seven-day prison sentence in Perth. In October, after being ejected from a meeting in Edinburgh's Synod Hall, she marched into the classroom of the male teacher who had been responsible and attacked him with a dog whip. In December she was arrested in Aberdeen for causing a disturbance and gave her name as Mary Humphreys; she went on hunger strike but was released on paying part of her fine after four days. At the end of January 1913 she threw cayenne pepper into the eyes of a police constable in Leven and was arrested under the name of Margaret Morrison. She caused havoc in Cupar police cells and was then sentenced to thirty days' imprisonment in Perth, but was released after serving only two days because she had been hunger striking since her arrest.

By this time Ethel Moorhead was being referred to as the 'leader' of the suffragettes in Scotland. She was never that but she was certainly very well known, not only for her many and varied activities but also because of her flamboyant defiance of authority. In July 1913, as Margaret Morrison, she was sentenced to eight months' imprisonment for attempted fire-raising but was released under the so-called Cat and Mouse Act after a five-day hunger strike. In 1914 she was re-arrested and became the first suffragette in Scotland to be forcibly fed (in Calton gaol, Edinburgh); she was released after contracting pneumonia. She escaped from the house of the doctor caring for her and was not recaptured before the war, though it seems certain that she was Fanny Parker's accomplice in attempting to burn down Robert Burns's cottage in July 1914.

Militancy was renounced by the Pankhursts after war broke out and, in common with many other suffragettes, Ethel was active in relief work during the early stages of the war, working with Fanny Parker for the National Service Organization, initiated by the other militant suffrage society, the Women's Freedom League.

After the war Ethel sold her house in Dundee to another artist and spent some time drifting, before settling in France in the 1920s where she launched and co-edited a literary journal, *This Quarter*, with a young Irish-American poet, Ernest Walsh. In *This Quarter*, no. 3, 1927, she recorded that the journal had been founded 'on the strength of a legacy left me by a friend, Frances Mary Parker'. Contributors to *This Quarter* included Ezra Pound, Ernest Hemingway, Gertrude Stein, and James Joyce. Ethel at that time was later described by American novelist Kay Boyle as having

> short bobbed hair, with only a little grey in it, and the pince-nez she wore gave her an air of authority; but there was at

the same time something like shyness, or wariness in her small uneasy brown eyes and her tense mouth. (McAlmon, 194)

Ethel had a love-hate relationship with Kay Boyle, who, bursting on the scene, had a passionate affair with her co-editor (and possibly lover), and bore his child. Walsh died of tuberculosis in October 1926. In 1934 Ethel edited his works for an American publisher.

Ethel Moorhead died on 4 March 1955 at 14 Booterstown Road, Blackrock, co. Dublin, and was buried at Dean's Grange cemetery, Dublin. LEAH LENEMAN

Sources L. Leneman, *A guid cause: the women's suffrage movement in Scotland* (1995) • L. Leneman, *Martyrs in our midst: Dundee, Perth and the forcible feeding of suffragettes*, Abertay Historical Society Publication, 33 (1993) • NA Scot., prison records, Scottish home and health department, HH16/40, HH16/41, HH16/44, HH55/336, HH12/63/12 • *Votes for Women* (4 March 1910) • *Votes for Women* (16 Dec 1910) • *Votes for Women* (24 March 1911) • *Votes for Women* (8 March 1912) • *Votes for Women* (5 April 1912) • *Votes for Women* (20 Sept 1912) • *Votes for Women* (8 Nov 1912) • *Votes for Women* (6 Dec 1912) • *Votes for Women* (13 Dec 1912) • *Votes for Women* (7 Feb 1913) • *Edinburgh Evening Dispatch* (7 Sept 1912) • *Edinburgh Evening Dispatch* (5 Oct 1912) • *Edinburgh Evening Dispatch* (2 Nov 1912) • *Edinburgh Evening Dispatch* (30 Jan 1913) • *Edinburgh Evening Dispatch* (5 Feb 1913) • *Edinburgh Evening Dispatch* (8 March 1913) • *Edinburgh Evening Dispatch* (8 April 1913) • *Edinburgh Evening Dispatch* (25 Feb 1914) • *Edinburgh Evening Dispatch* (5 March 1914) • *Edinburgh Evening Dispatch* (14 March 1914) • *Edinburgh Evening Dispatch* (17 March 1914) • *Dundee Advertiser* (14 Oct 1912) • *Dundee Advertiser* (2 Dec 1912) • *Dundee Advertiser* (30 Jan 1913) • *Dundee Advertiser* (5 Feb 1913) • *Dundee Advertiser* (6 June 1913) • *Dundee Advertiser* (28 July 1913) • *Dundee Advertiser* (30 July 1913) • *Glasgow Herald* (9 Sept 1912) • *Glasgow Herald* (28 July 1913) • *Glasgow Herald* (19 Feb 1914) • *The Scotsman* (16 Dec 1912) • *The Scotsman* (30 Dec 1912) • *The Scotsman* (9 Jan 1913) • *The Scotsman* (22 Feb 1913) • *The Scotsman* (2 March 1913) • *The Scotsman* (25–31 July 1913) • *The Scotsman* (11 March 1914) • *The Vote* (21 Oct 1911) • *The Vote* (16 Nov 1912) • *The Vote* (8 June 1915) • Dundee Art Society records • M. Henderson, *Dundee women's achievement trail* [forthcoming] • R. McAlmon, *Being geniuses together, 1920–1930* (1938); rev. with additions by K. Boyle (1968) • *Celtic Annual* (1918–19), 16 • private information (2004) [Dr Ann Prescott] • E. Crawford, *The women's suffrage movement: a reference guide, 1866–1928* (1999) • E. Moorhead, 'Incendiaries (work in progress)', *This Quarter*, 2 (1925) • b. cert. • d. cert. • *Irish Times*

Archives FILM Scottish Screen Archive, Glasgow, 'Ethel Moorhead', 1995

Likenesses portrait, Criminal RO, M/19433

Moorhouse, James (1826–1915), bishop of Melbourne and bishop of Manchester, was born at Sheffield on 19 November 1826, the only son of James Moorhouse, master cutler, and his wife, Jane Frances, evangelical daughter of Captain Richard Bowman, of Whitehaven. Intended originally to follow his father, he was educated privately and at St John's College, Cambridge. After a period of doubt he underwent a mystical conversion. He was ordained priest in 1854.

After serving curacies at St Neot's (1854–5), at Sheffield (1855–9), and at Hornsey, London (1859–61), Moorhouse was appointed perpetual curate of St John's, Fitzroy Square, London, in 1862, and vicar of St James's, Paddington, in 1868. Lord Salisbury was a parishioner at St John's and became Moorhouse's patron. A forthright, vivid preacher, by this time Moorhouse had been the first curate ever appointed select preacher to the University of Cambridge, in 1861; he was also Hulsean lecturer in 1864, and Warburton lecturer at Lincoln's Inn in 1876. In 1874 he was made chaplain-in-ordinary to the queen and prebendary of St Paul's. He married on 12 September 1861 Mary Lydia (d. 1906), daughter of the Revd Thomas Sale, vicar of Sheffield. There were no children of the marriage.

In 1876 Moorhouse was consecrated bishop of Melbourne, having refused the see of Calcutta. At Melbourne his eloquence, leadership, administrative abilities, and physical strength flowered. He played the bluff Yorkshire gentleman, smoked a pipe, drank wine, walked a bulldog, attended football matches, and won deep affection. His public lectures—historical, philosophical, and theological—were conventional and simplistic, but they drew audiences of up to 4000 people.

In 1878 Moorhouse started a new building for the theological faculty at Trinity College in the University of Melbourne. In the 1880s he oversaw the building of a cathedral designed by William Butterfield, costing £100,000, and in 1882 he presided over the synod which framed the constitution of the Church in Australia. As chancellor of Melbourne University from 1884 to 1886, he defended the traditional education in the classics and opposed the foundation of a women's college. He made strenuous journeys to distant parishes and out-stations for three months in each year, and he stimulated the religious life of priests and settlers.

To the consternation of those in Melbourne, Moorhouse was called to the see of Manchester in 1886 (he was about to be offered Southwell in 1884, but Gladstone changed his mind). Besides the ordinary activities of a very extensive diocese, to which he devoted himself wholeheartedly, he continued the Victorian practice of personally visiting each of his 600 parishes, entering each church and inspecting each church school. His most notable public efforts were a sermon to the British Association in 1887, an address to the church congress at Manchester in 1888, a reply to Cardinal Vaughan's assertion of Roman Catholic claims in the Manchester diocese in 1894, and, consistent with his policy in Victoria, attempts to protect religious instruction and church schools. He retired from Manchester in 1903 and died at his home, Poundisford Park, near Taunton, on 9 April 1915. He left an estate of over £54,000.

Moorhouse was a broad-churchman, outwardly tolerant, but invariably a fierce defender of scriptural authority and protestantism. His earliest published lectures included an attack on Baden-Powell's contribution to *Essays and Reviews*. He read German biblical criticism in translation and reproduced ill-digested conflations of it in his sermons. Moorhouse upheld the authenticity of miracles in the apostolic age, but allowed that scientific laws obtained in the post-apostolic era. He took a mystical view of the incarnation and of atonement, and conceded that parts of the Old Testament were morally indefensible. Moorhouse supported Christian working men's clubs and church missions to the urban poor, but he opposed independent working men's political and trades-union activities as threats to social order and property. He was an orthodox believer, sustained by his inner light and his will to believe. E. A. KNOX, rev. F. B. SMITH

Sources E. C. Rickards, *Bishop Moorhouse of Melbourne and Manchester* (1920) · C. R. Badger, 'Moorhouse, James', *AusDB*, vol. 5 · G. Serle, *The rush to be rich* (1971) · F. B. Smith, 'Religion and freethought in Melbourne, 1870 to 1890', MA diss., University of Melbourne, 1960 · Gladstone, *Diaries*
Archives LPL, corresp. with E. W. Benson · LPL, letters to A. C. Tait · University of British Columbia Library, Vancouver, letters to Hugh Reginald Haweis
Likenesses G. Reid, oils, c.1903, Man. City Gall. · Barraud, photograph, NPG; repro. in *Men and women of the day*, 3 (1890) · G. Bonavia, portrait (aged thirty-eight) · photograph, NPG
Wealth at death £54,317 5s. 3d.: probate, 28 June 1915, *CGPLA Eng. & Wales*

Moorman, John Richard Humpidge (1905–1989), bishop of Ripon and ecumenist, was born in Leeds on 4 June 1905, the younger son and second of three children of Frederic William Moorman (1872–1919), professor of English at Leeds University, and his wife, Frances Beatrice Humpidge (1867–1956). His father died when Moorman was fourteen. He was educated at Gresham's School, Holt, and Emmanuel College, Cambridge, of which he was made an honorary fellow in 1959. In 1926 he obtained a second class (division two) in part one of the history tripos and in 1928 a second class in part one of the theology tripos. At Cambridge, Professor F. C. Burkitt encouraged him to make the first of what became almost annual visits to Assisi, thus prompting a lifetime's interest in St Francis. He gained his BD with *The Sources for the Life of S. Francis of Assisi* (1940); and followed this with the more popular *Saint Francis of Assisi* (1950); his *magnum opus*, *A History of the Franciscan Order*, in 1968; and his final work, *Medieval Franciscan Houses*, in 1983. His library of Franciscan books (later given to St Deiniol's Library, Hawarden) numbered well over 2000 volumes, and Moorman himself achieved international recognition as the leading English Franciscan scholar.

Moorman's scholarly interests, however, were pursued not in an academic context but in the parishes and diocese he was to serve. He trained for ordination in the Church of England at Westcott House, Cambridge, under B. K. Cunningham, of whom he was later to write a memoir (1947). In 1929 he was ordained to a curacy at Holbeck in his native city of Leeds. In 1930 he married Mary Caroline Macaulay (1905–1994), an authority on William Wordsworth, daughter of George Macaulay *Trevelyan, regius professor of modern history at Cambridge. They had no children.

Moorman served his second curacy at Leighton Buzzard from 1933 until 1935, when he was appointed rector of Fallowfield, Manchester, where he remained until the early years of the Second World War. His innate pacifism, coupled with a concern to do work more obviously connected with the war effort, led him to resign his benefice and take employment as a farmhand in Wharfedale. At night, by the light of an oil lamp, he completed his *Church*

Life in England in the Thirteenth Century, which gained him a doctorate of divinity at Cambridge in 1945.

Moorman's deep interest in the spiritual and scholarly training of Anglican clergy was first recognized in his appointment early in 1945 to Lanercost Priory, where men could be trained for the rural ministry. In the following year, however, Bishop George Bell invited him south to reopen Chichester Theological College. Here Moorman restored both the financial fortunes and the academic standing of one of the oldest of Anglican theological colleges, serving at the same time as chancellor of Chichester Cathedral. In 1953 his best-known work, *A History of the Church in England*, was published: it illustrated well the clarity of his mind, the independence of his judgements, and also his concern, like that of his father-in-law, that history should be both well written and enjoyable to read.

In 1956 Moorman resigned an appointment for the second occasion in his life, this time to concentrate on his Franciscan writings. The invitation in 1959 to become bishop of Ripon was both timely and inspired. Not only did the diocese include the great city of Leeds with its university, of which both he and his wife were to receive honorary doctorates, but also the dales which they enjoyed as keen walkers, bird-watchers, and lovers of rural life in general. The pastoral care of the clergy, their housing, pay, and continuing ministerial education, were paramount concerns of his sixteen-year episcopate and he saw administrative efficiency as subserving these ends.

The most significant development in Moorman's life, however, came in his appointment by Archbishop Michael Ramsey as chief Anglican observer at the Second Vatican Council from 1962 to 1965. His fluency in the Italian tongue, coupled with his warm gift of friendship (not least his personal friendship with Cardinal Montini, who was to become pope in 1963), and his deep knowledge of church history marked him out as one of the best-known visitors to Rome in those years. He thus became in 1967 the Anglican chairman of the preparatory commission which led to the setting up of the Anglican–Roman Catholic International Commission, of which he was a member from its inception in 1969 until 1981. During this time he was also the driving force in establishing the Anglican Centre in Rome and personally assembled books for its library.

Although Moorman was slight of stature and reserved by nature he had an authoritative presence. He was an accomplished pianist and a keen gardener. From his mid-teens Moorman kept a diary, making daily entries until a week before his death on 13 January 1989 at Dryburn Hospital in Durham where he had retired fourteen years earlier. He was cremated and his ashes were interred in Adel church in Leeds.　　　MICHAEL MANKTELOW, *rev.*

Sources *The Independent* (18 Jan 1989) · private information (1996) · personal knowledge (1996) · *CGPLA Eng. & Wales* (1989) · M. Manktelow, *John Moorman, Anglican, Franciscan, Independent* (1999)
Archives LPL, diaries · U. Newcastle, Robinson L., family corresp. | BL, letters to Albert Mansbridge, Add. MSS 65255b–652556 · LPL, diary of Second Vatican Council · St Deiniol's Library, Hawarden, research notes relating to Franciscan order
Likenesses photographs, priv. coll.
Wealth at death £137,881: probate, 14 June 1989, *CGPLA Eng. & Wales*

Moorosi [Morosi] (*c*.1795–1879), ruler of the Ngwe (Putili) and warrior, was born, oral evidence suggests, at Mohale's Hoek in the south of what became Lesotho. His father, Mokuoane, Ngwe (Putili) ruler, became a vassal of the Sotho leader Moshoeshoe in the late 1820s. When Moorosi succeeded to the relatively small chiefdom some years later he acknowledged Moshoeshoe as his suzerain, but sought as much independence as possible, and in 1846 moved south of the Orange River. When that area was annexed by the British in 1850 he returned to the south of what later became Lesotho, to a rugged mountainous area close to the Orange River. He aided Moshoeshoe against the forces of Sir George Cathcart in 1851–2, and fought with the Sotho against the Orange Free State in the wars of 1858 and 1865, gaining a reputation as an able military leader, a good shot, and a skilled rider. Towards the end of 1865 he retreated to a natural fortress, a mountain with three almost sheer rocky sides which rises above the junction of the Quthing and Orange rivers. He soon found that his territory was part of the area which had come under British protection as Basutoland.

After Cape Colony took over Basutoland in 1871 Moorosi was at first little troubled by the magistrate of Cornet Spruit, but in May 1877 a separate magistracy was created at nearby Quthing. Early the following year the tactless new magistrate, Hamilton Hope, issued a writ against some subjects of Moorosi's son Lehana (Doda) who had not paid tax, then insisted on referring the matter to Moshoeshoe's successor, Letsie. That matter blew over, but later in the year Hope's successor, John Austen, arrested Lehana, this time on a trumped-up charge of stock theft. Lehana was jailed at Quthing prior to being sent away, but was sprung from gaol on his father's orders. Moorosi then refused to surrender him. In February 1879, anticipating that Moorosi would go into full-scale rebellion, Austen abandoned the magistracy, which Moorosi's men then pillaged.

Moorosi then mobilized his forces on his natural stronghold, to which Cape colonial forces laid siege. Numerous attempts were made to take the mountain, but Moorosi's people put up valiant resistance, which included a number of daring sorties from the mountain. In September Colonel Brabant of the Cape mounted rifles met Moorosi part way up the mountain to persuade him to end his resistance, and another such meeting took place the following month, when Sir Gordon Sprigg (1830–1913), the Cape prime minister, met Moorosi, but on each occasion the chief refused to surrender unconditionally. In late November the commanding officer of the Cape mounted rifles led the final assault, which began with artillery bombardment, took three days, and included the use of scaling ladders. Forty-three members of the colonial force were killed before the mountain was taken on 20 November. Moorosi himself died that day, along with most of the other defenders. His head was cut off and exposed on a pole, then sent to King William's Town. After protest from Whitehall it was returned for burial with his body on the mountain which still bears his name.

CHRISTOPHER SAUNDERS

Sources A. Atmore, 'The Moorosi rebellion: Lesotho, 1879', *Protest and power in black Africa*, ed. R.I. Rotberg and A. A. Mazrui (1970), 3–35 · K. J. Wilson, 'A forgotten war a century ago: the Morosi campaign, southern Lesotho', *Quarterly Bulletin of the South African Library*, 33 (1979) · S. Burman, *Chiefdom politics and alien law: Basutoland under Cape rule, 1871–1884* (1981) · E. Bradlow, 'Moorosi', *DSAB* · E. Bradlow, 'The Cape government's rule of Basutoland', MA diss., University of Cape Town, 1966 · G. Tylden, *The rise of the Basuto* (1950) · G. Lagden, *The Basutos: the mountaineers and their country*, 2 vols. (1909) · D. F. Ellenberger, *History of the Basuto* (1912)
Archives Cape Archives, Cape Town
Likenesses sketch, repro. in *The Graphic* (7 Feb 1880)

Moorsom, Constantine Richard (1792–1861), naval officer, was born on 22 September 1792 at High Stakesby, Whitby, North Riding of Yorkshire, the eldest son of Admiral Sir Robert Moorsom [*see below*] and his wife, Eleanor, *née* Scarth (1765–1828). William Scarth *Moorsom and Henry Robert Moorsom, who died in command of the sloop *Jasper* in 1826, were his brothers.

Sir Robert Moorsom (1760–1835) was born on 8 June 1760 at Whitby, the second son of Richard Moorsom (1729–1809), an influential Whitby shipowner, and his wife, Mary Ward (1729–1816), received an excellent education under the Revd Mr Holmes at Scorton grammar school, and joined the *Ardent*, commanded by Captain Constantine Phipps, in 1777. Having removed with Phipps to the *Courageux*, he took part in the battle off Ushant under Admiral Keppel, the relief of Gibraltar under Admiral Darby and Lord Howe, the action off Cape Spartel, and the capture, by Admiral Kempenfeldt, of part of Admiral Guichen's convoy to the West Indies. He passed the lieutenant's examination in 1784 and was appointed to the *Sphinx* and then the *Thetis* in the Mediterranean. After meetings with the prime minister, William Pitt, and Henry Dundas, later Viscount Melville, treasurer of the navy and member of the board for Indian affairs, he chose and commissioned in 1787 the sloop *Ariel* with confidential orders to examine potential harbours on the Bengal coast and report on the practicability of refitting ships there. When illness forced him to return to England in October 1790, Admiral Cornwallis, commander-in-chief East Indies, was 'extremely sorry' and expressed his 'great regard' for him (PRO, ADM 1/167/47063). Sir George Cockburn was a midshipman on the *Ariel*, and his biographer recorded 'the great kindness and attention shown him by his commander who constantly afforded him the best instruction … at the taking of the different surveys and observations' (*United Service Journal*, 2, 1835, 242), of great importance to his career.

Moorsom was made post captain in November 1790 and married on 14 June 1791 Eleanor (1765–1828), daughter of Thomas Scarth of Stakesby, near Whitby; they had three sons and a daughter, who married the Revd Henry Longueville Mansel. When war against France broke out in 1793 he was appointed first to the frigate *Niger* to ascertain the

enemy force in Brest, then to the frigate *Astrea*, and in 1795 to the *Hindoostan*; but when she was converted to a troopship and her destination changed, Captain Moorsom resigned a command he felt he could not retain with honour.

Moorsom remained ashore until 1804, when Pitt returned to power and Melville became first lord of the Admiralty; he was appointed to the *Majestic*, and in April 1805 he commissioned the newly built *Revenge*, joined the Channel Fleet and then Admiral Collingwood off Cadiz. At Trafalgar he 'bore a distinguished and active part' (J. Ralfe, *Naval Biography of Great Britain*, 1828, 33). The *Revenge* was engaged for two hours with the *Prince of Asturias* and four other ships until they were driven off by British vessels. She was severely damaged and suffered twenty-eight killed and fifty-one wounded, including the captain who 'fought his ship as coolly as if at dinner' (Revd John Greenly, chaplain of the *Revenge*, to his father, 21 Oct 1805, Royal Naval Museum, Portsmouth, documents 1984/14 [130]). Moorsom carried the great banner at Nelson's funeral.

After resigning his command in 1806, Moorsom was in 1807 made private secretary to Lord Mulgrave, first lord of the Admiralty; in 1809 he became a lord of the Admiralty, honorary colonel of the marines, and MP for Queenborough. He was particularly well suited to his appointment in 1810 as surveyor-general of the ordnance: his introduction of the turning lathe instead of the grindstone for finishing gun barrels saved many lives. He was appointed rear-admiral (1810), vice-admiral (1814), and KCB in 1815. At his retirement from the ordnance in 1820 personal letters record the respect and affection with which he was regarded. He was commander-in-chief at Chatham (1824–7) and was promoted admiral in 1830. 'Distinguished by his scientific and professional acquirements' (*Annual Biography and Obituary*, 20/2, 1836), he retired to Cosgrove, Northamptonshire, and died at his residence, The Priory, Cosgrove, on 14 April 1835. He was buried at Cosgrove parish church on 21 April 1835.

Constantine Moorsom's name was on the muster roll of the *Revenge* at Trafalgar but he was actually at school at the time, and in July 1807 entered the Royal Naval College, Portsmouth, newly organized by James Inman. He gained the college's first medal and three mathematical prizes, and in November 1809 was appointed to the *Revenge*, employed off the coast of Portugal and at the defence of Cadiz. He returned to England in May 1812 in the *Warspite*, passed the lieutenant's examination on 6 June, and was appointed to the *St Alban's* and in October 1812 to the *Superb*, employed in the Basque Roads, on the coast of Brazil, and on the coast of North America. He was promoted commander on 19 July 1814 of the sloop *Goree* in Bermuda, in June 1815 to the bomb (mortar) vessel *Terror*, which he took to England, and in July 1816 to the bomb vessel *Fury* for service in the expedition against Algiers under Lord Exmouth. In the bombardment on 27 August 1816 the *Fury* threw 318 shells in nine hours, nearly twice the number thrown by any other bomb vessel. An Admiralty inquiry attributed this to the fitting of the mortars on a plan devised by Moorsom himself and subsequently adopted for general service. But he did not receive the anticipated promotion until 7 December 1818, after commanding the *Prometheus* on the home station.

In April 1822 Moorsom was appointed to the *Ariadne* and carried out a series of experimental cruises, with the *Racehorse* and *Helicon* under his orders. Built as a corvette, the *Ariadne* was converted to a frigate by the addition of a quarterdeck and six guns. This increased her draught and seriously affected her sailing qualities, but Moorsom, by readjusting her stowage and ballast, made her as fast and seaworthy as could be expected. He took her out to the Cape of Good Hope and was senior officer at Mauritius for some time. Negotiations with King Radama of Madagascar and contact with Captain William Owen strongly influenced his support for the abolition of slavery. On the death of the commander-in-chief, Commodore Nourse, in December 1824, Moorsom took command of the *Andromache* and hoisted a broad pennant until relieved by Commodore Christian. From December 1825 until the summer of 1827 he was captain of the *Prince Regent*, bearing the flag of his father, commander-in-chief at Chatham. He had no further service at sea, but was promoted rear-admiral on 17 August 1851 and vice-admiral on 10 September 1857.

Moorsom married, on 12 March 1822, Mary (1796–1877), daughter of Jacob Maude, of Selaby Park, co. Durham. They lived with their five sons and three daughters at Highfield, Edgbaston, near Birmingham. In 1830 he was engaged by the directors of the London and Birmingham Railway Company; he was appointed joint secretary with Richard Creed in May 1833, and a director in 1839. He became a director of the London and North Western Railway Company on its formation in 1846, and chairman from January 1861 until his death. Exacting, and renowned for his 'inflexible integrity' (*The Times*, 28 May 1861, p. 9), he was intolerant of others' failings. 'I am so angry I can hardly hold my pen', he wrote in 1834 (PRO, rail 384/278, XC 12492). He was chairman of the Birmingham and Gloucester Railway from 1841 to 1843. In 1849 he chaired a committee to determine the basis on which the gross tonnage of ships should be calculated: 'Moorsom's rule' is in use to this day. As executive director of the Chester and Holyhead Railway he was particularly concerned with steam navigation: he addressed two papers to the British Association and was appointed chairman of the steamship performance committee. He published *The Principles of Naval Tactics* privately in 1846. He considered that his naval services were not properly recognized, continuing to request appointments and (in one letter) to be nominated CB. His persistence contributed to the award of the Algiers medal, in 1849, to those officers commanding at the battle. He died suddenly on 26 May 1861 at his residence in Montague Place, Russell Square, London, and was buried at Kensal Green cemetery, London, on 1 June.

Constantine Moorsom's first cousin **William Moorsom** (1816–1860), naval officer, was 'Shell Moorsom', inventor of the percussion fuse. Born on 7 February 1816 at Airy Hill, Whitby, the son of Richard Moorsom (1758–1831),

shipowner and marine merchant, and his wife, Barbara, *née* Craig (1780–1832), he attended the Royal Naval College, Portsmouth (1829–30), gaining the first medal, and passed the lieutenant's examination in June 1835 but was not commissioned lieutenant until 1842, with the *Cornwallis* in the First Opium War. In 1854, in the Crimean War, he was appointed captain of the *Firebrand* but served ashore with the naval brigade, having a large share in its organization. Wounded and twice mentioned in dispatches, he was a CB, a chevalier of the Légion d'honneur and a knight second class of the Mejidiye. Known as Black Will when shaving was compulsory in the navy he was, on his return from the Black Sea, 'the first captain who had the temerity to invade the sacred precincts of the Admiralty with hirsute "fixings"', to be met with 'the cutting remark: "Horseguards next door!"' (Clowes, 6.211–12).

William Moorsom was described fifty years afterwards as 'an officer of high scientific attainments' (Garbett, 30). His 'Moorsom percussion fuze' of 1850, though obsolete fifteen years later, was the first satisfactory metal percussion fuse for the navy. He also invented the 'Director', an instrument for concentrating a ship's broadside, perfected and in use forty-five years later. He was the author of *Remarks on Concentrating the Fire of Ships' Guns* (1846), *Suggestions for the Organisation and Manoeuvres of Steam Fleets* (1854), and *Remarks on the Construction of Ships of War and the Composition of War Fleets* (1857). In 1857 he was appointed to the screw frigate *Diadem* in which, while recovering from a severe attack of smallpox, he was sent to the West Indies and to Vera Cruz, where he contracted a fever. On his return to England he was compelled to resign his command in October 1859. He died suddenly on 4 February 1860 at Vernon Terrace, Brighton, Sussex, and was buried a week later at Cosgrove, Northamptonshire, where there is a stained-glass window to his memory in the church.

ELAINE DRAKE

Sources E. Drake, *Admiral Sir Robert Moorsom and his family* [forthcoming] · priv. coll., Moorsom MSS · *Annual Biography and Obituary*, 20 (1836) · J. Ralfe, *Naval biography of Great Britain* (1828), 33 · O'Byrne, *Naval biog. dict.* · DNB · *Memoir of Captain William Moorsom* (privately printed, 1860) · W. L. Clowes, *The Royal Navy: a history from the earliest times to the present*, 7 vols. (1897–1903), vol. 6, pp. 211–12, 226–31, 445–7, 468 · *The Times* (28 May 1861) · *The Times* (30 May 1861) · *The Times* (8 Feb 1860) · *GM*, 3rd ser., 11 (1861) · PRO, ADM 1/167/47063 · H. Garbett, *Naval gunnery*, repr. (1971), 30, 274 · PRO, rail 384/278, XC 12492, London and Birmingham railway summary, 17 Feb 1834 · PRO, ADM 50/171 · R. H. Mackenzie, *The Trafalgar roll* (1989), 106 · R. Kemp, ed., *The Oxford companion to ships and the sea* (1988), 559 · Whitby parish records [Robert, Constantine, and William Moorsom] · Cosgrove parish records [Robert and William Moorsom] · E. Fox-Thomas, *History of freemasonry in Whitby, 1764–1897* (1897) · N. Yorks. CRO, Parkin papers, TD19 4/11, 4/12 · letter signed Constantine Moorsom, Wordsworth Trust, Grasmere, Moorsom papers, 63/1/9 · priv. coll., Moorsom/StH MSS · P. J. Long and W. V. Awdry, *The Birmingham and Gloucester railway* (1987), 50, 60, 74 · Mulgrave archives, Mulgrave Castle, Whitby, boxes 6 and 7 · private information (2004)

Archives Mulgrave archives, Mulgrave Castle, Whitby, letters [Robert Moorsom] · priv. coll., MSS | BL OIOC, Moorsom collection, letters to or concerning R. Moorsom, MS Eur. E 299 [LM36/1–2, LM.45/1–23] · priv. coll., Drake papers [Robert Moorsom] · PRO,

corresp. with Robert Fitzroy, BJ7 · Wordsworth Trust, Dove Cottage, Grasmere, papers, 63/1/9, 33/1
Likenesses P. Jean, miniature, watercolour on ivory, c.1784 (Robert Moorsom), priv. coll. · oils, c.1805 (Robert Moorsom), Freemasons Lodge, Whitby · oils, 1838 · B. Holl, engraving, pubd 1839 (after oil painting, 1838), NMM · G. Richmond, pastel drawing, 1851, priv. coll.; photographic reproduction Bromsgrove Museum, Worcestershire · retouched photograph, c.1854 (William Moorsom), priv. coll.; photographic reproduction, NMM · group portrait, coloured print, pubd 1855 (William Moorsom: one of a series, *The Naval Brigade before Sebastopol*), priv. coll. · J. Lucas, group portrait, engraving, 1858 (*Conference of engineers at the Menai Straits*), National Railway Museum, York · oils, c.1860, priv. coll. · E. W. Wyon, stone bust, 1862, priv. coll. · B. R. Haydon, group portrait, oils (*The Anti-Slavery Society Convention, 1840*), NPG · marble bust (mounted on piece of *Revenge*; Robert Moorsom) · watercolour, chalk, pastel, gouache over photograph (of P. Jean, miniature; Robert Moorsom), NMM
Wealth at death £14,000: probate, 25 June 1861, *CGPLA Eng. & Wales* · under £25,000—Robert Moorsom: probate, 1 June 1835 · under £30,000—William Moorsom: probate, 24 Feb 1860, *CGPLA Eng. & Wales*

Moorsom, Robert (1760–1835). *See under* Moorsom, Constantine Richard (1792–1861).

Moorsom, William (1816–1860). *See under* Moorsom, Constantine Richard (1792–1861).

Moorsom, William Robert (1834–1858), army officer, was born on 24 June 1834 at the home of his grandfather Admiral Sir Robert *Moorsom [see under Moorsom, Constantine Richard], Cosgrove Priory, Northamptonshire, the eldest son of Captain William Scarth *Moorsom MICE (1804–1863), army officer and railway engineer, and his wife, Isabella Ann Morris (1808–1860), daughter of Judge Lewis Wilkins of Nova Scotia and his wife, Sarah. Two younger brothers also served with distinction in the army: Colonel Henry Martin Moorsom (1839–1921), rifle brigade, present at Lucknow, chief constable of Lancashire in 1880–1909, and Major-General Charles John Moorsom (1837–1908), who commanded the 30th regiment. Willie Moorsom was the brightest light in a loving family of nine children, remembered for his dark good looks, open countenance, and happy smile. Brought up in the Church of England, his deep Christian faith was a constant source of spiritual strength, remarkable to those around him. He was educated under the Revd William Borman Jacob, headmaster of Calne School, Wiltshire, and at Harrow School (1847–52), where he excelled in drawing maps and the classics.

Commissioned ensign (by purchase) in his father's regiment, the 52nd (Oxfordshire) light infantry on 17 August 1852, lieutenant (by purchase) on 10 June 1853, Moorsom embarked with the regiment for India. On the annexation of Oudh in 1856 the 52nd were ordered to Lucknow, where Moorsom was commissioned to make a military survey. With the aid of only four or five Indians he completed, in five months, the triangulation and survey of a city of 300,000 inhabitants extending more than 25 square miles, daily traversing the streets in the summer heat and the torrential monsoon rain. He received the commendation of his commanding officer and the chief field engineer. In March 1857 he obtained leave to join his father, who

William Robert Moorsom (1834–1858), by McLean, Melhuish, Napper & Co., 1853

was making a government survey for a railway in Ceylon. On receiving news of the outbreak of the mutiny he hastened back to Calcutta. While trying to rejoin his regiment he was commissioned to repair the telegraph between Benares and Allahabad, once marching 32 miles in twenty-five hours. He joined General Sir Henry Havelock's column from Allahabad, and was appointed his aide-de-camp, taking part in the action at Fatehpur without uniform, armed only with a stick. Present at the actions of Auong, Pandoo, Nuddee, and Cawnpore, where his horse was shot under him, he and a sergeant of the 78th were the first to enter the 'charnel house' at Cawnpore. After Moorsom was appointed deputy assistant quartermaster-general to Havelock, Lieutenant-Colonel North wrote, in the context of his temporary bridge and defences over the Ganges, 'an officer of extraordinary promise, his capabilities … seem inexhaustible' (W. S. Moorsom, 403). As deputy assistant quartermaster-general of the division, he was in the battles of Mungerwar and the Alambagh. Very happy in his many activities, he yet longed for his beloved family and the peace and pleasures of home and countryside.

At Havelock's relief of Lucknow, Moorsom rendered important services, as a daring and intelligent guide, gallantly driving the enemy out at bayonet point, leading the relieving parties to the residency and establishing a coded telegraph. A letter to his mother, rolled in a quill and hidden in the beard of a Sikh, was smuggled out of the beleaguered city and published in *The Times* of 15 December 1857: 'we relieved Lucknow from its instant peril and now ourselves occupy a more extended position in the town …

we have grub abundant, ammunition, good quarters, plenty of fighting men, stout hearts and our God on our side ... Had we not many women and children, and sick and wounded, we could walk out of the town at any moment' (Lucknow, 27 Oct 1857, priv. coll.). He planned the withdrawal of the garrison under General Outram.

After Havelock's death on 24 November Moorsom was appointed quartermaster-general to Sir James Outram, and laid out the entrenched camp of the Alambagh, successfully held by 4000 men for three months against an enemy varying from 50,000 to 80,000 men with 100 guns. At the final taking of Lucknow he accompanied Outram as quartermaster-general in the assault on the north side of the fortified city. He was killed, on 11 March 1858, aged twenty-three, while leading an attack.

An officer close to Moorsom wrote, 'sudden death was sudden glory to him ... a good soldier of his Queen ... equally a good soldier of the Cross of Christ' (Lieutenant C. A. Dodd to Mrs Laurence, Camp Nawabgange, Fyzabad Road, 24 Nov 1858, priv. coll.). 'One of the very ablest men in the service' (*Bombay Mail*, 12 March 1858), his survey and knowledge of Lucknow were of immeasurable value to its relief and capture during the Indian mutiny. 'Modest, unselfish, gentle and affectionate, brave as the brave, clever, accomplished and witty, your son was admired, respected and beloved by all ... a friend who possessed my warm regard' (Sir James Outram to Mrs Moorsom, Lucknow, 15 March 1858, priv. coll.). He had been engaged in nine pitched battles and numerous skirmishes, twice wounded, honourably mentioned thirteen times in dispatches and in the thanks of the government of India, and, unknown to him, promoted to a company in the 13th light infantry six days before his death. He was buried on 12 March 1858 by the River Gumti, and later reburied in the residency cemetery, Lucknow. Officers of the 52nd placed a memorial to him in Rochester Cathedral and the 1st division a lancet window—destroyed in the Second World War—in Westminster Abbey. ELAINE DRAKE

Sources E. Drake, *Admiral Sir Robert Moorsom and his family* [forthcoming] · H. M. Moorsom, 'The Moorsoms of the 52nd', *Oxfordshire and Buckinghamshire Light Infantry Chronicle*, 23, 210–24 · W. S. Moorsom, ed., *Historical record of the fifty-second regiment (Oxfordshire light infantry), from the year 1755 to the year 1858* (1860) · BL OIOC, Moorsom MSS, MS Eur. E 299 · *Bombay Mail* (12 March 1858) · *Description of the memorial and other painted glass windows in Westminster Abbey*, *Historical description of Westminster Abbey, its monuments and curiosities*, 19th Century Editions, Westminster Abbey (privately printed), 1, 2, 5–7 · priv. coll.
Archives BL OIOC, personal and family papers, MS Eur. E 299 | Regimental Museum of Royal Green Jackets, Winchester, Hampshire · Wellcome L., letters to Rosalie Longmore
Likenesses oils, 1852, priv. coll.; reproduction, Royal Green Jackets Regimental Museum, Winchester · McLean, Melhuish, Napper & Co., photograph, 1853, BL OIOC [*see illus.*] · A. Ali Khan, double portrait, 1856 (with G. Hallam), BL OIOC · A. Ali Khan?, portrait, 1856, BL OIOC · Dickinson, pencil and colourwash, *c*.1858, priv. coll. · T. Jones Barker, group portrait, oils, 1860 (*The relief of Lucknow and triumphant meeting of Havelock, Outram and Sir Colin Campbell*), NPG
Wealth at death under £1000: letters to his father, 6 Sept 1857; BL OIOC, Moorsom MSS, MS Eur. E 299/24; proceedings of Supreme Court of Judicature Fort William, Bengal, 1 May 1858; will, BL, microfilm, 20 Feb 1858

Moorsom, William Scarth (1804–1863), civil engineer and soldier, was born at Upper Stakesby, near Whitby, Yorkshire, the youngest of the four children of Admiral Sir Robert *Moorsom (1760–1835) [see under Moorsom, Constantine Richard] and Eleanor (1765–1828), daughter of Thomas Scarth, of Stakesby. He entered the Royal Military College, Sandhurst, in 1819, where he distinguished himself, particularly in fortification and military surveying.

In 1823 Moorsom was appointed an ensign in the 79th highlanders regiment, then stationed in Ireland. While there he spent his leisure time on a trigonometric survey of the Dublin area. After purchasing a lieutenancy in the 7th fusiliers in 1825, he was transferred to the 69th regiment in 1826. He was only with this regiment a few weeks before exchanging his post for one with the 52nd light infantry, then serving in Nova Scotia. There Moorsom found himself in his element, surveying the province. His observations were published as *Letters from Nova Scotia* (1828) and the survey of the harbour and surroundings of Halifax remained the standard work for the next half century. In recognition of Moorsom's abilities he was appointed deputy quartermaster-general by Sir Peregrine Maitland, lieutenant-governor of Nova Scotia, and in this capacity he compiled a large amount of data relating to Nova Scotia and New Brunswick. Despite distinguishing himself in this office, Moorsom was unable to purchase a suitable promotion; he returned to England and on 2 March 1832 bought his release from the army.

Moorsom met his wife, Isabella Ann Morris (d. 1860), in Nova Scotia, where her father, Lewis Wilkins, judge, was head of the supreme court. The couple had six boys and three girls. On their return to England, Moorsom and his wife went to live with his father at Cosgrove Priory, near Stony Stratford, until the latter's death in April 1835. At that time his eldest brother, Constantine Richard *Moorsom (1792–1861), was secretary of the Birmingham committee of the London and Birmingham Railway, and Moorsom took an interest in this work. He suggested an alternative alignment for the line across the Ouse valley which avoided the need for a large volume of expensive embankments. At the end of 1833 he was asked to survey the route for a proposed Birmingham and Gloucester Railway by Messrs Sturge, corn merchants of Gloucester and Birmingham.

The railway directors were almost exclusively concerned with trade between Birmingham and Gloucester, and Moorsom was instructed to survey the most direct route. Unfortunately this bypassed many of the main towns, and included the severe Lickey incline near Bromsgrove. The directors accepted Moorsom's report, believing it was the cheapest option. In 1835–6, while the scheme was promoted, Moorsom toured railway and canal works in progress and also assisted Robert Stephenson on work associated with the London and Birmingham Railway. He surveyed the line of the Cheltenham, Oxford, and London and Birmingham Union Railway in 1835, and gave evidence against the rival Cheltenham scheme of the Great Western Railway in 1836.

Work began on the Birmingham and Gloucester in 1836. The Lickey incline was considered too steep for locomotive working and it was originally intended to work it by stationary engines. Tenders were so high that Moorsom was instructed to place orders for locomotives. Edward Bury, the original locomotive consultant for the line, and many of his contemporaries regarded the idea as impractical, but Moorsom seems to have resolved to prove them wrong. The allegedly successful performance of the American-built Norris locomotives on inclines was widely reported at the time Moorsom met their English agent, William Gwynn, and agreed to purchase them subject to satisfactory performance in trials. Although the heavier Norris locomotives proved capable of climbing the incline, the section of line was expensive to work, and Moorsom's direct route proved a false economy. His susceptibility to American technology was evident elsewhere in his work: the Birmingham and Gloucester line featured timber lattice bridges based on the Town truss, which, although widely used in the USA, were the first to be employed in Britain.

Life in Moorsom's office at this time is well documented by F. R. Conder, whose *Personal Recollections of English Engineers* (1868) highlights Moorsom's faults as an engineer and manager. The philosopher Herbert Spencer gives a gentler portrait in his *Autobiography* (1904), describing Moorsom as a kind man, although he felt that he had treated some subordinates meanly. The latter may have been due to the financial pressures of bringing up a large family, combined with working for companies which had limited financial resources.

Moorsom's work on the Birmingham and Gloucester was completed in 1841. By that time he had other commitments. In 1840 he began work on several railway surveys in Cornwall, including the Cornwall, and West Cornwall railways. In both these cases he was eventually replaced as engineer by I. K. Brunel. In the railway mania period he was engineer for a large number of schemes, often in association with Robert Stephenson or Sir John Macneill. The most important to be built were the Southampton and Dorchester and Waterford and Kilkenny railways. Moorsom was dismissed from the latter, in part because his fees were considered excessive. He described the timber lattice viaduct over the Nore on the Waterford and Kilkenny line in a paper to the Institution of Civil Engineers (*PICE*, 11, 1852, 426–34). His attendance at meetings continued, and he became one of the most prolific contributors to its early *Proceedings*. He had already been awarded a Telford medal for his paper 'Description of a cast iron bridge over the Avon, near Tewkesbury, on the Birmingham and Gloucester Railway' (*PICE* 3, 1844, 60–62), which described an early use of concrete-filled iron caissons for bridge foundations.

The latter part of Moorsom's career was full of disappointments. In 1850 he won the Prussian government's engineering prize for his design for a bridge across the Rhine at Cologne, with 600 ft wrought-iron spans, but the design was not used. In the 1840s he had perhaps been associated with too many schemes: some of his surveys were criticized, and it was felt on occasion that he did not spend enough time on individual projects. This led to his replacement by other engineers, his reputation suffered, and in the years after the railway mania he found it difficult to obtain work. His attempts to extend the Southampton and Dorchester line were unsuccessful. In 1852 he became involved with short-lived schemes to extract gold from British ores, but the idea was abandoned as uneconomic.

In 1856 Moorsom was asked by the government to report on a proposed railway in Ceylon between Colombo and Kandy. His survey was conducted hurriedly in the early months of 1857, and his report was published in May. Reports by other engineers followed, and part of Moorsom's survey was found to be faulty. Although Moorsom revised his route and continued to press his case until 1861, he was unsuccessful in his attempts to be appointed engineer for construction of the line.

While carrying out the survey in Ceylon, Moorsom was joined by his eldest son, William Robert *Moorsom (1834–1858), on leave from the 52nd light infantry. The latter was killed during the Indian mutiny in the course of an attack on the iron bridge at Lucknow on 24 March 1858. Of Moorsom's other five sons, four pursued a military career and only his second son, Lewis Henry Moorsom (1835–1914), became a civil engineer.

In the latter part of his life Moorsom wrote on topics recalling his early career in the military and colonial service, including *Historical Records of the 52nd Oxfordshire Light Infantry* (1860), and *On Reorganising the Administration of India* (1858). In 1861 he went to Mull to report on the huge monolith at Tormore Quarry intended for an enormous obelisk to be a memorial to Prince Albert, to the design of Sir George Gilbert Scott; but the stone was later found to have a flaw and the project was abandoned. Moorsom died of cancer at his home, 17A Great George Street, Westminster, on 3 June 1863, and was buried at Kensal Green cemetery.

MIKE CHRIMES

Sources *The Engineer* (19 June 1863), 345 · *PICE*, 23 (1863–4), 499–505 · H. Spencer, *An autobiography*, 1 (1904), 140–86 · F. R. Conder, *Personal recollections of English engineers, and of the introduction of the railway system into the United Kingdom* (1868); repr. as J. Simmons, ed., *The men who built railways* (1983) · P. C. Dewhurst, 'Norris locomotives in England, 1838–1842', *Transactions* [Newcomen Society], 26 (1947–9), 13–45 · P. J. Long and W. V. Awdry, *The Birmingham and Gloucester railway* (1987) · d. cert. · J. Faithfull, *The Ross of Mull granite quarries* (1995) · private information [Elaine Drake, great-great granddaughter]

Archives BL OIOC, personal and family papers, MS Eur. E 299 | BL OIOC, records of Ceylon railway · HLRO, deposited plans and minutes of evidence · Inst. CE, membership records, MSS of two published papers, and publications of Moorsom · PRO, rail records, Birmingham and Gloucester Railway MSS, PRO/RAIL · W. Sussex RO, letters to duke of Richmond

Likenesses J. Lucas, oils, *c*.1850, priv. coll. · F. Talfourd, pencil sketch, priv. coll.

Wealth at death under £1500: probate, 26 Nov 1863, *CGPLA Eng. & Wales*

Mor, Anthonis [Antonio Moro] (1516x20–1575/6), portrait painter, was born in Utrecht, Netherlands, the son of a dyer. His name appears in various forms, and he is sometimes referred to as Anthonis Mor van Dashorst. He was apprenticed and about 1540 employed as the leading 'disciple' of Jan van Scorel, the city's principal artist. Mor's admiration for his master is demonstrated by a circular portrait that he painted in 1559 for van Scorel's monument in the Mariakerk, Utrecht (Society of Antiquaries, London). His *Two Canons* of 1544 (Gemäldegalerie, Berlin-Dahlem), belongs to a sub-genre of portraits of pilgrims to Jerusalem developed by van Scorel, but the characteristic combination of naturalism and abstraction, together with the prominent, unusual signature, indicates that he was by this date a fully-fledged, independent master. In October 1546 he was mentioned as 'painter and burgher in Utrecht' (Beaufort, 192). An undated document in the Archivo di Stato, Rome, provides evidence of a stay in Rome and his earliest biography, written by Karel van Mander and published in 1603–4, mentions that 'he also visited Italy and Rome in his youth' (van Mander, 1.180, 181; 3.232). This trip almost certainly took place before 1547, when Mor registered as a free master in the guild of St Luke in Antwerp. It may well have been before 1542, the date of a depiction of St Sebastian (Museum Boijmans-van Beuningen, Rotterdam), which is attributable to him and which reveals knowledge of the figure of one of the blessed in Michelangelo's *Last Judgement* for the Sistine Chapel in Rome, unveiled in October 1541.

In September 1549 Mor was described as 'painter to' the Habsburg statesman Antoine Perrenot de Granvelle, bishop of Arras, a position which involved him living in his patron's household. This connection, and the ceremonial visit to the Netherlands that year of the Habsburg emperor Charles V's son and heir, Philip of Spain, paved the way to a successful career as a portrait specialist at the Habsburg courts. Images of Granvelle, the duke of Alva, and probably Prince Philip (later Philip II) himself date from this period. They establish Mor's characteristic style of court portraiture as a subtle, unmistakably Netherlandish development of iconographic models associated with Titian, the principal portraitist of Charles V. In the summer of 1550 Charles's sister Mary of Hungary, governor of the Netherlands, sent Mor to portray her relatives within the Portuguese royal family. These included her niece Princess Maria, the intended bride of Philip, who was depicted in a seated pose similar to that used later for Mary Tudor, to whom Philip was eventually married (Convent of the Descalzas Reales, Madrid). Mor travelled to Portugal via Spain and remained there until at least April 1552 before probably returning to Spain. In a legal testimonial of 14 November 1553 he declared himself to be 'living here within the city of Brussels' and 'painter to his Imperial majesty' (Hymans, 42).

The following year Mor was commissioned by the Habsburgs to portray Prince Philip's recent bride, Mary Tudor, who was rumoured to be expecting his child. This important image employs an established iconography, derived

Anthonis Mor (1516x20–1575/6), self-portrait, 1558

from Raphael's *Joanna of Aragon* (Louvre, Paris), and ultimately images of the Virgin Mary, to represent the queen of England as a Habsburg consort. A letter patent of 20 December 1554 implies that Mor left Brussels for London at the beginning of the previous month. It seems quite probable that he travelled in the entourage of gentlemen that Charles V provided for Cardinal Reginald Pole, who was returning to England to reconcile the church to Roman Catholicism after many years' exile in Italy. Pole took his leave of the emperor on 12 November and arrived in England on 24 November 1554. On the journey to England, or later in London, Mor would have had the opportunity to establish a friendship with a compatriot, Pole's young secretary Dominic Lampson, who became an important humanist commentator on Netherlandish art. Lampson had his portrait painted by Mor and wrote several laudatory verses on his works, including the poem that appears in his self-portrait (signed and dated 1558; Uffizi Gallery, Florence).

The letter patent of 20 December, signed in London, documents Mor's formal appointment as painter to Prince Philip. As long as he remained at court, he was to receive an annual salary of 300 escudos, in addition to payments for individual works executed in the prince's service. After his return to Brussels in 1555, Mor worked on commissions for the Habsburg court and seems to have lived at the expense of the new king, Philip II, who granted him numerous favours. In 1559 he followed Philip to Spain but, for reasons that are not entirely clear, from

September 1561 he no longer received his salary and he abruptly left Spain, probably towards the end of that year. He never returned, despite Philip's requests, saying that it was difficult to travel *propter herniam* (Piquard, 141). However, he may have continued to receive a royal pension, since he executed a seminal portrait of Philip's fourth wife, Anna of Austria (signed and dated 1570; Kunsthistorisches Museum, Vienna), and a large *Crucifixion with the Virgin and Saint John* (Museo Sta Cruz, Toledo), bearing an inscription which reads in translation: 'Ant. Mor, painter to Philip king of Spain, made this in the year 1573'.

After his withdrawal from Philip II's court, Mor's hernia did not prevent him from dividing his time between Utrecht and Antwerp. However, in 1567 he seems to have definitively left Utrecht, in which he had maintained his family and property throughout his career. Van Mander says that the duke of Alva, who arrived in the Netherlands at the end of August 1567 to restore Habsburg authority, summoned him to his service in Brussels but the available evidence indicates that he was based in Antwerp. His decisive move south when aged about fifty and not in the best of health may have been motivated by the economic threat to painters posed by the iconoclasms of 1566, since in 1567 Mor was for the first time documented as in debt. He had also come into conflict with his profligate only son, the neo-Latin poet and Utrecht canon Philips Mor. In 1572 Mor was mentioned as the master of an apprentice in the Antwerp guild of St Luke and in August 1573 he was described as living in Antwerp. He may nevertheless have worked for the duke of Alva since, although there are no identifiable commissions, documents bear out van Mander's statement that the duke favoured one of Mor's sons-in-law with the lucrative receivership of West Flanders. Although Mor painted some religious and mythological subjects, such as a large *Circumcision* for Antwerp Cathedral that he apparently left uncompleted at his death, his reputation rests upon his extraordinarily powerful, subtle and acute portraits. He died in Antwerp in 1575 or 1576, one of the most renowned painters of his day, but in his homeland his close identification with the Spanish Habsburg regime soon undermined his position as a humanist artist. Van Mander's biography implies that he was motivated by honour and profit, rather than by love, the highest motive of the artist.

Mor is one of a series of northern European artists who worked at English courts in the sixteenth and seventeenth centuries, setting the standard for local production. There are numerous works erroneously ascribed to 'Sir Antony More' in British collections, although there is no evidence that he was ever knighted. Mor is well known for his unsympathetic, seated portrait of Mary Tudor (of which the best of three known examples is in the Museo del Prado, Madrid), painted in London in 1554. He also portrayed at least two English courtiers, most likely in Antwerp: the leading Catholic Henry Fitzalan, twelfth earl of Arundel (dated 24 December 1562; priv. coll., Gloucestershire) and Sir Henry Lee (signed and dated 1568; NPG), who became Elizabeth I's personal champion. Portraits by Mor

of Jane Dormer and Margaret Harrington, English Catholic noblewomen who married members of Philip II's Spanish entourage and ceremoniously retired to Spain on Elizabeth's accession, are also recorded in the portrait gallery at the Spanish royal palace of El Pardo (destroyed by fire in 1604). From the 1560s onwards quite a number of portraits of English sitters by other artists relate more or less closely to Mor's standard court portrait formula, in which intensely naturalistic surfaces and details are combined with an abstract conception of immobile, standing, life-sized figures in three-quarter view, placed high within an indeterminate space, strongly lit from the upper left, with a centrally placed eye fixed on the viewer.

Like Holbein, Mor also portrayed élite merchants and financiers, a clientele apparently connected with the valuable commerce between London and Antwerp. A report of 27 September 1564 that Mor was in Antwerp, 'making his profit by portraying the merchants [les marchantz]', may refer to the English Company of Merchant Adventurers, because there is a tradition dating back to the 1740s that Mor painted the financier Sir Thomas Gresham (Piquard, 141). His pendant portraits of a seated man and woman (Rijksmuseum, Amsterdam) have been identified as Gresham and his wife, Anne Ferneley, since at least 1792 and the man's likeness resembles the best authenticated image of Gresham, a portrait of 1544 in the Mercers' Hall, London. Three further images have traditionally been identified as Gresham and attributed to Mor, with less secure foundation (examples are in the Pushkin Museum of Fine Arts, Moscow; NPG; and the National Gallery of Canada, Ottawa). The Amsterdam couple forms the nucleus of a small group of similar works held in the North Carolina Museum of Art, Raleigh, the Art Institute, Chicago, and the David M. Koetser Gallery, Zürich (1974), which all have English provenances and may well also represent merchant adventurers. Mor's links with the English community in Antwerp were probably longstanding, since a legal testimonial of December 1553 relates that Hans Maes, who was one of Mor's principal assistants in Antwerp in the late 1540s and remained there after his master's departure for Brussels, frequented the houses of the leading merchants in the city, such as the ambassador of the king of England. The end of his contact with the English merchants seems to have coincided with the decline of trade between London and Antwerp in the mid-1560s.

JOANNA WOODALL

Sources J. Woodall, 'The portraiture of Antonis Mor', PhD diss., Courtauld Inst., 1989 · E. E. H. Groenveld, 'Een herziene biografie van Anthonis Mor', *Jaarboek van het koninklijk Museum voor Schone Kunsten Antwerpen* (1981), 97–117 · K. van Mander, *The lives of the illustrious Netherlandish and German painters*, ed. M. Miedema, trans. D. Cook-Radmore, 6 vols. (1994–9), vol. 1, pp. 180–84; vol. 3, pp. 221–34 · J. Woodall, 'An exemplary consort: Antonis Mor's portrait of Mary Tudor', *Art History*, 14 (1991), 192–224 · H. Hymans, *Antonio Moro: son oeuvre et son temps* (Brussels, 1910) · W. A. Wijburg, 'Mor van Dashorst', *De Nederlandsche Leeuw*, 72 (1955), cols. 230–31 · W. A. Wijburg, 'Antonie Mor van Dashorst "vermaard schilder van Utrecht" en zijn naaste familie', *De Nederlandsche Leeuw*, 76 (1959), cols. 230–48 · J. Puraye, 'Antonio Moro et Dominique Lampson',

Oud Holland, 64 (1949), 175–83 · J. Piquard, 'Le cardinal de Gran-velle, les artistes et les ecrivains, d'après les documents de Besan-çon', *Revue Belge d'Archéologie et d'Histoire de l'Art*, 17–18 (1947–9), 133–47 · R. F. P. de Beaufort, 'De Abdij Marienweerd', *Gelre. Vereeniging tot Beoeffening van Geldersche Geschiedenis, Oudheidkunde en Recht. Bijdragen en Mededelingen*, 56 (1957), 179–94 · tribunale del governatore, Archivo di Stato, Rome, miscellanea artisti, b. 1, fol. 78 · Contaduría mayor de cuentas, primera época, 1554, Simancas, legajo 1184 · W. A. Wijburg, 'Korte mededelingen: Antonie Mor van Dashorst', *De Nederlandsche Leeuw*, 104 (1989), cols. 32–6 · J. Woodall, 'Mor, Antonis', *The dictionary of art*, ed. J. Turner (1996) **Archives** Archivo di Stato, Rome, tribunale del governatore · Archivo General, Simancas · Stadsarchief, Utrecht **Likenesses** A. Mor, self-portrait, oils, 1558, Uffizi Gallery, Florence [*see illus.*] · line engraving, NPG

Moran. For this title name *see* Wilson, Charles McMoran, first Baron Moran (1882–1977).

Moran, David Patrick (1869–1936), journalist and Irish nationalist, was born in Waterford city on 22 March 1869, the youngest of twenty children of James Moran (*fl.* 1820–1890), building contractor, and his wife, Elizabeth Casey (*fl.* 1830–1890). An elder brother, Alexander, emigrated to America, where he became a lawyer and associate of the Fenian leader O'Donovan Rossa.

Moran was educated at the Christian Brothers' school, Waterford, and Castleknock College, Dublin. In 1887 he went to London to work as a journalist on T. P. O'Connor's evening paper, *The Star*. Moran went through a period of political disillusionment in the 1890s following the defeat of Parnell and realization of the vast disparity in economic power between Britain and Ireland. He joined the London-based Irish Literary Society and took a London University extension course in economics taught by Sidney Webb. After joining the Gaelic League in 1896 Moran developed his own version of Irish nationalism, based on Catholicism and Gaelic revivalism. He stated his views in *The Philosophy of Irish Ireland*, serialized in 1898–9 in the *New Ireland Review* and published in book form in 1905. He criticized nineteenth-century nationalists for emphasizing the protestant Anglo-Irish patriot tradition, which he called an ephemeral colonial phenomenon: 'The Gael must be the element that absorbs ... Once Ireland had Home Power, she could laugh at those who would deny her home rule' (Maume, *Irish Ireland*, 2). He also wrote a propagandist novel, *Tom O'Kelly* (1905). He returned to Ireland in 1899 and on 9 January 1901 married Teresa Catherine O'Toole (*fl.* 1900–1950), whose father, Thomas Francis O'Toole, a retired sea captain, was a former Parnellite mayor of Waterford. They had four sons and one daughter, Nuala.

In September 1900 Moran established a weekly, *The Leader*, assisted by the economist Father Thomas Finlay (who wanted a clericalist rival to Arthur Griffith's *United Irishman*) and a dissident faction of the Gaelic League. His vigorous, slangy style of writing made an immediate impact. He had a gift for sloganeering—he coined the phrase 'Irish Ireland'—and for derogatory nicknames. He developed an audience among Catholic graduates and white-collar workers by campaigns exposing protestant dominance in certain professions and the higher reaches of the civil service, and his publicity campaigns for Irish industries secured *The Leader*'s financial stability by attracting advertisements from firms which wished to appeal to an Irish Ireland audience. His economic ideas may have influenced Sean Lemass, whose family were close friends. He was also widely read by Catholic priests.

Moran saw separatism as an adolescent emotional disorder, and said Irish nationalists should unambiguously accept the British connection as inevitable in return for control of Irish internal affairs. Griffith denounced Moran as 'D. P. Hooligan, editor of the *Oracle*, who thinks Ireland can be saved by advertisements' while Moran ridiculed supporters of Griffith's Hungarian policy as 'the Green Hungarian Band' (Maume, *Moran*, 26). He was unsympathetic to the Irish literary revival, though he provided a platform for Edward Martyn's campaign to improve standards in Irish church art, and published the early journalism of Daniel Corkery. He particularly disliked W. B. Yeats, whom he lampooned as a snob seeking self-advancement and protestant supremacy through cultural mystification; Yeats saw Moran as symbolizing demagogic philistinism. Moran was also a lifelong campaigner for censorship of 'evil literature' in association with Catholic pressure groups.

The Leader's devaluation of political nationalism was most resonant in the years of tory dominance in British politics at the beginning of the century; it was increasingly marginalized as the Irish party revived and home rule returned to the political agenda. Moran supported the Irish Volunteers, broke with the party over Redmond's support of the British war effort, and endorsed Sinn Féin from 1917. The paper was suppressed by the British authorities in August 1919, but reappeared six weeks later (at first as the *New Leader*). Moran supported the Anglo-Irish treaty of 1921; though he criticized the Cumann na nGaedheal government of 1922–32 for its refusal to adopt industrial protectionism, he was generally more favourable towards it than to the Fianna Fáil government which succeeded it.

Moran suffered a cerebral thrombosis while leaving for work on 1 February 1936, and died a few hours later at his home, Beulah, Dublin Road, Sutton, Howth, co. Dublin. He was buried at Kilbarrack churchyard, co. Dublin, three days later. His wife inherited ownership of *The Leader*, and Nuala Moran took over the running of the newspaper, which survived until 1971.   PATRICK MAUME

Sources P. Maume, *D. P. Moran* (1995) · P. Maume, *The rise and fall of Irish Ireland: D. P. Moran and Daniel Corkery* (1996) · *The Leader* [Dublin] (1900–36) [continues after D. P. Moran's death until 1971] · D. Toomey, 'Moran's collar: Yeats and Irish Ireland', *Yeats Annual*, 12 (1996) · B. Leacock, 'Yeats and Moran', *N&Q*, 242 (1997), 355–6 · *The Leader* (3 Dec 1960) [Diamond Jubilee number] · *The Leader* (21 Oct 1950) [Golden Jubilee number] · *Waterford News* (7 Feb 1936) · *The Leader* (8 Feb 1936) · *The Leader* (15 Feb 1936) · *The Leader* (22 Feb 1936) · *The Leader* (7 March 1936) · *The Leader* (14 March 1936) · *The Leader* (28 March 1936) · *The Leader* (11 April 1936) · *The Leader* (25 April 1936) · *The Leader* (9 May 1936) · *The Leader* (2 June 1936) · J. Horgan, *Sean Lemass* (1997) **Likenesses** M. Healy, oils, 1902, priv. coll.; repro. in Maume, *D. P. Moran*, cover · photograph (in later life), repro. in *The Leader* (8 Feb 1936)

Wealth at death £1655 13s. 7d.: probate, 14 May 1936, *CGPLA Éire*

Moran, Michael [*performing name* Zozimus] (*c*.1794–1846), street entertainer, was born to poor parents in Faddle Alley, off Black Pitts, in the Liberties of Dublin. His age at death, given by a reproduction of his burial certificate in the *Memoir of the Great Original Zozimus*, implies that he was born about 1803, but the *Memoir* also states that he was born around 1794, and this date is regarded as being the more likely. Moran was blind from infancy, and he followed the well-established Dublin occupation of street entertainer, which suited his disability and temperament. He covered in his circuit an area from the river quays to the old city, where he lived with his wife and children. His nickname, Zozimus, was acquired in manhood from a character in the 'Life of St Mary of Egypt', which he recited in the verse version written by Bishop Antony Coyle. Although he was no great singer, he became well known for his song 'The Finding of Moses', which is included in *Songs of Dublin* (ed. F. Harte, 1978). It is uncertain whether he composed this song himself or adapted an existing poem to the mocking, sentimental tone that was his and was already regarded as typical of Dublin. With his nickname and reputation he remained a Dublin legend after his death.

Dublin comic magazines were named after Moran (*Zozimus*, 1870–72; *Zoz, or, The Irish Charivari*, 1876–9), a New York collection of Irish stories was fathered on him (*The Zozimus Papers*, 1889), and W. B. Yeats's *The Celtic Twilight* (1893), with a frontispiece painting of Zozimus by J. B. Yeats, subsumed him as 'the Last Gleeman'.

According to the *Memoir of the Great Original Zozimus*, published by Joseph Tully in 1871 under the pseudonym Gulielmus Dubliniensis Humoriensis, Moran married twice, and his second wife was a widow whose surname was Curran. They had one son, Patrick. Moran died on 3 April 1846 at his lodgings, 15 Patrick Street, Dublin, and was buried in Glasnevin cemetery. His wife, son, and stepdaughter emigrated shortly afterwards to America.

HUGH SHIELDS, *rev.*

Sources Gulielmus Dubliniensis Humoriensis, *Memoir of the great original Zozimus (Michael Moran)* (1871) · W. B. Yeats, *The Celtic twilight* (1893)
Likenesses H. Macmanus, oils · Millard and Robinson, photograph (after H. Nelson) · H. Nelson, portrait · J. B. Yeats, portrait, repro. in Yeats, *Celtic twilight*, frontispiece

Moran, Patrick Francis (1830–1911), Roman Catholic archbishop of Sydney, was born on 16 September 1830 at Leighlinbridge, co. Carlow, Ireland, youngest of the five children of Patrick Moran (d. 1841/2), businessman, and his wife, Alicia, née Cullen (d. 1831/2); for both parents it was their second marriage. His mother died when he was a year old, his father when he was eleven; his mother's Cullen relatives took care of him until in 1842, aged twelve, he was sent to Rome in the charge of his mother's half-brother Paul *Cullen, then rector of the Irish College. Cullen was to be the decisive and continuing influence on

the direction and style of his nephew's life: 'more than a father to me', said Moran. As a student in Rome, Moran gave immediate evidence of extraordinary capacity and diligence, initially in languages: by his early twenties he had mastered eight. His theological studies led to a doctorate from the Urban College of Propaganda Fide in 1852: the future Pope Leo XIII was among the examiners who acclaimed the brilliance of his work.

Ordained priest at the age of twenty-three on 19 March 1853, Moran's position at the Irish College, of which he was made vice-rector in 1856, placed him at the hub of an Irish missionary world with a Roman bureaucratic centre. His experience there brought him close familiarity with Vatican officials and their procedures which he used on behalf of Irish interests worldwide. Moreover, his involvement in furthering Irish overseas missions fostered a personal disposition in favour of the missionary vocation.

In Rome in 1857 Moran embarked on an academic career as professor of Hebrew in Propaganda College, where he also taught scripture; here too began his lifelong study of the early history of the Irish church. This issued in a procession of major publications which won him an international reputation in that area. His period of greatest productivity was between 1862, when he published his *Historical sketch of the persecutions suffered by the Catholics of Ireland under the rule of Cromwell and the puritans*, and 1884, when the third volume of his collection of Irish ecclesiastical documents, *Spicilegium Ossoriense*, was published. This work betokens prodigious industry and erudition and may be properly deemed scholarly, indeed pioneering, in the context of its time. But its bias was antiquarian and its general purpose that of disputing the protestant dominance then exercised over Irish history by Trinity College, Dublin. Moran made no attempt to disguise his Catholic purposes, which at times degenerated into polemic. Much later, his sole Australasian book, the enormous *History of the Catholic Church in Australasia* (1895), represented his achievement at its worst. It was a vast compilation of more than a thousand pages, an undigested assemblage of borrowed materials presented in a spirit of triumphalist edification. Yet despite their shortcomings and apologetic bias, Moran's histories and his embracing of scholarly and cultural pursuits in general played an important role in conditioning his church towards valuing such matters, a function of particular importance in the young Australian society.

In 1866 Moran went to Ireland as Cardinal Cullen's secretary. Since 1850 Cullen had enjoyed supreme influence over the Irish church, asserting the power of Roman-oriented religion over organization, discipline, education, public affairs, politics, and nationalism. Moran implemented Cullen's policies, first as Cullen's secretary in Ireland and then with appropriate adaptations in Australia, though not before mirroring them in Ireland itself. In 1872 he was appointed bishop of Ossory, a diocese centred on Kilkenny. From 1869 that diocese had been the centre of a celebrated and spectacular challenge to episcopal authority by Father Robert O'Keefe, which was expressed in his (unsuccessful) libel case against Cullen and Moran and which ended in 1875. Dealing with the case and the subsequent disturbance, and coping with the 'land war', a rural agitation to which Moran was initially opposed, absorbed much of his energies. Conversion to a nationalist viewpoint came too late to redeem a reputation as weak on Irish causes which was to cling to him for the rest of his life. In part it was merited, in that he remained a cautious constitutionalist, with a snobbish contempt for the underclass and its causes. Nor did his personality and demeanour attract confidence. Tall, shy, seeming to his fellow bishops colourless and of small ability, a pale shadow of his respected if disliked patron, Cullen, Moran appeared a virtual caricature of the typical Roman churchman. His popular reputation in the 1880s was that of an ecclesiastical autocrat servile to Rome, reactionary and pro-English in politics.

Moran's appointment as archbishop of Sydney in 1884 seemed appropriate in Ireland, where Australian affairs were regarded as of very minor importance: a dull man for a distant, inconsequential job. But Australian Catholics welcomed Moran with enthusiasm, as triumphal affirmation of their Irishness: he represented victory for those who had opposed the ecclesiastical governance of the English Benedictines under archbishops Polding, between 1835 and 1877, and Vaughan, between 1877 and 1883. Nor was Moran to disappoint them. He blended Irishness with his Australian environment. His first public words were, 'Becoming today an Australian among Australians'. At fifty-four Moran showed remarkable adaptability, determined to provide his church with integrationist leadership, its Irishness and Catholicity fitting harmoniously into national life; his ideal was a great national society enriched by religion. Within, his church would be marked by clerical control and lay pursuit of respectability. In all this he took a personal lead, supporting the movement for the federation of the Australian colonies, to the extent of standing, in 1897, in the public election of delegates to the Australian constitutional convention: he was defeated but polled significantly. From the maritime strike of 1890 he showed himself sympathetic to trade unionism, and by 1901 his support for the Labor Party was evident and increasing. He minimized the importance of that party's socialism, accepted it as the party natural to his working-class flock, and saw it as the only party above religious prejudice.

Moran's policy of community integration and harmony nevertheless conflicted with his determination to enhance the public status of Catholics and his capacity to rouse strong sectarian opposition. His frequent visits to Rome and his ambitious and energetic building programme, begun on his arrival and seen at its most grandiose in the seminary of St Patrick's College, Manly, opened in 1889, were inescapable witnesses to a Catholicism on the march—the cause of either delight or dismay. Similarly divisive was Moran's elevation to the cardinalate on 27 July 1885. Alarmed protestant elements saw Catholicism as advancing in power and prestige in Australia. Nor

was Moran, despite his calls for harmony, above provocative and sectarian point-scoring. Conflict came to a spectacular head in the citing of Moran's secretary, Mgr D. O'Haran, as co-respondent in the Coningham divorce case of 1900–01. O'Haran was acquitted but Moran's plans to make him coadjutor were frustrated. However, the major contradictions to Moran's integrationist ambitions were long-term. The greatest was the continued—and prodigious—building of a Catholic education system: 102 schools in 1884 and 306 in 1911, with a tripling in numbers in religious teaching orders. Moran envisaged this system as an adjunct to that of the state, the religious instruction only being Catholic, and thus as simply waiting for financing by a reasonable state. Such recognition was not forthcoming, and his passive policy generated Catholic impatience. Catholic protest was silenced by those characteristics of Moran's that also alienated protestants—his triumphalist style, air of rectitude, and autocratic personal bearing.

Moran ruled not only the Sydney but the Australian church, through force of personality and various centralizing initiatives. He constantly made his presence felt, visiting other centres and colonies. There were plenary councils of bishops, in 1885, 1895, and 1905, aimed at standardizing the governance of the Australasian church under Moran's reign. Major Catholic cultural initiatives, involving clergy and laity, were designed to affirm Catholic elements within national life—the Australian Catholic conferences of 1900, 1904, and 1911. Moran's ideas and presence were central and decisive in all this activity and he also made himself available to the press on the public issues of the day: he swiftly became a well-known public person. Behind the scenes he was the key figure in the appointment of bishops and other important church personnel save in the case of a coadjutor. Unable to have O'Haran, Moran was saddled with Michael Kelly (consecrated in August 1901), for whom he had virtual contempt.

Moran exercised power despotically, being a harsh master with an eye to unity achieved through prayer, discipline, and order, and working through emphasis on complete deference to the clergy and the organization of pious sodalities. A prayerful man, he was also tirelessly efficient in the administration which made his dominance possible. Yet despite his remarkable achievements in building—in both fabric and stature—he invites criticism as a mindless pragmatist, devoted to the short-term and obvious problems of his day. He seems to have been oblivious to deeper trends towards unbelief, and blind to fundamental neglects of the life of the mind. His greatness lay in attention to the immediate and to the outward show. His legacy was that style whose essentials—conformity as against confrontation—have underlain the major debates which have troubled Australian Catholism ever since.

Resting at his palace at Manly after a trip to Perth in Western Australia, Moran was found dead in his room on 16 August 1911. After an enormous public funeral he was buried in the crypt of St Mary's Cathedral, Sydney.

PATRICK O'FARRELL

Sources P. J. O'Farrell, *The Catholic church and community: an Australian history*, rev. edn (1992) • A. E. Cahill, 'Catholicism and socialism: the 1905 controversy in Australia', *Journal of Religious History*, 1 (1960–61) • A. E. Cahill, 'Cardinal Moran and the Chinese', *Manna*, 6 (1963) • P. Ford, *Cardinal Moran and the A.L.P.* (1966) • P. MacSuibhne, *Paul Cullen and his contemporaries*, 5 vols. (1961–77)
Archives Catholic diocesan archives, Maitland, New South Wales • Catholic diocesan archives, Melbourne • Catholic diocesan archives, Perth • Catholic diocesan archives, Dublin • Catholic diocesan archives, Kilkenny • Irish College Archives, Rome • Sacra Congregazione di Propaganda Fide, Rome, Propaganda Fide archives • St Mary's Cathedral, Sydney
Likenesses B. Mackennal, bronze statue, St Mary's Cathedral, Sydney • photographs, St Mary's Cathedral, Sydney, archives • portrait, St Patrick's College, Manly • portrait, University of Sydney, St John's College

Morande, Charles-Claude Théveneau de (1741–1805), writer and spy, was born on 9 November 1741 in Arnay-le-Duc in Burgundy, probably at 22 rue St Honoré, the eldest child of Louis Théveneau (*bap.* 1715, *d.* 1772), a notary, and his wife, Philiberte Belin (*bap.* 1714, *d.* 1792). Although his parents were bourgeois, by 1765 he had usurped the aristocratic title chevalier de Morande, by which contemporary texts and historians refer to him.

Morande was a large and charismatic man of great physical strength and presence, traits he used to bully and intimidate. Having received an education in Arnay-le-Duc and Dijon, Morande joined the French army and was possibly wounded serving in the Seven Years' War. His enemies allege he deserted and fought under Prussian and Russian banners (*Public Advertiser*, 5–6 Sept 1776). Having been demobilized after the war, Morande fled to Paris in mysterious circumstances. There he resorted to petty crime, confidence tricks, befriending and blackmailing wealthy homosexuals, and pimping for wealthy courtesans, whom he exploited and abused ruthlessly. He was arrested after a disturbance in a brothel in 1765, while undergoing mercury treatment for syphilis, and again in 1768 after his father requested a *lettre de cachet*. Having been released for good behaviour in 1769, he soon reoffended and in 1770 fled to London ahead of a new arrest warrant. He lived there, fêted as a refugee from French tyranny, for the next twenty-one years.

In August 1771 Morande published his most notorious work, *Le gazetier cuirassé, ou, Anecdotes scandaleuses de la cour de France*, a libellous attack on the ministry and court, which Voltaire denounced as 'a work of darkness' (Voltaire, *Questions sur l'Encyclopédie par des amateurs*, new edn, 9 vols., 1771–2, 9.224). Robert Darnton ranks the *Gazetier* fifty-third on his list of illegal best-sellers in pre-revolutionary France, and Morande appears fifth in his list of best-selling authors, though this placing rests on some dubious attributions (Darnton, *The corpus of Clandestine Literature in France, 1769–1789*, 1996, 196, 199). Although Darnton sees the *Gazetier* as the most corrosive and potent of all political *libelles*—the archetype of the whole genre, which hastened the desacralization of the monarchy without a positive alternative—there is much to suggest that, despite his criminality, Morande pursued a *patriote* reform

agenda throughout his works (Burrows, 'Literary low-life').

Morande followed the *Gazetier* with a campaign of extortion, targeting the marquis de Marigny, the comte de Lauraguais, and even Voltaire. Above all, he threatened Louis XV's mistress Madame du Barry with the publication of a scandalous biography. Louis XV determined to silence Morande, and, after a kidnap attempt failed, ordered Lauraguais, the chevalier d'Eon, and the playwright Caron de Beaumarchais to buy him off with a large payment and pension, in return for a contractual promise never again to libel the court or government, and the destruction of the manuscript and the entire edition. Morande apparently favoured a narrow interpretation of the contract, which soon became public and inspired further *libellistes*: later works attributed to him attack the regime, but avoid libelling senior government figures. Morande was almost certainly the author of *Remarques historiques et anecdotes sur le château de la Bastille* (1774), *La gazette noire* (1784), *Le bonhomme anglois* (1783), and *La vie privée* (1784), a scandalous attack on the duke of Orléans that was rumoured to have been commissioned by Marie-Antoinette. Other libellous works attributed to him include *Le portefeuille de Madame Gourdan* (1783), *Le désœuvré, ou, L'espion du boulevard du Temple* (1781), and, occasionally and highly improbably, *Anecdotes sur Mme. la Comtesse Du Barry* (1775), *Lettres originales de Mme la Comtesse du Barry* (1779), *Les joueurs et M. Dusaulx* (1781), *Le diable dans un bénitier* (1784), and *Le chien après les moines* (1784).

On 10 April 1771, Morande married Elizabeth Sinclair (1751–1807). His wife was the daughter of Jane Rowe, who was his landlady and the widow of Charles Sinclair, a lawyer. The marriage, initially a love match, produced three surviving children, but anecdotal evidence and the spouses' correspondence hint that Morande was habitually unfaithful and treated his wife with his customary brutality. Nevertheless, they did not separate.

From 1774 Morande worked for Beaumarchais, whom he alternately served and extorted, helping to supply guns to the American rebels. Together they also tried to persuade the mysterious d'Eon to reveal his true sex to them, to profit from wagers on the issue, and when he refused, attacked him in the press. D'Eon retaliated in print, tried to force Morande to fight a duel, which he repeatedly evaded, and brought a libel case, which was dismissed on the grounds that he too had libelled Morande. Morande later gave perjurious testimony that d'Eon was female in a court case over the wagers, claiming to have seen him topless.

After France declared war in 1778, the British ministry, aware of his links with Beaumarchais, ordered Morande to leave London. He retired to Stanmore in Middlesex until 1783, but from 1781 he earned £1000 per annum as a spy for the French naval ministry, after his predecessor, Henri de la Motte, was betrayed and executed. However, there is no evidence to sustain Louis-Pierre Manuel's allegation that Morande betrayed de la Motte—or suspicions that he was a double agent—and Manuel's circumstantial details are certainly erroneous. Morande continued spying on the British until May 1791, sending valuable weekly military and political intelligence reports, and seeking out *libellistes* in London, including, Morande alleged, the future Girondin Jacques-Pierre Brissot de Warville, whom he framed.

From 1784 to 1791 Morande edited the influential *Courier de l'Europe* newspaper, using it as a mouthpiece for Beaumarchais, a means of extortion, and, from 1787, to disseminate his personal reformist creed and 'the sacred principles of constitutional liberty'. His engaged essay journalism probably served as the model for Parisian revolutionary newspapers, but this role was never acknowledged, probably because of Morande's notoriety and continuing libels against, among others, the journalist Simon-Linguet, future revolutionary Mirabeau, former minister Charles-Alexandre de Calonne, and charlatan Cagliostro.

Morande left London suddenly on 14 May 1791 and travelled to Paris, where he established the *Argus Patriote* to defend the constitutional monarchy by denouncing extremists of both left and right, and to campaign unsuccessfully against Brissot's candidature for the legislative assembly. In 1792 Morande was briefly arrested after the September massacres, but released after his denunciation, presumably by Brissot or his allies, was judged malicious. On his release he retired to Arnay-le-Duc, where he was listed as a suspect during the terror. Nevertheless, he was proposed as a witness against the Girondins but was never consulted, and in 1797 he advised the Directory on British trade during abortive peace negotiations. Morande died peacefully on 6 July 1805, having outlived almost all his enemies, and the old regime he had exploited so successfully and hoped to reform constitutionally.

SIMON BURROWS

Sources J.-P. Brissot de Warville, *Réponse de Jacques-Pierre Brissot à tous les libellistes qui ont attaqué et attaquent sa vie passée* (1791) · S. Burrows, 'A literary low-life reassessed: Charles Théveneau de Morande in London, 1769–1791', *Eighteenth-Century Life*, 22 (1998), 76–94 · S. Burrows, 'The forging of a revolutionary, or the innocence of Jacques-Pierre Brissot' [forthcoming] · R. Darnton, *The literary underground of the old regime* (1982) · L. P. Manuel, *La police de Paris dévoilée*, 2 vols. (1791) · G. von Proschwitz and M. von Proschwitz, *Beaumarchais et le 'Courier de l'Europe': documents inédits ou peu connus*, 2 vols. (1990) · P. Robiquet, *Théveneau de Morande: étude sur le dix-huitième siècle* (1882) · C.-C. Théveneau de Morande, *Réplique de Charles Théveneau de Morande à Jacques-Pierre Brissot, sur les erreurs, les oublis, les infidélités, et les calomnies de sa 'Réponse'* (1791) · Archives Nationales, Paris, W 251, dossier 27; W 292, dossier 204 · PRO, TS 11/793, file 2 · état civil, Arnay-le-Duc, Côte d'Or, France · parish register, Westminster, St George, 10 April 1771 [marriage] · Bibliothèque de l'Arsenal, Paris, papiers de la Bastille

Archives état civil, Arnay-le-Duc, Côte d'Or, France, Archives Départmentales de la Côte d'Or, Dijon · Archives de la Mairie, Arnay-le-Duc, Côte d'Or · Archives du Ministère des Affaires Étrangères, Paris, corresp. politique, Angleterre, vols. 496–577 · Archives Nationales, papiers de Brissot, 446 AP · Archives Nationales, papiers du chevalier d'Éon, AP277/1 · Bibliothèque de l'Arsenal, Paris, papiers de la Bastille · Bibliothèque Municipale de Tonnerre, Yonne, France, papiers du chevalier d'Éon · BL, d'Éon papers, Add. MSS 11339–11341 · priv. coll., corresp. with Beaumarchais

Likenesses Lenain, engraving (after portrait), repro. in Robiquet, *Théveneau de Morande*; priv. coll.

Wealth at death moveable wealth valued at Fr1768.50: Archives Départmentales de la Côte d'Or, Dijon, 3Q1

PICTURE CREDITS

Meyrick, Frederick (1827–1906)—
© National Portrait Gallery, London

Meyrick, Kate Evelyn (1875–1933)—
© Science & Society Picture Library;
photograph National Portrait
Gallery, London

Meyrick, Sir Samuel Rush (1783–
1848)—© National Portrait Gallery,
London

Miall, Edward (1809–1881)—© National
Portrait Gallery, London

Micklem, Nathaniel (1888–1976)—
© National Portrait Gallery, London

Micklethwaite, Sir John (bap. 1612,
d. 1682)—by permission of the Royal
College of Physicians, London

Micklethwaite, John Thomas (1843–
1906)—© National Portrait Gallery,
London

Middleton, Charles, styled second earl
of Middleton and Jacobite first earl
of Monmouth (1649/50–1719)—
© Fitzwilliam Museum, University of
Cambridge

Middleton, Charles, first Baron
Barham (1726–1813)—© National
Portrait Gallery, London

Middleton, Conyers (1683–1750)—
© National Portrait Gallery, London

Middleton, John, first earl of
Middleton (c.1608–1674)—Phillips
Picture Library

Middleton, Nathaniel (1750–1807)—
unknown collection; photograph
Sotheby's Picture Library, London /
National Portrait Gallery, London

Middleton, Richard William Evelyn
(1846–1905)—© National Portrait
Gallery, London

Middleton, Thomas Fanshaw (1769–
1822)—© National Portrait Gallery,
London

Middleton, Yevonde Philone [Madame
Yevonde] (1893–1975)—© Yevonde
Portrait Archive; collection National
Portrait Gallery, London

Miers, Sir Henry Alexander (1858–
1942)—© Estate of Sir William
Rothenstein / National Portrait
Gallery, London

Miers, John (1789–1879)—© National
Portrait Gallery, London

Mifflin, Thomas (1744–1800)—
Historical Society of Pennsylvania,
Philadelphia / Bridgeman Art Library

Mikardo, Ian (1908–1993)—© National
Portrait Gallery, London

Milburn, Colin (1941–1990)—© Empics

Milburn, John Edward Thompson
[Jackie] (1924–1988)—Getty Images –
Hulton Archive

Mildmay, Anthony Bingham, second
Baron Mildmay of Flete (1909–
1950)—© reserved; private
collection. Photograph:
Photographic Survey, Courtauld
Institute of Art, London

Mildmay, Grace, Lady Mildmay (c.1552–
1620)—© National Portrait Gallery,
London

Mildmay, Sir Walter (1520/21–1589)—by
permission of the Master, Fellows,

and Scholars of Emmanuel College
in the University of Cambridge

Miles, Bernard James, Baron Miles
(1907–1991)—Getty Images – Hulton
Archive

Miliband, Ralph (1924–1994)—
© reserved; News International
Syndication; photograph National
Portrait Gallery, London

Mill [Taylor], Harriet (1807–1858)—
© National Portrait Gallery, London

Mill, James (1773–1836)—© National
Portrait Gallery, London

Mill, John (1644/5–1707)—reproduced
by permission of the Provost and
Fellows of the Queen's College,
Oxford

Mill, John Stuart (1806–1873)—
© National Portrait Gallery, London

Millais, Sir John Everett, first baronet
(1829–1896)—© National Portrait
Gallery, London

Milland, Ray (1907–1986)—Getty
Images - Hulton Archive

Millar, Gertrude [Gertie] (1879–1952)—
© National Portrait Gallery, London

Millar, James (1762–1827)—Scottish
National Portrait Gallery

Millar, John (1735–1801)—Scottish
National Portrait Gallery

Miller, Hugh (1802–1856)—Scottish
National Portrait Gallery

Miller, Max (1894–1963)—© Estate of
Russell Westwood / National Portrait
Gallery, London

Miller, Patrick (1731–1815)—© National
Portrait Gallery, London

Miller, Ruby Laura Rose (1889–1976)—
© National Portrait Gallery, London

Miller, Thomas (1731–1804)—
© National Portrait Gallery, London

Miller, William Allen (1817–1870)—
© National Portrait Gallery, London

Milles, Jeremiah (1714–1784)—Society
of Antiquaries of London

Millington, Sir Thomas (1628–1704)—
by permission of the Royal College of
Physicians, London

Mills, Annette (1894–1955)—
© National Portrait Gallery, London

Mills, Bertram Wagstaff (1873–1938)—
© National Portrait Gallery, London

Mills, Cyril Bertram (1902–1991)—Getty
Images – Hulton Archive

Mills, Florence (1895–1927)—Getty
Images – Hulton Archive

Mills, Frederick Percival [Freddie]
(1919–1965)—Getty Images – George
Konig

Mills, (William) Haslam (1873–1930)—
© The Guardian

Mills, John (d. 1736)—Garrick Club / the
art archive

Milman, Henry Hart (1791–1868)—
© National Portrait Gallery, London

Milne, Alan Alexander (1882–1956)—
© National Portrait Gallery, London

Milne, Sir Alexander, first baronet
(1806–1896)—© National Portrait
Gallery, London

Milne, George Francis, first Baron
Milne (1866–1948)—© National
Portrait Gallery, London

Milne, (George) James Henry Lees-
(1908–1997)—© reserved;
photograph National Portrait
Gallery, London

Milne, John (1850–1913)—Heritage
Images Partnership

Milner, Alfred, Viscount Milner (1854–
1925)—© National Portrait Gallery,
London

Milner, John (1752–1826)—St Mary's
College, Oscott, Birmingham

Milner, Violet Georgina, Viscountess
Milner (1872–1958)—courtesy Mrs
R. Q. Edmonds / The King's School,
Canterbury

Milnes, Richard Monckton, first Baron
Houghton (1809–1885)—© National
Portrait Gallery, London

Milnes, Robert Offley Ashburton
Crewe-, marquess of Crewe (1858–
1945)—© National Portrait Gallery,
London

Milton, John (1608–1674)—© National
Portrait Gallery, London

Misaubin, John (1673–1734)—
Wellcome Library, London

Mitchel, John (1815–1875)—© National
Portrait Gallery, London

Mitchell, Colin Campbell (1925–
1996)—© News International
Newspapers Ltd

Mitchell, Hannah Maria (1872–1956)—
Manchester Archives and Local
Studies, Central Library, Manchester

Mitchell, (James) Leslie (1901–1935)—
The Grassic Gibbon Centre

Mitchell, Leslie Scott Falconer (1905–
1985)—© National Portrait Gallery,
London

Mitchell, Sir Philip Euen (1890–1964)—
© National Portrait Gallery, London

Mitchell, Reginald Joseph (1895–
1937)—Heritage Images Partnership

Mitchell, Sir Thomas Livingston (1792–
1855)—La Trobe Picture Collection,
State Library of Victoria

Mitchison, Naomi Mary Margaret, Lady
Mitchison (1897–1999)—
© Wyndham Lewis Memorial Trust

Mitford, Algernon Bertram Freeman-,
first Baron Redesdale (1837–1916)—
© National Portrait Gallery, London

Mitford, Jessica Lucy Freeman- (1917–
1996)—© Mayotte Magnus;
collection National Portrait Gallery,
London

Mitford, John Freeman-, first Baron
Redesdale (1748–1830)—© National
Portrait Gallery, London

Mitford, John Thomas Freeman-, first
earl of Redesdale (1805–1886)—
© National Portrait Gallery, London

Mitford, Mary Russell (1787–1855)—
© National Portrait Gallery, London

Mitford, Nancy Freeman- (1904–1973)—
© National Portrait Gallery, London

Mitford, Unity Valkyrie Freeman-
(1914–1948)—© National Portrait
Gallery, London

Mivart, St George Jackson (1827–
1900)—by permission of the Linnean
Society of London

Moberly, Charlotte Anne Elizabeth
[Annie] (1846–1937)—by kind
permission of the Principal and
Fellows of St Hugh's College, Oxford

Moberly, Winifred Horsbrugh (1875–
1928)—© National Portrait Gallery,
London

Mocatta, Frederic David (1828–1905)—
© National Portrait Gallery, London

Moffat, Robert (1795–1883)—
© National Portrait Gallery, London

Moffatt, James (1870–1944)—
© National Portrait Gallery, London

Mohl, Mary Elizabeth (1793–1883)—
© National Portrait Gallery, London

Mohun, Michael (c.1616–1684)—private
collection; photograph National
Portrait Gallery, London

Moir, (John) Chassar (1900–1977)—by
courtesy of the family / Photograph
National Portrait Gallery, London

Moir, David Macbeth (1798–1851)—
Scottish National Portrait Gallery

Molesworth, Mary Louisa (1839–1921)—
© National Portrait Gallery, London

Molesworth, Robert, first Viscount
Molesworth (1656–1725)—© National
Portrait Gallery, London

Molesworth, Sir William, eighth
baronet (1810–1855)—© National
Portrait Gallery, London

Mollison, James Allan (1905–1959)—
© National Portrait Gallery, London

Molteno, Sir John Charles (1814–
1886)—© National Portrait Gallery,
London

Molyneaux, Thomas (c.1785–1818)—
photograph by courtesy Sotheby's
Picture Library, London

Molyneux, William (1656–1698)—
© National Portrait Gallery, London

Momerie, Alfred Williams (1848–
1900)—© National Portrait Gallery,
London

Momigliano, Arnaldo Dante (1908–
1987)—photograph reproduced by
courtesy of The British Academy

Mompesson, Sir Giles (1583/4-
1651x63)—© National Portrait
Gallery, London

Monash, Sir John (1865–1931)—
© National Portrait Gallery, London

Monck, Charles Stanley, fourth
Viscount Monck of Ballytrammon
(1819–1894)—National Archives of
Canada / PA-27931

Monck, George, first duke of
Albemarle (1608–1670)—Scottish
National Portrait Gallery

Monck, Nicholas (c.1610–1661)—by
kind permission of the Lord Bishop
of Hereford and the Church
Commissioners of England.
Photograph: Photographic Survey,
Courtauld Institute of Art, London

Monckton, Sir Philip (bap. 1622,
d. 1679)—private collection.
Photograph: Photographic Survey,
Courtauld Institute of Art, London

Monckton, Robert (1726–1782)—
private collection. Photograph:

Oxford dictionary of
national biography